EDITORIAL ASSOCIATES

LITERARY HISTORY
OF THE
UNITED STATES:

HISTORY

LITERARY HISTORY
OF THE
UNITED STATES:

HISTORY

Editors

ROBERT E. SPILLER · WILLARD THORP

THOMAS H. JOHNSON · HENRY SEIDEL CANBY

RICHARD M. LUDWIG · WILLIAM M. GIBSON

FOURTH EDITION: REVISED

MACMILLAN PUBLISHING CO., INC.
NEW YORK

COLLIER MACMILLAN PUBLISHERS
LONDON

Fourth Edition, Revised

Second Printing 1975

Published in Two Volumes

Macmillan Publishing Co., Inc.
866 Third Avenue, New York, N.Y. 10022
Collier Macmillan Canada, Ltd.

Library of Congress Catalog Card Number: 73–14014
Printed in the United States of America

ACKNOWLEDGMENT

Pᴇʀᴍɪssɪᴏɴ to quote copyrighted mate-
rial is acknowledged to publishers and authors as follows: Albert & Charles
Boni, Inc.—*Collected Works of Ambrose Bierce,* 1909–1912; Doubleday &
Company, Inc.—*The Octopus,* by Frank Norris, copyright, 1901, by Doubleday
& Company, Inc., and *The Responsibilities of the Novelist,* by Frank Norris,
copyright, 1901, 1902, 1903, by Doubleday & Company, Inc.; Harcourt, Brace
& Company, Inc.—*Collected Poems 1909–1935,* by T. S. Eliot, copyright, 1936,
by Harcourt, Brace & Company, Inc.; *Essays Ancient and Modern,* by T. S.
Eliot, copyright, 1936, by Harcourt, Brace & Company, Inc., *The People, Yes,*
by Carl Sandburg, copyright, 1936, by Harcourt, Brace & Company, Inc., and
Criticism in America: Its Function and Status, by Joel E. Spingarn, copy-
right, 1924, by Harcourt, Brace & Company, Inc.; Harper & Bros.—*Mark
Twain: A Biography,* by Albert Bigelow Paine (1929), and *The Mysterious
Stranger,* by Mark Twain (1916); Harper & Brothers and Edward C. Aswell

as Executor—*The Web and the Rock*, by Thomas Wolfe (1937, 1938, 1939);
Harvard University Press—*Literary Pioneers: Early American Explorers of
European Culture*, by Orie W. Long (1935); Henry Holt & Company, Inc.—
Collected Poems of Robert Frost, copyright, 1930, 1939, by Henry Holt &
Company, Inc., copyright, 1936, by Robert Frost, and *Chicago Poems* by Carl
Sandburg, copyright, 1916, by Henry Holt and Company, Inc., copyright, 1943,
by Carl Sandburg; Houghton Mifflin Company—*Mont Saint Michel and
Chartres*, by Henry Adams, copyright, 1905, by Henry Adams, *The Educa-
tion of Henry Adams*, by Henry Adams, copyright, 1918, by the Massachu-
setts Historical Society, *Letters of Henry Adams*, ed. Worthington C. Ford,
copyright, 1930, 1938, by Worthington C. Ford, *The Life of George Cabot
Lodge*, by Henry Adams, copyright, 1911, by Houghton Mifflin Company,
Journals of Ralph Waldo Emerson, ed. Edward W. Emerson and Waldo
Emerson Forbes, *Outlines of Cosmic Philosophy*, by John Fiske, and *Some
Imagist Poets*, by Amy Lowell; International Publishers, Inc.—the introduc-
tion to *Proletarian Literature in the United States*, by Joseph Freeman, 1935;
Alfred A. Knopf, Inc.—*Not Under Forty*, by Willa Cather, copyright, 1936,
by Willa Cather, *Imaginary Interviews*, by André Gide, 1944, and *Prejudices:
Fourth Series*, by H. L. Mencken, 1924; The Macmillan Company—
Collected Poems, by Vachel Lindsay, 1925, *Collected Poems*, by Edwin
Arlington Robinson, 1937, and *The Autobiography of William Allen White*,
1946; The *Nation*—"Individualism and the American Writer," by Newton
Arvin, Oct. 14, 1931; *Poetry*, Chicago—the article "Private Experience and
Public Philosophy," by Philip Rahv and William Phillips, *Poetry*, May, 1936;
Princeton University Press—*The Poetical Works of Edward Taylor*, ed.
Thomas H. Johnson, copyright, 1939, Rockland Editions, copyright, 1943,
Princeton University Press; *Publishers' Weekly* and Lovat Dickson—"The
American Novel in England," *Publishers' Weekly*, Oct. 29, 1938; Charles
Scribner's Sons—*Gondola Days*, by F. Hopkinson Smith, 1897; University of
California Press—*Singing for Power*, by Ruth M. Underhill, copyright, 1938,
by the Regents of the University of California; The Viking Press, Inc.—*A
Story Teller's Story*, by Sherwood Anderson, 1924; Yale University Press—
Collected Essays, by William Graham Sumner, 1934, *Notes While Preparing
Sketch Book, etc.*, by Washington Irving, ed. Stanley T. Williams, 1927.

Also acknowledgment is made for excerpts from Emily Dickinson's poems
1100 "The last Night that She lived" and 365 "Dare you see a Soul *at the
White Heat*," reprinted by permission of the publishers and the Trustees
of Amherst College from Thomas H. Johnson, Editor, *The Poems of Emily
Dickinson*, Cambridge, Mass.: The Belknap Press of Harvard University
Press, copyright 1951, 1955 by The President and Fellows of Harvard College; to John Dos Passos to quote from *The Big Money!*, copyright 1933,

1934, 1935, 1936, by John Dos Passos; to the editors of *Fortune* magazine to quote from the article on Thoreau, in the May, 1944, issue; to the Ralph Waldo Emerson Memorial Association and the Widener Library of Harvard University for the use of manuscripts of Ralph Waldo Emerson; to the Committee on Higher Degrees in the History of American Civilization, Harvard University, to quote brief passages from the MS *Billy Budd*, by Herman Melville; to the Library of Harvard University to quote from the Howells papers, Jan. 31, 1902, and from the Ticknor Letter Books, May 10, 1851; also to the Henry E. Huntington Library and Art Gallery to quote from the letters of Harriet Beecher Stowe; to The Executive Council of the Modern Language Association of America to quote from *The English Language in America,* by George Philip Krapp, 1935; to Mrs. Dorothy Pound and Yale University Press to quote from *Make It New,* by Ezra Pound, 1935; and to G. P. Putnam's Sons for "Herman Melville: Adventurer," preprinted by them with permission of the editors in *A Man's Reach,* ed. Thomas H. Johnson, copyright, 1947, by G. P. Putnam's Sons.

To the following publishers for permission to use copyrighted material in this fourth edition, acknowledgment is made: Little, Brown and Company, for a quotation from "Open the Gates" by Stanley Kunitz in *Selected Poems 1928–1958,* copyright 1929, 1930, 1944, 1951, 1953, 1954, 1956, 1957, 1958, reprinted by permission of Little, Brown and Company in association with the Atlantic Monthly Press; Little, Brown and Company, for "A Little Madness in the Spring," copyright © 1914, 1942 by Martha Dickinson Bianchi; Oxford University Press for a quotation from *Collected Poems, 1930–1960,* by Richard Eberhart, © Richard Eberhart 1960; reprinted by permission of Oxford University Press, Inc.: for two lines from "The Dance," by Theodore Roethke's *Words for the Wind,* © Doubleday & Company, Inc.; for six lines from the poem "The Ships are Made Ready in Silence," from *The Moving Target* by W. S. Merwin, copyright © 1963 by W. S. Merwin; reprinted by permission of Atheneum Publishers, Inc.; for five lines from "Corsons Inlet" by A. R. Ammons: *Selected Poems*; copyright © 1968 by Cornell University; used by permission of Cornell University Press.

PREFACE

Each generation should produce at least one literary history of the United States, for each generation must define the past in its own terms. A redefinition of our literary past was needed at the time of the First World War, when the *Cambridge History of American Literature* was produced by a group of scholars. It is now needed again; and it will be needed still again.

At mid-point, the twentieth century may properly establish its own criteria of literary judgment; indeed, the values as well as the facts of modern civilization must be examined if man is to escape self-destruction. We must know and understand better the recorders of our experience. Scholars can no longer be content to write for scholars; they must make their knowledge meaningful and applicable to humanity. As our part of that task, the editors, associates, and contributors have undertaken and completed this work.

Such a history could be the work of one or a few hands, or it could be a collaboration of many. But the United States, in its life of less than two centuries, has produced too much literature for any one man to read and digest. Its literary history can therefore be best written by a group of collaborators, whatever the risk of differences of perspective or opinion.

Those who have joined in this undertaking are historians and critics rather than specialists in a narrow sense. Their contributions are related to one another within a frame rather than separately composed essays. Each member of our company has a proportional share in the whole enterprise rather than an exclusive interest in his part of it.

The drawing of the design and the assignment of chapters took a year of conferences in which every point was discussed to a satisfactory conclusion. Seven men took part in this planning: the four editors and the three associates. Each of the additional forty-eight contributors had at hand a detailed outline of the entire work and a statement of basic principles before he agreed to write. Upon his acceptance, he was asked to meet, either individually or in group conferences, with the editors and associates and with the authors of allied chapters, and discuss the problems presented by his assignment. Three years were given to the writing; two more, to the editing and publishing. During this period each of the three editors who had undertaken major tasks of detail was granted a year of freedom from professional duties in order to give full time to the work, and in some instances contributors received grants-in-aid. All the bibliographical essays were written by one editor in close collaboration with the authors of relevant chapters.

A genuine collaboration requires some sacrifice of the individual in the interest of the group. The authorship of each chapter is given on pp. 1442–1445, but the chapters are unsigned in the text. Many of them have been substantially revised in order to fit them into the larger plan, and parts of some have been lifted and incorporated elsewhere. The editors have themselves written many chapters and have supplied necessary links; but individual opinions and styles have not been altered in substance. The result is, they believe, a coherent narrative, with valuable differences on individual points. Principles of orthography in quotations have been left to the judgment of the respective contributors.

The almost ideal conditions which made this procedure possible were created by The Macmillan Company and the Rockefeller Foundation, with supplementary aid from the American Council of Learned Societies, the American Philosophical Society, and the institutions with which several of the editors were connected—Swarthmore College, Princeton University, the University of Pennsylvania, and the Lawrenceville School. The disruptions of the war and postwar eras, far from presenting handicaps, have stimulated interest by emphasizing the need for cultural redefinition.

It would be impossible to make specific acknowledgment of indebtedness to the scholars who indirectly contributed to this work. In some instances, the debt was immediate and personal, but more often it took the form of dependence upon the great body of critical, historical, and analytical studies that the past quarter of a century has produced. The mere listing of names and books here or in footnotes would be meaningless. The bibliographical essays, which attempt to be critical both in their selection and in their arrangement of entries, must serve as confession of obligation on almost every point. There would be little reason for attempting again the task which the *Cambridge History* undertook for its generation were it not for the pioneering work of such historians as F. L. Pattee, A. H. Quinn, W. B. Cairns, P. H. Boynton, and V. L. Parrington; the stimulation of scholarship by these and other such teachers as Norman Foerster, J. B. Hubbell, R. L. Rusk, and H. H. Clark; the bibliographical work of E. E. Leisy, Gregory Paine, and their associates; the invigorating perceptions of such critics as W. C. Brownell, John Macy, Stuart P. Sherman, Van Wyck Brooks, and Edmund Wilson; and the specific investigations of a host of careful scholars.

The entire text of this book was prepared specifically for it under individual contracts with contributors for their respective parts of a single overall plan.

December, 1947

THE SECOND EDITION

A NEW edition of *Literary History of the United States* after five years and ten thousand copies suggests a few comments and reflections. As the possibility of reducing the text from two volumes to one was anticipated when the work was first planned, the form and pagination of the first edition have not been altered except in the correction of errors of fact or detail where they have been detected. For most such alterations, the editors are gratefully indebted to their readers.

The original plan of the book, including omissions for which the editors have been admonished and critical opinions for which they have been challenged, has therefore been kept intact. LHUS is the creative work of a group of scholars who will never be assembled again. Any extensive revision would have to be total, and the time has not yet come for that. Most of the critics who read it consecutively have found that, whatever other faults it may have, it is a solid whole. More than perhaps in any similar undertaking, the collaborators in LHUS really collaborated. The book they have written tells a single and unified story.

A few changes have been made in format and some new material has been added. In the listing of chapters, the titles of those which were designed to supply information about the history of thought and of the instruments of culture have now been distinguished from those which deal more directly with literature by being set in italics. The master plan of the work may thus be seen more clearly, it is hoped, as a literary history of the United States rather than as a history of American literature. The view of literature as the aesthetic expression of the general culture of a people in a given time and place was, from the start, an axiom in the thinking of the editors and their associates. Rejecting the theory that history of any kind is merely a chronological record of objective facts, they adopted an organic view of literature as the record of human experience and of its history as the portrait of a people, designed from the curves of its cultural cycles and the colors of its rich and unique life. LHUS is one kind of history of the United States.

The brief "Postscript" chapter has been added, not to provide a full literary history of the period 1945–1953 as a thing apart, but to carry some of the themes and motives of the larger story, already developed in the earlier chapters, forward past the century's mid-point and in this way to round out the account of the second literary "renaissance."

The new bibliographical essay has been designed for the general reader rather than for the scholar. It does not attempt, even in part, what the separate bibliographical volume does thoroughly. Some time in the future that volume too may be carried forward in time by the use of supplementary essays, but it also is too much of a single work to lend itself readily to partial revision. The two parts of LHUS, text and bibliography, still belong together.

May, 1953

THE THIRD EDITION

A<small>GAIN</small> another decade calls for another edition of *Literary History of the United States,* and again the temptation to alter the main text has been resisted.

The "Postscript" chapter of the Second Edition has, however, been completely revised and broken into two. The first of these, by Willard Thorp and Robert E. Spiller, deals with those authors whose careers were mainly in the period between the two world wars and who can therefore now be discussed with some historical perspective. The second, by Ihab Hassan, attempts a preliminary historical estimate of those authors whose careers began after 1945.

The bibliography for the general reader at the end of this volume, compiled in 1953 by Thomas H. Johnson, has been completely revised and brought up to date by Richard M. Ludwig. The more nearly definitive bibliography which was the third volume of the first edition of *Literary History* (1948) and the supplement, edited by Richard M. Ludwig in 1959, have been brought together and have become the second or *Bibliography* volume of this edition.

The Editorial Board, which first came together in 1940, assumes responsibility as a whole for all parts of this work although each member has throughout made his individual contribution. Robert E. Spiller has directed his attention mainly to policy and planning, Willard Thorp to editing the text, and Thomas H. Johnson to compiling and editing the bibliographies. Henry S. Canby contributed as senior adviser until his death in 1960 when Richard M. Ludwig joined the Board primarily as bibliographer. The Associates, Howard Mumford Jones, Dixon Wecter, and Stanley T. Williams, acted as consultants.

February, 1963

THE FOURTH EDITION

ONCE more a decade of steady demand calls for another edition of *Literary History of the United States*, with a second *Bibliography Supplement* incorporated into the *Bibliography* volume, and an updating of the *History* text.

At the close of its first quarter century, *LHUS* has belied its editors' original pronouncement that "each generation must define the past in its own terms." The election of William M. Gibson to the Editorial Board as an editor of the *History*, with Richard M. Ludwig as editor of the *Bibliography*, assures at least a substantial bridge into the next phase of our literary history.

Again the editors have resisted the temptation to alter the main text; but new scholarship has made imperative, and the coming of a new editor has made possible, a wholly new chapter on Emily Dickinson. The chapter on the "End of an Era," dealing with the writers who survived World War II, has also been virtually rewritten as time has cleared perspective; the "Postscript" section has been dropped and new chapters by Ihab Hassan, Daniel Hoffman, and Gerald Weales have brought the *History* into the new generation. Once again the "Reader's Bibliography" in Volume I has been updated by Richard M. Ludwig.

With this Fourth Edition, *Literary History of the United States* moves into a new period in the history of American literature.

October, 1973

CONTENTS

PREFACE   vii
THE SECOND EDITION   ix
THE THIRD EDITION   xi
THE FOURTH EDITION   xiii
ADDRESS TO THE READER   xix

I. THE COLONIES

1. *The European Background*   3
2. *Colonial Literary Culture*   16
3. REPORTS AND CHRONICLES   24
4. WRITERS OF THE SOUTH   40
5. WRITERS OF NEW ENGLAND   54
6. JONATHAN EDWARDS   71
7. WRITERS OF THE MIDDLE COLONIES   82
8. BENJAMIN FRANKLIN   101

II. THE REPUBLIC

9. *Revolution and Reaction*   115
10. *The Making of the Man of Letters*   122
11. THE WAR OF THE PAMPHLETS   131
12. PHILOSOPHER-STATESMEN OF THE REPUBLIC   146
13. POETS AND ESSAYISTS   162
14. THE BEGINNINGS OF FICTION AND DRAMA   177
15. THE AMERICAN DREAM   192

III. THE DEMOCRACY

16. *The Great Experiment*   219
17. *Art in the Market Place*   228

18. WASHINGTON IRVING   242
19. JAMES FENIMORE COOPER   253
20. DIVERSITY AND INNOVATION IN THE MIDDLE STATES   270
21. IN NEW ENGLAND   284
22. IN THE SOUTH   306
23. EDGAR ALLAN POE   321

IV. LITERARY FULFILLMENT

24. *Democratic Vistas*   345
25. RALPH WALDO EMERSON   358
26. HENRY DAVID THOREAU   388
27. NATHANIEL HAWTHORNE   416
28. HERMAN MELVILLE   441
29. WALT WHITMAN   472

V. CRISIS

30. *A House Divided and Rejoined*   501
31. *The People's Patronage*   513
32. THE HISTORIANS   526
33. THE ORATORS   541
34. LITERATURE AND CONFLICT   563
35. THE NEW ENGLAND TRIUMVIRATE: LONGFELLOW,
        HOLMES, LOWELL   587
36. MINORITY REPORT: THE TRADITION OF THE
        OLD SOUTH   607
37. HEARD FROM THE NEW WORLD   618

VI. EXPANSION

38. *The Widening of Horizons*   639
39. *Literary Culture on the Frontier*   652
40. *The American Language*   663

41. THE MINGLING OF TONGUES   676
42. THE INDIAN HERITAGE   694
43. FOLKLORE   703
44. HUMOR   728
45. WESTERN CHRONICLERS AND LITERARY PIONEERS   758
46. THE WEST AS SEEN FROM THE EAST   771
47. ABRAHAM LINCOLN: THE SOIL AND THE SEED   778

VII. THE SECTIONS

48. *The Second Discovery of America*   789
49. *The Education of Everyman*   798
50. DEFENDERS OF IDEALITY   809
51. PILGRIMS' RETURN   827
52. DELINEATION OF LIFE AND CHARACTER   843
53. WESTERN RECORD AND ROMANCE   862
54. REALISM DEFINED: WILLIAM DEAN HOWELLS   878
55. EXPERIMENTS IN POETRY: EMILY DICKINSON
        AND SIDNEY LANIER   899
56. MARK TWAIN   917

VIII. THE CONTINENTAL NATION

57. *A World to Win or Lose*   943
58. *Literature as Business*   953
59. THE LITERATURE OF IDEAS   969
60. FICTION AND SOCIAL DEBATE   986
61. THE EMERGENCE OF THE MODERN DRAMA   1000
62. TOWARD NATURALISM IN FICTION   1016
63. HENRY JAMES   1039
64. THE DISCOVERY OF BOHEMIA   1065
65. HENRY ADAMS   1080

IX. THE UNITED STATES

66. *The Hope of Reform*   1107
67. *Creating an Audience*   1119

68. THE BATTLE OF THE BOOKS   1135
69. EDWIN ARLINGTON ROBINSON   1157
70. THE "NEW" POETRY   1171
71. THEODORE DREISER   1197
72. FICTION SUMS UP A CENTURY   1208
73. EUGENE O'NEILL   1237

X. A WORLD LITERATURE

74. *Between Wars*   1253
75. *How Writers Lived*   1263
76. SPECULATIVE THINKERS   1273
77. A CYCLE OF FICTION   1296
78. AN AMERICAN DRAMA   1317
79. POETRY   1335
80. SUMMARY IN CRITICISM   1358
81. AMERICAN BOOKS ABROAD   1374
82. END OF AN ERA   1392

XI. MID-CENTURY AND AFTER

83. *The New Consciousness*   1415
84. POETRY   1426
85. DRAMA   1447
86. FICTION   1460

TABLE OF AUTHORS   1476
BIBLIOGRAPHY   1480
INDEX   1521

ADDRESS TO THE READER

THE literary history of this nation be-gan when the first settler from abroad of sensitive mind paused in his adventure long enough to feel that he was under a different sky, breathing new air, and that a New World was all before him with only his strength and Providence for guides. With him began a different emphasis upon an old theme in literature, the theme of cutting loose and faring forth, renewed under the powerful influence of a fresh continent for civilized man. It has provided, ever since those first days, an element in our native literature, whose other theme has come from a nostalgia for the rich culture of Europe, so much of which was perforce left behind.

It is not surprising that our own writers in the first three centuries of New World history were more often purveyors of this nostalgia than re-corders of the warmth of the American imagination kindling in novel scenes. They believed that their mission was to be importers and middlemen for America of this European culture. They encouraged nostalgia, even while spreading civilization, and they were often insensitive to the effect upon the imagination of the novel experiences developing upon this continent with extraordinary rapidity and force.

Yet the literature of the new country was to be shaped more by a hope for the future than by a clinging to the past. Observers from across the seas have noted from the beginning the buoyancy of our writing, its richness in spiritual conflicts, carried in such great writers as Poe and Melville, and in such moderns as William Faulkner, Ernest Hemingway, and Thomas Wolfe, to the bounds, and sometimes beyond the bounds, of neuroticism. They have been impressed by the vigorous self-assertion, expressed in the lesser men as naïve pride. The slow emergence of an articulate racial mixture—a race of races, as Whitman called it—had deeply interested them, for this was an experience not known in Europe since the Roman Empire; and they have seen that the remark of Michel Guillaume Jean de Crèvecœur, one of our most sympathetic immigrants, was true: English dogs after two or three generations in the new land became in habits and experience American; and so it was with men and with literature.

The first historians of American literature wrote of it as if they were describing transplanted English flowers and trees. A later school of historians discovered its democratic, psychological, and economic differentiations; but in their zeal for argument and their eagerness to establish our originality, they often left unemphasized the timeless values in our writing. The Emersons, the Mark Twains, the Whitmans emerged from the criticism of these historians with new depths of national significance; the Poes, the Hawthornes, and all writers who were primarily artists, and whose merits often did not depend upon the peculiar circumstances of American history, were less adequately estimated.

The time has now come, and the materials of research and criticism are available, to strike a balance between those who protested against European dominance and those who did not. To draw a new and truer picture of our literary tradition is the intention of the chapters that follow.

2

It is quite possible, and indeed necessary, to write of American literature in terms of its European, and especially its British, sources. That was the way in which Longfellow viewed our literature, the way in which Howells seems to have felt that it could be best understood. It was the approach of teachers, critics, and historians in general until the 1920's. From the academic point of view, American literature was simply a hoped-for extension of the great literature of the English-speaking peoples. And so it is; and such a history, as far as it goes, is entirely valid. Even the radical Walt Whitman insisted that in this new continent we should absorb, not discard, our European past. We could not discard it, if we willed to do so. The progenitors of our literature are in a European and usually in an Anglo-Saxon past. Chaucer, Shakespeare, the folk ballads, the great religious literature of the English seventeenth century, are as deep in our ancestral strain as in the genealogy of modern British writing. The English eighteenth century, English romanticism, the English novel of character, and all later and vital English literature, have a family resemblance to ours, and a family influence, with which any other source for the American imagination outside our own terrain is by comparison weak indeed. A history of American literature exclusively in terms of democracy or the frontier is no less false than a history of American writing regarded as a colonial extension. There is a blending of elements in our culture which is inevitable in a newspaper editorial or in *John Brown's Body* or the *Song of Myself*.

Obviously, our literature is a *transported* European culture, bringing with it the richness of its sources in the classical world, the Middle Ages, and the

Renaissance. Obviously, the roots of our literary culture reach down into British literature which itself has absorbed so long and so much. Yet it is equally true that our literature is a *transformed* culture. It has been written in a new continent, and under conditions definitely and impressively different in the vast majority of instances from the circumstances of Great Britain, or of Europe in general. Slowly, yet inevitably, it has found its own accent, as has American speech. But the divergence has been much greater than that between American and British habits in the use of the English language, because literature is speech made expressive of values, and from the very beginning the values, the expectations, the experience of life in America have been different, with a difference that would continue to increase were it not for the influence of America upon Europe, now making itself strongly felt.

Progress, for example, as a concept may have little general validity; but whether we call it progress, or change, or development, increasing power and vitality are extraordinarily characteristic of the American nineteenth century with which so much of this book is concerned. Never has nature been so rapidly and so extensively altered by the efforts of man in so brief a time. Never has conquest resulted in a more vigorous development of initiative, individualism, self-reliance, and demands for freedom. Never have the defeats which preceded and accompanied this conquest of nature led to more surprising frustration, decadence, sterility, and dull standardization. All this is in American literature, and the causes of both our successes and our failures are implicit, and often explicit, in our early national books. James Fenimore Cooper, for us, is more significant than Sir Walter Scott, although he only rarely equals Scott as a novelist. Melville and Whitman mean more to an American, and are more revealing for our own times, than Thackeray and Wordsworth.

The mobility of the Americans throughout their history has been another transforming factor in their life, and therefore in their literature. They moved across a continent, and continue to move, from habit as much as necessity. And although their speech is English and their political and social organization largely Anglo-Saxon they have assimilated millions whose cultural background was not English at all. Tradition in America is not the same as tradition in Europe. Our national tradition has been acquired by study and by imitation as often as by childhood inheritance of an environment. Thus the relation of what is called the American way of life—which really means the American way of thinking and feeling—to the national unity is extremely important. Our national unity does not and cannot depend upon blood or upon inherited tendencies. Thus very naturally our literature, which is a record of our experience, has been deeply, often subconsciously, aware of its responsibility in the making of a nation from a complex of peoples in voluntary union. It has been an inquiring, an exploratory, literature from the beginning—asking questions of the New World, challenging the effects of sudden release and expansion upon the spiritual nature, delighting in adventure, whether along the Indian borders or on the Mississippi or in the trek across the continent, easily elated in a Whitman, easily depressed in a Hawthorne or Poe. It has been a literature profoundly influenced by ideals and by practices developed in democratic living. It has been intensely conscious of the needs of the common man, and equally conscious of the aspirations of the individual in such a democracy as we have known here. It has been humanitarian. It has been, on the whole, an optimistic literature, made virile by criticism of the actual in comparison with the ideal.

All this has been transforming, and has given to American writing, even to American style, qualities which no Aristotelian criticism, no study of literary influences from abroad, can explain. Our contemporary literature, which from comic strip to satiric novel is really the adult education of most Americans, can be rightly understod only by readers who have followed the history of this American tradition.

3

Such readers of this book as are neither critics nor specialists in scholarship are probably more interested in the literature itself than in the vast historical changes which it reflects. Fortunately for them American literature is not merely in a state of becoming. Our national history is already long enough to have had its periods of maturing and fruition. We do not have to leave our readers confused and bored by writing in which imagination is only half formed and half worded. We are not dependent upon the topical and the timely, the imitative or the unconsciously intuitive, upon the halfgods of journalism, or the sprawlings or conventions of experimental or commercialized fiction. These are all in the background, but we have had a sufficiency of great writers representative of whatever in our history could in their time and by them be put into the forms of art. In this book the approach will be through the varied and extensive experience of a national culture on its way, but the objective of the history will be to record and explain the great men and women who have made this culture speak to the imagination. Literature as they have written it, and as the term is used in the title of this book, is any writing in which aesthetic, emotional, or intellectual values are made articulate by excellent expression. It is the record of man made enduring by the right words in the right order. It is a feeling or thought which by some inner necessity has created for itself a form. Literature can be used, and has been magnificently used by Americans, in the service of history, of science, of religion, or of political propaganda. It has no sharp boundaries, though it passes through broad margins from art into instruction or argument. The writing or speech of a culture such as ours which has been so closely bound to the needs of a rapidly growing, democratic nation, moves quickly into the utilitarian, where it informs without lifting the imagination, or records without attempting to reach the emotions. History as it is written in this book will be a history of literature within the margins of art but crossing them to follow our writers into the actualities of American life. It will be a history of the books of the great and the near-great writers in a literature which is most revealing when studied as a by-product of American experience.

Inside these margins are so many notable writers that the emphasis in the following chapters will inevitably fall upon men rather than upon movements and institutions, although these will not be neglected. There is available for discussion the enlightened common sense of Franklin, the first to make a modernizing Europe feel that there was a still more modern America. There are the astonishing intellects of a Hamilton and a Jefferson arguing great causes in documents and letters which became the political classics of their times. We have the communicable fire of Thomas Paine, the most effective propagandist of modern times before Hitler, and the antithesis of Hitler in the history of human liberty. In the youth of the nation the art of style was mastered by Irving, suave in a tumultuous commonwealth. In the same decades the equally great art of story-telling was enriched by Cooper, who added to the sagas of the world the heroic myth of Red Indian and pioneer. There is the somber beauty of Hawthorne, the moral romancer as Milton was the heroic poet of Puritanism; the fierce humor of Thoreau's individualism; the shrewd saintliness of Emerson, who spiritualized expansion; the soul-plunging adventures of Melville's imagination; the prophecy of Whitman, seeking and finding new rhythms in which to sing democracy and the future of the common man. We have had historians who were also men of letters, and statesmen like Lincoln who could say the word which makes aspiration articulate. There was Henry James, looking both ways across the sea from an Atlantis of his own creating; and Emily Dickinson who saw eternity through the windows of Amherst; and Mark Twain, tasting the bitterness of uncharted freedom while he told tall tales of an expanding America. There are the modernists of our twentieth century. Both in prose and in poetry they have pushed through the mists and illusions of romance and idealism and given us pictures of psychological oppression and moral divergence in a vast society transformed by industrialism. These and subtler strides of spiritual change have enlarged the boundaries of literary truth. The chapters that follow will be an account of such writers and their background and their associates and of a literature which must be known more fully in order to estimate their contribution to the country and to the world.

4

It may enlighten the reader of these introductory remarks to think of American literature as the record and analysis of a series of cultural waves beating in from across the Atlantic to our shores in a continuous series and changing their form and nature and sometimes their direction as they sweep over the New World.

The first waves that came with the explorers and the settlers of the seventeenth century retained their European characteristics with only slight modifications from circumstance. When the wilderness became new towns and organized communities, and immigration swelled into the floods of the eighteenth century, the waves became more numerous and more complex. For nearly two centuries they were dammed by the long walls of the Appalachians, yet their contour and content were subject to changes only less extensive than the novelties in the actual experience of millions of settlers now committed to a life in which opportunity, hardship, and danger were in equal proportions.

After the Revolutionary War and the establishing of independence, itself a modifying influence of tremendous force, the wall of the mountains was breached in a dozen places, and waves from the seaboard pool and new waves from across the sea swept into the Mississippi Valley and on toward the Western mountains and the Pacific. Here in this vast frontier the colonial culture of the East, and later the powerful literature of what was now an old New England and a mature East and South, were fertilized by pioneer experience, dynamized by the sense of a continent in unity, and transformed by the needs and new imagination of a people no longer European. Sectional literature became national literature. And while new ideas from abroad were continually absorbed, currents typically American in their influences began to roll back toward Europe and the rest of the world, a reversal that had begun with Cooper and Emerson in the early nineteenth century.

By the twentieth century and especially after the First World War, the United States was no longer a New World. Culture was now not immigrant here except on a basis of equal exchange, and the complex interactions of democracy and industrialism and the new struggle for economic democracy outweighed in importance any pressures from abroad. By the mid-century American fiction and the American drama of the screen were beginning to dominate the imagination of the masses throughout the world, although of this striking fact the American intellectual was as yet scarcely aware.

To write a simple account of these complex developments is not easy; and a chronology of writers and their books is obviously insufficient. But if a historian will view in perspective a century of this nation's history from any one place and time he will discover a logical pattern in its literary growth. He will see the raw and objective records of the explorers and settlers, usually our earliest writing, developing into documents of politics and religion. Gradually the sense of art awakes as primary needs become more certain of fulfillment; but art in this stage is either primitive or imitative. Not until the settler or his descendant is thoroughly at home in his new world can he create an art which is an organic expression of his experience. A century is not too long for the full cycle of this process, whether the place be New England, Virginia, Ohio, or California. Because this cycle unrolled in all regions, and because there was no single time schedule for the various parts of the continent, nor even a consistent tempo of westward movement, the historical account must be complex, however simple and oft repeated this formula of literary evolution.

Yet the imagination often discovers truths where complications of fact obscure it; and the imagination responds to two great movements in our literary history: the era of Emerson, Melville, and Whitman; and the age in which we are living today. The first epoch is evidently the climax of a long growth from colonial beginnings to a self-conscious and organized nation, but a nation on the brink of a destructive Civil War and a westward expansion transforming in its character. The other, the era of complete national fulfillment, shows its beginnings in the earliest hints of a country that was to be continental in scope and cosmopolitan in population, but that would not realize itself completely and make its voice heard and its power felt in the world at large until the twentieth century. These two main cycles of growth overlap and intervene, and one American author, Whitman, is clearly a pivot upon which sectional America swings into its continental phase. Yet they afford a pattern for marshaling facts and for tracing developments, and thus provide a ground plan for this book. The details will range far but find their organization in this view, which we believe to be an accurate view, of American literary history.

5

We shall tell in the following chapters the story of the importation into our New World of European ideas and shapes for the imagination. We shall show that American literature differs from all the modern literatures of Europe in that it depends both upon an imported culture and upon the circumstances of a New World radically different in human experience from the Old, and thus has a quality which will presumably be characteristic of the literature of the future in a world society more mobile and yet more integrated than our own. We shall discuss the instruments of our national culture as they existed and developed. We shall set in order the progress from colonies to republic, from republic to democracy, from East to West, from sections and regions to a national unity. We shall treat at length these regions and sections, and discuss the rise and fall of literary dominations, the schools and coteries, the prophets and mythmakers, the interactions of politics, economics, and religion with literary expression, and those strong impulses toward escape and refinement and toward revolt and the needs of the common man, so characteristic of the United States. We shall correlate American literature with the successive swings of this country, which sometimes have been toward an ideal of leadership in all human progress, and sometimes have been away from the world we have helped to make smaller by our own energy and into an isolationism where we hoped vainly to solve our own peculiar problems. And we shall pause where genius emerges; for this is a history of literature, and literature, unlike politics, can never be measured by quantity, but only by the crystallization of strong imagination in words.

THE COLONIES

--- importation and adaptation

1. THE EUROPEAN BACKGROUND

T<small>HE</small> world in which the mainland colonies in North America were founded and out of which American letters were to grow was a world at once incredibly remote from modern man and strangely like his own. In the sixteenth century "Europe" was a tiny island in a dim, gray universe. To all intents, "Europe" was Great Britain, the Low Countries, the Iberian Peninsula, France, Italy, and "Austria," with a few adjacent territories. The Scandinavias and Germany existed, one had commercial relations with them, but they existed as remote and savage parts of the world—travelers describing German inns, for example, as if they were writing about nineteenth century Siberia. Distant in the East, "Muscovy," a part of mankind even less known to western man than is Soviet Russia, loomed darkly; southward from it, the Turks pressed into Hungary and besieged Vienna in 1529. As late as 1602 Captain John Smith's travels in Wallachia had a remote, fantastic air.

Little vessels kept to the northern half of the Mediterranean to reach the Levant, avoiding, their masters hoped, the Moslem pirates of Tripoli. Southward from the Mediterranean stretched something huge and unknown called "Africa," where dwelt the anthropophagi and men whose heads do grow beneath their shoulders. Somewhere beyond was the flashing splendor, the brilliance intermittently revealed, of "Asia," where Prester John, Cipango, Kambalu, and the Spice Islands were all jumbled together. As for the western outlook, there was for Englishmen the savage and inhospitable land of Ireland, beyond which lay the gray Atlantic main and such legendary islands as O Brasil. Past these cloudy archipelagoes—and it was difficult to distinguish actual Iceland from mythical Cibola—there was perhaps something called America. Writing *A New Interlude and a mery of the nature of the .iiij. elementes* about 1519, John Rastell said that "westwarde be founde new landes," and thought they were "muche lenger than all christendome," but Englishmen were not overly eager to find them out.

Small groups of educated men labored throughout the century to inform themselves and their countrymen more accurately about the globe. But the efforts of Thorne, Barlow, Eden, Hacket, Dee, Hakluyt, and others to improve the knowledge of geography scarcely touched the general mind. We do not know the rate of illiteracy in the kingdom of Gloriana, but we know that the vast majority of Englishmen could not read. The art and mystery of chart reading was even more severely restricted by the regulations of the guilds, governmental policy, and the profit motive of merchants and mariners; in the next century, when John Donne was writing about the round earth's imagined corners and Milton could not make up his mind whether to be a Ptolemaist or a Copernican, it is probable they were picturing the general confusion of the English imagination. Most of the great library of travel literature available to middle-class readers, moreover, was not published until either very late in the sixteenth century or in the seventeeth.

In the art of landscape painting Tudor England lagged woefully behind the continent; and though New World flora and fauna began to appear on canvases painted in sixteenth century Italy or Spain, England had no comparable pictures. What was worse, the technique of landscape description in literature, by which the small reading public might have been familiarized with America was, even as late as Hakluyt's *Principal Navigations* (1598, 1600), still struggling to pass beyond the medieval stereotypes which had satisfied literary workmen from Chaucer through Spenser. The consequence was that only a few visualized America. When Jamestown was at last founded, the world was certainly wider and better known than it had been to Sebastian Cabot; but, so far as the average literate middle-class Englishman was concerned, it was a world still vague in outline, still filled with inexplicable miracles and stupefying terrors, an inhospitable world, in which only a dogged determination not to be swallowed up by Spain drove the English out of the bastions of their island fortress set in a silver sea. This determination explains why, for many decades, the West Indies seemed to Tudor statesmen far more important than the mainland. You could raid the Spanish silver fleet with vessels based on Barbados; the James River and the Charles were much too far north.

The four million Englishmen who inhabited the southern portion of Great Britain when Elizabeth came to the throne seemed to themselves to be greatly crowded together. The suppression of the monasteries, which ended the obligations of celibacy for about ninety thousand persons; the weakening of the guild system, a social pattern which had postponed marriage for apprentices; the prosperity of the towns and the contrasting poverty of the countryside—these and other causes had increased the number of inhabitants from an estimated two and one-half million in the fifteenth century to a probable four million in 1558. This increase in population had two important effects upon the image of America. The first was to increase the confidence of Englishmen in themselves, to make them feel that along with Spain,

Portugal, and France, England deserved a place in the New World sun. If the Queen was, indeed, the "Great Ladie of the greatest isle," that isle should be the center of an empire of her majesty's subjects

through the speciall assistance, and blessing of God . . . searching the most opposite corners and quarters of the world, and . . . compassing the vaste globe of the earth.

Hakluyt continued with Miltonic majesty:

For, which of the kings of this land before her Majesty, had theyr banners ever seene in the Caspian sea? which of them hath ever dealt with the Emperor of Persia, as her Majesty hath done, and obteined for her merchants large and loving privileges? who ever saw before this regiment, an English Ligier in the stately porch of the Grand Signor at Constantinople? who ever found English Consuls and Agents at Tripolis in Syria, at Aleppo, at Babylon, at Balsara, and which is more, who ever heard of Englishman at Goa before now? what English shippes did heeretofore ever anker in the mighty river of Plate? passe and repasse the . . . straigth of Magellan, range along the coast of Chili, Peru, and all the backside of Nova Hispania, further than any Christian ever passed?

These achievements were, however, principally the work of a dedicated few.

The second effect of the increase in population, together with the new economic forces at work in Europe, was to demand relief from poverty through emigration. The enclosure movement had followed upon the Wars of the Roses. When Henry VII put down livery and maintenance, he ended the necessity for great lords to maintain bands of followers through their connection with the land. And as mines in the New World poured gold and silver into Europe, coinage, agricultural prices, rents, and wages were thrown into confusion. The slow emergence of a spending economy led to the rise of a race of *novi homines* replacing the ancient nobility, whose ranks had been depleted by civil war and sectarian strife. The wool market boomed while new trade arrangements led to the growth of towns. The old common lands were obviously in better use for sheep grazing than for "strip" farming or the pasturage of occasional cows; and, moreover, sheep required fewer attendants. Said Latimer: "Where there have been many householders and inhabitants, there is now but a shepherd and a dog." The *novi homines,* wanting estates, got them by enclosure; and the villeins, no longer permitted their old pasture and farm lands, owning no acreage, unable to pay rent, and unhired as plow hands, were thrown upon the roads or crowded into the evil-smelling cities. They formed the race of sturdy beggars against whom statutes were passed, and for whom the Elizabethan poor law was written.

Some of these landless men were lured into the unprofitable enterprise of colonizing Ireland, and others were enlisted for service in the Low Countries. But in the opening years of the seventeenth century propaganda pictured a New World paradise where farms could be acquired by mere manual labor; and relieving the pressures of superfluous population became a standard theme in colonial promotion. Those who could not read listened to sermons.

Thus it was that the attractions of empire and the pressures of poverty operated to overcome the vagueness, the indifference, the parochialism, the prejudice, and the terrors of the Tudor world. Thus England eventually entered the colonial race to compete with the Latins. If the delay seems to many Americans inexplicable, we who are children of the colonial fathers must remember that we read into the records of their random enterprises a sense of importance subsequent to the event. The English did not consciously create the United States. If it is not flattering to think of Jamestown and Boston as being founded in fits of absence of mind, they were founded at least in fits of absence of plan, for the sufficient reason that neither Tudor government nor Tudor theory had any clear notion of "plantations." The astonishing thing is not that English discoveries were made at random or that colonies were nourished by neglect; the astonishing thing is that out of the social confusion of the Tudor world there emerged any colonial enterprises at all.

2

The social confusion of Tudor England was, then, great; great also was its cultural disharmony. Three opposed systems of life fought for supremacy over the Tudor mind and, in some degree, for supremacy in the New World— medievalism, the Renaissance, and the Reformation. Despite the brilliance of Spenser and Shakespeare, the massive structure of the medieval world order did not crumble at the discovery of America; on the contrary, even Marlowe's *Dr. Faustus,* with its immortal passage on the pagan Helen, contains the Seven Deadly Sins and a description of hell as vivid as that in Jonathan Edwards' famous sermon.

Tudor Englishmen in truth still looked upon the visible world as a bridge between two bottomless eternities. In relation to these the earth was but a fretful midge; but because the age of the world was less than seven thousand years the story of mankind was essentially without historic change, Troy being a town like London, and the relation of sinful poets to Christ being very like those of medieval vassals to their lord. As mankind marched across this narrow span, the chief concern of each individual was still that relation— in other words, the salvation of the soul. Catholicism may have been altered to the Church of England; Christian eschatology in the days of Ben Jonson was what it had been to St. Augustine.

History began when God, fulfilling an ancient purpose, called the visible universe into being and created Adam and Eve for his glory. These twain disobeyed him of their own free will; wherefore God placed the curse of travail and death upon their descendants from Cain and Abel to Sir Walter Raleigh, who, though he imagined he saw the grave where Laura lay, saw also heaven as a place where Christ, as an unfeed king's attorney, got his clients off. For God was not merely just, he was also kind, and offered to save some part of mankind, first through a succession of symbolic events like the preservation of Noah, and afterwards through the birth, ministry, crucifixion, and resurrection of Christ. History would come to a fitting end at the Day of Judgment, when the souls of the saved were to rejoice in the presence of God. If this be Christian orthodoxy in the modern Bible belt, we forget that it is a medieval inheritance.

Crossing the bridge of life, sinful man was surrounded by various supernatural beings of superhuman power. A great angel had instigated the original fall. This angel had evil companions, driven with him out of heaven. He was Satan or the Devil, whose chief purpose was to prevent as many human souls as possible from attaining salvation; he, with his confederates, therefore delighted to work mischief, both grotesque and terrifying. Though his power was less than God's, his followers were enabled to do magical things. These followers might be witches and wizards—human souls gone wrong; or they might be human beings who never had opportunity to go right. Such were, for example, the American Indians, whose origin could best be explained by supposing they were the offspring of Satan. Human history was (as conducted by Divine Providence) an enormous campaign between Satan and Christ; therefore colonial historians like Bradford and Winthrop anxiously examined and recorded special providences revealing the cosmic significance of striking events. Even a hard-boiled character like John Smith wrote that Lord De La Warr's coming to Virginia showed "how God inclineth all casuall events to worke the necessary helpe of his Saints."

Had the medieval world persisted unchanged in Europe, the governing concepts of a single church, a single state, and a single ordering of knowledge might have been transferred to the colonies there to shape a culture comparable to the culture of the Latin-American colonies south of the Rio Grande. In fact, nationalism, sectarianism, and the New Learning had already arisen to wreck the old unity. Yet elements descending from the medieval unity persisted, notably in New England. That human reason unaided by divine revelation could go but a partial way toward understanding the causes of things was a proposition no more unsympathetic to the New England minister than to his remote scholastic progenitor. The logic of Peter Ramus of Paris replaced Aristotelian traditionalism in the search for a lost accord; and, with the entrance into the United States of Roman Catholic education, the old scholasticism was in a sense reborn. So likewise the American colonial, though he hated the Pope, could think of the realm of the spirit as a *civitas Dei* or polity of God, as Augustine had taught, and differed chiefly from his Catholic contemporary by considering that Rome was in schism, not New England. Finally, the shadowy concept of unity in Christian society was not lost in crossing the Atlantic. All that Rome had to do was to turn Protestant.

In the feudal system man had status. Status consisted of the place he occupied in the social hierarchy, together with the rights and duties appropriate to his social function. This was his "calling." Status extended beyond military and political duties; it included the economic order, or that "practical life" which existed in order that man might fulfill his chief obligation, to glorify God and serve him. "Business" was therefore also a part of the great drama of time and eternity. Buying and selling were not something done by individuals for private personal gain, but occupations to be directed toward the great religious purpose set for mankind. This control emanated from the church, the feudal order, and various professional and occupational associations. The church, for instance, long frowned upon interest ("usury") as a violation of Christian charity, and church and state likewise denounced such forms of individual profit as "engrossing," or cornering the market. Economic life was supposed to conform to an ideal order; and since a part of this ideal was the assumption that everything had its just price or ideal value (fixed partly by custom and partly by the relation of the cost of production to the selling price) law and custom demanded and frequently secured a stabilization of price and wage. Guilds, furthermore, were organized to guard particular occupations; and as the guild (together with the town) might properly seek to fix the just price of anything, so it might also properly regulate the number of apprentices admitted to a calling. Fundamental to this system, so far as trade is concerned, was the tacit assumption that the town or community is the true economic unit. In Jamestown, in Plymouth, and in other early colonies, these assumptions had considerable vitality, and the communal idea of economic activity was for a time accepted as a matter of course.

The medieval notion of a community of goods cannot be pushed too far inasmuch as men have fallen from that state of innocence which alone would make possible a holy communism. The individual's desire for wealth is the result of man's imperfection since the Fall. But God so manages history that in commanding Adam to earn his living by the sweat of his brow and so sanctioning both private property and profit, he had still in mind his own glory. Only through property can the individual keep that status in society to which God has called him; only through the love of wealth can human industry increase the amount of private riches sufficiently to make charity possible. Only, in fact, through property can God's church be maintained from the gifts of the faithful. Communism was, indeed, the original ideal, reflected in the practice of the primitive church and in such institutions as the monastery, but over the institution of private property medieval doctors managed to throw a sacred veil; and private property thus indirectly received from the medieval world a sanction which in America it has not lost.

3

The most striking, influential, and permanent influence of medieval thought upon American development was, then, the concept that the primary values of life are theological. But the British colonies were founded after the European Renaissance and the Protestant Reformation, which obliterated some parts of the medieval inheritance, altered others, and added to that inheritance elements of their own. The gifts of the Renaissance to American development were manifold; here there is space to particularize only a few: scientific curiosity; a particular kind of individualism; and the concept of the commonwealth as an autonomous structure.

John Addington Symonds' haunting definition of the Renaissance as the rediscovery of the world and of man, despite repeated attempts to point out its inadequacy, will not down, because it contains a living truth. Doubtless Roger Bacon was not the only man of a scientific turn of mind in the Middle Ages. Doubtless if the New World had been discovered in the twelfth century, men's curiosity would have been as great as it was later, things would have had to be named, and despite metaphysical realism there would have been a pragmatic approach to problems arising from the discovery. But the New World was a Renaissance invention; and it was unnecessary to consult the schoolmen about its prodigious natural wonders. It was possible to catalogue its phenomena with a certain innocence of the eye, to describe things as they really were and not as they appeared in bestiaries—to begin, in other words, founding natural science in the United States. The reports of voyagers and settlers are strewn with specific observations, with lists of words, with careful documentation about river and cape, thunderstorm and iceberg, the increase of plants, the habits of animals, the life of Indians, manifestations of natural wealth, the operation of religion, anthropology, and much else to which we give our modern names. Medieval travelers could report, and report vividly; the Renaissance voyager was nevertheless by comparison of a more scientific habit of mind. The *Ymago Mundi* of Pierre d'Ailly, the excellent geographical compilation from the fifteenth century which fascinated the imagination of Columbus, begins by postulating nine spheres "according to the opinions of the astrologers," though Aristotle "admits of eight only." The heavens do not share in the four elements and possess none of their qualities; therefore they are neither generative nor corruptible. If we contrast this appeal to authority and dogma with Winthrop's experimental study of Atlantic weather as he went his way to Massachusetts, we see the immense distance men had come, even though Winthrop's contemporaries frequently appealed to authority and even though Pierre d'Ailly himself is capable of experimental observation.

If we turn from the thing observed to the observer, we are face to face with Renaissance man. The man of the Renaissance has been often and variously described, but always in terms of eminence, superiority, *virtù*, the conscious development of extraordinary capacities. This emphasis upon superiority and leadership is an important clue to understanding the history of the discovery and settlement of British North America, since, at least in its earlier phases, the history was to a surprising degree determined by men of *virtù*. The great names in this history—Lok, Frobisher, Gilbert, Raleigh, Drake, Smith are representative—share in greater or less degree the quality of *noblesse oblige,* even if they are of the middle class. Expeditions to the New World are, as it were, each a *posse comitatus*; one almost expects the giving out of gold rings as in *Beowulf,* so immediately does the personal capacity of the man in charge as statesman, mariner, economist, writer, and general fill the imagination. One forgets the humbler joint-stock enterprises that sent them forth. Products of a culture in which the old, rigid class structure was yearly less evident, these men, violent, capable, headstrong, command only by the sheer weight of personality; at that immense distance from England the authority of king or queen, parliament or city company, is meaningless, and they stand alone, confronting their mutinous and headstrong crews. What drove them forth? They thirsted for an immortality of fame which for them eclipsed a promised immortality of soul. The works of Captain John Smith open with complimentary verses comparing him to Moses, Caesar, Monluc, and Homer:

> Like *Caesar* now thou writ'st what thou hast done,
> These acts, this Booke will live while ther's a Sunne.

Shakespeare cannot promise more to the mysterious W. H. But these verses merely say what Hakluyt and Purchas have said, what Drayton repeated:

> Thy voyages attend
> Industrious Hakluÿt,
>   Whose reading shall enflame
>   Men to seek fame.

This individualism is, furthermore, a completely masculine individualism A few like Raleigh, when in England, were aware of the softer side of Renaissance culture, wrote sonnets to their mistress's eyebrow or capered to the lascivious pleasing of a lute; but for the most part elegance and scholarship did not cross the ocean main until the second third of the seventeenth century. The explorers, the founders, were men brought up in the turbulence of Tudor England, of a Europe torn by civil strife and religious warfare. They scarcely knew the humanitarian virtues, rationalizing the slaughter of Indians or papists with the sublime indifference they brought to the slaughter of the wild Irish. Their careers were under the guardianship of Fortuna, that survivor from the Middle Ages, who, after presiding over the destinies of Wolsey, Cromwell, and Lady Jane Grey, came as it were to preside over the destinies of Edward Maria Wingfield, Captain John Smith, the "Lost Colony" at Roanoke, or any other strange bit of early American history. In such a situation the Platonic Academy, Petrarchan amorousness, or nice differences about meter or prose style were meaningless; fortitude and statesmanship, a bravura recklessness, the kind of unlicensed egoism that fascinated Marlowe and Shakespeare, were the qualities needed for success. If these men read, their libraries were those of Captain Myles Standish: Plutarch, "Bariffe's Artillery Guide and the Commentaries of Caesar," and somebody on the art of war were more to the point, not Ovid.

But the personal qualities that will lead unlettered men into the wilderness are not necessarily the same as those that will create settlements; the fishing post yields to the plantation; the marauder is replaced by the statesman; and a colony is born. The most striking fact about these colonies is that they are states in little, autonomous commonwealths, miniature nations, not those dependent invertebrate settlements which to this day helplessly dot the African coast line. An older generation of historians traced the ancestry of the Mayflower Compact to the traditional liberties of the German *Volk;* it is more historical to note that Jamestown, Plymouth, Massachusetts Bay, Providence, Hartford, each of these little settlements is conceived in the spirit of *respublica,* even when (as in the instance of Maryland) one is studying a proprietary colony. The commonwealth may be tiny, but it is a commonwealth, a single state usually with its single church, in the best manner of Renaissance theorizing. If, as Louis Le Roy wrote only thirty years before Jamestown was founded, Providence guides the transition of prosperity from state to state, the colonial founders were conscious of an historic mission; the course of empire took its way westward in men's minds long before Berkeley wrote.

These little states followed current Renaissance theory. In them as in Europe the emphasis was long upon subordination. hierarchy, and order. It was assumed as a fact in nature that there must be a ruling class, the "people" being subordinate. Government was necessarily by a minority. Citizenship was not a right but a privilege; and the dwellers in a given community did not *ipso facto* become citizens of the state. Government was something divinely sanctioned, the necessity for order arising from the spiritual corruption of mankind whether in France or in Virginia, on the coast of Maine or in Italy. The contract theory, so far as it operated, was not as with Rousseau a compact of individuals mystically conscious of their natural rights; on the contrary, "contract" was characteristically a covenant between the ruling classes and Deity, to which such minor matters as royal charters or the directives of a trading company were but codicils. We misunderstand the early years of the American colonies if we read their history through the eyes of Locke, Samuel Adams, Freeman, or Theodore Roosevelt. They grew up, not in anticipation of the Glorious Revolution, the Declaration of Independence, or the "Germanic" theory of liberty; they were creations, imperfect, tiny, obscure, but typical, of Renaissance speculation about the nature of government and the commonwealth; and the transition from these postulates to nineteenth century liberalism was as painful in the New World as it has been in the Old.

4

To remark that the Reformation was also a basic factor conditioning American cultural development is surely a work of supererogation. The rest of this history is lengthy proof of the fact that the spirit of American letters is predominantly Protestant. To the disentangling of the many threads of this Protestant influence whole subsequent chapters are given. It would be idle here to argue such vexing questions as whether Lutheranism or Calvinism was the more democratic faith; whether there was a distinctive and unique American Puritanism; or whether the protest of Protestantism and the dissidence of dissent appearing in such nineteenth century faiths as Mormonism and Christian Science are lineal descendants of the European Reformation. It is a commonplace that colonial clergymen were learned men who continued the traditions of humanism, and who sought to found Christian utopias (strictly limited to godly of the right sort) up and down the Atlantic coast. Latterly, ink has been spilled to show that Puritanism had an aesthetic, that the Pilgrims liked strong liquors and were lusty fellows. For intellectual history these questions are not so important as is the realization that in northern Europe Protestantism conquered humanism in the degree that Calvin was no Pico della Mirandola and Luther was no Erasmus. The American colonies were the children of north European Protestantism.

If humanism was the rediscovery of a literature, Protestantism was the rediscovery of a book. American colonials, even in Virginia, became the people of that book. Displacing ancient Israel as the chosen of God, the founders of American plantations regarded themselves as divinely appointed to increase the kingdom of a Protestant Christ and to further the cause revealed by Deity in the Old Testament and continued in the New World. Bibliolatry took shape as an attempt to legalize in the wilderness the Mosaic code and to learn from the cloudy pages of the prophets the American signs of the times. A kind of *sortes Biblicae* aided the magistrate; whether at Geneva or at Salem, orthodoxy became the primary test of citizenship. One has only to study, as Otto Benesch has done, the Renaissance art in northern Europe to see how profoundly Protestantism alters values; out of this alteration of values America was born. Contrast portraits by Dürer, Cranach, and Holbein with canvases by Raphael, Titian, and Tintoretto. The difference is not that the Puritan is opposed to art and the Catholic embraces it, nor that the Teutonic world distrusted paganism and the Latin culture went out to meet paganism with open arms; the difference is that in the one culture life is the education of a character, in the other it is the cultivation of a personality. The grave faces which look out at us from the pictures of the northern masters are the faces of men of affairs, men whose integrity is a credit-making virtue, who do not deny that recreation has its place in life, but to whom pleasure is never spontaneous because they have read in the Book that there is an appointed time for everything. Theirs is, in sum, a Biblical culture, not, as in the Mediterranean world, a spontaneous one.

For such men, belief is an inner experience; seeking to evaluate that experience, they are filled alternately with enthusiasm and melancholy—not the sensuous melancholy of Da Vinci's portraits, but that melancholy which transcends all wit in Dürer's most celebrated engraving. Translate this melancholia into New England theology, it becomes the inwardness, the perpetual dubiety and concern for the symbolical significance of trifles that make the diary of a man like Cotton Mather so curious and remote. A world whose deepest significance lies within is not a world of pictorial splendor, architectural magnificence, colorful theater, or sensuous verse. In America baroque architecture appears only in the Latin colonies; the spare, geometrical lines of our seventeenth century houses are boundaries about a life within, not, as in the case of Spanish-American cathedrals, a reaching outward into the air and the sky. The Spaniards and the Portuguese found theaters, give concerts, produce architects, painters, poets who really rival Camoëns; in North America there are sermons, domestic architecture, the handicraft arts, political controversy, and the most erudite colonial literature the world has ever seen. But the erudition is principally theological and looks within. Life is not an artistic affair, it is sober duty; thrift, industry, carefulness, the qualities of Poor Richard, the economic virtues do not conceal this inwardness. The most characteristic production in stone of New England culture is the tombstone, on which the local cutter engraved an hourglass, a skeleton, or a winged head.

In sixteenth century Europe Protestantism was a fighting faith. In an either-or world there was no room for the tolerant grays of modern latitudinarianism; the century which saw the Massacre of St. Bartholomew was understandably suspicious of mere toleration. To modern readers the harsh, bounding line of any religious faith in the period is repellent and strange. It was, however, as necessary to be clearly and definitely an Anabaptist, a Quaker, a Lutheran, a Calvinist in that epoch as it is today to be definitely a Communist, a Fascist, or a democrat. He who was not for you was against you, and he who was against you was also against God and therefore capable of any wickedness. Elizabethan gentlemen undoubtedly treated Spanish grandees with the courtesies due to class and breeding, and there are records of the polite reception of even Jesuits in seventeenth century New England. We are, however, so bemused by the historical fame of Mrs. Hutchinson, Roger Williams, and other victims or examples of intolerance in an intolerant time that we overlook the darkest heritage of the Reformation in American history—the hatred of the Catholic faith. Not merely were Tudor voyages directed toward defeating Spain; not merely did Elizabeth encourage legends about Catholic plots against her life; but this prejudice also landed at Jamestown, at Plymouth, swarmed up the Shenandoah Valley, ended the well meant experiment of Baltimore in Maryland, and, save for a brief period during and after the American Revolution, still conditions the folkways of "old Americans" in dealing with their newer fellow citizens. It is also an unexpressed assumption of American literary history that Protestantism is intellectually more important than Catholicism, and that, for example, Jonathan Edwards or Emerson is of greater cultural importance than Bishop England of Charleston or Cardinal Gibbons of Baltimore. The United States derives from the Protestant Reformation a *Kulturkampf* like in kind, though not in present intensity, to that of sixteenth and seventeenth century Europe. It is one of the longest-lived and one of the most baffling inheritances to reach us from the sixteenth century world.

It has been already here remarked that the world which brought the first English colonies into being was a strongly masculine world. But among the most important legacies of the Reformation to the United States was the position of women. In the annals of Latin America women figure as poets, as religious mystics, as great ladies in colonial courts; but they figure always within the confines of customs that are both Catholic and Mediterranean. The

Protestant world being both mercantile and middle-class, women were primarily wives and daughters. In American legend Priscilla Alden is seated at her spinning wheel, and the heroic pioneer women engage in domestic economy. In a world without nunneries, without viceregal courts like those in Lima or Mexico, the Virgin was replaced by the mother; and the curious and singular purity of the history of womanhood in the United States is no less a product of the Protestant Reformation than is Woolman's *Journal* or Emerson's Divinity School Address. American culture produced no *belle dame sans merci* (until Hollywood); and it is characteristic of its mores that the first cabinet crisis of its first frontier President, Andrew Jackson, concerned a chivalric defense of Peggy Eaton. In the United States female wickedness comes from France—from, in other words, a Latin and Catholic culture. Classic American literature is without sexuality, but has domesticity; its most serious description of passion is *The Scarlet Letter,* a book taught in the public schools; and when the Protestant imagination of Longfellow finished with anthropological lore, Minnehaha was as properly a bride of Hiawatha as ever Mrs. Lapham was of Silas the paint king. Doubtless the domestic virtues are the middle-class virtues; but in the New World the middle class was originally Protestant, and when we seek the origin of their codes of conduct we are led backward to the world of the Reformation, which, in the name of domestic morality, attacked indulgences and replaced celibacy by the marriage of its prelates. From the point of view of the influence of feminine taste upon culture, the place of women in Protestant domesticity is one of the most important facts in our inheritance from sixteenth century Europe.

By the end of the seventeenth century the English mainland colonies, absorbing every other racial stock settling from Maine to Florida, were launched upon an autonomous cultural life. To the north and west the Catholic French were unabashed and defiant; from Florida and Alabama to the river Plate His Most Catholic Majesty of Spain held sway. Any map of the New World for 1700 shows only a ribbon of coast belonging to the English. If they were later to absorb most of the continent, the long delay allowed them time to adjust to new conditions, to put down roots, to adapt their heterogeneous Old World inheritance to a new environment. They developed colonial education, colonial books, colonial publishing, colonial literary art. Out of this came in time a national culture. The chronicle of this development now follows. It is the history of a complex European inheritance, by slow degrees and ceaseless experimentations becoming so unique a phenomenon that modern transatlantic observers have difficulty in recognizing its Old World roots.

2. COLONIAL LITERARY CULTURE

THE Protestant communities which sprang up in Virginia, New England, and elsewhere in America were much like country towns and villages of England. The people for the most part were hard-working, simple folk without much acquaintance with belles-lettres, and it would have been a miracle indeed if polite literature had suddenly bloomed in the American woods. The truth is that the majority of settlers had little or no literary background. They were a plain people faced with the task of subduing a wilderness.

Though some of the stricter Puritans and Quakers were actively prejudiced against many forms of imaginative literature, which they conceived to be idle and frivolous, they nevertheless placed a high value on certain forms of learning. The Puritans emphasized Biblical and theological learning; the Quakers stressed practical studies which served for the relief of man's estate. The significant fact is that colonial Americans cherished learning even when they did not share it, and in spite of great difficulties they fashioned instruments of culture which made possible a literary development in the eighteenth century.

Frontier conditions are rarely conducive to literary production, and the frontier of the seventeenth and early eighteenth centuries was particularly unfavorable. Some colonies, notably in the South, lacked the means of printing until well along in the eighteenth century. The lack of towns was also a serious deterrent in the South to the development of literary activity. Inspiration may come from vernal woods, but sustained literary production is a characteristic of urban rather than rural environment. Until the colonies along the Atlantic seaboard achieved settled towns, citizens with a modicum of leisure, and the paraphernalia of urbane life—such as schools, libraries, booksellers, lecture platforms, printing presses, and discussion clubs—literature was in abeyance.

But, from the very first, American colonists showed a deep concern lest their children grow up barbarous in the wilderness. This concern was equally great in New England and in Virginia, though the methods of meeting the danger varied with differing conditions. In New England villagers quickly set up schools for their children, and the Puritan fathers in 1636 established Harvard College to insure a learned ministry and provide a nursery of learning for their sons. In Virginia the wealthier planters hired tutors, and the less well-to-do organized plantation schools and shared the expense of a teacher; those who were able sent their sons, and sometimes their daughters, to England for more advanced education. In 1693 Virginians established the College of William and Mary from the same motives that had prompted the founders of Harvard.

By 1760 some cities, particularly Boston and Philadelphia, had excellent grammar schools, and throughout the colonies public-spirited citizens were laboring to increase educational opportunities. Stern Calvinists were convinced that education was necessary to combat the devil, and easy-going deists were equally certain that education was needed to bring about man's perfection. The doctrine of universal educational opportunity, which Thomas Jefferson was to advocate near the turn of the century, was already incipient, and movements were on foot which would transform the ideal of education into something akin to a religious fervor for Americans in the nineteenth century. Before 1760 the colonies could take pride in six colleges which freed them from dependence for higher learning upon the Old World. In addition to Harvard, and William and Mary, these institutions were Yale (1701), the College of New Jersey (1746—later Princeton), King's (1754—later Columbia), and the Charity School in Philadelphia (1740—later the Academy and College of Philadelphia, and eventually the University of Pennsylvania). Vernacular belles-lettres, it is true, had small place in formal education in this period; but classical rhetoric and the prose and poetry of Greece and Rome exerted a profound influence in the development of a literary consciousness.

2

Despite the laborious tasks faced by the earliest settlers, both North and South, they did not entirely neglect the benefits of letters. Indeed, the books which they brought with them were remarkable for their variety and significance, and the importance of little household libraries in the transmission of the literary tradition can scarcely be overemphasized. Seventeenth century inventories show a wide dispersion of books throughout the colonies. Before the end of the seventeenth century Boston had a half-dozen or more booksellers. One of the earliest of these was Hezekiah Usher, who at his death in 1676 left a comfortable fortune made in the book trade. Peddlers often carried books and pamphlets in their packs. Cotton Mather proposed to induce an itinerant hawker to "fill this Countrey with devout and useful

Books"—from Mather's own pen—but complained, years later, that peddlers were corrupting good manners by disseminating ballads and foolish poems. In the tobacco colonies, where local booksellers were virtually unknown, English factors supplied the literary needs of planters. Letters from Virginia and Maryland to merchants in London or Bristol contain frequent requests for specific books, though the planters sometimes asked their factors to send the latest things in the booksellers' stalls and left the choice of titles to the agents' discretion.

The subject matter of the books imported in the seventeenth and eighteenth centuries is indicative of the serious purpose of the colonists. In the broadest sense, their selections were utilitarian, and books designed merely for entertainment or amusement found small place in their household libraries. Picaresque narratives, jest books, ballads, and other literary frivolities were not unknown, it is true; but little money was squandered upon idle reading. This concentration upon "useful" books was as characteristic of Virginia planters as it was of New England Puritans.

Although the New England and the Southern colonists showed differences of emphasis in literary taste, they showed more striking—and perhaps more significant—similarities. The books having the widest circulation before 1760 can be broadly classified as religious and pious. Many of the same religious books were read by Calvinists in the North and Anglicans in the South. Though preachers and some laymen bought and read strictly theological works, the majority of readers preferred less controversial handbooks of piety. Books which had pleased middle-class Tudor and Stuart Englishmen remained standard reading in the colonies for generations. Lewis Bayly's *Practice of Piety* and the sermons of the Reverend William Perkins edified alike merchants and apprentices in Boston and Philadelphia and gentlemen in the region of Chesapeake Bay. Households possessing no other book might have a well thumbed copy of the King James Version of the Bible; a remarkable number had Foxe's *Acts and Monuments*. The appetite of the seventeenth and early eighteenth centuries for pious reading should not be discounted too cavalierly in appraising the cultural development of Americans. Many books of piety were written with a conscious effort at simplicity and clarity to appeal to the understanding of plain men. In such works colonial readers found not only lessons in ethics and good morality but patterns and forms of expression.

Historical works, both classical and modern, were second only to religious literature in the favor of colonial Americans. From Greek and Roman historians, they drew lessons of statecraft as well as facts about the ancient world. Tacitus was a favorite author, for example, and Thomas Jefferson, who read him in his youth, declared later in life that he was the wisest of all writers. Raleigh's *History of the World,* Bishop Gilbert Burnet's *History of the*

Reformation in England, and many another English work entertained and instructed colonial readers.

Books of conduct, instructions in domestic relations, political treatises, legal discussions and handbooks for the amateur as well as the professional lawyer, medical books, and sundry guides to farming, navigation, surveying, and other practical pursuits were among the useful books which colonists bought and treasured.

The most influential writers in the eighteenth century were probably Joseph Addison and Richard Steele. Countless Americans who bought and read the *Tatler* and the *Spectator* could not entirely escape the moral and social lessons which the authors intended. Neither could they avoid being affected by the style. Benjamin Franklin was not the only colonial writer who deliberately imitated the *Spectator* essays.

By the end of the seventeenth century, poetry and drama had come to have a larger place in colonial reading, and the appetite for belles-lettres gradually increased. A few men and women of advanced literary taste dipped into Spenser's *Faerie Queene* and Milton's *Paradise Lost*; considerably more read the poetical works of George Herbert, Francis Quarles, and Abraham Cowley. By the mid-eighteenth century, Shakespeare's plays were frequently found in gentlemen's libraries. By the same period, booksellers had discovered a considerable market for chapbooks, fiction something less than edifying, and other trifling works which serious folk still regarded as frivolous and perhaps iniquitous.

During the seventeenth century most libraries were gathered for the immediate utility to their owners; but by the end of the century book collecting in almost a professional sense had begun. Cotton Mather in Massachusetts and William Byrd in Virginia during the early years of the eighteenth century gathered substantial libraries; and at death each had nearly four thousand volumes divided among the various branches of learning. By 1751 James Logan had gathered in Philadelphia a library of approximately three thousand volumes, which he bequeathed to the city for public use. To the collecting instinct of the Reverend Thomas Prince of Boston, we are indebted for the preservation of many rare books and manuscripts of the period. Many other private libraries of substantial proportions were gathered during the colonial period and helped in the dissemination of learning. Records of book borrowing show that the influence of the private libraries extended far beyond the households of the owners.

Institutional libraries date from the founding of the first colleges. John Harvard's bequest of his books to the college at Cambridge established a library that continued to grow in importance and usefulness. By the middle of the eighteenth century Yale also had a respectable library, and the other colleges had working collections of learned books.

A systematic effort to foster piety and learning by the circulation of books was started near the end of the seventeenth century by the Reverend Thomas Bray, moving spirit in the founding of the Society for the Propagation of the Gospel in Foreign Parts. He devised a plan for sending parish libraries to the colonies for the use of the Anglican clergy and their parishioners. By his efforts it is estimated that approximately thirty-four thousand volumes reached America and were widely distributed, chiefly in regions where Anglicans were most numerous. In 1700 the provincial legislature at Charleston, South Carolina, made Dr. Bray's parochial library a public institution.

Public and semipublic libraries began to develop in the seventeenth century and by 1760 were fairly numerous. A merchant, Robert Keayne, by his will in 1653, established a public library in Boston which in some degree served the needs of the populace for several generations. In 1700 the Reverend John Sharpe, chaplain to the governor, bequeathed his books to found a public library in New York; although this benefaction was augmented somewhat, it made little impression until a group of citizens in 1754 took up a subscription, bought about seven hundred additional volumes, and rejuvenated an institution which eventually grew into the New York Society Library, a proprietary institution. Benjamin Franklin was instrumental in founding the Library Company of Philadelphia, incorporated in 1742 but actually started by subscription some time before. A few years later, in 1747, a merchant, Abraham Redwood, provided funds for the Redwood Library in Newport, Rhode Island; and a year afterward "seventeen young gentlemen" founded the Charleston Library Society in South Carolina. All of these institutions, which still exist, exerted an important influence. Benjamin Franklin, in his pride over the Philadelphia Library Company, wrote in his *Autobiography* that such libraries had made common tradesmen and farmers as intelligent as gentlemen elsewhere and had contributed to the ability of Americans to defend their privileges.

3

Before an indigenous literature could develop in the colonies, an adequate means of printing was essential. Massachusetts led all the other colonies in this endeavor with the press established at Cambridge in 1639 and operated by Stephen Day for the widow Glover. From this press came the Bay Psalm Book, the earliest laws of Massachusetts, and many religious and learned works. Day was succeeded by Samuel Green, whose descendants later carried the art of printing to several other colonies. Before the end of the century the Cambridge press had competitors in Boston, which soon became an important center for New England publishing. There James Franklin had his shop, and there his half-brother Ben learned the craft. After Boston, Philadelphia became the most important printing center, and by the middle of the eighteenth century it had equaled if not surpassed its northern rival. William Bradford, the first printer in Philadelphia, was also responsible for the establishment of a press in New York in 1693.

Printing got under way more slowly in the South, where royal governors took a sour view of printing presses and at first sought to suppress them (if Massachusetts Bay had not been virtually independent of royal interference for most of the seventeenth century, it is certain that the press there would have enjoyed much less freedom). In 1682 William Nuthead attempted to establish a press at Jamestown, Virginia; but he soon became involved with the authorities, and his efforts were suppressed by order of the governor. In 1685 he transferred his activities to the proprietary colony of Maryland. Thereafter no press was attempted in Virginia until 1730, when William Parks came over from Maryland to Williamsburg and set up a print shop. In 1731 three printers working separately tried to start presses at Charleston, South Carolina; but it remained for Lewis Timothy, a partner of Benjamin Franklin, in 1733 to become the first successful printer there.

By 1763 printing was firmly established in each of the thirteen colonies. Although censorship varied from colony to colony and from time to time, printers had achieved considerable freedom by the mid-eighteenth century, and had become potent influences in shaping public opinion. After the beginning of the eighteenth century nearly every printer aspired to be the proprietor of a newspaper, for newspaper publishing—along with the printing of official documents—was regarded as essential to a printer's prosperity.

A writer in the *Gentleman's Magazine,* in November 1796, observed that "the newspapers of Massachusetts, Connecticut, Rhode Island, Pennsylvania, and Maryland are unequaled whether considered with respect to wit and humour, entertainment or instruction." And he added that "every capital town on the [American] Continent prints a weekly paper; and several of them have one or more daily papers." The journalism that excited the admiration of this writer had not suddenly flowered after the Revolution, but had developed over a long period of years. Indeed, newspapers from the mid-eighteenth century onward provided a means of expression which had a far-reaching influence upon the literary, as well as the political, development of the country.

The first newspaper was Benjamin Harris' *Publick Occurrences,* which appeared on September 25, 1690, in Boston and expired four days later when the governor and council "disallowed" its further publication because Harris had presumed to make his venture without permission. The next endeavor of this kind was made in the same city by a cautious Scot, John Campbell, who, in 1704, founded the *News-Letter,* which lasted until the Revolution.

By 1735 Boston alone had five newspapers, and other cities of the Atlantic seaboard were not far behind. By 1750 the colonies were well provided with newspapers, published weekly and in some cases oftener.

Many of the early papers were partly literary in content. James Franklin, for example, mingled poems and humorous pieces with the news items in the *New-England Courant*. The stated purpose of this journal was to be entertaining, amusing, and instructive. Benjamin Franklin contributed anonymously his first literary efforts to his brother's paper. Many another American achieved a brief literary life in the columns of newspapers. Among the more literary papers were the Boston *Evening-Post*, the *Virginia Gazette*, and the *South Carolina Gazette*. The last-named paper published extensive selections from contemporary English authors as well as from the pens of local writers.

Benjamin Franklin and Andrew Bradford founded rival monthly magazines in Philadelphia in 1741, but both periodicals soon collapsed for lack of support. Magazines were to be a later development in American letters. Even earlier, Samuel Keimer, a visionary printer of Philadelphia, had endeavored to give a literary quality to the weekly paper which he founded in 1728 under the title of *The Universal Instructor in all Arts and Sciences: and Pennsylvania Gazette*. Besides attempting to reprint a contemporary encyclopedia, he started the serial publication of Daniel Defoe's *Religious Courtship*. The heavy instructional and literary quality of the paper was too much for Philadelphia, and Franklin bought it for a song the year after its establishment. The new publisher made the *Pennsylvania Gazette* more lively—if less consciously "literary"—and the publication flourished.

Of several attempts to establish foreign-language newspapers during this period, only two achieved success. Christopher Sower and Heinrich Miller published German-language papers, religious in sentiment, at Germantown and Philadelphia respectively.

An event of vast import for the freedom of expression in the colonies was the fight made in 1734–1735 by John Peter Zenger, publisher of the New York *Weekly Journal*, against the persecution by the governor's party. His imprisonment and trial for libel, and his vindication by the jury, made a great stir, not only in New York but in all the colonies, and quickened men's zeal to defend the liberty of speech and press.

4

The tradition of public discussion in the colonies was a strong influence in the training of men's intellects. Long before newspapers gave an outlet for written thoughts, colonial citizens were practiced in self-expression. In the legislative assemblies, political debate was not the exclusive monopoly of the rich and well born. An occasional speech or state paper, preserved in the records of the popular assemblies, is written in vivid and sinewy prose. The town meetings of New England and the political gatherings in the Southern colonies are more famous for their effect upon the development of democratic institutions, but their influence upon literary expression should not be overlooked.

The pulpit, particularly in the seventeenth century, was a forum for learned exposition on religion, ethics, sociology, science, politics, and almost any phase of the life of man. Puritan sermons are amazing in the variety of subjects treated directly or incidentally. Here and there preachers succeeded in putting their thoughts into moving prose; and even though the literary qualities of the clergy have been exaggerated by later historians they at least furnished a pattern of logical reasoning and taught their audiences useful lessons in formal expression. The Puritan clergy of New England were far more influential than ministers elsewhere, but an occasional Anglican clergyman in the middle and Southern colonies furnished intellectual stimulation in his region.

Informal clubs and discussion groups helped to foster literary as well as scientific interest. Most famous was Franklin's Junto in Philadelphia, the later American Philosophical Society, but nearly every town of importance had some sort of discussion club by the mid-eighteenth century.

Religious opposition to theatrical performances was widespread throughout the seventeenth century. Besides a prejudice against plays on moral grounds, a lingering belief among middle-class folk that stage productions were frivolous and wasteful of precious time helped retard theatrical progress. The first professional actors to perform in the colonies presented a play in Charleston in 1703. Within a year of production in London, George Lillo's sentimental drama *George Barnwell* (1731) was published serially in the *New-England Weekly Journal,* which recommended it to readers on the ground that it tended to promote virtue and piety, though Boston censorship forbade dramatic activity in the city for many years to come. Professional companies appeared in New York after 1732, and Philadelphia and Williamsburg witnessed mid-century performances, often written or acted by college students. But on the whole the theater was late in development, and its influence was relatively unimportant in this period.

During the first century and a half of settlement and development, the colonists spent their main energies in practical and utilitarian pursuits, as would be expected in a raw and unexploited continent. Although the colonial contribution to literature was small, these busy settlers salvaged time for intellectual interests and attached great importance to schools, books, libraries, and other influences above and beyond material considerations. The foundation for a later manifestation of remarkable intellectual and literary capacity was laid in the period before 1760.

3. REPORTS AND CHRONICLES

The earliest writing to come from the New World can be called literature only by stretching the meaning of the word. Before the English had settled their strip of coast, men of many nations had explored the continent from Newfoundland to Mexico and from the Atlantic to the Pacific. The records of their adventures, many of them crude and utilitarian, are our first literature. They are letters home, diaries written in the midst of dangerous actions, chronicles compiled while the memory of the actions was still warm. They were written in the languages of the explorers—Spanish, French, Dutch, and the Scandinavian—some were written in or translated into Latin, others English. Some were published at the time, some were excerpted for collections of voyages, some remained in manuscript for centuries. Together they form a body of documents recording one of the great adventures of man, the opening and settling of the western hemisphere. In them, American literature made a cosmopolitan beginning which was narrowed to the Anglo-Saxon cultural tradition only after two centuries. The story of these reports and chronicles is vast and complex; only its main outlines and principal documents can be noted. But unless it is told, our literature would seem more provincial in its origins than it was. The British colonial period was but an episode—a major episode to be sure—in our cultural history.

2

Suppose that one Leif Ericsson did sail west from Greenland about A.D. 1000, and suppose that ten years later one Thorfinn Karlsefne did the same thing—what reports of their adventures exist?

Three manuscripts, the *Flateyjarbók, Hauksbók,* and a document known as A[rna]-M[agnean] 557, which contains the story of Eric the Red, are in the Royal Library at Copenhagen. Written in the thirteenth or fourteenth century, these tell of events which had occurred about four hundred years earlier. They are the oldest extant writings containing traces of the reports on "Vineland"—which may have been anywhere between Labrador and Long Island. What these "sagas" have to tell did not get into print until Adam of

24

Bremen's "Ecclesiastical History" was published in 1595—more than a century after Christopher Columbus got his story into type. These sources have been often republished, translated and reproduced in facsimile, while critical works about them multiply, and authorities continue to agree vaguely, or disagree openly as to what they mean. It may be, indeed it has been said, that the history of America would be precisely the same if no Norseman had ever steered his Viking ship west from Greenland. As reports these manuscripts are not contemporary, and as chronicles they are not trustworthy. They are merely parts of that Scandinavian literature which has occasionally inspired American writers from Longfellow to the present.

3

Spain got a head start with respect to "voyages" to and through the "Newe Worlde." "It is therefore apparent that the heroical facts of the Spaniards of these days deserve so great praise that the author of this book (being no Spaniard) doth worthily extoll their doings." Thus Richard Eden, in his *Decades of the Newe Worlde* (1555), introduced the first collection of "voyages" to the English reading public in its own language. His magnanimity to Spain may have owed something to the fact that the English sovereign was the Catholic Mary who had temporarily forged a bond with Spain's Philip. More than sixty years had elapsed since the first printing of Columbus' own "Epistola" in 1493. Of that book, in which the discoverer published his own story, there were at least seventeen "incunabula editions"—but not one in English.

So let the literary history of the United States begin in Texas. Between 1528 and 1536, Alvar Núñez Cabeza de Vaca, Spaniard, walked across the present area of Texas, New Mexico, and Arizona and wrote a book about his wanderings. His *Relación* appeared in print in 1542, has been translated into many languages, and reprinted in every century since. Colored by the religious zeal of his time, it is not altogether the work of a mere superstitious observer though he lived in a day when impossible wonders found their way into the literature of travel. De Vaca's inaccuracies are gratifyingly few, and he provided the first report on two animals without which American literature would be the poorer: his opossum was to become a character in the writings of Joel Chandler Harris, and what would be the literature of the trans-Mississippi West without the buffalo?

The next "overland narrative" tells of Hernando de Soto, who between 1539 and 1542 marched his Spanish expedition from Florida to North Carolina, thence west to the Mississippi. There his death and dramatic burial in the Father of Waters ended his career. The chronicler of this exploit lives only as "The Gentleman of Elvas," an unknown Portuguese who accompanied De Soto and whose *Relaçam verdadeira* was published in 1557. His work was introduced to the English reading public by Richard Hakluyt (of whom, more, later) as *Virginia richly valued* (1609). Said Hakluyt, quite correctly: "This work . . . though small in show, yet great in substance, doth yeeld much light" upon the immensity of the area and resources of what was to become the United States.

In 1540 Francisco Vásquez Coronado started from Mexico into our Southwest. Searching for the "seven cities of Cibola," Coronado certainly got as far north as the present state of Kansas. His chronicler was Pedro Castañeda, who did not write the full and fascinating "Relación de la jórnada de Cibola" until twenty years after the expedition's return to Mexico. It lay in manuscript (occasionally transcribed by men who had no share in the original work) for more than three hundred and fifty years. Not until 1896 were the Spanish text and a translation into English printed for the first time. Partly because the region explored was sparsely settled (discoveries are still being made there), partly because of the ever-changing place names, and partly because the Southwest was not much exploited by European colonization at the time, the Coronado-Castañeda story has only recently assumed its proper place in the literature of the United States. The expedition was one of the last of those swashbuckling and panoplied raids for God, glory, and gold, wherein Cortez and Pizarro succeeded in Mexico and Peru, but Coronado failed because the gold was not found. The "Conquistador" has persisted in national legend.

Less well known than Coronado is Antonio de Espejo, who roamed the Southwest in 1582 and 1583. His work produced a book in English, the authorship of which is credited to him: *New Mexico: otherwise the voiage of Anthony of Espeio . . . translated out of the Spanish copie printed first at Madreel [Madrid], 1586, and afterward at Paris, in the same yeare* (London, 1587). The modern reader will find the elaboration in Hakluyt's *Voyages,* as these early Spanish and French editions are hard to come by and the English edition survives in a single copy in the Huntington Library; but translations and successive reprintings are some measure of the significance of a book.

4

The first Frenchman who wrote satisfactory reports on what is now the United States was Samuel de Champlain, soldier, explorer, and "Father of New France." He knew how to make bold decisions and to act with dispatch, suggesting a clearheadedness which, in turn, reveals itself in clarity of style. What he saw, he described vividly and in detail. In the 1613 edition of his

Voyages he first reports upon his mapping of New England and his celebrated "battle" with the Iroquois, which had far-reaching effects since it allied the French with the enemies of that all-powerful league. Champlain's powers of description are well illustrated by his reports on such matters as the effects of scurvy and by word pictures (often with engraved maps) such as that of Port St. Louis (Plymouth, Massachusetts). Despite the many printings of his works, it was 1922 before a complete and satisfactory edition in English began to appear; yet many a traveler has followed Champlain's routes, text in hand, and been able to check and verify the accuracy of his observations. The reader of Champlain's *Voyages* may be reminded of Caesar's "Commentaries." Both captains were dealing with a disorganized and semibarbarous foe. As Caesar played off the Gauls against one another, so Champlain allied himself with Algonquins against Iroquois. Both were able to view and to describe their enemies objectively, admiring their meritorious qualities while pointing out less desirable characteristics. Champlain's description of his attack on the Iroquois fort is a miniature of Caesar's siege of Alesia. Both writers seem fascinated by mechanical details, and enjoy describing them. At times a reader is apt to feel that Champlain had a more genuine sympathy for, and understanding of, the American Indians than Caesar ever had toward the Gauls. It is entirely possible, if anything may be inferred from such a comparison of their writings, that Champlain was more deeply and sincerely concerned with the glory of France than Caesar ever was with that of Rome. On the whole, a critic might well conclude that Champlain was the greater of the two. His report of wandering in upper New York State in 1615 appears in the 1627 edition of the *Voyages et decouvertes*. His personal explorations ended in 1616, and the final summing up of all his work appears in his longest and last book *Les Voyages de la Nouvelle France* (1632).

Promotion writing is sometimes literature. The annual reports of a commercial corporation, a government bureau, or a missionary society may be literature if they are well written, and if they are widely read throughout the years for more reasons than the original reporter anticipated. Such is that series which has come to be known as the "Jesuit Relations." They were originally prepared to tell the superiors of the Order what the Jesuit missionaries were doing in New France, to secure financial support, and to inform the pious of the great work "ad majorem Dei gloriam." The Jesuits covered the world, but the expression "Jesuit Relations" has come to designate the group of reports which came from the area of the Great Lakes in the seventeenth century, more particularly between 1632 and 1673 when they were being published by Sébastien Cramoisy in Paris. A substantial part of them recount what was going on in the areas of the present states of New York, Michigan, Illinois, Wisconsin, and Minnesota. The "Relations" tell of the folklore, the mores, the economic condition, and the daily life of an Indian people now practically vanished. They were written by men who combined the physical endurance of the athlete with the scholar's academic training, for these Jesuits had to be, and were, rigidly educated in rhetoric, the humanities, and what would today be called psychology. Although the driving force back of this writing was religious zeal, the intellectual curiosity of these missionary reporters led them to record all sorts of phenomena so that generations of readers have found the "Relations" a source of information in many fields. After enjoying a considerable and significant popularity, the "Jesuit Relations" sank into relative obscurity for two centuries, to be revived in the latter half of the nineteenth century, possibly because of their republication by the Canadian government (1858), the popularity of Francis Parkman's *The Jesuits in North America* (1867), and the publication of the series with translation into English by R. G. Thwaites in seventy-three volumes. The expression "Jesuit Relations" should not be permitted to obscure the fact that these volumes were written by individual authors, many of whom became martyrs to their faith at the hands of the Indians. Any consideration of them should record the names of Paul Le Jeune, Barthélemy Vimont, Jérôme Lalament, Paul Ragueneau, Claude Allouez, Claude Dablon, Jean de Brébeuf—and Jacques Marquette. They were trained men with a thirst for adventure, a zeal for Catholicism, and an unusual ability to express themselves.

A by-product of these writings was the "War of the Orders," the rivalry between the Jesuits and Franciscans (Recollects, in this case). The administrators, explorers, and traders of New France were inclined to favor the Franciscans because they were more tolerant than the Jesuits, particularly with respect to using brandy as legal tender to the Indians. Foremost among these Franciscans is Brother Gabriel Sagard, historian of the Hurons, whose first book appeared in 1632 with a dictionary of the Huron language. His *Histoire du Canada* (1636) sums up his previous works and first accounts for the arrival in the present area of the United States of one Etienne Brulé who probably reached Mackinac and the Sault a year before any Pilgrim got to Plymouth. Father Chrétien le Clercq's *Premier etablissement de la foy dans la Nouvelle France* (1691) is a compilation of original accounts of La Salle's voyages, especially that down the Mississippi, and particularly the writings of Father Zenobius Membré. But the most widely read of these Recollects was Father Louis Hennepin, whose *Description de la Louisiane* (1683) is a more reliable account of his work, particularly in the upper Mississippi Valley, than his subsequent *Nouveau Voyage* (1696)—story of a journey he probably never made but plagiarized from Membré's account in Le Clercq. Although Hennepin's writing is marked by the literary egotism characteristic of his day, his geographical observations and his comments on men and manners are excellent. It may be that something has been lost in the continued reliance upon the seventeenth century English translation. Does "This Calumet is the most mysterious Thing in the world among the Savages" express quite the same thought as "Il faut avouer, que le Calumet est quelque chose de fort mysterieux parmi les Sauvages du Grand Continent de l'Amerique Septentrionale"? Hennepin's books ran to thirty-five variant editions in five languages.

Among these Frenchmen was the charming Baron Louis-Armand Lahontan. While the Jesuits and Recollects were minutely describing the American Indian, Lahontan philosophized about him. The fifty-two editions of Lahontan's *Nouveaux Voyages* (1703), which appeared in five different languages, provide some quantitative measure of his work. A more subtle evaluation of his influence is suggested by a modern critic who has pointed out the significance of Lahontan's "noble savage" Adario. That imaginary Indian describes "man in a state of nature" in a manner which is a perfectly logical outcome of many descriptive writings by the Jesuits and the Recollects in the previous decades. French critics have been the first to point out that Montesquieu and Rousseau drew their inspiration from these French reporters and chroniclers of the Indian in New France, and have suggested that the French Revolution actually takes its origin in Huronia

5

In that seventeenth century when the Thirty Years' War eliminated Central Europe from the colonial game, the maritime nations played for high stakes—overseas. In America, two lost out. Both were Protestant, both apparently had the resources and energy for expansion. Both favored the region between New England and Virginia. But, while failing in North America, the Dutch succeeded in the other hemisphere, whereas the Swedes elected to attack Russia and lost out in the east as well as the west. England displaced both in the river valleys of the east coast of North America.

A Florentine, Giovanni da Verrazano, in the service of France, probably looked in at New York harbor in 1524. But from then until 1609 that water was relatively undisturbed by the white man. Emanuel van Meteren published the first account of Henry Hudson and his *Half-Moon,* which bore the flag of the Dutch West India Company. Said Meteren in 1610: "They reached 40° 45′ where they found a good entrance, between two headlands and entered on the 12th of September into as fine a river as can be found." With this, the Hudson River gets into American literature; but Meteren never came to America—he wrote that simply as a part of his story of the Netherlands. More important is the account given by Robert Juet, an English sailor on the *Half-Moon* whose story appears in 1625 in Purchas' *Pilgrimes*. Better than either is a book published in that year by Johann de Laet. He was himself a director of the West India Company, a learned business man, and an associate of the great publishing house of the Elzevirs with whom, under Abraham of that name, he published his *Nieuwe Wereldt* (1625), the first work devoted solely to these Dutch colonies of which New Amsterdam was only one.

So much for the "North," or "Hudson," River. A reporter of the "South," or "Delaware," River is David Pieterszoon de Vries whose *Korte historiael,* published in 1655, recounts his travels in the "four quarters of the globe"—which seem based on some sort of contemporary journals or notes. He went out to the previously abandoned Dutch settlement at Swanendael (near the present Lewes, Delaware), did a bit of trading, then went to the more promising settlement at New Amsterdam, where his descriptions cover the years 1633 to 1643. As a patroon he displays a natural prejudice in favor of that system and is often critical of the administration of the West India Company. His observations show him to have been a person of energy and ability, with a style that is both quaint and vivid. His book is illustrated by exceedingly well executed etchings on copper (including a portrait of the author), which like the narrative sometimes betray a naïve plagiarism.

A somewhat more reliable volume is Adriaen van der Donck's *Beschry-vinge van Nieuw Nederlant* (1655). The author was a Dutch lawyer who, as a young man, was brought out to manage the finances, particularly to collect the rents, on the patroonship of the great Kiliaen van Rensselaer. He got into difficulties with that worthy because he seemed to understand the point of view of the tenants who could not always meet their obligations. This led to his preparation of the *Vertoogh van Nieu-Neder-Land* (1650), one of the first of a long line of "remonstrances" stating the grievances of the tenant farmers in the Hudson Valley, a line which did not end (if indeed it is yet ended) until the days of the Anti-Rent War in the mid-nineteenth century. Although this book was begun under the approval of Governor Petrus Stuyvesant, van der Donck quarreled with that worthy, and when writing the *Beschryvinge* was refused access to the official records. His work is less a narrative than a description—and a very satisfactory description at that.

The short-lived colony of "New Sweden" follows the usual literary pattern —some books published at the time, and at least one important report which was not fully published until two centuries afterward, yet was drawn upon by later writers. Peter Mårtensson Lindeström, engineer, visited these Swedish settlements on the Delaware, 1653-1654, then returned home and spent the last years of his life compiling his *Geographia Americae* (published 1925). The first detailed chronicle was *Kort beskrifning om provincien Nya Swerige* (1702), by Tomas Campanius Holm. This author never came to America but composed his work from the journals left by his grandfather, Pastor Campanius Holm. The latter was for six years minister to the colony and made a translation of Luther's catechism into the Lenape Indian language that was printed in 1696. Possibly the best of these Swedish chroniclers was Israel Acrelius who was pastor of the church at Christina (Wilmington, Delaware) 1749–1756. His *Beskrifning om . . . Nya Swerige* (1759) is somewhat ecclesiastical but contains a good description of the land and people. Mention should also be made of a curious series of "theses" on America published at the University of Upsala in the eighteenth century, one of which, by Tobias Erick Biörck, may be accounted the first such "dissertation" about Pennsylvania by a native Pennsylvanian (1731).

6

The literature of the British conquest of America owes an inestimable debt to Richard Hakluyt. This scholar, collector, and editor introduced the English-speaking public to the American discoveries by the Cabots, Verrazano, and Ribaut in his slender volume *Divers Voyages* in 1582. Although he has been variously called a geographer and historian, Hakluyt was, above all, a collector of narratives in the time when it was most important to rescue them. In 1589 appeared *The principal navigations, voiages, traffiques and discoveries of the English nation,* a folio volume which through subsequent editions down to 1600 trebled in size. For America the work is supremely important as gathering the then known narratives of what the explorers were finding, and making these first-hand accounts available to posterity. Stylistically the sections are uneven, varying with their authors; but the value of the source material transcends any consideration of literary quality. At his death Hakluyt had a mass of unused material. By good fortune it was bequeathed to one with similar tastes, Samuel Purchas, who carried on the work by publication of his *Hakluytus posthumus; or, Purchas his Pilgrimes* (1625). Purchas used much material that he had himself gathered as well as what Hakluyt had left him. On the whole his editorial work is far less satisfactory than Hakluyt's, but even so posterity is grateful for it.

The first English book on the first English colony in what is now the United States was *A briefe and true report of the new found land of Virginia* (1588) by Thomas Hariot, professor of mathematics at Oxford. He was especially selected by Raleigh to go with the expedition of 1585 to observe and to report. The result was a slim volume which must ever be "Number One" in the literary history of the British colonies which form the present United States. It is an excellent illustration of the fact that a clear and precise thinker can produce an accurate and readable statement. The economic resources of the North Carolina coast, the manners and customs of the Indian inhabitants, and the possibilities for colonization are succinctly set forth. The book was promptly translated into Latin, French, and German and republished. But its pre-eminence in the literature of history lies also in the fact that Raleigh, besides sending out so expert an observer, sent with him an artist, John White, who painted scores of water-color drawings of what he saw. At the same time Theodore De Bry, publisher in Frankfurt-am-Main, conceived the idea of combining the text of discoveries currently being made with illustrations in full-page engravings made from the drawings the explorers were bringing back to Europe. These De Bry produced periodically, somewhat in the manner of the modern *Illustrated London News* or *Life*. The first "part" combined the text of Hariot and the pictures of John White (1590)—and it had to be reprinted at least nineteen times before 1625. The extent to which the Hariot text was borrowed and the White and De Bry pictures were plagiarized by subsequent writers and artists for the next two hundred years is evidence of the widespread influence of the volume. No other English colony in America ever produced anything comparable to it. De Bry did the same thing with René Goulaine de Laudonnière's *L'histoire notable de la Floride* (1586), the tragic history of the Huguenot colony in Florida, conceived by Admiral Coligny, and planted by Jean Ribaut, which ended in a general massacre by the Spaniards. Laudonnière was also accompanied by an artist, Jacques Le Moyne, whose paintings got back to France and were used by De Bry to provide illustrations for his edition of *La Floride* (1592).

Here let a distinction be made between "adventurers" and "planters." The former "adventured" (invested) their money, not their lives, wives, and labor. The latter "planted" homes as well as seed in the soil. The word "plantation" did not connote a lush growth of tobacco, sugar cane, or rice, but was used to characterize so agriculturally unpromising a place as "Providence Plantation." Thus advertising literature, designed to sell an idea to an absentee "adventurer," had to precede such a book as *Advertisements for the unexperienced planters of New England, or anywhere* (London, 1631), the author of which now enters the story.

For the Old Dominion of Virginia, there is, instead of the careful Hariot, that cheerful romancer and valiant soldier, Captain John Smith. The fact that he was "Governour in Virginia" has, rightly or wrongly, overshadowed the fact that he was also "Admirall of New England," and strove for most of the last years of his life to plant a colony farther north than Chesapeake Bay. The puzzle of his writings is well illustrated by the story of Joseph Sabin's *Dictionary of Books Relating to America*. That great work began publication in 1868, and foundered in 1892 when it reached "Smith, John." "Sabin" stayed on the rocks for twenty-six years before a combination of scholars, foundations, and book collectors pulled it off and arranged the works of John Smith in order. Critics and bibliographers alike have spent three hundred years trying to ascertain exactly what John Smith did write, and did publish—and, worse than that, just what he meant. In those Jacobean days writers did not always observe the canons of scholarship current in the twentieth century. If a traveler writing of what he has seen departs from accuracy, he is apt to be checked up and contradicted by some other member of his expedition. Cortez told his own story of the conquest of Mexico and provoked his companion Bernál Díaz to correct him with yet another book. But the curious thing about John Smith is the manner in which his contemporaries ignored rather than contradicted his yarns. Consider the Pocahontas story—and one cannot well avoid it. Smith's own account in 1608 is matter-of-fact. When he retold it in 1624, the story had become gorgeously and glamorously enlarged. Perhaps the 1608 text is history and the 1624 version is literature. Mark Twain characterized this kind of wisdom after the event in a single word: "embroidery." John Smith may have had that adventure with the comely Indian girl, but he does not mention it in his first account, and his companions, Edward Wingfield, Ralph Hamor, and Christopher Newport, did not record it. Then there is the story of the first Church of England service in America. It is told by others besides Smith, but Smith alone gives us a word picture of that rude first Episcopal church, in his *Advertisements for the unexperienced planters,* published in 1631 nearly a quarter-century after the event. One will never know whether his description is correct, but no artist, sculptor, or even dioramist would dare reproduce that memorable scene without putting in the hewn-log seats and the roof of "sayle" cloth, for the existence of which John Smith is the sole authority. Three of his books are "musts": *A True relation of . . . occurrences in Virginia* (1608); *The Generall historie of Virginia* (1624); and *New Englands trials* (1620). His descriptions of what he saw, what happened to him, his narrow escapes, his bad luck, his triumphs, and his unappreciated greatness give us a picture of an egoist who must have been thoroughly delightful if not always reliable.

7

During the seventeenth century a change came over the temper of the pioneers to the New World, and with it a change in their reports and chronicles. After 1607 the attempted settlements of the Atlantic coast began to succeed. The letters and diaries of the seventeenth and eighteenth centuries are records of hardships encountered and overcome, of plans for living that finally worked. Still contemporaneous in their interest, the stories of these permanent settlements—most of them British—become a more immediate part of our literature. They constitute the first step in our cultural tradition in its specific and dominant Anglo-Saxon phase.

Although Champlain described the harbor of Plymouth, it was Captain John Smith who, in 1614, put "Plimouth" on the map in the position it still occupies. Not until six years later came that band of English Separatists who produced and provoked some notable specimens of literature of their own. The first book about the "Pilgrim" colony seems to have been compiled from memoranda sent back by William Bradford and Edward Winslow in the returning *Mayflower*. But because the volume was seen through the press by one George Morton, of the original Scrooby congregation, he was credited with the authorship of *A relation or journall of the beginning and proceedings of the English plantation settled at Plimoth in New England* (1622)—a title so long that the book was at once dubbed "Mourt's Relation." Its importance lies in the facts that, unlike Bradford's own Journal, it was written at the time the events took place, that it contains the only contemporary account of the voyage of the *Mayflower,* and that it tells of what happened in the first few months of the life of the Plymouth colony.

Far better known are two journals: that of William Bradford, perennial governor of Plymouth, and that of John Winthrop, Sr., who was similarly persistent governor of Massachusetts Bay. Both journals remained in manuscript for a long time, Bradford's until 1856 and Winthrop's until 1790. None can deny the simplicity and sincerity of Bradford's literary style, nor the fact that he reveals the Puritan at his best. Winthrop's character was slightly more complex, and he did not always display the Christian charity of his contemporary at Plymouth.

These articulate founders of New England, and others who will be mentioned below, not only were educated gentlemen, but were well educated. Within certain narrowing limits of their religious beliefs, they were able to discern and to think clearly. They were "planting" as well as "adventuring" in a new country in which they proposed to make permanent homes. It was inevitable that they should want to write about what they were doing. To select the more significant of these men and generalize about them and their writings, would betray a lack of understanding. They were individuals and individualists—that is why they came to America in the first place. They displayed in common the pietism of their sect, and they thought in terms of their own consequent concept of the Deity. But it must be remembered that if occasionally they displayed intolerance, they had been the victims of intolerance; if they seemed inhospitable to other emigrants such as Quakers and Catholics, whose views were at variance with their own, this may well have been because the Puritans felt that America was big enough for all and that the dissidents ought to go elsewhere. The heterodox should find other open spaces even if the Puritans had to whip them or imprison them to make that point clear. True, they made a fetish of hard work; but that was not only because these people had work to do in making new homes in a comparatively un- fertile land with a chilly climate, it was also because they genuinely enjoyed hard work.

The language in which they expressed themselves was the language of their day, contemporaneous with the publication of the King James Version of the Bible, and all that that implies with respect to the standardization of literary expression and form. Because the King James Version is still readable, so are these Puritan books.

Although the literature of New England in this period is more fully treated in later chapters, mention should here be made of those reporters and historians whose works first chronicled the process of settlement. A thorn in the side of the serious people at Plymouth was Thomas Morton, "Gent.," who persisted in conducting a rum-and-gun-running house (even worse) at "Merrymount" between Boston and Plymouth. The Plymouth people threw him out bodily twice, whereupon he wrote *New English Canaan* (1637), which had to be printed in Amsterdam. In it he "reports" what was going on from a point of view quite different from that of the patient Governor Bradford who had to handle him. There was not likely to be any agreement with an author who always referred to Myles Standish as "Captain Shrimp."

A very different Morton was Nathaniel of that name, actually one of the original "pilgrim fathers," and a minor politician at Plymouth. He used the unpublished works of Bradford and Winslow in the preparation of his *New-England's memoriall* (1669), and reported from his own knowledge the pains- taking character of the life of his region. More readable is *New Englands prospect* (1634), wherein William Wood describes the natural features of the country with an easy grace and intersperses really meritorious verse in his prose. In contrast is Edward Johnson's *History of New England* (1654), which covers the period 1628–1652, and which he wanted known by its ponderous subtitle "Wonder-working providence of Sion's saviour in New England." This is a homely record of workaday facts to which other chron- iclers are apt to be superior. But to provide such facts was not Johnson's purpose in writing it. His design was to prove that the Deity in person ordained the success of the Bay Colony and that he took a personal interest in such matters as the price of cattle and the accuracy of Myles Standish's aim when shooting at an Indian. The book is revivalistic in style, and the text is garnished with original verse of questionable merit. Better balanced is John Josselyn, who hovered on the border line between herbalist and botanist, and whose *New Englands rarities discovered* (1672) was noticed by the Royal Society. This encouraged him to write *An account of two voyages to New-*

England (1674), which combines scientific lore with hints to settlers and sly digs at the Puritans.

Toward the close of the seventeenth century the colonies had become so firmly established that they had histories to be written. Among the historians whom New England produced, three—William Hubbard, Thomas Prince, and Thomas Hutchinson—wrote about their own day as well as of earlier times. Hubbard was a clergyman, and his *A Narrative of the troubles with the Indians in New England* (1677) is a graphic account of those wars which later came to be associated with the name of the Indian King Philip. Hubbard lived through those struggles, and though one feels that sometimes he agreed with General Sheridan that the only good Indian was a dead Indian he did interpret his own times. A more ambitious work was his *A general history of New-England from the discovery to MDCLXXX,* based on the previous works of Morton and Winthrop. It was not published until 1815, but the manuscript was drawn upon heavily by subsequent historians, notably Cotton Mather and Thomas Prince. Unlike Hubbard—an historian who happened to be a clergyman—Prince was a clergyman who made an historian of himself. He must have been a precocious youngster. He got into print by issuing sermons, which led to his writing an introduction to a life of Cotton Mather, thence to a deep collector's interest in Matheriana and the planning of his ambitious *A chronological history of New-England,* the first volume of which appeared in 1736. In this noteworthy work Prince seems to have outgrown his earlier subject-matter limitations and developed a style which was both lively and fairly objective. But his praiseworthy love for verifying details bogged down his history.

Thomas Hutchinson was a chronicler of a different and far broader experience than these clergymen. He was a cultivated gentleman, a merchant, a lawyer, a man of the world, and Governor of Massachusetts. The first volume of his *The History of the Colony of Massachusetts Bay* appeared in 1764, and although it is rather dull reading today, its reception encouraged him to continue work so as to bring his story down to 1750. His conservative position in the Stamp Act troubles led to disorders wherein his house was invaded by a Boston mob and his papers scattered. Rescuing them the next day from the mud (which may still be seen on the manuscripts) and undeterred by the ill manners of his fellow townsmen, he pushed his second volume to conclusion and wrote with facility and grace on happenings of which he himself had been a witness. On the losing side in the Revolution, he colored his third volume with his prejudices and displayed a failure to appreciate that his world was changing.

When the Dutch yielded New York to the British, two little books appeared which, because of their extreme rarity, are probably less known than they should be. Daniel Denton, a native Long Islander, published in 1670 *A brief description of New York: formerly called New Netherlands*. Since this is the first separate publication in English describing New York, it is noteworthy that the author insists he has "writ nothing, but what I have been an eye witness to all or the greatest part of it" and deliberately cries down the extravagant claims of both the Indians and the Dutch as to the possibilities of the real estate—yet he concludes with a not-too-subtle statement that the poor of the Old World will find haven here. In the next year appeared a tiny volume by the first American minister to have a charge in New York, Charles Wolley. His *A two years journal in New-York* (1701) is worth while if only for his anecdote on how he reconciled the pugnacious Lutheran and Calvinist ministers whom the Dutch had left behind. These two, says Wolley, "behav'd themselves one toward another so shily and uncharitably as if *Luther* and *Calvin* had bequeathed and entailed their virulent and bigotted Spirits upon them and their heirs forever."

Of the many published writings of William Penn, few deal with his great colony. His *Some account of the province of Pennsylvania* (1681) was written before he set sail—yet gives us this phrase: "Colonies are the seeds of nations." His *Frame of Government* (1682) suggests, "Any government is free to the people under it where the laws rule and the people are a party to the laws." This antedates by a century John Adams' adaptation from Jean Bodin, "to the end that it shall be a government of laws and not of men." After Penn reached Philadelphia, he reported to the "Free Society of Traders" in London, by *A letter from William Penn* (1683), a document which is largely descriptive but contains a priceless introductory paragraph in which he gently corrects the reports by his enemies in London about him, and explains that he is not dead and is not a Jesuit. Upon his return to London he published his *Further Account* (1685), wherein he sums up by saying to prospective emigrants, "Be moderate in Expectation, count on Labour before a Crop, and Cost before Gain"—than which no entrepreneur ever gave better advice.

As what Penn had to say about Pennsylvania was the least of his literary output, the investigator must turn to Thomas Budd's *Good order established in Pennsylvania & New Jersey* (1685), a delightful seventeenth century imprint wherein the author tries to summarize the entire book on the title page. Few specimens of colonial promotional literature state so succinctly that the capitalist system will do Christian work and produce 7 per cent:

Taking into consideration the distressed Condition that many Thousand Families lie under in my Native Country, by reason of the deadness of Trade, and want of work, and believing that many that have great Store of Money, that lies by them unimploy'd, would be willing and ready to assist and encourage those poor distressed People, by supplying them with Monies, in order to bring them out of Slavery and Poverty they groan under, if they might do it with safety to themselves, these Considerations put me on writing this small Treatise, wherein I hope . . . that the Rich may help relieve the Poor, and yet reap great Profit and Advantage to themselves by their so doing.

The practical tone of Budd's advice was predominant in all the reports and chronicles, as well as the other literature, of the Southern colonies discussed in the next chapter. Even indentured servants like John Hammond and George Alsop praised the pioneer life in a gay and worldly spirit reflected, in more serious vein, in the histories of Robert Beverley and William Stith. Characteristic of these writers are John Lederer and Thomas Ash.

Tourists of the future will become more and more familiar with the "skyline" drive along the Blue Ridge, Shenandoah Valley, and the Great Smokies, in the back country of Virginia and North Carolina. The earliest reporter of this country was one of whom little is known save his book, *The Discoveries of John Lederer in three several marches from Virginia to the west of Carolina* (1672). Lederer introduced the geology, botany, and native inhabitants to the English-reading world. Of German origin, he wrote in Latin, whence his book was rescued by a member of the Virginia "Council" and translated into English because the author was "a modest ingenious person, and a pretty scholar." There is reason to think that Lederer was first to climb the Appalachian Divide and look over into what was to become the Middle West.

For writing that is picturesque one turns to Thomas Ash who, as "T. A." in *Carolina* (1682), describes the synthesis of the elements of the social history of the region. Noteworthy among these are two derivatives of corn: hominy and a beverage wherein the corn is treated "by Maceration, and when duly feremented, a strong spirit like *Brandy* may be drawn off from it, by the help of an *Alembick.*" Both Ash and Governor John Archdale, whose *A new description . . . of Carolina* appeared in 1707, are careful writers within the limits of the scientific knowledge of their day. Archdale betrays the fact of his previous residence in the Bible commonwealths to the north when he suggests that it "pleased Almighty God to send unusual sicknesses amongst" the Indians since, in order to make room for the white man, "there seemed a Necessity of thining the barbarous *Indian* Nations." Yet he has misgivings and comforts himself with the assurance that the English colonists "in comparison to the Spaniard, have but little *Indian* Blood to answer for."

Thus the discovery, opening, and settlement of the continent was recorded by those who took part in the adventure. There is the charm of the primitive, not only in the expression but in the format of these old books. But their principal appeal lies in the fact that they present the feelings of the man who was there at the time the event took place and not what some later interpreter, however learned, may have felt. If the "end of all scribblement is to amuse," there are those who are entertained by these efforts at expression on the part of many a stout Cortez who was not content to remain silent upon a peak in Darien.

4. WRITERS OF THE SOUTH

THE earliest literature of the permanent English settlements came from the Southern colonies and was, for the most part, descriptive and factual, concerned in some fashion with the land itself. Less introspective than the Puritans of New England, the writers of the agrarian South turned their attention to the world outside their doors. Though verse writers frequently were imitators of conventional themes in poetry, a few devoted their efforts to describing their own milieu, sometimes satirically, but with attention to external life in the colonies. Southern writers of prose and poetry rarely, if ever, wrestled with their souls in the manner of Cotton Mather; to most of them, the exposure of one's innermost thoughts and feelings would have seemed indecent. Even when, like William Byrd of Westover, they kept diaries, they were more reticent about their thoughts than about their behavior; and their meditations were more often upon politics and social relations than upon metaphysics.

To its London readers the Reverend Alexander Whitaker's *Good News from Virginia* (1613) described an earthly paradise. In Virginia men might live in ease supported by the fruitfulness of the soil and take their pleasure in sport which the Creator provided, for the woods abounded in wild turkeys, swift as greyhounds, and with pigeons, ducks, geese, partridges, and other game birds, and the rivers teemed with the finest fish: "Shads of a great bigness, and rockfish . . . trouts, bass, flounders, and other dainty fish . . . [and] multitudes of great sturgeons, whereof we catch many." The author vouches for the abundance of the fish which he himself had caught— "with mine angle." Therefore, he advises his readers, "since God hath filled the elements of earth, air and waters with his creatures, good for our food and nourishment, let not the fear of starving hereafter, or any great want, dishearten your valiant minds from coming to a place of so great plenty." If Whitaker's book stirred the hopeful imaginations of Englishmen to contemplate the virtues of the New World, that was his intention. And that, indeed, was the purpose in one way or another of much of the writing in the colonial South.

The first strictly literary work, however, was an exception to this most characteristic type of colonial writing, for it linked the New World with the great cultural past and was prophetic of that interest in the classics which the educated groups in the colonies retained and fostered for many generations. The work was Ovid's *Metamorphoses,* translated into English verse by George Sandys, son of the Archbishop of York and brother of Sir Edwin Sandys, the noble-spirited secretary of the Virginia Company of London. Sandys came to Virginia in 1621 and remained seven years, taking an active part in the colony's administration and defense.

The more cultivated members of the colonial ruling class inherited something of Sandys' zeal for the classics. This tradition, a legacy of the Renaissance more evident in the reading and in the oratory of Southerners than in their literary productions, helped to modify and transmute some of the materialism which frontier conditions induced. Generations later, colonial gentlemen read Sandys' Ovid as they read another of his works, *A Paraphrase upon the Psalms of David* (1636), and they approved of both.

The contrast between the classical interests of Sandys and the literal record of Whitaker provides a revealing introduction to the study of Southern colonial writers. The same contrast is to be found in the person of the master of Westover, William Byrd the younger, most representative Southern colonial writer. A man of means and learning, he collected perhaps the finest private library of colonial times; but his own writing is a record of his life on his plantation and on his surveying expeditions into the interior. The Southern books that have come down to us from these early days are concerned with the things of this world rather than of the next. Behind Thomas Jefferson's *Notes on Virginia* (1784) there is a tradition of scientific, descriptive, and promotional literature unequaled in the colonies to the north.

2

To defend both Virginia and Maryland from traducers, John Hammond in 1656 published in London a little tract entitled *Leah and Rachel, or, the Two Fruitful Sisters, Virginia and Maryland: Their Present Condition, Impartially Stated and Related.* Hammond had lived for nineteen years in Virginia, he tells us, and for two years in Maryland, until dissensions during the Cromwellian period forced him to flee to England. This pamphlet, written after his arrival, describes nostalgically the goodness of the land in the Chesapeake region, where men and women can live in ease and plenty. By contrast England is an abode of misery. "And therefore I cannot but admire," Hammond declares, "and indeed much pity the dull stupidity of people necessitated in England, who rather than they will remove themselves, live here a base, slavish, penurious life, . . . choosing rather than they will forsake England to stuff Newgate, Bridewell, and other jails with their car-casses, nay cleave to Tyburn itself." Like Crèvecœur more than a century later, Hammond vividly emphasizes the opportunities of the new life in America, where everything is inviting, a country "not only plentiful but pleasant and profitable, . . . pleasant in . . . the brightness of the weather, . . . pleasant in their building, . . . pleasant in observing their stocks and flocks of cattle, hogs, and poultry, grazing, whisking, and skipping in their sights, pleasant in having all things of their own, growing or breeding with-out drawing the penny to send for this and that, without which, in England, they cannot be supplied."

A few serpents had invaded that Eden, notably Maryland, and Hammond is emphatic in his distaste for troublemakers, particularly one of the leaders of a turbulent faction, Will Claiborne, "whom ye all know to be a villain." The earlier tract, *Hammond versus Heamans, or, An Answer to an Auda-cious Pamphlet, Published by an Impudent and Ridiculous Fellow Named Roger Heamans* (1655), was a vigorous but less literary diatribe against the ship captain who had espoused the cause of rebels against the government and had helped to drive Hammond himself out of Maryland.

The most vigorous and original work of the middle decades of the seven-teenth century was George Alsop's *A Character of the Province of Maryland*, printed in London in 1666. The author, who had served four years as an indentured servant in Maryland, wrote in stout defense of life in that colony, even the life of a servant, which he found far pleasanter and more promising than the drudgery and the hopeless poverty of England.

Alsop's descriptions, written in colorful and idiomatic prose, have the rhythms of the Elizabethans and their zest for the world about them. His style is not unlike that of Thomas Dekker's pamphlets. With a boisterous humor that is sometimes coarse but never dull, he tells about the country and its customs, the Susquehannock Indians, and the mutual benefits of trade between England and Maryland. At the end of the book are several letters written to friends and kinsmen about his voyage to the New World and his experiences there. Occasionally Alsop inserts a poem, displaying an ease of versifying and a quality not often encountered among early writers in the colony.

That Alsop is a man of some cultivation appears from his literary allusions. He has read the prose of Dr. John Donne, and, when ill and threatened with death, he quotes from a sermon by the learned dean and includes a philo-sophic observation: "We are only sent by God of an errand into this world, and the time that's allotted to us for to stay is only for an answer. When God, my great Master, shall in good earnest call me home, which these warnings tell me I have not long to stay, I hope then I shall be able to give him a good account of my message."

Like certain Cavalier poets, Alsop's muse requires no theme of vast importance. When someone sends him a purple cap he lets his imagination range on the possible uses of this piece of velvet headgear. Perhaps it once graced Oliver Cromwell's head, which, Alsop is pleased to note, has lately been hoisted on Westminster's roof:

> Say, didst thou cover Noll's old brazen head,
> Which on top of Westminster'[s] high lead
> Stands on a pole, erected to the sky,
> As a grand trophy to his memory?
> From his perfidious skull didst thou fall down,
> In disdain to honour such a crown
> With three-pile velvet? Tell me, hadst thou thy fall
> From the high top of that cathedral?

Elsewhere in prose and verse, he is equally disdainful of Puritans and their kind. For example, he attributes the ready market of Maryland's pork with ship captains of New England to the stiff Calvinists' need for some kind of softening, "because their bodies being fast bound up with the cords of restrigent zeal, they are fain to make use of the liniments of this non-Canaanite creature physically to loosen them."

Alsop's little book reads less like a promotional tract than most of the descriptive works written in the colonies. He gives the impression of sincerity and truth in his descriptions, as in the passage defending the system of indentured servitude. Those who cannot pay their passage to Maryland, he writes, "may for the debarment of a four years' sordid liberty go over to this province and live there plenteously well. And what's four years' servitude to advantage a man all the remainder of his days, making his predecessors happy in his sufficient abilities, which he attained to partly by the restrainment of so small a time?"

Most of the descriptive prose of the early eighteenth century was less boisterous than Alsop's. Typical of a long series of such works was *The Present State of Virginia and the College* (1727), prepared by a committee of Virginians consisting of Henry Hartwell, James Blair, and Edward Chilton, who presented their report to the Board of Trade in London on October 20, 1697. The author of the portion describing the College of William and Mary was that institution's founder, the Reverend James Blair, an irascible Scot, who as "commissary" of the Church of England was the Bishop of London's personal representative in Virginia. He labored unceasingly to make the College of William and Mary a nursery of Anglican clergymen, and he was the author of a popular series of homilies entitled *Our Savior's Divine Sermon on the Mount,* five volumes, published in London in 1722. A second edition was called for before the author died in 1743, and the work attracted so much attention that it was translated into Danish and published in Denmark in 1761.

By the end of the seventeenth century, settlers in the oldest English colony were beginning to feel a maturity not yet manifest in the newer colonies. Writers began to display an incipient nationalism, a loyalty to the new land as their native region. An anonymous Virginian published in London *An Essay upon the Government of the English Plantations on the Continent of America* (1701) and in place of his name proudly subscribed on the title page the words "By an American." Some evidence suggests that the writer was Robert Beverley, or perhaps his father-in-law, William Byrd the elder. Certainly it was some member of the Beverley-Byrd group of planters. The tract is an earnest and clearly written plea for more intelligent understanding and administration by the colonial authorities in England, and it makes one of the earliest proposals of a plan of union for the English colonies.

Robert Beverley exhibited an originality and self-conscious pride in his Virginia origins that sometimes irritated his contemporaries, especially his socially ambitious brother-in-law, William Byrd the younger, who was pleased to hang the walls of his house at Westover with portraits of English noblemen. In 1705, a London bookseller brought out *The History and Present State of Virginia . . . by a Native of the Place.* On a handsomely engraved frontispiece, Beverley acknowledged the authorship with his initials. Writing with humor, and occasionally with biting sarcasm, he did not spare the feelings of his contemporaries. He was sharply critical of various royal governors, particularly Francis Nicholson, and he ridiculed the lack of enterprise of his fellow planters who had become utterly dependent upon tobacco and the English market. He also suggested somewhat satirically that his fellow Virginians would have been better off if they had followed John Rolfe's example and had intermarried with the Indians. Although the historical narrative for the early years is largely derivative from Captain John Smith and other chroniclers, the sections dealing with the Indians and with contemporary observations are an important contribution to history.

In 1722, the year of his death, Beverley finished and published a revision of the *History* which omitted the acerbities of the earlier version. The second edition, reprinted in the nineteenth century, is less colorful but more charitable. The *History* was translated into French and had four printings on the Continent by 1718. Beverley had written his book with one eye on prospective immigrants, especially French Huguenots, and he must have been pleased at its popularity abroad. It is an early instance of how the patronizing tone of British writers on the colonies could stir the "native" pride to reply.

3

The writer from the Southern colonies best known today is William Byrd the younger, author of the *History of the Dividing Line,* and of an extensive diary lately discovered and published. The son of one of the wealthiest planters in Virginia, Byrd received an English education and while a student of law at the Middle Temple cultivated the acquaintance of literary and social lions. A familiar friend of Wycherley and Congreve, he played with the idea of being a man of letters and wrote dainty or satirical verses, some of which found their way into an English miscellany. Since scientific speculation at the turn of the seventeenth century was both fashionable and appealing, Byrd determined to make himself a man of learning and a virtuoso in science. Flattered by an invitation to join the Royal Society, he submitted a paper describing an albino Negro and for the rest of his life prized his status as a corresponding member of the Society. Although Byrd was called back to Virginia in 1704 on the death of his father, he later spent considerable time in England as agent for the colony, and until the day of his death in 1744 he corresponded with titled and learned friends in the mother country.

His diary indicates a methodical devotion to classical learning; he is careful to record the daily reading of Greek, Latin, or Hebrew, interspersed with an occasional effort at literary translation. A free rendering of the tale of the Matron of Ephesus from the *Satyricon* survives. He also continued to write verses, a few of which are in existence, and he turned his hand to science and mathematics. Fancying himself something of an amateur in medicine, he dosed his household and neighbors when opportunity offered, and wrote *A Discourse Concerning the Plague with Some Preservatives Against It* (London, 1721). This forty-page pamphlet is the only complete work from Byrd's pen known to have been published in his lifetime.

Byrd's diary, kept in shorthand, probably through most of his adult life, is a significant and revealing document with occasional glints of humor. Three portions are known, two of which are now in print. The Virginia Historical Society, which owns a section covering the years 1717-1721, has declined to permit its publication. In this suppressed part Byrd describes with Pepysian frankness his amatory adventures in London, where he pursued without discrimination whores, chambermaids, and great ladies. Most of his diary, however, concerns the matter-of-fact and fairly decorous existence of a man intent upon maintaining his classical learning, managing his estates successfully, and fulfilling his responsibilities to the commonwealth.

Byrd's most important literary contribution is the *History of the Dividing Line Run in the Year 1728,* a narrative of the boundary survey between Virginia and North Carolina in which he commanded the party of Virginians. Although he was clearly ambitious to be regarded as a man of letters, he preferred to pursue his avocation in the genteel manner, without rushing precipitately into print. From a journal kept during the survey, Byrd made a draft of his well known narrative which he called *The Secret History of the Line*. This version, which contained fictitious names of the participants, the author revised, expanded, and polished; but he never brought himself to publish the finished text. Not until 1841 was any version of the narrative printed, though manuscript copies had circulated among Byrd's friends and had attracted their favorable attention, as did two shorter works, *A Journey to the Land of Eden, Anno 1733* and *A Progress to the Mines in the Year, 1732*.

These are all spirited narratives. Writing with the zest of youth and the maturity of a man of the world, Byrd conveys to the reader some of his own adventurousness and commands attention with his shrewd observation and commentary. He spices his story with humor, as in the passage describing the laziness of North Carolinians encountered in the back country:

They make their wives rise out of their beds early in the morning, at the same time that they lie and snore, till the sun has risen one-third of his course, and dispersed all the unwholesome damps. Then, after stretching and yawning for half an hour, they light their pipes, and, under the protection of a cloud of smoke, venture out into the open air; though, if it happens to be never so little cold, they quickly return shivering into the chimney corner. When the weather is mild, they stand leaning with both their arms upon the cornfield fence, and gravely consider whether they had best go and take a small heat at the hoe: but generally find reasons to put it off till another time. Thus they loiter away their lives, like Solomon's sluggard, with their arms across, and at the winding up of the year scarcely have bread to eat. To speak the truth, it is a thorough aversion to labor that makes people file off to North Carolina, where plenty and a warm sun confirm them in their disposition to laziness for their whole lives.

4

The defense of North Carolina, its products and its native people, was undertaken by John Lawson, a Scottish adventurer who landed at Charleston in 1700 and became surveyor-general of the colony. First published in London in 1709 as *A New Voyage to Carolina,* it is generally referred to as *The History of Carolina* from the title given to the second edition of 1714. Lawson's book, a brisk and readable account from first-hand observation, achieved considerable popularity. A third English edition appeared in 1718, and it was translated into German and published in Hamburg in 1712 and

1722. Like Beverley's *History*, it served as propaganda for immigration to the Southern colonies. "'Tis a great misfortune," Lawson observes in the preface, "that most of our travellers who go to this vast continent in America are persons of the meaner sort, and generally of a very slender education . . . uncapable of giving any reasonable account of what they met withal in these remote parts, tho' the country abounds with curiosities worthy a nice observation. In this point, I think, the French outstrip us." To correct the balance, Lawson expanded the journal of his travels; but he warns the reader that he has aimed at truth and accuracy instead of entertainment, "which is, indeed, the duty of every author and preferable to a smooth style accompanied with falsities and hyperboles."

The most readable part of his narrative is the description of the Indians and their customs, which attributes to them, particularly the women, many attractive qualities, albeit a lack of inhibitions shocking to a Puritan but not to John Lawson. Of a companion of his travels whose fair comrade of the night made off with her lover's shoes and personal possessions, Lawson remarks, "Thus early did our spark already repent his new bargain, walking barefoot in his penitentials like some poor pilgrim to Loretto."

Lawson's earthly and literary career was cut short in 1711 by these self-same Indians. In company with the Baron de Graffenried, a Swiss promoter of colonization, he made another journey into the hinterland and was captured by the savages, who put him to death. De Graffenried escaped to tell the tale and blame Lawson's rashness for the catastrophe.

The chief literary monuments during the remainder of the colonial period were descriptive histories or narratives. The Reverend Hugh Jones, professor of mathematics at the College of William and Mary, the author of the first American grammar of the English language, published in 1724 *The Present State of Virginia,* a brief factual account, which announced on the title page that the book was designed "for the service of such as are engaged in the propagation of the gospel and advancement of learning, and for the use of all persons concerned in the Virginia trade and plantation." Jones' book is simple and clear without any effort at rhetorical adornment.

The most voluminous historical work in the Southern colonies up to its time was William Stith's *The History of the First Discovery and Settlement of Virginia: Being an Essay towards a General History of this Colony* (Williamsburg, 1747). Stith's 331 pages of small type brought the narrative of Virginia down only as far as 1624. Though his detailed account of Virginia's early history proved tedious to the busy master of Monticello, the work exemplifies a new ideal of historical investigation and a zeal for accurate research hitherto unknown in the American colonies. His preface is a readable and significant landmark in the story of American scholarship, and the main body of the text is far from deserving Jefferson's censure. Like more recent historians, Stith found much to commend in Captain John Smith's own observations, but lamented the confusion of his work and deplored the inattention to documentary evidence displayed by Smith's successors. "And I can further declare with great truth," he says, "that had anything of great consequence been done in our history, I could most willingly have saved myself the trouble of conning over our old musty records, and of studying, connecting, and reconciling the jarring and disjointed writings and relations of different men and different parties."

Stith's uncle, Sir John Randolph, had contemplated an account of the development of the government of Virginia, and had collected many records and public documents which at his death he left still unused. Furthermore, William Byrd, who had procured a manuscript copy of the records of the Virginia Company, made this document available and encouraged Stith to pursue his research. "Neither could I well excuse myself," Stith comments, "if I did not likewise acknowledge with what humanity and politeness that well-bred gentleman and scholar not only communicated those manuscripts to me, but also threw open his library (the best and most copious collection of books in our part of America) and was himself ever studious and solicitous to search out and give me whatever might be useful to my undertaking." Stith's history, which he intended to continue to a later period, was an example of the newly awakened American point of view. For example, his interpretation of King James' interference with the Virginia Company as the machinations of a hostile tyrant—a view which grew ever more congenial under the mistakes of the Georges—became the traditional explanation until our own time.

Somewhat akin to the historical and descriptive narratives was a brilliant satire and an exposé of conditions in Georgia by a group of disgruntled enemies of the founder, General James Oglethorpe. Their tract, *A True and Historical Narrative of the Colony of Georgia* (1741), was published in Charleston, South Carolina. The authors—who announced themselves on the title page as Patrick Tailfer, M.D., Hugh Anderson, M.A., David Dougles, "and others"—had taken refuge there after antagonizing Oglethorpe's agent in Georgia. Prefaced by a dedication of mock deference to Oglethorpe, the book calmly and devastatingly ridicules the vanities and weaknesses of the philanthropist. Jonathan Swift himself need not have been ashamed of the satirical skill demonstrated in the dedication. After referring to the generous governments of certain colonies and the prosperity which commerce had brought, the authors comment that "your Excellency's concern for our perpetual welfare could never permit you to propose such transitory advantages for us. . . . You have afforded us the opportunity of arriving at the integrity of the primitive times by entailing a more than primitive poverty on us. The toil that is necessary to our bare subsistence must effectually defend us from the anxieties of any further ambition. . . . The valuable virtue of humility is secured to us by your care."

Among the grudges which the authors held against Oglethorpe were his injunctions against Negro slavery and the importation of rum. Although promotional tracts had lavished hyperboles on the wholesomeness of the air and water in the colony, they thought a little rum would be a benefit to health, for "the experience of all the inhabitants of America will prove the necessity of qualifying water with some spirit." They were particularly hostile toward John Wesley, whose residence in the colony had encouraged such "attendances upon prayers, meetings, and sermons" as to "propagate a spirit of indolence and of hypocrisy amongst the most abandoned" who by a show of religion managed to live in ease from the public stores.

Although the tract is plainly partisan, its authors display an urbane cultivation, a familiarity with contemporary literature, and a detachment unusual in eighteenth century controversial writings. That its barbs went home is evident from a solemn defense made by the Reverend William Best in a sermon before the trustees for the colony of Georgia, entitled *The Merit and Reward of a Good Intention* (London, 1742)

5

The muse of poetry inspired few Southerners in the colonial period to write from their hearts about their own world. When they wrote verse, the most formalized type of composition, they became self-conscious and imitative. Rarely could they escape the diction, the manner, the style, or the themes of the reigning dictators of poetry in England. Dryden and Pope had their slavish and uninspired disciples on the banks of the James, as well as the Thames. Even incipient democracy was sung in formal measures in the Southern colonies.

The verse with which George Alsop decorated his prose account of seventeenth century Maryland demonstrates that indentured servants were often men of considerable schooling. It is possible that another indentured servant was the author of one of the noblest poems of this period. The rebellion in 1676 of Nathaniel Bacon against Sir William Berkeley, governor of Virginia, inspired both a narrative tribute and a poetic one, which are preserved in a manuscript usually called the Burwell Papers (published 1814). The unknown prose narrator, clearly no partisan of Bacon's, inserted the poem at the conclusion of a passage recounting the rebel's death. The elegy ends:

Mars and Minerva both in him concurred
For arts, for arms, whose pen and sword alike
As Cato's did, may admiration strike
Into his foes; while they confess withal
It was their guilt styl'd him a criminal.
Only this difference does from truth proceed:
They in the guilt, he in the name must bleed.
While none shall dare his obsequies to sing
In deserv'd measures until time shall bring
Truth crown'd with freedom, and from danger free
To sound his praises to posterity.
   Here let him rest; while we this truth report;
He's gone from hence unto a higher court
To plead his cause, where he by this doth know
Whether to Caesar he was friend or foe.

Such praise was certain to bring forth an answer, and another unknown writer replied with a poem beginning:

Whether to Caesar he was friend or foe?
Pox take such ignorance, do you not know?
Can he be friend to Caesar that shall bring
The arms of Hell to fight against the King?

Thus in the midst of civil war and Indian forays, men of action could take time to express their emotions in verse that had a depth of feeling and sometimes a grace and ease of diction. Clearly the wilderness of Virginia was far from destitute of literary talent, though few examples have survived.

More in the realistic tradition of Southern colonial writing is a boisterous satire, *The Sot-Weed Factor* (London, 1708), which took for its subject of ridicule the contemporary scene in Maryland. Unfortunately for American literature, its author, who signed himself Ebenezer Cook, declared that he was an Englishman.

Condemn'd by Fate to wayward curse
Of friends unkind and empty purse,

he had been obliged to make a dismal voyage to a rude and ribald land. Twenty-one quarto pages of couplets relate the poet's unhappy adventures in Maryland, where he tried to set up as a tobacco merchant but was roundly cheated by the inhabitants. With his last lines he curses the country:

May wrath divine then lay those regions waste
Where no man's faithful nor a woman chaste.

Belles-lettres in Maryland and Virginia found a fresh stimulation after the arrival of William Parks, the printer, who by the spring of 1726 had established a press at Annapolis, and by 1730 had opened a printing shop in Williamsburg. Parks was more than a printer. He had literary taste and a flair for journalism. In 1736 he established the *Virginia Gazette,* which opened its columns to ambitious poets and essayists. They responded with an assortment of occasional verse and miscellaneous commentary.

The most important poetical work to issue from Parks' Annapolis press was *The Mouse-Trap, or the Battle of the Cambrians and Mice* (1728), a translation by Richard Lewis of Edward Holdsworth's Latin poem *Muscipula,* satirizing the Welsh. Lewis, who served as a schoolmaster in Annapolis, displayed a genuine talent for versification, and a learning which would have been a credit to Augustan London. His verse dedication to Governor Benedict Calvert concludes:

> Yet—hear me!—while I beg you to excuse
> This bold intrusion of an unknown muse;
> And if her faults too manifest appear
> And her rude numbers should offend your ear,
> Then, if you please with your forgiving breath,
> Which can reprieve the wretch condemn'd from death,
> To speak a pardon for her errors past,
> This first poetic crime shall prove her last.

Governor Calvert encouraged the translator by heading a list of one hundred and fifty Marylanders who subscribed for one or more copies of the book. Lewis was the author of a few later poems, but the translation was his most ambitious undertaking. His preface in prose to that work is an urbane, polished, and learned bit of literary criticism, worthy of an Elizabethan courtly scholar.

Two years after the publication of *The Mouse-Trap,* the Annapolis press issued *Sotweed Redivivus, or the Planter's Looking-Glass,* by E. C. Gent. [Ebenezer Cook?] (1730), written in obvious imitation of the earlier satire, *The Sot-Weed Factor,* which had proved popular; but the new work lacked the vigor and the robust humor of the original. The following year Parks brought out a volume bearing the hopeful title of *The Maryland Muse,* which, in addition to a versified account of Bacon's Rebellion, included a third edition of *The Sot-Weed Factor.*

Fittingly William Parks chose to publish as one of his first labors at Williamsburg, J. Markland's *Typographia, an Ode on Printing* (1730). With a panoply of classical allusion, Markland praises King George and Governor Gooch, and then pays tribute to Parks, the printer:

From whom Virginia's laws, that lay
In blotted manuscripts obscur'd,
  By vulgar eyes unread,
Which whilom scarce the light endur'd,
Begin to view again the day,
  As rising from the dead.
For this the careful artist wakes,
And o'er his countless brood he stands,
  His numerous hoards
Of speechless letters, unform'd words,
Unjointed questions, and unmeaning breaks,
  Which into order rise, and form, at his command.

If Markland's ode has no great originality it at least displays able craftsman-ship in a genre popular in the age of Pope.

Governor Gooch, to whom Markland dedicated his ode, was himself a man of no mean skill in letters. To popularize a new law regulating the inspection of tobacco, he wrote in spirited prose and had Parks publish *A Dialogue Between Thomas Sweet-Scented, William Oronoco, Planters, and Justice Love-Country, Who Can Speak for Himself* (1732). For lightness of touch and humor, Gooch's piece of propaganda surpassed the usual work of this type.

The Williamsburg press brought out in 1736 *Poems on Several Occasions,* by "a Gentleman of Virginia." The unnamed author was William Dawson, a graduate of Queen's College, Oxford, and professor of moral philosophy at the College of William and Mary who later became its president. Daw-son's statement in his preface that "the following pieces are the casual pro-ductions of youth" is confirmed by the quality of the poems. No verse in the volume shows the slightest glimmer of inspiration from the New World. Though Dawson's poems are not without skill, they can hardly be described as contributions to American literature, for they were most certainly written before he took up residence in Virginia.

A somewhat better claim for a small niche in the annals of American letters can be made for James Sterling, Anglican rector of St. Paul's Parish, in Kent County, Maryland. An Irishman who had already achieved a mod-est reputation in Dublin as a playwright and poet, Sterling is believed to be the author of an anonymous poem, *An Epistle to the Hon. Arthur Dobbs, Esq. in Europe, From a Clergyman in America* (London, 1752). This work in sixteen hundred lines is a display of patriotic verbosity glorifying the promoter of a voyage in search of the Northwest Passage. Other poems attributed to Sterling appeared in the *American Magazine* between October, 1757, and October, 1758. These ranged from "A Poem, On the Invention of

Letters and the Art of Printing" to "The Royal Comet," praising the King of Prussia as the champion of Protestantism. Sterling's muse inspired him to fluency rather than depths of feeling.

6

By the mid-eighteenth century, the Southern colonies had developed a considerable literary activity, thanks largely to the establishment of local printing presses and newspapers which gave an outlet. Much of the writing was far removed from belles-lettres, but it illustrated the needs and interests of the people. The argument over inoculation for smallpox, for example, precipitated a controversy in 1739 between James Killpatrick and Dr. Thomas Dale, which Lewis Timothy chronicled in pamphlets from his press in Charleston, South Carolina. Doctors in Virginia and Maryland likewise published their observations on various diseases in books which are of considerable interest for the history of American medicine, if not for literary history. Religious disputes often resulted in the publication of controversial sermons. George Whitefield's evangelical tour of South Carolina aroused the ire of Dr. Alexander Garden, rector of St. Philip's in Charleston, and called forth an exchange of letters between the two which Peter Timothy duly published in 1740. Three years before, Lewis Timothy had advertised an edition of hymns and psalms by John Wesley, earlier by nearly a year than Wesley's first London edition. Some of the most interesting bits of writing are to be found in old private letters, which now and then exemplify literary skill. Though they usually wrote about business, an occasional letter of William Fitzhugh or Robert Carter of Corotoman in Virginia, or of Eliza Lucas Pinckney of South Carolina, reads like a little essay on some theme of intrinsic interest.

The growth of an interest in belles-lettres was diverted after the middle of the century by the gathering storm of controversy over the colonies' relation to the mother country. From 1750 onward there was an increasing flood of political writing, and by 1760 literary effort was already being translated into the kind of oratory, satirical verse, and polemics which would occupy such a large place in the intellectual activities of the Southern colonies in the Revolutionary period. For those activities, the substantial and circumstantial accounts of such men as Byrd, Beverley, and Stith provided a solid background in the realities of life in the New World.

5. WRITERS OF NEW ENGLAND

With different motives for colonization from their Southern neighbors, the early settlers of New England wrote in order to guide in daily living, to educate and to edify, rather than merely to describe. It is extraordinary that colonists preoccupied with the great task of building a durable state in a new land found time to write so much and so well. But they did so because they were convinced that effective writing was a necessity for a healthy commonwealth. Books were useful tools for teaching. If they gave pleasure, well and good; but to write merely to please would have seemed to the northern colonists usually a dangerous waste of time. They left us no novels, no drama, and very little that can be classified as belles-lettres, not because they were aesthetically blind but because they were sure that there were better uses for their talents. Most of their work was designed to convey religious truth or to give sound instruction on immediate practical issues, political, social, or economic, because they were confident that such work was essential for the building of a vigorous and virtuous state.

If the modern reader is to appreciate colonial New England literature, he must have some familiarity with the state of mind loosely called "Puritanism." In general, the early writers of New England shared that state of mind, and although attitudes shifted quickly after 1700, many of the old ideas and the literary habits fixed by them persisted. Even the work of the few non-Puritan writers in colonial New England was affected by the prevailing intellectual tastes of the community.

The Puritan author, ever striving to make his books useful, recognized that they could be so only when they presented truth understandably and attractively. He chose his methods from those which seemed to have proved useful in practice and also to be in accord with God's laws. Art was a means, not an end; but the New Englander's realization that some degree of artistry was required if his writing was to be effective made him a careful workman and led him to develop a definite, although limited, theory of style.

The theory was shaped by his religious beliefs. He was an extreme Protestant, and saw the Reformation as a great victory of true Christianity over the man-made tenets of the Church of Rome. He was sure that the universe centered not on man, but on God, and that all man's energies must be devoted to God's service. God absolutely controlled all creation. Man was his creature, inherently sinful, and could be freed from evil only by the arbitrary gift of divine grace. Neither his own deeds nor the intercession of a church could help him—although he might do something to escape the fear of damnation by proving that he could persistently do God's will. That will he could best comprehend from the Bible, the precepts of which might be supplemented, but never challenged, by a patient study of God's operations in creating and controlling the world. To claim knowledge of the divine will by direct inspiration was arrogant and "enthusiastic" heresy. God did not speak directly in man's heart, but through the Bible and through the orderly plan of the universe. Those to whom he vouchsafed his grace could and should use their reason to learn what the Bible and God's creations meant; logic, metaphysics, science—any conceptions with which the mind could deal— were serviceable only because God had benevolently granted to some of his fallen children the power to reason. The would-be righteous must hope that God's grace was in them so that their reason might bring them knowledge of his truth. In this hope they must struggle to inform themselves, with all the aids of logic and philosophy, as to God's will and the means of carrying it out on earth. Inevitably they revered scholarship: to be good in any real sense they must learn; they needed both knowledge and faith. As John Cotton, a pioneer Boston divine, put it: "Knowledge is no knowledge without zeal"—that is, without religious conviction—but "zeale is but a wildefire without knowledge." The classics, the heathen philosophers, the teachings of Renaissance humanism were all grist to the Puritan's mill, all helps in his effort to use his reason for the carrying out of divine law.

Such thinking, in its essentials, was common to most Protestants in the sixteenth and seventeenth centuries. The elements in it which affected literary standards are therefore reflected in the writings of Anglicans and Puritans alike, in the religious artists of the Old World as well as the New. But the latter differ markedly from the former in content and style, because Puritanism, of the variety prevalent in early New England, gave special emphasis to certain tenets of Protestantism and developed accordingly some special points of view toward literature.

Starting from the idea that the Bible is God's word, to be believed even when its validity could not be demonstrated by human processes, Puritan and Anglican agreed that reason furnished arguments for the infallibility of Holy Writ. But the Anglican tended to supplement the Bible with other authorities, holding that it stated the fundamental Christian principles but need not be looked upon as a complete guide for every detail of life. Those details were regulated by reason, by the rules of a church taught by experience, and by the judgment of devout men. The Bible was not to be taken so literally as to leave no place for men to act freely when no essential Scriptural precept forbade. But the extreme Protestant—the Puritan—was more strict. If the Bible was God's word, and God was infinite, why suppose its authority to be less than infinite? Why was not its authority complete and binding, regardless of changing human conditions and aspirations, all of which were, after all, decreed by God? The Puritan took his Bible literally as a manual of instruction for every phase of conduct. In it he thought he found precise rules for the structure and polity of the true church, and he was sure that there should be nothing in worship or church government not specifically authorized by it. Inevitably he rejected many elements of the Catholic and Anglican service and polity because he could find no warrant for them in the sacred text. Thus he seemed to conservatives to be a rebel, not because of any basic theological unorthodoxy, but because his conception of a true church was unlike that of English ecclesiastics.

The New England Puritan's difference from the Anglican or Catholic in worship and polity dictated differences in literary theory. His literal attitude toward the Bible left little excuse for any religious art not somehow justified by its text; and the ardor of his Protestantism led him to reject anything traditionally associated with the Church of Rome. Organ music, stained-glass windows, incense, rich vestments, ornate altars, religious images —these were all adjuncts to Catholic, and to some extent to Anglican, worship. Their "Papist" associations were enough to make them anathema to the Puritan. Catholics commonly held that things which appealed to the senses could be fittingly used in the service of religion. The Puritan could not agree. He distrusted sensuous appeals in worship because they usually involved objects and practices not specifically endorsed by Holy Writ, because they smacked of Rome, and because he believed that "fallen man" was likely to become the prey of his senses, subject to the tyranny of passion rather than the dictates of right reason and faith.

This meant that the Puritan writer could not use, as his Catholic and Anglican contemporaries did, a body of material and a set of devices calculated to charm sensuously and to "adorn" his work—such charming and adornment seemed to him dangerous. He wanted to reach men's reason and to convince them of truth, not to lull them to acceptance by drugging their minds with potions all too likely to stir the carnal passions so powerful in the descendants of fallen Adam. The Puritan usually rejected imagery which served merely to delight, accepting only that which seemed to him to make the truth more easily understood, and preferring that which he could find in the Bible. He would rather talk of plain glass, letting in all the light, than of stained-glass windows, which seemed to him empty adornment symbolizing man's aptness to dim the light of truth. Anything which appealed to the senses so strongly as to endanger concentration on what must be grasped by reason, was dangerous. Good writing was to teach; its method must make directly and clearly comprehensible what man most needed to know.

Naturally, early New England writers of prose concentrated on sound and logical structure, and on clarity. The logic and rhetoric of Peter Ramus, the great French anti-Aristotelian logician of the sixteenth century, were adopted by Puritan pundits partly because they seemed to offer useful rules for good expository prose. But more immediately important than such rules was the Puritan's consciousness of the nature of his audience. It comprised men who were neither trained critics nor expert writers, but were, usually, earnest Christians, eager to learn. They were humanly fallible, and if a page, however clear, seemed dull, their thoughts strayed. Therefore the Puritan preacher and writer, although he advocated the "plain style" and objected to adornment for adornment's sake, seasoned his prose with imagery and used whatever literary devices seemed to him legitimate and necessary to make his instruction palatable. Anything in words which might rouse evil passions was forbidden, but picturesque phrasing and evocative images were allowable if their associations were innocent or if they had Biblical precedent.

The last point is important. The Bible had for the Puritan supreme literary value. It was the work of an omnipotent God, who used language perfectly because all that he did was perfect. Allegory, figures of speech—even frankly sexual imagery—crop up often in Puritan writing, sometimes in ways that are startling if we forget that its authors knew that men's "affections" must be charmed if their attention was to be held, and were sure that any literary method used in the Bible had divine sanction. New England authors avoided the rapturous expression of Catholic or Anglican mystics as too sensuous and too redolent of "enthusiasm"; they closed their eyes to much in the great religious literature of seventeenth century England because they did not want to tempt their readers' passions or to cloud their understanding of the truth by too elaborate rhetoric. Moreover, symbols and images, linked with the Mass and with ritualistic forms of worship, were suspect to the Puritan, and, in general, he looked coldly upon the ingenuities of style, the extended similes, the complicated metaphors (often sensuous or even sensual in suggestion), the elaborate prose music, and the rhetorical decoration, which characterized much of the best English writing in the late Renaissance. The Puritan was thus cut off from many sources of literary effect; but mercifully the Bible gave him others. He had no qualms about using its imagery, its rhythms, and its stylistic devices for his own pious purposes.

Part of his success with his audience depended on what he learned from Biblical style; he profited also by his understanding of other means by which he could hold his audience's attention without concessions to its baser appetites. He spoke and wrote principally for fishermen, farmers, woodsmen, shopkeepers, and artisans. However little they knew about classical literature or about rhetorical niceties in English prose and verse, they knew a great deal about the sea, gardens, village life, and the concrete concerns of pioneers busily establishing prosperous colonies in a wilderness. They enjoyed seeing an author drive home his point with a simile or a metaphor that touched their familiar experience; and their experience was rich with homely material. When Thomas Shepard wrote in his *Sincere Convert* (1655 edition), "Jesus Christ is not got with a wet finger," he meant, "Salvation cannot be had by mere study of books"; but his metaphor made a commonplace statement expressive and vivid for his readers by calling up the picture of an earnest student wetting his finger whenever he had to turn a page. Such metaphors and similes abound in Puritan writing. Their purpose is obvious; their effect is to give to pages which might otherwise be abstract and dull the taste of life.

Some New England writers broke away from the usual Puritan conventions of style. They were all to some extent influenced by non-Puritan ways of writing; many of them were English university men, well trained in literary traditions; and those whose work has merit enough to deserve mention today were individuals never completely subjugated by rigid convention. But the variations from orthodox Puritan practice are usually minor, and, so far as the work of any group can be summed up in a formula, the Puritans' can be. The formula called for clarity, order, and logic as supreme stylistic virtues. It admitted some concessions to the reader's liking for sensuous appeal, but limited that appeal to what was unlikely to stimulate man's baser nature and distract his mind from truth.

2

Nathaniel Ward, who came from England and preached at Ipswich, Massachusetts, in the early days of its settlement, is a useful example both of the Puritans' literary theory and of the permissible deviations from it. His *The Simple Cobler of Aggawamm in America,* a vigorously intolerant plea for Puritan orthodoxy, which was first printed in London in 1647 and ran through four editions in a few months, is full of word coinages, jingling phrases, and other forms of verbal display, and its style is certainly far less "plain" than that prescribed by strict Puritan theory. But Ward knew what he was doing. He defended himself against the charge of "levity" by writing:

> To speak to light heads with heavy words, were to break their necks; to clothe Summer matter, with Winter Rugge, would make the Reader sweat.

In other words, he was trying to make his style fit his material—and his audience. He virtually admits that he has now and then adorned his prose too much:

> I honour them with my heart, that can expresse more than ordinary matter in ordinary words: it is a pleasing eloquence; [I honour] them more that study wisely and soberly to inhance their native language. . . . Affected termes are unaffecting things to solid hearers; yet I hold him prudent that . . . will help disedged appetites with convenient condiments.

Ward wrote to teach, and he chose what seemed to him to be an effective method for his audience. If he offended against the strictest Puritan standard in using too many stylistic "condiments," he observed it in his reliance on homely imagery and in his exclusion of anything likely to stir sinful passions.

As for Cotton Mather who, in most of his work, departed from the plainest Puritan "plain style" by peppering his pages with allusions, quotations, and pedantic playings upon words, he knew quite well that he followed a fashion not universally approved in New England. He did so deliberately. He had thought a little about style, knew what he wanted to accomplish, and believed there were good ends to be served by varying from stylistic plainness. But even Mather, although he wrote his ecclesiastical history of New England, the *Magnalia Christi Americana* (1702) in the full tide of an enthusiasm for a prose encrusted with rhetorical eccentricities and learned allusions, in many another book used a style as simple and direct as the most conventional Puritan's. He could ape the new prose writers of the Restoration and the early eighteenth century in England, as well as the rhetoricians of 1630 or 1640. His *Political Fables* (about 1692) are in impeccably lucid prose; his *Christian Philosopher* (1721), an exposition of the arguments for Christianity to be found in the study of the natural world, has its flowery passages and is loaded with quotations and allusions, but the stylistic core is simple expository prose; his *Bonifacius* or *Essays to Do Good* (1710), beloved of Benjamin Franklin, was aimed at plain folk and is appropriately homespun in texture. So in all his voluminous writing—some four hundred and fifty books and pamphlets—Mather chose the kind of prose which seemed to him best suited to his purpose, without ever lapsing into a style so sensuously appealing as to be dangerous for fallen man. The *Magnalia,* he hoped, might reach the erudite abroad, and for such a book a style "richly trimmed" with learned trappings was appropriate. For less pretentious offerings he chose a simpler style, because he understood his audience and, like other good Puritans, held that his first task was to make truth intelligible to it.

The main stream of early New England literary practice is best shown in the chronicles and histories treated elsewhere in this volume, and in the sermons and other religious prose of Cotton Mather's generation and before. His own father Increase, for example, wrote numerous works chiefly striking for their typical Puritan emphasis on clarity and order; so did hosts of other New Englanders before 1700. Their zeal for ordered simplicity and their distrust of the sensuous too often makes their work seem to us cool and thin, colorless, and imaginatively tame. But with the faults went virtues—an effect of patterned dignity and, often, skillful use of homely realism.

This realism appears everywhere. Samuel Sewall, a Puritan layman, writes a paragraph about New England in *Phaenomena quaedam Apocalyptica,* a pamphlet on the Book of Revelation, and we hear of "the hectoring Words and hard Blows of the proud and boisterous Ocean," beating against Plum Island, of the salmon and sturgeon in the Merrimac, and of the "free and harmless Doves" perching in the "White Oak." And Sewall's famous diary is full of vividly realistic phrasing. How could the behavior of an angry man be more sharply pictured in a single phrase than in the diarist's account of the minister, who "with extraordinary Vehemency said, (capering with his feet)"? Even in the pages of a scholar as formidable as the Reverend John Norton, Augustine's "A good life is requisite in respect of ourselves, but a good name is requisite in respect of others" is pointed up by the observation "The gratefulness of the most excellent liquor unto the stomach depends in part upon the quality of the vessel." And elsewhere Norton remarks: "The hen, which brings not forth without uncessant sitting night and day, is an apt emblem of students." Roger Williams, although his advanced democratic ideas and his championship of complete religious toleration made him seem to many New Englanders a dangerous heretic, wrote with the authentic Puritan ring. He tells us of "the day of our last farewell, the day of the splitting of this vessel, the breaking of this bubble, the quenching of this candle." He reminds us that we are mere sojourners on earth, "strangers in an inn," "passengers in a ship," who "dream of long summer days." We "dwell in strange houses" and "lodge in strange beds," and pass like "smoke on the chimney's top" when the time comes for "the weighing of our last anchors." We are "poor grasshoppers hopping and skipping from branch to twig in this vale of tears."

The literary virtue stemming from the Puritans' insistence on order and logical structure as essential for conveying truth appears in a passage from

Samuel Willard's election sermon, *The Character of a Good Ruler* (Boston, 1694):

A People are not made for Rulers, But Rulers for a People. It is indeed an Honour which God puts upon some above others, when he takes them from among the People, and sets them up to Rule over them, but it is for the Peoples sake, and the Civil felicity of them is the next end of Civil Policy; and the happiness of Rulers is bound up with theirs in it. Nor can any wise men in authority think themselves happy in the Misery of their Subjects, to whom they either are or should be as Children are to their Fathers: We have the Benefit of Government expressed, 1. *Tim.* 2:2. *a quiet Life and a peaceable, in all Godliness and honesty,* and it lies especialy with Rulers, under God, to make a People Happy or Miserable. When men can injoy their Liberties and Rights without molestation or oppression; when they can live without fear of being born down by their more Potent Neighbours; when they are secured against Violence, and may be Righted against them that offer them any injury, without fraud; and are encouraged to serve God in their own way, with freedom, and without being imposed upon contrary to the Gospel precepts; now are they an happy People.

Or, to take a more complicated example, here is Thomas Hooker, in *The Application of Redemption* (London, 1659), expounding a point important both theologically and in its implications for literature:

It is by the Spiritual Operations and Actions of our minds that we meet with the Lord, and have a kind of intercourse with the Almighty, who is a Spirit. For al outward things are for the body, the body for the soul, the soul is nextly for God, and therefore meets as really with him in the Actions of Understanding, as the Eye meets with the Light in Seeing; which no other Creature can do, nor no action of a bodily Creature doth. Our Sences in their sinful and inordinate swervings, when they become means and in-lets of evil from their objects, they meet with the Creature firstly, and there make the jar: It's the beauty of the Object that stirs up to lust by the Eye, the daintiness of the Diet that provokes to intemperance by the tast, the harsh and unkind language that provokes to wrath and impatience by the Ear: But the Mind and Understanding toucheth the Lord directly, meets with his Rule, and with God acting in the way of his Government there, and when it goes off from the Rule as before, and attends its own vanity and folly, it justles with the Almighty, stands in open defyance and resistance against him.

In this the effect comes both from the structure and from the vigorous realism of such phrases as "there make the jar," or "justles with the Almighty." Samuel Willard's sentence, in his *Mercy Magnified* (1684),

There is a great deal goes to the eternal life of a soul, and thou hast none of it; thou wantest the love of God, which is better than life; thou wantest grace which is indeed the inward principle of life in the soul, thou wantest the promise which is the support of the soul here in this life,

hits its mark because of its balance and its flavor of simple speech. Hooker writes of "meditation," in *The Application of Redemption* (1659):

> The second End of Meditation is, *It settles it effectually upon the heart*. It's not the pashing of the water at a sudden push, but the standing and soaking to the root, that loosens the weeds and thorns, that they may be plucked up easily. It's not the laying of Oyl upon the benummed part, but the chafing of it in, that suppleth the Joynts, and easeth the pain. It is so in the soul; Application laies the Oyl of the Word that is searching and savory, Meditation chafeth it in, that it may soften and humble the hard and stony heart: Application is like the Conduit or Channel that brings the stream of the Truth upon the soul; but Meditation stops it as it were, and makes it soak into the heart, that so our corruptions may be plucked up kindly by the Roots.

The pattern is plain; its effect is enhanced because it is clothed with images thoroughly familiar to men and women who weeded gardens and treated one another's ailments.

3

Not only in his prose but in his poetry the Puritan displayed his fundamental literary creed. Early New Englanders wrote a great deal of verse, and in it, as in their prose, they chose the methods which seemed to them best adapted to their audience and most consonant with the Puritan view that all good writing must teach. Of course distrust of sensuous appeals does more injury to poetry than to prose, and the Puritan's verse suffered accordingly. Too often his poems are merely versified prose, expounding a useful lesson. Too often they are flat reiterations of pious truisms, adorned with some of the poetic artifices which the seventeenth century appreciated more than the twentieth. The devices were the more innocent ones sanctioned by the time, the ones least likely to arouse unruly and dangerous emotions; but some of them were intricate and "witty" to a degree uncommon in Puritan prose. The New England colonist gave a little more license to his verse writers than to the preacher or the writer of theological tracts, but he still kept them on a tight rein. The result is that their feeling, however genuine, too often quite fails to reach the readers of their verse.

That they wrote as much verse as they did, however, is sufficient refutation of the old heresy that Puritans were "hostile" to poetry. They were not. They found in it a way of expression necessary to them, but their theories limited their freedom in writing it. Also their utilitarian attitude toward all literature often put verse in the light of a luxury, since there was so much that needed to be said in sober prose. Most of the poetry written in New England before 1760 was never printed; most of it was circulated, if it was circulated at all, in manuscript, or committed to the pages of diaries or volumes of family memorabilia.

There were exceptions, though, and some New England verse found its way into print in the seventeenth and eighteenth centuries. The almanacs, indispensable to colonial farmers and fishermen, gave space to many stanzas, and there were even a few whole volumes of verse. Most famous of these is the "Bay Psalm Book," *The Whole Booke of Psalmes Faithfully Translated into English Metre,* printed in Cambridge, Massachusetts, in 1640, celebrated not for any poetic merit in its clumsy stanzas and tortured lines but because it was the first book issued in the English colonies in North America. Its authors, Richard Mather, John Eliot, and Thomas Welde, all devout and learned ministers and capable craftsmen in prose, knew that they were not writing poetry and said so. They wanted a literal translation of the Psalms which would fit metrically the tunes familiar to Puritan congregations. Accuracy and serviceability for worship were more important than literary excellence. The book was designed to be useful to ministers and their flocks, and was therefore a proper offering to God. If it was rough and graceless in form, it did not matter, since, as its authors wrote, "God's altar needs not our polishings."

Other New England books had more pretensions and more success as poetry. Most famous in its own day was Michael Wigglesworth's *Day of Doom* (1662), a colonial "best-seller." Its jog-trot ballad measure seems to us curiously inappropriate for an account of the Judgment Day, but it has a few flashes of sensitive poetic expression. So have some of Wigglesworth's other poetic efforts. But he was first of all a Puritan divine, and saw his main task as the teaching of sound Christianity. Therefore he chose a meter familiar to his readers, and versified standard Puritan doctrine, hoping that the rhyme and rhythm might make it more gratefully received and more easily remembered than it could be in prose. That he succeeded seems to be proved by the fact that *The Day of Doom* had at least ten editions before 1760.

Anne Bradstreet's verses were never as popular as Wigglesworth's; but they were well enough received to make possible three editions before 1760. The daughter of Thomas Dudley, steward to the Earl of Lincoln and, later, Governor of Massachusetts, she married Simon Bradstreet and came with him to Massachusetts in 1630, when she was seventeen. She had apparently read widely, and although she was a faithful Puritan wife, she could not always accept in entire docility the sterner aspects of the New England variety of

Calvinism. The last stanza of her little poem on the death of a grandchild is revealing:

> By nature Trees do rot when they are grown.
> And Plumbs and Apples throughly ripe do fall,
> And Corn and grass are in their season mown,
> And time brings down what is both strong and tall.
> But plants new set to be eradicate,
> And buds new blown, to have so short a date,
> Is by his hand alone that guides nature and fate.

The simplicity of the diction and the limited but accurate imagery carry a genuine emotional effect until, suddenly, Anne Bradstreet realizes that she is perilously close to writing rebelliously against God's decrees. She pulls herself up in the last line. It falls flat, even metrically, because it is dictated not by real feeling but by deference to orthodox doctrine. In other poems she is content simply to versify learning, sedulously imitating the pious French poet Du Bartas, whose work, in the English translation of Joshua Sylvester, she loved. Many of her pages are dull; many are merely "instructive" verse, using the devices of poetry but rarely rising above the attitudes of prose. But there are also pages in which she wrote simply and well of things close to her heart, and let her emotion, although always decorously expressed, warm her lines. Her *Contemplations,* for example, although overformal by modern standards, is a brave attempt to express poetically some sense of the physical beauty of Massachusetts; her lines in praise of Queen Elizabeth have defiant vigor and wit:

> Now say, have women worth? or have they none?
> Or had they some, but with our Queen is't gone?
> Nay Masculines, you have thus taxt us long,
> But she, though dead, will vindicate our wrong.
> Let such as say our Sex is void of Reason,
> Know tis a Slander now, but once was Treason.

Many a minor English poet of her day, more celebrated than Anne Bradstreet, wrote nothing that is better than her best, even though her best conforms to the Puritan's utilitarian view of art and to his distrust of the frankly sensuous.

A host of other New England colonial poets published only an occasional verse, or are known in print only by lines prefixed to books or collected by Cotton Mather in his *Magnalia*; but many of them left poems in manuscript. Mather says, for example, that the Reverend John Wilson, a pioneer divine in Boston, left at his death enough verse to fill a folio; but a very small book would contain all of it that was put into type for his contemporaries. He was a diligent anagrammatist, addicted to the then admired device of rearranging the letters of a man's name to make a phrase which could be used as the theme for a set of verses. Such contrivances seem to us mere ingenuity, but we should not forget that in Wilson's time anagrams were sometimes thought to have a mystic significance, and that to write verses on themes suggested by them was an intellectually reputable pursuit. Here, as in most Puritan poetry, the modern reader is handicapped by the fact that it is poetry written to meet outmoded standards. The great English poets who were publishing, and were winning applause, while the colonial New Englanders were constructing rhymes in the intervals of arduous lives in a "wilderness," adapted those standards to the uses of great poetry. The New Englander usually followed the convention expertly enough, but rarely made his finished work memorable for anything but competent craftsmanship. He was partially cut off from the tradition of great poetry by his specifically Puritan theories. He was reluctant to stir emotions too deeply, and he disliked the Anglicanism or Catholicism of many of the poets who might have taught him most. He was hampered by the lack of an artistically experienced audience, and he was too often blinded to poetic values by his intense concentration on the idea that the writer's first task was to put useful doctrine into the most immediately intelligible form. This is not to say that the Puritan was emotionally cold or poetically insensitive; there are proofs to the contrary in both Wigglesworth and Bradstreet. Nor is it to say that he could never write memorable lines; there are several in Urian Oakes' *Elegy upon the Death of the Reverend Mr. Thomas Shepard* (1677), and others in the usually awkward rhymes which Edward Johnson sprinkled through his *Wonder-Working Providence*. Any reader with a taste for good technique in expository or didactic verse will be rewarded in the pages of Benjamin Tompson or Richard Steere, who, for all their defects in imagination, were good enough workmen to give pleasure by the neatness with which they satirized New England's foibles or used the devices of Dryden and his school to make useful precepts and sound learning palatable to the colonists.

4

The greatest poet of New England before the nineteenth century was Edward Taylor, a Puritan minister of Westfield, Massachusetts, in the late seventeenth and early eighteenth centuries. His work, and his apparent attitude toward it, illustrate admirably the working of the Puritan theory of poetry, and his successes and failures are useful indices of the general poetic condition of the New England he knew. Very little of his verse was published in his day, but he left enough in manuscript to fill a large volume, with the request that it be not printed. We cannot be sure why this request was made, but Taylor probably knew that his poetry was not quite orthodox, and that it might seem to the more sober of his brethren a reflection upon his godliness or upon his understanding of man's sinful nature. His poetry is, in general, more sensuous, richer in luxurious imagery, and more daringly expressive of an essentially mystic emotion, than that of most Puritans. There are in Taylor decorated altars, jewels, spices, perfumes; tnere are strong echoes of such poets as John Donne and Richard Crashaw; there are whole poems which play more directly than most Puritans approved on men's love for color, gems, scents, and the delights of the flesh. Of course Taylor's poems were pious in intent; he was passionately devout—but he chose to express his pious devotion in terms which, as he may well have recognized, savored strongly of this world. He seems to have been not only more imaginatively endowed than his contemporaries, but also more defiant than they of the restrictions imposed on poets by the Puritan's fear of the passions of fallen man. For us his poetry gains by this. Where Bradstreet and Wigglesworth give hints of poetic power, Taylor gives proofs; where other Puritan poets rise only to ingenious expression or deft exposition in verse, lighted by very occasional flashes of imaginative insight, Taylor at his best writes poems so vivid in emotional evocation that they attain an artistic immortality quite independent of their doctrine.

Taylor's virtues do not stem merely from his enlargement of the limits of conventional Puritan practice; one source of strength in his work is his skill in using the kind of image most dear to Puritans—the homely image drawn from the simplest daily experience of simple folk. With this goes his adroit use of homespun diction, made more effective often by a contrast between the earthiness of a word (or a figure) and the loftiness of his theme. The soul is a "Bird of Paradise" in a "Wicker Cage," and there it "tweedles" praise to God. God "grinds, and kneads up into this Bread of Life, . . . the Purest Wheate in Heaven, his deare-dear Son." The result is "Heavens Sugar Cake." Man is to be a "Spinning Wheele" for God:

> Thy Holy Worde my Distaff make for mee.
> Make mine Affections thy Swift Flyers neate,
> And make my Soule thy holy Spoole to bee.
> My Conversation make to be thy Reele,
> And reele the yarn thereon Spun of thy Wheele.

The poem goes on to the weaving and dyeing of the cloth, until man is at last "Cloathd in Holy robes for glory."

The image is ingenious in the typical "metaphysical" mode, and is effective by virtue of its realism. No Puritan could have taken exception to it except possibly in so far as its ingenuity might seem to him to smack too much of current Anglican verse, and to be too apt to delight the reader to the point of distracting him from the truth the poem was written to express. But many Puritans might have had doubts about

> My Lovely One, I fain would love thee much,
>   But all my Love is none at all I see;
> Oh! let thy Beauty give a glorious touch
>   Upon my Heart, and melt to Love all mee.
> Lord, melt me all up into Love for thee,
> Whose Loveliness excells what love can bee,

or

> Shall I not smell thy sweet, oh! Sharons Rose?
>   Shall not mine Eye salute thy Beauty? Why?
> Shall thy sweet leaves their Beautious sweets upclose?
>   As halfe ashamde my sight should on them ly?

Was there not room for fear lest such lines work perilously on the carnal nature of sinful man? There might be offense, too, in

> But now my Heart is made thy Censar trim,
>   Full of thy golden Altars fire,
> To offer up Sweet Incense in
>   Unto thyself intire.

Censers, golden altars, and sweet incense had Biblical precedents, to be sure. But was not this verse too redolent of the ritualism against which the Puritans rebelled? There are other lines of the same sort in Taylor; others, too, in which love fills heaven, love runs over, blood is linked with love. The intensely emotional tone of many of Taylor's poems, and their specifically physical connotations, might well frighten critics who believed the senses could betray the reason, and had no use for the dangerous "enthusiastic" idea that man could ever achieve on earth a rapturous union with God.

Today, fortunately, no such scruples get in the way of our appreciation of Taylor's imaginative power and dramatic skill. His emotions may have been too strong for the tightest bonds of Puritan theory, but he adroitly used some Puritan literary conventions to give contrast and dramatic tension to his work. His constant use of homely and realistic diction and imagery brings ecstatic religious vision and the actualities of earth together in his verses, striking poetic sparks from the contrast. Again and again he makes articulate the drama inherent in man's quest for a beauty which is beyond earth but realizable only in images of earthly delights.

5

Taylor died in 1729. By then New England had changed greatly. The old religious fervor had abated; the concept of a universe centered in God had weakened before that of one centered on man; and more and more colonists, especially in the properous seaboard towns, were interested in trade and in aping the amenities of English society rather than in conquering new lands for Christ. They paid lip service to the old theology, and church membership was still a mark of social respectability; but the zeal for teaching and the fierce concentration on the dilemma of sinful man had lessened, and literature reflected the change. More and more the grace and urbanity of the English periodical essayists came to be admired; the robust vocabulary and rhetoric of the original colonists were toned down to the level of easy fluency; concrete realism often gave way to well turned generalizations couched in abstract terms. In verse Taylor's ardor and his love of dramatic contrast were replaced by smooth couplets and neat stanzas obviously reminiscent of Dryden, Watts, and Pope. Between 1700 and 1760 New England produced plenty of good prose and plenty of graceful verse; but much of it seems tame when compared with earlier work because the feeling behind it was less intense. "Good sense" was in vogue; "reasonableness" and "politeness" were more important than they had been to Puritan preachers and tract writers. Compare almost any line of Taylor, or almost any stanza, however clumsy, of *The Day of Doom* with this bit from a "Poetical Meditation" by Roger Wolcott of Connecticut, published in 1725:

> Vertue still makes the Vertuous to shine,
> Like those that Liv'd in the first week of time.
> Vertue hath force the vile to cleanse again,
> So being like clear shining after Rain.
> A Kind and Constant, Chearful Vertuous Life,
> Becomes each Man, and most Adorns a Wife.

True enough, any Puritan would have agreed; but few earlier Puritans would have put it so blandly, with so little sense of man's helpless vileness before God or of the miracle of God's grace vouchsafed to his elect. The change in attitude—and in style—from the earlier writers, shown in Wolcott and many eighteenth century New Englanders, illustrates some of the ways in which deism, the new rationalism, and changed English literary fashions affected the original Puritan outlook.

There were some literary gains. The newer theory flowered in Benjamin Franklin's best essays, skillfully written by a "sensible" man for "sensible" folk, with their eyes on this world more than on the next, and in the scientific and philosophical works of Jonathan Edwards. The brilliance of the prose in which the Reverend John Wise defended the original New England church polity in *The Churches Quarrel Espoused* (1710) and *Vindication of the Government of New-England Churches* (1717), shows how much he had learned from English stylists of the school of Dryden and Swift.

Furthermore the increasing secularization of society, the relaxing of the old dominant preoccupation with religion, opened the door to pleasant excursions in fields unvisited by the earlier Puritans. Mather Byles, for example, the nephew of Cotton Mather, was a minister, but achieved almost as much fame for his punning as for his preaching. He was also a rhymer, and an admirer of Pope and of the English poets of his day, and dashed off a few verses which his ancestors would have considered too trivial—or too frivolous —for a divine. The early Puritans had humor, of course—to take but two examples, Samuel Sewall in his diary and Nathaniel Ward in his *Cobler,* showed theirs; but usually the seventeenth century colonial preacher would have considered it a waste of paper and ink to display wit (in the modern sense) or humor in published writings. Nor were there, in the early days of Massachusetts, merchants like Joseph Green, ready to entertain themselves and their less pious neighbors with verses on the joys of drinking, or on the death of Mather Byles' cat, or with even more direct ridicule in rhyme of the minister of the Hollis Street Church. New England's notion of the purpose of literature changed fast after 1700. Good writing was seen no longer as simply a way of serving God by communicating divine truth as directly as possible; there was room for work designed merely to entertain. There was also an increasing interest in discussions of purely literary and stylistic matters. John Bulkeley, in 1725, wrote for Wolcott's *Poetical Meditations* a preface which is pious enough but devotes more attention than do most earlier colonial writings to purely literary values. Cotton Mather's famous essay on style, inserted in his *Manuductio ad Ministerium* (1726), a manual for theological students, takes a broader aesthetic view than the preface to the "Bay Psalm Book" or Michael Wigglesworth's unpublished "Prayse of Eloquence."

It is unlikely that more than a few pages of poetry and prose of New England before 1760 will ever achieve popular literary immortality. There are, none the less, memorable passages not only in the chronicles and histories, but in the great mass of sermons, tracts, essays, poems, and pious verse written by the colonists; and there are hundreds of other passages which lack the stamp of greatness but still have interest for, and may give excitement to, the modern reader who can read them with the understanding they deserve. That understanding involves first of all some knowledge of colonial conditions, some realization of the circumstances under which they were written and of the purpose and the audience for which they were designed. It involves, too, an appreciation of the literary conventions which were accepted by our fore-fathers and, in spite of serious limitations, had value. Order, logic, clarity, are still virtues in writing, even though the devices by which we try to achieve them are unlike the Puritans'. Homely imagery, earthy phrasing, and the use of simple and realistic figures to make abstract ideas or emotions concretely realizable are traits still characteristic of much of the best American writing. Emerson admired "language of nature." He found it in the speech of a "Vermont drover" and said that "in the 17th century, it appeared in every book." For an example he cited Thomas Shepard's "And to put finger in the eye and to renew their repentance, they think this is weakness." Obviously he was thinking of the homeliness so characteristic of Puritan prose; obviously too, much of his own best work shows the same quality. Emerson, and others, found in the Puritan's stylistic theory something adaptable to the needs of the idealist in any age. The early New Englanders' eyes were on God; but they were busy men with a wilderness to subdue and the divine will to carry out on earth.

Jonathan Edwards wrote on science and philosophy more effectively and more attractively, at least for modern readers, than most of his seventeenth century predecessors. Such men were exceptional, but they profited from some of the new methods in English prose popularized in the late seventeenth and early eighteenth centuries—methods by which many other New England writers before 1760 made their work palatable. The Puritans' literary prac-tice grew out of the search for some way to express both the spiritual emotion that controlled them and their vigorous desire to make practical use of it, and to teach others to do so, in daily life. They never succeeded, perhaps, in realizing their aim, either in literature or in life, but only those of us who are too limited in vision to see the gallantry of their quest will refuse them respect for what they did and wrote.

6. JONATHAN EDWARDS

THE East Windsor parsonage where Edwards was born October 5, 1703, was a rambling Connecticut farmhouse which easily accommodated the eleven children of Timothy and Esther (Stoddard) Edwards. In the gently sloping meadow at the rear, by a brook, the youthful Jonathan built the booth where he and his boy companions came to meditate and pray. It was in the immediate neighborhood that he observed the flying, or balloon, spiders in his twelfth or thirteenth year and reported on them in an account celebrated as the earliest natural history essay written on the subject. Timothy encouraged his only son in tasks that required painstaking accuracy, and the boy's imaginative mind responded to the discipline. The son was under the tutorship of a parent better remembered as a teacher than as a preacher, one who was especially successful in preparing students for Harvard and Yale. The power to evoke an "admirably rich and delicate description," as William James characterized *A Treatise Concerning Religious Affections* (1746), was foreshadowed in the youthful considerations of natural phenomena, of insects and rainbows, seen on a Connecticut hillside. Thus endowed, the boy entered Yale College in the autumn of 1716.

The pattern of Edwards' thinking was first displayed in the "Notes on Natural Science" and "The Mind." They were responses to courses in "natural philosophy," or physics, taken in the junior and senior years. This was the time when his conning of the new science, through the pages of Newton and Locke, bewitched him into self-discovery. The quiet young man, whose dependability won him the honor of a college butlership, as supervisor in the dining hall, was already a citizen of the realm of mind. The "Notes" pose the questions: What is reality? What are the metes of human knowledge? Wherein consists true liberty? And, most important of all, is it possible for a man to love anything better than himself?

Here Edwards first attempted to integrate the principles of morals, art, and being. The note on "Excellence" concludes:

Wherefore all Virtue, which is the Excellency of minds, is resolved into *Love to Being*; and nothing is virtuous or beautiful in Spirits, any otherwise than as it is an exercise, or fruit, or manifestation of this love; and nothing is sinful or deformed in Spirits, but as it is the defect of, or contrary to, these.

However technical as doctrine, this early attempt to set down a philosophical ideal on nine sheets of foolscap is the kernel of everything that later took root. It is Edwards' first effort to harmonize emotion and reason, mercy and justice, fate and free will. To read the world in terms of love was Edwards' unique contribution to the philosophic system of Calvin.

All his study of theology, undertaken in the two graduate years after he received his bachelor's degree in 1720, was now absorbed into abstract reflections, as were the scientific speculations. The idealism of "The Mind" and of the better known "Of Being" may or may not be traceable to the English idealist George Berkeley. One thing is sure. The stretch of Edwards' mind is observable from his youth. Rumors of new and exciting speculative theories were in the air: that the world of the senses is a direct expression of divine ideas; that mind and spirit are more important than their manifestation in matter. Such perceptions he had doubtless discussed, for they are convictions toward which he was moving.

The final and certainly determining event in his student years, described so charmingly in the "Personal Narrative" written twenty years after, was his mystical conversion at seventeen: "I often used to sit & view the Moon, for a long time; and so in the Day-time, spent much time in viewing the Clouds & Sky, to behold the sweet Glory of God in these Things: in the mean Time, singing forth, with a low Voice, my Contemplations of the Creator and Redeemer." All that he witnessed as manifestations of the sensible world became shadows of divine truths. The concrete image henceforth was to be the symbolic fact. From now on, nature was an analogy, as it has been felt by mystics from the beginning of time. Among American men of letters in the next century, Bryant came to express it in his own way; and Emerson, most articulately of all.

The apprentice preaching in New York during 1723 at a newly congregated church in William Street lasted but eight months. Edwards' haste to accept an invitation by a group in Bolton, Connecticut, may imply that the world of wharves and brick houses was not congenial to the New England youth now first separated from homestead, woodland, and meadows. The "new Sense of Things" as reflected in the universe round about, which had first possessed him at college, was never to alter.

A pressing community need released him almost immediately from his Bolton commitments. In 1724 his alma mater offered him the senior tutorship at a most stormy moment in the early days of the college, a position which Edwards held for two years, acting virtually as president. Then came the call as colleague pastor to his grandfather's church at Northampton. The aged "Pope" Stoddard, who dictated church polity in a manner no Boston minister dared emulate, would shortly retire. Edwards was settled in February, 1727, and in the same year married Sarah Pierrepont of New Haven, a woman of spirit and great sensitivity. These were the years when the burdens of raising a family and the task of preparing biweekly sermons and writing an occasional book occupied him fully. Indeed, the stately Mr. Edwards, spare of limb, was becoming an author of repute, though his townsmen would recall him walking, lost in thought, across the village common or riding with loose rein through the back pastures, his coat dotted with paper slips, notes set down lest he forget the ideas which absorbed him. It was Sarah Edwards that encouraged this life of plain living and high thinking, and uncomplainingly shared with her husband the heartbreaks of the later Northampton years. She accepted as he did, without self-pity or remorse, the humble missionary station after their transfer to the small Stockbridge Indian outpost in 1751.

2

The root of the Northampton trouble which led to Edwards' dismissal in his forty-seventh year from the most influential Connecticut Valley parish can be traced to the idealism implicit in the youthful notes on "The Mind." Edwards had been embroiled in "issues" from the day he matriculated in Yale College at the age of thirteen. His forthright honesty clearly produced them, and he was now willing to court his dismissal because any earlier doubts were resolved. The good of mankind was inseparable from the manner in which that good must be obtained. The *Farewell Sermon,* preached in July, 1750, spotlights the drama of his life in mid-passage. "You need one," he concludes, remarking of a successor, "that shall stand as a champion in the cause of truth and the power of godliness." And the opinion ruefully evaluates his administrative limits, not his principles.

The willingness of Edwards to accept into church membership only those who professed "renovation of heart," a conviction of spiritual regeneration, seemed intolerable to the majority. The shadow of his grandfather Stoddard, dead these twenty years, was yet upon the community, for Stoddard had taught his congregation to believe that under special circumstances the sacred seal of the Lord's Supper might in itself be a "converting ordinance." That is to say, Edwards was at last convinced that the sacrament was for those only who felt it to be the symbol of a conversion already achieved by the participant. His tragic realization of the place of evil in the scheme of things, his conviction of the irreversible reality of human isolation, were now fully reasoned. The revolution he was effecting in an attempt to abrogate Stoddard's decision, and the issue he joined, were to be made clear in the treatises he would soon write in the frontier settlement at Stockbridge during the remaining eight years of his life. For the moment he seemed an isolated reactionary, lost to the times because he would not compromise with them. Need religion be more than regular church attendance, profession of a reasoned belief in godly living based on good breeding and humanitarian interests in the welfare of one's neighbors? Edwards thought it should be. He was ready to express himself in a series of independent metaphysical speculations which have in fact given permanent direction to spiritual culture in America.

3

Edwards did not codify his analysis until after the apparent failure of his career in 1750. Of the five works which compass his scheme, only *Religious Affections* was written before he left Northampton. The remaining four appeared very late. *A Careful and Strict Enquiry . . . of That Freedom of Will . . .* was issued in 1754; *The Great Christian Doctrine of Original Sin Defended,* in 1758, the year of his death; and the *Two Dissertations* on "The Nature of True Virtue" and "Concerning the End for Which God Created the World"—capstones of his philosophical edifice—were brought out posthumously in 1765. The orthodox theology of Calvinism, on which Edwards had been nurtured in East Windsor and at Yale College, was not a shackle limiting the range of his ingenious faculties. Taking, as he did, all human nature for his province, he absolutely required some frame of reference. Calvinism served him admirably as material for the creation of a new idealism.

In a strict sense Edwards, like Emerson, did not construct a systematic philosophy; but the pattern of his interpretation of man's struggle is laid out in the early "Notes," and the later treatises expound the doctrine. From Locke he took the concepts that knowledge must be supplanted by faith, that man's ideas are derived from sense-impressions, even though he diverged widely from Locke in his exposition of the limits and value of knowledge. To Edwards the process was intuitive: man cannot achieve moral grace by an act of will or reason, but must passively receive it through the senses. From Newton, Edwards learned to observe how immutable natural laws, working harmoniously, reflect the great Geometrician. He began by attacking the problem of man's limitation and failure. His weapon was the language of Calvinistic theology.

Calvinism was never synonymous with Puritanism. Archbishop Whitgift, who crowned James I, was a Calvinist; but not so the men he drove to seek out a new plantation in the Bay Colony. Boston and Salem were not touched by Calvinism, nor the dynasty and followers of the Mathers. Edwards, better than any other spokesman, articulated it as a working philosophy, and this Connecticut Valley phenomenon was carried by his supporters into New Jersey and Virginia. Edwards as the first American Calvinist did not emphasize, like Thomas Shepard, Thomas Hooker, and other leaders among the seventeenth century Puritans, the covenantal relation between God and man, whereby the Sovereign was as fully bound by the contract as the subject. Edwards' Calvinism made the Deity more awesome and arbitrary. It emphasized sin as a property of the species. The "immensity and spirituality of the essence of God," in the words of Calvin, were not to be apprehended by an act of reason or bound by man in too legal a contract.

At great pains Edwards reasserted the reality of evil and the assurance of salvation, not to all, but to the "elect." Those so saved, he emphasized, are the regenerate: men and women infused by some external, supernatural grace which they are powerless to win by inclination alone. The regeneration is passively received by way of a new sense. Men may not be sure of election, but they must never cease yearning, with a heart laid passively open to receive the mystical grace. To see God in a rainbow or a buttercup is a reassurance and a challenge. Both the pantheism and the mysticism of Edwards are harmonized in a Calvinistic dogma.

In common with all Puritans, Edwards made clear distinction between the two activities of God, and set them forth in the "Treatise on Grace," written during the Stockbridge years but not published until 1865. There is first God's "common grace," working through secondary causes, to be seen in his providence—his decreeing will—observable in events; and in his commanding will—the Bible. There is secondly, and most important, his "supernatural grace," his regenerative power, an emanation, a new radiation reaching directly to man, overleaping regular channels. It is the supernatural grace that is peculiar to the elect, for it is an irresistible force depending on no antecedent condition or preparation. It reaches beyond the flawless regularity, the implacable justice of cosmic laws. Such mystic union cannot be rationalized. But this "Divine and Supernatural Light, Immediately Imparted to the Soul by the Spirit of God," as Edwards called it in the title of one of his earliest published sermons in 1734, is coexistent with God's common grace. Without the lesser, the greater cannot work. Since God's decreeing will is clear to all who will read their Bible, the preacher is under obligation to advocate hell-fire and brimstone now and then, in order to remind men forcibly that "conversion" is a matter of immediate urgency. The minatory sermon, though seldom used by Edwards in fact, is especially associated with the Calvinism he expounded, and was a traditional part of the Puritan ideology. Edwards' sermon on the sovereignty of God and depravity of man, *Sinners in the Hands of an Angry God* (1741), has fascinated and horrified succeeding generations of readers as much, apparently, as it did the hearers at Enfield, Connecticut, when it was first delivered; but, removed from its contextual place in the scheme of salvation which Edwards expounded, it tends to misrepresent him as one who despised men when in fact he loved them as fellow beings sometimes forgetful of the warnings of a compassionate Father.

The position of Edwards has thus far been stated in the language peculiar to Puritan theology. When it is reassessed as a living philosophy its idiom is seen to have universal truth. Edwards was Calvinistic especially in that he asserted the persistent reality of sin. Its existence, he felt to be inevitable and inescapable. Created free, with power of choice, man has yet one compulsion laid upon him: that he shall not, as a human creature, overstep the limits which his humanity had fixed. He must not seek to be as a god. The fruit of the tree of knowledge is not his to eat. For Edwards there was a twofold significance to the story of Adam's fall, and in both instances the implication, though tragic, was spiritually invigorating. Act and consequence are inseparable. For Adam's wrong act there must be an appropriate consequence which men call justice. Yet men know that as *human* beings their blindness and ignorance are so necessary that, if justice is to be satisfied, the doctrine of God's absolute sovereignty, with respect to salvation and damnation, can admit of no doubt. "The doctrine has very often appeared exceeding pleasant, bright, and sweet," Edwards remarks in his "Personal Narrative." "Absolute sovereignty is what I love to ascribe to God."

And the second implication is profounder still. Had Adam been allowed to remain forever in Eden where the fruits hung ripe for his picking and no physical problems taxed his ingenuity, what conceivable pleasure could he or his descendants ultimately have found in such virtual condemnation to the life of Lotus-Eaters and Struldbrugs? It is at this point that the concept of Mercy or Redemption is required, for were there no mitigation of justice somewhere, man could have no purpose in living. "Use every man after his desert," said Hamlet testily to Polonius, "and who should 'scape whipping?" No theme more surely postulates the issue of Being. Milton had chosen it for his great epics because he believed it the profoundest subject in the world. And Edwards as a Calvinistic metaphysician expounded the theme with originality. His efforts to uncover the roots of religious experience were greater even than those of William James, since James did not share his conviction that the roots were discoverable. The attempt schematically begins with the "Treatise on Grace," already mentioned, and with the *Freedom of the Will*. It concludes with the essay on God's end in creating the world. The projected *History of the Work of Redemption,* a vast design which was to have epitomized his philosophy by embracing all three worlds, heaven, earth, and hell, was left unfinished.

4

In order to understand *Freedom of the Will,* it is necessary first to know the problem Edwards had to meet. The fact that the treatise is a polemic, directed at certain contemporary "heresies," is today inconsequential except in so far as Edwards hacked at them to provide a clearing on which to establish his city of God. Any child of the eighteenth century knew that the proper study of mankind is man; and Edwards began and ended with man. His probing of the psychology of desire is a courageous facing of the rigors of existence, one that avoids the cosmic optimism of thinking mere flawless regularity is enough. *Freedom of the Will* is an essay on human liberty wherein the will and the emotions are seen to be indistinguishable: "And he that has the Liberty of doing according to his will," Edwards says, "is the Agent or doer who is possessed of the will; and not the will which he is possessed of." Morality, then, is an emotional, impulsive process, not a rational one. Edwards does not deny man's freedom, but states that it is qualified by man's "previous bias and inclination"—by such antecedent complexes as inheritance and childhood conditioning. Here are established both the basis of motivation—that is, self-love—and the limits of achievement. Shades of Mandeville and Hobbes! Had Edwards been their apologist he could hardly have argued their position more cogently. The fact that Edwards had never read Hobbes, though he considered him by way of secondary sources to be a "bad man," gives added force to Edwards' philosophical integrity. "Let [Hobbes'] opinion be what it will, we need not reject all truth which is demonstrated by clear evidence, merely because it was once held by some bad man." The will, then, is passive, the creature is "possessed" by it, and the doctrine of necessity equates with Greek fate. Both transcendentalism and pragmatism have roots in a Puritan past, and this essay with its insistence on passivity is one of them.

To follow the scheme of man's relation to the cosmic plan as it is seen to unfold in Edwards' analysis, one must note that he had established at this point the causal relationship of reason and emotion. A resolution of the struggle between justice and mercy must be attempted, and Edwards faced the issue in the essay on *Original Sin.* Though it was not completed until shortly before his death, it assembled material Edwards had long been pondering: What is the cause of evil? Where are its roots? The logical objection to the position Edwards assumed is that, since God is admittedly the creator of man's moral capacity, any apologist of "original sin" must find God the author of it. Edwards met the argument by contending that sin is original in the sense that it is a "property of the species," that God ordained a system which allows it, that therefore necessarily sin will come to pass. But the sin, Edwards contended, is man's act, not God's; hence the punishment is just. The system which God, the All-Good, ordained, is indeed desirable. Nothing but suffering will answer the Law. The thought is St. Paul's, and is integral with all Christian thinking. If this be tragic, it is the tragedy of an infallible nexus. Let more comfortable men stress the benevolence of Deity, Edwards insisted. Logic and the experience of mankind give no warrant for the assumption. Sin is a universal malady, common to all mankind, one which they must endure from their coming hence until their going thither. It is one illness definitely not contracted from rats, lice, and other vermin. Thus man is unique among creatures. To Edwards the story of the origin of evil, traced to our own hereditary taint, was beautiful as well as disturbing. The fact that it is disturbing should not lead us to deny its truth. Its beauty is manifest by the incentive which man is hereby given to contemplate the mystery of God's inscrutable design. Boldly to avow the reality of sin is to enhance the terror of God's sublimity and compel acknowledgment of humanity's dependence.

The essay does not make easy reading, but the conclusion justifies the labor. "It appears particularly, from what has been said," he remarks in final summary, "that all oneness, by virtue whereof *pollution* and *guilt* from *past* wickedness are derived, depends entirely on a *divine establishment.* . . . And all communications, derivations, or continuation of qualities, properties or relations, natural or moral, from what is *past,* as if the subject were *one,* depends on no other foundation." And here is the second of the elements which gave later transcendentalists a kinship with their inherited past: truth is forever and everywhere one and the same.

A Treatise Concerning Religious Affections has long been widely known as a notable discussion of the psychology of religion. It grew out of Edwards' concern for the problems of human destiny, and constitutes a minute observation of revival meetings when they were recurrent during the 1730's and 1740's. Indeed, his hospitable reception of George Whitefield, the most spectacular exhorter of the century, his endorsement of the many "awakenings," made him suspect among the more urbane ministers of the colony. Though Edwards' support made itinerant evangelism theologically acceptable for the next hundred years, the real importance of *Religious Affections* was not felt until later. Like William James, he was concerned with the psychology of religion in general, and with abnormal psychology in particular; and he analyzed the soul's experience with utmost acumen. The experience is emotional, not rational, Edwards believed; and he traced the steps and gave his witness to the workings of the Holy Spirit, reintroducing emotion as a valid shaper of the good life. He perceived the philosophic meaning which lesser exhorters overlooked: "that the essence of all true religion lies in holy love; and that in this divine affection, and an habitual disposition to it, and that light which is the foundation of it, and those things which are the fruits of it, consists the whole of religion." This was Edwards' pattern for living. What he later systematized in *Freedom of the Will*, he was accounting for in the emotions of men. The union of man and God lay through the mysteries of the heart, and Edwards' bold examination established him as a student of the psychology of mysticism. His care, here as always, is to avoid identifying mere intuition with the voice of God, or fusing God and nature into one substance of the transcendental imagination. The work in this respect is unique and remains an initial force in one cultural tradition, through Emerson to the present.

The Nature of True Virtue (1765), properly a sequel to *Religious Affections*, is something of an achievement, for it is mysticism shaped by dogma. It proceeds by contending that acts receive moral quality from the motives that inspire them. True virtue consists of love to Being in general and thus to God as the sum of being. Since no man, Edwards concludes, can have this love unless he is supernaturally charged by some immediately imparted agency, no man can actively work toward becoming truly virtuous. If such a doctrine seems to imply that man should be glad to be damned for the glory of God, it also presents a surpassing moral ideal. How supreme the love can be! How complete becomes the virtuous man's humility when he is able to love others rather than himself! The virtuous man is motivated by good emotions—good because of their beauty, not because of their usefulness or benefits. In the companion dissertation, *Concerning the End for Which God Created the World*, he pushes the implications to final limits. God created the world as the Supreme Artist or Genius, for the pure joy of creating. "It is certain that what God aimed at in the creation of the world, was the good that would be the consequence of the creation, in the whole continuance of the thing created, . . . aiming at an infinitely perfect union of the creature with himself . . . to satisfy his infinite grace and benevolence." God intended the emanation of his fullness, Edwards here states, since beauty, goodness, and existence are all manifestations of the same Principle. The union is one for man to establish, not by will or action, but through passive receptivity. The essay is written for those who would hear, in Milton's phrase, "the unexpressive nuptiall Song."

Edwards has been analyzing pure goodness in a manner no poet has successfully done. Milton and Goethe both succeeded in portraying evil. Edwards, believing that sin is inherent—that man, to the extent that he partakes of common humanity, is "possessed" as well by good will as by bad—is presenting the conclusion that the good man is the continent of Satan. The convincing symbol of goodness must *contain* evil—experiencing it, transmuting it, dissolving it. How could so magnificent a system, Edwards implies, be postulated without the damnation of sinner and election of saint? He has added to Calvinism the mystical and pantheistic overtones; and thus emerges a symbol of sensuous experience philosophically derived.

Each of Edwards' great treatises was written to answer the arguments of insignificant publicists. The issues concerned him, not the stature of the opponents. The recognition of the dislocation as extended to the social order, the tragic vision, though less central in Edwards' thinking than in that of novelists and poets who re-create human action, is none the less clearly present. "Dear children," he said, addressing the youth of the congregation assembled to hear him preach his Farewell Sermon, "Dear children, I leave you in an evil world, that is full of snares and temptations. God only knows what will become of you." Edwards' treatises are documents to which men may turn for enlightenment on a subject of inescapable concern to man. Most of them were composed in a frontier stockade, in a wilderness village beset by trivial bickerings, by one who, while he set spelling lessons for Indian boys, was giving shape to the American destiny.

As a writer of prose, alike in his sermons and in his treatises, Edwards was sensitive to the requirement of his aim. The dissertations hold to the integrity of the syllogistic method, the sermons avoid flights of oratorical fancy. His ear for prose cadence was developed by conscious attention, and he was expert in writing a "plain" style which, in those moments when he abandoned the syllogism to describe the memory of some boyhood experience, effectively communicates the glow of his own heart.

5

Edwards' call to the presidency of the College of New Jersey followed ten years of great productivity and increased renown. His almost immediate death in 1758 deprived the young institution of a celebrated name. "Edwards of New England," as Boswell refers to him, was better known abroad than at home, where he had never been intimate with the religious spokesmen of his time. Inevitably one contrasts him with Franklin, already something of a power, though by no means yet the world figure he was shortly to become. The two, born in the same decade, in the same province, are recognized counselors of their century. Might Edwards, who never did so, have enjoyed meeting Franklin? Neither of them, one suspects, would have understood the other. Both were speculative, ingenious, and basically concerned for the welfare of mankind. But Franklin, with a patriarchal wisdom never the birthright of Edwards, was the mediator. Taking men and things as he found them, he knew how to mold issues without sacrificing principle. Edwards was an austere logician whose compassion yearned toward mankind rather than toward men. He was a dweller in the Augustinian City of God, where the symbol suggests the meaning, where reason and emotion alike are disciplined by contemplation of the principle itself.

Edwards' mystic doctrines were variously reshaped in the nineteenth century; but the tragic intensity, the dwelling upon the reality of sin, the violent imagery, the concern with symbolism were downright shocking, as Holmes acknowledged, to the men of a later generation. To many, but not to all. One thinks first of Hawthorne who, though a skeptic, transmitted much of the essence of Edwards into fiction. Is there not the elf-child Pearl, humanized only when her mother's sin is expiated? Is there not the recriminatory violence of one Maule, and the minatory apostrophe of lonely Judge Pyncheon? And Hawthorne's friend Melville, darkly brooding of a summer's night in the Stockbridge hills, expressed similar aspects of man's incapacity, failure, and turbulent striving. Emerson dedicated Transcendentalism—which never fought Edwardean Puritanism, but absorbed it—to a new preoccupation with the old symbolism of nature. "We do not determine what we will think. We only open our senses, clear away, as we can, all obstruction from the fact, and suffer the intellect to see." Emerson too was well aware, as he speaks here in his essay on "Intellect" of the will's limitation, of the correspondence of the thing and the word, the object and the spirit. Whitman's bold language shot into fresh tangents, but he wrestled with good and evil, the flesh and the spirit, in poems such as "Chanting the Square Deific." Did the idealism within the pessimism of Henry Adams, intensely cultivating self-analysis, attempting to piece "the singulars" together into rules of art through the symbols of the Virgin and the dynamo, derive more than he would have conceded from a New England inheritance? The voice, through these many American years, is the voice of Hawthorne, and Melville, and Emerson, and Whitman, and Adams. But the hand is the hand of Jonathan Edwards.

7. WRITERS OF THE MIDDLE COLONIES

B<small>ETWEEN</small> the Wilderness Zion of the
Puritans and the plantation colonies of the South lay the provinces which for
want of any common characteristics save their intermediate location have
been known as the middle colonies. Yet the fact that these provinces—New
York, New Jersey, Pennsylvania, and Delaware—were not dominated like
New England by a single theological system or like the southern colonies by a
peculiar social system, was itself a most significant common characteristic.
By virtue of their linguistic and cultural variety, their relatively democratic
social and political institutions, their easy tolerance, and their material prosperity, they were the typically American region.

Few areas of the earth embraced such a conglomerate population. There
were Dutch patroons on the Hudson; Anglican, Jewish, Huguenot, and
Dutch Calvinist merchants in New York; English Quakers and transplanted
New England Puritans on Long Island and in New Jersey; English and
Welsh Quaker merchants and farmers in Philadelphia and the surrounding
counties; industrious German sectarians farming the fertile hinterland of
Philadelphia; hardy Scots-Irish Presbyterians on the frontiers; descendants of
Swedish and Finnish traders along Delaware Bay; Negro servants and slaves;
Iroquois, Delaware, and Susquehanna Indians. This mixed race, restless and
inquiring, was always on the move; by the middle of the eighteenth century
it could no longer be contained in the region drained by the Hudson and
the Delaware and had begun to spill over into the watershed of the Susquehanna, where it entered the arena of Anglo-French imperial conflict. Here
were the people from whom, as Crèvecœur was to write, "that race now
called Americans have arisen."

Most of the books produced in the middle colonies were concerned with
the topography and history of the inner and the outer worlds; few of them
were written with conscious literary intent. In the older towns, however,
where economic prosperity had created a stable society, a vital literary culture
was coming into being. In spite of a relatively late start among the English
colonies, the region advanced rapidly towards cultural maturity, and the
quarter-century preceding the Revolution witnessed in New York and Phila-

delphia a literary flowering which foreshadowed the intellectual leadership to be assumed by those centers in the early years of the Republic.

2

Over the greater part of the middle colonies religious freedom prevailed, resulting in a typically American babel of sects and churches. The most distinctive note was contributed by the Quakers, a religious minority whose ideas, operating as a leaven, have had an influence in American life quite out of proportion to their numbers. It was a note of persistent moral idealism, drawing its strength from a religion of pure inner experience, and manifesting itself practically in the quick response of a sensitive conscience to human suffering.

The central figure in early American Quakerism was William Penn, perhaps the greatest of colonial statesmen, who organized the colonies of New Jersey, Pennsylvania, and Delaware on the basis of religious toleration, political democracy, and pacifism. He was a prolific writer on theological, moral, and political subjects, but his chief claim to attention as a literary figure rests upon his moral and religious aphorisms, of which the most extensive collection is *Some Fruits of Solitude* (1693). A singular compound of devout Quaker and man of the world, Penn distilled into his maxims a morality which was at once intuitively religious and shrewdly utilitarian, prefiguring in its latter aspect some of the sayings of Poor Richard. In *Fruits of a Father's Love* (addressed to his children on the eve of a voyage to Pennsylvania in 1699) he described the Inner Light, the root principle of Quakerism, as

the Light of Christ in your Consciences, by which . . . you may clearly see if your Deeds, ay and your Words and Thoughts too, are wrought in God or not. . . . And as you come to obey this blessed Light in it's holy Convictions, it will lead you out of the World's dark and degenerate Ways and Works, and bring you unto Christ's Way and Life, and to be of the Number of his true self-denying Followers.

The characteristic literary expression of Quakerism was the journal or spiritual autobiography. There were in the colonies scores of obscure men and women of uncommon spiritual sensitivity who traveled in the ministry as "public Friends," and left these records behind not as monuments to their own spiritual achievements but as guidebooks to others on their inward odysseys. Concerned primarily with inner states rather than outward events, the journals followed a more or less uniform pattern, beginning with a record of divine intimations in childhood, followed by an extreme compunction over youthful frivolities, passing through the spiritual conflicts of adolescence to "convincement" of the truth of Quakerism, and conversion, in which the will was utterly surrendered to the divine leading. As if repeating one another, most of the journalists recorded the same turning-points in later life: entrance upon the vocal ministry, the adoption of "plain dress," the decision to curtail the volume of outward business, and the awakening of the social conscience.

As the structure of the Quaker journals tended towards uniformity, so did the style. Its keynote was an austere simplicity. "Ye that dwell in the Light and walk in the Light," George Fox, founder of the Society of Friends, had urged, "use plainness of speech and plain words." William Penn's advice was to the same purpose: "Affect not Words, but Matter, and chiefly to be pertinent and plain: Truest Eloquence is plainest, and brief Speaking . . . is the best." The emphasis on plainness had been part of the total Quaker revolt against the "world" of the mid-seventeenth century when English literary prose had been loaded with farfetched tropes, inkhorn terms, learned quotations, and other ostentatious rhetorical trappings. In pursuing the ideal of unadorned simplicity, the Quakers were careful to strip their writings of superfluities that served only to please the carnal mind. In their insistence upon plainness of diction, they fell in with, indeed they anticipated, the trend of English and American prose style. Failing to match in syntax the simplicity which they achieved in language, the Quakers retained in their writing an archaic structural element which was to distinguish the plain style of Woolman from that of his contemporary Franklin. Just as the "plain dress" of the eighteenth century Friend was essentially the costume of Charles II with its ornaments removed, so the basic sentence structure of the Quaker journals remained tortuous and intricate in the manner of Browne and Burton, while the diction had all the simplicity and plainness of Swift and Defoe.

The uniformity of the Quaker style blurred but could not wholly erase the individualities of its users. The robust piety of a seagoing Philadelphia Quaker was revealed in the *Journal, or Historical Account, of the Life, Travels, and Christian Experiences, of that Antient, Faithful Servant of Jesus Christ, Thomas Chalkley* (1749); for all its austerity, Chalkley's language retained a salty flavor as he related the nautical and spiritual adventures of a life spent in the triangular trade with the West Indies and England. With the *Journal of the Life, Travels, and Gospel Labours of . . . Daniel Stanton* (1772) the Quaker style showed signs of becoming stereotyped; after repeated usage expressions which had originally been vivid metaphors of spiritual experience—"to dig deep," "to outrun one's Guide," "to keep down to the root"—came to be colorless, drained of imaginative content. In the hands of the saintly John Churchman of Nottingham, Pennsylvania, on the other hand, the Quaker style could be a subtle and sensitive instrument. Thus in his journal (1779) he described the manner in which a religious "concern" to travel "in the love of the Gospel" to Europe had come to him:

One day walking alone, I felt myself so inwardly weak and feeble, that I stood still, and by the reverence that covered my mind, I knew that the hand of the Lord was on me and his presence round about, the earth was silent and all flesh brought into stillness, and light went forth with brightness, and shone on Great Britain, Ireland, and Holland, and my mind felt the gentle, yet strongly drawing cords of that love which is stronger than death, which made me say, Lord! *go before, and strengthen me, and I will follow whithersoever thou leads.*

The possessor of the sweetest spirit, the tenderest social conscience, and the purest prose style among all the eighteenth century Quakers was John Woolman, the tailor of Mount Holly, New Jersey. He was early convinced, as he wrote in his *Journal* (1774) "that true Religion consisted in an inward life, wherein the Heart doth Love and Reverence God the Creator, and learn to Exercise true Justice and Goodness, not only toward all men, but allso toward the Brute Creatures." Humanitarianism was in the air in the eighteenth century, but the source of Woolman's social concern lay deeper than the transient mood of an age. The poignant consciousness of God's infinite tenderness and love was constantly renewed in him, and these moments of mystical awareness were the wellsprings of his dedicated life, causing him eventually to realize that he was so "mixed in" with the mass of suffering humanity that henceforth he could not consider himself as a distinct and separate being. This realization impelled him, as he traveled to the southward, to labor lovingly with the planters, urging them to renounce slaveholding, which struck his sensitive spirit "as a Dark Gloominess hanging over the Land." It led him to travel unarmed on a visit to hostile Indians on the frontier that he might "feel and understand their life, and the Spirit they live in"; to sympathize with the poor brutalized sailor lads on the Atlantic crossing; and to seek the elimination of the seeds of war from society.

In *Some Considerations on the Keeping of Negroes* (1754, 1762), he spoke out clearly for racial equality, and called attention to the deleterious effects of slavery on the slave owners. His *Plea for the Poor* (published posthumously in 1793) and *Conversations on the True Harmony of Mankind* (first published in 1837) left no doubt that he was equally sensitive to other forms of social injustice, that he was conscious of the rift opening up even in the midst of provincial plenty between the wealthy merchant and the workingman. "To labour for a perfect redemption from this spirit of Oppression," he wrote, "is the Great Business of the whole family of Christ Jesus in this world."

The ideal of perfect simplicity by which his life was guided led him in his writings to strip away every superfluous word and phrase. The man who insisted upon traveling steerage to England because he "observed sundry sorts of carved work and imagery" on the outside of the more comfortable cabin, and "some superfluity of workmanship of several sorts" in the cabin itself, applied the same rigorous standards to his own prose, eliminating from it everything designed merely to please the "creaturely" mind. By banishing non-essential or merely decorative adjectives, adverbs, and modifying phrases, he laid bare the structure of the introspective process. His prose was lacking in warmth and grace and color, but it had a purity which enabled his essential meaning to emerge unclouded, uncolored, undistorted, like something seen at the bottom of a clear spring of water. Thus in spite of his indifference to art, or because of his scorn for the merely ornamental, Woolman created out of the plain style which was his inheritance a medium of expression that was a triumph of functional art. In its crystal purity it was, as William Ellery Channing was to perceive, continuous with the saintly simplicity of his life.

In the realm of purely religious writing the many sects and churches of the middle colonies produced nothing to match the distinctiveness and literary charm of the Quaker journals. But in the field of philosophical speculation, a field which was alien to the Quaker mentality, learned Anglican and Presbyterian divines exhibited notable intellectual acumen and vitality. American philosophy in general has tended to oscillate between the poles of absolute idealism and naïve realism, and it was characteristic of this region of diverse peoples and liberal intellectual climate that it should have fostered, almost simultaneously, both of these diametrically opposed systems—the one originating in Ireland and given currency here by an Anglican clergyman, the other stemming from Scotland and reformulated by a Presbyterian minister.

Samuel Johnson, a Yale graduate who took orders in the Church of England, was at one with the unphilosophical Woolman and with the young Jonathan Edwards when he wrote: "I must account it the greatest perfection and happiness of every intelligent creature to depend on a perpetual intercourse with the Deity for all his happiness and all his hopes." Reacting from the Calvinism of Yale, Johnson moved towards rationalism in religion, composing a "rhapsody" called "Raphael; or, The Genius of English America" in which he pleaded for the use of reason in the pursuit of truth. He drew back as the realization dawned that in the ordered universe of Newton and Locke there was no room for the idea of God as a sustaining presence. At this point the philosophical idealism of Bishop Berkeley came to his rescue, providing a rationale for the sense of the divine presence and a safeguard against skepticism and materialism. Johnson's *Elementa Philosophica* (1752), the first philosophical textbook written and published in America, was dedicated to the Irish bishop, whom he followed closely in insisting that spirit was the only substance, that matter existed only in the mind of the perceiver, and that nature was simply the succession of ideas that God presented to our minds. Johnson's textbook was used at King's College in New York, where he was President, and at the College of Philadelphia, where the Anglican William Smith was Provost.

Idealism enjoyed a brief vogue at the College of New Jersey; but it ended abruptly in 1768 when the Reverend John Witherspoon came from Scotland to be President, bringing with him the Scottish philosophy of common sense. As a theologian Witherspoon occupied a commanding position wherever the influence of Calvinism extended. Quite as much as Johnson he was concerned to vindicate the Christian religion from the corrosive attacks of rationalism and natural science. Dismissing idealism as "a wild and ridiculous attempt to unsettle the principles of common sense," he bluntly maintained that the existence of an object was completely independent of the mind that perceived it. Furthermore, as the external senses assure us infallibly of the existence of the material world, so through the "internal senses" we are made aware of the existence of God and the validity of Christian principles. This naïve realism was the more successful in combating the deists and materialists in that it made use of their own empirical methods. "It is safer," wrote Witherspoon, ". . . to trace facts upwards than to reason downwards." With its empirical methods and its uncritical acceptance of hard facts, the realistic philosophy which Witherspoon introduced into America found a congenial environment. Radiating from Princeton, its influence was to permeate American thought for a hundred years until it came to be regarded as "the American philosophy."

3

Although the broad region occupied by the middle colonies formed the keystone of the colonial arch, it was almost *terra incognita* to English-speaking people until the last third of the seventeenth century. The forested reaches of the Alleghenies and the Ohio River valley hardly entered the consciousness of Englishmen in the colonies or the mother country until the middle of the eighteenth century, when pioneer traders and settlers from the middle colonies came into fateful conflict there with outposts of the French empire. As each of these areas was successively opened for settlement, the colonists rushed into print with accounts of the lay of the land, its flora and fauna, its aboriginal inhabitants, and the momentous affairs being transacted there. These utilitarian reports and chronicles were in the oldest tradition of American literature; but they differed from the exuberant accounts of the Elizabethan sea dogs and traders in that they were informed with something of the scientific spirit that entered British thinking after the middle of the seventeenth century.

The earliest accounts of the region were sober, factual reports, designed to attract settlers but distinguished by accuracy in observation and moderation in language. Thus Daniel Denton in his *Brief Description of New-York* (1670) declared:

I . . . have writ nothing, but what I have been an eye-witness to all or the greatest part of it: Neither can I safely say, was I willing to exceed, but was rather willing the place it self should exceed my Commendation.

He did not hesitate to compare the New World favorably with the Old, both in economic opportunities and in natural beauties:

Yea, in *May* you shall see the Woods and Fields so curiously bedecke with Roses, and an innumerable multitude of delightful Flowers, not only pleasing the eye, but smell, that you may behold Nature contending with Art, and striving to equal, if not excel many Gardens in *England*.

William Penn, whose *Letter to the Free Society of Traders* (1683) was the first comprehensive report on Pennsylvania, was a Fellow of the Royal Society, and the scientific temper was apparent no less in his meticulous survey of the natural resources of his colony than in his first-hand observations on the culture of the Lenni-Lenape Indians. Fifteen years later, his account was expanded and brought up to date as *An Historical and Geographical Account . . . Of Pensilvania and of West New-Jersey* by the Welsh Quaker Gabriel Thomas, who added to Penn's sober and temperate language a certain Celtic sparkle and playfulness. With ebullient optimism he enunciated the theme of the promise of American life, setting over against the incredible bounty of nature on the shores of the Delaware a dismal picture of the laboring poor in England "half-starved, visible in their meagre looks, that are continually wandering up and down looking for Employment, without finding any, who here need not lie idle a moment." Only occasionally did Thomas' penchant for hyperbole or his enthusiasm for his new home lead him to transcend the facts, and when he did, it was in a manner that would be regarded in years to come as the typically American vein of humor:

There are among other various sorts of Frogs [he solemnly reported], the Bull-Frog, which makes a roaring noise, hardly to be distinguished from that well known of the Beast, from whom it takes its Name.

From these early reports and chronicles stemmed two types of writing—

natural history and political history—both dominated by a utilitarian purpose and both characterized by the spirit of careful observation and accurate reporting. These books stood in contrast to much of the contemporary writing in the other provinces in that they were the work not of clergymen, but of lawyers, physicians, teachers, and merchants—men of affairs with a cosmopolitan outlook limited neither by theological dogmatism nor by parochialism and excessive provincial pride. The historians among them wrote from a broad imperial point of view, and the writers on natural history were always conscious of belonging to the international community of scientists. Both groups wrote primarily for a European rather than a colonial audience.

Lieutenant Governor Cadwallader Colden of New York was both historian and scientist. Indeed he was a typical eighteenth century *virtuoso,* equally at home in history, medicine, botany, mathematics, physics, and metaphysics; he was a correspondent of Linnæus and Gronovius in Europe and of the leading members of the Royal Society in England. His *History of the Five Indian Nations* (1727) was drawn largely from Jesuit sources, eked out by his own experiences among the Mohawks. Using these same materials a century later, Francis Parkman was to create a magnificent historical drama. Colden lacked Parkman's historical perspective, his dramatic power, and his architectonic skill in relating incidents to a single overarching theme. His narrative consisted of a succession of apparently unrelated forays, council fires, and peace treaties. The chief distinction of style was contributed by the Indians themselves, whose formal orations, faithfully reproduced, were studded with picturesque and striking metaphors. However inadequate his achievement, there was grandeur in Colden's conception, nor was he unmindful of the momentous lesson implicit in his formless narrative; his avowed purpose was to demonstrate that the Five Nations were of crucial importance to British America as a buffer against the French and a means of holding the West.

"I have sometimes thought," Colden declared, "that the Histories wrote with all the Delicacy of a fine Romance, are like *French* Dishes, more agreeable to the Pallat than the Stomach, and less wholesom than more common and courser Dyet." Thirty years later, William Smith, Jr., an able New York lawyer, found himself in agreement with this dictum, although in politics he was ranged on the opposite side from Colden. Smith's *History of the Province of New-York* (1757), written to dispel British ignorance of colonial affairs, was a full-dress chronicle of New York under British rule, with a prologue on the Dutch period and a comprehensive concluding survey of the trade, religion, and politics of the province at mid-century. The narrative was written for the most part in plain, lawyerlike English, but it was punctuated and enlivened by a series of brilliant set-pieces in the form of mordant sketches of the royal governors. Smith's design, he confessed in his preface, was "rather to inform than please":

The ensuing Narrative . . . presents us only a regular Thread of simple Facts; and even those unembellished with Reflections, because they themselves suggest the proper Remarks, and most Readers will doubtless be best pleased with their own. . . . no Reins have been given to a wanton Imagination, for the Invention of plausible Tales, supported only by light Probabilities; but choosing rather to be honest and dull, than agreeable and false, the true Import of my Vouchers hath been strictly adhered to and regarded.

Animated thus by a scientific ideal which tempered his partisanship, Smith produced a work second among colonial histories only to Thomas Hutchinson's *History of the Colony of Massachusetts Bay*.

In Pennsylvania, historians were preoccupied with the problem of the Indian on the frontier, and scientific objectivity gave way before the emotions aroused by that ever-present reality. Another William Smith, Provost of the College of Philadelphia, enlisted his literary talents on the side of the aristocratic Proprietors, and launched two vigorous salvos of polemic history against the Quaker-dominated Assembly. In his *Brief State of the Province of Pennsylvania* (1755) and his *Brief View of the Conduct of Pennsylvania* (1756), he taxed the peace-loving Quakers with excessive republicanism and with having appropriated money for hospitals and libraries at a time when the frontiers lay open to Indian incursions. He exploited all the resources of the skilled propagandist, including cold statistics, gruesome atrocity stories, and charges that the Quaker opposition was "a factious Cabal, effectually promoting the French Interest." Charles Thomson, a teacher in the Friends school in Philadelphia, endeavored in his *Inquiry into the Causes of the Alienation of the Delaware and Shawanese Indians* (1759) to vindicate the Quaker policy of seeking the friendship and respect of the Indians. With sober and painstaking scholarship, though not without an obvious bias, he recounted the story of Indian relations in Pennsylvania, a story filled in his telling with fraud and .chicanery on the part of the whites and climaxed by the infamous "Walking Purchase" of 1737 by which the Indians had been deprived of a large portion of their patrimony. More than a century of dishonor was to pass before another American, Helen Hunt Jackson, would come forward with an equally strong and well documented plea for justice towards the dispossessed red man.

Lewis Evans, Philadelphia mapmaker, was, like Colden, both historian and scientist, although something of the polemic spirit infected the historical and political portions of his *Geographical, Historical, Political, Philosophical and Mechanical Essays* (1755–1756). These essays, written in the first instance as analyses of his own pioneer map of the middle colonies and the Ohio River valley, contained some of the earliest descriptions of the American landscape west of the Alleghenies. "To look from these Hills into the lower Lands," he wrote as he stood high in the Alleghenies gazing westward, "is but, as it were, into an Ocean of Woods, swell'd and deprest here and there by little Inequalities not to be distinguished, one Part from another, any more than the Waves of the real Ocean." As Evans had hoped, his essays attracted attention in England, where no less a personage than Dr. Samuel Johnson thought them an indication that literature was gaining ground in America. The treatises, Johnson pontificated, were written "with such elegance as the subject admits, tho' not without some mixture of the American dialect, a tract of corruption to which every language widely diffused must always be exposed." No doubt the lexicographer was distressed by Americanisms like *branch, fork, creek,* and *run,* his pedantry thus blinding him to a significant manifestation of the vitality of the English language in America.

Evans' companion on his first reconnaissance of the Appalachian plateau was John Bartram, a tireless collector of botanical specimens from the American forest. Natural history in the eighteenth century was an exciting adventure of identifying and classifying thousands of newly observed forms of life, and a whole continent lay open before the sharp eyes of this simple Philadelphia Quaker turned deist who corresponded with the leading scientists of Europe. The laconic style in which Bartram set down his observations was a product of the Quaker tradition of plain speech reinforced by the spirit of scientific accuracy and objectivity. Traveling through the verdant Susquehanna valley in the summer of 1743, he allowed himself to note only that

the land hereabouts is middling white oak and huckleberry land. . . . we went up a vale of middling soil, covered with high oak Timber, nearly west to the top of the hill . . . from whence we had a fair prospect of the river Susquehanah.

Even in the midst of the gorgeous exotic scenery of Florida, the taciturn Quaker naturalist, distrustful of emotion, permitted himself only a restrained scientific curiosity. He remarked in a letter to Franklin that his journal contained only his "observations of particular soils, rivers, and natural vegetable productions," adding in a revealing comment, "But there was no artificial curiosities in those provinces as temples, theatres, piramids, palaces, bridges, catacoms, oblisks, pictures." A century hence, more sophisticated writers like Hawthorne and Henry James would be regretting the absence of these "artificial curiosities" from the American scene. And within a few years Bartram's own son was to interpret the American landscape in a manner which required no reference to a remote and storied past to establish its romantic character.

William Bartram, who spent the years between 1773 and 1778 botanizing in the Floridas, Georgia, and the Carolinas, added to his father's scientific curiosity a sensibility to form and color, a rich and varied vocabulary, and a pantheistic philosophy, all of which were to make a strong impression upon the romantic poets of England. His volume of *Travels* (1791), which has attracted attention from literary historians chiefly as a document in the history of romanticism in England, deserves attention on its own merits as an authentic literary masterpiece of early American romanticism.

The younger Bartram was a painter in water colors as well as a poet. He looked upon the strange and beautiful tropical landscape with all the freshness and acuity of vision which had distinguished the earlier observers; but he had the priceless advantage of an artist's eye and a richly varied verbal palette. His style—the most distinctive and accomplished style developed by any writer in the middle colonies—was loose in structure, fluent in movement, heavily ballasted with Latin botanical names, equally apt for detailed delineation and for rapid narrative. Whether he was describing a furious battle of alligators or the flowering shrub which he named the *Franklinia Alatamaha,* a tropical thunderstorm or that "inchanting and amazing chrystal fountain" that was to meander through the wondrous landscape of Coleridge's "Kubla Khan," William Bartram wrote with conscious artistry. The measure of his success can be judged by this description of a fish observed in Georgia:

It is as large as a man's hand, nearly oval and thin, being compressed on each side; the tail is beautifully formed; the top of the head and back, of an olive green, be-sprinkled with russet specks; the sides of a sea-green, inclining to azure, insensibly blended with the olive above, and beneath lightens to a silvery white, or pearl colour, elegantly powdered with specks of the finest green, russet and gold; the belly is of a bright scarlet red or vermilion, darting up rays or fiery streaks into the pearl on each side; the ultimate angle of the branchiostega extends backwards with a long spatula, ending with a round or oval particoloured spot, representing the eye in the long feathers of a peacock's train, verged round with a thin flame-coloured membrane, and appears like a brilliant ruby fixed on the side of the fish.

Occasionally Bartram lapsed into rhapsodic ejaculations, full of pseudo-classic epithets and periphrases, revealing that, for all his romanticism, he was not wholly emancipated from eighteenth century conventions. His attitude towards the Indian owed something to his Quaker background, but probably more to the current literary stereotype of the noble savage; nevertheless, his observations on the culture of the Creeks, Seminoles, and Cherokees were anthropologically sound. His romantic pantheism, which so attracted Wordsworth, sprang from the union of his ancestral Quakerism, with its ideas of divine immanence, and the scientific deism which he absorbed from his father; he was probably unconscious of the degree to which the two influences merged in such a passage as this: "Let us rely on providence, and by studying and contemplating the works and power of the Creator, learn wisdom and understanding in the economy of nature, and be seriously attentive to the divine monitor within." With William Bartram the middle colony tradition of scientific observation and description reached a culmination. In his *Travels* the raw materials with which his predecessors had been struggling for a century were finally given form by the shaping hand of a scientific observer who was also a sensitive artist.

Not until thirty years had passed did any other American naturalist emerge to carry to greater heights the work of the Bartrams in what was to be a great American tradition of writing about nature. Starting also from Philadelphia, John James Audubon studied and painted the birds of the neighboring areas, extending his journeys eventually from the Alleghenies to the Mississippi and from the Cumberland Gap to the Louisiana bayous. He intended that his *The Birds of America* should include every American bird known to man. The great folio of beautifully colored plates was accompanied by five volumes of text, *Ornithological Biography* (1831–1839), in which species and their habits are set against romantically described landscapes and lively narratives of Audubon's adventures on the frontier. "My work," he said, "shall be not a *beacon* but a *tremendous lighthouse!*" And so it has proved to be. The light from it has thrown into undeserved shadow the pioneering work of his quiet Quaker predecessors, the two Bartrams.

4

Self-conscious literary life in the middle colonies was associated chiefly with the colleges established in the mid-eighteenth century. In two respects educational ideals in the middle colonies differed from those which had led to the founding of the older colonial institutions: education was conceived primarily as training for civic responsibility, and the English language was given a place beside Greek and Latin as a proper subject of college study. Both William Livingston in *The Independent Reflector* (1752–1753) and William Smith in *A General Idea of the College of Mirania* (1753) echoed Archbishop Tillotson's dictum that classical or speculative learning which had no practical usefulness was "but a more specious and ingenious sort of idleness, a more pardonable and creditable kind of ignorance." Regular opportunities for practice in English rhetoric and oratory were provided in disputations and literary exercises held in the college halls. The ideal college graduate in the middle colonies was thus not primarily the polished country gentleman or the learned minister but the useful and responsible citizen, skilled in the elegant and persuasive use of his mother tongue.

William Livingston, a brilliant lawyer and leader of the liberal party in the politics of provincial New York, did much by precept and example to foster this ideal. In 1747 he published a poem entitled *Philosophic Solitude,* a faint echo of *The Choice,* an enormously popular English poem written a half-century earlier by the Reverend John Pomfret. In correct heroic couplets, with a slight Miltonic flavoring, Livingston's poem described the simple felicity of life in a rural retreat, and culminated in a mild paean to a Deity whose existence was inferred, in typical eighteenth century fashion, from the beauty and harmony of the creation. Both the mood and the measure of the poem harked back to Augustan England. It is interesting chiefly for its revelation of the influences which had formed Livingston's mind and tastes. In enumerating the authors whose works he would chose for his library, he named the writers of classical antiquity; the French authors Fénelon and Montesquieu; Milton, Dryden, Pope, and Isaac Watts among the English poets; Raleigh, Swift, and Addison among the prose writers; and Bacon, Boyle, Newton, and Locke, chief architects of the eighteenth century cosmology.

Livingston's strong sense of social responsibility led him to place his literary gifts at the service of the liberal causes to which he was committed. He was the principal author of *The Independent Reflector* (1752–1753) and *The Occasional Reverberator* (1753), two series of periodical essays in the tradition of Trenchard and Gordon's *Independent Whig.* Although he denied any literary purpose ("In subjects meerly literary," he wrote, "I shall rarely indulge myself"), he achieved genuine distinction as a writer of prose. His style was formal and balanced, barbed with satire, full of carefully contrived antitheses and climaxes, rising occasionally to a pitch of stately eloquence. For vigor and trenchancy it was unsurpassed by any other periodical writing of the day either in the colonies or in the mother country.

Livingston left no room for doubt about the cause in which his literary talents were enlisted.

'Tis the cause of truth and liberty [he wrote]; what he intends to oppose is superstition, bigotry, priestcraft, tyranny, servitude, public mismanagement, and dishonesty in office. The things he proposes to teach are the nature and excellence of our constitution, the inestimable value of liberty, the disastrous effects of bigotry, the shame and horror of bondage, the importance of religion unpolluted and unadulterate with superstitious additions and inventions of priests.

Himself a Presbyterian and the descendant of Dutch Calvinists, Livingston nevertheless deplored sectarianism, and was suspicious of any interference by the church in secular affairs. In theology he was a liberal, believing religion to be "plain and simple, and to the meanest capacity intelligible." In politics he was a Whig, bent upon vindicating the authority of the provincial Assembly against the encroachments of the royal governors.

When it became known that the proposed college in New York was to be chartered by the Crown as an Anglican institution, Livingston launched a literary campaign to have it incorporated by the Assembly and kept free from denominational control. Returning again and again to the attack in successive numbers of *The Independent Reflector,* he underlined the importance of intellectual freedom, not neglecting the opportunity for animadversions upon Harvard and Yale where the tender minds of the future ruling classes, he maintained, were filled with illiberal Puritan doctrines that were bound to filter down through the whole of society. Behind Livingston's plea for academic and religious liberty one could detect stirrings of a more far-reaching revolt against authority that was to culminate before many years in a revolution.

Livingston's liberalism and literary skill made him something of a hero to the undergraduates at the College of New Jersey who gathered in Nassau Hall every afternoon at five under President Witherspoon's direction to hear orations declaimed by their fellow students. Livingston's essays were frequently used for declamations, and one of the two undergraduate literary societies at the College was named after Livingston's pseudonym, "The American Whig." The leading figures in the American Whig Society were three young men destined soon to take prominent parts in the founding of a national literature. As undergraduates Philip Freneau, Hugh Henry Brackenridge, and James Madison expended their literary energies chiefly in directing coarse and vigorous satires against the rival Cliosophic Society.

For the Commencement of 1771 Brackenridge and Freneau composed a long poem in blank verse called *The Rising Glory of America.* Their imaginations were fired by the same imperial vision which had inspired Colden and Evans. They foresaw new towns springing up along the Ohio, and "nations" on the Mississippi, American poets arising by the Susquehanna, in the Alleghenies and the Tuscarora hills, a new civilization burgeoning on the Appalachians, in the Carolinas,

> and the plains
> Stretch'd out from thence far to the burning Line.

Moved to hyperbole by their regional pride, they celebrated New York as the "daughter of Commerce" hailing from afar

> her num'rous ships of trade
> Like shady forests rising on the waves.

And Philadelphia they hymned as

> mistress of our world,
> The seat of arts, of science, and of fame.

At the College of Philadelphia Provost William Smith held sway as a sort of provincial Great Cham of literature. Like Dr. Samuel Johnson, his English contemporary, he is remembered not so much for his writings as for his personality and his influence on younger writers. The little circle of poets which he gathered around him in the fifties and sixties was the first self-conscious poetic "school" in America, the first group of American writers who regarded poetry not as a handmaid to ethics and religion but as a craft to be practiced for its own sake. The *American Magazine and Monthly Chronicle* (1757–1758), which Provost Smith edited, served as a vehicle for their literary efforts, establishing itself in the brief twelve months of its existence as the most brilliant and original literary periodical in colonial America. The artistic vitality of the group was further manifested by the fact that it included the first American composer of secular music, Francis Hopkinson; the first American dramatist whose work was professionally performed, Thomas Godfrey; and the first American painter to achieve international recognition, Benjamin West.

Even before the founding of its college the Philadelphia region could boast of considerable classical learning. Between 1718 and 1730 David French, Prothonotary of the Court of Newcastle in the "Lower Counties" (Delaware), had rendered into English verse some of the frankly pagan and sensual odes of Anacreon. The Quaker James Logan, who had come to Philadelphia as William Penn's secretary and had remained to become Pennsylvania's most distinguished scholar-statesman, published a translation of the *Moral Distichs* of Dionysius Cato in 1735 and of Cicero's *De Senectute* in 1744. His publisher, Benjamin Franklin, hailed the former as "the first translation of a classic which was both made and printed in the British Colonies," and the latter as "a happy omen that Philadelphia shall become the seat of the American muses." The classics were not neglected at the College of Philadelphia; but by the fifties the tide was beginning to set in another direction.

The college poets of Philadelphia were caught in the same crosscurrents and confusions of taste that affected English verse in this transitional period between the decline of the classical ideal and the emergence of full-blown romanticism. It is instructive to compare them with their English contemporaries, Collins, Gray, and the Warton brothers. There was the same devotion to the Pindaric and Horatian ode-forms and to the youthful poetry of Milton;

the same addiction to the stock epithets and personified abstractions of the Augustans mingled with glimmerings of sentiment that forecast the Romantic mood; the same scholarly urbanity alternating with effusive sensibility. If the poetry of Philadelphia was derivative, so was the best English poetry of the day. Before condemning these provincial poets out of hand for seeking their literary inspiration abroad, one should reflect that they regarded themselves after all as English poets, that they had no indigenous poetic tradition to draw upon, that they lived and wrote in an academic atmosphere, and that, like many later American poets, they felt, or professed to feel, radically out of sympathy with the bustling mercantile society in which their lot was cast. The day of appreciative patrons is past, lamented Nathaniel Evans, young Anglican clergyman,

> And we are in a climate cast
>   Where few the muse can relish;
> Where all the doctrine now that's told
> Is that a shining heap of gold
>   Alone can man embellish.

The artificialities of the moribund pastoral tradition exercised a singular fascination over the Philadelphia poets. Thomas Godfrey and Francis Hopkinson were at one with Nathaniel Evans in his resolution to naturalize the eclogue in America, to

>   wake the rural reed
> And sing of swains, whose snowy lambkins feed
> On SCHUYLKILL's banks with shady walnuts crown'd.

Streams bearing the names of Schuylkill and Delaware appeared in many of their poems, but the landscape through which they flowed was always the conventional bucolic backdrop derived from Theocritus, Virgil, and Pope, further conventionalized by the persistent use of such "poetic" epithets as "spicy vales," "gay, enamell'd groves," "the finny brood," "the feather'd tribe."

No doubt Provost Smith must be held partly responsible for the vein of academic classicism in the poets of his circle, but he also encouraged them in the expression of an inchoate Romanticism. His own principal literary contribution to the *American Magazine* was a series of essays written under the pseudonym (itself a typical pre-Romantic stereotype) of "The Hermit," in which a didactic purpose was invested with an atmosphere of romantic melancholy and awe at the sublimity of nature. In praising the work of his special protégé Thomas Godfrey, the untutored son of a glazier, he employed phrases which betrayed his sympathy with the emerging Romantic conception of poetry. He wrote of the young poet's "poetic warmth," his "elevated and daring genius," and cited Godfrey's own lines as descriptive of his work:

> In beautiful disorder, yet compleat,
> The structure shines irregularly great.

Godfrey's "Night Piece" (1758), written in the stanza of Gray's "Elegy," was redolent of the atmosphere of contemporary "graveyard" poetry; and his *Court of Fancy* (1762) and "The Assembly of Birds" (1765) reflected the current revival of interest in Chaucer. Francis Hopkinson's "Description of a Church" (about 1762) was an American echo of the current English vogue of Gothicism. All three of the major poets of the group shared their generation's adulation of Milton, and paid him the homage of imitation. They were in their happiest vein when they took their inspiration from the Elizabethan and Caroline lyrists. In his lines "To Celia," Thomas Godfrey succeeded in capturing something of the gay *insouciance* of Waller and Herrick:

> When in *Celia's* heav'nly Eye
> Soft inviting Love I spy,
> 'Tho you say 'tis all a cheat,
> I must clasp the dear deceit.
>
> Why should I more knowledge gain,
> When it only gives me pain?
> If deceiv'd I'm still at rest,
> In the sweet Delusion blest.

Both Evans and Godfrey died young, and Provost Smith, suspected of Loyalist sympathies, was under a cloud in the seventies; but Francis Hopkinson was to live on into the first years of the Republic, providing a link between the literary life of the provincial metropolis and that of the political and cultural capital of the new nation. This "pretty, little, curious, ingenious" man, as John Adams described him, was the most versatile of the group: he was a musician and composer, an amateur portraitist, a poet, satirist, and writer of graceful Addisonian essays, as well as a dabbler in science, a lawyer and judge, and a member of the Continental Congress. During the Revolution he exploited the satirical vein first revealed in the pungent humor of his burlesque fragment "Dirtilla" a decade earlier. To the patriot cause he contributed a number of rollicking ballads like "The Battle of the Kegs" (1778) and a series of political allegories in verse and prose of which *A Pretty Story* (1774) and "Date Obolum Belisario" (1778) were the most effective.

Combining in his own person a gift for pure literature and a readiness to devote his talents to the public weal, Hopkinson carried into the literary life of the Republic the ideal which had flourished in the college towns of the middle colonies. In 1787 he celebrated the adoption of the Federal Constitution with a ballad called "The New Roof: A Song for Federal Mechanics," employing an elaborate metaphor which he had used earlier in prose to defend the Constitution against its traducers. In vigorous and homely images he sang:

> Come muster, my lads, your mechanical tools,
> Your saws and your axes, your hammers and rules:
> Bring your mallets and planes, your level and line,
> And plenty of pins of American pine:
> *For our roof we will raise, and our song still shall be,*
> *Our government firm, and our citizens free.*

In 1788 he dedicated to George Washington a volume of songs of which he had composed both words and music. In these stanzas, with their Shakespearean echo and their romantic imagery, the lyric note which had been intermittent with the poets of colonial Philadelphia finally reached clear and sustained expression:

> The traveller benighted and lost,
>   O'er the mountains pursues his lone way;
> The stream is all candy'd with frost
>   And the icicle hangs on the spray,
> He wanders in hope some kind shelter to find
> "Whilst thro' the sharp hawthorn keen blows the cold wind."
>
> The tempest howls dreary around
>   And rends the tall oak in its flight;
> Fast falls the cold snow to the ground
>   And dark is the gloom of the night.
> Lone wanders the trav'ler a shelter to find,
> "Whilst thro' the sharp hawthorn still blows the cold wind."
>
> No comfort the wild woods afford,
>   No shelter the trav'ler can see—
> Far off are his bed and his board
>   And his home where he wishes to be.
> His hearth's cheerful blaze still engages his mind
> "Whilst thro' the sharp hawthorn keen blows the cold wind."

Already the various race which inhabited the middle colonies was revealing through its spokesmen certain traits which were to become constants in the American character. A strain of idealism, of stubborn faith in a higher law and a deeper reality behind appearances was combined paradoxically with a shrewd realism, an insistence upon hard facts and utilitarian values. The literature that came out of the experience of these archetypal Americans, a literature which achieves first rank in the writings of Benjamin Franklin, expressed something of the freedom and newness of the American continent with a freshness of feeling tempered by the objective spirit of scientific inquiry. And around the newborn colleges of the region was springing up a promising literary life that was to reach its flowering in the early days of the young American republic.

8. BENJAMIN FRANKLIN

B̲ENJAMIN FRANKLIN, though he was born in Boston, was little affected by its earlier, sterner traditions. His father was a tradesman who had come from England in 1683, and the son grew up in a generation to which the theocratic concepts of the founders of New England seemed remote if not preposterous. He enjoyed *The Pilgrim's Progress,* particularly because it "mixed narration and dialogue," and he read other books by Bunyan; but the inquiring boy soon tired of his father's "books of dispute about religion" and preferred Plutarch's *Lives* and Xenophon's *Memorabilia.* Neither the polemic habits which Franklin first picked up nor the Socratic method to which he turned during his juvenile disputatious period stayed with him long. Reading the orthodox arguments against the deists when he was fifteen, he was converted to a lifelong deism. Reading the arguments in favor of natural religion at nineteen, he set out to prove that whatever is is right, in a pamphlet called *A Dissertation on Liberty and Necessity, Pleasure and Pain* (1725). As he did not linger with theology, neither did he with metaphysics. He burned all but a few copies of his *Dissertation,* and would not bother to print a short treatise on prayer which he wrote at twenty-four. "The great uncertainty I found in metaphysical reasonings disgusted me, and I quitted that kind of reading and study for others more satisfactory."

Yet here and there in Franklin traces of theology, New England and older, appear. From either or both of two epitaphs printed by Cotton Mather in his *Magnalia* Franklin probably took for his own *Epitaph,* written at twenty-two, his often repeated image which compares the resurrection of a man with a new edition of a book; and he was certainly indebted to Mather's "Essays to Do Good." In Franklin's *Articles of Belief and Acts of Religion,* composed in 1728 for his own spiritual guidance, there is a strain of Puritan self-searching as well as a philosopher's code of morals. In his efforts to attain moral perfection he made laboratory notes on his daily successes and failures in a manner much like that prescribed by Loyola in his *Spiritual Exercises,* which Franklin may not have heard of. In one of his electrical papers, where he speaks of "adoring that wisdom which has made all things by weight and measure," he seems to be quoting from Augustine. Years of experience brought Franklin to the conviction that "God governs in the affairs of men." But the divine government, Franklin held, was a vast order to be studied, not a mystery to be sought in ardor and torment. However intense his youthful perturbations were, he soon mastered them and thereafter lived at reasonable peace in his spacious universe.

2

His life was one of the great lives of all time, and his writings are full of great, if fragmentary, autobiography. It is hard to distinguish between the plans Franklin made and the instincts which impelled him. In his boyhood he wanted to go to sea, disliked his father's trade of tallow chandler, and at twelve was apprenticed to his brother James, a Boston printer. While the younger brother was speedily learning the printer's trade, he was also teaching himself the writer's art. He began with broadside ballads, now lost, on contemporary incidents, then took to prose in painstaking and skillful imitation of Addison's *Spectator*. Franklin was "extremely ambitious" to excel in writing prose, which he afterwards said had been "a principal means of my advancement." His *Dogood* papers, contributed to James Franklin's *New England Courant* in 1722, were Addisonian but also Franklinian, remarkably precocious for an apprentice of sixteen. Before Benjamin Franklin had completed his apprenticeship he had outgrown his status, and he ran away from his brother-master in 1723 to Philadelphia, thereby committing an act which in a tradesman of that age was almost as culpable as desertion in a soldier.

In Philadelphia, and in London in 1724–1726, Franklin worked at his trade as a journeyman. During his voyage home, recorded in a lively *Journal* which is the earliest of his autobiographical writings, he drew up a Plan for his future conduct as if he were making a "regular plan and design" for a poem. He resolved to be frugal, industrious, and strictly truthful, and to speak ill of nobody. That he made such resolutions seems to indicate that he thought he then lacked such qualities, at least in a sufficient degree. His self-discipline had begun. This discipline, and the impassioned inner life of his next few years, did not interfere with Franklin's swift and simple success in business, but did enlarge his mind in preparation for his subsequent career on wider stages. In 1729 he acquired a newspaper, the *Pennsylvania Gazette,* and in 1733 he began to publish an almanac called *Poor Richard* which was soon famous throughout the British colonies. In 1736 he was chosen clerk of the Pennsylvania Assembly, and in 1737 appointed Postmaster of Philadelphia.

One of the least solitary of geniuses, Franklin, while striving to perfect his own character, had been no less busy in his efforts to improve the society in which he lived. The Junto, the club of young tradesmen whom he brought together in 1727, founded in 1731 the subscription library which has survived as the Library Company of Philadelphia; and in 1736 the Union Fire Company, the first in the town. From these Junto beginnings, Franklin and its members and later a widening circle of public-spirited men, particularly after he was elected to the Pennsylvania Assembly in 1751, went on to reform the city watch, encourage the paving and lighting of streets, propose the Academy which was to become the University of Pennsylvania, establish the Pennsylvania Hospital, organize the armed defense of the Quaker province, and generally to develop in Philadelphia the forms of active and enterprising life which made it long the chief city of America.

Philadelphian and Pennsylvanian, Franklin was at the same time American. His *General Magazine, and Historical Chronicle, for All the British Plantations in America* lasted for only six months in 1741; but the American Philosophical Society, which he initiated in 1743 in the hope of uniting American scientists everywhere in a common effort, is still the first of American learned societies as it was the earliest. In 1753 Franklin became the Crown's joint deputy postmaster general for North America. In 1754 his Plan of Union was adopted by the Albany Congress which had been called by the Crown in the desire to see the English colonies united against the French power in Canada. The Plan of Union having been rejected, Franklin had to go back to affairs in Pennsylvania, where he was a leader in the struggle of the people of the province against the British proprietors. That struggle was for Franklin a rehearsal of the part he was afterwards to play in the struggle of the United Colonies against the British Parliament.

In brief intervals snatched from business and politics Franklin incredibly found time to perform the experiments in electricity, mostly in the years 1747–1753, which made his the first great name in that branch of science and produced, in his successive volumes of *Experiments and Observations on Electricity* (1751–1774), the principia of electrostatics. In 1752, apparently in June, he flew his famous electrical kite; in October of that year he announced in *Poor Richard* the invention of the lightning rod. These achievements brought him the official thanks and compliments of Louis XV of France, the Copley gold medal of the Royal Society in London and election to the Society, and honorary degrees from Harvard, Yale, and William and Mary. When, in 1757, Franklin was sent to London to manage the appeal of the Pennsylvania Assembly from the proprietors to the King, he went not only as Pennsylvania's agent but also as, what David Hume called him, America's "first philosopher, and indeed the first great man of letters, for whom we are beholden to her."

For the years down to about 1757 Franklin's *Autobiography* (first published in Paris, 1791) tells the story that is known round the world. But in countless letters and other private and public papers written afterwards it is easy to find as full, if not so formal, a record of his later life. He returned to America for a short stay in 1762-1764, only to go back to England with Pennsylvania's petition to be made a royal, not a proprietary, province. He returned again in 1775-1776, to serve in the Second Continental Congress, and by it to be sent to France as commissioner—and in time minister—from the rebel colonies which had declared themselves the independent United States of America. Everywhere his renown grew, as wizard in science and wit in letters, philosopher and sage, beloved friend to men, women, and children. Yet his method in dealing with affairs remained essentially what it had been in Philadelphia. By deft and tireless persuasion he sought to draw like-minded people together to bring a just political order out of the confusions of prejudice and special interests. The English thought him too American, the Americans thought him too English. As he had risen from local to intercolonial concerns in America, so he rose in England to imperial concerns, and worked year after year for a broader conception of the British Empire. When his vision of that Empire as "the greatest political structure human wisdom ever yet erected" was ruined by the outbreak of hostilities between the parts on the two sides of the Atlantic, he turned himself with all his weight and charm to the business of uniting America and France, not only in resistance to England but also in support of the rights of man in any nation. What he did was of less importance than what he was. When at last, in 1785, he left Europe for America again, he was the most famous private citizen alive. His life had roused the universal curiosity with which his *Autobiography* was greeted the year after his death by contemporary readers, and its record has ever since been cherished in virtually every language that has a printing press. He had written his biography, so far as it went, as well as he had lived his life.

3

Not only his final *Autobiography* but also a large part of his written work had followed the steps of his life, recording it. In his youth, whether as Mrs. Silence Dogood in the *New England Courant,* or as the Busy Body in the *American Weekly Mercury,* or as Richard Saunders in *Poor Richard,* Franklin assumed a fictitious role and wrote in the first person. When in time he put off these disguises and wrote as himself, he continued to write more or less autobiographically, whether in his accounts of his scientific experiments or in his records of his diplomatic activities or in his statement of the various ideas upon which he hit in many fields of speculation. Though he wrote always with care, drafting and revising, he looked upon writing as his means, not as his end. With all his inventive gifts he invented no new forms of writing, but was satisfied with those ready at hand, and with the fresh uses he could put them to.

When late in 1732 Franklin issued his first *Poor Richard,* for the year 1733, he was simply a printer risking his money and labor on an almanac, as many other printers were then doing in America and Europe. His brother James, now removed to Newport, had an almanac called *Poor Robin.* An earlier English almanac, *Appollo Anglicanus,* had been compiled by an actual Richard Saunders. Benjamin Franklin, taking over the name of Richard Saunders for himself as compiler, and adapting the title *Poor Robin* to *Poor Richard,* fell smoothly into step with a familiar tradition. His circumstantial prophecy that a rival almanac-maker, Titan Leeds, would die on the coming October 17, merely imported to Philadelphia the hoax played by Jonathan Swift on John Partridge in London twenty-five years before. *Poor Richard's* forecasts of sunrises and sunsets, high and low tide, lunations and eclipses through the year were mathematical and naturally the same as those in any other almanac. What was new in Franklin's almanac was the humorous character of Poor Richard the philomath, and the range of laconic wisdom tucked in along the margins of the crowded pages.

Poor Richard, in his annual appearances from 1733 to 1758, did not in reality tell much about himself. He lived in the country, made some profit out of his almanac but had to share it with the printer, engaged in altercation with his wife Bridget, and was pestered by people who wanted him to tell their fortunes. Yet the brief strokes with which he was displayed, year after year, were drawn with a skill which could have made Franklin a first-rate novelist if he had cared to write novels. The earliest well-known character of fiction created by an American, Poor Richard, though only an outline, is still as amiably, eccentrically alive as ever.

The marginal Sayings of Poor Richard are some of them in character, more of them not. For they come from Franklin's, not Poor Richard's, reading and reflection during that formative quarter-century. He drew upon such identifiable sources as Rabelais, Bacon, La Rochefoucauld, Dryden, Swift, Pope, Prior, Gay, anthologies of verse, and collections of proverbs. Besides sayings in English, there are also a few in Latin, Spanish, French, German, and Welsh. Now and then Franklin set down one of his own recent moral conclusions, as in 1739: "Sin is not hurtful because it is forbidden, but it is forbidden because it is hurtful. . . . Nor is a duty beneficial because it is commanded, but it is commanded because it is beneficial." La Rochefoucauld's "Cunning and treachery are the offspring of incapacity" became, either directly or through some intermediary version, in 1751 Franklin's "Cunning proceeds from want of capacity." Franklin, returning to the matter in 1754, spoke more definitely in his own idiom: "A cunning man is overmatched by a cunning man and a half." In 1749 he formulated his thoughts about revenge with a neatness found in none of his predecessors: "Doing an injury puts you below your enemy; revenging one makes you but even with him; forgiving it sets you above him." In one of the most characteristic of all his sayings, not yet traced to any earlier source, Franklin in 1752 summed up his principle of tolerance for erring mankind: "The brave and the wise can both pity and excuse when cowards and fools show no mercy."

So many of Franklin's sources remain unidentified that it is impossible to tell with precision how much he only passed on, and how much he added to, the stream of proverbial wisdom which flows down from the past through him into the living human language. But it is easy to see that he bettered most of the sayings which he reworked, thanks to his genius for terse clarity and his delicate ear for cadence. For example, since 1572 a common English-Scottish proverb had been put by several writers into as many forms: "A gloved cat can catch no mice"; "Cuffed cat's no good mouse-hunt"; "A muffled cat was never good mouser." In 1754 Franklin gave it the form which it has since kept: "The cat in gloves catches no mice." The Scottish "Fat housekeepers make lean executors" became in Franklin, in 1733, "A fat kitchen, a lean will." A saying as old as Chaucer or Shakespeare, in one set of words or another, and printed in 1670 as "Three may keep counsel, if two be away," was pointed up by Franklin in 1735 to "Three may keep a secret if two of them are dead." As far back as Plautus it had been said that no guest is welcome longer than three days. Lyly in *Euphues* and Cervantes in *Don Quixote* had compared guests with fish as soon ill-smelling, and Herrick in his *Hesperides*. Franklin may have come upon the saying in John Ray's *English Proverbs* (1670) as "Fresh fish and new come guests, smell by they are three days old"; or in James Kelly's *Scottish Proverbs* (1721) as "Fresh fish and poor friends become soon ill sar'd"—that is, ill savored. In Franklin's handling the proverb settled in 1736 into its vernacular idiom and cadence, "Fish and visitors stink in three days," which sensitive editors print with a politer verb.

If the merely prudential maxims of Poor Richard, which are in fact fewer than the others, are better known than all the rest put together, this is partly an accident of printing. In July, 1757, when Franklin was crossing the Atlantic to London as Pennsylvania's agent, he wrote a preface, longer than usual, for the next year's almanac, which was to be the last edited by him. That preface, known as *The Way to Wealth,* has since then been reprinted more often than anything else by Franklin except his *Autobiography*; while the less specialized sayings have lain unread in the original almanacs or have had to be content with few and limited reprintings. Consequently the prudential part of Poor Richard's counsel has been mistaken for the whole of Franklin's wisdom. But it must be remembered that in *The Way to Wealth* the imaginary speaker, Father Abraham, is an old man at a country auction urging people not to pay more for things than they are worth, and quoting Poor Richard as his authority. Of course he restricts himself to the economical maxims, and has no occasion to quote Poor Richard on all the larger topics with which he had concerned himself. Franklin, for whom frugality was discipline, not nature, had insisted too much on pennysaving and so left behind him a reputation which belies his character and is contradicted by his career.

4

Though Franklin early made up his mind that any writing, in order to be good, ought to be "smooth, clear, and short," and though his own writing from first to last invariably had those merits, he experimented with more different styles than have been commonly noted. They ranged from the sly bawdry of his letter of advice to a young man on marriage (dated June 25, 1745, and called by Franklin *Old Mistresses Apologue*) through the homespun splendor of the opening paragraph of his neglected *Some Account of the Pennsylvania Hospital* (1754) to the elevated and harmonious prose of certain of his later political papers, not to mention the varied tones of sharp wit and easy candor and warm affection in his private correspondence. Slow and hesitant in speech, in English as well as in French, he was at his best only when he could write what he had to say. He is immensely quotable, yet never annoyingly sententious. His years of practice at adapting and perfecting maxims for *Poor Richard* no doubt bred in Franklin the habit of felicity, but it was his felicity, not something borrowed from other writers.

"If you would not be forgotten as soon as you are dead and rotten, either write things worth reading or do things worth the writing," Franklin said in *Poor Richard* for 1738. In his own life he aimed to do both, though his writing, as the pressure of affairs upon him increased, frequently lagged behind his living. By the end of 1741 he had invented the Franklin stove, which he described in his *Account of the New-Invented Pennsylvanian Fire-Places* (1744). This was at once a promotion pamphlet written for a Junto friend to whom Franklin had given the right to manufacture the stoves and also, in effect, the first published contribution to science by a member of the new American Philosophical Society. Franklin, secretary of the Society, found its members less active in general science than he had hoped they would be, and he himself turned aside in 1747 to the special electrical studies which brought him fame. His originality in research was equaled by the force and grace with which he reported his discoveries to the learned world and to general readers alike. It never occurred to them, or to him, that such writings did not belong to literature in the large true sense of that term.

Nor did it occur to Franklin that he was free, however well his electrical studies were under way, to confine himself to them in the midst of the public troubles which beset Pennsylvania and the rest of America. Though he retired from business in 1748, his interests expanded rather than contracted. In August, 1750, he had observed that the pigeons in a dovecot on the wall of his house increased in number as fast as he provided room for them. From this he proceeded to his germinal idea, expounded in *Observations concerning the Increase of Mankind, Peopling of Countries, etc.* (published 1755), that population depends on subsistence and will grow as long as supplies hold up. His idea developed into a confidence that the people of America must before long outnumber the people of the British Isles, and the conviction that the coming change in the balance of population must demand a new organization of the British Empire in respect to its dominions overseas. This confidence and this conviction guided Franklin in all his political and diplomatic efforts down to the American Revolution, and were implicit if not explicit in his Canada pamphlet called *The Interest of Great Britain Considered* (1760), *The Examination of Doctor Benjamin Franklin* (1766) before the House of Commons, *Causes of the American Discontents before 1768* (1768), and many of his more casual pieces. Though he had to suit himself in his particular actions to events as they came, he was remarkably consistent in his major principle.

His fundamental political consistency is sometimes lost sight of in the bewildering, if charming, variety of his scientific, moral, and humorous utterances. He did not cease to seem a wizard and a wit while he became a more and more important politician. In 1769 he brought together a "corrected, methodized, and improved" edition of his *Experiments and Observations on Electricity . . . To which are added, Letters and Papers on Philosophical Subjects*; and in 1773 he aided in the publication in French, at Paris, of a still more extensive collection of the *Œuvres de M. Franklin*. In the scientific papers there were then bound to be many "conjectures and suppositions," as Franklin had earlier insisted. "I own I have too strong a penchant to the building of hypotheses; they indulge my natural indolence." But to his readers it appeared that here was the evidence of a tireless mind inquiring with masterly ease and success into all the mysteries of nature. They could only wonder, since they could not know which of his guesses (in fact the majority of them) would be confirmed by later experiment, and which would turn out to be inadequate or erroneous

While it might seem strange that a politician was also a scientist, it seemed stranger still that he could moreover be so delightful a humorist. Humor, with a satirical intent, was one of Franklin's social and political methods. His specialty was the hoax. As early as 1730, in his fictitious account of *A Witch Trial at Mount Holly,* he ridiculed the witchcraft superstition. In *Exporting of Felons to the Colonies* (1751) he gravely proposed that as a kind of return for the felons the Americans might export rattlesnakes to Britain. In a letter *To the Editor of a Newspaper* (1765) he made fun in London of tall tales about America with his comment on the pursuit of the cod by the whales into American fresh waters: observing, with unquestionable though elusive accuracy, "that the grand leap of the whale in that chase up the Fall of Niagara is esteemed, by all who have seen it, as one of the finest spectacles in nature." In 1773 he parodied the British claim of a right to rule America in *An Edict of the King of Prussia,* wherein Prussia made what Franklin offered as a parallel claim on Britain. In 1782 he printed in Paris his *Supplement to the Boston Independent Chronicle* purporting to prove that the British commanders in America had paid regular bounties to Indians for scalps from American settlers they had killed. Readers fooled at first by such hoaxes might soon see through them, but they would also see these matters in a new perspective, and would remember Franklin's serious meaning as well as his witty expression of it.

The bagatelles with which Franklin amused himself and his circle at Passy, near Paris, while he was Commissioner or Minister to France, were merely a further, lighter application of his hoaxing method. Because Madame Brillon smilingly refused his smiling request that she be more than daughter to him, he wrote, and printed at his little private press, *The Ephemera* (1778), a fantasy on the passage of time and philosophic resignation. When Madame Helvétius declined his proposal of marriage, Franklin in *A Notre Dame d'Auteuil* (1778?) lightheartedly told her how he had slept and gone to the Elysian Fields, where he had found her former husband now married to Franklin's former wife. "Here I am; let us avenge ourselves." If gallantry was expected of a diplomat in France, Franklin could be a master in that pleasant art; just as, if he was expected to be a sage, the Solon of the New World come back to the Old with news of a Golden Age ahead, he could be sage and Solon. These were not disguises he put on, as with Poor Richard, but his own character touched up with deft dramatic art. The years had taught him how to become fully what he was.

The most substantial writings of his later years, outside his *Autobiography,* belong to the literature of diplomacy, in which no other writer has surpassed him. Even his routine dispatches, if any can be called that, were written with a statesman's grasp of the diplomatic situation, a philosopher's insight into the minds and motives of the persons involved, and a wit's happy knack at making everything alive and intelligible. About two of the most interesting chapters in his diplomatic history Franklin was too busy to write much: the passage and repeal of the Stamp Act, and the negotiation of the treaty of alliance with France. But he told as much as it was then possible for any one man to know about three other important chapters, in his *Tract relative to the Affair of Hutchinson's Letters* (1774), *An Account of Negotiations in London for effecting a Reconciliation between Great Britain and the American Colonies* (1775), and *Journal of the Negotiation for Peace with Great Britain* (1782). For the first two of these affairs Franklin remains the chief and almost the sole authority: of all of them he is the classic chronicler in whose pages the bones of those old controversies get up and walk in convincing flesh and blood.

For writing out these chapters at such length Franklin had different specific motives. His narrative of the Hutchinson affair was his vindication of his conduct though it had cost him his Crown office. His story of his negotiations with the British ministry during the winter of 1774-1775, set down on his voyage home while those events were still fresh in his memory, was his testimony that he had done everything he thought possible to avert hostilities. His detailed record of the early peace negotiations in Paris was intended not only for the Continental Congress but also for his fellow commissioners, not one of whom was in Paris when the first moves were being made. But in every case Franklin wrote autobiographically because he had already begun his *Autobiography,* and knew that these recent events must have a place in what was yet to be written.

5

He had begun the *Autobiography,* which Franklin himself never called anything but his Memoirs, at Chilbolton, the house of Bishop Jonathan Shipley near Twyford in Hampshire, in August, 1771. Shipley, pro-American among the British bishops, had a large family which was devoted, young and old, to Franklin whom they regarded as a modern Socrates. They asked him for anecdotes of his childhood, so different from theirs, in far-off Boston. They insisted, at least the older among them, that he owed it to the world to tell the story of his life. Their suggestion seems to have roused a responsive impulse in him, and the unusual expectation of "a week's uninterrupted leisure" furnished him an opportunity. In "the sweet retirement of Twyford, where my only business was a little scribbling in the garden study," as Franklin later put it, he wrote the first part of his *Autobiography* in the thirteen days of his visit, and probably less than that. Since no form of writing was so natural to him as autobiographical letters, and since he had written many of them to his son William, now royal Governor of New Jersey, the father cast his Memoirs in the form of an autobiographical letter to the son. On the first day of writing, it appears, Franklin began with a rush of family anecdotes about his ancestors, his parents, and his early childhood; then, again it appears, he resolved to write "more methodically" and drew up the Outline which thereafter he followed, not too methodically, through all four parts down to the year 1757. The first part is the happiest and sunniest of them, with its carefree recollections of one of the best known of all boyhoods.

After that August, 1771, Franklin for thirteen years found no time, or impulse, to resume his story. On his voyage home in the spring of 1775 he was expected, by his eager friends at Twyford, to do it, but he chose instead to write for his son about the past winter's unsuccessful negotiations. The outbreak of the Revolution interrupted any plans for the Memoirs that Franklin may have had. Not till 1784 did he turn back once more to his youth and go on with the narrative. He had left the manuscript of the first part in America, and could not remember exactly where it broke off. Estranged from his son, who had sided with the British government in the late conflict, Franklin would not now write as to him, and did not feel disposed to give so much space as before to "little family anecdotes of no importance to others." What he wrote in 1784 was "intended for the public" which, through certain of Franklin's close friends and advisers, was demanding that he recount the instructive adventures of his rise to world renown.

Yet even in the congenial air of triumph at Passy, after the peace, Franklin wrote only a short second installment of his Memoirs. Living so richly in the present as he did, he found it difficult to relive the remote past. For that he needed a more pressing personal vanity or literary ambition than he had. His last voyage home to America, in the summer of 1785, he spent on scientific speculations which interested him more than his own history. And at home, where there was no such leisure as he had looked forward to, he put off his Memoirs, in spite of many urgings, till August-October, 1788, when he wrote the third part. He was now too old and infirm to plan, or hope, to do much more. In November, 1789, he sent revised (and somewhat formalized) copies of Parts I-III to friends in France and England, asking their advice whether to publish the work at all. After that he wrote the few pages of the fourth part, probably in the last weeks of his life. The final lines of the manuscript are crooked, as if he were writing in bed.

Because Franklin had delayed so long, his Memoirs met with strange fortunes for so desired and desirable a book. It first appeared in 1791, in an unauthorized and unexplained French version, promptly retranslated into English by some unknown London journalist. That version was often reprinted, even after Franklin's grandson in 1818 printed an authorized version from one of Franklin's revised copies of 1789. Not till 1868 was the original manuscript discovered in France, and the *Autobiography,* including the hitherto omitted fourth part, printed as Franklin had written it.

This bungling introduction of a masterpiece did not too seriously handicap it. The meat of the matter was there in any version, as it was in time to be in any language. This was of course not the earliest of autobiographies. Augustine had told of his struggles between flesh and spirit, Benvenuto Cellini of his fiery life as artist and lover, Rousseau, very recently, of his career among raptures and neuroses. Franklin, telling his straightforward story in a language so transparent that few readers noted his amazing art, seemed to them hardly to be writing a book. This was a life. The book fixed the mode which most realistic autobiographers have since then followed. Franklin is still known to the world at large for his *Autobiography,* which is a fragment, and for *The Way to Wealth,* which is only a selection from his memorable sayings. Probably he will always be best known by these pieces of himself he left behind. Posterity can hardly be trusted to fit the whole of him together in one record if he could never do it. Nor has posterity a good excuse for asking that a man who did so much should have somehow managed to do less in order to write and publish more.

Franklin, summing up his world and at ease in it, left behind him the essence and living image of colonial America in the years when it was realizing its power and achieving its independence. The first to be called the father of his country, he came, after the rise of Washington's fame, to be thought of rather as his country's grandfather. In America, more than elsewhere, he has been popularly remembered for his grandfatherly qualities of prudence, geniality, humor. But the history of his fame has been notably marked by the rediscovery, decade after decade, of his other qualities of originality, audacity, and searching wit. One after another his prophetic forecasts have been justified by events. It increasingly appears that he conformed to the revolutionary spirit in his age, not to its complacency. Revolutionary as well as prophet, he helped shape the future. If he was full of contagious energy in the eighteenth century, so is he in the twentieth. No other early American writer is anything like so well known as he, so often reprinted, or so widely read and enjoyed. A large part of the American character lay in him as in a seed, and it has gradually unfolded by a process not unlike that of his own individual growth. Some great men cast a shadow over posterity. Franklin throws a light, which has affected American life, literature, and science ever since his own day and is still undimmed. He survives as a tremendous national symbol, and yet has never ceased to be a familiar and beloved person.

THE REPUBLIC

---inquiry and imitation

9. REVOLUTION AND REACTION

By 1763 the British colonies on the North American continent had attained a degree of political and economic maturity which ill fitted them for the restraints and prohibitions of British colonial policy. Moreover, the conquest of French Canada by the combined forces of Great Britain and her colonies produced in America an exuberant confidence and expansionism which led Benjamin Franklin to urge the extension of the British Empire—and the liberty for which he believed it stood—around the globe. This lusty sense of power and freedom constantly overset the best-laid schemes of British imperialists who sought, after 1763, to curtail the liberties of Americans with direct taxation by the British Parliament and a stricter enforcement of the Navigation Acts. Balked in their efforts to bend the Empire to their ideals, Americans directed their new-found feeling of unity and strength into the struggle for independence from the mother country.

In order to protect their liberties from the efforts of English administrators to centralize in London power over the Empire, Americans turned—as they had repeatedly done in the past—to Locke, Harrington, and other philosophers of the natural rights school. Their first line of defense against British tyranny was natural law, upon which, they contended, the British constitution itself was based. "Who," asked John Dickinson of Pennsylvania, "are a free people? Not those over whom government is reasonably and equitably exercised but those who live under a government so constitutionally checked and controlled that proper provision is made against its being otherwise exercised." By this philosophy, King and Parliament could not do what God and Nature had clearly forbidden. Above all, they could not impose taxation without representation. God and Nature, to Americans, were Reason; and they sought to apply the cardinal principles of the Enlightenment—the faith in reason and human perfectibility—to the British Empire. Until 1776, far from seeking to destroy the Empire, they strove to ensure its prosperity and perpetuation by bringing it into harmony with the laws of nature. But what the laws of nature were, Englishmen and Americans could not agree: "Were my countrymen now in England dipped once in the River Delaware," remarked an Englishman, "I dare say, that it would make an almost miraculous change in their opinions." Americans stoutly insisted upon the privilege of interpreting natural law—which, Englishmen objected, was to submit the laws of the Empire not to God or Nature, but to a "Jury of Bostonians" with Sam Adams and James Otis as judges.

Because of its universality, natural law became a bond of union among Americans, giving New Englanders and Carolinians alike a common ground upon which to rest their case against British oppression. As a philosophy of the liberty of the individual against the state, natural law was one of the most fruitful sources of democratic ideas. Whether debated by the Rev. John Wise as determining the proper form of government for New England churches, or by Robert Beverley as determining the relationship of the Virginia planters to the mother country, the issue of natural rights *vs.* civil authority was familiar to thinking Americans at least a century before the Revolutionary War.

When applied to the problems of empire, Americans' interpretation of natural law led to decentralization and the exaltation of local liberties. Fearful of the authority of the government at Westminster, they glorified their provincial assemblies into local parliaments, bound to the mother country only through a common king. In the opinion of Englishmen, these ideas pointed not so much to liberty as to provincialism and isolationism—in short, to the break-up of the Empire. When compromise failed, Americans declared their independence—and in so doing inherited the problem which the English government had been unable to solve: how local liberty in the Empire could be reconciled with the existence of central government.

2

Conflicting ideologies gave rise to a war of words which raged for ten years before Americans and Englishmen resorted to blows to settle their differences. During the decade before Lexington, the colonists sought to persuade the British government by means of arguments, reinforced by non-importation agreements directed against British merchandise, to respect their rights. Literature became a weapon in the struggle for liberty: the art of whipping up public opinion by propaganda became the chief study of many American writers. As the conflict grew more embittered, less attention was paid to the niceties of the constitutional argument as developed by James Otis and John Dickinson: British atrocities, the wickedness of the ministry of Lord North, and the depravity of the English people increasingly became the subject matter of American pamphleteers and newspaper writers. This literary outpouring materially helped to prepare public opinion for the

Declaration of Independence and to sustain American morale during the days that tried men's souls. Edmund Burke said that Americans sniffed tyranny in every tainted breeze: it would be more exact to say that they read about it in their newspapers.

As long as the revolutionary movement remained an effort to win for Americans the rights and privileges of Englishmen within the Empire, the colonists were united and "Toryism" was relatively unimportant; but when the goal of independence and Republicanism was held up to Americans early in 1776 by Thomas Paine, it became apparent that the revolution was to be a civil war in which Americans fought Americans. A large number of colonists—perhaps one-third of the population—continued loyal to Great Britain, not merely out of love for King and Parliament and veneration for the mother country, but because they feared that a democratic upheaval would be the first result of American independence. The Declaration of Independence gave these conservatives no comfort. In pronouncing that "all men are created equal," Jefferson seemed to have opened the floodgates of revolution at home; it was now certain that the patriot leaders intended not only to sever the connection with Great Britain but to usher in a new order based upon the principle that government was created for the welfare of the common man.

Not all conservatives took the hard and thorny road that led to Toryism and exile; many threw in their lot with the patriots and, in consequence, the revolutionary party itself became a battleground between radicals and conservatives. Conflict centered on the questions of who should rule at home and how democratic the United States was to be. Some patriots resisted all reform and strove to confine the revolutionary movement within the narrow channel of resistance to Great Britain; others wished utterly to sweep away the old aristocratic order and to turn the country over to the new men— chiefly from the small-farmer class—who boldly promulgated the right of the majority to rule. But neither radicals nor conservatives won a clear-cut triumph: it was rather the moderate reformers who carried the day. Over the protests of the embattled reactionaries, the state churches were disestablished and the principle of religious freedom avowed; primogeniture and entail were swept away; slavery was abolished, usually by gradual means, in the Northern states; and the preambles of the new state constitutions proclaimed that the people were the source of all political power. Yet in most of the states "the people"—in the sense of those qualified to vote and to hold office—remained essentially the same; and the West was denied its fair share of representation lest it should seize control of the state governments from the conservative East.

These reforms were the most important achievements of the Enlightenment in the United States during the revolutionary period. The eighteenth century was the era of enlightened despots: for a brief span in European history, philosophers were kings. It was a period when ideas, long germinating in the minds of philosophers, began to bear fruit in the form of humanitarianism. Thus the United States was conceived in an age of reform—but it was reform from above, the work of paternalistic and arbitrary rulers. The American patriots of the revolutionary generation proved that republicans were not less enlightened than despots and that the people themselves could do, and do better, what kings and philosophers sought to do for them.

The changes introduced by the Revolution did not destroy aristocracy in the United States. In abolishing primogeniture and entail, Jefferson believed that he was striking a blow at the roots of aristocracy; but he soon found that he had merely lopped off one of its limbs. Privilege had yielded only a few of its outer defenses to the democrats: its citadel remained unshaken. Moreover, the Revolution spawned its own aristocracy: the *nouveaux riches* created by privateering, profiteering, and speculation, having already moved into the houses of the departed Tories, quickly adopted their manners and ideas. These beneficiaries of the Revolution became the backbone of the Federalist party and the most redoubtable enemies of the "principles of 1776."

Perhaps the greatest service rendered by the Revolution to the cause of democracy in the United States was throwing open the West to settlement. Quite rightly, many British statesmen had foreseen that, once Americans were permitted to stream unimpeded across the Alleghenies, the cause of authoritarian government would be gravely weakened. But the westward advance was too powerful to be long held in check by any governmental fiat: the Federalists sought to oppose the growth of the West and, like the British government before them, went down to defeat. The party of Jefferson, on the other hand, allied itself with the West and thereby with the future of American democracy.

If the American Revolution seemed to many democrats an "unfinished" revolution, it likewise fell short of the expectations of those who wished to establish a powerful national government. During the darkest hours of the Revolutionary War, these patriots had been sustained by the hope that the United States would emerge from the struggle a strong and united nation. But under the Articles of Confederation, the republic was weak, disunited, and seemingly drifting into anarchy. To alarmed nationalists, the United States seemed a certain victim of hostile European states; yet the mass of Americans remained unconscious of their danger, unheedful of warnings that weakness was an invitation to attack.

Instead, the American people, spurred on by a postwar depression, attempted to apply the ideals for which they had fought to conditions at home. They demanded laws for the benefit of debtors, fair representation for the West, office holding open to all, manhood suffrage, and curbs upon the power of wealth—in short, Jacksonian Democracy fifty years before Jackson became President. The small farmers gained control of many state governments and proceeded to enact legislation in their own interest; and where the conservative, privileged class refused to yield, as in Massachusetts, the people rose in armed rebellion.

These events produced a sharp reaction in favor of strong government. The people, who in 1776 had been hailed as the source of wisdom and virtue, now began to be regarded as a "great beast" which must be kept securely under leash. To reconcile order with liberty and to create a strong central government capable of resisting foreign foes and American populists alike, plans for "a more perfect union" were drawn up at the Constitutional Convention held in Philadelphia in 1787. Here was contained the answer of American statesmen to the problem that had wrecked the British Empire: how local liberty could exist alongside strong central government. It was also the answer of Americans to the age-old problem of whether man lives for the state or the state is his servant, created for his benefit. Despite the strong feeling against popular "licentiousness," the framers of the Constitution made clear that Americans were not to be mere creatures of the state but citizens endowed with inalienable rights beyond the reach of government.

3

If a nation had been created by the American Revolution and the Federal Constitution, the question remained: What kind of nation was it to be? Was the United States to become an industrialized country of cities, with an aristocracy of wealth looking to the federal government for bounties and protection, or was it to be a country of small farmers, led by an aristocracy of talents, and with the fostering of individual liberty the paramount concern of the states? Herein lies the crux of the struggle between Jefferson and Hamilton, between Republicans and Federalists—the struggle that was to preoccupy the American mind until, merging with the slavery question, it produced the elements of civil war.

The contest between Jefferson and Hamilton, involving as it did the future of American civilization, was intensified by the outbreak of the French Revolution. In the United States, discontented democrats hailed the work of French revolutionaries and began to clamor for a second American revolution, to be based upon the principles of "Liberty, Equality, and Fraternity" and directed against the home-grown brand of aristocracy and privilege. Conservatives rallied to the defense of the established order, resolved to resist any change whatever lest it prove the opening wedge for revolution.

In this struggle, Thomas Paine's *The Rights of Man* became the Bible of the radicals while conservatives found an arsenal of arguments in the counterrevolutionary writings of John Adams and Alexander Hamilton. The New England clergy—the "black regiment" of war days that had given its congregations rebellion and theology in approximately equal measure—now fulminated against the infidelity and license of the French Revolution, picturing the horrors that awaited Americans if they followed in the footsteps of the French. "Shall our Sons become the disciples of Voltaire and the dragoons of Marat," exclaimed the Reverend Timothy Dwight of Connecticut, "or our daughters the concubines of the Illuminati?" But American democrats staunchly upheld the cause of revolution both at home and in France: in their eyes, opposition to the French Revolution was "a war of Kings and Nobles against the equal Rights of Men" and the Federalists were reactionaries who sought to deny the American people the freedom that was their birthright.

4

It is significant that even before the Constitution had been adopted, an ardently nationalistic school of American writers had appeared: the so-called Hartford Wits. The idea that the United States was to be the new Athens of the arts and sciences had been frequently expressed during the Revolution: as long as they remained British colonists, it was said, Americans had reflected all the prejudices and insularity of Britons, but now, as free men, they stood prepared to embrace the world, drawing inspiration from all cultures and all men. In the eyes of some patriots the separation had come just in time: another generation of British rule, said an American, and the colonists would have "learned to eat and drink, and swear and quarrel like Englishmen." Happily, their eyes had been opened in time and they could now perceive that France, for example, was "the most enlightened nation in the world" and its people the most civilized and polite. France had polished and refined Europe: the next step was for this gifted nation to remove the last vestiges of colonialism from the United States. To Thomas Paine, the alliance of the United States with France was like a breath of fresh air stirring among the dead leaves of provincial America, promising a golden age of American literature. "We see with other eyes," Paine exclaimed; "we hear with other ears; and think with other thoughts than those we formerly used. . . . Every corner of the mind is swept of its cobwebs, poison and dust, and made fit for the reception of generous happiness."

In this frame of mind, Americans rushed into print to proclaim their declaration of intellectual independence, grimly determined to stand and die in the literary trenches rather than submit to any return to colonial bondage in things of the spirit. Inevitably, they were led to use American scenes and materials—and thus helped prepare the way for the American Renaissance of the nineteenth century. If America had not come of age in literature— and the work of these early writers is the best evidence that it had not—at least the first stirrings of a vigorous and promising adolescence were evident.

Yet polemics continued to engross the American mind: Philip Freneau, the most promising poet of his generation, spoke as Jefferson's champion against Hamilton and devoted to politics talents that belonged to literature. Party warfare tended to make the American a "newspaper reading animal," to borrow the phrase of an English traveler, and to make American writers propagandists and pamphleteers. Seemingly a grave disservice was thereby done to the cause of literature; but, by developing a great mass of readers, the newspapers made possible a wide and expanding market for books.

By 1820, the triumph of democratic ideals and the ending of the menace of foreign intervention enabled Americans to turn their attention to the business of settling and developing the continent. The purely polemical phase of American literature was passing, and writers could give literary expression to something more enduring than the political passions of the day. America, it began to be recognized, in its size, color, and diversity furnished the man of letters with a wealth of material for his pen. No longer wholly concerned with hewing out a livelihood from a forest wilderness, and now imbued with a desire to exploit the literary resources of their country, Americans were prepared for the long awaited, and long delayed, American Renaissance.

10. THE MAKING OF THE MAN OF LETTERS

E<small>DUCATION</small> was the first need, and the colonial schools and colleges had made a good start toward providing it. The early colleges survived the era of revolution and maintained well into the following century their modified classical curricula, their small and socially selected student bodies, and their emphasis on preparation for the law, the ministry, and public life. To the eight colonial colleges were soon added Virginia and many others. The church drew fewer of their graduates, and the law and politics more. Gradually there was less temptation to send likely youth to Oxford or Cambridge, London or Edinburgh, for the fundamentals that make a gentleman.

On the other hand, the habit of going abroad for advanced study in medicine, the fine arts, science, and still to a large extent the law became even more firmly established in the first half-century of independence, and, particularly in science, continued to our own day. The American-born president of the British Royal Academy, Benjamin West, spread his giant historical canvases on the walls of Windsor Castle and Greenwich Hospital, and trained almost all our early painters in his London studio, at least until one of them, Charles Willson Peale, broke the tradition and helped to found in 1805 the Pennsylvania Academy of the Fine Arts. Similarly our early physicians went as a matter of routine to Edinburgh and London for their training until they in turn could establish medical schools at home. And the study of language and literature took George Ticknor, Longfellow, and many another young professor to England and Germany during the years that followed. The former colonists were typically adolescent in their attitude toward their parent cultures. They cultivated the strut of independence in voice and manner while sedulously learning from and aping their elders.

On other levels of education, this attitude brought good results. The rampant nationalism of the lexicographer Noah Webster and the geographer Jedidiah Morse did much to popularize a more genuine and less traditional system of elementary and secondary schooling, combating the limitations of the colonial grammar schools, dame schools, and private tutors of the socially privileged. The district and "charity" schools which, after the Revo-

122

lution, provided the democratic foundations for our modern system of public instruction, were slow of development. Although Massachusetts had had a public-school law since 1647, most of the state constitutions made no such provisions, and even the federal constitution was silent on the subject. During the eighteenth century, the training of youth was still a responsibility of the home.

Into this situation, Webster in 1783 injected his "blue backed speller," a challenge to traditionalism and complacency. On the principle that learning must be close to experience, it proclaimed an American language and set out, by properly training the youth, to make this country "as independent in *literature* as she is in *politics*—as famous for *arts* as for *arms.*" The campaign was carried forward by his own reader, grammar, and dictionary, by Morse's *The American Geography,* "calculated early to impress the minds of American youth with the idea of the superior importance of their own country," and by Jefferson's proposal of 1817 for a comprehensive plan of mass education, starting with county schools and culminating in a university in which should be taught "all the useful sciences in their highest degree."

It was a century or longer before natural democratic man took his place in the councils of the colleges. In spite of the liberal and rational views of such planners as Franklin, Jefferson, and even the American Samuel Johnson, first president of King's College (Columbia), the classical and theological ideals of the colonial period, born of sedulous loyalty to the tradition of Oxford and Cambridge, persisted through early national days. Our first literary men had a colonial training and a colonial heritage. They were the select few, presumably masters of Latin, Greek, logic, rhetoric, theology, mathematics, and perhaps science in its early form of natural philosophy. In college, "that temple of dullness, that roost of owls," as Joseph Dennie described it, discipline was strict and learning carefully divorced from life. Occasionally the more spirited students were rusticated for misbehavior as was Dennie, or dismissed outright, as was James Fenimore Cooper when, it is reported, he opened the door of a friend's room by a miniature blast of gunpowder tucked into the keyhole.

Other and better outlets for youthful spirits were the literary and debating societies, such as the Linonia and Brothers societies at Yale, the American Whig Society in which Freneau and Brackenridge were active at Princeton, and the Philomathean and Zelosophic societies at Pennsylvania. These groups were usually paired, and their rivalries provided the focus of undergraduate life. They supplemented the classroom by promoting debate on current topics in politics and literature, sometimes so successfully that the resulting pranks and brawls led to petty bloodshed. But, most significant for our purposes, their surviving libraries show a preponderance of the currently imported and popular books, which must have compensated for the narrowly academic collections built up by the administrations. It was out of them rather than the formal classroom that the modern American college grew, and it was in their meetings that the combative and creative interests of our later political and literary leaders were formed and nurtured.

2

Once out of college, the American youth found even less stimulus to a purely literary life. If he had learned to read, analyze, and declaim in the classroom, he had also learned in his societies to debate current issues and to enjoy current English and American books. His mind might be stored with Latin and Greek, theology, logic, rhetoric, and mathematics, but his veins secretly pulsed with the gentle rhythms of Addisonian prose or the emphatic couplets of Pope while his ears rang with the phrases of Patrick Henry and Samuel Adams. It was all very confusing and thwarting if one wished to write, as college graduates do. The simplest answer to the problem was to read for the law, and then to enter the political or business world, saving literature for the idle moment and watering it down to belles-lettres. There were so many immediate issues to be settled; there was so much work of the pioneering world to be done!

For one thing, there were no publishers in the modern sense, and few printers would take a chance on a book by an American when English authors could be pirated at will. Franklin had republished *Pamela* in 1744, and the example had been followed with no qualms by later printers. These printers, of whom there was a steadily increasing number in all the coastal cities, were primarily equipped to issue broadsides, currency, pamphlets, newspapers, and occasionally a magazine. Until about 1825, American authors published their own books, taking all or the greater part of the financial risks. Most of our printers had learned from the example of Hugh Gaine, of wartime notoriety, to change their opinions with the weather and to seek out such business as the market afforded. Our first publishers in anything like the modern sense—Isaiah Thomas and Mathew Carey, who had ambitions and ethics of their own and the initiative to implement them— were exceptions. Yet even these two were primarily printers, only incidentally publishers.

The reading public, which grew rapidly during this period, was also in part responsible for hampering the immediate encouragement of native work because the prestige of English authors more than satisfied the increasing demand for popular forms of literature. Colonial libraries had been composed of the works in the classics, history, philosophy, and theology which their owners had learned to value in college; and the stock-holding subscribers to the libraries of pre-Revolutionary days like the Philadelphia Library Company, the New York Society Library, and other athenaeums and library societies from Providence to Charleston, merely extended the pattern to New Orleans (1805) and to Boston (1807). Even though these societies bought generously from the lists of native printers, their subscribers demanded even more urgently the London imprint and the standard or popular work.

The craze for novel reading which hit the British public toward the close of the eighteenth century, and the subsequent popularity of the Romantic poets and the familiar essayists of the early nineteenth, soon found reflection in this country. American presses were reprinting English novels in quantity before 1790, and long listings of "new books (mostly travel and fiction) by the ship Electra from London," sales of private libraries, and offerings of "books, fancy articles, &c. for Christmas" were occupying almost as much space in the newspapers as were announcements of importations of gloves, cotton goods, wine, tea, salt, and soap. Cooper could not hope to find a publisher who would pay him adequately for his first success, *The Spy,* in 1821; but when it appeared, in December of that year, there were four booksellers in New York City alone ready to advertise that they had it for sale.

The novelist Charles Brockden Brown was the first American, and the only one before Cooper and Irving, to attempt the literary profession by reliance on the book market alone; and he failed. He experimented with a bookseller as well as with local printers as publishers for his American Gothic tales. The list of fiction in the circulating library of one William Caritat (1804) supplies the causes of Brown's failure with both, and the reason why he, like so many of his fellows, turned from writing to magazine editing for subsistence. Caritat, a fashionable bookseller, in that year had some two thousand French and English novels on his shelves, reprinted in this country or directly imported. A study of this list reveals why Brown was hopeful of the popular moral tale of horror as a medium for his literary ambitions; but it also explains why his inspiration dried up so suddenly in the face of foreign competition.

3

Our printers were quicker than our authors to learn how to profit by the unequal situation. By the time *Waverley* appeared in 1814, the war was on, and Scott became its principal victim. John Miller, a hack publisher of London, acted as agent for his most successful American counterpart, Mathew

Carey in Philadelphia. It was his task to see that the sheets, or even the proofs if he could get them, of any potential British success were in Carey's hands by fast packet (about thirty days) almost before the bound volumes had appeared in the London bookshops and well before any of them could be imported. Carey paid Miller, not the British author or publisher, for this service. "We have rec'd *Quentin Durward* most handsomely," he writes Miller on June 17, 1823, "and have the same completely in our own hands this time." He had won the race if he could be first to get sufficient copies to the local booksellers and into the van of the picturesque Parson Weems, peddling his wares through the countryside and fiddling his way to the hearts of his customers.

When the sheets of a new book were received, they were at once divided among three or four typesetters who worked night and day in shifts and sometimes produced a reprint in twenty-four hours. Even one or two days' priority assured financial success. It is perhaps significant that when this traffic was at its height, about 1815, popular books of American authorship were virtually nonexistent. The first group of writers had given up the struggle and were depending on a precarious magazine market to issue the literary by-products of their more substantial pursuits, while the second had not yet overcome the increasing obstacles to success. It is also significant that almost all the prominent early American printers of books—the Wileys, Appleton, the Harper brothers, and the Careys, as well as other and lesser men—were violently opposed to any form of international copyright.

The problem remained unsolved until about 1825, when Irving and Cooper discovered the cause of the difficulty. They were the first to realize that Noah Webster's patriotic zeal had overreached itself, for the Copyright Act of 1790 allowed protection only to American authors, whereas in England protection could be claimed under common law or gentlemen's agreement on the basis of prior issue and regardless of the author's nationality. For an entire literary generation this legal difference had remained unnoticed and merciless pirating gone unchecked on both sides of the water. Both British and American authors suffered; but British prestige made the lot of the American hopeless. "What publisher," wrote Cooper to Carey, "will pay a native writer for ideas that he may import for nothing?"

Great as this temporary sacrifice of native talent may have been, perhaps it was a necessary preparation for the writers who were still to come. However unethical the copyright situation, it built up and educated a reading public in a great European literary tradition, and it taught American writers that they could not compete with that tradition by imitation alone. The full force of this education would not be felt for another generation, when the spirit rather than the mere forms of older cultures had been absorbed and the values rather than the bare facts of the American experience had begun to be understood by native writers.

4

If the book market was, in this transition period, practically nonexistent for the American author, the outlets for his work provided by the magazines and the theater were little better. The four principal post-Revolutionary magazines of the eighteenth century—the *Columbian*, Carey's *American Museum*, the *Massachusetts Magazine*, and the *New-York Magazine*—all were addicted to the scissors and the paste-pot, although they occasionally published original essays, poems, and tales with scrupulous anonymity. Dennie's *Port Folio* occupied the central place among American literary magazines during the first quarter of the nineteenth century and achieved the longest run of any such journal up to that time. It offered safe harbor to John Quincy Adams and Richard Rush when their impulses turned from diplomacy to poetry and essay, and to men like Charles Brockden Brown and Dennie himself, for whom writing was an end in itself. The ambitious "Knickerbocker" authors, Irving, Paulding, and their friends, long before the *Sketch Book* days, relied on the newspaper and the pamphlet rather than on the book or the magazine for their Addisonian *Salmagundi* essays, as did Dickinson and Paine for their political tracts during the Revolution and Halleck and Drake for their verse satires, *The Croaker Papers*, in 1819. Yet even the scant market provided by the magazines and newspapers, by an ironic paradox, may have had some bearing on the cultivation of the tract, the essay, the short story, and the lyric poem by American authors at a time when novels were obviously the choice of their readers.

The theater too afforded little encouragement to native talent. Probably there was no time during colonial days when some form of play-acting had not been practiced, however primitively or secretively. The problem of what to do about it was among the first of the agenda of our forefathers. As early as 1610 it had seemed wise to Virginian authorities to forbid the immigration of actors from England because of the evils associated with them. In 1665 three young men of Virginia were charged with "acting a play of ye Bare and ye Cubb." New England's hostility toward the drama has been proverbial, yet in 1712 Samuel Sewall was disturbed by "a Rumor, as if some design'd to have a Play acted in the Council Chamber, next Monday." In Charleston, South Carolina, the "Court room" was used for theatrical performances (in 1735) long before a regular theater was established. In the meantime New York had probably had its first taste of professional acting about 1700 when Richard Hunter apparently was granted a license to present plays. By 1732 there was some sort of "play house" in New York. Strolling players turned up from time to time in many of the major towns and cities of the Atlantic seaboard: Boston, New York, Philadelphia, Annapolis, Williamsburg, Charleston. Sometimes a nucleus of professional actors (generally British) worked in conjunction with local amateurs. In the absence of adequate theaters, performances took place in coffeehouses, stores, or barns. Occasionally, to avoid arousing the ire of municipal authorities, a flimsy, impermanent structure was devised or adapted on the outskirts of a town.

The more consecutive history of the American theater begins about the middle of the eighteenth century. In 1749 a "Company of Comedians" presented the tragedy of *Cato* in Philadelphia. New York was accorded its first notable Shakespearean performance on March 5th of the next year when, with the permission of his Excellency the Governor of the Province, the "Comedians" presented *Richard III*—"Wrote originally by *Shakspere,* and alter'd by Colly Cibber, Esq." Another notable "first" was the presentation of *The Merchant of Venice* at Williamsburg, Virginia, on September 15, 1752, by the "American Company." This occasion was the more historic because it marked the first American production and performance of the Hallam family, among them Lewis Hallam the younger, who was to dominate "the stage of the New World" for "nearly a quarter of a century." It was this initial performance of which John Esten Cooke wrote a glamorous (and not entirely accurate) account in his *Virginia Comedians* (1854). From about this time on, the record indicates a rapid expansion of the theatrical activities, professional, amateur, and "unofficial." When authorities frowned, plays were sometimes advertised as "readings" or "lectures." Private performances, which were hard to censor or suppress, whetted the appetite of play lovers. Students at some of the colleges began to put on performances despite administrative disapproval. In a moment of irritation one former tutor of Yale College complained to the president (in 1777) that students had "left the more solid parts of learn^g & run into Plays & dramatic Exhibitions chiefly of the comic kind & turn'd College . . . into Drury Lane."

The professional theater slowly acquired confidence and prestige. The establishment of more or less permanent buildings was a material gain. The first of these, the Southwark Theater on South Street, Philadelphia, was built in 1766. A brick-and-wood structure painted "a glaring red," it lasted fifty-five years as a theater before becoming (what the opponents of playgoing did not fail to mark) a distillery. The John Street Theater (opened in 1767) in New York was of the same general type as the Southwark. In Annapolis a theater was built in 1771; and Charleston's "elegant" new theater, larger than either the Southwark or the John Street Theater, was opened on December 22, 1773.

With the erection of substantial buildings, the play business became more and more institutionalized. A common practice was to have performances on

Mondays, Wednesdays, and Fridays, with the bill changed for each night. Performances generally began at six or seven o'clock, and the standard bill included a regular play and an "afterpiece," which might be a farce or ballet or a comic opera. The "society" which attended was of course mixed, but it was by no means riffraff. In the South, ladies of the better families were often seen at public amusements, as Josiah Quincy of Boston noted to his astonishment when visiting Charleston in 1773. The frequency and virulence of tirades against the theater everywhere lessened in proportion to the increasing social distinction of its patrons. When General Washington himself attended dramatic performances—as, the records indicate, he did on scores of occasions —who should presume to say that the theater was an altogether degrading and iniquitous place? Alert managers learned to advertise the fact that he would be present, sometimes with a party including brilliantly appareled ladies. Surely on occasions such as these the theater had "arrived." But the best that can be said of it in this period is that it was not a bad imitation of the British. Where Byron and Keats failed, American poets can hardly be blamed for inadequacy. It produced a successful actor in John Howard Payne, whose fame rests equally on his playing of Young Norval in Home's *Douglas* and on the perennial "Home, Sweet Home" from his own *Clari*; but it failed to make a playwright out of himself or his friend Washington Irving, however hard they tried.

5

For self-protection as well as for sociability, these writers gathered together in mutual encouragement societies. The most famous of such groups was the "Hartford Wits," originally composed of four men of varying political views —Joel Barlow, John Trumbull, Lemuel Hopkins, and David Humphreys— but later to include Timothy Dwight, Elihu Hubbard Smith, and many others who shared with them either an enthusiastic patriotism, a religious conservatism, or a love of rhyming couplets. When Dr. Smith moved to New York City in 1793, he became the center of the Friendly Club, a group composed of William Dunlap, Charles Brockden Brown, Dr. Mitchell, and Noah Webster. The fellowship which gathered about Dennie's *Port Folio* in Philadelphia, known as the Tuesday Club, and Peter Irving's Knickerbocker group on the *Morning Chronicle* of New York, were not dining and writing clubs in as strict a sense; but they performed similar functions, as did the later Bread and Cheese Club which forgathered with Fenimore Cooper in the "Den" back of Charles Wiley's bookshop in the City Hotel, and which survives as the Century Association in its dignified home off modern Fifth Avenue.

Under such circumstances, the false literary dawn of the nineties and the "dark ages" which followed seem to lend themselves to ready explanation. Not only was the creative genius of our best minds channeled into politics and practical affairs, not only were we intellectually dependent on England long after we obtained political independence, but we had as yet inadequate means for producing a literature of our own. The struggles of Poe, Cooper, Irving, Halleck, and Bryant did not meet with even modest success until well after 1825; the first half-century of our national life was spent mainly in preparing for the writers and readers to come.

11. THE WAR OF THE PAMPHLETS

Even though excellence in the deliberately "literary" forms of literature had to wait more settled times, the Revolutionary era was ideally suited to the pamphlet. The writer of 1776 might have said of his book, as George Gascoigne said in 1576 introducing Humphrey Gilbert's *New Passage to Cataia:* "It is but a Pamphlet & no large discourse, & therefore the more to be borne withall: since the faults (if any be) shalbe the fewer, because the volume is not great."

The first three hundred years of American history coincided with the age of the pamphlet. In these centuries, pamphleteering became a distinct profession with its own techniques and forms, the pamphlet the dominant vehicle of propaganda and debate. Promotion of colonies in the sixteenth century and the rise of contending religious sects, political revolutions in the seventeenth century, the issues of imperial organization and national wars in the eighteenth century, finally the American and French revolutions at the end of the pamphlet era, were episodes perfectly suited to brief, controversial, and popular treatment.

The literary controversies of the American Revolution were conducted in little books—books inexpensive to print (though well printed), cheap to buy, easy to read, and, more significant, easy to write. About nine thousand books, newspapers, and broadsides were emitted by some two hundred American presses between 1763 and 1783; of these, perhaps two thousand were pamphlets on the political issues of the day. This is the corpus of literature of the American Revolution—a couple of thousand little books with their pretentious and formidable titles, intended for instant circulation, designed to change men's minds, addressed to urgent problems, sometimes touching the universal issues that confront men everywhere, any time, in civil society.

In a literature of such fugitive productions and such voluminous mass, individual dimensions were likely to be slight. The man and his book had to be considered in relation to a host of men and their books which, taken together, expressed the thoughts and feelings of two million Americans embroiled in a common experience of appalling magnitude. The pamphlet, even a great one like Dickinson's *Farmer's Letters* or Paine's *Common Sense,* never stood alone. It took its place in the stream of action and the stream of thought. Nor did its influence end with its publication. Often an essay would have prepublication readings, as did Otis' *Rights of the British Colonies* before the Massachusetts Assembly, and Governor Stephen Hopkins' treatise on the origin and nature of law before the legislature of Rhode Island. Sometimes, too, it would have public readings after publication, around a drumhead in a militia camp or in meetings of the Sons of Liberty. Some loyalist tracts received public burnings after being heard. Frequently, a little book had appeared first in a newspaper, or was reprinted in news columns afterward. Moreover, it was the nature of the pamphlet to evoke other pamphlets— rejoinders, refutations, responses of all kinds. Samuel Seabury's five "West-chester Farmer" tracts explain and are explained by the prodigious rejoinders of young Alexander Hamilton. One little book did not make a literary figure, nor a political leader. Only when a man had written several pamphlets, and developed in them a reasoned, coherent program of thought and action, did he rise to personal eminence as a writer among writers.

Some men did just that. A few pamphleteers—Otis, Dickinson, Paine, Franklin, Jefferson, Hamilton, Seabury, Galloway—wrote so effectively and so often that for them the little book became a literary career. Each had something more than ordinary to say; each, through special insights or unusual learning, saw in discrete instances of political conflict the permeating principles of universal application that enabled Americans to feel their cause akin to the historical purpose and destiny of man.

The pamphleteers of the Revolution received their training in local political struggles in each colony before 1765. There were American political pamphleteers before there was any unifying American point of view. The Parson's Cause in Virginia had produced the early tracts of Patrick Henry; Daniel Dulany argued a taxation question in Maryland; the prolonged attempt to overthrow the Penn family's proprietorship in Pennsylvania occasioned pamphlets from the famous Franklin and from men like Joseph Galloway and John Dickinson who were not yet so famous; in Boston James Otis, Josiah Quincy, and a brace of Adamses became the leaders of a radical faction in Massachusetts politics. All these writers developed in their partisan little books the contentious tone familiar to America from the religious polemics of the Great Awakening; but the orientation of their thinking before 1765 was narrowly provincial. A sense of purpose common to all America was lacking. After 1765, however, provincial issues were swallowed up in imperial polemics. When the British government embarked on its program of reforming the Empire, American writers rose from local squabbles to general political principles. The Stamp Act and the laws of Parliament which followed

not only forced the several colonies into a kind of union; they also obliged
the American pamphleteers to rise above their local orientation and become
philosophers. The philosophy of the pamphleteers gradually won Americans
from fundamentalist attitudes of colonial political thinking to secular attitudes
of revolution.

2

The literary career of James Otis comprehended the early stages of the
movement (1761-1769). Massachusetts-born and Harvard-trained, Otis in
1761 was a successful lawyer in his middle thirties. His sister, Mercy Otis
Warren, was a playwright, poet, and historian, whose *History of the Rise,
Progress, and Termination of the American Revolution* (1805) was to stimulate the patriotism of a generation. Otis had published a textbook in Latin
prosody and composed another in Greek, but his tastes were not really
academic. He was by nature partisan and worldly. An eloquent courtroom
speech against the new parliamentary measures made him the chief spokesman of the local radicals, and as leader of this faction he wrote the five
pamphlets on which his great reputation rests. They were controversial and
intemperate works, reckless and sometimes coarse, but they stated tersely and
vividly (if not always logically) an American constitutional theory. The first
tract, *A Vindication of the Conduct of the House of Representatives of the
Province of Massachusetts Bay* (1762), written in angry tone on a trivial
issue of local politics, developed the principle of representative taxation as a
basic requirement of constitutionally limited government. The second, *The
Rights of the British Colonies Asserted and Proved* (1764), marked Otis'
transition from local to imperial issues. Written "amid the continual solicita-
tions of a crowd of clients," after "one single Act of Parliament has set people
a-thinking, in six months, more than they had done in their whole lives
before," this pamphlet was a testament of fundamental political faith.
Supreme power, Otis asserted, was *"originally* and *ultimately* in the people."
The people delegated power to whom they pleased, but only as one man gives
another a possession to hold in trust for him. Thus government was a fidu-
ciary trust. "The *end* of government being the *good* of mankind, points out
its great duties: It is above all things to provide for the security, the quiet, and
happy enjoyment of life, liberty and property." The tract, conservative in
spirit, was designed to justify opposition to Parliament. Otis hoped to persuade Americans "to behave like men, and use the proper legal measures
to obtain redress." The next year, in an acidulous pamphlet, *Considerations
on Behalf of the Colonists* (1765), he retorted to the English writer Soame
Jenyns, stressing the dependence of the colonies on Britain but warning:

"Revolutions have been. They may be again." In later pamphlets the violence of his writing increased, at times approaching "a mere shriek," and the contours of his thinking failed to alter with changing issues. After 1769 he was silent, living in a disordered half-world until he was struck down by a bolt of lightning in 1783. But his work had really reached fruition, for in his virile tracts he had exhibited the literary technique of resistance, and had given, in Moses Coit Tyler's words, "a conservative and law-respecting race, a conservative and lawful pretext for resisting law, and for revolutionizing the government."

A large amount of James Otis' fame is due to the repeated encomiums heaped upon him by John Adams, from whom we have the only contemporary description of Otis' Writs of Assistance speech. Although Adams continued to praise the older man as long as he lived, he produced himself four essays on the Stamp Act more profound than anything Otis was capable of, treating the new measures as episodes in the ageless struggle in western civilization between corporate authority and individual rights. These essays, originally published in newspapers, were issued in pamphlet form as *A Dissertation on the Canon and Feudal Law* (1768)—the first of a long series of distinguished works by Adams which are more properly considered as philosophical literature than as political pamphlets. To Adams also is due much of the reputation of the Rev. Jonathan Mayhew, whom he termed a "transcendent genius." Author of a dozen significant published sermons and tracts, Mayhew represented the spirit of the Enlightenment in New England dissent, and epitomized the combination of religious leadership with political emancipation. Just before his death at the age of forty-six he published *The Snare Broken* (1766), a sermon on the repeal of the Stamp Act in which he justified civil disobedience even to the point of rebellion. The "great and primary law of nature" was self-preservation, he averred, and the measure of political action (as of spiritual truth) was now as always private rather than public judgment.

A bewildering number of little books by a host of young men had appeared before the Stamp Act controversy was over. One, by an older hand, appealed to readers in all provinces. Daniel Dulany, eminent Maryland statesman whose gracious personality and immense learning had placed him, in the Chesapeake colonies, at the very summit of the newest American profession, the bar, wrote a brilliant, persuasive tract against the power of Parliament to legislate for the colonies, *Considerations on the Propriety of imposing Taxes in the British Colonies* (1765), which went through many editions and endured as a strong influence in American constitutional thinking. "No taxation without representation" had been a slogan to Otis; to Dulany it became the foundation principle of free government.

3

The Stamp Act also marked the beginning of John Dickinson's leadership as a writer of the little book. Dickinson was thirty-three years old in 1765, a product, like Dulany and so many other leaders of the middle colonies, of the wealthy farm-proprietor group of the Chesapeake Bay region. He had prepared for three years at the Middle Temple, and had built a conspicuously prosperous business as lawyer, merchant, and landowner. Studious, frail, modest, diffident, he lived elegantly in the most polished Philadelphia society; he wrote with good humor and poised assurance. "The cause of *liberty* is a cause of too much dignity to be sullied by turbulence and tumult," he observed. "Those who engage in it should breathe a sedate yet fervent spirit, animating them to actions of prudence, justice, modesty, bravery, humanity and magnanimity." Dickinson's literary career extended over forty years and ranged over many subjects. The basic principles of his philosophy were broad enough and his mind was fluid enough to adapt to the successive crises of revolution, constitution, nationalism, and democracy. Dickinson stood between extremes. He was moderate in all things. He presented the picture of the thoughtful legislator, the adroit political manipulator, the able administrator, moving slowly but firmly toward well defined goals. His extensive learning, his ever keen sense of political conflict, his winning style as a writer, his analytical ability, and his impelling moral convictions gave his books immediate popularity and imposing stature. Tyler has called the appearance of the *Farmer's Letters* "the most brilliant event in the literary history of the Revolution."

The early pamphlets of Dickinson on Pennsylvania politics—he wrote eight in five months—not only reveal his mastery of this technique of propaganda, but also reveal how ephemeral the tract on transitory issues could be. When he turned to the greater questions of colony and empire he explored permanent values of freedom and order. His powerful state papers and pamphlets on the Stamp Act made his voice the most effective of the resistance movement, since he wrote for a broader audience than Otis had reached. Dickinson described all the various classes of colonial society and their relations with one another, analyzing the economic situation of each class, and the meaning of freedom for each. He warned that while the colonists were instinctively loyal, oppression would undermine that loyalty: "we never can be made an independent people, except it be by *Great-Britain* herself," he declared, "and the only way for her to do it, is to make us frugal, ingenious, united, and discontented."

When the Townshend Acts were passed, Dickinson wrote his *Letters from a Farmer in Pennsylvania* (1767-1768), which were published in all but four of the twenty-five American newspapers, and in eight book editions; Richard Henry Lee edited them in Williamsburg, Otis in Boston; in England Franklin wrote a preface for the first of two editions; in France also two editions were published, translated and edited by a noted liberal. Dickinson made a triumphal tour of England, was awarded an honorary degree by Princeton, was toasted in John Wilkes' prison lodgings in London; he was to be known for the rest of his life as "the Pennsylvania Farmer." He formulated the American interpretation of the British constitution in terms of the principles of liberty.

For WHO ARE FREE PEOPLE? [he asked]. Not *those,* over whom government is reasonably and equitably exercised, but *those* who live under a government so *constitutionally checked* and *controuled,* that proper provision is made against its being otherwise exercised.

He developed a theory of imperial federation in which colonies and empire were perfectly balanced. In such an empire, Americans could "support the character of *freemen* without losing that of *faithful subjects.*"

From 1774 to 1776 Dickinson led the moderate party in the Continental Congress; and he wrote many of the state papers of that body. As chief executive of two states, Delaware and Pennsylvania (1781–1785), he wrote proclamations and messages on the nature of political power, on the suppression of vice and immorality, on social inequality, and on free governments as the expression of the American spirit. He participated in the Constitutional Convention, wrote the *Letters of Fabius* (1788) urging ratification, and in 1797, when American politics turned upon the axis of the French Revolutionary Wars, produced his most reflective and most eloquent pamphlet, another series of *Letters of Fabius* (1797), in which he recommended the French cause, enioining his countrymen:

Let us assert and maintain *our true character—sincerity* of thought, and *rectitude* of action; and convince the world, that *no man,* or *body of men,* whatever advantages may for a while be taken of our *unsuspecting confidence,* shall ever be able to draw this nation out of the direct road of an honest, candid, and generous conduct.

The length of Dickinson's career, and the distinction of his writing, made him one of the most constructive and successful pamphleteers of his generation—among them all, one of the surest of his ground. In a "chaos of politics and morals, in which strength and weakness, safety and ruin, virtue and iniquity, strangely met together, and wrought in wild conjunction," he strove for order and principle, for intellectual integrity. "I am acting a very small and a very short part in the drama of human affairs," he told his critics. "I shall little trouble myself how your applause or your censures are bestowed."

4

The year 1774 was the watershed of Revolutionary literature. The meeting of the First Congress gave continental expression to all the various bodies of opinion. Production of pamphlets increased, and the state papers of the Congress, instead of emphasizing the areas of agreement among the American writers, polarized the elements of disagreement. Three parties appeared: moderates like Dickinson, loyal extremists of the right, and the independence party of the left. The loyalists were among the ablest literary figures. They had a worthy cause, and they were as American in their orientation as the moderates and independents, expressing—only with different emphasis—the same intellectual and emotional currents that moved in the revolutionists. There was a loyalist philosophy, akin to the fundamentalist conservative philosophy of all social crises. Jonathan Boucher, Virginia clergyman, developed in bold sermons the theme of a natural aristocracy and a divinely ordained government. Robert Proud, pedantic Latinist and schoolmaster, argued in almost medieval spirit that men were born to obey. But not all Toryism was backward-looking. By more realistic men a positive reform program was developed, which can be seen in such spirited essays as *A Friendly Address to all Reasonable Americans* (1774) by President Myles Cooper of King's College, and the five great "Westchester Farmer" pamphlets (1774-1775) of Samuel Seabury. Most original of the loyalist writers was Joseph Galloway of Pennsylvania, whose plan for union between Britain and the colonies was first presented to the Continental Congress where it was rejected, then published in various pamphlets, and after Galloway's migration to England developed through three more stages, the last appearing as late as 1788. Galloway's productivity included more than a score of the little books. His nobly conceived plan of a federal empire was one of the significant intellectual achievements of the American mind of this period.

Meanwhile, after 1774, the extremists on the left steadily gained adherents, and with the beginning of hostilities in April, 1775, independence tracts secured an ever widening audience. The war itself was the cradle of a more exuberant literature, in which the poetic careers of Philip Freneau, Francis Hopkinson, and John Trumbull were nurtured. These satirists as well as radical leaders like John and Samuel Adams continually urged independence; but at the end of 1775 America was still paralyzed by indecision. Then in January, 1776, a new little book appeared in Philadelphia, by a writer theretofore unknown, who with this work began to assume international significance as a pamphleteer of revolutions. The pamphlet was *Common Sense,* its author the one-time English artisan, Thomas Paine.

Paine belonged to no country, his doctrines to no age. Of all the writers of the American Revolution, he was the least American in background, in spirit, and in purpose. He had not participated in the fifteen years of constitutional debate that had qualified the colonial mind for contention and produced such achievements as Galloway's simple federalism and Dickinson's complex matrix of constitutional limitations, for throughout these years he had been still in England. His cause was not America; it was revolution. He differed in every essential respect from the major writers who had preceded him: his learning was slight, his personal standing inconsequential, his ability in systematic philosophy or organized presentation of argument almost nonexistent. Still, having missed the previous debates with their constitutional metaphysics, he was uninhibited by them. He felt, he sensed, he reacted. He did not complicate his emotional processes with intellectual refinements. He was the exotic radical, the revolutionary prototype. He wrote with urgency, excitement, and bold simplicity; he furnished straightforward, uncomplicated guidance for artisans, mechanics, and farmers. He carried the new philosophy to the masses of the American people, and turned the resistance movement into revolt.

Once a corset maker of Thetford in Norfolk, later a sailor, then a careless exciseman, later still a teacher, successively a tobacconist, a grocer, and once more a crown servant, Paine had lived a singularly disorganized and unfulfilled life before he came to America in 1774 at the age of thirty-seven. Possessed of a lively intellectual curiosity but lacking the capacity for sustained application, he had learned a little about a great many subjects. He became an editor in Philadelphia just as the cumulative force of the resistance movement was supplied with a national focus, the Congress, and in Pennsylvania was entering a proletarian phase. He responded both to the aspirations of the lower classes and to the humanitarian zeal of such enlightened men of position as Benjamin Franklin and Dr. Benjamin Rush, who were his patrons. His newspaper articles on abolition, women's rights, dueling, titles, and the freedom of British India constituted a significantly different preparation for writing revolutionary tracts from that furnished by local political contention and legal study to Henry, Otis, Dickinson, Dulany, and Galloway. The battle of Lexington awakened Paine to the magnitude of the Revolution in a way that constitutional arguments and congressional papers had not. Deciding that, "in a country where all men were once adventurers," his recent arrival did not preclude his uttering opinions, he set out to win America's thoughts from dependence to independence. He concluded that the issue had passed beyond the subtleties of constitutional law, had indeed become a matter to be solved "by man's instincts for truth, decency, and fairness"—that is (Dr. Rush suggested the title), by *Common Sense*.

The impact of the pamphlet was amazing. In a few months more than a hundred thousand copies were published in America and four European editions appeared. The total number eventually circulated was not much less than half a million. Every contemporary felt its effect. Washington found it "working a powerful change in the minds of many men." A South Carolinian declared it had made independents of a majority of Americans. Seldom if ever had a book enjoyed such an immediate popularity. Paine rejected all political theorizing over sovereignty and federalism; he scoffed at loyalty to George III. Instead, he presented the doctrine of separation as inevitable: a continent could not remain subject to an island. "The period of debate is closed," he wrote. "Arms, as the last resource, must decide the contest." In violent language he attacked "the royal brute of Britain" and ridiculed the institution of the crown. "Of more worth is one honest man to society, and in the sight of God, than all the crowned ruffians that ever lived." He painted the picture of three million Americans "running to their seacoast every time a ship arrives from London, to know what portion of liberty they should enjoy," and he contended that the colonies had reached a maturity that made their state of pupilage both farcical and dangerous. Finally, he challenged America to build a freer state than existed anywhere in the world:

O ye that love Mankind! . . . Every spot in the old world is overrun with oppression. Freedom hath been hunted round the globe. Asia and Africa have long expelled her. Europe regards her like a stranger; and England hath given her warning to depart. O! receive the fugitive; and prepare in time an asylum for mankind.

Paine was, like Jefferson and Rousseau, a master rhetorician. In this lay the strength of his appeal. His arguments were crudely simple, his presentation of issues blandly elementary. The canons of good taste scarcely applied to his works; he was not above referring to the stricken George III as "His Madjesty," and he approached the subtleties of politics with blundering passion. But his very simplicity and the heat of his febrile writing brought him the attention of masses of readers whom the careful, reasoned arguments of others had not touched. "The world is my country; to do good my religion," he exclaimed, and in the confident way of inspired agitators he proselyted for his faith.

That faith contained two stable and enduring elements: a belief in the ability of natural reason to govern, and a conviction that all men everywhere were united in the fellowship of freedom. Neither idea was original, nor had Paine as profound an appreciation of their meaning as had certain of his greater contemporaries. But he proved better able than anyone else to translate them into the vernacular of the common man, and his books were then and have ever since been range-lights of liberalism.

Common Sense made Paine the spokesman of the independence party. *The American Crisis* (sixteen papers he contributed at irregular intervals to the *Pennsylvania Journal* during the next seven years) made him the journalist of the Revolution itself. The first *Crisis* opened with the famous words that became a battle-cry:

These are the times that try men's souls. The summer soldier and the sunshine patriot will, in this crisis, shrink from the service of their country; but he that stands it *now*, deserves the love and thanks of man and woman. Tyranny, like hell, is not easily conquered; yet we have this consolation with us, that the harder the conflict, the more glorious the triumph.

He attacked the complacency of those who wished for peace in their day, if it meant war for their children's generation; and he praised the sturdy resolution of the patriots who had endured the defeats of the first year of campaigning.

I love the man that can smile in trouble, that can gather strength from distress and grow brave by reflection. It is the business of little minds to shrink; but he whose heart is firm, and whose conscience approves his conduct, will pursue his principles unto death.

Later numbers dealt with the threatening issues of the war years: financial chaos, loyalist opposition, military conspiracy, national union, a just peace, and adequate government. Busy with minor offices and with many essays besides the *Crisis,* Paine became enmeshed in the details of political life. His essential philosophy remained, but he did not again achieve the originality, the vitality, the unifying definition of the American overcause that had in *Common Sense* helped to make "thirteen clocks strike together."

But there was no confusion in his philosophy of freedom. "My own line of reasoning is to myself as straight and clear as a ray of light," he wrote; and as he watched the slow and painful victory of the American people he developed the concept of revolution as the emancipation not of Americans alone but of common men everywhere from the worship of their antique idols in their antique symbolism. Revolutionism became Paine's basic faith. It had little application in American politics after the peace, even less after the reforms in government of 1787-1789. In this country, the Revolution was over. In Europe it was just beginning, and Paine, who went abroad in 1787, was its self-appointed evangel. Like Archimedes, he felt that, "had we a place to stand upon, we might raise the world." The French Revolution gave him his platform. Ineffectual in his efforts of personal leadership, he gave all his intense convictions and restless energies to his writings. *The Rights of Man* became a textbook for world revolution, and has remained the democrat's breviary of two continents. *The Age of Reason,* confronting the connection between political and theological doctrine—always present but never before so explicit in his thought—stated the case of deism crudely but so overtly that Paine incurred the enmity of hosts of the common people who had once been his admirers and followers. *Agrarian Justice* was an examination of the problem of poverty. Could civilized man, who begat poverty, eliminate it by social action? To answer this question in the affirmative, Paine proposed a system of state taxes and pensions. He had moved from the democracy of the seventies to the nationalism of the nineties.

The French Revolution ended, as the American had; France entered a constructive, aggressive phase, to which Paine had little to contribute. He returned to a strange America in 1802, spent a few pitiful years, poor, ill, and outcast; he died in 1809. Thriving on social turmoil, he languished in times of peace; apt to stir emotions, he affronted sober judgment; yet he had wrought marvelously in the processes that undermined the ancient pieties of men; he had crystallized the conviction that reason, rather than accepted authority or revelation, is the surest guide in politics, religion, and morality; and he had added to the vocabulary of politics stirring phrases of courage, determination, and faith that have not lost their magic in the passing years. If doubt still lingers as to which nation should take Paine unto itself, there is at least no doubt that, in giving memorable expression to American life at its most decisive moment, he made his place in the formative literature of the new republic.

5

There was only one Otis, one Dickinson, one Galloway, one Paine; yet the age of the little books produced many other notable literary careers. There was, for example, gentle Anthony Benezet, whose humanitarian ministry of good works included five sensible tracts on abolitionism, the slave trade, temperance, Quaker doctrine, and the treatment of the Indians. There was the vain, half-educated mountaineer, Ethan Allen, who wrote pamphlets on the Vermont controversy, an account of his captivity during the war, and shared in a barbarous presentation of deism, *Reason the Only Oracle of Man* (1784). Most copies of this tract were accidentally destroyed by fire and some were burnt on purpose; but enough remained to cause a brief uproar among orthodox clerics, and it has unaccountably received serious attention by historians since. There was Benjamin Rush, scientist, philosopher, reformer, statesman, and educator, whose great works on chemistry, diseases, medicine, and madness do not entirely eclipse the scores of essays and tracts he wrote on social and political questions. And there were many more. But for several years after the peace (1783) fewer pamphlets emerged from the run of little books to achieve either literary distinction or a wide audience. Controversy scarcely abated, but the issues of controversy were not so often the great universal issues of political experience. Religious contention, social reform, currency problems, and economic ills were the subjects of the little books, while larger books were appealing to the dominant moods. War-nurtured nationalism was gratified by the publication of military journals and patriotic histories of the Revolution. These were noncontroversial works that were not part of the literature of propaganda and debate.

The proposal of the new Constitution in 1787, however, was the occasion for another spate of pamphlets, in volume second only to that the independence controversy had caused. The debate on ratification extended over twenty months, and produced examinations of first principles of political organization as searching and as significant as any of the revolutionary pamphlets of the previous decade. Historical traditions have conferred such an accolade upon *The Federalist* that other tracts of literary merit, particularly those opposing the Constitution, have been all but forgotten. Yet writers of ability, reputation, and learning, in little books simpler and more popular than the great classic of Madison, Hamilton, and Jay (which was "not well calculated for the common people"), laid the cases for and against the Constitution at the bar of public opinion. Elbridge Gerry's *Observations . . . By A Columbian Patriot* (1788), criticized the new plan as a scheme "of military combinations, and politicians of yesterday." In New York the partisan leader George Clinton attacked the proposed frame as tyranny and corruption, in *Letters of Cato* (1787–1788), to which Alexander Hamilton, as *Caesar,* replied. Albert Gallatin, Luther Martin, James Monroe, Patrick Henry, George Mason, and Samuel Chase were among the pamphleteers who wrote little books and newspaper essays against the Constitution; but the most effective antifederalist tract, and one of the most persuasive pamphlets of the whole period, was Richard Henry Lee's *Letters of the Federal Farmer* (1787–1788), which went through four editions in as many states in three months, and became a handbook of the opposition to the new frame of government. It evoked vigorous rejoinders, among them an elaborate refutation by Timothy Pickering. Lee's writing was spare and firm. He preserved a calm dignity. His arguments were careful and thorough. He was neither narrow nor contentious in spirit, but earnest and constructive. "We are making a constitution, it is to be hoped, for ages and millions yet unborn," he wrote, and warned that the defects in the proposed instrument would doom it to failure. Lee spoke for what he termed "the honest and substantial part of the community," as Henry and Gallatin spoke for the lower income groups. His *Letters* were a powerful influence in bringing about the first ten amendments (the Bill of Rights) which as Senator from Virginia he helped put through Congress in the following year (1789). The pamphlet also deserves notice as the principal literary achievement of this sturdy, quiet, somewhat austere character who had been throughout a long public life above the reproach either of interest or of enthusiasm. Ever since his bold oration against slavery in the House of Burgesses in 1759, Lee had been in the forefront of the resistance movement. His stately petitions and official papers had been on a plane with Dickinson's. He it was who had written and introduced the resolution of independence in 1776; he had shared in composing the North-West Ordinance, had served long in Congress as member and for a while as president. Above all the Virginia statesmen, Lee represented what the classically trained revolutionary generation meant when it spoke of Roman virtues.

On the other side of the ratification question were writers equally distinguished and apparently even more effective. Dickinson's *Letters of Fabius,* published in a Wilmington newspaper, helped to make Delaware the first state to ratify. Noah Webster, John Jay, Edmund Randolph, Alexander Hamilton, James Iredell, Hugh Henry Brackenridge, Hugh Williamson, and Tench Coxe joined the lists of the Constitution's champions, under a bewildering array of pseudonyms. James Wilson, ineradicably Scotch, inordinately learned, incurably romantic, had led the Convention through its most tortuous philosophical difficulties. To the ratification polemic he contributed a precise explanation of the principles he had concocted, *Address to a Meeting of the Citizens* (1787), pronouncing the Constitution "the best form of government which has ever been offered to the world." Trained in law by John Dickinson, associated with him in opposition to the Stamp Act and later regulations, author of the *Considerations on the Nature and Extent of the Legislative Authority of the British Parliament* (1774) and other pamphlets, Wilson had always represented the opinions of the Philadelphia mercantile and professional classes. His style was sober and heavy, his arguments sometimes turgid, but he had attained a very extensive influence. His lectures on law at the University of Pennsylvania mark the beginning of the public study of jurisprudence in America. His brilliance as a thinker and writer and his effectiveness as a statesman were alike marred by his immoderate speculations in land companies. Perhaps because his life closed amid sordid scenes, his substantial contributions to American literature and statecraft have been insufficiently valued.

6

Of all the little books of 1787–1788, none has a stronger claim upon the student of literature than *The Federalist,* written by Madison, Hamilton, and Jay. These papers formed the best exposition of the principles of the new government, and after its adoption gained the authority almost of constitutional law. They appeared first in New York newspapers, and were issued in two volumes in March–May, 1788; republished in many American cities and in two French editions during the nineties; praised by German reviewers; and reprinted on the occasion of South American and Central European revolutions in the nineteenth century. *The Federalist* occupies a unique place in American journalism, for it summarizes the most original contributions the revolutionary generation of pamphleteers made to the discussion of government. As Paine's *Common Sense* marked the height of revolutionary radicalism, so *The Federalist* signalized the success of the conservative, constructive, consolidating processes which shaped the new nation in postrevolutionary molds. The ideas of distributive powers, checked by correlative limitations upon power, the colonists had found in their political texts: Montesquieu, Harington, Sidney, and Locke. They had given their own expression to these ideas in their first pamphlets on imperial organization in the Stamp Act year. Dulany, Wilson, Dickinson, and especially Galloway had proposed a federal scheme for the empire, and Galloway had developed his proposals into a well articulated structure of administrative and legislative units. The members of the Constitutional Convention, though young men, had in one sense been truly as Gerry had charged "politicians of yesterday," for they were directed by the writings and experience of the previous two decades. *The Federalist* papers, written by a strangely assorted trio—a conservative New York lawyer, a convinced monarchist and nationalist, a pedantic constitutional theorist— were the result not so much of the discussions behind the closed doors of Independence Hall during that hot summer of 1787, as of all the American experiments, literary and actual, with federal forms since the dimly remembered days of the Confederation of New England. This book was a sort of codification of American conservative thought. It signalized as much the end of an era as the beginning of a nation.

The ratification controversy was the last great American chapter in the age of the pamphlet. The form itself did not disappear; every national election and every national issue for many years was to see a flood of the little books. But American writers were already by 1790 presenting larger and longer works to an expanding reading audience. The pamphlet, a ready instrument in conflict, was being relegated to a minor place in the currents of reconstruction and nation building. The literary career of Tench Coxe, our first original economic thinker on a national scale, bridged the two eras. Most of his score of works (1787–1820) were pamphlets, varying from thirty-eight to one hundred thirty-five pages in length; but his *View of the United States* (1795) ran to more than four hundred pages, and was popular enough to appear in three editions in one year. Coxe and his contemporaries had to be more than pamphleteers, because the processes of thought and opinion set in motion by the pamphlet literature of the Revolution had been completed. The techniques of communicating major ideas in simple words had been refined to a point where the philosopher, the political leader, the reformer had an almost instantaneous hearing in the public forum. The newspaper and the magazine at one level, the printed book at the other, took the place of the pamphlet. The age of the little book, like the American Revolution itself, had come to an end.

12. PHILOSOPHER–STATESMEN OF THE REPUBLIC

N<small>O LESS</small> contemporaneous in its inspiration than the writing of the pamphleteers, but far more substantial and enduring, was the writing in all forms of those philosopher-statesmen who did most by thought and action to bring the First Republic into being.

The founding fathers were men of remarkably broad interests with an uncanny aptitude for political analysis and for the adaptation of theories to practice. There are some who describe this phenomenon as no more than the heritage of humanism which the American enlightenment merely reembodied. Certainly the statesmen who shaped the Republic in its first form were confronting essentially the same issues as those formulated by the Renaissance humanists: the attempt to reconcile speculative thinking on the nature of man with the immediate task of creating a new political and social order. But these modern humanists differed from More and Erasmus in being under more pressure to apply their theories to the urgent task at hand. Yet there is something breath-taking about the reembodiment of broad humanist principles in a struggling and relatively unsophisticated people, beset on every side by the problems of living. The "fathers" therefore deserve either spontaneous admiration or informed respect, whether we study their ideas and actions as we find them, or trace their intellectual heritage to another age.

Of the first statesmen of the Republic, four—Jefferson, Madison, John Adams, and Hamilton—trained their sights higher than any of the others. Addressing themselves to more than practical considerations, they seemed to be genuinely inspired by the historical uniqueness of the experience open to them, to launch a new civilization on a large scale. In final outcome, they proved equal to the challenge of planning republican government, and they could only have become so because they tried to understand not only the buried sources of power, but the moral objectives of good government. In a sense they were, as Hamilton once contemptuously declared, "speculative" thinkers and "empirics." Even Hamilton belonged to the company he criticized, for he, with the others, assessed what he already found in existence as social habit and political tradition; he built upon that which was already "given," and recommended, according to his lights, the best direction of change.

Jefferson, the greatest of them all, was conspicuously devoted to the theory and practice of good government. Further, he was actively critical of his own methods of establishing political judgments, and he was intellectually prepared to examine the logical, philosophical, scientific, or sentimental elements in his views of society. He learned to style himself an "ideologist," identifying himself with his friends the French philosophers, who had founded a school of thought known as "Ideology" in the Napoleonic period. Hamilton, Madison, and Adams as well as Jefferson contributed characteristic ways of thought, individual tempers of belief which were to be important not only in the era of the Republic but for America thenceforth. The principles of the four philosopher-statesmen taken together almost define the range of our national ideology—our objectives, our character as a people, our economic and social patterns, our "Americanism."

The challenge of creating a new form of government gave rise to an atmosphere of intellectual adventure, in which the Platonic vision of the philosopher-king could for one brief period take on American reality. "Until philosophers take to government, or those who now govern become philosophers," Plato had boldly written, "so that government and philosophy unite, there will be no end to the miseries of states." In the timeless analogy of the cave in the *Republic,* the philosophers who struggle to free themselves from the chains of ignorance and superstition make their way to the light outside. They see the truth. Loving its clarity, they would bask in its light. But the thought of the chained multitude below gives them no rest, and they understand, as Platonic seekers of truth must, that they cannot fail to carry glimmerings of light to the poorer minds who inhabit the cave.

The four great philosopher-statesmen of the American "Enlightenment" conform admirably to the Platonic pattern. They grope in authentic Platonic fashion for the true principles of social order, accepting the responsibility of administering the affairs of their less farsighted fellow men; yet they reject the Platonic ideal as an explicit inspiration. They are willing to exemplify it if they must; but justify it, direct from its ancient source, never. Plato, even for Jefferson who had the most developed philosophic predilections of the group, was too full of metaphysical flights and trances to prove sympathetic to the common-sense orientation of the new nation. Yet the double drive of philosophy and leadership, thought and action, vision and its fortifying concrete detail is heeded by Jefferson, Madison, Adams, and even Hamilton. From the time of Franklin to the present this double drive, common to all humanity but intensified by life in a new continent, has dictated a double destiny for the American nation and a dualistic orientation for its literature. In the great period of American political literature, both forces were present without fatal conflict, and lend a peculiar divided charm and predictive importance to this body of writing.

2

In its literary guise, the issue faced by the philosopher-statesmen was the reconciliation of potent ideas with traditions of style formalized by eighteenth century English writers and imitated by our early writers of fiction, essay, and poetry. The methods of belles-lettres were inadequate to the urgent demand for clear and effective expression. These public-minded men wrote their state papers, their reports, their tracts, and their letters with some care for the form as well as the content, but they subordinated the formal demands of art to the immediate need for communication. John Adams, who was himself a tyro in the "literary" essay, had made it all too plain: "substance" was to take precedence over "elegance." He had written: "The simplest style, the most mathematical precision of words and ideas, is best adapted to discover truth and to convey it to others, in reasoning on this subject [politics]." That Adams himself, who once boasted that he had never had "time" to compress his written pieces nor to prune them of repetitions, did not always live up to the severe criteria of clarity and communicability he invoked, in no way affects the importance of the ideal. Amusingly enough, some of Adams' most notorious departures from this standard produced his best prose, the nervous and animated passages so eloquent with his erratic brilliance. Jefferson and Madison never quite forsook the rounded and urbane prose line which by now seems characteristic of the Virginia political dynasty with the notable exception of George Washington, who strove, not always successfully, to restrict himself to a "plain stile." Yet even the Virginians never hesitated to put communication and content above consideration of style or form. Madison, ever judicious and temperate, best conformed to the utilitarian ideal. In criticizing a political pamphlet, he commented that it would have been "much improved by softer words and harder arguments," and he found the style attractive in that it had "the artless neatness always pleasing to the purest tastes." Hamilton, in the calculated fixity of his desire to convince, to silence the opposition by a brilliant show of fire before an enemy gun could shoot, did not hesitate to employ rhetorical ornament and insistent, obvious rhythm. Although he too agreed that "our communications should be calm, reasoning, serious, showing steady resolution more than feeling, having force in the idea rather than in the expression," he often lapsed into purple passages whose melodramatic tones are as trying as they are insincere.

Throughout, the unorthodoxy of this political literature is a consequence of the fact that these statesmen were primarily devoted to the issues and principles growing out of a serious national undertaking. The motivation of interest seems to have been so compelling that communications tended to become direct colloquial exchanges, discussions of ideas, selfless presentation of the "argument" without stopping for artifice or formal discipline. For this reason it is a great pity that the most often quoted of their political "classics" have tended to come from the public documents and official papers of the nation's archives, rather than from the enormous correspondence which more truly characterizes this age of statesmen. This correspondence, in fact, should be the mainstay of our knowledge of the political thought and of the social continuum of the early Republic. In a sense, its excellence may be regarded as the nation's unearned reward for having once lived in an age with inadequate media of communication. It is hardly an exaggeration to say that there is no Jefferson, no Adams, and no Madison without the body of letters they left. To understand Hamilton and Madison, notes for their speeches in the Constitutional Convention and elsewhere must be added to the justly famous papers they separately contributed to *The Federalist* (1787–1788).

All the statesmen had been trained in Congress or had read deeply in the law. None in the country knew better than they the amount of power that could be borrowed from the logical ordering of material, the legal-rhetorical habit of defining terms. A truly impressive endurance also marks the longer writings of Jefferson and his colleagues, as they patiently investigate detailed charges and sternly cleave to the political issues under discussion. Their writing is suffused with a kind of lofty passion born of the consciousness of the cosmic importance of the "infant nation" with which they identified themselves so intimately. What a terrible disaster it would be, they seem to say, if the "ark, bearing as we have flattered ourselves the happiness of our country & the hope of the world" (Madison's phrase), should be shipwrecked! It is not surprising that an earnestness of moral tone is the keynote of this literature which in general is neither original in metaphor nor polished in style.

On occasions, the utilitarian limitations upon expression are conceived of as a moral question, intimately related to the simple and severe needs of republican society. Jefferson, gentle lover of the fine arts, was keenly aware that America differed from Europe in being not yet ready for the highest and most cultivated art-forms. His journals of travel through Italy and France conscientiously record technical improvements in agriculture and contain long passages on how to make wines and cheese. This attitude is at war, all through Jefferson's varied European sojourn, with such projects as the adaptation of Palladio's Villa Rotunda to his plan for the second Monticello and his general enthusiasm for the ancients in literary form and moral leadership, and to the highest expression of what was then "modern" music, painting, "beauty" in general. John Adams, prone to state reasons for his actions, epitomized the stage of American literary and artistic needs by declaring:

It is not indeed the fine arts which our country requires; the useful, the mechanic arts are those which we have occasion for in a young country as yet simple and not far advanced in luxury, although perhaps much too far for her age and character. . . . The science of government is my duty to study, more than all other sciences. . . . I must study politics and war, that my sons may have liberty to study mathematics and philosophy, geography, natural history and naval architecture, navigation, commerce, and agriculture, in order to give their children a right to study painting, poetry, music, architecture, statuary, tapestry, and porcelain.

Jefferson had clearly announced that in "a republic nation, whose citizens are to be led by reason and persuasion, and not by force, the art of reasoning becomes of first importance," and had recommended the speeches of Livy, Sallust, and Tacitus as "pre-eminent specimens of logic, taste and that sententious brevity which, using not a word to spare, leaves not a moment for inattention to the hearer." Amplification, he thought, was the "vice of modern oratory," and he avoided speech-making when he could. But it was Jefferson who developed that flowing and "felicitous" line for which John Adams, the Continental Congresses, and all America since came to know him—the rhythmic yet thoughtful line that moves unchecked in our most famous public *Declaration,* in our early official papers and documents, and in that remark-able corpus of Jefferson letters with which no subsequent political corre-spondence can compete.

Madison we have noted as the advocate of the tightened composition of logical demonstration. He felt that the "only effectual precaution against fruit-less and endless discussion" was the definition of our political terms. Hamil-ton nursed a notorious and constitutional fear that republican government would not weather the storm; but in his *Federalist* essays, when he was promoting the cause of the new constitution, he shared the general excitement over political innovation.

The people of this country, by their conduct and example [he wrote], will decide the important question, whether societies of men are really capable or not of establishing good government from reflection and choice, or whether they are forever destined to depend for their political constitutions on accident and force.

Adams, paternal watchdog of his beloved New England, had further called attention to the specific virtues found in the self-government local to his region. These virtues he kept in mind from his early directives on government in his influential letters, "Thoughts on Government" (1776), to his last review of the revised constitution of Massachusetts, half a century later. Madison added to his theoretical contribution a practical demonstration of superior journalism in the unique service he performed by reporting the Constitutional Convention. Demonstrating selfless honesty, patience, and comprehension, he early set a high standard for American political reporting. Thus, in different ways, the statesmen of the American Republic demonstrated their sense of a supreme political mission, and it was this dominant aim of constructing a government compatible with freedom which gave unity to their writing— not in the sense of formal arrangement or style, but in the homogeneous conviction which flowed from their dedication to political ends.

The very issue of English versus American idiom adds the final touch to the thesis that there was a separate quality in American political writing as early as the formative years of the new Republic. The British critics who mocked American writing for forsaking "purity" of standard English form and style were met with singular equanimity. Jefferson, for example, whose use of the word "belittle" in *Notes on Virginia* (1784) had been the occasion for reproof by the *Edinburgh Review,* was unperturbed. Languages, he explained, had always grown by innovation. They fattened on flexible adaptation and change. Who would expect a vast new American nation, with its very different regions, to bind itself in an iron cask of ready-made English speech and prose? No, "neology" must clearly replace purism, since the price of purism was stagnation.

Had the preposterous idea of fixing the language been adopted by our Saxon ancestors, of Peirce Plowman, of Chaucer, of Spenser, the progress of ideas must have stopped with that of the language . . . what do we not owe to Shakespeare for the enrichment of the language, by his free and magical creation of words? [To be sure] uncouth words will sometimes be offered; but the public will judge them, and receive or reject, as sense or sound shall suggest.

No matter how often the debates in Congress, or the individual statesmen in writing, might call upon the eloquent models of antiquity; no matter how much the balanced sentence of the English essayists, Addison and Steele, or the English political theorists of the seventeenth and eighteenth centuries might be copied—a sense of the American scene in all its heady potentialities was so strong in the minds of these architects of the Republic that they could scarcely avoid giving direct expression to nascent American culture. In the authentic idiom of American thought and speech the statesmen of the greatest experimental democracy in history put pen to paper.

3

The ideology of American democracy began its career with a set of political principles termed "Republican." Although John Adams was quick to warn of the shifting meanings of "Republic," the term became a fixed pole of reference in American political theory, directly contraposing that other pole, Monarchy, against which the Revolution had been waged. Adams himself believed in republican doctrine and, like the other political leaders of his day, made standard references to the ancient republics as the historical alternative to monarchy and to feudal hierarchic society. Almost everyone in early America agreed on the minimal connotation of the term, either explicitly or by implication. Like late eighteenth century philosophers elsewhere, they understood that a republic was a government which derived its power from the people "originally," referred back to the people for an ultimate court of appeal in "crucial" questions transcending the ordinary affairs of legislation, and exercised its granted powers through representatives chosen by a majority of the voting citizens. In theory, at least, these voting citizens were further supposed to represent the "will of the people"; and, while they confided specific powers to their representatives, it was understood that a republic was essentially a government of laws rather than of men.

Were one to try to locate the maximum adherence to this republican ideal, one could project an imaginary political line with the left terminal point designating "maximum faith" and the right terminal point "minimum faith." We should then have to place Jefferson at the left and Hamilton at the right. John Adams accordingly must occupy the middle ground, to the left of Hamilton and the right of Jefferson; but he is also to the right of Madison, who is closer to Jefferson on most fundamental political matters—although it is important to note that Madison is sometimes closer than either Adams or Jefferson to Hamilton in economic questions.

Had Jefferson written no more than the initial draft of the *Declaration of Independence* he would probably have earned his place on the radical left of our American political line. The achievement of the *Declaration,* if it proves nothing else, certainly establishes its author's title to the greatest pen in the patriotic cause. Certain contemporaries, either through faulty judgment or through jealousy of his ability to fashion a line of fundamental national policy that could sing itself into the country's ears, challenged the author on the score of "originality." Madison was incensed, for he knew that it was absurd to cavil thus.

The object [he protested] was to assert not to discover truths, and to make them the basis of the Revolutionary Act. The merit of the Draught could only consist in a lucid communication of human Rights, a condensed enumeration of the reasons for such an exercise of them, and in a style and tone appropriate to the great occasion, and to the spirit of the American people.

But if the content of the *Declaration* alone is not enough, Jefferson is established in his preeminence on the left by his *Notes on the State of Virginia* (1784), the first American book to become an accidental "expatriate," published in England and France in pirated versions before it reached print in the country of its origin. This series of informal essays ranges far and wide over disputed questions in philosophy, science, politics, and morals, and is the natural discourse of a born humanistic rationalist. Proud of his friend's prowess as a thinker, Madison once observed that Jefferson was "greatly eminent for the comprehensiveness and fertility of his genius, for the vast extent and rich variety of his acquirements; and particularly distinguished by the philosophic impress left on every subject which he touched." And then, as if the *Notes* had come to mind, Madison hastened to add: "Nor was he less distinguished from an early and uniform devotion to the cause of liberty, and systematic preference of a form of Government squared in the strictest degree to the equal rights of man."

Although Madison had been a friend, follower, and co-worker of Jefferson's for many years when he wrote this tribute, it is notable that in all the advancing and receding waves of historical interpretation the residual significance of Jefferson's contribution to the American tradition has grown rather than diminished. Of American Presidents, this statesman of the "Enlightenment" most closely approximates the Platonic philosopher-king. No other incumbent of the Presidency, and no other of the liberal philosophic spirits of his age—many-sided men like Franklin, Benjamin Rush, and Thomas Cooper—could match Jefferson's happy union of learning, independence, and competent judgment in diverse fields such as social morality, government, education, natural science, agriculture, and the arts. What Washington began to do for the American personality by example and by the sheer weight of personal decency and leadership, Jefferson molded into an intellectualized ideal of social order. The entire development of American affairs, as the definition of our national ideology, is consequently more indebted to Jefferson than it is to any other single man.

This is not to say that Jefferson was an illustration of that cliché, the crusader of eighteenth century enlightenment who preached the gross "goodness" of man and the inevitable rational progress of society. Jefferson, who never wearied of reading history—he knew excellently the classical and the best of modern historians—had come to recognize the hazards of evil in human as in social affairs. He had so acute an awareness of the consequences of entrenching evil men in public positions that he concluded no society would be safe without an informed, alert citizenry participating actively in government. Devoted to human possibilities of growth, he outdistanced the faith of the other philosopher-statesmen—although Madison and Adams both had their areas of hope and solid, if less generous, funds of good will. Another way of viewing the difference between Jefferson and all others is to recognize his philosophy of education for what it was—a conscious "ideological" program to create right-thinking, tolerant citizens whose management of local affairs would be but a neighborly orientation for their wise judgment and activity in the affairs of the Union. It was a program fitted to practical needs and political responsibilities, and yet attuned to the highest cultivation of the arts, the sciences, and belles-lettres.

If it was Jefferson who recommended the fullest participation in political control, just as he sustained the greatest confidence in the educability of the American people, it was Hamilton who had most concern for government as a force, who saw little to worry about in its suppressive intrusions upon local or personal rights. It must be understood that the whole of the political line ranging from Jefferson to Madison to Adams and to Hamilton operated within realistic limits. Each statesman feared different contingencies, each phrased his hopes in typical or unique terms, each seized upon symbols of approbation or aversion sympathetic to his own personality and to the range of his ideational life. One might almost conclude: therefore, the republic was made possible—through the very variety and divergence of the founders' visions, ideas, and wishes.

Hamilton, for instance, saw very clearly the vast economic potentialities of America if the government would ally itself with the possessors of large fortunes and legislate in the direction of the expansion of financial and commercial activities. In the "people" Hamilton held virtually no stock. He thought they might listen to a debate and repeat with fair accuracy another man's line of argument, but were by and large susceptible to the flatteries and the manipulations of natural politicians. When left to his own selfish and irrational devices, the "great beast" might actually retard the productive energy of the nation, rather than build it up.

It was some time after Hamilton's memorable project of the *Federalist* (1787-1788)—that lucid exposition of constitutional republican government, not always consistent in its internal logic, but always impressive in its powerful defense of the need for national unity—that he began to voice his gloomiest thoughts about the survival of the republican experiment in self-government. "It is yet to be determined by experience whether it be consistent with that stability and order in government which are essential to public strength and private security and happiness," he wrote in 1792, having already tasted the strength of Jefferson's principled opposition. He seemed eager to give voice to his fear that republicanism might not "justify itself by its fruits." His progress Tory-wise, away from what he had called "the fair fabric of republicanism . . . modelled and decorated by the hand of federalism," was complete. In this shortsightedness Hamilton showed himself less of a philosopher and less of a statesman than one would desire. Were it not for the towering importance of certain of his administrative and governmental principles, his temperament and the transparency of his self-interest would hardly qualify him as a philosopher-statesman. But there is great penetration in his theory that the extension of national prerogative is indispensable for achieving internal uniformity and efficiency in a genuinely "central" government. And there is undeniable truth in his perception that this is the first essential of defense against foreign powers. Another realistic principle of capitalist development appreciated by Hamilton early in the nation's life was that it was a direct obligation of the government to foster the development of the productive resources and activities of the nation—by whatever combination of interests might prove effective. The first of these principles figures in Hamilton's masterful *First Report on the Public Credit* (1790), when he unhesitatingly decides, "If the voice of humanity pleads more loudly in favor of some [classes of creditors] than of others, the voice of policy, no less than of justice, pleads in favor of all." The second principle is the key argument of his classical treatise on protectionism, the *Report on Manufactures* (1791).

By a peculiar concentration of interest, Hamilton attained a definiteness in the body of his belief which sounds surprisingly modern in tone. Read today, his justification of strong, efficient government comes close to a native American defense of totalitarian political management. But, clever though his analysis was, it did not succeed in reconciling the two inseparable demands of prospering republicanism: national power, exercised to the full by an unimpeded, energetic central administration, and mature responsibility vested in the people of a free society.

The conservatism and legalism of John Adams and Madison explain almost as much about the success of the American Republic as they do about the absence of their names from most of the emotional appraisals of the early American tradition. Adams was a testy man, given to incalculable fits of temper that could shake his soul and harden his behavior to the utmost expression of stubbornness. Madison was naturally prudent, neither commanding in person nor captivating in his imaginative vistas. He did not permit himself the occasional exaggerations of the genius which he himself detected in Jefferson, while Adams, unlike Hamilton, kept steadily in view his high duty to guard the national interest and subordinate his own political welfare to the paramount needs of the American Republic. Adams was therefore saved from the extravagances of Hamiltonian ambition. Since the "mean," in politics, is not golden—not, at any rate, in the "memory of the race"—both Adams, the unorthodox Federalist, and Madison, the conservative Republican, paid the political price of hewing to the Aristotelian middle. Without Adams, the preservation of the dignified ideal of lawful, responsible government and a great example of Bolingbroke's ideal "Patriot King" who comes to guard like an "angel" the destiny and the long-range interests of his country might not have been realized. Without Madison, the amelioration of factional (including "class") strife would not so early have been made a governmental objective; nor would the allocation of sovereign power in the federal and in state contexts have found so subtle an expositor.

The surety of republican foundations, one might say, depended upon the Jeffersonian "left," with its key insights that the preservation of individual freedom and the moral development of cooperative society were the ultimate objectives of free society. It depended upon the Hamiltonian "right" with its knowledge that governments need effective organization and the power which comes from having the substantial productive and financial forces in the nation solidly united behind the administration. The stability of the Republic and its true course depended much upon the labors of Madison, with his realistic conviction that the main purpose of a government is the protection of the many and diverse economic interests into which every country is divided—and with his belief that this protection can be accomplished through a limited, federal republic capable of preventing the monopolistic dictation of one faction or combine over the people of the nation. The experienced conclusion of the elder Adams, that republicanism would not dispel the disparities of wealth and station and their attendant aristocracies, was a grave note of warning. When Adams added that the chief function of wise governors would be to protect the separate but "balanced" powers delegated to them, by compact with the people, and thus prevent tyranny, chaos, or the anarchy of the impassioned mob, he further safeguarded the Republic from what the ancients had been pleased to characterize as the "inevitable" degeneration of the good society.

The main task of republican government, in the long view of John Adams, appeared to be the prevention of excessive power in the hands of any one group. Believing that "vice and folly are so interwoven in all human affairs that they could not, possibly, be wholly separated from them without tearing and rending the whole system of human nature and state," Adams had to put his trust in the rare statesmanlike leaders who would possess wisdom to formulate just laws, and discipline to abide by them. Adams thought the network of checks and balances would defeat the ambitious and power-hungry few who might design to capture government for their private ends, and would insure fair representation of the interests of every region in the nation, thereby allowing the propertied and "responsible" citizens who were the mainstay of each region a voice in governmental affairs. By these devices, he thought he could make the most of fallible human nature. A republic, devoted to the interests of the people and operating through their own representatives, should be the outcome of these precautionary mechanisms. Adams accordingly thought his own republicanism as firm as that of anyone, including the leader of the Republican party, his good friend and occasional enemy, Thomas Jefferson, who, in Adams' opinion, differed from himself only in that he was for "liberty and straight hair. I thought curled hair was as republican as straight."

Madison's starting point was less psychological and more sociological. It began with the observed differences in group interests, differences which he took to calling "factions." Factions for Madison were special-interest groups arising out of the fundamental conflict present in every society between those who are rich and maintain their riches, and those who are poor and struggle to relieve their condition.

All civilized societies are divided into different interests and factions [he wrote in the crucial year 1787], as they happen to be creditors or debtors—rich or poor— husbandmen, merchants or manufacturers—members of different religious sects— followers of different political leaders—inhabitants of different districts—owners of different kinds of property, etc.

The advantage of modern republicanism over other governments Madison expected to find in its ability to impede the full force of factional combinations, preventing them from controlling the state, and from usurping the rights of one or more minorities. Madison as a Virginian feared the added danger that the majority (the North) might suppress the rights of the minority (the South), and contended in a letter to Jefferson:

Where the real power in a government lies, there is the danger of oppression. In our Governments the real power lies in the majority of the Community, and the invasion of private rights is chiefly to be apprehended, not from acts of Government contrary to the sense of its constituents, but from acts in which the Government is the mere instrument of the major number of the constituents.

Madison thus called to the attention of all men the inflexible requirement that democracies protect the civil rights of minorities from the real or reported "will" of the majority.

Madison and Adams made more of property rights than Jefferson did, but neither of them deserted the democratic theories of natural rights, popular sovereignty, limited government, antimonarchism, and antiaristocracy. Nor did the two conservatives ever approach Hamilton's justification of plutocracy. Both Adams and Madison inclined to the ideal of a republic which was economically agrarian at base, but supplemented by mercantile and manufacturing interests. Madison perhaps a little more than Adams realized the vital role of credit and of government-financed expansion of the country's natural resources and communications—the role which John Adams' son, John Quincy Adams, was to develop fully in his program of "Internal Improvement." Theoretically, therefore, it was Hamilton, of doubtful birth, who thought most exclusively of the moneyed interests of the country, partly because he saw in them the source of national strength, while Jefferson, graceful and learned "landed squire," cared most deeply about the widespread independent well-being of the "people," farmers and laborers included. Adams and Madison, aristocratic in taste in the typical styles of Massachusetts and Virginia, but far from dazzling in the family fortunes to which they were born, were actively promoting a scheme of society favorable to widespread middle-class prosperity and power.

4

The ethical theories of these men had pronounced influence upon the political and economic views they maintained. As character is the inner side of habit in the individual, so in society its outward crystallized structure is government. Save for these four philosopher-statesmen of the Republic, the American character might never have been given more than haphazard or perfunctory significance. Jefferson, Madison, and John Adams all understood the importance of character for those who would be leaders in a republic, and Hamilton sometimes did but sometimes paid only lip service to the ideal. Jefferson and Madison and Adams advocated that "the purest and noblest characters" (Madison's phrase) should serve as the people's representatives, since they alone would do so from the "proper motives." Because these men dedicated themselves to the cause of their country before they consulted their immediate personal needs, the inceptive principles of the American republic betoken seekers of truth and wisdom, and good citizens in the Roman sense, rather than mere men of office.

Jefferson, perceiving that government was necessary for the release of man's fullest potentialities, liked to speak of it as of secondary or instrumental value—a habit which was later perversely construed to mean that government was evil. The range of realistic political choice for Jefferson lay entirely between repressive government and republicanism, and he identified the essence of republicanism as "action by the citizens in person in affairs within their reach and competence, and in all others by representatives, chosen immediately, and removable by themselves." For this reason, a republic was the "only form of government that is not eternally at open or secret war with the rights of mankind." To achieve republican freedom, citizens must pay a price, the wakefulness of "eternal vigilance," and therefore a citizenry trained in the principles of government, an educated citizenry, is the indispensable support of freedom.

Thus, subtly and indirectly, a moral climate had been postulated for the America in which republicanism was to be tried. Benevolence and moral sense, self-created will rather than coercive force, are the dynamic daily agents in free society as well as the purely theoretical factors of its ethics. "Natural" moralism is opposed to the reputed "natural" rule of force, which Jefferson saw as the breeder of authoritarian society, whether of "kings, hereditary nobles, and priests" or, in the language of a later day, of leaders, demagogues, and commissars. Jefferson's agrarianism, so often made the catchword for his variety of democracy, is in reality a by-product of an almost sentimental preference for the simplicity of classical republicanism joined to the supposed purity of "primitive" Christianity. Yet when Jefferson realized that the evolution of his nation demanded the self-sufficiency and expansion of her manufacture and trade—when he perceived that free society would be jeopardized if it were unable to defend itself on the high seas—he protested that "he . . . who is now against domestic manufacture, must be for reducing us either to dependence . . . or to be clothed in skins, and to live like wild beasts in dens and caverns. I am not one of these; experience has taught me that manufactures are now as necessary to our independence as to our comfort." Despite this, Jefferson's instinctive trust reposed in the fair and free interchange of nation with nation, as in citizen with citizen—which is to say that he was a man of peace, conceiving productive society basically as a peaceful society, an earnest judgment in which he was fully joined by James Madison.

Economically and politically, to Hamilton's expert eye, the softer fringe of social morality was not a subject for enthusiasm nor even for belief. "The seeds of war are sown thickly in the human breast," Hamilton had written, and the rivalry that precipitated wars, in his view, stemmed partly from "the temper of societies," and partly from the human disposition to "prefer partial to general interest." Coming to terms with self-interested reality was accordingly Hamilton's basic preoccupation, whether that "reality" meant strong armies and navies for defense against foreign powers, or a strong system of national credit. His ultimate separation of himself from his idealistic associates, whom he termed "political empirics," finds expression in an important unfinished paper called "Defence of the Funding System" (about 1795), where he identifies the "true" politician as one who "takes human nature (and human society its aggregate) as he finds it, a compound of good and ill qualities, of good and ill tendencies, endued with powers and actuated by passions and propensities which blend enjoyment with suffering and make the causes of welfare the causes of misfortune." Afraid to warp this fundamental human complex by urging a happiness not suited to it, the true politician supposedly aims at the social measures designed to "make men happy according to their natural bent, which multiply the sources of individual enjoyment and increase national resources and strength." The great objective of the statesman should thus be to find the cement for compounding diverse elements of a state into a "rock" of national strength.

Governments would not need to be afraid to take power, Hamilton believed, could they strip themselves of false attitudes of modesty. In the logic of economic stability and national expansion, of credit and appropriations and "sound policy" versus the misguided pleadings of "common humanity," Hamilton saw an unanswerable imperative: to wit, that the "sacred" right of property must be defended by the laws and by the constitutions of the land, and that even the non-propertied groups in the community should protect property rights lest the "general principles of public order" be subverted.

John Adams, the self-styled "John Yankee" who could not bear to kowtow to "John Bull"—nor for that matter to any foreign power—seems more at home in Jefferson's and Madison's company than he is with Hamilton, the "boss" of his own party. Without Adams, the democratic precedent of the New England meeting hall, the training green, and the system of self-support for local schools, churches, and cultural institutions might have spoken only with muffled voice in the American tradition. The political "virtues" of Massachusetts even Jefferson commended, pointing to that state as the best exponent of the theme that knowledge is power. In Adams' championship of New England there is a nucleus of national pride useful and perhaps necessary to a rising nation. To this Adams personally added the dignified appeal that, however much republican government consisted of equal laws justly administered, it further required consistent benevolence and encouragement for the arts and sciences. Almost a humanist but never quite freed of a Puritan sense of guilt and sin, Adams privately reveled in the classics just as Jefferson did. The late correspondence which flourished between the two aged statesmen as they enacted the roles of sages in retirement, with great éclat, is a phenomenon of tireless learning and peppery jest, joined in a correspondence the like of which is not known in the annals of American statesmen.

5

Such were the philosopher-kings of the American Enlightenment. However often they may have erred—in description, in prognosis, in emphasis, and sometimes in behavior as statesmen—they seem to have possessed that rare wisdom about human and political affairs which never quite exhausts its power to suggest. On occasion, it restores its own original vitality and suffices to sanction an important change in national or international policy. We know that in the curious reversals of history, the truths of an age are likely to suffer sea change. As Lincoln pointed out, the maxim "All men are created equal," once thought a self-evident truth, is termed a "self-evident lie" once we have "grown fat, and lost all dread of being slaves ourselves." So it may be with the far-ranging insights and veridical principles of the philosopher-statesmen of the Republic. Since the advent of the Jacksonian age—a "calamitous" Presidency in Madison's prediction—the objectives of tempered democracy have been often ignored or ingeniously misinterpreted. As the letters and state papers of the Republican era again come under review, it is apparent that democratic ideology can still benefit by its own very articulate original. The foundation of our national literature is present here, in the practical literature of ideas, as well as in the imitative experiments of the deliberately "literary" work of the day.

13. POETS AND ESSAYISTS

THE writing of the pamphleteers and of the philosopher-statesmen thus frequently rose to the level of literature, but it did not satisfy the demand for a national expression in that first of the arts. Independence to be complete, declared the poet-politician Freneau and many another young man, must produce for America its own Miltons and Addisons and Swifts, its Popes and Goldsmiths and Wordsworths. The times that tried men's souls demanded iron purpose, tempered to the single task of creating the framework of a strong republic; but the coming of peace brought the need and the desire for fuller expression of the national "genius."

Here was a paradox: On the one hand, patriotism demanded a national literature; on the other, the urgency of events made its creation seem an idle and unworthy occupation. The difficulty, of course, lay in the sophistication of art developed by the English neo-classical writers and as yet unsuccessfully challenged by the romantics. The standards and forms for the epic, the pastoral, the novel, the essay, the comedy, the tragedy, which had evolved in the self-conscious literary atmosphere of eighteenth century London, could not easily be bent and stretched to contain the ideas and the experiences of the young republic; yet bent and stretched they must be if that republic were to have a literature of its own. Imitation of established or current literary modes contended therefore with the unruly spirit of nationalism during the first half-century of independence in an effort to create overnight an American literary tradition.

Young men all over the new nation fumbled for words to explain themselves and the busy tumult about them. None were more active than the group in Connecticut, known as the "Hartford Wits." But practical considerations often sprawled into the path of literature. John Trumbull would have liked nothing better than to be allowed to become a man of letters, an "American Swift," the sting of whose satire reminded contemporaries of their comic inadequacies. Couplets came easily to him. He liked the tone of Prior and Churchill, the quick cantankerousness of Pope. Such satirical pose allowed him to correct without seeming pontifical, to flick incisive little wounds into complacency and pretense:

> Were there no fools beneath the skies,
> What were the trick of being wise?

He could do this kind of thing rather better than he could write seriously in the mood of Milton or Gray, though the notebooks in which he experimented privately indicate that he did not easily convince himself of his own limitations. It was gratifying to be admired, as he was admired, to be compared publicly with Pope, applauded as equal to Samuel Butler and Jonathan Swift. But the young man was also a Trumbull, with reputation to maintain and his way to make in the world. Satire, even when good-naturedly modulated, hurt people, and people who were hurt turned in anger. Their humorless opposition made difficult, perhaps impossible, the road to judgeship and political renown which a sensible young man should follow.

The lesson was learned early, when Trumbull's sprightly, but corrective essays, first called "The Medler" (1769-1770) and then, less truculently, "The Correspondent" (1770-1773), led him into controversy. It was learned most pertinently when *The Progress of Dulness* (1773) landed him in the midst of distressingly public quarrels. Today the poem seems innocently amusing, well worth an evening's reading. There is good humor behind Trumbull's probings into the aspirations and hapless adventures of the dullard ministerial student Tom Brainless, of the fop Dick Hairbrain, and of the modish young belle Harriet Simper. Idiosyncrasies of manners, dress, and education, religious bigotries and reading habits are dissected with such impish skill that we chuckle as we remember similar small absurdities among our own neighbors. We recognize Tom, Dick, and Harriet as ancient literary types, long familiar in England, but livened by Trumbull's deft wit into characters whose foibles seem distinctively American. The author's contemporaries read more knowingly into the poem to discover local men or favorite local institutions impiously ridiculed, and they struck back at him viciously in print and with ominous threats of violence. He replied manfully, denying what he could of personal intention, but affirming the satirist's traditional responsibility to expose incompetence and dishonesty wherever he found them.

Such undignified public wrangling certainly could not be permitted to continue. Little was accomplished, except that a young man's career was jeopardized. Thus Trumbull learned to soften his stroke: his next, and most popular, satire, the Revolutionary *M'Fingal* (1776), was so cautious in ridicule both of Tory and of Patriot that it could be reprinted in London without apparently causing a ripple of comment. Perhaps Honorius, who ranted pompously at the town meeting with which the poem opens, was intended to represent John Adams, with whom at the time Trumbull was studying law; certainly no such satirical intention could be openly expressed. *M'Fingal* is effective burlesque of the bombastic oratory of the early Revolution; it is ironical in analysis of Tory argument, but is not pitched in a key calculated to incite vacillating men to action. Even in 1782 when Trumbull lengthened the poem, he reached his now more strongly patriotic climax only with the tar-and-feathering of Tory M'Fingal and the ignominious hoisting of his ally, the constable, to the "sublimest top" of a liberty pole. The verse is competent, objectively humorous, sometimes quotable:

> No man e'er felt the halter draw,
> With good opinion of the law.

Such moderation helps explain the enormous post-Revolutionary popularity of *M'Fingal,* which went through some thirty editions and was frequently quoted in political campaigns and school readers during the next half-century. Avoiding extremes, it became a well of good-tempered ridicule into which later countrymen of whatever political persuasion could dip for aptly phrased commentary on affairs of their own times. John Trumbull seems to have been little moved by the American Revolution: he viewed it dispassionately, not quite as a disinterested spectator, but as one who allowed himself neither shrill cries of triumph at patriot successes nor thunderous encouragement when victory seemed remote. *M'Fingal* is the least topical of Revolutionary satires, and the best worth reading. We may overlook its literary debts to Swift and Butler, accept its impertinent burlesque of Virgil and Milton, forget even the minor position to which it must be assigned in the history of the English mock-epic, and still enjoy what it has to say of our ancestors and, obliquely, of us.

Though by 1782 Trumbull had virtually abandoned literature for a more respectable career as a jurist, his influence remained pervasive among contemporaries in New England. As tutor at Yale until 1773, he had led friends and students to an examination and imitation of modern English authors—to Addison, Pope, and Milton. "I have learned more about English style from Jack Trumbull," said one of his students, "than from any other man." David Humphreys probably expressed the opinion of many of his Yale friends when he playfully blamed the "ill company" which he kept with Trumbull for having induced him to "turn scribbler." Trumbull's was a witty and intellectual leadership which appealed to young men. When he looked forward to the literary future of America in his *Essay on the Uses and Advantages of the Fine Arts* (1770), he struck a spark which glowed to fine imitative fire among his younger friends:

> This land her Steele and Addison shall view,
> The former glories equall'd by the new;
> Some future Shakespeare charm the rising age,
> And hold in magic charm the listening stage.

It was not for lack of trying that Trumbull's protégés failed. Literature to them was the hallmark of superiority, a method of instruction whereby men who knew the way pointed it clearly to their less fortunate fellows. Such a guide was David Humphreys, whose armload of solid volumes taught industry and patriotism and humble recognition of the wisdom of one's betters. Such, too, was Timothy Dwight, who grew to be one of America's giants, created in the image of his own honest ambition. One of Yale's great presidents, a teacher whose solidly authenticated theological doctrines spread through all the expanding young country from the close-written notebooks of his students, he became an oracle whose voice inspired no one so greatly as himself. People like his brother-in-law, William Dunlap of New York, who read William Godwin and wrote plays, found him narrow and censorious. They called him the "Protestant Pope of New England," but they squirmed under the confident vigor of his disapproval.

At nineteen Dwight conceived a poem, an epic of high moral purpose which would combine the sublimity of Milton and Fénelon with more modern notions of what a great poem should be. Its rhyme would be the heroic couplet of Pope's Homer. Its theme would be Biblical—Joshua's hard-won entry to the promised land. When fourteen years later *The Conquest of Canaan* (1785) appeared, readers had little trouble convincing themselves that patriotic analogy was intended, that Joshua was Washington, and that other American heroes strode thinly disguised through its eleven tedious books. "He who would learn," suggested William Cowper in England, "by what steps the Israelites possessed the promised land, must still seek his inspiration in the Bible." Another Englishman, Thomas Day, whose *Sandford and Merton* was a best seller on both sides of the Atlantic, defied "the most resolute reader to wade through" Dwight's poem "without yawning an hundred times." The elements so storm in sympathetic energy with the martial strivings of its heroes that Trumbull suggested it be provided with lightning rods. In it also, says the best and most sympathetic of Dwight's critics, stalwart eighteenth century Americans with Hebrew names talk like Milton's angels and fight like prehistoric Greeks.

After 1785 Timothy Dwight left literature almost as completely as did John Trumbull. His single subsequent trial at belles-lettres was a charming bucolic and didactic poem called *Greenfield Hill* (1794), which represents the landscape and the people of a small Connecticut village. The scene is perhaps less familiar to one who knows New England than to one with some acquaintance among the poets of England. Lines are so admittedly imitative of Beattie, Dyer, Gray, Goldsmith, Thomson, and Pope that any reader, if he pause at all over the poem, may simply hold in one hand a copy of, say, *The Deserted Village* and, with *Greenfield Hill* in the other, completely deflate Dwight as a creative artist. He was not essentially a creative artist:

he was a moralist, a powerful and successful teacher, a righter of great wrongs. With a practical job to do, he did it effectively by taking what he could where he could find it. Yet the America of his day, with his concurrence, accepted him as one of her principal men of letters. The fault was as much with America as with Dr. Dwight.

As a moralist, Dwight was most persuasive in his sermons, where he could undisguisedly correct to his own pattern. He is strongest in protest, as in *The Triumph of Infidelity* (1788) which attacks what Dwight interpreted as the influence of Voltaire in America. It is a bitter and a coarse poem, published anonymously and never, even in the face of public accusation, acknowledged by Dwight. As a clergyman, he was fond of talking of the "Duty of Americans," "The Genuineness and Authenticity of the New Testament," and "The Nature and Danger of Infidel Philosophy," and he simplified, explained, and defended his theology in a series of sermons delivered to many college generations at Yale. Outsiders found him an autocrat who talked so much they could get no word in themselves. He puttered every day in his garden for his health's sake, and he spent the long college holidays exploring byways of northeastern America. His wanderings are recorded—where he had been, what he had seen, what needed correction—in a journal which, published as *Travels in New-England and New-York* (1821–1822), preserves not only delightful pictures of countryside and people but also a candidly revealing self-portrait of its author.

Other men from Yale turned in other directions. Younger than Trumbull and Dwight, Joel Barlow grew in New England under the influence of both until search for livelihood took him to Europe. There, always impressionable, he found in new masters exciting new sources of enthusiasm. He was to move familiarly among the liberal political circles of Horne Tooke, William Godwin, and Joseph Priestley, to absorb the intoxicating doctrines which promised rights to all men. He would advise with Lafayette on the future of France, with William Hayley on the future of poetry, or with Mary Wollstonecraft on the future of women. Futures fascinated him, and he overflowed with optimistic good talk. His friends remembered him as "so far gone in Poetry, that there is no hope of reclaiming . . . him."

As one of the international gadflies attracted by the bright promise of the French Revolution, Barlow joined in the attack on Edmund Burke, until that stout-hearted statesman brushed him off contemptuously as "Joel the Prophet." His *The Conspiracy of Kings* (1792) unleashed a young man's best store of conventionally rhymed invective against the designs of scheming and undemocratic men. Less heatedly, his *Advice to the Privileged Orders* (1792) defended in prose the superior claim of human rights over property rights and sounded the revolutionary's traditional warning that a better day must dawn. Fox applauded the pamphlet in Commons, but the Pitt ministry ordered it burned and the author arrested. Thereafter, like his friend Paine, Barlow became a marked man, for people were attracted by his simple logic and paused to think—nothing seemed more dangerous. The French Assembly voted him an honorary Citizen of the Republic. But friends in New England were shocked: they wished there were some way to "relieve him of his enchanted castles"; Barlow's brains, they thought, needed settling. Sober Noah Webster could not understand what maggot gnawed at his old schoolmate. John Adams considered even Tom Paine "not a more worthless fellow."

Before this, as a young man at Yale, Barlow had also conceived an epic. He hurried it to completion as *The Vision of Columbus* (1787), in nine rhapsodic books which told of the past, but particularly of the future of the brave, new American world. A young man's poem, and choked with little of the pedantry of Dwight's epic, it nevertheless breaks down in spite of—or perhaps because of—its breathless verve and easy patriotism. Barlow had dashed off page after page at single sittings, and neither his imagination nor his control of verse was equal to the strain. Yet failure in poetical technique and confusion of thought never quite dull the *Vision's* assertive enthusiasm. Foreshadowings of Barlow's later and less restricted notions of human freedom are there, sufficiently submerged beneath conventionalities to allow his conservative friends to greet the poem with hosannas of loud praise. That more precise critics in England found it pretentious, as they found Dwight's epic pretentious, was unimportant; that critics in England noticed it at all was a sign of success.

Within a year after publication of the *Vision,* Barlow had left New England to become the apostate whose change-of political coloration increasingly distressed old friends. He poured out his heart in long letters to his young wife, as he was to do every time they were separated during the next thirty years—in letters which Ruth Barlow faithfully preserved and which re-create today an idyl of married love which is, quite inadvertently, among the finest monuments of her husband's career. There is humor and playfulness in Joel Barlow, sincerity, and a great fund of often completely impractical idealism. Homesick for New England and corn-meal mush (though he detested the word), he composed the mock-epic *The Hasty Pudding* (1796), a completely American adaptation of an ancient gastro-literary theme, and a poem so admired by anthologists that it sometimes promises to be all that remains of Joel Barlow.

Barlow developed into one of the most cosmopolitan and useful Americans of his generation, Minister Resident to Algiers, Ambassador to France, adviser and confidential friend to Jefferson and Madison. He worked with

Fulton on the steamboat; thrilled to the promise of the age of canals. As he grew older his enthusiasms were more controlled, but he never lost them. Nor did he ever forget the epic which had not been exactly right as he first presented it. When he had mulled over it for twenty years, it was ready again, rewritten and expanded for second publication as *The Columbiad* (1807), and heralded by public fanfare such as no American book had received before. It was a beautiful volume, a credit to American printers and bookbinders, a collector's item enhanced by engravings from his friend Robert Fulton. It is better articulated than the *Vision,* more mature and more correct in versification; but *The Columbiad* is best known today as one of America's great failures, the book nobody reads, the tin-plated epic.

The tragedy of Joel Barlow is not that he is not remembered, but that he is remembered for the wrong thing. Every textbook pauses for a paragraph to review the epic failure of *The Vision of Columbus* and *The Columbiad.* Few remind us of the armor of bright prose with which this early American Lochinvar girded himself as he crusaded for doctrines which never quite spread from the new Western world. Like Timothy Dwight, Barlow was a greater man than his writings ever reveal him. Like too many others of his time he still awaits the biographer who will detail his sincere and whole-hearted small contribution to the articulation of democratic thought.

These three—Trumbull, Dwight, and Barlow—are traditionally listed as outstanding among the larger group, variously called the Hartford Wits, the Yale Poets, or the Connecticut choir. There were others: Humphreys for the bulk of his earnestly patriotic verse is sometimes admitted as a fourth; Richard Alsop, Noah Webster, Lemuel Hopkins, Mason Cogswell, and Theodore Dwight, to list them in an arbitrary, rough order of excellence, were the principal remaining members—not to forget the younger Elihu Hubbard Smith, never completely of their company, who extracted from them generously when he edited our first all-American anthology in 1793. The aim of the Wits was chiefly political and remedial: in one combination or another they produced *The Anarchiad* (1786–1787), *The Echo* (1791–1805), *The Political Greenhouse* (1799), and other serviceable satires directed against the absurdity of anyone disagreeing with solid, New England views. Such barbs more often than not found tender marks and called for retaliation, until the acrimonious exchange produced some of the most readable, if not the most refined verse of those times. It was a rough-and-tumble battle of poets with shirt sleeves rolled, the effects of which lasted long enough for Fenimore Cooper half a century later to throw his weight in satire against the New Englanders, not realizing perhaps that another man of letters from the Middle States, Philip Freneau, had already done the job very well indeed.

2

"The writings of an aristocratic, speculating faction at Hartford, in favor of monarchy and titular distinctions," wrote Freneau, "are sufficient to convince any candid person that the old *insular* enemy to independence and prosperity in America has her hired emissaries at work in that part of the union." The Wits, he continued, openly profess the same principles as the "old, defunct Tories of 1775." His statement, of course, was not quite true, but the men of Connecticut had found in this hard-bitten veteran an opponent who could stand to them blow for blow. Freneau represented, as did the apostate Joel Barlow, the democratic principles of Jefferson, even of Thomas Paine. Therefore he was an enemy, subject to attack as a party tool and, in contrast to the epic poets of New England, a "mere writer for newspapers": by others far less original than he, he was ridiculed as an imitator, a plagiarist. Literature had so become the handmaiden of politics that, "amidst the mutual clamours of contending parties, not one reader in a thousand cares three cents about the literary honour of his country."

It was not, as James Madison said more pointedly, the time for poetry. Nor perhaps could it be expected to be. Men in leather aprons rose early to insure expansion of American commerce; hands toughened at the plow were raised in committee room or assembly; come-uppers were coming up, and there was no time for dallying. Literature was for ladies, for clergymen with leisure, or for young men who had not yet found more proper and productive work. But America had then among her young men one poet whose talent, caged within the utilitarian necessities of his times, was allowed frequently to beat itself to doggerel. Might-have-beens have no place in literary history, but the early promise of Philip Freneau, displayed in the Keatsian insight of "The Power of Fancy" (written in 1770) and the philosophic searching of "The House of Night" (written possibly in 1775), foretold achievement which could have placed him among our greater poets. Even thwarted, he developed the most original, though not consistently original, poetic voice of his generation. He sang of American men and American achievements, of his fine hope for America, and of the bitterness of his disappointment that she seemed so often to fail. He had none of the mellow inclusiveness of Walt Whitman, and he wrote more often in anger than in understanding, but not before Whitman was his country to produce a poet more completely or more devotedly her own.

As a young man at Princeton Freneau had also written prophetically of the future of his fair Western world. With his classmate Hugh Brackenridge he composed *A Poem on the Rising Glory of America* (1772) as a commencement piece which, like Trumbull's, looked forward to more than a march of material progress.

> I see a Homer and a Milton rise
> In all the pomp and majesty of song, . . .
> A second Pope, like that Arabian bird
> Of which no age can boast but one, may yet
> Awake the muse by Schuylkill's silent stream, . . .
> And Susquehanna's rocky stream unsung, . . .
> Shall yet remurmur to the magic sound
> Of song heroic.

This was not only a schoolboy's poem of optimistic augury. It was the personal dedication of a young poet, steeped in the lore of his calling. Freneau would be a poet, and he would sing a clear new song. Where are the glories of yesteryear? he asks in "The Pyramids of Egypt."

> —all, all are gone,
> And like the phantom snows of a May morning
> Left not a vestige to discover them!

Vast and unexplored, filled with promise such as the modern world had never known, America would be his theme, she and the opportunities she offered for fulfillment of the ideals of which great poets had always sung. An apprentice to the art of these, his masters, Freneau soon developed his own elastic lyric idiom which, avoiding much of the stereotyped pattern of his contemporaries, contained echoes of young Milton and promise of young Keats. Thus at eighteeen he invoked his muse in "The Power of Fancy":

> Wakeful, vagrant, restless things,
> Ever wandering on the wing,
> Who thy wondrous source can find,
> Fancy, regent of the mind; . . .
> Come, O come—perceiv'd by none,
> You and I will walk alone.

This was the kind of poetry for which busy America could make no room, and it was what Freneau most wanted to write. Nevertheless, when revolution broke over America, he dutifully put poetry behind him, though not without hesitation and false starts, to enlist his talent for rhyming in the shrill war of words which played accompaniment to military and political maneuverings. Mercurial, sensitive, quick to speak in anger, Freneau in his satire showed neither the moderation of John Trumbull nor the infectious good humor of Francis Hopkinson. He spat derisively at every enemy, whether among the faint-hearted in America or among the false-hearted abroad. He wrote jubilant songs on patriot victories, spurred laggard spirits when defeat seemed most certain, and denounced the "gorged monsters," "infernal miscreants," "foes to the rights of freedom and of man" who "spare no age, no sex from lust and murder." He became the authentic "Poet of the American Revolution," who wrote of what he had known at first hand as a militiaman, of what he had suffered in his poet's pride as a prisoner of war. With the memory of his experience hot within him, he wrote *The British Prison-Ship* (1781), as intensely bitter a poem as America has ever produced. He called on his countrymen to "glut revenge on this detested foe" which pants "to stain the world with gore." Banish them forever. "Defeat, destroy and sweep them from the land." Then only might America be free for, among other things, the kind of poetry which Freneau wanted most to write.

This hatred for England, bred of his war years, colored the rest of Freneau's life and his literary production. What had been America's crime, except that she had raised her arm to stay an assassin's knife? Pride, greed, lust, avarice, each cruelty which kept mankind in chains was exhibited by that same land from whose poets he had drawn his early poetic vision. As the Revolution dragged through its last weary phases, Freneau, now editor of the *Freeman's Journal* in Philadelphia, found it necessary to combat not only the foreign tyrant but new tyrannies of compromise with and imitation of England which appeared within his own country. Drawn ever deeper into petty quarrelings, he became increasingly disillusioned. How many fine sentiments were on people's lips, how few in their hearts! With what faint courage men of letters in America faced their future! He ridiculed David Humphreys who seemed sycophant in seeking literary honors, just as he later ridiculed Washington Irving for seeking reputation abroad. Would America ever be truly independent of England?

> Can we ever be thought to have learning or grace,
> Unless it be sent from that damnable place?

One of Freneau's unique characteristics was complete sincerity in meaning exactly what he said. His were no catchwords designed to rouse the rabble to defense of special privilege. He had learned to speak plainly, in simple idiom, of simple things which common men understand, about things like liberty and the right of every man to happiness. When, after ten years of patriotic satire, he retired from controversy in 1785 to become a sea captain plying between New York and Charleston, he avoided the grandiose schemes, the epic attempts which had attracted him as a collegian. He turned to simpler subjects, less traditionally poetic—to rugged, unpretentious themes like "The Virtue of Tobacco," "The Drunken Soldier," "The Pilot of Hatteras," "The Roguish Shoemaker," and, best loved of all, "The Jug of Rum." He wrote of "the red-nosed boy who deals out gin," "the quack that heals your negro's bruise," the ranting evangelist, native Americans all, "who did as they pleased and who spoke as they thought." No poem was very long, none very serious, and all were greatly popular among men who read their newspapers quickly.

Here was what America seemed to want, simple songs of American things, in stout American idiom, brightened with humor which recognizes even its own shortcomings. No moth-wing aspiration here for the sentimentalist, no learned claptrap for the intellectual. These were clearly stamped as of domestic origin, songs of and for the people. The pity is that the more finely wrought poems that Freneau produced during these busy years were unrecognized and virtually unread. In England Sir Walter Scott purloined a line from the elegiac stanzas "To the Memory of the Brave Americans" who fell at Eutaw Springs; Thomas Campbell took another from the contemplative "The Indian Burying Ground." But "The Wild Honey Suckle" (1786), which surpassed them all, was seldom reprinted during the poet's lifetime. The tone of muted wonder and the fresh clarity of diction which here consider the "frail duration" of beauty amid American swamplands place Freneau chronologically at the head of America's poets. Burnsian it is, and written in the year which greeted the Kilmarnock edition of the Scotch poet; Wordsworthian, too, and twelve years before *Lyrical Ballads*. America cannot afford to forget "The Wild Honey Suckle," for here at last were fused the two elements of native scene and native expression, and here, too, was poetry.

Moods productive of poetry were seldom allowed to Freneau again. When principles for which the American Revolution had been fought seemed threatened and democracy held in contempt among his countrymen, he emerged once more as a partisan propagandist who lashed out courageously, even boisterously, to defend rights of the common man, the poor soldier fleeced of his earnings, or the farmer crowded to poverty by greed of industrialists. Hard-headed and sharp-tongued, he became the first powerfully effective crusading newspaperman in America, and lost, as editor of the *National Gazette* (1791–1793), much of his reputation as a popular poet. Plain people still understood him as he reduced national issues to their own plain language, but men in power struck back with blows that left permanent marks. Alexander Hamilton wrote him down publicly as a liar. Washington damned him as a rascal. The Wits of New England, when they could not withstand the logic of his argument, attacked him as a poet. But he saved our Constitution, said Jefferson, when it was "galloping fast into monarchy." Few men have done more, and with less reward. When defeat of John Adams in 1800 made the place of the common man seem at length secure, Freneau retired again, to the sea, finally to a "few sandy acres" of homestead in New Jersey, to re-phrase, more quietly now, his tenacious convictions. He continued to publish volumes which sold poorly, or unnoticed verses in obscure periodicals, even after he was seventy; but America passed him by. Bryant remembered him only as "a writer of inferior verse . . . distinguished by a coarse strength of sarcasm."

Freneau's coarse strength can be better understood and better treasured today. His stubborn refusal to compromise seems even admirable, as he extended it to include "such rhyming dealers in romance" as Joel Barlow, who failed to forge their songs to the simple, democratic temper of America. As editor of the *Time-Piece, and Literary Companion* (1797–1798), Freneau had offered its columns for the display of poetical wares from his countrymen. And what had he received? Echoes of English verse, sentimental and sac-charine, as beaux and bluestockings parried traditional compliments, prettily phrased and insipid. Where was American virility, the solid, self-assertive strong phrases in which a new country should sing herself to the world? Nothing was more popular than the limpid lines with which young Joseph Brown Ladd, as "Aroeut," addressed his fair "Amanda," or which Robert Treat Paine as "Menander" exchanged in Boston with the "American Sappho," Sarah Wentworth Morton, known to each reader of sensibility as "Philenia," the "warbling eloquence" of whose harp stirred such polite, such sad and sweet response. The air was filled with melancholy strains inspired by Goethe's *The Sorrows of Young Werther,* with liquid rhapsodies distilled from Ossian, with inconsequential nonsense hung—so spoke one critic—with "garrish ornament and tinsel decoration, which are necessary to satisfy expec-tation." Against this background, Freneau's unpretentious work stands out, homespun among faded satins, durable, woven of native fiber to a pattern adapted to native requirements.

Like his verse, Freneau's prose became progressively more indigenous. During the Revolution he had been satisfied with that stock figure of the eighteenth century periodical essayist, the learned hermit who surveys the world from a quiet, woodland retreat. The voice with which "The Pilgrim" (1781–1782) pleaded for simplicity or railed against bestial servilities of Eng-lishmen was a deep-throated expression of Freneau's new-found national creed, but the words were old, and the mood and the setting. "Tomo-Cheeki, the Creek Indian in Philadelphia" (1795–1797), an unidealized American aborigine who found strange foibles among his white neighbors, represented an advance, but along trails already clearly marked by Goldsmith and Mon-tesquieu; "Hezekiah Salem" (1797), the defrocked Yankee deacon who spoke variously and sometimes amusingly in ridicule of domestic eccentricities, was more genuinely a home-grown product; but most American of all was "Robert Slender." As first presented in 1788, he was a stocking weaver who liked to record sly observations on such things as young men in love, the frustration of garret-pent poets, or the peculiarities of American businessmen; but he grew as Freneau grew until, when resurrected in 1800 to comment on the upheavals which brought Jefferson to power, he had become a native type whose literary and political descendants have been numerous among us. He was the simple country boy, who knew nothing of affairs except what he read in the newspapers. His rustic interpolations and naïve misgivings, his optimistic assurance that everything must come out right are in the best tradition of American political burlesque.

Freneau's failure is most simply explained by his headstrong refusal to compromise his conception of a literature divorced completely from "that damnable place" which had threatened American liberties. He had few followers, no imitators, for he was not quite respectable. He was a radical who, even when right, went too far. He addressed the wrong people, and proper people scorned him. His strictures on the writings of contemporaries went unnoticed or were explained as grumblings of a disappointed man who prostituted his own talents to politics. His nativism thus became an undercurrent which was seldom to emerge during the next fifty years, and never in the pristine and unworkable state in which he conceived it. In person he was known as an opinionated gaffer, eccentric in insisting on smallclothes and cocked hat long after they were out of fashion. So also in poetry he refused the easy sentimentality which became popular in America. His stark and didactic idiom, founded on rational principles of human justice, seemed old-fashioned and harsh in the 1820's beside the smooth, more modern phrases of Fitz-Greene Halleck and Rodman Drake. His prose, for all its sturdy independence, was seasoned so strongly with reference to local events that it repelled all but the most expertly trained palates. Forgotten in his own time, too seldom remembered in ours, he left as his testimony:

> To write was my sad destiny,
> The worst of trades, we all agree.

This worst of trades attracted few experienced workmen. Almost everything presented as literature was apprentice work by young men who later in self-protection turned to other things. We read copybooks in which students painstakingly traced moods and themes in which other men had succeeded. Scott, Byron, Moore, even Gray and the older poets were eagerly read in America: in what better manner might young men write if they too wished to be read? "Piddling poetasters," their practical countrymen called them, and this they were, swaying sensitively, as young poets must, to every breath of influence. They sang of solitude, of broken harps, and of genius—how they liked the word!—allowed to wither unrecognized. Theirs were juvenilia beside which Freneau's simplest "newspaper verse" seems extraordinarily mature.

3

Americans were proud of their newspapers. What other country on the face of the globe could boast a larger proportion of readers? This was America's literature—she had no time for more. Almost every newspaper or short-lived magazine had its poets' corner, and had also its essayists dressed in motley patched with shreds of Addison, Swift, Goldsmith, or Johnson. Noah Webster's homely "The Prompter" (1790) was popular and inspirational. Brockden Brown's "The Man at Home" (1798) contained the first draft of scene and incident later to find place in his novels. William Wirt's "Letters of the British Spy" (1803) was panoramic in literary learning. Each was corrective, some were pointedly satirical. Thomas Greene Fessenden was "Christopher Caustic"; New York had its "Tobey Tickler," Boston its "Tim Touchstone," and Philadelphia its "Tobey Scratch-'em," all lampooning with the conventionalized audacity of their English betters. Following them came the Irvings and James Kirke Paulding who in *Salmagundi* (1807-1808) simply did so much better what had often been done before.

Satire was condoned as a useful occupation, but polite literature was something quite different. William Wirt inquired of St. George Tucker whether being known as an author would harm his legal reputation and seemed not at all surprised at the older writer's answer that it very well might. At best, what sensible men liked to call "scribbling" was what they also liked to dismiss as "an avocation of idle hours," something almost surreptitious, certainly anonymous, for one dared not acknowledge many hours idle. Only a few hardy souls attempted literature as a livelihood; and they failed, like Freneau, and like Brockden Brown who capped his brilliant brief successes as a novelist with hack work little above that of an almanac maker.

Fresh from brilliant journalistic triumphs in New England, Joseph Dennie was also resolved to make writing a profession. He was equally resolved to create a standard for native literature in no degree inferior to that demanded in England. In fact, to this young Harvard man the standards were the same. His own prose rang so true that Timothy Dwight could claim him as the "Addison of the United States, the father of American belles lettres." Hawthorne recalled him as "once esteemed the finest writer in America," and Irving began his career in the contagion of Dennie's influence. It was as "Oliver Oldschool," a precise and opinionated champion of tradition, that he first edited the *Port Folio* (1801-1808) in Philadelphia, just as it was as

"The Lay Preacher" who restrained American folly that he had made his earlier reputation. Like Freneau, he was contemptuous of the sentimental and the extravagant: "a childish taste prevails and childish effusions are the vogue." Unlike Freneau, he refused even by implication to accept inferior products just because they were linsey-woolsey from homemade looms.

A critic rather than a creator, Dennie himself produced little that recommends him to our day. His essays seem prim, crotchety, sometimes sophomoric. His humor is condescending. His occasional easy familiarity is that of a well informed superior who stoops self-righteously to instruct. Above all else, however, he did love literature and had a sound, sure taste when his prejudices allowed him to exercise it. He printed long extracts from his favorite English authors. He solicited original verses from Thomas Campbell. He recognized and helped promote the early promise of Leigh Hunt. He was the first American critic to notice Wordsworth. He spent charming hours with Thomas Moore, who contributed to the *Port Folio* and remembered his visits with Dennie as among the "few agreeable moments" of his American tour. He gathered young men about him, and many a fine, literary talk they had together. "Mr. Dennie," said Moore, "has succeeded in diffusing through his cultivated little circle that love of good literature and sound politics which is so rarely characteristic of his countrymen."

Someone like Dennie was necessary to America—after him came the *North American Review* (1815) and the flowering of literary New England. He helped draw together, bind up, and package for many generations a conception of literary purpose irrevocably tied in with politics and respectability: authoritative sanction was given for lifting the literary embargo against England; standards were reimported and the level of excellence set high. He supplied an atmosphere in which Irving could grow to favor and Cooper to favor and disfavor, in which Freneau could be disregarded and Bryant hailed as a fresh, clear American voice; which made it possible for Longfellow to flourish, and necessary for Emerson to sweep aside the debris of tradition in clearing a path for Whitman.

Not everyone was convinced: "Dependence is a state of degradation, fraught with disgrace; and to be dependent on a foreign mind, for what we can ourselves produce, is to add to the crime of indolence, the weakness of stupidity." But, for all the protest of Freneau or anyone else, literary independence was as unrealized by 1820 as when Trumbull had called for it half a century before. After Campbell published *Gertrude of Wyoming* in England, Rodman Drake rephrased in the twenties the old complaint:

> No native bard the patriot harp hath ta'en,
> But left to minstrel of a foreign strand
> To sing the beauteous scenes of nature's lovliest land.

14. THE BEGINNINGS OF FICTION AND DRAMA

THE history of fiction and of the drama during this period runs parallel to that of poetry and the essay. Here too the impulse to produce an independent, indigenous literature vied with the natural tendency to carry on a distinguished European tradition.

The vogue of the novel, so pronounced in England during the latter half of the eighteenth century, was reflected in America by imported reading until about 1790. Then native authors began suddenly to write stories of their own in the three current British fashions: the sentimental (or domestic), the satirical, and the Gothic. The first to succeed was the sentimental. Its usual theme, seduction, not only permitted the discreet exploitation of thrills but lent itself to those moral lessons which made fiction acceptable. Thus William Hill Brown's *The Power of Sympathy* (1789), usually reckoned the first indubitably American novel, was designed "to represent the specious causes, and to expose the fatal consequences, of seduction . . . and to promote the economy of human life." This formal reassurance prefaces a story compounded of seduction, narrowly averted incest, abduction, rape, and suicide. The main plot tells of a young man who, upon learning that his sweetheart is really his half-sister (by a liaison), shoots himself—a copy of Goethe's *The Sorrows of Young Werther* lying on the table beside him. The secondary plot tells of an unprincipled Lothario who triumphs over the virtue of his wife's sister. The victim dies by taking poison. The diction employed by Brown is decorous to the point of obscurity, and the episodes are only obliquely described; but between the lines lie the very elements against which moralists were inveighing as likely to inflame the passions if not corrupt the heart. Still, the story was, as the title page made clear, "founded in truth." The secondary plot was so patently based on an actual case in contemporary Boston that Brown was prevailed upon to suppress his book.

Connecticut and New York soon received similar lessons—and thrills. Susanna Rowson's *Charlotte Temple* (London, 1791), one of the most popular novels ever written, relates the tragic experiences of a young English girl lured to New York on the promise of marriage, only to be abandoned there by her lover and to die in childbirth. Old-fashioned in its rhetoric, the story is nevertheless told with a sincerity and power that can be felt even today; and indeed the novel still sells. Like *The Power of Sympathy,* this narrative is based upon an actual history, that of Charlotte Stanley whose mortal remains (according to legend) lie in Trinity Churchyard under a tombstone now inscribed "Charlotte Temple." Whether as love story or as a moral emblem, *Charlotte Temple* has attracted millions of readers; it went through some 160 editions (many of them incredibly garbled) before 1860.

The Connecticut Valley also had its lurid fictional warning when Hannah Foster published *The Coquette* (1797). The novel closely followed the case of Elizabeth Whitman, daughter of a trustee of Yale College, who put her confidence unwisely in a "gentleman" speculatively identified by some as Aaron Burr and by others as Pierrepont Edwards, son of Jonathan Edwards. Her death in childbirth occurred at a tavern in Danvers, Massachusetts. In the novel the heroine (Eliza Wharton) is the victim partly of her own vanity and partly of the unscrupulousness of a glamorous military man. The narrative is quietly unfolded by means of letters, but the moral is inescapable, and Eliza's tragic end added to the mounting calendar of advice to young women.

All three of these novels are in the general stream of Richardsonian fiction in that they picture females in distress. Two of the three are told in letter form with a great deal of analysis of the "heart." All are at times heavily didactic in tone, but since the same lessons could have been conveyed by straight prose, it must be inferred that the authors preferred to be novelists rather than moralists. The quality of fiction they represent is not high. Settings are almost negligible, and dialogue sparse and generally inept. *Charlotte Temple* is the most touching as a story; *The Coquette* is the most finished as a novel; *The Power of Sympathy* is the most uncompromising as a tract.

2

The satirical novel was not so prolific as the sentimental, for its irony was disturbing to the Calvinistic mind, and its humor, often arising from sordid picaresque episodes, was objectionable. Yet the use of satire is one of the first signs of intellectual maturity, of the writer's consciousness of his art. Hugh Henry Brackenridge's *Modern Chivalry* may therefore be listed as among our more important achievements in the last decade of the eighteenth century. This massive work—as long as four or five average-length novels—was published in installments between 1792 and 1815. In outward form it is a picaresque or "rogue" novel; its intellectual core consists of a satire on bad government.

As a picaresque story *Modern Chivalry* contains many of the stock elements and devices of eighteenth century British fiction. Chief of these is the framework of roadside adventures experienced by a master and his servant—a parody, in effect, of Don Quixote and Sancho Panza. In *Modern Chivalry* the protagonist is a fifty-year-old Squire, Captain Farrago, who is described as a "peripatetic philosopher" engaged in a trip through Pennsylvania. His servant is the Irishman, Teague O'Regan, a blundering, conscienceless, irrepressible oaf who passes ingloriously from one ludicrous scrape to another, to be rescued and lectured (vainly) by his master on each occasion. Some of these scrapes are of a low order; on one occasion Teague tumbles into bed with a chambermaid, who resists his advances. When she screams for help, Teague manages, with what the author ironically calls presence of mind, to cast suspicion on a Presbyterian preacher. Urged to confess so that an innocent man should not suffer, Teague at first refuses; and he finally consents to do so only if the minister pays him "smart money": it "is a thankless thing to do these things free, you know."

But *Modern Chivalry* is no mere sequence of rogue incidents related for amusement. Teague is a walking embodiment of some of the ills of a raw republic, and his crude actions stimulate Captain Farrago's (i.e., Brackenridge's) analysis of governmental abuses. The author's basic intention was serious: he proposed to examine the state of American "democracy" as he had seen it in operation. For years a judge in Pennsylvania, he knew at first hand the rough politics of democracy; yet his point of view in *Modern Chivalry* is generally that of an objective observer.

Modern Chivalry has often been called a satire on democracy; but Brackenridge was not opposed to democratic government. Indeed he explains that to him it is "beyond all question the freest." His target in *Modern Chivalry* is not democracy itself but rather its incompetence and corruption. Teague is the fulcrum on which his satire turns. Crude and illiterate as he is, Teague is everywhere invited to assume positions for which he is totally unqualified except by a certain good-natured acquiescence. Had it not been for the interference of Captain Farrago, he would have become a preacher, a member of the Philosophical Society, and an Indian treaty maker. When on one occasion he disappears, the Captain not unnaturally fears that he will find him speaking in the Congress or lecturing at a university; but this time Teague is employed as an actor, a post for which he is as little fitted as any. Before he has finished, Brackenridge has touched satirically upon legislation, the practice of law, the ministry, higher education, the press, dueling, scientific research, political chicanery, and Jeffersonion economy. His general method is to show Teague in an incongruous situation from which he is somehow extricated by the Captain, and then to pass on to appropriate philosophical reflections regarding government and society.

But incompetence is only one of the threats to democracy; the other is corruption in high places. The untutored and arrogant masses are themselves vulnerable to exploitation from above:

The demagogue is the first great destroyer of the constitution by deceiving the people. . . . He is an aristocrat; and seeks after more power than is just. He will never rest short of despotic rule.

Thus Brackenridge thrusts at Hamiltonian politics and at the excessive power of the courts. The "rage of mere democracy" and the aristocratic urge toward domination are the Scylla and the Charybdis between which a democracy must sail. "The great moral of this book," he concludes, "is the evil of men seeking office for which they are not qualified." It was this lesson—urged when the air was full of theories of the natural rights of man—which Brackenridge tried to teach his countrymen. To him liberty is neither an abstraction nor an inalienable right; it is something sought and worked for intelligently. Because he loved democracy, he became one of its sternest critics.

Brackenridge was a deliberate craftsman with a definite theory of writing and a calculating eye on his public. He set a high value upon clarity, and he quoted with approval Swift's injunction concerning style—proper words in proper places. Embellishment for its own sake he frowned upon, and he believed that the proof of good writing is "that when you read the composition, you think of nothing but the sense." Yet he enriched his own page with many an allusion to the Greek and Roman classics, which more than any modern models (excepting *Don Quixote*) influenced his writing.

At the same time he thought of himself as an American writer. Occasionally oppressed by his lonely existence in a western wilderness, he "sighed for the garrets of London," but he was in general reconciled to his environment, and he never became (like his contemporary Joseph Dennie) an outright Anglophile. Although he seldom referred specifically to American writers, he once asserted that English is better written in America than in England, and his own prose could stand comparison with most of the best that eighteenth century England produced. He said that he intended *Modern Chivalry* for "Tom, Dick and Harry in the woods"; but its quality was such as to appeal primarily to the intelligentsia. His was one of the ripest minds of the era. While the lady novelists were dispensing simple, serious lessons in morality for young folk, Brackenridge was teaching his fellow men how to be good citizens. His was the harder task. To it he brought not only the wisdom of observation but also his wide reading from Plato to Swift.

3

Charles Brockden Brown, exemplar of the American "Gothic," was the first of our writers to make a profession of literature and the first to approach the stature of a major novelist; few have failed of "greatness" by so narrow a margin. Powers, Brown indubitably possessed; his failure lay in his inability to focus and sustain them. His work drew praise from a wide diversity of other writers as well as from critics domestic and foreign. Shelley was fascinated by him; in the opinion of one of his biographers, "nothing so blended itself with the structure of his interior mind as the creations of Brown." Keats found *Wieland* "a very powerful book." Applause came from many other foreign writers, including Thomas Hood, Godwin, and Hazlitt. In America his gifts were recognized by Poe, Cooper, Neal, Dana, Hawthorne, and others. The scene depicting the maniacal frenzy of Wieland deeply impressed Whittier, who wrote: "In the entire range of English literature there is no more thrilling passage. . . . The masters of the old Greek tragedy have scarcely exceeded the sublime horror of this scene from the American novelist."

The common factor in most of the tributes to Brown is their recognition of his originality: there was no writer quite like him even among the contemporary pre-Romantics to whom he was in some ways akin. The nature of Brown's power eludes exact definition, but its property is to compel the reader's attention irresistibly not only to the exciting narrative but also to the gravity of whatever philosophical or moral problem is implicit in it— whether it be religious obsession (as in *Wieland*), criminology (as in *Edgar Huntly*), philosophic anarchism (as in *Ormond*), humanitarian reform (as in *Arthur Mervyn*), or marriage (as in *Clara Howard* and *Jane Talbot*). His fiction was outwardly sensational, yet no device for heightening the reader's interest in tense action—and Brown commanded Gothic devices—completely effaces the reader's awareness of his high seriousness as a student of mankind.

Brown took himself seriously too. He was a writer of great ambition— perhaps too much so for the good of his health. During his bookish boyhood and effervescent youth he conceived (partly under the stimulus of Elihu H. Smith and William Dunlap) the most grandiose schemes. He would write a trilogy of epics. He would analyze the basic causes of man's misery and propose remedies. He would serve the cause of perfectibility. He would classify all knowledge. He would found important magazines—on a scale suggested by the prospectus of one of them: "to extract the quintessence of European wisdom; to review and estimate the labours of all writers, domestic and foreign." He was in fact attracted by so many ideas that his work suffered from the dispersion of his energies. The air was full of liberal theories which he brought to his desk for eager observation. He was excited by ideas which he could not finally or fully endorse, yet he acquired the reputation of a radical, for in his fiction he discussed the most "advanced" theories: freer divorce laws, political rights for women, deistic religion, a more humane treatment of criminals, amelioration of the lot of the peasant class. Many of these ideas he probably first encountered in Godwin's *Political Justice* (1793), but even less than Godwin could he implement radical thought. He was less interested in machinery than in motives. He never devised a coherent program of reform because he lacked the final qualification of the true crusader, a dynamic urge to act. He remained a liberal Utopian dreamer, resting his hopes for mankind somewhat vaguely in the rule of reason, the rejection of the incubus of Calvinism, and an appeal to benevolence in the human spirit.

In *Wieland* (1798), his best novel, Brown seems to have used for his plot an actual case of murder committed under the influence of hallucination in Tomhannock some years before; but the tone, coloring, and motivation are his own. The action is laid in the environs of Philadelphia, where Theodore Wieland has lived in pastoral tranquillity with his wife and sister until events begin to play havoc with his delicately poised mental health. He becomes the victim of a religious melancholia and hears a mysterious "voice." Actually this voice is at first the voice of a wandering, experimental ventriloquist, Carwin, who uses his special powers some eight times altogether in situations ranging from the trivial to the tragic. Finally Wieland, far gone in a religious psychosis (for which Carwin's experiments are only partially responsible), hears a heavenly "voice" (not Carwin's this time) which commands him to slay his wife and children. This he does. He is prevented from extending his dubious benevolence to his sister Clara only by the intervention of Carwin, who calls upon him to "hold!" This command brings him back to reality; but his realization of his deed converts him into a "monument of woe," to be delivered from ineffable remorse only by death.

The story, despite serious structural defects, is intrinsically as well as historically important. On the derivative level, it is obviously Richardsonian in its presentation of a persecuted heroine (Clara) carrying on in the face of incredible difficulties. Gothic terrors beset her, for she lives in seclusion in a house architecturally ideal for nocturnal terrors. Yet these horrors take on a degree of reality because of the seriousness with which Brown treated— apparently for the first time in American fiction—a case of dementia. In addition there is a Faustian motif: the ventriloquist's chief trait is his appetite for knowledge, and he pleads that his "only crime" is "curiosity." His dismay in contemplating the tragedy that he in part induced may have given Mary

Shelley the idea for her Frankenstein. Says Carwin: "Had I not rashly set in motion a machine, over whose progress I had no controul, and which experience had shewn me was infinite in power?" *Wieland* derives its strength not merely from the exploitation of sensation, but from the blending of the Gothic method with philosophical, psychological, and moral implications to create a powerful, even if unbalanced, book.

Like his own Carwin, Brown had a vast curiosity. In *Ormond* (1799), as chaotic a book as he ever wrote, he presented a glamorous, superman-like villain with a high intelligence and a low opinion of bourgeois conceptions of good and evil. His principles he has absorbed in part through contact with the secret society of the Illuminati on the Continent. He scoffs at the conventions of marriage, religion, and private property. His conduct is commensurably extravagant and violent. Yet opposite this almost caricatured villain Brown placed Constantia Dudley, who seemed to Shelley "a perfect combination of the purely ideal and possibly real." In *Arthur Mervyn* (1799–1800) there is a serious study (with emphasis on civic responsibility) of the problem of yellow fever, which Brown had observed in epidemic proportions in Philadelphia. In *Edgar Huntly* (1799) he provided his country with its first detective novel. The story has thrilling moments, but its action is finally bungled. At the same time it reflects Brown's interest in the Godwinian theme of morbid curiosity and its relationship to crime. Its "cave scene" may have inspired Edgar Poe as a source for "The Pit and the Pendulum," and Cooper, who at first scoffed at *Edgar Huntly,* later imitated its author.

Clara Howard (1801), Brown's next novel, is relatively free from the violence of the preceding stories, being mainly a love story told with emphasis upon an ethical dilemma. *Jane Talbot* (1801) treats of the problem of a sensitive young lady who makes a loveless marriage although she has met her real affinity before the wedding. The problem is handled with a finesse that surprisingly adumbrates certain stories of Henry James. The relative quietness of these last two novels reflects Brown's awareness of the relationship between a writer and his public. He was a conscious craftsman. His first three novels had made him a reputation, but they had not sold well. In April, 1800, he wrote, "Book-making . . . is the dullest of all trades." When his brother suggested that perhaps the public would find more interest in novels less devoted to "the prodigious or the singular," he gloomily agreed, and he promised less extravagance and more emphasis on "daily incidents" of the sort that the public presumably cared for. Yet he never succeeded in becoming a popular writer, and indeed produced no novels after 1804.

A late eighteenth century novelist, Brown was inevitably influenced by foreign models, for American models were almost nonexistent. Yet he was keenly aware of his position as an American writer. Even as the author of Gothic fiction, he bravely attempted to use native materials. He prided himself on the fact that in *Edgar Huntly* he had opened new sluices of power:

Puerile superstition and exploded manners, Gothic castles and chimeras, are the materials usually employed for this end. The incidents of Indian hostility, and the perils of the Western wilderness, are far more suitable; and for a native of America to overlook these would admit of no apology. These, therefore, are, in part, the ingredients of this tale, and these he has been ambitious of depicting in vivid and faithful colours.

Europe's example was to him by no means an unmixed blessing, for, he said in *Clara Howard,* "Our books are almost wholly the productions of Europe, and the prejudices which infect us are derived chiefly from this source." A substratum of American democratic thinking underlay his romantic theorizing and his moral speculation.

Without being overtly doctrinaire, Brown was unquestionably a moralist in his fiction: idea and scene coalesced to form art. His most sensational narrative episodes were the artistic counterparts of his philosophic probings into the causes of man's unrest. Even those of his characters who (like the protagonist in *Ormond*) were antisocial in act and creed revealed the basic problems of humanity. Final remedies Brown did not in most cases propose: he was not a "didactic" writer. He merely described the human tragedy with a skill great enough to enable him to produce many memorable scenes of high seriousness and compelling interest. Constantly interrupted by illness and the exigencies of business, he wrote rapidly during the time available to him, and he revised little. He rose brilliantly to heights of eloquence and as suddenly bogged down in bombast, bathos, or incoherence. Had he been able to sustain his flights, he might have been a great tragic novelist.

4

In this period the novel could experiment, with relatively few restrictions, but the drama suffered under enough handicaps and discouragements to founder any ordinary enterprise. Legal statute, clerical frowns, the exigencies of war, yellow fever, the copyright bogy—these and other factors operated to prevent the conception and hinder the growth of the American theater.

Moralists might indict the theater as the "House of the Devill," and lawmakers might legislate against it as contrary to the public good; but no amount of opposition could effectively stamp out a form of entertainment based on the virtually instinctive will to "make-believe." Not that the opposition ever capitulated completely or permanently—it was renewed, for example, during the Revolutionary War—but its severity was relaxed from time to time. At the end of the eighteenth century the American theater was pretty well established, but original American drama was far from arrival. Repertories were mainly foreign; it would have been folly to expect a native drama to compete with royalty-free plays such as *Richard III* or Dryden's *Amphitryon* or Farquhar's *Beaux' Stratagem*.

In the beginning, however, there was no thought of an American drama. To be sure, many Americans experimented with the dramatic form; but they had little hope of seeing their plays professionally produced. Out of some forty plays written prior to 1787 fewer than a half-dozen were even intended for production on the regular stage, although many of them were presented by amateurs. The first complete and unquestionably American play to be performed publicly and professionally was presented in 1767. Gradually more American writers entered the field, and between 1790 and 1820 the variety and vigor of native production was so great that our failure to bring forth a single great dramatist or a single great play is the more remarkable.

The first American play of record acted on the American stage was Thomas Godfrey's *The Prince of Parthia,* written before 1763, published in 1765, and produced at the "New Theater," Philadelphia, April 24, 1767. That the play was a tragedy was perhaps consonant with the prevailing sobriety of our national thinking at the time. That it was Elizabethan in pattern and Oriental in subject matter is not to be wondered at. The population of this country at the time was in effect that of Englishmen transplanted, but scarcely rooted, in a new land. Given the circumstances, it was natural for a playwright to utilize the tested and the universal rather than the new and the local. *The Prince of Parthia* is a reasonably good play. It tells of dark passions and violent action in the ancient and remote kingdom of Parthia. Epic enterprise and fierce personal tensions combine in melodrama sincerely conceived. Brother fights brother; father and son compete for the favors of the same woman; wife instigates the murder of husband—these are some of its bloody data. At the end the heroine, falsely told that her lover is dead, takes poison; it remains for the hero to dispatch himself on his sword. Plot elements and language from Shakespeare, and Beaumont and Fletcher, obviously inspired but did not completely dominate Godfrey's work. In *The Prince of Parthia,* tradition was put to good use by the first native American dramatist.

There was a good deal of interest in the drama during the Revolutionary War. The British, who were active in promoting it, converted Faneuil Hall for a time into a theater. Some plays were written, and a few of them remain as interesting mixtures of colonial art and politics. Tory views were sometimes dramatized, as in the anonymous farce *The Battle of Brooklyn* (1776 *)

* Except as noted, dates of plays are those of first production.

which lampoons General Washington and his officers. Notable among patriotic plays were Mrs. Mercy Warren's *The Adulateur* (published 1773), a satire on Governor Thomas Hutchinson, and *The Group* (about 1773), which bitterly satirized those persons who acquiesced in the abrogation of the Massachusetts charter. It is possible that Mrs. Warren also wrote *The Block-heads,* a coarse satirical answer to Burgoyne's satirical farce, *The Blockade,* which had been played in Boston in 1776–1777. These plays by Mrs. Warren and others are not of sufficiently high quality to command enduring interest, but they are reminders of the fact that the Revolutionary War was one of the factors responsible for the awakening of interest in the drama.

5

By the time Royall Tyler wrote *The Contrast,* the nation had emerged as an independent political unit; but its social pattern was still equivocal. *The Contrast,* the first American comedy to be presented in America, was performed at the John Street Theater in New York on April 16, 1787. It was and is an excellent acting-play. Its universally interesting theme of urban sophistication vs. rural naïveté had a peculiarly appropriate application in post-Revolutionary America, when the British, having lost political control, were still able to patronize us culturally.

The central situation in *The Contrast* shows an English cad maneuvering for the hand of a pure American girl while at the same time he is making dishonorable overtures to another intended as a "companion" to his wife. Of course he loses out ignominiously. The characterization of the "fashionable" elements in the dramatis personae is done with the authentic tone of a writer who knew his Sheridan—for *The Contrast* has much in common with *The School for Scandal*—but the prologue sounded a national note that was well sustained:

> Why should our thoughts to distant countries roam
> When each refinement may be found at home?

Patriotism was further emphasized when "Yankee Doodle" was sung during the performance. Beyond this, the action was made interesting to Americans by local references and the celebration of the American character. Colonel Manly's success in breaking up a sinister stratagem (and in his suit of the young lady he has saved from a Chesterfieldian fop) constitutes an endorsement of the American way of life in 1787. Our own social institutions must set the standards of individual behavior.

The success of *The Contrast* on the stage was probably due also to the adroitness with which Tyler manages his dialogue and to the introduction, for the first time on the American stage, of a fine example of Yankee rustic, Jonathan, whose combination of sturdy, though not inflexible, New England morality and childlike innocence makes for rollicking comedy, especially in the scene in which he unwittingly attends a theater and tries to carry out the foreign servant's instructions as to how to succeed in an amour. The play scene is almost worthy of Fielding, whose Partridge is a literary cousin of Jonathan. Jonathan's attempted amour ends in a rebuff which helps to clarify his thinking: "If this is the way with your city ladies, give me the twenty acres of rock, the Bible, the cow, and Tabitha, and a little peaceable bundling."

The Contrast was a lusty embodiment of American ideals in a play which, without pointedly ignoring English tradition, made its own way. Subscribers to its publication included, among other eminent people, George Washington and General Humphreys. Tyler also wrote other dramatic pieces, including a musical farce (a popular type at the time), but his fame as a dramatist remains vested in The Contrast.

The mixture of opportunity and handicap that confronted early American dramatists is further illustrated by the production of James Nelson Barker, who experimented with masque, domestic comedy, topical (political) drama, romantic comedy, and historical play. His Tears and Smiles (acted 1807), a sentimental comedy, reopens a vein which Tyler had mined profitably in The Contrast, with the foreign menace to our native institutions—this time French instead of British. Barker had "never even seen a Yankee," but at the request of the actor Jefferson he supplied Nathan Yank. The play was a moderate success. His next play, The Embargo (acted 1808), illustrates a current trend toward realistic political discussion. Its text has been lost, but when it was produced at "Old Drury" (the Chestnut Street Theater) in Philadelphia, a riot was instigated by those of the merchant class who objected to Barker's pro-administration bias. The drama was evidently becoming a social force to be reckoned with.

Barker's The Indian Princess (1808), the first "Indian play" written by an American and produced on the stage, told of the adventures of John Smith and Pocahontas, with perhaps less emphasis upon the dangers threatening Smith than upon the romantic love between Rolfe and the Princess, as well as among the lesser personnel. Realism was here no major aim of Barker. The outcome of events is happy: a conspiracy to kill the white men is quashed, and there comes (as Lord Delawar puts it) a "pairing time among the turtles." John Smith survives to envisage a time when "arts, and industry and elegance shall reign" in "this fine portion of the globe." Called a "melodrame" (a sign of increasing French influence on our theaters), The Indian

Princess is a light, actable play, with music and a masque added in deference to popular taste.

Superstition (acted 1824), Barker's most ambitious work, is a carefully wrought drama based on an aspect of the Regicide Judges' story, a very creditable early treatment of a theme later used by Cooper, Hawthorne, Paulding, Longfellow, and others. It is a sober and serious study of a solemn chapter in American history. If it fails to be really memorable, the reason is that Barker's derivative language was not quite equal to sustaining the mood in which the play was pitched.

Barker led an extremely active public life, and his plays form only one expression of his constant concern for the public good. He was no blind believer in an untutored democracy. He realized, as his use of the witchcraft theme in *Superstition* showed, the havoc that might be wrought by an "unthinking crowd." Yet he was basically American and republican. He was furthermore a proponent of an American theater even though he seems to have connived at manager William Wood's ruse of passing off one of his plays (*Marmion,* acted 1812) as by a British dramatist. Without being fanatically nationalistic, he staunchly did his part in building a native tradition in the drama. Compared with Tyler, he seems more earnest but less of an artist. Compared with Dunlap, he seems less significant by reason of the latter's more voluminous production and more intense devotion to the cause of the drama.

6

One of the most influential names in the earlier cultural history of America is that of William Dunlap. He fell short of genius in any single category, but he achieved distinction in several. Playwright, theatrical manager, painter, historian of the drama and of the arts of design, novelist, biographer, diarist, periodical writer, entrepreneur, he escaped the obscure fate of many men who have exhibited so much versatility. Called the Vasari of America for his services to painting, he might also be called the father of the American drama and theater. His devoted service to the drama was motivated by his conviction, "The rise, progress, and cultivation of the drama mark the progress of refinement and the state of manners at any given time and in any country." All the arts were having their troubles in America at the time of Dunlap's ascendancy, roughly from 1790 to 1820. When a man like John Adams could say, "I would not give sixpence for a picture of Raphael or a statue of Phidias," there was obviously much missionary work to be done. Dunlap objected to the practice of singling out the drama for attack. He believed that "the fine arts [are] all connected, and must stand or fall together . . . if the drama is injurious to a state, so are literature and the arts." As manager, designer, producer, and writer of plays, he exerted an influence which helped to elevate and stabilize the theater in a chaotic period. If as a writer he lacked imaginative powers of the first order, he was extremely useful to the young nation at a time when it greatly needed standards of taste and technique.

The plays Dunlap presented were both a reflection and a cause of conditions in the theater. As producer he responded to public demand; if he frequently presented Shakespeare, he also presented many of the mediocre plays of Kotzebue, that darling of the Continent as well as of the American theater about 1800–1805. But even in his partial concessions to public demand, he knew good taste and good technique even though he did not always exercise them. He himself wrote and adapted some sixty plays. If one failed to succeed, he could be ready with a new one in ten days to two weeks. He had the advantage of his own versatility; he could keep control of most of the production factors himself. First and last he experimented with many varieties of drama: comedy, farce, melodrama, tragedy, heroic plays, romantic drama, opera, domestic drama, and patriotic "spectacles" lying between drama and pageant. The scenes of his plays include America, England, Germany, France, Russia, Italy, and South America.

His first play, *The Father, or American Shandyism* (acted 1789), was a creditable but not really distinguished work written under the influence of *The Contrast.* Dunlap himself thought that the best of his plays was *The Italian Father* (acted 1799), for which he used as a model Dekker's *The Honest Whore.* Considered critical opinion now points to *André* (1798) as probably his best. It is a tragedy based on the last days of the British officer. Dramatic tension is established by a young American's attempt to save André out of gratitude for the latter's generous behavior to him. But General Washington, to whom young Bland applies, denies the appeal on the ground of patriotism. Complications arise when the British threaten to execute Bland's father (their prisoner) if André is hanged. Since the outcome of the action was known to the audience in advance, the success of the play depended on the power of Dunlap (and the actors) to invest the drama with high seriousness of mood and resourcefulness in episode. High seriousness the play does attain, but the action tends to crumble away into a diversity of separate scenes which, despite unity of time, fail to cohere. The blank verse in which the play is written is mobile and not without apt echoes of Elizabethan dramatists. The public did not greatly favor the play in its original form; but Dunlap thriftily revamped it and presented it as a patriotic spectacle with music. In this form, known as *The Glory of Columbia,* it was a commercial success. But as a dramatist Dunlap exhibited more craftsmanship than high art. To him the text, in any case, was only one of the elements upon which the prosperity of the theater depended.

All the factors of production and management interested Dunlap. He frequently inveighed against the star system, for he sensed the danger that playwrights would be guided by the whims of the star instead of the principles of sound, balanced drama. He studied the physical conditions of the theater as well as the use of appropriate sets and properties. He observed that an overlarge theater could affect a play adversely, for besides making it impossible for actors' facial expressions to be seen, it "requires an exertion of the actor's voice which destroys its melody, and renders variety of intonation impossible." He was extremely meticulous in working out details of staging, especially for Shakespeare. He once searched "several books" in order to find out what were the right banners to use for "the Britons under Cymbeline." His intelligent interest in the merging of the theater arts was exemplified when during a production of *Hamlet* he painted an interpretation of the play scene. Harassed by practical production problems and beset by the temptation to pander to the masses, Dunlap never really relinquished his high ideals.

As a producer-playwright Dunlap was not unduly concerned to stress American themes. Indeed he even queried "how far we ought to wish for a national drama, distinct from that of our English forefathers." He thought that the process of Americanization should be gradual rather than hasty and arbitrary, but in one sense he did wish the drama to be "national": he believed that most of the ills of the theater—which he attributed to the "necessities and cupidity of managers"—could be removed by a system of government patronage, citing in support of his view the experiences of Germany and France. Time and again in his *History of the American Theatre,* he reverts to this possibility of saving the drama. Perhaps such a system would have made his own career more tolerable, for he was in constant difficulties and went into bankruptcy at one time.

In his later years Dunlap had very little active connection with the theater, returning to painting and to miscellaneous writing for his somewhat precarious livelihood. In 1832 he produced his *History of the American Theatre,* a work which, despite evidences of hasty composition, remains a monument to a man who did more than any other one person in his time to promote the welfare of the American theater and drama.

7

During this period the novel fared better than the drama: Brackenridge's *Modern Chivalry* and Brown's *Wieland* probably reached a higher level of achievement than any of the plays that appeared. Yet for a long period the harvest is singularly meager in both forms. The familiar explanations of this condition are the lack of affinity between Puritanism and art, and the overinfluence of Europe. Probably the latter factor was the more deleterious. Puritanism was a direct deterrent, but it waned to a point at which it should have ceased to hamper a real artist. The influence of Europe, particularly England, was more subtle and pervasive, taking various forms. England provided us with a language and a tradition. With a ready-made literature at hand, was it not natural for us to defer our efforts? Long after we had won our political independence we remained, as Barker said, "mental colonists." A kind of provincial snobbery prevented many Americans from seeing such merit as there was in national productions. Certain critics, as he noted in the preface to his *Tears and Smiles,* had coined the opprobrious term "Columbianism" to apply to "every delineation of . . . American manners, customs, opinion, characters, or scenery. . . . They can never pardon the endeavor to depict our national peculiarities, and yet they will listen with avidity to Yorkshire rusticity, or Newmarket slang." Such an attitude was fostered by the British who, having lost the war, continued to belittle our cultural progress.

There were notable exceptions: John Howard Payne, for example, had a considerable success as an actor at Drury Lane, and his tragedy *Brutus* ran fifty nights in one season. Yet he was later to be the victim of "much prejudice" and "persecution" because of his American principles. During the first two decades of the nineteenth century an inglorious literary warfare was carried on between England and America. It was Irving's purpose in "English Writers on America" to allay this ill-feeling. He reminded England that it was beneath her dignity to attack us; and he bade Americans think indulgently of England as a "perpetual volume of reference." Yet perhaps it was unwise to seek to end this literary war by appeasing both sides. Perhaps it was necessary that we should fight for our literary independence too.

15. THE AMERICAN DREAM

Wᴴɪʟᴇ the citizens of the United States were thus struggling to create a literature fitting to the assumed grandeur of the national destiny, the idea of America was becoming itself a part of the cultural tradition of Europe. As a state of mind and a dream, America had existed long before its discovery. Ever since the early days of Western civilization, peoples had dreamed of a lost Paradise, of a Golden Age characterized by abundance, absence of war, and absence of toil. With the first accounts of the New World, it was felt that these dreams and yearnings had become a fact, a geographical reality fraught with unlimited possibilities. The first navigators had landed, not on the rocky coast of the northern part of America, but in islands swept by balmy breezes, inhabited by natives of peaceful dispositions, living without toil or industry on the natural productions of a generous soil. Their nakedness, their disconcerting absence of shame, their simplicity seemed to indicate that in some incomprehensible way they had not been as much tainted by original sin as had the peoples of Europe.

From the very beginning travelers' relations provided an inexhaustible store of material and arguments in the great debate, opened since the early days of the Renaissance, between the enemies and the defenders of the European form of life. Critics of a society which was becoming every day more closely knit, more sophisticated and artificial, never tired of comparing the simple, virtuous, and "natural" life of the Indians with the complicated, restless, and greedy existence of civilized men. Undoubtedly Shakespeare had these people in mind, when he made the honest old Counsellor Gonzalo, in *The Tempest,* draw a picture of the ideal commonwealth he would establish in an island if he were "king on't":

> All things in common nature should produce
> Without sweat or endeavour: treason, felony,
> Sword, pike, knife, gun, or need of any engine,
> Would I not have; but nature should bring forth,
> Of its own kind, all foison, all abundance,
> To feed my innocent people.

This is the "soft primitivism" also found in the French poet Ronsard or in the story of *El Villano del Danubio* retold by the sixteenth century Spanish writer Antonio de Guevara or even later in Cervantes' description of the Island of Barataria under the rule of good Sancho. To a philosopher like Locke it offered a true image of a condition which had existed before personal property and compacts had laid the foundation of human society such as we know it, for then "all the world was America." But though neither Locke, nor Vico, nor Montesquieu intended to use their praise of the savages as an argument destructive of our form of society, such was clearly the purpose of the Frenchman Lahontan, in his *Dialogues between an American savage and the author* (1703), and to a lesser extent of Jean-Jacques Rousseau. Whether they intended it or not, these advocates of a more or less complete return to nature were the forerunners of some of our modern anarchists and communistic utopians.

Admirers of a harder form of primitivism also found abundant material in the travelers in the northern parts of America, particularly in the Jesuits' relations. The good Fathers were steeped in the classical tradition, and they were delighted to find in the Indians replicas of Greek and Roman exemplars of stoic and republican virtues. On the other hand, it is no less certain that Hobbes derived from travelers' accounts his unsympathetic reconstruction of the natural state of mankind. But such pessimistic views were exceptional; what prevailed was the picture of a boundless and generous land, preserved from the evils of our modern society, and it is significant that Thomas More in 1516 set a precedent followed by countless imitators in locating his ideal state of Utopia in the newly discovered world.

This dream of an Earthly Paradise was, of course, a mirage—but it was more; it was a revolutionary force, let loose in the Western world, because it proved that the whole of mankind had not been irremediably condemned by some inherent vice to toil, suffering, oppression, war, famine, and misery. Man's faulty organization of society and not man's nature was responsible for his unhappiness. America as an idea was already at work pointing the way in the never-ending and hitherto chimerical quest of happiness.

If it had not been confusedly felt that the New World held out a hope to the whole of mankind, the indignation against the atrocities committed by its European conquerors might have been less vehement. The first eloquent outburst of indignation came from a Spanish missionary, the famous Las Casas, as early as 1552. His *Brief Relation* was translated into English in 1556 and into French in 1579, and in the Latin original was circulated throughout Europe. It marked the beginning of a long protestation in the name of humanity against the use of unjustified violence and the enslavement of innocent peoples. It was the proclamation of the rights of the so-called inferior peoples, echoed again and again during the eighteenth century. From the very excesses of the conquerors rose a new conception of the right of conquest and the right of colonization.

2

The implication was clear: what our civilization had failed to accomplish would perhaps find its fulfillment in the newly discovered lands. This "infant world, still quite naked and at the breast" suddenly presented to a senescent world another chance, perhaps the last one, to build anew the city of man.

By the middle of the eighteenth century, despite the vogue of the primitivistic dream in literature, this view had become singularly definite. The American Indians occupied a larger place than ever on the stage, in poetry, and in works of fiction, and more than ever their simple and natural virtues were opposed to the corruption of civilized men. It was only too plain that any reform in Europe would entail an enormous effort, and that new structures could not be erected without destroying the buildings still sheltering a discontented society; but in America persecuted peoples could find not only a refuge but an opportunity to lay the foundations of a better society. This dream was not limited to the British colonies, for the French had attempted in Brazil and in Florida about the middle of the sixteenth century to establish such settlements. Whether the Jesuits had succeeded or not in doing it in Paraguay was a moot question among the philosophers. At any rate, it was known that the French Huguenots, after the Revocation of the Edict of Nantes, had found a refuge in New England, on the banks of the Hudson where the Palatines had joined them, in Pennsylvania, and in the Carolinas. New England as well as Virginia had been the subject of a considerable body of "promotion literature," intended to counteract the recital of the trials and sufferings of the first colonists.

Among the British colonies, Pennsylvania occupied a privileged rank. Even the wildest dreamers among the philosophers never entertained seriously any scheme which would bring man back to a stark state of nature. The real problem was to find a form of society which would enable man to preserve his native qualities while enjoying all the benefits resulting from his association with his fellow beings; and such was the formula proposed at the end of the century by Godwin in his famous *Enquiry concerning Political Justice*. But long before Godwin the French *philosophes* thought they had discovered such an ideal commonwealth in the "republic" of Pennsylvania. To a large extent, the propaganda carried on in Europe by William Penn, in order to attract desirable immigrants, was responsible for that impression.

Pamphlets and leaflets containing enthusiastic descriptions of the advantages offered to the colonists were printed in English, Dutch, German, and French and distributed among the would-be immigrants. The Quakers, themselves a persecuted people, had substituted purchase from the Indians for conquest by force; they were true republicans using the equalitarian "thee" and recognizing no man as their master; they were philosophers who had abolished all the artificial trappings of religion, and who worshiped God in their hearts. The noble Quakers inherited all the virtues of the noble Indians, and Voltaire could declare, in his *Lettres anglaises* (1734), that Penn had brought to this earth the Golden Age, hitherto believed an invention of poets but now existing in Pennsylvania. Thus was developed through the eighteenth century a semiphilosophical and semisentimental body of literature dealing with the good Quakers and culminating in the *Histoire philosophique des deux Indes* of Abbé Raynal, in which the author contrasted the humane and philosophical development of the republic of Pennsylvania with the atrocities committed by the Spanish, the Portuguese, and all the European nations in the course of their colonial conquests.

Even admitting that the British colonists had not succeeded in establishing everywhere the city of the philosophers, the fact remained that liberty in America was much more the result of conditions inherent to the soil than the product of reasoned efforts. Such was the conclusion reached in 1774 by the editor of the *Gazette de France*, the official journal of the Court:

Those of our navigators who have studied this half of the Northern American Continent, maintain that an inborn love of liberty inherent to the soil, the sky, forests, and lakes prevents this still young country from resembling the other parts of the Universe. They are convinced that any European transported under this climate will be affected by this particular condition.

Whether through some providential design or, as Montesquieu and his disciples would have said, because of the "nature of things," the stage was already set for an unprecedented political experiment. During the earlier part of the eighteenth century, Voltaire and Montesquieu had represented England as the classic land of liberty. But Montesquieu himself had admitted that he had described not England as he had seen it, but England as it might be if the principles of the British constitution were integrally applied. American liberty, however, did not rest upon ancestral institutions and traditions; it was a new revelation, and as such it was described by Thomas Pownall, a former colonial governor and a friend of Benjamin Franklin, in his *Memorial addressed to the Sovereigns of America* (1783). It was a

New System of Things and Men, which treats all as they actually are, esteeming nothing the true End and perfect Good of Policy, but that Effect which produces, as equality of Rights, so equal Liberty, universal Peace, and unobstructed inter-communication of happiness in Human Society. . . . This is a Principle in act and deed, and not a mere speculative theorem.

This was the burden also of Crèvecœur's *Letters of an American Farmer* (first printed in English, then in French, and broadly circulated between 1780 and 1790), and of Thomas Paine, who came to Philadelphia to tell its citizens in January, 1776, that theirs was much more than a quarrel with the King of England:

The cause of America is, in a great measure, the cause of all mankind. Many circumstances have and will arise which are not local but universal, and through which the principles of all lovers of mankind are affected, and in the event of which their affections are interested.

To the enemies as well as to the friends of the Anglo-Americans, it appeared from the very beginning that from the Revolution would come answers to the problems affecting the future development of Western civiliza-tion. It was generally conceded by clear-sighted observers, even in England, that the revolt could not be crushed once for all by force. Sooner or later, the colonists would win their independence. Furthermore it would be utterly impossible to limit the conflagration, which would spread from the British colonies to the other colonies of the new world and to all European colonies, all over the globe. This meant the disappearance, or a deep transformation, of economic factors on which rested the economic structure of Europe. It meant the end of monopolies, of exploitation of colonies for the sole benefit of the metropolis; it meant also that the trade of all nations might enter hitherto restricted areas. It meant eventually the freedom of the seas and consequently the complete reorganization of international life.

This was clearly perceived in England and explains the exclamation of Horace Walpole upon hearing the "black news" of Saratoga: "Nothing will be left of England but the vestige of her grandeur." In France it was hardly less keenly felt by Turgot, Vergennes, and even such a liberal as Abbé Raynal, who dreaded the consequences which would follow the collapse of the colonial system.

Even more important and fundamental was the answer given to the social and political problem which had become acute during the eighteenth cen-tury and was simply the problem of government. Very different were the forms of government adopted by the former colonies; but all rested on the doctrine of popular sovereignty proclaimed in the Declaration of Independence and developed in the declarations prefixed to most of the state constitutions. The theory was not new, but the undertaking was unprecedented. It was an attempt to form a society in which essential natural rights would be preserved, and government from above be reduced to a minimum. Such a form of government was not to be granted by sage legislators more or less divinely inspired or by an impersonal state substituted for the monarch; it was to be determined by the decisions of the citizens, whose collective body constituted "the people." It cannot be said that all the implications of the initial expression of the Constitution, "We the people," were at first fully understood even by the philosophers. The Italian-born citizen of Virginia, Mazzei, had to explain to the French in 1788 that "the people" was not the rabble, but was constituted of all the inhabitants of the land. Mirabeau fought in vain to make the deputies in the National Assembly meet and proclaim the Declaration of the Rights of Man in the name of "the people." The old prejudices prevailed in 1789: the Deputies preferred "Nation" to "People" and the "French people" was recognized only in the preamble to the Constitution of 1793. Joel Barlow, friend and disciple of Jefferson, had to remind the French in particular and the Europeans in general in his *Vision of Columbus,* published in Paris in 1793, that the people was this

fraternal family divine
Whom mutual wants and mutual aids combine.

Condorcet himself, who, because of his efforts in favor of the rebels, had been made a "citizen of New Haven" with several members of the philosophical group gathering around Madame d'Houdetot, was puzzled to know how the will of the people could be ascertained and wrote to his colleagues of the American Philosophical Society of Philadelphia to inquire what mathematical computations would enable the Americans to have a true representation of the people. Despite these reservations, the magic words uttered in Philadelphia echoed, to quote Condorcet again, "from the Guadalquivir to the banks of the Neva." Enthusiasts like Lafayette hailed the beginning of "the American era," and Dr. Richard Price, Benjamin Franklin's old friend, could declare in 1785:

.Perhaps I do not go too far, when I say that, next to the introduction of Christianity among mankind, the American Revolution may prove the most important step in the progressive course of human improvement.

Even before the final success of the Revolution, its first repercussions were felt in Europe. Nowhere were they more direct and more instantaneous than in Ireland, where ever since 1763 the progress of independence had been anxiously followed. "Look to America," cried Grattan two months after Yorktown, and already, on June 14, 1782, Henry Flood had proclaimed in the Irish House of Commons:

A voice from America shouted to Liberty, the echo of it caught your people as it passed along the Atlantic, and they renewed the voice till it reverberated here.

This fervor reached its maximum in France. It has often and justly been pointed out that the French Revolution was in fact the daughter of the American Revolution. The French Declaration of the Rights of Man follows very closely the Virginia "Bill of Rights" of 1776. The American precedent was quoted in the National Assembly and in the different assemblies which vainly tried to establish a permanent regime during the ensuing years. If later Fench historians have attempted to trace the main principles of the Declaration of Independence to Montesquieu and Rousseau, it does not seem that such indebtedness ever occurred to the French contemporaries of Jefferson. Yet, as Chamfort, the French moralist, pointed out, Louis XVI had acknowledged the legitimacy of popular government and signed his abdication when, in February, 1778, he signed a treaty of alliance with the young United States. Almost a hundred years later, Lamartine, at the end of his career, was no less justified in declaring with poetical emphasis:

One would need the discernment of God himself to distinguish America from France after their respective causes had been fused together during and after the American Revolutionary war.

3

The fight for independence had been won and a stable government established through the countless efforts of obscure American citizens, but popular imagination is fond of heroes who seem to embody all the characteristics of a people and an epoch. From the Revolution emerged two towering figures, living symbols of the country they had created: George Washington and Benjamin Franklin.

The Virginia gentleman called by Byron, after the first abdication of Napoleon,

the first—the last—the best—
The Cincinnatus of the West,

enjoyed from the early days of the American Revolution an extraordinary popularity. He was celebrated in epic poems; he appeared as the main character in patriotic dramas; no novel dealing with the Revolution was complete without some episode in which he appeared as a stern, sad, reserved, dignified figure, a great man without personal ambition, entirely devoted to his country, at all times conscious of the tremendous responsibility he was bearing on his mighty shoulders.

To him young Alfieri, in Italy, dedicated one of his odes on America in December, 1781, and seven years later he repeated his tribute "Al chiarissimo e libero uomo il Generale Washington," in the dedication of his tragedy *Brutus*. In a gesture of defiance to the Tories, young Coleridge drank Washington's health in a public inn in 1792. The French volunteers who joined the Americans unanimously acknowledged in him a military genius of the first order. Frederick II was anxious to obtain information on his tactics. Berthier, who later was to become Napoleon's chief of staff, made it a point to visit all the places where the American general had fought, and drew elaborate maps of his battles. In him they saw an organizer who had revolutionized modern warfare by leading to victory against professional soldiers an army of volunteers without any military training, poorly armed, without uniforms, "without shoes and without bread." His fame grew immensely in later years when the French, during their Revolution, had to resort to the levy in mass in order to defend their frontiers, and when Kosciuszko who had served under him attempted to repeat the tactics of his old chief during the insurrection of Poland. When the news of Washington's death reached France, young Bonaparte, then First Consul and still a republican hero, ordered a week of mourning for all the French Army and had his eulogy delivered in the "Temple of Mars" before the veterans of the campaigns of Italy and Egypt.

The foreign officers who served under Washington, the foreign visitors who saw him at Mount Vernon, when under his vine and fig tree he was living as a private citizen, readily acknowledged in him a sterling character, an impressive dignity, and a sort of melancholy most striking in a man who had had such a glorious career and had lived to enjoy the completion of his task. The only discordant notes to be heard in this unanimous praise are found in the correspondence of some French and British ministers during the troubled years between 1793 and 1797.

Of his achievements as a statesman, of the part he played in the making of the Constitution, little was known and little was said. Outside America, the names of his victories were soon forgotten, with the exception of Yorktown. His military glory was eclipsed by the fact that, once the victory was won, he had disbanded his army and resigned his commission to the hands of Congress. As the years passed, the comparison with Napoleon became unavoidable and almost obsessing, and Washington stood more and more as the prototype of the republican hero.

For obvious reasons, the tributes paid to Washington were more frequent and more persistent in France than in any other country; but they were not limited to France. The Italian Carlo Botta, writing in 1809 a *History of the War of Independence of the United States of America,* concluded his account with Washington's resignation as commander-in-chief, a significant and bold allusion to the very different course followed by Bonaparte. According to his memorialist, Napoleon himself sighed at St. Helena, "They wanted me to be another Washington" and attempted to explain that conditions in Europe did not permit him to keep his republican faith. In his "Ode to Napoleon Bonaparte" as well as in the "Age of Bronze," Byron gave Washington as a "watchword" to would-be dictators. Traveling in South America in 1817, H. M. Brackenridge found everywhere translations of Washington's Farewell Address, and at the same time the political magazine published by Chateaubriand deplored that everywhere on the Boulevard were seen portraits of Washington and Bolívar as a sort of tacit protest against the Bourbon restoration. No more eloquent tribute has ever been paid to the republican leader than the pages in which the author of *Atala,* recalling the short visit he had paid to the President of the United States in 1792, contrasted Washington and Napoleon, the man who had built a country and the conqueror who had left only ruins behind him.

The Washington hero-myth persisted throughout the nineteenth century and into the twentieth. Less eloquent than the praise of Chateaubriand, but no less striking, is the chapter at the close of *The Virginians* (1857–1859), in which Thackeray pictures Washington taking leave of his army at Whitehall Ferry, on the Hudson. More qualified and typical of many English appreciations was the estimate of Matthew Arnold, who spoke of Washington as if he had been an Englishman accidentally living in America, and maintained that Americans should think of him as a good model of the English country squire. In France admiration for Washington remained throughout the century a form of opposition to dictatorship and arbitrary power, as may be seen in the lectures delivered at the Collège de France during the Second Empire by Edouard de Laboulaye. Washington appeared again to proclaim "Liberty to the World" in *Le Nouveau Monde,* a play written by Villiers de l'Isle-Adam to commemorate the centennial of the Declaration of Independence. Again, in 1882, when France was obsessed by the fear of a dictator, Joseph Fabre in his book *Washington, libérateur de l'Amérique,* hailed the soldier-citizen. More recently, when many French liberals were seriously alarmed at the progress of totalitarian ideology and the growing popularity of Mussolini and Hitler, Louis Ferrier produced a play on Washington, to revive the old patriotic faith and, in the name of the great American, to preach the republican gospel.

Of an entirely different order has been the fame of Benjamin Franklin in Europe. His mission to France (1776–1784) marked the apogee of his European popularity, but he would not have taken Paris by storm if his reputation had not already been firmly established. His experiments in electricity were known in England through his friend Collinson as early as 1749; the French physicist Dalibard made them available to the French in 1752; and translations into German and Italian soon followed. European scientists saw in him a skillful observer and experimenter, but popular imagination magnified the American "doctor" into a modern Prometheus, a man able to control and play with a force of nature which had filled with awe countless generations.

During his lifetime, Franklin's fame extended throughout Europe even to Austria, the Scandinavian countries, and Russia. He corresponded with the most famous philosophers and scientists of his age, received from them and from monarchs the most flattering messages. He felt as much at home in Paris, although his knowledge of French was far from perfect, as in Philadelphia. After the partial publication of his *Autobiography,* printed in French and in Paris during the Revolution, he appeared as the most striking illustration of the unlimited possibilities residing in the "people," a living demonstration of the fact that in a republican society, where class distinctions do not prevent recognition of talent and genius, a poor boy may seize opportunities and rise to positions reserved to privileged classes in the Old World. No wonder the German historian Georg Forster in his *Reise um die Welt* (1784) saw in Franklin a prophet chosen to inaugurate the Golden Age of humanity, and Chamfort in his *Tableaux de la Révolution Française* (1793) hailed him as the herald of the new era of the common man. Thirty years later, the "child of poverty" who was to become a great South American leader, Domingo Faustino Sarmiento, treasured equally the only two books he had in his possession, the Bible and Franklin's *Autobiography.* As late as 1845, the French historian Mignet included a life of Franklin in a collection issued under the auspices of the *Académie des Sciences Morales et Politiques.* It was reprinted again in 1865 under the same auspices

as a biography which makes live again a good man, a master of wisdom adapted to every age, every condition, every society, and one of the founders of that American liberty which is not the privilege of a race, or of a given form of government, but pure and simple Liberty.

Franklin had not kept to himself the secret of his extraordinary success in life. Eighteenth century philosophers had vainly attempted to establish a practical code of morality which would not rest on a religious foundation and would be acceptable and accessible to the common man. In Franklin they found no metaphysical speculations, but sound and homely precepts of conduct. "The Science of Good Man Richard," the title generally given to the translations of *The Way to Wealth,* provided a sort of civic catechism soon incorporated in elementary textbooks and still to be found in fragmentary form in many of the readers used by children in the public schools of France and Italy. There is no young European who in his school days has not become familiar with the story of the whistle and anecdotes from the *Autobiography.*

Franklin also contributed another important element to the composite picture of America as it appears to European eyes. He stood, even more than Fulton, as the embodiment of the spirit, bold in its aims and yet practical, which characterizes American science; and the great English physicist Humphry Davy praised his work as justifying not only pure scientific research, but the application of science to the service of man. Franklin was the first to give the impression that through science America could achieve the impossible. Thus was established a popular tradition which was reinforced through the pseudoscientific tales of Poe and carried out in the novels of Jules Verne, in which Americans conquer the interstellar spaces and travel to the moon. Later the tradition, already well established, received a new confirmation in the inventions of Edison, "the wizard of Menlo Park," celebrated by Villiers de l'Isle-Adam, in his *L'Ève Future* (1886) not only as the man who had invented the phonograph but as a sorcerer who through mechanical devices had succeeded in creating an automaton endowed with all the manifestations of a living organism, including feeling and thought.

4

General as this admiration for America was in the days of the Revolution and later, it was accompanied in many quarters by reservations and misgivings. By comparison with the discoverers whose imaginations were haunted by visions of a recovered Earthly Paradise, many eighteenth and early nineteenth century travelers seem particularly unimaginative and "unromantic." To them, as well as to most of the settlers, nature was essentially an obstacle to colonization: it had to be tamed and subdued in order to make room for civilization and provide a living to man. As late as 1770, Oliver Goldsmith in his *Deserted Village* represented Georgia as a "dreary scene":

> Those matted woods, where birds forget to sing,
> But silent bats in drowsy clusters cling; . . .
> Where crouching tigers wait their hapless prey,
> And savage men more murderous still than they.

Occasionally happier notes occur in the accounts of foreign travelers who were sincerely interested in nature, and particularly in botany, like the Swede Peter Kalm, or in glowing descriptions of the Ohio published in Paris shortly before the Revolution and intended to attract French immigrants; but with the exception of Chastellux, who was a philosopher and a poet, the officers who accompanied Rochambeau failed to be impressed by the American scene, and Lafayette was completely blind to the beauties of nature.

British travelers generally deplored a country defaced by unsightly settlements and by forest fires leaving behind them bleached skeletons of trees and horrible stumps. They compared the scarred spaces surrounding the farms, the dreary and unhealthy swamps, and the eroded hills, with the well kept and humanized European countryside. Very few of them showed any real appreciation of American scenery; Isaac Weld was one of the first foreigners to perceive the beauty of autumn foliage, of the majestic landscape of the Hudson between New York and Albany, and of Niagara Falls. Here and there scattered notations could be collected. John Davis, in his *Travels in the United States* (1803), was probably the first European to celebrate the mockingbird. A disciple of Rousseau, he should take first rank among the romantic observers of America.

Frequent as the unfavorable comments of disgruntled travelers may have been, their effects were largely canceled by the works of two writers, the American botanist William Bartram and the French prose-poet Chateaubriand. Bartram's *Travels* was widely reprinted in Europe and was used as a source by Coleridge in "Kubla Khan" and "The Ancient Mariner," by Wordsworth in "Ruth," by Southey in "Madoc," by Thomas Campbell in "Gertrude of Wyoming" (County in Pennsylvania), by Mrs. Hemans, by Shelley, and even by Tennyson in *In Memoriam*.

Bartram's influence was multiplied in a measure difficult to ascertain because he was the chief source of the descriptions inserted by Chateaubriand in *Atala* and *Les Natchez* (1802 and 1826). In many respects, the famous prose-poem of Chateaubriand may be considered not as a revelation of an unknown world, but as a final and perfect expression of the various sorts of exoticism which had flourished during the previous three centuries. Atala and her simple lover are no longer children of nature; they are torn between the traditions, customs, and prejudices of their tribe and a new and higher code of ethics. Unable to solve the conflict, they can only suffer and die; Chateaubriand's poem sounds the funeral dirge of a disappearing race.

A generation later, the novels of Fenimore Cooper were to revive European interest in the Indians and to start a very different tradition. Whatever may have been the intentions of the author of the Leatherstocking tales, the

French public saw in them primarily exciting adventures, with Indians lurking behind the trees, tracking their enemies with uncanny skill, scalping and slaying the white settlers. Balzac, who was a fervent admirer of Cooper, drew abundantly from him to portray not only the half-savage peasants ambushing the Republican soldiers in *Les Chouans,* but also both the criminals and the detectives constantly at war in the jungle of the Paris underworld. Thus gradually through a long series of popular novels and particularly through the many stories of Gustave Aimard, the noble savages of the early discoverers and philosophers underwent a curious evolution to become finally the *apaches,* or gangsters, of the French capital.

At the beginning of the nineteenth century, the success of Chateaubriand's *Atala* could be attributed to the magnificent descriptions of the "scènes de la nature": the Falls of Niagara, the Mississippi, the virgin forest, and the tropical swamps which serve as a frame for the melancholy love story of Chactas and the half-breed Atala. Whether or not his descriptions were embellished and magnified by his poetical imagination matters little here. They were accepted as authentic, for the author had dreamed of the American solitude, he had heard the voice of the desert, he had seen or imagined, with the assistance of Bartram, the swarming life of the swamps, the majestic cedars and the towering magnolias (*grandiflora*). He had done what many of his less gifted successors had confessed themselves unable to do, from Thomas Moore who was content to observe that the sight of the Niagara was "sad as well as elevating," to Frances Wright, who admitted that the Falls "acknowledge at once their power and immensity, and your own insignificance and imbecility." Neither the much more precise descriptions of Volney, in his *Tableau du Climat et du Sol des Etats-Unis* (1803) nor the scientific and minute accuracy of the great British geologist Charles Lyell could modify the deep and lasting impression made by Chateaubriand's little book, translated at once into all the languages of Europe and accepted as a model of description even by several South American writers. This extraordinary popularity was strengthened by Longfellow's *Evangeline* which helped further to arouse, in European travelers, exaggerated anticipations followed by an almost general disappointment when they were confronted by the actual countryside of the Eastern United States.

More serious than this concern for the contemplation of nature was the effort of European observers to find out whether natural conditions in the United States would permit and favor the development of a great civilization. During the last half of the eighteenth century, the French naturalist Buffon and the Berlin academician Cornelius de Pauw answered negatively. Judging from the accounts of travelers, they found the climate enervating, and nature itself so weak that the natives were unable to do any sustained work. Only unfavorable natural conditions could explain the fact that the New World, despite its reported fertility, had never developed a population comparable in density to the populations of Europe or Asia. The creoles (whites born in the colonies), as well as the domestic animals they had brought with them, showed signs of physical degeneration, and the wild species were decidedly smaller than the corresponding animals in the Old World. This was more than an academic question, and its political implications grew apparent as the British colonies progressed towards independence and finally formed a new nation. What faith and what hopes could be placed in the mission assigned by European liberals to the United States if this "young" people was condemned by the laws of nature ever to remain small and comparatively weak? Many of the French officers who had suffered from the extreme cold of a Rhode Island winter before being exposed to the semitropical temperature of the Virginia seashore had come to the conclusion that America was unfit for human beings. La Rochefoucauld-Liancourt and Volney, who spent several summers in Philadelphia, between 1794 and 1799, could but agree with them and insist upon the unhealthy features of the climate and the frequent epidemics.

These were some of the notions that Franklin and later Jefferson attempted to refute; but they did not succeed in convincing their opponents. The controversy found a last echo in Schopenhauer. Facts, however, spoke louder than theories: it was soon discovered that, despite certain unfavorable circumstances which could not be denied, the population of the United States increased at a regular rate independently of immigration, thus justifying the optimistic calculations of Franklin. Malthus provided an explanation: in the rapid development of the new nation he saw a confirmation of his theory that population invariably increases with the increase in the means of subsistence. The native population had remained practically stationary because of the Indians' lack of industry. It had increased as new territories were opened to cultivation and, because new land was practically limitless, it would continue to grow with the progress of agriculture.

Doubts nevertheless persisted concerning the quality of the civilization which the Anglo-Americans, as they were still called, would succeed in establishing. The first reports were far from favorable. French refugees remembering the exquisite life of the Old Regime, supercilious Britishers still considering America as a wayward child, criticized sharply or with indulgent scorn the uncouth manners of the people. In New York, Philadelphia, and Boston they missed the literary and artistic coteries, the salons, the concerts, the frivolous and yet intense intellectual life of the great capitals. Some, like the poet Thomas Moore, were so deeply disappointed as to doubt the soundness of the liberal creed in which they had placed their hope. Even the best intentioned among them fell into the common mistake of judging American society by European standards, and were disillusioned by this unexpected contact with a harsh reality. Once again was confirmed the curious separation between America as a geographical, political, and social entity, and America as a state of mind. Never perhaps had it been more strikingly expressed than in the words of Goethe in *Wilhelm Meister,* when one of the characters declares after a disappointing experience in America:

I shall return, and in my house, on my land among my home people, I shall repeat: Here and nowhere else is America. *Hier oder nirgends ist Amerika.*

But as Europe grew constantly weaker, torn by continuous wars and domestic strife, while the strength of the United States increased rapidly, the optimistic predictions concerning the future development of the United States made on the eve of the French Revolution seemed amply justified. Already in 1795, during the third year of the French Republic, Pictet of Geneva, summing up the observations of European travelers and the data found in Jedidiah Morse's geography, thought he was justified in examining "the causes of the greatness of America." His was not a great book; but it contained a summation of all the material available at the time, and his conclusion contrasted the country whose inhabitants had been wise enough "to submit themselves to a strong government in order to preserve their liberty," with a Europe apparently doomed "to oscillate between the cheerless tranquillity of despotism and the stormy fury of anarchy." At the same time (1793-1799), impelled by the same considerations, Christoph Daniel Ebeling published in Hamburg an enormous compilation on the United States which was to serve as the main source-book of information for several generations of German scholars.

Even more emphatic were the views presented by the Reverend John Bristed after the fall of Napoleon, the Peace of Ghent, and the reorganization of Europe. In the world of 1818, this British clergyman who had spent many years in America could see only two countries susceptible of growth: the giant Russia and the giant United States. He was too much attached to the European tradition to admire without restrictions the American ways of life; but he had to admit that the sun of Europe was setting, that none of the old nations could compete with a country capable of supporting ultimately a population of five hundred millions through its agriculture, commerce, industry, steam navigation, and mechanical inventions. It was not that the soil was extraordinarily fertile—America was "neither the Garden of Eden, nor the Valley of Tophet"—but a practically unlimited extent of territory which could be reclaimed through the tremendous energy and industry of the inhabitants offered possibilities undreamed of by the crowded populations of Europe.

Very similar was the conclusion reluctantly reached by Abbé de Pradt, the former chaplain of Napoleon, in his study *Des Colonies et de la Révolution actuelle de l'Amérique* (Paris, 1817). The contagion predicted by Jefferson and dreaded by Turgot and Vergennes had reached South America. The Spanish and Portuguese colonies, following the example of the United States, were shaking off the yoke of Europe. Thirty years after the conclusion of the Treaty of Versailles, the revolutionary influence of the United States extended over the whole New World. Considering "What is the future of the United States?" De Pradt answered that according to Franklin's calculations, which so far had proved to be correct, the United States would support 138,400,000 inhabitants by 1919. Nothing comparable had ever happened in ancient or modern times. The American flag was already everywhere, and everywhere the very existence of the United States placed monarchies in jeopardy. Going even further than Bristed, De Pradt concluded:

No human power can now stop the march of a nation destined to exert its influence all over the world and perhaps to dominate it.

In fact, it was not an influence, it was an "invasion."

Less emphatically, but no less positively, ten years later, Barbé-Marbois reiterated the warning. In the eyes of the old diplomat who had served Louis XVI and known Washington; who, acting for the First Consul, had "sold" Louisiana to the United States and remained in the diplomatic service under Louis XVIII,

the United States, even without participating actively in the affairs of Europe, will exert through their example, an influence to be reckoned with by the imperial and royal cabinets of Europe. The Prince, whether he be called a king, magistrate, or people will no longer be able to rule without paying due regard to the political liberties of the citizens.

This extraordinary prediction was intended as a lesson to the future ruler of France, since it was dedicated by the old Royalist to the heir apparent of the French throne, "Monseigneur le Dauphin."

Once again Europe was discovering America. All the predictions and misgivings of Montesquieu and his disciples had proved to be false. It was no longer possible to maintain that a republican system of government was inherently weak and that it could survive only in a small territory. Not only was America a powerful country which had recently repelled aggression, but it was the only country that had been able to establish "a stable government, standing without props, while most governments in Europe maintained a precarious existence through measures of expediency."

5

Far more extensive and pervasive than the influence exerted in Europe by the American Revolution proper, and consequently not so easily traced, was a new force, symbolized in the magic word "America" and felt throughout the Old and the New World. This new force was Democracy. All the subterranean activities which neither Napoleon nor the Holy Alliance had been able to suppress completely had slowly prepared the violent explosion which shook all the nations of Europe in 1830. To determine the part played by the American example in the elaboration of the ideas and the fostering of the movements which came to fruition at that time, would require detailed studies which are not yet available. It would be particularly desirable to ascertain the influence of Jefferson, exerted directly and personally through his extraordinarily large correspondence with the lovers of liberty in Europe.

The author of the Declaration of Independence never enjoyed during his stay in Europe the extraordinary popularity carefully exploited by Franklin in the interest of his country. The *Notes on the State of Virginia* (1784), printed in Paris and in London, were not widely circulated, and Jefferson's other writings very seldom appeared in the public papers. But to the *philosophes* he was known as the man who had drafted the "Bill for establishing Religious Freedom," who had proposed a comprehensive plan of public education. By the members of the Committee on the Constitution of the National Assembly he was eagerly sought as a wise counselor. By the Physiocrats he was highly esteemed as a practical philosopher and farmer, interested in developing the agricultural resources of his country. He became later the man who had befriended Volney, Priestley, Thomas Cooper, and Thomas Paine, and was represented as the champion of the oppressed and the protector of political refugees fleeing their country to escape prison, persecution, or worse. As long as he stayed in office he was compelled to observe great prudence in the communications he addressed to his European friends. After his retirement he spoke more openly. He did not conceal the fact that he hated Bonaparte, the man whose ambition had changed Europe into a charnel house. He applauded the first efforts of the South Americans to achieve their liberty and the attempt of the Cortes to establish a more liberal regime in Spain. He advised the Greek Coray, the Portuguese Correa, the Pole Kosciusko, the Spaniard De Onis, and encouraged even more strongly his French friends, Lafayette, Du Pont de Nemours, and Destutt de

Tracy. He corresponded with British liberals like Major Cartwright, and with philosophers like Dugald Stewart, and political and human geographers like Alexander and Wilhelm von Humboldt. He was fully aware that his letters circulated secretly among his friends, but he showed a genuine iritation when his confidence was betrayed and they were printed, on several occasions, in the public papers. He was in fact, and perhaps unknowingly, the leader of a secret resistance movement in Europe during the Empire and the Bourbon Restoration.

The few and still superficial investigations of Jefferson's influence hitherto undertaken are singularly revealing. It seems that at the origin of the Italian *Risorgimento* is to be found a combination of eighteenth century philosophy and French revolutionary theories, with Jeffersonian Americanism acting as a sort of catalytic agent. It may be shown that under the combined influence of Jefferson's theories of government and Destutt de Tracy's *Commentary and Review of Montesquieu's Spirit of Laws,* the Russian "Decembrist" Pestel wrote his book on *Russian Justice* (1825), which led to the promulgation of the first Rumanian code of laws, worked out in collaboration with the representatives of the Rumanian people in 1832. In France again, Auguste Comte acknowledged his debt to the man who had attempted to found the science and practice of government irrespective of theological and metaphysical assumptions. A selection of Jefferson's letters and speeches published in Paris in 1832 led to a long discussion of his political philosophy in Armand Carrel's *National.* The great French critic Sainte-Beuve advised the young French generation to take as a leader and master the man who had proved that one of the first functions of government was to respect the rights of the "individual." No less emphatic and enthusiastic was the *Edinburgh Review,* in October, 1837, proclaiming Jefferson "the recognized leader of the party which had effected the first, possibly the most remarkable of those revolutions, and the one that has had the greatest influence upon the fortunes of mankind." Two years earlier, Richard Cobden had already declared that the time had come to draw lessons from the American example, in words calling for a complete reorganization of the social structure:

We fervently believe that our only chance of national prosperity lies in the timely remodelling of our system so as to put it as nearly as possible upon an equality with the improved management of the Americans.

Shortly before the Revolution of 1830, the French "doctrinaire," Royer Collard, had declared, "La démocratie coule à pleins bords," and indeed Democracy seemed to be on the point of overflowing its banks and of sweeping through Europe like an irresistible flood. But "Democracy" was now a battle cry rather than a definite program, as "Liberty" had been some fifty years earlier. Even its most enthusiastic apostles had no experience with the working of a democratic system of government. At a time when a complete transformation of the European system was impending, the Americans were the only people who had somehow managed to control and to direct through well laid-out channels this apparently unmanageable force. The United States stood no longer as engaged in an unprecedented and venturesome experiment: the experiment had been conducted in a gigantic laboratory, and it was an undeniable success.

6

Such were some of the thoughts which filled and haunted the mind of the young French magistrate who, in the spring of 1831, crossed the ocean with the official mission of studying the penal system of the United States. Born of a noble family, Alexis de Tocqueville was the grandson on his mother's side of M. de Malesherbes, the fearless lawyer who had presented the defense of Louis XVI before the Convention. Recently appointed to a modest position in the judiciary, he seemed little prepared by his education and family tradition to become, if not an apostle, at least a theorist and an exponent of democracy. He did not venture on his expedition without misgivings and hesitations. He was, as he has told us himself, "under the impression of an almost religious awe" caused by the sight of that irresistible revolution, marching for so many centuries through countless obstacles and now advancing in the midst of the ruins it had accumulated. To determine whether this "phenomenon almost fatal or providential" could in some degree be limited; to discover through what means democracy could be dedicated to the great task of enabling people to govern themselves; to find out some of the reasons which had made it possible for America to avoid the pitfalls into which the French people had fallen—these were the momentous problems that this young man, twenty-seven years of age, had undertaken to solve.

This utilitarian preoccupation, this eagerness to serve his country and the cause of civilization, have secured for Tocqueville a unique place among the critics and historians of America. He had no desire to prove or disprove any theory or system. He had no preconceived idea or prejudice, but as a judge he had been trained to look for the evidence and the facts of a case. His training largely accounts for both the judicial quality and the shortcomings of *Democracy in America* (1835).

That he was an alert and keen observer, susceptible of spontaneous reactions, is amply proved by his recently published journals. He traveled extensively in the United States, interviewed many statesmen and scholars, slept in the huts of the pioneers, and even visited some Indian tribes. But he strove to rise above contingencies; he looked for what is permanent and durable under the changing surface of changing phenomena. To use again Montesquieu's phrase, he was more interested in the "nature of things" than in things themselves. He used observation to establish principles from which, through an extensive deductive process, he could derive logical consequences and ultimately lessons in the art of self-government for the use of his fellow countrymen.

The consequence and perhaps the weakness of this method is that *Democracy in America* does not present a vivid and complete picture of American life, but rather a sort of diagram of what American life might become if the principles which directed its development continued to apply. A not inconsiderable number of Tocqueville's predictions have proved to be false, but for three-quarters of a century his book was accepted as fundamental and authoritative in America as well as abroad, and even today it can be read and studied with profit.

Tocqueville concluded that the pillars on which the structure of American civilization rested were separation of church and state, and an almost excessive decentralization. Obviously, in emphasizing these features of American life, the author had always present in his mind reverse conditions and tendencies in his own country. His conclusion was that the American experiment could not be repeated in Europe, and least of all in France, without a deep moral transformation. His picture of American democracy was presented as an object lesson and not as a pattern to be exactly reproduced.

Two problems, however, were common to Europe and America. The first was how to preserve the liberty of the individual against all tyranny, whether it be the tyranny of the state or the tyranny of the majority. The second problem, no less pressing, was raised by the irresistible leveling and lowering tendencies of modern peoples. As the old aristocracies were doomed and had amply demonstrated their political incapacities, as an aristocracy of riches would entail no lesser evils than those of the old system, as on the other hand, the common people were incapable of solving directly the problems of modern life, the main question was

for the partisans of democracy to find means of getting the people to choose the men capable of governing and to give them in addition enough power to direct the latter in matters as a whole, but not in the details of their work nor the means of execution.

And in discussing, in a letter to John Stuart Mill, the first part of his work, Tocqueville concluded: "That is the problem. I am fully convinced that upon its solution depends the fate of the modern nations."

One of the unavoidable consequences of this unavoidable leveling was the disappearance of many of the features of the old civilization which were dearest to Tocqueville and most of his French contemporaries. Among them was, first of all, the gradual pauperization of intellectual and artistic life, which can thrive only where a distinct and semipermanent aristocracy is maintained. In common with almost all of the travelers and observers of American life, Tocqueville not only refused to recognize that America had made any distinctive contribution to arts and letters, but asserted that conditions in America were so adverse to the development of the arts that an acceptable mediocrity was the most that could be expected. It was an old quarrel and an old contention against which Franklin and Jefferson had protested in the eighteenth century, and which had aroused the ire of the American public on several occasions during the first third of the nineteenth century. In vain David Warden, for a long time Consul General in Paris, and later Eugène A. Vail in his book, *De la Littérature et des Hommes de Lettres des Etats-Unis d'Amérique* (Paris, 1841), had attempted to counteract the supercilious criticism of American literature published in the *Edinburgh Review,* the *Quarterly Review,* or the *Revue des Deux Mondes.* At most it was granted that in some "minor" fields like history, oratory, perhaps natural history with Bartram, Audubon, and Agassiz, American authors had attained some distinction. But even if Irving, Cooper, and later Longfellow were names ranking high in literature, their indebtedness, real or assumed, to the literatures of the old world was such that they could hardly be regarded as the leaders of a truly original and American school.

Such was the price that America had already paid, thought Tocqueville, and that sooner or later Europe would have to pay; such as it was, it was not too high. With all its imperfections and deficiencies America remained to him and to his many followers the only place on earth where a new science, the science of government, could develop with a minimum of interference from internal troubles and foreign wars. Europe had already lost its leadership. In the world of 1830, there remained only two great powers with undeveloped and practically unlimited resources, America and Russia—one representing, despite many deficiencies, an ideal of liberty and a promise to respect the rights of the individual, the other centering all the authority of society in a single arm:

The principal instrument of the former is freedom; of the latter servitude. Their starting point is different and their courses are not the same; yet each of them seems marked by the will of Heaven to sway the destinies of half the globe.

Tocqueville had made his choice early and never departed from it. Only six

years before his death in 1859, when the Union was on the eve of being torn
by a civil war, he reiterated his faith in the mission of America:

I earnestly hope that the great experiment in self government which is carried
out in America will not fail. If it did, it would be the end of political liberty in
our world.

The lasting influence of Tocqueville's book can hardly be overestimated.
It was translated into Danish, English, German, Hungarian, Russian, Serbian,
Spanish, and Swedish and went through many editions in France, England,
and America. There is little doubt that John Stuart Mill, who reviewed the
first part of *Democracy in America* a few months after its publication, would
never have written his great book *On Liberty* (1859), and would not have
insisted as he did on "individuality" and the dangers of government interference, if he had not had always present in his mind the picture of democracy
presented by Tocqueville. This impact was felt in many different quarters.
Tocqueville strengthened the faith of the European liberals by insisting upon
the checks to which popular government should be submitted, while
Proudhon in France, Max Weber in Germany, and more recently Harold
Laski in England saw in him a prophet, proclaiming the doom of the
bourgeoisie and the necessity for drawing leaders from the mass of the people.
In some respects, and particularly as an analyst of the American form of
government, he was not only complemented but superseded by Lord Bryce.
But the influence of Bryce's *American Commonwealth* (1888) was far more
limited both in time and in space, while for many generations *Democracy in
America* has remained, if not the bible, at least the handbook of liberals in
most countries of the world.

One of the most obvious shortcomings of Tocqueville was his failure to
give sufficient consideration to the new economic forces and to the industrial
revolution then taking place before his eyes. To a large extent his work was
supplemented by two of his fellow countrymen, Michel Chevalier and Guillaume Tell Poussin. Both of them were civil engineers, and both of them
foretold the gigantic industrial power of the United States. Michel Chevalier's
Lettres sur l'Amérique du Nord (1836) was somewhat overshadowed by the
success of Tocqueville's book. In common with many of his contemporaries,
he entertained a gloomy view of the future of Europe. As did so many of
them, he accepted the historical theory of the westward march of civilization
and of the decline of old societies. He was too patriotic a Frenchman to admit
that Europe was irremediably doomed, but he admitted that preponderant
influence in world affairs would soon pass to the young peoples of Asia,
among which he included Russia, and to the young peoples of America. His
only hope was that ultimately the East and the West, the civilizations of

Europe and those of the young nations of Eastern Europe and Asia, would meet on the American continent not in a death struggle, but "to join hands and mix together, and this will be the greatest fact in the history of mankind."

His contemporary, Guillaume Tell Poussin, whose ambition was to write "a complement to Tocqueville's great book," emphasized, even more than Chevalier had done, the extraordinary development of applied science in America. In the railroads and steam navigation he foresaw the end of economic isolationism and a sort of industrial democratization of the world originating in the United States. In a book significantly entitled *De la Puissance Américaine* (1845), he foretold the triumph of world democracy, following great struggles in which America would be called upon to participate. Her strength and power, which could no longer be questioned, were consequently a matter of international importance. Nor was this view limited to the French. In the Introduction to his *Philosophy of History,* Hegel, some twenty years earlier, had admitted that

America is therefore the land of the future, where, in the ages that lie befcre us, the burden of the old world's history shall reveal itself . . . perhaps in a contest between North and South America. It is the land of desire for all those who are weary of the historical lumber-room of Europe. Napoleon is reported to have said: "Cette vieille Europe m'ennuie." It is for America to abandon the ground on which hitherto the History of the World has unfolded itself.

It remained for a disciple of German thought, Edgar Quinet, in an article published in 1831 in the *Revue des Deux Mondes,* to trace the decay and death of the religions of the Old World accompanying the decline of Old-World civilizations and to predict:

A new idea of God will surge from the lakes of Florida and the peaks of the Andes: in America will begin a new religious era and will be born a new idea of God.

To a certain extent, but with an interesting modification, this was also the view expressed by the Prussian historian Friedrich von Raumer, in 1845 (*America and the American People*). In the prodigious growth of the United States he saw an almost divinely inspired achievement of "the Germanic stock marching irresistibly forward." Having little faith in the future development of Asia and Africa, unable to distinguish any indication of a rejuvenation of a sickly Europe, he concluded:

If we were forced to despair of the future progress of the Germanic race in America, whither could we turn our eyes for deliverance, except to a new and direct creation from the hand of the Almighty.

7

Such were some of the dreams to which America was giving rise. As much as during the eighteenth century, it was, in the early years of the nineteenth, still a Utopian land, or rather a land where Utopias became realities. It was the land where Lezay-Marnesia had hoped to establish a refuge for the French aristocrats and where a few years later Coleridge had planned to establish his Pantisocracy. It was the land where Robert Owen after his unsuccessful experiment in England came to build his New Harmony and where the German Rapp established his communistic village of Economy, sixteen miles from Pittsburgh. The Napoleonic exiles, after Waterloo, had come as "soldier farmers" with General Bertrand to plant "the vine and the olive" in the wilds of Texas and Alabama. It was known that, while the theories of Fourier could not be put to the test of experience in Europe, a group of New England writers managed to conduct a famous if inconclusive experiment at Brook Farm. America was the only country on earth where the French socialist Cabet could attempt to organize colonies of Icarians, because nowhere else could small groups, advocates of a new order, establish and govern themselves locally and practically without any interference from a central government. It was the land where Priestley and Thomas Cooper from England, Comte de Noailles, Talleyrand, and Volney in the troubled last decade of the eighteenth century, General Bertrand, Jérome Bonaparte, and Achille Murat after the fall of Napoleon, had found an asylum. It was the land where the Germans, the Irish, and the French after 1848 were again to come as refugees to seek a liberty which they despaired of establishing in their own countries. It was also a land of hope in another respect. It was an irrefutable demonstration that the representatives from all the nations of the world, thinkers, reformers, and generous poets who had been called to attend an International Peace Conference under the presidency of Victor Hugo, in 1848, were not wild dreamers. The United States of America was a "commonwealth of nations." It had proved the truth of one of Hegel's chief axioms, that Unity dominates the diversity of elements. As long as the United States stood, there was hope that ultimately the peoples of the Old World could be redeemed from themselves. The American dream had become part of the cultural tradition of Europe.

THE DEMOCRACY

. . . the meaning of independence

16. THE GREAT EXPERIMENT

During the years from the nonpartisan reelection of James Monroe in 1820 to the Compromise of 1850, the United States lived very much to itself. Contacts with Europe were slighter than at any time before or since. Transportation by steamship was initiated in the thirties, but it was irregular and unreliable. Communication by cable had not yet been attempted. Consular and diplomatic exchanges were few. As compared with the rate of increase from births, the increase in population from immigration reached the lowest point since 1607. For three decades, Washington and New York and even Boston moved westward across the globe—farther from Europe, nearer the Rocky Mountains.

In the period of the Revolution, American liberals had put into execution European ideas; during the early years of the Republic, conservatives had been equally willing to accept foreign thought. Now, in partial isolation, a new generation adjusted Old World concepts to their own activities and began to create indigenous symbols to represent their own experiences. Out of this ferment there emerged a way of life dominated by the two forces of self-trust and expansion. Each advanced the other, yet at the same time each contravened the other: the thrust of expansion drove individuals and the states farther apart while the pull of self-trust held them together in one nation. More often expressed in action than in words, this diversity within unity found fragmentary utterance in the speeches of Clay, Webster, and Calhoun, and in the social criticism of Bryant of the New York *Evening Post* and of Cooper. In these crosscurrents of opinion, the generation of Lincoln and Emerson came to maturity.

Self-trust, when exercised by a people, is nationalism—in this instance, the brash yet healthy assurance of a youthful country secure in its achievements and its potentialities. Born in the political and philosophical debates of eighteenth century Europe, the doctrine had first taken on a negative form in America, that of hostility to England. Later it had become a self-conscious demand for native arts, native customs, and even a native language—to be created *de novo*. Now, as the frontier moved toward the Pacific, geography gave nationalism a new context. Not only was the United States the first nation founded on the novel principle that the boundaries of a nationality should coincide with those of a sovereign state, but it was also the earliest example of a nationality taking root in the rich soil of an unexploited continent. It is true that the enthusiasm of Americans for national symbols and holidays, for native scenery and customs, and for their own past often paralleled similar enthusiasms in Europe. But the impact of a new world, with its tremendous resources and its ever-present frontier, gave to nationalism in the United States a fresh and gusty incisiveness which sometimes angered and always amazed foreign observers.

This nationalism of the thirties and forties was often provincial, and it was often noisy—never in American history were patriots more vocal. It was at the same time realistic. Statesmen in Washington, as they watched the continental European powers withdraw from the Americas, discovered that the United States could rely on the Atlantic Ocean and on the self-interest of Britain as guarantors of American independence. In 1823 President Monroe was shrewdly capitalizing on the geographical self-sufficiency of the United States and on the foreign policy of Britain when he announced that the young republic had become the protector of a hemisphere: "The American continents . . . are henceforth not to be considered as subjects for future colonization by any European powers," and any attempt of a foreign power to control any independent state in the American hemisphere will be viewed as "the manifestation of an unfriendly disposition toward the United States." It should be remembered that the President and his advisers, Jefferson, Madison, and J. Q. Adams, did not commit the United States to this bold policy until they were assured of the support of Britain. Self-confidence for Americans in that day was confidence not only in themselves but in the only foreign power which maintained a navy capable of striking across the Atlantic.

Meanwhile the American people were congratulating themselves on the success of their experiment in republicanism. The division of opinion in the later eighteenth century between monarchists and republicans now disappeared, and monarchy became a symbol of all that Americans hated. Their republic, on the other hand, was neither the mirage nor the chaos that European reactionaries had anticipated; it was a practical, going concern. Out of the older concepts of natural law and natural rights, American liberals developed the new doctrine of popular sovereignty. Then they defended the republic as the only form of government consistent with that doctrine. (Popular sovereignty was not at that time generally associated with "democracy" because the latter term was not yet in general use.) Americans, as might be expected, were confirmed in their faith by the emergence of each of the French republics, by the founding of the South American republics, by the turmoil in Europe in 1830–1831, and particularly by the revolutions of 1848–1849. Whenever a foreign political experiment collapsed, Americans congratulated themselves again on the happy state of their own nation.

A steadily increasing respect for and reliance on the idea of the Union, one and indivisible, further strengthened egocentric Americanism. Jackson made his position dramatically clear at the Jefferson Day dinner of 1830, when he repudiated a series of toasts from the nullifiers by proposing: "Our federal Union: it must and shall be preserved." Likewise unequivocal was his reaction when in 1832 South Carolina declared that the federal tariff was null and void, and that the state would leave the Union if it were coerced. Jackson issued a proclamation in which he denied that the Union is a league of independent states and insisted that it is sovereign and perpetual. He let it be known also that he would use troops to enforce national laws. Respect for the Federal Constitution continued to grow until that instrument and the doctrine of the Union became, in the minds of nationalists, the two great bulwarks of the Republic.

A people as successful as the Americans considered themselves to be, and as religious as a majority of them were, inevitably credited their triumphs to God as well as to themselves. Reinterpreted in terms of the nineteenth century, the Puritan thesis that God's hand had been evident in every incident in the colonization of New England became the cult of manifest destiny. The United States had been set apart by divine Providence or by fate as the scene of a great, and perhaps a final, experiment in free government. The success of this experiment now made it evident that Americans were indeed a chosen nation. As such, they were destined to bring self-determination and republicanism to Texas, to California, and perhaps even to Canada and Cuba. They were chosen, likewise, to exemplify the ideal state for the imitation of rebels against monarchy in Europe. The honest concern of the American people for the welfare of all mankind gave a certain dignity to this theory of manifest destiny and a comfortable feeling of self-righteousness to its exponents.

The pervasive self-trust of these decades was announced, both by single citizens and by the nation, in a variety of terms. On the frontier, Davy Crockett shouted: "I kin lick my weight in wildcats!" In the White House, the President announced the nation's coming of age in state papers. In office and countinghouse, men said: Much as we owe to Europe, that continent is merely the exhausted past from which our fathers escaped; we find it expedient and profitable to be Americans. Among the older men of letters, Irving and Cooper groped for security, now abroad and now at home; but the young men put their trust in themselves and their new world. Emerson, speaking in 1837 for his egocentric contemporaries both in the United States and in Europe, declared: "If the single man will plant himself indomitably on his instincts, and there abide, the huge world will come round to him." And speaking for all high-minded nationalists of his century, he announced: "Our day of dependence, our long apprenticeship to the learning of other lands, draws to a close. The millions that around us are rushing into life, cannot always be fed on the sere remains of foreign harvests. Events, actions arise, that must be sung, that will sing themselves."

2

The spirit of expansion, at once result and cause of self-trust, wrote its own history across the map of the United States. In the years from the Revolution to 1820, the area of the Union had doubled. From 1820 to 1850, the westward migration pushed on into Texas, into Oregon, and to the Golden Gate; the territory of the United States increased by half; and the Americans were masters of three million square miles of land—an empire thirty times the area of the British Isles. The people themselves at the same time were growing with a swiftness unparalleled in history. During the two centuries from 1650 to 1850, their rate of increase per decade maintained an average of 35 per cent—that is to say, the number of inhabitants doubled every twenty-five years. Thus the population rose from nine million in 1820 to twenty-three million in 1850, when it was all but equal to that of the British Isles. American brag may have offended foreign ears, but it was often confirmed by history.

Under the thrust of expansion, no new cleavages appeared among the American people, but old frictions were intensified. Sectionalism, for example, in the 1780's had delayed the Federal Constitution and during the War of 1812 had provoked New Englanders to threaten secession. By 1840 not only the East but the South and the West were actively promoting their own interests. In New England sectionalists campaigned for protective tariffs, a centralized monetary system, and a strong federal government. In the South Hayne and Calhoun defended free trade, easy money, and states' rights. In the West, where self-interest coincided now with the interests of the South and now with those of the East, local patriots stood for easy money, a strong federal government committed to internal improvements, and free land. No one section commanded enough votes to win a national election. The South and the West in alliance were rarely able to control national affairs; only a coalition which included the East could dominate the nation. When the three sections came to a realization of these facts and of the futility of any attempt by a single state to exercise its rights through nullification, the only question which remained was this: Have the territory and wealth of the United States become so great that one of its sections is prepared to withdraw from the Union and form a new nation?

Certain of these sectional differences reappeared in the pattern of the agrarian-industrial conflict of the period. The nation was still predominantly rural, for only 7 per cent of the population in 1820 lived in towns of more than twenty-five hundred, and in 1850, only 15 per cent. The value of farm property was moved upward, exceeding three billion dollars in 1850, but the rate of increase was soon to fall off. In 1820 manufacturing ranked third as a source of national income, surpassed by shipping as well as agriculture. But the value of industrial property was doubling every ten years; the annual value of manufactures rose to over a billion dollars in 1850; and American industry was well launched on its spectacular career. Humanitarians and the early spokesmen of labor were already attacking Eastern industrialism as undemocratic. Southern planters feared its power and damned it as a peculiarly unenlightened variety of slavery. Western farmers in general agreed that industrialism was dangerous, but they were too busy with their own affairs to make an active assault on the factory. Apologists for capital remained on the defensive, content to emphasize the democratic nature of an industrial order which offers every man an equal opportunity to earn a living, to invest his savings, and to climb to the top of the ladder. The factory itself was glorified by capitalists as a Utopia where young men and women from the back country took on urban culture—an interpretation endorsed by Davy Crockett after a glimpse of the mills at Lowell, Massachusetts, and by the mill girls themselves in their literary organ, the *Lowell Offering*. But the American people as a whole remained agrarian-minded.

Deepest and widest of the cleavages in the era was that between aristocracy and democracy. In the South, where the past retained its greatest influence, Jefferson's theory of a natural aristocracy flourished but the democratic elements in his thinking were neglected. In their place, Calhoun proposed a "democracy" modeled after the society of pre-Christian Greece, in which a large population of slaves supported a small population of enlightened freemen. Moneyed aristocrats in the East (especially in Cooper's New York) adhered to the stake-in-society theory, arguing that men should participate in government to the same extent that they own property. Less materialistic patricians continued to put their trust in family; others, in the learned professions; and still others (as the Brahmins of Boston), in both. The stronghold of democracy was the new West and its new states. Here backwoodsmen and farmers kept alive the radicalism of the left-wing Jeffersonians and of Shays' Rebellion, until in 1828 their man Jackson went to the White House.

A prelude to this defeat of the patricians was the gradual extension of suffrage: by 1828 only Virginia and Rhode Island retained property qualifications on the ballot. This expanded electorate, free but of course not unanimously democratic, chose as President a frontiersman skilled in swapping horses and land, in wrestling and dueling, in killing Indians and British—the first man to reach the highest elective office in the nation without benefit of family or learning or wealth. This event threw many of the well bred into a frenzy: the young gentlemen of Harvard College burnt Andrew Jackson in effigy, and their elders fulminated against this "millennium of minnows" and the enthronement of "King Mob" in the White House.

To Jackson and his followers, the one institution which most clearly symbolized wealth, privilege, and aristocracy was the National Bank. He did not rest until it was destroyed. He also gave his support to such equalitarian practices as frequent elections, the increase of elective offices, and rotation in office, on the ground that "the duties of all public officers are, or at least admit of being made, so plain and simple that men of intelligence may readily qualify themselves for their performance." Then followed the demand of party members that the rewards of office should also rotate, and the spoils system was established. But the theory of Jacksonianism remained noble, for it proposed to achieve equality not by leveling but by raising. Andrew Johnson, the Tennessee tailor who became President at Lincoln's death, could declare in 1865:

Man can be elevated; man can become more and more endowed with divinity; and as he does he becomes more God-like in his character and capable of governing himself. Let us go on elevating our people, perfecting our institutions, until democracy shall reach such a point of perfection that we can acclaim with truth that the voice of the people is the voice of God.

3

In religion, the result of self-trust was diffusion in the form of voluntarism, secularization, and sectarianism. The process of separation of church and state, which had been initiated in the eighteenth century, came to its conclusion in 1833 when Massachusetts broke all official ties between government and religion. Legal regulation of religious practices, especially Sabbath observance, declined. Church membership and church support were now a matter of choice, and the success or failure of all religious activity became the responsibility of individual sects and their individual members. At the same time authoritarianism was weakened. In the Congregational and the Baptist churches, every man had a right to speak and hold office; in the Episcopal and the Methodist churches, secular authority increased; and among the Disciples of Christ, unpaid lay preachers filled the pulpit on Sunday and earned their own living during the week. As the nation expanded, minority groups among the Baptists, the Methodists, and the Presbyterians split off from the mother churches, to create new schisms. Even more symptomatic were the "come-outers" who devised their own religions, some as early as the eighteenth century: the Shakers, the Harmonites, William Miller and his Millerites (who announced that the world would end in 1843), the Fox sisters and the spiritualists, John Humphrey Noyes and his Oneida Community, Joseph Smith and his Mormons, and many more. During these lively years, creeds multiplied as rapidly as the swiftly multiplying population.

The success with which minorities shaped new religions to fit their own needs is illustrated by the history of transcendentalism. Its exponents were a small group of New England intellectuals who, after rejecting both rationalism and Calvinism, built their own faith around the divinity of man. Their nucleus was the informal Transcendental Club, their organ was the *Dial,* and their most influential spokesmen were William Ellery Channing and Ralph Waldo Emerson. Channing announced the fundamental principles of Transcendentalism: God is all-loving and all-pervading, the presence of this God in all men makes them divine, and the true worship of God is good will to all men. Emerson pointed up its individualistic tendencies by stressing intuition, Platonic idealism, and self-reliance.

The fashion in which less intellectual Americans cultivated their own variety of emotionalism in religion is evident in the history of the revival on the Western frontier. In the equalitarianism of the camp meeting, every man had as much right as his neighbor to renounce his sins, square his accounts with God, and choose a new way of life—all on his own volition. The Congregational church offered equality in church government, but its college-trained and college-founding ministers offered little excitement at the mourners' bench. More successful was the Baptist faith, especially among Negroes and pioneers who derived particular satisfaction from the rite of immersion. Most popular of all was Methodism, which prospered mightily in the West under the apostolic Francis Asbury and the rough and ready Peter Cartwright. A few nights of the singing and shouting, the holy laughter, holy jerks, and holy rolling of a revival gave emotion-cramped pioneers new faith in their country and their sect.

Humanitarianism in its broadest aspects may have helped to unify American society, but in the daily living of individuals it provoked dissent and acrimony. The theory and the practice of doing good, which had received their impetus in eighteenth century sensibility, were now sustained by American democracy and by nineteenth century pietism. The theory, as interpreted by the prophet Emerson, was all-inclusive: Let us not capitulate to the lie of one idea or of one reform; let us destroy, not one prison, but all prisons. Men who attempted to put this doctrine into practice—Lyman Beecher, William Ellery Channing, Theodore Parker—were hailed as universal reformers. But even those expansive souls could not cure literally all the ills of mankind; they could only give their support to certain favored causes and withhold it from the rest. And the leadership which translates good intentions into good deeds came in most instances from zealots devoted to a few related reforms or a single issue.

An instance was the temperance movement, which by 1825 enlisted more than a million Americans in a crusade directed not toward temperance but toward total abstinence. Those friends of all good causes, Beecher, Channing, and Parker, blessed the movement and made converts in the upper reaches of the electorate—important people but a minority on election day. Such universal reformers as the Sweet Singer of Hartford (Lydia Huntley Sigourney) and the staff of *Godey's Lady's Book* converted wives and mothers—but they cast no ballots. It remained for the men with one idea to bring in the votes: Timothy Shay Arthur, author of *Ten Nights in a Barroom, The Sons of Temperance Offering,* and a flood of tracts; the Washington Temperance Society, a group of reformed alcoholics; and the famous evangelist John B. Gough. These enthusiasts aroused the masses, and they in turn enacted prohibition legislation in thirteen states during the fifties.

In similar fashion, other crusades were led by men who concentrated their powers. Horace Mann and Henry Barnard were aware of more than one contemporary problem, but they specialized in educational reform. Emma Willard and Mary Lyon taught "females." Thomas H. Gallaudet, Samuel Gridley Howe, and Dorothea Dix befriended the deaf, the blind, and the insane. Lesser contemporaries, whose names are no longer familiar, organized municipal leagues, societies for prison reform, and similar agencies for amelioration. Unhappily, most idealists who were sufficiently tough-fibered to fight for a minority were too individualistic to get on with their fellows. Many a builder of the New Jerusalem erected with his right hand his own little structure of perfection, and tore down with his left hand what his neighbor had shaped.

While humanitarian movements clashed and rose or fell, one question grew more insistent: What shall be the final attitude of the United States toward slavery? As the years passed, the answer of the abolitionists gained in volume and insistence, until theirs was the loudest voice in the land. When the advocates of temperance bid for support in competition with the aroused antislavery men, the latter won and the temperance movement declined. When the campaign for women's rights ran afoul of abolition, only William Lloyd Garrison's radical minority accepted women as equals, and feminism receded into the background. The peace movement, pioneered by William Ladd and Elihu Burritt, flourished for more than a quarter-century; then it met slavery head-on, and even Theodore Parker finally admitted of war: "I hate it, I deplore it, but yet see its necessity. All the great charters of humanity have been *writ in blood,* and must continue to be for some centuries." The pressure of events thus made it evident that slavery was the one issue which could not be evaded.

4

Only a nation endowed with perfect wisdom could have effected a final reconciliation between the self-trust and the expansion of these years. Actually, the American people achieved a partial reconciliation in their thinking and a series of compromises in their public affairs. In their thinking, they brought together the familiar doctrines of the rights of man and his perfectibility, the expanding idea of democracy, and the new doctrine of progress. Out of these concepts, came their faith that by perfecting the individual they might eventually build the perfect state. Thus they reconciled the one and the many.

In the realm of public affairs, the period began and ended in compromise. The National Republican Party collapsed in the early thirties with the defeat of Clay. The Whig Party then emerged, an ill assorted band of former National Republicans, worshipers of Clay and Calhoun, nullifiers, and Antimasons, whose only common denominator was hatred of Jackson, living or dead. Jackson's party was itself in disagreement, West vs. South, over a variety of issues, particularly slavery. Men's minds were whirling with the claims of nationalism and sectionalism, industrialism and natural rights, slavery and the will of God, equality and a stake in society, revivalism, public improvements, the emancipation of women, manifest destiny, progress.

Of the three compromises which emerged from these conflicts, two involved the problem of slavery, and all three the problem of sectionalism. The first was the Missouri Compromise of 1820, whereby the South gained Missouri as a slave state and the East gained Maine as a free state, and slavery was prohibited "forever" in the greater part of the Louisiana Territory. The second was the Compromise of 1833, whereby Southern sectionalism was placated by a gradual reduction in the tariff and Unionists were appeased by the enactment of Jackson's Force Bill. The final and unavailing Compromise was that of 1850. The weary Clay, whose nationalism was ever stronger than his pronounced sectionalism, now urged the Whigs to make large concessions to Calhoun and the South in order to save the Union. The aged Webster, at last convinced that the preservation of the Union was more important than the liberalism of New England, supported Clay. By the legislation which they sponsored, the slave trade but not slavery was abolished in the District of Columbia, the reclaiming of runaway slaves was made easier, and the Missouri Compromise was repealed by the stipulation that new territories should come into the Union either slave or free, as their citizens might determine.

Compromise could go no further; civil war was inevitable.

17. ART IN THE MARKET PLACE

The era for the making of the new literature had arrived by 1820, but no one knew the rules or had the blueprints. The air was alive with energy and experiment. Writers were relying more upon journalism and the lecture and less upon the law, politics, and the church for their support. At the same time, American culture began to develop stronger regional characteristics and to strengthen such cultural centers as New Orleans, Charleston, Richmond, Baltimore, Cincinnati, Louisville, Philadelphia, Albany, New York, Concord, and Boston. But as the business of publishing and distributing books and magazines became better organized, these widespread centers looked more and more to New York for the stimulus of literary association and for the market place of literary wares.

The spirit of self-trust and expansion in this period found one form of expression in a zeal over all of America for the country to distinguish itself in the arts, to compel the critics as well as the common readers of England to think highly of the American book. That zeal was doubly felt in the South which, after about 1830, was concerned to justify itself sectionally against the North as well as nationally against Europe. The West as it expanded felt the same double defense to be necessary. Nationalism and sectionalism can hardly be distinguished; both stimulated the demand for "mental independence," both deferred to the critics of the older cultural center. The result was a ferment of literary activity.

2

New theories of education based on the concept of the natural man had already begun to develop a new generation of readers. The textbook reforms of Noah Webster and Jedidiah Morse were carried forward by the matter-of-fact "Peter Parley" (Samuel G. Goodrich) who insisted that cows give milk as well as jump over the moon, and that the first ideas of children "are simple and single, and formed images of things palatable to the senses." Starting with pictures and common experience, he took his imaginary charges over the globe, at the same time covertly attempting "to spiritualize the mind, and lift it above sensible ideas." He wrote or edited in the next twenty years 170 volumes and sold seven million copies. Emerson's philosopher-friend Bronson Alcott followed the same route from sense to spirit for the thirty children in his "Temple School" in Boston a few years later, although his climb from the sensory experience to the "spiritual" was aided by a school-room with "paintings, busts, books and not inelegant furniture," which provided "a prop round which tendrils may fasten"; while the Thoreau brothers accepted the conditioning provided by nature for their Academy and took their charges for long walks in the woods and fields of placid Concord.

The theories of Pestalozzi and of Jefferson, thus curiously mixed with sentimental idealism, were to require another century before John Dewey could urge their acceptance in a purer form, but meanwhile primary educa-tion developed rapidly. In 1827, when Peter Parley began to write, there were two "infant schools" and fifty-six primary departments in New York City, while a Massachusetts law in the same year required a high school in every town of five hundred families or more. But progress was slow, especially in the South, and it was not until 1850 that a campaign of propaganda and legislative reform, led by Horace Mann, succeeded in establishing, in principle at least, in every Northern state the provision of a common-school education for all children at public expense. "I have faith," wrote Mann, "in the im-provability of the race—in their accelerating improvability."

This faith in improvability led to the founding of some five hundred universities and colleges before the close of the century. There were two theories of state direction of higher education: that of New York which followed the French plan of administrative centralization of control over a distributed group of institutions, and the German plan of gathering the various schools of learning into one place and establishing a sprawling mammoth. The latter prevailed in most instances, and the states of the West and South almost without exception created universities within a few years of their admission to the Union. Even cities like Charleston and Louisville had by 1837 set up universities or colleges of their own on this pattern. At the same time, the various religious sects followed the advancing waves of migration and established small denominational colleges by twos and threes in each new state. The pattern of higher education for affairs as well as for ideas, which had been laid by Jefferson in the early years of national life, guided this entire period of expansion and became set as the distinctive form of organization for democratic institutions. Its chief characteristics were elas-ticity and a blind faith in "Veritas" and "Lux."

The colonial colleges adopted this pattern by a slow breakdown of the classical curriculum and of the close-knit control by the faculty over the students. George Ticknor, appointed the first teacher of modern foreign languages at Harvard in 1815, is spokesman and symbol for the changes which were national. Before taking up his duties, he spent several years of study at Göttingen—an example followed by Edward Everett, George Bancroft, and ultimately a hundred other young American admirers of the German awakening, including Longfellow and Lowell. Supplementing his studies by wide travel in England and on the Continent, he returned with books and ideas enough to overturn the settled ways of the provincial college. Long a friend of Jefferson, he admired the unrestricted freedom for intellectual exploration which the latter had made the guiding principle of the University of Virginia. Ticknor published a pamphlet in 1825 urging the adoption at Harvard of the departmentalized elective system, with a wide variety of offerings, the system finally achieved by Charles W. Eliot who became president of Harvard in 1869.

The education of women was a natural by-product of this tendency. Women were not full citizens under our original Constitution, but a few of them like Lucretia Mott, Margaret Fuller, and Elizabeth Peabody began agitation in the forties which ultimately brought them most of their "rights." In 1821 Emma Willard had established at Troy, New York, a "Female Seminary" which provided not only religious and moral, but literary, domestic, and what was called "ornamental" instruction for girls. Although the force behind this movement was moral zeal, its social implications were not long in making themselves felt. Other seminaries followed, but years passed before the education of women reached the college level on a par with that of men.

This widespread intellectual hunger produced the Lyceum and other systems of popular lectures. The surviving Lowell Institute of Boston, one of the earliest and most influential of these organizations, has been providing free public lectures in all branches of human knowledge for more than a century. The Peabody Institute of Baltimore and the later Cooper Union of New York were and are similar bodies. Supplementing the wider Lyceum movement, these local agencies soon offered a career to traveling lay preachers like Emerson, and a modestly remunerative side line for newspaper editors like Horace Greeley, as well as innumerable writers including Simms and Thoreau, Dickens, Thackeray, and later Matthew Arnold. Even museums like the Smithsonian Institution at Washington used the lecture as well as the display of their treasures as means "for the increase and diffusion of knowledge among men," and exponents of pseudosciences like mesmerism and phrenology or of causes like abolition and temperance gained an audience by combining entertainment with knowledge.

The rage of Boston has turned from parties to lectures [wrote W. W. Story in 1840]. What with Waldo Emerson and Useful Knowledge, and Lowell Institute and Grammar and Temperance, the whole world is squeezed through the pipe of science. All go to be filled, as the students of old went with their bowls for milk.

This movement owes much to Josiah Holbrook of Derby, Connecticut, peripatetic lecturer on geology and mineralogy. In 1826 the *Journal of Education* carried an outline of his plan for a national adult system of popular education. Every town was to have its own lyceum, with a library, a collection of minerals or other specimens of natural history, courses of lectures given by members, and groups for the study of science, history, and art. County lyceums were to be formed by delegates from the town societies, and in turn state lyceums and finally a national or even a world lyceum. Holbrook gave his life to the development of this vast corner in the adult education market and might have succeeded but for the rivalry of American copies of the Mechanics' Institutes of England and other local movements originating in trade and guild schools, local academies and colleges, women's clubs, and extensions of the great universities. Nevertheless, Holbrook's crusade created a hundred branches of the American Lyceum in two years and spread to nearly every state in the Union. By 1834, when the movement was at the crest, there were some three thousand local lyceums in the nation. The American Lyceum, a national federation of local units, had been organized in New York City three years earlier and held annual meetings until 1839. It influenced popular education from the common school to the college, and no one can tell how close was the connection between its popularization of knowledge and the explosive anarchy within every type of formal educational institution during this period. Whether cause or result of the forces of uncontrollable freedom in our early educational history, it did more to shape American literary history than any other agency. Not only in the East but throughout the North and West, it created a vast army of readers, listeners, and students and developed the new literary form of the popular lecture, although in the South the tradition that gentlemen could give themselves most fruitfully to politics delayed the democratization of literature.

3

New York City became in these years, by sheer mercantile superiority, the literary capital of the nation, making virtual provinces of the South, the West, and even New England. But in Boston and its environs there were literary stirrings which depended on other than mercantile factors. From the glitter of lower Broadway to the calm of Concord or Cambridge is a journey longer in mood than in miles. To discover the significance of the cultural renaissance which flowered in these New England villages in the forties and fifties, one must turn backward or forward a few pages in this book and forget the descriptions of bustling and mercantile New York. Boston, with its *North American Review* and its Harvard College, had succeeded more than any other American city in keeping aloof from the market place even though the materialism of its State Street was shocking to some. Prosperity did not avoid it in blessing the commerce of all American seaboard towns from Charleston north, but Bostonian pride succeeded in using material gains to foster rather than to overwhelm the things of mind and the spirit. The mystery of this contrast can probably never be completely resolved; with the same instruments of culture at its hands, Boston developed great orators, great teachers, great writers; and Concord, some twenty miles to the west, was her conservatory for the cultivation of her finer fruits.

Two closely related institutions, the Town Meeting and the Congregational Church served, as they had since the founding of New England, to maintain the distinct character of the region. The Congregational and Unitarian ministers, although few of them retained either the theological rigor of early Puritan days or the fiery enthusiasms of the Great Awakening, still exerted great influence. Aside from their spiritual and religious functions, they were New England's chief representatives of the intellectual life. They almost alone had leisure for study, for thought, and for thought's full expression. They were, in fact, "delegated minds" in a sense more exact than that in which Emerson could use the term in speaking of his ideal American scholar, and indeed he might never have used that term if he had not been familiar from childhood with the duties and prerogatives of the New England clergy.

In trying to estimate the probable influence of these clergymen we should have in mind not only men of exceptional ability, powerful preachers such as Joseph Stevens Buckminster, intrepid leaders such as William Ellery Channing, or scholars and thinkers like Frederick Henry Hedge, but also the far more numerous run-of-the-mill ministers who spoke from country pulpits week after week in tones none the less authoritative because they had little to say. Fair examples of this ordinary preaching are to be found in the sermons of Ezra Ripley still preserved by the hundreds in Concord's Old Manse, some of which were heard by Ripley's young kinsman, Ralph Waldo Emerson, when he was making up his mind to leave the ministry. The Reverend Mr. Ripley was undoubtedly a stout laborer in the vineyard of the Lord, but it must be said that the sermons he preached for nearly sixty years in Concord can have done very little to advance the culture of that town or, one may add, the Christianity. His sermons were empty and dull, laboriously conventional and elaborately superficial. While struggling to read them one is often reminded that their author was, as he said, a "natural Unitarian," so that he never had the intellectual discipline of thinking down into the "cast-iron logic of despair" called Calvinism nor yet that of thinking his way out of it. Compared with the rock-ribbed sermons of the great Puritan past written by men such as Thomas Hooker, Thomas Shepard, and the Mathers, these of his are woefully deficient in "fundamental brain-work." Indeed, they all but justify one of the severest remarks ever made by Emerson about any human being: "This afternoon the foolishest preaching—which bayed at the moon. Go hush, old man, whom years have taught no truth."

With such leadership the New England culture that began to be aware of itself in the third and fourth decades of the nineteenth century was inevitably conservative, moralistic, and tinged with an unimpassioned piety. Often erudite but seldom creative, it was largely a matter of reading and bookish talk, doing little to lessen that unwholesome predominance of literature and oratory over the other arts which had characterized New England from the start. And even with regard to literature a culture thus dominated was somewhat timorous and spinsterish—inclined to doubt, for example, whether Goethe could be really a great poet in view of what was known or surmised about his illicit amours. Worst of all, this culture was not an indigenous growth but a plant imported from foreign lands to take its chance among the native flora.

The prevailing mood of New England was as conservative as that of her clergy. In her detestation of Jefferson's Embargo and her lack of enthusiasm for the War of 1812 she revealed, at least among her more prosperous classes and in the vicinity of Boston, an Anglophile tendency. Members of the Federalist Party, retaining power in Massachusetts long after the party elsewhere had died out, exerted an influence out of proportion to their numbers. At the Hartford Convention in 1815 they expressed their belief that New England might at need become independent. Longfellow's father attended that convention as a delegate, and it seems likely that the fathers of Lowell and Holmes would willingly have done so.

The chief intellectual center of the region, from which most of the Congregational clergy were sent forth, was, and from the start had been, Harvard College, an institution almost two centuries old when Holmes graduated there in 1829. With fewer than two hundred undergraduates, a faculty of some fifteen permanent members, and a library of less than forty thousand volumes, Harvard did not make an extensive educational offering. The curriculum, rigidly prescribed, laid primary stress upon Latin, Greek, and mathematics, although increasing attention was given to the modern languages and science was recognized in a few lectures and "demonstrations." Courses in English composition were conducted, with signal success, by Professor Edward Tyrrel Channing, who in his many years of teaching read and castigated the "themes" of Emerson, Holmes, Lowell, Dana, Motley, Thoreau, Sumner, Parkman, and Edward Everett Hale. Compulsory chapel exercises were held twice a day.

The college was not remarkably stimulating to lads of fine intelligence, and the ordinary undergraduate probably gained less information there than is commonly acquired in a good high school of the twentieth century. On the other hand there was at Harvard a serious concern for things of the mind to which even a dullard could scarcely fail to respond. In a time and place almost exclusively concerned with crude "practical facts" it managed to inculcate an interest in abstract ideas and in knowledge for its own sake. It had a character, an idiosyncrasy of its own, which it stamped upon all its sons indelibly. There was a hint of ancient Rome and Athens in this Harvard character, and through the barnlike classrooms and dormitories there blew as it were the bracing air of Plutarch's "Parallel Lives." Most of all to its credit, the place was hospitable to odd and unclassified individuals who did their own thinking and boldly spoke it out. In training most of the New England clergy Harvard had done her share, producing a conventional and conservative culture; but now she was slowly making ready for a different kind of leadership.

4

The pulpit and the lyceum did not supersede other and more traditional agencies for the making of the literary man. The increase in population, the spread of literacy, the improvement in means of communication, the growing sophistication of both urban and rural society, and the technical advances in printing and book production conspired to build up a substantial reading public. George P. Putnam of New York, the first of the great publishers in the modern sense, estimated that in 1845 the combined college libraries in the country contained 600,000 volumes and public collections almost 900,000. "Besides these," he added, "there is scarcely a town of any importance in the Union, but has some sort of a public library, reading-room, lyceum, or athenaeum."

The effects of inventions on the spreading of the printed word soon became apparent. The old methods of hand-set type, handmade paper, and the screw-pressure press had already been superseded by the principles of levers and cylinders when in 1825 the Napier steam-driven press made its appearance. The production of 2,000 copies an hour of the New York *Daily Advertiser* seemed a miracle until in 1847 the Hoe rotary press stepped production up to 20,000. Type casting and hand setting continued, however, for editions of most books, which in 1832 averaged 1,000 copies. Stereotyping of plates was known in this country as early as 1813, but was applied mainly to Bibles and textbooks until about 1830 when the Harpers adopted it as a regular practice for their "omnibus editions" of English reprints and Carey began to use it for Cooper's novels. Paper- and ink-making processes, machine type casting, and new methods of binding and embossing kept pace with these other improvements, and the process of steel engraving in the forties started F. O. C. Darley and others on careers of book illustration which would have been altogether impractical with the less durable wood block, the copper plate, and the lithograph.

Important by-products of these improvements were the appearance of the annual or gift book and of the giant anthology or cyclopedia of literature, scenery, or other matter suitable to fine printing, binding, and illustration. Goodrich attributed the sudden vogue of such annuals as *The Token, Friendship's Offering,* and *The Atlantic Souvenir* to the invention of steel engraving. "Under such seductive titles," he wrote, "they became the messenger of love, tokens of friendship, signs and symbols of affection, and luxury and refinement; and thus they stole alike into the palace and the cottage, the library, the parlor, and the boudoir." Similarly, R. W. Griswold raised the literary anthology to new levels of luxury if not of discrimination with *The Poets and Poetry of America* (1842) and his subsequent collections of prose and of the work of "female poets." And the Duyckincks produced their ten-pound, two-volume *Cyclopaedia of American Literature* in 1855.

Mechanical improvements in book making led in two quite contrary directions. They made it possible to produce far more elaborate books at no increase in cost, to illustrate them more copiously, and to bind them more sumptuously; but competition was so acute that mechanical improvements could not be generally applied until the middle of the century, when the Townsend *Cooper* and the Putnam *Irving* appeared, dignified gentlemanly rows of stocky volumes, with clear type on heavy paper, steel-engraved illustrations, and embossed ornaments on substantial cloth covers. Such books could look down on the humble, paper-bound parts of the 1819–1820 *Sketch Book* as a well disciplined, modern regiment might view ragged mountain guerrillas.

On the other hand, competition called for a continuously increasing quantity of production and lowering of costs. This tendency reached its climax in the late thirties and the forties, when Cooper's novels began appearing in paper wrappers at twenty-five cents instead of a dollar a volume; when mammoth newspapers, four feet long and eleven columns wide, began to print the complete novels of Dickens, G. P. R. James, or Lytton in "extras" of some seventy closely printed pages at ten cents a copy; and when the editor of the New York *Herald,* one of the first great penny newspapers, could write:

What is to prevent a daily newspaper from being made the greatest organ of social life? Books have had their day—the theatres have had their day—the temple of religion has had its day.

The effect of the situation on the book market is stated by Goodrich. According to his estimates the gross amount of trade in books in the United States in 1820 was $2,500,000, of which one million was in books of kinds other than educational, classical, theological, legal, and medical. By 1850 the total had mounted to $12,500,000, or an increase of 500 per cent, of which $4,400,000 was in the miscellaneous category. And, with the general lowering of cost and quality the actual number of titles issued may have shown as much as four times this increase. At the same time Goodrich estimates the ratio of books of American authorship to those of British at 30 to 70 per cent in 1820 and at 70 to 30 per cent in 1850. Throughout the period, the Southern market remained a major outlet for Northern booksellers, and the markets of the Ohio River valley grew in importance.

"American authors," writes Putnam, "are not always deprived of just remuneration for their writings." In this respect, progress was fairly rapid, and, in the period of inflation prior to the panic of 1857, royalties were as high as they are today. But the struggle of Poe to earn a livelihood by his writing is reflected in the experiences of many others in the earlier group. Cooper offered Carey the rights to an edition of his *Notions of the Americans* in 1828 for $1,500 and usually got $2,000 for an American edition of his novels. But even with his reputation made Poe could get no return for his *Tales* in 1839 and only eight cents a copy for the small 1845 edition. Emerson followed the common practice of paying for the manufacturing of his books and let booksellers handle them on commission. It was apparently Putnam who developed the royalty method of payment, offering 10 per cent to American and even to exploited British authors in 1845–1846. The shock was almost too much for them. Carlyle, with characteristic pomp, exclaims, "Such conduct was that of men of honour." The usual method of distribution was a barter system among publishers, which, without national advertising, tended to restrict sales and so cut the return from royalties, however high their rate might be.

Book publishing was financially unrewarding unless the British market was played as well as the American and the absence of an international copyright law or protocol was thus circumvented. Cooper and Irving together found at least a temporary solution to this problem. Irving's *Sketch Book*

(1819–1820) marks the real beginning of American literature in more ways than one, in that it was the first book by an American to bring its author financial returns on both sides of the Atlantic. The formula which he stumbled upon by his presence in London and his urgent financial need was learned by Cooper when he visited England in 1827, and it became an important means of support for most of our mid-nineteenth century writers. It was, briefly, the trick of residence or of prior publication in England.

The reason for this curious situation was that the American copyright law allowed protection for their work only to *American* authors, whereas the English law based its protection on priority of publication or on residence without regard to the nationality of the author. British publishers were often willing to pay an American author cash in advance for first publication rights, whereas citizenship made prior publication unnecessary for protection at home. Thus the American author could sell his manuscript to an English publisher, have advance sheets, or pages, shipped by fast packet to America, and, by timing the issuance of the books in the two countries with an interval of a few days or weeks, outwit the pirates and obtain double returns. An English author, on the other hand, because of his foreign citizenship, could not obtain protection in the United States and was free spoil for the American publisher until, toward the middle of the century, a sense of fairness on all sides tended to equalize the situation.

The fight for international copyright stretched on for a century with both British and American laws frequently altering but never correcting the situation. For a long time authors fought almost alone, but they were slowly joined by the publishers under the leadership of Putnam. The paper and other collateral industries seem to have furnished the bitter-enders, aided and abetted by the reading public which unthinkingly wished its books to be many and cheap. The passage in 1891 of an American law providing for international copyright brought to an end a century of controversy.

Meanwhile, the magazines managed to pay sufficiently to keep both major and minor authors in pocket money by offering modest fees for original work and by allowing advances to authors in need. The vogue of the short story, the familiar essay, and the lyric poem in America may be attributed to this cause. The *North American Review* marched sedately through the period, publishing mainly critical articles; but there were many other magazines of more popular and literary caste. Among the earlier ones were the *Casket* (1826–1840) of Philadelphia, the *New England Magazine* (1831–1835), and the *Southern Review* of Charleston (1828–1832). Later the field was taken over by the *Knickerbocker* (1833–1865), the *United States Magazine and Democratic Review* (1837–1859), the *Southern Literary Messenger* of Richmond (1834–1864), and *Graham's* (1840–1858) of Philadelphia, the last two of which Poe edited for short periods. Margaret Fuller and Emerson published the distinctive organ of the transcendentalists, the *Dial*, in Concord from 1840 to 1844 while *Harper's* started publication in 1850 and the *Atlantic* in 1857. *Godey's Lady's Book* set the pace for women's magazines in 1830 with its colored fashion plates and its sentimental fiction and poetry, and continued its prosperous career almost to the end of the century; while Willis' *New York Mirror* (1823–1857) exploited the possibilities of the weekly, and for many years was supreme in that field.

Graham's, for its period, seems to have created almost a monopoly, and entered into contracts with authors for regular and exclusive rights to contributions. Its circulation in 1843 was over 100,000 copies, and Hawthorne was content with the arrangement "on account of the safety of your Magazine in a financial point of view." Its editor, R. W. Griswold, offered Mrs. Frances S. Osgood $25 each for stories and $10 for poems in that year, and about the same time Park Benjamin wrote Graham: "Would you like to have an occasional poem from Professor Longfellow? I think I could get him to write for you at $20. He asks $25." Still some minor authors wrote for love and there is no record of their offers having been rejected, but a professional attitude was becoming more common. A contemporary guess set N. P. Willis' annual earnings in four magazines at $1,200 to $1,600 a year, and Paulding contracted to write a five-page article for every issue of *Graham's* at $10 per page. "My terms," wrote H. W. Herbert, "are necessarily in these hard times cash on delivery." Even as late as 1851, the dramatist George Henry Boker could write to a friend, "Alas! Dick, is it not sad that an American author cannot live by magazine writing?"

Writing for the stage was an even less secure profession. Prior to the passage of the Copyright Act of 1856, which gave the playwright, "along with the sole right to print and publish the said composition, the sole right to act, perform, or represent the same," the only hope for protection was to keep a play out of print. Early managers and actors like Dunlap, Hackett, and Wallack sometimes rewarded their authors with a benefit "third night," but the return in any case was insufficient to encourage native talent, especially as most acting companies came direct from London with their casts and their repertories complete. Gradually American actors and managers took over, and the tendency of companies to travel less and to become identified with specific theaters encouraged local talent without providing any regular returns. Forrest's system in the forties of offering cash prizes for new plays did much to dignify the position of the playwright, but it reacted unfavorably as it meant the outright sale of the manuscript. The story of Boker's *Francesca da Rimini* is now classic: the best play by an American in the nineteenth century, it was withdrawn in 1855 after a few performances and had to wait twenty-seven years before it was revived by Barrett, when its author was too old to be stimulated to new effort by its popularity. Boker seems to have earned no more than $1,500 in all for five plays produced between 1849 and 1856. Robert Montgomery Bird, after selling several plays to Forrest for $1,000 each, turned from drama to the writing of fiction.

There were a few efforts to better the position of the writer. In 1836 a joint stock company of lawyers and literary men, called the Stationers' Company of Boston, was organized to promote the publication of more serious work. It issued Prescott's *Ferdinand and Isabella* and Hawthorne's *Twice Told Tales,* but it was not financially successful. Yet recognition was coming to authors by 1855, the year of the Duyckincks' *Cyclopaedia.* On September 27, there was held in the Crystal Palace, "the Complimentary Fruit Festival of the New York Publishers' Association to Authors and Booksellers." It "was one of the most gratifying and suggestive occasions I ever witnessed," wrote a visitor from Boston, and Everett, Sumner, Bryant, and Beecher were present to raise their voices in praise, while James T. Fields read a poem.

A word should be added for the publisher-bookseller, for he often encouraged an author when other agencies failed. Putnam did much to promote the sale of American books in his London shop, and Hawthorne wrote to his friend Fields in 1862, "My literary success, whatever it has been or may be, is the result of my connection with you." It was Fields who had suggested in 1849 that he rewrite *The Scarlet Letter* as a novel, with the result that it had three times the circulation of the book of Tales from which it was taken. The Old Corner Bookstore in Boston was Hawthorne's favorite haunt even though he sat apart from the distinguished group of men and women who made of the shop a literary club in the days of Emerson, Holmes, Harriet Beecher Stowe, and Lucy Larcom. Cooper and Irving formed similar groups in the shops of New York and Philadelphia, and by 1856 William Gilmore Simms had gathered such a group in Russell's bookshop in Charleston.

More even than Fields and other publishers, the two anthologist-editors, Rufus W. Griswold and Evert A. Duyckinck, shaped the course of literary history in the forties and fifties. Their choices became the choices of the ever widening reading public, and authors were quick to court their favor and enjoy their friendship. Griswold, whom Lowell accused of plucking alive and feeding on his literary flock, became Poe's successor as editor of *Graham's Magazine* in 1842, and later his literary executor, and with his many anthologies developed into a kind of "chief herdsman" of the "Parnassian fold" of younger writers including Thomas Buchanan Read, George Henry Boker, Bayard Taylor, and Richard Henry Stoddard. *The Poets and Poetry of America* (1842) and the companion volume of *The Prose Writers of America* (1847), together with a half-dozen other anthologies and introductions to editions of the poetry of Scott, Milton, Praed, Béranger, Bryant, Hemans, Campbell, and others, made him a sort of court of appeal in matters of taste; but he abused the authority this gave him in his treatment of Poe's life and reputation, and otherwise exercised it with breadth rather than discrimination.

Duyckinck was a man of sounder scholarship, finer taste, and broader human sympathies. Unlike his rival, who fought with Poe, he encouraged Melville when the author of *Typee* was beginning his career and most needed the kind of aid that an editor could give. A graduate of Columbia College in 1835, Duyckinck spent more than a year (1838–1839) in Europe in the expectation of a professorship of literature; when the appointment failed to materialize, he became a sort of *ex officio* professor to countless literary men, many of whom gathered weekly for far-ranging conversations over Roman punch and cigars in the basement of his New York residence. Bryant, Irving, Lowell, Simms, Taylor, and Hawthorne were his close friends. They and many others borrowed books from his well chosen library of some eighteen thousand volumes. As editor, after 1845, of Wiley & Putnam's Library of Choice Reading and Library of American Books, he was a major influence in introducing European classics to American readers and in helping American authors to find an audience. Hawthorne advised him to publish Emerson's poems because he thought Emerson's reputation still "provincial, and almost local, partly owing to the New England system of publication." Simms sought him out on a visit to the North and became one of the distinguished group of contributors to the *Literary World*—as brilliant a literary journal, under Duyckinck's editorship, as this country has known.

The *Cyclopaedia of American Literature* (1855) immediately became and still is a standard reference work. Written and edited with the aid of his brother George, it reflects his comprehensive reading, his widespread acquaintance with living authors, his extensive research in both books and manuscripts, and his indefatigable correspondence in search of facts, as well as his taste and his critical judgment. Here and in his critical articles he declared the superficiality of the popular N. P. Willis and of much of the poetry of even Longfellow and Lowell. Although out of sympathy with the principles of transcendentalism, he never doubted Emerson's greatness and was disappointed in not obtaining some of his work for New York publication; and he unqualifiedly proclaimed Hawthorne and Melville the literary titans of his day. Like most New Yorkers, Duyckinck felt ill at ease in Boston; but his friends included writers from all sections, and his home—like his native city—was a national meeting ground.

Thus mercantile giants like John Jacob Astor and Stephen Girard were not alone in learning before the middle of the century the art of focusing the diverse material of a democratic laissez-faire economy upon their own fame and profit. James Gordon Bennett, Horace Greeley, and William Cullen Bryant became powerful as editors by so marshaling these forces; George Palmer Putnam, E. A. Duyckinck, and James T. Fields did the same for book making; Willis, Graham, and Lewis Gaylord Clark, for the magazine; Edwin Forrest and William Niblo, for the theater; and finally Cooper, Irving, Emerson, Kennedy and many lesser men, for literature. Cooper, Irving, and Willis, by playing their cards with cunning and care, made possible the career of the professional man of letters in America; Emerson did the same for the popular lecturer, as Edward Everett stamped out the pattern for the occasional orator by making of his art a career. By mid-century the American literary man had come into his own.

The increasing millions of new readers created by education and migration could thus be supplied with literary fare only because there was corresponding progress in importing, producing, and circulating the printed word. At first glance one wonders, not why there was suddenly a new generation of native authors, but why this group was relatively small and why it struggled with financial obstacles almost as great as those of an earlier day. The answer to these questions is clear. In a competitive mercantile economy, the writer is in the position of the farmer, a producer of raw materials without protective tariff. Power and profit pass him by unless he too can find ways to play the game. "Democratic literature," wrote De Tocqueville in 1835, "is always infested with a tribe of writers who look upon letters as a mere trade"; Dickens spoke of the "present abject [moral] state" of the American newspaper press; and the elder Longfellow wrote sorrowfully to his son in college, "There is not wealth and munificence enough in this country to afford sufficient encouragement and patronage to merely literary men." Wealth was growing, but for many years it was to be widely distributed and was to fall for the most part into the hands of the literary manufacturer and middleman rather than into those of the author.

18. WASHINGTON IRVING

T<small>HUS</small> America was ready for a man of letters: the lights were on; the audience assembled. The mediums for the new culture were exciting. In all those interests of man which we call cultural there was a stir, the unmistakable promise of a future. A few of our writers, a Hawthorne or an Emily Dickinson, were to live "beyond time," that is, not without aloofness to the dust and heat of their own eras. This man of letters, however, for whom the theater, the magazine, the novel, the more civilized society, and the new nationalism called so imperiously, was not to be, like Edwards or Emerson, timeless, but temporal, an inevitable creation and adroit user of those cultural mechanisms and moods; it could not, in this adolescence of our intellectual life, be otherwise. Without a skillful manipulation of these instruments of culture, success in writing was impossible; and without measurable public renown of some kind, any author might hope in vain for readers.

Naturally some of our first men of letters were men of affairs who discovered in themselves surprising talents with the pen. Before he published *The Sketch Book,* at the age of thirty-six, Washington Irving had been a lawyer, a businessman, and a soldier; in his contemporaries' eyes the crown of his career was not this famous volume, but his appointment as minister to Spain. Although at heart a dreamer and a deliberate artist, he was fascinated by these new playthings of culture, and became an urbane participant in the clubs, coteries, and literary and theatrical circles which formed a graceful backdrop to his own preeminence. In spite of his long residence abroad, his links with the "Knickerbocker Group" were real. No writer gauged better than he the demands of contemporary readers, at home and abroad; his essay of manners was not unaware of that of Joseph Dennie in Philadelphia, of Miss Mitford in England, and of Fernán Caballero in Spain. His creative life prospered not in the study, but in the drawing room, the theater, or John Murray's publishing house.

Washington Irving was our first classic. Even in his own time his sketches found their way into the schools and into the libraries beside the English masters; and he early demonstrated his mastery of the form and temper of the nineteenth century essay. Byron, Coleridge, and Scott were among his admirers; he stands on the shelves with Addison, Goldsmith, and Lamb. Yet, contrary to the myth, he never imitated these essayists, nor even Scott; his own style is authentic, born of a temperament, taste, and subtlety of mind which were peculiarly his own. Hawthorne, who worshiped him, and whose writing resembled his in its singular unity of tone, felt, as did all his peers (save the bristling Cooper), the union in him of a sensitive personality and the power to express this completely. His good sense and amiability undoubtedly enhanced his prestige, as Cooper's truculence diminished his; if Irving is now unread, this may be partly the reason. Yet his place, apart from his literary pioneering and his personal charm, is secure.

For Irving is classic not only as a stylist but as a poetic interpreter of legend—local, European, and universal. The monument at the entrance of "Sunnyside" commemorates his triple achievement, in the three figures of Diedrich Knickerbocker, King Boabdil of Granada, and Rip Van Winkle. If we dismiss the romantic story of his life, that of the son of middle-class Scottish parents rising to eminence as a famous American, or if we set aside his brilliant workmanship in prose, there still remains his extraordinary intuition concerning America's heritage of world legend, his fulfillment of his early determination to enrich his country with the "colour of romance and tradition." The tendrils of Irving's finest stories lie deep in human memories and feeling. Rip Van Winkle's return is a symbol of his concept of mutation, an all-pervasive theme in his writings:

With what singular unanimity [says Thoreau] the furthest sundered nations and generations consent to give completeness and roundness to an ancient fable.

2

In retrospect, Washington Irving's golden career as a man of letters seems the result of a happy convergence of circumstances: the rapidly growing social and literary life of Manhattan; European fashions of writing; his own alert, plastic mind. Spanning the period between the Revolution and the Civil War (1783–1859), he read successively, as they came from the press, the writings of Burns, Campbell, Byron, Scott, and later, with some misgivings, those strange new books of Emerson, Poe, and Hawthorne! The early nineteenth century romantics, particularly Scott, oriented his taste, as the clubs, periodicals, and theaters of the gay, civilized little city directed his talents toward satire, the essay, the drama, and the short story.

Indulged by parents and innumerable friends as the youngest and most gifted child of a large family, he let himself drift in the pleasant currents of parties, gossip, and tea-table authorship. By his twenty-sixth year he had already composed light verse; a life of Thomas Campbell; essays and biographies for the *Analectic Magazine,* of which he was for a brief period the editor; a dim little volume of dramatic criticism (*The Letters of Jonathan Oldstyle, Gent.,* 1802); a symposium of satiric pieces, in collaboration with his brother William Irving and James K. Paulding (*Salmagundi,* 1807); and that energetic burlesque, *Diedrich Knickerbocker's A History of New York* (1809). This was our first remarkable piece of comic literature. Old New York shook with a roar of laughter.

In these years Irving knew the blessing of a light heart which defied his strain of latent melancholy. Of medium height, with chestnut hair, blue eyes, and a peculiarly pleasant, husky voice, he was friendliness itself; never as a person does he seem more winning than in these casual years when he squired the damsels of New York and Philadelphia, journeyed on a holiday trip to the Canadian frontier, played with the study of law in Judge Hoffman's office, or frolicked with *Salmagundi.* He "makes his travels go far," said his friend Henry Brevoort, alluding to a two years' grand tour of Europe bestowed upon Irving in 1804 by his fond brothers. He had returned still less in love with the family hardware business or with the bar; instead he was enamored of his little vellum notebooks, reminiscent of his wandering and germinal of many a later essay and story. Thus he had become almost the habitual dilettante when in 1809 the remarkable satire by "Diedrich Knickerbocker" (one of Irving's many *noms de plume*) revealed to discerning eyes, among them Scott's, his exceptional powers as a satirist. Yet in this very year occurred the great sorrow of his life, the tragic death of his fiancée, Matilda Hoffman; a period of doubt and uneasiness ensued, accentuated by the uncertainties of his future. During the War of 1812 he served as a staff colonel, and in 1815 he again sailed for Europe: he did not know that he was to remain abroad for seventeen years, or that he would return as "Geoffrey Crayon," the famous author of *The Sketch Book* (1819–1820).

After *Bracebridge Hall* (1822) and *Tales of a Traveller* (1824), and a winter in Dresden, he collaborated unsuccessfully in play writing in Paris with John Howard Payne. In 1826 he was on his way to Madrid to translate, at the request of A. H. Everett, Navarrete's history of Columbus. The following three years, mellowing his natural vein of romance, saw him a scholar in the ancient libraries of Madrid (where Longfellow called on him), a dweller with Andalusian peasants in the courts of the Alhambra, and a friend of the German antiquarian Böhl von Faber, and of his daughter Fernán Caballero, the Spanish novelist of manners. Such a life, seminomadic, was entirely congenial. Nevertheless, in 1829, bowing to his brothers' wishes, he accepted the post of Secretary of the American Legation in London. Three years later he returned to his own commonplace country, but not before he had published or prepared for the press four works memorializing his experience in the Spain of a century ago (*The Life and Voyages of Columbus*, 1828; *The Conquest of Granada*, 1829; *The Companions of Columbus*, 1831; *The Alhambra*, 1832).

For Irving this break with European life and thought was momentous. Though only fifty and at the height of his powers, he returned to an America appreciative of his fame but suspicious of his extended exile abroad and of his truancy to European themes. He now permitted a belated Americanization of all his interests. After a pilgrimage to the wild Southwest, he celebrated the wonders of the Osage frontier and other Western explorations in three elegant volumes for the parlor tables of his countrymen (*A Tour on the Prairies*, 1835; *Astoria*, 1836; *The Adventures of Captain Bonneville*, 1837). He was now the friend of Astor and, some said, his factotum; he dabbled in the stock market; and he was discussed for political posts. Most dismaying, he ceased, so far as we can tell, to read or to write for his craft, and on one occasion he admitted to John Pendleton Kennedy that, like most of his contemporaries, he regarded the creation of literature as merely a gentleman's avocation.

Living on at "Sunnyside," except during the years when he was the popular Minister at the court of Isabella II (1842–1846), he became an arbiter of our letters, a benevolent despot of our writers, a symbol of our thin literary culture. Uncomprehending, he beheld the rise of the great New Englanders and uttered pontifical platitudes on Poe's tales and *The Scarlet Letter*. He himself could only rifle again his old notebooks to produce biographies of Goldsmith, Mahomet, and Washington. His work was long since done; the age in which men read eagerly of the romantic wanderer in Europe already belonged to the past. Yet in the pathos of his decline we must not forget the adoration of Poe and Hawthorne; through Washington Irving, writing as an art had been born in America.

3

On all the historic events occurring within his long life of more than three-quarters of a century Irving sets down in letter or essay shrewd comment; but in his pages we look in vain for sustained wisdom concerning the movements of thought behind such events, for penetration of the intellectual life of his epoch. He wrote graphically of many famous episodes, of Waterloo or of the War with Mexico; but of Anglo-French relations or of American imperialism he has nothing to say worth hearing. He lived in England during the ferment culminating in the Reform Bill; but he merely laments the passing of the stagecoach and the yule-log Christmas. From the unrest in England and the democratic upsurge in America he acquired only a sentimental Toryism. On the meaning of democracy, of sectionalism, of the frontier he offers only pretty paragraphs communicating his personal distaste. He was simply a lover of old ways, of the romantic past.

Likewise, on more spiritual problems Irving was properly silent. His personal religious history includes his childhood with Deacon Irving, a Scotch Covenanter, his rapid progress toward skepticism and indifference, and finally, in the later years at Tarrytown, his identification with the Episcopal Church; the story reflects his natural remoteness from religious introspection. On the turmoil of Unitarianism, transcendèntalism, evangelicalism, he let fall no word; he merely found New Englanders uncongenial, and popular religions vulgar. His notions on current trends of thoughts had their origin not in an analytical mind such as Melville's, nor even in a passionate partisanship such as Cooper's, but in an indolent temperament and an incurably conservative taste.

Irving's first books, *The Letters of Jonathan Oldstyle, Gent.* and *Salmagundi,* are distinguished by little save high spirits. Yet the other "youthful folly," as Irving ruefully called it, *A History of New York,* is still breathing. Prolix, repetitious, and, in consequence, mercilessly revised by Irving for later editions, it boils over with his boisterous ridicule of Swedes and Yankees, Dutch ponderosities, the pedantry of histories, and Jeffersonian democracy. It is written with gusto, on one occasion breaking into blank verse, and with such an avalanche of satiric allusion, from Cervantes and Rabelais to Walter Scott, that the latter's sides ached, so he wrote Irving, from laughing at its fantasy. In particular, the Dutch personalities of Wouter Van Twiller, William Kieft (a cartoon of Jefferson), and Peter Stuyvesant have crept into tradition, painting, and into the imaginations of subsequent generations of readers. The tough old mock epic may live; it proclaimed not only the breadth of Irving's self-cultivation, but also the vigor of mind that underlay his apparent languor.

Even as Irving corrected the proof sheets of his comic history, lovely Matilda Hoffman lay dying. The decade beginning with the publication of Diedrich Knickerbocker's learned indiscretion and ending with the appearance of *The Sketch Book* changed Irving from a callow youngster to a man; he was still amiable, still shrewd, but he was now meditative, a participant in human suffering. "I know," he wrote, "what it is to be sick and lonely in a strange land." As a refuge he turned again to writing. From boyhood he had faithfully kept journals and notebooks, and now, after his arrival in Europe in 1815, he continued to set down the titles of books, quotations, anecdotes, travel incidents, and his moods of depression; in the blurred pencil lines we may read of his unhappiness in the Liverpool office, of his study of German, of his ecstatic hours with Walter Scott: "Ah," he exclaims, "I knew happiness then!" On March 3, 1819, he forwarded to New York the first number of *The Sketch Book*.

"Crayon is very good," remarked Byron. Some even believed that he was Walter Scott. To us halfway through the twentieth century, all the virtues of *The Sketch Book* seem pallid; we can endure but not applaud the unevenness of the thirty-two pieces, the sickly pathos of such an essay as "The Pride of the Village," the naïve records of Irving's travel in England, the appropriation of the familiar legends. This last weakness in particular has attained an unpleasant emphasis in the scholars' discovery that even "Rip Van Winkle" is dependent on a literal translation from a tale in Otmar's *Volkssagen,* and that "The Legend of Sleepy Hollow" has origins in Bürger's *Der wilde Jäger* and one of the Rübezahl tales. Superficially at least, *The Sketch Book* appears to be dated, embalmed beyond all hope of a resurrection.

Yet beneath Irving's insipidities burned one strong response to life, his sadness or romantic melancholy in the presence of the law of change. The underlying idea in all Irving's best essays is that of flux. The old, forgotten books in "The Mutability of Literature"; the silence of the Boar's Head Tavern, once alive with the mirth of Falstaff; the tombs of Queen Elizabeth and Queen Mary; the grave of Shakespeare; the aged Rip Van Winkle— all declare the terrible brevity of life, the transiency of Man. Wistfully, recalling the tragic alterations in his own life, Irving dwells repeatedly in his public and private writing on "the dilapidations of time":

How [he lamented in a notebook] the truth presses home upon us as we advance in life that everything around us is transient and uncertain. . . . We feel it withering at our hearts . . . in the funeral of our friends and written on the wrecks of our hopes & affections—when I look back for a few short years, what changes of all kind have taken place, what wrecks of time and fortune are strewn around me.

Perhaps the gossamer loveliness of these sketches suffers under precise interpretations. Their symbolism is probably unconscious, involuntary; the essays' indefinitiveness of emotion may be felt as we read, but not explained. In "Rip Van Winkle" this connotative meaning is the secret of its hold upon our imaginations; in it are all the implications of the grim but romantic theme of *tempus edax rerum*. In retrospect or in prospect, Rip's free youth, prolonged sleep, fanciful dreams, and disillusioning return are all ours. The fragile piece deserves study for its debt to German literature, to American legend, to Thomas the Rhymer, to Walter Scott, and to Irving's own boyhood; for its arresting adaptation in the theater, in song, or in Spanish or

Russian translation, for its revelation of a great stylist. But its soul lies in the symbolic distillation of a universal mood. All of Irving's literary manipulation of his reading, his wandering life, and his melancholy were concentrated in a passion which made him compose the tale during a single night, pouring into it all that he had ever felt concerning man's ceaseless enemy, "time": the German romance of Otmar, stories heard from the lips of Dutch friends, memories of the shadowy Catskills and of the blue Hudson. However outworn, by familiarity, jest, and parody, "Rip Van Winkle" still belongs to the indestructible literature of all peoples.

The depths of Irving's melancholy were not meant for repetition. As the climax of ten years of uncertainty and bereavement, his sadness had nearly spent itself in "Westminster Abbey" and "Rip Van Winkle." In a sense he had spoken; never again was he to recapture the spiritual tension of these essays, even in the moonlight scenes in "St. Mark's Eve," in *Bracebridge Hall*, or in the reveries of *The Alhambra*. A professional writer, bent on consolidating his reputation, he was now destined to do *The Sketch Book* over and over again, for the most part on its lower levels. After a season as "the most fashionable fellow in London," with Gifford, Rogers, Moore, and Scott as his friends and Byron and Coleridge as his admirers, he became the author of the fifty-one miscellaneous tales and sketches known as *Bracebridge Hall* (1822). "The fault of [this] book," said Maria Edgeworth justly, "is that the workmanship surpasses the work. There is too much care and cost bestowed on petty objects."

4

Meanwhile Irving was exploring the vein which was to link his books with the more macabre studies by Poe and Hawthorne. Long before 1817, when he sat in Scott's library and watched the novelist take down from his shelves his copies of Fouqué, Grimm, Bürger, Tieck, and Hoffman, he had shared the popular passion for what Scott called "the supernatural in fictitious composition." His approach to the tale of horror, despite his laborious study of the German masters, was characteristically light; he was fond of pointing his eerie stories with a question or a whimsical smile. Was the specter bridegroom an actual being? Was not the rumble of the Catskill bowlers a thunderstorm? After all, the head on Brom Bones' saddle was a pumpkin! He understood the practical value of success in this lucrative field, but his interest in the supernatural had causes deeper than those of expediency. Late in life he declared that the essential stuff of his life had been reverie. Dreams he could express in his versions of German romantic tales; these stories of the supernatural fed his restless, playful imagination, and in addition, as in "The Spectre Bridegroom," offered provocative problems for his craftsmanship. It is not surprising to hear of him during the winter following *Bracebridge Hall* writing, so rumor had it, a "German novel."

If so, this novel was never finished, and only one of the four sections of *Tales of a Traveller* (1824) showed directly the harvest of Irving's prolonged curiosity concerning the supernatural, from his youthful days in New York through this unlucky winter in Dresden. Beginning in an intensive study of German language and folklore, this had been expended in Saxon balls, skating parties, boar hunts, and an unhappy love affair with the English girl, Emily Foster. Tenacity of purpose was not the dominant trait in Irving's nature. So the ghost stories and the robber tales, at best marionettes, were supplemented with three other sections, one on Italy (rehabilitated from the notebooks of 1805), "Buckthorne," a shallow, semiautobiographical novelette under the influence of Goethe's *Wilhelm Meister,* and flaccid tales of cabbage-growing Dutchmen and of Captain Kidd. Gothic novelists, German romancers, Italian robber stories, legends of old New York—*Tales of a Traveller* is an empty cave of echoes.

The ensuing Spanish episode was to be far more felicitous than the German. In the Madrid libraries and in the matchless collection of the bibliographer, Obadiah Rich, he lingered long, indulging his love of old books and manuscripts. His original plan of translating Navarrete's history proved difficult; finally he abandoned the translation in favor of his own free dream of the great navigator. *The Life and Voyages of Christopher Columbus* (1828), in its eighteen books and one hundred and twenty-three chapters, is a strange compilation of theatrical personages (Columbus is a "man of sensibility"), pageantry, Gothic thunderstorms, treacherous Spaniards, noble savages, mermaids, seas of milk, and careful documentation. Its tantalizing hesitation between history and romance evidently created in Irving—a natural *colorista* in his treatment of Spanish material—an indecisiveness which reached a culmination in the next year in *The Conquest of Granada,* a book which no critic has ever been able to classify. It translates the chronicles but poetizes episode and character. Professedly the work of an old monk Fray Antonio Agapida, it craved respect as history. Yet the two long volumes are really romances, beautiful in their tone and even in their monotonous, flowing style. That such things never happened, we may be sure. Yet few admirers of Irving would cancel, as part of his total achievement, the lofty, melancholy personages of Columbus and the fair-haired "El Chico," Boabdil, the last Moorish king of Granada.

In *The Alhambra,* Irving's "Spanish Sketch Book" as Prescott christened it, the frail Boabdil reappears, the legendary king living happily in the palace or pausing sadly at *El Suspiro del Moro* for his final glance backward at his "city of delights," *bellissima Granada*. In its pages Irving was more at ease; he was not a scholar nor even a historian, despite his myriad footnotes; he was an antiquarian romantic. Released from a pattern of writing which had never won his complete devotion, he was again the easy student of folk-lore, through the black-letter books he had studied for his histories, through his friendship with Fernán Caballero, and through his intimacy with Andalusian peasants in the palace, Dolores and Mateo Ximénez. So he described in the leisurely fashion of *The Sketch Book* the Court of the Lions and the gallery of Lindaraxa; so he revived the ancient myths of mysterious caverns, buried gold, clashing scimitars, and phantom Moors. History, legend, and the ways of Granada blend in a reverie like those inspired by the dim, blue Catskills. Instead of homespun Dutchmen, paynim cavaliers; instead of the pumpkin, the pomegranate. In the book is the gorgeous tapestry of the Moorish past; such stories as "The Legend of the Arabian Astrologer" in Irving's most civilized manner perpetuate the enduring fascination of opulent, barbaric Spain.

If Irving was, as Robert Southey declared, no man to write of the wars of Granada, it is equally true that his books on the Western frontier, which after his return to America in 1832 he published as a capitulation to popular demand, show the same incapacity to set down facts unadorned by sentiment. H. L. Ellsworth's literal record of adventures in the Oklahoma country, on this same journey, reveals by contrast Irving's prettifying of buffalo, wild horses, and the customs of the Osage Indians. *A Tour on the Prairie* (1835) is a drawing-room version of, to do Irving justice, a rough experience, in which he forded streams on horseback and dined uncomplainingly on skunk. Yet in the waving trees of the forest he saw the Gothic arches of the Europe for which he was still homesick; and as he rode with Ellsworth through the blackjack, he reminisced on his creation of *The Sketch Book*. The glimmering lights of the campers, the picturesque dress of the ranger, the bee hunt, the hostile Indians, the undulating reaches of prairie and forest, he refined into a Europeanized idealization of the wilderness.

Sensing the gentle wave of excitement roused by *A Tour on the Prairie* in readers who had never seen a bison or an Indian, he sat in John Jacob Astor's library, and from the diaries of trappers, authentic writing of the frontier, he spun out in *Astoria* an agreeable epic of the overland journey to the Pacific outpost and the voyage around the Horn of the *Tonquin*. In both *Astoria* and the *Adventures of Captain Bonneville, U.S.A.,* also under the patronage of Astor, he relied upon just the right composite of general reading and citation from original sources, upon velvety narrative, upon that "singular sweetness of composition" which had captivated even the hard-bitten Francis Jeffrey. These frontier narratives were not really history, though scholars quoted from them; nor were they humbug, for compared with the actual events they depicted no dream world; they merely reflected the born romancer exploiting materials which belonged to the historian.

However popular, the Western narratives proclaimed one fact: the famous Washington Irving had written himself out. Surrendering in 1839 to Prescott the great theme of the Spanish conquest of Mexico, he attempted little more until, in 1848, he revised his collected works. He now, as he said, read little, and during the four years in Spain as Minister he did not even keep a notebook. He still loved everything Spanish, even the odor of the kitchens, but his beautiful letters to his nieces concerning the court of Isabella II and Espartero remain the sole record in these years of a talent that had gone to seed. Instead of legend, his thoughts were of politics, gossip, and his return to dear Sunnyside and his nieces. Reestablished there, in the last decade of his life, he wearily replundered the old notebooks until Longfellow, who owed so much to the inspiration of *The Sketch Book,* protested at this deterioration. These articles for the *Knickerbocker,* the miscellanies, such as *Wolfert's Roost,* or the third-rate biographies of Goldsmith and of Mahomet hardly bear analysis; little remained but the worn-out themes and the perfunctory grace of the master's style. Of his decline he was conscious, and just before his death he spurred himself to one last effort; but the five huge volumes of his *Life of Washington* mirror in his tired prose merely a stolid marble bust of the founder of the Republic.

5

More and more in retrospect, Irving emerges as both the beneficiary and the victim of the adolescent American culture of the first three decades of the nineteenth century. In this period he formed standards of literary taste from which, for good and ill, he never afterward deviated. To the pre-Victorian drama (he boasted he had seen every actor of his time), to the periodicals, to contemporary idols (not Addison and Steele, but Byron, Moore, Campbell, and Scott), to literary clubs, to growing libraries and still unexhausted private collections of manuscripts, and to lax copyright laws he was heavily in debt. Although he was occasionally capable, as in the libraries of Spain, of almost monastic devotion to learning, yet constructive thought, such as that of the Concord group, was alien to him. His satire, his short stories, his personal essays, were the easy products of his travel, his life in society, his endless casual jottings in his notebooks. Tirelessly he collected these literary *morceaux;* skillfully he amplified them into story or essay; and tactfully he introduced them into the most apropriate cultural medium—the periodical, the annual, or the timely book. He was a superlative literary adventurer.

This is the first, most obvious Irving, the caterer to public taste, hardly more than the hack writer hand in glove with such eminent publishers or editors as John Murray or Lewis Gaylord Clark; this is the Irving cannily alert to fluctuations in literary fashions and sales. Yet from such habits of mind, evident to readers of his self-revealing correspondence with Murray concerning the *Columbus,* developed a second Irving, the man of affairs, the successful American, the substantial citizen of New York (mentioned as candidate for the mayoralty), the grandee of Sunnyside, the Minister to Spain. From the days of Aaron Burr, Irving had hated the sweaty nightcaps of the mob; his Tory soul shrank before Jacksonian democracy. Yet if not openly on the political stage he remained in the wings of this theater. The same disarming tact, the same shrewdness, the same comprehension of public opinion so influential in his literary career, did not harm him in this related role of the observer of American life. These two careers were intimately joined. The America of the forties loved to canonize its literary men, such as a Bryant or an Irving—and so destroy them as poets or essayists. Literary fame might mean public eminence and, turn about, public distinction might enhance literary reputation.

Yet still another Irving—there were really three—commanded the homage of younger American writers who resisted more effectually than he the corrupting influences in our callow culture. If Hawthorne and Poe beheld in their inspirer a journeyman or political meddler, they never said so; in Irving's *Sketch Book* and even in his trifles they perceived the penetrating observer, and his aspirations and his craftsmanship as an artist. This Irving they revered. This Irving wrote tolerable verse and sketched so well that for days in Rome Washington Allston pleaded with him to turn painter. This Irving's notebooks blossomed with delicate sketches; his writing was deeply in debt to this related art; the pictorial quality of his prose is evident both in its metaphors of the brush and in its transference into the drawings of Leslie, Darley, and others, and into the weird beauty of John Quidor's paintings, from "Rip Van Winkle" to "Wolfert's Roost." For this nobler Irving, no self-imposed discipline for the sake of the image or sentence was, as the notebooks prove, too arduous. Ceaselessly he rewrote; indefatigably he revised; his was, in his best moments, the happy, blessed labor of the true artist.

19. JAMES FENIMORE COOPER

M<small>EANWHILE</small>, James Fenimore Cooper, a tyro in the more subtle aims of the novel, assumed in the history of our literature an almost giant stature. More casual than Irving toward literary craftsmanship, he triumphed by his interpretation of romantic and realistic life on the frontiers of the forest and the sea, of the development of democracy, and of the meaning of America. A man of action whose career as a novelist was superficially an accident, in him genius was "mainly an affair of energy." In preface, pamphlet, history, and novel he poured out his convictions concerning his era, employing to the full, like Irving, all (except the theater) of the new instruments of culture. Cooper's was not properly a "literary" spirit; he was Agamemnon at a desk (and in the fray, too). Yet his genius left some thirty novels, several volumes of enduring social criticism, and two or three immortal characters. The resiliency of his masculine mind defied in his time devastating attacks from his critics; and his vitality is still contagious. As we read, we breathe the air of ocean and primeval lake; we hear the crack of Leatherstocking's rifle. Not only is Cooper an indispensable critic of growing, bumbling democracy, but a golden story-teller, the creator of our own Arabian Nights of the frontier.

Born in Burlington, New Jersey, on September 15, 1789, of English, Swedish, and Quaker antecedents, he enjoyed a vigorous youth in his father's village, Cooperstown, New York, not far from the edge of the eighteenth century frontier. Here he learned, from the example of Judge Cooper, to restore the traditional right of property to the Revolutionary prerogatives: life, liberty, and the pursuit of happiness. After two years at Yale College, from which he was dismissed for some obscure disciplinary reason, after serving as a midshipman in the United States Navy, after his marriage in 1811 into the family of the aristocratic Westchester De Lanceys, he began, virtually on a wager, his career of the man of action turned fiction writer. His rise to fame seems incredible. Within four years he had written four novels that placed his name second in popularity at home and abroad to that of the author of *Waverley*.

After these preliminaries, after his first fame in literary New York, after the incomparable *Last of the Mohicans,* we may follow him for seven years through England, France, Switzerland, and Italy. His was now a triple role: the cultivated American, with his family, in quest of the traditional experiences of European life; the distinguished author consorting in London and Paris with other notables; and the aroused critic of political and social institutions abroad and, indirectly, at home. Hazlitt saw him "strutting" down the streets of Paris; he was, in contrast to Irving whom he already despised, an unabashed observer in this older civilization.

Before Cooper returned to America in 1833, he had found time, besides aiding Lafayette in the French budget controversy and composing his invaluable commentaries on Europe and a defense of America against the attacks of foreign critics, to publish seven novels, of which three concerned the past of Europe, two the life of the sea, and two that of the frontier. Human energy could hardly do more. When Cooper, refusing an invitation to a dinner of welcome by his countrymen, set foot again on American soil, he was alive with a critical spirit which was to mold his career in America until his death in 1851. His was to be a boundless and often misdirected fervor. For eighteen years he instructed his unwilling countrymen through preface, novel, and libel suit; he lived his full life as country squire and critic of democracy; and he gave to the world his flow of novels. At virtually the height of his powers he died, his personal unpopularity obscuring his brilliance as a romancer of wilderness and sea.

2

An orderly and chronological or a sharp and topical classification of Cooper's writings is almost impossible. He had begun, after his unsuccessful novel *Precaution* (1820), modeled upon Jane Austen or Mrs. Opie, with three types of American subject (the Revolution, the frontier, and the sea); these themes he was to discuss throughout his life. Almost simultaneously he had begun in *Notions of the Americans* (1828) that downright defense of American life which was to animate *A Letter to His Countrymen* (1834) and his many prefaces and articles. In particular, his first frontier novel, *The Pioneers* (1823), explored the subject in which his genius was to find its noblest expression; it began the Leatherstocking series. The five novels in this series were composed over a period of eighteen years, and their chronology, in reference to the prolonged life story of Leatherstocking, is at variance with the order of composition and publication. At the same time the Revolution, the frontier, and the sea crossed and recrossed one another in these and other tales; and through them all crackled the fire of Cooper's criticism of America.

One fact is clear, a by-product of the truism that Cooper's writings are a paradise for the intellectual historian: he cared little for literature as litera-ture. For him, writing was primarily an implement for his convictions about America. Some of his ideas, such as those concerning the Navy or the antirent laws, are as obsolete as those in Melville's *White Jacket or Mardi*; but others anticipate the persistent problems of democracy which now meet our troubled eyes in the newspapers. We should be aware of those which recur: his belief in the moral quality of liberty; his nationalism; his conviction that an aris-tocracy of worth was not inconsistent with the democratic ideal; his notion that native human character received its most valid self-expression in Amer-ica; and his concept of the relation of all these ideas to the natural world of forest and sea. With infinite variation in detail these great themes reappear in all his books.

Thus in Cooper's writings we may see America in the early stages of introspection and self-evaluation, America trying to explain its origins and growth and to prefigure its far-off future, and America struggling for a commensurate cultural independence. In his novels and tracts may be found the optimism and fatalism of the frontier, the growth of class-consciousness, the beginnings of imperialism, the stubborn resistance of property-ownership, and a hundred other battles of a century ago. The desire to record these drove Cooper to his pen instead of to the forum; through writing he hoped to resolve these elements into some kind of unity. Having become an author, he was subject to literary influences, but his fundamental conception of writing is suggested in his statement in 1837:

It is high time not only for the respectability but for the safety of the American people, that they should promulgate a set of principles that are more in harmony with their facts.

Nevertheless he can never be dismissed as a social novelist. Despite his "literary offences," as Mark Twain called them, he stands with Dumas and Scott as one of the great romancers of all time. Thackeray, for example, paid tribute to his heroes:

Leatherstocking, Uncas, Hardheart, Tom Coffin, are quite the equals of Scott's men; perhaps Leatherstocking is better than anyone in "Scott's lot." *La Longue Carabine* is one of the great prizemen of fiction. He ranks with our Uncle Toby, Sir Roger de Coverley, Falstaff—heroic figures, all—American or British, and the artist has deserved well of his country who devised them.

Here is a puzzle: the contrast between these "great prizemen" and Cooper's own disregard of his famous novels, at which he was accustomed to laugh as "light literature." His attitude toward such fiction was, of course, typical of an era which considered writing a medium for saying what had to be said; even Irving came to believe that he must not take belles-lettres too seriously. Most of our early nineteenth century men of letters disdained, at least outwardly, the aims of the "artist."

Yet Thackeray uses this very word, and not too hastily or too flexibly. If we turn to Cooper's letters or his prefaces we shall find only simple literary principles, such as a story-teller's right to take a poetical view of his subject, or the novelist's definitions of types. Such do not seem, in the deepest sense, to be the reflections of an artist. Yet their simplicity is misleading. The fact is that Cooper cherished unconsciously an allegiance to the traditions of English fiction, precisely as he felt a deep but unanalytical devotion, especially in later life, to one of the traditional churches. We should reconsider his associations with writing not immediately concerned with "American opinions" or "American things."

Such a reexamination discovers in his reading the positive, somewhat naïve tastes which adorned his living. Certain economists and geologists he studied meticulously; he did first-hand historical research for both his fiction and his nonfiction; and he was steeped in Shakespeare. Yet deep literary intimacy, comparable to Hawthorne's understanding of Milton, is absent. His critical opinions were violent, impressionistic; throughout his letters we encounter few penetrative judgments on books, and though there is real dependence on the substance of literature, extremely few allusions occur, except for the poetic captions of his chapters. In his youth he read the lucid poetry of the eighteenth century (Pope, Gray, and Thomson); and he afterward shifted to such popular narrators in verse as Byron, Scott, and Long-fellow. We do not need his sarcasms to learn what he thought of the more introspective nineteenth century poets. Shakespeare he held dear, but the writing of other Elizabethans had for him little meaning. Verse of intellectual weight bored him; he was fond of saying that Shakespeare should have written *Paradise Lost*!

Whenever the broader philosophic thought of Shakespeare or Scott touched his own simple code of living, he approved; but he was evidently less moved by such wisdom than by the power of the well told story. Here was a gift which, though he never says so precisely, must have stirred him deeply, like the bold art of historical or biographical narration. Such vital creation was worth a man's attention. Let us not be deceived by the petulance uttered not long before he composed *Precaution:* "much as I dislike writing in general." In the prefaces he sets down theories on the technique of narration. In such matters he was interested.

Thus by reading and by temperament Cooper acquired a devotion to a leading art form of the nineteenth century; namely, narrative. No definition

of his work is just without recognition of this interest, however incomplete
he was in the exposition of his theories. Perhaps this representation of action
was an escape; certainly his study of it as an art form was amateurish; but
his intuitional grasp of its methods was impressive. His love of books centered in the depiction of moving events and large natural emotion. His
writing, says his daughter Susan,

was simply the outpouring of his own nature, the expression of his own inmost
train of thought, the current of real feeling in his own breast.

Had not his early experiments in verse revealed his incapacity for rhyme,
he might well have attempted narratives like Byron's, for poetic feeling, as
Balzac pointed out, was a strong element in his mental constitution. Since
he loved narrative, he drew his literary life from the English novel. He
swallowed it whole, with all its vices, devoting himself to its main purposes
of eventful record and broad characterization.

For like reasons he admired the basic characteristics of the English novel
form: realistic action, unrefined psychology or character, luxurious description, comfortable denouements, and the use of all these elements for the
communication of social ideas. This last function of the English novel, which
enjoyed such vogue in the first decades of the century, he emphasized, often
to the detriment of his literary reputation. His great original contribution
was the theme of the frontier, but this he adapted to the standard concepts
of the novel form, concerning which he harbored no misgivings. Rebellion
and criticism he reserved for the affairs of his country. In the movements
which prophesied the break-up of the novel form or in those which strove
for an American literary independence he showed no interest whatever:

It is quite obvious [he remarked] that, so far as tastes and forms alone are
concerned, the literature of England and that of America must be fashioned after
the same models. . . . The only peculiarity that can, or ought to be expected in
their [the Americans'] literature is that which is connected with the promulgation
of their distinctive political opinions.

Accepting, with a surprising docility, a form later used by Hawthorne
and Melville, Cooper made the most of its time-honored conventions. With a
heavy, humorless style, often drawn into a terrible prolixity, he repeated in
novel after novel all the threadbare formulas. He exploited heroic action in
battle or single combat; he described secret escape and breathless pursuit;
he played with disguises and rejoiced in true love rewarded. So objective
was he, so fixed in purpose, so lacking in self-criticism, that he never foresaw
how absurd his subservience might appear to later writers, so ridiculous,

indeed, that he became a target for satire not to the intellectuals of New England but to other frontier writers such as Mark Twain and Bret Harte. He romanticized famous personages such as Washington or John Paul Jones, and for characters he often created bright-uniformed officers and high-bred maidens, strange blends of musical comedy and convent. In contrast to the natural conversation of his best characters, he frequently penned a dialogue so artificial that we read it with suppressed laughter; such diction represents not life but only the false taste of the novel readers of his generation. Everything suggests his obtuseness to what was happening in the craftsmanship of the novel.

3

Cooper's literary career, beginning with *Precaution* in 1820 and ending in 1850 with *The Ways of the Hour,* covers a period of thirty years during which he issued more than fifty books and pamphlets, exclusive of his articles and communications in periodicals. The main line of his development is difficult to trace; and in it Cooper himself had no interest. He obeyed merely his changing impulses to write on European subjects, on the bad manners of the Americans, on the United States Navy, or on frontier themes to which, had he been more sensitive to the true meaning of his genius, he would perhaps have wholly consecrated his unique powers. For convenience we may let chronology furnish us with an artificial division into three periods. The first includes Cooper's venture into fiction in his thirty-first year, his sudden triumph in his historical novel of the Revolution. *The Spy,* his comparative failure with a similar subject in *Lionel Lincoln,* and his success in special historical material of two distinct kinds—the sea and the frontier.

The second period, which includes the journey to Europe (1826–1833), beginning with *The Prairie* in 1827 and ending, according to our arbitrary division, with *The Deerslayer* (1841), consummates the novelist's richest, most varied performance. From his thirty-fourth to his fiftieth year he bestowed upon his puzzled countrymen his travel sketches, his social criticism, his satirical and allegorical novels, his romances of Europe, additional sea tales, and the three supplementary volumes of the Leatherstocking series. In the third period, which equates the last decade of his life, he played, with strength but with less inspiration, on the now familiar themes. Surveyed in this broad fashion, the three periods tell a fascinating story of his alternate blindness and vision in the creation of fiction.

Cooper's uncritical dependence upon the traditions of the English novel is evident not merely in his first novel, *Precaution* (1820), but in his second, *The Spy* (1821), in which the conventional patterns of mysterious disguise, the near-supernatural, sensibility, realistic comedy, and the mercurial rise and fall of human fortunes in chase or battle create all the surface faults and virtues of this version of a Revolutionary legend. The differences between *The Spy* and its feeble predecessor are real enough, but less so than some critics lacking the courage to finish *Precaution* have admitted. In both novels is the same Cooper, trying an increasingly deft hand at the tricks of story-telling. What delight must have filled his energetic mind as he found in the tale of "neutral ground" opportunities to use the devices culled from his wholesome but unprofessional habits of reading! Halfway through the composition of *The Spy* he must have known himself for a master of his new trade; likewise he must have realized that he had stumbled on themes suited to his unique powers.

One of these themes, invisible in *Precaution,* we may call, for want of a better name, patriotism. Often clumsily handled in *The Spy,* as in his anxious justice to the loyalists as opposed to the predatory skinners, or in his too composed, too benevolent "Mr. Harper"—George Washington transformed into a kind of fairy-godmother—this is basically a profound, almost religious emotion concerning the destiny of America. This feeling he was to express in many different ways, from the petulance of *Home as Found* to the sublimity of certain scenes in *The Prairie.* The feeling seems at best a tenuous, inconclusive weapon for a novelist, but it served Cooper well; indeed, it sheds today a glory on his writings. His meaning is inadequately conveyed in the starched words of Washington, as, at the end of *The Spy,* this Olympian figure attempts vainly to reward Harvey Birch for his unrecognized loyalty:

That Providence destines this country to some great and glorious fate I must believe, while I witness the patriotism that pervades the bosoms of her lowest citizens.

We smile and rephrase the sentiment for ourselves; yet there remains the sincerity of Cooper's emotion. Consistently throughout his life it led him to expound and defend a Platonic theory of democratic society which, he felt, Europe needed and America did not appreciate.

Less nebulous, but equally suggestive of directions in Cooper's development, is his mastery in *The Spy* of native background; his powers of observation were remarkable. Intimate friends stressed this gift, now suddenly so apparent in these splendid scenes of the river country in autumn. Whenever Cooper's eyes fell on forest or stream he saw much; such details of nature he recombined endlessly for the settings of his novels. Thus the picturesque haunts of Harvey Birch on hillside or in mountain cavern are almost as fascinating as the spy himself.

In this portrait of the peddler-patriot we apprehend another talent of Cooper's, dim in *Precaution* and, like his intuitional sense of America, only intermittently revealed in, for example, Magua, Chingachgook, Leatherstock-ing—or now, in Harvey Birch. This talent is his capacity for creating truly original and *natural* character. So beset is Harvey by lay figures, such as the bewildered Mr. Wharton or the "lovely maniac" Sarah, that we are likely to lose sight of the unique qualities in the spy himself. This special insight of Cooper's is evident in Harvey, rather than in the tedious Smollettesque echo Dr. Sitgreaves, or even in the robust Betty Flannagan, who excited the admira-tion of Maria Edgeworth. In fact, Harvey Birch is not imitative at all, except in his incidental resemblance to the Yankee peddler type. Daringly conceived, inviting the contempt of his readers by his avarice, timidity, and meanness, he wins them in the end by the selflessness with which he faces his leader and his God. On this legend of the mysterious patriot who served Washington directly as a spy Cooper first employed that understanding which found fulfillment later in another conception, that of Leatherstocking. Thus he early revealed his comprehension of such natural men; Harvey Birch transcends the conventional formulas which control the hundreds of manikins in his novels.

It is characteristic of Cooper's experimental temper in this early period and also of his restless energy that, instead of following this successful historical novel of the Revolution with others like it, he essays in *The Pioneers* (1823) a fresh approach to American subjects. Conscious perhaps of his newly dis-covered skill in narrative, he now tells a negligent tale of Oliver Edwards and Elizabeth Temple, and of their union after the heroine is rescued from a forest fire by her lover who is finally revealed as the grandson of old Major Effingham. Jejune devices reappear, but Cooper's interest now centers on a reproduction of the frontier settlement in Otsego County, so dear to him in his youth. In an illuminating preface, written seventeen years after the first publication of *The Pioneers,* he reveals a conflict in his mind, still unresolved prior to the Leatherstocking tales. On the one hand, he is attracted by the imaginative creation of character, as in a Harvey Birch, and, on the other, by a literal accuracy tempting him in this novel to set down a true record of the life and environment of Judge Marmaduke Temple:

This rigid adherence to truth [he admits], an indispensable requisite in history and travels, destroys the charm of fiction; for all that it is necessary to be conveyed to the mind by the latter had better be done by the delineation of principles, and of characters in their classes, than by a too fastidious attention to originals.

Such in 1823 was Cooper's uncertainty; from it resulted a compromise between a dependable record of his own father's life-history on the New York frontier, and a romance destined to be third in fictional chronology in the series of five great novels dedicated to the life of the forest. Yet he had hit it at last. He had implemented his patriotism, his descriptive power, and his exploration of human character (apart from his innumerable conventional figures); he had begun his long task of memorializing the American frontier experience. Dreamlike indeed, even with their basis of fact, were the clearings of the Otsego settlement, and heroic was the gaunt, angular Leatherstocking in his middle age. Yet these were living places and persons; at least their prototypes had lived in the past. Cooper hoped, as he said later, to show them without "too fastidious attention to originals" and "by the delineation of principles," that is, by the full sweep of his imagination. If he could do this, he would re-create one of the poetic yet essentially true experiences of developing America. He was adjusting his realism and romance in the treatment of native themes. He now trod the actual frontier and there brought to life one authentic inhabitant, a human being susceptible of continuous growth in his imaginative re-creation of the wilderness.

During this same year he had written and published *The Pilot,* a further capitalization of his own experiences. It is easy to attribute the novels of this period to minor incidents: *Precaution* to his annoyance at a weak English novel; *The Spy* to a tale told him by the brother of Mr. Jay; or *The Pilot* to a dinner party at which was discussed the nautical inadequacy of Scott's *The Pirate.* The causes lay deeper. His first novel of the sea was a consequence of his intense interest in the two frontiers; the sea and the wilderness, the water and the forest, were always intimately associated in his mind—witness, in particular, the aqueous quality of *The Pathfinder.*

In *The Pilot* (1823) we may disregard the complicated plot: the love affairs of the lieutenants Barnstable and Griffith with Cecilia Howard and Katherine Plowden, the nieces of the loyalist Colonel Howard; the schemes and ghastly death of the villainous Christopher Dillon; the usual soufflé of escapes, rescues, and pursuits. With variations, such are always staples in Cooper's novels. Beneath the veneer rests the solid oak of *The Pilot*: the passage of the straits by the schooner in the storm; the battle between the frigate and the British man-of-war; and the accurate transcripts of life on the ocean during the Revolution. Cooper's novels of the sea have more authenticity than those of the frontier; he never knew well an Indian warrior. His two years in the Navy, apart from his reading in the sea tales of Smollett and Marryat, enabled him to write with precision of sheet, jib, and compass. The sailors' dread of the land, their love of the open water, their management of schooner and frigate make *The Pilot* an event in the history of the novel of the sea.

Cooper's growth toward the mastery of his "art" is evident not only in this wider frontier of the Atlantic, but in two characters. The pilot himself, a favorite of our school days, is the second in Cooper's gallery of fictionized historic figures. This misty representation of John Paul Jones reminds us of the earlier portrait of George Washington; Cooper never learned that dimness of outline and an aura of mystery did not in themselves create a heroic character. In this man without a country he attempts a tragic hero; instead he achieves a Byronic ghost, a man with secret sorrows, darkened brow, mysterious devotions, and almost comic mannerisms. From our first sight of him in his "calmness bordering on the supernatural" until he waves adieu wearing "a smile of bitter resignation" he is as vague as his platitudes on liberty, of which Cooper evidently hoped to persuade us he was the ardent defender.

Long Tom Coffin is otherwise. He is as real as the *Ariel* itself, whose first timbers he saw laid and whose death he shared. Tom's every salty word, every vigorous action with cannon or harpoon, every simple feeling, reveal these perceptions demonstrated by his creator in Harvey Birch and Leatherstocking; himself a sailor and a man, Cooper could delineate a man of the sea. We welcome Long Tom's entrances as we dread uneasily those of the Gothic pilot, and his death (surely a mistake if we consider the possibilities for him in later sea novels of Cooper's) is closer to our human sympathies than that of Captain Ahab, in Melville's greater novel. Brief as is Long Tom's literary life, he ranks with Leatherstocking.

Presumably we must attribute the unevenness of Cooper's novels to the sluggishness of his self-critical faculty. Such disparities are almost ludicrous in the last two novels published before his journey abroad, that is, the final two in the first period of his writing and the fifth and sixth in his swiftly moving career as a novelist. Few if any novels in his later work, and relatively few from the pens of other writers, have equaled in pompous dullness *Lionel Lincoln* (1824–1825), a well informed but preposterous melodrama told against an oddly contrasting background of Boston on the eve of the Revolution. No character in the novel makes common sense—neither the priggish hero, nor the mysterious father, nor "Ralph," nor the hideous, unconvincing Mrs. Lechmere. *Lionel Lincoln* is a harlequinade of absurd scenes unredeemed save by the two or three battle pieces. Momentarily Cooper throws over us his old spell as the embattled farmers drive the redcoats down the Lexington road or as they release their sheet of fire from the crest of Bunker Hill. Yet such flickers of life are hardly to be mentioned except as hints of the unfaltering genius of the sixth volume, the second in order of publication of the Leatherstocking series, *The Last of the Mohicans* (1826). Here at last was mastery; more profound studies of his great frontiersmen were to come, but never was Cooper, now thirty-five years old, to attain such unerring control over the only technique of art which really interested him; never was he to tell another story with more triumphant suspense.

For many—and this represents one real level in the book—*The Last of the Mohicans* is a breathless, unrelenting chase, unbroken save when Alice and Cora are captured by Magua, and Leatherstocking, Uncas, and Duncan Hayward, thus far the pursued, become the pursuers. Who does not, like Mark Twain, discern extravagances in the plot? Yet the pauses between the climactic rifle shots of "La Longue Carabine" are so brief; the moments of security, so insecure; the very rustle of the leaves in the red man's forest, so ominous that the reader has no peace—nor desires it. This acceleration of event is a convincing indication of the novelist's development: gone is the jerky Cooper, backing and filling between tense incident and dreary moralizing. In this novel too there is time for frontier wisdom, but from the bitter struggle of Hayward and the Indian on the rock until the deaths of Uncas and Magua, action is all!

To this unflagging suspense *The Last of the Mohicans* probably owes its universal fame and its innumerable translations into foreign languages. The student of Cooper will also observe his skill in showing the civilization of the white man through the eyes of the Indians and through the mind of the partly Indianized Leatherstocking. In *The Pioneers* we have glimpses of the wilderness; in *The Last of the Mohicans* we live there. In this novel Cooper is less interested in the trapper than in the Indian, and the latter he counterpoises not so much against his enemies, the whites, as against other types of his own race. The noble young brave Uncas, his father, the honorable chieftain Chingachgook, the treacherous Magua, the venerable patriarch Tamenund—all such commemorate Cooper's first sustained exploration of the Indian's soul. In no other of his novels do we live so intimately with the folk ways of the red man and appreciate so sharply the inevitable conflict of those ways with encroaching civilization.

Aside from their value as studies of the Indian character, in whose depiction Cooper has been so maligned and eulogized, Uncas and Magua epitomize fairly the virtues and vices which Cooper thought worthy of portrayal in human nature: in the former, loyalty, unselfish love, and kindness; in the latter, treachery, hatred, and cruelty; in both, bravery, endurance, and intelligence. Cooper had never seen such Indians, but he had known, with modifications, such men. Intensifying and magnifying these human traits, he placed them in their frontier setting; authentic, Uncas and Magua retain permanent places in the history of fiction. As for Leatherstocking, he has grown younger since his somewhat grumpy role in *The Pioneers*. Wise counselor of the forest, chivalrous protector of women, ruthless enemy, provocative if by no means succinct philosopher, he has now reached full stature, although he is to be younger and more adventurous fifteen years later in *The Deerslayer*.

4

The appearance in the next two years in our second period of two strongly contrasted novels of respectively the sea and the prairie (on which Cooper never laid eyes) is an illustration of the vigor of his imagination. The *Red Rover* (1828) offers a magnificent drama of sailing ships in combat on the vast ocean; *The Prairie* (1827), though not deficient in incident, breathes upon us the peace of Nature and of Leatherstocking's old age and death. The story of the seaman in the Royal Navy who killed an officer and became the notorious pirate, but who loved America, flags and ends in the usual revelations of mistaken identities; the antics of Fid and Scipio Africanus cannot excuse its conventional episodes. Only the storm—perhaps the most titanic in all Cooper's writings—survives, the storm in which the *Royal Caroline* is beaten to a naked hulk.

More slow-moving than *The Last of the Mohicans, The Prairie* tells an adventurous tale in which a kidnaping, a buffalo stampede, and a prairie fire cannot divert our interest from Cooper's powerful conception of the immigrant family of Ishmael and Esther Bush and their sons. These squatters, the villainous Sioux, Mahtoree, or the benevolent Pawnee, Hard-Heart, are subordinate to the noble delineation of Leatherstocking, which, Cooper honestly believed, was to be the last glimpse of his frontier hero. This book, he wrote—not divining the future—

closes the career of Leatherstocking. Pressed upon by time, he has ceased to be the hunter and the warrior, and has become a trapper of the great West. The sound of the axe has driven him from his beloved forests to seek a refuge . . . on the denuded plains that stretch to the Rocky Mountains.

Enfeebled in arm but not in mind, Natty is still the "philosopher of the wilderness"; he dies as he has lived, serenely, calling out to his Maker, "Here."

Although in this period Cooper published ten more novels, all save the two which recalled Natty from his grave on the prairie (*The Pathfinder*, 1840; *The Deerslayer*, 1841) were marred by that pedestrianism which was so characteristic of him when absorbed by some general aspect of tradition or afflicted by his heavy enthusiasm for reforming his countrymen. Thus *The Wept of Wish-ton-Wish* (1829), clumsily aiming to "perpetuate the recollection of some of the practices and events peculiar to the early days of our history," is a melodrama of King Philip's War enacted against a superficial background of Puritan Connecticut; Cooper alluded to these New Englanders' "very quaint and peculiar dogmas." He was more at home but not more convincing in *The Water-Witch* (1830), set in New York in the same century; instead of the assault on the blockhouse of the previous novel, he offered the pursuit of the pirate, "The Skimmer of the Seas." This book he wrote in Italy, while, with his fatal fertility, he was already at work on a series of three novels with European themes. This trilogy *(The Bravo, The Heidenmauer, The Headsman)* attempted to meet Scott on his own ground, by portraying European society as it would appear to an enlightened American, liberalized by his intimacy with democracy.

Some savage attacks from American newspapers on *The Bravo* crystallized his latent intention: in 1834, he published his vituperative *A Letter to His Countrymen,* in which he assailed these criticisms and prematurely announced his retirement as a novelist. He now embarked upon that fierce warfare of preface, satire, and libel suit which makes the reappearance of Leatherstocking nearly a miracle. His anger found expression in an experiment in allegory, *The Monikins* (1835), and in two complementary novels *Homeward Bound* and *Home as Found* (1838). These latter are ambitious efforts to portray contemporary American manners; the first, spiced with the usual chase and battles, shows a group of cultivated Americans returning to their country in company with less estimable members of society; the second examines American social life in town and country. Cooper's success is debatable; the elegant Effingham brothers, who represent his conceptions of the American gentleman, are as unnatural as his caricatures of our clodhoppers, Mr. Steadfast Dodge and Aristabulus Bragg. Through such charcoal sketches Cooper solidified the growing enmity of his countrymen, earned the nickname of Effingham, became involved in the famous "Effingham" libel suits, and seemed to justify his irritable decision (to which he did not adhere) that he would write no more fiction. Yet in *Homeward Bound* and *Home as Found* he bequeathed to historians sovereign documents of the social issues of the day.

About the year 1840 he had reached the peak of his activity, not only in his quarrels with his countrymen, but in his power over the written word. Since his return to America he had published, besides the works already described, four volumes on his life in Europe, his political primer for his countrymen *The American Democrat* (1838), various reviews, the pioneer history of the American Navy (1839), a masterpiece of tediousness *(Mercedes of Castile)* in the form of a novel on Columbus; and in a demonstration of the fertility of his genius, he completed the Leatherstocking series with *The Pathfinder* (1840) and *The Deerslayer* (1841). These two novels were the immortal answer, had his angry contemporaries only realized it, to all denunciations of Cooper as a man and writer. Once again he moved freely amid forest and lake; forgotten were the self-conscious allusions to his own experiences (as in *Home as Found*), and even the moralizing, which he could never entirely abandon, took on dignity from Leatherstocking's life in the wilderness. Again, all is action; and once more we share his beautiful insight into simple, strong characters, so amazing after the grotesque portraits of the Effinghams.

The Pathfinder is absorbing for its union of the two themes most natural to Cooper in fiction—adventure in the forest and adventure on the water; and in this novel the water is an inland lake, enriching the beautiful panorama of the Ontario frontier. Moreover, he obtains a secondary contrast in Cap, the salt-water sailor, watching with reluctant admiration the exploits of young Jasper Western, the fresh-water pilot of the *Scud*. No other frontier novel of Cooper's attains the variety of episode of *The Pathfinder*; even the standard blockhouse scene is pleasantly off-pattern through the character of the Indian woman, Dew-of-June; and there are no mistaken identities! Only the suspicion concerning Jasper, with his final vindication, reminds us of Cooper's stock artifices. The great central character of the series is in his prime now, like his creator; and the woods are his sanctuary as well as his battleground. Cooper wishes us to feel the deepening influence of the frontier upon this natural man, this true democrat living simply with other men. Possibly some of Cooper's own Quaker heritage enters into the scout's relations with God and Man. Leatherstocking is capable of grief in the loss of Mabel Dunham. Yet Cooper's blessing lies on the idyllic happiness of Mabel and Jasper; united at last, the lovers bid the scout farewell:

A tread whose vigour no sorrow could enfeeble soon bore him out of view, and he was lost in the depths of the forest.

Thus at this apex of Cooper's intellectual and emotional powers, sustained in *The Deerslayer,* we may observe not only his control over his material—stock characters are few in this final novel of the series—but also his deeper intuitions concerning the moral nature of the scout. In renouncing Mabel Dunham (in *The Pathfinder*), he dedicates his life to the meditative moods of the forest, and because of his conviction, already latent in *The Deerslayer,* the love of Judith Hutter finds him unresponsive. Younger now, if we follow the chronology of Leatherstocking's spiritual development, the affair prepares us for his unwillingness to wed Mabel. In his increasing imaginative grasp on the character, Cooper emphasizes Deerslayer's essential loneliness and his kinship with the forces of nature. Thus he now depicts him in its early years, the brother-in-arms of Chingachgook, taking human life for the first time and acting with youthful energy and intensity. We thrill at the fight for Tom Hutter's "castle" or mourn for the death of Hetty or shudder as Deerslayer awaits the torture; but in this culminating novel we perceive, in particular, Cooper's preoccupation with the spiritual meanings of his immortal character.

5

In *The Deerslayer* Cooper had, unaware of the precise nature of his post-humous fame, made his ultimate bid for immortality through enduring works of fiction. Nevertheless, in the dozen or so novels which were to follow, in our third period, from *The Two Admirals,* in April, 1842, until *The Ways of the Hour,* published in 1850, a year before his death, he retained his zest for narrative. Moreover, in the trilogy of antirent novels, the Littlepage Manu-scripts, he reached the zenith of another talent; he became the acute social observer. Thus there occurred no real decline of his innate force as a writer, but only, according to the laws of advancing years, a hardening of prejudices, a narrowing of opinions, and insulation from the new generation in the America he loved so dearly. It is pointless to enumerate the topics which clogged more and more his narratives and aroused his didacticism as his social vision was dissipated into concern for particular and sometimes petty causes: revelation and reason in *Wing and Wing*; Dutch and English land grants in *Wyandotté, Afloat and Ashore,* and *Miles Wallingford*; Christian conversion in *The Oak Openings*; or trinitarianism, against the odd Arctic backgrounds in *The Sea Lions.* Religion, as he himself drew more closely to its supports, and social injustice, as he realized its persistence, were now perpetually the subjects of his lectures to his readers, but his other obsessions were infinite: the Yankees, English pronunciation, or the Bay of Naples. Yet if to these crotchets we oppose a patience unknown to their possessor we may, in such a novel of adventure as *Jack Tier* (1848), learn much concerning Cooper's mind. In *The Two Admirals* (1842) the maneuverings, not this time of single ships, as in *The Pilot* and *The Rover,* but of fleets, make engaging episodes; and, despite the theology and the ever present villainous Yankee Ithuel Bolt, Cooper's complacence about *Wing and Wing,* which appeared only a few months later, is pardonable. Against a blue and gold Mediterranean back-ground, this tale of a privateer and an English frigate is enthralling—more so, indeed, than the standard blockhouse siege in *Wyandotté.* In contrast to Hawthorne, who distilled his study of Puritanism into delicately balanced interrogations, Cooper's exposition of the ideology he detested is opinionated and superficial, though hardly more so than his favorable delineation, in the same novel, of Anglicanism.

It is on his mature mastery of an impartial approach to social history in the guise of fiction that the distinction of his next two novels rests. Published within a year, told in the first person as the recollections of their hero, and relating a continuous story, *Afloat and Ashore* and *Miles Wallingford* are really one novel. The first part is in Cooper's best narrative manner, the action on the sea equaling in suspense that of *The Pilot* or *The Red Rover,* and throughout both parts we take pleasure in Cooper's own autobiography (for the lovely Lucy is assuredly Susan De Lancey, and Miles is Fenimore Cooper). Yet apart from an undeniable subacidity of manner, the two novels are remarkable for their temperate portrayal of eighteenth century life in orchards, meadows, fields, river valleys, and substantial buildings of such American farms as Clawbonny. Here is a serene picture of this solid, almost idyllic America then hardly known at all to European critics of our civilization. Here, as in *Satanstoe* and *The Chainbearer,* is the novel of manners, the fictional re-creation of the best in American society, which Cooper had always hoped to accomplish, blended imperfectly with the romance of action which he did with such natural ease.

This panorama of American life is integrated with the succeeding trilogy, *Satanstoe* (1845), *The Chainbearer* (1845), and *The Redskins* (1846). In the antirentism controversy, now a forgotten issue, Cooper saw the crisis of American idealism, and characteristically aligned himself on the side of the landlords and the rights of property. His now nostalgic patriotism had finally turned him against the equalitarian society of Andrew Jackson's America. Again, in the first of the three novels, and to a lesser degree in the second, he tells a good story, though this virtue is stifled in the preachy *Redskins.* In any case the sequential elements of the three books, as he says in a Preface, depend upon his study of "principles." The romance of Cornelius Littlepage and Anneke Mordaunt, with the usual reticulations of plot and with a black-hearted pedagogue from Danbury, Connecticut, ranks high among Cooper's plots. At the same time the social novelist diverts us from the action to the scenes themselves, to the patroons and the English in the eighteenth century, or to colonial New York, with its "Pinkster" or Dutch Festival. Such interests dominate the trilogy, even in the symbolic character of Thousandacres, the New England squatter, and in the long debates concerning the ethics of this upstart and that of the heroic figures admired by Cooper. The tone of the first two books is judicial; only in *The Redskins* does the controversy dissolve in Cooper's incoherent rage at the impending defeat of what he held so dear.

With the beguiling confession of the Littlepage Manuscripts, really Cooper's own memories related in his late fifties, and with these adventures of the trilogy, it may be said that Cooper's career as writer of the creative imagination began its decline. His five remaining novels show little weariness; they include lightning flashes of his art, as in the careful symbolism of *The Crater* (1848) or the battle between the sloop-of-war and the brig in *Jack Tier* (1848). Yet toward the close of his life his disgust with the stupidities of civilization narrowed his literary horizon; his general underlying thesis concerning the blindness of mankind to his ideal of controlled liberty was not enough. Into *The Crater,* for example, our first important Utopian allegory, he poured his dismay about humanity's need for authority; into *The Oak Openings,* his fears concerning its insensibility to conversion; into *The Sea Lions,* his ideas on the Trinity; into *The Ways of the Hour,* his hatred of trial by jury; and into all that he wrote, the thousand little familiar petulances which we still associate with Cooper's temperament. Though he fled to the mysterious island in *The Crater* or to antarctic realms in *The Sea Lions,* yet he was still harassed and stung by these gnats of the mind. It is a strange, and in retrospect, almost a comic spectacle. His powers had not failed; the old narrative skill and the social idealism were still strong, but they were cluttered by the foibles of the society in which he lived so critically.

After all, as we look back on Cooper's career, we may well be lost in wonder at the magic which this American civilization, with all its follies and grandeurs, held for him, at once its enemy and its lover. He criticized it, satirized it, and abused it, but he never ceased to find it fascinating; for him its interest long outlived his intermittent experimentation with literary craftsmanship. All his writing after *The Deerslayer* indicates that he cared less and less for form and method and more and more for what he could say through the novel as a medium. To only one phase of art he remained loyal, to the talent which he could not have abandoned had he wished, the art of telling a story; this art he never quite fused with his devoted but often misguided patriotism. Thus, estimating Cooper, we should note again that in his writing America was first indeed and the novel for its own sake a bad second. Therefore in scope and in passion, it is barely possible that Cooper the social critic will outlive Cooper the novelist of the many novels, but never Cooper the romancer, Cooper the teller of the Leatherstocking tales. Yet even those tales could never have been so passionate, so profoundly and originally American, had he not probed relentlessly beneath the surface of facts to the principles of American society and of human conduct.

20. DIVERSITY AND INNOVATION IN THE MIDDLE STATES

B ETWEEN the extremes of New England on the one hand and the South on the other, New York and Pennsylvania, as the leaders of the group of middle Atlantic states, were distinguished at this time by their "middleness," as Henry Adams put it—their practical and sagacious aptitudes for compromise and the blending of interests. Uniting now with New England, now with Virginia and her Southern neighbors, serving as a balance wheel, they provided the force that in politics made a nation and in intellectual and artistic activities was ultimately to fuse divergent elements into a national culture.

Cooper and Irving were, of course, the major literary figures, with Bryant joining them in 1825 after a New England youth, and Poe later, after struggling to make his career in Richmond. It is perhaps significant that these four writers, thus drawn to a center, became recognized, when they spoke for the region, as the first literary spokesmen for the whole Republic, both at home and abroad. A region that boasted the political and commercial capitals of the nation would have little incentive to develop a strong regional characteristic in its culture. Only in its minor writers, like Paulding, Willis, Barker, Halleck, or Bird, does the too insistent influence of a Dutch, a Quaker, or a patrician British ancestry, a naïve coffeehouse or greenroom sophistication, a patriotic fervor, act as a restraint on creative power. This was the hub of the national literary life—and a wheel is small but solid at the hub.

These minor writers created in the metropolitan centers of Philadelphia and New York—and to a lesser extent in the smaller cities of Albany, Baltimore, and Washington—something of the spirit of a provincial eighteenth century London. These were the men and women who gathered in salons and clubs for literary conversation; who supplied the magazines and the stage with acceptable offerings, patriotic in accent but usually British in form and tone. They were the logical inheritors of the earlier group (Freneau, Brown, Dennie, Hopkinson, Brackenridge, Tyler), but more numerous and more successful. Many of them managed, where the earlier group had failed, to make a substantial living by their pens. Poe caught their dominant characteristic when he called them the "Literati"; N. P. Willis, their tone when he titled his essays *Pencillings by the Way.* There was scarcely an accepted literary form that escaped them, but they naturally ran to the short story, the essay, and the lyric poem because there was a market for such writings in the new magazines, or to the social comedy or the melodrama because there was a call for such plays in the new theaters.

2

James Kirke Paulding, throughout his life identified with New York State, was perhaps the most typical writer of his time and place—of the diversity and innovation so characteristic of the writings of these middle states. In his voluminous writings over several decades, he showed affinities with more literary movements and styles, even with more individual authors, than any other figure of the early nineteenth century. His virtues and his faults were those of a new nation just coming to self-awareness. He was a Cooper without Cooper's gusto, an Irving who stayed at home. His versatility, his impetuous enthusiasm for a wide variety of subject matter, his willingness to experiment with poetic epic, short story, novel, drama, literary criticism, humorous sketch, moral and social and political criticism of a Swiftian stamp—all these phases of his ever alert inclusiveness perhaps explain better than any lack of talent or perspicacity his failure to achieve the stature of a truly great writer. He was "middleness" personified, and "innovation" was his greatest virtue; he was as well a devout though sometimes noisy champion of democracy, but realistic, with his feet on the ground, and without metaphysical subtlety.

Except for minor contributions to Peter Irving's *Morning Chronicle* as early as 1802, Paulding's literary career properly began in 1807, with the publication of the first series of periodical essays entitled *Salmagundi; or the Whim-Whams and Opinions of Launcelot Langstaff, Esq., and Others,* jointly produced with William and Washington Irving, who had been his friends and literary cronies since his arrival in New York City from his native Dutchess County some ten years before. Though the collaboration of Irving and Paulding was so close as to make individual assignment problematical, Paulding is generally given credit for having first sketched the characters of the Cockloft family, modeling one of them on his own uncle. The second series of *Salmagundi,* issued in 1819, was entirely Paulding's work.

The Diverting History of John Bull and Brother Jonathan (1812), published as by one Hector Bull-us, set the tone and indeed to a large degree the pattern for a series of nationalistic political satires. This work, originally in sixteen chapters but later more than doubled in length, looked backward to Francis Hopkinson's *A Pretty Story* (1774) and forward to some of the later sections of Melville's *Mardi* (1849) in its intention and method. Bullock

Island, representing England, and the thirteen farms of Jonathan, representing the United States, are the chief locales of action, though activities are reported from the Manor of Frogmore of Lewis Baboon (Louis XVI) and Beau Napperty (Napoleon), "called Beau because he was no beau at all." The theme of the British traveler in America, which reappeared in Paulding's *John Bull in America; or the New Munchausen* (1825), is embodied here in Corporal Smellfungus. The sequel of this early work, though its inferior, *The History of Uncle Sam and His Boys* (1835), pictured Jonathan as now become Uncle Sam, with twenty-four sons (states), mostly large, though a few, "shrunk in the boiling," were "rather conceited and jealous, as most little people." Paulding's two plays—*The Bucktails; or Americans in England* (written about 1815) and *The Lion of the West* (which won a prize in 1830)—reflect this tendency of nationalistic caricature, though the major figures deserve more serious consideration as realistic character portrayals.

For most of Paulding's later serious work—whether epic poetry or fiction or drama—the keynote was sounded and the intention stated in his article on "National Literature," in the final issue of the second series of *Salmagundi,* August 19, 1820. Here, in discussing "rational fiction," Paulding attacked "servile imitation," "the ascendancy of foreign taste and opinions," "the aid of superstition, the agency of ghosts, fairies, goblins, and all . . . antiquated machinery," and advocated dependence on nature and "real life" where "events, however extraordinary, can always be traced to motives, actions, and passions, arising out of circumstances no way unnatural, and partaking of no impossible or supernatural agency." Though Paulding sometimes used foreign settings for his tales—rarely with much success—and occasionally introduced supernatural elements, for the most part he lived up to his creed. Some aspects of American life he saw through rose-colored glasses; he shared with his contemporaries an ill founded hope that pioneering and frontier life would develop only "doric simplicity" and strength of character, rarely noting that it might also develop crudity and cupidity.

Paulding's epic poem of some sixteen hundred lines, *The Backwoodsman* (1818), is less romantic than Crèvecœur's account of Andrew the Hebridean and foreshadows some of the ideas expressed in Frederick Jackson Turner's famous essay on the frontier three quarters of a century later. The story of Basil's westward trek from the banks of the Hudson to "the poor man's long-sought, new-found promis'd land" in the Ohio River valley, Paulding told "with homebred feeling, and with homebred fire," though the fire of the ruthlessly mechanical eighteenth century heroic couplets has dimmed. Indicating the success of Basil's Western career by sending him to Congress as reward is a fault more national than personal—merely another evidence of the common American belief that virtue and industry inevitably bring material reward. The descriptions of natural scenery, the pictures of the Moravians in Pennsylvania, the interspersed accounts of the Wyoming Massacre and of various historical figures—Arnold, André, Greene, Marion, Franklin, Washington—as well as the central narrative, make the poem intrinsically American.

The tales or short stories and the novels are Paulding's most important work. His leisurely manner of writing, his inclination to introduce personal comment and opinion, and his variety of interests are best adapted to happy expression in prose fiction. Assuredly the Dutch stories are the best—and Sybrandt Westbrook of *The Dutchman's Fireside* (1831) is probably his most successful full-length characterization—but settings and characters other than Dutch are also effectively handled. Woodsmen and frontiersmen, whether Sir William Johnson in *The Dutchman's Fireside* or Ambrose Bushfield in *Westward Ho!* (1832), are drawn with veracity and compulsion. Paulding's first novel, *Koningsmarke* (1823), introduced the Long Finne as a character against a background of the Swedish colonies in Delaware; his fifth and last novel, *The Puritan and His Daughter* (1849), shifted from Cromwellian England to New England, portraying Puritanism in its two main environments. *The Old Continental, or the Price of Liberty* (1846) used the background of New York during the Revolution to tell a story of the vicissitudes of Whigs in a Tory community—a theme echoed in the account of the origin of the ancestral curse that haunted the melancholy Dudley Rainsford in *Westward Ho!*

In his zealous and often self-conscious efforts to build an indigenous literary tradition, Paulding took himself and his work seriously, emphasizing throughout accuracy and morality. As he took pains to point out, he frequently used original sources, such as Mrs. Grant's *Memoirs of an American Lady* (1808) for *The Dutchman's Fireside* and Timothy Flint's *Recollections of the Last Ten Years* (1826) for *Westward Ho!* He no doubt fully agreed with the publisher's (Harper's) preface to *The Dutchman's Fireside* setting forth the moral duty of the novelist to supply to his reader

without the bitterness and danger of experience, that knowledge of his fellow-creatures which but for such aid could, in the majority of cases, be only acquired at a period of life when it would be too late to turn it to account.

By characterization, depiction of the mores of other times, dialogue, and direct auctorial comment, he inculcated the values of "doric simplicity" (a frequent phrase in *The Dutchman's Fireside*), rationality, common sense, and tolerance—the latter notably in his attack on the sadistic dogmatism of the itinerant preacher in *Westward Ho!* Sometimes he used broad satirical portraiture suggestive of Sheridan or Royall Tyler to reduce the qualities he abhorred to the absurd. The Obsoletes in *The Bucktails* are caricatures of this type, as also the suitors of Catalina Vancour in *The Dutchman's Fireside*: Barry Gillfillan, a "combustible gentleman," with "the truly Irish propensity for falling in love extempore," and Sir Thicknesse Throgmorton, the impecunious peer of "dignified stupidity." Less frequently, and most often less successfully, he embodied the admired virtues in a model character, like Sir William Johnson, also of *The Dutchman's Fireside,* or Virginia Dangerfield or Father Jacques, of *Westward Ho!*

In characterization and in handling of plot, Paulding was occasionally the equal of Simms and Cooper. Resemblances between *The Dutchman's Fireside* and Cooper's *Satanstoe* (1845), both dealing with the region near Albany during the French and Indian War, have often been pointed out. *Satanstoe* is a more compact and unified story, but Corny Littlepage's rescue of Anneke from the ice break in the Hudson was no more vividly described than Sybrandt Westbrook's saving Catalina Vancour when a violent storm flooded the island where the young people were picnicking. Cooper's hero had much in common with Paulding's: both represented the ideal fusion of Dutch and English blood; both saved the heroine's life on more than one occasion when she was threatened by a natural calamity or by Indians; both found their chief rivals in Britishers visiting the colonies. But Paulding's Sybrandt was less idealized, more bashful and lacking in assurance, less suave (indeed, even awkward), more credible thus in confronting the situations the plot involved him in, and withal more human and appealing. The author's understanding of his psychology was on occasion profound, particularly in the relations of Sybrandt and Sir William Johnson. Catalina, also, was in her womanly spirit and perversity more credible than Anneke. Paulding did not, however, produce any character so vividly compelling as Cooper's Guert Ten Eyck.

Though more fluently written, *Westward Ho!* which was published only a year later is less realistic, even less honest. Paulding did not know or understand the Virginia plantation owner type, which Colonel Cuthbert Dangerfield of Powhatan represented, as he knew and understood the New York Dutch. He was also less familiar with the topography and mores of Kentucky in the days when it deserved the name "dark and bloody ground." In his fascination for the psychological quirks of Dudley Rainsford, whose perverted guilt-consciousness is a major determinant of the plot, Paulding was on the track of profoundly dramatic material, but he was beyond his depth—unwilling to treat his character according to the superficial romanticism of Poe's practice and unable in realistic terms to understand and describe the aberrations of Rainsford's diseased mind. Thus he fell short of Charles Brockden Brown in picturing a situation reminiscent of *Wieland* (1798), when Rainsford feels religious compulsion to make a blood sacrifice of his fiancée, Virginia Dangerfield, though in a detailed transcription of the hell-fire sermon which immediately provokes the delusion, Paulding prepared the way for intense tragedy. In the character of Ambrose Bushfield he was more on his own ground. The burly and uncouth woodsman who is Colonel Dangerfield's executive officer in the conduct of the expedition down the Ohio to Kentucky and in the building of a new community is an inveterate Indian-hater, made so by the Indian massacre of all of his family in which he miraculously escaped. "Transcendent" is his favorite adjective, and he invariably desires to make the object of his wrath "smell brimstone through a nail hole." Woodsman's rodomontade—suggestive of the speeches of Nimrod Wildfire in *The Lion of the West,* which Paulding got ready for the stage about the same time—comes frequently from Bushfield's lips. Despite his eccentricities of dress, speech, and action, Bushfield is a well rounded, credible character exemplifying Crèvecœur's theories of the effects of life on the cutting edge of the frontier.

Of the Dutch short stories, "Cobus Yerks" and "Claas Schlaschenschlinger" —both included in *The Book of St. Nicholas* (1836)—are typical. The first, in mood and material suggestive of Irving's "Legend of Sleepy Hollow" though the situation described more nearly resembles that in Burns' "Tam O'Shanter," is the account of Cobus' return one night from a tavern presided over by a "bitter root of a woman." He is chased by a black dog turned "devil," and learns the fallacy of "the doctrine that spirit and courage, that is to say whiskey and valour were synonymous." In "Claas Schlaschenschlinger," the two main events are supernatural interventions by St. Nicholas; but the details of the plot and the characterizations are realistic. The psychological stories are best represented by "The Dumb Girl" and "The Ghost," though both might also be classified as stories of character or of plot. In the first, Phoebe Angevine, the title character, living a frustrated existence with her mother and idiot brother, Ellee, is attracted by the stranger, Walter Avery, allows herself to be seduced, and is deserted. Though some critics have made extravagant comparisons with Hawthorne and *The Scarlet Letter,* Paulding's tale lacks the fullness and depth to give conviction to the handicapped heroine's psychology or reality to the pathos of the story. "The Ghost," first published in both *The Atlantic Souvenir* and the New York *Mirror* in 1829, is the story of one William Morgan, who perversely delights in playing ghost, thereby occasioning trouble for others as well as himself. Paulding's characterization of Morgan and of Tom Brown—the chief victim of Morgan's pranks—and his handling of suspense and narrative are effective, direct, and convincing.

Restless like the young nation itself, Paulding was busy with political office as well as with writing—too busy ever to criticize and revise, too eager to be doing other things that also needed to be done ever to do anything quite to the best of his abilities. But he frequently did first what other writers—New Yorkers, or New Englanders, or Southerners, or Westerners—were later to do better and more memorably. Poe's comment, "Paulding owes *all* of his reputation as a novelist, to his early occupation of the field," is unjust. In his range of interest and materials, in his capacity for "innovation," in the breadth of his view of the resources out of which America could build her own literature, and in his formulation and practice of a literary creed, Paulding represents the catholicity and inclusiveness, the fusion of divergent strains, for which the whole body of literature produced in the middle states from 1810 to 1860 is most distinguished, and by which it is best characterized.

3

Closely allied with Paulding in the novel—and like him showing common traits with Cooper and Simms—was the Philadelphia physician Robert Montgomery Bird. After two novels with a Mexican background, *Calavar; or The Knight of Conquest* (1834) and *The Infidel; or The Fall of Mexico* (1835), as well as the earlier plays for Edwin Forrest which also used foreign settings, Bird turned to native material. *The Hawks of Hawk-Hollow* (1835), which Poe condemned as too much like Walter Scott, is the story of a Tory family in Pennsylvania in the year after Yorktown. *Sheppard Lee* (1836), to cite Poe's complimentary term, is a *jeu d'esprit* about a New Jersey farmer whose passage through numerous incarnations affords Bird opportunity to comment satirically on contemporary conditions ranging from fashionable life to plantation slavery. His most popular and best novel is *Nick of the Woods* (1837), the story of Nathan Slaughter, an uncompromising Indian-hater, like Paulding's Timothy Weasel and Ambrose Bushfield in many respects but a better realized character than either—or, for that matter, than any character Paulding or Simms or Cooper ever drew. Nathan the Quaker is called "Bloody Nathan" in derision for his refusal to join his fellow Kentuckians of 1782 to fight the Indians. In spite of his miraculous exploits and his weird dependence on his little dog Peter, who smells Indians and other danger afar off, he is a credible human being, the victim at times of a powerful monomania, but a consistent personality, whose actions and speech and personal appearance all fit into place. *Nick of the Woods* is a good novel, as good as any produced in America in the 1830's, with narrative directness and a skillfully handled complex plot. Bird's conception of the Indian is based on the belief that "in his natural barbaric state, he is a barbarian." Not believing the myth of the noble savage, as he affirmed in the preface to the 1853 revision of this novel, he "drew his Indian portraits with Indian ink."

Like *The Old Continental* by Paulding and *The Hawks of Hawk-Hollow* by Bird, *Greyslaer* (1840) by Charles Fenno Hoffman, a novel of the Mohawk valley during the Revolution, presented the favorite theme of the conflict between Whigs and Tories. This novel, which Hoffman based at least in a general way on the well known murder of Sharp, the Solicitor General of Kentucky, by Beauchamp, changing the locale and many other details, seemed to Poe less effective than Simms' treatment of the same event in *Beauchampe* (1842); and he thought both novels less impressive than the real events. Hoffman's talent lay chiefly in journalism. Thus one may understand the purposes and methods of the greater Fenimore Cooper by seeing his work as a part of a national movement in the novel.

4

In poetry, the field where Paulding was least successful, Fitz-Greene Halleck takes first place after Bryant. Poe in his *Literati* sketch so rated him a hundred years ago, with Nathaniel Parker Willis third. Griswold would perhaps have saved the third place for Charles Fenno Hoffman, best known for the martial lyric "Monterey" and occasional poetry like "The Mint Julep"; but Poe's ranking seems sounder. After Freneau's death in 1832, the middle states had no important poet until Whitman's emergence in 1855, except as New York could claim Bryant.

In 1819, the *Croaker* pieces, a series of humorous and satirical odes published pseudonymously in the New York *Evening Post,* launched Halleck and his friend Joseph Rodman Drake in popular poetry. Beside this joint production, Drake's fame must rest on "The Culprit Fay" (1819), a conscious attempt to utilize American scenery for poetic purposes, which though not altogether successful, hardly deserved Poe's label of "puerile abortion." The younger poet's death the following year occasioned the lines of Halleck "On the Death of Joseph Rodman Drake" (1820), by which Drake is now chiefly remembered.

Steeped in Thomas Campbell, Samuel Rogers, Byron, and Walter Scott, Halleck often seemed more a part of English literary romanticism than a native American product. True, the materials of *The Croaker* and of his own long poem "Fanny" (1821), also in the vein of social satire, were local. "The Field of Grounded Arms" (1831), about the Battle of Saratoga, "Red Jacket" (1828), eulogizing the Indian chief of the Tuscaroras, and "Wyoming" (1827), all used American settings, characters, or events, but are not distinctively American. Halleck's interest in the banks of the Susquehanna was derived from an appreciation of Thomas Campbell's *Gertrude of Wyoming* (1809); the eulogy of the Indian chief afforded opportunity to lament the good old days; the vanquished at Saratoga appealed more romantically to him than did the victors, because they represented an older tradition. His poem "Young America" (1865) was about a fourteen-year-old boy, but it was a "bonny" boy who dreamed of Titania and Diana—American, if at all, only in his desire

> to settle down in life
> By wooing—winning—wedding A RICH WIFE.

The unfinished "Connecticut," despite such intrusions as "the San Marino of the West," "delicate Ariels," and "the Rhine song," was in thought and feeling, as well as in material, the most native of Halleck's poems. Though identified in both business and literary career with New York, Halleck retained a nostalgic loyalty to his native state:

> Hers are not Tempe's nor Arcadia's spring,
>   Nor the long summer of Cathayan vales,
> The vines, the flowers, the air, the skies, that fling
>   Such wild enchantment o'er Boccaccio's tales
> Of Florence and the Arno; yet the wing
>   Of life's best angel, Health, is on her gales
> Through sun and snow; and in the autumn time
> Earth has no purer and no lovelier clime.

His love for "Greece, the brave heart's Holy Land," could make a hero of the title figure of the justly celebrated "Marco Bozzaris" (1823); a "wild rose of Alloway" could inspire a masterful appreciation in "Burns" (1827) of the poet and the Scotland that gave him birth; a visit to the "home of the Percy's high-born race" could produce his masterpiece, "Alnwick Castle" (1822)—and these three poems were their author's selection as his best work—but it commonly took the far away in time and place to evoke the poetic muse in Halleck. Employed most of his life by John Jacob Astor, he found ample occasion to lament, as he did in "Alnwick Castle," that

> The power that bore my spirit up
> Above this bank-note world—is gone;
>   .   .   .   .   .   .
>
> These are not the romantic times
> So beautiful in Spenser's rhymes,
>   So dazzling to the dreaming boy:
> Ours are the days of fact, not fable,
> Of knights, but not of the Round Table.

Out of a "bank-note world" and "days of fact" Halleck was unable to make poetry. Though he lived past Emerson's pronouncement in "The Poet" (1844) and into the days of Whitman's fulfillment, his outlook and habits were fixed in an earlier period, and he could not agree with Emerson that

banks and tariffs, the newspaper and the caucus, methodism and unitarianism, are flat and dull to dull people, but rest on the same foundations of wonder as the town of Troy, and the temple of Delphos, and are as swiftly passing away.

In Nathaniel Parker Willis, Poe's choice for the third most significant poet of the New York group of this period, there was generally the same failure to treat American materials with seriousness and poetic depth. Perhaps poetry is, by its nature, the last form of literature to become thoroughly indigenous; but one is tempted to agree with Lowell that

> For some one to be slightly shallow 's a duty,
> And Willis's shallowness makes half his beauty.

Willis was polished, urbane, sophisticated, but never—in poetry, plays, or prose—profound or great: a talented, versatile, and prolific writer.

As a poet, Willis seems today inferior to Bryant or even to Halleck. In bulk his poems on scriptural subjects loomed large; but a comparison of his "Absalom" with a masterpiece like Browning's "Saul" establishes the justice of Poe's verdict that though "quite 'correct,' as the French have it," they were "in general tame, or indebted for what force they possess to the Scriptural passages of which they are merely paraphrastic." In his poem "Parrhasius," the story of the Athenian painter who subjected his aged Olynthian captive to extreme torture that he might better from this living model paint the agony of Prometheus, the dramatic values somehow fall flat, and Willis shows himself unequal to the tragic theme. Of the serious poems, the "Dedication Hymn" (1829), sung at the consecration of the Hanover Street church in Boston, is simple and direct and owes its force to these qualities. "Unseen Spirits" (1843), Poe's choice as Willis' best poem, showed clearly that Willis' talent lay, not in picturing profound passion or tragedy, but in wistful sentiment. The contrast between the beauty who married for wealth and the woman who loved without marriage vows is effectively pointed by the final well known lines:

> But the sin forgiven by Christ in heaven
> By man is cursed alway.

"To M——, from Abroad" (1834) and "Birthday Verses," written to his mother, are charming examples of sentimental poetry, better suited to Willis' abilities, and, with his religious lyrics, account for much of his contemporary fame.

The bulk of Willis' prose writing was in a dozen volumes of letters of travel and personal reminiscence, beginning with *Pencillings by the Way* (1835) and extending to *The Convalescent* (1859), mainly collections of letters written for the New York *Mirror* and other periodicals of which Willis was at one time or another an editor. The earlier letters recorded excitement about Lady Blessington and her circle and the conventional tourist haunts and shrines of the Old World, but from *A l'Abri; or Thè Tent Pitched* (1839) onward, Willis' country estates, Glenmary and Idlewild, and his ramblings in the areas near by formed an important part of his subject matter. As he once said of an exploratory walk to the Chemung River, so it might be said of many a poem or letter or essay he wrote: "It was done *à l'improviste,* as most pleasant things are." For most of the results, in collected form, Lowell's opinion of the best known title still holds:

> Few volumes I know to read under a tree,
> More truly delightful than his A l'Abri.

At his best, Willis was, like many earlier pilgrims to the English literary scene, "a casual writer for dreamy readers." One is inclined to smile now at his more serious ideas, such as his pronouncement in 1839:

In literature we are no longer a nation. The triumph of Atlantic steam navigation has driven the smaller drop into the larger, and London has become the centre. Farewell nationality! The English language now marks the limits of a new literary empire, and America is a suburb.

Willis' short stories often showed the "casual" quality of his other prose and the sentiment of his best verse. Most of them deal in a moral tone with highly artificial situations and characters. Only in "The Lunatic's Skate" from "Scenes of Fear" (1834) did he show real depth of feeling and sense of character. Though the story elicited from Willis' biographer, Henry A. Beers, a comparison with Poe, the treatment of the material here was more realistic than Poe would have given, and without stagy romanticism or generalized sentiment. Willis' approach to the psychotic skater was more like Paulding's in Dudley Rainsford of *Westward Ho!* though the story of Larry Wynn is more concise, better written.

Late in life, in *Paul Fane* (1857), Willis attempted a psychological novel about a young American artist who determined, after being shunned by a cold English girl, to make the noble and high-born women of England accept him on a basis of equality by whatever methods were available. Though several women fell in love with him, he spurned them. Since Willis proved unable here to sustain the keenness of insight of "The Lunatic's Skate," the novel failed to come off.

5

In keeping with the diversity and innovation of the middle states literature of this period, four writers well known for fiction or poetry were also leading playwrights: Paulding, Bird, Willis, and Mathews. The two main themes of the native drama produced in New York and Philadelphia during these years were the glorification of American nationality or distinctiveness, and a romantic escape into the far away or the long ago. The most successful plays often combined these two motifs, though the best of them, Mrs. Anna Cora Mowatt's *Fashion* (1845), was frankly an American comedy of manners much influenced by Sheridan, in which Adam Trueman was something of a cross between the Yankee type inaugurated by Jonathan in Royall Tyler's *The Contrast* (1787) and the serious-minded patriot represented by Colonel Manly in the same play. Mrs. Mowatt's villain, Count Jolimaitre, was also a variation on Tyler's Dimple, though more ingenious and more dramatically effective. There was considerable penetration in Poe's assessment in the *Broadway Journal,* March 29, 1845, that "*Fashion* is theatrical, but not dramatic," and in his elucidation, perhaps too tartly expressed:

The drama has not declined as many suppose: it has only been left out of sight by everything else. We must discard all models. . . . compared with the generality of modern dramas, it is a good play—compared with most American dramas, it is a *very* good one—estimated by the natural principles of dramatic art, it is altogether unworthy of notice.

Notable among the plays with a foreign setting were N. P. Willis' *Bianca Visconti; or the Heart Overtasked* (1837 *), whose action took place in fourteenth century Milan, and his *Tortesa the Usurer* (1839), dealing with medieval Florence; Robert Montgomery Bird's *The Gladiator* (1831), a story of Rome in 73 B.C., and his *Broker of Bogota* (1834), which used a setting of the South American city in the early Spanish colonial days; and *Charles the Second; or The Merry Monarch* (1824), written by John Howard Payne with assistance from Washington Irving.

Plays on native themes which used material from the past included James Nelson Barker's *Superstition* (1824) and Cornelius Mathews' *Witchcraft* (1846), both set in late seventeenth century New England; a host of plays about Indians, by George Washington Parke Custis and John Augustus

* The dates of plays cited here are of production.

Stone; Mathews' *Jacob Leisler, or New York in 1690* (1848) and Elizabeth Oakes Smith's *Old New York, or Democracy in 1689* (1853), both of which made use of the same incident in the early history of Manhattan.

In *The Lion of the West* (1831), introducing a character suggestive of Davy Crockett, Paulding presented a salient aspect of contemporary American life not touched on in a play like Mrs. Mowatt's *Fashion*. Earlier, in *The Bucktails; or Americans in England* (not published until 1847), he had made an important contribution toward defining the American character by showing his countrymen against a European background. *The Bucktails* was a comedy of manners, often exaggerated into farce, designed to dispel the myth that all Americans were Wildfires or Crocketts. Among the few notable plays using contemporary American materials was Cornelius Mathews' *The Politicians* (1840).

Of the plays here named, only Payne's *Charles the Second* was without relevance to characteristic American themes and interests. It was an adaptation of a French play by Alexandre Duval and was originally produced on the London stage during Payne's long residence abroad (1813–1832), but was free enough of its original to be considered as part of American literature. Willis' *Tortesa, the Usurer* had a tenuous connection with the American theme of the rise of the underdog, in the success of the poor painter Angelo in winning not only the noble and beautiful Isabella de Falcone in marriage but also, through the sudden and largely inexplicable generosity of Tortesa, a sizable fortune along with her. But Willis' interest was less in American ideology than in the age-old theme of the triumph of true love over seemingly insurmountable obstacles, and more especially in effective theater.

In *Bianca Visconti,* the central character was Francesco Sforza, at the time of the action in high-pitched rebellion against the Italian dukes who were using him to fight their wars against each other while he himself was personally despised and trifled with. Sforza attracted Willis in part at least because of the dramatist's concern for democracy and the dignity of all men. Willis' interest in this character was similar to Bird's interest in Spartacus and his revolt against brutal Roman tyranny over conquered peoples, though Bird approached the subject of *The Gladiator* differently. Stone's sympathetic portrayal of the title character in *Metamora* (1829) was in the same vein, though here the dramatic impact was sharper since the oppressors of the chief of the Wampanoags, son of Massasoit, were the New England colonists of the seventeenth century, the ancestors of the audience now applauding the Indian's struggle for freedom. Jacob Leisler, in the plays by Cornelius Mathews and Elizabeth Oakes Smith, was another hero in revolt—the champion of an abortive democracy in New York of 1689–1690. The same theme appeared in Bird's *The Broker of Bogota* in the struggle of the bourgeois Baptista Febro to get his rights against people of noble birth.

It becomes apparent then that, like the essay and fiction and poetry of the day, the American drama prior to Boker's notable *Francesca da Rimini* (1855) reflects not a matured but an adolescent indigenous culture. The leading writers of the middle states between 1820 and 1850 were realistic at their best rather than merely picturesque, tolerant of variation and originality within the boundaries of intelligibility, well informed about European literary traditions and current vogues though disinclined to be swept away by passing fads, lacking in intellectual unity but thriving on diversity and innovation, catholic in interests though caring "but little for the metaphysical subtleties of Massachusetts and Virginia." In the middle of the road in opinions and tastes, the literature of this section during the decades preceding the Civil War became the unifying core of an American national culture.

21. IN NEW ENGLAND

DURING the years when Bryant, Irving, and Cooper were the major figures in American letters and the Concord-Cambridge galaxy were still schoolboys, authorship in New England was by no means confined to eastern Massachusetts. The editors of the *North American Review* and their chief contributors, it is true, were Boston men; but in that day the poets of Connecticut outranked the Bostonians and the most popular novelists lived in the Green Mountains, the Berkshires, and Maine. Thus literature in New England was shaped by the life not of any single community but of the entire region—the half cultivated, half primitive homeland of William Ellery Channing and Richard Henry Dana, Sr., of Daniel Pierce Thompson and William Cullen Bryant.

The literary tradition of Boston and its back country was overwhelmingly English, for New England at the opening of the century was closer in spirit as well as in fact to the British Isles than any other section of the United States. This is to say that the heritage of Pope was still strong, and that American romanticism was chiefly imitative. Where the great romantics in England wrote on English and Continental themes, early romantics in America copied, not American life, but English copies of English life. This literary colonialism focused the attention of New Englanders on decorum and sensibility, on the legends and history of Europe, on Old World religious and political concepts, and on both the substance and the style of the eighteenth century novelists and of the nineteenth century romantic poets. Thus the lesser New England authors were moved hither and yon by the backwash of classicism, the main current of derivative romanticism, and the ever increasing pull of indigenous American romanticism. In the poetry of William Cullen Bryant, New England found its authentic voice, not because Bryant was a rebel against the past and Europe, but because he absorbed tradition and made it his own. Other writers of his day were less successful either because they rebelled more violently or because they were swept too easily with the currents of foreign influence.

2

Boston, according to James Fenimore Cooper, was populated by hardened provincials, incapable of speaking either the English language or a kind word for the rest of the United States. Although the members of the *North American* group were friends—professional men in Boston and faculty men in Cambridge—with the same cultural heritage, they never actually reached the agreement concerning the national scene which Cooper attributed to them.

Provincial devotion to New England was exemplified by the first editor of the *Review,* William Tudor, who traveled in Europe and South America but wrote only one significant book: *Letters on the Eastern States* (1820). Despite his promise that the *North American* would "avoid the narrow prejudice of locality," he gave so much attention to his college, his city, and his New England that readers in other sections dubbed his periodical, the *North Unamerican.* A sane nationalism animated Tudor's friend Jared Sparks, who during his two terms as editor of the *Review* was concerned with everything American—not only North but South. As professor at Harvard, he outlined an ambitious program in the history of the United States. As author, he wrote biographies of John Ledyard, Gouverneur Morris, and Benjamin Franklin as well as many of the briefer sketches in his *Library of American Biography* (first series, 1834–1838). Even though twentieth century historians find his work inaccurate, they still honor Sparks as the man who won recognition for American history in American colleges. But it was Europe that filled the mind of Edward Everett during his years as editor, and came near to filling the pages of the *Review.* The first American to receive the Ph.D. degree from the University of Göttingen, he and his fellow student in Germany, George Ticknor, were busily reshaping Harvard College along German lines. The facile Everett later turned to American affairs and defended nationalism in his oration at Gettysburg; but in his *North American* days he was an apostle of that inverted provincialism which flourishes among the colonially minded.

Even ardent nationalists uncritically continued to evaluate their own literature in European terms; to them, a native author was successful if he could do what a foreigner did. But in 1830 one of the most distinguished of this Boston group proffered a formula for creating a genuinely American literature. William Ellery Channing brought to the criticism of belles-lettres in the United States a sound knowledge of European authors and a fine capacity for generalization. In his "Remarks on National Literature" in the *Christian Examiner* (1830), he reached these conclusions: First, we have not yet produced an American literature because, even while we protest against "dependence on European manufactures," we continue to import the "fabrics of the intellect." Secondly, the American faith in "the essential equality of all human beings" is highly favorable to creative activity. Finally, when this new world begets "great minds" and breeds "a nobler race of men," we shall then write books of the first magnitude. At the time, Bryant was moving toward the same position in his reviews of American authors, but not until Emerson delivered his Phi Beta Kappa oration in 1837 was cultural nationalism defended more cogently.

Morality bulked almost as large as public affairs, and was indeed a public issue, in the writings of the *North American* authors. Channing, for example, declared in his "Remarks" that the only force which can elevate American literature to its full potentialities is "the religious principle." Fortunately for America, his faith was a particularly enlightened variety of the Boston religion. Combining whatever was congenial to his mind in the beliefs of Separatists and Deists, Rousseau, the French Revolutionists, Godwin, and Wollstonecraft, he devised his own brand of Unitarianism. He announced, in his ordination sermon for Jared Sparks and in other addresses, that God is infinite (too great to die on a gallows) and God is love (too beneficent to predestine men to eternal flames). Man like God is good—and divine. The natural relationship between such a man and such a God can only be good; to worship God, therefore, is to live the good life. As God recognizes the inalienable rights of man's personality, "the only God . . . is the God whose image dwells in our own souls." Thus Channing laid the moral foundation for an egocentric yet devoutly religious romanticism which, in so far as it was truly self-reliant, was truly American.

Such a man as Channing found it easy to love that "outer garment of God," the physical universe. The Atlantic Ocean, the White Mountains, the forests of New England he knew and cherished, both for themselves and for their Creator. In reading these physical transcripts of deity, he was aided by Schelling and Coleridge, and by his favorite among living poets, Wordsworth. When he visited Wordsworth, the two men exchanged ideas while riding in a farmer's cart on the road from Dove Cottage to Grasmere. "We talked so eagerly," said Channing, "as often to interrupt one another, and I descended into Grasmere near sunset, with the placid lake before me, and Wordsworth talking and reciting poetry with a poet's spirit by my side."

Boston's most severe critic of outmoded classicism and its most extravagant champion of romanticism in the English manner was Richard Henry Dana, Sr. Sensitive and high-tempered, distrustful of his contemporaries and himself, he was lonely in New England. As a contributor to the *North American,* he insisted that Pope could not write poetry but that the poets of the Lake School were masters. Thereupon he was violently attacked by the reactionary majority among the Boston literati and warmly defended by his friend Bryant; he failed of election to the editorship of the *Review*; and thereafter he refused to contribute to its pages. Eager for public recognition, he was hard hit by the cool reception of his essays and tales in *The Idle Man* (published in parts during 1821–1822), of his long poem, *The Buccaneer* (1827), and of his collected *Poems and Prose Writings* (1833, 1850). In middle life, he withdrew from the world which would not recognize his genius.

Dana's heart was not in this present "age of improvement" but in that golden day when, he fancied, "all was rustic and unforced" and "the relentless curiosity of modern times had not . . . soiled and torn asunder the flower." Past-minded in politics, he remained a Federalist long after the party had disappeared, and he even argued the superiority of monarchial to republican government. He was likewise an ardent Trinitarian and, during the twenties, an outspoken foe of the heterodoxy of Channing and Bryant. In his poetry and prose, as might be anticipated, he followed many masters: in *The Buccaneer,* eighteenth century sentimentalists, Coleridge, Wordsworth, and Byron; in his tales, especially "Paul Felton," the same Englishmen and Charles Brockden Brown. Dana expressed much sympathy for Brown's "loneliness of situation," his isolation as a man of sensibility in a mechanical age, and his ultimate success in escaping from "free thought" and becoming "a true believer." Didactic as Dana was at times, his extreme romanticism entitles him to a reprieve from Poe's sentence to death by hanging for all the *North American* men. The fact remains, however, that Dana was throughout his life an ardent exponent of the inverted provincialism which colored Edward Everett's earlier years. Except for Channing, this Boston group did little to break away from England or her literature and to discover the roots of American life.

3

Connecticut, according to Washington Irving, was populated by onion eaters, hog stealers, bundlers, improvers, and slab-sided schoolmasters. Such witticisms are an index not only to the complacency of New York, but to the dilemma of genteel men of letters in Connecticut during the early century. Cut off by distance from the intellectual stimulus of Boston, and by choice from the earthy stimulus of life among hog stealers and onion eaters, they too turned directly to Europe for precedents, as had the earlier Hartford wits. Thus it happened that the most enthusiastic medievalist of the period and the most complete romantic solitary were products of Yale—and the most shameless sentimentalist was a Hartford woman. The poets were no longer stirred by the old themes of religion and politics; the graces and amenities of life took their place.

The medievalist was James Abraham Hillhouse. In "A Discourse . . . on

Some of the Considerations Which Should Influence an Epic or a Tragic Writer in the Choice of an Era," he rejected the "heathen" world of the ancients for the glorious Christian era of chivalry ("Its spirit was pitched to enthusiasm, imagination was the ruling power, and the whole tenor of its actions was extraordinary"). America, he added, is an admirable residence, but it has no past and the American writer of tragedy or epic must therefore rely on our "indefeasible . . . portion in the fame of Arthur and Alfred." These principles he put into practice in three blank-verse dramas: *Percy's Masque* (1819), based on Thomas Percy's original ballad, "The Hermit of Warkworth"; *Hadad* (1825), a melodrama of the days when there was "intercourse between mankind, and good and evil beings from the Spiritual World"; and *Demetria* (1839), a "horrid" tragedy of Italian cavaliers and ladies. Always self-consistent, Hillhouse introduced nothing of the epic or the tragic into his American poem, *Sachem's Wood* (1836), but pictured his home in New Haven solely in terms of the sentimental and the comic.

The romantic solitary was James Gates Percival. Elegant steel engravings of distinguished authors, hanging on the parlor walls of America, honored him through the twenties as the nation's chief poet, and many reviewers gave him the same rank; but the public left him to starve. He met nothing except disappointment as a tutor, a lecturer on anatomy and later on botany, a physician, an editor, a surgeon in the Army, a professor of chemistry at West Point, a lexicographer, and the author of four volumes of poetry—all within the span of twelve years. Wounded, and too timid to mix with the herd, he next voluntarily secluded himself for a decade in three unswept rooms in the state hospital at New Haven. He spent his last years on the frontier in Wisconsin, where he died in solitude.

The world of poetry into which Percival escaped from New Haven was compounded of his own undisciplined emotions and his emulation of the English romantics. When a young maniac in "The Suicide" shouts, "Give me the knife, the dagger, or the ball," he echoes his creator Percival, who in youth attempted to destroy himself in a variety of ways; but the same maniac echoes Byron when he cries, "O, hell to me is nothing,—nothing's hell." When Percival generalizes windily in "Prometheus," he follows Shelley; but his condemnation of Prometheus for sacrilegiously rending "the veil Religion hung around us" voices his own pietism. Although the mountains which rise on many of his pages are dim copies of Wordsworth's first-hand observations, it should be added that Percival could write delightfully of the American scene when, on rare occasions, the charms of Seneca Lake or a landscape in New England caught his eye.

Percival's chief weakness was loquacity, but of it he made romantic virtue. "The highest interest of a poet," he declared, is "to write only, when

he feels inspired, when his subject has gained full possession of him. . . .
Then . . . his language will flow abroad without effort." It is too evident
that his long poems and his flood of lyrics—there are more than four hundred of them—did indeed flow abroad, with all the ease of divine madness
and little of the anguished effort which Bryant, for example, was putting
into his best lines. Thus Percival, instead of expending his slender talent
with caution and discretion, scattered it with a prodigal hand.

Sentimentalism came to a dead end in the verses of Lydia Huntley
Sigourney. She offered the public neither the violence nor the abstractions
which alarmed them in Percival; instead, she gave them literalness and propriety, convention and elegance. As her reward, she was editing an annual,
contributing to a half-dozen more, and selling her work to a score of magazines while Percival was hiding himself in a hospital. She knew something
of the humanitarian movements of the day, but all that she did for Negroes,
Indians, the poor, and the insane was to embalm them in the amber of her
tears. Until Longfellow came into his own in the fifties, the most widely read
American poet (she published sixty-seven volumes) was "The Sweet Singer
of Hartford."

4

Even the ruggedness of the hinterland could not wean New England
writers from conventional European modes. The simple realities of contemporary life in Vermont, in the Berkshires, and in Maine helped bring
national and international recognition to three novelists; but the hand of the
past lay so heavily on all three that they capitulated to traditional melodrama
or to traditional propriety and rejected, in varying degree, the region which
made them famous. They too failed to achieve the nationality or the universality of an indigenous art.

Least original of the three and least appreciative of his resources was
Daniel Pierce Thompson. In a day when native novels were few, *The Green
Mountain Boys* (1839) was famous as a classic of Vermont life. But its author,
a rural lawyer with no literary standards and no literary conscience, was less
concerned with recording New England character than with imitating the
blood-pudding school of romancers. Actually, the book is not a document
in social history but a violent yarn of a villain who slinks, muttering, down
the valleys and a hero who strides up the mountains with the heroine held
high in one arm and her Indian maidservant in the other. *Locke Amsden*
(1847), frequently praised for its account of education in early Vermont, is
likewise so filled with clichés and stereotypes that it has little meaning as
a record of local manners.

Catharine Maria Sedgwick, like Maria Edgeworth to whom she dedicated her first book, was at first keenly interested in the manners of her own region; and in her early novels she described those manners with naïve and convincing honesty. When she recorded the meanness of Yankee rustics and defended the Friends' religion in *A New-England Tale* (1822), her brother reported, "The orthodox do all they can to put it down, . . . and New Englanders feel miffed." Thin-skinned New Englanders were miffed again by the pungent, self-willed spinster, Miss Debbie, in *Redwood* (1824); Shakers protested that the novel treated them with "irreverence and derision"; the austere Dana in Boston charged Miss Sedgwick with lack of good taste; but her friend Bryant praised *Redwood* "as a conclusive argument, that the writers of works of fiction, of which the scene is laid in familiar and domestic life, have a rich and varied field before them in the United States." Thereafter she grew more interested in the chitchat of her ladies and gentlemen than in the homely ways of Berkshire countryfolk—she was now a distinguished authoress who wintered in New York and only summered in the Berkshires. She was also so infected by the vogue of historical romance that she deserted contemporary American life for seventeenth century Massachusetts (*Hope Leslie,* 1827) and Revolutionary New York (*The Linwoods,* 1835). Thus propriety and a new fashion in novels smothered Miss Sedgwick's innate realism and made her at last an apostate to her region and a purveyor of sentimental romance to genteel females.

The most colorful and original of the trio was John Neal of Portland, Maine, a Quaker and a tempestuous individualist, a shrewd down-Easter and a citizen of the world, and withal a strident prophet of Americanism in literature. With no education beyond elementary school, he went into trade with John Pierpont in Boston and was left penniless when their branch in Baltimore failed. For a few years he studied law, wrote for the Baltimore newspapers and the *Portico,* and dashed off one novel after another—now in six or seven weeks and again in twenty-seven days: *Logan* (1822), *Errata* (1823), *Seventy-six* (1823), and *Randolph* (1823). In his first novel, *Keep Cool* (1817), he attacked dueling; he enlivened *Randolph* by biting comments on American authors and public men, among them William Pinkney. Pinkney's son challenged Neal, who refused to fight. From 1824 to 1827 Neal lived in England, where he was the first American to write regularly for the great reviews. To *Blackwood's* he contributed a series of essays on American authors—sharply critical but no more severe than his comments written in the United States for *Randolph*. Eyed with suspicion in Portland after his return to America, Neal let it be known that he was a trained boxer and fencer (he had now been read out of meeting by the Friends for knocking a man down), founded the *Yankee,* a literary journal, and in due course was accepted as a leading citizen. In the thirties Neal was one of the first to praise Poe; in the sixties he wrote dime novels for Beadle.

The young law student who turned off a novel with one hand and a review with the other had no time to search for original characters or themes. He snatched high-minded villains from Godwin and low-minded heroes from Byron, then sent them roaring and murdering through the hackneyed routines of cheap melodrama: Logan, who sheds tears and blood with equal ease; and Harold, "whose very breath is poison." The public which supped deep and often on these horrors is well represented by an Englishwoman who, according to Neal, read his novels until "the high seasoning and wild flavor of these fierce and extravagant stories had rendered all other literary aliment unpalatable," and she "died with 'Seventy-Six' in her hand."

Unlike Miss Sedgwick wintering in New York, John Neal living in London developed new respect for our native character and speech. When he took stock of American books, he concluded: "Our best writers are English writers, not American writers. . . . Not so much as one true Yankee is to be found in any one of our native books: hardly so much as one true Yankee phrase." Adapting to his own ends the romantic doctrine of uniqueness, he declared: "It would not do for me to imitate anybody. Nor would it do for my country. Who would care for the *American* Addison where he could have the English?" Neal therefore proposed to abandon *"classical* English" ("It is no natural language—it never was") for common American speech, and to plow deep into American soil. American authors, he believed, would find "abundant and hidden sources of fertility in their own beautiful brave earth, waiting only to be broken up."

Although it remained for later generations to put these precepts into full execution, Neal at least attempted to observe them in his later novels. In the early chapters of *Brother Jonathan* (1825), he reported Yankee manners and diction with extraordinary fidelity, then relapsed into melodrama. In *Rachel Dyer* (1828) he dealt honestly with the witchcraft delusion and two of the unfortunate women sentenced to death by Judge Hathorne, then wandered off into polemics. In the opening pages of *The Down-Easters* (1833) he etched a striking series of Yankee portraits, then degenerated into bombast. Neal's most significant account of the resources of our "beautiful brave earth" is his lively autobiography, *Wandering Recollections of a Somewhat Busy Life* (1869)—his most distinctly American and, as a result, his most memorable book. Here was a romantic individualist who under more favorable circumstances might have exemplified Emerson's theory that any American who writes with full self-trust becomes a true voice of America. In him, as in Paulding and Cooper, belligerence served where art was inadequate to break the ties with the past and with Europe.

5

The interest in reform which had led Mrs. Sigourney into excessive senti-mentalism was more vigorously pursued by another group of New England writers. During the two decades which followed 1820, they fought what Emerson described as "a war between intellect and affection." The war was won by affection, as exemplified by humanitarians who believed that "the nation existed for the individual, for the guardianship and education of every man." When a call went out in 1840 for a Convention of Friends of Universal Reform, all manner of men and women presented themselves at the Chardon Street Chapel in Boston. With as much approval as amusement, Emerson catalogued them as "madmen, madwomen, men with beards, Dunkers, Muggletonians, Come-outers, Groaners, Agrarians, Seventh-Day Baptists, Quakers, Abolitionists, Calvinists, Unitarians, and Philosophers." Among the members of the older generation who contributed to this re-orientation of the New England mind were Channing, John Pierpont, and Lydia Maria Child. As reform was their ultimate concern, their lives speak more loudly than their books. And their books, lacking in literary distinction as they are, speak more loudly of America than do the more polished writings of their bookish contemporaries.

After Channing had analyzed the relationships between the members of the Trinity and between God and man, he turned to those between men and men. Translating into contemporary terms his "high estimate of human nature," his "reverence . . . for human rights," and his faith in "the essential equality of men," he warned his wealthy parishioners in Boston that "justice is a greater good than property, not greater in degree, but in kind." He told Southerners that a man cannot be held as property, because he is both a rational and a moral being—but he told Abolitionists that they were too violent. He attacked intemperance as "the *voluntary extinction of reason*"— but he rebuked temperance agitators for their irrational attempts at coercion. He lectured against war as incompatible with a proper recognition of "the worth of a human being" and helped organize the Massachusetts Peace Soci-ety. He declared that "it is a greater work to educate a child, in the true and larger sense of the word, than to rule a state" and gave his support to Horace Mann. He rejected Franklin's dictum that a man should improve himself to increase his earning power, and urged self-improvement as a means of self-perfection. And the perfection of society through the perfecting of each citizen was, of course, Channing's goal.

John Pierpont brought to the role of universal reformer less elevation but no less devotion than Channing. He sold dry goods and went bankrupt with his partner John Neal, wrote his widely popular *Airs of Palestine* (1816), and pawned the family silver to pay the printer; studied divinity and was ordained as a Unitarian clergyman. American-minded, he wrote "Warren's Address to His Soldiers at Bunker's Hill" for generations of schoolboys to recite and edited *The American First-Class Book* (1823) and *The National Reader* (1827). A friend of universal reform, he opposed war, slavery, imprisonment for debt, and intemperance. When his church in Boston leased its cellar to a rum merchant as a warehouse, after a "Seven Years' War" against the enemy, he resigned in protest and was fully vindicated by an ecclesiastical council. Pierpont lived on to serve briefly as chaplain in the Civil War and to see the Negro emancipated, but not to write a line of truly memorable prose or verse.

From patriotic romances of New England to tracts in defense of humanity was an easy transition for Lydia Maria Francis Child. Encouraged by her brother, a Unitarian clergyman, the youthful Miss Francis published two novels: *Hobomok* (1824), a story of a noble red man, spawned by eighteenth century sentimentalism, and *The Rebels; or, Boston Before the Revolution* (1825), another misalliance of propriety and melodrama. "My natural inclinations," Mrs. Child confessed, "drew me much more strongly toward literature and the arts than toward reform"; but in 1833 she dedicated herself once for all to humanitarianism with *An Appeal in Favor of That Class of Americans Called Africans,* which was the most widely read of her books. It won considerable and important support for abolition, but it also killed her journal, the *Juvenile Miscellany,* reduced the sale of her novels, and deprived her of membership in the Boston Athenaeum. Mrs. Child, with occasional assistance from her husband, edited the *National Anti-Slavery Standard* from 1841 to 1849, and in 1843–1845 she sharply condemned the current scale of income and wages in the United States (*Letters from New York*). As Lowell remarked in doggerel,

> Yes, a great heart is hers, one that dares to go in
> To the prison, the slave-hut, the alleys of sin,
> And to bring into each, or to find there, some line
> Of the never completely out-trampled divine.

But there was doubtful honor and no money for her in social reform and quiet realism; until *Uncle Tom's Cabin* established a precedent, it was more profitable for the authors of New England to romanticize an unreal past than to explore the actualities of a controversial present.

The absorption of humanitarian reform into a larger view of man and society—so vital an element in the work of Emerson, Thoreau, Melville, and Whitman—was at least hinted by Richard Henry Dana, Jr. With the publication of *Two Years Before the Mast* (1840), a new generation took its place in New England letters. Dana paused midway in his college career to strengthen his eyes by a two years' ocean voyage on the brig "Pilgrim," then graduated from Harvard and became a lawyer. Out of his voyage to California came a narrative of the sea as sober and honest as his father's *Buccaneer* was extravagant. To readers of the forties who still doubted, in spite of Cooper's success with such romances, that it was possible to fill a volume with life on the sea, the book was a revelation. To a generation of patriotic Americans who found high satisfaction in the achievements of Yankee captains and Yankee crews sailing the seven seas, this account of the daily duties and the daily boredom of seamen was exciting. To humanitarians of the Chardon Street persuasion, Dana's account of flogging and other severities on shipboard was a sound indictment of the petty tyrants of the American merchant marine. And to sea-smitten boys, the book was and is a classic. For readers who know *Typee* and *Moby Dick*, *Two Years Before the Mast* is most significant as a specimen of the kind of raw material out of which Herman Melville created his great romances of the sea. As for Dana the lawyer, he lived quietly on in Massachusetts, where he befriended sailors (his manual, *The Seamen's Friend*, became their bible), longed for more years before the mast, and was sensibly content with a vacation in the West Indies (*To Cuba and Back*, 1859). Once a month he dined at the Parker House in Boston with Holmes, Lowell, and the other immortals of the Saturday Club.

6

It remained for the quiet poetry of William Cullen Bryant to express the unity of past and present, of America and Europe, which underlay the work of these seemingly diverse writers. On November 3, 1794, he was born into the primitive society of Cummington in Hampshire County, Massachusetts—the home of Ebenezer Snell and his daughter Sarah Bryant. Grandfather Snell was a figure from the past: a Federalist in politics and an extreme Calvinist in religion. Sharp-tongued and austere, he meted out harsh justice as squire in the town of Cummington, deacon in the Congregational Church, and head of the house of Snell and Bryant. To him, the chief temporal duties of man were thrift and industry. His grandson, he taught to plant potatoes and hoe corn. In raking hay, he put the boy in front of him; if Cullen did not make enough speed, his grandfather's rake dropped on his heels.

William Cullen Bryant was born also into the Massachusetts of his father Peter Bryant, M.D., who wrote verse in the manner of Pope but bought for his library (one of the best in Hampshire County) the poems of the late eighteenth century romantics. An able physician and an active public servant, he journeyed often to Boston as a member of the state medical society and of the state legislature. His friends in Boston and his own reading early converted him to Unitarianism. Kindly and democratic during his life, Peter Bryant at his death was mourned throughout western Massachusetts as "the beloved physician."

From the conflicting worlds of Peter Bryant and the Snells, Cullen early escaped into his own New England. To Sarah Snell, the physical world was wind and rain to be noted in her diary; to Dr. Bryant it was an herb garden for his medicines. But their son was from his earliest years "a delighted observer of external nature—the splendors of a winter daybreak over the wild wastes of snow seen from our windows, the glories of the autumnal woods, the gloomy approaches of the thunderstorm, . . . the return of spring, with its flowers, and the first snowfall of winter." Near his doorstep he found yellow violets and fringed gentians, growing beside a rivulet and in a wood. To the eastward, he roamed down the hill-meadows to the noisy Westfield River. To the west, his eyes followed the dim ranges of the Berkshires. And when he walked with nature, he declared:

> I was with one
> With whom I early grew familiar, one
> Who never had a frown for me, whose voice
> Never rebuked me for the hours I stole
> From cares I loved not.

Out of the Federalism of both Squire Snell and Dr. Bryant came Cullen Bryant's first notable publication, *The Embargo, or Sketches of the Times; a Satire*, printed in Boston in 1808 as the work of an anonymous "Youth of Thirteen." The boy's earliest lines had been pious jingles written with the approval of the Snells and sometimes rewarded by a coin from Ebenezer. Lampoons on his schoolmates followed. Then, encouraged by his father, he aimed his shafts at that "imbecile slave," the President of the United States. His angry couplets repeated current libels on Jefferson, among them the accusation that he was intimate with a Negress on his plantation, and demanded his resignation. In Boston the *Monthly Anthology*, organ of William Tudor, George Ticknor, and William Ellery Channing, and predecessor of the *North American Review*, found in *The Embargo* "no small amount of fire and some excellent lines." Such a satire by a boy of thirteen would have been in 1758 an auspicious beginning for a literary career; but in 1808 it was a piece of belated classicism to be outgrown.

Out of the religious liberalism of Peter Bryant and out of Cullen's exploration of his own New England came "Thanatopsis"—the bridge over which the youthful poet moved from Pope toward Wordsworth. The autumn of 1811 found Cullen in a somber mood. He and his father had hoped that he might attend Harvard College, where Peter Bryant had once expected to study medicine and where Sparks and Everett were now undergraduates. The Snells, however, favored the orthodoxy and the economy of Williams College, where he entered as a sophomore—only to leave before the year was out, exasperated by the intellectual poverty of Williamstown. Then he thought to transfer to Yale, where Percival was a student; but Yankee thrift again defeated him, and he attended college no more. Thrice disappointed, Cullen now rambled over the "lone and still and unfrequented" Hampshire hills, meditating sadly on life and, more particularly, on death. Sixteen years earlier, he had been born across the road from a burying ground. He had been frail, and the neighbors predicted that he would not live. As he grew older, his grandfather's prayers of death and his mother's biblical tales of death made the grave a terrible and an imminent reality. As he walked, Cullen asked himself, How shall I face death? The answer was "Thanatopsis."

Back of "Thanatopsis" lay not only long years of fear but long hours of reading among the poets in Peter Bryant's library: Robert Blair, Beilby Porteus, Henry Kirke White, Erasmus Darwin, Southey, Cowper, Milton. Back of "Thanatopsis" lay also Volney's *Ruins* and Dr. Bryant's Unitarian journals from Boston, and Cullen's knowledge that his father testified to his Unitarian belief by refusing to stand when the Trinitarian doxology was sung in the Cummington church. Behind the poem lay also the boy's exploration of nature. In the second edition of *The Embargo* (1809) he had published three crude pastorals in which he attempted, without success, to express his incipient romanticism in the diction of Pope. Now as he wandered "in the gloom of the thickets" and "the twilight of mountain groves," among the "deep-cloven falls" and beside "the rush of the pebble-paved river," he found, without benefit of Wordsworth whom he had not yet read, a vocabulary fit to voice his conception of the physical world.

Ignoring Christ and Calvin, conversion and immortality, Cullen stoically announced in "Thanatopsis" (in early texts of the poem, his own "better genius" speaks, not nature) that every man shall go to the grave serene in his own particular faith—and what that faith is, the poet does not particularize. Here he broke with the more rigorous aspects of the religion of the Snells, accepted the deistic elements in Peter Bryant's religion, and turned in death, as he had already turned in life, from mankind to nature. As this was no poem for the eye of Ebenezer Snell, Cullen hid it away for a time, meticulously revising its lines as his father had taught him.

The economic pressure which had kept him from Yale now sent him over the hill to Worthington to study law. Here he was concerned with people; he lounged in grogshops and danced in taverns; he read Byron and rhymed Byronically of maidens and love. But whenever he returned to the homestead nature spoke to him again, and he lived in his private world of stream and forest. What he heard he set down in "The Yellow Violet" and "Inscription for the Entrance to a Wood." Already professing to be weary of men, he concluded that nature is "the abode of gladness" where the birds "sing and sport in wantonness of spirit" and the wind

> That stirs the stream in play, shall come to thee,
> Like one that loves thee nor will let thee pass
> Ungreeted, and shall give its light embrace.

At Worthington Bryant read Wordsworth's poems and drew from them new symbols to express his conception of the universe; but the romanticism which was emerging in his poetry was neither English nor American; it was both.

7

At the age of twenty-one, Bryant left Cummington to make his own way in the world. During the decade which followed, his ideas, his emotions, and his poetry took on the conformations which were to mark them until his death at eighty-five. First, he came to terms with God and religion. Late one afternoon in December, 1815, he set out from the homestead to open a law office in the crossroads hamlet of Plainfield, to which he resigned himself when it became evident that there was no money in the family purse to send him to Boston. As he walked down into the gathering shadows, uncertainty crowded upon him. Very much alone, he remembered his father's God, to whom he had of late given little thought. Then his eye was caught by a waterfowl sharply outlined against the evening sky—nature's confirmation of the existence of omnipotent Goodness. Deeply moved, Bryant put himself into the keeping of nature's Deity:

> He who, from zone to zone,
> Guides through the boundless sky thy certain flight,
> In the long way that I must tread alone,
> Will lead my steps aright.

Thereafter he was a religious liberal, associating himself particularly with the Unitarians, who to the mind of the Snells and most New Englanders, were a Christless lot.

"Thanatopsis" was given to the public by the *North American Review* after Bryant had left Plainfield, not for Boston, but for Great Barrington among the Berkshires. The town had been settled by the Dutch and was now in closer contact with Albany and New York than with eastern Massachusetts; but the influence of Boston still followed Bryant. On a visit to Cummington, he left the manuscript of "Thanatopsis" on his father's desk, and the latter took it to Dana and Channing. Both were profoundly moved by the poem—the Anglophile Dana so deeply that he protested to one of his editorial colleagues: "Ah, you have been imposed upon. No one on this side of the Atlantic is capable of writing such verses!" When the *North American* printed "Thanatopsis" anonymously in 1817, it attracted no particular attention, and the world was not aware that an obscure lawyer in the Berkshires had published what was then the finest of American lyrics.

Bryant's first critical pronouncements on poetry were in close accord with his own practices. In an essay on versification, commenced when he was writing the early drafts of "Thanatopsis," he revealed that his preciosity in poetry was no accident; at sixteen, he had already concluded that the use of trisyllabic feet in iambic verse "is agreeable to that kind of measure, as well as to the habits of our language." Reviewing Solyman Brown's *An Essay on American Poetry* in 1818, he condemned the American Augustans for their "balanced and wearisome regularity." And in his own poetry he had long since freed himself from the chains of Pope and was now exploring, with true romantic delight, the varied resources of meter. No American during the twenties matched Bryant in the diversity and the refinement of his measures.

The problem of nationalism in literature also occupied Bryant's mind. He pointed out in the *North American* that contumely abroad and complacency at home were equally unjustified. So, likewise, was American subservience to foreign opinion: "We do not praise a thing," he protested, "until we see the seal of transatlantic approbation upon it." He admitted that an American author "must produce some more satisfactory evidence of his claim to celebrity than an extract from the parish register," but he insisted, despite British and American pronouncements to the contrary, that the United States was "a rich and varied field" for literature, and that authors who dealt honestly with the American landscape and the diversities of American character would deserve well of their countrymen. He was soon able to point to the novel *Redwood,* by his friend Catharine Sedgwick, as an example of honest nationalism.

An opportunity to review the history of the human race and at the same time to make a name for himself in Boston came to Bryant in 1821, when the editors of the *North American* secured for their contributor an invitation to deliver the Phi Beta Kappa poem at Harvard. For that occasion, Bryant wrote "The Ages"—a pedestrian defense of the doctrine of human perfectibility. In heavy Spenserians, he traced the progress of mankind from the early days of barbarism, through the glory of Greece and the darkness of the Middle Ages, on into modern times, and at last to America, where man shall come to ultimate fulfillment:

> Here the free spirit of mankind, at length,
> Throws its last fetters off; and who shall place
> A limit to the giant's unchained strength,
> Or curb the swiftness of his forward race?

Nothing in this familiar interpretation of history impressed the Harvard faculty, nothing in Bryant's quiet delivery caught the fancy of the public, and no one offered him a good berth in Boston. But he met Dana, and with Dana he formed the longest and closest friendship of his life. And he found a publisher for his *Poems* (1821), which included among its eight items "Thanatopsis," "The Yellow Violet," "Inscription for the Entrance to a Wood," "To a Waterfowl," and "Green River." The volume sold slowly; no important journal in New England praised it except the *North American*; and its most enthusiastic reviewer was a New Yorker, Gulian Verplanck. Although Bryant was in reality the foremost American poet of the day, he was still an unknown.

In Great Barrington, Bryant was moving toward the same stability in his affections and in his politics that he had already attained in religion. During his days as a student of law, his fancy and his pen had often toyed with love. Now he gave his heart to a young woman reared beside his Green River; in Frances Fairchild's honor he produced, after agonies of revision, the graceful lyric, "Oh Fairest of the Rural Maids"; and the two were happily married. As for his political beliefs, Bryant had been from boyhood an advocate of human liberty and of republicanism. Now he spoke out for the emancipation of Greeks, Waldenses, and Spaniards in Europe and of Negroes in the United States. He was converted to free trade by his reading in the English economists Adam Smith, Ricardo, and Thornton, to whom he was introduced by the Sedgwick brothers of Stockbridge and New York. Thus, when the Federalist Party disappeared and no antislavery party offered itself to the electorate, he was prepared to turn from the conservative majority in New England to the Democrats and free trade. Thereafter he remained a political liberal, in one party or another, until old age overtook him.

A systematic testing of his capacity for writing poetry followed in 1824–1825. From Boston came an invitation to contribute to each issue of a new semimonthly magazine, the *United-States Literary Gazette*. In response, he wrote more poetry than during any comparable period in his life. As the Berkshires and he were now intimate friends, his favored theme was nature:

"A Winter Piece," "The West Wind," "A Walk at Sunset," "March," "Summer Wind," "After a Tempest," "Autumn Woods," "November," "To a Cloud, "A Forest Hymn," and others. Bryant's regular appearance twice monthly in a new literary journal had its effect: his poems were reprinted, critics commented on them both here and in England, and his reputation grew. But in Massachusetts comment was often unfavorable, for Bryant was an America scion of the Lake School of poets and the Lakers were still anathema to most Bostonians.

At the age of thirty, Bryant left New England. Respected in Great Barrington but not universally liked, he himself was sharply annoyed by the factiousness of village life. "It cost me," he complained, "more pains and perplexity than it was worth to live on friendly terms with my neighbors." In this unwelcome atmosphere, he was

> forced to drudge for the dregs of men,
> And scrawl strange words with a barbarous pen,
> And mingle among the jostling crowd,
> Where the sons of strife [are] subtle and loud.

Practicing only in the civil courts and occupied chiefly with trivial suits for the collection of debts, he never earned more than five hundred dollars for a year's toil for the dregs of men, while the *Literary Gazette* paid him two hundred dollars a year for a hundred lines of poetry per month. In financial matters, Bryant possessed too much practicality to starve in a garret for the sake of the muse. But a salary of a thousand dollars as joint editor of the *New-York Review and Atheneum Magazine* was a conclusive argument for abandoning both the law and Massachusetts. In 1825 he became a "literary adventurer" in New York.

8

The adventurer soon found security as editor and part-owner of the *Evening Post*. There Bryant for a half-century shaped American public opinion, took on prestige and patriarchal dignity, and eventually became one of the first citizens of New York. Yet the characteristics of the New York editor all had their origins in the character of the Massachusetts lawyer. Thriftily he invested his earnings, not from profitless poetry but from his newspaper, in real estate; then the growth of New York made him a wealthy man. Once a caustic young satirist and later a hot-tempered lawyer, he horsewhipped Editor Stone of the *Commercial Advertiser* and refused, under any and all circumstances, to speak to Editor Weed of Albany, N.Y. Then he learned to curb his wrath—but even in his last years dull flames occasionally smoldered under his heavy brows. The man who had fled from men to the fastnesses of the Berkshires was in New York as shy as "a sensitive young girl"; his polished contemporary from Boston, Edward Everett, found him as nearly helpless in polite society as any famous man he had ever met. To cover all this, Bryant developed a highly formal manner ("One would as soon think of taking a liberty with the Pope as with BRYANT," said John Bigelow) and cultivated an austere silence ("Not a soul can get a word out of him without cart and horses to fetch it," complained Bret Harte). Uncritical observers soon mistook this mask for the man, and in the forties young Lowell was so far misled by externalities as to write:

> There is Bryant, as quiet, as cool, and as dignified
> As a smooth, silent iceberg, that never is ignified.

But in Bryant's last years his emotions did indeed atrophy under this rigid self-discipline, until the man whom Harte met in the seventies was truly a cold and silent iceberg.

Bryant of the *Post* was a hard-working and capable editor, but brilliance was not to be expected from a quiet country lawyer turned city journalist. When the *Post* finally became a money-maker, its prosperity came not from any superlative ability of Bryant as a newsman but from increased public endorsement of the two beliefs which he had brought with him from Massachusetts: faith in liberty and faith in democracy. In New York he was an early and often a lonely advocate of abolition, free speech, and the rights of labor. In 1836 he defended a group of tailors who formed a union and were thereupon fined for conspiracy in restraint of trade. "If this is not SLAVERY," he thundered in the *Post*, "we have forgotten its definition." When a mob murdered Lovejoy in 1837, Bryant wrote a noble plea for freedom of speech: "The right to discuss freely and openly, by speech, by the pen, by the press, all political questions and to examine and animadvert upon all political institutions, is a right so clear and certain, so interwoven with our other liberties, so necessary, in fact, to their existence, that without it we shall fall at once into despotism or anarchy." He made the *Post* an organ of the Free Soilers, of the Barnburners, and, after the Kansas-Nebraska Bill was enacted in 1854, of that radical new party, the black Republicans. He damned the Fugitive Slave Law as "the most ruffianly act ever authorized by a deliberative assembly," glorified John Brown as "one of the martyrs and heroes" of human liberty, and sponsored Abraham Lincoln on his first appearance in New York. When further compromise with the South became impossible, Bryant repudiated his youthful belief in the right to secession and became a hot advocate of relentless war upon the rebels.

Too level-headed to become a universal reformer, Bryant gave the support of the *Post* only to those movements which seemed to him both sane and urgent. In municipal affairs, for example, he campaigned with varying degrees of success for a central park, improved police and fire protection, and against corrupt politics. In international affairs, he continued to back free trade, and he became an advocate of free cultural, as well as economic, exchange between the old world and the United States. Moral considerations were never forgotten in his editorials. Although his conception of democracy is more reminiscent of Peter Bryant than of the Snells, he attributed his adherence to "the great rule of right without much regard for persons" to the influence of his mother, whose conduct taught him "never to countenance a wrong because others did." Thus when Editor Bryant pilloried such national figures as Harrison, Clay, and that "sordid apostate" Webster, he was dealing with wrongdoers just as Sarah Bryant and her female colleagues had dealt with a notorious wife-beater of Cummington when, one election day, they rode him out of town on a rail. Industry, good sense, moral purpose, honesty, courage—these made Bryant one of the great figures in American journalism.

During his early years in New York, Bryant turned his hand to prose tales on romantic themes which he had earlier treated in verse: Indians and pioneers in the manner of Cooper ("The Indian Spring," "The Cascade of Melsingah," "The Skeleton's Cave," "The Marriage Blunder"), fantasy and legend in the manner of Irving ("A Border Tradition," "A Pennsylvania Legend," "Reminiscences of New York," "The Legend of the Devil's Pulpit"), and the literature and customs of Spain ("Recollections of the South of Spain," "Early Spanish Poetry," "Phanette des Gantelmes"). From his travels in the prairie states (where his mother and brothers found a new frontier) and in Europe and the Near East, he brought back solid cargoes of fact: *Letters of a Traveller* (1850), *Letters of a Traveller, Second Serie.* (1859), and *Letters from the East* (1869). When his contemporaries among the romantics died, he reviewed their careers: Thomas Cole, Cooper, Irving, Gulian Verplanck. But Bryant's prose, whether fantasy or funeral oration, was heavy, and in his later years he wisely employed verse as a vehicle for his excursions into fairyland: "Castles in the Air," "The Little People of the Snow," "Cloudland," "Stella."

9

Bryant was also a pioneer in American literary criticism; his was our earliest systematic study of the nature of poetry. From "Lectures on Poetry" (delivered in 1825; published 1884) to "Poets and Poetry of the English Language" (introduction to *A Library of Poetry and Song,* 1871), he consistently defined poetry in the same familiar terms: morality, imagination, originality, emotion, simplicity. Thoroughly committed, like the entire *North American* group in Massachusetts, to a moralism at which New Yorkers were beginning to smile, Bryant never doubted that the poet should teach "direct lessons of wisdom." At the same time, he believed that poetry, as a suggestive rather than a mimetic art, addresses itself to the imagination of the reader. Then the reader, in turn, contributes to the poetic experience by sending his own imagination along "the path which the poet only points out." Admitting that every artist takes up his art where his predecessors have left it, Bryant insisted that the poet, if he is to "deserve the praise of originality and genius," must go on to discover "new modes of sublimity, of beauty, and of human emotion." And emotion, Bryant declared, is "the great spring of poetry." From this principle, it follows that "poetry which does not find the way to the heart is scarcely deserving of the name." And again: "The most beautiful poetry is that which takes the strongest hold on the feelings." Finally, he was an advocate of clearness and simplicity, particularly as they are exemplified in the "luminous style" which is "one of the most important requisites for a great poet." As for the origins of these views, young Cullen Bryant met them in his father's library in Cummington, stated explicitly or through implication by certain of the eighteenth century rhetoricians and critics who precipitated the romantic revolution in Great Britain.

General recognition of Bryant the poet came belatedly, on the heels of recognition of Bryant the editor. In 1837, Poe wrote: "Mr. Bryant's poetical reputation, both at home and abroad, is greater, we presume, than that of any other American. British critics have frequently awarded him high praise; and here, the public press have been unanimous in approbation." These superlatives were not entirely justified, for American critics were by no means unanimous in recognizing Bryant as the chief American poet. An English edition of his poems, sponsored by Washington Irving in 1832, was well received, and in the United States he reached the apex of his reputation in the thirties—only to be overshadowed at once by the next generation of romantic poets, Poe, Longfellow, Whittier, and Lowell. It is a further irony of literary history that during the years of his greatest fame, he wrote only a handful of significant poems ("To the Fringed Gentian," "Song of Marion's Men," "The Prairies") and during the four decades which followed, hardly more ("Oh Mother of a Mighty Race," "Robert of Lincoln," "The Planting of the Apple-Tree," "The Death of Lincoln"). Although he was at times too hard pressed by editorial duties to compose poetry, he had at other times considerable leisure. His scanty output is therefore to be explained on the ground that he possessed only a modest vein of genius, which he early discovered and soon explored to its full extent. From the first, he was obliged to mine that vein with the utmost industry—revising, discarding, reworking, and revising yet again. To his credit, these revisions were almost invariably fortunate. Likewise to his high credit is the fact that, despite these limitations, he earned for himself a secure place among the American poets.

Even though Bryant's early readers found his poems complex and difficult, he is in the present century read, as he would prefer to be, as a poet of simplicity. His ideas are few and familiar. God he interpreted as truth and love, justice and liberty. Man is, in terms of the immediate, a creature of "sorrows, crimes, and cares"; in terms of the ultimate, man is moving steadily toward that great day when "love and peace shall make their paradise" on earth. Nature is a serene temple for worship and a reservoir of health and joy to which Bryant continually invited his reader to escape, from

> all that pained thee in the haunts of men,
> And made thee loathe thy life.

Bryant's emotions seem to readers of the present day to be equally limited: reverence for God, wrath for all despoilers of humanity, pity for their vicitims, love for wife and child (who, to Bryant's mind, never despoil), devotion to native land (which rarely despoils), and affection for the physical world (to whose despoilings Bryant closed his eyes). But his most successful transcriptions of these ideas and these emotions are marked now by a quiet charm and again by a dignity unsurpassed, of their kind, in American poetry.

Bryant would wish to be, and should be, read also as a poet of America. His nationalism was more consistent than that of Catharine Sedgwick or John Neal and more solidly grounded than that of any contemporary New Englander except Channing. His affection for the American landscape exceeded Irving's and equaled Cooper's. As a New Yorker, he capitulated to the beauty of Long Island and the Hudson. He and Thomas Cole, the romantic painter of magnificence and grandeur, were particularly charmed by the Catskills; they are, very appropriately, the only human figures in Asher Brown Durand's painting of a Catskill landscape ("Kindred Spirits"). But Bryant, like his friends among the Hudson River School of painters, was more successful in introducing American materials into his work than in creating an American manner. Unlike Whitman in the next generation of romanticists, he was prepared neither to announce nor to put into practice the brave dictum, "The expression of the American poet is to be transcendent and new." Closely related as the substance of many of Bryant's poems is to the life of America and especially of New England, his voice was to the end the voice of an Anglo-American.

Bryant should be read, finally, as a poet of the eternal procession of mankind. He followed the march of men and of time in the ancient classics, which in boyhood he translated for pleasure and in old age, for consolation (*The Iliad of Homer,* 1870; *The Odyssey of Homer,* 1871–1872). In the Bible and in science, he traced "the great Movement of the Universe." In Massachusetts and in New York, he mourned as his family and his friends joined

> The innumerable caravan, which moves
> To that mysterious realm, where each shall take
> His chamber in the silent halls of death.

Then he drew on the events of history to trace the great procession in "The Ages" and "The Past." In terms of the physical world, he charted the progression of the universe in "The Planting of the Apple-Tree," "The Song of the Sower," and employing an even more figurative idiom, in his many poems of the winds. Drawing on his own memories, he retold the story in "A Lifetime" and "The Flood of Years." Here, with fourscore years behind him, the poet asked for the last time the question which he had first posed at sixteen: How shall a man approach the grave? And the aged Bryant replied: Go serenely, with an unfaltering trust in "the never-ending Flood of Years," a trust in that "eternal Change" which unites all men, all times, and all events in "everlasting Concord."

22. IN THE SOUTH

By 1826, when Cooper, Irving, and Bryant were making for themselves the first great names in American literature, Poe was an unknown student at the newly established University of Virginia, and the most notable author in the South was George Tucker, the Charlottesville Professor of Moral Philosophy and Political Economy. Tucker was born in 1775 in Bermuda. He came to Virginia as a youth to study law at William and Mary College under his cousin St. George .Tucker, himself a native Bermudan, a famous lawyer, and an occasional author.

George Tucker's career may be taken to reflect the state of literary culture in Maryland, Virginia, and the Carolinas during the 1820's. A man of inquiring mind and conservative temper, he was led by his legal training into a serious study of the agrarian economy upon which the political philosophy of the South was deeply based, and to the publication, while a member of the National Congress, of *Essays on Subjects of Taste, Morals, and National Policy* (1822). But when he turned to the writing of literature as such, he looked for models to the London of the past century rather than to the contemporary New York of Irving and Cooper or the New England of Bryant. As a lawyer in Richmond, he is reported to have put an end to card playing among refined people by a poetical satire, and his novel, *The Valley of the Shenandoah* (1824) combines his memories of Richardson's *Clarissa* with observations of sparsely settled Virginia. After his fanciful, pseudoscientific *Voyage to the Moon* (1827), his writings both in Charlottesville and in Philadelphia, where he resided after 1845, a vigorous and productive figure, were for the most part historical and sociological.

Even more than Tucker, William Wirt, though long inactive in literature, was generally held during the late twenties to be the most important author in the South for his popular *Letters of the British Spy* (1803) and other Addisonian essays on Southern manners. A Marylander born in 1772, Wirt had married into a prominent Virginia family and moved to Richmond to practice law, where he gained repute as one of the leading orators of his day. There he wrote a life of Patrick Henry, and prosecuted the extremely sensational trial of Aaron Burr. In 1817 he became Attorney General of the

United States. From that date, through the year of his declining to become first president of the University of Virginia, till his death in 1834, he resided in Baltimore nearly all of the time that he was not in Washington. Wirt's tastes were aristocratic and conservative; in the manner of the day, he divided his energies sharply between the light satiric essay and the serious efforts of the court of law and the world of affairs.

There was surely little love lost between Wirt and his older, mercurial Baltimore fellow citizen, William Pinkney, a perennial diplomat, often esteemed the greatest lawyer in America; and of Pinkney's son, Edward Coote Pinkney, even more mercurial than Pinkney the elder, the always temperate Wirt must have entertained a poor opinion indeed. This poet was born in 1802 in England, when his father was there on a diplomatic mission, and he spent more than half of his twenty-six years either with his father abroad or in the United States Navy, which he joined at thirteen and, proud and quarreling, abandoned at twenty-two. In 1823 he published *A Serenade Written by a Gentleman of Baltimore* ("Look out upon the stars, my love") reminiscent of the Elizabethan lyrics, and *Rodolph: A Fragment*; and in 1825 he published a slight volume, *Poems,* containing "A Health":

> I fill this cup to one made up of loveliness alone,
> A woman of her gentler sex the seeming paragon.

All of this time, especially after his marriage in 1824, he was desperate for money, but his poetry, echoing Byron in morals as well as in melody, was too unconventional for sedate people, and did not help him with his law practice. What it did help him with was an appointment to the unsalaried Professorship of Rhetoric and Belles-Lettres in the University of Maryland, and later, the editorship of a political paper, which he held for a few months before his death. For its fiery spirit and its flowing rhythm, Pinkney's poetry, though scant in volume, has come to be recognized as the purest product of the romantic and conservative Old South of the twenties.

The friendship that Wirt enjoyed with another young man in Baltimore must have delighted him as much as the Pinkney phenomenon dismayed him. John Pendleton Kennedy, the patron of Poe and the Maecenas of Southern letters for fifty years, was the son of an immigrant father and a mother from the distinguished Pendleton family in Virginia. In his youth he was probably more at home on the Shenandoah Valley plantations of his mother's relatives than in his native town, where he attended school and college.

Of bookish disposition, Kennedy contributed to the newspapers at an early age, and, as an advancing young lawyer, helped publish at irregular intervals an anonymous little magazine. Though this magazine was somewhat impish, it was trenchant enough to win the mild, solicited applause of Edward Everett at Harvard. In 1820 Kennedy was in the Maryland legislature, and early in 1822 Wirt proposed him, without his complete assent, for a diplomatic post in South America. In his mid-thirties, about the time when in Baltimore Poe at twenty-one was living in poverty and Pinkney at twenty-six was dying in poverty, Kennedy inherited a considerable sum of money and married the daughter of a prosperous and literary-minded Baltimore manufacturer. From that time, he devoted himself less and less to the law and more and more to writing, politics, and public affairs.

Kennedy's presence made Baltimore a literary center to be rivaled only by Charleston, which was in the meantime becoming notable in letters mainly through the unimportant writings of a society-wit who had come from Massachusetts and of a transcendental painter who was bound for Massachusetts. In the late 1820's, however, a vigorous and thoroughly native group asserted themselves and William Gilmore Simms, then a slightly schooled young man of twenty, but soon to become the most prolific and popular of Southern authors, published two volumes of poetry. And two prominent fellow citizens of his, plantation men both of them—the aging banker and botanist Stephen Elliott, and the maturing lawyer and traveled scholar Hugh Swinton Legaré—inaugurated the *Southern Review* in 1828. This recondite publication was an adaptation to the Old South of the great quarterlies then current in Britain. But its collapse after four years suggests that the editors' calculation of the degree of adaptation needed was something less than adequate.

Always a little ponderous, inflexibly honest, Legaré was a phenomenon of industry and learning in his own subject, the law, and in most phases of European history. He was too earnest and fastidious to be interested in anything but the most classic classics, and he had little respect for American literature; that is, for American creative literature. His own essays, whether published in the *Southern Review* or in the *New-York Review,* testify fully that he was ready to tolerate critical literature that was American in authorship if not in subject. The brevity of his service in Congress indicates how gravely his opposition to Calhoun injured him as a politician at home, and his appointment as Attorney General of the United States in 1841 and Acting Secretary of State in 1843 indicates how little that opposition injured him elsewhere. His death in 1843 at the home of his long-time intimate friend George Ticknor in Boston was celebrated in a memorable poem by his kinsman, James Mathewes Legaré; and in 1846 his sister edited two volumes of his writings in Charleston.

As the national Congress, a sort of haven for Southern authors, had received Legaré and George Tucker, it received in 1818—and intermittently until 1835—Richard Henry Wilde of Georgia. Wilde was born in Ireland in 1789 but grew up in Augusta. He was a lawyer at nineteen, and the author by 1815 of a long poem dealing with the Indian wars in Florida and containing the lyric "My Life is Like the Summer Rose." This widely popular, lugubrious, Byronic plaint was the center for a long time of a storm of charges and countercharges as to its originality. A Greek translation of it, passed off as a newly discovered fragment of the verse of Alcaeus, and an outright claim to its authorship by an Irish impostor kept confused an issue that was cleared up in 1871 to its true author's complete credit.

In 1834 Wilde bestirred himself valiantly in Augusta in connection with the inauguration of the Richmond magazine, the *Southern Literary Messenger,* writing articles for it and procuring a hundred subscribers. But he was disillusioned with democracy; he could find no political party that did not "require of its followers what no honest man should and no gentleman would do." In 1835 he quit America for Italy. There for five years he occupied himself with a study of Renaissance Italian literature; and in 1842 he published a book on Tasso. The severe contemporary judgments passed on his "shirking abandonment" of America for Europe—"delight to the senses, but mildew to the heart"—and his own freely expressed poor opinion of the literary potentialities of America did not cool the adulatory nature of his welcome when he returned home. He had already to some degree refuted and, it was hoped, might further refute the charge that the artistic life in America was sterile, and somebody proposed that the people of Georgia should set up a monument to him. The proposal was not carried out, and Wilde left Augusta for New Orleans, a change which he came to think a further step into the cultural badlands. Before his death from yellow fever in 1847, he taught and practiced law, contributed to Southern magazines, and made occasional trips to New York where at times he encountered his friend Simms of Charleston.

2

In 1832 Kennedy in Baltimore published as by one Mark Littleton *Swallow Barn*—not a novel, he explained, but "a series of sketches linked together"; and Southern literature to some extent broke its tie with the classical and chivalric traditions of the Old World to recognize its kinship with the young writers to the North. Whatever its species, *Swallow Barn* is highly suggestive of Irving in style and spirit. It deals with Virginia plantation life in the first quarter of the nineteenth century. The really Great Days of Virginia, Kennedy thought, had already vanished; but he presented the remains of greatness there in such a fashion as to suggest that the time and place were inexhaustibly romantic. Kennedy's scenes and characters are uniformly "aristocratic," so that the credit as an early realist goes to Augustus Baldwin Longstreet for his humorous and earthy *Georgia Scenes,* published three years later. Yet it is important to remember that the way of life which is pictured in *Swallow Barn* is more simple and casual than that represented by the alabaster columns, with human and other appurtenances, which later novelists reared in battalions all over Virginia.

Swallow Barn was well received throughout the country, and its author was recognized as the literary heir of the aging Wirt, to whom the book was dedicated in time for him to know of the compliment before his death in 1834. In 1833 Kennedy was one of a committee of three who awarded to Edgar Allan Poe, then almost wholly unknown, a prize in a literary competition for his short story "MS Found in a Bottle." Poe's talents and his poverty and general emotional wretchedness stirred Kennedy deeply, and it was through him that Poe in 1835 obtained the position with the year-old *Southern Literary Messenger* in Richmond that in a sense "made" both magazine and editor. During the rest of Poe's life Kennedy entertained the most cordial feeling for him. He helped him at times with money and oftener with what Poe indeed more truly needed but was reluctant to accept, counsel that was wise and kindly and as understanding as a man like Kennedy could devise for a man like Poe.

Two years after the appearance of *Swallow Barn,* a physician, William Alexander Caruthers of Savannah, who was almost surely a follower of the *Messenger,* published his novel *The Kentuckian in New York.* His birth in Virginia in 1800 and his schooling at the college in Lexington, if no more, made him refer to himself always as a "Virginian"; but he was also a self-conscious protagonist of the "West," of which Georgia was in his mind a part. He said that he could see Savannah in his time outstripping New York and Philadelphia, and the United States by 1870 a nation of 168,000,000 people—all of whom, he hoped, would eschew both rum and Romanism.

The Kentuckian in New York is made up of letters between two young South Carolinians and a Kentuckian, who are visiting New York, and a young Virginian who is visiting in South Carolina. The final effect is that of a voluble, high-spirited travel book, with long but interesting digressions devoted now to the tender passion, now to historical, economic, or philosophic commentary. In spite of the author's belief that there was a Northern conspiracy against Southern writers, the main thesis of his book is that if Northerners and Southerners could be brought to know one another they would inevitably love one another.

Caruthers was an affable, too credulous, but earnest and candid patriot. He deprecated the big-plantation system in the South and city "mobocracies" in the North, and he wished for the entire country, apparently with hope of realizing the wish, an economy based predominantly on small farms operated by their white owners.

In an epilogue to his first novel, he declared that he had created his talkative, Jackson-worshiping Kentuckian primarily as a humorous enticement for readers, and that his true interest lay in a historical romance that he would publish soon. This book, *The Cavaliers of Virginia* (1834–1835), though it deals with Bacon's Rebellion in a way deeply sympathetic with Bacon, is high-flown in its style, and generally saturated with the theory that Virginians are a race considerably apart—and apart wholly in the direction of excellence. His last novel, *The Knights of the Horse-shoe* (1845), maintains the same theory in its treatment of the Old Dominion under Governor Spotswood, who led the first expedition into the Shenandoah Valley and the Appalachians.

An actual and not a merely philosophic intersectionalist was William Gilmore Simms of Carolina. Born in Charleston in 1806, he began to publish very early; but when his first widely read work, the novel entitled *Guy Rivers,* appeared in 1834 he had been living in New England and New York off and on for a year or so.

Simms' mother died when he was an infant, and his father soon afterward migrated to Mississippi, leaving the boy to be brought up by his impoverished maternal grandmother. She gave her charge a casual schooling, put him to work in a drugstore, fed his mind with her memories of the Revolution, and attempted vainly to curtail his vast reading. The visit East in 1816 of Simms' father, by then a bona-fide frontiersman and an Andrew Jackson veteran, doubtless added its weight to the boy's discontent with life as a druggist. By 1824, when he readied himself to visit his father in Mississippi, he was a neophyte lawyer engaged to be married. He remained in the West for several months, observing much that he never forgot; but, for all of his father's appeals to him never to return East, he was again in Charleston by 1825.

In that year he published a dirge in heroic couplets to celebrate the death of a local Revolutionary patriot; and in 1827 he published a volume of poems largely patterned on Byron. During 1828, while Legaré and Elliott edited the august *Southern Review,* Simms edited his ephemeral magazine, the *Tablet.* That failing, he transferred his energies to a newspaper called the *City Gazette,* which he edited with such vigorous anti-Calhoun ardor that the Calhoun victory in the next elections went very hard with him. For other reasons, too, the last of the 1820's and the first of the 1830's in Charleston were a momentous time in his life. He continued to publish poetry, one generally neglected offering after another, and he suffered the deaths of his wife, his father, and the grandmother who had reared him.

Bereaved and frustrated, politically rebuffed like Legaré, he left Charleston for the North, doubtless in a mood similar to that in which Legaré about the same time undertook a diplomatic post in Belgium. In New England and in New York City, he formed warm and lasting friendships with a number of people, the most notable of whom was William Cullen Bryant; and there he published his first prose tale, *Martin Faber* (1833), and his most important poem, *Atalantis* (1832), written in Massachusetts but having to do with the love affairs of a somewhat southerly sea nymph.

With *Guy Rivers* (1834), an action tale of gold-mining then being carried on in the wilds of North Georgia, Simms achieved his first success in romantic fiction on a native theme. After it was published he returned to South Carolina; but for the remainder of his life he made regular, frequent, and extended visits to New York. In 1835, he published *The Partisan,* a novel of the Revolution, and *The Yemassee*—always the most popular of his works—an exciting South Carolina "Border Romance" which provided, next to Cooper's more idealized portraits, the most influential fictional study of the Indian.

Simms exploited various aspects of Southern life in his many novels. *Guy Rivers* was the first of a series dealing with the Southwestern border, which he had learned about chiefly from his father; and *The Partisan* was the first of a similar series dealing with the Revolutionary War, which he had learned about chiefly from his grandmother. *Pelayo, a Story of the Goth* (1838) and its sequel, *Count Julian* (1845), both unsuccessful romances, were his response to the feeling current about him that America was in the end not a fit setting for noble literature. The story "The Loves of the Driver"— it was a Negro driver—and the two novels *Beauchampe* (1842) and *Charlemont* (1856), both turning on the same notorious Kentucky murder that Poe and Chivers set into drama, were considered offensively direct about matters best approached circuitously. But in Simms' case so very much was always happening that few could hold against him for long his occasional brief sallies, in writing, across the frontiers of what was esteemed to be propriety.

After his second marriage in 1836, Simms shifted fairly promptly and very thoroughly his political outlook to accord with that of his wife's estimable planter-father—just as in Baltimore Kennedy shifted his outlook to accord with that of his wife's estimable manufacturer-father. Both men have been blamed as craven for these sins. Both have been defended, on good grounds, for having shifted, not because of personal venality, but because the little worlds about them changed.

At length a great planter, resident at his wife's plantation, Woodlands, Simms was the head of a vast household—he became the father of fifteen children—and a host whose guest list grew always more and more voluminous. Like many other Southerners, everywhere and unremittingly harried on the score of slavery, he now found it increasingly easy to take fully to heart the ingenuous doctrine, fascinating at a moment when everything Greek was fashionable, that the South was a "*Greek* Democracy"—with a few Christian modifications. In such a society, it was maintained, any freeman might with virtue aspire to any height, and no Negro slave might so aspire, ever; but every slave could expect always, as many a "wage slave" in Boston could not expect, all of the basic necessities of existence plus a recognition of his humanity, of his brotherhood in God.

This theoretical recognition of every freeman's unlimited right to any development he can legitimately achieve is always precarious and all too likely at any moment to flicker out. For a number of reasons, it managed in the Old South to maintain itself somewhat more generally than it did in many other places. One of these reasons was the continuing existence of frontier influences. Another, apparently, was the existence of the slaves, a submerged class that could always be made to absorb readily any anti-equalitarian impulses that might assert themselves.

Simms became one of the most powerful exegetes of the Greek Democracy point of view, and it is safe to believe that as the South's position became the more dangerous and his own fame the more impressive, the one-time drug clerk was more acceptable to his fellows. There is a story of a British grandee visiting Charleston who replied to his host's question as to what he would most like to see, that he would like to see some of the great men of the place—for example, Simms. When the host indicated that at home Simms' greatness was not generally accepted, the grandee is said to have inquired who, if not Simms, was a great man in Charleston. All this may have happened; but it is probable that the phenomenal man was extolled at home quite generously, that even the more discriminating talk about him as a writer turned not so much on the carelessness of his style as on his torrential gusto and energy, on his kinship to Cooper (whom he excelled in characterization) in his treatment of the Indian, on his kinship to Scott in his heroics, on his kinship even to Shakespeare in his epic portrayal of an American Falstaff, the Revolutionary soldier Lieutenant Porgy.

The same year, 1835, that saw the publication of Simms' *The Yemassee* and *The Partisan* saw Poe become editor of the *Southern Literary Messenger,* and Wilde exile himself in Italy. In this year, also, were published Longstreet's

Georgia Scenes and a second book by Kennedy. Kennedy's novel, *Horse Shoe Robinson,* a story of the western Carolinas during 1780, was a deliberate effort to contribute to the Grand American Legend by way of romantic fiction. The central character, a veteran of the Revolution, made a living as a blacksmith; but his main business was apparently the unconscious fulfillment of the dream of the "natural man." The story was that of a man whom Kennedy had met on a trip to Georgia in 1819, and who survived long enough to vouch for most of the narrative as Kennedy set it down. Not so vigorous as Simms' stories of the Revolution in the South, the book is more seemly and precise. It was widely read and highly regarded, and in spite of its author's conviction that really important people do not care for literature, it furthered his name and fame to very practical effect throughout the seaboard states.

Kennedy celebrated the year 1838 by being elected to Congress and by publishing *Rob of the Bowl,* a loosely organized, romantic novel of Catholic and Protestant feuding in Maryland in 1661. During the forties and the early fifties politics and public affairs largely engrossed him. He published *Quodlibet,* a sharp and still very readable satire on Jacksonian Democracy, and, nearly ten years later, a biography of William Wirt. By then, he had almost come to feel that really important people care even less for politics than for literature. Accordingly, though he was flattered to serve as Secretary of the Navy, 1852–1853, and to meet and to charm the great Thackeray when he visited here, he felt that all of this was decidedly not enough.

Simms till he was a mature man, and Caruthers and Kennedy for most of their lives, were little touched with suspicion of the North. But in Williamsburg, Nathaniel Beverley Tucker, son of George Tucker, looked out when he was fifty upon a world that seemed to him heavy with malign conspiracy. Always at heart a Virginian, in spite of his residence in Missouri from 1815 to 1833, he returned home at about the time of the death of his cherished half-brother, John Randolph, to teach law at William and Mary College.

He had believed since 1820 that the South would at last resort to secession. In 1836, when his friend Thomas Dew, an irreconcilable like himself, became president of the college, he published a novel, *The Partisan Leader,* which embodied his hope for a free South unexploited by Northern tariffs. Dated twenty years after its real time of publication, the book describes a War of Southern Secession successfully concluded around 1850. The author's style was patterned upon that of Sir Walter Scott, and his conjectures as to military science were notably bad; but as a prophet within a large framework he was tragically accurate. His novel *Gertrude* appeared serially in the *Southern Literary Messenger* (1844–1845), and another, *George Balcombe* (1836), based on his memories of Missouri, stirred Poe to write, "There have been few books of its peculiar kind . . . much its superior."

3

Poe was in the North during most of the late thirties and the forties, but he was none the less a dominant figure in the Southern literature of those years. Feeling himself still a Southerner, he established relations with most of the people then writing below the Potomac. Kennedy, Tucker, Simms, Chivers, and many others were beholden to him for favorable judgments.

Because he too was a poet, the work of Thomas Holley Chivers is most closely linked to that of Poe. The son of a wealthy Georgia planter, divorced before he was twenty, Chivers was by profession a doctor of medicine. He was also a mystic poet, familiar with innumerable angels. Like Poe, he was much in the North in the late thirties, and he married a Massachusetts girl. In 1837 he published his volume of poems, *Nacoochee,* with a long preface defining Poetry as "that crystal river of the soul which . . . empties into the sea of God." Two years later he wrote his second dramatic version of the sensational Kentucky murder of 1825 used by Poe in his drama *Politian* and by Simms in two novels.

The association between Chivers and Poe began in 1840 by correspondence, and included a controversy over a pronouncement in which among other things Poe said that Chivers was "at the same time one of the best and one of the worst poets in America." The object of this verdict protested that such talk seemed likely to confirm an already widespread rumor of his insanity.

In 1842 his oldest daughter died and he memorialized this and other recent sorrows in a group of poems that both in theme and in technique were a just reflection of his own basic taste, and that were a fairly just reflection, at least, of the basic taste of Poe. These plaints were published in 1845 in *The Lost Pleiad and Other Poems.* In the same year Poe and Chivers met in New York. They were for a while intimate friends, Poe testifying to his adulation of Chivers, and leaving the avenues completely open for Chivers to advance him money. All this while Chivers, for his part, offered Poe much counsel and recurrent but vain invitations to come to Georgia as a kind of lifetime house-guest.

After Poe's death, Chivers in 1850 published his *Eonchs of Ruby* containing the much debated "Isadore," probably written in 1841, but reminiscent (or anticipatory) of "The Raven":

> While the world lay round me sleeping,
>   I, alone, for Isadore
> Patient Vigils lonely keeping—
> Some one said to me while weeping,
>   "Why this grief forever more?"
> And I answered, "I am weeping
>   For my blessed Isadore!"

The general charge, made immediately to the effect that the volume was wickedly plagiarized from the dead Poe, was met by Chivers with the charge that it was the dead Poe who had wickedly plagiarized from him. This dispute, now nearly a hundred years old, continues active among the critics. In 1853 Chivers published three volumes of verse, one of them, *Virginalia, or Songs of my Summer Nights,* carrying his metrical effects, his refrains, his suiting of sound to sense, to a point that Poe would surely have marveled over. Of far less worth than that of Poe, or even of Pinkney, Chivers' verse carries forward the interest in rhythm as such which seems to have been a dominant characteristic of Southern poetry.

Another whom Poe befriended was Philip Pendleton Cooke, author of some poetry in the *Knickerbocker Magazine* and a series of articles on early English poetry in the *Southern Literary Messenger.* His lyric "Florence Vane" —"you who were beautiful are now dead"—which appeared in *Burton's Gentlemen's Magazine* in Philadelphia in 1840 while Poe was editor, made him famous everywhere. His many prose romances were perhaps chiefly effective in establishing a domestic atmosphere in fiction that encouraged his younger brother to become a writer. John Esten Cooke was already at eighteen an inveterate writer of poetry and prose for the magazines; and at twenty-four (1854), he published two books, the first of the thirty-one volumes he achieved before his death in 1886. The most notable of all his writings are the two romances *The Virginia Comedians* (1854), dealing with Williamsburg in 1765, and *Surry of Eagle's Nest* (1866), dealing with the just concluded war.

The Southern world of the Cooke brothers was so very full of a number of enthralling things, including weather and natural prospects and field sports,. that both of them always found it hard to remain for long indoors, inactive and contemplative. Yet the elder of the two loved the "fever fits" of composition, the music "coming from God knows where," the excitement of the "rapid writer," and "the gallant dash" to "round off the stanza." He affected narrative verse because that was best for reading aloud to his hunt-companions after dinner.

One of those companions actually said to him, after the success of "Florence Vane": "I wouldn't waste time on a damned thing like poetry; you might make yourself, with all your sense and judgment, a useful man in settling neighborhood disputes and difficulties." Yet Cooke continued to live in both worlds, and he was as fond of his hunting friends as he was proud of the encouragement Poe gave him. They were to him "good, kindly men, rare table companions . . . great in field sports . . . rather deficient in letters than mind . . . people whom he loved and was beloved by."

Not all of the writers whom Poe esteemed necessarily esteemed one another. Simms, for example, was too robust to care for Chivers. He thought that Chivers imitated Poe too closely, and told him so; and he admonished him, for good measure, to "be manly, direct, simple, natural." Chivers denied that he imitated Poe, and in general proclaimed himself the only American writer who had freed himself of transatlantic influences and who was absolute in his originality. This originality he said Poe himself admitted; and it is sure that Chivers, for all of Simms' condemnation, must be included among the American writers who have been influential abroad.

During the forties Poe sounded Simms' praise on every possible occasion, and in truth Simms' energy, however that alone may have impressed Poe, was enough to make him notable. In addition to his constant trips between Woodlands and Charleston and between Charleston and New York, in addition to his constant flow of novels, poems, dramas, articles, lectures, and histories, he edited the apocryphal plays of Shakespeare and wrote biographies of Francis Marion, Captain John Smith, the Chevalier Bayard, and General Nathanael Greene.

He edited during 1845 the *Southern and Western Monthly Magazine and Review*—a title that is itself indicative of his conception of himself as a kind of political strategist for the South. In that magazine he published much written by himself and much written by his other self, "Adrian Beaufain," and, when he could extract it, material by other Southern writers, one of whom lived as far inland as Arkansas.

In 1849 he took over the editorship of the *Southern Quarterly Review,* which he carried on manfully for little besides love and affection till 1856. One of the chief fruits of this work was increased association with John Reuben Thompson, the poet and editor (1847-1860) of the *Southern Literary Messenger,* which in 1845 had absorbed Simms' *Southern and Western Monthly Magazine and Review.* Thompson was a friend and memorialist of Edgar Poe, but that was less interesting to Simms than what seemed to him Thompson's bounden duty to be more aggressively Southern. Another fruit of this work with the *Southern Review* was the association it furthered between Simms and the venerable Beverley Tucker, who in turn was much interested in what he thought was Simms' bounden duty to be more aggressively Southern. Simms did his best to comply. He exulted over Tucker's never fulfilled plan to write a biography of his kinsman John Randolph, and published Tucker's scathing review of the accomplished biography by H. A. Garland. And at Tucker's death in 1851 he fruitlessly planned himself to write a biography of Tucker. But by that time the old Southern chivalric ideals were being swept aside by the impending crisis in contemporary affairs.

4

The younger group of Southern writers which made its appearance on the eve of the Civil War was torn between the old traditions and the urgent ironies of the present. Only the youngest of them, Sidney Lanier, born in 1842, survived into the period of reconstruction; but even his latest work echoes in some respects the Elizabethan and Byronic modes of his predecessors. To those who could not forecast the future, the year 1856 in Charleston seemed to hold the promise of cultural maturity. In that year there came together a sort of informal club made up of gentlemen who were somewhat formal, highly esteeming one another—highly, in fact, estimable. Most of the members, already prominent in the professions or in business, were concerned with scholarship and literature chiefly as admirers and patrons. Simms, the Nestor of the group, was primarily a writer, as were three other members, Henry Timrod, Paul Hamilton Hayne, and Basil Gildersleeve, the oldest of them only twenty-seven.

In 1857 these men inaugurated a publication which continued for three years, *Russell's Magazine*. Aside from the contributions of Simms, Timrod, and Hayne, possibly the most notable articles that this journal carried were those on political affairs written by William John Grayson. This Charleston lawyer and planter, a one-time Congressman, was turning seventy as the magazine took form. He had published in 1854 a poem in heroic couplets, *The Hireling and the Slave,* to show that the wage slavery of the North was worse than the chattel slavery of the South, and to suggest that at last the slaves would be returned to Africa.

The most enduring of prewar Southern poets, with the exception of Poe, were Henry Timrod and Paul Hamilton Hayne. Timrod was the grandson of a German immigrant and the son of a bookseller who was himself a poet. He grew up in Charleston in hard circumstances, attended briefly the college which was to become the University of Georgia, and later supported himself as a tutor. To the more notable Southern journals he contributed verses that were reminiscent of Wordsworth and Tennyson; and in *Russell's Magazine* he published some critical articles on poetry which maintained, peace to the ghost of Poe, that poems do not have to be "short" and that poetry must be powerful and true as well as beautiful. A number of his nature poems were brought together in a volume published in Boston in 1860, but he did not achieve his full stature until he was stirred by the issues of the war.

Hayne, a year Timrod's junior, was endowed more generously than his friend with apparently everything except genius in poetry. His verse even more than Timrod's was influenced by their great English contemporaries and immediate predecessors. His connection with *Russell's* was not his only experience in editing a magazine; and he published poems in the *Southern Literary Messenger* and in three independent volumes in Boston (1855, 1857, 1860).

When civil war imminently menaced the continent, there were left alive only a few notable Southern writers who had been active in the thirties. Outside the Charleston group, George Tucker was filling out his fifteen years of residence in Philadelphia, fated to die in 1861; and Kennedy and Longstreet, though they would live till 1870, were old men long since absorbed in practical affairs.

During the War, Timrod and Hayne proved incapable of extended service in the Army, and both of them poured all of their fervid spirits into martial and patriotic verse for the Confederacy. Timrod was ever exhilarated and dejected in turn: up because of his marriage in 1864, down because his verse was not, after all, published in England as he had expected it to be; up because of his appointment as newspaper editor in Columbia, down, down, utterly crumpling at last, in 1867, before the actuality of the South's defeat and of his own wretched poverty and illness. Some of his verse was noble in performance as well as in aspiration, and if Hayne's verse was always great in aspiration chiefly, his personal character was by any gauge exalted. In his memoir accompanying the *Collected Poems of Henry Timrod* (1873), this very earnest, very ambitious, indefatigable craftsman and experimenter judges and without ado declares his friend superior to himself as an artist. Certainly the militant spirit of the Confederacy is nowhere more vitally memorialized than in the ringing lines of Timrod's "Carolina":

> The despot treads thy sacred sands,
> Thy pines give shelter to his bands,
> Thy sons stand by with idle hands,
> Carolina! . . .
>
> Thy ancient fame is growing dim,
> A spot is on thy garment's rim;
> Give to the winds thy battle hymn,
> Carolina!

Hayne with Simms' help befriended Timrod to the limit of their very limited powers during 1866–1867. Immediately after the war, Simms had resumed his relationships in the North, and through him there were efforts on the part of some people there to be of practical help to Timrod and Hayne also. Timrod could not meet a prospective benefactor because he could not command the expenses of a trip to New York.

Hayne owned a small tract of land in the pine woods on the Georgia side of the Savannah River, and it was there, with his mother and wife and young son, that he retreated at the war's end. He swore a vow to make a living as a poet and as a poet alone, in Georgia, in the last third of the nineteenth century, and the audacity of that oath, even if he had not fulfilled it, would have made him remarkable. Timrod visited him twice shortly before his death. Simms also visited him, and when Simms died in the summer of 1870 Hayne could not, he said, accept the news; he had somehow come to fancy that Simms would live forever.

Notwithstanding Simms' regular visits to New York, and for all of Hayne's associations there after the war, both men in the last years of the sixties doubtless thought themselves unreservedly inimical to the late enemy. They must have sorely blamed Kennedy, in Baltimore, for the part he had played in the great conflict.

Over many years Kennedy had drifted into a position that made his anti-Southernism mandatory, and his *Letters of Mr. Paul Ambrose on the Great Rebellion in the United States* gave only added evidence of what was already understood. While south of the Line people cringed in poverty, Kennedy walked proudly in Maryland. He supervised the munificent Peabody Fund for the benefit of Baltimore. Or he made extended journeys to Europe. Or, agreeing perhaps with his friend and biographer Tuckerman that the war had happily ended an eagerness for mere wealth in America, he meditated on the blessings of a stable aristocracy of intellect and taste. Or, a master grievance to the South, he made a progress through that land, reporting—the same Kennedy who lately with his guest Irving had scoffed at tales of cruelty to slaves—the most wanton and direful abuses against the new freedmen.

Yet, loyal as Simms and Hayne were to their defeated Confederacy, there is something ominous from the standpoint of the Old South in the fact that both men seriously entertained the idea of moving North. A number of their peers made that move to good account for themselves. John Reuben Thompson of the Richmond *Messenger,* for instance, became literary editor of the New York *Evening Post.* It is even more ominous that before the War was twenty-five years gone, countless other Southern paladins were looking back upon the conflict more through Kennedy's eyes than through Simms'. The new upsurge of nationalism following the war with Spain carried this process further. By 1909 an influential Tennessee educator could admit that the literature of the Old South was as poor as one might care to call it. And, most ironically, a lady who was a high official in a great Confederate patriotic society could find it in her heart to apologize for Thomas Jefferson's preferring the open country of Virginia to the sidewalks of Paris.

As time ran on, notable people in the South as well as in the country at large were the agents of this reconciliation; in fact, it sometimes seemed that eminence away from home was the first condition of local eminence. But a number of brave and strong and large-dimensioned men lived on, proclaiming the old shibboleths faithfully, to go down at last quaintly regarded as doctrinaire persons by even their closest and most kindly neighbors.

23. EDGAR ALLAN POE

Concerning none of the major American authors of the nineteenth century has there been anything like the critical disagreement that still surrounds the name of Edgar Allan Poe. Even his central position in Southern literature has been disputed because of his later importance to the literary and cultural development of the middle states. Nearly a hundred years after his death the lines are still as sharply joined as when Tennyson thought him the most original American genius and Emerson pronounced him "the jingle man." He has always been a great poet in France, but to Henry James an enthusiasm for Poe was "the mark of a decidedly primitive stage of reflection." In our own day Yeats has found him "always and for all lands a great lyric poet," and Valéry has believed that Poe made an unrivaled contribution to literary method, in prose no less than in verse. But no major American poet has yet affirmed his living value in such high terms, and many have echoed the charges of Emerson and James.

The controversy even about the facts of Poe's life has been almost as violent ever since Baudelaire visualized him as the young aristocrat, "le Byron égaré dans un mauvais monde," while the Reverend Rufus Griswold pointed to his career as a satanic example and warning. A succession of scholars has at last corrected Griswold's falsifications. These began with the venomous memoir which he produced at Poe's death, where he went to the length of incorporating a passage in which Bulwer had described his morbidly egotistic villain in *The Caxtons,* and which Griswold allowed to appear to be his own characterization of Poe. As literary executor Griswold was soon to go much further by forging passages in Poe's letters to him in order to show the poet in the most unfavorable light. But the corrected version is hardly less far from Griswold's monster who exhibited "scarcely any virtue in either his life or his writings" than from the romantic legend that Baudelaire conceived, and many details of which Poe himself had done his best to foster.

The psychological insecurity that was deep in Poe's nature becomes pathetically apparent through these fabrications. Toward the end of his forty-year life he wanted to appear younger than he was, and used to give his date of birth as two or four years after that winter of 1809 when, as the son of traveling actors, he had first opened his eyes in Boston, the city of "the Frog-pondians" upon whose pretensions to dominance over American literature he was to pour out so much scorn. In his desire to give himself roots in Southern stability, he liked to state that his Baltimore grandfather Poe had been a general. He did not dwell on the fact that David Poe had started life as an Irish immigrant wheelwright, and that the title of general had been largely complimentary, the result of his having helped, as a dry-goods merchant, to supply the Revolutionary army. Poe naturally did not mention that his chief inheritance from his father may have been his high-strung liability to dipsomania, nor that when his frail and talented English mother died in poverty in Richmond when Edgar was two, his father had already permanently disappeared. Poe's description of John Allan, the tobacco exporter who then took him into his family without formally adopting him, made it sound as though Allan's connections were more with the plantation gentry and less with the merchant class than they actually were.

The poet also liked to remember from his youth the years between six and eleven that he had spent with the Allans in England, and how after his return to Richmond, while preparing for college, he had, though slight in frame, been notable as a boxer, and had swum half a dozen miles in the James—as though already to challenge the comparison with Byron. His later account of his career at Jefferson's newly founded university assumed that he had passed three years there, and had graduated with high honors. In point of fact, although he had shown marked distinction in Latin and French, the two fields which he was pursuing, he had been withdrawn by Allan at the end of a year because of gambling debts. These, Poe insisted, he had con-tracted simply because his foster father had not allowed him enough money to live on. Even before this the tension between the two had become so acute that, whether justly or not, Allan could say, "The boy possesses not a spark of affection for us, not a particle of gratitude for all my care." In his dealings with his foster father, Poe was to show himself at his most unstable, alter-nately arrogant and self-pitying, like a sick boy. But after his return from Charlottesville he determined on a break, and at eighteen he ran away from what he could hardly call home, to make his own way in the world.

This was the period which he later tried to conceal most thoroughly beneath the bright colors of legend. He spoke of having set off to join the Greeks in their struggle for liberty, but of having gotten instead into diffi-culties, somewhat unaccountably, at St. Petersburg. Actually he had gone no farther than Boston, where he managed to publish his first small volume of poems, and, having no means of subsisting, he had soon enlisted in the Army. He always played down his two years as a soldier—though he had risen to be a sergeant major—in order to play up his brief experience as a West Point cadet. He gained appointment there at the time when he had become temporarily reconciled with Allan through his grief over his foster mother's death. But when Allan married again Poe set out to get himself expelled, since he finally realized that he could not hope to be Allan's heir, and concluded that the Army was no career for a poor man.

If Poe had been the young aristocrat he liked to fancy himself, this expulsion would have been the last dramatic step of reckless youth. Even though disinherited he would doubtless have found some support among his wealthy connections. He had stressed to Allan his talent and his ambition. He could envisage himself as a heroic conqueror: "Richmond and the United States were too narrow a sphere and the world shall be my theater." But in cold truth he was to be faced, from the age of twenty-two, with a life of struggle and incessant poverty, for which his overwrought nervous system was desperately ill equipped.

2

His early poetry still accorded with the legend of how a young romantic poet should behave. The title piece of *Tamerlane and Other Poems* (1827), which recited the folly of risking love for ambition, was not much more than an echo of Byron's narratives. Poe was soon to speak of himself as "irrecoverably a poet," but few even of the ten short lyrics that made up the rest of this small book show any special promise. Yet his later accents can be overheard here and there, in the fervor with which he says, "Oh! that my young life were a lasting dream!" or in the characteristic image with which he ends his account of "the happiest day, the happiest hour." For even on that hour's fluttering wing there falls a "dark alloy."

His second venture, *Al Aaraaf, Tamerlane, and Minor Poems* (1829), was published in Baltimore during the interval between his release from the Army and his appointment to West Point. He had turned hopefully to Allan to underwrite the small cost of printing, but to this letter Allan had replied, "strongly censuring his conduct and refusing any aid." Poe had tried to assure him that he had "long given up Byron as a model"; but, if so, he had merely substituted the Moore of *Lalla Rookh*. Poe's narrative takes its name from the Mohammedan realm intermediate between heaven and hell, and its somewhat more than four hundred lines constitute the longest poem he ever attempted. It is also the vaguest of his many celebrations of unearthly beauty; and since a poet's theory of poetry inevitably relates to his own practice, it is not surprising that Poe should later declare that no such thing as a long poem can exist. Among the half-dozen new lyrics here, two begin to show his mature quality: "To Science," which dwells, like Keats' "Lamia," upon its withering limitations; and "Romance," which Poe himself thought "the best thing" in the volume. Here he first enunciated how his heart would feel it a crime to give itself up to the delights of music "unless it trembled with the strings."

The *Poems* of 1831, dedicated "to the U.S. Corps of Cadets" just after his dismissal from their midst, marks a great advance. He has revised much of his earlier work, as he will continue to do meticulously throughout his life, usually to its distinct improvement. But the impulse through which he has now found his own lasting direction can be discerned in the preface, his first piece of criticism. He may seem to dismiss Wordsworth far too airily, but his mind has become saturated with Coleridge. He is drawn more to *Biographia Literaria* than to *Aids to Reflection,* upon which the transcendentalists were later to build so much. In fact, Poe is later to state, after he has declared war on New England, that Coleridge has "aided Reflection to much better purpose in his 'Genevieve.'" Yet it is a remarkable tribute to Coleridge's seminal vitality that such different writers as Emerson and Poe were alike indebted to the same rich source for the immediate stimulus to their theories of language and expression. Without Coleridge the romantic movement in America would not have had the shape by which we know it.

The extent of Poe's debt may be judged by the definition of poetry with which he ends his preface. When he says, "A poem, in my opinion, is opposed to a work of science by having, for its *immediate* object, pleasure, not truth," he is giving what is to remain his opinion, but he is also following Coleridge, almost word for word. As Poe completes his brief definition, he stresses "music" and "indefiniteness," hints for both of which he has also found in the *Biographia,* though he makes them even more essential to the poetic effect than Coleridge did.

Poe completed only six new poems for this collection, but four of them are among his best known. "To Helen," he said later, was his commemoration of his first love, for Mrs. Stanard, who had died when he was fifteen. It has become probably his chief anthology piece, though its classical references are of a sort that made Baudelaire call it a pastiche. "Irene," which Poe was subsequently to name "The Sleeper," and was to regard for "the higher qualities of poetry" as "better than 'The Raven,'" is most akin to the incantation of "Christabel," in its irregular tetrameter as well as in its vision by liquescent moonlight of a strange lady from afar. "The City in the Sea" takes the stock romantic theme of the city of the dead, exploited by Byron in "Darkness," and transforms it, by means of Poe's unique command over the details of horror, into a realm where we can actually feel how Death "looks gigantically down," with an intensity unlike anything in Byron. "Israfel," the disjointed stanzas which have become the symbol for Poe's career, tells how he gained this intensity—through suffering.

With this book Poe came of age as a poet; but he was not to publish another volume of poetry for fourteen years. His work had attracted little critical attention, and he had to live. The next few years in his annals are still very obscure, though he seems to have spent them mostly in Baltimore, with his aunt Mrs. Clemm. He wrote to Allan, in the fall of 1831, in an agony of fear that he was going to be imprisoned for debt; and his final letter to his former protector, in the spring of 1833, cries out that he is "absolutely perishing for want of aid." But Allan had made up his mind that Poe's was a "debased nature," and remained unreconciled to him at the time of his own death the following year. Meanwhile Poe, determining to live by his pen against whatever odds, had turned from poetry to fiction.

3

He competed for a prize offered by the Philadelphia *Saturday Courier*, which awarded the hundred dollars to Delia Bacon for her tale "Love's Martyr" but, during the course of 1832, printed five of Poe's stories. The first of these, "Metzengerstein," already shows what was to be a characteristic feature of his fiction: it not only tells a story, but also develops an idea. Poe began here with the doctrine of the transmigration of the soul, and worked it out through a plot wherein a young baron is destroyed by a horse in which his dead enemy's unrelenting soul has become incarnated. Poe himself pointed to its source when he reprinted it with the subtitle: "A Tale in Imitation of the German." The other four are "grotesques," the intended and contemporary tone of which is not so easy to catch. They are "The Duc de l'Omelette" and "Bon-Bon," two ludicrous bargains with the Devil; "A Tale of Jerusalem," in which the offering to the scandalized Pharisees turns out to be a pig; and "Loss of Breath," wherein, applying that phrase literally, Poe demonstrates the series of disasters, culminating in premature burial, that befall the unfortunate Mr. Lacko'breath. Poe took his own humor seriously, which is a dangerous sign, and it seems never to have kindled much enjoyment in others. Putting it against its immediate background, we can see that he was dealing in some of the familiar devices of American humor: the wild exaggerations and violent destructiveness of the tall tale, the literal play on words pushed to the verge of idiocy, the gravely sustained frozen-faced manner. But Poe's handling of these devices was singularly without the saving warmth of mirth.

He had a very clear notion, however, of what he was about. He was not writing straight humor but various species of burlesque, as we can tell by glancing at his outlined scheme for *The Tales of the Folio Club,* into which he intended to fit all his early pieces. The names of some of the members of that club, who were supposed to recite the tales, may convey the tone, since they are such worthies as Mr. Blackwood Blackwood, Mr. Horrible Dictu, "who had graduated at Göttingen," and Mr. Solomon Seadrift, "who had every appearance of a fish." Furthermore, Poe was outspoken as to some of his targets. He was to give "Loss of Breath" the subtitle, "A Tale neither in nor out of 'Blackwood,'" and to say that he had been satirizing the "extravancies" of that magazine's bloodcurdling fiction. He described several of his stories as being "half banter, half satire," and in "Lionizing," a slightly later piece, he seems at once to have been quizzing the vogue for lions like N. P. Willis, and to have been burlesquing Bulwer's "Too Beautiful for Anything." When Thomas White, proprietor of the *Southern Literary Messenger,* wrote him in 1835, objecting to his taste in "Berenice"—the story in which Poe extended his horrible details to the length of making his obsessed hero rob a corpse of her teeth—Poe replied with an explicit account of the aims of his early fiction.

He agreed that his subject had been "far too horrible," but stated that the question of bad taste was "little to the purpose," since "to be appreciated you must be *read.*" He had followed current English writing very closely, and knew what had made a sensation were such productions as "MS Found in a Madhouse," "The Man in the Bell," and *Confessions of an Opium-Eater.* He had formulated the nature of such successful work:

You ask me in what does this nature consist? In the ludicrous heightened into the grotesque: the fearful coloured into the horrible: the witty exaggerated into the burlesque: the singular wrought out into the strange and mystical.

If four of Poe's first five stories had exploited the brittle possibilities of the first or third of these alternatives, the story with which he won, in the following year, the fifty dollars offered by the *Baltimore Saturday Visiter* was a very different departure. Poe may possibly have thought of having "MS Found in a Bottle" recited by Mr. Solomon Seadrift, but here his imagination had been caught, as he dealt with both the fearful and the strange. The opening sentences struck his peculiar note: "Of my country and my family I have little to say. Ill usage and length of years have driven me from the one, and estranged me from the other." From start to finish he sustained "the presentiment of evil," the terror and wonder mounting to "a feeling for which I have no name," as his narrator's helpless craft rushed to destruction "down the unfathomable ocean."

Poe referred in 1835 to the existence by then of sixteen *Tales of the Folio*

Club, which he hoped, unavailingly, to publish as a book. He prided himself on their variety, and among the other new types that he had struck off were "Morella," his first treatment of the death and terrifying rebirth of a beloved woman; and "The Unparalleled Adventures of Hanns Pfaal," the earliest of his hoaxes, in which he sought to give the most ingenious verisimilitude to a balloon flight to the moon. An instance of how he could now take the Byronic hero and make him his own is "The Assignation." The scene opens at the Bridge of Sighs, but the slender hero, with his "singular, wild, full, liquid eyes" and his "forehead of unusual breadth" beneath lustrous black hair, is an idealized self-portrait. This is the earliest story into the texture of which Poe wove one of his lyrics, the haunting melody of "To One in Paradise." In his death speech the hero declares that "like these arabesque censers, my spirit is writhing in fire," and so introduces the term that Poe was to balance against the grotesque, as his imagination balanced his fancy.

4

Through John Pendleton Kennedy, who had been one of the judges of his prize-winning story, Poe formed a connection with the *Southern Literary Messenger,* and late in 1835 he went to Richmond to become White's editor. A letter from there to Mrs. Clemm is swept by the gusts of uncontrol to which he was to be increasingly subject. He has heard that his aunt and her daughter Virginia are deserting him, and he cries out that he will live no longer. This recently recovered letter also gives evidence that he did not marry his cousin as a matter of convenience, since it is filled with passionate messages for her. Mrs. Clemm soon came and set up their little home in Richmond, and Poe and Virginia were married the following spring. He was twenty-seven, and she was not quite fourteen.

Another phase of his legend, begotten by those who disapproved of his habits, was that Poe was one of the discoverers of Bohemia. Nothing could be further from the truth. He did not drink convivially to shock the bourgeoisie, but because he could not help it. His insecurity became ingrained. As he was to say a decade later, "the irregularities so profoundly lamented were the *effect* of a terrible evil rather than its cause." Although later Bohemians have liked to believe that Poe worked best under the release of alcohol, there is no evidence to support them. The cycle of his life from now on consisted of periods of intense industry broken off by neurotic melancholia, which sought its anodyne in drink.

His more than a year with the *Messenger* sets the pattern. He wrote its reviews, an immense number, on the average nine or ten a month and generally of essay length. He also did all the editorial drudgery, for a total pay of about eight hundred dollars a year. His work was of such caliber that it first brought both the *Messenger* and Poe to wide attention. Despite the persistent notion that he lived "out of space, out of time," his reputation in his own day, until he produced "The Raven," was almost entirely as a magazine critic. He dealt with science no less than with romance, with books on navigation and classical history and phrenology as well as with all the current literature. He won his spurs by the thoroughness with which he could excoriate the pretentiously second-rate, and he became known primarily for "cutting and slashing," in the tradition of the British quarterlies. Yet, as he pointed out in summing up his first year's work, his laudatory reviews had greatly predominated; and if we look through them now we are more likely to think that when he went astray it was through overpraise of some lady poet like Mrs. Hemans or through such a remark as "Woman is the only proper Scheherezade for the fairy tales of love." And when we find him saying, "There *may* be men now living who possess the power of Bulwer," the thought occurs that the dark clothes which became habitual with Poe may have taken their model from Bulwer's dandy-hero Pelham.

But, whatever his vagaries in taste, Poe brought to his reviews a probing intelligence such as no other American critic had shown. He made a unique stress upon "design" and "keeping," "upon a strict subordination of the parts to the whole." He was concerned from the start with a term he found in Schlegel, "the unity or totality of interest." He noted Coleridge's exceptional appreciation of "the value of *words*," and was soon making a rigorously detailed analysis of the defects in Simms' diction. The point of view from which he undertook to criticize is outlined at the opening of the most ambitious of these early reviews, the long essay in which he demonstrated, again under the aegis of his chief master, that Drake and Halleck were not poets of imagination, but merely of fancy. What most disturbed Poe in the American literary scene was the replacement of our earlier subservience to British standards by a form of provincialism that he deemed even worse, by the blatant determination to like "a stupid book the better, because, sure enough, its stupidity is American." In opposition to both extremes, Poe was to take his stand on the proposition that "the world at large" is "the only proper stage" for both writer and reader.

To be sure, he sometimes betrayed a provincialism of his own. He was so eager to prove himself a Virginian that he followed Allan's tradition, which was that of Marshall and not that of Jefferson. Poe went so far as to deplore the French Revolution, to defend slavery as "the basis of all our institutions," and to assume the scorn held by the propertied class for the democratic "mob." But, whatever his prejudices, he often showed the resilient critic's capacity to appreciate a talent far different from his own, as when he greeted with enthusiasm the frontier humor of *Georgia Scenes*. Most importantly, he demonstrated from the outset his devotion to the first principles of art. As he was to declare in his *Marginalia*: "It is the business of the critic so to soar that he shall *see the sun*."

Through his work for the *Messenger* he had learned what he could do with a magazine. But he had had several bouts with drink, the slightest amount of which could destroy his nervous control. Although he declared, "I have fought the enemy manfully," both White and himself grew dissatisfied with their relationship, and early in 1837 Poe decided to try to make his way in the North, and left for New York.

His duties as editor had yielded him no time for new creative work, and his *Tales of the Folio Club* had been rejected by Harper's as being "too learned and mystical." Another objection of the publisher's, that there would be no vogue for a collection of short tales, may have caused him now to undertake *The Narrative of Arthur Gordon Pym* (1838), whose seventy-five thousand words constitute the longest piece of work that he produced. His account of the disasters that overwhelmed a Nantucket vessel which had started out for the South Seas reveals his sustained fascination with the imaginary voyage, and his ability to conjure up the kind of realistic details in which as a boy he had rejoiced in *Robinson Crusoe*. On one level these adventures of young Arthur and his friend Augustus, who survive mutiny and delirium and the sight of sea gulls gorging themselves on human flesh, are merely the last word in adolescent fantasy. But the imaginative effect of the compulsive horror of whiteness, as the voyagers are driven at the close farther and farther into the uncharted Antarctic, relates back to Coleridge's albatross and forward to Melville's "whiteness of the whale," and is on a level kindred with both.

Pym met with no particular success, and Poe seems not to have been able to find a foothold in New York, for a few months later he moved his family to Philadelphia. He turned again to short stories, and within the next year he produced three of his most original: "Ligeia," "The Fall of the House of Usher," and "William Wilson." An interesting feature of the rhythm of his production is that he was writing at the same time such pieces as his burlesque of "How to Write a Blackwood Article"; "The Devil in the Belfry," for which he took a hint from Irving's old Dutch material for a farce about the clock that struck thirteen in the borough of Vondervotteimittiss; and "The Man That Was Used Up," another drearily literal working out of a play on words. Poe perceived that his stories fell into two main groups when he gave his first collection of them in 1840 the title, *Tales of the Grotesque and Arabesque*. He managed to place this collection of twenty-five pieces, all that he had written up to then, with a Philadelphia printing-house, but only on the basis that it was to take all profits. The title may have been suggested by Scott's famous essay, "On the Supernatural in Fictitious Composition," but Scott had used both "arabesque" and "grotesque" interchangeably to suggest the bizarre quality of Hoffmann's imagination. In Poe's collection his "grotesques" slightly outnumbered his "arabesques," though it is the latter that are still read.

Concerning these latter, Poe raised the crucial issue in his brief preface when he maintained that their "terror is not of Germany, but of the soul." Upon the reader's felt acceptance or rejection of the truth of that statement seems to depend whether he regards Poe's work as mainly a meretricious fabrication or as a compellingly imaginative creation. Even Poe's most hostile critics have generally made an exception for some of these tales. "William Wilson," with its uncannily thorough handling of double identity, forms a sustained allegory of a man's murder of his own conscience, even if for the use of allegory Poe ordinarily had not one good word to say. "Usher" is generally rated as Poe's best, though he preferred "Ligeia." The two together present the contours of his peculiar world. Roderick Usher is the distillation of Poe's isolated, dreamy, and introspective heroes. Absorbed in occult learning, he is consumed with nameless fears, which he articulates through his poem, "The Haunted Palace," a hidden allegory on his dreaded loss of reason. The heroine matched to such a hero is Usher's sister Madeline, whose delicate beauty is heightened by disease. Or, in her fullest development, she is Ligeia, whose dangerous erudition is a match for that of the husband with whom she inhabits a remote and decaying castle. Through her Poe expressed his acceptance of Bacon's doctrine, "There is no excellent beauty that hath not some strangeness in the proportion." Through her likewise comes his most intense expression of the wild desire "for life—*but* for life," as by her naked strength of will she rises after death in brief resurrection to seize upon the body of her hated rival.

Poe said that this story had been suggested by a dream, and those who believe that he was a drug addict point to the hero's confession of being caught in the trammels of opium. But on this question, unlike that of Poe's drinking, there is no sure external evidence. It would certainly have been possible for him to imagine these sensations, as he imagined those of catalepsy or premature burial, without being subject to either. And it is interesting that, like most of its first readers, he took the *Confessions of an Opium-Eater* to be fiction. The important issue about a story like "Ligeia" is whether Poe's fantasies were merely abnormal, or whether, as Paul Elmer More believed, they had authentic roots in the same "haunted mind" that troubled Hawthorne, in the strained preoccupation with evil that had formed an inextricable strand in American experience from our Puritan beginnings.

Poe's *Tales* were favorably reviewed, but fewer than seven hundred and fifty copies were sold within three years. He had to undertake a great deal of miscellaneous hackwork for *Burton's Gentleman's Magazine* and other Philadelphia periodicals, but during the next half-decade, especially in 1841 and 1842, he displayed an access of energy in several directions. By 1845 he had more than doubled the number of his stories, and had added distinct new types. The most popular of these was the "tale of ratiocination," as inaugurated by "The Murders in the Rue Morgue." Poe, who was presently to make quite a stir as a solver of cryptograms, showed a lively enjoyment of analysis, and created in his detective Dupin a very different hero from Roderick Usher. In describing Dupin's extraordinary grip over the mind's processes of association, Poe again applied Coleridge to uses now entirely his own. For Dupin's "rich ideality" was a startling combination, both "resolvent" and "creative"; he held that "the ingenious are always fanciful, and the *truly* imaginative never otherwise than analytic." Poe had been a good student of mathematics at West Point, and in his further incarnations of Dupin, in "The Mystery of Marie Roget" and "The Purloined Letter," he attributed his hero's powers of reasoning and his ability to apprehend general truths to the fact that he was both mathematician *and* poet.

Another development of the tale of ratiocination, and Poe's most popular story in his own day, was "The Gold Bug" which, in contrast to the ten dollars he could usually expect for a story, won in 1843 the hundred-dollar prize offered by the Philadelphia *Dollar Newspaper*. "The Gold Bug" combined the fascination of cryptography with that of buried treasure. Its fresh description of Sullivan's Island near Charleston is a reminiscence of the days when Poe was stationed there in the Army, and in dealing with Captain Kidd he made use for once of an American legend.

Quite a different kind of development is apparent in such pieces as "The Philosophy of Furniture" and "The Landscape Garden," wherein he worked out his theories of taste and design. In considering the ideal interior he insisted that "an aristocracy of dollars" was far inferior to "an aristocracy of blood," that taste was ordinarily corrupted by wealth. He maintained that "keeping" was as important in a room as in any other work of art, and presented in detail such a room, the character of which was determined by a profusion of crimson and gold, wrought into "arabesque devices" in the pattern both of the wallpaper and of the carpet. Poe's longing for luxury and magnificence was in part that of a man who had been starved of them. Letting his fondness for the bizarre run riot in "The Masque of the Red Death," he devised those seven rooms of different colors, the last of which, with its tapestries of black velvet and its scarlet window panes, was a masterpiece of ballet décor for the dance of death. Taking hold of the contemporary interest in landscape gardening, he also designed his fabulous domain of Arnheim, an artificial paradise of fantastic vegetation, crowned by a mansion of "semi-Gothic, semi-Saracenic architecture." Such scenes vibrated for Baudelaire "d'un frisson surnaturel et galvanique."

Still another departure is found in his dialogues after death, such as "The Colloquy of Monos and Una," in which he first made open his scorn of the utilitarians and his rejection of the doctrine of progress, and ridiculed, "among other odd ideas," that of "universal equality." Here also he began the speculations, which were to culminate in *Eureka,* on identity after death, and conceived of a state in which the senses blended into one another and all man's perceptions became "purely sensual."

In "The Black Cat" and "The Imp of the Perverse" he enunciated the belief that sadistic cruelty "is one of the primitive impulses of the human heart," that we respond to the promptings of the perverse "for the reason that we should *not.*" In these stories, as in "The Pit and the Pendulum" and "The Case of M. Valdemar," he developed to the full his ability to convey hallucinated horror by making it immediately physical, as when rats crawl across the lips of the imprisoned man. In such stories he showed too what a thin line may separate a "grotesque" from an "arabesque." When the material treated in the two is the same, the difference depends solely on the shift in tone, whereby the ludicrous "Angel of the Odd" may become the deadly serious "Imp of the Perverse."

It is interesting also that after 1840 the proportion of "grotesques" declined to hardly one in four. He seems to have come to perceive more clearly the limitations of the genre. He stated that harmony predominates in the workings of the imagination, whereas novelty predominates in those of the fancy, novelty that may quickly turn from beauty to deformity and thus pass over into the realm of humor. In analyzing Thomas Hood's grim "struggles at mirth" he gave an unconscious definition of his own: "the result of vivid Fancy impelled by Hypochondriasis." The best of his later "grotesques" have a concrete object for satire, just as the plausibility of his balloon flight across the Atlantic hoaxed New York for a day. In "The Business Man" the quality of his mockery is obvious, but in "Diddling Considered as One of the Exact Sciences" his satire of knaves and fools has a sustained bitterness kindred to Melville's in *The Confidence-Man.* Yet to the last year of his life Poe would still be capable of the wasted ingenuity of "X-ing a Paragrab."

Another sphere of his energy during his Philadelphia years was an ambitious plan for a magazine of his own. He was among the first to discern the tendency of the age toward "the curt, the condensed, the pointed, the readily diffused," away from "the detailed, the voluminous, the inaccessible." Against those who deplored this trend as a sign of American superficiality, Poe urged that men might not think "more profoundly" than they had thought half a century ago, but that they must think "with more rapidity," since they had so many more facts at their disposal. For this reason they needed "to put the greatest amount of thought in the smallest compass": "Hence the journalism of the age." Poe often thought of himself as "essentially a Magazinist," and planned to make his journal an organ of "an absolutely independent criticism."

The money that he hoped to raise by subscription was not forthcoming, and during 1841–1842 he took the job of editor for *Graham's Magazine*. Here he reached his peak as a critic. He opened the volume for 1842 with an exordium on the proper method of reviewing. He repeated his attack on all forms of narrow nationalism, and stated that he would "limit literary criticism to comment upon art." With "the opinions" in a book, "considered otherwise than in their relation to the work itself, the critic has really nothing to do." He followed up this statement of principles with a series of masterly essays. He was the first to mark so clearly the inescapable limitations of the "pioneers," the generation of Bryant, Irving, and Cooper. He helped to establish the reputations of his own generation, while continuing to expose the mediocrity of most of our best sellers. In his resolvent analysis of the plot of *Barnaby Rudge,* in which he unraveled the mystery before the last installments had been printed, he also pointed out the common error of trying to separate practice "from the theory which includes it." "If the practice fail," Poe contended, as no one else in American criticism had done, "it is because the theory is imperfect." In his most balanced treatment of Longfellow, he objected to the "too obtrusive nature" of his didacticism, and went on to develop his own theory of poetry as the product of "supernal" longing, as "the rhythmical creation of beauty." In recognizing Hawthorne as one of our "few men of indisputable genius," he formulated his famous conception of the short story, which must be designed for "a single effect," and every word of which must be made to count.

Poe's imperfections as a critic have often been dwelt upon. Just as he was overimpressed by such pseudo sciences as phrenology and mesmerism, his tastes in literature were oppressively contemporary. When he had protested against being withdrawn from the University of Virginia, he had told Allan how far he still was from "a liberal education"; and gaps in his understanding of the past remained very apparent. Unfortunately he acted as he always did when he felt insecure. He made pretensions to erudition that he did not possess, and backed them up with quotations borrowed from some such source as D'Israeli's *Curiosities of Literature.* His critical temper was often unsteady. He was capable, as in his dealings with Lowell, of withdrawing his praise when Lowell ventured a few strictures upon his work. He exaggerated the conspiracy of New England to venerate only its own, he was vicious in his attack upon poor Ellery Channing, and his obsession with Long-fellow's alleged plagiarism grew into a mania. Yet he also fought steadily to improve the conditions of American authorship, and his own near-starvation had taught him "the irreparable ill" that the absence of a copyright law wrought upon our native culture, even upon our writers' bare survival. His originality as a critic resulted from his refusal to rest upon any authority, from the way he considered *de novo* the capabilities of whatever art he examined. His greatest contribution was that he always insisted upon "the application of a rigorous *method* in all forms of thought."

5

After the plans for his magazine had failed for a second time in 1842, Poe underwent a period of hopeless depression. In that winter Virginia, who had now matured into womanhood—a fact usually overlooked by those who speak invariably of his "child-wife"—had ruptured a blood vessel while singing, and her condition from then on was always precarious in the extreme. Looking back to this period, Poe said that the continual uncertainty, her partial recovery followed by relapse, made the recurrence of his desperate anxiety more than his nerves could stand. "I became insane," he said, "with long intervals of horrible sanity." He also added that his enemies attributed the insanity to his drinking, "rather than the drink to the insanity." His relations with the proprietors of the magazines, with Burton and Graham, followed a variant of the pattern of those with the *Messenger*. During his editorship, the circulation of *Graham's* rose fabulously, from fifty-five hundred to forty thousand; but that brought no rise in Poe's fortunes. By 1844 he had become thoroughly dissatisfied with any further prospects in Philadelphia, and moved to New York, wandering, as Baudelaire conceived it, once again restlessly in the American desert. Poe himself had now come to believe that in America, "more than in any other region upon the face of the globe, to be poor is to be despised." But his New York years did not alleviate his condition. He became even less prosperous than he had been.

That remained true even after "The Raven" made an instant stir upon its appearance in the New York *Evening Mirror*. He wrote to a friend that for popularity his "bird" had beaten his "bug" "all hollow," and yet, "I am as poor now as ever I was in my life." It may be impossible any more for an adult American to have a fresh reaction to "The Raven," since it has become such a classic of declamation and its once original tones have been drowned out by parodies. Its repetitions and refrain, the impulse for which Poe may have received from Chivers, and which were so startling upon their first hearing, have long become so expected as to allow Aldous Huxley to take it for one of the showpieces of "vulgarity in literature." The suspicion of its being fabricated was given some color by Poe himself, who proceeded, in "The Philosophy of Composition," to deliver a cool account of every step in the process of designing the poem to "suit at once the popular and the critical taste." Poe spoke of this essay as being his "best specimen of analysis," but many readers have been bothered by its mechanical exactitude. Baudelaire, who delighted in Poe even as a *farceur,* detected a deliberate undertone of impertinence, whereby Poe wanted to scandalize again those who talked only of inspiration and refused to admit the necessary dependence of genius upon talent. It is possible that Poe wrote with his tongue in his cheek, since he had a fondness for what he called "funny criticism": but he also believed that an artist should possess the fullest consciousness of all the stages of composition, since "to originate, is carefully, patiently, and understandingly to combine."

As a result of his new fame Poe was able to issue, in the summer of 1845, a selection of a dozen of his tales, with a royalty of eight cents a copy on a small edition, and then a collection of his poetry for a flat payment of seventy-five dollars. This was the first time his earlier poems had any considerable audience. Griswold's widely circulated anthology, *The Poets and Poetry of America,* had included in 1842 three pieces by Poe, "The Coliseum," "The Haunted Palace," and "The Sleeper," as against seventeen poems by Lydia Sigourney and forty-five by Charles Fenno Hoffman. Poe dedicated his book to "the noblest of her sex," Miss Elizabeth Barrett Barrett, whose line, "With a murmurous stir uncertain, in the air the purple curtain," he had most certainly echoed. He said in the preface that there was "nothing in this volume of much value to the public, or very creditable to myself"; and, indeed, he had succeeded in composing scarcely ten new lyrics since 1831, the best of which, with the exception of "Dream-Land," had been incorporated into his tales. The only large addition lay in the scenes from his unfinished tragedy *Politian,* which dated from 1835 and were flatly undramatic. Yet the depth of Poe's concern over this book was apparent not only in the care with which he had revised many of his poems, but particularly when he said: "Events not to be controlled have prevented me from making, at any time, any serious effort in what, under happier circumstances, would have been the field of my choice. With me poetry has not been a purpose, but a passion." The reviews were prevailingly unsympathetic.

He was trying again to establish his magazine, and contrived for a few months to get control of the *Broadway Journal*; but the project blew up for want of funds, and because of his instability. From now on his ambition for a magazine seems to have become more overmastering as it grew less and less likely of realization; and he spoke of it in 1846 as "the one great purpose of my literary life." But in this year he had instead to undertake for *Godey's* his hack-work series dealing with thirty-eight of "the Literati of New York City." The announcement of this series fluttered the dovecotes because of Poe's reputation as "the tomahawk man," but the essays, as Poe himself knew, turned out to be hardly more than "critical gossip" of a prevailingly flattering kind.

Virginia was finally dying from tuberculosis, and sometimes there was not even enough money for a fire in their cottage at Fordham. After her death, in the winter of 1847, Poe went rapidly to pieces. One medical diagnosis at this time was that he had a "lesion on one side of the brain." He could not endure his loneliness, and threw himself into one emotional affair after another. He often behaved as though he hardly knew what he was doing, since at the very time he was trying to marry Mrs. Helen Whitman, he was torn also by his longing for the companionship of his "Annie," the wife of Charles Richmond. The only escape seemed to be suicide, and he swallowed an ounce of laudanum; but this acted as a violent emetic.

The Griswold legend was that Poe had now become diabolically possessed, and that he walked the streets with his lips moving "in the indistinct curses" of one who felt himself "already damned." Poe himself spoke of his "terrible agony." But the remarkable thing about these last years is the amount and variety of work he still managed to accomplish. Even in the midst of Virginia's final crisis, he had rallied himself and had written to Willis: "The truth is, I have a great deal to do; and I have made up my mind not to die till it is done."

Eureka was the fulfillment of prolonged meditation. In "Mesmeric Revelation" (1844) he had used the device of a trance to purvey his own doctrine of immortality, and had argued that matter is indivisible, that God "is but the perfection of matter." *Eureka,* upon which he was working through 1847, was advanced as "an Essay on the Material and Spiritual Universe." But he also called it "a Prose Poem." He was completely in earnest about the importance of his ideas, but he emphasized the beauty in their truth, and addressed himself "to the dreamers and those who put faith in dreams as in the only realities." He dedicated his book to Alexander von Humboldt, and showed himself well read in that naturalist's *Cosmos,* as well as in the nebular hypothesis of Laplace. Despite his rejection of progress, Poe shared with Emerson the contemporary concern with speculative science. He was finally giving, in *Eureka,* a full-length example of what he meant in saying that "the *highest* order of the imaginative intellect is always preeminently mathematical." Some critics have made much of the point that Poe's theories about the attraction and repulsion of atoms, and about "the stage of progressive collapse" of the universe, seem to anticipate twentieth century science. But at best these are lucky guesses of a mind untrained in physics and astronomy, and it would seem wiser to follow the course Poe urged in the last sentence of his preface: "It is as a Poem only that I wish this work to be judged after I am dead."

He started out by rejecting, in an oddly facetious passage, both deductive and inductive methods as too confined, and affirmed that for creative discovery "only Intuition can aid us." Poe's reliance upon the imagination as the discerner of truth, as the supreme faculty that brings man's soul to "a glimpse of things supernal and eternal," indicates again, despite his professed rejection of "immateriality," a belief curiously akin to Emerson's—as they both had adapted it from Coleridge. Poe once commented upon his tales of ratiocination that "people think them more ingenious than they are—on account of their method and *air* of method." The "air of method" is astonishingly sustained throughout *Eureka,* so that, whatever its originality or substance, it is a masterpiece of finesse, of intelligible and lucid exposition. At one climax, after expressing his awed admiration for the structure of the universe, he showed what kind of metaphor came most naturally to him when he added: "The plots of God are perfect. The Universe is a plot of God."

Poe ends on the note that was to become so prevalent in nineteenth century individualism, that he cannot believe "that anything exists greater than his own soul," that if God is to become "all in all," each man must recognize his own existence "as that of Jehovah." After such colossal egotism it is not surprising that Poe put an immense significance upon *Eureka,* and liked to talk of the metaphysical revolution that it would inaugurate. He had reached the stage where he was living a double identity, though not that of his William Wilson. It was as though the tortured and plunging chaos of his love letters were compensated by the way he proved that he could still conduct his intellectual processes with balance and decorum.

6

In his final years he also produced his *Marginalia,* that magnificently fertile series of suggestions on literary method. Here he condensed his leading principles of art. He gave recurrent attention to the similarities between music and mathematics, and found the basis of rhyme in our "appreciation of equality." He made his most original exploration of the unconscious by examining the images that well up at "the point of blending between wakefulness and sleep." These hypnagogic images are what surrealism has seized upon as its peculiar province; but Poe balanced his interest in them with a proposition that separated him also from most of the romantics of his day. He affirmed, "Man's chief idiosyncrasy being reason, it follows that his savage condition— his condition of action *without* reason—is his *un*natural state."

In "The Poetic Principle," which he delivered as a lecture during 1848-1849, he made a survey of contemporary poets and brought to its final stage his theory of "pure poetry," which we have already seen in formation. He betrayed again the limitations of his taste in speaking of Tennyson as "the noblest poet that ever lived," not on the grounds of depth or of intensity, but because he "is, at all times, the most ethereal—in other words, the most elevating and the most pure. No poet is so little of the earth, earthy." After such a passage one understands better why Poe thought the best conceivable subject for a poem was the death of a beautiful woman, and why both his poetry and his stories are so lacking in sensual body.

Other weaknesses in Poe's theory are manifest. The lyric, not the epic nor the dramatic poem, becomes the only norm. His occupation solely with supernal beauty risks turning even the lyric into a sustained tone, and nothing else. Atmosphere becomes not merely the envelope, but the content. The chief deficiency is owing to Poe's brittle terminology—in such contrast to Coleridge's resilience—which leads him into making mechanical and far too exclusive separations between the spheres of beauty and truth. He was so determined to root out "the didactic heresy" that he barred truth from poetry, and confined it to science and prose. In "The Philosophy of Composition" he had at least granted truth a subsidiary role in the total effect of poetic beauty, and in *Eureka* he had operated from a much broader basis and had held that "symmetry and consistency are convertible terms:—thus Poetry and Truth are one." But whatever its limitations and lapses, Poe's theory held firmly to his central conception about art, that it was not a spontaneous overflow of genius, but a designed effect. This separated it from all romantic theories of expression, and made it, in turn, the catalytic agent that quickened the French reaction from romantic disorder back to classic control of their forms.

Poe's production in fiction amounts to about seventy stories, only seven or eight of which were written after 1845. "The Cask of Amontillado" (1846) is one of the most compact illustrations of his belief that plot is not a "simple *complexity*," but "that in which no part can be displaced without ruin to the whole." "Hop-Frog" is one of the last of his "grotesques," the savage energy of which transforms it. Its story is that of a deformed dwarf who as court jester has been made drunk against his will and has watched a brutal injury to his girl. In the account of his revenge, by burning the king and his councilors to death, Poe's imagination became luridly destructive, as though in savage response to his own frustrations. In the winter of 1849 he devised the last of his hoaxes, "Von Kempelen and His Discovery," which purported to be a scientific description of how lead might be turned into gold. Poe's aim was to act as a sudden even if "temporary check to the gold-fever" of that year.

His growing bitterness to his times poured itself out most fully in "Mellonta Tauta," which looked back on that world from the vantage point of a thousand years. It defined a New York church as "a kind of pagoda" for the worship of the idols, Wealth and Fashion; but it reserved its harshest scorn for the notion that "the ancient Amriccans governed themselves." Poe traced their absurd course to its "abrupt issue" when "a fellow by the name of Mob took everything into his own hands and set up a despotism." In the latest installments of *Marginalia* he continued his attack on the pressures against the solitary thinker. He denounced "the modern reformist Philosophy which annihilates the individual by way of aiding the mass." He was still a Southerner looking at New England when he said:

The fact is, that in efforts to soar above our nature, we invariably fall below it. Your reformist demigods are merely devils turned inside out.

After "The Raven" Poe composed about a dozen poems to bring the total number to scarcely fifty. "The Bells" is a case of onomatopoeia pushed to a point where it would hardly be possible or desirable to go again. "Ulalume," appearing in the year after the death of his wife, voices a strange collision of passions, and Poe is reported to have said that its ending "was scarcely clear to himself." This poem presents all the paradoxes that have so divided Poe's critics. It uses again the hypnotic repetitions that he inaugurated with "The Raven," and subordinates meaning to music. Mallarmé deemed it "perhaps the most original and the most strangely suggestive of all Poe's poems," but Huxley thinks that its "walloping" dactyls are "all too musical." Furthermore, those whose musical tastes are severer than Poe's declare that, despite his challenging analogies between music and mathematics, he showed little technical knowledge of the subject, since he so readily confused the musical with the vaguely indefinite. Again he professed to be a craftsman devoted to perfection, and was capable of rhyming "vista" with "sister." He was a superrational analyst, the meaning of whose poems often eludes any analysis. The limitations of his terminology are apparent once more, for he declared that "a passionate poem is a contradiction in terms." He tried rigidly to restrict "passion" to "sexual desire" in contrast to "ideal love"; but those who respond to "Ulalume" are stirred by a deeply compulsive passion.

In "Eldorado" Poe voiced the pursuit of the ideal which should supplant "the gold-fever," and in revising now one of his earliest lyrics he added the lines,

> *All* that we see or seem
> Is but a dream within a dream.

But his latest poetry was by no means all escape. He became more directly personal in his sonnet for Mrs. Clemm, whom he called his "mother," in token of his dependence upon her after Virginia's death. His stanzas "For Annie" were torn out of his knowledge of tragedy. "Annabel Lee" raises the same issue that he raised in the preface to his *Tales*. For some readers it evokes merely an imitation Gothic "kingdom by the sea." But Poe knew that his longing for remote beauty could not be divorced from mortal sadness. His prevailing theme was ruin, and the intensity of his imagination could transform even the thinnest trappings of romance into the moving climax:

> And so, all the night-tide, I lie down by the side
> Of my darling, my darling, my life and my bride,
>   In her sepulchre there by the sea—
>   In her tomb by the side of the sea.

This poem did not appear until just after Poe's death. He had gone back to Richmond in the summer of 1849, still in the hope of founding his magazine, and turning away again from a harsh North to a South that was actually even more indifferent to his ambitions. He spoke for the first time of "an attack of *mania a potu*." But he found some happiness, and after a swift courtship became engaged to his boyhood sweetheart, Elmira Royster, now a widow. At the end of September he started North to attend to some literary hack work and to see Mrs. Clemm. Nothing is really known about what happened during the next week until he was picked up unconscious near a polling booth in Baltimore. When he regained consciousness, he passed into a violent delirium, and kept crying out for "Reynolds"—the man whose concern with the importance of exploring the South Seas had stimulated the composition of *Pym*. Perhaps Poe's fevered mind had returned to such details as he had conjured up in "MS Found in a Bottle," the first instance when he projected his inner world through the horror of his sensation that he was "hurrying onwards to some exciting knowledge—some never-to-be-imparted secret, whose attainment is destruction." He died of acute congestion of the brain, and was buried near his grandfather in the Presbyterian cemetery. He had recently written in *Marginalia*: "There are moments when, even to the sober eye of Reason, the world of our sad humanity must assume the aspect of Hell." He was one whom "unmerciful disaster" had "followed fast and followed faster" to the end.

7

Poe's final value may hardly be judged apart from the many traditions to which his work gave rise. French Symbolism, with its desire to attain the suggestiveness of music, began at the moment when Baudelaire recognized in Poe's logical formulas for a poem his own half-developed thoughts, "combined to perfection." But Baudelaire was indebted to Poe for more than form. He took the title for his intimate journal from a phrase in *Marginalia*, "my heart laid bare," and attributed to Poe's reaffirmation of evil the recovery of human dignity from the shallowness of the optimistic reformers. Another note in *Marginalia*, "The orange ray of the spectrum and the buzz of the gnat . . . affect me with nearly similar sensations," led to Baudelaire's epoch-making sonnet, "Correspondances," and in turn to Rimbaud's further development of this same doctrine of the interpenetration of the senses. Rimbaud's masterpiece, "Le Bateau ivre," also confirmed the degree to which Poe's image of man's destiny as a frail boat out of control on the flowing waters of life was to become a major symbol for the age. Meanwhile, Gautier and the Parnassian group had found in "The Philosophy of Composition" their conception that the form creates the idea. The relevance of all these complex developments to American poetry lies in the profound attraction that T. S. Eliot and Wallace Stevens were to discover in symbolism, and thence to bring Poe back to American art by way of France.

Poe's introspective heroes begat a long line of descendants. As Edmund Wilson demonstrated so brilliantly, the remote castle that Villiers de L'Isle-Adam's Axel inhabits was inherited from Roderick Usher; and when Huysmans voiced through his Des Esseintes the doctrines of decadence, almost every artificial detail of his shut-in paradise was borrowed from Poe's interiors, as was the disordered preoccupation with what Usher himself had called "a morbid acuteness of the senses." The furthest possible withdrawal of the hero from the responsibilities of a hostile world might seem to be that in Proust, and although nationalists in criticism now view with alarm any effect in America of such European influences, the feeling that the artist is at war with a business civilization was as much Hart Crane's as it was Poe's.

This may still seem to leave Poe remote from the main currents of American thought. And although Hawthorne admired the originality of his tales, and Lowell had been quick to recognize his double gift for imagination and analysis, the first generation of realists passed Poe by. Both Howells and Twain found his method as "mechanical" as Henry James did; and for the belated dedication of his tomb in 1875, Mallarmé wrote his great sonnet, but Whitman alone among important American writers attended—and Whitman judged Poe to belong finally "among the electric lights of imaginative literature, brilliant and dazzling, but with no heat." Yet his ultimate effect upon our most popular literature was enormous. As much as anyone ever invents a genre, Poe invented the detective story. He also inaugurated the vogue for the pseudoscientific romance and for that of adolescent adventure.

Jules Verne, Stevenson, and Conan Doyle are equally in his debt. "The Gold Bug," "The Pit and the Pendulum," and "The Murders in the Rue Morgue" have now been read by millions oblivious of their author's aesthetic theories.

The notion has sometimes been advanced that the materialism of so many of Poe's interests, his fondness for inventions and hoaxes, and his special flair for journalism made him more "representative" than Emerson or Whitman of ordinary Americans. His more serious importance was noted by the Goncourt brothers, who declared in their journal for 1856 that here was "the literature of the twentieth century," an analytic literature that would be more given to what passes in the brain than in the heart. That distinction may be as brittle as some of Poe's own, but the intense investigation of the roots of Gothic horror in morbid states of mind has been part of American fiction from Brockden Brown and Poe through Ambrose Bierce and William Faulkner.

Poe wrote at a time when America was producing more real and alleged transcendental geniuses than maturely wrought poems or stories. In opposition to the romantic stress on the expression of personality, he insisted on the importance, not of the artist, but of the created work of art. He stands as one of the very few great innovators in American literature. Like Henry James and T. S. Eliot, he took his place, almost from the start, in international culture as an original creative force in contrast to the more superficial international vogue of Cooper and Irving.

LITERARY FULFILLMENT

24. DEMOCRATIC VISTAS

IN quality of style, and particularly in depth of philosophic insight, American literature has not yet surpassed the collective achievement of Emerson, Thoreau, Hawthorne, Melville, and Whitman. Having freed itself in these writers from its earlier tendencies either blindly to imitate or blindly to reject European models, American literature here for the first time sloughed off provincialism, and, by being itself—by saying only what it wanted to say and as it wanted to say it—attained, paradoxically, the rank and quality of world literature, a literature authentic not only in America but everywhere the English tongue is understood.

The release was both material and social. There was, to begin with, the increasing social fluidity of the mid-nineteenth century in the East, with its accompanying sense of unlimited cultural possibilities. While the West was expanding and experimenting, those parts of the country which had by now been settled for more than two hundred years began to lose their sharp social and regional contrasts and to settle into a cultural homogeneity more like that of the older civilizations of Europe, though built firmly on a democratic base.

The social stratification of the seaboard colonies, with their mercantile and landed aristocracies, their small farmers, their squatters, and their slaves, had begun to disintegrate during the Revolution, but was not yet reshaped into the industrial class structure of the future. Regionally, colonial distinctions had also broken down with the mounting pressure of populations to the eastward—from Europe to the Atlantic seaboard and from the seaboard to the frontier. The slow process of eroding these regional differences, so important in colonial assemblies, had already achieved, by the intermingling of ideas and of local customs, the national feeling which was to culminate later in a simpler, more inclusive, division of the country into the North, the South, and the West.

Moreover, this flux of institutions and people was marked not by a sense of loss or confusion but by a sense of potentiality and expectancy. The era of good feeling following the War of 1812—a war which at first seemed lost but was miraculously retrieved—had affected all levels of the national life and, blinding men to the risk of the American experiment, revealed only its adventure. And this spirit of self-confidence had been fed by other fires: by the material promise of timber, land, and waterway, convertible at a touch into ready wealth; and by the technological promise—already apparent—of American mechanical and social invention.

Yet neither the general confidence nor the manifold promises of the period can alone explain the peak reached by American literature at this time. For this we must turn to a third and more decisive factor: the reorientation of literature under the influence of New England transcendentalism. For, by reawakening—even among its critics—an interest in the great problems of human nature and destiny, transcendentalism conferred upon American literature a perspective far wider and deeper than that proposed by its own formulated doctrines, the perspective of humanity itself. This perspective it is which gives common purpose and meaning to the otherwise divergent achievements of Emerson, Thoreau, Hawthorne, Melville, and Whitman, and accounts in great part for their manifest superiority to precedessors like Irving and Bryant whose interests were less profound and more superficially literary.

2

Transcendentalism emerged as a full-fledged movement of New England thought between 1815 and 1836. The first date marks the maturing of the liberalizing ministry of William Ellery Channing; the second, the publication of Emerson's *Nature,* the original—and probably the best—systematic expression of the transcendentalist philosophy. Thereafter the movement continued to expand, first as a revolt against the sterile Unitarian orthodoxy, then as a protest against the continuing cultural dependence of America on Europe, and finally as a profound exploration of the spiritual foundations and moral implications of the new democracy. From the beginning it attracted eccentrics no less than men of genius, and after the Civil War it gave way to weaker forms of idealism. But at its zenith in the writings of Emerson, Thoreau, and Alcott—and by its challenge to fresh speculation in Hawthorne, Melville, and Whitman—its vitalizing effect upon American art and literature and, indeed, upon the development of American democracy as a whole, remains unrivaled.

The source of this vitality lies in the intellectual background of transcendentalism: in its appropriation of certain insights of Puritan, Quaker, and other colonial theologies as they had been refracted through the secular and equalitarian ideology of the Revolution; and in its reexpression of these insights in the vocabulary of contemporary European philosophy. For in spite of its oft proclaimed rejection of authority and its frankly nationalistic bias transcendentalism was rooted both in the American past and in the Europe of that day.

To Puritanism in the broadest sense, for example, it owed among other things its pervasive moralism. Like all those early pioneers who sought freedom of conscience in a new land, the transcendentalists were ever disposed to interpret life ethically, to subordinate the aesthetic, intellectual, and even political and economic aspects of human nature to man's significance as a moral agent. Once again, after two centuries and more, this conception was used as a means of dignifying all phases of human activity, even the most humble. Thus, just as the Mathers, Edwards, Penn, Woolman, and even Franklin had alike maintained that each man is "called" to perform as faithfully as he can the duties of his particular station in life, so Emerson argued that every act of the individual springs from his inner nature as a unique embodiment of humanity, and hence no occupation is inherently ignoble.

A similar affinity may be discovered between transcendental "intuition" and the doctrine of the "inner light." For each of these theories interpreted material nature mystically as a "veil" or symbol of the divine; and each maintained that every individual can penetrate the veil to discover divine truth for himself without the aid of traditional authority or even of logic.

But none of these doctrines had been transmitted in its original form. The Puritan orthodoxy of New England had from the earliest times been subject to the filtering process of dissent, and had finally succumbed as a rigid and dominant system to the less precise and more rationalized theology of the Unitarians. The tendencies thus manifest on the level of religious thinking were even stronger on that of secular radicalism during the Revolutionary epoch. The worldliness and "common sense" of a Franklin or a Jefferson had apparently made a clean break with earlier orthodoxies while retaining their zeal for moral enlightenment; and the same tendency had but recently moved even further from theological sanction in the equalitarian theory of Jacksonian democracy. These latter-day and transplanted expressions of the Reformation and the Enlightenment, which had coalesced in the preachings of William Ellery Channing and other predecessors of the transcendental movement in New England, had in some instances added to, but in all instances had transformed, the orthodox teachings of the early religious and secular leaders.

This is illustrated in the new meanings given to the old doctrine of the sovereignty of ethics. For one thing, the equalitarian implications of the doctrine were secularized and broadened to a degree hitherto unknown in this country. Whereas in the orthodox Puritan interpretation the doctrine of the equality of man with man was largely theoretical—being restricted to a mere hypothetical equality before God and the law—and, even in the political philosophy of the Revolution, had accepted social stratification, Jacksonian individualism demanded that it be applied as a practical principle of social reform calling for local autonomy, free public education, and universal suffrage on a scale undreamed of even by Jefferson. Coincidentally, the scope of the principle had been broadened. In place of the old invidious distinction between the elect and the damned which had suggested that only a chosen few were to be admitted to spiritual equality, the Unitarian and Universalist emphasis on the brotherhood of man proclaimed the perfectibility of all.

Still more subtly, this leveling process reoriented the very concept of ethics itself. For although it was still insisted that moral obligation is transcendent in origin—is determined by more than personal whim or habit—that obligation could no longer be construed in abstract universal terms or continue to be rooted in the will of an arbitrary God. Under the influence of Unitarianism, Deity was reduced to a kind of immanent principle implicit in man everywhere, and man himself thereby was made the true source of the moral law. Also, instead of continuing to conceive moral obligation legalistically—as a kind of ritualistic observance of a general code—it was now argued that no single code fits all situations adequately and that each individual must be left perfectly free to judge for himself what his actual duty on any given occasion is. Thus theology made its final effort to provide religious sanction for equalitarian tendencies inherent in the republic from the start.

Equally radical was the transformation of the doctrine of the inner light brought about by the acknowledgment of the autonomous power of secular reason, in part aided by the accelerating conquests of natural science. For this acknowledgment—validated anew by the role of reason in formulating the principles of the Revolution, and manifested concretely both in the rationalism of Unitarian theology and in the pragmatism of frontier thought—had undermined belief in the inner light at two points.

In the first place, it challenged the theoretical competence of the inner light. Although often authoritarian in spirit itself, the new emphasis on reason was wholly antiauthoritarian in implication. Holding with Locke that all knowledge is perceptual in origin, it demanded that every truth be held subject to the test of experiment and observation. And this was a test which, with its implicit mysticism, the doctrine of the inner light as the word of God could not hope to sustain.

In the second place, the new emphasis on reason challenged the doctrine of the inner light on the score of its immediate utility. For while the older doctrine could promise only the quietistic value of bringing man face to face with God, the reason, practically applied, promised a control of nature itself and thereby the immediate satisfaction of human needs.

Yet neither the period generally, nor Unitarianism and democracy in particular, was so pragmatically inclined as to deny the possibility of religious insight entirely. The hold of the Christian tradition upon belief and imagination was still too strong. Nevertheless, certain changes in the conception of the inner light were effected. One of these was to restrict the scope of the inner light to the moral and speculative sphere and to concede to observation priority in the understanding of nature. Another and more important change was the transformation of the inner light into a wholly natural organ. Instead of being dependent, as in the early orthodoxies, upon divine Grace—upon a kind of flooding of the mind by light from without—the power of the inner light was now grounded in the nature of the mind itself, becoming merely one mental faculty among others and subject, therefore, to the same degree of individual control. It was converted, in other words, from a "revelation," an act and agency of God, into an "intuition," an act and agency of man.

It is doubtful whether these transformations of the Puritan ethic and theory of knowledge ever could have become more than vague intellectual tendencies of the time or could have achieved the degree of articulate formulation they subsequently did without the stimulus of contemporary European philosophy. There had emerged in Germany an intellectually sophisticated movement elaborately embodied in the systems of Fichte, Schelling, Schleiermacher, and Hegel, and—at a further remove—in the thought of Coleridge, Carlyle, and Victor Cousin. This movement, idealistic in nature, had its specialized formulas and idioms, its accepted premises and methods. In literature it took the form of romanticism.

It was also a movement whose influence began to be felt in New England about 1820. New England interest in German thought generally goes back much further: to William Bentley who acted as cultural ambassador between the merchants of Hamburg and of Salem in the late years of the eighteenth and the early years of the nineteenth century; and, beyond Bentley, to the correspondence of Cotton Mather with the Pietistic theologians of Halle. The interest was not widespread until after the War of 1812, when it became intellectually fashionable for younger New England to make the grand tour or to enroll in German universities, and when particular notice began to be taken of German philosophy as reflected in the writings of its English and French disciples. Later, many of the transcendentalists were to make some pretense of studying German philosophy directly; but their initial—and probably most enduring—impression of the movement was derived from such secondary sources as Marsh's edition (1829) of Coleridge's *Aids to Reflection,* Linberg's translation (1832) of Cousin's *Introduction to the History of Philosophy,* and Carlyle's *Sartor Resartus* (1836).

What was important in this influence was the fact that it made available to the New England writers and through them to American writers generally an elaborate symbolic construction capable not only of expressing the general metaphysical hesitancy of the period—its inability either to retreat into frank supernaturalism or to advance to a bold materialism—but also of providing principles and distinctions whereby this midway position could be explored and defended.

Thus, the doctrine of human individuality as both self-transcending and self-asserting—as both acknowledging its oneness with and obligation to something higher than itself, and yet ever cherishing its uniqueness and independence as a distinct being—and the further conception that individual happiness depends upon the successful synthesis of these twin tendencies, provided an almost perfect theoretical framework for a new effort to discover supernatural sanction for the swift-moving and constantly changing panorama of American life.

Similarly, the distinction found in Coleridge and Emerson alike, between the reason and the understanding—which, by a curious distortion of terminology, identified the reason with intuition and imagination, and the understanding with logic and induction—could express and justify the transcendentalist's desire to retain both the mysticism of the past and the empiricism of the present, and to assign each a sphere in experience proper to its character.

Finally, the idealistic view of the universe as an embodiment of a single, cosmic psyche, now manifesting itself as man, now as nature, and achieving through the interaction of the two in history its own secret intent, permitted the self-asserting impulse of the individual—his determination to be himself at all costs—to be explained as the consciousness of his identity with the world-psyche, while his self-transcending or outgoing impulses could be attributed to the consciousness of his own finitude, to the fact of his awareness that he is only one fragmentary expression of the world-psyche among others. The theory could also account for and validate the distinction between the intuitive and the inductive, interpreting the first of these faculties as the necessary condition for conscious union with the world-psyche, and the second as the necessary condition for survival as a separate expression of that psyche.

The initial function of this movement was thus to act as a kind of model and repository of ideas from which American, and in particular New England, writers could borrow in their self-imposed task of creating a new metaphysic for democracy out of the theological and intellectual materials of the American past. Without slavishly imitating this model, but still inspired by it in various degrees, Emerson, Thoreau, Whitman, and even, by contraries, Hawthorne and Melville were able to achieve a curious blending of the alien and the native, a blending in which specific traditional conceptions were adjusted to specific American use. This fusion is apparent, for example, in Emerson's appeal to the Over-Soul as a sanction for Yankee self-reliance, in Thoreau's discovery that Walden recapitulated the universe in small, and—by its very failure—in Melville's ambiguities. It is also apparent in Whitman's *Democratic Vistas,* which preached a new brotherhood of man in terms of the mystic unity of creation, "the divine central idea of All."

But European idealism was to act as more than a mere model for New England transcendentalism. For, working in and through transcendentalism—and reinforced a little later by the influx of roughly similar teachings from the Orient—its influence leavened American literature as a whole, including even the writings of men like Hawthorne and Melville who were actively opposed to transcendentalism proper. The general leavening consisted not so much in the transmission and implanting of specific borrowings—although this also occurred—as it did in the setting of problems and perspectives like the nature of the universe, the origin of evil, and the meaning of experience, which were destined to give American literature a universal import and eventually swing it into the orbit of world literature.

3

At first sight, Emerson, Thoreau, Hawthorne, Melville, and Whitman seem to differ from one another more than they agree. For one thing, they are divergent in temperament. Thoreau, Whitman, and—above all—Emerson are prevailingly optimistic. Hawthorne, on the other hand, is at least fatalistic in point of view; while Melville seems to have run the entire emotional gamut from optimism through pessimism to final resignation. Again, all of them differ widely in their choice of subject matter and literary form. Primarily novelists, Hawthorne and Melville are concerned with the psychological and allegorical analysis of certain types of human personality and moral situations; primarily poets and essayists, Emerson, Thoreau, and Whitman focus, each in his own way, upon the underlying relation of man to nature.

Most widely of all, they differ in their interest and capacity for sustained philosophical thought. None of them could be described as interested in philosophical theory for its own sake—not even Emerson, who is less intolerant of abstract reasoning than the rest. But even within these limits their divergency is still great. For although we can find at least traces of a comprehensive philosophical system in Emerson, the traces become progressively more rudimentary in Thoreau, Melville, and Whitman, until at last in Hawthorne they almost disappear.

Yet this incommensurability is not absolute. Common to them, as to all great writers, is a profound sense of the human predicament, of the questions that beset man as man, and of the relation of these problems to man's defects and potentialities. Their common concern surmounts all differences, as may be seen in Emerson's and Hawthorne's treatment of the problem of evil. When Emerson proclaims the non-existence of evil in an ultimate form and Hawthorne rejects this conception as tragically blind, neither writer is proceeding on the assumption that the problem of evil itself is unreal or trivial. For Hawthorne, as we know, it is the most pressing of all problems, while for Emerson—as the haunting overtones of "Experience" intimate—it is a problem which can be optimistically resolved only after the most desperate of inward struggles and only after attaining a serenity almost stripped of emotion. In other words, the difference between the two lies not in their conception of the importance of the problem but only in their conception of its proper solution.

Common also to all these writers is the framework of ideas within which they seek to understand the problem of man. Even when it provides quite divergent solutions the framework or perspective is in all instances radically humanistic.

Its basic premise is that man is the spiritual center of the universe and that in man alone can we find the clue to nature, history, and ultimately the cosmos itself. Without denying outright the existence either of God or of brute matter, it nevertheless rejects them as exclusive principles of interpretation and prefers to explain man and his world so far as possible in terms of man himself. This is expressed most clearly in the transcendentalist principle that the structure of the universe literally duplicates the structure of the individual self, and that all knowledge therefore begins with self-knowledge. But it is no less evident in the moral earnestness of Hawthorne and Melville, which leads them to dwell ceaselessly upon the allegory of the human soul and to personalize impersonal nature itself as an allegory of human experience. It is because of this, for example, that few incidents in their plots ever turn out to be wholly fortuitous or to be without symbolic significance for the characters involved in them.

This common perspective is also, in all cases, radically universalized. Its emphasis is almost never upon man as particular—as European, say, or as American—but almost always upon man as universal, upon man as freed from the accidents of time and space as well as from those of birth and talent and reduced to his common humanity. It is apparent not only in Emerson and Thoreau but also in Hawthorne, Melville, and Whitman; none of them even in the most concrete and practical moments can ever quite forget that the drama of man is clothed with the aspect of eternity. Thus, for Emerson, the "American Scholar" turns out to be simply "Man Thinking"; while, for Whitman, the song of himself merges imperceptibly into a song of all the "children of Adam," where "every atom belonging to me as good belongs to you." Thus also, in spite of a frequently high degree of individualization, the characters and situations of Hawthorne and Melville are fundamentally impersonal, emerging at their best as a fusion of particular and type but at their worst as types only.

This turning away from the current scientific view of the world and regression under the impetus of European idealism to the Neo-Platonic conception of nature as a living mystery full of signs and portents, revives a conception with which some of the five were already familiar from their reading in the literature of the seventeenth century and of religious mysticism. At the same time, a principle of correspondence is evolved which promises the reconciliation rather than the rejection of science.

Nor can we overestimate the practical importance of this conception from either the literary or the social point of view. In terms of literature, for instance, its construing of nature as inherently symbolic invests the natural faculty of imagination with a new prestige, dissolving the older literary emphasis upon wit, sentiment, and rationality, and preparing the way for the symbolist literature to come. Even more far-reaching are the social implications of the conception. For by postulating, as it does, an identity between the categories of impersonal nature and the categories of human psychology— and thereby also the unity of creation—the conception provides a metaphysical basis for the belief in democratic equality to which the social philosophy of Emerson, Thoreau, and Whitman can and does appeal.

The second assumption common to all five writers is the belief that individual virtue and happiness depend upon self-realization, and that self-realization, in turn, depends upon the harmonious reconciliation of two universal psychological tendencies: first, the expansive or self-transcending impulse of the self, its desire to embrace the whole world in the experience of a single moment and to know and become one with that world; and second, the contracting or self-asserting impulse of the individual, his desire to withdraw, to remain unique and separate, and to be responsible only to himself.

The current theory of self as expounded by Coleridge and other Europeans was adaptable here, and its importance was more than theoretical because it stated in universal terms the central goal and problem of democracy itself. On the one hand, democracy as a moral and political doctrine implied an ethic of extreme individualism, one which preserved to the individual a maximum degree of freedom and self-expression. On the other hand, the democratic self was divided. There was, first, the conflict between its traditional sense of duty to God and its new-found sense of duty to man. There was, second, the conflict between the duty to self as implied by the concept of liberty and the duty to society as implied by the other two concepts of the revolutionary triad, equality and fraternity. Hence, a doctrine which recognizes the divisions in the self and insists that their reconciliation is necessary for true self-realization defines not only the democratic ethic in general but also the specific hope of democracy that the self can be realized without sacrificing any side of its nature, altruistic as well as egoistic.

There can be no doubt that all five of the writers define the ethical ideal in these terms, although, characteristically, they disagree both on *how* the ideal is to be actualized and on the degree to which it is actualizable. Thus Emerson, Thoreau, and Whitman, who accept its actualization as a real possibility because they have assumed to begin with that the self and the cosmos express one and the same spiritual force, disagree on what specific course of action will convert their inner harmony into an outward fact. For while Emerson and Thoreau believed the harmony can be fully realized by the simple, though paradoxical, expedient of forgetting the world and being true only to oneself, Whitman seems to hold that there is needed an unlimited love of creation as such, a love that will include the self and the world as one.

In contrast to these three stand Hawthorne and Melville, who doubt whether a genuine harmony between the individual and his cosmos is possible at all. For although both assume that the destiny of man is ever to seek such a harmony, they are also deeply convinced that the self and the cosmos are victim to tragic flaws which prevent their ever realizing it. Hawthorne discovers the flaws both in the spiritual pride and spiritual weakness of the individual and in the intractability of his social environment. And Melville identifies them with a defect in the universe at large, symbolized in the inscrutability of the white whale.

But both writers hold that the flaws, in all cases, effectively block a final rapport between the individual and the world. For although the conflict between these two protagonists is sometimes susceptible of an emotional resolution—either by a daemonic assertion of the will, as in Captain Ahab, or by the will's abnegation, as in Hester Prynne and Billy Budd—the resolution is only partial since it is at the cost of eliminating either the world or the self from final moral consideration. In other words, where Emerson, Thoreau, and Whitman discover in the romantic theory of self-realization grounds for ultimate hope, Hawthorne and Melville draw from it only tragic irresolution.

The third assumption common to the five writers is that intuition and imagination offer a surer road to truth than abstract logic or scientific method. It is a corollary to their belief that nature is organic, and corresponds to the technical distinction between the reason as intuition and the understanding as logical analysis. In the specific form of this distinction, the assumption appears frequently in Emerson. But as a general principle underlying both theory and practice it is present in all.

It is illustrated by their emphasis upon introspection—their belief that the clue to outer nature is always to be found in the inner world of individual psychology—and by their constant interpretation of experience as in essence symbolic. For both these stresses presume an organic relationship between the self and the cosmos of which only intuition and imagination can properly take account.

Finally, in terms of the third assumption, all five writers were able to deduce a consequence of immense practical importance not only for their own work but for the subsequent course of American literature as a whole. Not only could the belief in the primacy of imagination be used to justify their own tendency toward the concrete, the metaphorical, and the didactic; it also had the wider implication of attaching greater significance to the craft of literature generally. Once the faculty of imagination is placed on a par with the faculty of reason, the writer as the primary exponent of the imagination acquires an importance in society at least equal to that of the scientist, the philosopher, and the theologian. All equally can then claim to be engaged in the same pursuit: the search for truth.

It is undoubtedly their faith in the imagination and in themselves as practitioners of imagination that enabled Emerson, Thoreau, Hawthorne, Melville, and Whitman to achieve supreme confidence in their own moral and metaphysical insights. It is this also that led them to conceive of the writer as a seer, and thus to exemplify in their attitude toward literature the emphasis upon its responsibility to life which is characteristic of our own day.

4

The close affinity between the idealism of contemporary European philosophy and the romanticism of Emerson, Thoreau, Melville, Hawthorne, and Whitman must not be pressed to the point of identity or to the exclusion of other influences. The sharing between European and American thinkers of common concepts and a common idiom for their expression is merely one more evidence that the young nation was beginning to lose its provincialism and to take its place in the main flow of Western culture. American philosophical thinking had remained true to its own origins, which were of course European in the first instance, through the periods of settlement, early development, and now a first maturity. Once more it could look to Europe for a confirmation by parallel of its own conclusions.

There were, however, significant differences as well as similarities. Where the Europeans of the eighteenth and nineteenth centuries were predominantly intellectual and aesthetic in their interests, the Americans were predominantly moral; and where the Europeans often tended to underscore the role of hierarchy and institutional stability in human affairs, the Americans stressed the ideas of equality and freedom from state interference.

Nor was European philosophy the only such force to act as a catalyst on the nineteenth century American mind. Its importance was taken for granted even though it was not fully understood by the earlier critics of New England transcendentalism. Recently there has been a tendency to underestimate it in favor of the obvious influences of Neo-Platonic and Oriental kinds of idealism in giving new forms and a new vocabulary to American thinkers. Historians have demonstrated the catalytic effect of Plato and Plotinus on Emerson and of the Bhagavad-Gita and other Oriental tales and poems on Emerson and Thoreau. But more often than not such influences out of the past were shared by American writers with their European contemporaries, and the precise channels or directions of their flow can be distinguished only with the greatest difficulty. The minds of Emerson, Whitman, and Melville were characteristically American in their willingness to appropriate usable ideas wherever they might be found, without too much concern for logical consistency, and it is safer to assume that these men obtained many of their principal assumptions—or at least the language in which such ideas found expression—through their alert interest in the dominant intellectual movements of the time rather than from any single source in the past.

Whatever the sources or channels of their common feeling, the fact remains that there existed between these five Americans and their European contemporaries a community of interest based upon the use of a common philosophical idiom and upon the discovery, as a result of the common vocabulary, of a common set of problems approached in a common spirit. This community helps explain the promptness with which Emerson, Thoreau, and others of the group were "discovered" and acclaimed abroad. It also helps explain the almost proprietary sense these writers themselves had in European literary and philosophical movements.

Of even greater moment was the fact that contact with European philosophy and literature established a spiritual continuity not only with their contemporaries but with the great literary and philosophical traditions of the past. For in rediscovering such fundamental conceptions of Western culture as the correspondence between man and nature and the doctrine of the poet as seer, these writers acquired something more than a set of inert principles. Rather, by means of these ideas—by accident of the fact that the ideas had been perennial to Western thought—they acquired that spirit of universality which has characterized Western literature at its greatest moments, even making it capable of absorbing the best of the Orient. Thus the preoccupation with local customs, local legends, and local scenes characteristic of the earlier writers in the seaboard states, and again of those of the frontier, was generalized, at least for a moment of literary fulfillment, into a profound concern with human nature, while democracy itself instead of continuing to be construed as a mere experiment in government was now subjected to a more thorough examination of its fundamental moral and metaphysical meanings.

In other words, European philosophical theory, acting as a primary catalyst for forces already deeply indigenous to the American mind, had effected and accelerated a reorientation of literature which was tantamount to raising it to a new plane. Having revealed the American character and experience as identical in form and substance with the character and experience of man everywhere, it had created the conditions whereby American literature without ceasing to be national could become a part of world literature. And it is one measure of the genius of Emerson, Thoreau, Hawthorne, Melville, and Whitman that they were able to transmute this possibility into an opportunity.

25. RALPH WALDO EMERSON

F ROM these currents of thought and feeling Emerson emerged as the delegated intellect—his own "Man Thinking." "There are periods fruitful of great men," he wrote, "others barren . . . periods when the heat is latent,—others when it is given out." A half-century had passed since the United States had been baptized in political independence; the time had now come for confirmation in freedom of the soul. Ralph Waldo Emerson, of Concord, Massachusetts, declared the ceremony performed and became spokesman for his time and country.

His preeminence has caused our literary historians some embarrassment. America was ready for a Shakespeare, a Dante, or a Dostoevski to give literary voice to her achieved majority. She was given an apologist—an Aristotle, a Paul, a Bacon. In the wise and temperate Emerson, the heat became radiant light. It was he who brought into its first sharp focus the full meaning of two centuries of life on the Atlantic seaboard of this continent; of the economic and spiritual revolutions which had unsettled the Old World and settled the New; of the experiment in democracy which was to make a Holy Commonwealth into a world power.

He did this in two ways: by carrying to its ultimate statement the individual's revolt from authority, which marked the transition from the medieval world to the modern; and by formulating the dichotomy between the vision of a Jonathan Edwards and the common sense of a Benjamin Franklin, a conflict and a balance which has always provided the creative tension in American life. But he translated these discoveries neither into formal philosophy nor into fully formed art. His logic and his metaphysics remained without system; his art, like that of all great American romantics, retained its organic freedom.

As Emerson had no Boswell, he must speak for himself, and he spent his life in doing so. Upon an audience he played with the sure hands of a master organist; but the oft shuffled manuscripts in his study were cold. "We do not go to hear what Emerson says," wrote Lowell, "so much as to hear Emerson." A tall blond figure in black, he leaned forward across the reading desk in shy

Yankee awkwardness and searched the hearts of his hearers with sincere blue eyes and controlled voice.

"Where do we find ourselves?" he asks in his essay on "Experience," and he gives his answer: "On its own level, or in view of nature, temperament is final." The inner wholeness of the man is his true self; his life "is a train of moods like a string of beads"; temperament, the iron wire on which the beads are strung. Striving to give expression only and always to this central self, Emerson has left a handful of essays and poems which are to many an essential part of their religious literature; but the man himself evades discovery. "So much of our time is preparation," he explains, "so much is routine, and so much retrospect, that the pith of each man's genius contracts itself to a very few hours."

Preparation—routine—retrospect; these are the entries on the calendar, the frame of life for a reticent New England man who is Emerson the seer. He devoted thirty-three years to what he thought of later as "preparation" before he published his first book in 1836; some two decades provided the "very few hours" when his genius was at high pitch and all of his great work was produced from the essential stability and calm of "routine"; and finally there were almost thirty years of "retrospect" before his death in 1882. The central twenty years have left us our impression of a man who always stood firm on moral ground and admonished his fellows to turn their eyes from evil, to have faith in themselves and in one another, and to seek God through Nature. But the Emersonian confidence and calm were not achieved, nor were they maintained, without struggle, doubt, and self-examination.

2

The chronicle of Emerson's preparation may be reconstructed from letters and journals; it would have been alien to his temperament to leave an autobiography of the soul such as *Sartor Resartus, Dichtung und Wahrheit,* or the *Confessions* of Rousseau. But the romantic pattern of introspection, doubt, and psychological crisis found in a Carlyle or a Goethe was his as well, marked by the familiar circumstances of poverty, loneliness, illness, idealized love, and the discovery of death.

Poverty was the lot of his youth. The second of four boys, he was only eight years old when his father died in 1811 and the congregation of the "Old Brick" Church in Boston granted the "pious and amiable" widow home and subsistence for a few years, while the boys shared one winter overcoat and the housework, studied their grammar, and ended the "toils of the day," as Ralph reports to his Aunt Mary, with their private devotions.

During Ralph's school and college days this diminutive aunt, appearing suddenly out of her private wandering for visits at the Emerson home or writing admonitory letters to her adopted spiritual orphans, became the substitute for both father and conscience. Her life, writes her nephew, "marked the precise time when the power of the old creed yielded to the influence of modern science and humanity." The zeal and consecration of Puritan ancestors was mingled in the latter-day sibyl with shrewd common sense and an insatiable intellectual curiosity. Mary Moody Emerson lived this life in preparation for the next, but she lived it with gusto. The correspondence between her and her nephew charts his course as his mind and spirit grew. There is solemn thought and wiry humor in the letters of both, even though the boy's sophistication is sophomoric, that of the little old lady crisp and intricate. For Aunt Mary was both mystic and critic, Calvinist and skeptic; Ralph could laugh at her because he profoundly respected her. To her he took both his doubts and his discoveries. She sharpened his wit and deepened his perceptions. Here is at least one source for that mixture of insight and common sense which characterized his thought, that aphoristic directness which sharpened his style.

During these early years, Emerson learned the habit of introspection. His intimate experience with people seems hardly to have extended beyond the family. "The friends that occupy my thoughts," he wrote at Harvard, "are not men, but certain phantoms clothed in the form and face and apparel of men by whom they were suggested and to whom they bear a resemblance." But his intimacy with his brothers, William, Edward, and Charles, was close. The journals which he, and apparently Charles as well, kept from an early age have not all survived, for the first is now dated 1819 from Harvard; but even in these we can see the somewhat affected litterateur gradually recede and the true man emerge. By 1824, the journals have ceased to be a "motley diary" and have become a "soliloquy," a "savings bank" where he can deposit his earnings. Here is the workshop, with saw, hammer, and plane, where the raw lumber of thought, reading, and experience is stored and worked. There is a vast difference between the early and late volumes. The first four or five constitute a moving autobiography of the spirit, but the others may be read in almost any order and are most enjoyable when dipped into. Between 1820 and 1836, when his inner life was growing steadily, the record of his progress has dramatic conflict and movement. Thereafter the journals gradually become to the reader what they were to him, a mine to be worked rather than a journey to be taken.

To poverty and introspection was added a struggle with sickness and adversity sufficient to supply a romantic hero with all the sorrows he might need. For the shadow of the white plague lay across the Emerson household, and Ralph barely escaped its doom. It carried off his two younger brothers, the one more eager and self-consuming, the other less robust than he; and, if we accept his own theory, he avoided certain death when a depression and cough racked his chest only because of a "sluggish" passivity of temperament which allowed him to give in to the malady and take the rest and care which brought his recovery. But Edward's sudden mental breakdown in 1828 followed Ralph's trip to Florida in search of health by only a year, and the frailty of Charles, "the friend and companion of many years . . . whose conversation . . . has been my daily bread," kept the minds of both in secret morbid contemplation to be confessed only to private notes. "I read with some surprise the pages of his journal," wrote the elder brother after the death of Charles in 1836. "They show a nocturnal side which his diurnal aspects never suggested,—they are melancholy, penitential, self-accusing; I read them with no pleasure: they are the creepings of an eclipsing temperament over his abiding light of character."

It would be a mistake to overemphasize the similar traits in Ralph's character, but the tone of penitential self-accusation is strong throughout the college and following years, driving him in upon himself when external adversity made the way dark. Like Charles too, but again not to the same degree, this mood cultivated an insistently skeptical habit of mind which fought throughout these years a losing but bitter battle with the native optimism of his character and resulted in a strengthening of his affirmation.

Love likewise came to him in somber garb. Within parentheses he confided in 1827, "I am a bachelor and to the best of my belief have never been in love"; but the next year when he took Edward to Concord, New Hampshire, to hasten his recovery, he confessed to William: "The presumptuous man was overthrown by the eye and ear, and surrendered at discretion. He is now as happy as it is safe in life to be. She is seventeen years old, and very beautiful, by universal consent." Ellen Tucker's illness—the same as his own though more acute—had made her already an invalid and emphasized the ethereal qualities that so appealed to suppressed but dreaming youth. Delicate, deeply religious, and altogether devoted, she awoke his protective manhood, spurred ambition, inspired poetic tribute. The marriage lasted a little over a year, and her death left a "miserable apathy" rather than the morbid depression of adolescent sorrow. As pastor of the Second Church of Boston, he had meanwhile become a man. Yet Ellen remained the one great romance of his life, a dream of purity the easier to maintain because illness had protected it from the rigors of living.

Eager for experience and thwarted by his shyness, Emerson sought in books the reality he craved. His tastes were formed in early childhood. Aunt Mary had seen to it that the fatherless boys should grow up in the family tradition of religious zeal and the love of letters. She herself read beyond orthodox theology, and she encouraged her nephews to follow her devious course. Through her, Ralph discovered Milton and Bacon, Shakespeare and Burke, who were to remain through life close friends on his expanding shelves.

As he grew older and moved away from her influence, the eclectic quality of his reading increased. For the formal Harvard curriculum he had little use, and he was content to remain in the middle of his class rather than seek academic distinction. A good sermon from W. E. Channing, or an oration from Everett or Webster gave him more pleasure than the rhetorical instruction of Edward Channing or the cold rationalism of Locke. The influence of the Scottish rationalist Dugald Stewart can be traced in his later writing; but, at the time, the *Elements of the Philosophy of the Human Mind* seemed all cottages and shops after entering the gate of splendor and promise. Doubt knocked at his door in the form of Pyrrhonism, the current undergraduate fashion. Slowly, as he took over his own education, he added Plato (in the translation of Thomas Taylor), Montaigne, Newton, Swedenborg, and Plutarch (both the *Lives* and the *Morals*), to his list of imperatives. More commonly he turned to histories, anthologies, and translations as short cuts to usable ideas: Gérando, Schlegel, Staël, Cousin, Hammer's translations of Persian poetry into German, and Taylor's translations of the Neo-Platonists. Newton's *Principia* and Lyell's *Geology* opened his mind to both the old and the new science. He could read both French and German slowly, but he would "as soon think of foregoing the railroad and the telegraph" as of avoiding translations when they could save time.

In all of this reading two trends are clearly marked. He hoped to learn from the skeptics, the rationalists, and the scientists a common-sense basis for moral truth; and he hoped to meet in the mystics and romantics a validation immediate, instinctive, and final. The one brought him closer to experience, the other to God. He was feeding his moral imagination rather than disciplining his mind. The two-pronged nature of his quest was a reflection of his two-sided temperament and led to a suspended dualism, the necessary creative tension for literary expression. Always Emerson strove to make one of two; but in his own early thinking he did not clearly distinguish between the logical and the intuitive roads to truth. This distinction he owed largely to Coleridge, but it was not to become clear to him until his spirit had been melted and reforged.

The romantic crisis in his life came with his retirement from the ministry in 1832. The independence of spirit to which he had responded in the books he had read was now focused on an issue which had its roots in his own temperament, his traditions, his times. "Whoso would be a man," he wrote later, "must be a non-conformist. . . . Nothing is at last sacred but the integrity of your own mind." The choice lay before him, raw and urgent. He must renounce his own world in order to find himself.

The earnest young clergyman had chosen his profession deliberately. In one of the most remarkable passages of self-examination in all literature, he stated his prospects to his journal on April 18, 1824:

I am beginning my professional studies. In a month I shall be legally a man. And I deliberately dedicate my time, my talents, and my hopes to the Church. Man is an animal that looks before and after . . . and this page must be witness to the latest year of my life whether I have good grounds to warrant my determination.

In the following inventory a strong imagination is balanced against a proportionally weak reasoning faculty, but theology requires, in its highest form, the moral imagination rather than the "reasoning machine" of a Locke, Clarke, or Hume. Lack of self-confidence in society is a serious handicap in the ministry and entirely precludes the law; he finds in himself no taste for medicine; but "in Divinity I hope to thrive." An inherited "love for the strains of eloquence" makes "entire successs" in public preaching a reasonable expectation, even though relative failure in the functions of private influence may dull the triumph. As a teacher—he had assisted in the girls' school which his brother conducted—he had experienced little satisfaction. But his trust is that, by discipline of his weaknesses, his profession may be the "regeneration of mind, manners, inward and outward estate."

Three points emerge from this inventory, which are central to an understanding of the later Emerson: his faith in the moral imagination rather than the intellect, his lack of self-confidence, and his choice of eloquence as his natural medium of expression. At this time, he seems to have had none of the doubts about his ability to conform to the requirements of an organized church that later were to invalidate his choice.

His rebellion, when it finally came, was twofold: against the last vestiges of ecclesiastical authority over the spiritual life of the individual, and against the eighteenth century rationalism which had killed spirituality, he thought, when it denied revelation. The first pointed to a final schism in which each man becomes his own church; the second sought to provide the rules for a new and personal orthodoxy. In the end, self-reliance was sanctioned by submission to the "Beautiful Necessity." As, long before, Jonathan Edwards had paradoxically sought to bring the straying Arminians back to orthodoxy by a personal appeal to the heart as well as to logic, so Emerson attacked the intellectual liberals of his day.

For the faith of the fathers had by the early 1800's once again cooled in the growing Unitarianism of William Emerson and William Ellery Channing of Boston. The new sect had not yet declared itself, but a small company of New England clergymen, liberal in their theology, were "discarding Calvinism by silently ignoring it" and appealing to the intellect, to sentiment, and to literary taste rather than to dogma or revelation. The next step toward heterodoxy, which Emerson heard preached in the "sublime sermons" of Channing, was the doctrine of truth discoverable by the mind rather than the heart. But the spirit of Calvin stirred once more when the boy wrote to his aunt and mentor, "It would assuredly make us feel safer to have our victorious answer set down in impregnable propositions." A new orthodoxy was implied by direct appeal to the God within. His own version of the new revelation was framed in *Nature,* and elaborated in his lectures and poems. It was an indigenous growth in nineteenth century soil, but the seed was found on a high shelf of the family cupboard.

The inner drama of this struggle is written between the lines of more than 160 sermons preached between 1826 and 1832, a selection of which has been published as *Young Emerson Speaks.* In these sermons, we find most of his later and characteristic doctrines expressed in a voice straining for conviction and leaning upon logic and authority where uncertainties still cling. In his first sermon, "Pray Without Ceasing" (1826), man is declared "the architect of his own fortunes"; conscience, the predecessor of the "moral sentiment" of the later essays, is "God's vicegerent"; "the preexistent harmony between thought and things" anticipates the later convictions of correspondence between moral and natural law; and nature "helps the purposes of man."

These central ideas together with others equally characteristic are developed more fully in the sermons which follow, while other ideas, expressed perhaps with less confidence, were later modified or rejected. The painful effort to account for "Miracles" (1831) as a special "means by which God can make a communication to men" was scratched out and rewritten only to have its main argument denied in the confident "Divinity School Address" of seven years later. His wife's death made faith in personal immortality an urgently needed "Consolation for the Mourner" (1831), a doctrine which his later pantheism modified to the point of rejection. And his effort to find his vocation within the frame of the Church made him not only acknowledge the importance of the public functions of prayer and preaching, but the validity of the formal sacraments of marriage, baptism, and the Lord's Supper.

The young preacher struggled with these doubts and contradictions as long as he could; but he sensed his main difficulty from the start. With conformity in spite of conscience, he was determined to have nothing to do. In his first personal talk to his congregation he announced that he would not "be so much afraid of innovation as to scruple about introducing new forms of address, new modes of illustration, and varied allusions from the pulpit." The desire of his hearers for sanctity in style and solemnity in illustration would not deter him from the study of secular as well as scriptural wisdom and its use in his ministry. His revolt from formal sacraments might then have been predicted. Not the administering of the Lord's Supper alone, but the whole structure of formal worship was challenged.

It is perhaps ironic that the man who was to free Unitarianism from the last vestiges of dogma and from reliance upon the authority of logical argument should himself have contrasted so sharply in his discourse with the eloquence of his predecessors, W. E. Channing and Henry Ware. These sermons are cold, and the earlier of them follow careful outlines. They remain on the level of the mind and contain no evangelical buoyancy. Gradually, as personal conviction grew, a new form and a new style asserted themselves. As his personal and theological difficulties became more pressing, his heart seemed to awaken. The need for self-justification in the lonely path which was inevitably opening before him brought an emotional power to his discourse which no evangelical technique could supply. His farewell sermon on the Lord's Supper (1832) was his last effort to rest a case upon the principles of logical analysis. His real farewell came a month later in his final sermon to his congregation on "The Genuine Man," who "parts with his individuality, leaves all thought of private stake, personal feeling, and in compensation he has in some sort the strength of the whole. . . . His heart beats pulse for pulse with the heart of the Universe." With this new strength, a new eloquence was born. Hereafter Emerson would start on the plane of the commonplace and raise his hearers with himself to that of the ideal. In "The Miracle of Our Being" (1834) the form of all his later work is declared. From "the fitness of man to the earth" this sermon rises by swift ascent to "an infinite and perfect life." The seeker has become the leader and guide, with conviction in his message and confidence in his medium.

Many volumes have been written to prove that Emerson's final position was based on Neo-Platonism, German idealism, or Oriental mysticism; but a study of these sermons and of his early reading indicates that he never departed from his loyalty to the faith of his fathers, the Christian tradition as developed by Christ, Paul, Thomas Aquinas, and Calvin. Essentially romantic by disposition, he took his place with the rebels and seekers and, like Coleridge and Goethe, sought both confirmation and refreshment from all ages and quarters.

It was this growing romanticism which made the bondage of formal religion insufferable. For his final searching of the soul, he retired to Ethan Crawford's in the New Hampshire mountains, where "life is reconsidered."

There the hours passed on, bearing him to the crisis of his fate. "How hard to command the soul, or to solicit the soul." Struggling with "indignation at this windmill," recognizing that "without accommodation society is impractical," he confronted at last his inevitable choice of path: "I cannot go habitually to an institution which they esteem holiest with indifference and dislike." The issue was not one of doctrine or of form; it was a private matter of his conscience. He would not abolish the institution of the Lord's Supper if it had meaning for others; but he could no longer administer it. When he returned to Boston and once more faced his congregation, he had left all conformity behind, for he had at last grappled with himself and conquered. Fears of his own inadequacy could not block his path, for personal success no longer mattered. The self-reliance which he had preached to others was now to be his.

3

This, as Carlyle was writing at the time, is the "Everlasting Yea," the crisis and resolution of romantic doubts. But before full achievement, it must be preceded by a "Center of Indifference." Divorce from circumstance must be complete, that the inner man may expand to full self-recognition.

The way was not clearly charted when he was on the brig *Jasper* bound for Malta in January, 1833. In spite of his lifelong aversion to travel as a means of escape or refreshment, he spent most of that year in Europe. At thirty, his life lay behind him, apparently a succession of failures with no positive accomplishment to show for his efforts and a state of health and mind which promised little for the future. His mood sank to self-disgust and despair: "What under the sun canst thou do, pale face? . . . I did not put me here; yet God forbid I should therefore decline the responsibility into which I am born." With himself he was relentless: "It is doubtless a vice to turn one's eyes inward too much, but I am my own comedy and tragedy." When he warned later that the traveler "carries ruins to ruins," he was doubtless thinking of his own experience; and on his return, he sighed, "I am very glad my travelling is done. A man not old feels himself too old to be a vagabond."

Such moods were occasional only. He gave various reasons for the trip, among them illness and the desire to see great men: "to learn what man can,—what is the uttermost that social man has done." But his obvious purpose was to be alone, to confront himself, and if possible to find a new vocation unfettered by the formalities and expectations of others or by his own shortcomings. "I am thankful that I am an American as I am thankful that I am a man." His quest ended with a pledge, "if health and opportunity be granted me, to demonstrate that all necessary truth is its own evidence; that no doctrine of God need appeal to a book; that Christianity is wrongly received by all such as take it as a system of doctrines,—its stress being upon moral truth; it is a rule of life, not a rule of faith."

But his discoveries were not all moral or religious. Much to his own surprise, he was startled and ensnared by Old World culture. His senses and emotions were stirred by the incense and the music of St. Peter's, by the calm beauty of Raphael's Transfiguration, by the Sistine frescoes and the Moses of Michelangelo. He warmed to the monuments of Catholicism, but found no charm in Geneva, the home of his inherited faith, other than the surrounding mountains. In Paris, he was astounded by the collection of birds, beasts, and other specimens in the Jardin des Plantes. "I am moved by strange sympathies; I say continually 'I will be a naturalist.'" His confessed lack of human sympathy and ease of approach to strangers was belied by his friendliness with fellow Americans, the sculptor Greenough, the traveler Dewey, and innumerable others whom he joined for part of his way. But with Landor at Fiesole, Coleridge at Highgate, and Wordsworth at Rydal, his hope to discover greatness in the great was disappointed. Carlyle alone fulfilled his expectations. Emerson had come upon "the latest and strongest contributor to the critical journals" in 1827–1829 when Carlyle's articles in the *Edinburgh Review, Fraser's,* and *Blackwood's* were scorching their pages. He sought him out in his lonely farm at Craigenputtock, listened to his wry and revealing comments on the ingenuity of a pig and the immortality of the soul, and entered into a correspondence which continued through life and ultimately filled two volumes. These two met and talked through the night because they were exploring the same caverns, not because they had come out into the same sunlight. When it appeared finally that Carlyle preferred to remain a struggler in the darkness, the sympathy waned, and Emerson emerged alone into the affirmation of his middle years.

That affirmation was most intense during the ten years between his return and the *Essays, Second Series* in 1844. In that short time he delivered from carefully prepared manuscripts over seventy-five lectures, most of them in series of ten or twelve at the Masonic Temple in Boston; a dozen occasional addresses, and many sermons. His letters to Carlyle whom he met only at wide intervals of years, to Sterling whom he never saw, and to nearer friends like Margaret Fuller, Caroline Sturgis, Samuel Gray Ward, and Henry Thoreau, were platonic essays in friendship. The pages of his journal were filled regularly and fully, and poems were wrought with care at frequent intervals. Yet only *Nature* and the *Essays* from this mountain of manuscripts were prepared for the press at the time. This was to be his capital upon which he could draw with interest for the rest of his life. A few poems and essays found print in the *Dial*, the *Western Messenger*, the *Massachusetts Quarterly*, and later the *Atlantic*, and there only to help his friends and the cause of enlightenment which they shared with him, not because he wished to publish. He had found his new profession. His was to be the living message, the spoken voice. The town hall was his new church, the Society for the Diffusion of Useful Knowledge his sect.

With this rededication he discovered a new way of life. Within three years after his return from Europe all his major decisions had been made, his life put in order. In the winter of 1833–1834 he began his lectures; that summer he made Concord his home; the next year he married Lydia Jackson of Plymouth, bought the Old Coolidge house on the Cambridge Turnpike—regrettably in a meadow rather than on a hill—and delivered to his townsfolk an "Historical Discourse" on the occasion of their second centennial. In 1836 he published *Nature* and his son Waldo was born. He had home, wife, family, career, friends, and associates. "The lonely wayfaring man," as Carlyle was later to call him, was once more a citizen of this world.

But the spirit of revolt did not die in him so abruptly as these facts might suggest. He had dispersed the morbid clouds of introspection and uncertainty. He had chosen his point of issue with his age. He knew what he must accept as well as what he must reject. He was ready to speak and to act. There are two phases of romanticism, that of doubt and seeking, that of revolt in equilibrium. Emerson had reached the second phase by 1834, and his productive tension showed no sign of breaking for at least ten years.

The immediate release of that tension was *Nature*; the key to its understanding is what he called "the First Philosophy." "I endeavor to announce the laws of the First Philosophy," he wrote in June, 1835. "It is the mark of these that their enunciation awakens the feeling of the moral sublime, and great men are they who believe in them. Every one of these propositions resembles a great circle in astronomy. No matter in what direction it be drawn, it contains the whole sphere. So each of these seems to imply all truth."

The source of this cornerstone of his reconstructed philosophy may have been, as he himself implied in *English Traits*, his discovery that "Bacon, capable of ideas, yet devoted to ends, required in his map of the mind, first of all, universality, or *prima philosophia*." But it is likely that his inheritance of Christian mysticism then drew him to sympathy with the Quakers, the Swedenborgians, and the Methodists, tempered and extended by his early absorption of Neo-Platonism and Oriental insight.

In announcing these laws, Emerson, who rejected all established doctrine, formulated a new doctrine composed of assumptions which experience had taught him were vital. With logic he could have nothing to do, declaring that "a foolish consistency is the hobgoblin of little minds." As has been pointed out, his propositions constituted for him, as it were, the persons in a drama of the mind, not the steps in an argument or system; they have also been likened to equations. They are based on the definitions of a few key words used by Cousin, Coleridge, Sampson Reed the Swedenborgian, and Thomas Taylor the Neo-Platonist, which these writers derived in turn from German metaphysics, Scottish rationalism, and the literature of romanticism in general. The similarity of Emerson's thought to that of Kant, Hegel, Schleiermacher, and Schelling is deceptive; such influences usually came to him at one or more removes. His attitude toward his assumptions had the quality if not the rigidity of the dogmatism he had rejected. He had discovered a way of setting down his victorious answers in impregnable propositions, in laws which describe relationships rather than essences. They are the stuff of ethics and faith rather than of metaphysics, theology, or logic.

Nature (1836) is the gospel of the new faith rather than, like Thoreau's *Walden*, a record of an experience of earth. Lifted by the excitement of recognition to the plane of prose-poetry, it is nevertheless a concise statement of the "First Philosophy." The primary assumption of this essay is that man, whether regarded individually or generically, is the starting point of all philosophic speculation. His functions, his relations, and his destiny are its only concerns. The self-reliance which results from this assumption is essential to vital experience. Whatever truth lies beyond or outside man can be reached only through him and by him.

Emerson opens his essay with the current distinction between the Me and the Not Me, the Soul and Nature, thereby establishing the first of his provisional dualities. The Me is consciousness, or that part of man which partakes of divinity, the Not Me is the objective of consciousness, that with which the Me is in relation. But Nature, or the Not Me, also partakes of divinity in that "outward circumstance is a dream and a shade"; its reality lies in its being "a projection of God in the unconscious." A second duality is thus established between Nature and God; and a third, between God and Man. Here is a triangle of relationships, the value of which lies not in the absolute identity of Man, God, or Nature, but in the common relationship between any two of the factors. Man may learn to worship God through the contemplation of Nature. The stars, the flowers, the animals, the mountains reflect the wisdom of his best hour, first as that which is outside of his consciousness, then as that which shares with his consciousness a "vision of original and eternal beauty," an awareness of a divine principle.

The ability to view experience in this twofold manner is the essential quality of the First Philosophy. Emerson's position, in so far as it approaches the statement of final verities, is monistic; his method invariably dualistic. He declares in the opening paragraphs of his essay that he will use the word "Nature" in two senses: the common sense in which it refers to essences unchanged by man, and the ideal sense in which it is the phenomenal expression of the soul. The possible ambiguity "is not material; no confusion of thought will occur." It is necessary to set up a provisional dualism in order to explore the ultimate unity. This method, established in the opening paragraphs of his first published book, is implicit or stated again in every word that Emerson ever wrote. As he is wholly concerned with the process of thinking rather than with the objects of thought, his position is often declared to be dualistic; it is so only in its method, but its method is very nearly all there is to it.

From Sampson Reed, and later from Swedenborg himself, Emerson borrowed the doctrine of correspondence between the natural and moral laws to validate this primary assumption. "The spiritual part of man is as really a substance as the material; and is as capable of acting upon spirit, as matter is upon matter." In each sphere there is a law the study of which may be reduced to a science; but the law in the one sphere exactly corresponds at every point with that in the other. Thus natural and moral laws are distinguishable from each other but are actually correspondent at every point. "Matter," concludes Emerson, "is a phenomenon, not a substance." "There is a law for man and a [parallel] law for things." This assumption that the one law may be treated in practice as two allowed him complete and open-minded acceptance of the progress of physical science without fear that its findings would invalidate religion. With one stroke he swept away the major controversy of the age by linking it to the persistent Christian synthesis of faith and works.

Emerson came to describe the faculty whereby man might explore the realm of the spirit as "the moral sentiment," and most of his value judgments on men and experience depend ultimately upon the presence or absence of this faculty. It is the capacity of human nature to discover the moral law by means of intuition. In *Nature* and his early essays he more commonly calls it the "Reason" as distinguished from the "Understanding," another instance of his habit of dividing in order to conquer—this time probably borrowing from Coleridge, who had stated in his *Aids to Reflection*: "Reason is the Power of Universal and necessary Convictions, the Source and Substance of Truths above Sense, and having their evidence in themselves. . . . The Judgments of the Understanding are binding only in relation to the objects of our Senses, which we *reflect* under the forms of the Understanding." "Heaven," echoes Emerson from the *Aids to Reflection*, "is the name we give to the True State, the world of Reason, not of the Understanding; of the

Real, not the Apparent." He uses these two terms specifically in this sense throughout his writing as he similarly makes distinctions on two planes between Imagination and Fancy, Talent and Genius, in common with English romantic philosophers. He thus again clearly distinguishes between the lower and the higher faculties of the mind: Understanding, Fancy, and Talent are means of dealing with immediate experience, but each has a nobler counterpart in Reason, Imagination, and Genius by which man may climb from the plane of the natural to that of moral law.

From these two assumptions, the centrality of man in his own universe of experience and the exact correspondence between the planes of material and spiritual law, Emerson developed the other principles which constituted his working philosophy. From them he derived his law of compensation or balance of conflicting forces in experience, his theory of good and evil, and his beliefs in the inevitable vocation of each man, in the idea of progress, in unimpassioned love among men, and in the Over-Soul. From the same source he developed his characteristic method for lecture and essay, starting in most cases on the level of common or material experience and rising to that of spiritual realization. From them too he derived his theory of art and poetry as an intricate system of symbols or "language" expressing through human agency an organic moral harmony.

Here was a new covenant of the spirit, built upon the foundation of Puritanism, tested by the rigors of American experience, and shaped by the architecture of romantic theory and the democratic ideal. All materials available were carefully studied and built into the structure if they could prove of use; from the past, the wisdom of Plato and his followers, the inductive method of Bacon and Montaigne, and the mysticism of Oriental religion and poetry; from the future, the naturalism of science and the rampant materialism of a growing industrial nation. The result was a tentative organization of opposing forces into a dynamic harmony rather than a static unity, a philosophy of growth and change rather than one of certainty and system. In a single essay Emerson made himself the apologist of a people because he had discovered a formula in which temperamental contradictions were reconciled if not logically resolved. The theological mystic Jonathan Edwards could speak through him across the centuries to the political idealist Woodrow Wilson; Benjamin Franklin could send through him to William James the message that pragmatism was merely "a new name for some old ways of thinking"; and the American habit of testing truth simultaneously by intuition and by action could seem to be merely a rounding out of experience, not a division of personality.

Even though *Nature* was Emerson's first formulation of his position, it was only a beginning. In spite of its organization into topics proceeding on an ascending scale from Commodity through Beauty, Language, and Discipline, to Idealism and Spirit, it asks rather than answers questions, it is a cry of astonishment at the possibilities of life rather than a record of achievement. There was much work to be done, and its author immediately set about the doing.

When Emerson stood before the Phi Beta Kappa Society at Harvard on August 31, 1837, to define the American Scholar, he was delivering an annual address on the conventional topic. Men far more prominent than he had spoken on the same subject from the same platform many times before. Current journals had for a quarter of a century been sprinkled with pleas for a national literature. There was nothing in the announced subject, the mood of the audience, or the appearance of the speaker to suggest an unusual occasion. Yet when the address was concluded Lowell declared it "an event without any former parallel in our literary annals," and Holmes pronounced it "our Intellectual Declaration of Independence." His hearers realized, as we today cannot, the depth and force of his revolt against his times.

In a series of occasional addresses between 1837 and 1844 he announced to his old associates—writers, scholars, clergymen, and men of thought in general—the revolution that had taken place in his conception of his own function and of theirs. The occasions were seized as offered, the Commencement of his old divinity school, convocations of the Dartmouth and Waterville college literary societies, meetings of library associations, or merely sponsored evening lectures at a public hall. In all of these he is eager, excited, defiant, but firm, clear, and relentless. He knew that he was issuing a challenge: "Amidst a planet peopled with conservatives, one Reformer may yet be born."

He anticipated, especially from the clergy, the violence of the inevitable response. He was speaking with deliberate intention to shock, but in carefully considered language. Each of his thrusts was strong and sure, aimed at the heart. To the scholar he said: "Translate, collate, distil all the systems, it steads you nothing; for truth will not be compelled in any mechanical manner." And again, "Man Thinking must not be subdued by his instruments. Books are for the scholar's idle times. When he can read God directly, the hour is too precious to be wasted in other men's transcripts of their readings." To the writer: "All literature is yet to be written. Poetry has scarce chanted its first song." To the student of divinity: "All men go in flocks to this saint or that poet, avoiding the God who seeth in secret. . . . Let me admonish you, first of all to go alone; to refuse the good models, even those which are sacred in the imagination of men, and dare to love God without mediator or veil," even Christ himself. And in discussing "The Times": "Our forefathers walked in the world and went to their graves tormented with the fear of Sin and the terror of the Day of Judgment. These terrors have lost their force, and our torment is Unbelief, the Uncertainty as to what we ought to do; the distrust of the value of what we do, and the distrust that the Necessity (which we all at last believe in) is fair and beneficent." The intention of all these overstatements was the same. They were designed to shock complacency into recognition that each dawn opens a new day. They did not deny the past; tradition must serve the present as one kind of experience rather than as authority. Emerson was challenging his audiences; not announcing measured and final truth.

For the present and the future he had high hope, granted that self-reliance could be restored and assured. "I speak of the politics, education, business, and religion around us without ceremony or false deference." The new literature must be neither Classic nor Romantic: "I embrace the common, I explore and sit at the feet of the familiar, the low. Give me insight into to-day, and you may have the antique and future worlds." This, he announced, is a Reflective or Philosophic age; its concern is with itself. He did not shrink from the abounding energy and the inexhaustible resources of his time and place. "Railroad iron is a magician's rod, in its power to evoke the sleeping energies of land and water." "It seems so easy for America to inspire and express the most expansive and humane spirit; new-born, free, healthful, strong, the land of the laborer, of the democrat, of the philanthropist, of the believer, of the saint, she should speak for the human race."

Emerson was not blind to the dangers in all this rampant energy. He accepted an economy of abundance based, like that of Adam Smith, on a moral law which allows self-interest full play. He believed in a natural aristocracy, in property, in immigration, in trade, and competitive industry. A laissez-faire Yankee materialist on the level of the senses, he relied on the moral sentiment to transcend and resolve all conflicts. "The materialist takes his departure from the external world, . . . the idealist . . . from his consciousness." The transcendentalist accepts both views; because his dualism is a provisional state only, he can "take his departure" from the level of the senses in full confidence that, at the same time, he is also operating from the level of the spirit. "He believes in miracle, in the perpetual openness of the human mind to new influx of light and power; he believes in inspiration, and in ecstasy."

Ecstasy is not always apparent in Emerson's own life during these ten years, nor in the many lectures which he delivered. A substantial number of them still exist, however, in manuscript, and most of them are listed or abstracted in the appendix to J. E. Cabot's *Memoir*. Their uniform emphasis upon the moral law is evident from the titles of the series: "Biography," "English Literature," "The Philosophy of History," "Human Culture," "Human Life," the "Present Age," "The Times," "New England." With the journals, these lectures bear the relationship to the *Essays* that an artist's sketch does to his finished painting. They were written out with care, but their style has the rhythm of speech, the loose phrase, the colloquial and often humorous turn.

The energy and eagerness, the security and peace which Emerson conveyed to his audiences had roots at home. His marriage and family life were steady, rich, and rewarding. Lidian, as he asked permission to call her because the *n* smoothed transition to the new name, had the qualities of a Madonna rather than of a St. Cecilia. In 1836, Waldo was born,

> Boy who made dear his father's home,
> In whose deep eyes
> Men read the welfare of the times to come—

bringing completion during his five years of life and a sorrow when he died more calm than at the deaths of Ellen Tucker and Charles. Emerson gave to his two daughters the names Edith and Ellen; to his second son, Edward. "In the dwelling-house," wrote the father, "must the true character and hope of the time be consulted," for there a man may "stand on his feet."

The town of Concord was a larger home and the circle of friends that gathered in the Emerson drawing room was but an extended family. Near-by towns had succumbed to industry, but the Musketaquid was still navigable only to canoes, and:

> Bulkeley, Hunt, Willard, Hosmer, Meriam, Flint,
> Possessed the land which rendered to their toil
> Hay, corn, roots, hemp, flax, apples, wool and wood.

The Thoreaus, Hoars, and Ripleys were native citizens, but Alcott, Ellery Channing, and Hawthorne were later comers; Margaret Fuller, Elizabeth Peabody, the mystic Jones Very, and many others of the transcendental set were never more than visitors. The Social Circle which met frequently at the Emerson home on Tuesday evenings consisted of "twenty-five of our citizens: doctor, lawyer, farmer, trader, miller, mechanic; solidest men, who yield the solidest gossip."

A very different group had formed the habit of gathering at one another's houses for an afternoon of serious conversation, whether in Boston or Concord, and so the "Transcendental Club" came into being without deliberate intention or constitution. It was, as one facetious member remarked, "like going to heaven in a swing," and Emerson himself at times mocked their earnest aspirations. "Perhaps they only agreed in having fallen upon Coleridge and Wordsworth and Goethe, then on Carlyle, with pleasure and sympathy. Otherwise, their education and reading were not marked, but had the American superficiality, and their studies were solitary," like his own. Bronson Alcott, the Orphic philosopher, existed in an ethereal sphere which he shared with Plato; Thoreau came fresh from the woods and fields; Emerson from his study; Parker, "our Savonarola," and Brownson from their churches, the one a Unitarian, the other inclining toward Rome. Margaret Fuller and occasionally Hawthorne's sister-in-law Elizabeth Peabody shot bolts of aggressive femininity into the company with their radical notion that women are people, seeking friendship on a plane transcending sex.

One such friendship, violent on Margaret's part, acquiescent but at times disturbing on Emerson's, produced "the modest quarterly journal called *The Dial*," organ of the movement for four years. George Ripley, inspired by Owen and Fourier, attempted the most famous of all communistic experiments at Brook Farm, even though the stars of the movement took only a casual part, preferring to shine each in his own sphere. A third practical—if we may stretch the word—result was the Concord School of Philosophy, founded in 1879 by Alcott in his own back yard, a highly successful pioneer of the American summer session. For at least a quarter of a century, the idyllic town was the intellectual seed pod of the nation.

In so stimulating an atmosphere, largely of his own making, Emerson expanded and matured, producing the *Essays, First and Second Series* in 1841 and 1844. These in a very real sense were new works, dependent no more on the lectures he had delivered than on the pages of the *Journals*, for he drew from both sources, running a pencil line across the chosen passage, lifting it from the page, and remolding it to its new purpose. Lectures in form and spirit still, they are written for a larger audience than any that ever could be assembled in one place. Though they retain their quality of voice, they are not meant to be spoken. In every line and every paragraph they bear the evidence of loving workmanship.

The new form which Emerson developed is neither wholly essay nor wholly lecture. Its unit is the carefully wrought sentence, "pure, genuine Saxon"; as Carlyle immediately recognized, "strong and simple; of a clearness, of a beauty." Each contains in crystalline suspension the whole meaning of the essay, of the book, an art learned perhaps in part from the gnomic sentence of Bacon or the *pensées* of Pascal, as simple and direct as the familiar style of Montaigne. "Nature will not have us fret and fume." "All things are double, one against another." "Life only avails, not the having lived." Sometimes they are but a single image: "Life is a train of moods like a string of beads, and as we pass through them they prove to be many-colored lenses which paint the world their own hue, and each shows only what lies in its focus." Longer sentences are broken and rugged, retaining their staccato quality: "The death of a dear friend, wife, brother, lover, which seems nothing but privation, somewhat later assumes the aspect of a guide or genius; for it commonly operates revolutions in our way of life, terminates an epoch of infancy or of youth which was waiting to be closed, breaks up a wonted occupation, or a household, or style of living, and allows the formation of new ones more friendly to the growth of character."

Carlyle sought coherence in the paragraph and found rather "a beautiful square *bag of duck-shot* held together by canvas." Even less closely are the paragraphs knit to their foregoers and followers, the essays to one another to make a book. But it would be a mistake to conclude that form is lacking. Each paragraph, each essay, has the structure of the circle containing smaller circles within it and itself contained in larger circles. "The eye is the first circle," wrote Emerson in the shortest of his essays; "the horizon which it forms is the second; and throughout nature this primary figure is repeated without end." His method is organic, a reflection of the structure of the universe as he sees it.

But if the movement of logical sequence is lacking, that of direct communication to faculties beyond the reason is not. The units of his style are built upon one another into a rising structure of thought and feeling. Always there is the sense of a man speaking to his audience, catching their attention, focusing it on a central meaning, expanding it to furthest limits of experience, raising it to highest levels of recognition, bringing it back to the center. Each essay opens with a challenge, either by quiet reference to ordinary experience or by sudden shock of overstatement. With text thus supplied, homiletic rather than logical principles elaborate, illustrate, and slowly unfold the theme as writer and reader are borne onward together. In most of the essays, there is a sense of rising intensity in both meaning and form, which suggests Emerson's own images of the spiral, the ladder, the swift flight upward. The conclusion brings a quiet sense of completion, of exhausted possibilities, of whole vision which has the dramatic finality of the curtain of a play.

A similar sense of structure is not discernible in the arrangement of the essays in the two companion volumes, although the first series has more coherence than the second. The wholeness of Emerson's thought is such that, touched at any point, it immediately embraces experience. The differences between the essays lie in their varying points of emphasis; each includes all. Their unity lies in the "First Philosophy" expressed, not in its expression.

The points of departure are roughly of three kinds: description of the universe and its laws (Self-Reliance, Compensation, Spiritual Laws, the Over-Soul, Circles, Experience, Nature, and Nominalist and Realist); analysis of the moral faculties in human relationships in general (Love, Friendship.

Prudence, Heroism, Character, and Manners); and studies of more nearly particular problems of experience (History, Art, The Poet, Politics, and New England Reformers). But even such broad categories soon break down as the elaboration of the primary point of any one essay includes those of all others.

The resulting unity of approach to living is the key to Emerson's hold on his own and later generations. Henry Adams called it "naïf," and others have put it away with childish things. His disregard rather than denial of evil, his lack of logical system, his staccato crispness of style, his didacticism, his appearance of being above torment and suffering, have provided blockages for many. But his morning quality of recognition and confidence, his power of distilling essences that all know to be true, his gift of innumerable texts for the problems of living and thinking, his accurate reflection of the American mind and heart in its moments of aspiration, have made these essays a book in our modern bible. "It is not yet art," wrote the sophisticated Comtesse d'Agoult when she discovered them for her people, but "the mingling heretofore unknown, of the protestant spirit of individualism, or self-reliance, with the pantheistic spirit which inspires this book, the combination and harmonizing of these two antagonisms in a superior intellect forms, incontestably, a new element from whence may be born an original art." For a moment the tensions and contradictions of American experience were held in vital suspension and, in Emerson, found their first clear and authoritative voice.

4

The "new art" of Emerson is contained in five volumes—all, except some of the poems, written within the decade 1844-1854, none published immediately. They are *Poems* (1847), *Representative Men* (1850), *English Traits* (1856), *The Conduct of Life* (1860), and *May-Day* (1867). That in this period he passed from a state of romantic tension to one of "classic" or organic restraint more suitable to the New England disposition is attested by his own statement in a lecture on "Art and Criticism" delivered in 1859:

"The art of writing is the highest of those permitted to man as drawing directly from the Soul, and the means or material it uses are also of the Soul. . . . Classic art is the art of necessity; organic; modern or romantic bears the stamp of caprice or chance." Even though he retained the doctrinal foundations of his thought in historical romanticism, Emerson developed his arts of poem and lecture-essay in this, his own, definition of the classic, by admitting the need for moral restraint in art.

His poetry was written in his own study, the product of walks in the Concord fields or to his "garden," the wood lot on Walden Pond which he allowed Thoreau to use for his cabin. The prose was a reworking of lectures delivered in England (1847–1848) and in the "West" from Pittsburgh to Cincinnati, to St. Louis and Chicago (1850–1853). During these years he was away almost as much as he was at home, and Lidian made out as best she could, caring for the children and the big white house, aided by the townsfolk and by Henry Thoreau, the master's delegate in residence to tend the fires and the garden.

Had he never written a word of prose, Emerson's achievement as an experimental and epigrammatic poet would give him a primary place in our literature. In his youth he was the admitted poet of the family, but even he refrained from taking his nonsense and imitative verses too seriously. When the time came to woo Lydia Jackson, not only to himself but to Concord, he had attained to better perspective. "I am a born poet," he wrote, "of a low class without doubt yet a poet . . . in the sense of a perceiver and dear lover of the harmonies that are in the soul and in matter, and specially of the correspondence between these and those"; but he was "uncertain always whether I have one true spark of that fire which burns in verse."

A born poet he most assuredly was, in theory as well as fact. Before the publication of his *Poems* in 1847, the United States had had but one true student and experimenter in the art, Edgar Allan Poe. Bryant, Halleck, and Freneau either had shown no deep interest in the theory and technique of poetry or had conformed to the romantic modes of Wordsworth and Byron, and to the traditions of the English lyric. The early verse of Whittier, Simms, Longfellow, Lowell, and Holmes had accepted similar models without fresh exploration of anything but the American scene. Poe alone had sought to rediscover the nature and function of poetry in itself. Emerson's originality is as profound as that of Poe, and the theories of the two supplement each other. Poe sought an aesthetic base for the art; Emerson, a moral. Poe explored mainly the possibilities of rhythm; Emerson, of symbol. Together they directed the course of American poetry since their time by turning from borrowed conventions and by seeking once more the springs of poetry. Walt Whitman and Emily Dickinson were further to exploit these breaks with the past; others would follow.

Part of Emerson's sense of inadequacy was caused by his high ideals for the poet. He is the seer, but he is more. He is also "the sayer, the namer, and represents beauty. He is sovereign and stands on the center. . . . He is a beholder of ideas and an utterer of the necessary and causal." His office is that "of announcement and affirming." He does not make his poem, "for poetry was all written before time was. . . . The men of more delicate ear write down these cadences." By characteristic overstatement, Emerson would thus make the role of the poet seem almost passive. He is an Aeolian harp that "trembles to the cosmic breath" (a favorite image). But he is also Merlin, the traditional bard, the wise man, the magician, whose "blows are strokes of fate." In the distribution of functions among men, he is the man speaking, the scholar who has an assigned course of action—to express the message he receives. By this test Plato at times seems almost to qualify as poet, and Sir Thomas Browne, Zoroaster, Michelangelo, and the authors of the Vedas, the Eddas, the Koran. George Herbert stands the test and Milton, next to Shakespeare the prince of poets because his genius is "to ascend by the aids of his learning and his religion—by an equal perception, that is, of the past and the future—to a higher insight and more lively delineation of the heroic life of man." And the Persian Saadi becomes for Emerson the prototype of the poet because

> He felt the flame, the fanning wings,
> Nor offered words till they were things.

Herein lies the insight which caused his spontaneous acceptance of *Leaves of Grass* in 1855. Whitman's words were things.

If the recording of celestial music had been to Emerson the only function of the poet, his verse might have been more melodic than it is. Rather in his prose, especially when it was prepared to be spoken, he came closest to achieving rhythmic freedom, as did Melville, whose philosopher in *Mardi* chants only when he is seized with the frenzy of prophetic vision. Before it was pruned and sharpened by gnomic insight, Emerson's style might flow with the current of his eloquence and climb by the measured but open periods of the Song of Solomon, the Sermon on the Mount, or Whitman's sweeping rhythms. In an unpublished passage from the introductory lecture to the early course on "Human Culture," he used the techniques which Whitman was later to exploit. Freed from the paragraph of prose as well as the meter of verse, his periodic lines are held to a frame by parallel phrasing, assonance, alliteration, and return:

The philosopher laments the inaction of the higher faculties.
He laments to see men poor who are able to labor.
He laments to see men blind to a beauty that is beaming on every side of them.
He laments to see men offending against laws and paying the penalty, and calling it a visitation of Providence. . . .
He laments the foreign holdings of every man, his dependence for his faith, for his political and religious estimates and opinions, on other men, and on former times.
And from all these oppressions is a wise Culture to redeem the Soul.

But Emerson asked more than this of the poet. The active function of poetry, as he saw it, was to make manifest and specific the correspondence between the real and the ideal, a task which rhythm alone could not accomplish. From the English metaphysical poets in prose and verse, Herbert, Donne, Milton, Browne, he learned the connotative value of the individual word, the possibilities for luster and surprise in the image. He turned to them rather than to the contemporary romantics who had acquiesced too easily in a passive pantheism. Milton and Herbert rather than Wordsworth and Coleridge felt God intensely and struggled to restore him to this world. These elder poets had striven, as did Emerson, to reconcile an intense religious faith with an equally intense challenge of science, and his method was theirs. In this, he stood alone in his times among British and American poets, for not even Matthew Arnold appreciated the full worth of the symbol, however much he struggled with the "two worlds" between which he stood. The mystic and the scientist must become one, and the symbol is the only means for the accomplishment of the union. This Emerson fully appreciated, and it is his gift to modern poetry. From Bacon he took the Aristotelian view that "poetry, not finding the actual world exactly conformed to its idea of good and fair, seeks to accommodate the show of things to the desires of the mind, and to create an ideal world better than the world of experience." To this he added the Swedenborgian view that nature must serve man for symbols, that by seeing through the phenomenon to the essence, the poet might transform the evidence of his senses to a higher use and reestablish the correspondence between the natural and the moral laws. "The act of imagination is ever attended by pure delight. It infuses a certain volatility and intoxication into all Nature." The poet is "an exact reporter of the essential law," but he is active rather than passive because he restores the harmonies of the Over-Soul through the counterpoint of experience; he supplies from his intuition the true, rather than the apparent, natural image. "The mind, penetrated with its sentiment or its thought, projects it outward on whatever it beholds." The result is a beauty not of the senses but of the moral sentiment.

The critic should not be misled by Emerson's frequent references to poetry as music, for his own verse rarely sings. "That which others hear," he confessed, "I see." Even in his poem on "Music," the images are almost all visual, and "Merlin's Song" is "of keenest eye" before it is of "truest tongue." His dissonant rhymes and limping rhythms are parts of a deliberate effort to achieve freedom of movement, and they receive at least some authority from their models. Butler used "slanted" or imperfect rhymes, Milton incomplete lines, and Shakespeare, in his later plays, a roving accent. Emerson asked for all these freedoms together. He made excessive use of rhyme, because to him it was the favorite instrument of rhythm in Nature (although again his examples are visual: reflections in a pond or the repeating forms of shadows). He also adopted the eight-syllable line because he was convinced by the theory of O. W. Holmes that periodicity in poetry is determined by human respiration. He never broke loose in his poetry as did Whitman, into the more natural freedom of colloquial speech. But within his limits, all of which he believed are imposed by Nature rather than tradition, he trusted the song as he heard it, even though his hearing was not always true. His rhymes are often little more than assonances; his meter, counted syllables that sometimes miss the count, letting the accent fall where it may.

With the visual image, Emerson's muse can safely be trusted. In his "Mottoes"—verses distilled to provide texts for his essays—he committed Wordsworth's fault of trying to deal too directly with thought. But where the image is given full play, as in "The Sphinx" (his own favorite), "Days" (perhaps his most successful), "Hamatreya" (his most direct), "Uriel," "Brahma," "The Snow-Storm" and the first part of "Merlin," it achieves an intricate pattern of conceit worthy of Herbert or Donne, but fresh from his own experience. Here the poet exerted his full prerogatives with volatile nature, using the evidences of the pines, the sea, the stars to its own purposes and revealing the correspondence of the law of things to the law of God. In other poems like "Woodnotes," "Threnody," and his odes, he achieves sureness and freedom in some passages, but falls into rhymed prose in others; and sometimes, as in "The Rhodora," the message is too explicit, the effect didactic.

At his best, Emerson's keen sensitivity to the larger aspects of nature, his mastery and daring with the visual image, his deep appreciation of the connotative value of single words (a gift not shared even by Poe and not approached by any other contemporary except Emily Dickinson who followed his course in both theory and technique), place him among the most original and provocative if not the most even poets in the language. Add to these qualities the intrinsic value of what he has to say, and his poetry becomes one of the treasures of our literature, greater in some respects than his essays because, when he allows himself full scope, he speaks from and for himself a universal language, without reference to a particular audience even by inference. His art is organic in that it reproduces the organism of moral law as reflected in nature; it is classic, as he would have it, only when his daring experiments achieve unity and, as in "Days," his intricate and climbing images merge into a single symbol of revelation.

The same quality is achieved in the prose of his maturity, *Representative Men, English Traits,* and *The Conduct of Life.* Derived from specific lecture courses, each has a distinguishable central theme upon which the parts play variations: the uses of great men; the values in modern civilization; the principles of individual action. The wise Emerson now speaks in his own church, of his own people, and to his own people. He is on sure ground, no longer defiant; the fight has been won, and he knows that he is heard.

His themes are not new. Back in 1835, in his first lecture series, he had spoken on "Biography" and examined the tests of a great man: Has he an aim to which he gives his whole soul? Is it broad and unselfish? Is it based solidly on fact? Does it set in motion the minds of others? Has it divine sanction? Two of these lectures, "Michael Angelo" and "Milton," were published in the *North American Review* and have come down to us virtually intact. The other three, "Luther," "George Fox," and "Burke," together with the introductory lecture, are unpublished or absorbed into other writing. The design for the series was his own, perhaps suggested in part by Plutarch's *Lives,* where a man's actions and distinctions are judged for their moral values; strengthened by Carlyle's *Heroes and Hero Worship,* which he welcomed in 1841—"a good book, and goes to make men brave and happy," because, from these cases, it describes and evaluates a whole system of conduct. But Carlyle's confusion of worldly with moral power was beginning to show through his transcendental intensity. On this point Emerson was clear. He did not test men for their control of others. "He is great who is what he is from nature, and who never reminds us of others." "Men are also representative; first, of things, and secondly of ideas." In contrast to Carlyle's, his criteria were the measures of democracy: self-reliance, the moral sentiment, experience, intuition.

For *Representative Men,* Emerson chose his cases carefully, each to represent a way of thinking and acting: Plato, the philosopher; Swedenborg, the mystic; Montaigne, the skeptic; Shakespeare, the poet; Napoleon, the man of the world; Goethe, the writer. All of these ways he had to some degree tried. They were tests for himself and for his hearers rather than essays in criticism. He was asking: By what measures may a man judge his own ambition? He was answering: By these I have judged my own. Only as they guide you and me in our private and single lives by their examples are great men of use.

The first four, "Plato," "Swedenborg," "Montaigne," and "Shakespeare," were written from the heart. These men had given Emerson personal aid as he emerged from the doubts and uncertainties of youth into the calm confidence of his later years. Each he had finally found lacking, incomplete for his purposes, because there is no such thing as a wholly great man. No man but one has succeeded in resolving the dualities of the law of things into the unity of the moral law, has finally identified faith and works. And Emerson did not choose to write directly of Christ, who had succeeded in fact; or of himself, who had striven in theory. But the book begins and ends, by implication, with these two. For Napoleon and Goethe he has less perfect sympathies. They were added to complete the list, for he must include at least one man who did not write, and one whose greatness depended almost wholly on the fact that he did. Carlyle had used Napoleon as the symbol of worldly power, the hero in action; Emerson through him analyzed the values in "experience" and, by revealing the dangers inherent in democracy, made one of his finest statements of the democratic faith.

In each lecture the same series of questions is asked: What is this man? What did he make of his life, and why? Are his values sound? The final test in each case is the moral sentiment, the ability to rise from the many to the one. Unlike essays on more abstract topics, these do not themselves rise except in the questions asked. Each finally records a partial failure which brings the special case back to the central thesis. Except that the weaker essays are at the end, the book thus achieves a greater unity than did the earlier *Essays*; but the individual judgment is warped to the pattern. For true perspective on the misleading final paragraphs on Shakespeare, for example, one must turn to the fragmentary tercentenary address of 1864, where, without reservation, Emerson declares that he is "the one resource of our life on which no gloom gathers . . . the most robust and potent thinker that ever was." In *Representative Men,* Shakespeare serves as a means for discussion of values beyond his own; in the later address he is confronted for himself. There is no confusion of moral with aesthetic values as some critics have affirmed.

This lecture series was delivered in Boston in 1845–1846, but it served Emerson as the chief item of his repertory while in England. On his return he prepared no single series on his impressions, but many of his lectures between 1849 and 1856 drew upon this experience to illuminate his social views. *English Traits,* in the latter year, was a book freshly written, but it drew ideas and paragraphs from both journals and lectures. At the same time he was offering his series on the "Conduct of Life" particularly to audiences in the West, the first draft of the book on the same subject.

Emerson did not enjoy himself on these travels, but they were enriching experiences both to him and his audiences. He was now carrying wisdom to wisdom, not "ruins to ruins." He was known for what he was and what he would say. In England he was guest of honor at the Grand Soirée of the Manchester Athenaeum, where he addressed several thousand people, among them such notables as Cobden, Bright, Cruikshank, and Blackwood. A few years later he faced in Cincinnati a "vast assembly, which sat for two mortal hours . . . lecture hungry," in anticipation. He met the great now on their own level: among them Dickens, Tennyson, and Carlyle again. He heard Chopin play: "Could the denying heaven have also given me ears for the occasion!" Between lectures, he traveled in the new steam trains or in ruder conveyances, was entertained in unfamiliar homes, or sat in lonely hotel rooms. He found Paris "a place of the largest liberty that I suppose in the civilized world," and "the great sweeps of the Mississippi . . . the loneliest river." In Europe, he studied people and society; in the West, he bought maps and learned geography. The demand for him was so great that he was forced to write new lectures on the road. Seldom were his audiences large— nor was he uniformly successful with them—but there were many, sometimes two within twenty-four hours, and the returns from any one were small. In one course in Chicago the "gate" for Bayard Taylor was $252; for Emerson only $37—an extreme instance. In spite of the industry and enthusiasm of Alexander Ireland who made the arrangements, the English trip apparently did not cover expenses; the American did somewhat better. But the real and enduring profit of these journeys lay in his two ripest and roundest books, *English Traits* and *The Conduct of Life*. If he had written nothing else, by these two he would deserve to be called our most representative man.

His report on British civilization was, like all the work of this later period, the fruit of years of study and speculation. For one of his early lecture series, he had chosen the topic "English Literature" and in preparation had read Warton's *History of English Poetry*. The English classics had always been favorites, but his first visit to England was a disappointment. Only when he returned in 1847 did the past become a living part of the present and the meaning of the British character become clear. "England is the best of actual nations," he wrote, "London is the epitome of our times." *English Traits* was the first record of an American's return to "Our Old Home" to achieve critical detachment without loss of sympathy; but it was also an analysis and judgment of the civilization of which America was as much a part as England. This book takes its place of fulfillment in our travel literature with ease and grace; but it marks in Emerson's own work the turn from a personal to a social perspective. In studying the English, he was concerned for the first time with the problem of man functioning en masse.

Set in the frame of his own journey, it opens with accounts of his first visit and of his voyage, and concludes with his trip to Stonehenge, his personal reception, and his speech at Manchester. The intervening chapters constitute an analysis of contemporary British civilization against a background of history. "If there be one test of national genius universally accepted," he writes, "it is success; and if there be one successful country in the universe for the last millennium, that country is England." His curiosity is piqued, and he seeks the answer in geography, ethnology, moral philosophy, economics, politics, education, religion, and literature. He finds it in a never-failing "reserve of power in the English temperament," a Saxon inheritance strong enough to absorb and use other racial strains, to profit by a favorable location, to rise above mistakes without denying them, and to exploit material resources without losing moral integrity. The mother of human liberty, England in her age is perennially young "with strength still equal to the time." She may pay absolute homage to material wealth, she may retain and develop her aristocracy, she may have her established church and her revered universities, she may cling to her traditions and rituals without great harm because she can laugh at her own mistakes and forever hold on to her "original predilection for private independence." As long as she can produce both steam engines and poets, she is sound and safe in spite of her faults.

Like Cooper and many another American traveler, Emerson returned to his own country with renewed respect for her potentialities, but sharp criticism of her crudities. The glamorous faith of his Boston lecture on "The Young American" (1844) was dulled by a keener critical sense when he began working on *The Conduct of Life* soon after his return. Not, like *English Traits,* an overt analysis of a specific civilization, this book was nevertheless his counsel to his own people in contrast to his earlier advices to men in general. He felt himself swept into the current of analysis of "the times." "By an odd coincidence," he began, "four or five noted men were each reading a discourse to the citizens of Boston or New York, on the Spirit of the Times," during the same winter. Carlyle had published *Past and Present* in 1843, and reform was in the air. "To me, however," he warned, "the question of the times resolved itself into a practical question of the conduct of life." The conflicts in prevailing ideas could only be resolved by reference to larger contexts than those of the here and now. Once more he must write a summary statement of the First Philosophy, but this time its generalizations were to be tempered by experience with the actual forces at work in contemporary society, the conduct of men at court and in the wilderness.

Now for the first time he planted his feet solidly on the ground and looked critically about him. His new task was to evaluate civilization in his day with the tools and criteria he had spent a lifetime in perfecting. No part of his earlier position, as defined in *Nature,* was denied, but no longer did he confuse what he saw of men and things with the perfection of which he believed life to be capable. The critical realism of this third period followed the balanced tensions of his earlier work with a more sharply defined duality of view: keener observation of the world as it is, on the one hand; firmer convictions of the unity of the ultimate moral principle, on the other. His conclusions and inconsistencies are now intellectual more than emotional. His equations have almost the certainty of the formula; his art is firm rather than fluid. To those who enjoy his work for its romantic fervor, this is a loss; to those who look for restraint and form, there is positive gain in firmness of texture.

The Conduct of Life marks the culmination of Emerson's work. He has become social critic as well as moral philosopher. He is willing to explore the pragmatic as well as the ideal test of conduct, and to evaluate men as well as man. Inconsistencies between the material and the ideal are the more glaring, and the ascent from the one plane to the other can no longer be made with the careless abandon of *Nature* and the *Essays*; but made it must be. A wiser and firmer spirit wrote these chapters on "Fate," "Power," "Worship," and "Beauty," because temptation, conflict, and suffering are recognized. The old optimism is not dimmed—we must still build our altars to the "Beautiful Unity" and the "Beautiful Necessity"; but the difficulties of the way are sympathetically explored before they are waved aside. "The young mortal enters the hall of the firmament. . . . On the instant, and incessantly, fall snow-storms of illusions. . . . And when, by and by, for an instant, the air clears and the cloud lifts a little, there are the gods still sitting around him on their thrones,—they alone with him alone."

5

The clouds of the Civil War were already gathering when the lectures on the conduct of life were being written; the War broke in the year the book appeared. It marked a fourth and last phase in Emerson's development, a time for retrospection. His literary powers had reached their meridian; during the last thirty years of his life, they were slowly undermined by the distractions of the times, which led him into reluctant participation in public and national affairs, and later by increasing demands and weakening powers, which made for less care in composition.

Never up to the moment of his death in 1882 did he equal the achievement of *The Conduct of Life*. He gathered together one more collection of his essays, *Society and Solitude* (1870), but a second, *Letters and Social Aims* (1875), was too much for him after the shock of the burning of his home in 1872. His friend James Elliot Cabot took over the task and completed it under Emerson's wandering supervision. Cabot culled two more volumes from the stock pile of shuffled manuscripts, and Edward Emerson a third after their author's death. In bulk, these five volumes represent almost half of his published prose; but at best they are fragmentary, however studded they may be with brilliant passages.

Part of the difficulty lies in a new habit of workmanship rather than in declining power. In his early years, Emerson borrowed freely from his own previous writing; but he always copied and revised the borrowed passage, leaving the original manuscript intact. Later, when the demands upon him grew too heavy for this practice, he took to lifting pages bodily, with the result that few of his later manuscripts were whole when the editors set to work on them. No canon of his work during these years can therefore be established, except as Cabot has done it in the listing by title of his lecture series. The lectures themselves as he delivered them are lost. The one collection that he himself prepared, *Society and Solitude,* is on a more familiar level than are his earlier essays, but it has much of the old charm and eloquence. Emerson had settled, after the war, more contentedly into the enjoyment of domestic life, farming, books, clubs, art, and old age, and he gathered together what he had said on these topics, as early as 1841, as late as 1862, to make a single book. "The central wisdom, which was old in infancy, is young in four-score years, and, dropping off obstructions, leaves in happy subjects the mind purified and wise." This is what his mind would be; and this is what it had become.

In 1870, his lifelong wish to develop "a new method in metaphysics, proceeding by observation of the mental facts, without attempting an analysis and coordination of them" seemed gratified by an invitation to deliver a course of sixteen lectures to the students in philosophy at Harvard. But his mind was too tired to undertake so great a work as the reformulation of his theory of the law for man and the law for things, and he drew upon old lecture courses for most of his material.

His *novum organum* remained unwritten at his death. The fragments of the course which survive were published under the title he had chosen for the whole, *The Natural History of the Intellect.* In them he attempts once more to harmonize the powers and laws of thought, instinct, inspiration, and memory with the findings of natural science. The ideas are not new, but the tone is cold and clear like the atmosphere of a late autumn afternoon. Three years before, he had written:

> As the bird trims her to the gale,
> I trim myself to the storm of time,
> I man the rudder, reef the sail,
> Obey the voice at eve obeyed at prime.

The distinction in experience between the moral and natural laws, and their ideal identity, remained the primary message of that voice. It had been a long struggle from youthful doubt to wise serenity, but faith in the "each and all" had not wavered. He had defined and revealed the eternal human verities in the conflicting demands of the new man in the new world.

26. HENRY DAVID THOREAU

WHEN in 1872 the town of Concord was dedicating its fine new library building, Ralph Waldo Emerson was the natural choice for speaker. A river of thought, he said, is always flowing from the invisible world into the minds of men. And he named over Concord's makers of books. "Henry Thoreau we all remember as a man of genius, and of marked character, known to our farmers as the most skilful of surveyors, and indeed better acquainted with their forests and meadows and trees than themselves, but more widely known as the writer of some of the best books which have been written in this country, and which, I am persuaded, have not yet gathered half their fame."

Thoreau had then been dead ten years. While he lived, only a meager miscellany of his poems, essays, and reviews had appeared in newspapers and magazines; only two books had been printed, *A Week on the Concord and Merrimack Rivers* (1849), and *Walden* (1854).

Given this history of publication, and considering the peculiar man himself, there was bound to be a confusion of appraising voices—a babble taking years to blend into anything which approximates a chorus. To William Ellery Channing, Thoreau's companion on many walks, he was the poet-naturalist. Amos Bronson Alcott believed him the finest possible example of the native New Englander—a rugged, independent, inventive Yankee to show Europe with pride. To the village selectmen, at the time of John Brown's trial, he was a meddlesome troublemaker. Nor, though they employed him as the town's surveyor, could they quite forgive him for once accidentally setting their wood lots afire, on the day of Town Meeting, of all things, when he should have been mindful of his civic obligations. In South Africa, Mahatma Gandhi, editing *Indian Opinion,* found in Thoreau's "Civil Disobedience" the way to resist tyrannical government. Though leaning heavily on Thoreau in his own life and writing, Robert Louis Stevenson labeled him a skulker, dodging the responsibilities of living. A twentieth century critic, remarking on Thoreau's immensely busy practical and creative life, characterized him as "one of the masters of English prose, purer, stronger, racier, closer to a genuine life rhythm, than any one of his contemporaries, in England or America." John

Burroughs, after scolding Thoreau for scientific errors, concluded that he was, first and last, a moral force speaking as a literary naturalist. George Eliot, in the *Westminster Review,* called *Walden* "a bit of pure American life (not the 'go a-head' species, but its opposite pole), animated by that energetic, yet calm spirit of innovation, that practical as well as theoretical independence of formulae, which is peculiar to some of the finer American minds." James Russell Lowell pronounced him an imitator of Emerson, an unpleasant egotist, and a failure. And Emerson himself spoke of him as *the* man of Concord.

Many of these opinions appear to be based on Thoreau himself as much as on his writings. That is readily explained, for he lived what he wrote. When his subject was nature, his intensest effort was to transfer directly to the page what each of his senses and his mind and spirit told him. When he wrote on controversial questions, he knew his thoughts were true since he had lived them—however difficult, inconsistent, or absurd they might seem to others. The electric impulses, the vital blood of his brain and body, gave life to the spirit and matter of his books. Probably more than with any other American, his acts, opinions, and literary work are one. Any attempt at comprehension, including why he wrote as well as what, begins and ends with the man himself.

2

When Emerson, still a comparative newcomer there, hailed young Henry Thoreau as *the* man of Concord, he had not long known him—though he was acquainted with his mother, for Mrs. John Thoreau, like many gentlewomen of modest means, took in boarders, among them Mrs. Lucy Brown, Emerson's wife's sister. Concord thought of John Thoreau as one of its less successful mercantile citizens. Even after the repeal of Jefferson's disastrous embargo and the close of the War of 1812, the number of merchant-bankrupts was far from small. John had failed in his storekeeping at Concord, where, on July 12, 1817, his son Henry was born. He had tried his hand in Boston and elsewhere. When Henry was five, the family had moved back to Concord, and was doing reasonably well in the manufacture of pencils. There were four children: Helen, the eldest, John, Jr., two years ahead of Henry, Henry himself, and Sophia.

Henry soon showed a bent for studies, and, with Concord township for his background, developed a liking for the country as did most New England boys who could shoulder a fowling piece, though he never became a hunter, preferring to tramp or fish. An affectionate, close-knit family, the Thoreaus pinched to send both boys to Concord Academy, not satisfied with the standards of the town school; then chose Henry as their candidate for college.

When Thoreau was at Harvard he never bothered to stand higher than the middle of his class, though his fellows soon came to think of him as a scholar. He spent many hours in the alcove of the library where Chalmers' *English Poets* were shelved—twenty-one packed volumes in which he continued his reading already begun at Concord. It was not in his nature to follow the narrow highway of the college curriculum. He preferred to cut across lots. The careful reading of books became the basis of his education.

Though content with average work in most of his courses, he was good enough in his second year to be assigned a role in Greek dialogue. Shortly after this, in the long winter vacation, he taught a term of school at Canton, Massachusetts, living with the Unitarian minister there, brilliant, erratic Orestes Brownson, who interested him in the German language and some of its literature, and perhaps in his own radical notions.

By the time Henry was a senior, he had jotted down in copy books many passages and verses from his reading—not with any definite intention, but because he wished to keep them. These were sentences the sight and sound of which he liked; these were ideas about which he wished to think.

The copy books, too, served in the composition of classroom exercises for Edward Channing, Boylston Professor of Rhetoric and Oratory. It was Channing's aim to teach his students how to express their ideas logically and in order, in a natural, lucid style. Thoreau's mind was intuitive, not logical, and there was sure to be trouble. Not that he disliked doing essays—he loved to write—nor objected to Channing's methods of teaching. Far from it—he averred this was his one beneficial orthodox experience at Harvard. But harm came with the good. Essay topics encouraged by Channing were of a sort bound to produce didactic, prosy exposition, a type of writing alien to Thoreau's better genius, yet lingering in his poorer passages.

In his extracurricular reading he had discovered certain modern British authors: Coleridge, guide to German transcendentalism; Wordsworth, whose thoughts in poems like the "Intimations" ode flowed sympathetically into the stream of Thoreau's thinking; and Carlyle. He found Carlyle highly provocative. This was the richest prose style he had met. Here also was an antidote to Professor Channing's emphasis on logical didacticism. Here was a gospel of individualism for the encouragement of young men. Thoreau enjoyed Carlyle's vigorous humor, his rank exaggeration, his readiness to burst through conventional barriers. But the Carlylese which Emerson found infecting most of the Scotsman's young American readers also took its toll of Thoreau's early prose. Before reaching maturity, he had to get rid of it.

His interest in the Elizabethans and in British authors of the seventeenth century deepened as his knowledge increased. Prose writers like Sir Thomas Browne and metaphysical poets like Donne, Vaughan, Crashaw, and Herbert became his favorites. Their eccentricity caught his fancy. But what kept his attention was the way they strove to picture with all their senses what they felt and did. The lines he liked best to repeat were these from Elizabethan Samuel Daniel:

> Unless above himself he can
> Erect himself, how poor a thing is man.

His explorations in the Harvard library also led him to old travel books like Josselyn's *New-Englands Rarities Discovered*. Aside from his interest in the. subject, he valued the strong, straightforward, practical language of these cultivated men of action.

With some additions, these tastes were to remain Thoreau's favorites, and his absorption made him one of the most deeply educated of American authors. In his maturity he would tolerate no master; but books form one solid part of the foundation beneath him. The greatest impact came from his native village when, in the fall of 1836, Emerson's *Nature* was published. Our age in America, wrote Emerson, suffers from retrospection. "The foregoing generations beheld God and nature face to face; we, through their eyes. Why should not we also enjoy an original relation to the universe? Why should not we have a poetry and philosophy of insight and not of tradition?" Here was a precept to win the most from existence. Books themselves must change to drops of water in this stream of living. Nothing must impede its flow. Thus advised, Thoreau could enter into the American Renaissance directly.

On August 16, 1837, as one of the better scholars, Thoreau took an active part at Commencement, picking the negative side in a debate on the merits of the Commercial Spirit. Man's absorption by that spirit, he declared, made him turn his eyes from the world's beauty and from life's best purposes.

3

College over, he was going home. Full of joy at the thought, he was convinced he had been born in the most estimable place in the world, and in the very nick of time. "If I forget thee, O Concord, let my right hand forget her cunning," he boyishly affirmed in his class book. "To whatever quarter of the world I may wander, I shall deem it good fortune that I hail from Concord North Bridge."

To live fully, vitally, was his intent, to keep himself always at the top of his condition. But given the workaday world, how best bring this about? He was making himself useful to his family in the house and garden—no son in the village was handier—and helping his father in the pencil shop. The family meant him to be a scholar, and did not question his use of his time. He paid for his keep, like the other boarders. He continued his walks and his reading. Presently he took on the Grammar School, having taught before. But the committee's interference when he would not flog—though the discipline he kept was good—caused him to resign within a fortnight. Perhaps he would try for another school in Maine, in the South or West. Still casting about while his Harvard classmates settled down to business or the professions, he was restless, a little ill at ease, and with his back up.

Meanwhile, Emerson invited his friendship.

In his thirty-fourth year, and at the top of his intellectual powers, Emerson was delighted with this youthful scholar, deeply read in those authors whom he also found stimulating. Moreover Henry was able to read in many languages—Greek, Latin, and French with ease, Italian, Spanish, and German with more effort. He had a curiosity about the structure of language, was acquainted with Anglo-Saxon, and relished Chaucer. Though Emerson of course recognized the kinship between Thoreau's thinking and his own, he saw and hailed at once this erect, independent mind, bent on testing the truth and worth of everything it met with.

At Cambridge that August, before the Phi Beta Kappa Society, Emerson had delivered "The American Scholar." Was not this young friend the Free American he had imagined—versed in great books, responsive to nature, fit for doing as well as thinking? The better Emerson got to know him, the more he valued this firmly built man, his hands strong and useful with tools, his brain meshed beautifully with his capacity for action.

The world Thoreau entered when Emerson opened the doors of his house could be matched in few other times or places—an extraordinary intellectual universe within which Emerson and the group around him moved familiarly and with command. Easily and soon, admitted as an equal, Henry, the youngest, became a member of the circle. Sometimes, especially when the inevitable cranks were present, he rudely turned on his heel and walked out. Yet citizenship in this Athenian society was of greatest value in his development, strengthening the growth of his faith in intuitive thinking.

This group set up one target for his shafts. Farmer-friends in the village—simple, shrewd, elemental, earthy Yankee philosophers—furnished another.

"Do you keep a journal?" Emerson asked him. No, not regularly. So he began. "What are you doing now?" Emerson also inquired. Even at this experimental stage, Henry could probably never have brought himself to go permanently to Maine or the West, but he did give one more test to teaching. His brother John and he took over the old Academy and kept it for three years, incidentally using part of the summer vacation for an excursion on the Concord and Merrimack rivers. But when John's health failed Henry decided

against continuing alone. The toll exacted on his freedom was out of proportion to the income. He needed more winter, as well as summer, for observation and study. Nor would he go on teaching just for a livelihood, since in
his honesty he admitted that his primary objective in doing so was not the
good of his fellow man.

He liked home, but a boarding house can be noisy and distracting. Sensing
Thoreau's need, Emerson saw a way to gratify needs of his own. He still
greatly missed his dead brother Charles, who had lived with him, and he
longed for another such companion. In a letter to Carlyle, he was soon able
to report: "One reader and friend of yours dwells now in my house, and, as I
hope, for a twelvemonth to come,—Henry Thoreau,—a poet whom you may
one day be proud of." He was finding Henry as full of buds of promise as a
young apple tree. He had already presented him as a writer, having persuaded
Margaret Fuller, the *Dial*'s editor, to print Thoreau's poem, "Sympathy," in
the first issue along with an essay on the Roman satirical poet Flaccus. It was
for introducing young men like Henry that Emerson chiefly valued the *Dial*—
not to multiply writing in the old tradition, but to report life, newness, and
the dreams of youth.

A young poet had one duty—to be a poet—and Emerson never doubted
Thoreau's obligation. Thus encouraged and given an outlet, Henry was soon
in a mid-sea of verses. But the question of how to live while writing still
needed resolving, though Emerson's household arrangement gave a temporary
answer. Emerson's business of lecturing seemed a possible solution, till Henry
tried it. In his first year out of college he had spoken gratis before Concord's
Lyceum, his subject, significantly, "Society." But offers had not poured in to
speak for money. Like all Emerson's young men, Thoreau lectured with
Emersonian intonations—but not with Emerson's skill nor his rich, compelling voice; and what he said was muffled to the neck in Harvard rhetoric.

A Carlylean doctrine Thoreau heartily approved of was the insistence that
each man search for that one work which fits him best, then enter wholeheartedly into it. "I must confess," he wrote, "I have felt mean enough when
asked how I was to act on society, what errand I had to mankind. Undoubtedly I did not feel mean without a reason, and yet my loitering is not without
defense. I would fain communicate the wealth of my life to men, would really
give them what is most precious in my gift. I would secrete pearls with the
shellfish and lay up honey with the bees for them. I will sift the sunbeams
for the public good."

Thoreau's concentration first on poetry is not surprising, since the *Dial*
carried on its pages some of Emerson's best: "The Problem," "Woodnotes,"
"The Snow-Storm," "The Sphinx." And much of his early prose caught
Emerson's manner, but little more. Margaret Fuller rejected his essay, "The

Service," for though she found it rich in thoughts, they were so out of any natural order, so choked with mystical symbolism, as to make painful reading. When Emerson took over the editorship, his protégé had better luck. "Our tough Yankee must have his tough verse," wrote Emerson to Miss Fuller when Thoreau refused to make a suggested change. He had his criticism, too, for Henry's prose. Emerson had sent "A Winter Walk" to the printer with some misgivings, he confessed, notwithstanding its fine sketches of the pickerel fisher and woodchopper. The trouble, he repeated, was Henry's *mannerism,* as if one could get the trick of rhetoric through shock; to call a cold place sultry, for example; a solitude, public; a wilderness, domestic. But Henry, developing his own style, was learning what to do. In its amended form, "A Winter Walk" is characteristic. More and more his manner sprang from and suggested the solid matter on which he based what he wrote; yet, when he wished, he could take flight thence into the realms of his imagination and thinking.

Emerson wrote to his brother William, at Staten Island, about his new housemate, praising his scholarship and poetry, his partnership in the garden and in walking. This firmly built, light-complexioned, healthy-skinned boy, his gray-blue eyes strong and serious, seemed indefatigable when bent on any labor. With Emerson's support, he had served as curator of the Concord Lyceum and, though the town meeting proved niggardly in its grant of money, had assembled as interesting a slate of speakers as the people had thus far listened to. While Emerson was away, he edited the *Dial.* Full of inventiveness and strong common sense, this young man, thought Emerson, could give judicious advice in the gravest affairs; would prove competent as leader of any Pacific exploration.

In the woods, Thoreau's spirits were most elastic and buoyant. He was developing, Emerson noticed, a passion for observation. He was furthering an intense conviction that the keys to life's secrets could be found in Concord's fields. Yet none perceived better than Henry that it is not the fact that imports, but what lies behind it. For Thoreau, every least thing, like the greatest, lay in glory, a symbol of the order and beauty of the whole.

At Emerson's or the Harvard library Thoreau was rereading the English poets. He was studying Audubon, whom he had chanced on, with delight. While a Harvard undergraduate, he had found, in Chalmers' collection, Sir William Jones' "Essay on the Poetry of the Eastern Nations," with some examples in translation. Emerson, deeply interested in the sacred books of the East—the Laws of Menu, for example, setting forth the religious ethics of the Hindus—was drawing the attention of his friends to them. Thoreau soon knew them well. But it was probably not until he left Emerson's, by 1844, that he got acquainted with the Bhagavad-Gita, which Emerson was then enthusiastically recommending. It came to be Thoreau's greatest find, as important to him as Emerson's *Nature*. What attracted Emerson was its mystical speculation. The possibility, through asceticism, of uniting contemplation and action became for Thoreau a further guide toward fulfillment.

These explorations in Hindu philosophy naturally drew closer the bond between Thoreau and Emerson. A more immediate and poignant sharing came through the sudden presence of death. In the first winter at Emerson's, Henry's brother John, whom he loved with silent intensity, unexpectedly and horribly succumbed to lockjaw. Two weeks later, Emerson's first-born son, Waldo, died. These losses make their mark in the writings of both.

Emerson had very early recognized Henry's affection for children—how heartily, like a child himself, he threw himself into their play. This affinity was like a confession that Henry was not so independent of human sympathy as he pretended. Emerson knew better than to take too seriously his friend's militant nature, though Thoreau could be prickly as a hedgehog and touchy as a snapping turtle. It seemed as if Henry's first instinct on hearing a proposition was to controvert it—a habit somewhat chilling to the social affections. But, valuing Henry for his integrity and peculiar worth, Emerson never really lost patience. Indeed, wishing Thoreau's light to become a beacon, he cast about for means to let it shine more widely than was possible in the *Dial*.

With papers like Horace Greeley's *Tribune,* New York was the nation's journalistic center. No writer of poetry, few of prose, Emerson was painfully aware, could make enough to live on in America. Still, with a letter introducing him to Greeley, Henry in New York might profit more than was possible in the village. The city might further his growth. Emerson had not seen what Henry had written in his journal: "I think I could write a poem to be called 'Concord.' For argument I should have the River, the Woods, the Ponds, the Hills, the Fields, the Swamps and Meadows, the Streets and Buildings, and the Villagers. Then Morning, Noon, and Evening, Spring, Summer, Autumn, and Winter, Night, Indian Summer, and the Mountains in the Horizon."

Sent ostensibly as tutor to William Emerson's son, Thoreau set out to explore and perhaps conquer New York. Nathaniel Hawthorne, who liked him, had also tactfully given him a lift, introducing him to John Louis O'Sullivan, editor of New York's *Democratic Review*. Horace Greeley took to young Thoreau, and began quietly to look after his literary welfare. This relationship he continued through Henry's life. For O'Sullivan's journal, Thoreau wrote an unimportant essay, "The Landlord," and a significant review of an extraordinary book by a German immigrant in Pennsylvania named Etzler who foresaw a technological age which would give man an opportunity, with a minimum of labor, to make a paradise of earth. Like a good Yankee interested in mechanical devices, Thoreau read Etzler with an open mind; but he quarreled outright with the prophet's materialistic aim. This "paradise (to be) regained" would be mechanistic and nothing else—offering an easy, hedonistic life through super-gadgetry. There was a speedier way, wrote the critic, to diversify the land, drain the marshes, secure a pleasant environment. That way must rely on the power and rectitude of the best human behavior. In his own attitude, this faith never lost its dominance over Thoreau.

New York had opened few doors, and Henry was homesick. "Am I not made of Concord dust?" he wrote to Lydian Emerson. "I carry Concord ground in my boots and in my hat." By November, 1843, he had brought it home.

4

Twenty-six years of age, Thoreau found himself again at a crossroads. Soon after leaving college, he had written: "The world is a fit theatre today in which any part may be acted. There is this moment proposed to me every kind of life that men lead anywhere, or that imagination can paint." South African planter, Greenland whaler, soldier in Florida, navigator of any sea. Now, in the summer that followed his New York venture, this proposal was repeated, literally. His friend Isaac Hecker, another explorer in living, suggested that the pair, taking nothing with them, work their passage across the Atlantic, and so through England, France, Germany, and Italy.

Henry, having weighed it, turned the proposition down. "The fact is," he replied, "I cannot so decidedly postpone exploring the *Farthest Indies,* which are to be reached, you know, by other routes and other methods of travel." Instead he would go to Walden Pond. In the metaphorical, imaginative, vigorous prose he could now command, he made a final comment on the offer. "I have been surprised when one has with confidence proposed to me, a grown man, to embark in some enterprise of his, as if I had absolutely nothing to do, my life having been a complete failure hitherto. What a doubtful compliment this to pay me! As if he had met me half-way across the ocean beating up against the wind, but bound nowhere, and proposed to me to go along with him! If I did, what do you think the underwriters would say? No, no! I am not without employment at this stage of the voyage. To tell the truth, I saw an advertisement for able-bodied seamen, when I was a boy, sauntering in my native port, and as soon as I came of age I embarked."

Emerson offered him his wood lot and field at the pond. There he would be secure of his leisure for work and study.

"I went to the woods," Thoreau later reported, "because I wished to live deliberately, to front only the essential facts of life, and see if I could not learn what it had to teach." The suspicions forming in his college days had become convictions. The mass of men led lives of quiet desperation, complaining of the hardness of their lot or of the times, when they might improve them. With man's industry and invention, when these expressed the man himself, uninfluenced by greed, Thoreau had no quarrel. It was man's exploitation of sovereign man which he deplored; man's self-delusion as to life's objectives. Everywhere, in shops and offices and fields, men appeared to be doing penance in a thousand remarkable ways. Henry was well aware that his own father, bred to the mercantile system, had worked hard only to suffer repeated failure, like so many merchants of his times. Or if they made money, they used it to ignoble ends. In his review of Etzler's book, Thoreau had pointed out that its chief fault, like that of the age itself, lay in taking for granted the idea that gross comfort is the greatest good—not the free, serene, unhampered growth of the individual. It would continue to be his purpose to dwell with a minimum of hindrance as near as possible to the channels in which his life flowed; to be in as perfect correspondence with his natural environment as possible, so as to be at home with nature. Thus he could sample and report on life with all his senses.

Not that he wanted others to follow his pattern; nor did those need advice who were already well employed. This was his present, personal answer to the problem of how to create, be happy, yet not lack food or shelter.

In the summer of 1845, in his twenty-eighth year, significantly on Independence Day, he started living at the cabin. From its door he could see the sun rise, watch the moon shine over Walden. On quiet evenings, alone in his boat under the stars, he could play his flute. He could search devotedly for images and phrases to describe the songs of birds. A master of reading, he could read more deeply.

He amused himself by keeping a record of his frugal housekeeping. He cultivated his philosophy and a patch of beans. He continued to study his world's fellow inhabitants: the otters, the foxes; Therien, French Canadian woodchopper, a primitive, Homeric man; the Irish, who, throughout sixteen hours of the day, for a pittance of sixty cents, were toiling, about one hundred rods south of his cabin, on the new railroad to Fitchburg. He often passed along the cut where they lived in stylike shanties, their bodies permanently contracted by the long habit of shrinking from cold and misery—the development of all their limbs and faculties checked. In one's prospect of society, it was certainly fair to consider that class by whose labor the distinguishing achievement of the century was being built. The sight of this slavery and exploitation outraged him, though his indignation was matched by his disgust at the human stupidity that let itself be thus imposed on. He was fascinated and repelled by the fact that, save for its wastefulness and squalor, this Irish shanty life perversely resembled the efficient simplification he was after. He turned with relief to thought of the primitive Indians, whose way of existence represented a healthier adjustment. Yet the endurance of these Irish won his admiration—especially the cheerful courage of the children, facing this new America as the earlier pioneers had faced it.

Frequently—almost daily—Thoreau visited the town, using the railroad tracks as the shortest way. The men on the freight trains waved as to an old acquaintance. And Henry liked to watch the laden cars pass, through storm and snow, a symbol of man's enterprise and adventurous spirit. In town, he called at the new house his father and he had built. He came drawn by a wish to see his family and by a typically Yankee taste for apple pies, much to his mother's pleasure, who baked them with a flavoring of herbs that was her special secret.

On request, he lectured, without pay, to the Lyceum—his subjects, the trip on the rivers, or his life in the woods. Almost daily he wrote in his journal—on his discoveries, on books, on his adventures with people, on life and its purpose. Detached somewhat from the village, he could study it the better. Though so intense an individualist himself, Thoreau favored the ideal of communal living as in keeping with the spirit of America. But this limping actuality, he condemned. Why should a village stop short at a pedagogue, a parson, a sexton, a parish library, and three selectmen, because our pilgrim forefathers got through a cold winter once on a bleak rock with these? "It is time that villages were universities, and their elder inhabitants the fellows of universities, with leisure—if they are, indeed, so well off—to pursue liberal studies the rest of their lives." Let us have noble villages of men, Thoreau pleaded. "If it is necessary, omit one bridge over the river, go round a little there, and throw one arch at least over the darker gulf of ignorance which surrounds us."

In addition to his far travels in Concord, he made two excursions: one to Maine, the other a venture into the realms of State, which ended in prison. The trip to Maine, where he climbed Katahdin, was the first of three to the north woods. He greatly enjoyed brief excursions from Concord—to Cape Cod; to Fire Island; to Canada; to see Walt Whitman in Brooklyn. On each, he kept careful records, storing up materials for future books. The trip to prison in 1846 followed the road of immediate circumstance. Negro slavery outraged Thoreau's every principle. His friends deplored it too, but most did little about it. Not so he and his family. They sheltered runaways at home, and at Walden he had already harbored one fugitive on the way to Canada. As he watched the conduct of the nation, it seemed to him that daily the slave power became more arrogant and grasping. The North, still greedy, though glutted by profits spun from cotton grown by the black man, became daily more pusillanimous and appeasing. His quarrel, he saw, was not with far-off foes but with those hundred thousand merchants and farmers, near home, who though declaring themselves opposed had their hands in their pockets, doing nothing. For himself, he was more than ever conscious of his obligation to act at any time as he thought was right. Here was a moment when truth and the Constitution were in conflict. When war broke out with Mexico during Thoreau's second summer at Walden, he saw it as an iniquitous plot by the slavery interests to control more votes through the acquisition of Texas. If government acted without principle, he must refuse it his allegiance. So he would not pay his tax.

His friend Sam Staples, the constable, did not wish to lock him up. "I'll pay your tax, Henry, if you're hard up." But Henry explained his one-man revolution. That night, much to Thoreau's disgust, someone short-circuited his protest by paying. Nothing could be done about it, so he returned to the pond. But his night in jail had developed further his ideas on the relation of the individual to the State.

At Walden he was completing, from his journals and lectures on the subject, the physical and spiritual history of the excursion on the rivers which he had taken with his brother John. He finished an essay on Carlyle and saw it printed in *Graham's Magazine*. He entertained visitors. On Sundays, sometimes half a dozen railroad construction engineers—healthy, sturdy workers in clean, white shirts—would drop in for a neighborly talk.

Sometimes the hut and little hillock above the cove was lively with children—little Hosmers, little Alcott girls, who drifted out as naturally as a breeze from the village. Ellery Channing also frequently called. Henry was as close to his aim, thought Channing, as the bark of a tree. Emerson came, and Alcott. He had never known a man, thought Alcott, so thoroughly of the country. He seemed one with things, of Nature's essence and core, knit of strong timbers, most like a wood and its inhabitants. One evening, Henry read him some passages from the rivers manuscript. Fragrant with the life of New England woods and streams, Alcott found it, purely American. It could have been written nowhere else in the world, yet it profited by its author's wide knowledge of other men's books. It should become popular, Alcott decided, "winning at once the reader's fancy and his heart, inspiring a natural piety for nature and natural things, as surprising as it is refreshing."

Most works of major importance have been gestated with the aid of more than average love, sorrow, hate, or other emotion—experienced singly or in combination. Because to more than a usual degree what Thoreau wrote came out of how he lived, it was bound to be so with the *Week*; would be so with

Walden—though their backgrounds demanded and received a serenity of spirit which testifies to the power of creative sublimation.

Outwardly Henry's trip with his brother seems as tranquil as the river-ways it followed in 1839. Inwardly there was emotion which, in recollection, was to lend beauty and strength to the writing. Henry could not jot down a single word about the excursion without the recollection that John, a year later, was dead. And thought of that loss, in itself still an anguish, was made even more poignant by the curious fact that when the brothers set out on the river, each was in love with the same girl, though probably neither ever really discussed with the other this disturbing complexity.

The girl was Ellen Sewall, daughter of a prominent, conservative New England family. She had come briefly to Concord on a visit. It is clear that she liked both boys, with whom she walked or went boating. John was the first to propose, but was rejected—Ellen probably not certain of her feelings and mindful of family misgivings. Henry, thus given his chance, at last tested his fortunes. "There is no remedy for love but to love more," he wrote in his journal, but so great was his regard for the emotion, and on so high a plane, that he expected the sensitive though altogether normal Ellen to recognize his love without his telling her. "Love is the profoundest of secrets. Divulged, even to the beloved, it is no longer Love." But the realistic acuteness of his feeling forced him at last below his transcendental level—what had begun so idyllically had become confused, painful, and needed resolving. So he proposed by letter, with little expectation, apparently, that she would take him. There is testimony in support of the notion that Ellen found it difficult to turn Henry down. And thus the affair ended. Then his brother died. At Walden, some four years later, Thoreau as he wrote lived over his feelings.

Had Ellen accepted him, it might have proved very embarrassing. Marriage, he must have seen, would have demanded compromise with his ideas, and compromise had no place in Henry's make-up. But Ellen Sewall had played her unconscious part in shaping the writer and thinker. Immediate result of this love affair was his charming poem, "To the Maiden in the East." Deferred result was his philosophy of love and friendship. After the *Week* was finished, he added to it an essay—one of the fine things in it—setting forth his idealized, spiritual conception of the affinity of friend with friend and the high, impossible requirements of love.

On September 6, 1847, after two years, two months, and two days at the pond, Thoreau left it. His friend Emerson was going abroad to lecture, and wished Henry to look after the household. That was one reason, but of course there were others, though Henry himself was not sure he could name them. He was fond of Lydian Emerson, whom he called a "mother-sister."

With Ellen Sewall, she was a factor in shaping his transcendental, Platonic philosophy of friendship. He had other lives to live; there was more day to dawn.

At the pond, he had indeed traveled far, through time and geography. With Captain John Smith, William Bradford, Josselyn, and other chroniclers, he had visited a wilder, fresher America and talked with Concord's first settlers. He had conversed with the priests of Brahma and Vishnu and Indra in temples on the sacred banks of the Ganges. He had lived closer than ever to nature. He had added to his oneness and integrity of spirit. Practically, without that stay by the cove, there would have been no *Walden,* and very possibly no *Week.* Had Thoreau lived as other men expected him to, he would not have been Thoreau, and the world would have lacked his books.

Because his mind and his journals were full of it, he wrote out and delivered a lecture, "Civil Disobedience," first given under the title of "Resistance to Civil Government," protesting against the cowardice of people who would not deny their government when it sinned against justice and eternal law. Conscience, even of the minority, must decide what is right or wrong.

5

Having finished revising the *Week,* Thoreau was seeking a publisher. Forgetful that originality has a dubious commercial value, his friends, sure that the book would find a ready market, could not understand the delay. On his travels in Britain, Emerson was full of praise for author and manuscript. "Pastoral as Isaak Walton, spicy as flagroot, broad and deep as Menu." Yet all this enthusiasm persuaded no publisher to bring the book out at his own risk.

Thoreau had waited long enough. By concentrating on the manufacture of pencils, he could meet the expense. Early in the summer of 1849, one thousand copies of the *Week* were printed. But the so-called publisher, being promised his money, made little effort to carry the book to the reader. Few critical journals noticed its existence. Only two reviews of any importance appeared. Horace Greeley carried a notice in the *Tribune*; in the *Massachusetts Quarterly Review,* James Russell Lowell, well on the way toward fame as a critic, gave the book a well meant, patronizing boost. He had obviously read with pleasure the account of the actual excursion, though he complained he had thought himself bid to a river party, and not to be preached at. Nevertheless he conceded that the writer was both a wise man and a poet.

It was not the first time Lowell had referred to Thoreau. In the witty *Fable for Critics,* he had dressed up the discovery that first had struck him when, a bored, sophisticated Harvard senior rusticated at Concord, he noticed that Thoreau seemed to be picking up the windfalls in Emerson's orchard. There had been justification for the suspicion then. Full of admiration for Emerson's *Nature,* which was contributing life and strength to his creed, recognizing his kinship with Emerson, appreciating his friendship, Thoreau, like many able young men still groping their way, quite unconsciously and naturally followed Emerson's light. But in maturity Thoreau was nobody's man but his own. Emerson himself was always surprised and hurt when anyone failed to perceive this.

The *Tribune* review, by George Ripley, might have given the *Week* a further boost, for the critic had written with that objective. But as a former Unitarian minister, though a liberal, Ripley was offended by what he called Thoreau's adherence to the "dubious and dangerous school" of the transcendentalists, and his "misplaced Pantheistic attack on the Christian Faith." In the nineteenth century, such a charge was sure to warn many away. It is hardly surprising that Thoreau's first book fell stillborn from the press. Of the thousand copies printed, most were presently returned to the author as unsalable. Close to one hundred he gave away.

At Emerson's suggestion, one copy had gone to a young Englishman to whom he had spoken of Thoreau's uncompromising life—James Anthony Froude, Fellow of Exeter College, Oxford, earnest, hard-pressed author of the reviled *Nemesis of Faith,* that "wild protest against all authority, Divine and human." "When I think of what you are—of what you have done as well as what you have written," wrote Froude, "I have the right to tell you that there is no man living upon this earth at present whose friendship or whose notice I value more than yours." Obviously not just for a book about a short excursion; from Thoreau, Froude drew strength to stand by his guns.

A Week on the Concord and Merrimack Rivers has for its architectural framework a scheme of seven chapters, one for each day. Though the trip lasted considerably longer, Thoreau's artistic judgment caused him to condense the itinerary. Nor did it suit the author's purpose to admit only observations made on the actual journey. He dipped into the journals both before and after, and drew on his work in the *Dial.* Most of his comments on the Hindu scriptures had entered his thinking later—in Emerson's library and at Walden. The book's numerous digressions—like the essay on friendship—are inserted with an unequal skill, so that Lowell's complaint that collisions with them were like bumping into snags on the river can be justified. Yet, as Lowell admitted, one would hate to miss many. With an exuberance not sufficiently controlled, Thoreau poured into his account the stream of his reading—more than three hundred references and quotations—nearly swamping his little boat. There is no denying that the *Week* is bookish, for Thoreau had not solved the problem of the artistic use of his reading, a charge that cannot be leveled at *Walden*. Yet even in the *Week*, what Thoreau read and the journey he is describing blend with the river's flow. A first venture, in which the author goes beyond basic purposes and patterns, the book inevitably displays a certain lack of know-how. It is easy to contend that the *Week*, hung together on the simplest of schemes, loses through its discursiveness any claim to artistic unity. Yet with equal validity, it can be argued that the leisurely and discursive current suggests the very spirit of Concord River, which for Thoreau and Emerson alike served as a symbol of the invisible stream that bears life on. Day slips into dreamy August day from morning to sunset, as many of the topics give the illusion of fitting the varied scene. The ending brings definite terminus. September sharpness has driven off summer's drowse, and tonight there may be frost.

The manuscript of *Walden*, Thoreau's maturest record of his life and thinking, was ready for printing as the first book appeared; but, chilled by the reception of the *Week*, no publisher would now touch it. Henry had to wait. Yet the mental and emotional incentives that created *Walden* were the guarantors of its ultimate success. Henry's devoted love of life at the pond and in Concord township, his intense religious feeling for nature (on the alert for the God behind it), his protest at the waste of life through misdirection by the code of the mercantile system, his feeling for his friends, his interest in men—all this and more enter into *Walden*. "We cannot write well or truly but what we write with gusto," he noted. "The body, the senses, must conspire with the mind." Thoreau considered no pains wasted to achieve excellence, nor resented the labor which writing cost him. His journals were the broad fields where he seeded his books, which grew to maturity at last after infinite cultivation. In composing, he profited by what he had learned of conciseness from the Greeks; but he used also his knowledge that the raciest, shrewdest, most compressed, typically American language was that spoken by farmer-friends like George Minott and Edmund Hosmer.

Thoreau's intuitional process of thinking led to the minting of individual sentences. But these often came to him in a form not yet finished for printing, nor yet perfect for apprehension, and he would copy them over and over, shaping them, thrusting them this way and that, gathering them together, finally fitting them into his plan and texture. Before *Walden* was ready for the press, he had scribbled quantities of work sheets. Several times he laboriously recopied most of the sections of the first draft.

Through the five years that *Walden*, like a chrysalis, lay dormant, Thoreau hovered over it, alert for a fault in even the most insignificant word. Meanwhile, he continued making pencils to pay for the *Week*, and, for what little extra money he needed, he practiced surveying because he enjoyed it, rather than dipping indiscriminately into his miscellany of manual skills—garden-ing, masonry, house painting, laying walls, carpentry. Even though Apollo was serving King Admetus, his tasks now took him into the groves and fields he loved. Daily he pursued his fluvial and terrestrial explorations.

Though nature was still religion to him, something of a change had taken place. Harvard's famous scientist, Louis Agassiz, author of the "Essay on Classification," had become his friend. Agassiz imparted to Thoreau his own absolute passion for minutely detailed description—which came naturally enough to Henry. But this approach, typical of nineteenth century science, brought no philosophy to release its practitioners from an ever-increasing rubble of facts. With Gray's *Manual of Botany* in his pocket, Henry some-times lost sight of the God in the wood. In the early days of their friendship, Emerson had warned his friend never to find that mysterious night warbler which had always eluded his vigilance. Thoreau never made that mistake. But he now had less time for the quest, loading himself instead with a mass of detail—on depths of snow, on tree rings, and grasses, and lichens--facts he did not know quite what to do with.

Thoreau was seeing less of Emerson now than in the early days of their friendship. Forgetting Henry's manuscript of *Walden,* the gathering treasures of his journals, Emerson kept on hoping that his friend would complete the equation set forth in "The American Scholar": would prove himself the man of major action. Full of this wish, Emerson for the time being lost sight of the fact that Thoreau was making of himself a consummate artist, the native American master of expression Emerson was hoping would soon appear. Henry's prayer, in his poem of that title, that he might greatly dis-appoint his friends, seemed all too literally realized at that moment when Emerson confided to his journals: "Thoreau wants a little ambition in his mixture. Fault of this, instead of being the head of American engineers, he is captain of a huckleberry party."

Fortunately nature remained the common ground on which he and Emer-son could meet. Like so many highly intellectual men, Emerson, though drawing inspiration from the woods, was awkward in them. When Henry took him for a walk, or boating, it was the rarest of privileges. There was not a fox or a crow or a partridge in Concord, Emerson believed, who knew the ground better than Henry. So Emerson followed as best he could his friend's striding figure, Thoreau clad in efficient homespun to brave the shrub-oak thickets: in his coat pocket, made big enough for the purpose, his notebook and pencil; under his arm, an old music book to press plants in. For birds, a spyglass; for flowers, a pocket microscope; for utility, a jackknife and twine. One must submit abjectly to such a guide, for the reward would be great.

Early in August, 1854, *Walden: or, Life in the Woods,* at last was pub-lished. A packed book, beautifully and economically written; among many things the autobiography of a mind and body in cooperation enjoying fullness of living. The structure of the whole is based on the framework of the author's life at the pond; its sense of time established by the passage of the seasons, through summer, autumn, and winter to triumphant spring—the year itself a symbol of man's lifetime. As in the *Week*, and with like purpose, Thoreau did not stick to the chronology of his stay, but considerably shortened it. Its many topics and reflections, arranged with a skillful eye on contrast or agreement, are joined with neatly managed links and transitions.

The worthy burghers of the village, oblivious to much else, fixed on Thoreau's economy and marveled that one could live so cheaply. They suspected the author's honesty, and looked for signs of cheating, recalling Mrs. Thoreau's delicious pies. This literal approach has spread far beyond the bounds of the village. Many readers, attracted by its easy concreteness, take too seriously Thoreau's account of his housekeeping, as though it represented the author's whole purpose, instead of being a diverting aside, a means to an end. In sly amusement, to catch literal minds, he attached sundry fractions to his figures, down to three-fourths of a cent, and succeeded all too well, sidetracking readers from greater matters. Channing, Emerson, Alcott, and other friends, knew better what to look for. Emerson must have loved the flashes of mystic writing, the beauty and truth of his friend's descriptions. "The little pond," he wrote, "sinks in these very days as tremulous at its human fame." Alcott, of course, fastened on Henry's social theories, and his account of the day he ran amuck against the State. "This man is the independent of independents—is, indeed, the sole signer of the Declaration, and a Revolution in himself—a more than '76—having got beyond the signing to the doing it out fully." And a boy wrote from Harvard College: "We who at Cambridge look towards Concord as a sort of Mecca for our pilgrimages, are glad to see that your last book finds such favor with the public."

Hesitant favor, however, with reviews still few and far between. Thoreau must wait for his fame. Ninety years after *Walden* was published, this appraisal could be written: "We read *Walden* as notes toward a philosophy of human happiness, with digressions into the movement of ponds, the flight of hawks, the patterns of snow, and the habits of owls. But it is most triumphant in the superb grace with which it joins the life of man to the life of nature. Its woodland jottings fold into its condemnation of greed and insincerity like the pauses of a prayer."

6

Shortly before *Walden* was published, government again ran amuck against Henry Thoreau. In 1850, the Fugitive Slave Law had been passed, turning Thoreau into a criminal, along with other like-minded New Englanders, since like them, he refused to comply with its prohibition against aiding black men. In 1854, the *Walden* year, public opinion in town meeting was strong enough to call for a discussion of the slave power. But when Henry showed up to speak on the duty of Massachusetts, he found the meeting concerned only with what was happening in distant Nebraska. On Independence Day, however, at Framingham—succinctly, jarringly, with the fearlessness habitual to him when roused by a moral concern—he gave the speech, declared out of order at Concord, attacking the complacency and complicity of Massachusetts. Only conscience and principle concerned him—to the disgust and despair of the practical-minded.

Three years later, when John Brown visited Concord, Thoreau met a man ready to act his belief. When Brown was condemned to hang for the raid at Harpers Ferry, Thoreau at once dared to defend him. The local Abolitionist Committee, the committee of the newly born Republican Party, his closest friends even, sent word it was premature. "I did not send to you for advice but to announce that I am to speak"—and he did so, first at Concord, then at Boston. Because of this initial push, Henry Thoreau must be acknowledged one of the movers when Massachusetts finally shifted to an antislavery stand.

While this question was fevering his mind, it was hard for Thoreau to recall that wood ducks still dived in the Assabet. It was an actual effort to remember he had other lives to live, with further essays and possibly books to be written. In these final years, another barrier was his sense of obligation to his family. When his father died, Henry took over John Thoreau's business, shifted from the manufacture of pencils to the more profitable grinding of graphite. Yet the occasional essays continued: "Ktaadn," an account of his first trip to Maine, printed in the *Union Magazine*; in *Putnam's,* a description of his visits to Cape Cod. And, at James Russell Lowell's request, he was preparing for the new *Atlantic* the story of his second Maine-woods journey, "Chesuncook." It was to appear, during 1858, in the June, July, and August issues.

When Thoreau opened the July number, he was amazed to discover that Lowell had cut out from a passage describing a pine tree one sentence: "It is as immortal as I am, and perchance will go to as high a heaven, there to tower above me still." Thoreau had met with editorial tampering before, but not of this particular sort. Lowell had struck into Thoreau's very spirit. Hawthorne once jokingly remarked that Henry prided himself on coming nearer the heart of a pine tree than any other human being. But it is only needful to recall his love of the Hindu Scriptures to realize this was not just a matter for jesting. "I do not ask anybody to adopt my opinions," wrote Thoreau, "but I do expect that when they ask for them to print, they will print them, or obtain my consent to their alteration, or omission." This deletion seemed to imply that he could be hired to suppress his ideas. "I am not writing to be associated in any way, unnecessarily, with parties who will confess themselves so bigoted and timid as this implies." Was this the avowed policy of the *Atlantic*? The Editor never replied.

During Lowell's tenure, Thoreau sent no further essays. But when James T. Fields took over, and asked for more, he sent them—"Walking," "Autumnal Tints," and "Wild Apples." But Thoreau, correcting the proof of the first one, was a very sick man, destined never to see it in final print. Consumption, the scourge of his family, had at last struck him down—its attack postponed perhaps by his outdoor life, then aided by a heedless exposure; perhaps also by the unhealthy, dust-filled atmosphere of the graphite shop.

He had just returned from a trip to Minnesota made in quest of health and because the West always attracted him. By winter's end, he lay dying. Even in this final confinement, the outdoorsman remained serene. He was drawing up a list of what he had written. He was setting his journals in order. He was enjoying his friends. The porcupine quills that had guarded his independence were no longer needed. Beneath was his essential kindliness. Perhaps his one sorrow was the civil strife that was bleeding his country; while it lasted, he said, he could never get well.

He had grown to be admired and revered by many of his townsmen who had at first known him only as an oddity. Sam Staples remarked he had never seen a man dying in so much pleasure and peace. His neighbor, Reverend Grindall Reynolds, found him working over a manuscript. Thoreau looked up cheerfully, and whispered, for his voice was nearly gone, "You know it's respectable to leave an estate to one's friends."

"Henry, have you made your peace with God?" asked his pious Aunt Maria. "Why, Aunt, I didn't know we had ever quarreled!" On May 6, 1862, at nine A.M.—Henry always liked best the morning—he died in the forty-fourth year, ninth month, and twenty-fourth day of his living.

Soon after, Emerson wrote a brief biography of him—one of the finest things of its sort in the language. As for Alcott, he could hardly bring himself to realize that this oldest inhabitant of the planet had not chosen to stay and see it dismissed into Chaos—had instead slipped so quietly away from the spaces and times he had adorned with the truth of his genius. Eagerly Alcott had awaited one final work, a sort of all-inclusive "Atlas of Concord." But, had time and strength been granted, the book which Thoreau might more probably have written would have had the American Indian for its subject. In the year of his death his mind had been full of this topic. George William Curtis had seen him for the last time in the autumn of his final illness. "His conversation fell upon the Indians of this country, of our obligations to them, and our ingratitude. It was by far the best talk about Indians I have ever heard or read; and somewhere among his papers, it is to be hoped, some monument of his knowledge of them and regard for them survives." It does—but in amorphous form.

7

After Thoreau's death, further books, compiled from his periodical writings and from his journal, were brought out by his friends. The first of these was *Excursions,* in 1863, made up of such pieces as Henry's sister Sophia could readily collect. The volume included "Walking"—perhaps the finest brief statement of what he lived for—from the *Atlantic,* and the much earlier "Natural History of Massachusetts" and "A Winter Walk" from the *Dial.* In it also, among other things, appeared "The Succession of Forest Trees," a final lecture given before the Middlesex Agricultural Society. Here Thoreau set forth the results of his investigation into silviculture. Though written in his own fashion, it prompted the chairman for the day, George Boutwell, Governor of Massachusetts, to congratulate the audience on having heard an address so plain and practical.

In 1864 *The Maine Woods* appeared, bringing together Thoreau's accounts of his three expeditions into New England's northland. Not really a book, nor in the form in which Thoreau might finally have cast his material; yet here at its finest is Thoreau's zest for outdoor adventure and delight in it—save for hunting, which, as a sport, he regarded as a degradation to the human spirit. Here is his admiration for men of the wilderness like Joe Polis, the Indian guide; for Uncle George McCauslin and Tom Fowler, rivermen and pioneers, as native to the Penobscot as a brace of salmon. Because of its objectives, the book is not discursive like the *Week.* While less provocative or inspiring, it contains fewer pitfalls for the uninitiated. Henry wished it to be of help to campers. *The Maine Woods* makes excellent reading for men of action and for boys getting their earliest taste of Thoreau.

Cape Cod (1865) brought together what he had written on this subject. Unlike *The Maine Woods,* this book, departing from literal fact, has an architectural plan; but, like his travel literature in general, it is a reporter's record rather than an artist's finished product. The *Week,* thanks to the time granted at Walden, is the only one of Thoreau's excursions which escapes the limits of observant narrative. For his rudimentary scheme, Thoreau has used the record of his first trip to Cape Cod as his outline, working it into his later ventures. More than anything else he wrote, *Cape Cod* explores people along with the land and ocean. There is a warmth, a humor, a sympathetic understanding which keeps it a favorite with many readers.

Letters to Various Persons, collected and edited by Emerson, was also issued in 1865.

Thoreau, who had published only two books during his lifetime, was becoming an established author, with a lengthening list of works on each successive title page. Yet, before the next appeared, a check occurred in the march toward fame foreseen by Emerson and Alcott. In 1865, James Russell Lowell said his final say about Thoreau and the transcendental group with which he linked him. As Lowell ranked high, what he wrote carried weight. His *obiter dicta,* covering eleven pages in the influential *North American Review,* bear only minor resemblance to the opinions advanced, sixteen years earlier, in his review of the *Week.* Praise of Thoreau's artistry remains; little else. Lowell is perhaps the most intelligent commentator who chose to take very seriously Thoreau's "experiment" at Walden, looking eagerly for cheating and failure. He found Thoreau "a man with so high a conceit of himself that he accepted without questioning, and insisted on our accepting, his defects and weaknesses of character as virtues and powers peculiar to himself." Here, be it said, the critic exercises the age-old privilege of unfamiliarity with what his victim had actually written. Thoreau was indolent, continues Lowell, and excused his laziness by holding the normal activities of man unworthy. But then, Lowell had never tried to match strides with Thoreau in the woods, had never carried his surveyor's chain for him nor perambulated the bounds of Concord, had never laid walls, nor ground graphite, had not written *Walden* or the *Week,* nor seen the accumulated journals. Thoreau's solitary life, Lowell contended—having never joined the groups that gathered even at the Walden hut—cut him off so completely from men as to disqualify him as an observer of them. Thoreau, said Lowell, attacked success—as Lowell understood that word—because he lacked the qualities to achieve it. Selfish, and doing no man any good—the critic added—Thoreau lived for himself alone. But Lowell could not know about the day when a skinflint farmer claimed the prize which an Irish laborer in his employ had won, in the spading match, and Henry made up a purse to right this injustice, and burned the Yankee's ears with his blistering comments. How could Lowell know what strength Thoreau had lent to fighters in the battle, from James Anthony Froude in England to the Harvard undergraduates who acknowledged themselves heartened by what he wrote?

Alcott, who liked Lowell, was grieved by this review. Lowell, he felt, should never have written it—Thoreau and his class were so wide of his range and perception. "There is truth at the root of his estimates, and just enough to give credibility to them; but Henry's merits will survive all disparaging criticism, and justify his life and writings to unprejudiced minds." Yet, as Alcott foresaw, Lowell's strictures cannot be so readily dismissed.

There is a legitimacy about them. Thoreau stamped on the corns of worthy, public-spirited, philanthropic, hard-working, respectable men—men highly successful by average standards. He still does so. Lowell has become the spokesman for such as these. To realists, Thoreau's position will never make sense. He had a quixotic disregard for facts as they are in aiming for the right as it should be. "Either this man is joking or he's too impossible for words," scribbles one twentieth century student on the margins of a college library's copy of "Civil Disobedience." "But you don't grasp what he's driving at!!" scrawls another. Both protest and answer deserve to be weighed.

Thoreau's work kept coming out. In 1866, *A Yankee in Canada*—three chapters of observations first printed in *Putnam's*; the rest of the volume a catchall for such social and political essays as "Civil Disobedience," "Slavery in Massachusetts," and "A Plea for Captain John Brown." In it also is "Life Without Principle," given as a lecture in 1854. Only life lived *with* principle and purpose, Thoreau insisted, was worth living. Next, the manuscript journals: *Early Spring in Massachusetts* (1881), *Summer* (1884), *Winter* (1888), and *Autumn* (1892)—each book made up of appropriate selections from Thoreau's comments on nature, irrespective of the year in which written. Six years after the turn of the century, appeared a collected edition which included the journals in their chronological sequence. The first, ten-volume edition of the *Works* alone had preceded this issue by fifteen years. And in 1895, about half his verses were published under the title of *Poems of Nature*. A collection of "every available piece" of his verse appeared in 1943.

Both in composition and in reception, Thoreau's poetry has had a checkered career. Because of its unevenness, because his friends, when their first enthusiasm faded, persuaded him that prose was his higher medium, his verse had been relegated to a place of little importance. But the second quarter of the twentieth century has witnessed a revival. Thoreau's poetry, say its recent advocates, belongs not with the past but with the present—has no kinship, in its conscious and militant heterodoxy, with standard patterns such as Whittier, Longfellow, Bryant, and Lowell established. "Thoreau, like Emily Dickinson, . . . anticipates the bold symbolism, airy impressionism, stringent realism, and restless inconsistencies of twentieth-century poetry." Like these scholar poets, he too was searching for suggestions from all schools and times which he approved of—among them the classics, Chaucer's age, Ben Jonson's, and that of the seventeenth century metaphysicals, right down to Emerson's terse and gnomic didacticism. From the Greeks, of course, comes the sense of form so strikingly in evidence in "Smoke," perhaps his finest poem. Yet he loved to experiment with meters, searching for those most fitted to his moods.

When Emerson remarked that Thoreau's biography was in his verses, he meant, of course, his inner history. Thoreau's abrupt, rugged, image-crowded verse sprang from his effort to express the truth of a moment. Certainly, in the brief period during which he wrote it, Thoreau was deeply in earnest over his poetry. It is valid to argue that much of it is better than his own day supposed; that had not Emerson's advice turned him from it, Thoreau's poetry might have attained further importance. As it is, many readers will probably prefer to agree with Emerson's dictum: "The gold does not yet flow pure, but is drossy and crude. The thyme and marjoram are not yet made into honey."

With most of his work published, Thoreau's stature kept increasing through the years. His fame has grown like that heap of stones which marks where his cabin stood—a cairn begun from a single pebble picked up by Alcott at the margin of the pond, then added to by countless pilgrims from many lands. By dedicating his genius with such entire love—as Emerson put it—to the fields and hills and waters of his native town, Thoreau has proved them universal. Gone full-circle at the farthest Ganges, his Yankee words, blending even with the East, helped set up passive resistance. Translated into many tongues, his speech has reached many people. Scandinavians and Germans can read *Walden*; Czechoslovakians, Hollanders, Frenchmen, Russians, and Japanese. In England, toward the turn of the century, British liberals were carrying *Walden* in their pockets, as a spiritual sword and buckler against materialism and imperialistic sway. Indeed Thoreau must be held partly responsible for the revolt, as much social as political, of the British Labor Party. Under the title of *Life and Friendship,* pertinent selections from his writings were printed in London, to form a lay bible for its members—a pulp-paper edition cheap enough to put no great strain on the purses of such young pioneers as George Bernard Shaw, Beatrice and Sidney Webb, Edward Carpenter, and Ramsay MacDonald. Other Englishmen, of a somewhat different stamp, also discovered *Walden*. "The one golden book in any century of best books," wrote W. H. Hudson.

In Russia, during the Tsarist days, young revolutionaries found in Thoreau strength for endurance. And, in Europe and America, Thoreau speaks to a twentieth century sure to be known as the age of critical battle between the State and man's private integrity. He remains a David armed and ready to fight for himself and all men whenever government threatens to become a tyrant Goliath. Men often read meanings into classic writings which the authors could not possibly have intended—one explanation why, in a changing world, such books last. Thoreau himself countenances the practice when he advocates "sentences which suggest as many things and are as durable as a Roman aqueduct." So there is justification for reading into his attack on mercantilism, and into his one-man revolution against his government, a plea for the reappraisal of life's values in the modern industrial state, and a ringing challenge to totalitarianism. How the integrity of the individual is to be preserved within the structure of our nationalistic, intermeshed, highly mechanized, contradictory world is the twentieth century's problem, not Henry Thoreau's. But he will always speak to those who passionately love the elusive ideal of liberty; will remain "one of the prophets of that struggle for moral independence that is the deepest and most permanent of American conflicts."

To those thinkers who insist on the worth of the common man, Thoreau has become something of a hero. "When, in some obscure country town," he wrote, "the farmers come together to a special town meeting, to express their opinion on some subject which is vexing the land, that, I think, is the true Congress, and the most respectable one that is ever assembled in the United States."

8

How Thoreau lived and what he lived for is indeed the gist of all his writing—all the more reason for the reader to turn to the books themselves. Thoreau's style at its best is vigorous, terse, pungent; often epigrammatic, often racy and even colloquial, yet at the fit moment capable of a soaring beauty. Lover of spicy mountain blueberries, he had the knack of conveying that flavor to his prose. Sometimes his forcefulness betrayed him into outrageous paradox and overstatement, but he learned control of this quality as he grew older, till it became one source of his excellence. He had a remarkable gift for metaphor, and aimed, through pictures, to suggest thinking. He liked to deal in quaint, arresting comparisons, as when he spoke of a dog with a noseful of porcupine quills as the Arnold Winkelried of its race. He loved Indian names, and liked to work them, when he could, into his classic prose with a startling yet symphonious effect, like wildflowers decorating an urn in a Greek temple. In plebeian passages he was not above puns, rhymes within sentences, and other lighthearted tricks, and he was fond of alliteration, which he used for its music with a subtle skill. He spoke of the white-throat's whistle as a wiry sound. Such was the wealth of his truth, declared Emerson, that it was not worth his while to use words in vain.

Much that Thoreau wrote found its first expression in casual speech. Leaning against a fence and discoursing of the shortness of time since the supposed creation, he remarked to a friend, "Why, sixty old women like Nabby Kettle"—an ancient crone in the village—"taking hold of hands, would span the whole of it." This he repeated later in the *Week*, adding, "a respectable tea-party merely—whose gossip would be Universal History." Sentences like these in his journals, pieced together and filled out with descriptive and discursive matter, he gathered for his lectures. These frequently became essays, and then books. Like Emerson he was an intuitive thinker, and his best statements are in the sentences his craftsmanship built to hold them. Yet it does not do to underestimate his power with longer passages. In his best paragraphs, it would seem as if he had taken the hermit thrush as his model. Their intricate phrasings and rhythms flow with the pure and spiritual beauty of its song, and with its perfect unity.

Though Thoreau did not read fiction, because he disliked it, the portraits of people scattered through his work are as three-dimensional as reality itself. To see them one need but read what he has to say of Therien, the wood-chopper, of one-eyed Goodwin shooting muskrats from his flat-bottomed skiff, of Hugh Quoil, soldier of Wellington, drinking himself to death, an outcast in Concord. When he wished to, he could tell a story straight, with an arrowy directness, giving immediacy through the present tense—taking the reader with him.

Thoreau's stature as a critic of literature has steadily grown. "As good as anything ever written upon the subject," G. W. Curtis called the chapter on reading in Walden. "Books must be read as deliberately and reservedly as they were written," wrote Thoreau, and this attitude became habitual practice. Some of his enthusiasms suffer through his love of paradox, but the initiated can make their own adjustments. Characteristically, he is reported to have carried Whitman's Leaves of Grass around Concord "like a red flag." finding it "very brave and American"; and though he made the deductions he deemed necessary, he was, with Emerson, among the first to appreciate the genius of the new poet. Could he have arranged them, his comments on poetry would have made a significant essay. His critical articles are informative, analytical, and provocative. His essay on Carlyle is a clear-headed appraisal; what he says is still good after a hundred years. Furthermore, it contains some of the most perspicacious remarks on style to be found in American writing. His more occasional comments on books and reading are scattered like seasoning throughout his works.

As his life story reveals, Thoreau's absorption in nature began gradually, through a period of imperfect knowledge, till, at Concord, it developed into a religion, with the visible world as a symbol of the invisible. The force of this attitude, so fundamental to his thinking and feeling, never really weakened till toward the end, under the guidance of such classificationists as Agassiz and Gray—and here is a typically Thoreauvian inconsistency—he was led into the dry deserts of nineteenth century science. These deserts were probably never really dull to him, but they were wide enough to prevent his reaching that fruitful region in which scientists, seeking more significant answers than facts, at last allow the validity of intuition.

Yet the latter period of his observing is far from wasted. Particularly in one department of geographic exploration, Thoreau is a discoverer rather than just a pioneer. His detailed study of the behavior of natural bodies of water was a first move toward a region of scientific investigation which has not yet reached its full development. Very indirectly, the inhabitants of the Mississippi watershed owe a debt to Thoreau.

The purpose of the first editor of Thoreau's journals helped fix more firmly the American belief that his major contribution was as a naturalist. It has taken fifty years or so to modify that notion. Strictly regarded, Thoreau remains the expert amateur of nature. John Burroughs described him as so much more than a naturalist merely that he is to be thought of as a naturalist only in the largest sense. He had the philosopher's perception of identity, declared Emerson; "he referred every minute fact to cosmical laws." Sometimes, in a blinding flash or quiet revelation, his approach to comprehension fashioned mystical passages like that, in "Chesuncook," on the pine tree.

"I heartily accept the motto, 'That government is best which governs least,'" Thoreau wrote in "Civil Disobedience." Like many Americans, he noticed government mainly in times of crisis, and, like his fellow Americans, he blamed it for its iniquities. But those who hold that his political doctrine is mere anarchy do not analyze his import. His attacks on government are Thoreau keeping himself and mankind at the topmost bent, refusing compromise for expediency, demanding and expecting the noblest and best. "Seen from a lower point of view, the Constitution, with all its faults, is very good; the law and the courts are very respectable; even this State and this American government are, in many respects, very admirable, and rare things, to be thankful for, such as a great many have described them; but seen from a point of view a little higher, they are what I have described them; seen from a higher still, and the highest, who shall say what they are, or that they are worth looking at or thinking of at all?" Though he will remain the representative American in his insistence on the individual's right to self-determination, he never denied the value of enlightened communal action. He never gave up hope. The muck of man's imperfect institutions, his wars and outrages against himself, Thoreau compared to the mud at the bottom of Concord River; the water-lily became his symbol for man's emergence.

His quixotic protest against flogging, which terminated his two weeks' tenure as grammar-school instructor, has become unnecessarily famous. Much more significant is his statement that an experiment performed before the eyes of students, and with their active participation, is worth weeks of conventional teaching. As conducted by the Thoreau brothers, Concord Academy employed pioneering methods which the passage of a century has made common. Finally, he believed there should be no such thing as graduation, and held it a fault that in his day there was no adequate system for adult education.

Thoreau was among the first in America to recognize the rightness and validity of functional architecture, and, in *The Maine Woods,* he praised, as the most honest dwelling, the lumberman's log cabin. But he also foresaw the evil results that must inevitably follow what the lumberjack was hired to do. Written in a day when there still seemed no end to America's resources, this becomes a significant statement: "We shall be reduced to gnaw the very crust of the earth for nutriment." It would be worth while, he thought, in each village to appoint a committee to see that the beauty of the town receive no detriment. Highways must not be left narrow. "The road should be of ample width and adorned with trees expressly for the use of the traveller. There should be broad recesses in it, especially at springs and watering-places, where he can turn out and rest, or camp if he will." He believed that natural resources, like beneficial ideas, should be free as air; should belong to mankind inalienably.

For all these things, and others, Thoreau has become one of America's great. Yet among his various claims, perhaps his greatest value will remain his power to open magic casements on the verities of nature. As the lava flow of our material civilization licks up the natural beauty of earth, Thoreau's poetical, pictorial writing may become increasingly the greatest gift he bears. Each day brings its fresh discoveries, its wonder, which he delights to impart.

27. NATHANIEL HAWTHORNE

M<small>EANWHILE</small>, Nathaniel Hawthorne, endowed with a more earthy nature than Emerson and a more realistic mind than Thoreau, watched, not without misgivings, the divine madnesses of Concord. Toward the circle of aspiring young men at the feet of Emerson he was critical, and though he admired Thoreau's independence (together they had boated on the Concord River) he was aware in himself of no response to what he called the "wild, original strain" in this experimenter with life. In "The Celestial Railroad" he was to satirize the dreams of transcendentalism, and in *The Blithedale Romance* he was to delineate the follies of humanitarianism as he had witnessed them during his stay at Brook Farm. His boredom in the society of Bronson Alcott deepened in that of Margaret Fuller to active dislike. The celestial vagaries of Concord confirmed in him his own somewhat sardonic studies of a moral law which offered no millennia but only bitter proofs of its operation in the sufferings of human beings. He retreated hastily from Brook Farm; he never contributed to the *Dial*; and he remained silent in Emerson's study and at the meetings of the Saturday Club. That his writings as a whole aimed to refute or annotate the current gospels of self-reliance, the oversoul, intuition, and similar fantasies, no proof exists in his prefaces or in his fiction itself. Yet there in Concord he dwelt, a neighbor down the street, writing the romances which Emerson thought lacked "inside"; there in the midst of the transcendental storms he meditated quietly; he was silent, serene, almost quizzical. For he was, so he must have thought to himself, no prophet, no reformer, no diver into the God within him, even if he was himself in love with the invisible landscape.

Soon after Hawthorne's birth in 1804, circumstances intensified his innate Puritan characteristics: his analysis of the mind, his somber outlook on living, his tendency to withdraw from his fellows. Yet if, from the first, in the quiet household of his widowed mother at Salem, during a period of lameness which kept him out of sports, or throughout the summers in remote Raymond, Maine, he became increasingly introspective, he had few personal problems of mind or spirit. Already he was detached, and if the most characteristic paper in his juvenile magazine, the *Spectator,* concerned his own solitude, we must not conclude that melancholy had claimed him as its victim. Quite the contrary. During the four years at Bowdoin College (1821–1825) appeared that self-command which intimated that his ways of loneliness were the result of a positive choice. He had already learned to contemplate cheerfully subjects which other men as normal and healthy as he avoided. Unlike his classmate, the social, gregarious Longfellow, he was no prize winner in the curriculum; though he loved cards, wine, fishing, and shooting, his conviviality was distinctly limited, subordinate to a love of quiet. Yet these "accursed habits" of solitude, as he once called them, failed to make him unhappy. In them, as a matter of fact, lay the origins of his life of the intellect and spirit. Out of such habits, formed in the first twenty-one years of his life, were to be born Ethan Brand, Hester Prynne, Zenobia, and the other lonely children of his imagination.

This secret space in his mind, to which he ever afterward returned, and which sheltered him from the turmoil of contemporary America, had early become the center of his being. Though we cannot regard the meditative creations in his first fiction as accurate self-portraiture, it is demonstrable that he had devoted some of his early leisure to writing. He had already at Bowdoin, mentally at least, limned the college for the prose of *Fanshawe,* his first novel. There remained only one step to fix him in this course of life; and this he took on his return from Brunswick: he became a "Salemite." For, he said, "I felt it almost as a destiny to make Salem my home." The quiet streets, the lonely house, the necessity for solitude, and his innate passion for the written word, all counseled a procedure whose continuance for twelve long years has never been satisfactorily explained. Probably the reasons are not really mysterious: presumably, he had experienced no romantic disillusionment nor grief. Those eyes which Bayard Taylor said could flash fire, never viewed coldly men's lives in the busy world. Perhaps, as he wrote Longfellow later, he merely drifted into this role of recluse. Or perhaps—why not, if we think of his satisfaction in his later fame?—he meant in this Philistine America to glean the rewards of his painful solitude; namely, independence and literary success. At any rate, here he sat long in his "accustomed chamber," writing, revising, and burning the sketches and tales; perfecting his delicate craft of the symbol, of allegory, of the few themes and oft repeated character-types which were to haunt forever the minds of those who know New England.

When in 1837 he emerged from the chamber where his "fame was won," in his hand was his first published collection of prose, *Twice-Told Tales,* and primarily in his heart the image of Sophia Peabody, to whom he was married five years later, with enriching consequences to his personal life and to his writing. Neither his recognition as an author (by Poe, among others) nor his new, happy companionship in a solitude which he never really relinquished, altered his literary aims. He was, like his own Holgrave in *The House of the Seven Gables,* deepened and softened; but his broadening through associations with the workaday world as a measurer in the Boston Customhouse, as a laborer in the Brook Farm Community, and as a surveyor in the Salem Customhouse seems, in retrospect, illusory.

His daily world was real enough, of course. Few writers comprehended better the shallow objectives of the contemporary magazine; as contributor and editor, and in association with Samuel Goodrich ("the moralistic, sentimental Peter Parley"), he knew the quality of American readers. His long apprenticeship in fiction was served chiefly as a contributor of short pieces to magazines and annuals; this modified his theory of the romance and the novel and presumably influenced his techniques as a writer. By writing he earned his bread, even composing stories for boys and girls. He worked hard at Brook Farm, and in both customhouses, and he manifested a shrewd interest in local politics. Yet in spite of these concessions to everyday affairs, of an acquisitive strain in money matters and a fondness for a strong cigar or an oath, his thoughts were elsewhere. Dearer to him than these associations with the common man, in whom he was mildly interested, dearer even to him than his near-transcendentalist Sophia, who never quite entered the shadows of his darkest imaginations, dearer than all these, were his ancient vows in the lonely chamber. In 1849 he sat down and, using the craft he had learned in silence, wrote, hardly blotting a line; in four months he had finished *The Scarlet Letter.*

The mid-century mark and the two following years beheld the apogee of Hawthorne's art *(The Scarlet Letter, The House of the Seven Gables,* and *The Blithedale Romance,* as well as his best collection of tales); and the decade was rounded out by his exquisite, if rather tired, study of Puritanism in a Latin environment, *The Marble Faun* (1860). The lacuna of eight years in his formal writing we owe to a sudden dislocation in his New England life: his appointment by President Franklin Pierce to the American consulship in Liverpool, with a subsequent sojourn in Italy. Even during the English interlude Hawthorne's pen and notebooks were busy with writing fated to be posthumous: *Septimius Felton; The Dolliver Romance; The Ancestral Footstep;* and *Dr. Grimshawe's Secret.* Thus, unlike Irving, he never renounced his youthful dreams; the *English Notebooks* tell the story of his busy life but also of literary hopes deferred. Moreover, the salty vigor of this exegesis on England was an admirable substitute for a novel. As we read *The Marble Faun* and ponder over the lethargy of Hawthorne's last years, it is difficult to avoid the conclusion that in his speculations he had reached a baffling wall. Over and over in fragmentary first drafts he turned to the jejune symbols of spider and bloody footstep. Indeed, his sudden death, during a walking tour with Pierce in 1864, seemed a natural ending for a mind which could go no farther in the moral labyrinth it had entered a half-century earlier as a dreaming boy in Salem.

2

In any study of Hawthorne's art, his life story must be regarded as causative. Fixed from birth in his Puritan attitudes, he would, we may believe, have been Hawthorne had he lived for many years upon the *rive gauche* or the banks of the Mississippi. It was so in Rome; Italy failed to alter the underlying mechanisms of his Puritan mind. For he was completely integrated, until his fiftieth year, with the soil and spirit of a New England which had bred and indoctrinated his introspective forebears. He was not unlike Major William Hathorne, that "grave, bearded, sabled-cloaked and steeple-crowned progenitor,—who came so early [to America], with his Bible and his sword," or his ancestor Judge Hathorne, the persecutor of witches. Such antecedents continued to be a powerful influence in his character as a writer. We can understand New England without Hawthorne; yet Hawthorne without New England we cannot comprehend. She was literally of his blood and brain; her scenes and her people form the stuff of his romances, and his own forefathers revisit the upper shades in his pages. What he wrote of New England was not merely "local color"; rather it was the subconscious mind of the New England Hawthornes vouchsafed a voice in this unregenerate descendant of theirs.

Yes, it was the breath of his nostrils, this study of an invisible world, of whose existence he was in his way as firmly convinced as were Emerson and Thoreau. Refusing traffic with philosophic thought, both of the past and of his New England contemporaries, he clove his own path through the trackless realms of the moral life; his Puritan mind easily understood the introspective processes which made Emerson certain, Thoreau skeptical, and himself judicial concerning the meaning of life. That curiosity concerning the two fundamental relationships, of Man to God and Man to Man, which motivated the literature of New England, he shared, though his conclusions were neutral, inconclusive, even pessimistic. For he experienced with a peculiar intensity the transcendentalists' continuance of Jonathan Edwards' exploration of moral meanings. The light was the same; only the lens of Hawthorne's mind was different. Thus the spiritual questioning of his tales and novels far outweighed their ballast of New England history and background; it even subordinated his beautiful craftsmanship.

It was this memorable art of his which distinguished him from Emerson and Thoreau, an art which included his distillations of historical episodes into moods; soft color schemes of red, white, and black; rhythms of sentence and phrase which echo the harmony of his unified and reposeful life; symbols, sometimes inadequate and even absurd, but more often coefficients of the unseen moral laws which he was trying to communicate; and unforgettable case histories of men and women afflicted by guilt, or, as he called it, by "a stain upon the soul." Little of this he drew from books, apart from his beloved Bunyan, from Milton, or from Spenser, who inspired some of his allegory and even the name of one of his daughters, Una. From common incidents and from common men he wove his intricate web of the seemingly inevitable involutions of the moral pattern. Yes, except for an excusable contamination of the didactic in a few tales which he composed during his period of apprenticeship, he maintained toward all his laboratory researches into the human heart a singular detachment. His were grave and acute reflections upon the way in which the Puritan mind worked; it was, for almost the first time in American literary history, as the devoted Henry James was quick to see, the judgment of the artist upon familiar Puritan material. Thus he was akin to Poe; he anticipated James himself; and he was really the founder of the psychological novel in America.

This is a matter for mild marvel, this calm of Hawthorne amid the winds of literary doctrine. He seems to have been little affected by the conventions of the nineteenth century English novel; his indifference to the prevailing passion for the full, discursive narrative is particularly notable. In this sense, it may be argued that he never wrote what Dickens and Thackeray would have called a good story. In his beautiful letter of homage to Irving there is no trace of imitation, and his links with Charles Brockden Brown are tenuous; whatever he learned from the Gothic School he assimilated for his own precise objectives. Though different in nearly every other respect, he resembled Emerson in reading chiefly for confirmations of his own meditations: for example, his interest in the downfall of aspiring human beings through their higher natures found reassurance in Bunyan's compelling hint of the bypath to hell from the very gate of heaven. He was moved neither by the literary modes of the day nor by its criticism of his own aims. The pity recently bestowed upon him because his exposure to European culture was so belated; because, save for his sketchy intercourse with Herman Melville, fifteen years his junior, he worked alone without the give-and-take of literary peers; such pity for himself he never felt. Indeed, it may be questioned whether richer cultural influences than those of Salem and Concord would have altered either his themes or his art; these were predestinate, consecrated to his semiscientific study of the whorls of man's moral impulses.

"A most unmalleable man" he was, as he told his wife, thinking presumably of the concentration of his interests in his family, his work, and the dear lump of earth that he called New England. Yet, in a deeper sense he was, unlike Irving (or even Melville), unductile. He was a Toledo steel which bent, as in his sensibility during the writing of *The Marble Faun,* to an ancient culture, or suffered damascene ornamentation, as in his planned use of the Gothic plot in *The House of the Seven Gables*; but still steel he remained in his undeviating preoccupation with his quest for moral mysteries. This aim was the compass of his artistic life; this he followed unswervingly in his hundred-sixteen-odd tales and sketches and in his four great novels. Therefore we are not deceived by his indolence, his petulance, his intolerance of fools, or even by the deceptive softness of his prose. Our first artist in the novel had in him this vein of iron, this conscious dedication to the fulfillment of a few aesthetic-moral principles which so moved to admiration his disciple Henry James.

His is the record of a man pledged from youth to a special quest: the history, regardless of Hawthorne's provincial background, of the artistic mind. Modern scholarship has tried valiantly to right the balance, to show Hawthorne as a normal citizen of greedy, striving America. Some important readjustment of opinion has resulted: we understand better his interests in Brook Farm, the Civil War, or his own pocketbook. We certainly see him more clearly as a person, an enigmatic presence, in his dark cloak pacing the streets of Salem, but changed to robust flesh-and-blood. He was, we know, self-assured, sardonic, hardheaded. Such revaluations bring us closer to him as a man but only reaffirm the cryptic nature of his preoccupation. What was it? Sophia could not define what lay behind the veil, and his friends alluded to another Hawthorne hidden within the stalwart, outward man. He himself spoke of depths in his mind which he could neither fathom nor explain. In this transalpine region he heard the music, like Thoreau, of his own distant drummer. This intuition marked him out as a product of the New England Renaissance. In any case, no outward event in Hawthorne's biography is so important as this secret place in his mind of solitude and meditation; within this refuge, he drew the breath of life itself. When this failed him, he died.

3

The exact date of the composition of *Fanshawe* (1828), at once a culmination of Hawthorne's boyish experiments in writing and the beginning of his career as a romancer, is unknown. His later contemptuous destruction of all his amateurish work rendered this novelette—it contained only two hundred pages—a bibliographical rarity and helped to focus attention on its theme and character as a key to the origins and development of his early technique. Incidents in the awkwardly told story suggest Scott and the Gothic novel. The characters are thin and two-dimensioned, the dialogue pretentious; but a contemporary was right in declaring that in *Fanshawe* we may easily detect the weak and timid presence of all of Hawthorne's peculiar powers.

These powers were less apparent in young Hawthorne's style, which was still insecure, or in his use of plot, which was never distinguished, than in an instinctive predilection for certain basic character-types which were to reach fulfillment in a Phoebe, a Chillingworth, and a Dimmesdale. Indeed, in embryo, Phoebe, the sunny heroine of *The House of the Seven Gables,* as well as the villain of *The Scarlet Letter,* Chillingworth, and, in a lesser degree, the sullied idealist, Dimmesdale, are in this first novel. Had Ellen Langton, as has been asserted, a prototype beloved by Hawthorne in his youth, which endeared to him this type of woman, this antithesis of the sable Hester, Zenobia, and Miriam? Ellen is unmistakably the precursor of Phoebe, Priscilla, and Hilda. Another preliminary sketch is that of the "fiend-like" Butler, whose Satanism is probably derived from Hawthorne's persistent study of Milton. This crude anticipation of Roger Chillingworth confirms Hawthorne's early interest in the genus of the heartless villain, a type which he never succeeded in making altogether natural. In the end we are fascinated by the central character itself, an alloy of Byronic arrogance and Gothic gloom which Hawthorne spared his later characters. For, akin to Dimmesdale in his idealism, Fanshawe has none of the tremulous, lovable weakness of the unhappy minister:

The expression of his countenance was not a melancholy one: on the contrary, it was proud and high, perhaps triumphant.

Fanshawe is a forerunner of Hawthorne's long line of idealists (Fanshawe, Aylmer, Dimmesdale), and, though blurred by conflicting traits, the portrait reminds us of young Hawthorne himself, taking his lonely walks and imagining himself to be this solitary being, this high-minded man of thought.

Who would not desire, for an understanding of Hawthorne's art, a day-by-day record of his twelve years in the chamber while he was "the obscurest man of letters in America"? Of about sixscore pieces written during this period some were lost, some were burned, and some, he said in 1851, "might yet be rummaged out (but it would not be worth the trouble) among the dingy pages of fifteen- or twenty-year-old periodicals, or within the shabby morocco covers of faded souvenirs." All such apprentice work was unsystematic, desultory, essential to the delicate development of the artist's perceptive processes. We may deduce much from lists of the pieces in their order of publication: that about seventeen antedated the important commencement, in 1835, of the *American Notebooks;* that the rapid increase in such publications in this and the following three years (fifty-two essays, tales, and sketches) indicates a consciousness of power; that in the early years the essay seemed to be his favorite form. Yet, since the dates of composition are unknown, those stages by which Hawthorne's self-disciplines reached perfection in the few classic studies of isolation must, for the most part, remain conjectural.

4

Hawthorne's selection of nineteen pieces for the first series of *Twice-Told Tales* (1837) he based upon some fifty published contributions, and the second series (1842) upon some seventy-three; but these facts do not mean necessarily that the second volume included only later work. The third volume (*Mosses from an Old Manse*, 1846) completed, to all practical purposes, the canon of the Hawthorne short story or sketch; but five other collections, including *The Snow Image* (1852) and two posthumous volumes, were to appear before all the known fragments and bagatelles were available, and even now an occasional relic of "the accustomed chamber" is unearthed and republished.

Studying this period, we must abandon the idea of a consistent intellectual progression; we may note only over-all characteristics, and later relate these, if we can, to the more complex and sustained performances of his novels. In the sketches we detect unevenness in quality through the author's sensibility to the standards of the wretched magazines to which at first his literary fortunes were unhappily bound, and also in his early reliance upon bookish sources; and we are sometimes tempted to date the compositions according to the degree of their emancipation from these influences. Certainly after the establishment of his own unique savings bank, the first of the series of notebooks, he must have determined to lean almost wholly on those earthy observations, so characteristic of him, concerning the bizarre or the psychologically interesting:

The search [he wrote in 1844] of an investigator for the Unpardonable Sin; he at last finds it in his own heart and practice.

Here is a germ of "Ethan Brand." Indeed, in the rich soil of the notebooks may be found the seeds of many of Hawthorne's concepts concerning man in relation to man; he was no debtor to the platitudes of libraries.

The tales anticipate themes and characters in the longer narratives. If we look backward momentarily from novel to tale, the agonized, introspective Dimmesdale is in essence Parson Hooper; Chillingworth, subtly diabolized, is Rappaccini, brewer of poisons; and the perfectionist Hollingsworth carries us back to the folly of Aylmer who destroyed his wife's birthmark—and her life. Here, too, in the tales, are specimens of sins destined to reappear in the novels; in "The Gentle Boy" the Puritans cruelly persecute the Quaker child; in "Ethan Brand" the self-centered intellectual, slain in the limekiln, is found to have a marble heart; in "Roger Malvin's Burial" the youth leaves his friend to perish in the forest and is tormented by remorse. Our privilege in this early laboratory is to inspect each vial itself instead of the devil's brew in which are stirred the complicated relations of, for example, Hester, Dimmesdale, and Chillingworth.

Besides their exegetical service to the novels, the tales emphasize Hawthorne's matchless delineation of Puritanism in the seventeenth century. They constitute a minor compensation for the fact that only one of his novels deals with this epoch, with which, by reason of reading and temperament, he was so deeply familiar. "The Maypole of Merrymount," "The Gray Champion," "Howe's Masquerade," all historical pieces, give us the fruits of his profound knowledge of his ancestors' world, and intensify our regret that only *The Scarlet Letter* (though this is much) exists, among his major writings, to demonstrate his extraordinary gift for re-creating the world of the Winthrops and the Mathers. These seventeenth century tales are relatively few, but they have come to be a precious frame of reference for the great novel. Because of them we view it with more understanding, and had they never been written it assuredly would be less. Hawthorne pondered much on these Puritan precursors of his; he even wondered whimsically what they would have thought of him, their renegade romancer-descendant. Why in 1850 after the publication of *The Scarlet Letter* he wrote no more novels concerning seventeenth century Puritanism remains an enigma. The deeper Hawthorne resided in this period, and the tales concerning it are essential to our understanding of him.

Finally some of these short writings of Hawthorne's have a classic dignity —and perhaps an immortality—of their own, apart from their illumination of his craftsmanship or their record of his fealty to the seventeenth century. The number of the elect is few indeed; on the fringe of the large collection are such inanities as "Little Annie's Ramble" or such sentimentalities as "The Wedding Knell"; it is more difficult to discover divinity in Hawthorne's tales than in the early fiction of Irving or Poe. Many savor of the provinciality which seldom infects the novels. Undoubtedly the conventions of gift-book and annual shadow some of these pieces. They offer, too, very little advance in the technique of the short story; in their leisure, indefiniteness, and absence of precision they are reminiscent of Irving, whose influence over many a contemporary was no less real than it was subtly hidden. Yet for the creation in us of a single poignant mood (the quality recognized in them by Poe) they are perhaps without parallel. The utter loneliness of Parson Hooper wearing perpetually his black veil, of Young Goodman Brown who believes himself sharing the dark secrets of his friends, of Roger Malvin who deserts his comrade in the wilderness, or of Ethan Brand; the selfish perfectionism of Aylmer; the almost intolerable exposition of cruelty in "The Gentle Boy": all these moral distempers, through his special language of symbolism, Hawthorne makes us share.

In 1849 Hawthorne wrote in effortless fashion, after his long indenture to such themes and characters, *The Scarlet Letter,* his lovely novel "of human frailty and sorrow." It is too easy, from the moment that we mingle at the prison door with the women in hoods and the men in gray steeple-crowned hats until we stand beside Hester Prynne's grave, to undervalue Hawthorne's superb interfusion of fact and fancy in this tale of New England seventeenth century life: sincere in its way and aspiring, but brutish too, and often debasing, save as it could provoke the "spiritual warfare" in Hester's breast. What Hawthorne conveys of the olden time is less literal—though this element is also present, for example, in the portraits of Governor Bellingham or Mistress Hibbins—than might have been predicted from his skillful distillation of history in "The Maypole of Merrymount." Such modes of thought, our reading and the Puritan inheritance in our own minds confirm as true. There is no heavy-handed intrusion of theological doctrine or of local custom. Church priest, sermon, court of justice, and meetinghouse are here, but all are incidental to a persuasive reality of mind. Pearl could have passed an examination in *The New England Primer* or the Westminster Catechism; but Pearl is a living child, not an animated monograph on the nature of Puritan children. All that Hawthorne had heard by word of mouth of this past, all that he had read in the Mathers or Thomas Prince, and all that he had divined through his own mind of the Puritans, make the background of *The Scarlet Letter* as accurate as a town record but also as alive as the grim beadle himself or comely Hester Prynne. Perhaps the primary virtue of *The Scarlet Letter* is stylistic: its unity and perfection of tone.

This story of Hester Prynne, this slender thread of narrative in Hawthorne's most famous novel is no great affair as to originality or complexity. When, after our introduction to her and her memories on the scaffold, she recognizes on the skirts of the crowd the then slightly deformed figure, we perceive readily that it is her wronged husband bent on his revenge. What are to be the exact terms of the punishment of Arthur Dimmesdale, Hester's lover, or what will be the ultimate fate of each of the three in the triangle (or of little Pearl), we do not know. Nor do we care particularly, so surely has Hawthorne fascinated us by his clinic, in which three superior minds exhibit the deepening stains of guilt: in one freely confessed and ennobling, in another reluctantly unconfessed and debasing, and in the third deliberately concealed and poisonously malignant, until its owner is transformed into a monster. Thus the story pauses, resumes, and pauses; it is less a narrative than a problem discussed and rediscussed by many regroupings of all the characters. One fancies a resemblance to a play by Chekhov. Even the few incidents, such as Chillingworth's harrowing interviews with Dimmesdale or the proposed flight of Hester and Arthur, are merely prolongations of Hawthorne's diagnosis of the mortal hurts of his patients. The sins of these three are assumptions merely; we are not present at their commission, but, appalled, we watch the slow, relentless fires of subsequent remorse and revenge sear them all. How strange it seems, in contrast to the luxuriance of the letter and of Hester's nature, that this writer coolly turns his back on youth and desire to show us only the complex consequences of guilt! Yet in the tales, too, the initial violations of the moral law were hypotheses.

Nevertheless, as fellow students with Hawthorne of these moral maladies we are entitled to know something of their causes. With much more amplification than in the tales he tells us all that we need to know to understand how the natural sympathy between Hester and Dimmesdale—for their temperaments are complementary—deepened into passion. On the scaffold Hester recalls her home in England, and Pearl is the ever-present reminder of her lost youth; in similar fashion Dimmesdale remembers the happy days of his scholarly renown at Oxford. We see them clearly, these lovers, and Chillingworth too, the keen-eyed seventeenth century Casaubon who married Hester to mitigate his loneliness. All such memories, so delicately conveyed, give body to the story without altering the emphasis upon the later years. We think, of course, of Shakespeare. How well we seem to know by his similar double-time schemes the early days of a Hermione or a Falstaff! This presentness of the past, suggestive of Henry James and T. S. Eliot, one of Hawthorne's oft reiterated themes and the central idea in his next novel, *The House of the Seven Gables,* prevents *The Scarlet Letter* from being a mere truncated study of the arid years of middle age. Amid the other evidences of Hawthorne's subtlety of art we should never forget this delicate balance between the present and the past.

This long foreground, woven of reminiscence and allusion, this wholeness of the story, lifting it out of the stark framework of Winthrop's Puritan colony, strengthen our conviction that we are studying no timid trio reared in a fantastic theology but rather three high-minded persons facing dilemmas as ancient and as recurrent as all common experiences. The Puritan mechanisms, such as the emblazoned **A**, are not inherent in the tragedy, but represent only an era's fashions which might have counterparts in twentieth century conventions. The sting lies not in church laws, which receive no special emphasis, but in the pangs of conscience, which have never been monopolized by any particular group, not even by the Puritans. The sin, the consequences, and the resultant quandary are of all time. The "cool familiar stare" rebuking Hester, the festering wound of Dimmesdale's hypocrisy in the pulpit, the self-torment in Chillingworth's revenge, all these human emotions transcend the seventeenth century setting in which Hawthorne has chosen to pose his questions concerning the moral law.

If the issues ring true, unconditioned by the Puritan system, they also ramify into innumerable aspects of Hawthorne's inquiry into evil and isolation. Herein lies the superiority of Hawthorne's novels to his tales. Subtle moral questions are intertwined in complex interaction. We must phrase these as questions, and, characteristically, Hawthorne obliges with no definite answers: Was Chillingworth's capitulation to a marriage for which he was unsuited a sin? If so, is not his punishment in hideous discrepancy with his small fault? Or was his anterior absorption in learning, like that of Ethan Brand, his cardinal error? Why does his plan of revenge upon Dimmesdale, upon whom his hate battens, grow into an abnormal love? How can we explain the fact that Dimmesdale's descent to folly seems to begin, in accordance with Hawthorne's favorite quotation from Bunyan, at the gate of heaven, in a spiritual attraction for Hester? Why does his cowardice in not acknowledging his fault exalt him to heights of moral counsel to his people? Why does the confession of guilt free Hester from remorse? Indeed, why does the entire experience enrich and dignify her nature? Contemplating this regenerative power of sin, which so absorbed Hawthorne in his later study of Donatello, can we wish the evil undone? One could study endlessly other chemistry in Hawthorne's experiments: the telepathy between father, child, and mother, or the mysterious violation of Dimmesdale's personality by the leech. Thinking of such crude early tales as "Egotism or the Bosom Serpent," we marvel at the foliations of Hawthorne's ideas concerning guilt as a "stain upon the soul."

In his exposition of these complicated problems Hawthorne frankly employed fiction to study psychic case histories; in him, as already hinted, was a tough, cold streak, tempting him outside the personal relationships of his characters into indefatigable analysis of these specimens of moral experience. It is true that this semiscientific study sometimes chills the characters themselves, even in the richly human *Scarlet Letter*; at times, for example, the diabolized Chillingworth seems an incarnation of the passion of revenge. Yet in other instances Hawthorne loved the people whom he had created; like the great novelist he was, he relived their experiences as persons, and he had compassion upon them. "On Hester Prynne's story," he said quietly, "I bestowed much thought." In discussing the theme which always engrossed him, the violation of one personality by another, he was as tender toward Dimmesdale under the cruelty of Chillingworth as toward Ilbrahim in "The Gentle Boy." The fact is that *The Scarlet Letter* is a nobler book than the other novels partly because we remember these four troubled characters as individuals long after we have forgotten the rise and fall of their moral temperatures.

Thus Hester Prynne has the quality of the great characters in fiction who step from the pages of a book as living, breathing human beings. She is as real as Becky Sharp or the heroines of Shakespeare's plays. Reminiscent of Beatrice in "Rappaccini's Daughter," she is also the fully formed predecessor of the dusky, strong-souled women in the other novels, Zenobia and Miriam. Tall, regal, somber-eyed, black-haired, her presence spells calm and strength, especially beside the less stable Dimmesdale, or in contrast with the thin, cold personality of the scientist Chillingworth. If in her nature there is a hint of the voluptuous, this is absorbed in the complete naturalness of her longing for the domestic life of which she has been so cruelly deprived. In her skill with the needle, in her reposeful guidance of Pearl, in her wifely (so to speak) control of the minister's hysterical emotions, in her interviews with him, with her child, or with both—interviews which seem like satires upon the fireside scenes for which Nature designed her—she is a true woman, born to comfort and command. Her tragedy is not altogether in the loss of public respect which she has learned to evaluate accurately or in that of private remorse which she has expelled in good works for others, nor even in the loss of Dimmesdale himself, but rather in the frustration, through the customs of the world, of her deep affections. Hawthorne's exposition of her spiritual development is admirable; from the timid, erring wife, shrinking before her husband, she becomes a dreamer of a new moral order, a free spirit almost disdainful of the feverish obsessions of Dimmesdale and Chillingworth.

Dimmesdale himself enjoys no such resurrection of the spirit. Yet his lineage as a character-type seems longer than Hester's: into him entered Fanshawe, Parson Hooper, and the scholar-idealists of the tales; never again was Hawthorne to paint this portrait so well. Weaker physically than Hester, he seems to demand her maternal strength. His nervous uncertainty is balanced against her repose and the intellectual assurance of the iron Chillingworth. He has the intuition, the sensitivity to moral values, which was the finest flower of the Puritan preoccupation with the invisible world; all the more terrible are the consequences of his brief concession to grosser laws. An early torment has been the corroding concealment which the stronger Hester repudiated: *vitum crescit aliterque tegendo.* The next state in this decline is his subjection to the domination of Chillingworth, until, as in the scene in the forest, he is a broken spirit, craving, unlike Hester who desires more abundant life, only release and peace. "Hush, Hester, hush, the law we broke . . ." On his breast, in effect, is the letter; gone, dead, is the dreamer of the old Oxford days; such is the penalty of guilt upon the highly wrought nature of the idealist.

Hester Prynne and Arthur Dimmesdale leave little to be desired; they are complete. The two other major characters, Roger Chillingworth and Pearl, lack finish. They suggest the benefits which Hawthorne might have received from the wise criticism of a circle of peers; there is a provincial air about them, which reminds us of the shadowy figures in the tales. The truth is that in neither of these did Hawthorne's love of the character itself transcend his interest in the abstract moral state symbolized. Chillingworth is more convincing than his prototypes, but he is still an exercise in Hawthorne's study of the process of degeneration. He is theatrical too; in him recurs Hawthorne's weakness for melodrama, which sometimes runs wild in the other novels in drowning or murder. The physical correspondence to the spiritual nature, well integrated in the studies of Hester and Dimmesdale, is in Chillingworth more rudely done, and even verges on the absurd, in the gradual growth of his hump, and the baleful red light from his eyes. Hawthorne's debts to Milton's Satan and Spenser's Archimago are apparent in this creation of an agent who must force the minister to confession. Chillingworth is a pathological study of revenge.

It is curious that Pearl too seems a product of the clinic rather than of the world of human beings in which Hester and Dimmesdale move so naturally, for she alone of the four characters is born of Hawthorne's own personal experience; Pearl is his little daughter, Una, adapted to the purposes of The Scarlet Letter. Her health, her elfin ways, her life and grace find parallels in the notebooks; we might expect her, for she was not the first of Hawthorne's many studies of childhood, to realize the same perfection of technique which distinguishes, for example, the portraits of the scholar-idealist. This is not so. In her beautiful union of the qualities of earth and air, in her precocious awareness of the dark currents of passion about her, she does indeed provoke reflections on the sensibilities of childhood; we think of a subtler treatment of the same theme in the story of Mamillius, in The Winter's Tale, who died of "thoughts high for one so tender." We are interested in the tension aroused in Pearl by the unnatural relations existing between her father and her mother, and in the strange emancipation following the latter's confession: "A spell," Hawthorne says, "was broken." Yet, as a child character, Pearl is often tedious and sometimes preposterous. Perhaps we could not give her up; her symbolic value is far from negligible; in Hawthorne's phrase she stands for "the rank luxuriance of guilty passion" and, at other times, for the youth and happiness which her mother has forever lost.

Any survey of *The Scarlet Letter* returns us ultimately to the ever-present inner compulsion in Hawthorne toward that frontier of human experience which is so close to the supernatural. In one way or another all of these unhappy persons relate their sufferings to things in heaven and earth not dreamt of in our philosophy. As the modern view has emerged of Hawthorne as realistic and even sardonic, we incline to find in his writings a half-sarcastic condescension toward man's wishful belief in a divine interference in his affairs. Certainly he seems to echo, with the implication of a negative answer, Cotton Mather's oft-repeated query: "What can I see of the glorious God in these occurrences?" From his comments upon his own tribulations, and indirectly from the novels and tales, we know that he thought living a basically grim business. It is possible that occasionally he is ironically treating as a fantastic illusion the hope that our petty fortunes elicit any attention from an indifferent, impersonal universe. There is, for instance, an air of mockery in his point of view toward Mistress Hibbins, and this skepticism he may have easily extended to the weak Dimmesdale's infantile trust in a divine guidance. Was Hawthorne at heart a realist, or even an incipient naturalist, secretly scornful of a man's attempt to ascribe his knaveries to the stars?

Though such a temper exists intermittently in his writing, it seems senseless to believe that Hawthorne's adumbrations of the occult are merely targets which he himself set up for derision. Rather, he shared a general disillusionment of the age, and often expresses an irony which links him with the pessimism of Herman Melville and Henry Adams. His iconoclasm was profound. He reflected what his age thought of the decaying Puritanism, and his skepticism forced him back upon a kind of meliorism not unlike George Eliot's or even the ambiguous reconciliation of Melville in *Billy Budd*. Indeed, Hawthorne and Melville introduce into American literature a spirit of tragic irony. For about these mysteries Hawthorne is uncertain; he does not know, he cannot say; he repeats the eternal questions which no amount of so-called "realism" ever quite silences. He is careful not to declare his credence in divine agencies; he never, for example, is more than vaguely suggestive about the transference of Hester's badge of shame to the anguished breast of Dimmesdale. In fact, the temper of the book hints at the fatuousness of such fancies, even of the vision of the **A** in the heavens; as in the other novels, the fulfillment of Maule's curse in the death of Judge Pyncheon or the reincarnation of the faun in Donatello. He hints rather that these are objectifications or delusions held by tormented souls. So Hamlet, but no one else, sees his father in his mother's chamber. Yet Hawthorne does not deny these possibilities either. Were the portents there for Dimmesdale? Or if not there, does it matter, if to him they seemed to exist? Symbol melts into fact. Through *The Scarlet Letter* flit these phantoms, either real or the creations of the characters' dreams. Everywhere bordering on New England is another land, whose geography human beings imagine but cannot chart.

5

The Scarlet Letter was published in the spring of 1850, and in August Hawthorne moved to the "Red House" in Lenox, Massachusetts. He was now forty-six years old. Though weariness from his supreme intellectual effort and sadness from the death of his mother in the preceding year had induced a lowered tone of body and mind, he was revived by the almost immediate recognition of his novel. "Mr. Fields tells me," he set down in his notebook May 5, 1850, "that two publishers in London had advertised *The Scarlet Letter* as in press." Yet so deeply had he drawn upon his inner strength that a revulsion of feeling came over him toward the book itself.

Before him lay the most active literary period of his career, as well as his seminal friendship with Herman Melville. If we include *A Wonder Book for Girls and Boys* (1851) and his campaign biography, the *Life of Franklin Pierce* (1852), he was to publish, before his appointment in the following year to the Liverpool consulate, no fewer than five volumes. With two of these, *The House of the Seven Gables* (1851) and *The Blithedale Romance* (1852), we now leave the shadows of *The Scarlet Letter*.

"Evil will bless and ice will burn," sang the blithe Emerson. Only for the strong, Hawthorne might have replied: only for a Hester Prynne or perhaps a Holgrave. On the contrary, evil not only destroys the weak with a terrible swiftness, as in the cases of Dimmesdale and Chillingworth, but it lays its dead hand on remote generations. Maule's curse, "They shall drink blood," was uttered in the seventeenth century; the guilt of the Pyncheons—this time the hypothesis is far off—had its sequel in the nineteenth century in the marred spirits of Hepzibah and Clifford Pyncheon and in the darkened lives of Holgrave and Phoebe. *The House of the Seven Gables,* appearing only a few months after *The Scarlet Letter,* is in some ways a reaction against the sustained tragedy of the latter; and its events are spread on a vaster canvas of space and time. By comparison *The Scarlet Letter* seems but a brief episode; *The House of the Seven Gables* emphasizes the infinite reaches of retributive action from the unseen world, from the Puritan settlement to this contemporary, friendly Pyncheon garden. Hawthorne shows the ultimate wrong done the Maules (of whom the daguerreotypist Holgrave was the descendant) in the persecution of Hepzibah and Clifford by the hypocritical

Judge Pyncheon. "Shall we never," says Holgrave in a striking speech, "have done with this corpse of the past?" Hawthorne's negative is implicit; the book is a modern cancellation of the freedom of the will. In contrast to Emerson's easy "The sun shines today also," Hawthorne shows us the present as frozen, moving slowly in the inexorable glacier of past actions. In its masterly presentation of this difficult theme, this novel, despite obvious mannerisms, may well justify preference for it over *The Scarlet Letter*.

Why did Hawthorne consider this book, as he wrote to Bridge, "more characteristic of my mind, and more proper and natural for me to write"? He could hardly have referred to his plot, so obviously indebted, even in the intermezzo of Alice Pyncheon, to the Gothic romance, and so artificial in its denouement as to invite a smile at his playthings: ghostly music, manuscripts, and hidden panels. His narratives, such as the essential one in this "romance" of the Pyncheon and Maule families, are apt to be merely regroupings of characters, with solutions easily prefigured by the reader. The melodrama in Judge Pyncheon's demise is like the sensational deaths in the other novels, typical of a weaker phase of his art. What did he mean by his preference? Perhaps its quiet temper of contemplation? Perhaps the everyday events and scenes which differentiate this book from *The Scarlet Letter* and make its predominant tone as peaceful as his own tranquil days in Salem and Concord? It is a reposeful record of places and persons studied with an intimacy denied him in his imaginary companionship with Dimmesdale, Chillingworth, and Hester Prynne. Thus, in spite of ancestral curses, a theatrical villain, and a gloomy thesis concerning the past, the romance exhales a spirit of happiness as fresh as Phoebe's roses. Hawthorne's craft of the symbol now has a light, shyly humorous cast, alien from that of the macabre, crimson letter; Hepzibah's hens, the blue Davenport china, the tinkling shop bell are far from the baleful world of Chillingworth. *The House of the Seven Gables* owes little to the darkness of the Puritan past; it is "a legend prolonging itself, from an epoch now gray in the distance, down into our own broad daylight."

"The curtains are more drawn," wrote Herman Melville of *The House of the Seven Gables,* "the sun comes in more." Yet Hawthorne's recurrent themes, concerned only tangentially with the disintegration of old families and with the decay of an ineffectual New England aristocracy, suffered the usual laboratory tests through the characters. Each person in the story represents a culmination of interests explored in early writing and each is also (unlike *The Scarlet Letter*) a composite of living individuals. Here is the innocent and happy Phoebe, halfway between Ellen Langton in *Fanshawe* and Priscilla and Hilda of the later novels; Judge Pyncheon with his evident kinship to Chillingworth, Westervelt, and "the model" in *The Marble Faun*;

and, in particular, Clifford the artist, reminiscent of Owen Warland (in "The Artist of the Beautiful") or of Dimmesdale, without the latter's Puritan fiber. Hawthorne's investigations are, as always, double-edged; he studies not merely evil itself but its effect upon various textures of mind. The ancient wrong engraves itself in different degrees of indelibility upon different characters. "Let the black flower blossom as it may." Over the two contrasted women, the faded Hepzibah and the blooming Phoebe, the shadow of the past shifts uneasily. In poverty and loneliness the spinster is broken by the tragedy of Clifford, while Phoebe experiences a mild, nameless sadness in the aftermath of a sin in which she had no part. The range of Hawthorne's experimentation is well illustrated in this particular antithesis between the two novels: the impact of evil on Hester Prynne is direct and personal; upon Hepzibah and Phoebe it is remote, indirect, impersonal.

After the contrast of Holgrave with Judge Pyncheon—that is, of a robust goodness with a robust evil as responses to life—we are drawn irresistibly to the most memorable character in the book, Clifford Pyncheon, the hypersensitive artist, the man with his skin inside out. Disregarding the temptation to connect Clifford's suggestibility with a strain, well controlled, in Hawthorne's own nature, we observe the author's persistent interest in weak souls doomed to combat frustrations which even the strong might bear with difficulty. The nature of this unstable being is delicately suggested; he bursts into tears at the sight of a monkey, aghast at spiritual and physical ugliness. Perhaps the episode of Clifford's thirty years in prison is unfortunate; the ordeal intimates that Clifford's weakness may conceal an inner strength. He is Hawthorne's only complete neurotic; at times almost revolting, he elicits the tenderness of Hepzibah, the cruelty of Judge Pyncheon, and the wisdom of Holgrave.

Possibly the first three novels (excluding *Fanshawe*) exhibit progressively an abandonment by Hawthorne of all objectivity in the novel form. As *The House of the Seven Gables* is a step removed from the austere world of *The Scarlet Letter,* so *The Blithedale Romance* is a bolder revelation of Hawthorne's own experiences, and of his own methods as a psychological novelist. For in the pages of this tale appear, despite his denials, Hawthorne's memories of Brook Farm, and also his confessions concerning his role as a spiritual "Paul Pry":

It is not [he remarks] a healthy kind of mental occupation, to devote ourselves too exclusively to the study of individual men and women.

The personal tone of *The Blithedale Romance* is due to such autobiographical asides, to the reader's suspicion that Zenobia (and perhaps Hollingsworth and others) have actual Concord prototypes, and to Hawthorne's use, for the only time in a novel, of the first person singular. No one can positively identify Miles Coverdale as Nathaniel Hawthorne, an alienated member of the Brook Farm community. Yet his shy, thoughtful ways so closely resemble his creator's that, for good or ill, we are unable to think of Coverdale as merely the apotheosis of the observer type so dear to Hawthorne from the early sketch of "David Swan" to *The Marble Faun*. Presumably *The Blithedale Romance* is Hawthorne's most intimate study of the mind; there is something shameful, as he suggests, in knowing so well "the diseased action" of the hearts of Priscilla, Hollingsworth, and Zenobia. In fact, the tragic dialogue between the two last-named characters, like the drowning of Zenobia, comes as a shock against the quiet friendliness of the episodes at the farmhouse or at "Eliot's Pulpit."

Thus, in spite of the disarming preface, and the fact that only special traits of Margaret Fuller or of Emerson are exploited, it seems likely that Hawthorne was easing his bosom of the perilous stuff of Brook Farm. "I saw," Coverdale says of Hollingsworth, "in his shame nothing but what was odious." This portrait of a fully rounded Ethan Brand, of a humanitarian who, says Zenobia, is all "self, self, self," is not lacking in bitterness, even as the description of the Blithedale crops is not wanting in humor. The neighbors, who remarked that even the cows laughed at this spectacle, added that the Blithedale farmers

hoed up whole acres of Indian corn and other crops, and drew the earth carefully about the weeds; and that [they] raised five hundred tufts of burdock, mistaking them for cabbages; and that, by dint of unskilful planting, few of [their] seeds ever came up at all, or if they did come up, it was stern-foremost.

Certainly the book has not lessened our curiosity concerning Hawthorne's relations with the Brook Farm experiment, and his covert speculations about Emerson, Margaret Fuller, or Orestes Brownson are more exciting than his flimsy plot of mistaken identity, secret marriage, hypnotism, and suicide.

Besides studying the naïve story of *The Blithedale Romance* and its secret satire on contemporary persons and doctrines, we should look through Hawthorne's microscope at the souls of the four characters. The gold-toothed, ludicrous Westervelt is not an unworthy colleague of Hawthorne's other villains, and Coverdale is something of a prig. From his arboreal or urban perches he sees and hears more than he deserves; even if he is, as he announces in the ridiculous last line of the book, in love with Priscilla, he is, unlike Kenyon in *The Marble Faun,* a rather absurd Nosy-Parker. Yet the exposition of Hollingsworth's hardness of heart bears the imprint of Hawthorne's best work. This delineation of the reformer is too explicit, but the character is a magnificent supplement to the other investigations of those men who have surrendered themselves to an overruling purpose. Never, repeats our analyst, is the devil more ingenious than in developing egotism under the guise of philanthropy. Hollingsworth injures Priscilla, kills Zenobia, and is himself "a cold, heartless, self-beginning and self-ending piece of mechanism!" Thus we travel again the old bypath described by Bunyan; Hollingsworth's hypocrisy and selfishness began in a dream of virtue.

The Blithedale Romance depends for body and warmth upon one character. Zenobia, as imperial as her Palmyran namesake, is a freer study of the nature of women than Hawthorne elsewhere permitted himself, even in her sister-characters, Hester and Miriam of The Marble Faun. The three novels containing this type of Oriental, passionate woman are richer in tone, for this very reason, than The House of the Seven Gables, which lacks even guarded exploration of questions which could not have been absent from his singularly complete investigation of the moral impulse. The two alternating stage sets, of idyllic countryside and crowded city, are really only backgrounds for the stormy emotional experiences of this commanding character. Wearing her symbolic crimson flower, remembering some mysterious liaison with Westervelt, Zenobia is a complex of veering queenly moods, of arrogance and pity toward Priscilla, of condescension toward Coverdale, and of tempestuous love and hatred toward Hollingsworth. Zenobia is the lifeblood of the somewhat anemic Blithedale Romance. Into her Hawthorne poured his reflections concerning the future of woman; in her Hester's freedom of speculation becomes dynamic. Our curiosity about her kinship with Margaret Fuller is secondary to the fact that Hawthorne would create such a character. She suggests, like Miriam, his scrutiny of more violent human passions than those regarded as legitimate material for a novelist of the nineteenth century.

6

Several influences conspired to render The Marble Faun, Hawthorne's last work of fiction published during his lifetime, far more different from the previous novels than were these three from the preparatory sketches and tales. The Scarlet Letter, The House of the Seven Gables, The Blithedale Romance, all issued within a period of three years, were an inevitable culmination, in temper and technique, of this apprenticeship. Yet a space of seven or eight years, of whose nonproductivity Hawthorne is acutely conscious in his illuminating Preface, had intervened since he had meditated on Hollingsworth and Zenobia. He was older, and his age is evident not merely in the tone of The Marble Faun, in its note of tranquillity or resignation, but in the stiffening of his prejudices toward the novel form. We observe, in particular, his indifference to plot in his contemptuous evasion of a solution for this story, his disdain of adequate motivation in the obscure allusions to Miriam's past, and his speculations concerning the twilight land of the supernatural even to the point of ironic fantasy in the implications concerning the reincarnation of Praxiteles' faun in the modern Italian gentleman Donatello.

Secondly, the penetrating experience, not of Concord but of ancient Rome, dyed his mind even in these later years, with tints of an older civilization. Basic change in his outlook on life there could not be, but forum, campagna, and Italian peasant stirred his sensibilities, creating a conflict of ideologies in this novel absent in those rooted in the New England scene. He was now writing, as he says in the Preface, "of a sort of fairy or poetic precinct." Looking back toward the years in America, he set down the familiar, revealing, ironic words:

No author, without a trial, can conceive of the difficulty of writing a romance about a country where there is no shadow, no antiquity, no mystery, no picturesque and gloomy wrong, not anything but a commonplace prosperity, in broad and simple daylight, as is happily the case with my dear native land.

In addition, *The Marble Faun* received the benefits of a long incubation. He began it in Florence in 1858, but he revised the entire work on the "broad and dreary sands of Redcar, with the gray German Ocean tumbling in upon me, and the northern blast always howling in my ears." Thus he created these "Italian reminiscences" out of complete maturity, out of a new life, and out of a perspective of quiet afterthought. *The Marble Faun* was inevitably different.

For these reasons, like a quiet river flows on the tale of Miriam, beloved of Donatello, the child of nature and Italian antiquity; restful as a happy dream. Sometimes, it pauses in the slack water of the guidebook descriptions of Rome, which so endeared the book to contemporary Americans but which bore a generation more familiar with the scenes, readers uninterested in the forgotten travel books of a Nat Willis or a Washington Irving. In its way *The Marble Faun* is identified with Rome as *The Alhambra* is with Granada. In the catacombs, in the Forum, in the Italian plains, the book lingers, turning to action only in the arresting episode of the Tarpeian rock when Donatello, obeying, doglike, the bitter, unspoken wish in Miriam's eyes, hurls her persecutor to his death.

It is disturbing to discover how the passages in Hawthorne's notebooks on fountain, statue, and gallery, have found their way, almost unrevised, into the novel, and how frequently the analysis of the characters is retarded by this enchiridion of ancient Rome. Yet, in the end, we must return to his study of the moral problems of New Englanders astray amid the Latin civilization. Here are once more the old, unanswered questions: Hawthorne has changed his skies but not his riddles. Against the backdrop of the Italian campagna or the Roman carnival (instead of Boston, Salem, and West Roxbury), Kenyon, Hilda, Miriam, and Donatello experience and discuss the ruthless influences of the past, the blight of wrong upon the completely innocent, the fellowship of sinners, and the regenerative power of sin. Between the New England characters and the Roman setting exists a marked incongruity; Hawthorne's transference of his themes to Italy proclaims the persistence of his obsessions.

One unique quality of the book depends upon Hawthorne's special use of these foreign instruments to support his reasoning concerning the moral law. The splendor of the Catholic church leaves our New Englander merely curious, but in the device of the confessional he finds confirmation for his own psychological convictions; to the priest Hilda lays bare her troubled soul. In particular, since the faun belongs to the race of primitive peoples, we may study natural innocence. In Donatello's loss of the virtues of Eden by the sin of Cain, Hawthorne poses again the problem of his New England ancestors, the "Fall of Man." Not only does he study the effects of gross evil upon utter innocence, but for perhaps the only time he asks directly questions concerning the origins of evil, a kind of speculation which, for the most part, he left to his friend Herman Melville.

Whatever the causes, Hawthorne's age, his exhaustion of the normal problems in evil, or the influence of this Latin civilization, in which he must have apprehended moral depravities incommunicable to his New England readers, it is certain that in *The Marble Faun* he conveys to us by implication dark aberrations of the human spirit. Kenyon the observer, like Coverdale, may reasonably be Hawthorne himself, and Hilda is, with her exaggerated horror of "moral evil," an idealized portrait of Sophia Peabody Hawthorne. These two are as normal as Coverdale and Phoebe, whom they strongly resemble. The other three persons, however, the theatrical "model," Miriam, and Donatello, lead us into moral caverns measureless to man.

The model, least motivated of Hawthorne's motiveless villains, never, in spite of his conversations with Miriam, quite emerges from his supernatural world. Was Hawthorne thinking of the Wandering Jew? He hints that this persecutor of Miriam has a kind of immortality, that he is demonic, and that with him Miriam has been guilty of some nameless crime. Such hints and the otherwise pointless allusions to Beatrice Cenci intimate that Miriam's sin is incest, already considered obliquely by Hawthorne in one of the tales. This may account for the hopelessness of Miriam, and for the barrier between her and the reader, who never knows her with pity and understanding as he knows Hester and Zenobia. Again we reflect on the extent of Hawthorne's studies in evil, and again we speculate on possible discussions between him and Melville, in which Isabel of *Pierre* and Miriam Schaeffer, or their counterparts, may have found mention. It is unlikely that either writer refrained from frank consideration in his own mind of the depths of human iniquity.

The problem of Donatello, if more savory, is hardly less occult, except for the study of his miserable spiritual union with Miriam after the murder. As in "Young Goodman Brown," Hawthorne surveyed with puzzled excitement the wretched, almost joyous partnership of guilt. The study of Donatello's "transformation" from primitive innocence to "withering, sad, self-knowledge" is conditioned by a long preparatory definition of traits which leaves us poised in the usual uncertainty between the natural and the supernatural worlds. Did Hawthorne mean that Donatello was really a pre-Roman faun in modern dress, complete with pointed ears? The idea hardly bears phrasing; it is Hawthorne's middle world turned to fantasy, even to the whimsical. For Donatello's antics, his animallike fidelity, are not always felicitous; at best he is a heavy-footed sprite of nature. Only in his awakening experiences of sin does he take on reality, and unfortunately Hawthorne was now too explicit, explaining his parable as flatly as one of his preaching ancestors. He himself epitomized the effect on us of this beautifully written, yet unconvincing book, when he referred to it as "figures in a dream."

7

Thus Hawthorne fulfilled the impulse felt on April 22, 1858, as he stood before the faun of Praxiteles:

A story, with all sorts of fun and pathos in it, might be contrived on the idea of their [the fauns'] species having become intermingled with the human race.

To accomplish this he had laid aside a curious manuscript now known as *The Ancestral Footstep,* whose central idea was that of an American returning to the home of his English forebears. This postponement, though it yielded the rich recompense of *The Marble Faun,* was typical of the frustration of the last six years of Hawthorne's life, during which period he began without completion no fewer than four novels, until on January 1, 1864, he exclaimed bitterly:

I have fallen into a quagmire of disgust and despondency with respect to literary matters. I am tired of my own thoughts and fancies, and my own mode of expressing them.

This fatigue had a tragic outcome in his failure to finish any one of the four books; few American authors have left so incoherent a tangle of first drafts and preliminary sketches as the fragments of the posthumous novels known as *Septimius Felton* (1871), *The Dolliver Romance* (1876), and *Doctor Grimshawe's Secret* (1883). Sad indeed was this decay of the strong, sensitive mind, hopelessly retracing old paths, clumsily venturing into new ones. The artist's hand had lost its cunning.

Old dreams, old fancies! How they tormented him as he vainly sought a focus! Leaving the ancestral footstep and the tiresome old magician Grimshawe, he returned to his beloved theme of immortality. The *elixir vitae* on which Doctor Grimshawe had been working had had a long history in Hawthorne's mind, from Thoreau's legend of the deathless man and from his own story of Doctor Heidegger, until now—was this really possible?—he himself approached the fatal bounds at which a man renews his interest in the question. As one never finds in Hawthorne a personal application of his speculations on the unknown, perhaps in these years he himself was weary of life rather than eager for its continuance. It is idle, perhaps, to point out, as one example, the resemblances of the character of Septimius to other scholar-idealists, particularly to that of Fanshawe (as if the wheel had now come full circle) or, in the various fragments, of Rose Garfield to Phoebe Pyncheon, or of Sibyl Dacy to Priscilla or of Aunt Keziah to Hepzibah Pyncheon. All is repetition, uncertainty, chaos. These four novels reveal a mind whose work was done.

In the end, our study of Hawthorne leaves us with an abiding sense of the integrity of his mind and art. Few American writers have obeyed so implicitly as he the imperious, unconscious dictates of genius. In him dwelt no impatience for effect, no diversion to extraneous themes, either by emulation of other writers or by the pressures of the stormy world just outside Salem and Concord; he never strained beyond himself. From the writing of his first sketches until *The Dolliver Romance* his art, however narrow, remained supremely natural, without pretense, defying imitation. In the center of his being, deeper even than his passion for perfect expression, lay a microcosm of the New England Puritan mind; its ways of thought were integuments of himself. Indeed, he had never needed to learn how the Puritan mind worked, for to him by the time he had written *Twice-Told Tales* the revelation of its meaning was complete.

Hawthorne's quiet, independent implementing of his own beliefs concerning the objectives of the novel is remarkable if we remind ourselves of the growth and wide discussion of this form of art in the nineteenth century. Alone he achieved a pattern of high artistic excellence; alone he won the homage of Poe, Melville, and Henry James, even if, apart from his exposition of the differences between a "romance" and a novel, he bequeathed no sustained definition of his theory of fiction. At first, his idea of making it an illustration of moral concepts strongly recalls the old Puritan idea of literature as the handmaid of religion; but his freedom of speculation emancipates it from this naïve view of the art of writing which lay like a blight over such American nineteenth century poetry as that of Bryant and Longfellow. His convictions concerning these matters seem to have been unexpressed, but innate and unalterable. His imperviousness to literary fashions, to new principles, to any departure from his own instinctive way of writing is emphasized by his aloofness during his stay in England from men of letters. He had, it appears, neither desire nor need of their counsel. When we consider his long road to recognition, his loneliness in these purposes, except for the brief companionship of Herman Melville, the strength of his personality and the "unmalleable" character of his mind appear even more amazing. His was a resolute fulfillment of private artistic principles.

Yet in the America of the nineteenth century, Hawthorne's consecration to artistic purposes was not an uncommon experience. Those who live in the desert must find in their own souls secret springs. Some of our most powerful writers have been those who looked intensely within at the spiritual experiences induced by their very isolation. So Emerson himself as he walked through the snow puddles of Boston Common was "glad to the brink of fear"; and so Emily Dickinson in the brick house on the village street fell in love with Eternity—and described it, too. Possibly, then, it was Hawthorne's poverty which begot his riches. In the Puritan experience, so austere that it still moved men to fear or anger, he discovered, with his artist's eyes turned inward, the enduring fabric of art.

28. HERMAN MELVILLE

In the midsummer of 1850 Herman Melville, then thirty-one and a novelist with a considerable popular following, read, lying on the hay in his Pittsfield barn, *Mosses from an Old Manse* by his neighbor Nathaniel Hawthorne. (The two novelists were soon to meet and become friends.) As Melville read on, he was oppressed by the fact that his countrymen had not acknowledged Hawthorne's genius. Presently, in a long critical article, he tried to make American readers see that they had in their midst an inimitable man, one of "the new and far better generation of writers."

"Hawthorne and his Mosses" is a remarkably perceptive judgment of its subject, but it is more than that. In it Melville unconsciously describes his own aims as a writer. What he says of Hawthorne's work could have been said of his. "If you travel away inland into his deep and noble nature," he wrote, "you will hear the far roar of his Niagara." There is no one writing in America in whom humor and love are so developed "in that high form called genius." As the indispensable complement to these, there is in Hawthorne a "deep intellect, which drops down into the universe like a plummet." If Americans would confess the power in this man, they would "brace the whole brotherhood. For genius, all over the world, stands hand in hand, and one shock of recognition runs the whole circle round."

At the moment when Melville felt in Hawthorne the kind of genius he could admire, he was in the midst of his most ambitious work, *Moby-Dick*, a novel far greater in scope and meaning than his earlier and popular sea tales. There would be few readers who would hear in it the far roar of Melville's Niagara. For the kind of appreciative understanding which he accorded Hawthorne in 1850, Melville had to wait until the twentieth century caught up with him.

Why was it that in the years after 1852 Melville's fame was even less than that which his countrymen granted to such outragers of conventional thought as Thoreau and Whitman? Why was it so long before he joined the pantheon of American writers? His was, to begin with, a most complex nature in which divergent impulses were at war. His "ruthless democracy," as fervent as Whitman's, could make him bleed with "keenest anguish at the undraped spectacle of a valor-ruined man"; yet he was born a patrician, and all his life he loved what Thoreau despised, the company of mellow men, their champagne and cigars, their old folios and rare engravings. Even his friend Hawthorne he found lacking in the necessary "plump sphericity" of a man. "For the sake of argument," he was willing to call Emerson a fool for being so full of "transcendentalisms, myths, and oracular gibberish"; but he would rather be a fool, at that, than a wise man, and he loved all men, like Emerson, who dive. In his own plunges for truth he got into deeper and more dangerous waters than Emerson cared to dive in. As ardent a nationalist as Whitman, he shared with him, after 1865, fear for the future of American democracy.

While the other four men worked toward solutions from which they drew strength for their art, the civil war in Melville's nature grew more intense and divisive. The issues of that war came to be of greater importance to him than his art. In his quest for certainty he left the readers of *Typee* and *White-Jacket* far behind. In an age which increasingly believed in the rightness of material success and was content with the compromise of agnosticism, this spectacle of a once popular novelist who permitted his mind to "run riot amid remote analogies" was, to say the least, bewildering. Even the more troubled spirits of the day preferred the certitudes of Melville's four great contemporaries to his ceaseless search for the general equation which would solve all the relativities of his nature.

2

When the *Acushnet* put to sea from New Bedford on January 3, 1841, she had in her crew of twenty-six a new hand, twenty-two years old, who would make her voyage, transformed by his art, the most famous ever undertaken by a whaler. This was not the first time young Melville had gone to sea. In 1839 he had shipped on a merchantman bound for Liverpool. The story of that voyage he would likewise record, apparently with an equal disregard for fact, in *Redburn*. Why he was again at sea and on a whaler is no mystery. It is true that he was the son of a once prosperous New York merchant, and that his mother was a member of the distinguished Gansevoort family of Albany. Men with such a lineage did not commonly ship on whalers, for whaling was a dangerous and dirty business. But Herman Melville's father was dead, and his mother had a numerous brood to look after. The young man had his way to make in the world. He had tried and abandoned school teaching. Fortunes were sometimes made in whaling by lads who signed on at sixteen and became captains and part-owners before their beards were grown. More persuasive was the fact that Melville was tormented all his life with an "everlasting itch for things remote." A sea-captain uncle and two naval-officer cousins had told him stories of South Sea marvels, feeding his desire to "sail forbidden seas and land on barbarous coasts." Since he abominated "all honorable respectable toils, trials, and tribulations of every kind whatsoever," it bothered him not at all that he must put his hand in the tar barrel.

The *Acushnet's* voyage out was tame enough and did not at all resemble that of the *Pequod* in *Moby-Dick*. She followed the usual route of whalers bound for the Season-on-the-Line in the Pacific, touching at Santa, Peru, in June, cruising off the Galápagos Islands (of which Melville later made fictional use in "The Encantadas") in November. Captain Pease had his troubles. An unusually large number of men jumped ship before he arrived in the Sandwich Islands in June, 1843. Among the seven was Melville, who, with his friend "Toby" Greene, had dropped overboard in the romantically beautiful Anna Maria Bay on Nukuhiva, one of the Marquesas, on July 9, 1842. More than likely Melville had planned all along to look in on this South Sea paradise, well known to sailors and missionaries but still incompletely explored and described. The natives were not very friendly, and one tribe, the Taipis, were said to be practicing cannibals.

Later, in writing *Typee,* which purported to be an autobiographical record of his stay in the Marquesas, Melville mixed in plenty of fiction and a good deal of circumstantial information filched from earlier accounts of the islands; but some, at least, of the personal details are true. Toby was with him in their accidental descent into the unfriendly instead of the friendly valley. In the end Toby got away first, though Melville did not know until after his story was published whether his companion was still alive or had been killed. To make his readers believe what he tells them, Melville says he lingered against his will for more than four months. Actually he was the honored guest of the cannibals for only a few weeks, probably not more than four.

He made his escape on a decrepit but fast-sailing Sydney schooner, the *Lucy Ann,* degraded in her old age into whaling. The story of his next adventures, of a mutiny in which he was a ringleader, of beachcombing in Tahiti, that much visited but no longer sinless Pacific Eden nearly a thousand miles from the scene of *Typee,* he later set down with considerable veracity in *Omoo.* It is a skylarking book, though its high spirits were in some places achieved at the expense of several respectable persons who, after its publication, declared in print that the novelist was a libeler.

Perhaps it was homesickness, as he said, which caused Melville to leave Tahiti. We hear of him next acting as clerk and bookkeeper for a "dealer in general merchandise" in Honolulu to whom he had contracted himself for a year's service beginning July 1, 1843. A few weeks earlier the *Acushnet* had arrived in Hawaiian waters, and her captain was making affidavits about deserters. Perhaps Melville feared the arm of maritime law might snatch him back into whaling servitude. For this or some other reason he put himself under the protection of the American flag by signing on as a common seaman for the homeward voyage of the frigate *United States,* which became the *Neversink* of still another book of Pacific adventures, *White-Jacket.*

For fourteen months the *United States,* with Melville in the afterguard, cruised homeward, putting in for long periods at Callao, Peru, and Mazatlán, Mexico. The future castigator of brutalities in the American navy, as he had witnessed them on the *United States,* missed nothing of the degradation and the heroism to be seen daily around him. The man-of-war sailed into Boston Harbor on October 3, 1844, and Melville, though he had half his time yet to serve, was discharged with the rest of the crew.

The long voyage, the most momentous in literary annals, was over. Melville had seen much that other travelers had also seen and set down; but none of them—scientist, explorer, missionary, or merchant—had so clearly understood what the white man's greed and vice, and his charity, too, were doing to the primitive peoples who welcomed the pocky sailor as hospitably as the missionary's wife in her Mother Hubbard. Life on a man-of-war had helped to make him an unconditional democrat in all things. He could imagine no nobler hero than Jack Chase, captain of the maintop, to whom, in his old age, he dedicated his last work, *Billy Budd.* The impressions of these years stayed with him all his life, surviving undimmed those conveyed in later years by foreign travel and the ceaseless reading of many books.

It was inevitable, in that day when every publisher advertised a Travelers' Library in his list, that Melville should write about the wonders he had seen. He settled down to his congenial task at his mother's home across the Hudson from Albany. In 1846 *Typee, a Peep at Polynesian Life* was published by Murray in London (as *Melville's Marquesas*) and by Wiley & Putnam in New York.

Critics and readers were in the main delighted with *Typee.* Some objected to the warmth of the descriptions of Typeean women, and the franker passages on this engaging subject were removed in the new edition which was soon required. To some the story seemed too good to be true. Adventures so delightfully told and scenes so beautifully described could scarcely be trusted as the work of a deserter from the crew of a whaling ship. Actually Melville had produced a book the like of which had not been known before.

The art of *Typee,* which takes it out of the class of Stewart's *A Visit to the South Seas* (1831) to which it owes much, is evident in the first chapter. What reader can resist turning to Chapter Two after his appetite has been piqued by the anecdote about the scandalous treatment the Marquesans accorded the wife of a missionary and the account of the behavior of an Island Queen which so astounded some French sailors that they fled from the scene of so shocking an exhibition? For more than half of his story Melville keeps his readers in suspense over the fate of the two adventurers. Will they make good their escape from the whaler? Will they survive the perilous descent into the valley? Will the natives prove to be the dreaded Typees? When the adventurers find themselves among the Typees in fact, a new complex of fears arises. Will they be killed? Have they unwittingly eaten human flesh at a native feast and not the usual "puarkee" (pork)? When Toby escapes and does not return, Melville worries, needlessly, for both of them. The smoked head of a white man is whisked from his view before he can discover whether it is that of his black-haired friend.

The reader's anticipatory thrills are not always fearful. Halfway through the book Melville begins to make use of a hint he drops casually near the beginning: "I have no doubt that we were the first white men who ever penetrated thus far back into their territories." Who in 1846 could fail to read on, that he might be among the first to learn about the Marquesan marriage system (a variety of polyandry which Melville did not completely understand) and the goings-on at the Feast of the Calabashes. Melville shows in these chapters with which he fills out the middle section of his story his ability to make detail fascinating by humanizing it. It was an art he would perfect in *Moby-Dick*.

It should be noted, too, that just as Defoe makes the teller of *Robinson Crusoe* into a veritable person, so the "I" of *Typee* is not merely a reporter, but an enterprising young man, full of spirit and curiosity, and also somewhat shrewd and sly. For contrast Toby (whether Richard Tobias Greene had such a temperament or not) is represented as given to bursts of anger and moody fits. Nor are these two the only carefully drawn characters in the book. Mehevi, the chief; the aged leech; the faithful Kory-Kory; Marnoo, in masculine beauty an Apollo—all are touched into life with the finger of their creator. As for Fayaway, she was everything a romantic generation could imagine and desire a Polynesian nymph to be.

Melville's second book, *Omoo,* formed from his beachcombing adventures in Tahiti, appeared in the spring of 1847. His first publishers had turned it down, evidently fearing what the missionary world would say to Melville's attack on the Protestant stations in the South Seas. Harper, who took him on, published his next six books, and thus had the honor of putting the firm's imprint on *Moby-Dick*.

Though *Omoo* lacks the calculated element of suspense which teases along the readers of *Typee,* it is in many respects more of a novel. In place of suspense Melville uses a sequence of episodes, each one of which is naturally introduced and finished off with the self-confidence of a professional writer,

The hilarious opening chapters describing the fourth-class mutiny on the *Julia* are followed by the even more amusing pranks of the mutineers while they are confined in the open-air British jail, the Calabooza Beretanee. After their release Melville and his companion-in-idleness, the renegade Doctor Long Ghost, see the sights. This episode gives Melville his opportunity to describe "Tahiti As It Is" and to get in a word about the missionaries. His quarrel with them arose from their preposterous claims of having rescued many savage souls from the devil. He was willing to admit that they had mitigated the evils of drink, gonorrhea, and greed imported by their fellow white men, but he also knew that the missionaries had done irreparable harm in destroying the taboos which cemented the social structure of these island societies.

After the missionaries have been given their due, Melville and the Doctor move on to the island of Imeeo where for a brief time they help a Yankee and a Cockney on their potato farm. But even with three hours out each day for "nooning," work is not to be endured. They are off again on a grand tour which ends in their climactic court visit (without an invitation) to barefooted Queen Pomaree Vahinee I, who receives them surrounded by cut glass and porcelain, sabers and fowling pieces, laced hats, candelabras and decanters (all gifts from European royal cousins), and eating her fish and poi out of her native calabashes.

Beyond his new skill in developing episodes, the advance in Melville's art is evident in two qualities possessed by *Omoo*. In writing it he made almost no use of books by other travelers, depending with confidence on his own invention. He has progressed, too, in the power to characterize. In the throng of amusing characters who help to give *Omoo* its tone of irresponsible gaiety, more than twenty are sketched with a master's hand, whether Melville uses a few sentences, all he required for Old Mother Tot, or several chapters, which were needed to polish off Wilson, the blustering and high-handed deputy consul.

The third book which Melville made out of his years in the Pacific is *White-Jacket or The World in a Man-of-War*. Again as in *Typee*, Melville had novelty to offer his readers, this time in the authenticity of his picture of life at every human level on board an American warship. What he had done (in the opening chapters of *Omoo*) as the chronicler for exploited whalemen he was now doing, with much more serious intent, for the common seamen of the American navy. His faith in the innate dignity of man had been outraged by the brutal floggings and the scenes of petty tyranny he witnessed on board the *United States*. At heart a pacifist, he had been revolted by the naval laws and usages which supposedly must be enforced to make fierce fighting men out of American farm boys and mechanics. His hatred of rank could not endure without protest the parade of authority which the presence on board of a commodore required. *White-Jacket* is in places straight propaganda, and it had its small share in the reformation to which the old Navy soon had to submit in the mid-century. Melville was able to write to his friend Evert Duyckinck six months after his book appeared: "I am offering up devout jubilation for the abolition of the flogging law."

Only in a few chapters is Melville's propagandist purpose obtrusive. *White-Jacket* is the most mature book of the five which appeared before *Moby-Dick*, and ranks next to it in the completeness with which the theme is realized. It is no inconsiderable tour de force to keep the reader interested, for four hundred pages (without a plot to help), while the author explains every rite and remote compartment, every duty and activity, on a man-of-war.

Though there is no plot, there is what happens to White-Jacket, the teller of the story, whose canvas surtout makes him a marked man among his five hundred shipmates. As in *Typee,* the "I" is a person whom we like and whose fortunes we follow with sympathy. White-Jacket is "of a meditative humor," an expert lounger and time-killer, fit to be a member of the Forty-two Pounder Club to which belong the *aristoi* of the ship. He possesses an uncommon gift of satire, a gift which his creator had hitherto been able to exercise only on missionaries and pettifogging colonial officials. Subjects were rife on board the *Neversink*: the transcendental sermon of the Chaplain; the ceremonious visits of state made by the Commodore when the ship was in harbor; the rank-pulling of the five-foot midshipmen, too soon escaped from the posterior discipline of the nursery and infant school; and, most vulnerable of all, that toothless and hairless butcher of men, Surgeon-of-the-Fleet Cadwallader Cuticle, M.D.

The logbook of the *United States* has fortunately survived, so that it is possible to see what Melville transcribed from life and what he invented. Actually the last three months of the voyage home, the period which the novel covers, were so uneventful that they supplied only one important incident which he could transfer to his book. The rest is invention: Surgeon Cuticle's ghastly operation on the foretopman; the fragrant story of how eau de cologne was substituted for grog when the stores gave out; the Great Massacre of the Boards; White-Jacket-Melville's narrow escape from a flogging. The most exciting episode of all, the story of how the white jacket caused its owner to fall from the weather topgallant yardarm into the sea more than a hundred feet below, Melville coolly lifted from Nathaniel Ames' *A Mariner's Sketches,* thus causing his future biographers much pain when they discovered that he had assumed another man's death agony and passed it off as his own —or as White-Jacket's.

When Melville set to work on *Moby-Dick,* one of his main concerns was to raise the voyage of his whaler to a higher level than that of ordinary experience. His readers must find significance in a hundred routine activities. Only by investing them with universal meaning could his mighty theme be supported. In *White-Jacket,* published in the year he began writing his masterpiece, Melville experimented with this method of poetizing shipboard experience. Life on board a man-of-war had furnished him with an image of the great world. In his ship microcosm he had run the gamut of character upward from Scriggs with the picklock eye to noble Jack Chase, and of human experience from the horrors of flogging through the fleet to the pitiful moment when the "last stitch" must be sewn through his nose before a sailor may be decently buried at sea.

The world-frigate, Melville concludes, sails under sealed orders—"we ourselves the repositories of the secret packet, whose mysterious contents we long to learn." From our first embarkation its violent rolling makes every soul of us seasick, though in after life the motion becomes endurable through gradual habituation.

Oh, shipmates and world-mates, all round! we the people suffer many abuses. Our gun-deck is full of complaints. In vain from Lieutenants do we appeal to the Captain; in vain—while on board our world-frigate—to the indefinite Navy Commissioners, so far out of sight aloft. Yet the worst of our evils we blindly inflict upon ourselves; our officers can not remove them, even if they would. From the last ills no being can save another; therein each man must be his own savior. For the rest, whatever befall us, let us never train our murderous guns inboard; let us not mutiny with bloody pikes in our hands.

3

The popular success of *Typee* and *Omoo* induced Melville to make writing his profession. On this assurance that he and the reading public, in England as well as America, could get on together, he married, in the fall of 1847, Elizabeth Shaw, daughter of the Chief Justice of Massachusetts. They settled in New York where Melville was soon a member of the circle of writers whose center was Evert Duyckinck, editor, critic, and adviser to publishers. With this group, the "Knights of the Round Table," whose punch parties offered the best literary conversation in New York, the young novelist exchanged stories about South Sea wonders for talk about art, literature, philosophy, and politics. His friends and reviewers expected him to go on spinning yarns. Though *White-Jacket* (1850) had overtones which only the more sensitive of his readers could hear, Melville continued in this, his fifth book, to oblige his public with the sort of writing which it demanded of him.

The year before, in *Redburn,* Melville had gone back to his memories of his Liverpool voyage at the age of nineteen. He despised, or affected to despise, this moving tale of the sufferings of a gentleman's son who sails under a hard captain and sees for the first time the filth of a foreign seaport. Shortly after *Redburn* appeared Melville wrote to his friend Duyckinck: "[It] seems to have been favorably received. I am glad of it—for it puts money into an empty purse. But I hope I shall never write such a book again—tho' when a poor devil writes with duns all round him, and looking over the back of his chair . . . what can you expect of that poor devil?—What but a beggarly 'Redburn'!" The economics of publishing being what they were at the time, not even a writer who had lived among the cannibals, and had come home to America to tell his experiences, could support a growing family by his craft.

Yet there were signs that Melville might some day risk what security he had and strike out into a kind of writing which it was very unlikely his readers would care for. *Moby-Dick* would be in its entirety such a book, and he had premonitions of disaster while he was writing it. To Hawthorne he confided as he was slaving away on his "Whale": "What I feel most moved to write, that is banned,—it will not pay. Yet, altogether write the *other* way I cannot. So the product is a final hash, and all my books are botches." Before *Moby-Dick* he had tried to compromise—offering in part what his public wanted, in part what he wanted himself. Possibly Melville was thinking of *Mardi* (1849) as he wrote this letter to Hawthorne. His words fit it well, for it is a hash of adventure, romance, satire, and jejeune philosophizing; an annoying botch, yet to one interested in the necessary waywardness of genius, a most revealing book.

The first fifty chapters of *Mardi* reel off like those in his earlier books. This time we follow the adventures of the narrator and his companion Jarl who desert from a whaler, suffer horribly in an open boat, board and stalk a mystery-shrouded native-built ship which is later sunk in a gale. In the open boat again, they meet new adventures which are curious but not improbable. They rescue from a priest whom they kill a snow-white maiden with Golconda locks. Her story—of her more than mortal birth, of a strange captivity in the Island of Delights, of her reincarnation and deification at the temple of Apo—suggests a hand-me-down from Blake or a prose rewriting of a poem by Thomas Holley Chivers. Still, the unwary reader might suppose he was hearing a South Sea legend. He might believe, too, that the narrator was actually received as the demigod Taji at the island of Odo, even as Captain Cook was supposed by the Hawaiians to be their war god Lono. But when Taji undertakes a journey round the archipelago of Mardi in the company of a king named Media, a philosopher with the suspiciously allegorical name of Babbalanja, the historian Braid-Beard, and the poet Yoomy, at this point in the story (Chapter Sixty-six) the cat jumps out of the bag. The reader knows that Melville's little preface to *Mardi* is telling the truth: "Having published two narratives of voyages in the Pacific, which, in many quarters, were received with incredulity, the thought occurred to me of indeed writing a romance of Polynesian adventure, and publishing it as such; to see whether the fiction might not possibly be received for a verity: in some degree the reverse of my previous experience."

Into *Mardi* Melville poured the ferment of his mind in 1848. During the past seven years he had discovered the world of ideas, as he read his way through ships' libraries and the volumes in Evert Duyckinck's large collection. His new literary friendships stimulated his interest in contemporary political issues, especially the slavery impasse and the American imperialistic thrust toward Mexico and the Northwest. With the confused but insatiable curiosity of one who has had no academic training in philosophy, he delighted in juggling the technical terms of Stoicism, Idealism, Necessitarianism, Christian theology, and even Transcendentalism, though he did not heartily respect his Concord contemporaries.

Mardi is clogged with recondite allusions; with the vapid poems of Yoomy (Melville's first attempts at verse), with little essays on everything from "Time and Temples" and royal wines to the polysensuum and the physiology of genius. In spite of the intoxicated language and the amateurishness of most of the philosophical meditations, there is a new power here, and Melville is evidently exulting in the consciousness that he possesses it. The best episodes are the satirical passages about philosophers and pedants and the sequence of chapters in which Taji and his court companions explore Dominora (England) and Vivenza (the United States) and the lesser nations which made up the Mardian world in the year 1848.

Though everything which interested Melville in this American year of decision was tossed into the book, *Mardi* has a perceptible plan. The credible adventures of the first part yield to the fantastic story of Yillah. Taji's quest for her after she is stolen from him furnishes the motive for this strange voyage through the world of politics and the world of mind. The earlier satirical chapters of this section, written in a Rabelaisian vein and on traditional and universal subjects, lead to the excellently controlled satire on the superstitions, the corruptions, and the unending battle of the sects which have disgraced the Christian church for nearly two thousand years. After this long interlude Melville describes the Christian state which might be, the land of Serenia where the laws are bred, not of vengeance, but of love and Alma (Christ).

Though there was no need for him to be explicit since his chief purpose is clear enough, Melville declares in the chapter called "Sailing On" that this chartless voyage through the world of mind is as bold as that of Columbus:

That voyager steered his bark through seas, untracked before; ploughed his own path mid jeers; though with a heart that oft was heavy with the thought, that he might only be too bold, and grope where land was none.

So I. . . .

But this new world here sought, is stranger far than his, who stretched his vans from Palos. It is the world of mind; wherein the wanderer may gaze round, with more of wonder than Balboa's band roving through the golden Aztec glades.

But fiery yearnings their own phantom-future make, and deem it present. So, if after all these fearful, fainting trances, the verdict be, the golden haven was not gained; yet, on bold quest thereof, better to sink in boundless deeps, than float on vulgar shoals; and give me, ye gods, an utter wreck, if wreck I do.

What was Melville's quest? What landfall in the "world of mind" did he hope to sight? Who is Yillah, the elusive phantom whom Taji follows off the final page into an endless sea? Who is the dark and sinister Hautia who pursues the pursuer, offering him the voluptuous pleasures of this world? The symbols are vague and tritely romantic, but, in the light of the themes of *Moby-Dick* and *Pierre,* with both of which *Mardi* is affined, Melville's meaning can be discerned. He was off on his long quest for the ultimate truth. He would have an answer from the inscrutable mask of the universe. The appearance of things must be made to dissolve into the reality beyond.

When *White-Jacket* was published in London in January, 1850, Melville's fifth book was in print. He had just returned from a trip to England to which had been added a few delightful days on the Continent. Though he was abroad on business—in those days of reciprocal Anglo-American literary piracy American authors could only appeal to the generosity of their English publishers—he had filled his days and nights with pleasure: rummaging in bookstalls and, as usual, buying more than he could afford; dining with literary lions, sight-seeing, and attending the theater. London was a very different place to the now successful author of *Melville's Marquesas* from the Liverpool which had received the anonymous deck hand of nineteen. He was a full-grown literary lion himself. In his last days in England the Duke of Rutland honored him with an invitation to Belvoir. Melville reluctantly declined, so that he might return sooner to his family.

The literary society of New York had begun to disgust him. Even his faithful friends the Duyckinck brothers were deep in the business of promoting writers whom he no longer admired. In Book XVII of *Pierre* he satirizes, with some transparent allusions, this amiable society: ignorant publishers who flatter a youthful writer by bidding for the privilege of issuing his "complete works," lecture committees who beg him for an oration on any subject of his choosing (though the subject of Human Destiny is respectfully suggested), magazine editors who demand a daguerreotype to aid promotion, attar-of-roses young ladies asking for autographs.

In *Mardi* one of Babbalanja's favorite subjects for discourse is the pain of writing well. Melville makes his philosopher say that men who think deeply are giants in their genius, but dwarfs when they try to speak what they know. With his new awareness of the mysterious springs of creative power and the realization of what adventures he might experience in the world of mind, was born a contempt for the kind of fame which was already his. Of what use is fame unless it is wedded to power, money, or place? Fame is an accident, in any event, but merit is absolute. He would yet write something which would be, in its absolute excellence, beyond reach of the critics who are mules "so emasculated from vanity they cannot father a true thought."

Early in 1850 Melville embarked on a book with a mighty theme which he hoped would please himself, whether or not it pleased the critics. As if to signalize his break with the literati in New York, a few months later he moved his family to "Broadhall" near Pittsfield, Massachusetts. It was now a boarding house; but it had once belonged to a favorite uncle, and he had happy childhood memories of the region around it. Soon he found a house and farm near by which he wanted to own. For his own pleasure he added a porch to "Arrowhead" on the north where he could pace up and down and look across the meadows to the peak of the majestic mountain, Greylock, twenty miles away. When winter came he was deep in *Moby-Dick* and so full of plans for future works that he wrote in jest to Evert Duyckinck to ask if he could send him fifty fast-writing youths who could help him with his labors.

4

In the reckless mood of *Mardi*, Melville sent Ahab and his biographer Ishmael on a more fearful voyage than Taji's into the "world of mind." Readers who looked into *Moby-Dick or the Whale* on its publication in the fall of 1851, may have covered the first few chapters in all innocence, supposing they had bought just another account of a whaling voyage. Books describing the adventures of whalemen, books about the whaling industry, about leviathan himself, his anatomy and physiology, were then a staple of the book trade. But a reader could not have got through many chapters of *Moby-Dick* before suspecting that it was a very different sort of book from Frederick Bennett's *Narrative of a Whaling Voyage* (1840) or J. Ross Browne's *Etchings of a Whaling Cruise* (1846).

Moby-Dick opens properly in New Bedford, greatest of whaling ports, and the voyage of the *Pequod* begins in the most ancient home of American whalemen, Nantucket. What happens to young Ishmael while he is waiting for his ship could well have happened to any landlubber who had signed on for his first voyage—except that the details of his first hours in port are told with a livelier humor than such matter-of-fact narrators as Bennett and Browne could command. Yet there are signs even in these early chapters that the *Pequod,* that "cannibal of a craft, tricking herself forth in the chased bones of her enemies," is destined for no ordinary voyage, the end of which might be a hold crammed with casks of sperm oil transmutable into gold. Doom hangs over the ship from the start. The dark words of a prophet in faded jacket and patched trousers (his name is Elijah) beget in Ishmael all kinds of "vague wonderments and half-apprehensions." The sermon of the nautical Father Mapple, who preaches from a kind of maintop pulpit in the sailors' bethel, throws a strong beam ahead on the wayward path which, deliberately and wantonly, Captain Ahab will soon take. Like Jonah who fled from the hard command of God, obeying his own will instead, Ahab will yet know the torment which a just God visits on those who cannot say in their last breath: "O Father—chiefly known to me by Thy rod—mortal or immortal, here I die. I have striven to be Thine, more than to be this world's, or mine own. Yet this is nothing: I leave eternity to Thee; for what is man that he should live out the lifetime of his God?"

It was a bold stroke on Melville's part to draw his cast of characters from American whalemen, whose counterparts he had known on his own voyage on the *Acushnet* ten years before. His mighty theme is the equal of any attempted by Sophocles or Shakespeare, yet his cast acts it out on the oil-soaked decks of a whaler. It is his art, of course, which transforms this setting into a background worthy of the theme. But there was hidden power in the setting itself. The whaling years form one of those great episodes in our national life when thousands of Americans have been lured—by the surge of the westward migration or by the cry of "Gold in California"—to risk life and fortune on the triple hope of adventure, gold, and glory. Whaling was at its peak when Melville wrote *Moby-Dick*. The American fleet was then three times the size of the whole European fleet. We supplied the world with most of its illuminating oil, candles, and whalebone. The heroic exploits of the fishery were passing into myth, and there was at hand for Melville's use a rich literature on whaling going back even to classical times. Leviathan, most powerful and mysterious of God's creatures, had for centuries engaged the imagination of writers. All that was true and all that was myth in the lore of whalemen Melville had in his mind as he wrote in his workroom at "Arrowhead." Joined to what he had read and heard were his memories of the spirit-spout jetted into the clear moonlight, of cutting in, and of the hell-smoke of the tryworks. He would use fact, myth, and things remembered for the "honor and glory of whaling" and thus body forth the tale he had to tell of Captain Ahab, who brought destruction on his crew and on himself by pursuing private vengeance against the White Whale for the leg torn from him in their last encounter.

Such a malicious whale had in fact haunted American whalemen for years. As Mocha Dick he was described by J. N. Reynolds in the *Knickerbocker Magazine* for May, 1839. Melville himself had talked with the son of Owen Chase, whose *Narrative of the Most Extraordinary and Distressing Shipwreck of the Whaleship Essex* (1820) tells how such a ferocious whale as Moby-Dick sank the *Essex* just south of the equator in longitude 119° W. This *Narrative* may be the germ of Melville's novel. He had read it first when outward bound on the *Acushnet*.

But Ahab's White Whale is far more than a natural phenomenon to be shunned by whalers desirous of reaching home port. Ahab hates him as "the monomaniac incarnation of all those malicious agencies which some deep men feel eating in them, till they are left living on with half a heart and half a lung." He has resolved to pit himself, all mutilated, against his antagonist. In Moby-Dick he sees all evil "visibly personified and made practically assailable." He has piled on the whale's white hump all the resentment and rage felt by his race from Adam down against the divinely permitted suffering in the world.

Nor is this all. When the mild-mannered first mate, Starbuck, good Christian that he is, calls it madness, blasphemy even, to be enraged with a dumb brute, Ahab turns on him with his deeper motive. Moby-Dick may be the evil principle itself or he may be the agent of evil, but how is man to know unless he strikes through the mask of the whale's whiteness? Sometimes Ahab thinks there may be nothing beyond, but he must know for a certainty. What he chiefly hates is an inscrutable malice sinewing the White Whale's strength. Is it blasphemy to demand an answer? He would strike the sun if it insulted him: "Who's over me? Truth has no confines."

There is no one on board who can call Ahab back to sanity and divert the destruction to come, once he has nailed the gold piece to the mast and aroused the frenzy of the crew to win it by hunting down the White Whale. Ahab pauses once in his mad course to confess to Starbuck his momentary regret for the happiness with his wife and child which he wills to forgo, and to cry out at the "nameless, inscrutable, unearthly thing . . . the remorseless emperor" who commands him. But Starbuck has no power with him and, "blanched to a corpse's hue with despair," he steals from his captain's frightening presence.

Though there is no one to hold back the doom, there is one on board who apprehends its steady approach. Young Ishmael speaks for Melville. He alone survives the ship's destruction to bring back to civilization the story which he tells. It is fitting that he should be the sole survivor since he is the only man aboard who sees Ahab's monomania in its true light. At the moment when Ahab reveals his purpose to the crew, Ishmael feels himself drawn into his Captain's "quenchless feud," but as time passes he comes to realize that the mad old man's "special lunacy" has stormed his "general sanity" and "turned all its concentrated cannon upon its own mad mark." Musing on the Loom of Time one cloudy, sultry afternoon, while his cannibal companion Queequeg is weaving a mat, Ishmael decides for himself that the web of life is made up of the straight warp of necessity, the free-willed movement of the shuttle, and the play of chance which "has the last featuring blow at events." Ahab has willed his own destruction. He is not, as he believes, turned round and round in the world by the handspike of Fate.

The truth about Ahab strikes Ishmael most clearly one night when he is at the tiller while the fire and smoke from the tryworks lick the intense darkness. Stupefied by gazing too long on the face of the fire, Ishmael lets the tiller slip from his grasp. Aroused by the blow, he awakens to see that whatever swift, rushing thing he stands on is "not so much bound to any haven ahead as rushing from all havens astern." He faces back just in time to prevent the vessel from flying up into the wind and capsizing. The meaning is clear, but Ishmael points it up for us. Ahab, from gazing too long on the artificial hell-fires of his own kindling, has permitted the "wisdom that is woe" to be inverted into the "woe that is madness." At another time, seeing Ahab burst from his cabin, driven from his intolerable dreams like a man escaping from a bed of fire, Ishmael prays to himself: "God help thee, old man, thy thoughts have created a creature in thee; and he whose intense thinking thus makes him a Prometheus; a vulture feeds upon that heart for ever; that vulture the very creature he creates."

Seen as Ishmael comprehends it, Ahab's astounding struggle to wrest from heaven the secret of human woe looks like the purest tragedy. But the tone and the intent of the book are not tragic. For one thing Melville is too much in sympathy with the Promethean mood of his villain-hero, and he sends him to his death on the third day of the chase still unreconciled to the power which suffers evil to exist. And in Ishmael himself we find mutinous thoughts which border on blasphemy and worse. In the chapter called "The Whiteness of the Whale" he meditates, close to the edge of atheism, on the "heartless voids" covered by the sinister and universal whiteness. Is there nothing but the charnel house within? Can it be that there is neither agent nor principle of good or evil behind the material, white mask? Ishmael can himself go no farther along the road to submission than to say: "For this I thank God; for all have doubts; many deny; but doubts or denials, few along with them have intuitions. Doubts of all things earthly, and intuitions of some things heavenly; this combination makes neither believer nor infidel, but makes a man who regards them both with equal eye." It is with no such faint heart that Hamlet speaks his farewell to Horatio and the world; with no such doubt does Oedipus, with blinded and bloody eyes, face his subjects and confess his unwitting crimes.

When Melville wrote in "The Whiteness of the Whale," "Though in many of its aspects this visible world seems formed in love, the invisible spheres were formed in frigh',," he had not said his final word about the hyperborean regions to which enthusiastic Truth will lead a mind fitted, as was his, for fearless thought. Leviathan was not the biggest fish in the sea of ideas. He had heard of krakens. He was off on his new hunt before the critics had time to express their bewilderment before *Moby-Dick*. The new novel he called *Pierre; or, the Ambiguities*—a "rural bowl of milk," as he described it, jesting grimly about the fallen innocence of his country-bred Hamlet-hero from whom the book receives its name.

The plot is as fantastic as a bare recital of it suggests. Pierre Glendinning, son of an aristocratic father now dead and a proud and adoring mother, is about to marry Lucy Tartan, a match for him in innocence and beauty. Suddenly there appears to disturb their Eden of young love the dark-haired Isabel who persuades Pierre, by hints from her mystery-veiled past, that she is the natural daughter of their father. She must be protected, and Pierre believes he must be the one to atone for the sin his father committed. To acknowledge her as his sister would undo his mother and blacken the name of his father whose memory he holds sacred. A false marriage is the only solution. This leads in the end to his mother's death and to Pierre's murdering his cousin Glen Stanly, who tries to prevent Lucy from following the hapless couple and living with them in New York. In the last act of the tragedy Lucy dies of shock and Pierre and Isabel take poison.

Melville was not writing a paper-backed thriller for "Wonder and Wen" or "The Captain Kidd Monthly," firms which sought the talents of Pierre while he was trying to live by writing a novel about Vivia who is also struggling to write a novel, the theme of which is the "pursuit of the highest health of virtue and truth." The lurid episodes of the plot and the tortured characters are intended to instruct us in what happens to a young enthusiast to Duty, who in seeking to live by heavenly absolutes discovers that he steps deeper into grief until he brings down his world around him. Like Titan, the demigod, Man is born of an incestuous union between Heaven and Earth. But the marriage was made in Heaven, and it was there that the corruption of evil first touched our nature. Innocence struggles to regain its divine birthright even by fierce escalade, but it is doomed to be thrown from the heights even as Titan was.

The theme of *Pierre* may have taken root in Melville's mind at the time he worked at *Mardi*. When the travelers arrive at the church-state of Maramma, they meet on their way to the inner shrines a youth of open, ingenuous aspect. He has refused a guide, declaring that he must seek the right way for himself. Though he may have to act counter to all monitions of wisdom, he must follow the divine instinct within. This youth who still clings to the "legend of the Peak" may well be Pierre, the Fool of Truth, of Virtue, and of Fate, in his first incarnation.

The chief of the ambiguities which the novel seeks to discuss is the sinister aspect of the visible world which breeds in the man who thinks deeply the paralyzing fear that in the Truth of Heaven the Demonic Principle has some part.

Ah, if man were wholly made in heaven, why catch we hell-glimpses? Why in the noblest marble pillar that stands beneath the all-comprising vault, ever should we descry the sinister vein?

But the word of the novel's subtitle is plural, and other ambiguities start from every chapter. Once the love idyll of Lucy and Pierre is disrupted, there is no natural love in the novel, only relations which are ambiguous indeed. Pierre and his mother are bound by a silver cord and converse with the gallantry and coquetry of old-fashioned lovers. Pierre's false marriage to Isabel soon goes beyond the brother-sister relationship which he intends it shall mask. Melville implies that it becomes incestuous, in desire if not in fact. He plays effectively, and with surprising awareness for one writing in the mid-nineteenth century, on the normal-abnormal boy friendship of Pierre and Glen which turns later to fierce jealousy over Lucy. And Lucy herself, when she succeeds in her plea to be taken as a lodger by Pierre and Isabel, transforms the strange union under the eaves in their miserable little flat into a still stranger triad.

Melville did not invent these ambiguous sexual relationships to startle such readers as may have noted them in that pre-Freudian era. They are evidently related to a theme which he states early in the book, though he does not develop it or in any other passage tie it to the theme of the ambiguous nature of ultimate reality. The passage comes just after Pierre goes to make his morning call on Lucy. It is a kind of Benedicite in praise of young love, but in its deeper meaning it declares that Love, natural love, drives the demon Principle which is the sire of Want and Woe further and further back into chaos. "All this Earth is Love's affianced; vainly the demon Principle howls to stay the banns." When Pierre deserts Lucy and love to do what he thinks is his heaven-directed duty, his chance for happiness departs. The demon Principle enters his earthly paradise.

It has often been said that an author's second novel is the turning point in his career. His first book he writes out of his experience; his second must come from his imagination. It tests whether his powers are really creative or only reportorial. In a sense *Pierre* was Melville's second novel. His earlier books, including *Moby-Dick,* came from the sea life which he had mastered as no writer who lived before him had done. Much of what had not come from his own first-hand experience, he had found in the writings of other seafarers. The books which precede *Moby-Dick* were preparatives for its greatness. But with *Pierre* he began over again. Aside from some recollections of his boyhood years among his Gansevoort relatives in Albany and his Melville relatives at Pittsfield, the novel is largely invention. He could not fall back on his endlessly delightful sea anecdotes or on his ability to interest his readers in the business of keeping a ship afloat and running before the wind.

Pierre is not a perfect book. It is not even a good one, judged by any standards. But in writing it Melville took, not altogether by accident, a road which other novelists would take thereafter. We who read *Pierre* now, with benefit of Henry James and Virginia Woolf, D. H. Lawrence, and James Joyce and the century-long tradition of symbolism, can have some idea of what his intentions were. *Pierre* is a "primitive" and will be read—by those who do not take to fiction as a substitute for life—as one of the earliest attempts to use in a prose narrative devices which before had been considered appropriate to poetry. Melville had little use for the shallow fiction of his time, novels in which "every character can, by reason of its consistency, be comprehended at a glance." Human nature, he believed, is far more complex than fiction writers then supposed it to be. Motives for action lie deep in the accidents of childhood. They cannot be directly stated and neatly reconciled but must be shadowed forth by the light projected upon them from dreams and symbols and myths.

The discordances of *Pierre,* in consequence, arise from the fact that Melville attempted to accomplish by new methods more than any novelist had previously undertaken. He was unfortunate in his choice of an incestuous relationship for the central situation of the novel, though this was probably forced on him by his allegorical theme of the incest between Heavenly Truth and the Heaven-born evil of Earth. Overt incest is too theoretical a sin to engender any terror in a modern audience. In abandoning his usual methods of narration, the autobiographical form or the device of the narrator who is close to the events yet not a whole-souled participant in them, Melville also made further difficulties for himself. Sometimes the narrator speaks as "I"; sometimes as "we." Usually the tone is that of the omniscient novelist, but occasionally a sort of chorus of pities or of ironies seems to comment on Pierre's acts or thoughts.

But these faults of method a less experienced novelist might commit or amend. Melville's greater failure is in his inability to bring his symbols together into a harmony of tone and to use them so that one can move through them deeper and deeper into his characters and the profundities of his theme. Some of the symbols are almost ludicrous in their effect, as is, for example, Isabel's guitar from which she plucks a dark music that is to Pierre infinitely significant but (as to the reader also) utterly unintelligible. The symbolic intention of the two portraits of Pierre's father is fully conveyed. The myth-dream of the Mount of Titans is admirable in conception, but its Enceladus theme will not quite square with the genealogy of Pierre's "heaven-aspiring but still not wholly earth-emancipated mood." Similarly the pamphlet of Plotinus Plinlimmon, which is supposed to furnish symbolic comment on Pierre's behavior, is so hedged round with satire and enigma that the critics will argue its significance perpetually.

In one magnificent section of the novel Melville uses symbolism with a power which shows us what the book might have been had he been expert enough to reach this level all the way through. Young Pierre, as a boy, had often played in the woods near a great stone, huge as a barn yet balanced so delicately on a single point of contact that it was a breathless thing to see. Pierre called it the Terror Stone. In the moment of his agony when he must decide what he is to do with Isabel, he goes to the stone, stands under it and bids it fall on him if life is a cheating dream and virtue meaningless. As his hero stands waiting for the answer which does not come, Melville transforms the Terror Stone into the Memnon Stone, built by the subjects of "that dewy, royal boy, son of Aurora, and born King of Egypt, who, with enthusiastic rashness flinging himself on another's account into a rightful quarrel . . . met his boyish and most dolorous death beneath the walls of Troy." But Pierre is not only Memnon. The symbol widens to include Hamlet and all ship-wrecked royal youths whose tragedy is that of the "flower of virtue cropped by a too rare mischance."

5

In *Moby-Dick* and *Pierre* Melville had made his bid for the kind of post-humous fame he wanted to have. Each novel fulfilled the requirements for a great and original work, as he would later define them in three chapters on the theory of the novel interjected into *The Confidence Man* (XIV, XXXIII, XLIV). He had sought to provide entertainment, but, as well, "more reality than real life itself can show." He had given his readers novelty and he had given them nature too, but "nature unfettered, exhilarated, in effect trans-formed." Pierre, as well as Ahab, was an "original character," as Melville asserted the hero of a great work of fiction should be: one who, "like a revolving Drummond light, raying away from itself all round it—everything is lit by it, everything starts to it (mark how it is with Hamlet), so that, in certain minds, there follows upon the adequate conception of such a character, an effect, in its way, akin to that wl.ich in Genesis attends upon the beginnings of things."

But there were not enough of such "minds" to praise these two novels or to buy them. *Moby-Dick* puzzled Melville's friends, though some were discerning enough to suspect that there was great power in it. Even friends and friendly critics were dismayed by the ambiguities of *Pierre,* while the simpler sort were content to be disgusted with the theme of incest. The measure of the public's desertion of Melville can be taken in the fact that his next novel, *Israel Potter,* published three years after *Pierre,* received scarcely any critical notice. Seldom has a successful author been dropped so suddenly from his pinnacle of fame.

The years between *Pierre* and Melville's removal to New York in 1863, where soon he took a job as a customs inspector, must have been the bitterest of his life. How to get enough money to support his family (which included his mother and sisters) was a constant worry. Since he was in debt to Harper's until 1864, he drew no royalties from the books which bore their imprint. The writing which he did between 1853 and 1856 could not have brought in more than $240 a year. Putnam, who issued *Israel Potter,* was forced to sell the plates in the panic of 1857. Dix & Edwards, who published *The Piazza Tales* (1856) and *The Confidence Man* (1857), went bankrupt.

Like most of his literary contemporaries, Melville tried lecturing; but his income from this source between 1857 and 1860 did not average more than $423 a year. Influential friends failed to get him a consular appointment, the quest for which took him to Washington and, incidentally, into Lincoln's presence, in March of 1861. Ill health dragged at his spirits, and there is truth in the family tradition that a breakdown soon after *Pierre* was published caused fears for his sanity. If Melville's father-in-law, Judge Shaw, had not tactfully eased matters the situation would have been desperate.

There is not very much to put into the biographical record of these years, but out of the stories and essays which he was writing one can read Melville's moods. The theme of charity recurs often enough to hint that his need of it and his resentment at having to receive it were constantly in his mind. "Maternal charity nursed you as a babe," he makes the narrator say in "The Two Temples." "Paternal charity fed you as a child; friendly charity got you your profession, . . . You, and all mortals, live but by sufferance of your charitable kind; charitable by omission, not performance."

In spite of the humiliations of these harrowing years, Melville continued to look on himself as a professional writer until 1857, the year of *The Con-*

fidence Man. He did not turn out work at the prodigious rate of the period between 1846 and 1852, when he published seven novels as well as some incidental literary criticism, but the production in five years of two novels, *The Piazza Tales* (a collection of six stories), and ten other stories and essays, is a substantial body of writing even for so fecund an author. Nor should it be forgotten that some of this writing was still of a high level. *Israel Potter*, the story of the "Revolutionary beggar" which Melville enlarged from a chap-book autobiography, is for the most part a pleasant picaresque tale, but the episode of the sea fight between the *Serapis* and the *Bonhomme Richard* is carried off with great spirit. "Benito Cereno" moves the reader step by step toward unmentionable and unimaginable horrors. It was reported to Melville that James Russell Lowell thought one of the episodes in "The Encantadas" "the finest touch of genius he had seen in prose." "Bartleby" lifts the allegorical tale above what Hawthorne could do with it to the fusion of fantasy with serious meaning which Henry James achieved in such a fable as "The Beast in the Jungle." Even *The Confidence Man*, though its narrative does not move and its tone is baffling, is redeemed by passages of sharp satire.

What one notices first in reading the work of these years is the great variety of style and theme. Possibly Melville was trying to find forms and subjects which editors would accept. "The Lightning Rod Man," for example, is close to the kind of tale with an evident but unlabored moral which made Hawthorne famous. The narrator in "The Piazza" muses learnedly and romantically on the beauties of the Berkshire countryside somewhat as the "I" of D. G. Mitchell's *Reveries of a Bachelor* (a best seller of the fifties) daydreams about his existence.

If Melville was trying to please a new public, he was also trying to release the tensions of his life in these stories. He returns again and again to themes and situations which are concerned with fears of isolation or incarceration, the dislike of taking charity, the inviolable sanctity of the human heart (his own, perhaps, in "I and My Chimney"). His narrators are men of a persistent, sometimes a perverse, integrity who hold on in spite of the contempt of the genteel world. Sometimes the teller of the tale is a moody, inquisitive fellow, withdrawn but observant, reaching out from his isolation to the poor who are, in spite of their poverty, kind, intrepid, and to a degree happy, because they have learned how to live by illusion.

As one reads these autobiographical passages one gains the impression of a man who is trying to achieve detachment and equilibrium; to be aware but not dangerously involved. The Promethean mood of *Moby-Dick* is gone, and so is the Titanism of *Pierre*. Melville seems to be struggling to stave off the disenchantment to which he finally gave way in *The Confidence Man*.

The character of Hautboy in "The Fiddler" may well be, *mutatis mutandis,* Melville as he wished to be in the year 1854. Once a famous violinist, Hautboy now "walks Broadway and no man knows him." Yet he is the most admirable of men, "honest and natural," able to hit intuitively "the exact line between enthusiasm and apathy."

It was plain that while Hautboy saw the world pretty much as it was, yet he did not theoretically espouse its bright side nor its dark side. Rejecting all solutions, he but acknowledged facts. What was sad in the world he did not superficially gainsay; what was glad in it he did not cynically slur; and all which was to him personally enjoyable, he gratefully took to his heart. It was plain, then—so it seemed at that moment, at least—that his extraordinary cheerfulness did not arise either from deficiency of feeling or thought.

From all this autobiographical writing "Bartleby" and *The Confidence Man* must be singled out for special comment, the first because it bears importantly on Melville's attitude toward his art at this time, and the second because it is the last prose work he published. After that came the long silence of thirty-four years, broken only by the four avocational volumes of verse.

Bartleby is a furtive law-scrivener, the third assistant copyist to a prosperous Master in Chancery. At first amenable enough for all his eccentric ways, Bartleby soon grows obdurate and refuses to carry out the many trivial tasks assigned to him. He will not even copy documents. He refuses, also, to be dismissed. His contrariness disrupts the whole office and at length forces his employer to change quarters in order that Bartleby and his influence may be left behind. But Bartleby stays on in his old place. Disgusted with such goings-on, the landlord has him removed to the Tombs as a vagrant. Here he dies; and all that his distressed employer can learn about him is that he had once been a subordinate clerk in the Dead Letter Office in Washington. Before a change of administration put him out, he had spent his days in opening letters full of hope "for those who died unhoping; good tidings for those who died stifled by unrelieved calamities."

From signs along the way it is clear enough what Melville means by this fable. The lawyer, we notice, declares that though he belongs to a profession proverbially energetic, he is content with his great volume of routine business; he never addresses a jury or in any way "draws down public applause." His first clerk, the overenergetic Turkey, is dangerously reckless after twelve o'clock. Yet he is invaluable to his employer in the morning, accomplishing a great deal of work in a style not easily to be matched. Nippers, the second clerk, is the victim of ambition and indigestion. Impatient of the duties of a mere copyist, he occasionally lets his imagination run wild when he should be drawing up legal documents. The Master in Chancery keeps the two clerks in his employ because "their fits relieved each other, like guards. When Nippers' was on, Turkey's was off; and vice versa. This was a good natural arrangement, under the circumstances."

"Bartleby" was the first magazine short story which Melville published. The new kind of writing he was attempting in *Harper's* and *Putnam's* resembles that of his Master in Chancery, dull business but (possibly) profitable. He is of three minds about it. Like Turkey he can keep at it until noon. Like Nippers he can be steady enough until his ambition gets the upper hand. In the character of Bartleby Melville prefigures what this new life may ultimately come to. Will its trivialities, the conventional nature of his task, impel him to follow the lonely scrivener's decision to "copy" no more? This possibility was certainly in Melville's mind in 1853. But the decision to abandon his profession, to "go to the Tombs" if that were necessary for his peace of mind, was put off until after *The Confidence Man* was published four years later.

This strange series of conversations among the passengers on a Mississippi steamboat—*The Confidence Man* cannot be called a novel—certainly does not deal with trivia, and Melville could hardly have expected it would be bought by the readers who subscribed to the family magazines in which his stories had been appearing. *The Confidence Man* begins cryptically with the emergence on deck of a deafmute who bears before him a shieldlike slate on which he has written "Charity," followed, after several erasures of the scriptural phrases belonging to the word, with his final version: "never faileth." While this is going on, the ship's barber puts up his sign—"No Trust." The ironic theme of the book has been stated, and the action, or what there is of it, begins.

A crippled Negro shuffles on, seeking alms from the crowd. Asked if there is anyone who will vouch for his poverty, he obligingly (for the reader) enumerates the eight kind "ge'mmen" who will speak a good word for him. Each is the confidence man as he will appear in one of his disguises. Every time he reenters he is a plausible fellow trying to get money or moral support out of the victims of his con game for such beneficent institutions as the Seminole Widow and Orphan Asylum or the World's Charity or the Black Rapids Coal Company. Those who are taken in are as stupid as the confidence man is vicious.

The devices of the ship-microcosm, which Melville had used in *White-Jacket* and *Moby-Dick,* and the series of episodes in each of which the confidence man makes his suave approach and fleeces his catch or is rebuffed, provide Melville with opportunity to loose his satire on missionaries, stock jobbers, universal reformers, transcendentalists, romantic nature lovers, believers in industrial progress, worshipers of the machine. He is able, through the amplitude of his structure, to work off some private grudges, as, for instance, his stab at Fanny Kemble Butler (as Goneril in the "Story of the Unfortunate Man") whose marital difficulties were the scandal of the day.

The Confidence Man is a fascinating book, in what it reveals about Melville's state of mind, for the strength of its satire, and its allusive wit. If it is a failure as a whole, it succeeds superbly in places. But one must be deeply read in Melville's earlier works to penetrate its secrets.

The clue would seem to be that Melville, having abandoned, in the course of writing *Pierre,* his confidence in the moral order of the universe, has now come to the point where he must abandon his humanist faith in the decency and dignity of man. It will be noticed that the stories written after *Pierre* deal almost exclusively with human relationships, not with metaphysical considerations. The point of *The Confidence Man* is in its title: the workers of con games make fools of those who have the wrong kind of confidence, who are, that is, made gullible through greed and softheartedness. Where can one find in the world the mutual trust and esteem, the charity, the love, which are the cement of society? In Chapter X Melville sends into the cabin "a somewhat elderly person, in the quaker dress," who distributes copies of a broadside poem "rather wordily entitled": "Ode on the Intimations of Distrust in Man, Unwillingly inferred from repeated Repulses, in Disinterested Endeavors to Procure his Confidence." If even the Quakers must give up, then it is time for all men to quit.

When Melville visited Hawthorne in England in November, 1856, after this book was completed, they talked—or Melville did—"of Providence and futurity, and of everything that lies beyond human ken." Melville informed his old friend that he had "pretty much made up his mind to be annihilated" —to become, that is, a materialist. But Hawthorne noted that he did not "seem to rest in that anticipation" and shrewdly guessed that he would not rest until he got "hold of a definite belief." Slowly and at first very tentatively, trying out the possible paths in his Civil War poems and in *Clarel* (1876), Melville worked his way to the solid ground on which he finally stood when he wrote *Billy Budd.* It was finished in April, 1891, five months before he died.

6

It is not altogether surprising that Melville should have turned, after his decision to write no more prose, to the writing of poetry. *Mardi* contains discussions of the nature of the poet's mind and art, and Yoomy is permitted to recite some of his own wobbly verses, composed in the sentimental style of the mid-century. By 1859, as Mrs. Melville notes in a letter to her mother, possibly with some dismay, "Herman has taken to writing poetry. You need not tell anyone, for you know how such things get around." When Melville left in 1860 for a voyage around the Horn with his sea-captain brother, he had a volume of verse ready for the printer. It found no publisher, though some of the verses included in it were, apparently, distributed in the privately printed volumes issued in 1888 and 1891.

The Civil War affected Melville profoundly, cured his lethargy, gave him a sense of participating in a common cause, and, above all, purged the saturnine mood of *The Confidence Man*. Like Whitman he looked on as a civilian, harrowed by the suffering and the heroism of the soldiers, brothers of a house divided. It was good for him to be lost for the time being in the joy at Northern victories and the common grief of both sides. That this was a war between Wrong and Right he did not doubt, and the steady assurance was medicine to his soul. Yet his heart went out to the misguided South, and in *Battle Pieces* (1866) he is as much the poet of the Confederate forces as of the victorious soldiers who fought for the Union. (In many of the poems the speaker is a Southerner.) But the Northern cause was indubitably the just cause. He exults as wholeheartedly as Seward or Sumner must have done in the outcome of the battle of Lookout Mountain. Many fought, he believed, in the reckless mood of Ahab.

> As men in gales shun the lee shore,
> Though there the homestead be, and call,
> And thitherward winds and waters sway—
> As such lone mariners, so fared they.

The section of *Battle Pieces* entitled "Verses Inscriptive and Memorial" tells us how constantly he brooded on the instances of individual heroism and how he desired to say in marmoreal verse the final word for those who fought with a whole heart.

However strongly Melville may have felt that in the Northern triumph there was a "type and victory of Law," he was not deluded into thinking that the Union had been saved by its success in arms. He feared the aftermath of conquest. His prose Supplement to *Battle Pieces* is a warning and a prophecy: "The years of the war tried our devotion to the Union; the time of peace may test the sincerity of our faith in democracy."

The war healed his private hurts, restoring his faith in the "Knights and Squires" of democracy whose "immaculate manliness" he had believed in while writing *Moby-Dick*. It also made him willing once more to wrestle with the metaphysical antagonists whose malign strength had finally thrown him down. The old themes appear again in *Battle Pieces*, as, for example, in the poem entitled "Commemorative of a Naval Victory":

But seldom the laurel wreath is seen
    Unmixed with pensive pansies dark;
There's a light and a shadow on every man
    Who at last attains his lifted mark—
    Nursing through night the ethereal spark.
Elate he never can be;
He feels that spirits which glad had hailed his worth,
    Sleep in oblivion.—The shark
Glides white through the phosphorous sea.

But now there are suggestions of a way out for those who hesitate perpetually before the inextricableness of good and evil. The note of reconciliation is sounded for the first time in his writing. Nature, inexhaustible and ever renewing, heals in time some scars. What say the elms of Malvern Hill which surround the dead, grimed faces in those bloody cypress glades?

    We elms of Malvern Hill
      Remember everything;
    But sap the twig will fill;
    Wag the world how it will,
    Leaves must be green in Spring.

Melville began to see, too, "that the 'throes of ages' may rear the 'final empire and the happier world.'" No man struggles alone. All those who have known bewilderment and despair over the nature of things are his comrades. Time, he had said in *Mardi,* is the great philanthropist. If history is fate, it may "also prove to be redemption." For Melville the road was open again. There might be refuge at its end.

In 1856–1857 Melville had made the journey to the Holy Land looked forward to by every devout or agnostic Victorian. He saw something, too, of the rest of the Near East and of Europe and England, but his record of the journey, *Journal up the Straits* (1935), proves that it was Judea which struck deep within him. His meditations on what he had seen were as decisive in his quest for certainty as the emotions aroused by the Civil War. *Clarel,* the poem which grew from them, had revolved for a long time in his mind before it was published in 1876. We know from a letter of his wife's with what anguish it was completed.

In form *Clarel* is a pilgrimage like the *Canterbury Tales.* A company of strangely assorted men journey from Jerusalem to Bethlehem, conversing as they go, their conversations provoked by their mild adventures and the odd characters, guides, monks, and other pilgrims, met along the way. The thread of narrative is attached to Clarel who, having fallen in love with Ruth, a

Jewess, leaves her for the pilgrimage when, according to Jewish custom, he is forbidden to see her for a time after her father's death. The slight story reappears at the end, with the news of Ruth's death.

Though Clarel gives his name to the poem, he is the least important character in it. As Melville's deputy he listens to the others, who are more violent in their hates or stronger in their faiths. On one side is ranged Mortmain, Swedish by birth, a disillusioned political idealist who once shared the ardor of the European revolutionaries. He has become "oblivion's volunteer" and asks only that he may die in one of the gray places of the earth. He has his wish when death comes to him in the desert. His place in the story is taken by Ungar, another of civilization's dispossessed. Blighted by the defeat of the Southern cause for which he had fought in the Civil War, he rails at the new Democracy. Having spurned the past, what can it promise for the future?

> Behold her whom the panders crown,
> Harlot on horseback, riding down
> The very Ephesians who acclaim
> This great Diana of ill fame!
> Arch-strumpet of an impious age,
> Upstart from ranker villanage,
> 'Tis well she must restriction taste,
> Nor lay the world's broad manor waste:
> Asia shall stop her at the least,
> That old inertness of the East.

Over against these lost, violent souls Melville sets the suave optimist Derwent, a Church of England clergyman. The character most fully outlined in the poem, he is as much the object of Melville's scorn as Mortmain and Ungar are of his pity. There are no issues between science and religion, Rome and modernism, paganism and Christianity which he cannot reconcile. Melville seems to dislike him most because he uses the remnants of a once strong faith to patch up his specious gospel.

Through the character of Rolfe we see most clearly the direction of Melville's own thought when he was writing *Clarel*. Impulsive, intellectually acute, he is the pilgrim who takes the widest view of all the questions which are debated on the journey. Though at first Clarel recoils from Rolfe's strength, he is soon drawn to him. Like his creator, Rolfe feels a deep regret that the Christian mysteries have not proved strong enough to stand in the modern world. But he knows well enough that civilization has lived through other times when faith was dim. Christ came at last to impious Rome where, to believe,

Except for slave or artisan,
Seemed heresy. . . .
The inference? the lesson?—come:
Let fools count on faith's closing knell—
Time, God, are inexhaustible.

Amid all the conflicts of opinion which bewilder the reader of *Clarel*, Rolfe's declaration stands out clearly as Melville's own conclusion to the debate. That he sides with Rolfe is plain from the eloquent epilogue to the poem.

Then keep thy heart, though yet but ill-resigned—
Clarel, thy heart, the issues there but mind;
That like the crocus budding through the snow—
That like a swimmer rising from the deep—
That like a burning secret which doth go
Even from the bosom that would hoard and keep;
Emerge thou mayst from the last whelming sea,
And prove that death but routs life into victory.

The faith which Melville longed for while he was writing *Clarel* and finally achieved when he wrote *Billy Budd* was not the faith of his fathers. He did not receive it in a moment of conversion to any inherited system of belief. He had to construct it for himself. But it was complete and it was sufficient to satisfy him at last. That he had to make the faith by which he could live—and that he succeeded in his long effort to do so—suggests why he has been so appealing a figure to many later writers whose struggles resemble his own. War and economic chaos and the new fears aroused by atomic power have been as unsettling to men of sensibility as were the issues of Melville's day to men of his kind. Writers like Yeats and Auden, unable to rest in any traditional faith, had—even as Melville did—to construct their own. Modern man must believe or he is lost. That is the meaning of *Clarel*.

If Luther's day expand to Darwin's year,
Shall that exclude the hope—foreclose the fear?

The running battle of the star and clod
Shall run for ever—if there be no God.

7

At his death Melville left a mass of manuscript prose and verse sufficient to fill nearly three hundred pages in the standard edition of his works. Little of this merits attention from the literary historian. The one exception is *Billy Budd, Foretopman,* the most expertly wrought of all his stories, a tale so satisfying in the way its tragic theme is explored that it takes its place among the really great works of fiction. With good reason *Billy Budd* has been called "Melville's testament of acceptance," for much of its power comes from the fact that here at last he came to terms with the "mystery of iniquity," content to acquiesce in what he could not, as no mortal can, fully resolve.

The time is 1797; the place, the deck of a British seventy-four, H.M.S. *Indomitable.* Memories of the recent mutiny at the Nore and the hanging of the mutineers "for an admonitory spectacle to the anchored fleet" haunt officers and men alike. The Captain, the Honorable Edward Fairfax Vere, known through the Navy as "Starry Vere," is prepared to put down sternly any incipient revolt, though he is compassionate by nature. Given to dreaminess of mood, so modest in manner that if he had been on board as a civilian one might have taken him for "some highly honorable discreet envoy on his way to an important post," "Starry Vere" is nevertheless a man of positive convictions. Deeply read in history and biography, he has come to his settled views by means of those writers who, "free from cant and convention . . . honestly, and in the spirit of common sense, philosophise upon realities." Through his acts and thoughts we come upon Melville's meaning. It is young Billy Budd, innocent, fair to look upon, the victim of foulest treachery, whose death we mourn; but the tragedy falls equally upon Captain Vere who has the mind to comprehend it, as well as the heart to feel.

When the story opens, Billy Budd has just been impressed from a merchantman, the *Rights of Man.* He takes his impressment cheerfully, though he had boldly jumped up in the bow of the boat carrying him away, to salute his ship as his sorrowful shipmates look down from the taffrail: "And goodbye to you, too, old *Rights of Man.*" His new mates love him for his happy-go-lucky air and his willingness to work. But he has from the start one enemy, Claggart, the Master-at-Arms. The motives which engender his dislike of Billy, Melville explains with great care, for in them lies much of the inner significance of the story.

By indirection, Claggart tries to draw Billy under the suspicion of mutiny, but the "handsome sailor" is so innocent that he does not understand the hints dropped to him. Claggart then goes to Captain Vere and accuses Billy openly. Astonished and unbelieving, Vere calls Billy to hear the accusation. This time Billy understands clearly enough. Unable to protest his innocence in words, because he is a stammerer, he speaks with his fist. The blow kills Claggart. In time of war a sailor who kills another seaman must die. Vere might take the case to the Admiral, but he chooses to accept the responsibility for a decision. A court is held, the other three officers are summoned to it and with some reluctance, yield to Vere's decision that the law must take its course. Billy dies at dawn, crying out before the rope strangles him: "God bless Captain Vere." At the moment of his death the cloud hanging low in the east is "shot through with a soft glory as of the fleece of the Lamb of God seen in mystical vision, and simultaneously therewith, watched by the wedged mass of upturned faces, Billy ascended; and ascending, took the full rose of the dawn."

When *Moby-Dick* and *Pierre* were conceived Melville was incapable of writing tragedy, though both novels have tragic implications. It was otherwise when he came to the writing of *Billy Budd*. In the story each of the central issues of tragedy is resolved, so far as human insight will permit, and all are harmonized in Captain Vere's speech to the doubtful officers who scruple to condemn Billy. Yet it is Melville's own version of tragedy, constructed after years of painful thought, and the chief enterprise of his maturity and old age.

Claggart is the representative of evil, but this time Melville knows whence evil comes and why it is loose in the world. Men like Claggart are sick with a "depravity according to nature." They are not normal men, and in passing over to the world they inhabit one must cross "the deadly space between." Their depravity is not universal. It does not involve "total mankind." "Civilization, especially if of the austerer sort, is auspicious to it." Those who, like Claggart, are naturally depraved seem often to be subject to the law of reason. Actually they use reason to accomplish aims which "in wantonness of malignity, would seem to partake of the insane." Melville, we see, has struggled free of the fetters which once bound him to the fear that good and evil are so inextricably interlocked that men like Pierre in seeking to do good involve themselves and others in the foulest deeds.

Most men, like Billy Budd, are by nature innocent. Their sins are little sins, resembling those of sailors everywhere whose "deviations are marked by juvenility." We must not miss the significant fact that Billy is impressed from a ship named the *Rights of Man* and that he is as innocent as Adam before the fall. The ship which impresses him is named the *Indomitable* (at one time Melville thought of calling it the *Bellipotent*). Billy has left behind him the natural state of man and has entered a world at war, our world, where monomaniac depravity like Claggart's is free to roam and subvert but where, too, men like Captain Vere are sometimes in command.

Melville drops the mantle of tragedy on Billy. He gives him a tragic flaw in his symbolic inability to speak and thus throw Claggart's accusation in his teeth. Billy goes to his death manfully with a cry of blessing for Captain Vere. Melville permits him as well some recognition of the reasons for his plight, though he shuts the door upon the healing words the Captain spoke to Billy in their closeted interview.

The agony is Billy's, but only Captain Vere is capable of understanding the law which compels his suffering. To the perplexed officers of the court he expounds the law under which they live and by which they must act as its responsible agents.

Now can we adjudge to summary and shameful death a fellow-creature innocent before God, and whom we feel to be so?—Does that state it aright? You sign sad assent. Well, I too feel that, the full force of that. It is Nature. But do these buttons that we wear attest our allegiance is to Nature? No, to the King. Though the ocean, which is inviolate Nature primeval, though this be the element where we move and have our being as sailors, yet as the King's officers lies our duty in a sphere correspondingly natural? So little is that true, that in receiving our commissions we in the most important regards ceased to be natural free agents. When war is declared, are we the commissioned fighters previously consulted? We fight at command. If our judgments approve the war, that is but coincidence. So in other particulars. So now, would it be so much we ourselves that would condemn as it would be martial law operating through us? For that law and the rigour of it, we are not responsible. Our vowed responsibility is in this: That however pitilessly that law may operate, we nevertheless adhere to it and administer it.

"We fight at command. If our judgments approve the war, that is but coincidence." Here Melville sets up his everlasting rest. He will not obey the first commandment. He cannot upon compulsion love the God who created the moral order in which we live. But to the rest of the decalogue he at last subscribed.

29. WALT WHITMAN

THE United States in which Emerson, Melville, and Walt Whitman spent their formative years was a group of commonwealths, loosely joined together in spite of the Constitution which was supposed to have made them one country. The federal principle had not yet been really tested, and, within Whitman's own lifetime, was temporarily to break down.

Walt Whitman was born in the intermediate land of Long Island on May 31, 1819, near the great harbor and westward-leading river of New York, with Dutch and Yankee, Quaker, and Calvinist in his ancestry. He was bred an enthusiast for the unity of his country. From his childhood in a patriotic family, he was taught to regard all men within the boundaries of the Republic as Americans like himself, differing only in their labors, fortunes, and separate personalities. In contrast to Emerson, Thoreau, and Melville, he was an American and an expansionist on a new model. Less wedded to class or region, he saw America as a whole.

There was, however, a cleavage in self-interests, in hopes for the future, or in temperament among these New World men and women more significant than the contrasts between New England and South Carolina, a cleavage which Walt too easily overlooked. In every state, and most visible of all in near-by New York, the capital of Walt's youth, an observer was sure to comment upon the difference between the settled society of Eastern merchants and landowners, and the multitude whose thoughts and energies were engaged by the great undeveloped West. Some of this multitude of the unsettled were recent immigrants on their way to new homes. Some were native Americans who, by the nature of their livelihood, or the turn of their imagination, were dominated by the idea of expansion into an unconquered continent. Many an expansionist remained where he was born, yet shared the dream of a continental, cosmopolitan state, a true New World. Such a man was Walt Whitman, and with the expansionists of geography and of politics, of body and of soul, he definitely belonged from his earliest maturity to death.

Walt Whitman was born on a farm in Long Island. a remnant of the five-hundred-acre estate of the Whitman family long settled there, near the marine village of Huntington. Just before his fifth birthday, he was taken with the family to Brooklyn, where his father, a carpenter-builder by trade, established his business. But for the next thirty years Walt was to return again and again to ramble and loaf in the fields and on the beaches of Long Island. In Brooklyn, he went to elementary school, his only formal education, and was soon apprenticed to the printing trade; there and in New York he got ink in his blood, and had opportunities to journalize on his own. From printer he grew into reporter and editor (with politics on the side), and in 1846 was given his "best sit," by which he meant situation, as editor on the *Daily Eagle,* the leading Brooklyn newspaper of his day. Here for nearly two years it was his job to round up the news of the town, of America, and of the world for local readers, and to preach to them daily on Democratic politics, morals, civic virtues, and the tendencies of the times.

He was at home in Brooklyn, a respectable member of a growing community, and placed in a typical framework of American small-town life. But the great bay of New York lay just beyond Brooklyn Ferry, crowded with shipping that swarmed with immigrants on their way to the West, especially after the opening of the Erie Canal in 1825. And New York itself was just across the ferries, already a great metropolis, cosmopolitan, turbulent, rich, incredibly growing. From Brooklyn Heights, the young Whitman could and did look at the symbol of American expansiveness, the port of New York, from which, even though art and literature still looked largely to the Old World for patterns, the trade, industry, and energetic imagination of thousands of Americans were already viewing westward expansion in terms of a continent.

The youth was a dreamer and mystic in his inner life. But as a young editor, a spokesman for the party of the plain people, he was actively concerned with the nation, and its problems which had become acute as a result of the expansions of the Mexican War, fought while he was editing the *Eagle.* As a reporter (and Whitman both in prose and in verse was always a reporter), he left daily his pleasant stall in Brooklyn to roam New York, to frequent its theaters in the years of great Shakespearean actors, and to drink in its operatic music while he watched the capture of vast audiences by the art of poetic oratory. As a Bohemian (and Whitman, who seldom lived with his family and never married, was always a Bohemian), he delighted in the crowds of Broadway, studied the "en-masse," as he called it, without prejudice, preferring workmen, farmers, the vitality of the common people, to the static and the complacent in American society. "Remember, the book [the *Leaves of Grass*] arose," he said to his friend Dr. Bucke, "out of my life in Brooklyn and New York from 1838 to 1853, absorbing a million people, for fifteen years, with an intimacy, an eagerness, an abandon, probably never equalled."

Whitman's education was partly self-education and partly vocational education, with great variety in both and few frames of reference in either. The former came by reading, the second was a by-product of his occupation as a journalist. It is difficult and unnecessary to separate the two, for while, as he grew older, he read more and more to enrich the *Leaves*—as before he had read because he was an editor and needed information—yet he read as a journalist always, finding nothing about mankind alien to his purposes and hence absorbing always the handiest books. Journalism, and especially political journalism, canalized his otherwise indiscriminate perusal of the many books that came for review into the *Eagle* editorial office, directing his attention toward all that fed his inner life, or that dealt with the rights, the opportunities, and most of all the potentialities of the common man.

We have abundant records of Whitman's reading in his many notes, not easily dated, but extending back into the formative years of the *Leaves*. As a child, he was nursed on romance, especially Scott; but when books in quantity became accessible to him and his own purposes had focused on the "long journey" of man toward personal freedom and full self-development, he foraged in history, science, general literature, and what he could take of philosophy. No year passes that some scholar does not discover a new source for the *Leaves,* in Michelet, Hegel, George Sand, Carlyle. A hundred more sources will be found, for the range, though not the depth, of the knowledge recorded in Whitman's notebooks is extraordinary.

These sources, as such, are not very important. The young man was seeking confirmation for the impulse of his inner being to become the voice of the common man who had been given at last, and on a new continent, his opportunity. Yet it is clear from the notes that, unlike the popular sentimentalists and indeed most "literary" writers of his youth, he was furnishing his imagination with facts, to be used as tools and weapons and poetic symbols. While feeding his dreams, he was collecting an intellectual arsenal for democracy, although it is probable that his first intention was to use it in editorial combats, for which, with his meager education, he had been none too well prepared.

By 1849, the Democratic Party, confused and split by the issues of slavery, no longer offered his independent mind a career in political journalism. Then he definitely turned to another objective, which was to capture not so much the opinions as the emotions and the imaginations of Americans. While still supporting himself by miscellaneous journalism, he gave his energy, his ambitions, and his deepest life to poetry. But this poetry, the *Leaves of Grass,* got much of its relevance to American life and to democracy from his reporter's training in observation and the editor's duty to be prepared for public debate on political and social issues of his day and time.

2

Although known until 1855 only as editor, or free-lance writer for the magazines, Walt Whitman had heard the call to the vocation of serious literature from his earliest youth. At first it was the wrong call, or (for him) the wrong kind of literature. Beginning at a very early age, he had endeavored to make a reputation in the conventional modes of the day—sentimental and melodramatic stories such as were being published by second-rate authors in the annuals and the magazines, orthodox poetry in the usual rhyme and meter schemes, and essays in the rhetorical-personal style then fashionable. He was successful enough to make a little place for himself in the better magazines, such as the *Democratic Review,* but, without exception, his work of this kind, including a novel on the dangers of intemperance, was commonplace, empty of real literary values, imitative, often banal, and definitely inferior to his journalism. Either the man's creative imagination had very little to say, or he could not say it. Until the late 1840's, when he was nearly thirty years old, both statements seem to have been true. Beside Emerson and Thoreau, who wrote for the same magazines, he seems shallow, facile, and ignorant. Yet in ten years Emerson was to hail him as author of *the* American poem.

The change had taken place when his inner life began to push to the surface and become articulate. We know that Whitman had been a dreamy boy, absorbed and absorptive to the point of apparent languor, so that he was often accused of laziness. Sometime in the forties, when he was most active in journalism and most prolific in attempts to be literary in the current modes, his maturing imagination began to draw upon experience lying at deeper levels. Strong influences of his childhood made it easy for him to believe in his own inspiration. The intense egoism of a young man in an expansive time encouraged him to put on the mantle of a prophet. His reading, as his notes show, supplied him with examples of the power of poetic leadership. And all this reacted upon his professional reporter's vision of the active millions of Americans around him engaged in one of humanity's great experiments. Being a writer already by profession, he began to try to make his vision articulate in poetic prose and adequate poetry, and with laborious difficulty finally succeeded.

This is not guesswork. As early as 1847, while Walt was in his "best sit," editing the Brooklyn *Daily Eagle* and lecturing the town, he began a notebook, now in the Library of Congress, which contains mingled prose and poetry, some of the poetry probably copied in from earlier records. By this time, Whitman had become completely self-expressive in good newspaper prose, and could exhort to good politics and sound morals as well as any of the journalistic tribe. Yet in this notebook is a mass of confused, apocalyptic prose writing, oracular, rhythmic, even when not written as verse, transcendental, evangelical in its earnestness. This writing, in style and subject matter, has no obvious relationship to his good if conventional editorials, or to anything known in his letters, or his personal communication with his associates. And it is definitely imperfect and experimental. The poetry in the notebook, which is written as such, is highly symbolic, rhythmic but not metrical, often unfinished, but recognizable as a first, or early, version of a part of the *Leaves of Grass*. Indeed, the dominant ideas of both the Preface and the poems of the first edition of the *Leaves* can be disentangled from the prose and verse of the first and immediately succeeding notebooks.

It is impossible to explain by any final analysis this remarkable phenomenon of the unveiling of a genius and prophet (however unformed) in the mind of a busy and successful journalist. Whitman's later friend, the Canadian alienist Dr. Richard Maurice Bucke, asserted that here was a remarkable instance of direct inspiration functioning through what he called cosmic consciousness, and many an early admirer of Whitman (and perhaps Whitman himself) was convinced by this theory of spiritual intuition. A more modest statement seems nearer the truth. There was a genius for absorption in this youth so sensitive to both his physical and his spiritual environment, and this genius became creative as soon as his rich but inchoate inner life felt the pressures of experience. His dreams became compelling and sought an expression for which his training so far was entirely inadequate. The notebooks not only record his early experiments, but show that these dreams, wherever derived and however inarticulate, had already taken form as a religion of divinity in the common man, which called for a new poet and prophet. Many of these earliest records of his inner being are meditations upon what such a poet should be like, how he should proceed, what should be the nature of his success. And it is made clear that the poet was to be himself.

Therefore, when Whitman's career as political journalist was frustrated by events, it was natural that the poet should take over the center of his life. Indeed, as one reads these notebooks, it is clearly inevitable that sooner or later this should happen. What had been a painful experiment to express the deepest in his belief and his desires, became his immediate and settled ambition. In a few years he set the motto, "Make the works," on his desk, and made ready for publication the first *Leaves of Grass*, which seems an incredible achievement for a politician and a journalist only because its long deep roots stretching back into childhood were known only to Whitman himself. This is a reasonable if not a complete explanation of one of the most surprising outbursts of genius in early middle age known in literary history.

3

But what was this *Leaves of Grass?* Whitman himself defined it many times, not always in the same terms:

An attempt . . . of a naive, masculine, affectionate, contemplative, sensual, imperious person to cast into literature not only his own grit and arrogance, but his own flesh and form, undraped, regardless of models, regardless of modesty or law; and ignorant, as at first it appears, of . . . all outside of the fiercely loved land of his birth. . . . The effects he produces in his poems are no effects of artists or the arts, but the effects of the original eye or arm, or the actual atmosphere, of tree, or bird.

I saw, from the time my enterprise and questionings positively shaped themselves (how best can I express my own distinctive era and surroundings, America, Democracy?) that the trunk and centre whence the answer was to radiate, and to which all should return from straying however far a distance, must be an identical body and soul, a personality—which personality, after many considerations and ponderings, I deliberately settled should be myself—indeed could not be any other.

Leaves of Grass . . . has mainly been . . . an attempt . . . to put *a Person,* a human being (myself, in the latter half of the Nineteenth Century, in America,) freely, fully and truly on record. I could not find any similar personal record in current literature that satisfied me.

After half a century these definitions still ring true, but they apply to the extended later editions, rather than to the original poem out of which all the *Leaves* grew, and which was crudely outlined and partly written in the 1847 notebook. This is the "Song of Myself," by no means Whitman's greatest poem, though probably his most characteristic. It is a true microcosm, and one of the most self-revealing poems in literature. He must have been working on the "Song" from the dawn of his resolve to be the poet of the New World in the "strange, unloosen'd, wondrous time" of the earlier nineteenth century—say, from about 1846 to its publication in 1855—and he heavily revised it in later editions. It is the key to an understanding of Walt Whitman.

When the "Song," the Preface, and the accompanying shorter poems were ready, Whitman became printer as well as writer. Knowing well what publishers would and would not accept, he decided to become his own publisher, fell back on his knowledge of the printing trade, laid out a book of unusual size and typography, set up some of it himself, and brought out the first edition of the *Leaves,* now a collector's item. Of this the "Song" was the outstanding feature, and was so recognized by the reviewers.

The "Song of Myself" in its final arrangement is a poem of fifty-two groups of long lines, each group a paragraph introducing a turn in the thought. Sometimes the break is abrupt, and the only reference is back to the brooding, oracular imagination of the author.

The poem begins with an assertion intended to challenge contemporary (and earlier) literature, which Whitman regarded as "class poetry" representing a world where literature had spoken for the exceptional man, not for the simple, separate person or the en-masse:

> I celebrate myself, and sing myself, . . .
> For every atom belonging to me as good belongs to you. . . .
> I loafe and invite my soul. . . .
> I harbor for good or bad, I permit to speak at every hazard,
> Nature without check, with original energy.

In an early manuscript he was more specific:

> I am your voice—it was tied in you—in me it begins to talk.
> I celebrate myself to celebrate every man and woman alive; . . .
> And I say that the soul is not greater than the body,
> And I say that the body is not greater than the soul.

This is the key passage in the poem. He proposes to be the voice of the democracy, and he intends to speak at all hazards what he finds in himself as representative of the "divine average." What does he find there?

He discovers that there is a world of sense perception in every man that is part of the eternal time stream and is far more important than what he calls the "latest dates" and the routine of daily living. Through love and its instrument, the senses, comes the knowledge that all men, with God also, are brothers. This cannot be argued, any more than the question, "What is grass?" can be answered. Yet it is certain that life and death are part of one continuous process in which every phenomenon has its importance. So leave discussion, and look at the pageant of life—wives, old maids, drivers, farmers, hunters—the Yankee clipper under her staysails, the clam digger, the trapper, the runaway slave, beautiful young men bathing and the woman who joins them in fancy, the Negro drayman with polished muscles—all these to the caresser of life are part of himself, part of a continuum both physical and spiritual. They are kin to the grass that grows wherever the land is, the common air that bathes the globe.

Therefore the self-dramatized Walt Whitman speaks for all this, sees himself in all people and all life, speaks for woman as well as man, for evil as well as good, and walking with the tender and growing night feels unspeakable passionate love for such beauty. He accepts time absolutely; in the long run, he says, it is without flaw. He accepts science which explains reality. He trusts the en-masse:

> I speak the pass-word primeval, I give the sign of democracy.
> By God! I will accept nothing which all cannot have their
>   counterpart of on the same terms.

Therefore, through him, long dumb voices of prisoners and slaves, the diseased and the despairing, the forbidden voices of sex and lust, speak at last, are clarified and transfigured. *"Walt,"* he says, *"you contain enough, why don't you let it out then?"* Which he does, first telling what he hears in the exciting world of his senses, then what he touches, both in intricate sexual imagery.

Now Whitman goes afoot with his vision. Over America, its work and festivals, he wanders, pleased with all he meets, then lifts his imagination to the past. He walks with Christ on the hills of Judaea; he is a free companion, a hero, a slave hounded by pursuers; he was at the Alamo; he fought with Paul Jones. He will save the depressed and the dying by the power of his love, outbidding those old hucksters, the heathen gods:

> I know perfectly well my own egotism,
> Know my omnivorous lines and must not write any less,
> And would fetch you whoever you are flush with myself.

Immense have been the preparations for this robust soul of his which symbolizes the soul of a new society. Nothing can stop its evolution. He will hook each man and woman around the waist and show them the endless road onward which each must travel for himself. Long enough have we dreamed contemptible dreams. As for himself, having given his message, he will depart, bequeathing himself to the dirt to grow again from the grass he loves. Somewhere, and notably in these poems, he waits for you.

This brief outline of the "Song of Myself" shows what many a reader has failed to see because of the profusion of detail and of imagery, that in spirit and exhortation, and in its long catalogues of activities, it is an expansionist poem, as expansionist as its country and its century. It is also a prophetic poem in the Old Testament sense, for Whitman is urging a vigorous country to spiritualize its energy and demanding that a society whose culture is intellectual shall find new sources of power in beautiful blood, in the ardors of sex, in a harmony, like the harmony of animals, with the physical universe. Furthermore, it is a dramatic poem. The author plays a histrionic role, like a revivalist. If he contradicts himself, he says, paraphrasing Emerson, well, then he contradicts himself. He is large, he contains multitudes. He can and does project a man of this age, great enough to feel with all, to love all, and to point them down the long brown road to full self-development. And this is the heart, though not the totality of Whitman's message. He will say it in separate poems more completely and far better, but he will never unsay any of it.

With all its extravagance, its artistic imperfections, and its incoherences (which are more apparent than real), this is an amazing poem to have come from the pen of a journalist whose literary publications hitherto had been conventional and often inferior. What was the long foreground which the wise Emerson, in his letter of greeting to the 1855 edition, intuitively felt lay behind it? What were its roots? In what spiritual and intellectual climate was it incubated? What was this "personality," this "identical body and soul," which was its dramatic center, and which Whitman deliberately settled should be himself? We can give some of the answers, without attempting to account for the essential genius which fed on the sap of environment, influence, and personal traits.

Whitman had been born in a household where radical liberalism was already familiar. His father, Walter Whitman, had been a disciple of Frances Wright, protégée of Lafayette, feminist, lecturer, and writer in behalf of labor and the common man. Walter Whitman was an intense individualist, who, though of landed stock, worked with his own hands, and liked to sleep, as he said, on floors of his own making. The family were Democrats when to be a Democrat meant specifically to vote for the rights of man and for the power of the masses against vested interests. The philosophy of this Democratic Party under Jefferson and Jackson was still revolutionary. Indeed, it was American Democrats who were to carry on a social revolution which our political Revolution had only begun. And the democracy of the Democratic Party was also a triumphant cause, never more vigorous, more hopeful, more potential than in America in the decades of the great expansion westward. A transference of the political ardor of the young political editor to the imaginative enthusiasm of a poem in which he wished to speak for the common man was natural, and carried confidence with it. Thus the background of the *Leaves* was the whole revolutionary process from eighteenth century "enlightenment" onward. For its author, the cause of the common man was a conquering religion, in which he had begun as a worker and became a priest.

It is not therefore surprising that Whitman's first characteristic poetry is not propaganda, or argument, but a chanting of victory and aspiration, in which he celebrates himself as a symbol of the "divine average." Nor that he addresses it to the "simple, separate person," the common man on common ground, who best represents a New World where oppressed human nature has already found successful release.

Yet one doubts whether the young Whitman, still so inarticulate, as his notebooks show, in the things which concern him most, would have been so confident of his inspiration or so determined to find a way to communicate it, if it had not been for his indoctrination in the mystical assurance of Quakerism. He was, of course, never a Quaker by profession; he was not made, as he said, to live within a fence. Yet he grew up in a Quaker strong-hold, his mother's family were Quakers, his father was an admirer of the great Quaker heretic, Elias Hicks, and Whitman himself was not only personally familiar with, but deeply impressed by, a religion whose only authority was the Inner Light. The essential fact is that he lived as a child and youth among men and women who took inspiration with the utmost seriousness, believing that, no matter how simple and unlearned was the voice that spoke of God, what was said was worthy of regard and should never be suppressed. He was familiar with the distinction which every Quaker made between the "I" which did the daily business of life, and the "soul" which, feeling a concern to report on the inner life of the spirit, might speak out in meeting, no matter how crudely, in the language of inspiration, a language usually rhythmic. The young Whitman had no inhibitions to overcome in writing as one inspired.

It must not, of course, be forgotten that the influence of transcendentalism, so pervasive and so powerful upon idealists, and also expansionist in its nature, was at its height in the years when the "Song of Myself" was forming in Whitman's imagination. How far this powerful transcendentalism, emanating from New England in the thirties and forties, gave form and logic and philosophy to Walt's celebration of himself, will always be in controversy. There can now be no question that Whitman absorbed from Emerson be-fore he wrote the *Leaves*. Not only is there record of essays read and lectures heard, but in the "Song of Myself," which represents the earliest stratum of his real poetry, there are echoes and paraphrases of Emerson. Whitman was definitely a fellow traveler with both the Quakers and the transcendentalists, as can be seen in the extraordinary meditations in his first notebook. Yet he was never a transcendentalist in the restricted Concord sense. Like the Quaker Hicks, he carried the ideas of man's intuitive knowledge of God and the spiritual significance of all phenomena to an ultimate conclusion, disregarding all metaphysical difficulties.

But Whitman's transcendental tendencies, though obvious, united with other tendencies much more personal to him, and emerged as a philosophy which neither Thoreau nor Emerson could accept as identical with their own, although they recognized the affiliation.

If, as Whitman learned both from the Quakers and from Emerson, a man could be God's mouthpiece, then God, so Whitman felt, must be manifest through man's body and all its impulses as well as through his soul. Soul and body were indissolubly interdependent, and blood and spirit were equally important in a true democracy. The common man, lusty, full-blooded, living, especially in America, upon hearty and varied experience, was as important as the saint, the intellectual, or the aristocrat, and in history likely to become more important. The vigorous sexual instinct which keeps the race alive was not merely a means for breeding new candidates for the Heavenly Kingdom, nor was it, as the Concordians thought, an animal remainder to be sublimated into a love transcending the flesh. No, if the soul was God, so was the body, and if democracy, and man himself, was to reach an ideal society, then the senses must have their full self-development as part of the expression of the soul. Here was an extension of transcendentalism, adapting it to the needs and the facts of an expanding democracy in a new land. When Whitman called Emerson "master," he may have meant that Emerson first gave direction and authority to his vague Quakerism. And when, later, he asserted that he was now his own master, he must have meant that he had carried his conception of God and man, body and soul, far beyond the limits of transcendental orthodoxy.

Of the personal traits which are reflected in his poems—and especially in the "Song of Myself"—one was his strong capacity for self-dramatization. Throughout life, as any careful biographer must see, he found it easy to differentiate between the "I," who was the Walt of daily relations, and the "soul," which was dramatized as Walt Whitman in the poems. The "I" was simple, natural, affectionate, often diffident and modest. The "soul," especially in his first decade of real poetry, was aggressive, brash, self-confident, violently assertive, and intensely egoistic—in addition to having many nobler qualities. Here he was representing, perhaps unconsciously, the brag and exaggeration of the frontier, the vanity of the self-taught leaders, the almost paranoiac desires of a new country aiming at greatness and clamoring for recognition. And his long and often tiresome catalogues of occupations (inventories of America, Emerson called them) are like the answers to the curious questions so frequent among immigrants and pioneers. In his vatic moods Walt clearly regarded himself as two persons, one of them under the influence of inspiration. Psychologically this, of course, was not true; but for him it had a pragmatic truth.

This accounts for the personal, prophetic element in Whitman's brand of transcendental thinking, which gave it a warmth that orthodox transcendentalism too often lacked. But the strong sensuality of the "Song of Myself" and many other poems, the deep sympathy with carnal man, indeed Whitman's whole argument for a democracy of the emotions, and particularly those emotions which are primarily sexual, unquestionably were all much influenced by his powerful body and strong but highly complicated sexual nature.

In his young manhood and early middle age, six feet in height, ruddy, not athletic, but an outdoor man, he radiated health and vigor. His best known pictures, which were taken in later years and show him "buffalo-haired" and full-bearded, a combination of Santa Claus and Father Time, give a false impression of the man in his prime. Health, vigor, lustiness are words that occur or are paraphrased throughout the *Leaves*. When most mystical, most prophetic, Walt most insists that it is his "beautiful blood" as much as his soul that is speaking. The affinities he found in his country were not among intellectuals, professional men, scholars (though these were his associates), but workmen, fishermen, farmers, pioneers, as hearty as himself, who did the work of God without analyzing. How well he knew them (and he did know them well) is not the question. It was the physical health and energy of his America in its great expansive period which stirred his imagination because he felt it in himself.

In this cult of triumphant physical vigor, Whitman was in accord with the continent-conquering energy of the mid-century, and out of accord with its most literary literature—whether the ghost-haunted narratives of Hawthorne, the polished romance of Longfellow, the febrilities of Poe, or the anemic sentimentalism of the annuals and the magazines. Most of the other writers of the age—Emerson, for example—were busy with sublimating or intellectualizing the crude energy of American physical life. Even Thoreau, who once wished to eat a woodchuck alive, was more disturbed than excited by what he regarded as the turbulent rush across the continent for land or gold. These writers were analyzing, criticizing, and portraying the first maturity of American culture. They were little concerned with the muscle, not much with the heart, except as an organ of refined or repressed passion. Though an observer and dreamer rather than forest feller and prairie breaker, Whitman had a zest for magnificent bodies, stimulated by his admiration for his own, which made him recoil from the intellectual and refined and gloat upon such manifestations as the full-bloodedness of New York—"turbulent, fleshy, sensual, eating, drinking, and breeding." He admired the immigrants bringing their muscles and little else to the new land, and was fascinated by the immense labors of pioneering, and the pageant of America at work. When, on his trip to New Orleans in 1848, he saw some of his frontiersmen along the Ohio, he was a little disillusioned by their idleness and the effects of malaria, but this did not change his dream. He believed he had more blood than his fellow writers, and better than they could feed his imagination on the strengths of the common man set loose in a free world, an aspect of America from which, he thought, literature had turned her face away, and so missed the reality of democratic advance. In an expanding democracy, the senses, he felt (and responded with his own), must take on new patterns of expression to represent the nature and needs of the "divine average," of common man on common ground of human unity.

These were some of the roots, and this was part of the foreground of this book which shocked, puzzled, amused, amazed, or profoundly impressed its few readers. But there was another source for its most challenging quality not easy to analyze. If the "Song of Myself" was symbolic of the release and expansion of democratic man, neither Whitman himself, nor some of his most characteristic poetry, was entirely representative of his fellow Americans. Physically and psychologically, Whitman was not typical of this "divine average" to which he wished to give, and did give, a voice. His love poetry was not always or often the expression of a normal sexual man. Nor was the difference merely in genius speaking, nor in a sublimation of body with spirit.

This ruddy body of Whitman's, with its electric senses, and its quick perception of passion, was not the body of an average man. Sexually, it and he (for his imagination of course was involved) belonged in the vague regions that lie in the hinterland of what a doctor or a psychiatrist would call a normal man or woman. He was physically sympathetic, mentally interpretive, for both sexes, richer perhaps than either taken alone. There is not one particle of evidence that he was actively homosexual, and when he was challenged in old age he recoiled from the idea with a horror whose sincerity is convincing. Yet from the records of his life and the testimony of the imagery of his poems, it is clear that his love went out more readily, more frequently, though not more passionately, to men than to women. With the boys he loved and cared for in the Civil War hospitals, and with young friends like the streetcar conductor, Pete Doyle, this love seems paternal. But there was often a perturbation, as he called it, a sexual arousing that does not differ from the passion between man and woman. Also, women readers of the *Leaves* have long since recognized an approach to passion that is often more feminine than masculine. Yet his love poems to women are too aglow with fervor to let one doubt that he knew also the love of women, and here in full sexual release. And to this must be added a curious worship of his own body which a psychiatrist would call autosexuality. There are patent instances in the "Song of Myself."

This sexual oversensitiveness is supernormal rather than abnormal. It made him a writer of great love poems. It made him an apostle of the love of comrades, which he believed alone could insure a durable democracy. It made it easy for him to dramatize himself as a symbol of the lusty vigor of expansionist America and of a sexuality fully developed and expressed and indispensable to the growth of a perfect society. It made it fatally easy for him to carry his sexuality beyond the bounds of reason and good taste.

Thus he became a target for the prudish; and he confused and sometimes disgusted his simpler readers, who did not like their sexual instincts discussed in terms of a religion; and he shocked beyond measure the bourgeoisie whose favorite reading was moral or sentimental novels in which sex was not so much ignored as bought off with hypocritical or lascivious hints.

4

The first *Leaves of Grass* was put on sale in Brooklyn and in New York at the shop of his friends Fowler and Wells, publishers of phrenological literature and of *Life Illustrated,* a popular magazine for which later Whitman did a series of articles. A number of copies were sent out for review and to men of influence. It was the reviews of the *Leaves,* and not the sales (which were negligible) that made American, and also English, readers aware of the appearance of a new poet, who was original if also shocking, bold if egoistic, powerful even if, in the opinion of most of the critics, powerful in wrong directions.

The first *Leaves* contained a brilliant Preface, stating a theory of poetry for democracy and for America. It contained also twelve poems, of which the first, "Song of Myself," was obviously an attempt to describe a symbolic man of the nineteenth century. This symbolic man was named in the poem, Walt Whitman, although there was no author's name on the title page of the book. Of the other poems, the most significant were (using their later titles) "I Sing the Body Electric," which was the most shocking, and "Who Learns My Lesson Complete," in which the poet steps onto the platform to explain his idea of life.

A second edition was published the next year, 1856, with new poems, some of them among Whitman's best, such as "Salut au Monde!" "Song of the Broad-Axe," "Crossing Brooklyn Ferry," "Song of the Open Road," in which his scope is notably extended. This edition failed with the buying public as completely as the first.

In 1860, Whitman issued a much more extensive volume, heavily revised, and with important additions, especially under the headings of "Chants Democratic," "Enfans d'Adam," dealing with the love of women, and "Calamus" inspired by the love of men. The outbreak of war cut short a promising sale for this edition. The Civil War, however, found its best expression in literature in *Drum-Taps,* of 1865, and the Lincoln poems, both groups included in an edition of 1867. Some of the finest of *Drum-Taps* came from Whitman's experience as a professional visitor to the sick and wounded in the hospitals in Washington where he cared for and comforted thousands of men. Though he never saw a battle, he knew soldiers intimately, and it was in the hospitals, as he said, that he first came to know from first-hand experience the virtues of the American en-masse.

In 1876, three years after his paralysis (in 1873), from which neither Whitman nor his poetic faculty ever entirely recovered, he published the sixth edition of the *Leaves,* containing the farewell poems of his creative period, "Passage to India" (separately printed earlier), "Prayer of Columbus," and "Song of the Redwood Tree," with other new poems. In 1881, the *Leaves* were given their final rearrangement in a definitive edition, and in 1892, the year of his death, got their final text in a ninth edition.

Even this briefest of bibliographical notes should make it easier to understand the unusual composition of the *Leaves of Grass.* It is not at any time, even in its ninth edition, a complete, articulated book. It is a becoming, in which the imaginative concept of the whole is to be found in the beginning, a whole which expands and gains power and control like a man's body, and which ceases, not because there is no more growth possible, but because death ends it.

Unfortunately, the courageous reader who proposes to go through the *Leaves of Grass* from cover to cover is confused not only by Whitman's occasional verbosity and frequent repetitions, but also by the aging man's rearrangements of the poems, by which a chronological order was destroyed, and poems of little vitality were inserted among the works of his great creative period. He intended to make a coordinated structure like a cathedral, but succeeded only in imitating an American World's Fair, such as the International Exposition in New York in 1853, which deeply stirred his imagination. No major author so thoroughly needs an editing as Whitman, such an editing as Arnold gave to the poetry of Wordsworth. He forbade it in his own lifetime because, with the genteel age against him, he felt that his lesson must be learned complete. There is no such necessity now for what revivalists used to call a "protracted meeting."

The first *Leaves* of 1855, which, it must be emphasized, was only the nucleus of the extensive final work, began a long battle for recognition, fought first by Whitman and then by his devoted friends. Its importance was much more generally recognized by critics in America than has been supposed, though it got plenty of blows. The selections which W. M. Rossetti made for England in 1868, from earlier editions, established Whitman's reputation there much sooner than at home. This was because the sexual poems, which had confused the prudish judgment of mid-nineteenth century America, were not included. And also, the English were naturally not offended, in fact the opposite, by what Americans regarded as a rough and raucous representation of their democracy.

The *Leaves of Grass* was one of those documents of the human spirit which appear at intervals in time, and which arouse both violent opposition and (though not always) unmeasured praise. Such documents are always the work of a pioneer, and, like the efforts of geographical pioneers, are often incomplete, defective, as full of faults as of genius. They meet with extraordinary opposition for several reasons. Even though the ideas they express may be familiar to thinkers, or drawn from the actual practice of the age, these books give these ideas their first emotional impact, take them out of philosophy or the current mores, and force them upon the imagination. It was thus with *The Prince* of Machiavelli, and the works of Rousseau. Also, it is often necessary for the writer to find, like the early Elizabethans, a new idiom in which to make his imagination articulate, and this idiom is often unfamiliar, and therefore not liked. So it was with the music of Wagner. Furthermore, if the document is literary and deals with human behavior, it is quite sure to run counter to the moral conventions, though not necessarily to the moral practices, of the locality of production. It offends because it asks for a reconsideration of what we have agreed to accept and live by. So it was with the New Testament.

All this was true of the first *Leaves of Grass,* and unfortunately the shock and clamor with which the relatively few greeted its "arrogant" verses redoubled when in the 1860 edition Whitman included his "Calamus" and his "Children of Adam," poems which, so the outraged critics thought, were only incentives to sexuality and perhaps to perversion. They neglected (with a few exceptions) new poems of moving beauty and emotional depth, such as "Crossing Brooklyn Ferry." Critics of later editions did not recognize the deepening of Whitman's religious feeling and his far saner intuitions of human nature in such superb poems of the late fifties and the sixties as "Out of the Cradle Endlessly Rocking," "When Lilacs Last in the Dooryard Bloom'd," and "Passage to India." Nor did they note, again with a few exceptions, a growth in artistry, until what had been an experiment in "Song of Myself" became in these later poems the technical excellence of a great and original creator of prosody. They let slip with faint praise (there was no general reading) the dramatic portraiture (begun in the "Song of Myself") which in *Drum-Taps* produced some of the best etched, most realistic, yet most uplifted poetry of war in English. Still confused by the outcry over Whitman's indecencies, they failed to see that democracy, which in the "Song of Myself" is only an emotional reaching toward the health and vigor of the common man, had become in "So Long!" of 1860 a religion of development, which, through the love of comrades, could make a society of realized physical and spiritual power. Nor was the profound acceptance of the will of the universe in Whitman's great poems, "Song of the Redwood Tree" and "Prayer of Columbus" (1876), adequately recognized until after his death. The critics were still discussing his sexuality, his egoism, and his exuberant optimism, while these poems, with their Hegelian antitheses of optimism, lifted faith above hope, and asserted the dream as the ultimate master of reality.

This deepening of Whitman's mind, like his growth in art, is easier to explain than the origins of his genius. His autobiographical writings, both in prose and in verse, show with painful clarity what had happened to the cheerful, confident caresser of life in the years between 1850 and 1870, so momentous to the nation. He was, it must be remembered, intensely patriotic in the most religious sense of that word. The United States, for him, was the haven of democracy, the hope of the common mass. Its unity on a continent was the great fact of the nineteenth century, and now, in the fifties, he saw his country rent apart by factions, governed by weak or corrupt politicians, hopelessly divided by the conflict over slavery, unable to meet the great emergency because of greed and selfishness in the North and arrogance in the South, and the incapacity of its leaders in both sections. When war was declared, his morale rose because the challenge to unity had been accepted, and he was soon aware of the emergence of a great man in Abraham Lincoln. But in Washington, where he arrived in 1862, he was a witness to the corruption, the self-seeking, the chaos of a government which survived only because the faults of the South, though different, were as great. Consolation was to be found only in the courage, the love, and the simple goodness of the great majority of common men as he watched over them, sick or dying, at the hospitals. In his bitter poem "Respondez" (1856–1871) he frees his heart:

> Let the people sprawl with yearning, aimless hands! . . .
> (Stifled, O days! O lands! in every public and private corruption!)

His later recollections, printed in *Specimen Days and Collect* (1882–1883), and *The Wound Dresser* (1898), tell of his own distresses. Only the common man and a statesman with the best virtues of the common man kept him faithful to the idealism of the earlier *Leaves,* but no longer egoistically confident. And to the disillusions of history must be added personal griefs and frustrations, their exact source unknown, though love and loss were evidently their source.

No one, for example, can fail to note the deepening of every noble emotion in "Out of the Cradle Endlessly Rocking" (1859). This poem, which is a reminiscence of childhood, when the "tongue's use was sleeping," is a record of loss and love far too passionate and too mature for a child's mind. The ardent sensuality of the "Song of Myself" has been sublimated in this great chant into "the unknown want, the destiny of me," and the solution is the "strong and delicious word," death, the continuum of life, the only answer to the insatiable.

Or the depth of "When Lilacs Last in the Dooryard Bloom'd" (1865), his elegy on the death of President Lincoln. This is no patriotic poem in the usual sense, nor such a triumphant celebration of the achievements of "beautiful blood" and a noble spirit in a man of the people as Whitman might well have written ten years earlier. Actually, like the far less elevated "Calamus" poems, it chants the love of comrades, which is the spiritual binding of democracy, and also the death of a "great companion," "the sweetest, wisest soul of all my days and lands." The gray-brown bird in the shadowy cedars supplies the elegiac commentary. The "powerful, western, fallen star" (Lincoln) was not extinguished with its light. The poem praises the "strong deliveress" death, and its message is always love.

Or of "Passage to India" (1871), which contains his most eloquent idealism. The theme is in the question asked by the feverish children of the modern age, "Whither, O mocking life?" The marriage of the seas in the Suez Canal, the crossing of the continent by steel, do not satisfy, they are but shadows of a greater dream. There must be passage to more than India. The soul, "that actual me," must voyage beyond its material successes in order to amplify its love, its ideals, its "purity, perfection, strength." So "sail forth—steer for the deep waters only."

Or of "Chanting the Square Deific" (1865–1866), not a great poem but an interesting commentary on Whitman's philosophy. Here is described the stern morality of a Jehovah, Christ the consolator, the Holy Spirit inspiring, and, for the fourth boundary of truth, Satan, the comrade of criminals, brother of slaves, despised, proud, equal with any, "nor time nor change shall ever change me or my words." As body and soul are aspects of the same verity, so are evil and good.

What Whitman acquired in these years when he knew, almost equally, distress and exaltation, was wisdom. Passion he had before, and more experience of varied human contacts and man's daily work than usually comes to a poet of mystic love. But his philosophy of living in the years of the first *Leaves* was what the eighteenth century would have called enthusiastic. That was its strength, the poet's exuberant faith in the onsurge of life as an end in itself and an evidence of God come from the depths of his consciousness, where it beat with his blood, and was as real as his blood. One had only to loaf and invite one's soul to know that there is not any more heaven or hell than now. It was a dangerous philosophy for a hot-blooded man who adored action as much as loafing, in a period of excited expansion like that of his youth. It was easy to oversay his philosophy, easier to shout it than to make it conform to reality, just as it was easier to describe the en-masse of America than to know the American as a fellow worker and fellow sufferer. Whitman's earlier poems have the faults of rhetorical overemphasis even though he tried so hard to make them unrhetorical. They are aggres-sive as a debater is aggressive who talks for points. And furthermore, as his cryptic passages too often show, he had not yet squared his own personal problems with his religion of simple and passionate love.

He needed to be broken away from his egoism by blows from without, as the enthusiast in religion needs to encounter irremediable sorrow or in-explicable sin. He needed to take into his imagination death as well as life. And being Whitman, this extension, for it was only an extension of his philosophy, had to come through no intuition of kinship with God, which was too easy for his expansive nature, but by "crises of anguish" for all who believed as he did that America was the last best hope for their fellow men. There was first the

> Year that trembled and reel'd beneath me!
> Your summer wind was warm enough, yet the air I breathed froze me,
> A thick gloom fell through the sunshine and darken'd me,
> Must I change my triumphant songs? said I to myself,
> Must I indeed learn to chant the cold dirge of the baffled?
> And sullen hymns of defeat?

And after that and equivalent experiences, a transcendence of the ego was needed, a sounder because a wiser religion, and a better understanding of "the potent, felt, interior command stronger than words," which compelled him to accept death with all it implies as passionately as life. His poetry deepened because his imagination, always sensitive to spiritual values, now reached out of his too physical world as he heard another song "covering the earth and filling the spread of the heaven."

Death began to seem as important as life, religion more important than self-expression, for only death with its extensions of spiritual continuities growing closer to the mystery of God, solved the irreconcilable contradictions of earthly life. His poetry deepened because his imagination, always aware of spiritual values, now was chastened into reaching far beyond and beneath his sensory experiences.

5

Since Walt Whitman is poet first, and an apostle of democracy and love and death only because of his poetry, the growth and maturing of his art is of the first importance in any history of the man. To understand this art it will be necessary to go back to the beginning of his career when he turned from what he called useful errands for humanity, his journalism, his surface writings, to making "the works."

Endless disputes have raged over Whitman's prosody. The truth is best ascertained by inquiring what he was trying to do, and what he actually did with the English language.

Two statements may be categorically made. What Whitman sought (and he said so more than once) was a medium in which he could express satisfactorily the expansive soul and the expansive mind and body of democratic man developing in a new continent and forming a new and different society. That a more orthodox technician could have made the conventions of rhyming or metrical verse do this, is not the question. Whitman could not, as his early verse shows. Also, his conviction that he had something new to say and describe impelled him to break away from orthodoxy in order to get an idiom which was fresh on his tongue and so could be personal and sincere. He needed to be free and lavish like his subject matter.

He did not, as he asserted, get rid of outworn poetic diction, though he refreshed it with the bold frankness and realism of his speech. He did not get much closer to the colloquial language of the people than Bryant or Longfellow. No one of his devices to achieve a unity of poetic music is original with him. Yet the result, which means the style, is unmistakable. It can be parodied and imitated, but not reproduced. It is original because it is Walt's own.

For sources, one need go no further than the flowing rhythms of the Old Testament, which, in debased form, was the emotional language of the people of Whitman's generation. And also the oratory of Shakespeare's blank verse in its more rhetorical passages, which he had heard declaimed again and again by the best actors of one of the great ages of Shakespearean presentation. Here he got his elaborate sentence structure. And, finally, the French and Italian opera, of which he was a devotee, a mixed art, both lyric and declamatory, rhythmic in both words and music. Here he found a form for many of his finest poems.

An analysis soon shows the technical contrivances of his long rolling lines, his catalogues, his exhortations, his lyrics, and his dramatic dialogues with himself. If meter and rhyme are to be discarded, some other means must be devised of securing that intense unity of impression which is an essential in poetry. Even a superficial study shows Whitman's extensive, sometimes tiresome, use of alliteration, both along the line and down the line beginnings. It shows assonance and internal rhyme, often most skillfully contrived. It shows a general trochaic and dactyllic pattern (unusual in English poetry, though not in American speech). It reveals a subtle use of the caesura, breaking the long lines into parts of differing lengths. And also a very effective play upon repetition of rhythmic patterns and of words. Rolling his lines (as we know) over and over on his tongue, until they were ready to set down, building his poems slowly with revisions that kept on until his death, he slowly perfected his use of these and other devices, the governing principle being a rhythmic pattern in his mind, which was his style.

If one reads with analytic care the extraordinarily skillful "Out of the Cradle Endlessly Rocking," it is easy to note its alliterations and its use of assonance and internal rhyme. Equally obvious, when looked for, is the structure of the whole, which is that of an opera—overture, recitative, musical meditation, and the song of the bird as lyric, until (as he says himself) "the aria sinking," the poem concludes with a finale. The verse technique of this poem or of "When Lilacs Last in the Dooryard Bloom'd" should be compared with the sprawl and pull-together of the experimental "Song of Myself," which is usually taken as the point of reference in attacks on Whitman's verse. He never wrote better than in some brief passages of the "Song," but its new prosody required the firm grip of the later poems to demonstrate its success.

The advantages of this new style (idiom, he called it) were various. Such diction responded easily to his ambitious attempt to make a voice for multitudes. It made easy rather than difficult his endeavor to put into poetry what current fashion regarded as prosaic, and what seemed, even if it was not, out of place when carried by the current forms of literary verse. It was very flexible, stretched (too readily) to any scope, and enabled him, like the makers of new literary languages, Chaucer for example, to say first and best what no one had endeavored to put into literature before, at least no one in his own land and time.

Most of all, since his personality flowed freely along these rhythms, there was an easy transference to them of the dramatized ego which he called his soul, and which was the symbol of the inner life of Walt, and also of his century and his environment as he felt them. When he "let it all out," he flowed, not into the stereotyped elocution of the orators whom he envied, but into a flexible mold already prepared.

Thus in a true sense Whitman's style may be called functional. It was admirably adapted to describe the immigrant and emigrant American on the move, the still unshaped landscape of a new continent, the energy and the romance of pioneering, the dreams of a nation sure of an illimitable future, and the revolutionary ideas of modern civilization finding their greatest release in this same America. It was also an excellent medium for his passionate nature, so often uncontrolled, and responded with a lift toward the sublime when he wrote of religion and of death.

His diction had great disadvantages also. It encouraged the occasional prose writer and the frequent preacher in the man. It tugged always at restraint, making it easy to reiterate, expand, forget the beginning in the end. In the best controlled poems, the technique became sometimes annoying because artificial. It favored ranting, encouraged padding, for anything could go in almost anywhere, and indeed Whitman frequently switched passages from one poem to another. Worst of all for him (though unavoidably) it offended good readers bred in the great tradition of poetry in English, and made his reception so difficult that in obstinate reaction he sometimes turned what was after all only a technique into an eccentricity.

Yet Whitman's poetic style must be judged by its best passages, and there it is not only as characteristic of the writer as was Shakespeare's late blank verse, but it is also a new style and often a great one.

One more commentary should be made on the growth of Whitman's art. If his own nineteenth century did not quickly rise to the flies he cast across its swirling water, one reason was that from the beginning he was often symbolic by choice and perhaps sometimes by necessity in his poetry to a degree equaled only by the much later surrealists. His endeavor was to convey the unexpressed, or the inexpressible except by indirect means, which we now recognize as a trend in modern art. One result was that his symbols were discussed in terms of their direct and prosaic (and often indecent) meanings, rather than of their indirect (Walt's favorite word) and poetical significance.

Whitman's youthful imagination was strongly absorptive, and fed upon vast, vague emotions, and upon generalized ideas about love and the varied and active reality of expanding America. He could not analyze, could not (and sometimes dared not) express himself except by finding symbols of experience which would suggest his inner meanings. There was an incapacity here which a greater artist in words, a Milton or a Tennyson, might have overcome. Yet Walt's determination to "let it all out" somehow, like his struggle to get an idiom, has given some of his best lines a symbolic force which is now recognized by world-wide quotation. In his early poetry especially, he is sometimes merely fantastic in his symbolism. Some pages could readily be added to this chapter on Whitman's lack of any true sense of humor, and his frequent absurdities in word, phrase, image and symbol—

like the "budding bibles" he hopes to find on his passage to India. Absurd, if you take him seriously, as you must, is

> By my life-lumps! becoming already a creator,
> Putting myself here and now to the ambush'd womb of the shadows.

In his early poetry he is also, and especially in sexual matters, cryptic in his symbolism beyond easy interpretation:

Is this then a touch? quivering me to a new identity,
Flames and ether making a rush for my veins,
Treacherous tip of me reaching and crowding to help them,
My flesh and blood playing out lightning to strike what is hardly different from
    myself,
On all sides prurient provokers stiffening my limbs, . . .
Deluding my confusion with the calm of the sunlight and pasture-fields,
Immodestly sliding the fellow-senses away,
They bribed to swap off with touch and go and graze at the edges of me.

He could also, in sexual reference, and elsewhere, be magnificent:

Bridegroom night of love working surely and softly into the prostrate dawn,
Undulating into the willing and yielding day,
Lost in the cleave of the clasping and sweet-flesh'd day.

How much of his sexual imagery, which is much more abundant in his earlier than in his later poems, was a subconscious protection against the onslaughts (from which he so heavily suffered) of the prudish, or the hypocritical purity of so-called Victorianism, psychologists may decide. But it must be clear that, for him, symbolism was a native language of his poetry.

In his later poems his symbolism is no longer eccentric, and seldom erotic, and seldom confused. It should be studied in "When Lilacs Last in the Dooryard Bloom'd," which is conducted throughout by powerful and beautiful symbols, profound in their significance, so that even the imaginations of children can feel them, though they may not penetrate the meaning. The fallen western star, the perennially blooming lilacs, the thrush (it was not a thrush, but no matter) warbling death's outlet song in the pines and cedars, the pictures of active America for the walls of the burial house, the long black smoke trail of Lincoln's funeral train drifting over the daily usages of the land, "lilac and star and bird" twined with the chant—this symbolism is confident, controlled, expressive, and beautiful.

6

Walt Whitman's importance and place in American literary history can be approximately stated, although of his absolute merits it may be too soon for definitive judgment. It is clear that he was one of the significant voices of the nineteenth century, expressing in his symbolism its creative, its transitional, and its revolutionary character. Probably in poetry he will come to be regarded as its most prophetic, if not its perfect, voice. Certainly he must be named as the first powerful celebrant of the upsurge of the masses and the potentiality of the "divine average" in terms of an ideal democracy. His impulses are close to modern times—particularly in his insistence upon the vital importance of sex in human relationships, which is Freudian in its perceptions. Yet here and elsewhere his mind and style are deeply involved in the rather romantic science of his own period, and even more in that era's evangelicism and its oratory.

In trying to decide whether Walt Whitman was as prophetic as he believed and as influential as he hoped to become, it is essential to consider his prose as well as his poetry. In the poetry, a dominant theme is not so much democracy in any of its usual senses, as sex the life force which, escaping from the suppression of a false morality, revitalizes love, and makes an enduring democratic society possible, something no institutions or political or economic methods can guarantee.

In Whitman's important prose, however, the ruling theme is democracy as we all know it, and how it can get leadership and be maintained and made to grow. The powerful prose Prefaces are revealing here, especially the Preface to the first edition of the *Leaves,* afterward disintegrated and worked into the poetry of "By Blue Ontario's Shore," and now seldom reprinted and much too little read. Of the first importance also is the *Democratic Vistas* of 1871, one of the great American pamphlets, to be compared for its ideas, though unfortunately not for its style which has too much of the parentheses of conversation, with *The Federalist* papers.

In the first Preface, in singing, epigrammatic phrases, Whitman proclaims what the American poet and his poetry should be like, and his duty, which is to give voice and leadership to the dream of a fully developed man in a continent mastered for the benefit of the people as a whole. That the poet's work will be literature is only incidental. Whitman's point is, that it cannot be literature unless it makes articulate essentially American life and hopes and dreams, however conducted and wherever derived. The best American literature had too little concerned itself with the American democracy so far, and therefore is too often sterile for our own experience, and unable to speak for our New World experiment. For "America is democracy." His own hope was to become the first effective spokesman for a new race of races in a democracy, and to begin a literature for a new continent which would burst the bounds of region and class and cult. He wished to chant to the world.

Democratic Vistas was written at the end of one crisis, the Civil War, and at the beginning of another, the threatened capture of the nation by oligarchies and monopolies. In it, he carries on his theme. Democracy is not to be defined as majority rule, which may become tyrannical; it is the possibility of individual self-development, in which body, mind, and soul all proceed toward spiritual ends without loss of the material functions of living, which are as divine as the immaterial. Only a government which provides for the free functioning of every individual in every way necessary for complete being can be regarded as democratic, and such a government must rest ultimately upon the fraternity of comrades. Only such a government—and here he is more prophetic than clear—can meet and survive the difficulties of a new age in which nature has become the servant of man and can be used either to elevate or to destroy. He is realistic in describing the diseases and the collapses of our own democracy (after all, he had been a "practical" politician before he was a practicing poet). Centuries, not decades, will be required in order to mature democracy, but he has his faith.

What claim have Whitman's *Leaves of Grass,* his Prefaces, his *Democratic Vistas* to be regarded as interpreting the chief social significance of a century? The reader, too often distracted by rant and rhetoric, overwhelmed by inventories of American activities, will at first be skeptical. Yet, as gradually the lucid and powerful passages in both poetry and prose rise out of a seeming confusion, and as the self-assertive individual who calls himself Walt Whitman becomes more and more symbolic of indisputable qualities in the age of expansion, the faults begin to seem less important. Here is no typical or even representative man of the expansive age, but here, unquestionably again, is a writer of extraordinary intuition and unusual powers of expression, who could have lived in and been a product of only such a time. Whitman was quite right in saying that most of his contemporaries in authorship were running temporary errands for their fellow men, while he (so he implied) was out for immortal service. It was true that he was the bard and seer of a great idea and a great hope—even though he had some of the improvisation of the bard, and some of the extravagance in prophecy of the seer.

Was he a great poet? Many of his contemporaries, including William Dean Howells, denied that Whitman wrote poetry at all. They usually meant poetry in what they regarded as the proper form, or written upon subjects which they felt to be poetic. Even so the charge is hard to understand. His verse is sensuous and passionate and at its best simple, thus according with

Milton's famous definition. It does not fail (again at its best) when judged by the severer requirement that its form should convey its sense. True, it is difficult to find a poem in the *Leaves* which is one perfect chrysolite, yet still more difficult to deny the attributes of great poetry to "When Lilacs Last in the Dooryard Bloom'd," or "Passage to India," or many another poem or part of a poem even more characteristic of the chanter of democratic man.

The most satisfactory test of permanent value in poetry is not rhetorical, but pragmatic. If it enters into the common consciousness, exercising there the function of poetry, which is to lift the emotions by its rhythms, and to enliven the imagination by its final statements of the essence of experience, then there is not much room left for argument. This, Whitman's best lines and a few whole poems increasingly do, while the catchier meters of so many of his American contemporaries are already dropping out of memory. But even more significant is the remarkable extension of the influence of his poetry, and the welcome of that poetry itself both in its original form and in translations through so many lands and languages. This began early in his career, and has increased with each decade. He not only took his place beside revolutionary poets, his contemporaries in nineteenth century Europe, but has proved to be more expressive and more lasting.

Walt Whitman as poet and artist undoubtedly suffered from his too urgent sense of the importance of his self-appointed mission. His transcendental belief in the worth of original inspiration made him leave many a line in its first crudity, perhaps because he felt that what had come to him was inspiration, even though imperfectly caught, like radio music in a storm. His taste, too—and this was a result of self-education and a democratic disdain for refinement—was defective, as Poe's was so often in his prose. Again, in spite of powerful lines where every word was right, his feeling for words was often inferior, more often experimental, and sometimes plain bad. In this, as in his dislike of "polishing," he was a true American, with the frontiersman's disdain for too much learning or art. It was unfortunate also that Whitman's native expansiveness should have flowered in a period of literary romanticism that favored extravagance and discouraged restraint. Yet every writer should be judged by what he tries to do, provided it is worth doing. With Walt it is certain that his chants, like his favorite operas and his favorite Shakespearean plays, were never intended to be absolute art. They were written to capture his fellow men in his own time by any relevant means.

When Whitman died on March 26, 1892, his century was concluding its last quarter. The prejudices of the genteel age in America which spread burrs and prickles over his poetry were beginning to wither. A vigorous period of poetic experimentation was not far ahead, in which his rebellious rhythms were to be influential. His verse no longer offended the ear except of the most orthodox, for the industrialized world, where almost no one is illiterate, was full of new rhythms to which readers easily adjusted their senses. Shakespearean blank verse is more difficult for a schoolboy of the twentieth century than the irregular roll of Whitman's lines. After the Spanish War of 1898, national self-consciousness became the rule rather than the exception, and it was not long before Whitman, whose success (at home, if not abroad) had been a notoriety of sexual sensationalism, took his rightful place as the first poet of continental America and as the bard of democracy. The decline of religious dogmatism, so marked in this latter end of the century, also made his acceptance easier. The assumption of Godlike intentions, which had seemed blasphemous, now was seen to be only an assertion of the God in every man. Furthermore, the rising social consciousness of the early twentieth century, the acknowledgment of the rights of labor, and the emergence of the en-masse as the new factor of power in the Republic, made much of the humanitarianism and the political philosophy in the *Leaves* timely and relevant to great issues now clearly understood. Not until later, with the capture of European governments and their corruption by what Whitman had called "invaders"—those exploiters of democracy, the Mussolinis and the Hitlers—was it revealed that his fears for democracy as well as his faiths were truly prophetic.

It is still difficult to separate the gold from the mud (this is his own figure) in the heaped-up and shoveled mass of the *Leaves of Grass*. Yet the gold is easy to find, and it has become a currency which provides a common exchange of poetic ideas throughout the democratic world. We may repeat and paraphrase with confidence Emerson's remark to Moncure Conway after the publication of the now famous first edition: Americans who had been seeking abroad for some powerful expression of their phase of earth history could now come home—unto us a man had been born.

CRISIS

. . . conflict, refinement, success

30. A HOUSE DIVIDED AND REJOINED

THE average citizen of the United States in 1850 held certain truths to be self-evident. Whenever he heard them uttered, from flag-draped platform or in the echoing chambers of a still-unfinished Federal Capitol, he applauded almost by reflex. He believed that God had created man with certain rights and dignities, and given him a moral law for his guidance—what Emerson in 1854 called "the constitution of the Universe." This law underlay our own Constitution, making it a document almost as sacred as the Bible, and affording us Americans the best government in the world. Mankind, in fact, was watching our experiment in democracy, to see whether it ultimately succeeded or went to smash. This government, rather than our resources of coal and iron or illimitable fields of wheat and cotton, had already made us a great people. Liberty bred self-sufficience and achievement. Liberty was greater than Equality, because it comprehended the latter—in giving every man the opportunity to rise until he became the peer of any man.

It was a fine gospel, so long as humility tempered it against smugness, and sincerity against mere lip service. If at times the behavior of average citizens—as they confronted the immigrant, for example, arriving in the Land of Promise, or the Negro long domiciled in the Land of the Free—seemed to deny some of these postulates, that contradiction merely showed that an individual, like his nation, might be a house divided. And here, as always, a split personality meant tension, frustration, unhappiness.

A conviction that their nation enjoyed a special revelation of light made some citizens look down their noses at "the old and moth-eaten systems of Europe," as young Whitman saw them from the vantage point of Brooklyn. Senator Stephen A. Douglas, pride of the Illinois Democrats, announced that, in comparison with ourselves, Europe "is a vast graveyard." In fact, the great commercial city of New York, and the new metropolis of the prairies, Chicago, from their lead in the van of materialism tended most loudly to voice this bumptiousness. But Philadelphia with its seasoned wealth, and still more Boston with its Europeanized culture, regarded such swagger with a faint distaste. Their gentry and scholars, while admitting the national genius for enterprise and invention, still granted the Old World primacy in arts and letters. James Russell Lowell, savoring a leisurely holiday in Europe in 1851–1852, reflected that our predilections were less Greek than Roman. "I cannot help believing that in some respects we represent more truly the old Roman power and sentiment than any other people," he wrote his friend John Holmes. "Our art, our literature, are, as theirs, in some sort exotics; but our genius for politics, for law, and above all, for colonization, our instinct for aggrandizement and for trade, are all Roman." Reconciled to the *fait accompli* of Manifest Destiny, the Mexican War, and California, Lowell could not help paying tribute to the expansive vigor of the great Republic, like that which had once girdled Europe, North Africa, and Asia Minor with the Pax Romana. To a few Americans, the cult of vulgar self-satisfaction was no more reprehensible than the contrary mania for cultural flunkyism. That proud Brahmin, Francis Parkman, while fretting against the commerce which in the fifties was making America powerful—grumbling that there was "no sanctuary from American enterprise"—still refused to fall a victim to the "John Bull mania, which is the prevailing disease of Boston in high places and low."

The existence of two Englands, two Europes—aristocratic and proletarian, absolutist and liberal, with very different sets of interests in the New World—became much clearer to Americans after the onset of the Civil War, with the French Emperor and the Court of Queen Victoria as frankly pro-Southern as Karl Marx, John Bright, and the mill hands of Manchester and Lyons were pro-Union. In the fifties, these demarcations had been latent but less plain. While the leisured classes of the Eastern seaboard turned more and more to the social rites of London and the elegances of Paris, in love with antiquity and the glitter of coronets, Americans in the mass were prone to sympathize with Cuba under the Spanish heel and cheered wildly for Louis Kossuth, symbol of revolt against the Hapsburgs, when as the nation's guest he visited these shores in 1851. A localized minority might share the nostalgia of Lowell's grandmother—who used to dress in black on the Fourth of July "and loudly lament our late unhappy difference with His Most Gracious Majesty" —but the majority of Americans applauded constitutional revolutions such as their ancestors had fought.

Toward economic revolution their attitude was much less friendly. Why pull down, level, destroy, when every man himself expected to be a property holder some day? Hence the arrival of Marxist socialism in the fifties, with some German immigrants, and at least one short-lived attempt to found a "Proletarierbund," roused little support. In fact, the presence of radical elements among the new immigrants, joined to prejudice against the Irish Catholics, lent fuel to the flame of nativism. From these fears and suspicions the Know-Nothing Party sprang, gathering such strength that it won the 1854 state elections in Massachusetts and nearly carried New York. For two or three years it threatened the civil liberties traditional to America. "When the Know-Nothings get control," wrote Lincoln to a friend in August, 1855, the Declaration of Independence "will read 'all men are created equal, except negroes, *and foreigners, and Catholics.*' When it comes to this I shall prefer emigrating to some country where they make no pretense of loving liberty." As he intimates, Know-Nothingism tried to link its racial prejudices with those of the slaveholding South—a move that soon cost it the roving Northern support vital to any third party's success, and so the movement collapsed.

The task of ameliorating the lot of labor, in ways less revolutionary than those of the Communist Manifesto, meanwhile engaged the attention of thoughtful Americans. Growth of the factory system in New England had shortly contrived the end of that benevolent paternalism fairly common at the dawn of Fall River industrialism—under the new hurly-burly of immigrant toilers, competitive low wages, sweatshop conditions, and quick profits. The old American fluidity of opportunity was threatened by the freezing of working classes into lasting depression. Lincoln objected to the "mud-sill" theory, that "whoever is once a hired laborer, is fatally fixed in that condition for life." In self-defense American labor began to organize, although its efforts proved feeble until man-power scarcities in the Civil War lent new leverage to its bargaining power. Up to the outbreak of war, ironically enough, the sharpest critics of the Northern sweatshop were apologists for slavery, as will be seen: writers with an ax to grind, a cause to foster, that could hardly be described as pure humanitarianism.

Other crusades and enthusiasms, platforms and shibboleths, did flourish in the North in the fifties. "Marriage reform" looking toward more liberal divorce laws and property rights, and woman suffrage as championed by Lucy Stone, Lucretia Mott, and Elizabeth Cady Stanton, enlisted minority sympathy. The opposition of the rigid minds in the male sex might be typified by Parkman the historian. Having admired the Middle Ages for their religious faith and the cult of chivalry, he caustically remarked that American vulgarity had resuscitated the one under the guise of "spirit-rapping," and the other in the form of "woman's rights, Heaven deliver us." Yet feminism found hearty endorsement from men like James Russell Lowell, husband of the poet and gentle reformer Maria White, and Henry Ward Beecher, clerical brother of Harriet Beecher Stowe. Espousing the new development of coeducation in the *Atlantic* in 1859, Thomas Wentworth Higginson, abolitionist and man of letters, argued that "woman must be a subject or an equal: there is no middle ground." Still another crusade sought to curb intemperance. Maine enacted the pioneer prohibition law in 1851; by 1855 every Northern state save New Jersey had some form of liquor control on its statute books, although aid from the courts and the machinery of enforcement often proved weak, and the experiment yielded much ground during the next decade. Wendell Phillips and Mrs. Stowe sought alike to rouse moral boycotts against wine served at public dinners. The march of the "Cold Water Army" spread propaganda through the Mississippi Valley in the fifties, invading even "the land of Dixie and whisky." By and large the South distrusted Yankee fads, rejecting them with pride and dignity, and more than a little fear of the most powerful ism of them all—abolitionism.

2

In the century's early years, the native region of Jefferson had been prone to apologize for slavery, an expedient evil that time would prune away. But from about 1830 on, following the party battles of the Jackson era, the exacerbation produced in the South by abolitionists like Wendell Phillips and William Lloyd Garrison, and the economy forged ever more tightly upon these states by King Cotton and the tribute he drew from world markets, slavery ceased to be regarded as transitional. The South's "peculiar institution" was a lasting good, vindicated by history in the glory that was Greece, and sanctioned by the wisdom of God who had created blacks to serve their white superiors. The South never tired of quoting Jefferson's praise of agrarianism, while treating with more and more neglect his devotion to natural rights, public education, and the religion of human progress. While a growing solicitude for the black man prevailed in Western Europe and the Northern states —regions where slave economy was unprofitable, as Southerners loved to point out—the spirit of Dixie moved back toward the past, taking avenues of escape into medieval chivalry, race myths, and cultural isolation. While glorifying her Anglo-Saxon stock over the mixed bloods and unassimilated immigrants of the North, and her claim of descent from Cavaliers rather than Puritans, the South increasingly regarded herself as distinctive, unique, and her way of life as the American way.

Others of course held contrary views about the essence of true Americanism, and put up strong arguments. But these rebuttals fell upon Southern ears growing more deaf through the years—as antislavery books like Hinton R. Helper's *The Impending Crisis* (1857) were suppressed south of the Mason and Dixon line, while during the fifties large numbers of Southern lads were withdrawn from Princeton, Harvard, Yale, and similar institutions, to enroll in "orthodox" colleges at home. To discussion, debate, dissent, the South began to shut its mind, fearful of apostasy among the whites, insurrection among the blacks. Its people began steadily to shift their loyalties from the nation to state and section. Under the spell of their own logic, many

Southerners in the fifties began to demand that the slave trade be reopened, and still more that slavery be spread to the Pacific. With an agrarian system and a static population (in which four million blacks had no right of franchise), Southerners saw themselves disadvantaged against a North steadily recruited by industry, immigration, and westward expansion. Short of war, only two reinforcements of their position seemed possible. The first was the safeguarding of minority rights, and the second, the establishment of slavery upon fresh soil to capture the voting strength of new states in the Union.

Thus the old wedge of the tariff yielded to the new one of slavery in threatening irreparably to split the Union along the thirty-ninth parallel and the Ohio River. And the oldest economy in the world (a staple crop agriculture on a base of slavery) found itself pitted against the newest (industrial capitalism grounded upon the wage system) within the frame of the same democratic government.

A sense of popular relief, similar to that after Munich in 1938, first greeted the Compromise of 1850 and lasted long enough to achieve the election of easy-going Democrats to the White House, Pierce in 1852 and Buchanan in 1856—the "filthy presidentiads" whose time-serving maddened the disillusioned Democrat Walt Whitman. The Kansas-Nebraska Act of 1854, referring the issue of free soil versus slavery on the Great Plains to local decision ("popular sovereignty"), looked like another victory for appeasement—although Kansas was soon won for the antislavery party by aggressive infiltration of settlers. Certainly the Dred Scott Decision of 1857, upholding property rights of slaveholders even on free soil, was a thumping Southern victory which captured that august symbol of government, the Supreme Court. In the next year, Abraham Lincoln was the Illinois Senatorial candidate of the new Republican Party—a coalition of antislavery elements, free from the old cumbering garments of Whiggism, and rejoicing in an idealistic zeal tempered by the presence of some shrewd politicians. But he was defeated by a fairly close margin, after a series of debates with his opponent, Stephen A. Douglas, through the prairie towns. Although he lost the election, these speeches helped to win Lincoln the leadership of this new party.

Despite compromise and political victories for the Southern bloc, the storm of opposition was rising steadily. In 1852 the most influential novel in all history, Mrs. Stowe's *Uncle Tom's Cabin,* was published, selling 300,000 copies in its first year. Unhappily for its cause, the South found no penman who served it with such power and persuasion as the North possessed in Mrs. Stowe, not to mention Lowell and *The Biglow Papers,* the abolition poetry of Whittier, and the fiery utterances of Emerson and Thoreau late in 1859, when John Brown stepped from the gallows into martyrdom and the battle songs of the future.

For the drift of war appeared inevitable. It was now plain that the party and leader able to unite the West with the North—as the seaboard statesmen seemed powerless to do—would win the next election and, as promised by Southern hotheads, infallibly split the Union. William H. Seward of New York, statesman of moderation, coined the phrase "the irrepressible conflict." It reverberated in the mind of the nation, along with the saying of another moderate, Abraham Lincoln, about a house divided, in his prophecy of 1858 that "this government cannot endure permanently half slave and half free." Neither then nor upon his nomination and election to the Presidency in 1860 —with hardly a single ballot from the South—did Lincoln propose to force emancipation upon the slave states. But upon two things the new President and his party were determined. There was to be no spread of slavery farther into the West, whose pioneers (in Lincoln's vivid speech) deserved "a clean bed, with no snakes in it." And the Union must be preserved. Upon this last issue the Civil War was joined—after a procession of states, led by South Carolina, seceded in the winter of 1860–1861, as the promised answer to Lincoln's election, and on April 12, a Federal expedition to relieve the garrison at Fort Sumter drew fire from the Charleston shore.

3

The leaders of North and South, most writers and thinkers, and masses of the rank and file, felt the justice of their respective causes with peculiar intensity.

The Southerner, repelling invasion from across the Potomac, fought for hearth and home, his right to freedom and self-government, and pride of race against a widely assumed threat of insurrection, rapine, and murder. Stirring songs like "Maryland, My Maryland," poems like Dr. Francis Ticknor's "Little Giffen of Tennessee" and Henry Timrod's "Ode to the Confederate Dead," exalted the spirit of self-sacrifice, often the heroism of common men. The finest poet in the South, Sidney Lanier, served through the war in uniform, was captured and imprisoned near its close. Yet under this mortal crisis, intellectual and creative life tended still more to stagnate. "Wait until you have saved your country before you make preachers and scholars," Colonel James Chesnut told some theological students seeking draft exemption. "When you have a country, there will be no lack of divines, students, scholars to adorn and purify it." Long before Appomattox, many of the best libraries had been scattered and destroyed, most colleges closed, and such vestiges of public education as the South possessed now obliterated. In the heat of war, the Southern gentry were sometimes led to exalt ideals not only of aristocracy, but autocracy as well. In a Boston speech in 1863, Oliver

Wendell Holmes seized upon a recent editorial from the Richmond *Examiner*, avowing that the embattled Confederacy had withdrawn from "the whole course of the mistaken civilization of the age. For 'Liberty, Equality, Fraternity,' we have deliberately substituted Slavery, Subordination, and Government." As the war lengthened and reversals multiplied, rifts of disillusion and disunity appeared, not only among crackers and hillbillies, but in the multitude of non-slaveholders (for, as the census of 1860 reported, out of eight million whites in the South, only four hundred thousand owned slaves). They began to say it was "a rich man's war, and a poor man's fight." The last act of the tragedy, at Appomattox, found the South bruised and bleeding, fissured geographically and spiritually, but still proud, and magnificent in her downfall.

The utterances of Lincoln, upon war aims and ideals of the Union side, made those of Jefferson Davis seem petulant and narrowly partisan. Beyond question, the man from Illinois was spokesman for the clearest thoughts and wisest judgments in the North, and became the voice of idealists throughout the world. Lesser men at first often disagreed with him; generally swung round in the end to his conclusions. The morale of the North at war is essentially the story of Lincoln's growing and deepening influence, as he thought things out for himself and expressed them, with simplicity and clarity—knowing the unimportance of malice, working all the while through the medium of democratic government, waiting for public opinion to ripen, with patience and rare skill in timing.

How literary men fell into line, and added the reinforcement of their art to his argument, may be shown by one or two instances—for, during the war, even as in its prelude, the North was richer than the South in the literature of persuasion. The pacifism with which the New England temper had opposed the Mexican War quickly yielded to the holy crusade of Sixty-one, as utterances of Thoreau, Lowell, and even Whittier the Quaker bear witness. The essayist or scholar, coaxed from his lamplit study by the controversy that heralded the war, hailed its outbreak as a great regenerative experience. A veteran like Emerson, a newcomer like Henry Adams, exulted alike in this test of strength. Typical of the New England mind in crisis was Lowell, with his second series of *Biglow Papers,* expressing in homely idiom the tenderness and pride of a nation in its costly sacrifice. Or the New England Loyal Publication Society, led by Charles Eliot Norton and other men of scholarship and letters, which undertook to mold public opinion in favor of the Union by broadsides and other propaganda angled toward small-town newspapers and border-state citizens. A kindred organization in New York, also called the Loyal Publication Society, scattered tons of pamphlets assailing both secession and pacifism. Its guiding spirit was Francis Lieber, who had left the uncongenial South in 1856 to take a professorship at Columbia University and lend his pen to glorifying the organic unity of the United States and the wisdom of her constitutional government.

Indeed the unity of this nation, and its significance in the eyes of the world, was the deepest concern of Lincoln and those who followed his leadership. It became the basic argument for the war—preservation of the Union. Lincoln had so interpreted the struggle, even before the first gun spoke. In Philadelphia's Independence Hall, en route to his inauguration in 1861, he appealed to the Declaration of Independence "which gave promise that in due time the weights should be lifted from the shoulders of all men, and that all should have an equal chance." World-wide democracy had a vital stake in the salvation of the Union. If this nation were destroyed by its domestic feuds, as Lincoln told Congress and the people time and again through the war years, the whole theory of popular self-government would be discredited forever. All nations were anxiously watching us, serfs as well as kings. The last best hope of earth here trembled in the balance.

Even after the Gettysburg dedication, some factions, of course, envisaged the war in ways less heroic than the spirit of that occasion. Certain Unionists— for example, Longfellow's great friend Charles Sumner, the eloquent senator from Massachusetts—reduced it to an invidious sectionalism, every bit as narrow as that which motivated so many Southerners. Some praised war itself as a fine, exhilarating thing. Parkman, regretting that bad nerves and eyesight kept him at home, wrote letters to the newspapers reminding Americans that "Rome grew colossal through centuries of war." Still others lost all sense of balance in sheer vindictiveness—like Parson Brownlow, the Tennessee firebrand, and Thad Stevens, the embittered Pennsylvania Congressman. But wiser, more temperate citizens in the North kept coming back to Lincoln's assertion that this was a fight not only for the Union but for world democracy, and that the only fit spirit for waging it was one of charity for all.

A second war aim, whose announcement came later, and most effectually identified the aspirations of the Union with those of world liberalism, was Emancipation. A Union reconstituted by blood and tears, in which the anachronism of slavery was still allowed to linger, was not likely to satisfy those who had sacrificed so much for victory or to enlist world sympathy. Gradual emancipation, with compensation for slave owners, which Lincoln had once favored, also became untenable in the heat and passion of war. Every passing day made compromise more improbable. "The moment came," Lincoln said, "when I felt that slavery must die that the nation might live." And so, in his cabinet meeting of July 22, 1862, he projected the Emancipation Proclamation for New Year's Day, 1863, drafting in September an announcement of the impending act. Without bating a jot of his concern over saving the Union, Lincoln saw that this new infusion of idealism would revive liberal sentiment in the North and overseas as nothing else could do. Federal acquiescence in Southern theories about the inherent superiority of whites over blacks now ended. (In the year of the Proclamation, 1863, Charles Loring Brace, pioneer New York social worker and friend of Emerson and Darwin, set forth the scientific evidence against the separate origin of races in his book *The Races of the Old World*.) Reverberations of the Proclamation were world-wide. Charles Francis Adams, American Minister to Britain, who had long breasted the current of aristocratic sympathy for the Confederacy, now felt even stronger tides flowing in favor of Lincoln and the North. His son, young Henry Adams, after attending a mammoth rally of London trade unions on March 26, 1863, organized by Karl Marx and addressed by John Bright to consolidate public opinion, wrote: "I never quite appreciated the moral influence of American democracy, nor the cause that the privileged classes in Europe have to fear us, until I saw directly how it works."

After Gettysburg and the collapse in 1863 of Lee's summer invasion of Maryland and Pennsylvania, the fall of the great Confederate river fort at Vicksburg, and in 1864 Sherman's relentless sweep through Georgia to cut the Confederacy in two, the war's outcome grew more and more apparent. Despite "Copperhead" schemes to appease the South, and counterplots by Radicals thirsting for more vindictiveness, Lincoln won overwhelming reelection in November, 1864, under the steadily growing affection of millions for Father Abraham. The assault continued, with Grant's sledge-hammer blows raining upon Lee's Army of Northern Virginia. Months before Appomattox, Union victory seemed a foregone conclusion. And, with the premature celebration so typical of American impulses, a mood of false armistice began to settle upon the North, notably in the big cities of the seaboard—with the resurgence of prosperity, extravagance, and selfishness. Moralists of press and pulpit reminded the North that her boys were still fighting and dying, but the fervent crusading spirit had already passed its peak. In the South, an almost religious exaltation—heritage of Stonewall Jackson, sustained by Lee— settled at length into grim desperation, then crumbled into the apathy of exhaustion when on April 9, 1865, Lee surrendered.

In the North, victory brought wild jubilation, and to the thoughtful, a reconsecration of patriotism. Lowell wrote to his friend Charles Eliot Norton, on April 13, that he wanted to laugh and cry at the same time, but "ended by holding my peace and feeling devoutly thankful. There is something magnificent in having a country to love. It is almost like what one feels for a woman. Not so tender, perhaps, but to the full as self-forgetful." (His feelings obviously were unlike those of the battered Johnny Reb who threw down his gun at Appomattox, and reportedly said, "Damn me if I ever love another country.") The day after Lowell wrote these words, the assassination of Lincoln transformed the jubilee of the North into a mass sorrow such as Americans had never known before. To Whitman, threnodist of the tragedy, Lincoln's death was a climax on the stage of universal time, to "close an immense act in the long drama of creative thought, and give it radiation, tableau, stranger than fiction."

4

The memory of Lincoln and the half-million war dead, North and South, lingered a little while like a benediction. Sermons, orations, poems, folklore, enshrined together in a mystic reverence the sacrifice of the nation's bitterest war and the greatest American of the century. That ardor was still strong upon Lowell when, in the summer of 1865, he was asked to write a Commemoration Ode for the war dead of Harvard College—a roll that included the poet's three favorite nephews. "So rapt with the fervor of conception as I have not been these ten years," as he confessed, Lowell read his noble poem on July 21, and before its publication in September added its most famous strophe, praising the dead leader—

New birth of our new soil, the first American.

Lowell's allusion in this Ode to "the Promised Land that flows with Freedom's honey and milk" tarnished into irony within a few years, when he wrote another poem with a bitter gibe (suppressed at the instance of friends) about "the Land of Broken Promise." For, with the backwash of postwar selfishness, the spirit already latent in the closing months of the struggle now found itself ascendant. President Andrew Johnson's attempt to carry out Lincoln's promise of charity toward the prostrate South was wrecked by the vindictive Radicals, and Johnson himself barely escaped removal from office on flimsy charges.

A stronger federal Union had been achieved, but its powers suffered abuse, as military government fastened its shackles upon all the defeated states. The carpetbagger, and his antidote the Klansman, added turmoil and violence in the later sixties. Slowly and painfully, the South began to tread the flinty road to reunion. At first, the sense of disaster seemed all-engulfing, with poverty acute among both whites and blacks, the means of production destroyed, and chaos everywhere. Speaking for the economic casualties, Sidney Lanier, the now consumptive poet who symbolized the artist's privations in those days, remarked: "With us in the South, pretty much the whole life has been merely not dying."

Emancipation was achieved, but a permanent race problem remained. Probably the most encouraging sign of the times was the zeal which the Freedmen's Bureau and Northern philanthropy brought to the education of the Negro. Within a short time, universal public education for whites as well as blacks was seen to be one of the wisest, most tangible, goals of postwar endeavor. To some observers it seemed as if that idealism which formerly had been poured into the cause of abolition now streamed into the channels of popular education, over the nation at large. A few months after Appomattox, the idol of the South, General Lee, accepted the presidency of Washington College in the foothills of Virginia, believing that education was the most important task of peace in knotting the broken threads of Southern life and enterprise. In 1867 the Massachusetts-born banker George Peabody set up an endowment of $3,500,000 to promote education in the South among all peoples.

Over the vanquished ideal of a plantation aristocracy—with its gracious manners but illiberal point of view, its appreciative but sterile humanism—arose the philosophy of success, the cult of the businessman. In the early postwar years, as the urgencies of commerce began to rebuild the first bridges of intercourse over the Mason and Dixon line, this philosophy began to infiltrate the South. But its abiding home was of course the Northeast, among the great centers of industrial capitalism. The census of 1870 revealed that the per capita wealth of the North had doubled in ten years. Some few thinkers now began to recall the wartime arguments of Lysander Spooner—Massachusetts lawyer and nonconformist—that the war had been largely a struggle for economic power, with Northern capitalism moving in to dominate the markets of the South. Ironically enough, the Fourteenth Amendment, by its "due process of law" clause, ultimately afforded more aid and comfort to the preacher of the gospel of wealth than to the poor black child—so that it seemed, by a strange jugglery of words, that Lincoln had lived and died that the giant corporation, rather than the Negro, might become a person. Though lip service to democracy survived, corporate industry—railroads, factories, oil and mining leviathans—began to arise from the demands of war and postwar technology. Organized labor, in the glut of demobilization and the short but sharp depression of 1866–1867, visibly lost ground. The immigrant, now badly needed in the expanding factories of North and West, was welcomed with open arms; the ghost of Know-Nothingism remained temporarily laid. But another concern of ante-bellum liberalism, rights for women, did not fare so well, although gains continued in higher education. Despite notable work in the war, in groups like the Sanitary Commission, women failed to win the ballot as their reward, and had to bide their time till the aftermath of the First World War.

The balance of power in America had subtly shifted. The traditional rivalry of New England with the South, in ideas and culture, as well as politics and wealth, was effectually destroyed. The defeated South was obviously in eclipse. Victorious New England had undergone changes more intangible but no less real. The Civil War had not been the pure consecrating experience that her idealists had wished for her. Its end seemed to set a term to the high noon of New England's prestige and creative power—her plain living and high thinking, her passion for reform and her literary florescence. Her culture now entered a Silver Age, when she began to produce more critics and competent editors than novelists and thinkers, more politicians than statesmen, more conservers of inherited wealth than adventurers or entrepreneurs. The new alignment—corresponding to the new flow of the nation's lifeblood of trade East and West along the rails, instead of the old North-South circulatory system along the waterways—now balanced New York against Chicago, Pennsylvania coal and iron against Minnesota wheat and Nebraska corn. The Great West had come into being. It had taken such a lion's share in raising, equipping, and feeding the vast Union armies, under pilotage of the man from Illinois, that the Middle West felt it had won the war. At any rate, its challenge in basic production, commerce, politics, and the intellectual life of the nation had now been squarely delivered.

31. THE PEOPLE'S PATRONAGE

Even before the onset of the Civil War, the Middle West had become a crude power, a quantitative if not a qualitative force, in the collective life of the nation—and a mission field ripe for the eager, if at times momentarily discouraged, evangels of culture from the East. Emerson at St. Louis in 1852 doubted that there was a "thinking or even reading man" among 95,000 souls; and in 1866, in an Iowa town, he perceived that, though here was "America in the making, America in the raw . . . it doesn't want much to go to lecture, and tis pity to drive it."

This impression was confirmed by some of the newspapers. Cleveland was scornful that this "perpendicular coffin" should talk to the West about the "law of success," and Detroit reported that he was palming off the "sayings of old almanacs and spelling books; . . . putting transcendentalism on stilts for the admiration of natives." Quincy, Illinois, described him as "Another Bore," and Bloomington as "Ralph Cold-Dough Simmerson." Yet, year after year, in late autumn, he set off wearily to the land of promise, pushing as far and as fast as the new railroads would take him, for like all professional lecturers he knew that he must now seek his market west of the Hudson. And year after year listeners continued to come. Perhaps they hoped that next week John Godfrey Saxe would turn up with funny verse, or Bayard Taylor with his genius for bringing Persia to Peoria, or John B. Gough to give them a near-view of a reformed drunkard. It was significant, however, that though an Iowa town might, one week, listen to Emerson on "Power" and, next week, to "Professor" Oscanyan (dressed in Turkish costume and accompanied by three females in harem pajamas) on "The Domestic Life of the Turks," it was Emerson who derived his basic income from lecturing for thirty-five years, not the "Professor." Emerson once explained, "In every one of these expanding towns is a knot of loving New Englanders who cherish the Lyceum out of love of the Charles and the Merrimac and the Connecticut rivers," but this was a limited and insular version of the truth. The fact was (and Emerson knew it) that the cultural isolationism and localism of the old Northeast was breaking down: the whole of the North, from Boston to the Mississippi, with Baltimore, Pittsburgh, and Cincinnati as a southern boundary, was becoming a cultural unit.

The key to this momentous development was the railroads which spread from the Alleghenies to the Mississippi Valley between 1850 and 1870—ten thousand new miles of them before the war. Any observant trainman (on the run from Albany to Cleveland, for example) could have seen the symbols. In the coaches were not only Emerson, but Horace Greeley, George William Curtis, and Anna Dickinson, all with lectures newly tried out in New York or in New England villages; Dion Boucicault's road company taking the successful *Colleen Bawn* from New York to the hinterland, probably unaware that in so doing they were revolutionizing the American stage; James R. Osgood, Ticknor & Fields' first traveling representative, carrying the firm's fall list to bookstores in Detroit and Cincinnati (another innovation); and subscription agents with handsome sample volumes from New York or Hartford. As they rode, many of these passengers passed the time by reading paper-covered volumes produced specifically for railroad travelers—Putnam's Semi-Monthly Issue for Travelers or Appleton's Popular Library. In the baggage car were bundles of the weekly edition of Greeley's New York *Tribune*, of Bonner's New York *Ledger*, of *Harper's Weekly* (cheaply carried in bulk under the postal regulations of 1852). In the freight train just behind were packing cases of Harriet Stowe's latest volume, a special shipment of Holmes' *Autocrat* bearing on its title page a Cincinnati book dealer's imprint along with that of the Boston publisher; and even bigger boxes of novels by Augusta Jane Evans, Miriam Harris, and Mary Jane Holmes; and certainly a consignment of *Hiawatha,* for by the middle of 1856 one-tenth of all copies printed had been bought by one Chicago jobber.

Such passengers and such freight had been moving out of the East for decades, but they had been subject to the uncertainties of river currents and floods, and to the slow plodding of horses on canal tracks and mired roads. The difference now was in quantity, speed—and direction. Northeastern migrants having moved West rather than South, Northeastern cultural goods flowed to Western bookstores, lecture halls, art galleries, and theaters. More important, perhaps, than either speed or quantity was the fact that these goods were blocked by none of the cultural embargoes and tariff walls that were appearing along the Mason and Dixon line.

What had happened to the Southern market? Up to 1840 it had been a major outlet for New York and Philadelphia book and magazine publishers, whose alliances with booksellers in large Southern cities were certain evidence of the cultural homogeneity of the Atlantic seaboard. Even in the early fifties, few Northern publishers dared to alienate Southern buyers, or failed to apply pressure to writers who were indifferent to their prejudices. In 1845, for example, a Philadelphia publisher removed Longfellow's antislavery poems from a collected edition because they would damage his Southern business. The popular "Grace Greenwood" (Sara Jane Lippincott) was warned by her Boston publisher in 1851 that the question whether her remarks on slavery would cut off the sales of her work south of the Mason and Dixon line was "one of some importance to a writer whose reputation should make her books sell extensively thro'out the country." But the lady had better business sense than her publisher. Not at all concerned about Southern opinion, she begged him to see to the distribution of her books in Western towns, where there was a constant and unsatisfied demand for them. Within a year another Boston publisher turned down *Uncle Tom's Cabin* because it would not sell in the South; when a competitor took a chance with it, the new North bought 100,000 copies in eight weeks. James T. Fields saw the point when he removed the *Southern Literary Messenger*, the most important of all Southern magazines, from his review-copy list in 1849; so did G. P. Putnam when he ignored dire threats from Southern readers of his *Monthly*: its entire sale in the South was smaller than that in Ohio alone. The fact that the enormous development of the popular lecture after 1850 took place almost exclusively in the North enforced the moral: as a literary market, the South was dispensable. As its screen against Northern thought became finer and finer, its purchasing (and therefore its cultural) power became less and less.

The Midwest not only mattered—its cultural, as well as its economic and political, influence was by the fifties beginning to be crucial. Predisposed, like the Northeast, to a threefold economy—agriculture, commerce, and manufacture—it offered no serious barriers to cultural penetration from the coast. Committed, like the Northeast, to the ideal of universal, free, and eventually compulsory education, it was destined to produce an ever larger percentage of the literate adults of the nation. Once tied by railroads to New York, Boston, and Philadelphia, the centers of cultural production and the meccas of the nation's talent, the Midwest became an integral and influential part of that powerful civilization known as "the North" which was to dominate the nation thenceforward.

The accessibility of the Western market to publishers depended as much upon urbanization as on railroads. Newspapers and magazines could reach isolated farms by mail, but the bookstore, which could flourish only in fair-sized towns, was still the publisher's chief outlet. If, now, Cincinnati, Buffalo, and Cleveland book jobbers served ever-growing clusters of towns capable of supporting bookstores, they were merely belated beneficiaries of an economic phenomenon which had been characteristic of the industrial Northeast for decades. In New England, countryfolk were flocking to Lawrence and Pawtucket, Fall River and Hartford; in New York to Albany and Troy,

Schenectady and Elmira; and in Pennsylvania to Harrisburg, Reading, and Allentown. With markets geographically so concentrated, the publishers of Boston, New York, and Philadelphia had been able to achieve a leadership in book production which they have never lost.

For the literary man, Boston had importance far out of proportion to the volume of its publishing business. New York in the fifties had 107 publishers —twice as many as either Boston or Philadelphia; but its biggest houses specialized in British and in nonliterary writings, as did its biggest magazines —*Harper's Monthly* and *Harper's Weekly*. When G. P. Putnam (the most "literary" of the New York publishers), and his *Putnam's Monthly* (the best literary magazine of its time), dropped out of the running in the middle fifties, Boston firms had few important rivals in the publishing of American belles-lettres. Admittedly, the best printing (especially of poetry) and the best proof-reading were done in Cambridge by the University Press; and the best cloth binding was done in Boston by Benjamin Bradley. Ticknor & Fields was hospitable to poets and essayists; Little, Brown & Company, to historians; James Munroe, to philosophers; John P. Jewett, to popular novelists; and Phillips, Sampson & Company, to writers in general.

Constantly improving railroad connections with the West via Albany, and the enterprise of the younger publishers (Jewett, Harriet Stowe's publisher, had a branch office in Cleveland) reduced somewhat the disadvantages of Boston's geographical position. Even so, Boston publishers could rely upon a local public long accustomed to buying and reading books, and it was a common belief among American poets that verse sold better in New England than elsewhere. Moreover, the New England public accorded to the writer a prestige which he enjoyed nowhere else in the nation; and properly introduced authors from other sections were sure of a cordial reception and good literary fellowship in dozens of homes, bookshops, and editorial offices in and near Boston. When the *Atlantic Monthly* was founded in 1857 (two months after *Putnam's Monthly* had expired), its success was assured—not only because there was enough local talent to keep its pages full (one explanation of its reputed provincialism), but because it was backed by the money and influence of publishers long accustomed to dealing with literary materials and with creative writers. Such factors as these had much to do with the renaissance of the fifties.

2

Important as were material factors in the growth of the power of the new North, education was the social foundation on which the region was building a culture radically different in quality, depth, and extent from the patrician culture which had prevailed in the old urban centers and in the South. If time devoted to formal education is an index to consumption of print, the accelerated growth of mere literacy in the North was a phenomenon of some import to the literary world. Between 1850 and 1870 the population of the country increased about 68 per cent, but attendance at public schools almost doubled—to six and one-quarter million. Educational methods, equipment, and teaching personnel may have failed to keep step with this growth, but ability to read well was an educational goal more faithfully kept in view than it is now. In spite of brave attempts in some Southern states to combat difficult conditions, the great majority of these readers were being trained in the North. Illiteracy among South Atlantic whites in 1850 was five times as great as in New England; and in the relatively new South Central states it was three times as great as in the Middle West.

A presumably more sophisticated class of readers was being produced during the period (both in the North and in the South) at an even greater rate, for enrollment in academies, liberal colleges, and other private schools more than tripled to almost a million. The academies, now for the first time enduring strong competition from public high schools, were in 1850 a far greater influence in the literary market than the colleges, which enrolled a mere 27,000. It was not only that the enrollment in academies was ten times as great, but that they were hospitable to women, as most Northern colleges were not, and to "modern" courses, of which the majority of colleges were still suspicious. Like the public high schools (during the period some sixty-five of these were established in large towns, only four of them in the South) they tended increasingly to offer a terminal education rather than a merely preparatory course. Inasmuch as the South in 1850, with a relatively small white population, had 40 per cent of the nation's private schools (Kentucky had twice as many academy students as Indiana) it is no wonder that Northern publishers resented the alienation of Southern readers.

Few colleges (total enrollment was only 56,000 on the eve of the Civil War) were doing much to improve the old classical curriculum. There was some progress in the teaching of science, modern languages, and the newer social sciences, but sectarian influence was still strong, and higher education still awaited the thorough shaking-up it was to get under new, young, German-trained presidents within a decade after the war. It was largely because the established colleges, committed to an academic program of what Veblen later called "conspicuous waste," were slow to respond to the needs of industry and agriculture, that during this period technological schools sprang up as separate entities or as independent affiliates of older institutions. Most of the twenty-two technological schools and state universities founded in the sixties got federal support through the Morrill Land Grant Act (1862), the purpose of which was "to carry the advantages of education to those engaged in manual industries." Though the South before the war had sent an even larger proportion of its white population to college than had the North, the war delayed the development of technological education in the region. At any rate, higher and "useful" education for the many, like literacy for the masses, was a typically Northern idea, one which was steadily undermining the old tradition of an exclusively classical and British culture for the few.

Paradoxically, increasing material prosperity was the major factor in the education of the most potent class of readers in the nation—women. Though few people as yet believed that women were worth educating beyond the elementary level, something had to be done with girls who did not have to become household drudges as soon as they were old enough to work. The solution was the female academy. Census figures for secondary education of the sexes before 1870 are lacking, but in that year more than half of all academy students were girls. As for women's colleges, the striking fact is that in 1870, though those in the Northeast were the best in the country, the number of girls enrolled in them was negligible; whereas the South, which had forty-two of the fifty-six women's colleges established during the period, was giving higher education to almost as many women as men. Except in normal schools, technical and professional curricula were intended for boys, with the result, momentous for the literary market, that education for the enrichment of life, as opposed to education for a job, was monopolized by girls. No one knows what percentage of the readers of poetry, fiction, and essays was female, but the signs are many that by mid-century most of the consumers of imaginative literature were women of the upper and middle classes. Whether, at this date, the younger female audience was made up of "vivid, responsive intelligences, which are none the less brilliant and admirable because they are innocent" (according to Howells), or whether it constituted an "Iron Madonna who strangles in her fond embrace the American novelist" (according to Boyesen), it was a force which affected literary history.

Of the informal varieties of education, the most characteristic of the period was the "popular lecture," which, though it grew out of the lyceum system, must not be confused with the typical lyceum lecture. By the fifties, the superior man was no longer sharing his cultural wealth, in the local lyceum, with his less fortunate townsman; he was selling it to large groups of critical strangers who demanded their money's worth. Young Men's Associations and Library Societies, which (particularly in the West) were displacing the lyceums, now paid fees of from $50 to $100 to "names" who invariably had made their reputations in activities other than lecturing, and the reappearance of these on any platform depended on their ability to talk "interestingly" on foreign travel or on social and ethical topics. This test of popularity was not necessarily corruptive. Emerson, who made only the indispensable compromises with his audience, by much effort could earn as much as $2,000 for a season. Bayard Taylor, with his popular travel lectures, often made $5,000, and magnetic personalities like Henry Ward Beecher, Anna Dickinson, and John B. Gough earned much more. Although, inevitably, such sums tempted lecturers to cheapen their wares, the public rarely tolerated charlatanism. Dr. Holland (writer of best sellers and, later, editor of *Scribner's*), who declared that "the public do not accept of those who are too openly in the market," believed that at its zenith the popular lecture was the champion of liberty and the foe of bigotry in politics and religion. From the forties until 1865 the platform was a medium for the expression of social opinion; and as such it served the great purpose of ameliorating prejudice; and, like the radio of today, it was a nationalizing force.

But the end of the war brought about a rapid if temporary degeneration of social and intellectual tone, one of the permanent effects of which was the destruction of the popular lecture. Commercial lecture bureaus, under the inspiration of publicity geniuses like James Redpath and Major J. B. Pond, quickly transformed it into "amusement business," and by 1870 the platform was reserved for exhibitions of the newly famous, "readings" by the latest or the oldest literary idol, and what Bayard Taylor called bitterly "non-intellectual diversion." In a little more than forty years a great cultural institution had outlived its usefulness. Thereafter the serious-minded turned to the Chautauqua for edification and enlightenment.

3

Journalism proved even more adaptable to social change. As business and industry destroyed the slow tempo of the old agrarian culture, American life speeded up. The great mass of literates produced by the schools sought reading matter attuned not to the ages but to the day, the week, and the month. Increasingly, writers were trained to write and readers to read, by periodicals. Not only literacy but inventions and improved news-gathering techniques enabled daily newspapers during the period to more than triple their circulation, though the war was responsible for a good part of the total of two and a half million.

Of these, much the most significant from the point of view of Northern culture was Horace Greeley's New York *Tribune*, which sold over half of its huge weekly edition outside the city, and which, according to Bayard Taylor, ranked next to the Bible in popularity in the Midwest. It is of some significance that Greeley thus sent into the hinterland the book and lecture reviews of George Ripley (who was kindly to social radicals like Emerson), the travel letters of Taylor, Curtis, and Clemens, and the more popular verse of the New York poets. But even Greeley could not counterbalance the weight of the scores of cheap weekly magazines and "Sunday newspapers" which flooded the nation in mid-century. The historian of our magazines has well said that the descending curve of illiteracy seems to have been matched by the ascending curve of popularity of the weeklies, for by 1870, 4,295 of them had a circulation of ten and one-half million—one copy for every two or three adults in the nation. Many of them, it is true, were insignificant religious and agricultural papers of small circulation, but some of those that emanated from New York were known in every downy hamlet in the land. Among those with circulations of over 100,000 were the *New York Weekly,* whose serials were the foundation of the Street & Smith dime-novel dynasty; the somewhat more respectable New York *Sunday Mercury,* which specialized in the J. H. Ingraham and "Ned Buntline" thrillers, and in the new popular humor of Ward, Billings, and Kerr; and the New York *Ledger,* which topped them all with a circulation of 400,000 in 1860. Robert Bonner, the owner of the *Ledger,* was, like Barnum, a master of the recently born art of publicity. His amusing use of gold—and brass—to lure such "names" as Henry Ward Beecher, Edward Everett, and Longfellow into the domain of "Fanny Fern" (Sara Payson Willis Parton), Mrs. E. D. E. N. Southworth, and Sylvanus Cobb, Jr., gives an intimate view of new cultural mutations.

Bonner's success was rivaled only by that of illustrated news weeklies such as *Frank Leslie's Illustrated* and *Harper's Weekly.* The latter, like the illustrated *Harper's Monthly,* were of less direct importance to American writers than weeklies of the *Ledger* type because they printed little American fiction. Nevertheless, the editorial policies of Bonner and the Harpers had considerable influence upon literature. Before the establishment of *Harper's Monthly* (1850), few American novels were serialized. By that date Cooper had serialized one of his last romances, the other major writers none. But by 1870 almost all recognized novelists were selling their work first to magazines and were making the necessary compromises in matters of chapter division, construction, arrangement of incident, style, and moral and social prejudice. In their new venture the Harpers had intended only to get ahead of their competitors by reprinting foreign novels as fast as they appeared in serial form abroad, but they soon discovered the potency of the phrase "to be continued." When other magazines like the *Ledger* (1850) and the *Atlantic* (1857) began to serialize American novels, the writer had a new and tempting source of income, for he could sell each novel twice—three times if he could get an English magazine to serialize simultaneously, four times if he could also sell to an English publisher.

Only slightly less important were other policies of the new magazines: they popularized the illustration of fiction, a development which was later to affect the work of novelists like Howells and James; they raised the rate of pay for magazine work and thus not only helped to stabilize further the literary profession but made New York the center of literary magazine production; they protected the copyright of their periodicals and thereby helped put a stop to the wholesale scissoring which in the forties had deprived Poe and Longfellow of the major rewards of their popularity; they helped break down the custom of literary anonymity, which had also militated against the author's interest; most important of all, by appealing to a national audience, they helped to destroy the narrow localism which damaged such respectable and even superior competitors as *Putnam's* and the *Atlantic Monthly*. The influence of these popular periodicals on literary production shows that, though Emerson may have been justified in his faith that "water and intelligence work down," it is just as true that popular influences work up.

4

The same forces were at work in the book world. The opening of railroad transportation in the Midwest, the campaign against illiteracy throughout the North, the habit of reading which was encouraged by lecturers, newspapers, and magazines, served to increase the sale of books on all levels. The schools contributed directly to publishers' prosperity, not only through textbooks and juveniles, which were the backbone of many a firm's list, but through district-school libraries, whose holdings increased from two and one-half to three and one-half million volumes. By mid-century these libraries had become so important in the literary market that the standard Harper contract included a clause covering school editions.

The contribution of religious education was little short of spectacular: church and school libraries in 1850 owned six hundred thousand volumes; in 1870 the number was almost ten million. The ancient alliance between the church and literary culture, inevitable in colonial and early national days when the clergy wrote much of what got into print, was perpetuated up to the Civil War by close relations between the major publishers and specific denominations—Harpers with the Methodists, Appleton with the Episcopalians, Ticknor with the Baptists, Munroe & Francis with the Unitarians. But if the churches stimulated the appetite for books they also satisfied it to some extent by doing much publishing on their own account. There were bitter complaints that such organizations as the American Sunday School Union, the Presbyterian Board, and the Methodist Book Concern, all subsidized by charity funds, were publishing and distributing general literary works of a religious cast in competition with "legitimate" houses, and that authorship suffered because copyright was paid only rarely and reluctantly.

The cycle of business expansion completed the process by which literature became an important article of commerce. The enlarged book market led printers to buy improved and expensive machinery, and publishers to compete with one another by paying higher royalties, sending agents out on the road, and advertising nationally. Increased overhead made larger sales necessary; so that publishers could no longer afford to be hospitable to the elite few who absorbed a thousand copies of a "good" book. G. W. Curtis in 1854 wrote the publishers to whom he was adviser that "nowadays a book seems hardly to be launched until it has a circulation of 5000."

For authors who were willing to consult the tastes of the five thousand the rewards were increasingly great. The almost universal royalty of 10 per cent and/or "author's risk" of the forties became, in the early fifties, 15 per cent, often 20 and sometimes 25 per cent if the writer paid for his own stereotype plates. Indeed, the years between 1850 and the panic of 1857 saw a boom of authors' profits unequaled in the whole nineteenth century, and royalty offers reached a high of 33⅓ per cent before the panic. During the sixties, they tended to slip back to a norm of 10 to 15 per cent, where they remained until the nineties. Authorship suffered during the Civil War, for new literary works were not in demand unless they had some special relation to the conflict, and the doubling of the cost of living about 1864 left many writers in bad straits. But retail book prices doubled too, and since deflation did not reduce them all the way to the old level, authors were left better off than they had been before.

Meanwhile, publishing methods had improved. By 1850 the old barter system by which bookseller-publishers exchanged their imprints for those of shops in other towns had been displaced by techniques of publishing for a national market. Booksellers were now encouraged to move their stocks through generous publishers' discounts which were adjusted to the salability of individual titles. Nation-wide newspaper and magazine advertising (Ticknor & Fields, publishers of the Brahmins, did not spurn the columns of the nationally circulated *Leslie's*), and new promotional methods undermined the vicious local review clique which had done great harm to professional authorship in Poe's day. Publishers learned how to exploit potential reader-markets more thoroughly by adjusting format and price to differing income levels. The difficulty of reaching readers in rural areas was overcome to a certain extent by the development of subscription publishing. It was chiefly biography, history, and travel that was thus issued by such firms as the American Publishing Company in Hartford and Scribner's in New York, but Harriet Stowe in 1870 daringly contemplated sending agents into the South with an illustrated edition of *Uncle Tom's Cabin*. As she wrote her publisher, "Books to do anything here in these southern states must be sold by agents. . . . Yet *there is* money on hand even down to the colored families, and an attractive book would have a history." Mrs. Stowe's experiences illustrate another comparatively new development: the growth of intimate and trusting relations between author and publisher. Many a house like Putnam, Scribner, and Ticknor & Fields now inspired such loyalty as Emerson's, who called his publisher "the guardian of us all."

Among the new duties of the friendly publisher was arranging for simultaneous publication of his titles in England. Author and publisher alike studied British copyright, so that in spite of unfavorable decisions in the House of Lords in the early fifties, shrewd writers like Mrs. Stowe made better bargains with English publishers than Irving, Cooper, Prescott, and Melville in earlier days. Setting up a few days' residence in Canada at the time a new book was published in London was one method by which American authors acquired a kind of standing in British courts, but careful preliminary arrangements with a reliable foreign house frequently sufficed to turn the trick. Publishing relations with Canada were excellent, though they were destined to degenerate in subsequent decades. A Canadian law of 1849 removed all tariffs on American books; another of 1850 permitted the importation of American reprints of British copyright works, with the provision that a 12½ per cent royalty for the benefit of the English author be collected at the border. In 1852 a correspondent reported that low-priced American books had almost destroyed the Canadian-English book trade, and that New York had displaced London as the purchasing center for the Dominion.

On the American side, reckless competition in the printing of English books had produced its own partial cure by mid-century: a system of courtesy by which a publisher who bought and announced a foreign title was let alone by other houses. Such arrangements raised the price of American editions of foreign works and gave native productions a better chance than they had had before. By 1860, at any rate, many American writers were deriving an adequate income from the home market, which had not been possible during the first half of the century even for such well established authors as Irving, Cooper, and Willis. During this period writing ceased to be a part-time avocation and became a profession capable of supporting authors in middle-class respectability.

5

The forces of education and business having combined to make the popular patronage of literature an economic fact, it was inevitable that readers and publishers should exert a shaping influence upon literary work. Bald logic would suggest that such influence must have been destructive of pure creative ideals, and that the success of T. S. Arthur, Sylvanus Cobb, Susan Warner, and Josh Billings during the period of the decline of Melville, Hawthorne, and George Henry Boker was not merely coincidental. Common sense would indicate that increased literacy might have brought the new group into being without destroying the old. Between logic and common sense lay a fact: that even the best of the older writers recognized the new reading class as a force and attempted to adjust themselves to it without compromising their integrity. Unsophisticated readers throughout the North required that writers and lecturers present themselves not on the ground of their local (if impressively urban) reputations, but on the ground that they had something interesting to say to "nonliterary," "nonintellectual," but intelligent people. The prerequisites for such an appeal were then what they must always be: simplicity, concreteness, lightness, eloquence, freshness, and a distinctive (if not distinguished) personal style. If the writer's ideals included also imagination, power, and relentless truth, so much the better: the public required only that he communicate and that he be interesting.

Emerson, who derived his living not from a little group of transcendentalists in Boston but from a public which extended from Bangor, Maine, to Davenport, Iowa, saw the validity of such standards. When Thoreau remarked in 1853 that any lecture which pleased an audience must be bad, Emerson demurred. "I am ambitious," he said, "to write something which all can read, like *Robinson Crusoe*. And when I have written a paper or a book, I see with regret that it is not solid, with a right materialistic treatment, which delights everybody." Melville recognized the requirements when he sought better terms from his publisher for *Pierre* because its "unquestionable novelty" would make it popular, it "being a regular romance, with a mysterious plot to it, and with all, representing a new and elevated aspect of American life and stirring passions at work"; and for *Redburn* because it was "a plain, straightforward, amusing narrative of personal experience . . . no metaphysics . . . nothing but cakes and ale."

It was the mark of younger and lesser writers of the period that instead of striving, like Emerson and Melville, to adapt their best gifts to the needs of their audience, they attempted a false dualism: that of subsidizing their unprofitable "art" by grinding out commercially successful work of which they were contemptuous. Bayard Taylor was humiliated that on his lecture tours women swooned, and cried, "There he is! That's *him*!" And he complained that lecturing, which built him a fifteen-thousand-dollar country house, was destroying his poetry, which he never wrote for money. Similarly, Stedman, in 1869, was conscience-stricken because he had "lately written so much poor stuff for the money's sake"; and a year later he reported that the public taste was being led astray "after burlesque, the grotesque, the transitory."

There was indeed a bigger market for "poor stuff" than ever before; but those who had genuine faith in democratic man knew that the crowd were ready for better stuff if only one would learn their idiom. Whitman and Emily Dickinson did not; Mark Twain did, and reaped his reward. Melville, who never mastered it, said bitterly in 1851: "This country . . . is governed by sturdy backwoodsmen—noble fellows enough, but not at all literary, and who care not a fig for any authors except those who write those most saleable of all books nowadays—i.e.—the newspapers and magazines." Yet he added, more hopefully: "This country is at present engaged in furnishing material for future authors; not in encouraging its living ones." But it was Emerson, as usual, who saw in true perspective the dilemma of the author in this age of Barnum, Beecher, and Bonner. When a "stout Illinoian" walked out on his lectures, he reflected that "the people are always right (in a sense), and that the man of letters is to say, These are the new conditions to which I must conform . . . he is no master who cannot vary his forms, and carry his own end triumphantly through the most difficult." The time was, indeed, a difficult one for the artist, but it was not impossible. He needed only faith and humility to see that though he himself must serve Mammon as well as God, the people served God as well as Mammon.

32. THE HISTORIANS

THE effort of mid-century writers of the patrician East to meet popular taste and popular interest with important books is nowhere better illustrated than by Irving's turn, in his last years, to a many-volumed life of Washington, and in the monumental historical works of Prescott, Parkman, and Motley.

"Literary" history—when it has not meant, as it does elsewhere in this book, the history of literature—has still meant different things at different times in different countries. In the United States the adjective "literary" has generally been confined to the work of three historians, William Hickling Prescott, John Lothrop Motley, and Francis Parkman, who wrote in the middle decades of the nineteenth century. Limited in this way, the "literary" historians may be identified as men who chose themes of sweeping dimensions, collected their materials by enormous and skilled research, were concerned with a dramatic story of leaders and ideas rather than the workaday life of ordinary people, and built works of such artistic attractiveness that they have been read with pleasure by the educated public ever since. Another and more elusive quality was given to such literary history by the fact that all three of its major exponents were patricians.

2

Prescott, Motley, and Parkman began to write amid the encouragement of a boom in historical interest. By the time that the oldest of the three, Prescott, started his first book in 1829, the new nation had reached a state of self-consciousness which made its past seem exciting. Shoddy national histories and better biographies and state histories written by the previous generation were attracting an ever widening audience; a scaffolding was being built for new histories. In the early part of the century, Peter Force, a politician and printer-journalist working in Washington, was only the most important of a considerable group of documentarians who were editing and publishing materials concerning the whole period from the beginnings of colonization on the American shores to the adoption of the Constitution. They were convinced, as Force put it, that "the tendency of the present age has been justly and philosophically designated as historick," and the interest in their work—including Federal funds of more than $200,000—justified his view. The historic tendency of the age also showed itself in the critical journals. Both in its editors and in its articles, the principal critical journal, the *North American Review,* was almost as much a historical publication as a literary one from the twenties through the Civil War. In 1857 the literary historian, Prescott, helped found the *Atlantic Monthly,* and from its beginning the magazine showed a history-mindedness similar to that of the *North American Review.*

All kinds of history and biography poured from the presses, especially in Boston, the center of the new enthusiasm. There Prescott, Motley, and Parkman were joined by three quite different authors to complete the list of the period's most important historians. Of the latter group, two were literary only in the most limited sense; the other was belligerently antiliterary. The most prolific of the three, Jared Sparks, managed to produce nearly seventy historical volumes despite periods as a Unitarian minister and as president of Harvard. During Sparks' lifetime more than 600,000 Americans bought works bearing his name either as author or as editor—especially the ten-volume *Works of Benjamin Franklin; with Notes and a Life of the Author* (1836–1840), which probably contained his best writing, and *The Library of American Biography* (1834–1838), which was certainly his most skillful editorial enterprise. But Sparks' writings can claim no permanent place either as literature or as history. His research was marred by a patriotic tendency to overlook or alter facts which he considered injurious to the reputations of the great, and his writing was distinguished only by clarity.

Much more pretentiously literary was George Bancroft, whose reputation was based on a twelve-volume *History of the United States* (1834–1882). When Bancroft's first volume appeared in 1834, many a guardian of current literary taste hailed it as a classic. Edward Everett, in a review typical of many, said: "You have written a work which will last while the memory of America lasts." Almost until the time of his death in 1891, Bancroft's *History* was accepted as standard, and his prestige as a literary figure grew until Chester Arthur could say that the President of the United States is "permitted to accept the invitations of members of the Cabinet, Supreme Court judges, and—Mr. George Bancroft." A century's perspective now makes it plain that the critics and the country had been beguiled into extraordinary overpraise by Bancroft's flamboyant declamations about Liberty, Democracy, and the Nation. The best literary taste of the mid-nineteenth century was hardly represented by rhapsodies about a work from which it is quite fair to quote these sentences: "With one impulse the colonies sprang to arms. With one spirit they pledged themselves to be ready for the extreme event. With one heart the continent cried, Liberty or Death."

Bancroft's floridity produced a direct reaction in the shorter *History of the United States* (1849–1852) of Richard Hildreth, which is as matter-of-fact as a railroad schedule. Hildreth's irritation at "centennial sermons and Fourth-of-July orations" combined with an enthusiasm for English Utilitarian thought to produce history that was consciously antiliterary. Many a later historian, seeking "scientific history," hailed Hildreth as the most important American historian of the nineteenth century; his contemporaries were inclined to ignore him as a churlish fellow who reduced everything to his own dull level.

However different Hildreth, Bancroft, and Sparks were, all three were alike in having grown up outside the wealth and aloofness of patrician Boston. They lived their lives with no sense of remoteness from the hurly-burly of politics and economic change around them. Bancroft was an active Democratic politician, Hildreth an active Whig, and both operated for considerable periods at the grubbier level of politics. When they picked a theme for history they chose the history of the United States, of a United States close to them in time and in problems. They were so concerned with contemporary issues that their histories plainly voted on tariffs, central banks, land, slavery, and other public questions of their day. Even the least present-minded of the three, Jared Sparks, had served for two years as Chaplain of the House of Representatives and persistently thought of history as a kind of sermon to politicians and voters.

This sympathetic interest in their age, this sense of moving with it, Prescott and Parkman did not have; and Motley shared it only to a small degree. The background of the literary historians put them on an aloof social plateau, from which they could come down to the level of common life only by a conscious effort. All three were heirs to great wealth, and disengaged from the trading by which it had been amassed. Socially, they belonged to a circle which had hardly admitted a new name since the Revolution. Theirs was the Boston patrician routine: the gentleman's excursion at Harvard, the *Wanderjahre* in Europe, and then the return home to an exclusive social life and equally exclusive literary societies. There they discussed one another's papers over a sound supper of widgeons and teal and generous claret brought in by a ship which one of them probably owned but had never seen. None of them came to grips with contemporary economic life; the closest any of them approached to active politics was Motley's one term in the Massachusetts legislature, which revolted him, and his short periods as a diplomat, the least rough-and-tumble of government services. They varied only in the degree to which they were repelled from their age and from present-minded history by a raw industrialism and the "vulgar" politics of factory hands, small farmers, and trades-people.

Yet this Boston was too much New England, too close to its conscience-lashed past to be satisfied with fashionable dilettantism. The merely graceful life was unthinkable to the grandsons of men who had believed that idleness was sin and who had, on their own road to heaven, wrung wealth out of rocky soil and stormy oceans. The answer, the most natural answer under the circumstances, was the writing of serious books. As Prescott put it,

A person in our country who takes little interest in politicians or in making money—our staples you know—will be thrown pretty much on his own resources, and if he is not fond of books he may as well go hang himself, for as to a class of idle gentlemen, there is no such thing here.

When Prescott, Motley, and Parkman thought of writing books, a special circumstance inclined them to books of literary history. Hostile as their Boston was to raucous new America, it was alive and open to the literary interests, enthusiasms, and standards of western Europe, where the brightly colored history of dramatic men and events was the current enthusiasm. Even without the European influence, no kind of writing could have seemed more con-genial. What else was so far removed from the drab factories that were ruin-ing the charming little rivers of Massachusetts or the ragamuffin hordes that toppled over punch bowls at Andrew Jackson's inauguration? With a happy sense of escape, Prescott turned to the glamorous Spanish conquerors, Motley to the dramatic Dutch struggle for liberty, and Parkman to the technicolor story of the American forests.

3

Tall, graceful William Hickling Prescott was one of the gayest figures of young Boston, but there was never any question in his mind that he must become "habitually industrious." The loss of one eye in a Harvard frolic and the rapid inflammation of the other, which rendered him nearly blind for the rest of his life, brought no weakening of the compulsion to work. At first the industry went into sentimental short stories for his literary society "The Club"; then into carefully worked critiques of English literature for the *North American Review*. Prescott was not satisfied; none of these projects was big enough to match his conscience or his ambition. He toyed with the idea of writing a history of Italian literature, a history of Rome, and with various biographical possibilities. Meanwhile, an interest in Spain, set off by Napo-leon's raids on the Peninsula, was intensifying in Anglo-American literary circles. As Prescott entered his thirties, George Ticknor, another member of the patrician set, returned from Europe eloquent with the possibilities in Spanish subjects. Prescott listened entranced to some lectures Ticknor had prepared for a Harvard course, browsed though Ticknor's extensive Spanish library. In 1826 he made his decision. He "subscribed" to the subject of the reign of Ferdinand and Isabella.

"Subscribed" is a weak word for the dedication Prescott actually gave. To conquer the scholarly and literary problems involved and the handicap of his near-blindness, he systematically employed every kind of aid available. To overcome his love of leisure, he budgeted his life as a pauper budgets his pennies. He had his servant pull away his bedcovering at a set hour; he made bets with his secretary that he would write the allotted number of pages that day; even on his daily horseback ride he made sure that he composed history in his head. From this intense concentration came, with notable rapidity, Prescott's four major works: *A History of the Reign of Ferdinand and Isabella* (1837), *A History of the Conquest of Mexico* (1843), *A History of the Conquest of Peru* (1847), and *A History of the Reign of Philip the Second* (1855–1858)—the last incomplete at his death.

Into each of these works Prescott poured enough research to produce a hundred learned monographs. After generations of criticism, the general verdict is that his scholarly use of the sources then available leaves little to be desired. But Prescott himself would be even more pleased by the fact that after a hundred years his *Mexico* and *Peru* are still in print in several inexpensive editions, for he thought of himself primarily as a literary craftsman. As such, he carefully studied the existing models before writing a word of his first major literary history. Of course, Sir Walter Scott, whom he considered "the master of the picturesque," was given close attention. From Voltaire, Prescott took the idea of a topical rather than a chronological matrix. He found in *De l'étude de l'histoire* of Voltaire's contemporary, the Abbé de Mably, a congenial notion of the "necessity of giving an interest as well as utility to history, by letting events tend to some obvious point or moral; in short, by paying such attention to the development of events tending to this leading result, as one would in the construction of a romance or drama." Prescott also acknowledged his debt to French disciples of Scott, who heightened the readability of their histories by freely paraphrasing from colorful documents. In his general approach Prescott followed contemporary European romantic history, which sought, above all, unity of theme embellished with striking facts, a dramatic arrangement of these facts, and elaborate attention to the characterization of leading personalities. Basically, his conception of the structure of literary history was also that of Motley and Parkman.

Prescott's style at first shunned the flexibility encouraged by European romanticism and showed more of the eighteenth century English emphasis upon clarity, use of balance, antithesis and metaphor, and abstention from "low diction." When his first important work, the *Ferdinand and Isabella,* appeared, one reviewer roundly condemned him as "always on his best behavior, prim, prudish, and stiff-necked." The critic had a point. *Ferdinand and Isabella* is overfull of the balanced sentence, the studied antithesis, and the elaborate parallel; women are invariably "females," a gift is a "donative," people are married by "having nuptials solemnized," a name is an "appellation," and people are buried by being "consigned to their kindred dust." Prescott's immediate reaction was to say that the reader had to take his style for better or for worse, but he did admit that it was not as simple as it might be. As he went on writing, he simplified it a great deal and he repudiated more and more consciously the eighteenth century theory that there is only one good style. "The best rule," he came to believe, "is to dispense with all rules except grammar and to consult the natural bent of one's genius." In only one stylistic idea did he remain so rigid that he would have pleased Samuel Johnson on the Doctor's most dogmatic day; he belligerently insisted on writing English, not American. As chary of the new language as he was of the new America, he warned against "innovations, liable to spring up in a country where an active, inventive population, less concerned with books than with business, is very likely to corrupt the pure waters of 'English undefiled.'" How artificially he wrote English is suggested by the contrast between his books and his letters, which bounce along with such downright Americanisms as "whopper-jawed," and "take it easy."

Because of his tendency to use literary starch, the extraordinary effect of Prescott's writing comes largely from his successfully dramatic structure, his precision in language, and his striking ability to adapt that language to the demands of his subject matter. His military descriptions march in staccato sentences of parallel structure which are as devoid of ornament as a troop train. In a philosophical or a generalizing vein, his use of metaphor gives attractive clarity to abstruse thoughts. His paragraphs of general history vary from the lush to the spare, and are as arresting either way because the materials seem to demand just that treatment.

As literature, the *Conquest of Mexico* is undoubtedly Prescott's masterpiece. Here was a subject ideal for the medium. One man, Cortés, strides through the story in a way that would be spectacular in the coldest recital of the facts. As Prescott said:

The natural development of the story . . . is precisely what would be prescribed by the severest rules of art. The conquest of the country is the great end always in view of the reader. From the first landing of the Spaniards on the soil, their subsequent adventures, their battles and negotiations, their ruinous retreat, their rally and final siege, all tend to this grand result till the long series of events is closed by the downfall of the capital. . . . It is a magnificent epic, in which the unity of interest is complete.

As Prescott conceived the work, it presented only two serious problems of form. To describe the conquest without describing the Aztec civilization it conquered was obviously superficial; and yet such an introductory section could easily disrupt the unity of the whole work. Prescott also felt that he had to tell Cortés' life after the Conquest, and he was only too aware of the dangers of an anticlimactic effect in doing this. It was in the difficult introduction and in the difficult close that Prescott demonstrated his supreme artistry. Far from disrupting unity, his "View of the Aztec Civilization" builds into an attractive foreground a mass of facts which needed telling but would have clogged the story of the Conquest itself. Moreover, the opening, by emphasizing the barbarism of the Aztec civilization, makes its overthrow seem the more glamorous an enterprise. Far from being anticlimactic, the later life of Cortés is handled in such a way that he is made to seem fascinating even when his main work is done, and the total interest in him is thus heightened.

The earlier work of Prescott, *Ferdinand and Isabella,* offered less opportunity for dramatic unity than the *Mexico,* but Prescott did as much as could be done for literary effect by weaving the story around the theme of progress out of a "barbarous age" to a powerful and unified Spain. The work that followed the *Mexico,* his *Conquest of Peru,* presented still more tortuous literary problems. Pizarro is neither so dominant nor so attractive as Cortés. The main action, the subduing of the Incas, comes to an end long before the close of the narrative, and the rest of the story consists mainly of squabblings among the conquerors until the supremacy of the Crown is finally established. Prescott sought his unity by making the narrative a series of steps leading to the "great result" of the domination of the Spanish Crown, but, as one of his critics has remarked, this solution was more logical than convincing. The conquest of a humane people by a group that Prescott had to call the "scum of [Spanish] chivalry" could hardly be called progress toward a "great result," and the vanquished, unlike the Aztecs, were so feeble that their submission offers only sporadic drama. The story moves and shimmers, but the movement is mostly the whirl of little men and the shimmer is often the effect of artificial lighting. Prescott's last work, covering the reign of Philip II, would have taxed even his normal powers to the fullest, since its subject matter was the worst possible for a literary historian—a mass of disparate facts adding up, if they added up at all, to decay and dissolution. As it was, most of the volumes were written against the doctor's orders; and they emerge only as a collection of charming or spectacular episodes.

4

As Prescott was working on his *Philip the Second,* he received a worried communication from a young fellow Bostonian, John Lothrop Motley. Motley had started to write a history of the revolt of the Dutch against Philip II, and when he heard of the famous Prescott's project he was afraid of being completely overshadowed. In the spirit of gracious scholarship, Prescott invited Motley to a conference and encouraged him to go ahead on the basis of a division of emphasis. Prescott would use the focus of the whole reign of Philip, and Motley would concentrate on the development of the Netherlands. The field was, Prescott assured the younger man, big enough for two plows. Big enough it was, especially since there were differences between the two men's conceptions of literary history.

Not that Prescott and Motley arrived at their methods by very different routes. Motley also was born into the Boston elite; he graduated from Harvard; he went on to the inevitable travel and study abroad; and he returned to Boston contrasting the "naked and impoverished" past of the United States with Europe, "where fable and romantic legend have lent a name and a charm to every forest, mountain, rock, and river." Motley's first attempts to put this kind of charm on paper were two novels that stumbled under the burden of bad plots. Restless and in magnificent physical vigor—he was the only one of the three literary historians not to suffer serious eye trouble— Motley then tried a minor diplomatic post in St. Petersburg and one term in the Massachusetts legislature. But bleak St. Petersburg brought only homesickness and, after two years in the Massachusetts House, he recoiled from all active politics with lugubrious reflections on "rule by the dismal mob."

Meanwhile, a piece of literary criticism that he wrote for the *North American Review* led him to a more congenial field. What started as a critique of two books about Russia ended as a brilliant piece of literary history sketching the reign of Peter the Great. In a chorus Motley's friends advised him to turn to history on a large scale. The advice was sound. History did not require what Motley found it hardest to do—invent a plausible plot—and it used to the fullest his talents for picturesque language and sweeping generalization. Although he could not down the feeling that any kind of history was a job for "sappers and miners" compared to the novel-writing "lancers," Motley took the advice of his friends, and in his mid-thirties began intensive preparation for writing history. Later in life, he paused for some gentlemanly politics as United States Minister to the Austrian Empire and to England, and did considerable nonhistorical writing on the American Civil War as a struggle for a quite abstract "liberty." But the core of Motley's life was the many-volume literary history he wrote around that same thesis of liberty, worked out, by a wise choice, in terms of the history of the Dutch. Over the years, his carefully wrought volumes carried the story of the Dutch all the way from the struggle for freedom from the Spanish Empire to the struggle to reconcile freedom with nationhood. The story was told in *The Rise of the Dutch Republic* (1856), the *History of the United Netherlands, from the Death of William the Silent, to the Synod of Dort* (1860–1867), and *The Life and Death of John of Barneveld, Advocate of Holland* (1874).

Fundamentally, Motley's conception of the structure and style of literary history was the same as Prescott's. He sought above all to cut through the "confused mass of particulars" to a unity of theme, and to develop that theme by "startling and brilliant pictures." But Motley, who had spent his boyhood building miniature theaters and declaiming in and out of season, sought the dramatic so avidly that his work takes on a different tone from Prescott's. In characterizing even Cortés, Prescott preserved a certain calm and balance. Motley, imitating the "magnificent" Carlyle, made his heroes all heroic, and when he disliked a man he could write of him, "If there are vices—as possibly there are—from which he [Philip II] was exempt, it is because it is not permitted to human nature to be perfect in evil." Motley also contrasts with Prescott in belligerent didacticism. The older man was careful to insist that, while all history should flow into a unified theme, the theme should never shape the facts. Of a more simple mind and with his emotions under less restraint, Motley consciously wrote history as tract. With full-throated dogmatism, he preached the virtues of "noble," "grand" Protestant liberty as opposed to "ruthless," "decadent" Catholic absolutism.

Motley's first work, *The Rise of the Dutch Republic,* is far more sure of permanence in the national literature than anything else he wrote. Here the subject, the struggle of the Dutch for independence, lent itself to the dramatic unity of a liberty-versus-absolutism thesis; the fight of a small nation against a powerful empire made heroic language natural; and the leader of the Dutch, William of Orange, was, in fact, a character of almost Carlylean perfection. Once the Netherlands were free and William was dead, Motley himself saw literary trouble ahead. "It is difficult to scare up another William of Orange," he observed ruefully. Moreover, the action was no longer neatly confined within the Netherlands, but had to pass through most of western Europe and even push along the routes of navigators who were daring many oceans. The *History of the United Netherlands* is at best only brilliant episodes, and at worst it is grossly overwritten. In *John of Barneveld,* Motley was able to recapture dramatic unity by pitting two strong personalities against each other and by giving the outcome of their struggle tragic inevitability. His work regains some of the power of the *Dutch Republic,* though in making these men focal symbols he had to distort more than when he made William of Orange an idea incarnate.

Motley's overdramatization and didacticism, combined with research less intense than Prescott's or Parkman's, have cost his works in staying power. Scholars have largely rewritten the story of the Dutch Republic; it is the rare modern who would, for pleasure alone, read Motley from cover to cover, even his *Rise of the Dutch Republic.* But particular characterizations and episodes in his writings—notably the portraits of William of Orange and Philip II, and the descriptions of the Siege of Leyden, the abdication of Charles V, and the assassination of William—are not excelled in American literature for glint and lift and thud of language.

5

Neither Motley nor Prescott has been the subject of a full-length biography since 1905, but as late as 1942 an ambitious life of Parkman appeared, and more about him is always on the way. This interest is not surprising. Not only is Francis Parkman generally accepted as representing the literary historians at their best, the man himself is as arresting as any page he wrote.

A lanky, sensitive boy, scion of the most settled Boston, Parkman was not through Harvard when, as he says, he contracted "Injuns on the brain." Before graduating, he was off on vacation trips to the forests lying north and west of Boston. Only a few months after getting his degree, he left on horseback for a seventeen-hundred-mile trip along the Oregon Trail. In the forties, such a venture was as dangerous as crossing the Atlantic in a small boat, and Parkman reveled in the danger. Out of the trip came *The California and Oregon Trail* (1849), which, in addition to being one of the few authentic accounts of primitive Indian life at that date, is still widely read by lovers of the literature of adventure. Out of this trip also came some of the maladies that were to cut seriously into his working efficiency for the rest of his life. Medical scholars still argue exactly what was wrong with Parkman, and how much of his illness was neurotic. He certainly was afflicted for long periods with a painful arthritis, and, between near-blindness and fierce headaches, the day was rare when he could write more than a few pages.

Fighting illness, Parkman, like his admirer Theodore Roosevelt, developed an extreme hate for "weakness." To Parkman, nothing was a plainer confession of weakness than arguments for democracy, and the mores of commerce and industry were accorded equal scorn because they seemed a departure from the blunt, virile ways of an earlier world. He once called himself "a little medieval," and the description catches well his feudal disdain for the market place and the ballot box. Politically, this disdain made Parkman one of the most sweeping reactionaries in all American letters; as an author, it gave him ideological impetus to write the history of the frontier to which he was so emotionally attached. Here was a wide-open opportunity for a story of raw forces, unrestrained by strivings for democracy and, at least in Parkman's view, comparatively unaffected by the traffickings of commerce. Before he was out of his twenties, Parkman had found his way to his natural outlet—"a history of the American forest," which, more specifically, meant the struggle of France and England for the mastery of North America. Eight different works, running to a total of eleven volumes and published over the long period from 1851 to 1892, were required to complete the whole of this vast design. The series is known by the title *France and England in North America.*

Of the three literary historians, Parkman was easily the least self-conscious as a craftsman, though his preparation for his task was as conscientious as that of the others. He studied all the classics, historical and otherwise, and carefully worked out a method and style which he thought best suited to his purpose. But he had an aversion to the intricate theorizing about literary method which was characteristic of the romantics, just as he shied away from much of their ebullience. Only from occasional remarks, his prefaces, the internal evidence of his volumes, and his reviews for the *North American Review* and other journals, can the fundamentals of his conception of history be reconstructed.

Parkman believed that the facts should be collected by the most painstaking and persistent research—whenever possible, in first-hand documents and by personal visits to the scenes of the incidents. The writer was to go at his material with a determination "to imbue himself with the life and spirit of the time," to avoid moralizing and philosophizing, and, above all, to get at "the truth." The work was to be constructed on the principle of dramatic unity of theme, and both the integrity and the artistry of the book were to be safeguarded by the utmost care about proportions. The style should be "manly" and "direct," distinguished by "freedom from those prettinesses, studied turns of expression, and pretty tricks of rhetoric, which are the pride of less masculine writers."

With this conception of history, Parkman's volumes are naturally similar in many fundamentals to Prescott's and even, though in lesser degree, to Motley's. But parts of Parkman's ideal of history produced significant differences. His emphasis upon the integrity of materials ruled out Prescott's and

Motley's use of color for color's sake, particularly Prescott's tendency to prefer a chatty chronicle to a rationally determined set of facts. Parkman's aversion to philosophizing would have killed many a paragraph in Prescott and required a reconstruction of Motley's whole work. In style, his predilection for the "direct" and "manly" made him both less eighteenth century and less romantic than the other literary historians, as little disposed to balance and antithesis as to glossy adjectives and hyperthyroid verbs.

Each of Parkman's variations from the other men, perhaps intentionally, gave greater permanence to his volumes. Prescott's and Motley's conceptions of what is colorful, Motley's philosophizing, and both men's highly stylized styles have all tended to date; but the past is immortal, and Parkman's whole method may be accurately summarized as an attempt to bring back the past just as it was. To more than one critic he has recalled the remark of Michelet, that history is not narration as Thierry thought, nor analysis as Guizot thought; it is "resurrection."

Parkman's success in historical resurrection has, by general recognition, never been excelled. Time after time the reader comes close to the sense of being able actually to see and hear the incident. It is not difficult to tell from Parkman's writings that he preferred English civilization to French, the Protestant religion to the Catholic, and many features of the old regime to democracy. The discovery of additional materials has rounded out some episodes he described, such as the French explorations, and changed in important ways other incidents, like the story of Braddock's defeat. Many modern historians feel that he seriously underrated the importance of economic factors. But his research was so prodigious, his use of materials so coolly rational, and his language so objectively precise that the main body of his work has stood immune to the criticism of modern scholarship. Parkman's practice of making trips to the scenes of incidents gave his work one type of authority which no amount of modern scholarship could possibly have, for in his day many of the physical scenes were very little changed from the period of French-English rivalries. And what he learned he set down with the most timeless type of art—dramatic organization restrained by disdain for melodrama, and clarity enlivened by a sure sense of the picturesque.

The achievement of Parkman has such majesty that many a critic has overlooked the fact that his style is of uneven quality. At times the past does more than live again. It lives bombastically, as when "that savage river [the Missouri], descending from its mad career and a vast unknown of barbarism, poured its turbid floods into the bosom of its gentler sister," or when the French Revolution became "blazing hamlets, sacked cities, fields steaming with slaughter, profaned altars, and ravished maidens." This turgidity virtually disappeared as his art matured. The style which has made his writings the manual for many a wise young author is more accurately exemplified by his description of the death of Wolfe at the battle on the plains of Abraham (in *Montcalm and Wolfe*), where the drama inherent in the event reveals itself through straightforward narrative prose.

As Parkman looked back at his volumes over nearly seventy years, he was satisfied with the style he had wrought by infinite hard work. It was another literary feature of *France and England in North America,* its organization, which troubled him. According to the literary historians' ideal of structure there is a flaw, for the organization of the work is not consistent. From the dramatic point of view, the French and English conflict should revolve around the clash between dominant men and ideas. From the logical point of view, the story should move in a cause-effect series, with men and ideas subordinated to that series. Sometimes dramatic and sometimes logical, *France and England in North America* shifts perspective both within the series and within particular books of the series. Parkman, always the perfectionist, was bothered by this inconsistency, and only his death cut short a plan to revise the whole massive work.

One may wonder whether the flaw did not seem more serious to Parkman than it actually is, whether it is not more technical than real. After all, the struggle of France and England for North America was a sprawling, inchoate conflict in which the dramatic and the logical blended and clashed. Perhaps Parkman's instincts served him better than his intellect by loosening his structure in a way that approximates the wobbling of human affairs. At any rate, only a few of his most critical readers have been bothered by the organization of his work. Even Populist-minded Vernon Parrington, whose pen reached for acid as soon as it approached a Brahmin, was ready to accept *France and England in North America* as a permanently great work. The full stature of this nearly blind historian, tortured by sickness and imaginings of sickness, is suggested by the fact that no man has attempted to do again the full story of the struggle for mastery of the North American continent.

6

Well before Parkman died in 1893, the writing of history in the United States had swerved away from the Parkman concept. There were, of course, attempts to write in the tradition of literary history. John Bach McMaster, a civil engineer with the ambition to be "the American Macaulay," made the effort quite consciously in his *History of the People of the United States* (1883–1913). McMaster's bulky green volumes earned a prominent place in historiography because of their attention to the activities of ordinary people, and many a contemporary critic hailed their "vivacity"; but a ramshackle

organization and an awkward style cost them any permanent place in literature. Theodore Roosevelt's *Winning of the West* (1889–1900), modeled after
Parkman's work, continued the Parkman story through the Louisiana Purchase. Here again the attempt at history as literature was decidedly inferior
to the earlier masters both in research, which was too often skimpy, and in
style, which was frequently tumid.

More popular than the historical writings of either Roosevelt or McMaster
were the eleven scattered volumes of John Fiske. Lucid and lively, his written
history showed the same flair for popularization that made him one of the
most successful lecturers the American platform has ever known. But even
the book to which Fiske gave the most research and the most thought, his
Critical Period of American History, 1783–89 (1888), was little more than
an ingenious arrangement of well established materials. Of all the historians
writing toward the end of the century, the only one who produced volumes
that are incontestably literature as well as important history was, appropriately
enough, a latter-day Boston Brahmin, Henry Adams. His *History of the
United States During the Administrations of Jefferson and Madison* (1889–
1891) is a triumph of research, thought, and art.

Yet even Henry Adams did not hold the ideal of literary history. He
wrote his nine volumes, as he put it, to try to fix "a necessary sequence of
human movement" by the "severest process of stating, with the least possible
comment, such facts as seemed sure, in such order as seemed rigorously
consequent." In short, Adams, like most of his generation, wrote as a
"scientific historian." The American Historical Association, organized in 1884,
was dominated by a group of men who believed that history could and
should be converted into a science by the most objective statement of the
most critically determined facts. This "scientific history" denied to the historian the right to impose on his facts any pattern, either literary or ideological, or to add color and movement to the narrative by an imaginative handling
of the materials. The American predecessor on whom "scientific history"
lavished its praise was Richard Hildreth, who had shillelagh words for any
historian seeking literary effects.

The lessening importance of the patrician in the historical field also
undermined interest in literary history. By 1900 the overwhelming number
of American historians were the sons of middle-class families who shared
relatively little (when they shared it at all) the patrician type of revulsion
from commercial and industrial America. Moreover, the reform enthusiasm
sweeping the United States in the early twentieth century found sympathy
in many professors. With this sympathy came a tendency to use the major
intellectual weapon of the Reform movement, an economic interpretation
of past and present affairs. Even historians unsympathetic to the reformist

social program and hesitant about rigorous economic interpretations were, for the most part, in revolt against a romantic apotheosis of an undemocratic past. They too were turning to history which focused on the undramatic, workaday activities of masses of little men. The older literary history, with its emphasis upon the powerful few and the colorful incident, was ruthlessly squeezed between the "scientific" and the "social" history, both of which were combined in the typical new history.

The new history soon brought a radical change of audience. Prescott, Motley, and Parkman had been and continued to be read by the general educated public. With a few exceptions, the footnote-fettered "scientific historians" were read only by one another. Their triumph in the early decades of the twentieth century meant that the public interest in history had to be served largely by popular writers who had neither the high artistic standards of the old school nor the high scholarly standards of the new.

Obviously it was only a question of time before a still newer type of historian combined some features of both traditions. Beginning in the 1920's, the educated public was offered a rapidly increasing output of history which could challenge the work of the literary historians in readability and that of the "scientific historians" in method. Most of these books were written outside the universities; the Professor of History generally kept his eye to the microscope of monographic treatment. But, in or out of universities, these men and women wrestled, often successfully, with a problem that is fundamentally literary. It was a problem made ever more tortuous by the increasing mass of materials, the increasing demands of historical scholarship, and the increasing sophistication of historical interpretations.

This newer new history has been called a revival of literary history but it is hardly that in the sense in which the term has been used in this chapter. The newer historians of high readability chose different kinds of subject matter, treated it with a modern concern for social and economic analysis, and built their books along essentially different lines of structure and style. The literary history of Prescott, Motley, and Parkman came from a particular milieu which has never reappeared in the United States. Although many another Brahmin group has appeared, with an equal attachment to books and even an equal aversion for commercialism and "the mob," there has been only one Brahminism stirred by those cross winds of the eighteenth and nineteenth centuries which swirled through Boston at the mid-century. Men and women will always go on writing history that is also literature, but the work of Prescott, Motley, and Parkman is as unique as it is permanent.

33. THE ORATORS

ORATORY has always been a proud American tradition, a national habit. The tradition of more than three centuries links Thomas Hooker preaching in his pulpit at Hartford, Connecticut, on *The Soules Humiliation* with Franklin D. Roosevelt halting a national debacle with the sanative words of his First Inaugural: "Let me assert my firm belief that the only thing we have to fear is fear itself." We have produced oratory robustly in mass, volume, and diffuseness. In times of crisis we have also produced addresses of compelling thought and enduring beauty.

The art which the orator practices—the art of rhetoric—was defined by Aristotle as the faculty of observing (not necessarily of using) all the available means of persuasion. Our orators who have practiced this art have been men who by logical proof and emotional appeal, reinforced by all the resources of their established prestige, have persuaded large groups of their fellow citizens to adopt certain beliefs or to pursue certain policies. In America, oratory has been the great creator of loyalties. The pervading tradition of our literature, written or spoken, is a tradition of revolt, but the orator, even when leading a revolt, has always sought to arouse the indifferent or dissuade the hostile in order that he may secure the loyalty of a group. He has attempted by direct address to compel that same kind of devoted response which may come to novelists or poets only after generations of readers have read their works.

It has been said that "oratory is partly an art, partly a power of making history, and occasionally a branch of literature." Oratory concerns chiefly the public life of society, but literary critics select for survival those passages of the oration which show something of the private life that a public life preserves. To the literary critic Lincoln's Gettysburg Address is a great prose passage written by a man who brooded much in solitude, and who rose above a particular occasion to speak to the ages. But we should remember that he also seized the occasion with its powerful emotional associations to dedicate his audience to carrying on the Civil War.

We call the criticism of the work of the orators rhetorical criticism. It is not primarily concerned with permanence, nor beauty, but with effect.

Rhetorical criticism carries on near the boundary line of literature and politics. Its atmosphere is that of public life rather than the quiet of the library. It is concerned with the ideas of masses of people as influenced by their leaders rather than with the ideas of solitary thinkers or poets. It examines the wielder of public opinion as one handling a technique of power. For rhetorical criticism the personality of the orator, the history of the issues he debated, the nature of the opposition he faced, the character of the audiences he addressed are at least as important as his artistic ability to lend interest to matters whose practical importance has vanished. Necessarily, then, the critical approach of this chapter will differ somewhat from that of other chapters which are concerned with the works of thinkers or poets whose audience never crowded close around them to hear their voices.

In no period of American history was the orator so influential as during the fifty years before the Civil War. The age produced a steady stream of able speakers who by their superior eloquence attained the stature of orators and profoundly affected the direction of public affairs. Many, like Emerson and Phillips and Parker, were notable writers as well as lecturers and orators. It is appropriate, therefore, that the chapter of this history devoted to American oratory should appear at this point in the story of the development of American literature, and that it should be concerned mainly with the great figures of the golden age of American oratory. But to make the account complete, the chapter must look before and after, backward to the great Puritan preachers and forward to the day when the radio would make it possible for a national leader who was also an orator to speak directly to millions of his countrymen and move them to act.

2

The first American orators—the preachers, the colonial governors and legislators—were men well trained, as they needed to be, in the art of rhetoric which they had learned in the English universities, the Inns of Court, or the infant colleges of the New World. At Harvard in 1655 students were required to make public declamations twice each month. Lectures on rhetoric were given on Friday mornings, and all the members of the college spent the rest of the day in rhetorical exercises based on the logic of Peter Ramus and the rhetoric of Talon.

The Puritan preacher had special need of this elaborate training. The Covenant Theology which he expounded was intricate and most difficult to make plain. Too much depended on the truthfulness and clarity with which he set it forth to permit him to exceed by much the bounds of the "plain style." Curious as the sermons of Increase Mather and Urian Oakes may seem to modern readers, they were wonderfully effective instruments for explaining great mysteries to simple men.

The colonial legislatures were closed assemblies until the middle of the eighteenth century; but within the small chambers in Boston or Williamsburg the great debate between the Crown and a rebellious America had already begun. Governors sometimes spoke sharply to the people's representatives in their opening addresses, but they usually tried to argue the Crown's case well—if relations were still cordial enough to induce them to speak at all. Once the people were admitted to the galleries, the legislators learned soon enough to speak beyond the heads of the governor and their fellow representatives to the larger audience outside the walls of the statehouse.

Until the third decade of the eighteenth century most of the orators were trained in the rhetorical tradition which the Renaissance inherited from Aristotle and Quintilian and remade for its own purposes. But a new age in America in which an ever increasing audience of the plain people was eager to hear religious and political issues debated before it, now demanded a more emotional style. The preachers who induced the Great Awakening in the 1730's were bent on arousing their hearers to the dangers of their sinful state. Their instrument was enthusiasm rather than logic. When ministers of the established churches refused them their pulpits they went to the people in the open air, as George Whitefield did when Franklin heard him speak from the Courthouse steps in Philadelphia. The power of his voice on this occasion impelled Franklin's belief in the newspaper accounts of his having preached to as many as twenty-five thousand in the fields. The great orators of the Revolution likewise knew how to sway the emotions of their hearers, an art which they had learned by belaboring their opponents in law cases and by appealing to reluctant juries. Burke spoke the truth when he said in his speech On Conciliation that the American legislators were all lawyers or men endeavoring "to obtain some smattering in that science," and that their training had made them "prompt in attack, ready in defence, full of resources."

John Adams complained of the tediousness of the sessions of the Continental Congress in which "every man upon every question must show his oratory, his criticism, his political abilities"; but most of the other members agreed that he, as well as George Wythe, James Wilson, and a dozen others who spoke frequently, was good in debate and easy to listen to. Even John Witherspoon, whose voice was so low that it did not carry to the back of the room, received close attention because of the weight of his frequent speeches. Jefferson, Franklin, and Washington did not indulge in oratory but kept strictly to the issues. The great orators of the Congress, as most Americans still know, were Patrick Henry and Richard Henry Lee.

When presently the fateful issue of the Constitution was before the people, the skill of the orators who rose to defend it in the several states equaled that of the pamphleteers who also helped to secure its ratification. John Jay and Alexander Hamilton were ingenious and indefatigable in their arguments for adoption before the convention in New York State, as were C. C. Pinckney in South Carolina and Oliver Ellsworth in Connecticut. In Virginia the passionate opposition of Patrick Henry seemed at the time dangerous but was ultimately matched and defeated by the logic and lucidity of James Madison, the chief architect of the Constitution.

3

Throughout the years of the early national period there were many voices and multitudes of attentive listeners. They spoke and were heard in farm surroundings, village squares, and town halls, and only here and there in what we now call cities. For in 1830 a bare sixth of the people lived in places of over 8,000 population. It was a period, however, when men everywhere were eager to learn, eager to speak and take sides, eager to reach decisions. "The traits of intelligence, rapidity, and mildness seemed fixed in the national character as early as 1817," observes Henry Adams. And he significantly adds: "Another intellectual trait . . . was the disposition to relax severity." New horizons were ahead. The people were shifting, restless, youthfully optimistic, ambitious for better life and happier living. Literacy and learning were not widespread, but the capacity to listen to speakers and to criticize them knew no bounds.

The most important addresses of the period were made before legislative bodies, especially the United States Senate, before courts and juries, and at great patriotic ceremonies before vast audiences, like those assembled at Plymouth, 1820, Bunker Hill, 1825 and 1843, and Faneuil Hall, 1826, to hear Daniel Webster. His magnificent addresses on those occasions are without equal in the history of ceremonial oratory.

The pulpit, the lecture platform, and the election campaign likewise offered variety of subject matter ranging from instruction to entertainment. Audience taste, speech form and style, the educational equipment of the speaker combined to produce in the early years, from 1815 to as late as 1850, a characteristically ornate and diffuse kind of speaking. The same was true of the writing. By 1858, for instance, a writer in the *North American Review* took pains to explain:

It pleases our English critics to charge upon American writers in the mass— particularly upon our historians, orators, essayists, and lecturers, and the after-dinner speakers of our frequent celebrations and commemorations—what has come to be designated as "the spread-eagle style,"—a compound of exaggeration, effrontery, bombast, and extravagance, mixed metaphors, platitudes, defiant threats thrown at the world, and irreverent appeals flung at the Supreme Being. Now it is a simple slander upon us to generalize this charge, and to visit it upon American writers and speakers as such. There has been, as we all know, too much of this inflated and braggadocio utterance among us. . . . This habit of speaking, however, is now visiting the force of its own ridicule upon itself, and that will banish it sooner than will any protest of those aggrieved by it on either side of the water.

The prophecy proved correct. A youthful country may produce, it is true, a blatant and bumptious kind of oratory. But as individual speakers matured— Webster and Lincoln in particular—the powerful, simple, straightforward kind of address that befits a better educated and cultivated citizenry slowly emerged.

What kinds of subjects occupied men's minds? Wendell Phillips, the most famous of the antislavery orators, spoke during his lifetime on woman's suffrage and equal rights, temperance, capital punishment, treatment of the Indians, religious topics, education, prison reform, money and banking laws, and better wages and working conditions for labor. His consuming interest, however, was in freeing the slaves. He was typical of the age. From 1820 until Lee surrendered at Appomattox slavery was the dominating political issue. All other causes including the war with Mexico and the expansion of the West are dwarfed by the volume of speech-making produced by slavery. It carried with it, of course, discussion, debate, and dissent on the doctrines of States' Rights, Popular Sovereignty, Nullification, the Compromise of 1850, and eventually in 1860, Secession. Year by year until the Kansas-Nebraska Bill of 1854 and the Dred Scott Decision of 1857 the intensity of feeling and the convictions of evil and good mounted in the hearts and minds of men. When Lincoln and Douglas staged their joint debates in 1858 they were the final-act characters of a drama that had been playing with accelerating tempo and heightening action for fully forty years.

Throughout the process of erecting a superstructure on the foundation of the Fathers three orators were preeminent. In the beginning they were sectional figures. Daniel Webster was the North, John C. Calhoun the South, and Henry Clay the New West. But all were also nationalists, and Clay and Webster outgrew their sectionalism. Their principles came not from the inner light, nor from systematic political philosophy, but from an understanding of their constituents. Their ideas changed with changing times and interests. If they are to be criticized for having their eyes on the Presidency, they should be credited with able attempts to state ideas upon which the greatest number of conflicting interests could unite. Their power rested fundamentally upon their ability to state those ideas persuasively and impressively, and to convince their constituents that they were the ablest advocates before the bar of public opinion.

These men did not need an Emerson to remind them of "the meal in the firkin, the milk in the pan." They lived in their country homes at Marshfield, Fort Hill, and Ashland with something of the dignity of Washington at Mount Vernon or Jefferson at Monticello. They were not only attached to their lares and penates, they were practical directors of their agricultural pursuits. Their education was classical in background, and they all possessed an ardor for *respublica*. In the loyalties inspired by them the economic and political history between 1815 and 1850 may be understood, and in their devotion to country and section patriotism often rose above economics and politics.

4

Henry Clay was the first of these new leaders to talk himself into national prominence. "Harry of the West" was born in Virginia, and nurtured in Jeffersonian agrarianism. He migrated to Kentucky, absorbed the spirit of speculative expansion, entered the State Legislature, and was appointed to the United States Senate in 1806. Henry Adams notes that the twenty-nine-year-old Senator had been in the capital only two weeks when he introduced a new style into American politics by rhetorical references to the Union and the Fathers. George Washington and his contemporaries had previously been conceded greatness and had occasionally been hailed as venerable, but from now on American orators were to vie with one another in deifying them.

Clay, however, was as quick to defy Washington as to deify him. The policy of the older men had been prudence and peace, and under such a policy our army had been reduced to a small police force to guard against the Indians. Clay, as one of the sixty new youngsters sent to Congress, was determined to show what the boys could do, and he led a country without an army to attack a country whose army had been commanded by Wellington and whose navy had been trained by Nelson. "Sir," he exclaimed in the Senate two years before the War of 1812, "is the time never to arrive when we can manage our own affairs without the fear of insulting his Britannic majesty? Is the rod of British power to be forever suspended over our heads? . . . Whether we assert our rights by sea, or attempt their maintenance by land—whithersoever we turn ourselves, this phantom incessantly pursues us. Already has it too much influence in the councils of the nation."

The War Hawks, Clay included, deserved Josiah Quincy's characterization of them as "young politicians, with the pinfeathers yet unshed, and the shell still sticking upon them—perfectly unfledged." But the "Western Star," elected to the Speakership of the House immediately upon his entrance in 1811, had behind him the whole Mississippi Valley, bitter over a depression which it laid to the British Orders in Council, and the South, eager to wrest Florida and Mexico from England's ally, Spain. New England, still making profits in spite of the invasion of seamen's rights, had no desire to have its pride avenged, but its wrongs also furnished battle cries in the crusade of the West and South for war. Clay's Liberty Boys were determined to fix a national character by a second declaration of independence which should separate us from the governments of Europe. Clay had a vigorous two years of organization as well as of oratory before he could overcome the opposition of the Federalists. In his debates on the need for a navy, for a militia, for frontier mounted rangers, for equipment and supplies, he learned what a task it was to organize America's resources and create a national spirit capable of maintaining independence. The difficulties were so great that Clay and his colleagues may well be accounted foolhardy. Their policy, by all the laws of probability, should have brought defeat and ruin, but the net result, in spite of military disasters, was to establish the self-confidence of the nation, and win for it European recognition as an independent power.

Clay's expansive thinking led to large plans for the creation of a balanced economy for the United States, which he summarized as "The American System." It has been charged that it was a blind for a policy of high tariffs, but this is to fail to consider the system in its entirety. Clay's tariff was protective and it did build up manufacturing interests, which was a departure from his early Jeffersonianism. But, he argued, this would make the country self-sufficient in war, and would support a large industrial population, which in turn would provide a market for the produce of the expanding West and the plantations of the South. A substantial part of the tariff revenue was to provide funds for internal improvements in the West, thus distributing the benefits of the system to the whole nation. If the selfishness of sectional, class, and occupational interests could have been controlled, and the balance preserved, the American System might still be a tribute to Clay's powers of persuasion. But the blindness of the supporters of the National Bank, the uncompromising hostility of Jackson and the frontiersmen, and the demands of Calhoun for the South led to the Nullification Crisis of 1833. Clay saw that it was his American System against the Union, and he sacrificed what he regarded as his greatest contribution to American statecraft in order to introduce a compromise tariff.

From 1833 to 1842, during the years when Clay's powers were at their greatest, he was a leader of the opposition, and achieved little that will be remembered. His position as candidate for the Presidency in 1844, when the bitterness over the annexation of Texas compelled him to announce that he considered the preservation of the Union the paramount issue, was regarded as an unheroic straddle; his preference for the middle ground was thought to be dictated by his consuming desire for the Presidency. But when, after six years of retirement at Ashland, he was returned at the age of seventy-two to attempt again his old role of pacificator, he could remind the Senate that he was beyond ambition, could seriously deprecate the violence of party spirit, and could solemnly urge the necessity for compromise:

The final result [of Civil War] would be the extinction of this last and glorious light which is leading all mankind, who are gazing upon it, in the hope and anxious expectation that the liberty which prevails here will sooner or later be diffused throughout the whole of the civilized world.

The debate upon Clay's compromise proposals is one of the great debates in American history, or in the history of any parliamentary body. Clay, Calhoun, and Webster, all old and ill, were still the giants of the Senate, although a fiery and impetuous younger generation, including William H. Seward, Salmon P. Chase, Jefferson Davis, and Stephen A. Douglas were asserting themselves. But the older leaders symbolized their cause as no younger men could. Harry of the West was now the Great Pacificator. His sunken cheeks, pinched nose, bald head, and long fringe of gray hair falling to his shoulders, showed his age, but he profoundly moved the crowded galleries. His speeches gained in power from the fact that he was the author of the compromise proposals. He knew the extremists of both sides. He knew the temper of the nation, and no one could accuse him of ambition when he declared:

I go for honorable compromise whenever it can be made. Life itself is but a compromise between death and life, the struggle continuing throughout our whole existence, until the Great Destroyer finally triumphs. All legislation, all government, all society, is formed upon the principle of mutual concession, politeness, comity, courtesy; upon these everything is based. . . . Let him who elevates himself above humanity, above its weaknesses, its infirmities, its wants, its necessities, say, if he pleases, I never will compromise, but let no one who is not above the frailties of our common nature disdain compromises.

Clay was in his own time esteemed as the greatest orator of the day, but his speeches have had little effect as literature. His outlook on human affairs was eminently practical, and his speaking had a highly utilitarian purpose; but he understood the American mind, and he typified more than any other man of the age its strength and its shortcomings, its emotions, hopes, and ambitions

5

Daniel Webster attained his oratorical eminence during the period 1818–1830. Elected to Congress in 1813, at the age of thirty-one, he attracted attention in his maiden speech by his historical learning and power of illustration. Chief Justice Marshall writing to a friend shortly after the speech predicted that Webster would "become one of the very first statesmen in America, and perhaps the very first." Had his career stopped short with the Second Reply to Hayne in 1830 his immense fame would have been secure. By then he was known for a score and more of speeches which made history. He had become a highly successful courtroom pleader both at the bar of the Supreme Court, as in the Dartmouth College Case (1818 *) and before criminal juries, as in the White Murder Trial (1830). But Webster's even greater reputation is based on his ceremonial speaking—the Plymouth Oration (1820), the First Bunker Hill Address (1825), the Eulogy of Adams and Jefferson (1826). These were addresses which furnished declamations for generations of American schoolboys up to the Civil War and it was that final solemn sentence of the Second Reply to Hayne, "Liberty *and* Union, now and forever, one and inseparable," that became the rallying cry of Union troops in 1861.

In appearance, in learning, in temperament and action Webster was the ideal orator. But it was his legal turn of mind, his ability to cast large ideas into musical language, and his remarkable gift of imagery that set the man apart as a speaker. Clay was the better debater and campaign orator; Calhoun was the better reasoner and political thinker. Webster was the epideictic orator par excellence. He lays down his own formula for good speaking in his Eulogy of Adams and Jefferson delivered at Faneuil Hall on August 2, 1826:

When public bodies are to be addressed on momentous occasions, when great interests are at stake, and strong passions excited, nothing is valuable in speech farther than as it is connected with high intellectual and moral endowments. Clearness, force, and earnestness are the qualities which produce conviction. True eloquence indeed, does not consist in speech. . . . It must exist in the man, in the subject, in the occasion. Affected passion, intense expression, the pomp of declamation, all may aspire to it; they cannot reach it. It comes, if it comes at all, like the outbreaking of a fountain from the earth, or the bursting forth of volcanic fires, with spontaneous, original, native force.

It was Webster's reply to Hayne in the Senate session of 1829–1830 that raised his reputation to the highest pitch. Senator Foote of Connecticut had

* Unless otherwise noted, dates of speeches in this chapter indicate the year of delivery rather than of publication.

introduced a resolution asking for an inquiry into the practical effects of limiting the sale of government land in the West. Senator Hayne of South Carolina had forcefully argued that the East had always tried to oppose the development of the West. Webster rose to defend the charge. His exordium beginning, "Mr. President, when the mariner has been tossed for many days in thick weather and on an unknown sea," is easily the most famous in American parliamentary address. The speech itself completely demolished the attacks made on Webster's character and his motives. By a strong argument the orator demonstrated his reliance upon the supremacy of the Constitution. Hayne on the other hand, Webster held, was deliberately expounding ideas which would surely lead to disunion and civil war. The final paragraph suggests in farseeing language what came to pass thirty years later:

When my eyes shall be turned to behold, for the last time, the sun in heaven, may I not see him shining on the broken and dishonored fragments of a once glorious Union; on States dissevered, discordant, belligerent; on a land rent with civil feuds, or drenched, it may be, in fraternal blood!

The popular acclaim of the Second Reply to Hayne was extraordinary. The speech marked the zenith of the orator's career. In succeeding years Webster made many speeches, some good and a number lacking in quality. He reached a peak again, but with bitter result, in his Seventh of March speech (1850), when he deserted the abolitionist cause and in effect justified the South's stand on slavery.

The evidence now shows that the Union was in imminent danger of armed conflict in the spring of 1850. General Winfield Scott wrote General Sherman that the country was "on the eve of a terrible civil war." Similar testimony is available from such varied observers as Alexander H. Stephens, Francis Lieber, and Horace Mann. Late in February, 1850, Edward Everett wrote that "the radicals of the South have made up their minds to separate, the catastrophe seems to be inevitable."

It was with this knowledge that Webster planned the oration he called "The Constitution and the Union," but which history has named the Seventh of March speech. His opening sentence set the tone of the address: "I wish to speak today, not as a Massachusetts man, nor as a Northern man, but as an American."

The address proper required more than three hours in delivery and its published form takes up forty-one pages in the National Edition of Webster's works. In the main section the speaker calmly reviewed the grievances of the North and the South. He admitted that the North had failed to live up to its constitutional obligations to return fugitive slaves. He conceded that the abolition societies had only served to inflame feeling without effecting anything "good or valuable." He did not deny the irritating results of the resolutions to abolish slavery as drawn up by legislative bodies in the North. But the North objected to the institution of slavery which the South wished "to be cherished, preserved, and extended." And the only basis for solution, Webster argued, rested on new understandings—"a better feeling and more fraternal sentiments between the South and the North." Any attempt at "peaceable secession is an utter impossibility," he proclaimed as he turned and faced Calhoun.

With respect to an economic solution of the problem Webster announced his willingness to support a project for transporting freed slaves "to any colony or any place in the world." He also favored paying Texas a fair sum for deeding to the United States the lands adjoining New Mexico, an area always claimed by Texas as its own.

In his final appeal the orator counseled that "instead of speaking of the possibility or utility of secession" the nation should try to enjoy "the fresh air of Liberty and Union," and to preserve the Constitution and "the harmony and peace of all who are destined to live under it."

In general, it was a wise and temperate speech, not impassioned or emotional. And therein lies its strength. Webster assumed a statesmanlike position, and history has vindicated him; but his New England friends at the time, the Abolitionists in particular, never forgave him. Soon the Quaker poet, Whittier, gave to the once great Daniel the name of Ichabod and mourned for him in cutting verse as one dead:

> Let not the land once proud of him
> Insult him now,
> Nor brand with deeper shame his dim,
> Dishonored brow.
>
> But let its humbled sons, instead,
> From sea to lake,
> A long lament, as for the dead,
> In sadness make.

But the Union was preserved for another decade. If only another orator could have spoken again and preserved it, let us say, until 1870, economic forces, which we now comprehend, might have prevented the bloodshed.

6

The third of the triumvirate, John C. Calhoun, was in his prime a little later than Clay and Webster. His best speeches are in the Senate debates from 1833 to 1843 and again shortly before 1850. The most important are Against the Force Bill (1833), In Support of States' Rights (1833), Against Incendiary Publications (1836), those denouncing the Expunging Resolution and the Abolition Petitions (1837), Against the Ten Regiment Bill (1848), and his last speech, delivered just before he died, on The Slavery Question (1850).

As these titles suggest, Calhoun was generally in the opposition; as the spokesman of the South, he was against the long succession of measures designed to limit or abolish slavery. He argued in 1837 that slavery was a positive good, and he fought valiantly in the Senate to his death to maintain the balance between the slave and free states. On these issues Calhoun's excellent education at Yale, his first-class legal training under Judge Reeve at Litchfield, his lifelong reflective habits, and his analytical mind made him intellectually more than a match even for Clay and Webster.

For years Webster, the symbol of the New England manufacturing interests, and Calhoun, representing the slaveholding aristocracy of the South, were direct antagonists. (At the time of Webster's reply to Hayne, however, in 1830, Calhoun was serving as Vice President, and the Great Nullifier yielded to Hayne as the first expounder of the doctrine.) In simplest terms, Calhoun argued that a state reserved the right within its own borders to impede or to attempt to prevent the federal government from enforcing a law of the United States.

Emerson says: "There is no true eloquence unless there is a man behind the speech." Calhoun is perhaps the shining example among statesmen before the Civil War of the classical definition of the orator: the good man skilled in speaking. Even his political opponents admired his character, freely acknowledged the absence of corruption in his personal life. His voice and learning could not be bought. It is this intellectual honesty of the man that we must fix in mind to form a true estimate of Calhoun.

But I take higher ground. I hold that in the present state of civilization, where two races of different origin, and distinguished by color and other physical differences, as well as intellectual, are brought together, the relation now existing in the slaveholding states between the two is, instead of an evil, a good—a positive good. I feel myself called upon to speak freely upon the subject, when the honor and interests of those I represent are involved. I hold, then, that there never has yet existed a wealthy and civilized society in which one portion of the community did not, in point of fact, live on the labor of the other. Broad and general as is this assertion, it is fully borne out by history.

Thus spoke Calhoun before the Senate in 1837 on the question of receiving petitions in Congress for the abolition of slavery in the District of Columbia. The whole speech is typical of his style and logical structure. Unlike many speakers of his day he was not given to extensive use of emotional appeal. His use of ethical proof, the relation of the orator's character to the larger treatment of the subject, is awkward and generally not effective. But his arguments, well planned and supported, are readily followed. He is a master of cause-to-effect reasoning, and he frequently uses specific examples, analogies, and authorities to buttress the framework. The total effect is one of cold rigidity rather than of smooth persuasive appeal. Calhoun's language is not florid or effusive, as Southern oratory often is. Nor could anyone ever say of him, for example, as John Quincy Adams on a certain occasion wrote of John Randolph:

His speech, as usual, had neither beginning, middle, nor end. Egotism, Virginian aristocracy, slave-scourging, liberty, religion, literature, science, wit, fancy, generous feelings, and malignant passions constitute a chaos in his mind, from which nothing orderly can ever flow.

"The cast-iron man who looks as if he had never been born," Harriet Martineau called Calhoun. The impression explains why Calhoun never rose to the popular esteem of Clay or the brilliant eloquence of Webster. He seldom swayed votes on the issues he opposed, and his influence, not his interests, seldom went beyond sectional range. He was too severe, too humorless, too strait-laced to be a great public idol. Nevertheless his speeches deserve wider reading than they have enjoyed. They are neither dull nor ponderous, and they furnish the clue to the constitutional principles upon which the South defended slavery as an institution for the three decades before the fateful first shot at Fort Sumter.

7

In the summer of 1850 a young lawyer, Abraham Lincoln of Illinois, compiled some notes for a law lecture. What he wrote, concisely stated his character and foretold his own career:

Extemporaneous speaking should be practised and cultivated. It is the lawyer's avenue to the public. However able and faithful he may be in other respects, people are slow to bring him business if he cannot make a speech. And yet there is not a more fatal error to young lawyers than relying too much on speech-making. If anyone, upon his rare powers of speaking, shall claim an exemption from the drudgery of the law, his case is a failure in advance.

Within the next ten years Lincoln became by his own formula of diligent study and fluency in debate the people's chosen leader and the successor to the tradition of Clay, Calhoun, and Webster.

Ask any American today which of Lincoln's writings he remembers, and he will usually reply, "The Gettysburg Address and the Second Inaugural." If he happens to be a student of Speech or History he may add the Lincoln-Douglas Debates (1858), the Cooper Union Address (1860), the Farewell Address at Springfield (1861), the letter to Colonel Ellsworth's parents (1861), the letter to Mrs. Bixby (1864), and possibly others. These letters and addresses have established Lincoln as one of the masters of prose style in the English language.

Like Webster before him, Lincoln gradually came to see the strength and power of the plain style. As a young politician he was used to the ornate overspeaking of the day. But during the Zachary Taylor presidential campaign of 1848 he heard William H. Seward, later to be his Secretary of State, speak in Boston, and was impressed with his logical argument and conversational manner of delivery. We see the signs of a maturing speaker in the Peoria Speech of 1854, in the famous House Divided Against Itself Speech delivered before the Illinois Republican State Convention in 1858, and especially in the address at Cooper Union on February 27, 1860.

For this speech Henry Ward Beecher had first invited Lincoln to his Plymouth Church in Brooklyn; but the scene was later changed to accommodate the larger audience. A good share of Lincoln's argument went to answering the charges of Stephen A. Douglas that the writers of the Constitution had denied the government control over slavery in the territories. The speech did much to gain Lincoln the nomination for the Presidency. Joseph H. Choate later described its impact: "That night the great hall and the next day the whole city rang with delighted applause and congratulations, and he who had come as a stranger, departed with the laurels of a great triumph."

The Lincoln we know as President is less the orator and more the writer of masterful prose. He then habitually read his speeches from manuscript, and for this reason probably prepared and revised more carefully than ever before. The final wistfully hopeful sentences of the less often read First Inaugural Address reveal the glow of polish:

I am loath to close. We are not enemies, but friends. We must not be enemies. Though passion may have strained, it must not break our bonds of affection. The mystic cords of memory, stretching from every battlefield and patriot grave to every living heart and hearthstone all over this broad land, will yet swell the chorus of the Union when again touched, as surely they will be, by the better angels of our nature.

Edward Everett was the first to recognize the dignity of Lincoln's address at Gettysburg. He wrote to the President the next day from Washington:

I should be glad if I could flatter myself that I came as near to the central idea of the occasion in two hours as you did in two minutes.

And Lincoln courteously replied:

In our respective parts yesterday you could not have been excused to make a short address, nor I a long one. I am pleased to know that, in your judgment, the little I did say was not entirely a failure.

The general recognition of the exalted beauty of the Gettysburg Address was late in coming. So it was with the Second Inaugural Address. Yet British critics who had previously berated American literary efforts were quick to praise the poetry of the lines:

With malice toward none; with charity for all; with firmness in the right, as God gives us to see the right, let us strive on to finish the work we are in; to bind up the nation's wounds; to care for him who shall have borne the battle, and for his widow and his orphan—to do all which may achieve and cherish a just and lasting peace among ourselves, and with all nations.

Gladstone proclaimed:

I am taken captive by so striking an utterance as this. I see in it the effect of sharp trial, when rightly borne, to raise man to a higher level of thought and action. It is by cruel suffering that nations are sometimes born to a better life. So it is with individual man. Lincoln's words show that upon him anxiety and sorrow have wrought their full effect.

Here we have the judgment of an orator who has turned literary critic. His opinion is of interest because it reminds us that Lincoln is the one American orator who survives as a literary artist. His literary instinct was so true that we tend to forget his rhetorical skill. But whenever he spoke Lincoln was a persuasive man, an orator, as a study of the effect of his addresses reveals.

8

For forty-odd years before his death in 1865, Edward Everett was the great scholar-orator whose reputation was for a time on a plane with Webster's. Everett's published addresses were best sellers a century ago, and they reached a ninth edition in 1878. His famous oration on The Character of Washington was delivered nearly 150 times, and from its proceeds he donated a large sum to the Mount Vernon Ladies Association, an organization formed about 1856 to preserve Washington's estate. In all his addresses Everett exhibited the power of his classical learning both in content and in form. He was not profound, but he was never superficial. Indeed, the very weight and variety of his literary and historical illustrations add up to his greatest fault. But the audiences of his day did not object. They admired the man and devotedly gave him their attention.

Emerson complained of Everett: "He is all art, and I find in him, nowadays, maugre all his gifts and great merits, more to blame than to praise. He is not content to be Edward Everett, but would be Daniel Webster. This is his mortal distemper." Everett himself admitted in his later years the need for pruning some of his floweriness, and he added: "This operation might have been carried on still further with advantage; for I feel them [the speeches of his 1849 edition] to be still deficient in that simplicity which is their first merit."

The truth of the self-criticism is confirmed for those who have taken the trouble to read Everett's two-hour-long oration at Gettysburg. But it was far from a failure on the day of delivery. The audience received it with prolonged applause, and it is unfair to Everett's ability to inspire audiences to end a criticism of him by contrast with Lincoln. Emerson later and more wisely said of Everett that he "had a great talent for collecting facts, and for bringing those he had to bear with ingenious felicity on the topic of the moment." He was the most erudite speaker of his time, a great disseminator, before thousands of relatively unschooled Americans, of the lofty sentiments for which they hungered.

Preachers in pulpits, professional agitators, women orators, and a host of lesser persons took up the struggle against slavery. Not all of the speaking on these issues was done on the floor of Congress. A mere list of those active would include scores of names. Foremost of the preachers who were also reformers at heart were Theodore Parker, Henry Ward Beecher, and Phillips Brooks. They were all important antislavery figures, and the influence of Beecher and Brooks reached into the Reconstruction Era.

Theodore Parker espoused what came in time to be popular causes, but he helped to make them popular. He opposed the sterile rationalism of established Unitarianism; he fought the social abuses of his day; and in the fifties he spoke daringly, and acted also, against slavery. He attacked unceasingly the dominant powers in Boston: the strong remnant of Federalism, the cotton Whigs, the Democrats who accepted without a qualm the Fugitive Slave Act, the influence of Webster whom he had loved but whom he denounced the Sunday after his death in one of the strangest funeral sermons ever preached

No living man [he said to his congregation] has done so much to debauch the conscience of the nation, to debauch the press, the pulpit, the forum, and the bar.

. . . He poisoned the moral wells of society with his lower law, and men's consciences died of the murrain of beasts, which came because they drank thereat.

From the time Parker left his church in West Roxbury to shepherd a new congregation of three thousand, in the old Music Hall in Washington Street, he was the keeper of the public conscience of Boston. He said he was the most hated man in the city, and he was often in danger of physical violence; but Emerson was near the truth when he declared him to be one of the four great men of the age.

In his theology Parker was a transcendentalist. His sermon On the Transient and Permanent in Christianity, preached in 1841, occupies a place in the history of transcendentalism comparable to that which William Ellery Channing's Baltimore Sermon of 1819 holds in the history of Unitarianism. Parker's transcendentalism was of a more logical, though much less subtle, kind than Emerson's. For this reason his presentation of the new faith reached listeners whom Emerson could not touch. He announced the "new views" with an unostentatious but careful rhetoric in which simple words and homely allusions were enriched with metaphor. In all his speaking, but in none of his causes more boldly than on the issue of slavery, he was Emerson's "Man Thinking," a great soul strong to live as well as strong to think, but one who never sacrificed "any opinion to the popular judgments and modes of action."

For tenacious persistence in conquering a hostile audience there are few better examples than Henry Ward Beecher's speech defending the North, delivered at Liverpool in 1863. The orator here adapted his arguments to his immediate hearers with amazing skill. He used luminous and convincing illustrations, historical facts and statistics, pleading all the time for fair play and the right to be heard. The speech began amidst catcalls and heckling but ended in a vote of thanks.

Beecher's Memorial Sermon on Abraham Lincoln (1865), his oration on Raising the Flag at Fort Sumter (1865), and his Yale Lectures on Preaching (1872), have survived in interest to this day. Though the gift of argumentative reasoning was not wanting in the man, his real power lay in imaginative appeal. The key to his method is made clear in his own words:

There are in any community probably six to one who will watch for the emotional and impassioned part of the sermon, saying, "That is the preaching I want; I can understand what I feel." They are fed by their hearts. They have as much right to be fed by their hearts as others have to be fed by their reason.

Among the lesser political speakers we should not neglect "Old Bullion," Thomas Hart Benton of Missouri, the defender of the rights of settlers upon the public lands and the advocate of gold and silver in preference to a paper currency; Thomas Corwin, who opposed the war with Mexico in a brilliant prophetic speech; John Quincy Adams, the ex-President, who skillfully kept alive the discussion of slavery and won permission in 1844 for antislavery petitions to be heard in the House of Representatives after a six-year period of tabling; or Stephen A. Douglas, to whom Lincoln lost a senatorship, but who established himself as "an exponent and interpreter of the essence of democracy."

The more significant individual orations dealing with the Civil War include The Crime Against Kansas (1856), by Charles Sumner; The Irrepressible Conflict (1858), by William H. Seward; On Withdrawing from the Union (1861), by Jefferson Davis; and On the Confederate Constitution (1861), by Alexander H. Stephens. Other Southern orators who gained more than sectional attention were Robert Y. Hayne of South Carolina, William L. Yancey, the "orator of secession," and Seargent S. Prentiss, a native of Maine but an adopted son of Mississippi.

Wendell Phillips, perhaps more than any other of the orators before the Civil War, typifies the mighty force of the spoken word. Neither statesman nor preacher, he was essentially a professional agitator. His famous speech on the Murder of Lovejoy (1837) was classed by George William Curtis with Patrick Henry's The Call to Arms and Lincoln's Gettysburg Address as one of the greatest American public utterances. In the fifties Phillips was preeminent among an eloquent company—Douglas and Lincoln, Seward and Sumner, Chase and Choate. His lecture, Toussaint L'Ouverture, spoken more than a thousand times during the war years 1861–1865, fascinated and enthralled even those bitter with race prejudice. Designed to show the potentialities of the colored man, it served to improve understanding of the Negro and to instill a sympathy for him as a freeman.

Nor can the effect of the women agitators during the forties and fifties be underrated. Many of their best speeches have not been preserved, and until recent years their contribution has escaped the historians. But Frances Wright, the Scotchwoman lecturing on free inquiry, Angelina Grimké, the refined South Carolinian speaking out against slavery, and Abby Kelley, the New England schoolteacher turned Abolitionist, were persuasive personalities a century ago. Even more influential in a slightly later period were those earnest and skillful platform speakers, all trained at Oberlin College, Lucy Stone, the advocate of women's rights, Antoinette Brown and Sallie Holley, crusaders in the antislavery cause.

The law, too, contributed distinguished speakers during these years. Rufus Choate was a foremost jury orator; Jeremiah H. Black was a defender of civil rights before the Supreme Court; and William M. Evarts was government counsel in privateering cases and other litigation following the Civil War.

Choate is known also for his Eulogy of Webster at Dartmouth College (1853). The speeches of Black and Evarts are not literary masterpieces, but as speakers both men were effective legal thinkers dealing with complex issues and adapting them by artful use of invention in the best Aristotelian tradition to the audience at hand, whether it was composed of trained jurists or common-sense citizens.

Viewed in the mosaic of history, political and literary, American oratory of the period 1815–1865 deeply influenced our national destiny. We now know that many of the mighty movements that have affected the common man began in obscure places. Likewise many of the speakers in this distinctly oratorical age began as obscure persons. They became known and gained leadership by the greatness and intensity of the issues they discussed and by their mastery of the rhetorical art. But behind those we have briefly considered were thousands, now forgotten, who within their own small spheres commanded respect, created loyalties, and moved men to action.

Oratory was a political instrument. In fact, the national consciousness was created and established, policies for the development of the West were formulated, the rise of the common man was effected, the slave power was consolidated and then broken, all through the democratic processes of public address—ceremonial, controversial, deliberative. As we glance back we realize that the effect of even inspired speaking is often transient. The speech is heard and forgotten. But Americans of the years before the Civil War heard, mulled over, read aloud, and committed to memory their favorite orators. "It was the noble passages from Webster learned in school by Northern boys that prepared them to respond, with arms in their hands, when Lincoln called them to support the National Government and to save the Union."

9

The Radical leaders in the Republican Party were the victors in the Civil War. For twenty years after 1865 the Republicans controlled the life of the nation so absolutely that they had little need of orators to defend their rule. All that was required of a political speaker was ability to wave the Bloody Shirt at the climactic moment. For political rallies and anniversary dinners the speakers most sought after were Civil War generals, whose mere presence was sufficient to revive memories of Gettysburg and Atlanta and bring audiences to their feet singing "Marching Through Georgia." In consequence, the tradition of political oratory declined during these years to its lowest point. James G. Blaine is the only political leader whose ability as a speaker is remembered. A master in debate rather than an orator, his strategy of attack, surprise, and sarcasm often overreached itself.

As the Democrats slowly regained power, new issues, such as populism, free silver, imperialism, and the power of the trusts, replaced the problem of reconstruction, and a new generation of orators came forward to debate them. For thirty-seven years William Jennings Bryan carried the arguments of the Democrats to the American people with his rich and tireless voice. As one historian has noted, probably Samuel Adams alone excelled him in the power of manipulating the masses; and Adams never spoke as Bryan did to audiences of fifteen thousand, making sometimes as many as thirty appearances in one day. Bryan's effectiveness as a speaker came from the biblical simplicity of his language and from his appeal to the emotions of his listeners, who saw in him a great champion of the West and the South against the money power of the East. He said little that was new and he did not deign to argue. He simply assumed the wisdom of the cause he was advocating and used all his oratorical powers to enlist the faith of his hearers.

Matched against Bryan for ten years after 1896 were two Republicans who became the leaders of the Progressive movement, Theodore Roosevelt and Albert J. Beveridge. Both were great "spellbinders," but as they matured in public address they adopted a more blunt and conversational style without losing any of the vigor for which they were noted. The listener's initial astonishment at T. R.'s squeaky voice, which often broke in moments of great excitement, was soon forgotten in admiration of his sharp, driving style and the energy with which he attacked the "interests" and defended his ideal of a militant imperialistic America.

If, with few exceptions, great political orators were lacking between Lincoln and Wilson, there were many able men who spoke eloquently for particular causes, and certain of their speeches created historical moments in the life of the nation. The Atlanta Exposition Speech (1895) of Booker T. Washington won him wide support among whites, North and South, who approved his proposal that the Negro should "put brains and skill into the common occupations of life." This policy, ably set forth in the Atlanta speech, aroused at the same time the opposition of the militant Negroes and defined an issue which still divides the race. The Atlanta editor Henry W. Grady achieved a national reputation with his adroit speech on The New South delivered before the New England Society of New York in December, 1886. There are few occasions in the history of American oratory to match this one when a suspicious audience, made up of men who wielded great financial and political power, was won over completely to the speaker's side. Grady proved not only that the loyalty of the New South to the Union could be trusted but—what may have been more important to J. P. Morgan, Russell Sage, and other capitalists at the table—that its business capacity warranted the investment of Northern capital in the reconstructed South.

During these years Samuel Gompers, organizer of the American Federation of Labor, ruled and advanced the power of the organization in large part by speeches which played upon the discontent and frustration of labor. Revolt within the Federation he controlled by blunt speaking and invective. Workingmen still hear of his momentous speech at the Convention of 1903 when he headed off a strong Socialist offensive organized to seize control of the American Federation of Labor.

Of all the pleaders for special causes in this era, none had so large a popular following as Robert G. Ingersoll—to millions of the pious a notorious infidel, to other millions the preacher of a new gospel which had released them from superstition and bigotry. Ingersoll was an effective trial lawyer, and as a political orator he helped to elect three Republican Presidents; but he will be remembered as the great agnostic, impressing his vast audiences as terribly in earnest, a humane, big-hearted man who sought to rescue the reputation of the Deity from "the aspersions of the pulpit." Redpath, the lecture-manager, declared that he was the "best card" in America, and that his last house in San Francisco had "more money in it than any lecture ever yielded since lecturing began."

Though there were some giants in the years between 1865 and 1912 to carry on the oratorical tradition of Clay, Calhoun, Webster, and Lincoln, admiration for the art of oratory declined year by year. Professors of Rhetoric and Oratory in the colleges were looked upon as little better than teachers of elocution, which, indeed, most of them were. Their once proud profession was despised by their academic colleagues. The college debating societies, which had trained many of the great orators, and in whose activities students had found more intellectual stimulus than in their regular classes, fell to low esteem among extracurricular campus organizations. Yet it was a new national leader, nurtured in this matrix of the American orator who restored confidence in the art. From his boyhood Woodrow Wilson aspired to lead men by his eloquence. His father, who read the orators with him, trained him in precise speaking. At Princeton, Johns Hopkins, and Wesleyan he led in organizing student debating and speaking. As a professor at Princeton he was voted the most popular lecturer, year after year; and he believed that no teacher, no matter how learned, can stimulate young men unless he is an orator. At the time Wilson became President he was already nationally known as a speaker. When the country faced the crisis of war, he was able to lift the nation to the level of his ideals, even as his masters, Burke, Bright, and Gladstone, had done in critical moments of British history. It is a fact to be remembered that if Wilson's eloquence had not so thoroughly convinced his countrymen that they were engaged in a great crusade to make the world safe for democracy, the disillusionment which followed the shattering of his ideal of a world government would not have been so profound and pervasive.

The invention of the radio brought to the orator a great access of power. It also tested his resources severely. Voices effective before ordinary audiences sometimes came over the air ruinously distorted. Gestures and facial expression did not come over at all. Some political speakers, like Governor Alfred Smith, acquired additional force when faced by the microphone. Few who heard him, in the 1928 campaign, attack the Republican misdeeds with his nightly "Let's look at the record" will forget how even his East Side New York accent helped him as a radio orator. The radio also created a new profession for the public speaker, that of news commentator. Each listener had his favorite, but the one most admired was Raymond Swing, who, night after night during the Second World War, brought comfort to millions here and in England. His grave and measured words were adequate to the issues and events which he analyzed for his anxious listeners.

But the master of all the radio orators was President Franklin D. Roosevelt. The radio technicians who set up the equipment for his speeches and fireside chats marveled at his imperturbability under all sorts of difficult conditions of delivery. To the millions who listened to him his humanity came through as well as his power. No nuance of humor or sarcasm or emotion was lost. When speaking from fireside to fireside he seemed to be near by, beside the listener. This sense of his having been, time and again, in one's home accounts in large measure for the personal loss which his fellow Americans felt when he died. It was well known that he had expert assistance in the preparation of his speeches, as do most men in public life; but the tone and the watchwords were always his. Quite as much as Wilson, he contributed memorable phrases to American life. The barbs of irony stayed in the hides of his opponents, as he intended they should, but he could also lift the nation with his eloquence. Most telling of all was the sense he conveyed that he was speaking to and for the whole nation, seeking to unite and fortify its strengths. In this respect he belongs with the orators of the golden age, with Clay and Webster and Lincoln who would recognize their hope for a united America in words which Roosevelt spoke during the presidential campaign of 1940:

We are a nation of many nationalities, many races, many religions—bound together by a single unity, the unity of freedom and equality. Whoever seeks to set one nationality against another, seeks to degrade all nationalities. Whoever seeks to set one race against another seeks to enslave all races. Whoever seeks to set one religion against another seeks to destroy all religion. I am fighting for a free America—for a country in which *all* men and women have equal rights to liberty and justice. I am fighting, as I always have fought, for the rights of the little man as well as the big man—for the weak as well as the strong, for those who are helpless as well as for those who can help themselves.

34. LITERATURE AND CONFLICT

T HUS historical writing and oratory rose to perhaps their greatest literary heights in those troublous mid-century years when national feeling was both intensified and strained by civil war. But on literature less immediately connected with domestic issues, the effect was not so clear-cut. Many writers like Emerson and Hawthorne lost power or died; others like Lowell and Whittier turned their energies and their arts at least temporarily to the service of the cause of the day.

When President Lincoln greeted Harriet Beecher Stowe with the words, "So you're the little woman who made the book that made this great war," he was speaking as a political realist who had learned by experience to respect the power of the pen. It was not for him to refer slightingly to "mere literature." Without *Uncle Tom's Cabin,* in the opinion of Sumner, there would have been no Lincoln in the White House.

But the historian must avoid hyperbole. In spite of the enormous vogue of Mrs. Stowe's novel, it is doubtful if a book had much power to change the course of events. More persuasive than her tender pleadings was the harsh propaganda carried on by Abolitionists for over thirty years. And mightiest of all was the trend of liberal opinion through the nineteenth century, which was bound to sweep out of existence even the most beneficent and patriarchal of feudal survivals. In the last analysis slavery was abolished because men could no longer endure the thought of it. Shrewd common people were the first to sense how the tide was running.

2

"A small, shallow, and enthusiastic party preaching the abolition of slavery upon the principles of extreme democracy"—so John Quincy Adams in 1835 appraised the Abolitionists. He was not one of them. At that date few people of social standing were numbered in their ranks. The protest against the wrong of slavery was not initiated by men of wealth, or politicians, or the clergy, who were the customary molders of opinion. It was begun by humble men who, though living by the work of their hands, did not let their minds lie fallow. A journeyman printer and newspaper editor, a shoemaker poet, and a Yankee peddler were promoters or convinced adherents of the first anti-slavery societies. Their names were William Lloyd Garrison, John Greenleaf Whittier, and Bronson Alcott. Intellectual aristocrats came later.

The early Abolitionists were plain people who took their Christian and democratic convictions seriously. They believed in the power of moral suasion, and hoped to sway the policy of the nation by appeals to reason and right principles. The small cost of establishing a four-page weekly newspaper made it easy for them to place their ideas before the public. As early as 1821 an Abolitionist journal, the *Genius of Universal Emancipation,* was started by the Quaker reformer Benjamin Lundy, and thereafter was issued at irregular intervals whenever the peripatetic editor could avail himself of a printing press. Ten years later Garrison, who had been jailed in Baltimore while working as Lundy's partner, founded in Boston the most intransigent of antislavery organs, the *Liberator,* which sounded an uncompromising demand for the immediate freeing of the oppressed. After the formation of the American Anti-Slavery Society in 1833 at least a score of journals of opinion dedicated to the cause of emancipation sprang up throughout the Northern states.

The proslavery element, which insisted on a strict construction of the Constitution where its own interests were concerned, had no scruples about denying to its opponents the constitutional guarantees of free speech and a free press, the right of assembly and the right of petition. Abolitionist agents and speakers were mobbed on numerous occasions, and meetings broken up by violence. But the attempt to muzzle opinion brought important recruits to the antislavery cause. John Quincy Adams waged a bitter struggle in the House of Representatives to prevent the petitions of his constituents from being laid on the table without a hearing. When Elijah P. Lovejoy, the editor of the Abolitionist *Observer* of Alton, Illinois, was killed while defending his printing plant, it became dramatically evident that slavery and the free discussion of slavery could not exist side by side. The indignation meeting in Boston inspired by Lovejoy's death brought out the most effective of antislavery orators in the person of Wendell Phillips. Prominent clergymen, scholars, men of letters, lawyers, and statesmen were gradually drawn into the movement.

Only when such recruits as Theodore Parker and William Ellery Channing, Edmund Quincy, Lowell, Emerson, Longfellow, and Charles Sumner were secured from the educated classes did the Abolitionist propaganda overflow to any considerable extent into literature. Even then its staple remained direct and practical, taking the form of manifestoes, resolutions, petitions to legislative bodies, newspaper paragraphs, circular letters, tracts, lectures, speeches, sermons, and political songs. Its tone may be represented by some lines written by Garrison to be sung to the tune of "Auld Lang Syne":

> I am an Abolitionist!
>   The tyrant's hate and dread—
> The friend of all who are oppressed—
>   A price is on my head!
> My country is the wide, wide world—
>   My countrymen mankind:
> Down to the dust be Slavery hurled:
>   All servile chains unbind!

The first men and women of letters who became interested in the cause of the slave were at once deflected from their literary careers. The hope of reforming the world, leading to emotional identification with the downtrodden, proved to be then what Robert Frost has since called it, "poetry's great anti-lure."

Mrs. Lydia Maria Child may be cited as a typical example of what was happening to many minor writers. Born in 1802 into a family of Boston intellectuals, a sister of the transcendental Convers Francis, this lady when hardly out of her teens was producing successful historical fiction by the simple device of confronting herself with a quire of blank paper. She also made a promising start with a magazine for children. But marriage to the Reverend David Lee Child, a serious thinker, turned her mind to social problems. In 1833 she shattered convention by issuing a forthright *Appeal in Favor of That Class of Americans Called Africans,* in which emotional fervor and common sense, sound economics and fanciful anthropology, were equally harnessed to the cause of emancipation. Thereafter Mrs. Child was marked as a dangerous woman. As Thomas Wentworth Higginson recalled, "She seemed to be always talking radicalism in a greenhouse." Though she was fertile in devising all sorts of antislavery propaganda, she lent herself freely to other causes, such as the movement to abolish capital punishment, in her popular *Letters from New York* (1843, 1845). Only toward the close of her career did she succeed in fusing philanthropy and literature in the belated Abolition novel entitled *A Romance of the Republic,* which did not get into print until 1867.

But poets and novelists were, on the whole, slow to turn their attention to slavery. In the North it was long considered bad form, and also unprofitable, to expose the skeleton in Freedom's closet. The Negro might be sketched as a comic figure, as by Fenimore Cooper in *The Spy,* or a certain romantic pathos might be extracted from the picture of the untamed savage doomed to a bondage which he is too noble to endure, as in Bryant's early poem, "The African Chief." But even stanch opponents of the extension of slavery like Bryant kept their controversial sentiments out of their poetry. Edmund

Quincy, an editor of the *Liberator*, though he composed a small group of polished tales dealing with servile insurrections and the devotion of slaves to their masters, yet preferred to amuse his fancy with the elegances of bygone days in his chief novel *Wensley*, which preserves as if under glass a picture of colonial society.

Soon after 1840 several prominent New England poets followed Whittier's lead in the production of antislavery poems. Longfellow on a stormy return voyage from Europe conjured up seven of the eight lyrics contained in his tiny paper-covered pamphlet, *Poems on Slavery* (1842). Eight years later his fears for the safety of the Union inspired his much quoted apostrophe, "Thou, too, sail on, O Ship of State." His relation to the abolition movement was never more than that of a sympathetic bystander. Emerson likewise remained somewhat apart, saving his strength for the freeing of souls from a more universal bondage than that suffered by the Negro.

Lowell, though serious workers for the cause considered his tone regrettably playful, took a more than passing interest in the subject of slavery. Over fifty editorials from his pen appeared in Abolition journals at the time when the annexation of Texas was being debated, and in the first series of *The Biglow Papers*, begun in the Boston *Courier*, June 17, 1846, he voiced with homely effectiveness the protest of New England idealists against a war in the interest of the slaveholder. The resolute expression of Lowell's democratic and pacifistic principles in the mouth of the rustic Hosea Biglow was partly obscured by the swathings of prose commentary written in the character of Parson Wilbur. But enough wit penetrated the prolixity to make the satire count. Nothing that Lowell wrote with more serious intent on questions of the day, and nothing in the revived *Biglow Papers* which dealt with the Civil War, equaled the first impromptu outbursts of his indignation.

Hosea Biglows in the flesh were not wanting. In vigorous protest against the government's official policy of appeasing the South by permitting the expansion of slavery into the lands newly wrested from Mexico, Bronson Alcott declined to pay his taxes and was briefly lodged in Concord jail. A little later Henry Thoreau followed his example. The latter's "Civil Disobedience," written as a result of this experience and delivered as a lecture in 1847, has become the classic defense of the individual's integrity against the moral degradation of the state. The hard intellectual intransigence of Thoreau in this essay and in his "Plea for Captain John Brown" is in sharp contrast to the sentimental humanitarianism of much Abolitionist literature.

Until after the spectacular success of *Uncle Tom's Cabin*, antislavery novels hardly existed. The only one of possibly half a dozen examples that calls for mention is *The Slave: or Memoirs of Archy Moore* (1836) by the Federalist historian Richard Hildreth, which recounts representative vicissitudes in the life of a light mulatto, at once son and slave of an aristocratic Virginia colonel. All the stock cruelties are visited on Archy, and in particular the sexual abuses incident to slavery are handled with considerable freedom. But the first-person narrator of the story is all too clearly a New England intellectual.

A flood of fiction attacking or defending slavery was released by Mrs. Stowe. Most of the Abolition novels made the mistake of selecting an exceptional situation, as of a white child kidnaped into slavery, or of presenting an impossibly idealized hero or heroine. The "anti-Tom" novels, which originated less often in the South than in Philadelphia, were hardly more impressive. The blandest of the many counterblasts was Mrs. Mary H. Eastman's *Aunt Phillis's Cabin* (1852), a book rightly described as insipid.

In the South slavery remained a debatable issue until about 1830 at the latest. Opinion then crystallized, and the allegiance of the region to its "peculiar institution" remained unshaken. The social philosophy of the plantation owners, first formulated by such men as Thomas R. Dew and William Harper, was given persuasive political application by John C. Calhoun and glorified with golden oratory by William L. Yancey. By 1854 George Fitzhugh, the author of *Sociology for the South,* could confidently predict, "Slavery will everywhere be abolished or everywhere be reinstated"—and the first of these alternatives was evidently unthinkable. Firmly assured that their social system would be envied and imitated the world over, Southern leaders paid no heed to protests in the name of the poorer farmers and landless whites such as Hinton R. Helper's *The Impending Crisis of the South* (1857). The wide circulation given this work by Northern reformers only added to the fury directed against the Abolitionists.

But it is important to note that the antislavery crusade was almost as much resented in the North as in the South. Many Northern leaders were perfectly content with the compromise embodied in the Constitution. Slavery was not more ardently defended by the Charleston intellectuals Hugh Swinton Legaré and William Gilmore Simms than it was by Washington Irving's friend, James K. Paulding of New York. Even in Boston the circle of George Ticknor viewed with extreme disfavor the promoters of social agitation on this subject. Francis Parkman could write in 1850:

> For my part, I would see every slave knocked on the head before I would see the Union go to pieces, and would include in the sacrifice as many abolitionists as could be conveniently brought together.

This latter sentiment was cordially endorsed by William J. Grayson of South Carolina in his sizzling verse-satire *The Hireling and the Slave* (1854) and by John Beauchamp Jones, a Southern journalist, in *Wild Southern Scenes*

(1859), a fantastic picture of an imagined civil war fought over the issue of slavery. Even after the outbreak of hostilities a Boston antiquary and temperance reformer, Lucius M. Sargent, a "late George Apley" of his day, could write in *The Ballad of the Abolition Blunder-buss* (1861) a scathing Hudibrastic satire in the best doughface tradition. It was not the comfortable classes, North or South, who took pity on the slave.

3

"An afflatus of war was breathed upon us," wrote the young Confederate private Sidney Lanier in *Tiger-Lilies* (1867), a first novel largely composed while the writer was in camp:

> To obscurity it held out eminence; to poverty, wealth; to greed, a gorged maw; to speculation, legalized gambling; to patriotism, a country; to statesmanship, a government; to virtue, purity; and to love, what all love most desires—a field wherein to assert itself by action.

In the North, Robert Gould Shaw's sister, at seventeen, felt the same ebullience, even after the Union forces had recoiled from Bull Run:

> These are extraordinary times and splendid to live in. . . . This war will purify the country of some of its extravagance and selfishness, even if we are stopped midway. . . . We, as a Nation, are learning splendid lessons of heroism and fortitude through it that nothing else could teach.

At the outbreak of hostilities the emotional pressure on both sides demanded instant outlets. Pure chance rather than intrinsic merit settled upon the music-hall song of "Dixie" and the camp-meeting chorus of "John Brown's Body" as the vehicles of opposing sentiment. Hardly less fortuitous was the later choice of Julia Ward Howe's "Battle-Hymn of the Republic" and James Ryder Randall's "Maryland, My Maryland" as the supreme expressions of the North's crusading zeal and the South's defiance. Each of these poems was destined to become the one piece by its author that posterity has cared to recall. Entirely forgotten are such fervently patriotic songs as William Ross Wallace's "The Sword of Bunker Hill" and "Keep Step with the Music of the Union," which as marching songs attained a wide popularity in 1861. These and many other ephemeral outpourings hurling heated epithets filled the pages of the early anthologies of war poems, Union and Confederate alike. Not until the publication of Francis F. Browne's *Bugle-Echoes* (1882), the prototype of later collections of Civil War poetry, were the memorable occasional poems of the war separated from the chaff and arranged in relation to the episodes that inspired them.

The established poets of the North responded variously to the emotional impact of the war. Bryant was startled out of his calm to write two stirring lyrics in "Not Yet" and "Our Country's Call." Thereafter he contented himself with a single poem on "The Death of Slavery." Emerson likewise celebrated the emancipation of the slaves in his "Boston Hymn." Longfellow's single utterance, on the loss of the sloop-of-war *Cumberland,* ranks with the finest of patriotic elegies. Holmes, who had previously written little on public questions, scattered his fire, and neither his marching songs for Armageddon nor his furious invectives against traitors and stay-at-home rangers attained distinction. Lowell, besides his rather labored revival of *The Biglow Papers,* expressed the dark forebodings of the early war days in "The Washers of the Shroud."

On the Confederate side the coming of war and the invasion of the Southern states by Federal troops had a profound effect on Henry Timrod, the leading poet among the younger writers of Charleston. At its best his early verse was scholarly and overdelicate, at its worst derivative and formal. But the war made him the spokesman of a nation struggling to be born. Though he opposed secession, Timrod was fervidly loyal to South Carolina. His "A Cry to Arms" paralleled Bryant's "Our Country's Call" as a tocsin of patriotic feeling. His "Ode" sung at Magnolia Cemetery holds the same relation to the Confederate dead as Lowell's "Commemoration Ode" to the fallen soldiers of the North. The contrast between its twenty chiseled lines and the orotund amplitude of Lowell is impressive.

> In seeds of laurel in the earth
>   The blossom of your fame is blown,
> And somewhere, waiting for its birth,
>   The shaft is in the stone!

Fewer than a dozen poems contain Timrod's poetic response to the war, but they remain a monument to the Southern ideal of classic grace united with deep emotional fervor.

Paul Hamilton Hayne of Charleston, whose memory is kept fragrant by his chivalrous devotion to his section, was a poet of lesser stature and was seldom at his best when writing of the war. Though he duly celebrated the sacrificial zeal of the Southern arms, his gentle nature inclined him to pursue a beauty detached from the hard realities which he uncomplainingly endured. After the war he was able to prepare the way for the reconciliation of the North and the South through his cordial relations with Whittier, Taylor, and other literary men. More notable than any collection of his own verse was his edition of the poems of Timrod.

As the war dragged to its close the sufferings of Southern womanhood were epitomized in *Beechenbrook* (1865), a popular narrative poem richly freighted with sentiment by Margaret Junkin Preston, the Pennsylvania-born sister-in-law of "Stonewall" Jackson. A proud allegiance to the lost cause throbbed in "The Conquered Banner" by Father Abram Joseph Ryan and "The Land Where We Were Dreaming" by Daniel Bedinger Lucas, to mention only two of the many dirges for the Confederacy. Long before the end the soldier songs lost all traces of vivacity. The plaintive melody of "Tenting on the Old Camp Ground" expressed the most pervasive emotion of both camps, weariness of the protracted struggle and an overmastering desire to go home.

The factual record of the Civil War in diaries and narratives of personal experience was extremely voluminous, but seldom reached a literary level or even the level of expert reporting to which the two world wars of the twentieth century have accustomed us. The Confederacy produced a minor Pepys in John Beauchamp Jones, who deliberately prepared for posterity the account of life in Richmond, published as *A Rebel War Clerk's Diary* (1866). Gamaliel Bradford has not unaptly likened the commonplace and average temper of the war clerk's mind to the conventional choral figure of Greek tragedy. Money troubles and an increasing dissatisfaction with political leaders form the burden of his testy plaint: "Never before did such little men rule such a great people."

Theodore Winthrop, the writer of several novels, should have pictured the war from the Union ranks, but his brilliant sketches were soon terminated by his untimely death in battle. Walt Whitman's graphic but inconsecutive impressions convey the feeling of war-torn Washington. Perhaps the palm for literary reporting should go to Thomas Wentworth Higginson for his *Army Life in a Black Regiment* (1870), though almost as readable is the realistic *Camps and Prisons* (1865) by Augustine J. H. Duganne, a writing colonel who elsewhere undertook to memorialize each important clash of the armed forces in indifferent rime. Henry Howard Brownell gained eminence as a "Battle-Laureate" for his accounts of the naval actions at New Orleans and at Mobile Bay written under the immediate impulse of the occasion in facile but stirring verse. Of some thirty poems dealing with the war his best are "Bury Them," a tribute to Robert Gould Shaw, and "Abraham Lincoln," which pictures the long file of the nation's dead passing in review before the martyred President while the review of the Grand Army sweeps through the capital. Brownell owes his place in American literature entirely to his poems inspired by the struggle.

Previous to the war the prevailing tone of polite fiction had been tearful and sentimental, while a vigorous school of backwoods humorists created realistic sketches of illiterate rascals of the Simon Suggs and Sut Lovingood type. The humorists of the war years, however, specialized less in character than in opinion. Like Lowell in *The Biglow Papers* they wrote what were in effect editorials from behind the mask of a comic personality. David Ross Locke ("Petroleum V. Nasby"), Robert H. Newell ("Orpheus C. Kerr"), and Charles G. Halpine ("Miles O'Reilly") for the North, and on the other side Charles H. Smith ("Bill Arp") did much by their witty comment on current happenings to sustain the morale of men whose nerves were worn ragged by the stresses of the hour.

Meanwhile fiction discarded the trappings of sentiment and tended to become more realistic. Though the war novels of John Esten Cooke were still of the romantic cloak-and-sword type, he made an effort to introduce actual characters and incidents and to report verbatim the words spoken by Jackson, Jeb Stuart, Ashby, and other Southern immortals. Still more authentic was the picture of the sufferings of Union sympathizers under the Confederate regime as presented by William Mumford Baker, the manuscript of whose *Inside: A Chronicle of Secession* (1866) had several times to be buried to keep it from falling into the wrong hands. A much more powerful treatment of the Southern Unionist was written by the Alabama politician Jeremiah Clemens in *Tobias Wilson* (1865), a novel which deserves to be rescued from the oblivion that has befallen it.

But the best of the Civil War novels and one of the most notable achievements in American fiction is John William De Forest's *Miss Ravenel's Conversion from Secession to Loyalty* (1867), a book that for lifelike portrayal of scenes of action, firm grasp of character values, and penetrating interpretation of the issues of the time can hardly be too highly praised. Considering the fact that the novelist was a Union officer, he maintained a remarkable objectivity in his picture of high purposes mingled with inefficiency and corruption at the North and of chivalry badly flawed by moral laxity at the South. De Forest was a pioneer realist too honest for his own good in an age that expected conventional falsifications in works of imagination. In particular his habit of treating his women characters as responsible human beings who must make their own decisions and abide by the consequences was not popular. In *Kate Beaumont* (1872) and *The Bloody Chasm* (1881) he again drew unsparing pictures of Southern scenes and characters, while in *Honest John Vane* (1875) and *Playing the Mischief* (1875) he exposed the vicious deterioration of political life in Washington.

Reflective interpretation of the meaning of the war was carried to an ultimate contemporary extent in Walt Whitman's *Drum-Taps* (1865) and Herman Melville's *Battle Pieces* (1866). The brief prose supplement appended to the last-named has been likened to Lincoln's "Second Inaugural" because of its noble perception that "the glory of the war falls short of its pathos—a pathos which now at last ought to disarm all animosity." Melville states that his poems "originated in an impulse imparted by the fall of Richmond," and that they record the variable moods induced by memories of the conflict much as a harp placed in a window might respond to wayward airs. But beneath the temporary heightening of emotion and the sense of dedication to a great cause which *Battle Pieces* shares with much other war poetry there may be detected an undernote of apprehension, even in the moment of victory. Musing on his country's ills, "On the world's fairest hope linked with man's foulest crime," Melville cannot convince himself that a spiritual regeneration will necessarily follow the resort to the sword. It may be that the war will bring only a release of "power unanointed," a triumph of sheer Mammonism before which "the Founders' dream shall flee" and "the Dark Ages of Democracy" be ushered in. Oppressed by thoughts like these, Melville like another Prospero cannot still his beating mind.

No such prescient fears afflicted Whitman. Though he knew more immediately than many of his contemporaries the terrible cost of the war in human suffering, he was possessed by visions of apocalyptic grandeur, seeing

How DEMOCRACY with desperate vengeful port strides on, shown through the
    dark by those flashes of lightning!

"I have lived to behold man burst forth, and warlike America rise," he jubilates. "Never was average man, his soul, more energetic, more like a God." For America, the mistress, he was ready to chant a greater supremacy, confident that "affection shall solve the problems of Freedom yet." Even while exulting in these affirmations of upsurging power, Whitman could still pause to caress the grief of stricken families in "Come up from the fields, father," and to write for the dead Lincoln the tenderest tribute that any statesman has ever inspired.

Melville's brooding concern and Whitman's passionate love of country were fused, though somewhat diluted, in the exalted sentiment of Lowell's "Commemoration Ode," admittedly the finest example of official poetry in the literature of the United States and the inevitable epilogue for a discussion of the writing inspired by the great conflict:

> O Beautiful! my Country! ours once more!
>   .   .   .   .
>
>   What were our lives without thee?
>   What all our lives to save thee?
>   We reck not what we gave thee;
>   We will not dare to doubt thee,
>   But ask whatever else, and we will dare!

4

After Appomattox the development of realistic fiction was carried on chiefly by writers associated with the North and West, like William Dean Howells, and by the few Southerners who along with George W. Cable found a congenial refuge in the North. The prevailing mood of Southern fiction for a full generation was nostalgic and sentimental, a turning back to what had been. The vogue of local color and dialect stories only slightly modified, as in Joel Chandler Harris' Uncle Remus tales, the fond recollections of ante-bellum days on the old plantation.

Fiction dealing with the problems of Reconstruction was written chiefly by De Forest and by Albion W. Tourgée, both Northerners with first-hand experience of life in the South. Women realists such as Rose Terry Cooke and Rebecca Harding Davis also drew upon the war and its aftermath for subjects. The latter, though straining too hard to impress her message, barely missed creating a great novel in *Waiting for the Verdict* (1868), which pictures the helpless predicament of the Negro when the North, after emancipating the slaves, turned its back on the social problem it had brought into being. A bitter arraignment of the collapse of Southern integrity under the shock of defeat and poverty was composed by John S. Wise, the son of a former governor of Virginia, in *The Lion's Skin,* but this book was not published until 1905.

The most persistent efforts to embody in fictional form a review of the breakdown of the slaveholders' empire and the chaos that followed were made by Tourgée, a Union officer born in Ohio who returned to the South after the war. As a political judge in North Carolina he soon earned the hostility of his fellow citizens, a sentiment which he cordially reciprocated. His novels, consequently, are colored by violent partisanship, especially in their opposition to Ku Klux activities in the reconstructed states. At no time did Tourgée reveal any comprehension of the complex psychological strains that Southerners were forced to undergo.

In the order of the events they dramatize, Tourgée's polemical novels begin with *Hot Ploughshares* (1883), which deals largely with the efforts of a conscientious slave owner to emancipate his Negroes in defiance of sectional prejudice. *Figs and Thistles* (1879), a fictional treatment of the career of James A. Garfield, is set in Ohio during and after the war and pictures the relations of a rising politician to the manipulators of finance and industry who are his backers. *'Toinette* (1874), rechristened *A Royal Gentleman* (1881), is a sentimental exploitation of the dilemma of a nearly white Negro woman who cannot marry her lover, a patrician Southron, because of his ingrained horror at any pretense of equality between the races. *A Fool's Errand* (1879) and

Bricks Without Straw (1880) analyze the political and social problems of Reconstruction, particularly the plight of the Negro who has been left without adequate provision for his free development. The novelette *John Eax* (1882) develops a story of Southern family pride in conflict with the hero's vigorous individualism. Tourgée's plots have elements of the sensational, and his books are overweighted with didactic passages, but the backgrounds are drawn with an instinctive faithfulness to actuality that gives these novels some importance as social documents.

Tourgée was by no means unique in desiring to impress a partial interpretation on the events of history. Ex-Confederates felt an even stronger compulsion to make palatable by dialectic the bitter blow to its pride that the South had experienced. The long process of glorifying the lost cause and explaining away its defeat, a process which still continues, was begun by the brilliant Alexander H. Stephens, the former Vice President of the Confederacy, in his *Constitutional View of the Late War Between the States* (1868–1870).

The Southern man of letters who most gallantly faced the facts of Reconstruction and tried to find a remedy for the economic ruin of the South was Sidney Lanier. This young poet, who had proclaimed himself "a full-blooded secessionist" at the beginning of hostilities, recorded in half a dozen poems written in 1867–1868 his agonized awareness of the complete prostration of his section: "We lie in chains, too weak to be afraid." In urging a greater diversification of crops in "Corn" and other poems Lanier may seem to have adopted a grotesque expedient; but when men harnessed themselves to the plow for want of draft animals it was not altogether inappropriate that the muse should be similarly employed.

What has often been called an American renaissance took place at the time when the Abolition movement was gathering strength; but it is doubtful if the increased tensions due to public agitation had any demonstrable effect on the concurrent production of literature. In general, national convulsions are not favorable to the arts. The strong emotions they arouse are exhausting rather than stimulating. So much fuel is used up for heat that little remains for light. The antislavery crusade may be held directly responsible for *Uncle Tom's Cabin,* which in its stage version has become a part of America's folklore. Out of the Civil War came some stirring lyrics, two or three fine volumes of poetry, and one first-rate piece of fiction. When one considers the sacrifice of blood and treasure, the surges of passion, the heroism, and the broken lives, the disproportion between the great conflict and its immediate results in literature seems to indicate that the war tended to stifle the creative expression, at least of relatively minor writers.

How participation in controversy may channel a vigorous writer's energy in a single direction, and so limit the full rounding of his nature, may be shown by an examination of the careers of Whittier and Mrs. Stowe. The Civil War and the agitation that preceded it have often been pictured as a conflict between Union and Secession, between North and South, between slave and free. The literature of the struggle, however, reveals most emphatically an ideological difference between plain and privileged people. The Abolitionists in all sections of the country were revolting against aristocratic and conservative leadership. It was not inappropriate that the movement should find its major literary spokesmen in a homespun poet and a daughter of Puritan levelers, both of them gifted with uncommon powers of expression.

5

In the course of his eighty-five years John Greenleaf Whittier, though deprived of most advantages that foster a writer's labors, managed to produce well over forty books of prose and verse, in addition to a large quantity of journalistic writing which remains uncollected. He came of New England farmer stock, was largely self-educated, and after his early thirties could seldom count on two successive weeks of good health. Yet within a long lifetime he ran through several literary careers, turned out an amount of work that would have done credit to a robust man, and maintained a level of good craftsmanship that commanded the respect of his peers.

Between 1826 and 1832 Whittier was primarily an editor of country newspapers and a writer of newspaper verse. Except for three early books, which he would have gladly disowned in later years, little of the product of this period has been preserved. From 1833 to 1860 he was engaged in the antislavery campaign as an active agent, an editor of reform journals, and a writer of polemics in prose and verse. His antislavery poems and his political prose constitute an important section of his collected works. Finally from about 1850 until his death in 1892 Whittier's chief interest was again centered in poetry. During this period he wrote the majority of the pieces for which he is best known.

Whittier's prose is subsidiary to his verse. His Abolitionist pamphlet *Justice and Expediency* (1833) is of biographical importance as announcing his decision to throw in his lot with the unpopular friends of the slave, but it does not stand out above the level of antislavery tracts as his polemical poems rise superior to most productions of the sort. *Margaret Smith's Journal* (1849) is a charming sketch of life in colonial New England as seen through the eyes of a descendant of Quakers. The remaining biographical, historical, and miscellaneous papers included in his works are of slight importance. His letters, which remain largely in manuscript, show that he possessed a gift of personal humor which rarely appeared in his public writing. But as an American poet Whittier is remembered for three kinds of poetry: his antislavery poems, his New England ballads and idyls, and his personal and religious lyrics.

The most vigorous and formative years of Whittier's life were so bound up with his activities as an antislavery agitator that the poet himself was inclined to rate his part in the great humanitarian crusade as his chief claim to distinction. He was prouder to have signed the Declaration of Sentiments adopted at the first convention of the American Anti-Slavery Society than to see his name on the title page of any book. In the modest "Proem," written in 1847 for a forthcoming collection of his poems and retained in all subsequent editions, he denied that his verse possessed any "rounded art" or "seer-like power," but emphasized his unqualified devotion to freedom and human brotherhood. "I am a *man*," he wrote to his first biographer in 1883, "and not a mere verse-maker."

But one may protest too much. Poets are not normally reluctant to accept whatever share of glory may fall to their lot. Whittier's repeated disclaimers of "a selfish pursuit of literary reputation" rouse the suspicion that he was constrained to seek compensation in the cause of Abolition for some secret disappointment.

It is remarkable that about one-third of Whittier's total poetic output, measured in terms of number of poems, was written before he was twenty-five and was published in newspapers. Some of these pieces were jocular or trivial, but most of them were serious exercises in exalted rhetoric, the work of a young man who considered literature as a realm of ideal values apart from and superior to the commonplace of daily existence. At this time Whittier was apparently dreaming that in some vague way he might attain through poetry the kind of sudden fame that had come to Burns and Byron. But verses in the poet's corner brought him neither renown nor a livelihood. There was clearly no future for him as a man of letters. Under the sting of this disappointment he renounced literature, writing with just a shade of bravado to his friend Jonathan Law: "I have knocked my Pegasus on the head, as a tanner does his bark-mill donkey, when he is past service, and the crows—alias, critics—may have the picking of his bones."

But if poetry was closed to Whittier there remained the vocation of newspaper editing, for which he had shown a considerable aptitude. He entered journalism as an awkward and ill educated youth from the country, but he had tact and modesty and the ability to learn quickly by experience. He proved to be a vigorous and able editor, and no doubt would have remained an editor had his health permitted. He was also a natural politician whose astuteness made him a useful though prickly ally of Caleb Cushing, the Whig, and Robert Rantoul, the Democrat, and later a discerning friend of Charles

Sumner. As an ardent supporter of Henry Clay and the American System he had learned how to gauge public feeling and how to make effective use of key phrases and striking incidents to enlist the popular imagination. This ability acquired in the tough school of Essex County politics Whittier brought to his work as a writer of rhymed propaganda for the Abolition cause.

His antislavery poems are not literary in the bookish sense, though they contain biblical echoes. They are packed full of explosive slogans: "Our fellow-countrymen in chains!" "No fetters in the Bay State!" The several poems are skillfully adapted to a variety of readers. "The Yankee Girl," for example, is purely the equivalent of a campaign poster, using the gaudiest colors and appealing to vulgar sentiment. On a higher level "Clerical Oppressors," written to castigate the clergy of Charleston, and "The Pastoral Letter," reproaching the Congregational ministers of Massachusetts for failing to bear witness to the evils of slavery, sound a note of Hebraic indignation. "A Sabbath Scene" makes a vigorously effective contrast between the Christian doctrine of brotherhood and the hunting down of fugitive slaves. The seizure of an alleged runaway in Boston was the occasion for an outburst of genuine local pride in the powerful "Massachusetts to Virginia." And when Webster betrayed the hopes of Northern idealists in his notorious "compromise" speech, Whittier's withering scorn in the incisive lines of "Ichabod" brought invective to the level of high art. Few of the antislavery poems are more than earnest propaganda, but in writing them Whittier learned to crystallize his meaning in clear and sharp-edged phrases. As an Abolitionist agitator he attained a power of expression that he could never have reached as an imitator of Mrs. Hemans and Mrs. Sigourney.

But his advance in power was not achieved without cost to his development in other directions. Thirty years of intense absorption in humanitarian reform left their mark on Whittier. He had little time for general reflection and his principles, once adopted, remained fixed. Beneath his temperamental tolerance and sympathy one can sense a trace of the stiffness that showed itself most baldly when he decided not to marry a Quaker woman whom he had been fond of for many years because of divergences in their religious views. His *Songs of Labor* are innocent of any such comprehension of the problems of the American workman as Orestes A. Brownson, for example, possessed. He had no such suspicion of material progress and invention as Thoreau. To the end he apparently remained unaware that the Industrial Revolution created situations which could not be solved in terms of a simple personal morality. It was in part an evidence of limitation that Whittier turned to the New England past and to religion as the favorite subjects of his late maturity.

More than most poets Whittier was identified with the region that produced him. When he was born in 1807, the second child and eldest son of a farmer in the township of Haverhill, Massachusetts, he had behind him four generations of Whittiers who had occupied the same spot. The family homestead, later pictured in *Snow-Bound,* had been built in 1688 by the Thomas Whittier who, some fifty years earlier, had left his native Wiltshire and had prospered and begotten ten children in the new land. The house had been passed down, in defiance of primogeniture, from youngest son to youngest son until it came to John Whittier, the poet's father, who worked the farm jointly with a bachelor brother. In his boyhood Greenleaf heard, from the elders of the household and from rare visitors, tales of adventure and hardship, of witchcraft and persecution, that made up the lore of the countryside. There was no trace of either clerical or mercantile leanings among Whittier's forebears. They were plain Yankee farmers rooted in the soil of Essex County.

In only one respect was the family not typical of New England yeomanry. For three generations the Whittiers had professed a sturdy adherence to Quaker principles. The fact that they belonged to a minor and once persecuted sect encouraged a certain critical detachment in the poet when he contemplated the New England past, and at the same time it encouraged a habit of "inwardness" which deepened his inherent tendency to mysticism.

Both incidents in Quaker history and traditions of colonial days in general furnished Whittier with material for local ballads and narrative poems. He did not attempt, as Hawthorne did, to inject symbolic meanings into historic episodes, but contented himself with reviving the atmosphere of a bygone time and portraying scenes and characters as vividly as possible. He seldom made alterations in the stories as he found them. His revisions were generally amplifications. He was no antiquarian and seldom took pains to verify his information. Consequently a highly successful piece of poetic craftsmanship like "Skipper Ireson's Ride" wrings from the professional historian the acid comment: "In 1808 occurred the regrettable incident of Skipper Benjamin (not Floyd) Ireson, for his crew's cowardice and lying (not for his hard heart), tarred and feathered and carried in a dory (not cart) by the fishermen (not the women) of Marblehead." But Whittier chose to tell the tale as he heard it from the lips of a schoolmate from Marblehead, partly because in its oral form it was already on the way to acquiring the quality of folklore.

Along with his historical and legendary narratives Whittier produced a number of country idyls, of which "The Barefoot Boy," "Maud Muller," and "Telling the Bees" are familiar examples. As early as 1847, in reviewing the poems of his Abolitionist friend William Henry Burleigh, he had deplored the lack of "Yankee pastorals" and had called attention to "the poetry of human life and simple nature, of the hearth and the farm field" as a type of writing that might well be attempted, not by the "amateur ruralist," but by one who was himself part and parcel of the country life of New England. He thus became a pioneer in exploring the ground which in our own time has been more expertly cultivated by Robert Frost.

He also celebrated in verse the sea beaches at the mouth of the Merrimack, the landscape of ridges and pleasant valleys around Haverhill, and the loftier mountains of the interior. But he was not well equipped to be a nature poet. Too color-blind to distinguish red from green, he was not by temperament a man who lived a full life of the senses; nor did he possess the Wordsworthian faculty of finding thoughts too deep for tears in a wayside flower. His impulse was to value external nature purely in terms of its human associations; as in "Monadnock from Wachuset,"

> We felt that man was more than his abode,—
> The inward life than Nature's raiment more.

Only rarely, as in the later poem "Sunset on the Bearcamp," did he even approximate a feeling of identity between the light of setting suns and the mind of man.

His interest in public affairs made it inevitable that he should comment in verse on various aspects of the Civil War. At its outbreak he regarded the resort to arms as a spiritual disaster. "The sad war drags along," he wrote in a letter of November, 1861. "I long to see some compensation for its horrors, in the deliverance of the Slaves. Without this, it is the wickedest war of the nineteenth century." Yet he was patriotically stirred by the legendary heroism of Barbara Frietchie, which he recounted in a highly successful ballad. The most heartfelt of his war poems, however, was the fervent "Laus Deo," which sang itself as he heard the bells ringing to celebrate the passage of the constitutional amendment abolishing slavery. His long campaign was finished, though not by the means he would have chosen.

The death in 1864 of his sister and companion Elizabeth, who in some measure shared his poetic gift, left Whittier solitary and by the same token turned his thoughts back to the close-knit family life of his boyhood. Out of his loyalty, not alone to vanished faces, but to the fulfillment of personal relationships which his boyhood home symbolized, he wrote *Snow-Bound* (1866), the finest of his Yankee idyls, a faultless integration of precisely remembered detail and tender devotion. In a general way this poem is the New England analogue of Burns' *The Cotter's Saturday Night,* with which it compares favorably both for its wealth of homely description and for its genuineness of sentiment. But against the background of a nation fast adapting itself to urban ways the poem appears something more than a cold pastoral. It is a quiet tribute to a form of civilized living that was passing. Here embodied in glowing terms was the Jeffersonian dream of the virtuous small landholder and his household, beholden to no one and winning an honest, laborious livelihood from the soil. Long before the Presidency of Grant this ideal pattern of a good life that might have been realized on an unpre-empted continent had been shattered; but it still continued to haunt the minds of country-born dwellers in the expanding cities whose simple upbringing had not prepared them for the complex problems of an industrial era. In Whittier's idyllic picture of an existence totally untroubled by the fevers of getting and spending, many Americans recognized with wistful regret an Eden from which they were forever debarred.

Significant also of a quality of mind that was rapidly becoming old-fash-ioned was the naïve directness of Whittier's poetic technique. With no obeisance to the method of suggestiveness illustrated by Whitman in "Out of the Cradle Endlessly Rocking," where a reminiscence of childhood is analyzed into its component sensuous images and then freely recomposed into a globed and harmonious work of art, Whittier developed *Snow-Bound* by a linear or melodic progression of one image after another. Very little is conveyed by hints or implications, but each mood and moment is defined with stark integrity. Behind this way of writing may be felt, not merely personal inno-cence, but a deep-seated racial conviction of the virtue of plain speaking, a conviction that for Whittier was reinforced by his Quaker breeding. As a man of undefeated spirit, he was not concerned to explore the devious hinter-land of consciousness that could only be expressed by innuendo, suggestion, or symbol. What he felt he could say.

Not all of Whittier's poems are limited to a New England setting. He took an interest in the struggle for freedom all over the world, in Italy, in Brazil. He found many subjects for ballads in Scandinavian or Oriental stories drawn from his wide reading. Hardly less intrinsic than *Snow-Bound* in its simplicity and genuineness is his account in *The Pennsylvania Pilgrim* (1872) of the pious German community established by Pastorius near William Penn's newly settled Quaker colony, with which it soon merged in religious affiliation. From this group of perfectionists came the first protest against slavery made by any religious body. Whittier himself considered *The Pennsylvania Pilgrim* "as good as (if not better than) any long poem" he had written, and surely no poem in the language has succeeded better in evoking a sense of the charm and sweetness of social intercourse that becomes possible when for a brief moment men have managed to reconstitute some semblance of a Golden Age.

The virtue of Whittier's poetry at its best lies in its firm texture of sincerity. He wrote about things that he knew intimately. His feelings were based on sentiments tested by the strains of life and driven down until they rested on bedrock conviction. His religious perceptions especially rested on a very real sense of divine immanence.

For these soundings, these often meditated inward truths, Whittier could find compact, simple, moving, and very nearly ultimate phrases. Much as he concerned himself with the outer world of politics and men's daily occupations, his deepest resources were of the spirit; in the poems which he called "subjective and reminiscent" and in his religious lyrics is his most distinguished writing. The autobiographical stanzas from "My Namesake" might be cited as a high point; but more fervent and more touching are the lines from "My Triumph," in which the poet foresees his own fulfillment in the eventual perfection of human society.

> The airs of heaven blow o'er me;
> A glory shines before me
> Of what mankind shall be,—
> Pure, generous, brave, and free.
>
> .   .   .   .   .   .
>
> I feel the earth move sunward,
> I join the great march onward,
> And take, by faith, while living,
> My freehold of thanksgiving.

With equal honesty Whittier recorded his occasional religious doubts and his more characteristic seasons of transcendent confidence. His vital experience of God's nearness inspired such devotional lyrics as "The Eternal Goodness," "Trinitas," "Our Master," "Questions of Life," "The Over-Heart," "The Meeting," and "My Psalm," to mention only some of the best loved. Though Whittier was specifically a Quaker and a Christian, his faith was as free as any man's can be from the trammels of formalism. He turned to God with a childlike passion of trustfulness that needed no support or creed. Among the finest hymns of the nineteenth century is that beginning "Dear Lord and Father of mankind," a selection of stanzas from "The Brewing of Soma." Stronger than the local attachments that led Whittier to join with Hawthorne and Longfellow in awakening a romantic interest in the New England past, and deeper than his humanitarian dedication to the relief of the oppressed among men, was his sense of "the silence of eternity interpreted by love" and the beauty of God's peace.

6

Unlike the homespun Whittier, Harriet Beecher Stowe was a product of the intellectual aristocracy of New England. Her father, the Reverend Lyman Beecher, a militant evangelist in the pulpit and a diligent promoter of multifarious good causes in his spare time, followed Jonathan Edwards as a stalwart upholder of Puritan orthodoxy. Six of his sons became clergymen, four of them nationally known. His eldest daughter, Catharine, after the untimely death of the professor of mathematics she should have married, devoted her life to the higher education of women. A younger daughter was an early advocate of women's rights. Any of the Beechers, if cast away on a cannibal island, would have been capable of organizing a church, a school, a temperance movement, and a ladies' aid society before help could arrive. They were all public characters.

Harriet, the second daughter of the family, was born while her father was pastor of the important church at Litchfield, Connecticut. She never outgrew the effects of her upbringing under the rigid restraints of Puritan discipline, which turned her nature inward upon itself and left her acutely imaginative and morbidly introspective. To such a nature the experience of religious conversion occurred with hardly a perceptible shock. She had absorbed Calvinistic doctrines from her earliest years, and all her days were full of upward strivings and self-abnegations. This program of austere improvement was only slightly mitigated by country outings, by some acquaintance with the novels of Scott, and by the liberal teachings of an uncle, Samuel Foote.

At sixteen Harriet went to Hartford to become a pupil and shortly a teacher in her sister Catharine's school for young ladies, while her father, translated to Boston, stirred the dry bones of Unitarianism by his rattling revival sermons at the Hanover Street Church. In 1832 he accepted a call to Cincinnati, Ohio, to establish Lane Seminary in order that ministers and home missionaries might be trained to cope with the alarming heathenism of the American frontier. With him went the whole "Beecher caravan," and once in possession of the ground they proceeded to act very much as though Cincinnati were the hypothetical cannibal isle. Catharine and Harriet attended to the school part. It was while she was living in virtual exile from her girlhood home that Harriet began writing for the religious press little tales of the New England life that she passionately loved and of the village people whom she had known. A collection of these stories, which were about equally compounded of conventional piety and sharp factual observation, was issued as *The Mayflower; or, Sketches of Scenes and Characters Among the Descendants of the Pilgrims* (1843).

Meanwhile Harriet had found a husband in the Reverend Calvin E. Stowe, her father's colleague at the seminary, a widower at once childlike and incredibly learned, a kind of theological cherub in a frock coat. The Stowes had six children. Mrs. Stowe as a busy mother and frontier housekeeper had little time for writing, but under the most adverse circumstances she was always able to produce a thin trickle of copy for the sake of adding a few dollars to the family income. She made a brief visit to Kentucky, in the course of which she saw something of slavery in its gentlest form. In Cincinnati she had become aware of the help afforded to runaway slaves by the "underground railroad," and without committing themselves to an unpopular position in public she and her husband had both become sympathetic to the antislavery agitation. Her brother Edward Beecher was an out-and-out Abolitionist, a friend and associate of the martyred Lovejoy.

In 1850 the Stowes' long exile ended when Professor Stowe was appointed to the faculty of Bowdoin College in Brunswick, Maine. Surrounded again by the decencies of New England village life, Harriet brooded in her apocalyptic way over the tales of violence and oppression that she had read in antislavery tracts and had in small part heard confirmed from the lips of fugitive Negroes. A letter from Mrs. Edward Beecher besought her to dedicate her fluent pen to the deliverance of the dusky Israelites. Filled with deep and vague emotions while attending a communion service, Mrs. Stowe unexpectedly saw unrolled before her as in a vision the scene of Uncle Tom's pathetic death and Christlike forgiveness of his persecutors. In that exalted moment the greatest of American propaganda novels was conceived.

Uncle Tom's Cabin (1852) was great in its social effects rather than in its artistic qualities. Its author's resources as a purveyor of Sunday-school fiction were not remarkable. She had at most a ready command of broadly conceived melodrama, humor, and pathos, and of these popular elements she compounded her book. In spite of the intensity of her feelings while writing, Mrs. Stowe showed admirable tact in refraining from attacks on the people of the South. All the villains of her story are Northern renegades. Her emphasis was clearly placed on the unavoidable evils of slavery, the separation of Negro families by sale and the brutality inseparable from the pursuit and recapture of fugitive blacks. Abolitionists at first considered her book too gentle, and Southerners saw no reason to resent it—until the extent of its effect on the public became evident. Nothing attributable to Mrs. Stowe or her handiwork can account for the novel's enormous vogue in the Northern states, in England, and throughout the world. When she went abroad, the reception accorded her was little short of hysterical. She had become a symbol.

In her second antislavery novel, *Dred: A Tale of the Great Dismal Swamp* (1856), she conscientiously attempted to construct a story complementary to her first, in that she now focused attention on the effects of slavery on the slaveholders. But she was betrayed by weaknesses which had somehow been overcome by the sheer fervor of her vision when she wrote *Uncle Tom's Cabin,* a fervor that could not be indefinitely sustained. Her plot is a tissue of unlikelihood. She was unable to fuse into any sort of unity the double story of the sensitive Nina Gordon and her lover in their efforts to prepare the way for eventual emancipation and of the defiant Negro insurrectionist Dred, who lurks in the swamps to provide a refuge for runaways. The novel alternates between scenes of fantastic melodrama and stretches of too-conscious homily.

Mrs. Stowe had now said all she had to say on the subject of slavery. Even before the outbreak of the war, which in Lincoln's eyes she had done much to provoke, she turned to other themes. After a second trip abroad marked by scarcely less acclaim than the first, she settled down in Andover, Massachusetts, and later in Hartford, to continue her career as a popular author. She did an immense amount of journalistic and pietistic hack writing, some of which found its way into published books. From the mass of indifferent and hasty scribbling her New England novels stand out.

In *The Minister's Wooing* (1859) she returned to the subject most suited to her capacities, the delineation of the mind and manners of New England village folk during the period when its clergymen, like Jonathan Edwards when he left his Northampton pulpit, were led to follow theological counsels of perfection without regard to the temper of the time or the vital needs of their people. The ensuing collapse of Calvinistic dogma may have inspired Holmes to write his mischievous parable of "The Deacon's Masterpiece, or the Wonderful One-Hoss Shay." But Mrs. Stowe knew better than anyone else how much earnest striving and high-minded self-discipline had been consecrated by descendants of the Puritans to the cause of spiritual perfection —and what the effort had cost in human terms. Particularly she understood what repressions women had undergone in the vise of uncompromising convictions, and what psychological adjustments they had been obliged to make in the struggle to survive and keep their sanity. *The Minister's Wooing* with its plot based on a succession of fine-spun renunciations is not a great novel, but it is a masterly revelation of the springs of Puritan character. The light it throws on the inner life of an intensely native New England poet like Emily Dickinson can never be too insistently brought to the attention of readers who have not cultivated a historical imagination.

A plot that suffers from idealistic manipulation is combined in *The Pearl of Orrs' Island* (1862) with Dickenslike portraits of well weathered characters on the Maine coast. Mrs. Stowe knew human nature instinctively and thoroughly, but she was constantly hampered in her presentation of the figures that she could create at will by her desire to make them illustrate the moral prepossessions that she had been brought up to regard as sacred.

This handicap was less in evidence when she undertook to embody in fiction her husband's recollections of his boyhood in the little Massachusetts town of Natick. The resultant leisurely exposition of New England ways in *Oldtown Folks* (1869) crowned her work as the interpreter of a peculiar people whose institutions and habits of thought had for nearly two centuries suffered little by abrasion from the rest of the world. The descriptive chapters in this novel and its varied gallery of village characters place Mrs. Stowe at the head of the school of New England realists. Her later transcriptions of local material in *Sam Lawson's Oldtown Fireside Stories* (1872) and *Poganuc People* (1878), the latter a re-creation of the Litchfield of her childhood, confirmed her control of background and character without in any way improving on the penetrating insights that she had already recorded.

In a certain sense Mrs. Stowe has been a victim of her own enormous success, since the world-wide celebrity of *Uncle Tom's Cabin* has tended to distract attention from the field where she was most at home. The merits of her New England novels should be rediscovered. It is doubtful, however, if Mrs. Stowe was capable of realizing the limitations of her talent. Her Italian novel, *Agnes of Sorrento* (1862), was simply an unqualified mistake. Her embroilment in a minor but acrimonious controversy over Lord Byron's marital troubles led to the ill considered publication of *Lady Byron Vindicated* (1870), a book which demonstrates both the author's conscientious officiousness and her indifference to worldly prudence. Though her society novels published in the seventies achieved a contemporary success, they are ephemeral in quality. A Freudian analysis of them, however, might cast a startling light on long repressed urges in Harriet Beecher Stowe.

Conflicts between the rigid standard of conduct in which the Beechers had been reared and the desires natural to opulent and creative personalities were not infrequent and sometimes led to amusing evasions of the code. Mrs. Stowe, for example, concurred in her father's view that the theater was the devil's instrument; but when a dramatic version of her own *Uncle Tom's Cabin* visited Boston in the winter of 1852 or 1853, she could not repress a wish to see it. Francis H. Underwood escorted her to the manager's box—"and we entered privately, she being well muffled." Mrs. Stowe was entranced. "I never saw such delight upon a human face as she displayed," said Underwood; but the New England conscience must have received a mortal wound. Less clandestine but equally funny was the *Atlantic* dinner when women contributors were for the first time invited. Mrs. Stowe agreed to attend with the ironclad stipulation that no wine should be served, and then, according to the report of one of the thirsting guests, made her appearance wearing "vine-leaves" in her hair. Mrs. Thomas Bailey Aldrich, finally, records a delicious anecdote of Mrs. Stowe's early arrival at an afternoon party on a sweltering day, of her innocent partaking of a refreshing punch and feeling a subsequent drowsiness, and of the hostess' horror when she had to receive her guests in the small drawing room close to the alcove where on a sofa, in hoop skirt and lace mitts, the author of *Uncle Tom's Cabin* lay sleeping off her potations.

Obviously Harriet Beecher Stowe was neither a great personality nor a great artist; yet the words set down by her hand appeared to convulse a mighty nation. She herself solved the paradox with charming simplicity by saying of her world-famous book, "God wrote it!" She was only the amanuensis of the Eternal. To a mind grounded in Hebrew Scripture, there was nothing impossible in the thought that God should choose the foolish things of the world to confound the wise, and the weak things of the world to confound the things that are mighty.

35. THE NEW ENGLAND TRIUMVIRATE: LONGFELLOW, HOLMES, LOWELL

NEITHER the issue of slavery nor the fact of civil war could stir very deeply the peace which pervaded the country town of Cambridge, near Boston, in the middle years of the century. Around the disorderly College Yard and its seven red-brick "Muses' factories" sprawled the "Village," which Lowell was to describe in one of his sprightliest essays, "Cambridge Thirty Years Ago." It was in fact a country town, quite separate from Boston, and though perhaps not beautiful, certainly not ugly. To the casual visitor it would have seemed to differ from other New England towns mainly in its vivid recollections of the Revolutionary War and in the pride it took in the college. On closer acquaintance one would have found it a place in which scholarly attainments outshone every sort of worldly success. Democratic enough for the president of the college to serve happily as major in the company of militia of which his own manservant was the colonel, it possessed and highly respected its own intellectual aristocracy.

Cambridge was also a friendly place, a true society, in which the loneliness endured by most American thinkers and creative workers could have little excuse. The intensity of the Puritan past, now sluiced into other channels, was still evident there. Somewhat provincial the place may have been, and a little out of the main American current; yet one would be at a loss to say where or when America has provided a pleasanter residence for a scholar, a thinker, or a man of letters. Even a young poet, if by chance he should turn up there, would not be laughed or frozen into silence.

Three young poets—Henry Wadsworth Longfellow, Oliver Wendell Holmes, and James Russell Lowell—lived there and in Boston in the thirties. The good fortune that was to persist throughout their long lives began with the time and place of their birth. The New England of their early years was a rural and agricultural region, yet strongly sea-minded. It was remarkably homogeneous in population and had a history and tradition of its own. In two centuries of toil this region had accumulated a moderate, well distributed wealth. Nowhere in the world had the elements of education been made more accessible. At no time since the great age of Athens had any community worked out a better balance of individual liberty with the sense of social and political obligation. This New England was composed not so much of states and cities as of towns, and of towns so nearly independent, so stoutly supported within by citizens fully aware of their rights and duties, that a clear-eyed foreign observer, Alexis de Tocqueville, could regard them in 1835 as almost perfect examples of democracy. Such a New England town was Cambridge—with the difference that it had an ancient college.

In such surroundings, a poet could be in harmony with the present and at the same time devote his energies to the exploration of the past. Cooper and other early American writers had complained that the young nation could not produce a really great literature until it had a cultural tradition of its own, rooted deeply in the past. Only then would there be a society of readers who had assured and common thoughts, and emotions with which to respond. In Longfellow, Holmes, and Lowell such "great writers" seemed to be in the making.

With equal success these three poets managed to reconcile the conflicting demands laid upon the scholar, the creative writer, and the gentleman. One and all, they were sound literary craftsmen, industrious and fluent and prolific in prose and verse. They were good men in nearly every sense that the word "good" can bear. Each of them descended from dignified and long-established New England stock, they were highly respected in their day and so could do much to make literature "respectable" in a country preoccupied with quite other things. Their inheritance of New England's version of the eighteenth century, during which the more acrid juices of Puritanism had considerably mellowed, made them optimistic, serene, and sweet-tempered, so that the widespread admiration they won in their time was always warmed by affection. Although their unquestionable patriotism was deeply rooted in their native region, each of them in his way was a transplanter of Old World culture. Moreover, they moved in the same circles, heard the same talk, and read the same books for half a century. They even read and liked and praised one another's books, and often met as members of the Saturday Club of Boston, which came to be called a "mutual admiration society."

In writing deliberately for an audience which they knew and which they wished to address in terms that would be widely understood, Longfellow and Holmes and Lowell had good and numerous company. To oversimplify an intricate matter, many poets of the years after the First World War talked to themselves not so much because they despised a larger audience as because they despaired of one. But the Cambridge and Boston triumvirate had no reason for any such despair. Their natural and easily defensible wish to be understood, to be liked, to be even influential, was fully gratified. They were as sure of their audience as a minister composing his Sunday sermon, and out of this assurance came the tone of public address that we hear in much of their verse. Thence too, no doubt, came the platitudes and sentimentalities, the threshing of thrice-tossed straw, the smooth slipping along old greased grooves, that have lowered the repute of their verse with a later generation; but in counting the cost we should not forget that much was gained when these men showed that poetry of a sort could be written in America and made intelligible, even enjoyable, to common and workaday understandings.

2

Longfellow was twenty-nine years old when, in 1836, he took up his duties at Harvard College as Smith Professor of Modern Languages. His preparation for those duties had not been of the sort that provides severe mental discipline or produces what would later be called accurate scholarship. Born in 1807 at Portland in the District of Maine, the son of a successful lawyer and grandson of a patriarchal hero of the Revolution, he had graduated at Bowdoin College in the same year as Nathaniel Hawthorne and then had spent three years of random travel and study in Europe. There had followed five years of teaching at Bowdoin, his marriage to a Portland girl, a second stay in Europe, and the death of his young wife. By the time he arrived in Cambridge he had written and published a number of conventional poems, several magazine articles, certain textbooks for the use of his college classes, and a slight volume of travel essays in Irving's manner entitled *Outre-Mer*. It was clear that he was quite determined to succeed in some as yet unspecified way, but nothing he had yet done showed remarkable originality or creative power.

Short in stature but good-looking and graceful, quiet and modest in manner but not unduly reticent, very careful in matters of dress, laughter-loving and with plenty of humor though not much wit, highly appreciative of creature comforts, always sociably inclined, the young professor made friends easily and held them long. He had enough personal dignity to command respect but not so much as to prevent affection. His colleagues and students liked him from the start, even though there might be something slightly exotic about his florid waistcoats and flowing hair. His unconcern with the contemporary American scene could easily be explained to his credit as the result of his two long sojourns abroad. Though so young and gay and accessible, he brought with him into the provincial college town a hint of romantic distances. He had walked the Rialto and the streets of old Madrid. He had lingered long among the "last enchantments of the Middle Age" as they were to be found— or so young America was beginning to surmise—at Göttingen and Heidelberg and along the castled Rhine. "The Old World," as he had written years before in his neatly kept private journal, was to him "a kind of Holy Land"—a feeling which would by no means impede his success in a Cambridge and a New England in which the old Hebraic sanctities were slowly giving way before a Europeanized culture. And indeed it was impossible to regard him as an outsider. His father and his grandfather had been Harvard men, and four of his maternal ancestors, including John Alden, had "come over in the *Mayflower*."

Professor Longfellow performed his college duties faithfully but without enthusiasm. He was neither a brilliant teacher nor a dull one. His lectures on the literatures of modern Europe, quiet in tone yet warmly appreciative, contributed less to the scholarship of his auditors than to their "general culture." There was a suggestion in them that a gentleman would no more flaunt his scholarship than he would his bank account, and for criticism Longfellow had little taste or ability. "Doubtless criticism," he was later to remark in his *Table Talk*, "was originally benignant, pointing out the beauties of a work, rather than its defects. The passions of men have made it malignant, as the bad heart of Procrustes turned the bed, the symbol of repose, into an instrument of torture."

Several passages in his early letters show that Longfellow had acquired, probably in Europe, a theory of higher education in advance of anything to be found in practice at Bowdoin or Harvard, but this did not make the routine of classroom teaching any the less irksome to him. Before he had been two years at Harvard he confided to his Journal: "Perhaps the worst thing in a College Life is this having your mind constantly a play-mate for boys . . . instead of stretching out and grappling with men's minds." These words have an odd sound as coming from a man who seldom grappled with anything and was never remarkable for "stretching out." They are as surprising as the line "Let us, then, be up and doing" in "A Psalm of Life," his most famous but perhaps least characteristic poem. For Longfellow was in no sense a man of action. His life and work seem to have been actuated by two diverse desires. On the one hand he emphatically wanted to make and to leave his mark, to succeed in the world's opinion; but on the other he wanted, perhaps less consciously, to spend his life in the leisurely reading of old books and in the kind of rumination and reminiscence that went to the making of his poem "My Lost Youth." His problem was, how to satisfy both of these apparently contradictory wishes, and rather early in life he found the answer: by success as a poet. His work at Harvard could not satisfy either one of them. In 1854 he resigned his professorship.

To meet the objection that this view of Longfellow's career suggests a cool calculation, not to say an opportunism, seldom found in poetic minds, one might easily cite a number of instances in which he showed himself an astute manager of his worldly affairs while at the same time closely guarding the treasure of his dreams. His choice and rejection of poetic themes, the timing of his publications, his dealings with publishers, and most of all his accurate knowledge of the public taste, show that the tendency to what he called "daydreaming" which he seems to have inherited from his mother was well balanced by the practical gifts that had made his father a successful lawyer and politician.

Longfellow, moreover, was not a poet by compulsion of inward and innate necessity. Year after year in his early manhood he wrote verse hardly at all, and his first collection of poems was not published until he was thirty-two. There is of course no doubt that he loved poetry and delighted to write it; but he had to be assured that the writing of it would amount to something more than mere "daydreaming." When at last that assurance came, when he saw that poetry would provide a dignified and leisurely way of making his mark without the necessity to be "up and doing" or to "be a hero in the strife," he settled down to become America's first professional poet—a phrase which involves a contradiction in terms.

An interesting example of Longfellow's ability to advance his worldly fortunes while serving the needs of the heart is seen in his long courtship of Frances Appleton. One would not suggest that his love for this charming woman was alloyed by any materialistic consideration, and yet it is at least worthy of record that she was a daughter of one of the wealthiest merchants in Boston and that when, in 1843, she finally became his wife, she brought him as a wedding gift the handsome Craigie House and grounds in Cambridge, once the headquarters of General Washington.

In asking himself whether he ought to allow his daughter to marry a man who, besides being a college professor, was known to have written verses, Nathan Appleton, the prosperous merchant of Beacon Hill, had to consider that by 1843 Professor Longfellow was rapidly becoming a famous man. His first volume of poems, *Voices of the Night,* published in 1839, had sold 43,000 copies, and several poems in it, such as "A Psalm of Life" and "The Reaper and the Flowers," were already widely popular. Such success would assuage the wound caused by Longfellow's prose romance *Hyperion,* also of 1839, in which the professor had shown definitely bad taste by narrating, under a thin disguise, the early stages of his affection for Nathan Appleton's daughter. In 1842 there had appeared *Ballads and Other Poems,* considerably more vigorous than the first book and including two well told tales of the sea, "The Wreck of the Hesperus" and "The Skeleton in Armor," which any businessman could understand. Here, too, was the sweetly sentimental "Maidenhood," the platitudinous "Rainy Day," and "The Village Blacksmith" with precisely the right tone of gentlemanly condescension toward the laboring classes. These lines were fitted out at the end with a moralistic tag which, though its relation to the main substance of the poem was slight, would mitigate the curse of poetry for those who preferred sermons. In short, there seemed to be something in the little book for almost every taste, and the poem called "Excelsior" was really a masterpiece in the profitable art of pleasing everybody at once. For the youth who bore "the strange device" in that poem might, if one pleased, be thought of as climbing toward heaven, toward the summit of Parnassus, toward the full development of his own powers, or, equally well, toward the presidency of a bank, a railroad, even a college. At any rate he was climbing, hoping, aspiring, and so could be taken as the perfect symbol of a young ambitious country that hardly knew as yet where it was going but felt sure that it was on the way.

The poems in these first two books of verse sank so deep into the national memory, soon attaining there almost the currency of proverbs, that we usually think of them even today when we remember Longfellow at all—and then perhaps decide that he is not worth remembering. The deeper reasons for their popularity, though not recondite, may be left to the historians of American culture. Perhaps the most charitable thing that the literary critic can say about them is that they were, in the language of seventeenth century musicians, hardly more than toccata pieces written to try out the range and sonority of the instrument. In other words, a mind in which there was little of its own that was really burning for utterance was here trying to find out, by trial and error, what themes, what moods, what literary effects, would be acceptable to a reading public with which no one as yet was familiar. It was engaged in the task of discovering about America certain basic things which America herself did not know. Little wonder that for a while it fumbled and groped almost blindly here and there, trying all things but determined to hold fast what it found good.

Longfellow's love for Frances Appleton brought him an experience of passion, and also, for a time, of pain and apparent failure, which deepened and strengthened his whole nature. Its successful outcome brought him inward peace and released him from the need, real or imagined, to strive for the approval of everyone. During the long and mainly serene remainder of his life, his writing in verse gradually developed admirable qualities of which the early poems had not given clear promise. Completely happy at home, surrounded by friends such as Lowell, Sumner, Norton, and Agassiz, with his fame steadily spreading through the two Americas and England and Europe, he poured forth his poems with an almost effortless ease. *The Belfry of Bruges and Other Poems* (1845) contained, besides such popular things as "The Bridge" and "The Old Clock on the Stairs," a really fine sonnet called "Mezzo Cammin" in which he surveyed his past accomplishment with characteristic modesty and manly candor. Two years later his *Evangeline,* a long and rambling narrative in loose hexameters, gave notice that here was an American poet, at last, who regarded the making of poetry as his life's work. The luster of its success was undimmed by the appearance of *Kavanagh* (1849), an unfortunate excursion into prose fiction which showed how inadequate the poet's thought appeared when the cunningly woven veil of his verse was drawn aside. Longfellow reached the height of his powers in extended versified narrative in *The Song of Hiawatha* (1855) and *The Courtship of Miles Standish* (1858), both of which, like *Evangeline,* did something to stay if not to satisfy America's hunger for a past, a legendry, a body of myth, of her own. So, in part, did the *Tales of a Wayside Inn* (1863), bringing together stories from many lands, including New England, in a "framework" suggested by Chaucer and Boccaccio, and relating them as though through the mouths of New England speakers round the fireside of a Massachusetts tavern.

Not only the narrative methods but also the themes of these *Tales* illustrate what one may call the antiquarian habit of Longfellow's mind. A few of the stories, like the inaccurate but highly effective "Paul Revere's Ride," are American and almost "local," though everything possible is done to make them look old. All the rest deal with the far away and the long ago, and the "Saga of King Olaf," the best item in the series, has an air of all but mythological antiquity.

One need not urge the absurdity of the supposition that a group of nineteenth century Americans would tell such tales to one another while sitting at ease round a New England fireside, for it is obvious that Longfellow was little concerned with verisimilitude either here or elsewhere. He had almost none of the respect for concrete fact that gives body and verve to the work of Chaucer, his chief model in the composition of the *Tales,* and apparently it never occurred to him that the poetic imagination might and should be used not for escape from the facts of life, as he used it, but for penetration and inward illumination of them. At any rate, nothing seemed poetical to him until all taint of modernity had been cleansed or hidden away. When he did occasionally single out a recent event for imaginative treatment his first and instinctive act was, so to speak, to dip it in "time's ever-rolling stream." Thus in writing "The Wreck of the Hesperus," less than two weeks after the incident it describes and within fifty miles of its scene, he made it sound as much as possible like a medieval popular ballad. The scenes of his three long narrative poems with an ostensible American setting might almost as well have been laid in ancient Arcadia, so devoid they are of sharp factual detail and contemporary reference. Only once, and then reluctantly, at the request of his friend Charles Sumner, did he make an approach to a living national issue. The unsatisfactory result was his *Poems on Slavery* (1842).

This antiquarian habit was of course by no means peculiar to Longfellow.

We see it clearly in Irving and Hawthorne, and it is a familiar characteristic of the Romantic Movement throughout its long course. Yet, in American literature at any rate, Longfellow is an extreme example of this "devotion to something afar from the sphere of our sorrow." His homesickness for the glamorous twilights of the past is often attributed to the influence of his early wanderings and random readings in Europe, especially in Germany where the Romantic Movement began and lingered longest. But this is to confuse cause and effect. Longfellow's romantic tendencies were already well developed when he first went to Europe, and if they had any literary source it was probably Irving's *Sketch Book*—a work he read with delight in his boyhood, began at once to imitate, and never outgrew. More probably, however, his romanticism was fastened upon him by the choice he made between his mother's "daydreaming" and his father's clear-eyed worldliness. For the latter he never lost respect; but he saw that it involved a vigor and persistence in action "still achieving, still pursuing," which was not congenial to his nature. Poetry or daydreaming, on the other hand, required no coarsening contacts with the world's work. In the words of Ossian, one of the favorite poets of his boyhood, it was to him "a tale of the times of old, the deeds of the days of other years."

The source of Longfellow's antiquarianism, however, is not nearly so important as the fact that the true habitat of his thoughts was neither America nor Europe but the past, and not the past as reconstructed by historical scholarship or as revived by an alert historical imagination but an unchanging and timeless and quite unbelievable epoch of his own creation. This has meant that Longfellow's writing, for all its great vogue, has done nothing to correct but rather much to confirm a notion to which America has long been prone—the notion that poetry and the other arts have no bearing upon actual life and that, like "religion," they may be consigned to rainy Sundays and to otherwise unoccupied females.

After the dreadful death of his wife, by fire, in 1861, Longfellow "took refuge," as he wrote to a German friend, in the work of translating Dante's *Divina Commedia*. The result, published in three volumes from 1865 to 1867, was an adequate rendering of the Florentine's words but not of his cramped and fiery force. Longfellow was not using his developed powers and what should have been the most fruitful years of his life to advantage, either in this quite uncreative task or in his several attempts at poetic drama. His *Christus: A Mystery* (published as a whole in 1872) is a loosely connected trilogy of "closet dramas" in verse which, we are told, he regarded as his most important work. Only the second part, entitled "The Golden Legend," is today easily readable, and it reads like an extremely mild dilution of Goethe's *Faust*. Longfellow was working closer to his true vein in the simple and dignified "Morituri Salutamus," which he wrote for the fiftieth anniversary of his class at Bowdoin College.

Old age brought Longfellow a quiet culmination. His last two collections of verse, *Ultima Thule* and *In the Harbor* (1880 and 1882), had in them a number of poems far better than anything in his first one. He was, and modestly knew himself to be, the most popular poet in America or in the world. He was as widely beloved as he was famous, and must have been aware that he had done much good for multitudes of people. Letters of praise and gratitude, always courteously answered, poured in upon him from many lands, in many languages. His seventy-fifth birthday was celebrated in every school-house in the United States. Two weeks later he wrote his last poem, "The Bells of San Blas." Ten days later still, on March 24, 1882, he died.

The perennial question with regard to Longfellow's "Americanism" is not so difficult as it has been made to seem. Surely the best proof that a man belongs to his people is given when they accept him as their representative and beloved voice. By this test Longfellow is the most American poet that America has ever had. He is so much of our kind that a close reading of him helps our understanding of ourselves, not always in a flattering way. The sentimentalities, the platitudes, and the lugged-in moralisms that mar his earlier writing are faults that he came by, as we say, "honestly." He reminds us of deep-drawn traits in the American character by his antiquarian delight in the shadowy past, by the superficial melancholy that never really darkens his essential optimism, and perhaps most of all by his occasional awaking from daydreams with the injunction that one must "act,—act in the living Present." One would say, therefore, that not to know Longfellow, or to be contemptuous of him, is to lose some part of one's national heritage.

Yet after all it is not a poet's main business to represent his time and his country, to have witty or profound ideas, or even to hold sound opinions. The elementary but oft neglected fact that a poet must make poems was fully understood by Longfellow, and in his best work he showed himself a conscientious and deliberate artist. He was a master of the orthodox technique of versification, ranging easily and with a skill that concealed itself through a wide variety of meters and stanzaic structures. He could versify a long story like *Evangeline* with many a subtle modulation in the verbal music and the mood. He could narrate a short story like "Paul Revere's Ride" in a verse that races and rings. In later life he made a dozen or more sonnets, notably the one entitled "Nature" and the six composed to accompany his translation of Dante, that give the effect of massive and grandly modeled bronze. His expression, moreover, was always as clear as he or anyone could make it, and whatever he wrote, well or ill, he always seemed to write easily, without the least strain or strut. To borrow a metaphor from Thoreau, he struck not with the end but with the middle of his stick. Thus he sometimes achieved, especially in old age, a grand simplicity of style which seems the perfectly natural expression of his own essential goodness, his serenity, and his peace of heart.

3

Longfellow took twenty-nine years in reaching Cambridge, but Oliver Wendell Holmes saved time, as he himself might have said, by being born there, in an old gambrel-roofed house between the common and the college. He remained a Cambridge boy to the last of his many years, notwithstanding the fact that he was also emphatically a Boston man. In 1829 he graduated from Harvard College at the age of nineteen, and in the following year, while "yawning over law books," wrote the vigorous poem "Old Ironsides" which carried his name for a time far beyond the confines of New England and saved the old battleship *Constitution* from threatened destruction. Soon abandoning the law, he took up the study of medicine, at first in Boston, and in 1833 he went to Paris for two and a half years of close application to anatomy, surgery, and medicine under the foremost teachers that the world at the time afforded. These were the years, as his letters show, in which Holmes grew up. With a purpose far more precise than that with which Longfellow had gone to Europe some years before, he got more definite results. Besides a solid grounding in his chosen profession, he gained enough knowledge of Parisian life, and saw enough in brief glimpses of England, Scotland, and Italy, to prevent him from ever becoming in fact the provincial Bostonian that he sometimes humorously pretended to be.

During the first year, 1836, after his return from Europe, Holmes took the degree of M.D. at the Harvard Medical School, began his medical practice, published his first volume of poems, became a member of the Massachusetts Medical Society, published a dissertation on Intermittent Fever in New England, won a Boylston Prize at Harvard, and wrote for the Harvard Commencement a Phi Beta Kappa Poem that filled—allowing for the applause—an hour and ten minutes in the recitation. This year, except that it represented only a few of his later acquirements and activities, was a swiftly drawn sketch of the always eager, gay, and multilateral life that Dr. Holmes was to lead in Cambridge and Boston for more than half a century.

And yet neither in youth nor in age were his interests merely miscellaneous. They had a center, a burning focus indeed, from which not even the later fame of his prose and verse could deflect him. First of all he was, and he remained, a doctor, although he interpreted that title in a sense more inclusive than the one it usually bears. His medical practice, never extensive, was abandoned before he reached middle age, and he was never eminent in original medical research; but as a teacher he did his most completely devoted, enthusiastic, and influential work. It was said of Lowell that he sometimes yawned when entering the classroom, and one fears that Longfellow's students occasionally did the same in the midst of a lecture; but the wit, the Yankee common sense, and the completely humanized erudition of Professor Holmes were a prophylaxis against the germs of boredom. First at Dartmouth from 1838 to 1840 and then at the Harvard Medical School from 1847 to 1882 he taught anatomy and physiology with a deep, abiding sense of the teacher's privilege and obligation. One judges from the testimony of his pupils that his teaching was actuated by an unmistakable intellectual passion for what he proudly called "Science," and also by a keen aesthetic delight in the intricate order and symmetry of Nature, especially of the human body, which science was in his time slowly revealing.

If therefore we find that Holmes' prose and verse lack intensity, we do well to infer not that the Doctor himself was quite without that quality but that it had been directed elsewhere. Diminutive in stature, chronically adolescent in appearance, charmingly egotistical and avid of praise as a schoolboy, bestrewing his long path through life with puns and quips and bons mots, always cheerfully convinced that the main thing about a cloud is its silver lining, the doctor and professor and poet and prose-master called Holmes was a little hard for people who saw only the surface of him to take seriously; but to those who knew him well it was observable that when he sallied forth to assail bigotry in any of its forms—it might be the bigotry of medical doctors of the old school against which in 1843 he launched his fierce and brilliant essay on "The Contagiousness of Puerperal Fever," or that of Calvinistic theologians whom he attacked again and again, as in his essay on Jonathan Edwards and his poem "Wind-Clouds and Star-Drifts"—his works carried the concentrated force of a hornet. His hatred of disorder and confusion and darkness and cruelty was the inevitable antithesis of his strong love of order and clearness, that intellectual light and beneficence which he believed modern science was offering to mankind. We are right, no doubt, in calling him a conservative, and he called himself that; but at the core of his caution and temperamental dislike of change there was an ardency, an audacity of the kind by which revolutions are made. One of the public testimonials of which he may well have been proudest was a vote taken by the members of the Massachusetts Medical Society after he had read his paper on "Currents and Counter-Currents in Medical Science." In that vote it was "resolved that the Society disclaim all responsibility for the sentiments contained in this Annual Address."

What Holmes chiefly brought back from Europe and strove to transplant in the soil of American culture was a resolute and unqualified faith in Science.

The word "faith" is here exact, for he felt and thought and wrote about Science—a word he habitually capitalized—as New England ministers of the past had done about religion. He held it to be nothing less than a new revelation of the divine mind, in terms of which all real or alleged foregoing revelations would have to be reconsidered. "The attitude of modern Science," said he, "is erect, her aspect serene, her determination inexorable, her onward movement unflinching; because she believes herself, in the order of Providence, the true successor of the men of old who brought down the light of heaven to men."

Holmes' faith in Science led him more than once out of his natural conservatism and into the ranks of the reformers. It was partly with scientific weapons that he fought his long battle with the lingering representatives of Calvinistic theology, although he did not neglect to put on also the whole armor of his learning, reason, common sense, and wit. He used scientific methods and data to show that criminals, vicious persons, and "sinners" in general, because they were not wholly responsible for their evil doing, ought rather to be educated than punished. His three novels, *Elsie Venner* (1860–1861), *The Guardian Angel* (1867), and *A Mortal Antipathy* (1885), were written with this primary intent. In fact he laid so strong an emphasis upon heredity and environment that he often seemed to be teaching a materialistic determinism no less binding than the Calvinistic predestination which he ridiculed.

But Holmes was never completely a materialist. He left some room for the freedom of the will and never lost his belief in a beneficent Deity. According to his chief biographer, John T. Morse, Jr., who knew him intimately, he was always more attracted by theology than even by literature and medicine. To those who regard him as merely an amiable jester, his theological lore is likely to be the most surprising item in his accurate and various learning. His own religious beliefs, to be sure, were neither precise nor numerous, and he once said that he could sum them all up in the first two words of the Lord's Prayer, yet he apparently found them sufficient. For all the little man's bustle and bristle, it was clear that he had in his heart the peace of God which passed even his understanding. In this regard he reminds one of certain minor poets of England's eighteenth century—men like Parnell and Gray, the Warton brothers, and William Shenstone, who were so careful to avoid all outward show of "enthusiasm" that their real religious faith seldom came to the surface.

Holmes recalls England's neo-classical period in several ways. Like Addison and Steele, he based his admirable prose style upon the best of the talk—and that would be largely his own—that he could hear in his time. In verse his favorite form was the heroic couplet. Like Pope, although not to the same extent, he depended for his effects chiefly upon wit—a term within which he would have included both reason and good sense. His feeling for Boston, where a faint aroma of the eighteenth century still lingered when he was young, was like that of Dr. Johnson for London. Moderation, urbanity, and serene self-control meant as much to him as to Lord Chesterfield. He might have excelled in the writing of satire like that of Swift if his convictions had been more fervid and his heart less warm. Even his devotion to science makes one think of the eighteenth century Deists who saw in the laws of nature a second revelation of the Creator's mind and purpose. His prevailing optimism, based upon an assurance that the human mind can comprehend and in some degree control the physical world in which it finds itself, closely resembled that to be seen in the immediate followers of Sir Isaac Newton.

One of the few outstanding events in Holmes' life was the request that came to him when he was nearing fifty that he contribute to the newly founded *Atlantic Monthly,* edited by his friend James Russell Lowell. At that time, in 1857, Holmes was little known outside the Boston region, and even there his reputation was that of an able physician and teacher who, as an amateur of letters, could be counted upon to turn out at short notice a string of amusing verses for the annual meeting of his Harvard class or almost any other such festive occasion. In *The Autocrat of the Breakfast Table* (1857–1858), however, he established his own fame and that of Lowell's new magazine at one stroke.

American literature had never before been suddenly enriched by an extended piece of writing at once so wise and gay, so felicitous in swift mingling of fact and fancy, so crackling with wit while remaining so warm, so kind. For this work and its two successors, *The Professor at the Breakfast-Table* (1860) and *The Poet at the Breakfast-Table* (1872), Holmes developed a literary form admirably calculated for the exhibition of his own powers. By combining the techniques of prose fiction, drama, and the essay, he made for himself a literary method by means of which he could sketch character, tell stories, present his favorite ideas and prejudices, parade his erudition, praise Boston, smite stupidities, and indulge in an endless monologue without fear of interruption. It was a method that made miscellaneousness a virtue and changed what might have looked like ostentatious egotism—for in fact it was something rather like that—into pure charm. And yet in admiring the method or form of the Breakfast Table series one must not ignore the contribution of Holmes' prose style, elastic and delicate and strong as a strand of spider's web. There is little to subtract from the statement made long ago in the Boston *Advertiser* that it has "the spring of the hickory, the smack of the cider, the tonic of the climate, and the vigor of the type of men hardened by the struggle that has formed our national character."

The Autocrat of the Breakfast-Table is one of the most highly civilized books ever written in America. It is a book in which the seeds of factual knowledge spring up into thought, and thought bears the fruit of wisdom. It is the product of an epoch and a place. It is a masterpiece, a triumph, of wit. One sees this mainly in the blaze of the metaphors with which it is, so to speak, encrusted. Yet they are never used for mere display. One laughs at them, if at all, in pure admiration, sharing Holmes' own manifest delight and surprise at their aptness. For he himself was amazed at his own discoveries of this kind. "What happens," he asks in *Mechanism in Thought and Morals,* "when one idea brings up another? . . . What is this action which . . . in men of wit and fancy connects remote ideas by partial resemblances? . . . There is a Delphi and a Pythoness in every human breast."

Holmes contained in himself the man of wit, the man of imagination, and the man of science, and all three of them were continually diving into what he calls "the infinite ocean of similitudes and analogies that rolls through the universe." No doubt it was this triple equipment that enabled him to make his unerring gannetlike plunges out of the skies of abstract thought upon the one minute and distant object that could best illustrate and drive home his meaning. For he was quite wrong, of course, in implying that everyone can do this sort of thing. He came near the truth when he said, "Just according to the intensity and extension of our mental being we shall see the many in the one and the one in the many."

Whatever may be thought of Holmes' intensity, he had a remarkable mental extension. He was erudite not only in medicine and anatomy, in theology, and in the English literature of the eighteenth century, but in the dialect of New England, the records of trotting horses, pugilism and photography and rowing, rattlesnakes, elm trees, prenatal influences, heredity, the Harvard Class of 1829, and microscopes. Nothing Bostonian was alien to him. He was at the same time bookish and social, a hard worker and a man of endless leisure who loved to have his talk out. He could talk with any man on any man's own topic while holding back large reservoirs of professional knowledge to which few others could pretend.

One may suspect that Holmes was kept from being in the full sense a poet by what the French would call a "defect of his qualities." He tried to be one, but laughter was always breaking in. He reaches full-throated song perhaps only in "The Chambered Nautilus." He wrote a large number of "occasional poems," all highly successful, no doubt, when first read by him in public but now for the most part lifeless. He really excelled in a dozen or fifteen tiny masterpieces—"The Last Leaf," "Dorothy Q," "Contentment," "Aunt Tabitha," and "The Organ-Blower" among them—as ingeniously wrought as a Chinese ivory carving.

Dr. Holmes knew his limitations. He accepted, he obeyed, and he even enjoyed them, often making them look like positive advantages. Thus, realizing that his profession and the asthma with which he suffered all his life would confine him to the region of Boston, he assured himself and the world that "identification with a locality is a surer passport to immortality than cosmopolitanism is," and also that the "Boston State-House is the hub of the solar system." In the same way he made his peace with the boundaries that nature had set for his intellectual and artistic aspirations.

4

The symmetry of Holmes' career is even more apparent when one compares it with that of James Russell Lowell. More versatile than Holmes by far, more deeply and highly gifted, Lowell did not willingly accept any limitations, any discipline or routine whatever. Although he gained a remarkable erudition from a lifetime of reading in half a dozen languages, he never was subjected, by himself or by others, to an arduous training. This may be one reason for the fact that he makes a blurred impression, and that one rises from a study of his manifold life, his brilliant essays, his verse of many kinds, and his wholly delightful letters, with the feeling that he was, in both the good and the bad sense, "a man of parts."

Like Holmes, Lowell was a native of Cambridge and the son of a Congregational clergyman. He was born on February 22, 1819, in a substantial pre-Revolutionary house called "Elmwood," standing in ample grounds about a mile west of Harvard College. On the paternal side he came of New England stock already distinguished and destined to be more so. His father was a man whose political and social opinions made it appropriate that he should live in a part of the town known as "Tory Row." His mother, from whom he derived his poetical talent, was descended from families that had lived for several generations in the Orkney Islands.

After a happy childhood in which he unconsciously gathered from the natural beauty about him many of the poetic images that were to enrich his later writing, Lowell entered Harvard at the age of fifteen. The letters of his college days show him as a scatterbrain, eagerly enthusiastic, devoted to his friends, gay, and averse to hard work. Toward the end of his senior year he was rusticated for a breach of college discipline and was required to spend the following six weeks at Concord. There he met Emerson, of whom he reported to a college friend: "He is a good-natured man in spite of his doctrines."

In 1840, having graduated at Harvard College and also at the Harvard Law School, Lowell became engaged to Maria White, a highly intelligent young woman of poetic talent who seems to have increased his already nascent interest in the current liberal and humanitarian movements, including Abolition. His first book of verse, *A Year's Life and Other Poems,* appeared in 1841; and when it was followed by *Poems,* three years later, his reputation was such that N. P. Willis could speak of him as "the best-launched poet in America." Meanwhile he had begun his varied editorial career with a short-lived journal called *The Pioneer,* published in Boston. After his marriage he lived for a time in Philadelphia, contributing to various liberal journals. In 1848 he put forth a two-volume edition of his poems, *A Fable for Critics,* the first series of his *Biglow Papers,* and *The Vision of Sir Launfal,* thus establishing his fame before he reached the age of thirty. There followed a long period of travel in Europe, shortly after which his wife died. This event, as he said in his old age, broke his life in two. It deprived him of the only companion and guide who was ever able to give direction to his random energies and miscellaneous interests.

Lowell fell back, as Longfellow had done under similar circumstances, upon the literary past. Since boyhood he had been a bold adventurer in the wilderness of books, but now he became, as he said, "one of the last great readers." In 1855 he accepted the professorship at Harvard recently vacated by Longfellow, thus turning his addiction to old books into a duty. He taught his classes faithfully though not with all his strength, and in 1857 became the first editor of the *Atlantic Monthly.*

Far more public-minded than Holmes or Longfellow, Lowell was profoundly stirred by the tragedy of the Civil War, in which he lost three beloved nephews. It roused him to write a second series, more mature than the first, of *Biglow Papers* (1867), and to contribute a number of deeply thoughtful articles on the topics of the times to the *Atlantic* and the *North American Review.* Thus he returned to the concern with social and political questions which he had shown in his younger manhood, gradually acquiring reputation as a public figure. He was one of the first American men of letters to recognize and proclaim the greatness of Abraham Lincoln. The noble sixth section of his *Ode Recited at the Harvard Commemoration* (1865), devoted to Lincoln entirely, may well outlast all his other writing.

Lowell's central thought with regard to democracy was that it can be saved from its tendency to "level downward" only by the constant presence and pressure within it of an aristocratic leaven. This was approximately Thomas Jefferson's position, but Lowell probably reached it through acquaintance with the New England scene. In his address on the two hundred and fiftieth anniversary of the founding of Harvard he spoke a vivid paragraph or two in praise of the early ministers of New England, asserting that they composed "a recognized aristocracy," and that "never was there an aristocracy so simple, so harmless, so exemplary, and so fit to rule." If this is a conservative opinion, then Lowell was conservative all his life, and the attempts sometimes made to divide his political and social thinking into several "periods" do not reach to the ingrained and possibly innate habit of his mind.

In spite of the disgust he felt at the political corruption of the North in the postwar years, Lowell continued to write extensively. A long poem called *The Cathedral*, one of his most ambitious, appeared in 1870. In the next year he published *My Study Windows*, a delightful collection of familiar essays. The two series of essays entitled *Among My Books* (1870 and 1876), with their extended studies of Dryden, Milton, Wordsworth, Dante, Spenser, and Keats, established his reputation as a literary critic and as one of America's foremost men of letters.

But literary fame could not satisfy this mind that never found its own center. In 1877 Lowell gladly accepted from President Hayes an appointment as Minister to the Court of Spain, and from 1880 to 1885 he served as American Minister in England. He was highly successful in both countries as a diplomat and as a spokesman for America, keenly enjoying his work, making many friends, and gradually abandoning the tendency to heckle John Bull so evident in the second set of *Biglow Papers* and in the political essays he had written before and during the Civil War. England, indeed, became to him almost a second home, and he returned to that country four times in the last five years of his life. The loss of his second wife in 1885 left him a lonely and heartbroken man. His health, which had always been remarkably robust, was destroyed by successive attacks of gout. On August 12, 1891, he died at "Elmwood," in the house of his birth.

The more one knows about this brilliant career, in so many ways so decidedly successful, the more one is inclined to call it a failure. What Lowell most deplorably lacks is coherence—and this not merely in the style of his prose and verse, but in his life, his thought, his beliefs, even his character. Lowell's mind was certainly one of the most brilliant that America has produced; but it was brilliant in the way of a shattered mirror, or, let us say, in that of the vividly colored bits of glass in a kaleidoscope that give the effect of a new geometrical pattern at every slight turn of the tube. "He did not, indeed, make one impression upon me," said William Dean Howells, "but a thousand impressions, which I should seek in vain to embody in a single presentment." Continually while reading Lowell, and even when most delighted by the incessant glitter and glint of his style, one is perplexed and vexed that a man with such powers could not draw them together and so make more of them.

Lowell was himself aware of his failure, and wrote in his old age: "I feel that my life has been mainly wasted—that I have thrown away more than most men ever had." For this failure he gave, early and late, a number of reasons. Thus, he felt that his teaching at Harvard, his work as a literary editor and critic, perhaps even his erudition, tended to inhibit his creative faculties. "I know so well how certain things are done," he told a friend, "that I can't do them." Now and then he complained that the necessity of making his livelihood with his pen had left him little continuous leisure for doing his best work. He knew also that his remarkable fluency in composition, or what he called his tendency to "improvise," was hostile to real excellence. More than once he inveighed against his penchant for "preaching." But he comes closer to the truth when he confesses the natural "indolence" which underlay his random bursts of last-minute energizing. The number, bulk, and variety of his "Works" do not conceal the fact that we seldom find him really working. He postpones the labor of the mind with such experienced grace, he veers away from it with such a veteran skill, as almost to persuade us that labor has been done; but one need only watch him closely for a typical page or two in order to see how prone he is merely to quote and paraphrase and remember when he ought to be thinking.

Another source of Lowell's failure may have been that incorrigible youthfulness which he, like many of his countrymen, seems to have mistaken for a virtue. "I continue as juvenile as ever," he wrote to his daughter at the age of sixty-nine. "I was passing a Home for Incurable Children the other day, and said to my companion, 'I shall go there one of these days.'" "Happy the young poet who has the saving fault of exuberance," said Lowell, "if he have also the shaping faculty that will sooner or later amend it." But Lowell himself never acquired that faculty. His intellectual life was not a development but a long vagrancy. His poetry shows nothing like the growth to be seen, for example, in that of Longfellow.

At the end of his life Lowell did not overestimate the value of his own verse, but he often saw and said, quite truly, that it contained "good bits," or "a good strain here and there." These were usually connected in some way with the vivid sensuous images he had gathered in childhood, before he had loaded his mind with other men's words or thought it necessary to be witty or wise or persuasive. Occasionally he has the courage to let these "invitiate firstlings" stand alone, as in "The First Snow-Fall," "To the Dandelion," "The Courtin'," and "Sunthin' in the Pastoral Line," and at such times he is likely to make a good poem. For the most part, however, he embeds them in oddly incongruous contexts. In "The Vision of Sir Launfal," surely one of the worst constructed poems in English, he foists upon a story about a medieval knight a lavish description of June in Massachusetts; and he begins his poem about the Cathedral of Chartres still more "doubtfully and far away" with a hundred admirable lines about his childhood in Cambridge.

The *Biglow Papers,* written from the Yankee point of view and partly in a carefully studied Yankee dialect, owe their unmistakable vitality and tang to Lowell's deep love of home. The poems of the two series are uneven in quality, and some of them, now that the once-burning issues they discuss are nearly forgotten, are positively dull. There is little poetry in them. Their rattling verse, though often clever, is in no way distinguished. The rustic dialect often seems to be overlaid, as a veneer, upon habits of thought and feeling that are by no means rustic. Yet the *Biglow Papers* have more life in them than most of Lowell's work in verse because they give free play to his learning, his humor, and that inveterate provincialism which he had in common with Holmes.

Most of Lowell's more ambitious poems are products of a nimble, well stored, but undisciplined mind in quest of a topic and a poetic emotion. His "Rhoecus" and "Columbus" and "Endymion" leave no definite impression. The "Agassiz," though warmer, is also more garrulous. "The Present Crisis," once widely popular and often quoted in American pulpits, is a noisy and platitudinous declamation which owes as much to Emerson's thought as it does in versification to Tennyson's "Locksley Hall." The famous "Commemoration Ode" is superb versified oratory designed for a solemn public occasion.

Lowell's prose at its best, as in his always admirable letters, has a sparkle and effervescence. Like the prose of Holmes, it has the virtues of excellent talk. Yet it lacks continuity, and the effect of steady purposeful march. Of his criticism there have been conflicting opinions. J. J. Reilly concludes a book on the subject with the statement that Lowell is not a critic at all. Norman Foerster asserts that he had "the sanest and most comprehensive conception of literature formed in America prior to the twentieth century." These two opinions do not necessarily contradict each other, for it takes more than a sane and comprehensive conception of literature to make a critic. Lowell's theory of literature was undoubtedly sound, but his practice of it in his own writing and in his estimates of other writers was spasmodic, impressionistic, and inconsistent.

Lowell's influence upon literary scholarship and criticism in America has been deep and pervasive, but it has not been the influence of a mind that reaches firm conclusions and renders consistent judgments in accord with them. It has been the influence of a sensitive and volatile temperament indulging itself in a lifelong intellectual vagabondage. In the sheer enjoyment of literature—hearty, robust, and, at any rate with regard to writers of the past, open-minded—Lowell has only such men as Lamb and Hazlitt for equals, and he has no superiors. His love of books was his nearest approach to a passion, and his devotion to them came nearer than any other of his enthusiasms to giving his life a shape and a focus. Moreover he did a great deal, by precept and example and by the contagion of his own delight, to spread the love of books in America. This was his main contribution to the task of "transplanting European culture." Thus, like Longfellow and Holmes, he did in his own way the indispensable work of all sound conservatism—conservation.

36. MINORITY REPORT: THE TRADITION OF THE OLD SOUTH

If the New England poets seemed to be engaged in a literary exercise when they borrowed an Old World glamour to cast over the American myth they were attempting to create, Southern writers seized upon the romance of feudalism with desperate seriousness in constructing their counter myth. As an earlier chapter has noted, the literature of the plantation South began in the 1830's as the expression of far-reaching changes in the Southern economy. The Industrial Revolution, creating an apparently limitless market for cotton in England and New England, had revived the declining institution of slavery, given fresh momentum to the expansion of the plantation system into the Southwestern interior, and transformed the South into one of the largest colonial areas yet seen in the world. The dominant note of these processes was rapidity of change. The whole history of that Old South which has survived in popular memory lasted only about thirty years before it was cut off by the outbreak of the war in 1861.

The literature of this society was evidently not allowed to reach fruition. Many of its impulses failed to develop beyond the stage of manifestoes and critical discussions. Furthermore, Southern writers were forced to struggle against a number of hampering influences, all of them noted by contemporary Southern critics. The most serious was the absence of cities that might have functioned as literary centers. If it is not quite true that the arts are a product of overcrowding, at least literature depends in modern times upon certain urban institutions—magazines, libraries, publishing houses. But the plantation economy of the South did not produce cities. This was a consequence of the colonial nature of that economy, which in another direction imposed upon the Southern writer a severe psychological handicap. No section of the United States had been able to develop enough self-confidence before 1820 to emerge from intellectual and literary dependence on Britain. In the South this state of affairs was indefinitely prolonged. Regardless of political forms, the region was a colony of Britain and of New England down to the Civil War. Jefferson Davis, in his First Inaugural, drew an explicit parallel between the position of the seceding Confederate States and that of the British colonies of 1776. One does not have to be a very energetic believer in economic causation to perceive

607

the relationship between the South's economic position and its dependence on British and Northern literature.

Another consequence of the structure of Southern society was the exclusion of a majority of its peoples from the ranks of potential readers of books and magazines. The slaves were excluded as a matter of course. In addition the meagerness of popular education in the South kept a large fraction of the white population illiterate. And the remaining potential audience, an often highly cultivated, aristocratic minority, had archaic tastes and was inclined to give the English classics preference over fumbling and uncertain writers like William Gilmore Simms who were trying to develop an American or a Southern literature. A writer in Hugh S. Legaré's *Southern Review* in 1831 deplored the growing evidence of a spirit of American literary nationalism, declaring, "We have no need of a separate literature." As for Southern writers, the critic was devastating:

The general feeling of aversion to authorship in the South, may be said to prevail, for the greater part, precisely in proportion to good education and cultivated taste.

To mention only one other difficulty in the path of the man of letters in the Old South, when he was given any encouragement at all he was usually exhorted to write according to a stated program. The critics who came to support the idea of a Southern literature made every effort to enlist the literary imagination in the service of a rigidly prescribed social goal—the defense of slavery, or at any rate of Southern society, against outside attack. While no important Southern writer rebelled against this imposed discipline —all of them, from Poe to Simms and John Esten Cooke, were defenders of slavery—one can at least guess that the steadily increasing sense of crisis and urgency, of the need to mobilize all forces to repel attack, interfered to some extent with free play of the imagination.

2

During the period 1830–1860, what were Southern writers able to achieve within these limitations? It can be said at once that the often demanded literary defense of the slave society was never adequately provided. When *Uncle Tom's Cabin* appeared in 1852, Southern critics winced. Here was no assault that could be met by analytical power or oratorical skill in the halls of Congress. The only defense, they realized, would be a comparable achievement on the plane of the imagination. But there was no Southern writer or school of writers capable of making this defense. The South lost the literary battle before actual hostilities began.

On the other hand, if the demand for a literary defense of slavery was not satisfied, Southern society between 1830 and 1860 did produce a far from negligible literature. Even more important was the fact that it set in motion certain trends which were pregnant with consequences for American literature and thought in later periods.

The most important literary achievement of the Old South was of course the work of Poe. The nightmare quality of Poe's recurrent symbols can be read—if one is so disposed—as testimony from the unconscious of a poet to the Southern sense of despair, of a lost battle and an imminent doom. Much of this quality proved capable of being transmitted to Europe, so that some imaginative energy originating in the experience of the Old South outlived the destruction of the slavery system as an element in French symbolism and its English and American consequences. Yet the work of Poe is not a finished achievement. In addition to its archaic strain of Gothicism and its cult of a rationalism derived from the Enlightenment but stripped of social implication, Poe's work shows a straining after effect, an ostentation of learning, in a word the touch of "vulgarity" noted by Aldous Huxley, that mark it as provincial.

The other permanently valuable literary achievement of the Old South makes a virtue of provincialism and vulgarity by pursuing them to their ultimate consequences in an intense localism of language, characters, and setting. The humor of the Old Southwest, product of the turbulent frontier of the cotton economy as it moved out into the Gulf plains of western Georgia and Alabama and Mississippi, overshadows the contemporary development of "Down East" humor both in imaginative power and in influence upon the future course of American literature. This frontier humor contained the germ of an American literary prose based upon the vernacular instead of upon a literary tradition. It likewise adumbrated the invention of local color literature after the Civil War. Most important of all, because embracing these impulses and going beyond them, was the contribution of Southwestern humor to a folk tradition destined to flower in Mark Twain. In assessing the potentialities latent in the Old South one must remember that Mark Twain grew up in a slaveholding community, that he served for a brief period in the Confederate Army, and that his greatest book, *Huckleberry Finn,* derives its central theme from slavery and is laid in slave territory. If Mark Twain meant to denounce the South, as at least on certain levels of his mind he did, his would not be the first instance of an artist formed by his gesture of protest against the society which produced him. It would probably be more discerning to see in him an ambivalence of attitude, a ferocious but artistically fruitful interplay of attraction and repulsion not unlike William Faulkner's attitude toward the South.

Except in a dozen poems of Poe, the vein of lyricism that runs through

Southern literature of this period is not often interesting. It produced a few poems that leave an odd impression of being happy incidents, yet the imposing presence of the sentimental Mrs. Hemans hovers everywhere over the scene. But in historical fiction the Southern achievement was more notable. The Southern disciples of Cooper include his principal American follower, William Gilmore Simms, and such epigoni as William Caruthers, John P. Kennedy, Philip Pendleton Cooke, and his better known brother John Esten Cooke. Indeed, the line of filiation that connects Cooper with the rebirth of historical romance near the end of the century in Maurice Thompson, Mary Johnston, and Winston Churchill is precisely this Southern succession. Cooper's adaptation of the Scott formula to American materials evidently had a special meaning for the South. For other regions Cooper was important because he discovered landscape and adventure in the American forest; for the South he was important because he discovered the past.

3

The best known early Southern novels in the Cooper tradition, such as Simms' and Kennedy's tales of the Revolution, were not markedly sectional in tone. Like the frontier, the Revolution was usually a national theme. The historical romance could not be made into an expression of sectional feeling unless some peculiarly Southern symbol could be discovered in the past. Such a symbol was the Virginia Cavalier. The development of the cult of the Cavalier on the plane of polemic discussion can be illustrated in the writings of Nathaniel Beverley Tucker, Professor of Law at William and Mary College, and one of the first generation of fire-eaters. When George Bancroft of Massachusetts began publishing his *History of the United States* in 1834, Tucker conceived the notion (a mistaken one, as it happened) that the historian had represented the seventeenth century Virginians as going over to the side of Parliament after the execution of Charles I. This seemed an intolerable insult, for Tucker took great pride in his ancestors' unswerving loyalty to the Stuarts.

There are those [he wrote] who will say that there is great arrogance in thus claiming for them a place among the generous and brave and faithful. Others will call it folly to insist, *at this day,* on their fidelity to a *king,* and especially to one who had lost all means of rewarding, or even of using their zeal.

But he demanded to be "allowed to speak of our fathers as they were." And the account of what they were is taut with meaning:

If we know anything (and we think we do) of the character of the early settlers of Virginia, they were a chivalrous and generous race, ever ready to resist the strong, to help the weak, to comfort the afflicted, and to lift up the fallen. In this spirit they had withstood the usurpation of Cromwell while resistance was practicable, and, when driven from their native country, they had bent their steps toward Virginia, as that part of the foreign dominions of England, where the spirit of loyalty was strongest. We learn from Holmes . . . that the population of Virginia increased about fifty per cent. during the troubles. The newcomers were loyalists, who were added to a population already loyal. Could *they,* without dishonor, have been hearty in favor of the new order of things? *They* whose principles had driven them into exile? *They* who, had they remained, would have fought and fallen with Montrose?

The bare facts were commonplace; Abiel Holmes of Cambridge, father of Oliver Wendell Holmes and author of *The Annals of America* to which Tucker refers, states that the increase in the population of Virginia from twenty to thirty thousand during the Civil War in England was due to the emigration of "cavaliers." But in Tucker's mind the fact has acquired portentous overtones. His Cavaliers are not merely chivalrous and generous; they are loyal with the crazy but pure loyalty of men devoted to a lost cause—perhaps for the precise reason that it is lost.

The character of the seventeenth century Cavalier is a crucial matter because it accounts for "those peculiarities which, at this moment, form the distinctive features of the Virginian character." The Virginian character is unique, and it is doomed:

How long it shall be before the *"march of mind,"* as it is called, in its Juggernaut car, shall pass over us, and crush and obliterate every trace of what our ancestors were, and what we ourselves have been, is hard to say. It may postpone that evil day, to resist any attempt to impress us with false notions of our early history, and the character of our ancestors.

It is important to keep in mind, finally, that the object of the Virginia Cavaliers' devotion was not intrinsically good:

None can feel more deeply than we do, how utterly unworthy of this steady and passionate loyalty, was the wretch who was its object. But they knew not his faults. They only knew him in his lineage and his misfortunes. . . . We are more proud to be descended from the men who stood forward in the business of that day, than we should be to trace ourselves to Adam, through all the most politic and prudent self-seekers that the world has ever seen.

The politic and prudent self-seekers are the New England descendants of the Cavaliers' Roundhead enemies, penny-pinching children of this world who will always triumph in their generation over the children of light. The Virginian's loyalty to the past, even though the past may be embodied in an indefensible institution like absolute monarchy (or slavery), isolates him in a modern world moving in a wrong course: the march of mind leaves him to one side and makes of him a more and more helpless minority. The Virginian's honor, in fact, reaches its full development and becomes entirely pure only as it binds him to a lost cause and a drooping banner. From this point of view, the economic prosperity of the North was simply a tradesmen's vulgarity.

Although Tucker's thought was centered in Virginia, the symbol of the Cavalier could easily be expanded to shed its glory on all the South. In 1843 an anonymous writer in the *Southern Literary Messenger* announced:

A chivalrous daring—a spirit that may break but never bend—an estimate placed upon individual honor which counts all else as dust in the balance—virtues, such as these, are the peculiar birthright of the Southern people. They hold them as a direct inheritance from that bold race of cavaliers who emigrated from all parts of Europe and settled in the Southern colonies. Nor have they been impaired in the transmission.

The myth of the Cavalier lent itself admirably to literary use through the historical romance; indeed, the suggestion has often been made that it was an outgrowth of historical fiction in the first place, especially the novels of Scott and Bulwer-Lytton, so that the adaptability of the symbol to literary use is hardly surprising. At any rate, the Virginia Cavalier makes his entrance into fiction in the 1830's, concurrently with the general antidemocratic revolution in Southern thought. The first historical romance exploring the theory of Cavalier origins was William Caruthers' *The Cavaliers of Virginia* (1834-1835), dealing with the period of Bacon's Rebellion, a determined but wooden effort to say through the mechanism of plot and characters what Tucker was saying through his expository treatment of seventeenth century history. Yet if the historical novel in the Cooper tradition gave ample scope for swashbuckling adventure in the remote past, it was not an ideal form for celebrating the virtues of a contemporary society based on slavery. The value to be defended was not physical courage or aristocratic swagger, but a system of social relationships—the pastoral bliss of an orderly feudal regime. To this end the sentimental tradition was much more efficacious. The mood of Irving had somehow to be incorporated into the narrative framework of Cooper.

The sentimental treatment of the Southern plantation, without the narrative framework of the historical romance, made its first significant appearance in Kennedy's loosely constructed, Irvingesque sketches grouped under the title

Swallow Barn (1832). Given some development by Tucker in his *George Balcombe* and *The Partisan Leader,* both published in 1836, and by Philip Pendleton Cooke, as in his novelette "The Two Country Houses" (1848), the theme of the social unit of the plantation comprising devoted slaves, gallant masters, and spirited heroines was ready for merging with the historical romance of adventure in John Esten Cooke's novels. In a single year, 1854, Cooke brought out three novels—*Leather Stocking and Silk* (with a "stalwart mountaineer," John Myers, "the living type of the old border past," as an explicit reference to Cooper), *The Virginia Comedians,* and *The Youth of Jefferson.* Stilted as these romances seem to a modern reader, they carried great conviction to an age accustomed to a constant seasoning of sentimentalism in its fiction, and above all they had a pointed relevance to the sectional tensions that dominated the public mind in the year of the Kansas and Nebraska Act. Cooke merely glances at the institution of slavery, but it is everywhere presupposed, whether the setting be eighteenth century Williamsburg or the Virginia back country a hundred years later; and the glimpses of it that we get always reveal happy, indolent slaves bound to their masters by the strongest ties of affection.

Cooke's career, bisected by the Civil War, carried the plantation formula on down into a period of intensified nostalgia when a new generation of Southern writers captained by Thomas Nelson Page found a national audience for fiction dreamily recounting the virtues of the institution of slavery which the nation had just spent four years of agony to destroy. A close examination of this paradoxical phenomenon will suggest the final contribution of the prewar Southern tradition to American literary and intellectual history. For the pleasure which readers in all sections during the seventies and eighties took in stories about a vanished Golden Age in the South seems almost certainly a reaction against the ugly adolescence of Big Business. The theme of the plantation embodied graces and social harmonies to which an urban industrial society could not aspire. Although the point was obscured in the sentimental haze of plantation fiction, the feudal and now defunct Old South had embodied the only serious challenge to the triumph of finance and industry in American society.

4

It was true, as antislavery propagandists declared, that slavery was an unendurable anachronism in the modern world, a wickedness outmoded for more than a thousand years. The affirmations of Southern social theory were of little consequence because they were exercises in rationalizing an indefensible institution. But the negations implicit in the Southern tradition were much more valid. The apologists for slavery called attention to weaknesses in the Northern position that were likely to go unnoticed precisely because they were a part of the dominant "march of mind." For Northern thinkers as well as Southern were victims of the sectional rivalry. Few of them could resist reading in the depravity of the South a contrasting virtue in their own section. If the issue was between slavery and free labor, and if slavery was wrong, then free labor was right. And free labor implied the entire system of industrial capitalism.

But was the Industrial Revolution indeed an unqualified blessing, the glittering goal of the march of mankind up from the jungle? The Southerners were prepared to say no. Reports of Parliamentary hearings on the appalling misery of British industrial workers during the thirties—which were to provide so much of the documentation for the denunciatory passages of Karl Marx's *Capital*—and the scattering accounts of comparable conditions in American cities published by pioneer philanthropists in the same decade threw a somber light on the outcome of industrialization. It was not yet time for an American to declare that progress brings poverty, but the most astute apologists for slavery were beginning as early as the forties to proclaim "the failure of free society."

On the other hand, they were far from being in agreement with the Northern reformers who were likewise pointing to the evil consequences of industrialism. Southern thinkers considered all Utopian schemes for social reform futile and dangerous. Horrible as the ills of free society might be, they could not be alleviated by the remedies proposed in philanthropic programs. George Fitzhugh, the Virginia lawyer who proved to be the most fertile Southern polemicist, perceived that when the reformers denounced industrial society in the name of the "sovereignty of the individual," they were but carrying to an extreme the ideas which the school of Adam Smith had taken over from John Locke. Their programs, however various, could be enacted only after they had "dissolved and disintegrated society, and reduced mankind to separate, independent, but conflicting monads, or human atoms." An argument similar to that of Fitzhugh's *Cannibals All! or, Slaves Without Masters* (1857) was directed especially against Herbert Spencer's *Social Statics*, by George Frederick Holmes in *DeBow's Review* of the same year. The Southern case against industrial capitalism rested on exactly opposite premises. In its most telling form it proclaimed an alternative to the anarchy of individualistic competition in an organic theory of society. This Aristotelian insight lay at the base of what was permanently interesting in Calhoun's political theory, as distinguished from his fantastic checks and balances. Fitzhugh, with the not always happy aid of Carlyle, fumbled toward it once or twice.

Man, and all other social and gregarious animals [he wrote], have a community of thought, of motions [sc. emotions?], instincts and intuitions. The social body is of itself a thinking, acting, sentient being. . . . The great error of modern philosophy is the ignorance or forgetfulness of this fact.

But the thinkers of the Old South did not carry through their repudiation of liberalism, perhaps because it constantly led them against their will toward the general position of the Utopians. After the Civil War, the leaders of Southern thought were even less inclined to challenge the business economy. In return for the tacit but important Northern surrender of the problem of the Negro to Southern handling, the New South group led by Henry W. Grady took over the doctrines of Northern capitalism and energetically set about industrializing the South. The ideas of most articulate Southerners became indistinguishable from those of official Republican spokesmen except for an occasional polite difference of opinion about the tariff.

The logic of Southern dissidence was nevertheless still there, and after the War it was acknowledged by some of the most perceptive minds that appeared in this country during the nineteenth century. In order to throw into relief the corrupt political practices of Senator Silas P. Ratcliffe of Illinois, "The Prairie Giant of Peonia," Henry Adams chooses as the hero of his novel *Democracy* (1880) John Carrington, a Virginian "of the old Washington school" and a veteran of the Confederate Army. Carrington exposes Ratcliffe to Mrs. Lightfoot Lee, the heroine, and at the end of the novel receives the author's stamp of approval by being designated as a probably successful suitor for Mrs. Lee's hand. It is clear that Adams found in the Southern tradition some support for his repudiation of the politics of postwar America. Henry James' *The Bostonians* (1886) also has a Southerner for a hero. Basil Ransom of Mississippi succeeds in rescuing the heroine Verena Tarrant from the "mediums, and spirit-rappers, and roaring radicals" who are the heirs of the New England tradition of social reform. The conservative Southerner's freedom from shallow fads masquerading as philanthropy is held up as a saving principle of health. The reformers of the second generation are, by implication, either frauds or neurotics.

Most interesting of all is Melville's use of the Southern point of view in his long narrative poem *Clarel* (1876). Through the lips of Ungar, "the clouded man," an expatriate and unreconstructed Southern soldier of fortune, the author utters the bitterest of his diatribes against American society in a period of "sordid mercenary sin." In turn Ungar denounces mill owners who destroy children for the sake of profits, social reform, the idea of democracy ("Arch strumpet of an impious age"), and universal suffrage. When another character urges technological advance as evidence of Progress, Ungar exclaims,

> Your arts advance in faith's decay:
> You are but drilling the new Hun.

In the future Ungar sees "a civic barbarism," with

> Man disennobled—brutalized
> By popular science—atheized
> Into a smatterer—

a "dead level of rank commonplace," "an Anglo-Saxon China" which

> May on your vast plains shame the race
> In the Dark Ages of Democracy.

Without raising the question whether a society based on Negro slavery would be preferable, one can readily acknowledge that Melville's Ungar is the intellectual heir of the Tuckers and Holmeses and Fitzhughs of the Old South.

5

The implications of the Southern tradition which Adams, James, and Melville perceived were phases of a minority protest—a suspicion of humanitarian enthusiasms, a revulsion from the practical politics of democracy, a skepticism concerning the outcome of scientific and technological "progress." Its affirmations—its concern for intellectual distinction and for a religious view of man—were not so fully worked out.

One of the first evidences that the tradition of the Old South was thus moving in postwar Southern writers themselves from a nostalgia for a lost era to a protest against an industrial economy appeared in the poems of Sidney Lanier, "Trade" and "The Symphony." Lanier reflected both aspects of the tradition, as well as the concern for technique that seems, in some unexplained way, to have been its constant by-product from Poe to the present. There were, however, too many romantic elements in Lanier's agrarianism to make it more than a portent.

The tradition as a mature cultural phenomenon came to the surface in the twentieth century in the Nashville Agrarians. The Agrarian movement had its inception soon after the First World War in a group of teachers and students associated with John Crowe Ransom at Vanderbilt University who called themselves "Fugitives" and devoted themselves to writing and discussing poetry. The Fugitives were not consciously sectional in their program, but several of them later became leaders in an effort to restore an economy of subsistence agriculture in the South as a means of escape from the ills of industrialism. Besides a manifesto published in 1930 under the title *I'll Take My Stand,* the Agrarians have written such books as Ransom's *God Without Thunder* (a critique of "liberal" Christianity), Allen Tate's *Reactionary Essays on Poetry and Ideas,* and Donald Davidson's *The Attack on Leviathan.* Although it is difficult to conceive of a Southern movement of any kind that is not in some way political, the Agrarians have found a much wider audience for their theories of literary criticism than for their political ideas. In the *Southern Review,* edited at Louisiana State University by Cleanth Brooks and Robert Penn Warren during the later 1930's, the Agrarian program for the South was overshadowed by a nonsectional concern with aesthetics, especially with the interpretation of "difficult" contemporary poetry. The *Southern Review's* successor, the *Kenyon Review,* edited by Ransom since 1939 at Kenyon College in Ohio, could not be called Southern in tone.

Although by the middle forties many of the Agrarians had left the South and were dispersed as teachers in colleges in the North, they and their allies had by that time published a body of writing which for its consistency of tone and intention is unique in American literature. In the novels of Robert Penn Warren and Caroline Gordon and in the poems of Tate, Warren, and Ransom, voices from the Old South are heard again eighty years after the surrender at Appomattox. If to the work of these writers is added the fiction of William Faulkner and Katherine Anne Porter and of a host of lesser figures, it becomes evident that the South too has had its literary renaissance, though it was long delayed.

37. HEARD FROM THE NEW WORLD

By the end of the Civil War most literate Americans were beginning to be aware of the fact that there was already in existence an American literature. There was no longer need for protestations of cultural independence or demand for the appearance of native authors. A cycle of literary growth, coincident with the rise of a Romantic Movement and deriving its chief inspiration from the matured civilization of the Atlantic seaboard, had reached the stage in which its authors were recognized for their intrinsic worth rather than merely as spokesmen for an experiment in political theory. The reputations of Irving and Cooper were secure. Hawthorne, who had died just before the war ended, had his first measure of fame. Emerson's followers were often idolaters. Even Poe, dead at forty in 1849, had ceased to be notorious and was beginning to look like a classic. It was evident, too, that the younger men—Longfellow, Holmes, and Lowell—were carrying on what had by now become a tradition. The niches in the pantheon of American authors were filling rapidly.

Certainly this sense of achievement and fulfillment was strengthened by the change of attitude toward American writing on the part of European critics, creative writers, and even the mass of readers. In the early part of the century European liberals who wished America well could only hope that some day the magnificence of our experience would find its poets and novelists. By the time of the Civil War their hope had been justified.

A library not yet written would be needed to contain the history of the reception and influence in Europe of the classics of nineteenth century American literature. Thus far European scholars have had more will and energy for the task than have English or American scholars. It is a story that involves both the excitement and the apprehension of Europe and England over our democratic experiment, and it goes beyond the world of letters into every world of the mind. Of the digesting of reviews and articles, of bibliographical inventory, of the influence of one author on another, we have much; but we must have more before coherent literary history can be written. Here an outline alone can be laid down, from the evidence thus far collected.

At the beginning of the century the European, however he might be engaged by the spectacle of the political experiment across the Atlantic, could feel little obligation to deal with American literature, for he found none— practically none—to deal with. The British critics were not alone in their denial of our possession of a literature. In Tocqueville, Chasles, and lesser commentators there persisted a graver speculation: perhaps a democracy, by definition, cannot produce a literature. Not, at any rate, until it achieves a society. America had thoughts for poetry, yes, but the poetry that America wrote was European.

Carlyle wrote to Emerson of the lean tough Yankee settlers steering over the Western mountains with unsubduable fire in their bellies, and every eager European critic felt the splendor of the American myth. If he were English, he was inclined to discount its possibilities for literature; if he were continental, he would deplore our Anglophile timidity, and remind us that until we should throw off our mother ties, we could have no hope for a literature of our own.

As has been said in an earlier chapter in this work, the great fact to the European was not what America wrote, but what America was. It was fixed in the general imagination as the land of great forests and mighty rivers where the Red Man still contended with the pioneer. It was also fixed, in Goethe's words, as "the Eldorado of all who found themselves restricted in their present circumstances." Brighter than the promise of romantic scenery was the promise of a decent life, lived in innocence and freedom. Was America's democracy workable? Could the dignity and worth of the common man find there its true chance for fruition, unblighted alike by political tyranny and the sharper tyranny of caste? This was the great question. It was not for beautiful letters that Europe looked to America; it was for a better life.

For this reason the books and pamphlets of the new country, the countless travelers' reports (more than three hundred from England alone up to 1860) the flooding stream of letters from emigrants, were scrutinized not as literature but as documentation. If Europe was done with, as Jefferson had thought, and America was indeed the symbol of freedom, then our derivative literature need not matter. This was a shortsighted view, and Emerson was not the first to see that the whole inner strength of a people is revealed in its imaginative genius; but in the beginning criticism was bound to turn to our political and social expression. Even Cooper declared that the only peculiarity of American literature was its distinctive political opinion, and that in taste and form English and American literature must be fashioned after the same models.

As political expression American literature received high praise from the time that Lord Chatham admired the papers of the American Congress of

October, 1774. Before the War of 1812, American histories, state papers, and congressional reports had good sales in England, and biographical studies of the founding fathers were eagerly sought. Washington and Franklin were Europe's heroes—the choice of Goethe, her greatest poet, and Sainte-Beuve, her most influential critic. Political judgment of course controlled the British magazines. The *Edinburgh Review,* brilliant and caustic, was actually less harsh toward American literature than toward more immediate targets at home. Its Tory rival, the *Quarterly Review,* like the *Anti-Jacobin* review and the *Literary Gazette,* deliberately baited all things democratic. *Blackwood's* and the *Athenaeum* were tolerant but patronizing, and the *Westminster Review* could be even extravagant in praise. Organs of the Established Church were stand-offish, and the dissenting journals were inclined to be friendly. Literary opinion was party opinion.

This is not to say that Europe and the mother country were wholly oblivious of a native literature. On the contrary. The Connecticut Wits who had set out to furnish it were rated in England beyond their strict desert. Joel Barlow's inflated *Columbiad* received respectful British reviews, and so did Timothy Dwight's *Conquest of Canaan,* although the English knew it to be feeble stuff. John Trumbull's *M'Fingal* had the best hand of all, as it deserved. Charles Brockden Brown won European praise early, the London edition of his works calling forth a good deal of talk about neglected American genius. Brown was an author's author. Percy and Mary Shelley fed on his romances, Keats praised him, Scott admitted his "wonderful powers," Hazlitt thought him a real genius. John Neal, American journalist extraordinary, creating his own "American literature" in his *Blackwood's* articles of 1824 and 1825, was proud to say that only Brown, Paulding, and himself were the genuine American article. A true forerunner of Hawthorne, Brown was read widely in Germany and France where his best work was recognized as "a conscientious study of the heart of man, of its mysterious raging, its resistless flights."

2

By the end of the War of 1812 American literature was already enough of an entity to pose the great question of its real existence, a question over which was to rage an unholy war whose fires were dampened but not extinguished in the burgeoning years from 1820 onward. It was largely England's war, not Europe's, for only a parent could take the issue so to heart. The English, alarmed alike by our competitive power and their own loss from emigration, were quick to impugn our nationalism, quick to see our almost morbid desire to have it confirmed. On our side the issue of a native literature at once became confused with the issue of patriotism. The quarrelsome aspects of the problem, with its jaded and tedious history of English abuse and American deference, need not detain us here. Across the Atlantic too much talk came from bookmen who had little information about America, and wanted none. In this country too much came from aroused patriots. Therefore most of it had nothing to do with genuine critical insight, which would have been concerned with the effect of the American experience upon imaginative expression.

The major documents in the case—Irving's "English Writers on America (1820), Bryant's "Lectures on Poetry" (1826), Channing's "On National Literature" (1830), Longfellow's "The Defence of Poetry" (1832), Emerson's *American Scholar* (1837), Melville's "Hawthorne and His Mosses" (1850), Thoreau's essays, Whitman's *Democratic Vistas* (1871), and the whole import of their other writings—are evidence that these men understood how vital it was to evaluate American literature in terms of the forces which shaped it at home. The writers of magnitude were nourished more by their differences from anything in Europe than by their similarities; and foreign influence upon them was powerful only as it accorded with native purpose. They could not but question what the European took as a matter of course, and instead of showing that American literature is only English literature written in America, their work shows that all influences which make the total experience of a nation must shape its expression.

They were in the current of the future, but against them were opposed powerful countercurrents. One was the persistent American nostalgia for the old European culture, for the institutions and forms of a traditional society with its high civilization and picturesque accompaniments. This adoration of the old was so plain in the pages of Irving and Willis that Englishmen were amused by the American worship of ways which they were passing by. In later years Howells spoke contemptuously of those American romancers who tried to be little Londoners. The little Londoners were rife in American cultural centers, especially in the colleges where American literature was largely ignored until the end of the century.

The copyright problem, of course, accentuated our dependence on the foreign market. One of Emerson's English friends remarked, "As long as you do not grant us copyright, we shall have the teaching of you"; and he was right, for the lack of an effective international agreement meant that not only the English rights of American authors were ignored, but the American market was flooded with pirated English books, many of them reprinted in cheap "mammoth" newspapers. In vain did both American and English authors protest. Under piracy the printers made money, and from them came the specious cry of free books for free men and the foolish charge that international copyright would turn the native business to foreign control. Not until 1891 was a comparatively decent copyright act written into American law.

Despite the injustice there were gains. American authors, injured in the book market by pirated English competition, turned to the American magazines, which not only developed the short story to a superb technique but became so stimulating that they were frankly imitated in England. Unquestionably, the international reputation of authors like Poe, Willis, and Longfellow was immeasurably increased by piracy, which also made possible the enormous traffic in English reprints of "cheap book" series of American authors by British publishers. The same story held true on a lesser scale in France, and in Germany where the Tauchnitz series swelled the account.

Irving was the first American author to interest all Europe. We are inclined to forget how powerfully he influenced his time, how he set in motion a whole school of imitators—Willis, Paulding, Longfellow, Kennedy, Cooke—but his contemporaries knew it, even those who, like Emerson and Poe, felt his limitations.

Salmagundi and *A History of New York* had delighted Coleridge, Byron, and Scott; but neither they nor Irving's other English readers were prepared for the spectacular success of *The Sketch Book,* which in 1820 precipitated the mood of an age. Samuel Rogers could cry, "Addison and water!" as Melville was later to cry, "An appendix to Goldsmith!" but Irving had really found a manner that was never to lose its adjustment to the popular response. The British were surprised that he could write so pure an English, and the Americans were proud that he did. *The Sketch Book* was the beginning of Irving's international reputation. John Murray, who had refused it, offered 1,200 guineas for its successor *Bracebridge Hall* (1822), and both books were quickly translated into French and German. Presently Irving found himself admired as a great man of letters in London, Dresden, and Paris.

Goethe read him although he preferred Cooper; Heine praised him, the Queen of Saxony hoped he would do a "Bracebridge Hall" for her own country. Irving hoped so, too, and tirelessly collected the legends which were to go into the *Tales of a Traveller* (1824). The Germans, who had regarded him as an English purveyor of English legends, were pleased that the *Tales* was allegedly indebted to Teutonic sources, but the English critics damned it so heartily for the same reason that Irving found little comfort in Murray's 1,500 guineas. The *Tales* was indeed a flawed performance, but now no single failure could halt the momentum of Irving's reputation. The *Collected Works* began to be edited in Frankfort by 1826, and in France the translations mounted steadily, thirty-eight separate editions being published by

1842. There were dissenting voices, of course—critics who thought he made the most of "a small talent and a small spirit." Nevertheless Irving was a standard author, and on European terms. This was his chief glory to many Americans, though not to Cooper, who thought him a sycophant.

In Spain, from whose history five of his books were to come, and where his skill as a diplomat was greatly respected, he had a surprisingly slight audience. *The Alhambra* (1832) did not appear in a complete Spanish version until 1888 although some of its tales, as well as adaptations from *The Sketch Book*, appeared in separate translations. Both *A History of the Life and Voyages of Columbus* (1828) and *The Conquest of Granada* (1829) were agreeably received, but the fact is that Irving's Spanish editions make a small showing, and Spanish knowledge of him came largely from French translations. The Spanish admired Irving, but they do not appear to have read him. Nevertheless, Irving has continued to live in all the European countries, even in Russia where his books have been popular since the Revolution.

Irving's European reputation began under English auspices and thrived on English prestige, but Cooper's began with the rejection of English imitation and disdain of foreign opinion. He resented the charge that his success at home was owed to his success abroad, and he resented even more the label of "The American Scott," which became a stereotype not only of English but of French, German, Spanish, and Italian critics as well. For six years he carried a chip on his shoulder through Europe, and when he returned it was still there. He was a social critic, who wanted Europe to know the characteristics of the American man, and America to know those of the gentleman. It was ironical, then, that his prodigious renown rested only upon the spell of his forests and prairies, his Indians and pioneers, but it was a powerful enchantment. From the first he appealed to the European as a great teller of tales, whose stylistic blemishes were lost in translation, and whose readers cared nothing for the opinions of critics.

When Cooper went to Europe in 1826 to get foreign rights for his books he was just in time. By 1829 all his first six novels had been published in England and translated into French and German as well as Italian, Danish, and Swedish. Four years later he was being marketed in thirty-four European cities. He was mighty on the Continent, but in England he ran into stormy weather. His honest *Notions of the Americans* (1828) pleased neither the English nor the Americans. Where Irving had been suave he was militant. He exulted that the American people cared no more for a lord than a woodchuck, and in his *Gleanings in Europe* (1837) he continued to offend. Despite the critics' war, Cooper never lost the regard of England's authors who, from Scott to Conrad, have praised his creative power. At least fifty editions of his work appeared in England in the last twenty years of the nineteenth century, and generations of English schoolboys have played Indian because they read Cooper.

In Germany his novels confirmed in young minds the romantic America of Chateaubriand. After *The Spy* and *The Pioneers* appeared in 1824, the translations multiplied until by 1850 there were more than a hundred, and a whole school of German novelists were influenced by him. In France there was the same ardent appreciation, especially from Balzac, and the mystery of Cooper's forests, the outlawry of his savages has been felt in the pages of Hugo, Dumas père, and many other French romancers. Although *The Bravo* (1831) was bitterly attacked in Italy as misrepresenting the tyranny of Venice, both this novel and others were read by Italians who took their knowledge of America from Cooper's stories. In Spain, where his novels were taken from French versions, he received little serious criticism, but he was read more widely than Poe. His full fame, arriving with the Madrid publication of *The Red Rover* in 1839, lasted for two decades. In Russia, where he was hailed by the powerful critic Belinsky in 1839, he has long been standard, thirty-two Russian editions appearing by 1927. To Russia, as to all Europe, Cooper's fame rests on his entrancing portrayal of a primeval America.

3

In mid-century, 1852, the fabulous reception of *Uncle Tom's Cabin* began in piracy and exploded into unequaled drama. Mrs. Stowe had herself prepared it by sending copies to England's great—Prince Albert, Dickens, Macaulay, Kingsley, and others—and kept it at top pitch by her triumphal tours abroad. One publisher among the forty who issued it in England estimated the aggregate English sales at a million and a half copies, most of them unauthorized. In fact, the book's phenomenal success inaugurated the bestseller era in England. British song writers flooded the market with tearful lyrics about slavery, and queues lined up at London theaters to see *Uncle Tom* dramatized—"Tom-mania," pronounced the *Spectator*. In England both *Uncle Tom* and *Dred* (1856), which sold 100,000 copies in four weeks, became arguments in the campaign for the emancipation of English labor that ended in the Reform Act of 1867. Even Mrs. Stowe's notorious attack on Lord Byron, the most widely discussed article in nineteenth century England, could not halt her march. She herself thought the French had a finer appreciation of her "subtle shades of meaning" than the English. And no wonder. George Sand dismissed the question of talent to call her a genius. Alfred de Musset cried, "This leaves us all behind—all, all, leagues behind!" Turgenev was charmed to meet her in Paris where *Uncle Tom* was serialized daily. At the same time a dozen other European countries were taking it up, and the exiled Heine avowed that he knelt with his black brother in prayer. From Sweden Fredrika Bremer wrote to Mrs. Stowe of its serialization in the Stockholm press. The authorized biography of Mrs. Stowe lists translations of *Uncle Tom* in twenty languages from Armenian to Welsh, omitting Hindu and Javanese which also exist. In Russia no other foreign book has enjoyed such a sympathetic audience as *Uncle Tom,* which first appeared in 1857, and has had many stage versions, including Communistic adaptations.

Mrs. Stowe moved the heart of Europe, but Emerson moved its mind. He knew that "the soul makes its own world," and his profound individualism absorbed whatever in European thinking confirmed his own faith. He had responded to the muscularity of seventeenth century English literature, and to Coleridge and Carlyle. He read Kant as early as 1820, Goethe in 1834, Böhme and Swedenborg by 1835, Jacobi, Schleiermacher, Schelling, Hegel, and Michelet in the thirties and forties. All these were voices to be listened to, but to be obeyed only at the soul's prompting. His own voice was demanding its listeners.

In England the listeners were at first the ardent younger men who had set forth or were about to set forth upon their own crusades: Carlyle, who through the long years could never forget the "clear high melody" of the American voice; Matthew Arnold, who heard the voice at Oxford, and who was to call the *Essays* the most important work done in prose during the century; Clough, who thought Emerson to be the only profound man in America; Froude, who credited Emerson with breaking from him the fetters of the church; John Sterling, to whom he was "the teacher of starry wisdom"; Spencer, who wanted Emerson's judgment on his philosophy; Tyndall, who avowed, "Whatever I have done the world owes to him." And there were others equal to the giants in their discipleship, such as George Searle Phillips, whose 1855 study of Emerson—*Emerson, his Life and Writings*—was the earliest in print, and Alexander Ireland of Edinburgh whose insistence brought on the famous tours of 1847 and 1848 that introduced Emerson to the English. In twenty-five towns Emerson lectured sixty-four times to audiences largely composed of the members of the Mechanics' Institutes. Along with the wealthier sponsors were the rank and file, the unprofessional people whose support was more significant than the fashionable following in London. In the long run Emerson's English reputation was solidly grounded among the dissenters—the Unitarians and the Reformists, who read him as sacred literature.

On the Continent Emerson's influence was felt from the time the Polish revolutionary poet Mickiewicz lent *Nature* in 1838 to the brilliant French historian Edgar Quinet; and when these two men, together with Michelet, began attacking Jesuitism at the Collège de France a few years later, they found in Emerson's principles a powerful ally. Mickiewicz also inspired the Countess d'Agoult, who published in July, 1846, the first French estimate entirely devoted to Emerson, although Chasles and Montégut were already discussing him in their reviews. A generation later another woman disciple, Marie Mali, who belonged to an advanced coterie in Brussels including Maeterlinck, Verhaeren, Verlaine, and Vielé-Griffin, initiated a Belgian vogue for Emerson. Her *Sept Essais d'Emerson* (1894), introduced by Maeterlinck, was a weapon against European pessimism. Emerson's power over French thought is widely dispersed—in the meditations of Amiel, in the creative philosophy of Bergson, in French liberal Protestantism, even in the desperate attempts of Baudelaire to find a guiding principle. Some of this influence carried over to Spain, where no editions of his work were published before 1900, but where he was read in French translation. The best Spanish criticism of Emerson belongs to the twentieth century, particularly Cebriá-Montoliu's introduction (1910) to the Catalan version of *Self-Reliance* and *Friendship*.

In Germany where Emerson was studied by many scholars his most loyal disciple was Hermann Grimm, his most influential was Friedrich Nietzsche. Grimm published an essay on Emerson six years after he first came upon the writings where he found his "own secret thoughts." There followed a warm correspondence between the two men, culminating in a meeting at Florence in 1873. Nietzsche, exiled at Pforta, came upon Emerson's essays in 1874, and, like Grimm, found thoughts he could not distinguish from his own—the gay wisdom of his own Zarathustra. Tolstoi felt Emerson's force in Russia, and from Indian leaders came testimony of the closeness of his thought to Hindu philosophy. The light from Concord had gone round the world.

Emerson traveled and lectured abroad; Thoreau, who traveled much in Concord, stayed at home. Nevertheless the light of his *Dial* essays and the later lectures was visible across the Atlantic, and *Walden* was to be often reprinted in England and translated abroad. Hawthorne rejoiced that it was one of the few works he could recommend to the English as having original American characteristics. The book became a bible of the English labor movement, deeply influencing Blatchford's *Merrie England* (1895), which sold two million copies; and Gandhi, a half-century after Thoreau's death, found his "Civil Disobedience" to be a weapon in his hand.

Foreign criticism rarely made Lowell's mistake of regarding Thoreau as a lesser Emerson. Tolstoi marked nearly every page of *Walden*; George Eliot found plenty of sturdy sense in his unworldliness; Stevenson, trying to reduce him to one word—"skulker"—confessed that he could scarcely write a sentence which would not show the influence of Thoreau; Froude saw in his pages hope for the coming world; and Thoreau's English biographer A. H. Japp could not but regard him as a sort of nineteenth century St. Francis. Yeats tells how his father's reading from *Walden* induced the boyhood dream of Innisfree, and in France Proust wrote of his admirable pages. It was an Englishman, Thoreau's friend Thomas Cholmondeley, who gave him his most valued gift from abroad, a library of Hindu classics, and another Englishman, H. S. Salt, who in 1890 published the first sound biography of Thoreau.

There were hostile gestures too. Thoreau was a strange bird to others besides Stevenson who, like Watts-Dunton, thought him as bizarre as Hawthorne's Donatello. Yet his strangeness and his strength alike have cut across boundaries in a way that his own time, not fully aware of his edge, could hardly predict; and it is not surprising to learn that, of all writers in English, Thoreau translates with least loss of value into Chinese.

No European critic of Hawthorne had the fiery penetration into his work of his own countryman, Melville, but both of them found perceptive readers abroad. To Europe Hawthorne has been from the beginning a man of high artistry whose prose has been analyzed with delight by minds as diverse as Arnold, Trollope, and George Moore. In the fifties he sold rather better in England than at home, his novels creating the high excitement there that the Brontës had aroused but a few years before. By 1851 five English editions of *Twice-Told Tales,* three of *The Scarlet Letter,* and two of *The House of the Seven Gables* had appeared. Only *Our Old Home* (1863) was to displease the English, a reaction surprising to Hawthorne, who thought his occasional sardonic reflections had not concealed an underlying affection. But abroad he was, like Cooper, a sensitive provincial who half resented the undeniable attraction of Europe. He was really never happy abroad, he especially distrusted the Italian scene, and his one novel about Europe, *The Marble Faun* (1860), while it sold better in England than in America, was felt to be a disappointment, though an admirable guide to Italy.

The French were also reading his stories in the fifties, one of them being plagiarized by the elder Dumas. Among early critics the most acute were Montégut, who felt Hawthorne's melancholy, and E. D. Forgues, who especially admired *The Scarlet Letter.* In him as in Poe the symbolists were later to find provocations to fantasy. The Spanish translated him early and enthusiastically, relying for once not on French hack work, but deriving their versions from Germany where *The Scarlet Letter* and *The House of the Seven Gables* appeared in 1851. For many years *The Wonder Book* has been read in the primary schools of Argentina and Chile; and it is also popular in Russia. Almost all of Hawthorne appeared in Russia in the ten years following 1852, and the evidence is clear that Dostoevski felt his influence as a great explorer of the conscience.

About Melville has grown the erroneous legend of a hostile reception both here and abroad. Actually *Typee* (1846) and *Omoo* (1847) were acclaimed in England as lively travel fiction; and when Melville went there in 1849, having published *Mardi* and *Redburn* and about to publish *White-Jacket,* he was entertained by the celebrities of the literary world. Only the sectarian journals had not liked *Typee* and *Omoo* because these tales had satirized the South Sea missionaries. *Mardi* troubled some of the critics with its allegorical thrusts at English imperialism, *White-Jacket* pleased nearly everybody, and so did *Redburn.* Across the channel Chasles and Forgues wrote of him in the *Revue des Deux Mondes.* Melville was being "typed" as a writer of adventure stories, and nobody was prepared for the monstrous apparition of *Moby-Dick.* In England it was called *The Whale,* and although the book was bowdlerized it was still monstrous. The critics on both sides of the Atlantic were dismayed, but of three friendly reviews one was English —the *London Leader* asking, "Who knows the terrors of the seas like Herman Melville?" But as Melville reached the height of his powers, the critics fell away. With the affronting *Pierre* (1852) his following disappeared, and he was never to know its inevitable return, although he continued to have a subterranean reputation among discriminating readers.

On the Continent Melville had been neglected, the first full study of him in a foreign language—K. H. Sundermann's *Herman Melvilles Gedankengut* —not appearing until 1937. But in England, as more belatedly in this country, his genius has demanded its followers, who have passed their discovery on to others. In this way, he has been sought and praised by a company of English admirers whose words are worth seeking out: Thomson, Morris, Salt, Dobell, Birrell, Lucas, Forster, Tomlinson, Meynell, Woolf—others. Melville's Pierre had learned that mediocrity and commonplace "hath its fire and sword for all contemporary Grandeur." Melville was in this respect Pierre, but time has revenged him.

4

Melville was a candidate for the future. Not so Longfellow, who was the poet—in Whitman's words—of the mellow twilight of the past in Italy, Germany, Spain, and northern Europe. New England's other bards—Lowell, with his immense prestige in the fashionable world; Holmes, who shared with Lowell first honors as a transatlantic wit; Whittier, who followed next in English popularity; and Bryant, whom Irving introduced to Englishmen as belonging to the best school of English poetry—had their strong roots in English affection, but Longfellow's following was incomparable.

The statistics are staggering: more than seventy British publishers, largely piratical, nearly three hundred editions in England alone in the second half of the century, at least a hundred separate book translations into eighteen different languages by 1900, and in Latin America at least eighty-seven of his poems in one hundred seventy-four separate versions by fifty-three translators. He surpassed Tennyson as the household laureate; and *Evangeline* (1847), *The Golden Legend* (1851), *Hiawatha* (1855), and *Miles Standish* (1858) became the common property of Englishmen everywhere, from the British Isles to the Antipodes. English criticism was polite before this phenomenon—more polite than Poe and Margaret Fuller in America. But his faults did not go unnoticed. Lockhart, the Rossettis, the Earl of Lytton, Harrison, and Swinburne, among others, complained of his didacticism, his sentimentality, his lack of original force. Trollope admitted that of the poets of the day he was "the last that I should have guessed to be an American." None of them denied his skill. The last word was with the general reader who, after all, was responsible for the Oxford and Cambridge degrees and the bust in Poets' Corner.

On the Continent his popularity was unmatched—even by Poe. In France his poems, especially *Evangeline,* were widely dispersed. In the northern countries he was a favorite—"Tell him," the word came, "that Iceland knows him by heart." In Spain where his books came untouched by French influence, both from Spanish America and directly from the United States, he was more influential than Poe, who was regarded mainly as a story-teller. In Italy his foreign editions outnumbered those of France. But Germany took him over as a German poet. There his works went into more editions than anywhere else in Europe, except England. The poet Freiligrath, with whom Longfellow corresponded affectionately after their first meeting in 1842, assured him that his German popularity increased daily. "There is no anthology in which you are not plundered to an excess." Freiligrath translated *Hiawatha* in 1858, a year after Elise von Hohenhausen had translated *The Golden Legend*; and many other translators followed suit. In Russia, where with Mark Twain and Cooper, Longfellow has long been standard, Ivan Bunin has transposed his *Hiawatha* with great distinction. In Latin America Longfellow, at the height of his vogue between 1870 and 1900, is now slowly losing ground to Poe and Whitman. He remains the poet of the common reader, for whom he made a legendary past.

Longfellow's gift is an inheritance, but Poe and Whitman provided a working capital of such potential that the history of their influence is still largely unwritten. Only the barest outlines can be indicated here. Of our poets they are the most seminal because both had innovating genius, and both thought through and announced the principles from which grew their practice.

Much European criticism of Poe is affected by half-truths—that his genius was independent of his environment, and that he died unappreciated. Actually, he was a skilled professional in the current of his time, alive to events, and drawing on the Gothic fashion to not inconsiderable applause. Griswold's slander confirmed error, and "genius allied to vice" was a common British formula for Poe before John Ingram rehabilitated him with his admirable biography of 1880, preceded by the faithful editing of his works.

Nevertheless the praise of English writers was early and unstinted. Swinburne delighted in his "short, exquisite music"; Lang pronounced him America's greatest literary genius; Tennyson thought him to be our most original writer; the Rossettis recited him; Stevenson, Conan Doyle, and others reflected him in their fiction; George Bernard Shaw, characteristically, expressed amazement that America could produce him; and with the Poe Centennial of 1909 the British voice was heard in full chorus, "We offer tribute to one of the great artists of the English language."

But France has taken Poe for one of her own ever since Baudelaire found in him the enchanted mirror of his own daemon. In a remarkable essay published in 1852 and revised to preface his translations *Histoires extraordinaires* (1856) and *Nouvelles Histoires* (1857), Baudelaire, excoriating the gaslighted barbarity of America, saluted the neglected genius who "writes for our nerves." Thus he set a pattern—genius amid neglect—which, while it did not affect the judgment of Taine or Sainte-Beuve, was taken over by many critics, including d'Aurevilly and Villiers de L'Isle-Adam. Baudelaire's sensual genius was not, after all, Poe's, and it is often forgotten that before his powerful identification, E. D. Forgues had already (1846) subjected Poe's work to penetrating analysis. Poe's logic attracted Forgues, and it is the logic of Poe, more than any other quality, which accounts for his French prestige. The Parnassians adopted his brilliant theorizing in aesthetics; the decadents and the surrealists found in Poe what they were looking for—the night side of the mind; and the symbolists studied his power of rhythmic suggestion. Mallarmé's adaptations of Poe's "Raven" and other poems have greatly stimulated French experimentation in free verse. The French have never regarded Poe as a jingle man.

It is impossible here even to indicate the scores of French writers who have been drawn to Poe, or to trace the influence evident in Baudelaire, Verlaine, Rimbaud, Villiers de L'Isle-Adam, Huysmans, Schwob, Maeterlinck, Valéry, and others. The problem is under constant review, and Poe has commanded brilliant criticism in recent years from men like Lauvrière, Lemonnier, and Mauclair. Even before the end of the century nearly fifty critical studies of Poe came from France.

Baudelaire's translations were the chief means of introducing him to Spain, where in 1858 they excited the novelist Alarcón, who wrote an essay full of enthusiasm and misinformation. Spanish interest in Poe, mounting with the modernist movement, has not abated, but in Spanish America, where the lyrics are preferred to the tales, Poe's influence has been more profound than in the mother country. The Spanish-American poets—among them Bonalde, Díaz, Darío, Silva, and Nervo—have devotedly translated him. Still awaiting full study is his influence upon such important Spanish writers as Villaespesa, Carrere, and Baroja.

In Germany Baudelaire also served as Poe's intermediary for readers who found in him the macabre vein they loved in Hoffmann. The novelist Spielhagen pondered his structural principles, Elise von Hohenhausen, Strodtmann, and others translated him, and "The Raven" was almost as popular in Germany as in France. The Russians read Poe by the late 1830's, long before he was taken up in France. Dostoevski called attention to the psychological penetration of his tales in his magazine *Wremia* (1861), and the Poe influence is manifest in *Crime and Punishment,* as it is also in the work of Chekhov and Andreev, who knew Poe and studied his technique. But Poe's foremost spokesman in Russia has been the poet Balmont, who began translating the complete works in 1906, and whose ardent but uncritical praise has played in Russia the Baudelairean role.

5

In foreign regard the name of Poe has meant craftsmanship, the name of Whitman has meant a message. To Europe Whitman is a symbol, even a myth, and the myth consists both in the projection of himself, the lover and encourager, and in the dream of man's brotherhood. In avowing him to be the prophet of man's aspiration toward a better society, the testimony of foreign criticism is overwhelming. His "literary" performance has abundant recognition, its skill and power affirmed by the poets from Swinburne to Hopkins and Lawrence and his prosody elaborately analyzed by scholars like Jannaccone in Italy and Bazalgette and Catel in France, but it is his redeeming force, a religious more than an aesthetic ascendancy, that is insistent in Whitman criticism.

Not even the outlines of his story abroad can find room here; but when it is written it must embrace the whole theme of the interaction of European and American thought, for Whitman's origins are in Europe as well as in America, and Europe's hopes are found in him. It is not yet a story of the great audience Whitman had adumbrated, but of scholars, intellectuals, and poets drawn by a genius too baffling for the common reader. In Europe Whitman became a classic, not a best seller. Yet this truth needs qualification, for his following was unconventional and dispersed.

His English reception, often cited to American disadvantage, glittered with the names of Dowden, Rossetti, Symonds, Buchanan, Rhys, Saintsbury, Ellis, Carpenter, but he was also a "penny poet" in England, available in cheap reprint and influential among Blatchford's labor disciples and the fellowship groups of industrial centers. In Germany, where Freiligrath discovered Whitman in 1868, translating rather ineptly from the Rossetti edition, many scholars and poets spread his word, most notably Johannes Schlaf (1907, 1919), who became the center of a Whitman cult, and Hans Reisiger (1922), for whose admirable translation Thomas Mann expressed his gratitude. But here too, as in England, Whitman has been the inspirer of the dispossessed and the ardent young—such worker-poets as Engelke, who fell in the First World War, Bröger, Grisar, and Lersch.

In France early criticism of Whitman was mistrustful until the symbolists—La Forgue, Vielé-Griffin, Mallarmé, and others—began to translate and make available the accurate text of *Leaves of Grass* as an innovating experiment in form. Closer to Whitman's own emphasis was Bazalgette's influential biography of 1908, followed in 1909 by his translation (of which Gide was critical), and in 1921 by his analytic study. To Bazalgette Whitman was an evangelist, and his discipleship affected the earnest group known as the Abbaye—Romains, Vildrac, Duhamel, and others for whom Whitman became the poet of the new age. French soldiers took *Leaves of Grass* into the trenches; in 1926 a "Comité Walt Whitman" was founded; and such later interpretation as Catel's psychoanalytic study of Whitman's personality and his "vocal style" has strengthened a recognition which finally eclipsed that of Poe.

In Russia Whitman was frankly turned to Soviet doctrine, the Moscow poet Chukovsky's translation of *Leaves of Grass* reaching a sixth edition by 1923. After the Revolution his poems honoring "humanity" and the "machine" were declaimed all over the country, and such class-conscious poets as Mayakovsky, Meyerhof, and Gastev own his kinship. In earlier days Turgenev had thought of translating him, Tolstoy deemed it necessary to criticize his lack of clarity, the poet Balmont translated him in a mood of mystic ecstasy, misinformed biographical sketches appeared in the press, and Chukovsky's own first translations were censored by the police. His influence spread irresistibly, and carried over to Hungary where Pasztor, Gaspar, and others translated him, and such poets as Kosztolányi, Babits, and Margit Kaffka were affected by him.

The mounting list of Whitman's partisans may not even be sketched here —merely instanced: Jensen and Schyberg in Denmark; Gamberale, Jannaconne, Praz, and Nencioni in Italy; Mann and Werfel in Germany; Verhaeren in Belgium; Brossa, Guerra, and Cebriá-Montoliu in Spain; Darío in Spanish America. Like Thoreau's *Walden* and Emerson's *Essays,* Whitman's word has been procreant in the Orient—in India, China, and especially Japan, where *Leaves of Grass* has been regarded as a text of Western democracy. It may be, as Whitman hoped, that he will reach, more than any other American poet, to "the bulk-people of all lands."

6

At Whitman's own urgency Europeans had made a mythic figure of him— a bearded divinity, compelling and resolute, who, if not representatively American, was what America ought to produce. Something of the same expectancy was operative in the foreign reputation of the Western writers who emerged after the Civil War: Artemus Ward, Miller, Harte, Bierce, and —above all—Mark Twain. Their "aura" was theatrical and flamboyant, as befitted travelers from a region of fantasy; and they were all indiscriminately assigned to the tradition of humorous exaggeration which went back to the early coon songs and yokel buffoonery of the comedian Charles Mathews, to Haliburton's Sam Slick, to Davy Crockett's exploits, to countless pirated collections of Yankee drolleries, and on to the *Biglow Papers* of Lowell, the wit of Holmes, and Leland's Hans Breitmann.

The list is partial: the point is that when Artemus Ward faced his first London audience on the night of November 13, 1866, it expected the kind of performance it got. All England was being flooded with Western humor by enterprising publishers, chief of whom was the pirate Hotten who issued all of Ward he could steal, one compilation selling 250,000 copies. The English loved Ward's gentle absurdity, the highly personal art that shone from his letters to *Punch,* and the wonderful lectures that wore out his brief life. They were also taken, the fashionable world in particular, with the red shirt and gusty verse of Joaquin Miller (*Pacific Poems,* 1871, *Songs of the Sierras,* 1871, *Songs of the Sun-Lands,* 1873), whose appeal was elemental—and brief. Upon his final visit in 1878, England, whom Miller had publicly thanked for her noble treatment, turned a cold shoulder. Ambrose Bierce, who hated humor, enjoyed repute as a wit and raconteur during five London years (1872–1877) as a journalist and staff writer for Hood's *Fun.* His first three books, all published in England, won praise, even from so important a man as Gladstone, but Bierce needed better criticism than his Fleet Street confreres could give him. His Western air suffered a sea change in London, acquiring a Tory cast.

Bret Harte's triumphal progress eastward upon the phenomenal success of "The Luck of Roaring Camp," "The Outcasts of Poker Flat," "The Heathen Chinee" was marked in England as the emergence of a new trans-atlantic genius. Hotten's pirated edition of his works sold heavily, and when Harte later turned up in England (1879), his American prospects fallen away, he found a ready audience whose interest in his performance lasted until death ended his exile in 1902. "England never got tired of that lariat," said Aldrich. Harte thought he could say some new things of England, but he never did. He remained to the English a mercurial and puzzling fellow who could combine sentiment and humor in the right proportion. In Germany, where Harte had been consul at Crefeld in 1878, his vogue was extraordinary; and it was the conspicuous success of the German edition of *Tales of the Argonauts* (1873) that persuaded Harte's Leipzig publisher to chance the first publication of Mark Twain. Up to the end of the century Harte's German editions actually outnumbered those of his great compatriot.

Mark Twain went to England in the summer of 1872 with two purposes: to protect his copyright, and to deal as freely with English manners and customs as the "Innocent" had dealt with Europe. He assailed Hotten satisfyingly enough, but his second purpose, which had been common talk among the English themselves, was never achieved. Why? His own answer was that he could not write critically of people whose hospitality he had accepted, an excuse that had deterred neither Emerson nor Hawthorne. The real answer seems to be that his immense success in England—the endless sales of his books, the crowded lectures, the innumerable occasions when his wit played across the festal board, the friendships with England's great, the impressive honors culminating in the Oxford degree—forced him inevitably into the role of international jester. More than this, he fitted with consummate grace into the role of unofficial ambassador to England from America.

It was a great service he performed because he had the gift of remaining himself, of actually being what he seemed to be. His experience abroad simply confirmed and accentuated his national characteristics because he carried with him, as one critic said, the same habits of life that sufficed him in Connecticut. Yet the discerning were uneasy that he should play the amiable part merely. Men like Bernard Shaw and Thomas Hardy saw in him more than the entertainer; they saw his kinship with Cervantes and Swift. Had they seen his notebooks they would have been reassured, for here his private rages, his resentment against the hypocrisies of hereditary privilege, boiled over. But publicly Mark Twain tilted only against England's medieval institutions— as in *A Connecticut Yankee in King Arthur's Court* (1889), which was criticism in motley. The English public did not like the *Yankee,* but it liked nearly everything else of Mark Twain's, tending, like the American public, to praise most what most complied with conventional taste.

All over the world Mark Twain's "place" was that of public entertainer. He had always hunted, he told Lang, for bigger game, for the masses; and to the masses everywhere he became a legend. In Germany, where his popularity, associated with Harte's, was cultivated by the publishers' campaigns of the seventies, interest in him was enormously stimulated by his personal appearances. Mark Twain's translations in Germany have sold beyond the million; in Soviet Russia they have sold beyond three million; in Spanish America he is still the most popular American author. To these millions of readers he has, it may be guessed, passed into the province of children's literature. Has he, then, in foreign judgment, lost interest for mature minds? Not so. In the year of Mark Twain's death the Danish critic Johannes von Jensen called for a more serious interpretation of his genius. German criticism has stressed his value as a symbol of American vitality; Schönemann, his most thorough continental appraiser, has protested against the injustice of regarding him as a humorist merely; and the Swedish Liljegren has stressed his anti-romanticism. In its estimate of the democratic tradition Europe will always have Mark Twain to deal with.

7

By the turn of the new century the actuality of American literature was not a question to Europe but a portent. From America the Atlantic bore a vast freight of popular literature, of which this brief survey has taken no account —the stories of Louisa Alcott, Frank Stockton, Thomas Bailey Aldrich, Susan Warner, Elizabeth Phelps, E. P. Roe, Marion Crawford, many others. It bore, amid the flood of sentimental romance, the more distinctive art of the regionalists—not alone the robustious stuff of the Western school but the richly diverse materials of Mary Murfree in Tennessee, Sarah Orne Jewett and Mary Wilkins Freeman in New England, George W. Cable in New Orleans, Hamlin Garland in the Middle Border, Joel Chandler Harris in Georgia, Edward Eggleston in Indiana. It bore, too, the quickening social vision of Henry George and Edward Bellamy.

In the nineties England became conscious of a new wave of American literary migration. Henry James, of course, had been settled there since 1876, absorbed in the fine art whose "international style" would never obscure its American center. Both James and Howells, who stayed at home, were published in England and disseminated abroad by Tauchnitz and others. Their studious realism, committed to a contained and well mannered world, was shaded by the light of their bolder followers—Harold Frederic, whose *Damnation of Theron Ware* (published in England as *Illumination* in 1896) was a sensation; Stephen Crane, whose *Red Badge of Courage* (1895) seemed to younger writers like Wells and Conrad to herald a new genius quite free of the English tradition; and Frank Norris, whose *McTeague* (1899) prefigured the rude strength of Dreiser and London.

Thus, in spite of some European and English recognition of American writers as artists, American literature was interesting to Europe and England throughout the nineteenth century mainly as the voice and character of democratic man, and its wide popularity seems to have been a reflection of curiosity about a new way of life rather than about a new art. With the vogue of Henry James, America began to seem, in European eyes, capable of teaching something about art itself. But that is another story, and one which cannot be told until the literature of the continental nation has come under full review.

EXPANSION

. . . new perspectives

38. THE WIDENING OF HORIZONS

AMERICAN literature to the end of the Civil War, the literature of the First Republic, presents a pattern of growth, maturity, and decline. By the seventies the Golden Day was dwindling to the mild glow of the Chautauqua Institution; and although the official standards of culture and "ideality" remained ostensibly dominant to the very end of the century, they came to seem more and more irrelevant in the face of the violent, crude, and formless energies generated by American society—in the westward movement across the continent, the development of mechanized industry, the attraction of immigrants from every corner of Europe.

The First Republic had been agrarian, with a few scattered commercial centers; the Second Republic, that was created by the Civil War, was focused on an industrial economy moving rapidly toward integration. The First Republic had been a relatively unimportant member of the community of nations occupying the shores of the North Atlantic basin. The Second Republic was different in scale and in geographical orientation; by 1900 it had emerged as a major world power and was on the point of becoming a First American Empire, dominant in the Caribbean and expanding into the Pacific.

If the transforming forces of the nineteenth century destroyed the tradition on which the First Republic had been based, at the same time they widened cultural horizons and laid the foundations for a new flowering of American literature in the twentieth century. It will therefore be expedient to depart from chronology at this point in our survey in order to glance at some of the expansive influences that were brought to bear upon the American people.

The famous portrait of American society in 1800 which opens Henry Adams' *History of the United States During the Administrations of Jefferson and Madison* emphasizes the conservatism and inertia which were all but universal. The South had of course produced its statesmen, but despite the influence of Jefferson interest in science and letters had declined since the time of William Byrd. New England was dominated by an alliance of clergy and magistrates who feared nothing so much as new ideas. "From 1790 to 1820," asserted Emerson, "there was not a book, a speech, a conversation, or a thought" in Massachusetts. Even in Philadelphia, which in Franklin's time had been the most enlightened and tolerant city in America, Joseph Dennie's *Port Folio* devoted most of its efforts to reproducing the attitudes of England a generation before. Among American men of letters, Philip Freneau, Charles Brockden Brown, and Hugh Henry Brackenridge indicated that some fresh viewpoints were struggling against convention; but they were isolated and on the whole ineffectual figures. The dominant tradition was one of provincial narrowness and sterile intellectual orthodoxy.

2

Yet forces were already at work that were destined to revolutionize American society. The first of these to make itself felt was physical expansion. Even before the Revolution, the frontier of settlement had begun to press against the Appalachian barrier. With the end of hostilities the first great wave of westward migration began to pour through the Cumberland Gap. Kentucky, with one hundred thousand inhabitants, was admitted to the Union in 1792. In 1820 there were three million people west of the mountains, and the frontier had crossed the Mississippi to advance two hundred miles up the Missouri. By 1848 the frontiersmen had pushed all the way to the Pacific Coast, occupying Texas and Oregon in their stride, and had rounded out substantially the present boundaries of the United States.

In the vast area between the Appalachians and the Pacific there appeared, as the frontier advanced, a society with fewer ties to bind it to the mother country. The Westerner, as contemporary observers described him, was restless, enterprising, and devoted to money-making. He had a pathetic desire for culture, in the abstract, coupled with a scarcely veiled contempt for impractical and effete representatives of older civilizations. He considered himself aggressively democratic, but his democracy often took the form of a refusal to acknowledge superiority of any kind. Eastern observers called Westerners barbarians; and from a certain point of view the charge was justified, for despite the efforts of pioneer men of letters in rising centers like Lexington and Cincinnati the West had lost contact with the cultural tradition of Europe and had not yet developed a civilization of its own. Yet it was the West that held the balance of power in the sharpening contest between North and South. In Jackson and Lincoln it furnished the only strong Presidents between the gentlemen of the Virginia dynasty and Grover Cleveland.

When the pioneer reached the end of the Overland Trail on the Pacific, he found that numerous other Americans had been there before him. Fur traders had come by sea to the Puget Sound area before 1800, and the droghers, or hide-trading ships, on one of which Richard Henry Dana sailed before the mast, had frequented the California coast in the twenties and thirties. As soon as the establishment of independence freed American mariners from the restrictions of the monopoly granted by Britain to the East India Company, they had set out for the Orient. *The Empress of China,* of New York registry, anchored off Macao in 1784. By 1790 the *Columbia,* of Boston, had explored the Northwest Coast, discovered the river that bears the ship's name, and begun the development of a complicated but profitable trade route from Atlantic ports around Cape Horn to Puget Sound, thence by way of the Sandwich Islands to Canton and home by way of the Cape of Good Hope.

Overseas trade charted paths which missionaries soon followed. The American Board of Commissioners for Foreign Missions began its work in Bombay in 1812 and in Ceylon in 1816. By 1840 it was maintaining 283 foreign missionaries, including some fifty in twenty-nine Oriental stations, from Bombay to Macao. These evangelists showed little interest in the civilization of the Far East, but they did set about learning the Oriental languages so that they might translate the Scriptures into the speech of their mission congregations. The joint effect of commercial and religious activity in the Orient was to keep at least a fraction of the American people aware of the strange and remote countries beyond the western sea.

American familiarity with the Pacific was also increased by the whale fishery. Many seamen followed the missionaries into the islands of Polynesia and Melanesia, and by the forties Melville was able to draw upon an extensive literature of Pacific travel and exploration in his *Typee* and *Omoo.* The needs of the whaling industry led in 1838 to the United States Exploring Expedition under the command of Charles Wilkes, U.S.N., which touched at Tahiti, Samoa, and Australia, engaged in Antarctic exploration, and visited the Oregon coast before returning home by way of the Philippines, Singapore, and Capetown. The acquisition of Oregon and California intensified the desire for the development of trade with the Orient and dictated the series of efforts to penetrate Japan which culminated in the Perry expedition of 1852–1854 and its commercial treaty. But the fifties represented a peak of interest in the Orient which was not reached again until 1898. The Civil War, the decline of the American merchant marine, and the absorption of the nation's energies in the West and in industrialization led to almost complete neglect of the far Pacific.

The decades following the war were, in fact, a period of introspection, during which the reunited nation seemed to be taking account of itself. For the national reading public, there were two domestic frontiers to be explored—not only the Trans-Mississippi, which was going through its greatest boom in the seventies, but also the South, which had been isolated from the North during the bitter decades of antislavery agitation and was now for the first time opened up to the forces making for economic and social integration under Northern leadership. The discovery of the South by hundreds of thousands of soldiers in the invading Union armies was reflected both in the popularity of factual narratives like Edward King's *The Great South* (serialized in *Scribner's* with numerous illustrations in 1874) and in the surprising Northern vogue of fiction and poetry elaborating the myth of the Southern plantation.

3

Even more important than expanding frontiers in transforming American society and altering perspectives were the related phenomena of industrialization, the rise of great cities, and immigration. Beginning with the use of steam power in transportation and manufacturing, which reached a significant scale in the thirties, the technological revolution went forward at a rate never before equaled. By the sixties, when the Atlantic cable was put into commercial operation, the characteristic rhythms of modern life were established: mass production of basic commodities, instant transmission of news, rapid and relatively cheap transportation on land or water.

The swiftly developing economy of the United States drew across the Atlantic millions of European peasants and artisans who saw in the New World a Utopian hope of economic betterment. During the first half of the nineteenth century the principal European immigration came from distressed Ireland and the Rhine provinces of Germany. By 1840 Irish peasants were crowding into Boston cellars and displacing the farmers' daughters who had made up the first labor force of the New England textile mills. The slum as a constant feature of urban society quickly came to seem inseparable from the idea of the immigrant. Faced with conditions having no precedent in the United States, leaders like Theodore Parker were forced to improvise or to adapt from British experience the modern techniques of case work and social service.

The German immigrants before the Civil War tended to move toward the Middle West, where they gathered in the growing cities, or, more often, bought out the improvements of American pioneer settlers and established compact, stolid, hard-working farm communities. Many of them, proud of the culture of their homeland, sought to preserve it in the New World through German-language schools and periodicals; and in the Midwestern cities they established beer gardens, *Turnvereine, Männerchore,* chamber-music societies, and even an occasional symphony orchestra. Another illustration of German influence in the West was the group of Hegelian philosophers who founded the *Journal of Speculative Philosophy* in St. Louis in 1867.

During the early decades of the century, Americans were usually proud to conceive of the Republic as a haven of refuge for the oppressed subjects of European monarchs. This attitude bore some relation to the chronic shortage of labor; it was especially marked in the West. In 1839, for example, the *Hesperian* (of Columbus, Ohio) proclaimed that "the gates of our entrance are never shut against the stranger and the foreigner; but stand wide open forever for the persecuted of every nation and tongue under heaven." Yet even as the West was welcoming foreign immigrants, the crowding of the Irish into cities of the Atlantic seaboard had begun to arouse opposition to them. Hostility to the Irish was increased by religious differences: the Know-Nothings, who advocated restrictions on the naturalization of immigrants, charged that the Pope was conspiring with the House of Hapsburg to overthrow American republicanism. Furthermore, the fact that, both before and after the Civil War, most immigrants settled in the North and West led Southerners to include the immigrant in their condemnation of Northern society.

Know-Nothingism disappeared as a political force in the realignment of the fifties, and eventually the rural immigrant vote, mainly German and Scandinavian, went over to the Republican Party. This made assimilation easier. The absence of a language barrier and inherited anti-English feeling in the United States similarly helped the Irish to gain acceptance in some parts of the country. But the industrialization which followed the Civil War created a new state of affairs. Although many European farmers were sent by railroads and land companies to the Western plains, by far the greater part of the "new" immigrants became factory workers and formed compact colonies in the great industrial cities, where they played an important if indeed not a dominant role in the increasingly class-conscious labor unions. After 1880, furthermore, most of the immigrants came from areas in Southeastern Europe whose languages and cultural traditions were much more remote from the American pattern than had been those of the earlier immigrants from Northwestern Europe. The unfortunate result was that toward the end of the century immigrants came more and more to be thought of as a distinct class, a well defined and perhaps unassimilable segment of the industrial proletariat. A protracted debate concerning the problem of "Americanization" and the "melting pot" occupied increasing space in magazines and newspapers; a cult of "Anglo-Saxon" superiority appeared, especially after 1890; and many of the contributors to the discussion revealed an irrational fear of the newcomers which was to find expression in the restrictive laws of the twentieth century.

It is not easy to determine exactly what effect these successive waves of immigration had on American thought and culture. The cosmopolitan character of the large cities was already pronounced by the end of the century. One factory in Chicago, in 1909, numbered among its forty-two hundred employees representatives of twenty-four nationalities; and in 1900 there were almost a thousand foreign-language periodicals and newspapers in the United States, published in twenty-five different tongues. Altogether, some twenty million aliens entered the United States during the nineteenth century. The census of 1900 showed more than ten million "foreign-born" in a total population of about seventy-six million. If persons whose parents were foreign-born were included, this number would perhaps be doubled, and would amount to more than one-fourth of the whole population.

From artists and scholars to illiterate peasants, all the immigrants brought with them an invisible baggage of cultural tradition: folklore, crafts, religions, patterns of the family and the community, foods and drinks. Much of this cultural baggage disappeared in the process of Americanization, but much of it was absorbed into the American way of life. Especially in the arts has the role of the immigrants and their descendants been important. It is worth noting also that the presence of many groups with a vital interest in European problems helped to offset the isolationism and provincial nationalism that were so powerful in nineteenth century America.

4

Such social and economic influences widened the cultural horizons of American society by adding increments of experience and proposing new topics of concern. But the century also brought many explicitly intellectual stimuli to bear upon the United States, just as it did upon Europe. The American people shared in all the major transformations of man's realm of ideas which took place during this period.

The first of these was the discovery of the past, the growth of the historic sense. Irving and Cooper early showed what richness of overtone could be added to familiar landscapes by weaving about them historical legends. Cooper's demonstration of the narrative interest of the American Revolution coincided with the growing spirit of nationalism, which in sanctifying the Revolution gave rise to the first efforts at systematic investigation of the American past. Around 1830 two Washington journalists began publishing collections of source materials for American history: Jonathan Elliott's *Debates* (in state and federal conventions on the Constitution), published 1827–1845, and Peter Force's ambitious *American Archives* (nine volumes, 1837–1853), comprising a documentary history of the British colonies in America. Thirty-five local and state historical societies were established between 1820 and 1850. (Only three, Massachusetts, New York, Pennsylvania, had been established before 1820.) In the same period collectors like John Carter Brown of Providence and James Lenox of New York began to form libraries of Americana. The fruition of these stirrings of interest in the American past came in the group of distinguished historians who dominated the mid-nineteenth century: George Bancroft, Jared Sparks, Richard Hildreth, and Francis Parkman.

The development of historical writing owed much to Americans who had studied in Germany during the first half of the century and had participated in the renovation of German scholarship that followed the nationalistic uprising against Napoleon. The new "philosophical" approach to classical antiquity, especially to Greece; textual criticism of the Scriptures; scientific study of the literatures of modern Europe—these enterprises drew a brilliant company of young Americans to German universities. Not only Bancroft's *History of the United States,* but George Ticknor's masterful *History of Spanish Literature,* John L. Motley's *Rise of the Dutch Republic,* and Longfellow's *Hyperion* and *The Golden Legend* developed out of impulses received at Göttingen and Heidelberg and Berlin.

But there was more in the transaction than scholarship. It was an important moment in the history of American culture when young Ticknor, the son of a wealthy Boston merchant, made a pilgrimage in 1817 to Wetzlar and experienced the emotions which he recorded in his journal as follows:

On the way I imagined that we passed the valley where the scene between Werther and Charlotte's distracted lover happened, and the chilly wind which blew as we went through it gave me a sensation of sadness such as I have seldom felt. I was still quite alone. A little farther on, I mounted the rocks, where Werther passed the dreadful night after he had left Charlotte—and in the village itself, I needed no guide to show me the red church—the lime trees—the burying ground, and the village houses which [Goethe] has described with such fidelity. On returning to the city, I stopped again on the rocks—read the description of his despair and stayed until the departing sun had almost descended behind the hills.

The American cult of Goethe, of which this is one of the early evidences, not only introduced a new generation to the complicated emotions of the *Sturm und Drang,* but led to a prolonged controversy on the subject of morality in art which helped to undermine the genteel tradition and to prepare the way for the eventual acceptance of realism in literature. German thought reached America more circuitously but with equal force in the transcendental philosophy transmitted to Emerson and his circle by Coleridge and Carlyle. The dimension of the self, of subjectivity, which transcendentalism set out to explore, was often described by critics of the movement as a morbid German invention.

Closely associated with transcendentalism, although not identical with it, was the ferment of social reform in New England during the thirties and forties. If all established institutions and usages were to be called before the bar of intuition and made to give an account of themselves, there was likely to be a great holocaust, as Hawthorne perceived. The young men and women of Brook Farm considered that they had come out from civilization, which they found too confining, and were engaged in building the society of the future on the principle of association. Together with Fourierists and Icarians and Owenites and Perfectionists scattered from New Jersey to Texas and Wisconsin, they were exploring the dimension of utopianism, and although presently the movement to free the slaves swallowed up many of the other reforming crusades that had flourished in the forties, there remained a leaven of willingness to experiment which never wholly disappeared from American life. A generation glorying in its gospel of "the Newness" had made it impossible for any future conservative to oppose change merely on the score of the wickedness of all "innovation."

5

While transcendentalists and reformers were voyaging strange seas of thought and tampering with the institutional foundations of American society, less radical writers and thinkers were undertaking an inventory of the actual conditions of life on the American continent, especially in the vast interior that had been so recently occupied by white settlers. The most striking symbol of the non-European factors in the new environment was the Indian. Although there was a tradition of exotic interest in the red man dating from the time of Columbus, the accounts of missionaries were the most reliable factual reports available when Cooper began his Leatherstocking series in the twenties. But the scientific impulse to collect and organize data was soon to yield tangible results. Beginning with Lewis Cass' criticism of Cooper's depiction of the Indians during the late twenties, the *North American Review* established a policy of publishing in almost every volume at least one solid article on the subject; and Albert Gallatin in his old age contributed to the *Transactions* of the American Antiquarian Society (1836) a "Synopsis of the Indian Tribes . . . in North America" which virtually created the science of American linguistics.

Less disciplined projects were going forward at the same time—perhaps because Andrew Jackson's policy of forcing the Eastern tribes beyond the Mississippi dramatized the Indians as a vanishing race. George Catlin, a Pennsylvanian who deserted the law for painting, began in 1832 a series of journeys that took him to every part of the United States, from Florida to the Yellowstone, where he might observe and paint the natives. His gallery of Indian portraits and his collection of costumes, weapons, and ritual objects were exhibited to large audiences in American cities of the East and in Europe. Catlin's *Manners, Customs, and Condition of the North American Indians* (1841) is strongly primitivistic in flavor, but it contains valuable accounts of the author's travels. Henry R. Schoolcraft married an Ojibway wife and lived for thirty years among the Indians of the Great Lakes region. His numerous books (published from 1839 to 1857, sometimes with subventions from the federal government) represent a design even more far-reaching than Catlin's to set down everything that could be learned about the aborigines. Schoolcraft's work provided the "source" for *Hiawatha,* but it was too unsystematic to endure as a scientific influence. Lack of method likewise impairs the sumptuous collection of Indian portraits with biographical sketches compiled by Thomas L. McKenney, Superintendent of Indian Trade in the War Department, and the Cincinnati writer James Hall, which was published in three folio volumes, 1836–1844.

During the forties the American Ethnological Society (founded in 1842 under Gallatin's leadership), and after 1848 the Smithsonian Institution, gave consistent attention to American ethnology; and by the seventies the discipline was assuming its modern form. Frank Hamilton Cushing, who lived from 1879 to 1882 in the pueblo of Zuñi, wrote a series of articles on his experiences for the *Century* (1882–1883) which are a landmark in the sympathetic yet accurate study of American Indian cultures. John Wesley Powell, after securing the establishment of the Bureau of American Ethnology in 1879, issued an important series of reports prepared by a professional staff. An equally enthusiastic student of the Indian was John G. Bourke, an officer of the regular army who fought in campaigns against the Plains Indians in the seventies. In addition to a pioneer monograph on the Snake Dance of the Hopi (1884), he wrote many scientific papers, and a half-dozen books designed for a more popular audience. The first half-century of work on the Indians was synthesized in H. H. Bancroft's *Native Races of the Pacific States* (1876–1882). American archaeology, in its early stages hardly to be distinguished from ethnology, had meanwhile been placed on its modern footing through the pioneer investigations of the Swiss-American Adolph Bandelier, whose classic papers on the art of war, land tenure, and social organization of ancient Mexico appeared between 1877 and 1879.

Like the study of buried American civilizations, the growing interest in folklore enriched men's understanding of the possibilities of life in the New World. British and Continental efforts to collect the tales and songs of the uneducated folk were not imitated immediately in the United States, perhaps because there was no obvious equivalent for the European peasant traditionally attached to the soil. But there were nevertheless some minority groups, isolated from the main currents of American life, which had retained or developed an authentic folklore. In the Southern Appalachians were mountaineers who had preserved into the nineteenth century the social patterns of the eighteenth; as collectors discovered with delight in the eighties, they sang ballads which their ancestors had brought from the British Isles. Interest in ballads had been aroused in the United States through the efforts of Professor Francis J. Child of Harvard, who had begun his study of the English and Scottish ballads before 1850; his great work eventually appeared in five volumes from 1883 to 1898. Appropriately, Professor Child became the first president of the American Folklore Society in 1888.

The richest find of the collectors was the songs of the Southern Negro, first recorded for publication by Northern Abolitionists and officers during the Civil War. James M. McKim of Philadelphia and his daughter Lucy (later the wife of Wendell Phillips Garrison) encountered spirituals among freed slaves of the South Carolina Sea Islands in the early sixties, and T. W. Higginson collected songs in the same area from soldiers in his colored regiment. In his pioneer article on "Negro Spirituals" in the *Atlantic* (1867), Higginson says that he was drawn to the project because he had been "a faithful student of the Scottish ballads, and had always envied Sir Walter the delight of tracing them out amid their own heather, and of writing them down piecemeal from the lips of aged crones." But the Northern collectors also wished to create cultural prestige for the Negro. This purpose is evident in the first book setting down words and music of the spirituals, *Slave Songs of the United States*. Published a few months after Higginson's article, it was compiled by Lucy McKim Garrison, Charles Pickard Ware, and William Francis Allen, a Northern teacher who went South to help the freed Negroes during the war. The same influence appears in the career of the Fisk University student singers who began touring the North in 1871 to raise funds for their school. Joel Chandler Harris' Uncle Remus stories in the Atlanta *Constitution* in 1879 were the first significant notice of Negro folk tales.

6

Despite the importance of the forces already mentioned, the most drastic changes in American thought during the nineteenth century came from another source, the impact of natural science. Geological speculation concerning the age of the earth, in the early part of the century, and the Darwinian theory of organic evolution in the latter part, called in question the infallibility of the Scriptures and weakened the widely prevalent faith in the governance of the universe according to an intelligible divine plan. The result was a lessening of emphasis upon the supernatural aspects of religion with a corresponding growth of interest in its ethical and especially in its social implications. As the supernatural conception of sin lost force, evil was projected from the individual soul into the environment. Here it was attacked by men who sought to apply a "social gospel" to American society as a remedy for urban poverty and for the tensions between employers and laborers that had resulted from the growth of large-scale industry. The social gospel was being discussed as early as the seventies, and its influence was eventually felt in every Protestant denomination—although of course with varying intensity. But if the idea of organic evolution thus indirectly strengthened humanitarianism in the evangelical churches, it could also have a contrary effect: the notion of the survival of the fittest was often interpreted as giving scientific sanction to the fierce competitive struggles of the closing years of the century.

The emphasis on adaptation to environment implicit in evolutionary biology influenced literature by calling attention to the varieties of man's efforts to accommodate himself to terrain and climate. Not only in the flood of travel books which described the various regions of the country—especially the Far West—but even more strikingly in the local color fiction which flourished in the eighties was evident an insatiable curiosity concerning the land and the people of the different parts of the United States. This new preoccupation with the physical conditions of life in the New World, with the unpredictable novelties of American experience, played a great if not easily definable part in the reorientation of American literature after the Civil War.

One of the most tangible evidences of the new point of view is the changing attitude of writers toward language. In the twenties Americans had been delighted to hear Irving's elegance of diction and avoidance of Americanism praised by the British, but much of the best writing of the period after the Civil War shows little regard for "correctness." The revolution had been prepared by the humorists of the thirties and forties—by books like A. B. Longstreet's *Georgia Scenes* and T. B. Thorpe's *The Hive of "The Bee Hunter,"* with their loving attention to the illiterate dialect of the frontier. Even the Brahmins of the great period had done their share to bring the vernacular into literary use. As George Philip Krapp remarks:

How tantalizingly near this rustic native speech [of New England] lay to the cultivated speech is evidenced by the use of the native speech which was made by writers like Holmes, Lowell, and others, who endeavored to express homespun character in homespun speech. Though this native speech was felt to be vigorously expressive, may even have been felt to be the real speech of New England, yet it was always used with a reluctant admission that the reality was not good enough for the highest purposes. It is doubtful, however, if Lowell ever expressed himself more sincerely than he did in the *Biglow Papers,* and time and again in Holmes, when he good-humoredly permits himself to forget the literary pose, glimpses of the essentially local, provincial New Englander, wise, kindly, and simple, show in the language he uses.

The intrusion of the vernacular into consciously literary usage had been preceded by a linguistic discussion dating from the eighteenth century. Noah Webster, asserting that "a *national language* is a band of *national union*," protested in 1789 that an "astonishing respect for the arts and literature of their parent country, and a blind imitation of its manners," were preventing Americans from establishing their intellectual independence of England. He predicted that American speech would grow entirely away from English. Although Webster was a Federalist, most conservatives in politics were opposed to the acceptance of Americanisms. The *Port Folio,* for example, reprinted with approval a pseudonymous attack on Webster's project for an American dictionary which took the familiar position that "it is incumbent on literary men, to guard against impurities, and chastise, with the critical lash, all useless innovations. . . . Colloquial barbarities abound in all countries, but among no civilized people are they admitted, with impunity, into books."

Official prejudice against the use of the vernacular in literature continued strong for more than half a century. As late as 1878 a critic in the *Atlantic* objected to a historical novelist's use of "the dialect supposed to have been spoken by the rude forefathers of the New England hamlets" on the score that the "wanton distortion of sounds and a hardy disobedience to grammar," characteristic of the speech of "the unrefined," were "wholly base." It was not until the appearance of Bret Harte after the Civil War that a writer could be generally praised for capturing "the robust vigor and racy savor of the miners' vernacular."

Whitman, however, had already advanced far beyond Harte's attitude toward the native speech. Whereas Harte continued to exploit his gambling and mining terms for comic purposes only, Whitman used the vocabulary, if not the rhythms, of American oral speech for the most elevated occasions.

American writers are to show far more freedom in the use of words [he declared in the late fifties].—Ten thousand native idiomatic words are growing, or are to-day already grown, out of which vast numbers could be used by American writers, with meaning and effect—words that would be welcomed by the nation, being of the national blood—words that would give that taste of identity and locality which is so dear in literature.

Leaves of Grass thoroughly bears out Whitman's theory; indeed, so important did he consider the question of diction that he once described his work as "only a language experiment . . . an attempt to give the spirit, the body, the man, new words, new potentialities of speech." But it was Mark Twain, in *Huckleberry Finn* (1885), who proved to America at large that the vernacular was adequate to meet any demand a serious writer might make on it.

As the quotation from Whitman suggests, the use of American English was closely bound up with the choice of vividly localized characters and incidents. Despite frequent exhortations by critics who urged the use of native materials, American writers during the first half of the century found it difficult to disentangle themselves from the notion that "low" scenes and characters could appropriately be dealt with only as comic. The humorists who created Major Jack Downing and Sam Slick and the Davy Crockett of the almanacs made an important transition from the conventional contempt for illiterate characters by endowing their creatures with an engaging shrewdness and a vein of poetry growing out of the folk experience. As Walter Blair points out, their work reached a wide and enthusiastic audience, although most critics, and for that matter the humorists themselves, would have been astonished to learn that posterity would consider their tales as the starting point of a truly American literature. Longstreet's *Georgia Scenes* went through twelve editions between 1835 and 1894; Benjamin P. Shillaber's *Life and Sayings of Mrs. Partington* sold fifty thousand copies within a few weeks of its publication in 1854; and William T. Thompson's *Major Jones's Courtship* went through thirteen editions between 1844 and 1855. The popularity of the *Biglow Papers* was a part of the same trend: no one could doubt, by 1860, that strongly localized characters had an appeal for the American public.

Closely related to the native humorous tradition, but more self-conscious and more superficial, was the local color movement. The demand for an American literature had often been understood to mean no more than the use of peculiarly American materials. As *Hiawatha* and *Evangeline* indicate, the writer's duty was taken to be simply the application of traditional techniques to native scenes and characters, usually of the past. The principal change evident in the local colorists after the Civil War was the use of contemporary "regional" materials. These writers had an astonishing vogue. Within ten years after Bret Harte's original success in 1869 the reading public was familiar with a long list of specialists, each of whom had identified himself with a given locality, from New Orleans to the Maine coast. By the end of the eighties no literate American can have failed to become acquainted with a score of formerly isolated and self-contained regions.

In the course of the nineteenth century, a variety of expansive forces completely altered the scale of American life and thought. The new national culture was in many respects raw and crude, but it had great vitality, and despite the variety of social patterns embraced within the national synthesis the parts were related to one another in a whole. In the future, although regional cultures would become increasingly significant, it would be impossible for an important writer to deal with his own area of experience in isolation from that of the entire society.

39. LITERARY CULTURE ON THE FRONTIER

I<small>N</small> recent years, it has become conventional to attribute these cultural changes to the "frontier." Nathaniel Ames, with an almanac maker's gifts of prophecy, foretold as early as 1758 that "Arts and Sciences will change the Face of Nature in their Tour from Hence over the Appalachian Mountains to the Western Ocean." While the settler was destined to transform the frontier, it was clear from the start in an equally real sense he would be transformed by it.

These interactions happened at successive times and places—as white settlement after the Revolution flowed first into the great meadows of Kentucky and the fertile wilderness of the Ohio Valley, then early in the new century pushed on to the Illinois country and began to explore the vast Mississippi Valley, while another tongue from Virginia and the Carolinas thrust itself into the then Southwest frontier of Georgia, Alabama, and Tennessee. Eddying around points of earlier settlement like New Orleans and St. Louis, the wave of migration that had surged so promptly into the territory of the Louisiana Purchase—the "choice country with room enough" promised by President Jefferson—began before long to encroach upon Mexican dominion in Texas and later in the Far West, until both vast regions had fallen to the Federal Union by 1848. Meanwhile in 1846 the United States, by treaty with Britain, gained undisputed title to that Pacific Northwest which for a decade had been the journey's end of the famous Oregon Trail. This, in brief, is the story of the frontier, whose march rounded out the continental expanse of the nation before the nineteenth century was half done—although areas and pockets of unsettled land remained for many decades, and the frontier was not declared officially closed until the Census of 1890. The cultural institutions and tools which shaped the mind of this frontier, through printing, reading, and writing, deserve examination.

Within a few years after the winning of independence, hosts of settlers —carrying seeds, a few tools, and one or two indispensable books like the Bible—had begun to cross the Alleghenies toward "the meeting point between savagery and civilization," as the historian Frederick J. Turner called the frontier. It has been defined as that zone, facing the trackless public domain, where fewer than two persons lived per square mile. Socially and culturally, it was a laboratory of mixed races and folkways from the start. Success came to the young and vigorous, rather than to the heir of wealth and prestige. Even book learning mattered less than brawn, daring, and the earthy lore of soldier, woodsman, and farmer.

In those early days, the valves of influence opened chiefly westward. Receiving from the Eastern seaboard almost all the culture it knew, the frontier gave little or nothing in return. Once a settler made the western traverse, he rarely went home. The mind of the East, in general, felt little more than casual curiosity about the rude frontier, save as a terra incognita of romantic novelists. Soon after the dawn of the nineteenth century, travel grew easier, thanks to the building of turnpikes into the West, and the steamboats that pioneered its great rivers, and the canals that linked its waters. In the thirties and forties came the first railroads, and conquest was assured.

Over these roads and watercourses eagerly streamed the advance agents of civilization. One such courier was the itinerant revivalist, missionary, or circuit rider. He helped break the shell of frontier loneliness, as the grim homiletics of Cotton Mather and Jonathan Edwards gave way to the warmth of backwoods exhorters like Lorenzo Dow and Peter Cartwright. "When I hear a man preach," said Lincoln, "I like to see him act as if he were fighting bees." Emotional oratory from the pulpit, and reading matter like missionary tracts, henceforth became a powerful element in frontier culture, shaping its imagination and daily idioms. From the preacher, also, much backwoods education stemmed. As early as 1800, the Methodist General Conference made its circuit riders agents for books published under direction of the church; the greatest of its Western missionaries, Bishop Francis Asbury, shortly became an evangel of popular education. The Baptists, who shared with Methodists the primacy on the frontier, presently followed suit. From early days, Presbyterians and Congregationalists, whose Yankee traditions demanded learning in the pulpit and literacy among the flock, tended the vineyard of knowledge. Biblical scholars like Lyman Beecher and Calvin Stowe—father and husband, respectively, of Harriet Beecher Stowe—transplanted their educational interests, with powerful effect, to the Ohio country.

Secular education in the West owed most to that hardy perennial, the wandering schoolmaster. The first historian of Kentucky and introducer of Daniel Boone to the world, in 1784, was a Pennsylvania pedagogue, John Filson. On the frontier, this profession was no sedentary calling; the first master of a log-cabin school at Lexington, Kentucky, began one day's tasks by strangling with his bare hands a wildcat in the schoolroom. First in the South, later in the Southwest, the New England schoolmaster grew proverbial for qualities of enterprise, rather than for the cloistered pursuit of knowledge.

He charged what he could get, and boarded around, while holding classes in a cabin of mud-daubed logs, where boards served for desks and shingles with bits of charcoal for slates and blackboards. Little beyond "readin', writin', and cypherin' to the rule of three" was expected of him. Nevertheless, he inducted his charges into the mystery of the printed word—chiefly by means of those aggressively American textbooks that came after Independence, like Noah Webster's blue-backed speller, Jedidiah Morse's geography, and Nicholas Pike's arithmetic ("more suitable to our meridian than those heretofore published").

Such books, and others on law, medicine, surveying, biography, history, and fictional subjects, were carried into the West by that humble pollinator of culture, the itinerant peddler. Like the greatest of his tribe, Bronson Alcott, this type was commonly Yankee. That New England wrote, published, taught, and sold the majority of books on the frontier, in the first generation of settlement, is a fact of much significance in the shaping of the western country's neo-Puritanism.

Free education was one of the pioneer's cherished ideas. The Land Ordinance of 1785 set aside section sixteen in each township for public schools; that of 1787 promised, "Schools and the means of education shall forever be encouraged." As a matter of sober fact, the dream of a great public educational system in the West did not come close to realization until the 1830's, when the taxes necessary to its support were at last levied.

Colleges, however, made early headway. Transylvania Seminary in Kentucky, the pioneer west of the Alleghenies, started in 1785 as little more than a grammar school; it began to confer degrees in 1802, amassed an important library, and grew to considerable prestige before sectarian quarrels sapped its usefulness. Ohio University at Athens, set up by act of the state legislature in 1804, drew sustenance from federal land grants. It bred a notable generation of schoolmasters in the New England tradition. Its president during the Van Buren era was William Holmes McGuffey, whose Eclectic Readers taught three generations of Americans good English and sound morals. Most pioneer colleges, by the yardstick of modern times, were poor in books, scholarship, and mental stimulus; but their spirit, like that of the region itself, fed upon hope. Naturally enough the fount of intellectual America remained in the East, whence came the best educators, and where backwoods sons with ambition and luck were prone to gravitate. Thanks to the religious orthodoxy of the frontier, the shadow of Yale, in the land of steady habits and Trinitarianism, and likewise that of safely Presbyterian Princeton, loomed larger across the Ohio Valley than did the influence of more liberal, heretical Harvard.

Mechanics' institutes, local lyceums, lecture and study courses, museums featuring exhibits and talks, all promoted Western education upon the adult level. Moreover, here and there, nuclei of utopian communities—such as New Harmony, Indiana, on the lower Wabash, which drew the English socialist Robert Owen, the feminist Frances Wright, the French naturalist Charles Lesueur, and others who taught in its school—served as intellectual beacons on the prairie, even though geographically the radius of their light was small.

Under great handicaps—indeed with an appetite whetted by privation—the westering pioneers cherished the crumbs of book learning and culture. In an address in 1859, Henry Ward Beecher picturesquely described these emigrants: "They drive schools along with them, as shepherds drive flocks. They have herds of churches, academies, lyceums; and their religious and educational institutions go lowing along the western plains as Jacob's herds lowed along the Syrian hills."

2

Subscription libraries sprang up before public ones. Amid the isolation of the frontier, books were prized for their rarity as well as their companionship. One Ohio pioneer, subscriber at $10 a share to the Belpre Farmers' Library, tells how he regularly made the twelve miles' round trip necessary to borrow books, and usually spent the winter evenings reading aloud by the light of pine knots, while his wife carded or spun. In the same state, Ames township in 1803 started its famous "Coonskin Library," whose members paid their dues in furs and skins which the factor sold in Boston to buy books. Free libraries began to develop in the next decade. Louisville gained its public library in 1816, while smaller settlements were grasping the idea. Henry R. Schoolcraft, student of the Indians, following the Wabash in 1821, found at Albion "a library of standard books, accessible to all, and much attention is paid to the improvement of the mind as well as the soil." That astute young Frenchman, Alexis de Tocqueville, exploring the backwoods in the early thirties—and discovering in a typical pioneer's cabin "a Bible, the first six books of Milton, and two of Shakespeare's plays"—reflected upon the paradox of the frontiersman:

> Everything about him is primitive and wild, but he is himself the result of the labor and experience of eighteen centuries. He wears the dress and speaks the language of cities; he is acquainted with the past, curious about the future, and ready for argument upon the present; he is, in short, a highly civilized being, who consents for a time to inhabit the backwoods, and who penetrates into the wilds of the New World with the Bible, an axe, and some newspapers.

The printing press, carried in the wake of the pioneer, made the frontier more self-reliant. Although Filson in 1784 had to journey back to Delaware with his manuscript about Kentucky, in the lack of a single printer's shop west of the mountains, two years later the trans-Allegheny country produced its first newspaper, the Pittsburgh *Gazette*—sometimes printed on cartridge paper borrowed from Fort Pitt. Its publisher, John Scull, in 1793 printed the first book west of the Alleghenies, the third volume of H. H. Brackenridge's novel *Modern Chivalry*. Meanwhile a printing press, carried from Philadelphia by wagon and boat into Kentucky, in 1787 enabled John Bradford to start the second Western newspaper, the *Kentucke Gazette*. Copies stowed in the saddlebags of postriders penetrated far into the wilderness; staleness of news mattered little, and neighbors often gathered around a stump to hear the paper read aloud. In 1810, as the Postmaster General reported, Western newspapers made up less than a tenth of the total published in the nation; but by 1840 they comprised more than a quarter of the total.

Dearth of news, national and international, often proved to be a boon for literature. Amateur essayists, still under the spell of Addison and Steele and Dr. Johnson, revealed the timidity of a consciously bookish culture on the frontier. Also popular was the local poets' column, styled "The Parnassiad," "Seat of the Muses," or "Poetical Asylum," where fledglings attempted the flights of the English Augustans, and a little later Scott or Byron. Those two absorbing passions of the frontier, politics and religion, sired a great deal of verse, partisan and pietistic, which seldom rose above mediocrity, but encouraged the habit of versifying.

More exclusively the preserve of literature was the magazine. The pioneer in the West was Daniel Bradford's *The Medley, or Monthly Miscellany,* which lasted but one year, 1803, at Lexington, Kentucky. After the lapse of sixteen years, a successor appeared on the same spot, in William Gibbes Hunt's *Western Review*. History, biography, sentimental fiction, poetry, synopses of English novels, and an important series on science by Constantine S. Rafinesque, made up the bill of fare. (The work of that naturalist, along with the still more important findings of John James Audubon and Alexander Wilson, stirred keen interest upon a frontier which loved the outdoors and knew its natural history to be so largely unique.) If the purely literary complexion of these magazines seems pallid, beside the daily adventure of life in the West, at least the aspiration was in the making. Timothy Flint, romantic Yankee missionary who launched another *Western Review* in 1827, and Judge James Hall, planter of two literary magazines in Illinois in the next decade, both were fierce champions of Western culture against the effete East. Yet, significantly enough, the most distinguished magazine to come out of the West in this era, the *Western Messenger*—begun in 1835 by the Reverend James Freeman Clarke and other intellectual Unitarians—drew most of its sustenance from the taproot of Concord and Boston. Liberal and transcendental, it was the first periodical to publish Emerson's poetry; and thanks to George Keats, brother of the poet and a citizen of Louisville, John Keats' "Ode to Apollo" first appeared in its pages. Breasting strong currents of anti-Unitarian prejudice, the *Messenger* never made much headway in the West, and expired in 1841. In fact, most magazines in this region died young, after struggling against local poverty, the scarcity of gifted contributors, and competition for subscribers with imported Eastern and British reviews.

In forms less professedly literary, the printed word did flourish. The firm of Truman & Smith, founded in Cincinnati about 1830, presently became the largest schoolbook publisher in the world—in the first decade of its existence turning out more than 700,000 copies of texts like the McGuffey Readers, Ray's Arithmetic, Miss Beecher's Moral Instructor. Also in heavy demand were songbooks sentimental or patriotic, and almanacs, specially the comic almanac which salted its weather forecasts with funny stories about frontier favorites like Mike Fink, king of Mississippi keelboatmen, and Davy Crockett, that ring-tailed roarer of the woods. Humor in fact became the great medium for home-grown literature and art in the back country. Joke books, comic balladry, black-face minstrels, and the tall tales men told at frontier outposts or around the campfire, to beguile time and solitude—all added something to an art of humor that reached perfection upon the lips of such true frontiersmen as Abe Lincoln and Mark Twain.

This art flourished with special flavor in the Southwest. Its frequent appeal to slapstick, horseplay, and belly laughter should not lead one to hasty conclusions. Aside from the autobiography purported to be written by Davy Crockett and published in 1834—in which the hero's lack of book larnin' is somewhat proudly displayed—the most representative specimens of this humor did not spring from illiterate men. Augustus Baldwin Longstreet, a Georgian educated at Yale, and future Methodist clergyman, published in his small-town newspaper, the Augusta *Sentinel,* many of the droll sketches later collected as *Georgia Scenes* (1835). In the midst of such backwoods crudities as gouging matches and gander pullings, the author steps aside to quote Horace, or dress in classical mythology his account of a fox hunt. The sketch called "The Debating Society" suggests another cultural resource of the frontier, which enlivened Fourth of July barbecues and political campaigns, produced its finest flower in the oratory of Henry Clay, and led a wag to observe that speakers kept the American Eagle so constantly in flight that his shadow wore a trail across the Mississippi Valley. Another minor classic of the old Southwest, *Flush Times in Alabama and Mississippi* (1853), was written by Joseph G. Baldwin, a lawyer steeped in history and classical literature, who yet could savor the brawling and practical joking of the buckskin frontier.

The old Southwest, from Georgia to the Mississippi, was in fact a frontier with its own hallmark—settled by a more homogeneous population, largely Virginians and Carolinians, than that of the Northwest, and hence strongly molded by Southern influences, whether in the love of outdoor sports or in its code of honor. Culturally, its most characteristic instrument of education was the "academy" on the Southern plan, a secondary school somewhat more democratic than the Latin schools of the larger New England towns, but less so than the high schools which developed later. Sometimes this institution was called a county academy, and looked to the state for support; more often it was maintained by a religious denomination, private subscription, and tuition fees. With almost fanatic zeal, the South and the old Southwest trimmed the lamp of eighteenth century scholasticism in the lonely backwoods. They clung to Latin and Greek as the essence of gentlemanly discipline, supplemented by a smattering of mathematics and English grammar, while literature and history went begging. Rude in equipment and poor in staffing, the frontier academy still served as the chief implement of organized education in a region where elementary schools as well as colleges were still exceedingly sparse. But that no very vigorous thinking or writing, or even much constructive reading, sprang from that thin, derivative culture is not surprising. Sport, politics, gossip, and conviviality were the chief fruits of leisure in the old South, as the minor Georgia poet Henry R. Jackson observed plaintively in 1840, adding:

As compared with the North, there are with us more individuals of leisure not engaged in the busy avocations of life. . . . Nature has given them temperaments demanding strong excitement! Unaccustomed to seek it in the more ennobling pursuits of literature, they too often resort to the short-lived stimulus of the intoxicating cup.

3

A cultural map of inland America, in the first half of the nineteenth century, would show "islands" of more exotic and sophisticated tradition. For, flowing west, the Anglo-Saxon tide first met the French culture of the Mississippi Valley, and then flowed on to encounter the Spanish influence of the new Southwest and the Pacific slope.

Catholic folkways differed from Protestant in the indulgence of a gayer Sabbath and pre-Lenten carnival, in the Latin passion for warmer colors and franker delight in the senses. From Canada to the Gulf, the *voyageur* carried his boat songs and folklore, and his French speech. That tongue won considerable popularity among the new schools and academies of Ohio, Indiana, Illinois, and Missouri. St. Louis, founded by French trappers, remained the insular center of Gallic culture in America; and its leading educational institution, St. Louis University, chartered by the Jesuits in 1832, from the start influenced the intellectual life of this region and drew students even from Mexico and South America. But the heart of France *in partibus infidelium* was New Orleans, whose gentry prized their Epicurism and courtly manners and education founded upon Continental and parochial models—for, until the Constitution of 1845, common schools were unknown in Louisiana. Most Anglo-Saxons who settled there were insensibly wooed by the charm, the apparent paganism, of the place, and those who came to convert often remained to conform. The effect of the Crescent City upon such tarrying birds of passage as Walt Whitman and Lafcadio Hearn, or upon a native son of alien stock like George W. Cable, proved of high import to literature.

In the westward current of empire, other whirlpools of culture appeared German immigrants into Illinois after 1848, and Scandinavian settlers in Wisconsin and Minnesota in the middle years of the century, brought with them new languages, cultures, and nostalgias to the cabins and sod houses of the prairie. Foreign-language presses turned out many newspapers and a few books. Most such immigrants were sturdy, simple, hard-working folk rather than artists or scholars; but literacy ran high among them, with a craving for advancement, of which "the America fever" (as Selma Lagerlöf called it) was symptomatic. Among groups of old American stock, but sharply set apart from their neighbors by mores and theology, the Mormons drew most attention. Finding their promised land, after trials and tribulations, in the basin of the Great Salt Lake, the Saints fabricated a life of their own that culturally was somewhat bleak, but typically American in its accent upon enterprise and self-improvement—notably in the decree of compulsory education for all children, in secular schools that were tuition-free to the poor.

The Spanish civilization of the Pacific coast was too thin in population, too indolent, to make a concerted stand against the Anglo-Saxon. Within a short time it underwent absorption into the cultural complex of the New West—along with Southern New England, Midwestern, European, and Oriental elements—while lending the mass some of the richness of its pigment. Spanish language newspapers, sermons in Spanish and a few quaint remains of liturgical drama, and the inflow of a modest quota of books from Mexico City and Spain, were persistent enclaves in the midst of a speedy English-speaking conquest. The cultural history of the frontier beyond the Rocky Mountains, therefore, was written anew after Manifest Destiny turned the page.

When Americans began seriously to think about pushing the nation's western boundary to land's end, two main trails led from the middle border into the West. The older was the Santa Fe Trail, from the Mississippi Valley through Kansas into the highlands of New Mexico—a path of trade rather than of folk migration, at least prior to the California Gold Rush. Younger but of greater importance was the Oregon Trail, from the woodlands of Missouri northwestward across the Great Plains and mountain passes to the forests of Oregon and northern California. Its ground breakers, the preacher Samuel Parker and the medical missionary Marcus Whitman, had been sent to work among the Nez Percés and Flathead tribes. Lean years following the Panic of 1837 sent legions of dispossessed men and their families over the Oregon Trail. Though traveling light, many carried a few of life's amenities. Joel Palmer, off to Oregon in 1845, wrote in his journal while encamped on the Trail:

At two of the tents the fiddle was employed in uttering its unaccustomed voice among the solitudes of the Platte; at one tent I heard singing; at others the occupants were engaged in reading, some the Bible, others poring over novels.

To west-coast ports at this time, sizable shipments of books from New England and New York were already being brought around the Horn, in the course of the hide and tallow trade. While the almost bloodless deliverance of California from Mexico was being won, other cultural developments appeared. The *Californian,* first newspaper in that state, appeared at Monterey in August, 1846, but shortly moved to San Francisco to merge with a junior rival as the well known *Alta California.* The Public Institute, an educational enterprise, opened in San Francisco's Portsmouth Square on the eve of the Gold Rush; in 1849 the new state constitution promised free education to all.

Discovery of gold forced the early flowering of northern California. (As a touch of bookishness worth remark, the finders of ore in Sutter's millrace carefully read the article on gold in the *American Encyclopedia* before believing their luck.) Now the Pacific trek began in earnest. President Everett of Harvard might exhort Boston emigrants to go "with the Bible in one hand and your New England civilization in the other, and make your mark on the people and country," but influences here were too diverse to permit any such distinctive impress of culture as New England had left upon the early Ohio Valley. This was a novel kind of frontier. Footloose and ambitious men from all the states, and most nations, flocked to the diggings. The intelligent and sophisticated mingled with the rough and ready. The unsuccessful were apt to lay aside pick and pan, to try their hand at trade, politics, journalism, literature. The Civil War and its aftermath sent thousands more to California, in a passage from the East that the years had made successively easier by clipper ships, the Nicaragua passage, the overland stage and pony express, and finally the transcontinental railway in 1869.

Unlike earlier frontiers, that of northern California enjoyed both the wealth to patronize art and the cosmopolitan spirit to create it. In literature, for instance, the best talents seemed to spring from young expatriates of staid communities and various brands of provincialism: Sam Clemens from Hannibal, Missouri; Bret Harte from Albany; Joaquin Miller from Liberty, Indiana, by way of Oregon; Ambrose Bierce from Horse Cave Creek, Ohio; Edward Rowland Sill from Windsor, Connecticut, and rural Ohio; Charles Warren Stoddard from Rochester, New York; Prentice Mulford from Sag Harbor, Long Island; George Horatio Derby ("John Phoenix") from Dedham, Massachusetts, and Ina Coolbrith from Illinois, by way of Los Angeles. Flung into the heady life of the frontier, they were immensely stimulated—often reaching powers they never attained before or afterward. Reading and writing flourished on a scale never before seen in any frontier environment. As early as 1850, San Francisco was keeping fifty printers at work. By the middle of that decade the city boasted more newspapers than London, more books published than all the rest of trans-Mississippi put together. Magazines of belles-lettres—the *Pioneer, Golden Era, Hesperian, Californian, Overland Monthly* —sprouted, flourished, and even in dying left a literary humus from which successors sprang. Here also the average newspaper, metropolitan or rural, favored high-flown essays, humorous skits, and "Poets' Corners" to which tradesmen and brokers alike contributed. Around the Comstock Lode, red-shirted miners (especially when in their cups) loved to hold hot argument over the merits of rival bards like Joe Goodman and Rollin Daggett, or solemnly ballot in a poet-of-the-day contest. The first slim collection of California verse, *Outcroppings* (1865), made by Bret Harte, recognized only nineteen poets and overlooked so many "thousands" that it caused a literary riot. A sequel, *The Poetry of the Pacific* (1866), extended the list to seventy-five and, among writers of repute, omitted only Harte.

Moreover, a bent toward practicality so characteristic of all frontiers fostered in the West many types of writing other than "mere literature." At their best they are represented by Clarence King and John Muir on geology and natural science, Henry George on economics and social reform, and Hubert Howe Bancroft on California records and history; at their mediocre bulk, by innumerable political speeches, orations, legal works on mining and riparian rights, and the early propaganda of the booster.

Other instruments of culture were not neglected. Seven years after the start of the Gold Rush, San Francisco was supporting three public libraries, twenty-four public grade schools, and one public high school; outside this orbit of new wealth and population, Los Angeles had no free library, and only one public school of elementary level, in addition to parochial schools. The College of California, soon to become the University at Berkeley, was founded in 1855. The system of public support, assured for technological and agricultural education by the Morrill Act of 1862, rapidly became the keystone of all higher education in the Midwestern, Rocky Mountain, and Far Western regions. Lacking the colleges and universities of private endowment traditional in the East, the West built its collegiate and university structure, for cultural and vocational training, upon the base of state and federal aid. While certain amenities were missing, the gains for democracy were evident.

San Francisco's gilded age witnessed an almost frenzied enthusiasm for the drama, opera, and music. Lectures—given in theaters, churches, billiard saloons—were vastly popular. The effect of certain visiting celebrities upon the style of Western humor and sentiment, and the development of young journalists like Mark Twain and Bret Harte, proved notable. A passion for entertainment and culture radiated from the Bay region into remote mining camps. Miners supported a lively theater circuit from Rabbit Creek to Mariposa, and drew the best that gold dust could buy. On Sundays, miners held their own debating societies. Often, of course, the yearning of the parvenu was naïvely earnest—among a generation of provincials who had sometimes heard, and resented, the sneers of Mrs. Trollope and Charles Dickens. Wealth meant a new stake in gentility. It is reported that the first miner to strike gold at Gregory's Gulch in Colorado, in 1859, flung down his pick with the exclamation, "Thank God! Now my wife can be a lady—and our children can have an education!"

A tincture of social vanity, mingled with a sincere wish for the good life, set the tone for aspiration on this Western frontier. If the prospector, mountain man, or cattle king be scorned because he reckoned culture by weight and bulk, or recognized beauty only when certified by convention, it must be added that he was faithfully striving for better things. By the building of schools and colleges and free libraries, the West was trying, according to its lights and with admitted future success, to enhance the cultural perception of its children.

40. THE AMERICAN LANGUAGE

It was the great movement to the West that finally fixed the character of the American language, preserving as it did the Elizabethan boldness which characterized the speech of the first settlers. "Our ancestors," said James Russell Lowell in his "On a Certain Condescension in Foreigners," "unhappily could bring over no English better than Shakespeare's." This, of course, was mere rhetoric, and its aim was only to confute the English chauvinists who for more than half a century had been howling against American speechways. As a matter of record, not many of the colonists who stumbled ashore during the seventeenth century were steeped in the poetical glories of the Elizabethan age, and four-fifths of them, in all probability, had never so much as heard of Shakespeare. But if we dismiss the exact meaning of Lowell's words—often a safe plan in dealing with a literary critic—and consider rather their underlying drift, it turns out that a good deal of truth was in them. The newcomers to the wilderness, if they lacked both information and taste, were at least Englishmen, and they shared with all other Englishmen the enormous revolution in the national language, as in almost every other cultural trait, that had gone on during the forty-five years of Elizabeth's reign.

Those years saw the disappearance of the last trace of medieval resistance to change. The English, once predominantly insular and introspective, became an eager and expansive race, full of strange curiosities and iconoclastic enterprises. They began to investigate the world beyond the sky rim; they made contact with outlandish and inexplicable peoples; they looked with sharp and disillusioned eyes upon many of the ideas and ways of life that had sufficed them for centuries. All this ferment of fresh concepts and unprecedented experiences had its inevitable effect upon the language in which they expressed their thoughts, and it began to burgeon in a manner truly amazing. The last of the bonds that fastened it to the other tongues of the Indo-European family were loosed, and it settled into a grammatical structure so slipshod that, in more than one detail, it suggested less the related German, French, Latin, and Greek than Chinese. Simultaneously, there was a sudden increase in its vocabulary, with new words and idioms coming in on all levels, from that

663

of the street boys of London to that of the court poets and university illuminati. The contribution of Shakespeare himself, whether as inventor or as introducer, was heavy, and in part at least it was lasting. Not infrequently, to be sure, he failed to find a market for his novelties, as when he launched *to happy, to child,* and *to verse,* but his successes were quite as numerous as his failures, and it would be hard to imagine English today without some of the terms he introduced, e.g., *to fool, disgraceful, barefaced, bump, countless, critic, gloomy,* and *laughable*; or without the swarming coinages of his contemporary poets and dramatists, e.g., *dimension, conscious, jovial, rascality, scientific, audacious,* and *obscure.*

All these locutions are now universally accepted, and no one apparently has ever challenged them. But as Tudor license began to succumb to Puritan dogmatism, there was a tightening of the whole English *Kultur,* and the language did not escape its effects. Grammarians arose, and efforts were made to break English to the patterns of Latin. All novelties in speech were received hostilely, and the doctrine was launched that there were enough words already, and no more were needed. The Restoration had but little corrective effect upon this foolishness, and it went roaring into the eighteenth century when Samuel Johnson became its chief fugleman. No man who ever undertook to write a dictionary knew less about speechways. He was all theory— and nine-tenths of his theory was nonsense. It may seem incredible today, but it is nevertheless a fact, that he tried to put down *touchy* and *to coax*; what is more, *stingy* and *to derange*; what is yet more, *chaperon* and *fun.* Nor did he battle alone; for example, Jonathan Swift had frowned upon *banter* and *sham, bubble* and *mob, bully* and *to bamboozle.* Under such attacks English became again a highly policed language, and lost almost altogether its Elizabethan hospitality to novelty. The writer who thought of a new word kept it to himself, for the penalty of using it was infamy. The tony English style became an imitation of Johnson's quasi-Latin, and no term was countenanced by the elegant that was not in his dictionary. Thus the old libido for word making went underground, and there it has remained in England, to this day. Ardent neologists, of course, have arisen since Johnson's time—notably Thomas Carlyle—but they have had but little influence upon the language, and a good three-fourths of the novelties it has adopted in our own time have come from the United States, and have been on the level of the vulgar speech.

Why the people of America, despite their general subservience to Puritan ideas, have preserved the Elizabethan boldness of speech remains a bit mysterious; perhaps it is mainly because the life they have led has continued to be predominantly Elizabethan. They had, during their first two centuries, an immediate and menacing wilderness to subdue, and the exigencies of their daily lives did not favor niceness, whether in language or otherwise. It was not until the early years of the nineteenth century that the influence of English purism began to be felt here, save only upon the higher levels, and by that time the great movement into the West had begun—a movement that seems to have fixed finally the character of American speech. Moreover, it is not to be forgotten that, to the immigrants who swarmed in during the century following, life in the United States continued to be a sort of frontier life, even in the East, and that niceness was beyond their powers, even if they were aware of it. Whatever the chain of causes, American English refused to be policed, and it continues in a kind of grammatical, syntactical, and semantic outlawry to this day. The schoolma'am has tried valiantly to bring it to heel, and only too obviously in vain. Most of the native grammarians of any sense have long since deserted her, and the rules they now propagate tend to be more and more inductive. If she continues to war upon *ain't, it's me,* and the confusion of *will* and *shall,* it is only because most of the supergogues who train her are apparently unaware of this collapse of the old-time grammar. New words and idioms swarm around her in such numbers that she is overwhelmed, and her function as an arbiter of speech withers away. In this great free Republic the verdict of life and death upon a neologism is not brought in by schoolma'ams, whether in shorts or step-ins, but by a jury resembling a *posse comitatus,* on which even schoolboys sit. In brief, the American language is being molded by a purely democratic process, and, as on the political level, that process is grounded upon the doctrine that any American is as good as any other.

2

The first Americanisms, naturally enough, were nouns borrowed from the Indian languages, designating objects unknown in England. Some of them reached the present bounds of the United States by way of the older colonies to southward or northward, e.g., *tobacco, canoe,* and *potato,* but the great majority entered the colonial speech directly, and nearly all the earlier ones came from the Algonquin dialects, e.g., *hickory* (1634*), *hominy* (1629), *moccasin* (1612), *opossum* (1610), and *pone* (1612). The colonial chronicles are full of such loans, and though many of them survive mainly in place names or have become obsolete altogether, e.g., *cockarouse* (1624), *sagamore* (1613), and *tuckahoe* (1612), others remain alive in the general American speech, e.g., *moose* (1613), *persimmon* (1612), and *raccoon* (1608). Not a few, indeed, have been absorbed by standard English, e.g., *tomahawk* (1612)

---

* The dates here and hereafter are of the earliest examples found by the searchers for the *Dictionary of American English.*

and *squaw* (1634), and even by other languages, e.g., *totem* (1609). "The Indian element" in American English, said Alexander F. Chamberlain in 1902, "is much larger than is commonly believed to be the case. . . . In the local speech of New England, especially among fishermen . . . many words of Algonkian origin, not familiar to the general public, are still preserved, and many more were once current, but have died out within the last one hundred years." *

At later stages American English was destined to receive many loans from the languages of non-English immigrants, especially the Dutch, French, Spanish, and Germans, but before 1700 they seem to have been relatively small in number. *Portage,* from the French of Canada, has been traced to 1698 and is probably somewhat older, but *bureau, chowder,* and *rapids* are not recorded until the time of the French and Indian War, and many other familiar French loans, e.g., *prairie* and *gopher,* did not come into general use until the Revolutionary era. The same time lag is observed when Spanish loans are investigated, and there was no appreciable infiltration from the German until the middle of the eighteenth century. Even the borrowings from Dutch, save in New York, were very few before 1700. *Scow* is traced to 1669, and *hook* (as a geographical term) to 1670; but most of the loans now familiar are later, e.g., *sleigh* (1703), *stoop* (1755), *span* (of horses, 1769), *cooky* (1786), and *coleslaw* (1794). It was not, indeed, until after Yorktown that there was any considerable infiltration of Dutch into the common speech, and some of the loans now known to every American are surprisingly recent, e.g., *spook* (1801), *cruller* (1805), *waffle* (1817), *boss* (1818), and *Santa Claus* (1823). John Pickering omitted all these save *scow, sleigh,* and *span* from his pioneer *Vocabulary* of 1816, but by 1859 John Russell Bartlett was listing *boss, cooky, hook, stoop,* and *cruller* in the second edition of his *Dictionary of Americanisms. Yankee,* perhaps the most conspicuous contribution of Dutch to American English, was at first applied to the Dutch themselves, and it was not until the years immediately preceding the Revolution that it came to signify a Northern American.

Of far more importance than these loans were the new words that the colonists made of English materials, mainly by compounding but also by giving old words new meanings. *Snowshoe* is traced by the *Dictionary of American English* to 1666, *backlog* to 1684, *leaf tobacco* to 1637, *statehouse* to 1662, *frame house* to 1639, and *selectman* to 1635. By the middle of the eighteenth century the number of such neologisms was very large, and by its end they were almost innumerable. Many were invented to designate natural objects not known in England, e.g., *bluegrass* (1751), *catbird* (1709), *tree frog*

---

* *Journal of American Folk-Lore,* XV (1902), 240. The best account of such loans is to be found in the etymologies by Joseph Coy Green in *Webster's New International Dictionary,* 1934.

(1738), *slippery elm* (1748), *backwoods* (1784), *salt lick* (1751), and *garter snake* (1775), and others were names for new artifacts, e.g., *smokehouse* (1759), *ball ground* (1772), *breechclout* (1757), *buckshot* (1775), *shingle roof* (1749), *sheathing paper* (1790), *springhouse* (1755) and *hoecake* (1755). But not infrequently, as if delighting in the exercise, the colonists devised novel appellations for objects that were quite well known in England, e.g., *broomstraw* (1785), *sheet iron* (1776), *smoking tobacco* (1796), *lightning bug* (1778), and *bake oven* (1777), and almost as often they gave old English names to new objects, e.g., *corn, shoe, rock, lumber, store, cracker, partridge,* and *team*. Some of the latter were extended in meaning, e.g., *rock,* which meant only a large mass of stone in England, and *barn,* which meant only a building for storing crops, with no accommodations for cattle; others were narrowed, e.g., *corn,* which indicated any kind of edible grain to the English, and *boot,* which indicated any leather footgear; and yet others underwent a complete change in significance, e.g., *freshet,* which the English applied to a small stream of fresh water, and to which the Americans gave the meaning of an inundation, and *partridge,* which the English applied to *Perdix perdix* and the Americans to *Bonasa umbellus, Colinus virginianus,* and various other birds.

By 1621 Alexander Gill was noting that some of the new words bred in America were coming into recognition in England, by 1735 Francis Moore was denouncing one of the most vivid of them, to wit, *bluff,* in the sense of a precipice or escarpment, as "barbarous," and by 1754 Richard Owen Cambridge was suggesting that a glossary of them would soon be in order. But so far as the studies of such philological historians as Allen Walker Read, M. M. Mathews, and W. B. Cairns have revealed, there was no attempt at an orderly treatise upon them until 1781, when John Witherspoon printed a series of papers on the subject in the *Pennsylvania Journal and Weekly Advertiser* of Philadelphia.* This Witherspoon was a Scots divine who came out in 1768 to be president of the College of New Jersey (Princeton). When the Revolution shut down his college he took to politics, was elected a member of the New Jersey Constitutional Convention, got promotion to the Continental Congress, and signed both the Declaration of Independence and the Articles of Confederation. But though he was thus ardently for independence as a political idea, he was outraged by its appearance in speech, and denounced not only the common people for daring to exercise it, but also the bigwigs who showed signs of it "in the senate, at the bar, and from the pulpit." His animadversions, in the main, were only echoes of the pedants then flourishing in England, and they had but small effect. Thus

* They appeared under the heading "The Druid." They are reprinted in full in M. M. Mathews, *The Beginnings of American English,* Chicago, 1931.

when he protested against the peculiar American use of *to notify*, as in "The police were notified"—"In English," he said, "we do not *notify* the person of the thing, but the thing to the person"—he roared in vain. The politicians, lawyers, clergy, and journalists of the time paid little heed to him, and the generality of Americans never heard of his attempt to improve their speech.

Of much more potency were the English reviewers who began, after the Revolution, to notice American books. They were, with few exceptions, bitterly hostile to the new republic, and their hostility often took the form of reviling Americanisms. Thomas Jefferson was one of the first victims of this crusade, which went on violently for almost a century and is not infrequently revived in our own time. When he used the verb *to belittle*—apparently his private invention—in his *Notes on the State of Virginia,* the *European Magazine and London Review* showed as much dudgeon as if he had desecrated Westminster Abbey, and during the years following nearly all the other contemporary American writers were attacked almost as savagely, notably John Quincy Adams, John Marshall, Noah Webster, and Joel Barlow. It would be too much to say that all this fury had any substantial effect upon the national language, but it undoubtedly shook some of the national literati. Even Noah Webster was influenced more or less, and in his earlier writings he was extremely polite to English opinion. As for Benjamin Franklin, he yielded to it with only the faintest resistance.

3

This complaisance was broken down at last by the War of 1812, but there were still signs of it in the first formal study of American speech—the beforementioned *Vocabulary* of John Pickering. Pickering was no dilettante like Witherspoon, but a diligent and learned student of language, and Franklin Edgerton has described him as "one of the two greatest general linguists of the first half of the Nineteenth Century in America." * His observations on Americanisms first appeared in a paper he read to the American Academy of Arts and Sciences of Boston in 1815. This paper attracted so much attention that in 1816 he expanded it into a book that is still well worth study, for it is admirably documented and contains a great deal of valuable matter. Unhappily, it is mainly devoted to the objurgations of the English reviewers, and even more unhappily, it shows a lamentable tendency to yield to them. Though he might produce some English authority, says Pickering, for many of the Americanisms he lists, "yet the very circumstance of their being no-

---

* "Notes on Early American Work in Linguistics," *Proceedings of the American Philosophical Society,* July, 1943, p. 27. The other was Peter Stephen Du Ponceau.

ticed by well-educated Englishmen is a proof that they are not in use at this day in England, and of course ought not to be used elsewhere by those who would speak correct English." This position was fatal to any really rational discussion of them, and in consequence Pickering's book probably did more harm than good. Its influence hung over the discussion of the national speech for a long while, and is not altogether thrown off today. A number of American writers, during the thirty years following its publication, dissented sharply from its thesis, notably James K. Paulding; but many more acquiesced, and it was not until 1848, when Bartlett brought out the first edition of his *Dictionary of Americanisms,* that American English found an anatomist willing to take it for what it was, without any regard for what Englishmen or Anglomaniacs thought it ought to be.

Pickering was thoroughly the scholar, and showed some of the deficiencies that occasionally go with that character. His outlook was rather narrow, and he was more than a little cautious. He omitted all mention of Indian loans from his *Vocabulary,* probably because they were predominantly uncouth, and he dealt only gingerly with the common speech. The great movement into the West was already under way as he wrote, and was already coining the gaudy neologisms that were to give color to the national language, but he seems to have been either too pained to deal with them or unaware of them altogether. By Bartlett's day they were everywhere visible; indeed, they were so numerous after 1840 that all novelties in speech came to be called Westernisms. Bartlett not only listed hundreds of them; he obviously relished them, and he found the same relish in a large number of readers, for his *Dictionary of Americanisms* had to be brought out in a revised and expanded form in 1859, again in 1860, and yet again in 1877, during which time its bulk doubled. It is still on the shelves of most public libraries, and copies often turn up in the secondhand bookstores. Bartlett, unlike Pickering, was not a schooled philologian; but he had a fine feeling for language, and in his preface to his fourth edition he discussed the sources of Americanisms with great perspicacity. Most of them originated, he noted, in the argots of the more raffish trades and professions, and entered the common speech as slang. There they entered upon a struggle *à outrance* for general acceptance, with no assurance that the fittest would survive. Some of the best succumbed, and some of the worst gradually took on respectability, were passed by lexicographers, and became integral parts of the language. Such was the history, for example, of *to lynch, squatter, to hold on,* and *loafer.*

There were various other writers on American speech in the period between the Revolution and the Civil War—for example, Jonathan Boucher, David Humphreys, Charles Astor Bristed, James Fenimore Cooper, Robley

Dunglison, and Adiel Sherwood—but their studies were fragmentary and not of any importance.* Noah Webster, though he was an ardent reformer of spelling and believed in the future autonomy of American English, gave relatively little attention to Americanisms, and did not list them in any number until his *American Dictionary* of 1828. The first discussion of them on a large scale by a man trained in language studies was in Maximilian Schele de Vere's *Americanisms: The English of the New World* (1871). Schele was a Swede educated in France and Germany, and was brought out to the University of Virginia to profess modern languages. He arrived in 1844, and save for four years in the Confederate Army, held his chair until 1895. In his book he attempted a classification of Americanisms, and was the first to give adequate attention to the loan words among them. After him there was a hiatus until 1889, when an Englishman, John S. Farmer, published *Americanisms, Old and New,* a useful compilation but not altogether free from English prejudice. A year later the American Dialect Society was formed, and the publication of *Dialect Notes* was begun. The ostensible field of the society was narrow, but it soon branched out into wider studies of the national speech, and there is a vast richness of material in the files of its journal. Its projectors included many philologians of sound distinction—for example, Charles H. Grandgent, E. S. Sheldon, E. H. Babbitt, J. M. Manly, and F. J. Child; and in the course of time it attracted the interest and collaboration of many younger scholars of ability, including especially Louise Pound, who became the first editor of another valuable journal, *American Speech,* in 1925. But the Dialect Society, though it had a profound influence, flourished only feebly, and the publication of *Dialect Notes* was often delayed by lack of money.

Next to the appearance of *Dialect Notes* the event that had most to do with putting the study of American English on a scientific basis was the publication of Richard H. Thornton's *American Glossary* in 1912. Thornton was an Englishman who migrated to the United States in 1874. He was a lawyer by training, and died in 1925 as dean of the Oregon Law School, but a good part of his leisure of half a century was given over to an attempt to produce a really comprehensive dictionary of Americanisms. Pickering, Bartlett, and Farmer before him had introduced the practice of illuminating the subject by dated quotations, but he went much further than any of them. Among other things, he seems to have read the whole file of the *Congressional Globe,* along with a multitude of early newspapers. The result was a work of wide range and very high merit. There were a few slips in it, but not many. Unhappily, no American publisher would venture to publish it, and

* Humphreys, Cooper, Dunglison, and Sherwood are reprinted by Mathews in *The Beginnings of American English.*

Thornton had to turn to a small firm in London.* He continued his researches afterward, and between 1931 and 1939 the printing of his posthumous materials went on in *Dialect Notes*. His work was not only valuable in itself; it also paved the way for the much more comprehensive *Dictionary of American English*, edited by Sir William Craigie and published between 1938 and 1944 by the University of Chicago Press. Meanwhile, a *Linguistic Atlas of the United States and Canada* was begun in 1939 under the supervision of Hans Kurath.

4

"For some two centuries, roughly down to 1820," said Craigie in 1927,† "the passage of new words or senses across the Atlantic was regularly westward; practically the only exceptions were terms which denoted articles or products peculiar to the new country. With the nineteenth century, however, the contrary current begins to set in, and gradually becomes stronger and stronger, bearing with it many a piece of drift-wood to the shores of Britain, there to be picked up and incorporated in the structure of the language." This eastward current, at the start, was resisted with the utmost violence, partly because of the lingering English suspicion of all neologisms, but mainly because of an increase in the political hostility that had begun with the Revolution. From the turn of the century until after the Civil War, the Americans, to all right-thinking Englishmen, were the shining symbols of everything infamous. "They have," wrote Southey to Landor so early as 1812, "acquired a distinct national character for low and lying knavery; and so well do they deserve it that no man ever had any dealings with them without having proofs of its truth." To which the Very Reverend Henry Alford, Dean of Canterbury, added in 1863:

Look at those phrases which so amuse us in their speech and books . . . ; and then compare the character and history of the nation—its blunted sense of moral obligation and duty to man; its open disregard of conventional right when aggrandisement is to be obtained; and I may now say, its reckless and fruitless maintenance of the most cruel and unprincipled war in the history of the world.

The literati—for example, Dickens—were in the forefront of this fray, for they had a special grievance: to wit, the refusal of the United States to make a copyright treaty with Great Britain, and the consequent wholesale piracy of their works by American publishers. But there were also deeper and

* The J. B. Lippincott Company of Philadelphia brought out 250 sets of the London sheets in 1912; but they sold slowly, and there was never a genuinely American edition.
† *The Study of American English* (S.P.E. Tract No. XXVII), Oxford, 1927, p. 208.

more general considerations. The population of the United States had grad-ually overtaken that of the United Kingdom during the first half of the century, and in the fifties it went bounding ahead. American commerce and manufactures began to increase at a rate which offered an alarming menace to English world trade, American agriculture and mining developed in al-most geometrical progression, and the discovery of gold in 1848 and of oil in 1859 gave promise of new and almost illimitable floods of wealth. Thus the English, once only contemptuous, began to view the republic with a mixture of envy and dread, and it is no wonder that most of their chosen augurs hoped (and predicted) that the Civil War would wreck it.

The insular hostility to American ways of speech hardly needed any fresh fillip; it had been active and violent, as we have seen, since the palmy days of the English reviewers. But now it was augmented by a gathering sense of futility. What could be done to stay the uncouth novelties that so copiously barged in? Apparently not much. Every returning English traveler brought them in his baggage, and every American book bristled with them. In 1820, at the precise moment fixed by Sir William Craigie for the turn of the tide, Sydney Smith could still launch his historic sneer at American literature; but only a few years later Cooper and the early American humorists were begin-ning to break down the English barrier, and they were soon followed by authors of greater heft and beam. The English purists, of course, did not surrender without a bitter fight. Moreover, they had some successes, especially against such shocking Westernisms as *gone coon, semioccasional, to scoot, to skedaddle, to stay put,* and *to shell out.* But when they encountered the more decorous and plausible American novelties, e.g., *outdoors, telegram, anesthetic, presidential, to belittle, to progress, reliable, mileage,* and *caucus,* they objected in vain. These words were sorely needed, and England itself had nothing to offer in place of them—nothing so logical, so apt, so good. The Elizabethan gift for bold and vivid neologisms had been transferred to this side of the water, and here it has remained. The dons of Oxford, perhaps, still make some show of clinging to the waspish precepts of Johnson, but the English plain people, ever since the Civil War era, have exhibited an increasing and, in late years, overwhelming preference for the novelties marked "Made in America."

It was the American movie, of course, that gave the final impulse to this revolution. When the first American-made films reached England, in 1907, they were too few and too crude to attract the attention of the guardians of the national speech; but this age of innocuousness did not last long. By 1910 the English newspapers began to print an increasing spate of letters from Old Subscribers protesting against the new words and phrases that the silent legends were bringing in, and during the fifteen years following, the protest gradually mounted to a roar. In 1927 legislation was adopted limiting the influx of American films, and it was hoped that the onslaught might be stayed. That hope was renewed on the advent of the talkie, for most authorities declared that the patriotic English people would never tolerate the abomination of American spoken speech. Even the American movie magnates seem to have been of that mind, for they showed a considerable perturbation in the talkie's early days, and even got out English versions of their master-pieces, manned by proper English actors. But within a short while they had trained their native performers to give a tolerable imitation of English speech, and soon afterward they began to discover that English audiences really did not object to what remained of the Yankee twang. By the middle thirties a wholesale imitation was in progress, and on December 14, 1930, a woman contributor to the London *Evening News* was writing:

An American, coming over to England for the first time, was struck by the fact that English children in the streets of London and elsewhere talked exactly the same as children in the United States. An American impresario came to this country to make films. He was anxious to secure a crowd of English-speaking children, but he utterly failed to find English children who could talk English, and he had to abandon that part of his programme.

To which D. W. Brogan, of Cambridge University, added in 1943:

There is nothing surprising in the constant reinforcement, or, if you like, corruption of English by American. And there is every reason to believe that it has increased, is increasing, and will not be diminished. If American could influence English a century ago, when the predominance of the Mother Country in wealth, population and prestige was secure, and when most educated Americans were reverentially colonial in their attitude to English culture, how can it be prevented from influencing English today, when every change has been a change of weight to the American side? *

5

There was a time when most Americanisms originated in the Western wilds, but by 1940 their source was mainly among city sophisticates, many of whom were devoted professionally to inventing them. They appeared in the compositions of gossip columnists, comic-strip artists, sporting reporters, press agents, advertisement writers, and other such subsaline literati, were quickly gathered into the movies, and were then on their way. They were first adopted in England, as at home, on the lower levels of speech, but if they had the requisite pungency they gradually moved upward. It is curious to note

* "The Conquering Tongue," London *Spectator*, Feb. 5, 1943.

that the very few Briticisms that enter American take a different route: they appear first on pretentious levels, and then sink down. But not many of them ever really survive. English speech seems affected and effeminate to the 100 per cent American, and he would no more use *civil servant, liftman, luggage van,* or *boot shop* than he would stuff his handkerchief into his wristband.

American spelling and pronunciation, like the American vocabulary, have departed considerably from English standards. Efforts to simplify and rationalize the spelling of the language were begun in English so early as the sixteenth century, but it remained for Noah Webster, the American, to work the first effective reforms. It was he who induced Americans to drop the *u* in the *-our* words, the redundant consonants in *traveller, jeweller,* and *waggon,* and the final *k* in *frolick* and *physick*; and to change *gaol* to *jail, plough* to *plow, draught* to *draft, barque* to *bark,* and *cheque* to *check.* In the first flush of his enthusiasm Webster advocated a large number of other reformed spellings, including such bizarre forms as *bred, giv, brest, bilt, relm, frend, speek, zeel, laf, dawter, tuf, proov, karacter, toor, thum, wimmen* and *blud,* but by the time he came to his first dictionary of 1806 he had abandoned them. To the end of his days, however, he had a weakness for *cag* (keg), *hainous, porpess,* and *tung,* and it remained for other lexicographers to dispose of them. Two pets of his later years were *chimist* and *neger,* but they never got a lodgment. Perhaps his partiality for them arose from a desire to change the common American pronunciation. *Neger,* which seems to have been borrowed by the early colonists from some Northern dialect of English, survived until the nineteenth century, though *negro* had been challenging it from the start, and *nigger* has been traced to 1700.

The Simplified Spelling movement, which was launched by Francis A. March, W. D. Whitney, F. J. Child, and other eminent philologians in 1876, languished until 1906, when Theodore Roosevelt, then in the White House, gave it his imprimatur and Andrew Carnegie financed it. In its heyday, during the fifteen years following, it brought out long lists of proposed new spellings, including *corus, giv, stomac, brekfast, harth, bluf, activ, hostil, giraf, ar,* and *wer*; but the country would not have them, and after 1919, when both Roosevelt and Carnegie died, it ceased to trouble. Its efforts, however, succeeded in reducing words of the *programme, catalogue,* and *quartette* classes to their *program, catalog,* and *quartet* forms, and in giving *tho, thoro,* and *thru* a certain amount of countenance. It also promoted the exchange of the last two letters in words of the *theatre* class. In England the reform of spelling at the turn of the century was chiefly furthered by the brothers Fowler. Their *Concise Oxford Dictionary,* which first appeared in 1911, retained the *-our* ending; but it abandoned the English *-ise* for the American *-ize,* and the *y* in *cyder* and its analogues for *i*, and made various other concessions to American practice.

The first Englishmen to observe American speechways all reported that there were no dialects in this country. This was an exaggeration; but it remains a fact, as John Witherspoon wrote in 1781, that "there is a greater difference in dialect between one county and another in Britain, than there is between one state and another in America." More painstaking investigation has revealed three major speech areas. The first includes the New England states, the second the South, and the third all the rest of the country. These areas are divided into subareas more or less narrow, and the speech of Boston differs from that of New England in general just as the speech of the Southern tidewater differs from that of inland regions. But these differences, which mainly have to do with the pronunciation of *a* and the treatment of terminal *r*, are not important, and even on the most ignorant levels an American of one speech area readily understands an American of another. Noah Webster based his recommended pronunciations upon the cultivated usage of New England, and for many years this practice was inculcated by the school-ma'am; but it has been losing ground since the Civil War, and most authorities seem to believe that what is commonly called General American or Western American will eventually prevail everywhere. It is, on all counts, an admirable form of English, and its great superiority to the Oxford form fashionable in England is manifest. A great many educated Englishmen, indeed, denounce the Oxford form as affected and absurd, and it shows no sign of spreading hereafter. General American is much clearer and more logical than any of the other dialects, either English or American. It shows a clear if somewhat metallic pronunciation, gives all necessary consonants their true values, keeps to simple and narrow speech tunes, and is vigorous and masculine.

41. THE MINGLING OF TONGUES

So rich and diverse is the great body of writing by Americans who use tongues other than English that it is difficult to generalize about it in any precise terms; yet, when it is examined in detail, certain recurrent patterns emerge. Prior to 1870 the immigrants to America, however different their backgrounds and the impulses which moved them to migration, underwent in the United States similar emotional experiences and found similar means for their expression. The pattern bears close resemblance to that of the English colonists when they first settled on the Atlantic seaboard, and it was repeated again and again in the westward movement of the frontier.

There was first a pioneer period of diaries and letters. The departure from the old country, the crossing of the ocean, the first steps on the new soil seemed to each traveler an experience of special significance; it demanded to be recorded.

Next came the expression of ideas, religious and political—advanced ideas most of them, though the preponderant immigrant influence has been steadily on the side of conservatism; the majority of the newcomers were democrats only in the sense that they considered the American brand of government best suited to the acquisition and maintenance of property and position. The organizers of communistic experiments, on the other hand, and the intellectuals, sent out by the abortive European revolutions of the early nineteenth century, though few compared to the multitude of laborers, peasants, and artisans, were earnest and articulate social crusaders, journalists, or litterateurs. They were determined to avoid a repetition in the new land of the stresses and suppressions that had driven them from the old. They wanted a perfect America. Each of these men with a mission, as soon as he set foot in the United States, bought a press or secured access to one, and Volume I, Number 1, appeared. Many of these journalistic ventures barely survived their launching; others drifted along for years; a few are prospering today.

The reading class of each racial or national group—of the Germans in Milwaukee, the French in New Orleans, the Mexicans in San Antonio, the Poles in Chicago, the Chinese in San Francisco, the Jews in New York—soon had its own monthly, weekly, or daily paper. Even the smaller and scattered groups had their periodicals. It was not uncommon to find the publisher of an English paper willing, sometimes eager, to allow a German or Norwegian to use his shop to print a sheet that would not compete with his own. The small capital outlay and the scissors and paste-pot editorial method in common use made these foreign language journals practicable if not always of first-rate quality, and they served a dual purpose, giving recently arrived immigrants news from the homeland while offering them opportunities to record their new experiences or express their views. Gradually the space devoted to the news of the mother country and clippings from European periodicals decreased, but the distant continent was never wholly forgotten. Marcus Lee Hansen reminds us that in the years before 1914 the American citizens best read in international affairs were probably the older generation of immigrant farmers in the Middle West. The gradual process of Americanization can be traced, almost measured, by the lengthening columns of American news and the increasing space devoted to the local activities and interests of each immigrant group.

Clumsy and crude as the early attempts at journalism often were, they fostered a taste for expression among both readers and contributors. Simple letters or reminiscences soon developed into memoirs and histories. Essays and polemics followed, and then came the third stage of immigrant writing: stories, novels, and plays, usually with a strongly romantic cast and obviously imitative of Scott, Irving, or Cooper.

2

After 1870 the literary patterns changed. The vast increase in the number of immigrants—nearly a million arrived each year—caused them to concentrate in urban areas where they suffered sharper pains of readjustment than their predecessors of the earlier decades, the majority of whom were absorbed by the land. The new immigrant writers, increasingly conscious of social and economic issues, began to criticize their environment in realistic novels, as the American-born writers of the period were doing.

An important change took place at the same time in the immigrant's attitude toward his native culture and his native tongue. During the nineteenth century he had subscribed to the melting-pot theory, assumed since the time of Crèvecœur and translated into a crusade by such men as Israel Zangwill and Theodore Roosevelt. The immigrant's native gifts and his language would, he had supposed, be distilled into the new American race that was being formed. By the time of the First World War it began to be apparent that no such assimilation was taking place, that the spontaneous play of natural social forces was not achieving the expected fusion of alien cultures. The older Americans took alarm and launched the strident Americanization movement which produced the Immigration Act of 1924. Designed to stabilize the foreign elements in the United States at their current proportions, the Act succeeded in virtually stopping all immigration. It succeeded also in allaying among the "natives" the fear of "foreigners" and in quieting the agitation against them.

Among the foreigners themselves its immediate effect was an intensification of racial and cultural pride. An attitude of mind that had long been growing among the more thoughtful now became general. The national groups ceased to feel that they must abandon as quickly as possible their native language and their native customs. They began to take pride in their racial characteristics, to exploit and cultivate their folklore and folk literature. The reading public in each foreign language increased. At the same time the writers began to translate their work into English so that it might reach a larger audience and America as a whole might come to understand their nation's special characteristics and contributions.

It was at this point, too, that novelists who, though American-born, had grown up in close proximity to one of the cultural islands began to write about their friends and neighbors. Such pictures as George Washington Cable's of the New Orleans Creoles, Willa Cather's of the Nebraska Czechs and Germans, and Harvey Fergusson's of the Spaniards of the Southwest bear eloquent evidence that the regional cultures have enriched American literature.

3

In the work of German-American writers, the most considerable body of non-English writing produced in the United States, many of the lines of the pattern of development we have indicated are clearly and easily discernible. Sooner even than the French in New Orleans, the Germans in colonial Pennsylvania and New York became articulate.

The first exponents of ideas were animated by religious zeal: Francis Daniel Pastorius, founder, in 1683, of Quietist Germantown, whose contribution to colonial literature deserves to be better known; Johann Kelpius, the hermit of the Wissahickon; Conrad Beissel and his monastic brothers and sisters in the Ephrata Cloister in Lancaster County, Pennsylvania, who composed and edited two large collections of hymns (1739, 1766). Benjamin Franklin printed hymn books for the Ephrata Dunkers as early as 1730, and Sauer's press, established in 1738, brought out later editions as well as a complete Bible in German and a German newspaper which reached four thousand readers scattered from Pennsylvania to Georgia. Henry Miller, printer to Congress, founded in 1762 the *Philadelphische Staatsbote* and published many German books. German presses in the United States were soon able to handle anything written here except voluminous works like the *Hallesche Nachrichten* (1787) of the Lutherans, the *Nachrichten* (1735-1752) of the Salzburgers, the diaries of the Moravian missionaries, or the travels of Mittelberger (1756), Achenwall (1769), and Schöpf (1788). Such books, too elaborate for the German-American presses, publishers in Germany were glad to print.

In the second and third decades of the nineteenth century, when the heavier flow of German immigration set in, a stream of travel literature began, much of it designed to attract or direct immigrants. Some of these books had considerable literary power; the immigrants not only studied them before they crossed the ocean but reread them with pleasure in America.

Critical accounts of the New World began to appear at about the same time. In the form of essays or fiction they ranged from extravagant idealization to fierce indictment of everything American, with attempts, by the revolutionaries of 1848, to reshape the United States into something closer to their dreams. Men like Heinzen, Hecker, and Weydemeyer joined with such older liberals as Körner, Weitling, and Münch to form strong German-American blocs bent on reforms which looked to their contemporaries "radical" and "subversive." Others, like Nikolaus Lenau, whose American experience is the basis of Ferdinand Kürnberger's *Der Amerikamüde* (1855), thought improvement hopeless and contented themselves with denunciation of the "philistines of these hog-besotted States, scoundrels all, who in their horrible vacuity cannot conceive that there can be any gods higher than those struck in the mint." If they had circulated beyond the German reading public, books like *Der Amerikamüde,* Karl Büchile's *Land und Volk der Vereinigten Staaten,* and Friedrich Gerstäcker's *Nach Amerika!* (all published in 1855) would have roused quite as much anger as Dickens' *American Notes.*

Somewhere between the extremes of delight and disillusion stood Charles Sealsfield, the first important German-American writer to devote himself to fiction. He was an enthusiastic republican, ready to overlook some cultural deficiencies in the United States because he believed in the rugged virtues which he saw pushing on the construction of a new social order. He was also the sworn enemy of oppression in any form, a fiery defender of liberty, who would swing into action his full battery of satire, ridicule, and abuse whenever he encountered human slavery, political corruption, or commercial opportunism.

Sealsfield cloaked his true identity so effectively during his lifetime that he kept the editors and critics of two continents guessing as to his true nationality. When he died in Switzerland in 1864 his last will and testament revealed that "Charles Sealsfield," "C. Seatsfield," and "C. Sidons" were all of them Karl Anton Postl, a runaway monk from a Bohemian monastery. In 1823 he landed in New Orleans as a German immigrant and traveled extensively through the Mississippi Valley region and the Southwest, possibly as far as Mexico City, gathering experiences and impressions which went into a long shelf of books, essays, and stories published in Germany, in Switzerland, and, sometimes simultaneously, in London, Philadelphia, and New York. In the United States, Sealsfield made Kittanning, Pennsylvania, his headquarters; but he shuttled back and forth across the Atlantic, maintaining precarious connections as a newspaper correspondent and a private political agent in London and Paris. Hobnobbing with people as various as Lord Palmerston, Joseph Bonaparte, and Stephen Girard, he had a hand in a variety of picturesque international intrigues. His books were widely translated and reprinted (with and without his permission), adapted, imitated, and plagiarized, and he enjoyed a considerable international reputation before he was much read in America outside German-American circles, where he was popular from the first. He acquired and proudly maintained American citizenship and, while carefully preserving his anonymity, claimed to be "America's Most Famous Author."

His earliest works were *The United States of North America As They Are,* published in 1827 in Stuttgart and in London, and a book on Austria which attacked the reactionary policy of Metternich. His first novel, *Tokeah, or the White Rose* (1829), recast in *Der Legitime und die Republikaner* (1833), though a rather wooden performance, was a prototype of the genre at which he became so successful—the "ethnographic" novel, where the hero is a whole people. The characters are typical shapers of the new republic, frontiersmen and pioneers. They are portraits, Sealsfield insisted, from life, and they move against a background of magnificent scenery described in realistic detail.

From 1834 to 1841 Sealsfield produced in quick succession a series of novels based on American themes. He grouped them under such collective titles as *Lebensbilder aus beiden Hemisphären* or *Transatlantische Reiseskizzen.* The setting is usually the Southern or Southwestern states, where he was most at home, and where the panorama of river and plantation life, racing, fishing, hunting, and adventures in forest, swamp, and prairie gave his powers of observation and imagination ample scope. The best of these collections is *Das Cajütenbuch* (1841), stories told by a company gathered at a retired sea captain's house (built in the shape of a ship's cabin, hence the title). The tales are most of them dramatic incidents of the Texas War of Secession. "Die

Prairie am Jacinto," with which the book begins, is considered to be Seals-field's best piece of work.

The later books are inferior to the earlier, partly because, during his absence from the United States, Sealsfield lost touch with the rapidly changing American scene, partly because he began to blur his realism with clouds of romantic phantasmagoria. He came to believe that it was impossible to write realistically of a society that no longer existed; so he burned the manuscript of an autobiography together with all his memoirs and personal papers, and retired to Switzerland, poverty, and seclusion.

In addition to his popularity with readers in Europe and the United States, Sealsfield put his impress on American letters through his influence on native American writers. Longfellow spent entire evenings reading his "favorite Sealsfield" and reread the Louisiana portions of the *Lebensbilder* while he was working on the second part of *Evangeline*. A. B. Faust has shown that William Gilmore Simms borrowed a telling episode for *Guy Rivers* from *Ralph Doughbys Brautfahrt,* that Helen Hunt Jackson's *Ramona* bears striking resemblance to *Tokeah,* and that the third, and best, part of Mayne Reid's *Wild Life* is filched outright from Frederick Hardman's translation of *The Cabin Book*.

There were other popular novelists who, like Sealsfield, made literary capital out of their own picturesque adventures in the New World. Friedrich Armand Strubberg was a hunter, soldier, rancher, merchant, physician, and entrepreneur of German colonization ventures before, at fifty-two, he began to turn out, under the pseudonym "Armand," sensational novels with such titles as *Sklaverei in Amerika* (1862) and *Der Sprung vom Niagarafalls* (1864). He was quite uninfluenced by Sealsfield or anyone else, and his unliterary straightforward prose gives his wildest tales an air of authenticity. His *Carl Scharnhorst: Abenteuer eines deutschen Knaben in Amerika* (1872) was long one of the most popular German stories for boys.

Friedrich Gerstäcker, after adventures that led him through both Americas, produced some hundred and fifty books of travel and adventure, half fictional, half true, to become, during the fifties, the most popular of German-American novelists. His best known and in some respects his best work is *Nach Amerika!* (1855), a realistic account of the fortunes of a shipload of German immigrants who land in New Orleans and make their way up the Mississippi.

More skillful as a writer—his best *Erzählung* is *Der Pedlär* (1857)—was Otto Ruppius, who came to the United States as a refugee in 1848 and worked as a journalist in New York and St. Louis until 1861, when the Prussian proclamation of amnesty permitted his return.

Heinrich Balduin Möllhausen, sometimes called the German Cooper, came to seek not political refuge but adventure. He served as artist and topographer for the Smithsonian Institution on expeditions charting transcontinental railway routes across the mountains, and turned his experiences into some fifty novels and travel books which were translated into English, French, Dutch, and various other languages.

Though all these writers returned eventually to their native land, they are to be considered not German travelers but actual German-Americans. They shared the hazards of migration and the hardships of the frontier, and their point of view is always that of the immigrant and settler, never of the European observer merely.

More brilliant as a writer than any of the adventure novelists was the German-born polemicist and poet Robert Reitzel. He was educated for the ministry but turned freethinker. In the United States he wandered about the country lecturing, writing, and lending a hand to any agitation fomented in the Midwest by German radicals. He propagandized for *Sozialdemokratie, Weltbürgertum, Materialismus, Arbeiterbewegung, Turnerei, Freimännerei,* defying arbitrary power wherever he met it and loving truth even to a pose. In 1884 his friends and admirers set him up in Detroit as editor of a weekly literary paper, which he named *Der arme Teufel,* and into which he poured, for the remaining fourteen years of his life, his wit, irony, and fierce philippic. He recognized revolutionary spirits when he found them and by excerpt and translation did much to familiarize readers on the frontier with the ideas of Emerson and Thoreau.

The nineteenth century German-Americans were of course prolific writers of lyric verse. Thousands of poems chant praise of the adopted home or sigh for the distant fatherland, and the range beyond these obvious themes is wide. There is a considerable body also of German-American epic poetry, and there are some interesting poetic narratives based on immigrant and frontier experience. The poets tried valiantly, too, to familiarize their countrymen with the poetry which was being read by their new fellow citizens. German translations were made of *Evangeline, Hiawatha,* "The Raven," *Snowbound,* and *Leaves of Grass,* as well as of the English poets most popular in the United States. Chicago was long the poetic capital: at least half the High German poetry written in America was published there.

The German theater in America began in New York in 1840, and by 1854 the city had two houses devoted entirely to German plays. The famous Germania Theater opened in 1872; the Thalia in 1879; and the Irving Place in 1888. Philadelphia, Milwaukee, Chicago, St. Louis, and Cincinnati also had important theaters, and in at least a dozen other cities with large German populations the drama flourished. With rare exceptions the plays presented were classics of the German stage, for the actors were far more interested in performing great roles like Wallenstein and Hamlet than in encouraging new playwrights, but there are a few notable instances of plays by German-Americans reaching and holding the boards. Those plays that succeeded best had such titles as *Ein lateinischer Farmer* and *Der Corner Grocer aus der Avenue A,* though, unlike the novelists, most of the playwrights sought to dramatize events of grand proportions or to tell romantic stories against exotic backgrounds.

After 1870 the use of German in speech and writing declined. The once popular *Erzählungen* survived only in the moralized tales of church periodicals; by 1900 the German theater had almost disappeared; and lyric poetry grew weak and thin. By the twentieth century not more than two or three writers of importance were using High German. Literature in German dialects, on the other hand, especially Pennsylvania German, increased steadily as cultural pride and racial consciousness grew. The dialects lent themselves readily to humor, and popular verse appeared in Hessian, Swabian, and Palatinate as well as in *Plattdeutsch.*

Less defensible linguistically, though amusing to a larger audience, were Karl Adler's *Mundartlich Heiteres* (1886) and Charles Godfrey Leland's *Hans Breitmann Ballads* (1856–1895), written in a kind of *Kauderwelsch,* a mixture of broken English and German dialect, not to be confused with Pennsylvania German. Hans is a huge, bearded, good-natured rogue, who gorges and guzzles his way through a roistering and checkered career, speaking a tongue and portraying a character which German-Americans say is a libelous caricature. Much later, in the twenties and thirties, Kurt M. Stein succeeded in amusing both Americans and Germans with the same sort of linguistic exaggerations.

4

Pennsylvania German, or Pennsylvania Dutch as it is often called, is more nearly a language than a dialect. It is the tongue of the emigrants from the Palatinate and the upper Rhine who settled in Pennsylvania in the seventeenth and eighteenth centuries. During the long colonial period, Pennsylvania German literature, most of it religious, was written in literary German, but there was a decade between 1830 and 1840 when dialect stories, poems, and columns filled the newspapers and magazines. After the Civil War, High German receded while English advanced, but the trilingual Pennsylvania German clung tenaciously all the while to his vernacular. The language ceased to be funny, and men like Henry Harbaugh and Henry L. Fisher used it to preserve "in simplicity, dignity, and loveliness" all phases of life from the cradle to the grave and beyond. Legends, tall tales, anecdotes of rural and small-town life, huskings, apple butter bees, and quilting parties, gentle satire of pretenses, and superstitions are the common themes of Pennsylvania German poetry. More and more dialect was written as the century wore on; probably nowhere else in the United States were so many average citizens trying to express themselves in verse. Newspaper letters were followed by newspaper columns and then by dialect radio programs. The dialect short story flourished. Also, like the High Germans, the Pennsylvania German poets translated for their audiences the currently popular American poems. Toward the middle of the twentieth century, as knowledge of the written language waned, dialect plays became increasingly popular.

Exploitation of the Pennsylvania Germans in American literature began as early as 1869 in the novels of Mrs. Phebe Gibbons and has continued ever since. Most widely read of the exploiters is Mrs. Helen Reimensnyder Martin, whose *Tillie: A Mennonite Maid* (1904) went into twenty editions. She followed it with a score or more of novels and short stories, some of which were dramatized and others made into movies. The Pennsylvania Germans themselves think Mrs. Martin's pictures defamatory, and generally prefer those of the even more prolific novelist Elsie Singmaster (Mrs. Elsie S. Lewars).

5

French literature did not begin to blossom in Louisiana until that region had been separated from the mother country for more than half a century. Starting timidly when Louisiana was transferred to Spain in 1762, it grew vigorously only after the annexation of the territory by the United States (1803). Scarcely any of the work of the early period survives, and what importance it has is not literary but historical.

After 1820 the number of French writers in Louisiana is large. Edward Larocque Tinker's bibliography lists three hundred fifty in a population of less than a quarter of a million Creoles, as the descendants of the original French and Spanish settlers were called. The ability to write either prose or verse was a necessary accomplishment for a Creole gentleman whatever his occupation, and leisure for writing increased when the admission of the territory to statehood (1812) and successive waves of immigration from the North brought a rise in land and slave values. The Creoles now had means for travel and study abroad, generally Paris, which strengthened their cultural ties with France. At the same time, as the number of Anglo-Saxons about them multiplied, the Creoles became more aggressively conscious of their language and culture, and more determined to preserve them. It was in this period, from 1840 on, that the most significant French works appeared, Gayarré's histories, the lyrics of the Rouquette brothers, Canonge's plays, and Testut's historical novels.

Charles Etienne Arthur Gayarré was a Creole whose ancestors had for generations been prominent in the colony—his maternal grandfather was host to the Duke of Orléans during his visit to Louisiana in 1798. Educated in New Orleans and trained at law in Philadelphia, Gayarré entered politics and held several important elective and appointive positions, including that of United States Senator in 1835, an office which he resigned for reasons of health soon after his election. Very wealthy, he was able to spend eight years of travel in Europe collecting material and documents for his history of Louisiana. His first survey was the *Essai historique sur la Louisiane* (1830) which, enlarged and documented, became *Histoire de la Louisiane* (1846–1847). Later he published in English several series of lectures which, collected into four volumes, formed his *History of Louisiana* (1866).

Gayarré was ambitious also to become Louisiana's Walter Scott. He wrote novels and one play, and in his histories took some poetic liberty with strict fact. He took care also in the course of his historical narrative to point out good subjects for fiction, such as the expedition of the Chevalier Saint-Denis into Mexico in 1714. His suggestions were seized upon by a number of novelists and playwrights. Charles Testut drew on Gayarré for two of his three historical novels; so did Louis-Armand Garreau for his *Louisiana* (1849), a tale of the anti-Spanish conspiracy of 1768. That same conspiracy inspired a poetic tragedy by Auguste Lussan and a prose drama by Louis-Placide Canonge. Canonge, the best of Louisiana dramatists, was the author of *Le Comte de Carmagnola* (1856), which is said to have had a run of one hundred performances on the Parisian stage.

The only Louisiana poetry of importance was written by the Rouquette brothers, sons of a French father and a Creole mother, who idealized the noble savages of the St. Tammany forest near New Orleans. Their admiration of the Indians was no mere product of theory and imagination, like that of their French contemporaries. As small boys they perpetually ran away from home to live with the Choctaws, and each of them spent a large portion of his mature life in the woods.

François-Dominique Rouquette, the elder and the better poet of the two, was educated in New Orleans and Paris and, as long as the family fortune permitted him to live as he pleased, alternated residence in Paris with sojourns in St. Tammany. Forced eventually to support himself, he engaged in a variety of unsuccessful ventures ranging from the direction of a *lycée* in New Orleans to the running of a grocery store in Arkansas. He finally ceased to worry about practical affairs or to feel any obligation to society, while he extolled in his poetry the simple primitive life of the Indians and

Negroes, the beauties of solitude and of nature. His *Meschacébéennes* (Paris, 1839) was praised by Hugo and Béranger, and *Fleurs d'Amérique* (New Orleans, 1857) was also well received by Parisian critics. His social attitude is made plain in a Civil War poem: "If I don't fight, the State has me shot; and if I fight, Uncle Sam will hang me."

The younger Rouquette, Adrien-Emmanuel, had been so fascinated by the life of the Indians that when he completed his education in France, he went back to his Choctaws and, like a proper romantic, fell in love, from reports of her beauty, with an Indian chief's daughter whom he had never seen. (She died of consumption before their marriage.) Like his brother, Adrien-Emmanuel traveled back and forth between Paris and New Orleans, and it was in France that he published his first collection of poems, *Les Savanes* (1841). Barthélemy and Sainte-Beuve praised it; Brizeux hailed the author as "the American Ossian," and Thomas Moore called him "the American Lamartine." On his return to Louisiana, Adrien-Emmanuel entered a seminary and was ordained priest. For fourteen years he served as vicar-general of the Archbishop of New Orleans, longing always for the solitude of the forest and the society of the Indians, feelings he expressed in his prose work *Le Thébaïde en Amérique* (1852). Eventually he obtained permission to go as a missionary to the Choctaws, with whom he spent the rest of his life, identifying himself with them so completely that they called him Chahta-Ima, "One of Us." He died in 1887 while working on a dictionary of the Choctaw language. His books include *Wild Flowers* (1848), a collection of his English poems, and *La Nouvelle Atala* (1879), an Indian legend which was highly praised by his friend Lafcadio Hearn. He wrote also some delightful poems in gombo, the Negro-French dialect.

The Civil War was a fatal blow to the French language and French literature in Louisiana. It ruined the Creoles, like the rest of the wealthy South, and cut the umbilical cord that had connected them with France; they could no longer afford Parisian travel and education. During the Reconstruction period, also, there was strong government hostility to French culture, partly because it was alien, partly because of the uncompromising loyalty the Creoles had shown to the Confederacy. In 1868 it was decreed that laws and documents in Louisiana must be published in English only; and the teaching of French was forbidden in elementary and frowned upon in secondary schools. Children of Creole families speaking the French they had learned at home were taunted by their schoolmates as "kiskeedees" ("Qu'est-ce-qu'il dit?"). Older writers like Gayarré and the Abbé Rouquette continued for a time to publish in French, but few young men rose to take their places and carry on their work.

Most important of the small group who fought the losing battle was Dr. Alfred Mercier, who combined novel and poetry writing with his medical practice. With eleven other intellectuals he founded in 1876 the Athénée Louisianais, a cultural association, whose bulletin, the *Comptes Rendus*, was for a time the sole medium of publication for French writers in Louisiana. Dr. Mercier himself contributed more than sixty items. One of the later contributors, Alcée Fortier, made the first attempt at a survey of French litera- ture in Louisiana and composed also a *History of Louisiana* (1914), which equals Gayarré's in importance.

Twentieth century scholars have made interesting studies of the interplay of French and American culture, and in both the nineteenth and twentieth centuries the Creole has furnished material for American fiction. The best pictures of French New Orleans are in the novels and stories of George Wash- ington Cable, Kate Chopin, Lafcadio Hearn, and Grace King.

6

During the period of Spanish exploration and conquest of the American Southwest and during the Mission period that followed, reports, histories, diaries, and memoirs were written by government officials and by members of the religious orders. Some of these were published in Spain or Mexico and were later printed in English versions by American historians.

The literature that survives today among the descendants of the early colonists is an oral literature of plays, songs, ballads, and folk tales brought from old Spain. In 1598 missionary priests in New Mexico began to perform religious mysteries and pantomimes as a way of teaching Christianity to the Indians, and the tradition has survived. Every year at the recurrence of certain festivals, especially during the Christmas season, local casts in most of the Spanish settlements produce religious dramas. Most popular of these are *Los Tres Magos, Los Moros y los Christianos, Los Pastores, La Aparición de Nuestra Señora de Guadalupe,* and *Los Comanches.*

Of other writing there was little. The theocratic rule of the Mission period was hostile to profane knowledge. Scientific books were sometimes publicly burned, and not until 1833 was a printing press brought to California. Then it published almost exclusively official documents. The first volume printed in Texas, in 1829, was in English by an American immigrant. The seculariza- tion of the Missions (1833-1834) might have created an atmosphere more favorable to literature, but it was accomplished only a few years before the annexation of California. The Gold Rush followed almost immediately, bringing a large American immigration and a period of lawlessness which impoverished the Spanish settlers. The rancher class could not acquire the wealth and leisure with which to do for Spanish literature what the Creole planters of Louisiana had done for French.

In the twentieth century, Spanish-American culture, both early and contemporary, furnished material to such American-born novelists as Gertrude Atherton, Willa Cather, Harvey Fergusson, and John Steinbeck.

7

Long before Italian immigrants came in large numbers to America, Italian explorers, political exiles, and adventurers visited or settled in the United States. Their number was small—3,645 in 1850, 16,766 in 1870—not large enough to form a reading public, and the literary men among them wrote consequently in the languages spoken by the people with whom they lived—English, French, Spanish—rather than in their native tongue. One of the few early works in Italian is a series of articles on the political problems of the colonies in 1774, written by the physician, trader, farmer, and diplomat Filippo Mazzei. It was translated into English by Thomas Jefferson and published in Pinckney's *Virginia Gazette*.

The political exiles who came to America between 1815 and 1861 either published in English or had their Italian works published in Italy. The only notable exception was Lorenzo Da Ponte, author, before he came to America in 1805, of many librettos, including Mozart's *Le Nozze di Figaro* and *Don Giovanni*. Settling in New York, he became the first professor of Italian at Columbia University and published numerous Italian works in prose and verse, most of them ephemeral. His only surviving book is an autobiography, republished several times in Italy and translated into French and English.

After 1880 the huge increase in Italian immigration created an American market for Italian writers, but, since most of the immigrants were of humble origin, their literary requirements were satisfied by the daily and periodical press and the propaganda literature published by labor groups and the Protestant churches who tried to evangelize them. The better writers soon began to use English as well as Italian, partly to reach the American reading public, and partly because the majority of the children of the immigrants were unable to read Italian.

8

Scandinavian culture in the United States is nineteenth century history, but its pattern of development bears close resemblance to those of the earlier migrants from Southern Europe. More easily than the Germans or Latins, the Norwegians, Swedes, and Danes adjusted themselves to the new land. They had had at home some schooling in democratic processes; they had not been much hampered by class distinctions; and they gravitated toward the broad expanses of the American Northwest where they took natural and sturdy root. Their numbers increased with such rapidity that there were, for example, more Norwegians in the United States at the end of the nineteenth century than there had been in Norway at its beginning. The Swedes, too, are numerous and have to their credit a considerable body of literature in the United States. The earlier writers were either journalists or ministers, but a professional literary class developed toward the end of the nineteenth century, producing a great quantity of work in the familiar forms, some of it excellent in quality. But no Swedish-American author emerged of the stature of the American-Norwegian Rölvaag.

The growth of Scandinavian-American literature is closely associated with the vigorous development of the Scandinavian periodical press, but before long the writers were using English even when treating Old World themes. The first Norwegian-American novel, Hjalmar Hjorth Boyesen's *Gunnar*, was written in English and published (1873) by William Dean Howells in the *Atlantic Monthly*. The material is all Norwegian. It is the story of a little goatherd and a mermaid, and the trolls play important parts. Some of the later novelists wrote successfully in two languages, but most of them used English whether they were dealing with Scandinavian themes or with pioneer struggles against Indians and the wilderness.

In the twentieth century the social novel became a distinctive feature of this literature. It reached its highest point in O. E. Rölvaag's novel of Norwegian-American life, *Giants in the Earth* (1927). Rölvaag, who was born of Norwegian fisherfolk, came to America in 1896 when he was twenty years old. He worked for three years on his uncle's farm in South Dakota and then determined to get an education. Without funds, with scant knowledge of English, struggling against illness, he put himself through three years of school and matriculated at St. Olaf College in Northfield, Minnesota. His determination, his ability, and his fine integrity of character endeared him to his professors who, after his graduation in 1905, made possible for him a year of graduate study in Norway and then called him back to St. Olaf to teach Norwegian.

Rölvaag found the transition from the Old World to the New difficult, but exciting and rewarding. He analyzed the process thoughtfully and became convinced that, to make a good American, a Norwegian must be surely rooted in his own culture. He believed that the United States needs the stability and mature richness of the old civilizations. All his life—it was cut short at fifty-five—he taught this doctrine with passion, in his classroom, on the lecture platform, in societies organized in the Northwest for the preservation of Norwegian culture, and in the many novels he wrote in Norwegian from *Amerika-Breve* (1912), so autobiographical that he published it under a pseudonym, to *Peder Victorious* (1929) and *Their Father's God,* published in

1931, the year of his death. Most effective of all was *Giants in the Earth* (1927), which, translated like most of his work and widely read in both Norway and the United States, fulfilled the ambition Rölvaag had cherished from his college days to become the spokesman of his people, to tell the story of the immigrant's part in the making of the great new nation.

9

Jewish-American literature, one of the richest products of the mingling of tongues, has developed in some respects in ways similar to those followed by the Latin, German, and Scandinavian. In other respects the divergence is sharp, for Jewish immigration derived from all parts of the world, and each Jewish immigrant brought with him not only the racial and religious traits which united him with other Jews but also many of the manners and customs of the people among whom he dwelt before migrating. Thus the Jews in the United States form not one composite group but rather a congeries of many groups, at once individualistic and generic. Hebrew, traditionally the national language of the Jew, is spoken by relatively few of the Jews outside Palestine, while Judaeo-German, commonly called Yiddish, as the mother tongue of some seven million, is the nearest approach to a Jewish language. German and French, Greek and Syrian Jews often spoke the language of their fellow nationals, while Russian and Polish Jews, hedged about by restrictions in the old country, spoke mainly Yiddish. Many a Jewish immigrant, landing in the United States, had to submit to a double process of assimilation: first to find his place in the ghetto, and then to make his way in the New World. In spite of these handicaps and other difficulties, Jews, who in 1825 numbered only 16,000, increased until a century later there were more than 4,000,000. Approximately half this number lived in New York City, making it the largest Jewish community in the world.

The literature of the Jews in the United States, as in almost all European countries, began with Hebrew writings of a religious nature and branched out either into the special national dialects used by the Jews among themselves or into Yiddish. They have considerable bodies of literature not only in Hebrew and Yiddish but also in German, English, French, Spanish, Portuguese, Italian, Dutch, and Russian. Sharply divided by factions, often splitting on one issue while combining on another, they are subject not merely to linguistic cleavages but also to such a variety of social, religious, and economic strains and stresses that valid generalizations are hard to make.

The love of Zion, which found early supporters in America in individuals like Mordecai Manuel Noah, Emma Lazarus, and Henrietta Szold, has always been indissolubly linked with religious orthodoxy and the Hebrew language. The plight of Jews in Europe shortly before and after 1900 won support for "political" Zionism from many Jews in America hitherto untouched by the Zionist program; and after the First World War Zionism, under Louis D. Brandeis, appealed to a larger American following than ever before. Brandeis approached Zionism through Americanism, explaining that, to be good Americans, Jews must be better Jews; and, to be better Jews, they must become Zionists.

The movement was marked from the beginning by a fervent faith and high idealism; but faith and idealism were not enough to attract and hold the masses, who were moved by social forces in the ghetto, by hard working conditions, and by the struggle for existence to look for leadership to the labor unions and the radical Yiddish press, both of which were largely antireligious and anti-Hebraic.

Then there were many who, holding to the melting-pot theory of social-racial assimilation, broke with their cultural heritage and sought, by obliterating the Jewish element within them, to become altogether "American," or tried, by the annihilation of all national differences, to promote an unrealistic internationalism or an impossible cosmopolitanism. Between these extremes were all possible variations and gradations, so that no racial or national group in the United States presents a greater range of conflict and complication than the Jewish.

The literary import of this complexity is indicated by such a compilation as A. S. W. Rosenbach's *An American Jewish Bibliography . . . [to] 1850* (1926). The complexity is increased by the remarkable activity, first of the Yiddish writers following the great Jewish migration from Eastern Europe that began in 1881, and second, by American Jews writing in English, from Mordecai Noah and Emma Lazarus to Waldo Frank and Ludwig Lewisohn or George Jean Nathan and Elmer Rice (Reizenstein), to say nothing of Jewish personalities in the related fields of the cinema and the radio. In many instances the American Jew who expresses himself in English has written, consciously or unconsciously, in a manner to make his product almost indistinguishable from the main stream of Anglo-American literature. This tendency on the part of Jews who write in English has become so marked that one prominent Jewish critic, Ludwig Lewisohn, has insisted that whatever the medium or the subject, a book is Jewish only when it is written by a Jew who "knows he is a Jew." But even this simple distinction fails to identify satisfactorily all books produced by Jews. It classifies Abraham Cahan's *Rise of David Levinsky* (1917) as "Jewish," though written in English, but it does not dispose as patly of Mary Antin's autobiography, *The Promised Land* (1912), a lyric, ecstatic apostrophe to America as the golden land of opportunity for the persecuted immigrant child from the Pale of Settlement.

One of the strongest forces in arresting the assimilative process of the Jew has been the ancestral language, which, in turn, was kept alive even during the darkest days of Jewry by the fact that Jewish religious observance remained largely identified with the Hebrew language. As might be expected, the earliest Hebrew books produced in the United States were almost exclusively rabbinical works like "responses" on disputed points of religious law or practice, commentaries on parts of the Talmud, and homilies. Of strictly literary books in Hebrew virtually none appeared until after the profound effects of the First World War quickened popular interest on the part of American Jewry in the Hebrew movement. Where earlier periodicals had seldom survived beyond a year or two, the new Zionism aided in the establishment and maintenance of new journals, notably the monthly *Hatoren* (founded in 1913), the *Miklat* (1917), the *Hadoar,* a Zionist weekly (1921), and the *Bitzaron* (1939), a monthly of high standards. The establishment of the Histadruth Ivrith, or Hebrew Organization, which serves as a central agency for the dissemination of Hebrew culture in America, aided in the founding of the *Hadoar.* This same organization, through its publishing company, has issued some fifty books and pamphlets, including an anthology of American-Hebrew poetry. While not devoted exclusively to the propagation of Hebrew, the Jewish Publication Society, taking as its motto "More Jewish books in Jewish homes," has reinforced the work of the Hebrew Organization. It encourages authors to devote their attention to Jewish subjects. It has published some two hundred titles. In 1940 it sold 52,844 volumes to numerous persons throughout the country, including many of its 6,357 members. It is estimated that through its efforts three and a half million copies of Jewish books have reached the homes of Jews and of Gentiles interested in Jewish knowledge.

There is a considerable body of Hebrew poetry, and there are a few novels, short stories, and essays, but American-Hebraic writings are still primarily rabbinical, and the writers are still essentially East-European immigrants. The development of a genuine American-Hebrew literature, indigenous to the country and rooted in American soil, remains contingent upon the crystallization of an American Judaism and an American Jewish tradition.

Yiddish, or Judaeo-German, literature in the United States began slowly. The educated refused to recognize Yiddish as a literary language, and the masses, driven by toil and grinding poverty, bought few books. But with the rapid increase of immigration, the gradual recognition of Yiddish as a legitimate vehicle for literary expression, and the establishment of periodicals, Yiddish authors began to find support. By 1916 the Yiddish daily press in New York was reaching 537,982 readers; after that it hovered between three and four hundred thousand. In Chicago, Philadelphia, Cleveland, and other cities, Yiddish periodicals flourished.

It was Abraham Cahan of *Vorwärts* (*Forward,* founded 1897) who did most to make newspapers the principal literary outlet and source of support for Yiddish writers. By consistently maintaining high standards for the fiction and poetry published, he raised the level of literary appreciation among Yiddish readers; and he was as assiduous in discovering new talent as in maintaining established writers. Such men as Sholem Asch (whose *Kiddush Ha-Shem,* 1926, is usually considered the greatest Yiddish novel), Abraham Weissen, and Jonah Rosenfeld were contributors to the paper. While doing the normal daily chores of newspaper work, they were permitted to create what they pleased in whatever way they pleased. Metropolitan editors and editors in other cities followed Cahan's leadership in this respect, so that the rise of Yiddish literature has been closely identified with the development of Yiddish journalism. This relationship is one of the important reasons for the use by Yiddish writers of the *Skitze* and the short story rather than the full-length novel. Most important of *Skitze* writers are Solomon Libin (Israel Hurewitz) and Solomon Rabinowitz (Shalom Aleichem), sometimes called the Jewish Mark Twain.

Yiddish writers, who made almost no progress in the drama while they were in Europe, found in America the conditions they needed for developing their talents. Their earlier and crude dramatic workmanship underwent a reformation at the hands of the producer Jacob Gordin, who, while not himself a playwright of the first class, recognized excellence when he met it in the work of others. By the end of the nineteenth century he had lifted Yiddish drama from cheap popular entertainment to the dignity of legitimate art. His insistence that acting was an art, demanding serious study and hard work, did much to raise the level of dramatic performance and undoubtedly contributed to the preeminence which the Jews have enjoyed in the twentieth century American theatrical world. The Yiddish theater in America, which began as early as 1883, reached its high point in the twenties with the organization of the Yiddish Art Theater under, successively, Emmanuel Reicher, Ben-Ami, and Maurice Schwartz.

The study of other foreign literary cultures in the United States—of such groups as the Icelanders, Finns, Poles, Czechs, Portuguese, South Americans, and Asiatics—has only just begun, but it is evident that the patterns they follow are similar to those that have been examined in detail. Something of the nature of this cultural amalgamation may be discovered by following the leads suggested in the bibliographical essay on "The Mingling of Tongues." The early desire to cast the Old World into a mythical melting pot has given place to a conviction that the immigrant serves his adopted country best when he is steeped in the traditions of his fatherland; that various and lively regional cultures increase the vitality of the culture of the United States.

42. THE INDIAN HERITAGE

Nοτ until the nineteenth century was well on its way did Americans begin to look upon the Indian as a cultural asset. The English colonists on the Atlantic seaboard usually felt that the best Indian was a dead Indian, and whole tribes were extinguished without any record of their inner life. If Indian traditions became known, they were romanticized and dressed up in cultural-white literary modes.

Interest in the Indian, even on the part of Cooper, was more in the individual than in his traditions or arts. It was not until the time of Henry Rowe Schoolcraft that any adequate attempt was made to gather the tales and songs of any American Indian tribe.

Schoolcraft was a good workman, and in the 1830's he collected a large amount of authentic traditional lore from the Ojibwa tribes around Sault Ste. Marie. But he lived in a romantic age, and there seems to be little doubt, in the light of more recent collections, that he not only changed and prettified, but actually invented some of his material. He certainly mixed the traditions of various tribes. In spite of all this, however, he did a fine service in bringing to the American public some acquaintance with the interesting legends of our Indians. It is also fortunate, of course, that Schoolcraft's work should have fallen into the hands of Longfellow at a favorable moment. For it is through *Hiawatha* that most Americans even now learn what little they know about the American Indian story.

The remarkable group of ethnologists who worked in the last decades of the nineteenth and the first of the twentieth century achieved at last an adequate record of Indian life and lore. They set themselves at all times an ideal of verbal accuracy in reporting, and they tended increasingly to take material down in the original language. With the perfection of phonograph recording it became possible to preserve not only words and phrases but also the actual tone and emphasis of oral delivery; thus it is as an oral art that American Indian song and tradition must be considered.

There is really no such thing as a written literature among the Indians of the United States. Such picture writing as appears on rocks and on birch bark or skins is nothing more than a kind of sign language, sometimes serv-

694

ing as a crude historical record and sometimes as a device for remembering the details of ceremonial. The most ambitious "literary" production of the Indians of the United States is a historical record of the Delaware Indians known as the Walam Olum. The text, apparently taken down by dictation, is accompanied by illustrative pictographs. Its value is entirely linguistic and historical, not actually literary.

All traditions of artistic value among our Indians are oral. These are handed down by word of mouth and are retained by individual and collective memory. Such expression is analogous in many of its details of form and substance to the genres familiar to students of European literatures. It serves and has served for a very long time the same needs for its unlettered folk as the literature of manuscript and printed page has served for its readers.

Somewhere among American aboriginals examples of nearly all of the familiar literary patterns are to be found. The lyric, always as a song; the chant; the incantation; the myth; the fairy tale; the humorous anecdote; occasionally even the riddle and the proverb—all these have been widely practiced from the time when we first meet the Indians shortly after the Discovery. The small amount of change observable in their traditions suggests that many of these patterns must be very old. We read tales in the Jesuit Relations of the 1630's and find them told three centuries later with insignificant change. But there has also been a continual importation of the new and an adoption of material from neighboring tribes, and the far traveler has always carried alien material and transplanted it in distant regions. This folk literature of the natives of the United States is therefore a complex structure, the result of the mingling of many influences and of centuries of ripening and refining.

It is not possible to consider the Indians of the United States in complete separation from those of the rest of the continent. Our present political boundaries have no practical bearing upon the traditions of these people. The coast tribes of Washington and British Columbia form a unit, while those of Oregon and California do not. Our Pueblo culture extends far into Mexico, and the Blackfeet are equally at home in Montana and Alberta. A thorough study of the American Indian must be made with the whole continent as a background. We may well assume that the high culture of the Incas in Peru and the Mayas in Yucatan produced their correspondingly fine myths and ceremonial songs, and perhaps other literary forms. But, except for some poor fragments preserved by early Spanish colonizers, this literature has perished and left no trace in tradition.

2

Both because of the wealth of available collections and the wide geographical distribution which they display, myths and tales have always been given more attention than other aspects of American Indian folklore. In contrast to the students of a half-century ago, recent scholars no longer expect to find hidden meanings, symbolism, or dream interpretation in them; nor are they concerned with determining just what is tale and what myth. They find that these narratives not only are interesting in themselves, but afford an excellent opportunity for studies of the distribution of narrative material from one culture area to another and for a comparative examination of narrative patterns. Any reader of American Indian tales becomes impressed with a certain uniformity in the story plots throughout the continent; but further examination always brings out significant differences dependent not only upon geography but also upon many obscure facts of history. For the nine well recognized culture areas north of Mexico present not only their characteristic tale patterns but interesting differences in stylistic emphasis and in the social milieu of story-telling.

In accordance with the definition of mythological tale here suggested, a considerable number of the stories coming from all these regions can be thought of as myths. They give accounts of origins, and their action lies in a world different from the present. As for the actual myth of creation, it is hardly present at all. Perhaps the nearest approach to it is to be found in California and the Southwest. A number of the small tribes still surviving in California have rather elaborate accounts of the formation of the earth and its features and of the beginnings of human culture. But the "creator," usually conceived of in animal form, already floats about on a primeval water and sends down one animal after another to bring soil from the bottom. When the muskrat or some other animal succeeds in bringing a little soil, the creator works upon it and makes the earth. But the initial problem of where the primeval water and the muskrat came from, as well as how the creator himself came into being, remains as unanswered by these people as by our own theologians.

Somewhat less naïve, though perhaps even more difficult for the mind to grasp, and somewhat similar to traditions of other Southwestern groups, is the account of beginnings reported from the Zuñi of New Mexico. Here the world is considered as an emanation of the creator's thought. As Cushing has it, he "thought outward in space, whereby mists of increase, steams potent of growth, were evolved and up-lifted." * This vague world-stuff was consolidated by easy stages and through many cataclysmic changes into the earth as we now know it.

In other parts of the continent all the so-called creation myths assume the existence of the earth and are concerned primarily with the origin of the tribal culture hero or demigod, and with the ways in which he changes shapes and

* Report of the Bureau of American Ethnology, No. 13, p. 379.

conditions of objects and animals on the earth. We thus find the Iroquois telling how the mother of their twin gods fell from the upper world onto the backs of water birds, and how the earth originally rested upon the shell of a great turtle. Much of this tale is shared by the Algonquian peoples around the Great Lakes. In the Plains and Plateau the interest is primarily in the transforming activities of the culture hero, and this is true to an extent among the Northeastern tribes. But with the latter the hero is almost completely humanized instead of being essentially an animal. The nearest approach to an origin myth in the Southeast is usually an elaborate history of migrations of the tribe from some fancied original home. These migration legends are also present in Southwestern mythology, usually consisting of the ascent of the people from a series of lower worlds.

If well integrated mythologies are rare, it does not follow that our aboriginals in general are uninterested in explanations. Every tribe has a number of separate stories used to account for particular phenomena. Especially widespread over the continent are the tales of the thefts of light and of fire. In spite of some superficial resemblances to the Prometheus myth, these stories are certainly indigenous. They are especially popular in the western half of the country. As ordinarily told, the animal culture hero learns of the presence of fire in possession of some monster. By some trick he is able to steal it. The whole point of the story usually consists of an elaboration of the trick employed. Sometimes, for example, he turns himself into a particle and is swallowed in water by the monster's daughter. He is magically reborn and, as a child in the house, succeeds in stealing the fire. Other well known mythical incidents concern the regulation of the seasons, the origin of death, the placating or conquering of monsters or of some unruly natural forces—strong winds, high tides, floods, or the like.

No sharp line can be drawn between such explanatory tales and the large number of simple anecdotes to which explanations have been added almost at random. Earlier scholars were inclined to overestimate the importance of these explanatory tags and to assert that they were the essential part of the anecdote. More recent studies have shown, however, that it is the anecdote rather than the explanation which has permanence in tradition. There is no one story about how the chipmunk got his stripes, though that explanation has been appended to several different anecdotes. Some tribes do have the habit of sprinkling explanatory remarks at many places in the tales, appropriate and inappropriate.

In nearly all parts of the continent a considerable portion of the native narrative repertories deals with situations thought of as humorous by both teller and audience. These are usually known as trickster tales, since the point of the anecdote is nearly always some clever act of a half animal, half human being, conveniently referred to as a trickster. From region to region his name and nature vary. On the North Pacific Coast he is Raven or Blue Jay or Mink, according to the location of his tribe. By far the most widely known of all tricksters is Coyote, whose cleverness and foolishness are celebrated from the Eastern Plains to the California coast. With such tribes as the Ojibwa the culture hero and the trickster are the same person. In religious contexts, at initiation ceremonies and the like, Manabozho (Longfellow's Hiawatha) is the bringer of culture and livelihood to his people. But in everyday gatherings the stories told about Manabozho are much the same as the trickster tales related farther west concerning Coyote. The ducks that the trickster lures into dancing blindfold so that he can kill them, or the race which he wins by pretending lameness and getting a handicap—these illustrate the simple tricks which show him in his clever aspect. But the same trickster on other occasions is a buffoon or dupe. He buries his feast in the sand while he climbs a tree in order to stop the limbs from rubbing each other. Then he is caught between the limbs and looks on helplessly as the ducks are stolen.

These trickster incidents are humorous. Many of them are distributed over half or two-thirds of the continent, and they are probably known to more individual tale-tellers than any other kind of story. Their inconsistencies seem not to matter. Coyote is at one moment an animal, at the next he is obviously a person; Manabozho appears at one moment as a demigod, at the next as a buffoon; and all tricksters are uncertain mixtures of cleverness and foolishness.

As in our own culture, these humorous or near-humorous anecdotes are usually short and have little narrative elaboration. At their best they are witty and pointed; at their worst, silly and stupid. The only way in which they are given any length is by the process, familiar to all story-tellers, of stringing independent incidents together into an acceptable sequence.

Our aborigines do, however, have a number of stories of substantial compass. Some of these take a half-hour in the telling, and they are usually recited on more formal occasions than the trickster anecdotes. Of the longer tales, many are widely known, sometimes from ocean to ocean. Others belong to one or two culture areas. Rarely does an elaborate story remain in a single tribe unborrowed by neighbors. The process by which the rather elaborate tales have spread over the American continent is extremely interesting to the folklorist. For here he sees the principle of diffusion of oral narrative freely at work without interference from writing and literature.

Of the more popular of these longer stories among the American Indians there are some forty. About a dozen can be spoken of as "hero" tales, since they recount conflicts between a hero, often weak and unpromising, and a monster or at least a frightful adversary. Some of them remind one of the

European cycle in which the father-in-law puts the son-in-law through almost impossible ordeals. Another series, known as Lodge-Boy and Thrown-Away, current primarily in the Plains, has fortuitous resemblance to the medieval romance of Valentine and Orson. A woman is killed by a monster who takes twin boys from her body, leaves one in the lodge and throws the other into the bushes. Eventually Lodge-Boy and Thrown-Away find each other and go together on heroic adventures.

Frequently the hero tales come as a sequel to events which have taken place in the upper world. These other-world stories are not numerous, but they are among the most popular and best told of all our native tales. Particularly well known is "The Star Husband," which recounts how a girl goes to the star world, marries a star, is forbidden to dig, but disobeys and is overcome by longing to return home. Sometimes she has borne her supernatural husband a son. In any case, she makes a rope, and on it begins a descent to the earth. In some versions she succeeds in returning, but in others it is only the son who survives. Among the Plains tribes this boy becomes the hero of an elaborate series of adventures.

A tale like "The Star Husband" must be old. It has had time to develop three different characteristic forms, each with a clear-cut geographical distribution. It is known from Alaska to Nova Scotia, from California to Alabama.

A detailed account of American Indian stories is impossible in a short sketch. But even a cursory acquaintance shows that they have about them a considerable degree of narrative skill, a rather wide range of interest, and large scope for the imagination of both story-teller and audience. Most tribes recognize certain individuals as especially endowed with the gift for narrative. The stylistic resources of such artists, their repertories, their social status, and their relation to other gifted persons—all of these remain largely unnoticed in the available collections; but folklorists are becoming increasingly aware of the importance of learning more about such problems.

3

To the person with a background of European or white American culture, the tales of the North American Indians are, for the most part, interesting and clear, even in fairly literal translations. But this is not true of some of the other literary forms. The riddle and proverb are present but are scarce, and when approached through translation they lose much of their point. We know also that there have been many renowned Indian orators, and several of their orations have become famous. Students of American history are familiar with the remarkable oration attributed to the Mingo chief Logan after the massacre of his family in 1774: "There runs not a drop of my blood in the veins of any human creature. This called on me for revenge. I have sought it—I have killed many—I have fully glutted my vengeance. For my country I rejoice at the beams of peace; but do not harbor the thought that mine is the joy of fear. Logan never felt fear. He will not turn on his heel to save his life. Who is there to mourn for Logan? Not one." Yet it is extremely difficult to know just what the chief actually said, since it appears that the speech as we have it was composed only from rough notes. Something of the original in this and other orations doubtless remains, but it is natural that, in the excitement of debate, no one would think to record the orator's exact words.

Though they are not a part of literature themselves, the ceremonials of many American Indian tribes have served as a framework for several literary forms, particularly for the myth and the song. Intimately connected with both is the religious dance. In many groups the ceremonial life is so important as to be the mainspring of practically all artistic activity. This is especially true of the Southwestern group, which has a tendency to draw everything into the ritualistic pattern. The externals of such ritualism are clear and interesting to the observer, even to the casual traveler, but the esoteric significance of the dances and songs remains hidden, and of course unappreciated.

Generalizations about the poetry and songs of the American Indian are difficult, for these vary considerably from tribe to tribe. It is a long way from the elaborate chanted ritualistic poems of the Southwestern peoples to the short and often inarticulate miscellaneous songs of the Plains. In the latter particularly, the actual words seem unimportant in comparison to the music. Frequently there is little more than a succession of meaningless syllables, and always an excessive repetition. The musical idiom varies, but it almost never becomes pleasant to the unaccustomed ear unless profoundly modified by some professional composer. The range of subject matter of the songs is considerable and it varies with their use: for particular parts of a ceremonial, for dances, for gambling, for magic incantations, for war, for children's games, for love making, for lullabies, or for other events of ordinary life.

The ritualistic chants of such peoples as the Navaho or Iroquois, though they are naturally filled with repetition, usually fourfold, and are likely to tire the listener from outside the group, often contain excellent imagery and in their proper setting are truly impressive poems. An adequate appreciation of their literary value is only now becoming possible with the publication of the more extended texts. It is certainly going too far to assert, with Mary Austin, that these elaborate poems have had any profound influence on the rhythm of American poetry.

Perhaps the best opportunity which the American Indian had for the exercise of an individual poetic gift is in the short magic song. These songs are usually alleged to have been learned in a dream, and they are undoubtedly a combination of suggestions received from poetic patterns already well known with an observation or emotion of the moment. In such songs we find described a situation such as the singer wishes it to be. He expects by singing the song to bring this about. Thus in a song from the Papago of Arizona, preserved by Ruth M. Underhill, the corn is encouraged to come up:

> The corn comes up;
> It comes up green;
> Here upon our fields
> White tassels unfold.

> The corn comes up;
> It comes up green;
> Here upon our fields
> Green leaves blow in the breeze.

> Blue evening falls,
> Blue evening falls;
> Near by, in every direction,
> It sets the corn tassels trembling.

Or the rain is called down from the clouds after the long desert drought:

> Where stands the cloud, trembling
> On Quijotoa Mountain,
> The cloud trembling,
> There lies my heart
> Trembling.

> Within Quijotoa Mountain
> There is thunder.
> I looked through it and saw
> In every direction
> Light!

> Wind came, clouds came.
> I sat above them.
> Underneath, the mirage glittered.
> Rain fell,
> The mirage was gone. . . .

At the edge of the world
It is growing light.
The trees stand shining.
I like it.
It is growing light.

At the edge of the world
It is growing light.
Up rears the light.
Just yonder the day dawns,
Spreading over the night.

The oral literature of the Indians of the United States has served for these peoples in much the same way as the written literature has contributed to the civilization of Europe. In the contact between Indian and white these traditions have largely remained unassimilated and even unknown by the dominant group. But they were here long before the whites came and they remain, even in an age of books and radio, the artistic outlet for our increasing Indian population.

43. FOLKLORE

THE same stirring of the historic sense which turned attention to the lore and culture of the American Indian began, by the middle of the nineteenth century, to stimulate exploration of the riches of American folksong and folklore. The Negro spiritual was "discovered" in the North at about the time of the Civil War. The collection of folk tales was seriously undertaken in 1888. By the twentieth century, scholars were at work in delighted earnest collecting, collating, and comparing.

Strictly speaking, folklore is that congeries of knowledge (beliefs, customs, magic, sayings, songs, tales, traditions, etc.) which has been created by the spontaneous play of naïve imaginations upon common human experience, transmitted by word of mouth or action, and preserved without dependence upon written or printed record. Practically, since printed matter has become cheap and easily accessible, and reading and writing have become common-place accomplishments, folklore is not easily distinguishable from "popular" (or oral) literature, and vice versa.

In 1849 thousands of men trekked across the continent in the Gold Rush, encountering danger and hardships, suffering disappointments. Folklore handles the historical fact in the ballad of "Joe Bowers," humorously recount-ing the fate of a Forty-niner who left Pike County, Missouri, to raise a stake for his Sally. Who composed the song—whether one of the Argonauts and his pals, on the trail, or a professional comedian—no one can say with cer-tainty. But it was sung on the stage of a San Francisco theater, spread to the mining camps, was brought back to the South to become a favorite of Con-federate soldiers in the Civil War, and eventually achieved almost nation-wide diffusion. Today, nearly a century later, it is still sung in many variants throughout the United States. It has become folklore—current for a con-siderable period of time among the people, owing its preservation and cir-culation to word of mouth, not the printed page, and existing in numerous variants.

Thus folklore has its origin in an imaginative attempt to relate events, express feelings, and explain phenomena according to a graphic and remem-berable pattern. This attempt, normally begun by an individual, is transmitted to other individuals by word of mouth or by action. Through repetition and unconscious variation, it loses its original individual traits, if it has any, and becomes a common possession of a group.

The group best qualified to make and keep folklore is one that "has preserved a common culture in isolation long enough to allow emotion to color its forms of social expression." Examples are the Southern Highlanders, once cut off from the rest of the country by difficulty of communications; the Pennsylvania Germans and the Louisiana French, with linguistic and cultural heritages different from those prevailing around them; and cowboys, sailors, lumberjacks, and miners, unified by occupations. In a sense that may still be true of most European nationals, the people of the United States are not a folk, and "traditionalist" folklorists have therefore denied that there is an American folklore. But such theorists have minimized or left out of account the culturally unifying memories of several profound experiences peculiar to the American people. Most of these are embraced in the frontier heritage. Though for millions of the foreign-born and the urban-dwelling this is not a memory, still it is an inescapable tradition, coloring manners, speech, song, story, and social attitudes. To an important degree it has produced a likeness of mind, a homogeneity of character, and an accent of expression which constitute the real test of a folk. Furthermore, regional consciousness, the ties of a common occupation, and other integrating principles have shaped our people into groups capable of preserving folklore, and have tended to stimulate the creation of it. Obviously, too, whatever folklore is imported into a country remains folklore *in* that country as long as it is remembered. The extent to which the people of the United States have created a considerable body of folklore will appear from examination of types and examples of what has been preserved.

Folklorists recognize four main types. Three of these circulate by word of mouth: the "literary," including folk poetry and such varied prose forms as legend, myth, and tale; the "linguistic," including speech, proverb, and riddle; and the "scientific," including cures, prophecies, witchcraft, weather lore, and other forms of belief. The fourth, circulating by action or practical imitation, includes arts and crafts, custom, dance, drama, festival, game, and music. For obvious reasons, this chapter is chiefly concerned with the literary and the linguistic, leaving, however, some of the categories, speech and myth, to other more appropriate chapters, but noting a few action types—e.g., drama and games—in their relation to song and story. The scientific and most of the action types will be passed by as belonging more to scientific folklore, anthropology, sociology, and general cultural history than to literary history. Although the subject matter of folksong and ballad frequently overlaps that of the folk tale, verse and prose forms will be treated separately.

2

The framework and the patterns of our folklore are in the main British. The linguistic medium by which it has largely been preserved and transmitted is English. The types thus established are those closest to the experience of our people and most intimately related to our print-recorded literature. For these reasons, aside from incidental references and comparisons to the other three largest pockets—the French, the German, and the Spanish—the illustrations will be taken from folklore of British types and type modifications expressed in the English language as spoken in the United States.

The first type of "Relics of Old English Folk-Lore" named by the first editor of the *Journal of American Folk-Lore* (1888) as an object of research was "old ballads." "The prospect of obtaining much of value," he wrote, "is not flattering." At that time Francis James Child of Harvard had been collecting the English and Scottish ballads for over thirty years, chiefly from British sources, and was in process of publishing his monumental work. The harvest of over fifty years of collecting in the United States has proved that the "prospect" was greatly underestimated; more than one-third of the 305 ballads in Child's *The English and Scottish Popular Ballads* (1882–1898) have been found in oral tradition among the people of the United States.

These old ballads, stories told in song, are the bluebloods of folksong in the United States. Their narratives illustrate all the major themes of ancient balladry. The favorites are romantic love stories like "Barbara Allen," "Lord Thomas and Fair Annet," "The Maid Freed from the Gallows," and "The Gypsy Laddie." Domestic tragedies are well represented by "Edward," "Babylon," "The Two Sisters," and "Lord Randal." Riddles and wit contests are exemplified by "Riddles Wisely Expounded" and "Captain Wedderburn's Courtship." Medieval romance is echoed by "The Marriage of Sir Gawain" and "Thomas Rhymer." Saints' legends and sacred stories are recalled by "Sir Hugh, or, The Jew's Daughter," and "The Cherry Tree Carol"; jests and fabliaux, by "Our Goodman" and "The Wife Wrapt in Wether's Skin"; the Robin Hood cycle, by nine pieces. The supernatural is impressively handled in "The Wife of Usher's Well" and "Sweet William's Ghost." Two superb sea ballads are "The Sweet Trinity" and "Sir Patrick Spens," the latter found of late in Virginia and Tennessee.

Such ancient song stories, couched in language and style of an archaic flavor and set to the older musical modes, ministered to the need in the New World for a view of the romance, the tragedy, the comedy, the heroism, the adventure of life shaped into easily remembered patterns. That they have been remembered so well is due to continuation of that need in isolated and socially undeveloped sections of the country, as well as to the inertia of folk memory. Yet they are far from being an exclusive possession of the ignorant and the illiterate. Many of the best texts have come from educated and locally prominent people who learned them in the traditional way. Great Americans outside the ranks of literary scholars—John Randolph of Virginia, Abraham Lincoln, Woodrow Wilson—have been fond of them and have sung them. The metrical patterns have been well preserved. Though most of the ballads have deteriorated by transmission, a few have been improved. Unfamiliar words have been corrupted or lost, names of persons and places changed, strange customs or beliefs dropped or rationalized, feudal possessions exchanged for homely goods. One editor has remarked that these old ballads have been made as thoroughly American as anything not Red Indian can be. They are aristocrats in homespun.

Of foreign ballads known to oral tradition in the United States, those most comparable to the group just discussed are Spanish *romances* of the Southwest. About a score of these, dating from the sixteenth and seventeenth centuries, have been found in New Mexico. Most of them belong to the novelesque type, treating of love, honor, fidelity and infidelity, war, legends originating in Arabic traditions, and religious emotion. They have undergone little change since they were transplanted. Among them are "Delgadina," telling the old Apollonius of Tyre story of an incestuous father; "Gerineldo," relating the love of Emma, daughter of Charlemagne, and Eginhard, the Emperor's steward; "Un Angel Triste," describing the intervention of the Virgin to save a condemned soul; and "Estaba el gato prieto," a burlesque story of a lovesick cat. The French ballads "Le Prince d'Orange" and "Le Prince Eugène" have been sung in sections contiguous with French Canada, and "Malbrough," "Montez, la Belle," and "Sept Ans sur la Mer" are known in Louisiana.

Referring to the old traditional legendary and romantic ballads, the editor of the *Journal of American Folk-Lore,* previously quoted, complains: "In the seventeenth century, the time for the composition of these had almost passed; and they had, in a measure, been superseded by inferior rhymes of literary origin, diffused by means of broadsides and song-books, or by popular doggerels, which may be called ballads, but possess little poetic interest." It may have been such "foolish songs and ballads," hawked and sung in every town, that annoyed Cotton Mather. As a matter of fact, even today these pieces, of later and more plebeian rise, and other comparable types like the Irish come-all-ye's, are more current than the legendary and romantic ballads. Not all of them, however, are distinctly inferior. Exception must be made for such as "The Babes in the Wood," described by Addison as "that darling song of the English common people," and almost equally a favorite in America; "Shooting of His Dear," "The Yorkshire Bite," "The Pretty Fair

Maid," "The Bugaboo," "Foggy, Foggy Dew," and nursery favorites like "Cocky Robin" and "The Three Jolly Huntsmen." More typical of the broadside are "The Butcher Boy" (an American amalgam of two or three British broadsides), "The Bramble Briar" (naïvely relating an analogue of Keats' "Isabella," previously treated by Boccaccio and Hans Sachs), "The Drowsy Sleeper," "The Silver Dagger," "The Sheffield Apprentice," and "The Wexford Girl"—the last three gory murder stories that established a pattern for many native ballads on that theme. In their relations to the older balladry and in their inferior quality, such pieces are paralleled by Spanish ballads of the Southwest like "La Esposa Infiel" and "Lorenzo Gutiérrez" (a murder ballad), by French ballads of Louisiana like "On a resté six ans sur mer," and by the Pennsylvania German "Wie ich von Frankreich komm" (perhaps an old Huguenot ballad transformed into an accumulative song), and "Der Tod von Basel."

Many of the nursery songs known in this country are perhaps as old as the ballads, and most of them are likewise traceable to British or Irish origin. Of such, besides "The Babes in the Wood" and "Cocky Robin," are "The Jolly Miller," "The Miller and His Three Sons," "The Carrion Crow," "Shule Aron," "Three Jolly Welshmen," and "The Frog's Courtship." The English-derived "Paper of Pins," "Billy Boy," and "Sleep, Baby, Sleep," have their counterparts, respectively, in "Te donnerai un papier d'aiguilles" and "Charmant Billi," sung by Louisianians of French descent, and the Pennsylvania German

> Hei-yo Bubbeli schlof,
> Der Dawdy hüt die Schof.
> Die Mommy hüt die rote Küh,
> Un kummt net heem bis Morge früh.

Bound up with the ballads in origin and transmission are the game songs and rhymes. The oldest of these early found use in such children's games as "Here Comes a Duke," "Green Gravel," "King Arthur Was King William's Son," and "Ring Around Rosie." Out of these games and the square dance, with its songs and calls, developed the unique American social fête known as the play party. Deemed an innocuous substitute for the square dance, which was interdicted by Protestant religious sects, the play party took over many of the old children's game songs and developed new ones, giving them an American flavor. Favorites have been such songs as "All Down to Sleep," "Hog Drovers," "Buffalo Girls," "Circle Left," "King William Was King James's Son," "Miller Boy," "Shoot the Buffalo," and "Skip to My Lou."

3

Of early native American ballads few have survived in popular tradition. "Lovewell's Fight," narrating an Indian fray of 1725, was remembered into the nineteenth century. Perhaps "Springfield Mountain" (originally a dolorous story about the death of a young New Englander from the bite of a rattlesnake, gradually burlesqued into a nursery tale) is the oldest and sole survivor from colonial times. The incident on which it was based happened in 1761, but there is "no evidence that the ballad is of earlier date than the second quarter" of the nineteenth century. From the period of the Revolution, "Yankee Doodle," "The Bombardment of Bristol, R.I.," and a few others, mainly of broadside origin, survived to some extent in oral tradition. It is known that there was one on Shays' Rebellion, but it has been lost. The War of 1812 produced "The Constitution and the Guerrière," "James Bird" (connected with the Battle of Lake Erie), "Andrew Jackson's Raid" (celebrating the campaign against the Creek Indians in 1813–1814), and "Ye Hunters of Kentucky" (known to a few folk singers of the present century). Regardless of their exact origins, "Springfield Mountain" and "Young Charlotte" (by Seba Smith), are perhaps the best exhibits of native balladry, their chief rivals for popularity being the later "Jesse James" and "Casey Jones," and a flock of low-life ballads, of which "Frankie and Albert" is the prize piece.

Other types of folksong may be characterized without regard for origins or strict distinction between ballad and lyric. The arbitrarily drawn distinction between these two genres is that the ballad tends to be narrative, romantic, and impersonal; the lyric (without story content), to be emotional, passionate, and personal, more often than not on an amatory theme. Folk singers are not conscious of the difference. A better principle of classification, for the remainder of what is to be said on the subject, is the functional relationship of folksongs to the singers' interests and activities.

Functional classification, however, convenient as it is for exposition, to some extent distorts the facts of relationship. Practice of the folk-singing art is closely interwoven with all the actions, interests, and moods of everyday life, not merely with its ordinary avocations. A few incidents from collectors' field experiences will illustrate the point. In a Virginia cabin, Maud Karpeles listened to the singing of "The Green Bed" by a mother of thirteen children, all present in the room. "Then almost as though impelled by some unseen power" the children "softly joined in the singing of this beautiful air . . . the haunting loveliness of their young voices subdued to an overtone so as not to disturb their mother's singing." A Mississippi informant said she had learned "Sir Hugh" as a lullaby sung by her mother. An Alabama family, father, mother, and son, sang "The Gypsy Laddie" dramatically, in character. Cecil Sharp found among the Appalachian mountaineers that aspect of "an ideal society" in which every child developed the inborn capacity for song and sang the songs of his forefathers "in the same natural and unselfconscious way in which he now learns his mother-tongue." Folk singing functions spontaneously in most of the singer's relations to himself and to his fellows. All folksongs are broadly "social."

A large body of songs have to do with the events and movements of American history. Besides the historical ballads already mentioned, a few, like "Plains of Mexico" and "Buena Vista," adaptations of earlier songs, relate incidents of the Mexican War. During the Civil War songs in the folk idiom, like "John Brown's Body," were modeled on more stately pieces, like the "Battle-Hymn of the Republic," and old favorites like "We'll All Take a Ride" were adapted into such pieces as "The Union Wagon." "Grafted into the Army" was perhaps the first of many comic treatments of conscription. "I Would Not Be Alone" is a more scornful handling from the point of view of a high-spirited Southern woman. "Come in Out of the Draft" may be the first pun on the word. "Tenting on the Old Camp Ground" and "Just Before the Battle, Mother" achieved wide circulation on both sides of the line, but not "Marching Through Georgia." On their side the Confederates sang "Dixie" in the folk version, not in the words of Albert Pike's "bastard Marseillaise," revamped "Wait for the Wagon," and started "The Bonnie Blue Flag" and its tune sharer "The Homespun Dress" on careers that practically made them folksongs. "The Southern Oath," composed perhaps by Rose Vertner Jeffrey in 1862, was still traditionally known in Missouri as late as 1906. The gaiety of Southern spirits was best expressed by "Goober Peas," "The Captain with His Whiskers," and "The Rebel Soldier" ("I'll eat when I'm hungry"). Finally, the "unreconstructed" spirit of the South proclaimed itself in "I'm a Good Old Rebel." From the Spanish-American War emerged "There'll Be a Hot Time in the Old Town Tonight" and a few picturesque pieces about the girl-kissing naval hero Hobson, but no songs achieved long or extensive circulation. The First World War produced several soldier songs, of which "Hinkie, Dinkie Parlez-vous (Mademoiselle from Armentières)," indubitably composed communally, on the model of the British Army "Skiboo," is *facile princeps*.

The stirring presidential campaigns of the forties were marked by extensive use of political songs in the folk style, published in *The Harrison and Log Cabin Song Book, The Clay Minstrel, The Polk Songster, The Rough and Ready Songster,* and the like. The Harrison campaign song "What Has Caused This Great Commotion?" was sung to the tune of "Little Pig's Tail." "Frémont Campaign Song" has a stanza beginning, "Old Ten-Cent Jimmy is no go." "Henry Clay," sung to the tune of "Old Dan Tucker," survived in Mississippi as late as the 1920's—

> Henry Clay came riding a jack,
> He rode on his belly to save his back;

and "Harrison Campaign Song," celebrating the farmer who left his "tidy log cabin" to drive out the occupants of the White House, and "When the Old Hat Was New," praising Harrison and Clay, were known in Missouri in 1912. These are early illustrations of an American political tradition continued in the transient popularity of such songs as "Happy Times Are Here Again" and "The Sidewalks of New York," and climaxed by the use of hillbilly music and song in state campaigns in Texas and Louisiana during the late 1930's and the early 1940's.

One of the most characteristically American bodies of songs, in content if not in originality of form and style, is that reflecting the Old West. Three groups of these may be illustrated.

The Gold Rush of 1849 and the conditions of life in the mining towns produced a considerable number of songs. "The Dying Californian" was modeled on an older tear-jerker, "Ocean Burial." "Joe Bowers," alluded to at the beginning of this chapter, has a less tragic conclusion. After enduring hard work, privations, and perils for his Sally, Joe received a letter from brother Ike stating that Sally had married a butcher with red hair—

> And what was worse than that—
> I almost wisht I was dead—
> That Sally had a baby,
> And the baby's hair was red.

The companion piece to "Joe Bowers" is "Sweet Betsy from Pike":

> Oh, don't you remember sweet Betsy from Pike,
> Who crossed the big mountains with her lover Ike,
> With two yoke of oxen, a large yellow dog,
> A tall shanghai rooster and one spotted hog?

Several romantic and circumstantial accounts of the origin of "Joe Bowers" have been published, from which the most probable fact seems to be that the singing of the ballad at the old Melodian Theater in San Francisco, in 1849, by a comedian, John Woodward, member of Johnson's Minstrels, gave impetus to its currency. The origin of "Betsy from Pike" seems to be unknown. Similar pieces, sung to folk and popular tunes, were broadcast among Californians by songsters, of which John A. Stone's *Put's Original California Songster* (1854) is an example. Among the favorite pieces with folksong antecedents are "An Honest Miner," "Days of Forty-nine," "Sacramento Gals," "Hog Eye Man," and "What Was Your Name in the States?" Two or three of these are still traditionally known. "The Dreary Black Hills," relating to the gold strike in Wyoming in the sixties, is a pendant to these ballads of the Forty-niners.

A second major contribution of the West is the cowboy song. In John A. Lomax's and most succeeding collections, there are two types. Songs transmitted by purely oral tradition are exemplified by "The Old Chisholm Trail," "Git Along, Little Dogies," and "Old Paint." What Howard Thorp describes as "songs originally printed, clipped from a local paper or magazine, fitted to a familiar air, and so handed down from one cowboy to another, becoming genuine folksongs in the process," are exemplified by "The Glory Trail" (reshaped and sung as "High-Chin Bob"), "The Cowboy's Christmas Ball," and "The Texas Cowboy." Among the best and most memorable modeled upon older songs are "The Dying Cowboy" ("Oh, bury me not on the lone prairie"), based upon "Ocean Burial"; "The Cowboy's Dream," on "The Sweet By-and-By"; and "The Cowboy's Lament," on an Irish broadside, "The Dying Rake." Comparable Mexican pieces known in Texas are exemplified by "La Corrida de Kiansas," relating the heroic death of a vaquero. However the cowboy songs may have originated, they were adapted to the needs of the lonely men who rode night herd, drove the steers from range to range or to market, and forgathered around campfires, in the ranch houses, or at the saloons. They have a distinctively American accent, and they splash the palette of American folksong with bright colors.

A third group of Western songs describes pioneering. "Starving to Death on a Government Claim" and "Dakota Land" typify the usual themes. These are supplemented by a considerable number of Norwegian emigrant songs and ballads.

Songs of the sea, the canals, and the rivers are variously adapted to the work, the interests, and the sentiments of men whose business has sent them upon the waters. The chanteys flourished in the glorious era of American shipping following the War of 1812, and their heyday coincided with the supremacy of the clipper ships. Though some of them are traceable to the Elizabethan period, the first description of chantey singing on an American ship is said to be R. H. Dana's, written in 1834. Critical opinion awards equal merit to British and American sailors for developing them. The true chanteys, directing the movements of sailors at work, followed a definite pattern in which solo and chorus were adjusted to the practical purpose in hand. Four types are represented in standard collections: the short-drag, exemplified by "Haul Away, Joe"; the halyard, by "Whisky Johnny" and "Blow the Man Down"; "any song with a long 'chorus' and swing," by "Shenandoah" and "Santy Anna"; and the "Forecastle Song," by old traditional English ballads like "The Golden Vanity," and broadsides of the War of 1812 such as "The *Constitution* and the *Guerrière.*" The whalers sang both the chanteys and a number of ballads and songs especially related to their experience. Among these were "Reuben Ranzo," the success story of a tailor who "shipped on board a whaler" and made up for his landlubberly deficiencies by marrying the captain's daughter; "Jack Wrack," a moralistic piece on spreeing; and "Blow, Ye Winds" and "Greenland Whale Fishery," describing the hardships and perils of whaling.

The mingling of the waters by the construction and operation of the canals resulted also in the mingling of folklores. Besides scattering the Irish laborers and their songs and tales from Rome to Buffalo, the Erie Canal became a five-hundred-mile folk festival. "Paddy on the Canal" describes the digging of the ditch. Other ballads celebrate races and fights, and numerous songs issue warning about the business end of a mule, satirize the hotels, and detail the accommodations of jails. "The Raging Canal" is a rhymed tall tale on the perils of navigating a four-feet-deep ditch. "Boatin' on a Bull-Head," however, describes a real danger—"The bowsman he forgot to yell, 'Low bridge, ducker down!' " The classic is "Low Bridge, Everybody Down" (I've got a mule and her name is Sal), called by Sandburg "the Volga Boat Song of America."

Of even greater variety than the songs of the sea and the canals are those sung by paddlers of canoes and bateaux, polers of keelboats, steersmen of flatboats and steamboats, pilots, roustabouts, and passengers on the river. The "rouster" and the "soundings" songs are the closest river counterparts of the sea chanteys. These and sprawling song narrative like *"Katie* and the *Jim Lee* Had a Little Race," and bits like "The Gold Dust Five," are the most distinctive river pieces. "Steamboat Round the Bend," dating from the Civil War, is known throughout the length and breadth of the land. Except for fragments about such steamboats as the *Stacker Lee,* the *Lovin' Kate,* and the *City of Cairo,* most of the river songs are remembered only by the river people. Like the cowboy songs, they are local and topical in content, loose and rambling in structure.

As the lumber industry moved westward from the Atlantic seaboard toward the end of the eighteenth century, the industrial woodsman (lumberjack, raftsman, sawmill hand) began to appear. The invention of the circular saw and the demands of the West for building material brought on the golden age of the industry in the North Central states and produced the shantyman as an industrial and folk type. By 1900, when the industry spread to the South, most of the romance and glamour had disappeared as the Irishman, the Scotchman, and the French Canadian gave place to the native hired hand in the woods. It was during the years between 1850 and 1900 that most of the songs of the shantyboy were composed and first sung around the deacon seat. Most popular of all was "The Jam on Gerry's Rocks." "Jim Whalen" relates a similar story of death in a log jam. "Shanty Boy and Shanty Girl" and "The Little Eau Plaine" develop romantic episodes. "The Little Brown Bulls" is a delightful yarn of a pulling contest between ox teams. Paul Bunyan, the mythological hero of the lumberjacks, is celebrated in a few ballads, but these are overshadowed by the tall tales about him.

Railroad construction produced the Negro hero John Henry, who looms gigantic in a cycle of ballads. The functional aspects of this ballad, setting the rhythm for hammer or pick, are complemented by a host of other work songs most fully developed by Negroes. But accidents and disasters incidental to operation supply the most dramatic and picturesque themes. The best ballads of train wrecks have come out of the South and West. "Casey Jones," for instance, was probably composed on older models by a Negro roundhouse worker, Wallace Saunders, about John Luther Jones, engineer of the Cannon Ball Express, who died at the throttle in a collision at Vaughan, Mississippi, in 1900. The ballad owes much of its present form and wide diffusion to vaudeville rehandling of the earlier song by Saunders. "The Wreck of Old '97" is well known in Virginia and the Carolinas.

Linked to the balladry of the nation's canals, lumber camps and railroads, but dashed with a Celtic infusion, are songs growing out of the mining industry. The best of these have come from the anthracite region, where Irish and Welsh immigrants, with their old-country songs and tunes and their communal gatherings on the green, a part of every "mine patch," developed their own minstrelsy. Some of the pieces recall the troublous days of the Molly Maguires, Irish laborers who terrorized the anthracite region in the seventies; but the most characteristic treat of mine work, disasters, and strikes: "Pat Dolan" and "Thomas Duffy," two Molly Maguire ballads; "The Shoofly" and "Down, Down, Down," on the fears and hopes, the hardships and mishaps, of the industry; and "My Sweetheart's the Mule in the Mines."

4

Realization of the varied wealth and cultural significance of religious folksongs in the United States is comparatively recent and is still somewhat confused by controversy. Curiously enough, the story begins in the forties with minstrel-show capitalization of plantation melodies. Stimulated by this interest, Northern writers during the period of the Civil War "discovered" the spiritual. Allen, Ware, and Garrison's *Slave Songs of the United States* (1867) is a landmark. It was followed by other books devoted to spirituals. In the seventies the Negroes themselves at Fisk University and Hampton Institute, with their far-journeying troupes of singers and their published collections, began to take a hand in exploitation of the spirituals. Until recently it was generally assumed that the Negro originated the spirituals; but it is more probable that he "borrowed themes, song patterns, and tunes from the white man, and adapted or reshaped them, investing them with his own mental, emotional, and vocal mannerisms." Thus, each race has an honorable and not necessarily invidious claim: the white, for primacy of the spiritual as a folksong type; the black, for the distinctiveness of the Negro spiritual.

As a result of almost a century of collecting and a quarter-century of controversy over origins, we do not have agreement among the scholars, but we do have a great and beautiful host of spirituals from both the blacks and the whites. Examples of songs shared by the two races, the white versions being the older, are "Old Ship of Zion," "When the Stars Begin to Fall," "Roll Jordan," "Old-Time Religion," "Poor Wayfaring Stranger," "Swing Low, Sweet Chariot," "Go Down Moses." In time-hallowed association and power of emotional evocation and expression for millions, the spirituals have no serious rival among the types of American folksong.

Vying with the spirituals in distinctiveness are several other types of Negro songs. First to attract the attention of the whites were the plantation songs, like "Zip Coon" and "Ole Virginny Nebah Tire," which were sung all over the country by such companies as the Ethiopian Serenaders and the Virginia Minstrels. "Massa Had a Yaller Gal," "Uncle Ned," "Oh, Susanna," and "Run Nigger Run" are examples of pieces ultimately traceable to plantation melodies but adapted to minstrel use by white composers, and given a currency still persistent in both Negro and white oral tradition. Recent collections of Negro folksongs recognize and abundantly represent a large variety of work songs, including those of pick and hammer sung by labor gangs, and those sung in farming and miscellaneous other types of work. Besides these occupational songs, there are those that have to do with animals, recent events, and sex relations. As a result of a mayoralty campaign in Memphis, Tennessee, in 1909, in which W. C. Handy, a Negro singer, played a prominent part, the blues began to sweep the country. In contrast with the spirituals, which are communal and choral, the blues are individual and lyrical. Their common themes and moods are best described in their own phrases—"a good man feelin' bad," "a woman on a good man's mind," and

> De blues ain't nothing
> But a poor man's heart disease.

As with the ante-bellum plantation songs and as with the "coon songs" a half-century later, commercialization and popular fad have made the blues a dubious expression of the Negro folk mind. But they and the other Negro song types are among the most characteristically American contributions to folklore.

5

From the beginning of American literature through the Romantic Period, connections between art poetry and folk poetry were incidental and more or less consistent with British precedent. Until well into the nineteenth century broadside and newspaper ballads were staple provender. Franklin and, later, Bryant and Cooper wrote ballads used by newspapers and itinerant singers and peddlers. Royall Tyler's "Ode Composed for the Fourth of July" (1796) gives a gusty list of folk customs, including game songs and dances. Freneau occasionally used folksong patterns, as in the come-all-ye "Barney's Invitation" and the ballad "The Battle of Stonington." Bryant, as in "Song of Marion's Men," and Poe, as in "Annabel Lee," show general influences of the literary vogue of popular poetry; but in Longfellow and Whittier treatment of American material in the ballad goes somewhat beyond the conventions established by British Romantics. "The Wreck of the Hesperus" and "Paul Revere's Ride" are authentic in their traditional form and in their native substance. Both qualities are less pronounced in Whittier's idyllic "Maud Muller" and "Telling the Bees," but more so in "Skipper Ireson's Ride," with its tarry and salty folk speech. Oliver Wendell Holmes would have relished the irony that his "Ballad of the Oysterman," parodying the pseudo-ballads of the time, has been adopted by the folk themselves. Form and mannerisms characteristic of folk poetry, well known to Lowell, as well as Yankee dialect and shrewdness, help to explain the raciness of *The Biglow Papers*, especially in pieces like "The Courtin'." "I hear America singing, the varied carols I hear," declared Whitman. He showed a passionate awareness of folksong, and its refrains and rhythms pulsate in his orchestration; but it did not exert a strong formal influence. Author of one of the most eloquent tributes to the old ballad, Sidney Lanier wrote at least two fine imitations, "The Revenge of Hamish" and "A Ballad of Trees and the Master." His dialect pieces, like "Uncle Jim's Baptist Revival Hymn" and "Thar's More in the Men Than Thar Is in the Land," though inferior, are closer to current American folksong.

With Bret Harte and John Hay, vernacular poetry in the United States plants its feet solidly on the ground of American folksong. Tickled by "Joe Bowers," they established the vogue of the Pike County ballad with such pieces as "The Heathen Chinee" and "Jim Bludso." Shortly after this innovation, Irwin Russell, a young Mississippian, showed the possibility of a more authentic poetic treatment of Negro life and character than had hitherto appeared in pseudo-Negro poetry, even at its best in the songs of Stephen Collins Foster. Such poems as Russell's "Christmas Night in the Quarters" owed a part of their effectiveness to their undertones of Negro song and dance. Dialect verse exhibiting the inspiration of folksong and affinities with it constituted an important part of the local color movement. Among the chief practitioners were Will Carleton, James Whitcomb Riley, Eugene Field, and the Canadian Robert W. Service.

The quiet simplicities of folksong, and frequently its forms, appear in much twentieth century poetry. Edwin Arlington Robinson's ballad "Miniver Cheevy" is an early example. Robert Frost has played with both folk material and form in such pieces as "Brown's Descent, or the Willy-Nilly Slide," characterized by Louis Untermeyer as "a tart New England version of 'John Gilpin's Ride,'" and "Paul's Wife," a bit of apocryphal Bunyaniana. Nursed on *Uncle Remus,* Negro songs, and pioneer traditions, and later roaming the country as a minstrel, Vachel Lindsay reflected his heritage in such poems as "The Congo," "General William Booth Enters into Heaven," "My Fathers Came from Kentucky," "The Statue of Old Andrew Jackson," and "Preface to 'Bob Taylor's Birthday.'" Carl Sandburg, singing minstrel, distinguished folksong anthologist, owes little to the form but much to the feeling and the phrase of folk poetry. The best illustrations of the influence of all elements are to be found in the poetry of Stephen Vincent Benét. "The Ballad of William Sycamore" is the incarnation of the pioneer spirit set to a perfect American transposition of the old ballad music. "The Mountain Whippoorwill . . . (A Georgia Romance)" is a capital ballad on a fiddlers' contest. Echoes of spirituals and dance songs and the exquisite ballad beginning "Love came by from the riversmoke" enrich the harmonies and color the texture of *John Brown's Body.* Both American folksong and Benét's poetry show how irrepressible the American spirit is:

> They tried to fit you with an English song
> And clip your speech into the English tale.
> But, even from the first, the words went wrong,
> The catbird pecked away the nightingale.

"Folk-songs," remarked Constance Rourke, "have been set like rosettes on the surface of plays and novels." In early American drama and fiction this use was decorative, as Miss Rourke's simile suggests: chapter tags from the old ballads, as in the Waverley novels, an occasional song by one of the characters in a play or novel, *entr'-acte* singing. Many of the famous old actors—

e.g., Edwin Booth and Joseph Jefferson—grew up singing folksongs. The development from vaudeville solo to duet, duet to dialogue, dialogue to play is characteristic of the history of the theater in America. *Old Lavender* (1877), "growing out of a vaudeville sketch [about a] genial drunkard" is an illustration. The capital examples of dramatic use of folksong occur in the 1930's— Marc Connelly's *Green Pastures,* woven of religious fantasies and spirituals of the Negro; such operatic pieces as DuBose Heyward's *Porgy and Bess*; Lynn Riggs' *Green Grow the Lilacs,* which flowered into *Oklahoma.* A study of the use of folksong in fiction descriptive of the Southern scene shows that between 1923 and 1932 thirty-one writers (among them James Boyd, DuBose Heyward, Elizabeth Madox Roberts, Thomas Wolfe) utilized over two hundred folksongs in more than twoscore novels and short stories. The songs afforded bright threads for the tapestry of history, primary colors for genre painting of folk scenes, and character-revealing high lights and shadows for the chiaroscuro of individual personality; thematic and choral music to suggest the moods and signalize the stages of dramatic action; and the spirit and substance of action itself. Fiswoode Tarleton, in "Curtains," and Olive Tilford Dargan, in *Call Home the Heart,* handled climactic episodes by representing the process and the results of communal composition through the characters.

6

The collecting and preserving of folktales in the United States was not seriously undertaken until 1888, when W. W. Newell declared that scarcely a single nursery tale had been recorded in America. He was hopeful, however, that something might be done to save from oblivion the great store of fairy tales, beast fables, and jests still alive within the memories of nurses and mothers only a few years before the time of his writing. During the next fifty years Newell's hopes were abundantly fulfilled. In addition to thousands of examples of the types he named, other richly illustrated types were discovered and collected. Among these are legends transplanted and naturalized, new legends invented, and, notably, the tall tale. The latter has the strongest claim to being an indigenous American invention. It exhibits a tendency toward cyclic evolution around representative American heroes which approaches the familiar pattern of Old World cultural myth.

The store of collected Old World *Märchen* remembered in the United States is now large. Examples in English from white people are "The Wolf and the Pigs," "Bluebeard," "How Jack Went to Seek His Fortune," "Johnny Cake," "Lazy Maria," "The Three Brothers and the Hog"; adaptations of the ancient Mak-the-sheepstealer episode; and a whole cycle of "Jack Tales" (giant killing, dragon quelling, and the like). Congaree River Negroes in

South Carolina have stories explaining why jaybirds are not to be killed and why the skin of the ox is used to whip the mule. Gullahs on the Sea Islands tell traditional versions of Rumpelstilzchen, of "Rescue of the King's Daughter," and of the doings of Ber Rabbit, Ber Fox, Ber Wolf, and the rest of the hierarchy of the Uncle Remus stories. Independent versions of many of the last-named cycle have also been recovered from Mississippi and published in a delightful book, *The Tree Named John*. Louisiana French tales, early collected by Alcée Fortier, include Compair Lapin's exploits with animals, fairy stories, and vaudevilles of song and prose story. An extensive collection from a pocket of French-speaking people in Missouri falls into somewhat similar categories; Compair Lapin is an important figure, and there is also the French Canadian hero P'tsit Jean. Collections made in the Southwest illustrate the range of the Spanish folktale. Almost every major Old World tale type, including such international examples as "The Tar Baby" and others in the Uncle Remus cycle, is exemplified in American folklore.

Of the other prose narratives falling within the classical folklore categories, the legend is also well represented. Literary treatment of legendary material by Irving, Hawthorne, and Cooper called attention to its existence in the East. It has since been found to be widespread. Stories of treasure hidden by Captain Kidd, Blackbeard, Teach, and other pirates have been recovered from Money Cove, Maine, to the North Carolina Banks. On Chappaquiddick, Martha's Vineyard, have been found stories of the Phantom Ship, the Blue Rock Treasure, the Haunted Hollow, and the Little Man. In the Bayou country of Louisiana flourish stories of Jean Lafitte, of the Acadians, and of old plantation houses. Among the people of the Middle West have sprung up countless legends like "The Lone Tree" (commemorating the birth of a baby to a pioneer Iowa couple), "Providence Hole" (relating the escape of a child from Indians), and "Lovers' Leap" (a story, current in many versions throughout the country, of a death pact kept by tragic lovers). The most characteristic and widely diffused legends of America are those about seekers after treasure and wealth. The Southwest abounds in these tales of lost mines and hidden, sometimes forgotten, hoards.

Tending also to be localized are tales of witches, ghosts, devils, and phantoms. In number, popularity, and variety, they form one of the most considerable groups of folktales. They also reflect some of the most ancient and deeprooted superstitions of the American people. "De Witch 'Oman an' de Spinnin' Wheel" from Louisiana, "Old Skinny" from North Carolina, and "Out of Her Skin" from South Carolina Gullah Negroes illustrate the belief that witches slip out of their skins in order to do mischief. "The Bell Witch of Tennessee and Mississippi" combines the vampire and the poltergeist in a story of the supernatural persecutions visited by the "witch" of a murdered overseer upon a North Carolina family who moved to the lower South early in the nineteenth century. Dating from the eighteenth century and localized in New Jersey, "The Leeds Devil" relates the horrendous acts of a witch's offspring. "The Death Waltz" from the Southwest exemplifies the return of the ghost of a dead lover to interrupt the wedding of the surviving mate. Traffic with the devil motivates "Jack-o'-My-Lantern," a Maryland tale of a clever Jack who outwits the Evil One. The impulse which created tales of the supernatural is still alive. Automobile accidents on lonely roads have given rise to a widespread story of a traveler who picks up a beautiful hitch-hiker, to discover in the denouement that she is the ghost of a girl killed at the spot where he was accosted.

"Skitt's" (H. E. Taliaferro's) *Fisher's River Scenes and Characters,* published in 1859 but containing North Carolina stories said to be current in the twenties, is perhaps a fair sampling of pioneer tales. These include hunting yarns by Uncle Davy Lane, who "became quite a proverb in the line of big story-telling"; tales about panthers, bears, horn snakes and buckmasters, frontier fights, and eating exploits; anecdotes about greenhorns and local characters; and a localization and vernacularization of Jonah and the whale. Such stories, also preserved in old newspapers, almanacs, county and church histories, personal memoirs, and the like, and still current where memories of the frontier linger, are largely anecdotal.

Pioneer yarns and anecdotes began early to cluster around two types of the folk character—the hero as philosopher and the hero as man of action. The evolution of the first includes the Yankee, recognized in Royall Tyler's *The Contrast* (1787), and Seba Smith's *Jack Downing* (1834); the backwoodsman; the Irishman, the Negro, and the Jew; and the old farmer. It is an exaltation of homely wisdom and shrewdness applied to comment upon men, manners, and events. The other type, beginning with the backwoodsman, develops the epic or mythological hero. Its chief narrative medium has been the tall tale, defined as "an exuberant combination of fact with outrageous fiction."

Already shaped by oral tradition, the backwoodsman was publicly recognized in 1822 at a theater in New Orleans, when Noah Ludlow, a comedian, sang "The Hunters of Kentucky" to a pit full of flatboatmen. The "half horse, half alligator" described in the ballad at once suggested the Gamecock of the Wilderness. Davy Crockett, who best personified the type, was apotheosized in stories about him and in his own writings and speeches. "Cradled in a sap trough, clouted with a coonskin," he became "the yaller blossom of the forest . . . all brimstone but the head and ears, and that's aquafortie. . . . I'm that same David Crockett, fresh from the backwoods, half-horse, half-alligator, a little touched with the snapping turtle; can wade the Mississippi, leap the

Ohio, ride a streak of lightning, slip without a scratch down a honey locust; can whip my weight in wildcats—and if any gentleman pleases, for a ten dollar bill, he may throw in a panther,—hug a bear too close for comfort, and eat any man opposed to Jackson."

The man who thus declared himself became the "coonskin Congressman" from Tennessee, figured prominently in the politics of the Jacksonian period, led in the conquest of the West, and died in glory at the Alamo. It has been averred that the Crockett myth was deliberately fabricated in Washington for frankly partisan purposes. On the other hand, no one has identified the inventors or connected them with the almanacs published by Crockett or under his name between 1835 and 1856. In these, as in the tales that flourished in the Old Southwest and still linger in Tennessee, Texas, and the Ozark country, the Indian fighter and hunter, with his long rifle Betsy, his dogs Grim and Soundwell, and his bear Death Hug, grins coons out of trees, wrings the tails off comets, thaws and greases the frozen axis of the earth, and returns to his neighbors with a piece of sunrise in his pocket.

A contemporary and rival in fame, who appeared in Crockett's *Almanac,* was Mike Fink, King of the Mississippi Keelboatmen. Early printed tales about him dating from 1828 are close to oral tradition. Gigantic in stature and strength, the peer of Crockett as a marksman, and a whimsical roisterer, Mike lined up in his sights a deer and a pursuing Indian and killed both with one bullet, shot the scalp lock off a brave, and raised shindies at Natchy-under-the-Hill.

Similar stories began to appear in print in Porter's *Spirit of the Times,* a sporting journal published in New York between the thirties and the sixties; in numerous Southern and Western newspapers; and in books like *The Big Bear of Arkansas* (1845).

Meanwhile, new types, both comic and heroic, were emerging. From authentic folk manners and characters the theater and the minstrel show created Jim Crow and Old Dan Tucker. In the logging camps the Paul Bunyan legend, crossing over from Canada, was burgeoning. Loggers of the United States later gave Paul the Blue Ox (who was "forty-two ax handles and a plug of chewing tobacco between the eyes"), the mythical logging camp, and many of his associates. They set him up as inventor, orator, and entrepreneur. They devised a chronology and a meteorology—the Winter of the Blue Snow, the Spring that the Rain Came from China. Wisconsin raftsmen told stories about a hero of their own, Whisky Johnny, who once worked for Paul but left camp to escape a monotony of prunes, and who practiced his own version of the Crockett coonskin trick. American sailors laid the keel of Old Stormalong, "fourteen fathoms tall," deep-water sailor-man and whaler. His greatest feat was sailing the *Courser,* which was too big to turn around in the North Sea. Out of dialogue, tale, and tune was woven around the swamp squatter the cycle of "The Arkansas Traveler."

Anecdotes and tall tales arising from later economic and social conditions have polarized about new folk types and modified the older ones. Blood brother to Paul Bunyan was Pecos Bill, a creation of the cowboys. He was a "killer of the bad men . . . taught the bronco how to buck . . . staked out New Mexico and used Arizona as a calf pasture." The Southern Negroes developed the saga of John Henry, the steel-driving titan, localizing his birth-place, his *enfances,* and his exploits all the way from Cape Fear to the Missis-sippi Delta, and celebrating, in ballad and tale, his triumphant death in com-petition with the steam hammer. Texas oil workers imported Paul Bunyan to the pipe line, and American soldiers brought him to the fighting fronts of the Second World War. A twentieth century hero is Joe Magarac, the Slav steel man of the Pennsylvania mills.

Folk fancy has created now the saint, now the bad man. Parson Weems' inventions about Washington, the beautiful pioneer legend of Johnny Apple-seed, some of the yarns (dashed with humor) about Lorenzo Dow and other pioneer preachers, and the elaborate myths about Lincoln gathered by Lloyd Lewis illustrate the hagiological impulse at work in the New World. The opposite impulse has found expression in tales about such ogres as the Harps of the Old Southwest, the Murrell gang, Quantrell, and the Daltons. Most of the technically bad men, however, like Jesse James, Billy the Kid, and Wild Bill Hickok, have been heroized as expressions of the innate American ad-miration for courage and violence. One of the recent discoveries in literary history is that the ultimate source of the humorous writings that emerged from the East and the South in the thirties was such popular oral narratives as have just been noted, especially anecdotes and tall tales. While conscious literary exploitation of this material was going on, it was being purveyed, often in more naïve form, in such periodicals as Porter's *Spirit of the Times* (1831–1861) and such books as *The Big Bear of Arkansas* (1845), T. B. Thorpe's *The Mysteries of the Backwoods* (1846), T. A. Burke's *Polly Pea-blossom's Wedding* (1851), and the Philadelphia firm Carey & Hart's Library of Humorous American Works.

The influence of this indigenous material upon the form and substance of twentieth century American literature has already been noted by critics and historians of our culture. Among the examples cited are Wayman Hogue's *Back Yonder,* autobiography grounded on folklore and folkways; Lloyd Lewis' *Myths After Lincoln,* showing "the primitive myth-making faculty at work among us"; and Roark Bradford's *John Henry,* "a little epic, half fan-tasy, stripped to the core of tragedy." H. W. Odum's *Rainbow Round My Shoulder* and Opie Read's *I Remember* show interesting variations of the folklore foundation for autobiography, imaginative in the one, factual in the other. Stephen Vincent Benét's *The Devil and Daniel Webster* and Wilbur Schramm's Windwagon Smith stories illustrate the refinement of the tall tale, and such stories as William Faulkner's "The Bear" and Marjorie Kinnan Rawlings' *South Moon Under* demonstrate the effectiveness of the hunting yarn.

7

Englishmen coming to America in the colonial period brought their folk plays and continued to act them for several generations. The old St. George Christmas Play was as familiar to Bostonians of the eighteenth century as it was to Thomas Hardy's Wessex peasants. A Mummers' Christmas Play and a Plough Monday Play were remembered by Kentucky mountaineers as late as 1930. The most elaborate example of folk drama in the United States is *Los Pastores,* a dramatic representation of the birth of the Savior, enacted by the inhabitants of the Lower Rio Grande, in Texas, as late as 1907. Native examples of folk drama are few and rudimentary. The best, perhaps, is *The Arkansas Traveler,* little more than a skit. A more elaborate but less definitive example is *Easter Rock,* a pagan rite "clothed in Christian symbolism," of choral and dramatic nature, traditionally practiced by Negroes in the lower Mississippi Delta.

The chief, if not the only, purely native American dramatic entertainment is the minstrel show. Its basic character was, of course, the Negro, in person or impersonated. Although the Negro had appeared on the stage as early as 1795, it was not until 1828 that the minstrel type exploiting folklore was successfully presented. Thomas D. Rice, a popular actor of the period, having observed an old and deformed Negro singing and dancing "rockin' at de heel," learned song and dance, introduced Jim Crow to a Louisville, Kentucky, audience, and entered upon a career that won for Jim Crow international fame. From this innovation, Rice proceeded, by collecting Negro melodies and weaving them into medleys, to develop "Ethiopian Opera." These "operas" were the elaborate precursors of the sketches which became characteristic of the minstrel shows established during the forties. *Bone Squash: A Comic Opera,* by Rice and Charles White, is a good example.

The first public presentation of the minstrel show as such is thought to have taken place at the Bowery Amphitheater in New York in 1843. The priority of companies rests between Christy's Minstrels and the Virginia Minstrels. Other early companies were the Kentucky Minstrels, the Ring and Parker Minstrels, and the Congo Melodists. These stereotyped the minstrel-show form. The heyday of the minstrel show was the period 1850–1870. It has been estimated that in the eighties thirty companies carried this form of dramatic entertainment by wagon, stagecoach, steamboat, and railroad train to practically every center of population in the United States. Until the movie developed, it remained the most popular form of indoor public entertainment.

Though indisputably originating from Negro folksong and folkways, often incorporating genuine Negro songs, the minstrel show cannot, of course, be regarded as pure folklore. Yet it continued to utilize many of the folklore types—dance, song, spiritual, folktale, tall tale, proverb, riddle, jest. It "created a *genre* which cannot be regarded as a folk-song, although it has the folk-song feeling, nor as an art-song, nor yet merely as popular ballad." Its reflex effects upon folksong have been considerable. While the minstrels made their entertainments out of folksongs, the people also made folksongs out of what had originally been minstrel compositions by known individual authors. Foster's "Oh, Susannah," and Rice's "Ol' Virginny Never Tire" have histories illustrating the cycle.

During the fifty to sixty year span of its popularity (about 1870–1930), American vaudeville drew more largely upon urban folklore and folkways than did the minstrel show. Yet vaudeville bills show considerable folk stuff of racy rustic origin. For example, in the eighties the Chicago Clark Street Museum put on a black-face song-and-dance act entitled "Arkansas." As with the minstrel show, so with vaudeville—banjo music, dance, and songs were standard. In "The South Carolina Home," a rheumatic old darky interpolated banjo music and a song about "'mancipation proclamation" into a dialogue with a plantation owner about the ol' Marster, who was suddenly revealed sitting in his privy. The "racial comics" of the eighties (Negro, Irish, German, Italian, etc.) resembled those of the minstrels. Some of the songs sung in them (e.g., "The Roving Irish Gents" and "The Lackawanna Spooners") touch upon occupations. "Drill, Ye Terriers" has gone into folklore as far south as Florida. The comedian J. W. McAndrews impersonated the old Southern darky in dress, speech, and action in a way that made Southerners nostalgic. Goss and Fox, a famous blackface team of the eighties, used plantation and camp-meeting melodies almost exclusively. In general, however, the stuff of the later variety programs was urban and sophisticated, treating such topics as politics, baseball, the Army and Navy, trades and professions, and immigrant types.

In legitimate American drama of the twentieth century, artistic use of other types of folklore than songs is so common that a few examples will suffice. In *Lightnin'* (1918), the hero tells a tall tale about driving a swarm of bees across the prairie in dead winter without losing a bee, but—"got stung twice." Percy MacKaye's *This Fine-Pretty World* (1923) presents the Kentucky mountaineer Sprattling, the "lie-swearer who follies the Oninvisible and the Onbeheerd-of" and runs afoul of the law into seventeen jail sentences. *Ile,* treating with dramatic intensity the material found in whaling folklore, and *The Emperor Jones,* utilizing motives like the beat of the tomtom, the chorus, the silver bullet, and the "boogers" of superstitious terror, illustrate Eugene O'Neill's notable practice. Jack Kirkland's dramatization of Erskine Caldwell's *Tobacco Road* exhibits an intimate knowledge of folkways and folk speech of Georgia Crackers, dedicated to the purpose of shocking and spicing a jaded popular appetite. A sharp contrast in point of view is afforded by *Porgy and Bess,* the folk opera shaped out of Dorothy and DuBose Heyward's *Porgy,* a moving and sympathetic dramatization of the life of Catfish Row in old Charleston.

More sympathetic exploitation occurs in the work of what might be called a school of folk drama. Early in the 1920's appeared Lula Vollmer's *Sunup* and *The Shame Woman,* plays about mountain folk. In similar vein were Hatcher Hughes' *Hell-Bent fer Heaven* (Pulitzer Prize play for 1923–1924) and *Ruint* (1925). While these plays were enjoying success as regular theatrical productions, a fundamental program was established at the University of North Carolina. This had a twofold aim: first, to discover the stuff of drama in the lives of primitive folk removed from urban and sophisticated centers and to shape it into simple plays; second, to take folk drama to the people. The leader was Frederick H. Koch; his instruments were his classes in folk drama and the Carolina Playmakers. The early plays dealt in the main with the North Carolina scene—the fisher folk on the Banks, the mountaineers, Piedmont tenant farmers and mill hands, moonshiners, outlaws, picturesque or romantic character types among the Negroes and the Croatans. The plays were first produced at Chapel Hill and then taken on tour to all quarters of the state and to large centers in near-by states. Since then, Koch's pupils have extended the scope of quest for material and of treatment by writing folk plays representative of life in more than half of the states and in all of the major regions of the nation. One pupil, Paul Green, who began in the Carolina Playmakers' tradition, has transcended it in plays which have won for him a national reputation. Others, as actors, playwrights, and teachers, have disseminated the idea of a people's drama throughout the nation.

8

Of the "linguistic" types of folklore current in the United States, the proverb records common human experience most pungently. It has been extensively collected from several language groups—English, German, Spanish, Yiddish, etc., but no extant collection can claim to be nationally representative. The collections we have show that most of our proverbs came from Great Britain. For example, "An apple a day . . ." is traceable to the English

> Eat an apple on going to bed
> And you'll keep the doctor from earning his bread.

Of one collection of 199 proverbs from the Northeast, 70 per cent were in use in England two hundred years ago. A few, however, are definitely American in origin, e.g., "A sitting hen never grows fat," "Don't kick a fellow when he's down," "It pays to advertise," "The bigger they are, the harder they fall," and "Paddle your own canoe." Most of the proverbs collected from the various foreign-language groups originated in the Old World.

Since the time of *Poor Richard's Almanack,* American public speakers and writers have salted their discourse with homely proverbs. Two Presidents have given currency to possible American coinages: Lincoln with his figure about swapping horses in midstream; Franklin D. Roosevelt with his allusion, in a war-bond address, to "an old saying about sticking to the plow until you have reached the end of the furrow." Mark Twain used proverbs freely in his works. The dialect humorists have cultivated the homely aphorism and invented new ones, as, for example, Josh Billings (Henry Wheeler Shaw) in his *Allminax* and "Kin" (Frank McKinney) Hubbard in *Abe Martin, Hoss Sense and Nonsense.* Some of these have become folklore. E. W. Howe's similar predilection earned for him the epithet "the modern Poor Richard." Platform humorists and columnists like Will Rogers have used the proverb as stock in trade. In Carl Sandburg's *Good Morning, America* (1928) it became art.

With a few exceptions, the minor linguistic types of folklore, great stores of which have been gathered, have only slight significance for literature. Because of its pert tone and compact form, the riddle has been well preserved in parts of the country where riddling, the oldest extant form of humor and intellectual exercise, is still a fireside amusement. It exists in simple forms like

> Runs over fields and woods all day,
> Under the bed at night sits not alone,
> With tongue hanging out,
> A-waiting for a bone;   [shoe]

and

> De dia con la boca llena de carne
> y de noche con la boca al aire.   [*zapato*—shoe]

A more elaborate form frames the riddle in a story relating how a condemned man saves his neck by riddling. North Carolina mountaineers have sought to cure burns, and the Pennsylvania Germans to keep off bumblebees by the use of charms. The counting-out rhyme, characteristically traditional and rural or small-townish, sometimes shows distinctly urban traits, as in this one:

> The people who live across the way
> At nineteen-eighteen East Broadway—
> Every night they have a fight,
> And this is what they say:

> Icky-bicky soda cracker,
>   Icky-bicky boo,
> Icky-bicky soda cracker,
>   Out goes you.

One of the most delightful bits of urban folklore is the street cry, heard in Charleston, New Orleans, New York, and other of the older cities, and even in some of the new ones. A Louisiana Negro was heard chanting this cry on a Chicago street:

> Watermelons fresh and fine,
> Watermelons right off the vine.
> Come and get your nice, sweet watermelons,
> Only a dime.

9

This account of types of folklore in the United States has made incidental mention of various modes of transmission and diffusion. For folklore in its purest state, the individual singer, story-teller, or speaker is of course the primary medium. Often his calling gives him preeminence in this function. Before the development of the railroads the wagoner was frequently a spreader of songs and tales. So have been the peddler, the fruit-tree seller, the sewing-machine agent, the canal worker, the railroad man. But these natural and spontaneous agencies were supplemented by print and by professional entertainers. The broadside continued to be commonly printed well into the nineteenth century; it is still occasionally struck off by country presses. In the nineteenth century hundreds of songsters and almanacs that flooded the country gave currency to folksongs as well as recent hits. More important than the almanacs were newspapers. Even city editors followed the practice of the country sheets in devoting columns to old songs and stories. All this printed material worked side by side with the minstrel shows, the Negro college spiritual singers of Fisk, Hampton, and Tuskegee, and the professional singers like the Continental Vocalists and the Hutchinson Family, in making nationally popular folklore that might otherwise have been confined to one region or locality.

In the twentieth century the phonograph, the radio, and the sound movie enormously multiplied the means of diffusion, so that a story or a song like "Praise the Lord and Pass the Ammunition," inspired, it is said, by a chaplain in the Pacific during the Second World War, might overnight become, for a few weeks at least, a sort of national folk possession, and the millions of a continent might share an experience comparable to that of a Scottish Border community learning for the first time one of the old riever ballads.

Folklore in the United States is a massive, vital, and portentous heritage. At first the unreflectively possessed memory of an ancient mother and an antique land, it has begun to achieve an unselfconscious expression of the experience of a continent that has wrought deep changes in human habits, attitudes, and outlooks. In its relations with literature it has been both borrower and lender. Indeed, present-day means of communication and record are so swift and so nearly universal that they tend to sweep away the criteria of differentiation. Phonograph, radio, and sound movie now expand indefinitely the range of oral transmission. At the same time, with universally accessible print intelligible to a literate people, they diminish the need for memory. Folklore may instantly become literature, and literature may speedily travel the road to folklore. Their interaction may threaten to invalidate the "traditional" folklorist's criteria, but it will be beneficial for both. Thomas Mann makes Mai-Sachme, Joseph's wise and humane jailer, say: "There are, so far as I can see, two kinds of poetry: one springs from folk-simplicity, the other from the literary gift in essence. The second is undoubtedly the higher form. But in my view it cannot flourish cut off from the other, needing it as a plant needs soil."

44. HUMOR

MORE effectively even than folklore—
from which it has persistently borrowed—American humor from colonial
days to the present has acted as a catalytic agent for the changes in our
expanding nation and its mingled peoples. It has been said that humor is born
of incongruities—and of these we have always had plenty. But at every stage
of our awkward and uneven growth, our humorists have spoken to our
extravagances and helped us appreciate our common humanity. In their
writings are often to be found the most distinctively American strains in our
literature.

It is the recognition of unity amid differences, the addition of imaginative
sympathy to a sense of reality, the acceptance of a common denominator in a
people of innumerable origins and widespread regions that makes American
humor important, not only for a student of what Whitman called "These
States" but for the student of mankind.

That there are differences between American humor and that of other
nations, in subjects and in technique, has been recognized at home and abroad
for more than a century. As long ago as 1838, a puzzled Englishman in the
London and Westminster Review wrote, "The curiosity of the public regarding the peculiar nature of American humor seems to have been early satisfied
with the application of the all-sufficing word exaggeration." Evidently
burlesque and the tall tale then seemed the principal types; then as now, exaggeration was regarded abroad as our funniest gift to literature.

But from whom did we learn to exaggerate? Lucian, a Syrian-born wit
writing Greek in the second century after Christ, composed a preposterous
True History about a trip in a Mediterranean whale, and Rabelais could have
held his own on the deacon seat of any American lumber camp. And it is
probable that in the past century Americans have owed as much to the Baron
Munchausen as to any English drawer of the long bow. That suave and
poker-faced master of lies represents the cosmopolitan sources of one brand
of American fun. By 1835 twenty-four American editions of the Baron's
adventures had been published—according to a title page of that date. An
early New York edition includes a tour through the United States in the year

728

1803, and this transatlantic trip appeared also in the Philadelphia edition of 1832; so Munchausen was a welcome immigrant. Many of his stories have been collected (and sometimes published) by American folklorists from New England to New Mexico; others appear with changes that somewhat disguise the original narrative. The favorite, the story of the stag shot with cherry pits and later growing a cherry tree from his antlers, has at least fourteen American variants; doubtless scholars will uncover many more. What Americans have done with the Baron is to improve upon his stories by adding local settings and dialect, and by expanding short comic tales into richly humorous yarns of our oral tradition.

What has been suggested regarding "American" exaggeration could also be applied to other favorite devices or forms. The trickster is found in the Yankee hero of the nineteenth century down to the hoss-trading David Harum, but he is also a favorite with the Red Indians as Manabozho or Coyote, with the Negro as Br'er Rabbit or Jack, with the Jew as Herschel or Motke. An essay could be written on the fable from Aesop to George Ade and James Thurber. How much have we borrowed? Nobody knows. Certainly Americans are not necessarily sharp dealers because they like tricksters, or childish because they like their wisdom in fables; but in folklore and in humor they are as certainly the heirs of all the ages.

Even though there is this continuity in our humor, there is also a difference between its early and late forms. Artemus Ward and Clarence Day are of different ages. Some time between 1860 and 1875, American humorists began to draw less upon the incongruities of an expanding nation and more upon those of a heterogeneous people struggling with internal problems of adjustment. The story may therefore be roughly divided by the pivotal work of Abraham Lincoln and Mark Twain into a first phase which developed mainly out of frontier conditions as civilization moved from the Atlantic to the Pacific, carrying the memories of the Old World with it, and a second phase which gave expression to the absorption of immigrant strains, the progressive industrialization and urbanization of our society, and the increasing complexities of modern living. No single generalization can therefore describe the American brand of humor. We laughed as we grew.

2

The distinguishing characteristics of the first phase of "American" humor were already defined by the time of the appearance of the professional humorist in the second quarter of the nineteenth century. In it were combined —in a combination distinctively American—the traditional satire of the learned sophisticate with the traditional exaggeration of the folktale and hero legend. The idea that it is exclusively "Western" has been pretty well dispelled. Such types as the "crackerbox philosopher," the "Yankee," and "Gamecock of the Wilderness," and the Negro minstrel are symbols of the national character. More accurate is a broader classification into main groups and types, such as the humor of the New England crackerbox philosopher, of the frontiersman, of the Old Southwest, and of the literary comedian.

Our first coastal frontier set the patterns. Even in Massachusetts, gaiety was not entirely lacking. The anti-Puritan Thomas Morton, with his maypole at Ma-re Mount, sang his "songe" beginning, "Drinke and be merry, merry, merry boyes," and lampooned Miles Standish as "Captain Shrimp." Here we have the humor of contrast with a vengeance. There is plenty of humorous incongruity also in the Puritan diaries, especially that of Master Samuel Sewall at the opening of the eighteenth century, with his autumnal, parsimonious, and ineffectual wooing of Madam Winthrop, as well as in the comments of Mistress Sarah Kemble Knight, who in 1704 took an October junket from Boston to New Haven, jotting down in her journal the whims and perils of the way. In Virginia we find the best example of the Queen Anne wit in the person of William Byrd II, master of Westover. Byrd was an aristocrat but an easy one with interest in all classes and races. He is perfectly willing to apply his satire to his own class, as when he gives a summary of the history of his colony and of the early settlers, who were "most of them reprobates of good families." He loves folktales like the one about a North Briton who found his way out of the great swamp by the aid of a fat louse from his collar, or his stories of comical adventures with bears. Perhaps he started the traditional jests about the men of Lubberland, the poor whites of North Carolina; but they sound like folklore too.

With the Revolution came an outburst of political satires, for which the way had been prepared by such earlier works as Ebenezer Cook's *The Sot-Weed Factor*, which had much of Byrd's gusto and a command of Hudibrastic rhyme. When political issues finally broke into open war, American ridicule, sarcasm, and irony poured forth in newspapers, periodicals, broadsides, and pamphlets in every literary form known to a surprisingly literate lot of writers. More than three hundred satires in prose and verse have been studied, a third of them never reprinted. The most humorous seem to have been modeled upon ballads and popular songs, or upon *Hudibras* or periodical essays or fables. Swift, Dryden, Pope, Churchill are the inspiration from English literature, but Aristophanes, Juvenal, Horace, Claudian, and Rabelais are easily traced also; in other words, our urban wits like Benjamin Franklin and H. H. Brackenridge knew both their folk and their classics.

Similar use of folk material or manner is found in the numerous songs that parodied "Chevy Chase," "Hearts of Oak " "The Vicar of Bray"—not to mention the jovial "Yankee Doodle" in all its variants. An example of the blending of folk tradition with urban humor is "The Battle of the Kegs" by the variously gifted signer of the Declaration, Francis Hopkinson, who was also the composer of several love songs that Arne might have signed. In this case the tune used may have been "Yankee Doodle," as the opening stanza will show:

> Gallants, attend, and hear a friend
>   Trill forth harmonious ditty;
> Strange things I'll tell, which late befell
>   In Philadelphia city.

John Trumbull's burlesque epic, *M'Fingal,* now almost forgotten except for a Hudibrastic epigram or two, in its day evidently seemed the apex of American satire, and we are still amused to find the rough-and-tumble of colonial Connecticut resembling frontier humor of later days. As Sir Walter Scott explained to Washington Irving, the character of a nation is to be found in its plain people—the gentry are much alike everywhere. One must turn, therefore, not to such city wits as Irving and Holmes, but to the plain people of post-Revolutionary days to find humor that can be called characteristically American.

Trumbull's kinsman, Governor Jonathan Trumbull of Connecticut, is sometimes given credit for furnishing the name of the first important type-figure in American humor, the Yankee Jonathan, though Yankee Doodle of the song had suggested the comic rustic ignorance sometimes found in this type. New Englanders in the eighteenth century and thereafter enjoyed a rich local lore about greenhorns as well as about smart tricksters and assorted "originals," and the Yankee's humorous wisdom was a staple of New England's second bible, the almanac. The Yankee peddler became a familiar figure, not only in the Northeast but also in the South and the Middle West, where he gained a reputation for being not only brisk and funny but a master of sharp business methods, a vender of wooden nutmegs, pit-coal indigo, and "Yankee notions." Jonathan made his first appearance on the American stage in the middle of the second act of Tyler's *Contrast* (1787) and thereafter furnished the chief fun in a thoroughly sentimental and patriotic play.

For some years his imitators continued to play minor parts on the stage, while dialect poems filled the newspapers, often in celebration of comic Yankee love—as Lowell knew when he later wrote "The Courtin'." Actors like G. H. (Yankee) Hill recited monologues between the principal play and the farce, just as actors sang Negro songs before the days of the minstrel shows. Finally in 1825 Jonathan Ploughboy in Samuel Woodworth's *The*

Forest Rose showed that this Yankee type could furnish forth a principal role; and thereafter such actors as Hill, Marble, and Silsbee starred in similar parts.

Washington Irving was too busy building the comic figure of the Dutchman to contribute very much to the characterization of the Yankee for whom, as a Yorker, he used rather contemptuous satire in his *Knickerbocker History*; but Ichabod Crane shows that the amorous type was certainly within his acquaintance. Similarly Cooper was much more interested in the frontiersman of New York than in Yankees, though he shows some of them unsympathetically in *The Pioneers, Lionel Lincoln,* and *The Last of the Mohicans.* If the type did not fare well in more pretentious fiction, by 1830 it was famous in folklore, in almanacs, in newspapers, and on the stage.

Other type-characters were slower of development and never reached the stature of the Yankee and his lineal descendant, the frontiersman. The only funny fat man of the era was the Dutchman of Washington Irving, whose *Knickerbocker History,* as a burlesque, was compelled to feature the humor of exaggeration. Irving gave his own native mood of good-natured indolence to Governor Wouter Van Twiller, and later, minus the burlesque exaggeration, created a village counterpart of the type in Rip Van Winkle. The minstrel Negro was the Northern white man's conception of the happy-go-lucky "darky," who was comical in love and in retort but at the same time was a singer of sentimental nostalgia. Later the combination of humor and pathos was to be a staple of local color tales and the movies; in the case of the minstrels the ever-present burlesque blurred the pattern. Thus the basic types of American humor are discoverable well before the West was opened to settlement.

3

At this point enters the "crackerbox philosopher," introduced by Seba Smith, creator of the Jack Downing Papers, which date from 1830 in the era of Jacksonian Democracy. Descended from English immigrants of the seventeenth century, Smith was born in a log cabin in Maine and, in true Yankee fashion, left school early to work in a grocery, a brickyard, a foundry, and a little school—all this before he managed to graduate with honors at Bowdoin at the age of twenty-six. Literary historians think of him as a journalist, but folklorists remember him as the author of a ballad still widely known and sung about "Young Charlotty," the girl frozen on the way to a dance. He won from Poe the title of "worst of all wretched poets" when he composed a lively broadside ballad about Sam Patch, a folk hero from Rhode Island who in 1829 jumped 120 feet from Goat Island into the eddy below Niagara Falls and later killed himself in the attempt to leap the Genesee Falls at Rochester.

"Some things can be done as well as others," was Sam's motto, and it might well have been Jack Downing's.

The first of the Downing letters were written for the Portland *Courier*, founded by the young Bowdoin graduate as an independent journal. In Letter I, Jack comes down to Portland from his native Downingville with a load of ax handles and his mother's cheese for market, but he blunders into a session of the Maine Legislature (which first met in Portland) and reports in rustic wonder the struggle to organize a government. Fired by political ambitions, he fails to obtain a nomination for governor but resolves to try his luck at Washington where, he is informed, the Cabinet has "blown up." He finds that people carry on in Washington "like old smoker." After showing his mettle in dispersing a turbulent crowd which "marches away as whist as mice," he is commissioned a captain, and after freeing (without bloodshed) some American prisoners on the northern border, he is made a major. "I and the President" (Jackson) see their country through the threat of Nullification, though at times the major is "wamble-cropt" with fear at the idea of military action. "I'd sooner let nullification go to grass and eat mullen," he says. He attends the President on a grand tour to the North, assisting as a handshaker:

I took hold and shook for him once in a while to help him along, but at last he got so tired he had to lay down on a soft bench, covered with cloth, and shake as well as he could; and when he couldn't shake, he'd nod to 'em as they came along. And at last he got so beat out, he couldn't only wrinkle his forehead and wink. Then I kind of stood behind him, and reached my arm around under his, and shook for him for about a half an hour as tight as I could spring.

In similar fashion Artemus Ward was to interview Lincoln after his first election, and Will Rogers was to describe his visit to the White House in the Presidency of Calvin Coolidge. All three humorists show how "common" and how comically harassed the Chief Executive can be. The result is the sympathy of democratic humor.

Between 1833 and 1847 there is a gap in the genuine Downing Papers of Smith, though other journalists borrowed the hero's name. (At one time he said he knew himself only by the scar on his left arm.) Then we find the major in the reign of Polk, struggling with the problem of annexation during the Mexican War. Jack has a dream in which Polk, as captain of a ship, decides to take Europe and Asia and Africa—"don't stop for bird's-egging round among the West India Islands; we can pick them up as we come back along." Manifest Destiny was never more genially displayed.

There is folk wisdom also in the parable that Jack tells to show that peace has not really been won. When they were boys the major and Bill Johnson undertook to conquer a hornets' nest, expecting to get lots of honey. Bill smashed the nest with a club but found that it "wasn't conquered, only scattered." "Darn it all," says he, "if I hain't got no honey, I knocked their house to pieces; I've got that to comfort me."

Curiously enough, the comic New England character that ranked close to Major Downing in popularity for a score of years was the creation of a Nova Scotian judge, Thomas Chandler Haliburton. Still more curious is the fact that the creation of Sam Slick of Onion County, Connecticut, was the result of the Judge's desire to contrast Yankee industry and inventiveness with Blue-Nose indolence and indifference. Inasmuch as Haliburton's ancestors on both sides came from New England, he probably knew something about Yankee ways; but he owed quite as much to print as to observation, and he never had the sure touch of Seba Smith.

The first series of *The Clockmaker,* which appeared in 1836 (Halifax), introduces Sam as a tall, thin peddler with hollow cheeks and twinkling black eyes, riding upon a fast stepper called Old Clay. Sam boasts to a Nova Scotian squire (the author): "I guess we are the greatest nation on the face of the airth, and the most enlightened too. . . . We are a 'calculatin' people, we all cypher." Yankees are "actilly the class-leaders in knowledge among all Americans." Sam attributes his own success to that knowledge of "soft sawder and human natur" which enables him to dispose of a clock worth six dollars and a half for forty dollars. He mollifies the cross hostess at a tavern by praising and kissing her children, who have "mamma's eyes." "Any man that onderstands horses," he says, "has a pretty considerable fair knowledge of women, for they are jist alike in temper, and require the very identical same treatment. *Incourage the timid ones, be gentle and steady with the fractious, but lather the sulky ones like blazes."*

Sam's wise saws and modern instances are derived principally from the folk; he says: "Brag is a good dog, but Hold-fast is a better one"; "A nod is as good as a wink to a blind horse"; "Power has a nateral tendency to corpulency." He likes such proverbial comparisons as "deff as a shad"; he and his countrymen are "spry as a fox, supple as an eel, and cute as a weasel." He has a vivid set of figures such as, "I'll send your tongue a sarchin' after your teeth." He knows folktales such as the one about the Yankee's wooden nutmegs, and folk heroes like Sam Patch. All these features amused millions on both sides of the Atlantic; in *Portraits of the Sixties,* Justin M'Carthy said, "I can remember the days when Sam Slick was as well known in England as Sam Weller." Old Walter Savage Landor addressed verses to the "witty head of Haliburton,"

> Wherein methinks more wisdom lies
> Than in the wisest of our wise.

Like the boasters of the frontier Sam is said to have claimed, "I'm half fire, half love, and a little touch of the thunderbolt!" He has the best shooting rifle in all Virginia and declares himself to be a "free and enlightened nigger-whipping Peddlar as ever was raised, and no soft-sawder." Evidently the English were acquainted with more than one type of American humor and liked to have all varieties at once.

In his later years Haliburton had some theories regarding varieties. In the preface to an anthology which he called *Traits of American Humor* he observed that the humor of the middle states, like that of the English, is "at once manly and hearty, and, though embellished by fancy, not exaggerated"; humor of the West is like the Irish, "extravagant, reckless, rollicking, and kind hearted"; that of the Yankees is like the Scotch, "sly, cold, quaint, practical, and sarcastic."

Both Sam Slick and Major Downing owe much to the earlier tradition of the type-Yankee, but Jonathan realized his full possibilities only when Lowell embodied him in Hosea Biglow. Until 1846 the humor of the Yankees had never been recorded with any great range except in folktales which got into print, and had never engaged the talents of a first-rate writer. Then Lowell started the First Series of his *Biglow Papers* during the Mexican War and later continued his success during the Civil War in a Second Series. Like Seba Smith he was a true Yankee himself, reared in Cambridge in days when that little university village was set in farming country. In an Introduction written for the complete Papers he said of the Yankee dialect:

When I write in it, it is as in a mother tongue, and I am carried back far beyond any studies of it to long-ago noonings in my father's hay-fields, and to the talk of Sam and Job over their jug of *blackstrap* under the shadow of the ash-tree which still dapples the grass whence they have been gone so long.

This homely speech Lowell had found "fuller of metaphor and of phrases that suggest lively images than that of any other people I have seen." In his Introduction he follows this remark with a series of proverbial sayings and comparisons that have the sap of humor in many of them. As for exaggeration, thought to be typical of American humor, it seemed to him "that a great deal of what is set down as mere extravagance is more fitly to be called intensity and picturesqueness, symptoms of the imaginative faculty in full health."

For his wartime satires Lowell required more than a single Yankee. In creating Hosea Biglow, he says, "I imagined to myself such an upcountry man as I had often seen at antislavery gatherings, capable of district-school English, but always instinctively falling back into the natural stronghold of his homely dialect when heated to the point of self-forgetfulness." Parson

Wilbur was added to express "the more cautious element of the New England character and its pedantry"; he was to be "the complement rather than the antithesis of his parishioner"—there would be a humorous element in the "real identity of the two under a seeming incongruity." Birdofredum Sawin was to be the clown of the puppet-show: "I meant to embody in him that half-conscious *un*morality which I had noticed as the recoil in gross natures from a puritanism that still strove to keep in its creed the intense savor which had long gone out of its faith and life." He was to be the incarnation of "Manifest Destiny," of national recklessness as to right and wrong. In presenting these three characters, moreover, the satire was to be generalized so far as was possible.

The humor of Parson Wilbur derives from learned sources and has had few successors except in the familiar essays of capering professors. The humor of Birdofredum, the unmoral trickster and rascal, has deep origins in folklore and appears often in the Southwest. It depends for effect not only upon characterization through monologue but also upon Sawin's actions as he goes to the Mexican War, which he finds as disillusioning and uncomfortable as all our war humorists have done down to Bill Mauldin; as he loses one leg, one eye, his left arm, and four fingers on his right hand; as he fumbles with the idea of becoming a politician; and, in the Second Series, as he spends some time in a Southern jail for a crime of which he is innocent. At the end he is freed, joins the Southern cause, marries the Widder Shennon—for whose sake he would like a divorce from his Yankee wife—and settles down comfortably.

> An' here I be ez lively ez a chipmunk on a wall,
> With nothin' to feel riled about much later'n Eddam's fall.

He may, as some have thought, show moral degeneration, but after all there was not much of the moral nature to degenerate, and he has earned his place among America's most amusing rogues.

Hosea likewise shows some development of opinion and character from the radical idealism of the forties to the sad mellowness of Civil War days when his creator lost many relatives in a war which he did *not* call murder. The poet and humanist in Lowell replaced the witty zealot; like Hosea, he could say:

> I sometimes think, the furder on I go,
> Thet it gits harder to feel sure I know . . .

Men of good will who wish for unity in the nation and in the world may regret some of the sharp propaganda inevitable in wartime satire, but the fundamental sympathy for human rights is forever valid. We cannot neglect the humor which opposes those who say,

> I *don't* believe in princerple,
> But O, I *du* in interest.

So *The Biglow Papers* are the high point of Yankee humor, solidly based upon principle and folk wisdom. Lowell added to the Second Series his "The Courtin'," a poem which has nothing to do with war and everything to do with sincere though comical love; the addition was in a long tradition and it was a happy symbol.

4

After the Yankee, a second type-figure, that of the frontiersman, embodied American humor. The most famous exemplar, Colonel David Crockett of Tennessee, was taught to look upon the people of New England as "a selfish, cunning set of fellows, that was fed on fox ears and thistle tops," though when he visited them he changed his mind. When need arose at home, he managed to trick a "gander-shanked Yankee" into selling him ten quarts of liquor for a single coonskin which Davy deftly stole between quarts.

To find the first examples of this second type we must go back to those famous Injun-killers of New York State and Pennsylvania whose more romantic features were used by Cooper for Leatherstocking. There was, for example, Tom Quick, the Avenger of the Delaware, who cut his teeth on an arrowhead and shortly after his death made up the tally of a hundred Indians whom he had aspired to kill in vengeance for his slain father; Tom's body was dug up and sent in pieces to various villages of red men who did not know that he had died of smallpox. He was a trickster; like Daniel Boone he is said to have caught seven Indians in a cleft log which they generously agreed to help him split before putting him to torture. Tom just knocked the wedge out while Indian hands were pulling. There was also Tim Murphy of Morgan's Rangers and the York militia, who bent his gun to shoot an Indian chasing him around a boulder, and who made leggings of Indian skins. There was Nat Foster the trapper, who is said to have called himself Leatherstocking long before Cooper wrote; he referred to his killings as "taking the filling out of a blanket." When the Yorkers laughed at exploits of Colonel Crockett in the twenties and later, they had the pleasure of identifying him with sons of their own, all of whom shared the opinion of Artemus Ward that "Indians is pizen wherever found."

Long before Davy published his autobiography in 1834 or furnished material for the narrative of his tour of the North, the War of 1812 had glorified those "Hunters of Kentucky" in whose honor a popular song to the tune of "The Old Oaken Bucket" was first sung in 1822 at New Orleans, the scene of their greatest battle. "Half man and half alligator" was the subtitle of the Boston broadside version of the song, and for these dashing frontiersmen other names were devised—"the gamecock of the wilderness," "the ring-tailed roarer," "the yaller blossom of the forest." Mighty deeds as well as names were invented; after his death at the Alamo, Crockett of popular almanacs was made into the tallest myth before Paul Bunyan. The thirties saw exaggeration enthroned.

Davy's autobiography is still read with delight, not only for its comical self-portraiture and its tallness but for the gift of oral narrative and humor that he had learned from the folk. He is full of proverbs: liquor is like the Negro's rabbit, "good any way"; in making love he practices "salting the cow to catch the calf"; he escapes from Indians "like old Henry Snider going to heaven, 'mit a tam tite squeeze'"; when he wins an election he remembers, "A fool for luck, and a poor man for children"; he reminds corrupt financiers that "what is got over the devil's back, is sure to be spent under his bellie"; he thinks that the denizens of a city's slums are "too mean to swab hell's kitchen." Perhaps the Scots-Irish strain in such frontiersmen as Crockett, Boone, and President Jackson explains their love for the picturesque as well as occasional supernatural fantasy. What Davy likes is "a regular sifter, cut-the-buckle, chicken-flutter set-to." He always sees pictures: "I didn't think that courage ought to be measured by the beard, for fear a goat would have the preference over a man."

The tall tales and high boasting lived on in the legend of Mike Fink and in Mark Twain's boatmen; for that matter, you can hear them from almost any Adirondack guide. Crockett's rather thin vein of romance filled a number of plays that held the boards in the memory of men now living. Hamlin Garland saw Frank Mayo play the title role in Frank Murdoch's *Davy Crockett, or, Be Sure You're Right, Then Go Ahead*. Paulding is thought to have had the Tennessean in mind when he invented Colonel Nimrod Wildfire in *The Lion of the West*. The Yankee actor, Dan Marble, won applause in *The Gamecock of the Wilderness*. Much more important, some of Davy's funny traits were fused with the humor of the Old Southwest.

5

This humor of the Old Southwest (Georgia, Tennessee, Missouri, and the Deep South) deserves to be called a third principal type, though it was never embodied in a single picturesque figure like that of the Yankee or the fron-

ersman. Americans visualized for the Yankee a figure and costume which
ave survived in our cartoons of Uncle Sam; for the frontiersman they saw
"gamecock" in deerskin shirt and coonskin cap. Perhaps the "cracker" of
835 was as close to a single type as the Southwest achieved, but even for the
racker there was no single stereotype. Certainly the shiftless, pasty-faced,
dirt-eating" cracker does appear, but he is not in the majority. Major Jones,
ne of the most popular heroes of Southwestern humor, is represented in one
olume as wearing the striped trousers and swallow-tailed coat of Uncle Sam,
ut so, for that matter, are certain Negro minstrels depicted on the covers
f sheet music a century ago. No, the Southwest did not furnish a single
icture but rather a number of individual portraits whose humor shows certain
ommon traits.

Its writers usually found publication in local newspapers, but for a national
udience they were deeply indebted to William Trotter Porter, a Vermonter
vho lived in New York and often visited the South. Brought up in a family
hat owned much land and many horses, he was a lover of sports—angling,
unting, horse racing, and even cricket. The *Spirit of the Times,* which he
dited from 1831 for a quarter of a century, was a sports magazine that became
he receptacle for masculine anecdotes and humorous sketches sent from
very part of the country. At times he gathered these contributions into such
ooks as *The Big Bear of Arkansas* and *A Quarter Race in Kentucky,* and
nost of his principal contributors brought out books of their own. The quality
f their humor has already been suggested by the word "masculine"—the
umor of sports and those circuit courts where Lincoln polished the great
rt of oral anecdote. The trickster and the practical joker are much in evi-
lence. Most of the writers were men of varied professional experience; for
xample, Augustus B. Longstreet, a Georgian of Yale's class of 1813, was in
urn a lawyer, a legislator, a judge, a Methodist minister, and the president
f two colleges (Emory and Centenary) and of two universities (Mississippi
nd South Carolina).

Longstreet's *Georgia Scenes* (1835) had for its subtitle *Characters, Incidents,*
&c., in the First Half Century of the Republic; in other words, his tales are
f less civilized times in the back country. "They consist," he said, "of noth-
ng more than fanciful *combinations* of *real* incidents and characters. . . .
ome of the scenes are as literally true as the frailties of memory would allow
hem to be." The remark applies to nearly all the other writing of this type;
ere realism found its most entertaining expression before the Civil War, and
he realistic charm of oral narrative is what keeps this kind of humor alive.
The first "scene" in Longstreet's book tells of a young man who practiced
ll alone the frontier art of gouging while he shouted the emotions of two
ontestants. The most spirited of the narratives concerns a fight started by

one Ransy Sniffle, a dirt-eating cracker, between two champions who bite noses, ears, and cheeks to the vast entertainment of a vividly realized crowd. Other sketches include a gander pulling, a militia drill, a fox hunt, a horse race, and a shooting match. (All these subjects are duplicated in current folklore of New York State.) Before the Civil War the Negro played small part in Southern fiction; but Longstreet does use him occasionally, with careful reproduction of dialect; he even satirizes the attitude of a lady who remarks, after seeing a Negro rider killed in a race, "I declare, had it not been for that little accident, the sport would have been delightful."

The softer side of life in back-country Georgia is found in Major Jones, the creation of William T. Thompson who had some of his early experience as a journalist with Longstreet on the Augusta *States Rights Sentinel*. (Later he handed on the leadership in Southern humor to the creator of Uncle Remus when Harris worked on a Savannah newspaper.)

Major Jones's Courtship, the first and best of three books about this hero, shows the folkways of kind and fun-loving people in a back country that still existed in 1843; the major himself is an amiable innocent who woos and wins, presenting himself as a Christmas gift in a large bag at his sweetheart's door. Before his marriage the best scene shows him tricked at what folklorists call a play party; with the aid of his fiancée he turns the tables on his tormenter, who falls into a tub of water. Thereafter we see the cares of a young father and the humors of domestic life. In *Major Jones's Sketches of Travel* the hero makes a tour to Washington, Baltimore, Philadelphia, New York, Boston, Lowell, Niagara Falls, and Canada, falling into such embarrassments as various generous men of feeling had endured in eighteenth century novels. The epistolary form helps build up the character of a Southern innocent at home and on his travels in such a way that a Northerner feels the humor to be not narrowly local but sympathetically American. Loyal Georgian as he was and defender of slavery, Thompson was born in Ohio of a Virginian father and an Irish mother, and, like Joel Chandler Harris, he was a lover of Goldsmith, whose *Vicar of Wakefield* he dramatized.

The best example of the genus rogue in Southwestern humor, and the most spirited before Twain and H. T. Lewis, is *Some Adventures of Captain Simon Suggs,* by a lawyer and journalist named Johnson J. Hooper, who was to be Secretary of the Provisional (Confederate) Congress. Hooper was born a Tarheel but migrated to the Gulf States when twenty and identified himself with Alabama. Leader of the "Tallapoosy Vollantares," more accurately known as the Forty Thieves, his Simon had a single principle, "It is good to be shifty in a new country." In a series of picaresque tales, remarkable for gusty dialogue and a rowdy humor that Smollett would have enjoyed, Suggs cheats his own father at cards to get a horse, and thereafter dupes everyone

whom he meets. Perhaps the most famous chapter tells how he gets religion—
and the collection—at a camp meeting where, under the inspiration of the
Reverend Bela Bugg, the crowd exhibits all the ecstasy of emotional religion,
shouting,

> I rode on the sky,
> Quite ondestified I,
> And the moon it was under my feet.

Some readers would prefer Simon's tearful trick to escape from a prison
sentence, or his adventures at a faro game. Almost as amusing is a later sketch
in which Simon does not appear, called "Taking the Census," a remarkable
piny-woods study in genre.

If Simon Suggs is the rogue par excellence, the prince of coarse practical
jokers is the hero of *Sut Lovingood's Yarns.* The author, George W. Harris,
was born in Pennsylvania, was apprenticed to a jeweler, was captain of a
river boat, worked in metals, and after the Civil War was the superintendent
of a small railroad in Tennessee, the scene of his yarns. His first full-length
sketch for the *Spirit of the Times,* in 1845, was "The Knob Dance," which
shows the gusty loving and fighting then popular in the Great Smokies.
"I'm agoin to marry Jule, I swar I am, and *sich* a cross! Think of a loco-
motive and a cotton gin! Who! Whooppee!" That is the tempo of Sut
Lovingood also, the bad boy who attended Sicily Burns' wedding, where he
jerked the handle of a basket over a bull's horns with violent and confused
results when the critter backed "agin the bee-bainch." Beside his somewhat
sadistic practical jokes and rough fighting Sut enjoys sniggering about sex, a
subject taboo in nearly all other American writings of the period. "Rare Ripe
Garden Seed," a fabliau about a first baby that arrived too soon, would be
considered too broad by almost any modern magazine editor.

Many other humorists of the Old Southwest are worth reading for a story
or two. T. B. Thorpe's "The Big Bear of Arkansas" is a masterpiece of oral
narrative, tall and imaginative, supposedly told on a Mississippi steamboat.
Henry T. Lewis, in "The Harp of a Thousand Strings," parodied a ranting
sermon in a manner which inspired imitations. Joseph G. Baldwin, whose
Flush Times of Alabama and Mississippi appeared in 1853, would have made
his boastful Ovid Bolus, Esq. much funnier if he had not tried to be an
essayist recapturing the faded elegance of the eighteenth century.

6

In the decade before the Civil War the most popular humorous writers
were the literary comedians, authors and lecturers whom it is convenient to

group together as a fourth general class. Some of them were as well known to the public as the heroes of comic strips or the leading radio comedians of today. Most of them conducted columns in newspapers, but all preserved the qualities of oral address. To the techniques of predecessors they added certain literary devices or brought them into greater prominence: dead-pan solemnity, meandering stream of consciousness, burlesque, anticlimax, puns, bad spelling, and skillful timing. Manner was more than matter; the grand aim was to entertain—not to record types or vanishing manners. Each writer adopted the character of an eccentric individual.

It was from the writings of Artemus Ward that President Lincoln is said to have read before presenting to his Cabinet the draft of the Emancipation Proclamation. The creator of Ward, Charles Farrar Browne, was "born in the State of Maine of parents." (Imagine the pause after the word Maine.) He learned the printer's trade and got on so fast that at twenty-three he was city editor of the Cleveland *Plain Dealer,* in which the first Ward letter was published three years before the Civil War. Four years later *Artemus Ward: His Book* was as huge a success as the lectures which brought a telegraphed message from San Francisco, "What will you take for forty nights in California?" The reply was, "Brandy and water," and Browne had plenty of that spirited beverage when he met young Sam Clemens and other local humorists in Virginia City, Nevada. It was Artemus who helped Mark Twain get a hearing in the East with his "Jumping Frog." The English enjoyed Browne so well that he sailed in June, 1866, to lecture and contribute to *Punch*; but less than a year later Fate played its cruel "goak" on him and the admiring public when he died of tuberculosis.

Browne's creation, Artemus Ward, was a Yankee crackerbox philosopher with a difference, a mixture of apparent simplicity and shrewd showmanship which suggests the great P. T. Barnum, who had opened his American Museum of curios in 1842. Artemus operated on a smaller scale, of course, with a few "Wax Statoots" and certain "Sagashus Beasts" which included "three moral Bares" and a "Kangaroo (a amoozin little Raskal)." His motto was, "Cum the moral on 'em strong." A feature of his written style was comical spelling; for him a critic was a "cricket" and Boston was the "modern Atkins." He had trouble with his verbs: "I asked her if we shouldn't glide in the messy dance. She sed we should, and we Glode."

Politically Artemus was slyly neutral, as the entertainer for the entire country needed to be: "My perlitical sentiments agree with yourn exactly. I know they do, becawz I never saw a man whoos didn't." He was, however, decidedly unsympathetic toward "Our Afrikan Brother" whom he regarded as "a orful noosance." At the opening of the war his "Interview with Lincoln" ridiculed the job hunters and advised the President to fill his Cabinet with showmen who would know how to cater to the public. During the course of the war, Artemus satirized not the South principally but the rascals at home in the North—the hypocrites who whooped about enlisting, the sixteen able-bodied citizens who bought a stage line because stage drivers were exempt, the young patriot who sold disabled cavalry horses as beef—and throughout was loyal to the core. To be sure, at the outbreak of the war, Artemus had a "narrer scape from the sonny South" after a struggle with a Secesher who "put his nose into my mouth." In May, 1865, he went to Richmond and found a remarkable amount of alleged Union sentiment:

I met a man to-day—I am not at liberty to tell his name, but he is a old and inflooential citizen of Richmond, and sez he, "Why! we've bin fightin' agin the Old Flag! Lor' bless me, how sing'lar!" He then borrer'd five dollars of me and bust into a flood of tears.

However, Artemus was equally irreverent at Washington: "The D.C. stands for Desprit Cusses, a numerosity which abounds here, the most of whom persess a Romantic pashun for gratooitous drinks."

Any popular butt he was safe in attacking—the Shakers, the Spiritualists, the Free Lovers, the contenders for Women's Rights, the "Mormins," and even the necessary harmless college students. Of Harvard he wrote, "This celebrated institootion of learnin is pleasantly situated in the Bar-room of Parker's, in School Street, and has poopils from all over the country." Even in the best of the interviews, such as the one with Brigham Young, there is such flat "goaking" as talk about the "Scareum," though nobody else would have thought to ask so mildly upon learning of the Prophet's eighty wives, "How do you like it, as far as you hev got?" Nobody else would have repulsed an offer of Mormon marriage with the cry: "Awa, you skanderlous femaile, awa! Go & be a Nunnery!"

A thoroughly partisan literary comedian was Petroleum Vesuvius Nasby, the creation of an upstate New Yorker, David Ross Locke. The son of Abolitionist parents, he was editor of the Toledo *Blade* at the opening of the war. His Nasby is a rogue in the tradition of Suggs and Birdofredum. At home in Ohio he is a Copperhead who, when drafted, escapes to Canada and then to the South. When drafted there, he escapes again to found churches in the North until the close of war, when he manages to get the postmastership of "Confedrit X Roads" in Kentucky. Later he tries running a grogshop in New York, fails because he drinks too much, and finally retires to Kentucky.

When drafted in the North, Petroleum finds ten reasons why he should be exempt, including:

1. I'm bald-head'd, and hev bin obliged to wear a wig these 22 years.
2. I hev dandruff in wat scanty hair still hangs around mv venerable temples.

One of the sharpest of these satires is dated from Saint's Rest in New Jersey and begins: "The nashen mourns! The hand uv the vile assasin hez bin raised agin the Goril—the head of the nashen, and the people's Father hez fallen beneath the hand uv a patr—vile assasin." If this seems crude, like all the rest of Nasby, we might remember that according to Charles Sumner, Lincoln had said of Nasby, "For the genius to write these things I would gladly give up my office." Lincoln just did not talk that way—the rhythm is wrong, but he certainly enjoyed Petroleum, as Grant and Lowell did. After all, he was attacking cowards and traitors and rogues in the North.

On the Southern side there was one effective literary comedian, the Bill Arp of a Georgia lawyer, Major Charles H. Smith, son of a Massachusetts father and a South Carolina mother. The tone reminds the reader of Major Jones; except for its references to "niggers" the letters are restrained, reasonable, and toward the close rather plaintive but not unmanly. The first epistle to "Abe Linkhorn" in April, 1861, asks for a little more time before obeying his proclamation—the boys in Rome, Georgia, are in a sizzling mood: "A few days ago I heard they surrounded two of our best citizens, because they was named Fort and Sumter." Bill politely asks that the President "let us know whereabouts you intend to do your fitin." At the end of the war, Arp writes to Artemus Ward to remind him, "If we ain't allowed to xpress our sentiments, we can take it out in *hatin*; and hatin runs hevy in my family, shore. I hated a man so bad onst that all the har cum off my hed, and the man drowned himself in a hog waller that nite." The whites "aint a shamed of nuthin"; as for the blacks, "Sumboddy have drawed the elfant in the lottery, and dont know what to do with him."

The last of the important literary comedians of Lincoln's era was Josh Billings. When an Englishman was preparing to bring out a British edition of Josh, he guessed that the author might be Hosea Biglow or Horace Greeley, but was solemnly assured that it was President Lincoln himself. The honor properly went to Henry Wheeler Shaw, a native of western Massachusetts, whose father and grandfather were both members of Congress. In later years young Shaw used to say, "Hamilton College has turned out a good many fine men—it turned me out." The tradition is that Shaw left because he stole the clapper of the chapel bell, but a roving disposition is the better explanation; at any rate another alumnus is right in saying, "Thus, at the age of fifteen, Josh had much more than most men acquire in a lifetime—a sense of humor and a year's schooling at Hamilton College."

Shaw was forty when he abandoned farming, steamboating, and varied wandering to settle down as an auctioneer at Poughkeepsie. In the following year he wrote his essay on the mule, beginning, "The mule is haf hoss and haf Jackass, and then kums to a full stop, natur diskovering her mistake," and ending, "I herd tell ov one who fell oph from the tow path, on the Eri kanawl, and sunk as soon as he touched bottom, but he kept rite on towing the boat tu the nex stashun, breathing thru his ears, which stuck out ov the water about 2 feet 6 inches; i didn't see this did, but an auctioneer told me ov it, and i never knew an auctioneer tu lie unless it was absolutely convenient." Generously appreciative of a rival's talent, Artemus Ward helped secure a publisher for *Josh Billings, His Sayings* in 1865, at which date Josh was already a national figure.

Not unexpectedly Shaw was a successful lecturer in the dead-pan style; in some seasons he spoke as often as eighty nights in the wandering, solemn manner so acceptable. He made a greater hit with his annual *Farmer's Allminax* for the decade following 1870 when Bret Harte and Mark Twain were the other most popular humorists. Anyone acquainted with almanacs will enjoy the burlesque upon that American perennial, but the "affurisms" are the enduring part, with their blend of folk wisdom and mellow irony:

Most people repent ov their sins bi thanking God they aint so wicked as their nabers.

There may cum a time when the Lion and the Lam will lie down together—i shall be az glad to see it as enny boddy—but i am still betting on the Lion.

Dont never trust a man at the rate ov 50 cents on a dollar—if you kant confide in him at par let him slide.

Josh knew that "yu hav tew be wise before yu kan be witty," and he went on interspersing his wisdom of middle and old age between daft little "characters" of men and such critters as "The Frequent Fly," or his receipts, riddles, advice about planting, and prophecies about "windy winds" and "liquid rains." He died in 1885 while sunning himself on a hotel veranda in California. With him passed the last great literary comedian whom Lincoln had enjoyed.

7

Lincoln appreciated these comedians because he was a humorist at heart himself. The wisdom that directed a people through a civil war was close kin to wit. In him and in Mark Twain our early types of humor matured and formed a tradition; for both of these men realized that, as Mark Twain said, "humor is not enough."

As they understood the era that was passing, so likewise they sensed the forces that were at work in the era that was to come. Lincoln died before he could put all of that knowledge into expression, but Mark Twain lived on and wrote. Master of the oral tradition, both Negro and white, his early humor was radiant with youth. It is first as the poet of childhood's unsearched possibilities that he is to be remembered in comparing him to other humorists. When he and the era grew older and more disillusioned, it is to him again that we turn for comparison with the more ironic and sophisticated wit of a later day.

Perhaps it was the success of *Tom Sawyer,* perhaps there are deeper reasons for the vogue of humorous childhood stories in the latter years of the century. Six years before Mark Twain's classic was published, Thomas Bailey Aldrich explored the humors of childhood in an autobiographical book called *The Story of a Bad Boy* (1869). Tom Bailey, who is of about the same age as Tom Sawyer and Tarkington's Penrod, lives in the "rusty, delightful old town" of Rivermouth (Portsmouth, New Hampshire) where he and his companions engage in such pranks as burning an old stagecoach and firing off a battery of old cannon. There is an amusing club called the Rivermouth Centipedes; there are theatrical performances such as delighted Penrod; instead of the dogs so comically important to Tarkington's boys there is a pony, and instead of the companionable, funny Negroes of Twain and Tarkington there is the droll sailor Ben Watson who woos Kitty Collins, a maid descended from Irish kings. The girls of Primrose Hall play minor parts, and Tom has a short season of love for Miss Nelly, aged nineteen. "It was a great comfort to be so perfectly miserable and yet not suffer any." Except for the tragic loss of one boy at sea the tone of realistic comedy is well sustained, though the author shows a didactic preference for the sort of manly lads exhibited thirteen years earlier in *Tom Brown's Schooldays* by the Englishman Thomas Hughes—to whom Aldrich refers as the author of "one of the best books ever written for boys." Of course there is a bully, properly and comically trounced by the hero.

Stephen Crane's *Whilomville Stories* (1900) carried on the tradition of Aldrich and Twain, though in the author's somewhat dour style. To Crane, children often seemed "little blood-fanged wolves," just as their mothers were a "company of latent enemies," infatuated by affection for their offspring. He realized that "in the jungles of childhood . . . grown folk seldom penetrate," but he had insight into the psychology of boys sore beset by ridicule, humiliation, and hostility. Again there is a genial and companionable Negro servant; there is also comical gormandizing and showing-off. The harassed father, the Angel Child daughter, and the screaming mob of children with their damnable iteration were hints for the more genial Tarkington.

More in the spirit of Tom and Huck is Booth Tarkington's Penrod. When well-born Tarkington graduated from Princeton, he went to live in that mildly Bohemian New York of the nineties whose young writers looked upon Crane with awe—but not for his humor. After success as a writer of romance

Tarkington finally came home from Paris to the "tranquil, friendly life of the people," in this case the people of his home town, Indianapolis. There in the year in which the First World War broke out, he found himself as a humorist and wrote *Penrod*. From his autobiography, *The World Does Move,* we know that he regarded war itself as a "herd mania . . . one of the adolescent disorders of undeveloped mankind"; we know also that he was as suspicious as Sinclair Lewis of "the tremendous universal respect for respectability"; but in his best humorous books he accepted the world of his own youth in which, as the milkman told him, "Pretty much everybody is either a church member or at least abiding." As a consequence, in recent years owlish historians of literature have regarded him as a *farceur,* whereas he was one of the two American humorists who have seen farthest into our childish hearts.

For his three most durable studies of childhood's humors—and there are several others—Tarkington chose a boy in his eighth year as the hero of *Little Orvie*; one in his twelfth for *Penrod*—about the same age as Tom Bailey, Tom Sawyer, and Crane's Whilomville set; and a high-school adolescent, Willie Baxter, for *Seventeen*. Each age has its special trials and humors, carefully discriminated. "Look how I do! Haw Poot!" is the slogan of Orvie and his destructively buoyant peers; what makes him comically puzzling to adults is the simple fact that "not many older people transform all their impulses into action."

Penrod Schofield has reached the romantic age of adventure; he is the ardent author of "Harold Ramorez the Roadagent or Wild Life among the Rocky Mountains." He has moments of soaring reverie and can extemporize tall tales of embarrassing realism. Lovely Marjorie Jones can give his heart a squeeze, but he is so far from the Court of Love that "little gentleman" is the most abusive of epithets. His world is still so separate from that of adults that punishment and clemency are alike inexplicable.

Willie Baxter is at the age of romantic posturing, with a sense of his own picturesqueness, a fear of derision, and devastating love for Miss Pratt, "a howling belle of eighteen who talked baby-talk even at breakfast." He lives by a code that is not without dignity and decency; his griefs are real enough to answer the charge that Tarkington is incapable of humor deeper than farce.

Tarkington's three heroes are surrounded by a variety of companions individually characterized. They inhabit a world of well-to-do midlanders in the last tranquil period of American history, they are true of American children everywhere. Though they may not seem so elemental as Mark Twain's boys and certainly lack his grandly romantic setting, they are as prophetic of the adult human comedy. Like all great humorous creations they reconcile us to other men by reminding us that we are all comical—and on the whole decent—boys.

8

As Mark Twain moved from the study of a small boy to that of his world, and salted the whole Midwest with his humor, so his contemporaries like Bret Harte, Edward Eggleston, and Joel Chandler Harris exploited local customs, dialects, and other regional characteristics in story and verse. "Local color" was humorous as often as it was serious in the decades following the Civil War, and when developed in a racial idiom like that of the Negro, the Irishman, or the Jew, as well as in the idiom of a region, it provided the dominant tone of the literature of the post Civil War period.

Most successful in combining sentimental with humorous interest in the local story was Joel Chandler Harris. His *Uncle Remus: His Songs and His Sayings* (1880), was the first of eight notable volumes that gave America one of its half-dozen finest humorous characters and its best example of artistically treated folklore, "befo' de war, endurin' de war, en atterwards."

He insisted that his own stories of the "old-timey" Negro were "uncooked," that he aimed only at "honesty, sincerity, and simplicity" in their telling. A shy man himself, though fond of pranks and practical jokes, he took easily to animal tales in which the trickster element is almost always prominent. He also had, possibly from his Celtic ancestors, a fondness for myth, the supernatural, and the picturesque proverb. He liked such funny language as "How does yo' copperositee segashuate?" He had the wisdom to know that "You er what you is, en you can't be no is-er." Once again the shrewd American views life, this time through the eyes of a benevolent, aged Negro who instructs the world in such humorous tales as "The Story of the Deluge." For Harris as for Mark Twain, humor was not enough; but unlike Twain he did not despair of the "damned human race." He went on sanely in the Remus tales, and in such other books as *The Chronicles of Aunt Minervy Ann,* always instructing through laughter.

The first Negro American to learn the literary lessons of Harris was Paul Lawrence Dunbar, who was equally skillful in dialect, having studied it in the white Hoosier poetry of James Whitcomb Riley, an Indianapolis journalist whose *The Old Swimmin'-Hole and 'Leven More Poems* came out three years after the first Remus book. Five years after Riley's poems had taken the nation's favor, Dunbar was born at Dayton, Ohio, the son of former slaves. After graduating from high school he sold his own first volume to passengers on an elevator which he operated for four dollars a week. Two years later, in 1895, his second book of verse, *Majors and Minors,* was reviewed by Howells, who appreciated the value of humorous folkways found in such poems as "The Party." When *Lyrics of Lowly Life* came out in the following year, Dunbar's poetry took first place in Negro literature. Like James Weldon Johnson of later fame, he realized that humor and pathos are the "two stops" of dialect; but instead of leaving those stops undrawn, as Johnson and Countee Cullen did, he mingled their sweetness in verses about children (white and black), love making, frolics, and religion. If he occasionally permitted himself such tragic notes as "We Wear the Mask," he was usually content to be the sympathetic humorist of the folk.

In the third and fourth decades of the twentieth century, three young Negro poets showed that laughter was still not drowned in tears or wrath. Countee Cullen's *Color* includes such sharp epigrams as "To a Pessimist," "For a Mouthy Woman," and "For a Lady I Know." As he said of Dunbar,

> Born of the sorrowful of heart,
> Mirth was a crown upon his head.

While Cullen avoided dialect, Langston Hughes used it for poems often in traditional folk form, such as his "Po' Boy Blues." As folklorists have observed, the mood of the blues is a curious mingling of humor with self-pity. In *Southern Road,* Professor Sterling A. Brown of Howard University tried further experiments with the blues and other folk rhythms; he also started a series of humorous poems about the adventures of Slim Greer, a wandering Negro whose odyssey is full of tall tales and sly satire. In verse Brown proved himself the most accomplished Negro humorist since Dunbar, partly because of his sympathetic vision and wide range.

In prose depicting the humor of Negro life the outstanding writer of her race is Zora Neale Hurston, an anthropologist as well as a creative writer. Her *Mules and Men* (1935) was called by Alan Lomax "the finest single book in American folklore"; one of her novels, *Jonah's Gourd Vine,* is equally full-blooded in humor. When she describes the life of colored people in Florida, she never loses humanity and zest in the quest of science.

If the Negro has given unique turns to American humor, others not of the old English stock have also made their mark. "The last one over" has always been cause for mirth, like the new boy in any school. Before the Civil War the Irishman was already a comic figure on the stage, and after the great immigration of the "famine forties" books of humorous Irish songs were popular. The first really great Irish figure, however, did not appear until Finley Peter Dunne triumphed in the late nineties with Mr. Dooley, the most popular literary comedian and crackerbox philosopher between Artemus

Ward and Will Rogers. Born of Irish Catholic parents in Chicago, Dunne started newspaper work at the age of sixteen, was a city editor at twenty-one, thereafter was one of the first baseball reporters, and by 1898 had held good positions on every Chicago paper except one. From two of his colleagues, Eugene Field and George Ade, he may have learned tricks of journalistic humor, but from the time when he started to write Irish pieces for the *Sunday Post,* he broke ground for himself.

For his early articles he created the character of McNeery, suggested by a saloon-keeper named McGarry; but when McGarry objected to the rather obvious identification, the name was changed to Dooley and the saloon was moved to "Archey Road." To ask Dooley questions and to represent the prejudices of an ignorant day laborer, the character of Hennessey was added. In 1898 a volume of sketches in which the two cronies had appeared was published with the title of *Mr. Dooley in Peace and in War;* in the next year this was followed by *Mr. Dooley in the Hearts of His Countrymen,* with a dedication to the English publishers who had pirated the first book. Other books appeared annually through 1902, and the five volumes represent the best of their author's writing, though he continued to publish for a long time. In all, Dunne wrote more than seven hundred dialect essays, about a third of which were republished in eight books.

Though some of the early essays contained a considerable amount of Irish sentiment and pathos, those remembered now are nearly all political commentaries by a "scourge of princes" who satirized affectation and corruption at home, toadying and imperialism abroad. Most of our crackerbox philosophers have been famous for common sense; when his own prejudices were not involved, as in the case of Woodrow Wilson, Dunne wrote from the uncommon sense which derives from intelligent and humane principle. Before the *Maine* disaster Dooley tells Hennessey: "Ye cud niver be a rale pathrite. Ye have no stock ticker in ye'er house." After Dewey's victory at Manila, the Irish sage announces that the Admiral is a member of his own family and prophesies that he will be king of the Philippine Islands, "Dooley th' Wanst." Dunne paraphrases Lodge's slogans as "Hands acrost th' sea an' into somewan's pocket" and "Take up th' white man's burden an' hand it to th' coons."

The most amusing of the early sketches is a review of Theodore "Rosenfelt's" account of exploits of the Rough Riders: " 'Tis th' Biography iv a Hero be Wan who Knows! . . . But if I was him I'd call th' book 'Alone in Cubia.' " Great politician that he was, Roosevelt thereupon invited Dunne to pay him a visit. It is said that President McKinley used to have Dooley's remarks read at weekly meetings of his Cabinet, evidently forgiving such barbs as occur in an account of the President's visit to Chicago: "Th' proceedin's was opened with a prayer that Providence might remain undher th' protection iv th' administhration."

At the time of the Boxer insurrection in China imperialism was castigated again and again. To Hennessey's smug observation that the "Chinnymen" would be civilized by the war, Dooley replies: " 'Twill civilize thim stiff. An' it may not be a bad thing f'r th' rest iv th' wurruld. Perhaps contack with th' Chinee may civilize th' Germans." If Americans consider themselves anti-imperialists, we may owe more to Dooley in this regard than to the rage of Mark Twain and the noble indignation of William Vaughn Moody.

Comments on domestic problems were equally frank and pungent, particularly at the time of the anthracite coal strike in 1902 when a winter without fuel threatened. "The rich can burn with indignation, thinkin' iv th' wrongs inflicted on capital, th' middle or middlin' class will be marchin' with th' milishy, an' th' poor can fight among thimsilves an' burn th' babies." When Hennessey asked Dooley what he thought of a man in Pennsylvania who said that the Lord and he were partners in a coal mine, Dooley asked, "Has he divided th' profits?" When the twentieth century's perennial suggestion for a "business administration" was first heard, Dooley agreed ironically: "We must injuce th' active, conscientious young usurers fr'm Wall Street to take an inthrest in public affairs." When Hennessey defended high tariffs on the ground that the foreigner paid the tax anyhow, Dooley said, "He does, if he ain't turned back at Castle Garden." He described the elder Rockefeller as "a kind iv a society f'r th' prevention iv croolty to money. If he finds a man misusing his money he takes it away fr'm him an' adopts it." In the era of muckrakers he deplored the American method of cleaning a house by burning it down, "but I want to say to thim neighbors iv ours, who're peekin' in an' makin' remarks about th' amount iv rubbish, that over in our part iv th' wurruld we don't sweep things undher th' sofa."

Of the other national strains that have had interpreters in humorous dialect, none has produced a philosopher of the stature of Uncle Remus and Mr. Dooley; but the Jews have fared well in sympathetic characterization. Before the twentieth century they were usually presented as tricksters and money grabbers; but a devoted schoolteacher in New York, Myra Kelly, showed them and children of other immigrants in more amiable light when, at the opening of the century, she wrote her *Little Aliens* and *Little Citizens*. Adults have always enjoyed the books for their dialect and for the humorous contrasts in civilizations. In 1910 Montague Glass, an English-born Jew who knew intimately the cloak-and-suit trade of New York, began a series of books about Potash and Perlmutter and other businessmen who were both as sharp and as kind as David Harum, the Yankee Yorker. These stories reached both the popular magazines and the stage. In 1937 the *New*

Yorker published a series of sketches later collected in a book called *The Education of Hyman Kaplan*. The author, Leonard Q. Ross (Leo C. Rosten), took for his hero a puzzled, genial, and patriotic member of an "American Night Preparatory School for Adults." Part of the fun derives from Kaplan's struggle with the English language, but more of it is due to the creation of an enthusiast who is a real person. As the author says, there was "something sacrilegious in trying to impose the iron mold of English on so unfettered an intelligence." He is perhaps the most amusing immigrant in our literature and one of the most amiable.

Funny German dialect appeared in the Hans Breitmann ballads of Charles Godfrey Leland, a Philadelphian who studied at Heidelberg and Munich. "Hans Breitmann's Barty" started the series in a magazine in 1857, and a collection was made for a volume as late as 1914. In the 1930's the radio comedian Jack Pearl popularized again the Baron Munchausen in a program not entirely limited to tall tales. As for the Italians, T. A. Daly of Philadelphia wrote sympathetically humorous verses in their immigrant dialect from the year 1906, when his *Canzoni* was published; in prose the important book is *Mount Allegro* (1943) by Jerre Mangione, who writes about the gusty folkways of Sicilians in Rochester, New York.

Meanwhile humorous figures bearing English names have found places in the American gallery. In what has been called the "B'Gosh School," a favorite is David Harum, hero of the single novel published at the turn of the century by Edward Noyes Westcott. Member of a prominent family in Syracuse, New York, the author began his book after tuberculosis had compelled him to leave the world of finance. Though a friend has declared that David is a composite portrait, his character is undoubtedly based upon that of David Hannum, a small-town banker and horse trader in Homer, New York. Certainly he is as true to the type of central New York Yankee as Irving Bacheller's Eben Holden is to the North Country hired man of the same era. Part of the time David is a crackerbox philosopher whose sayings have become proverbial: "Do unto the other feller the way he'd like to do unto you, an' do it fust." "A leetle too big's about the right size." "A reasonable amount o' fleas is good fer a dog—keeps him from broodin' over *bein'* a dog, mebbe." Part of the time he is a trickster, but secretly he is a generous man of feeling.

A Southern counterpart of Harum in the twentieth century will be found in *Back Home* (1912) and Irvin S. Cobb's other tales about a Confederate veteran, Judge Priest. Cobb himself, the sage of Paducah, was a "character," and his funny face was as welcome in a movie role as at a banqueting board. Such rambling essays as *Speaking of Operations* are proofs that Cobb was one of those numerous "columnists" of his generation who always knew what would make his countrymen laugh. So did Frank McKinney ("Kin") Hubbard of Indiana, whose "Abe Martin" ran in syndicated columns and collected volumes for almost forty years before 1930. Abe was a crackerbox philosopher who reached out from Hoosier land to almost all the country.

Of course the philosopher who has held highest place since Dooley is Will Rogers of Oklahoma, inheritor of Cherokee Indian blood and proud of it. He was born bowlegged, "so I could set on a horse," and knew that life of the range which was popularized at the end of the nineteenth century by *Wolfville* (1897) and other tales of Alfred Henry Lewis, as well as by John A. Lomax's great collection of cowboy ballads in 1910. After touring the world in Boer War days as a rider and rope thrower, Rogers progressed through vaudeville to the Ziegfeld Follies. Thereafter he played in silent movies, then in the "talkies," in which he was starred as the Connecticut Yankee and David Harum. From 1919 he published a number of books, including *Letters of a Self-Made Diplomat to His President.* His syndicated newspaper column was said to reach 40,000,000 readers; his talks certainly were heard by everyone who owned a radio.

Will's mottoes were, "We are all ignorant, but not about the same things," "All I know is what I read in the papers," and "I'm always agin the party that is up." As he said, "There is no credit in being a comedian, when you have the whole government working for you. All you have to do is report the facts." He insisted that there were 120,000,000 in the American kindergarten, and he addressed these infants in a slow, friendly drawl that usually carried over into his books and columns. The irreverence of the Southwest sometimes shocked the well bred, as when he referred to the Supreme Court as "nine old men in kimonos" or when he wrote for a popular magazine a burlesque account of his visit to President Coolidge. The older comedians all lived again in him; he reminded the American people that "there is a big country west of the Hudson River."

9

By the turn of the century, American humor was no longer a reflection of a nation in the making. It had gained a sophistication, an urbanity, of native origin. It was wit, not humor. One thing that had happened west of the Hudson and elsewhere in America after the Civil War was the shift of population to the cities, with a consequent change in our humor. As early as 1879 humor of the suburbs appeared very successfully in *Rudder Grange* by Frank R. Stockton, who was born in Philadelphia and spent most of his writing life in suburbs of New York. His most popular story was suggested by the sight of a family living on a ruddered canal boat in the Harlem River;

its most entertaining character, Pomona, was patterned after an orphan maid who had worked for the Stocktons. Pomona is incurably romantic before her husband takes her on her honeymoon to a lunatic asylum where she meets people whose imagination has carried them a little further than she is willing to go. The competent hero and his wife Euphemia are the sort of pleasant young married people whom Howells was using for his "parlor farces" and are not unlike those whom Christopher Morley was to make so agreeable in all his early works. The style is as well bred and felicitous, though not so original, as Morley's; and like Morley the earlier author is able to mix fancy with realism. At least once again Stockton got his mixture right in the following decade, when he wrote *The Casting Away of Mrs. Lecks and Mrs. Aleshine.*

Much of the urban humor of the late nineteenth century appeared in three weeklies: *Puck* (1877–1918), of which Henry Cuyler Bunner was editor from its second year until his death in 1896; *Judge* (1881–1939), founded by seceders from *Puck*; and the older of two magazines called *Life* (1883–1936), started by two young Harvard wits, J. A. Mitchell and E. S. Martin. Bunner composed familiar verse and parodies which included a clever set on "Home, Sweet Home"; he also wrote stories collected in *Short Sixes* and other volumes.

Oliver Wendell Holmes and John G. Saxe had written admirable light verse in the mid-century, but Bunner, John Kendrick Bangs, and a host of others made *vers de société* even more popular in the nineties. This form of urban humor continued and had a greatly increased vogue again in the 1920's, when its irony and frequent tone of comic depression complemented the angry disillusion of the novelists. Any collection of such verse might well include all of the following books and more: Guy Wetmore Carryl's *Fables for the Frivolous* (1898); Franklin P. Adams' *Tobogganing on Parnassus* (1911); Arthur Guiterman's *The Laughing Muse* (1915); *A Few Figs from Thistles* (1920), by Edna St. Vincent Millay in the flippant mood of Greenwich Village; Samuel A. Hoffenstein's *Poems in Praise of Practically Nothing* (1928); Dorothy Parker's *Not So Deep as a Well* (1936), collected from three earlier volumes; Christopher Morley's *Poems* (1931), including some of the best sayings of the character called the Old Mandarin; Morris Bishop's *Spilt Milk* (1943); and Ogden Nash's *The Face Is Familiar* (1940), selected from earlier volumes. Practically all these writers are Horatian in some degree; all have gaiety, irony, and a command of technique that ranges from Guiterman's flashing triple rhymes to Nash's deliberately bad and funny ones. All have the tang of New York.

In prose certain individuals have stood out for some special theme or themes which the twentieth century found funny. George Ade's *Fables in*

Slang (1899) vied in popularity with Mr. Dooley. To be sure, Ade's had been preceded by many comical or satirical fables from the day of Franklin and had to compete in 1899 with the mordant *Fantastic Fables* of Ambrose Bierce, whose *The Devil's Dictionary* (1881–1906) is an American masterpiece of cynical wit. (We still remember that "positive" means "mistaken at the top of one's voice.") But it was the slang that gave Ade preeminence, as it did O. Henry's stories a little later, a slang that gave America a common speech in those days before the radio.

Don Marquis caught the dafter features of the twenties. His *The Old Soak,* from which a popular play was made, is the comic monument to the Prohibition Era. In the persons of a cockroach and an alley cat his *archy and mehitabel* satirizes the frustrations of the little man and the gay sexual amorality of the "liberated" woman. Almost as funny are his *Hermione and Her Little Group of Serious Thinkers,* his *Sonnets to a Red-Haired Lady,* and the book of verse entitled *Noah an' Jonah an' Cap'n John Smith.*

The gold-digging "babes" of the same period are exploited in Anita Loos' *Gentlemen Prefer Blondes* (1925) and its sequel, *But Gentlemen Marry Brunettes.* The illiteracy of these ladies is matched by that of the baseball players in Ring Lardner's *You Know Me Al* (1916) and by that of various other conceited and inarticulate people who are castigated in other volumes of the same author down to the time of his death in 1933. No other American humorist except Bierce, Mark Twain in his last years, and H. L. Mencken in his Booboisie period has shown such contempt for those whom he satirized; few have equaled Lardner's savage mimicry and the slang which was nicknamed "Lardner's Ringlish." The more genial tone returned with the work of another sports writer, Damon Runyon, whose *Guys and Dolls* in 1932 was the first of several volumes which told in illiterate, imaginative slang about the adventures of gamblers and other sporting characters of the big city.

A New Yorker from a very different social stratum was Clarence Day, educated at St. Paul's and Yale, a writer who began the fashion of accounts of ebullient parents, told from the point of view of their offspring. As early as 1920 he had published *This Simian World,* in which the types of mankind were broken down into their animal resemblances and the irony completed without pointing a moral. In the same decade he began to publish his famous studies of a financier and his family that afterwards became known as *Life with Father* in the most successful play of the turn of the forties. *God and My Father* and *Life with Father* were published in book form in 1932 and 1935. His unformed but mordant drawings in illustration of his text set a style which James Thurber developed toward fantasy.

Day, who began his career in *Harper's Magazine* and the *Literary Review* of the New York *Evening Post,* became one of the valued contributors to the

New Yorker, founded in 1925 by Harold Ross, who gathered the most notable group of urbane writers since the early years of the *Atlantic Monthly* and the Saturday Club. Of them, Ring Lardner was the most influential in setting the sophisticated tone with undernotes of an irony which was often savage. These writers included E. B. White, Alexander Woollcott, Robert Benchley, Dorothy Parker, James Thurber, and many others who could properly be called the New York Wits. Their urbane knowingness was often accompanied by an almost naïve wonder at their mad and beautiful city. The style of all was deliberately easy and conversational. As writer and actor for the screen, Benchley specialized in the sort of nonsense which only literates achieve; *My Ten Years in a Quandary, and How They Grew* is a typical example of his titles. Woollcott's wit, arrogance, sentiment, and wonderful command of an audience made him the First Gentleman of the Radio; even the best of his books, *While Rome Burns* (1934), and the book of his letters would give an imperfect idea of his flashing personality if he had not found the perfect biographer in Samuel Hopkins Adams. Mrs. Parker, in the humorous verse already mentioned, specialized in the comically woeful war of the sexes; in such prose sketches as *Laments for the Living* (1930) and *After Such Pleasures* (1933) there is still plenty of mordant wit but also such penetration into the grief of being woman that she is obviously a good deal more than a pert humorist.

E. B. White, who was a chief contributor to the *New Yorker* at the beginning, and again much later to its editorial section called "The Talk of the Town," was known for his *One Man's Meat* (1942), a collection of essays published elsewhere, but indicative of the best qualities of his anonymous editorial writing. Here was an ironic mind holding up the mirror of Nature and her simplicities, which he loved, to the noisy, thoughtless life of the metropolis, where the rush for publicity and profits had warped the desirable values of living. He was, indeed, a sophisticated Thoreau come to preach Concord to the town, and by many of his contemporaries he was regarded as the best essayist, the best writer of prose of this kind in a time when the personal essay as a literary form had almost disappeared. It is noteworthy that from the beginning, but particularly in the heavy years of the Second World War, his unsigned leaders in the editorial section, light in style but deeply incisive and with powerful emotional undercurrents, performed the same function as the commentators who had overshadowed the editorial writers of the newspapers. His comments were unsigned, but his style made them personal. Many were republished in *The Wild Flag* (1946).

James Thurber brought to the *New Yorker* another strain of American writing, but transformed almost out of recognition. A Puckish genius, his skits and stories depended upon burlesque and exaggeration for their impact;

but, as with Mark Twain, a whimsical realism (in his case often fantasy) sheathing a deadly satire, gave them quality. He was as much in love with contemporary life as Mark Twain was with the Mississippi Valley; but where Mark's rancor against human inconsistency finally broke into tragic despair Thurber was content if all would see, either in word or in picture, that his world was more mad than bad. He is best represented in *The Thurber Carnival,* a cumulative collection made in 1945, and in his later work, *The White Deer* (1945).

The wits and essayists mentioned in the paragraphs above evidently belong in that marginal area which can be called either journalism or literature, or both. Yet in many instances, as, for example, the light verse of F. P. A., the ironic and affectionate character sketches of Don Marquis, the subtle period studies of Clarence Day, or the essays and skits of E. B. White and James Thurber, the end result is clearly a literature of sophisticated humor. Not news of events, which is the staple of journalism, but news of life prepared for the discriminating reader, and addressed to his imagination, defines this literary journalism, especially in its creative period in the early 1920's.

So our national humor, which began with university wits, has strengthened itself on folklore and various emerging types, often crude but nearly always sympathetic and kind and wise, until it has returned to the wits of the city. On the way it has joined arms with the Yankee, the frontiersman, the Southwesterner, the children, the Negroes, the Irish, the Jews, the Italians, and such genial folk heroes as David Harum, Judge Priest, and Will Rogers. It has taken innumerable literary forms, from the fable and the anecdote and the tall tale and the trickster story to the parlor farce, light verse of the wits, and the playful retelling of classical legend. It has recorded all our follies, especially those of politics but also Prohibition, the snares of the gold digger, and the cantrips of the underworld. It has gone deep into satire of the kind of human nature shaped in our society. It has not been afraid of dialect or slang; it has glorified them. And always it has been democratic; it has made us one.

45. WESTERN CHRONICLERS AND LITERARY PIONEERS

Thus in language and ethnological change, in folklore and humor, can be traced the widening horizons of culture as the United States grew from a confederation of former British colonies to a cosmopolitan and continental nation. The record of this growth is further and more explicitly manifested in the literature of the frontier itself—or rather, the two literatures, one written on the ground, the other from the point of view of the East. The present chapter picks up this story where an earlier chapter on "Reports and Chronicles" (Chapter 3) left it, and describes a representative selection of some two dozen books written by explorers and travelers in the frontier West, or by literary pioneers who made the earliest efforts at artistic use of Western materials. Because these books are important primarily for the experiences they record, they group themselves naturally according to the phases of the westward movement: the Franco-British struggle for empire; the American agricultural advance into the trans-Allegheny; early exploration of the Louisiana Purchase; American contact with New Spain in the Southwest; the great lunge across the Plains and over the Rocky Mountains to Oregon and California; and the integration of the West with the nation in the period following the California Gold Rush.

2

The chronicle literature dealing with the Mississippi Valley during the first six decades of the eighteenth century reflects the dramatic contest between France and Britain for control of North America. The French point of view is well represented by a young Parisian Jesuit named Pierre François Xavier de Charlevoix who, sent out in 1720 on a tour of inspection by Louis XV, traveled from Quebec to New Orleans along the well established highways of Bourbon imperialism. In the course of time he pieced out his own notes with descriptions of the flora, fauna, and native inhabitants drawn from such sources as the Jesuit Relations. The resulting *Journal of a Voyage to North America,* published in Paris in 1744 as part of an ambitious *History of New France,* shows a clear intelligence and a gift for style. Charlevoix's comments on the Indians are almost devoid of religious dogmatism and are even tinged with a respect for natural man that hints at the coming Enlightenment. In the French-Canadian colonists he discerned many traits that came to characterize the English settler in the New World: love of danger and hardship, and of a wandering life; an "excellent genius for mechanics"; an impatience of discipline even in war, combined with a general capacity for "managing the greatest affairs." Yet, like the British administrators whom Burke criticized on the eve of the Revolution, Charlevoix failed to read the lesson offered by the character of the colonists, and proposed to direct the settlement of the Mississippi Valley through a centralized administration in Paris. He could not foresee that the advance of European settlers into the great wilderness would shatter all efforts at control from a remote metropolis.

Although of course he did not know it, Charlevoix was writing the end of a chapter in the history of the West. The future of North America belonged to the British. Twenty years after the urbane Jesuit floated down the Mississippi an advance guard of fur traders from South Carolina was firmly established on the eastern bank of the river. Among these was James Adair, a younger son of a Scotch-Irish baronet who left a unique record of the southern Mississippi Valley before the Revolution in a book published in London under the title *The History of the American Indians, Particularly Those Nations Adjoining to the Mississippi, East and West Florida, Georgia, South and North Carolina, and Virginia* (1775).

Although Adair wastes a regrettable amount of energy in trying to prove that the American Indians are descended from the Jews, his discussions of Indian ritual, government, oratory, and modes of warfare are still valuable sources of ethnological data. He took an aristocratic delight in wilderness life, fighting and all, and had a backwoodsman's contempt for city-dwelling officials. Into the mouths of the Indians he puts a scathing satire of the "young, lazy, deformed white men, with big bellies," idling their time away in Charleston. With its love of the forest, its stern warrior's ethics, and its rejection of the norm of "civilization," Adair's *History* is the first important book written from the point of view of the American frontier.

Jonathan Carver's journey westward to present Minnesota in 1766-1768 was made during the brief interval between the destruction of French power in America and the outbreak of the Revolution. Carver was a subordinate of the famous, or notorious, Robert Rogers, sometime commandant of Detroit, whom Kenneth Roberts has celebrated in *Northwest Passage*. But the *Three Years Travels through the Interior Parts of North-America* (London, 1778), which went into more than thirty editions, made Carver better known than his superior officer.

The New England traveler viewed the trans-Mississippi in a grandiose mood. Proclaiming that the seat of Empire moves toward the West, he predicted that stately palaces and solemn temples would one day adorn the wilderness where at that time only the savage's hut gave evidence of the handiwork of man. But the most noted part of his book is his long essay "Of the Origin, Manners, Customs, Religion, and Language of the Indians," a compendium of information, much of it secondhand, that gained for the *Travels* a greater international reputation than any other book of American authorship in the eighteenth century. Chateaubriand drew upon it for his *Voyage en Amérique,* and a German translation of 1780 furnished the source for Schiller's famous "Nadowessiers Totenlied."

3

With the settlement of Kentucky, a new phase begins in the history of the West. Charlevoix, Adair, and Carver had been primarily representatives of European empires, but the American Revolution divorced the problem of the American frontier from Europe. The two most important books dealing with the post-Revolutionary West, John Filson's *The Discovery, Settlement and Present State of Kentucke* (1784) and Gilbert Imlay's *Topographical Description of the Western Territory of North America* (1792), suggest how the Mississippi Valley was to be occupied during the next hundred years. The Daniel Boone of Filson's account already bears much of the significance with which the folk mind was to invest him during the next half-century: he is a Long Hunter, a woodsman, an Indian fighter who can beat his enemies at their own game. It is significant that the illiterate hero cannot write his own story, but must dictate his reminiscences to a schoolmaster who clothes them in stilted language. The "cutting edge" of the frontier has all but lost contact with the cultural tradition of Western Europe.

Gilbert Imlay, probably a native of New Jersey, served in the American forces during the Revolution. In 1784 he appeared in Kentucky as a land speculator and surveyor; he may have dabbled in intrigues with the Spanish. After a couple of years he left America for London. Here his *Topographical Description* appeared in 1792, and a novel laid in part in Kentucky, *The Emigrants,* in 1793. In that year he was in Paris, where he formed a temporary liaison with Mary Wollstonecraft. His subsequent career is obscure: he seems to have lived in Europe until his death in 1828.

Imlay's description of Kentucky is permeated by ideas of the Godwinian Enlightenment. In a state of exalted sensibility, he finds the beauty of nature bound up with political ideas:

Everything here gives delight; and, in that mild effulgence which beams around us, we feel a glow of gratitude for that elevation our all-bountiful Creator has bestowed upon us. Far from being disgusted with man for his turpitude or depravity, we feel that dignity nature bestowed upon us at the creation; but which has been contaminated by the base alloy of meanness, the concomitant of European education.

Passing over the tedious details of settlement, Imlay takes it for granted that within a hundred years the entire continent will be peopled by republicans and governed according to the highest dictates of reason. The ingredients of Manifest Destiny are already present.

But the occupation of the trans-Allegheny was not carried through by rhetoric alone. The often repeated phases through which the frontier passed as it moved steadily westward have been described by Frederick Jackson Turner: first the fur trader and Indian fighter; then the hunter-farmer who clears a small patch of the forest, puts in a crop or two, and moves on when the country begins to fill up; then the more substantial farmer who buys out the preemption rights and "improvements" of the first settler; and finally the "men of capital and enterprise," the first market towns, banks, a rudimentary industry, and so on.

Of the characteristic figures shaped by the successive stages of the frontier, only the fur trapper and Indian fighter seemed heroic and glamorous. As a result, pioneering experience in the trans-Allegheny has left its mark upon imaginative literature almost exclusively in fictional versions of the character of Daniel Boone. The most famous of these is of course Cooper's Leatherstocking, but even here the imaginative synthesis is incomplete: Leatherstocking is half Noble Savage and Forest Philosopher, half illiterate backwoodsman inferior in social status to the "straight" heroes and heroines of the novels. Writers in the Ohio Valley who tried to use frontier materials in literature were unable to improve on Cooper's formula. The *Legends of the West* (1832) of James Hall, a Philadelphia lawyer who settled in Cincinnati, were intended to celebrate "the gallant men who . . . conquered for us the country of which we are so proud." But although Hall occasionally makes valuable notes on what he saw around him—trappers from the Missouri, missionaries boating down the Ohio, camp meetings, border crime—his backwoodsman is as stilted and unreal as his genteel characters. The other early novelist of the Mississippi Valley, Timothy Flint, who came out in 1816 from Massachusetts as a missionary, was more ambitious than Hall but even less successful. With a valid perception of the literary opportunity offered by the early West, but with a notable lack of imaginative power, he wrote long, tedious, and now justly forgotten novels dealing with fur trapping in Oregon, the maritime trade of the Pacific Northwest, and Mexican revolutionary intrigue against Spain in the Southwest. Flint's rambling *Recollections of the Last Ten Years* (1826), despite some rather self-conscious passages of nature description in imitation of Chateaubriand, is a much more valuable record of the early West because of its first-hand observations of life along the rivers.

Only here and there in contemporary writing do we get a glimpse of the period when a semiagricultural population began to arrive in the footsteps of the Indian fighter. The most vivid reports are those of travelers like Henry R. Schoolcraft, who, as a youngster of twenty-four, came out from upstate New York in 1818 to make a geological exploration of the Ozarks. On the headwaters of the White River he encountered the Coker family, living within three miles of the farthest white settlement.

These people [Schoolcraft noted] subsist partly by agriculture, and partly by hunting. They raise corn for bread, and for feeding their horses previous to the commencement of long journeys in the woods, but none for exportation. . . . Gardens are unknown. Corn, wild meats, chiefly bear's meat, are the staple articles of food. In manners, morals, customs, dress, contempt of labour and hospitality, the state of society is not essentially different from that which exists among the savages. Schools, religion, and learning, are alike unknown. Hunting is the principal, the most honourable, and the most profitable employment . . . a man's reputation is measured by his skill as a marksman, his agility and strength, his boldness and dexterity in killing game, and his patient endurance and contempt of the hardships of the hunter's life.

A later stage of agricultural settlement is depicted in Morris Birkbeck's *Notes on a Journey in America, from the Coast of Virginia to the Territory of Illinois* (1817) and his *Letters from Illinois* (1818). Birkbeck was an English farmer (that is, an agricultural entrepreneur leasing a large tract of land). He brought to early Illinois a determination to set up in America something equivalent to the well kept farms he had conducted in Surrey. His freedom from frontier prejudices enabled him to see the advantages of prairie lands at a time when most backwoodsmen were convinced that land too poor to grow trees was worthless for farming. For the benefit of other Englishmen who, disgusted with political reaction at home, might be induced to join him in republican America, he presented an eloquent record of his expenditures and his profits, emphasizing the fact that within a few years he expected to have clear title to a valuable property.

With the advent of settlers who regulated agriculture by cost accounting, the trans-Allegheny was ready for the boom days of town planners, real estate brokers, lawyers, and promoters of wildcat state banks. The advance of the plantation economy into the Gulf Plains is described in two collections of sketches that are famous as landmarks in the development of American humor: Augustus Baldwin Longstreet's *Georgia Scenes* (1835) and Joseph G.

Baldwin's *Flush Times in Alabama and Mississippi* (1853), both rich in the local color of lawyers' circuits, frontier brawls, "groceries" (whisky), and tall tales. A similar period in the Old Northwest is depicted with less masculine gusto but with a feminine wit and an eye for detail by the New York mistress of a young ladies' seminary, Caroline Kirkland, who went out to southern Michigan in the 1830's and lived there for several years until her husband's venture in town promotion was ended by the panic. *A New Home —Who'll Follow?* (1839) is marred by obvious efforts to impose conventional plots on Western material; but the author had a sense of humor, and her notations concerning squatters and their wives, small-town society, and the imaginative finance of Western bankers constitute an all but unique historical record.

4

The acquisition of the vast area between the Mississippi and the Rocky Mountains through the Louisiana Purchase (1803) meant that the cycle of frontier advance had to begin again with exploration of country that was still almost a blank on the maps. Even before Napoleon's unexpected decision to sell Louisiana to the United States, Jefferson had planned an expedition overland to the Pacific with his secretary and fellow Virginian Meriwether Lewis at its head, and Lewis had chosen William Clark, a boyhood companion who had gone out to Kentucky, as second in command. The party was in camp on the east bank of the Mississippi near St. Louis when Louisiana was formally transferred to the United States on March 9, 1804.

Despite the fact that Jefferson had devoted years of study to the geography of the trans-Mississippi, Lewis and Clark had no more than vague conjectures about the country they were to traverse. Besides the two officers, the party consisted of fourteen soldiers, "nine young men from Kentucky," two French-Canadian *voyageurs,* an interpreter, a hunter, and Clark's Negro slave York. Blending the French and American traditions of wilderness travel with what they could learn from the Indians, Lewis and Clark at a single bound carried the advance guard of the westward movement to the Pacific Coast.

A series of misfortunes, climaxed by the mysterious and violent death of Lewis in the Tennessee forest in 1809, delayed publication of the narrative of the journey *(History of the Expedition Under the Command of Captains Lewis and Clark to the Sources of the Missouri, Thence Across the Rocky Mountains and Down the River Columbia to the Pacific Ocean)* until 1814. The book, prepared by Nicholas Biddle of Philadelphia from the manuscript journals, is one of the great travel narratives of the world. The editor had the good sense to let the hard, compact prose of the journals stand with a minimum of tidying up. The result is a day-by-day record of things done and seen, of physical toil and hardship, of the country and the Indians, of conjecture and increased knowledge. Only from the whole does the grandeur of the accomplishment emerge: the discovery of a new world in the Far West, by a party that never numbered more than fifty men.

The Lewis and Clark expedition immediately stimulated the fur trade up the Missouri. Within five years the river had become almost a thoroughfare, and a restless young man with literary ambitions could make a trip up to the Mandan Villages in present North Dakota simply as a tourist. Henry Marie Brackenridge, son of the author of *Modern Chivalry,* had grown up in Pittsburgh and was making gestures toward the practice of law in St. Louis. The journal of his travels with one of Manuel Lisa's fur-trading brigades appeared in 1814 as an appendix to a little book called *Views of Louisiana,* and was published separately in an enlarged version in 1816. It is a charming document. Exempt from either the labor or the responsibilities of the journey, the author was free to stroll along the bank thinking of Ossian, Fénelon, Ariosto, or the Arabian Nights Entertainments. He read *Don Quixote* in Spanish with Lisa's help. He set himself literary exercises in rendering the landscape—the sky "as clear as that represented in Chinese painting," "the flowery mead, the swelling ground, the romantic hill, the bold river." Or he picked up a local tradition and composed "Lines on an Unfortunate Female Maniac, Seen on the Missouri, Beyond the White Settlements." But Brackenridge was more than a sentimental poseur. He made shrewd notes on the Indians, and at this early date he perceived the role which the West would play in restraining the sectional bitterness of North and South.

While Lewis and Clark were wintering at the mouth of the Columbia, Captain Zebulon Montgomery Pike was in northern Minnesota carrying out another part of Jefferson's plan by trying to find the source of the Mississippi. Hardly had he got back to St. Louis when General James Wilkinson ordered him out across the Plains to the headwaters of the Arkansas in the Colorado mountains. Here Pike, according to plan, allowed himself to be arrested by Spanish troops and returned to the United States under guard by way of Texas.

Pike's journals, published in 1810 under the title *An Account of Expeditions to the Sources of the Mississippi, and Through the Western Parts of Louisiana* . . ., afford an attractive picture of a young and enthusiastic professional soldier. He carried with him Volney, Shenstone, and Pope, and occasionally remarked upon the picturesque features of a landscape. His flair for rhetoric not only gave an Elysian coloring to his description of the Kansas prairies, where his "warm imagination" pictured "the future seats of husbandry, the numerous herds of domestic animals, which are no doubt destined to crown with joy those happy plains," but also led him to exaggerate the sterility of the Great Plains farther to the West, which he compared to the Sahara so vividly as to establish the myth of a Great American Desert east of the Rockies.

The second major American effort to explore the upper Arkansas was made some fifteen years after Pike's expedition, under the command of Major Stephen H. Long, with an elaborate scientific staff. Setting out up the Platte in June of 1820, the party traveled out to the mountains and returned down the Arkansas. The voluminous narrative of the expedition, published in 1823, was compiled from several manuscript journals by Edwin James, a young Vermont physician and geologist. It touches upon portions of the Mississippi Valley as widely separated as Pittsburgh and the Royal Gorge in Colorado, and is filled with careful observations, especially concerning the public domain beyond the frontier. The scientists' opinion confirmed the gloomy report of Pike. James describes a "Great Desert at the Base of the Rocky Mountains" five or six hundred miles wide, stretching from north Texas to the Canadian border.

5

In Josiah Gregg's *Commerce of the Prairies* (1844) the American advance along the Santa Fe Trail toward the outposts of New Spain produced a work that ranks with the Lewis and Clark narrative as a literary monument of the westward movement. The author grew up on the Missouri frontier, but the life of the trails across the Plains became so thoroughly a part of him that even this primitive society came to seem overcivilized:

Scarcely a day passes [he wrote later] without my experiencing a pang of regret that I am not now roving at large upon those western plains. Nor do I find my taste peculiar; for I have hardly known a man, who has ever become familiar with the kind of life which I have led for so many years, that has not relinquished it with regret.

Gregg had little formal education, but he had the vocation of a scientist. The Plains and the strange Latin civilization lying beyond were his library and his laboratory; the keeping of his journal, his professional work. In form his book is an apotheosis of the familiar traveler's diary. Gregg calls it "The Journal of a Santa Fé Trader." But although he adopts the narrative framework to describe one trip out of Santa Fe, one southward to Chihuahua and Aguas Calientes, and one back to Missouri, the entries are enriched with the fruits of observations made during four trips out and back in his nine years in the trade. In addition, separate chapters discuss such matters as the history and government of Santa Fe, animals and plants, and Indian tribes. The effect is that of a systematic monograph devoted to the new Southwest that was rising over the American horizon.

In George W. Kendall's *Narrative of the Texan Santa Fé Expedition* (1844) the outlines of the coming war are plain, and the tone is quite different from that of Gregg's tranquil picture of the 1830's. The fantastic expedition which Kendall accompanied set out in the belief that the people of New Mexico would welcome Texan aid in securing their independence from Mexico, and that a trading route from Austin to Santa Fe could be developed in competition with the trail out the Arkansas from Missouri. But when the half-starved travelers reached the Rio Grande settlements the Mexican authorities arrested them as armed invaders, shot two of them, and marched the rest to Mexico City as prisoners.

The early part of the narrative offers gruesome evidence of the sanctions which the West could exact of travelers who tried to substitute enthusiasm and courage for the ancient skills of the fur trader. Their horses were stolen by Indians, they suffered agonies of thirst, their baggage was burned in a prairie fire, stragglers were scalped. Yet Kendall, who was editor of the New Orleans *Picayune,* maintained his professional poise and was capable of noticing the landscape of the Staked Plains or telling a tall tale in the midst of his sufferings. The book is an admirable expression of the society which was about to go to war as an outlet for its rhetorical expansionism, its contempt for ignorant Catholic Mexicans, and its young sublime confidence in the American (that is, the Western) idea.

The war, when it came, was not in all respects adequate to the rhetoric in which it had been conceived. But one campaign, Alexander W. Doniphan's march into northern Mexico, proved to be the all but incredible audacity which the Western imagination demanded. There are several journals of this venture, of which the fullest is John T. Hughes' *Doniphan's Expedition,* published in Cincinnati in 1847. Doniphan set out down the Rio Grande in December of 1846 with something less than a thousand of his Missouri volunteers. They cut themselves loose from any base of supplies, and after two battles occupied Chihuahua. Then the column turned eastward for the seven-hundred-mile march across the Bolsón de Mapimí to join Wool's army at Saltillo. No professional soldier would have risked his reputation by such foolhardy behavior, but the Missourians made it plain that they wanted nothing to do with professional soldiers. They threw sheep's entrails into the tent of a West Pointer who tried to get them to drill. Hughes describes them as they emerged from the desert.

Their dishevelled hair, their long-grown whiskers, their buck-skin apparel, their stern and uncouth appearance, their determined and resolved looks, and their careless and nonchalant air, attracted the gaze, and won the admiration of all people. Though they were somewhat undisciplined, yet they were hardy, unshrinking, resolute, independent, chivalrous, honorable and intelligent men.

It was the very ideal of the frontier made flesh.

The best book growing out of the exciting winter of 1846–1847 is Lewis H. Garrard's *Wah-to-yah, and the Taos Trail.* The author, a native of Cincinnati and a stepson of Justice John McLean of the United States Supreme Court, was only seventeen years old, but despite the war he persuaded his parents to let him make a trip out to the Rocky Mountains. He accompanied a Bent, St. Vrain & Co. caravan to Bent's Fort on the Arkansas in present southeastern Colorado and spent the winter with trappers and Indians. *Wah-to-yah* (the title is taken from an Indian name for the Spanish Peaks near Fort Bent) appeared in 1850, when the author was twenty-one years old. Garrard had a rare natural ability to record the rich metaphors of the trapper language, compounded as it was of Kentucky, Spanish, and Indian elements. A long passage describing John Hatcher's dream of his visit to hell is the richest single item in the lore of the mountain men. Garrard also remembered happy hours passed in a Cheyenne camp—"the bright faces of the girls . . . the dancing eye of 'Morning Mist,' . . . the low chuckle of the young men, as they gained a triumph in the favorite game of 'guess' "—and other pretty girls in Taos, smoking shuck cigarettes, "their magically brilliant eyes the meanwhile searching one's very soul."

6

Although the military invasion of the Pacific Coast in 1846 followed a southern route by way of the Gila River, American settlement of Oregon and California had begun earlier along the more northerly trail of the fur traders which went out the Platte and through South Pass. Wide public interest in the Oregon Trail dates from the report of Lieutenant John Charles Frémont on his trip to South Pass in 1842. Frémont's role in the history as well as the literature of the West was the outgrowth of his marriage to the daughter of Senator Thomas Benton of Missouri, who secured a Congressional appropriation for the mapping of the trail, caused Frémont to be selected as commander of the party sent out, and saw to it that the report (judiciously edited, if not in large part written, by Frémont's wife) received wide circulation as a government document. Frémont became a symbol, and the myth-making faculty of the people read into his Western journeys a vast extrinsic interest derived from the heightened public emotions of the period of Manifest Destiny.

The *Report of the Exploring Expedition to the Rocky Mountains in the Year 1842* (1843) seems to a modern reader somewhat routine. But thousands of Americans in the 1840's experienced an aesthetic glow upon reading such comments as:

My horse was a trained hunter, famous in the west, under the name of Proveau, and with his eyes flashing, and the foam flying from his mouth, sprang on after the [buffalo] cow like a tiger.

If this seems to derive too directly from Delacroix, there are other entries in the mode of Defoe, such as Frémont's description of how he made a new tube for his broken barometer from a powderhorn. The passages establishing the guide Kit Carson as a faithful retainer of the chivalrous hero made Carson the first mountain man to attain national celebrity. Like Filson's life of Boone, Frémont's report contributed a figure to the national folklore.

After the explorers came the settlers. To this group belonged Edwin Bryant, a Kentucky newspaperman headed for California. His skillfully written *What I Saw in California* (1848) records a typical covered-wagon journey across the Plains: the gathering of prospective travelers near Independence, Missouri, in April; ceremonies of farewell with the indispensable speeches; the election of officers and drafting of by-laws; the nightly corral; the bugle at dawn. With the arrival in California Bryant stops his journal in order to recount the ghastly fate of the Donner party of the emigration of 1846 who, caught in their late crossing of the Sierra by winter snows, were sealed up in a fetor of starvation and cannibalism that has remained the most revolting chapter in the history of the Overland Trail. Later, as a member of Frémont's California Battalion, and as alcalde of San Francisco under the American military occupation, he describes the comic opera of the conquest.

Bryant's book is a sufficiently vivid reminder that the American advance to the Pacific Coast did not begin with the discovery of gold. The Forty-niners merely swelled the number of emigrants on trails across the continent, and their narratives add little to the picture of the crossing available in earlier chronicles. Among contemporary journals of the Gold Rush, one of the best is Alonzo Delano's *Life on the Plains and Among the Diggings* (1853). Delano, a resident of Illinois, recorded the hardships of the 1849 migration which resulted from exhaustion of the limited supplies of grass, water, and game by the greatly increased traffic across the Plains. As emigrants had to lighten their loads they dumped food and other supplies by the side of the trail.

We . . . found sugar on which turpentine had been poured [wrote Delano], flour in which salt and dirt had been thrown, and wagons broken to pieces, or partially burned, clothes torn to pieces, so that they could not be worn, and a wanton waste made of valuable property, simply because the owners could not use it themselves, and were determined that nobody else should.

7

During the first half of the nineteenth century all observers regarded the trans-Mississippi as a region remote from the normal patterns of American society. But when the Gold Rush brought a large population to the Pacific Coast almost overnight, the Far West was suddenly recognized as the area within which lay the destiny of the American people. The narratives of Western travel between 1849 and 1869, when the Union Pacific Railway at last connected New York and San Francisco, accordingly emphasized the need for integration between West and East, or announced its achievement. Most of them were written by newspapermen who felt an obligation to interpret the West for a national audience.

The beginnings of the new attitude are evident in Bayard Taylor's *El Dorado, or, Adventures in the Path of Empire* (1850). Taylor, already a professional travel writer, was sent out by Horace Greeley to cover the Gold Rush for the New York *Tribune*. Traveling by steamer via Panama, Taylor reached San Francisco in July of 1849, and set out at once on mule back for the diggings. It was at the height of the boom, when miners were warming canned lobster over campfires and drinking champagne at tables made of packing cases. Taylor witnessed the spontaneous creation of local governments for mining camps and the first convention which met to draw up a state constitution. He also described the pistol battles, the gambling dens, the theaters, and the Stephen Foster songs that have ever since been associated with 1849.

Horace Greeley's *An Overland Journey, from New York to San Francisco* (1860), based on the editor's letters to his famous paper, devotes two or three chapters to the Pikes Peak rush of 1859, but gives greatest emphasis to Republican politics in Kansas and to agricultural settlement beyond the Mississippi. As a New England farmer's son, Greeley was interested in the Western soil and climate, and was distressed both by "the infernal spirit of land speculation and monopoly" and by the widespread frauds in the patenting of public lands. In California he saw the early stages of hydraulic mining and wrote the tribute to Yosemite Valley which was henceforth to be obligatory in all tourists' books. He also made a substantial contribution to the already vigorous California boosters' tradition by recording corn twenty feet high, squashes like brass kettles, and two-year-old steers larger than three-year-olds in the East.

The integration of West and North which Greeley so earnestly desired was cemented by the Civil War. When peace finally came, the triumphant Republican Party was aware that it had secured a vast theater for the expansion of Northern industry. Within six weeks of Appomattox, Schuyler Colfax, Speaker of the House of Representatives, set out on a triumphal tour beyond the Mississippi that symbolized the official commitment of the party to the development of the West. He was accompanied by Samuel Bowles, influential editor of the Springfield (Massachusetts) *Republican,* who described the trip in his *Across the Continent* (1865, reissued in 1869 with additions based on a later trip, as *Our New West*). Bowles was as confident as Gilbert Imlay had been that the West would undergo prodigious development. He saw in the trans-Mississippi, as Imlay had seen in Kentucky,

an aggregation of elements and forces that . . . will present on the North American Continent such a triumph of Man in race, in government, in social development, in intellectual advancement, and in commercial supremacy, as the world never saw,—as the world never yet fairly dreamed of.

46. THE WEST AS SEEN FROM THE EAST

Before the Louisiana Purchase the people of the United States had little knowledge of that as yet foreign region which was to become the western half of their country; they lacked indeed any special reason for interest in it. Once that area had been acquired, interest sprang up quickly, but knowledge came more slowly. Gradually, however, some information was disseminated—by actual travel in the West, by word-of-mouth reports of such returned travelers, by fugitive articles in newspapers and magazines, and by books. Inevitably there was another lag before such information could be absorbed and reexpressed in writing which may be described as "the West as seen from the East."

The process of informing the East was gigantic in proportions. The book titles alone constitute a formidable list. The West was described to the East in numerous volumes based upon the notes of official explorers—Lewis and Clark, Pike, Long, Frémont. Many other notable accounts were written of the journeyings of travelers and unofficial explorers—Brackenridge, Catlin, Leonard, Gregg. Some highly interesting books, like James Pattie's *Personal Narrative* (1831) and D. H. Coyner's *Lost Trappers* (1847), lay along the line between fact and fiction. Other writers, such as Emerson Bennett, wrote novels or romances. Some of the interpreters of the West were not Americans at all. They might be British like Ruxton and Marryat; or from the Continent, like Sealsfield and Prince Maximilian of Wied.

The present chapter passes by these interesting but scattered writers, in order to concentrate upon a few of the most important literary figures. The work of such men has a double interest, being an interpretation both of the West and of the men themselves. In general, moreover, their attitudes toward the West show the variations characteristic of the less important writers and of the country as a whole.

Doubtless along the frontier the chief source of information about the farther regions was always actual travel and the talk of returned trappers and Indian traders. For the rest of the country, newspapers and magazines were perhaps most important. The literary men, however, were readers of books, and their ideas were largely shaped by such reading. In fact most of the sources of their writings about the West can be found in a few books. Of these the most important were Biddle's redaction of the journals of Lewis and Clark (1814), the narrative of Long's expedition (1822–1823), and Frémont's report (1843).

2

Among our early writers, the two who most strongly felt the influence of the West were Cooper and Irving. In addition, these two deserve first and fullest attention because their books in turn became strong influences upon later writers. The melodramatic tradition of Western fiction may be said to spring directly from Cooper.

The Prairie (1827) appeared at the height of Cooper's popularity. It was widely read by a public which as yet had little real information, and was therefore unable to separate fiction from actuality. The book can thus be set down as one of the most important single documents in producing a picture of the West in the American mind.

The novel itself shows that Cooper had read Biddle and the Long report, and perhaps a newspaper account of the Santa Fe trade. So far so good, for Biddle and Long were authoritative. From Biddle, for instance, Cooper took the names for his Sioux chiefs, Mahtoree and Weucha; Hard Heart and most of the other names were from Long. The trouble was that Cooper went no further, and seems to have read nothing else. He did not, like Irving, actually visit the West. Instead, with this slight smattering of knowledge, he merely let his romancer's imagination have free play. The result, however luring as romance, is a farrago of absurdities as a picture of the West.

For illustration, a single example of Cooper's method must suffice. In a romance, he needed heroes and villains. With his Indians, he had already worked out a formula. The Indians on our side shall be noble Red Men (Mohicans); the opposing Indians shall be Red Devils (Mingos). In *The Prairie* he cast the Pawnees as the heroes, and the Sioux ("Siouxes," he wrote originally) as the villains. In reality there was little difference between the two tribes; each had its good and bad points. (Curiously, in Irving's *Tour on the Prairies* the Pawnees have the villain role.) One detail of Cooper's traducing of the Sioux is his constant attribution to them of all the horrors of practicing torture upon their captives. Probably he did this because he assumed them to be like the Iroquois and some other Eastern Indians. The Sioux themselves, however, have vigorously denied the charge, and the fact apparently is that, being a primitive people, they killed their captives outright. Torture thrives among more sophisticated peoples who have learned artistic restraint, such as the Iroquois or the Italians of the Renaissance.

In one instance Cooper unconsciously made a remarkable prediction of the future by taking covered-wagon emigrants out on the plains. In 1827 only a few Santa Fe traders had traversed the plains with wagons. But in spite of this triumph of intuition *The Prairie* spread misinformation broadcast.

Fortunately the next important Eastern writer to approach the subject set a higher standard and subscribed to the sometimes forgotten principle that a writer should, when possible, collect some first-hand knowledge on a subject before setting himself up to write about it. In short, Washington Irving went to look at the West for himself.

There has been of recent years a tendency to sneer at Irving's Western writings. Many moderns, their own knowledge gained of necessity chiefly from books, seem to have forgotten that Irving learned about the Old West from actual sight and sound. He crossed the swollen Arkansas in a bullboat; he saw Sublette come home wounded from the epic fight at Pierre's Hole; he knew the terror of the cry "Pawnees!"

A Tour on the Prairies (1835) may be called a simple and factual record of an expedition across what is now Oklahoma. There is, of course, artistic omission and shaping. Critics point out that Irving suppressed some incidents which would have made him seem ridiculous, that he developed an unfortunate and unwarranted dislike for the half-breed Beatte, that his polished style is not cousin to the roughness of the Cross Timbers. But there is no traveler's narrative which does not show such distortions. Certainly Irving's narrative is much more detailed and interesting than the two others still extant upon the same expedition. In many ways it is more alive than any of his other works.

An actual background of Western experience must have given Irving confidence, and must have helped to make *Astoria* and *Captain Bonneville* the solid books that they are. Inspired, they are not; and yet they still remain the authoritative works on their subjects. The chief charge that can be brought against *Astoria* is that it is not what it purports to be. Irving in his Introduction mentioned "the journals, on which I chiefly depended," but listed also six published works of which he had availed himself "occasionally." Actually the reverse was true, and many parts of *Astoria* are nothing more than paraphrases of the accounts of Bradbury, Brackenridge, or one of the other earlier writers.

Granted, however, that his acknowledgments are not what they should be, Irving shows up well as both scholar and writer. Like many a modern professor, he hired a research assistant to do the spadework. Then from the half-dozen different accounts he drew his own conclusions as to what most probably had happened, and wrote a reasonably well unified and certainly a readable account. To produce solidity of background he had his own experiences, and he also culled information from such basic work as that of Lewis and Clark. *Astoria* is neither profound scholarship nor brilliant writing, but it is at least that somewhat rare combination of good scholarship and good writing.

Captain Bonneville is more difficult to appraise. It is perhaps not so well constructed or well written as *Astoria*. On the other hand, it is a much more original contribution, based upon now lost documents and upon conversation with Bonneville himself.

Astoria was the subject of a highly laudatory review by Poe in the *Southern Literary Messenger* for January, 1837. The book apparently stimulated Poe's interest in the West, and one may note, as details, that in the *Narrative of A. Gordon Pym* (1838) the hero selected for his reading "the expedition of Lewis and Clark to the mouth of the Columbia," and that his comrade Peters is described as a "hybrid" Upsaroka Indian.

Poe's only extended piece of writing about the West appeared in 1840. He saw fit to masquerade the "Journal of Julius Rodman" as "an account of the first passage across the Rocky Mountains." Probably, however, it deceived few people. In writing it, Poe seems to have followed the Lewis and Clark narrative chiefly, but also drew material from *Astoria, Captain Bonneville,* and probably other works. Since *Astoria* itself often echoes the words of its sources, it is difficult to be dogmatic about whether Poe was borrowing from it or directly from the earlier books. In order to make the story more reasonable, he adopted the device of understatement—"in every point, Mr. R[odman]'s account *falls short* of Captain Lewis's." Such a method naturally did not produce an exciting story, and in the end Rodman, like Pym, merely petered out and left his story unfinished. The *Journal* is thus of little importance in itself, although it remains a document of some interest as another indication of the turn of attention westward near the end of the thirties.

3

The transcendentalists concerned themselves more with the Far East than with the Far West, although the mountain men indeed were skilled practitioners of self-reliance and really lived the kind of life which Thoreau played at living when he camped by Walden Pond. The practical or Yankee side of Emerson appreciated the expansive, go-ahead spirit of the frontier, but his earlier experiences with it and most of his scattered statements about it deal with Middle Western rather than Far Western conditions. He read Frémont, but his comment in his journal is a shrewd one upon the Pathfinder's own self-consciousness, not upon Western scenes or characters.

One might expect Thoreau to display an interest in the great opening

Western land. He seems rather, however, to have reacted by contraries. Extensive passages in his journal were devoted to the fur trade and the California Gold Rush. He conceived both primarily in economic terms, and made his judgments on what he would probably have called "moral grounds." There must always, of course, be an argument as to how largely the economic factors loomed in such frontier movements. Yet anyone reading a few of the genuine Western books can notice that hope of profit was seldom the sole motive, or even the first one. There were plenty of volunteers, for instance, to go with Lewis and Clark, but none of them could have expected to make money in addition to wages. Among the motives often mentioned in reminiscences are desire to go adventuring, to see strange country, and to live a free life removed from the restraints of civilization. Thoreau, however, saw in the mountain men only "the loafing class tempted by rum and money," and exclaimed, "What a pitiful business is the fur-trade!" He thought that the rush to California reflected "the greatest disgrace on mankind," and there is a hint of jealousy in his antagonism toward the West. The trappers were gloriously shooting the rapids of a hundred uncharted rivers while he floated upon the placid Concord; they made Homeric revelry and battle at Pierre's Hole, but he raised beans within the sound of the home-town dinner horn.

The poets also paid the West little attention. Bryant's famous "where rolls the Oregon" apparently sprang from his reading of the Biddle version of Lewis and Clark, as is shown by his use at first of the spelling "Oregan." * The next few lines beginning, "Yet the dead are there," were probably suggested by the vivid descriptions of Memaloose Island and the other Indian burial grounds along the Columbia. Bryant's "Prairies," although showing his familiarity with Far Western conditions, actually sprang from his own experiences in Illinois and describes scenery of that state. A few minor poems also show Bryant's continuing interest in the West.

Section IV of Part Two of *Evangeline* opens with a sweeping scenic passage:

> Far in the West there lies a desert land, where the mountains
> Lift, through perpetual snows, their lofty and luminous summits.

Most of its details can be traced to Frémont, even such a touch as the juxtaposition of "luxuriant clusters of roses and purple amorphas." Although well handled, the passage does not necessarily show much reading on Longfellow's part. Most of the allusions can be found in the first few chapters of the book,

* The Biddle volume appeared in 1814. But even if a version of "Thanatopsis" was written in 1811, there is no proof that the Oregan-Oregon passage was written very long before its first publication in 1817.

and the fine geographical coup d'œil with its place names is suggestive of the inspection of a map.

Two young New Englanders went to see the West for themselves. Richard Henry Dana, Jr., chose to call his book *Two Years Before the Mast* (1840), but it might equally well have been *A Year in California*. Francis Parkman, like Irving, took a trip upon the plains with a view to utilizing his experiences in writing. His *California and Oregon Trail* (1849) was misleading in title, for he never got near to either California or Oregon. Doubtless many a Forty-niner cursed the book as a worthless catchpenny, but it has survived as a juvenile.

Dana was an excellent factual reporter upon the West. Parkman was more likely to be carried away, and to interpret upon the basis of his own insufficient experience. Both the youngsters carried with them their Bostonian traditions. Dana had a raised eyebrow for frontier immorality; Parkman, although rejoicing in Western spaciousness, curled a snobbish Brahmin lip at uncouth covered-wagon emigrants.

This sketch of early writings about the farther West can naturally be brought to an end around 1850. By then the Gold Rush of '49 had stirred the whole country. In the new desire for information, *Two Years Before the Mast* was rescued from obscurity; Frémont gained thousands of new readers; because of the name California in its title, Parkman's little volume became a best seller; and dozens of now forgotten books about the West came sliding from the presses. Casual references to the West began to crop up everywhere. Poe wrote his "Eldorado." Melville adorned the pages of *Moby-Dick* with some half-dozen Western allusions—"the black bisons of distant Oregon." Even Hawthorne's dimly lit world of dream and allegory was not wholly insulated; the Introduction to the *Scarlet Letter* (1850) contains a reference to digging gold in California, and Chillingworth is stated to have "dug into the poor clergyman's heart, like a miner searching for gold."

4

Thus, by 1850, the Eastern writers all knew something about the Far West, or at least had some vague notions about it. What was this knowledge—or what were these notions? Most typically, they conceived the Far West as a very strange country. The American tradition, and the English tradition before it, assumed that a well watered and well forested country was the natural state of the earth as God had created it. (Actually, vast regions are desert or steppe, and only comparatively small areas are well watered and thickly forested; the misconception, however, is easily understood.) Early descriptions of the West emphasized again and again treeless plains unbounded as the ocean, bare rocky buttes like ruined castles, dry earth half encrusted with salt, endless buffalo herds that shook the prairie. The "scoriac rivers" of "Ulalume" could have been derived from some description of a Western lava flow. Certainly Julius Rodman described the scenery in not dissimilar terms; for example, "The whole descent towards the stream has an indescribably chaotic and dreary air. No vegetation of any kind is seen." There is no need to multiply examples; the strangeness of the country was notable then, by experience or through descriptions, just as it is still notable to any born and bred Easterner making his first transcontinental trip.

If this first acquaintanceship with the Far West had begun during the middle eighteenth century, no one can doubt that the new land would have been judged altogether hideous and repulsive. But even before the "perioques" of Lewis and Clark first cut the muddy current of the Missouri, the spirit of Romanticism was abroad in the land. People had begun to love deep romantic chasms and forests decaying but never decayed more than well trimmed sylvan parks and enameled meads. As Poe wrote of Julius Rodman: "He stalked through that immense and often terrible wilderness with an evident rapture at his heart which we envy him as we read." Such a sentence is almost a textbook demonstration of Romanticism, and it might also be quoted of Frémont, Jedediah Smith, and other actual Western explorers.

This rapture at the heart, sometimes combined with advertising zeal, led to the build-up of the West as a land of beauty. First perhaps the strangeness stirred the heart, and when the heart was stirred the eye saw beauty. Thus, by grace of Jean-Jacques Rousseau, our poets and novelists came to see the West as a strange but beautiful land of vast spaces where a man could live freely—and so, as dream and partially as reality, it has been ever since.

47. ABRAHAM LINCOLN: THE SOIL AND THE SEED

There is one man in whose words, spoken and written, the West of vast spaces and the East of many peoples are subsumed under one meaning. It is no accident that a hero myth has sprung up about the name and person of Abraham Lincoln as earlier such a myth grew about George Washington. In Lincoln the people of the United States could finally see themselves, each for himself and all together.

Abraham Lincoln had many styles. It has been computed that his printed speeches and writings number 1,078,365 words. One may range through this record of utterance and find a wider variety of styles than in any other American statesman or orator. And perhaps no author of books has written and vocalized in such a diversity of speech tones directed at all manners and conditions of men.

This may be saying in effect that the range of the personality of Abraham Lincoln ran far, identifying itself with the tumults and follies of mankind, keeping touch with multitudes and solitudes. The free-going and friendly companion is there and the man of the cloister, of the lonely corner of thought, prayer, and speculation. The man of public affairs, before a living audience announcing decisions, is there, and the solitary inquirer weaving his abstractions related to human freedom and responsibility.

Perhaps no other American held so definitely in himself both those elements: the genius of the Tragic—the spirit of the Comic. The fate of man, his burdens and crosses, the pity of circumstance, the extent of tragedy in human life, these stood forth in word shadows of the Lincoln utterance, as testamentary as the utter melancholy of his face in repose. And in contrast he came to be known nevertheless as the first authentic humorist to occupy the Executive Mansion in Washington, his gift of laughter and his flair for the funny being taken as a national belonging.

Three short pieces from his pen are kept as immemorial possessions of the American people, each keyed to a high tragic note. These are the Letter to Mrs. Bixby, the Gettysburg Speech, the Second Inaugural.

The War Department records showed a Boston woman to have lost five sons in combat actions. The number was less than five, as later research revealed, but Lincoln spoke through her to all families that had lost a boy or man in the war. "Weak and fruitless must be any words of mine which should attempt to beguile you from the grief of a loss so overwhelming," he wrote. "But I cannot refrain from tendering to you the consolation that may be found in the thanks of the Republic they died to save." He poised his quill pen for the final sentence of the letter, he on whose initiative, action, and responsibility the war had begun and had been carried on for nearly four years, and he wrote: "I pray that our heavenly Father may assuage the anguish of your bereavement, and leave you only the cherished memory of the loved and lost, and the solemn pride that must be yours to have laid so costly a sacrifice upon the altar of freedom."

In a photographer's studio eleven days before delivering the speech at Gettysburg, Lincoln had held in his hands the lengthy address of Edward Everett, the designated orator of the day, the printed two-hour discourse covering nearly two sides of a one-sheet supplement of a Boston newspaper. To a young newspaper correspondent from California he said his own speech at Gettysburg would be "short, short, short"—as it proved to be, ten sentences spoken in less than five minutes. In its implicative qualities, it stands among the supreme utterances of democratic peoples of the world. "A new nation, conceived in liberty and dedicated to the proposition that all men are created equal"—for the perpetuation of this men were dying on battlefields, he said. And, having so died, they would be forgotten men and their deaths of no use unless the living dedicated themselves to the unfinished work for which the dead had given "the last full measure of devotion."

Virtually the Gettysburg Speech is one of the great American poems, having its use and acceptation far beyond American shores. It curiously incarnates the claims, assurances and pretenses of republican institutions, of democratic procedure, of the rule of the people, and directly implies that popular government can come into being and can then "perish from the earth." How he would have defined "a new birth of freedom," at length, must be sought elsewhere in the body of his utterance. No accusations, no recriminations, no lash of invective, not even a mild outspoken reproach of the enemy. Some have detected in haunting echoes of the Gettysburg Speech a quiet summons to those of the South reluctant to let go of national unity: Come back into the old Union of states and let us make of it what those Virginians, Washington and Jefferson, envisioned. Apart from its immediate historic setting it is a timeless psalm in the name of those who *fight* and *do* in behalf of great human causes rather than *talk,* in a belief that men can "highly resolve" themselves and can mutually "dedicate" their lives to a cause, in a posture of oath-taking that "these dead shall not have died in vain."

As one may delve endlessly into the restless implications of the Gettysburg Speech, so also one may ponder the Second Inaugural and the intricate derivations to be made from it. A cry for merciless and further war, so some took it, while others read it as a benediction, a prayer, and a fathomless hope set to music. How did the war begin? He would try to tell it in two sentences, one long and one short: "Both parties deprecated war; but one of them would make war rather than let the nation survive; and the other would accept war rather than let it perish. And the war came." The peculiar sobriety of judgments pronounced on both of the warring sections of the country has had wide discussion and keeps a permanent value:

Neither party expected for the war the magnitude or the duration which it has already attained. Neither anticipated that the cause of the conflict might cease with, or even before, the conflict itself should cease. Each looked for an easier triumph, and a result less fundamental and astounding. Both read the same Bible, and pray to the same God, and each invoked his aid against the other. It may seem strange that any men should dare to ask a just God's assistance in wringing their bread from the sweat of other men's faces; but let us judge not, that we be not judged. The prayers of both could not be answered—that of neither has been answered fully.

In like pitch and key was the often quoted passage from the First Inaugural four years earlier:

Suppose you go to war. You cannot fight always; and when, after much loss on both sides, and no gain on either, you cease fighting, the identical old questions as to terms of intercourse are again upon you.

The Bixby Letter, the Gettysburg Speech, the Second Inaugural, these were widely reprinted and went to increasingly large readerships as decades passed. Yet there was another utterance of Lincoln that did not come to any immense audience until the Second World War. This consists of passages from the President's Message to Congress, December 1, 1862. In this message, Lincoln was using to the limit his powers of persuasion to get the Congress to enact legislation enabling "compensated emancipation," the Federal government to buy the slaves and set them free. Also in this message he presented the cause of national unity in new phases.

A nation may be said to consist of its territory, its people, and its laws. The territory is the only part which is of certain durability. "One generation passeth away, and another generation cometh, but the earth abideth forever." It is of the first importance to duly consider and estimate this ever-enduring part. . . . Our national strife springs not from our permanent part, not from the land we inhabit. . . . Our strife pertains to ourselves—to the passing generations of men;

and it can without convulsion be hushed forever with the passing of one generation.

Having presented his plan for compensated emancipation he appealed for united action as between Congress and Executive:

We can succeed only by concert. It is not "Can any of us imagine better?" but, "Can we all do better?" Object whatsoever is possible, still the question occurs, "Can we do better?"

Then came his pleadings wherein it is seen that he was sensitively aware of how momentous was the hour and of the need for each man to make his personal record such that it would stand the scrutiny of remote generations:

The dogmas of the quiet past are inadequate to the stormy present. The occasion is piled high with difficulty, and we must rise with the occasion. As our case is new, so we must think anew and act anew. We must disenthrall ourselves, and then we shall save our country.

There have been long-time students of Lincoln who place among his sublime passages the one that closed this 1862 message:

Fellow-citizens, we cannot escape history. We of this Congress and this administration will be remembered in spite of ourselves. No personal significance or insignificance can spare one or another of us. The fiery trial through which we pass will light us down, in honor or dishonor, to the latest generation. . . . We shall nobly save or meanly lose the last, best hope of earth. Other means may succeed; this could not fail. The way is plain, peaceful, generous, just—a way which, if followed, the world will forever applaud, and God must forever bless.

That the Congress paid little heed, that it balked at the legislation suggested, that it had a low or indifferent opinion of Lincoln's language and persuasions, is part of the record. That the Congress, save for a remnant of two or three members, had any dim vision that possibly eighty years later, in another national crisis of world scope, there would be global circulation of sentences from this message of Lincoln, there is little or no indication. Not until the Second World War did there come wide circulation, in print and in radio broadcasts and in musical composition, of cadenced declarations from this message. A grim fighting insistence was found in such lines as, "The fiery trial through which we pass will light us down, in honor or dishonor, to the latest generation."

Lincoln, it would seem, practiced his mind in private, rehearsed by himself the method of the abstruse, lofty, cogent reasoning he would apply to the materials of public discussion. Among memoranda written about the time of the debates with Douglas is the following piece of dialectic:

If A can prove, however conclusively, that he may, of right, enslave B, why may not B snatch the same argument, and prove equally that he may enslave A? You say A is white, and B is black. It is *color,* then: the lighter, having the right to enslave the darker? Take care. By this rule, you are to be slave to the first man you meet with a fairer skin than your own. You do not mean *color* exactly? You mean the whites are *intellectually* the superiors of the blacks, and therefore have the right to enslave them? Take care again. By this rule, you are to be slave to the first man you meet, with an intellect superior to your own. But, say you, it is a question of *interest*: and if you can make it to your interest, you have the right to enslave another? Very well. And if he can make it his interest, he has the right to enslave you.

The ancient cry, "Against stupidity even the gods struggle unavailing," had a manner of paraphrase from Lincoln before a Midwest audience.

If a man will stand up, and assert, and repeat, and reassert, that two and two do not make four, I know nothing in the power of argument that can stop him. I think I can answer the judge so long as he sticks to the premises; but when he flies from them, I can not work an argument into the consistency of a maternal gag, and actually close his mouth with it.

2

The tragic note, the fateful event at hand or to come, the screen of mist and cloud behind which Providence wrought his designs, the drama of man in shadowy and portentous deeds, this enters in the Bixby Letter, the Gettysburg Speech, the Second Inaugural, and other instances given. Of another color are Lincoln's many forensic passages where his purpose is the achievement of inexorable and unanswerable logic. The most celebrated example of his style in this field is his letter in the summer of 1862 to a New York antislavery editor who continuously attacked Lincoln as slow, indecisive, and vacillating in emancipation policy. In clarity and as a definition of political and military aims in the turmoil of civil war, the letter has curious dignity and the self-possession that cheers adherents.

The editor had addressed a vehemently critical letter to Lincoln, and without sending a copy of it to him had published it in his newspaper. Lincoln's reply began:

If there be in it any statements or assumptions of fact which I may know to be erroneous, I do not, now and here, controvert them. If there be in it any inferences which I may believe to be falsely drawn, I do not, now and here, argue against them. If there be perceptible in it an impatient and dictatorial tone, I waive it in deference to an old friend whose heart I have always supposed to be right.

Of his policy he would not leave anyone in doubt, wrote the President, as he proceeded:

I would save the Union. I would save it the shortest way under the Constitution. . . . If there be those who would not save the Union unless they could at the same time save slavery, I do not agree with them. If there be those who would not save the Union unless they could at the same time destroy slavery, I do not agree with them. My paramount object in this struggle is to save the Union, and is not either to save or to destroy slavery. If I could save the Union without freeing any slave, I would do it; and if I could save it by freeing all the slaves, I would do it; and if I could save it by freeing some and leaving others alone, I would also do that.

Equally fateful, and as widely known and discussed at the time of its delivery, was the House Divided Speech of 1858. This was the preliminary to the nine debates with United States Senator Stephen A. Douglas that year, from which Lincoln emerged a national figure, and the Cooper Union Speech of February, 1860, which dramatized Lincoln as a possible presidential candidate. Out of the tumult and troubled horizons of '58 came the tall Illinoisan with his relentless, "If we could first know where we are, and whither we are tending, we could better judge what to do, and how to do it." The slavery agitation would not cease, he declared as his opinion, until a crisis should have been reached and passed. He quoted, "A house divided against itself cannot stand," and proceeded, "I believe this government cannot endure permanently half slave and half free. I do not expect the Union to be dissolved—I do not expect the house to fall; but I do expect it will cease to be divided. It will become all one thing, or all the other."

Perhaps nothing else that Lincoln ever wrote or spoke brought so many inquiries as to what he meant as did the House Divided Speech. Some construed that he favored war, wanted war. Before he became President and afterward, these queries came. He intended to be plain-spoken, he would reply to these questioners, and the speech meant what it said. To one puzzled correspondent he wrote, after quoting the opening paragraph of the speech: "It puzzles me to make my meaning plainer. Look over it carefully, and conclude I meant all I said, and did not mean anything I did not say, and you will have my meaning." His final counsel in this letter ran: "If you will state to me some meaning which you suppose I had, I can and will instantly tell you whether that was my meaning."

Plain reasoning to reduce the opponent's position to absurdity was often

Lincoln's aim and method as writer and speaker. Into grim fantasy could he carry it, as in 1856 when he sketched a cultural apparatus arrayed and a climate of opinion generated toward the chattel slave:

All the powers of earth seem rapidly combining against him. Mammon is after him, ambition follows, philosophy follows, and the theology of the day is fast joining the cry. They have him in his prison house; they have searched his person, and left no prying instrument with him. One after another they have closed the heavy iron doors upon him; and now they have him, as it were, bolted in with a lock of a hundred keys, which can never be unlocked without the concurrence of every key—the keys in the hands of a hundred different men, and they scattered to a hundred different and distant places; and they stand musing as to what invention, in all the dominions of mind and matter, can be produced to make the impossibility of his escape more complete than it is.

3

Thus we have considered, or touched in degree, the brooding and speaking figure of Lincoln in the human Tragedy. How he moved and spoke as part of the human Comedy became vivid mouth-to-mouth folklore while he was alive, and his quips and drolleries went beyond his own country and began the process by which he was internationally adopted by the Family of Man.

A paradox was seen. Year by year came the stream of photographs reporting the face of the Chief Magistrate in the Executive Mansion. Camera craft had developed. The carte de visite was more than a vogue. Millions came to know the Lincoln face as though they had seen it in life. There it was, gaunt, fissured, melancholy, tragedy scrawled over it as on no other that had moved with authority among the doors and rooms of the Executive Mansion. "A Hoosier Michel Angelo," wrote Walt Whitman. And yet this man was the source and wellspring of a current of folklore and humor that widened and grew, that still exists and has its periodic accretions of newly found authentic material and its apocryphal and gratuitous contributions.

Among ten-cent books in paper covers published in the latter half of Lincoln's administration, one was titled "Old Abe's Joker" and another "Old Abe's Jokes—Fresh from Abraham's Bosom." It could be taken as part of a trend in American literature. The horse-laugh school of American humor had come into its own with its preeminent pen names of Orpheus C. Kerr (Robert H. Newell), Artemus Ward (Charles Farrar Browne), and Petroleum Vesuvius Nasby (David Ross Locke), vulgarians all, with their potshots at pomposity, and a meat ax for frauds, hypocrites, and snobs. Friends and compatriots of the President, they supported him and his cause with their satire and gibes. It was a country and a people warmly receptive of these jesters, whose persiflage often carried a razor edge, that gave its response and understanding to the byplay and humor that came to be known as "Lincoln stories."

Several facets had the Lincoln humor. His generation and his kinsfolk had their story-tellers who could "spin a yarn" to pass the time and to brighten the pioneer corners where they lived. He could tell a story for the sake of merriment, a medicine to his bones. Or again he would use a story as illustration of an argument or point of view, or as fable and allegory. Or again what he was saying could be veiled in a delicate irony. And there were phrasings and pithy utterances that came to be known as "Lincoln sayings," such as, "You can fool all of the people some of the time and some of the people all of the time, but you cannot fool all of the people all of the time." Or: "It is not best to swap horses while crossing the river." And: "Broken eggs can not be mended"; "Bad promises are better broken than kept"; "We shall sooner have the fowl by hatching the egg than smashing it"; "A jury too frequently has at least one member more ready to hang the panel than the traitor"; "No man knows so well where the shoe pinches as he who wears it."

Of the authenticated stories that Lincoln used for illustration, one seemed to have been reported by callers and visitors more than any other. Often his duties required him to be furtive and secretive beyond what he liked in political affairs. And he would tell of the Irishman in the state of Maine, where the sale of alcoholic liquor was prohibited. Having asked a druggist for a glass of lemonade and having the glass as ordered set before him, the Irishman whispered, "And now, can ye pour in just a drop of the creeter unbeknownst to me?" In a discussion of his use or misuse of constitutional prerogative Lincoln once said, "I am like the Irishman, I have to do some things unbeknownst to myself."

To make a point, Lincoln could mention, in passing, the two gentlemen who met and fought themselves out of their overcoats, each into the other's. To the query of an old neighbor from back home, "How does it feel to be President of the United States?" he could answer, "You have heard about the man tarred and feathered and ridden out of town on a rail? A man in the crowd asked him how he liked it, and his reply was that if it wasn't for the honor of the thing, he would much rather walk." One verbose man had the rating, "He can compress the most words into the smallest ideas of any man I ever met." A rural orator from the Southwest "mounted the rostrum, threw back his head, shined his eyes, and left the consequences to God."

The Lincoln vocabulary ranged from the plainest of street vernacular to hoary and archaic Anglo-Saxon terms. The enemy had "turned tail and run," he told a crowd on the White House lawn in 1865, to the dismay of various purists. And again he would trust to be understood in the ancient form of the noun "burthen" or the verbs "holden" and "disenthrall." His influence on the styles of other speakers and writers has been vast. The extent of it is incalculable. His use of the gift of laughter has been better emulated than the depths of his desire to mislead no man by act or word. This latter lay at the root of his counsel to the Congress in the 1862 Message:

In times like the present, men should utter nothing for which they would not willingly be responsible through time and in eternity.

Human solidarity, unity of action and feeling, may rise from a leadership knowing somewhat of both soil and seed; a leadership knowing somewhat of the dynamics Lincoln believed he could see at play among men and political states and civil factions when in 1862, he wrote to a New Orleans man:

I shall do nothing in malice. What I deal with is too vast for malicious dealing.

THE SECTIONS

--- tradition and experiment

48. THE SECOND DISCOVERY OF AMERICA

THE defeat of the Confederacy in the Civil War preserved the Union, but at the same time transformed it from a federal aggregate of sections into a national state dominated by the industrial and financial power concentrated along the axis Boston to New York to Chicago. After the opposition of the Southern plantation class had been eliminated, the leaders of the Republican Party were to carry through their program with only minor concessions to the rapidly developing agrarian West. Beginning with the Pacific Railway subsidies and the National Banking Act during the early years of the war, the Republican majority in Congress enacted a remarkable series of laws designed to aid finance and industry. The tariff was increased, the war debt was manipulated in the interest of investors, and the greenbacks were redeemed at par. Even the public-land system, ostensibly intended to favor the penniless settler, was administered in such a way as to transfer vast portions of the public domain to mining, lumbering, and stock-raising corporations.

In this favorable environment, the scale of business enterprise rapidly increased. Principles of management which had been developed in order to maintain the Union armies were applied to private undertakings of comparable scope. Improved transportation enabled raw materials to be carried great distances and made markets accessible for the mass-produced goods of the new factories. Technological improvements, like the introduction of the Bessemer process for making steel and the use of refrigeration in meat packing, revolutionized traditional types of manufacturing; and new major industries were developed on the basis of petroleum and electricity. Industrial expansion created the modern cities: by the 1890's New York, Philadelphia, and, miraculously, Chicago had grown beyond a million inhabitants each. New York, with three millions, had outstripped Paris and Berlin and had attained half the size of London.

These and similar factors determined the main trends of American literature during the thirty years following the Civil War. Despite the work of Henry James and Mark Twain, it was an age of transition rather than of fulfillment. The prewar enlightenment which had so variously and richly expressed the insights of transcendentalism was fading; and although there was no lack of new ideas, none appeared that was capable of providing the impetus for a literature commensurate with the nation created by the war. The dominant American intellectual tradition had been a creation of New England. Explicitly theocratic in the seventeenth century, it had been secularized into a program of humanitarian reform by the middle of the nineteenth, and after the formal enactment of abolition it was left with no more than minor political goals like civil service reform. The civic zeal of former abolitionists was frustrated by their commitment to a Republican Party controlled by Roscoe Conkling, James G. Blaine and Mark Hanna. And since the official tradition with its emphasis on ideality took little account of economics, it was powerless to understand, much less to direct, a society which subordinated everything to business. Even such a well informed conservative as E. L. Godkin, editor for thirty years of the influential weekly *Nation,* who considered himself a political economist, could only resort to moralistic invective against critics of the business system who rejected his dogma of the automatic beneficence of free competition. Men like Godkin continued to invoke an ill defined code of values which they called Civilization, Culture or Refinement. But the code was based historically upon a theology, and their position became increasingly confused as the new deterministic ideas of Darwin and Spencer undermined the old supernatural sanctions and made necessary a restatement of all the accepted theological doctrines.

Here then were the problems which faced American writers during the decades after the Civil War: the New England tradition was to be transformed, or if necessary supplanted by ideas adequate to the task of interpreting a continental nation that embraced a South and a West—indeed, a succession of Wests—in addition to the regions from which had come the first flowering of American letters. At the same time, the Industrial Revolution was to be confronted. Attitudes derived originally from an uncentralized agrarian social pattern were to be replaced by attitudes relevant to an integrated society dominated by huge metropolitan centers. Values formerly based on supernatural sanctions were to be restated in terms of natural law or to lose their authority entirely. None of these problems was fully solved before the end of the century, but a beginning was made toward solving all of them. Literary interpretations of the South and the West were devised; a critique of Big Business was begun; and American literature was launched upon an exciting exploration of nontraditional materials, forms, and assumptions. The new realism, imported as a literary method from Europe, became the radical implement of interpretation for an expanding America; the old ideality became its unrelenting foe, the defender of all the threatened values and memories.

2

The inauguration of Hayes in 1877 symbolized the end of Reconstruction in the South. Democratic and Liberal Republican protests against the corruption of Grant's administration, which had forced the nomination of Hayes instead of Blaine or Conkling, were reinforced by the fact that the popular vote for the Democratic candidate Tilden had actually exceeded the Republican total. The carpetbag period was over, and Hayes quickly withdrew the remaining troops from the South. But it was still necessary to formulate the intellectual terms on which the South could be received back into the nation. This task was undertaken by a group under the leadership of the Atlanta editor Henry W. Grady, who adopted the slogan of the "New South."

Economically, the New South movement sought industrialization, with slogans and aspirations already familiar in Britain and the Northern states; a minor theme, emphasized by Sidney Lanier, was development of diversified farming to replace the single-crop system of the plantation. For literature, the New South movement implied a rapprochement with the Northern publishing houses and magazines which were creating and guiding the new national audience. The Southern writers of fiction who for a decade all but dominated the American magazines—George W. Cable, Joel Chandler Harris, Thomas Nelson Page, and to a less marked extent Mary Noailles Murfree—were committed to the New South point of view. The strategy was explained to them by J. G. Holland and his successor R. W. Gilder of *Scribner-Century,* who in many instances took the initiative in discovering and developing Southern writers. "A sane and earnest Americanism," a calculated desire "to increase the sentiment of Union" were the principles imposed upon the Southerners, and accepted by them, even to the point of editorial deletion of phrases or ideas that were not sufficiently reconstructed. Only by accepting the new order and the principle of integration did these writers achieve a national audience; but once this major position was established they found in the romance of a no longer dangerous South an inexhaustible storehouse of themes related to the prewar plantation for which readers all over the country showed an apparently insatiable appetite. To take a single example, the Negro, presented in fiction according to the Southern conception of an inferior race happily adjusted to a feudal class structure, became a stock literary character of the first importance. If the Southern writers conceded to the nation the fact of union, the nation conceded to the South its view of the race problem, and by the 1890's it was possible for such a former Abolitionist as T. W. Higginson to sit dissolved in tears over the death of a slave owner in Page's "Marse Chan."

3

If the South, during the twenty years from 1876 to 1896, seemed to be transformed from a menace into an opportunity for the industrial and financial metropolis, the West developed in almost exactly the opposite direction. From a numerous army of journalists who set out along the Union Pacific in the late sixties and seventies, Eastern readers learned to think of the trans-Mississippi as a boundless treasure house of natural resources waiting to be developed through the investment of Eastern capital. L. P. Brockett's encyclopedic *Our Western Empire* (1881), which compiled all available information in an apotheosis of the Emigrant's Guides of the first half of the century, adequately represents prevailing attitudes toward the "Goodly heritage, with which God has endowed this Nation." Brockett emphasized economic matters like the new bonanza farming, the cattle industry, mineral resources, railway construction, and the astonishing growth in population beyond the Mississippi. Yet he was apprehensive lest the innumerable Westerners of the future, forced to live "without opportunities of education, and far from civilizing influences," might fail to show proper "reverence for law and order" and might, through pride and fullness of bread, become easy victims of demagogues. The prophecy, although based on widely held opinions, was wide of the mark. When the demagogue did appear, to proclaim the abomination of free silver, he derived his power not from fullness in his hearers but from hunger. The inability of the East to perceive this basic fact about the Populist West had a great deal to do with the misunderstanding between the sections in the eighties and nineties.

The literary discovery of the Far West came soon after the Civil War in the widely acclaimed work of Bret Harte, Joaquin Miller, and Mark Twain. The sudden vogue of Harte, especially, suggests that the American audience was hungry for literary experience beyond the somewhat narrow confines established by current critical theory with its emphasis on ideality. Confronted with the fact of Harte's popularity, the critics at first were inclined to concede that his heart-of-gold formula was an adequate device for palliating the introduction of prostitutes, sluice robbers, and gamblers into fiction. His work, wrote a critic for *Putnam's Magazine* in 1870, showed "the capability of our American experience of an original and fine artistic treatment." With "the eye and the sympathy of genius" the Californian had been able to bring his characters and events, in themselves commonplace and often repulsive, "out of their vulgar relations, and transplant them into a realm of beauty." But as the original freshness of Harte's materials was staled by too constant repetition, and especially when a more sensational exploiter of Western materials appeared in Joaquin Miller, the doubts about morality which had lurked in the background again came to the fore. William Dean Howells predicted in 1882 that readers would not care for "the huge Californian mirth, when the surprise of the picturesquely mixed civilization and barbarism of the Pacific coast has quite died away." Harte dealt, after all, remarked James Herbert Morse in the *Century,* with "passion . . . in its original, natural conditions, released from the decencies of social restraint, and subject only to the instinctive laws of the heart." The *Atlantic* itself, which in 1871 under Howells' editorship had welcomed Harte to the East with the unprecedented offer of ten thousand dollars for his next year's work, had decided by 1882 that sentiment alone was the motive force in his stories; that his heroines had lost their honor, his men their principles; and that at best one could speak of his "unmoral treatment of immoral subjects." Joaquin Miller's more daring exploration of a sentimental, as opposed to a theocratic, code of ethics had already suggested the true leading of his precedessor's "easy optimism," as *Appleton's Journal* had perceived as early as 1876. Bret Harte's effort to find "something good even in the worst of men and women—gamblers, *roués,* border-ruffians, harlots, etc.," remarked the critic for this magazine,

is one thing; but it is quite another to laud these people as, by reason, apparently, of their very "primitiveness" and "savagery," an exceptionally praiseworthy species of the genus man. Mr. Miller makes a parade of condemning everything that civilized and decent men hold in respect; and his social code seems to be that men are "noble," and "grand," and "earnest," and "sincere," and admirable, in exact proportion to their barbarism.

An open and avowed sentimental ethics, then, was going too far. Conservative opinion, accustomed to finding literature heavy with explicit moral judgments, was not prepared to see the moral weight of fiction thrown into the scales on the side of clear violations of the social code. Yet a compromise was possible. If immorality could not be forgiven, certain other less central aspects of barbarism, such as incorrect speech, illiteracy, and uncultivated manners, could be condoned and even enjoyed as picturesque, provided the author demonstrated the inner moral purity of outwardly crude characters. In this milder version, the heart-of-gold formula became the stock in trade of the local-color movement and furnished the framework on which dozens of industrious authors could drape the representations of new landscapes, new provincial types, and new dialects that filled the magazines during what have been called "the local-color eighties."

The influence of the West was felt not only in the development of local-color fiction, but also in a reversal of the westward movement by small but significant numbers of back trailers, sons of pioneers who were impelled eastward by disenchantment with the epic dreams of the earliest frontiers and by the broader opportunities of the metropolitan centers. Lincoln himself was a back trailer, after a fashion. His election directly involved John Hay's translation to Washington and eventually to a diplomatic post in Paris from what Hay considered a "dreary waste of heartless materialism" in Warsaw, Illinois; and was indirectly responsible for sending the young Ohioan Howells, who had written a campaign biography of Lincoln, to a consulate in Italy. Howells presently emerged as editor of the *Atlantic* and close associate of the Cambridge Brahmins, while Hay moved into the charmed inner circle of "The Five of Hearts" (the Henry Adamses, the Hays, and the geologist Clarence King) in Adams' drawing room. Bret Harte and Joaquin Miller likewise followed the back trail as far as Europe. Mark Twain settled in Hartford and, like Godkin and Howells, married an Eastern wife. In other fields men like John W. Powell, who had made their careers in the West, were climbing paths of increasing authority and influence to positions comparable with Powell's directorship of the United States Geological Survey. The name "Back Trailers" is a creation of the Middle Westerner Hamlin Garland, who followed Howells' footsteps to Boston two decades later, returned for a time to Chicago in a rather self-conscious effort to establish a literary center independent of the East, and when this effort failed migrated to New York.

Some of the Back Trailers managed to adapt themselves to the newer industrial America, as Howells did, and retained a certain sweetness and poise as the century drew to a close. But some of them, like Garland, seemed unable to establish a satisfactory relation with either the East or the West; and some, like Hay, despite successful careers, took over the gloomy social outlook of leading Eastern intellectuals. The novelists E. W. Howe and Joseph Kirkland, who remained in the Middle West with their own kind of disillusionment at the failure of the high hopes of the first waves of settlement, prepared grim reports of small-town life that contributed much to the consciously if mildly antiromantic "realism" of the 1880's. A new literary mood was being created.

4

The new mood was even more plainly evident in the protests against the industrial order which were nourished both by Western farmers' resentment of railroads and moneylenders, and by the growing awareness of poverty and suffering in the cities. A significant if not a representative ex-Copperhead, Henry Clay Dean of Iowa, whose nickname "Dirty Shirt" anticipated the "Sockless Jerry" Simpson period of Populist spellbinding, declared in his impassioned *Crimes of the Civil War* (1868) that the East had used the Republican party to "enslave" the Mississippi Valley under the pretext of freeing the Negro slaves, and pleaded for a union of West and South against the "eastern capital and manufacturing machinery." In the late sixties "Gentleman George" Pendleton, another former Copperhead leader, sponsored the Ohio Idea of repaying war bonds in greenback currency—the earliest of many Western inflationary schemes. A succession of third-party movements leading up to the Populism of the nineties tried in vain to bring about political cooperation between farmers and urban laborers. Humanitarian clergymen in the cities, appalled by conditions in the slums, developed a "social gospel" which proclaimed, in the words of the Congregational minister George D. Herron, that "the Sermon on the Mount is the science of society."

Such movements gave rise to a vast body of writing, both imaginative and expository, denouncing the plutocracy in the name of an older American equalitarianism. Henry George, the most influential critic of the existing order, constructed his single-tax theory in protest against the monopolies in land he had observed being formed during the sixties in California. The most important novelists of the dissident group—Edward Bellamy, the early Hamlin Garland, and William Dean Howells in his Utopian phase—different as they were in detail, were alike in their refusal to accept either the standards of value or the practical consequences of the economic revolution.

The critics of Big Business were unable to find support in the conservative New England literary tradition. The great Bostonians were gentlemen, well descended and almost to a man independently wealthy. Longfellow, Lowell, Holmes, Norton—such men belonged to an aristocracy that could hardly be called even middle-class, and it was difficult for them to conceive of a literature not produced in an atmosphere of refined leisure. The dominant literary figures of New York, such as Edmund Clarence Stedman, Charles Dudley Warner, and Richard Henry Stoddard, strove to keep literature unsullied from the world of politics and economics. "There were certain subjects," remarked Stoddard's literary executor, "which remained wholly foreign to the atmosphere of the poet's library. He lived in New York, but the omnipotent name of the stock market was never heard"—despite the fact that Stedman, one of Stoddard's most intimate friends, was head of a firm of brokers.

Nevertheless, the stock market existed, and in the last decade of the century, men who studied American society became increasingly aware that changes were under way whose end no man could see. The historian Frederick Jackson Turner's famous paper on "The Significance of the Frontier in American History," read in the year of the Panic of 1893, ominously announced "the closing of a great historical movement" with the imminent disappearance of the frontier of settlement in the West. In an essay on "Industry and Finance" contributed to the three-volume symposium *The United States of America* edited by the Harvard geologist Nathaniel S. Shaler in 1894, the economist F. W. Taussig noted the decline in the rate of growth in population since 1860 and predicted it would continue. Like Turner, he asserted that the good farming lands of the public domain were nearing exhaustion, and drew the inference that "The conditions of the future must be different from those of the past." Other contributors to the symposium alluded to the many problems that industrialization and urbanization had brought: the "new immigration" from Southern and Eastern Europe, the slum, the approaching exhaustion of forests and other natural resources, corruption in municipal government, trusts and monopolies. Dr. D. A. Sargent of Harvard, the noted expert on physical training, described the nervousness resulting from the pressures and stimuli of modern urban life and asked, "Can we stand it?" He believed that Americans would learn to adapt themselves to the new conditions, but the question itself would have sounded strange amid the optimistic predictions made at the opening of the Philadelphia Centennial Exposition of 1876, when Progress was the watchword and official spokesmen unanimously foresaw a new age which would outshine even the glorious first century of the Republic.

The somber tone of the early nineties was brightened somewhat by the success of another world's fair, the Columbian Exposition at Chicago. Here, in the white neoclassical columns and the majestic esplanades, was evidence both that the supposedly materialistic West had grown upward into aesthetic expression and that American art in general need no longer be called weak and pretentious in comparison with the best work of Europe, as it had so unmistakably seemed at Philadelphia two decades earlier. Even Henry Adams, who made two visits to Chicago and found there "matter of study to fill a hundred years," was willing to acknowledge that the West had at least known how to hire its art made for it. Sitting on the steps before Richard Hunt's Administration Building, he was tempted for a moment to wonder whether it was indeed as impossible as he had imagined for "the new American world to take this sharp and conscious twist towards ideals." "Chicago," he wrote, "asked in 1893 for the first time the question whether the American people knew where they were driving."

But on his return to Washington late in the summer, he found his answer in the repeal of the Sherman Silver Purchase Act. He interpreted the establishment of the gold standard as the final decision of the American people to abandon the past, the eighteenth century, the Constitution of 1789, the world of the Adamses, and to accept the leadership of business.

A capitalistic system [Adams continued] had been adopted, and if it were to be run at all, it must be run by capital and capitalistic methods; for nothing could surpass the nonsensity of trying to run so complex and so concentrated a machine by Southern and Western farmers in grotesque alliance with city day-laborers, as had been tried in 1800 and 1828 and had failed even under simple conditions.

If Adams overdramatized the year 1893, at least his analysis of the outcome of the Industrial Revolution in America suggests the future that faced the nation on the eve of the twentieth century: "Once admitted that the machine must be efficient, society might dispute in what social interest it should be run, but in any case it must work concentration." And concentration meant

the protective tariff; the corporations and trusts; the trades-unions and socialistic paternalism which necessarily made their complement; the whole mechanical consolidation of force, which ruthlessly stamped out the life of the class into which Adams was born, but created monopolies capable of controlling the new energies that America adored.

49. THE EDUCATION OF EVERYMAN

JAMES A. GARFIELD, last of the log-cabin candidates to sit in the White House, declared at Lake Chautauqua during his campaign in 1880: "We may divide the whole struggle of the human race into two chapters: first, the fight to get leisure; and then the second fight of civilization—what shall we do with our leisure when we get it." Sitting there in the lake breeze, his audience knew what Garfield meant, these prosperous farmers with leathery faces and gnarled hands, retired merchants and small-town bankers with palm-leaf fans, women who had left their summer canning and jelly making to come and hear about books and ideas. Most of them were middle-aged or over, for leisure had come late and dearly bought. Even so had success come to the speaker—scion of a poor pioneer family "hungry for the horizon," who had reversed their westward march to work his way through Williams College, and become schoolmaster and politician.

The setting of the speech was significant. In southwestern New York State in 1874 an experiment in adult education had begun. Lewis Miller, agricultural inventor and Sunday-school teacher, here joined forces with a onetime circuit rider, John H. Vincent, who as a youth had gone preaching with "a few very good books" in his saddlebags. These two Methodists started with the idea of a camp meeting for Sunday-school teachers. Thanks to their own inclinations and the link which bound the church to social life and serious entertainment in most middle-sized American towns, they soon found themselves sponsoring a cultural program called the Chautauqua Assembly. Lectures on the Bible and Palestinian geography quickly expanded into study courses in history, literature, science, art, and music. In 1878, gratified by the popular demand, Dr. Vincent extended "the Idea" to include a winter's program of reading at home, the Chautauqua Literary and Scientific Circle. The circle offered a four-year study course, like that of the regular colleges, appealing to middle-aged women for whom the establishment of Vassar, Smith, and Wellesley had come too late. Members studied European and American history, classical civilization, and modern science. Those who persevered to the end won a diploma and marched on Recognition Day through the Golden Gate, while flower girls strewed their path—in a quaint blending of academic with nuptial pageantry. By 1892, one hundred thousand were currently enrolled in the circle. The advent in 1883 of William Rainey Harper, future president of the University of Chicago, as educational director, attracted to Chautauqua some of America's best university lecturers, such as the historians John Fiske and Herbert B. Adams, the economist Richard T. Ely, the psychologist G. Stanley Hall. William James might stand appalled before these "earnest and helpless minds," but his Harvard colleague George Herbert Palmer saw the colony of summer tents and tabernacles as the expression of a folk impulse, idealistic, hopeful, bizarre, but vital, comparable to the Crusades or the Greek Mysteries.

From the shores of this lake the Idea spread far and wide in the eighties. Hosts of local Chautauquas each summer drew their hundreds of thousands, sending them home to study over the winter months, to earn "seals" for their diplomas. The ranks of those who "wanted to know" were swelled by young men and women seeking bonds of acquaintance, housewives and shut-ins, pastors and congregations, a myriad farm and village families caught in the doldrums of loneliness between the husking bee and house-raising of frontier days and the undiscovered future of motorcar, radio, and movies. Above all, in this generation Chautauqua helped allay the thirst of those middle-class Americans who had had too little book-learning in the rude schoolhouses and poor libraries of their youth, and now felt an urge to come within hailing distance of their children. The gospel according to Chautauqua proclaimed that study was no longer drudgery, but radiant opportunity; that education did not end when a boy went to work or a girl got married, but persisted forever. It also asserted that knowledge was no closed preserve or class monopoly, but lay open to squatters' rights by Everyman.

The breaking of barriers between scholar and common citizen, scientist and mechanic, specialist and layman, is a corollary of that Jeffersonian democracy which needs many generations to work out all its implications. But no era in American history saw more speeding of the process, in the diffusion and popularization of knowledge, than the seventies and eighties. The Civil War and Reconstruction had been distracting to adults of military and business age, even though education for the young had advanced steadily. The Panic of 1873 induced, if not an about-face to plain living and high thinking, at least some inkling of values more durable than Wall Street stocks. Even more important in the long run was a growing mass awareness of the new science and its miracles—if not Darwin and Huxley, then the visible wonders of chemistry and electricity—with the consequent stirrings of curiosity in many, hostility among a few. Moreover, this same science purchased freedom from toil and a broader margin of leisure, for farmer as well as city dweller.

And finally, the technique of publishing had begun to bombard the average citizen with the printed word. From newspapers he might pass tentatively to the cheaper magazines and paper-backed novels, thence to books of better quality, until he began imperceptibly to educate himself. From the other side of the barrier, seeking to make easy his ingress into the garden of knowledge, were both the idealists, like Chautauqua's founders, and entrepreneurs like James Redpath the lecture agent, Thomas J. Foster the founder in the eighties of the International Correspondence Schools at Scranton, and a little later Elbert Hubbard the author of chapbooks inspirational and informative.

Popularization had a dark and a bright side. On the one hand, it often meant a cheapening of standards that spread from adult mass education into other compartments of American life, such as schools, colleges, and pulpits. A smattering took the place of scholarship, while intellectual distinction faded in the glare of novelty and notoriety. On the other hand, it helped keep the savant from isolation and intellectual snobbery, and the common man from sullen suspicion of these mysteries. The Wisconsin novelist Zona Gale called the phenomenon of the eighties "a homely renaissance, not of learning, but of study." Whether for good or ill, it helped to make us the greatest popularizers of knowledge on earth. Our shrewdest observer, Lord Bryce, recognized this fact in 1888, reporting in his *American Commonwealth* that "the average of knowledge is higher, the habit of reading and thinking more generally diffused, than in any other country."

Kindred symptoms, in the post-Appomattox period, had antedated Chautauqua. The women's club in America began in 1868 with the Sorosis in New York and the New England Women's Club in Boston; by 1889, when the nation-wide General Federation of Women's Clubs was organized, uncounted thousands of women were conning Robert's *Rules of Order,* or preparing papers on English flower gardens and the poetry of Robert Browning. Also in 1868, the journalist Redpath from Boston revamped the old lyceum into a commercialized lecture bureau. Attended by greater publicity, and featuring more humor, color, and sheer entertainment, the Redpath Lyceum Bureau quickly raised the modest $25 and $50 fees for which Emerson and Thoreau had once spoken, to the $400 to $500 commanded by John B. Gough the reformed drunkard or Thomas Nast the cartoonist, or the $1,000 sometimes paid Henry Ward Beecher or Henry M. Stanley (just back from darkest Africa). Almost equal in popularity were Anna E. Dickinson the crusader and feminist, John L. Stoddard with stereopticon views of his travels, and funny men like Petroleum V. Nasby and Mark Twain. When some old favorites dropped out, and lectures began to pall, Redpath turned first to magicians, then to musical soloists and quartets, small opera companies, and programs verging more and more upon the domain of the circus. The edifying lecture, which had driven a wedge in Puritan America for opera and drama, slowly crumbled in the later years of the century, after long-continued profit from the quest for culture.

2

"I never made a success of a lecture in a church yet. People are afraid to laugh in a church," wrote Mark Twain to Redpath early in the seventies. But inspirational speakers easily bridged the chasm between lyceum and pulpit. One of the most celebrated was the Reverend Russell H. Conwell of Philadelphia, who delivered his "Acres of Diamonds" some six thousand times. "Opportunity is in your own backyard," was the theme. A religion of success, old as Cotton Mather and popular enough before the Civil War, now flourished with renewed vigor. Its great practitioner in fiction was Horatio Alger. A neurotic Unitarian clergyman, timid and solitary, he lived in a newsboys' hostel in Manhattan and wrote more than a hundred books of pluck and luck, beginning with *Ragged Dick* (1867) and *Tattered Tom* (1871), together with inspirational lives of Lincoln and Garfield. Like many exemplars of the success cult, these books were products of the author's own morbid awareness of failure. But beyond question they mirrored a naïve hopefulness, a passion for self-improvement, characteristic of the times. Their blend of morality with riches can be found in scores of nonfiction books throughout this period, all pointing the way to wealth and happiness.

In this age of many aspirations, the church found itself a house divided. Too often it yielded to the blandishment of riches, ultimately to lose prestige both as spiritual and educative force in American life. Some ground it recovered through the gospel of social service, trying to satisfy the query propounded in the nineties by Charles M. Sheldon's immensely popular novel *In His Steps*—"What would Jesus do?" The success of two other best sellers in this generation, *Ben Hur* (1880) and the Revised Version of the Bible (1881–1885), gauges the breadth of religious interest. More radical departures from orthodoxy appeared in the cult of Christian Science, stemming from Mrs. Eddy's *Science and Health* (1875), and flowering into churches, reading rooms, lecture courses, and literature of nation-wide distribution; the Theosophical Society, established in New York by Madame Blavatsky in 1875; and Dr. Felix Adler's Society for Ethical Culture, founded in 1876. Meanwhile, the rapid increase of Roman Catholic power, notably through the new immigration, stirred forebodings in rural Protestant minds and led to the foundation in 1887 of a secret order, the American Protective Association, which, like the Know-Nothing movement of the fifties, for a while aligned farm belt against city, Anglo-Saxon against Irish and Latin culture.

A more important battle front in the zone of religious loyalties lay between supernaturalism and science. Within a few years after the Civil War, the real impact of Darwin's theory regarding the descent of man was first felt in American thought. The New York *World* published John Fiske's Harvard lectures on Darwin and Comte; in 1871 James Freeman Clarke's popular *Ten Great Religions* introduced the public to the subject of comparative religions and myths; in this year Edward L. Youmans, a self-taught farm boy from upper New York State, established the International Scientific Series, to which Tyndall, Darwin, Huxley, and Helmholtz soon contributed, and in 1872 Youmans launched his *Popular Science Monthly*. The hypotheses of science found perhaps their ablest champions in the seventies in President Andrew D. White of Cornell, whose famous Cooper Union speech, "The Battlefields of Science," was embodied in the book *The Warfare of Science* (1876); and in Dr. John W. Draper, physicist, physician, and author of the widely read *History of the Conflict between Religion and Science* (1874). Almost from the first, certain liberal clergymen like Henry Ward Beecher proclaimed that geology no less than Genesis was a revelation of God's purpose, that the animal origins of *homo sapiens* no more impeached his dignity than did the "mud man" theory of Creation. Citadels of the old-time religion could not be expected to strike their flags in instant surrender. "Harvard's raid on religion" was fiercely resented in the Corn Belt; young Vanderbilt University in 1878 dismissed a professor of geology for "untamed speculation," and within the next six years similar purges occurred in at least three other academies in the South. More thoughtful men meditated an emergent paradox deeper than these conflicts—between survival of the fittest and the law of love and solicitude, with even science (cast in the role of healer) seeking to arrest the harsher operations of nature. As time went on, popular curiosity about the new biology and anthropology increased, reaching some kind of truce with the old dogmas of supernaturalism. When in 1893 a series of lectures on evolution by Henry Drummond was the feature of that Chautauqua summer, the *Nation* called it "a sign of the times which no observer can neglect."

3

Beside this harvest of new ideas, fruitful of debate, questioning, and final assimilation, one must set the more tangible instruments of culture which aided the sowing of those ideas through the Republic. Reading, writing, school teaching, travel, and bookmaking advanced in a manner befitting a literate and technical-minded democracy. For not even the Fundamentalists opposed the new efficiency of applied science.

In 1876 Alexander Graham Bell invented the telephone, a boon to communication and the breaking down of rural isolation, while doubtless contributing to the decay of letter writing as a fine art. Of vast import to the literary man and journalist was Christopher Sholes' invention of the typewriter in 1868. Mark Twain and a few other pioneers took it up with alacrity; most creative writers lagged behind businessmen in its adoption. Its ultimate effect upon literature—in promoting fluency and speed, while perhaps discouraging niceties of revision—can hardly be measured today, when most writers have become very centaurs of the machine age, half man and half keyboard. The practice of dictation, common in American business life after the spread of the Pitman system; popularity of the new Eclectic method in the seventies, and introduction of the Gregg system at the close of our period, appealed to only a few literary men—notably Henry James in his later years—and its effects upon style were consequently sparse. A greater aid to the average man came in 1884, with Lewis E. Waterman's invention of the fountain pen, enabling one to write wherever he went. Also universal were the innovations wrought in the reading and writing habits of Americans by the steady improvements in gas illumination through the seventies, and the final triumph of Edison's incandescent light early in the eighties. In the multiplication of books, no other achievement of modern times surpasses Ottmar Mergenthaler's invention of the linotype in 1885.

4

In general the phenomenal growth of the city during the quarter-century after Appomattox meant concentration of the demand for culture and amusement, bigger and possibly better newspapers, magazines, publishing houses, and bookshops. It also meant more local wealth for the taxgatherer's sickle, with correspondingly improved municipal art galleries, museums, concert halls, public libraries, and schools. Such interplay quickened the educative and creative spirit within the focus of city life.

Illiteracy declined from 17 per cent of our population in 1880 to 13 per cent in 1890, despite the influx from Ellis Island. Compulsory school laws, beginning in the North and West in the early seventies, embraced nineteen states at the start of the next decade. Free textbooks were first offered in New York City in the eighties, then spread to other cities, and were presently demanded for back-country schools by crusaders like Minnesota's Ignatius Donnelly. In the farm belt, groups such as the Farmers' Alliance and the Grange agitated for better schools; the Grange itself, through its circulating libraries and homely debates on politics and economics, built civic intelligence. In 1878 high schools numbered less than 800 throughout the nation;

twenty years later, 5,500 were reported. This increase in turn fed college attendance enormously, making higher education less a class luxury and more the birthright of all Americans with ambition and ability.

Between the common school and the college, vocational education was spreading its vast ramifications. In the wake of the Morrill Act of 1862, trade and technological schools in the East were prone to stress engineering; in the Midwest and the South, agriculture; in the Rocky Mountain and Far West, mining and metallurgy. Other institutions fitted themselves for new service. In the seventies the Young Men's Christian Association had begun to assume cultural as well as spiritual and recreational tasks; in the eighties it set up evening classes in crafts and skills which proved popular. This latter decade also saw the dawn of university extension courses, through lectures and correspondence methods, under the inspiration of British example and the labors of Herbert B. Adams from Johns Hopkins.

Among the universities, innovation flowed from the Harvard of Charles William Eliot. In the *Atlantic* in 1869 he had blown the reveille whose echoes sounded through the next generation: the elective system, shattering the old predestined regimen of ancient languages and disciplines, giving play to free will. In consequence, modern languages and history, science, applied mathematics, economics, and English literature came virtually to dominate the field. The new state universities, seeking broad programs of study, welcomed this change with as much alacrity as they showed respecting another innovation, coeducation. Women's work in the Civil War had accelerated recognition of their rights in higher education and the professions, just as their services in a later war sped the award of the ballot. By 1880 the United States counted 154 mixed colleges and universities, in addition to those exclusively the property of women, pioneered by Vassar in 1865, and Smith and Wellesley ten years later.

Graduate study was another marked development of the times. At Yale and Harvard organized graduate work began about 1870, though a few doctorates on the German model had been given in the sixties. Johns Hopkins opened in 1876 as an institution of purely graduate study. Private endowments, upon a scale of generosity hitherto unknown, led to establishment of new and powerful universities—of which Stanford, founded in 1885—is representative. The eighties also witnessed a flow of American students toward German universities, where Virchow, Mommsen, Harnack, and other teachers of world fame had set up the highest standards of research then known. An estimated two thousand American candidates for degrees were constantly in residence there throughout the eighties. By 1886, with due acknowledgment of past benefits, James Russell Lowell began to voice alarm lest Prussian pedantry widen the breach between mere erudition ("the new dry rot of learning") and true culture of the spirit. Men of his persuasion turned increasingly for their ideal toward Oxford and Cambridge, where a balance was held between extremes in a manner befitting the cardinal maxim of humanism, "nothing in excess." But just now, in an age of avid specialization, they found themselves outvoted.

5

For the great mass of Americans, the printed word remained their chief instrument of culture. A most significant development, therefore, was the burgeoning of public libraries. Subscribers' libraries, as has been seen, flourished from colonial times. In many a city, ambitious mechanics and laborers pooled modest resources for a common lending library. But free public libraries supported by taxation were comparatively late, beginning in communities of New Hampshire, Massachusetts, and Maine around the middle of the nineteenth century. In 1865 several other states began to follow, until the whole nation swung into line. By 1875 the number of free libraries owning upwards of a thousand books was 2,000; by the century's end it had grown to 5,400. Early arguments for the cause strike a modern mind as rather naïve: for example, that studious workingmen will absent themselves from "haunts of vice and folly," while the unemployed "are much safer with a book in the library than elsewhere." Thus, as if to appease a lingering scruple of Puritan capitalism, many Americans have always found hardheaded arguments for mass cultivation and recreation. Greatest of private benefactors was the steel king Andrew Carnegie. In 1881 he began to donate library buildings to those towns which would provide the site and promise maintenance. Before the end of this era, the continent was studded with Carnegie libraries. Meanwhile, to promote efficiency of cataloguing and other services, the American Library Association had been organized in 1876.

Magazines were growing in number from 200 at the outbreak of the Civil War, to 1,800 by the end of the century. Highest literary prestige still clung to the *Atlantic,* which in 1871 passed into the editorial hands of young William Dean Howells from Ohio. Boston Brahmins, like Holmes, who impressed him with solemn remarks about apostolic succession and the laying on of hands, had picked their man with much astuteness: Howells deferred to his "Holy Land of Boston" and its literary mores, while injecting into his job the earnest enthusiasms of the West. Despite all his efforts, the *Atlantic* was far outstripped in the race for circulation by *Harper's,* which prospered steadily under the editorship of Henry Mills Alden. The really spectacular successes were reserved for the *Century* under Richard Watson Gilder, which in 1885 topped 200,000, eventually helping to draw Howells himself to the brighter lights of New York; and on less literary levels, the *Ladies' Home Journal,* with 270,000 circulation in this same year, and the *Youth's Companion* with 385,000, as a record-breaker of all previous time. Artificial aids to circulation in these days were the news-stand traffic of organizations like the American News Company, and the awarding to new subscribers of premiums ranging from lithographs to sewing machines. Small but influential was the *Nation* under E. L. Godkin, begun in 1865, whose ideas were cribbed by innumerable liberal preachers, lecturers, and editors throughout the country. Thomas Nast's cartoons against the Tweed Ring and later corruptions buttressed the crusading prestige of *Harper's Weekly.* In 1877 *Puck* appeared, the first durably successful magazine of humor in America, fashioned somewhat on the model of the London *Punch*; *Judge* followed in 1881, and *Life* with more subtle satire in 1883. When set beside an ante-bellum specialist in misspelling and rustic horseplay like Shillaber's *Carpet-Bag,* such magazines reveal the coming-of-age of American tastes in comedy.

In the book trade, New York clearly overshadowed every other center of production, as early as 1865 excelling Boston and Philadelphia put together. In the eighties Chicago began to challenge these runners-up, with San Francisco continuing her prosperous regional business. Certain developments within the trade promoted the circulation of books. Rescued from the obscurity of certain back shelves in drug and mercantile stores, or casual newspaper racks, the bookshop declared its independence in scores of middle-sized American towns, and by window display sought to make its wares attractive. Circulating libraries, often as adjuncts of these shops, continued to multiply. With even greater enterprise, book agents became an increasingly common sight, canvassing from house to house in town and suburban communities, or jogging along country roads from farm to farm. They were the heirs of Parson Weems and the Yankee peddler of Bronson Alcott's youth, but unlike their forebears dealt almost exclusively in books. In the first years after Appomattox they vended encyclopedias, dictionaries, illustrated books about battles and leaders of the Civil War, and sets of standard authors. Soon they began to purvey series—like the Seaside Library, Standard Library, Leisure Hour Series, Library of American Humor, Town and Country Library, fiction and nonfiction, of variable quality, in cheap cloth and paper—which issued from presses in an unending stream. Foreign titles abounded, in the lack of international copyright. The obviously heavy profits for publisher, but small royalties to author, of a canvassing concern like the American Publishing Company of Hartford, led Mark Twain early in the eighties to set up his own firm, C. L. Webster & Company, and to achieve a dazzling success by selling over 300,000 sets of General Grant's Memoirs at $9 to $25 a set. Other ventures, like a life of Pope Leo XIII which Twain assumed all good Catholics would buy, proved far less lucky, and the ultimate crash of that firm is well known. Nor was the effect of "subscription sets" upon literature itself a very happy one. To take an example from the same author, Twain's *Life on the Mississippi*, written for James R. Osgood of Boston and his impatient canvassers, had been hurried along and padded out, to bring it up to cubic specifications, at the cost of inspired art.

The greatest disservice which publishing methods inflicted upon this generation of authors came from a lack of international copyright laws. Every author was likely to be without profit save in his own country, and even on native ground had to bear an unfair competition with foreign authors which did not even benefit them. In the sixties and early seventies a "courtesy of the trade" convention, among American publishers of European books, for a while curbed excessive reprints. But it collapsed in the latter seventies and eighties, as new firms multiplied and competition in paperbacks grew fiercer. Abroad conditions were no better. John Camden Hotten and other Britons flew no flag but the Jolly Roger. By 1878, as G. H. Putnam reported, one out of every ten books printed in England was an American book. Typographers, binders, and printing management in general opposed international copyright, masking their greed in pious words about the cheap dissemination of good books. Needless to say, the basis of their selection was not quality, but often quite the reverse. On their side, authors and magazine editors fought for new legislation, banding together in 1883 as the American Copyright League, to bring pressure in Washington. The Berne Copyright Convention in 1887 found the United States still isolationist. Not until 1891 was the first major battle won, when a workable law (though not so stringent as the Berne Convention) finally passed Congress.

Culturally this was a generation of parvenus—naïve, exuberant, in the main self-satisfied. Vastly impressed by the wonders of applied science and the material gains for which it thanked Edison and Bell, the average American was oblivious of Willard Gibbs and looked somewhat askance at Darwin and Huxley. Yet his awareness of economic and intellectual problems and dilemmas was not without significance, nor was the talisman, increasingly prized everywhere, of a college education and a nodding acquaintance with "the best books."

The primary stage of American culture, literacy, which had gone hand in hand with the primary era in our material production—of corn and cotton, coal and iron—had absorbed majority interest and effort prior to the Civil War. Now a secondary stage had begun. Upon the material plane industrialization of a once agrarian nation laid new stress upon manufactures, their technology and quantitative output. Meanwhile, in the sphere of mass culture, a more than literate citizenship sought to fuse the inspirational with the utilitarian, sensing in education and books the means to an end of worldly success and happiness. A tertiary stage—which might witness the emergence of fine craftsmanship upon the one plane, and a corresponding concept of quality upon the other—had hardly begun to develop.

50. DEFENDERS OF IDEALITY

Between 1870 and 1890, therefore, the older tradition in American literature—the tradition which found its origins in Franklin and Edwards, its fulfillment in Emerson and Melville and Whitman—seemed suddenly the articulation of a vanished era. Only its ideals survived, but without their familiar bearings. Painfully the American writer must start over again the gigantic task of national self-discovery and expression, of reducing elemental experience to the discipline of art. The securities of Concord and Cambridge were gone, even though Longfellow and Lowell, Holmes and Emerson, lived on. Plainly the culture for which so much effort had been expended, and which now seemed so close to perfection, must be preserved. Mark Twain and William Dean Howells, already becoming the spokesmen for the new realism, felt its power and hurried East on the morning of their first fame. The issue was sharply drawn: if one wished to write, one must choose to defend the old order or to throw in one's lot with the new. There was no easy blending of ideality with reality in these uncertain times.

From the time of the Civil War until past the turn of the century, the writing and the criticism of poetry were largely in the hands of a group of friends bound by many personal and literary ties. Presenting a united front to the materialism of the age, resentful of the claims of the realists, they self-consciously proclaimed themselves the champions of Ideality in literature. Their influence was so persuasive that when their control over editors and publishers was broken by the writers of the newer generation, the naturalistic revolt was the more violent because they had held it in check for more than a quarter of a century.

At the center of the group were five close friends—Stoddard, Taylor, Boker, Aldrich, and Stedman. They had made their way up together, and during the early years in New York they were constant companions. They praised one another in their correspondence and occasional verse; they reviewed one another, dedicated books to one another, and cajoled editors to help along their common cause. Surrounding them were a dozen writers, obedient to the same canons of criticism and allied to them through friendship.

Their common denominator was Richard Henry Stoddard. New England born, the son of a sailor, as a boy and young man he was scarred by a poverty which left him the least sophisticated of their company. Not until he was over fifty could he support himself completely by writing. The meeting place of their company—"the band," as they called themselves—was Stoddard's house at the northeast corner of Fourth Avenue and Tenth Street. His ardor and sympathy and the critical acumen of his moody wife, whose forgotten novels show her to have been gifted with an imagination finer than that of any member of the group, were the ties that drew them to Dick and Lizzie.

The first to join Stoddard was Bayard Taylor, eventually the most widely known of their company. Taylor's first fame had come when he reported in *Views A-foot* (1846) how he made the European grand tour on less than five hundred dollars. His ambition was to be a great poet, and his published verse eventually filled a dozen volumes. But his insatiable public wanted from him only new accounts of exotic lands. In twenty years' time he surveyed the world. Between excursions he wrote three creditable novels on social themes, built himself a lavish house at his native Kennett Square, near Philadelphia, and served as secretary of legation at St. Petersburg. His friends could not have been surprised when, at the moment of his greatest triumph as newly appointed Minister to Germany, the body which ambition had pushed beyond endurance refused to obey his will any longer, and he died at fifty-three.

Even closer to Taylor than Stoddard was the handsome, aristocratic millionaire, George H. Boker, whose house at 1720 Walnut Street was the Philadelphia rendezvous of the group. Each moved gracefully in the company of European diplomats and writers. Boker had the means to indulge his connoisseurship of good living; Taylor did not have the means, but he lived well all the same and sometimes let Boker lend him the money. Less feverishly active than Taylor's, Boker's life was a crowded and useful one, in business, in literature, in the affairs of his native city, and in diplomacy.

Thomas Bailey Aldrich, the Tom Bailey of his *Story of a Bad Boy* (1870), was destined for Harvard, but his father's death forced him to try business in New York. Deserting Pearl Street for journalism, he flocked with the Bohemians at Pfaff's restaurant in the basement of 647 Broadway. Though he soon repudiated these early companionships, the attenuations of Boston life never effaced his early dandyism. Safely in New England in 1865, he was glad to forget the stridencies of New York; he wondered that he had got out with his English tolerably correct. The act was symbolic: he would be withdrawing the rest of his life—from his editorship of the *Atlantic,* from Boston, even, to the Maine seacoast and to the indolence of travel.

New Yorkers spent the month of October, 1859, laughing over "The Diamond Wedding," a poem in the *Tribune* which satirized the well advertised vulgarities of a courtship in what was called society. The poem brought the young poet, Edmund Clarence Stedman, the threat of a duel and a lawsuit, but it also made him a member of the band. Taylor, meeting him in the *Tribune* offices, invited him to the house which he and Stoddard were sharing. The next year, through Stoddard's connivance, Scribner's issued Stedman's first collection of verse. In time he would become the member of the group whose criticism most thoroughly expressed their ideals. He would evangelize for them in Philistia itself, for Stedman earned his living in Wall Street, and his contemporaries thought it a wonderful thing that a poet could also be a broker.

Around this loyal band of five, who thought and felt as one, must be grouped their outriders, if one is to gauge their influence. It is indicative of their early prestige that the Southern poet, Paul Hamilton Hayne, sought them out by correspondence in the late sixties in order that he might find his way back into the society of writers. As Hayne came into their circle, Thomas Buchanan Read, now remembered only for his "Sheridan's Ride," dropped out. By the late fifties he had forsaken poetry for portrait painting and wrote his friends condescendingly from London, where Patmore undid him by declaring that his "Closing Scene" was superior to Gray's "Elegy" and where the Brownings sat to him. In contrast, William Winter was their most faithful adherent. During the forty years he was dramatic critic on the *Tribune* he preached their law against the heresies of Ibsen. Exiled in California and later in Ohio, Edward Rowland Sill, who would not let editors print his name under his poems, reached Eastward for the advice of Aldrich: "I have no friendly sage at hand to help me judge of my things. . . . So I have to send and trouble you." Richard Watson Gilder, editor of the *Century,* 1881–1909, must be counted in this company. So should Louise Chandler Moulton, Boston poetess and dealer in discreet literary gossip, and Richard Grant White, a gentleman always, and a critic occasionally. This is only the beginning of the roll. The lesser names, or shall we say, the names of the less well known, the curious may find in the 1,292 pages which the official biography of Stedman requires to tell the story of his literary friendships.

The members of the band of five and their satellites were sure that they represented the continuing tradition in poetry and criticism, yet they saw that the Civil War was a great divide separating the older New England generation from theirs. In their efforts to renew the tradition and keep its aims high, they felt they were contending with the depravity of a public which for ten years had been fed on the literature of sensation and propaganda generated by the war. They had also to make their way against the continued popularity of Longfellow, Holmes, and Whittier, who still charmed but were now, so they said, "running in grooves."

Their attitude toward these elder poets is ambivalent. They were tied to them by many acts of kindness received at their hands. Aldrich acknowledged that Longfellow made him a poet. Stedman wrote Whittier in 1890: "You have put your hands upon my head and blessed me." Taylor was grateful to Lowell for having been the first to give his poetry respectful criticism. Even Stoddard, who occasionally got out of line and wrote disparagingly of his elders (the band was distressed by his irreverent review of Lowell's *Under the Willows*), remembered the day when Hawthorne received him, an unknown young poet, and took him up to himself as an equal and a friend.

In the band's relations with Lowell one begins to see that there were flaws in this filial regard. They submitted meekly enough to his epistolary lectures, and time and again they humbly accepted honors first offered to him: Taylor in 1876, when he took the commission of the Centennial Ode after Lowell (as well as Bryant, Longfellow, Holmes, and Whittier) had refused it; Stedman in 1891, when he delivered the first series of Turnbull Lectures on poetry at Johns Hopkins in place of Lowell who had declined. But as their reputations increased, we can see from angry outbursts in their letters that they chafed under this gentle domination by their elders—all except Aldrich, of course, who was, as he said, if not genuine Boston, at least "Boston-plated."

This determination to assume their rightful place is evident also in their attitude toward their English contemporaries. They believed that at last poetry and fiction were on the same level in the two countries. They accepted the friendship of English writers with no trace of humility or bluster. Not even Aldrich who idled around Europe in his last years had anything of the expatriate about him. Though they spoke constantly of the difficulty of their fight, they never felt, as did some of their later disciples, that it would be lost and that escape from American vulgarity was the only possible retreat.

Without possessing George W. Curtis' zeal for reform or Henry Adams' cosmic insight, they were appalled by the dislocations of American society. The holy show the *arrivistes* made of themselves from Nob Hill to Newport, the antics of what Stedman called the "champagne aristocracy," the pretentiousness of its Fifth Avenue *palazzi,* its toadying to bogus titles of nobility, moved them to oppose to this vulgarity the ideal world of their poetry. Economically illiterate, as most intelligent Americans have been until recently, they could not fathom the changes in the nation's life. Even if they could have followed the sinuous legal line by which, under the Fourteenth Amendment, the sacred American doctrine of individual rights had been twisted into sanction for the unlicensed greed of great corporations, they would have rejected the evidence. They saw nothing incongruous in their friendship with such comparatively civilized plutocrats as Andrew Carnegie and Collis P. Huntington.

They proposed to reduce the fever of the age by means of a poultice of Ideal Poetry. What exactly they meant by the phrase is not easy to say since they used it passionately. All they disliked about the era of Grant they summed up under realism—its materialism, the extravagant rewards it offered men of action, its faith that science would soon answer all questions. From this world of immediate reality poets faithful to their noble calling must try to lure men to the ideal world of the artist's creation. Two stanzas in Boker's *Book of the Dead* sum up their position:

> We poets hang upon the wheel
>   Of Time's advancement; do our most
> To hide his inroads, and reveal
>   The splendors which the world has lost.
>
> Science and Avarice, arm in arm,
>   Stride proudly through our abject time;
> And in their footsteps, wrangling, swarm
>   Their own begotten broods of crime.

What happens in this ideal world? Who inhabit it? Obviously it is not the Platonic heaven of ideas; nor is it a spiritual kingdom, since these poets share in the passive agnosticism of their age. Stoddard, in his "Castle in the Air," locates it within the heart, but shows that he does not mean by his trope the complex consciousness of modern man. It is, evidently, the world of dreams in which the poet's spirit wanders, unfettered from the False and free to seek the (ideally) True. Here we have it. The ideal world of these poets can only be achieved in dreams from which all base desire, all action (except heroic action), all speculation have been purged. Stedman, as usual, most clearly shows us what they were aiming at. Speaking of Tennyson's "Lady of Shalott" and "A Dream of Fair Women," he calls them "those peculiar, delicious, ideal —*intensely ideal* and elevated productions."

When one understands that this is the kind of poetry they desired to write, it is easy to account for certain of their principles and prejudices. Their objection to dialect poetry, for example, is subsumed from their belief that the deeds and words of Harte's gamblers and Kipling's soldiers are not the stuff from which poetic dreams can be distilled. Or consider their stand on sex as a fit subject for poetry. The prevalent notion that they were prudes is, of course, absurd and is derived apparently from the editorial allergies of the squeamish Gilder who was not a charter member of their band. The youthful poetry of all of them is warmer than that of Keats who inspired it. Sex as the naturalists presented it they kept out of their later poetry, but not because they could not "abide carnation" (Boker, according to his biographer's surmise, had three mistresses, *seriatim*). They kept it out because Love's dream but not Love's act is admissible in ideal poetry.

Stedman's discussion of poetry and sex, in his study of Whitman (*Poets of America*), will be found illuminating by any who wish to fathom their view of this troublesome aesthetic problem. We should have to answer Stedman that, in spite of his fine words about the idealization of sex, he reveals an attitude which in the modern view betrays his whole argument. He accuses Whitman of taking away the "sweetness and pleasantness of stolen waters and secret bread. *Furto cuncta magis bella.*" Even to an enlightened Victorian, sex at best was illicit.

The aesthetic aims of the group explain in part such features of their humanism as their excessive idolization of the artist and the decline in their poetry of the earlier romantic enthusiasm for nature. The ideal world of the poet is not revealed to him by contact with nature; it is not the natural world transformed. It obeys its own laws, which are aesthetic. The poet, as the creator of this ideal world which men desperately need as an anodyne to soothe the pain caused by Huxley, Tweed, and Zola, should be cherished by society. The desire of these poets to be useful had something to do, too, with their adherence to what Stedman spoke of as "our Canon—the law of fidelity to form in poetry." They wished to be influential not only in their own time but with posterity; and the "things that have lasted," Aldrich declared, "are perfect in form."

Although the aesthetic principles of the band prevailed by the end of the century, at least in the criticism of poetry, they had not had things entirely their own way in the earlier years. The strongly ethical but witty critical essays of E. P. Whipple lightened the pages of the *North American Review* until his death in 1886. Even though Lowell's last years were largely given up to diplomacy and after-dinner speeches, he wrote criticism in the eighties and most readers would still have considered him the first of American critics. The name of Henry James, Jr., was frequently signed in the seventies and eighties to critical papers, chiefly on French and Russian authors, in the *Atlantic* and the *Nation*. In the camp of the realists, Howells and his Norwegian-born friend H. H. Boyesen, novelist and essayist, kept up a truceless war against the criticism and poetry written by the band.

As the years went by, the connections which the group formed with magazines and publishing houses multiplied until their names were spoken and seen everywhere, and they formed a kind of literary interlocking directorate. In time their influence infiltrated even into the colleges. There the teaching of literature was still preempted by the last of the professors of belles-lettres or had just passed to the alert young "scientific" scholars trained in Germany and determined to substitute for the sweetness of Blair's *Lectures on*

Rhetoric the light of Sievers' *Angelsächsische Grammatik*. None of the band accepted an academic post, though Stedman in particular was wooed by the universities. But they were frequently honored visitors to academic lecture platforms, however, and in the next generation disciples like Woodberry of Columbia, Wendell of Harvard, and van Dyke of Princeton would challenge the philologists on their home ground.

2

Though Edmund Clarence Stedman was by no means a great critic he uniquely represents his generation and may here speak for it. His industry was prodigious. Despite the financial upheavals of his Wall Street life and the hypochondria which often kept him from attempting still huger tasks, Stedman signed his name so frequently to long reviews and thick books of criticism that there was no escaping his opinions. By constant study he became really learned in English and American literary history and in Greek poetry. Most unusual of his qualifications were his catholicity of taste and his courage. If his enthusiasms were rather too numerous, they were usefully contagious. Many readers were persuaded by his gusto to a just view of Poe and to an acceptance, at least, of Swinburne and Whitman.

Stedman developed for himself a set of critical principles that were, if not very original or profound, at least consistent and workable. He adhered to them in *Victorian Poets* (1875) and *Poets of America* (1885). His two poetry collections which served as companions to these works, the immensely popular *Victorian Anthology* (1895) and *American Anthology* (1900), were made with these principles as the guide. After several partial attempts at definition, he stated his principles fully in *The Nature and Elements of Poetry* (1892).

Stedman's eclectic method at first diverts the reader of his *Victorian Poets* from the fact that it was written to amplify, by illustration, his poetic beliefs. He liked to call himself a judicial or philosophical critic, and such he was, in the main. But since he was eclectic in his methods as well as in his ideas, he moves vigorously from the discussion of the historical background of literary figures to impressionistic rhapsodies stimulated by their work. Though he shifts his method constantly, he keeps his eye on his main objective, the illustration of his theories.

The book was of slow growth. Stedman summarized the story of it:

This book grew out of a study of R. H. Stoddard's "Late English Poets" [an anthology]—a review of which I contributed, at Mr. Lowell's request, to the *North American Review* in 1865 or '66. Five years later I made the study of Tennyson and Theocritus (see Chapter VI) which appeared in the *Atlantic Monthly*. The interest excited by it led me to write the other essays, mostly for *Scribner's Monthly*, which I afterwards revised and collected in "Victorian Poets." The *prefix "Victorian" had not previously become familiar.*

Stedman stated in a letter to Theodore Watts that his real purpose in both the *Victorian Poets* and *Poets of America* was "to give the author's *views* and *canons of poetry* and the *poetic art*, and to study a *poetic era* and *poetic temperaments.*"

Stedman's tact and ingenuity were abundantly needed in writing *Poets of America*. Holmes, Lowell, and Whittier were still alive; Bryant, Emerson, and Longfellow, only recently dead. Though partisans faced him on all sides, he contrived to write a book which pleased his generation and survives in ours. He wished to demonstrate to Americans by means of his book that our ideal and intellectual progress, which was gaining speed, warranted less deference to Europe, and to assert, against such critics as Lowell and Richard Grant White, the "distinctive national character" of our poetry.

As in the *Victorian Poets,* Stedman applied his canons throughout the work; yet in contrast with the earlier volume there is much less technical criticism and more discussion of the "poetic temperament and the conditions that affect it; more of poetry as the music of emotion, faith, aspiration, and all the chords of life." Stedman may have pursued this method in order not to be too explicit in condemning certain works of poets who were admired in every American home. The reader is fascinated, nevertheless, in following the turns by which he managed to say what he believed, even when the truth was likely to shock. If we peel off his elaborate praise of the elder poets as kind neighbors and good citizens, we come, time and again, on the hard core of a valid judgment. In his essays on Poe and Whitman, Stedman was at his best, since, as a strategist, he preferred attack to defense. To praise Poe required some courage but no magnanimity on his part since Poe, like Swinburne or Rossetti, was to him a poet of the Ideal. His generous criticism of Whitman shows more clearly than anything else he wrote his superiority to the other critics of his time.

As has been said, Stedman's criticism of poets and schools was always guided by the principles he had worked out for himself. These he tentatively set forth in three systematic essays: "Elements of the Art of Poetry," "Genius," and "What Is Criticism." *

When in 1891 he was asked to be the first Turnbull Lecturer in poetry at Johns Hopkins, he took on the labor of preparing *Nature and Elements of*

---

* *Galaxy*, I, 408–415 (July 1, 1866); *New Princeton Review*, II, 145–167 (Sept., 1886); *Epoch*, I, 108–109, 131–132 (Mar. 11 and 18, 1887).

Poetry (1892) as a chance to do battle in the war of the Idealists against the corrupting influences of science, realism, and journalism. Poets are born with special insights and should rule by divine right. The age of economics and physics and prose fiction had forgotten this and should be made to acknowledge poetic sovereignty. The volume is not only a recapitulation of Stedman's leading ideas on aesthetics, but a history of poetry and poetic theory as well. Always inclined to overwrite, he felt the occasion to be so momentous that he sought to cover every conceivable idea and argument as thoroughly as he knew how. But when the digressions and excessive illustration are stripped away, the thesis of the book stands as the one complete defense of literary Idealism which the age produced.

What it owes to the Platonic tradition in criticism and to Poe and Emerson especially is evident throughout, but Stedman's awareness of how far on the defensive he and his friends had been driven by the new forces operating in men's lives compelled him to modify the tradition. He saw clearly that the discoveries in the physical, biological, and psychological sciences and the new positivism based on them had sapped the position of the Idealist in art as well as religion. Poetry's chief enemies were the realists who had capitulated to the spirit of the age. In his essay on "Genius," written five years earlier, Stedman had tried to take them into his camp by the genial method of convicting the best of them—Howells in particular—of unwittingly seeking the "ideal which is the truest truth, the absolute realism," which the poets also sought. But this maneuver by transvaluing values had not succeeded. In these lectures, therefore, he tried a different attack by which he might destroy the realists from a superior position.

The crux of Stedman's argument is found in his chapters on "Beauty" and "Truth." Beauty is ever the object of the poet's search—and, as well, of the transcendentalist's, the impressionist's, and the realist's. Beauty exists, though it cannot be measured: in the mind of the poet it is a "quality of his imagined substance." By an argument which owes much to Emerson, Stedman proceeds to equate beauty with truth, of which it is the "unveiled shining countenance." All natural things "make for" beauty, and the poet, having insight into the soul of truth (i.e., "natural things") expresses the beautiful. But a given truth, to be beautiful, must be complete. The fallacy of the realist is that he deals only with things that are seen; the rest which remains to complete the truth, he ignores. Hence he can never produce beauty.

At this point in his argument Stedman introduces an idea which shows how far he had come from his early Poesque aestheticism and the degree to which he had unconsciously yielded to the realistic and utilitarian spirit of the times. In essence his next argument is an assertion of the functionalism which has dominated American aesthetics from Emerson and Greenough (whose theories of art are more impressive than his sculpture) to Louis Sullivan and Frank Lloyd Wright. He concedes that beauty does accord somewhat with use; the essence of beauty, in fact, lies in conformity to the law and fitness of things. But Stedman draws back from a complete acceptance of the functionalist theory of art in time to save his idealism. His compromise here is instructive. That ideal beauty "lies in adaptation of the spirit to the circumstances" is true, but this adaptation need not always be to the "apparent material exigencies." It is a function of ideal needs rather than of mundane necessities.

Stedman's Turnbull Lectures must have comforted those who wished to believe the realists could be beaten back and the supremacy of poetry, the most ideal and comprehensive of the arts, reasserted. His own confidence that this could be done was supported by his belief that a new age of ideal poetry was about to begin. Genius, he had tried to make Howells understand, is a fact; the spontaneous poet is born when least expected. The poetry he brings into the world is of the highest kind, heroic in tone and dramatic in form. Stedman was sure that the signs indicated the advent in his time of this kind of poetry. He discerned it, remarkably enough, in the work of Swinburne and Whitman. He found it significant, too, that our poets had ceased to be landscape painters and were becoming figure painters, turning to "human life with its throes and passions and activity."

Stedman's hierophantic attitude toward poetry, which he shared, of course, with such Victorian critics as Arnold and Pater, ultimately repelled rather than attracted readers. In his zeal to claim all for poetry, he lost the ground he hoped to reclaim from the realists. The irony is that having made, as he thought, generous, even dangerous concessions to the claims of science and utility, he and his kind should have been reviled by the next generation as timid, genteel, and reactionary.

Though Richard Henry Stoddard wielded influence equal to Stedman's, his contemporary reputation as a critic is now difficult to understand. The reader who looks through the mass of his introductions to anthologies, scans his numerous literary biographies and his reviews will come on little which he can call criticism. In the preface to his most substantial volume of literary essays, *Under the Evening Lamp* (1892), Stoddard acknowledges that in these studies of authors who were "worsted by misfortune" he was more interested in their lives than in their writings.

Stoddard was chiefly responsible for the great popularity in the last quarter of the century of decently intimate pictures of poets and novelists at home. N. P. Willis was our first dealer in the table talk of literary celebrities, and the form into which much of this sort of writing was cast had been devised by the authors of the sumptuous *Homes of American Authors* (1854). Though he did not invent the "pilgrimage" to the "shrine" of the man of letters, Stoddard made the appetite which craved this sort of thing. His Bric-a-brac Series, anthologies of reminiscences of writers, sold over 60,000 copies in eighteen months.

When Stoddard occasionally ventured beyond anecdote and platitude, as a critic he could be disconcertingly incisive. He never publicly deflated any of his poet friends; he was a faithful member of the *Brüderschaft*. In his letters, however, one comes on acute judgments of his contemporaries, such as these remarks about Taylor's verse.

When [his poems] are only fairish or middling, they are always well written, and in their way, faultless. You will see his "Sunken Treasures" in Put[nam's] for Septr. I can't find any verbal fault with that piece, but somehow it don't leave any marked impression on my mind. It seems *built*; it wants simplicity; it is more artificial than natural. The artifice of rhetoric is second nature with Bayard.*

Such bull's-eye criticism makes one believe Stoddard could have taken the palm from Lowell and Stedman if he had cared to be a public critic.

3

Though the last of the chief defenders of Ideality had died by 1910, a group of their heirs carried the tradition into the age of Dreiser, Mencken, and Anderson. Three of them were professors of literature: George Edward Woodberry at Columbia, Barrett Wendell at Harvard, and Henry van Dyke at Princeton. The fourth member of the group, Hamilton Wright Mabie, literary editor of the *Outlook*, whose inspirational messages on ideals and literature comforted hundreds of audiences up and down the country, served the new naturalistic generation as a symbol of everything from which they scurrilously dissented.

Twenty years before his death, in 1930, Woodberry felt that the cause was lost. Toward the end he spent as much time as he could in his favorite Italy, venturing occasionally into the Western wilderness to lecture at the summer sessions of various state universities. Not even the admiration of the large circle of his one-time students reconciled him to modern America.

At first glance Woodberry's criticism seems to echo that of Stedman, Stoddard, and the others, but important differences appear. He worships beauty, as do they, but its pursuit eventually so obsessed him that only in the Greek past or the Italian present could he find it. The war which Stedman made on realism had been a vigorous counterrevolution. The plaintiveness of

* Quoted in Schultz, *Unpublished Letters of Bayard Taylor* (1937), pp. vi–vii.

Woodberry's protest shows how much narrower is his humanism than that of the earlier Idealists. In his criticism, refinement rather than Ideality is the key word.

In his attitude toward American literature Woodberry also stands apart from his predecessors. His first important work was his collaboration with Stedman in their edition of Poe, a by-product of which was his own biography of the poet (1885; revised 1909), and he had also written biographical studies of Hawthorne (1902) and Emerson (1907). But as time passed he grew doubtful of the status of our writers. As his disgust with the materialism of his native land increased, he spoke bitterly of the future of the arts in America. It was bad enough to have to admit that what we had produced was merely a backflow from Europe. Prospects for the future were even worse: they were rooted in Mark Twain and Missouri.

Immured by his Harvard professorship, Barrett Wendell saved himself from Woodberry's melancholy over the state of our national culture. A more robust spirit, he hedged himself from the new vulgarity by means of his New England lineage, his Tory prejudices, and his wit. Unlike Woodberry, who as a young man shared the nativism of the Idealist critics, Wendell at no time in his life thought very highly of the accomplishment of American writers. His depreciatory *A Literary History of America* (1900) tries them at the bar of the tradition of English letters and finds them guilty of so many literary crimes that the reader wonders why he wished to write the book at all. In the nineties he was already quite reconciled to the "provincial obscurity" into which his class and kind were vanishing; it cost him little pain to observe twenty-five years later that "this age of ours [in England as well as America] grows literally obscene—thrusting into sight everywhere the foulnesses which are better ignored."

The other two members of this group of latter-day disciples never gave up. Mabie rallied the supporters of the waning cause by overpraising his friends. His method of dealing with the new naturalistic literature was to ignore it. To the end, Dr. van Dyke of New York's Brick Presbyterian Church and Princeton, never missed a chance for a scrap—ecclesiastical, political, or literary. At the age of seventy-eight, when the international blue ribbon was pinned on the triumphant naturalists by the award of the Nobel Prize for Literature to Sinclair Lewis, van Dyke was ready for one fight more. Addressing the Germantown Business Men's Luncheon Club, he deplored the act as a backhanded compliment to America and so gave Lewis a chance to tell off the Idealists in his acceptance speech at Stockholm, by declaring that the American Academy of Arts and Letters, which the Idealists had founded and still controlled, represented only Henry Wadsworth Longfellow. Dr. van Dyke hit back, but the ring was empty.

4

None of the poets among the band and their associates—and nearly all of them attempted poetry—so ardently longed for literary fame as Bayard Taylor. From his correspondence one can see that he thought constantly of his "place" as a poet. His works are "slowly gaining ground"; his biography is wanted for a German *Konversations-Lexikon* ("That seems almost like fame, doesn't it?"); his appointment as Minister to Germany shows, at last, that "the world *does* appreciate earnest endeavor."

Taylor's instinctive doubts of his poetic talent, which these constant references to his reputation reveal, do him credit as a critic. Despite the novelty of his "California Ballads" and the popularity of his gushing *Poems of the Orient* (1854) and the hopeful labor he bestowed on *The Picture of St. John* (1866), despite the many poems in praise of the poet's calling, he was a verse-maker, as Stoddard said, and not a poet. His lines will not stick in the mind. Invariably, as one reads, a tolerable passage sinks to bathos. His gift for parody induced echoes of other poems in his verse. Even the "Bedouin Song," which some provincial soprano is carolling at this moment, is the offspring of Shelley's "Indian Serenade." It is significant that Taylor, unlike his friend Aldrich, rejected or revised little of his early poetry, but carried most of it along into later editions

Of all his volumes of verse, Taylor's *Home Pastorals* (1875) alone is intrinsically as well as historically valuable. Here, for once, he lays aside his usual bardic disguises and speaks movingly of his predicament as man and artist, clear to him at last; the clearer perhaps because he had just finished his translation of Goethe's great metaphysical poem. Sated with visions, he pictures himself as one who wishes to come home after wandering over the world. His predicament is sharper than that of other American poets who, starved in the Present, are weary of singing only the Future. His Quaker neighbors, whose lives he wishes to poetize, are suspicious of him and his work. He cannot really be at home among them. Here, as in every other corner of America, "the form of Art abides as a stranger."

The *Home Pastorals* also reveals the struggle of a typical American intellectual of the time to find a tenable philosophical position. Taylor had earlier subscribed to the conventional romantic Nature worship, but Nature, the "indifferent goddess," no longer inspires him. He is glutted with physical beauty and Man is now more to him than the suns and rains and "the plastic throes of the ages." He repudiates boldly the various Victorian religious compromises and is satisfied to be shadowed by the Angel of Unfaith. These themes he carries over into his ambitious Faustian drama, *Prince Deukalion* (1878), in which the Prince and Pyrrha, guided by Prometheus, reject in turn the solutions of Medusa (Roman Catholicism) and Urania (Science), to accept the doctrine contained in the following lines:

> Seek not to know Him; yet aspire
> As atoms towards the central fire!
> Not lord of race is He, afar,—
> Of Man, or Earth, or any star,
> But of the inconceivable All.

These two poems show that the poetical maturity Taylor had longed for was at last evincing itself. He died a month after the publication of *Prince Deukalion.*

The kind of fame Taylor had so wistfully sought was his, actually, in December, 1870, when his translation of *Faust,* Part I, was issued by Fields, Osgood & Company in a volume uniform with Longfellow's *Dante* and Bryant's *Iliad,* the second part appearing in March, 1871. This great moment of his career was marked by Fields' ceremonial dinner at which the coveted praise of his New England masters was cordially given. There was, indeed, little dissent from their opinion that Taylor had made a handsome contribution to American culture. In Germany it was said that he had assimilated to himself the German "mode of thinking and feeling." Taylor's *Faust* still leads the procession of forty-four translations of Part I, and sixteen of Part II, and seems certain of permanence, in spite of passages which are neither German nor English in style and of occasional misinterpretations of Goethe's meaning.

Taylor's devotion to *Faust* was so great that without effort he came to know by heart almost all of it. A man without academic training, he had mastered the Goethe literature, extensive even at that date, and had made "lateral studies" to complete his comprehension of the drama. He industriously consulted German scholars and men who had known the poet. He was the first enthusiast in England or America to comprehend Goethe's intention in the second part of *Faust,* which even G. H. Lewes, his foremost English biographer and *Dolmetscher,* had called "an elaborate mistake." Particularly eager to counteract the prejudices created by the two "stupid translations" then existing, Taylor analyzed in his Introduction the development of Part II act by act, and correctly asserted the unity of the poem.

Taylor discussed his theory of translation in his prefaces to the two parts. Sensitively aware of how much of the *Stimmung* of the poem is communicated by its varied rhythms, he set himself the task of reproducing Goethe's meters. Though he did not always succeed, there is no doubt that his bold attempt gives his version scope and weight lacking in the work of his many rivals. Since he had wisely relied less on his intuitions of Goethe's meaning and more on the painstaking search for the exact word, no critic, paraphrasing Dr. Bentley, could tell him his *Faust* was a "pretty poem" but not Goethe. The translation is not a great poem, but it is still after seventy years as much of Goethe as a reader with small German can hope to have.

Like his friend Taylor, George Boker longed for poetic fame. "My theatrical success I never valued," he wrote Taylor. "I had not, nor have I, any ambition to become a mere playwright. . . . If I could not be acknowledged as a poet, I had no further desire, and no further active concern in literature." His poetry never caught on with the public, though one volume, *Poems of the War* (1864), was popular, fittingly enough, since he had founded the motherhouse of the Union League Clubs and had exhorted his fellow poets to turn propagandists for the Northern cause. His longer poems, like "The Song of the Earth," "The Ivory Carver," and the autobiographical *Book of the Dead* (1882), written to answer the slanderers of his father, exhibit the defect most characteristic of the minor poetry of his time. The form revolves like the musical phrases repeated in the groove of a victrola record when the needle is stuck. The images change but the metaphorical dimension does not expand.

Taylor was the only one of Boker's friends who knew he had written a sequence of 313 love sonnets, probably intended for publication but not issued in his lifetime. Together with fifty-eight printed in his *Plays and Poems, II* (1856), the first 282 of these sonnets commemorate a prolonged and passionate affair with a "golden-brown beauty well known in his native city." The remaining thirty-one sonnets were inspired by two subsequent love affairs.

As it was Boker's misfortune that he wished to write Elizabethan dramas in a most un-Elizabethan time, so it will always be the fate of these love sonnets to invite comparison with Shakespeare's sequence. The echoes are troublesome. Occasionally, too, the modes of Victorian love-making interfere with one's pleasure in reading, although it is possible that these conventions may in time seem no more quaint than Petrarchan conceits. Yet unfinished and imitative as they are, these sonnets surpass anything written by the poets of Boker's generation. Sufficiently the artist to distinguish emotion from its communication, he worked to achieve the *parlante* quality which the sonnet form demands.

Of the poets of his generation Aldrich was the most conscientious artist. We may now find the emotions displayed in his verses decorative and their inspiration trivial, but we must admit that the trivia are his own. The shades of Chatterton and Keats, Tennyson and Hafiz loom over the early poems, and a devotion to Herrick is continuously evident in them, but Aldrich worked away from these masters to a recognizable idiom of his own. He eliminated the Victorian lumber from his lines and he is seldom guilty of the bathos of Taylor or the sentimental vulgarity of Stoddard. An exception must be made, of course, for the enormously popular "Ballad of Babie Bell," the tale of whose ethereal birth and gratuitous death made strong men in Western barrooms break down and weep, remembering home and mother But then no nineteenth century poet could be trusted with a baby.

Though Aldrich's forms and subjects are traditional, his interest in impressions conveyed through the clear image anticipates the later style of the Imagists of the generation of 1910. Either because he shrank from indecently exposing himself in his verse or because he was seldom deeply stirred, Aldrich worked as they did, on the surface. Even when the reader suspects the mood may be personal he finds it hidden behind a Persian or Italian or medieval pseudonymity.

From the beginning Aldrich rigorously educated himself to be a poet of the Ideal. His first volume, *The Bells* (1855), swoons and pulses with extravagant emotion. Aldrich never reprinted anything from this volume. From the next, *The Course of True Love Never Did Run Smooth* (1858), a perfumed tale of a Caliph who permits Giaffer to marry the Princess Abbassa but not to enjoy her, he saved a few of the chaster lines. This process of rejection and revision continued relentlessly from volume to volume until the canon was established in 1897.

What survives of Aldrich's poetry now that Time has completed his own winnowing? Not the picture poems and idylls which the taste of his age so much approved. Nor the society verse which his friends admired: "Pepita" and "In an Atelier" seem to this post-Freudian generation arch rather than daring. There is left a handful of lyrics of the kind the poet especially labored to perfect, the quatrains he called "Footnotes"—

> Four-line epics one might hide
> In the hearts of roses.

There is a place, too, for three fine elegiac poems on the Civil War dead: "December," "Spring in New England," and a sonnet, "By the Potomac." Aldrich thought topical poems were not worth the effort because they would not survive!

It is significant that most of Aldrich's remarks on the poetry of his time are condemnatory. When he became editor of the *Atlantic* (1881) he wrote to Stedman: "Our old singers have pretty much lost their voices, and the new singers are so few! My ear has not caught any new note since 1860." By 1900 he had grown completely despairing of the art. The vogue of dialect poetry and especially the enthusiasm for the unspeakable Kipling ("a narsty little brute") had completely vitiated all literary taste. The demand for mediocrity had given America a ragtime literature as well as a ragtime art. Worst of all, the dark night of realism was closing in and those who were still faithful to Beauty were twilight poets, groping alone.

> The mighty Zolaistic Movement now
> Engrosses us—a miasmatic breath
> Blown from the slums. We paint life as it is,
> The hideous side of it, with careful pains,
> Making a god of the dull Commonplace.
> —"Funeral of a Minor Poet"

5

Despite Aldrich's gloomy view of the state of poetry, contemporary readers and critics were in the main pleased with his *Friar Jerome's Beautiful Book* and Stedman's *Blameless Prince,* Stoddard's *The Book of the East* and Hayne's *Legends and Lyrics* and spoke of their verses as noble and elevated. One heretic in their midst, Elizabeth Stoddard, the "Pythoness" as the band called her, penetrated the grace and rhetoric of their poems to the emptiness within. Boker records a session in July, 1874, when Lizzie exploded the terrifying truth: "George, you, Dick, Bayard, Stedman, Aldrich, Read, the whole lot of you youngsters, have all been dreary failures as poets. . . . It was not time that you lacked . . . but poetic ability."

The situation was more complex than even she, wise woman though she was, could comprehend. It should be plain from what has been said in this chapter, that the band held firmly to a set of standards which permitted them to write only "ideal" poetry. They did not suspect how completely this literary asceticism had devitalized their imaginative powers and cut them off from the modern world. So disgusted were they with realists in verse like Harte and Riley that they suppressed what talent of this sort they had. Classical themes they had grown weary of. Because they were humanists and city men, they found little to inspire them in nature. Small wonder that Stedman, writing to Winter in 1873 about the discouragements of their literary generation, should conclude by saying: "You may be sure that whatever failure such men as you experience grows out of the *only* difficulty in our literary life—want of *themes* suited to *our* tastes and aspirations."

Inflexible in their belief that only the traditional forms of verse were suitable vehicles for the few themes which they found worthy, they were little interested in the experiments in free forms carried out in their time by Arnold, Whitman, Emily Dickinson, and Stephen Crane. Their reverence for the great masters made them deplore the vogue of ballads and villanelles and the preoccupation with form for form's sake which this vogue encouraged. All of them, except Boker, repudiated the romantic introspection of their early poetry, preferring, as Stoddard put it, "objective creation to subjective meditation in verse."

Forced deeper and deeper into a blind alley by these exclusions and rejections, their imaginative scope narrowed until their poems became merely daydreams. For polite readers to whom poetry was an institution to be maintained this dream poetry sufficed. To earnest folk perplexed in the extreme by the dilemmas of the age and to the more stalwart who were exhilarated by the prospects opened up by science and the material progress promised by the Corliss engine and the dynamo, their poems were, what Lanier called them, "dandy kickshaws of verse."

51. PILGRIMS' RETURN

THE historians have had much to say about the influence of the idea of the West on the American mind and imagination. They have neglected an equally powerful force operative during the years between 1850 and 1900, a force which, incidentally, helped to maintain the dominion of the "defenders of Ideality" in poetry and criticism. During this half-century Americans discovered Europe, with results which were culturally quite as significant as the discovery of the West.

In ever increasing numbers travelers returned home to record what they had seen and felt in the Old World. From this migration came a superlative travel literature and a new type of fiction, the "international novel." Ultimately this exodus was also responsible for a shift in attitude which, on the eastern seaboard and with the more literate classes, transformed the chauvinism of the forties into the cosmopolitanism of the 1900's.

The causes of this great exodus are not obscure. There was, of course, more money and more leisure for travel. After the *Great Western,* marvel of the age, made its first voyage in 1838, the terrors of the Atlantic were converted into pleasures, even for the invalids on their way to European spas. The revolutions of 1848 drew patriotic Americans to Italy and France that they might be on hand when monarchical Europe was republicanized. Though their hopes were betrayed, liberals continued to arrive in order to learn why the revolutions had been abortive. The various European countries wooed American tourists by providing them with special objectives for their holiday, such as the Great Exhibition at the Crystal Palace in 1851 and the Paris exhibitions of 1855 and 1867.

More powerful than any other persuasive were the books written by the pioneer generation of travelers. Irving's *Sketch Book* (1819) and *Bracebridge Hall* (1822), though they imaged an England which scarcely existed in actuality, inspired his countrymen to search for it. N. P. Willis' *Pencillings by the Way* (1844), his collected travel letters contributed to the New York *Mirror,* enchanted the subscribers to the five hundred newspapers which made excerpts from them. Longfellow's *Hyperion* (1839), Irving's *Conquest of Granada* (1829), and more factual but equally influential books, such as Silliman's *A Journal of Travels in England, Holland and Scotland* (1810), induced thousands of Americans to go in quest of the holy places of Europe these pioneers had so eloquently described. In the time of Irving and Willis the casual tourist, who was abroad chiefly to absorb as much as he could in a short time, was the exception. After 1850 he is the type.

2

Few Americans in the fifties went to Europe without a sense of the momentousness of their journey. They often apologized for leaving home, knowing that many of their countrymen believed that one's Americanism could be corrupted by foreign travel. It was possible to enjoy Europe too well, and a good American had to be on his guard. W. W. Story, an early expatriate, spent the winter of 1849–1850 in Berlin, which seemed to many Americans the most nearly like Boston of European cities, as a kind of expiation for his excessive enjoyment of Italy. As Henry James says of this visit, he had not yet burnt his ships; "he was to saturate himself . . . but he was somehow, by the same stroke, and in some interest to be felt better than named, to be protected against that saturation." Few of the apologists were so philosophical as C. A. Bartol in *Pictures of Europe, Framed in Ideas* (1855), which is more a transcendentalist treatise on the theory of travel than a book about Europe, but invariably, at some point in his narrative, the traveler in these earlier years reassured his readers that he had come home undamaged.

There was much to disapprove of in Europe: the power of the Roman Church, the beggars, the indifference to social reform of the British upper-classes, the evils of the land system in the Papal states, the lax morals of Parisians and Florentines, the absence of a "go-ahead" spirit. Some patriotic travelers were so disturbed by what they saw that they considered it their duty to indict Europe. Julia Ward Howe, for instance, decided that even art study hardly justified a prolonged residence abroad. "The Prometheus of the present day is needed rather to animate statues than to make them."

The professional humorists warned their countrymen against losing their native common sense among the ruins and becoming monarchists or aesthetes. The devotees of Artemus Ward, Petroleum V. Nasby, and Samantha Allen, of J. M. Bailey (the Danbury News Man) and Mr. Dunn Browne (of the Springfield *Republican*) were eager to hear such undeludable Americans inform against Europe. Unfortunately the calculated candor of the humorists seldom goes beyond a scornful paragraph on the battered noses of the Elgin Marbles or a tempered insult aimed at the British royal family. Their books are, on the whole, as mild as milk, possibly because they had a profitable public in England. Two or three, Locke's *Nasby in Exile* (1882) for example, comment shrewdly on European manners and morals, but the only masterpiece of this genre is Mark Twain's *The Innocents Abroad*.

After the failure of the revolutions in the mid-century made Americans less sure that democracy was predestined to triumph everywhere and after our own Civil War had sobered their chauvinism, they were more open to the persuasions of travelers like E. C. Benedict, who asked them to believe, in his *A Run Through Europe* (1860), that an acquaintance with the Old World "must be of great value to our national character . . . letting some of the gas out of our conceit, and some of the hyperbole out of our vanity." Readers of G. S. Hillard's *Six Months in Italy* (1853), the most widely quoted of all the travel books, were at length ready to submit to his advice that they must leave notions of progress behind, and "learn to look on churchmen and church rites as a pageant."

The gradual aesthetic education of Americans during these earlier years is fascinating to watch. What they knew of European art they had learned from line drawings, engravings, bad copies in oil of Raphael and Guido, plaster casts of statuary in a few sepulchral galleries. Ruskin had taught them to admire Gothic art and to despise that of the High Renaissance. Some of them debated whether a preoccupation with aesthetic matters was not debilitating. There was always a searching of the conscience when the tourist confronted the nudity of the Venus of the Tribune in the Uffizi and turned to gaze on her even more unabashed sister smiling from Titian's canvas across the room. This cabinet, remarked one traveler, might be called a public boudoir.

No one worked harder to diffuse artistic knowledge in America than James Jackson Jarves, world traveler, editor of the first paper published in Honolulu, art critic, connoisseur, and collector. Jarves is remembered now because he was forced in 1871, because of poverty, to relinquish his magnificent collection of Italian primitives to Yale; but he should be known also as the author of four delightful European travel books (which will be discussed later in this chapter) and for *Art Hints* (1855) and three other pioneer works of this sort notable for their acuteness. In all these books his announced purpose was to convince Americans that their moral and utilitarian prejudices blinded them to what they had gone to Europe to see.

Equally independent are the aesthetic theories and judgments advanced by a Philadelphia amateur, Horace Binney Wallace, whose *Art, Scenery and Philosophy in Europe* was issued posthumously in 1855. One of the first to propose a functional theory of architecture, Wallace discusses in "The Law of the Development of Gothic Architecture," one of the best essays in his book, ideas which are far in advance of his time. In another chapter he describes with great perspicuity the aesthetic effect produced by various European cathedrals, an achievement which is not a little remarkable when one considers how firmly he held to the requirement of functionalism in architecture.

One is likewise interested to watch the progress in aesthetics of certain better known Americans. In all three of his travel books Edward Everett Hale shows an extraordinary open-mindedness. Possessing the usual prejudices in favor of the later Gothic style, he worked his way back, by study and contemplation, until he could enjoy primitive painting and Romanesque and Byzantine art. Hawthorne struggled with art while he was in Italy even though he was often weary and sometimes disgusted. He went back to certain pictures and statues time after time, trying to find—not what his friend Powers, the sculptor, told him was to be found in them—but what he might experience by himself. His *Italian Note Books* show him "improving" day by day. His persistence bore fruit in *The Marble Faun,* whole pages of which are observations from the *Note Books* transformed for the purposes of fiction.

These amateurs, indeed, often returned home better instructed than the scholars and critics whose profession it was to interpret European civilization. Charles Eliot Norton, Harvard's Professor of the History of Art from 1875 to 1898, was, for example, strangely limited by his American prejudices. As friend and disciple of Ruskin, a founder of the Archaeological Institute of America, the School of Classical Studies at Rome, and the *American Journal of Archaeology,* Norton might have been expected to comprehend and treat sympathetically various schools of painting and styles of architecture. Actually few American travelers in Europe were so narrow. His lifelong hatred of Catholic institutions—he once wrote Lowell that he thought he could roast a Franciscan with pleasure and that he would only need a tolerable opportunity to make him stab a Cardinal in the dark—constantly interfered with his aesthetic judgments. With a zeal worthy of a member of the Know-Nothing party (whose principles he approved) he sets forth his detestation of the Roman Church in his early *Notes of Travel and Study in Italy* (1860) and permits it to intrude on his observations about art.

3

There was scarcely a professional writer of this period who did not furnish his public with his impressions of Europe. Grace Greenwood (Sara Jane Lippincott) in *Haps and Mishaps of a Tour in Europe* (1854) satisfied her readers, for whom she was the arbiter in matters of sentiment, with long meditations inspired by famous paintings or historical scenes. Mrs. Stowe, celebrated as the author of *Uncle Tom's Cabin,* described in *Sunny Memories of Foreign Lands* (1854) her royal progress through the drawing rooms of England and the Continent. Bayard Taylor's fate was settled when his *Views A-Foot* (1846), the naïve raptures of a twenty-year-old boy, captivated the nation. Twenty editions were required in the next ten years. Taylor would be fifty before he could cease traveling up and down in the world as a professional weigher and gauger of culture for his countrymen. Year by year he pushed into new lands: Africa, Asia Minor, India, and Japan, the Scandinavian countries, Iceland. "I am led," he wrote, "into these wanderings without my will; it seems to be my destiny."

The less imaginative of the professional writers soon evolved a sort of standard pattern for the travel book. The author must begin with the excitements of the ocean voyage itself and devote at least a portion of a chapter to the thrill, so long anticipated, of setting foot on foreign soil. From this point on he should mix architecture and scenery with comment on philanthropies, skillfully work in a little history cribbed from Murray's guides, taking care to add a touch of sentiment or eloquence when the occasion permitted. If the essay or book required a little padding, it was always possible to retell an old legend or slip in an account of dangers surmounted in crossing the Alps.

Soon there would be interesting deviations from this pattern, but in the fifties and sixties the reader wanted a series of variations on a theme. It did not matter to him that he had read forty descriptions of the hallowed places —Shakespeare's tomb, the Burns country, Warwick Castle, and the Tower of London, the vale of Chamonix, and the Roman Campagna. He listened with delight to any new variations which Edward Everett Hale or Helen Hunt Jackson could compose.

In the sixties this predominantly sentimental approach begins to yield to the kind of book which offers chiefly information and advice. Tourists were in a hurry and they wanted to know how to get over the ground without wasting any time in unprofitable expeditions. The books such determined travelers found most useful were those represented by J. H. B. Latrobe's *Hints for Six Months in Europe* (1869) and C. C. Fulton's *Europe Viewed Through American Spectacles* (1874) which supplied, in addition to 310 double-columned pages of fact, an appendix of "Hints to European Tourists."

Soon the more sophisticated began to shun the spots where their meditations might be disturbed by the rushing hordes to whom such books appealed and fled to haunts whose charms had not yet been defiled. As early as 1852 W. W. Story complained to Lowell, "We must take some untravelled paths which the English have not spoiled, and go into the wildest fastnesses of the Abruzzi, perhaps to Sora." Eugene Benson, whose *Art and Nature in Italy* (1882) is caviar for the élite, traveled to Ferrara not for the sake of Tasso and Lucrezia Borgia whom the vulgar pursued there, but to seek out the work of an obscure painter named Scarscinello [sic]. It was a mistake to let such secrets out. Henry James knew well enough what always happened. Writing in 1903 of W. W. Story's *Vallombrosa* (1881), he lamented that the dense Etrurian coverts to whose secluded beauty Story had unwisely given publicity, would by then be "scarred and dishonoured by the various new contrivances for access without contact and acquaintance without knowledge."

These books unlocking the secret charms of particular regions are sufficiently numerous to constitute a subdivision of travel literature, but the sophisticates who produced them were also responsible for another kind of book. This is the detailed study of some city already repeatedly described but never so minutely nor by a traveler so devoted and so learned. W. W. Story, for example, knew Rome as few Americans have ever known it, and he found in Italy, and in Rome especially, an antidote to the ugliness of the rest of the world. It is not surprising therefore that some of the chapters in his *Roba di Roma* (1862)—on *villeggiature,* on games, ceremonies, and holidays—are unexcelled.

One book of this type, F. Marion Crawford's *Ave Roma Immortalis* (1898), possesses a distinction which almost makes it great. Son of the Italian-trained sculptor Thomas Crawford, convert to Catholicism, after 1883 a resident of Italy, Crawford was in every way fitted to write the perfect book about Rome. Accurate, swift, adroitly planned, heightened in the right places by a careful rhetoric, his *Ave Roma Immortalis* achieves the totality of impression which eluded scores of novices. Crawford's Rome is not the Rome of Garibaldi or of Pio Nono, but his description fulfills the ideal toward which many writers, baffled by the beauty and mystery of the city, had struggled. Here at last the glories of the fourteen "regions" and the immensities of St. Peter's are adequately reduced to words.

Before the century ended, the travel writers had devised yet another sort of book designed for tourists who went to Europe to escape. Too sophisticated to ration their days to the Blue Grotto at Capri and the castle at Heidelberg, and too well traveled to need hints and helps, they were in Europe in search of the picturesque. Stevenson's *Travels with a Donkey in the Cévennes* (1879) had delighted them, and for them the Pennells drew and wrote the series of "pilgrimages" beginning with *A Canterbury Pilgrimage* in 1885. F. Hopkinson Smith in *Gondola Days* (1897) describes the mood of these latter-day travelers.

In this selfish, materialistic, money-getting age, it is a joy to live, if only for a day . . . in a city the relics of whose past are the lessons of our future; whose every canvas, stone, and bronze bear witness to a grandeur, luxury, and taste that took a thousand years to perfect, and will take a thousand years of neglect to destroy.

All that had vexed the first generation of European visitors—ecclesiastical corruption, feudal survivals, filth, indolence—was now dissolved in a glow generated by acceptance. Smith, noting the toppling of jamb and lintel in Venice, is full of thanks to the little devils of rot and decay. They are, he says, really "the guardians of the picturesque."

4

Among the hundreds of Americans who attempted travel books, at least a dozen theorize about what they are doing and strive to give shape and character to their observations. In "Leaves from My Journal in Italy and Elsewhere" * Lowell wrote at length on modern travelers. They see nothing out of sight, are skeptics and doubters, materialists reporting things for other skeptics to doubt still further upon. With every step of the modern tourist "our inheritance of the wonderful is diminished," and year by year more and more of the world gets disenchanted. Lowell's own travel book was written in emulation of the elder navigators to whom the world was a huge wonder horn.

The young George William Curtis, returning from abroad in 1850, sought in his *Nile Notes of a Howadji* (1851) to re-create for his readers—and he soon had a host of them—the "essentially *sensuous,* luxurious, languid and sense-satisfied spirit of Eastern life." No one, he noted, had ever sought to do this. He accomplished his aim so successfully that his family was terribly shocked, especially by his voluptuous description of an Oriental dancer whose style descended from Salome's. The spirit of this book, Curtis wrote to his aggrieved father, is "precisely what I wish it. I would not have it toned down, for I toned it up intentionally."

Several later writers, determined to do more than furnish guidebook information colored intermittently a deep purple, throw a challenge to their readers. John Hay ironically warns in *Castilian Days* (1871) that he does not belong to the "praiseworthy class of travelers who feel a certain moral necessity impelling them to visit every royal abode within reach." Charles Dudley Warner in *Saunterings* (1872), the first of ten travel books, suggests to his audience that, as a compromise, "we shall go somewhere and not learn anything about it." Thomas Bailey Aldrich in *From Ponkapog to Pesth* (1883) complains of another restriction on the freedom of the travel writer. He is not vexed, like Hay and Warner, by the requirement that he be informative, but he does reject the convention which decrees that he may be "aesthetic, or historic, or scientific, or analytic, or didactic, or any kind of ic, except enthusiastic."

* *Graham's Monthly,* 1854; published in *Fireside Travels,* 1864.

Aldrich indulged in nostalgia rather than enthusiasm, but his chapters have a characteristic quality. This is compounded partly from his humorous picture of himself as a provincial American, awed though not cowed by Europe; partly from his conveyance of that disturbing desire which American travelers have always experienced, a longing to possess Europe, to stave off disenchantment, to carry home, in Signor Alinari's sepia photographs or by act of memory, some of the age and beauty of the Old World.

Because these authors took care to organize their impressions and to infect their readers with their discoveries, the travel books of Lowell, Curtis, Hay, Warner, and Aldrich are still alive. But they do not reach the level attained in the records left by Emerson, Hawthorne, Jarves, Twain, Howells, De Forest, and Henry James. The difference is not explained by simply noting that the men in the second group are better writers. The point is that they were more concerned to find a valid answer to the question which was, in some degree, in the consciousness of all traveling Americans: What shall I, as an American, do about Europe?

The first of these records, in point of time as well as in absolute excellence, is Emerson's *English Traits* (1856). The book gave him much trouble and did not appear until nearly ten years after his second visit to England. In his anxiety to make it deep and accurate, he invited the young Clough to stay with him for two or three months at Concord to "answer a catechism of details touching England, revise my notes on that country, and sponge out my blunders." This plan did not go through; but Emerson expended an unusual amount of labor on his book, and it was much on his conscience before the printers finally got the first chapter in October, 1855.

The first printing of 3,000 copies sold quickly, and a second printing of 2,000 was required within a month. Emerson's countrymen sensed that here, at last, was the true and perfect answer to the British travelers who for a half-century had sneered at the nascent American civilization. The liberal British reviews gave the book serious attention; the conservative journals conjured it away by ignoring its existence.

English Traits is less a travel book in the ordinary sense of the word than an essay in cultural anthropology, undertaken years before the science was named. Only a civilized man like Emerson who understands the interaction between ideas and institutions can judge wisely the faults and achievements of a civilization alien to his own. He had little to say about architecture and scenery, but much to say about the English character. He did not admire it with a whole heart, and though, as Richard Garnett observed, there is not a sneer in the book it is full of a wonderful irony. England lacked, for Emerson, what the best civilization must have, spirituality; but England was a success, and he wished to know why. His proposition is stated in the first paragraph of the chapter called "Result."

England is the best of actual nations. It is no ideal framework, it is an old pile built in different ages, with repairs, additions, and makeshifts; but you see the poor best you have got. London is the epitome of our times, and the Rome of to-day.

A fact of such importance for the nineteenth century needed to be explained, and so Emerson probed his way through chapters on Land, Race, Ability, Manners, Truth, Character, Wealth, and pondered the influence exerted by the aristocracy, the universities, the Anglican Church, and the *Times*.

The marvel of the book is how much of it is still true, a tribute both to Emerson's penetration and to the unchanging characteristics of the English people. Page after page could be reprinted as the record of an observer living in our time. Admirers of English unity and courage during the desperate nights of 1940 understand what he means in saying, "In politics and in war, they hold together as by hooks of steel." Though it is now less true than it was in the fifties that "man in England submits to be a product of political economy," England's rivals, as Emerson noted, are still irritated because the English have found out how to unite success with honesty. What he has to say about England's dealings with other nations, particularly those she rules, still needs no amendment.

They assimilate other races to themselves, and are not assimilated. . . . The English sway of their colonies has no root of kindness. They govern by their arts and ability; they are more just than kind; and, whenever an abatement of their power is left, they have not conciliated the affection on which to rely.

Such is their tenacity, and such their practical turn, that they hold all they gain. Of these memorable judgments, none goes so far in explaining the equipoised character of English civilization as Emerson's conclusion to his chapter on "Literature." There are, he says, two nations in England, not Norman and Saxon, or Celt and Goth, but the perceptive class, and the practical finality class. These

are ever in counterpoise, interacting mutually; one, in hopeless minorities; the other, in huge masses; one studious, contemplative, experimenting; the other, the ungrateful pupil, scornful of the source, whilst availing itself of the knowledge for gain; these two nations, of genius and of animal force, though the first consist of only a dozen souls, and the second of twenty millions, forever by their discord and their accord yield the power of the English State.

While Emerson labored at the composition of *English Traits,* Hawthorne, his Concord neighbor, serving as our consul at Liverpool, was keeping a 300,000-word record of his impressions. The experiences of these years between 1853 and 1857 affected him profoundly. If his health had not failed, he would have transmuted them into a novel. It was mainly for this purpose that the *English Notebooks* (completely published in 1941) were compiled. In two abortive romances, *Dr. Grimshaw's Secret* and *The Ancestral Footstep,* he attempted to tell his story, the theme of which was the symbolic return to England of an American whose ancestor in Cromwellian times had violently broken his ties with the homeland. Fortunately, before his creative powers weakened, Hawthorne distilled the more significant passages from the *Notebooks* into *Our Old Home* (1863).

To one who knows something of Hawthorne's state of mind in his last years, his apprehension over the imminence of civil war in America, his struggle to find himself at home in England, the shift in his thinking from the belief that England and America might complement each other, the one supplying the deficiencies the other lacked, to the view, which was also Emerson's, that the two civilizations could not be reconciled and that the future lay with America; to one who perceives how these and related themes return again and again in the pages of *Our Old Home,* the book becomes the most moving autobiographical record left by any of the travelers.

His best chapters are built from the themes related to the all-engrossing question: How shall an American come to terms with England? In the chapter on Leamington Spa these themes emerge most insistently. The little resort city evidently attracted him because it is a "home to the homeless all the year round," though no man has reared a house there wherein to bring up his children. From this theme Hawthorne moves on to his disquiet in trying to picture the influence of hoar antiquity lingering into the present daylight; then to the theme of the illusion to which Americans are constantly subject in England, of having been there before, the result of the print of a recollection in some ancestral mind, transmitted with fainter and fainter impress, through several generations, to the descendant who returns to our old home.

5

James Jackson Jarves resembles Emerson as a travel writer in at least one respect: both men were concerned to describe only those particulars which illustrate general propositions. Because, either unconsciously or by intent, Jarves usually succeeded in going to the heart of the matter in his books about France and Italy, the modern reader who discovers them will be impressed with the significance as well as the prodigality of the details of life in Paris, Florence, and Rome which pour from his pages. His four books are valuable "documentaries."

Parisian Sights and French Principles Seen Through American Spectacles

(1852) takes us, in the fashion of the earlier travel books, to the favorite tourist haunts—the Morgue, Père-Lachaise, the Madeleine; but already Jarves evinces the wit and the independence of judgment which make his books the most amusing of the group now under discussion. He likes to begin a chapter with an informing idea, often epitomized by a symbolic building or a Parisian type, and then to describe the ceremony or process or institution or social class about which he has generalized. Occasionally the details swamp the generalization; but the reader is none the poorer, for he is permitted to see Paris as it was in 1852, recovering from the coup d'état by which Louis Napoleon undid the Second Republic, gay and splendid in its new boulevards, squalid in its attics and slums. Jarves has already begun to discuss freely subjects hinted at by other travelers. What, one wonders, did the family circle think of Chapter VIII, "Something Curious for Moralists"—an unsentimental account of prostitution in Paris and of the French code of extramarital behavior? In the second series of *Parisian Sights* (1855) Jarves even more consistently follows his own bent, poking his nose into dubious alleys and hitherto unvisited places.

In *Italian Sights and Papal Principles Seen Through American Spectacles* (1856) Jarves was again under the necessity of reporting on the usual tourist places. But he saw in his rounds so much more than any of his contemporaries that the reader's interest never diminishes. His incomparable chapter on Pompeii is a tour de force of historical reconstruction. As he went deeper into his subject, Jarves became increasingly reflective. Few Americans meditated with such profit, for instance, on the comparative influence of Romanism and Protestantism on the societies in which each predominated. He ridiculed the mummeries of Holy Week in Rome; but he was no bigot, and, as always, he told his fellow Americans what it was good for them to hear. In this early book, as in the later and mellower *Italian Rambles* (1883), he warned them against the false and meretricious, and encouraged them to carry home a desire to make a civilization in which the artist could exercise his function freely and fully.

Mark Twain's *The Innocents Abroad* (1869) was, in its day, the most famous of American travel books. At last his fellow countrymen, long deceived by the sentimentalities of the guidebooks, were to have the truth about the Old World fraud. He would convince them that the pictures they had rhapsodized over were now too dingy to be deciphered, and the tales of chivalry were actually records of cruelty and avarice. Some of his impieties were shrewdly calculated, but most of them sprang from a deep suspicion of Europe. A success Europe could never be, Italy least of all, for it is the "heart and home of degradation, poverty, indolence, and everlasting unaspiring worthlessness."

Everything Mark saw on his first trip abroad affected him too immediately to permit any historical or aesthetic detachment. Napoleon III, bowing to the plaudits of the crowd and watching everybody with cat's-eyes to discover incipient treason, was no nearer to him in time than the Medicis who required their hireling artists to drag pride and manhood in the dirt for bread. In funereal Venice thoughts of its hidden trials and sudden assassinations crowded out the splendor of St. Mark's. He hurried past frescoes and altarpieces because his anger was still hot from the sight of the gold hoard in the *trésor*.

In these satiric attacks on the easy, un-American acceptance of what is esteemed to be culture we find the Mark Twain we know in his other books: the hater of pretense, resentful of all forms of tyranny, defender of the Jews and other oppressed minorities, tender toward women, the extravagant admirer of what is new and progressive. One enjoys this book, chiefly perhaps, as one does *A Tramp Abroad* (1880), for these sudden fires kindled by the ardor of his prejudices. For the sake of them we indulge him in the crudities of his humor—his fondness for burlesquing venerable legends (a hint here of *A Connecticut Yankee in King Arthur's Court*), his tiresome fun with the intricacies of foreign languages, his set pieces of comic meditation, such as the doing-up of a spectacle in the Coliseum as a Barnum might have produced it.

As compensation for these barbarisms we receive passages which move us strangely, for Mark was not always without reverence. The monuments of Greece and of Rome (before it became Peter's seat) could stir him to write descriptive prose of an unexpected quality. His unlawful visit to the Acropolis by moonlight, the silence of the streets of Pompeii, which he peoples with the oblivious workaday citizens soon to be stricken, Damascus as the type of immortality, such sights and moments impelled him to drop his clown's false face.

The chapters on the new pilgrims in the Holy Land are the best of the book, though they must have pained many churchgoers in the seventies. This climactic episode in the *Quaker City* excursion was Mark Twain's meat. Ill at ease when confronted by a cathedral, he was specially created to satirize the grim willingness with which his pious countrymen endured heat and risked filthy diseases in order that they might follow in His steps. One gets more than delight from these chapters. In no other book is the psychology of the modern pilgrim so clearly exposed, his determination to find a Presbyterian or Baptist Palestine, his ruthless lugging off what of Judaea was not trampled into mud. As for Mark himself, if he had met the Queen of Sheba on the way to Solomon, he would have said to himself, "You look fine, madam, but your feet are not clean and you smell like a camel."

6

Remembering William Dean Howells as the novelist of social change in America, *Atlantic* editor, and convert to Socialism, we forget that he was from 1861 to 1865 our consul at Venice and that out of this experience came some of his first work in prose, *Venetian Life* (1866) and *Italian Journeys* (1867). Nor do these and his other travel books, *Tuscan Cities* (1886) and *A Little Swiss Sojourn* (1892), contain the sum of his impressions of Europe. In his early years he was as much an "international novelist" as his friend Henry James, delighting in contrasts between the fresh innocence of young American girls and the deviousness of Europeans. His first novel, *Their Wedding Journey* (1872), is more travel book than novel, and *A Chance Acquaintance* (1873) furnishes a better portrait of Quebec than of its heroine. He saw Europe as a novelist might be expected to see it. The life of Lucca in the past, the life of Venice in his years there—this is what he has his eye on. We notice before we have read far how frequently these sketches turn into fiction. The patriarch of Capri is as engagingly introduced as if he were to be the leading character in a novel; episodes blossom inevitably into dialogue. Passages from these travel books turn up, only a little transformed, in the novels themselves. (In the twentieth century Howells wrote six travel books.)

No travel writer of these years gives us a fuller sense of how it felt to be in Pisa in 1883, in Vevey in 1887. His attention soon loses its grip on church and statue, but, to our profit, it fixes on what the average tourist, nose down in Hare, would have thought trivial: the little steam tram snuffling through the Piazza Santa Maria Novella; his Holiness hawking into his handkerchief during Mass; the guide in the Baptistry at Pisa who could howl so ably that he has to perform twenty times a day for the tourists who have read about him in the guidebooks.

Howells' observations on architecture and painting are prejudiced, but at any spot where men have been moved to great actions, he was willing to be entranced. "At home," he says, "one may read history, but one can realize it, as if it were something personally experienced, only on the spot where it was lived." To effect this realization, Howells believed, was the prime use of travel. Henry James, the perfect travel writer, saw that the problem for the artist in this genre was to fuse the past and present, the monuments of unaging intellect and the politics of the moment. This fusion Howells could not effect; and he admits that he cannot. For him there was a "sweet confusion" in travel. When we try to lose ourselves in the past, our modern dreariness intrudes. Yet if we were less modern we should be the more indifferent to the antique charm. He cannot bring the two worlds together.

This division of interest between the present and the past is everywhere apparent in his books. *Venetian Life* concentrates on the present. Howells had resolved to tell as much as possible about the everyday life of the Venetians and to develop a just notion of their character. He studied the social structure of Venice and the effect of the weight of the past on its inhabitants. He penetrated every quarter of the city, festival, and gathering place where he might observe them advantageously. In the end he thought he took on a little of the Venetian tone himself, the dispiritedness and the sense of loss and helplessness. His method in *Tuscan Cities* accords with his equally compelling purpose as a traveler: the "experiencing" of history. He lounges in some memorable square or court until the thought of its great moment drives out all other impressions, and the story follows. In telling it he strives for the circumstantial minuteness, the air of simple truth he so much admired in the old Florentine gossipers, in whose tales "the passions are as living, the characters as distinct, as if the thing happened yesterday."

Howells' predilections as a traveler changed, as did those of his countrymen, between the sixties and the nineties. Beneath the ingratiating manner of *Venetian Life* one detects the seriousness of the generation of Americans for whom Europe was a problem to be solved. The tone of *A Little Swiss Sojourn* is very different. Howells is content now to escape for a time, imagining how pleasant life might be in a certain noble *château meublé à louer* by the Rhone. If one had daughters to educate or were wearing out a heavy disappointment, this great house would suit very well. For many Americans, as for Howells, Europe was becoming a château to be rented for a season of self-indulgence.

Like Howells, who was his admiring critic and sponsor, John W. De Forest first practiced the art of the novelist in his travel books. His *Oriental Acquaintance* (1856) is lifted above the usual accounts of the tour to the Holy Land by its descriptions of the antics of the enraptured tourists. An even better book is his *European Acquaintance* (1858). In his conversation De Forest, so he would have us believe, indulged in the usual banalities of tourists who felt it was their duty to compare the canvases of the Venetian painters to gorgeous sunsets; but his book is almost entirely about the wonderful eccentrics he met by the way. Twelve chapters are devoted to those who endured with him the savage water cure at Gräfenberg and the more effeminate wettings and purgings and freezings at Divonne, near the Swiss border. More valuable than Norton on Orvieto cathedral is his account of the horrors of the Curd Cure, and the Straw Cure, and, most terrible of all, the Wine Cure, so barbaric that patients and doctors, when the prescribed tortures were relaxed each Saturday, all got drunk together.

In the travel essays of Henry James, collected in three volumes—*Transatlantic Sketches* (1875), *Portraits of Places* (1883), and *A Little Tour in*

France (1884)—the genre attains its highest development. One thinks regret, fully in reading these neglected books of the misfortune of the hundreds of James' countrymen who carried their prejudices abroad in their baggage. And not Americans only. In a devastating attack on Ruskin's inadequate percep- tions (*Portraits of Places*, pp. 64–69), James defines by implication his own qualifications for this sort of writing. "Instead of a garden of delight, [Rus- kin] finds a sort of assize-court, in perpetual session. Instead of a place in which human responsibilities are lightened and suspended, he finds a region governed by a kind of Draconic legislation." For James travel was an immense pleasure. Perpetually going a journey, he was willing to permit the scene to take hold of him and "speak"—to use the word he often uses himself.

For each experience he returns a picture which is harmonious and com- plete. Having sorted out and related the multitude of separate impressions, he builds his essay around a dominant idea or object or mood, so that the reader may grasp the essence of the scene. At Lichfield his theme is the commonplaceness of the little city looked down on by the wonderful cathedral whose great towers overtake in mid-air the conditions of perfect symmetry; at Wells it is the perpetual savor of a Sunday afternoon. In Venice what most impresses one is the way one lives "in a certain sort of knowledge as in a rosy cloud," which "certain sort of knowledge" James exquisitely defines.

What moves him least is scenery. There is a limit to the satisfaction with which one can sit staring at a mountain. Even the liquid sapphire and em- erald of Leman and Lucerne suffer when compared with firm palace floors of lapis and verd-antique. He retreats in haste from literary shrines too much possessed by tourists. What pleases most is a great English country house like Haddon Hall, where the incommunicable spirit of the ghost-haunted scene strikes with almost painful intensity; or the brooding villas of Florence whose extraordinary largeness and massiveness are a satire on their present fate. For him a great building is the greatest conceivable work of art, because it represents difficulties annulled, resources combined, labor, courage, and patience. A great building has been, and still may be, inhabited by men and women, and James relishes above all a human flavor in his pleasure.

These essays fascinate for another reason than their superb art. Whether James is contemplating the façade of Rheims cathedral from his stage-box window at the Lion d'Or or abstracting the French character from the dis- play of bathing manners on the *plage* at Etretat, the scene is always, to him, a drama. "To travel," he says, is "to go to the play, to attend a spectacle." Sometimes the gestures and murmured conversation of actual persons supply the plot; sometimes it rises from the contrast between past and present, as when he is struck with the insufferable patronage of the culture-seeking tourists toward Young Italy, preoccupied with its economical and political future and heartily tired of being admired for its eyelashes and its pose. Often it is the conflict of ideas implicit in the scene before him which transforms it into a psychomachia. Thus, in the midst of his enjoyment of the tranquil grandeur of Rheims he is overwhelmed with the realization that the hierarchy which erected this magnificent structure is now the go-between of Bona-partism. "How far should a lover of old cathedrals let his hands be tied by the sanctity of their traditions? How far should he let his imagination bribe him, as it were, from action?"

If the modern world obtrudes in these sketches more insistently than one might have expected, the past is always there as a continuous present, made palpable by the endless devices of James' art. He hated the restorers of the nineteenth century, professional vandals like Sir George Gilbert Scott and Viollet-le-Duc, the more, perhaps, because their licensed depredations deprived him of his chance to evoke and reconstruct. To James a great ruin was a great opportunity. Mark Twain fled from ruins because he did not have the skill to make them speak. James was impelled to them by a kind of aesthetic hunger. Though only a beautiful shadow remain (as he said of Leonardo's "Last Supper" and of the hoary relics of Glastonbury), that "shadow is the artist's thought." This thought was James' quest; it gave him each time new proof of that most pertinent lesson of art, "that there is no limit to the amount of substance an artist may put into his work."

52. DELINEATION OF LIFE AND CHARACTER

There was living substance in the land that spread in three directions from the New York of Stedman and James, but it was a substance largely unrefined and undisciplined. To discover and develop the values and the order within it required perhaps a greater tolerance, more empirical knowledge and a freer spirit of literary experimentation than the defenders of ideality could supply. Once again the old patterns were being repeated; once again a new literature was evolving spontaneously from close contact with new ways of life and new lands at the same time that familiar forms and modes were being put to fresh uses. This time, the new land was a continental nation, the literary modes were the modes of realism and romance. Those writers who so enthusiastically rediscovered the life of the old America of the East and South or the new America of the Middle and Far West might, like naturalists from William Bartram to John W. Powell, put it directly into descriptions of nature, or might like writers of romantic tales from Fenimore Cooper to Bret Harte, strive to find literary forms adequate to what they wished to say. If they chose to make short stories and novels and poems and plays of the new material, whether it be the life of the Southern Negro or that of the California prospector, realism and romance vied with each other to create satisfactory forms.

When Harriet Beecher Stowe published *The Minister's Wooing* in 1859, Lowell welcomed her return from the intersectional triumph of *Uncle Tom's Cabin* to her true literary ground, the delineation of New England life and character. No other writer, said he, was so capable of perpetuating, through the medium of prose fiction, the fast vanishing essence of Yankeeism. Mrs. Stowe confirmed her welcome with *The Pearl of Orr's Island* (1862), and although it was not flawless, it glowed in a warm light of native affection. Without visible effort, Mrs. Stowe showed that she was capable of sharp genre painting; she got the feel of Kennebec Island life among the Pennels and Kittridges; she proved once again the importance of localized environment to verisimilitude in fiction; and she got inside common people like Aunt Roxy and Aunt Ruey as if she had never left them for Topsy and Legree. *Oldtown Folks* (1869) was an even more deliberate study of village character, manners, and social organization, this time in her husband's birth-place, South Natick. She took the task seriously. "It is more to me than a story," she said. "It is my résumé of the whole spirit and body of New England." In the *Oldtown Fireside Stories* (1872) she used the dialect yarns of the philosopher-raconteur Sam Lawson to lighten the darker aspects of the New England spirit, and her *Poganuc People* (1878), in which she condensed her recollections of girlhood in Litchfield, Connecticut, might have been written to Lowell's order.

Mrs. Stowe's work reflects the limitations, as well as some of the positive virtues, of the literary movement to which her name thus early lent prestige. Dedicated to the exploitation of the most anciently settled America, the coastal plain and the adjacent mountains from Maine to Florida and along the Gulf to the Mississippi Delta, the movement gained momentum in the East and South during the years of war and reconstruction. Under the double impact of foreign and Western influences it reached a production peak after the third quarter of the century, and continued, with various modifications and interruptions, as a prominent force in American writing for a good fifty years thereafter. Long before Mrs. Stowe's return to the New England scene, a democratic regionalist tradition had begun to take form and amass sub-stance both in the North and in the Deep South. All the elements Mrs. Stowe employed were ready to her hand in the literary record: exploitation of rural character and manners in the immediate or the colonial past, using dialect, local coloring, or any other devices which would produce, at the literary level, the kind of realism represented in the visual arts by genre painting, where the aim was to render truthfully, though always selectively, a picture of ordinary life as it was being lived or had been lived in times not too remote. Partly because of her own limitations as a writer, Mrs. Stowe fell heir also to the main weaknesses of the tradition: structural deficiencies, labored histrionics, sentimental didacticism.

In the year of *Poganuc People* appeared books by two other Connecticut Yankees. Rose Terry Cooke's *Happy Dodd* and Annie Trumbull Slosson's *China Hunters' Club* indicated that the tradition was not to be allowed to languish. Mrs. Cooke's profound religious feelings and her love of the in-dustrious poor found expression in *Happy Dodd,* the life chronicle of a plain little cripple. The ensuing years saw other volumes, of which the stories in *Huckleberries Gathered from New England Hills* (1891) are among the best. Mrs. Slosson reached full stature only with *Dumb Foxglove and Other Stories* (1898), studies in the psychology of religious emotion among the lowly. If the three middle-aged ladies from Connecticut did not establish a school, they fixed upon the writing of the period the mark of their own gentle and generous personalities, and proved that in the proper hands the democratic regionalist tradition was still capable of development.

Meantime a doctor's daughter in South Berwick ("a Maine borderer," she called herself) was quietly commencing what would become the most distinguished career among all the writers of regional fiction. Sarah Orne Jewett developed her gifts more rapidly, maintained them at a higher level and employed them with greater dexterity and control than did any of her predecessors in the field. After a period of apprenticeship to children's magazines she entered adult fiction at twenty with a story in the *Atlantic* (December, 1869), and in eight years had accumulated enough others to take Howells' advice and collect them in her first book, *Deephaven* (1877). In that year Mrs. Stowe was sixty-five, Mrs. Cooke fifty, and Mrs. Slosson thirty-nine. Miss Jewett was only twenty-eight, and her youth may have had something to do with the fact that *Deephaven,* for all its faults, has a certain distinctive newness and brightness beside which *Poganuc People, Happy Dodd,* and *The China Hunters' Club,* all issued in the following year, seem dull and old-fashioned. But *Deephaven* was only a start. Through the next twenty years she published in the best monthlies, and then collected, a succession of stories which showed a steadily deepening insight into the complexities of human character, and a steadily growing technical skill. Her masterpiece, *The Country of the Pointed Firs* (1896), is the best piece of regional fiction to have come out of nineteenth century America.

Yet this great book is not her only claim to admiration. Nearly all the stories she wrote after 1880 show the distinctive quality of her work: that particular combination of deep and tender insight with technical resilience and toughness which none of her contemporaries in the field learned to match, chiefly because they were unwilling to work as hard as she. She took very seriously her own Arnoldian maxim: "Study the work that the best judges have called good and see *why* it is good." Occasionally she was capable of being deceived by her respect for men like Tennyson into thinking them greater than they were; but her letters repeatedly show the rightness of her judgments about Henry James and the French and Russian novelists. She read Balzac with discernment, admired Zola's "shrewdness of workmanship," borrowed two leaves from Flaubert as a counsel of perfection, and even grew to comprehend what Tolstoy, her antithesis in most ways, was attempting to do. Yet of Miss Jewett one might repeat what someone said of George Sand: although she had the deepest veneration for the aristocracy of the intellect, the democracy of suffering touched her more. Even as a child, making sick calls with her father, she had learned how to get in among the people of York, Wells, South Berwick, and the surrounding countryside, and when she became a writer they still received and trusted and confided in her—these "village people—not the new ones, but those to whom in their early days Berwick was the round world itself." The quiet towns and the weathered farms gave her all her best stories—"The White Heron," "Marsh Rosemary,"

"The Only Rose," and a great many others—and she felt only an occasional need to look farther afield. "People talk about dwelling upon the trivialities and commonplaces in life, but a master writer gives everything weight, and makes you feel the distinction and importance of it."

What gave her writing weight was her ability to combine a rightness of observation with an intuition that looked beneath surfaces. In the precision of her feeling for natural objects she resembled, and knew she resembled, Dorothy Wordsworth. The reader is often brought up sharp by the clean, poetic accuracy of her epithets: the westering sun, for example, is said to light up schooner sails, far on the eastern sea, like "golden houses." But Dorothy Wordsworth could rarely develop her scattered observations into a total pattern; whole stories of Miss Jewett have this quality of breathless delight, or display that equally compelling sense of thoughts that lie "too deep for tears." One recalls the picture of the deserted farmhouse in *Deephaven*:

that fireless, empty, forsaken house, where the winter sun shines in and creeps slowly along the floor; the bitter cold is in and around the house, and the snow has sifted in at every crack; outside it is untrodden by any living creature's footstep. The wind blows and rushes and shakes the loose window-sashes in their frames, while the padlock knocks—knocks against the door.

Miss Jewett's landscapes had always figures in the foreground, for people were always in the foreground of her consciousness. "You must write," she told Willa Cather, "to the human heart, the great consciousness that all humanity goes to make up. Otherwise what might be strength in a writer is only crudeness, and what might be insight is only observation; sentiment falls to sentimentality—you can write about life, but never write life itself."

To such ideas she had triumphantly adhered throughout her writing life, though not at first with so deep a sense of either tragedy or comedy, or so complete a dominance over her material. The growth between *Deephaven* and *The Country of the Pointed Firs* can be measured by seeing how observation has matured to insight, and how her attitude toward both her people and her art has subtly deepened. In the early book the narrator seems (though she was not) a summer resident in search of the quaint and unique; without looking down on the people she is never quite at one with them, and her experiments with scenes are sometimes tentative and unsure. By the time of the *Pointed Firs* and its epilogue-story *The Dunnet Shepherdess,* she knows how to understand and therefore how to present her people; she has learned the great trick of true realism: to combine depth of sympathetic involvement with artistic detachment, reaching unity through the establishment of a point of view. Deeply responsive to a look or a word from people like Almira

Todd the gatherer of pennyroyal, or William Blackett the taciturn islander, she can still see that look or word as only one thread in the fabric of her total impression. An emotional experience is thus never felt to be the end in view, but only an indispensable contribution to that end. One could cite among dozens of examples the farewell to Mrs. Todd, soon followed by the distant prospect of the same Antigone-like figure descending the profile of a hill as party to a walking funeral. One hears that Miss Jewett's was a limited and muted art. But the significant point—in an age of realism for social history's sake, or regionalism strongly dependent for its force on mere local color, where characters were sometimes embarrassed and stereotyped by being saddled with the responsibility of representing a particular region—is that her stories were works of art, and of a high order.

Two of Miss Jewett's contemporaries, Rowland Robinson and Celia Thaxter, showed what could happen to regionalism and local color when other motives than those of the serious artist were predominant. Robinson was a Quaker farm boy from Vermont who invented the fictional village of Danvis as a theater of operations for characters like Lisha Peggs, Sam Lovel, and the French Canadian, Antoine. According to its author, *Danvis Folks* (1894) "was written with less purpose of telling any story than of recording the manners, customs, and speech" in vogue in Vermont during the early nineteenth century. At the other extreme stood Celia Thaxter, whose deservedly popular sketchbook, *Among the Isles of Shoals* (1873), ran through seventeen editions in twenty years. Her subject matter is that of the poet-naturalist, and she writes as a pure local colorist determined to describe, in the closest detail, her own well loved region: the lonely islands, flower-studded and peopled with birds, the landsmell wafted eastward after rain, the cries of terns, the breathing sound of whales in the bay at night. The few Shoalers who appear in her pages are gingerly handled; her interest is in the setting.

If Robinson and Mrs. Thaxter are preoccupied with extensions of the exploitational idea, the work of Mary Eleanor Wilkins, a native of western Massachusetts, is close to the center of the tradition. Her best work was done before 1902, when she married and henceforth wrote as Mary E. Wilkins Freeman. At the top of her form, she was a finer artist than any of her contemporaries except Miss Jewett, and there was a sharpness of line and directness of purpose about her first two collections which even Miss Jewett could not match. The fifty-two short stories in *A Humble Romance* (1887) and *A New England Nun* (1891), represent about a quarter of her total short-story output. The locus of her interest is always the proud, reticent, stoical people. Descriptive passages are spare and apposite, and the local customs, like the local idiom, are used for high-lighting and never for substance. In these respects she resembles Miss Jewett, but hers is on the whole a more objective art. On one occasion the narrator in *The Country of the Pointed Firs* notices how "a narrow set of circumstances had caged a fine able character and held it captive." But Miss Jewett rarely stresses, as Miss Wilkins so frequently does, the caging environment, the captivity of circumstance, and there seems, accordingly, a larger measure of modern realism in the work of the younger writer. Yet her grimness has been overemphasized; she is not primarily the expositor of social conditions, the iconoclast of country codes, and if she has not the tenderness and humor of Miss Jewett, she has a saving sense of the comic. In "A New England Nun," where Louisa Ellis finds herself unable to admit her aging fiancé to the gentle rhythms of her spinster's domain, there is suggestion of hidden sublimations of which a Freudian might have made much. In the complex jealousies of "A Village Singer" or the inherent hardnesses of "A Village Lear," similar opportunities present themselves. Miss Wilkins' refusal to overplay her hand is a sign of control rather than lack of courage. Yet she was unable to sustain the high level thus early achieved in these stories, and later collections are far less admirable, although one observes, even in the first two volumes, that little effort has been made to distinguish the mediocre and repetitious from the fifteen or twenty stories which are her real contribution to the tradition.

2

The regionalist impulse in one form or another accounted for the emergence of almost every prominent writer in the Middle Atlantic states and the Deep South in the last quarter of the century. By 1887, fourteen years after Hayne had supposed that Southern literature could not survive, a score of young writers were vigorously engaged in the exploitation of native materials, for which many of them found a ready market in the section-conscious magazines of the North. When the reading public discovered, somewhat belatedly, an insatiable interest in prewar planters and country gentlemen, poor whites of mountain, piedmont, tidewater, and bayou, and the plantation Negro, whether enslaved or emancipated, the writers were ready to supply the demand, and the number of stories and articles about the South reached proportions formerly undreamed of.

That prominent driving force among the Northern regional writers, the desire to preserve in print a vanished or vanishing past, reappears most strikingly in the plantation literature of Virginia where it often leads to an idealization of former times far more marked than one finds in New England writing of the same period. The tendency was hard to resist, as was shown in the career of Dr. George W. Bagby. In 1859 this Lynchburg journalist had sought half seriously to accomplish what he called "The Unkind but

Complete Destruction" of that well known romancer, John Esten Cooke, who kept his eye steadily fixed on the glories of the Old Dominion. Bagby was tired, he said, of hearing his ancestors cracked up as the topmost top-sawyers of all creation, and he called for a man who could effectively paint the real Southern life around him. Bagby's own contribution was the "Mozis Addums" letters, where the common-man humor of overstatement, the slap-stick practical joke, and the barbaric spelling indicate that Mozis is another in the long queue of broadly humorous commoners, like Hosea Biglow, Jack Downing, and Simon Suggs. But nostalgia ultimately triumphed even over Bagby. The huge success of his lecture "Bacon and Greens," a lengthy and discursive panegyric on rural life in prewar Virginia, led him to undertake other similar experiments, of which his idealized and intensely localized por-trait of "The Old Virginia Gentleman" is a prime example. In a note to this lecture Bagby recalled that during the life of the Commonwealth he had been at pains to satirize its shortcomings. "But our Mother," he added, "is dead." Now, without shame, he could mourn the loss of that beauty, simplicity, purity, uprightness, cordiality, warmth, grace, and lavish hospitality which had undoubtedly distinguished country life in old Virginia.

Neither his good friend Cooke, whose romances he had satirized, nor the young lawyer Thomas Nelson Page took Bagby to task for this reversal of his former position. Page, indeed, saw in the old tidewater Virginia a mature and deep-rooted civilization upon which he was presently to draw. After Cooke, the gentleman cavalier tradition found its most articulate exponent and apologist in Page. The *Century* in 1884 accepted his "Marse Chan," a retrospective piece in the dialect of an aging Negro body servant who still loyally guards the dog of his late master, a gallant war casualty. This and five other tales form *In Ole Virginia* (1887), the success of which drew Page away from his Richmond law practice into the profession of letters. The Page formula is revealed in stories like "Marse Chan," "Unc' Edinburg's Drown-din," or "Meh Lady." Forlorn ex-slaves yearn for the good old times—"de bes' Sam ever see"—or worshipfully recall the great dark eyes and blushing cheeks of those goddesses in crinoline, the plantation ladies; or remember how they stood by as sympathetic servant-observers when dashing young soldiers left for the wars, or galloped back under cover of darkness to pluck a rose from the bush under milady's window. "That the social life of the Old South had its faults I am far from denying," says Page in a characteristic echo of Bagby's words. "But its virtues far outweighed them; its graces were never equalled. . . . It was, I believe, the purest, sweetest life ever lived." Page's faults—overidealization of character and melodramatic emphasis in his management of incident—are at least matched by his virtues: genuine descrip-tive skill, as in the lingering and loving account of a Christmas feast and dance in the plantation washhouse, or the sinister swamp atmosphere of "No Haid Pawn"; an eye for significant detail and an ear for the niceties of dialect which gave him in these respects a marked superiority over Cooke and Bagby; and enough appreciation of the realities of war and reconstruction to enable him to shrug off the charge that he was totally immersed in what Bagby had called "the golden patriarchal days that shall come no more."

By 1884, when Page was getting his start, James Lane Allen had decided to make a career of the central Kentucky plateau around his native Lexington, and to use the landscapes of this single neighborhood as the locale of all his work. But it was characteristic of him that he rejected the selective realism of the genre painters in favor of synthetic prose tone poems about Kentucky's "soil and sky and season"; and that he depended heavily, as Bagby and Page did not, upon a mannered and heightened style, designed to lift his work above the common run of localized writing. His first collection, *Flute and Violin* (1891), showed where his theories led in practice—to the bizarre heroics of Palemon, the insurgent Trappist monk; or the sacrifice of Sister Dolorosa, gone from Kentucky to die among Damien's lepers; or the idealization of the tramp King Solomon, redeemed from disgrace in a cholera epidemic. The sense of the actual flows away in this never-never land of Allendom. Nor is it totally regained in the famous and popular idyls, *A Kentucky Cardinal* (1894), and its sequel, *Aftermath* (1895). We should now apply differently the remarks of those contemporary reviewers who compared these books and *Summer in Arcady* (1896) to pressed flowers smelling faintly of lavender, exuding sweetness, moral fervor, and light. *The Choir Invisible* (1897), Allen's novel of late eighteenth century Kentucky, sometimes gets closer to reality. Yet its hero, John Gray, is too much the feudal knight in the garb of a frontier schoolmaster to seem more than remotely credible. What Allen missed, even in so marked an advance as *The Reign of Law* (1900), was that deep belief in the importance of earthy character which strengthened and sustained those regionalists who were in other ways his inferiors.

Yet Southern writers discovered other values than those of the plantation aristocracy, and with the appearance of Charles Egbert Craddock's *In the Tennessee Mountains* (1884), the Southern poor white, described here and there by earlier writers, began to look like a subject for exploitation. Little was known about the author of these sketches, except that this was probably not his real name, that he wrote a bold, black hand, and that he was apparently well acquainted with the regional idiosyncrasies of the hill dwellers in the Tennessee Cumberlands and the Great Smokies. "Possibly not since George Eliot's time," wrote Charles Coleman in 1887, "has there been so great a literary sensation as that created by the discovery" that Craddock was the pseudonym of a well educated, partially crippled Tennessee spinster named Mary Noailles Murfree. This young lady's love of mountain topographical features was such that huge blocks of scenic description were allowed to obstruct the flow of her narrative, and her desire to produce phonetically exact transcriptions of the local dialect was so strong that the reader, as with Rowland Robinson's Vermonters, must overcome his objections to the orthography before he can read the dialogue with any pleasure. A patience durable enough to survive these obstacles finds its reward in the generally realistic tales of moonshiners and posses, fist-fighters and hunters, pointed up with graphic accounts of courting, dancing, eating, drinking, plowing, and card playing among the human neighbors of brooding old peaks like Chilhowee. One finishes books like *The Prophet of the Great Smoky Mountains* (1885) and *In the "Stranger People's" Country* (1895) with an authoritative knowledge of backwoods life in Tennessee during the Reconstruction period.

Although Miss Murfree was among the earliest of the regionalists to gain fame through the fictional treatment of mountaineers, she had no corner on the Southern poor white. Henry Watterson's anthology, *Oddities in Southern Life and Character* (1882), showed that in the humorous writing of the old Deep South, particularly that which originated in Georgia and Alabama, there was a strong rural democratic tradition. Watterson's collection came late enough to include samples of the work of two Georgians, Richard Malcolm Johnston and Joel Chandler Harris, who plainly occupy the tradition of Longstreet, Hooper, and Thompson. What chiefly distinguishes their achievement from that of the raucous elder humorists is a combination of the rugged virtues of the old with a new and pervasive sympathy and a restrained use of sentiment.

Johnston was almost fifty when his Dukesborough stories first gained wide recognition and he had become an old man by the time people began to talk about the Uncle Remus stories of the young Atlanta editor, Harris. The antetype of Dukesborough was Powelton, Georgia, near which stood Johnston's plantation birthplace, "Oak Grove." By the time he died in 1898 he had published some eighty tales and three middling novels, all of them centered in or near the Georgia he had known as a plantation child, or as lawyer and educator among the villages of the state. A gifted raconteur in the leisurely manner, he brought both ebullience and charm to his accounts of Dukesborough school life, family feuds, and red-letter days in the village calendar, often employing the native idiom of a special narrator, old Mr. Pate. The accent was on a particular terrain, and the Dukesborough people: their suspicions of the local witch, their excitement over the weasels in the chicken house, the nervous mother's caution to her children when the World-

Renowned Circus parades through town: "Stay behind there, you Jack, and you Susan! You want to git eat up by them camels and varmints?"

Like his fast friend, Colonel Johnston, Harris had grown up among small planters and impecunious villagers from whose mode of life the grand manner was conspicuously absent. Like Johnston, too, he preferred to picture Georgia country life as it was, not as a lost paradise through which the rustle of angelic wings could be heard, but as a democratic society. This is not to say that Harris employed naturalistic techniques, or that he habitually painted Southern poor-white life as Caldwell and Faulkner were to do. But he contrived to show that the annals of the poor are neither short nor simple, and there is an air of complete naturalness about everything he wrote. His characteristic approach lay somewhere between that represented by Goldsmith's *Vicar of Wakefield,* his favorite novel, and the work that he regarded as the most characteristic American story thus far written, E. W. Howe's *The Story of a Country Town.* He shared the opinion (however one may disagree with it) which underlay all the best genre writing of the period: "No novel or story can be genuinely American unless it deal with the *common people,* that is *country people.*" And he held boldly forth against a strictly regional emphasis:

What does it matter whether I am Northern or Southern, if I am true to truth? . . . My idea is that truth is more important than sectionalism, and that literature that can be labeled Northern, Southern, Western, or Eastern, is not worth labeling at all.

That Harris' merits were not totally comprehended in the songs and sayings of Uncle Remus became evident in 1884, when he published the volume *Mingo, and Other Sketches in Black and White.* The struggle between the stalwart moonshiners of Hog Back Mountain in North Georgia and their inadequate foes the revenue agents, provides the substance of the novelette, "At Teague Poteet's," longest and best of the four stories in this volume. The gay mountaineer, his taciturn cracker wife, and his daughter Sis, whom Harris cannot resist idealizing a little, are all worthy to stand beside Uncle Remus. "Trouble on Lost Mountain" in the next collection, *Free Joe and Other Georgian Sketches* (1887), is a tragic variation on the same theme, less successful as a story, but excellent in the vitality of characters like Abe Hightower with his healthy and breezy but deep-founded affection for his daughter Babe. Among the lowlanders, one remembers especially Mingo's sour companion, the embittered Mrs. Blivins, cracker rebel against the shortcomings of her "restercrat" kinfolks; and the stoical yellow-faced Emma Jane Stucky, the piney-woods tacky of Harris' sandhill novelette, "Azalia." The most striking aspect of Harris' writing, the quality that destroys his often reiterated avowal that his work was valueless as literature, is the apparently effortless ease with which he convinces the reader of the truth of what is being read. If the Negro Balaam's wealthy master is a sensual good-for-nothing, Harris refuses to idealize him; if Colonel Flewellen was so much a gentleman that he was willing to live on what the ex-slave Ananias could steal for him, Harris gives the facts and lets the reader judge. Had he done nothing beside the stories in these and several later collections, Harris would still stand out as a minor master among the Southern genre writers.

Harris' picture of the Georgia Negro is his foremost achievement. Those who do not easily surrender to the charm of Uncle Remus or complain that there is too much honey and too little gall in the animal stories can turn for variety to the portraits of the dignified Mingo, the abject Ananias, the splenetic Mom Bi, Aunt Fountain, Balaam, Free Joe, or Blue Dave. Harris' characteristic respect for the truth, and his close knowledge of the Georgia Negro as he existed under slavery and reconstruction, gave his Negro stories an authority which few of his contemporaries could approach.

The Negro had need of Harris, if only to explain his variety. The slave Hector in Simms' *The Yemassee* (1835), Jupiter in Poe's "The Gold Bug" (1843), and Mrs. Stowe's Uncle Tom (1852) hardly presented an adequate composite picture of a minority group which in 1860 numbered close to 4,500,000. Nor were the songs of Stephen Foster of any great value in filling out the picture of what the Southern Negro was like. Not only was Foster a native of Pittsburgh, but he was also preeminently a showman, looking for marketable material, and lacking in what may be called the deeper literary motives. For all his enviable hold over the singing habits of a nation, in his own day and ever since, Foster had little first-hand knowledge of the Negro, and his songs merely perpetuate a stereotype of the melancholy plantation "darky." Closer to the real thing were the dialect poems of the Mississippian, Irwin Russell, who once remarked of *Uncle Tom's Cabin* that it gave no more true idea of Negro life and character than the Nautical Almanac. Russell's death in 1879 at the age of twenty-six was lamented throughout the reading South, and Harris stated, in introducing a posthumous edition of his *Poems* (1888), that Russell was among the first of the Southern writers to appreciate the literary possibilities of the Negro character, which he represented with great accuracy. Russell's poems are too few to make sound judgment possible. Yet the often praised "Christmas-Night in the Quarters" is certainly a minor triumph, a Southernized version of Burns' "The Jolly Beggars," which has all the vivacity Bagby could have wished. One of the recitativos, a localized retelling of the Noah story ("'Dar's gwine to be a' ober-flow,' said Noah, lookin' solemn") uses a method since widely popularized in the work of Roark Bradford.

Harris' *Uncle Remus, His Songs and His Sayings* (1880) was the first collection of Negro lore, plantation song, and country anecdote to reveal at all comprehensively the possibilities for genre painting inherent in the Negro life and character. One could best measure the value of Harris' contribution, said Professor William Baskervill, pioneer historian of Southern letters, by comparing Uncle Remus with the ideal Negro of "My Old Kentucky Home," *Uncle Tom's Cabin,* "Marse Chan," and "Meh Lady" or with the impossible Negro of the minstrel show. Beside such visionary types or clownish, plug-hatted caricatures, thought Baskervill, Uncle Remus stood out, largely because Harris knew whereof he spoke. His protagonist was a composite picture of old Uncle George Terrell and half-a-dozen other workers to whom Harris had listened during the early sixties when he was a youthful protégé of Joseph Addison Turner at the "Turnwold" plantation, not far from his birthplace in Putnam County, Georgia. After some years of newspaper work in Macon, New Orleans, and Savannah, Harris had settled down permanently in 1876 as a staff member of the Atlanta *Constitution,* and about a year later had begun to realize that his home-grown knowledge of the Negro was a valuable possession. Although Harris undoubtedly overworked Uncle Remus, and although he disclaimed literary pretensions, the ten Uncle Remus books which he (or his executors) published between 1880 and the First World War showed appreciable merit; a skillful variation of materials, a love of ironic implication, a mastery of the short dramatic form, and a sure grasp of humorous idiom and the natural rhythms of folk speech.

During the latter years of the century the most noteworthy followers in the wake of Harris were the Negro writers Charles Waddell Chesnutt and Paul Laurence Dunbar. Both happened to be Ohioans, but Dunbar's mother (to whom he owed the idea for his best known poem, "When Malindy Sings") was a native of Kentucky who had grown up in slavery, while Chesnutt's legal training involved a number of years in North Carolina. The *Atlantic Monthly* accepted several of Chesnutt's stories in the late eighties, and in 1899 he selected seven tales for his volume *The Conjure Woman.* These were unified through their common subject matter, Negro magic, and through the character of Uncle Julius McAdoo, an elderly colored man who suggests Remus, and is his closest rival. With his second collection, *The Wife of His Youth* (also 1899), Chesnutt forthrightly considered the tragi-comic implications of the "color line," and his career included also three novels which expose the consequences of racial prejudice.

Dunbar's early work in verse caught the attention of Howells, who wrote an introduction for *Lyrics of Lowly Life* (1896) in which he praised Dunbar's "refined and delicate art," his objective study of the Negro, and his conviction that there is or ought to be an essential unity among human beings which has nothing to do with skin color. Dunbar's first collection of short stories, *Folks from Dixie* (1898), employed dialect successfully, and although two or three of them follow too closely the lead of Page, others are original and apparently authoritative. Before his early death in 1906, Dunbar published four novels, three other collections of short fiction, and several more volumes of verse. If as writers of fiction he and Chesnutt sometimes derived suggestions from other analysts of Negro character, both brought to their work the stamp of their persuasive personalities, and both enriched that branch of nineteenth century literature which relates to the old-time Southern Negro.

3

Nowhere else in the literature relating to the older America does one find the particular flavor which distinguishes the regional writing of New Orleans. Elsewhere plainness and homeliness are the rule; New Orleans writing inherits from its setting an Old World patina. Elsewhere the stress is on the rural, the lonely; but the sprawling city of New Orleans teems with life. Elsewhere the Americanness of the characters is unmistakable; in New Orleans, even the eccentric "Posson Jone" (who would have been quite at home in Dukesborough) seems like a foreign interloper, that is to say, an *Américain*. Elsewhere one observes a certain unanimity of thought and language among the inhabitants of a particular region; in the polyglot New Orleans of George W. Cable, French, Spanish, Irish, and Dutch mingle with American boatmen from the upper reaches of the Mississippi, West Indian refugees, and sailors of fortune from every quarter of the globe; the quadroon demimondaine lingers on the edge of society; Choctaw women vend sassafras along the banquettes; the levels of thought and the details of action, like the divisions of speech, are as various as the tongues of Babel.

At the time of Cable's emergence, New Orleans and the delta region of Mississippi was in a sense virgin territory for fiction. A French literature had flourished in colonial and early nineteenth century Louisiana, and a few American writers had tentatively scratched the ground. But a full-fledged literature of New Orleans and the bayou country did not appear until the 1870's.

Cable's struggle for fame was long and arduous. He had gone to work as a boy of fifteen, served in the Confederate cavalry, and worked for a cotton wholesaler. But he remarked that although the cotton business was pleasant enough, he could not help striking higher, and "trying for an honourable profession." For a time it seemed that reporting for the New Orleans *Picayune* would do, but when the newspaper discharged him he was not sorry. "I wanted to be always writing," said he, "and they wanted me to be always reporting. This didn't work well . . . and I went back to bookkeeping." The books he began to keep in 1871 were those in the counting rooms of Black and Company, cotton factors, and for the next ten years he handled the firm's financial transactions with accuracy but without enthusiasm. At last he was able to tell Howells that he had resigned his secretaryship, closed his office, and now stood armed with nothing "for offense or defense but my grey goose quill."

That goose quill had been busy for the better part of the preceding decade. During the sweltering days when the countingroom was ahead of schedule, Cable used to slip away to the municipal archives. There he read hundreds of old newspapers, and soon knew more about the New Orleans past than anyone else in town. But he also found, among the yellowing items, stories that cried for fictional development. "It seemed a pity," he explained later, "for the stuff to go to waste," and in off hours he tried his hand with three or four: "'Sieur George," "Bibi" (later rewritten and incorporated in *The Grandissimes* as "The Story of Bras-Coupé"), and one or two more. When Edward King, on contract to *Scribner's Monthly* for a series of articles on the South, visited New Orleans in 1872, he met the slight, black-bearded book-keeper, read his tales, and enthusiastically recommended them to the Scribner editors, Holland and Gilder. Although they rejected half of the stories Cable submitted (they cared nothing for "Posson Jone" and found the subject of "Bibi," as they said, "unmitigatedly distressful"), they had accepted and printed four others by the spring of 1876, and Edward King's "discovery" was being mentioned as a coming name in Southern literature. By 1878 Scribner's had invited him to do a serial novel *(The Grandissimes)*, and had agreed to bring out a volume which Cable thought of calling *Prose Idyls for Hammock and Fan,* but which bore, on its appearance in 1879, the familiar title, *Old Creole Days.*

American letters had previously seen nothing quite like these seven fresh, though hardly faultless, stories—the old city of mellowed brick and mildewed stucco, with bustling streets over the wall from fragrant gardens; or, on the purlieus, doomed plantations like the Belles Demoiselles; or, in the French Quarter, the *Salle de Condé* where young bloods went to dance with well chaperoned quadroons; the languor, femininity, gaiety, or knife-wielding ferocity of the Creole caste, from General Villivicencio down to Mazzaro of the Café des Exiles; the invariably beautiful women, demure in bearing but strong in will, like Madame Délicieuse, or Madame John, 'Tite Poulette's guardian; misfits like Poquelin or Monsieur George; mild-mannered young men like Dr. Mossy or Kristian Koppig. The whole was projected poetically, with care for precision of simile, and a certain allusive richness; yet it carried, too, a sly humor which touched with acid some of the Creole portraitures.

Still, it fell short of first-rate writing. A certain desultory clutter inhibited the forward march of the narrative; the use of Creole dialect was overzealous; characters were often merely eccentric; and there was a fondness for the smash ending which soon dated the stories of 'Tite Poulette, Jean-ah Poquelin, and Madame Délicieuse. What one noticed as a leading quality was the gentle love of mystification, a diffusion—not of syntax but of total effect—which seems to be the chief source of Cable's charm.

This charm accounted partly for the success of *The Grandissimes,* a leisurely, discursive, densely populated, panoramic, high-colored, witty, and complicated novel which Cable brought out in 1880. The book had shape, movement, richness of texture, and a kind of subdued violence, and it was crammed with living portraits; the two Honorés (one a quadroon); Frowenfeld the German apothecary (another of those young foreigners whom Cable delighted to put into his books); the beautiful Nancanous, mother and daughter, on whom Cable lavished his best talents; Palmyre Philosophe, the fierce and unpredictable *voudou*; the fabulous Negro prince, Bras-Coupé, and a dozen others. The elements of romance were there in plenty: the simmering feud, the stolen inheritance, the half-brothers separated by the laws of caste, the triple love story, the visitation of yellow fever, the mob assault, the knife in the dark, the hamstrung slave, the trapped and screaming Negress in the cypress swamp, and behind all the slow spectacle of a proud Louisiana, sold over the heads of its citizens, blunderingly resisting Americanization. But there was also a strong infusion of the actual, and Cable knew how and when not to take himself seriously. The Creoles were the "Knickerbockers of Louisiana," relentless reactionaries who had called caste and slavery right, and then "sealed the whole subject." In reopening that subject, Cable did not hesitate to impale these dark butterflies, to borrow a phrase from Hawthorne, upon the iron rod of social ethics; but it was plain, in this and later books, that Cable loved the Creoles, too, and his laughter at their expense was not loud enough to conceal his admiration for their better qualities.

Succeeding years showed Cable's versatility and staying power. *Madame Delphine,* published in 1881 and added to later editions of *Old Creole Days,* was a deft novelette, a variation of the theme of "'Tite Poulette," but more subdued and controlled, suggesting *The Scarlet Letter* translated to the New Orleans milieu. *Dr. Sevier* (1885) was another thronged and complex novel, more straightforwardly told than *The Grandissimes,* in which were detailed the struggles of a serious young married couple against poverty and despair in ante-bellum New Orleans. In the idyllic *Bonaventure* (1888), a trilogy of novelettes, the hero was a Creole schoolmaster, living among the Acadian peasants.

Despite his continued exploitation of Creole character, Cable lived in the

North for the last forty years of his life. When he collaborated with Mark Twain on a series of lecture tours, he found audiences as ready for his stories and songs as for Twain's drolleries. He denied the charge that he had fled the South through social pressure arising from his Creole portraits and his ably reasoned social essays on the predicament of the Southern Negro, and before his death in 1925 he often happily revisited his native city, gathering more material for stories about a region which he, more than any other writer, had indelibly engraved upon the map of regional literature.

About the time Cable moved to Northampton, Massachusetts, Creole enmity toward him was pronounced, and the allegedly injured group soon found a genteel champion. Grace King, daughter of a New Orleans lawyer, assured Gilder in 1884 that Cable had proclaimed his preference for colored people over whites, and for quadroons over Creoles. Gilder icily suggested that if Cable were such a traitor, someone had better try writing better. What Miss King produced in response to the challenge was not spectacular, but it was respectable. *Monsieur Motte* was a girlish, theatrical piece, but the four long stories of Louisiana which she collected in 1892 as *Tales of a Time and Place* displayed a distinguished style, a prose deliberate and cool, illuminated with splashes of color, and filled at the end with climactic passages of action. Both here and in later works Miss King carefully avoided controversial matters, stepped softly, and sought everywhere to tone down the more garish, but always more interesting, portraits which Cable had drawn.

The writing career of Kate Chopin, one of the shortest in the annals of the ordinarily long-lived regional writers, began in 1899 with some indifferent poetry and followed a meteoric course which ended a year or two before her death in 1904. What she did in that time had, however, an intensity, courage, vigor, and independence which sets her work in sharp contrast to the pale antidotes to Cable which Miss King had chosen to offer. An exact contemporary of Miss King, Katherine O'Flaherty was born in St. Louis of Irish and French parents, was graduated from a convent into the active life of a Missouri belle, married Oscar Chopin at nineteen, entered New Orleans society, bore six children, moved to a Red River plantation, saw her husband die of swamp fever, returned to St. Louis, fended off several potential suitors, and in 1890, at the age of thirty-nine, published her first novel. She subsequently wrote nearly a hundred short stories, about half of which were collected in two volumes, *Bayou Folk* (1894) and *A Night in Acadie* (1897). The best of these describe the Acadians in the mid-Louisiana parishes of Natchitoches and Avoyelles, regions with which Mrs. Chopin had become acquainted during her plantation days. Many of them (and there is possibly a connection here with Mrs. Chopin's own mild unconventionality) turn upon acts of rebellion: Zaida's attempted elopement during the Cajun ball at Père Foché's; the refusal of Athenaise to settle into a dull marriage; young Polydore feigning rheumatism to escape work; Chicot, the *neg creol,* whose professed paganism contradicted his Christian practice. At their best the bayou tales displayed a clean economy of line, and were rounded off with a kind of Gallic finesse which suggested that Mrs. Chopin's study of Maupassant had not gone unrewarded. She knew, better than many of her contemporaries among the regionalists, how to begin, develop, and conclude a story without waste motion or observable self-consciousness. Her feeling for character was supported by an almost instinctive grasp of form and pace. Like Miss Jewett, she knew how to use dialect for flavoring; with her it never became an obstacle. Miss Murfree might have learned from her the art of subordinating environment to character. Like Harris and Johnston, she knew where sentiment ends and sentimentality begins. Yet many of her stories fell short of excellence because she wrote too swiftly and impulsively, leaned too heavily upon the suggestions of the moment, and impatiently shrugged off the burden of correction and revision. She rarely resorted to mere trickery, though it is a trick which mars her frequently anthologized (and not very typical) study in race relations, "Désirée's Baby," which satisfies the reader's sense of justice while disappointing him with a contrived conclusion. Even her failures are readable, and at her subtle and economical best, she challenges the workmanship of Mary Wilkins Freeman, analyzing the more exotic and passionate Cajun character or painting the humble romances of canebrake and cotton field with something of that control and candor which her Northern contemporary brought to her studies of New England nuns and village choristers.

4

The regional movement in the East and South, for all its scope and variety, produced few writers of the first magnitude. The best work of Miss Jewett and Mrs. Freeman, like that of Harris and Cable, shows a wholesome originality, a masterly dominance of difficult materials, a devotion to problems of structure and texture, a feeling for character and motivation, a love of the actual and a hatred of the artificial, the bathetic, and the cheap which raises it far above what one usually thinks of as run-of-the-mine local color writing. Many of the lesser writers succeeded often enough so that if a patient editor were prepared to read hundreds of sketches and short stories, he could select, even after applying the most rigorous standards, a group of two or three dozen short stories worthy to stand beside the best short fiction of the period, whether in America or abroad.

Modern critical opinion has divided sharply on the question of the value of regional fiction. One side of the argument is represented by Botkin's assertion that "regionalism marks a trend away from the belletristic—pure literature and absolute poetry—toward a social and cultural art." The other side would follow Tate in believing that regionalism at its worst leads to "a falsification of the creative impulse with the motives of social action." A fair judgment of the achievement of the genre writers would follow a middle path between these extremes. The limitations are clear enough, although they have been somewhat overemphasized: absorption with the picturesque for its own sake (as variously observable in Mary Murfree, James Lane Allen, Celia Thaxter, or sometimes in Cable); the curious pursuit of the unique, idiosyncratic, or grotesque in local character (as *passim* in Ruth McEnery Stuart, Johnston, Mrs. Freeman, Mrs. Cooke, Miss Jewett, Mrs. Slosson, and others). One finds also a noticeable though not universal tendency to gloss over the uglier aspects of the human predicament; an occasional lapse into mere formula writing; a reactionary glorification and sentimentalization of a wealthy and powerful plantation *aristoi* (as in John Esten Cooke, T. N. Page, or sometimes in Bagby, Mrs. Stuart, and Grace King); an equally deplorable tendency to overdo the "common man" motif until one is led to the apotheosis of the mediocre. One could see, over all, an attempt to petrify and monu-mentalize that which in all classes and castes was petering out through its own internal weakness or decadence—the sort of effort which can usually be trusted to produce a negative and static art, unmoved from within and therefore unmoving. The predilection for dialect (it was then the fashion, however irritating it may be to modern readers), in which authors played at amateur phonetics under the mistaken impression that the use of heavily apostrophized contractions, barbaric misspellings, and other desperate expedi-ents would be useful to future linguistic historians, is distressing, as is the tendency to introduce extraneous social detail, which sometimes led in prac-tice to the refusal or failure to compress the sprawling sketch into the tighter limits of the bona fide short story.

The faults are probably outweighed by manifest virtues, whether one is a social historian, a student of literary history, or a plain reader in search of entertainment and instruction. The best of these writers, and even the worst, were aware of a usable past. They were deploying for the attack on the monster bulk of America, like their literary brethren in the Middle and Far West, and they were everywhere showing that earlier critics had been correct in believing in the richness, abundance, and variety of the American scene as a field for literary exploitation. They were proudly displaying and defending such native traits as individualism, ingenuity, sectional or clan loyalty, charity, humility, shrewdness, toughness, and stoicism. They were apologizing for, frankly deploring, explaining, or sometimes trying to explain away such prominent American vices as moral opportunism, social or economic inequality, slavery, racial prejudice, caste divisions, ignorance, indolence, shabby gentility, hypocrisy, mob law, and violence.

It is too easy to deride these writers for their preoccupation with the past, as if the backward look were necessarily a mark of reaction. Like most blanket condemnations, this one neglects the genuine liberalism of Harris and Cable, the forward-looking aesthetic of Jewett, Freeman, or Chopin, or the over-all democratic orientation of a movement deeply devoted to the common people, and to those fundamental integrities of mind and heart which in dangerous days have strengthened and saved the American republic. It is too easy to become supercilious over the "minor triumphs" of the "chroniclers of decay." Regional exploitation per se drove writers to deal with life as they directly knew or had known it. It has never been satisfactorily proved that the example of regionalist fiction was not as effective in the development of the short story and the American novel as the influence of foreign models. The occasional leavening of romance did not invalidate the rule that the movement was fundamentally realistic and that its basic attempt was the analysis of homespun character. Much effort was profitably brought to bear upon the correction of stereotypes—the shrewd Yankee trader, the shiftless mountaineer, the plantation darky, the Kentucky colonel—and what resulted was not another battery of types, but a series of highly individualized people whom one can classify as old maids and dewy maidens, moonshiners and mariners, crackers and sandhillers, Cajuns and Creoles, but who in practice are no more limited by these categories than Falstaff is limited by his resemblance to the *miles gloriosus* of Latin comedy.

Even without these achievements, the regionalists and genre writers of the East and South made their contribution to the history of American culture. At a crucial period in American history, when old faces, manners, customs, recipes, styles, attitudes, and prejudices were undergoing rapid change or total extirpation, they seized and perpetuated, through the medium of fictional character, the cultural landscape: the native idiom, the still unravished rural peace, the feel and flavor of things as they were, and would never be again.

53. WESTERN RECORD AND ROMANCE

WESTERN literature in the generation after the Civil War was a literature of discovery. Peace released grand energies, scattered fortune hunters and land-hungry veterans westward, heightened the sense of national oneness, gave Americans their first real notion of what it meant to be a continental nation. The transcontinental railroad linked the social and cultural variants thus far formed in the West—the farming Midwest, the Mormon commonwealth in the Rocky Mountains, and the mining and ranching world of California—and tied not only them but the Indian and Spanish societies of the West into the national fabric. Now began the final filling-in of the continent westward from the Missouri and eastward from the Pacific. Now American writers began to explore their country; now Americans began to know themselves as a single people and at the same time a diverse people, one large pattern full of endless variations.

The literary exploitation of the West was simultaneous with that of the older sections of the country, but its spirit was very different. It was equally sectional, equally national, but the newness of the material made it more adventurous, more romantic. Picturesque sections of the continent were thrown open; all the sections were tied into one. And all through the period after the Civil War explorers and writers and travelers and geologists were enthusiastically recording their own versions of what life in the West came to.

There were in general two kinds of people who wrote this literature: those who knew what they were talking about, and those who did not; those who aimed to tell the truth, and those who aimed to dress it up. At their extremes, these two tendencies are represented on the one hand by the scientific report and on the other by romantic local color fiction. But it would be a mistake to assume that only scientists told the truth about the West and only storytellers glamorized it. The same new country, the same new experiences, were encountered by all sorts of people, and were reflected from different surfaces.

One may discuss these writings in either local or national terms. The two distinct schools of Western literature, one centered in Indiana and one in California, were distinguishable not only by geographical but by temperamental qualities. Earthy realism more like that of the East, stemming from Edward Eggleston, was dominant in Indiana; when Indiana writers strayed into more romantic paths they were likely to take the way of folksy sentiment, and a flavor of piety was in most of what they produced. The local colorists, on the other hand, stemmed from Bret Harte; their piety, like their concern for the truth of social patterns and customs, was less demanding, and both their materials and their methods were altogether more gilded than those in style in Indiana. Yet currents of cross-fertilization flowed back and forth. Both Indiana and California were on the main street of America, and their very localism gave them something in common. Between them, they produced not only two vigorous schools of regional literature, but a type of American literature which derived strongly from native soil and native character. The scientific writings of the period can hardly be said to belong to either school; they deal primarily with the more recently opened trans-Missouri West, and thus have close links with California, but their objective scientific approach is closer to the realism of Indiana.

The writer who knew both Midwestern and Western life most fruitfully was Mark Twain. In him, various strains met and fused; but in the lesser figures the same strains are observable separately or in other combinations. It is the function of this chapter to detail who they were, what of America they discovered, what literary tendencies they created or followed.

Their discoveries may be listed: They discovered first the romantic Past, though antiquarian delvings produced more for Eastern and Southern imitators than for the Westerners themselves. There was a bloom over two areas of the Western past—over the French settlements around the Great Lakes, and over the drowsy Lotus Land of Spanish California. Both were exploited.

They discovered also the Present. A society with a character of its own was forming in the Midwest, maturing first in Ohio and Indiana. It was not a highly developed society: Maurice Thompson compared it to a boy whose voice was changing. But it provided a succession of realistic writers from Eggleston on with a chance to paint the unposed face of inland America. The tradition that Eggleston began would flower later in other Midwestern realists, in Garland and Dreiser and Cather and Sandburg and Lewis. And what might be called its dialectic strain would become the homespun tradition of sentiment and folksy philosophy, the subliterary but immensely popular poetizing of Carleton, Riley, and Field.

At the other end of the West, Bret Harte, Mark Twain, and Joaquin Miller also discovered a social order, a fleeting and picturesque one, in the world of the frontiersman and miner. These characters had practically passed before they broke into serious literature; and by that time they had acquired the romantic patina of time. But for a brief moment in the fifties and sixties,

Angel's Camp and Red Dog were reality of a startling kind. Another heroic and almost as transitory society, that of the cattlemen, was later in finding chroniclers except on the dime-novel level. It was the end of the century before Andy Adams and Owen Wister and Alfred Henry Lewis made the cattle frontier the subject of serious fiction.

These discoverers were all literary men—poets and novelists and short-story writers. Quite as important in their way were a group of men whose primary interest was the country itself, the superb physical endowment of the nation. A good part of the best writing done in the West in these postwar years was done by geologists, explorers, surveyors, mountain climbers, naturalists. Sometimes, like George Horatio Derby (John Phoenix) of an earlier generation, they were geologists with one hand and writers with the other. Sometimes they blended geology and scenery with action and ideas and produced literature of a special kind, as did Clarence King, John Muir, John Wesley Powell, and Clarence Dutton.

There were also the frontiersmen of the mind, explorers of ideas. Henry George looked gloomily upon the Pacific Railroad, prophesying that it would bring wealth to a few, poverty to many, and out of his observations built a new economic philosophy. Major Powell studied the arid regions and told the nation explicitly how it would have to settle that country if it wanted to avoid erosion, droughts, floods, and the ruin of the land. And William Gilpin, who has been called the first geopolitician, dreamed mighty dreams of the global mission of the American people. Because people have gone on reading the books of these men, and because their ideas have been of incalculable influence, all three men deserve inclusion in any literary survey of the period.

Finally, the postwar discoveries must include the basic American, the common man. He had appeared in print before, but usually on the level of the sporting magazine. He was brother to the Hoosier and the poor white and cousin to the Yankee farmer or peddler; but in California his name was "Pike," and he dominated Western literature for almost two decades. He was named for Pike County, Missouri, but he came from Illinois, Arkansas, or North Texas quite as frequently: in practice, Pike County was as large and vague as Los Angeles County is today. At the eastern extension of his range, the Pike merged imperceptibly into the Hoosier and poor white of Indiana, Ohio, and Kentucky. His literary portraits show him as anything from the "acclimated man" of Mark Twain's *Gilded Age* to Abraham Lincoln; anything from the "Missouri Pukes" who massacred Mormons in the forties to Jim Bludso or Huckleberry Finn.

Bayard Taylor defined the Pike as "the Anglo-Saxon relapsed into semi-barbarism." But relapsed or not, his discovery by writers of the sixties, seventies, and eighties was something tremendous and wonderful for native literature. And when Pikes began *writing* books, we had for the first time a literature that mass America could feel in its bones. Ultimately, the biggest discovery of the whole period was the Pike, the common man.

2

A country and a people, a forming society in a newly opened land, were thus before the writers of the West, who fell upon both land and people as the gold seekers fell upon the placer sands of California's rivers. Neither scientific observer nor literary exploiter, realist nor romantic, had precedence. Discovery was simultaneous in several directions, so that when we look at the beginning of the seventies we find every major element already there. Bret Harte's first unheralded mining-camp story, "The Work on Red Mountain," which was to be rewritten as "M'liss," had come in 1860; and Twain's *Celebrated Jumping Frog of Calaveras County and Other Sketches,* in 1867. But with the linking of the rails in 1869 the stage was set for more spectacular things. Harte's "Luck of Roaring Camp" and "Plain Language from Truthful James" appeared in 1870. John Hay's *Pike County Ballads,* in the same dialect vein as Harte's poems, came in 1871, as did Joaquin Miller's *Songs of the Sierras.* The year 1871 also saw Edward Eggleston's *Hoosier Schoolmaster,* a realistic study of Midwest village life, and the first volume of Will Carleton's homespun verses. And in that same year came Clarence King's *Mountaineering in the Sierra Nevada,* in many ways the most delightful book of its decade, though written by a geologist.

None of these discoveries—local color, dialect, homely sentiment, realistic rural life, or the grandeur of natural scenery—was actually a discovery. Writers had done local characters and local dialects before, dug into the national past; for example, Theodore Winthrop's *John Brent* (1862). Though this Western country was new, it had been written about by Lewis and Clark, Pike, Frémont, Marcus Whitman, and others. The local scene in California had been exploited by newspaper and magazine writers from the time when Sam Brannan unloaded his boatload of Mormons and uncrated the press machinery for the *California Star* in 1846. Even before that, Dana's *Two Years Before the Mast* had told the world something of the Spanish towns strung from Yerba Buena to Guaymas. Earlier still, the wild life of the Mississippi and Ohio had been caught by Timothy Flint and James Hall. Even the Pike was no fire-new character. The *Alta-California* had advertised a romance, "Pike County Bill, or the Maid of the Mountains," in 1854, and by the next year the Pike was having his malarial phiz sketched by several newspaper humorists, including "Old Block," "Jeems Pipes from Pipesville," and "John Phoenix." Wagon trains were already rocking westward to the strains of "Sweet Betsy from Pike"; the ballad saw print as early as 1858 in *Put's Golden Songster.* The Pike was thus almost a stereotype in California before Harte ever took him up. Back of California there were earlier versions of the general type in the Beowulfian humor of the Mississippi, the nameless newspaper exchanges, the *Spirit of the Times,* the *Georgia Scenes* of Augustus Longstreet and the *Autobiography of Davy Crockett of Tennessee.*

Drawing more than they knew on traditions, a handful of innovators at the beginning of the seventies remade Western literature, and in a real sense the literature of the United States. Harte, Miller, Eggleston, Hay, King, and Carleton (and of course Mark Twain, who is discussed in a later chapter) gave the literature of a whole generation its directions.

3

Bret Harte was no Argonaut. He came to California from Albany, New York, in 1854 to join his mother, not to seek gold. Though he worked at several jobs—teaching school at La Grange in the gold country, setting type for the *Northern Californian* in the town of Union, compounding pharmaceuticals, contributing to and editing various journals, especially the *Golden Era* and the *Alta California,* and acting as secretary of the mint—yet he never quite became a participant. Essentially he was a civilized man, a bookish man. In San Francisco, by dedication and hard work, he made himself the leader of a brilliant group that at various times included Twain, Henry George, Ambrose Bierce, Prentice Mulford, Charles Warren Stoddard, Joaquin Miller, Clarence King, and Ina Coolbrith. His appointment in 1868 to the editorship of Anton Roman's new magazine, the *Overland Monthly,* was recognition of the position he had won. In the three years of his editorship he not only made the magazine the most brilliant of all Western periodicals, but made himself a national figure.

He had had triumphs of a minor and local kind, written occasional poems and Irvingesque sketches with legendary and Spanish themes, had parodied popular novelists in a clever series called *Condensed Novels* (1867). His first big success came with the *Overland's* second issue, which carried "The Luck of Roaring Camp." The stir was tremendous; the *Atlantic* wired extravagant offers for stories of the same kind, fan mail poured in. Harte followed "The Luck" with others, among them the best stories he was ever to write: "The Outcasts of Poker Flat," "Tennessee's Partner," "Miggles," "The Idyl of Red Gulch," and "Brown of Calaveras." He scored a second triumph as great as the first when he printed, rather dubiously, the dialect poem called "Plain Language from Truthful James." This was reprinted in magazines, newspapers, broadsides, and spread in store windows, all over the nation. Together with other "Pike" poems, it was reissued as "The Heathen Chinee" in 1871.

"The Luck of Roaring Camp" is the father of all Western local color stories; "The Heathen Chinee" begot a progeny of dialect poems. Both represented something new to sophisticated audiences: a romantic, picturesque world; characters as striking as the characters of Dickens and perhaps in part derived from Dickens; a trick of neat paradox that gave scoundrels Raphael faces and endowed bruisers and hard cases with a saving spot of sentiment; a method of story telling that was lean, unpadded, finely calculated. Harte had served a long apprenticeship. He was a finished writer by the time "The Luck" appeared. He was destined to have an influence as great as that of the greatest.

But when Harte left San Francisco in 1871, bound for Boston and the larger world, he had already done all his best work. Money pressures, the demands of a public that always wanted "more like 'The Luck,' " and perhaps a drying-up of his inspiration, forced him into a mold. He went on, the rest of his life, imitating himself. The last twenty-four years of his life he lived abroad, in Germany, in Scotland, and in London where he died. At the end he was a tired, skillful, dependable hack, turning out stories to order and adding a volume every other year or so to his collected works. The best of his achievement lay far back in the seventies.

Talent, Harte certainly had; but he lacked Twain's fecundity, and he was farther from reality. Reading through his twenty volumes, one has a feeling of deadly sameness. The characters are Dickensian types: never a gambler who is not Jack Oakhurst, never a stage driver who is not burly and "squar' " like Yuba Bill, never a miner who is not a rough soul with a vacuole of sentiment pulsating in him somewhere, like Tennessee's Partner or the heroically sentimental gift bringer in "How Santa Claus Came to Simpson's Bar."

Yet this last story, like earlier ones, illustrates Harte's strengths. Dick Bullen's wild ride is a masterpiece of dramatic action reporting. A story such as "Mrs. Skagg's Husbands," though ruined by an impossibly bad ending, has a beginning as sharp and clean and modern as John Steinbeck at his best might have written. Harte was no prude; he drew no morals and preached no sermons; he painted prostitutes and foul-mouthed children and drunken sots without apology. His children are always sympathetically and convincingly drawn. He had humor, a good ear, a style that was disciplined and clean. Yet through all, even his best work, runs a thread of something theatrical and false.

Hobos have a word for anyone who pretends fellowship in the fraternity of the road. Such an impostor they call a "scenery stiff." In spite of the trained brilliance of his best stories, Harte was a scenery stiff. It is safe to apply the same term to Joaquin Miller, who in the year of Harte's first success was in London peddling his poems to various publishers. Born in Indiana (as he said, "in a covered wagon headed West"), he had traveled the Oregon Trail with his family, had snatched a handful of education here and there, had taught school, and had edited a newspaper which was closed for its Copperhead sympathies at the onset of the war. He had, so he asserted, lived and fought with the Modoc Indians, had begotten at least one little half-breed Miller, and finally had married an Oregon girl whom he left behind while he bore his poetic ambitions to San Francisco. There the literary were not impressed.

Neither were the London publishers impressed. Never one to be over-modest, Miller printed *Pacific Poems* at his own expense and sent them to the reviews. The result was startling: somehow the barbaric, uneven verses took the British fancy. W. M. Rossetti wrote a glowing review, the Pre-Raphaelites welcomed Miller to themselves. In cowhide boots and sealskin coat he dined with London celebrities; in red shirt and Stetson he knocked the eye out of Britishers eager to support a tame frontiersman. With help from Rossetti and others, Miller revised *Pacific Poems* and reissued them as *Songs of the Sierra*. When he went home to the United States the next year he was an international figure, self-made.

Except for his influence, which was not lasting, and his reputation, always slightly tainted with ridicule, Miller seems of little account today. His long verse dramas, his panoramic and tempestuous narratives of the Indian country, Nicaragua, the mountains, and the deserts, are mainly sound and fury. The poet's own posturing, his bald self-aggrandizement, made him a character, though he was only in flashes a true poet. He wrote through a long life many books, but a very large proportion of what he wrote is chaff. Of the dramas, only *The Danites of the Sierras* offers much to a modern reader; and of his prose writings, cluttered with incredible lies, there is nothing likely to live except *Life Among the Modocs,* a fragment of what he called autobiography. Of his shorter poems, the anthologists neglect everything but "Columbus."

In the wake of Harte and Miller—especially of Harte—came a whole generation of lesser local colorists mainly female. They are worth a summary statement, hardly more. In general, they approached local habits and local characters as a tourist would approach them. It is fair to say that as a group they avoided the commonplace, concerned themselves chiefly with the unusual, were incurably romantic, obsessed with the picturesque, and accurate only to the superficial aspects of their chosen materials. The spirit of the West almost inevitably escaped them because they wrote from outside, not from within. Constance Fenimore Woolson and Mary Hartwell Catherwood dug industriously into the past and present of the Great Lakes settlements and the romantic history of New France. Alice French (Octave Thanet) exploited Davenport, Iowa, and Black River, Arkansas, though with a greater understanding and a stronger impulse to realism. Mary Hallock Foote brought readers back to the mining camps of Idaho and Colorado and to some of the materials first publicized by Bret Harte.

Though there are fine passages and fine single stories among these writers, especially in the work of Miss French and Mrs. Foote, their reputations are likely to dwindle further rather than revive. But one reputation will last. It is that of Helen Hunt Jackson, who after a prolific career of romantic hack writing became interested in the fate of the Indians and, in her honest indignation, wrote two books. One, *A Century of Dishonor* (1881), was a bitter indictment of the federal policies toward the Indian. The other, *Ramona* (1884), was calculated to be for the Indian what *Uncle Tom's Cabin* was for the Negroes, but wound up as a romance about the dying Spanish society of southern California. It is hard now to read *Ramona* and realize that Alessandro is Indian at all, or Ramona a half-breed. But people still read it; there is hardly a library in the land without several copies; it has hit the millions in Technicolor. Part of that enduring charm is in the principals and in the backgrounds and in the theme of thwarted love, but the greatest strength of the novel is the portrait of Señora Moreno, guardian of the old Spanish ways against the encroaching Americans. In her practice of duty without love, justice without kindness, she dominates the first half of the book. It is not so good a book when she leaves it.

It would not do to omit mention of the Indiana romancer Maurice Thompson, who began in his literary career with a volume, *Hoosier Mosaics* (1875), in the realistic vein of Eggleston, but quickly gave up realism for more colorful story telling. None of his books, either in poetry or in prose, achieved marked success until *Alice of Old Vincennes* (1900) crowned his career with a best seller. This romance about George Rogers Clark and the Northwest Territory served, with Mary Catherwood's New France novels, as a model for most of the later writers of historical novels. Yet, popular as they were in their day, these romantic local color writers are not the people to whom we would go for pictures of their own times. Rather we must consult the school of Edward Eggleston, which began, like most of the trends of the period, in 1871.

4

Edward Eggleston came to writing not by way of a long literary apprenticeship and a sense of dedication, as Harte did, but by way of the Methodist ministry and the editing of Sunday-school papers. Until he was well grown he had never even read a novel.

Yet he had had encouragement from his old teacher in Vevay, Indiana; and though his schooling had been irregular he had had access to his father's good library, and was well read in the Bible, history, and the classics. For a time he was a circuit-riding minister in southern Indiana: his health broke down in six months. After a period of settled pastorates in Minnesota he took the editorship of the *Little Corporal,* a Chicago children's paper, going later to the *Independent,* and finally to *Hearth and Home* which he made—as Harte had made the *Overland*—with his first contribution, a serial version of *The Hoosier Schoolmaster*. He justified his tale to himself and his employers on the ground that, though a novel, it contained valuable moral lessons.

Eggleston's method was quite different from Harte's. Led to picture local manners and local speech by his reading of Taine's *History of Art in the Netherlands,* he produced something as realistic as Dutch painting, touching with love and care the homely details of living. From his childhood and his experience as a circuit rider, he knew the Indiana backwoods intimately; and only a year after Harte had set a romantic fashion Eggleston turned the fashion back. He never changed his method, though he learned a great deal about writing novels after his first attempt; and even when in later life he turned to writing history he adopted the same aim and the same method as in his novels.

Mechanically *The Hoosier Schoolmaster* (1871) is a bad novel. Its villain is unmotivated, its incidents syncopate like a badly patched film, its style is lumbering, it preaches. Eggleston did better in *The Circuit Rider* (1874), *Roxy* (1878), and *The Graysons* (1888). He did much worse in *The Hoosier Schoolboy* (1883), a curious recession in style and tone. Altogether, he wrote seven novels of the West, as well as a good many juveniles and two solid volumes of history. Like Harte, he was the author of a philosophy of composition, the cornerstone of a school. It is a proof of the validity of his method that, even when he is clumsy, he can still be read without boredom.

Two other dialect writers, both poets, deserve a place beside Eggleston as early painters of the local. One is John Hay, whose *Pike County Ballads* (1871) numbered only six poems, tossed off in a hurry and regretted ever after. Probably they were stimulated by Harte's dialect poems, though Mark Twain thought they had been written before Harte's "Truthful James." Whether influenced by Harte or not, Hay tapped a purer vein than Harte. He had been born in the Midwest, had attended school in Pike County, Illinois, had read law in Springfield next door to Lincoln. As a result, his Pike poems have a ring that Harte's lack, a depth of character not all paradox and surprise. "Jim Bludso" and "Little Breeches" have become virtual folk possessions; and of the six poems only "Golyer," the tale of a no-good stage driver who redeems himself by shielding a child from robbers' bullets, is in the Harte vein. It is the worst of the six.

Hay's only other connection with Western literature comes through his collaboration with Nicolay on the ten-volume life of Lincoln; but the crude little ballads he was ashamed of are likely to prove quite as durable as the monumental biography. Jim Bludso was too real to die.

In the same year that Hay and Eggleston tackled real Midwestern themes and people, a Michigan poetaster, Will Carleton, published the first of a long series of volumes. Carleton's name is not usually spoken when the literary markers are counted, and there is no irresistible reason why it should be; yet he cannot be quite overlooked either. Limping as to meter and simple as to sentiment, his poems were widely read, and still are. He was the first "People's Laureate" in the Midwest, and poems like "Over the Hill to the Poorhouse" and "Gone with a Handsomer Man" have as solid a place in subliterary America as any of James Whitcomb Riley's. Tear-jerking situations, happy endings, the celebration of homely virtues, were the stock in trade of both Carleton and Riley, though Riley was both a smoother versifier and a better showman than his predecessor. Along with a grasp of the plain emotions of plain people (which in literature often means the stereotyped emotions of stereotyped people) Riley had a wit, an aptness of phrase, an acuteness of observation, that give his work for all its conventionality a frequent lift. Though he was in many ways, like Carleton, completely unrealistic in his pictures of Midwestern farm life, also like Carleton he was triumphantly common; and commonness has been part of a magic formula for popularity for a long time, at least in America.

The "Hoosier School" begun by Eggleston, forwarded by Thompson's *Hoosier Mosaics,* and modified by the work of Carleton and Riley, went on producing writers pretty much according to its original patterns. Eggleston's uncompromising realism did not flower until later, and farther west; but his influence touched every Midwestern writer. Booth Tarkington and Meredith Nicholson both exhibited in curious ways the mixture of realistic, romantic, and commonplace that went into the making of the earliest Indiana literature. In *Monsieur Beaucaire* (1900) Tarkington was as romantic as Thompson; in *The Gentleman from Indiana* (1899), *The Magnificent Ambersons* (1918), *Alice Adams* (1921), and other novels he exhibited the moral earnestness and seriously realistic intent of Eggleston; in the Penrod series he showed the sharp eye, the humor, the delight in the commonplace that distinguished Riley. In the same way Nicholson swung between romantic and realistic, between *The Port of Missing Men* (1907) and *A Hoosier Chronicle*

(1912), between *The House of a Thousand Candles* (1905) and *The Poet* (1914).

Something of that same blending of realistic and romantic is to be found in the best of the cowboy novelists. Least romantic of these was Andy Adams, whose solid, Defoe-like books are so underplayed and accurate that they pass for history. The best of them, *The Log of a Cowboy* (1903), is really the synthesized record of the many cattle drives Adams took from the Texas range to the cattle country of Nebraska and Montana. Others, equally honest, are *The Outlet* (1905), *Reed Anthony, Cowman* (1907), and *Cattle Brands* (1906), a collection of short stories.

Another cowboy writer, Alfred Henry Lewis (Dan Quin), is notable as the author of the whole series of Wolfville novels, the first of which was published in 1897. Probably one of that series is enough for the average reader, but the literary flavor of the cowboy West has not been fully sampled without at least one of the Old Cattleman's drawling yarns.

Lewis as well as Adams had been a cow hand, and wrote of what he knew inside and out. But the most readable of all cowboy novels was written by a visitor from Pennsylvania and Harvard. Owen Wister began with short stories of ranch life, collected in *Lin MacLean* (1898) and *The Jimmyjohn Boss* (1900), and followed them with *The Virginian* (1902) which, in spite of some romantic goings-on that Adams would have scorned, has held its place as a literary milestone. It is still immensely readable, full of action and humor, and the ring of authenticity. Wister's ear for lingo was unusually keen, and he had apparently absorbed ranch life through his pores. "When you call me that, smile!" is still standard for young Americans playing cowboy, and the situation between the buckaroo and the schoolmarm has become stock equipment for horse opera. But the book from which many horse operas derive has a dignity and strength not shared by its imitators. Adams, Lewis, and Wister made the cowboy a respectable character for serious literature. Though their lead has been followed since by Eugene Manlove Rhodes and others, their performance has not yet been bettered. All came when local color as a coherent movement had about played itself out; all owe as much to the honest realism of Eggleston as to the flossy melodramatics of Harte.

5

The authentic cowboy writers and the novelists of Eggleston's school had one great virtue in common: they knew what they were talking about. So did the geologists and nature writers who all through the last three decades of the nineteenth century were busy building a literature out of observation and facts. The taste for that literature was national. In a career that lasted fifty years, John Burroughs was establishing it in the East as a writer of essays that mingled the philosophy of Emerson and Whitman with careful observation of the birds, trees, and flowers of the Catskill Mountains. His readers shared in the work, reporting their observations in letters and in pilgrimages to "Slabsides."

The first of the Western nature writers, Clarence King, was for a short time a member of the *Overland* group in San Francisco, and in 1871 his *Mountaineering in the Sierra Nevada* sketches were sharing the *Atlantic*'s pages with Bret Harte's writings. It is not customary to give King credit as an innovator or source of anything; yet *Mountaineering in the Sierra Nevada* was very widely read and has been persistently reprinted, and he had dozens of friends, among them Hay and Henry Adams, who admired him extravagantly. He was the first Western nature writer to find a public.

Mountaineering in the Sierra Nevada is a completely charming book, exciting, gay, vigorous, witty, and written in polished and perceptive prose. If he had chosen, King could probably have been a major writer; but, even though he wrote only the one book outside the geological field, his reputation will last. In the chapter "The Newtys of Pike" he gives us a Pike family with an odd, sidelong sympathy, one of the best and subtlest portraits of the Pike in our literature. A romantic chapter like "Kaweah's Run" does the Bret Harte sort of thing as fluently as ever Harte did it. In "Cut-Off Copples's" he paints a hilarious portrait of a self-taught, garrulous Pike artist. And the core of the book, concerned with climbs up Tyndall, Shasta, and Whitney, is personal experience narrative and nature description of top literary quality. The short story "The Helmet of Mambrino," so cherished and overpraised by King's friends, has no connection with Western literature except that it was written as a letter to a friend in San Francisco.

Of all the men who followed King in writing about Western scenery, John Muir is unquestionably the most important literary figure. Though ten years of residence in Yosemite identified him with that spot, he knew the continent as few did, had walked over it lengthwise and crosswise and cornerwise, had explored the Alaskan coast and the Sierras and the Great Basin ranges and the Midwest and Florida. When he talked about North America, he knew whereof he spoke.

Though he seems never to have met King, their histories are entangled. Muir's first paper, a piece of Yosemite glaciers, appeared in the New York *Tribune* in 1871, while King's mountaineering sketches were running in the *Atlantic*. Maintaining that the Yosemite was glacier-formed and not formed by cataclysmic splitting, as King and his chief Whitney had supposed, Muir started a controversy that ended in Whitney's complete discomfiture. Muir knew glaciers had formed the valley: he had followed their tracks all over the range.

During the course of an energetic life Muir established himself, without academic or governmental aids, as an authoritative geologist and naturalist. He was invited on the Harriman Expedition to Alaska and toured the nation's forests with eminent scientists. Emerson, Theodore Roosevelt, the great of the world, beat a path to his door in Yosemite. To his understanding and love for natural things we owe much of our national forest and national park program. Busy as he was, he wrote many articles and kept voluminous journals; but most of his books were put together in later years, and his journals did not appear until 1938, when a selection was published. Between 1894 and 1918 he wrote nine books which have become a part of our literature—among them *The Mountains of California* (1894), *The Story of My Boyhood and Youth* (1913), and *Travels in Alaska* (1915).

On the strength of these writings Muir must rank as the very best of the nature writers who followed the paths earlier explored by Thoreau. Indefatigable, dedicated, enthusiastic, single-minded to the point of bullheadedness, he wrote only what echoed the freedom and delight of his life. His writing is full of exclamations and glad shouts, and though he wrote slowly and his ideas are not, on examination, of extraordinary variety, yet his words have an air of the most sprightly spontaneity. They bubble and dance; occasionally, as in the essays on conservation in *Our National Parks* (1901), they are hot as flying sparks. A kindly, friendly, open-souled man, Muir made friends by the score and won many to the wilderness he loved. As the years pass he will win more.

Not every one of our areas of stupendous scenery has its *genius loci,* as Yosemite had its Muir. But the Grand Canyon of the Colorado has two, both geologists and explorers. One, the last great explorer of continental America, was a one-armed veteran of Shiloh, Major John Wesley Powell, who in 1869 and again in 1871 ran the Colorado River by boat from Green River Crossing, Wyoming, to the mouth of the Grand Wash, just above the present Boulder Dam. The account of the first trip, which took from May until the end of August and covered over a thousand miles of wild and terrible river sunk in canyons sometimes more than a mile deep, was published for the Smithsonian Institution, which had sponsored the expedition, in a cumbersome quarto, *Exploration of the Colorado River of the West* (1875). It is one of the best adventure stories in American literature.

As director of the United States Geographical and Geological Survey of the Rocky Mountain Region, and later as the second director of the United States Geological Survey (succeeding Clarence King), Powell gathered around him a corps of able men, one of whom, W. H. Holmes, is an unpublicized

Western painter for someone to discover. Another, Captain Clarence E. Dutton, was assigned through more than a decade of field work to most of the grand parts of the West--first to Utah, then to the Grand Canyon, then to the extinct volcanoes of Oregon and the desert near Mount Taylor in New Mexico. Of Dutton's books and monographs, two deserve reading not merely as geology but as nature writing of a fine and sensitive sort. *The Geology of the High Plateaus of Utah* (1879–1880) and *The Tertiary History of the Grand Canyon District* (1882) are not likely to attract readers either by their ponderous format or by their formidable titles, and neither has been reprinted. Yet both are delightful and rewarding books, the geological exposition livened constantly by powerful descriptions. In country so bizarre that orthodox notions of color and form were inapplicable, Dutton learned to know and love what has merely startled most observers. His descriptions of the Grand Canyon and its surrounding plateaus and canyons are certainly the best that have appeared in print—and literally hundreds of writers have essayed the task of getting that chasm into words. Both Muir and Burroughs leaned heavily on Dutton when they came to write of the Grand Canyon, and Charles Dudley Warner borrowed freely and without enough quotation marks. Within the canyon Dutton is remembered by the dozens of names he gave to amphitheaters and buttes; but his two books about that region deserve far wider reading than they have had.

6

Midwestern and Western life—the developing farms of Indiana and Ohio and Illinois and Iowa, the fleeting world of miner and cowboy, the past of the Spanish and the French black-robes—were reflected with varying degrees of accuracy in the literature from 1870 to the end of the century. But there were attempts at forecasting the future, and those too are of literary importance. It is appropriate to close a discussion of this period with the stargazers.

One of these, Henry George, is discussed at length elsewhere in this volume. His observation of the ways in which land ownership in a new country patterned itself led him to the writing of *Progress and Poverty* and to economic conclusions that have brought him millions of readers in the past sixty years. He prophesied the slow revolution which has concentrated land ownership into fewer and fewer hands, and as the burning advocate of the single-tax system he became a figure of international importance.

Another, William Gilpin, who visited the Northwest with Frémont's expedition in 1842 and got the continental vision earlier than most Americans, never became an international figure; but he thought in international terms. An officer of the Missouri Volunteers in the Mexican War, first territorial governor of Colorado, and the man who saved Colorado for the Union, he spent much of his life developing one big dream, foreshadowing the geopolitical thinking of Mackinder and others of a later time. Within what he called the Isothermal Zodiac, Gilpin thought he had found the area where all high civilizations must develop. Most of the United States lay within that straggling belt, and because of this and the favorable unifying influence of North American topography, America must become the first and best example of peace and prosperity and unity, and must teach those lessons to the world. Full elucidation of Gilpin's theories would take pages; those theories were both extravagant and prophetic. Many of the things he said in *The Central Gold Region* (1860—reprinted, 1875, as *The Mission of the North American People*) and in *The Cosmopolitan Railway* (1890) have been verified by later geopolitical studies. Even his pet notion of intercontinental railways linking America and Asia by way of Bering Strait, and Europe and Africa by way of Gibraltar, was in its way perfectly logical. The opening of the West, which both George and Gilpin lived through, was a mighty explosion of forces; it is appropriate that it should have produced not merely a new theory of property and a new economic philosophy, but the first geopolitical theorizing, the first global thought.

Modern geographers are not likely to go back to Gilpin's books as to a bible, interesting as they are. But modern regional planners have gone back again and again to Major Powell's *Lands of the Arid Region* (1878). An innocent-looking government report on land and irrigation surveys in the West, this book contained the germs of far weightier things. Though the program recommended in it, including a sharp revision of the public-land system in the arid belt, never won out against the opposition of Western Congressmen, these surveys were the first step in the formation of the Reclamation Service which has remade whole sections of the West. Moreover, from his own studies of Western land and resources, Powell knew that the whole American pattern of settlement would have to be altered if the arid lands were to be settled without disaster. The homestead laws were inapplicable, size of farms had to be enlarged, probably government had to control what and how much land was to be plowed up. The whole region had to be opened carefully, with long-range planning. Powell demonstrated methodically the effects of breaking sod where there was scant rainfall; he showed the effects of overgrazing, water wastage, and destruction of timber and grass on the watersheds. Earlier than almost anyone else, and more thoroughly than any, he sensed what colossal engineering, both social and mechanical, would be necessary if we were to prevent large parts of the nation from becoming deserts as bleak as Palestine. He prophesied dust bowls, foretold floods and soil erosion and the social erosion that accompanies them. In this one volume is outlined an enormous amount of the federal government's reclamation and conservation program. Here in 1878 is the blueprint for all the still-to-come valley authorities; for reclamation dams, flood control, forest reserves, and reforestation programs and the practice of withholding certain lands for planned social reasons.

By the middle of the twentieth century, little by little, grass could creep up the hillsides again and the dust bowls come back to relative fertility. None of the waste need have happened if Powell's program of 1878 had been applied then. He was the last of the explorers and the first of the great regional planners, and though he would have been the last to claim consideration as a literary man, it is somehow right that the book which was in many ways the most important single volume of the whole period should have been a handbook on how to settle and conserve what Manifest Destiny had tossed in our laps. Many of the writers considered earlier gave us pictures of how life was lived, or might have been lived, in the West. Powell gave us an uncannily accurate picture of how it would have to be lived. And, in writing without literary intent, he wrote more vital literature than did many a story teller or poet of the West.

54. REALISM DEFINED:
WILLIAM DEAN HOWELLS

O<small>NE</small> answer to the literary dilemma of the seventies and eighties was thus to waive literary intent, as Franklin and Jefferson and Lincoln had done in earlier times; but the story teller and poet will not be so easily silenced. For every Franklin there is an Irving, for every Jefferson a Cooper, and for every Lincoln a Whitman. And in these later times, there appeared a William Dean Howells, a Henry James, a Mark Twain, each in his own way ready to grapple with reality and reduce it to literary terms.

Realism is as old as fiction itself. Though often considered the antithesis of romance, it was actually developed by the romancers to make their creations plausible. In the nineteenth century it received its greatest stimulus from Sir Walter Scott's descriptions of scenery and costumes, his effort to depict dialects and manners, especially in characters from humble life. Balzac began the Comédie Humaine after reading the Waverley novels, and Galdós, Merezhkovski, Tolstoy, and many others besides the English novelists acknowledge Scott's influence. As early as 1826 the word *réalisme* was used in France to describe a literary method that attempted the faithful imitation of originals found in nature; it was contrasted, not with romanticism, but with classicism, which tended toward the imitation of art rather than nature. Both romanticist and realist tried to give detailed transcripts of the world about them. The romanticist wanted a background picturesque, yet real enough to be plausible, against which to display the subjective passions that were his main interest, while the realist's aim was an accurate, objective reproduction of scene and character for its own sake. The difference lay less in their choice of material than in their intention.

This affords the best criterion for distinguishing local color writers from true realists, though the impossibility of determining intention forbids dogmatic classification. Realism must always be a relative term, varying with the author's view of reality. To Stendhal it meant the effort to state truly and precisely "what men are in the world that is." George Eliot showed a Wordsworthian influence with her emphasis on homely subjects; her principle of "the faithful representing of commonplace things," enunciated in *Adam Bede*

(1859), is identical with that of William Dean Howells. "Ah! poor Real Life, which I love," he wrote in 1872, "can I make others share the delight I find in thy foolish and insipid face?" His definition is well known—"Realism is nothing more and nothing less than the truthful treatment of material"—but the seldom quoted conclusion of the sentence, "and Jane Austen was the first and the last of the English novelists to treat material with entire truthfulness," reveals his limitation.

Many parallel definitions might be cited (Trollope's "faithful reproduction of the manners of real life," and Eggleston's "correct portrayal of life and manners," for example) to demonstrate that American realism in the nineteenth century was part of a world movement. Through mistaken patriotism, historians have too often treated our literature in isolation. One has only to open an American magazine of, say 1850, to see how much of our reading came, in the absence of a copyright law, from the pens of the most popular English authors. The English periodicals circulated in America, too, reaching Howells in Ohio and Harte in California, and played a significant part in the education of our realists. None of them was college-bred: De Forest, Howells, Eggleston, Mark Twain, even Henry James escaped the possibly stultifying effect of a conventional education. Most of them traveled widely. De Forest lived abroad six years before he began his novels, Howells for five, and James spent much of his life there. The dominant realism of the seventies and eighties was closely related to that across the Atlantic.

Certain native factors doubtless favored its development. A strain of transcendentalism is apparent. Like Whitman, the realist (as Howells remarked) "feels in every nerve the equality of things and the unity of men"; he "finds nothing insignificant," "nothing that God has made is contemptible." The growth of the democratic spirit made it easier for writers to accept the low and the common as suitable literary material, and the Civil War, mingling men from widely separated regions, stirred interest in local peculiarities and violently destroyed certain romantic misconceptions. Yet the assumption that realism was brought into American literature from the Western frontier cannot be supported by fact. While the excitement over Bret Harte's California stories stimulated genre writing everywhere, New England writers had for decades been describing curious characters in their native surroundings. Harte was brought up in New York, wrote with his eye on the East, and returned there as soon as his success permitted. De Forest, the first professed realist, and in many respects the stanchest, lived on the Atlantic seaboard. Howells and Eggleston followed the same pattern: born west of the Alleghenies, drawn toward a literary career by youthful enthusiasm for the romantic and sentimental, they became realists only after settling on the East coast. Eggleston was living in Brooklyn when Taine's *History of Art in the Netherlands* inspired him to write about the Indiana of his childhood. Howells, more fastidious in some respects than his Cambridge friends, turned from mediocre romantic verse to realistic fiction with the encouragement of Lowell, James, and others of the *Atlantic Monthly* circle. The early realists were all in one way or another innocents abroad; like Mark Twain, they found their impulse to write in the contrast between their native manners and those of a longer established, more cosmopolitan culture. They were back trailers, thrown by circumstance into an older, more sophisticated society.

2

Some of them moved only from a rural community to a great city. Eliza beth Drew Barstow Stoddard, for example, who came to New York after hei marriage to Richard Henry Stoddard, drew her first novel, *The Morgesons* (1862), from memories of her childhood in Mattapoisett on Buzzards Bay. She herself was the rebellious, passionate heroine Cassandra, and many other characters in her books were recognized by their originals. Veronica Morgeson, the sensitive and eccentric young recluse, is both strange and lifelike; Colonel Higginson certainly had her in mind when he wrote his wife that she would understand what Emily Dickinson was like if she had read Mrs. Stoddard's novels. Even more remarkable are the repressed, middle-aged women, intense and yet restrained, memorably portrayed in Sarah Auster in *Two Men* (1865) and Roxalana Gates, "the passionless soul," in *Temple House* (1867). The men fall into two types: fascinating, dissipated, Byronic wanderers like Desmond Somers and George Gates ("as handsome as Romeo, as dissolute as Antony"); and stalwart, middle-aged, homespun heroes like Jason Auster and Argus Gates, who marry the young heroines at the end. Of the three novels *The Morgesons* is the best because it has fewest of the romantic obtrusions that mar Mrs. Stoddard's realism. Her emphasis on suppressed or abnormal emotion and her abrupt and obscure narrative method give her novels a curiously modern tone. Though her descriptions of everyday manners are minutely realistic, the emotional relationships are too strange to pass for truthful transcriptions of life. On the surface the characters seem exact and varied portraits; within they are no more typical of New England than the inhabitants of Wuthering Heights are of Yorkshire.

Realism is mingled with sentiment in the work of Rebecca Blaine Harding Davis, a prolific writer of novels and short stories, who consciously sought her material in "this commonplace, this vulgar American life." Born in southwestern Pennsylvania, she moved to Philadelphia after her marriage; as a child she had lived in Alabama and in Wheeling, West Virginia, where she observed the industrial conditions that comprise her most original contribution to realism. In "Life in the Iron Mills," published in the *Atlantic* in 1861, Hugh Wolfe, a consumptive iron puddler with a talent for sculpture, and his sister Deb, a hunchbacked cotton-mill worker, are favorably contrasted with the rich mill owner and his dilettante friends. In her effort to rouse pity in the manner of Dickens, Mrs. Stowe, and Kingsley, Mrs. Davis violates her own rule of the commonplace. Few mill workers are hunchbacks, and except in a reformer's tract no consumptive could long be an iron puddler. In *Margret Howth* (1862), a study of slum life, the same romantic contrasts are drawn in the struggling young manufacturer who gives up a rich heiress for the poor but earnest Margret, and the same deliberate pathos surrounds the death of the crippled Negress, Lois Yare. Sentimental propaganda for the Negro distorts *Waiting for the Verdict* (1868). The earlier stories like "John Lamar" (*Atlantic,* 1862) with its fine description of the bewildered slave Ben are closer to the truth. At the farthest extreme are tales like "Volcanic Interlude" (*Lippincott's,* 1880) in which two girls brought up with the greatest luxury in New Orleans learn as they are about to come out that their mother was a Negress. Of her numerous novels *John Andross* (1874) is the strongest; in an atmosphere of political corruption in the Pennsylvania state capital Mrs. Davis studies Anna Maddox, one of the best of those seductive and ruthless women who lead men to ruin in the novels of the period. Unfortunately, the faults of melodrama and didacticism mar even her best work.

3

The first American writer to deserve the name of realist was John William De Forest, who treated the Civil War, the freed slave, the female lobbyist, and other aspects of contemporary life with a complete objectivity he seems to have developed abroad. The son of a prosperous manufacturer at Seymour, Connecticut, he spent two years (1848–1849) traveling in the Near East and four more (1851–1854) in France, Germany, and Italy. During a nine-month stay at Divonne, where no one else spoke English, he came to know Europeans of every shade of opinion and read deeply in French literature. Wide experience of foreign life made him neither a blatant Yankee nor a sycophant. His first book, *History of the Indians of Connecticut from the Earliest Known Period to 1850* (1851), a pioneer study, manifests the realistic tendency of his mind. His first novel, *Witching Times* (*Putnam's,* 1856–1857), brings a cool rationalism to bear upon the religious delusions of Salem during the witchcraft persecutions. Though the background of common life is created with well drawn details, the sentimental plot destroys what realism had been achieved in the minor characters, and De Forest judged wisely in not reprinting the story. Realism contends more successfully with melodrama in the contemporary story *Seacliff* (1859). Again the most original characters are the minor ones, old Warner and Ma Treat, in whom De Forest catches to perfection the authentic Connecticut flavor.

After his marriage in 1856 he lived part of each year in Charleston, South. Carolina. He was there when the war broke out, escaping with his wife and child on the last boat. Having organized a company of volunteers in New Haven, he served as their captain in the Louisiana campaigns and later in the Shenandoah. His rhymed accounts of certain episodes, "Under the Colors," collected with earlier verses in *Poems: Medley and Palestina* (1902), are labored and wooden. De Forest was no poet. The long, descriptive letters to his family, however, provide the most vivid picture we have of army life. From these he made seven articles such as "The First Time Under Fire" and "Forced March" which appeared during the war; and with eight new chapters he made of the whole series an absorbing narrative, *A Volunteer's Adventures,* which was not published until 1946. At the cessation of hostilities he was placed in charge of the Freedmen's Bureau at Greenville, South Carolina, where he observed at close range the difficulties of Reconstruction. Parts of his account of this experience appeared in the magazines of the day.

By the end of 1865 he had completed the ineptly named *Miss Ravenel's Conversion from Secession to Loyalty* (1867), his finest novel and quite the best story of the Civil War. War had never been depicted so truthfully. Instead of a chivalrous romance of Blue and Gray, De Forest tells of the wearisome struggle against mud, filth, sickness, stupidity, red tape, and graft. Fear and panic, the anguish with which the bravest face battle, such horrors as the field hospital are all described uncompromisingly. In the characters good and bad traits mingle as in real life. Colonel Carter, one of the most vigorous portraits in American fiction, combines great personal courage and professional skill with an unfortunate flexibility of moral principles. Tender affection for his wife continues during his affair with Mrs. Larue. The generous motive of providing for his family overcomes his deep sense of honor and tempts him to misuse army funds. When he dies during battle, declining the chaplain's ministrations, a friend justly observes, *"Il a maintenu jusqu'au bout son personnage."* Mrs. Larue is another character long without equal in our fiction. A "child of Balzac's moral philosophy," she shocks the young New Englander Colburne (whose military experience coincides with De Forest's) by declaring Don Juan "a model man." To her, love is a game, pleasant, and even necessary, but "she would not have isolated herself from society for any man." De Forest studies her unflinchingly, concealing neither her immorality nor the undeniable goodness in her nature. Left at the end of the story more prosperous than before, she is the first profligate woman to escape retribution in an American novel. Lillie Ravenel is also an innovation. Unlike the pious.

submissive heroines of the age, she has a mind of her own; she disagrees openly with her father, usually getting her own way. In spite of his disapproval she married the magnetic Carter. De Forest shows how much of her attraction to him was unconsciously physical; it mastered even her prejudice against Yankees. Her feelings after discovering his infidelity and on learning of his death are subtly delineated. If the account of her widowhood and eventual marriage to Colburne is a little reminiscent of Thackeray's Amelia and Dobbin, it is done with a firm, masculine hand. At the start Colburne is almost too perfect, but in the army he grows more credible and by the time he returns to civilian life, wasted by fever and fatigue, he is a completely natural character. Like De Forest he was mustered out a captain, while the promotion went to the arrant coward Gazaway, a political boss whose hold over the Governor eventually secured him a colonelcy and a safe command of a conscript camp, where he made $2,000 a month by letting substitutes escape.

Political corruption is the theme of two other novels, *Honest John Vane* (1875) and *Playing the Mischief* (1876). John Vane, a shallow fellow in whom honesty is mere policy, finding it impossible to live in Washington on his $5,000 Congressional salary, sells his vote for the "Great Subfluvial Tunnel Road" (a satire on the Crédit Mobilier) but escapes ruin during the investigation by declaring that he had bought the stock, not knowing it was a fraud. As an exposure of lobbying the story is more effective than *The Gilded Age.* De Forest's zeal to denounce the scandals overshadows his interest in the characters; John's wife Olympia is as shallow as he, and many of the others are only flat figures in an allegory. The Vanes and Senator Ironman reappear in *Playing the Mischief,* a longer and more carefully constructed novel. The central character, Mrs. Josie Murray, a clever and beautiful female lobbyist, has come to Washington to press a $100,000 claim for her father-in-law's barn, destroyed in the War of 1812! Using her charms without scruple, she cheats Pike the lobbyist out of half his share of the spoils and is left at the end ostensibly triumphant. The bribery theme here is subordinated to the study of Washington society, in which De Forest includes such varied types as the doting senator Old Jake Hollowbread, and an amusing Bloomer girl, Nancy Appleyard, known as "the Jael of California," very feminine in spite of her trousers and pistols.

Howells considered *Kate Beaumont* (1872) De Forest's best novel. It describes a feud in South Carolina, but except for the sensational opening episode, Frank McAlister's rescue of Kate from the burning steamer, a high level of realism is maintained. Kate's father, Peyton Beaumont, a low-country planter aristocrat, scarred in many a duel, beginning each day with two cocktails, hot-tempered and profane, yet with a lofty honor that commands the reader's respect, is easily the best character in the book. His children are well differentiated. Nellie, the elder daughter, is married to the handsome drunkard Randolph Armitage, whom she can't help loving in spite of his abuse. He represents the seamy side of Southern chivalry; returning from a cracker ball in the cabin of the "lone women" (a picture of poor white degradation that anticipates Faulkner and Caldwell), he beats his wife and threatens her with a knife for hiding his whisky. The daring of these scenes is striking when one recalls the timidity with which Howells a decade later described Bartley Hubbard's coming home drunk. The McAlisters, less carefully detailed, represent the more democratic, upcountry Scotch-Irish aristocracy that supported the common schools and the electoral system. The story holds interest throughout; even the happy ending, in which marriage terminates the feud, fails to destroy the reader's impression of having observed real life.

The reading public, however, preferred not to look at real life, and De Forest was forced to turn his hand to more popular formulas. *Overland* (1871), written for the *Galaxy* in the lurid style of Theodore Winthrop's *John Brent* (1862), combines De Forest's hobbies of ethnology and military tactics, and employs realism, as do his later novels, to bolster an impossible plot. The descriptions of the crucifixion of the maid Pepita by the Apaches and the trip down the Grand Canyon in a canvas boat are tours de force quite wasted on the juvenile mind the story aims at; De Forest had never been in the West, but collected all his information in the Yale Library.

In 1886 after some years abroad, he began a novel to be called *A Daughter of Toil* which treated the problems of lodgings, wages, and cost of living in the vein of Howells' *The Minister's Charge,* then appearing serially. Noting that Howells' story was taking the same line, he wrote to disclaim any intention of stealing his thunder. The manuscript has disappeared, and one can only speculate as to whether it marked any further development in De Forest's realism. There is no sign of that in *A Lover's Revolt* (1898), a contribution to the wave of historical romances about the Revolution, which concludes the list of his novels. The military maneuvers of Bunker Hill interest him more than the frail love story. He must have known that to make his heroine turn Tory and abandon the Yankee hero would insure the book's failure with women, who form the greatest part of the novel-reading public. Essentially a man's novelist, he could never flatter the feminine mind. Howells' explanation of his failure to attain popularity cannot be improved:

Finer, not stronger workmen succeeded him, and a delicate realism, more responsive to the claims and appeals of the feminine oversoul, replaced his inexorable veracity. In the fate of his fiction, whether final or provisional, it is as if this sensitive spirit had revenged the slight it felt, and, as the habit of women is, overavenged itself. It had revealed itself to him as it does only to the masters of fiction, and he had seemed not to prize the confidence.

4

Astute knowledge of the feminine oversoul and his own delicate taste made William Dean Howells the most popular exponent of realism. Both as novelist and as editor of magazines he consistently advocated "poor Real Life" as the artist's material, and he came to be considered the leading spokesman of the movement in America. In the calm perspective of time it may seem that he simply gave a name to a kind of writing that others in some degree had been doing for years. Like most critical theories, his was derived from his own practice, and it suffers from his limitations. But there is no doubt that he formulated the principles of realism about which the prolonged debate raged in the eighties. He had a strong ally in Henry James; and in England other discerning critics like J. A. Symonds were advancing much the same arguments. If the champions of romance, among whom Andrew Lang and Stevenson were the most vocal, appeared to be victorious, their triumph was only temporary; for when American fiction reached the peak of its influence soon after Howells' death, the realistic strain was dominant.

The view of the realist as a back-trailer to a more sophisticated society is illustrated perfectly in the case of Howells. He was born in Ohio, the son of a Pennsylvania German mother and a Welsh father, who had been compelled to turn his hand to many trades, of which printing was the chief. After an unsuccessful attempt to found a magazine, he moved when William was three to Hamilton in southwestern Ohio, where friends lent him money to buy a newspaper. Howells describes the life of those days with humorous candor in *A Boy's Town* (1890), *My Year in a Log Cabin* (1893), *Years of My Youth* (1916), and, thinly disguised as fiction, in *New Leaf Mills* (1913). "I do not know when I could not set type," he wrote. At the age of seven he set up an essay of his own writing; at twelve he was a swift compositor, working regularly in the shop. After several business failures, his father moved to Jefferson in the Western Reserve, a Free Soil community more sympathetic with his principles, where the family found a permanent home. In "The Country Printer," the best essay in *Impressions and Experiences* (1896), Howells recalls his work on the newspaper there. "The printing office was mainly my school," he said.

He got what formal education he had during the earlier years in Hamilton. His most vivid recollection of school was the discovery at the back of his reader of the rules of prosody, which set him to writing verses modeled on those his father read aloud from Scott and Moore. He learned most from the books that came to his hand by chance. Goldsmith's *Greece* and Jarvis' translation of *Don Quixote* were his earliest favorites. They were soon followed by Irving's *Conquest of Granada,* which, with Longfellow's *Spanish Student,* fired his ambition to learn Spanish. A printer of some literary taste interested him in Shakespeare and joined his self-conducted inquiries into Latin, Greek, and German. A Yankee machinist inspired a brief enthusiasm for Macaulay, and an English organ builder and house painter introduced him to Dickens and Thackeray, deploring his preference for the latter.

Each author in turn became for a time Howells' favorite, to be read and imitated to the exclusion of all others. His unreserved account in *My Literary Passions* (1895), tracing the development of his mind through this eclectic course, reveals the defect of the method in the gaps it left. Richardson, Fielding, and Smollett, from whom the future realist might have learned so much, he missed altogether. Though Tennyson shared his heart with Longfellow, the "divine poet I have never ceased to read," he could never force himself to read Wordsworth, and, despite his interest in German, he saw no greatness in Goethe. In the Howells household the works of Swedenborg replaced the Bible.

In the village of Jefferson, Howells passed for something of a youthful prodigy. Both his knowledge of languages and their number were exaggerated in local report, and late in life he confessed that he had probably been less fond of study than of the effect it created. His final judgment on his blind struggle for an education was the rueful one, "Self-taught is half-taught." There emerges from the autobiographical accounts the image of an undersized, oversensitive youngster, earnestly doing a man's work, shy and aloof from boys of his own age, intolerably homesick when away from his family, and haunted by horrible fears. In 1855 overwork and overstudy brought on a serious nervous breakdown, of which the worst symptom was an obsession that he had hydrophobia. An intense fear of dogs, which he never overcame, figures in several of his novels.

In 1856 his father was appointed a legislative clerk in Columbus, and Howells went along to write daily letters on the proceedings for several newspapers. Offered the city editorship of the Cincinnati *Gazette,* he gave it a brief trial before the usual homesickness and the unpalatable duty of reporting police-court cases made him abandon the lucrative post. "My longing," he wrote, "was for the cleanly respectabilities." After a second period of nervous prostration he returned in 1858 to Columbus to be city editor of the *Ohio State Journal,* recently reorganized to serve the growing Republican Party. The society into which he was now introduced made an impression that can be felt throughout his novels. Governor Salmon P. Chase, ambitious for the

Presidency, befriended the bashful young reporter, and Howells soon found himself at home in a congenial circle, of which he gives a vivid account in *Years of My Youth*.

For him it was largely a feminine society, and with the zeal of a diffident convert he adopted its most delicate refinements of etiquette. Since early childhood he had despised the coarse crudity of frontier life; he longed to be a dandy and dressed with extreme fastidiousness. His literary taste also turned naturally toward the genteel. With the young ladies of Columbus he read the English periodicals, discussed the novels of Thackeray, George Eliot, and Trollope as they appeared, and fed on the soft praise of his own rhymes in the manner of Tennyson and Heine. "Ah! if I only could write something worthy of the *Atlantic*!" he exclaimed. His first contribution, a poem called "Andenken," was held for months while Lowell made certain that it was not a translation from Heine.

With John J. Piatt, Howells published his first volume, *Poems of Two Friends* (1860). His verses, painstakingly modeled on Tennyson, Heine, and Longfellow, have been justly forgotten. Only "The Pilot's Story," which had appeared in the *Atlantic,* achieved any popularity, and that was rather for its lurid account of a slave girl's plunge to death in the Mississippi than for the awkward hexameters in which it is written. The newspapers, to its author's chagrin, sometimes reprinted it as prose. With his first profits Howells made a literary pilgrimage to New England, described in glowing detail years later in *Literary Friends and Acquaintance* (1900). He liked Hawthorne, but could not understand Thoreau and got on badly with Emerson. His Ohio publisher next commissioned him to write the *Life of Abraham Lincoln* (1860), who had just been nominated for the presidency. Howells himself would not go to Springfield to interview the candidate, but sent a law student to gather material for him. Though his failure to sense Lincoln's greatness at that time is quite pardonable, the reader of the *Life* feels a discord between the honest, manly subject and the flashy style in which it is presented.

After the election Howells' friends suggested that he apply for a consular post abroad; and, recommended by all the prominent Ohio Republicans from the Governor down, he secured the consulship at Venice. His five years there affected him less profoundly than one might expect. For an appreciation of the *Divine Comedy,* which he studied with "an ingenious priest" (the original of Don Ippolito in *A Foregone Conclusion*), his education had hardly fitted him; and he says plainly that much of the poem bored him. The only result of his study was a long effort in *terza rima* about the Civil War, which no editor would print. His reading soon turned to more modern authors, especially Goldoni and the later dramatists. Through the Tauchnitz editions he kept up with English fiction; *Romola* in particular was a profound ethical revelation that he never forgot. In Paris in 1862 he married Elinor Mead of Brattleboro, Vermont, whom he had met in Columbus. She came of a talented family and was a second cousin of President Rutherford B. Hayes, to whose campaign in 1876 he contributed a biography.

Under the skies of Venice he toiled vainly to invoke the Muse; he should have been writing realistic stories instead of romantic idyls in hexameters. One of these poems, "No Love Lost: A Romance of Travel" (1869), a gentle satire of Americans in Italy written in 1862, is cast in what was to be the typical Howells pattern: a pair of lovers kept apart for a time by too delicate scruples are at length united. Failing to interest English or American editors in his poems, he turned to writing short prose sketches of Venice, which, after their appearance in the Boston *Advertiser,* were reprinted as *Venetian Life* (1866). While the book leans inevitably on standard works of history and travel, it is notable for the fresh, personal style of a polite but quizzical observer. The realist's aim to represent ordinary things truthfully is plain in his resolve to tell "as much as possible of the everyday life of a people whose habits are so different from our own." How well he gauged public taste is attested by the book's success. A second edition was called for the next year, when he also published *Italian Journeys,* a similar collection of sketches reprinted from the *Nation* and the *Atlantic.*

For a few months after his return to America, Howells worked as a free lance in New York. His literary ambition, however, was centered in Boston, and when Fields offered him the assistant editorship of the *Atlantic* he accepted gladly. For $50 a month he agreed to sift the manuscripts, correspond with contributors, write many of the book reviews, and read all the proofs. It was not kept from him that his experience as a practical printer was "most valued, if not the most valued, and that as proof-reader I was expected to make it avail on the side of economy." His Italian connection brought him an invitation to Longfellow's Dante Club, where among the great of Cambridge he found a heaven higher than the *Paradiso.* His literary taste had been so formed on the *Atlantic* model that when he was made editor-in-chief in 1871 he took over the wheel without perceptibly altering the course. The success of the Italian sketches prompted him to turn to similar themes at home; his colored cook, an organ grinder, a beggar, and even a stroll through the dullest outskirts of Cambridge are invested with an interest Howells rarely fails to invoke. "If the public will stand this," he told Henry James, "I shall consider my fortune made." Collected as *Suburban Sketches* (1871), they passed through many editions.

His novels grew from his travel sketches. *Their Wedding Journey* (1871), he wrote to his father, is "the story of our last summer's travels, which I am giving the form of fiction so far as the characters are concerned." Most of the book consists of descriptions of the American scene—the night boat, the sleeping car, the parlor car (which never ceased to fascinate him), the sordid New York streets, the Hudson and Mohawk rivers, "romantic Rochester," Niagara Falls (at excessive length), Montreal, and Quebec. Except for a minor steamboat collision, the book is without incident. But Howells' theory of realism is already defined; he avoids "the heroic or occasional phases," seeking man "in his habitual moods of vacancy and tiresomeness," in "his vast, natural, unaffected dulness." Apology for the rawness of America contends with his pride in its native honesty and beauty. Basil March, who reappears in seven other stories, is the scarcely disguised projection of Howells himself, commenting on the new scenes as he had on those in *Venetian Life* and *Suburban Sketches*. Isabel March, vivacious, humorous, illogical, and charming, is the first of his subtle feminine portraits.

5

With *A Chance Acquaintance* (1873) his work as a novelist properly begins. Though the "scenery" element is not yet wholly fused with the dramatic, Howells made some effort to subordinate it to the social conflict that was to serve as his major theme in nearly a score of novels: the story of a sensitive country girl or boy thrown into a more sophisticated society. It is, of course, his own experience. Kitty Ellison, like her creator the child of a Free Soil editor in the Middle West, has grown up in democratic ignorance of social differences. On an excursion to Quebec she meets a cultivated Bostonian, Miles Arbuton, the first of Howells' coolly superior and impossibly refined young men, who could hardly be expected to understand the culture of Erie Creek; indeed, he is a mere foil for its homely virtues, and Howells admitted to James that he was "a simulacrum." But Kitty really comes to life. In her homemade dress, naïve, fresh, natural, and sincere, she is the first of those girls who were to demonstrate the superiority of American simplicity to the conventions of a Europeanized society.

In the succeeding novels Howells transports his heroines to Italy to be studied with varying degrees of realism against a romantic background. Florida Vervain in *A Foregone Conclusion* (1875) is brought to Venice, where the watchful young artist-consul Ferris protects her from the hopeless love of the priest Don Ippolito, a variety of sentimental romance that Howells did not repeat. In Venice also, Lydia Blood, the charming heroine of *The Lady of the Aroostook* (1879), focuses the conflict of three cultures. Reared north of Boston in simple ignorance of such customs as chaperonage, she sails for Italy, the only woman aboard the *Aroostook*. Attracted by her beauty, two "cultivated Yankees," aware that the upcountry ideal of propriety is "very different from ours," resolve to "preserve her unconsciousness" of the anomal ous position her friends have placed her in. So scrupulous is the Bostonian Staniford that he refrains from telling her he has fallen in love with her until she is properly in her aunt's charge. Such delicacy merely perplexes Lydia, though she is gravely shocked by Sunday opera and the easy immorality of Venice. She is humbler and less sophisticated than her contemporary, Daisy Miller, but more genuinely American—a quality emphasized by contrast with her aunt, who toadies to the English colony. Howells' faculty foi writing dialogue as direct and natural as conversation overheard in real life reaches full pitch in this novel. Lily Mayhew, the heroine of *A Fearful Responsibility* (1881), is another country girl who comes to Venice to visit her aunt. But Howells had exhausted the theme; the only noteworthy thing about the book is the deliberate avoidance of a happy ending.

He had already begun to exploit native material. *Private Theatricals,* laid in a country boarding house, originated in the summer of 1874, which he spent at Jaffrey, New Hampshire. Published in the *Atlantic* (1875–1876), it was not reprinted until after Howells' death, when it appeared as *Mrs. Farrell* (1921). That Howells studied his originals closely is suggested by an un-authenticated legend which says that the family with whom he boarded at Mountain Farm recognized themselves in the Woodwards and "threatened him with the law" if the story were reprinted. If the charm of the flirtatious young widow is not quite convincing, some of the minor characters are drawn with Howells' maturest art. In a sentence he sketches the meeting of two old neighbors, who,

when they had hornily rattled their callous palms together, stand staring at each other, their dry, serrated lips falling apart, their jaws mutely working up and down, their pale-blue eyes vacantly winking, and their weather-beaten faces as wholly discharged of expression as the gable ends of two barns confronting each other from opposite sides of the road.

It is ungracious to remark that this superb realism is largely external. The Woodward family are revealed only through the eyes of their boarders, who observe such details as Mrs. Woodward's "large, toil-worn, kitchen-coarsened hand, with its bony knuckles and stubbed, broken nails," without penetrating far into her mind. Howells had not yet attained his deepest understanding of the silent granite of New England character.

In *The Undiscovered Country* (1880) he turns for a fresh setting to the Shakers, who, except for Hawthorne's brief glances, had not been used in fiction. The community at Vardley (a composite of Harvard and Shirley, where Howells stayed in 1875) serves merely as a picturesque background for the love story, varied with spiritualistic phenomena, of which Howells and the Shakers both take a skeptical view. Shakers are the principal characters in two thin volumes published in 1896, *A Parting and a Meeting* and *The Day of Their Wedding,* highly implausible triumphs of celibacy over young love, in which the tradition of local color is stronger than realism. Another of Howells' favorite settings is the seaside hotel, which he uses first in *Dr. Breen's Practice* (1881). No one has recorded the trivial and malicious conversation of the rocking chairs with more accurate realism. The book solicits interest from the current debate between allopath and homeopath and the problem of medicine as a suitable profession for women. Neither issue is treated more than superficially. The true issue is whom Grace Breen shall marry. A Puritan conscience had turned her to medicine as a sort of atonement for wealth and ease. By nature, however, she is completely feminine and, having refused the attractive young man who has been camping on the beach to be near her, finally proposes to him herself.

Marcia Gaylord, the heroine of Howells' only study of married life, *A Modern Instance* (1882), behaves even more passionately. Bartley Hubbard, the husband on whom she throws herself against her father's advice, is a shrewd, enterprising young journalist drawn, as Howells perceived years later, from himself. The village paper in Equity, Maine, where the story opens, could hardly hold a man of his talent; in Boston he quickly wins his way as a free-lance writer and with borrowed money secures an interest in a weekly magazine. But like George Eliot's Tito Melema, who had obviously impressed Howells deeply, Bartley was created to serve as a horrid example of moral decay. Though the progressive disintegration of his character has been praised, there is really no change in him beyond a growing stoutness, the result presumably of drinking beer. From the start he was self-seeking, self-indulgent, unscrupulous, with "no more moral nature than a baseball." In real life these qualities would not necessarily have prevented his becoming a successful journalist, and, if his destruction were not foreordained, marriage might have improved his morals. The Marcia of the opening chapters, whose "elemental" and "animalistic" qualities troubled contemporary reviewers, might well have become a mate worthy of his early ambitions. After their marriage, as Howells steadily blackens Bartley, he reveals in Marcia an unexpected strain of moral delicacy incompatible with her fundamental possessiveness. Ben, the sensitive, lame, pious, and incredibly noble hero, with more than a reminiscence of *Romola,* sends her back to Bartley: "No man can be your refuge from your husband!" Ben's love for her increases unaccountably as the reader's sympathy declines. With all her inconsistency Marcia is Howells' most notable attempt to portray a complete woman. No reader can fail to admire his skillful drawing of such minor figures as Judge Gaylord, the perfectly wrought background of the village in winter, and the Boston boarding houses.

Resigning from the *Atlantic* in 1881, Howells spent the following year in England, Switzerland, and Italy. Besides such work as *Tuscan Cities* (1885), illustrated by Joseph Pennell, his only novel was *A Woman's Reason* (1883), which suffers from fatigue and remoteness from his material. It is a transitional book, marking a change in Howells' attitude toward Boston society, to which he returned in *The Rise of Silas Lapham* (1885) with a new perspective.

The Laphams are the first *nouveaux riches* to be studied sympathetically in our fiction. A poor farm boy who has made his million in paint, Silas was (like Howells himself) building a house on the water side of Beacon Street. With complete mastery Howells notes the distinctive traits of the American; his massive physique inherited from generations of laborers, his casual dress, his love of speed, and wholehearted dedication to business are observed and recorded kindly. Persis, his plain, unpretentious wife, adapting herself to the city less easily, is helpless to guide her daughters' social life. Against the background of a preposterous drawing room or calamitous dinner party, Howells can describe their perplexities without rousing ridicule so much as pity. Through it all they keep a kind of simple dignity bred of solid worth that makes one forgive mere ignorance of manners. The Coreys, "a little beyond the salt of the earth," but studied more critically than Howells' earlier Bostonians, serve as a foil to the Laphams' homely virtues: "stalwart achievement against sterile elegance." Tom Corey, the link between the old order and the new, combines grace with an energy his father lacks; and though his behavior before he proposes to Penelope is so discreet that every one, including the young lady herself, believes him in love with her prettier sister, he is one of the most likable of Howells' heroes. For those days the business ethics that make Silas prefer poverty to a legal sale that would have saved him are perhaps somewhat idealized. But the episode was necessary to complete his "rise," and it gives the book a symmetry of form Howells seldom achieved. In contrast with *A Modern Instance,* the setting, masterfully rendered, is completely fused with the action. On the whole, popular taste has judged well in declaring this his best novel.

Indian Summer (1886) may be a finer technical achievement. Here Howells keeps well within his range, writing mostly about women, in this case cultivated Middle Westerners living in Florence. The germ of the story seems to come from memories of his early days in Columbus. Colville, one of our first expatriates and a curious forerunner of James' Strether, is a middle-aged hero who falls into an ambiguous intimacy with Mrs. Bowen, a widow whom he had known years before, and with her young protégée Imogene

Graham, who imagines herself romantically in love with him. Like many of Howells' men, Colville is slow to perceive his own happiness. When at last he proposes, Mrs. Bowen, out of pride and pique, refuses him with a woman's "No" that is quickly reversed. The conflicting motives in her mind are traced with great subtlety, and Colville, for all his obtuseness, is drawn sympathetically. While it lasts, the spell wrought by a rare unity of tone conquers the reader; it is only on analysis that one sees the frail structure of the book.

6

Howells' reviews in the *Atlantic* and *North American* constantly praised the merits of De Forest, James, and others who were striving to make a faithful transcription of the world about them. In "The Editor's Study," which he conducted in *Harper's* from January, 1886, to March, 1892, he waged a crusade for realism that roused violent opposition on both sides of the Atlantic. A group of these articles, too carelessly assembled, make up the little volume called *Criticism and Fiction* (1891). The critic's function, he says, is like the scientist's, "to discover principles, not to establish them; to report, not to create." He has only to ask if a novel is "true to the motives, the impulses, the principles that shape the life of actual men and women." While Howells professed to see little difference between *Literature and Life* (as he declares in a collection of articles published under that title in 1902), what he calls Life sometimes seems to the reader merely Literature. His theory omits several important phases of human experience. Tragedy is excluded because it is rare in the United States: our novelists "concern themselves with the more smiling aspects of life, which are the more American"; Romance is also barred because it is exceptional; and Sex is banished completely for the inconsistent reason that interest in it is all too common.

The genteel atmosphere of Boston has been unfairly blamed for Howells' extraordinary prudishness. His letters show that Lowell, James, and others steadily urged him toward a stronger realism and stimulated an interest in social problems, which the *Atlantic* had fostered before Howells joined it. His autobiographical books yield ample evidence that his squeamishness about sexual relations and the nude in art was fully developed in his boyhood on the Ohio frontier, which, as Mrs. Trollope observed in 1832, was ridiculously sensitive about such matters. He is not quite candid, then, in attributing the necessity for reticence to the young lady reader—the "Iron Madonna," as Boyesen called her. His own sensibility dictated it. There was also another reason. Though an *Anna Karenina* can be printed as a book and locked up from the children, no American (or, he might have added, English) magazine would publish anything that "a father may not read to his daughter, or safely leave her to read for herself. After all, it is a matter of business."

Business and prudishness combined to make Howells' practice incompatible with his theory of realism. His income came chiefly from the magazines, and, like the modern writer, he had to accept their limitations. The damage done his art by serial publication was serious, though there is no sign that he was restive under the restrictions. Despite his insistence that realism "prefers to avoid all manner of strange coincidences and dire catastrophes," his books abound in them. Three plots turn on train wrecks, three on fires; two characters are removed by brain fever, a number by sudden sickness; two commit suicide with poison; one hero is shot, another knocked down by a horsecar, and two others killed by locomotives. Yet realism is determined less by choice of material than by intention and method of treatment; if Howells seems now to have conceded too much to his public, he also sacrificed a good deal for his principles.

His reviews widened America's literary horizon, introducing such foreign authors as Galdós and Valdés, Ibsen and Björnson, Turgenev, Tolstoy, and Dostoevski. Howells' increasing concern with abnormal states of mind like the jealousy of the half-insane husband in *The Shadow of a Dream* (1890) or the remorse of the embezzler in *The Quality of Mercy* (1892) may have been quickened by the reading of Dostoevski. Tolstoy, however, whom he first read when *War and Peace* was translated in 1886, he considered the supreme influence of his life. While his literary method remained unchanged, his ethical outlook was profoundly affected; he began to regard the poor with a new sympathy.

In his next novel, *The Minister's Charge; or the Apprenticeship of Lemuel Barker* (1887), moral problems occupy him more than manners. The central theme is "complicity," the responsibility every one in society shares for the deeds of every one else. The story is written from the point of view of Mr. Sewell and the Corey family of earlier books, but the poor factory girls Statira Dudley and 'Manda Grier are depicted truly and without sentimentality; they are low because they like to be. Lem Barker, the humorless country boy who rebukes conventional insincerity by his dogged honesty, has little else to recommend him. The reader welcomes even so palpable a caricature as Miss Vane, distributing bouquets to the poor to prevent crime. *Annie Kilburn* (1888), a slightly less uncomfortable book, teaches the Tolstoyan lesson that money is useless without the sympathy that comes from suffering. Through the stern and uncompromising young minister Mr. Peck, the heroine learns that the prosperous, since they are agents of the system that causes poverty, cannot help the poor. The grim theme is lightened with some amusing satire on the vapid society ladies' futile efforts at charity. There is no such relief in *An Imperative Duty* (1892), Howells' worst violation of the commonplace, where he applies Tolstoy to the Negro problem, evading the obvious difficulties of mixed marriage as Mrs. Stowe did by shipping the couple off to live in Europe.

The influence of Tolstoy was soon reinforced by a more immediate acquaintance with socialism. In the fall of 1887 he heard Laurence Gronlund lecture in Buffalo and was led to read his book, *The Co-operative Commonwealth* (1884), Kirkup's article in the *Encyclopædia Britannica,* the *Fabian Essays,* and some of William Morris' tracts. The "civic murder" of the Chicago Anarchists, November 11, 1887, stirred him to active protest and greatly increased his discontent with the shallow Boston society he was dissecting in *April Hopes* (1888). Since his resignation from the *Atlantic* in 1881, his novels had been serialized in the *Century* and *Harper's*; the center of his interests had shifted, and in 1889 he moved to New York, where *A Hazard of New Fortunes* (1890) is laid. On a canvas of Tolstoy's panoramic dimensions he strives to include all the groups involved in the class struggle: the established aristocracy, the new plutocracy elbowing their way in, the business and professional classes, and the poor of the lower East Side. Though the point of view is necessarily Howells' own in the person of his *alter ego,* March (who has relinquished the moribund refinement of Boston to edit a New York magazine), the poor are studied realistically but compassionately. Their spokesman is the patriarchal socialist Lindau, a refugee of 1848, who lost his left hand in the Civil War and lives by choice in the slums "among my brothers"; he was drawn from the bookbinder who taught Howells German. Dryfoos, recently enriched by the discovery of natural gas on his Ohio farm, has come to New York to watch his money breed more money in speculation. Created to play the villain, greedy, an avowed enemy of labor unions, domineering over his family, Dryfoos is depicted without the sympathy that illuminates Silas Lapham; his melting after Lindau's death is improbably sentimental. His ignorant, pushing, and vulgar daughters are described with a more authentic realism than the hero, Conrad, sensitive, continually blushing, holding at the age of thirty ideals of "virginal vagueness" about women, and longing, if he dared, to join an order of Protestant celibates. Amidst philosophies ranging from Dryfoos' free enterprise to Beaton's aesthetic indifference, Howells stands close to Lindau, who proposes by orderly political action to achieve state control of resources and a program of social security. The streetcar strike of 1888 brings the plot to a melodramatic close.

New York's social contrasts are treated more mildly in *The Coast of Bohemia* (1893), which depicts the struggles of a talented Ohio girl studying art. *The World of Chance* (1893) is a better novel. The hero Shelley Ray, a "neat, slight, rather undersized" Ohio newspaperman, who is clearly autobiographical, has come to New York with the manuscript of a romantic novel, which succeeds only because a reviewer took it home by mistake. The best character in the book is the old socialist David Hughes, who had lived at Brook Farm; he probably speaks for Howells in criticizing Tolstoy's "eremitism": "Society is not to be saved by self-outlawry. . . . The way to have the golden age is to elect it by the Australian ballot."

Howells seems to have known nothing of Karl Marx except what he picked up from Gronlund and younger men like Hamlin Garland. In *A Traveller from Altruria* (1894) and its sequel *Through the Eye of the Needle* (1907), Aristides Homos disrupts an American summer hotel by helping the servants with their work and, in a lecture arranged by the rattle-brained Mrs. Makely, describes Altruria, where inequality and competition have given way to what seems a rather dull life. The utopias of Bellamy and Morris had preceded Howells', and parallels for many of his ideas have been pointed out in Gronlund's *The Co-operative Commonwealth*. Though he called himself a socialist and was troubled by inequality and poverty, Howells never actively revolted against the established order. He wrote Henry James in 1888:

After fifty years of optimistic content with "civilization" and its ability to come out all right in the end, I now abhor it, and feel that it is coming out all wrong in the end, unless it bases itself anew on a real equality. Meantime, I wear a fur-lined overcoat, and live in all the luxury my money can buy.

He was always sensitive to changes in literary fashion. As realism deepened in the nineties into naturalism and veritism, his own work took a stronger tone. In *The Landlord at Lion's Head* (1897) the tubercular Durgin family on their lonely New Hampshire farm make his bleakest picture of New England life. The country people in *Private Theatricals,* a sort of preliminary study for *The Landlord,* were subordinated to their boarders; now Howells develops them more fully. Mrs. Durgin is a thoroughly lifelike character, one of his masterpieces. Westover, the artist who comes to paint Lion's Head and suggests to her the possibility of a summer hotel, acts as a sort of Jamesian reflector throughout the story; the social problem of a hotelkeeper's son at Harvard, on a picnic with the summer boarders, or in Boston society, bothers him much more than it does Jeff Durgin. In Jeff, his only character in whom passions are not blinked, Howells comes closest to creating a real man. Before the ruthless male had been popularized by the apostles of the strenuous, Jeff is given the iron will of a Nietzschean superman, a powerful, masculine physique, and a magnetic attraction for women. He holds weakness the only sin. His flirtation with the Boston society girl is more convincing than the absurd scruples of his fiancée, a waitress at the hotel, who finds a worthier mate in the overrefined and much older Westover. The reader is repelled by her preternatural delicacy, while Jeff's imperfections, so honestly owned, evoke a sympathy Howells did not mean us to feel. In spite of its flaws, *The Landlord at Lion's Head* is one of Howells' best books; it has been undeservedly neglected.

Few novels of his last two decades demand consideration. *The Kentons* (1902) shows how a love affair affects a whole family, exiled from their comfortable home by one daughter's unhappiness. Without unkind satire Howells portrays Judge Kenton's nostalgia and the whole family's lack of interest in foreign countries, which they judge by comparison with Ohio. The fifteen-year-old Boyne is Howells' best study of adolescence. Among all his works *The Kentons* seemed to James the perfectly classic illustration of Howells' spirit and form. *The Son of Royal Langbrith* (1904), a novel of richer texture, is less true to the commonplace but more absorbing to read. The chief interest lies in the autumnal romance of Mrs. Langbrith, nineteen years a widow. There is only one obstacle to her marriage: her son Jim has never been told that his father, whose memory he idolizes, was really a drunken brute, who beat his wife and kept a mistress. Jim, an undergraduate at Harvard, has enough influence over his mother to make her delay her decision, and while she hesitates, Howells deliberately removes her fiancé by typhoid fever.

From 1900 until he died Howells conducted "The Editor's Easy Chair" in *Harper's,* though he continued to contribute to other magazines, notably the *North American Review*. His encouragement of young writers—Howe, Crane, Garland, and Norris—is well known; it is not always remembered, however, that his advice to more famous contemporaries was often important. James acknowledged his gratitude warmly:

You held out your open editorial hand to me at the time I began to write—and I allude especially to the summer of 1866—with a frankness and sweetness of hospitality that was really the making of me. . . . You showed me the way and opened me the door.

A talk with Howells in England in 1897 revived the desire to write novels that flowered in his greatest work. More than anyone else Howells stimulated and directed Mark Twain's genius, which he recognized at the beginning. Without Howells there might have been no *Life on the Mississippi*. Antipodal in personal habits, they maintained for forty years the friendship of which *My Mark Twain* (1910) is an intimate record. Howells has been unjustly blamed for imposing a prudish gentility on Mark Twain's native genius; his advice was generally sound, and the replacement of "hell" and "damn" by milder expressions is editing no more drastic than a modern film scenario or radio script must undergo today.

As the years passed, Howells received honorary degrees from Yale, Harvard, Oxford, Columbia, and Princeton; he was elected the first president of the American Academy of Arts and Letters. In 1920, the year of his death, a realistic novel, *Main Street,* became a best seller. His long crusade was at an end. The realism for which two romantic generations had abused him was already being ridiculed as timid by new realists whose art owed more to Howells than they cared to admit. Although he embraced too narrow a segment of human experience, few of his successors surpassed his power to draw exactly what he saw.

55. EXPERIMENTS IN POETRY:
EMILY DICKINSON AND SIDNEY LANIER

Prose played the largest role in the literary exploration and exploitation of the new America. By the year 1870 all the arts, however, felt the onrush of contemporary events, and among the resultant fresh ideas poetry played its part. Poets born in the latter half of the century, even Henry Timrod who died in 1867, felt the impact of the new science and the new industrialism and the shattering war between the North and the South.

One may detect, faintly, even in the poetry of the 1860's the rumble of the approaching storm. Many poets experienced merely the uneasiness of the times, but all sensed the moral problems posed by the new science, and all were excited by the national spectacle which Lanier celebrated in his "Psalm of the West." Walt Whitman, whose *Leaves of Grass* (1855) was almost without imitators before the end of the century, had at any rate spoken out. Meanwhile the fact of war had elicited the harsh truthfulness of Melville's verse and had prepared a fraction of the public for Stephen Crane's grim *Black Riders* (1895). A few poets had begun to recognize the power of fresh, realistic material communicated by blunt, experimental methods. To this low groundswell of change we owe the adventurous poetry, greater and lesser, of Emily Dickinson and Sidney Lanier.

This conflict between the new realism and the old conservatism encouraged experiment by a few poets such as Dickinson and Lanier—experiments with new attitudes and techniques which were still contained within the straining old patterns. To embrace the new utterly, like Whitman, was publicly fantastic; to retire completely into the old, like Aldrich, was irrational. In addition to these two more daring experimenters, we occasionally find a few others who thought poetically ahead of their times. In the seventies, for example, Frederick Goddard Tuckerman, recluse and dreamer, was writing sonnets and other verses which, though his more conventional side pleased Longfellow and Lowell, exhibited the restless search for a new technique. Here were the heralds of great changes impending in the poetry of America.

2

Of these conservatisms and of these stirrings toward a new poetry, Sidney Lanier sometimes seems a feverish epitome. For sixteen years after the Civil War he enunciated and practiced a dynamic but tryingly inconclusive doctrine of the identity of poetry and music; and he became an almost fanatical experimenter in the techniques of verse. Yet in spite of his stimulating theory concerning the two arts, not one of his adventures with irregular lines and far-fetched metaphors had the daring concentration and the natural symbolism which inhere in Emily Dickinson's stanzas. It is pertinent that the rude salt spray of Walt Whitman's poetry really shocked Lanier, though it also refreshed him.

Likewise, though he clasps nature in strange embraces, proclaims the sacredness of art, worships the sun, and denounces "trade," he is at heart curiously orthodox. He never, like his two now famous contemporaries, Whitman and Dickinson, strips himself of old beliefs before he starts to build a new universe. On the contrary, he clings to the familiar concepts of nineteenth-century romantic Christianity; and he tries to adjust the evil world and its subversive science to his "crystal Christ." He is not remote from the Southern Christian-cavalier tradition to which the poets Chivers and Poe belonged. Thus his moral world remained a narrow one; from first to last he was evangelical. In the emergence of the new poetry he typifies its uneasiness rather than its rebirth. Like Dickinson and Whitman, he felt the trammels of established verse, but unlike them he never fully initiated new forms.

Yet Lanier, like some "bearded meteor trailing light," moved through the course of poetry after the Civil War persuading by the intensity of his feeling and the complexity of his melody and counterpoint, until we can hardly conceive of the postwar epoch without his enriching influence. His opulence was needed in an age reared on Longfellow and Whittier. His fame, enhanced by his gallant war against poverty and disease and by his distinguished career as a musician, began slowly and reached a climax at about the time of his premature death in 1881. In its recent revival, induced partly by his alleged anticipation in his social ideas of Southern agrarianism, his reputation rests less upon his chivalric war novel *Tiger-Lilies* (1867), or upon his volumes of impressionistic literary criticism (in which for example he refers to Fielding as that "muck of the classics"), or even upon the striking *Science of English Verse* (1880) than upon a dozen poems. Unique in the story of poetry, these probably insure him against oblivion, for they add to our literary history Southern landscapes richly depicted by a fine sensibility which was the mainspring of his genius. Throughout his periods of poetic activity Lanier was a sick man; the fact is more than a partial explanation of his ardors and ecstasies. Though we may shake our heads over his cloying extravagance and though we may talk of the need for restraint or for criticism from poets wiser and more demanding than his friends Paul Hamilton Hayne and Bayard Taylor, his passionate hurrying eloquence, so reminiscent of Shelley's, forms Lanier's own peculiar charm.

The excitement of Lanier's poetry is matched by that of his tempestuous life; "the hottest of all battles," he called it. Born in Macon, Georgia, on February 3, 1842, he inherited from the Elizabethan Laniers, and more directly from his mother, his golden legacy of music: "he could not remember the time when he could not play almost any musical instrument." While undecided, after his graduation from Oglethorpe University, between the careers of music and law, he was swept into the Confederate Army; the war, the deeply shaping experience of his youth, bestowed upon him memories of battle and prison, the companionship of his beloved flute and of Father John Banister Tabb, and tuberculosis. This affliction was to make his remaining years a struggle to maintain the integrity of his art and his individuality in the face of certain extinction.

In the confused and broken South in the "dark raven days," as he called them, he essayed many trades and professions; hotel clerk and lawyer were but two of his occupations. His weak lungs made him travel; like John Sterling, of whom he sometimes reminds us, every year he survived demanded new attitudes of body and spirit. Yet his persistent consecration to his "twin-goddesses" of music and poetry brought fruition in the 1870's when he became first flutist of the Peabody Orchestra of Baltimore. In this decade he wrote "Corn," "The Symphony," "The Marshes of Glynn," and his "Centennial Cantata." There followed misdirections of his talent, among them the lectureship in English literature at the Johns Hopkins University and his immersion in literary criticism—an inconclusive effort except for *The Science of English Verse*. It is pardonable to dramatize the conclusion of his heroic effort within his "living egg of pain"; he died in 1881, at the age of thirty-nine, shortly after finishing one of his finest poems, "Sunrise," written when he was suffering from a temperature of 104 degrees.

Lanier was an undergraduate when *On the Origin of Species* appeared. He admired Darwin intensely, and carefully annotated his copy of the book; for him, as for many young poets of the era, it was less a revelation of the organic world than a culmination, a symbol, a harbinger of the future. At Oglethorpe, the brilliant German-trained tutor, James Woodrow (grandfather of Woodrow Wilson), had opened to him the portals of scientific study. These Lanier never closed. Before he delivered his lectures at Johns Hopkins in 1878 on "The Physics of Poetry," he checked not only with the sixteenth-century precursor George Puttenham, but also with his friends in the department of physics, to assure himself that the science of sound and the "arte" of poetry were kindred. The implications of science drove him into fresh views of nature, but not out of the old faith which haunted him to the end, in a tangled congeries of paganism, amateurish learning, and Christianity as he understood it.

Thus he could write of

> Th' indifferent smile that nature's grace
> On Jesus, Judas pours alike.

Yet in the next moment he was kissing the "friendly, sisterly, sweetheart leaves" or celebrating the Saviour in his "A Ballad of Trees and the Master." Like Tennyson, but with far less success, he attempted to reconcile the warring claims of science and of personal religion in some far-off event. In the same vague fashion, he was aware of the social upheavals of the age; Carlyle was an enduring influence, and he has often been called Ruskinian. Yet his apostacies from childhood beliefs were intellectual rather than moral. He took shelter under the illusive adjustments of the nineteenth century, in "progress" and in the "somehow good." For all his dislike of "trade," one senses his buoyant hope that all may yet be well with men in an America so remarkable for material prosperity.

3

The Science of English Verse is a mature recapitulation of Lanier's formal experimentation in poetry. Its origins lie not only in his passionate interest in his craft and in the pedagogic streak in his nature but also in the inquisitiveness of the nineteenth century artist about the interrelation of the arts. Through his dual allegiance to music and poetry, Lanier's entire life had been an exploration of the laws governing each; gradually he had convinced himself that these laws were identical. It is not demonstrable that Lanier's faults as a poet arose from this oversimplified notion of an esthetic link; but his growing belief in theory affected deeply the quality of his verse. His climactic study remains a challenging exposition of a theory, now less definitive in the light of modern studies in prosody than provocative in its minor perceptions concerning a difficult subject.

Since, according to Lanier, the organic principles of music and poetry are the same, and since therefore sound relations are the essence of both,

when we hear verse, we *hear* a set of relations between sounds; when we silently read verse, we *see* that which brings to us a set of relations between sounds; when we imagine verse, we *imagine* a set of relations between sounds.

He then proceeds to study scientifically (he thinks) such elements in sound relations as duration, intensity, pitch, and tone color. He then discusses accents, phrases, lines, and stanzas, but he regards these as subordinate elements. In the end we must feel that, however stimulating to the study of prosody, *The Science of English Verse* is too forced, too artificial, to alter finally principles in either the creation or the reading of poetry.

Such poems as "Corn," "The Symphony," "The Psalm of the West," and others written during the last seven years of his life, reflect a conscious though belated attempt to make such workmanship serve his crystallized belief in the identity of the two arts. Apart from the elaborate theory and its relation to practice, however, we may perceive the instinctive master of his craft in his flowing cadences, in, say, these lines from "The Marshes of Glynn":

> Emerald twilights,—
> Virginal shy lights,
> Wrought of the leaves to allure to the whisper of vows . . .
> Of the dim sweet woods, of the dear dark woods . . .
> Ye held me fast in your heart and I held you fast in mine . . .
>   As the marsh-hen secretly builds on the watery sod,
>   Behold I will build me a nest on the greatness of God.

What remains is his matchless pattern of sound, even to the overreaching of the sense, a fact even more arresting than the sudden, beautiful simplicity in his dialect poems or in "The Revenge of Hamish," one of the best modern ballads. When we yield uncritically to his throbbing music in the rose-leaf passage in "The Symphony," or in that on the live-oaks in "The Marshes of Glynn," or in the sun-passages of "Sunrise," we feel a power transcending both his theories and his practice.

4

Though W. D. Howells rejected Sidney Lanier's early poem "Corn" for the *Atlantic*, he recognized at once Emily Dickinson's quality in her *Poems*, 1890. Comparing her "singular and authentic spirit" to Emerson and Blake, he argued that in her strange poetry New England had made a "distinctive addition to the literature of the world," that Dickinson formed a moment in the national life, and "could as well happen in Amherst, Mass., as in Athens, Att." She was, Howells implies, America's Sappho. Howells' remarkable acumen also appears in his confident surmise that Dickinson wished her poetry finally to be published, because she could not have made it without knowing its singular worth. But no one in 1891 could have predicted the bizarre struggle that ensued, over six decades, to publish her "letter to the world." The record of this struggle bears essentially on any effort to place Dickinson in literary history and to understand her poems.

The poet who died in 1886 at the age of fifty-six wrote more than 1,775 poems, most of them finished in fair copy but some still in the formative stage. Like an Elizabethan poet, she sent copies of poems to her friends. But only seven poems appeared in print in her lifetime, partly because Colonel T. W. Higginson, her mentor after 1862, thought she should not publish such rough verse. Then, after her death, her sister Lavinia persuaded Colonel Higginson and a sympathetic young neighbor, Mabel Loomis Todd, to prepare the best of the poems for publication. The editors put together and "polished" three series of *Poems* in 1890, 1891, and 1896, and a selection of *Letters* in 1894, all of which sold widely. Perhaps ten volumes of poems might have appeared if Lavinia had not sued Mrs. Todd, successfully, to regain a strip of meadowland Austin Dickinson had earlier given her in token compensation for Mrs. Todd's long service to his sister and to Apollo. The act left Mrs. Todd embittered and silent. Then in 1914, Martha Dickinson Bianchi, daughter of Emily's much-loved sister-in-law Susan Dickinson, who had lived next door to her, published the poems of *The Single Hound* from manuscripts which the poet had sent her mother. Mrs. Bianchi also published *Further Poems* in 1929. Mrs. Todd edited an enlarged and corrected *Letters* in 1931. Mrs. Bianchi came up with *Unpublished Poems* in 1935. Mrs. Todd's daughter, Millicent Todd Bingham, published *Bolts of Melody* in 1945 from her mother's hoard of originals—still more unpublished poems. So the verse trickled out for sixty-five years, its slant rhymes "improved" by Higginson and Mrs. Todd, its force hidden by genteel titles in genteel categories, the spidery handwriting miscopied by Sue and her daughter, and the still puzzling dashes and capital letters reduced to conventional pointing. Only after the death of the warring factions in the Dickinson family was it possible for Thomas H. Johnson to present accurately from the manuscripts and to set in order of composition the whole body of Dickinson's verse in his three-volume *Poems of Emily Dickinson* (1955). With Theodora Ward, he performed the same kind of invaluable service in *The Letters of Emily Dickinson* (1958).

What sort of life produced so distinguished a body of semi-private poetry? Much has been made of Dickinson's withdrawal in her early thirties into the family grounds, the house, and her own bedroom, like a nun or a character in a Hawthorne tale. She dressed in white, like fastidious old Samuel Clemens. She talked to visitors through a half-closed door. She came to be considered eccentric, if not cracked. Her mother surely failed her if only in her entire acquiescence to Edward Dickinson, the father whose heart was uniquely "pure and terrible"—so the daughter believed—and who presented himself to God and the Congregational church of Amherst finally at the age of forty-seven. But Emily Dickinson, devoted as she was to parents and brother Austin and sister Lavinia and eventually Austin's ambitious wife, Susan, grew up normally enough with good schooling, much letter writing, beaux and comic valentines and gardening and household chores. She showed her special quality first, perhaps, at eighteen, in the middle of a religious revival at Mt. Holyoke Female Seminary where she was a student. When the headmistress, Miss Lyon, asked all those students who wished to be Christians to rise, only Emily remained seated. "They thought it queer I didn't rise," she is reported as saying; "I thought a lie would be queerer." She must have shown this same piercing love for the truth in the poetry she was sharing, still in her eighteenth year, with Benjamin Newton, her father's law student. He was "the first of my own friends," she said; he was also her first mentor, who gave her a copy of Emerson's *Poems*. To her third mentor, Higginson, she confessed, in 1862, "My dying Tutor told me that he would like to live till I had been a poet." Higginson saved her life, she was convinced, by saying yes to her desperate inquiry if "my Verse is alive?": he answered that the verse she enclosed was indeed poetry, however flawed, faulty, imperfectly rhymed, and unpublishable. The second mentor was the man who created the crisis of Dickinson's life, in 1862, the miraculous year when she wrote 366 poems. Though the identity of the "Master" may never be finally determined, it is likely that he was the married Philadelphia clergyman Charles Wadsworth, who preached before her in 1855, met her twice in Amherst, and corresponded with her until his death. It seems likely too that she fell in love with him in a New England variety of the psychological pattern once called courtly love, he being unaware or carefully unconscious of her passion. "I had a terror—since September—I could tell to none—" Dickinson wrote to Higginson in 1862, "and so I sing, as the Boy does by the Burying Ground—because I am afraid." Wadsworth had moved to California in 1861.

Her grand passion passed over, the day to day life of Dickinson cannot be understood in such simple terms as neurotic withdrawal. The house where she lived was filled with relatives and visitors throughout the year, not to speak of college faculty and students. She cooked and cleaned and gardened, playing Martha to Lavinia's Mary. She composed, drafting and revising, letters to a wide circle of friends. Crucially, with the backing of Austin and Benjamin Newton and Susan, she came early to know what she was for— she was a poet; so that when the crisis came, in 1861 and 1862, she sustained herself writing a poem a day; and from 1861 to 1864 she wrote over 750 poems. Such a rate of composition not only demands a heavy spending of psychic energy: it constitutes a life. Moreover, as Howells guessed, it must in these years have yielded her "a radiant happiness" within the heart of her misery.

5

Efforts have been made to interpret Dickinson's poems chronologically, or by her own "packet" groupings, or in terms of her relation to the "Master" during the Civil War, or of an increasing firmness, despite lapses, in her belief in immortality, or of a natural slackening of poetic economy and fervor in the verse after the 1860's. Most evaluation however still follows the categorical approach of Dickinson's first editors, considerably refined, with recent emphasis on key terms and basic metaphors, such as "circumference," in the poems. The major concerns of Dickinson's poetry early and late, her "flood subjects," may be defined as the seasons and nature, death and a problematic afterlife, the kinds and phases of love, and poetry as the divine art. (Poems are referred to hereafter by first line or by the number in the 1955 Johnson edition.)

Manifestations of change fascinated Dickinson both in the natural world and in human life, and the pomp of the passing seasons excited her like an endless menagerie passing through Amherst. Thus "Winter is good," she says (1316) because his chilly pleasures give an "Italic flavor" to "Intellects inebriate / With Summer, or the World." The hemlock tree likes to stand near a snowbank (525) just as men feel the need to slake their instinctive thirst for wilderness. The poet who views everything "New Englandly" is raised to a state of ecstatic *hubris* by the "Bronze—and Blaze" of the northern lights (290), only to acknowledge in a sharp reversal of feeling that her "Splendors" (her poems, that is) are as various and impermanent as the creatures in a traveling zoo; whereas the "Competeless Show" of the aurora borealis will go on for centuries after she lies in a neglected grave. "It sifts from Leaden Sieves" (311) is Dickinson's rendering of a New England snowstorm as "Artisan," in the vein of Emerson's "The Snowstorm" and Whittier's "Snowbound." Winter, however, as frost is a "Visitor in Marl" whose kiss is deadly (391). He can be a "blonde Assassin" lopping off the heads of flowers (1624) before an "Approving God." Even more painful and sinister is Dickinson's vision in the poem, "There's a certain Slant of light, / Winter Afternoons" (258), for this light oppresses the beholder, hurts him internally, makes him despair, even as he realizes that it is "Heavenly" and "imperial." When the light comes, the "Landscape listens"; when it goes, one feels as if he were looking on the face of the dead, encountering that mystery of translation which figures again and again in Dickinson's poems.

Spring and especially its first tokens Dickinson greets with all the warmth of the romantic poet she was, as in Poem 140, where "Nicodemus' Mystery / Receives its annual reply!" It is "the Period / Express from God" (844), and in striking, perhaps intentional, contrast to Poem 258, above, she insists, "A Light exists in Spring / Not present on the Year / At any other period" (812). Like Wordsworth's "light that never was, on sea or land," Dickinson's light in March has a color not to be defined, illuminative, almost speaking, and when it goes it affects us as if Trade had suddenly "encroached / Upon a Sacrament." But Dickinson was sceptical as well as romantic. She warns (1333):

> A little Madness in the Spring
> Is wholesome even for the King,
> But God be with the Clown—
> Who ponders this tremendous scene—
> This whole Experiment of Green—
> As if it were his own!

Dickinson brilliantly creates the feeling of summer in "The Trees like Tassels—hit—and swung" (606), its insect sounds, sun and shadow, birdsong and flower-odor, and concludes that "Vandyke's" delineation of a summer day would prove mean to "those that see." In a familiar poem (569), she "reckoned" Summer as third only to Poets and the Sun. But the heat and light and glory of the season are precious to the poet finally because they form a flawed series of passing "nows" and not a forever. It is for this reason that Dickinson's season of seasons is Indian Summer, the mild hazy weather following the first heavy frosts when the maples and oaks of the Connecticut valley are all ablaze. This "June when Corn is cut" (930), this second beginning of summer (1422), is almost peculiarly her subject, for she wrote more than twenty poems about it from 1858 to 1883. Of these four are distinguished: "These are the days when Birds come back" (130), "As imperceptibly as Grief" (1540), "Further in Summer than the Birds" (1068), and "The murmuring of Bees, has ceased" (1115). Despite its duplicity and dissembling, the season appears to be sacred, with the crickets singing their "spectral Canticle" in praise of its beauty, and all nature enhanced by a "Druidic Difference" (1068).

Beyond the cycle of the year, Dickinson recreates the cycle of the day as in "The Red—Blaze—is the Morning" and dozens of other poems depicting the sunrise or sunset. The cycle of the single human life and its end is, as will be seen, her profoundest concern. As a poet of her age, she could not but be affected also by notions of geological and sidereal time. So, in "It's easy to invent a Life— / God does it—every Day," she is speculating about Darwin's concept of evolution, the ephemeral individual, and even the "Perished Patterns" of extinct species. In all these cycles of change, Dickinson longed for certainty and stasis. How deeply, Poem 1056, wherein all cycles merge, envisions. Noon and summer coalesce and reach entire peace in the consciousness of the poet. *Revelation* 22:5 may have inspired her: "And there shall be no night there; and they need no candle, neither light of the sun; for the Lord God giveth them light; and they shall reign for ever and ever."

Dickinson loved the natural world, her earthly paradise, for its winds and storms, black bees with "gilt surcingles," the robin who eats his worm raw, the bobolink who swung upon the Decalogue and shouted "Let us pray," the snake in his boggy acre, bats and rats and spiders, the hummingbird, and fifty other creatures, sights, sounds, and sensations. In any attempt to summarize the poet's eclectic responses, however, wonder rather than ecstatic identification is probably the word. "What mystery pervades a well!" is a late poem in which images of the deep well and the "floorless sea" precipitate the comment:

> But nature is a stranger yet;
> The ones that cite her most
> Have never passed her haunted house
> Nor simplified her ghost.

That is, scientists and transcendentalists alike risk knowing nature less the nearer they get to her. The conclusion seems plain. Dickinson took particular delight in the green earth and all its avatars. She called it Eden and Paradise. But she did not pretend ever to have solved its *mysterium tremendum*.

6

The great mystery extended for her, as well as for Whitman, into the reaches of outer space. That Dickinson is a cosmic poet a number of important poems, such as 290, 502, 721, and 738, will witness. "Behind Me—dips Eternity" (721) presents an astronomer's setting for the traditional voyage of the human soul from the blank before birth to the blank after death. The soul in its brief ocean voyage between Eternity and Immortality appears sailing toward death and the promise of dawn in the East, although the light is of the faintest. The goal of the voyage "they say" is the "Dateless" kingdom of heaven and its monarch, God, whose son, Christ, was fathered by no mortal man, yet who in man diversified himself in "Duplicate divine." The miracle before and behind is the kingdom of God, Alpha and Omega, the first and the last—the Lord God who is and was and who is to come (*Revelation* 1). The East-West North-South axes may represent the four corners of the earth, as in *Revelation* 7. "A Crescent in the Sea" is an image of the "I" actor of the poem. The last image is truly apocalyptic: the tiny figure drifts toward the gray East, with no light behind it in the West, absolute midnight prevails to North and South, and a maelstrom or hurricane rages overhead in the sky. The poem is thus pictorial on a Miltonic scale and comparably terrific in revealing the crescent soul surrounded in every direction except the East by the blackness of darkness. A revealing gloss may be cited in Venerable Bede's comparison of the life of man, according to the pagan view, to the sparrow that flies from the storm of winter into one window of a warm bright mead hall and out another window into the black snow-filled night again. The difference of course is that Dickinson's vision is informed by terror as well as pathos.

It was Dickinson's love poetry that first established her fame, with the mostly adventitious help of gossip and speculation about the identity of her lover; though inevitably some of the love poems have faded as the unknown lover image has given way to the honorable preacher, Charles Wadsworth, or conceivably to Austin Dickinson's closest friend, Samuel Bowles, vigorous extraverted editor of the Springfield *Republican*. Put differently, the biographical facts may never be finally determined; but the consequence of Dickinson's first love, whether it was fulfilled or reciprocated or largely self-generated, was poetry.

The love verse begins with the youthful conviction that "the Earth was *made* for lovers" (1) and that love is "Necromancy Sweet" (177), then deepens in the crisis years into the passionate particularity of "Wild Nights —Wild Nights!" (249). "There came a Day at Summer's full" initiates the sacramental motif of lovers separated and suffering, looking forward to a new marriage in heaven "justified—through Calvaries of Love" (322). "The first Day's Night had come" (410), which may well refer to the same day of meeting and parting, presents the split view that the soul may endure so terrible an experience by singing, but that the brain simply balks, mumbling foolishly, in potential madness. The climax in this phase of the love-poem sequence Dickinson reached with Poem 640, the longest she ever wrote and one of the strictest in its poetic development. "I cannot live with You" the speaker declares; "I could not die—with You," "Nor could I rise —with You" because you "served Heaven" and "I could not." "And were You lost," she cries, "I would be," "And were You—saved" separate from me, "That self—were Hell to Me." So, the narrator concludes: "So We must meet apart— / You there—I—here— / With just the Door ajar / That Oceans are—and Prayer— / And that White Sustenance— / Despair—." The personal reference may be to Charles Wadsworth, who "served Heaven" in Philadelphia and then in Calvary Church in San Francisco, but the whole effect is impersonal: it is like that of the lovers' fate in *The Scarlet Letter* or of Dante's Paolo and Francesca. After "I cannot live with You," Dickinson in varying moods will admit that "We outgrow love" (887), or will reassert despair, in the metaphor "Bountiful colored, my Morning rose / Early and sere, its end" (913), or return hotly to the claim that "Title divine—is mine! / The Wife—without the Sign!" (1072). But her force as a love poet is strongest when she embues physical passion with religious feeling, like John Donne and the English metaphysicals before her, and when she grounds spiritual awe in sensation. Her power arises also, necessarily, from her knowing the psychology of hatred. Purely in the spirit of Blake she observes that "Anger as soon as fed is dead— / 'Tis starving makes it fat" (1509).

Though poems of earthly and divine love form a melodic line throughout Dickinson's poetic career, the diapason of her verse is death, and life after death. It is a theme to which in one degree or another she devoted some five hundred of her poems. The motif is linked, of course, to nature and the existence of God, to the little death of friends' or lovers' parting, to justice in heaven for separated earthly lovers, and to the poet's immortality in his verse. It varies in tone from elegiac despair, or horror at bodily decay, to exalted and confident belief, to resignation before an unsolvable mystery. It begins early in the poetry and persists late.

Many early poems embody the progress from life to death, traditionally, as voyaging, the exultant going of an "inland soul to sea" (76), or the royal status which "simple You, and I" achieve by dying (98). "How many times these low feet staggered" (187) is weightier and more original, however. It pictures the amazingly still body of a once busy domestic woman with a kind of tender irony. Her mouth is soldered; the hot forehead is cool; the fingers are "adamantine," never more to wear a thimble; and so the "Indolent Housewife" now pays no heed to the cobwebs or the "freckled pane" of an unwashed window. The coolness of this poem gives way within the same year, 1860, to an expression in Poem 193 of hot pain which only Christ in heaven will be able to justify. Basically Christ the teacher will explain to the "I" pupil at his death the reason for his suffering, in the lovely (and just) schoolroom of heaven; then, by comparison, Christ's woe at Peter's betrayal of him and the pain from his blood-dropping crown of thorns will make the pupil's hot tears coursing down his cheeks seem trivial. But the whole effect is rather less of future consolation than of present anguish, because the repetition of "scalds me now" and the nine times repeated diphthong "ai" tip the balance toward pain. Where pain is the prime motive of this poem (193), madness is the anticipated end-state of "I felt a Funeral, in my Brain" as "I" falls through space into unconsciousness (280). Frustrated failure of the senses concludes "I heard a Fly buzz—when I died" (465). And corrosive doubt fills Poem 338, whose speaker turns from certainty of future Bliss to a suspicion that the glee might "glaze— / In Death's—stiff—stare."

Sheer wonder at the growth of the human soul is also characteristic. It is "A Solemn thing within the Soul," the poet asserts, to feel itself ripen as an apple does in the orchard, and a wonderful thing to feel the Sun at work ripening the cheek and glancing into the Core; but it is "solemnest" to consider that every day one moves nearer to "Harvest," and that every day is the last day in some lives (483). Almost always Dickinson works best from real, domestic, New England experience, here apple-picking. The well-known poem "Because I could not stop for Death" is also homely in metaphor: Death is a suitor taking a girl dressed as if for a wedding on a buggy ride in the country (712); the carriage takes them to a House in the Ground and empty centuries of eternity, all shorter than the vital day of courtship. Dickinson it must be admitted had a taste for "obituary eloquence" and graveyard poetry, like Mark Twain's Emmeline Grangerford; but she is also capable of noting "the gravity / Of every Citizen" in the curious Town of the dead (892) and the silence of the "meek members of the Resurrection" once so sagacious (216). She attempted often to reassure herself that death was no more than a dialogue between the Spirit and the Dust wherein the Spirit had the final word (976). Christ had told her, incontrovertibly, that "Death was dead" (432). She could even argue that an "ignis fatuus" in an age when God is not to be found is better than no faith at all.

All these dramatic responses to her conviction that "all but Death, can be Adjusted" (749) form an amazing spectrum of feeling and belief. The dominant color in that spectrum is surely the effort itself to know the "stirless" truth, shaded with the awe that death inspires. "The last Night that She lived" (1100) may be cited to illustrate the contention. Those who go in and out of the dying woman's "final Room" discover that they see nature differently; they feel a touch of guilt at living, a touch of envy of the "so nearly infinite," and a jostling in their very souls. Then, the focus shifts back to the dying:

> She mentioned, and forgot—
> Then lightly as a Reed
> Bent to the Water, struggled scarce—
> Consented, and was dead—

What Hawthorne observed of Melville's long internal debate on annihilation can be said of Dickinson too. She could "neither believe, nor be comfortable in [her] unbelief," and she had "a very high and noble nature . . . better worth immortality than most of us."

The poetry of death and immortality is thus Dickinson's prime subject. Nonetheless, she wrote at least fifty poems on the subject of art; and indeed, poetry itself may rival mortality as her deepest preoccupation, if the measure is a high level of poetic performance. If Dickinson could never reach a consistent solid faith in the immortality of the soul, she had few doubts about

Shakespeare's living in his work, or the conviction that "in black ink" her love might "still shine bright." Like the poetry about death, the poetry about art begins early and persists; in witness to its depth and variety, four poems —307, 365, 505, and 569—may be cited. The first of them asserts that "The One who could repeat the Summer day" or "reproduce the Sun— / At period of going down— / The Lingering—and the Stain—I mean" would be greater than the immense phenomena themselves; and even if he were physically minute, his name would outlast all the cycles of nature. The verbal mastery here—Sun, Stain, mean, Name, remain—is as subtle as it is beautiful. The second poem rivals William Blake and his "Tyger."

> Dare you see a Soul *at the White Heat?*
> Then crouch within the door—
> Red—is the Fire's common tint—
> But when the vivid Ore
> Has vanquished Flame's conditions,
> It quivers from the Forge
> Without a color, but the light
> Of unannointed Blaze.

Every village blacksmith with his hammer and bellows, she avers, stands a symbol for the "finer Forge" within, the creative soul, which in the end can produce a light so pure as to "Repudiate the Forge," its origin. The third of these poems about art presents poetry as an "awful" and shattering art that combines the forces of painting and music. The verse is especially witty, since the speaker insists that she prefers the role of looker and listener and appreciator to that of creator; but in the end she wonders how she would feel if she possessed the art to "stun" herself with "Bolts of Melody." In this mock-modest fashion, she denies her ability to wield the thunderbolt of poetry in the very act of dazzling her reader with sound and light.

The poet's subjects, or her "Visitors" in the house of possibility (657) provide a summing up in Poem 569. With cool logic and a shocking disregard for the world's opinion, the soliloquist rates Poets first and God's Heaven fourth, only to decide that the Poets "comprehend" (circumscribe and understand) the Others. In the second half of the poem Dickinson proves that the poets' summer is permanent, that their sun surpasses nature's, and that God's Heaven could scarcely be more beautiful than the heaven of poetry.

7

Dickinson's ways of defining the matter of poetry and the process of poetic creation are richly varied. Poetry is a frostless garden (2). It is a lamp that burns on after Aladdin is dead, each age a lens disseminating the original light (233, 883). It is local and provincial (285). It is a ballet (326) or a tune like a brook able to "Set bleeding feet to minuets" (83). It is the "Territory Argent" of stars, never yet consumed (469). It is the truth, to be achieved only indirectly (516, 1129), "slant." It demands the exact word (581, 1126), and that word may "infect" a reader at the distance of centuries (1261). It is magic (177). It is the distillation of amazing sense—and scents —or "essential oils" from ordinary flowers, by painful effort (448, 675). It combines the arts of painting and music. It is coeval with love (1247). As for the poet, he is a forger, a carpenter (488), a gentian blooming only after frost has come (442), a phoebe neither more nor less (1009), and a lover of truth and beauty (449).

The figures of carpenter and blacksmith and "expresser" of essential perfumes illustrate Dickinson's belief that art requires a craftsman's skill as well as inspiration or a compelling need for compensation. Quite as seriously as Flaubert or Mark Twain, Dickinson searched long for the right word, as certain unfinished poems show, in which the poet had not yet chosen among as many as sixteen "candidates." Then after searching, if she could not find the word she wanted, she might simply invent one. She speaks of "Death's immediately" (1420), or "illume" (1551), "gianture," a smile that "meagres Balms" (1531), and in a letter writes, "your absence insanes me so." It follows that such a connoisseur of words might develop a taste for serious word-play, and Dickinson does, often with sharp awareness of older residual meanings. So, in the line "Essential oils—are wrung" essential means both necessary and of the essence. Or in Poem 520 the young woman who visits the Sea admits that "no Man moved Me" from the water's edge, though thereafter, the tide-god, Neptune, makes her retreat even as he moves her emotionally. The justification for such close attention to the word, for Dickinson, lay in her conviction that since language is itself metaphorical, to tell the truth one must tell it metaphorically.

In the matter of total form, Dickinson appears to be limited to short poems and to the quatrains of the Isaac Watts hymns; but looked at more closely and read aloud, the poems display greater variety, in the internal music of assonance, alliteration, pause, and in line length and stanzaic patterning as well. She uses six-line stanzas and varies the length of lines from one foot to five as it suits her (155, 285). One strategy by which she contains her poetic force is to construct a triad of quatrains or double quatrains, developing a metaphor in each, and to close the poem with a summarizing statement or question. Poem 414 grows this way. It was like a maelstrom; it was as if a goblin gripped you; it was as if you were led to the gallows after trial, and then reprieved: which anguish were utterest, then—to live or to die? Dickinson created this form presumably as her variation on the Shakespearean sonnet. She also uses a triad of triplets with great economy, as in "A Spider sewed at Night" (1138). Also, she worked out free forms when the traditional ones would not answer, only once abandoning rhyme or half-rhyme. Generally, however, she was less original in the physical features of her verse than in the adaptations she made of genres or rhetorical patterns. As a student of the dictionary, for example, it is natural that she should make definition a category. "Success is . . .", "Exultation is . . .", "'Heaven'— is . . .", "Exhilaration—is . . .", "The Brain—is. . . ." In much the same way she wrote a number of poems as letters, like "Bee! I'm expecting you! . . . Yours, Fly," the form originating in the comic valentine letter-poems of the early 1850's. Another pattern she put to use was the Anglo-Saxon riddle turned into puzzle poems, like "A Route of Evanescence" (1463) about a ruby-throated hummingbird, or "A Visitor in Marl," which is a killing frost (391). Less definable traditionally but very impressive are Dickinson's dream poems (mostly nightmares), which are filled with mixed metaphors and synesthetic effects, and often end in falling or unconsciousness or madness. Examples are "In Winter in my Room," "It was not Death," "The Soul has Bandaged moments," and the "sonnet" poem already cited, "'Twas like a Maelstrom." Finally, Dickinson wrote a small number of memorable elegies, to Emily Brontë, to Benjamin Newton, and to her father, among others.

By the end of the Civil War, Dickinson had passed through the crisis years of her life, which were also the years most productive of poetry. Higginson, as we have seen, had thrown her a life-line, not quite aware of what he was doing, but the opportunity to send him poems occasionally and to be assured that they were quick with life was enough. Much like other New England spinsters, she withdrew from contact with all but family and a group of close friends. But unlike other spinsters, she continued to feel ecstacy in the act of living, to think life still the "finest secret," to keep up her large correspondence, and to write twenty poems a year. In the early 1870's Dickinson made a new friend in the popular poet and novelist Helen Hunt Jackson, who published "Success" (67) anonymously in *A Masque of Poets* (where it was widely thought to be by Emerson) and who said flatly "You are a great poet." Dickinson must have taken keen pleasure in such earnest assurance, though Mrs. Jackson could not persuade her to change her mind about publishing other poems. Dickinson's last and most important friend was Judge Otis P. Lord, a good friend of her father for many years, eighteen years older than she, and happily married. At the death of her father in 1874, a shattering event, Dickinson drew comfort from the friendship of Judge Lord. After the death of Lord's wife in 1877, their friendship developed into love, ardent and acknowledged, which would probably have led to their marriage had not the Judge died of a stroke early in 1884. With his death, the spring of Dickinson's life was broken. She had lost Bowles in 1878 and both Wadsworth and her mother in 1882. But in April of 1882, her rare spirit still shows when she writes to Lord, "In Heaven they neither Woo nor are given in wooing—what an imperfect place!" The disclosure, in fact, of Dickinson's tenderness for Otis Lord and his for her has rendered her whole life more real, credible, and human.

8

The attempt to place Dickinson at a given bend in the stream of American art and thought is difficult: she insists on turning up elsewhere, partly at least because she is an original Protean force. Many of her critics call her a Puritan. In the degree that she believed death to be the goal of life, often seeking to learn the manner of a particular friend's dying moments, she certainly was. But once she had decided to remain true to herself—all the rest being "perjury"—the doctrines of New England Calvinism seem to have affected her inner life scarcely at all. Heaven and Hell became, for her, states of mind and consciousness. Somewhat more plausibly than "Puritan" she may be termed a "Transcendentalist by native essence," as an early reviewer said. Her ties to Emerson are identifiable and strong. Newton had given her Emerson's *Poems* early; she quotes "The Snowstorm" and refers to "The Humble-Bee," and dubs *Representative Men* "a little Granite book." She believed in her mind and conscience as the ground for self-reliance; her idea of compensation was Emersonian; her theory of poetry, like Emerson's, rests on a language theory; and she was intoxicated by glimpses of divinity in the world around her. Rather like another spiritual heir of Emerson, Walt Whitman, she was capable of seeing women going to work in the Amherst morning carrying their children as "Madonnas . . . carrying Saviors." When Emerson died, she wrote to Otis Lord, "My Philadelphia [i.e., Wadsworth] has passed from earth, and the Ralph Waldo Emerson—whose name my Father's Law Student taught me, has touched the secret Spring. Which Earth are we in?" Plainly, to her Emerson belonged in sacred company. Of her possible borrowings from Emerson for her own poetry, some are verifiable and persuasive; but even when she borrows, she transforms. Thus Emerson makes his poet, Merlin, render back "artful thunder"; but Dickinson endows her poet with the power to stun herself with "Bolts of Melody." As Mark Twain might say, the almost right metaphor to the right metaphor is as the lightning bug to the lightning.

Dickinson is Puritan and Transcendentalist, but also the contemporary

of Mark Twain, Sarah Orne Jewett, W. D. Howells, and Henry James. Inevitably she is a writer of her own day, who shares the impulses and talents
of the local-color story-tellers, and their taste for the provincial. Though the
warp may be spiritual or cosmic, the woof of her poetry is the common, the
near, even the low, quite particularly the domestic. Her taste for wild
exaggeration comes from her early love for the tall-tale humor of the Southwest. Thus one of her wittiest verses boasts that she finished two sunsets
(Poems 307 and 308 presumably) while day was making one. The day's was
"ampler," she admits, but hers is "more convenient / To Carry in the
Hand." She took her idea, it seems probable, from one of Davy Crockett's
adventures on a frigid winter morning. Finding the January sun frozen
fast in sweat on its axis at the top of Daybreak Hill, Crockett breaks it loose
with the help of hot bear oil, and walks home "introducin' people to the
fresh daylight with a piece of sunrise in my pocket." Most specially, Dickinson shares with her contemporaries an intense concern with consciousness, in
life and after death. "Captivity is Consciousness," she writes, "So's Liberty"
(384). The soul cannot rid itself of this "awful Mate" any more than it could
secrete itself "Behind the Eyes of God" (894). Its "Adventure" is "unto
itself," attended by the single hound of consciousness, or identity (822).
Consciousness and the soul tend to fuse, in Dickinson's poems, in the end;
so that the absolute of solitude, of "polar privacy," is embodied in "A soul
admitted to itself— / Finite infinity" (1695). Awareness, sensibility, consciousness—these were the subjects of Henry and William James as well as
of the poet of Amherst.

It was this awareness in Dickinson that may, primarily, have made her
a popular poet in the 1890's, and that certainly led to her wider, more lasting
reputation in the second American renaissance of the 1920's and to her present fame. She is a confessional poet. She makes a drama of her will to believe. She is subtle and proficient technically. In all these respects she possesses
a sensibility comprehensible and attractive to poets who have followed her
in the present century, like Carl Sandburg, Genevieve Taggard, Hart Crane,
Archibald MacLeish, Louise Bogan, Richard Wilbur, Adrienne Rich, and
Ramon Guthrie. Dickinson wrote of her father after his death, "Lay this
Laurel on the One / Too intrinsic for Renown." Scorning the notion of
popularity, she might well have written so classic, so truthful, an epitaph
for herself. But she also knew the counter-truth, and spoke it to Higginson,
"If fame belonged to me, I could not escape her." She has not escaped, to our
beatitude.

56. MARK TWAIN

"I AM persuaded," wrote Bernard Shaw to Mark Twain, "that the future historian of America will find your works as indispensable to him as a French historian finds the political tracts of Voltaire." By his own participation, no artist in our literature save Lincoln spans so broad a segment of typical American experience in the last century. Samuel Langhorne Clemens, known by the most famous pen name that an American ever bore, is a matchless annalist of his times. His life makes those of literary men in Boston and Concord and New York resemble (in Hawthorne's phrase) the flowering of talents that blossomed in too retired a shade. He knew the greatest river of the continent as Melville knew the high seas. He witnessed the epic of America, the westward tide at its full, with perception keener than the shallow appraisals of Bret Harte and Joaquin Miller. When in his *Autobiography* Mark Twain recalls after forty years the tragedy of an emigrant lad stabbed to death by a drunken comrade, and adds, "I saw the red life gush from his breast," we are reminded of Whitman's affirmation, "I was there"—with the difference that Walt's immediacy was imaginative, Mark's actual. In the activities of the external man as well as in character and temperament, Mark Twain was a representative American— from idyllic ante-bellum boyhood in a river town, to maturity enmeshed in the cross-purposes of the Gilded Age which he christened, and thence to the sunset years of mingled hope and disillusion in the Progressive Era. Despite his own avowal, "There is not a single human characteristic which can be safely labeled as 'American,'" Mark Twain is stamped unforgettably with the national brand. If he failed finally to reconcile reality and ideality, he absorbed and gave expression to both. That failure was not his; it belonged to his generation.

In old age his incurably Calvinist mind saw all the events of his life, from birth on November 30, 1835, in the village of Florida, Missouri, as a chain of causation forged by some power outside his will. Like his Connecticut Yankee he was led to reflect upon heredity, "a procession of ancestors that stretches back a billion years to the Adam-clam or grasshopper or monkey from whom our race has been so tediously and ostentatiously and unprofitably developed."

His father, an austere restless Virginian, bequeathed the family a vain hope of fortune from "the Tennessee lands," like Squire Hawkins in *The Gilded Age*; he also gave his son an object lesson in failure like the example set by the father of a genius whom Mark the Baconian once rose to challenge, Shakespeare of Stratford. The wife and mother, Jane Lampton Clemens, of Kentucky pioneer stock, sought by her strong Presbyterianism to balance her husband's village-lawyer agnosticism; their famous son inherited the self-tormenting conscience with the latter's will to disbelieve. As for derivations more remote, Twain the romantic relished his maternal tie with the Earls of Durham through "the American claimant," while Twain the democrat reserved his sole ancestral pride for a Regicide judge, who "did what he could toward reducing the list of crowned shams of his day."

In 1839 the Clemenses moved to Hannibal, on the west bank of the Mississippi, and set the conditions of boyhood and youth from which flowed the wellspring of Mark Twain's clearest inspiration. Thanks to *Tom Sawyer* and *Huckleberry Finn,* its aspect in the forties has become the property of millions: the wharf giving upon the turbid waters where rafts and broad-horns, fast packets and gay showboats passed endlessly, the plank sidewalks where Tom and Becky trudged to school, the tanyard where Huck's drunken father slept among the hogs, the steep slope of Cardiff (really Holliday's) Hill, the surrounding woods of oak and hickory and sumach, and a few miles downstream the cave where Injun Joe met death. Hannibal lay in its halcyon summer between frontier days and the convulsions of the Civil War, the latter forecast in the mobbing of an occasional abolitionist and the tracking down of runaway slaves. On the whole, happiness outweighed grief; prized in retrospect was the large freedom of a boy's life, with the swimming hole and woods full of game, jolly playmates banded against a world of adult supremacy, and dinner tables groaning with prodigal hospitality. "It was a heavenly place for a boy," Hannibal's first citizen remembered.

Sam Clemens' schooling ended early, when he was about twelve. After his father's death the lad was apprenticed to a printer's shop—"the poor boy's college," Lincoln called it. Lack of formal education doubtless gave the later Mark Twain an eagerness to have his genius certified by convention, and also led him occasionally to discover shopworn ideas with a thrill impossible to sophisticates; but it also delivered him from those cultural stereotypes into which the genius of New England, for example, for generations had been poured. Fatalist that he was, Twain liked to date his career from certain accidents. The first of them came one day on the streets of Hannibal, when the young printer picked up a stray leaf from a book about Joan of Arc, and for the first time saw magic in the printed word. Henceforth the itch of scribbling was strong upon him. His earliest known appearance in print, a crudely humorous sketch called "The Dandy Frightening the Squatter," appeared in the Boston *Carpet Bag* of May 1, 1852. He left Hannibal the next year, wandering on to New York and Philadelphia, and began to send home-town papers the first of those facetious travel pieces which he wrote sporadi-cally for the next half-century. In 1857, after tarrying awhile in Cincinnati, he set out for New Orleans with a notion of shipping for the Amazon. But, lacking funds, he became a steamboat pilot under the tutelage of Horace Bixby. That veteran gradually taught him the ever changing aspects of the Mississippi, by sun and starlight, at low water and in flood.

For two years after that Clemens turned his wheel atop the texas deck, drawing a licensed pilot's high wages, while he gained postgraduate schooling in human nature. Oft quoted is his later assertion: "When I find a well-drawn character in fiction or biography I generally take a warm personal interest in him, for the reason that I have known him before—met him on the river." A born worrier, he felt the responsibility that lay within a pilot's hands as he steered past narrows and snags and sand bars, or for the sake of prestige raced his rivals until the boiler nearly burst under its head of steam. His old master, many years later, stated that Clemens "knew the river like a book, but he lacked confidence." One may speculate whether a very human incertitude, deep in his being, did not chime with a classic type of humor in his constant self-portrayal as the man who gets slapped: the bumptious yet timid cub of *Life on the Mississippi*; the fear-bedeviled soldier of "The Campaign That Failed"; the tenderfoot of *Roughing It,* setting forest fires and just missing wealth through sheer stupidity; or the harassed traveler losing his tickets, browbeaten by porters and shopkeepers, falling foul of the authorities, who appears in a long sequence from the juvenile Snodgrass letters to *A Tramp Abroad.*

2

Clemens' career on the river ended in the spring of 1861 with the outbreak of hostilities. With brief enthusiasm he joined a Confederate militia band, savoring the boyish conspiracy of war in its early stages. In the lack of dis-cipline the band soon broke up; and Sam, with qualms about fighting for slavery, yielded to persuasion from his Unionist brother Orion, lately ap-pointed Secretary of the Territory of Nevada. In July, 1861, the two set out for the West. The outlines of the story told in *Roughing It* are true enough: the nineteen-day trip across the plains and Rockies to Carson City; an attack of mining fever that left Sam none the richer; his acceptance of a job on the Virginia City *Enterprise*; a journalist's view of San Francisco in flush times; and a newspaper-sponsored voyage to the Sandwich Islands. His dream of becoming a millionaire by a stroke of fortune never forsook him; lingering in his blood, the bonanza fever made him a lifelong victim of gold bricks, quick-profit schemes, and dazzling inventions. But his return to journalistic humor—the vein he had worked in his late teens and early twenties, imitative of such professional humorists as Seba Smith, J. J. Hooper, and B. P. Shillaber, in whose productions every newspaper office abounded—proved to be his really lucky strike. In 1863 the Missourian of twenty-eight met Artemus Ward on the latter's Western lecture tour, and watched a master storyteller in action: the adroit timing, change of pace, and deadpan obliviousness to the point of one's own wit. Twain's "How to Tell a Story" (1895) acknowledges these profitable lessons.

It was Ward who encouraged him to seek a wider audience than the red-shirted miners of Washoe and nabobs of the Golden Gate. The first fruit of this encouragement to appear in the East—a piece of jocular sadism against the small fry who made day and night hideous at resort hotels, "Those Blasted Children"—was printed early in 1864 by the New York *Mercury.* Meanwhile in 1863 Clemens had begun to imitate current funny men like Ward, Orpheus C. Kerr, and Josh Billings, by selecting a pen name, the river-boat man's cry for two fathoms, "Mark Twain." Clemens stoutly maintained he appropriated it soon after an eccentric pilot-journalist of New Orleans, Captain Isaiah Sellers, relinquished it by death. No contribution in the New Orleans press, however, has ever been found under that name; also, Sellers' death occurred a year after Clemens adopted this pseudonym. Whether original or borrowed, the name served an important purpose. It created an alter ego, a public character, which Clemens could foster through the years while doffing it in private as he pleased. It set definable limits to his role of being what the age called a "phunny phellow." A speculative critic might guess that his abiding interest in transposed identities, twins, and Siamese prodigies mirrored a dualism which self-observation would have shown running like a paradox through his nature: gullible and skeptical by turns; realistic and sentimental, a satirist who gave hostages to the established order, a frontiers-man who bowed his neck obediently to Victorian mores, and an idealist who loved the trappings of pomp and wealth. Incessantly he contradicted himself on a variety of subjects. His was not a single-track mind, but a whole switch-yard. The creation of two more or less separate identities—Clemens the sensitive and perceptive friend, Mark Twain the robust and astringent humorist—springing from the same trunk of personality, helped to make him like those ligatured twins in *Pudd'nhead Wilson,* Luigi and Angelo, "a human philopena."

Under the name of Mark Twain the wild-haired Southwesterner began to contribute to the press yarns swapped about the legislative halls of Carson

City, the bars and billiard parlors of San Francisco, and the hot stoves of miners on Jackass Hill. From these last, about February, 1865, he first heard the old folk tale of the Jumping Frog. To the anecdote he added the salt of human values which the genre usually lacked, in garrulous Simon Wheeler and simple Jim Smiley the Frog's owner. Published in the *Saturday Press* of New York, November 18, 1865, it was swiftly broadcast. The author grumbled in a letter home about the irony of riding high on "a villanous backwoods sketch," but already he was tasting that sense of popularity which soon came to be his elixir of life. In October, 1866, back from Honolulu and planted on a San Francisco lecture platform, he first encountered another powerful stimulant, the instant response. Early in 1867, at Cooper Union in New York, he won his eastern spurs, and began to be hailed as rightful heir to Artemus Ward, lately dead of tuberculosis in England. Soon, as his friend William Dean Howells phrased it, Twain learned "all the stops of that simple instrument, man." The lecturer's effect upon the writer was great. Increasingly Twain came to write by ear, testing his books by reading aloud, while making the expanded anecdote or incident the unit of his literary composition. Sometimes, of course, without benefit of his infectious personal charm, that mane of fiery red hair and hawklike nose, the gestures of an artist's hands, and the inflections of that irresistible drawl, a reader of cold print missed qualities which on the platform redeemed humor of a perishable sort.

"When I began to lecture, and in my earlier writings, my sole idea was to make comic capital out of everything I saw and heard," he told the biographer Archibald Henderson. After his first volume, of chiefly Western sketches, named *The Celebrated Jumping Frog* (1867), he reinforced this reputation by distilling a humorous travelogue out of the letters sent back to the *Alta California* from his cruise to the Mediterranean and Holy Land on the *Quaker City* in 1867. Comic capital was readily furnished by the flood of tourists, affluent merchants and their wives, war profiteers, former army officers on holiday, and clergymen for whom Jerusalem justified the junket, which swept over the Old World after Appomattox. Knowing themselves to be innocents, they faced down their provincialism by brag and cockalorum, and haggling over prices. Mark Twain gladly joined them, joking his way among the shrines and taboos of antiquity, comparing Como unfavorably with Tahoe, bathing in the Jordan, finding any foreign tongue incredibly funny, and pitying ignorance, superstition, and lack of modern conveniences. *The Innocents Abroad* (1869) helped to belittle our romantic allegiance to Europe, feeding our emergent nationalism. Instantly a best seller, it delighted those Americans in whom "the sense of Newport" (as Henry James later called it) had never been deeply engrafted. A slender minority like James himself felt that Mark Twain amused only primitive persons, was the Philistines' laureate. Years later, in 1889, in a letter to Andrew Lang, Twain would glory in this charge:

Indeed I have been misjudged, from the first. I have never tried in even one single instance, to help cultivate the cultivated classes. I was not equipped for it, either by native gifts or training. And I never had any ambition in that direction, but always hunted for bigger game—the masses. I have seldom deliberately tried to instruct them, but have done my best to entertain them. . . . Yes, you see, I have always catered for the Belly and the Members.

3

Yet this is not the whole story. From an early date, Mark Twain, the playboy of the Western world, had begun to feel the aspirations of an artist, to crave deeper approval than had come to the cracker-box humorist like Sam Slick and Jack Downing. In Honolulu in 1866 the diplomat Anson Burlingame gave him advice by which the aged Twain avowed he had lived "for forty years": "Seek your comradeships among your superiors in intellect and character; always *climb*." On the *Quaker City* voyage the Missourian fell under the refining spell of "Mother" Fairbanks, wife of a prosperous Ohio publisher, and tore up those travel letters which she thought crude. Always enjoying petticoat dominion, he eagerly sought her approval of the revised *Innocents* and was enchanted when she pronounced it "authentic." "A name I have coveted so long—and secured at last!" he exclaimed. "*I* don't care anything about being humorous, or poetical, or eloquent, or anything of that kind—the end and aim of my ambition is to be authentic—is to be considered authentic." In a similar thirst for higher recognition he told Howells, reviewer of *Innocents* in the *Atlantic*: "When I read that review of yours, I felt like the woman who was so glad her baby had come white." Nevertheless, as Twain found to his intermittent chagrin, his reputation throughout life kept returning to that of a "phunny phellow," turning cartwheels to captivate the groundlings—until at length he built up the defensive attitude expressed to Lang. At *Atlantic* dinners, the author of "Old Times on the Mississippi" and *Tom Sawyer* found himself seated below the salt, ranked by Longfellow and Lowell and Whittier, as well as by such adopted sons of Boston as Howells and Aldrich. Despite the new decorum of his life and the growing richness of his art, the wild man from the West was expected, some time, somehow, to disgrace himself. And, by the meridian of Boston, he eventually did so, when at the celebrated Whittier birthday dinner on December 17, 1877, he made his speech of innocent gaiety about three drunks in the high Sierras who personated Emerson, Longfellow, and Holmes. The diners were shocked, refusing their laughter while he stood solitary (as Howells said) "with his joke dead on his hands." The next day or so, when Twain's haunting distrust of himself and his own taste had induced a penitential hangover, he sent apologies, writing characteristically: "Ah, well, I am a great and sublime fool. But then I am God's fool, and all his works must be contemplated with respect." He then begged Howells to exclude him from the *Atlantic* for a while, in the interest of readers' good will. The gravity with which both the saints and the sinner regarded this incident reveals the massiveness of the genteel tradition in New England and the probationary status upon which Mark was kept for so many years.

Between the publication of the *Innocents* and this indiscretion, Clemens had taken a wife whose remolding influence has been the subject of much debate. The story of their courtship is familiar: his first sight of her delicate face in a miniature carried by her brother on the *Quaker City* cruise; Twain's meeting with the original, Olivia Langdon, ten years his junior, a semi-invalid who had turned to faith healing; their two years' betrothal while her father, the richest businessman in Elmira, and her kin were slowly won over; and their wedding early in 1870, with Clemens the bridegroom trying unsuccessfully to establish himself as a solid newspaper editor in Buffalo, but moving to Hartford in 1871 to resume a free-lance life. His veneration of women and their purity was almost fanatical. "I wouldn't have a girl that *I* was worthy of," he wrote "Mother" Fairbanks before his engagement. "*She* wouldn't do."

About the sexual make-up of Mark Twain speculation has been indulged since the Freudian era. In that famous sophomoric sketch *1601*, written in mid-career to amuse his clerical friend Joe Twichell, he had Sir Walter Raleigh describe "a people in ye uttermost parts of America, y^t copulate not until they be five-&-thirty yeeres of age." This, it happens, was the age when Clemens married a semi-invalid wife, as if some inadequacy in himself, some low sexual vitality, made such a woman his fitting mate. And yet respecting their physical love for each other and the fruitfulness of their union, with its four children, no doubt can be raised. What illicit experience might have come to a boy growing up in the accessible world of slavery, and passing his green manhood upon river boats and in bonanza towns, can only be guessed at. In later years, respecting the idealized Hannibal of his boyhood, he went so far as to deny the existence of sexual irregularities; and by confining his two great novels about Hannibal to adolescence he was able in a manner to carry his point. Obviously certain taboos about sex, personal as well as conventional, appear in his writings from beginning to end. Unlike his friend Howells, he attempted no probings of desire, no analysis of the chemical affinity between man and woman beyond the calf love of Tom and

Becky and the implausible treatment of Laura the siren of *The Gilded Age*. Only under the protective shield of miscegenation, in the person of the warm-blooded Negress Roxana in *Pudd'nhead Wilson*, does he venture even to approach passion which overleaps the bounds of society. Joan of Arc, a virgin of exquisite purity, plainly is the heroine after his inmost heart. A certain fear of sex, like the shrinking of primitive races and some adolescents from carnality as if it meant degradation of the body, seems to lie at the root of Mark Twain's nature. The exceptions of his occasional bawdry—in *1601* and a few unprinted works like his speech before the Stomach Club in Paris and his manuscript "Letters from the Earth"—but prove the rule, in ridiculing the body and its ways sufficiently to suit the most fanatic Puritan.

Yet Twain was in no sense a misogynist. He loved the company of women, of the refined women whose tastes and restraints fitted his own presuppositions about them. His understanding of the feminine mind has left no more delightful evidence than "Eve's Diary," written in 1905 shortly after Olivia's death, so that Adam's final bereavement becomes the epitaph of his own loss: "Wherever she was, *there* was Eden." In summary, Mark Twain's personal make-up and the conventions of gentility surrounding the kind of success he aspired to, joined to suppress the recognition of sex as a key motive in human actions—leaving woman not an object of desire but of reverential chivalry.

The effect of his wife upon Twain the artist has provoked latter-day discussion. One school of thought holds that Clemens was forced, first by his mother and then by his wife, to "make good," i.e., to make money and be respectable. Moreover, thanks to the censorship of his wife, they say, he became not the New World Rabelais but a frustrated genius incapable of calling his soul or vocabulary his own. It is clear, however, that proof of Livy's "humiliating" dominion rests largely upon Twain's letters to Howells: that pair of devoted husbands married to invalids who made a gallant little joke over being henpecked. The notion that women exercised a gentle tyranny over their menfolk, for the latter's good, always appealed to Mark Twain, schooled in Western theories that man was coarser clay and woman a rare and special being (as among the Washoe miners in *Roughing It,* who chipped in $2,500 in gold as a gift at the miraculous sight of a live woman). All his life he encouraged women to reform him, improve his taste and manners. His three little daughters who shared in the family rite known as "dusting off Papa," and the "angel-fish" of adolescent girls in his Bermudian Indian summer, were among the youngest of the sex whose devoted slave he rejoiced to be. It was a kind of game in the feudal tradition, which he adored. But to assume therefore that Twain the genius was henpecked, baffled, unmanned by women in general and Livy in particular is to convert a jest into a cry of anguish.

About the converse influence of husband upon wife something deserves to be said. For Twain's vitality rescued her from abysses of timorous living, his banter relaxed her serious disposition, and his religious skepticism destroyed her Christian faith.

As for the specific question of censorship, we know that Twain liked to read aloud *en famille* the results of his daily composition, usually meeting the approval he craved, sometimes encountering a chill disfavor to which he was equally sensitive. He was a poor self-critic and knew it. He plunged into writing without much plan or foresight. Livy's judgment in matters of simple good taste and in pruning wordiness and irrelevance was clearly superior to his own in the heat of incubation. A careful examination of his manuscripts shows that Mrs. Clemens, like that other long-standing adviser William Dean Howells, objected to certain vivid words and phrases— "wallow," "bowels," "spit," "rotten," and realistic allusions to stenches and putrefaction which always tempted Mark Twain, so that he grumbled about her "steadily weakening the English tongue"—but that in mild profanities (like Huck Finn's "comb me all to hell") and in rare inclinations toward the risqué (such as the farce of "The Royal Nonesuch") the author on second thought was his own most attentive censor. He was not above playing an occasional hazard with his critics to see how far he could skate on thin ice; then doubled on his own track back to safety. Just as he dreamed of the unabashed nakedness of a boy's freedom on a raft floating down the Mississippi, now and again he yearned for the lusty old ways of medieval speech, "full of unconscious coarsenesses and innocent indecencies," "good old questionable stories," as the Connecticut Yankee says. But quickly he reminded himself, as he observes in *A Tramp Abroad,* that the license of the printed word had been "sharply curtailed within the past eighty or ninety years." To this curb in the main he gave unstinting consent.

4

Up to the time of his anchorage in Hartford in 1871, the most important facts about Mark Twain are the things that happened to him, shaping his development as an artist and filling the granaries of memory. After that date the chief milestones are the books he wrote out of that accumulation. His maturity and self-assurance can be gauged, growing from book to book through the next two decades, as he lectured at home and abroad, met the captains of literature and politics and finance, read widely if desultorily, and perfected his early journalistic manner until it became one of the great styles of American letters—easy, incisive, sensitive to nuances of dialect, rich in the resources of comedy, satire, irony, and corrosive anger.

One group, of secondary importance, consists of his travel books. Between *The Innocents Abroad* (1869) and *Roughing It* (1872) he learned, under emancipation from newspaper reporting, to take greater liberties with fact for art's sake. Both books owe such structure as they have to a rough chronology. Upon this thread Mark Twain the raconteur strings one story after another. The latter volume offers us almost all the classic types which Americans in general, frontiersmen in particular, had long since favored: the tall tale, the melodramatic shocker, the yarn of pointless garrulity, malapropian humor, the canard of impossible coincidence, the chain of free association that wanders farther and farther from its announced subject; the comedy of man in his cups, the animal fable, and the delusions of a lunatic. Paradox, surprise, and understatement often heighten his effects. Anecdote continues to be the fiber of those later travel books, which show more fluency in repeating the essential pattern, but grow in world-weariness after the early gusto of the Innocents and the Argonauts. They include *A Tramp Abroad* (1880), with more travesty of European languages, guide books, and art criticism, and *Following the Equator* (1897), which reports Twain's lecture tour in Australia and India. Inevitable become his burlesques of sentimental poetry, parodies of romantic situations, yarns picked up in new places or recollected from the limbo of years. In this last book, however, flippancy at the expense of peoples and customs vanishes when the traveler reaches the threshold of Asia, as if the ancient disillusioned torpor of that continent had stricken the satirist dumb. These travelogues do not show Twain's gifts to greatest advantage. Flashes of notable writing occur, but intrinsically they are the potboilers of a master improviser.

The earliest novel he attempted was *The Gilded Age,* in collaboration with Charles Dudley Warner, published late in 1873, just as the panic was ringing down the curtain upon the worst excesses of that age. It harks back to their common knowledge of Missouri, where Warner had been a surveyor, and to Twain's passing observation of Washington in the winter of 1867–1868, when after return from the Holy Land he had served briefly and unhappily as private secretary to pompous Senator William Stewart of Nevada and more successfully had begun to write humorous commentaries on the news (anticipative of the late Will Rogers) for the *Tribune* and the *Herald* of New York. This phase left him with an abiding scorn for politicians, their intelligence and honesty. ("Fleas can be taught nearly anything that a Congressman can," is as characteristic as the remark that we have "no distinctly native American criminal class except Congress.") Beside the bungling amateurs of Carson City, these were graduates in graft, scrambling for the spoils of what a later critic termed the Great Barbecue. This same spectacle of post-bellum Washington which sickened fastidious Henry Adams and led even Whitman the

optimist to pen the darker pages of *Democratic Vistas,* gave Mark Twain his
first shining target for satire.

Warner supplied conventional plot elements of romance, gentility, pluck
and luck, harmonized with the theme of material success, which the novel
debunks at one level but praises fulsomely at another, when it is sanctioned
by what passes among the majority as honesty. Twain himself was always
dazzled by the romance of fortune, especially if it followed the ascent from
rags to riches, as he shows in a story like "The £1,000,000 Bank Note" (1893).
Yet he was aware of the ironies and unhappiness springing from the root of
all evil, as revealed in "The $30,000 Bequest" (1904) and most superbly in
"The Man That Corrupted Hadleyburg" (1899). In *The Gilded Age* the
authors' wavering purpose resembles a mixture of Jonathan Swift and
Horatio Alger. Satiric punches are pulled by the constant impulse to strike
out in all directions but follow through in none. The vulgarity of a chromo
civilization and the urge to keep up with the Joneses mingle with churchly
hypocrisy, pork-barrel politics, high tariff, oratorical buncombe, abuse of the
franking privilege, bribery, personal immorality in high places, profiteers of
"shoddy," and the wider degradation of the democratic dogma.

The Gilded Age is clearly a world of optimistic illusion, proudly putting
its best foot forward though the other limp behind in a shabby mud-bespat-
tered boot. In the backwoods, stagecoaches with horns blowing enter and
leave town at a furious clip, but once out of sight "drag along stupidly
enough"—even as steamboats burn fat pine to make an impressive smoke
when they near port. Credit is the basis of society; a typical parvenu boasts:
"I wasn't worth a cent a year ago, and now I owe two millions of dollars."
Most engaging specimen of this psychology is Colonel Sellers, a New World
Micawber, who deals in imaginary millions while he and the family dine off
turnips and cold water (man's best diet, he loftily assures them), and warm
themselves at a stove through whose isinglass door flickers the illusory glow of
a candle. Drawn from Twain's Uncle James Lampton, the Colonel is an
epitome of the American dream that remains a mirage—impulsive, generous,
hospitable, scheming to enrich not only himself but relatives and friends,
and incidentally benefit all humankind, a colossal failure who basks forever
in the rushlight of the success cult. Not dishonest by nature, in the heady
milieu of Washington he begins to apologize for bribery ("a harsh term"),
while hitching his wagon to the baleful star of Senator Dilworthy, drawn
from the lineaments of Kansas' notorious Pomeroy. In certain passages Mark
Twain's irony is whetted to a cutting edge, but the book's total effect is far
from mordant. In many ways both authors were children of the Gilded Age,
with hands too unsteady to strike a mortal blow of parricide.

Like everybody else Twain grew fond of Colonel Sellers and tried to resuscitate him. The modest laurels of a dramatic version of *The Gilded Age,* produced in 1874, led Twain and Howells to attempt in 1883 an hilarious sequel which, however, the stage Sellers of the earlier script, John T. Raymond, declined to play because that character had been exaggerated to the brink of lunacy. The plot, as embalmed in Twain's novel, *The American Claimant* (1892), justifies the actor's verdict. It is one of the humorist's most strained and least successful efforts.

5

Three years after *The Gilded Age* Twain published *Tom Sawyer,* the first of three great books about the Mississippi River of his youth. Beyond question, *Huckleberry Finn* (1885), *Life on the Mississippi* (1883), and *Tom Sawyer* (1876) are, in that order, his finest works. The reasons for their superiority are not far to seek. In plotting a book his structural sense was always weak; intoxicated by a hunch, he seldom saw far ahead, and too many of his stories peter out from the author's fatigue or surfeit. His wayward technique, as Howells recognized, came close to free association:

So far as I know, Mr. Clemens is the first writer to use in extended writing the fashion we all use in thinking, and to set down the thing that comes into his mind without fear or favor of the thing that went before or the thing that may be about to follow.

This method served him best after he had conjured up characters from long ago, who on coming to life wrote the narrative for him, passing from incident to incident with a grace their creator could never achieve in manipulating an artificial plot. In travel books and other autobiography written under the heat of recent experience, Mark Twain seemingly put in everything, mixing the trivial, inane, and farcical with his best-grade ore. But in the remembrance of things past, time had dissolved the alloy, leaving only gold. The nostalgia for a youth's paradise "over the hills and far away," for the fast-vanishing freedom of the West, appealed deeply to the age of boyhood sentiment enriched by Longfellow and Whittier. It also led to Mark Twain's strength; namely, the world of the senses and physical action. What he felt was always better expressed than what he had thought or speculated about. A boy's world freed him from those economic and political perplexities, adult dilemmas and introspections, where in rages and knotty casuistries he lost the sureness of touch that came to him through the report of his five senses, or through the championship of justice when the issue was as simple as the conflict between bullies and little folk.

In his heart Mark Twain must have realized that essentially he was a man of feeling, too sensitive to serve merely as a comedian, too undisciplined to be the philosopher he sometimes fancied himself. His forte was to recapture the sheer joy of living, when to be young was very heaven. A great river flowing through the wilderness set the stage for a boy's own dream of self-sufficience, of being a new Robinson Crusoe on Jackson's Island. In the background moved the pageantry of life, colored by humor, make-believe, and pure melodrama; but the complexity of the machine age and the city lay far, far away.

Mark Twain did not write his first books about this dream world, but let the haze of ideality collect about it, reserving it luckily for the high noon of his powers. Apparently the first hint of this motif comes in one of his New York letters to the *Alta California,* in the spring of 1867, in which he happens to recall the town drunkard of Hannibal, Jimmy Finn (destined to return as Huck's father), and also the Cadets of Temperance which Sam Clemens joined in order to march in funeral processions wearing their red scarf. This latter incident crops up in *Tom Sawyer*. Shortly afterward in *The Innocents,* among the pleasures and palaces of Europe, Twain interpolated other boyhood memories. In February, 1870, on receiving a letter from his "first, and oldest and dearest friend" Will Bowen, one of the flesh-and-blood components of Tom Sawyer, he sat down under the spell of the past and wrote a reply calling up some eight scenes which later appear in *Tom Sawyer* and *Huckleberry Finn*. Around this time he wrote a nameless sketch about a romantic lovesick swain who beyond question is Tom Sawyer. Designated as "Boy's Manuscript" by Twain's first editor, Albert Bigelow Paine, it was not published until 1942 in Bernard De Voto's *Mark Twain at Work*. Some four years later Twain made a fresh start, scrapping the earlier diary form in favor of third-person narrative. By midsummer, 1875, it was done, and off the press late in the next year (a few months after Clemens with his usual inconsistency had written Will Bowen a stern letter on August 31, 1876, bidding him dwell no more in the sentimental never-never land of boyhood, denying that the past holds anything "worth pickling for present or future use"). In this latter year Twain began *Huckleberry Finn* as a sequel, laid it aside during six fallow years, went back to the story after his visit to Hannibal in 1882, and published it a little over two years later.

The first reader of *Tom Sawyer,* William Dean Howells, disagreed with the author that he had written a book for adults only. He quickly persuaded Twain that it was primarily a story for boys, which grown-ups would enjoy by reading over their shoulder. Twain therefore withdrew a few gibes against Sunday schools and tamed several phrases that smacked of backwoods frankness. Nothing of importance, however, was altered, nor did Tom suffer transformation into the neat, obedient paragon which fiction for the young so long had held up to their resentful gaze. The first chapter announces that Tom "was not the Model Boy of the village. He knew the model boy very well though—and loathed him." The only resemblance Tom bears to the fictional creations of his time is in sensibility: he yields to self-pity, relishes every neighborhood tear shed over his supposed drowning, and almost faints upon hearing that even a villain like Injun Joe has been sealed in the cave. Otherwise, our hero is of very different mettle. He steals from and outwits Aunt Polly, luxuriates in idleness, misbehaves in church, huffs and brags, and like his friend Huck employs lying as protective coloration in a world of adult tyrants. Consequently, in some American homes the new book was read by grown-ups, then tucked away out of a boy's reach; its successor, *Huckleberry Finn,* soon after publication was ejected from the town library of Concord, Massachusetts (where, a generation before, John Brown had been welcomed by Thoreau and Emerson), because Huck elected to "go to Hell" rather than betray his friend, a runaway Negro.

In 1870 Thomas Bailey Aldrich had published his mild *Story of a Bad Boy;* twenty years later Twain's friend Howells would reminisce of adolescents not too bright or good for human nature's daily food in *A Boy's Town;* a little later came Stephen Crane's recollections of Whilomville and William Allen White's of Boyville. They helped maintain the tradition of realism. In extreme recoil from priggishness, a line beginning with *Peck's Bad Boy* in 1883 flaunted incorrigibility above all. It is possible to overstress the picaresque intent of *Tom Sawyer* in turning upside down the world of Peter Parley and the Rollo books, or its analogues with that still greater novel, Cervantes' *Don Quixote,* in which some critics find the model of Tom the dreamer and Huck his commonsense henchman. Mark Twain's verisimilitude should not be overlooked in this search for "purpose." He wrote about boys from having been one in the Gilded Age, in a river town before the war.

To a stranger in 1887 he described this book as "simply a hymn, put into prose form to give it a worldly air." These lads no more resemble Peck's Bad Boy than they do the model children of that improving story-teller, Jacob Abbott. Within a framework of superb dialogue and setting, of sensitive perceptions that turn now and again into poetry, against a background where flicker shadows of adult humanitarianism and irony, Tom and Huck grow visibly as we follow them. The pranks and make-believe of early chapters—whitewashing the fence, releasing a pinchbug in church, playing pirate in *Tom Sawyer,* and in its sequel the rout of a Sunday school picnic under the guise of attacking a desert caravan—are dimmed as the human values deepen and occasional moral issues appear. The Tom who takes Becky's punishment in school, and testifies for the innocent Muff Potter at risk of the murderer's revenge, parallels the development of Huck from a happy-go-lucky gamin to the epitome of generosity and loyalty. Mark Twain makes no account of rigid consistencies in time. His boys vary between the attitudes of nine-year-olds and those of thirteen or fourteen, despite the fact that *Tom Sawyer*'s time span is one Missouri summer, and that of *Huckleberry Finn* a few more unbroken months. Like the creator of perennial comic-strip characters, Twain arrests or syncopates the march of time as he pleases. In the latter novel he also ignores the fact that Nigger Jim could have escaped by swimming across to the free soil of Illinois early in the book, and commits other sins against literalism which he would have ridiculed unmercifully in the pages of his *bête noire* James Fenimore Cooper.

Huckleberry Finn is clearly the finer book, showing a more mature point of view and exploring richer strata of human experience. A joy forever, it is unquestionably one of the masterpieces of American and of world literature. Here Twain returned to his first idea of having the chief actor tell the story, with better results. Huck's speech is saltier than Tom's, his mind freer from the claptrap of romance and sophistication. Huck is poised midway between the town-bred Tom and that scion of woodlore and primitive superstition Nigger Jim, toward whom Huck with his margin of superior worldliness stands in somewhat the same relation that Tom stands toward Huck. When Tom and Huck are together, our sympathy turns invariably toward the latter. A homeless river rat, cheerful in his rags, suspicious of every attempt to civilize him, Huck has none of the unimportant virtues and all the essential ones. The school of hard knocks has taught him skepticism, horse sense, and a tenacious grasp on reality. But it has not toughened him into cynicism or crime. Nature gave him a stanch and faithful heart, friendly to all underdogs and instantly hostile toward bullies and all shapes of overmastering power. One critic has called him the type of the common folk, sample of the run-of-the-mill democracy in America. Twain himself might have objected to the label, for he once declared "there are no common people, except in the highest spheres of society." Huck always displays a frontier neighborliness, even trying to provide a rescue for three murderers dying marooned on a wrecked boat, because "there ain't no telling but I might come to be a murderer myself, yet, and then how would I like it?" Money does not tempt him to betray his friend Nigger Jim, though at times his conscience is troubled by the voice of convention, preaching the sacredness of property— even in the guise of flesh and blood—and he trembles on the brink of surrender. Nor can he resist sometimes the provocation offered by Jim's innocent credulity, only to be cut to the quick when his friend bears with dignity the discovery that his trustfulness has been made game of. Even as Huck surpasses Tom in qualities of courage and heart, so Nigger Jim excels even

Huck in fidelity and innate manliness, to emerge as the book's noblest character.

Sam Clemens himself (who in the first known letter he wrote his mother, on the day he reached New York in August, 1853, had indulged the easy sarcasm, "I reckon I had better black my face, for in these Eastern States niggers are considerably better than white people") learned in time, much as Huck learns, to face down his condescension. In later years he became a warm friend of the Negro and his rights. He paid the way of a Negro student through Yale as "his part of the reparation due from every white to every black man," and savagely attacked King Leopold of Belgium for the barbarities of his agents in the Congo. Mrs. Clemens once suggested as a mollifying rule to her husband, "Consider everybody colored till he is proved white." Howells thought that as time went on Clemens the Southwesterner was prone to lose his Southern but cleave to his Western heritage, finding his real affinities with the broader democracy of the frontier. On other issues of race prejudice, Twain looked upon the Jew with unqualified admiration, defended the Chinese whom he had seen pelted through the streets of San Francisco, and confessed to only one invincible antipathy, namely, against the French—although his most rhapsodic book was written in praise of their national heroine.

The final draft of *Huckleberry Finn* was intimately bound up with the writing of Twain's third great volume about his river days, *Life on the Mississippi*. Fourteen chapters of these recollections had been published in the *Atlantic* in 1875; before expanding them into a book Twain made a memorable trip in 1882 back to the scenes of his youth. In working more or less simultaneously on both long-unfinished books, he lifted a scene intended for *Huckleberry Finn*—about Huck and the raftsmen—to flavor the other book, but the great gainer from his trip was not the memoir but the novel. The relative pallor of *Life on the Mississippi*, Part II, is due in a measure to the fact that so much lifeblood of reminiscence is drained off into the veins of *Huckleberry Finn*. The travel notes of 1882, written up soon after Twain's return home, are suffused with some of the finest situations in his novel: the Grangerford-Shepherdson feud, Colonel Sherburn and the mob, and the two seedy vagabonds who come on-stage as the Duke and the King, with a posse in their wake, who "said they hadn't been doing nothing, and was being chased for it."

Mark Twain's renewed contact with life among the river towns quickened his sense of realism. For *Huckleberry Finn,* save in its passages about the peace and freedom of Jackson's Island, is no longer "simply a hymn," and so dim has grown the dream of adolescent romancing that Becky Thatcher reappears but perfunctorily under the careless label of "Bessie" Thatcher. The odyssey of Huck's voyage through the South reveals aspects of life darker than the occasional melodrama of *Tom Sawyer*. We are shown the sloth and sadism of poor whites, backwoods loafers with their plug tobacco and Barlow knives, who sic dogs on stray sows and "laugh at the fun and look grateful for the noise," or drench a stray cur with turpentine and set him afire. We remark the cowardice of lynching parties; the chicanery of patent medicine fakers, revivalists, and exploiters of rustic ribaldry; the senseless feudings of the gentry. In the background broods fear: not only a boy's apprehension of ghosts, African superstitions, and the terrors of the night, nor the adults' dread of black insurrection, but the endless implicated strands of robbery, floggings, drowning, and murder. Death by violence lurks at every bend of road or river. Self-preservation becomes the ruling motive, squaring perfectly with the role of the principal characters, Huck the foot-loose orphan and his friend Jim the fugitive—puny in all strengths save loyalty, as they wander among the Brobdingnagian boots of white adult supremacy. The pair belong to the immortals of fiction.

Never keen at self-criticism, Mark Twain passed without soundings from these depths to the adjacent shallows of burlesque and extravaganza. The last fifth of this superb novel, *Huckleberry Finn,* brings back the romantic Tom Sawyer, with a hilarious, intricate, and needless plot for rescuing Jim from captivity. The story thus closes upon the farcical note with which the Hannibal cycle has begun, in the whitewashing episode. On the same note many years later Mark Twain tried to revive his most famous characters, in *Tom Sawyer Abroad* (1894), with Tom, Huck, and Jim as passengers of a mad balloonist and their subsequent adventures in Egypt. Though inferior to its great predecessors, this book does not lack humor, gusto, and rich characterization. *Tom Sawyer, Detective* (1896) dishes up a melodrama of stolen diamonds, double-crossing thieves, and that immortal device of Plautus and Shakespeare, identical twins, whose charm custom could not stale for Mark Twain. Here haste, artifice, and creative fatigue grow painfully apparent.

Uneven quality appears in *Life on the Mississippi,* even though it came at the high tide of his powers. Chapters IV–XVII were written for the *Atlantic* after Twain's chance reminiscences led his friend Twichell to exclaim, "What a virgin subject to hurl into a magazine!" Fresh, vivid, humorous, they recall the great days of river traffic: the problems of navigation, the races, the pilots' association, the resourcefulness and glory of the old-time pilot. The addenda, which came after Twain's return to the river for "copy," sometimes attain the former standard—the description of Pilot Brown the scold, or the account of the *Pennsylvania* disaster and Henry Clemens' death—but more often prove disappointing after the white heat of the book's inception. The first two chapters on the history of the river are merely an afterthought; the later ones too often wander among irrelevant yarns, like the revenge of Ritter the Austrian, or vignettes of picturesque New Orleans. Sam Clemens' year and a half as cub pilot are followed by almost no mention of his two years as a licensed skipper. Instead we are treated to such vagaries as Twain's famous theory about Sir Walter Scott, whose "Middle-Age sham civilization," he claimed, inspired the chivalry of the Old South, which in turn provoked the Civil War.

Yet with all its flaws of disunity and untidiness, *Life on the Mississippi* remains a masterpiece. Its communicable delight in experience, its rich picture of the human comedy and tragedy on the river (which Melville alone among great artists had tried to bring into focus in *The Confidence Man* in 1857), lend it real durability. Howells believed that the author long regarded it his greatest book—pleased with assurance to that effect from the German Kaiser and also from a hotel porter, whose praise he accepted with equal satisfaction. In other moods, toward the end of his life, Twain favored *Joan of Arc,* in part because it cost him "twelve years of preparation and two years of writing. The others needed no preparation, & got none." Thus again he displayed the blindness of self-appraisal. The book that required probably least effort of all, drawn from a brimming native reservoir, *Huckleberry Finn,* unquestionably is his finest, with *Tom Sawyer* and *Life on the Mississippi* as runners-up.

6

Mark Twain's later years show a drift toward the remote in time and place, in a fitful quest for new themes, new magic—a search that proceeded apace with a growing sense of personal dissatisfaction, frustration, and heartbreak. While the aging artist began to lose much of his creative fire, Clemens the generous, erratic, moody, and vulnerable human being remained, standing at bay against the disillusions and disasters that gathered to ring him around and mock his fame as the world humorist of the century. The development of this last phase is worth tracing.

From recollections of his Hannibal boyhood he gravitated toward a new but distinctly artificial romanticism, "the pageant and fairy-tale" of life in medieval Europe. His earliest treatment of the theme is *The Prince and the Pauper* (1881), a story mainly for children, built upon the old plot of transposed identities. Here to a degree, and still more in *A Connecticut Yankee in King Arthur's Court* (1889) and *Personal Recollections of Joan of Arc* (1896), the romantic's fascination with knights and castles is counterbalanced by the iconoclast's itch to shatter that world of sham and injustice, where crown and miter lorded it over the commons. The savage indignation which Twain so loved to unleash found hunting that gratified him: the prey bore some resemblance to the contemporary, without committing him to the consequences of a frontal attack upon modern authoritarianism, convention, and orthodoxy. *A Connecticut Yankee,* best of the cycle, shows just such an ingenious mechanic as Clemens must often have met on visits to the Hartford shops of Pratt & Whitney, a Yankee who is swept back in time to Camelot. With one hand he transforms Arthurian England into a going concern of steam and electricity; with the other, seeks to plant the seeds of equalitarianism. He remarks that in feudal society six men out of a thousand crack the whip over their fellows' backs: "It seemed to me that what the nine hundred and ninety-four dupes needed was a new deal." This passage, as the late President Roosevelt testified, furnished the most memorable phrase in modern American government. The Connecticut Yankee asserts that the mass of a nation can always produce "the material in abundance whereby to govern itself." Yet the medieval mob is shown collectively to be gullible, vicious, invincibly ignorant, like the populace of Hannibal or Hartford, so that the Yankee sets up not a true democracy but a benign dictatorship centering in himself and his mechanical skills—a kind of technocrat's utopia. Dazzled by the wonders of applied science, Mark Twain always hoped for social as well as technological miracles from the dynamo.

Twain's apotheosis of the Virgin—in terms of Henry Adams' dilemma—of spiritual forces in conflict with materialism and the stupid cruelty of organized society, appears in *Joan of Arc.* The Maid was his favorite character in history. But as Twain's imagination is better than his knowledge of medieval life, the result at best is a *tour de force.*

Joan was published anonymously, in hope of giving this book a head start free from a reputation which the world had come long since to regard as synonymous with comedy. Indeed, most people continued to hail with uproarious mirth Mark Twain's explosive attacks upon power politics, imperialism, malefactors of great wealth, hypocrisy in morals and religion, and other manifestations of what he increasingly came to call "the damned human race." They refused to forget "The Celebrated Jumping Frog," or his reputation for convulsing any crowd whenever his mouth was opened. Meanwhile, as the satirist gained upper hand over the humorist in his nature, and age diminished his ebullience, Mark Twain not only yearned vainly for a serious hearing but also came to flinch from the role of platform zany.

Lecturing, however, became a need more urgent than ever. For, beginning with the Panic of 1893, the tide of Mark Twain's luck suddenly changed. The famous writer, with ample cash in hand and enviable royalties rolling in, still vigorous in health and self-confidence, the adoring husband and beloved father of three charming daughters—this self-made "jour" printer and riverboatman whom the world delighted to honor—upon him fortune suddenly began to rain blow after blow. The first losses were financial. The Paige typesetting machine, brain child of an erratic inventor who came close to anticipating the fabulous success of Mergenthaler's linotype, failed after years of costly maintenance from Clemens' pocket; instead of making millions, he lost hundreds of thousands. Then the publishing firm of Charles L. Webster (named for the son-in-law of Mark's sister, but backed by the author himself through suspicion of the big commercial publishers) crashed into bankruptcy. Twain's new friend Henry H. Rogers, Standard Oil magnate and by the lights of the muckraking age a robber baron, advised him that the ethics of literature were higher than those of business, and "you must earn the cent per cent." Mark's own conscience fully acquiesced. Even though his old exuberant energy was flagging, he set out in 1895 on a world lecture tour, after giving a statement to the press:

The law recognizes no mortgage on a man's brain, and a merchant who has given up all he has may take advantage of the laws of insolvency and start free again for himself. But I am not a business man, and honor is a harder master than the law. It cannot compromise for less than 100 cents on the dollar and its debts never outlaw.

The profits, together with royalties and the astute management of Mr. Rogers, eventually enabled him to pay the last dollar to these creditors and add an American parallel to the case of Sir Walter Scott.

Twain's last notable book about American life, *Pudd'nhead Wilson* (1894), written on the brink of financial disaster but before the onset of deeper tragedies, is about a nonconformist who is too witty and wise for the backwoods community where his days are spent; miscalled "Pudd'nhead," he at last wins recognition by solving a murder mystery through his hobby of fingerprints. In so doing he also unravels a case of transposed identities for which the Negress Roxy—a character of magnificent vigor and realism—had been responsible. The novel is a daring, though inconclusive, study of miscegenation. Significant of Mark Twain's growing pessimism are the cynical chapter mottoes ascribed to Pudd'nhead's "Calendar," such as: "If you pick up a starving dog and make him prosperous, he will not bite you. This is the principal difference between a dog and a man." Or, still more typical of the aging Twain: "Whoever has lived long enough to find out what life is, knows how deep a debt of gratitude we owe to Adam, the first great benefactor of our race. He brought death into the world."

These notes—the ingratitude and folly of man, the vanity of human wishes, the praise of death as the nepenthe for life's tragedy—echo increasingly through the later writings of Mark Twain. This drift was no new departure, but the accentuation of a lifelong trend. In youth he had been subject to fits of melancholy and disillusion. In Cincinnati at the age of twenty he had listened avidly to a homespun philosopher expound the gospel of scientific determinism; as a cub pilot he read Tom Paine "with fear and hesitation." Later, in San Francisco, Mark said he had come within a trigger's breadth of suicide, and in 1876 for obscure causes yielded to a bad season of the blues. Still later he discovered Jonathan Edwards, brooding for days over the "dominion of Motive and Necessity," and was powerfully drawn to the agnosticism of Huxley, Haeckel, and Ingersoll. As a boy he had been terrorized by the fickle and vindictive Jehovah of Sunday schools; as a youth he graduated to the God of scientific law, impersonal but just; as an old man he returned to the cruel God, now stripped of anthropomorphic whims, but no less terrible as causation and fate. As early as 1882, in an unpublished dialogue between Negroes written on his river trip, Mark Twain sketched out the logic elaborated sixteen years later in his "wicked book" *What Is Man?*—not printed until 1906, then privately and anonymously because he thought it so blastingly incontrovertible. Its argument, developed between an earnest Young Man and a cynical Old Man, is that self-interest and self-approval are the mainsprings of human conduct, however cleverly they mask themselves as honor, charity, altruism, or love. Hunger for self-esteem is the master passion; under this demon of the ego, free will is nothing but illusion.

While Mark was lecturing around the world for "honor," news reached him that back home his favorite daughter Susy had suddenly succumbed to meningitis. Would the girl have died if her parents had not deserted her? It was perhaps a foolish question, but natural to a self-accusing heart like Clemens'. Unpublished papers bear witness to his bitterness in those days, savage reflections about how God gives us breath and bodies only to undermine us with the million plagues of disease and heartbreak, to show what Twain calls His "fatherly infatuation" toward us. Meanwhile Mrs. Clemens sank deeper and deeper into a hopeless invalidism that ended only with the mercy of her death in 1904; and their daughter Jean, whose moods had long puzzled them, was discovered to be an incurable epileptic. Mark Twain's own robust health was beginning to crumble, and—as a still more tragic circumstance to the artist who had begun to use hard work as an anodyne for grief—his magnificent creative powers were now sadly on the wane. His unpublished papers are full of fragmentary stories and novels that simply would not come out right, and were endlessly reworked, rewritten, finally abandoned. Many are reminiscent, in plot and character, of his golden period; the magician fell back upon his old repertory, made the same passes, but somehow failed to pull off the trick. They are also eloquent with personal revelation. Twain in old age kept tormenting himself, in a dozen allegorical disguises, with the problem of "guilt" which (as his Calvinist conscience whispered) must somehow be antecedent to punishment, the cause of all the failures and bereavements fate had inflicted upon him. The artist keeps asking himself: Was I to blame, for something I did or left undone? The motif of a doting father with a dead or missing child is frequent, and of course transparent.

One such story concerns the dream of a man who has fallen asleep after gazing at a drop of water, swimming with animalculae, beneath the microscope. He dreams that he is on shipboard in the Antarctic seas pursuing his lost child who has been carried off by another ship, in a chase that continues like some nightmare in a fever, while terrible creatures arise to roam the deep and snatch passengers off the deck. The captain of the ship is called the Superintendent of Dreams, and it is his cunning to destroy the seafarers' sense of reality, while they circle toward the ultimate horror of the Great White Glare —actually the beam cast through the microscope's field by the reflector—a vortex of death into which all things, including the craft with the missing child, are being drawn. Seldom has determinism found a grimmer symbol.

The greatest story of Mark Twain's later period, too often neglected in the appraisal of his work, wins at last the personal answer for which he sought so desperately. In the light of those unfinished manuscripts among the Mark Twain Papers, it attains true perspective. This is *The Mysterious Stranger,* begun in the gloom of 1898 after Susy's death and Jean's hopeless prognosis, but not finished until several years later and published posthumously in 1916. Like the last act of a Greek tragedy, or *Samson Agonistes* with "all passion spent," it achieves a wintry serenity beyond despair. The story is that of some boys who are really Tom Sawyer's gang in medieval dress, in the Austrian village of Eseldorf, who strike up acquaintance with a supernatural visitor able to work miracles and juggle with lives. Calling himself "Satan," he claims relationship with the prince of fallen angels, but appears to live in a sphere beyond both good and evil. Laughter and tears, joy and torment, saintliness and sin, to him are but as the sound of lyres and flutes, and at last he grows bored with his own wonder-working caprices. He then tells the wide-eyed Theodor:

It is true, that which I have revealed to you; there is no God, no universe, no human race, no earthly life, no heaven, no hell. It is all a dream—a grotesque and foolish dream. Nothing exists but you. And you are but a *thought*—a vagrant thought, a useless thought, a homeless thought, wandering forlorn among the empty eternities!

And in his heart of hearts the boy knows this is true. Here, in the closing pages of *The Mysterious Stranger,* Mark Twain solved his riddle of grief and self-reproach, and clothed his soul in the only invulnerable armor of desperation. Good and evil, like reality itself, are only illusions, such stuff as dreams are made on, and our little life is rounded with the best gift of the Artist who saves it to the last—extinction.

Like Halley's comet in 1835 and 1910, whose appearance Mark Twain saw as setting the beginning and the end of his life, the luster of his genius flashed forth now and again against this darkened sky of fatalism. He wrote and spoke with sparkles of his old wit, and few were aware of the encircling gloom. Oxford gave him her degree of Doctor of Letters in 1907, and his birthdays became national events. In his famous white clothes he seemed a kind of ghost from America's buried life, recalling the nostalgia of her youth, revisiting these glimpses of the modern city and its vast industrialism. But his great creative genius had almost gone—that energy which he spent and squandered so freely, when he had it, with the recklessness of the Old West. For Mark Twain the artist had always been a kind of pocket miner, stumbling like fortune's darling upon native ore of incredible richness and exploiting it with effortless skill—but often gleefully mistaking fool's gold for the genuine article, or lavishing his strength upon historical diggings long since played out. If latterly he seemed to deny his role as America's great comic spirit, perhaps the key can be found in his last travel book: "Everything human is pathetic. The secret source of Humor itself is not joy but sorrow. There is no humor in heaven."

THE CONTINENTAL
NATION

--- disillusion, reform, definition

57. A WORLD TO WIN OR LOSE

THE forces that stirred within that huge, loose-jointed America of the latter half of the nineteenth century came to focus in the life of Mark Twain as in probably that of no other man of his generation. With his generation he groped his way in a world of thought made unfamiliar by ideas born of science that flowed into America from across the Atlantic. To follow the trail of Mark Twain is to traverse America in one of its decisive epochs.

It was a period of change, change that increased in tempo with each passing decade. In the nineties when Clemens, well past sixty, had already sketched the outlines of his pessimism, his fellow countrymen were pressing hopefully forward into a new world whose landscape was already becoming clear. The frontier that started at Jamestown and Plymouth made its final advance against the wilderness as wheatgrowers fenced in the eastern Dakotas, cattlemen established permanent ranches on the High Plains, and settlers laid out farms on the terraces of the Snake Valley.

Life moved fast enough on this last frontier to develop before the outbreak of the First World War a rudimentary sense of history. "Charlie" Russell, ex-cowboy, made himself a kind of folk hero of the Montana cattle country when he set down on vigorous and authentic canvases, in order that it might be preserved for posterity, the life of the old free range where as a young man he had punched longhorns. Through Russell's home town, Great Falls, ran one of the four new railway systems that, surmounting the continental divide, had united the Pacific coast with the economic life of the Middle West and East. Trade caused the cities from San Diego to Puget Sound to surge with new life. On the western slopes of the Sierras, in such communities as that of Mark Twain's Calaveras County, the mood of living for a moment in a town that might play out tomorrow gave way to a sense of responsibility as Californians took steps to preserve the groves of giant sequoias and the majestic valley of the Yosemite. Colorful seaports grew beside Pacific harbors and sleek orchards covered the interior from Oregon to the Imperial Valley. A sense of history brought in California a revaluation of the Spanish period, now seen as a picturesque prologue that gave the dignity of tradition to a state escaping from a somewhat uncouth frontier chrysalis.

History also filled the thoughts of saddened and impoverished ex-Confederates for whom "the War" and Reconstruction had brought an epoch to a close. Although by the end of the century the Union had been reestablished in spirit as well as in form, the surviving soldiers who surrendered at Appomattox and their sons looked back to a romantic and romanticized plantation culture. At the same time, however, they busied themselves laying the foundations of a New South in what was in fact a new nation. By 1900 even the South, wrecked by war, had begun to feel the effects of that scientific and technological advance that, starting in the late eighteenth century, was now, a hundred years later, bringing about an industrial revolution in that portion of America that lay east of the Mississippi and north of the Ohio and the Potomac.

Scarcely had the Civil War ended when America, leaving behind the wooden waterwheel and sailing ship, entered upon an age of steam and steel in which the nation's bituminous coal fields powered an expanding industrialism. In the *fin de siècle* years electricity and the internal combustion engine that drew power from the oil pools of America further transformed the material foundations of the national life. Cities located at the crossroads of commerce grew vastly. In Chicago and New York, pioneer skyscrapers marked out new sky lines where before there had been only the dead level of flat-roofed, six-storied buildings, pierced here and there by church spires. Each year the new steamships that plied the oceans brought to the sidewalks of these sprawling urban centers a confusion of strange faces, as immigrants poured in from the four corners of the world. The cross, lifted above an increasing number of Catholic schools and churches, forecast a future in which Catholicism would assume a place of power and importance beside a dominant Protestantism in American civilization. Henry Adams, whose New England family tradition ran back beyond the beginnings of the Republic, declared that he and his generation were witnessing change that had accelerated to a pace without precedent. Change is the inevitable starting point for a consideration of American civilization at the turn of the century.

Not many years before the entry of the United States into the First World War the imported word *Zeitgeist* appeared in the conversation of more thoughtful Americans. A few made a conscious effort to discover the spirit of the kaleidoscopic age in which they lived. Henry Adams, William Graham Sumner, Lester Frank Ward, and William Dean Howells were among the more important analysts of the scene contemporary to them. The middle years of the twentieth century give perspective on that yesterday when the horse-drawn carriage was about to give way to the Model T. Its *Zeitgeist* seems to have been a blend of three basic moods: a sense of security, a belief in progress, and a malaise arising out of the impact of scientific naturalism and rampant materialism upon traditional ideals of the good life.

2

Security is the basic aspect. It was associated with a new spirit of nationalism emerging as the memories of Gettysburg and Cold Harbor grew less distinct and the wounds of fratricidal conflict healed. The hundred-day war against decadent Spain disturbed only for a moment the feeling that America had little to fear in the world. No powerful potential enemy crouched beyond either of the land frontiers of the Republic. The Atlantic, in spite of its crossing by Cervera's fleet, seemed to hold Europe at arm's length, while the interminable Pacific washed on the west a continent that even after 1898 and the acquisition of Hawaii and the Philippines remained a blurred and indistinct image in the American mind. So subtle and so pervasive was this sense of security that only a few recognized its importance. Americans as a nation looked upon themselves as free to make what they could of the continent which they and their forefathers had reclaimed from the wilderness. They were free as individuals to plan their lives without hedging their liberties to meet the demands of military necessity.

Theodore Roosevelt practically alone in his day feared that this sense of security might lead to trouble and perhaps disaster. Yet in the first decade of the twentieth century even his thought did not run so much to the danger of foreign war as to that of internal degeneration. Strength had enabled Americans to conquer the continent and to accumulate wealth surpassing that of the Indies. The enjoyment in security of this wealth, he thought, might well cause that moral decay, that flabbiness, which would bring down American civilization to the low estate of Spain. Stirred by such apprehensions, Roosevelt reminded his fellow countrymen that Fate had cast the United States in the role of a great power and that they must choose whether the part would be played well or ill. In a day when Thorstein Veblen was caustically pointing out the phenomenon of "conspicuous consumption" among the new lords of industry and finance, Theodore Roosevelt urged the ideal of the "strenuous life." The former rancher and Rough Rider made himself one of the great preachers in American history. His colorful personality and the White House sounding board gave currency to his message in the most remote corner of the nation. He succeeded in catching the ear of his fellow countrymen primarily because his philosophy of the strenuous life ran with, rather than against, the main current of American life. We were an active rather than a contemplative people. Roosevelt gave verbal expression to a firmly held folk ideal. Americans had been on the move since the *Susan Constant* dropped anchor before Jamestown. The pace had grown immeasurably faster by the time that Roosevelt was elevated to the Presidency.

> Afoot and light-hearted, I take to the open road,
> Healthy, free, and the world before me,

Whitman had written many years before. The mood still held as Americans set forth confidently into what they believed would be a glorious twentieth century.

It is true that Americans at the turn of the century, for all their sense of safety, were troubled by insecurities within their national life. Western farmers, the Grangers, and the Populists, frightened by what they looked upon as ravening corporations whelped by industrialism, organized popular fronts of resistance. Eastern capitalists feared the crackpot economic theories of the Populist horde that formed in 1890 in the upper Mississippi Valley. Industrialists watched with a deepening apprehension a succession of labor revolts—1877, 1886, 1892, 1899—whose tradition of violence culminated, in 1911, in the dynamiting of the Los Angeles *Times* building. Washington Gladden, statesman-preacher who achieved national stature as an advocate of unity among the Christian churches and as a conciliator in labor disputes, feared in the nineties that centrifugal forces in American life were about to overcome the forces tending to hold American society together. In this and the following decade the muckrakers sounded the alarm that municipal corruption and corporate greed were threatening both the political and the economic foundations of democracy itself.

Josiah Royce, philosopher who knew America from California to Cambridge, rejected what had become a popular thesis of European commentators that American civilization was engulfed in a tide of materialism, and insisted that materialism and idealism were evenly balanced in the national life. He, the last of great nineteenth century idealists, sought to turn the energies of his fellow countrymen toward the creation of a richer culture by his doctrine of regionalism, by his consideration of the problems of Christianity, and by his philosophy of loyalty. The work of Royce, of the muckrakers, and of a growing army of urban citizens who were spurred to action by a sense of social responsibility illustrated that malaise, arising out of the tension between new forms of materialism and idealism and adapting itself to a new social scene. But these domestic apprehensions were blunted by the sense of security from foreign aggression, which made possible the comforting belief that in due time Americans could and would set their house in order.

3

Never before in the history of the Republic had the idea of progress been so influential in American thought as in that period beginning in the early nineties and ending in 1917 which American historians have come to call the Progressive Era. The completion of the occupation of the continent, the overseas expansion following the defeat of Spain, the swift transformation, after Appomattox, of a civilization built on agriculture and commerce into an industrial culture, all combined in an American dream of a rosy-hued future.

Underneath this dream was the conviction that advance in the natural and biological sciences would make possible the creation of a new world. To the common man, science expressed itself most simply in the machine which each year grew more complicated and more important. Two events in particular in the first decade of the twentieth century dramatized for the average citizen the augmented role of science in the age in which the fortune of birth had placed him. Walter Reed in Cuba, making use of the new knowledge of bacteriology, discovered the secret of the dread yellow fever; and at Kittyhawk the Wright brothers began the conquest of the air. Such achievements broke ancient fetters binding the imagination.

At the same time students of the ways of man, pioneers in emerging social disciplines, began to dream of the possibility of a science of society that would become in the realm of social action the counterpart of the new technology. The prestige of the words "science" and "scientific method" and the universality of the new faith in the potentialities of the sciences were evidence that a cult had appeared and that the man of the laboratory was threatening to replace the minister as the accepted guide to human salvation. In the Progressive Era, August Comte's positivism reached its American apogee. New thinkers in the emerging social sciences substituted for the certitudes of theology what they thought to be the certitudes of science. Herbert Spencer, whose name ranked second only to that of Darwin, was their patron saint. He persuaded thousands of Americans, who thought of themselves as forward-looking, that society is an organism, that there is a law of progress leading in social as in biological development from the simple and homogeneous to the complex and heterogeneous, and that evolution ends in a state of peaceful and happy "equilibration." Spencer taught that society moves upward from the primitive hunting stage to the final triumph of the industrial stage, passing through the stage of the military society on the way. Behind the forward push is force, working through laws that science reveals. The social world of August Comte and of Herbert Spencer rested squarely on determinism. At the end of the scholar's road lay certainty. Spencer's was not the optimism of hope but of assurance.

Henry Adams dissented. Like his generation he saw the importance of the new technology, but he stood relatively alone when he suggested, in the face of the current optimism, that the harnessing of natural energy was putting men in chains as well as setting them free, and that malevolent as well as beneficent forces were being loosed in the world. He spoke of the modern man as being made to dance by the live wire he grasped, unable to let go his hold, and suggested that in the twentieth century men were being educated by bombs doubling each decade in number and power. Adams, historian and philosopher, was one of the ablest among a new and small group of naturalists appearing among American men of letters.

The position of the atypical Adams suggests a basic conflict in American thinking. His pessimism stemmed from what seemed to him the implications for society of the new physics that was modifying the old Newtonian conception of the cosmos. The pessimism of Clemens began with Darwinian identification of man with the animal world. What seemed to many Darwin's degradation of human nature found support in Ernst Haeckel's biological dictum not only that man arises ultimately from the most primitive forms of life but that the child before birth recapitulates the course of evolution. It was a hard doctrine. Spencer with his intellectual device of the Unknowable, the domain of religion, had compromised with long-held beliefs. But the German Haeckel and his Darwinian contemporary Nietzsche seemed to destroy the ancient theological canon that God had created man a little lower than the angels and had set the beasts of the field under his feet. There were some Americans too for whom the harvest of the new biology was frustration, futilitarianism, and despair.

4

As the end of the nineteenth century came and passed, Americans faced another tension in social thought. They sensed that the frontier ideal of the self-sufficient individual must be modified to make it accord with a new understanding of the community. Josiah Royce, protagonist of individualism, yet insisted that men are "saved by the community." He symbolized in his effort to combine in his philosophy individualism and collectivism a conflict in American social thought that grew more intense with each decade. The idea of the importance of the individual was an aspect of American tradition too important to be quickly abandoned even as a result of the vast social changes of the end of the century. In fact, individualism reached a new apogee in the triumphs of those men of finance and industry who created the prominences in the landscape of the new industrialism. Individualism was implied in the sobriquet robber barons, justly applied later to some of them.

Yet economic power proved to be a sobering influence in the lives of many of the new capitalists. Andrew Carnegie, master of steel and of trade, took the lead in formulating a philosophy of stewardship which he called the Gospel of Wealth. He declared that the individual who has demonstrated his superiority to the common crowd by his skill in building new economic structures and amassing economic power must assume a compensating responsibility to extend his leadership to a broader social field and to do for the average man those things which mediocrity prevents the commoner from doing for himself. This new and revolutionary doctrine of stewardship was expressed, among other ways, in hospitals, museums, libraries, new or enlarged universities, and in that novelty in American life, the endowed foundation. Big business, whose ruthlessness and lawlessness were responsible for much human suffering between 1885 and 1917, made at the same time contributions of the first importance to the advance of the finer aspects of American culture.

Individualism in the American tradition had always expressed itself in inequality. As the nineteenth century drew to a close, the men and women of the United States became increasingly aware, particularly in the swollen cities, of the contrast between Veblen's conspicuous consumption and that conspicuous destitution for the amelioration of which Jacob Riis led a ten years' war on Manhattan Island. The sentiment and practice of humanitarianism, old in American life, manifested themselves in new institutions, and the career of Jane Addams suggested that the relief of suffering was perhaps the most important field in which the genius of American women could express itself. For a time after Appomattox, humanitarians, spurred to great efforts by the definitive victory over slavery, believed that poverty could be destroyed with a similar finality. Nor throughout the entire period to the entrance of the United States into the First World War did they completely give up their faith, although each year hundreds of thousands of the world's poor crowded as immigrants hopefully into American communities to undertake in a new life the individual's struggle to better himself. The cities of the Republic became expanding reservoirs of the defeated and the exploited and of the morally and physically diseased. Poverty also marred the countryside of the South, emerging from tragedy, and of the Western plains where men gambled with the forces of nature and lost. Beside the humanitarians appeared a group of American men of letters for whom the realities of American life were the biographies of the demoralized and the defeated.

Individualism flourished, as it had previously, partly because no serious external threat forced American nationals into sacrifices of some of their liberties in the interest of protection. Internal insecurities caused the emergence of new ideas, ideas that remained for the most part in the speculative stage before the First World War, but which were to become important in the middle years of the twentieth century. Trade unionism, after the collapse of the idealistic dreams of the Knights of Labor in the eighties, continued the fight to establish the practice of collective bargaining. Lester Frank Ward, challenging the prophet of individualism, William Graham Sumner, assumed intellectual leadership among a growing company who would abandon laissez faire and establish the social service state. Ward, scientist and government servant, foresaw the state undertaking social experimentation to provide a part of the necessary data for social planning. He believed that a lumbering and somewhat haphazard democracy could be made to evolve into an efficient and scientific "sociocracy." Simon Patten, economist, denied the traditional assumptions of an economy of scarcity and insisted that science could be made to provide for all men an abundant life.

Neither Ward nor Patten had great importance for even the liberal politicians of the age. These latter, calling themselves Populists, Insurgents, or Progressives, contented themselves for the most part with battles to achieve governmental supervision of business and the conservation of the nation's resources. The new horizons suggested by such pioneers as Ward and Patten, together with the actual achievements of the reforming statesmen, bred such hopes for the future as to make it difficult for Marxian socialism to establish itself as a significant force in American life. Equally important in creating a blockade against the influence of Marx was the tradition of individualism carrying on in an expanding economy. This tradition tended to channel in America what the author of *Das Kapital* had described as the inevitable class struggle into individual efforts on the part of the natural leaders of the proletariat to escape from the class to which they were born and to achieve the dignity and power inherent in management. It is true that Marxism appeared and that its doctrines were disseminated by a political party and by a press that, about 1912, was surprisingly large. But even in its heyday before the First World War, it remained for the vast majority of Americans a foreign thought pattern imported by immigrants and of little relevancy to American life. Suggestive of the exotic nature of Marxism were the pains taken by its protagonists to minimize or even to deny the challenge of Marxian materialism to traditional Christianity.

5

But the "old-time religion" of the frontier group camp meeting did not go unchallenged. Geology, historical criticism applied to the Bible and, above all, Darwinism brought first rage and then consternation to the theologians of Protestant orthodoxy. When Andrew D. White published in 1896 *A History of the Warfare of Science with Theology in Christendom,* the theologians were in full retreat. Out of the struggle emerged new and somewhat vague patterns that came to be known as modernism, representing efforts to reconcile religious affirmations with science and objective scholarship. By 1917 modernism seemed to have triumphed in American Protestant circles. But the victory had been won at a price that was nothing less than the loss of that old sense of religious and moral security that the common men in a previous age had gained from the doctrine of the literal inspiration of the Scriptures. After the First World War a crusading fundamentalist revolt was to attempt a recovery of the old religious certainties. But before that conflict, Protestant leadership had sought to minimize and perhaps forget the new difficulties in the field of theology by turning to a social gospel. Influenced by the growing humanitarianism in an age of tension and suffering, they proclaimed the "law of love." In harmony with the optimism of the day, they declared the possibility of the establishment of the Kingdom of God on earth. Walter Rauschenbusch, clergyman and professor of church history, became the Isaiah who held up to scorn the smugness of the well-to-do urban church members and who took the lead in bringing a new social consciousness to American Protestantism.

William James, psychologist and philosopher, was disturbed by that religious insecurity that impaired the prestige and authority of modernism. In his *Will to Believe* he gave a pragmatist's reason for faith in a beneficent, if not omnipotent, God. Belief in a Power striving for good in the universe with which man can associate himself, James argued, makes for optimism, and optimism releases human energy. Faith, therefore, is justified by its results. Protestant leadership in the Progressive Era found comfort and even inspiration in the Jamesian formula. But pragmatism, the work of Peirce, James, and Dewey, had more significance than the reduction of the anxieties of theologians. The pragmatists' concept of an open and unfinished universe, conditioned by no fixed and eternal pattern, seemed to many men of the age a liberation from old absolutisms of both religion and science and a challenge to creation. Their definition of the good as that which works not only was a rationalization of changing customs in changing culture, but helped in the process of transformation. Pragmatism launched industrial America into an age of ethical relativism, an attitude of mind that was to be of importance in the period between 1918 and 1941.

The instrumentalism of the early Dewey and his gospel that man, through the use of ideas, can create his own world became the orthodoxy of education and helped to raise the American faith in the educative process almost to the level of a national religion. Dewey's instrumentalism was, from another point of view, merely a projection into philosophical thinking of the inherent optimism of the age. Pragmatism, as a philosophy of practicality, harmonized with the American genius for getting things done. Like Theodore Roosevelt's gospel of the strenuous life, pragmatism stimulated Americans to action rather than to thought. The emphasis of the pragmatists on experimentalism put them in the cult of science. The devotees of the new philosophy, however, mistook experimentalism for the scientific method, failing to recognize that only logical and criticized theory makes possible the formulation of the questions that are answered in the laboratory.

It was no accident that pragmatism appeared in the Progressive Era. It gained immediate and widespread popularity because in it practically all the moods and the trends of the time found expression. Change, swift and confused, was the central fact of the period from 1865 to 1917; the pragmatists affirmed that flux is the ultimate cosmic reality and distilled from change a philosophy for America. Liberal political thinkers seized upon this philosophy for assurance that the transition from the old agrarian to the new industrial nation could be made without destroying the sense of security and the belief in progress of the old ways. The evils in the new ways could be corrected by reform. From the Populist movement of the nineties to the Square Deal of the first Roosevelt and the New Freedom to come, liberal political leadership held a straight course through the flux of intellectual, moral, and social change.

58. LITERATURE AS BUSINESS

AT the same time that traditional individualism was being challenged by the development from rural America into urban and industrial America, changes in intellectual outlook were raising doubts about many venerable assumptions that directly affected the business of writing and publishing. Once again, as in the period immediately following the Revolution, the American writer found himself permitted—and indeed required—to deal directly with the facts and ideas of American life. Not only the experience out of which literature is made, but the conditions under which authors live and write, were undergoing a revolution.

The writers who in 1910 pleaded pathetically with the editor of the *Century Magazine* for "another damn" were winning a battle which had begun in earnest only twenty years earlier. In 1890 "damns" were forbidden rather than rationed; yet in that year Richard Harding Davis' "Gallegher" was rejected by the *Century*—not for its profanity but for its slanginess. Only a few years before, the *Century* had stopped the presses because of a reference to dynamite (in relation to labor troubles) in Howells' serial *The Rise of Silas Lapham*; and the same author had been scolded by the editor of *Harper's Monthly* for reviews too friendly to Mrs. Humphry Ward's "anti-Christian" *Robert Elsmere* and to Zola's *La Terre*. Scribner rejected a novel of Hamlin Garland's (which probably deserved no better fate) on the ground that it contained slang, profanity, vulgarity, agnosticism, and radicalism; *Harper's* dropped a chapter of James' translation of Daudet's *Port Tarascon* as offensive to Christian readers, and in 1892 warned Constance Woolson against unrelieved pessimism. Yet many of the rejected works got into print in book form. In 1895 Scribner was unable to accept Harold Frederic's *The Damnation of Theron Ware* as a serial, but offered to publish it as a book. Stephen Crane's *Maggie* got nowhere with editors, but Appleton printed four thousand copies of it between 1896 and 1900. *Harper's* bowdlerized Hardy's *Jude the Obscure,* but seductive or sensual novels like *She* and *Quo Vadis* were best sellers. Howells claimed that in this last decade of the nineteenth century any slightly dirty novel, which magazine editors would not touch, could get a substantial sale as a book.

It would be easy to arrange such evidence as this to show, first, that in the space of two decades our wall of taboos—aesthetic, social, moral, religious, political—crumbled to the ground, leaving only scattered bricks to be hammered to bits in the Jazz Age; and second, that a major cause of this phenomenon was the transfer of critical and selective authority from the once omnipotent monthly magazines to the publishers of books. There is some truth in both suggestions, but true enlightenment in neither. The repressive forces continued in operation, but they somehow lost, as the years passed, their power to block every channel in the literary market. By 1910 there was a welcome, in the book, magazine, and newspaper world, for every shade of opinion and every grade of excellence; and if only a faint chorus greeted the writer whose method, purpose, or message appealed only to a small minority, it is demonstrable that this minority was growing larger daily. The fact that Americans were buying wood pulp by the ton should not obscure the equally significant fact that in 1900 Scribner gave Henry James an advance of $2,000 for the book rights to such caviar as *The Sacred Fount,* and that *Harper's Monthly* offered him $5,000 for the serial rights to *The Ambassadors.* The Comstockery of the period was pernicious, but Dreiser's *Sister Carrie* finally found both publisher and audience. One may well ask how the magazines' taboos against the subjects of capital punishment and anarchism could prevail in a period which began by making best sellers of *Looking Backward* and *Caesar's Column,* and ended in a wave of muckraking journalism. From the publishing point of view, the key to the period is the diversification of the American reading classes, the breaking up of once solid cultural and social groups, and the readiness of enterprising editors and publishers to feed or exploit new audiences.

2

Basic, as always in American social mutations, was the advance of education. Granted that mere literacy was and is potentially as much a threat as an aid to high culture, by 1910 there were only 5,500,000 Americans (about 8 per cent of all people over ten years of age) who were not possible buyers of print. Of the schoolgoers in 1902 more than 500,000 were moving on to public high schools which had tripled in number during the nineties. Whether the adoption, in the public schools, of educational theories which stressed preparation for "life" rather than for college led also to preparation for independent thinking and reading is a question still unsettled. Mass education on the higher levels was still in the future, for in 1900 only 11 per cent of all high-school students were preparing for college; and in 1904 not many more than 100,000 students were enrolled in higher institutions. Graduate study, begun in the seventies, was growing rapidly. In 1901 there were some 6,300 graduate students, about three-quarters of them in the humanities; and in 1903 a total of 266 doctorates were conferred. Significantly, a Western institution, the University of Chicago—rich, progressive, and only twelve years old—was second only to Yale in the number of degrees granted. The effects of expanding higher education on literary production and consumption were necessarily intangible—except in one respect: the nineties saw the first full development of university press publishing, which was eventually to contribute importantly to the diversification of the book market. During the period, presses at Harvard, Johns Hopkins, Columbia, Chicago, Princeton, and Yale began to serve as outlets for subsidized scholarly studies which were of no commercial significance except to the popularizers who soon learned to ransack them for salable facts.

In a period when the average schooling of Americans was only five years, adult education had much to offer. The Chautauqua system, at its peak at the end of the century, brought the subject matter of the liberal arts curriculum—through its publications and summer schools and the mails—to adults in every state in the Union. Under the leadership of President William Rainey Harper of the University of Chicago, it grew beyond its original connection with the Sunday school movement, and became a force for general culture. Equally successful was a movement begun by the New York City Board of Education in 1888 to provide lectures for working people, many of them immigrants, at public expense. Attendance of seven million in the first fifteen years of the New York program revealed an appetite for cultural advancement which had not been equaled, except by Chautauqua, since the great days of the town lyceum. The idea that school buildings might be of use to adults after the children had departed, quickly spread not only to other cities, but to universities as well, for extension courses were also an innovation of the period.

Equally, perhaps more, important for the encouragement of the reading habit among the population at large was the growth of the free public library. The states had been passing ineffective permissive library laws since the Civil War, but it was not until 1893 that a new departure was made by New Hampshire, when it passed the first state law requiring its townships to create libraries. By 1900 there were 1,700 free libraries which owned more than five thousand volumes. The existence of many of these was made possible by Andrew Carnegie's gifts of buildings—300 by 1904. It may have been, as Mr. Dooley remarked, that these were for the dead authors, and that live authors stood outside and wished they were dead; but there is no question that Carnegie's Gospel of Wealth was taking tangible form. Live authors like Mark Twain might complain that librarians had arbitrary powers of censorship when time after time *Huckleberry Finn* was banned from the shelves, but many were likely to feel, with Frank Norris, that the growth of the reading habit was the important thing because it must lead ultimately to more liberal views and better taste.

In a period extraordinary for philanthropy only 2 per cent of all private gifts of money were for libraries, compared to 43 per cent for education, 37 per cent for charity, and 9 per cent each for museums and religion. Much of the money for education was poured into institutions of higher learning; in fact, benefactions, the rate of which tripled in twenty years, kept step with the growth of national wealth. The Carnegie and Rockefeller foundations, which distributed money not only for general college use but for research and teachers' pensions, did much to stabilize and improve higher education and to broaden its functions. If, as Veblen and others thought, industrial wealth controlled as well as subsidized many of our universities, its influence was neutralized by the people's willingness to help themselves. During the period, total university income from city and state increased almost twenty-four times, and from tuition fees almost six times. Of a total income of eighty millions in 1910, only eighteen millions came from private benefactors.

A more immediate influence in the American writer's milieu during these years was middle-class women—as readers, as guardians of the family, and as representatives of religion. The two best paymasters in the magazine world in the nineties were *Harper's Monthly* and the *Century,* both of which often and frankly explained to contributors that they were pledged not to offend religious sensibilities and not to print anything that could not be read by the women of the family circle. But the American woman was changing, and the family in the old sense was disappearing. The employment of women (five and a third million were at work in 1900, half of them under twenty-five years old) was rendering them more independent and less willing to reduce their standard of living by early marriage and large families. College education seems to have had the same effect. Other tendencies, such as migration to the city, the popularity of apartments and boardinghouses, birth control, and divorce (except for Japan's ours was the highest divorce rate in the world) resulted in the decline of the family from an average of four in 1890 to less than three in 1910. The shrinkage took place chiefly among the urban middle classes which constituted the richest book market.

At the same time, the horizon of the women of these families was widening. By 1898, 70 per cent of the colleges of the country were coeducational, and by 1902 women made up 25 per cent of the undergraduate, 26 per cent of the graduate, and 3 per cent of the professional enrollment of all colleges. Women's colleges, 128 of which had been founded by 1901, had only 25,000 students in that year, but 37,000 more were enrolled in normal schools, and almost 400,000 in secondary schools, where they were in the majority. Small as these numbers were in a nation of 76,000,000, they were relatively large in relation to the groups which bought and read books and magazines of literary quality. Presumably, also, these women were prominent in the culture clubs, which had a membership of perhaps 1,000,000 in 1910.

Increasing education and freedom for women must have tended to relax the rigid codes of propriety and morality which men had always inflicted on them. When Edward Bok of the *Ladies' Home Journal* began his columns of advice for girls and young mothers, he was generally ridiculed; but these columns were born of his conviction that women had been kept in enforced ignorance of the facts of life, and their response helped run his circulation above the 750,000 mark by 1900. Henry Mills Alden of *Harper's* had sensed the emancipation, for in 1894 he justified his acceptance of Du Maurier's *Trilby* on the grounds of "the increasing tolerance of our moral judgments as a people." He seems to have been right, for this story of the Latin Quarter became the greatest serial success of the decade, and Saint-Gaudens is said to have remarked, "Every other woman you meet thinks she could be an artist's model." When, in 1900, the police raided Clyde Fitch's adaptation of *Sapho* because the leading man carried the heroine upstairs, many women signed a public protest against the closing, and women stormed the theater when the play reopened. It is likely that the decline of the *Century Magazine* toward the end of the period was due in part to the quiet refusal of women to agree with the editors' ideas of what was good for them.

A comparable phenomenon was the growing liberality of religious groups. The social historian finds it easy to collect a distressing amount of evidence of narrow orthodoxy, sectarianism, and bigotry in the nineties, but such reactionary thought must have been inspired by opposite tendencies. The evangelist Moody's cry that the Bible was not meant to be understood was the sign of a widespread desire to understand. The popularity of Washington Gladden's *Who Wrote the Bible?* (1891) and its use by Bible and Y.M.C.A. classes show that the Higher Criticism was no longer a merely scholarly preoccupation. The sectarianism of the time must be balanced against the vogue of such novels as Margaret Deland's *John Ward, Preacher* and Mrs. Humphry Ward's *Robert Elsmere* in 1888, and against interest in the Parliament of Religions at the Chicago World's Fair. Orthodoxy could not have been too powerful in a period when Henry Drummond, as a Chautauqua lecturer, expounded Darwinism. Blue laws were still a live issue, but the circulation of Sunday newspapers and attendance at Sunday baseball games showed that the Sabbath was no longer monopolized by the churches. Protestantism may have been primarily the faith of the comfortable middle classes, but Christian Socialism was a Protestant phenomenon; and the millions of readers of the Reverend Charles M. Sheldon's *In His Steps* (1896) could not have been entirely indifferent to the problems of poverty and labor. Certainly the prolabor statements of the Federal Council of Churches in 1908 were the climax of steady change rather than a new departure.

For the writer and publisher the pertinent question was the extent of the power of religious sects and organizations to inhibit free expression and to dictate standards of propriety. Confusing as are the statistics of church membership in the period, it would seem that half the population were churchgoers. The fact that in these decades thirty-one new schools of theology were opened, as against thirty schools of medicine and twenty-four women's colleges, and that they were given two or three times as much money as these others, is evidence enough that the age of religious enthusiasm had not yet passed. But the power of sectarian groups to influence the general literary market was waning. On the publishing side, a major tendency was the shift of religious books from the general publisher to specialists like Fleming H. Revell or to the organizations set up by the Presbyterians, Methodists, Congregationalists, and Baptists. Moreover, the traditional ties between publishers and denominational sects, like that between Harper and the Methodists, were breaking because the economic motives for such connections were no longer strong; and the tendency of denominational publishers to invade the fields of general literature occasioned much bitter criticism.

There were changes in the magazine world also. Rose Terry Cooke said in 1885 that she sold a story to a religious magazine because it paid better than any other periodical except the *Youth's Companion*; by the end of the century, commercial magazines were no longer subject to such competition. General magazine editors, who had once lived in terror of attack by the sectarian press, now apparently were taking the point of view that the unreasonably prejudiced minority of religious readers and editors—always the most vocal—were too insignificant to affect seriously the great national literary market. Similar considerations were weakening the ancient prejudice against the theater. Of what avail was the Methodist Discipline against the drama-hungry crowds and the enterprising producers of the nineties?

3

The fact was that publishing had become big business, a force so great that it could no more be seriously hampered by minority groups than the growing automobile industry could be frustrated by lovers of horses. Especially in the so-called "merger prosperity" of 1898–1903, publishing boomed, along with other forms of enterprise. In the twenty years preceding 1910, the national wealth tripled, while population increased only 50 per cent. In the same period, the value of printed materials increased from less than $480,000,000 to well over $1,000,000,000. As a big business, publishing was falling into current industrial and financial patterns and sloughing off its antiquated habits and techniques in the struggle to survive. Two dips in the business cycle, the panic of 1893 and the silver campaign depression of 1896–1897, tended to put publishing, like other businesses, under the control of finance capitalism, with the result that the banks and investment trusts, which supplied it with capital, insisted on greater efficiency in the interest of surer profits. The reorganization in the nineties of great firms like Harper and Appleton reflected this tendency. The history of Harper is a case in point: a company which, as a close family partnership, had enjoyed a dominating position in the book world for almost three-quarters of a century, became at the end of the century an impersonal corporation under the temporary guidance of a bank.

Nor was the book business exempt from the movement toward consolidation and near-monopoly. As early as the eighties the American News Company had become so powerful as a distributor of reading for travelers that it was accused of dictating policy to some of the publishers from whom it bought extensively. In 1890 the American Book Company absorbed five other publishers of school texts, and for a while had a practical monopoly in its field. The cheap reprint business went through two such phases—once in 1890 when the United States Book Company came into control, and again about 1900, when Grosset & Dunlap proved that they could handle cheap editions more efficiently than regular houses. Publishing was also directly affected by combinations of manufacturers. During this period the American Typefounders Company absorbed twenty foundries; and in 1906 the Department of Justice was impelled to break up a powerful paper trust.

Technology was the basis of many profound changes. The perfection of the Mergenthaler typesetting machine in the mid-eighties, and of rounding, backing, case-making, gathering, and other machines for the manufacturing of books in the early nineties, solved so many problems that soon after the turn of the century a completely mechanized production schedule was practicable. By the nineties photoengraving was so well developed that the older illustrated magazines like *Scribner's* and the *Century* no longer had an advantage over the rising ten- and fifteen-cent periodicals which could not stand the expense of woodcut techniques.

Distribution, still the chief problem of the publisher, was modernized somewhat. The old-fashioned wholesale auction or "trade sale" was dropped in the nineties when it was obvious that it served little purpose except the getting rid of slow-moving stock. By 1900 booksellers' and publishers' organizations had succeeded to a certain extent in stabilizing retail prices and discounts, but as the department store developed into an important outlet for books, it created new problems of price control. The subscription-book business which, except in the case of Mark Twain's books, had never been very successful in the distribution of literary works, entered a new phase. Such magazines as *Collier's* began to distribute books as premiums and as low-priced sets got up for subscribers. In spite of new methods, however, books were not easily available to most of the population. W. H. Page estimated in 1905 that only 2 or 3 per cent of the people lived near bookshops. Nevertheless, by 1910, 46 per cent of all Americans lived in towns large enough (2,500) to support shops which could stock books, and the rest had been rendered more accessible to publishers by the inauguration of rural free delivery routes in 1897. For periodicals the latter was important. By 1908, 64 per cent of the total weight of mail consisted of newspapers and magazines.

That mechanization and improved distribution did not result in cheaper books was due to other business factors. As manufacturing costs went down, other costs went up. Royalty rates, for novels especially, reached an all-time high between 1900 and 1905. Outlay for traveling agents and salesmen mounted steadily. Long-term credits to booksellers made necessary increased capitalization. But the most conspicuous increase was in the cost of advertising and promotion. Competition for authors and readers led publishers to spend fortunes on publicity. Many of the big promotion campaigns for best sellers seem to have had the same object and effect as the advertising of "loss leaders" in department stores: advertising costs sometimes killed the profit on a particular book, but the publisher earned prestige with authors and booksellers. Of the "free" publicity which inheres in the news value of book-and-author gossip, there was as yet comparatively little. Edward Bok's syndicated column of literary chat had some popularity in the late eighties and nineties, but the modern weekly newspaper review did not begin until 1896 when the New York *Times* instituted its Saturday literary supplement. Even so, newspaper book reviews in general were still the province of over-worked desk men who contrived to "cover" twenty to thirty volumes in an hour's time.

The centralization of publishing and printing in a few cities was another sign of the new age. In spite of the denials and protests of such enthusiastic Westerners as Hamlin Garland and Frank Norris, New York was now definitely the center of the industry. In 1905 the total value of its book and job printing was $44,000,000; that of Chicago, $26,000,000: Philadelphia,

$14,000,000; St. Louis, $8,000,000, and Boston, $7,000,000. Though New York had the lion's share of literary publishing, Boston and Philadelphia were maintaining their great tradition of book and magazine production. Chicago had an enormous printing and book wholesaling business, but though in 1894 fifty-three of its firms published 243 titles, few of these were new literary works, and by the end of the decade even the Chicago authors were taking their business to New York publishers. A few firms like Stone & Kimball did some distinguished literary publishing for a while, but they did not long survive. Nevertheless, the civic enthusiasm which created the University of Chicago in 1890 and the great World's Fair of 1893 kept that city in the front ranks as a cultural center.

4

The differences between publishing and other big business were as important as the similarities. Fundamentally the publisher neither was nor is a producer. His "goods" are "made" by the writer and the printer, and his own essential function is to publicize and distribute. The status of his goods as property is complicated. Ordinarily he does not own what he sells: he buys the right to sell from a producer who loses his property after a period of time fixed by law. Durable as his product is in one sense, he cannot ordinarily build up a permanent demand for it. Hence his advertising problems are special. These problems are inherent in his business. Certain others were solved, or moved toward solution, between 1890 and the First World War.

Up to 1891 American publishers had been forced, by the lack of an international copyright law, to sell both foreign and native goods which were in competition with each other. If the difference in the cost of the two had consisted merely of the amount of royalty paid to the American author, this competition would not have mattered; but because competition for new uncopyrighted material among publishers forced down the price of foreign books and at the same time vastly increased the number and the variety of commercially attractive titles, the American writer was at a double disadvantage. Ordinarily he could not allow his books to be sold at the prices of foreign reprints—ten to fifty cents—because, unless the sale was enormous, even high royalties brought him small returns.

Generous and idealistic as many publishers were in the long fight for an international copyright law, their real motive was self-interest. Lack of clear title to literary property gave impetus to disorderly competition which proved fatal to many publishers. Trade courtesy had served as a restraint for a time in the mid-century, but when business morality degenerated in the Gilded Age, courtesy ceased to be effective. In the final successful struggle for copyright, moral force, exerted by those who believed that our theft of foreign property was a national crime, stood in the same relation to economic force as abolitionism stood to Northern industrialism before the Civil War: moral force could prevail only when economic conditions were right and ready. The evils of competition broke down the resistance of even the reprint publishers, and the manufacturing clause requiring the printing of foreign copyright works in the United States procured the support of manufacturers and of labor. In the political dynamics of the campaign, the influence of the International Typographical Union was crucial, as was the confusion of Congress about the nature of literary property and its relation to tariff. The trick seems to have been turned by personal pressure cleverly applied to lawmakers who did not feel that copyright mattered very much one way or the other.

Although by the end of 1892, nineteen thousand copyrights had been granted to foreign authors and composers, the results of the law were obscured by the depression of 1893. Perhaps the earliest repercussion was the unmourned death of the old reprint companies, some of which had been hastily organized in the late eighties in order to strip British lists while there was still time. Among salutary effects was the decrease in the reprinting of the trashiest English fiction, the publication of the good British works in reliable texts, and a general reduction in the price of standard foreign works. The most significant result for the author was that in 1894, for the first time, more American than foreign novels were published in the United States. That British titles continued to be well represented in our best-seller lists after 1891 is evidence that lack of copyright was not the only factor in Anglo-American competition in the nineteenth century; but the fact that American titles soon won and kept a majority on these lists shows how quickly our production of commercial literature was able to develop once fair conditions were established.

Whether or not James Bryce was justified in hoping that copyright would enlarge the horizon of English and American authors by broadening their market, the new law had the effect of internationalizing the publishing business. In 1896 three great English houses incorporated in New York—the Oxford University Press, John Lane, and Macmillan (which had founded its New York House in 1869); and many large American firms which had not set up English agencies earlier, rushed to do so. The law also probably helped to bring about a revival of good printing in America. In a period ripe for reaction against the horrors of Victorian taste, publishers now had the opportunity to offer attractively printed works to a public increasingly able to afford the necessarily higher prices. Among the designers, printers, and publishers who opened new paths, the most distinguished were Daniel Updike, who established the Merrymount Press in 1893; Bruce Rogers, whose work at the

Riverside Press began in the nineties; Thomas Bird Mosher of Portland, 1891; Stone & Kimball of Cambridge and Chicago, 1893; and Copeland & Day of Boston, 1895. It was not long before the work of these pioneers was emulated by large general publishers, who found that the public was willing to pay for well bound, well printed books.

5

One of the new conditions of the period was the change in the status of the publisher as a buyer of manuscripts and interpreter of reader demands. He had always had to compete not only for readers but for authors, but he had rarely exercised more than a negative control over the kind and quality of manuscripts that he bought. Competition now forced him to develop authors as well as readers, and to persuade writers to direct their energies into profitable channels. Frank Norris, who was a reader for Doubleday, wrote:

No one not intimately associated with any one of the larger, more important "houses" can have any idea of the influence of the publisher upon latter-day fiction. More novels are written—practically—to order than the public has any notion of. The publisher again and again picks out the man . . . , suggests the theme, and exercises, in a sense, all the functions of instructor during the period of composition. . . . Time was when the publisher waited for the unknown writer to come to him with his manuscript. But of late the Unknown has so frequently developed, under exploitation and by direct solicitation of the publisher, into a "money-making proposition" of such formidable proportions that there is hardly a publishing house that does not now hunt him out with all the resources at its command.

Correspondence of the day shows that publishers begged for "b'gosh" fiction when *David Harum* (1898) proved successful, only to warn authors away from it when Irving Bacheller's *Eben Holden* (1900) soaked up the market; that when one theme of historical fiction had been overdone, they suggested new ones; and that established authors were under constant pressure to produce in quantity the kind of work which sold best. The better publishers were careful not to force their authors too much, but some of the newer magazines and syndicates were relentless. George Ade wrote Howells in 1902 that he had determined four times to write "no more of this sickening slang," but that each time his publisher had weakened him by figuring the cash return from syndication in seventy newspapers. At the turn of the century the heaviest pressure was on novelists; the proportion of novels to all titles published was 1,278 to 6,336, or 20 per cent.

In spite of the great expansion of the book market (the number of titles published in 1910 was 13,470—three times the size of the output of 1890), the book continued to be an appendage to the magazine. The magazine in America had profited by the lack of a copyright law; the postal system took care of its distribution problem; ever increasing circulations enabled it to buy the best literary and editorial talent in the country; it offered much in the way of names, variety, and pictures for very little money; and it adapted itself to a stratified reading public. When a reader bought a magazine addressed to his level of interest and opinion, he received, as Howells said in 1893, literature with "the warrant of a critical estimate"—the warrant of editors and critics far better trained than the average publisher or his "readers."

For the novelist of the period, to quote Howells again, the reward was "in the serial, and not in the book." Established writers were paid $1,500 to $10,000 for serials, which apparently helped rather than hindered the book sale. Some magazines like *Harper's* could pay especially high prices because they published large editions in England. Young publishers like Stone & Kimball, who owned no magazine, frequently had to buy and sell serial rights in order to get book contracts. Situations like this encouraged the use of literary agents, and it was evidence of the increasing impersonality of the publishing business that such agents as A. P. Watt, Paul Reynolds, and J. B. Pinker were resorted to by authors who shrank from the growing financial complexity of the business of writing. Business seemed to many authors to be dominating art. Henry James complained bitterly of being "condemned to the economy of serialisation," which subordinated the writer to "catch-penny picture-books" by putting arbitrary limits on the length and number of installments. Other writers, like Harold Frederic, cheerfully submitted serials set up in blocks of ten thousand words, much as later writers designed their novels for easy transformation into movie scenarios.

As for illustrations, though there is little evidence that magazine fiction was chosen primarily as a vehicle for expensive artists, it is clear that authors of the stature of Howells, Lafcadio Hearn, and James Branch Cabell were sometimes engaged to write the text for a projected set of pictures. Generally speaking, the literary integrity of the standard magazines was carefully protected by the admirable editors of the day—Henry Mills Alden of *Harper's*, Horace Scudder, W. H. Page, and Bliss Perry of the *Atlantic* (which was not illustrated), Richard Watson Gilder of the *Century*, and Edward Burlingame of *Scribner's*. Inasmuch as all these magazines were the property of general book publishers, who asked for book rights when they accepted serials, it is obvious that the judgment of these editors is a key to the literary tone of the period, and that the decline of the circulation of their magazines about 1910 was an omen of a cultural change.

Robert Underwood Johnson of the *Century* crystallized the problem in a letter to his publisher in 1910. His magazine was not prospering, but the new ten- and fifteen-centers, "the cheap, illustrated all-story periodicals [were] making money hand over fist." His solution was to emphasize the *Century's* old policy of appealing to women, religious people, and the West, "where the American reading public is to be found." Unfortunately for him, all three seemed to prefer the cheaper periodicals created by journalistic editors and publishers like Bok, McClure, and Norman Hapgood of *Collier's,* who were not committed to nineteenth century notions concerning women, religious people, and the West. *McClure's, Munsey's, Cosmopolitan, Everybody's, Collier's,* and the *Ladies' Home Journal* were discovering new interests and tastes in American readers; and by 1905 they were taking their pick of American authors who could no longer afford to write exclusively for the editors they revered.

The new readers were more interested in facts and diversion than in principles and art. The reform campaigns of Gilder and Alden seemed stodgy compared to the solid factualism of muckraking articles about matters that touched the common people everywhere; and the fiction of O. Henry, Jack London, and George Randolph Chester seemed less like literature than like life. The financial heart of the new magazines was advertising, and when Bok decided in 1896 to run his stories back among the advertisements, he was merely being realistic about the relation of one to the other. General literary weeklies in 1909 had a circulation of almost 6,000,000 an issue.

The syndicates were equally realistic. The Sunday supplement was the only magazine for myriads of readers, and the economy of selling the same matter to scores of newspapers was obvious to the author. Bok, Bacheller, McClure, and Dana of the New York *Sun* had discovered the possibilities of this new market in the eighties, and by 1900 it was an important outlet for fiction. Howells thought that for second-rate literature the syndicate offered the best pay, but that though it had "enlarged the field of belles-lettres," it could not foster good fiction because newspapers were read not by women but by men and boys who wanted only to beguile their leisure. By the time his statement got into print, a Chicago newspaper had found it necessary to reprint installments of his own novel *The World of Chance* (1893), and by 1900 he was thinking of starting an international syndicate which would pay authors thousand dollar advances.

As it turned out, the Sunday newspaper, as a vehicle for literature, proved ephemeral; but if Howells was right about newspaper readers, and if the success of O. Henry's stories (in the New York *World,* for example) was symptomatic, it is probable that syndicates helped to spread the reading habit by bringing good if not profound fiction to people who had been reading nothing else of literary quality. If, as many claimed, the syndicates also tended to vulgarize the talents of men like Stephen Crane, Frank Norris, Jack London, and Richard Harding Davis, they deserve credit for doubling the rates for serial matter in the nineties and for offering sometimes the security of a salary.

Security was a new element in professional authorship. Literacy, new business methods, the rising standard of living, the adjustment of reading matter to diverse levels of taste, all helped to broaden and stabilize the literary market and thus to make writing income not only large but predictable. It is not very important that eighteen books of the period sold over a million copies each, but it mattered very much that the competent professional writer was finding an increasing number of outlets for his work. Novels and some other types of prose could by 1910 be serialized in newspapers, weeklies, or monthlies at prices which were usually higher than the total of book royalties. Royalties for American cloth editions rose from an almost universal 10 per cent on the retail price in the eighties to a fairly normal 20 per cent (for established authors) after 1900, though after that date there was a definite trend toward graduated royalties. Fifty-cent paper editions, and special cheap cloth editions made up for large jobbers, brought smaller royalties but bigger sales; and an author as popular as Richard Harding Davis could expect generous rates on sets printed as magazine premiums. In 1913 new horizons opened in the reprint field when Sears Roebuck printed from Harper's plates of Lew Wallace's *Ben-Hur* an edition of one million at a royalty of twelve cents. In the foreign markets, English, Canadian, colonial, and German rights could be counted on for small sums. Dramatic rights, which had been generally ignored earlier, became important in the nineties when producers began to scramble for every successful novel. Most book contracts granted the author one-third or one-half of the dramatic proceeds, which in the case of *Ben-Hur* totaled over half a million dollars in twenty years. Still larger vistas were appearing in Hollywood; but story-telling on the screen was not common until 1908, and the application of copyright laws to the movies was not clarified until some years later when a movie producer tried to get the rights to *Ben-Hur* from a theater producer who was trying in turn to get it from the publisher in order to cash in on the movie rights.

By 1914 a writer might have sold his novel in ten or twelve forms to as many different audiences, if he knew and did not spurn the common denominator by which they were all divisible. What was the result for literary culture? Was the contemporary success of Harold Bell Wright the goal toward which writers and educators had struggled for a century? Had financial security for authors been achieved at the expense of artistic integrity? Publisher Page in 1905 took a gloomy view of rapacious authors and of public taste. "It is a hard world," he said, in which *When Knighthood Was in Flower, Graustark,* and *Alice of Old Vincennes* "make fortunes," while Howells and James "write to unresponsive markets and even Mr. Kipling cannot find so many readers for a new novel as Mr. Bacheller of 'Eben Holden.' "

6

It is not easy to compare the taste of one era with another, and it is almost impossible to compare eras which differed vastly not only in literate population but in the proportion of educated to uneducated readers. Yet the facts about the popularity of authors from decade to decade are instructive. In 1872 the Public Library in Boston, a city of comparatively high culture, reported that the authors most in demand were the now forgotten Mrs. E. D. E. N. Southworth, Mrs. Caroline Lee Hentz, and Mary Jane Holmes. Fifteen years later things were not much better: the order books of a Midwestern wholesaler showed that the equally insignificant E. P. Roe led the same group in popularity, but that Cooper and Hawthorne stood tenth and eleventh.

But in the nineties something was happening. A survey of libraries in 1893 showed that only Alcott and Roe of the old group were still high on the lists, and that Dickens was first, with Scott, Cooper, George Eliot, Hawthorne, O. W. Holmes, and Thackeray close behind. Of the novels, *David Copperfield* was first, with *Ivanhoe, The Scarlet Letter, Uncle Tom's Cabin, Ben-Hur, Adam Bede, Vanity Fair,* and *Jane Eyre* following in order. As the century wore away the best-seller lists contained more and more books that have won a permanent place in literature. Page seemed not to have noticed that in the lists of the top ten, from 1895, were works by J. M. Barrie, Stephen Crane (*The Red Badge of Courage* ranked eighth in 1896), Kipling, and Finley Peter Dunne ("Mr. Dooley" ranked eighth in 1899). In 1904 Ellen Glasgow's *The Deliverance* ranked second (two years earlier she had assured her publisher that her "big," "deep," human documents could never be popular). In 1905 Mrs. Wharton's *The House of Mirth* ranked eighth. In 1906, a banner year, Winston Churchill's *Coniston,* Upton Sinclair's *The Jungle,* and novels by Margaret Deland, Mrs. Wharton, and Ellen Glasgow were among the top ten. With Howells in twenty-sixth place (in the 1893 list), Hardy in forty-sixth, and Henry James and the Russian novelists nowhere at all, Americans had little occasion for smugness; but the fact that both James and Howells were making comfortable, sometimes handsome, incomes shows that the better magazines and their readers were willing and able to support the better writers.

All things considered, the business of literature, which Howells called an infant industry in 1893, had come of age by 1910. Certainly it had been weaned from the mother country, and was self-supporting. Still more important, in the perspective of time, the democratic patronage of literature was proving its potentialities. It was still possible for the "venal novelist," as Frank Norris said, to gull the many who "for the moment . . . have confounded the Wrong with the Right, and prefer that which is a lie to that which is true." But Norris' faith that "The People, despised of the artist, hooted, caricatured and vilified, are after all, and in the main, the real seekers after Truth," and Howells' steadfast conviction that "Democracy in literature . . . wishes to know and to tell the truth, confident that consolation and delight are there" were finding their justification in the ever-increasing popularity of good literature.

59. THE LITERATURE OF IDEAS

THE group of writers that most courageously dealt with the new issues—social, economic, and philosophical—of America after the Civil War were those who addressed themselves in plain prose to the philosophy of change and to the problems it raised in American life. Broadly speaking, this "literature of ideas" falls into three main categories: that which justified traditional individualism in terms of traditional ideas; that which justified the older individualism, economic and philosophical, in terms of rising ideas and conditions; and that which endeavored to provide a synthesis of the old and the new. But any such classification is, at best, rough indeed and fails to do justice to the varied nuances of thought in these writers.

The individualism that had served as a primary assumption for Emerson, Whitman, and even Melville and Poe, was undoubtedly threatened. It was becoming increasingly clear that sporadic, unplanned efforts on the part of individuals to advance knowledge could no longer meet the needs of a more complex society. Well before the year 1900 government agencies, industrial corporations, universities, and philanthropic foundations were all contributing to knowledge through specialization, planning, and cooperation. It was no longer so apparent as it once seemed that the individual alone is the only or even the chief source of knowledge and light. Knowledge, in other words, was in part at least a social product. It might, moreover, be used not merely for the well-being of the individuals possessing it or controlling it, but for society as a whole. Such was the implication of the new movements for public health, the conservation of natural resources, and the application of science to business, agriculture, and government itself. At the same time that an ever larger company of men and women questioned the idea that individual effort and genius alone explain additions to knowledge, a rising group of economists maintained that wealth is likewise a social rather than an individual product. It was consequently plain to them that society might and should assume a responsibility for the just social use of wealth.

The intellectual revolution was even more profound than these changes suggest. To many the Darwinian theory seemed to rob man of his essential divinity by associating him with the lower animals, to despoil him of his freedom of will by reducing him to a mere automaton responding in a mechanistic way to the stimuli of his environment. The related philosophy of Herbert Spencer was frequently interpreted as materialistic or deterministic, as robbing man of divine impulse, of God Himself. The very method of science now seemed to many devout men far more dangerous than they had supposed: it threatened to destroy the validity of the intuitive approach to truth, an approach long regarded in some circles as the most satisfactory, if not the only adequate, justification of spiritual values, of man's universality and permanence—of all, in short, that made life worth living.

The Darwinian theory did not altogether militate against the older individualistic body of thought. In fact, it reenforced it at many points. This was particularly true in economic and social theory. Certain economists and an even more impressive group of business leaders used the doctrine of survival of the fittest to justify the process by which weak economic competitors were driven to the wall by the more competent monopolists. The free enterprise aspect of classical economic theory seemed, indeed, to gain a new scientific validity thanks to the findings of the Darwinists. Likewise individualism profited, or seemed to profit, when social theorists applied the whole concept of evolution through struggle and survival to society itself. Such applications of scientific theory to economic and social issues posed problems for the plain people and their intellectual champions who were trying to develop a new program in which cooperation, social responsibility for the individual, and sustained planning for the public good figured prominently.

2

The considerable body of literature which held that new conditions and problems might best be solved by the reassertion of traditional faith and ideas may be illustrated by the writings of John Lancaster Spalding. This brilliant and gifted son of well-to-do Kentuckians was, by the 1880's, a recognized leader in the Catholic Church. At the seat of his bishopric in Peoria he wrote, besides several volumes of regional and patriotic poetry, a half-dozen books widely read in Protestant and Catholic circles alike. His *Lectures and Discourses* (1882), *Means and Ends of Education* (1895), *Thoughts and Theories of Life and Education* (1897), and *Socialism and Labor* (1902) contain the essence of his thought.

Sensitive to the ways in which the new science challenged religious faith and authority, and aware that what passed for the modern temper was not to be brushed aside, Bishop Spalding argued with force and clarity for the thesis that the Catholic Church must enter into the living controversies of the time. The church must not only prove to Protestants that notwithstanding

its reliance on tradition and authority and its untutored immigrant following, it was in no sense opposed to science, learning, and culture. It must
actively contribute to American thought and literature, and so reflect the
faith that the evils of American life could be remedied solely by Christian
character, ideals, and values. The moral power of the church, its divine and
mystic character, could incorporate much of modern life, could mitigate the
materialism of science, could come to grips with the new age. Christian character, values, and ideals alone, insisted Spalding, could preserve the dignity
and integrity of the individual, could bring him into harmony with the permanent and the universal, could direct him to his proper destiny. This it
could do, not by denying modern knowledge, but by interpreting it and
directing the uses to which it was put.

Among the specific evils in American society which Bishop Spalding
especially deplored was the exploitation of immigrants in city slums. His
valiant efforts guided many newcomers into carefully planned colonies in
the Western states. The ill effects of cutthroat competition, of the power of
business monopolies, and of the sacrifice of human values for property rights,
disturbed the Bishop of Peoria no less than the degradation of immigrants
in city slums. The press, the public school, such legislative devices as the inheritance tax, and such organizations as the trade union could do something
to remedy all these evils. But at best, Spalding urged, such agencies and laws
could do very little. The true remedy for the "tyrannous sway of commercialism" and for "the ignorance and misery" of urban slums lay rather in the
primacy of Christian character. The social gulf between the steady, thrifty
laborers and the loafers and criminals was not economic but moral, and consequently "all real amelioration in the lot of human beings depends on religious, moral, and intellectual conditions."

Although Spalding denounced socialism as a mechanical device ruinous
to the liberty of men, although he preached class collaboration in the name
of religion and reason, he forthrightly condemned the avarice of employers.
"Only those who look above property to the peace of society, and strive in all
earnestness to live in the infinite and permanent world of truth, beauty, and
goodness, can hope to rise to the full height of a noble manhood." The captains of industry, mere mechanical men, mere victims of their own success,
could, like the poor whom they exploited, truly live only in those "inner
goods which make men wise, holy, beautiful, and strong." In preaching a
gospel the effect of which was in large measure to make the lowly and poor
content with their lot, a lot they could spiritually enrich by will and faith,
and in calling on the rich and powerful to seek God, Bishop Spalding argued
with engaging charm for the primacy of spiritual values in the here as well
as the hereafter.

The respect for authority and for the past which sets the tone of Bishop

Spalding's inspirational essays is also reflected in the writings of a non-Catholic educational leader and philosopher, William T. Harris. The son of a New England textile manufacturer, Harris rose rapidly in St. Louis to the superintendency of the public schools. In this position and subsequently as United States Commissioner of Education, Harris became the leading educational philosopher of his day. At the same time he wrote voluminously on philosophy, on literary criticism, on the arts, and on political and economic questions. Coming under the influence of a picturesque German-born thinker, Brockmeyer, Harris accepted Hegelianism. In 1867 he established and edited for a quarter of a century the *Journal of Speculative Philosophy*. The first American periodical devoted exclusively to philosophy, the *Journal* familiarized Americans with philosophical writings, old and new, European and American. As a close student of Hegel's *Larger Logic* and popularizer of his philosophy, and as an essayist who took the whole range of culture as his own, Harris expounded his ideas with authority and with force. He took an active part in the Concord School of Philosophy, an informal summer group before which the lingering transcendentalists and younger philosophical minds discussed Plato, Kant, Hegel, and their disciples.

In Hegelianism Harris found a thoroughly optimistic and idealistic philosophy which infused the world with a divine purpose and which, like Christianity, endowed the individual with a noble and immortal destiny. At the same time it justified the existing order and authorities by assuming that whatever exists is an inevitable stage in the unfolding of objective reason or the world spirit and is, consequently, right. Without sacrificing the individualistic ideals of self-help and "self-activity," Hegelianism seemed to lift the individual to a higher plane of self-realization. At the same time it subordinated him to existing social institutions by maintaining that his true, spiritual self, which was constantly subjected to conflict with his natural or physical self, could be realized only by adjusting himself to the divinely appointed environment and the social institutions that actually existed. What Harris thus did was to provide cogent arguments for regarding the individual and the solidarity of society as one and the same. The individual, according to Harris, could realize himself only through the family, school, church, and state.

In the mind of Harris, no conflict existed between the values of capitalism and those of the mind and spirit. Under capitalism the mass of men were destined to enjoy, not only competence and security, but leisure time for the cultivation of "the good life." Hegelianism, in his writings, served to reconcile any dichotomy between the material and practical and the intellectual and spiritual. Harris saw no threat in monopoly, or in technological and seasonal unemployment, to the realization of individual potentialities.

In justifying the ethics and practices of capitalism, Harris explicitly attacked as fallacious and as socially subversive the single tax, the utopianism of Edward Bellamy, and the "scientific socialism" of Marx, Engels, and their American disciples. No one can say in what degree Harris strengthened bewildered individuals by his assurances that their security and destiny lay in willingly subordinating themselves to the dominant aspects of the society in which they lived. Nor can anyone measure the effects of his teachings in reenforcing the conservative tenor of much American thinking. It is reasonable to assume, however, that he was one of the most influential intellectual leaders of his time. The very fact that his ideas found expression, not in elaborate and lengthy books, but in a vast number of essays and lectures, tended to increase his influence in his own day.

The writings of another absolute idealist, Josiah Royce, were less widely known than those of Harris, but they are even more important. The distinction of Royce's work rests only in part on the literary style in which he clothed his ideas. Occasional brilliance, humor, and imagination are apparent in Royce, but there are grandiose sentences and a kind of verbose dullness. Nor was it a particularly original thing to espouse Hegelianism, already becoming popular. But Royce gave it a new turn, and his distinction rests on the answers he thus gave to some of the perplexing problems of the individual in American society.

True to the doctrines of absolute idealism, Royce held that all reality is the idea, experience, or act of the mind and that there is but one Mind to which all others are related as parts to a whole. The Absolute has, however, endowed the individual with a moral will and independence which can be realized only through the community. Each individual, being thus a necessary part of the Absolute, makes his unique, indispensable contribution to the whole.

Here was a philosophy which restored to the individual the purpose and dignity of which Darwinism and the new interdependent society of urban industrialism seemed to so many to rob him. Here, too, was a system of thought serviceable to an older individualistic democracy which was being threatened by new aggregates of mass power, whether in the form of overwhelming corporations or a national state forced to wield more and more direction over the common life in the interest of common well-being. The individual's salvation in such circumstances, Royce believed, was in loyalty to a cause—to some cause to which the community, through which he could alone realize his moral independence, professed allegiance. It was not surprising that Royce commended the cause of regionalism. For regionalism had already found expression both in political movements and in the engaging local color school of literature. In loyalty to one's section or province,

Royce held, was to be found the needed training for the larger loyalties to the nation and to humanity itself.

In *The Philosophy of Loyalty* (1908) Royce developed the thesis that inasmuch as conflict of loyalties is inevitable, the individual must escape such conflict by loyalty to loyalty. Thus the individual, in the indirect support he gave to the whole realm of causes through his loyalty to loyalty, found his needed adjustment to life. He found it by coming into a closer relation with the Absolute, whether this be regarded as God or as the Absolute Idea or as the Ideal Community. In *The World and the Individual* (1900, 1901) Royce formulated this general position in maintaining that nature is a social product necessarily resulting from stable and cooperative intercourse. In thus emphasizing the voluntary and active aspects of absolute idealism, in making room for individual purpose and choice, and in laying stress on the individual's appreciative capacities and values, Royce gave direction to those Americans who were trying to relate their lives to a society and a universe that presented on so many levels obstacles and vexing conflicts. It is not hard to see why, in an America beset with class and regional tensions and with conflicts between the authority of science and that of religion, a philosophy at once empirical and idealistic, activistic and voluntaristic, a world view which found integrity of the individual in the community without in any way weakening the individual, appealed to thoughtful men in search of support for the traditional individualism.

3

Another group of writers sought to validate traditional individual values in terms of new currents of thought. The most challenging of these currents was the theory of evolution which gradually, in the sixties and seventies, won converts among scientists, social philosophers, and ethical and religious leaders. No single figure in this group was more representative or more influential than John Fiske. As the author of delightfully written popular histories of the American colonies and the American Revolution, as the interpreter of American political ideas, as a highly successful lecturer, and as a philosophical writer, Fiske was one of the most widely known American intellectual leaders of the last quarter of the nineteenth century. In many respects he and his Harvard associate Royce stood far apart, for Fiske was a disciple of Herbert Spencer and had no traffic with absolute idealism. But like Royce he offered reassurance to men and women to whom Darwinism seemed a repudiation of the dignity of the individual and a denial of Christian faith. In his engaging interpretations of American history he developed the theme that a guiding Providence had from the very start directed America on her successful course.

In his equally popular lectures on philosophy he brought to thousands of people the essential message of his book, *Outlines of Cosmic Philosophy* (1874).

In the last chapter of the *Outlines* Fiske asserted that there is no necessary conflict between Christianity and the doctrine of evolution.

We are not the autocrats, but the servants and interpreters of Nature; and we must interpret her as she is,—not as we would like her to be. That harmony which we hope eventually to see established between our knowledge and our aspirations is not to be realized by the timidity which shrinks from logically following out either of two apparently conflicting lines of thought—as in the question of matter and spirit—but by the fearlessness which pushes each to its inevitable conclusion. Only when this is recognized will the long and mistaken warfare between Science and Religion be exchanged for an intelligent and enduring alliance. Only then will the two knights of the fable finally throw down their weapons, on discovering that the causes for which they have so long been waging battle are in reality one and the same eternal causes,—the Cause of truth, of goodness, and of beauty; "the Glory of God and the relief of man's estate."

Although other intellectual leaders, including Henry Ward Beecher, Francis Abbot, and James McCosh, reconciled religion and the theory of evolution, no one appealed to so wide an audience as the versatile John Fiske. What he did in the religious and philosophical sphere William Graham Sumner did in the social and economic. The justification of the free competition of individuals in economic life by invoking the sanctions, not of traditional orthodox ideas, but of the new evolutionary theories, gives Sumner a prominent place in the group of intellectual leaders in the last quarter of the nineteenth century. Like Fiske and Harris, he sought to provide a formula which would give order and stability to an America torn by agrarian uprisings and labor troubles. In epigrammatic language, characterized by an appealing and homely wit, Sumner popularized from his chair of political and social science at Yale his essentially Darwinian version of laissez faire, his opposition to all notions of community responsibility for individual well-being, his denunciations of what appeared to him to be the soft sentimentality of reformers and radicals. Both as a celebrated teacher and as a widely read essayist, Sumner insisted that when social abuses appeared they must be met only by scientific procedures sponsored by competent authorities.

Sumner's individualism was the stark and somewhat questionable application to social issues of Darwin's doctrine of the struggle for existence and the survival of the fittest. This is clearly evident in "What Social Classes Owe to Each Other" (1883) and "The Absurd Attempt to Make the World Over" (1894), and "Commercial Crisis," to cite three of many essays.

The "strong" and the "weak" are terms which admit of no definition unless they are made equivalent to the industrious and the idle, the frugal and the extravagant. . . . If we do not like the survival of the fittest, we have only one possible alternative, and that is the survival of the unfittest. The former is the law of civilization; the latter is the law of anti-civilization.

The influential *Folkways* (1907) emphasized the doctrine that human sanctions lack rational validity and are relative to time and place. In this notable contribution to social theory Sumner still further lent support to an economic conservatism that found the security of the individual in the acceptance of his lot as both necessary and, in the larger scheme of things, good. The fact that he spoke in the name of the new evolutionary conception lent all the more weight to his justification of competitive individualism. This had resulted in great economic inequality, in widespread social insecurity, and in the preservation of a laissez faire philosophy which militated against the advance of the social legislation on which industrial societies in the Old World had already embarked.

The great limitation of Sumner's social thought was, of course, that with no understanding of the fact that government is a function of the groups able to exert power, he assumed that Jefferson's doctrine of "free men in a free society" was as valid in a highly interdependent and increasingly stratified America as it had been in the simple agrarian economy of the early nineteenth century.

In this assumption, to be sure, he was not alone. E. L. Godkin, editor of the New York *Evening Post* and of the *Nation,* a brilliant and witty Irish immigrant, represented, in the fashion of John and John Quincy Adams, the doctrine of an intellectual elite devoted to public honesty. Champion of property rights and critic of agrarianism and of organized labor, Godkin in true laissez faire spirit condemned the protective tariff as unwarranted favoritism to a special interest. His writings, largely editorials in the *Nation* and the *Evening Post,* advanced his social philosophy in pungent phrases and ironical twists of contemporary slang. His pen made even the driest subjects lively and memorable. His distinguished literary style showed no falling off as he became older; but his conception that the individual might, through exposing error and battling for decency, purge American society of its grossest faults, failed him in the end. The future came to seem to him too dark for his ideas to win their way.

In one notable respect both Sumner and Godkin differed from many writers who, like them, justified the traditional individualism in terms of evolutionary theory. Neither accepted the doctrine of the white man's burden in advancing a superior civilization among the more backward peoples of the globe. On the contrary, they stoutly opposed the growth of military and naval force and the imperial path which the country took during and after the Spanish-American War. They refused to be beguiled by the arguments of the Reverend Josiah Strong in *Our Country* (1885). They denied that Strong was justified in invoking the theory of evolution in support of a militant Protestant imperial program. Godkin and Sumner also vigorously condemned the doctrine of navalism popularized by Captain Alfred Mahan in his widely read and cogently written book, *The Influence of Sea Power upon History* (1890)

4

It is, of course, impossible to draw a hard and fast line between adherents of traditional doctrines and those who dealt with the new movements of thought and the new forces in American life. Yet in the last quarter of the nineteenth century and in the first decade of the twentieth a more or less clearly defined group did try to work out a synthesis between the older values and concepts of individualism and the newer concept of social responsibility for all individuals. In a general sense, this group was convinced that the root of the trouble in America, the great threat to the old-fashioned society in which individuals enjoyed relative security and freedom of opportunity, lay in the economic dislocation incident to the exhaustion of the open frontier and the startling growth of monopolies with their ruthless methods of competition and their strangle hold on government. Without giving up the conviction, cherished by Godkin, that public enlightenment is indispensable, the exponents of various types of radicalism were convinced of the ineffectiveness of the unorganized individual approach in reform, and favored some measure of collective action and the expansion of the functions of the government over private interests.

Yet the Marxist doctrines of economic determinism, class struggle, and the abolition of private property formed no part of the ideology of this group. As individualists anxious to restore waning individual autonomy they took their stand on the natural rights philosophy and insisted that they were merely extending it and giving it fresh applications which new economic conditions necessitated if the great creed of the Declaration of Independence were not to become a mere dead memory.

Among the significant writings which illustrate this general body of thought, Henry George's *Progress and Poverty* (1879) takes high rank by reason of its content, style, and influence. The central question posed in the book is: Why should increasing poverty accompany increasing civilization; in other words, how was it that more men had less of worldly goods as the country became more and more settled, and as more and more railroads, cities, and other instruments of civilization might logically be expected to ease man's lot? The central idea in the book is that every man has a natural right to apply his labor to land and to enjoy the full fruits thereof, and that this natural right had come to be greatly curtailed by the dominance of landlords. The increasing value of land in settled communities, George insisted, is created, not by the effort of the individual who had invested in it, often for mere speculative purposes, but by the contributions of the whole community. Therefore landlords in exacting economic rent—the "unearned increment" or the margin between the original outlay and the value of improvements he had made on the one hand and the market value on the other—are in effect robbing the user of the land of a part of his labor and the community of its social contribution to the increased market value.

This idea had been anticipated by the physiocrats, by Thomas Paine, by John Stuart Mill, by Herbert Spencer, and by a half-dozen less well known British and American land reformers. But George, a self-educated, poverty-stricken California journalist, had read none of their writings and had come to the idea as a result of his own observations and experiences. In relating it to American conditions he gave it an original turn. The central solution which *Progress and Poverty* proposed was to tax the unearned increment of land, to take back for the community that part of its value which the community, as it developed, had created. Such a tax, George maintained, would relieve industry and labor from all other taxes, inasmuch as it would be ample for the functions of the state: hence the term "single tax" readily became attached to his program.

The wide appeal of *Progress and Poverty* can be understood partly because of its clarity and its persuasiveness. George wrote simply but eloquently. He spoke with the conviction of a prophet. His trenchant indictment of speculation in land, of ownership by absentee landlords, and of monopoly of the earth, captured the imaginations of countless Americans. Its appeal was related to the fact that Americans were finding it increasingly hard to take up good land near channels of communication, and were feeling the pinch of high freight rates and dear prices for goods produced with less and less competition by larger and larger corporations.

The book went through a hundred editions before it was a quarter of a century old. It expressed the feeling of frustration of innumerable tenants, small businessmen, workers, indebted farmers, and struggling professional people. It cast its spell over Hamlin Garland, Brand Whitlock, and, to a certain extent, William Dean Howells. It provided a sort of corroboration for the drama depicted by Frank Norris in *The Octopus*. It inspired a few single-tax colonies, such as that in New Jersey where Upton Sinclair lived for a time.

The single-tax doctrine did not succeed in its larger purposes. Nor could it have done so in view of George's failure to implement the movement by building an organization capable of wielding political power; in view, above all, of its oversimplified economic theory, its failure to comprehend fully the nature of the new capitalism with its endless ramifications. Yet no one can deny that the book inspired, or at least accentuated, general awareness of the evils of land monopoly and the bearing of this condition on the relative autonomy so many Americans had once enjoyed. *Progress and Poverty* is of its time and place, but it is more than this. It is a great human document, a powerful statement of popular indignation and popular aspirations. It is a classic in the literature of American ideas.

Even when its greatness is fully recognized, the appeal of *Progress and Poverty* can hardly be understood without recalling that it was only one book among many which passionately protested against the encroachment of great aggregates of wealth on the ordinary individual. Two years after its publication William Dean Howells accepted for the *Atlantic Monthly* an article which had already been rejected by more conservative editors. It was entitled "The Story of a Great Monopoly." Its author was Henry Demarest Lloyd, a free-trade enthusiast and free-lance Chicago journalist. It portrayed succinctly and dramatically the methods by which the Standard Oil Company had risen to power by pushing its competitors to the wall by any methods, however unethical, so long as they "worked." It brought home to its readers the idea that business, hitherto either applauded or ignored by most men of letters, possessed antisocial characteristics: thus it heralded the essential message that Thorstein Veblen was later to develop. If any single piece of writing may be said to have inaugurated a new movement, this article did. "The Story of a Great Monopoly" introduced to America "the literature of exposure," or, as Theodore Roosevelt called it at its height, some twenty-five years later, "muckraking."

The *Atlantic* piece was followed by other writings in which Lloyd exposed the acquisitive and antisocial practices of the grain elevator magnates and manufacturers and the railroad men who trafficked in rebates. But Lloyd's writing was in no sense merely negative. He defended the interests of small businessmen, consumers, organized workers, even the Haymarket anarchists, whose belief in direct action he deplored. His impassioned plea for industrial justice in *A Strike of Millionaires Against Miners* (1890) indicated a sympathy with labor far stronger than Henry George's. *Man, the Social Creator* (1906) approached in quality the writings of the Christian Socialists. In this work Lloyd emphasized his faith in the ability of struggling, suffering humanity to achieve a common well-being through fusing economic cooperation with Christian ethics. It reflected his basic conviction that since men are sufficiently intelligent and honest to manage the business of other men for them, they are likewise intelligent and honest enough to be entrusted with the commonwealth of society—its mines, mills, and stores.

Lloyd will be remembered not so much for these later writings as for an elaborate documentation of the little article on Standard Oil which had launched his career. *Wealth Against Commonwealth* (1894) undermined much classical economic doctrine by showing the gulf between prevalent laissez faire theory and actual practice. Its facts were challenged at the time and have been challenged since; but the picture he painted of powerful men accumulating riches through an unfettered acquisitive bent and by the molding of government, churches, and education to their purpose, has, at any rate, the broad essentials of truth. Here Lloyd proved, whatever else he demonstrated or failed to show, that it was possible to present the findings of Congressional committees and court decrees with such clarity and human appeal that writing on economic issues could rise to a high level.

Lloyd's wit and skillful turning of phrases, his startling antitheses, the passionate depth of feeling revealed even in his most factual statements, gave to *Wealth Against Commonwealth* a distinguished place in the literature of ideas of the last quarter of the nineteenth century. Although Lloyd's work was continued by the muckrakers, who, during the Presidency of Theodore Roosevelt, exposed evils in the industrial and political life of the nation, *Wealth Against Commonwealth* remains the classic in "the literature of exposure."

Perhaps one reason for this is the sustained and positive conviction of its author that the individual can achieve earthly salvation only through cooperation with his fellows for economic and social well-being. The theoretical basis of this conviction was elaborately explored and systematized by Lester Frank Ward, government employee and natural scientist, who ranks with Spencer and Comte in the founding of modern sociology. Ward was profoundly influenced by the doctrine of evolution, just as were Fiske, Sumner, and others, but he drew from it more than Sumner's justifications for laissez faire and rugged individualism. To him evolution is not merely a blind, mechanistic, trial and error process, in which planned foresight and intelligence are negligible, but rather a cosmic force in which the active efforts of men's minds have played a decisive role. Ward urged that, whatever differences there may be between individuals in their innate gifts, or between the sexes or the races, every individual can realize his potentialities far more effectively than is supposed possible by people who accept the prevailing laissez faire theory. Thus Ward advocated a new type of education on a mass scale, an education in which the scientific spirit and method figured in a large way. Above all he favored the use of the government as an active, creative agency in such economic and social planning as might best achieve men's highest possibilities.

Ward invented a whole series of obscure, strange terms and these, together with his ponderous and often opaque style, kept his lengthy treatises, *Dynamic Sociology* (1883), *Outlines in Sociology* (1898), and *Pure Sociology* (1903–1918) from being widely known. The most readable of his books, *The Psychic Factors of Civilization* (1893), remains an arresting and significant statement of his beliefs. Its distinction lies in its forceful insistence that within a monistic and activistic universe the human mind has been and can be in the future in even larger degree, a creative force for the democracy and humanitarianism without which only a handful of individuals can truly live.

Among those who were particularly indebted to Ward, the most important figure is Thorstein Veblen. His skeptical and iconoclastic mind owed something to the Populist fever, which publicized the attack on "predatory" Wall Street in the Middle West where Veblen was born and reared; it owed at least as much to his revolt against the conservative Norwegian-American community he was part of and to his failure ever to feel thoroughly at home outside it. After graduating from Carleton College in Minnesota, Veblen studied at intervals at Johns Hopkins, Yale, and Cornell. Although some of his early work reveals the germ of his theories, these were not fully presented until 1899, when *The Theory of the Leisure Class* appeared. In 1904 *The Theory of Business Enterprise* carried his social theory still further.

Veblen approached the economic institutions and values of modern capitalism from evolutionary, anthropological, and psychological points of view. In his mind the production and distribution of goods had been, from the earliest times, subject to a struggle between the predatory and the industrious: the modern captain of industry was a lineal descendant of the robber baron, the hard-working laborer of the old-time artisan. Modern business, which Veblen regarded as something very different from industry, ruled through the price system—a system which, with modern machinery, frustrated the instinctive creative urge in the worker to see and enjoy the fruits of his toil. Modern business, moreover, covered its wastefulness with all sorts of rationalizations which, Veblen believed, infected religion, education, and every aspect of society. In his later life he sought to demonstrate that war and patriotism had become functional to business and equally hostile to the interests of mankind; and he was much impressed by the Russian Revolution and by the possibility of the direction of industrial life by engineers and technologists in the interest of all individuals.

Veblen's style is verbose and at times turgid. He makes use of elaborate anthropological analogies, and resorts to baffling phrases and to the twisting of conventional meanings. In its irony this writing is frequently powerful, even devastating; but it is too heavy to attract many readers.

Veblen failed to revolutionize orthodox academic theory, but he presented a sweeping and profound indictment of production for profit and of its impact on individuals. The social and economic theory of no other American writer is so original. In time a younger generation was, consciously or unconsciously, greatly influenced by his basic theories.

5

Yet it was not, after all, Veblen to whom, among all the writers of the literature of ideas, the future really belonged. Although it probably cannot be said to have belonged to any single one, William James presents the best synthesis of the ideas of his time and presents them in a literary style which no other, not even Henry Adams, surpasses in directness and clarity.

In the first place, James brought together and harmonized in a new working relationship the conflict between religion and science. Inheriting from his Swedenborgian and philosophical-minded father a deep and abiding interest in spiritual values and in religious ideas, James as a young man felt poignantly the conflict between these and the scientific theories he came to accept. It was, above all, the apparently deterministic implications of science, especially Darwinism, that troubled James. The result of his reflections on the conflict between the doctrines of free will and determinism was at length presented in *The Varieties of Religious Experience*. The meaning of this book cannot be understood apart from his philosophical thought, which was comprised in *The Will to Believe* (1897), *Pragmatism* (1907), *A Pluralistic Universe* (1909), and *Essays in Radical Empiricism* (1912).

Acknowledging his indebtedness to Charles S. Peirce and to the whole tradition of British empiricism, James maintained that the test of the truthfulness of ideas is to be found in the relationship between these ideas and their practical consequences in action. Ideas, even so-called supernatural ideas, are to be regarded as instruments subject to constant retesting in the hazardous experiment which all life in essence really is. If in this process, ideas provide personal and emotional satisfaction, then they are to be regarded as true in the sense only that they enable the individual for the time to deal satisfactorily with concrete problems. An idea "true" at any given time for any given person may not be true for others, or even for that person under different circumstances. This is necessarily so since the universe itself is an unfinished experiment, so rich and varied in its meanings for each individual that no final, absolute "truth" is possible.

Such a position enabled James to hold, as he did in *The Varieties of Religious Experience,* that any item of religious faith is true for any individual for whom it provides emotional satisfactions. This position could not satisfy the craving for final truth, for the Absolute, but for those who could accept it, it provided a working equilibrium of satisfactions: it harmonized faith with scientific knowledge and method by denying any necessary conflict in the never-finished open universe.

In his later philosophical thought James carried the implications of pragmatism even further. In the spirit of the experimentalist he gave the connections between sense experience a psychological status on a par with whatever was actually connected. The way was thus opened still further to the reconciliation of faith with the scientific method: the data of faith, the ideas men have about things, become true and important in themselves by virtue of the status given to relationships.

It is impossible to separate James' philosophy from his psychology. More than any other American, he pioneered in the application of the concept of evolution to the explanation of mind. In so doing he came to the conclusion that mind cannot properly be regarded as the antithesis of body: that it must rather be thought of as the function by which the human organism, like all organisms, adjusts itself to its environment. This was the basic position in his great *Principles of Psychology* (1890). James' emphasis was, it is true, on the individual as an adjusting mechanism, rather than on his environment. Thus the role of instincts and habits played a major part in his psychological thinking. Nevertheless his functional conception of mind as an instrument of adjustment enabled him to reconcile such "deterministic" forces as heredity and biology with effort, choice, and, properly defined, with "free will" itself. Toward the end of his life James argued for a functionalism which sees in the term "mind" not an entity different from the body, but a general name for certain types of symbolic adjustment. It was James' psychology that, extended by Dewey and others, influenced the great majority of American educators to adopt, in theory at least, the ideal of education as training for adjustment to life. Education became psychologically based. The school became child-centered. Individualism was reenforced; but individualism in terms of adjustment to environment. Above all, James' psychology provided ammunition against the lock step in the classroom.

What were the larger implications of James' thought for the conflict between the traditional emphasis on the autonomy of the individual and the demands of the new interdependent society for cooperative living? Hating all forms of tyranny, power, bigness, loving the infinite variability he detected in the universe, convinced that human nature could mold a better future, James celebrated the energies of men, actual and potential. In his scheme men are morally free agents determining their own destiny. He emphasized the "instincts" of competition, acquisitiveness, and freedom of action; and his social attitudes were largely those of the traditional laissez faire school of his political mentor, E. L. Godkin. "Religiously and philosophically," James wrote, "our ancient doctrine of live and let live may prove to have a far deeper meaning tnan our people now seem to imagine it to possess." Though he had not lived in any part of the country which had recently borne the impact of the frontier, James' social philosophy in a considerable measure expressed that democratic individualism which Frederick Jackson Turner in his famous essay on "The Significance of the Frontier in American History" made the key to American experience. To James there was something heroic and exhilarating in the struggles of the poor man against all sorts of material odds. The assumption was, of course, that such struggles breed character, bring out all one's potentialities, and add true zest to life.

In all this there was much that was traditionally American. The philosophy of James was optimistic, melioristic, individualistic. It postulated faith in newness, in beginnings, in youth, in the freedom to make mistakes, to pick up and start over again. There was something very American in this cosmopolitan's insistence on an open universe, on the active and voluntary nature of human behavior, and, most important of all, in his rejection of absolutes and his doctrine that hypotheses help to make the truth they declare—if they prove effective instruments in living. He spoke for the faith of the old America in disparaging system makers and systems, in taking his stand on the broad ground of experience, concrete realities, tolerance for dissidents, and the glories of choice and risk. What was more American, more democratic, indeed, than the pragmatic conviction that beliefs *become* true by *making good?* What was more American and more democratic than the insistence that philosophy must give satisfactions to the emotional, the temperamental needs, not only of the philosopher, but of the common man? Here was the reassertion of Emerson's emphasis on self-reliance and of Whitman's song of the open road.

Yet James offered more than the reassertion of the traditional values of the democratic individualism for which his fellow countrymen longed, had faith in, but knew not exactly where to find. Although he could see good in the existence of inequalities in wealth, he also on occasion declared that if the odds in the struggle were too great, the human spirit might be broken rather than tested. Although he believed that the pugnacious instinct made war "natural," he maintained that this "instinct" need not necessarily express itself in war. In his famous essay on "The Moral Equivalent for War" he advocated the channeling of man's "instinctive" love of a fight into a cooperative attack on the obstacles of physical nature in behalf of the public good; he envisaged bands of youth fighting forest fires and drought, building hazardous highways over and through mountains, reclaiming physical environment for the commonwealth. In other words, James sensed, and explicitly said in his last years, that the society of the future would become, by necessity, more socialistic. He tried to show how at the same time the traditional American values of self-help, initiative, competition, and the zest for living might also survive. This was the synthesis of the old and the new that James offered his fellow countrymen.

The ideas of William James, especially some of his social opinions, betrayed the limitations of his personal experience as a member of the advantaged class. Many Americans, even democratic and individualistic Americans, rejected his philosophy on the score that it justified an opportunism and a narrow expediency. In denying the possibility of fixed moorings, he may have opened the gate to the confusion, drift, and ineffectiveness which, according to some writers, characterized the modern man who has rejected ultimates and absolutes. James does, indeed, open himself to these and to still other charges. But he himself would have admitted as much. He would have insisted that the risks and chances so characteristic of his philosophy are necessary unless life is to be so restricted and ordered that the joy of individual living is lost altogether.

The idea of an open universe was unquestionably deeply related to American experience and faith, and time has shown that it was not to be lightly laid aside. In James it found its most brilliant and engaging champion. In demanding a world that left plenty of room for effort and that made effort the most valued of man's activities, and in relating this demand to the confident faith that the individual need not be defeated by nature or by his fellows or by himself, James was epitomizing the dominant theme in the literature of ideas that made his generation a pivotal one in American intellectual development.

60. FICTION AND SOCIAL DEBATE

F<small>OR</small> these direct traders in ideas, literary form presented no problem; but for writers of poetry, drama, or fiction, the problem was one of altering old structures so that they might contain the new views of man and his universe. It was the problem, in a new form, that had beset Brockden Brown, Cooper, and Melville in their turns.

Whatever their ideologies, the novelists of social debate generally understood the craft of fiction as it had been conventionalized in the nineteenth century. From its very beginning, the novel in England had disseminated ideas as well as stories, and had served to instruct and illumine as well as to entertain. As the industrial revolution matured in the United States, it provoked here, as previously in England, a vigorous critical movement in which men like Henry George and Edward Bellamy wrought at the same tasks that occupied such great Victorian critics as Carlyle, Dickens, and Morris; and as in them, it suggested the use of story for the illumination of ideas.

The American social and economic novelists knew and practiced the narrator's fundamental business, that of getting an interesting story under way and keeping it going. Their plots follow the old, established patterns, adapted with considerable skill to the portrayal of the American industrial scene and to the illustration of the authors' ideas. It is their scenes and characters—particularly their characters—that reveal how much they enlarged the area of awareness known to the American novel. For better or for worse, their pages throng with a miscellany of types hardly anticipated in the era of Irving and Hawthorne: the abandoned urban poor as a class, the corrupt walking delegate, the prostitute, the old-fashioned middle-class businessman, the business adventurer, the capitalist's henchman, the venal politician, the social climber, the wealthy dilettante, the reformer, idealist, and settlement worker, and, far from least, the great capitalist himself, prime mover in the whole upsurge of industrialized big business.

The problem novel of the eighties and nineties was an instrument of the still powerful middle classes whose civilization was threatened by the disruptions of the machine age and particularly by the dominance of big business. Though uneasily aware of the proletariat, the typical middle-class author felt the essential conflict of his times as a struggle, not between capital and labor, but between the plutocracy and the people; and it was in relation to this central conflict that he tried to interpret the many subsidiary debates over the currency, immigration, the slums, the idle rich, the Populist movement, and the manipulation of the government by big business. Yet the novelist could not, if he would, have sorted his ideas into watertight compartments and thereby have isolated these economic issues from others. A story of economic struggle was likely to become also a story of politics or marriage or prostitution; and if the writer were aware of Spencer and Darwin, it might easily pass on to the profounder issues of chance versus teleology, of science versus religion, of the material versus the ideal.*

Curiously enough, the novel of politics, which might well have flourished among a people so politically minded, was long in outgrowing a narrow scope of experience and a limited philosophy. The usual subject of the political novelist was the corruption of the government, whether municipal, state, or federal; or, at the least, the manipulation of the government by special interests. It matters little whether these interests derive from the Pennsylvania whisky ring, as in Rebecca Harding Davis' *John Andross* (1874); or from the traction enterprises of a great city, as in Charles K. Lush's *The Autocrats* (1901); or from the railroads, as in Winston Churchill's *Mr. Crewe's Career* (1908). In all, with a few exceptions such as Henry Adams' *Democracy* (1880), the plot arises out of the struggle between the general public on the one hand, and the corrupting forces of special interest and privilege on the other.

The novel of economics, while more various than the novel of politics, developed despite its variety a fairly clear-cut intellectual pattern. Ideologically, the majority of economic novels occupy a position just left of center; that is, they look toward the exposure and reform of the abuses of private enterprise, not to the abolition of private enterprise itself. Overwhelmingly middle-class, these novels are in effect weapons forged for use in the struggle for class survival; but they are also a great deal more. They are an expression of the middle-class economic code of productive work, prudence, thrift, and honesty. They are a product of the continuing American quest for a better life for each one among all the people; they embody the American version of that nineteenth century liberal philosophy—lingering twilight of the Enlightenment—which seeks social justice as a prelude to the limitless development of the individual. While they occasionally reveal influences and illuminations from abroad, they are chiefly a creation of American social idealism working upon American materials.

* Four novelists who explored the philosophical implications of this conflict—Garland, Crane, Norris, and London, are discussed in Chapter 62.

Within the intellectual pale of the left center, there was scope for vigor and keenness in treatment, and for abundance and variety of subject matter. The economic novelists could, and did, make fiction out of such issues as the humanitarian's effort to alleviate suffering, the corrupting influence of big business, the trust problem, widely debated issues such as the currency and Populism, and impulses toward Christian Socialism or the Social Gospel. Among the subjects most frequently and ably handled was that of the emptiness of merely financial or merely social "success." The bourgeois folly of acquiring wealth and position without values is exposed in dozens of novels, including Charles Dudley Warner's *A Little Journey in the World* (1889), H. H. Boyesen's *Social Strugglers* (1893), and Robert Grant's *Unleavened Bread* (1900).

Ideologically, the novelists of the left center are at their best in destructive criticism; their examination of the evils of laissez faire capitalism is wide-ranging, informed, and vigorous. They abound in specific illustration of the knaveries of business; they dramatize unforgettably the splitting of a relatively homogeneous, democratic people into sharply defined classes of the rich and the poor. But, representing no single self-conscious movement or literary school, they failed to agree on any single program of reform. Their constructive energies are dissipated in miscellaneous proposals for slum clearance, settlement work, profit sharing, labor organization, or the gradual Christianizing of the social order.

In the critical examination of capitalism, the few novelists of the middle-class left were in general agreement with those of the left center. In the advocacy of radical reform, they might be found either in the individualistic camp of Henry George, as was Garland in *Jason Edwards: an Average Man* (1892), or in the collectivistic camp of Edward Bellamy, as were many of the lesser utopian romancers who were drawn along in the powerful wake of *Looking Backward*. More numerous than the radicals, and on the whole an abler group of writers, were the moderate conservatives, whose position was right center rather than definitely to the right. From the conservatives proceeded a few vigorous defenses of old-fashioned "solid" individual enterprise, such as Alice French's story of the economic education of John Winslow in *The Man of the Hour* (1905), and a somewhat larger number of attacks on organized labor, including John Hay's popular but superficial treatment of the labor organizer in *The Breadwinners* (1884), and F. Hopkinson Smith's ably written study of union-conducted persecution in *Tom Grogan* (1896).

But the best and most characteristic product of the right center was the romance of economic conflict, in which the author, unconcerned with social justice, satisfied with the status quo, uses as a narrative framework the conflict of business, force with force or man with man. Among others, Will Payne in

The Money Captain (1898) and of course Frank Norris in *The Pit* (1903) cleverly developed suspense and dramatic tension out of the incidents of business struggle. From the hesitant beginnings of J. G. Holland and others in the seventies down through the vigorous portrayal of the self-made Harrington in Robert Herrick's *Memoirs of an American Citizen* (1905), the characterization of the big businessman advanced from conventionality and moral primness toward original comprehension and adequacy; so that the studies done by Payne in *The Money Captain,* by Norris in *The Pit,* and by Herrick in the *Memoirs* are worthy forerunners of Theodore Dreiser's massive Cowperwood trilogy.

2

In the words Goethe once applied to Carlyle, Edward Bellamy was, first of all, a moral force. The matrix of his character was the moral idealism which he developed amidst the liberal Christianity of his childhood home at Chicopee Falls, Massachusetts. As a youth, he nourished a Miltonic sense of dedication to high and noble ends, along with a non-Miltonic vein of mingled gentleness and melancholy. Except for a certain dearth of robust energy, Bellamy's was the personality of a major creative artist. He had imagination; he had emotional elevation and intensity; he had, above all, the curiosity, the intellectual élan which urged on his wide-ranging inquiries into history, biography, philosophy, military science, languages, and mathematics.

The focus of Bellamy's life work, and indeed of the whole movement of latter nineteenth century liberalism in America, is the Utopian *Looking Backward, 2000–1887* (1888). Few books appear, on the surface, more deceptively simple; only the greatest represent, actually, the confluence and creative fusion of more numerous and widely disparate forces. From young manhood, almost indeed from childhood, Bellamy had been sensitively aware of social injustice, and had felt that the most fundamental of all reforms would be a more equitable distribution of wealth. During the seventies, as reviewer and columnist for the Springfield *Union,* he had vigorously criticized child labor, the "caste" system in society, and the "feudalism" of industrial organization. During the eighties he could not have avoided, even had he wished, the currents of fresh new thought that were blowing in America over the subject of social reform; but one cannot yet say with certainty just when, or from just what causes. he experienced his conversion to socialism. In all likelihood he was affected by his knowledge of the Inca civilization of old Peru, and no doubt he was deeply impressed by the possibility of using for industrial ends the principle of universal military service. Nevertheless, the decisive turn in his thinking (although the matter is still controversial) appears to have come with his reading of Laurence Gronlund's *The Cooperative Commonwealth* (1884), and from the blending of Gronlund's modified Marxism with his own previous democratic, humanitarian, and Christian philosophy.

Meanwhile, although Bellamy had written one social novel, *The Duke of Stockbridge* (serially published, 1879), his chief experience in fiction had been in the genteel romance—in the subdued but finely imagined stories, *Dr. Heidenhoff's Process* (1880) and *Miss Ludington's Sister* (1884). Although this kind of story might appear ill-suited to provide the narrative frame for a significant Utopia, the unlikely combination had already been made, successfully, by John Macnie in his futurity story, *The Diothas* (1880), some elements of which, through Bellamy's conscious or subconscious memory, reappear in the pages of *Looking Backward*. Altogether, the complexity of the sources that contributed to Bellamy's Utopia is only less remarkable than the creative effort by which his imagination fused them into harmonious and almost organic life.

As a romance, *Looking Backward* relates how its hero, Julian West, awakens from a century's mesmeric sleep in Boston of the year 2000, and, utterly alone in that alien though splendid century, finds companionship in the love of Edith Leete. As an essay in Utopian thought, it relates how Julian West is instructed both in the advantages of the new cooperative commonwealth and in the evils of the abandoned system of competitive capitalism. For the Utopian form of fiction has remained true to the patterns employed by Plato and More; it is more than a dream-vision, it is a keen-edged knife of critical attack, and as such Bellamy employs it in penetrating exposure of the weaknesses of private enterprise: the wastefulness and inefficiency in production, the creation of futility among the rich and misery among the poor, and the fatal attrition, at all levels of society, of the finer human values. How different, all this, from the felicity of the cooperative state of the twenty-first century, from which poverty and exploitation have been forever banished. There, the Machine gives man the mastery over nature and creates for him an economy of abundance; and the State, through its command of production and distribution, guarantees that all share equally in the opulence they have helped create. Nor has this socialistic state been purchased at the cost of violent revolution; it has come into being in the course of the natural evolution of middle-class democracy from the political realm into the economic.

The end of that evolution is not to be material prosperity alone; it is to be, rather, the building of a vaster spiritual home, for the habitation of a progressively finer race. Leisure and abundance find their proper fruitage not merely in universal comfort, but in universal higher education, in learning, in creative art, in the fulfillment of the loftiest spiritual aspirations. Above all, the institution of marriage, freed from its ancient economic clogs, is to foster progressively in the race the finer virtues of love and awareness, and is to improve them, by sexual selection, from generation to generation. The cooperative commonwealth is therefore to be more than just an economic system; it is to mark "the rise of the race to a new plane with an illimitable vista of progress." "Humanity has burst its chrysalis. The heavens are above it."

The artistry of *Looking Backward* is essentially that of romantic contrast —not, of course, a contrast of moods or scenes or even of personalities, but that of two great systems of living, the competitive system of the past and the cooperative system of the future. Almost from the beginning, the intellectual conflict between these two is felt. As scene follows scene, the conflict heightens, like the tightening suspense of Elizabethan drama. At the last it culminates in the hero's return, in sickening dream, to the hideous slums of a competitive metropolis, and his sudden awakening from this nightmare into the clear, free morning of the new cooperative world. And yet, carefully wrought as is the artistry of *Looking Backward,* the book as a whole is more—far more— than that. More successfully than any previous work, it carries our American democratic ideology over from politics into economics. Alongside the Marxian collectivism of class conflict and revolutionary violence, it sets up an American collectivism of orderly democracy and peaceful evolution. The huge potentialities of the Machine it assimilates, imaginatively, into the ancient aims and uses of humane culture. In its optimism, its expectation of progress, its democracy, and its spiritual pioneering, it is one of the major expressions of nineteenth century liberalism; and in its blending of these with a hundred other mental and spiritual resources, it achieves one of the great modern syntheses of humane values.

Along with certain repercussions abroad—notably William Morris' *News from Nowhere* (1890)—*Looking Backward* initiated in the United States a vogue of Utopian debate that lasted until after the turn of the century. The book became all but universally known, and its immense popularity overshadowed and determined Bellamy's later work. With the formation of numerous Bellamy clubs, with the rise of the amorphous Nationalist "party," Bellamy felt it his duty and opportunity to lead in the reform movements directed toward the realization of his own dreams. Instead of continuing the romancer and artist, he became the publicist, the propagandist, the editor of the reform journals, the *Nationalist* and the *New Nation.* Evidently he felt it his duty, too, to make his case for the cooperative commonwealth as systematic, as logically impregnable, as it was emotionally satisfying. Toward this objective, largely, he directed the elaborate sequel to *Looking Backward, Equality* (1897), a closely argued, informed, and ingenious treatise, but one whose elaborately buttressed arguments are, after all, no substitute for the art and the emotional power of its predecessor.

3

The middle-class novel of social debate, though it developed a discernible consensus of interest and opinion, was never a clearly defined, highly integrated genre. It is reflected in novels as widely different from Bellamy's as were those of Harold Frederic, whose writing anticipates the mingled realism, naturalism, and disillusion of the twentieth century. Frederic's first novel, *Seth's Brother's Wife* (1887) anticipates Garland's *Main-Travelled Roads* in its removal of the false glamour with which the romantic era had invested rural life, and in its curiously provocative study of passion touches deep instinctive motives which the genteel novelists of the period preferred to avoid. *The Lawton Girl* (1890) is akin to the typical middle-class social novel in its awareness of the capital-labor conflict, but differs in its unsentimental and unconventional treatment of sex.

It was in *The Damnation of Theron Ware* (1896), however, that Frederic most appealed to his contemporaries. *Theron Ware* is a strongly imagined, vigorously developed story of a Methodist minister who, while increasingly aware of the crudeness, even the coarseness and hypocrisy necessitated by his evangelical environment, is nevertheless unable to make a successful escape. In its unsympathetic study of small-town Methodism the novel anticipates Sinclair Lewis, but without Lewis' distortions and exaggerations. Quite different from *Theron Ware,* Frederic's later novels, such as *Gloria Mundi* (1898) and *The Market Place* (1899), products of his residence abroad, disclose his interest in English society and in the romance of financial intrigue.

As Frederic's atypical writing suggests, the novel of social debate was losing, even before 1900, the clearness of focus which it had possessed as an expression of nineteenth century liberalism. From 1900 on, problem novels, while increasing in numbers, had still less cohesion as a genre. Temporarily, the novel advocating liberal reform declined in favor of the amoral story of economic or political conflict. After a time, the reforming energies of the middle class once more found expression, though of limited scope, in the work of the "muckrakers" and in the "progressive" attitudes associated with Theodore Roosevelt. Class-conscious spokesmen for the proletariat were appearing, meanwhile, in the persons of Jack London and Upton Sinclair.

The muckrakers were by no means the first writers to expose the scandals of business and politics. They differed from their predecessors, however, in the specific, personal direction of their attacks, and in their intimate liaison with popular journalism. The discovery of the mass appeal of exposure was made by the publisher S. S. McClure, who assembled for *McClure's Magazine* such brilliant writers and investigators as Ida M. Tarbell, Ray Stannard Baker, and, ablest thinker of them all, Lincoln Steffens. With little of the broad general philosophy of a Bellamy or a George, the muckrakers wrote out of a simple code of individual effort and honesty, and rested their hope of reform on the power and popularity of exposure. Although their chief medium was the feature article, they affected fiction through their provision of milieu and materials for stories of a "progressive" slant, such as those of Winston Churchill and William Allen White.

Perhaps the ablest novelist associated with the muckrakers, David Graham Phillips, served his apprenticeship as a journalist with the New York *Sun* and *World* in the nineties, and emerged as free-lance writer and novelist shortly after 1900. Phillips was a talented writer—artistically serious, somewhat didactic, capable of sustained hard work, and, above all, equipped with a certain rugged integrity. His scheme of values, while not so inclusive as Bellamy's, was a substantial one, firmly held. Genuine success, genuine fulfillment, meant to him "the exaltation that comes through a sense of a life lived to the very limit of its possibilities; a life of self-development, self-expansion, self-devotion to the emancipation of man." Most of his stories deal with the quest for success, in which only a few of his people discover the genuine thing, while the majority arrive only at the specious rewards of acquisition, power, and social prestige.

In the earlier novels of Phillips, economic and political themes are primary, while the impact of social forces on sex and marriage is secondary; in the later novels, the proportion is reversed. His first novel, *The Great God Success* (1901), relates how a young journalist finally sacrifices his integrity to the winning of worldly "success"—a term which Phillips later sarcastically defined as meaning "the accumulation of riches enough to enable one to make a stir even among the very rich." Others illustrate the destructive effect of great wealth on a family, the working of the money power in politics, and the notorious insurance scandals of the times. But in *The Second Generation* (1907) Phillips' theme has deepened from mere exposure to the moral renaissance which a wealthy young brother and sister experience when subjected to hard work and responsibility; and, in the subplot of Adelaide Ranger and Dory Hargreave, he approaches those problems of marital adjustment which he examines more fully in the complementary studies *The Hungry Heart* (1909) and *The Husband's Story* (1910). The latter of these, especially, in the firmness of its handling and in the sustained objectivity with which the husband-narrator is made to reveal not only his wife's personality but his own, is a worthy creation of the same vigorous talent that elaborated the immensely detailed pages of *Susan Lenox, Her Fall and Rise* (1917).

Less the journalist, less the teacher than Phillips, his contemporary Robert Herrick was at once the humanist, devoted to the discovery and statement of values, and the artist, striving to realize imaginatively his world. Surrounded by an industrio-capitalistic society, drawing his materials almost wholly from it, he neither defended it nor tried directly to reform it, but, instead, in story after story assayed its possibilities for creative, civilized living. For, to Herrick, the civilized life was, at bottom, the creative life, whether the creative talent wrought itself out in the work of farming, or of merchandise, or of the professions, or of the fine arts. True creation, he felt, requires of the individual a firm sense of personal responsibility, an austere integrity. The ideal life would balance in supreme tension the utmost adventurousness with the utmost order. For an American, it would be lived with vigorous realism in contemporary America, but it would be illumined by an awareness of the long European experience in civilized living.

Of Herrick's characters, those with whom he is most in sympathy struggle to live themselves into some such experience of humane values. His hero or heroine strives to build, within the conditions imposed by modern American society, a fine adult personality. The antagonist is seldom an individual; it is usually the crass Philistinism of society as a whole, the coarsening and enervating influence of a vast system of competition for a wholly materialistic "success." The conflict between these two forces seldom ends "happily." Herrick's characters either sacrifice integrity for profit, or develop lives of tragic emptiness, or at best arrive at the severe calm of renunciation. His indictment of society is, then, simply that it makes fine living so tragically difficult and rare.

Herrick's earlier novels, such as *The Common Lot* (1904), illustrate this conflict between creativeness and acquisition; but the *Memoirs of an American Citizen* (1905) is a realistic story of the rise, work, and character of a self-made executive and capitalist, Edward Van Harrington. Acting on the Nietzschean principle, "the strong must rule," Harrington competes and bribes without scruple, yet remains true to his own tough-minded code of personal responsibility and productive work. Credible, finely imagined, told with a consistent detachment that almost attains objectivity, the *Memoirs* is the most impressive American picture of the great capitalist prior to Dreiser's *The Financier.*

Clark's Field (1914), one of Herrick's happiest efforts, is a remarkably successful blend of fantasy and realism, at once a delicately beautiful Cinderella story and a study, which would have delighted Henry George, in the social effects of unearned increment. Unlikely enough in itself, the plot of *Clark's Field* takes on, under Herrick's full, even-toned, and consistent elaboration, the texture and the credibility of fine fiction. *Clark's Field* was the last of Herrick's writings to be cast largely in the nineteenth century mold. For, between this and his next major novel, he lived through the tumultuous years of the First World War, the Versailles Conference, and America's return to "normalcy" in the early twenties. During these years, he witnessed the rise of the "new poetry," the sudden popularity of such adventurous spirits as Lewis and O'Neill, and the vogue of a social criticism concerned less with injustice than with the limitations of our total culture.

Within this fresh, invigorating milieu, Herrick returned to the theme of certain of his earlier novels—the rebellion of a sensitive professional mind against the life-destroying forces of commercialism; but now he was able to treat that theme with less reserve, upon a larger canvas, and with the assured power of practiced maturity. In *Waste* (1924), the engineer Jarvis Thornton, who has found in the Progressive Movement only disillusion, whose marriage and liaison are both wrecked because of the excessive property sense of society, comes to feel in that society "a sense of corruption working at the very roots of life, turning it into some obscene joke, a meaningless tale told in the void. . . . Waste! All waste!"

Herrick did not again achieve the richness and the tragic scope of *Waste*. In *Chimes* (1926), he disposed against an academic background, suggestive of the University of Chicago, a number of deft characterizations illustrating the interaction of the higher learning with the pressures of a moneyed society. In *The End of Desire* (1932), he exposed the decadence latent in the new cult of sexual freedom. And in his last full-length fiction, the Utopian *Sometime* (1933), he expressed his despair of present American civilization and his hope of a remote future in which men will begin the search for the good life not by accumulating possessions, but by building personalities at once governable and creative.

If fine fiction required only acute observation, significant ideas, integrity, wisdom, and craftsmanship, then it would be difficult indeed not to regard Robert Herrick as America's foremost social novelist. But these resources, however indispensable, are not, in themselves, quite enough. Within them and above them must be also the elusive tension, emotional and imaginative, which fuses and kindles the novel into an actively experienced delight. This dramatic tension was low-keyed or lacking in Herrick; and the effect of his novels is often, in consequence, not that of artful and kindling story, but that of intellectual analysis, frequently static and sometimes dull.

4

Unlike Herrick, his younger contemporary Upton Sinclair had the born story teller's knack of swiftly moving action; and as a young writer of pulpwood fiction he developed also the knack of mass appeal and of enormously prolific production. As a novelist of ideas, Sinclair is first of all the product of his family, whose aristocratic connections had their share in the forming of his generous though somewhat self-conscious culture, and whose financial insecurity was one source of his proletarian sympathies. His early Christianity survives, too, in his sturdy clinging to immaterial values in a materialistic age, and in an ethical earnestness which has been inaccurately labeled as "Puritan." His own youthful temperament, first fully manifest during his college days, was one of intensity, of overpowering energy. Careless of classroom routine, he educated himself by voracious reading, during which he grew passionately devoted to the prophets and poets of rebellion and social justice—to Isaiah and Jesus, to Milton and Shelley. He sought the good life actively, in dynamic pursuit, and he continued to seek it. The inquirer, the searcher for values, was never wholly absorbed in the propagandist.

Sinclair's first novels, apart from hack-writing, grew out of a deliberately chosen struggle to express himself as a creative artist and to survive by means of his creative work. The struggle was heartrending; and the bitterness of it helped turn the potential poet into the rebel and partisan controversialist. Of these early writings the best is *Manassas* (1904), a historical novel in which much of the mature Sinclair appears in the germ. Here history is treated not romantically, after the fashion of the times, but ideologically, as seen now by Sinclair himself, now by the Southern-born hero who deserts his own class to fight in behalf of the slave. And it is also treated powerfully; the unsparing battle scenes come alive with a sense of reality equal to those in Crane's *The Red Badge of Courage.*

Meanwhile, Sinclair was finding, through his contact with Socialists such as George D. Herron and his reading in *Wilshire's Magazine,* an explanation of and sanction for his own battles with an unfriendly world. Socialism came to him as more than an intellectual conviction; it came as a magnificent discovery, as a combined religious conversion and revelation, in the light of which he saw clearly the ends for which he might live. It came also as a stimulus to action, in the form of an assignment from the Socialist *Appeal to Reason* to study the Chicago stockyards area and to use his findings in a serial. Out of his studies there, and also out of the emotions born of his own bitter struggle with poverty, came *The Jungle* (1906), the most powerful novel associated with the muckraking movement, and one of the very few actuated by forthright proletarian sympathies.

A victim-of-society story, *The Jungle* delivers a hard-hitting, ruthless indictment of the exploitation which destroys a family of Lithuanian immigrants—all except the hero, Jurgis, who belatedly finds help and instruction with a group of Socialists. Coarse, ungenteel, unsparing, heavily documented with brutal detail, *The Jungle* develops a cumulative power; its luridly melo-dramatic climaxes come alive with the grotesque conviction of nightmare. Little in Zola or Dostoevski surpasses the nightmarish strength of the scenes where the penniless Jurgis is befriended by a young drunk, or where he haggles with a reluctant midwife while his helpless Ona lies dying in child-birth. Yet for all its power, *The Jungle* is not quite "the *Uncle Tom's Cabin* of wage slavery," as Jack London called it. Too angry, too furiously imagined, it lacks the flair for racy characterization, the humor, the humanity, that enrich the older book, while its fierce partisanship estops it from being the fine naturalistic novel implied by some of its philosophical premises.

The reception of *The Jungle* caused Sinclair chagrin, for the public appeared more interested in the problem of a corrupted meat supply than in that of the exploited worker. But the book brought him fame, and the royalties relieved him of financial pressure. Nevertheless, the quality of his writing temporarily declined. He was absorbed in his Helicon Hall project for co-operative living, he was undergoing the strain of the gradual breaking down of his first marriage, and he was suffering the ill health of nervous tension. These conditions passed, in time, with his divorce, his remarriage, and his permanent settlement in southern California. Yet the weakness of his next novels was probably owing less to external disturbances than to a lack of the absorbing enthusiasm he had felt for *The Jungle*; for during the same general period of his life he was able to produce another strong novel in the autobio-graphical *Love's Pilgrimage* (1911), which contains—in its passages on the capitalistic distortion of religion and education, of the press and the arts—the germs of much of his later writing.

The full development and documentation of these ideas took form pres-ently, not as fiction, but as the series of expository, historical, and propagandist works which Floyd Dell calls "the great pamphlets": *The Profits of Religion* (1918), on the church; *The Brass Check* (1919), on the press; *The Goose-Step* (1923) and *The Goslings* (1924), on the schools; and *Mammonart* (1925) and *Money Writes* (1927), on the arts. In all six books Sinclair endeavors to show how agencies of learning and of culture are affected by economic pressures, and how, in our own time, church and press and university are made over into instrumentalities of capitalism. With dramatically told illustration, with abundant documentation, Sinclair makes an impressive case; too glaringly impressive, perhaps, for it becomes apparent that just as economic forces have often controlled the American press, so they control the controversial works of Upton Sinclair. The proletarian bias is as obvious in the one case as the capitalistic is in the other. As a consequence the author is repeatedly drawn into the fragmentary or partial statement of truth or into misleading simpli-fications, as in his tendency to transform Jesus of Nazareth into a proletarian rebel. Yet the pamphlets remain the most noteworthy essay yet made in this country toward a complete Marxian interpretation of culture, and their very partisanship contributes to their power to stimulate and to awaken.

Hardly was the series of pamphlets complete before Sinclair revealed, in *Oil!* (1927), new and larger resources as a novelist. *Oil!* is, technically, the story of the development of Bunny Ross, son of a big California oil operator, of his education in the ways of love and of business, and of his abandoning the interests of his own class in order to aid the workers; but it is much more than that. It is the story of the Harding era, with its industrial warfare, its oil scandals, its pervasive corruption, and of southern California society, from its glamorous movie stars to its lurid popular evangelists. And it is also in all ways a big, finely conceived novel, dramatically imagined, abundant in incident, rich in the lightly stated *obiter dicta* of an urbane and mellow conviction.

Boston (1928), based on the Sacco-Vanzetti case, is weaker; but *American Outpost* (1932) tells of the writer's first thirty-five years with the same urbanity he had displayed in *Oil!* At the time of its publication America was already struggling in the trough of the great depression, an event to which Sinclair presently responded with his unsuccessful candidacy for governor on the famous EPIC platform—End Poverty in California. That the Democratic party should have sponsored a Socialist platform and candidate is sufficiently astonishing; but already forces were stirring abroad which were to drive these and other American groups still closer together. The rise of the Nazi-Fascist coalition in Europe, equally a threat to American Left and Right, tended to force both toward rapprochement. In the midst of this new unity of resistance to Fascism, and under the shadow of the Second World War, Sinclair designed his most ambitious work of fiction.

The Lanny Budd series—so called from Sinclair's versatile hero—is a sequence of novels, or, rather, one vast novel under several titles, giving a Marxian interpretation of the course of history from the eve of the First World War into the midst of the Second. Seven volumes of the series appeared by 1946—*World's End* (1940, also the title of the series), *Between Two Worlds* (1941), *Dragon's Teeth* (1942), *Wide Is the Gate* (1943), *The Presidential Agent* (1944), *Dragon's Harvest* (1945), and *A World to Win* (1946)—and later ones, continuing the story to the downfall of Mussolini and Hitler, were then projected. The series is planned, apparently, not merely on a vast but on too vast a scale; all but the first three volumes document a familiar theme with needless iterations and with decreasing credibility, and the first of the volumes alone has an impressive unity within itself. In *World's End* as in *Oil!* the narrative proper is the story of a young man's growth into sophistication in business and in love, into self-possession and knowledge of the world. But the real subject is the "World" itself, the *grand monde* of early twentieth century aristocratic and capitalistic power. Paradoxically, yet truly, the appeal of the book lies in the author's evocation of the variety and interest, the beauties and the graces, of this very order to whose destruction he himself is committed. There is a charm reminiscent of Burke, but more various, in the portrayal of this later *ancien régime*; and there is real tragic intensity in the picture of its disintegration in its very nucleus at the Versailles Conference, for want of intelligence, moral responsibility, and realistic leadership.

Between Two Worlds and *Dragon's Teeth,* though they never reach the high tragedy of *World's End,* have their own rich and varied interests, carrying Lanny Budd through the intricacies of *la vie à trois* and of marriage, and carrying also the political story through the diplomatic futilities of the early twenties, the economic collapse of 1929, and the rise of the Fascists and Nazis. By no means all of even the political story, however, dwells on the level of high intellectual interpretation. In *Dragon's Teeth,* for instance, Lanny Budd's negotiations with the Nazis for the release of his friends Johannes and Freddi Robin tend rather toward the anti-Nazi melodrama of Hollywood and the popular magazines, and in that resemblance show how completely Sinclair had come to share the mass feeling of his wartime America. Thanks to the author of *Mein Kampf,* the author of *The Jungle* had achieved, at last, respectability. Faced with the threat of arbitrary power abroad, American socialist and American capitalist could be, at least temporarily, united.

Regarded as art, the social novels of the later nineteenth and early twentieth centuries appear neither better nor worse than other novels of the period. Most of them are merely run-of-the-mill fiction; the genre achieved momentary fusings of art and idea only when it was employed by some mind of superior creative power. It achieved that superiority in Mark Twain's blasts at man's inhumanity and stupidity in the *Connecticut Yankee.* It achieved it fleetingly in some of the finer stories of Hamlin Garland's *Main-Travelled Roads,* and more abundantly in Frank Norris' vigorous stories of economic conflict. It achieved it in William Dean Howells' clear-eyed analyses of the ills of free enterprise, and in the best work of Howells' strangely gifted friend and fellow socialist, Edward Bellamy. But in most of the specifically problem novels of the period, ideas were mixed rather than fused with art, with the resulting production of many good rather than a few great works.

61. THE EMERGENCE OF THE MODERN DRAMA

WHILE popular fiction was taking on a more realistic and a more controversial character, which at once served and flourished upon the social and philosophical issues of the day, the stage continued to thrive upon revivals of old favorites in the romantic or heroic vein. The impressive activity of the stage in Europe and the United States during the middle of the nineteenth century produced very little living art.

The Civil War was neither the beginning nor the end of an epoch in American drama. The demand for popular theatrical entertainment, which actually increased in the North during the war, produced only variations upon such established traditions as the comedy of eccentric character, domestic melodrama, and the sensational play. The stage continued to be dominated by a generation of great actors—Edwin Forrest and Edwin Booth, Charlotte Cushman, Clara Morris, Lester Wallack, E. L. Davenport, and James E. Murdoch—who kept alive the literary masterpieces of the past, especially the plays of Shakespeare, by their inspired if sometimes grandiose performances. Most of the new plays, by contrast, were ephemeral, sensational, or sentimental legerdemain evoked by the huge popular demand for entertainment or escape. Thus by contrast is emphasized the importance of James A. Herne, Bronson Howard, David Belasco, Augustus Thomas, Clyde Fitch, and William Vaughn Moody, who were the principal progenitors of the vigorous modern American drama.

Between 1860 and 1890 there had occurred certain changes in the "show business" which deeply influenced dramatic authorship. Even though in 1890 the stock company still persisted, it depended in a large measure upon visiting stars on tour who were unlikely to pay royalty for new American plays while they could pack the houses by offering Shakespearean revivals or pirated translations of foreign works. The laws of copyright were inadequate even within the nation before 1856, and afforded no international protection until 1891. Subject to constant piracy, a play had little value as literary property unless an actor took it into his repertory under terms forbidding the author to publish it. Thus *Metamora* and *The Gladiator* became identified with the reputation of Edwin Forrest, while the authors, John A. Stone and Robert

Montgomery Bird, were forgotten. A dramatist could hope for a career only if he was also a producer or actor, as were William Dunlap and John Howard Payne in the earlier period or Boucicault, Daly, Herne, and Belasco at a later time.

After the Civil War the traveling company, stimulated by the development of the railroads, tended to replace the old stock companies. Although the change produced new problems, like that of the monopolistic syndicate, its ultimate effect was to encourage dramatic authorship. While fewer plays could be performed under such conditions, they remained longer upon the stage and assured professional income for such dramatists as could overcome severe competition. The result was the establishment of a new profession of dramatic authorship attractive to talented writers, of whom Bronson Howard was the earliest.

Against the romantic traditions of the older actors and the inertia of popular taste this movement made at first but slow headway. Until the end of the century the older conventions lingered on. The plays of Robert Montgomery Bird, *The Broker of Bogota* and *The Gladiator,* introduced by Forrest in the thirties, continued after Forrest's death to be performed to enthusiastic audiences by John McCullough until 1884—indeed *The Gladiator* was persistently revived until 1893. Robert T. Conrad's *Jack Cade* was acted by Forrest, McCullough, and Edmund Collier until 1887. Boker's *Francesca da Rimini,* introduced by E. L. Davenport in 1855, became a standard repertory play of Lawrence Barrett in 1882, and was revived for a year's run by Otis Skinner in 1901.

2

The older tradition of romantic and heroic tragedy is best represented in the work of George Henry Boker who gave our literature its most original plays of the type. The earlier heroic play, as befitted the literature of a country recently born of a democratic revolution, had shown a marked preference for the theme of popular revolt against the oppression of a ruling class or a foreign despot. From Dunlap to Bird it mattered little whether the protagonist were an American patriot, Peruvian Indian, Greek slave, or British commoner, so long as he struck for freedom. Boker was the first American playwright to enlarge this concept and to deal with the tragedy of the great individual at desperate odds with society, with his own nature, or with malign destiny.

Like so many writers of his generation, Boker was in revolt against his own environment. In devoting himself to poetry in a society which measured achievement only in terms of the financier or scientist, and in reacting earnestly against the materialism of urban society, he resembled his fellow poets, Stoddard, Taylor, and even the younger Aldrich and Stedman. Yet Boker's poetry retained a firmer grasp on actuality than that of most of his associates, and his tragedies were swiftly paced portrayals of real men and women, written in a blank verse which evoked the poetry inherent in the speech of life.

Of Boker's eleven plays, the tragedies if not the comedies deserved a robust life on the stage. Yet the first of them, *Calaynos* (1851*), played in the United States only about two weeks altogether even though it ran for one hundred performances in London without its author's knowledge, consent, or profit. No producer could be found for *Anne Boleyn,* a good play on Henry VIII and the tragic fate of his second Queen. *Leonor de Guzman* appeared for ten nights during the winter of 1853–1854; and *Francesca da Rimini* was thought by E. L. Davenport to be worth just a week's run in 1855. In the face of such apathy Boker, like Bird, gave up the stage. In 1882 when Barrett triumphed in *Francesca* and added the play to his permanent repertory, the author wrote pathetically, "Why didn't I receive this encouragement years ago? Then I might have done something." He tried to write again for the stage but the fire that animated his earlier tragedies had waned.

This fire was the inextinguishable integrity of a great human spirit embodied, in each play, in the protagonist. Calaynos, an austere and patrician scholar of ancient Spanish lineage, came from his seclusion to take up arms against the licentious court which had connived at the betrayal of his young wife. Boker's Anne Boleyn rebelled against the cynicism of a court society which would spare her life in return for a false confession of adultery in order that the King might remarry as he wished; but her sacrificial stubbornness assured the rights of succession for her child, who became England's great Elizabeth. Leonor de Guzman, mistress of Alphonso XII of Castile, sacrificed her life in conflict with a debased and materialistic society, in order, after the King's death in battle, to secure the succession of her illegitimate son whom the King had designated in preference to the weakling son of the Queen.

In *Francesca da Rimini,* the story of Dante's star-doomed lovers, Boker found his masterpiece. Of seven plays on this theme in four languages, his is the only one to conceive the pathos of the deformed husband, Lanciotto, without sacrificing the enduring appeal of the young lovers, Paolo and Francesca, and to understand that callous society, not fate, was the agent of the tragedy. As a result of this interpretation, Lanciotto hides his deformity on the battlefield, sends Paolo to woo in his stead, and finally, because of an inexorable code of social honor, kills the young lovers even though he "loved

* The dates attached to titles of plays in this chapter refer to the year of production in each instance.

them more than honor, more than life." With this play, romantic tragedy in America achieved the dignity of art.

3

This type of drama was not the only survival from the prewar theater. Conventional types of comic character made popular by such native comic actors as James H. Hackett, Joseph Jefferson, and J. S. Jones, who preferred to portray country bumpkins, still continued to flourish, urbanized by Edward Harrigan. Harrigan's comical and sympathetic interpretation of the plight of the immigrant in the American city made him, both as author and actor, a popular figure on Broadway until the turn of the century; and even now a reference to the "Mulligans" will recall the shanty Irish immigrant of the last century, and his colorful influence on the life of the large American cities, especially New York.

The domestic melodrama, long associated with the presentation of eccentric types of character, usually rustic, now became increasingly citified, but no less conventional and sensational. While a number of forces were stimulating a new art of the drama, the bulk of the theatrical fare, except for the revival of older masterpieces, continued until about 1885 to be composed of tear-jerkers, side-splitters, and hair-raisers. Nor was the situation improved by the vogue of adaptations from foreign plays and from novels foreign and American. Bad taste dominated the theater in France, Germany, and England, which, with popular fiction, afforded an inexhaustible reservoir of plots and stories for adaptation to the demands of a voracious American audience. Daly brought to the stage at least ninety plays, and Boucicault produced 132 or more. Yet only five or six of Daly's plays are thought to be wholly original, and even the best of Boucicault's were recent French plays transferred to Irish settings and given Irish characters and humor. As a result of the indiscriminate preference of the popular audience for sensationalism, Daly was only following an inevitable practice in turning Reade's *Griffith Gaunt* into a melodrama. If a novel happened to be sentimental in the first place, the results of adaptation were certain to be excruciating, as in the stage versions of *The Old Curiosity Shop* or *Uncle Tom's Cabin*. Even playgoers whose initiation occurred in the present century will recall the death of little Eva, and her visible ascent toward heaven on not quite invisible wires from the loft, while an inconsolable Uncle Tom prayed with her family.

Dion Boucicault, whose associations with the theater were international, could write a historical drama so substantial as *Louis XI,* which for a half-century held the stage as a favorite of Charles Kean, and later Henry Irving, who selected it for his farewell appearance in London in 1905. Yet his popular appeal for a half century was based on such plays as *The Poor of New York* (1857), in which a financial crisis and the failure of the banks provide a contrast between crafty villainy and impoverished and deserving virtue. The concern of the age with the theme of seduction led the same playwright to adapt French plays like *Mimi*; and the theme recurs in his popular *The Octoroon* (1859), in which the villain attempts to secure Zoe, the beautiful octoroon, by ruining her widowed mistress and forcing the sale of the plantation. The ending, in which Zoe drinks poison while an Indian retainer pursues the villain on a flaming steamboat, provides a curtain that is unforgettable, if nothing else.

Augustin Daly's productions of Shakespeare won him international fame but his few published plays reveal a master of theatrical technique whose works remained subliterary. *Horizon,* his best original play, gave a new realism of setting and atmosphere to the frontier drama; *Divorce* and *Pique* were early approaches to the social problem play; but even such plays made only a feeble and losing struggle against melodrama and sentiment. It was plays like *Under the Gaslight* (1867) that really packed Daly's Theater after the Civil War. This is a crook melodrama involving the kidnaping of an heiress, the mistaken identity of a changeling child, and the heroic endeavor of a one-armed newsboy to save the heroine. She, in turn, rescues him when he is overcome and bound to the railroad tracks in the path of the express, by chopping her way out of the baggage room with an ax.

4

Such examples not unfairly suggest the conditions of the popular stage when James A. Herne and Bronson Howard entered upon careers which were to prepare the way for the modern drama. The development of Herne from the domestic melodrama of *Hearts of Oak* (1879) to the domestic tragedy of *Margaret Fleming* (1890) reflects the improvement of popular taste. At that Herne was obviously ahead of his times, for those of his plays which discriminating criticism now most approves—*Drifting Apart, Margaret Fleming,* and *Griffith Davenport*—were all financial failures.

Herne was educated in the earlier theater of sentiment in eastern stock companies and on tours through the West. Such plays as *Uncle Tom's Cabin, The People's Lawyer, East Lynn,* and sentimental versions of Dickens were then preferred by the playgoers of San Francisco where Herne became a stage manager and leading character actor in the seventies. There he began to collaborate with David Belasco, a youth of barely twenty-one. The principal product of this association was *Hearts of Oak* (1879), which became one of the most famous plays of the century in the hands of the Herne family who played it over and over for a score of years. The play is remarkable among domestic melodramas for its fidelity to character and to its rural setting, surpassed only by *Rip Van Winkle,* which entranced audiences of the twentieth century long after all the famous Rips, like Charles Burke and Joseph Jefferson, had taken their last curtains.

Unlike *Rip Van Winkle,* Herne's play does not stand the test of discerning criticism, even though it is vastly better than the domestic melodramas of Boucicault and Daly. Yet uncounted thousands wept as the blind and dying father, unrecognized by his little daughter, talked to her in the churchyard beside the shaft erected in his memory by his wife and her new bridegroom, whose nuptials are then being celebrated with music in the adjoining church. The domestic melodrama of eccentric character or humble life survived also in Steele MacKaye's *Hazel Kirke,* and Denman Thompson's *The Old Homestead,* which are inferior to Herne's play, even though they both outlived it. *Way Down East* (1898) ran for a full year before becoming a permanent possession of the rural stock companies. Winchell Smith's *Lightnin'* (1918) was the most popular play in this tradition until *Abie's Irish Rose* (1922) began a six years run.

Herne himself did not follow this path further. Instead his growing interest in realism produced the unpopular masterpiece *Margaret Fleming,* in 1890. This is a grim study of the effect of a husband's infidelity on a wife who loved him deeply. It seems curious that playgoers who manifested a high degree of tolerance for the romantic treatment of seduction should have balked at the realistic treatment of the theme. There were objections to Margaret's taking into her family the child of her husband's affair, and instinctively preparing to suckle it as the curtain descends. Her repeated request for a lamp in a room flooded with afternoon sunshine reveals the agony of soul beneath her outward calm, for she had been warned that blindness would result from any emotional strain. In *Shore Acres* (1892) Herne again appealed to the popular affection for the rural setting and "the old homestead," but without the sentimentality which usually beset this type of play. It deals with the struggle of a successful and hardheaded father to control his daughter's life, while his brother, the unworldly Uncle Nat, quietly brings about her freedom, her marriage, and her ultimate reconciliation with her father. The play remains a satisfactory domestic comedy, even if the social life which it depicts has passed from the American scene. Herne had brought realism to the theater.

5

Bronson Howard restored the social comedy as a civilized art in the United States, a form which had lapsed in the middle years of the century, and it was he who chiefly prepared the way for the social comedies of Clyde

Fitch, Augustus Thomas, and the playwrights of the present century. At the same time the social comedies of Howells, for the most part one-acters, though not produced, were widely read, and no doubt played their part in broadening the area of good taste.

Howard addressed himself to the social consciousness of the new audience produced by the growing urbanization and sophistication of American life. While his older contemporaries had often simply translated foreign plays for the American stage, Howard based his plot for *Wives* (1879) on two plays of Molière, but kept his characters truly American. Daly's social comedies in the same period, like the popular *Divorce* and *Pique,* broke down into melodrama. This defect Howard learned to avoid. His early plays, *Moorcroft, Only a Tramp* (1874), and *Lillian's Last Love* (1873), are problem melodramas; but his revision of the last of these produced a convincing and well developed drama in *The Banker's Daughter* of 1878. In the earlier version, Lillian's marriage to an older man saves her father's banking business during a panic, but the reappearance of her former fiancé causes her husband to leave her, taking their child with him; and the youthful lover is killed in a duel. This was no more than the favorite situation of continental melodramas like the famous *Frou-Frou,* which Daly had just adapted for American audiences. In the revised version of his play Howard made living people of both husband and wife, and gave their behavior an American meaning. Rejecting the male code of honor of their French friends, the husband now proclaims his faith in his wife's virtue and helps her to face the death of her former fiancé. The convincing truth of the subsequent reconciliation is attested by the number of plays, down to Barry's *Paris Bound* and Crothers' *As Husbands Go,* in which the long comradeship of shared experiences between husband and wife proves stronger than romantic infatuation.

Howard's mature social comedies reveal his knowledge of American society, and that growing awareness of international social contrasts to be found in the contemporary novels of Howells and Henry James. *Young Mrs. Winthrop* (1882) presents the mid-channel crisis in modern marriage caused by a husband's absorption in his professional interests while his wife takes refuge in social affairs. In *One of Our Girls* (1885), Kate, a forthright and independent American girl, arrives in France among her aristocratic relatives in time to save her cousin, Julie, from a marriage *de convenance* and to enable her to marry the middle-class lad whom she really loves. Unlike her prototype, Daisy Miller, whose story James had dramatized two years before, Kate survives the inevitable suspicions concerning her own character, to marry the awe-stricken English aristocrat of her choice.

Even in *Shenandoah* (1888), the elements of social comedy contribute vitally to the effect, although this, Howard's best play, is remembered chiefly as the first fully successful drama of the Civil War. Only Boucicault's *Belle Lamar* (1874) had earlier attempted to use the war as dramatic material, and it failed, both artistically and at the box office. William Gillette's *Held By the Enemy* had appeared the year before Howard's play, but it held interest primarily by its taut, hair-trigger action. The same might be said of Gillette's later and more famous *Secret Service* (1895). The action of *Shenandoah* is intense, yet Howard preserved the elements of comedy in his portrayal of four diverse sets of lovers whose lives and loyalties are curiously snarled by the war. In all of his social comedies, Howard made excellent use of broad elements of comic relief: in *Shenandoah,* Jenny Buckthorn and her ridiculous but likable suitor, Captain Heartsease; in *The Banker's Daughter,* the first American business "go-getter" on the stage, the absurd George Washington Phipps; and in the *Young Mrs. Winthrop,* the breezy Mrs. Chetwyn, who had been married so often that her several husbands became a blur in her mind. The later plays of Howard represent a decline of his powers, but he left play writing a profession and the American social comedy an art.

6

The really spectacular development of the social comedy, however, did not occur until the complexities of the present century furnished dramatic materials for such playwrights as Langdon Mitchell, Rachel Crothers, Gilbert Emery, Philip Barry, George S. Kaufman, George Kelly, Sidney Howard, and S. N. Behrman, whose work falls beyond the scope of the present chapter. While Augustus Thomas and Clyde Fitch devoted perhaps their best talents to this form, their earlier, and some of their most famous plays, were inspired by the romantic tendencies which still flourished at the end of the century, at the very time when Herne and Howard were contributing to a vital realism.

This *fin de siècle* romance influenced fiction as well as the drama, and provided a spate of romantic novels for dramatic adaptation. At the same time there appeared a new generation of romantic actors, like Lawrence Barrett, Richard Mansfield, E. H. Sothern, Julia Marlowe, and Otis Skinner, who revived the older heroic plays and especially Shakespeare, while at the same time encouraging the new tendency. Barrett's appeal as an actor was established by the success of *Pendragon* (1881), by William Young, whose *The Rajah* (1883) ran for two hundred and fifty performances, and whose dramatization of Lew Wallace's pulsating romance, *Ben-Hur* (1899), held the stage for three years before becoming a perennial of the stock companies and the films. Mansfield wrote, or sought from other playwrights, dramas which presented types of romantic character agreeable to his talents as actor and popular with his audiences. In Henry Guy Carleton's *Victor Durand* (1884) he played a quixotic lover who sacrificed himself for the woman whom he loved hopelessly. His own play, *Monsieur* (1887), portrayed a poverty-ridden music master who sacrificed his life for his art, to die of starvation amid the luxuries of a great house where he was playing for the entertainment of guests. These two situations were skillfully united by Clyde Fitch in his first play, *Beau Brummell* (1890), written to order for Mansfield. The latter meanwhile had played *Dr. Jekyll and Mr. Hyde,* and he continued to exploit the interest in the romantic "bad man" in a succession of plays like *Don Juan, Nero, Napoleon Bonaparte,* and Booth Tarkington's *Monsieur Beaucaire* (1901).

Another actor-author of the period who popularized a romantic character conception suited to his own temperament was William Gillette. His Sherlock Holmes is the most familiar example of the cool, shrewd man who steers a safe course through overwhelming complexities, perplexities, and dangers, physical or social. This character was suggested in his first play, *The Professor* (1881), and reappeared with profuse variations in such dramas as *Drum Taps* and *Secret Service,* his spy plays of the Civil War; in *Esmeralda,* in which the country suitor outwits sophistication; and in mad and merry farces like *The Private Secretary, Mr. Wilkinson's Widows,* and *Too Much Johnson.*

David Belasco is also most properly considered in connection with the romantic revival of the century's end. Belasco came to New York in 1882 after twelve years of tempestuous experience in the West, including a variety of associations with such actors and playwrights as Herne, Boucicault, and Bartley Campbell. He wrote or adapted almost every type of play that flourished after 1870. In his sensitiveness to popular taste he was chameleon, prophet, and phoenix. His collaborators were many, and all but one of his more important plays resulted from these associations. Among the seventy-five plays in which he is known to have had a hand one may find domestic melodramas, crook melodramas, farces, domestic problem plays, Civil War plays, frontier plays like *The Girl I Left Behind Me,* historical dramas, and exotic romances of spiritual revolt in semipoetic language, such as *Madame Butterfly, The Darling of the Gods,* and *Adrea.* Apparently without collaboration he wrote a fine romance on the nature of death, *The Return of Peter Grimm.* Two of Puccini's operas derived their librettos from *Madame Butterfly* and *The Girl of the Golden West.*

All of Belasco's plays are romantic in nature and his valuable contributions to stagecraft in details of setting, costume, and lighting were romantic in effect, however realistic in theory. He was a master of the theater, and it is probable that he contributed more than any other producer of his times to the mechanical perfection of the modern stage and playhouse. He continuously struggled against the monopolistic theatrical trust, supported courageous experiment, and promoted the talents of such actors as David Warfield, Mrs. Leslie Carter, Frances Starr, and Blanche Bates.

As a man of letters, however, his record is less impressive. His plays were "smash hits" in their own day, eminently satisfactory between the first and last curtain; but few of them are literature. Exceptions may be *The Darling of the Gods* (1902), *Adrea* (1904), and *Madame Butterfly* (1900), written in collaboration with John Luther Long, and his apparently independent play, *The Return of Peter Grimm* (1911). The first two are romantic tragedies in each of which a beautiful high-born woman, in revolt against the outrages of society and fate, gives all for love and counts a world well lost. Both of these plays present a never-never world, while their language, though passionate and often poetic, is so highly stylized as to intensify the sense of unreality. More can be said for *Madame Butterfly,* the tragic story of the little Japanese girl who made the mistake of falling in love with the American naval officer who bought her, according to the custom of the country. Cho-Cho-San's toy world is destroyed by her lover's marriage to an American girl; her suicide is an inevitable and thoroughly moving consequence. *The Return of Peter Grimm* has remained familiar by virtue of revivals on the screen and in radio performances. Its theme, the survival of personality beyond physical death, has retained its vitality in this century of world wars, and its characters give a sense of reality.

In its mixture of romantic and realistic impulses, the work of Belasco is typical of the American theater even beyond the end of the century. While American writers of fiction progressed from the realism of Mark Twain and Howells to the sterner naturalism of Stephen Crane and Hamlin Garland, the American dramatist was inclined to compromise. The same phenomenon may be observed in British literature. The sentimental and sensational *Saints and Sinners* of Henry Arthur Jones was typical in 1884, and Pinero's well named *Sweet Lavender* was not deemed old-fashioned in 1888. It was not until 1896 that Jones attempted a play like *Michael and His Lost Angel,* and no play of Pinero satisfies the modern sense of realism before *Iris* of 1901. Wilde's plays have the modern temper, but he was not influential in America until the late nineties, and the same must be said of Shaw. Our modern theater has responded strongly to the realism, the delicate symbolism, the analysis of psychology and social forces achieved by a number of modern continental dramatists. Various factors, but principally that of moral censorship, restricted Ibsen's influence on the English-speaking stage until late in the nineties. It was not until after the nineteenth century that the modern continental theater made its influence felt through the work of such playwrights as Strindberg, Chekhov, Gorky, Hauptmann, Sudermann, Schnitzler, and

Maeterlinck. These considerations increase one's appreciation for the contributions to the theater made by Howard, Thomas, and Fitch, especially when one compares them with such British contemporaries as Pinero and Jones.

7

For example, Augustus Thomas, like Howells and Bronson Howard, was reared in the Midwest, yet contributed to social comedy through his hard-won understanding of American life in various localities. His picture of American life is broader than that of Howard. He had the journalist's perception of the striking local characteristics of American regions so diverse as Alabama, Missouri, Arizona, Colorado, and the cities of New York and Washington. These, among other localities, he observed during his roving youth as Congressional page, transportation agent, lawyer's clerk, box-office man, amateur producer, dramatic critic, manager for Julia Marlowe, and agent for a mind reader. His mature work began when he succeeded Dion Boucicault as adaptor and revisor at the Madison Square Theater in May, 1890, where Mansfield was then presenting Fitch's first play, *Beau Brummell*. His *Alabama,* a romance of the Reconstruction, was ready for the stage at the Madison Square Theater the next year and once more dramatic authorship, unsupported by other enterprise, furnished a career.

Thomas wrote or adapted at least sixty-four plays. They fall into two groups which illustrate the development of the American stage of his day. All his best plays are social comedies in the larger sense. His earlier plays, like the earlier work of Clyde Fitch, belong to the *fin de siècle* romance. Later Thomas' preference was for a more sophisticated metropolitan society, sometimes involving international contrasts.

His *In Mizzoura* (1893) provided the famous character actor, Nat Goodwin, with the role of an uncouth Western sheriff who wins the love of a gently bred girl, an example of the persistence on the stage of the heroic Western "bad man" or the seemingly crude character who proves his worth in the supreme test. Bret Harte's stories had popularized such characters as John Oakhurst the gambler, and "Tennessee's Partner." Their stage progeny was legion, the poor relations of the more sophisticated characters portrayed by Mansfield. Variations of the themes are found, for example, in Daly's *Horizon* (1871), Fitch's *The Cowboy and the Lady* (1899), Belasco's *The Girl of the Golden West* (1905), and even in Moody's *The Great Divide* (1906). The motif still flourishes abundantly in the movies. In Thomas' *Arizona* (1899) which vividly portrayed the life of the ranch and army post, the "bad man" whom the girl loves is really the victim of a set of suspicious circumstances which have caused him to resign in disgrace from the army.

After 1900 Thomas produced a series of light social comedies, almost farcical in situation, but so lively in wit and dialogue that the best of them. *The Earl of Pawtucket* (1903) and *Mrs. Leffingwell's Boots* (1905), suggest comparison with Wilde. In 1907 appeared the first of his realistic dramas of character, *The Witching Hour,* in which the mysteries of human personality are investigated in a tense episode involving hypnotism, thought transference, and the control of fear. *The Harvest Moon* (1909), less popular, but even better than its predecessor, again deals with the power of the individual to control his personality by the force of his will. In this case it is a father who teaches his daughter to gain control of her life and her love, by conquering the haunting doubts of her own stability implanted in her by the bitter woman who brought her up. *As a Man Thinks* (1911) involved a social problem and a broader sweep of life than Thomas had hitherto employed. It portrayed the effort of an intelligent woman to indemnify herself for an infidelity of her husband by seeking a love affair of her own, and her discovery that a man's assurance of his fatherhood, and in consequence the whole structure of his society, rests upon his confidence in the virtue of his wife. This play was probably a retort to Rachel Crothers' first important play, *A Man's World* (1909), and together they introduced a question which was to be debated on the stage for a quarter of a century. Maurice Barrymore, in *The Burglar* (1889), was the first actor to make a professional appearance in a play by Thomas; his son Lionel starred in Thomas' last important play, *The Copperhead* (1918). In this convincing Civil War play his ability to reproduce local color united with his practiced command of the character problem.

8

Herne and Howard foreshadowed the modern realistic theater, but four plays of Thomas and the latest plays of Fitch, in the first decade of this century, constitute the actual beginnings of what we now recognize as contemporary realism. Clyde Fitch, like Thomas, began to write under the spell of the romantic theater, but ended his short career with a number of realistic character-problem plays. He wrote about sixty plays in twenty years, most of them comedies of manners and social comedies; he became, next to Belasco, the most spectacular figure in the international theater of his day; he had six plays on the stage in New York or London in the winter of 1901. It is a wonder that a dramatist producing at that rate the popular hits of each season could contribute to the permanent advance of the drama.

Yet even the romantic social comedies, melodramas, and period plays which gave Fitch an international eminence during his first decade were decidedly in advance of their times. The appeal of a play like *Beau Brummell* (1890) is enduring. This was written for Mansfield, who made famous on the stage the character of the late Georgian fop and dandy. The portrayal of his personality involves the artificial court life during the Regency, and a love story in which the Beau sacrifices himself and his favor with the Prince in order to give the girl whom he so hopelessly loves to the man of her choice.

Fitch surpassed his mid-century predecessors in such romantic or even melodramatic situations by his wit, and by the appeal of the characters whom he has projected upon scenes so obviously idealized or exotic. *His Grace de Grammont,* for example, gave Otis Skinner a quite memorable opportunity to act the gracious cavalier, and *Mistress Betty* (later called *The Toast of the Town*) afforded Modjeska, and afterward Viola Allen, a part redolent of eighteenth century manners and the glamorous theatrical life of that period. *The Moth and the Flame* is one of the best of the many romantic melodramas on the theme suggested by its title, and its popular success gave its author his first real financial security. In *Barbara Frietchie* Fitch caught the morning freshness, if not the power, of the Romeo and Juliet situation which he so obviously imitated, and the play had sufficient vitality, twenty-eight years after its first performance, to furnish the libretto for one of the most successful of modern operettas, *My Maryland*.

The character problem plays of his last decade no doubt constitute Fitch's more lasting contribution to the literature of the stage. *The Climbers* (1901), for example, is a social satire dealing with the perfervid aspirations for the material rewards of life on the upper levels of a city like New York. His last play, *The City* (1909), dealt somewhat less successfully with the same theme, although both plays are remembered. This satire is touched at all points with compassion. *Lovers' Lane,* however, is mordant satire in its portrayal of a wise and liberal clergyman confronted by the petty intolerance of the small-town mind, especially in its female manifestations. A world removed from this scene is that of *Her Great Match*. In depicting the refusal of an American girl to accept a morganatic marriage with the young prince whom she loves, Fitch revealed the subtle national variations in gentle behavior without suggesting the necessary superiority of one to another, and especially without apologizing for the American variety.

A number of Fitch's plays demonstrate a similar mastery of the delicate art of social comedy. Their success upon the stage is evidence of the rapid advance in taste in those urban communities where, only a score of years before, the preference was decidedly for slapstick and sensationalism. Even lesser dramatists might now sometimes approach his competence in this field. One of them, Langdon Mitchell, surpassed him in lightness of touch if not in depth of meaning, in *The New York Idea* (1906), in which the kaleidoscopic divorces and remarriages among a group of well bred but bored social leaders afford the dramatist an opportunity to reveal his delight in the human comedy. In all of his plays Mitchell proved his ability to portray convincing characters amid the artificialities of social life, but his earlier *Becky Sharp* and his later *Major Pendennis* have not the vitality of the social comedies of Clyde Fitch.

Fitch's best plays are *The Girl with the Green Eyes* (1902) and *The Truth* (1907). Again with compassionate understanding, he presents in each play the problem of a girl who has been conditioned in youth to a psychopathic reaction destructive of personal and social relations—in the first case, jealousy, and in the second, falsehood. His dramatic instinct was to avoid the intense clinical examination which weakens certain European dramas on such themes. Some critics have felt that the author manifested a fatal weakness in not pursuing the logic of these situations to the tragic conclusions ordained by the conventions of modern naturalism. Perhaps, however, there is another logic in the power of love to cancel the predetermined consequences of heredity or environment. Jinny Austin and Becky Warder have each been driven to the brink of a disaster from which she is saved by her husband's discovery, in a violent climax of action, that she is suffering from a profound and early spiritual injury which only his love and sympathy can heal.

9

The early death of William Vaughn Moody cut short the career of a poet already distinguished, and probably robbed our dramatic literature of a playwright who might have contributed more than any other, save Eugene O'Neill, to the modern symbolic drama of spiritual struggle in which romantic and realistic tendencies are blended. Fine humanist and university teacher that he was, Moody retained as artist a profound understanding of everyday life, and the ability to interpret its complexities in simple and passionate symbols of action. Moody's trilogy of poetic dramas was never produced; yet his two plays in prose, which were successfully presented, can be fully understood only in the light of his poetic *Masque of Judgment*. All of his dramatic work, in prose and poetry, through a variety of human situations, relates to a central problem which has persisted as a major theme in every period of American expression.

This theme is the sense of sin and, more particularly, its destructive power upon the freedom and expression of the human soul. The distinction is intended between evil, which may be an absolute, and the sense of sin or evil, which may have no absolute sanction, and may spring, indeed, from hereditary inhibitions, or from prohibitions which bear little or no relation to truth and justice. It is a commonplace of American history, and a principal clue to American behavior, that this sense of sin which Moody attacked in all of his plays was sharpened by the persistence of the Puritan inheritance, the Calvinist conception of the original sin and total depravity of mankind. For more than a century this problem has engaged the profoundest efforts of writers so diverse as Hawthorne, Whitman, Melville, and Edwin Arlington Robinson.

Thus the philosophical significance of Moody's plays is greater than their practical merits on the stage, although the two prose plays, *The Great Divide* (1906) and *The Faith Healer* (1909), continue to hold their own for the reader and in revivals on the stage and screen. The three poetic dramas of *The Masque of Judgment* present such a sweeping Miltonic canvas that generalization must prove unsatisfactory. Yet it seems clear that the central meaning of the first play, also called *The Masque of Judgment,* lies in Raphael's belief that God blundered in allowing sin and then ordaining its punishment. In this play the God of Wrath, conceived by the ancient Hebrew and worshipped by the modern puritan, is finally defeated by the Serpent for his mistake in punishing man for following his natural impulses instead of teaching him the full use of his powers. In the second play, *The Fire Bringer,* the classical story of Prometheus is given messianic meaning, as mankind through suffering learns the religion of rebellion against all that prevents man's service to man and his full expression of himself. In the unfinished *The Death of Eve,* the last of the trilogy, Eve was to bring back Cain and Adam to Eden, the place of original sin, and to find the sense of sin vanquished by the love of her descendants.

This brief analysis cannot show the wide range of these poems, their richness in secondary motivations, the interest of their action, and the nobility of their language, but their meaning is consistent with that of the two prose plays. *The Great Divide* presents a modern girl of New England, stunted in her expression of life by puritanical inhibitions. On a Western trip, alone in the wilds, she submits, in order to save herself from the others, to the best of three men who attempt to attack her. Ghent falls in love with her and she with him, but while he rises strengthened and purified to a successful life as mining prospector, Ruth tortures herself with his statement that he was brought to her by "whiskey, the sun, and the Devil." Impelled by her conviction that they must cleanse themselves by abnegation, she flees to her home where Ghent follows her to wage a difficult but finally successful battle against her lantern-jowled Puritan ancestors whose portraits line the walls.

The Faith Healer, a better play, presents an accurate study of a Midwest farming community, and a large number of convincing characters. The central story deals with Michaelis, a mystic who has come up on a mysterious mission from a hermitage in the grazing country of the Southwest. He has healed Mary Beeler, invalid aunt of Rhoda, a young girl, and news of this has brought a host of seekers to his door. In the midst of his work of healing he discovers his love for Rhoda, to whom sex has meant only sin, in her former experience of seduction. Their mutual sense of guilt causes Michaelis to lose his power of healing with almost tragic results for those whom he is helping until their great discovery, in this crisis, of the unity of the flesh and the spirit.

10

The story of the development of American drama from Boker to Moody is that of the formative stage of an art. The subliterary theatricality of the period, by illustrating the popular and prevailing taste, particularly in urban America, emphasizes the importance of those playwrights who gradually created, in spite of overwhelming handicaps, a native drama which gave deeper meaning to the theater, portrayed modern character and life with fidelity, and pointed the way toward imaginative maturity.

In the older period of romantic drama, Boker had rejected the prevailing heroic themes of national idealism, and had devoted his art to great tragic crises of the personality. This impulse has always afforded the themes for the noblest tragedy. The modern drama has drawn its strength from the ability of dramatists to find such subjects in the stuff of everyday life. Possibly this characteristic finds its point of origin, historically, in that series of Ibsen's dramas which began with *A Doll's House* in 1879. In American drama, Herne's *Margaret Fleming,* in 1890, marks an epoch. In the first years of the new century, the dramas which best stand the test of time are concerned with the mysteries of the human mind and spirit, or with some struggle of the will of the individual to overcome a fate that seems ordained in destiny or human frailty. That the important dramatists of the period were still entranced by the human miracle which Moody called a "mystical hanker after something higher" is demonstrated by such plays as Fitch's *The Truth,* and *The Girl with the Green Eyes*; Thomas' *The Witching Hour,* and *The Harvest Moon*; Belasco's *The Return of Peter Grimm*; and Moody's entire work.

Theatrical and melodramatic plays persisted until the end of the century, yet a new vitality was discernible after 1880. Stimulated in part by native forces and later by the experimental European theater, American drama gradually acquired social responsibility and seriousness, a surer grasp of psychological and spiritual realities. Enriched by the complexities of life in the twentieth century, these same convictions later found a more masterful statement in the dramatic symbolism of Eugene O'Neill.

62. TOWARD NATURALISM IN FICTION

Even at the close of the nineteenth century the realistic tendency in the American drama had thus failed to respond to the European discoveries and theories of science which, by demanding a new definition of nature and its part in human destiny, had given philosophic depth to the plays of Ibsen, Strindberg, and Hauptmann. But in American fiction there was evidence of an increasing effort to find new techniques with which to reinterpret the unchanging central issues of human experience in terms of naturalism.

In France, Emile Zola had carried the realism of Flaubert and De Maupassant to depths of sordidness and bitter criticism that defied even a tragic solution. In Russia, Dostoevski, Tolstoy, and Turgenev, each in his fashion, had proposed views of life which at least made the catharsis of tragedy possible. In England, Hardy was discovering a new tragic intensity in the simple lives of the Wessex folk. Although Howells and others report that all of these foreign writers, as well as the popularizers of science who gave them their view of man, were being read in the United States soon after they appeared in Europe, the full force of the movement in this hemisphere was dulled by a traditional optimism reinforced by prudery. Naturalism—an old word for these new ways of thinking—could not take root here as quickly or as firmly as it could in the richer soil of Europe. Zola had demanded in 1880 that "a novelist must be only a scientist, an analyst, an anatomist, and his work must have the certainty, the solidity, and the practical application of a work of science," but until Dreiser's *Sister Carrie* (suppressed in 1900), no American novelist took this prescription seriously and produced a wholly original work of pure naturalism. In the closing years of the nineteenth century the influences of Darwin and Spencer, of Zola and Turgenev, took no single form. One can discover many phases of naturalism in American fiction—in the moral confusion and dismay of Mark Twain and Harold Frederic, in the harsher forms of realism of E. W. Howe and Hamlin Garland, in the robustious action tales of Frank Norris and Jack London, or in the bold miniatures of Ambrose Bierce and Stephen Crane. But there was no single writer who could be described as a naturalist, no one wholly devoted, before Dreiser, to the philosophy, the material, and the method of Zola.

The writers who came nearest to practicing the formula of naturalism at the turn of the century are four: Hamlin Garland, Stephen Crane, Frank Norris, and Jack London. Each of these in his way made a significant break with the literal realism of Howells or the unthinking romance of F. Marion Crawford; each attempted to apply to art some part of the method or the meaning of the physical and biological sciences. Mainly in the work of these four the technique and the philosophy of serious modern American fiction took shape.

2

As Howells had defined the literal form of realism in his essays gathered together as *Criticism and Fiction* in 1891, so Hamlin Garland expounded the next step in the movement in his *Crumbling Idols* (1894). Howells was concerned only that the novelist be faithful in his work of representing reality as he knew it, and he limited the range of permissible material by conventional standards of taste. He failed to raise the question of the metaphysical nature of the reality which he thought should be described, and he formulated no theory of art beyond its function as record.

Although Garland in later life became narrower in his sympathies while the mind of his mentor opened, in the nineties the poor boy from the Iowa prairies was the spokesman for the young radicals gathering in Chicago and New York. His new theory, which he called "veritism," raised many of the issues which Howells had avoided. His wide but superficial reading in popular science, his personal bitterness at the harshness of his own boyhood, and his casual knowledge of the French impressionists in both writing and painting carried him beyond some of the limitations of literal realism. He asked that American fiction divorce itself from tradition and imitation, that it explore truth to its underlying meaning, that it deal with the unpleasant as well as the pleasant aspects of life, and that it develop a form based on the moment of experience, acutely felt and immediately expressed. A sensitive observer and chronicler rather than a great artist, he failed to realize in his own stories the possibilities of his theory. But in *Crumbling Idols* he made himself the public apologist for such younger writers as E. W. Howe, Henry Blake Fuller, Harold Frederic, and Stephen Crane, who were not afraid to discuss poverty, hardships, and the problems of society and religion, and who were working toward an instrument of expression which would interpret as well as record.

Garland's early life was a bitter struggle to extort the promised plenty from a rich but plague-ridden soil. The conflict between his soldier-father's consecration to frontier hopes and the wasting poverty and toil of his mother gave him his one great theme. Even in his first published writing, *Boy Life on the Prairie* (1885, 1899), he exploited the poverty and hardships of his boyhood at West Salem, Wisconsin, and in Iowa, as well as the zest of rolling hills and open prairies.

This was to be the material of all his best writing, but at twenty-four he thought he had left it behind him. In youthful rebellion he rejected his father's move to Dakota when the chinch bugs drove the family on, and with his brother Frank worked his way to Boston. There he sought out alone a rented room, and blindly struggled on toward his goal of becoming a writer and orator. Soon he was teaching at the Boston School of Oratory and reading Taine's *History,* Véron's *Aesthetics,* Henry George's tracts on the single tax, and the exciting new ideas of Spencer and Darwin. He had renounced the frontier except as literary material, and had taken to the back trail as Irving and Cooper had before him, and as Mark Twain and Howells were doing in his own day.

The turn left a sense of guilt at his heart, and his lifelong nostalgia was to be concentrated on the lot of his mother. His new life was dedicated to expiation for the old. There must be a Garland homestead somewhere, and where better than West Salem, his mother's childhood home? A peaceful old age could be found for her there, if his father would admit defeat. The Oedipus complex was here no deep source of buried tragedy; it shaped the life of a family and created a chronicler.

Main-Travelled Roads (1891) and the volumes of poems, plays, tales, and essays which clustered about it in the next few years are simple, honest, and sharp impressions of life as he had lived it. Howells urged him to tell his story straight; a Kansas editor, E. W. Howe, had set an example of how to treat the narrowness of a small community in *The Story of a Country Town* (1883); Joseph Kirkland had written two novels of the Middle West, *Zury* (1887) and *The McVeys* (1888), and encouraged Garland to exploit the same material. From Taine he had learned to blame environment rather than the dark soul for the hardships of the human lot; from Henry George he had learned that those hardships were attributable to the mishandling of resources in land; from Spencer he had concluded that all life is a part of a single physical and biological process working upward and outward from simple to complex forms, from homogeneity to variety, from the mass to the individual. His life confirmed these teachings.

The tales in *Main-Travelled Roads* and in its first sequel, *Prairie Folks* (1893), tell of the unadorned hardships, lightened by occasional small pleasures and made meaningful by the power of nature, that fill the lives of the people of the coolly country and the prairie. Predominantly bitter like "Lucretia Burns" or pathetic like "Mrs. Ripley's Trip," there is courtship and family loyalty to ease the burdens, prairie spaces and sunsets to give joy and hope, minor follies of men to add a touch of grim humor. Throughout all, the exploitation of the farmer by the social system and the tragic lot of the pioneer woman bind the stories to central themes. Several of these tales were expanded into short novels, the best of which, *Rose of Dutcher's Coolly* (1895), conjectures the life of Garland's older sister as it might have been had she not died after her first move toward a larger life. But by 1899, in spite of the encouragement of B. O. Flower and the receptive pages of the radical *Arena,* his vein was nearly exhausted.

After his marriage to Zulime Taft, sister of the sculptor, and his mother's death in 1900, New York became the Garland headquarters and his writing changed in subject, purpose, and style. He now published with the successful firm of Harper and the romances of the next decade bear little superficial resemblance to the early work. In their genre, however, they stand reasonably high, even though they have suffered by contrast with the Middle Border books, as well as with the more vigorous action tales of Harding Davis and Jack London. Based on trips to the peaks and high plateaus of Colorado, Wyoming, and Montana and to the Klondike, each has serious purpose, swift action, and balanced though often conventional plot. When adventure and prosperity came into his experience, his emotions changed color and he celebrated the admirable. Biology acclaimed the independent man of vigorous action, and Garland followed the path of Roosevelt, Frank Norris, and Jack London toward the brute-man as he had previously followed that of Eggleston, Howe, and Howells toward the influence of environment. It was the other half of the same equation.

The third and last phase of his work was ushered in by *A Son of the Middle Border* (1917). Nostalgia had crept upon him again and as his daughters grew older he turned back, but in a softened mood, to his boyhood memories. Life was different for them from what it had been for him—and he intended that it should be so, but they and their contemporaries should know their cultural inheritance. In four books he told the whole story: in *Trail-Makers of the Middle Border* (1926) he followed his father from Maine to Wisconsin; in *A Son of the Middle Border* (1917) he continued the migration to Iowa and Dakota, and back to the purchase of the homestead in West Salem, again proving that this was the richest and most fruitful period of his life; in *A Daughter of the Middle Border* (1921) he told of the dividing claims of his middle years to the death of his parents and through the early years of his marriage; and in *Back-Trailers from the Middle Border* (1928) he carried his story to New York and London and told of his literary compromises and successes and of the careers of his daughters. Here was the story of an American family through three generations, a domestic chronicle of the frontier, a cycle in biological sociology, a chapter from an American Taine.

There only remained in the later years the narrowing stream of his literary reminiscences which filled several large volumes but which are now of interest mainly to his biographer. One other book of this period, *Forty Years of Psychic Research* (1936) was a by-product of his pseudoscientific romanticism. In an early novel, *The Shadow World* (1908), based on notes he made immediately after sittings and on his reports to the American Psychical Society, he states his position in the character of a young chemist:

I am a scientist in my sympathies. I believe in the methods of the chemist and the electrician. I prefer the experimenter to the theorist. . . . I am ready to go wherever science leads, and I should be very glad to *know* that our life here is but a link in the chain of existence.

In forty years it failed to lead him past the great divide.

Thus Garland turned to nature to solve and harmonize all the problems of man. He shared the hope of his contemporaries that science, especially chemistry and biology, would answer the riddle of an increasingly complex civilization of which the old idols had crumbled. Not a profound thinker nor a wide reader, he accepted the current dogma of the evolutionists and attempted, like Zola, even though he rejected and resented Zola's preoccupation with sex, to use his art as a means of illustrating the theses of the most radical scientists of his day. The result was a new movement in art which was to go far beyond these beginnings as they in turn had moved beyond the literary recordings of De Forest, Howe, Eggleston, and Howells. That movement was to leave Garland behind because he failed to accept his own challenge to an open mind.

3

Garland's instant recognition of Stephen Crane is tribute to his literary theory, for the boy practiced instinctively and with ease the impressionistic veritism of *Crumbling Idols*. As Emerson had defined the man of nature and the poet only to discover the actualities later in Thoreau and Whitman, so Garland found in Crane the artist he could describe but could not himself become. When the younger man tramped the four miles from the Bowery out to Garland's flat in Harlem in 1893, the "nice Jesus Christ" fed him, introduced him to Howells, helped him sell a story to B. O. Flower, and lent him money to have *The Red Badge of Courage* typed. It was the beginning of Crane's short and colorful career.

"Let it be stated," wrote his biographer Thomas Beer with acute understanding, "that the mistress of this boy's mind was fear." Poverty, innate cruelty, war, and death are the themes of all his best work as they were in Ambrose Bierce, yet there is little in his life or reading to account for the pessimism and the sensibility of his tales and poems. The poverty, illness, and early death of this member of one of the oldest and most respected families in Newark, New Jersey, seem to have resulted from the pressure of nervous energy rather than circumstance. He lived intensely a life of his own choice.

The record of that life is confused and shrouded in myth, for, like Poe, he threw himself into his fiction and was not unwilling to become a part of it. His own reticence and the jealousy of lesser "Bohemians" conspired to distort into a legend of drink, drugs, and petty social crimes the simple facts of a small-town boyhood as the Methodist minister's youngest son, a few years of slumming in New York City's nascent artist colony, another few of reporting the color of the West and South as far as Mexico for a newspaper syndicate, involvement as correspondent in the Cuban and Greek comic-opera wars of independence, and a final attempt to find in English manor-house life the haven that his country was too busy to supply. It is the familiar story of romantic youth seeking escape from life into art and achieving a fleeting mastery before the overtaxed body gives way. The term of twenty-nine years, the late marriage to an older woman, and the death by consumption at a health resort follow an almost classic formula. Mastery was achieved in a half-dozen short stories and novelettes, near mastery in three short novels and in innumerable sketches, but two more ambitious novels failed. His slim volumes of epigrammatic and symbolic verse give him a minor but significant place in American poetry.

The appearance of an original artist, springing without antecedent into life, is always illusion, but the sources of Crane's philosophy and art are as yet undeciphered. Neither the cold-blooded determinism of his belief nor the sensuous awareness of his writing can be without source, but nowhere in the scant record he has left is there evidence that he, like Garland, read widely in the current books on biological science. A direct influence of Darwin, Spencer, Haeckel, or their American popularizers cannot be established. Rather he seems to have absorbed these influences at second hand through Russian and French writers. For Tolstoy's *Sebastopol* and *War and Peace* he confesses an early enthusiasm, but probably because of his interest in war rather than for deeper reasons. Of Dostoevski and Turgenev he admits no knowledge, yet internal evidence makes such knowledge possible. His tales, in theme and form, bear a striking resemblance to those of De Maupassant and he knew

Flaubert early in *Salammbô,* even though he resented its length. There is no doubt that he took direct inspiration from these French realists, and even more certainly from Zola, for *L'Assommoir* probably provided the plot for *Maggie,* and *La Débâcle* bears a close resemblance to *The Red Badge of Courage,* though he denied ever having read it. His work shows the stamp of European naturalism and contributed to the break of American literary history with the English tradition. With Zola he shared the philosophy of the *roman expérimental,* with De Maupassant and Turgenev the sensory acuteness, the brevity, and the repressed intensity of impressionistic art.

This can be said even though the superficiality of his acquaintance with these writers be acknowledged. It is probable that discussions with fellow artists—mostly painters—who shared the makeshift lodgings at the "Art Students League" on East Twenty-third Street in 1891–1892 had more direct effect on him than had any reading. Such sources can never be traced with accuracy, but the selection of an impressionist painter as hero of his semi-autobiographical novel, *The Third Violet* (1897), is revealing. The adolescent love story is Crane's own in essential respects and he tells it as a painter in prose. Monet's paintings he knew.

Maggie (1893) and *The Red Badge of Courage* (1895) came directly from these associations, the first a Bowery story based on observation, the other a wholly imaginative analysis of a boy's first battle experience in the Civil War. Yet the difference between them is not as significant as some critics have averred. Both are impressionistic studies of elemental fear, the one as shame, the other as failure of courage in action. Each takes as central character a youth, impersonal and typical (their names were assigned later), facing life at its crisis, and each analyzes the profound emotional forces bearing upon a point in time by presenting the color and movement of circumstances governing events from the outside and the strong psychological drives from within. To Crane, Maggie Johnson and Henry Fleming are elemental woman and man in the first moment of meeting with death.

In *Maggie* the mind is not entered; the crisis is presented only by swift and ironic reconstruction of environment and surrounding characters. By sheer sincerity the story rises to a conviction in which Howells could detect the "fatal necessity which dominates Greek tragedy" and the simplicity of effect of true art. Naïve and overwritten, it flung Crane's challenge to his times by its unprecedented candor of theme, its sense of fate, and its directness in dealing with sordid material. Its lack of sensuality makes it seem almost pale today, but the fire in its unsold paper-backed copies smoldered until the acclaim accorded to his next work made a new edition possible. With that republication (1896), modern American fiction was born.

In *The Red Badge of Courage* Crane marks his artistic advance by moving easily from the description of the countryside, the advance and retreat of armies, the din of battle, and the color of the sky to the alternating hopes and fears of his boy soldier. Because he can now reveal both inward and outward forces, his determinism carries its own conviction, and Henry Fleming's realization that, "He had been to touch the great death, and found that, after all, it was but the great death," strikes to deeper levels of reality than does Maggie's suicide. From books, from the tactical lore of his brother William, and from conversations with veterans like his teacher at Claverack Academy, General Van Petten, he could now transcend the realism of Howells and Garland because the fear that Henry Fleming felt was in his own heart.

Even in these early stories Crane was far in advance of the psychological knowledge of his contemporaries. His understanding of the effects of environment and instinct on the individual anticipates the theories of the behaviorists, the social psychologists, and the psychoanalysis of a decade or more later. Henry James, the leading current exponent of the psychological novel, had accepted the theory of association, depicting an almost molecular movement of ideas, without defined motivation, on the clear plate of the mind. Crane probed deeper into the problem and, especially in his analysis of Henry Fleming, gives us the anatomy of fear.

Here is a naturalistic view of heroism unknown to the war romances of the time, with the possible exception of those of Bierce, but its bitterness was lost on most of its readers because the hero seemed to be following the usual formula and discovering his manhood by violent action. The story was a success, but it transcends itself by its dismaying revelation. With less plot than *Maggie* it avoids the pitfall of melodrama, but its mood is so intense and its imagery so overwrought that it is led to the brink of another. The reader who can, like Joseph Hergesheimer, feel a sudden revelation in the image, "The sun was pasted in the sky like a wafer," is prepared for its repressed violence of conception and style. True restraint was to come later.

Crane was already familiar with newspaper work when he sold his Civil War novel to the Bacheller syndicate. As a boy he had worked for his brother's press bureau in Asbury Park and he had been the local correspondent of the New York *Tribune* during his year at Syracuse University. He had even held a job on the *Herald* for a short time when he went to New York at the age of twenty, only to lose it and become a free-lance reporter for the rest of his life. His best stories are reports, more successful as illustration than as news, because he could not, like his popular contemporary Richard Harding Davis, stop short at the action and the event. Life came to him in its primary colors, blue, red, and yellow, and he asked its meaning. The newspaper is not interested in such notions.

His reportorial art achieves its maturity in "The Blue Hotel," the scene of which is laid in a Nebraska town in midwinter. Crane, as "the correspondent," is gathered in by the cheerful Irish host as he steps from the train with a cowboy, a quiet Easterner, and a Swede. The tone of the action is set by the light blue of the hotel "always screaming and howling in a way that made the dazzling winter landscape of Nebraska seem only a grey swampish hush." The premonition of the Swede that he will be murdered is but the inner reflection of this screaming blue, the manifestation of Crane's own tense fear. His murder by the professional gambler is an act of necessity; the force which makes it inevitable is beyond any single person in the action. "This poor gambler isn't even a noun," comments the Easterner afterwards. "He is a kind of an adverb. Every sin is the result of a collaboration . . . the apex of a human movement." Crane has now grasped, in a minor incident, the meaning of fear and death, which had eluded him in his earlier and more fully written stories.

The "correspondent" again appears with three companions in "The Open Boat," this time the captain, the cook, and the oiler. A simple record of the actual wreck of a filibustering vessel off the coast of Florida, this story, Crane's masterpiece, achieves its effect by understatement. Its opening sentence, "None of them knew the color of the sky," exactly describes the negative mood of the men in the dinghy. The blue of the sea is slaty, canton-flannel gulls fly overhead, brown mats of seaweed float by to measure movement and distance, the black and white of trees and sand mark the near but unobtainable shore line, and when at last the carmine and gold of morning is painted on the waters, it seems that the impending fate of drowning within sight of help must come to them all. The lone death of the oiler, strongest of the group, is the culminating irony. "When it occurs to a man that nature does not regard him as important . . . he at first wishes to throw bricks at the temple, and he hates deeply the fact that there are no bricks and no temples." This is the meaning of life, in so far as it has a meaning. In no other story does Crane understand his fear so clearly and state it so effectively. Yet here he is apparently recording merely an event which happened to him, without altering a fact or a sequence.

In these and other Western, Mexican, and Cuban tales and sketches where he is recording his mature observations on life in moments of crisis, Crane achieves that instantaneous balance between reality and imagination which makes for great art. Tales in lighter mood like "The Bride Comes to Yellow Sky," "His Majestic Lie," or "The Lone Charge of William B. Perkins" prove that he is capable of comic as well as tragic treatment of his theme. His irony runs the entire gamut from sentimental melodrama, through tragedy and comedy, to travesty like "The Second Generation." Lewisohn feels that "An Experiment in Misery," the bleak account of a night in a flophouse, is his best work because here his "impassiveness" is most extreme, and he himself preferred the drunken shooting spree of "The Bride Comes to Yellow Sky," but both these tales are too slight to give him full scope. In neither his purely imaginary Civil War stories like "A Mystery of Heroism," a distillation of the theme of futile bravery, nor in the more literal accounts of London and the Irish countryside in "The Reporter Errant" does he strike the necessary balance as effectively. Critical consensus returns to "The Open Boat."

In his memories of childhood the mood is less intense, but the tone is still bitter, the meaning dark. The earlier story, "An Ominous Baby," had made a direct statement of his belief in the essential and dispassionate cruelty of childhood, on the theory that the cycle of the individual is the cycle of the race and that the truth of experience is most stark in the infancy of either. But the *Whilomville Stories* (1900), based on his adventures in Port Jervis, New York, as a small boy, are somewhat more mellow. Jimmie Trescott relives the shame and adventures of childhood with a starkness and a sincerity lacking even in much of Mark Twain.

His two longer tales based on early memory, *George's Mother* (1896) and *The Monster* (1899), are less incisive but explore psychological problems even more deeply. The first is only remotely autobiographical, but it suggests, in its analysis of the degenerating effects of too solicitous a mother for the last of her many sons, a possible clue to the emotional complex at the core of Crane's fears. The second is the most horrible of his tales. Though it has been erroneously linked to the school of Poe and Bierce, horror is not its primary purpose. The reaction of a small town to the imbecile Negro who has saved Jimmie Trescott from fire, only to have his face burned away and his mind destroyed, is Crane's major experiment in social satire. The sin is communal, but it appears inevitable as convention conspires with natural law to reject its own morality.

As the *Whilomville Stories* were Crane's last work, it cannot be said that declining health and the social demands of life in his old manor house at Brede, England, where his wife's "biscuits" lured innumerable uninvited guests, killed the art of which he was still capable. In spite of an encroaching consumption, aggravated probably by the fever which he had contracted in Cuba and which haunted him in his last journalistic filibuster to Greece, he could still write sharply and vividly of the fears within the human soul and their reflections in the primary colors of life. But he could not successfully stretch his art into a popular novel, as he attempted to do in *Active Service* (1899), nor into the swashbuckling Irish romance of *The O'Ruddy,* left unfinished at his death. He was still best at the vignette, the finely studied record of a moment, the swift thrust to the meaningless meaning of experience. His vivid impressions of life, with their linking of instinct and circumstance to chain the individual will to its own tragic issue, had provided a pattern for the writing of the next generation. He gave to the naturalistic short story its characteristic form, later to be exploited by Hemingway, Steinbeck, and a host of others.

4

Among the few to join Howells and Garland in critical appreciation of *Maggie* was a young man in San Francisco, Frank Norris of the *Wave*. "Stephen Crane has written a story something on the plan of the episode of Nana in *L'Assommoir*. . . . I think that the charm of his style lies chiefly in his habit and aptitude for making phrases—sparks that cast a momentary gleam of light on whole phases of life." Yet he finds that, "The author is writing . . . from the outside. Mr. Crane does not seem to *know* his people." The kinship and the contrast in the work of these two pioneers of American naturalism are both revealed in this comment. Norris instantly recognized the common debt to Zola, but he objected to Crane's aesthetic objectivity, his feeling for style rather than for "life."

Other critics were not slow in linking the names of the two men when Norris' *McTeague* finally appeared in 1899, three years after *Maggie* became known. In spite of temperamental differences and the span of a continent, they were working toward the same goal, experimenting with the same methods; and they were almost of an age—Norris was born in 1870 and Crane in 1871. Yet they met only once—as fellow correspondents on the tug *Three Friends* off Santiago when they were doing their part to avenge the sinking of the *Maine* by reporting, the one to McClure, the other to the *World*. To Norris, Crane then seemed a seasoned correspondent, the equal almost of his fellow correspondent Harding Davis, for he had "been in peril of his life on a filibustering expedition, was tanned to the color of a well-worn saddle." But natural reserve on both sides prevented a friendship between the "Bohemian" and the tall, serious, well dressed young college man from California, Harvard, and the Julian atelier. Norris was made of different stuff. Actually less deeply immersed in life than Crane, he had thrown himself into college high jinks whereas Crane had retreated, hurt, from his hazing; he had gone to Paris to study painting whereas Crane had merely associated with painters in New York's east side; he had rejoiced, on a grand tour of Africa, to be caught in the Boer uprising whereas Crane snarled and scoffed at the Greeks and Turks; he had never seriously lacked money—his father was a wealthy jewelry merchant—whereas Crane had early known poverty. These two could not talk of their art, their failures and successes.

The most striking fact about Norris and his work is that by temperament, education, and written statement of his philosophy of art, he denies kinship with the realists and allies himself with "Romance." Such easy generalizations as that of Irvin Cobb, "He was a pioneer of the modern school of native realists," can be true only if reconciled with his own statement: "Realism stultifies itself. It notes only the surface of things." In the year before his death, 1901, he proclaimed his creed to be derived from Zola and Kipling, denying the fiction of Howells as "respectable as a church and proper as a deacon." Accepting Howells as spokesman for the method, he rejected his limitations in so far as he could. In thus aligning himself with the romantics, according to some critics, he read himself out of the society of naturalists entirely.

But the conflict is largely a matter of definition. "Romance," he says, "is the kind of fiction that takes cognizance of variations from the type of normal life. . . . [It] may even treat of the sordid, the unlovely." To find her, you need not take her "a weary journey across the water—ages and the flood of years"; rather you should take her "across the street to your neighbour's front parlour," or to Fifth Avenue or Wall Street. She would note details to be sure, on the way, but she would find the heartache or the memory beneath the surface facts. Such searching for truth rather than for reality is quite respectable and may even resort to the ugly and the violent when safely removed to "the castles of the Middle Ages and the Renaissance châteaux." May it not also be used as "an instrument with which we may go straight through the clothes and tissues and wrappings of flesh down deep into the red, living heart of things?" This is the veritism of Garland in the hands of a man who plunged directly from feeling into action and then paused briefly afterward to think out his reasons. His critical terms may not be carefully weighed and his logic not always perfect, but he gave American fiction another dimension. When he said, "Life is not always true to life. . . . In the fine arts we do not care one little bit about what life actually is, but what it looks like to an interesting, impressionable man," he was speaking, like Crane, as the painter, but also as the dramatist. He was a novelist because of his passionate conviction that the novel "expresses modern life better than architecture, better than painting, better than poetry, better than music." The novel can speak directly to the people, as all art should, because the people will read and reread it. At her best, "the muse is a teacher, not a trickster." The realist who stops short at the surface fact, or the "Bohemian" who loses himself and his sincerity in the intricacies of style, tone, and effect, are equally at fault. To Norris, fiction was a vital, two-fisted art, the art of the future.

He did not reach this position at once, nor did he hold to it consistently. His work does not show a steady advance; in some ways, he came nearer his purpose at the start than at the close of his short career. He never achieved the discipline of the school to which he was instinctively allied, that of scientific naturalism, because his love of the story for itself was too likely to run away with his ideas about it. Although he tried to reject the conventions and the sentimentality of popular romance, his critical distinctions were not sufficiently clear to keep him out of the traps against which he warned others. Furthermore, as he did not publish his work in the order in which it was written, the progress which some critics have attributed to him is an illusion.

Nevertheless it is possible to trace his development with a fair degree of accuracy. It falls into four stages: his youth when he was completely immersed in the far away and the long ago; his college years when, under the spell of Zola, he did his best work; his years as a newspaper man and social dillettante when, in trying to find his own métier and at the same time to gain a hearing, he wrote his romances; and the last years of his life when, as publisher's reader and free-lance novelist, he undertook his trilogy of wheat. A further confusion arises from the fact that most of his short stories and sketches were potboilers, and many of them were gleaned from novels already written. Few are useful to the critic either as sources or as representative art. Unlike Crane, Garland, and London, Norris was a novelist, and he cared for no other prose form.

His first published work, *Yvernelle* (1891), a long narrative poem on a medieval theme, is the enthusiastic effort of a boy of nineteen who had spent long childhood hours playing lead soldiers with his younger brother and who had later immersed himself in Froissart and the *Chanson de Roland*. His interest was in medieval armor during his art-student days in Paris—the days of Zola, the Goncourts, and De Maupassant—and there is no evidence that he even then knew of the existence of these later masters. For the time, the Musée de Cluny held more life for him and his artist friend Ernest Peixotto than did the streets of Paris. Let it not be forgotten that when Norris made his final plea for romance, he was offering a justification for his own deepest nature.

Why then his sudden discovery of the first and greatest of the naturalists when he was a student at the University of California? Sensitive, acute, energetic, he instinctively turned to life rather than to books for his learning, but Zola gave his love of romance a present anchorage in the world he saw and felt and smelled, and about which he speculated with eager interest. "Naturalism, as understood by Zola," he wrote later in the *Wave*, "is but a form of romanticism. . . . Everything is extraordinary, imaginative, grotesque even, with a vague note of terror quivering throughout like the vibrations of an ominous and low-pitched diapason." To his early enthusiasm for Scott, Dickens, and Stevenson, instilled by his mother, Kipling was added. The British teller of tales had easily blended science with adventure, and his American disciple was off on a South African exploration when a return of "the attack of Harding Davis" seized him. It would be hard for him to disentangle the threads of science and popular romance, but a way would be found if sincere effort could find it.

McTeague (1899) was his first sustained experiment in fiction. This novel and *Vandover and the Brute* (1914), written during his year at Harvard when in Lewis E. Gates he found his first real teacher, follow the Zola formula strictly but, in spirit if not always in execution, are sincere explorations of his own experience rather than imitations. The one a story of a Polk Street dentist, the other of a privileged youth of his own class, they are both studies of slow degeneration through an overwhelming of the finer instincts and aspirations by the suppressed brute nature. McTeague has all the physical and mental characteristics of the brute, but he is harmless—almost admirable —in his childish acceptance of life. But he and Trina, his "mate-woman" as Jack London would have called her, relapse atavistically into avarice, as Norris notes step by step the slow inroads of poverty, the creeping degeneration of all his principal characters. The inherent ugliness of life, the gold symbols of aspiration—false because merely material—the dual nature of man, are examined with ruthless power. Up to the magnificently restrained scene of the murder the novel is a unified masterpiece of naturalism, superior in execution to *Maggie,* unequaled for a generation in American literature. Even Dreiser is less successful in fundamental grasp of motivation and in sensuous description of significant details.

There are romantic flaws: The love story of Old Grannis and Miss Baker, introduced into Norris' original plan with the valid intention of providing contrast but sentimentalized in the conventional fashion, and the melodramatic conclusion of pursuit and death in the desert—added later after the manuscript had long lain fallow—are the most striking. Both, however, are so well presented that they do not offend, and the total effect of the story is unified and powerful.

Vandover takes its theme as well as its method from science. It is autobiographic in the sense that it studies the form of atavism to which a young man of wealth, pliable disposition, and sensitivity like Norris would be subject. In Vandover the typical naturalistic weakness of will and consequent dissipation take the form of a recognized ailment, lycanthropy, a type of insanity in which the patient imagines himself a wolf or other animal and imitates its actions. Norris had experimented with the theme of reversion to primitive type in "Lauth," a short story in which a scholarly youth is awakened to his savage nature by the sight of blood of his own taking. But in *Vandover,* by following Zola into clinical realms, he violates his own warning that actuality is sometimes not artistically convincing. In the early part of the story, when the suppressed brute is merely an idea, a horrible fear, there are brilliant passages of narrative description and psychological subtlety; but when Vandover actually goes down naked on all fours the result, however sound medically, verges on the grotesque. Norris doubtless recognized this weakness, for he failed to complete his story and it was not published until long after his death; but it must now take its place beside *McTeague* as an early and daring example of naturalistic fiction, far more authentic than any of London's later and more acceptable treatments of the same theme.

If there is a mystery as to why the boisterous romance, *Moran of the Lady Letty* (1898), rather than either *McTeague* or *Vandover,* was Norris' first published novel, it is dispelled merely by taking his cheery little love story *Blix* (1899) as autobiography. The same mild vices of party-going and card-playing that led Vandover into degeneration are in Condy Rivers, the hero of *Blix,* diverted into success as a popular novelist and virtuous husband by the "thoroughbred" Travis Bessemer. "Blix," as Condy calls her, is the "new woman" on the Charles Dana Gibson pattern. She has an independence of mind that makes her all the more feminine, even though the reviewers objected when Norris described her as tall and solidly built as a man, radiating health, with small, twinkling, brown eyes. In a civilized way, she is the Viking type that Norris so much admired rather than the conventional heroine—an accurate portrait of his wife Jeannette Black, and the summer idyl of comradeship was his own love story. For the stories of Norris and of Condy are one. The suggestion for *Moran* is to be found in a letter, probably authentic, that Condy received from a New York publisher with the return of a manuscript of collected short stories. "The best-selling book just now is the short novel—say thirty thousand words—of action and adventure." Condy took the suggestion and pulled himself out of the inertia of Sunday supplement editing and the debilitating association of the Bohemian Club in which he was caught. Norris wrote *Moran.*

The story of Condy's novel was suggested by Captain Jack, an old sea dog that he and Blix had discovered in their harmless adventuring. Ross Wilbur of *Moran* is again Norris, now to be shanghaied from a season of "afternoon teas, pink, lavender, and otherwise," and carried by the schooner *Petrel* on a shark-hunting expedition with a crew of Chinamen and a beach-combing captain to Magdalena Bay. The education of Ross into manhood is started by the Captain's fist and continued by the Viking maiden Moran when a series of accidents with a derelict leave the two young people in command of the ship and its coolie crew. Here is the theme which London later developed more fully in *The Sea Wolf,* but Norris turns attention rather to "action and adventure." The naturalistic theme of Moran's awakening to womanhood and the sensuous wealth of descriptive detail aroused the enthusiasm of even the vigilant Howells, and Norris' career was assured.

He was summoned to New York, the "literary center" which he was soon
to deny, and put a winter of effort into reading for Doubleday and expanding
a story of Arctic adventure into another naturalistic romance of primitive
love, *A Man's Woman* (1900), "grinding out the tale, as it were by main
strength." But the bread had no yeast and his powers were being wasted on
the secondhand adventures of Captain Jack. The one significant event of the
winter was his discovery of Theodore Dreiser, his instant appreciation of the
manuscript of *Sister Carrie*.

Suddenly there came to him "an idea that's as big as all outdoors," and
McClure agreed with him that "the big American novel is going to come out
of the West." The trilogy of wheat which he was never to finish had been
conceived, and he hastened back to San Francisco and the San Joaquin Valley
for local color. "It involves a very long, a very serious, and perhaps a very
terrible novel," he wrote a friend.

The Octopus (1901) is usually studied as our first great economic thesis-
novel, but to Norris it was "the big, epic, dramatic thing." His literary problem is written into the poet Presley who goes to live on the Los Muertos
ranch in Tulare County in preparation for his epic of the West.

> Just what he wanted, Presley hardly knew. On the one hand, it was his ambi-
> tion to portray life as he saw it—directly, frankly, and through no medium of
> personality or temperament. But on the other hand as well, he wished to see
> everything through a rose-coloured mist—a mist that dulled all harsh outlines,
> all crude and violent colours. . . . He searched for the True Romance, and, in
> the end, found grain rates and unjust freight tariffs.

Presley accomplished no more than his poem "The Toilers," an idea modeled
on Markham's "The Man With the Hoe," but Norris, putting his vast idea
into more versatile prose, wrote *The Octopus* and very nearly achieved the
masterpiece he visioned. Since *Moby Dick*, by then virtually forgotten, there
had been nothing like it in American literature.

In sheer spread of canvas *The Octopus* achieved all that Norris hoped
for it, but as a work of art it has obvious faults. With romantic fogginess of
mind, Norris resolved none of his major issues, artistic, economic, or philosophic. His main story of the decline of Magnus Derrick, the master of Los
Muertos, follows the course of those of McTeague and Vandover, although
outside circumstance as well as moral weakness undermines the structure of
character. This in itself is an advance in naturalistic understanding, a recognition of the force of environment as well as that of biological defect, a movement away from the merely psychological to the sociological novel. But the
story of Magnus is intertwined with the primitive and tragic love of the

rancher Annixter for his milkmaid Hilma Tree (again the mating of Moran but now on a more civilized and restrained level), and with the mystical romance of the shepherd Vanamee with the spirit of his dead Angèle, reminiscent of *Trilby,* a book which Norris scorned. These three strands, together with lesser ones, are woven by an epic theme and a common philosophy into an intricate pattern—or at least it was Norris' intention so to weave them. Presley abandoned his Milton and Homer for Mill, Malthus, Henry George, and Schopenhauer.

He trembled with excitement as the relations between the [Railroad] Trust and the [Ranchers'] League became more and more strained. He saw the matter in its true light. It was typical. It was the world-old war between Freedom and Tyranny.

All these personal stories became merged in one impersonal conflict between the Life Force, as symbolized by the Wheat, and the Machine, as symbolized by the Railroad. Magnus, as leader of the wheat growers, and the potbellied S. Behrman, as spokesman for the railroad, became primary antagonists in the struggle. The vigorous California story teller saw the tragic issue of the time and place as the New England recluse Henry Adams saw it: the Wheat and the Railroad were the Virgin and the Dynamo, less subtly and profoundly understood.

The climactic scene where the ranchers meet the representatives of the railroad at the irrigation ditch more than satisfies Norris' requirement that a novel build up to a "pivotal event" and explode in a "rush of action," but the somewhat fortuitous conclusion—S. Behrman buried by his own wheat in the hold of his own vessel—fails to achieve the effect of naturalistic determinism which it was obviously designed to produce. "Men were naught," Presley had finally decided, "death was naught, life was naught; FORCE only existed." But the traditional idealist in Norris would not down so easily and he pushes past this force to the "primordial energy flung out from the hand of the Lord himself, immortal, calm, infinitely strong." Hence the fecundity of earth may find its expression equally in the warmth of Hilma Tree or the unreality of Angèle; the shepherd Vanamee may conquer death while the impersonal Force is crushing out the lives of his friends; and the demon behind it all, Shelgrim, the president of the Pacific and Southwestern Railroad, may plead that he, too, is a puppet in the impersonal drama of natural law. Dramatic it all is on a grand scale, both epic and tragic in its power, but logical it is not. The book finally fails as tragic drama because Norris has no consistent position on the vast economic and metaphysical problems he raises. Fiction need not provide answers to such problems, but its angle of view must be consistent. Norris shifts with his poet Presley from sympathy with the capitalistic ranchers to support of the "reds" and back to excuses even for the railroad, from mechanistic determinism to mystical theism and back. The principles at the foundation of the book were never thought through.

A great failure is akin to a success. *The Octopus* is the most ambitious novel of its generation. Though planned as the first of a trilogy which was to follow the Wheat through the three stages of growth, marketing, and export to famine-ridden Europe or Asia, it must stand alone, for its sequel *The Pit* (1903) is a relapse into the conventional novel form, and the third work, *The Wolf,* was never written. In *The Octopus,* the wheat itself could be the central character, for it was ever present. "There it was. The Wheat! The Wheat! In the night it had come up. It was there, everywhere from margin to margin of the horizon." But in the Chicago grain pit, it is off stage, a column of figures in a ledger, a few miles of ticker tape, an object of man-made speculation rather than of elemental force. Nevertheless, Norris' contemporary reviewers were not far wrong in greeting the story of the rise and fall of Curtis Jadwin as his most mature novel. Its theme is of profound social significance; the characters of Jadwin and his wife Laura Dearborn, like those of McTeague and Trina, studies of degeneration through greed, achieve sympathy through understanding and powerful treatment; and the plot, in spite of its unfortunately happy ending, has originality within its conventional frame. Anticipating Dreiser's *The Financier* (1912) and *The Titan* (1914), it is a sincere and impartial study of the meaning of American capitalism, of the degenerating influence of greed in high places. In this last novel Norris finally blended what he understood of naturalistic fiction with the romance of contemporary life. The result is not his most impressive work, but it is sound, and it was acceptable to his readers. He had proved, at least to his own satisfaction, that romance could find the truth in contemporary life as well as could realism.

5

Many of the abortive pseudoscientific trends in Frank Norris found their popular apologist in Jack London, author of forty-nine volumes of fiction, drama, and essay, who published his first book two years before Norris died. The illegitimate son of an itinerant astrologer and of a spiritualist, London preached the more obvious radicalism of his day in romantic fiction that, during sixteen years (1900–1916), raised him from obscurity and poverty to fame and wealth, brought him all the rewards of adventure, love, learning, and worldly possessions that his insatiable body and mind craved, and led him to egocentric despair and probable suicide. The personification of the romantic impulses of the new century, vigorous, naïve, and prolific, he provided his magazine readers with unstinted fare, and left a small body of writing which, for sincerity and vitality, deserves to be rescued from the oblivion to which his artistic faults threaten to condemn it. Primarily a skillful teller of tales, he achieved originality and significance by enthusiastic acceptance of the new doctrines of society and science that made a ferment of the popular mind.

"There is an ecstasy that marks the summit of life," he wrote, "and beyond which life cannot rise. . . . This ecstasy comes when one is most alive, and it comes as a complete forgetfulness that one is alive." It was this spirit, here ascribed to the dog Buck of *The Call of the Wild,* that drove him relentlessly through his forty years, as it drove his elder contemporary Theodore Roosevelt. Before reaching the age of nineteen, according to his own account, he had lived a life "raw and naked, wild and free" as an oyster pirate in San Francisco Bay, he had shipped as an able-bodied seaman on the schooner *Sophie Sutherland* for Japan, he had worked sixteen hours a day at a cannery and in a jute mill, he had hoboed his way across the United States with Kelly's "industrial army" in its march on Washington, and he had spent thirty days in the Niagara Falls jail for vagrancy. In spite of confessed abhorrence for alcohol he had proved his manhood by meeting the sociable John Barleycorn on his own terms.

Always a haunter of libraries as well as of saloons, he had as a boy devoured popular fiction, and, suddenly in 1895, he decided that he would sell brains rather than brawn. He would climb the class barrier with the aid of "the books." Like the hero of his semiautobiographical novel *Martin Eden* (1909), he identified the upper class and the university with all that was noble, and he diverted his burning zeal into a program of reading and writing which covered high-school studies and a term at the University of California in two years; then dropped it all and was off to the Klondike. Returning after a year to Oakland as poor as when he left, he began selling stories, jokes, light verse, and essays to the struggling *Overland Monthly,* to many a lesser journal, and even to the remote *Atlantic,* pawning his overcoat and his bicycle between checks to pay for his rented typewriter and boasting that he worked nineteen hours out of every twenty-four. In 1899 the unaccountable whirlwind of success that he describes in *Martin Eden* brought him fifteen checks from magazines and the acceptance of his first collection of tales, *The Son of the Wolf* (1900). His hero Martin brushed success from him and sought morbid peace by drowning; London, like Melville and many another, sublimated his restlessness in writing.

Eight years had to pass before he could understand this crisis well enough to record it. Those years saw his best work but none is so revealing nor so powerful as *Martin Eden*. The chronicle of a sick ego, this thinly screened confession, with its fidelity, its misunderstanding of naked tragic forces, and its failure of resolution, is the central document of his career. Martin's defeat was the tragedy of his times because in him the emotional and intellectual conflicts of the new science were brought to a focus.

Jack London was a confessed Spencerian evolutionist and Marxian socialist. He had familiarized himself with evolution and socialism by undisciplined and voracious reading, and by constant talks with men more learned than he was or ever cared to be, but he knew both movements as the ultimate consumer, the people, rather than as the scholar or critic. From Spencer and his popularizers he accepted the thesis that man evolved from lower forms of life, differing from them in degree rather than in kind, and he followed the doctrine of the "synthetic philosophy" through to a positive faith in progress and a benevolent anarchy of Anglo-Saxon supremacy that would allow both social harmony and complete individualism. His mind rejected the Nietzschean doctrine of the superman, but his temperament accepted it with a deeper logic. From the *Communist Manifesto,* which he had read while on the road, and from the writings of American socialists rather than from *Das Kapital,* he drew the doctrines of class warfare, revolution, and the ultimate triumph of the working class over the capitalists. He resented the socialists' demand for political action as a threat to individual prerogative, but he fell in with their program and became an active worker in their cause. Such inconsistencies were enough to tear him apart, but the real source of his sickness, an intense and inhibited egocentricity, he revealed with complete candor and total incomprehension.

These three issues, biological evolution, socialism, and psychological inhibition, became one in Martin Eden's attempt to win fame, fortune, and love by determination. The original of Ruth Morse of the novel was Mabel Applegarth, a college friend who at once symbolized for him the ideals of upper-class culture and the dream woman of the male animal. When he discovered the bourgeois conventionality, dishonesty, and materialism that he had mistaken for ideality in her and her set, he rejected both illusions, and with them the dying literary code of ideality. In his own life, London turned without love to the "companion" and "mother-woman" Bess Maddern, but he allowed Martin no such escape from his crisis. His divorce, after two years of marriage and two daughters, had taught him the fallacy of this solution, an argument that he worked out with the help of another "companion," Anna Strunsky, in *The Kempton-Wace Letters* (1903). His second marriage in 1905 to his "mate-woman" Charmian Kittredge had seemingly solved his own problem and had provided him with sufficient perspective to tell Martin's story; but he gave Martin suicide rather than a mate. His own crisis was deferred in his "Valley of the Moon," a pretentious but never completed ranch in Sonoma County, California, where success, wealth, and love brought with them recurrent alcoholism and a deep despair that belied his healthful buoyancy of spirit. The unwritten chapters of *Martin Eden* are added by his most sincere book *John Barleycorn* (1913), a personal analysis of the power of drink, where he confesses to "roaming with the White Logic through the dusk of my soul," and by *The Little Lady of the Big House* (1916), a "design for living" in which jealousy defeats the supreme experiment of free mating and brings the old and inconclusive answer, suicide.

In *The Sea Wolf* (1904) the failure of the amoral superman is illustrated with even more clarity. Wolf Larsen is London's most fully conceived character. Captain of a sealing schooner, he knows only the primitive law of survival through predatory ruthlessness. He is a wolf in fact as well as in name, with the shrewd intelligence as well as the brute power of the wolf. But he, like London, has grappled with "the books" and become conscious of his motives and deliberate in his actions. His awakening of the dilettante Humphrey Van Weyden provides a magnificent theme for a great novel, and the first half almost realizes the possibilities by showing in a parallel situation what Norris might have done with the opening chapters of *Moran of the Lady Letty*. But the sudden appearance of the "mate-woman" Maud Brewster, afloat in mid-ocean, throws the whole plot off balance and turns a study in naturalism into a desert island romance. Larsen's fall is caused by the accident of blindness rather than by a tragic flaw in his character or philosophy, and the island sequences, with their absurd mixture of Victorian prudery and primitive law, their painful stretching of probability, leave the novel a worse wreck than the vessel the *Ghost* or its master.

The two dog stories, *The Call of the Wild* (1903) and *White Fang* (1906), are more successful because they are uncomplicated by the problem of sex in society. The love of dog and man may be studied in primitive terms more readily than may that of man and woman. In the one book a dog breaks with the codes of civilization and reverts, step by step, to its wolf origins; in the other a part-wolf is gradually weaned from the wild and takes his place in the world of his man-god. *The Call of the Wild* is London's most satisfying work. The theme and action are in tune, the character of Buck is fully realized, the story proceeds with the economy and sure strokes of a writer in full command of his material. But never again, except in occasional short stories where the task is easier because less ambitious, did he so sharpen his focus and so completely realize his biological thesis in fictional form.

There is of course an underlying social significance in the rejection or acceptance of civilization by the primitive individual in all studies of atavism and its contrary, but the message of social revolution is expressed better in essay and tract than in any of his fiction. His contribution to the muckraking movement, *The People of the Abyss* (1903), is a study of English rather than American, economic rather than political, degradation. It is the narrative of his own experiences when he donned old clothes and lived in London's East End in order to study poverty and crime at its worst. A patronizing tone is not sufficient to injure the graphic realism of his account. In the essays of *The War of the Classes* (1905), *Revolution* (1910), and *The Human Drift* (1917) he states with passion but without philosophic depth the position of the American social revolutionist and his faith in the rise of the working class. Only once did he attempt to garb his thesis in fiction, in *The Iron Heel* (1908), a terrifying forecast of Fascism and its evils.

In the title essay of *The Human Drift* London comes to grips with his problem and realizes that social revolution is only an incident in the process of evolution. Returning to Spencer with the intellectual comprehension of a Garland and the emotional acceptance of a Norris, he declares that "man, the latest of the ephemera, is pitifully a creature of temperature, strutting his brief day on the thermometer," driven onward by his need for food—a thought that once occurred to Benjamin Franklin. All the red-blooded eagerness and purity of the open life, which had been honestly his own at the start but which had by now become merely his marketable product, had faded into a cynical negation. He had felt and thought deeply enough to be able to cry with Richard Hovey, "Behold! I have lived!" but he had come finally, in spite of his buoyant temperament, to the pessimistic conclusions of the philosophy of biological and mechanistic determinism. It remained for Henry Adams to define and for later naturalists like Dreiser, Hemingway, Farrell, and Steinbeck to grapple more significantly with the problems which he, Norris, and others had raised. Jack London had become story teller extraordinary to William Randolph Hearst.

With London's failure to realize its possibilities, naturalism as a movement in American fiction reached the end of its first and experimental phase. When Dreiser published *Jennie Gerhardt* in 1911 and republished *Sister Carrie* in 1912, it entered its second.

Thus the demand of science that human life be reconsidered as the manifestation of natural laws had led these experimental story tellers in two quite contrary directions. The method of science suggested a further development of realism toward analysis of data, and the frank discussion of all—and especially the abnormal, the sordid, and the socially unjust—aspects of experience. On the other hand its attendant philosophy of dispassionate force stimulated new generalizations and created new symbols to represent the basic drives in man and in nature—thereby developing a new form of romance. Neither impressionistic realism in Garland and Crane nor the romance of power in Norris and London proved adequate to its demand.

The movement succeeded, however, not only in this country but abroad.

in forcing the artist to confront once more the fundamental issues of human destiny, and because it chose the novel and the short story rather than the drama or poetry as its principal forms of expression, it gave them a depth and a sincerity which they had seldom before achieved. The faith in the possibilities of naturalistic fiction, which Garland and Norris preached with the zeal of fanatics, was not yet justified in their day, at least in the United States. Only once before had an adequate philosophy been put into the hands of the American teller of tales, when Poe, Hawthorne, and Melville wrote of sin, free will, and fate. When the new view of the universe proposed by science could develop a metaphysic and an ethic in harmony with it, the way would again be open to these fundamental issues. What the twentieth century held for the American writer of fiction, no one in 1910 could even guess.

63. HENRY JAMES

On the level of the ideal—on the level of art—American fiction achieved in the novels and short stories of Henry James a kind of reality different from both the literal record of a Howells and the philosophical naturalism of a Zola. This reality was his response to the human predicament of his generation, which James felt with unusual acuteness because of the virtual formlessness of his education—the predicament of the sensitive mind during what may be called the interregnum between the effective dominance of the old Christian-classical ideal through old European institutions and the rise to rule of the succeeding ideal, whatever history comes to call it. To express that predicament in fiction no education could have been more fitting than his, for it excluded him from assenting to the energies of social expansion, of technology, of the deterministic sciences, and of modern finance and business. Unconscious assent to these forces, over and above any rebellion against their moral values, caused most active minds in his day to conceal the fact of interregnum. James' mind reacted only to the shadows of those forces as revealed in human emotion and in social behavior and convention. With his abiding sense of the indestructible life, he expressed the decay and sterility of a society pretending to live on conventions and institutions but lacking the force of underlying convictions. He described what he saw, and he created what lay under what he saw.

They tell a story of Henry James which cannot be verified as to fact, but one which is so true and just in spirit that we may take it as the scriptural text for this chapter. Once, in the nineties, while James was staying in an English country house, the only child of a neighbor died of a sudden illness; and although James had quarreled with the neighbor and they had not been on speaking terms he announced to his host that he would attend the funeral of the little boy. His host argued that, in the small church in the small village, it would be conspicuously unseemly for him to go—the bereaved parents could only take it as an affront; but James was obstinate. When he returned, his host asked him how on earth he could have brought himself to go, and to sit, as he had, in the pew directly behind the mourners. James brushed all argument aside and, with that intensity in his eyes which made his face seem naked, stated firmly: "Where emotion is, there am I!"

All his life long, and in all but his slightest work, James struggled to use the conventions of society, and to abuse them when necessary, to bring himself directly upon the emotion that lay under the conventions, coiling and recoiling, ready to break through. So to bring himself, and so to see, was for him action in life and creation in art. "Where emotion is, there am I!" If he could find the emotion he could for himself realize life, and if he could create the reality of the emotion in his art, in terms of actual characters and situations, he could make his art—in James Joyce's phrase at the end of *The Portrait of the Artist As a Young Man*—the uncreated conscience of his race. The story of that struggle to realize life as emotion and to create it as art is the abiding story of Henry James, as near as we can come to the Figure in his Carpet.

With the events of his life we have here little to do except see how their conditions, both those imposed upon him and those which he imposed upon himself, led him to an increasing devotion to that struggle, and to the final decision at full maturity that in the very passion of pleading for full life in others, for him life had to be sacrificed to art. As he sometimes put it, his own life had to disappear into his art just to the degree that he was a successful artist. The conditions imposed upon him were freedom of sensibility and conscience and the emotional insecurity that is apt to accompany that freedom. His was a minimum financial security and the curious need to prove one's own value that in responsive natures sometimes goes with that security. His also was so wide a variety of social and educational exposures, which had in common only their informality, that he was left the most social man in the world but without a society or an institution that could exact his allegiance. His, further, was an accidental injury by a slip or a fall in early manhood which seems to have left him with the sense of a physical uprootedness and isolation that only aggravated, as it fed upon, his emotional isolation. Like Abélard who, after his injury, raised the first chapel to the Holy Ghost, James made a sacred rage of his art as the only spirit he could fully serve.

2

Henry James was born in New York City, April 15, 1843, the second son of Henry James, Sr.—a peripatetic philosopher and dissenting theologian of considerable means, a friend of Emerson and Carlyle, and a great believer in a universal but wholly informal society. It was he who on his deathbed directed that the only words spoken at his funeral should be: "Here lies a man, who has thought all his life that the ceremonies attending both marriage and death were all damned nonsense." To his sons William and Henry he gave a kind of infant baptism after his own heart by taking them abroad before they could speak and dipping them generously in the font of Europe: a rite which was to mark them both with particular strength and weakness for life. After Europe in 1843 and 1844, the family alternated between Albany and New York. The children were sent to at least three schools before 1855, when in June they went to Europe for a three-year educational experiment at Geneva, London, Paris, and Boulogne. The year 1858–1859 was passed at Newport, Rhode Island; 1859–1860, at Geneva and Bonn. Thus the boys learned languages and manners and fragments of many systems of formal education; but more important were the incalculable effects of years of exposure to the sights and sounds and tones of "other" worlds than that in which by birth they might have been expected to grow up. Part of their father's intention was to give them, by keeping them safe from any particular soil, the richest and most varied human soil to grow in. When he had given them as much of Europe as possible, he removed them to what was at that time the least American of all towns, and for two years they lived again at Newport. There they came under the influence of a young man who was to become the least American of all American painters, John La Farge. Then, in 1862, Henry James made his one attempt at formal education, in the Harvard Law School, a venture which seems to have had no effect on him at all. It was at this time that he sustained his injury and was kept out of the Civil War, the great historical action of his time.

The young James then turned to literature, at first uncertainly and as a "possible" occupation but within four or five years firmly and fully as a profession. His earliest story appeared in the *Atlantic Monthly* in 1865, when he was twenty-two, and he published stories, sketches, and critical reviews frequently thereafter in that magazine, in the *Nation,* and elsewhere. In the fiction and sketches the writing was easy to the point of facility, romantic in tone except where it was humorous, and distinguished chiefly by its competence; in the criticism, it was high-toned and even captious. It showed the influences of Dickens and Hawthorne, Washington Irving and perhaps a little Balzac, in short the dominant literary influences of his time. The American scene, as characterized by Boston and New York, kept him alive but did not provoke reaction or experiment in his writing.

In 1869 he went abroad again, this time to literary as well as social Europe, and for ten or twelve years paid visits to America rather than to Europe. Abroad he alternated between London and Paris, London and Italy. London was to live in, Paris was to learn in, Italy to love; America had become chiefly something for his literary and social sensibility to react on. London gave him the support of an institutionalized society which made for security and position. Italy gave him color and form and warmth, and the ideal satisfaction of all his romantic nostalgia for those qualities. But Paris gave him his profession; for there he met Turgenev, whom he called the "beautiful genius," and Flaubert, whom he found vulgar in person but perfect in writing. It was in Paris that he learned that the novel was an art and that art was the mastering, all-exacting profession that alone made life tolerable by making it intelligible. He learned also that the art of literature, like the art of painting or of music, was an international art, however locally rooted it might have to be in inspiration, and for himself he made the decision that his inspiration might well be as international as the art. It was a decision for which his education had prepared him, just as was his decision to live in London but to keep up his American and French connections. Perhaps it was the very informality of his education that made him grasp for safety at the formalism of English society and the form of the French novel of Flaubert and the Russian novel of Turgenev who was himself a result of the French influence. Formalism and form were for him the means of understanding the formlessness which was life itself; but he never confused the two, though he sometimes made the mistake of refusing to see the life, either in America or in the novels of "disorderly" writers like Dostoevski and Zola, if the form was not within the habit of his perception.

The effect of these years of discipleship and decision was triple. They transformed James from one more American writer working at his trade to an addicted artist working to perfect the form of his chosen art. They gave him his three themes: the international theme, the theme of the artist in conflict with society, and the theme of the pilgrim in search of society. And through his work, the form of the novel in England and America was developed to a new maturity and variety and responsibility. In 1881, with the publication of *The Portrait of a Lady,* the European novel as a form became part of the resources of the English language, and James himself a great novelist, for in that novel his three major themes were for the first time combined in a single objective form.

These years ended the first long period in James' literary life with a high climax, at the same time that they ended the actually international aspect of his personal life. Perhaps his father's death in 1882 helped diminish his sense of personal American connection. Perhaps his loss of popularity after *The Portrait of a Lady,* which was the last book to sell really well in his own lifetime, forced him into the more private reality of his English connection. Perhaps he had merely finally made up his mind. At any rate, he remained in England without visiting America until 1904 (when he made the tour which is recorded in part in *The American Scene*), and in the nineties he established himself in the nearest he ever had to a real home, at Lamb House, Rye, in Sussex.

The "middle period," from 1882 to 1897, when he published *The Spoils of*

Poynton, was one of experimentation, refinement of medium, exacerbation of sensibility, and extreme sophistication of perception. Nothing written during that period reached the stature of *The Portrait of a Lady;* much of it was water in sand that only rearranged the grains, though much of it was exquisitely molded. It was then that he earned his reputation for finickiness, difficulty beyond the necessities, unreality, and remoteness. His disappointment was so great that, during the latter part of this period, he succumbed to the temptation to write deliberately "popular," deliberately "well made" plays, none of which did well, and one of which, at its London performance, brought him the humiliation of personal hisses when he appeared on the stage at the call for author. Yet he had finally mastered the art that was to make it possible for him to write, in the third period, from 1897 to 1904, first-rate novels and tales, among them the series of three great novels, *The Ambassadors, The Wings of the Dove,* and *The Golden Bowl.* Perhaps his failure in his one effort at treason to his high calling when he turned to drama, and the personal humiliation of that failure, jolted him back with new strength by reaction to his old conception of the novel; perhaps he had merely needed the long time of experiment for secret incubation; in any case, preparation was necessary for maturity of technique and, more important, for maturity of sensibility.

The fourth period began with a visit to America in 1904 and 1905 and might well have prepared him, had he lived longer or had the First World War not intervened, for the still greater art of which we can see the signs in the volume of stories called *The Finer Grain,* collected in 1910. These years were spent in the revision of his novels and tales for the New York Edition, in the volume on *The American Scene* (1907), and in the writing of several volumes of memoirs. After 1910 two experimental novels were begun but never finished, *The Ivory Tower* and *The Sense of the Past.* War and sickness prevented their completion and they were published as he left them after his death in the winter of 1916. At his life's end he had a number of friends but none close, many acquaintances but none important to him, and considerable influence on the younger writers of his time, though nothing commensurate to the influence he was later to exert when the luxury of his sensibility and the rigors of his form became increasingly necessary to a larger number of readers and writers. Howells, Bennett, Wells, Ford Madox Ford, Conrad, and Edith Wharton gained by his example, and the last three avowedly made use of his method—Conrad notably in *Chance* and *Under Western Eyes,* Ford in *The Good Soldier* and his remarkable tetralogy about the war, of which the first volume was *Some Do Not,* and Mrs. Wharton in all but her early work. Of the later generation, Virginia Woolf and Dorothy Richardson would have been impossible without him, as less directly

Faulkner and Hemingway and Graham Greene would also have been impossible without the maturity to which he had brought their craft. But essentially he died, as he had lived, lonely both in art and in life, a very special case indeed.

3

Yet he is no more special than Swift or Donne or Proust. He is merely one of those writers in whom succeeding ages find differing values and to whom each age assigns a different rank; nor is it likely that within a particular age he will ever escape violently opposed opinions as to the character of what he wrote. He is thus a perpetual anomaly. How he came to be so, why he must remain so and for what literary good and ill, it is the purpose of this chapter to inquire. For in the stresses and oppositions and active conflicts that make him anomalous, we see what he stood for and we measure the varying stature of what he did.

He stood for that universal human society which is held to underlie any and all existing forms of society; and what he did was to attempt to express the supremacy of universal society over the very narrow existing society he fed on for material. What he stood for was deep in him, a shaping part of his nature; but for what he did he was ill equipped with the conventional kind of sensibility, though excellently equipped with the passion—the suffering readiness and tenacity—of extraordinary sensibility. He was therefore driven to excesses of substitution and renunciation and refinement (in experience and morals and style) beyond warrant of any other successful author's use. Yet in these very excesses lay the virtue of his fundamental insight. Given the broad poverty and intense riches of his known world, it was his insight that forced upon him his excesses. He had to go out of the world to judge the world.

That necessity, the privations which caused it, and its consequent excesses were almost family traits. They show in William as well as in Henry, and pretty much combine in their father. Each of the three suffered in youth a central damage from an experience of the immanence of overwhelming evil and its menace to the self, a damage which was never repaired and never forgotten, so that life always remained perilous. But each was able to balance his experience of evil by an experience of something like religious conversion. None of these conversions except that of the father were on Christian terms; none left its subject attached permanently to any particular form of religion or to any particular form of society. Each of them was left rather with the sense of access to the very center of society itself. William James gives an account of his own conversion anonymously in *The Varieties of Religious*

Experience; Henry gives his, in adumbration, in the story called "The Jolly Corner," and in a manuscript note of a New Year's visitation of his Genius which Lubbock prints in his edition of James' *Letters*. But the version which the elder Henry James gives will do for all three. The last book he himself published, *Society the Redeemed Form of Man,* suggests the works of his two sons as well. There the old man, thirty years after the event, said that in his own religious conversion he had been "lifted by a sudden miracle into felt harmony with universal man, and filled to the brim with the sentiment of indestructible life." Such experiences left all three with what the younger Henry was to call in his old age that "obstinate finality" which had made him an artist in spite of all privations.

If the nature of those privations remained always vague, like an obscure and spreading hurt, and if the experience of conversion was always vague, a force from outside that compelled him to go on beyond and in spite of the hurt, nevertheless the result in Henry James' written works is as clear as need be. There is everywhere in it the presence of a deep, almost instinctive, incentive to create the indestructible life which, to his vision, must lie at the heart of the actual life that has been hurt. He began at once to cultivate what his father had planted in him, the habit of response across any barrier—the more barrier the more response. His peculiar education had given him the straight look, acute ear, keen touch, and receptive mind. In his writing life, that mind received so much and reacted so constantly that it became itself a primary and trustworthy sense. This is the hallmark of the homemade mind, and it serves pretty well for home affairs, but in the affairs of the wide world it drives its victims partly to makeshift and partly to reliance upon naked humanity. To the elder James, such a mind was enough, because he never had any real intent to do more than goad and gad the society he lived in. To William James it was not enough, but he was partly able to make up his losses by the systematic study of physiology and philosophy. To Henry James it was not enough either, and he was driven all his life long, without ever acknowledging it, to make substitutes pass for the real thing. It was perhaps that necessity that made him an artist. At any rate the eloquence and passion with which he made the substitutes, rather than the act of substitution, pass for the actual, were what gave his writing stature a kind of contingent or inner reality. Not until war came in 1914 did he see that the true forces of society had all the time been leading to a final treachery to the values its conventions could no longer defend. He had seen it in his art, but not in his life. His immediate response was to throw himself into the war and to become a British subject. The British gave him the Order of Merit; but his response had been lifelong and was already recorded time after time in book after book.

There, in his "International" books, he set the two kinds of society he knew against each other for balance and contrast and mutual criticism. There are two kinds of society which demand writing like this of James: the society of Europe where the vital impulse has so far run out that all its meanings are expressed by the deliberate play of conventions and their refinements; and, second, the society of America where the original convictions and driving impulse have not yet matured in conventions adequate to express them on high levels. James belonged by birth and primary exposure to the second (New York and New England so far as he could deal with them by instinct), and he had a vision—alternately ideal and critical, alternately discouraged and disillusioned—of the first in the Europe of France and Italy and particularly England. Each gave him the means of dealing with the other; each kept the other from seeming the only society on earth; and together they gave him, at his best, great formality and passionate substance.

The International Theme, in short, was what his education had led to. It was the machinery at hand, and in the lack of anything else it had to provide momentum for everything else. Unlike most writers of his time, but a precursor of many who came to maturity after the First World War, he was barred from the help of religion and history, and a perverse critic might say barred even from the help of literature. He could not use religion because he knew nothing of the Christian Church, hardly even so much of its language as remains alive in the speech of those outside it. He did not know what had happened either to the institutions or the practice of religion; he had only the core of religion within him, and it got into his work only by indirection. He could not have written, like his brother, *The Varieties of Religious Experience,* because he was so obstinately a central form, beneath all varieties, of the religious experience itself. He was an example of what happens to a religious man when institutional religion is taken away. What happens to Maggie Verver in *The Golden Bowl,* to Milly Theale in *The Wings of the Dove,* to Isabel Archer in *The Portrait of a Lady,* to George Stransom in "The Altar of the Dead," are examples of religious experience outside a creed, just as what happens to John Marcher in "The Beast in the Jungle" is an example of the privation of religious experience, and just, too, as what happens to the governess in "The Turn of the Screw" is an example of what happens when positive evil inverts religious experience. James would have been wholly unable to relate any of these affairs in formal Christian terms; where for once, in "The Altar of the Dead," he tried to invoke the experience of the Catholic Church, he saved his story to actuality only by the eloquence of his hero's emotion.

As with religion, so with history, only the other way around. If religion was in James an inner primal piety, history was a felt objective residue. He cook his history in a single jump from the living man to the ancestral Adam. He was contemporary to an extreme. He took his tradition almost entirely on its face value; yet because he knew so much must have been behind that face, he actually felt more continuity, more unity, than had ever been really there. In that feeling lay the intensity of his sense of history. He lacked historical imagination because his mind lacked historical content; he had never been inside any history but his own; but he had the sense of history because he saw all around him in Europe how he himself came at its end, and all around him in America how he came at its beginning. He felt in himself, so far as history went, the power to represent the flash between the two eternities.

The strangest privation in James, and one that troubled him even less than the others—though it has caused much trouble for many readers—was the privation of his relation to the whole body of literature. He was, as Santayana ironically said of himself, "an ignorant man, almost a poet." It was because he knew so little great literature in quantity that to many he seemed excessively literary in manner; there were not enough professional barriers between himself and the printed page to prevent his mere unredeemed idiosyncrasy from now and then taking over. He knew well enough the things read around the house as a boy—Dickens and Scott and Hawthorne; he knew even better his chosen masters, Balzac and Turgenev and Flaubert; but it is not an exaggeration to say that he had no organized command of any of the possible general traditions of literature a writer living in his time might have taken up. There is very little evidence of reading in his letters, except for the books of his friends; and when his brother complained that he ought to read more, he answered that he had no time. His critical writing, even when it was not frank book reviewing, was almost entirely contemporary, of narrow range and narrower sympathies; it is worth reading chiefly as an illumination of his own mind and writing. Only when he tackled the technical problems—by the very narrowness of his solutions of which, in his own work, he so greatly stretched the scope and responsibilities of the novel as a form—was he critically at home and master in his house.

He was indeed virtually an ignorant man, actually a poet; but he had, besides that sense of the human which he shared with his father and brother, only the two natural weapons of a direct eye and an expert knowledge of surfaces. He had thus everywhere to depend more on his method than—in Plato's sense—on his madness. Only by resources of method which he had often to develop and sometimes to invent could he get his poetry into the objective form of novel or tale; for example, put another way, his use of dialogue is an example of development from illustration to substance; his use of an active consciousness interposed between the story and the reader, as in *The Ambassadors,* is almost an invention. He had to find means to get around the problems which trouble most novelists—as war and lust, love and God, troubled Tolstoy—in order to get at the problems that troubled him. Between him and the world he knew he had to interpose the story of the story, the passion of the passion, the problem of the problem; otherwise he could not aesthetically possess the story, the passion, the problem.

So central were morals to James, even though he was a dissenter to the forms in which morals are abused, that there was not ever quite enough for him in any part of the world either to fall back on or to go forward with. It was so in his own mind; his convictions never matured as ideas, but as images or metaphors, as aesthetic creations, always to be created afresh. As he never went backward into the full Christian tradition, but tapped his sense of what underlay it, so he never went back into the whole force of love, only into so much of it as could be conceived morally. It is for reasons such as these that, though he aimed always at the full picture, the full drama, James had to resort successively to the lesser forms of the allegory, the fable, the ghost story, and at the end, where he was nearest his target, to a kind of cross between the drama and the fairy story; for this is the journey James made between "A Passionate Pilgrim" and "The Madonna of the Future," through "The Turn of the Screw" and *The Sacred Fount*, to *The Golden Bowl* and "The Bench of Desolation," where the last two are almost pure Cinderella and Ugly Duckling dramatized and made haunting for every reader who can see himself in their terms. This is the reverse of what happens in novels wholly dramatized. Whereas great drama seems to rest on the driving power of myth, the thing deeply believed and subject to change and criticism only in externals, the fairy tale seems to rest on an insight anxious to prove itself ideal and therefore dependent on externals for access to essentials. In the fairy tale the skeleton is on the outside, sometimes so much so that there is nothing else, while in the drama the skeleton is always fleshed. This is what Edith Wharton meant when she asked James why he left out of his novels all the fringes of what really happened to his people; to which James answered that he didn't know that he had. James leaves the reader relatively everything to put in; all his density and richness develop in the details of his chosen skeleton. The big things are all fairy tale, with that threat of sudden dark illumination at the edge of which the fairy tale, even more than the fable or the ghost story, so often hovers. The bones that articulate the skeleton can be named. Candor, innocence, aloneness, the pure intelligence on one side, and mendacity, unspecified corruption, crowdedness, and a kind of cunning rapacity on the other are given at equally high value; but are given always at a point where each is about to break down, in the contest with actual life, either into renunciation (which to James as to Emily Dickinson was a "piercing" virtue) or into some deep and ambiguous kind of capitulation of good to evil and evil to good—as in the end of *The Wings of the Dove* or of *The Golden Bowl,* where the capitulations are mutual, affirmative, abysmal, shifting. At that point of capitulation, the dramatized fairy tale becomes the instrument and substance—form united with content—of revelation and judgment. This was the prodigy James made of the novel.

4

If this account of privations and defects is any way correct, James' accomplishment in the art of fiction was certainly a prodigy. No writer in the England or America of his time surpassed him, whether with or relatively without his defects, and his peers—Stevenson and Hardy and Moore and Meredith, Mark Twain and Melville and Howells—played in different fields. He had the extraordinary luck to come on a whole baggage of themes and conventions and situations in the same process by which he himself lived, and the luck, too, that made them suited to replenish each other in his chosen forms of the fable and the fairy story; he had had the luck to find a garden which he could cultivate, and did. He deliberately undertook, and invoked for himself, the profession, the role, the vocation of what he called "that obstinate finality" of the artist. As a profession, art gave occupation to his habit of omnivorous curiosity and to his knowledge of surfaces, and it made the sacrifice of other forms of life acceptable for the sake of good practice. As a role, it gave him both an inner independence and the protection of an outer identity no matter what sacrifices and failures might come his way. As a vocation, it overrode or made negative all sacrifices and failures whatever with the conviction of purpose, and so put him in unassailable relation with that universal man and that indestructible life which he felt under any society, no matter what any society in existence might think of his feelings about it. Art was his pride of energy. So much so that the profession and role of artist—both for themselves and as foils and ideal contrasts to other professions and roles—provided the major obsession for his fictions, as did the obsession of the International Theme, of which it was only another, and equivalent, version.

Where the International Theme showed the American against the European, whether as pilgrim or victim, the theme of the artist showed the writer or painter or actress against the world. The underlying theme which he used perhaps first in *Daisy Miller* (1879), but first clearly in *Washington Square* (1881), and at the last made his chief overt theme, was that of the innocent, loyal, candid spirit at the mercy of the world but reacting to it with high intelligence and spiritual strength, precisely with the artist's perception of what for good and ill it actually was. These stories of young

American girls smirched or driven out of society by the cruel stupidity of its conventions alternated with stories of artists who were also smirched or driven out. In James' imagination the two themes became identical. Perhaps this is again a sign of the interregnum in the thinking of modern man: that the artist should suddenly come to have exorbitant value as subject matter—should seem a hero or a traitor to his proper heroic role—and should seem so to the artist himself and not merely to his biographer. In this James is not alone; he is followed by Mann and Proust and Gide and Pirandello and Joyce, to all of whom the artist became the type of hero most precious; but James was first and most copious and most intransigent in moralizing the desperate straits through which the artist pursued his role—sometimes as if he had chosen it, as in "The Figure in the Carpet" (1896), sometimes as if he had been condemned to it, as in "The Lesson of the Master" (1892), and sometimes, as in "The Middle Years" (1893) as if he had accepted it.

In all these stories the fate of the artist is somehow the test of society. As a consequence he finds his own value so high that he cannot assent to society as it is, but has a great craving to assent to it as it ought to have been, for he knows that his very being declares, or is prevented from declaring, its possibilities. The degree of self-consciousness in these tales is equal to this conscious sense of self-value, and it is hard to say which overcomes the other. In "The Figure in the Carpet," the author Hugh Vereker has a secret pattern to his work that, when he dies, no amount of fanatic frenetic work can reveal. In "The Middle Years," on the contrary, the dying author leaves such a sure consciousness of his essential value that his disciple, a young doctor, gives up the certainty of a fortune to remain in the presence of the master to whom in his disciple's "young voice" is "the ring of a marriage bell." To them both, without "the madness of art," which both share, life is frustration. In "The Lesson of the Master," the Master urges the disciple to give up everything, marriage, money, children, social position—all the things to which the Master has himself succumbed—for the sake of his art. The artist is not a man, declares the Master, but a disfranchised monk, and the rarity of his art must be his only passion. To this teaching the disciple is true; he makes his retreat, and writes; but when he returns he finds that the Master, having become a widower, has married his girl, "partly" to make sure that the disciple sticks to his art, and has himself given up writing. James ends his fable with the remark that the disciple felt himself dedicated by nature to intellectual, not personal, passion. One hardly knows whether society or the artist is worse flayed in this brilliant story; but one knows certainly that the moral of the fable, and of that final remark, lies in the representation of the artist's life as the fullest possible human profession.

James thus raised his profession to a vocation—a calling from beyond himself by a familiar within himself—which, as he followed it, was a virtually continuous conversion, for strength, for identity, for piety to life, of his whole being. Who will say that it was not an invoked obsessive device, a ruse to transform life otherwise intolerable? But who will say, in the conditions of his life, that he had an alternative? To him the sense of his vocation was a predominant part of his sense of the animating truth, as anyone can see who reads his own invocation to his own genius, quoted by Lubbock in his edition of James' *Letters*. Unlike his friend Henry Adams, who thought that if anything he sat too much in the center of the whole world, James knew himself actually at the periphery, and had therefore to make himself a center in invoked reality. As an individual he felt himself to be so many *disjecta membra poetae*. But by raising his profession to a vocation, he celebrated, like priest and prophet at once, a rite in his own chapel of the true church. He became thus the individual who knew best how little individual he truly was, and was therefore able to overcome the dead weight of all those who merely thought themselves individuals because they wielded power and direction and routine to society by the accident of rank or privilege or money. The difference lay in the presence of the sense of vocation; and the only profession James could by nature see as vocation was that of artist; and he saw the artist as alternately cheated and blest in his vocation regardless of his immense task.

But he went further; the sense of vocation is primary in most of his fiction. He made a dramatic transposition of the artist's sense of vocation and he saw it as motivating rare and precious conduct everywhere. James habitually envisaged people as either with vocation in an extreme devoted sense—Isabel Archer in *The Portrait of a Lady* no less than Miriam Rooth in *The Tragic Muse* or Fleda Vetch in *The Spoils of Poynton* or Lambert Strether in *The Ambassadors*—or as without vocation, as in the foils to the characters just named, and more or less brutally against those who had it. He did not deal with the much greater numbers of people who are merely occupied as confused human animals. That is the difference between a writer like James and writers like his masters, Balzac and Flaubert. Hence perhaps his failure to understand the degree of remove at which the conventions of society actually work out (at some distance from where any of us are sitting) and how much of human energy other than the animal is merely manipulated rather than absorbed by the conventions. His novels have no ordinary people, except as barriers to the extraordinary; his people feel either the passion of the passion, or they feel nothing.

As an instance of the extremity to which James carried his transposition, one might take that great and beautiful tale "The Altar of the Dead" in which the hero devotes his life to the cultivation of the memory of his loved dead and is led finally, at the moment of his own death, to celebrate also the memory of the one dead man he hated, who seems suddenly to have been equal in need and just obligation to all the rest. But perhaps an example more sharply drawn may be exhibited in the bare bones of "Maud-Evelyn." Here a young man named Marmaduke, after being as he mistakenly thinks half jilted, goes off to Switzerland where he falls in with an elderly American couple named Dedrick. The Dedricks had some years since lost their daughter Maud-Evelyn, and now, to salvage their loss, take up the new young man in the role of imaginary son-in-law. The young man so far falls in with the fantasy that the role becomes as good as the thing itself, and he proceeds to realize it, stage by stage, for all it is worth: that is, as a vocation. Thus he passes through courtship, wedding, married life, into widowerhood and mourning till finally the Dedricks—whose fantasy he had authorized in the transformation of his own nature—die at peace. Shortly afterwards he himself dies, leaving, as his one gesture toward his erstwhile life, all his money to the girl to whom he had been originally engaged. Perhaps the theme is like Proust's, that the past, brooded on, grows and grows. What the old couple wanted was to get from the past what they would have wanted of the future. They made a temple of death in order to profane it, to stretch its precincts to cover the living world. To the young man—otherwise, by James' assertion, empty of clear intent—it was a chance to seize on the offered backward pattern with the intensity of vocation, in full belief that he might make out of it a true self. Thus, in this story, obsession with the dead reaches hallucination and hallucination reaches the new reality of art.

5

Further than this James never went, though in "The Friends of the Friends" he went as far, for he was eager to perfect his mastery of substance as well as of form. In that story an ordinary ghost is made into something monstrously human, and presides over one of those deep abortions of the human spirit which are yet, in their catastrophe, but "a response to an irresistible call": that is, are acts performed in the assumption of vocation. Had he gone further James would not have been so much unreadable—as this last example nearly is—as silly. He was content with his handful of dark fables of unassayable devotion, because they complemented and hinted at the filling out of such clear dramatic fables as *Washington Square* (1881) and *The Tragic Muse* (1890). The first of these is a light piece, done on the side, to show the opposite case to that of *The Portrait of a Lady,* which was published the same year. Catherine Sloper is the only one of James' heroines who is all round dull and plain, the only one whose intelligence is not equal to her innocence. Without intelligence, she is unable either to reject or to assent to her gradual exile from society at the hands of an egocentric father and a casually mercenary lover; she merely sticks it out. Her story is not there, and neither are the stories of her father and her lover. If anything carries the book along it is the atmosphere suggested in the title, neither of which—atmosphere nor title—have anything except accidentally to do with the theme of the book: which is that human decency, even when unaware of its grounds and its ends, can, if it is taken as a vocation, come cleanly through any soiling assault. It would have taken the passion of a Flaubert for working the riches of ordinary and inarticulate things to have made excellence out of this Madame Bovary in reverse; and perhaps James was trying to do so; but he did not have that skill, and his book remained in the deep sense only an intention.

Miriam Rooth in *The Tragic Muse,* on the other hand, has at least a real struggle because she has the weapons of beauty and intelligence and a vocation as artist to fight with. She makes the center (together with the bright figure of the aesthete Gabriel Nash a little off center for fun) of a brilliant account, in large scale, of the perpetual struggle between the artist of any sort and society of any sort. But there is more gaiety, more business of the great world and the studio without the concrete representation of the underlying perception of and reaction to it, than a novel can stand and still ring true. James himself thought it moved too fast, and certainly the values asserted are far ahead of the values rendered. As a result, the validity, whether for triumph or assault, of Miriam Rooth's or Nick Dormer's vocation is not so much proved as it is by its own self-insistence impugned. In short, it is very much the same sort of relative failure, but at the opposite extreme, as *Washington Square.* But it is often in his relative failures that an artist's drive is most clearly defined; if only because in his purest successes there is the sense of the self-born, self-driven, and self-complete and these qualities escape definition.

What we can see in these novels which relatively fail, and indeed in a full ten of the nineteen novels which he published in his lifetime (as in perhaps a greater proportion of his hundred-odd shorter pieces), is that James' work constitutes a great single anarchic rebellion against society—against the laws of society—in the combined names of decency, innocence, candor, good will, and the passionate heroism of true vocation. His work as a body is the dramatized or pictured exhibition, at those chosen points most familiar to him in his own society, of the revolt implied in the title of his father's book, *Society the Redeemed Form of Man.* Both Jameses were basic dissenters to all except the society that was not yet; and in both cases the rebellion or dissent was merely eccentric or extravagant in life and manners, but central and poetic in work and insight. That is why in these tales of people who renounce or ignore so much of life which to other eyes would have been precious and even necessary to living, the last legitimate cry is still: Live, live all you can! James was compelled to accomplish his rebellion of the ideal through the very conventions he meant to re-create; they were the given medium in which the underlying reality and the invoked ideal could meet and, in dramatic actuality, merge; conventions were what he knew.

The importance of this is worth any amount of reemphasis; for James is only an exaggerated instance of the normal author, and his works are only a special case of what always goes on in the relations between an artist and a society whose values have become chiefly secular without having quite lost the need or the memory of values divinely ordered. His case is representative of literature in America, whenever it has been ambitious, to a degree greater than we care to say; in their necessary addiction to external conventions, Hemingway and Dos Passos, for example, are no less representative than James. But, granting the addiction, we are here concerned with what the conventions were and what happened to them in James' imagination.

With the *haut monde* and the *beau monde,* somewhat of Italy and France, and particularly of England, together with their high Bohemias—to none of which did he actually belong—James had the expert familiarity of the observer. He knew the dinner table and drawing room, the country house and tea table, the library and smoking room, the city square and the estate park, the spas and hotels and promenades, and all the means and times and ceremonies for moving from one to another. They were the straps the people he knew swung on, and with which they held against the lurches which proved that their society was a going concern. Similarly, he knew how they got married, or jilted, or cheated; and he knew beautifully how they made cads and swindlers and lackeys of themselves almost as often as they made berths for themselves. To all this he turned first as to the form of a living society. Then he saw, rather, that this was but the mechanical arrangement of a society, that it was but the reflected tradition of values which the society might not otherwise possess and which indeed it often possessed only to soil and sully— though it could not destroy them. Those who ought to have embodied the truth of tradition in living conventions were in fact those who most demeaned it. He saw through the people, but what he saw was still the convention: the ultimate decency between human beings that could be created or ruined, equally, only by convention.

Thus James knew expertly what people's superficial obsessions were. If he did not know what their ordinary day-to-day preoccupations were, nor what, in consequence, they were likely to do, he did know the basic preoccupations of all people without regard to country or manners: he knew at what point of value men or women wanted, regardless, to live or die and what barriers they could put between themselves and affirmation. Hence he had, as a writer, to combine his two knowledges and jump the ignorance that lay between. Like a child, also a moralist, he had to use fables as the means of the jump.

Sometimes, of course, James tried to make his fables carry more than they could bear. We have touched on two examples in "The Figure in the Carpet" and "Maud-Evelyn." "The Great Good Place" is another, in which the heavenly world is seen as resembling an unusually comfortable club. But *What Maisie Knew* (1897) and *The Awkward Age* (1899) are better and fuller examples still, for in each a major use of social convention was attempted, and in each the failure was virtually, but not actually, saved by the bounty of the author's sensibility and the fertility of his technical invention. In the first the question is asked, what will happen to a little girl exposed to the breakdown of marriage in a succession of increasingly shabby divorces and liaisons? James was able to give so much through the innocence of his beautiful little girl's exposed consciousness that his story constantly both winces and cries out because the conventions through which Maisie is compelled to see her situation prevent the rest of the story, the whole story, the true story, from being told. In *The Awkward Age* the primary question is, what will happen to the publicly exposed relations of a set of people when the daughter of the house comes of social age and first takes part in those public relations? It is sometimes said that the relative failure of this book comes about because James restricted his presentation of his answer to a masterly use of scene and dialogue. But that argument would reduce Congreve to the stature of Wilde. The true cause of failure would seem to lie in the inability of all the characters in the book, including its presumably fresh and plastic young heroine, to bring into the conventions to which they restrict themselves the actual emotions and stresses that the conventions are meant to control, but of which they were never, in a living society, meant to be the equivalent.

In short, neither the domestic economy of social conventions nor the vocation of the artist was ever enough to bring out in James a mastery of substance equal to his mastery of form. What he seems to have needed was either an enlargement of the theme of the artist into terms of ordinary life, an enlargement of the social conventions into the International Theme, or a combination, in the press of one composition, of the artist and the international and the ordinary. At any rate, within these three fields lie his great successes, in which are to be included some fifteen or twenty tales as well as six or seven novels. The International Theme in its simplest form is the felt contrast of Europe and America. But it is a very different thing from the internal American contrast between New England and Virginia, and it resembles the contrast between the Old East and the New West only to the limited degree that, during James' lifetime, the Old East had digested and reversed its contrast with Europe. For the prime purpose of the contrast to James was that it furnished him with a reversible dualism which created as well as adjudicated values. It was not just a question of American girls marrying European men and of European women never, or seldom, marrying American men, though that question suggested many others having to do with the relative values of the maternal and the paternal in the conventional great world. Nor was it only the question of why American men went to Europe for culture, except in the secondary question of whether or not they could apply what they got in Europe to the American scene. It was these and much more. It was a dualism of right and wrong, of white and black, home or exile; and like any true dualism, before it becomes lost in an institution, its terms were reversible, without impairment of their reality. Reversed, right and wrong became fresh and stale, white and black became decent and corrupt, home or exile became integrity or destruction. With these reversals in mind, the questions at the heart of the International Theme can be put afresh. What happens to Americans in Europe? What does Europe do to them? bring out of them? give them, by threatening its loss, to struggle for? And, on the contrary, what happens to Europeans under impact of Americans? What new source do they find to make up for the loss which the exposure has laid bare? And so on.

In the beginning the American is conceived as having in him a dead or unborn place, and is, in moral perception if not in moral nature, gray or black; the European, in contrast, is conceived as alive with inherited life as well as his own and is all gold and pearls in moral perception, however black he may be in moral nature. Thus the gain of the European adventure ought, for the American, to be greater than the loss risked: James never quite rid himself of this speculative frame of mind and could supply, at the peak of his writing life, in the novel he cared most for, *The Ambassadors* (1903), an example in which one American gains every possible strength for his own moral nature through immersion in European moral perception. But he became increasingly forced to draw from his chosen examples the opposite conclusion, and in so doing he was only carrying one great step further the conclusion drawn in his best early work. In *The American* (1877) and in *The Portrait of a Lady* (1881) Newman and Isabel Archer are victimized by Europe; Europe is the disillusion for Newman, and for Isabel the evil and treachery, which overcame them; if they are left intact they are also left shrunk; their strength was in the strength to renounce. But in *The Wings of the Dove* (1902) and in *The Golden Bowl* (1904), the two American girls, Milly Theale and Maggie Verver, although victimized by Europe, triumph over it, and convert the Europeans who victimized them, by the positive strength of character and perceptive ability which their experience of treachery only brings out. Neither Milly's death nor Maggie's re-creation of her adulterous marriage is an act of renunciation or disillusion; they are deliberate acts of life fully realized and fully consented to, done because it is necessary to keep intact the conviction that life has values greater than any renunciation can give up or any treachery soil. By these means, in the figure of the American girl, candor, innocence, and loyalty become characteristic though not exclusive American virtues which redress the deep damage done by a blackened Europe. Thus James dramatized a reversal of the values in his International Theme so full as to make of the American's necessary journey to Europe a pilgrimage reversed. It was as if in his writing life he had made a series of withdrawals into a waste in which he assumed there must be an oasis, only to find himself strengthened, on each return, to meet the high values which had all along flourished at home.

It might be said that James had taken for his text the verse from the Sermon on the Mount, "For where your treasure is, there will your heart be also," and used it alternately, first just as it is and then with a reversal of the two nouns, so that a man might expect to find his treasure where and when he had discovered his heart. If we ask by what means he had come to be able to do this, an answer which is at least possible suggests itself: by merging the dynamic dualism of his International Theme with the static, if tragic, insight of the theme of the artist in stories of people extraordinary only for their unusual awareness of life and their unusual liberty to maintain their awareness. Putting it more strongly, if less certainly, James by combining his obsessive themes managed to equip his central insight into the indestructible life of man with a genuinely contingent body of morals and living tradition, regardless of the privation of his life, his education, and his times; and further, in so far as he was able to do this, he found released for use the inexhaustible wealth of felt life in quantities and qualities capable of receiving, and filling out durably, the stamp of form.

The stamp of form was itself a prodigy of accomplishment—and we shall come to it directly—but first it ought to be reemphasized how difficult it was for a writer like James to get hold of life in a way amenable to that stamp. Having no adequate tradition to fall back on for morals (values) or ethics (decision or judgment), James had to make the intelligence do for both, had to make it do as the equivalent of order and law in operation; and, not finding enough of intelligence in the world, he had to create it, and in creating it, had to put it in conflict with facts and stupidities it could not face without choice. For to James the height of intelligence was choice; intelligence was taste in action, and the utmost choice taste could make was the choice to live or die. It was by taste that James got hold of, valued, and judged the life to which his intelligence reacted. If this is so, it explains why his readers divide into such hostile camps of repulsion and attraction. Those who are repelled think the result, in the face of actual life, drivel; those who are attracted seem to find that taste and intelligence operate through his various themes and combinations of themes to drag into being a kind of ultimate human decency which expresses all the values a given soul can stand.

To those who recognize that decency in his work, James was full of the terrible basic ambition—but stripped of its ordinary ordeals—to create characters who meet the conditions of society so as to choose to live or choose to die. Thus his characters take on the heroism and the abnegation, as alternative and equivalent roles, of the artist and of the man or woman who ought to have been an artist in life itself. Isabel Archer in *The Portrait of a Lady,* Milly Theale in *The Wings of the Dove,* Maggie Verver in *The Golden Bowl,* and Lambert Strether in *The Ambassadors* are all clear examples of human decency operating through taste and intelligence to confront life heroically and with success. One is divided between thinking that the force of this decency is a transformation of the force of sex, and that it is a new kind of vocation in morals; in either case specially designed for the novelist to represent in the figures of ideally normal human beings; for such, in the four great novels named, he has created his three American girls and his one American man.

6

But the explanation of how James harmonized his substance and his art had better be put on a little lower plane. Just twice in his life was James able to lift his work to major stature, once at the age of thirty-eight in *The Portrait of a Lady* and once again for a five-year period beginning at the age of fifty-eight, when he produced beside the other three great novels just spoken of, two characteristic projections of the artist's faith, *The Sacred Fount* (1901) and *The American Scene* (1907). The first set up the conscience of the artist to act as the conscience of people who did not have enough for themselves; the second demonstrated the record of that conscience in action during his American visit—the first in over twenty years—of 1904. The period before the *Portrait* was no doubt the normal period of the growth and formation of his own character as a writer; the novels of that time could almost as well have been written by someone else, for they were carried forward by a combination of the existing institution of literature and the élan of first impressions. Then, suddenly, in his seventh novel, James added to the institution a momentum or élan which was his own; the character and fate of Isabel Archer were greater than both the social and the novelistic conventions through which she was exhibited. James had combined his themes for the first time, and for the first time told a story that demanded of him his full powers. Not until he again combined his themes, in *The Ambassadors* (1903), did he again reach full power. It is further notable that the best of the novels that came in between, *The Spoils of Poynton* (1897), is really only an elongated tale or *nouvelle*, like "The Turn of the Screw" or "The Altar of the Dead," and that it lacked the American or International Theme. Its story remains a melodramatic fable and never reaches the state of dramatized fairy tale in which the novels of full power are so strangely happy. Otherwise, aside from *The Awkward Age, What Maisie Knew,* and *The Tragic Muse,* which have already been discussed, there are two experiments in a genre of which James never became a master, *The Bostonians* and *The Princess Casamassima* (both dated 1886).

On their faces both Balzacian novels as modified by the general current of French naturalism, they were actually inhibited from becoming naturalistic by certain elements in James' own character as a writer, and so were partially transformed into something else. Each of these novels plunged him into centers of human conduct and motivation and obsession—into conditions of behavior—of which he was only superficially aware. In *The Bostonians* he made his center the infatuation of a grown woman for a young girl, with its havoc in each of them, and its final destruction by a violently conventional "rescue." In *The Princess Casamassima,* the center is the equally disastrous infatuation of the Princess for the little bookbinder's clerk, Hyacinth Robinson, against a general background of conspiratorial, underground, bomb-throwing revolution, ending in the violence of Hyacinth's suicide in the shabbiest, blackest room in London. Being fascinated by such subjects, James tried to make what he could see stand for what he could not; and if his attempt had been on a lesser scale—on something not the scale of a naturalistic novel—he might well have succeeded.

What did happen to his attempt in these two books suggests a general conclusion about all his work: his repeated argument that the artist should be released from the burden of things as they were ordinarily understood to happen, probably came from his ignorance of ordinary things in general. It also suggests a rudimentary principle for the art of fiction; that if you want the surface to stand for the whole you must put in enough specifications to make sure it is the surface of the thing wanted and not merely the surface of the writer's mind. In shorter forms this certainty may be provided by intensity of form or perception, but the full-length novel requires extensiveness of form and perception, and extensiveness requires knowledge and specification all around. Then James' argument against naturalistic detail would be sound; economy of strong specification would persuade the reader to put in, out of his own stock of perception, all else that was required. Then, too, the further argument would have been sounder still, that most of what we know deeply comes to us without ever fitting the specifications we had prepared for it. If we deliberately free ourselves of all specifications except those that lay us open to experience, who knows what of the vast unspecified actual will not press in?

It is this last question that must have lurked under James' practice, and this inviting risk he must often have felt he was taking. In *The Bostonians* and *The Princess Casamassima* he made a misjudgment of what detail he could do without and of what he needed, as a carpenter says of his tools, to do with. It is not that he left out the details that clutter but that he omitted to put in those that would lay his readers, and in effect the novels themselves, open to respond to the pressure of the actual—the special shabby underground menacing actual that presses inchoate at the threshold of the stories without ever getting in; so that the novels have a strangely transformed air of protecting themselves from what they are really about.

In the four great novels this is not so. There the unspecified actual does press in as the general menace of folly, inadequacy, or sheer immanent evil. Whatever it is, it ruins loyalty, prevents love, sullies innocence. It is the morass in which some part of every human being is in a nameless mortal combat, and which is felt as the dumb part of despair, the horror at the nether end of boredom, or the futility no bigger than a man's hand in any perspective of effort looked at; it is the menace of life itself. To measure, to represent, to reenact the force of that menace is one extreme of the moral feat of art; as the other extreme is to reenact the equally nameless good that combats it. To reenact both in full measure required of James his combined sense of the reversible dualism of Europe and America, the heroism of the artist's vocation, and the two focused in an otherwise ordinary set of characters. In the shorter pieces, intensity of form and relatively limited perception are enough to give the sense of the menacing, altering force without need of any further articulation. It is its intensity that gives the sense of the jungle to "The Beast in the Jungle," of the corner to "The Jolly Corner," of the screw to "The Turn of the Screw," of the dead to "The Altar of the Dead," and of desolation to "The Bench of Desolation." Each of these tales, if you asked for articulation, would fall flat, but when inarticulated, each shows an indestructible habit of growth into at least the hallucination of actual experience.

The one occasion on which James at all successfully tried for full articulation by direct means was in that testamentary novel *The Sacred Fount*. There the nameless narrator records the passage of the force of life through half a dozen people, with himself as the medium whereby they become conscious of the exchange, and, gradually, conscious of the nature of the force exchanged. He is their conscience and their creator because he is their intelligence; he makes them see what they are. In the end they reject his intelligence, and the reader is left with the ambiguous sense either that the author is crazy and had merely invented his perceptions or that he was right but his creations had now taken over the life with which he had endowed them, with a quite human insistence on mutilating and battening on each other as they themselves chose. The halves of the ambiguity shade into each other interminably in that indestructible association of the moral life in which evil is ignorance but actual, and good is knowledge created real.

Such success as *The Sacred Fount* has is by tour de force; but it is the essential tour de force of James' sensibility; it is the represented hallucination of what, as artist and as man, he wanted to do for life; it is the poetic equivalent, the symbol and example, of what, on his own shaking ground, he wanted to stand for. If he could not say what it was, that is because it was so deeply himself that he could only show it in action, like a man in love or deadly fear. But read with good will and with a sense of the title kept turning in the mind, *The Sacred Fount* becomes the clue to the nature of the intent and to the quality of the achieved substance of the novels and tales, and then in turn becomes clear itself. If there is a secret in Henry James and if there is a way in which we can assent to that secret, both may be found in *The Sacred Fount*. It is the secret of why he was obsessed with the story of the story, the sense of the sense, the passion of the passion. He wanted, in all the areas of life he could reach, to be the story, the sense, the passion not just of the life itself but of the conscience he could create for it. So deep and hidden were the springs of conviction within him, and at the same time so sure the credit he gave to his actual perception, that he could not help believing what he created to be the conscience of truth as well as the reality of art. The being was one with the seeming.

7

In such a life work, making so little call on the ordinary means whereby we symbolize the struggle for our relations with God, society, and ourselves, it was necessary for James to make extraordinary demands upon the formal resources of the institution of literature. His essential subject matter compelled him to transform not only the English novel but also the French and Russian novel from something relatively loose and miraculous to something relatively tight and predictable. Neither *The Sacred Fount* nor *The Golden Bowl* could have been written within anything resembling the form of *Madame Bovary* or *Vanity Fair*. His own view of what magnificence his transformation amounted to may be found in the critical prefaces he wrote for the collected edition of his novels and tales. Perhaps the best sense of it is contained in the single phrase: "the coercive charm of form," and perhaps its best aspiration is found at the end of the preface to *The Ambassadors*: "The Novel remains still, under the right persuasion, the most independent, most elastic, most prodigious of literary forms." For, in James' argument, form coerced true freedom upon the novel; form freed the novel for independent prodigies which, without the force of that form, it could not undertake. For his own work, that is what his rules of form did. He developed out of the resources of the old novel, and by invention of new resources, what we now call the James novel.

Since other novelists have used and misused the James novel and since by contagion it has modified the actual practice of many novelists who never read James at all, we had better try to say what the James novel is. It is consistent to its established variety of skeleton forms; it is faithful to its established method of reporting; and it insists on its chosen center of attraction. To do these things it first of all gets rid of the omniscient author; the author is never allowed to intrude directly or in his own person; the story is always some created person's sense of it, or that of some group of persons, so that we see or feel the coercive restriction of someone's conscious experience of the story as the medium through which we ourselves feel it. Secondly, the James novel uses device after device, not merely to invite the reader's ordinary attention, but to command his extraordinary attention. For example, the dialogue in all the later work is as close in structure and in mutual relationships, and as magnetic upon the reader's mind, as an essay in mathematical logic. The scenes between persons are dramatized as substance, not as ornament; true action is in speech and gesture; and thus the dialogue creates a new form of attention, in which we always sail close-hauled or trembling on the tack. As the command to attend is obeyed, the reader learns a new game which, as it seems to partake of actual experience, he can take for truth; and which, as it shows a texture of sustained awareness never experienced in life, he knows to be art. To gain that effect, to make art truth, is the whole object of James' addiction to the forms of fiction; it was the only avenue to truth he could recognize.

Hence he was compelled to be tight, close, firm, restrictive, and extraordinarily conscious in the process of his art; and had to pretend to be so, like any believer, when he was not, because to an unexampled degree he was unconscious of all the other machineries of the mind and of many of the forces to which the mind reacts. He could not think otherwise, as he grew older and lonelier, than that only the most restrictive possible form could stamp his vision of life as recognizable truth and transform the fine conscience of his imagination into recognizable art. That he wrote both novels and tales only less than the very greatest, and that he added permanently to the scope and resources of his art in the process of doing so, was for him only the achieved act of his nature, the "obstinate finality," as he called it, of what he was—an artist. For us, the finality is equally obstinate, but it is also, as he thought the novel was, independent, elastic, prodigious; a version, not the vision, of life; a language, which, as we learn its beauty for his purposes, we can adapt and develop for our own—especially when we are in those moods he has himself created in us—those moods when taste is intelligence, intelligence is conscience, and the eloquence of conscience is heroic truth. Then he is the special case of our own point of view: he is one version of the story of our story, the sense of our sense, the passion of our passion—to be satisfied nowhere else.

James seems to inspire intoxication either of taste or disgust. But these opposite reactions come to the same thing. Born in 1843, designed by his father to be a perceptive luxury in a society whose chief claims to luxury lay along singularly imperceptive lines and whose institutions during his life-time grew predominantly deterministic, he took to himself the further luxury of expression as a profession. So long as he expressed chiefly, or at any rate superficially, what was taken for granted, he had a fair share of popularity: he was taken as a smart if somewhat overrefined young man. As his expression came under control and exhibited deeper perceptions, he lost most of his small audience. As the quality of his work not only enriched but became characteristic and informed with passionate taste, his work was positively disliked and regarded as a luxury no one could afford.

This was about 1890. Exiled and alienated as well as dispatriated, he was stung to a new and powerful reaction by his failure with the well made play. He became again a novelist, and in this second life, beginning in 1896, more than any other writer, he was ever consciously himself; it was his self that had grown, and was more fully and formally a luxury of expression than ever, so that fewer and fewer could afford to read him. At the same time, he had become an institution, by no means ignored but not in much resort. There were always those who read him, some as a cult and as a means of escape, others because he added to the stature of their own perception. He visited America, after twenty years, not as a triumph but as a venture in discovery. Then he revised and collected his work, deepening his tone and making a cumulus of his weight, and began a new career, partly in the form of memoirs, partly in what promised to be a new form of fiction of which the only finished examples are the stories in *The Finer Grain* (1910) where he began to show a remote intimacy, through the poetry of his language, with the preoccupations of ordinary men and women. That same year—1910—his brother William, then in England, fell ill and he went with him to help him die in America. On his return to England, his own health weakened and he finished nothing but memoirs and short essays in the remaining five years of his life.

But he was more an institution than ever. On his seventieth birthday he was presented by three hundred friends with his portrait by Sargent. In July, 1915, he became a British subject; in the following New Year Honours, he was awarded the Order of Merit; and in February, 1916, he died, still a luxury of perception and expression. Gradually that luxury has become an institution of increasing resort for those who require to find upon what assumptions, in a society like ours, unconscious of any unity and uncertain even of direction, the basic human convictions can yet grow—whether for life or for the judgment of life in art.

64. THE DISCOVERY OF BOHEMIA

Out of the *beau monde* of Europe and the "good society" of New York and Boston and Newport, Henry James had fashioned his novels and tales on the International Theme. This had been his way of responding to the predicament of a society which did not yet know that it had to be redeemed. A further phase of the disenchantment of the late nineteenth century was a turning aside from the materialism of the modern industrial world, the conflict of science and religion, in the quest for a happier land of carefree life and impressionistic art of a mythical Bohemia.

A dominant movement in the literature of Western Europe, a minor but clearly distinguishable trend in the English Pre-Raphaelites and the contributors to the *Yellow Book*, this quest for Bohemia never achieved the form and focus of a literary mode in America. Writers here and there, in this respect or that, reflected one or another of its characteristics. A few like Saltus and Hearn succeeded in living its life of detachment without making notable contributions to literature; others like Garland or Henry Adams caught up its spirit for a moment, only to relapse into more sober methods of dealing with life and its problems. But our literary history would not be fully recounted without a sketch of its more striking manifestations, even though the method must be that of holding up a mirror to catch only the more obvious reflections. Sporadic as its direct influence was on our literature, it helped to reform our naïve criticism of the arts.

Notoriously vague are the boundaries of Bohemia. "Is it a state, not of soul, but of the purse?" asked Huneker. As a way of life it is evidently both; it involves both social and psychological consequences; it offers both the vicissitudes of a precarious career and the adventures of an enlivened sensibility. Its earlier devotee, in both respects, was Poe. But, though his work met affinities among the Pre-Raphaelites in England and even became the object of a cult among the Symbolists in France, he founded no aesthetic school among his countrymen. His campaigns against didacticism and his experiments with technique were continued in the United States, not in organized movements, but by isolated figures. Whitman may seem, when we view the fifties in retrospect, to have dominated the writers that forgathered at Pfaff's beer cellar under Broadway; but the official record of those forgatherings is Bayard Taylor's "Diversions of the Echo Club" (1872), a faint echo of mild diversions. A heartier atmosphere of literary conviviality was exhaled by San Francisco during the sixties, but within another decade its Bohemians had become lions: Mark Twain, Bret Harte, and Joaquin Miller had drifted eastward. Oscar Wilde, carrying the gospel of Ruskin and Morris to the American lecture platform in 1882, merely created advance publicity for the Gilbert and Sullivan *Patience*. For Howells, under the spell of Cambridge Brahminism, Bohemianism was "a sickly colony, transplanted from the mother asphalt of Paris, and never really striking root in the pavements of New York."

The *vie de Bohéme* was deeply rooted in the interstices of European society, in the rift between artists and Philistines, between a radical intelligentsia and a predominant bourgeoisie. In America where expansion left further room for individualism, the tensions were less explicit and the protests more superficial. When artistic flowering required intensive cultivation, however, Americans still sought training and encouragement on the other side of the Atlantic. What the Latin Quarter was to Parisians or Soho to Londoners, the whole of Europe was to them: a seacoast of Bohemia. Some of them, like Whistler, were destined for fabulous exploits within that international domain. Henry Harland, having tried unsuccessfully to catch the local color of Manhattan in his earlier stories, later emerged as editor of the *Yellow Book* and one of the arbiters of English aestheticism. Francis Vielé-Griffin and Stuart Merrill were naturalized into the innermost circles of French poetry, and Merrill completed the cycle by translating a selection of Symbolist prose into his native language. But the contributions of the expatriates—unless, like Henry James, they were still preoccupied with American themes—belong to the foreign cultures they embraced. We are more concerned with repatriates, with the new ideas and attitudes they brought home from the Old World, with the enrichment—or, at any rate, the sophistication—they brought to the nineties, which transcended the range of more genteel criticism by looking beyond England to the continent and beyond the art of literature to music and the plastic arts.

Thomas Beer has suggested that mauve, which Whistler defined as "pink trying to be purple," is the shade that characterizes this decade. It is an apt characterization of the popular blends that a domesticated Bohemianism produced. With the success of *Trilby* (1892), the Franco-English Du Maurier reinforced that picturesque and sentimental conception of the artist's life which the German-French Murger had popularized a generation before. The quizzical hedonism of Omar Khayyám, bound in crushed leather, made its appearance on many a parlor table. The Boston Irishman, John Boyle O'Reilly, tossed off a maudlin lyric, "In Bohemia" (1885), which was endlessly reprinted and parodied. Richard Hovey, after some translation from Mallarmé, collaborated with the Canadian poet, Bliss Carman, in the breezy series of *Songs from Vagabondia* (1894–1901). A vagabond pose, congenially flouting the lesser conventions, was becoming respectable and even profitable. Elbert Hubbard, reversing the process of William Morris, converted art into industry; his personal literary organ, with conscious and unconscious irony, was called the *Philistine*. Up-and-coming cities now boasted of their Bohemian clubs; the oldest, established at San Francisco in 1872, has outlasted the rest; its businessmen, to be sure, have long outnumbered its more professionally Bohemian members. It was in this club that the poet George Sterling committed suicide in 1926. Though he was a disciple of Ambrose Bierce, he was in his own right the leader of Bohemia in California. Sterling lived into the age of imagism and naturalism, still faithful to the kind of poetry which conveys a "sense of the remote, the mysterious, the sadly beautiful." A year before he took his life he mourned the solemnity of the new era in which there was no more "make-believe, no more masks and garlands." Of all these symptoms the most significant was the eruption of "little magazines" throughout the country. Many of these were hardly more than manifestoes, but a few survived long enough to introduce lively talents and open exciting horizons—notably the San Francisco *Lark*, the Chicago *Chap-Book*, and the cosmopolitan *M'lle New York*.

To distinguish a clear-cut direction or a guiding coterie behind these fads and trends would be to oversimplify. Yet they point to the growth of a class of self-educated intellectuals, whose characteristic form of expression might be described as aesthetic journalism. As a cultural influence it differed from its European counterpart, by striving rather to educate than to shock the middle-class reader. As a means of education it was not addressed to a privileged few or concentrated upon the past, but eager to spread a wide awareness of contemporary developments in taste and thought. Despite this world of difference between the academic and the journalistic, the lines were occasionally crossed. Charles Warren Stoddard, whose South Sea vagabondage terminated in religious conversion, assumed the first professorship of English at the Catholic University of America. Harry Thurston Peck, sometime professor of Latin at Columbia, subsequently edited the *Bookman* and championed the moderns. Henry Adams, abandoning both a professorial and an editorial chair, could look down from the lonely eminence of his leisure; whereas the aesthetic journalists, enunciating views which often paralleled his, had to write for a living. Though their American market—to judge from George Gissing's account—was not quite so discouraging as Grub Street, they inevitably wasted a good deal of talent in boiling the pot. Free lances for better or worse, they accepted the conditions of their profession. Much of their writing was bound to prove ephemeral; some of it remains worthy of reconsideration.

2

The militant independence of the free lance is personified in Ambrose Bierce, the earliest American author after Poe to reflect the recognizable qualities of the movement. Resisting all other affiliations and categories, his restlessness finds its appropriate haven in Bohemia, which—according to his definition—was the "taproom of a wayside inn on the road from Bœotia to Philistia." A youthful veteran of the Civil War, a belated Argonaut to the west coast, he relived his affrays and disillusionments in the rough-and-tumble of the San Francisco press. Joining the American invasion of London during the seventies, he mingled with the cockney wits, published some grimly facetious books under the pseudonym of Dod Grile, and even broke a lance in defense of the exiled Empress Eugénie. Failing to capture the British public that lionized Clemens and Harte, he retreated to California where his later career linked the bygone frontier generation with younger writers like Jack London and George Sterling. His principal employer was the up-and-coming William Randolph Hearst, who was wise enough to give him free rein. His most effective journalistic coup was to prevent Collis P. Huntington from lobbying a railway-refunding bill through Congress. Bierce's separation from his wife, and the tragic deaths of their two sons, embittered his private life. After the turn of the century he made his home—in so far as he had one—in Washington, which afforded increasing scope to his misanthropy. At the age of seventy, after supervising the publication of his collected works and revisiting the battlefields of his youth, he disappeared across the Mexican border, leaving biography to trail off into legend.

No reader, thumbing through those twelve volumes of *Collected Works,* can avoid being struck by their monumental disproportion. As if in a last effort to compensate for the good books he might have written, Bierce padded the set with outdated editorials and stale hoaxes and forgotten polemics, disregarding his habitual distinction between journalism and literature. Frequently the degree of animus seems disproportionate to the issue, and usually the style is disproportionately superior to the subject. *Black Beetles in Amber* (1892) aims at the kind of elegant preservation that Pope accorded his enemies in *The Dunciad,* but Bierce's fluent verse seldom rises very high above its occasion. His prose, on the other hand, has a crisp precision which is almost unparalleled among his contemporaries; his puristic standards of usage, which he may have brought back from England, are set forth in his little handbook, *Write It Right* (1909). America needed, but did not want, a Swift. It needed the sharp reservations of the satirist, armed like Bierce with the weapon of wit. It wanted only the blunt affirmations of the humorist. "Nearly all Americans are humorous; if any are born witty, heaven help them to emigrate!" exclaimed Bierce. Though many of his satirical sketches suggest that Gulliver might have discovered another Brobdingnag in California, one of his serious essays laments "The Passing of Satire." His points were too fine, his targets too ubiquitous. His phobias included millionaires, labor leaders, women, and dogs. His values were ultimately the negative values of war.

Though *The Monk and the Hangman's Daughter* (1892) is still readable, though it skillfully handles the ironic situation of Anatole France's *Thaïs,* it is merely Bierce's revision of G. A. Danziger's translation of a German romance by Richard Voss. And, though *The Devil's Dictionary* (1906) is still quotable, it is no more than an alphabetical compendium of Bierce's deadliest witticisms and most philosophical epigrams. His securest achievement is concentrated in two volumes of short stories. "Denied existence by the chief publishing houses of the country," he informs us, *In the Midst of Life* was published privately in San Francisco under the original title of *Tales of Soldiers and Civilians* (1891). The second collection, *Can Such Things Be?* attained a New York publisher two years later. There is no padding here. Defining the novel as "a short story padded," Bierce preferred the abbreviated form for its totality of effect. His technique of directing suspense toward a dramatic crisis is modeled on Poe, but Bierce's horrors are more realistically motivated: thus premature burial, in "One of the Missing," becomes a war casualty. Sometimes his settings encroach upon Bret Harte's territory, but Bierce's miners are far from sentimental, and even his "Baby Tramp" comes to a macabre end. Most of his denouements take place at graves. Editors, comprehensibly, were frightened away from these tales. Their violent obsession with sudden death cuts through the conventional twists of fiction to a mordant sense of reality. Dreams, flashbacks, hallucinations, as in "The Mocking Bird," provide irony but no escape.

Bierce's heroic theme, which Stephen Crane undertook a few years later, was not the Civil War in its strange grandeur, but its impact upon the individual consciousness. Every story is a single episode of conflict: son against father, lover against rival, a house—one's own—destroyed, a spy—one's brother—shot. Underlying them all, evoked in vivid imagery, is the contrast formulated in "An Affair of Outposts" between the civilian's preconceptions of military glory and the soldier's experience of ugliness and brutality. In "Chickamauga," an excruciating study in point of view, a child's idyl turns into a battle and the child turns out to be a deaf-mute. Further tales seek a moral equivalent for war in claim jumping and psychic experiment, ghoulish practical jokes and pseudoscientific fantasies. Naturalism did not exclude the

story teller's concern with the supernatural, and Bierce's rationalism operates
to lend credibility to his ghost stories. Peculiarly haunting is "The Death of
Halpin Frayser," with its interpolation of Bierce's own recurrent dream, its
Kafkaesque nightmare of the poet lost in the wood, its Freudian realization of
"the dominance of the sexual element in all the relations of life." But his most
nostalgic reminiscences are reserved for Chickamauga and Shiloh and Kenne-
saw Mountain. He himself is the lone survivor of "A Resumed Identity," a
Rip Van Winkle of the Civil War to whom everything afterward is an anticlimax. Even when he describes the Sierras, in "The Night-Doings at Deadman's," it is with the eye of a former topographical officer in the Union Army:

Snow pursued by the wind is not wholly unlike a retreating army. In the open
field it ranges itself in ranks and battalions; where it can get a foothold it makes
a stand; where it can take cover it does so. You may see whole platoons of snow
cowering behind a bit of broken wall. The devious old road, hewn out of the
mountain side, was full of it. Squadron upon squadron had struggled to escape
by this line, when suddenly pursuit had ceased. A more desolate and dreary spot
than Deadman's Gulch in a winter midnight it is impossible to imagine.

3

Lafcadio Hearn is not less completely the Bohemian for having remained
a foreigner, a transient contributor to American literature. On his devious pilgrimage from the Old World toward the Orient, he spent more than twenty
years in this country, and nearly all of his work encountered its audience here.
Born in 1850 on an Ionian island to a Greek mother and an Anglo-Irish father,
he had been educated sporadically in Ireland, England, and France. Emigrating in 1869, he was appalled by the grinding mechanisms of New York; he
sought out connections in Cincinnati, and there obtained his earliest newspaper assignments. He was estranged from his friends, however, when they
opposed his marriage to a mulatto. By 1877 he was glad to move on to the
Latinized environment of New Orleans, where his journalistic and literary
activities exfoliated. Always drawn toward the tropical and the primitive, he
served for the better part of two years as correspondent in Martinique and the
neighboring islands. Travel sketches in various periodicals and two or three
miscellanies of exotic lore established his reputation, and he went to Japan in
1890 under the auspices of *Harper's Magazine.* When the customary misun-
derstandings arose, he was forced to seek other employment: he taught
English in government schools, wrote editorials for the Kobe *Chronicle,* and
lectured for a while in the Imperial University at Tokyo. Meanwhile he had
fallen in love with the country, married a Japanese woman, and been adopted
into her Samurai family under the name of Yakumo Koizumi.

The striking paradox of Hearn's career is that so deracinated a personality should ultimately sink his roots into so conventionalized a civilization. In one of his innumerable essays on "Ghosts" he refers to himself as

the civilized nomad whose wanderings are not prompted by hope of gain, not determined by pleasure, but simply compelled by certain necessities of his being,—the man whose inner secret nature is totally at variance with the stable conditions of a society to which he belongs only by accident.

Was it his hyphenated origin, his diminutive stature, or his disfigured eye that compelled him toward the Tennysonian vision of a summer isle, a savage woman, and a dusky race? Certainly, as his letters reveal, he was ill at ease among the so-called improvements of the Occident, and out of sympathy with "the Whitmanesque ideal of democracy." Murger's Bohemianism counterpoised the ideal of art for art's sake, and Wilde's derided lecture tour—which Hearn defended in the New Orleans *Item*—was an "acute provocative to the consideration of estheticism in the United States." From first to last he professed himself a romanticist; his boyish solace from the commonplace realism of city life had been the public library; afterward, when he gathered together a small collection of his own, he boasted that every volume was quaint or curious. Valuable by-products of this wayward bookishness were his graceful translations from Gautier, Flaubert, and Anatole France. Loti's *Madame Chrysanthème* was his prospectus for Japan.

Knowing that I have nothing resembling genius, and that any ordinary talent must be supplemented with some sort of curious study in order to place it above the mediocre line, I am striving to woo the Muse of the Odd, and hope to succeed in thus attracting some little attention,

he had frankly resolved. Because he was never at home in America, he retained a traveler's perception of its strange corners and colorful survivals. As a reporter he specialized in the romance of reality; lurid murders and artist's models, madhouses and carnivals, voodoo rites and Creole cookery His Louisiana friend, Père Rouquette, had lived among the Choctaws and written a *Nouvelle Atala*; the most charming memento of Hearn's sojourn in the West Indies was *Chita: A Memory of Last Island* (1889), which also embodies localized memories of *Paul et Virginie*. Local color, heightened by his imaginative strokes, blends into exoticism. The intense expressiveness of his own style is attributable to the quality he admired in Poe: "the color-power of words." American cities made him yearn for "a violet sky among green peaks and an eternally lilac and lukewarm sea." The Japanese tones of his later writing are more subdued. The suggestiveness of the word "ghostly" was for him an incantation; for him, as for many agnostics, fantasy replaced belief. Believing that ghosts represented ancestral experience, now banished by steam and electricity, he tried to recapture them in books like *Kwaidan* (1904).

"The dominant impression made by his personality," Huneker remarked of Hearn, ". . . is itself impressionistic." A posthumous title, *Diary of an Impressionist* (1911), subsumes his entire work, which—fragile and casual though it be—has extended since his death into a seemingly endless sequence of volumes. The books by which he is most likely to be remembered are the twelve that deal with his adopted country, from *Glimpses of Unfamiliar Japan* (1894) to *Japan: An Attempt at Interpretation* (1904). Their naïve charm has tended to fade in the light of more recent years. Hearn was anything but a shrewd observer of mores or politics, and his ignorance of the language disqualified him from interpreting the literature. His most memorable episodes are descriptions of shrines, gardens, fans, insects, and bric-a-brac. "A land where lotus is a common article of diet," where everything is marshaled in aesthetic order, where egotistical individualism is conspicuous by its absence— as *Kokoro* (1896) reminds us—does not lack attraction. But Japan was already becoming aggressively and mechanically Westernized; while Hearn, who continually warned his students against this unholy synthesis, was swept from his university post in a rising wave of hostility toward Westerners. Tired of lotus-eating, he might have gone back to America if ill health had not finally overtaken him. He never escaped from what he had never found: himself. "Ironically," as Katherine Anne Porter points out, "he became the interpreter between two civilizations equally alien to him."

4

Since Hearn had departed from the United States at the very outset of the nineties, he could only help from a distance to set the scene. And Bierce, though he heard "the note of desperation" sounded in the final decade of the century, had been shaped by a more rugged period. It was left for Edgar Saltus to play the sophisticate, to dramatize the cut-glass brilliance of the *fin de siècle*. Where the others were intellectually sequestered, he belonged to society in the exclusive sense of the term. Scion of a New York family, brother of a minor poet, he responded more fully to literary and philosophical studies in France and Germany than to the Columbia Law School from which he was graduated in 1880. His fellow student, Stuart Merrill, was enabled to function in an artistic milieu by remaining abroad; by returning home, where art was hardly more than an ornamental plaything, Saltus cast himself in the part of a dilettante and a dandy. His sobriquet, "the pocket Apollo," implies a varied endowment, and his legend is seasoned by three marriages and two divorces. His career on various newspapers was less sensational than his career in them. He traveled widely, gravitating in later years to southern California. Toward 1900, under the pressure of hack writing, his work begins to repeat itself; his earlier books best preserve the leisurely skepticism and nonchalant preciosity of his once fashionable manner. By the time of his death in 1921 it was thoroughly outmoded.

When Saltus is recollected, he is sometimes regarded as an American disciple of Oscar Wilde, to whom he devoted a succinct memoir. Actually he parallels, rather than emulates, the English aesthete, who was his junior by a year. In *Love and Lore* (1890), a year before the preface to *The Picture of Dorian Gray,* Saltus defended fiction against the prudishness of Anthony Comstock by recognizing only two kinds: "stories which are well written and stories which are not." Two years before *Salomé* he had touched upon the same subject, which was common property since Flaubert's *Hérodias.* Saltus, like Wilde, derived his critical outlook from France, as he duly acknowledged in one of his poems:

> I chat in paradox with Baudelaire,
> And talk with Gautier of the obsolete.

His first book, an anecdotal monograph, shows that he was also on speaking terms with Balzac. From these and other French writers, including Mérimée and Barbey d'Aurevilly, he translated extensively. German metaphysics, in its realistic and pessimistic phase, was a further influence. *The Philosophy of Disenchantment* (1885), a pocket exposition of the doctrines of Schopenhauer and von Hartmann, jauntily concluded that life was an affliction. *The Anatomy of Negation* (1886) followed logically as well as chronologically; it proceeded down the ages with the iconoclasts, pausing here and there to admire a shattered idol; Jesus, to cite the crucial instance, was "the most entrancing of nihilists but no innovator." Long afterward, reenchanted by theosophy, Saltus strolled through the museum of the world's religions in *The Lords of the Ghostland* (1907).

But philosophic doubt and religious denial were the starting point for epicurean pastimes. The next stage was history, and the ideal theme was Rome, not in its grandeur so much as its decadence. *Imperial Purple* (1892), a scandalous chronicle of the Caesars, luxuriated in passages that matched its title. Saltus, considering it his most sumptuous triumph, subjected the Tsars to a similar treatment in *The Imperial Orgy* (1920). Among his potboilers loomed a three-volume survey of great lovers, and *Historia Amoris* (1906) gave full indulgence to his rather prurient sense of the past. Under the guise of historical documentation it was possible to discuss matters still too delicate for fictional handling, and Saltus was well versed in those authorities that booksellers classify as erotica and curiosa. An unexpurgated library of such works, "everything, in fact, from Aristophanes to Zola," is catalogued in *Mr. Incoul's Misadventure* (1887). This piquant novel, the first of sixteen, observes an amoral code whereby murder and adultery are far less heinous than cheating at cards. A typical intermingling of pornography and hagiography, which reads like a collaboration between Flaubert and General Lew Wallace, is *Mary Magdalen* (1891). How it was received by Henry James, to whom it is dedicated, tempts speculation. Other novels, set against modern backgrounds, are spun out increasingly thin. Their mounting reliance on artifice and sensation, on perfumes and poisons, on bejewelled luxury and operatic vice, points directly to the detective story.

Not content, as a stylist, to contrive epigrammatic phrases, Saltus coined experimental words: grammatical audacities like "longly" or "parallely," imported novelties like "fatidic" or "lascive," along with other pedantries and Gallicisms. This brief specimen, from *Daughters of the Rich* (1909), is suggestive of the general effect:

An agony made of a thousand wounds, each distinct, each more lancinant than the other, caught and enveloped him. The torture of it thrust into being memories long ablated.

Diction like this can only be justified by an ironic tone. If some university had been endowed with a chair of irony, Huneker declared, Saltus might have found his niche. A latter-day Bohemian, Carl Van Vechten, has credited him with giving New York a mythology: "harpies and vampires take tea at Sherry's, succubi and incubi are observed buying opal rings at Tiffany's." But these fantastic shapes could not linger in that worldly climate without partaking of its corruptions. Saltus' preoccupation with the imperial theme was an oblique commentary on the private scandals of contemporary empire-builders; he compared the Vanderbilts to Caligula, sketched Delmonico's as if it were situated on the Via Sacra, and underlined the analogy between Newport and Nero's Golden House. The "Gold Book" compiled by Bradstreet's, the "Gilded Gang" frequenting the society columns, the alliterative collusion of "Manners, Money, and Morals" were the stuff of his essays and tales. These, if taken seriously, illustrate Pater's refined epicureanism; otherwise, we can take them as a comic supplement to Veblen's *Theory of the Leisure Class.*

5

In contradistinction to those that cut dashing figures or enact poignant roles against the aesthetic backdrop, James Gibbons Huneker is less of an actor than a spectator. Whether before a stage or a table, whether at a piano or a desk, we think of him as comfortably seated. Owing perhaps to the advantages of this position, he was able to work out the implications of Bohemianism, both as a critical approach and as an attitude toward life, more explicitly than any other American writer. It was more than the warmth of a disciple that led H. L. Mencken to designate him "the chief man in the movement of the nineties on this side of the ocean." More precisely, Huneker protracted this momentum into the twentieth century; for his first book, *Mezzotints in Modern Music,* did not appear until 1899. But his long apprenticeship went back to the days when, as a Philadelphia schoolboy, he had escorted Whitman to concerts; when, as a musical student in Paris, Villiers de L'Isle-Adam had bought him a drink; when, as a pupil of Joseffy, he had taught piano for ten years at the National Conservatory in New York. His career as a critic, starting on the *Musical Courier* in 1887, continued through the *Sun,* the *Times,* the *World,* and other New York papers, interrupted only by occasional travels in Europe. Most of his twenty volumes were pasted together from magazine articles and newspaper reviews. He disliked being called a journalist, and styled himself with genial modesty "a newspaper man in a hell of a hurry writing journalese."

His rambling autobiography, *Steeplejack* (1920), introduces Huneker as jack of seven arts and master of none. Undoubtedly his interests ranged beyond his accomplishments, and he approached other fields with varying degrees of amateurishness; but he had qualified as a professional musician, and his criticism stays closest to the object when confronting the keyboard of his instrument. His most substantial book, *Chopin, the Man and His Music* (1900), for once subordinates biographical details to technical comments; while *Old Fogy: His Musical Opinions and Grotesques* (1913) playfully exposes romantic enthusiasms to classical prejudices. The Symbolist doctrine that conferred upon music the primacy of the arts was reinforced by Pater's dictum that all arts aspire to the condition of music. Thus encouraged to venture afield, Huneker recalls, he wrote of painting in terms of tone, of literature as form and color, and of life as a promenade of flavors. "I muddled the Seven Arts in a grand old stew. I saw music, heard color, tasted architecture, smelt sculpture, and fingered perfumes." In this pleasant state of synesthesia, the concertgoer became a gallery visitor, working "in the key of impressionism." His hurried critiques became, if not adventures of a soul among masterpieces, then *Promenades of an Impressionist* (1910). Taste, to so practiced an epicure, was no mere figure of speech; gusto was his canon, and degustation his critical function. His impressions of cities, in *The New Cosmopolis* (1915), were documented with menus. He would savor a painter, sip a composer, recommend an author, and announce, in *Variations* (1921): "There is no disputing tastes—with the tasteless."

To his axiom that the critic was primarily a human being, the corollary.

expressed in *Unicorns* (1917), was: "All human beings are critics." And, when the critical medium was a part of the daily news, timeliness was as important as human interest. Paul Elmer More, in asking where Huneker dug up "all those eccentrics and maniacs," indicated the cultural lag between journalistic and academic criticism. *Iconoclasts: A Book of Dramatists* (1905) and *Egoists: A Book of Supermen* (1909) were pioneering achievements which did much to direct the swirling currents of European modernism toward these shores. Huneker's pantheon was eclectic, if not eccentric; he exalted the individual above the type, the artist above the school; the dominating personalities were "Anarchs of Art" like Shaw and Nietzsche. If it seems incongruous that these image breakers should themselves receive hero worship, the incongruity is explained by a Nietzschean phrase which Huneker borrowed for one of his books, *The Pathos of Distance* (1913). Slyly he wondered whether the sordid circumstances of Gorki's *Night-Lodging* would be understood "in our own happy, sun-smitten land, where poverty and vice abound not, where the tramp is only a creation of the comic journals." But Europe had also a greater abundance of genius than his musical studies had trained him to expect from his compatriots. Poe, his father's acquaintance, was among his rare American admirations; but Poe, he thought, was no more American than English; and Poe, furthermore, would have been wiser if he had lived in Paris like Chopin.

The appropriate reward for Huneker's labors was that Rémy de Gourmont and Georg Brandes respected him as a colleague. Though he could not vie with the acumen of the one or the erudition of the other, he acted as a well informed and sympathetic American spokesman for the impressionism and the cosmopolitanism that they respectively exemplify. His style added a "personal note," an air of improvisation which now sustains the excitement of discovery and again diffuses into beery rhapsody and polygot exclamation. Names invite epithets, which bristle with additional names: Huysmans, for example, is "the Jules Verne of esthetics." Allusions are multiplied into virtual litanies: a single page on Flaubert contains references to nineteen other artists. Titles reflect the paraphernalia of symbolism: *Ivory Apes and Peacocks* (1915). Two volumes of short stories about art and its problems, *Melomaniacs* (1902) and *Visionaries* (1905), fall somewhere between Henry James and O. Henry. Huneker's novel, *Painted Veils,* written at the age of sixty, ushered in the twenties. "In it," he confided, "the suppressed 'complexes' come to the surface." Sex, heavily orchestrated in the manner of Richard Strauss, comes to the surface of the old Bohemian fable; the Seven Arts are symbolized by seven veils, which ambiguously drape the Seven Sins. The prima donna heroine is an up-to-date incarnation of the goddess Istar, and the critic-hero—an Irish-American steeplejack of the arts—resembles Huneker.

It is Rémy de Gourmont who advises him to return to America, and it is Edgar Saltus who tells him he should have remained in Paris.

6

To return was no mistake; for the age of innocence abroad was expiring, and the time was ripe for sophistication at home. The Exhibition of 1893 made Chicago an international point of distribution for the latest artistic fashions. Concurrently, in many large cities, art museums and symphony orchestras were acquiring a public which needed guidance. Men like H. E. Krehbiel, Henry T. Finck, and W. J. Henderson did helpful work, but seldom strayed from the field of musical reviewing. The theater and the fine arts had exponents, but they lacked Huneker's breadth. His collaborator on *M'lle New York*, Vance Thompson, could report literary gossip and editorialize against philistinism; but Thompson's *French Portraits* (1900) owed its ideas, as well as its illustrations, to Gourmont's *Livre des Masques*. Percival Pollard would chat about central European literature in *Masks and Minstrels of the New Germany* (1911); earlier, with *Their Day in Court* (1909), he had driven home an invidious comparison. "The case of American letters," as Pollard had stated it, stood less in need of judicial inquiry than of medical diagnosis. The feminine bias, the commercial motive, the other symptoms were analyzed to show how quantity had superseded quality. Yet a neglected Boston critic, Walter Blackburn Harte, was Pollard's example and authority for the statement that the United States scarcely contained half a dozen writers who pursued literature as a serious profession. Bierce was his culminating instance of neglect, Huneker the exception that proved his rule: "A cosmopolitan, who happened to live in America. But who was not, primarily, interested in American art."

But if the trouble could be traced—as Pollard argued—to "our lack of proper criticism," the establishment of criteria depended upon a groundwork of importation and translation. The opinions Huneker imported, the books Hearn and Saltus translated, did much to eradicate the taint of provinciality that Henry James had detected in Poe. Though traditionalists had kept in touch with England, the current stimulus came largely from France. And, though the importers and translators were equally versatile as creative writers, their accomplishment was largely critical. Its results may be counted in educated audiences, rather than achieved masterpieces. Where literature had been traditionally connected with oratory and theology, it could now be envisaged through its relation to purely artistic disciplines; hence the old-fashioned didactic presuppositions gave way to aestheticism. Art for art's sake was never a very positive credo, but it aided in releasing the artist from ulterior constraints—particularly the taboos of sexual reticence. Sometimes, it may seem to us, the prudery of the moralists was outmatched by the prurience of the aesthetes; the struggle between them, at all events, would be prolonged and embittered before the subject could be faced in frank simplicity. To turn from subject matter to technique is to note the paradoxical devotion of a group of journalists to the cult of style. Affectation and mannerism did not obscure their genuine feeling for the cadence and the nuance. If they no longer excite us, it is because their successors reaped the benefits of their imitations and experiments.

What these isolated stylists had in common was the endeavor to reproduce experience at the level of consciousness, to relay sensations in unimpeded immediacy, which is connoted by the term impressionism. It is this method which Stephen Crane applied to naturalistic fiction in *The Red Badge of Courage* (1895), and which Lewis E. Gates reconciled with academic criticism in his essay on "Impressionism and Appreciation" (1900). Since impressionists are by nature individualists, they cannot be herded very closely together within a concerted movement; their lasting achievements, such as Bierce's tales, are likely to be the fruits of solitude. A negative program, however, may be discerned in their consistent antagonism toward middle-class standards, toward everything that the popular lady novelists stood for, toward the distinguished—albeit inhibited—man of letters whom Bierce dubbed "Miss Nancy Howells." That the two men, born within a few years and a few miles of each other, should have ended so far apart emphasizes the divergence between the genteel tradition and the Bohemian protest. The latter developed, with the twentieth century, into a recognized opposition; it found a local habitation in Greenwich Village, and vociferous organs in *The Smart Set, Reedy's Mirror,* and *The Masses.* The Philistines were reduced by Gelett Burgess to Bromides, by Sinclair Lewis to Babbitts, and by Mencken to the *Booboisie.* The seacoast of Bohemia became the comic opera kingdom of James Branch Cabell's novels, and romantic bookishness was pushed to its illogical conclusion in his *Beyond Life* (1919).

Whether we glance ahead to Cabell and Mencken, or backward to Poe and Whitman, it is clear that Bohemianism has continuously oscillated between the poles of escape and revolt; between an imaginative retreat from, and an iconoclastic attack upon, the restrictions of the commonplace. That our means of cultural expression have gradually broadened to comprehend both extremes is due, in large measure, to the work of the aesthetic journalists. Edmund Wilson, paying his respects to Huneker and Mencken, has recently asserted that the heyday of the literary free lance is past; that such potentialities will hereafter be absorbed by staff-written periodicals, by educational institutions, or by Hollywood. If true, this terminates an epoch which goes back to the Civil War and reaches its height in the last years of the nineteenth century. The *fin de siècle* was confused by many contemporaries with the end of the world; Max Nordau's *Degeneration* (1895), which advanced pseudo-scientific reasons for disliking modern literature, was widely circulated and approvingly underscored in America. But Americans could not wreathe themselves in the laurels of decadence, as self-conscious Europeans were doing; for, regarding the new century as peculiarly theirs, they welcomed its innovations. They did not always realize that their own nineties harked back to the European sixties, to the ferment over impressionism, symbolism, naturalism, and nihilism. They chose instead to look forward to the American twenties, to a generation which would win the struggles they had initiated. In short, they were not victims of the romantic agony, but the couriers of critical realism.

65. HENRY ADAMS

E<small>VEN</small> an age of disillusionment must have, if not its prophet, at least its interpreter. Whitman and Emerson gave full expression to the regenerative hope of democratic man in a new world. Mark Twain recorded the first shock of discovery that human nature could not be so suddenly changed, and the confusion and despair of his latter years was reflected in all our serious writers as the nineteenth century came to a close. No one of them confronted the problem as a whole, however clearly an Emily Dickinson, a Henry James, a Stephen Crane, or a James G. Huneker might see a part of it. Henry Adams asked the central question of the age, and explored it with inexhaustible energy. Why had man once more failed? What new conditions made the hope for perfection again seem vain?

Just as the First World War was drawing to a close, a little old man died quietly in Washington, leaving a privately printed book which he had called *The Education of Henry Adams.* For it he wrote a preface which his friend and former student Henry Cabot Lodge obligingly signed, when the book was given to the public a few months later.

Here was the story of an eighty year search for the meaning of life in a modern world of machines, a story which professed to be a mere record of failure ending with a prophecy of universal dissolution. The tone was almost bantering, the mood dark. The public was slightly shocked, not immediately impressed, not at all amused.

In using the third person for his revelation, Adams had covered his inherent shyness but, whether deliberately or not, he had also created an impersonal voice. In the years that followed, a generation, younger but no less disillusioned than his, gradually discovered that voice to be its own. Like the age in which he lived, this man offered a new paradox at every turn. He spoke its contradictions and its dilemmas, its thoughts and its feelings; he arranged neat and balanced equations to expound its insoluble riddles; he set up contrary images that could nod to each other across the chaos. With its companion, *Mont-Saint-Michel and Chartres,* the *Education* became a testament of faith urgently needed rather than of faith achieved.

But was the strange power that these books came to exert tragic or merely morbid? Would they survive, would they grow in stature, as the particular problems with which they dealt became history, the dilemmas which they so clearly formulated resolved or forgotten? Had they, like *Paradise Lost,* the *Divine Comedy,* or *Faust,* bored to the subterranean rivers? At least once before this had happened in American literature when the flying turn of the harpooner's line caught Ahab about the throat and snatched him after Moby Dick into the sea. Had it happened again? If so, the little old man, sitting in his low chair alone among the exotic trophies in his big Washington home, would be the most surprised of them all.

2

As autobiography the *Education* is not altogether satisfactory. Like Walt Whitman, Adams sought to explore himself in order to discover the cosmos. He did not spare himself when he thought confession relevant to his theme, but when it suited his purposes to do so he completely suppressed important facts except by inference. Much must be read between the lines and between the chapters. Even with the aid of his many letters, subsequently published, the life story of Henry Adams is not easily told.

Like Whitman's also is the romantic pose assumed for dramatic intensification—here a pose of reticence and failure rather than one of vigor and success. Unlike the *Autobiography* of his brother Charles, this book is more than a memoir; it is a portrait thrown on a screen for analysis and study. Here, in effect Adams says, is a life—my life. What does it mean?

The reticence was real enough if not the failure. It was a trait common to all members of the Adams clan. Late in life, when rejecting the Buddhist retreat for the more active code of Brahma, he wrote:

> But we, who cannot fly the world, must seek
> To live two separate lives; one, in the world
> Which we must ever seem to treat as real;
> The other in ourselves, behind a veil
> Not to be raised without disturbing both.*

This inwardness was Adams' chief source of strength as an imaginative writer, and it made the *Education* "a book deep enough and strong enough to be a bible to some natures"; but it also makes it, as a more recent critic has noted, "a grand-scale study of maladjustment, of the failure of an exceptional individual to mesh with a prodigious civilization." The biographical critic could find no nicer problem. Strength repressed must burst forth somewhere

* *Yale Review,* n.s. V, 88 (Oct., 1915).

and somehow. In the repression, the maladjustment, must lie the clue to the power of the resultant expression. As Adams himself apparently hoped, the failure of the individual must stand for the failure of man. In recounting the impact of events, facts, and people he reveals the growth of an imaginative mind, an artistic consciousness searching through a long life for an adequate form of expression, and not recognizing it himself when at last he had found it. The account of the search is itself the end of the long trail, the achievement of his destiny.

To be an Adams was by definition to make history rather than to record it. The hand of the fathers lay heavily upon the young boy growing up in the old Adams homestead at Quincy, studying at Harvard and in Germany, accompanying his father to London to help guide the policy of a distraught country through a civil war. Doubtless the progenitors of many a man have shaped his course as much, but the shadow of two Presidents and almost a third in their line made the children of Charles Francis Adams more than usually conscious of their blood. With the Adams and Brooks, admixtures of Boylston, Bass, Quincy, and even Alden had assured a firm planting in Massachusetts soil. The White House was a family homestead like that at Quincy, and the Presidency a family habit. The pattern for Henry Adams was already set when he was born, February 16, 1838, on Boston's Beacon Hill, the third son of Charles Francis, third son of John Quincy, eldest son of John Adams—of the eighth generation of the name in Massachusetts. The Adamses were born to rule.

With so imposing an inheritance, life in Quincy and Boston could be upright and rewarding, but not joyous. Sprung from farmers rather than divines, the Puritan strain nonetheless ran strong in the blood. The father, coming home from fishing on Mr. Greenleaf's wharf on a summer day, records in his diary: "Perhaps this consumption of time is scarcely justifiable; but why not take some of life for simple enjoyments, provided that they interfere with no known duty?" Such comment was the product of "the only perfectly balanced mind that ever existed in the name," as the boy later records. The mother was a silent partner in this somber household, making no deep impression on his memory. Like Ruskin's, such parents provided much to admire, but little to love. Natural affection, with the exception of family loyalty, was turned inward. There it dwelt for the time with the souls of grandparents, living and dead.

Adams liked to think that he was a variant from the family norm and attributed this divergence to scarlet fever which left him even shorter and lighter in frame than was usual in the family, reticent, and sensitive in nerves although sound in health and vigor. But the "habit of doubt" was common to his brothers, if not "love of line, form, quality." Charles, in his *Auto-*

biography, confirms most of Henry's early memories, but he recalls most accurately from these days the gloom of the Boston house; Henry, the sunlight on the yellow kitchen floor at Quincy, the taste of a baked apple when he turned from sickness to convalescence, the smell of rotting peaches and pears on his grandfather's closet shelf, selected carefully for seed. More than any other Adams, Henry developed acute senses.

His habit of miscellaneous reading for enjoyment was also formed in these years when he lay on his stomach on a pile of Congressional documents and read Dickens, Thackeray, and Scott. Later he laid the novels aside and helped in the proofreading of his great-grandfather's *Works* or did his Latin in an alcove in his father's library. Such experiences, rather than his schooling, educated him both as the formal writer of history and as the informal seeker for truth, beauty, and goodness which he was to become.

Perhaps most important discovery of all, the contrast of the seasons, the severe and sharp winters of Boston Common against the warm indolence of the Quincy summer, suggested the habit of balancing of idea against idea, impression against impression. In thought and emotion, this pattern was to provide Adams with his substitute for singleness of drive, for logic leading to the inescapable conclusion. In its balance, life remained for him open to the end.

This trait was at once responsible for his lifelong sense of failure and for the distinguishing quality of his achievement. He became more aware of it during his Harvard years, acutely so during his years in Europe. Unable to reconcile his natural inclination to literature with the family directive toward action, he developed many of the characteristics of the dilettante unable to plan his path. The choice of a career was difficult. Even at college he had known that he must write. The essays which he contributed to the *Harvard Magazine* were carefully clipped and bound. They show a feeling for form suggestive of the classroom; their models are Macaulay and Irving. As index to his reading, they tell much. The interest in novels persisted, but to them he added the "literary" historians: Carlyle, Gibbon, Niebuhr, Grote. There is no evidence of concern for politics or contemporary problems; this was to come later when he went to Germany to study law and language. Gradually a single objective seemed to form: law would provide a living and at the same time a core for his study and his writing. "But how of greater literary works?" he wrote his brother in 1859. "Could I write a history, do you think, or a novel, or anything that would be likely to make it worth while for me to try?" And he adds later: "If I write at all in my life out of the professional line, it will probably be when I have something to say, and when I feel that my subject has got me as well as I the subject."

His brother replied by urging journalism as a more immediate occupation, and when he returned in 1860 he went willingly with his father to Washington, then to London. Although he had thus early formulated exactly what he was to make of his life, the path was not clear. He could not bring himself to enlistment in the actual fighting as could Charles—besides, his father needed him—yet in the thick of events, even he responded as an Adams and put his pen in the service of family and country. "Our Washington Correspondent" of the Boston *Daily Advertiser* became "Our London Correspondent" of the Boston *Courier* and the New York *Times*. The letters are lively and well written, with flashes of description interspersed with sharply reasoned argument. Irony plays lightly over them. The boy was earnest, and his moods of gaiety and despair alternate with the course of events. Primarily he hoped to support his father's efforts to keep England out of the war by giving out accurate information for consumption at home. In this task, he showed energy, fearlessness and skill, but little diplomacy. He did not always succeed in doing "good by sustaining papa at home."

3

But the role of "Special Correspondent" was too limited and too shallow to satisfy him for long. He was soon back on his main track with an article in the *Atlantic* and others in the *North American Review*. He wrote to his brother in 1862:

The more I see, the more I am convinced that a man whose mind is balanced like mine [the second of the name!] . . . cannot be steadily successful in action, which requires quietness and perseverance. . . . What we want is a *school*. We want a national set of young men like ourselves or better, to start new influences not only in politics, but in literature, in law, in society, and throughout the whole social organism of the country—a national school of our own generation.

In short, the Adams brothers and their friends henceforth would guide the country through the press rather than from the White House.

Chance and the audacity of a young college president, Charles W. Eliot, further opened the way for the writer in public life by offering respectively the editorship of the *North American Review* and an assistant professorship of history at Harvard. With hesitation as to his fitness and grave fear that he might be wasting his time, Adams accepted both in 1870. That these were steps along his chosen way was not as clear at the time as it appears from the vantage point of the finished career.

One of his students describes him at this time as "a small man, blue eyes, brown hair, pointed beard auburn verging to red, perfectly but inconspicuously dressed in brownish gray tweeds (as I remember), of easy and quiet movement and distinct but quiet speech." Another thought of him as "a man of pure intellect." Laughlin recalled that "his nature was positive, not negative. His smile had in it fellowship, welcome, and heartiness; but his laugh was infectious, preceded by a sibilant intake of the breath, with a gay twinkle of humor in his eyes and in the wrinkles at their corners."

To prepare for his courses, he read assiduously, but his scholarship in the Middle Ages was not yet profound. The syllabus of his course is a mere digest of facts. From medieval, he moved into general European history, and then into American; and his better students followed him. The climax of these seven years was his seminar at his home, 91 Marlboro Street, the product of which was *Essays in Anglo-Saxon Law,* four Ph.D. degrees for his students, and the real beginning of his original historical work.

The same independence of spirit marked his conduct of the *North American Review,* first alone, then with the help of Lodge. He wrote to David A. Wells upon accepting the post that he planned to make it "a regular organ of our opinions . . . which should serve as a declaration of principles for our party." This party was composed of the independents who were discontented with the conduct of both the regular parties and who were called together by Carl Schurz in 1875, shortly after Grant's reelection, when it became apparent that civil service reform was not in the offing. Here was Adams' "national school of our own generation."

The best of the essays from this period are closely reasoned and highly technical arguments in the economics of politics. Confronted by the anarchy of the Reconstruction period, with its rapid economic expansion, its wildcat finance, its government by deals and dickering, Adams made a valiant effort to apply to the situation the traditional family principles of conservative fiscal policy, stable currency, centralization of authority, civil service reform, and planned economic development. The task was hopeless, but he put acid and dynamite in his pen. Two of his essays, "Civil Service Reform" and his second essay on "The Session," were reprinted in pamphlet form from the *North American* as campaign documents even though, like his progenitors, he stood on principles rather than platforms and changed his party affiliations as leaders changed their policies. Other essays in the same and other journals studied the course of nineteenth century British finance by way of analogy and warning or exposed and attacked the breakdown of the American political and fiscal structures. Of them all, the most readable today is his account of the Erie Railroad grab, "The New York Gold Conspiracy," where ideas become actions and exposition becomes dramatic narrative.

During all of this discussion of contemporary problems, Adams was gradually forming his working philosophy of history. His reviews in the *North American* reflect his impatience with the narrative method of the English and

American schools, his growing admiration for the pioneer research of the German legal and institutional historians. History, he decided, should be both a science and an art. As science, it must examine the laws and institutions of the Middle Ages for in them rather than in the overworked theme of the "Discovery" are to be found the germs of modern American society. His medievalism was a fresh discovery rather than an inheritance from that of Keats or that of Longfellow. History must also be exact. "The Germans have these qualities beyond all other races," he wrote to Lodge. "Learn to appreciate and to use the German historical method, and your style can be elaborated at leisure." He would lead the younger historians away from the easy but unsound narrative method of a Bancroft.

From De Tocqueville and Michelet he learned the art of constructing his story about dominant ideas. Once, Thwing recalls, he boasted to his class that he never tried to remember dates; rather he remembered events, not in relation to time, but in relation to each other, as cause and effect. Laughlin reports that "his disposition to try out all possible points of view led him to say extravagant and fantastic things." This was a tendency which grew upon him and provided the framework for his more imaginative writing of later years.

Following his own precept, he moved from the study of Anglo-Saxon law to the documents of New England Federalism, a volume of evidence in the cases of Pickering, Otis, and others who had tried to separate Massachusetts from the Union in 1814–1815. From the Pickering manuscripts in the Massachusetts Historical Society, he was led to the papers of Albert Gallatin, Secretary of the Treasury under both Jefferson and Madison. Gallatin, though of Swiss origin and a Republican, had hewn close to the Adams line in his fiscal policy and had demonstrated that one could be a scholar as well as a man of affairs.

Here was man, theme, and exhaustive documentation for the kind of history which Adams had been preparing himself to write. The result, four heavy volumes, is the most thorough and Germanic work he ever did. He never again wrote with such sureness, such calm, such repression of personal bias. But only about one third of one volume is original work; the rest is a printing of the letters and essays of Gallatin.

As Adams himself might have put it, lines of force were bearing upon a single point—his *History of the United States of America During the Administrations of Thomas Jefferson and James Madison,* a task which required nine volumes and more than as many years. The work on Gallatin led directly to Washington and into the Jefferson and Madison papers, then in the State Department. From there, the trail took the historian to the archives of London and Paris where he spent the summer of 1879 attacking these new sources. Gradually the massive work took form. For the first time, Adams adopted a procedure which became habitual with him of printing his more important work privately in six copies only, interleaved for the corrections and comments of his friends.

To adapt the scientific method of the Germans to the problem of American democracy required first the definition of the problem, then the fixing of a segment of material to be examined.

The scientific interest in American history [writes Adams in his final volume] centered in national character, and in the workings of a society destined to become vast, in which individuals were important chiefly as types. . . . Should history ever become a science, it must expect to establish its laws, not from the complicated story of rival European nationalities, but from the economic evolution of a great democracy.

The point of focus alone remained to be chosen, not in terms of an individual like Gallatin, or even like John or John Quincy Adams, but rather as a segment of social and economic evolution. About such a trend, the art of history could construct a unified whole.

For this purpose, what period could be more suitable than that which lay between the Presidencies of the two Adamses when the new-formed democracy was undergoing its first major test? Here he could use all the material on which he had cut his eyeteeth as well as the vast store of manuscript which had recently come to hand. If one wished to understand the complex of the present, as well as the principles of relationship between the individual and society in the modern world, these sixteen years of Old World convulsion and New World expansion offered the best possible laboratory material.

Economic determinism had not yet been invented in the sense in which more recent historians have defined and applied the term, but the philosophical base of Adams' theory rests as firmly on its premises as does that of F. J. Turner. The central theme of his history is the incapacity of the individual to control his own destiny or to shape the course of events outside himself. The focus of the opening and closing chapters is upon the American character and the American environment. Individuals and events, whether in Congress, court, or battlefield, are given the fullest treatment in detail of fact and analysis. Leaders, silhouetted against this background, are followed with painstaking care through every step of their progress. But everything happens because it must. Jefferson, the dynamic and determined, left the country in near ruin; Madison, lacking in the gift of leadership, restored it by drifting with the current of events. The point of view is as naturalistic as is Dreiser's in *An American Tragedy,* and the two central figures of the story are as helpless in directing the world over which they preside as is Clyde Griffiths in controlling his minor destiny.

Intellectual exhaustion would be the natural result of so great an effort, and the other three historical works which followed were mere by-products. The *History* as a whole had been a study in the capacity of man to survive in spite of the stupidity and helplessness of individuals. The careers of the tempestuous John Randolph and the unprincipled Aaron Burr stood out as extreme cases of the whimsy of fate. Some perverse force within Adams urged him on to separate studies of these two men whom he thought despicable. The *Randolph* (1882) appeared during the course of writing of the *History*; the *Burr,* if ever completed, was never published and the manuscript is either lost, hidden, or destroyed. Basically unsympathetic, the former is nevertheless a vivid portrait and a unified miniature of the method used in the larger work; of the latter we have no real knowledge.

The final volumes of the *History* were yet to appear when Adams fled with his artist friend, John La Farge, to the South Seas in 1890. But he was not to escape so easily. Adopted into the family of Tati Salmon, a Tahitian chief of mixed Polynesian and English stock, his curiosity was aroused by the history of the island as recounted by its last Queen, Tati's sister Marau, and by her mother, "the Old Chiefess." Here was a third and an unexpected by-product of his investigations, for the competition of England, France, and Spain, which formed the backdrop for his drama of American struggle, had served the same function in this remote island. Here was the great theme of modern history in capsule form. The Queen herself became interested in the problem and long hours were spent in helping her mother to recall the family history. The written record Adams took home with him and fitted into the accounts of explorers and missionaries. From these sources he was able to reconstruct the story in outline from 1690 to 1846, when the memories of the Old Chiefess are edited from her own words. With this, Adams' work as an historian came to an end. His work as artist and philosopher had scarcely begun.

4

"The other in ourselves, behind a veil"—Adams was so eager to suppress the story of his inner life that he revealed its emotional power even more effectively than would an explicit statement. From the facts of his marriage and of his friendships, at least the outer form of that life can be distinguished, the inner significance conjectured.

The thirteen years of his married life and the seven years following the suicide of his wife are omitted from the *Education*. Adams claims that his education ceased in 1871 and that he began then to put it to practical uses. In 1892 his experiment was finished and his account with society settled. He was not impressed with the result.

But there were more personal reasons for this silence. Wordsworth omitted the French romance which determined the course of his emotional life from his account of the "growth of a poet's mind." Adams omitted the years when his emotional life was both most fulfilling and most dismaying from his account of his "education." The cases are closely paralleled: in both, the events struck too close for public discussion. They would throw emphasis upon the individual actor rather than upon the general principles of organic growth.

Such reasons for suppression, however sincere, are unsound, and the historical critic must supply the deficiency from letters and other available sources. Adams met Marian Hooper (of Boston) in London in 1866 and married her on June 27, 1872, shortly after he had begun teaching. During the preparation of the greater part of the *History,* she was with him in Washington where she made of their home on H Street a haven of Boston hospitality in a sea of national politics.

His facetious account of her to his friend Gaskell at the time of his engagement cannot be taken as evidence of coldness. He describes her as possessed of "a very active and quick mind . . . fond of society and amusement," accustomed to look after herself, and a Boston "blue" in spite of her protests to the contrary. Certainly the pair was well matched in family and personality, in common interests and tastes. He professes himself "absurdly in love," and her niece Mabel La Farge recalled from summer days at Beverly Farms "an impression of oneness of life and mind, of perfect companionship." Mrs. Adams' weekly letters to her father are filled with accounts of casual teas and formal dinners, of horseback rides and the adventures of the dog Boojum, of the repartee of men but not of women. There were no children. The strain of nursing her father through his last illness threw her into a nervous depression from which loving family care could not rescue her.

At her death by her own hand on December 6, 1885, Adams was plunged into a mood of despair which made him turn to friends, to books, to travel, and to introspection as sources of relief. Once before, when his sister died of tetanus in Rome in the summer of 1870, he had resorted to blasphemy rather than stoicism. The God who indulged in such cruelty could not be a person.

Flung suddenly in his face, with the harsh brutality of chance, the terror of the blow stayed by him thenceforth for life, until repetition made it more than the will could struggle with; more than he could call on himself to bear.

When tragedy next struck even closer home, it was greeted by stoicism.

These are the few given facts and one is left with the dangerous task of reading biography from fiction. Two novels, *Democracy* (1880) and *Esther* (1884), were the anonymous by-products of his married years. The work of an inspired amateur rather than a finished artist, they deal respectively with the two most pressing problems of the day, the corruption which resulted from the grasp of business upon government and the religious doubt which resulted from the attack of science upon established dogma. They thus help to fill the twenty years of silence in Adams' account of his life and give us at least some of the links of thought and feeling between his early and his late work. The one leads to the *Education,* the other to the *Chartres,* as he himself liked to call it.

In both, the central theme is the unwillingness of a woman of intelligence and feeling to seek fulfillment in marriage, the one with a senator who has sacrificed his moral integrity for political advantage, the other with a clergyman who has lost his right to faith by clinging to dogma and refusing to deal honestly with the questions which science proposed. In a political context, the trend toward disintegration in ideals and values had led to the corruption of the second Grant administration and called out the stinging satire of *Democracy.* In the context of the church, the same trend made it imperative that man reject traditional securities and accept as the working basis of a new quest for truth the provisional and morally discouraging terms of the new concept of nature. Both novels have many defects as art, but they stand comparison with the work of Eggleston, De Forest, and Frederic or even the early Howells or Henry James. In the handling of plot, incident, and character except for the principals, Adams is an inferior craftsman, but for psychological insight and for wit in expression he is superior to most of his contemporaries.

To draw a close analogy between these novels and the lives of Marian and Henry Adams, as some critics have done, is to oversimplify. Although Esther has many traits in common with Mrs. Adams, Madeleine of *Democracy* is more masculine, more nearly like Adams himself. The latter's motives for coming to Washington were his:

To see with her own eyes the action of primary forces; to touch with her own hand the massive machinery of society; to measure with her own mind the capacity of the motive power.

And there is nothing in the characters of Senator Ratcliffe or Stephen Hazard, physically, mentally, or emotionally, to suggest the self-effacing scholar that Adams had become. To push identification is to strain the evidence too far. If these novels are records of their author's emotional failure, they are evidence only of a failure of the ideal. Because the union was so great, it taught the inadequacy of all such meetings.

As studies in emotional failure they have nevertheless profound significance for their author. Adams has drawn on his own sensitive and suppressed inner life to depict the conflicts which these two women suffer, and he has applied his discoveries to human nature at large. Marian Hooper taught him to know himself, to admit that the riddle of life cannot be solved by the mind alone. In both novels, the theme is the conflict of the inner demands of the individual for unity and integrity with the requirements of a world which, in its materialism and its confusion, had substituted conformity for values. Whether the framework be politics or the church, modern man must accept doubt rather than faith in order to preserve his two remaining values, self-respect and the right to speculation. This is the final stage in the progress from an authoritarian to a pragmatic morality which might be followed down from Jonathan Edwards, through Channing, Emerson, and Whitman, to the passionate skepticism of Henry Adams. But the Puritan core is still there.

Whether viewed as a personal or an objective problem, the dilemma in which Adams found himself, when in 1892 he once more took up his "education" upon completion of the *History,* is not hard to define. "It belongs to the *me* of 1870," he wrote to Elizabeth Cameron from Tahiti; "a strangely different being from the *me* of 1890. . . . I care more for one chapter, or any dozen pages of *Esther* than for the whole history, including maps and indexes." *Esther* was suppressed even though the reason given was that he wished to experiment with the public—to see whether or not an unadvertised book would sell. He had written into it too much of himself, and he had not yet achieved the larger perspective which was necessary to an expression of his discoveries. The historian and commentator who could use his scholarship and skill to investigate and to influence the course of American democratic thought had died with his wife although he had still much unfinished business to complete; the poet who must use symbols to express the deeper meanings of the inner life had still much to learn.

His first experiment in symbolism was made by proxy in an art other than that of writing: the hooded figure which he commissioned Augustus Saint-Gaudens to place over the grave of his wife—and later of himself—in Rock Creek Cemetery, Washington. It is somewhat difficult to separate that which is Saint-Gaudens from that which is Adams in this profoundly mystical conception, as the specifications were purposely indefinite. Many of Saint-Gaudens' statues have a vague poetic quality; the figure of "Silence," for example, made for the Masonic Temple in New York, has the heavily draped anonymous head and figure of the Adams monument, but lacks its massive impassivity, its sexlessness, its timelessness, its power. The stark simplicity and the deeper meanings of the statue can safely be attributed to Adams.

From the moment of giving Saint-Gaudens the commission, Adams refused for five years to approve or disapprove the progress of the work. He spent the summer of 1886 with the artist La Farge in Japan. There he met the Americans, Ernest Fenollosa and his cousin Sturgis Bigelow, both of whom had renounced their native heritage for Oriental faith. No hint of Brahman or Buddist mysticism creeps through the skeptical and worldly tone of his letters, but the seed was planted. An early note in the sculptor's scrapbook reads: "Adams—Buddha—mental repose—calm reflection in contrast with the violence or force in nature." Photographs of Michelangelo's Sistine frescoes and other such objects were advised as inspiration, as were talks with La Farge, but no books. Hints were to be drawn from Chinese Buddhas; an early sketch shows the figure of Socrates.

Gradually the conception was transferred from the spirit of one man to that of the other. When this act had transpired, Adams left once more with La Farge for a year and a half in Honolulu, Tahiti, Sydney, and Singapore, and home via Paris and London, bearing with him the sorrow of the loss of both father and mother. When he returned to Washington in February, 1892, the statue was cast and in its place. He was being drawn to the East by the lure of the reopening Orient, as were Lafcadio Hearn and Sturgis Bigelow.

Meanwhile, Adams had journeyed to Anuradhapura in Ceylon to meditate under the sacred bo tree of Buddha on the mysteries of two thousand years and the ruined temple of a living faith:

> Life, Time, Space, Thought, the World, the Universe
> End where they first begin, in one sole Thought
> Of Purity in Silence.

From his now deeper knowledge of Asiatic religion, he was satisfied with the work he had inspired. "He supposed its meaning to be the one commonplace about it—the oldest idea known to human thought." Later he discovered that it was "a sealed mystery to the American mind." For him it was no more than a mirror to reflect what one brought to it, and the habit of returning to learn what it had to tell him became a ritual. That his contemplation, however abstract, was not impersonal is revealed in a letter to Gilder in 1896:

> The whole meaning and feeling of the figure is in its universality and anonymity. My own name for it is "the Peace of God." La Farge would call it "Kwannon" [the Japanese Goddess of Mercy], Petrarch would say: "Siccome eterna vita è veder Dio."

This is the opening line, "As to see God is eternal life," of the sonnet which, in his novel, had brought Hazard into his first rapport with Esther, and had made him feel "that to repeat to his Laura the next two verses of the sonnet had become the destiny of his life:

> So to see you, lady, is happiness
> In this short and frail life of mine—"

He was not alone on these pilgrimages to Rock Creek Cemetery, nor did he go merely to brood over a personal sorrow. His tragedy had become his secret index to the mystery of life and death. The burden of meaning which neither history nor fiction was strong enough to bear was beginning to find expression in symbol; but adequate symbols were yet to be discovered.

5

But first, the meaning itself must be explored, and the mind alone was insufficient instrument. Forced back into himself by the death of his wife, Adams turned once more to his friends and to his books.

The capacity for making and holding close friends was one of the most pronounced traits of this presumably cold and intellectual man. No idea, feeling, or experience was complete until it had been thrown back to him from the sounding board of another's consciousness. Because no thought or emotion ever settled into a fixed pattern for him, he awakened in others something of the questing spirit which was always his. Every important facet of his versatile personality is directly reflected in at least one other person. Such friends virtually lived in his home or he in theirs; they traveled with him to every corner of the earth; they suggested books which might satisfy his cravings and then had to submit to a complete experience with him in what such books offered. There were women as well as men in the group, artists as well as statesmen and historians. The only prerequisite was that they should share with him some part of the never-answered riddle of experience.

In his English friend Charles Milnes Gaskell, Adams found the connoisseur of life who, between 1863 and 1908, shared with him an ironic perspective on its strivings and its follies. His letters to Gaskell are his best, but he depended more for the closer intimacies of friendship on the American statesman John Hay and the geologist Clarence King. These two, with Mrs. Adams and Mrs. Hay, made up the "Five of Hearts" during the Washington years, the nucleus of a larger circle. Hay understood Adams thoroughly and confesses that he depended on him "to keep me in the straight path by showing me the crooked." It was he who commissioned Saint-Gaudens to make a caricature medallion with the wings of an angel and the body of a porcupine: "Henricus Adams Porcupinus Angelicus." Doubtless the mutual friendship with the leading geologist of his day, Clarence King, was the bond which held them most firmly, but in many respects, Hay accomplished where Adams failed: he met the nineteenth century world and put it to his own uses. His private life was a model of domestic happiness; his public, a triumph of international policy. The *Education* ends with his death, leaving the last of the trio in the "depths of Hamlet's Shakespearean silence."

For King had gone before, in some ways the closest of all Adams' friends. Adams wrote:

His only ultimate truth was the action, not the thought. To him all science and all life were in that law, which, after all, is the only result of his generation—the law of Energy. Those of us who gladly and carelessly gave ourselves up to his influence and let him swing us as he liked—those he loved.

It was largely under King's influence that Adams embarked upon his most profound exploration of human experience. While in London in the sixties, he had talked with Sir Charles Lyell and the door of scientific speculation had been opened to him. Later he reviewed the *Principles of Geology* in the *North American*. When, with this common interest already deeply rooted, he met King in Estes Park and, sharing room and bed, "talked till far towards dawn," it was "never a matter of growth or doubt." The friendship was sealed. King's pioneer work in geology was a mere starting point for a philosophy of energetic skepticism. Once more, in another's success, Adams had recognized his own failure. His mind and feeling went with his friend into the High Sierras and into the depths of emotional abandon with the defiance of personal danger, which his body could not summon. King expressed in action what Adams could experience only vicariously. But King did not stop to reason, to analyze, to explain. Adams was the historian of the adventure in books which contain scant if any reference to King by name. It was not Langley, but the spirit of inquiry awakened by King which sent him exploring the speculations of Stallo, of Karl Pearson, of William James, even though Willard Gibbs and Raphael Pumpelly helped. It was King who stood behind his shoulder when he wrote *A Letter to American Teachers of History* and who first prompted the final pages of the *Education*.

As King led Adams into the profundities of scientific speculation, so John La Farge, without benefit of passion, led him into the world of color and form and idealization which is art. Twice the historian sought the artist when the only answer to his sorrows and perplexities seemed to lie in travel. Both times they turned to the East, first to Japan, then to the South Seas and India.

The diary letters which he wrote to Elizabeth Cameron from these trips merely skim the surfaces of color and form of the sea and the islands; the naïveté and spirit of the native girls dancing their native dances; the hospitality of the queens and princes of a dying race of primitives. But such experiences led Adams out from his sorrow and spread a surface gaiety over his numbness. Under La Farge's tutelage he tried painting, but only learned to see color, not to reproduce it. Through borrowed artist eyes he awoke to the beauties of the physical world at their most brilliant, the gaiety and warmth of primitive people who knew how to live in the sun even when their European oppressors were closing in upon them. Vague stirrings of response to Asiatic religions sent Adams to books on Buddha, as earlier he had read Dante in a garden at Nikko, the sacred heart of Japan, while La Farge painted the fountain below his veranda. Here were the first tentative explorations of those depths which he had sighted in *Esther* and which he was to fathom with the aid of the Virgin of Chartres. But La Farge could not accompany him on these later journeys.

With La Farge, the story of Adams' formative friendships loses its sharper outlines except for his brothers Charles and Brooks. The first early helped him shape his career, the second debated with him during the summer of 1893 the collapse of the Exchange and the theory of history which made all civilization ultimately follow the exchanges into disintegration. Like Henry in many ways, Brooks was even more a solitary, even more a concocter of historical if not cosmic theories. "The two brothers could talk to each other without atmosphere" and together they worked out the theory of history which in the one became a law of decay, in the other a dynamic entropy.

But the deeper levels of experience were still to be explored. Perhaps Adams went on these journeys alone, perhaps his reticence kept him from acknowledging his companions. "Adams owed more to the American woman," he once wrote, "than to all the American men he ever heard of," and, especially in his later years, he formed the habit of turning to women for guidance. The book upon which he expended most of himself, the *Chartres,* was written for his "nieces." In these later years Elizabeth Cameron, niece of Senator Sherman, as well as Mrs. Lodge and visiting nieces, helped with the hospitality at 1603 H Street. To Mrs. Cameron he wrote the record of his travels for the broken circle of friends in Washington; with her and her husband he traveled to London and on the continent.

The other "nieces" were actual nieces of Mrs. Adams. One of them, Mabel Hooper, later Mrs. Bancel La Farge, has spoken for them all and has given his letters to print.

To them all [she writes], he was the *generic Uncle,* the best friend—to whom they not only could confide their innermost secrets, their perplexities, hopes and aspirations, but also at whose feet they could sit endlessly, listening to the most thrilling talk they had ever heard, or were likely to hear again.

It was to them and to such foster nephews, or "nieces in wishes," as Cecil Spring-Rice that the childless and lonely old man opened his home and his heart; and it was under the tutelage and care of Aileen Tone, an adopted "niece" and a Catholic, that he discovered, after his paralytic stroke in 1912, his last great enthusiasm, the music of the old French songs of which he had known the words for so long. Mabel La Farge and Mrs. Winthrop Chanler, who knew him well in these days, have expressed the belief that he was himself virtually a member of the church in faith, but most other Catholics do not agree with them. The Virgin of his *Chartres* was at heart a pagan.

6

On the assumption that Adams was primarily, if not wholly, a man of intellect, the majority of his critics have attempted to evaluate his final accomplishment as a logical statement of the philosophy of mechanism applied to history. With comparative ease they have pointed out fallacies in his premises, faults in his logic, and exaggeration in his conclusions and predictions. Some have argued convincingly that Brooks Adams, in his *The Law of Civilization and Decay* (1895), has made out a better case for the application of the thought of Newton, Comte, Darwin, and Marx to the history of Western civilization than did Henry. The result has been a tendency to discount the achievement of the latter almost as effectively as he did himself.

Throughout his life Adams thought of himself as a man of letters rather than primarily as a historian, scientist, or philosopher. He never lost his eager interest in the central and tragic conflict of man and nature; but he was thwarted, as all American writers have been until very recently, by the absence of a matured and autogenous literary culture. He instinctively knew, as Cooper and Melville and Mark Twain had each discovered in his own way, that American literature must be a reinterpretation of the eternal issues in human experience in terms of life in contemporary America. Politics, economic history, science, philosophy, and art itself were means and materials only. To the man of letters, no truth is new, its expression never done.

The discovery of an authentic and adequate medium of expression was his life's quest, and the recognition that form cannot be imposed, that it must result from understanding, made "education" for him the primary good. His confession of failure is merely, in its larger implications, his version of the failure which underlies tragedy from Æschylus to Eugene O'Neill.

For Adams was primarily a man of feeling, and his ultimate strength lay in his long delayed but overwhelming discovery of that fact. Before he could justify his choice of a career of writing in his own eyes or in ours, he had to rid himself of two assumptions that inhibited his development: that thought without action is void, and that thought without emotion is valid. He had to learn that living thought may be in itself a kind of action and that thought cannot live when divorced from emotion. His career as publicist and historian proved to him that writing could be a form of action; his personal tragedy and the release of his emotional life into friendships taught that no scientific truth could be final without imagination, no writing could be intrinsic action if it relied upon reason alone.

His transition from the man of thought to the man of feeling was, however, so gradual that the stages in the progress can readily be lost and the issue confused. In its last and crucial phase it centers on the application of the findings of science to history. But before science could produce original art, it had to become an instrument of the imagination rather than merely a method for the discovery and analysis of facts; history a record of man's whole development rather than merely a narrative of his past adventures and vicissitudes.

In the decade between the publication of the first volume of the *History* and his address to the American Historical Association in 1894, his view of the possible relationship between science and history had progressed far beyond the mere use of the inductive method and the assignment of historical evidence to man-made law. "The situation," he told his fellow historians, "seems to call for no opinion, unless we have some scientific theory to offer." From this day forward his energies were devoted to the search for that formula rather than to the writing of history itself according to established premises and rules. Although he does not seem fully to have appreciated the fact, such a quest was as romantic as those of Ahab for Moby Dick or Parsifal for the Holy Grail. As in those cases, it became a search for the symbol of the life force, an effort to wrest the meaning of man from a reluctant nature by sheer violence. The discovery of a new and scientific basis for history would mean the creation of a new religion.

The task of Adams' generation was not the completion of that creation. Rather they were to break down old structures by techniques which science had given them, to define issues, to set up working hypotheses for the new synthesis. Adams took as his particular task the discovery of an organic aesthetic form which could give expression to the significance of his age as he saw it. He proceeded direct from the experience to the expression because he had rejected all models. The result was the single gigantic but incompleted act of the imagination which resulted in the *Chartres* and the *Education*.

The final chapters of the *Education* state briefly the "dynamic" theory of history which Adams had adopted as his tentative instrument, a theory which is more fully expounded in *A Letter to American Teachers of History* (1910), his last important book, which his brother Brooks edited posthumously, adding the unpublished essay on "The Rule of Phase" and giving the whole his own unfair but provocative title, *The Degradation of the Democratic Dogma*.

The choice of the second law of thermodynamics, the law of dissipation of energy, as the needed formula was dictated by the stage to which physical science had developed by 1910. If the attempt were made today, Adams might equally well have adopted the law of relativity and developed a science of history in quite other terms. To him the important factor was the relation of the two components, science and history, to each other, not the final truth of the findings of either one. In the later and even more daring essay on the law of phase, he allows his imagination such range as to venture by computation to fix a date for the moment of dissolution. Impatience with the rapid progress of science and the stodgy conservatism of historians provoked heroic measures.

Adams' version of the more fully developed theory of entropy which he adopted for his two major literary works may, for convenience, be stated as two related hypotheses:

(1) Accepting force as ultimate fact, two kinds of force are recognizable in experience: an inner force which makes for unity and which man has traditionally known as religion or God, and an outer force which makes for multiplicity and which has come to be known as science or nature. Absolutely considered, both these forces may be traced to a common center in a mechanistic view of the universe, as in the past both were traced to a theistic center, but in human experience they have always been and probably always will be differentiated and in opposition to each other. This is no more than a restatement in modern terms of the classic theory of metaphysical dualism.

(2) Historically considered, experience shows that man reached the peak of his development in the era of medieval Christianity because he then succeeded through the instrument of the church in attaining the highest degree of unity; but the discovery of the inductive method of reasoning and its application to physical science in modern times introduced a new "phase" of evolution in which nature supplants man as dynamic center of the universe. Unity was then mortally challenged and the universe began to move toward disintegration by a law of accelerated entropy which should by now be reaching its culmination and which should be followed by complete dissolution or by new and unpredictable forms of life. Thus the historical framework is provided for the application of the theory of dualism.

These two hypotheses are complementary when treated in purely intellectual terms, but they present a fundamental inconsistency when viewed in the light of emotion. Adams thus also creates, perhaps unwittingly, a dichotomy between intellect and emotion which supplies the pattern for his art form, but which destroys the validity of his theory as an instrument for the logical explanation of the universe. Art alone could resolve this inconsistency because art records and evaluates rather than accounts for the evidences of experience.

Adams' creation of an arbitrary cosmology for his purposes suggests Milton's similar acceptance of the Ptolemaic system at a time when his own reason might have dictated the Copernican. Adams' acceptance of a modified Newtonian mechanism is a necessary premise to his artistic construction, and its degree of logical soundness has no bearing on its aesthetic validity. It was many years before Miltonic criticism could free itself from this difficulty and accept *Paradise Lost* as a great epic poem in spite of the fallacious cosmology upon which it is based. The criticism of Henry Adams has not yet reached that stage.

Only in the aesthetic expression of his position did he reach any degree of finality. To him the two major works of this period, the *Chartres* and the *Education,* formed a unified, albeit an imperfect, whole. The importance of their interrelationship is stressed by his quoting in his preface the key passage from Chapter XXIX of the *Education* when he finally decided that his time was up and he could bring his work no nearer to completion:

Any schoolboy could see that man as a force must be measured by motion, from a fixed point. Psychology helped here by suggesting a unit—the point of history when man held the highest idea of himself as a unit in a unified universe. Eight or ten years of study had led Adams to think he might use the century 1150–1250 expressed in Amiens Cathedral and the Works of Thomas Aquinas, as the unit from which he might measure motion down to his own time, without assuming anything as true or untrue, except relation. The movement might be studied at once in philosophy and mechanics. Setting himself to the task, he began a volume which he mentally knew as "Mont-Saint-Michel and Chartres: A Study in Thirteenth-Century Unity." From that point he proposed to fix a position for himself, which he could label: "The Education of Henry Adams: A Study in Twentieth-Century Multiplicity." With the help of these two points of relation, he hoped to project his lines forward and backward indefinitely, subject to correction from anyone who should know better.

The student who reads this passage ten times should need no further elucidation of these two books. He will not make the mistake that many critics have committed of assuming a finality in Adams' logical position; he will know that the two books in concept are one, a planned work of the imagination rather than an historical, autobiographical, or scientific record or argument; he will evaluate their timeless quality rather than their circumstantial reference.

As art, these books should therefore be approached only as companion studies in unity and multiplicity. As contributions to the philosophy of history, they may be accepted or discredited at will without invalidating this approach. Man's inner need for discovering a system of unity in his experience and his constant difficulty in reconciling this need to the multiple influences of the world outside of himself is the most persistent theme of all literature. It is the problem of Oedipus, Hamlet, and Faust, of Tom Jones, Ahab, and Ma Joad. Emerson discussed it for his age; Henry Adams did the same for an age when the conflict was infinitely more acute and the solution less apparently obvious.

We have seen at least some evidence that Adams at one time hoped to find his center of unity in Oriental art and religion and his symbol of that unity probably in Buddha. His poem "Buddha and Brahma," not published until 1915 but written earlier, reveals the failure of Buddhist quietism to make unity dynamic, of Brahmanism to achieve unity beyond action. When he turned from travels in the East to travels in France, he discovered in the arches and spires of Mont-Saint-Michel, Amiens, Coutances, Paris, and Chartres the symbol of unity which he sought, and communicated it in his only other known poem, "Prayer to the Virgin of Chartres." Not much more than adequate in technical skill, these two poems have an intensity of blended feeling and thought which gives them the dignity of art.

In exploring the nature of unity, Adams was led back to his study of medieval history, and he added to it a wide reading in chivalric poetry, works on medieval architecture, and the writings of Christian philosophers from Abélard to Thomas Aquinas. Again he was the inspired amateur rather than the documentary scholar or the conventional man of letters. He read books only when they "helped." Slowly he formed his pattern about the symbol of the Virgin—not Mary as person or as divinity, but the Lady of Chartres as creation of the medieval imagination. The selection of the century 1150–1250 was dictated by the facts because then the conception of the Virgin had become, for one moment in history, an effective symbol of man's eternal desire for inner and outer harmony, expressed both in art and philosophy. Just how this image evolved and what significance it might have not only for medieval but for universal man became one half of his life's concern. The result has served as a study of the medieval mind; it is only now coming to be recognized for its insight into the universal mind.

The structure of the book is apparent only when this central purpose is kept in mind. Adams' facetious statement that it is merely a tour de force for the entertainment of his nieces and "nieces in wishes" is obvious screening of its profound value to him. His light bantering tone persists throughout, but the careful unfolding of his plan is not hampered by it.

The book falls into three somewhat unequal parts: the preparation of the medieval mind for its gigantic effort of synthesis just before its collapse; its achievement of emotional unity in the first half of the thirteenth century as represented in the Cathedral of Chartres; and the translation of this process into the rational terms of medieval philosophy. For the first the Archangel Michael serves as personal focus, for the second the Virgin, for the third St. Thomas. Above them all, the Virgin becomes the symbol of unity achieved. The transition from worship of a masculine to that of a feminine deity is hinted at in the *Roman de la Rose* and acknowledged in the religious chivalry of Thibaut. Poetry, history, and architecture combine, with all their intricate details, in an aesthetic synthesis which makes manifest the sovereignty of the Virgin. Abélard, Bernard de Clairvaux, St. Francis, and St. Thomas add each his philosophy to emphasize the result and to translate it back from emotion to scholastic logic, from the supreme feminine intuition to the masculine approximation of truth through reason. For once, man's inner need for harmony seemed, at least in the perspective of later centuries, to have been partially supplied.

The truth which Adams here tacitly recognizes is that unity may be achieved through emotion even when denied by reason. His Virgin is completely irrational, her power nonetheless centripetal. Mary filled her church without being disturbed by quarrels because she "concentrated in herself the whole rebellion of man against fate. . . . She was above law; she took feminine pleasure in turning hell into an ornament; she delighted in trampling on every social distinction in this world and the next." Yet she answered the prayers of her suppliants because she judged by love alone. She could put in terms of positive symbolism what the hooded figure in Rock Creek could only permit by reflection. This is what Adams had learned from the American woman, but he had to trace it back to twelfth century France to find it unembarrassed and whole. Intuition is above reason; love may triumph over logic; art can speak deeper truths than science.

With the same detachment Adams then turned immediately to the other half of his problem: the study of multiplicity. Here the age of obvious choice was the present, the person of obvious focus himself. Even at the risk of being accused of merely writing his autobiography, he undertook *The Education of Henry Adams: A Study in Twentieth-Century Multiplicity.* The detachment of the third-person pronoun is not an affectation; it is an integral part of his scheme. He might have written of someone else had he known any other experience as well as his own. As the forces which he wished to examine are universal, as well as peculiar to the age, he would do as well as another for their point of impact. For the impersonality of the Ego, he turns again to Oriental thought. In a biographical testament of friendship to George Cabot Lodge, published in 1911, he states that the poet seeks unity in "some one great tragic motive." Lodge's

was that of Schopenhauer, of Buddhism, of Oriental thought everywhere,—the idea of Will, making the universe, but existing only as subject. The Will is God; it is nature; it is all that is; but it is knowable only as ourself. Thus the sole tragic action of humanity is the Ego,—the Me,—always maddened by the necessity of self-sacrifice. . . . In order to raise the universe in oneself to its highest power, its negative powers must be paralyzed or destroyed. In reality, nothing was destroyed; only the Will—or what we now call Energy—was freed and perfected.

Thus perhaps from the analysis of his own experience, Adams might witness the action of this tragic movement in the modern world and in harmony with the new concept of Energy which science had supplied. This he attempts in the *Education*.

This book also falls roughly into three parts: the inadequate and misleading preparation of a generation which reached maturity at the moment in history when the challenge of modern science became generally felt; the effort of one individual to adjust to this new and centrifugal world of multiplicity; and the translation of the result into a rational formula. The problem was more baffling because the perspective of time was lacking. On the other hand, the material was more familiar. Nor was a central symbol as easy to find. Frank Norris, at the same time on the same quest, adopted the railroad as symbol in *The Octopus*. Adams, in the high excitement of discovery, chose the dynamo which he saw first at the Chicago Exposition in 1893, later in Paris in 1901. Here was the outward image of his second kind of force, almost specific enough to excite worship if worship were due.

It would be dangerous to press the symbolic parallelism of these two books too far, but the temptation to explore it is great. As the power of the Virgin is humanity on the level of divinity, so that of the dynamo is mechanism raised to the infinite. In the one case, the power operated on an impassive and nonhuman object, the Cathedral of Chartres, which in a sense becomes a subordinate or reflective symbol; in the other, the object of the mechanistic force is human, is Henry Adams made impersonal and passive. From this perfectly balanced equation, the symbolism is developed on the one hand in terms of architecture, art, philosophy, persons and events (stained-glass windows, figures of saints, the rebellion of Pierre de Dreux, the poetry of Thibaut, the philosophy of Abélard); on the other in terms of politics,

science, philosophy, and again persons and events (Anglo-American diplomacy, the geology of Sir Charles Lyell, two World's Fairs, William Henry
Seward, and Lord John Russell).

Intricate and balanced as these imaginative elements are, it would be a
mistake to hold that Adams had perfected a new sort of epic or symbolic form.
The result gives the impression of work still in progress as Adams felt that it
was. The over-all form is massive and sprawling as are those of Melville or
Whitman, rather than balanced and finished as one knowing the man Adams
might expect. He was never satisfied with it, published the books privately,
allowed them reluctantly to be offered to the public. But they are thoroughly
American in that whatever order and discipline they achieve is organic. The
refined inheritor of Adams' energy had allowed his feelings and his understanding to mold their own form about them.

The pen works for itself [he confesses] and acts like a hand, modelling the
plastic material over and over again to a form that suits it best. The form is never
arbitrary, but is a sort of growth like crystallization, as any artist knows too well.

In his style, Adams came nearer to a classic restraint, but here too he
indulged in extravagance when the pen became willful. His revisions of his
historical essays when he collected them show a peeling off of the superfluous
phrase, a stripping down to clear and explicit statement. When he turned
from direct to imaginative writing, he deliberately created an *alter ego* and
from an oblique angle surveyed himself together with other phenomena, past
and present. The direct style would no longer do and he deliberately cultivated, even in his personal letters, the irony which had always been his. A
careful reading of Pascal, Montaigne, and Voltaire helped in this study. In
his final testament of futility and affirmation, his vein was comic in spite of
the tragic intensity of his feelings. Wit alone could bear the burden.

THE UNITED STATES

--- confidence and criticism

66. THE HOPE OF REFORM

By 1912 Eastern liberalism was swerving to the left. That year Walter Weyl championed the New Democracy—what with the New Nationalism and the New Freedom and even the New Republic, everything was new then—and his opening chapter furnished a mordant analysis of the "disenchantment of America." The revelations of the Pujo Committee furnished abundant support to the theory of disenchantment, and those who boggled at government reports could read the same story, with no perceptible improvement in style, in Dreiser's *The Financier.* The undismayed Roosevelt, always radical during election years, led his shouting followers out of the Grand Old Party to some Armageddon where they prepared to battle for the Lord, and for T. R. At Baltimore Woodrow Wilson, with the aid of the veteran Bryan, nosed out the noncommittal Champ Clark for the Democratic nomination, and that November the New Freedom officially supplanted the New Nationalism and the promise of American life seemed not hopelessly beyond fulfillment. The Eastern intellectuals—older men like Wilson and Brandeis and Villard, and younger men like Croly and Weyl and Lippmann—prepared to catch up with the homespun Western radicals after a lapse of only twenty years.

There was, to be sure, little that was new about the stirrings and strivings of the second decade of the new century, except the stage on which they were presented and the accent in which they were expressed. Even here the change was but relative. Jacob Riis, after all, had told how the other half lived, and Henry George had campaigned for the mayoralty of New York, and De Leon had taught socialism at Columbia University back in the eighties and nineties. Nor was there much the Pujo Committee could uncover that had not been known to Henry Demarest Lloyd, or much the *New Republic* could say that had not been anticipated by Flower's *Arena,* while men like Altgeld and Weaver and "Sockless" Jerry Simpson had known the realities of disenchantment long before Croly learned the meaning of the word. Indeed it is difficult to discover anything in the New Nationalism or the New Freedom that was not explicit or implicit in the Populism and the socialism of the nineties, except respectability. Otherwise, the distinction was quantitative rather than

1107

qualitative: whereas Bryan had persuaded but six and one-half million voters, Wilson, Roosevelt, and Debs, together, attracted more than eleven million. These figures dramatized the fact that public opinion had at last become aware of the problems that had confronted America ever since the decade of the nineties.

For in the second decade of the twentieth century the nation faced a crisis in the conflict of forces within itself that had first declared themselves in the nineties, and creative energies were released, with their doubts as well as their confidence, into literature and criticism. The outlines of that conflict had by then emerged clearly and even boldly. On the one side lay an America predominantly agrarian, concerned with domestic problems, conforming— intellectually at least—to the political, economic, and moral principles inherited from the eighteenth century: an America still in the making, physically and politically, an America on the whole self-confident, self-contained, and conscious of its unique character and of a unique destiny. On the other side lay the modern America, predominantly urban and industrial, inextricably involved in world economy and politics, troubled with the social and economic problems that had long been thought peculiarly the burden of the Old World, desperately trying to accommodate its traditional institutions and habits of thought to conditions new and in part alien.

2

The era of the New Freedom (1913–1921) and its subsequent disenchantment was the climax of the age of reform. That age (1890–1912) had been experimental rather than dogmatic, given to exploration rather than to the establishment of sovereign claims. It was a time of protest and reform, of the rejection of what was old and the championship of what was new, of speculation and experiment. There was boundless enthusiasm for good causes and endless tinkering with the political machinery. Armies of reformers advanced upon the battlements of vested interests, bands of humanitarians waged guerrilla warfare upon every form of social injustice, visionaries imagined felicitous Utopias and some even indulged in them, less felicitously. There was a youthful ardor to weed out abuses, democratize government, redistribute property, humanize industry, improve the lot of the workingman and the farmer, rescue the victims of social injustice, elevate the moral tone of society. It was the day of the music makers and dreamers of dreams, of world seekers—though rarely of world forsakers. The great figures in politics were all reformers, the great movements all reform movements. Bryan, La Follette, Roosevelt, Wilson, and Debs bestrode the national political scene; Altgeld, Tom Johnson, "Golden Rule" Jones, Hazen Pingree, Charles Aycock, Ignatius Donnelly, "Bloody Bridles" Waite, Tom Watson, Joseph U'Ren, gave color to state and local politics.

The era was ushered in by the Populist Revolt in the nineties, bowed out by the New Freedom and the crusade to make a democratic world. Agrarian reformers captured the Democratic party, and urban progressives the Republican; socialism became respectable and was taken up by the churches, and settlement houses blossomed in every slum. New England liberals emerged to take up the battle for the Negro and the Indian and, after Manila Bay, a crusade against imperialism enlisted the intellectual elite of the whole country. There were countless other crusades: for temperance, for conservation, for peace, for woman suffrage, for children's rights, for civil service reform. The conscience of the nation was troubled, and each exposure of sin or neglect brought contrition and penance. In those years Americans learned *How the Other Half Lives*, heard *The Bitter Cry of the Children*, were shocked by *The Shame of the Cities*, outraged by the *Treason of the Senate*, revolted by the fate of *The Daughters of the Poor*, initiated into the iniquities of *Frenzied Finance*, alarmed by *The Greatest Trust in the World*, came at last to understand the dichotomy of *Wealth Against Commonwealth*. As a result laws to clear slums, protect women and children, curb monopolies, supervise insurance companies, free the public lands, save the forests, frustrate corruption, and safeguard the ballot box crowded the statute books.

All this was eloquent of optimism. Despair leads to apathy or revolution, it is the incorrigibly hopeful who spend their energies in reform. Though the bright promise of American life seemed to be fading, there was no inclination to despair of the Republic, to abandon democracy, or even to challenge a capitalist economy. There was, on the contrary, an all but universal confidence in the beneficent workings of democracy and of the profit system—if only they could be operated honestly and by virtuous men. Carnegie's lyrical description of American material prosperity was, after all, entitled *Triumphant Democracy*. There was nothing fundamentally wrong with American institutions; it was merely that abuses had crept into them, that they had been exploited by shortsighted men to selfish purposes. What was needed was not the abandonment of democracy, but more democracy, not the abolition of private property, but the wider and more equitable distribution of property. "The evil," said Woodrow Wilson in his first inaugural address, "has come with the good, and much fine gold has been corroded." The task was to get rid of the evil and hold fast to what was good.

This is what explains the crusade for Social Justice, for the Square Deal, for the New Freedom, for all those catchwords and phrases which confessed a reassuring—and perhaps a naïve—optimism. Was democracy failing? The answer was to double the electorate by giving votes to women. Was there corruption at the ballot box? The Australian ballot, or formidable corrupt practices acts, would eliminate that. Were legislatures deaf to the voice of the people? The initiative and the referendum would once more give expression to that voice. Was the Senate a stronghold of privilege? Elect senators by direct vote, and that body would become a stronghold of democracy. Was Congress caught in its own cumbersome machinery? A revival of the Jacksonian doctrine of presidential leadership would make the cumbersome machinery of government work. Did bosses manipulate political parties? Direct primaries would circumvent them. Were wealth and privilege entrenched in the judiciary, as Jefferson had warned? The recall of judicial decisions, or even of judges, would assure a democratic interpretation of the Constitution.

In the economic arena, too, there was confidence in the soundness of institutions and the virtue of the majority of men. Roosevelt could talk of "malefactors of great wealth," but he distinguished sharply between "good" and "bad" trusts, and the moral distinction was carried over into the judicial realm as "reasonable" or "unreasonable" restraint of trade. The Grangers had denounced the railroads as the Great Monopoly, and the Populists had demanded that they be publicly owned; but these demands were easily watered down to regulation and supervision, and Roosevelt—who better than any other figure typified the optimism and opportunism of the reform movement —compromised even here. There was much ado about the maldistribution of wealth, but no attack upon wealth itself, and if the reformers were not quieted by Carnegie's confession that it was a disgrace to die rich they were willing enough to settle for income and inheritance taxes. Communism was not unknown, but it completely lacked the native roots of the earlier Utopian movements; and it was the Debs wing of the Socialist Party, not the radical De Leon wing, that won.

All this suggests that the reform movement was thoroughgoing in criticism, but opportunistic in its tactics. It formulated no logical system, subscribed to no universal principles. It accepted in practice Justice Holmes' dictum, "Legislation may begin where an evil begins," and put a touching faith in the efficacy of legislation. It was romantic in its philosophical implications, but realistic in its recognition of the economic basis of politics. It was, above all, secular—even the Christian Socialists seemed more socialist than Christian, more concerned, that is, with the material than with the spiritual welfare of men. It lacked, or rejected, the basic philosophy that had animated the reformers of the 1840's—the passionate religious conviction of the identity of man with God, of the infinite worth of every human soul. It was more concerned, indeed, with equality of income than with equality of soul, and demanded justice in the name of the Declaration of Independence and the Populist platform rather than of the New Testament.

There was disintegration, but no reintegration. Pragmatism, for all its merits, offered not stability but an open universe and the chance to make ideals truth; and most of the reformers were pragmatists even when they used the vocabulary of mechanistic determinism. Fiske, to be sure, illuminated history with Cosmic Philosophy, but Fiske's day was past, and Henry Adams had already traced the explosion of unity into multiplicity. Veblen was profound but scarcely constructive, and Lester Ward, who was constructive, was largely neglected. Holmes, greatest of American jurists, had no confidence in abstract notions of Law or Justice and no faith in reform, but merely an unassailable conviction that he was not God, and that in a democracy people had a right to make fools of themselves. Even criticism in the grand manner had lost its earlier assurance; it was significant that when Bryce came to portray America he was descriptive and tentative where Tocqueville had been analytical and magisterial, and that even Bryce seemed profound by comparison with native American interpreters.

By 1912 the reform movement began to seem curiously opportunistic and fragmentary. The agrarian reformers were not, on the whole, concerned with the welfare of the workers. Labor, especially after the demise of the Knights and the advent of the Federation, seemed completely self-centered and even boasted its opportunism; its leaders rejected Marxist philosophers and asserted: "We have no ultimate ends. We are going on from day to day." Many of the muckrakers were reformers only fortuitously, and few of them were inspired by ideals or sustained by convictions. It was not surprising that Ida Tarbell, who had laid bare the malpractices of Standard Oil, should later write a laudatory biography of Elbridge Gary; that John Spargo, who had first heard the bitter cry of the children, should end as an implacable opponent of the New Deal; that Burton Hendrick, who exposed the iniquities of life insurance, should celebrate the virtues of Andrew Carnegie. It was characteristic enough that Moorfield Storey should champion the cause of the Negro but bitterly oppose the elevation of Brandeis to the Supreme Court and the admission of Jews to Harvard University; that Tom Watson should fight for the tenant farmer and the mill hand, but inflame his followers against Negroes, Jews, and Catholics; that William Allen White should expose the corruption of politics and of wealth, but oppose Bryan, Wilson, and F. D. Roosevelt. Bryan was radical enough when it came to banks and railroads, but reactionary in matters of religion and education; Theodore Roosevelt enunciated reform principles, but exhibited distaste at their practical application; even Wilson, who spoke eloquently of the New Freedom, acquiesced in the suppression of freedom of speech and of the press during the war.

Because the reform movement lacked a pervasive and sustaining philosophy there is about it a depressing inconclusiveness. Many of the reformers lacked staying power; few of them were concerned with the whole scene.

They dissipated their strength, they wandered off on strange bypaths, they compromised. Their followers were even more unreliable. For most of them a touch of prosperity was all but fatal. With an increase in the price of wheat the agrarian revolt collapsed. Gold in the Klondike ended the free-silver crusade. Labor was persuaded by the argument of the full dinner pail. Southern deserters came trooping back to the ranks of the Bourbon democracy when the bogy of race equality was dangled before their horrified eyes. The succession of Roosevelt by Taft in 1908, the readiness to jettison La Follette for Roosevelt in 1911, the disintegration of the Progressive Party after 1913, all cast a curious light on the sincerity or the intelligence of the reform movement as it entered the new century.

3

Even before the opening of the new century the geographical center of reform had shifted from the Middle Border to the urban East. If, as Denis Brogan has observed, farmers confessed to few ills that dollar wheat wouldn't cure, the Eastern reformers recognized few that would not yield to Honesty and Philanthropy. These end-of-the-century reformers—men like Norton and Atkinson and Storey in Boston, like Gilder and Low and Roosevelt in New York—constituted a distinguished group. Their radicalism, however, was tempered by good manners and by a total inability to understand violence. They were the heirs of Godkin and Curtis rather than of Horace Greeley or Wendell Phillips. They had gone to the best schools—one sometimes feels that a degree from Harvard was a prerequisite to admission to their club—associated with the best people, read the *Nation* and the *Independent,* and knew poverty only at second hand. Their intentions were laudable, but their vision was limited and their interests narrow. They thought of reform almost exclusively in terms of politics, and they were inclined to think that honesty in politics was the sum of political science. Good government, they thought, would follow inevitably from the civil service system and gentlemen in politics. They had the same abiding faith in the efficacy of noble moral sentiments that Wells ascribes to the English liberals of the same period in *The New Machiavelli.* When they thought of the civil service they thought of England. When they thought of gentlemen they thought of one another, and though animated by no vulgar ambition for office, they were not unwilling, from time to time, to sacrifice themselves to the public good.

They had no interest in the agrarian crusade, little sympathy for organized labor, and they thought panaceas like the Single Tax or Bellamy's Nationalism as eccentric as Mormonism. Free silver they held to be simple dishonesty, and outbreaks like the Haymarket riot and the Pullman strike filled them

with horror. They were equally fearful of socialism, communism, and anarchism, and inclined to place any economic heresy indiscriminately in one of
these categories. For men like Bryan and Weaver they had only contempt;
Altgeld and Debs, they damned as un-American.

Yet they had both sympathy for the poor and the underprivileged and
a strong feeling of social responsibility. They were ready enough to remedy
injustice or alleviate misery, when made aware of them by a Jacob Riis or a
Jane Addams. Like the Western agrarians they opposed trusts and protective
tariffs, approved government regulation of railways, urged the conservation of
natural resources, and worked to wipe out slums, protect women and children, ameliorate race relations, humanize industry, and "socialize" Christianity. It was the humanitarian strain that was most pronounced in them.
Because most of them were economically immature, had been raised in a
Christian tradition of charity, and were heirs to the social tradition of *noblesse
oblige,* they turned instinctively to good works rather than to the state. They
engaged in earnest efforts to organize charity, help newsboys, maintain lodg-
ing houses, save delinquent girls, rescue homeless waifs, enforce Sunday closing hours, eliminate the sweatshop, mitigate the rigors of the penal code.

The best representative of this Eastern group is its most prominent member—the ebullient Theodore Roosevelt. He was, like most of the good-govern-
ment enthusiasts, primarily a moral crusader. His earliest venture into politics
had been on behalf of tenement house reform—reform nullified by the courts.
Under the tutelage of Jacob Riis he had seen Mulberry Bend and Poverty
Lane, the sweatshops, the vice and crime of the lower East Side. He had
fought the machine, and been rewarded with an appointment as civil service
commissioner. His enthusiasm for reform was temporarily dampened by the
radicalism of Bryan and then deflected into navalism and nationalism. Later,
as governor of the Empire State, he renewed his attack upon the bosses and
consolidated his reputation as a liberal.

In Roosevelt, even before he came to the Presidency, we see harmoniously
blended the qualities characteristic of the Eastern reformers: optimism and
opportunism; distrust of economic, and confidence in political, panaceas;
sentimentality and superficiality. Alert, zealous, and upright, he no sooner
saw an evil or an infirmity than he exposed and excoriated it. He was against
corruption, bosses, those who betrayed the public trust or looted the public
domain, he opposed trusts and monopolies, impure foods and drugs, the
exploitation of women and children; he was for honesty in politics and the
Square Deal and conservation and red-blooded Americanism. Elihu Root
once chid him for thinking that he had written the Ten Commandments.
Sensitive as he was to wrongdoing, he could never see that particular injustices
were the natural product of an inequitable economy or believe that any evil

was so deep-seated that it could not be cured by tinkering with the political machinery.

Because Roosevelt compromised on every important issue and evaded every dangerous issue, the transition to Taft seemed natural enough. Yet it was the Taft administration that brought home to the nation the failure of the reform movement. For while Roosevelt sounded like a progressive even when he acted like a conservative, it was Taft's misfortune to sound like a conservative even when he acted like a progressive. By the end of the first decade of the century it was clear that the Roosevelt-Taft brand of progressivism was inadequate to the needs of the day. With all the frenzy of trust busting, the trusts were stronger in 1910 than they had been in 1890 or 1900. With all the fever of railroad regulation, the railroads still managed to evade effective regulation of rates. With all the denunciation of malefactors of great wealth, the distribution of wealth was more inequitable at the end than at the beginning of the period. The protective tariff was untouched; centralized control of banking, unaffected; even conservation—the most sincere of all Roosevelt's reforms—proved woefully inadequate; the forests and soil of the nation disappeared with terrifying rapidity.

With the election of Wilson in 1913 the Progressive Movement reached such maturity as it ever attained. Both the country and Wilson had caught up with the radicalism of the nineties and were prepared to do, now, what should have been done twenty years earlier, as well as to make clear what had to be done twenty years later. Wilson, for all his academic antecedents, his passion for Mill and Bagehot, his curious reluctance to include Jefferson in his calendar of great Americans, his hostility to socialism and Populism, proved a far more realistic, thoroughgoing, and idealistic reformer than Theodore Roosevelt—and a far more effective one.

Like Roosevelt, Wilson was a moralist in politics, though his morality was more personal than that of his great rival, more a matter of principles than of good or bad men, more of the New Testament than of the Old. He was a Southern gentleman, brought up on the tenets of Manchester liberalism, Godkin respectability, and Virginian *noblesse oblige*. He had achieved a national reputation by playing the role of St. George with the dragon of corruption in New Jersey; and, except among those dazzled by the brilliance of T. R., the support of liberals and radicals throughout the country came to him almost by default. His mind was logical and consistent, and when he found himself cast in a democratic role he embraced the whole reform program much as he might have embraced the conclusion of a mathematical theorem. To a profound, almost a religious, conviction of the rightness of such causes as he espoused, he added an astonishing capacity for learning, genius in the manipulation of public opinion, and an iron determination to have his way. No wonder that he succeeded where Roosevelt had failed, and no wonder that his success, and the methods whereby he achieved it, outraged his critics and alienated his friends.

It is legitimate to personify the New Freedom in Woodrow Wilson, but a capital error to suppose that it was all Wilson's achievement. Without Wilson the New Freedom might have been inconclusive; without the support of public opinion it would have been impossible. Wilson had behind him not only the Bryan wing of the Democratic Party, but a substantial part of the Progressive Party. The nation, as a whole, was impatient for reform and ardent for leadership. As Wilson said, with characteristic eloquence:

The Nation has been deeply stirred, stirred by a solemn passion, stirred by the knowledge of wrong, of ideals lost, of government too often debauched and made an instrument of evil. The feelings with which we face this new age of right and opportunity sweep across our heartstrings like some air out of God's own presence, where justice and mercy are reconciled and the judge and the brother are one.

The country was ready, too, for a positive program which would translate these noble sentiments into constructive legislation.

That legislation came, the most comprehensive and effective program since the days of Polk, and under Wilson's driving leadership the progressive forces came closer to realizing their objectives than at any other time in our history. The Underwood Tariff, the Federal Reserve System, the Clayton Anti-Trust Act, the Federal Trade Commission Act, the Adamson eight-hour law, the income tax, farm relief, child-labor laws, the good-neighbor policy, all brought to a logical and impressive climax the agitation of a generation of reformers.

Yet even in its years of triumph it was clear that something had gone out of the reform movement. It had lost something of that elemental strength, that emotional fervor, that economic realism, which had characterized it in the days of Henry George and Peter Altgeld and Tom Johnson. Most of the leaders who had inspired it and molded its character had passed from the scene, or diverted their energies into different channels. Bryan, to be sure, retained his simple idealism; but he seemed to have lost touch with his old associates, and concerned himself increasingly with temperance and peace. Roosevelt, embittered by the spectacle of Wilson playing the role he felt rightly his, abandoned himself to vindictiveness and chauvinism. La Follette lingered on, harsh and irascible, flouted except in his own state. With the transfer of power from state to federal government, local reform movements diminished in importance. The shift was fateful. When the reactionaries moved in and took over, there were no local or regional groups powerful enough to counteract them or to maintain laboratories of liberalism in the states.

4

The First World War marked the end of the great reform movement which had set in about 1890. That the war, and the peace which followed, brought disillusionment is clear; what is not clear is why they should have done so. No historian has yet analyzed the anatomy of reaction after 1918, and the manifestations of that reaction are more obvious than its pathology. Just as the Civil War had canalized all the reform movements of the forties and fifties into the crusade against slavery and disunion, so the First World War canalized the reform movements of the previous decades into an all-embracing crusade for world democracy. After 1917 the interests and energies of the nation were deflected into new channels; prosperity, war, and the post-war problems of international order made most of the issues which had agitated the previous generation seem remote and unreal. Then, too, the inevitable idealization of the crusade for democracy brought an almost equally inevitable reaction into cynicism, while the identification of reform with Wilson himself involved it in the general repudiation of Wilson and Wilsonism. His collapse at Wichita undermined domestic liberalism as well as internationalism. Finally the wartime emphasis on national unity made it easy to distort even constructive criticism into obstructionism and disloyalty and seemed to justify not only the deportation hysteria and the Red scares but state and federal laws destructive of free thought and speech.

The details of the reaction are too familiar to justify rehearsal. President Harding in 1920 dedicated his administration to the return to "normalcy"; Coolidge in 1924, to the proposition that the "business of America is business"; Hoover in 1928 to the Spencerian concept of "rugged individualism." There was widespread hostility to foreigners and to foreign ideas: indeed, ideas themselves were suspect as somehow contrary to genuine Americanism. Aliens suspected of radical notions were rounded up and deported by the thousand; legislatures were purged; teachers were required to take loyalty oaths, and textbooks revised to conform to the concepts of Americanism entertained by the American Legion and the Daughters of the American Revolution. The Ku Klux Klan, which boasted a membership running into the millions, anticipated Nazi doctrines of Aryan supremacy, and its hooded Klansmen intimidated Catholics, Negroes, Jews, and radicals. Religious fundamentalists sponsored laws against the teaching of evolution in the public schools or the dissemination of information about birth control, and censorship laws emasculated moving pictures, plays, and books. In two notorious cases—those of Sacco and Vanzetti in Massachusetts and of Mooney and Billings in California —the victims were punished more for their radicalism than for any crimes proved against them. The Supreme Court, by its genial reinterpretation of the antitrust laws and its nullification of child labor and minimum wage laws, revealed its sympathy with the reactionary tendencies of the time.

There is no more representative figure in this whole period than William Allen White, of Emporia, Kansas. He tells us, in his charming *Autobiography,* how, in the 1920 convention, he led the Kansas delegation onto the Harding bandwagon.

I was too heartsick [he wrote] to rise and fight. . . . The whole liberal movement which had risen so proudly under Bryan, Theodore Roosevelt and La Follette, was tired. The spirits of the liberals who called themselves Progressives were bewildered. The fainthearted turned cynics. The faithful were sad and weary.

Not all of them, to be sure; there were some who fought on. Eugene Debs kept socialism afloat, and even from his cell in the Federal Penitentiary at Atlanta commanded almost a million votes. New parties arose in the Northwest, only to be paralyzed by the hostility of bankers and shippers. That sturdy oak, La Follette, refused to bend to the new winds howling out of the caves of Mammon and, in 1924, organized a party that won five million votes —and disappeared. The *Nation* and the *New Republic* kept up their shrill clamor for social justice; but only the faithful read them, and there were few converts. The liberal movement persisted—without it there could have been no New Deal—but it was a thin and shallow stream running beside the mighty torrent of reaction.

The whole intellectual atmosphere changed, too—more sharply perhaps than in any previous decade in our history. It was not that the artists and writers acquiesced in the new dispensation, but that their rejection of it was so desperate. The novelists and scholars and artists of the Bryan-Roosevelt era had been in revolt, but their revolt was not an expression of their alienation from or contempt for their society, but of indignation and pity. Their protests were designed not to display their own superiority, but to improve the common lot. No one could doubt their sincerity or integrity. When they spoke the language of the farm or the street it was because that language was rightly theirs, not because they wanted to deride it. They were not afraid of passion or indignation, and they directed these toward the oppressors, not toward the victims of oppression. Though they were often troubled by the contemplation of the helplessness of man, it never occurred to them that the only significant thing about man was his insignificance.

The intellectuals of the twenties revealed the same talent for exposure, the same revolt against the farm and the village, the same distaste for Mammon and for Mrs. Grundy, that had animated their predecessors. But they were more concerned with dissociating themselves from these things than with improving or changing them. They did not suffer, like Garland, with the farmers and villagers but, like Lewis, from them. They were not really rebels, but iconoclasts, which is a very different thing. They were too sure of their own superiority to be greatly troubled by the lot of the average man and woman, and their hatred of injustice was not nearly so lively as their hatred of vulgarity and spiritual decline. Others, like Willa Cather and Ellen Glasgow, turned to the past and celebrated the ideals, the achievements, and the failures of earlier Americans rather than attempting to reform their own times. They served art better than most of their predecessors, but lost force as propagandists for a new order. Where the writers of the nineties found it intolerable that a virtuous people should suffer, the literary rebels of the twenties found it intolerable that virtue should be so dull, and financial success so devoid of spirituality.

For all their rage and frustration, the writers of the twenties, with few exceptions, showed little concern for reform. They were not conspicuous in the fight for the League of Nations or the cleansing of politics or the improvement of the lot of the workingman and the farmer. There were no farm novels like Garland's *A Spoil of Office,* no labor novels like Sinclair's *The Jungle,* no political novels like Churchill's *Mr. Crewe's Career.* One might almost say that, even with the celebration of Freud, there were no sex novels like Crane's *Maggie* or Phillips' *Susan Lennox,* for the interest in sex, as in almost everything else, had become psychoanalytical rather than sociological. It was somehow appropriate that the 1890's should be ushered in with *How the Other Half Lives,* and the 1920's with *Main Street* and *This Side of Paradise.*

67. CREATING AN AUDIENCE

A NEW and vigorous nationalism, self-critical and analytic, was the underlying trait of both literature and journalism in the years immediately following the end of the First World War. It offset the lack of a reforming spirit of the times. Since the beginning of the twentieth century, new types of readers of books, and particularly of periodicals and great metropolitan newspapers, had been maturing; and the society thus formed now became self-conscious and avid for news of itself, its problems, its responsibilities, its humors, and its emotional needs. In the great cities, still rapidly increasing in population although the growth of the country as a whole was slowing down, Whitman's race of races had become a fact. The war had accelerated what the great depression of the 1930's was to complete, a breakdown of the formerly dominant social (and to a lesser degree intellectual) groups. The absorption of second and third generations of immigrants from all the North European races had also accelerated, and these no longer felt themselves less American than the so-called Anglo-Saxon stock. It was a mobile society, with a mobility very different from the westward streaming of the pioneers, a society urban rather than rural, national rather than sectional; a society ready—or almost ready—to support and encourage authorship.

Serious writers worked under greater financial handicaps in the period before 1910 than after it. It is true that authorship had already become a profession by which men lived; by which they even prospered like successful merchants. Book prices were low after 1900, at the most not more than $1.50 for a popular novel, but royalties were high by later standards; and very successful novelists expected to receive 20 per cent of the list price of every copy sold in the trade edition. Kipling was paid 30 per cent, which may be the highest royalty on record. Even at 20 per cent, authors could earn large sums from single novels; for example, Mary Johnston received more than $60,000 from the publishers of *To Have and to Hold,* not counting her income from other sources, such as magazine publication, second serial rights, and foreign rights. Gene Stratton Porter must have earned three times as much from *Freckles,* with its sale in the trade and reprint editions of nearly two million copies. Jack London had a yearly income of more than $75,000, most of it from magazines, which paid him $3,000 each for his more popular short stories.

With these rewards on the horizon, there had come to be a recognized path to preferment for younger writers. Those who followed the path attended an Eastern university, preferably Harvard, where they took Professor Baker's course in the drama; they came to New York with letters of recommendation; they worked as cub reporters for one of the metropolitan newspapers; and each of them, in his leisure time, wrote a novel, a play, or a book of short stories. If the book or play was successful, the author was launched on his career. But many of the young writers who appeared after 1910 had other aims than making a hit on Broadway or breaking into the list of best sellers; they were rebels and realists who could never be popular, so it seemed, and could scarcely even hope to be commercially published.

Two or three of the lucky ones had private incomes, like Amy Lowell; the rest supported themselves in fifty different ways. A few worked on the fringes of literature, either as newspaper reporters, in what had become the orthodox fashion, or else as hack writers or publishers' readers. Dreiser and Willa Cather were successful magazine editors. Others who would afterward have wide reputations earned their living outside the literary world; they included a farmer (Robert Frost), a struggling lawyer (Edgar Lee Masters), a suburban doctor (William Carlos Williams), a bank clerk (T. S. Eliot), an insurance executive (Wallace Stevens), a professional chess player (Alfred Kreymborg), a wanderer who read poems for bread (Vachel Lindsay), a paint manufacturer turned advertising agent (Sherwood Anderson), two secretaries to Socialist mayors (Carl Sandburg and Walter Lippmann), and a customhouse clerk. The last was Edwin Arlington Robinson, who was appointed to his post in 1905 after Theodore Roosevelt had read his early poems. Before that time Robinson had been an inspector in the New York subways, then under construction. The new literature in his time was also something under construction, and underground. As his fellow authors were doing symbolically, Robinson carried a real lantern, a prickle of light in what seemed to be an endless tunnel.

But the tunnel had exits, and the authors of his generation, even the poets, finally emerged into day. It was sooner than most of them had expected, but dangerously late in what should have been their literary careers. Robinson himself was forty-one years old before he felt able to resign from his clerkship in the Customhouse and fifty-eight before his poetry wholly supported him. Dreiser was almost forty when he resigned from the editorship of the Butterick Publications and devoted all his time to writing novels; Willa Cather was thirty-six when she resigned from *McClure's*. Frost was thirty-nine when he published *North of Boston*; Anderson, forty-three when he published *Winesburg, Ohio*; Masters, forty-six when he wrote *Spoon River Anthology* and abandoned the law for literature. In a sense all these men had gained by their apprenticeship to other crafts, for they brought something new into American letters, a sense of the world outside the Eastern universities and the polite magazines; a sense of bigness, rawness, loneliness. But they also lost by not having had time enough to practice writing or a chance for early contact with a cultivated audience. Of many of them it could be said that they were deficient in general knowledge, that their taste was uncertain, and that either they lacked technical skill or else—if they had begun by writing for the slick-paper magazines, like Hergesheimer and Lewis—they had too much skill of the wrong sort.

2

The new audience had been in the making since the opening years of the century, but in its earlier stages of development it was more notable for increase in size than for improvement in taste.

By 1910 there was in fact a larger public for books than would exist for many years after the First World War, provided that the books were of the sort this earlier public liked and could understand. It liked novels chiefly; it liked them if they were full of sentiment or swordplay, adventures in far places or local color; and if, at the same time, they moved by resolute steps toward an ending that satisfied the Protestant conventions. It liked Gene Stratton Porter, who by 1915 had written *Freckles* and four other novels with a total sale of eight million copies. It liked John Fox, Jr. (*The Trail of the Lonesome Pine*), Jack London (*The Call of the Wild*), Kate Douglas Wiggin (*Rebecca of Sunnybrook Farm*), and Harold Bell Wright (*The Shepherd of the Hills*). In all, between 1901 and 1915, it liked nineteen books well enough to buy more than a million copies of each, whereas there were only eight books, three of them nonfiction, with a sale of more than a million copies between 1916 and 1930.*

The early years of the century were an exciting time for publishers who could gauge the public taste. Men like Colonel Harvey of Harper & Brothers, George H. Doran, and Walter Hines Page had reached an eminence from which they looked down on literary critics and treated authors like children to be spoiled or birched. The same years, however, were a dull period for American literature. The public that adored Pollyanna and her sisters would have nothing to do with novels that denied its belief that virtue was rewarded in this world as well as the next. It would not attend serious plays; it would not read verse written in manners other than those of Ella Wheeler Wilcox

* *An Outline of History, The Story of Philosophy, The Sheik,* and five others.

and James Whitcomb Riley. It would not even read most of the authors whose reputations had been established late in the nineteenth century: the collected edition of Henry James had few buyers, and by 1915 even Howells described himself without much exaggeration as being "a comparatively dead cult with my statues cut down and grass growing over them in the pale moonlight." Younger men who hoped to write like James or Howells were advised by their publishers to choose a safer model, like one of Winston Churchill's historical epics—at any rate something big, colorful, and optimistic, with a plot that was easy to follow. During those flush years of popular fiction, there was an almost complete break in the literary tradition that had been founded in New England before the Civil War. If serious literature was to flourish again, a new beginning had to be made. Besides new writers, there had to be new magazines and publishing houses to present their work; and there had to be a new audience to support the authors and the publishers together.

The audience was at least partly created in the simplest manner, by formal schooling. Education above the secondary-school level developed rapidly in both quantity and quality after 1910, particularly in the prosperous twenties. Although the growth in population was being checked by a declining birth rate, and further checked after 1924 by restrictions on immigration, high schools and colleges attracted more students year by year. From 1910 to 1940, enrollment in high schools increased by 540 per cent, and that in institutions of higher learning by 321 per cent. During the twenties alone, enrollment at both levels doubled, and education, faced with crowded classrooms and inadequate equipment, sought new endowments, new buildings, and new methods. Public and private expenditure kept pace with expanding numbers of students by increasing 559 per cent, while colleges and universities pushed their endowments upward and built new buildings. A great deal of the increase was concentrated in special fields: notably in Southern universities, in city colleges, in Catholic colleges, and in graduate schools; also in junior colleges, of which more than four hundred were founded during the twenty years after the First World War.

Efforts to recapture some of the intimate quality of the earlier colleges led Harvard and Yale to institute "house" or "college" plans by which student bodies were broken up into complete residence and study units—a movement followed by a few other institutions where the necessary funds were available. Two major trends in educational method are noticeable. The Progressive Education Association, founded in 1918, and reflecting the influence of experimental and naturalistic thinking, began its reforms on the nursery and elementary-school levels and gradually advanced upward until it could challenge the traditional college entrance requirements and demand a more flexible and "child-centered" curriculum throughout the entire educational process.

On the other hand, colleges and universities, under the leadership of Woodrow Wilson, Frank Aydelotte, A. Lawrence Lowell, and John Erskine, began experiments with "Preceptorials" and "Honors" courses for small groups of selected students, tutorial systems, and "colloquia," in an effort to regularize once more the content of higher education and to individualize its methods. Although apparently similar in many respects to the Progressive Movement, such experiments reflected rather a tendency to develop humanistic and neo-scholastic influences. They allowed greater freedom of intellectual inquiry to the student, but at the same time they sought to raise standards and to liberate the mind through the newly developed disciplines of modern natural science, social science, and the humanities. Thus, while the educated reading public was rapidly increasing, intellectual leadership was stimulated by selective and intensive programs of higher education.

The growth of secondary and higher education not only created a potential audience for books larger than had existed before in any single country, or in all Western Europe, but also furnished new training grounds for writers. Until 1910 Harvard had graduated a disproportionate share of American literary men; after 1910 writers came in large numbers from other universities: first Princeton and Yale (with its brilliant class of 1919); then Chicago, Vanderbilt, Stanford, the Western and Southern state universities, and the new city colleges. Student writers who in the past had found little recognition in the academic system were once more given the stimulus and sympathetic atmosphere of the coterie. As during the literary revival of the early nineteenth century undergraduate clubs appeared, like the Elizabethan Club at Yale, devoted to good talk about books and writing.

About 1915, adult education began to be preached with enthusiasm and even practiced, if more tepidly; it was the new name for cultural activities that had continued in one form or another since colonial times. Some of the activities were now being institutionalized, while others were beginning to decline—among them the Chautauqua reading circles, which gradually disappeared from the two or three hundred cities where they had flourished. Their place was partly taken by university summer schools and extension courses, both of which were popular with grade-school teachers seeking academic credits. Most of the public lyceums dwindled away; indeed there was a temporary decline in the whole art and business of public speaking. The educational programs formerly offered by labor unions to their members were neglected or abandoned after the First World War, except by the two powerful unions in the garment trades; much later they would be adopted by the new unions of the post-depression years. Women's clubs all over the country increased rapidly in number and maintained a certain level of cultural effort; the level fell during the Wall Street boom, when Browning gave way to bridge; then it rose again in the depression and the early days of the New Deal, which was a period of self-education and general cultural activity.

The little-theater movement, beginning in this country about 1912 and reaching its height about 1924, was in one aspect a form of adult education. It created an audience for serious plays. Most of those plays, in the early years, were German or English or Irish or Scandinavian, so that the audiences became familiar with the ideas of the new European dramatists. Later, when there were more than a thousand little-theater groups, the audience learned to applaud American dramatists like O'Neill, themselves trained in the little theaters, whose work belonged to what had formerly been called the European current of thought. Pessimism, naturalism, lyricism, fantasy, expressionism, all these moods and methods were presented on the stage before they were embodied in any American novels that reached a wide public.

Motion pictures and radio, on the other hand, did little toward creating a literate audience; they might have been described in the beginning as forms of miseducation. The silent movies were, with few exceptions, written and directed to reach the twelve-year-old mind that was taken as the average of the population. Possibly they resulted in a leveling down of intellectual interests, while consuming time that had formerly been devoted to other cultural activities. It was not until after 1930 that the movies, transformed into talkies, began to have a positive effect on American reading habits. Radio at first was simply an electrical gadget; then it became a popular art that competed with wood-pulp fiction and, for a time, reduced the sales of confessional magazines like *True Stories*. Literary programs to which people willingly listened, like "Invitation to Learning" and "Author Meets Critic," were a comparatively late development.

With all the new claims on their time, of which the automobile was the most insistent, it is a wonder that Americans had time to read at all. Yet public libraries continued to be built and patronized; merely from the gifts of Andrew Carnegie, 1,677 library buildings were erected between 1896 and 1923, not to mention all those erected by states and municipalities. By 1935 there were in all 6,235 public libraries, serving 63 per cent of the population; they had more than 100,000,000 books on their shelves and a circulation for the year of 450,000,000. In general there was a steady increase in the number of books they lent, though most of the new readers belonged to special groups in the population: young people rather than adults, women rather than men, and—a point of interest—the working class as opposed to the business class. During the depression, when most public libraries were forced to operate on smaller budgets, the circulation of books grew larger year by year; in Muncie, Indiana (which the Lynds called "Middletown"), it more than doubled during the five years beginning with 1929. It reached a peak in

1933 and declined afterwards, although it remained far above the 1929 level. There was, in other words, a vast new audience that was ready to read good books as well as bad ones if it heard about them; that was ready to buy them, too, as soon as the publishers presented them in cheap editions.

3

After 1910 there was a great upheaval in the magazine world. Periodicals that seemed as fixed and predictable in their appearance as the days of the week were suddenly discarded like last year's calendars. The greatest mortality was among the muckraking monthlies. These had achieved great circulations for the time by exposing the sins of American business, government, churches, and social life, sometimes in merely sensational attacks, but sometimes, too, in sound and well documented articles written by the ablest journalists the country had so far known; a few of them, including Lincoln Steffens and Ray Stannard Baker, reached a higher literary level than the contemporary novelists. As for the magazines that published their work, *Everybody's, McClure's,* the *Cosmopolitan,* and *Hampton's,* all had circulations close to half a million copies a month in 1910. Two years later they all changed their editorial policies, and *Hampton's* had ceased publication— as had also the *Arena,* the *Twentieth Century, Success,* and *Human Life.* It was said at the time that the public had lost interest in muckraking; but later revelations by publishers and editors made it appear that the muckraking magazines had been ruined by their own success. They had frightened the business community, while at the same time they had become dependent on advertising and bank credit. When the advertising was withdrawn, page after page, and the loans were called, as if on a concerted signal, they had to stop their investigations or go out of business.

The great literary monthlies also changed or disappeared, but in a more leisurely fashion. *Harper's, Scribner's,* and the *Century,* with their elderly and, at the time, impoverished cousins the *Atlantic* and the *North American Review,* had exercised a long dictatorship over American taste; they were the guardians of the tradition of ideality, which, with the fabric worn shabby and more starch to conceal it, had become the genteel tradition. In 1910 the first three still had a combined circulation of more than half a million. All except the *Atlantic* lost readers during the next ten years, although *Harper's* would also revive after 1920 under new editors. The *Century* lived on until 1930, but only as a quarterly. *Scribner's* and the *North American Review* had a melancholy fate; both changed hands several times and ended (like *Littell's Living Age*) after coming under control of propagandists for Axis governments.

Other famous magazines disappeared during or after the First World War. *Harper's Weekly* was among the first to go, in 1916; brilliantly written in its last years under Norman Hapgood, but deserted by advertisers, it was merged with the *Independent,* which in turn was merged with the *Outlook,* which ceased publication in 1935. *Current Literature,* renamed *Current Opinion,* had been the best popular record of cultural life during the immediate prewar years; but it died from loss of circulation. The *Youth's Companion,* once the most successful American magazine, followed from week to week by adults as well as children, was defeated more by slipshod accounting methods than by lack of readers; it lived until 1929. The three humorous weeklies, *Puck, Judge,* and *Life,* starved to death on a diet of their own jokes. The *World's Work* was taken over by the *Review of Reviews,* which was taken over by the *Literary Digest,* which was laughed out of existence after its famous poll of presidential voters had revealed that Landon would sweep the country in 1936. The *Bookman* (like *Book Chat* and the *Book Buyer*), *St. Nicholas* (like the other established children's monthlies), the *Forum* (with all the periodicals intended to serve as open platforms for debates)—it was not only single magazines that perished, but whole families and groups. One after another they dwindled away, they vanished with their dignified names, leaving the field to new magazines less hampered by their own traditions.

These new periodicals were of many types. The *Yale Review,* founded in 1911, was the first of the university quarterlies to achieve a general reputation; it became the precursor of many others which provided a small but influential audience with a mixture of information, interpretation, and creative writing. The *New Republic,* founded in 1914, was the first of the new weeklies. With a brilliant editorial board, it tried to set a standard of intelligent discussion and good writing. The older *Nation,* founded in 1865, was transformed into a vigorous political organ after Oswald Garrison Villard became the editor in 1918; but it remained a literary organ, too, and its new critics supported the new generation of novelists. The immediate postwar years were the heyday of the "liberal weeklies," not all of which were either weekly or liberal; besides the *Nation* and the *New Republic,* there were also, for a time, the *Freeman,* which believed in good prose and the single tax, the radical fortnightly *Dial* (in the years 1916-1920), and the conservative *Weekly Review.*

Reviewing and criticism were the chief purpose of the *Saturday Review of Literature* (1924), which succeeded, under the same editorship, the *Literary Review* (1920) of the old New York *Evening Post.* Here a determined effort was made to bridge the gap between university scholarship and the interests of the educated public. In the years between 1915 and 1925, a group of teachers and scholars that included John Erskine and Carl Van Doren from Columbia, Henry Seidel Canby from Yale, and Stuart P. Sherman from the University of Illinois, migrated into the increasingly hospitable areas of literary journalism. Book reviewing in the Sunday supplements of the New York *Times* and the New York *Herald Tribune,* as well as in the *Saturday Review of Literature,* reflected this new vitality.

By an easy transition, the most skillful and powerful commentators on the political and literary weeklies slipped into the newspapers, where, over their own names, and often at variance with the editorial policy of the paper, they widened their audience and satisfied the demand of a society craving intellectual guidance. The career of Walter Lippmann is characteristic of the whole movement. Beginning on the staff of the *New Republic,* he became a writer of books (*Public Opinion,* 1922, *A Preface to Morals,* 1929), and finally the author of syndicated commentaries on national and world affairs which, thanks to his expert knowledge and the clarity of his exposition, gave him a national reputation and influence. Other commentators, when equipped with a good voice and the right background of experience, were able to flourish in the illimitable field of radio. During the thirties and forties they interpreted for the millions the complexities of politics, war, and international affairs.

As older periodicals lost their readers after the First World War, new ones were appearing year by year. In 1922 it was the *Reader's Digest,* modest in its beginnings but destined to have the largest circulation in the world. The next year it was *Time,* first of the news weeklies; in 1924 it was the *American Mercury,* edited by H. L. Mencken and George Jean Nathan; in 1925, the *New Yorker,* which tried not to be serious but didn't always succeed. Later there would be other magazines that helped to change the character of American journalism: *Esquire,* appearing toward the end of the decade with its luscious ladies reproduced in several colors; *Fortune,* in 1930, with its careful studies of American business and its beautifully drawn graphs which, for the first three years, showed only business declines; and the new *Life,* in 1936, first and most successful of the big picture magazines.

Time, Fortune, and *Newsweek* (1933) were, in one respect at least, a radical departure in American journalism. They proposed, at least, not so much to influence opinion as to supply facts for opinion. They were co-operative, collective efforts to cover the news, extending into science, literature, business, and the arts. Backed by staffs of researchers, they were not so much written as rewritten by a staff of subeditors. This procedure was the exact opposite of the personal journalism which elsewhere determined both the magazine and the newspaper worlds.

Some of the new periodicals had a level of technical competence never achieved before. Their reporters gathered more facts and better pictures; their editors had a better eye for lively stories and a surer judgment of the treatment they deserved; and yet—except sometimes among the staff of the *New Yorker*—there was not the same passion for discovering new writers or the intellectual curiosity often to be found in the stodgier magazines of half a century before; and magazine contributors were seldom given the freedom of opinion that the muckraking journalists had taken for granted. The new periodicals depended for much of their circulation on the public that also read serious books, but they had done less than their share toward creating that public.

4

When Harriet Monroe published the first issue of *Poetry: A Magazine of Verse* in October, 1912, she put a quotation from Whitman on the back cover: "To have great poets there must be great audiences too." Miss Monroe during the next few years was able to find a few great and many distinguished poets of all schools to print in her magazine. She was less successful in creating a great or at least a wide audience, for *Poetry* never had many more than 3,000 readers. This, however, was a much larger public than most of the poets it printed could have reached without its help.

Little magazines like *Poetry* become important in any era when there is a gulf between the tastes of the broad public and the aims of serious writers. They were especially important in the years after 1910 because they gave a first hearing to a whole rebel generation of poets and novelists. One after another they struggled through their usually brief span of life; but they printed more new authors, and sometimes better authors, than many magazines that lived for a financially profitable half-century. *Others,* the little magazine edited by Alfred Kreymborg, had three hundred subscribers and a life span of four years; but it printed William Carlos Williams, Alfred Kreymborg, Marianne Moore, Conrad Aiken, Wallace Stevens, and T. S. Eliot, when much of their work was being rejected even by *Poetry.* The *Little Review* had a longer history. Founded in Chicago in 1914, it moved first to New York and then to Paris, while moving intellectually from anarchism and feminism through a whole series of enthusiasms to cubism, surrealism, and tired cynicism, so that its files are an intellectual history of the period in which it flourished.

The *Masses,* founded in 1911, had its great period from 1914 to 1917; it was the organ of all the story-tellers, reporters, poets, and cartoonists who were criticizing the old society and trying to build a new one. *Reedy's Mirror,* in St. Louis, gave their first hearing to many of the new Midwestern poets, including Edgar Lee Masters; it printed most of his *Spoon River Anthology*. The *Smart Set* for the year 1913 was a little magazine in spirit, and almost in circulation. Willard Huntington Wright was its editor that year, and he had signed a contract giving him complete control of editorial policy. He celebrated his freedom by printing Joyce, Lawrence, Beerbohm, Wedekind, Schnitzler, and other authors unknown to most of his subscribers. Until his contract expired, to the owner's relief, after twelve monthly numbers, the *Smart Set* was the most interesting magazine in the English-speaking world. The *Seven Arts* was another successful experiment that lasted only a year. It assembled the best of the new American essayists, poets, and story-tellers; and it presented them in an impressive fashion, as if to say, "It is now time for these men to be publicly recognized." The recognition came, but not enough of it was pecuniary; and when the editors opposed our entrance into the war and their financial backer withdrew her support, publication had to be suspended. That was in the fall of 1917, when the *Masses* had been suppressed and its editors were standing trial for sedition.

After the war, most of the little magazines represented another generation of writers, more interested than their American predecessors in literary form and experiment. Some of them were founded by groups of critics or poets; the most interesting was the group at Vanderbilt University that published the *Fugitive*. In New York the principal spokesman for the generation as a whole was the monthly *Dial*, which was founded—or, better, re-created from the fortnightly *Dial*—in January, 1920. It was a well printed, dignified, but adventurous magazine that printed the best work it could find anywhere in the world; perhaps its most frequent contributors, among younger Americans, were E. E. Cummings, Marianne Moore, and Kenneth Burke. It started a tradition of technical as opposed to moral or social criticism that would be continued later by the *Hound and Horn,* and by at least three of the university quarterlies: the *Southern Review,* the *Sewanee Review,* and the *Kenyon Review.* But most little magazines of the twenties were printed in Europe, where costs were lower and many of the younger writers found it more convenient to live. *Broom, Gargoyle, Secession,* the *Transatlantic Review, This Quarter, Exile, Tambour*—there was a long succession of these magazines; but *transition,* which lived from 1927 to 1938, was the biggest and most influential.

5

In the early years after the First World War, newspapers rather more successfully than magazines adapted themselves to the new literate and sophisticated society of the great cities. It was an unsettled, uncertain, but in general a prosperous society, cheerful, good-humored, and seeking urbanity and information. It was a liberal society, even in the midst of the postwar political reaction. It was opposed to the genteel, the snobbish, the dogmatic, and the heavy materialism of business which dominated American politics and economics. Yet it was speculative and inquiring rather than radical, repelled by revolutionary action—since it liked its own world well enough—and was marked by none of the vindictiveness that accompanies a violent clash in ideologies. The intellectuals among this reading class cultivated tolerance for everything except the closed mind.

As a whole, this new society craved much more than ideas and information. It was a society in which loneliness was prevalent, the loneliness of the individual lost in great crowds of men and women in a city to which he had usually come from somewhere else. What he lacked was a sense of personality, of warmth, of the familiar if not the intimate. His desire for personal experience was frustrated in the standardized life that seemed to be the price of success. From the resulting loneliness, since there is no such thing as standardized friendship, from nostalgia for the intimate contacts of a small community, from the drabness of anonymity, the more intelligent sought escape in the highly personal journalism of commentators and columnists, where they could find kinship, at least on paper, among the like-minded. An analogy with eighteenth century London in the days of the coffee-houses and the periodic essays of the *Tatler* and the *Spectator* is not too remote.

The modern variety of highly personal journalism had, of course, begun long before these decades in the so-called yellow press, a creation of Joseph Pulitzer in his New York *World* of the 1890's. Pulitzer, an immigrant who had worked his way up, knew that the masses were hungry for news of human nature, and that a murder or a scandal or a sensation in public affairs warmed them into lively attention, where a narrative of colder events, no matter how important, passed over their areas of interest. The more sophisticated readers of books and magazines in the 1920's, particularly in the massed and lonely great cities, were equally hungry for more personality and more human interest in their journalism, but they had no taste for crude sensationalism. As the narrower group of intellectuals began to take their leadership less and less from the editorial columns and more and more from the signed commentary, so this urbane audience, college-bred most of them, asked for wits and satirists (on the stage and in books as well as in the press) to give them a sense of belonging to what they felt was a sophisticated civilization that was escaping from the stuffiness and tight morality of the Genteel Age.

What Artemus Ward and Petroleum V. Nasby and Mark Twain had done upon the lecture platform to release the lighter emotions of an earlier period now, in these 1920's of vast populations not yet accessible by radio, was paralleled by writers for the great newspapers, and institutionalized in what soon came to be called the column, with a columnist in charge. The column, satiric, lightly literary, pleasantly personal, and definitely sophisticated, became, with the comic strip, the recreational feature of the paper.

These columns, of which the earliest were written in the Middle West by Eugene Field and Bert Leston Taylor, were no longer mere collections of burlesque, smart anecdote, and horseplay, such as were common in the nineteenth century. Typical of the genre at the time of its greatest popularity among good readers was the "Conning Tower" of Franklin P. Adams, a transplanted Midwesterner who made his reputation on the New York *Tribune* and *World*. More of a true humorist, less of a wit, was Don Marquis, also from the Middle West, whose reputation was made on the New York *Sun*. He was an ironist, a creator of humorous characters, a keen observer of folly, who, at heart, was a romantic tragedian. The plays and the many sonnets he wrote from his inner being were more competent than distinguished, but this inner seriousness gave his humor an emotional coloring and often an ironic edge. His column also was a commentary on the news of the town, but he enriched it with creatures of his own fancy who spoke for his moods and for his philosophy.

Both these men, like Ring Lardner, could hear and reproduce the rhythms and vocabulary of the new American language, and their columns will be source books for the students of the city speech of their age. And, indeed, B. L. T., F. P. A., and Don Marquis and their columns were the taste-makers for the satire of such stories as Lardner's and F. Scott Fitzgerald's, and the ironic plays so popular on the stage in the twenties and thirties. They were essentially critics and observers rather than creators of life, and their success was to make the minds of their numerous readers more receptive to the new wave lengths over which American literature was being transmitted. Both mood and appeal were different from the writer-audience relationship of such earlier newspaper columns as, say, Eugene Field's "Sharps and Flats" in the Chicago *News*.

Another columnist of the later period, Christopher Morley, came from a different American environment, the academic-literary soil of the East, refertilized in his case by the ancient earth of Oxford. His column, "The Bowling Green," published first in the New York *Evening Post*, and afterwards in the *Saturday Review of Literature*, might have been called Adventures Among Books, and he was instrumental in giving a wide audience to many an author, like Joseph Conrad, who had been regarded as caviar for the public. He wrote many books, some very successful in the difficult field of fantasy, but his mark on his generation was made in a columnist's mood of the twenties. Alexander Woollcott succeeded him as what might be called a caresser of books, choosing the radio as his means of access to the public.

The column as a feature of the daily paper soon began to lose its literary qualities and its illusion of wits, artists, critics, and satirists in the heart of a materialist society. With each merger of newspapers some columnist lost his job and had to seek a new environment; and as journalism became big business, standardization and the rapid increase of syndicating cramped the finer talents. The good columnist needed to feel a well known community about him in order to do his best work.

6

New publishers likewise helped to create the new audience. In the years from before 1920 there were several of these, and, as a rule, they proved hospitable to the new poets and novelists whose work had not interested the long established firms. Mitchell Kennerley was the first of the new enterprisers; his business was founded in 1905. It was discontinued after 1916, but not without leaving behind it a record of literary as opposed to purely commercial publishing. B. W. Huebsch, another of the new men, paid special attention to European authors; he published Joyce, Hauptmann, Sudermann, Strindberg, Chekhov, and Gorky. In 1925 he carried many of his authors to the newly founded Viking Press. Alfred A. Knopf, after working for Doubleday, Page and for Kennerley, started his own business in 1915. He too specialized in European authors, including an amazing number of those who would later win the Nobel Prize; among the younger Americans, he published Cather, Hergesheimer, and Mencken.

There was beginning to be a conflict in the book world between the "old-line" publishers, who were accused of stodginess and commercialism, and the new publishers, who were accused of recklessness, bad taste, and financial instability. The new firm of Boni & Liveright, founded in 1917, sharpened the conflict by being the most reckless of all; it became famous for its advances to unconventional authors (including Dreiser, Anderson, Jeffers, O'Neill) and for the Roman banquets of its president, Horace Liveright. His cofounder Albert Boni retired in 1918 and his other associates were always leaving to start new firms of their own; so that Boni & Liveright became, in a sense, the parent of Albert & Charles Boni, Thomas Seltzer, Simon & Schuster, Random House, Julian Messner, and Covici-Friede—not to mention its relation to the Liveright Publishing Corporation, which acquired the copyrights of the parent house after the death of the founder. Another new firm, founded in 1919, managed to build a bridge between the old and the new: Harcourt, Brace began by publishing John Maynard

Keynes' *Economic Consequences of the Peace* and went on, in 1920, to publish *Main Street,* the first book by any of the new novelists to reach a sale of half a million copies. That same year Eugene O'Neill's first full-length play, *Beyond the Horizon,* was a success on Broadway. The rebel authors of the wartime years, having found their audience, were becoming the dominant authors of a new era.

One after another the established publishing houses began changing their policies. The chasm between new and old-line publishers disappeared after 1925; the fact was that some of the older houses, including Scribner and Houghton Mifflin, were showing more hospitality toward experimental writing than several of their younger competitors. The older houses, if not too strictly bound by their own traditions, had a better chance for survival in a highly competitive field. Some of them declined and a few went out of business, but most of them held their own or entered a fresh period of expansion. Of the fourteen large publishing houses each of which issued more than a hundred books in 1942—to carry our story ahead—only three had been founded after 1910, and the others included some of the oldest firms in the trade. Macmillan still published more new books than any other house; and Harper, founded in 1817, came second. Counting reprints as well as new books, however, the lead was held by Doubleday, Doran.

More and more the publishing trade was concentrated in New York City. There were two large trade-book publishers in Boston, one in Philadelphia, one in Indianapolis; but even these four maintained New York offices for contact with authors and agents. Most of the other publishers outside New York had special fields of activity; for example there were textbook publishers in Boston, medical-book publishers in Philadelphia and Baltimore, and reprint publishers in Cleveland and Chicago. Scholarly books —a few of which appeared as if by accident on the best-seller lists—were issued by the presses founded at more than a score of American universities. Either the Harvard University or the Johns Hopkins Press was the oldest of these—depending on how one interprets the records; while those issuing the largest numbers of books were at Columbia, Harvard, Chicago, Yale, and Princeton.

In New York the publishing trade had become more than ever a mixture of business, art, and profession. Perhaps its purely professional standards were lower than in the years before 1910, but its literary standards had risen. Many publishers tried to keep ahead of the public taste and were willing, at times, to spend money on books that would have no sale except in a problematical future. They listened to serious reviewers, where earlier publishers would have brushed them aside; they even read the little magazines; and they found scope to exercise their individual tastes and talents. The history of most of the newer publishing houses, and some of the older ones, during the interwar years, should be a study of individuals rather than institutions. To mention only a few names, it was individuals like Alfred Knopf, with his passion for well designed books that other publishers would copy; like Horace Liveright, with his disregard for finances and his arbitrary kindness to rebel authors; like Alfred Harcourt, with his intelligent interest in public questions; like Maxwell Perkins, of Scribner, with his support of Fitzgerald and Hemingway and his inspired editing of Thomas Wolfe; like Warder Norton, with his faith that the public would read scholarly books if they were well written—it was these and others like them who were directly responsible for changes in the publishing world.

Individuals, too, carried on the fight against censorship that reached a climax between 1915 and 1925. In the preceding years there had been comparatively few censorship cases involving reputable publishers; and one reason was that the publishers acted as their own censors. They refused to publish books that might have offended the public taste, including many books that deserved to be published; they omitted realistic passages from others—sometimes after publication, on the complaint of one or two newspaper reviewers—and if any conflict was threatened with the Society for the Suppression of Vice, they simply withdrew a book from circulation. As late as 1914, a chapter was omitted from the posthumous first edition of Frank Norris' *Vandover and the Brute* at the request of the publishers, who thought that readers might be offended.

Yet authors had begun to fight against censorship after the suppression of Dreiser's *The "Genius"* in 1916; and soon the new publishers were supporting them. Horace Liveright, Thomas Seltzer, and later James Henle of the Vanguard Press played important parts in the struggle. The authors whose books aroused the most violent objections were Dreiser, Cabell, Schnitzler, and James Joyce. Dreiser's experience with censorship, from the quiet semi-suppression of *Sister Carrie* in 1900 to the triumphant reception in 1925 of *An American Tragedy,* might stand as an epitome of the whole struggle. There was also, however, a great battle over Joyce's *Ulysses,* parts of which were published serially in the *Little Review*. Four numbers of the magazine were burned by the Post Office Department; and in 1920 the editors were fined $100 by the New York Court of Special Sessions. In 1933, however Judge John M. Woolsey of the United States District Court ruled that *Ulysses* was a serious work of art, that it was not obscene, and that it could therefore be admitted to the United States. Judge Woolsey's decision was interpreted at the time as a permanent victory for rebel authors, American as well as foreign; but it proved to be only a truce in a long struggle that would be renewed in the 1940's.

68. THE BATTLE OF THE BOOKS

O<small>NE</small> of the earliest signs of a maturing literature is the appearance of literary critics in force. Exploratory literatures like those of colonial times or of the frontier have little use for definitions, rules, and directions. But when a civilization becomes mature and its culture relatively settled it requires of its artists that they formulate their working principles. It asks: What is literature? What are the relationships between literature as expression and the life that it expresses? Upon what traditions is this literature based? What is the relationship between the literary artist and his art?

These are the questions which Poe attempted to raise early in our literary history; but he was too early, and there were no other critics to join with him. They are the questions raised with more success by Emerson, Thoreau, Whitman, Lowell, and others of the fifties and sixties, when American culture reached a temporary fulfillment. With the unsettled state of the modern mind and the expanding forces of American development at the end of the century, the efforts of Henry James, Howells, Norris, Huneker, and others to raise these questions again resulted in much critical activity with-out great results in systematic literary criticism or understanding of its own original artists like Emily Dickinson, Crane, Robinson, and Norris. Not until about 1910 did the intellectual and social ferment of these years take shape as a critical movement concerned with literary theory in and for itself. Not until then did the age become, in Emerson's sense, "introspective"—in the phrase of Van Wyck Brooks, "self-critical." Not until then was there a con-certed effort on the part of a large number of literary critics to reformulate the basic problems of art.

The sense of newness in the critical movement of the years 1910–1925 is of course illusory. Nothing then said was really new, because all of it had roots deep in the American soil and all of it partook of the general ferment of the modern mind. It was new only in its sense of sudden recognition, in its concerted effort at clarification. But in American literary history the battle of the books waged during those years is a phenomenon of major importance and assignable dates.

In essence, it was but one engagement in the perennial war between age and youth, between the ancients and the moderns, between conservatives and radicals. Efforts to classify these critics into schools—as naturalists, humanists, impressionists, idealists, etc.—usually fail because the critics themselves refuse to conform. They were inconsistent in their basic aesthetic positions; they could not answer the fundamental questions of literary criticism because the questions themselves had not been clearly reformulated in a modern American idiom.

The chronology of the movement is as hard to follow as are its schools to classify. The only developed school of literary criticism in the United States in 1910, the academic "defenders of ideality" (see Chapter 50), was united merely in its effort to avoid disturbing issues, to preserve a tradition from the great days, and to adapt it to modern usage. Alarmed at the inroads of materialism into American life and of skepticism into American thought, these critics clung to the old certainties with waning assurance. Conviction was less vigorous in Woodberry than it had been in Stedman, less confident in Stedman than it had been in Emerson and Lowell. The ground of American literary theory needed replowing.

The first critics to start this work were drawn from the ranks of the conservatives themselves. They were W. C. Brownell, Irving Babbitt, and Paul Elmer More. These men broke with the idealists as early as 1892 by refusing to accept without careful reconsideration the traditional moral assumptions underlying the popular literature of the day. Inspired mainly by Matthew Arnold and Sainte-Beuve, they demanded a restudy of the relationship between art and life, a revaluation of values. But they joined with the idealists in protesting the current breakdown of standards and of tradition. Too individualistic to form a school and too intellectual to gain much of a public hearing, their influence was limited to a narrow circle of devoted disciples until, in the thirties, their principles had become dogmatic and their methods combative under attack. Not until then did "neo-humanism," as a reactionary movement of power, declare itself.

In the meantime the self-styled "literary radicals" had issued their challenge to conservatism in all its forms. Young men like Van Wyck Brooks, H. L. Mencken, Lewis Mumford, Waldo Frank, and Randolph Bourne were drawn together in common protest against their elders rather than by a common aesthetic philosophy. To these young men the differences between the idealists and the humanists were not so significant as the similarities in their traditionalism and in their refusal to accept the inductive methods of thinking developed by modern science. The literary radicals demanded a complete and open-minded restudy of the whole relationship between literature and American life, past and present. In the excitement of the attack, they did not take time to formulate their underlying principles or to assure the accuracy of their statements. They merely threw in their lot with the swelling current of naturalism in fiction, poetry, and drama; and they denounced all of the accepted American tradition as false because they found parts of it stultifying.

By 1915, when Brooks sounded the tocsin in *America's Coming-of-Age,* the battle was on. Its issues and its outcome have not been clearly understood, because of the distracting brilliance of forensic skill displayed on both sides. Oversimplified, the main issue may stand thus: the literary radicals demanded a closer bond between literature and "life," in the sense of vital experience; the conservatives agreed, but they defined "life" as moral values established by tradition. There were also a few critics, like Joel Spingarn, who denied the importance of immediate connection between literature and life in any sense. These three groups, but mainly the first two, defined the complex pattern of modern American literature between 1910 and 1925 by their very antagonisms.

2

The demand for a new link between literary and social criticism was signalized by John Macy's *The Spirit of American Literature* (1913), but it was Randolph Bourne who became to rebellious youth the clear-minded leader and critic, then after his death the canonized saint. "I shall never forget my first meeting with him," wrote his closest friend Van Wyck Brooks, "that odd little apparition with his vibrant eyes, his quick, birdlike steps and the long black student's cape he had brought back with him from Paris." Successful in his struggle against both the middle-class complacency of his birthplace, Bloomfield, New Jersey, and his own physical deformity— his curved back was only one of his bodily distortions—he gained a serenity which allowed him to understand and to explain their bright new world without the inhibitions and fears that beset others.

While still a student at Columbia, Bourne lashed out against an elder generation whose values served only "to buttress a social situation." They could no longer think or feel or generalize. His essays, collected as *Youth and Life* (1913), suffered, as his friend Paul Rosenfeld pointed out, from "the gingerly *Atlantic Monthly* style, with its mincingness of persons perpetually afeared of stepping on eggs"; but they contained his central challenge. Radicalism for its own sake was to be his calling; irony—as he put it, the entering of the soul into iron—his method.

When war came to his country, and the liberal leaders to whom he had looked for inspiration—notably John Dewey and Woodrow Wilson—joined the vested interests with what seemed to him a false rationalization of the American cause, he turned from literature to oppose all those who would twist values to serve ends, and became a social critic. His essays for the short-lived *Seven Arts* magazine, collected later by James Oppenheim as *Untimely Papers* (1919), were timely enough. The energies of his last years were devoted to exposing the fallacy of service to the state rather than to the self. In a blind search for values in a distorted world, he died.

Van Wyck Brooks collected Bourne's papers as the *History of a Literary Radical* in 1920, the most important of which is a fragment of a novel. Here the young man Miro—Bourne himself—finds his escape from the "sweetness and light" which tainted the American tradition by the aid of the "abounding vitality and moral freedom" of Thoreau, Whitman, and Mark Twain. And Bourne, like Miro, turned to writers who were not afraid: to Dostoevski, because of his success in closing up the gap between the normal and the abnormal; to Cardinal Newman, because of his acceptance of skepticism; to Dreiser, because of his "revelation of a certain broad level of American life." Bourne's criticism had the negative virtue of exposing hypocrisy and cant rather than the positive virtue of formulating a doctrine and a program. But even in the few papers that he left he demonstrated his fearlessness, his irony, and his dialectical skill.

At Bourne's death Van Wyck Brooks more than anyone else took over the leadership of the radical cause and formulated its program. He had long been working closely with Bourne, for in *The Wine of the Puritans* (1909) he had diagnosed the causes of America's blindness and stupidity. Bourne had similarly warped the term in "The Puritan's Will to Power" to make it convey all the traits and none but the traits that these two young men disliked. Mencken and others accepted the thesis of the Puritan bogy as basic. The enemy was defined, and the battle could proceed. The issue was the fate of the American artist.

In order to create his straw man, Brooks used both psychological and historical criticism with acute insight but little regard for historical facts. The rational intensity of the Puritan ideal, he found, was a valuable trait for the starting of a new civilization; but as that civilization became extensive rather than intensive the social dominance of the New England mind fettered the growth of a new culture. By the fixity of his ideal for the inner life, the Puritan cut off the possibility of moral development and forced the "lofty and inspired sophist" Emerson and others into a formless transcendentalism. On the other hand, the Puritan settlement of all conflicts of the inner life made it possible to turn attention to the problem of subduing a wilderness and developed a practical materialism which tended to absorb vital energies. Moral inhibitions thus conspired with business success to divorce the American tradition from life.

The half-truth of this analysis was true enough to hurt, and it seemed to Brooks and his friends to be a kind of revelation. The weaknesses that Brooks found in contemporary American culture were real, even though his explanation of their causes was oversimplified. His own career as a critic is involved at all stages in this hypothesis: its statement (1908-1913), its application to specific cases (1913-1932), and its defense by a historical re-creation of the cultural past (after 1936).

In *America's Coming-of-Age* (1915) Brooks is on firmer ground because he is speaking of the present and the immediate past, and his historical distortion plays a smaller part in his analysis. In this book he sees the Puritan duality of view become a mere distinction between "Highbrow" and "Lowbrow." Literature had cast its lot with the thin moral earnestness of the "Highbrow" and had entered a sphere where life was rejected. There were two kinds of writing, and there were two publics. Each was only half human because of the rejection of the other. Only such a synthesis as Walt Whitman had attempted could bring them together and form a socialized individualism. America had a tradition if she would but recognize it.

The next step was to apply the thesis in detail to specific cases. After several lesser experiments, Brooks settled upon Mark Twain as the perfect American example of this dilemma; for he, more than any other, presented the case of the artist in the new, modern, and floating universe, a keen intelligence in a sturdy body, dragged down into the past by a moral tradition that his mind rejected, lured into the future by a chaos of forces in which he could discover no moral synthesis. *The Ordeal of Mark Twain* (1920) is the culmination of Brooks' thought on this problem, for Mark Twain faced the dilemma and succumbed to it, a noble but pathetic failure. To make his thesis tight, the critic deliberately dug out and then overstressed the buried psychological forces which had warped Twain's aesthetic career: the comparative cultural naïveté of the Mississippi Valley in which he was born, the Calvinistic inheritance from his mother, his bondage through his wife and his friend Howells to a false code of respectability in letters. His original genius, so the reader must infer from the evidence of his imperfect but powerful work, had been blighted in turn by each of the three factors against which the literary radicals were directing their attack: provincialism, Puritanism, and the "professors." With the defeat of the individual within him, he could only revert to his pioneer heritage and speak for the race character rather than for himself. "Has the American writer today," asks Brooks, "the same excuse for missing his vocation?"

Overdrawn as is this portrait, it is the most vigorous account to date of the curious and typical phenomenon presented in Mark Twain: the high-spirited humorist with the heavy heart, the bitter satirist who could not resist the temptation to torture himself with barbs meant for others, the sensitive artist who never developed a mature and formal art. In spite of the tirade of protest which the book immediately aroused, no critic of Twain has since been able to ignore this analysis. It has provoked others into an honest exploration and reevaluation of the American cultural inheritance.

Brooks survived the hubbub and brought out in a few years a "revision" in which he took back nothing. Doggedly he turned to Henry James as typical of a second possible reaction to the dilemma of the American artist. Mark Twain had surrendered; James tried the outward avenue of escape to Europe, in common with Howells, Henry Adams, and a whole company of lesser but no less sensitive spirits. *The Pilgrimage of Henry James* (1925) uses the same thesis of the blighted genius and the same method of psychological analysis to illustrate a second type of aesthetic failure. For James achieved his "high passivity" early in life when he was unable to participate in the Civil War. He would be the spectator rather than the manager of life. He would analyze, in innumerable expatriate Americans like himself, the division in his own soul. But the excesses of morbid psychology which had made his study of Mark Twain so unacceptable to many were now become pathological in Brooks himself. The dilemma was in command of the critic as well as of his subject, and a nervous breakdown resulted. The mirror was clouded beyond the possibility of a clear image.

It was this mirror which was next held up to the "lofty and inspired sophist," for Emerson's centrality in American cultural history must be explained if the thesis were to hold. The writing of this, Brooks' crucial book, was interrupted by its author's own breakdown, 1927–1932, when other American authors were migrating to Europe. *Emerson and Others,* containing six episodes, appeared in 1927. When its revision, *Emerson,* appeared as a completed study in 1932, a new note was struck in the final paragraph: "At last there was left only a sense of presence . . . the universe had become his house in which to live." Emerson alone of the prototypes of failure failed to fail. He had a narrow escape, but he emerged from the ordeal as a guide toward a possible solution rather than as the obviously planned example of defeat. Lofty sophistry had become dynamic idealism.

With the publication of the vigorous *Freeman* essays of earlier years as *Sketches in Criticism* (1932), the first phase of Brooks' work came to a close. His work as radical critic for the attack was completed. He believed that he had succeeded in presenting the case against aesthetic and spiritual sterility by exposing the falsity of the tradition of ideality and had opened the way for a reconstructed idealism. From now on he would devote his energies to the constructive spadework of supplying America with her "usable past." Lewis Mumford in *Sticks and Stones* (1924), *The Golden Day* (1926), and *The Brown Decades* (1931) had already demonstrated how this might be done by the application of a dominant thesis to the history of the arts and letters. In 1927 this would have been Brooks' method also, but in 1936, when *The Flowering of New England, 1815-1865* appeared, he was ready to take a more objective view—to let the past tell its own story. No nearer than he ever was to a systematic moral philosophy, he gives us in the person of his alter ego, in *The Opinions of Oliver Allston* (1941), his matured position as an idealist turning from the attack to the defense.

Because he was fresh from Emerson, the mid-century period was the obvious one with which to open his series of studies in cultural history. But his plan was chronological, extending from *The World of Washington Irving* (1944), through *The Times of Melville and Whitman* (1947) and *New England: Indian Summer, 1865-1915* (1940), to a projected volume on his own era to 1914. The Colonial period, with its Puritans, was omitted because nationalism rather than Puritanism now seemed to be the key to the American tradition; and the psychological method was abandoned in favor of an invented method of aesthetic sociology. These later books move swiftly and vividly across the surface of the cultural past, applying the techniques of critical biography to society, painting the moving picture of a composite national personality in its evolving configurations. By deliberately limiting his range and defining a single achievable task, Brooks has converted, for himself at least, the malaise of the twenties into a single original work of aesthetic and historical criticism. More literature than literary history—they even suggest the method of historical fiction—these books give full scope to his sense of personality, his love of the picturesque, and his delight in "the literary life."

3

The careers of Bourne and Brooks demonstrate that literary radicalism without a philosophic base or a constructive program is inadequate to form a movement. In the early stages of their attack they drew to themselves a substantial following; but their demand that literary criticism come to terms with modern American man and his society posited the need for a moral and social philosophy which they were not prepared to supply. Theirs was the hopeful but always inconclusive voice of liberalism *per se*. Even in the early twenties, when Brooks, like Ludwig Lewisohn and later Matthew Josephson—in his *Portrait of the Artist as American* (1930)—was concentrating on psychological criticism, strongly influenced by Freud, others in the group of literary radicals, like Waldo Frank, Max Eastman, and John

Reed, were moving toward the dialectical materialism of Marx and making it a social cause. All were being drawn away from traditional aesthetic and ethical bases of literary criticism to the study of man and society with the aid of the techniques of social science. In spite of Brooks' later assertion that he had always been an idealist, the method indicated by him and the other literary radicals was that of empirical criticism. If a new morality were needed, and if experience rather than tradition were to supply it, the new social sciences rather than the old philosophies must provide the dogma and the method. Brooks' rediscovery of idealism in Emerson, and Stuart Sherman's final and reluctant acceptance of Dreiser were but two sides of the same coin, both reversals of earlier positions. The root issue was philosophic; the choice between idealism and naturalism. Brooks, like Emerson, would rediscover the ideal by fresh and fearless analysis of living man and nature.

Meanwhile Theodore Dreiser was fumbling his way toward a naturalistic moral basis for art, and H. L. Mencken was his prophet. Like many another artist, Dreiser was himself very nearly inarticulate in his attempts at critical analysis. His one volume of criticism, *Hey Rub-a-dub-dub* (1920), does little more than echo the complaints of his fellows without their sustaining idealism. His chapter on "The Essential Tragedy of Life" echoes Mark Twain's despair in the helpless, hopeless state of arrogant man, protesting against the "truth" that he, like all other phenomena of the universal machine, is nothing more than a cog himself. That on "Life, Art, and America" is a bitter protest against the division in American life, so much more clearly defined by Brooks' terms, Highbrow and Lowbrow. Dreiser's work lay in the development of the new art of fiction initiated by Norris and Crane, not in criticism. His indignation sought and found a creative idiom.

But without adequate criticism it might well have remained unappreciated for at least his lifetime. Largely because of Mencken's essay (1917), the acceptance or rejection of Dreiser became the test of a literary critic's contact with his times. Mencken could perform this service only because he had long before worked out for himself a naturalistic philosophy which could serve as the tool of critical analysis. His book on *The Philosophy of Friedrich Nietzsche* (1908) is the key to his subsequent career. The German philosopher had given him a formula for dealing with metaphysical and ethical questions for which Dreiser had only an instinctive and unrationalized feeling. It also supplied him with a political and social philosophy which divided him sharply from those critics who found in the Marxian dialectic a similarly useful ideology with which to describe and evaluate the material universe. Although a literary radical like Bourne and Brooks, his social and political philosophy was more akin to the reactionary views of Brownell, More, and Babbitt than to those of Eastman and Frank.

In a deliberately naïve and charming series of reminiscences, *Happy Days* (1940), *Newspaper Days* (1941), and *Heathen Days* (1943), Mencken has given us an intimate picture of his boyhood and early manhood in Baltimore. His attack on the provincialism of his contemporaries was firmly rooted in his own attachment to the "immemorial lares and penates." He could never be long separated from Baltimore—was, in fact, Baltimore incarnate. The child of a German cigar maker, he knew creature comfort if not luxury, from his early years—a shoddy but none the less private school, summers in the near-by country, a home library of modest scope if not over-refined taste, a hand printing press of his own in the comfortable house on Hollins Street which was always his home to his later years. His years on the Baltimore *Evening Herald* merely intensified his sense of values in immediate experience and made it forever impossible for him to admit even the slightest divorce between life and books.

He soon knew that he was one of those people that are born to write, and he did fairly well around 1900–1902 with short stories in the *Criterion,* "the only solvent survivor of the literary movement of the nineties." Although he thus took his place in that movement, its lapse of vitality between 1900 and 1910 caught him in his third decade when his career as a writer would normally have taken shape. Instead of continuing with fiction, he tells us, he became interested in Shaw, and through him in Nietzsche. "After that I was a critic of ideas, and I have remained one ever since."

Most of Nietzsche's dominant concepts sank into his mind and remained his substitute for the decalogue. The issue, as he came to see it, lay between Dionysus and Apollo, between doubt and dogma. His own choice, both for himself and for his age, was clear: "The civilized world has disposed of supernaturalism and is engaged in a destructive criticism of the old faith's residuum—morality." A Puritan had arisen to challenge Puritans, a scholar to call the professors to account.

With the technique of doubt went other of Nietzsche's dominant ideas— the aristocracy of the Superman in a class-divided society, the antipathy for the proletariat, the deterministic biological approach to birth and love and death in a world in which man and woman have distinctive functions, and, most important of all, the fluent morality of power as a substitute for the codified morality of the Christian tradition. Thus Mencken had what most of his contemporaries lacked, a feeling that he stood on firm intellectual ground. His enemies too were sharply defined: the Marxists would hate him in spite of a common materialistic basis, and the Puritans, whether moralists who clung sincerely to the Christian code or "professors" who based an aesthetic ideality on that code, would be his sworn enemies for life.

Mencken's style changed from lucid exposition to shock and bombast when he had thus taken his stand. As the philosopher of doubt he joined the forces of the literary radicals and added to theirs a much louder and firmer voice than had yet been heard. Even his titles reflect his irony and his defiance: *A Book of Burlesques* (1916); *A Little Book in C Major* (1916); *A Book of Prefaces* (1917); *In Defense of Women* (1917); and *Damn! A Book of Calumny* (1917). Then came the first edition of *The American Language* (1919), with the first collection of the *Prejudices* (1919), and Mencken had found the two principal outlets for his message.

The *Prejudices* are the howls of a lone wolf in the wilderness of hypocrisy, a character equaled in historical picturesqueness in our literature only by the lone eagle of Whitman, and one adopted almost as calculatingly. It howled its way through six series, 1919–1927, and a supplementary one of *Selected Prejudices* in the latter year. It was heard from the pages of the *Smart Set,* which Mencken edited with George Jean Nathan from 1914 to 1923, and from those of the *American Mercury,* which he founded with Nathan in 1924 but carried on alone throughout most of its career to 1933. It even agitates the scholarly pages of *The American Language.*

This is the forensic voice of H. L. Mencken, especially in the middle years when he was taking an aggressive part in the battle of books and ideas. Those who heard it laughed, and he laughed with them, but it was the laughter of a Swift or a Voltaire. Rebellious youth in the postwar years took the *Prejudices* as its gospel of revolt, but unfortunately their very timeliness dates them. Mencken diagnosed the political, social, and cultural ills of his day, swiftly and with precision. His techniques are surgical, and his operations both sudden and major; but his patients usually survive unless they are deliberately murdered as indistinguishable from the diseases from which they suffer. Starting off bravely with a series of literary appraisals, the first volume of essays exposes the pretensions and the achievements of both small and great. But with the second series the *Prejudices* hit their stride. They are primarily political and sociological; only incidentally literary and aesthetic.

Mencken's major quarrels are two: with the Christian moral code whether in its pure state or in a diluted state, and with government by the people, whether under a democratic or a communistic form. These two themes are developed with every conceivable variation through the pages, and they finally emerge into books of their own. Nowhere in our literature is there so thoroughly damning an analysis of our political and social assumptions as in *Notes on Democracy* (1926). Is there any record that Hitler knew of it?

When he turns to "The National Letters" with his two measures, the morality of power and the government by aristocracy, he describes both the disease and his remedy for it with flamboyant challenge; the lack of "a distinguished and singular excellence, a signal national quality, a ripe and stimulating flavor," in our national letters; the lack of a "civilized aristocracy" in our society. In spite of the easy assumption of his critics, Mencken was never in his own eyes, or in truth, a clown. He was always in dead earnest, and his whiplashes are all from a single whip.

Mencken's essays may fade with time except for his occasional flashes of insight into the work of his contemporaries, but *The American Language* (1919), with its four revisions and its two supplements, will stand. Fortunately the partial suspension of free speech when the United States entered the First World War in 1917 turned his attention from his column on contemporary issues in the Baltimore *Evening Sun* and allowed him time to work on his long absorbing interest in American speech. For this work he combined the instinct of the scholar with the quick wit and shrewd insight of the journalist. The result was a book that, like the *Leaves of Grass,* grew by accretion and revision more in the manner of a living organism than of a card index. In itself a gigantic work of literature, it has given the American people their language as Emerson and Whitman gave them their literature by cutting the umbilical cord. Mencken does not deny the English, and behind that the Indo-Teutonic, origins of that language. He merely denies the authority of the historical scholar to legislate for the present as well as the past. By that simple device he has given new life to scholarship in one field of major importance. This is his final reconciliation with the "professors," some of whom like T. R. Lounsbury had been themselves working for the same ends by less sensational methods, but they came to him with the white flag. They found him at the old address on Hollins Street.

4

Literary radicalism could go no further in protest than Mencken took it. It was at this point that the conservatives, the followers of Apollo rather than of Dionysus, came back into the fray with armor refurbished. The death of Sherman in 1926 and of Brownell in 1928 seemed to signal the launching of the neo-humanist movement as a movement. Norman Foerster called the survivors together in *Humanism and America* (1930), and the defense took the offensive. The brief and belligerent course of the movement is subject for a later chapter, but its roots go back into the early part of the century.

These men were not "defenders of ideality"; they admitted the necessity for a new deal. With Brooks and Mencken they drew no sharp line between ethics and aesthetics, between conduct and beauty, and set to work on a critical analysis of the American tradition, rejecting, also, more than they accepted. But with the idealists they rejected the concept of an open universe, the inductive method. The twentieth century world, they agreed, with its scientific advances, its industrial and political upheavals, its confusion of directions and standards, must be freshly explored; but the guiding principles of that adventure must come from within, from what used to be called the conscience rather than from the impact of natural and social forces.

William Crary Brownell was their first articulate spokesman. As Brooks had given leadership to the radicals, so Brownell, as early as 1901, had formulated the principles which were to guide his own work and that of the conservatives. Although never connected with a university, he was, in the terminology of the young radicals, a "professor" of the deepest dye. He was academic in the sense of the founders of the American Academy of Arts and Letters in 1904, with membership limited to fifty. He believed that great literature is born of great rules, and great rules are born of trained minds. He was aristocratic and antiromantic by instinct, but he believed that literature is integral with life. No aesthetic could in his judgment be complete which did not stand on the Christian ethic of character, the Platonic doctrine of form, and the Aristotelian reliance upon reason.

Brownell's short period of training on the old New York *World* and the Godkin *Nation,* and his forty years as literary adviser to the Scribner firm, 1888–1928, were in a worldly sense almost completely uneventful. Living in the geographical and economic heart of American life, his temperament remained calm but not remote; he was his own university.

Brownell began his career as a critic with two books in praise of modern realistic art, *French Traits* (1889) and *French Art* (1892), and it is on this evidence that Stuart Sherman later assigned him to the "Party of Nature." But in spite of his apparently sociological and scientific premises, derived from his study of Taine and his admiration for the French, the germ of the later neo-humanist movement is present in his corollaries. He saw a renewed emphasis upon personality as humanity's natural response to the leveling effects of the modern impersonal view of nature. Even though he used the terms "temperament" and "personality" in a sense quite contrary to that of Babbitt and More, as descriptive of fundamental man rather than of individual eccentricities, he heralds rather than contradicts the later distinction between "humanism" and "humanitarianism" which became the battle cry of the movement.

It was in this emphasis upon personality that his humanism emerged. In two books, *Victorian Prose Masters* (1901) and *American Prose Masters* (1909), he attempted evaluations of British and American culture of the nineteenth century through analyses of outstanding writers. The idea of doing these studies of prose masters was doubtless suggested, as the parallel titles would imply, by Stedman's studies of Victorian and American poets; but Brownell's position is more judicial, his analyses more probing, his method much more objective than Stedman's. He took Arnold rather than the American for his guide.

The essay on Arnold is the core of the two volumes, for in evaluating the British man and critic he presents his own apology. The distinguishing quality of Arnold was that "he developed his nature as well as directed his work in accordance with the definite ideal of reason." The man and the writing were one, a carefully wrought work of art. Culture was identified thus with personality, and personality with an impersonal ideal that sought "first of all completeness of harmonious development" in the Greek and Christian inspirations. An apostle rather than an artist, Arnold stood alone among English critics for "his candor, his measure of disinterestedness, his faculty of extracting their application from the precedents indicated by culture." Brownell's prose masters are judged by the degree to which they achieved this standard, and the fact that they all fell so far short of it makes the reading of the essays depressing as well as illuminating.

In his last four books Brownell subordinated his judgments of individuals and developed his critical theory in general terms. *Criticism* (1914) and *Standards* (1917) state his case. Criticism is an art in itself, to be carefully distinguished from the techniques of creative art and of reviewing alike, both of which are particular and specialized. "It is its function to discern and characterize the abstract qualities informing the concrete expression of the artist." The critic should know history, aesthetics, and philosophy, but rely on no one of them to the exclusion of the others. With Sainte-Beuve, Brownell feels "that our liking anything is not enough, that it is necessary to know further whether we are right in liking it." As there is no universal taste, critical impressionism is inadequate, reason alone provides sound basis for judgment. The weakness in this exposition is the vagueness of Brownell's definition of his standards. In the two essays he merely asserts that standards are needed, that they exist always in impersonal personality—but he does not himself say what they are.

The Genius of Style (1924) and *Democratic Distinction in America* (1927) elaborate his position without further defining or developing it. They are a call to a "general spirit of order that is organic and of movement that is rhythm." Our democracy must cease to associate distinction with reserve, as did the Romans, and learn to associate it with development, as did the Greeks and the French. The "vice of sensation," as illustrated in Dreiser and the modern school, must give way to the style which is the expression of the inner and universal personality, thereby "supplying its helter-skelter of idioms and episodes with organic order, regularizing the eccentricities of its rhythms, rationalizing its artificial intensities, and elevating its grosser naturalisms."

5

Although Paul Elmer More and Irving Babbitt have been credited (or blamed) with founding the neo-humanist movement in American criticism, they did little more than develop and formalize Brownell's later position. Their thought, like his, stemmed from an enthusiasm for French culture; took inspiration from Greek and Christian ideals; linked literature with the graphic arts and music; battled both with academic classicism and with romanticism; called for decorum, harmony, and standards referable to the inner and moral man; combated the current naturalism in letters; like his, failed of finally reducing to a moral basis the judgment of art.

Against the literary radicalism of Mencken and the trend of thought reflected in the work of Dreiser, Lewis, O'Neill, Sandburg, Dos Passos, and the majority of the creative writers of the twenties and thirties, Babbitt waged relentless war. He could even descend from his professorial chair at Harvard and put on the gloves offered by Mencken, his leading adversary: "To reduce criticism indeed," he flung at him, "to the satisfaction of a temperamental urge, to the uttering of one's gustos and disgustos (in Mr. Mencken's case chiefly the latter) is to run counter to the very etymology of the word which implies discrimination and judgment."

The young men who, in the twenties, were delighted by the broadsides fired monthly from the pages of the *American Mercury* were equally delighted by this counterblast from so worthy an opponent on the side of the "professors." Secretly, no doubt, many of them distrusted the Mencken wit and resented the Mencken iconoclasm. They flocked to Babbitt's Harvard courses in French literature and the history of criticism as boys run to a good fist fight, for here they found wit and timeliness reinforced by the assurance of tradition. Here was a Brahmin—more truly than the now pale ghosts of Longfellow, Lowell, and Holmes—a worthy Brahmin come to battle with the confusion of the times.

Babbitt was a philosopher of literature, a student of its theory rather than an analyst of its product. His aim was to provide others with the means of judgment; he criticized criticism rather than creative art. His six major works, from *Literature and the American College* (1908) to his final collection of essays *On Being Creative* (1932)—the miscellany *Spanish Character* was posthumous (1940)—are elaborations and applications of a single thesis: that contemporary currents of aesthetic thinking must be corrected by a return to the classical concept of humanity as distinct from both God and nature.

The New Laokoon (1910) applies this thesis to the graphic arts and music, challenging the confusion of poetry with the other arts and the consequent breakdown of standards. *The Masters of Modern French Criticism* (1912), his nearest approach to a study of literary men in themselves and his best work as a critic in his own right, traces the anarchy of French romantic criticism from Chateaubriand to Renan, with Sainte-Beuve's development into judicial traditionalism as its solution. In *Rousseau and Romanticism* (1919) he came to grips with his dragon, naturalism (both sentimental and scientific), in an exhaustive analysis of the romantic fallacy as he saw it, and in *Democracy and Leadership* (1924) he extended his thesis, as did Brownell, to its political implications in the false theory of natural rights as opposed to the just theory of humanistic and aristocratic democracy.

Babbitt himself conceived these books as a single work and repeated his central dogma in each of his prefaces before proceeding to its special application. As readily as Van Wyck Brooks, he bent the past to his purposes. His theory of cultural history, in brief, is that the humanism of the Renaissance in its break with the authority of the church, attempting to give man his integrity as man by distinguishing him from God, had fallen into a counter error. The experimental method of Bacon, whom Babbitt took as a symbol of the fallacy of the whole scientific fraternity, had identified man with nature and had fallen into the error of naturalistic monism in trying to escape from theological monism. Specialization and technology were the results, and man was no longer man. Instead of mastering nature with the power and progress thus released, man had become a mere cog in the inhuman machine.

From the error of specialization and technology, the second error followed as an inevitable consequence—the error symbolized in Rousseau. In his effort to regain his place in the universe, man had developed his feelings rather than his mind. Sentiment was added to scientific naturalism, and the anarchy of the romantic movement resulted. Pity for humanity took the place of respect for self; humanitarianism was substituted for genuine humanism.

The terms romanticism, naturalism, humanitarianism, humanism—each defined clearly and used consistently—provide the basic structure of Babbitt's position, and were accepted in these meanings by his peers and his followers. The first three describe the progressive disintegration of modern man; the fourth describes the corrective. Only by reasserting the balanced belief of the Greeks in a dualistic universe could man stand free once more from his world and the error be corrected. But in one of his last attempts at definition contributed to *Humanism in America* (1930), even he admits that ethical self-control might be applied on the level of religion and, by a union of all faiths, might create a new faith. He died soon enough to avoid the necessity of conversion and so saved himself from becoming, at least in the technical sense, a saint.

Babbitt's earliest disciple was his contemporary Paul Elmer More—disciple only because the meeting with Babbitt, when they were both students of Hindu literature at Harvard, marked the major turning point in More's intellectual development, and his friendship with Babbitt held him throughout life to a strict acceptance of humanistic principles much less suited to his temperament than they were to that of his more vigorous friend. For More, if not a saint, was something more than a philosopher in the logical and dialectic senses; he was a secular monk. The cloister—whether his rural retreat at Shelburne, New Hampshire, where he formed his personality and his doctrine, or his final home at Princeton, New Jersey, where he exerted his greatest influence—was much more his natural habitat than the editorial offices of the *Independent,* the New York *Evening Post,* and the *Nation,* of which he was successively an editor from 1901 until 1914. Like Brownell, More made a hermitage of the metropolis.

But his mind had been cast at Shelburne even though his residence in that mountain retreat spanned only a little over two years (1897-1899). Like Walden, it became the symbol of an attitude rather than of a place, and it gave its name to a long series of critical essays, more than half of which are specific studies of authors, only a minority essays in critical theory. For, unlike Babbitt, More was a reader of books for the books' sake. He was a literary philosopher only because he felt the need of principles for judgment, a contender in the forum only when he felt that he had been attacked.

Appropriately the first volume of the first series of Shelburne Essays (eleven volumes, 1904-1921) opens with "A Hermit's Notes on Thoreau," for *Walden* was one of the earliest discoveries of More's retirement. Reading it on the banks of the Androscoggin, this "hermit after a mild Epicurean fashion of my own" learned the value of contemplation rather than of nature herself, for at the start of his serious thought about literature and life he was deeply immersed in the romantic doctrines that he and Babbitt were so violently to attack. Here are judgments of a mystic rather than of a humanist; More, at this time, was deeply engrossed in the translations which became *A Century of Indian Epigrams* (1898), and he was searching, like Emerson before him, in the Hindu rather than in the Greek or Christian tradition for confirmation of his romantic insights into the mystery of life.

The mood did not endure for long. Before the first volume of the Essays was complete, the lawgiver was crowding the poet. In Buddhism More found, not confirmation for the life of the soul alone, but the necessity for dualism.

Religion must not be confused with the ways of the world, the things of God with the things of Caesar; but it is not necessary to renounce either one. Reading into Christ's advice to the rich young man a relative rather than an absolute injunction (*If you would,* renounce . . .), he arrived at a position in which both levels of experience might be accepted and their interactions become the subject of a life's study. The long series of critical essays, many of which were first published in magazines that he edited, was thus launched in the terms which Babbitt later shaped into dogma.

More's method was his own. Each of the literary essays takes a single proposition in this relationship between the law for man and the law for thing, as discoverable in the work of a single author, and develops it into at once an insight and a proof. Often warped to their respective theses, these essays nevertheless are the most ambitious and often the most penetrating body of judicial literary criticism in our literature.

"We think," More quoted from Halifax in the ninth volume of the series, *Aristocracy and Justice* (1915), "that a wise Mean, between these barbarous Extreams, is that which self-Preservation ought to dictate to our Wishes." Even in these excursions into political and social theory, More retained his ideal of moderation and balance. Although in forensic combat he could deliver blow for blow with the best of his adversaries, his own temperament seems to reflect this moderation. His most dogmatic assertions seem mild because they are couched in the quiet tones of persuasion, irony, and sweet reason. The main thesis of an essay is insinuated rather than forced into the reader's consciousness, its supporting evidences and arguments are assembled with the casual ease of a limpid current, the style flows and bends to a conclusion at or near the point of starting. The proposition is round and apparently whole; it can be attacked only by exposing the premise.

More's semiretirement on the fringe of the Princeton campus—where he gave graduate courses and built up a devoted following—was spent mainly in the creation of a twentieth century neo-Platonism which would embrace the best of the Christian tradition but skirt the depths of religion itself. His series The Greek Tradition opened in 1917 with *Platonism,* closed in 1931 with *Christ the Word.* Yet in *Pages from an Oxford Diary* (1924) he tells us that, as a pretended don and philosopher, he sought God in "the universe as a manifestation of one comprehensive design," and learned "to walk humbly with God, never doubting, whatever befall, that His will is good, and that His law is right."

The New Shelburne Essays, which were initiated with *The Demon of the Absolute* (1928), bear evidence of More's development from inquiring sympathy for the individual writer to an organized attack on the naturalistic movement in modern literature, particularly American and French. Any creed which rests on the "absolute," he believed was false for that reason alone, and the effort of modern writers to identify man with nature invalidated their work as art. Thus Joyce's psychology was "nothing more than a theory of objective reality which will correspond to the inner stream of consciousness"; his literary work was therefore "in English a more or less exotic offshoot of a literary movement whose regular and logical development [occurred] in France"; and "the acknowledged fathers of the whole movement were the three Americans: Poe and Whitman and Henry James." To Babbitt's battle cry of denunciation of the dominant trend in modern literature, More thus brought the evidence of his wide and careful reading, but the result is no happier. The role of Jeremiah is not one to inspire affection even though it may create followers; and Paul Elmer More, by nature a man of quiet ways and sympathetic interest in books, men, and ideas, did not wear it any too comfortably.

On an impressionable young graduate student at Harvard in 1904, Stuart P. Sherman, the impact of Babbitt in person and of More in his essays came as a light and a way. No one of the younger disciples so wholeheartedly accepted the doctrine of the masters or echoed their ideas with more vehemence. But his loyalty sprang from enthusiasm rather than from mature conviction. In spite of Sherman's intense devotion for a time to the distinction between the law for man and the law for thing—reflected in his study of Matthew Arnold and in his first collection of essays, *On Contemporary Literature* (1917)—his career as a whole is that of an impressionist in temperamen· and in mind; hence his inconsistencies and the intellectual dilemmas which pursued him to the end of his comparatively short life. Let it be remembered that, before his confession of humanistic faith, he had espoused positivism and had soaked himself in the English romantic poets at Williams College; and at Harvard he had turned from the dry scholarship of Kittredge, which he later attacked openly, not at first to the criticism of Babbitt, but to the living drama of George Pierce Baker. Let it also be remembered that, long before he resigned from his professorship at the University of Illinois in 1924 to take the editorship of the New York *Herald Tribune* "Books," he had come out strongly (though with qualifications) for both Sinclair Lewis and W. C. Brownell. Too much has been made of his apostasy to the humanistic movement. What the situation called for, he wrote early in 1923 ("W. C. Brownell"), was a mediator who understood and valued that which both the "Party of Culture" and the "Party of Nature" desired, and who could "unite their complementary virtues in a common purpose." By temperament both an aristocrat and a literary radical (he became during the First World War almost what would later have been called fascist), he was drawn into extreme statements on both sides of the critical issues of the day. He attacked

Mencken, in *Americans* (1922), for his denial of an American tradition and pictured himself in the same book as remarking to More, "I am obliged to lean a bit forward to counterbalance the stubbornness of your Toryism."

Sherman, the natural aristocrat, the man of sensibility and taste, was as much as Bourne or Brooks or Mencken a literary radical throughout his life. His acceptance of the Babbitt-More role of Jeremiah was a passing phase; at the end he returned to his belief in vitality as a higher value than moderation. After having denounced Dreiser's "barbaric naturalism" in 1915, he had the courge in 1925 to accept *An American Tragedy* as "the worst written great novel in the world"—but none the less great for its moral integrity and its final mastery of the novel form. In those ten years, the critic had not changed —nor had the novelist. In spite of apparent difference in philosophy and art, they had been working, each in his way, for the "emotional discovery of America" which Sherman proclaimed in one of his last public utterances.

6

Between 1925 and 1930, the neo-humanist movement lapsed in the excitement of a growing creative literature and a giddy stock market; the battle of the books appeared to have been fought to a stalemate. The radicals gave evidence of rout; they had produced no philosophy upon which a critical movement could be based, and no method by which it could proceed. The conservatives had proved equally ineffective. Their warning had apparently not been heard, and their voices were becoming shrill—or silent. Yet it can readily be seen in the perspective of another literary generation that the critical ferment of these years marked a genuine renaissance of cultural interest and understanding. Old assumptions had been painfully dislodged, new forces had been submitted to scrutiny, the orientation of the American tradition to the twentieth century world had been undertaken. The stalemate was apparent rather than real.

The critical controversies of the thirties and forties were to turn on sharper issues and to form more clearly defined schools than were possible earlier. But the fact that literature and the theories about it seemed, by 1930, to be of public consequence was due in large part to the crusading years of Henry Seidel Canby, a professor who early broke from New England cloisters and entered the literary market place. Like Carl Van Doren of the *Nation,* and later Stuart Sherman of the New York *Herald Tribune* Books, Canby refused to share either the esoteric zeal of fact-finding literary scholars or the careless promotionism of much current magazine and newspaper reviewing. In the Literary Review of the New York *Evening Post,* and after 1924 in the *Saturday Review of Literature,* as well as in his own critical and autobiographical writing, he did more than anyone else to bring the scholarly standards of the university into working relationship with the productive energies of writers, publishers, reviewers, and critics.

In the universities themselves, the new lines of thought were already becoming manifest before 1930. The academic antecedents of the neo-humanist controversy of that year have already been traced, but those of socio-literary and purely aesthetic criticism, the dominant trends of the later decades, had been indicated mainly in the work, respectively, of two "professors," Vernon L. Parrington and Joel Spingarn.

Parrington's *Main Currents in American Thought* (1927–1930) was, he thought, a history of American literature even though his publishers assigned a more descriptive title when finally the exhaustive work came to press. The product of long years of reading and teaching on the West Coast, it ruffled academic waters—not so much by its author's somewhat forced effort to relate all that is good in the American present to the ideas and accomplishments of Jefferson, as by his success in reevaluating the entire American tradition in political, social, and economic rather than in aesthetic and moral terms. It demonstrated one effective way to relate literature to life in a historical context. The work of the new school of historians, from F. J. Turner to Beard and Schlesinger, seemed now brought to a focus on the problems of American literary history. The reconstruction of our "usable past" that Brooks had called for, and that Calverton, Mumford, and others had attempted, seemed here to have been accomplished by an obscure professor. There was mingled protest and acclaim as reviewers and scholars vied with one another in expressing astonishment. Meanwhile the author, now ready for the honor and the condemnation that were to be showered upon him, died with his third volume unfinished. It was left for later critics and historians to carry forward, in his idiom and by his method, the new synthesis of art and life, the past and the present—and either carefully to avoid the pitfalls of too narrow a social ideology or to accept and develop a criticism based squarely on the Marxian dialectic.

As socio-literary criticism was prepared by 1925 for an overhauling, so the "pure" criticism of art as art was revived and refurbished. To Joel Spingarn, Mencken gave a not too hearty welcome in his "Criticism of Criticism of Criticism" (1919). "Major Spingarn lately served notice upon me that he had abandoned the life of the academic grove for that of the armed array . . . his notions, whatever one may say in opposition to them, are at least magnificently unprofessorial."

Spingarn had been schooled by Lewis E. Gates of Harvard and by Benedetto Croce of Italy. His separation from the academic world in 1911 was complete in fact, but his notions were not so unacademic as Mencken thought.

Possessing a knowledge of critical tradition and method which none of the literary radicals could boast (he had written *A History of Literary Criticism in the Renaissance,* 1899), he did more than anyone else of his generation to supply rationale and method for the analytical criticism of Eliot and the critics of the thirties and forties.

His own work was slight in volume as he, like Babbitt, theorized about criticism rather than practiced it. An experimental poet and anthologist, he produced only one volume of his own essays, *Creative Criticism* (1917), revised and enlarged (1931). In the latter year he performed his greatest service to the critical movement in America by gathering the most significant critiques of his time into a volume *Criticism in America: Its Function and Status.* These essays span the period since his own "The New Criticism" (1910), and sum up the achievement of a generation. Brooks and Mencken speak for the literary radicals, Woodberry, Brownell, Babbitt, and Sherman for the reactionaries, and he, Eliot, and Ernest Boyd for the third, and as yet undefined, group.

The roots of Spingarn's theory in America must be sought in the philosophy of Santayana or in the aestheticism of Huneker and the "Bohemians," discussed elsewhere in this work, even though he denied kinship with any specific school. He differs from the Bohemians in denying their effort to validate aesthetic experience in biological science, and in so far allying himself with the humanists. But more truly he reverts to an earlier form of romantic aestheticism represented by Goethe and by Carlyle's essay on Goethe, both of which he approvingly quotes as his text: "The critic's first and foremost duty is to make plain to himself 'what the poet's aim really and truly was, how the task he had to do stood before his eye, and how far, with such materials as were afforded him, he has fulfilled it.'"

"This," says Spingarn, "has been the central problem, the guiding star, of all modern criticism"; but, he adds later, it has not been possible in America because we have had no critics sufficiently disciplined in aesthetics to achieve the exacting demands of close concentration upon the work of art itself. The disease of the age, materialism, has made critics "conceive of philosophy not as a self-creative and independent science, but as merely one, and a very subordinate one, among empirical sciences."

Spingarn's was the academic fault of spinning fine abstractions without engaging himself in the exacting task of doing what he advises. But he prepared the way for Eliot, Ransom, Tate, Blackmur, and a host of others, by objectifying the work of art for the analytical examination of the critic, by cutting away historical and circumstantial factors on the one hand and the critic's own emotional sensibilities on the other, and by stressing the intellectual and dispassionate sensibility to structure which Eliot in "The Perfect

Critic" (1920) defined as the essence of the critical function. But Spingarn's final position was one long step short of Eliot's. He developed no method of procedure. His break with the historical and judicial methods was complete, but he also denied the connection of art with life implicit in impressionism. He wrote despairingly in 1921:

> Critics are constantly carrying on a guerilla warfare of their own, and discovering anew the virtues of individuality, modernity, Puritanism, the romantic spirit or the spirit of the Middle West, the tradition of the pioneers and so on ad infinitum. This holds true of every school of American criticism, "conservative" or "radical"; for all of them a disconnected body of literary theories takes the place of a real philosophy of art.

Our criticism, he concluded, needs education in aesthetic thinking and a wider scholarship, "for taste is after all both the point of departure and the goal."

Spingarn's attempt to isolate literature from the moral and the natural experience of both its creator and its critic succeeded in avoiding, if not in solving, the problems of both the radicals and the conservatives, because for him, and in his judgment for literature, problems of conduct and of value, as well as problems of cause and effect, have no relevance to the analysis and judgment of expression. The work of art makes its own rules and must be judged by them alone. But Spingarn's Crocean formula, as Eliot was to discover, was a needed emphasis on a part rather than a definition of the whole of the critical function. Neither the waste land nor the cathedral could be so readily avoided. The battle of the books had been fought to a conclusion in which much had been revealed, nothing concluded. Before 1930 the renaissance in American criticism thus did little more than keep step with the forces at work in poetry, fiction, and drama which were giving new directions to American literature. The two great tasks of redefining the American cultural tradition and of developing a systematic literary criticism had scarcely begun.

69. EDWIN ARLINGTON ROBINSON

THE quiet, straightforward speech in Edwin Arlington Robinson's keynote book, *The Children of the Night* (1897), was first heard amid a babel of other poetic tongues both old and new. Here were the simple words of a great poet, inaudible among bold voices: those of the humanitarian singers, like Edwin Markham in *The Man with the Hoe, and Other Poems* (1899); those of the new naturalists in poetry, like Stephen Crane in *War Is Kind* (1899); or those of the intellectual nationalists in verse, like William Vaughn Moody in "An Ode in Time of Hesitation" (1900). Insistent, too, reverberated the many special accents, the songs of the Western farms (Hamlin Garland and James Whitcomb Riley); songs born of learning in the seventeenth century (Louise Imogen Guiney and Lizette Reese); and, still influential, the Victorian melodies of Gilder, Aldrich, and Stedman, all of whom published collections of their poetry not long after the stillborn *Children of the Night*.

That Robinson approved or disapproved of these "movements," no evidence exists. Nor had he convictions concerning the other cults whose creeds until his death beat against his independent mind, sometimes repudiating his techniques and themes, sometimes claiming both as their very own. He remained quiet, he went his lonely way. Denounce him the innovators could, for he never sloughed off the time-honored forms of the past; claim him they could, for though indifferent to group ideas he had discovered for himself principles dear to imagist or expressionist. To a few individuals he was in debt (as to a few great writers of the past): to Ridgely Torrence, dramatist and poet; perhaps to Richard Hovey, for his American pioneering in Arthurian legend; and to Moody for confirming in him his passion for poetic drama. But in his aloof dedication to poetry he was singularly unaffected by the tides of contemporary criticism discussed in the last chapter. Unlike Babbitt and most of the other controversialists who wrote about criticism without much practicing it, or about literature as an illustration of theory, he was solely interested in the creation of literature itself as an expression of his own soul.

Among the poets whose influence he seems to have felt, William Vaughn

Moody, many-sided, was indeed more than a poetizer of national problems. Born in the same year as Robinson (1869) he had, by 1900, won through his timely ode and by "Gloucester Moors" a public denied his obscure friend. Robinson revered him for his learning, his fine Puritan intelligence, and characteristically for his actual success. Acclaimed as a practical dramatist in *The Great Divide* (1906) and in *The Faith Healer* (1909), Moody still explored a dark transcendental world (Robinson called it "The Valley of the Shadow") in his incomplete metaphysical trilogy of poetic plays (*The Masque of Judgment,* 1900; *The Fire-Bringer,* 1904; *The Death of Eve,* 1912).

It may be said that two kinds of poets bordered the narrow path of Robinson and interested him, adversely and favorably: the "little sonnet men," as he called the faddist craftsmen of his day; and poets like himself under the spell of the enlightenment in reverse, of the melancholy of man's doom. That Robinson owed much to Crane or Moody or to later poets of despair or nihilism is doubtful. By 1897 he had acquired a naturalistic outlook then in its infancy in America, and to this by temperament and experience he remained in bondage all his life. Thus his apparent kinship with movements suggests not plan but accident. Robinson's poetic traits arose from the basic texture of his mind. *The Children of the Night* merely demanded bare and simple words; and no "renaissance" of 1915 can claim his poetry written between the years 1890 and 1896. For the same reasons his adherence to the sonnet, the dramatic monologue, or the narrative was a personal and inevitable choice suited to his psychological purposes. The "new poetry" eventually aided him by enlarging his circle of readers, but at heart he was an adroit adapter of the traditional. "Robinson," says Robert Frost, looking back in the year of his friend's death, "stayed content with the old way to be new."

Shunning, then, the tumult of the critics and the more worldly poets, Robinson wound his solitary horn before his dark tower, an intellectual Childe Roland in our twentieth century literature. Somber, introspective, he reminds us in temperament of his Puritan ancestress Anne Bradstreet and of other New England searchers in the ways of God. Hawthorne, to whose *Scarlet Letter* he was devoted, he resembled not only in his scrutiny of the delicate moral impulses and in his sensitivity to spiritual tragedy, but even in the reticence of his art. Akin to Emerson and Emily Dickinson in their individualism, their sensitivity to fact and thrift of expression, he was at the same time a landmark of the passing of the transcendental faith. Emerson's disregard of evil became in Emily Dickinson a qualified acknowledgment of its power ("the underside of God's divinity"), and now in Robinson a controlled despair at its mastery of life. Emerson's "dawn" faded to Emily Dickinson's light of winter afternoons to Robinson's faint gleam against a blackening sky. He is closer to these than to Crabbe and Browning, of whom he reminds us in his alternate bareness and explicitness, but all such debts, American and European, Robinson seems to cancel in the singular intensity of his art and inner life, which from his earliest to his last days were consecrated to poetry.

A man without a skin, as he admitted, he suffered acutely under poverty, obscurity, and misunderstanding. Finding no positive answer for himself, he still explored the enigmas in other lives, recording these in his verse stencils of souls warped by spiritual conflicts. Endowed with such a temperament, he led during his boyhood at Gardiner, Maine (he was born at Head Tide), and during his two years at Harvard (1891–1893) a life troubled by sensitivity to spiritual unknowns and also by the criteria of worldly success, to which he could never conform. Illness in his family, economic instability, and the tragedies of "Tilbury Town's" unfortunates, unveiled more bitterly through his own capacity for pain than to these individuals themselves, confirmed him in his misgivings concerning himself and human life. From the time when he sat on the kitchen floor of the Maine farmhouse reciting verse to his mother, his course was set. He would write. His compensations were his discovery of the release in creating poetry; the friendships of understanding spirits in Gardiner and Cambridge; and his dream, not without emulation as he watched Moody, that he would be, that he *was,* a poet.

Robinson needed courage. His "darkening hill" lay steep before him. The severe musing of *The Children of the Night* on the "faith within the fear" or the stern elevation of *Captain Craig,* the tale of a New England ne'er-do-well, would hardly convert readers who preferred, he said,

> Songs without souls, that flicker for a day
> To vanish in the irrevocable night.

Acceptance was slow, even after the advocacy of Theodore Roosevelt, who secured for him a position in the New York Customhouse where he struggled unhappily for five years. To keep body and soul together he had already checked loads of stone in the subway. New York, with its infinite drama of human lives, was essential to his art. Amid these and later, happier experiences such as a stay in England and many sojourns in the MacDowell Colony, he patiently stuck to his craft until he outstripped "the little sonnet-men." His unity with himself was complete; life now meant the creation of poetry.

Although his two plays, *Van Zorn* (1914) and *The Porcupine* (1915), were unsuccessful in establishing a poetical theater, *The Town Down the River* (1910) and *The Man Against the Sky* (1916) consolidated his fame. He now struck out boldly in longer poems, complex, psychological narratives, expansions of his research into the paradoxes in human character, into the "small, satanic sort of kinks" which betray us all. Some of these poems, like the later narratives, explored the twisted minds of men and women in the trap of modern life; others—*Merlin, Lancelot,* and *Tristram*—while grappling with similar problems, vivified intellectually the Arthurian legends. The precise quality of Robinson's eminence was, at the time of his death in 1935, still controversial, but no one challenged the nobility of his contribution, in both form and content. He had fulfilled himself and had asked in ways unlike those of any other poet the old unanswerable questions.

Attempts to connect Robinson, as a symbolist, with war, with the problems of society, or with the decay of our civilization have been generally unsuccessful, except in his very last poems. He absorbed much of our science and economics as well as our lore concerning the subconscious mind; yet his concern was with the individual in his relations to one or two other individuals, or, in one human personality, with the baffling connection with an inscrutable darkness in which, hardly visible, glimmered a crystal of light, a refraction of "The Word." All the dynamic forces of society's evolution are in his poetry, but they are concentrated in particular moral problems. His assimilative power was enormous; he was the thoughtful modern man, excessively sensitized, contemplating through the screen of a constitutional melancholy the twentieth century world.

Robinson offered no synthesis, no philosophy, but to formulate his teasing, repetitious questions he employed a genius which was more dramatic than lyrical or narrative. The reader may generalize, if he wishes, on his opinions concerning death, fate, time, "success in failure," love, marriage, frustration, and these he may transmute for Robinson into terms of society; but the poet himself merely poses endless interrogations on special cases. Hence he was never humanitarian, never proletarian, never national; and he was Puritan, like the most distinguished poetical descendants of the Puritans such as Emily Dickinson and Emerson (whom he deeply admired), as he faced moral riddles with the conviction that of all themes these were the ones most worthy of the poet.

2

In *The Children of the Night* (1897) first appeared the type of poem destined to be associated with Robinson's genius: the laconic, dramatic exposition of an individual's life history. The seemingly successful Richard Cory, who "glittered when he walked," in despair put a bullet through his head; the miser, Aaron Stark, with "eyes like little dollars in the dark," laughs at those who pity his avarice; Cliff Klingenhagen tosses off the draught of wormwood and, in renunciation of life, is happy; and Reuben Bright the butcher, in his excess of anguish at the death of his wife, tears down his slaughterhouse. Such are the observations of a mind which, like his own Merlin's, "saw too much" into human suffering and frustration. These hard little poems are specimens of human experience in a world in which agony is real and happiness but a wish. To this particular form of expression Robinson turned repeatedly: in all, he made up a vast file of spiritual dossiers. These are novelettes, cryptic one-act dramas of single persons: they reveal Robinson's dual powers as novelist and dramatist, fused in intense concentration, reticence, and implication. They are microfilms, needing only the illumination of the reader's experience to be projected as reality.

Their subjects vary; often these men and women are the apostates of society. Annandale is a derelict killed in mercy by his physician friend; Miniver Cheevy longs for the romantic past but cannot act in the present. Sometimes the characters are of bygone days or are the famous underdogs of literature: Crabbe, Hood, Zola, or Verlaine. The index moments on which the poet seizes with such skill are manifold. On his deathbed we see the wreck of Annandale, but we follow Miniver Cheevy into later life—he "kept on drinking." Sometimes the sardonic point is communicated in quaint invocation in the ballad form, as in the haunting reiteration of love's futility in the dialogue between John Gorham and his mistress; sometimes the narrator participates in the victim's disillusionment: puzzled, he drinks with Cliff Klingenhagen. Occasionally the medium is autobiographical, as in the mother's fond description of her worthless son in "The Gift of God." Irony, contempt, pity, questioning kindle these sketches till we forget their prosaic language and the detachment of the poet's narration.

The implement for these subacid portraits is primarily the dramatic monologue, though their ancestry includes the sonnet, with which Robinson often experimented, the ballad, and the orthodox quatrain. In any case, the final product is triumphantly his own. The closely packed, subtle reflections of the disillusioned wife of "Eros Turannos" are an excellent illustration of his complex condensation. "Why," the poet once exclaimed in answer to the charge of obscurity, "can't they read one word after another?" It is not the words or the syntax which lack simplicity but the intimations stirring in the poet's mind, which he conveys so indirectly. Sentences are clipped; dialogue hangs in mid-air; precise explanation is wanting. The "slight kind of engine," with which the doctor ends Annandale's agony, is a hypodermic needle, but the reader is often less fortunate in his divination. Robinson puzzles not merely by ellipsis but by periphrasis. Yet in their avoidance of the explicit lies the power of these short poems. They rejoice in the strength which in moments of emotion is exhaled from silence and the unspoken word. In "The Mill," a comparatively lucid poem, the explanatory word is not set down.

The miller's wife waits long for her husband until she is "sick with a fear that had no form." His suicide and hers we deduce from "what was hanging from a beam" and

> Black water, smooth above the weir
> Like starry velvet in the night,
> Though ruffled once, would soon appear
> The same as ever to the sight.

The beauty of the first two lines of this quatrain should caution us against the notion that Robinson as a poet was insensitive to nature, to color, or to light. The latter word is everywhere in his poetry. Even the grayness of these character portraits is pierced by lambent metaphors such as the familiar one in "The Gift of God" when the doting mother dreams of her son,

> Half clouded with a crimson fall
> Of roses thrown on marble stairs.

Robinson was not insensitive to nature, though his conclusions concerning life receive little aid from her sustaining counsel; and his early work, like the later epics, is enriched by such imagery as

> Dark hills at evening in the west,
> Where sunset hovers like a sound
> Of golden horns that sang to rest
> Old bones of warriors under ground.

This facet of his art should, by way of balance, be kept in mind. The terse sentences in Mr. Flood's dilemma or Luke Havergal's tragedy would mean less without the "silver loneliness" of the moon or the "crimson leaves upon the wall."

Early in these vignettes of character, Robinson committed himself to psychological subjects and to a technique of implication. His mind, though not insensible to the "poetry of earth," was primarily analytical and, for the time being, curbed by an iron reticence. That for such a mind the brief dramatic monologue would be inadequate was certain. He was not to be at his best, even in the Arthurian poems, when more than two or three characters were together; this fact he himself may have learned from the vignettes or from the failure of his *Captain Craig* (1902), tied, in spite of revisions, to the actual character of Alfred Hyman Louis. Yet he had to talk more; he could still play with riddles but there must be more words, amplifications of his introspection. Thus the volume contained, besides the verbose title poem, the long, refreshingly clear narrative of "Isaac and Archibald" (suggestive of Robert Frost) and the sixteen-page "Book of Annandale." Eight years later, in *The Town Down the River,* he was to enlarge his gallery of inarticulate "bewildered children," but he had now embarked upon an exhaustive consideration of the tragic problems merely adumbrated in a "Richard Cory" or a "John Gorham." This was well; it was, in fact, inevitable. In 1916 appeared, side by side with brief character portraits, the two noble poetic studies of man in an indifferent universe: "Ben Jonson Entertains a Man from Stratford" and "The Man Against the Sky."

Had Robinson adhered to his original method, he might have compressed the tragedy of Captain Craig into the usual quatrains or into the fourteen lines of the sonnet form. We might instead have lived through one important day in the life of the old man, the distinguished beggar, whose hands touched sleeves so significantly in Tilbury Town's streets; we might have read between frugal lines of his wise insight into life, his humor, and his sweetness, all travestied at his funeral by the blaring band's Dead March from *Saul.* Thus Robinson could have spared us many a tedious page of moralizing and some of the Captain's complicated relations with his six half derisive, half compassionate benefactors; the poet's preference for fifty-six pages and three long parts of some six hundred blank verse lines each was not wholly wise.

For even the later recognition of Robinson's talent for involuted intellectual patterns has never made *Captain Craig* popular; Robinson reproduced too ·accurately the garrulity as well as the wisdom of old age. Although the Captain's "inner peace" mocks "every smug-faced failure on God's earth," his death is an escape not only for himself but for the reader of the poem. Something in the character of the aged parasite is unattractive; despite the length of the poem, the hypothesis of anterior years is less persuasively conveyed than in the shorter portraits. What we derive from *Captain Craig* is incidental: the hard, brilliant photograph of the shallow, beautiful woman; or Robinson's provocative meditations, almost a defense of his own low tone of mind, on the perils of the "demon of the sunlight." As for Melville, the "light" for Robinson is fraught with a menace more terrible than darkness.

3

Yet *Captain Craig* is illuminating as Robinson's first extended homily on the searcher for light in an uncomprehending world. Fourteen years later the poet's language is more trenchant and the framework for sustained meditation happier in "Ben Jonson Entertains a Man from Stratford." Again the vein is reminiscent. To a friend of "our man Shakespeare" the clever dramatist Jonson pours out his memories, half irritated, half adoring, of the incomparably wise one, Shakespeare. Certainly Jonson's shadowy audience of Shakespeare's Stratford neighbor is a restful contrast to the sextet who gabble with Captain Craig. Two skillfully drawn portraits emerge, of which that of Ben Jonson is the less vital. Is this other really the best existent imaginative re-creation in verse of the mind and personality of Shakespeare, who

> Fills Ilion, Rome, or any town you like
> Of olden time with timeless Englishmen?

Is it not rather a conventional picture, echoing too carefully the familiar facts exhumed by scholarship and repeating the worn traditions concerning Shakespeare the Man, at once convivial and inscrutable? What interests us more is Robinson's expansion of his principle: instead of a sonnet on Erasmus (1902) we may now expect the carefully wrought "Rembrandt to Rembrandt" (1921). In addition, we encounter in this concept of the dramatist, the characteristic Robinsonian twist, now more detailed, toward darkness: Shakespeare's nature is clouded by despair:

> "No, Ben," he mused; "it's Nothing. It's all Nothing.
> We come, we go; and when we're done, we're done."

In the title poem of this same volume, "The Man Against the Sky," the dramatic setting has shrunk to a mere outline: the sunset-flooded hill crowned momentarily with its lonely demigod. The flame-lit slope darkens, and the figure vanishes; then follow the measured speculations of the poet on the destiny of Man, of whom in this golden instant the heroic figure seemed the incarnation. Like "Dover Beach" or other nineteenth century poems, "The Man Against the Sky" exemplifies an age-old poetic method, the prolonged tranquil reflection born of the moment of emotion. Such old-fashioned technique was to engage Robinson often, especially in the Arthurian studies; and it promised a more downright, a more elaborate expression of his judgments concerning "the life we curse."

After the magnificent opening stanza of the poem we follow our relentless searcher for answers to the riddle:

> Where was he going, this man against the sky?

To mystical experience of God? To a comfortable prosperity? To disillusionment? To become a world conqueror? Each section of the poem considers possible answers to the question. "Where was he going . . . You know not, nor do I." And now, as the metaphor fades, Robinson submerges us in waves of argument against the existence of any meaning whatever. All is darkness-save in the fact that we do *not* destroy ourselves! We live on; we cling to life. By 1916 all the strands in his thought were firmly interwoven. In the next year he wrote *Merlin,* which offers in profusion his psychological insight, his dramatic crises, his indirectness and directness of speech, his receptivity to the somber aspects of nature, his understanding of the complex characters of women, his flexible use of the symbol, and his deserts of prosaic introspection.

Before we invade this continent, of which the poems already studied seem to be the preliminary peninsulas, let us examine more precisely Robinson's definition of man's dilemma. Varied in countless individuals, one theme recurs endlessly, the tragedy of each human being; namely, that not to think is to be less than Man, while to think is to be far less than God. To covet dollars like Aaron Stark, or self-indulgence like Miniver Cheevy, or vice like Annandale, means a return to the beast; yet to be wise like Captain Craig, or to love unselfishly like the mother in "The Gift of God," means suffering. Most of all, to perceive and to understand the depths of anguish in our fellows is the supreme unhappiness. Robinson's pages are filled with men like Shakespeare, Merlin, Lancelot, and Tristram, who "see too much."

Here is a universe in which elevation of spirit entails agony and frustration, vision becomes a heavy burden. Each life, if it moves upward, mounts a "darkening hill." Some, like Miniver Cheevy or Mr. Flood, are defeated and no longer challenge the ascent. Others who "climb," like Flammonde, still fail. Why, Robinson cannot say; the reasons are obscure. Only one cause seems common to us all: a crinkle of temperament, a tiny cancer in the texture of the mind which came with us into the world. Flammonde breathed upon all whom he met his subtle influence; yet he missed fulfillment:

> What small satanic sort of kink
> Was in his brain? What broken link
> Withheld him from the destinies
> That came so near to being his?

The tragedy of life is its mystery; the power of Flammonde is mysterious; the reasons causing worldly success and spiritual failure or their opposites are forever mysterious; selfless love ("The Gift of God") and trivial, sensual vanity ("Veteran Sirens") are mysterious. Most of all, man's ultimate destination remains inexplicable. Is it also meaningless? Is the "light" an illusion? Robinson does not say. Certainly the connotations of his sense of mystery are not the wonder and joy found in other poets; he is neither optimist nor meliorist. Yet he never accepts utter Night as certitude, and to tag him pessimist is also inexact. Despite his talk of "nothing" and "nothingness," he is not convinced that, "after all that we have lived and thought," the sequel is a blank. His hope, if hope it may be called, is but a tiny flower in a dark forest, but this hope subdues his despair to mere doubt.

In this inscrutable world, in which no answer may be had, Robinson found at last his role, like that of his noblest characters, the role of Questioner. However fitful the light, he would essay to find it. Though Eternity hides too vast an answer for our time-born words, still he would seek that answer. Nor was this basically a moral quest, though it involved moral values. Robinson's search sprang from a kind of high intellectual curiosity; it was a fulfillment of his own "satanic kink." It was the realization of his function as a poet, a function deserving a definition better than that in his rather self-conscious verses:

> Dear friends, reproach me not for what I do,
> Nor counsel me, nor pity me; nor say
> That I am wearing half my life away
> For bubble-work that only fools pursue.

Robinson's attitude has been called transcendental in that he pursues a meaning unrevealed by empirical laws and based on the doubtful deduction that so much darkness predicates an underlying significance. Complementary to the poetry, hear his colloquial phrases concerning the world:

> I have always told you it's a hell of a place.
> That's why it must mean something.

That most men do not take their own lives, that the will to live persists, that the man against the sunset-tinted hill appears sublime, that a Shakespeare creates his timeless heroes, hint, though faintly, that we should cherish the "faith within the fear" that somehow "The Word" *may* exist.

4

This last idea, the true pivot of Robinson's poetry, animates his Arthurian poems, in which all his enigmas reappear in musings as calm and protracted as a summer day in immortal Camelot. Can the wise man, like this Merlin who shaves off his beard to be young again with Vivian, flee from the life of the intellect into that of the senses? Is the struggle of Lancelot between earthly passion for Guinevere and his impulse toward the Light a microcosm of the story of mankind? Is there a meaning in the love of this modern Tristram and Isolt, who are the creatures of no imperious potion on the bark from Tintagel, but who honestly realize a love transcending life and death? Nor is love the only problem analyzed; human qualities of character examined in the short poems, such as loyalty, hypocrisy, hatred, or cruelty, he now develops in a grand complexity. The "small satanic sort of kink" becomes in each of these human figures a moral labyrinth, and each problem is posed against a background of "Time" and against the insoluble mystery of the universe.

Since from his earliest days Robinson had been less interested in outward circumstances than in inward flaws impairing happiness, it was natural that, among the passions, the love of man and woman should win a central place in his poetry. In his three interpretations of Arthurian legends he invested this theme of love with a grace and majesty which rendered his trilogy more than comparable with other modern versions of these deathless tales. Here in the ease of his conversational blank verse we feel his irony, his pity, and— most surprising—the intensity of his emotion, in for example, his depiction of the sensuous black-and-red Vivian or the white-and-gold Guinevere. The *Tristram* (1927) in particular makes us view with critical eyes the analogous achievements of Tennyson, Arnold, Swinburne, and Hardy. Perhaps the ancient stories will offer new meanings to each succeeding century; perhaps our admiration is enhanced by our intimacy with the modern problems confronting these three pairs of lovers; at any rate the lovers are ourselves, the bewilderments are our own. For the unity of these poems resides not in Camelot, but in the poet's theme, his disillusioned study of the dilemmas of romantic love.

In these acres of blank verse are dusty corners, especially in *Merlin*. For our psychiatrist's thoroughness we pay heavily, his clinics are prolonged. *Merlin* is a tedious poem. With this story of the love of Merlin and Vivian, Matthew Arnold's Iseult of the Snow-White Hand beguiled her children; its moral—that even the wisest are deceived by passion—is not quite worthy of our subtle poet. Even if Merlin's meetings with the green-clad, amorous Vivian in her exquisite garden haunt the memory, the episodes of passion and satiety hardly justify Robinson's intellectualized elaboration. Only in the inner struggle of Merlin between his life of the senses and his consecration to wisdom is the poet entirely at ease. Presumably he already had in mind the higher levels in his problem of love; certainly *Merlin* takes on new meaning in its relation to *Lancelot* and *Tristram*. The three form one poem of which *Merlin* is the prelude.

Unlike Merlin, at best a shadowy figure, Lancelot is alive, a modern man, fevered, introspective, bewildered, doubtful of his way. At the end darkness covers Merlin, but Lancelot remains the searcher, and like his creator never renounces his quest for "the Light." The poem's analysis is mitigated, and its vigorous action reminds us of Robinson's petulant remark that he was "a disappointed dramatist." Readers who flag under his sustained introversion may find relief in the brutal episode of Lancelot's rescue of Guinevere from the pyre, an incident recalling Malory's primitive adventures. In the rage of Gawaine, in the plottings of Modred, in the battle scenes, in the anguish of Arthur, in the quarrels of the lovers, is good, if uneven, story telling. What dignifies the poem is the character of Lancelot, harassed by high love, loyalty, despair, and ceaseless questioning. Through him we hear again the authentic voice of the poet, as in *The Children of the Night* or *The Man Against the Sky*. In *Lancelot* recurs a moving exposition of "the faith within the fear":

> He rode on into the dark, under the stars,
> And there were no more faces. There was nothing.
> But always in the darkness he rode on,
> Alone; and in the darkness came the Light.

Tristram, also, is in simplest terms another study of two persons in love. Again we are engulfed in a vortex of lovers' thoughts and feelings, again the framework of the Arthurian court is nobly appropriate, and again we live amid profound darkness and faint light. Yet *Tristram* is different; Robinson (and better critics than the poet) regarded it as his masterpiece. Written with "precipitancy," it pulses with an energy wanting in *Merlin* and with an unfaltering ecstasy denied *Lancelot*. The self-abandonment of the poet to passion contrasts strongly with the silver grayness of his early work. All is feeling,

> Till terror born of passion became passion
> Reborn of terror while his lips and hers
> Put speech out like a flame put out by fire.
> The music poured unheard, Brangwaine had vanished
> And there were these two in the world alone,
> Under the cloudy light of a cold moon
> That glimmered now as cold on Brittany
> As on Cornwall.

Yet the essence of *Tristram* lies rather in the adjacent lines:

> Time was aware of them,
> And would beat soon upon his empty bell
> Release from such a fettered ecstasy
> As fate would not endure.

Robinson is not so much stressing experience itself, as if echoing Browning, as the relation of such "experience" to "Time," a word forever present in his poetry, but repeated relentlessly in *Tristram*. Can complete and intense spiritual experience defeat "Time"? Though no mystic, Robinson wonders whether such triumphant, elevated human experience as that of Tristram and Isolt links itself with the eternal. Is this the "Light"? He does not finally say.

5

During the decade (1917–1927) which produced the Arthurian trilogy Robinson issued half a dozen other books, among them *The Three Taverns* (1920); *Avon's Harvest* (1921), a penetrative study of fear and hatred; *Roman Bartholow* (1923), an analysis of a disturbed soul; *The Man Who Died Twice* (1924), the story of the waste of an artist's powers; and *Dionysus in Doubt* (1925), an examination of the relations of a materialistic society to the poet's office. Seven other poems, besides new collected editions of his works, appeared before his final, arresting *King Jasper* (1935), printed in the year of his death. In none of these volumes, nearly a score since *Merlin*, is evidence of a decline, though many of the long narratives, such as *Cavender's House* (1929) or *Nicodemus* (1932) hardly came to life. Over them rests the haze of oft repeated questions. King Jasper cries to himself (or, perhaps to Robinson):

> You were afraid of time, and you still fear it.
> Is it worth fearing, when so little is left?

In this later work such difference as exists is twofold, a deeper consciousness (as in *Dionysus in Doubt*) of social issues, and an experimentation with symbolism. Both of these variations should be studied in *King Jasper,* a poem built upon several levels of allegory. Not only do the disillusioned king and queen face the familiar Robinsonian problems of "success" and "time," but Hebron, standing for "Labor" as "Zoe" represents "Life," reflects the poet's attempt to rise above the personal into the philosophic contemplation of his enigmas.

What do we experience as we leaf again Robinson's fourteen hundred pages of poetry? Not sadness for all that he failed to see clearly, such as nature alive with meaning or men and women happy, but a stern invigoration from his uncompromising loyalty to his own "satanic kink." So he saw life: much darkness and a little light. Man is betrayed less by circumstances than by his own character. He is, like Robinson's character Clavering, one

> who for scant wages played
> And faintly, a flawed instrument.

So Robinson saw art: the communication of thought concerning the mysterious mind, in form austere, without the traditional poetic vocabulary.

From these concepts of life and art, though their possession caused him personal distress, he never deviated. His outlook, his unique "tone," his interests, his modes of expression were, from his boyhood, innate, predestinate; in no American poet more so, save perhaps Poe. He tried few experiments, yielded to no criticisms, followed no will-o'-the-wisps, remained tenacious of one aim. "I can't," he once said, "do anything but write poetry," and he was really our first professional poet. He might have added that he could write only poetry of one kind, for it is probable that the verse which he threw away when his schoolboy friends did not understand it was akin in quality to that of his last poem, *King Jasper*. From his simple honesty we have inherited a complete brief of his case against life. Knowing him through the worst, stated without mercy, we may trust the light which he still discovered in the predicament of man.

So we may see Robinson: the solitary poet who absorbed into his thought and art the best of the old in American poetry and became the first of his generation to understand, however darkly, the new. With the death of Moody in 1910, his voice alone was heard; five years later it was but one in a chorus. And not he, but rather his younger contemporary Robert Frost, who had perforce been silent all these years, seemed destined to compose the chorale of the new age.

70. THE "NEW" POETRY

As it turned out, 1912 was the *annus mirabilis* of American poetry. In the first place an enterprising publisher, Mitchell Kennerley, did an unusual thing. Genuinely interested in poetry, he issued late in 1912 *The Lyric Year,* an anthology of one hundred poems by one hundred poets, which the editor described as a kind of "Annual Exhibition or Salon of American Poetry." The three prizes offered in this poetry show totaled $1,000. In selecting his hundred best the editor had examined ten thousand poems by nearly two thousand writers. That so many versifiers existed whose work was worth considering proved that there was a public for poetry even among its makers.

As the editor read, he was sure he could perceive the Time Spirit at work among all these poets and poetasters. Its effect he detected in a more masculine quality than had been evident hitherto, a trend due to the ascendancy of the virile art of Norseman, Slav, and Anglo-Saxon over the decaying classical heritage. Twentieth century poetry was destined to be democratic, scientific, humane. It already showed the liberating touch of Whitman, "sweet with robust optimism." It reflected the exhilarating trend that was sweeping over Continental music, painting, and poetry.

Reading through *The Lyric Year* now, one notes that editor and publisher had not found more than a score of poets whose verse completely measured up to these new requirements. They had been compelled to depend in the main on the elder singers whose brief lyrics, usually on nature, love, and the goodness of life, were familiar to the devoted readers of the *Atlantic* and the *Century.* In the early 1900's every editor kept a handy drawerful of two- to ten-stanza poems of this kind. He used them to fill out a short page and to raise the tone of his magazine.

Eighty of the hundred poets who found a place in the anthology were "magazine poets." Typical of them was the Canadian-born Bliss Carman who, with Richard Hovey, had broken out of the dream world of the Idealist poets into a Bohemianism of the open road. Their *Songs from Vagabondia* (1894) had created a vogue. Among other contributors of the older school, Madison Cawein, Kentucky poet, still invited readers out of doors. Percy

MacKaye was still addicted to the ode, and Josephine Peabody could not forget Swinburne. Edwin Markham, whose anthology piece, "The Man with the Hoe" was a *lapsus naturae,* continued to write in the tradition of Tennyson and the "cosmic" poets. Clinton Scollard, more valiantly than any other contributor, carried on for the Idealists. In spite of its seeming serenity, the poetry of this elder generation of poets shows that they could maintain this mood only by ignoring the life around them. When they attempted to deal with it, their method was to knit up images borrowed from classical mythology into a poetical robe to drape over the sordidness of modern America. They felt no need for inventing forms which would adequately express the rhythms of the age of ragtime and the horseless carriage.

Some twenty of the contributors to *The Lyric Year* did give evidence of the working of the new Time Spirit which the editor asserted was a characteristic of the whole volume. The cleavage between these poets and their elders was noticeable enough to be commented upon by the reviewers of the anthology. Among these twenty were several whose names would be identified with the "new" poetry: Nicholas Vachel Lindsay, Sara Teasdale, Witter Bynner, Arthur Davison Ficke, William Rose Benét. The poem which most completely broke with the older order, "Renascence," was the work of a Vassar undergraduate, Edna St. Vincent Millay.

Those who recognized new cadences and themes in *The Lyric Year* had already been encouraged by the literary radicalism of a recently founded little magazine, edited in Chicago, which bore the plain title *Poetry: A Magazine of Verse.* This venture was destined to have a remarkable future. *Poetry* survives today, and it has "discovered" more good poets than any other magazine published in English.

The driving force of the enterprise came from Harriet Monroe, shy but determined, widely traveled, well read, and, as an entrepreneur, something of a genius. She had early decided to be a poet, and she worked hard at being one. When she learned that all the arts save poetry were to be lavishly honored at the World's Columbian Exposition, she resolved that the exposition should have a laureate, and she proposed to wear the laurel herself. The directors yielded. On the day the still scaffolded buildings were dedicated, 125,000 witnesses heard an actress with a powerful voice and statuesque presence recite Miss Monroe's "Columbian Ode."

She never forgot this moment. She was determined that poetry in America should no longer be the Cinderella of the arts. Architects were necessary to our civilization. Painters had their one-man shows, and more prizes went to them each year than the quality of the prize-winning works deserved. Poets must be permitted to feel that they also performed a function in our national life.

The means to this end would be a magazine of poetry. Chicago prided itself on the fact that it was taking the leadership in the arts. Chicago businessmen should therefore extend their patronage to poetry. Using her social connections and her local fame, Miss Monroe went from office to office, begging and upbraiding, until she found a hundred patrons who would guarantee $50 a year over a five-year period for the support of her magazine.

The first issue was ready in October, 1912. Miss Monroe's inaugural statement, "The Motive of the Magazine," spoke of the shameful neglect of poetry, asserted that there was a public for it in America, and assured readers that quality alone was to be the test for admission to *Poetry*. She concluded with characteristic grandiloquence: "We hope to offer our subscribers a place of refuge, a green isle in the sea, where Beauty may plant her gardens, and Truth, austere revealer of joy and sorrow, of hidden delights and despairs, may follow her brave quest unafraid." Her program was not defined beyond the desire to do good in the cause, but it was not long before she found coadjutors who were eager to provide her with a policy—with several policies in fact.

Miss Monroe possessed the essential quality required of an editor of a magazine of this kind—a willingness to be educated by her contributors. Though she was certain that the older order in poetry was passing, she but vaguely understood in 1912 what might take its place. She thought Americans should write about contemporary life, even if that meant poems about the slums of Chicago. She believed the traditional forms were played out, and she wanted poets to try freer rhythms. But it was no time at all before Ezra Pound, a young American who had expatriated himself in England, informed her that the new poetry would be far more revolutionary than she imagined. As a result of her solicitation of contributions from younger poets whose ability she had noted, two poems of Pound's appeared in her first issue. He assured her that *Poetry* would be the only magazine in America to receive his verse. In the second issue he had moved in as "foreign correspondent." Thereafter he wrote about as much of the editorial comment in each number as Miss Monroe herself.

Pound with others from abroad saved the magazine from parochialism and uplift. He brought Yeats and the "Imagistes" of London into its pages. His knowledge of verse technique, of Provençal and early Italian poetry, and of the French moderns enlarged the scope of *Poetry* and tied it to the new international movement in literature. During its first five years, the magazine published or reviewed translations from Belgian, Japanese, Chinese, Armenian, Peruvian, Hawaiian, and American Indian verse. It made much of the Bengali poet Rabindranath Tagore, who was the literary sensation of the day. Pound, Ford Madox [Hueffer] Ford, and F. S. Flint kept its readers up to the minute with developments in Continental poetry.

The pages of the early numbers of *Poetry* crackle with controversy: Chicago against Boston; the traditionalists (e.g., W. S. Braithwaite, Conrad

Aiken, Max Eastman) against the experimentalists. Pound takes command in the battle for the rights of Imagistes. Amy Lowell, with assistance, carries the day for *vers libre*. Echoes of these battles rolled into the newspaper offices of the country, and it was not long before the issues fought out on the pages of *Poetry* were the subject of newspaper editorials and of indignant letters from conservative readers. Poetry was news.

But the best proof of the magazine's usefulness was its ability to recognize promise and its readiness to support certain older poets who needed wider recognition than they had known. In its first year it published work by Pound, Richard Aldington, W. B. Yeats, Hilda Doolittle, Vachel Lindsay, Amy Lowell, and William Carlos Williams. During the second, John Gould Fletcher, D. H. Lawrence, Robert Frost, and Carl Sandburg were added to the roster. In 1914–1915 Wallace Stevens, Edgar Lee Masters, T. S. Eliot, and Marianne Moore made appearances. Young poets whose work would set the tone of the poetry of the twenties and thirties were cradled in Miss Monroe's little magazine. In still another way *Poetry* anticipated the future. Its reviewers frequently foreshadowed the critical attitudes of the next generation. Joyce was spoken of in *Poetry* as a significant modern. Rilke, Emily Dickinson, Hopkins, Hardy as poet, were given their measures of recognition.

Though Miss Monroe was in sympathy with this internationalism and gave the rein to her transatlantic assistants, she saw to it that the American poets whose careers she was nurturing had a place above the salt—quite literally so on one occasion. The issue was neatly pointed up when Yeats was given a congratulatory dinner during his visit to Chicago in March, 1914. He praised the new American poetry in his speech, but he warned the poets, critics, and editors present that they were too far from Paris: "It is from Paris that nearly all the great influences in art and literature have come . . . In France is the great critical mind." In the June issue of *Poetry* Alice Corbin Henderson, assistant editor, answered Yeats, asserting that Vachel Lindsay, who had read his "The Congo" at the banquet, did not have to go to France for it or for "General William Booth Enters into Heaven." He did not even have to cross to the eastern side of the Alleghenies. The traditions of the past are as open to the poet of Springfield as to the poet of Paris; the "tradition of the present is yet to make." Miss Monroe and Mrs. Henderson were certain that the poets of the "Chicago school," Lindsay, Masters, and Sandburg, would be the makers of the new tradition.

2

Even the receptive readers of the fourth issue of *Poetry* (January, 1913) must have got something of a shock when they found themselves swept along with the Salvation Army band rhythms of Vachel Lindsay's "General William Booth Enters into Heaven," which they were told to sing to the tune of "The Blood of the Lamb" with indicated instruments—bass drum, banjo, flute, and tambourine. Here was the "new" poetry with a vengeance, ecstatic with the responding shouts of the crowds at the street corner.

Who was this poet of thirty-four who soon had a following greater than that of any other of the Chicago group, the protégé of whom Miss Monroe was most proud? He certainly had a future: did he have a past? Actually he had been writing poems since his college days in the late nineties at Hiram in Ohio; but no publisher had issued them, and he was still hoping to make his way as an artist. His poems had only been attached to his spidery line drawings to help explain their "hieroglyphic" significance.

Born in Springfield, Illinois, a Southern boy in a Republican city, he was still tied to the strings of his energetic mother. The daughter of a Campbellite minister, she was hungry for Beauty and God and full of a thousand schemes for the religious and cultural regeneration of Sangamon County and its city, Springfield, the capital of Illinois. The indiscipline which always marked Lindsay can be traced to his parents' indulgence of his whims. They did not know what to make of their son; but they were themselves in love with beauty, and skeptically but hopefully they let him go his way. At college he schematized his future. Feeding his imagination on Poe, Blake, Swinburne, and Ruskin, he planned to roam and observe the world for twenty years; to be the great singer of the Y.M.C.A. Army; to reconcile culture and manliness; to be by 1905 the biggest man in Chicago. Whatever he might do, he would do in the service of Christ. "Curb your imagination; simplify your aim," he wrote in one of his voluminous notebooks. He paid no attention to his own advice.

In 1901 he went up to Chicago to study at the Art Institute. With a cream puff for breakfast, a lemon and a Uneeda biscuit for lunch, he dreamed in his classes and never learned to draw a face or figure. But by 1905 he was in New York, still asking for encouragement, this time from Robert Henri. The master painter was so farsighted as to praise his poems. Lindsay was now offering a few to the magazines. In a time of dire poverty, for the editors would not have them, he tried peddling his picture-poems up and down Third Avenue. The shopkeepers, annoyed or amused, sometimes paid him the asking price of two cents. At last Lindsay had begun to preach his gospel of beauty to a few startled hearers. The moment was significant. With a pack of poems he was off, the next year, on a vagabonding trip through the South.

When he could find an audience he lectured on art or recited poems. Otherwise he "traded rhymes for bread," sleeping in the hay, on the floor before the fireplace, or under the stars. He seldom worked with his hands.

If people would not give him life in return for the beauty in his poems, then he would starve. He was in dead earnest when he wrote in his diary: "If I cannot beat the system I can die protesting."

The poems for which his startled hosts gave him—sometimes—peach cider and corn pone were not in the least like the Booth poem and others of its kind which subsequently brought him fame. His principal stock in trade was "The Tree of Laughing Bells, or the Wings of the Morning." It is worth looking at, for hundreds of his poems, all but a few dozen in fact, are vision-poems resembling it.

On the Wings of the Morning (made by an Indian Maiden, from pansy buds and many morning-glories), the poet escapes to Chaos-night to find the Tree of Laughing Bells which

> Grew from a bleeding seed
> Planted mid enchantment
> Played on a harp and reed:
> Darkness was the harp—
> Chaos-wind the reed.

As he nears the Chaos-shore the red bells on the great tree sing beneath his wings "like rivers sweet and steep." He returns to the Indian Maid, bringing two bells which quench all memory in his breast. He gives the bells to her; she gives back one to him. She takes off the Wings of the Morning, and that is the end.

The reader would like to know what it means, just as he would like to know what Lindsay's Moon-Poems meant to him, and "The Comet of Prophecy," "The Spider and the Ghost of the Fly," "The Spice-Tree," and a hundred other poems. Almost any object, person, or passage in a book could set Lindsay dreaming, but his dreams were merely phantasms, lacking depth and congruity. He detached symbols encountered in his desultory reading in Egyptian, Chinese, and Christian lore and set them adrift through the aether of his fancy. As a worshiper of Swedenborg he no doubt believed, since all material objects have their spiritual correspondences, that his readers needed no guide to his visions except the "hieroglyphic" he provided. This word he constantly employed in speaking of his verse and of his pictures. What it meant to him is impossible to say. In practicing Egyptian picture writing and speculating on the "American hieroglyphic" which he proposed to evolve, he was struggling with symbols of some sort. But he never understood that poets who invent private symbols or adapt traditional symbols for their particular purposes must make their readers feel that the symbols are related and carry congruent meaning from poem to poem. Behind the mask there must be an order of a kind. Poe's "misty mid region of Weir" or Blake's Jerusalem or Yeats' Byzantium accumulates meaning from the other symbols which surround it and are related to it. There is no system behind Lindsay's hieroglyphics. His vision-poems do not even stir the irrational excitement generated by surrealist poetry. Because of his asceticism and his refusal to be a responsible man, Lindsay's unconscious was always as shallow as that of a child. Unlike the imagination of the mature poet who has loved and suffered, no dark and mysterious deeps opened into it.

Yet in his years of wandering and vacillation Lindsay was preparing himself to become the poet of a significant part of American life. He had soon tramped over most of the country, covering the South in 1906, the Middle States in 1908, the West in 1912. Though he talked with hundreds of Americans of all kinds, he returned from his adventures while preaching the gospel of beauty with no sociological statistics, nor even with memories of individuals and of individual tragedies from which the vagabonding Sandburg made poems. The people he understood were, like himself, the vision-haunted ones, the followers of his own heroes. And those heroes, one notices, are all champions and martyrs and leaders who were able to intoxicate the plain people with the hope of an America transformed and spiritualized: Alexander Campbell, who founded the middle-American sect, the Disciples of Christ; Johnny Appleseed carrying in his pack tomorrow's orchards; Old Andrew Jackson; the "eagle that is forgotten," Altgeld, who freed the Chicago anarchists; Booth leading boldly with his big bass drum, kneeling a-weeping before Jesus' face; and Bryan, Bryan, Bryan, Bryan, whose voice made the earth rock like the ocean until

> The angels in the flags, peered out to see us pass.
> And the sidewalk was our chariot, and the flowers bloomed higher,
> And the street turned to silver and the grass turned to fire.

Lindsay's first published volume, *General William Booth Enters into Heaven and Other Poems* (1913), introduced to America the Lindsay of his apocalyptic verses. Audiences soon demanded to hear him read them, and he was off on transcontinental tours which for years would be his chief source of income. With eyes closed, head thrown back, left hand on hip, right hand raised in ecstasy, he chanted and whispered "The Congo" from so many platforms that he came to loathe the sound of it. Yet, for all his protestations that he was debasing himself in these exhibitions of the "Higher Vaudeville," he exulted in his evangelical sway over his audiences. To one of his professorial admirers he wrote in 1922: "We have practically every University now in the U.S. for the asking, and we need worry about them no more. What we want now is the *whole public."* The capture of one editorial brain in each town would mean that converts would come down the aisle in droves. What they were to be converted to, Lindsay could never say, though half his poems and such books of prose as *The Art of the Moving Picture* (1915) and *The Golden Book of Springfield* (1920) were written to point the way to his Utopia. Perhaps it was enough that his proselytes were on their way.

O nowhere, golden nowhere!
Sages and fools go on
To your chaotic ocean,
To your tremendous dawn.
Far in your fair dream-haven,
Is nothing or is all . . .
They press on, singing, sowing
Wild deeds without recall!

The twenty or so poems which Lindsay's audiences demanded to hear again and again, the poems conveying the "camp meeting racket and trance," are as exciting as when they were first declaimed. Within them is the tumult of the Salvation Army rally and the Negro revival. They are tense with the joy of crowds enraptured by football games, Chautauqua lectures, and sky-painting political orations.

Each of them rises with wave on wave of rhythm until the Pentecostal moment arrives. For this kind of poem Lindsay used, beginning with "General William Booth," a four-stress line with dominant paeons. Deeply moved by the story of Booth's life, as it was told in the death notices in 1912, Lindsay brooded on the old General's heroism while the poem formed itself in the rhythms of the Salvation Army hymn:

Have you been to Jesus for the cleansing power?
Are you washed in the blood of the Lamb?

Within this measure, which became a unique instrument in Lindsay's hands, he could catch the cakewalk strut and revival shouts of "The Congo" and the toots of the autos whizzing by on the "Santa Fé Trail." He could also use his four-stress line with dignity and solemnity. Its effect on his readers has been so compulsive that it still echoes unexpectedly in modern sophisticated poets.

One must agree with the critic who said of Lindsay, three years before his suicide in 1931: "No other writer will have done so little with so much ability." Beside this potent handful of twenty poems possessing the "village apocalypse quality," there is not much left. In "A Rhyme for All Zionists" and "I Heard Immanuel Singing" he transfigured the gospel hymn. In *The Candle in the Cabin* (1926) one discovers a few fine poems which manifest normal human emotion. They were inspired by Lindsay's honeymoon in the Rockies. He had married at the age of forty-six.

3

The second of the Chicago poets to appear with a volume which gave him a national name was Edgar Lee Masters, a lawyer by profession—by avocation a poet. Before his *Spoon River Anthology* was issued in 1915, he had published eleven little noticed volumes of verse and prose, the first as far back as 1898. A friend and, later, the biographer of Lindsay, Masters was as different in temperament as one can imagine. Lindsay's Springfield is not far from Masters' boyhood homes in Petersburg and Lewistown, the villages from which he compounded his fictional village of Spoon River. While Lindsay saw visions of heavenly censers swinging above the old Courthouse dome in Springfield, Masters was turning over in his mind the life stories of the drunkards, skinflints, secret saints and private lechers, the dreamers, atheists, and idealists he had known as a boy and young man growing up beside two rivers in central Illinois, the Sangamon and the Spoon.

Several impulses generated the writing of Masters' collection of epitaphs spoken in self-justification, from the grave, by those who lie on the Hill above Spoon River. As early as 1906 he had told his father that he intended some day to write a novel based on his conclusion that the city lawyer and the country lawyer, the city banker and the country banker, have the same natures, "and so on down through the list of tradespeople, preachers, sensualists, and all kinds of human beings." In 1909 his friend William Marion Reedy of St. Louis, editor of *Reedy's Mirror* and an early champion of Masters' verse, had pressed on him a copy of *The Greek Anthology*. Under the spell of this tenth century compilation of epigrams and epitaphs reflecting on love, life, and death, Masters found that his hand "unconsciously strayed" to "Hod Putt" and "Serepta the Scold" and other sketches which would later become epitaphs in his *Spoon River Anthology*. Meanwhile he had taken note of Sandburg's success in using a new free-verse form for his poems of people. A visit from his mother in May, 1914, supplied the final impulse. As they gossiped about Petersburg and Lewistown, he determined to make a book out of the stories they knew of "Spoon River" people, "characters interlocked by fate," misjudged souls who should be given a chance to be justly weighed.

Masters was never a poet to dawdle over his verse, and by the end of the month he was turning in his epitaphs to his friend Reedy, whose Henry

George weekly was hospitable to unconventional literature. Masters often had as many as ten poems in a single issue of the *Mirror*. When the *Spoon River Anthology* appeared in book form in April, 1915, the poems numbered two hundred and fourteen. In the second edition, the next year, thirty-two new poems were added. The new epitaphs correct the overloading of sensationalism in the first form of the chronicle. Most of these speakers have kept the faith; some of them welcome "freedom from the earth sphere" after a lifetime of battle to be strong and true.

Several planets conjoined to make the book in its completed form one of the most momentous in American literature. As his autobiography *Across Spoon River* shows, Masters was, in retrospect at least, repelled by the meanness and hypocrisy of village life in southern Illinois as he had known it. But he could not forget what he had seen. His training as a lawyer helped him to look sharply into the lives of these village folk he half remembered, half invented. The epitaph form which he used in disclosing their secrets permitted the dead man or woman to give the lie to words or symbols carved on the gravestone. His fortunate choice of the epitaph form also required him to be brief and pointed. His device of contrasting characters who have exploited or hated or guiltily loved each other sets up ironic partials to the fundamental tones of sudden death, suicide, and isolated spirituality. The villagers who escape, pursuing or pursued, to the great world beyond Spoon River widen the scope of the chronicle. Some of the heroic dead have slept on the Hill since pioneering days. They cannot comprehend their degenerate descendants, and their reveries add the perspective of time.

Because he was himself a member of the generation of Dreiser and of Anderson, Masters is heard speaking through such characters as Jefferson Howard—

> Foe of the church with its charnel dankness,
> Friend of the human touch of the tavern.

He was most in sympathy with his libertarians in love, his freethinkers, and the idealists whom the money-perverted villains have defeated. Most successful as poems are the epitaphs spoken by craftsmen like Griffy the Cooper or Sexsmith the Dentist, each of whom reveals his important secret through the metaphor which encloses his life.

Thus it was that St. Louis scored on Chicago—"the one big hole in our record," as the editors of *Poetry* dolefully admitted. But Masters was soon an enthusiastic member of the "Little Room" which brought together Hamlin Garland, H. B. Fuller, the littérateurs at the University of Chicago, and the contributors to *Poetry*. After his astonishing popular success with his Spoon

River epitaphs Masters poured out verse, biography, novels, autobiography at the rate of more than one book a year; but he never again approached his achievement of 1915.

The stir caused by the *Spoon River Anthology* is in part explained by its timeliness. Americans had been made to see by the muckraking journalists and the novelists who labored beside them that Megalopolis had fouled and corrupted the part of America over which it sprawled. Writers like Sherwood Anderson and Sinclair Lewis were now ready to report that the infection had spread to the village where, so their countrymen wanted to believe, the democratic virtues still lingered. Masters' Spoon River was the first village to have its shroud of decency violently removed. Anderson's Winesburg and Lewis' Gopher Prairie were not spared for long.

4

Of the many poets whose careers *Poetry* helped to shape, none went so far on his own road as Carl Sandburg. He believed always that the best hope of the people is to be found in the men with "free imaginations, bringing changes into a world resenting change." Such a man he was himself, his ear laid to the heart of America. In his six volumes of poetry and in the six volumes of his great life of Lincoln (*The Prairie Years,* 1926; *The War Years,* 1939) he was a reporter of the dreams of the people, stronger than death; a champion of man the shaper and maker, man the answerer. Not even Whitman, with whom he is habitually compared, knew America as he knew it.

Whitman knew America, in part at first hand, in part intuitively, projecting what he experienced of it, through his imagination, into the vast spaces he had not crossed. Sandburg knew it along his senses. One is reminded as one reads his poems, from which pour all the occupations, classes, regions, types, races of America, of Lincoln shaking hands with the crowd which flowed ceaselessly through the White House, learning from each face some new thing about the people, and of how Lincoln believed, as Sandburg believed, that the collective wisdom of the people will see us through.

The struggle upward of his Swedish immigrant father taught the boy how death and despair are stood off by the foreign-born and poor in America. Galesburg, Illinois, a small prairie city filled with memories of Lincoln, was the right growing-up place for the kind of reporter and poet Sandburg was to be. He moved on from one job to another, driving a milk wagon, helping in a barber shop, a one-horse lunch counter, along the railroad, in the wheat fields. He liked to rove, listening to men talk, learning the songs the people sing. He paused to pick up a little education at Lombard College in his home town. By this time he had also been a soldier, briefly, in the Spanish-American War. From Puerto Rico he sent back to the Galesburg *Evening Mail* his first newspaper stories. He saw the inside of politics as an organizer for the Social Democratic Party. In 1913 he was in Chicago, making his way in journalism. By 1919 he had arrived as a feature writer for the *Daily News*.

His first poems were written, reporter-fashion, on rough copy paper and carried around in his pocket to be worked on when he could find a spare moment. Poetry, as he defined it in a series of thirty-eight definitions prefaced to *Good Morning, America* (1928), is "the report of a nuance between two moments, when people say 'Listen!' and 'Did you see it?' 'Did you hear it?' 'What was it?' "

His first volume, *Chicago Poems* (1916), hit genteel readers the way the butcher's maul hits the steer. Chicagoans were proud of their city's new poetical notoriety, but they did not at all like the opening lines of Sandburg's title-poem, "Chicago":

> Hog Butcher for the World,
> Tool Maker, Stacker of Wheat,
> Player with Railroads and the Nation's Freight Handler;
> Stormy, husky, brawling,
> City of the Big Shoulders.

What they had got was a completely American book and a new voice. The critics would see that he had been listening to the arguments in *Poetry* over Imagism; but there was not a poetical cliché in his book, and the style was his own.

Nor would his style change in subsequent books. There are no "periods" in Sandburg's career as a poet. His free verse is not far from prose. When one feels definite rhythmical recurrences in his lines, they are found to be of three or of four stresses, seldom longer. When they are longer, the rhythms tend to break down into prose, and Sandburg prints them as a cluster of images in a short, indented prose paragraph. His measure is seldom continuously iambic. To an ear trained to the predominant three-time of English poetry, the characteristic four-time movement gives his poems a slow pace. When Sandburg read his poetry aloud, unexpected rhythmical nuances emerged, a fact which proves that he had not constructed a form which communicates all he wished to say. Because his poems lack organic or traditional rhythmical form, the longer ones in particular do not linger in the memory. Yet for thousands of Americans the "new" poetry soon meant Sandburg. Even school children in the twenties possessed "Village in Late Summer," "Cool Tombs," "The Hangman at Home," "The Lawyers Know

Too Much." In such brief and remarkable poems the form adequately carries the vision; and the anger, tenderness, and irony.

The next three books—*Cornhuskers* (1918), *Smoke and Steel* (1920), and *Slabs of the Sunburnt West* (1922)—show no marked development. They revealed more and more of the life of the plain people, and, with hindsight, the critic can see that Sandburg was relying increasingly on the wisdom of the people, their metaphors and proverbs, for his materials. With *Good Morning, America* (1928) there comes a change. Significantly, fewer of these poems are about persons than about places. There is an undertone of brooding and pessimism, an evident indecisiveness. Symbols of mist, ashes, fog abound. Like the Methusaleh of one of these poems, Sandburg, the looker-on (even as we all are lookers-on), had seen too many "who died hungry and crying for their babies, many who died hungry and no babies at all to cry for." Having experienced so much of America, he seemed incapable of finding hope in what he had seen.

If Sandburg was full of doubt in 1928, when the rest of America was off on a wild joy-ride of financial speculation, he spoke in the midst of the depression years of his faith in the people. This testament, *The People, Yes* (1936), is a strange and powerful book which defies classification.

The poet hears someone say, "The people is a myth, an abstraction." He answers, "What myth would you put in place of the people?" The people will eat crow, but they don't hanker after it. They will suffer from the big owners, the lawyers, panderers, and cheaters who trade on their hopes.

> They will be tricked and sold and again sold
> And go back to the nourishing earth for rootholds.

But those who betray them,

> The tycoons, big shots and dictators,
> Flicker in the mirrors a few moments
> And fade through the glass of death
> For discussion in an autocracy of worms.

The people, only, are the builders. There are heroes among them, whose wise words become, as Lincoln's did, their folksay. By this wisdom they live—wary, resilient, discounting hope yet never losing it. Their dream of equity will win.

The People, Yes is one of the great American books. But, as so often happened in the history of our literature, its new matter required a new form, and the form is hard to name. Some of the one hundred and seven sections of the book are poems in the usual Sandburg manner, on such themes as the death of those who die for the people, or the common man as builder, wrecker, and builder again. Some sections merely assemble the collective wisdom of the people, on property, war, justice, and the law. One section puts together the best words of Lincoln, and it reads, as Sandburg knew it would, like the sections in which the people speak. Whatever may be the name you put to it, a foreigner will find more of America in *The People, Yes* than in any other book we can give him. But he will have to spell it out slowly.

5

From 1908 to 1912 a diverse company of English and American poets gathered in London were working out together a new verse-style and an aesthetic to justify it. Representing England were Richard Aldington (who years later became an American citizen) and F. S. Flint, master of ten languages and especially learned in French poetry. Among the Americans was the mercurial Ezra Pound who had fled from academic philology at home. Hilda Doolittle, daughter of an American astronomer and a graduate of Bryn Mawr, brought to the discussions of their company more than an amateur's knowledge of Greek verse. It was this group of writers, soon to be contributors to *Poetry,* who saved Miss Monroe's Chicago magazine from provincialism by bringing into it the current of new ideas and new work generated by the revolution in the arts created by Debussy and Stravinski, Chekhov, the Post-Impressionists, the performances of the Russian Ballet, and the philosophy of Bergson.

The dynamic force at the center of this group of London poets was T. E. Hulme, a young philosopher whose *Speculations,* as they were called when finally collected in 1924, were gospel to his friends. (A further compilation, *Notes on Language and Style,* appeared in 1929). Hulme was an antiromantic. Romanticism he considered as the final decadent stage of the humanism which had dominated Western thought for three centuries and had produced the vicious concepts of progress and human perfectibility. He reacted violently against the Victorian poetry which had contrived to fit the dogmas of evolution and the new faith in English imperialism into the master-idea of a gradual perfectionism stretching out to infinity.

To the cosmic poetry of the nineteenth century Hulme was determined to oppose a new style. "The particular verse we are going to get," he wrote, "will be cheerful, dry, and sophisticated." There must be no words which fail to contribute to the desired impression. Asking that poets consider their work as art and not vaticination, he said, "Poetry is no more nor less than a mosaic of words, so great exactness is required for each one." Style is simply a means for subduing the reader; hence it is the poet's business to subdue him with economic effectiveness.

Hulme's ideas owe something to Rémy de Gourmont's *Problème du Style,* but the movement he initiated was not to be narrowly imitative. Having begun to meet as a group in March, 1909, he and his friends set themselves the task of working out, in a series of exercises, a style which would present impressions precisely. Wherever they found a poetic style or form which confirmed their purpose, as in the severe and brief Japanese *tanka* (thirty-one syllables in five lines) and *hokku* (seventeen syllables in three lines), they advertised their discoveries. But their main interest, before Pound took over, was creation, not propaganda. Even Hulme himself produced five poems as copybook models. These Pound, half in jest and half in earnest, printed as a supplement to his own *Ripostes* (1915) as "The Complete Poetical Works of T. E. Hulme." The "Autumn" which heads these five pages, is said to be the first Imagist poem.

The first article in the Imagist creed asserted the dogma of the "pure" image. None of the impressions caught in the image should be allowed to escape through weak adjectives and needless connectives. All extraneous emotion or intellectual comment should be purged. To their detractors who said that Imagism was nothing new, that all poets are imagists by the nature of their medium, Hulme's followers replied, sensibly enough, that imagism had never been fully exploited as a technique.

The dogma of the "pure image" proved to be only a mild heresy. What alarmed the traditionalists and provoked a critical war was the abandonment by the Imagists of the song forms used by English poets since the Middle Ages. The issue was joined: Was free verse, the new medium of the Imagists, verse at all? Was it not merely prose cut up into varying line-lengths?

The Imagists demanded that poets should be freed from the requirement of subduing a unique impression to a traditional metrical pattern associated through long use with particular emotional states and attitudes. To do so was to impose an alien form on an experience which had already emerged in a form of its own. In the polemical writing of the Imagists the phrase "organic rhythm" began to appear. Although the new poets were only vaguely aware of the fact, they were working in a critical tradition which begins with certain poetic dicta of Coleridge and numbers among its adherents Emerson and Whitman.

But even if one granted that the free-verse poem written by an Imagist had found its appropriate form, how could one be certain that it was still poetry and not prose? F. S. Flint tried to lift his associates from the horns of this dilemma. He admitted that there is no way to draw a fast line between free verse and prose since both are rhythmical. The difference is noticeable at the extremes. The cadences which flow under impassioned utterance are of one sort and may be poetry; those which follow the pattern of the syllogism and are useful in setting forth facts or arguments, by general assent are prose.

Flint's argument gave the Imagists a new and precious technical term which they could use with effect—"unrhymed cadence." Their line of defense was now that the ear of the skilled writer of free verse instructs him how to vary the length and rhythm of his lines with precision to create cadences suited to his theme and total image. They talked of "rhythmic return" and of the inevitableness of the free-verse poem; of "thematic invention" in the rhythms of *vers libre,* of "concentrated stress" and the right use of "the poetic interval—the pause."

The most sapient observations on the quarrel over free verse were made by T. S. Eliot in an article in the *New Statesman* for March 3, 1917. The defenders of the new form could not admit the justice of his view because the pith of his argument is that free verse can be defended only in negative terms. *"Vers libre* does not exist," he declared bluntly, "and it is time that this preposterous fiction followed the *élan vital . . .* into oblivion." Its limit of effectiveness is attained when it reaches the farthest point to which it can depart from known patterns and still not slip into formlessness. Its strength comes from nothing within itself but from the pattern to which, to a greater or lesser degree, it approximates. In his own early verse Eliot proved the soundness of his remarks by using free rhythms when they suited his needs, but most often in ironic or emotional contrast to conventional metrical patterns revitalized by the new content with which he filled them.

In the history of English and American poetry there have been many battles, but none can compare in hilarity with the Imagist skirmish. At first all was harmony in the camp of the invaders; but after Ezra Pound irrupted among them in London peace departed. England and America were to be conquered at once. In England he captured two magazines. In America, as soon as he became foreign correspondent for Miss Monroe's venture, Pound could use *Poetry* pretty much as he wished. Every issue now discussed *Imagisme*—as it was first spelled.

The raising of the Imagist flag in *Poetry* had not escaped the notice of an American woman with poetic aspirations who was at that moment groping for a style. When Amy Lowell of Brookline, Massachusetts, saw in *Poetry* some verses signed "H. D. *Imagiste,"* she knew where she belonged, and she hastened to London to seek her kind. Miss Lowell's personality was as imposing as her physical bulk, her wealth, and the prestige of her name. She possessed the American talent for organization, and she would spend the rest of her life in organizing a great poetical offensive, conducted by means

of reviews which she browbeat editors to let her write, by her own books of
poetry announced by such a fanfare as only she could command, by lectures,
statements, interviews, dinners, always carried through with a storm of
hisses, applause, tears, violent exits, demonstrations, and eulogies. When she
collided with Pound in the summer of 1914, either the irresistible force or
the immovable object had to give way. Pound moved. He was ready to move
anyway, on to the company of Wyndham Lewis and Epstein and Gaudier-
Brzeska and T. S. Eliot, and to his newest discovery, "Vorticism."

He left one legacy of his generalship behind him, *Des Imagistes,* published in the spring of 1914. Pound threw into his anthology any poems of
his friends which could be called, by courtesy, imagistic. The one imagistic
poem Amy Lowell had thus far turned out, "In a Garden," went in too.

Such haphazard management would not do for a daughter of the Lowell
mills, who at the age of thirteen sold copies of her *Dream Drops, or Stories
from Fairy Land, by a Dreamer* at a bazaar for the Perkins Institution for
the Blind and netted $56.60 for the cause. Managing poets, living and dead,
was her business. On July 17, 1914, she entertained the battalion at an
Imagist Dinner at the Dieu-Donné restaurant in London. Through eleven
courses, from Norwegian hors d'œuvres to Bombe Moka, the issues of the
movement were fought over. But the rift appeared as soon as the dinner
was digested. Miss Lowell was determined that a new anthology should be
issued, to be the first of an annual series. The poets in it really must be
Imagists and not just friends of Pound's, and they must share equally in the
space. There should be a proper preface to serve as a program of action and
a declaration of independence. The poets lined up like participants in a
spelling bee. Aldington and his wife "H. D." stood with Miss Lowell. So
did F. S. Flint, D. H. Lawrence, and John Gould Fletcher, an Arkansan
who had been following the Imagist path at a distance from the rest of the
company.

Imagism became finally what Miss Lowell insisted that it was, and the
terms under which any poet who would call himself an Imagist must write
were emphatically set forth in a preface to the first of three annuals, *Some
Imagist Poets* (1915), written by Aldington and revised by Miss Lowell:

1. To use the language of common speech, but to employ always the *exact*
word, not the nearly-exact, nor the merely decorative word.

2. To create new rhythms—as the expression of new moods—and not to copy
old rhythms, which merely echo old moods. We do not insist upon "free-verse" as
the only method of writing poetry. We fight for it as for a principle of liberty. . . .

3. To allow absolute freedom in the choice of subject. It is not good art to write
badly about aeroplanes and automobiles; nor is it necessarily bad art to write well

about the past. We believe passionately in the artistic value of modern life, but we wish to point out that there is nothing so uninspiring or so old-fashioned as an aeroplane of the year 1911.

4. To present an image (hence the name: "Imagist"). We are not a school of painters, but we believe that poetry should render particulars exactly and not deal in vague generalities, however magnificent and sonorous. . . .

5. To produce poetry that is hard and clear, never blurred nor indefinite.

6. Finally, most of us believe that concentration is of the very essence of poetry.

One notices at once how much there is here which has been reiterated in every new poetic movement. Wordsworth desired in poetry to return to common speech. Kipling and Masefield and the Georgians again returned to it a hundred years after him. The Imagists, as a matter of fact, were less faithful to this principle than the Georgians. One has small chance of learning the sounds of common speech if one is born in Brookline and learns about the world from books. As to the Imagists' passionate belief in the artistic value of modern life, they actually showed a tendency to retreat from it—"H. D." and Aldington to ancient Greece, Pound to his troubadours, Miss Lowell to the newest historical curio on which her roving eye happened to rest.

When we come to the last three articles of the Imagists' program—the essentially imagistic articles—we recognize that we have come to the heart of the whole matter. We are back with Hulme and his original group in 1909. The real contribution of the Imagists was the exploration of a special technique which could be used to achieve certain ends but should not be expected to bear the weight of profound emotion or involved thought. By the determined evangelism of Miss Lowell other causes were dragged under the standard of Imagism.

After the smoke and tumult of the Imagist war cleared, it was possible to estimate how much new territory had been gained. Miss Lowell, the fugleman of the offensive, could not claim, finally, very much in her own name. With the alertness of a magpie she had fixed her attention now on the poets of the T'ang Dynasty, now on her cousin James' *Fable for Critics* which she brought up to date, now on Frost's New England tragedies which her *Legends* complimented by imitation. There is not much left of all this brave experimenting except a handful of anthology pieces. Similarly her most faithful disciple, John Gould Fletcher, expended his talent in "color symphonies" which compel poetry to drudge at tasks painting and music can more easily perform. With Hilda Doolittle the case is different, for she is the one poet of the Imagist faith who by her strict devotion to it brought forth good works. The second of the two poems entitled "The Garden," for instance, communicates perfectly in thirteen lines the oppressiveness of fructifying summer heat. The poem penetrates to essence much as Cézanne's painting of still life does. One can feel the solidity of the heat as one might expect to hear one of Cézanne's apples bump on the floor if it rolled off the table. It is not unfair to say that the chief service of the Imagists was to develop a technique which could be put to excellent use by the poets who followed them.

6

In the year *Poetry* was founded there arrived in England an American poet of thirty-seven who had tried with little success to persuade American magazines to take his verse. Between 1894 when the *Independent* printed "My Butterfly" and 1912, Robert Frost had disposed of fourteen poems. But he was still determined to be a poet, and he had gone to England in order that he might "write and be poor without further scandal in the family."

Born in San Francisco in 1875, he came to the New England with which he is now identified after his father's death in 1885. Twice he tried to make a go of college—at Dartmouth for a few months in 1892, at Harvard from 1897 to 1899. He farmed at Derry, New Hampshire, from 1900 to 1905. Twice he was a schoolteacher; but he had also worked as a bobbin boy in the mills of Lawrence, Massachusetts, as a cobbler, and as the editor of a weekly paper.

If he had lingered another year in America, the tidal wave of the "New" Poetry movement might have carried him to fame and perhaps to security. As it was, he found in England the companionship in craft and the appreciation for which he had waited so long. In his three years there he walked in the West Country, talking poetry with two of the Georgians whose aims were much like his own, Lascelles Abercrombie and Wilfrid Gibson. Among the new friends who admired and understood him was the critic Edward Thomas, destined shortly to die at Arras, whom Frost encouraged to turn to poetry.

In Gloucestershire Frost wrote poems about New England. There were soon enough of them for two books which David Nutt published: *A Boy's Will* in 1913, *North of Boston* in 1914. When Frost returned to America the next year, he brought with him a substantial English reputation. Norman Douglas had found in his first book "an image of things really heard and seen." Edward Garnett, in praising the second volume as containing poetry of a rare order, chid Frost's fellow Americans for their long neglect of him. "It would be quaint indeed," he warned, "if Americans who . . . are opening their hospitable bosoms to Mr. Rabindranath Tagore's spiritual poems of Bengal life, should rest oblivious of their own countryman."

The hint was acted on. Frost stepped off the boat into the hands of a reception committee. Though Miss Lowell had failed in her efforts to find a publisher for *North of Boston,* Holt issued it in the year of Frost's return. *Poetry* already knew his work, having published "The Code" in its issue of February, 1914. But Frost needed no impresario. The magazines which had once turned him down were now cap in hand asking for poems. He was known as one of the "new" poets, but he did little to identify himself with either the Boston or the Chicago branch of the movement. Always a lone striker, he still had need of being versed in country things. He found himself a farmhouse near Franconia in New Hampshire where he continued to meditate on the mysteries of birches and wild grapes, the sound of trees, and the dust of snow.

Frost was always, as any textbook will declare, a regional poet; and his region was New England, more particularly New Hampshire, "one of the two best states in the Union," the other being Vermont. Though he lived outside New England at intervals and moved in the larger world, he never had the slightest inclination to take all America for his province. However much he pitied his characters bound to the down-swing of a declining economy, he did not wish to alter their lives, never dreamed of Utopia as Lindsay did when he saw visions of his Springfield redeemed and spiritualized. Unlike Masters and Faulkner, Frost never sought to bring his characters into a regional unity. The men and women of his poems are isolated, like their farms and wood lots, or they are caught in a net which tragically or ironically encloses at most the fate of only two or three. His regionalism, in short, resembles that of Emily Dickinson and Sarah Orne Jewett. It gave him a place to stand where he could see what was close by in field or cellar hole, and, as well, a clear view above his hills to the "further range" beyond.

Politics he shunned, except to have his fun with the political poets of the thirties who reproached him for retreating from the problems of the day. He is not a religious poet, not even a nature mystic, in spite of all that nature meant to him. His verse is in the great tradition of pastoral poetry from Theocritus to Wordsworth, though his pastoralism is never, like Virgil's or Milton's, decorative or political. He is a learned poet but, as in Housman's poetry, his learning is muted to an echoic beauty. He was not the partisan of his plowmen, mowers, hired men, gatherers of huckleberries and tree gum, for all his sympathy with them and his gift of psychological penetration into their lives. He looked on them with a detachment which was ironic, humorous, or ruthful. He made of their toil and defeat what they would never have imagined for themselves.

Frost is a metaphysical poet in the tradition of Emerson and Emily Dickinson, with all that term implies of the poet's desire to go beyond the seen to the unseen, but his imagery is less involved than that of the older metaphysicals. Most of his poems fix on the mysterious moment when the two planes cross. Hasty readers, noting only the quiet beginning in what appears to be a simple anecdote about a person, event, or object commonly enough observed, fail to see how the commonness gradually disappears or, better, how it becomes transfigured. As in all great metaphysical poetry, the tension increases between the simple fact and the mystery which surrounds it, until the total meaning flashes in the final words. As one critic has observed, Frost's art consists in "his careful and deliberate laying of the material for a poetic bonfire." It has been noted often enough, and Frost commented on the fact, that poetry was to him essentially dramatic. Whatever his theme may be, he works to dramatize it for the reader, whether it is the tragedy of the hired man or the relation of the boy "too far from town to learn baseball" to the heaven-flung birches which he, one by one, subdues. The most dramatic moment in a Frost poem is the kind of anagnorisis or dénouement when the mundane fact achieves its full metaphysical significance.

Though Frost seldom strayed to alien country beyond the sight of his New England upland pastures and back meadows, his poetry widened in content and technique from book to book. Each volume disclosed a particular facet of his genius, some new attitude or tone or approach. Few modern poets have shown such a capacity for growth, on into old age.

Perhaps because Frost had long practiced poetry in silence, A Boy's Will (1913) was surprisingly free from the echoes of older verse which one expects to hear in a poet's first book. Three or four poems, "Storm Fear" for example, are authentic and memorable Frost. In his subsequent work there would be less dactyllic and trochaic movement (Frost's gait is usually a slow three-time); but the tone and content of the book were indubitably his and no other poet's. In North of Boston (1914), all the poems of which are on New England themes, there appeared for the first time his long dramatic monologues or dialogues, carefully set and lighted, and usually given, as in "The Mountain," a pervasive symbolic meaning. The marvel is that Frost could have so quickly mastered a genre which only E. A. Robinson had excelled in since Browning invented and perfected it.

Though three of the poems in Mountain Interval (1916) use this form, Frost had turned his attention to another kind of poem for which he became equally noted. This is a brief meditation prompted by an object or a person or an episode that seized his attention and compelled his wonder. As in the longer poems of the previous book, there is great drama in the elaborated situation, though there is no speaker and the play is done before the turning of a page. In "The Oven Bird" the starting point is an object, this mid-wood bird whose question, in all but words, is "what to make of a diminished thing." (Frost knew the answer.) In "An Old Man's Winter Night" thought moves out from a person, one aged man—one man, trying to keep a house, a farm, a countryside against ghosts, the moon, and the cold. The well known "Birches" turns on an episode: what it means, in several modes, to be a small-boy swinger of birches. But before the poem is finished it has become a meditation on the best way to leave earth for heaven.

With *New Hampshire* (1923) several new qualities emerged. The long, satirical title poem announced Frost's determination to prefer this state which has "one each of everything as in a show-case," to all others, except perhaps Vermont which lies beside it, the two of them wedged end to end. There is a new self-consciousness in the volume. The poet is willing to talk about himself and his art, somewhat defiantly. A sententiousness has crept into the longer dramatic poems, and some of the shorter ones, "An Empty Threat" for example, and "I Will Sing You One-O," are in a riddling manner which Frost sometimes carried to excess. These and the epigrams which appear in this volume for the first time anticipate the crypticism in which he would increasingly indulge. On the other hand, "Stopping by Woods on a Snowy Evening" and "The Need of Being Versed in Country Things" are as lucid and magical as anything he had written in his simpler style.

The title of his next book *West-Running Brook* (1928) has a special significance. (All the titles of his books should be pondered by those who would understand him.) Like the brook which runs west while all the other brooks flow east to reach the ocean, the speaker of the poem trusts himself to go by contraries. The black stream, striking a barrier, flings back one white wave. As it throws backward on itself, while it falls, so most of it is always raising a little, sending up a little. In this backward motion toward the source, against the stream, man most shows what he is. This stoic theme of resistance and self-realization is found in other poems in this book, in some of which there is even a suggestion of malaise. The tension between man and nature, hitherto always exciting and often harmoniously resolved, has loosened. Nature has grown more hostile, man more heroic. This increasing undertone of humanism is beautifully eloquent in the sonnet "A Soldier," one of Frost's greatest poems:

> But this we know, the obstacle that checked
> And tripped the body, shot the spirit on
> Further than target ever showed or shone.

In *A Further Range* (1936), published when Frost was sixty-one, there are two groups of poems which bear the significant captions "Taken Doubly" and "Taken Singly." The desire to sermonize had grown on him, and in the poems "taken doubly" he required the reader to keep his eye on the theme and the moral. "A Lone Striker" is a homily on individual freedom; "The Gold Hesperidee," a parable on pride. "Two Tramps in Mud Time" preaches the necessity of uniting avocation and vocation—

> Only where love and need are one,
> And the work is play for mortal stakes,
> Is the deed ever really done
> For Heaven and the future's sakes.

The poems in this group are delightful, full of an unobjectionable didacticism. Beside them the poems "taken singly" seem somewhat wan. The natural world, once a bringer of great joy to Frost, suggests to him now the closing in of age and winter.

> Petals I may have once pursued.
> Leaves are all my darker mood.

In his subsequent work he slipped the ties which had so long kept him earth-bound. He grew fonder of searching among abstractions. It was not surprising that on his seventieth birthday he should try, with only a moderate success, in *A Masque of Reason* (1945), to get a forthright answer out of God for his bewildering treatment of Job and the rest of the human race.

Before the desire to escape into pure thought overcame him Frost was above all a poet of nature. But, as has been said, for all that nature meant to him he was never a nature mystic. In his early verse one feels the joy in the sensuous pleasure which nature has given most modern poets; but Frost always knew where to find the line which separates nature from man. When tired of trees he sought again mankind; but if by noon he had too much of men, he could turn on his arm and smell the earth and look into the crater of the ant. In the earlier poems nature and man confront each other across the wall, as the buck and the doe in "Two Look at Two" face the wondering man and woman, each pair in its own pasture.

Though nature watches man, she takes no account of him. On the slope where a dozen boys and girls once played, the trees are again in the mountain's lap. Deep in the frozen swamp nature is taking back to herself, "with the slow smokeless burning of decay," the cordwood meant for a useful fireplace. This is nature's way: moving at a slower pace than man, destroying man's puny work for her own ends—to provide the manure for new growth.

Man has need of nature, though he should never make the mistake of crossing the wall into her pasture. The woods are lovely, dark and deep against the snowfall, a place to linger and forget duty; but to linger only, and not to stay. Man is most himself when he measures himself against nature's pace and the barriers she places before him:

> Well, there's—the storm. That says I must go on.
> That wants me as a war might if it came.
> Ask any man.

But in the end the bond between man and nature loosened, as Frost looked on. What had been strength and indifference in nature became for him brute force and hostility; what once was balance was now seen as struggle. Man rides bareback on the earth, but he knows some further tricks to try on his wild mount, his headless horse. Or, in the metaphor of "Sand Dunes," let the sea know that even though she rises into the town to bury in sand the living who have escaped her, she is ignorant of man—

> If by any change of shape,
> She hopes to cut off mind.

As C. Day Lewis wrote in the preface to the English edition of the *Selected Poems* (1936), the simplicity of Frost's verse "is the simplicity—not of nature —but of a serious and profoundly critical spirit." Frost was early aware that he wished to take the middle ground as a thinker, that he was a skeptic, a relativist, a "sensibilist" who would refuse to adapt himself a mite

> To any change from hot to cold, from wet
> To dry, from poor to rich, or back again.

As regards his art, he likewise knew very soon where he stood. Though he wrote little about the nature of poetry, he enjoyed talking about his art. From the considerable record kept by other participants in the night-long conversations which he delighted in, and from the poems themselves, one can outline Frost's theory of poetry.

An early well-wisher told Frost to give his days and nights to the study of Lanier's mellifluous verse. The young poet presently discovered what it was he so much disliked in Lanier's poetry: "All the tones of the human voice in natural speech are entirely eliminated, leaving the sound of sense without root in experience." Another friend had told Frost that the tone of his verse was too much like talk. With characteristic stubbornness, fortunately, the poet refused to change his style. He began to realize indeed that it was just this tone that he had been striving to get into his verse. When he returned from England in 1915, he was ready to formulate, in an interview given at the time, what he had learned about "sentence-sound" and "vocal gesture." Emerson, he remarked, had set forth in "Monadnock" the theory he was trying to put into practice:

> Now in sordid weeds they sleep,
> In dullness now their secret keep;
> Yet, will you learn our ancient speech,
> These the masters who can teach.
> Fourscore or a hundred words
> All their vocal muse affords;
> But they turn them in a fashion
> Past clerks' or statesmen's art or passion.

It was Frost's contention that what we get in life and miss so often in literature is the "sentence sounds that underlie the words." Whether the individual words carry to our ears or not, every meaning has a particular "sound-posture." The listener whose ear is attuned to the spoken language is "instinctively familiar" with the particular sound which goes with the "sense of every meaning." Since language only really exists in the mouths of men, the poet must write with his ear to the voice.

Though he was trying out his idea in the midst of the excitement over free verse, Frost did not abandon conventional metrical forms. He complicated his problem (and enriched his verse) by setting the traditional meters against the natural rhythms of his speaker's sentences. The spoken word and the verse pattern must fight out the issue between them. But the struggle when supervised by a skillful poet will end in reconciliation. As Frost said: "Meter has to do with beat, and sound posture has a definite relation as an alternate tone between the beats. The two are one in creation but separate in analysis."

As will be readily seen, the kind of poetry which would result from Frost's aim would be far from a simple imitation of New England farmer speech. At its best it would be extremely complex, though always seeming to be simple, and capable of carrying a variety of tones, ironies, and emotional gradations.

Unlike many modern poets who hold that a poem is an artifact, a thing deliberately constructed, Frost declares that a poem is "never a put-up job. . . . It begins as a lump in the throat, a sense of wrong, a homesickness, a loneliness. It is never a thought to begin with. It is at its best when it is a tantalizing vagueness." Yet the poem makes itself as it grows. It finds its thought; or fails to do so, and so there is no poem. What Frost stated as a generalization is borne out in his own poems. The reader's excitement is aroused by the slow unveiling, the inevitable approach of the moment of complete disclosure. He soon finds his comprehension advancing on more than one level as he recognizes that physical objects are changing into symbols, and that these are clues to the deeper meaning of the poem. Though Frost held with the romantics that a poem is an expression of an experience, his best poems are marvels of construction, the more exciting to the reader because their form seems to evolve before his eyes and ears.

The conversational tone and the dramatic manner of Frost's poetry strike one first. More than a second glance is needed to appreciate his expertness as a prosodist. He handles, as few modern poets except Yeats and Auden have done, a great number of English meters. More remarkable still is what he makes of the "strict iambic" and "loose iambic" in which most of his verse is written. One would not have supposed there was so much blood-pulse left in this ancient meter in which English rhythms most characteristically flow.

Though he was one of the "new" poets, Frost worked his revolution in the surest way. "It's knowing what to do with things that counts." For a poet the only things he has to do with are rhythm, sound, and sense.

71. THEODORE DREISER

W<small>HEN</small> Frank Norris read the manuscript of Theodore Dreiser's *Sister Carrie* in 1900 and urged Doubleday to publish this story of a poor girl who sought love and security in the city, the American novel faced a crisis in its development. Here was a painstaking and exhaustive study of what it meant to be alive in growing, grasping, exuberant Chicago, a story as free of moral inhibition as Zola, as detailed and literal as William Dean Howells. What he, Garland, Crane, Fuller, London, and many another had been urging the American novel to do, was here done with assurance and naïve crudity. Would the publisher publish and the readers read and accept? The answer for eleven years was, No. *Sister Carrie* was published without enthusiasm and then virtually suppressed. It remained largely unread until its third and first really public edition in 1912, a year after the appearance of the more carefully wrought study of the same theme, *Jennie Gerhardt*.

The author of these two forthright stories apparently was not disturbed by his rejection for a dozen years. He turned to other pursuits almost as though he knew he could afford to wait. He wrote for the newspapers, he edited a woman's magazine, he lived as he could. But he did not offer to pander to the public taste in romantic fiction, even in minor respects. After *McTeague*, Norris had largely forsaken the grim method of the realist who saw only the ugly things; after *Main-Travelled Roads*, Garland had preached "veritism" but had written romances of Colorado and the Yukon; after *Maggie*, Crane had gone off to real and re-created wars; even London's *Sea Wolf* had broken in the middle and become a romance on a Pacific isle. The American public in 1900 was not ready to see itself wholly and literally in fiction. The ugly things could not be revealed; the forbidden questions, asked. Edith Wharton's genteel satire and Ellen Glasgow's moral searchings were the strongest fare that it could take.

By waiting, Dreiser preserved his artistic integrity. Because he refused to compromise his materials or his purposes, he became the one novelist of what Mencken called "the literary movement of the nineties" who was fully prepared to take part in and to help shape the literary renaissance of the 1910's and 1920's. In him the two movements become one. Why he succeeded where others failed can only be conjectured. Certainly it was not because of confidence in himself or his art, for he paints his own portrait as a blind and stumbling seeker. Probably it was because he knew the one thing that he could do if he were to write novels at all; and he persisted in doing that thing because it was all he could do. His productivity between *Jennie* in 1911 and *The "Genius"* in 1915 is proof that failure of publication had no effect on his creative energy. All his major novels were apparently either conceived or written in those years of silence, even the two, *The Bulwark* and *The Stoic*, which were prepared for publication just before his death in 1945. With *The "Genius"* he bucked the censorship of the press and public opinion for a second time and again held back his novels except for *An American Tragedy* (1925), the story of a boy who, like Carrie and Jennie, failed to come to workable terms with American society.

These years were studded with collections of shorter works and with non-fiction. There were four collections of short stories in the years between 1918 and 1929, which in theme and treatment add little to an analysis of the novels and may be compared to a painter's sketches. There were also two volumes of poems (1926 and 1935), numerous essays in philosophic and social criticism (*Hey Rub-a-Dub-Dub*, 1920; *Dreiser Looks at Russia*, 1928), and his many volumes of autobiography; but his more ambitious stories often remained for long periods unfinished in manuscript. Was he oversensitive, or did he know, as master writers sometimes do, that he could afford to wait?

2

Of all American novelists, Dreiser limited himself most sternly to what he knew of life through his own experience, mainly in his youth. He was born in Terre Haute, Indiana, in 1871; he died in California on December 29, 1945. Many of the intervening years were spent in the three cities: Chicago, New York, and Philadelphia. He knew the United States because he had lived in it.

His father was an immigrant German workman, his mother the daughter of German parents who belonged to a small religious sect in a farming region of Pennsylvania. Dreiser has described his father as a fanatically religious man, honest, hard-working, plodding. He might have been an American success on a small scale but was devoid of will and too persistently concerned with trying to avoid the fires of a theological hell. In Dreiser's writing he emerges as a strangely appealing and rather pathetic figure.

For his mother, Dreiser felt a lifelong devotion. His description of her in *Dawn* reveals her as a deeply emotional woman who gave to her large family maternal affection, warmth, and security. But for her, his life might have been as ineffectual as that of some of his own characters. In boyhood he was shy, eager, timid, brooding, bewildered, slow to develop. He has himself confessed how important his mother's love and some measure of security were to him as well as to his brothers and sisters.

His childhood and youth were not happy. His father was almost continually poor, and this family moved constantly from house to house, from one Indiana community to another; they spent one period on the crowded West Side of Chicago. Besides poverty, they usually faced social ostracism. With each move, their hopes of economic and of social betterment reawakened, only to be disappointed, and again the Dreiser children were rejected by their fellows. Theodore's suffering was further aggravated, when he passed the age of puberty, by severe fears of castration and impotence, which intensified his shyness and caused sexual panic in the presence of girls. These difficulties, with the rigid conceptions of hell taught in the Catholic parochial school and reinforced by his father, played their part in his relative slowness of mental development. He was an inconsistent pupil, responding well only when his teachers took a sympathetic interest in him—a brooding, groping boy and youth who had to learn everything for himself.

The brooding and groping style which he often used in his novels was a reflection of these inner struggles, and they provided him with one of the chief motifs of his fiction: the conflict between what was then loosely termed "instinct" by the psychologists, and convention. The biological needs of his characters lead them to actions, particularly in love affairs, which result in infringements on the social code. His autobiographical writings tell us that he experienced this conflict constantly and poignantly in his own early life. The bewilderments of his teen-age period of drifting from job to job—he worked in a Chicago restaurant, drove for a laundry, collected for an easy-payment furniture company, helped in a real estate office, in the stockroom of a wholesale hardware company, and so on—suggest the later fictional wanderings of Clyde Griffiths in *An American Tragedy*. His characters usually receive their education in life itself, in a real and savage struggle for place, money, and social prestige, rather than in schools.

Dreiser was educated, like his characters, not so much by his schooling as by his repeated moves with their resulting contrasts of urban and rural life. From the farm lands and the many towns of Indiana, he came to know the vigorous young city of Chicago in the seventies and eighties. The moral and social consequences of the triumph of town over country were impressed upon him. In his early stories his characters, whenever they move to the city, find it an exciting adventure. The growth of cities is an integral motif of all his studies of youth. The decade of the nineties, when Dreiser was a youth in

Chicago, was a crucial period in its history. By the time of the World's Fair it was beginning to play an increasingly important role in national life, especially in finance and politics. No wonder he wrote, in *Newspaper Days*:

> To me Chicago at this time seethed with a peculiarly human or realistic atmosphere. It is given to some cities, as to some lands, to suggest romance, and to me Chicago did that hourly. It sang, I thought, and . . . I was singing with it.

There he saw the contrasts of grandeur and misery which he was later to describe so movingly; there his dreams and hopes of love, success, knowledge, prestige were born. It seemed to be a world city in the making, a center of gravity for the American Success Dream.

Dreiser as a boy absorbed this dream of social power and easy money as if by osmosis, at the same time that he saw poverty, failure, ignorance, and defeat all about him, even in his own family. Attending popular lectures and reading Eugene Field, he determined to understand it and to report it faithfully; to become a newspaperman. He inescapably was what Norris, Crane, and Garland envisioned the modern American to be.

3

There has been much debate among the critics as to whether Dreiser was a "naturalist" after the manner of Zola. If by this term is meant merely a franker acceptance of the ugly in life or a more faithful recording of personal experience, it can be accepted as a description of his art. If further it means a turning to the current findings of science for a philosophy with which to ask the fundamental questions about man in himself and in society, it can still be accepted. Only when it serves to confine creative genius within a formula must it be rejected, for Dreiser belonged to no school, studied no sources with intent to obey, knew little of literary movements at home or abroad.

He was an objective realist who gathered his facts impersonally, but he was more. He lived in his dreams, his hopes, his broodings. For this reason, he absorbed both the realistic method and the new conceptions of the universe from science into his thought and his writing. His views are loose in formulation, and inconsistent. For example, his theory of the relativity of morals is as inconsistent as it is challenging. But such views of man and nature as he had, however ill formed, are essential parts of his writing; without them, his works would be entirely different. They helped to deepen his imagination; they contributed toward the feeling of awe he creates concerning the condition of man; they served him in his very construction of theme, of story, of character. He was an artist, not a philosopher.

Dreiser's first two major novels, *Sister Carrie* (1900) and *Jennie Gerhardt* (1911), are stories of sensitive young girls who escape from poverty by forming liaisons with men of superior financial and social position. The salesman Drouet is but a step for Carrie toward the more attractive Hurstwood, and Hurstwood himself becomes important only as a means toward success on the stage. Jennie is similarly rescued from poverty, first by Senator Brander and then by Lester Kane. Superficially, both stories seem to be studies of struggle for the comforts and social position that money alone would bring, by thoroughly unconventional social means. But the plot in both cases is for Dreiser little more than the means for studying a more profound struggle: the struggle of an uneducated and unprivileged young girl for full realization of her own personality. Carrie's final rejection of Hurstwood because she could not love him and Jennie's final acceptance of Lester on any terms are but the two sides of the same coin. In the end and in spite of tragic circumstances, both girls achieve a degree of fulfillment that only their experiences could have brought them.

Dreiser remarks that Jennie's experience helped her to gain a "theory of existence." Perhaps the best way of describing Dreiser's total literary work is to state that he too was engaged on a lifelong search for a theory of existence. Like many another major American writer, he read to assimilate what were considered to be the best ideas of his time, to verify his own observations and brooding reflections. If there is a purpose which gives order and coherence to this spectacle, it is a secret and mysterious one. How to live in and to describe this spectacle? How to find some ideas, some values, some aims and purposes which might give more dignity, more sense, more pleasure, more human gratification to those who are a part of it?

Dreiser began his literary career when Social Darwinism was a main current of American thought, and he had, from his early years, absorbed it mainly, it seems, from Spencer, Huxley, and Loeb. Its central concept—which generally served as a means for justification of the practices of capitalism—was the equation of nature with society. It conceived the natural and the social worlds as continuous, subsumable to the same laws; in consequence, it attempted to give the status of social generalization to the conclusions of biological evolution. Dreiser, accepting this concept, developed from it an attitude of both personal and social determinism.

One of the major emphases in his work is therefore biological. Man is for him a creature with imperious biological needs. The "instincts" drive him to actions whose motivations he does not understand. Frequently, as in *The Financier* and *The Titan,* he characterizes these impulses as "chemisms," which in man are also expressions of some unapprehended force, or energy, purpose, or "God" in the universe. The universe, including the social world of man, is all of one piece, a product of unknown force, creative by nature, and resident in human organisms. Thus does man act in accordance with natural impulse. Sex, beauty, and a will to power or to dominancy are inter-related. Man seeks to satisfy himself. He seeks his mate or mates; he seeks beauty; he seeks power. The stronger personalities are best equipped to satisfy themselves; they crush the weaker, and themselves survive.

In Carrie and Jennie, Dreiser had studied the operation of these "instincts" in young women of almost no place in the social scheme. Their method of attaining a fuller life was the feminine one of exploiting the male animal to satisfy their deepest needs. In Eugene Witla of The "Genius," and more thor-oughly in Frank Cowperwood of the trilogy The Financier (1912, revised 1927), The Titan (1914), and the long delayed Stoic, he turned to the mascu-line version of the problem, already indirectly presented in Hurstwood and Kane.

On the character of Cowperwood, Dreiser exerted his greatest powers of observation and analysis. In this prototype of worldly success, modeled on the career of the street-railway baron, C. T. Yerkes, the primary instinct that drives the human animal forward and upward is the hunger for power. Wealth and sex are but means used by the individual to achieve mastery over the circumstances of his life and control of his own destiny. Cowperwood is a Social-Darwinian superman rather than a Nietzschean Zarathustra, for he is a victim rather than a leader. The author often mentions his personal magnetism, suggested in the look in his eyes, his manner of walking, his general appearance. It is as if universal force were planted in his very being. In paintings and in women he finds the most complete expression of beauty; he is a genius in financial manipulations; hence he is an artist, and his other satisfactions are related to his creativity.

Eugene Witla of The "Genius" is like Cowperwood in that he takes what he needs for his own satisfaction, but he is more emotional, more moody, less magnetic and forceful. He finds in sex the beauty which, as an artist, he seeks to recapture in his work; he feeds on women for inspiration. In the course of the novel, he has a near-breakdown and sinks into a dangerous condition of involutional melancholia. Cowperwood is an artist of power, Witla of beauty. The man of power is the stronger; and the novel of power is the greater.

The biological premise of Dreiser's writing is one side of a contradiction found in the conflict between instincts and the dictates of social convention. Man cannot harmonize the life of the body with the life of reason. He is not therefore, fully civilized, and it becomes increasingly difficult for him to attain harmony when society is organized on the basis of Puritanical mores and a rigid moral code. "America," Dreiser writes in Dawn, "and especially the

Middle West, was at that time miasmatically puritanic as well as patriotic, twin states bred of ignorance and what mental or economic lacks I am not able to discern." The dictates of conventional society tend to force man to repress his nature; the need to express and to satisfy his nature pushes him toward violating social codes and conventions. Life as a search for beauty, a quest for power, an effort to express creativity, becomes a struggle, on the plane of society, for money and position, and for sexual satisfaction. In this quest and rivalry, the strongest win out; the weak are crushed.

Thus to biological is added social determinism. As the stronger man has an advantage over the weaker, so organized groups are stronger than the individual. They punish those who oppose their dictations or seem to threaten their organization. Only those individuals who are strong enough to gain control over the levers of power have a good chance of resisting social pressure. In capitalistic society the struggle for power, for gratification, is expressed in the struggle for money. Woman, as the illustration of beauty, is bought. Carrie and Jennie are "kept women"; Cowperwood "buys" the women he wants. The absence of money means defeat; it means the lack of education, of beauty; it means that one is a victim, like Clyde Griffiths, of the rich, of one's relationships with others. Dreiser directly described the pitilessness and the hierarchical character of capitalistic society by showing that just as the poor are the victims of the rich, the weak of the strong, so are women, inferior to men, usually victims. American tragedy, like all tragedy, is the consequence of weakness. The impulses, the passions of man pitilessly drive him to satisfy himself; the force of social circumstance, the fierce nature of the social struggle, thwart him and produce both social and biological tragedy.

In *An American Tragedy* (1925), Dreiser provides a third approach to this all-absorbing social-biological problem. Clyde Griffiths is totally lacking in either the artistic gifts of Witla or the strong personality of Cowperwood. He is more like Carrie and Jennie in that his attitude toward life is passive; but he lacks their inner poise. From start to finish of his short career he is a victim of the social and biological forces which operate upon him. His instinct for fulfillment is not only thwarted by the forces without himself; his inner weakness makes even the development of a Carrie or a Jennie impossible. Thus, by choosing for his central character a boy who had practically no strength within himself through which mastery could be achieved, Dreiser in this novel throws all his emphasis on those forces of biological and social necessity which had shaped the careers of his stronger characters in spite of their protests. But by removing the only opposition that the individual can supply, the force of his own will for mastery, Dreiser here descends to the lowest possible plane of pure mechanistic determinism. The scene of the drowning of Roberta Alden is carefully planned in order to remove the factor of will as an instrument. Clyde plots his act with the greatest care and carries it to its climax with apparently self-directed intention. But his hesitancy at the final moment transforms the murder into an accident, and his swimming away makes his act passive. The description of this story as a "tragedy" is almost ironic, even though Dreiser probably intended no irony. For the Fate of classical tragedy there were now substituted the necessities of social and biological mechanisms. But the result is less tragic, in the classical sense, than are almost any other of Dreiser's novels because the opposition of man to his destiny, in whatever terms, is not even provisional. To raise necessity to the level of tragedy there must be at least the illusion of possible mastery. In Carrie and Jennie and Cowperwood this illusion is present; in Witla and Clyde it is not.

Dreiser portrays the social-biological struggle with a certain evenness or balance, an unflagging objectivity in which he is restrained from didactic condemnation. His works say that life as he has seen it is like this: it is a condition of joy and sorrow, of beauty, wonder, terror, and above all of mystery. Human destiny is a mystery. In his poems he offers a concentrated expression of this mystical feeling for life, and in his stories he frequently turns to the occult or to religion. Telepathy occurs often; Witla and his wife, at one period, are interested in Christian Science; and *The Bulwark* is a story of Quakers. The reliance of Solon Barnes upon the "inner light" throws him, as he grows rich, into a conflict of conscience. His children drift from him and from the ideals of Quaker simplicity. In the end, a sick, a dying old man, he finds consolation in mysticism. When a poisonous snake threatens him in his garden, he looks at it with the eyes of love. The danger is averted, and he is at one with the universe. The unknown creative force in life, the force that drove Cowperwood to the heights of power, that tore the soul of Eugene Witla, that sent Clyde to the electric chair, is now revealed as universal love. Like Solon, Dreiser died a mystic. Was it his intention to say at last that Solon Barnes was a giver of laws? If so, he had denied the purely mechanistic view of life in order to admit the further necessity of religion, a necessity which had always been implicit in his thought.

4

Equipped with a "theory of existence," however unsystematic, Dreiser was in a position to ask questions about American life more searching and profound than those of earlier realists like Howells, Garland, or even James. He dramatized in fiction the American success story; his world is one of growing cities where new careers, new fortunes, are made day after day. His characters, in their search for something better for themselves, take on the color of their milieu; they gain their ideals from experience. Occupation has much to do with their destinies. Usually they find their careers as the result of accident or circumstance. Carrie and Jennie drift into their fates; Jennie's lover inherits his career with his family position. Choice is allowed only to Cowperwood and Witla, the men of power and creative ability.

In these, and in minor characters, Dreiser reveals the plight of the individual in American society; but that society itself is not static. The span of years encompassed in his novels and short stories coincides with a period of tremendous social change in America. *The Financier* opens before the Civil War. In it, as in *Sister Carrie, The "Genius,"* and other novels dealing with an older form of American society, success comes early to those who use what abilities they have. There is no contradiction between their careers and their inner natures, because society itself is plastic. But Clyde and the younger generation in *The Bulwark* are their dialectic opposites. Clyde is the most pathetic failure in Dreiser—even more so than Hurstwood, Carrie's second lover. In order to get ahead, he has to pretend, to tell social lies, and to act deceitfully. In his time the path of opportunity is no longer open, there have been alterations in the American Dream. In the early works, this dream operates as a motivation to rise on the basis of one's talents, energies, and capacities; in the later, the dream becomes one of success by marriage in order to have a life of leisure and enjoyment. Clyde is an ambitious youth in an America more stratified than that of Cowperwood and Witla. Thus Dreiser not only reveals the meaning of American social ideals in his own lifetime and during the period immediately preceding his birth; his works also mirror the changes in those ideals, and the change in the social structure of American life.

Dreiser's methods of characterization are consistent with these attitudes and social revelations. Just as he does not conceive the individual as individual, so his characterizations are not mere representations of atomized men and women struggling in the American society of their time. They appear in their social roles, and their natures as well as their actions are involved in the functions which they perform in society. Carrie's first lover, Drouet, is one of the most successful and attractive of Dreiser's minor characters. He is jolly, genial, superficial, yet he is strikingly different from the salesmen of, for example, Sinclair Lewis. Drouet does not subordinate himself to the "fetish of commodities"; a successful salesman, he is concerned with a life of pleasure, he feels secure in his world. He appears in a social role which is an integral feature of his "individuality." Similarly, Hurstwood has the charm, the savoir-faire, the sophistication of the professional major-domo in a high-class saloon, concerned with meeting important personages. When he loses this position, he loses also the personality that goes with it. His character is social rather than individual, and his defeat is that of a man who has lost his function and place in society. The tragedy in Dreiser's novels is social tragedy. His characters do not merely represent themselves; they speak for their classes and their occupations. *An American Tragedy* would remain a tragic work even if Clyde and Roberta had not died; but it is tragic in a new sense. In Dreiser, the old terms of art are reset by the social thinking of his day.

Such characterizations as his are not mere types. Their traits are linked to occupation only as growth or decay occurs in relationship with occupation or sex experience. In the instances where sex is the dominant functional aspect of a life, we can observe his method of characterization from a primarily biological angle. Carrie, when she is a "kept woman," grows, expands in desire. She begins to realize her nature; she becomes more sociable, more sure of herself; the road is opened to her so that she can utilize her potentialities. Jennie as a mistress reveals a steady deepening of emotions and sympathies. But even biological impulses are social in their expression and development. The Social Darwinism of Dreiser's basic attitudes toward human nature is distilled into a social philosophy of determinism and change. Again, without formulation of a system (ironically, he became a communist only just before he died), he supplies the means by which basic questions about twentieth century American society may be asked.

5

Forgetful of the integrity and power of Dreiser's whole work, many critics have been distracted into a condemnation of his style. He was, like Twain and Whitman, an organic artist; he wrote what he knew—what he was. His many colloquialisms were part of the coinage of his time, and his sentimental and romantic passages were written in the language of the educational system and the popular literature of his formative years. In his style, as in his material, he was a child of his time, of his class. Self-educated, a type or model of the artist of plebeian origin in America, his language, like his subject matter, is not marked by internal inconsistencies. As a style, in the formal sense, it never developed at all, and he frequently permitted his novels to be revised by others before publication.

Dreiser has also been upbraided because of his auctorial comments. The newness of his material and method seemed to him to need explanation, and the censorship and rejection of certain of his novels did little to convince him that such explanation was not necessary. He had no model upon which to shape his attack on the formal middle-class conventions of the times. He needed to be extensive in his realism, rather than concentrated and intensive like Flaubert or Balzac or Zola, who wrote from a richer and deeper literary tradition, and for a more sophisticated and culturally sensitive public than America could supply.

There are many passages in these novels that rise to high levels of passionate writing. In Dreiser the subject matter is always more important than the expression. Because he reveals the very nerves of American society he has exerted a more profound, a more lasting influence than any other novelist on twentieth century realistic fiction in America. Several generations of writers are already his debtors. His influence is discoverable in a seriousness of approach to the material of American life, in a greater freedom of theme, in the parallelism of ideas and phenomena. Dreiser described the broad patterns of modern American experience; his successors have been more intensive in their treatment. Because he was faithful to his art and made no compromises with the censors and the prudes, his work gives a sense of totality and finality.

72. FICTION SUMS UP A CENTURY

THE other major writers of fiction of this period—even those whose first important books were published in the twenties—were not innovators of a new era, but belonged to the nineteenth century in which were their roots. They were prewar in inspiration or in their sense of fundamental values, and were summary, not iconoclastic, in their artistic purposes. The women were deeply concerned with the preservation of character, and especially with virtue—*virtus* in the Roman sense, but implying more emotion and less sheer virility than the Romans gave to the word. It was the decay or survival of ideals of living resulting from the great American experiment in nation making which most stirred their imagination.

With the exception of Edith Wharton, these novelists functioned as guardians of the race, and especially of its emotional life. The men drew equally from reservoirs of confidence stored up in the American nineteenth century, but their emphasis seems to be different. They saw, angrily, a machine-made materialism sheltering behind and perverting the Protestant-Christian code, turning it into a religion of success; and they satirized the victims of low objectives, and a generation which seemed to be losing the spiritual force and the virility of its ancestors. Both men and women, when the end of the war released energy for literature, were prepared to capture the imagination of a public much more ready to become self-conscious than in the confident years before the war. It was a classic moment, the end and summation of an era, a moment also when criticism and creation were equal in power. It was a brief pause to define and distill American values before new and sharper changes in our mores and our philosophy began.

2

Inevitably the confusion, not to say chaos, of values which followed the wide demoralization of the Civil War had been reflected in literature. But, unlike many postwar eras, our seventies, eighties, and nineties were decades of unprecedented expansion and multiplication of wealth. Writers—and they were numerous—who felt as Henry James said in the sixties, that America needed most of all refinement, found, it is true, dramatic themes ready-made for their not always competent pens. The great theme of crude human energy developing a continent of unequaled potentiality, which Whitman had proclaimed, did not appeal to them, because this energy was too rough for refinement, and, indeed, not perfect democrats, as Whitman hoped, but powerful millionaires were its most conspicuous by-product. Yet this impact of new wealth upon old, and of a new and aggressive materialism upon the different ideals of pioneers and old aristocratic societies alike, supplied conflicts in ways of life, and hence fascinating subjects for the novelist of manners.

New wealth, for example, in this land of opportunity did not manifest itself so much in the increasing riches of the possessing classes as in new candidates for what Veblen called the conspicuous waste of the socially prominent. It was not so much oil or iron or lumber money that appeared in the ballrooms of New York as new families whose unlimited spending power was more advertised than its sources. The crudeness of the newcomers and the limitations of the settled way of life of the old dictators of society and custodians of what they called culture, were equally exposed to the imagination in search of a story.

The "outsider" to all this rush for wealth and power, such as a Theodore Dreiser, interpreting the excesses of freedom as one of the masses, could see the whole in perspective, but made the protagonists seem like figures of melodrama. An intellectual aristocrat, an "insider," not committed to any vital part of the social drama of the secure and the ambitious—such an "insider" as Henry James—recoiled from the grossness of unrefinement, yet found in the new types and new situations rich materials for his consummate art, especially when transferred to the revealing light of a European background. But his so-called disciple, Edith Wharton, was an insider in another sense. She belonged, she was committed to, the idea of society in its narrowest sense, a wealthy and secure society, the plutocratic aristocracy of New York and its affiliated capitals of American social life.

Edith Wharton was born into this society, she married in it. She accepted its self-claimed necessity; she doubted the need of secure wealth no more than did Jane Austen. It was not the attacks of barbarian millionaires and monopolists upon such economic democracy as we had been able to achieve which disturbed her. It was the narrow culture, the rigid codes, and the lack of all but defensive vitality of this American aristocracy which stung her imagination. Her first important novel, *The House of Mirth* (1905), reveals nothing in the history of Lily Bart which wealth could not cure. This novel is the tragedy of a lovely woman without money, in a society where that is the only guarantee of security. The feeble hero of the story is unable to help her with his love because he too is poor. In Mrs. Wharton's greatest novel, *The Age of Innocence* (1920), written in her maturity and the new maturity of the country, the rebellious heroine, the charming Countess Olenska, is provided with money in order to enable her to escape Lily Bart's tragedy, and she does escape, but only to a more enlightened aristocracy abroad where good talk was possible, as it was not in New York. But her lover, even when he and she are both free, is too emasculated by his traditions of hothouse security to take even an easy step toward emotional reality.

Yet in spite of the stale air, the limited visibility of this society of more or less than four hundred which Mrs. Wharton chose for her studies of American life, there was an opportunity here for the kind of fiction which Stendhal had written in France—studies of significant manners in a group where worth as human beings had little relevance to the importance of their behavior as individuals observably conditioned by a uniform environment, the thing that Cooper longed for in an earlier age when he said Americans could not have a literature until they had manners. All that was needed was sufficient skill on the part of the novelist, an intimate knowledge, and some purpose deeper than the merely descriptive.

With Mrs. Wharton the last was supplied by the sharpening social conscience of the first decades of the twentieth century. Her stories are evidently preliminary to the obsession with the values of American experience which is so characteristic of the fiction of the summary period of the twenties and the work of the somewhat younger novelists discussed later in this chapter. She had the intimate knowledge, and she had the skill. It was she and another insider, Ellen Glasgow, who began the attack upon the idols of the social temples, North and South. Hers, in wealthy New York, still dominated society; but they were clay, and, what she did not see with any conviction, they were quite unimportant in the history of the great American experiment, since this aristocracy had nothing to recommend it except its security, and was even more irresponsible than the new millionaires who crashed its gates. But she belonged—as Sinclair Lewis belonged in Main Street—and this gave her satire authenticity.

As for her skill, it is part of the extraordinary advance in the craft of construction and emphasis which developed so rapidly in the American nineties, especially in the short story of which she was a master. It is not true, as has often been said, that she learned her technique from Henry James. That great craftsman is at the same time more subtle and more natural in the handling of situations. What she learned from him was what had been rare in America before his day, the infinite care of the artist who regards perfect expression as the hardest, if not the most important, part of his task. She was his apprentice, but she does not belong to his school. His influence, which undoubtedly formed her artistic conscience, was so strong because his favorite characters spoke her language, and belonged to an environment where no lack of refinement in the art of mere living prevented the free play of the subtler emotions or suppressed the adventures and obscured the rebuffs of the intellect.

The briefest consideration of Mrs. Wharton's other books will show how much she is at her best when, like a court painter, she accepts her characters' assumption of their own importance, and gives them her finest because her most intimate work. If, as in *The Old Maid* (1924), she works sympathetically instead of satirically within her little New York world, she is superb. When, as in that piece of perfect craftsmanship, *Ethan Frome* (1911), she gets her theme in the harsh stoicism of the New England hills, it is not Ethan, or his unhappy lover or still more unfortunate wife, who gives the story its final direction, so much as the horror of the final scene of sordid misery for an observer coming from a world where the spiritual effects of crude poverty are unknown. When, as in *Hudson River Bracketed* (1929), she chooses for her subject what her social New Yorkers called "writing people," her skill is manifest, but her book is unreal and out of focus, even in its satire, for she does not seem sufficiently to care.

Mrs. Wharton, indeed, if one of the first of the new critics of American society, was one of the last of the old regionalists. America as a nation was still unreal to her. She was closer to the great regionalists of an earlier New England than to the writers of the twenties who would consciously make their stories microcosms of what was most significant to them in a culture where North, South, East, and West were blending. Historically, she is likely to survive as the memorialist of a dying aristocracy. Yet the effect of her success upon the technical standards of popular fiction must have been great.

In the other novelists of manners who either began or came into full powers and appreciation in these earliest twenties, the same discontent with a lack of emotional vitality in American society is evident. Indeed, it gives to their novels an edge and a fire usually lacking in mere stories of romantic or eccentric behavior. With the exception of Ellen Glasgow, these novelists were unmoved by the spectacle of an aristocracy slowly fossilizing. It was in bourgeois or industrial or pioneer communities that they found their themes. For them, New York was only a center of amusement, easy morals, and high finance, although it is true that for the next decades the society columns and fashion commentators were to shed a cheap glamour on a "smart set" now rapidly shifting toward the promiscuousness of café society." The best of them saw America in a national perspective as Edith Wharton could not. They were writing the fiction of that race of races, that total democracy which Whitman idealized and romanticized. An example is the brilliant analyst Zona Gale, author of *Miss Lulu Bett* (1920), who wrote too little. In her books the conventionalism of the Middle West is defeated by impulse and passion. The most high-spirited moralist among women writers of the period, Dorothy Canfield Fisher, pleads always for emotional integrity anywhere and against any odds. While Mrs. Wharton deplores the corrosions of security, Ellen Glasgow fears only that the nobler aristocratic values will die out of America with her dying Virginians. And passion, nobly interpreted, is Willa Cather's chief theme. Indeed, it is Ellen Glasgow and Willa Cather, the two finest craftsmen and artists in this movement toward a summary literature of the secure and confident nineteenth century, who best illustrate the woman's contribution to American fiction at the end of an era.

3

Willa Sibert Cather, born in 1876 in mountain Virginia, was transplanted to the rolling grasslands of Nebraska in time to know a frontier. Sensitive to beauty, and quick to detect significance, she saw the great land make and break its people. She saw the full-blooded European immigrants, Czechs and Swedes, plowing the unbroken land, on the way up from peasants to proprietors. She saw their puzzled admiration of American culture, which was also immigrant in these wild plains, but grown successful and a little stiff and stale. She saw the break between the generations when the children of the foreign pioneers came to town, to become more smug, more conventional than their American neighbors. Yet the fresh blood she describes was still vigorous. What reader will forget the Czech and Danish servants and working girls in *My Antonia,* rash in love, warm in heart and body, still seeking passion in the small-town respectability of the settled Middle West!

Miss Cather was educated at the University of Nebraska. She taught, found her way back East, and became an editorial assistant on Samuel McClure's magazine, the periodical which torpedoed the great monthlies of the genteel age, then growing safe and dull. Raids against the corruption and decay of politics at the end of the nineteenth century were its specialty, but McClure opened his columns to the new literature appearing on both sides of the Atlantic. Either then or later, Miss Cather's creative mind ranged widely through literature, and she chose her tradition in craftsmanship, which was French, and her subject matter, which was the heroic but neglected *virtus* of the last pioneers of the unconquered West. In 1912 she left *McClure's*; in 1913 she published *O Pioneers!*; in 1915, *The Song of the Lark*; in 1918, *My Antonia*; in 1920, her brilliant short stories, *Youth and the Bright Medusa*; in 1923, *A Lost Lady,* her most skillful though not her most powerful work; in 1927, *Death Comes for the Archbishop,* her masterpiece; in 1931, *Shadows on the Rock.* These are her most important books.

Willa Cather, like the greatest of her predecessors among women in English fiction, Jane Austen, was extraordinarily consistent in her art from beginning to end. She did not experiment except within the limits of her purpose; she knew exactly what she wanted to do. And this can be described in her own words from a book *Not Under Forty* (1936), in which she recorded her admiration for her master in the art of fiction, Gustave Flaubert, and for her older contemporary, Sarah Orne Jewett. After learning to write the novelist must unlearn it, she wrote, for his material must go

through a process very different from that by which he makes merely a good story. No one can define this process exactly; but certainly persistence, survival, recurrence in the writer's mind, are highly characteristic of it. The shapes and scenes that have "teased" the mind for years, when they do at last get themselves rightly put down, make a much higher order of writing, and a much more costly, than the most vivid and vigorous transfer of immediate impressions.

Every fine story must leave in the mind of the sensitive reader an intangible residuum of pleasure; a cadence, a quality of voice that is exclusively the writer's own, individual, unique. . . . It is a common fallacy that a writer . . . can achieve this poignant quality by improving upon his subject-matter, by using his "imagination" upon it and twisting it to suit his purpose. The truth is that by such a process (which is not imagination at all!) he can at best present only a brilliant sham. . . . If he achieves anything noble, anything enduring, it must be by giving himself absolutely to his material. And this gift of sympathy is his great gift; is the fine thing in him that alone can make his work fine.

This is what Willa Cather proposed to do in her novels; she succeeded, thanks to a discipline in the absolute justice of the word, which she may have learned from Flaubert, and to an art of suspense, acquired probably from her own experience with the American short story, in which she was both critic and creator. Jane Austen let what "teased" her imagination flow along the framework of a conventional plot. She twisted neither plot nor subject matter to suit her purpose, and when her sympathy was discharged and her plot unrolled, was content to end with the handiest convention. Willa Cather discarded plot from the beginning. She yielded to her subject matter, content to evoke its cadences, its qualities, its stream of significant experience. Even the poignant death of the lovers in *O Pioneers!*, surely one of the notable scenes in English literature, is known only by its preliminaries and its evidences, as if to have made it a climax of a plot would have detracted from its perfect place in a chronicle of a land so immature, so hard that passion could find only a thwarted release.

Therefore, from beginning to end, the Cather novels are not stories of plot, but chronicles, given a depth and significance lacking in the merely historical chronicle by that "sympathy" which leads to a perfect interplay of environment and character.

Her art was essentially a representation of this reaction between the soul of man and its environment. That is why the best of her stories are told against the land—the sweep of red grass on the rolling plains of Nebraska, the hard warm mesas of the Southwest tempering the unconquerable spirit of the archbishop, shadows of the wilderness and the winter crowding in upon the tiny culture of France on the rock of Quebec. Her best characters are least at home in the fabricated cities which so stirred the naïve heart of Sinclair Lewis' Babbitt. Chicago as a city, to Thea when she is learning to sing in *The Song of the Lark,* means only trivial discomfort and an irrelevant confusion.

With *Death Comes for the Archbishop,* Willa Cather left even the semblance of fiction for pure chronicle. This novel is the *vitae* of two saints, a Paul and a Peter of the desert, and its story is a record of their minds and hearts and souls. So was *O Pioneers!* the story of a group of immigrants humanizing the land, so was *My Ántonia* the story of a great woman ennobling common things and a common struggle by elemental passion. But in the two obvious chronicles, of the archbishop and of the rock of Quebec, the narrative is distilled into biography. Here were lives working upon and wrought upon by a new land and its people. And the same was true of her late book, *Sapphira and the Slave Girl* (1940), with its unsatisfactory ending, where the teller of the tale does what Flaubert (so she says) never would do, enters herself upon the scene and "encourages familiarity."

If one asks how these chronicles are made evocative, comprehensive, and interest-holding, the answer is as easy to define as it is difficult to explain in detail. There is a selection of incident and appearance, and an inevitability of language (as with Flaubert and Turgenev) so careful that the result is a candid, if delusive, simplicity. It is candid because the author so evidently has given herself to the theme and found words for her experience; it is delusive because this simplicity is, of course, not easy but a fine art. And her own absorption in her people and her land creates the suspense that she herself has felt.

She was consistent in her craft, and also in her choice of character and theme. Like all the important novelists of this end of an era, she sought an emotional vitality great enough to break through stiffening conventions and repel the ideas of materialistic success. Her stories present the old case of the artist versus the people, the heart versus what the public calls success, the life of the spirit versus materialism, a case under trial for a century in prosperous America. But she offered an interesting variant in organizing her stories about the life of a good man or woman—that is, a human being intensely, often rapturously, devoted to the experiences of deep living itself. Alexandra in *O Pioneers!* is such a person with the emphasis upon a will to tame the American land for the needs of the future. Marie, the Bohemian girl, in the same book, is the essence of being alive, the very pulse of the blood personified, doomed to be the victim somehow of what we so justly call ill nature. Antonia is such a character, not too fine, not too nice in her ethics, determined upon happiness and getting it because she never counts the costs. Mrs. Forrester in *A Lost Lady* is not lost because of her adulteries. She is lost because her incomparable gift of charm cannot sustain itself by its own worth, but must feed on the gross sensualities of gross men. Her husband is the good man of this story, good because he understands that his wife is a precious jewel worth all the tribe about her, even though fibered with clay.

As Willa Cather grew older, she seemed to have exhausted her own best memories, and sought in history for subject matter less personal and more difficult. And so (influenced perhaps again by Flaubert) she left the present, left her own Middle West, and absorbed herself in the austere, ascetic, intractable beauty of New Mexico, and the Catholic culture of Quebec. Yet her characters have the same significance. The archbishop again is the good man endeavoring to make life and himself not more or less prosperous, but richer in spiritual passion, though he had no prejudices against the earthly variety. His good is *virtus*—character, love of experience, including emphatically the vitality of sensuous experience. He is a good man whose energy is challenged by the opportunities in a new land to create new and better experience for his followers. Thus, when he comes in the wake of American conquest to New Mexico he pioneers for his church with an almost sensual satisfaction. He is aware of the value of every genuine emotion, whether the gusto of the half-pagan priests of the old regime, or the Castilian decorum of his Spanish patrons, or the dark and true part-souls of his Indians. Only the cheap and the predatory rouse him to anger. With him is Father Joseph, a good animal irradiated by religion, a medieval saint saved from fanatical disaster by the finer intellect of the man he loves. The novel itself is the projection of these two lives against a compelling environment. It is good history, but it transcends history because its theme is the vitality of holiness. There is little to add in this respect of her later *Shadows on the Rock* which, with less power but equal purity, portrays the good life in conflict with worldly ambition and the wilderness in seventeenth century Quebec.

Thus Willa Cather usefully filled her niche in American literary history. Her youthful background in the unmade West, and her sensitiveness to the pervasive influence of new land upon European man, made her the summer-up of our long tradition of local color, now felt to be part of the history of the imagination of a great country. And her feeling for vital passion in any of its forms (passion, she says, is what she seeks in all her stories), gave her power over a theme unique in the nineteenth century, the overflow of vigorous men and women from the Old World into new country, after a thousand years of stability. She made personal history of Whitman's "race of races" in its formative century. Her art is not a big art. It does not respond to the troubled sense of American might and magnitude realized but undirected, and felt so strongly by such men as Sinclair Lewis in the same decades. It is national in significance, but not in scope. Her colleagues among the men "sweated sore" over that job, whereas her books rise free and are far more creative than critical. She is preservative, almost antiquarian, content with much space in little room—feminine in this, and in her passionate revelation of the values which conserve the life of the emotions. She knew evil, and suffered from the grossnesses of materialism and the smugness of cheap success, but preferred to celebrate the vitality of the good.

4

Ellen Glasgow was also from Virginia, and her ancestry is in the western mountain regions which were the first frontier of the tidewater aristocracy. But she remained in Virginia, and her impressive list of novels deals throughout with Virginians at home, or seeking new fortunes among the Virginia emigrants to New York. She spent a lifetime on deeply sympathetic studies of the end of an aristocratic culture, and the defeat of an agrarian people by their own misuse of the land. Both women were idealists, but Willa Cather was drawn to the dawn and Ellen Glasgow to the sunset. Both were concerned with values which should be conserved for the country. In Willa Cather's most characteristic novels the land is just beginning to yield its wealth to the settler, in Ellen Glasgow's it is worn out; yet in both mankind is in a state of becoming. Nor was either deflected in purpose by the current materialism which made satirists of the best of the men among their contemporaries. Ellen Glasgow's heroes and heroines triumph spiritually, Sinclair Lewis' do not.

Ellen Glasgow herself divided her novels into three groups, and discussed them in *A Certain Measure* (1943), which contains some of the best personal criticism written by an American novelist. Novels of the Commonwealth, novels of the Country, novels of the City, she calls them, the Commonwealth being Virginia, the Country being the rural and the mountain region west of tidewater, the City being Richmond. The grouping does not conform strictly to the chronology of her work. She began with Virginia history in the decades before, and in, and just succeeding the Civil War, so disastrous to Virginia. Then she moved upward to her own times, where two themes chiefly interested her: the endeavor to survive in and renew an exhausted land; and the struggle to preserve spiritual ideals of life and character in a prosperous and materialistic city. She is most colorful in her early historic novels, where, with an impassioned realism, she handles the story of the Lost Cause which the sentimentalists had made into a rosy legend. She is most profound and greatest in her stories of the land. She is most subtle, most ironic, and most critical in her novels of city life. Typical examples are *The Battle-Ground* (1902), *Barren Ground* (1925), and *The Romantic Comedians* (1926).

Ellen Glasgow chose for her motto, "What the South needs is blood and irony"; but there is less irony in her collected works than one expects, and more of the blood of a discriminating idealism. When she began to write at the turn of the nineteenth century, at the very climax of a confident age, the novelists of the South were capitalizing glamour and sentiment. Their favorite characters came from a never-never land of imagination, and they were compensating for the defeat of one way of life by another with whitewash tinted in rose, and success stories where, on such lines, there could be no success. Their realities were the memories of childhood, and their novels had a wide sentimental appeal but not much particular truth. Ellen Glasgow, even as a girl, determined to begin a "solitary revolt" against the formal, the false, the affected, the sentimental, and the pretentious in Southern writing.

The importance of this solitary revolt seems less now that the Thomas Nelson Pages and the other Southern novelists of glamour have faded almost out of memory. Yet a familiar and sympathetic culture which has not been made truly articulate is a challenge to the best powers of a novelist. "I had no guide," she says, and so, not desiring to imitate the "regimented realism" of William Dean Howells, then dominant in the North, she went, like Willa Cather, to the old masters of fiction, Balzac, Flaubert, De Maupassant, and the great English novelists. There she learned to define the art of fiction as the "assembling of material and the arrangement of masses," which has more of construction and perhaps less of art than Willa Cather's resolve to give herself utterly to her subject matter; and also to believe that fiction itself was "experience illuminated," with which Willa Cather would certainly agree.

Thus, and as might be expected, Ellen Glasgow's novels have the effect as well as the scope of social history. She is close to Dreiser and Howells and Sinclair Lewis here, though so different in her sympathies and her interests. And yet she was utterly uninfluenced by Dreiser, the most powerful of her contemporaries. In his massive, plodding defense of the unfortunate he was oblivious to the stoic ideals of character, the aristocratic virtues which, even in her stories of poverty, irradiate sordid experience. Where Lewis attacked with savage scorn, she used irony; and her leading characters, even her happiness seekers, as she calls them, are the morally successful, not the spiritually dead. "The spirit of fortitude has triumphed over the sense of futility" in her Dorinda in *Barren Ground,* and elsewhere in her lengthy gallery of portraits. Her women especially conserve, and were chosen to conserve, true values, not to destroy false ones. And she was like Howells only in this, that her purpose was not only to create life (the chief duty, as she says, of a novelist) but to reflect, as no Southern novelist had done before, the true movement and tone of a society and an age.

In describing Ellen Glasgow as essentially a novelist of social history, there is no intent to confuse her particular art with the historian's, or with the romancer's whose leading figures are only shadowy types. Ellen Glasgow, like Sherwood Anderson, begins always with the personality manifesting itself, and stirring the imagination with its hint of a story. The black-haired girl beside a whitewashed wall, seen in a fleeting glimpse, steps out into the sunlight, puts on identity, and is the cause, if not the purpose, of *Barren Ground,* perhaps her finest novel. Judge Honeywell in *The Romantic Comedians* "had endured the double-edged bliss of a perfect marriage" for thirty-six years, when his wife's death opened the gates of folly.

And yet the ultimate significance of all these novels is social, and we remember the struggle and its background and the form and pressure of the society better than the names of the characters. These books tell the story of the conflict of generations in Richmond. They show the vein of iron in the character of a strong stock which rusts but never softens at the core. They reveal, as in *The Battle Ground,* the moral destruction of war. So morally significant are these old aristocrats, lovely ladies, determined girls, that they illustrate the types to which they belong. They are rich in what she calls "the individual graces" of the past, "the perpetually escaping spirit of the thing we call life." History in its deepest sense always flows around them. Something they lose of unique personality by comparison with Willa Cather's figures, whom one always thinks of by name.

Like her fellow Virginian James Branch Cabell, Ellen Glasgow was young in the nineties when style as an achievement in itself was most in favor among the literary. Her careful workmanship, her "single artistic endeavor," saved her, as it did not save Cabell, from the rhetoric of that period; yet as a stylist she belongs with this literary period of time. The "old guard," as she called them, of her youthful day, although genteel and complacent, at least wrote with a professional care for beauty as they understood it. She had no sympathy, though she recognized the limitations of the old patterns, for the "amateurs," the experimentalists in force, vulgarity, and brutishness, practitioners of the unlovely, disdainers of form, who in the mid-twenties took over leadership in American fiction.

Her own style is classic in a good sense, but it is not the classicism of Willa Cather. It is a style of evident rhythms, a garment of flowing words, that describes rather than evokes, though in her descriptions of Virginia backgrounds she evokes also. It is a style which, like Thomas Hardy's, moves in masses rather than word by word, reflecting "the vision of the artist in the direct light of imagination" and playing upon life with "absolute fidelity of treatment." As with Hardy, it is an all-embracing garment that sometimes diverts or strains the attention of the reader. Her simpler, less stylistic books, dealing with the unsophisticated, like *Vein of Iron* and *Barren Ground* were most popular. But in her consciousness of style as such she summarized an era of American fiction soon to end.

5

The work of James Branch Cabell, another Virginian, born in 1879 at Richmond, Virginia, was once a cult for the literary, and is still significant in American letters. Aside from some newspaper experience in New York, his life was essentially that of a Virginia scholar and gentleman, such a life as Poe aspired to live. In his fruitful period, Cabell created a saga, a mythology, and a satire of a country of phantasy called Poictesme, which was medieval in appearance, chivalric in action, and satiric and cynical in spirit. His theme was ironic, romantic disillusion. Therefore it is biographically noteworthy that he sprang from one of the distinguished families of the old Virginian aristocracy which had been supplying myth and romance to sentimental novelists. Also, that in 1896–1897 he was instructor in French and Greek at William and Mary College, the two literatures from which he drew most of his materials for symbolism, both sexual and moralistic.

In the years when Cabell achieved fame, and when his style was the admiration of younger writers, he was engaged upon variants of one general idea. Beginning very early in his career, and continuing through *Figures of Earth* (1921) and *Something About Eve* (1927), the same females, prankishly disguised as nature myths, demons, or heroines of fable, and the same hero, whose *virtus* comes from a collaboration of moral skepticism with sexual might, appear and reappear in different blends and emphases. Many parts of these books are repetitive, confusing, mannered, and gross in their symbolism. But at least once Cabell's great power over expression, his talent for phantasy, and his carefully planned satire were combined in a moving and brilliant story which sums up his literary endeavor. This book is *Jurgen,* which was published in 1919, and got much useful publicity by its encounters with Philistia and the law. *Jurgen* did much to crack the taboo on sex in American fiction.

Jurgen himself was a nihilistic epicurean, better educated in philosophy and the art of living than Walt Whitman, but further away from the true ideals of epicureanism. He was endowed with what he calls cleverness, the only trait of which he is never skeptical. Anthropologists would call it that gift of curiosity which accounts for the intellectual progress of the human race. Jurgen is a paunchy pawnbroker of Poictesme married to a nagging wife who nevertheless keeps him comfortable; but his youth has been spent in amorous and romantic adventures, and his ideas of how to live are entirely aristocratic. By a shrewd bargain with the mythical mistress of disillusion, he gets back his youth stripped of its illusions, and begins a fantastic seeking through the imagination of the past for the kind of justice which will satisfy a sensual egotist who is too clever to be taken in by shams, too gross to be attracted by nobility, too skeptical to be content with anything short of an ultimate purpose revealed in things as they are. He finds none, although in his journey he visits all the famous seductive females, the engaging myths, and interesting heroes of history, and even enters hell and heaven.

He does discover two motives for existence which seem to have validity. There is love (not the amorous variety) which is to be esteemed, but is evidently impracticable for an aristocratic poet, so much of whose time is inevitably engaged by love of a more earthy kind. And there is pride which, if impossible for whoever created this sorry world, can be attained by a clever human whose curiosity is undaunted by disillusion. Yet, except for the satisfactions of curiosity, Jurgen views all revelations and all experience with skepticism.

Cabell's philosophy, as indicated by his choice of characters, and his conception of *virtus,* was fundamentally irresponsible, as has indeed been the philosophy of many ironists of the past. Life may be an idle dream, says Jurgen, shrugging his shoulders, but "what could I be expected to do about it?" This is not the irresponsibility of a later generation of writers assailed by Archibald MacLeish (in *The Irresponsibles*) and others, who were so obsessed with their diagnosis of the ills of their country that they failed to detect and encourage the idealism and the fortitude of American youth. Yet if one considers that Cabell's novels of Poictesme are one long attack upon the stale chivalry and the perfunctory religion of Virginia, and upon a bourgeois morality and an insensitiveness to beauty and to emotional truth in the American bourgeoisie in general—why, then it is fair to say that Cabell was irresponsible. For he belonged with Bernard Shaw in his prankish moods and Anatole France in his destructive ironies, and, following them, took more pleasure in putting a symbolic Galahad to bed with a symbolic Guinevere than in any attributes useful for the progress or the survival of the race. This, of course, is a description, not a condemnation. The satirist does not have to play ball with the future. But Cabell's local animosities often limited his truth.

In another aspect, Cabell was unquestionably a link between past and future in the transition of American literature. He was a romanticist, close in his subject matter and his incidents to the cloak-and-sword best sellers of the decades before *Jurgen*. But he was a romanticist with claws and teeth. He satirized his own aristocratic Main Street while sharing its tastes and habits of life. He was unread, and was perhaps unreadable, by a later generation which was forced into entire realism by a volcanic explosion of moral evil and efficient force, and was somewhat too doubtful of any craftsman in words. The stoic energy, the passion for life, the courage of Willa Cather's best characters seem now to have been truly valuable elements in American culture, over which Jurgen's contemporary swordplay (both sexual and skeptical) flashes like a comedian's trick. Yet Cabell's irony and his skepticism were clearly a first and necessary step toward the sarcastic realism of a Sinclair Lewis, and the escape from the prejudices, religious, philosophical, and sexual, of the dying nineteenth century. It would be too much to say that later writers acquired a necessary disillusion from him; but certainly he was the most adroit psychoanalyst of American complacency, and subtlest gadfly of American hypocrisy, among the intellectuals of our early 1900's.

His style is brilliantly allusive, ornate, pointed, yet flowing. Like much of the romantic style of the turn of the century (and its architecture also), it is a pastiche, yet it is conscious pastiche, in which Cabell, like Joyce a little later, uses imitation and pseudoromanticism for his own purposes. It is, to go back to Ellen Glasgow's remark, a professional style, and unlike the experiments of Thomas Wolfe and of Ernest Hemingway in that it fits life into a literary tradition instead of the opposite. Very seldom does it escape from preciosity.

As a symbolist in the American line, he was more self-conscious than Hawthorne or Melville, and less passionate than Whitman. Cabell's symbolism translated his disillusioned observations upon things as they are into a biographical dictionary of literary history. His figures and the regions he created for them are often exceedingly beautiful, but they melt conveniently one into another, and have to be retranslated by the reader before they persist in his memory. And when they are translated, which is not always easy, the result is often scandalous.

The charge of excessive sexuality made against Cabell was based on these figures of fancy, all of whom, except Jurgen and his variants, represent attributes rather than personality and unanalyzable life. The narrative about them is two-thirds made up of episodes of the approach to or the escape from fornication. But if Cabell's sexuality is extreme, it is also sophisticated beyond danger to the innocent, and indeed more truly a reaction against the South's sentimental deification of "pure womanhood" than a call to passionate experience. The excess, for it is sometimes a tiresome excess, is part of Cabell's self-appointed mission as a devil sent to torment the genteel age and especially genteel literature. He came too soon to write, like the novelists of the thirties, naturally of natural things. Yet he passionately wished to pull off the veils of convention and announce the native amorousness of women, even when they were Virginians, and to portray man with sexual experience as his most exciting occupation. All this his symbolism permitted, and when the law penetrated some of his disguises, his rage against prudery increased to the detriment of his art. He was best when suppressed—which may be true of all fiction writers who are abler in the criticism of mores than in the creation of character and personality.

6

Sinclair Lewis was born in 1885 in Sauk Center, Minnesota, in the farther Middle West, a region in which, as he often asserted, were the roots of his inspiration. His mind was as sensitive to the lakes, the land, and more particularly to the small towns and energetic cities of this region as Thomas Hardy's to Wessex, or Jane Austen's to south England and to Bath—but not so affectionate!

Educated at Yale, in the class of 1907, he was a brilliant misfit in an orthodox university. Nevertheless, he sucked much from men and books in an environment easy for conformists, yet tolerant of cranks, wild men, and geniuses. His early years as publisher's assistant and writer showed no more promise than a gift for clever journalism. But in 1920 his *Main Street* astonished, where it did not outrage, reading America. In 1922 his *Babbitt* gave a name and a local habitation to an American type, which, despite frantic denials, was recognized, both here and abroad, as having as much truth as satire requires. In 1925 he published *Arrowsmith,* the best, if not the first novel of science, where materialism versus idealism supplies the theme. It is also satiric, frequently unfair, but packed, like the best social history, with authentic information. In 1930, having refused domestic honors, he was chosen as the first American to receive the Nobel Prize for distinction in literature. Already he was the most publicized American novelist of the decade.

The Middle West of Sinclair Lewis is the Middle West of Willa Cather, but with the often heroic period of pioneering on the land further in the background. His characters have come to town. The land is conquered, and no longer concerns them except as income or profit. They are bourgeois, not agrarian. Complacency, meanness, and boasting have cheapened their way of life, which was true of the small-town folk who provide the irritant in Miss Cather's stories. Main Street in Gopher Prairie and the city, Zenith, are both confident that they represent the best of the new world to come.

And yet Sinclair Lewis, no more than Ellen Glasgow or Willa Cather, was a rebel against the advertised ideals of the nineteenth century, whose deplorable end in crassness he was to depict. The morals of Protestantism, the ideals of progress, the scruples of a Christian, and the manners of a liberal gentleman, are all implicit in his reforms. It was a decadence of spirit and a hypocrisy of morals in the midst of abounding energy which provoked him to distress and anger. The energy itself and the things, the gadgets, which it had created, fascinated him, and he was furious because they had been captured by a predatory materialism, where money and size were the only standards of success. He was not, as was thought when *Main Street* was first published, the herald of a new literature, but the satirist who felt himself to be part of a matured society, which he castigated with no more intent to destroy than if he had been criticizing himself. The shock of the war had aroused desire for society's self-improvement. That Greek-Christian culture was beginning to struggle for survival had naturally not occurred to him. He was still confident.

Thanks to the First World War, there had been a sharpening of American nationalism, and also a renewed consciousness of the European tradition whose values we had begun to forget in our energetic isolationism. Thanks to the same war, the United States was building economic supremacy. Thanks to the spread of American literacy, it was possible to write for, as well as of, a wide middle class which was both sensitive and vulnerable because its economic success had made it representative of America. Discarding the historical, the romantic, the sentimental, the symbolic, and the analytic approach, adopting that very familiarity which Flaubert condemned, choosing the new journalism which dealt with behavior as his guide (though not his master), Lewis took aspects of himself, a representative man, rather than a saint or artist or great lover, as the subject of his story, and so began his series of novels.

There, as always with these writers of the end of the age of security, the values of American living provided the theme. But it was not the ideal values (which he did not question) upon which his fiery spirit turned its pity and scorn, but the actual values which determined the careers of these overconfident men and women, whose lives, outwardly successful, rang hollow, or were wrecked in emotional crises or personal disasters. The crassly materialistic "villains" who are in the background of a Cather or a Glasgow novel, take the center of the stage in his work, and are more significant than his idealists who try to escape from them. For the rough task of faithfully representing the kind of society which his Middle West was making, irony was too delicate a weapon. He chose satire and sarcasm, for which he had more talent, and carried them to the edge of caricature. He was a novelist not writing *of* a situation, as Miss Cather had recommended, but *from* the inside of a situation of which he himself was part, and thus more eager to point than to prophesy, and more concerned with behavior, with which he was intimate, than with final interpretation.

Therefore, even as the dominant social class of nineteenth century England is most truly seen in the keen observation of the novels of Anthony Trollope, so the best social history of the "white collar" class of the United States at the high tide of its success is provided by these novels of Sinclair Lewis because of their almost naïve honesty and their accurate focus upon typical experience. That all of Lewis' important books deal directly or indirectly with the Mississippi Valley does not lessen their scope, for that is the heart of America, and his satire of Zenith needed only qualifications to be true for Los Angeles or New York.

Main Street, for example, begins like a novel by one of the women of the period, with a talented girl caught in a cramping environment, the small and ugly town of Gopher Prairie. Yet this is to be no story of a saint or a stoic or a creative artist. Carol Kennicott is a product of genteel education, and brings with her to Gopher Prairie a thin culture, vague in its objectives, and trivial in its requirements which seldom go beyond a pretty room to sit in and good talk. She proposes, nevertheless, to reform the town, socially, aesthetically, politically, and is broken, like the butterfly she is, because her intellectual and aesthetic frippery, sterile even in herself, cannot possibly function among men and women whose vulgar grossness (and kind hearts) require a new set of values, not new manners, in order to make a culture of their own. There is no reality in Carol, not even an emotional reality, though it is questionable whether Lewis in 1920 understood how artificial were her standards. She is cold, even in her sexual relations, and the best she can do toward adjustment to life is to escape for a year or so to Washington where she can talk, if not practice, intellectual improvement, and then to come back with enough tolerance to settle down as just another Gopher Prairie woman.

The town is the real subject and the triumph of *Main Street*—not Carol, who is, after all, an example of Lewis' somewhat naïve admiration in 1920 for the "intelligentsia." Lewis must have been well aware that a thousand communities in France and England were duller, meaner, less literate than this home of the second generation of westward-moving frontiersmen, where there was at least the belief that here civilization was on its way up. But his fierce idealism for America, and perhaps some defects in wisdom and perspective, make *Main Street* not only a picture but also a crusade against the cheapness of American ambitions. His men think in stereotypes. They profess the liberalism of their forefathers (as also in *Babbitt*), but practice economic domination of the poor farmers who are too dumb to live by their wits. Their conversation seldom gets beyond the twelve-year age level. The women live by gossip, and culture is a tepid circulating of stale and harmless ideas. Yet Lewis likes them as much as he hates their current values. Dr. Kennicott loves his furnace better than the Parthenon, but he does represent science heroically at work upon one of its frontiers. And if this friendly little society is almost elemental in the pleasures which it really enjoys, at least Main Street life has more gusto than the proposed activities of Carol's "city beautiful." Lewis is a distressed and disgusted idealist, not a cynic. His anger is worth while.

As a novel of character *Main Street* does not reach the highest rank, and as satire its edge is dulled because the author keeps changing sides. The book stirred America from coast to coast, not by its philosophy, but by the inescapable truth and remarkable intimacy of his picture of American behavior.

Lewis could not get his heart into Carol. He was too much a part of Main Street himself to think that she knew the answers. The significant American there was not the second-rate intellectual, but the back-slapping, boosting good fellow who had so much energy and good will, and only a secondhand morality and third-rate objectives toward which to steer his life. Lewis needed a man for his hero, an idealist like himself even if stunted and warped by a bad education and a set of false values. George F. Babbitt was his first great character creation, because Babbitt was as human as his author. He was a far more deadly instrument of satire than the somewhat sociological figures of *Main Street*.

And the book, *Babbitt,* branded the go-getting American, and burnt through his thick hide. George F. Babbitt could not be written off as a caricature, for he was a tragic figure. The man was kind; he was pathetic in his efforts to be both happy and successful; he was as sincere as he was ludicrous in his conviction that he served the community; he was completely devoid of self-knowledge except in brief, devastating gleams of the truth that he had never done what he really wanted; he was completely inconsistent in his morals, he could be both a strutting rooster and a runaway dog trying to sneak home. In fact, he was entirely male, completely bourgeois, and as much of a personality in his way as Falstaff, who was also created for satire.

To tell this man's story with scrupulous realism was inevitably to be satiric. Babbitt is living in the speed-up of the industrial revolution. Zenith is his wonder city, whose misty towers in the morning light provide his one concept of pure beauty—Zenith where automobiles breed faster and better than men. In Zenith everything except respectability is sold or bought for a price, and buying and selling are ends in themselves. In Zenith all boasts come true, because the Babbitts boast only of size and number, both of which science has made possible to very mediocre men. No souls are necessary in Zenith, for a lack of spiritual dignity is compensated by a pride in gadgets, which anyone who works hard enough where the money is, can possess. A new cigar lighter is a baptism into a faith, a new automobile a conversion. And to control and give objectives to all this activity is a code of individualism stereotyped from the heroic age of the frontier, when the pioneer's ability to produce made or broke him.

No one had to think about ultimates, for no one could doubt the religion of success which made a Zenith possible. Yet the society of Zenith was so efficient in its production of wealth and comfort that it had to be explained by something nobler than the ethics of profit on which its practice was based. Hence the accepted morality of "Root, hog, or die" was twisted to cover anything that made money. Profit was morality, for profit was clearly service, and service justified itself. Thus it became necessary for Babbitt and his kind to conform, verbally at least, to ideals of service, because, once you denied that the go-getter served the community and was himself truly successful, the whole show became immoral.

Babbitt, which begins with an ironical description of a perfect bathroom and the morning ritual of a gadget-minded man, soon passes into satire. The really vigorous faith of Babbitt himself in his Rotary clubs, his deals, his capacities for leadership, soon begins to threaten wreck on the reefs of personal experience not provided for by his philosophy. His world was like a river steamer, all flimsy top, built for quick profits, sailing down broad but treacherous currents, with the rudder set on the shortest course to wealth, and no pilot on the bridge.

Like so many characters of the novels of the era, Babbitt himself is a good man with tremendous vitality. But he is abysmally ignorant of everything but salesmanship. Like Lewis himself, he really cares for the success of his country, and for its ideals as he understands them. Lewis' immediate successors in a more irresponsible decade were not to care. Babbitt does not represent Babbittry, which, as is now evident, was an endemic disease, epidemic only in his generation. He is its victim, a victim of class pressure and his own mentality, a human being with close relationship to every American of his period, even though he has become a symbol of the false motives that got him down. And he is prophetic of nothing. All that he had learned from his experience was that you should do what you really like—and so he tells his son in the last chapter. But the next generation did not know what they

vanted, and were swept into the war, which recognized at least the true
values of necessity.

Sinclair Lewis was never to write a more memorable book than *Babbitt*.
However, in *Arrowsmith* (1925) he not only took a different grip upon the
same American problem, but also brought in new sets of values, true and
false. Babbitt seemed pathetic to Lewis. He was a man blown up till he burst
spiritually by subservient and erroneous ideas of how to be happy and successful. Martin Arrowsmith is much closer than Babbitt to Lewis himself.
His early environment is shoddy and materialistic, but he gets some real
education and has more self-knowledge at the beginning of his career than
Babbitt ever acquired. He chooses the hard way of science, and in his muddled
and inconsistent course, fights through the shams and compromises, the
temptations and false values, and finally the commercialized idealism of the
vested interests of the medical profession. Babbitt intended to be a lawyer
and to defend the rights of the poor. Martin does become the scientist he
wished to be, learning on the way what real service to the community means,
and the price that has to be paid by a searcher for the truth.

In *Arrowsmith* appears the first really likable woman in Lewis' novels.
His women are usually mischief makers, or are possessive, like Martin's
second wife from whom he escapes into the happiness of pure research, or
negligible, like Mrs. Babbitt. Leora, Martin's first wife, never wavers in faith
in her husband and the protection of his personality. Her values as a wife
are sound and genuine. She plays her man's game—is indifferent to anything
else. For Sinclair Lewis was no feminist. Indeed, a much later book, *Cass
Timberlane* (1945), contains some of the most violent attacks on women ever
written in America, and the thesis that American men are afraid of their
wives. Yet it is also a setting for Jinny Timberlane, one of his most engaging
characters.

Arrowsmith is Lewis' most informative book, and in it he again showed
that his scope was broader, if his searching less deep, than that of his contemporaries. He was so fascinated with America that he could not stop with
its values but rushed on to get the whole vast panorama, as he saw it, down
on paper. He gorged his reader on dramatic fact. The problem of Arrowsmith
was how to stay on the side of the angels. But Lewis did no cheek-turning.
He could not endure what he regarded as moral cowardice or hypocrisy.
This made him, sometimes, unjust and unfair.

He was the most powerful novelist of the decade when American fiction
in general matured in scope and in art. He was not so powerful as the
pioneer Dreiser, but was more accomplished in craftsmanship. He was not
so mellow as Ellen Glasgow, nor had he the evocative quality of perfected
art in which Willa Cather was a master. He had no trace of the passion of

beauty as such of the nineties. Yet the genteel critics of the twenties who called him a super-journalist invading the fields of literature were quite wrong. Like his elder contemporary, the great journalist H. G. Wells, he was a reporter of new problems and types emerging in a society rapidly transforming under the influences of science and industrialism. But for Lewis—a true man of letters—the qualities of that society were more interesting than its possibilities. He pledged himself to create in words a living America, and for that he saw, as Dreiser did not, that a style was essential. It is not a beautiful style, though it is capable of great beauty. It is a style of sharp-pointed description of the gadgets of the new materialism, and of most skillful dialogue and monologue which often carry the story and reveal the characters with only a push now and then by the author. *The Man Who Knew Coolidge* (1928) is a tour de force of this monologue, here used without the frame of a story. His ear was extraordinary. That this is the way Americans of his kind talk, no one has denied. But it was not at first realized that this revelation of a people by the rhythm and emphasis of their conversation is a style of a high order, such as Petronius Arbiter and Stendhal and Mark Twain, at his best, achieved for their times.

It is interesting, therefore, to note that *Main Street* was dedicated to two contemporary stylists of different schools, Cabell and Joseph Hergesheimer. Lewis was a rebel against the rhetoric of the nineties, and owed nothing to Cabell's style. But the Virginian's attack on the hypocritical Puritanism of the nineteenth century may have first suggested to him the discrepancy between fully sexed men and women as they appeared in life, and in American books about them. He was not much interested in sexuality as such, and so the frankness of his novels irritated rather than aroused the genteel. Here again he represented the balanced end of a period rather than the defiant emphasis upon sexual intercourse for its own sake which was to be a theme for the next literary generation. In *Cass Timberlane* he used for the first time, and to its furthest reaches, the frankness permitted by modern taste, but without a trace of pornography.

All of Lewis's later books can be described in terms of the analysis above, for they are variants and extensions of his first theme. The best is probably *Dodsworth* (1929), in which a far more sensitive and intelligent Babbitt escapes from a more sophisticated and ruthless Carol Kennicott who is determined to subdue man's soul to what she thinks is culture. The most abusive is *Elmer Gantry* (1927), which fluttered parsonages all over the United States. Here the go-getting clergyman, Elmer, carries Zenith's religion of success into the church itself. Gantry makes his deal with Mammon instead of the traction company, and exploits his God. In *Cass Timberlane* Lewis learned to strip his narrative to essentials and to substitute, without loss of unity, vignettes of parallel experiences for the digressive fullness of earlier stories. In *Kingsblood Royal* (1947) he chose the most sensational theme in America, the Negro question, and made a story which avoids all subtlety, though the violence of his treatment does not exceed the tragic drama of his plot.

7

Sherwood Anderson was born in 1876 in Camden, Ohio, his mother of Italian descent, his father an unsuccessful sign painter with a genius for self-dramatization. Anderson was self-educated after the elementary schools, a sensitive boy seeking answers which might explain human nature, more at home with Negroes, laborers, and hangers-on at livery stables and the race track than with the respectable and the ambitious. His best biography would not be the account of his career as manager of a paint factory, then as advertising writer, and afterward as short-story writer, novelist, and editor, but is to be found in *A Story Teller's Story* (1924), in which he wrote of his own life with precisely the impressionistic, introspective technique—psychoanalytic in character—which he applied to the personalities of fiction. "Having made a few bicycles in factories, having written some thousands of rather senseless advertisements, having rubbed affectionately the legs of a few race horses, having tried blunderingly to love a few women and having written a few novels that did not satisfy," he settled down at last in Marion, Virginia, where he edited two weekly newspapers, one Republican and one Democratic!

Sherwood Anderson's method of story-telling was even more consistent than Willa Cather's. He had one objective, and one technique, which is often loose, sprawling, and repetitive, though sometimes tightened, and particularly in his short stories, with very great art. His purpose was to get under the surface of everyday life in the America he knew best—the Ohio country and its small towns just below Lake Erie, with excursions to Chicago and New York. But his interests were very different from Miss Cather's or Sinclair Lewis'. It would be oversimplification to say that he worked in the subconscious of men and women whose conscious thoughts and feelings were commonplace, since the violent emotional lesions he reveals in his characters have often become conscious before the story begins. It would be more accurate to compare him with the students of abnormal psychology who were his contemporaries, although they did not influence him. His characters, however, are not pathological, but show what Anderson believes to be the normal results of emotional wounds in a sensitive mind. A disciple of either Freud or Jung would say that they are all subjects for psychoanalysis, yet Anderson was in no sense a scientific psychoanalyst. On the contrary, the spiritual lesions of his characters are precisely what make them important and valuable as human beings. His object was not to adjust the individual to a society which he regarded as dull, sterile, and insensitive, but to show how love in all its variants, and especially sexual love, will resist suppression by a mechanical and materialistic society, with such dynamic energy that it may crush or cripple the passionate woman or man.

It was Anderson's idea—and he wrote out of a rich experience—that something in the life of the Middle West he knew so well (though not only the Middle West) was inimical to love. "Suppose, I suggested to myself, that the giving of itself by an entire generation to mechanical things were really making all men impotent. There was a passion for size among all the men I had known. Almost every man I had known had a bigger house, a bigger factory, a faster automobile than his fellows." Were the factory workers who boasted of their sexual effectiveness doing so because year by year they felt themselves less effectual as men? "Were modern women going more and more toward man's life and man's attitude toward life because they were becoming all the time less and less able to be women?"

Sinclair Lewis felt all this, too (as did D. H. Lawrence in England). But Anderson, though his scope and his skill are less, is more intuitive, much more mystical, and far more concerned in his stories with the hurt girl or the warped man than with the apparatus and the traits of this mechanical civilization. His best stories, indeed, go back often to the horse-and-buggy age of his youth, and smugness, commercialism, respectability—anything that cramps emotion—will serve for his narrative as well as the industrial revolution.

All of Anderson's short stories and novels begin with a gesture, a look or an episode, however trivial, suggesting emotional tension and asking to be explained. Like the young reporter in *Winesburg, Ohio,* he was constantly being told stories, and in them one sentence would set his imagination going:

I was lying on my back on the porch, and the street lamp shone on my mother's face. What was the use? I could not say to her what was in my mind. She would not have understood. There was a man lived next door who kept going by the house and smiling at me. I got it into my head that he knew all that I could not tell mother.

This suggestive sentence is the germ of his long short story, "Out of Nowhere into Nothing," in *The Triumph of the Egg.* Such sentences (and scenes) were the "seeds" of stories. "How could one make them grow?"

And so, as Whitman rebelled against the conventions of meter and diction as not expressing his themes, Anderson rebelled against the current fashion of plot. "The plot notion did seem to me to poison all story-telling. Wha was wanted, I thought, was form, not plot. . . . Plots were frameworks about which the stories were to be constructed. . . . A new trick had been thought out." Willa Cather had meant the same thing when she urged the writer to give himself utterly to the situation. Both writers, as was natural at the end of a period when life seemed ripe for the imagination, spurned the half-gods of rhetoric and sought their own way of telling the truth. But a situation for Anderson contained no full-blooded woman conquering environment, or priest giving spiritual significance to a pagan landscape. Like his contemporary John Masefield, he preferred to write "of the maimed, of the halt and the blind in the rain and the cold," although for Negroes and race horses he had many a cheery word.

Confession stories, most of Anderson's tales might be called—a kind of story which, when cheapened and vulgarized, had great popular appeal. His novels are only expanded tales. As is true of so many American writers of fiction, the short story was his best medium, and there, in such stories as "I Want to Know Why" and "I'm a Fool," he did his finest work. Sometimes, as in the first of these two, it is a boy escaping from a restricted environment into the rich, easy life of the stables and track, where the Negroes take human nature and its pleasures as it comes, with no Protestant compulsions to bother them. And with the Negroes live the noble thoroughbreds, clean and courageous. How, admiring them, can human beings be so gross in comparison? (Whitman felt about animals much as he does.) Often the inspiration is neurotic but noble, as in the novel *Many Marriages* (1923), where a symbolic (and faintly absurd) nudity represents the ruthless stripping of convention necessary in order to begin a new emotional life. Sometimes the story explains the fluttering hands of a man in hiding, who had been a teacher with a gift for affection until his caresses had been misunderstood and his life broken. Nowhere is satire, everywhere sympathy, sometimes heated to anger. And if every story is a study of behavior, explained by a confession, the behavior is not for the sake of realism, though realistic enough, but is an index of thwarted or suppressed emotion.

Many of his narratives—notably *Many Marriages*—shocked readers by their sexual frankness. But it should be clear now that Anderson explored the sexual only because it is one of the chief paths to the secrets of the inner life. His courage in that still reticent time gave him a fictitious reputation as a breaker of taboos, which he did not really deserve. His true innovation was his sympathetic analysis of the inner emotional life of the victims of success in his Middle West.

He often fumbled in his narrative, which is always honest but sometimes truly artless. The style, however, is effective, and deceptively ingenuous and impromptu. Although, like Lewis, he dealt with familiar people in a familiar way, his prose is stylized. It has little of the colloquial, few differentiations between this man's speech and another's. What he did was to listen to his home-town folk with affectionate intentness, and then make out of their vocabulary and rhythms a style to express them. This is the precise opposite of sitting up nights with Addison. He resolved, as he says, to escape from the patterns of British prose as taught to his generation, and this is the way he did it. It is, nevertheless, a mannered style, supple, familiar, a little monotonous, but an excellent medium for the homely incidents he chose as revealing the inner life of seemingly commonplace people. Perhaps no American has more consciously made a personal style for his own needs.

Anderson's first book of importance was *Winesburg, Ohio* (1919), a collection of sketches of life in a small Ohio town. *Winesburg, Ohio* made a stir among the critics and pleased such writers as Dreiser and Carl Sandburg. It was rather widely attacked by the prudish, the general opinion being that the author was a pessimist whose morbidity was in sharp contrast to the healthy cheerfulness and good humor of Booth Tarkington's novels of much the same region. Actually, the difference was in selection. Tarkington was writing well for cheerful people, and, so far as they went, his portraits of the Middle West were true and excellent. He had been in Princeton, or lived far away from the railroad tracks of his home town, while Anderson was listening to the sordid tales of the village gossips at the livery stable. Born outside both Puritan and genteel traditions, Anderson felt no compulsion to make success stories of what he wrote. The somewhat stereotyped lives of the successful he took for granted as by-products of the American code of progress. Importance lay in what this emotionally sterile life of the small town and the impersonality of the big city had done to the individual. He found failures the most revealing.

His succeeding books were all built upon this theme, with no notable advance except in his growing power over the short story, which ceased to be a sketch and became organic and dynamic. *Poor White* (1920) is semi-autobiographic; *Dark Laughter* (1925) is another story of his own people with the dark laughter of the Negroes as a sardonic background and commentary. These indicate a widening of social observation. But *The Triumph of the Egg* (1921) and *Horses and Men* (1923), books of short stories, are most characteristic of his resources, his skill, and his quality—also of his faults, for each book contains narratives that do not "jell." "The Triumph of the Egg" itself, the story of an unsuccessful chicken farmer whose life is dominated by eggs until, in its grotesque, half-mad conclusion, one egg broken lifts the tale into significant tragedy, is a perfect example of Anderson's way of interpreting life.

Like the other novelists in this chapter, Sherwood Anderson did not belong with the postwar generation of writers who felt themselves to be pioneers in a new social structure and a new (but unformed) philosophy. He is to be placed, rather, in a Hegelian antithesis with Glasgow or Cabell. As part of the summary period of nineteenth century America, he wrote of its culture with the personal detachment of one who neither defends nor prophesies. His task was to explain a neglected aspect of an era of easy success. Without him and his people, the Middle West would have gone uninterpreted in an important area of emotional experience. He could not really create characters, except for boys'—perhaps one boy's—character. He lacked the power to synthesize a region as a society. He was less of a realist, more of a mystic than Dreiser; indeed, his realism was confined to the honesty with which he confessed personal experience, and to his descriptions. In these qualities he anticipated Saroyan and Steinbeck; and he explained, as Sinclair Lewis did not, why so many of the Babbitts became increasingly unsatisfied and hollow within.

His place in American literary history should be given further distinction by his very great influence in liberating the American short story from a petrifying technique. His own tales, appearing first in experimental magazines like the *Dial* and the *Little Review,* gradually acquired fame and were eagerly read by younger men and women trying to escape from the technical tradition of Poe, Aldrich, and O. Henry, which cramped expression even though it seemed to guarantee financial success. That the best and the most successful American short stories of the next decades—whether by Stephen Vincent Benet or Katherine Anne Porter or Eudora Welty—are in free forms where plot is subordinated to theme and form springs from the situation, must be credited in no small degree to the example set by Sherwood Anderson.

8

Ring Lardner was one of the least pretentious in a literary sense, and most interesting of the writers of this period. He was definitely transitional, carrying over into a more realistic age the surface good nature of the American humorists of the nineteenth century, their banter, and their evident affection for American types. And, like O. Henry, he had the nineteenth century American fondness for carefully constructed plots, ending usually with a reversal or a surprise, and as neatly made as a watch. Yet in content and in philosophy of character his writing forecast the irony and impatient disillusions of the later twenties, and a dislike for the current values of magazine-reading, bridge-playing, get-rich-and-spend-it American society as strong as the sarcasm of Sinclair Lewis, if far more skeptical and ironic. The smoldering hatred for possessive and dominating women as the enemy of the male, which was to be so characteristic of novels, stories, drama, and even comics of later American decades, is only half concealed beneath his surface good humor. The most influential magazine of the period among sophisticated intellectuals, the *New Yorker* (founded in 1925) had for its spiritual ancestor the ironical, realistic humor of Ring Lardner, with its notes of pity and its ruthless satire of dangerous human types.

Lardner was graduated into literature from the sports column of the American press, a department of journalism more influential, perhaps, than any other upon the growth of the American language. His work, like Sherwood Anderson's, was always close to reporting, and any one of his stories could have been printed as a human-interest feature containing news of life on the baseball field or in the home town, or in the suburbs of New York. Indeed, both men, regarded as journalists, were by-products of the shift from news of fact to "heart" interest, which transformed the American press in these decades, and swung its influence from ideas to emotions.

Ring Lardner and Anderson were both bored by normalcy and the respectable, and both were stirred to attack by the pressure of standardized thinking and feeling. But Anderson, an idealist of the emotions, was shocked and troubled, while the far more objective Lardner was, like his successors, uninterested in reform, and content to give his humor a cutting edge. He was at his best, not when his characters were most significant, but when they were most novel and alive. The dreadfully dull husband of "Anniversary," whom thrift and devotion to the ideals of business have reduced to the personality of a typewriter, is not so memorable as Alibi Ike, the greatest and most naïve liar of baseball. The horrifying effect of the brutality of Midge Kelly in "Champion" owes some of its effect to its satire on commercialized pugilism, but more to the carefully objective description of the man himself.

Indeed, it is probable that Ring Lardner's place as an American classic will be as a reporter of new phases of the American character, best seen through the satiric realist's eyes. In sports, particularly, there had come to be a new cohesion of American society, powerful over the imagination of millions. It had its own code, its own language, its own comedies and tragedies, its own heroes and buffoons. It was, indeed, the bourgeois equivalent of the fields of Troy, with many an uncertain Hector and boasting Thersites and sulky Achilles and wily Odysseus. Yet a corrupting commercialism, an inevitable accompaniment as elsewhere in American life, gave an opportunity to the realist that such a romantic of a previous generation as Richard Harding Davis would have been unable to take.

From sports Lardner turned to the gilded absurdities of the motion picture world, and to the deceit and cruelty which passed for humor in small-town life, as in "Haircut." His touch was light, and his victims might have read his stories without knowing that they were being damned out of their own mouths. Yet no intelligent reader could miss his ruthless summary of false values in the life he knew best. The best books are collections of short stories, *How to Write Short Stories* (1924) and *The Love Nest* (1926).

His stories are of major importance in their transcription of new American rhythms in speech, and phrases and words new at least to literature. Anderson stylized this language, Lewis used it to define his types, Lardner had no ulterior purpose except realism. It has been said that his own style is thin and often flat, and that the color and true style is taken from the mouths of his characters. This is at least relatively true. His baseball heroes talk a racy dialect which thousands of players, fans, and sports writers had shaped to fit the high excitements of the game. And he could make articulate without falsifying the shallow semiliteracy of his silly or predatory women.

Thus Ring Lardner, even if he had no obvious roots in the age of security and confidence, belonged in the summary group which firmly established the end-products of the nineteenth century in a satisfactory and expressive literature. If he also prepared for an era that liked to call itself more "realistic," meaning more concerned with the "is" and less with the "ought," his most praiseworthy quality is to have realized emerging character types of his own times.

9

This chapter makes no attempt to be inclusive of all the vigorous fiction of this rich period of American writing, which began to lose its summary character and give way to a new transition about 1925. It omits, in the interest of brevity, such brilliant achievements in the organization of American experience as Ernest Poole's *The Harbor* (1915), such new local color of the Negro South as Du Bose Heyward's *Porgy* (1925), such able records of increasing sophistication as Carl Van Vechten's novels. It leaves, for later treatment, the pioneers of a fiction with a changed philosophy of life behind it, such as Scott Fitzgerald in his pioneer study of postwar youth, *This Side of Paradise* (1920), a book more influential than excellent—his mature power was to be shown later; or the explorations in the changing mores of sex by Floyd Dell (*Moon Calf,* 1920), or the massive social studies of Waldo Frank (*City Block,* 1922). Some mention, however, must be made of Joseph Hergesheimer, to whom many novelists of the period, including Sinclair Lewis, owed new standards of descriptive accuracy. Hergesheimer was as much of an antiquarian as a novelist, and his books were rightly regarded as protests against the slovenly generalizations of popular romance. He was a naturalist writing of the past, who in later years applied the same scrupulous realism of detail to stories of the demoralized behavior of the Prohibition era. The research behind his novel of Pennsylvania ironmasters (*The Three Black Pennys,* 1917) or his story of Salem and the China trade (*Java Head,* 1919) was paralleled by the careful and laborious preparation made by Sinclair Lewis before each one of his novels of Middle America, who in *Arrowsmith* went as far as to use a research collaborator.

For it is clear that the most important fiction of the belated *fin de siècle,* which began in the early 1900's and ended in the late 1920's, when the young who had known no stability took over, was a study of the values which had already been established, for good or for ill, in American life. This study in Ellen Glasgow was ironic of the false, defensive of the true, historical in its point of view. In the stories of Willa Cather it was explanatory of the deep concordances between land and people, intensely creative in characters, an offering from a passing age to a new one. It was entirely ironic, egoistic, and almost wholly destructive in Cabell, an aristocrat's purge of a petrified morality. It was a seeking and a rescue of the life of the emotions in the tales of Sherwood Anderson. In Sinclair Lewis, it was a mirror held up to a whole society. He was the greatest social historian, though not the greatest artist or prophet of them all, and he was determined that his fellow countrymen should see in the light of his own fierce idealism what was happening in a country where body was out of mesh with soul. In Ring Lardner, it was the irony of the hardboiled reporter who suffers fools gladly when they supply him with good copy but never forgets that they are fools. He, with Sinclair Lewis, has left us the best transcription of the colloquial American speech of our time.

Edith Wharton gave to the local color cult of the regionalists, who were so successful from the seventies to the nineties, an edge and a social significance which that literature lacked. Ellen Glasgow and Cabell were also regionalist, but their books took the offensive against the decaying chivalry of the South, and prepared for the later work of Paul Green, Stark Young, and William Faulkner. Anderson's mood of confession was shared by his predecessor Dreiser and his contemporary Edgar Lee Masters, but with a transference of emotion stranger than in either of the other two writers.

Indeed, it is not too much to say that the air of the twenties was electric. It inspired the older writers, such as Glasgow, Cather, Wharton, Cabell, to their best work, and created new imaginations. Even Dreiser, who belongs in style and outlook upon life to the relatively barren first two decades of the new century, published his masterpiece, *An American Tragedy,* in 1925. And one reason, at least, is the summary character of all the best of this work. With these writers, the second great era of the Republic, from the Civil War to the Long Armistice, may be said to have got adequate interpreters in novelists who were conscious of their duty to give a final reality and a diagnosis of the results of a span of human experience. And they were fortunate, as their predecessors had seldom been, in finding an aware and receptive audience.

73. EUGENE O'NEILL

At no time during the eighteenth or nineteenth century was the drama a major department of American literature; and not until just before the First World War did it show any real promise of becoming one. It is true that the early years of our century had produced Clyde Fitch and Langdon Mitchell, popular playwrights whose works exhibited some increase in literary sophistication, and also more serious writers—notably Edward Sheldon, William Vaughn Moody, and Augustus Thomas—who made a cautious effort to treat themes which had some relation to contemporary life. But none of these men was permanently important, and the works of none achieved conspicuous excellence when judged in accordance with the standards set by the contemporary efforts of novelists and essayists, philosophers and historians. They pretty consistently consented to work within the limitations of a very narrow theatrical tradition, and that tradition tolerated no bold departure from long-established stereotypes both artistic and moral.

Eugene O'Neill is, on the other hand, held by many critics to be a major figure in American literature, and it is unquestionable that he was the first American to write a number of plays which still seem possible candidates for inclusion in any future list of native classics. He is, therefore, the inevitable central figure in any discussion of the new school of American dramatists. Moreover, there are reasons why he is a very convenient as well as an inevitable central figure. His work reveals both strong originality and the effect of forces in the world outside himself which sometimes help mold and sometimes actually distort the expression of his own talents. In him, therefore, may be observed both an individual creative writer and the effect of an intellectual milieu common to him and his fellows.

At least three factors determining that milieu are of major importance: the native, non-dramatic, literary revolution which produced Theodore Dreiser, Sherwood Anderson, Sinclair Lewis, and H. L. Mencken; the somewhat belated influence of Ibsen and the post-Ibsen playwrights of Europe; and the revolutionary "little theater" movement with which O'Neill was in the beginning identified.

The first of these factors is, of course, itself complex since it includes such superficially contradictory tendencies as that toward native realism and that toward an imitation of continental sophistication. It has already been discussed in previous sections of the present work and will be merely alluded to here. In this chapter O'Neill will be discussed chiefly in terms of his individual tendencies as they were modified by the European dramatic tradition and given opportunity to develop in an experimental theater.

2

Eugene [Gladstone] O'Neill was born in a Broadway hotel on October 16, 1888. He was the son of James O'Neill, a popular actor of romantic melodrama, and he spent his boyhood partly with his father on tour and partly in various boarding schools. As the result of a prank, he was suspended from Princeton at the end of his freshman year. He worked briefly in a mail-order house, and then, possibly influenced by Jack London, Conrad, and Kipling, as well as by his own restless rebellious spirit, he left in 1909 for a gold-prospecting voyage in Honduras. Another voyage took him as ordinary seaman to Buenos Aires, where he worked at odd jobs for a time before returning to play a small part in one of his father's productions in New York and work for about a year as reporter and columnist on a New London newspaper. In 1912 an attack of tuberculosis sent him for five months to a sanitarium, and it seems reasonable to suppose that the enforced idleness there brought him face to face with the self from which he had been trying to run away. He read Marx and Kropotkin as well as Wedekind, Strindberg, and Ibsen, and during the year of convalescence following his release from the sanitarium, he wrote his first one-act plays. In 1914 he attended for a time Professor George Pierce Baker's famous class in play writing at Harvard.

Next year, during the summer of 1915, a group of Greenwich Villagers vacationing at Provincetown, Massachusetts, unknowingly prepared the way for his introduction to the public by staging for their amusement four one-act plays in an improvised theater in a deserted fish house. By the next summer, some members of the group had heard somehow that the young O'Neill, also now living in Provincetown, had a trunkful of unproduced plays. He was invited to submit something, and the result was that the one-act romantic melodrama *Bound East for Cardiff* became the first of his works to be publicly performed. That same autumn the Provincetown group remodeled a stable on Macdougal Street in New York City, named the tiny theater Provincetown Playhouse, and opened in November with a bill of three one-act plays, one of which was again *Bound East for Cardiff*. The results were so pleasing to all concerned that between then and 1924 most of O'Neill's plays—including, besides a number of one-acters, *The Emperor Jones, The Hairy Ape,* and *All God's Chillun Got Wings*—had their premières on Macdougal Street.

These facts are of the utmost importance for understanding the atmosphere in which the new American drama began. The Provincetown group was one of two most directly responsible for creating a conscious conviction that such a new drama was possible, and the attitude of its members is highly significant. Not one of them was professionally connected with the theater. The two leading original movers were George Cram Cook, a Bohemian enthusiast, and John Reed, later to become a hero martyr of the Soviet Union. Others included Mary Heaton Vorse, labor journalist, Wilbur Daniel Steele, short-story writer, and Marguerite Zorach, a modernistic painter. One, Susan Glaspell, later became a professional playwright, and one, Robert Edmond Jones, a professional stage designer; but most of the members of the group, as well as most of the authors who wrote their plays, became famous, if they became famous at all, in some other field of activity. Thus, during 1917 and 1918, plays were produced by Floyd Dell, later a successful novelist; by Michael Gold, later a prominent radical journalist; and by Alfred Kreymborg, Harry Kemp, Maxwell Bodenheim, and Edna St. Vincent Millay, all to achieve in varying degrees reputations as poets rather than as playwrights. In other words, the prime movers in the enterprise were interested in art, literature, and politics rather than in the theater as such, and they were in revolt against the long prevailing assumption that play writing was a highly specialized, artificial, and essentially inartistic trade.

Beyond this, however, the Provincetown group, unlike the German Freie Bühne or the French Théâtre Libre, had no program. Various ferments including political radicalism, aesthetic experimentalism, and timeless Bohemianism were at work in differing proportions in most if not all of the members. But there was no unifying doctrine, and the group as a whole knew rather better what it did not want—namely, respectable, conventional, and commercialized entertainment—than what it did. Freud was a prophet hardly less important than Marx. A good playwright, they obviously felt, might be a prophet of social revolution, a romantic poet, or even merely an adept at the ancient Bohemian sport of shocking the middle classes. The one thing he could not be was one who complacently accepted the statement recently made by Eugene Walter, author of the sensational play *The Easiest Way* (1908 *), and one of the admired of Broadway: "In essence, play writing is a trade."

The Provincetown Playhouse did for O'Neill one thing which no commercial theater would at the beginning have done: it gave him an audience, though this audience was, and for some time remained, a small and very

* Dates in this chapter are of first performance rather than of first publication.

special one. Perhaps it is just as well that his sponsors had no definite pro-gram, for O'Neill was very susceptible to influence; he had not by any means found himself, and he might under different circumstances have been forced into a pattern alien to his own genius. As it was, his sponsors took gladly whatever he gave them; and even during these earliest years he gave them a number of seemingly quite different things. Among his early works only *Bound East for Cardiff* and the series of other one-act plays of the sea which followed form a unified group. Obviously to some extent products of his own experience as a sailor, they are poetic in tone, somewhat melodramatic in substance, and essentially romantic despite the fact that an avoidance of the more familiar romantic clichés and an insistence upon tragic implications led them to be called, as unfamiliar forms of romanticism so often are, "realistic." Their brevity and their relative simplicity enabled the author to achieve his intentions more completely than he was to do for a long time in more ambitious attempts, and for that reason some have always tended to give them a higher place in the hierarchy of his works than they really deserve.

O'Neill was, however, by no means content with either poetic or tragic melodrama. Passionately dissatisfied and restlessly seeking, he at times gave way to a sort of Strindbergian nihilism and at others sought answers to his questions in the doctrines of the political revolutionists or in those of the newly fashionable Freudians. It is easy to see in successive plays the pre-dominant influence of one doctrine or another. *Diff'rent* (1920), though theatrically very effective, is unmistakably a fable for Freudians; *All God's Chillun Got Wings* (1924) was, on the surface at least, a sociological problem play. On the other hand, *The Emperor Jones* (1920) was mystical rather than sociological or scientific, and two others, *Beyond the Horizon* (1920) and *Anna Christie* (1921), were given their first production in commercial theaters rather than at the Provincetown only because their method was that of a straightforward realism far less baffling to the general public than the poetry, the mysticism, and the preaching to some extent characteristic of his other work.

During this period O'Neill may be said to have had styles rather than a style, and philosophies rather than a philosophy. He was endeavoring with only partial success to adapt to his own uses available formulas provided by current intellectual movements, and he probably did not himself know how unsatisfactory for him each of them was. *The Hairy Ape,* produced in 1922, and the next to the last of his plays to have its première at the Provincetown Playhouse, is, in some respects, the most interesting because it is the one which most succeeds in fusing discordant elements into a new whole.

The story of *The Hairy Ape* is concerned with one of the stokers of an ocean liner whose previous contentment with his own primitive strength and humble indispensability is shaken by accidental contact with a female passenger representing a world of which he is totally ignorant. Arrived in port, he sets out to investigate this new world, discovers that he is not recognized as human by the more elegant of its denizens, gets thrown out of the hall where a group of self-conscious proletarians is meeting, and finally is crushed to death in the arms of a caged ape whom he has tried to hail as brother. The method of the piece obviously derives ultimately from that of Strindberg's *The Dream Play* and involves what the Germans had begun to call "expressionism"—one element of which is the effort to represent events, not as they would appear to a normal, detached spectator, but as seen through the distorted vision of a participant. The meaning of the fable (and this was to become a frequent characteristic of O'Neill's plays) was ambiguous in the sense that it lent itself readily to different interpretations. By the social revolutionist it was accepted as a protest against the brutalization of the proletariat. Yet in the text itself there is no suggestion that the hairy apes of this world could be humanized by any social system, and probably only the sociological preoccupations of an audience could suggest the conclusion that the author had affinity with the prophets of political or economic revolution. The nihilistic pessimism of the tortured playwright is the obvious source of its dramatic method.

When, however, we look back at *The Hairy Ape* and consider it in relation to O'Neill's subsequent development, we perceive that the real crux of the problem presented by the predicament of the central figure is not sociological, and we see also that the author is struggling with, rather than merely acquiescing in, the pessimism which has all but enveloped him. While the Hairy Ape was still content with his lot, he was content because he had faith that he was essential to his ship and that the ship had meaning. When he lost that faith, when he came to realize that the world which he served was unaware of his existence, and when he hence came to doubt that he had any function in a world he could not understand, he ceased to think of himself as a man and despised himself as an ape. "I belong" had been the recurrent phrase with which he justified himself. When he could no longer say that, he was lost; and the theme here for the first time clearly enunciated is the theme repeated with many variations in most of O'Neill's major works. Sometimes these works involve what appears to be a criticism of society. Sometimes they make use of a Freudian pattern. But at their most successful they are tragic rather than either sociological or psychological because at bottom the problem is, always, not what O'Neill himself has called the problem of man's relations with man, but the problem of man's relation to something outside himself, to that something to which he must "belong" if he is to feel himself more than the cleverest of the apes.

3

O'Neill's development long continued to be in zigzag or spiral rather than in a straight line, but *The Hairy Ape* marks a stage at which it is convenient to pause to consider the extent to which there was, by this time, a "new American theater," of which he can be considered a part. Certain of his contemporaries will be treated in a subsequent chapter. Here it is necessary to say only that the Provincetown group had failed completely, during the eight years which had passed since the production of *Bound East for Cardiff*, to discover any other American dramatist of importance. It had produced a long succession of pieces, usually in one act, by a considerable number of Americans. But not one of the latter was destined to become known as an important writer for the stage. Moreover, neither of the Provincetown's two rival "little theaters" had succeeded any better so far as the cultivation of significant native dramatists was concerned.

One, the Neighborhood Playhouse, which was operated in connection with a settlement house on Grand Street, was beginning to achieve a deserved reputation for its imaginative staging of poetic and fanciful productions, but had discovered no native playwright of importance. The other, the Washington Square Players—a semiamateur group founded in February, 1915, and at first not very markedly different in aims from its Provincetown rival—had achieved a somewhat more spectacular theatrical success, for under the changed name Theater Guild it had taken a full-sized uptown theater in 1919, and was soon (in 1925) to open its own newly constructed Guild Theater. It had progressed from bills of one-act plays to the increasingly elaborate and professional presentations of the major works of such established European dramatists as Benevente, St. John Ervine, Tolstoy, Strindberg, Molnár, and especially Shaw. By 1922 it had ceased to be a little theater and become instead almost a "commercial theater," specializing in the production of plays of a sort which had previously been considered impossible in commercial theaters. But it had not introduced a single American playwright destined either to conspicuous success or to enduring reputation.

What the three "little theaters" had accomplished was the discovery of an audience for a kind of play which was supposed to have none. The result was both to encourage a still unknown group to hope that it might write plays of similar quality and also to encourage the commercial managers to look with increasing favor upon works which tended more or less boldly to break with the timid conventions hitherto regarded as inviolable. Thus, while O'Neill still remained the only native dramatist of importance fostered by the little theater, certain plays either somewhat bolder or somewhat more sophisticated than had previously found a hearing on Broadway began to appear there—notably, Clare Kummer's series of "smart," "brittle" comedies beginning with *Good Gracious, Annabelle!* (1916); Zona Gale's realistic drama of small-time life, *Miss Lulu Bett* (1920); *Wake Up, Jonathan* (1921), a folk play dealing with the Southern mountaineers, by Hatcher Hughes and Elmer Rice; and *Dulcy* (1921), a comedy by George Kaufman and Marc Connelly, which pointed satire in a direction more familiar to readers of "sophisticated" writing than to frequenters of Broadway.

Almost precisely one year after the production of *The Hairy Ape,* the Theater Guild was to break new ground by presenting *The Adding Machine,* the first arresting independent work of Elmer Rice, who thus became the first "coming" playwright since O'Neill to find introduction as a "new" American dramatist through one of the "advanced" theaters. Within the next two or three years he had been joined on Broadway by several others, and the new school of play writing had been definitely launched with the production of *What Price Glory* (1924) by Laurence Stallings and Maxwell Anderson; *They Knew What They Wanted* (1924) by Sidney Howard; *The Show-Off* (1924) by George Kelly; and *Processional* (1925) by John Howard Lawson. No one of these plays could possibly have found acceptance on Broadway a decade before, and though the changed atmosphere created by the First World War no doubt had much to do with the fact that several of them were outstanding commercial successes, the spadework done by the Provincetown and the Guild counted for much.

Nevertheless it should be borne in mind that when *The Hairy Ape* was produced O'Neill was almost our only "advanced" playwright, and that the major part of the careers of most of the other important newcomers lie beyond 1925. On him, the chief immediate effect of the new developments in the theater was an expanding audience for work of a sort which had, up to then, been usually played on a tiny stage and before a few hundred spectators at most. His next two important plays were to be produced at the somewhat larger Greenwich Village Theater, which had been taken over by the management of the Provincetown; and then, in 1928, he gave *Marco Millions* to the Theater Guild, which produced the play at its own theater and has since sponsored all his New York productions, both at home and on tour.

These last facts must be mentioned because they indicate that his long struggle for a hearing outside the restricted group of consciously advanced intellectuals was by this time over; but, since O'Neill is conspicuously a writer more aware of himself than of his audience, they are probably far less important in his development than the steady growth within. To that growth we shall now again turn.

4

It would no doubt be generally agreed that since about 1915 the most conspicuous tendencies in the American novel, as well as in the American drama, have been toward realism, social satire, social protest, and what was commonly called "continental" sophistication. We have already noted that the influence of all these tendencies is observable in O'Neill's plays, but that they are essentially alien or at least peripheral, since O'Neill's chief concern had always been with the eternally tragic predicament of man struggling for some understanding and some justification of himself in a universe always mysterious and often seemingly inimical. For that reason, his work is actually less closely related to the work of most of his fellows than, superficially, it appears to be. While they have, for the most part, either adopted some form of satire or the problem play, or have, at least, taken one or the other as their point of departure, he has struggled persistently, if not quite consistently, toward the creation or re-creation of tragedy in the classic sense—toward a concern, as he put it, less with the relation of man to man than with that of man to God. Perhaps the most fruitful way to evaluate, as well as to understand the general character of his mature work, will be to consider his best plays in connection with their diverse ways of attempting to state in currently valid terms his conception of the human tragedy.

During the eleven years immediately following *The Hairy Ape,* thirteen of his dramatic pieces (two of them really trilogies and the others of normal length) were acted. He is thus a very prolific dramatist; but he is also an uneven one, and though there is considerable disagreement concerning the relative merits of certain of his works, few would deny that the most ambitious of his plays since 1922 are *Desire Under the Elms* (1924), *The Great God Brown* (1926), *Strange Interlude* (1928), and *Mourning Becomes Electra* (1931). *Ah Wilderness!* (1933) is interesting because it enjoyed considerable commercial success, and because it is a nostalgic comedy of youth, quite unlike anything else O'Neill ever wrote. Two others, *Dynamo* (1929) and *Days Without End* (1934), are also interesting, though failures commercially and perhaps artistically. Both deal more directly than any of O'Neill's other plays with the religious aspect of his problem, the first concerning itself with a man who thinks that he has found God in Force as it is symbolized by an electric generator, and the second with one who actually finds peace in an acceptance of the Roman Catholic Church. But to analyze successfully the four plays first mentioned would be by itself to gain a reasonably complete understanding of the whole sweep of their author's aims and methods.

Superficially no one of the four is like any other in respect to either the material dealt with or the dramatic method employed. Perhaps the best way to indicate their diversity, as well as the fundamental relationship among them, will be, first, to state briefly what each is, in the most obvious sense, "about," and then to point out how all are really concerned with the same theme.

The scene of *Desire Under the Elms* is rural New England in the nineteenth century. The method is strictly realistic, and the story revolves around a struggle for dominance between a son and his father—the father being a patriarch convinced that he is under the special protection of a "hard" Old Testament God, and the son competing with him for both his young wife and the ancestral farm. *The Great God Brown,* on the other hand, is contemporary in setting, fantastically "expressionistic" in method, and as completely subjective as the previous play was objective in its treatment of characters and fable. Dion Anthony, a genius, is dogged through life by Brown, a mediocrity, who assumes his mask and thus deceives his wife, appropriates the plans which he has drawn for a great public building, and all but usurps his identity. All the characters wear masks which they sometimes remove in soliloquies when they reveal their private, as opposed to their public, personalities. The symbolism becomes extremely confused; O'Neill's own explanation of his intentions is rather more obscure than the play itself; and one is left in doubt whether Anthony and Brown are not actually the two aspects of a single individual.

Strange Interlude (almost three times normal play length) has as its central character a beautiful woman who blames her emotional sterility on the death of a lover killed in the war, but nevertheless manages to dominate the lives of three men—her husband, a lover, and her feebly genteel bachelor uncle. The method is realistic except for the fact that long soliloquies are employed to reveal the unspoken thoughts of the characters. In *Mourning Becomes Electra* even this device, used in its two immediate predecessors, is abandoned in favor of a method which is, outwardly at least, essentially realism of the most familiar sort. The story, told in what is really three plays intended for performance on three different evenings, follows very closely the Greek story of Electra, Orestes, and Clytemnestra; but the scene is shifted to the time of the American Civil War, and the motives as well as the names of the central characters are so completely modernized that a naïve spectator might never suspect that the fable was not newly invented.

Each of these four plays enjoyed a considerable commercial success, and together they brought a large financial reward to an author who, before the first was produced, had spent almost a decade developing his talents with what appeared to be a contemptuous disregard for the tastes of his contemporaries. None of the four was, however, popular in the full sense that many other contemporary plays were popular, and it is difficult not to suspect that they owed some considerable part of the favor they enjoyed among intellectuals to a fact already insisted upon—the fact, that is to say, that each was to some extent interpretable in terms of a current intellectual fashion. To many, *Desire Under the Elms* was a contribution to the fashionable effort to "debunk" the nation's Puritan forefathers whom this play was supposed to present as tyrannical and lustful. Similarly, *The Great God Brown,* incomprehensible as much of it was, seemed, after its own fashion, to constitute a satire on the American ideal of "success" and thus to have some sort of relation to the novels of Sinclair Lewis and his imitators. *Strange Interlude* could be interpreted as the study of a Freudian complex, and even *Mourning Becomes Electra,* though more than any of the others it seemed to depend for its effectiveness upon the sheer power of the fable, also presented unmistakably Freudian motifs.

If, however, one has in mind when one approaches these plays not the intellectual patterns fashionable at the moment when the plays were written, but some hint of O'Neill's own preoccupations, it becomes evident that they represent four approaches to the same aesthetic and moral problem rather than four diverse attempts to exploit current interests or prejudices. Sometime during the years when they were being written, their author seems to have become for the first time clearly aware not only that what he wanted to write was tragedy, but that the stature necessary for a tragic hero was difficult to achieve unless that hero "belonged" to something—unless, that is to say, he had a relation to something felt to be larger than himself. But contemporary man has tended to lose the sense that there is anything in the universe with which he can establish a relation, and the realistic problem play accepts the fact when it consents to deal exclusively with the relation of man to man rather than concern itself with the relation of man to God. O'Neill, therefore, seemed to be faced with a dilemma. Either he must deal with the past when man still felt that something outside himself was of supreme importance, or he must be content with the only half-tragic frustrations which arise when a Hairy Ape or a Dion Anthony cries out for the gods he has lost.

"The playwright of today," O'Neill once wrote to George Jean Nathan, "must dig at the roots of the sickness of today as he feels it—the death of the old God and the failure of science and materialism to give any satisfactory new one for the surviving primitive, religious instinct to find a meaning for life in, and to comfort its fears of death with." *The Great God Brown* states that theme explicitly and deals with it in quite contemporary terms; *Desire Under the Elms* implies the theme and achieves artistic success only because in it O'Neill chooses to write of the past. Here the struggle between father and son can reach tragic proportions, can indeed achieve a quality which

immediately challenges comparison with classic treatments of this fundamental conflict: because the father never wavers in his conviction that
Jehovah is one of the protagonists, and because even the son has not lost all
sense of living in a universe more grandiose than any which can be known
to those who acknowledge only man-made laws. Moreover, the distinction is
clearly drawn in the last scene between these protagonists to whom the
possession of the soil can be the occasion of great passions, and the typical
modern, represented by the sheriff, to whom the farm is desirable merely
as a piece of salable real estate. *The Great God Brown* is, on the other hand,
concerned with moderns who have lost their faith, and the key is furnished
by the early scene in which Dion longs first for an earthly father and then
for a heavenly one, though he can find only a sensible parent and the now
trivial legend of an "old grey beard" in the sky. As art *Desire Under the
Elms* is strikingly successful, *The Great God Brown* conspicuously unsatisfactory, in part because one has a tragic hero, the other has only a hero who
is aware of his inability to give his failures tragic significance.

If these two plays represent the two horns of the dilemma between which
O'Neill felt himself caught, the two remaining represent efforts to escape
from it by two different routes. *Strange Interlude* is the demitragedy of a
group which neither believes in God, like Old Ephraim in *Desire Under
the Elms,* nor even, like Dion Anthony, wants to believe in God. In so far
as the individual members believe in anything larger than themselves, that
thing is the Freudian subconscious, some awareness of which seems to haunt
them, very much as others have been vaguely haunted by an awareness of
God. In so far as they "belong" to anything, they belong to the "complexes"
which force them into actions of which their reason would not approve.
And, whatever else may be said for or against Freudianism, *Strange Interlude*
does demonstrate that it is capable of adding a dimension to drama. Plays
which deal only with the relation of rational man to rational man are usually
thin. One in which the passionately irrational aspects of life are recognized
to the extent which Freudianism makes possible in *Strange Interlude* has
already recovered something of the psychological truth which, in some very
real sense, makes *Hamlet* more convincing than *Man and Superman.*

Strange Interlude is indeed completely absorbing. In many respects its
effect resembles that of a good psychological novel. But it ends "not with a
bang but a whimper." There is no satisfactory catastrophe, only a diminuendo,
as the characters, who have neither solved their personal problems nor made
defeat heroic, subside into the quiescence of age. They do not seem very
important; they have failed to achieve tragic stature because neither intellectually nor emotionally are they convinced of their own importance either to
themselves or to anything else. They are more interesting and complex than

the characters in even the best problem plays, but they are nevertheless interesting rather than tragically important.

O'Neill has already been quoted for the purpose of showing that he was consciously aware of at least the main outlines of the project which, as a dramatist, he had set himself. He is nevertheless a dramatist rather than a philosopher and owes his significance less to any absolute intellectual originality than to the forcefulness with which he has explored in dramatic terms "the sickness of today." Since he is, in the broadest sense of the word, a poet rather than a philosopher it cannot safely be assumed that he was himself always clearly aware of the pattern into which his successive efforts, now in one direction and now in another, seem to the critic to fall. Yet, whether or not he is fully aware of the fact, *Mourning Becomes Electra* does constitute another experiment which seems logically demanded by the pattern of experimentation already laid down. *Strange Interlude* served to demonstrate that modern characters can play out a richly interesting drama even though Freudian psychology furnishes the only spiritual universe, the only large thing outside their rational consciousness with which they are willing to admit relation. Only one question remains to be answered. Can such characters satisfactorily fill the roles, not in a psychological study, but in a tragedy? Can they be made to take on the necessary stature, can they work their way through to a catastrophe of tragic proportions?

Unwilling to accept finally the negative answer which his own previous work seemed to furnish, O'Neill posed the question again in *Mourning Becomes Electra*. Here is a series of events which become great tragedy when Æschylus represents them. So far as the incidents are concerned, they might have occurred as easily during the American Civil War as during the Trojan War. Suppose, then, we give them the local habitation and the names of our civilization. Suppose we avoid all the implications which depend upon the ancient ethos, and assume that whatever appears irrational has its source, not in the will of the gods, but in that layer of the human mind which lies below its consciousness. How close can we then come to achieving a tragedy, modern in the sense that it asks no suspension of disbelief in the gods, classic in the sense that its figures will seem large enough, and its catastrophe thrilling enough to stir real terror and pity? To what extent can we judge how much of any disproportion between Æschylus and O'Neill is due to the disproportion between their respective poetic gifts, how much to the possible fact that tragedy cannot happen in a world in which there is no supernatural moral order to be disturbed and then reestablished?

In so far as the play achieves a genuinely tragic effect, it not only vindicates the claim of O'Neill to importance as a writer, but at the same time tends to dispose of what has seemed to be his own conviction—namely, that contemporary man's failure to "belong" puts an insurmountable difficulty in the way of the dramatist who would make a tragic hero out of him. And without suggesting any weighing of the balance between Æschylus and O'Neill, it must at least be said that *Mourning Becomes Electra* was astonishingly powerful in the theater, to which it held large audiences through a second and a third part. By virtue of nothing except the passion with which he was able to endow them, the characters assume great stature. They come to seem important because those passions somehow make them important to themselves. And the catastrophe achieves something of the finality as well as the magnitude which genuine tragedy requires.

5

Since 1933 Mr. O'Neill has completed two tragedies and is said to be far advanced in the composition of a cycle of seven plays. By his own desire no productions were undertaken and none of the texts were published until the autumn of 1946 when *The Iceman Cometh* was presented by the Theater Guild. This long and somewhat grotesque tragedy has as its theme the attempt of a dipsomaniac to free himself from his last hopes and last illusions. It is less appealing than either *Strange Interlude* or *Mourning Becomes Electra,* but it exhibits much of the same tragic power.

From what has already been said it is evident that, if O'Neill is probably the most important playwright ever to arise in the United States, his development has been such as to make it difficult to consider him as a member— even as the leading member—of an American school of dramatists. That school doubtless owed a good deal to his pioneer efforts, which did so much to reveal an audience for unconventional plays. Moreover, as a subsequent chapter of this work will indicate, many members of the school have themselves shown a tendency to cultivate a style of play writing in which the didactic emphasis of the European problem play, so extensively cultivated during the late nineteenth and early twentieth centuries, disappears, and either comedy or drama, rather than demonstration or argument, becomes the chief effect aimed at. But O'Neill, nevertheless, remains all but unique in his persistent and increasingly more nearly exclusive attempt to deal with modern life in such a way as to achieve the effect of classic tragedy. In pursuit of that aim he has more and more completely avoided, as though he considered them trivial and irrelevant, the criticism of current social or political conditions or the characteristic features of contemporary manners. Certainly no other significant playwright has so persisted in the conviction that, if a drama is to achieve great excellence, it must deal with man's relation to God— or, if one prefers, with his relation to forces outside himself.

However he is classified, Eugene O'Neill is one more instance of the power and the maturity of American literature, which reached in the twenties a peak from which there was no dropping back. But unlike the majority of the important novelists and at least two of the most important poets of these twenties, his plays are not so much summary of an era as a new mode and a new theme for the American stage.

A WORLD LITERATURE

74. BETWEEN WARS

No period in American history is more eventful than that between the Coolidge-Hoover bull market of the twenties and the tragically sudden death of Franklin D. Roosevelt in 1945; and none furnishes greater contrasts and ironies.

From the boastful complacency of a boom era in which Americans thought that their wealth, technological power, and improved economic theories had lifted them to a plateau of absolute security, they were abruptly hurled into a whirlpool of perils, domestic and foreign. Two previous generations had endured similar periods of prolonged crisis. In the years 1775–1789 Americans had undergone a direful war, an uprooting of old traditions and loyalties, a severe depression, and all the quarrels that inevitably accompanied constitution making, state and national. In the years 1857–1873 they had experienced a panic, one of the most lethal wars of history, the bitter animosities of Southern Reconstruction, and the onset of a new depression. These were roller coaster generations—lifted high, flung far down, swallowing dizzy curves, rushing across sudden gaps. But the vicissitudes of this third period of crisis were even sharper. The panic was more savage, the war peril was deadlier, the internal discords were as harsh; while even Nature lent a hand in tormenting large sections with droughts, dust storms, and floods. The irony of the abrupt change from prosperity to poverty was grim. But it was another ironic fact that a nation which had finally adjusted itself to a chastened mood and a restricted economy suddenly in 1941 found war again spurring it to prodigies of effort, with a production that eclipsed its wildest dreams.

The political framework of the time was somewhat less simple than it seemed. The writers who speak of a Harding-Coolidge-Hoover epoch followed by a very different Roosevelt era hardly do justice to Hoover as a transitional figure. Both before and after his tardy adjustments to the Great Depression which began late in 1929, Hoover unlatched several doors which his successor simply flung wide. His principle of industrial self-government and his stimulation of the trade associations helped to usher in Roosevelt's grander experiment under the National Recovery Administration. He partially accepted Federal responsibility for relief. He was the first President to use a powerful government agency (the Reconstruction Finance Corporation) in a compensatory and balancing role in the national economy, thus setting a far-reaching precedent. In short, great innovations of government policy were beginning to take shape even before Franklin D. Roosevelt assumed control. And yet an old era did die, and a new era did open, in 1933.

The inauguration of Roosevelt, relieving the national tension at a moment of terrible crisis, seemed like the rolling up of a curtain on a brighter, more active scene. New forces, new doctrines, new characters all seized the public attention. The vibrant personality of the new President, sanguine, energetic, imaginative, and full of a zest for bold experiment which was encouraged by the legal philosophy of Justice Holmes and by the advice of the band of young men who gathered about the White House, did not cease for twelve years to dominate American affairs. For the same length of time a virtual farmer-labor coalition, reinforced by some small businessmen and many intellectuals, furnished the support which Roosevelt needed. A distinct and exhilarating atmosphere pervaded the period.

And yet the Roosevelt era, like that which preceded it, must be divided into distinct periods. It is more correct to speak of two New Deals, for example, than of one. At the outset the administration placed its emphasis on recovery combined with regulation, the National Recovery Administration and the first Agricultural Adjustment Agency (which was avowedly temporary) furnishing the cornerstone of the edifice. In the second phase the emphasis fell upon reform combined with regulation—the Labor Relations Act of 1935, the Social Security Act of the same year, and the second or permanent Agricultural Adjustment Agency (which provided for soil conservation) being the most important measures. Then came a third period. The progress of the second New Deal was being steadily braked down by conservative opposition when in the fall of 1937 Roosevelt's "quarantine speech" at Chicago heralded an increasing preoccupation with foreign affairs. Within two years the nation was almost entirely engrossed with the menacing situation overseas and the demands of national defense.

As in other crowded national eras, nearly every possible mood and trend of thought was discoverable somewhere and at some time. Fright, pessimism, fortitude, exaltation, selfishness, altruism, corruption, idealism—all these could easily be found. But a few elements of which there had been an unhappy superabundance in the days of Coolidge vanished completely. Placidity, complacency, and irresponsibility disappeared as the charwomen swept up the last ticker tape in bucket shops which closed in the fall of 1930, as Iowa farmers gathered with pitchforks to stop the sheriffs' foreclosures, and as hungry men peered into garbage cans in the streets of San Francisco and

Philadelphia. Our first impression of the fifteen years following the stock-market crash is that thought and emotion were highly chaotic: the psychology of unlimited opportunity swiftly giving way to the psychology of closed opportunity; the fascism of the pro-Nazi Bund clashing with the collectivism of Earl Browder's Communist party; the escapism of movies and radio balanced against the social earnestness of the Federal Council of Churches and the League of Women Voters; the static outlook of the Liberty League and the dynamic program of the National Resources Planning Board—where can we find a dominant trend?

Yet beneath all the surface crosscurrents and eddies a powerful trend did exist: a trend which psychologically brought together a great movement in home affairs and an irresistible reorientation in world relations. Americans learned in these stormy years that no type of security was attainable on the easy terms which they had taken for granted in the nineteenth century or in the 1920's. Security in the domestic sphere could be had only on a new social basis, through a broad governmental program of interference, regulation, and planning. It was no longer reconcilable with the stark individualism once regarded as an American birthright. Similarly, security in the world sphere could be had only on a collective basis, through courageous measures of world organization. It was no longer reconcilable with unfettered nationalism and unimpaired sovereignty. The new paths seemed strange and bewildering. Throughout nearly their whole history Americans had belonged to the go-it-alone school, which meant laissez faire in economics and isolation in diplomacy, and which seemed a natural expression of their history and genius.

Yet the change which so swiftly overtook the nation, and which came to millions as such a shock, had long been foreshadowed. For two generations progressive political leaders like La Follette, Altgeld, the first Roosevelt, and Wilson, with humanitarians like Jacob Riis, Jane Addams, Brand Whitlock, and John Spargo, had been preaching state intervention for social reform. For one generation a strong school of believers in international union—Root, Taft, Wilson, Cordell Hull—had been trying to draw the United States out of its old timidity and self-sufficiency. Now the irresistible pressure of events brought a decision. In both domestic and foreign affairs what we may call the social ideal triumphed.

What the American masses most wanted when the storms burst and the firmament trembled was security; but they had to find new paths to its attainment. The old economic formula of rugged individualism, which Hoover praised as if men still lived in Hebert Spencer's world, had proved to be not an immovable pillar, but the frailest of reeds. Other nations, caught in the Great Depression, were groping too. The fact that three great powers took refuge in Fascism or its like, which ultimately meant aggression, complicated the situation. For half a dozen years, 1930–1936, the country hoped that it need bother itself only with radical new solutions on the home front, and that foreign policy could be left unchanged. If the United States were to accept the crowding problems of modern industrialism and become a social service state like Britain and Scandinavia, that should be sufficient! In the middle thirties the spirit of nationalism and isolationism distinctly increased. But as the neglect of foreign dangers only heightened them, it was necessary to turn first toward foreign alliances, and then to flat and permanent acceptance of a world organization. By 1942 the social and collective paths toward security had been fairly adopted. It had been settled that the twentieth century road for America was not a continuation of the nineteenth, but a sharp divergence.

2

So much for the dominant trend of the fifteen years: a trend away from individualism and isolationism and toward cooperative solutions of both domestic and foreign problems. But the whole process had a rich complexity which cannot be grasped without some topical analysis.

The first impact of the Great Depression had its most obvious effect in a wave of exposure. In the wake of the Congressional investigating committees that were busy between 1930 and 1935, the press, drama, novel, pulpit, and pamphlet united to analyze and excoriate all the obvious abuses. When the mass of the population during the boom era had smugly worshiped false gods, the satirist had been more effective than the muckraker. Sinclair Lewis and H. L. Mencken had dealt with types, not individuals. But now the nation's mood was direct and grim, and the target was clearly identified. The erring bankers and brokers, the public utility magnates like Insull, the groups who wrecked such railroads as the Chicago, Milwaukee & St. Paul, the promoters of realty and stock-market speculation, came under heavy attack. Competent journalistic exposures of Southern illiteracy, poverty, and physical and intellectual anemia (the nation's Number One problem, said Roosevelt) found a literary reflection in Erskine Caldwell's *Tobacco Road*. The scope of the migratory labor problem, and the obduracy of economic royalists in the face of appalling misery, were laid bare in a monumental report by a California state commission, an impassioned sociological treatise by Carey McWilliams, and that memorable novel, John Steinbeck's *Grapes of Wrath*. From such works as these, dealing with whole sections and large populations, the literatuture of exposure ran down to attacks on labor baiters, on state and city bosses (for example, Huey Long of Louisiana and Frank

Hague of Jersey City), on racketeers, and on tax evaders. Even the chain gang had its official inquiry, its sociological reports, its motion picture, and its literary treatment in Paul Green's play *Hymn to the Rising Sun*.

An equally significant product of the depression was a new movement of economic and sociological analysis, definitely scientific in quality. In their bewilderment, the harassed population turned to the experts. Studies of industrial waste, like those of Stuart Chase; studies of labor, like Benjamin Stolberg's various books; studies of class and caste, like John Dollard's in his work on "Southerntown"; studies of the race problem in the light of anthropology, like Hortense Powdermaker's *After Freedom*; studies of agrarianism, like Arthur Raper's of the tenant farmer; studies of urbanization, like Lewis Mumford's *Culture of Cities*; cross sections of great typical communities, like J. C. Furnas' *How America Lives,* and the Lynds' *Middletown in Transition*—all these were evidence of a deeply felt impulse. Americans, long skeptical of the expert, now felt that their problems had attained a complexity which made it essential to mobilize the whole array of principles, facts, and ideas possessed by the social sciences. Much of the economic analysis was contradictory, for the old "orthodox economics" had been largely succeeded by a wildly confusing clamor. Much of the sociology was vague. But these new studies enriched American thought, banished much naïveté, broke down conventional assumptions, threw light on many hidden relationships, and defined such concepts as well-being, freedom, equality, and democracy with sharp realism.

That this more realistic and scientific approach to the problems of society would ultimately give a distinct coloration to literature could hardly be questioned. Southerners, for example, would have said in 1920 that they "understood the Negro"; but Howard W. Odum, Rupert B. Vance (*Human Geography of the South*), Gunnar Myrdal in his two volumes on the race problem, Spero and Harris in their book on the black worker, and many more proved that they did not. A still larger body of writers, like W. J. Cash in his *Mind of the South* and Clarence Cason in his gently corrosive *90° in the Shade,* showed that they did not even know themselves. Similar examples could be cited in the field of labor relations, of the urban and rural slum, and very conspicuously of the immigrant and his children. By such scientific approaches, greater depth of understanding and a fuller sense of complexity were ultimately conferred upon all letters. Already the impact of the new sociology was not difficult to trace in James T. Farrell's studies of the Chicago Irish, Albert Halper's labor novels, and even Marjorie Kinnan Rawlings' picture of the Florida cracker.

Meanwhile, the formulation of social security as a cardinal national ideal reached below political controversy to the very foundations of American thought. The discussion shook the country for half a dozen years as men who agreed that some recovery measures were essential and that some reforms were urgent, but who disagreed on basic principles, debated the question whether a philosophy of governmental provision could safely be substituted for the old philosophy of stern self-reliance. The ghost of William Graham Sumner struggled with the spirit of Supreme Court Justice Brandeis. The grim necessities of life in a crowded, highly industrialized, and overcompetitive society triumphed; by 1936 the revolutionary social ideal was victorious, for Landon no less than Roosevelt ran for President that year on a social security platform.

But the poignancy of the issue to tens of millions of people cannot be exaggerated. On one side stood a host of men who believed that true liberty was inseparably bound up with individualism, and true progress with unfettered initiative. They passionately desired to preserve the republic of Hamilton, Jackson, and Grover Cleveland: a republic of personal independence, courageous self-sufficiency, and automatic balances. On the other side stood a host of men who believed with equal passion that this old social and political framework was outworn, inhumane, and incalculably dangerous.

The deeper implications of the inevitable decisions were destined to be more slowly grasped in America than they had been in Great Britain when Lloyd George directed a similar plunge. The new social security state was a world removed in outlook, ideas, and spirit from our individualistic nineteenth century state, and its advent seemed appallingly abrupt. After all, many men still active in the thirties remembered when our industrial revolution had been brashly new in the seventies, and multitudes recalled the days when homesteading had remained a brisk reality in the eighties. The spirit of Davy Crockett's and Kit Carson's geographical frontier, and of Rockefeller's and Carnegie's manufacturing frontier, still exercised its spell over most Americans. Even as farmers took the benefits of the Agricultural Adjustment Agency they kicked at the attendant controls, while John L. Lewis' Congress of Industrial Organizations (not to mention some gangster-led unions) accepted government benefits with a fierce repudiation of government disciplines. The novel social ideals would naturally extend their sway but gradually, and they might well be slower still in affecting fiction, poetry, and criticism. Yet the new social security order was as firmly established after 1936 as the new independence had been after 1783, and the new race and labor relationships after 1865. The country had definitely committed itself to a transformed philosophy, which demanded not only a fresh relationship between government and society but a reshaping of society itself.

A new society: for the specifications of the social security state came to nothing less. They called for a drastic curtailment of wealth at one extreme, and a systematic attrition of poverty at the other. Henceforth nobody would be so poor, and nobody so rich; Fifth Avenue and Third Avenue would swing closer together. The specifications called for a society which would save less and spend more. By increasing both the income and the security of the masses, their "propensity to consume"—that is, their standard of living— would be healthfully raised. The millionaire would not needlessly save just to have the government take his money in surtaxes and death duties, while the poor man would not needlessly save to meet exigencies with which the state now dealt. And thus, while thrift lost something of its old standing as a Calvinist virtue, a greater taste for rational enjoyments should give a brighter hue to life. The new specifications implied that less planning would be done for society by the Rockefellers, Carnegies, and Morgans, and more by federal, state, and city governments. They involved, that is, a greater reliance upon that expert bureaucracy which Jacksonian democrats had distrusted, but which, first making its full debut under Theodore Roosevelt, had expanded with irresistible and beneficial rapidity. The specifications closed a good many of the old frontiers of effort, but they opened new ones. If we relied upon science and technology to furnish the foundations of an economy of plenty, as we now meant to do, individual talent would have ample scope in promoting the activities of both. Roosevelt gave one of his campaign speeches of 1936 the significant title, "The Period of Social Pioneering Is Only at Its Beginning."

The New Deal never succeeded in bringing back full prosperity or in banishing unemployment. At one time, in 1936–1937, it seemed about to do so; but a sharp recession during 1937–1938 called back the grimmest specters of the crisis. What the New Deal did accomplish was to plant in the nation a hopeful, aspiring spirit, and to conjure up before men's eyes a vision of national renascence. The rather artificial drives of the first Roosevelt administration to raise national morale did not achieve much; the feverish propagandist activities of various departments, the futile tail chasing of the National Recovery Administration, even the President's fireside talks, had but a transient effect. But as time passed the nation did feel a freer and far more bracing atmosphere. Nor were the principal elements of this atmosphere, by the date of Roosevelt's third election in 1940, difficult to define.

The components of the new spirit were half a dozen: (1) America felt once more that it was a dynamic, not a static, nation; that, in Roosevelt's phrase, it was "on its way" even if it did not always know just to what. Progress in the war against poverty made millions happier than they had been when, under Coolidge, they were told the nation had "arrived" and could now stand still. (2) Once they accepted the idea of the interventionist state, men took pleasure in learning how many objects of a desirable kind imaginative leaders could make the state promote. It conserved resources; it apportioned crops not hit-or-miss but by plan; it developed great valleys; not least of all, through the National Youth Administration it aided education, and through the Work Projects Administration it supported stimulating projects in writing, drama, painting, architecture, and sculpture. (3) A new humanitarianism, less sentimental and paternal, but more effective, had appeared. It recognized that government "economy" was stupid when it cut taxes but neglected human erosion, wasteful when it saved cash but did not save people from degradation. (4) The instinctive craving for national solidarity, the liberal idealism of the New Deal leaders, and advanced sociological and ethnological thinking, all united in a long overdue crusade against the intolerances which had defaced the Harding-Coolidge period, intolerances of which the Ku Klux Klan had been the special symbol. A new impatience of distinctions based upon class, creed, and national stocks took firm root, and the effort to erase them all was for the first time in American history vigorously sustained. (5) Roosevelt's own buoyancy visibly affected the people, as presidential leadership always affects them. (6) A conviction arose that the country was emerging from a careless, wasteful adolescence into a maturity that demanded prudence and planning, but that offered its appropriate rewards in confidence and vigor.

3

All this would have been enough to give intellectual interest to the period. But athwart the preoccupation with domestic affairs cut a sharp current of world perplexities. In 1933 the elevation of Hitler to power struck reflective men with apprehension. Year by year, the brutal drama of the Old World moved from scene to scene—Manchuria, Ethiopia, Spain, Shanghai, Austria, Czechoslovakia—its import to America grew plainer. The attitude of the country at large down to 1939 was far from creditable. The forces which would finally compel a new internationalism could hardly be ignored. But of genuine cosmopolitanism, a feeling for world culture, Americans showed all too little. Of regard for order and justice outside their own borders, and willingness to make sacrifices to promote it, they showed hardly more. Their main concern was simply for national safety. This might be given the dubious dignity of Charles Beard's special pleading in *The Open Door at Home,* or the franker selfishness of the America Firsters; in either event it was unworthy and unhappy.

The years of especially acute crisis, between Mussolini's attack on Ethiopia and the blow at Pearl Harbor, therefore constituted a remarkably dramatic period of education and conversion. In 1935 most Americans still rejected the international ideal. "Entanglements" meant war and all its accompaniments—propaganda, profiteers, repudiated debts, internal conflict, loss of civil liberties, general confusion. Americans had learned this lesson all too well, taught by the "exposures" which followed the First World War. Pacifists, reformers engrossed in home problems, liberals of the *New Republic* stripe, Russophiles (Russia herself being isolated), and Fascist groups all joined with the unthinking head-in-the-sand majority who wanted simply to play safe. But by 1941 the national attitude had completely changed. National safety was seen to lie in international union. It was one of the most dramatic and drastic *volte-face* in all American history. The fundamental reason for it again lay in stark necessity: playing safe had proved to be playing the aggressors' game. Twice in adult memory it had been demonstrated that the way to escape a prairie fire was not to retreat behind a few hasty furrows, but to join the neighbors in beating out the first sparks. Watching the house burn for the second time, Americans took a mighty resolve. They registered it at the Atlantic Meetings, Dumbarton Oaks, Yalta, and San Francisco.

This process of conversion, far from being confined to the political sphere, affected every department of American thought. From the beginning an unprecedented array of books by foreign correspondents and international experts had flooded the country. The newsreel and radio had made Americans feel that they were sitting on the very fringe of world events. Meanwhile, the nation's interest in world culture, the cosmopolitan tradition of Jefferson, Longfellow, and Ticknor, was being strengthened by a ceaseless irruption of refugee writers and artists. The Republic had gained much from refugees of the French Revolution, the German Forty-eighters, and the survivors of the Russian pogroms. But it obviously stood to gain far more from the tens of thousands of writers, scholars, painters, physicians, and composers who were cast on our shores by the Fascist terror. Some came temporarily, like Maeterlinck; most came permanently, like Einstein and Thomas Mann. A certain friction was visible in such professional fields as medicine. But in general the national welcome was warm; it became possible to staff an entire "university in exile"; and scientific journals, general magazines, and book lists soon showed the power of the new element in American life. Henceforth it would be a little easier for educated Americans to be at home in world culture.

An ideological emphasis upon democracy as a world force was an inevitable and notable accompaniment of the external crisis 1935–1945. Totalitarian and democratic ideals obviously stood in implacable opposition. As the United States finally moved toward guaranteeing its safety by membership in the United Nations, so it moved also toward the exaltation of democracy as an international gospel. Many diverse motives were bound up in the virtual Anglo-American alliance, in the Pan-American and Good Neighbor movements, and in Clarence Streit's Union Now program; but one of the most prominent objects was the protection and propagation of democratic ideas. In the nineteenth century America had consciously regarded herself as the exemplar of democracy; in 1917–1918 Woodrow Wilson had made her the crusading apostle. But after 1935 democracy became the basis for a grand world alliance. It was eventually made a veritable communion as against the hostile fellowship of Hitler, Mussolini, and Franco. A huge array of novels, plays, histories, and expository treatises, under the slogan "Books are weapons," was marshaled to the defense of democracy as a world force. The English-speaking peoples had long been close to one another; but now Ernest Hemingway discovered a brotherhood between the American and the Spanish rebel, and Pearl Buck a link between the Yankee and the Chinese—the brotherhood of democracy.

December of 1941 and January of 1942 were in some respects two of the darkest months in all American history. Half the battleship fleet had just been knocked out at Pearl Harbor; Japan was overrunning the Philippines; German submarines were littering the Atlantic coast with wrecks; the gravest danger existed that the Nazis would yet capture Moscow and break the spinal column of the British Empire at Suez. But out of defeat and distress, out of ten years of travail, a radiant dawn was beginning to light the national scene. America had fairly chosen its two new paths. Primarily under Roosevelt's leadership, but with the aid of Hull and Wallace, Willkie and Stimson, and many another leader in both parties, it had decided to seek domestic security in social measures, and world security in collective policies. National individualism and isolationism were seemingly forever dead.

It was dawn, moreover, in another sense. Just ahead lay such a display of power in the mass production of ships, airplanes, tanks, ordnance, and all the lesser paraphernalia of war, of skill in the mobilization and deployment of forces double those ever before put into the field, and of resolution in committing the country to colossal expenditures of money, effort, and if necessary blood, as would add fresh luster to the history of the nation. The early thirties had found the country half paralyzed; the early forties saw it exerting a giant's might. With this exercise of power in the war came a new mood of robust exhilaration—tempered, happily, at the war's end, by the sense of perplexity over still unsolved domestic problems and of the necessitated responsibility of sharing in world leadership.

THE society of the period between wars was curious about what Americans were, could do, might do, were doing. American literature and American journalism had grown up by the 1920's. By the 1940's, a host of serious writers, with the aid of publishers, foundations, universities, and the government, had learned how to make writing a profession, how to make a living at it, and how to get themselves read.

The best of these writers were able to work on a higher technical level than had their predecessors. They had fewer financial handicaps to overcome. They appeared at a time when magazine editors and book publishers were curious about the new generation, and also when its members, with their wartime adventures, their travels and their moral revolt, had something fresh to say. While waiting for literary recognition, they were able to support themselves without going far from their own field. Newspaper work had ceased to be a taken-for-granted step in the literary career, but a few of the younger writers became foreign correspondents, notably Ernest Hemingway and Vincent Sheean. Others were advertising copy writers (Scott Fitzgerald and Hart Crane); still others were teachers (Thomas Wolfe and Thornton Wilder); but more were book reviewers, free-lance journalists, junior editors of magazines, or book publishers' assistants. Literature was becoming a specialized field, almost like medicine, in which a man could spend his life from college to the grave.

All the younger writers of the twenties planned to go abroad, and either saved money for the trip or hopefully searched the woods for windfalls. In those days windfalls were fairly numerous: in addition to the Rhodes Scholarships to Oxford, there were the American Field Service Fellowships to French universities; after 1925 there were the Guggenheim Fellowships, which provided for a year and sometimes two years in Europe; and there were private benefactors, of whom the most widely known was Otto Kahn. Best of all, since they combined financial help with the prospect of publication, were publishers' advances against future royalties. Many publishers, including some of the oldest houses and more of the newest, were willing at the time to risk a few hundred dollars on any promising young writer who needed time to finish his first novel. The money could be used for a trip to France, where living was cheap and the writer could work, so he hoped, in ideal circumstances.

Sometimes the novel was written and published and was even a success. A distinguishing feature of the writers belonging to the interwar generation is the early age at which they became established in their profession. Scott Fitzgerald at twenty-three was already selling stories to the magazines. At twenty-four he published his first novel and earned $18,000 during the year. Fitzgerald was luckier in the beginning than his contemporaries; but his friend Ernest Hemingway had an international reputation after he published his second book at the age of twenty-eight. John Dos Passos, Thornton Wilder, Glenway Wescott, Louis Bromfield, and Thomas Wolfe—to mention only a few names—were all established writers before they were thirty. As men who could devote all their time to literary work and who, moreover, were fascinated by the problems of their craft, most of them became expert technicians.

2

Financially these writers suffered less than might have been expected from the depression. The sale of books decreased sharply in 1930 and continued low until after 1935. A large publishing house and four or five smaller ones went bankrupt, with a loss to their authors of accrued and future royalties. Several magazines suspended publication, while others stopped buying articles or stories and began printing the old manuscripts that had accumulated in their files; they were like bears in winter living on their fat. But new magazines were appearing even in the depression years; the Book-of-the-Month Club prospered; Hollywood was showing an interest in serious, even high-brow novelists, especially if they could write good dialogue; and in general the authors already known to the public found it not too hard to survive.

It was a different problem for the still younger writers, those born after 1905, who in 1930 still had their reputations to make. They had the bad luck to come forward at a time when there was no demand for college graduates with literary ambitions. The magazines, shrunk to half their former size, had no room for new writers; the publishers had no money to risk on first novels that might never be finished, nor had they jobs to offer on their now smaller staffs. "Wait a while," they said to the more promising applicants. "Perhaps next season . . ." But the young writers had to live while waiting; and their general difficulties were increased by the fact that many of them came from working-class families, without the financial resources or wide acquaintanceships or merely the air of assurance that helped the middle classes to keep afloat during the worst years. Once at a meeting of young writers an older writer asked from the platform, "How do you manage to keep going?" There was giggling in one corner of the hall, where half a dozen poets sat with their wives; then one of them rose to say, "We marry schoolteachers." That was in New York, where teachers received their full salaries even in the winter of 1932, and hence were regarded as persons of economic consequence. Young writers in general had no salaries; they lived on their wives or parents, brooded in cafeterias, found odd jobs; at one time there were hundreds of them on home relief—including some who later owned Hollywood villas with swimming pools.

In the early years of the depression, it was natural for young writers to believe that the best hope for American literature lay in a complete reorganization of society. They flocked by hundreds into the radical movement; and soon there were John Reed clubs—named for the author who died of typhus in Russia after helping to found the American Communist party—flourishing in all the larger cities. At least six of the clubs published their own little magazines devoted to the theory and practice of proletarian literature. In 1935 all the John Reed clubs were dissolved on instructions from the Communist Party, which condemned them as being too "leftist" and doctrinaire.

The organization that replaced them was the League of American Writers, which had no direct political affiliations, although there were some Communists on its executive board. The League was typical of the united front during the period when liberals and radicals were collaborating in all countries from Chile northeastward round the globe to China. It recruited more than eight hundred members, most of whom were professional authors, unlike the younger membership of the John Reed clubs. It held four writers' congresses in New York, all interesting affairs; it conducted a writers' school; it issued political statements, especially in favor of the Spanish Loyalists; and then it declined after 1940, in the midst of the political quarrels that followed the Moscow trials and the Russo-German Pact. By that time many of the younger writers had turned anti-Communist or had withdrawn from politics into a revived religion of art.

By that time, too, the Federal Writers' Project was dwindling away, although it would not be formally abolished until a year after Pearl Harbor. Founded in 1935, it employed at its peak more than six thousand writers and researchers, including some who would afterward be famous, like John Steinbeck, and even some who were famous already; a poet who had won the Pulitzer prize for his selected works was glad to receive a government check of about $25 a week for his researches into local history. One desirable effect of the Writers' Project—in addition to keeping writers employed through the later years of the depression—was that it encouraged them to stay at home. Since it was organized on a state basis, writers could be more easily certified to the Project if they lived in West Virginia or Idaho than if they moved to New York; thus, it favored the growth of regional centers. Its principal work was also regional, being the compilation of guides to the forty-eight states and Alaska, as well as to the principal cities, automobile highways, and national monuments.

Hollywood during those same years had served as a sort of auxiliary writers' project with chromium plate. There was a revolution in the studios when talking pictures replaced silent pictures after 1929. The producers had to recruit a staff of specialists in the written and spoken word. For a time they would hire almost any published novelist for twelve weeks at $300 a week, with a contract that could be renewed at a higher salary if his work proved satisfactory. Famous novelists received much more, sometimes as much as $1,500 a week for their first assignments. In the thirties scores and even hundreds of writers went to Hollywood and disappeared, like travelers in a rocket to the moon. Many of them joined the Hollywood proletariat that works for a few weeks a season at a splendid salary, then haunts the agencies looking for another job. A few of them made their way into the little circle of highly skilled motion-picture artisans whose names are familiar to income-tax collectors, but almost forgotten by the reading public.

In 1938 a Hollywood producer, talking with a visitor from the East, happened to mention Scott Fitzgerald. "Why, I thought he was dead," the visitor exclaimed. "If that's so," the producer said, "I've been paying $1,500 a week to his ghost."

3

At the end of the thirties, there was a boom in what was coming to be known as the literature business; and the boom continued until after the Second World War. Book and magazine publishing began to be organized as a mass-production industry. Most of the 11,806 professional authors—to borrow a figure from the 1940 census reports—were still insecure and underpaid; but those who had achieved or blundered into prosperity were living like speculators in a bull market.

The new era of best sellers had begun as early as 1931, when the sale of most books was hardly enough to pay the printer's bill. In that year Pearl Buck published her first novel, *The Good Earth,* which stood at the top of the bookstore lists for two years. It was reprinted many times at various prices, was translated into many languages, and had an American sale in all editions of probably more than a million copies, although its publisher has never released the exact figures. In 1933 and 1934, the best seller was *Anthony Adverse,* the first of the oversize historical romances. It had so wide a popular appeal that it became a sort of St. Christopher for the booksellers, lifting them on its back and carrying them through the slough of the depression; its sale during the next twelve years would be more than 1,200,000 copies. In 1936 and 1937, the book was *Gone With the Wind,* with a sale in its first ten years of over 3,500,000 copies in English; both at home and abroad it was the greatest publishing success of the century. All three of these novels had been issued to its subscribers by the Book-of-the-Month Club, which, with its competitors, was changing the history of the book trade in America.

Essentially the book clubs were companies engaged in the business of selling books by mail to various types of readers. By 1946 there were twenty-six clubs, with 3,600,000 subscribers, many of whom were buying books for the first time, and some of whom lived in villages more than fifty miles from the nearest bookstore. There were special clubs for Protestants, Catholics, radicals, children, executives, students of science, lovers of the classics, Sears Roebuck customers, and mystery fans; but two of the clubs that appealed to a general audience—the Book-of-the-Month Club and the Literary Guild—were the oldest and by far the most successful.

The Book-of-the-Month Club issued its first selection in April, 1926; at the end of the first year it had 40,000 members. Its growth was steady even during the depression, and phenomenal in the early wartime years; by 1943 it was setting a limit of 600,000 on its membership because of the paper shortage. In spite of difficulties with production, it was distributing nearly 300,000 copies, on the average, of the books it recommended, besides many other volumes ordered by the members from its monthly magazine; and it was then the third largest private customer of the Post Office Department, the first two being Sears Roebuck and Montgomery Ward. Obviously the members had learned to rely on the taste of the five judges who made its monthly selections. The judges never succeeded in choosing the twelve best books of the year in point of literary merit, but they almost always chose something of general interest, and they often took chances—that is, they voted for some out-of-the-way book which, without their approval, would have had no chance for success. The growing popularity of nonfiction books was a phenomenon of the years after 1930 when even the philosopher George Santayana became a best seller. Partly it was explained by the support that many of them received from the Book-of-the-Month Club.

The Literary Guild, which began to distribute books in 1927 after several years of discussion and promotion, had a more uneven history. At first it grew as fast as its rival; then for some years it fell behind, as a result of choosing books that were either too difficult or, in some cases. simply too dull for its audience; there were times when it teetered on the edge of bankruptcy. After 1937 it began a period of rapid growth under a new editor, John Beecroft, who also made the monthly selections for two other large book clubs owned by the same publishing house: the Doubleday One Dollar Book Club and the Book League of America. But the Guild received his special attention; it overtook and passed the Book-of-the-Month Club during the war, when it had a larger supply of paper; and by 1946 it had 1,250,000 members, as against 1,000,000 for its rival.

Paper stocks, however, were only part of the story. The more rapid growth of the Guild after 1937 was also the result of its having adopted an older, safer, and somewhat more cynical policy. Its selections were chiefly novels with a well constructed plot that was easy to follow: books that Beecroft was sure its members would like. The bookstore audience liked them too; and it was largely owing to the influence of the Guild that sales of more than a million copies for historical romances and local color novels once more became commonplace, as in the years before the First World War. Indeed, the best-selling novels of the new era—like *Captain from Castile* and *The Black Rose*—were almost on the same literary level as those of the period from 1900 to 1915; on the average, they were a little better than *Freckles,* a little worse than Winston Churchill's *The Crisis*; neither better nor worse, but only franker in sexual matters, than *The Trail of the Lonesome Pine*.

The publishing industry as a whole was growing in the wartime years; after 1942 the production of books was limited, not by public demand, which seemed to have no end, but only by the supply of paper and binding cloth and the time available on the printing presses. Some publishers, looking ahead, were taking steps to reach the wider market that had been created partly by the book clubs. Books had to be cheaper if they were to be distributed to a mass audience, but that was only part of the problem; they also had to be the sort of books the public would buy, and they had to be sold through stores that the public patronized. There were still only five hundred real bookstores in the country, and most of them were concentrated in the twelve largest cities. Some other machinery had to be found for mass distribution.

The answer that slowly developed was to issue reprints of best-selling novels and nonfiction, at prices ranging downward from $1.98 for illustrated biographies and travel books to 49 cents for clothbound popular novels; and to sell them through thousands of new outlets, including drugstores, stationery stores, and chain department stores. Pocket Books, Inc., founded in 1939, carried the process even further by finding a convenient, reasonably attractive, and highly salable format for books that could be offered for 25 cents at the corner news stand. It printed ten million copies of its books in 1941, twenty million in 1942; and it continued to expand until rivals crowded the field and there were more pocket-size books to sell than even the largest news stands had room to display.

Magazines also enjoyed a period of wartime prosperity when they could sell as many copies as their paper quota made possible. The market for literary products kept expanding; and yet there were whole categories and age groups of writers who gained nothing from the boom in the book and magazine trades. Most of the younger men were in the army; many of the women and the older men were in war work that took all their energies. Poets and scholarly critics, if they had time for writing, learned that it had become harder than ever to find a publisher for books that wouldn't sell. Even the great majority of novelists and general essayists had very little share in wartime profits. Lacking the art of salesmanship, or regarding its use as a dangerous temptation, they lived very much as before, on crumbs of income from a dozen different tables: now an advance from a publisher (who was likely to be more generous in wartime), now a story sold to a magazine, now a literary prize or fellowship (there were more of these than in the past), now a lecture or a summer of teaching at a writers' conference, now a book review or a manuscript to be reported on, now a few dollars for permission to reprint something of theirs in a textbook or anthology, now an invitation to spend a month or two writing at such endowed centers for creative work as Yaddo or the MacDowell colony—in general an irregular series of little windfalls that somehow kept them going while they waited to see whether the next book would pay for the publisher's advance on it and even yield them—for perhaps the first time—an actual royalty check.

Meanwhile a few scores or perhaps as many as two hundred of the most popular writers were earning money almost at the rate of war contractors. If they were lucky enough to have a book taken as its sole monthly choice by one of the two largest book clubs, they each received, in 1946, an advance payment of $50,000; and there was the prospect of further payments from the club if its members liked their work—not to mention the royalties from bookstore sales, certain to be larger for club selections than for other books. Magazines as a class had not raised their top rates for thirty years, and the successful magazine writers of 1940 were being paid rather less than Jack London had received in 1910; but this was another situation that changed during the war. All money was "hot" in those days because of income and excess-profits taxes; and magazines that were making profits subject to high taxation often shared part of the wealth with their collaborators by giving them bonuses or higher fees, at a cost to themselves of about 10 per cent of the sums advanced. The *Reader's Digest,* which was said to be printing eleven million copies a month, paid close to a dollar a word for most of the articles it published, and more than that to some favored writers.

The growth of reprint publishing had involved very little increase in the economic rewards of authorship. The various pocket books, for example, paid royalties of only one cent a copy, equally divided between the author and his original publisher; so that the author's share for an edition of 150,000 was only $750. On the other hand, the sale of foreign rights had begun to yield respectable sums; and the digest magazines gave high prices, in a few cases $10,000 or more, for permission to make a condensed version of a popular novel.

Two young ladies, overheard by a reporter for the *New Yorker,* were discussing the latest number of *Omnibook,* a monthly devoted to book digests. "It takes five or six books and boils them down," said one of the ladies. "That way you can read them all in one evening." The other said, "I wouldn't like it. Seems to me it would just spoil the movie for you."

The movie was not only more important for these young ladies; it was also the largest source of income for many writers. As much as $250,000 was paid for the motion picture rights to successful books; as much as $300,000 for plays that had run only three weeks on Broadway. There is one case on record of a Hollywood producer who paid $150,000 for a then unpublished first novel that the critics did not like when it finally appeared.

4

Besides commercialism, two other tendencies were transforming the literary world after 1930. To name each of them in a long word, they were institutionalization and collectivization.

Literary activities were coming more and more to be centered in the institutions that were powerful enough to support them. The government itself was the largest of these and, in the days of the Federal Writers' Project, it had also shown signs of becoming the most influential. There was at one time talk of establishing a bureau of fine arts with authority to undertake cultural projects and award prizes and fellowships. A conference held under official auspices in the spring of 1941 resolved that the government had an interest in supporting the fine arts, including literature, that went beyond the measures it had already taken to keep artists and writers employed during the depression. But our entrance into the war, and later the hostility of Congress and the change in government personnel, put an end to these plans. The only government support for literature after 1945 was through the State Department in the foreign field, and through numerous research programs maintained by the Library of Congress.

Many of the functions that might have been performed by a bureau of fine arts were gradually taken over by the American universities. With their vast endowments and, in many cases, their support by state governments (in addition to help from the Carnegie and Rockefeller foundations), they became the local centers of cultural activity. They maintained, generally speaking, the best American libraries for scholarly work. They offered extension courses and free lectures that took the place of the old-time chautauquas and lyceums. They were a refuge for the little-theater movement, which was declining in most of the American cities and continued to flourish only in summer resorts. To their student bodies they gave courses in creative writing, sometimes with the help of well known authors. Teaching and creative writing, in the early 1900's, had been two separate worlds; after 1940, however, it was no longer surprising to hear that a critic, an experimental poet, a successful biographer, or even a widely praised novelist was on the faculty at Harvard, Minnesota, California, Princeton or any one of a dozen other universities.

More and more writers in all fields had ceased to be independent craftsmen and instead had become officials in public or private institutions. Besides those who worked for the government or taught in universities, there were others who wrote on yearly salaries for magazine corporations, on three months' contracts for motion picture producers, or were hired by radio advertising agencies. They were sometimes very well paid; on the largest magazines they might earn salaries of as much as $25,000 a year (or even more, if they were among the top favorites of *Reader's Digest*); and there were a very few writers for the movies who earned $5,000 a week on short-term contracts. At the other end of the scale, salaried writers for wood-pulp magazines might be given less than the rate for cub reporters under a Newspaper Guild contract. Lavishly paid or miserably paid, salaried writers as a class did honest work, the best that was possible in the circumstances; but the work was not their own. It had become collective to a degree never achieved in Russia, where collectivization is set forward as an ideal. The Russians sometimes sent "shock brigades" of writers to report on a particular situation; at one time it was the industrial and agricultural progress of Tajikistan. The writers all made the same conducted tour; then afterwards each submitted his individual report. But American writers employed by a corporation might not only be assigned to the same collective task; each of them might be expected to perform only part of it, like a single worker on the production line. In Hollywood, for example, it was a practice of some companies first to buy a story, then to set three writers to work independently preparing it for the screen. Their three versions would be combined, usually by a fourth writer, and the completed script would then be subject to further changes by the producer, the director on the set, and the editor in the cutting room, not to mention changes in the course of production by virtually all those concerned, till at last the film emerged as a vast collective enterprise.

Writing for some magazines had become almost as purely a collective process. An idea might be suggested by one of the editors, adopted after a conference of executives, assigned to one or more researchers to gather the facts, then to a salaried writer (or sometimes two or three writers in succession) to put the facts together, then again to one or more editors to whip it into final shape. In the Luce magazines, most of the articles were unsigned, for one good reason, among others, that it would have been as difficult in some cases to assign them to any single authorship as it would have been to identify the man chiefly responsible for the ten-millionth Chevrolet to move down the production line.

Even in fields where the process was less advanced, much of current American writing had come to represent not a personal vision, but rather a trend, an imprint, or a decision taken at a board of directors' meeting. The literary world had undergone vast changes since the moral and aesthetic revolt that began after 1910. There was now a much wider audience for all writing, including some of the best, and a much larger body of writers trained to meet its demands. There had been a great elaboration in technique, so that American fiction in the forties was the most skillful produced anywhere in the world. Yet there was also a greater timidity among writers, of the sort that develops in any bureaucratic situation; and there was a tendency to forget that, although a great book expresses a whole culture and hence has millions of collaborators, including persons long since dead, in another sense it must finally be written by one man alone in his room with his conscience and a stock of blank paper.

76. SPECULATIVE THINKERS

In the twenty-five years that followed the death of William James in 1910, American speculative thought described a spiral movement. It began in idealism, swung rapidly to an opposite extreme, and then moved slowly back toward a philosophy which curiously resembled idealism but which had absorbed the results of the immense intervening progress made by science.

At the turn of the century the camp of idealism was thronged; nearly every philosopher of any standing in the country belonged to it. James began a revolt. Soon insurgents were springing up from behind every bush. Some of them were materialists, who were fortunate enough to have in Santayana perhaps the most eloquent spokesman that their ancient creed had ever found. Others gathered around John Dewey, who had picked up the weapons of James. The spread of his pragmatic revolt into the regions of educational, legal, and historical thought must form an important part of this chapter. A third rebellion came from the realists, though this ended in some confusion because of dissensions within the ranks. Another form of discontent broke out among the theologians, many of whom were repelled by the austere aridities of the appeal to reason. After all these alarms and excursions, it was curious, at the end of twenty-five years, to see thinkers from all points of the compass converging again, under the leadership of A. N. Whitehead, toward a philosophy strangely like the old and deserted idealism. The period begins with the emigration of Santayana from metaphysics and from America. It ends with a return to metaphysics led by an emigrant from Europe.

2

Santayana, Royce, and James belonged to the same department at Harvard, a department described by President Tucker of Dartmouth as not only the strongest department the country had known in philosophy, but the strongest in any field. Royce and James were Santayana's teachers; he knew them well; but almost from the beginning something within him rose in rebellion against them both. Indeed he reacted against nearly everything American. Born of

Spanish parents with New England connections, coming to this country an alien when he was eight years old, he remained throughout his life here an exotic and ill acclimated plant. It was as if there were something in his Latin blood that was determined to resist assimilation. He disliked American Protestantism and Puritanism and democracy and drive; he was always impatient to escape to Europe; and when, in 1912, it became financially practicable to give up his Harvard professorship, he abandoned it with a sigh of relief, boarded a ship almost immediately, and never set foot on American soil again.

Yet in a sense he never escaped America. "It is as an American writer that I must be counted," he says, "if I am counted at all." He adopted English as his exclusive medium; he avowed that he knew no other language well. For forty formative years New England was his home. Even his revolt against America was curiously American; it was almost as much the revolt of a sensitive American individualist like Henry James or T. S. Eliot as it was of an alien. Only by remembering how deep were his roots in American soil will one understand the animus of his criticisms. It has been pointed out that, though he regarded all religious belief as mythology, he reserved his sharpest strictures for "the genteel tradition of the Calvinists and the musty smell of duty over New England," and always treated Catholicism with gentleness and sympathy. For Santayana the thought of his past years was far indeed from a benediction; he sat singularly loose to his environment, wherever he was; and since New England was a peculiarly imperious environment, he hated it. At the same time it must be added that he was too genuine an individualist to be explained in terms of social or economic pressures, even by way of reaction against them. There are few figures in the history of American thought who, in their detachment from the scene around them, would offer to a historian of Marxist leanings a more awkward set of problems.

In some absorbing essays in autobiography (*Persons and Places*, 1944, *The Middle Span*, 1945), and still more perhaps in his single novel *The Last Puritan* (1935), Santayana revealed the source of his imperfect sympathies with New England. He believed that the Puritan character was "at enmity with joy." He therefore reacted against it with all the force of his Latin temperament and his Epicurean ethics. He appreciated the nobility of his Puritan hero, Oliver; but Oliver is a perfectionist ridden by conscience; he does everything—his work, his play, even his love-making—from an all-pervading sense of duty; and in the end it breaks him. Mario, his Latin-Catholic foil, can throw ultimate responsibilities on God and get on with his mundane hedonism. Puritanism, Santayana thought, served well enough for coarse, bluff minds who conceived of duty in the manner of good soldiers or good farmers. But when inherited by sensitive spirits, it is more than flesh can bear. It diffuses the sense of duty through all the capillaries of one's being, breeds a chronic feeling of failure, and spreads a creeping paralysis over the will. Man is not made for such self-torment. If he tries to live with his head continually in the clouds, he will only lose his footing on earth.

Santayana described himself as "a decided materialist—apparently the only one living." His materialism was not at all of the kind so often charged against Americans, that specifically moral materialism which consists in a preoccupation with the grosser goods. It was a philosophical doctrine; its "great axiom," he tells us, is "the dominance of matter in every existing being, even when that being is spiritual." This philosophy he expounded in two impressive and massive series, the five volumes of *The Life of Reason,* which formed the great achievement of his youth, and the four of *The Realms of Being,* which appeared at intervals from his sixty-fourth to his seventy-seventh year. In his own view these works expound a single coherent position. In the view of some of his critics, his early materialism underwent in the later volumes a transmutation into something richly and strangely Platonic.

According to *The Life of Reason* (1906), matter is all that exists. What then of thought and feeling? The answer is that they are by-products of the body, "a lyric cry in the midst of business," "a wanton music" babbled by the brain and wholly without efficacy in turning the wheels of the bodily machine. The life of reason is not, as it has been for so many philosophers, a life of free and speculative reflection; it consists rather in such judicious control and harmonization of our animal impulses as will secure for us most peace and satisfaction. To such mundane peace and satisfaction we shall devote ourselves if we are wise, for there is no other. The suggestion of free moral choice, uncontrolled by "the dark engine" of the body, or of a survival of the spirit beyond bodily disintegration, or of a God who presides over the course of nature and history, seemed to Santayana not so much a belief to be critically examined as the vestige of a primitive and pathetic mythology; he would say of religious creeds, as John Morley did, that they were less to be refuted than to be explained. Religion is not philosophy but poetry. If we would make the most of a brief and precarious life, let us rid ourselves of transcendentalisms, take stock of our little capital of impulses and powers, and make of it what we can. "Everything ideal has a natural basis and everything natural an ideal development." *The Life of Reason* is a leisurely and elaborate musing on that text as it applies to all the major branches of man's activity.

In the Santayana of later years there is a singular shift of interest. His preoccupation in *The Realms of Being* (1927–1940) is with the world of essences. And what are essences? We all know that when we say two and two are four, we are not saying something true at the moment merely, but something that is true always and everywhere. It never began to be true: it will never cease to be true; for twos and fours and the relations between them are not like apples that can decay or snowballs that melt; they are entities that are timeless and therefore beyond the reach of change. It is Santayana's doctrine of essence that everything we sense or imagine is in this position. We say that the odor of the violet is transitory. That, he insists, is false. To be sure, our sensing of it is transitory; we become aware of it and then cease to be aware; but that is another matter. The quality itself is as timeless as the twos and fours of our equations. So of all the colors and sounds, tastes and temperatures of actual or possible experience; all without exception are essences. Do they exist in the physical world? "No," he answers; "nothing given exists"; they are quite literally such stuff as dreams are made of. It is absurd to say that when we see or touch a chair, the shape and the hardness that we sense belong to the boiling mass of protons and electrons that is presumably out there; we may take them to belong there, and in favorable cases something like them may be there actually; but even of that we cannot be sure. In the end, philosophers, like everyone else, must rest their belief in the world around them on animal faith.

It might appear that Santayana in his age had come around to a point very close to the idealism he began by repudiating, and indeed the resemblance between his essences and the Platonic ideas is often remarked. But the resemblance is not in fact very close. Plato's ideas were also ideals; they descended into the stream of thought and action and made a dynamic difference there. Santayana's essences are "vestal virgins," beautiful perhaps to contemplate, but without issue in the world of events. All that we think, feel, or do is determined inflexibly by the distribution within our brains of a matter that even science cannot certainly know. All moral preferences, all scientific beliefs, all the dreams of the saints and the philosophers are at the beck and call of the material dynamics of nature.

The elaboration of this magnificent and melancholy philosophy was done in a prose that assures its writer of a permanent place in literature, whatever may be the fortunes of his theories at the hands of professional critics. It is a singularly quiet style, with a slow and meditative rhythm, exquisitely sensitive to the sounds and connotations of words as well as to their explicit meanings. Santayana is the conscious artist always. The words never tumble out as in informal talk; all is premeditated; dip into any page of his long row of volumes and you will find the same even flow of urbane and polished writing. It is as if a wise and traveled man of the world, released from entanglements with affairs, and free to contemplate the spectacle of life at somewhat elegant leisure, were discoursing over his tea in a world where it is always afternoon. For such a person to raise his voice or engage in logic chopping would not be seemly, and Santayana never does either. He will have it known that he is a gentleman and an amateur; he will have none of professors or their pedantic ways.

The not altogether happy result is that the professors have tended to take him at his own valuation. They have felt in him a certain lack of intellectual strenuousness, a reluctance to carry that agreeable flow of discourse into regions where the dialectical rocks in its bed might make it turbulent or turbid. It must be admitted that in his scorn of pedantry Santayana was content at times to forgo clearness and precision also. Sometimes, indeed not seldom, the reader bent on instruction feels a doubleness of purpose in his author, who, intent on catching all the fugitive lights and shadows as he strolls along, forgets that it is the philosopher's business to follow the straightest available path. Great philosophical prose is distressingly near to impossibility, for those very qualities of feeling that might give it a place in the literature of power may, by muddying its logic, exclude it from the literature of knowledge; and then it satisfies nobody. Philosophers are trained under an increasingly Spartan regime; and to persons in whom this training has produced a taste for spare and athletic writing, Santayana's prose seems lush and Oriental. Certainly he cannot be said to have solved the perhaps insoluble problem of the ideal philosophic manner. Still, there must be numberless persons who would ordinarily find a discussion of essence and existence the darkest sort of morass who have gladly pitched their tents in it because it was lighted, however dimly, by the glow of that iridescent prose.

3

Between Santayana and the next distinguished leader in the revolt against idealism there could hardly be a greater contrast. Santayana was an aristocrat, an artist, an alien among his own countrymen, a man who deliberately held aloof from the political and social movements of his time. John Dewey was a plebeian, both in his temperament—or absence of it—and in his writing. And he was an American through and through, as much at home in the Middle West, where he spent his early maturity, as in New England, where he was born into a society where homecrafts and manual skills still flourished. His philosophy was a philosophy of action rather than of contemplation, and it carried him into such crusading chairmanships as those of the League for Industrial Democracy and the committee that sought to vindicate Trotsky. Without the metaphysical gift of Royce, or the romantic and engaging personality of James, or the superb art of Santayana, he achieved a standing in American thought and an influence in the world that were probably unequalled by any of them. His life is an American success story. How is one to account for it?

Partly, no doubt, by the sheer volume of his output. Dewey sat thought-fully and indefatigably before a typewriter for a considerable fraction of his life, and in mere years this life was extraordinary. His grandfather was born before the American Revolution. He himself was born when Washington Irving was still writing at Sunnyside, and while Lincoln still had his shingle out in Springfield. He appeared in that *annus mirabilis* 1859, which produced, among much else that was notable, Bergson, Husserl, and Havelock Ellis, Mill's essay on *Liberty* and Darwin's *Origin of Species*. In his appearing in the world simultaneously with Darwin's great book, there proved to be a special propriety. One of his own books was entitled *The Influence of Darwin on Philosophy,* and some wag has pointed out that this is a good description of Dewey himself.

There are more solid reasons for Dewey's remarkable influence, three of which should be noted. First, in a time when the theory of evolution was still engaging the general thought, he used that theory as the basis for a reform of logic and ethics. Secondly, to a people distrustful of speculation and preoccu-pied with practical results, he offered a philosophy that seemed to justify both the distrust and the preoccupation. Thirdly, from this new philosophy he developed a set of corollaries about education that again suited in a singularly happy way the temper of the time. All these achievements were branches that sprang from the common trunk of his "instrumentalism."

The term "instrumentalism," which Dewey preferred to "pragmatism" as a name for his philosophy, is itself suggestive of the debt he owed to Darwin. He holds that in the course of evolution thought was generated as an *instru-ment,* an instrument of adjustment and survival, like running, flying, and climbing. It originated in practical necessity; it maintained itself because it was practically useful; and—here is the new departure—its right employment now as in the beginning is as a means of practical adjustment. The situation in which thought first arose is typified by that of primitive man when, chased by a bear, he came to the bank of a river. In such a pass, instinct has nothing to offer; habit also is helpless because the occasion is new; it is a case of think or die. If the violent impact of necessity could strike from the man's mind the spark of an idea—say the idea of pushing out into the stream on a log—then, and only then, he might save himself. Eventually he, or someone else, did. What sort of thing was this new and potent tool which we now describe as an idea? Essentially, says Dewey, it was a plan of action, a proposal to do this or that. If it worked, it was true, in the sense of fulfilling the purpose for which it was brought into being. If it failed to work, it was false. Now the essence of Dewey's instrumentalism lay in maintaining that this first purpose of thought has remained its permanent purpose, and indeed its only purpose. The nature and end of thought marked out by biological evolution, namely the survival, growth, and better adjustment of the organism, are its true nature and end.

This theory at first glance seems innocent enough. But as Dewey gradually unfolded it, it was seen to imply nothing less than a philosophical revolution. He first applied the theory to logic. Traditional logic had assumed that the world had the changeless structure of a pyramid, with a layer of concrete things at the bottom, fixed general classes in the middle, and a set of pure eternal abstractions at the top. Since it was the business of thought to understand this world, its own apparatus of genus, species, and so on, must correspond to these outer arrangements. Dewey brushed aside this whole conception of thought and its purpose. If thought was really a tool, produced to serve the needs of the organism, then it too was in course of change, with all its methods, laws, and concepts; there was nothing static about them. It followed that the very test and nature of truth must be reconceived. The test of a theory can no longer be self-evidence, or consistency with other facts or theories, for what seems self-evident or consistent today may no longer seem so tomorrow; the test lies in whether our theories, now seen to be plans of action, achieve their practical ends. Indeed, this is all that truth *means*. For if the aim of thinking is not to get a copy of the world but to get results in practice, then in achieving those results we are also achieving truth in the only sense that is open to us. Dewey went on to take a similar view in ethics. In conduct as in thought there can no longer be any fixed standards or absolutes. That is good which conduces to human growth. What is growth? Advance toward maturity. What is maturity? It is better not to define it; for any exact definition would set before us a fixed end, and that must at all costs be avoided. Growth is that which conduces to further growth in a world without end. We must be content with that.

In Europe this philosophy gained almost no adherents; its one important representative in England, F. C. S. Schiller, finally retreated in discouragement to America. But in this country it found a congenial atmosphere and throve. It was a philosophy of results. It looked at the elaborate metaphysical and theological systems of the past and put to them one sweeping question: "How much difference do you make in terms of practical human betterment? If you mean little or none, out you go." To persons engaged in the life of action, to students of philosophy who were weary of metaphysical subtleties, or not quite equal to them, and to theologians more interested in communal improvement than in ultimates and absolutes, the announcement of such a program by a philosopher of standing flung open a door of release. When Dewey went on, in his *Reconstruction in Philosophy* (1920), to indict metaphysics as the product of an aristocratic and leisure class, the expression of a desire to escape into another world instead of facing the responsibilities of the here and now, many persons felt that they were hearing for the first time the authentic voice of democratic philosophy.

They felt this even more strongly if they turned to Dewey's *Democracy and Education* (1916). This book contains the fullest statement of an educational theory that has had its influence in almost every schoolroom of America, and in many besides in Mexico, Russia, and China. The theory is based on the instrumentalist philosophy. According to this philosophy, intelligence is not a faculty like memory, to be trained through exercise, nor is it a pursuit of the vision of truth for its own sake; it is a process of making over one's environment into something more satisfactory to one's needs and desires. It involves action in its very essence. Hence in the ideal Deweyan school, rote learning would be banished, and pupils would confine themselves to problems whose solution made a difference in practice. Their interest would be maintained by dealing with those problems in the order in which they arose in the course of their own growth; prescription from outside would be reduced to a minimum and free experimentation encouraged; subject matter would be adjusted to the child rather than the child to the subject matter; the old distinction between cultural and vocational training would be abolished, for culture that is not a means to better activity is feudal and effete; and since that part of the environment consisting of other persons is in many ways the most important part, much of the child's education would consist of experiments in cooperating with his kind.

In these theses of Dewey the "progressive education" movement found its inspiration. Schools sprang up throughout the country in which children did their learning through play, mastering their arithmetic through keeping store, their biology through keeping pets and making gardens, literature through producing plays and stories of their own. Whatever else may have been the effects of such education, there is no doubt that it made the little red schoolhouse a more cheerful and inviting center for myriads of school children.

Dewey's break with tradition was so sharp and his influence in education became so dominating that a reaction was sure to occur. Its leader, when it came, was the young Robert Maynard Hutchins, president of the University of Chicago, who in a series of trenchantly written books (*The Higher Learning in America*, 1936, *No Friendly Voice*, 1936, *Education for Freedom*, 1943), challenged the whole Deweyan conception of education. His own opposing conception received the moral support of Alexander Meiklejohn (*Education Between Two Worlds*, 1942) and of Mark Van Doren (*Liberal Education*, 1943); and it was put to a sort of laboratory test at St. John's College, Maryland, whose leaders, Stringfellow Barr and Scott Buchanan, sought to embody Hutchins' ideals in practice. According to those ideals, intelligence is not, as it was for Dewey, merely a tool for nonintellectual needs; it has an end of its own in the understanding of its world; and education, at least in its higher ranges, should devote itself to this end exclusively. Such understanding means the grasp of the permanent principles governing nature, man, and society.

How far this revolt against the Deweyan program of education will go, it is still too early to say. But in one respect the reaction against Deweyan tendencies did clearly win out. In his later years the drift in higher education was definitely away from the elective system, with its freedom of experiment, toward a considered regimentation in which studies regarded as essential were required of all.

Dewey's influence in education was so extraordinary as to raise the question recurrently how it is to be explained. One explanation is merely that the man and the occasion happily met; but it should be added that, when we speak of the man, we mean rather the thought than the personality. Seldom has a great popular success owed so little to anything picturesque or dramatic in its author, or to any of the arts of advocacy. Dewey was unostentatious almost to self-effacement; when he appeared in public, his slow, abstracted, and somewhat sleepy delivery left his audiences respectful but unaroused; he lacked the impulse to self-advertisement, and he lacked artistic temperament.

He wrote as he spoke. The writing is invariably charged with thought; it always comes at first hand out of his experience; it is downright, unpretentious, transparently honest. There is a fair supply of illustration, usually homely and helpful, but the ratio of generality to particular fact is high. And the often-repeated charge that the style is dull and pedestrian must on the whole be sustained. It is not only that Dewey had no dexterity with the minor devices which the practiced writer could hardly dispense with for an hour— variation of sentence structure, smoothness of transition, climax, balance, relief through figure, humor, or quotation. The trouble lay deeper. Dewey had none of that feeling for the magic of words which saved the most difficult pages of Santayana. He had no ear. He lacked that sense, partly logical, partly aesthetic, of economy of word to thought, which hits an idea off precisely and memorably; there is strangely little that is quotable in all the vast volume of his writing. The literary censor was lax, so lax as to pass innumerable paragraphs and pages that are awkward, verbose, and shuffling.

Of course when one is opening up new country—and the great philosophers have all been pioneers—grace of utterance is not the prime matter, and for the good of his soul the literary man may well recall occasionally that the Aristotles, the Kants, and the Hegels have perpetuated themselves without benefit of form. But the old saying that it is style that preserves is probably still true of all minds except these mountainous ones. And if so, perhaps the representative of the pragmatic philosophy who will be most read fifty years from now will not be its most competent and thorough exponent, who is undoubtedly John Dewey, but the man who invested it with his own inimitable style and charm, William James.

4

Pragmatic ideas have crept into many fields outside philosophy proper. We have seen something of their influence in education. They also infiltrated into the law. Here their effect was most notable at the top, through the work of a friend of James who was also a justice of the Supreme Court, Oliver Wendell Holmes. Judges are not as a rule heroes of the people, but it is reported that when Holmes retired from the Court, he received an acclaim from liberals and conservatives alike that had not been accorded to a member of that Court since the days of John Marshall. His life became the theme both of a successful Broadway play and of a popular biography which, under the title *Yankee from Olympus,* was a best seller. The "Olympus" refers of course to his "Brahmin" background and his sonship to the famous Autocrat, a relation that embarrassed him in curious fashion during most of his ninety-four years.

From his Boston moorings Holmes drifted far in two important directions. For one thing he became a skeptic. In his youth he and James had tried their hands together at stripping some of the obscuring garments from "our dilapidated old friend the Kosmos," but he came to think that "certainty generally is an illusion," and that we must be content with working hypotheses. "The best test of truth," he said, echoing James, "is the power of thought to get itself accepted in the competition of the market." The implications of such a view for religious belief are disintegrative.

But Holmes also moved far from the social conservatism of his forebears. Together with Louis D. Brandeis, he became a precursor of that group of justices in the Supreme Court who, in the recurring conflicts of Franklin Roosevelt's administration between property rights and human rights, stood stanchly for the latter. Though he disliked dissent in the court as weakening its authority, he became known as "the great dissenter," and his tenderness for social experimenters made him a popular hero. The question arose repeatedly whether or not some new venture in legislation or practice regarding a minimum wage or the restriction of child labor or the toleration of soap-box radicalism in public places was in accord with the Constitution. It would have been easy enough to interpret the new venture as conflicting with the rights of property and to crush it beneath the enormous weight of the Constitution. Some of his colleagues, not without an impressive show of logic, favored this. Holmes would have none of it.

The true grounds of decision are considerations of policy and of social advantage, and it is vain to suppose that solutions can be attained merely by logic. . . . There is nothing I more deprecate than the use of the Fourteenth amendment . . . to prevent the making of social experiments that an important part of the community desires . . . though the experiments may seem futile or even noxious.

Such words from the Supreme bench put new heart into faltering liberals.

Though his words were weighty, Holmes had none of his father's gift for making them sing and scintillate. The style of his decisions and of his best known book, *The Common Law*—the Lowell Institute Lectures for 1880—is precise, as befits a jurist, but it is also involved and heavy. The first Oliver Wendell Holmes won a public by his manner rather than his matter. The second won it by his matter almost alone.

5

The movement culminating in the "New History" was not so much a product of pragmatic ways of thinking as a parallel development. Its leader was a colleague and friend of Dewey's at Columbia, James Harvey Robinson, whose course on the history of the intellectual class in Europe influenced historical teaching throughout the country. Robinson insisted that for the understanding and writing of history two things were essential which Dewey had also stressed as basic for understanding the advance of philosophy.

First was the genetic method. "In its amplest meaning," Robinson wrote, "history includes every trace and vestige of everything that man has done or thought since first he appeared on the earth." But history in that sense is impossible; most events of the past have vanished beyond recall, and of those that remain on record only a fraction are worth recalling. On what principle, then, is history to select its material? Robinson answers: "The one thing that it ought to do, and has not yet effectively done, is to help us to understand our fellows and the problems and prospects of mankind." And how is it to work toward such understanding? Certainly not by the old drum-and-trumpet tales; certainly not by making history biographic with Carlyle, or nationalistic with Bancroft, or propagandist with the Marxians, or even, with Freeman, by identifying it with "past politics." History is rather "the study of how man has come to be as he is and to believe as he does." What we should seek in the past is the causal explanation of the present. The method of the historian should be the genetic method; as another member of the group, Harry Elmer Barnes, put it, "Evolution should be to the historian what dynamics is to the physicist." Every important institution and event of our own day is only the last bead on a thread that runs back continuously into the past. The business of the historian is to seize that thread and follow it backward wherever it leads.

If he does so, he will be led in strange directions. Instead of following the track of royal genealogies, he will be taken into regions that would have seemed to the classical historian too dim and perhaps too sordid to invite exploration. The sanitary arrangements in Rome may have had more to do with its fall than the character of its emperors; the wages of medieval workingmen may have thrown more light on the crusades than religion itself; one of the new historians, Charles A. Beard, shocked his readers by arguing with much force that the American Constitution was set up by the propertied classes to give security to their own position. The lines of historic causation thus run out into medicine, economics, and psychology, into geography, statistics, and law; indeed there is no detail of the civilization he is studying which the historian can dismiss beforehand as irrelevant. The first point of the new history was that the past must causally explain the present. The second point was that if such explanation was to be achieved, the historian must leave the beaten tracks and get out into the alleys and hedgerows of the civilization he is studying; he must know its disease rates and death rates, the state of its coinage and the state of its housing, as well as its battles and princely marriages. It would be impossible for him to explain how the family, the church, and present social divisions came to be what they are without entering into the conditions of past life with a fullness seldom even attempted by earlier historians.

The most disquieting part of the new history was its account of human beliefs. People have generally regarded their beliefs as resting on reasons, and they have held this not less of beliefs about ultimate matters of philosophy and religion than of beliefs about everyday concerns. The new historians agreed with Dewey in holding that these larger beliefs generally spring from causes rather than reasons. They are accepted because others accept them, and these others accept them ultimately because they help to allay fear, or because they bolster self-respect, or because they justify one's own position and conduct. In short, they are not rational; they are only rationalizations. While Dewey was elaborating this theory for metaphysics in his *Reconstruction in Philosophy* (1920), Robinson was doing it for religion and social beliefs in his widely read *The Mind in the Making* (1921). These books were the more influential because there were at the time a wave of popular interest in Freudianism and a new burst of activity on the part of the anthropologists; Franz Boas, R. H. Lowie, Alexander Goldenweiser, Clark Wissler, and Margaret Mead were producing a row of interesting volumes on the formation of primitive customs and beliefs. An able book showing the influence of Robinson and Dewey, and written by a pupil of both, was John Herman Randall's *The Making of the Modern Mind* (1926), which was widely used as a textbook in American colleges. It undertook to show that the successive world views from Dante to Marx and Hegel, far from being examples of pure thought, working under the exclusive control of logic, were molded in numberless ways by the social conditions and technical knowledge of the time.

6

Of course all this was bound to create apprehension among those who took their religious beliefs seriously. For such beliefs were supposed to rest either on a revelation which could not conceivably mislead or upon reasoning that led to firm objective truth, and if they were now to be set down as by-products of the wish to believe, controlled not by the evidence but by non-rational pulls and pushes, then to put it plainly they were illusions, and all religion rested on something very like a mirage.

To the formidable challenge of this relativism, religious writers responded in various ways. Some of them, the humanists, accepted the new line of argument and sought to elaborate a religion virtually devoid of creed. At the opposite extreme, some sought to defend their orthodoxy by throwing doubts on reason itself. Catholics and Fundamentalists reiterated their traditional positions. And between the two extremes stood the religious liberals, troubled and divided.

The philosophical humanists—not to be confused with the literary neo-humanists discussed elsewhere in this work—included some academic teachers of wide influence, Dewey, Max Otto, Roy W. Sellars, Eustace Haydon, and Shailer Mathews. But the most effective writer among them was not a professed philosopher or theologian, but a journalist, Walter Lippmann. In his youth a precocious student at Harvard, gifted with a graceful and facile style, Lippmann burst into print in defense of socialism almost instantly upon graduation and continued to produce a stream of readable books on politics, religion, and international affairs while writing a daily column for the newspapers. His history was one of slow movement from the red end of the spectrum to a position approaching conservatism, first in politics, then in religion. His statement of the humanist outlook was made in mid-career in his *Preface to Morals* (1929).

In this book Lippmann holds that the entire framework of traditional theology has collapsed. The dogmas of a personal deity, of the incarnation and the atonement, the fall, original sin, the resurrection, the last coming, and the final judgment, have all been eaten away by the "acids of modernity."

It is not so much that they have been formally refuted as that in the bleak light of the modern world, with its scientific atmosphere, they have lost their plausibility and withered away. Lippmann views their disappearance complacently enough. What concerns him more is that for many centuries theological beliefs have provided the sanction and sustenance for moral idealism; men's hopes, their moral seriousness, the set of values that have guided their lives, have come in very large part from their religion. What will happen to this moral fruitage if the religious roots are pulled up? Can the godless naturalism that is superseding the old religion provide a rich enough soil for high-principled and generous living?

Lippmann thinks it can. The connection between moral idealism and religious belief he considered historical rather than logical. If men rate pleasure above pain, love above hate, and beauty above ugliness, it is because they, or the best of them, have seen that this order of value holds in the nature of things; there is nothing subjective or capricious about such judgment; pronouncements from on high may corroborate it, but they did not originate it; it rests on man's own authentic insight. And this insight is wholly independent of his creeds. With the disappearance of his creeds, he must review the case, dismiss the moral with the theological lumber, and retain only what his own perception can validate. In this process he will lose much that he prized, for he can no longer rely on the friendliness of the universe nor look forward with the old confidence to a life that endures; his life on earth is presumably his all. But it remains as true as before that some ways of living are noble and some debased, and there is no reason at all why a cultivated and disinterested mind should not find in purely mundane goods an end that can enlist its wholehearted devotion. That devotion will in truth be more stable than it was, because it does not now spring from precarious theological commitments, but is rational and free.

There was a cogency in this humanism that found a large response in the minds of thoughtful Americans and disturbed the peace of the orthodox. What were orthodox believers to do in the face of this continuing encroachment by the scientific and rational spirit? They could of course announce that the Church had spoken, that revelation and true reason could never disagree, and that if they seemed to disagree, it was not true reason that was speaking. This line was taken by a considerable body of neo-scholastics, but it was not widely persuasive. Many Protestant theologians were convinced that if religion threw down the gage to modern science and philosophy, with reason as its only weapon, the case was as good as lost beforehand; and the slow retreat of theology for the past three centuries seemed to them good evidence that they were right. To base faith on reason was in fairness to admit that it might be overthrown by reason. They held that a wholly different strategy must therefore be adopted. Faith must be cut loose from reason altogether. The believer may assure himself that in faith he has a certainty which reason can neither generate nor destroy, and which science therefore cannot endanger. His faith is a rock deep-based in nonrational reality, against which the shallow waves of intellectualism may beat noisily, but will always beat in vain.

This theology did not come in the first instance from America. It was the product of a line of European thought that began with the strange Danish genius, Kierkegaard, was developed in Germany by Karl Barth and Emil Brunner, and was imported into this country, with modifications, by Paul Tillich, Wilhelm Pauck, and the brothers Reinhold and Richard Niebuhr. In its purity, as represented by Barth, it is a bold attempt to turn the tables on all the pretensions of reason. God is; he reveals himself through the incarnation and the Bible; our contact with him is the most certain and the most significant thing in human life. Yet he remains, and must remain, an inscrutable mystery. There is nothing we can say of him that is true, not even, in the ordinary sense, that he exists, or is interested in us, or is good, for every attempt of our feeble thought to figure to ourselves his nature must fall infinitely short of its object. The philosopher cannot know him. Neither can the mystic, since his experience, however exalted, is shot through with finite passion and prepossession. No saint, not even the Christ who was a human being, can really embody his will, for God's ways are not as our ways, and he stands over against all we know or feel or aspire to as something "absolutely other."

How then make contact with him? The Barthians say frankly that we cannot—"There is no way from man to God." But God in his infinite power can come to man. And for reasons beyond our knowing he does come to some men, in the sense that he gives them grace to see, by a sort of supernatural insight, that in this or that passage of scripture, through this or that favored human vessel, perhaps oneself, the word of God is spoken. It is by no merit or effort of one's own that this insight is achieved, and when it comes, it is incommunicable to any other. Nevertheless it is certain. Those who have it have also a detachment from human vicissitude that they could not gain from the profoundest of human philosophies and of course a peace that "the world" cannot give.

Among American writers sympathetic with this theology, the most impressive was Reinhold Niebuhr, one of the few American thinkers who have been invited to the distinguished Gifford lectureship in Scotland. In the lectures he delivered in Edinburgh in 1939, published in two volumes as *The Nature and Destiny of Man* (1941–1943), he softened somewhat the sharpness of Barth's antithesis between the natural and the supernatural. Man himself is supernatural, in the sense that he has in him a power of looking before and after, and a power of judging his own thought and conduct, which cannot be derived from the natural order. History is the record of the conflict between his two natures. If history is tragic, it is because of human sin; and the root of human sin is pride, the refusal of the "creature" to judge of his creatureliness by the divine standard within him and the setting up instead of some "idol" of the natural man—some philosophy supposed to be final, or some pitiful social scheme with which Utopia is to be ushered in. Both idealism and naturalism are rejected by Niebuhr as thus idolatrous.

Fortunately Niebuhr's preoccupation with sin and his melancholy view of human achievement did not prevent his taking a vigorous part in social advance. He described his own history as a movement to the right in theology and to the left in politics, and he was an inexhaustible fountainhead of politically liberal books and articles. It says much for their content that these were widely read, for while he was a powerful speaker, his writing is graceless and heavily Teutonic. The same judgment would apply to the writing of many others of this school. There are those who think this fact symptomatic. If one holds that reason at its best is a murky rushlight, one has less motive for nursing it along into greater clearness than if one takes it, with all its feebleness and flickering, as the best illumination we can hope to have.

Between the humanists on the one hand and the neosupernaturalists on the other stood the bulk of liberal Protestants, divided after their manner into innumerable sects and schools. Among these schools a distinctively American one was personalism, whose speculative leader was Edgar Sheffield Brightman of Boston. Brightman's idealism held that the world is a society of persons of all degrees of development, with God, the divine person, presiding over all. His *Philosophy of Religion* (1940) made a bold and significant attack on the problem of evil by contending that God must be thought of as finite and limited in power rather than omnipotent, and as struggling against a nonrational factor in his own nature, somewhat akin to sensation in man.

Another school which is well-nigh perennial and whose thought cuts across all sects is that of mysticism. Its American leader in the first half of the century was Rufus Jones, the most considerable thinker that American Quakerism has produced. In his *Studies in Mystical Religion* (1909), *New Studies in Mystical Religion* (1927), *Some Exponents of Mystical Religion* (1930), and many other works, he developed a religious philosophy which was essentially that of Emerson. Human minds are fragments of an Oversoul, and so far as they succeed in embodying the great values—truth, beauty, goodness—it may be said of them literally that the divine mind is finding expression through them. Rufus Jones' service to his public lay not so much, however, in speculative acuteness or originality as in his advocacy of a practical mysticism, simple and somewhat homespun, yet elevated and serene, of which Americans of other days had caught attractive glimpses in Woolman and Whittier.

If Rufus Jones is to be described as a moralist rather than a dialectician, the same could be said with more obvious truth of another spokesman of liberalism, Harry Emerson Fosdick. In the great church built for him on Riverside Drive, New York, Fosdick remained during the twenties and thirties the most eloquent voice in the American pulpit. Misty and fluid in his theology, like so many other liberal Protestants who were the victims of their own groping honesty, he was inclined to elide the deeper difficulties in his sermons in order to deal more directly with the personal problems of his hearers; but he did this with such moral discernment and rhetorical skill, not only in the pulpit and on the radio where his audiences were enormous, but also in his many books, as to give him membership in that distinguished succession of American preachers which descends through Horace Bushnell, Henry Ward Beecher, and Phillips Brooks.

7

Thus in education, law, history, and religion, much the same "acids of modernity" were eating at the foundations of traditional American idealism. It will be recalled that both the naturalism of Santayana and the pragmatism of Dewey were reactions against the philosophy that held the stage at the turn of the century. Among the American thinkers who led the revolt against nineteenth century idealism, none have ranked with Santayana in literary stature or with Dewey in originality. But if success is measured by effectiveness in undermining an enemy, the most successful recent philosophers have been neither materialists nor pragmatists, but realists. There have been two schools of these, each of which has stated its case in a collaborative volume. *The New Realism* (1912) represents the extreme point in the anti-idealist movement. The idealists had held that the shapes and sizes, colors and sounds, of ordinary experience are all mental, in the sense that if there were no perceiver, they would not exist. The new realists sought to maintain the exact opposite, that they were all nonmental. What the mind contributed was only the act of attention, the beam of the flashlight that lit up the figures on nature's tapestry; the qualities and relations attended to were out there waiting to be perceived. This sounds at first like the merest common sense. But it soon appeared that if taken seriously, the view involved some very odd consequences. If what I see is always nonmental, then when I see converging tracks and spoons bent in water, these too are nonmental; the illusions of hypnotism and the snakes of the delirious toper are really out there, as truly as the Great Pyramid. And then the common sense of a moment ago begins to seem almost insane.

For the new realists such considerations proved in the end disastrous; they were the rock on which the school disintegrated. The six authors of the volume, unable to agree on how the problem of error was to be met, went their several ways. One of them, Walter B. Pitkin, abandoned technical philosophy altogether, devoting himself to fiction and to the popular applications of philosophy and science; his *Life Begins at Forty* (1932) achieved an extraordinary popular success. Another, William Pepperell Montague, remained in his Columbia classroom and produced much less, but the essays and volumes he did produce, notably *The Ways of Knowing* (1925), are models of lucid exposition. The member of the original six who reached the widest scholarly audience was Ralph Barton Perry. His *General Theory of Value* (1926) is the most ambitious work in its field that has yet appeared in this country; his vigorous defenses of democracy during both world wars made him a very useful public servant; and his massive *The Thought and Character of William James* (1935), partly by reason of its subject, but partly also because of the depth and sympathy of its interpretation, may be put down roundly as one of the best biographies in the language.

The other realist manifesto, *Essays in Critical Realism* (1920), attempted to introduce saving qualifications into the doctrine that the earlier volume had sought, with no great success, to render credible. In the enthusiasm of its first reaction against idealism, the earlier group had been led to maintain that the objects of delusion and dream were as independent of perception as tables and chairs. The second group reversed the argument. They said that tables and chairs, as directly perceived, were of precisely the same stuff as dreams; in ordinary life we take their shapes and sizes to belong to things out there, and sometimes they almost certainly do, or at least qualities like them do. But of this we can never be wholly sure; in the end we must fall back on "animal faith." This latter doctrine and phrase were contributed by Santayana, whose name turns up among the seven authors. Of the remaining six, the most notable was Arthur O. Lovejoy. Lovejoy was little known to the larger public, but his chief book, *The Revolt Against Dualism* (1930), is one of the most competent pieces of technical philosophizing yet produced by an American, and is also noteworthy for its style which, though intricate and subtle, is also remarkably clear; and his later work *The Great Chain of Being* (1936) is a classic study of the evolution of a concept. Lovejoy here provided a new technique for literary history by wedding philosophy to historical method.

8

It would be a mistake to infer that by all this belaboring the idealists were pommeled into silence or acquiescence. Few of them found plausible the naturalism of Santayana, with its tendency to belittle the part of mind in the conduct of life; most of them dismissed pragmatism as a somewhat freakish passing fashion; and as for realism, the more thoughtful of them had long been realists anyhow, if that meant believing in an outer world. What they insisted on, as against the naturalists, was that this outer frame of things was spiritual, and against the pragmatists, that it was the business of reason to trace its structure, and not merely to serve as a biological tool.

The most effective spokesman of this impenitent idealism was William Ernest Hocking, who inherited Royce's mantle at Harvard. Hocking was a Middle Westerner of great physical and mental vitality, who, after serving a youthful apprenticeship in railway engineering, made a pilgrimage to New England, fell under the spell of Royce and Palmer in Cambridge and later of Husserl in Germany, abandoned the Spencerian naturalism which was his first love, and moved on, as it seemed inevitably, to distinguished chairs at Yale and Harvard, and to the Hibbert and Gifford lectureships abroad. Hocking has suffered somewhat in concentration from the great range of his interests, which extend from logic and psychology to ethics, politics, and world religion, on all of which he wrote illuminatingly.

The central movement of his thought, however, is metaphysical. The business of reflection, he holds, is to understand its world. Now understanding proceeds through the linking of meanings. In mathematics, for example, it consists in seeing how one meaning, a triangle perhaps, implies another meaning, say the equality of its angles to a straight line. And meanings are ideal. The mathematician's triangle and line are not things that can be sensed, like red patches, nor are they material things in space. So of all the meanings with which the reasoner deals. Still, though they are ideal, they are not ideas merely: they do not live in our heads or minds alone; the mathematician discovers his relations, he does not invent them. What is more, the man who is trying to understand always assumes these relations to be intelligible, for unless they are, understanding would be out of the question. It is the first principle of Hocking's philosophy that for serious thinkers the world must be taken as a systematic whole of meaning, set to their understanding to construe. This is what he means by idealism.

So far there is nothing new; this is the view of all the great idealists from Plato down. Perhaps Hocking's most original addition was one made in his first major work, *The Meaning of God in Human Experience* (1912), in which he showed the importance of this outlook for the religious life. Religious experience is very largely feeling. Now feeling is "idea in process of being born." Our first intimation that an argument is unsound is normally a feeling of distrust; if analysis comes at all, it comes later; and where we are dealing not with abstractions but with concrete things and above all with persons, our analytic reason may never succeed in overtaking this advance guard of feeling. Nowhere does it fall so far behind as in religion. For religion, particularly in its purest form as mysticism, is an attempt to adjust oneself, not to this or that part of one's surroundings, but to the whole. The philosopher too is seeking such adjustment. But the mystic is the scout and pioneer of the philosophic enterprise; he does not know as the philosopher knows; he has not attained the end of the road; but his feeling is an "anticipated attainment" which the philosopher must take seriously. Indeed we should all take it seriously. It is one of Hocking's favorite doctrines that life, to achieve its best, must proceed by rhythm or alternation between vision and detail, life on the plains being rendered more meaningful by occasional withdrawals into the hills, and worship being saved from emptiness by embodiment in action.

Hocking's idealism was thus at a far remove from the frigid intellectualism of some of his predecessors. He remained close to fact; he was aware at every turn of the practical bearing of theory. It is significant that he was chosen by the American churches to head a commission of inquiry into their foreign missions, and that, with his colleagues, he wrote an admirably sane and large-spirited report, holding that in religious matters the process of enlightenment must proceed from east to west as well as from west to east. It is significant too that he was chosen as the leading member of a group of writers commissioned by the Armed Forces Institute to write a textbook on philosophy intelligible to men in camp and on shipboard (*Preface to Philosophy,* 1945). His style is singularly free from technicality and pedantry. Though a little discursive and lacking in emphasis, it is simple, clear, and flowing, with a command over example and analogy that could be exhibited only by a fertile mind.

Hocking did not, like Dewey, have a recognized school of disciples. This was due in part to the accidents of the time. Idealism, by 1910, had ceased to be a new thing, and idealists, however important the fresh insights they achieved, had to be content with a somewhat perfunctory attention, once the class label was attached to them. The great new event in the intellectual realm after the First World War was the recharting of physics, and therefore in a sense of all natural science, through the work of such frontiersmen as Einstein and Planck. This was an event which few idealists, nourished as they were on the humanities rather than on the sciences, were prepared to understand. And the younger philosophers wanted to understand it; they were impatient with thinkers who failed to take account of it, and they turned eagerly to those who were at home in the new science and competent to interpret it.

Preeminent among these were two visiting Cambridge mathematicians, Bertrand Russell and Alfred North Whitehead. Russell's visits to this country, though numerous, were temporary. Whitehead came to stay. Though his transplantation occurred at an age when most men would begin to think of retirement, he took so happily to the new environment, did so much of his important writing in America, and from his chair at Harvard achieved so large an influence on American thought that any review of the literature of ideas in this country must take account of it.

Whitehead came into philosophy from a profound study of mathematics and physics. His thought begins by eliminating one of the chief units with which previous philosophers had worked, and substituting another more in accord with the new science. He replaces substances by events. Einstein had shown that we cannot state precisely the place of anything without a reference to time; this holds equally of a stroke of lightning and of the Sphinx; both really are events, one short, the other relatively long. All things are in truth events; the universe is made of them. At present the most nearly elementary events with which we can work are the protons and electrons of physics.

The problem of the philosopher is not, therefore, to discover the stuff or substance of which things are made, but to find the laws or patterns in accordance with which events influence each other. Here Whitehead had some arresting things to say. Most physicists are mechanists in the sense that when they are explaining why iron filings leap to a magnet or why the earth goes round the sun, they would deny that purpose had anything to do with the matter. With this Whitehead disagreed. Every event, he held, is an activity which is essentially an urge, an appetition, an endeavor after greater fullness of being. And such an appetition is not a dead mechanical affair. It is a process best conceived in terms of sentience or experience. Thus in the foundations of his system there was a startling reversion to something very like idealism.

The resemblance is continued in his curious theory of "prehensions." Every event, he pointed out, is more influenced by some events in its environment than by others; the filings will leap to the magnet, for example, but not to a stick of wood. This is not totally blind; an elective affinity is involved; in the singling out of the magnet as a means by which their own activity may be furthered, the filings are showing something obscurely akin to man's selection of food and drink as a means of supporting life. Whenever one event acts upon or is influenced by another, it is "prehending" it.

And to prehend it is in the last resort to feel it. Let us now suppose that an event, or a group of events, such as an iron filing, displays a stable pattern of reactions to selected other events; we call such a patterned group of activities a "thing." Things are thus settled ways in which one set of events feels other sets of events.

It follows that to understand anything in isolation is a contradiction in terms. To understand what a cell in the nervous system is we must see how it interacts with other cells in that system. But of course that system itself must be understood in the same way; it, too, is a unit which is what it is because it maintains a fixed pattern of interactions with the organism as a whole, of which it is an integral part. And how understand the organism? By the same process again. The organism as a whole must be understood through its own design of interactions with a still larger environment.

Where is this to end? Are we to infer that according to Whitehead every cell in the body, every drop of water in the sea, is a pattern within a larger pattern, and that none of these can be fully made out except by discussing its place in the all-comprehensive structure of the universe? That seems to be what he meant by calling his world view "the philosophy of organism." If everything in the universe is seeking to maintain and perfect its own little structure, it is also maintaining, conjointly with everything else, an all-inclusive cosmic structure; and this structure it is the business of philosophy to disclose. Whitehead believed that the time had come for philosophers to leave the minutiae of analysis and take to speculation again in the grand style. And he was convinced that if they were to do so in earnest, the pattern that would gradually disclose itself would prove to be a rational pattern. He was moved by "the trust that the ultimate natures of things lie together in a harmony which excludes mere arbitrariness." The universal pressure toward rationality within the world of events is what Whitehead meant by God; God is "the poet of the world, with tender patience leading it by his vision of truth, beauty and goodness."

A man who thinks and writes in this vein is obviously not afraid to let himself go; if Whitehead was an acute mathematician, it is clear that he was also on occasion the dreamer of dreams. His writing is lighted up with epigrammatic flashes of insight. Unfortunately that writing is extremely uneven. Reading him is like listening to Coleridge's conversation as reported by Carlyle; one endures stretches of dreary obscurity for the sake of coming, as one ultimately and abruptly does, on "glorious islets of the blest and the intelligible." Among the chief sources of difficulty are his habits of coining words of his own: "prehension," "concrescence," "ingression," "concretion," not always clearly defined or even used in a single sense, and of giving familiar words and phrases—"object," "potentiality," "feeling"—new and strange significations. Unhappily these difficulties are at their worst in his major work, *Process and Reality* (1929); they are felt less in such semi-popular books as *Science and the Modern World* (1925), *Religion in the Making* (1926), and *The Aims of Education* (1929). Whitehead had probably a more profound mind than that of Russell, with whom he collaborated to produce one of the most impressive achievements of modern thought, *Principia Mathematica* (1910–1913). He was unfortunately far below Russell in that gift which is so peculiarly grateful in a philosopher, lucidity.

There is a sense in which the interval between these two remarkable co-workers is the interval between the beginning and end of the period under our review. Russell, like the naturalists, pragmatists, and realists who began the revolt against idealism, was suspicious of high flights of speculation, and inclined to think that all advance in thought must be by the scientific analysis of particular problems. Perhaps it was because Whitehead had given unquestionable proof of his prowess in such analysis that he commanded so much respect when he broke loose from it and began to paint again with the wide brushes and the full sweep of the great speculative periods. Dewey rose from reading *Process and Reality* with "the feeling that somehow the seventeenth century has got the better of the twentieth." Indeed the wheel of thought had come almost full circle in his own lifetime, moving from the whole-hearted metaphysics of idealism that was dominant in his youth to another metaphysics, equally wholehearted but more firmly grounded in science. Whether Dewey's own philosophy, which was so central to the period we have been studying, will appear to later historians of this highly irregular century as a peak between two valleys or a valley between two peaks it is perhaps safest to allow the future to decide.

77. A CYCLE OF FICTION

THESE currents of speculative thought found expression, of course, in the fiction, the drama, and the poetry of the years since 1925; but only when the despair of a "lost generation" is probed to its sources can they be recognized as providing the rationale of a literary era. It is not always easy to relate the specific work of art to its underlying inspiration—especially in so close a view. Artists are rarely philosophers or critics in the strict sense. But so much is evident: the literary work of these decades, taken as a whole, shows a more persistent search for values and a more competent control of forms than did that of the preceding decades.

If the weakness as well as the charm of the generation of the twenties lay in its indifference to its own past (for it was just then cutting its ties with the Progressive Movement in politics that had nourished it), there was at any rate a solid basis for its claims. Those were good years for American fiction. Chicago had been the center of the earlier days of the movement, and Dreiser and Sandburg and Sherwood Anderson, among others, had helped to establish its earlier tone—that initial revolt of the solid Midwest against both the pulpit and the stockyards. But now, as the literary current flowed east to New York and the "Little Renaissance" matured, its members seemed to represent every nook and corner of the country, from the Harvard of Dos Passos to the Michigan woods of Hemingway and the California coast of Robinson Jeffers. The South, too, was about to produce a whole host of Fugitives and Agrarians. Among the novelists and short-story writers Kay Boyle, like F. Scott Fitzgerald, came from Minnesota, Evelyn Scott and T. S. Stribling from Tennessee, Glenway Wescott from Wisconsin, Dorothy Parker from New Jersey, Joseph Hergesheimer from Pennsylvania, and James Branch Cabell of course—not to mention Ellen Glasgow or Pearl Buck—from Virginia.

Furthermore, the regional spread of this talent was matched by the variety of technical innovations it was using to commemorate the "Life of Realization." The ingenious new poets were not the only writers then continuously experimenting with the structure, the diction, the rhythms and the visual effects of their medium; for sheer technical virtuosity Elinor Wylie was to be matched in prose by Katherine Anne Porter, and T. S. Eliot by William Faulkner. This was the age of the craftsmen, and the complex interior monologue, for example, with its shifting elements of time and place and its purely personal framework of association, became a staple of the new novels. Between subjectivity and relativity all was flux for a while, and soon a novel which had a plot and related events in something like the normal order that events often take in life, a novel in which space was not time and time was not psychological, was almost a discovery in itself.

The sources of the new technique appeared to be chiefly European, and, among the Europeans, as Edmund Wilson suggested in *Axel's Castle* (1931), they were particularly the French symbolists and their heirs—although Proust and Yeats and Joyce led back in turn to Freud and Einstein. It was Gertrude Stein who was a chief intermediary for the Paris branch of the Lost Generation; yet it is interesting to notice that the cadences of Miss Stein's writing, mannered and self-conscious as they were and eventually pointing toward a sort of literary cubism or post-impressionism, had curious echoes of Midwestern talk. In Chicago, the urban center of the New American industrialism, Sherwood Anderson devoted his middle years to recalling the slow recurrent rhythms of the Ohio towns at the turn of the century—a language that was also at the base of Hemingway's. Those later "plain," "flat" tones, so laconic and ambiguous, brought to perfection a native style that had evolved from Thoreau to Twain. Like Ring Lardner, Anderson was aware of all the delicate grammatical intricacies and tonal gradations of the American language in its current forms, so thoroughly recorded by H. L. Mencken. These authors were joined in their determination to break the short story of fabricated action and a trick end. In such writers the most advanced European technical experimentation met a rich source of native material. As no other group of contemporary writers seemed more anxious to perfect their craft, so no other group had so much opportunity to do it.

It was the twenties, too, that had broken down the distinctions between schools of writing by producing outstanding individuals. Everybody was famous then, as Zelda Fitzgerald declared in *Save Me the Waltz,* and people were not concerned about the proletariat in a world where it was always teatime or "three o'clock in the morning"; while it was almost comic, again, to find H. L. Mencken, hot from denouncing the barren spirit of America, now complaining about the schools of fiction writing that were swarming in the land, and the hundred thousand secondhand Coronas that were rattling and jingling in ten thousand remote and lonely hamlets. By the time of *Prejudices: Fourth Series,* in 1924, even Mencken had to concede that the native literary spectacle had taken on an exhilarating aspect—that, in short, leadership in the arts "may eventually transfer itself from the eastern shore of the Atlantic to the western shore," since

no longer imitative and timorous, as most of their predecessors were, these youngsters are attempting a first-hand examination of the national scene, and making an effort to represent it in terms that are wholly American. They are the pioneers of a literature that, whatever its defects in the abstract, will at least be a faithful reflection of the national life. . . . In England the novel subsides into formulae, the drama is submerged in artificialities, and even poetry, despite occasional revolts, moves toward scholarliness and emptiness. But in America, since the war, all three show the artless and superabundant energy of little children. They lack, only too often, manner and urbanity; it is no wonder they are often shocking to pedants. But there is the breath of life in them, and that life is nearer its beginning than its end.

2

As early as 1924, F. Scott Fitzgerald had already given evidence that there was another aspect to all this glittering native pageantry. His *This Side of Paradise* was the generation's masculine primer, just as Edna Millay's *A Few Figs from Thistles* was the feminine, and as Ernest Hemingway's *The Sun Also Rises* was a second reader for both sexes. Irregular in exposition, broken in context, Fitzgerald's first novel set forth the apparently authentic observations of a typical young person of the period. "A chield's amang you taking notes"—and he printed them also.

Born in 1896, in St. Paul, Minnesota, Fitzgerald had gone to Princeton, "largely because of the Triangle Club," and had started work on *This Side of Paradise* (1920) during the week ends of his service with the armed forces in 1917. With the success of his first novel his "days of struggle were over," or at any rate the festive days had arrived. These were Fitzgerald's party days; the parties of *The Great Gatsby*; the big parties, as Edmund Wilson remarked, at which Fitzgerald's people "go off like fireworks and which are likely to leave them in pieces." This was the New York of the early twenties, of orchids and plush, which had "all the iridescence of the beginning of the world" with its young and disillusioned children who watched twilight fall, over cocktails at the Biltmore, and dawn strike the window of Childs' restaurant in Fifty-ninth Street. No other places were possible, for no other voices could whisper to the young Fitzgerald—and it was his gift to endow these rather unreal creatures with a peculiarly touching reality.

One took for granted the restlessness of these hotel children, their conviction that all Gods were dead, "all wars fought, all faiths in man shaken," their distaste for "the crude, vulgar air of Western civilization," their contempt for the "aliens" and the "masses" who contributed to "the heavy scent of latest America." And yet, triumphant as they were in their almost insatiable demands for wealth and glamour, the "visions of horror" also pursued these glittering narcissists of the Jazz Age. The sense of dark dissolution and of death "diffusively brooding" over *This Side of Paradise* and *The Beautiful and Damned* (1922)—over this whole lucent postwar panorama from absinthe to yachts—is at the center of Fitzgerald's work. Two of the four novels after *This Side of Paradise* attempt to deal with it, while it seems to form the hidden basis of the other two—and it splits his career in half. The corrosive vein in Fitzgerald's writing, the cry of suffering, the reverberations of the crack-up—these destructive accents become all too familiar and find their ultimate expression in those rich ruins and in those fugitives from justice who form the central group of *Tender Is the Night* (1934).

The true nature of that "misty tragedy played far behind the veil" which preoccupies the young Fitzgerald's mind remains obscure, although it was unquestionably sexual in origin. Fitzgerald's work, like Poe's, is colored by the imagery of incest. *Tender Is the Night,* psychologically perhaps the most interesting of all Fitzgerald's novels, deals directly with this theme, but, as the later Fitzgerald said about his friend Ring Lardner, "he had agreed with himself to speak only a small portion of his mind." What is certain, at any rate, is that he could never quite come to grips with the central inner conflict of his writing, and he moved to his outward and cultural studies of the American financial aristocracy at the cost of suppressing rather than resolving this problem.

It was not a complete defeat. Just as Fitzgerald had had "the conviction of the inevitability of failure" from the start, so at the end he had the insight of failure. During his entire later career, he devoted himself to his craft with something of the fanatical devotion of an anchorite expecting the collapse of the world, and here he reached a fulfillment that was not altogether granted to him elsewhere. And if *The Great Gatsby* fades a little with its last falling cadence, what an eloquent cadence it is! This is a deft and delicate tale, from the opening passages on the Buchanans' Long Island Georgian mansion, framed by its half-acre of deep, pungent roses, to the trip through the valley of ashes and the final passage on Gatsby's dream which had always been behind him—"somewhere back in that vast obscurity beyond the city, where the dark fields of the republic rolled on under the night." In the story of Jay Gatsby's illusion Fitzgerald caught the story of an age's illusion too, just as "The Diamond As Big As the Ritz" was a notable parable of our American ruling class, as "May Day" had all the faintly bitter fragrance of the age of wealth, and as *The Last Tycoon,* unfinished as it is, was still the closest an American novelist had come to the truth about Hollywood.

3

At various times Fitzgerald and Hemingway were in Paris together, when Fitzgerald had already achieved his early success, and even a certain notoriety. Gertrude Stein was said to have said that he had more talent than all the rest of the Lost Generation put together, while the younger man was still writing those early "sketches." Meanwhile, with "rather the aspect of an Eton-Oxford husky-ish young captain of a midland regiment of His Britannic Majesty," Hemingway pranced, as Ford Madox Ford tells us, among the young Americans from the limitless prairies who "leapt, released, on Paris."

Just as Fitzgerald had commented briefly on St. Paul, and as T. S. Eliot had passed lightly over St. Louis, Hemingway, a doctor's son born in Oak Park, Illinois, in 1898, had very early announced his verdict on commerce in the United States: "Let Hartman Feather *Your* Nest." He chose instead the Indians and the Michigan Woods—the idyllic scenes of youth in his first book, *In Our Time* (1925), that are contrasted so sharply with scenes from the First World War. He had been a reporter for the Kansas City *Star,* he had served with the Italian Arditi and had been wounded—and here his early experiences seemed to fuse: the flat yet equivocal Western tones, as well as the "innocence" of the provincial, were linked to that mode of "reporting" which, heightened by some altogether personal process of artistry, was to alter the rhythms of our contemporary prose. Perhaps, too, no other contemporary writer brought his readers so many vivid and almost unbearable impressions of the human temperament under the pressures of war. In a sense the war was made for him, and in a variety of stories—"In Another Country," "A Way You'll Never Be," "A Simple Enquiry," as well as in *A Farewell to Arms*—made the war his own.

In *The Sun Also Rises* (1926) the quality of this plain, factual recording of things became a little clearer. For it was only in a novel that a Lost Generation could feel its plight with such intensity and live out its fate with such meticulous perfection. Many tried but few could approach the disenchantment of Hemingway's little group of pleasure lovers, or seem quite so cunningly and even diabolically frustrated. He began to seem like a little more than another modern "realist," and, in the bulk of his work done between 1927 and 1937, the terms of Hemingway's "separate peace" were written out. For, while Scott Fitzgerald had largely allowed his own Western countryside to slip by, and had then walked a sort of intellectual tightrope between the élite and the masses, Hemingway had actually renounced his own society, as he stated in *The Green Hills of Africa* (1935), and he was through serving time "for society, democracy and the other things." America had been a good country, but "we had made a bloody mess of it and I would go, now, somewhere else as we had always had the right to go somewhere else and as we had always gone. You could always come back."

Such was the framework for the decade of dark stories collected in *Men Without Women* (1927) and *Winner Take Nothing* (1933). Some of them were notable, as were also certain sections of his rhapsody on the Spanish bull ring, *Death in the Afternoon* (1932), however much one might feel that there was something amiss in this safari of annihilation. For it was a curious world that Hemingway had taken to exploring: the world of the matador and the kudu in which the central trinity was the hunter, the hunted, and death; a world of deep and always fatally irrational feelings, in which the intellect pointed only to the method of destruction, and which was marked only by an increasing sense of dissolution, until all forms of action as well as all modes of thinking became merely another sort of opiate; a nihilistic spiritual world that reached its own perfection in such of his "first forty-nine" stories as "The Gambler, the Nun, and the Radio" ("Bread was the opium of the people") and "A Clean Well-Lighted Place." "What did he fear? It was not fear or dread. It was a nothing that he knew too well. *It was all a nothing and a man was a nothing too.*" Moreover, through the cheapened and coarsened texture of *To Have and Have Not,* in 1937, this all-consuming nihilism seemed to strike at last at the source of its own projection. Here, if only temporarily, Hemingway relinquished what had been his special gift among the American moderns: the gift of compassion which had modulated and given a kind of final harmony to the continuous play of the wounded psyche.

This was a step removed from the blind optimism of an earlier age of innocence; at times indeed it touched on a blind negation almost without parallel in the national letters, unless one finds it in Stephen Crane. But it is interesting to compare the increasing bitterness of Ring Lardner's work over the same period, the loss of that "abundant good humor" commented on in a previous chapter, and the almost continual omens and portents of disaster that also mark H. L. Mencken's work. Before passing a final judgment on Hemingway's "animalism" and "cynicism" it is well to remember that, if his researches into the darker instincts are limited intellectually, they are emotionally and aesthetically rewarding, and that the whole body of his work deals with a subject inadequately represented or almost misrepresented in our tradition, even in Melville and Hawthorne and Poe. In fact the best of these novels and stories—and the later stories like "The Snows of Kilimanjaro" and "The Short Happy Life of Francis Macomber" are among the best— are already part of the country's permanent literary heritage; whatever we may say about their shortcomings will not much affect their status. As Hemingway receded ever deeper into this interior sphere of the irrational death urges, he seemed to be drawing ever closer to the "real" world between two wars. For his portraits of a primitive and animal dignity in the face of suffering anticipated the dominant emotional pattern of this world, and described the last human heritage of thousands of similarly isolated and despairing individuals in the face of all the refinements of civilized viciousness.

4

Though *To Have and Have Not* was set in the Florida resort towns of the depression years, there was to be a still later development in the cycle of Hemingway's withdrawal and return. Meanwhile we are concerned with a very different sort of writer. If Hemingway dealt with the buried depths and the recessive impulses, John Dos Passos was the embodiment of the rational artist in our tradition—the conscious, moral, and progressive critic of our communal habits; and it is curious that both of these Americans should have started at a similar psychological and even geographical point. In the early Dos Passos, just as in the later Hemingway, there is the same central evocation of a detached and remote observer drifting on the tides of social renunciation. A grandson of a Portuguese immigrant, the young Dos Passos also found in republican Spain an apparent antidote to commerce under Harding and Coolidge: the Spain of Hemingway's fiestas and anarchists and ice-cold *horchata*. It was from a Spanish revolutionary writer, too, Pío Baroja, that Dos Passos gained his early intellectual concepts.

While Hemingway's *Death in the Afternoon,* in 1932, was still fixed on the matador, Dos Passos' *Rosinante to the Road Again,* as early as 1922, was already discussing the masses. And it was in Chicago, where Dos Passos was born in 1896, that his central trilogy, *U.S.A.,* would open: in the city which was the heart, or at any rate the nervous cortex, of the new American industrialism whose urban and strident rhythms also dominate Dos Passos' first major novel. In *Manhattan Transfer* (1925), too, we notice the early forms of those technical devices that would distinguish the later trilogy: the use of popular songs, of newspaper headlines, of the speech of the people as against the speech of the scholars, and of the actual figures from Woodrow Wilson to King C. Gillette—all these sociological indices which are fused into the panoramic view of our city culture, and, in *U.S.A.* itself, our national culture.

For the real "hero" of the trilogy—*The 42nd Parallel* (1930), *1919* (1932), and *The Big Money* (1936)—is of course the United States. Thus Dos Passos invented a series of technical devices in an attempt to widen the bounds of the novel: the "Newsreels," which form a running account of the actual events, as well as the crimes, fads, and follies of our society; the "Biographies" which form the record of our special personalities from Debs, "lover of mankind," who opens the trilogy, to Insull, manipulator of "power superpower," who closes it some fifteen hundred pages later; the "Novels" which form, by contrast, the record of the ordinary citizens in the great trading Republic of the West; and "The Camera Eye" which forms, as it were, the personal diary of the novelist as he writes the novel, the record of his shifting emotions in the face of this national scene which he is recording so brilliantly. These devices not only catch the more intricate patterns of industrialized society but also include all the real elements of the pattern by a stretching of every artistic resource to record "Nature." And while the aim was almost impossible the attempt was to a large degree successful.

Before Dos Passos, a score of American writers—including Norris, Fuller, Herrick, and Dreiser—had dealt with separate manifestations of the new industrialism, or in a series of novels had attempted to relate these manifestations. Of course the French from Balzac on were in a sense even closer to Dos Passos' aims, while Jules Romains suggested, in a later note, that the panoramic novel was *his* patent. But no one else had attempted to bring everything together at one moment and to set all the complexities of that "moment"—extending from the Promise of the American Century in 1900 to the Crash of 1929—within so sharp a focus; and perhaps none of them had understood so clearly the nuances of their own historical scene.

For Dos Passos was among the best informed and the most learned of the moderns—and this set him apart in a tradition that had been marked at once by its freedom from and ignorance of "ideas." And yet, though the exposition in *U.S.A.* was brilliant and its picture of American life was full and varied, the novelist's conclusion was simple, and not encouraging. Filled as the three volumes were with achievements of urban power in the land of power, the "Newsreels" became ever more sensational and chaotic, while the "Biographies" of our national heroes formed only the record of their disinheritance, the "Novels" recounted only the disintegration of these average lives, from the obscure merchant seaman Joe Williams to the publicity wizard J. Ward Moorehouse; and the reflections of the author in "The Camera Eye" became in turn increasingly desolate. Thus the immense national energy which had built up such a remarkable society within so short a period had apparently become centrifugal: the elaborate system was shaking itself apart. In fact, just as each novel of the trilogy was better than its predecessor, each was more despairing, and *The Big Money,* resembling in some respects Hemingway's *To Have and Have Not,* is a sort of apotheosis of stale horrors.

In one sense the basic view of life in *U.S.A.* defeats itself, for, if Dos Passos' people are really what he seems to think they are, there would be little value in the social revolution which is his central hope of redemption. A revolution implies the release of human traits which the older social order has been inhibiting. But what is there, in these grasping and empty American personages, left to release? The total picture is one of inherent human weakness rather than of chained power, of barely restrained human vicious-ness rather than of an inhibited human grandeur. Indeed *The Big Money* records the twilight of Dos Passos' radical hopes too, and here the revolu-tionary heroes who should perhaps reveal the promise of life most fully, show it least, while whatever vision of Paradise Lost lay behind the trilogy has turned into a sort of second-rate inferno. His two later novels, also possessing related episodes (*The Adventures of a Young Man,* 1939, and *Number One,* 1943) do not recover any of the vision.

5

As the literary paths of Dos Passos and Hemingway had separated in the early twenties, only to meet again in a common view of the time, another major figure was to carry this view forward in a rather special sense but in an even more extravagant form.

Born in 1897, a year later than Dos Passos and Fitzgerald and a year earlier than Hemingway, the young William Faulkner shared in the common experi-ence of his generation: he joined the Canadian Flying Corps and served with the R.A.F. in France. In him, too, the variety of its origins helped to explain the variety of the American genius. Faulkner was heir to a family of Southern governors, statesmen, and other public figures; early in his childhood he went to live in Oxford, Mississippi, and it was his home almost uninterruptedly thereafter. Perhaps these facts tell us more than those on Faulkner's European experience: this Southern home that is uninterrupted except by visions of ghouls, and these ancestral halls in which echo only the sobs of the possessed and the demented. Faulkner built his work on an even grander scale than Dos Passos. He related even his minor personages with one another, he elaborated their genealogy from generation to generation, he gave them a countryside: a deep land of Baptists, of brothels, of attic secrets, of swamps and shadows. "Jefferson," Mississippi, is the capital of this world which reaches backward in time to the origins of Southern culture and forward to the horrid prophecies of its extinction, and which ranges down in social strata from dying landed aristocracy, the Sartoris and Compson families, to the new commercial oligarchy of the Snopeses; down to the poor-white Bundrens of *As I Lay Dying,* to the pervert Popeye of *Sanctuary,* and to the Negro Christ-mas of *Light in August,* turned brute again by the society which had raised him from the animal.

It is typical of Faulkner's meteoric talent that the three years between 1929 and 1932 contain two of his major works, *The Sound and the Fury* and *Light in August.* Both novels are highly experimental in form. As a matter of fact, all of Faulkner's big novels are marked by a technical experimentation which adds to an already formidable ambiguity of content. *Light in August*

(1932), probably the most easily comprehensible to the average reader, seems to be written as an objective narrative; but it holds tale within tale and its meaning becomes clear only if you follow the story of Lena, the poor-white mountain girl—and a Faulknerian symbol of a rather appalling, blind, lower-class sexual fertility—to the story of Hightower, isolated, sterile, living in his memories of the Old South. Underneath, is the story of the New South: the murder in Jefferson, Mississippi, and the love affair of the northern spinster, Miss Joanna Burden, with the mulatto Christmas. Here finally Faulkner gives expression not only to the most bitter and profound cultural problem of the South, but to its dominant cultural phobia; and the nightmarish quality is matched only, perhaps, by one's sense of its reality in the haunted minds of the central figures.

The Faulknerian dialectic, which became reasonably clear in *Light in August,* had already been suggested in *The Sound and the Fury* (1929). The earlier novel is even more complex in its technique. It is an outstanding example of the interior monologue in our letters; and the skill of its architecture —the style moves from almost complete obscurity to the statement of prosaic fact—is evident in the use of the unifying symbols: the circus tickets, the river, the broken watch, the tolling clock, and, indeed, all the manifestations of dissolving time that pervade the novel. It is very different from *Light in August* in tone. In the Compson children, Faulkner caught the torment of childhood at the moment it reaches maturity—at the moment, that is, of the realization of sin and evil, the moment of the "Fall." Thus the "incestuous" love of Quentin Compson for his sister Caddy, which forms the central theme and provides the most eloquent passages of the novel, and which Faulkner handles with a peculiarly touching naïveté, is incestuous merely because these legitimate feelings of childhood—in a sense, the only true feelings of childhood—are judged from outside, from an adult framework of values. Indeed, filled as the tale is with all the pathetic devices and drives and tensions of infancy, and the intimations of those other lawless and poignant affections which color the better—or the worse—part of our lives, *The Sound and the Fury* is matched by few novels in its evocations of infantile origins. In spite of being specialized in form, rather self-consciously limited in appeal, it was a landmark of the new literature.

But the childhood here revealed is in a sense a double one. The drama of innocence and corruption takes place within a larger framework: there is the conflict, again, of a decaying landed aristocracy with the rising commercial classes. Avaricious and bigoted, the Jason Compson of *The Sound and the Fury* is the protagonist of the new economic order which, in effect, closes the novel. And, by contrast with Jason's "practicality," even the idiot Benjy Compson, whose obscure moaning and slobbering opens the novel, is an intelligible hero.

At least that is what Faulkner seemed to suggest, as he compared the youth of his culture with its misbegotten maturity. In the series of grotesque legends which followed, *As I Lay Dying* (1930), *These 13* (1931), *Sanctuary* (1931), and his later novels and tales, Faulkner dealt with the New South—with this modern stage, on which strut only those modern personages whose milieu is a cold and calculating corruption, whose single instinct is a lust for power, and whose lares and penates are the Faulknerian "Snopeses." It was only in *Absalom, Absalom!* in 1936, that Faulkner seemed to regain something of the tone of *The Sound and the Fury*; but there again he was treating the rise and decay of a landed aristocracy—and there, too, Quentin Compson proclaimed that he did not hate the South. " 'I dont hate it,' he said. *I dont hate it* he thought, panting in the cold air, the iron New England dark; *I dont. I dont! I dont hate it! I dont hate it!"*

With William Faulkner, the cultural pattern of isolation, of revolt, and of denial, the heritage of the American twenties lasting over and fully forming the American novelist of the 1930's reached an extreme. Here the two main elements of the pattern—the solitary and desperate individual of Hemingway's work, the acrid and despairing critique of contemporary society in Dos Passos' work—are given fullest expression, while even the shimmering flappers of Fitzgerald become a type of Faulknerian incubus. Indeed, the "misty tragedy" played far behind the veil becomes rather more explicit, and the sense of latent horror in the earlier evocation of the Jazz Age becomes acute. There is no denying Faulkner's real achievement. In the scope of his scene and the dimensions of his portraiture, in the complexity and subtlety of his emotions, as well as in the vivid and complex prose style, he is perhaps, as Gide remarked, "*the* most important of the stars in this new constellation." Nor is this Mississippi symbolist quite so esoteric as he may seem at first; for his picture of the Mississippi Valley and its people is the work of a realist even when, with the Representative Rankins, the Snopeses go to Washington. Those who praise Faulkner indiscriminately, *Sanctuary* as well as *The Sound and the Fury,* are in a sense unaware of how good Faulkner can be, and to what degree the history of this remarkable talent is also the history of its dissipation. The increasing stress on technical virtuosity, the sacrifice of content for effect, and of effect for shock—these, too, show the destructive element at work.

For this entire literary movement of the American twenties, fresh and promising, varied in talent and bold in achievement, seems to end almost everywhere on a note of negation and of exhaustion. Winesburg, Ohio, gave way to New York, and New York to Paris and Capri, and Capri to the Wasteland. This was the last resort, the true home of these innovators and rebels.

"My nerves are bad to-night. Yes, bad. Stay with me,
"Speak to me. Why do you never speak. Speak.
"What are you thinking of? What thinking? What? . . ."

I think we are in rats' alley
Where the dead men lost their bones.

So spoke the American poet of the twenties, T. S. Eliot, the poet from Sherwood Anderson's Middle West who turned East for his salvation to England, who turned still East. And the dominant note of aridity in Eliot, the evocation of a land without water, of rock and no water, found its echoes in the Gopher Prairie of Sinclair Lewis, the Manhattan Transfer of Dos Passos, the clean well lighted places of Ernest Hemingway, the Long Island suburbs of Fitzgerald, and even in the "George C. Tilyou smile" that floated above the spandangled bananas of Henry Miller's American Steeplechase, as well as in the deep and nightmarish shadows of Faulkner's Mississippi.

So, too, H. L. Mencken's own *Notes on Democracy,* which appeared in the middle twenties, marked what was probably a low ebb of the democratic belief in America. Here also, the first sense of gusto in Mencken's work was followed by a sense of black despair. Was the postwar malaise due primarily to the First World War itself? In a certain sense; but not in the sense that has usually been attributed to it. For what Mencken was tracing here, and what all these writers were describing in one form or another, may be more intimately related to "Faulkner's War"—it is, of course, the effect of the industrial change which began shortly after the Civil War: that age of disillusion foreshadowed in the gloomy Whitman and the dark Twain, whose impact colors the work of such figures of the "Middle Generation" as Dreiser, Cather, Glasgow, and Sinclair Lewis. As for the Lost Generation itself, its typical figure, Scott Fitzgerald, never saw action abroad, and Mencken himself, in some respects the worst war casualty of them all, was not in the Army. One notices, too, the curiously remote quality of the war novels of some of the writers who did see action: from the John Andrews of Dos Passos' *Three Soldiers* (1921), who devours *La Tentation de Saint Antoine* "as if the book were a drug in which he could drink deep forgetfulness of himself," or the still earlier Martin Howe of *One Man's Initiation* (1920), dreaming of his Gothic abbey, to the narrator of E. E. Cummings' *The Enormous Room* (1922), who prefers his prison camp to the outside world.

The First World War, which was after all a lesser war among our wars, and lasted barely two years out of the one hundred fifty of the Republic's history, completed the consolidation of the new industrialism in American life. It marked the triumph of the cartels, and the end of the older forms of agrarian democracy, if not, in fact, of free capitalism itself. Its extraordinary and disproportionate influence on the writing of a whole generation, now indeed lost, must be evaluated as the effect of this underlying cultural process. The war was the immediate cause; but the new economic order was the true cause of their discontent: this new money society which at the moment of its ascendance, seemed to render futile or grotesque the entire progressive movement, from the muckrakers to the trust busters, and from the Populist reforms to the New Freedom. This was the *causa sine qua non* of their despair. Whatever they suffered in a war which they had already felt was not their own, they sensed very early that they had lost the peace. And all the other revolts —against the Victorian gentility, against the Anglo-Saxon taboos, against the bourgeois virtues—were contained in the framework of this revolt.

In the forms of their opposition were they really, as they were later branded, the "Irresponsibles"? Certainly they had the limitations as well as the charms of youth; they had cultural innocence and ignorance. In their narrow range of values, too, and in their uneasy prejudices, in their fevered stress on pleasure and in the extremes of their despair, they often reflected the society they had repudiated: it shortly became clear that the "Aesthetic Man" was as dangerous a fiction as the "Economic Man." They, too, were living on borrowed time, and sometimes they believed it was eternity. But, without the solid affection for home and homeland that had marked the middle generation, in their unremitting devotion to their craft, at least, they carried forward an essential part of the older American life. Far more than some of their critics, they all sensed the real pressures of the period, and often they gave eloquent expression to the historical moment, as in *The Big Money*:

they have clubbed us off the streets   they are stronger   they are rich   they hire and fire the politicians the newspapereditors the old judges the small men with reputations the collegepresidents the wardheelers (listen businessmen collegepresidents judges   America will not forget her betrayers) they hire the men with guns the uniforms the policecars the patrolwagons

all right you have won. . . .

America our nation has been beaten by strangers who have turned our language inside out who have taken the clean words our fathers spoke and made them slimy and foul

their hired men sit on the judge's bench they sit back with their feet on the tables under the dome of the State House they are ignorant of our beliefs they have the dollars the guns the armed forces the powerplants

they have built the electricchair and hired the executioner to throw the switch

all right we are two nations

6

While the meaning of the lost generation became plain in the words of Dos Passos, the phrase itself was given a final twist by a new literary figure, who applied it to "those men of advanced middle age who still speak the language that was spoken before 1929, and who know no other. These men indubitably *are* lost. But I am not one of them." But with Thomas Wolfe, of course, we come to still another "younger generation," those who were raised on internal crisis. The impact of the depression years—"the unending repercussions of these scenes of suffering, violence, oppression, hunger, cold, and filth and poverty going on unheeded in a world in which the rich were still rotten with their wealth"—left a scar upon their lives, but a conviction in their souls. Since Wolfe was a primary figure among these new writers, his career may be used to summarize the entire shift of values that occurred in the thirties.

In Faulkner and Wolfe, too, were represented two poles of the modern South. Born in 1900, in Asheville, North Carolina, and descended from hill people, Wolfe was also caught up in the web of Southern emotionalism so pervasive in Faulkner's work. But while Faulkner seems to work steadily backward, Wolfe's movement is continuously forward; while the older writer explored the dissolving reaches of memory, the younger came to face the dimensions of the future. And while Faulkner marked the final full expression of the aesthetic nihilism that evolved out of the American twenties, Wolfe became perhaps the central spokesman for the artistic beliefs of the 1930's.

In a sense Wolfe's four huge novels, reaching well over a million words, may be considered as a single novel (or perhaps the beginning of a novel, since Wolfe rewrote the childhood episodes of the first volume in a later volume, and this, too, he considered still not a true beginning, but merely "something which led up to the true beginning"). *Look Homeward, Angel* (1929) deals with the early life of the Southern protagonist. *Of Time and the River* (1935) deals with his Northern adventures and first contact with the life of wealth and culture and sensibility: that life "so beautiful and right and good" toward which, as the young Wolfe felt, "all the myriads of the earth aspire"—or at least all the myriads of the American earth. For this was also the vision of a Mark Twain in Boston, and a Henry James in London, of Dreiser in New York, Cather in Nebraska, and Scott Fitzgerald on Long Island: this is the perennial fable in the national letters of the Provincial and the Magic City. And both *The Web and the Rock* (1939) and *You Can't Go Home Again* (1940) deal with the realization of this vision—and its final inadequacy—and with still another and a new beginning.

Moreover, this huge novel, multiformed and sometimes inchoate as it was, with its alterations always in progress, formed a central document of the period. Just as Dos Passos reinvigorated the naturalistic novel by means of the symbolist techniques, so Wolfe regenerated the whole tradition of native realism through the electric charge of curiosity, of lyricism, of anger and protest, and perhaps even of pure excitement which he put into it. In fact, he probably carried sheer energy to its highest pitch in the national letters, and this energy became matter. The emotional force of *Look Homeward, Angel,* for example, was materialized in its panorama of the general Southern scene, and, for all the obvious adolescent excesses and limitations of Wolfe's first novel, in the notable central portraits of the novel: those of Oliver Gant and Eliza Gant. Characters: that was one of Wolfe's plain contributions to the American novel—characters who, for all their idiosyncrasies, were by no means merely "eccentrics." It is interesting, too, that the weakest point of a national tradition based on "individualism" and the democratic character should be its indifference to individuals who are neither tycoons nor criminal cases—its indifference, in short, to character. Furthermore, the central conflict of the Gants, between Eliza's outrageous lust for property and Oliver's insatiable hunger for experience—a conflict that is not lacking in the American mind itself—became the central theme of the tetralogy.

The "Fame" which is sought by the artist-hero in *Of Time and the River* is nothing more than a barely sublimated form of Eliza's materialism. And the remarkable quality of Wolfe's unending evocations, descriptions, and evaluations of New York in *The Web and the Rock* is that he catches at once the fascination of the "Enfabled Rock" for the provincial mind, and the provincial's realization that this is not enough. Perhaps no other American has done so well with the first enchantments and terrors of the city. Both here and in *You Can't Go Home Again* Wolfe went, as Scott Fitzgerald never quite could go, beyond the whole glamorous pageantry of "that distant Babylon, cloud-capped and rosy-hued there in the smoke of his imagination."

There was never much doubt as to just whom Wolfe was talking about in these patently autobiographical novels; but the change of his hero's name from Eugene Gant to George Webber was more than a mere change of name. The mature Wolfe was no longer primarily concerned with one young man, however gifted, but with all young men; and not merely with his own experiences in society but with society's experience; not with the "superior individual" of Mencken and Fitzgerald but with Sherwood Anderson's "the general." So it was necessary to return and reevaluate his hero's youth and education—in fact to create a new youth and education. And in the world of the mountain grills in *The Web and the Rock,* or in the microcosm of Libya Hill during the boom and the bust of *You Can't Go Home Again,*

Wolfe did just that, while in the archetypal portrait of Judge Rumford Bland (one of his most memorable brief portraits) he seemed to present a local cousin of the Eumenides. Just as Wolfe's hero had been forced to renounce Esther Jack, the great lady of his provincial fantasies, since "love was not enough," he could now understand both the stature and the failure of the contemporary American writer, Lloyd McHarg, since "fame was not enough." And in the history of the Federal Weight and Scales Company, or in the portrait of "Mr. Jack at Morn," he displayed a notable increase in his satirical power. As a matter of fact, Wolfe would have been, and to a degree already was, a major social satirist.

Still, was it now claimed that he had lost his lyrical gift, by some of those who had earlier claimed that his only gift was the lyric? Probably he had done nothing more eloquent in his earlier works than the passages on New York ("Smoke-blue by morning in the chasmed slant, on quickening the tempo of the rapid steps, up to the pinnacles of noon") and on the rustle of the leaves across America:

'Promised, promised, promised, promised, promised,' say the leaves across America. . . . And everywhere, through the immortal dark, something moving in the night, and something stirring in the hearts of men, and something crying in their wild unuttered blood, the wild, unuttered tongues of its huge prophecies—so soon the morning, soon the morning: O America.

Nor had he done anything less rhetorical than the final words to that New York editor whom he had molded into his "Fox": "Man was born to live, to suffer, and to die, and what befalls him is a tragic lot. There is no denying this in the final end. *But we must, dear Fox, deny it all along the way.*" Where were the provincial accents now? Certainly the path that Wolfe took led him through all the heartbreaking detours that mark our literature from Melville to Dreiser. In July, 1938, after having delivered a new manuscript of more than a million words, he became ill with pneumonia. He died that September.

If he was ignorant and superstitious as the hill folks were, and stumbled into many gargantuan pitfalls—some those of his own making too—he had the persistence and cunning as well as the long legs of the hill people, and he walked with the mountain walk.

7

To some members of that original younger generation that was now the older generation, the Wolfean pilgrimage hardly seemed inspiring. "The stuff about the *Great Vital Heart of America,*" said Scott Fitzgerald in *The Crack Up* (1945), "is just simply corny." This little interchange of letters between Fitzgerald, as a sort of spokesman for the twenties, and Wolfe, for the thirties, forms an interesting footnote to our literary history. Maybe "corn" was a partial antidote to absinthe; at any rate there were many new literary figures who took up and supported Tom Wolfe's notions in one form or another. In a similar development over the same period, John Steinbeck moved from the primitive folk and the mystics of *To a God Unknown* (1933) and *Tortilla Flat* (1935) to the labor organizers of *In Dubious Battle* (1936). As the early tales, collected in *The Long Valley* (1938), had suggested, he was the most gifted of the writers surrounding Wolfe, and *Grapes of Wrath,* in 1939, confirmed his position in the new decade. It was chiefly an emotional facility and simplification of experience that kept Steinbeck's whole achievement from being as impressive as it was arresting. Nevertheless the story of the Okies' westward trek toward a New World—recalling as it did the historical meaning of the frontier in times of social crisis, even though the frontier was now an economic one—was a big and life-giving book. Similarly, Hemingway would soon announce his own return to a common humanity in *For Whom the Bell Tolls* (1940), while Dos Passos would take another look at the white pillars of the Republic in *The Ground We Stand On* (1941), and Fitzgerald himself would select, as the hero of *The Last Tycoon* (1941), a typical member of those odorous "aliens," a man who had moved up from the impoverished "masses" whom the earlier chronicler of the Jazz Age had described as "swarming like rats, chattering like apes, smelling like all hell . . . monkeys!"

It was indeed a new age, all over again—and even Edna Millay would desert her shining castles built upon the sand and beat a drum for mutual aid, while Muriel Rukeyser would voice the hopes of those other poets too young to see their funerals "in pantomime nightly before uneasy beds." Only William Faulkner remained an unreconstructed rebel. Furthermore, just as T. S. Eliot had earlier moved to England, W. H. Auden, perhaps the most gifted of the younger English poets, now moved to the United States. The obscure law of polarity seemed to be at work here as elsewhere. American literature, in its abrupt but rhythmic alternations between the opposing poles of the individual and of society, reflects the deeper process of cultural growth—the familiar oppositions of experiment and reaction—and the literary reaction in the thirties was historically almost inevitable. But the abrupt change of values in the new decade was more immediately connected, of course, with the financial crash of 1929—the sudden collapse of what Dos Passos had called "the great machine they slaved for" and what had seemed so recently more adamant, more unshakable than ever. In the stress of such quick and catastrophic change a Tom Wolfe might take up Sherwood Anderson's search for "the right place and the right people," while Steinbeck would carry forward the social criticism and something of the tone of Frank Norris and Jack London. And just as the larger literary figures carry within them both poles of the historical process, and are always classicists and romanticists together, so they seem at once more original as individuals and more deeply representative of their culture. Yet it was true also that the internal crisis had come as swiftly and unexpectedly upon the majority of the new writers as the First World War upon their predecessors. Under the new pressures, they were as guilty, in another mold, of the same excesses. They cut themselves off as completely from the twenties as the writers of the middle twenties had from the Progressive Movement of the 1900's. As a matter of fact, some of these New Dealers had hardly heard of the New Freedom, and believed that they were the first to initiate social progress in the United States—and they were not all New Dealers. Just as the new movement was primarily sociological in its orientation, some of its typical exponents, including Albert Maltz and Albert Halper, Leane Zugsmith, Fielding Burke, and even, it was rumored, Dorothy Parker (and also the talented mystery writer Dashiell Hammett), were avowed radicals; along with the revolutionary idealism they brought in revolutionary zealotry; very often the dogma got in the way of craft, and moral conviction became a substitute for artistic imagination. To some of these writers, indeed, the "Masses" became as formidable an abstraction as the "Individual" had been in the twenties; for a while, with the customary national intensity, it seemed that the age of the poets had been followed by the age of the pamphleteers. In America, as Sinclair Lewis remarked, a pendulum is not a pendulum; it is a piston.

This was part of the price of the American tradition under the stress of change—and in a world in crisis; but still, by contrast with the foreign scene, our own excesses were on the whole more ludicrous than vicious. By contrast with Dachau or Le Vernet, the Federal Writers' Project of the Work Projects Administration had even a certain grandeur—abused and vilified as it was— while in an extraordinary burst of studies, charts, reports, guidebooks, picture books, movies, plays, operas, and histories, these artistic leaf rakers on the "W. P. and A." brought forth an invaluable body of source material on the native scene. Their work, and a further group of related studies, such as Constance Rourke's *American Humor,* Carl Sandburg's *Lincoln,* and Van Wyck Brooks' *The Flowering of New England,* suddenly reestablished our sense of historical continuity, and if only through the Indians and the Negroes we seemed to gain a sort of racial unconscious, too. Many of these new journalists, historians, novelists, poets, and playwrights—and just as the Federal Writers' Project uncovered a richer past, so they helped to produce a richer present—also skipped the delicacies of their craft. If their work was sometimes crude, on the whole it was solid, and it could be built on. One of the best novels about the depression years, Ira Wolfert's *Tucker's People*, which appeared in the early forties, had been written during the thirties, and put away to mellow. Meanwhile a decade which saw, in addition to the works already mentioned, the plays of Clifford Odets or of Lillian Hellman, the movies of Pare Lorentz, and the popular historical novels of Walter Edmonds along with the tales of such an isolated and tragic figure as Hans Otto Storm —that decade was neither so extreme nor so barren as some critics have implied.

Nor was the break between periods and traditions, sharp as it seemed, altogether complete. The "nonpolitical" Southern Agrarians and Fugitives and their heirs went on their way unperturbed—although the members of the group, in their intense concern with purely "literary" values, and in their withdrawal from the more acute socio-economic issues of the decade, seemed to leave behind them the human problems as well, and to appear in their way quite as occult as the theoreticians of the class struggle. Essentially conservative also, such other Southern writers as Elizabeth Madox Roberts continued to display the virtues of a dissolving genteel tradition, which, by a greater boldness or a larger talent, Katherine Anne Porter had just escaped, and which, in the clinical morbidity of Evelyn Scott's work, or in that of Robert Penn Warren, seemed to be turning in upon itself. Yet all these writers were in one respect or another conservators of traditional values, and Willa Cather, who had by no means stopped writing over this period, or the Virginia radical of the nineties, Ellen Glasgow, who even put on a fresh burst of energy. In another area, near Park Avenue and Fifty-second Street, such a writer as John O'Hara continued to analyze the mores of the emancipated speakeasy set, and the polish of his phrases no less than the tone of his conversations recalled something of the lost elegance of the 1920's; in the neighborhood of Hollywood, too, James M. Cain brought the use of dialogue to a high gloss. And when such other skillful technicians and ex-expatriates as Kay Boyle, Glenway Wescott, and Frederic Prokosch turned their craft to the various phases of the world crisis it refreshed the entire tradition of sensibility.

The new "affirmation" of the American thirties, moreover, was not always accompanied by the vague sweetness and light that pervaded the tales of William Saroyan or by the rather murky violence of Edward Dahlberg's novels. In the middle ground also, along with Wolfe and Steinbeck, though not yet so firmly established, were writers like James T. Farrell and, a little later, Richard Wright. Considered as one of the most powerful and promising American novelists in the forties, Wright was also a leading representative of an established and versatile group of contemporary Negro writers and writers on Negro themes, including W. E. B. DuBois, James Weldon Johnson, Countee Cullen, and Claude McKay among the fiction writers; Roi Ottley, Zora Neale Hurston, Adam Clayton Powell, Chester Himes, Edwin Peeples, St. Clair Drake, and Horace Cayton, among a host of younger critics, poets, publicists, novelists, and scholars.

Both Farrell and Wright were working in the older and perhaps stronger naturalistic mold of Dreiser, although Wright, whose first important short story, "Big Boy Leaves Home," appeared in 1936, was still in a more formative stage. And, while Farrell relied chiefly on a cumulative effect of boredom with and disgust for the lives of his lower middle-class Irish people, and Wright relied on a cumulative effect of disgust for and horror at the existences of his Southern Negroes, both novelists had undoubted power. Their moral integrity, too, their determination to uncover all the unending viciousness and corruption of their environment—and perhaps the daily and hourly degradation of Farrell's people was as bad in the end as the moments of horror which marked the story of Wright's people—gave their work its solidity.

The limitations of Wright and Farrell, moreover, were just as revealing as their merits. In their work could be seen the real points of stress of contemporary American society—economic, racial, cultural; shaped by the pressures of the raw industrial cities in Farrell's novels, and by the blight of a diseased hinterland in Wright's. Here was the underlying social pattern that bound together both the aesthetic revolt of the twenties and the aesthetic conversion of the thirties. Showing the harsh prejudices and deep phobias of their milieu, these novelists also showed, through their own concentrated bitterness, through their refusal to accept even the catharsis of expression—through their indifference to the necessity of catharsis, the one reward of his art which the artist can always have, and which he can hardly afford not to have—they also showed, only too clearly, the harm that was already done. Thus Danny O'Neill, the "hero" of Farrell's tetralogy—and if Farrell's range was narrow, his architectonic concepts were certainly massive—was less convincing than Studs Lonigan, the "villain" of his earlier trilogy. The novelist's accent on personal emancipation hardly matched his earlier tones of blind cultural disintegration. Similarly, while Wright's autobiography, Black Boy (1945), was more moderate in tone than his earlier novel, Native Son, it was probably even more merciless in its impact—for the horrors one could tolerate in the life of a fictional hero, one could hardly accept in the actual life of an ordinary citizen.

No, those "latent atavistic urges" which a Thomas Wolfe saw everywhere around him in the disordered social arrangement of his time, as well as the Nazi Germany which exploited those urges, would not be eliminated by the liquidation of the German General Staff or by the atomization of Tokyo. They were strongly rooted also in the land of equal hope, and the imminence of a national future almost without limits seemed to revive all the fear and cruelty of the past. The Second World War also demonstrated the latent resources of a democratic order, since an average townsman from Abilene, Kansas, could become an outstanding military figure, while a patrician descendant of the Dutch landlords in the Hudson River Valley would best embody the common beliefs of the peoples of the world. These underlying cultural pressures still determined the shape of American life on the brink of another postwar era—and the shape of its literature—and whether the new age would burst in splendor or in terror.

78. AN AMERICAN DRAMA

I~ a previous chapter devoted chiefly to Eugene O'Neill, both the state of play writing and the general theatrical situation between 1915 and 1925 were discussed. The story is resumed at the end of that period, when three noncommercial "art theaters" testified to a widespread conviction that a "new" drama both could and should be brought to birth. However, except for O'Neill, no permanently important playwright was introduced through any one of these three theaters until the Theater Guild produced Elmer Rice's *The Adding Machine* in 1923. During the four or five years following that event, Rice was joined by various other "new American playwrights" destined to sustain their reputations through a series of plays, and it soon became evident that the new American drama—under discussion for at least ten years—was now a reality. The season of 1924–1925 * was especially notable for *What Price Glory* by Maxwell Anderson and Laurence Stallings, *They Knew What They Wanted* by Sidney Howard, and *Processional* by John Howard Lawson. .

The fact that *What Price Glory,* the most sensationally successful of these plays, was produced by Arthur Hopkins, technically a "commercial" producer, should serve to remind one that the "new drama," once it had actually come into existence, was by no means monopolized by the "art theaters." Indeed, it came more and more to be taken up by Broadway until there soon ceased to be any clear distinction between what was possible in an art theater and what was possible in a commercial theater. Thus, the new American drama had hardly begun to exist before it ceased to be the property of any coterie, and it was never at any time written exclusively by men who thought of themselves as belonging to any one group. Some of the most successful and esteemed playwrights would themselves have found it impossible to say how much they owed to the stimulus of the experimental producers of exotic drama and how much to certain predecessors in the American theater.

Long arguments have raged over the question whether the English drama of Shaw and Galsworthy owed more to Ibsen than to Tom Robertson. An equally long and equally futile one might be conducted concerning the

* Dates in this chapter refer to first production rather than to first publication.

relative importance to the new American playwrights of the European tradition and of that native one which had for decades been slowly evolving through James A. Herne, Charles Hoyt, Clyde Fitch, William Vaughn Moody, George M. Cohan, and the rest. Undoubtedly the most violent stimulus was provided by the revolutionary dramatists of Europe, and undoubtedly the "little theaters" contributed greatly to the playwrights' awareness of possible new horizons in the theater. But even as early as the season of 1924–1925, the three outstandingly successful plays mentioned above were the work of men who were less the disciples of any playwright, native or foreign, and less members of any theatrical cult, than they were simply talented writers eager to reach an American public for plays they found it in themselves to write.

When *What Price Glory* and *They Knew What They Wanted* appeared the names of the three authors responsible meant nothing to the average playgoer, although Anderson and Howard had each recently produced a first play without achieving commercial success. Both of the new works were theoretically shocking since the first treated in a frankly ribald spirit certain incidents in the lives of soldiers fighting the First World War, and the second had as its sympathetic heroine a young waitress whom a middle-aged Italian winegrower was willing to marry despite his knowledge of the fact that she was soon to bear an illegitimate child by a lover who had deserted her. Both plays were enthusiastically received, and it is evident that the large audiences which saw them were not actually shocked as the early audiences of Ibsen and Shaw had been; the reason is simply that by 1924 much of what had formerly seemed dangerously paradoxical had been assimilated not only by the intellectual but also by the whole sophisticated public. The two plays were not preaching a new doctrine. What they actually did was tell, for the first time on the American stage, dramatically interesting stories looked at from the point of view of the 1920's rather than from that of the mid-nineteenth century.

The same thing may be said of many of the other characteristic plays of the period. Laurence Stallings, coauthor of *What Price Glory,* abandoned play writing after failing to repeat his first success; but *Saturday's Children* (1927) and *Gypsy* (1929) by his collaborator, Maxwell Anderson, as well as *Lucky Sam McCarver* (1925), *Ned McCobb's Daughter* (1926) and *The Silver Cord* (1926), all by Sidney Howard, were comedies or light dramas which, without being directly didactic, told remarkably various stories always from the point of view of what may be called libertarian humanism—one conspicuous element in which is a protest in the name of common sense and kindliness against conventional respectability.

Some of these plays involved also an element which was the most important one in others of the time; namely, satire directed against materialism and the gospel of success, both of which libertarian humanism despised as aspects of Philistinism. Thus George Kelly's *The Show-Off* (1924) is a rather bitter satire in which the central figure, a blustering vulgarian, actually succeeds through a fluke in "pulling off the big deal" he has always dreamed of; and the long series of popular farces from *Dulcy* (1921) to *Once in a Lifetime* (1930), which George Kaufman wrote with various collaborators, represent a somewhat more frankly popular exploitation of the same theme.

Early in its career the Theater Guild, besides popularizing Shaw on the American stage, had produced the work of Molnár and other central European dramatists whose "Continental" treatment of the comedy of sex was widely regarded as a corrective to Puritanism. In *The Road to Rome* (1927) Robert Sherwood responded to the influence of Shaw by writing an amusing pseudohistorical comedy somewhat in the manner of *Caesar and Cleopatra*, and then, in 1931, achieved with *Reunion in Vienna* a comedy so perfectly in the Continental tradition that it might easily pass as a translation.

With the exception of *Reunion in Vienna*, none of the typical plays of the twenties so far mentioned exhibit foreign influence as their primary inspiration. Neither, of course, do Hatcher Hughes' *Hell-Bent fer Heaven* (1924) and Paul Green's *In Abraham's Bosom* (1926)—two folk plays, which are certainly among the best representatives of a genre that did not flourish as many supposed it would. On the other hand two plays held in high esteem both by critics and by a large public—Elmer Rice's *The Adding Machine* (1923) and John Howard Lawson's *Processional* (1925)—were directly inspired by those same expressionistic experiments which influenced O'Neill's *The Hairy Ape. The Adding Machine* is a theatrically effective exposition of a nihilistic fable concerning a certain "Mr. Zero," who remains hopelessly insignificant even after he has been transported to heaven. *Processional* professed (not too convincingly) to owe its method to vaudeville and the comic strip rather than to the European expressionists, and its rather vaguely but amusingly stated theme—that the true spirit of America is to be found in the exuberance of popular music and dancing rather than in the mouthings of its politicians or preachers—fitted well the mood of the moment.

To audiences of the time it seemed that all these plays were alike at least in that they were characterized by a sincere forthrightness, a realistically honest facing of the facts, and a liberal attitude toward moral questions. The present-day reader, particularly if he happens to be young enough to know the twenties only as a historical epoch, is more likely to be struck by the almost complete absence in these supposedly serious plays of any reference to what he has come to regard as the only serious problems, those of politics and economics. The explanation of this seemingly curious fact is that, theatrically at least, the twenties, though commonly described as years of disillusion (and so pictured by the novelists), were fundamentally optimistic and self-confident.

No doubt this fundamental self-confidence was hardly compatible with the current disillusion concerning the results of the great war from which America had just emerged. No doubt it was hardly less compatible with the contempt freely expressed for the exuberant materialism of those who were proclaiming the new age in which everyone was to get richer and richer without limit or pause. But no foreign enemy was feared, the normal expectation of the young adult was that he would find in the world a place ready to receive him in the trade or profession of his choice, and it was generally believed that advancing liberalism in the moral realm was gradually making possible for the first time not only the good but also the rich life. Only the most frivolous of youth really deserved to have the age in which they lived labeled "the jazz age." It was also quite as truly the age in which the drama, like many novels, poems, and essays, exhibited, even when the form was satiric and protestant, a fundamental confidence that a world which had grown secure and prosperous might rather easily be made beautiful and happy also.

This attitude of confidence produced a multitude of plays and stimulated experiments with both form and ideas. Only the four most influential trends can here be considered, with a single playwright representing each, as judgment of literature so nearly contemporary must always be arbitrary and largely personal. These four trends were: (a) Maxwell Anderson's experiments with tragedy which, unlike those of O'Neill, assume that verse is necessary if the highest effects are to be achieved; (b) S. N. Behrman's development of a comic style not wholly different from that of his predecessor Rachel Crothers or his contemporary Philip Barry, but seeming to be more consciously aware of the problem of adapting conceptions of the nature of comedy to the circumstances of American life; (c) the work of Clifford Odets as representing the most successful cultivation of the play intended to further a definite political and social ideology; and (d) the attempt on the part of several otherwise diverse writers to develop a dramatic form in which symbolism and fantasy definitely replace the realistic method.

2

Poetic tragedy found a convinced advocate in Maxwell Anderson. Born in 1888, he had written more than a score of produced plays before 1945. Among the earliest of these were *What Price Glory* (with Laurence Stallings) and several light comedy-dramas; but suddenly in 1930 he revealed an entirely new style in the formal tragedy in verse, *Elizabeth the Queen*. Though from time to time thereafter he wrote pieces in several different manners, it is probably with the formal tragedy, frequently historical in subject but in some instances dealing with a contemporary situation, that his name is most often associated. Plays of this kind include, besides the first just mentioned, *Mary of Scotland* (1933), *Valley Forge* (1934), *Winterset* (1935), *Key Largo* (1939), and *The Eve of St. Mark* (1942).

Maxwell Anderson was the only conspicuously successful dramatist except O'Neill who persistently attempted tragedy during the first four decades of the twentieth century; but the parallel between him and the author of *Mourning Becomes Electra* cannot be drawn any further. While the style and methods of O'Neill have been at times almost freakishly unconventional and his plays more fundamentally than superficially in the great tradition, Anderson began by choosing subjects which would have been regarded as suitable by any writer of tragedies since Elizabethan times and by treating them in a manner which may have been quite unfamiliar to the average playgoer but was actually closer to Bulwer Lytton or George Henry Boker than to any of Anderson's contemporaries or immediate predecessors. That these plays were theatrically effective is sufficiently proved by their popularity with large audiences despite the prejudice against verse in the contemporary theater. Two serious criticisms were made with considerable show of justification; one was that, by choosing traditional subjects and treating them in a traditional manner, Anderson created something which could be more accurately described as a theatrically successful pastiche than as a genuinely modern tragedy; the other was that his verse, while speciously poetic, was too often inflated, banal, and monotonous.

To the second of these criticisms it might be replied that at least the verse was theatrically practicable, that a contemporary audience could understand and would accept it, while—to take as an example one of the few other modern plays in verse to receive professional production—T. S. Eliot's *Murder in the Cathedral* proved to be in many passages extremely difficult to follow. The other serious charge Anderson himself met when he produced *Winterset* in 1935 and demonstrated that he could treat a modern theme in the manner which he had previously reserved for historical tragedies.

The subject was obviously suggested by the Sacco-Vanzetti case. Seven years before *Winterset* appeared Anderson had collaborated with Harold Hickerson on a play called *Gods of the Lightning,* in which the same famous case had been literally—one might almost say journalistically—treated in one of the earliest American attempts "to make art a weapon" after a fashion which was to be widely advocated in the early thirties. *Winterset* seems, on the other hand, to be a conscious effort to draw the distinction between the journalistic and artistic treatment of a contemporary subject and an equally conscious effort to demonstrate that such a subject can be made the basis of a formal tragedy.

Long before the play begins, a radical agitator has been railroaded to death by a court which shared the popular determination to fix the guilt of murder upon a man whom it had other reasons to hate. More recently a college professor, reopening the case, has pointed the finger of suspicion at a gangster just released from prison, and thus a ghost has been raised to plague those who had had a part in the now almost forgotten events. The key to the mystery is held by a young witness lost in the obscurity of the lower depths, and upon him converge all those most deeply concerned: the actual murderer, determined at all costs to prevent the truth from coming to light; the outcast son of the man who paid the penalty for the crime he did not commit; and, finally, the presiding judge, now driven out of his wits by the unsuccessful effort to convince himself that he had done only what duty compelled him to do. Obviously there is in all this no lack of exciting action or of opportunities for direct sociopolitical argument. But both are subordinated, as they would be in a classical tragedy, to a brooding and poetic treatment of the themes which the action suggests; namely, the nature of guilt and of justice, and the meaning of revenge. If *Gods of the Lightning* constitutes what Anderson had, as a citizen, to say about the Sacco-Vanzetti case, *Winterset* is what he had, as a poet, to say about the same thing.

This play was markedly less successful in the commercial theater than several of the author's more conventional poetic tragedies, and some spectators raised the rather curious objection that "gangsters don't speak verse." Since the appropriateness or inappropriateness of elevated speech depends (as Shakespeare will sufficiently demonstrate) not upon the speaker's social or even intellectual status but upon the success of his creator in endowing him with an intensity of feeling for the expression of which the best utterance is none too good, this objection seems frivolous enough. It can be more reasonably alleged that the irregular blank verse of *Winterset* sometimes exhibits the characteristic turgidity of its author; but, for all this, there are reasons for maintaining not only that *Winterset* is its author's best play, but also that it is a striking and original one.

Anderson's subsequent plays include pieces as diverse as *The Masque of Kings* (1937), a romantic tragedy about Rudolph of Austria; the extremely popular, but not very original, fantastic comedy *The Star Wagon*; a romantic verse comedy, *High Tor*; a musical comedy, *Knickerbocker Holiday*; and a patriotic war play, *The Eve of St. Mark*. They also include *Key Largo* (1939), the only other piece which suggests obvious comparison with *Winterset*. Like the latter, it was not among the author's most conspicuous commercial successes, and it perhaps comes less close to the full realization of its intentions than *Winterset*. The situation is nevertheless a powerful one, and the central character—an ex-soldier trying to justify himself for a failure to perform a duty at the cost of his life—has an obvious relation to the judge in *Winterset*.

Success was far more easily won by Anderson than it was by O'Neill. His originality is far less absolute; he generally seemed less eccentric to ordinary audiences, and either instinctively or through conscious design he adapted himself to the requirements of the modern stage instead of demanding, as O'Neill did, that the stage should adapt itself to him. The important fact that both have attempted to revive formal tragedy in the modern theater makes a comparison between them inevitable; but in every respect except this large general aim they seem to differ: Anderson showed, for example, the verbal facility which O'Neill so conspicuously lacked. Nevertheless, Anderson is to be ranked among the five or six most considerable playwrights of the two decades following 1925, and he represents one aspect of a movement which seemed, at least until the war arrested artistic development, likely to achieve something toward which the American drama had been struggling ever since the earliest of the "new playwrights" began to cultivate a "new drama"; namely, plays richer and more intense than the mere problem play can ever be.

3

At least at the beginning of his career, S. N. Behrman seemed to have dedicated himself to comedy as O'Neill did to tragedy, and pure comedy has been only somewhat less rare than genuine tragedy in the American theater. Sentimental folk drama tinged with comedy, and farce or melodrama tinged with sentiment had, of course, long provided one of the most popular genres. One may trace it from before the days of *David Harum* down through George M. Cohan's long series of plays with music and Winchell Smith's somewhat more sophisticated versions of the sentimental comedy which began in 1906 with *Brewster's Millions* and continued to achieve monotonously enormous successes until *"Lightnin'"* (1918) broke all previous records for length of run. But pure comedies—plays in which the comic spirit is recognized as something with which sentimentalism is fundamentally incompatible—had been so rare that when one has mentioned Langdon Mitchell's *The New York Idea* (1906) and Jesse Lynch Williams' very Shavian *Why Marry?* (1917) one has named the chief early examples. Behrman's *The Second Man* (1927) was, on the other hand, a drawing-room comedy which took as its theme the nature of the comic spirit here manifesting itself as the voice of a "second man" who whispers the witty counsels of common sense to the hero. As comedy it was "pure," both in the sense that it admitted no admixture of sentiment and in the sense that it so concerned generalized human nature rather than local conditions or customs as to seem almost abstract.

Two years later, Philip Barry, who had been producing plays at frequent intervals since 1923, turned aside from the rather whimsical style which had seemed his most characteristic one, to present in *Holiday* (1928) a witty drawing-room comedy somewhat closer than most of his previous works to high comedy in the usually accepted sense of that term; and two of his subsequent plays, *The Animal Kingdom* (1932) and *Bright Star* (1935), give him some claim to share with Behrman the distinction of being the most accomplished writer of comedy at once pure and smart. But in his writing he seemed to be a somewhat divided personality, so far from having dedicated himself to comedy that he could, on the one hand, revel in the rather cloudy mysticism of *Hotel Universe* (1930) and *Here Come the Clowns* (1938) and, on the other, purvey to an appreciative public the romanticism of *The Philadelphia Story* (1939). The result is that the impression produced by an attempt to consider his work as a whole is somewhat blurred and that, therefore, he seems less fit than Behrman to stand as our ablest exponent of the comic spirit.

Behrman was born in Worcester, Massachusetts, in 1893. Nothing in the quite ordinary details of his career—Clark University, Professor Baker's course in dramatic composition, work on the New York *Times,* and then as a theatrical press agent—helps to explain how he achieved at one bound the complete maturity of his powers and a mastery of the essential spirit of comedy. Nevertheless *The Second Man,* his first independent play, is as finished as anything he subsequently achieved.

His next important works, *Brief Moment* (1931) and *Biography* (1932), continued to cultivate the manner which he had just established. The hero of the first is a typical inhabitant of that intellectual world which its denizens have liked to call the Wasteland. But instead of gesturing magniloquently in the void and attempting to turn his predicament into tragedy despite the obvious absence of the necessary exaltation, he is content to analyze the situation intellectually and then to compensate for the absence of ecstasy by the cultivation of that grace and wit which no one can be too sophisticated to achieve. *Biography* is another vehicle for a comment made by the comic spirit upon one of the predicaments of modern life. Its heroine is a mediocre but successful portrait painter with a genius for comely living. Her dilemma arises out of the apparent necessity of choosing between two men, the one a likable but abandoned opportunist in public life, the other a fanatical revolutionary idealist. Her ultimate determination to choose neither is essentially a defense of her right to be a spectator and to cultivate the spectator's virtue—detached tolerance. The revolutionist says everything which can be said against her attitude. He denounces it as, at bottom, only a compound of indolence and cowardice, which parades as superiority when it is really responsible for the world's injustices. But the heroine sticks to her contention that neutrality is right for her. She may be useless while many persons less reasonable and less amiable than she are useful. But wit and tolerance are forms of beauty and, as such, provide their own excuse for being.

Such plays as these are obviously artificial, both in the sense that they deal with an artificial and privileged section of society and in the sense that the characters themselves are less real persons than idealized embodiments of intelligence and wit. Such actions as are represented could not take place, and such solutions to the problems presented could not seem valid except in a world fundamentally stable and comfortable because, as is usual in high comedy, all difficulties arise within the framework of the play itself and are solvable by common sense. If such a world seemed to many to exist during the twenties, it was already disappearing by the time *Biography* came to be performed, and the author himself soon felt the necessity of acknowledging in his plays the existence of forces with which the comic spirit is not capable of dealing. But instead of executing a complete about-face, as some of his play-writing contemporaries did, and attempting a kind of writing for which he had no gift, he devoted himself to exploring in dramatic terms the question whether the comic spirit could, while abandoning all attempt to present itself as a complete philosophy of life, nevertheless demonstrate that it had something to add to the discussions in which everyone was being compelled, willy-nilly, to take some part.

In *Rain from Heaven* (1934) we have what is basically the same situation as that in *Biography,* a wise and witty woman being brought into conflict with two men, each of whom is capable of a certain fanaticism incomprehensible to her. But in the earlier play, neither the Communist nor the practical politician is more than potentially dangerous; each is operating so nearly in a vacuum that the clash between them is chiefly a clash of temperaments and ideologies. In *Rain from Heaven,* on the other hand, another sort of crisis is near. One man, an aviator, is a popular American hero of the moment, being exploited by his brother in the interest of a vague Fascist scheme; the other is a German refugee. The scene has been moved to England, to an atmosphere charged with the possibility of proximate conflict. If the heroine elects again to remain to some extent "above the battle," there is, as there was not in *Biography,* a real battle to remain above. The exponent of the comic spirit is forced to approve the refugee's most uncomic decision to return to fight in his own homeland a dangerous battle over a matter of principle. When she attempts to defend the importance of "understanding" as opposed to even heroic passion, he replies that while you are trying to understand your enemy that enemy will kill you; and to this retort she can answer only that however useless people of her sort may seem now, some of them will some-how survive the storm and play a part in reestablishing the only kind of world worth having.

Had Behrman happened to live in a more stable society he would doubtless have written comedies more strictly in the great comic tradition than his later plays. As it is, *Rain from Heaven* established a pattern into which his best subsequent works—*End of Summer* (1936), *Wine of Choice* (1938), and *No Time for Comedy* (1939)—tended to fall. Faced with the problem of writing comedy in an atmosphere which many are ready to say makes comedy either impossible or impertinent, he thus invented something which might not improperly be called the comedy of illumination. This type of play touches upon the graver issues of the moment, but it differs from the Shavian problem comedy in two important respects: first, in its avoidance of Shaw's tendency to beg the question in order to favor one side of the debate; and second, in its persistent sympathy with those embodiments of the comic spirit who are described by one of their enemies as "inhibited by scruple and emasculated by charm." Behrman's wit enables him to make discussion really illuminating and hence to write comedies which are neither merely didactic nor merely trivial. Of the time in which he was fated to live, one may imagine that he has often said: "O cursed spite, that ever I was born to set it right!" Yet he wrote important comedies in an age which seemed to make them impossible.

4

In spite of the tendency of playwrights like Anderson and Behrman to treat the issues of the moment with full seriousness, the play intended to further a definite political and social ideology was slow in taking shape. During the twenties, the epoch dominated by libertarian humanism, the Com-munist party was of course beginning to be heard of. But even to its members revolution probably seemed pretty remote and the never widely attended Communist-inspired plays which began to be produced at the New Play-wrights' Theater—housed first in Fifty-third Street, later in Cherry Lane—were extravagant and dilettantish rather than grim. Outside the definite Com-munist group, criticism of society meant usually a criticism of morals, man-ners, and tastes, not a criticism of political or economic institutions. If Ameri-can life was denounced in the theater, as it often was, it was denounced as crass, puritanical, unsophisticated, and nonintellectual rather than as capi-talistic or fascist. Even political dissidence had little tendency to crystallize into doctrine. Plays like *The Adding Machine* or *The Hairy Ape* were some-what baffled considerations of the spiritual poverty of the underprivileged rather than revolutionary protests, and a change in point of view did not come until the crash of 1929. The depression which followed aroused widespread doubt concerning the adequacy of libertarian humanism as a philosophy of life.

Both Anderson and Behrman responded somewhat to the changed atmosphere though neither changed fundamentally either his convictions or his style. Most of the other established playwrights, except O'Neill, reacted much more violently to the shock by attempting a fundamental reorientation plainly evident in their plays. Thus Elmer Rice, who had just before written in *Street Scene* a completely nonpolitical though completely sympathetic tragedy-melodrama about life in the slums, came out with a series of propagandistic plays; John Howard Lawson, who had celebrated America's exuberant health in *Processional,* turned to a Marxian denunciation of American decadence in *Gentlewoman* (1934) as well as in other didactic dramas; and Sidney Howard, who had produced a whole series of studies in manners and morals, wrote *The Ghost of Yankee Doodle* (1937). Inevitably, any new insurgent group was a political group, and the Theater Union, definitely committed to the propaganda play, was (or at least tried to be) for the new age what the Washington Square and the Provincetown Players had been for the old.

It would probably be pretty generally agreed that, except in the cases of O'Neill, Anderson, and Behrman, the work done by the established group under the new dispensation was less successful than that which it had done in the twenties. Of such newly emerging playwrights as George Sklar, Paul Peters, and Marc Blitzstein, on the other hand, much was promised. "Art is a weapon" became a frequently heard slogan, and for a time the theatrical scene seemed all but dominated by the Theater Union, by the somewhat less exclusively political but still definitely leftish Group Theater, and, finally, by the various units of the Federal Theater which sponsored the technique of the Living Newspaper as permitting the most direct treatment of social problems in theatrical form. None of these three institutions survives, none had a history comparable to that of the Provincetown or Washington Square Players. Of the new playwrights who arose to supply them with plays only one, Clifford Odets, made a notable place in the theater, and even he migrated to Hollywood in the forties. However truncated his career seems to have been, he deserves serious attention in any study of the recent American drama.

Though born in Philadelphia, Odets was educated in the public schools of New York City. While still quite young he joined a junior acting company originally sponsored by the Theater Guild and soon to become the independent Group Theater. He never achieved any prominence as an actor, but like most of the Group members he began to take an interest in the current discussion of social problems; and early in 1935 the Group filled out a short bill by the production of his brief tour de force called *Waiting for Lefty.* The public reaction was extremely favorable, and about six weeks later the Group offered his first full-length play, *Awake and Sing.*

Waiting for Lefty is ingenious and forthright rather than impressive as play writing. The stage is assumed to be the platform at a labor union meeting, and the audience to be the assembled members of the union. A proposed strike of taxi drivers is under discussion, "plants" in the audience arise to interrupt or protest, and flashbacks present scenes from the lives of various persons concerned. Word finally comes that the "Lefty" for whom all are waiting has been killed, and the action ends with the cry of "Strike! Strike!" Characterization is in simple black and white, much of the didacticism is crude as well as blatant; but at least *Waiting for Lefty,* unlike most plays offered as "weapons," might actually serve effectively as such. It was perhaps a recognition of this fact that aroused enthusiasm for the new author.

Awake and Sing exhibits virtues of quite a different kind. It is said to have been begun before its author's conversion to Marxism, and to have been hastily provided with the concluding scene in which a "revolutionary" moral is drawn. In any event, the general effect is dramatic rather than didactic and most reviewers recognized immediately an interesting new talent. The scene is a Bronx tenement. Most of the characters are part of a struggling Jewish family, the various members of which are held together by intense loyalties even though a clash of conflicting ideals and desires is going on in an atmosphere embittered by poverty. The milieu is certainly not unfamiliar on the stage, but it has seldom been described so vividly, so compassionately, or with so striking a combination of emotional intimacy and intellectual detachment. Ostensibly the moral is a revolutionist's moral, for the play ends when the young son of the family frees himself from his obsession with a purely personal rebellion against the poverty which separates him from his girl and determines to throw himself into the class struggle. Actually the subject is less this specific protest and rebellion than the persistent and many-sided rebellion of human nature against everything that thwarts it.

Odets was soon publicly claiming kinship with Chekhov, and a comparison between the two is less grotesque than it might seem. Chekhov's decaying aristocrats are at the opposite end of the social scale from the proletarians of *Awake and Sing,* but they are astonishingly like them in their self-centered absorption in the bitterness of their individual frustrations. It may very well be that Odets learned from the Russian his most striking stylistic trick, the writing of brisk colloquial dialogue in which much appears to be irrelevant or random, though all is actually very much to the point. His characters, like most of Chekhov's, reveal themselves by their very inability to communicate with their fellows; and, again like the characters of Chekhov, they cannot communicate because each is too absorbed in his own misery even to recognize the similar state of all around him.

It was certainly not from Chekhov that Odets learned a certain fierce faith in his people. Other historians of the oppressed have pictured them as dumb, brutalized, inarticulate, and despairing; but his characters all lead vivid lives within the limitations which Fate (or the injustices of our society) has imposed upon them, and this fact not only makes the best of his plays exciting but also redeems them from fundamental pessimism, however calamitous the outward events recorded may be. Moreover his implied faith that the human spirit is never defeated is by no means so identical with his faith in the Marxian doctrine as he would perhaps have liked to believe. In *Awake and Sing*, the young son who turns revolutionist is directing his determination into one channel; but the play strikingly demonstrates that the same determination may be directed into any one of many channels. Perhaps this young man's aim is, for the moment, the most intelligent and useful one. But the real secret of mankind's success, the real hope for its future, does not lie in anything so specific as one crusade or one determination. It lies in the persistence of man's passion, his unwillingness to accept defeat for his desires. He can go on indefinitely insisting that he will be happy and free, tirelessly protesting against the fact that he is not; and if, by chance, one generation does surrender there is always another wanting the old things with a young determination to have them. Odets' characters are ignorant and crude; but his play is exhilarating despite its tragedies, because he makes it so clear that people like this are going to go right on demanding of life more than it will give them.

During the same year which saw the first production of *Awake and Sing*, the Group Theater produced two other plays by the same author: *Till the Day I Die*, an undistinguished if earnest drama of Nazi brutality; and *Paradise Lost*, which Odets professed to regard as his most important work, but which to most critics seemed a highly doctrinaire, rather than convincing, study of American society in the process of a disintegration closely in accord with the pattern laid down in Marxian prophecy. Possibly because neither of these plays achieved great success, *Golden Boy* (1937) attempted, not wholly in vain, to tell in terms of the popular theater a story capable of conveying to the attentive a moral for the politically radical; and it was not until the following year that *Rocket to the Moon* again gave convincing demonstration of the fact that its author was a man of more than mediocre talents.

Many critics have insisted that *Awake and Sing* is Odets' best play; but *Rocket to the Moon* is at least comparable in merit though somewhat different in method as well as tone. Once more the scene is that of lower middle-class American life, and the principal characters are again distinguished by the intensity of their rebellion. But the story is more that of a few individuals than that of a loosely connected group, and there is nothing explicitly doctrinaire in the emphasis upon poverty as a dominant fact in their lives. The failure of an arrestingly presented situation to work itself out to any conclusion as striking as that which the exposition seems to promise, leaves the play somewhat less than completely satisfactory, but does not prevent it from being absorbing and impressive. On the other hand, neither *Night Music* (1940) nor *Clash by Night* (1941) was commercially successful, and neither adds to Odets' reputation, although the second reveals flashes of the dramatic power which made both *Rocket to the Moon* and *Awake and Sing* memorable.

After the outbreak of the Second World War, most radicals, including finally even the members of the Communist Party, became convinced that it was advisable to form with "capitalism" a "united front" against the Axis powers. One result was an effective dampening of their enthusiasm for revolutionary social criticism, and the "revolutionary theater" as a recognizable entity rapidly dissolved. Many new plays of social import were written, and audiences became larger than at any time since the twenties; but between 1939 and 1945 no one kind of play was persistently cultivated, and no new theatrical movement became discernible.

Many of the most successful pieces were adapted from popular novels, apparently because original plays did not appear in sufficient number to keep the theaters filled; and, while certain writers continued to use the stage to comment upon the war or its implications, their comments were usually either patriotic melodrama or the defense of some specific ideological line— which inevitably made them less works of the imagination than sheer polemics. Thus Robert Sherwood's *There Shall Be No Night* (1940) was widely praised for its statement of the case of Finland against Russia. Yet its author evidently regarded it as above all a work of propaganda and, when the political situation changed, revised the piece to provide new heroes and new villains.

Lillian Hellman's plays, despite the critical acclaim and popular success which some of them have won, have a propagandistic element which makes it difficult to take her artistic pretensions with full seriousness. She began with a powerful drama centering in a malicious child and called *The Children's Hour* (1934). Soon she devoted herself exclusively to social themes, first with *The Little Foxes* (1939), whose raison d'être is an implied criticism of capitalist society, and then with *Watch on the Rhine* (1941), in which violent condemnation of Nazi Germany is the main motivating idea. Both of these plays, like *The Searching Wind,* which was produced after the German invasion of Russia, exhibit considerable theatrical dexterity but suffer from the extent to which they appear to be limited by immediate political considerations. *Another Part of the Forest* (1947) deals with the same family as *The Little Foxes* and is theatrically the most dextrous of her plays.

5

When the modern drama was born in Europe the assumption was commonly made that naturalism was its normal method In America, however, during the three decades after the founding of the Provincetown and the Washington Square Players, there was a strong tendency in an opposite direction, and even the Broadway audiences showed a willingness to accept fantasy, symbolism, poetry, and other deviations from the literal. This is surprising enough when one considers the supposed contemporary devotion to doctrinaire realism, or even when one remembers that the sentimental plays which dominated the late nineteenth and early twentieth century stages were usually presented in pseudorealistic terms. The least artistically self-conscious of audiences, during the second quarter of the twentieth century, accepted without surprise settings and methods of staging which would have seemed merely laughable to members of an earlier generation who had complacently accepted the box set and the convention of the fourth wall as the ultimate in theatrical art. What is much more important, general popular audiences accept, almost as readily, plays in which the imagination is given freer play than is possible in any work which confines itself to actuality.

Of the five modern dramatists given most extended consideration in this history, three, O'Neill, Anderson, and Saroyan, could not by any stretch of the term be called exclusively or even primarily realists. Marc Connelly's Negro fantasy *The Green Pastures* was tremendously successful in 1930, and Thornton Wilder's New England allegory *Our Town* won the Pulitzer Prize in 1938. Even the left-wing drama, though professing to be so practical in its implications, tended toward the expressionism cultivated by the earliest of the Communist-inspired groups and by John Howard Lawson in his *Processional* or, like many of the productions of the Theater Union and the Federal Theater, employed a symbolism which at times approaches the simple and directly translatable allegory of the old morality play. Moreover, a surprising number of isolated plays, presented in the commercial theater and directed, often with conspicuous success, toward a general audience, were frankly unrealistic and nonrepresentational; among them were *Our Town, On Borrowed Time, The Skin of Our Teeth,* and *The Glass Menagerie.* Moreover *Harvey,* winner of the Pulitzer Prize and one of the most successful plays of the 1944–1945 season, is realistic in method but highly fanciful in content. These sensational and sometimes merely eccentric deviations from the literal are possibly less significant as symptoms than the fact that O'Neill won success in formal tragedy or that Maxwell Anderson revived verse as the language of a genuinely popular play; but the various phenomena are not unrelated, and the ingenuities of the spectacularly nonrepresentational plays call unmistakable attention to a trend.

Among the symbolic plays which achieved conspicuous success during the forties, Thornton Wilder's extravaganza *The Skin of Our Teeth* (1942) and Mary Chase's engaging farce-comedy *Harvey* (1944) deserve special mention; but of the new playwrights who emerged between the debut of Odets and the middle of the forties only one, William Saroyan, has written often enough as well as originally enough to establish even a tentative claim to inclusion in any permanent list of American dramatists.

Saroyan's many plays are whimsical and symbolic to the extreme, yet he is only incidentally a playwright. For that matter he is also incidentally a novelist or short-story writer since he must be classed as a romantic egotist who lets himself go on paper. The fact nevertheless remains that he is gifted with an original vein of humor, sentiment, and fantasy which is delightful to those who can repress the irritation provoked by his adolescent pose of bumptious self-confidence. Born of poor Armenian parents in Fresno, California, he worked at various odd jobs, including that of messenger boy for a telegraph company; and in one of the many prose sketches which compose his spiritual—though presumably not factual—autobiography, he has described how a Mormon missionary converted him in the course of a few minutes to that "acceptance of the universe" which he has never lost. To the astonishment of a public accustomed to assuming that all serious young writers are bitter, disillusioned, despairing, and misanthropic, he volubly proclaimed his delight in a world so full to overflowing with a number of things that we should all be happy as kings if we would only, like him, relax, believe everything, and love the "beautiful people" all about us.

Of his several plays, only two, *My Heart's in the Highlands* (1939) and *The Time of Your Life* (1939), achieved any sort of conspicuous success; the second of these won the Pulitzer Prize and enjoyed a long run. Both are, however, a great deal more entertaining than any description is likely to seem, and both are perhaps best understood in the light of the author's complaint that the chief defect of American plays has been the lack of any "play" in them. *My Heart's in the Highlands* concerns a fantastically improvident and unsuccessful poet whose chief difficulty—getting something to eat for himself and his young son—is temporarily solved by the appearance of an old man who plays so sweetly on the bugle that the neighbors bring a tribute of eggs, fruits, and vegetables. In *The Time of Your Life,* a mysterious habitué of a waterfront saloon acts as deus ex machina in the lives of a group of fantastic unfortunates, and helps to rid the world of the only really ill disposed person in either play.

Inevitably the political- and the social-minded objected that such plays, far from being representative of reality, are merely fantasies, peopled by various projections of Saroyan's own personality who live in a daydream of their own. They are not impressed by such sly understatements as that at the end of *My Heart's in the Highlands,* where the poet's son brings the play to an end by remarking, "Don't say anything now but there is something wrong somewhere." Neither are they impressed by Saroyan's pervading implication that it is men who make "the system" rather than the other way around, and that if men were only happier they would make a better world to be happy in.

Technically the objection most often raised to Saroyan's plays is that, like his stories, they lack continuity, form, or unity. There is no doubt that they do, or that his later and less successful pieces like *The Beautiful People* and *Love's Old Sweet Song* were even looser and more inconclusive than the others. There is, however, a legitimate question whether or not the critics were wise when they urged upon the author a tighter theatrical form. Such form as he did achieve in *The Time of Your Life* was artificially imposed from without, and the more loosely written *My Heart's in the Highlands* is probably the better play of the two. The truth seems to be that Saroyan has composed daydreams, and that he is most convincing when the form is most dreamlike. The old man who plays the bugle does not come from anywhere. Like the Mock Turtle or Humpty Dumpty in *Alice,* he is simply there to be looked at before we pass on; and when, finally, he is "explained" as a fugitive from a home for superannuated actors, the explanation makes him less, rather than more, satisfactory—for reasons that are plainly Aristotelian. When he appears, asking for a drink of water and complaining that though he is present in California, his heart is as always in the Highlands, he is an example of the probable impossibility. As a runaway from an old men's home he is merely an example of the improbably possible. A good half-dozen of the fantastic personages in *The Time of Your Life* are similarly amusing, pathetic, and at least suggestive of certain realities which they do not literally imitate; and Saroyan is probably one of those authors who must be allowed, for good or ill, to go his own unorthodox way.

Saroyan is far too eccentric, both as a personality and as a writer, to be taken as typical of anything except himself. The fact that the theater of his day found some place for him does, however, serve to indicate how extremely eclectic that theater had become.

6

The revolution in the American theater which characterizes the twentieth century began when a group of new writers presented on the stage various stories told against the background of that new sophistication which not only the American intellectual but also a considerable part of the American population had somewhat self-consciously acquired from many sources, including more than a few European dramatists. Drama tended to remain up to date by treating themes current at any particular moment, and by treating them from current points of view rather than with the safe conventionality of most nineteenth century dramatists who, on the whole, were far more timid than essayists or writers of fiction. But this up-to-dateness, this topicality, imposes limitations even though it is, in itself and to a certain extent, a virtue. The brightly contemporary is often the transitory and journalistic, and most of the obviously outstanding dramatists were less topical than the general run, so that O'Neill wrote tragedy and Behrman wrote comedy while lesser men were inclined to stick closer to some immediate topic of the time.

Perhaps, then, the experiments with fantasy and symbolism and poetry so characteristic of the middle forties indicate a growing dissatisfaction of playwright and public alike with the limitations of a realistic treatment of current topics, and an obvious effort to gain intensity by exploring further methods not merely realistic and subject matter not essentially topical. On the whole, the novelists of these years were more successful than the dramatists in exploiting such subject matter, and the poets developed more highly experimental forms. But the drama, occupying a middle position, shared with writing unrestricted by the exigencies of stage and audience the creative vitality of the period, and the national theater was not wholly inhospitable to what the best playwrights could make of it.

79. POETRY

AMERICAN poetry in these years furnished the most serious evidence of a cleavage between what we have learned to call mass civilization and minority culture. Ignored for the most part by the large number of readers who hearkened to the novelists and playwrights, there were nevertheless more expert practitioners of the craft of verse during the twenty-five years before 1940 than during any other generation in our history. If we accept the proposition advanced by one of them, "Artists are the antennae of the race," the most sensitive registers of our spiritual and social well-being or malaise, we cannot ignore the poets' evidence, even though much of it may be disturbing. Indeed, in the view of the most influential poet of the 1920's, T. S. Eliot, one characteristic of authentic poetry, whether by Blake or by Æschylus, "is merely a peculiar honesty, which, in a world too frightened to be honest, is peculiarly terrifying."

Eliot's own career raises at once many of the most controversial issues. In some accounts of American literature he is omitted altogether on the ground that he lived in England during most of his maturity and became a British subject in 1927. Yet his work can no more be divorced from its American background than that of Henry James; and at a time when many European artists—including W. H. Auden, the leading English poet of his generation—are becoming American citizens, we must recognize that much of the future of art can only be international. Almost as controversial, however, is the value of Eliot's work, regardless of what country it belongs to. By 1940 he had already lived through two cycles of taste. In the early 1920's he was hailed as a revolutionary by the young survivors of the war, by "the lost generation" who read in him their feeling of the breakdown of tradition and their sense of being thereby liberated, if only into despair. But when he found his way out of the pit inhabited by "the hollow men" by means of a return to formal religion, he was dismissed by many of his followers as a reactionary. Yet his preoccupations, from first to last, show a singular consistency.

2

Before we can see his career in any perspective we must reckon with that of the craftsman to whom he dedicated *The Waste Land,* calling him, in

Dante's phrase, "il migglior fabbro." The fact that Ezra Pound became an accused traitor can easily blind us to his previous services to modern art. In 1916, when the renaissance inaugurated by Harriet Monroe's magazine *Poetry* was still new Sandburg remarked that Pound "has done most of living men to incite new impulses in poetry." The propagandist for the Imagist movement in London, he had abandoned it when Miss Lowell took it over and transformed it into what he called "Amygism." He then moved on to further blasts and instigations. But his career antedated his appointment as the original European correspondent for *Poetry*. It might be said to have been officially inaugurated on that occasion in 1909 when he read aloud to his Soho friends his sestina, "Altaforte," and, according to a witness, "the entire café trembled."

The young American who could adapt one of the most delicate of Romance verse forms had just then begun his siege of London. His ancestors had been in America since the seventeenth century. His grandfather had moved from upper New York State to engage in the lumber business in Wisconsin. The poet himself had been born in Idaho, though his father soon returned East and became assayer at the United States Mint in Philadelphia. After graduating from Hamilton College and taking his Master's degree at the University of Pennsylvania (1906), Pound spent a year abroad in further preparation as a teacher of Romance languages. But his one appointment, at Wabash College, ended after four months with the mutual recognition that he was too much "the Latin Quarter type." He departed again for Europe to work on a doctoral thesis on Lope de Vega, but by the time he had printed, in a hundred copies in Venice, his first book of poems *A Lume Spento* (1908), the thesis had been dropped, and he had decided to remain abroad.

Pound's earliest poetry is saturated with medieval literature, with Provençal and Italian verse forms, with Arnaut Daniel and Guido Cavalcanti, whom he adapted freely. In the preface to his first book of criticism, *The Spirit of Romance* (1910), which was devoted to these same authors, Pound delivered several propositions by which he was able to abide throughout his work:

What we need is a literary scholarship, which will weigh Theocritus and Mr. Yeats with one balance . . . and will give praise to beauty before referring to an almanack. . . . Art is a fluid moving above or over the minds of men. . . . Art is a joyous thing. Its happiness antedates even Whistler; apropos of which I would in all seriousness plead for a greater levity, a more befitting levity in our study of the arts.

He had found our current attitude toward the arts particularly grim and barren, and said that when he left this country "there was no one in America

whose work was of the slightest interest for a serious artist." His own attitude
had been affected by the Pre-Raphaelites and the English aestheticism of the
nineties; but he made his bridge from medieval to modern poetry mainly by
way of his enthusiasms for Browning and Yeats. The fusion that Pound contrived between such seeming opposites is suggested by the title of his second
book of verse—a title he also used for later collections—*Personae*. The word
means "masks of the actor," which suggests Yeats' doctrine that the poet
must objectify his emotions through finding his Mask or Anti-Self. It also
suggests Pound's direct inheritance from Browning's *Men and Women*.
Much of his work was to be monologue, in which, like Browning, he was
concerned with "verse as speech"; but his technique is far more indebted to
Yeats who, alone among his older contemporaries, was sufficiently concerned
also with "verse as song." Pound's double gift of the musical phrase and the
speaking voice is what challenged the admiration of so many other practitioners.

What he had to say was always less impressive. His view of his function
was adumbrated in "Grace Before Song," the opening poem of his first book:

> As bright white drops upon a leaden sea,
> Grant so my songs to this grey folk may be.

To the first issue of *Poetry* he contributed "To Whistler, American," whom
he hailed as "our first great," a sustaining force to the new generation:

> You and Abe Lincoln from that mass of dolts
> Show us there's chance at least of winning through.

But the masks Pound adopted were far less varied than Browning's. In "Altaforte" he was a medieval warrior; but he seemed far more in character in his
guise of the faun in "Tenzone" or as the by then traditional Bohemian in
"The Garret." In the course of his defense of Imagism, he defined an image
as "that which presents an intellectual and emotional complex in an instant
of time." Some of his best and shortest poems do precisely that, for instance
his two-line "L'Art, 1910," in which he imitated the compression of the
newly discovered Japanese poetry to convey another joyous discovery, that
of the newest French painters:

> Green arsenic smeared on an egg-white cloth,
> Crushed strawberries! Come, let us feast our eyes.

In *Lustra* (1916), whose title was borrowed from the offerings made by the
censors "for the sins of the whole people," he devoted a dozen or more poems
to the discussion of the role of his own work. He was at his best when he was

most light-handed, when he declared that his "chansons" had made "a considerable stir in Chicago," that they had been praised because they were really "twenty years behind the times," and concluded that their emotions were "those of a maître de café."

By then he had begun to make his most lasting contribution. He spoke of his translations as "but more elaborate masks," and demonstrated the accuracy of that statement with great fertility. His version of "The Seafarer" (1912), as subsequent poets recognized, was no mere tour de force; it reopened the possibilities for alliterative verse. On the basis of such poems as "The River Merchant's Wife" and "Exile's Letter" in *Cathay* (1915), Eliot declared Pound to be "the inventor of Chinese poetry for our time." Of course Pound did not know Chinese, and expressed his great indebtedness to the manuscripts of the late American scholar Ernest Fenollosa, for whose labors the poet gained wider recognition. When Pound produced his "Homage to Sextus Propertius" (1918) other scholars took him to task for inaccuracies in rendering the Latin; but his "more elaborate masks" are never strict translations. They are his most successful original poems.

That may be seen most clearly by contrasting his living version of the corruptions of Augustan Rome with "Mœurs Contemporaines" (1915), wherein his attempt to satirize his own surroundings seems thin and even smarty. In his discussions of the theory of poetry Pound may put an undue stress upon the importance of the "inventors," the discoverers of "a particular process" of technique, but it is natural for a man to exaggerate his own forte. When he had a subject matter provided for him, and could devote all his attention to his metrical and verbal inventions, he produced work of solidity as well as brilliance. When his masks were simply variants of himself, he often betrayed a human emptiness. The one great exception is *Hugh Selwyn Mauberley* (1920), where he was sustained by a major emotion, his reaction against the war, and was also challenged by Eliot's first dramatic monologues on the same theme. *Mauberley* is Pound's nearest approach to a criticism of his age. Its hatred of the futility of war is unforgettable, though Pound was far from being able to envisage any positive social goals. His versification is at its most accomplished here. He and Eliot had agreed to tighten up their verse by basing some experiments on the stanzas of Gautier, and when Pound let himself go again after this discipline, he created, in the flowing lines of his "Envoi," a masterpiece of subtle music.

In one of the last poems of this series he wrote as an epitaph:

> "I was
> And I no more exist;
> Here drifted
> An hedonist."

Though it may not have been apparent at the time, the Ezra Pound period was really over, the period in which he had been at the vortex of creative activity, had championed new poets as different as Frost and Eliot, and had helped to find an audience for Joyce and Lawrence. *Mauberley* was his farewell to London. He settled in Paris for four years and then went on to Rapallo. He kept up his interest in music, but was presently to be distracted by economics. In the meantime he had begun to publish his *Cantos,* the single poem with which he was concerned after *Mauberley.*

Two master craftsmen of the age spoke of the *Cantos* with great respect. Eliot cited them as the chief evidence that Pound's poetry "is an inexhaustible reference book of verse forms." Yeats accepted, at the end of the twenties, Pound's contention that when "the hundredth canto is finished," the whole would "display a structure like that of a Bach fugue." Certain recurrent themes, the Homeric descent into hell, one of Ovid's metamorphoses of men into beasts, passages from the history of Renaissance and Chinese courts and the American Revolution are meant to be counterpointed against passages dealing with the modern world to compose a musical pattern and to display persistent continuities between past and present. Pound kept repeating that "an epic poem is a poem including history," but neglected to remember that an epic poem also builds upon a narrative structure. On the basis of the seventy-one cantos that had been issued by 1940, it seems no longer necessary to believe that the whole could be more than the sum of the parts. And the parts are best described in the opening line of the eighth Canto, "these fragments you have shelved," a variant of the phrase Eliot used at the close of *The Waste Land.* Pound also revealed his initial conception in a sentence subsequently excised from the second Canto:

> the "modern world"
> Needs such a grab-bag to stuff all its thought in.

He further denoted his content as

> the usual subjects
> Of conversation between intelligent men,

and there is no denying the virtuosity of the sustained speaking voice, even though it divagated into seemingly endless monologue, and often left the reader dazzled by the surface texture of the language, but with the sensation that it was hardly saying anything.

Perhaps it would have been better if it had continued so, or if Pound had remembered his earlier declaration that he was "against all forms of oppression." But in the years of the slump he grew concerned with the problem of the distribution of wealth, and became a convert to Social Credit, which appealed as a panacea to several literary men. He perceived sharply the abuses of finance capitalism, though he seems never to have been greatly concerned with any poverty except that of the artist. He was increasingly isolated in Italy, less and less in touch with the actual state of society in either England or America. As a result of his interest in Chinese literature he began to believe that he could think in "ideograms," and worked out several fantastic equivalents, such as that if Jefferson had been alive in 1933 he would have acted as Mussolini had done. He also seems to have equated Fascist order with Confucian order, and to have allowed his hatred of "usury" to become a hatred of "international Jewry." He became a catastrophic instance of what can happen when the artist loses all foothold in his society. From the familiar position of the Bohemian thumbing his nose at the bourgeois he drifted to the point where, in pathological insecurity, he was obsessed with the question of monetary control to the exclusion of everything else. With no adequate equipment to judge such matters, he deludedly accepted Mussolini's kind of control as the answer. When the war came he was not a turncoat. He broadcast for the Fascists the same crackbrained ideas he had been expressing in prose and verse for more than a decade. But now they rendered him subject to the charge of the gravest crime in a nation's laws. Pound was finally brought back to America as a prisoner in 1945, and escaped trial only on the ground that his irresponsible judgment gave evidence of "a paranoid state."

3

Eliot arrived in London after the outbreak of the First World War. Like Pound he came abroad as a student engaged with a doctoral thesis; but his background and equipment were very different. Born in St. Louis, where his clergyman grandfather had been the pioneer in carrying the Unitarian church to that part of the Middle West, Eliot had studied philosophy at Harvard, and had also been influenced by Irving Babbitt's reaffirmation of classicism. He had spent a year at the Sorbonne, where he had listened to lectures by Bergson, and was in Germany when war was declared. He completed his thesis on F. H. Bradley's idealism, but did not return to Harvard to take his degree. His first published poem "The Love Song of J. Alfred Prufrock," appeared in Poetry in 1915; but his growing preoccupation with literary tradition as a necessary sustenance for mature art led him to settle in England. What he valued in tradition was represented by such a line of poet-critics as Dryden, Johnson, Coleridge, and Arnold, and he had found in his America, outside the special climate of the university, no living interest in any such succession.

His first book, *Prufrock and Other Observations* (1917), displayed a poetic orientation all his own. His chief masters were the Jacobean metaphysical poets and the French symbolists, not so unlikely a starting point for an American poet as might appear, since a taste for Donne and Herbert had been deeply rooted in New England from Emerson through Emily Dickinson, and Baudelaire and his followers had been inspired by Poe. The witty and ironic conversational tones of Eliot's earliest poems are most akin, among the symbolists, to Laforgue, but a graver spirit than Laforgue's can already be discerned beneath the surface of what seemed to most of its first readers to be a mocking vers de société. The epigraph to "Prufrock" was taken from Dante, about whom Pound had also been enthusiastic. But their divergence of interest in this master was the same as it was regarding Henry James. In both cases Pound was primarily occupied with pointing out the technical excellences. Eliot penetrated more deeply into the meaning of the texts. His predominant interest is suggested in his remark that James' "real progenitor" is Hawthorne, and that the essential quality common to both these Americans is their "profound sensitiveness to good and evil."

A much firmer critic than Pound, Eliot was to teach, through both his verse and his prose, a way of seeing and feeling to a younger generation. Pound may first have stimulated him to realize that the authors of the past and present should be judged with equal eyes, that a sense of the past is not "of what is dead, but of what is already living." But Eliot's ethical values gave him far more insight into the meaning of history, just as his projection of spiritual struggles endowed his monologues with a dramatic tension quite missing in Pound's. As a result his Prufrock, Sweeney, and Gerontion, sparely drawn as they were, became some of the most living characters of their time. Prufrock, the fastidious and futile middle-aged product of the genteel tradition, and Sweeney, the tough Irishman "assured of certain certainties," are Eliot's chief response to the decadent Boston he knew as a young man, when the gulf between Back Bay and the common life of the South End was so great as to cause him to say that the former's "society" was "quite uncivilized, but refined beyond the point of civilization."

In "Gerontion" (1920), the leading poem in his second book, Eliot presented, through the *persona* of the old man, the mood of disillusion most symptomatic of the postwar era. He also produced one of the most significant examples of his dramatic method. This poem makes clear why he believed that Baudelaire, by using "the imagery of the sordid life of a great metropolis" and by raising it "to the first intensity," had "created a mode of release and expression for other men." Such a belief divides Eliot sharply from the generation of Frost. Eliot did not see man in the country but in the city. He did not see the self-assured Emersonian individual, but men in a chaotic society consumed with doubt. He had been attracted to the metaphysicals because their poetry had also sprung out of self-consciousness, out of the need to express not merely lyric feeling, but likewise the "hard precision" of thought. While reflecting on the achievement of the school of Donne, he made one of the most revelatory statements of his own aims:

It is not a permanent necessity that poets should be interested in philosophy, or in any other subject. We can only say that it appears likely that poets in our civilization, as it exists at present, must be *difficult*. Our civilization comprehends great variety and complexity, and this variety and complexity, playing upon a refined sensibility, must produce various and complex results.

Such, in his view, were the compelling grounds for devising the compressed, elliptical, and allusive method of his dramatic monologues. Only in such a way could he suggest the real fusion between feeling and thought in living brains, and, at the same time, pass beyond the too narrowly personal masks of Pound to portraits of a more general and more significant relevance.

He was not interested in experimentation for its own sake, since he noted, while discussing Wordsworth, that "any radical change in poetic form is likely to be the symptom of some very much deeper change in society and the individual." The imagists were on a false track in their attempted loosening of form, since "no *vers* is *libre* for the man who wants to do a good job," and since "the very life of verse" consists in the "constant evasion and recognition of regularity," in the precarious balance between monotony and flux. He had thought as persistently about the question of language, and held that it was the poet's responsibility to be as aware as possible of the historical weight of connotation behind the words he was using, and to master a diction that could range from the most erudite to the most colloquial, as the mind of the educated man must range.

As he extended his technical resources from "Gerontion" to *The Waste Land* (1922), he also demonstrated what he meant by a poet's "sense of his own age." This is something very different from a sense of journalistic surfaces, since it involves a recognition of the permanent no less than of the changing. As an inheritor of the nineteenth century's determination to repossess all of history, modern man could often have the feeling, as Eliot remarked in Joyce, "of everything happening at once." The duty of the critic was to train himself to the point where he could embrace the whole of literature since Homer as having "a simultaneous existence" in his mind, and composing "a simultaneous order." The philosophical historian must discern the phenomenon of cyclical recurrence, and thus the contemporaneity of various cultures. But such an extension of knowledge could become an oppressive burden if it left man with the feeling of "being too conscious, and conscious of too much." As Gerontion had cried out in a memorable line, "After such knowledge, what forgiveness?" Eliot had been profoundly impressed by Frazer's *Golden Bough,* but he had realized that the effect of comparative anthropology is both a freeing and a destruction, that taboos are removed but sanctions wither.

He gave voice to this awareness in *The Waste Land,* the most ambitious long poem of the period. Its structure is the opposite of the diffusion of the *Cantos,* since Eliot attempted to compress the essence of an epic into a poem of hardly more than four hundred lines. He omitted logical connectives, and the reader must find his way through this "music of ideas" in a way somewhat analogous to associating recurrent themes in a symphony. Eliot was much attacked for this method, though it was in deliberate keeping with his reasons for believing why modern poetry must be difficult In the effort to give further coherence to his structure he borrowed a device from Henry James, and introduced Tiresias, the prophet who had "foresuffered all," as a central observer who *"sees,* in fact, the substance of the poem." *The Waste Land* may not succeed as a whole, it may exist simply as a succession of dramatic lyrics. But it interpenetrates the present and the past, it manages to treat on the same plane modern London and the world of primitive myth, and to probe thereby at the root causes of cultural decay. In discerning the imaginative possibilities in the use of myth, Eliot was at one with the leading creative minds of the age. He knew that he had found "a way of controlling, of ordering, of giving a shape and a significance to the immense panorama of futility and anarchy that is contemporary history."

Eliot could envisage the modern metropolis as an Inferno more affectingly than Pound could in the *Cantos,* since, as he observed, Pound's "is a Hell for the *other people,* the people we read about in the newspapers, not for oneself and one's friends." This complacency, this lack of feeling implicated in the struggle with evil, necessarily rendered much of Pound's observation of human beings "trivial and accidental." Eliot's peculiar intensity comes from his conviction that poetry must spring out of suffering. What excited the first appreciators of *The Waste Land* were its astonishing juxtapositions, its sudden transitions from the witty to the serious, its bewildering variety of literary allusions, its passages of satire and its passages of lyric beauty, and its unfailing expertness in phrasing. Few recognized sufficiently, even when Eliot reached the pit of his Inferno in "The Hollow Men" (1925), how terrifying an exposure he was making of the emptiness of life without belief, or that his main theme was how much of modern life is merely death. That his overwhelming sense of the need for redemption must finally transform Eliot into a religious poet was not apparent to many at that time.

4

The most striking evidence of Eliot's pervasive influence upon even the most vigorous younger imagination of the 1920's is provided by Hart Crane's *The Bridge* (1930). Crane's short life is a record of the disintegration that can result from modern rootlessness. Born in Garrettsville, Ohio, the son of well-to-do but incompatible parents, his high-strung nervous system was to display in its instability lasting scars from the tensions between them. No one seems to have paid much attention to his education, and he was allowed to be on his own in New York in 1916, nominally preparing for college, but actually immersing himself in the new poetry. He was soon to declare that he considered Pound second only to Yeats among living poets in English, and was then to share in the contemporary excitement about the symbolists and the Elizabethan dramatists, with a particular taste for Rimbaud and Marlowe.

His first poems, collected in *White Buildings* (1926), reveal the extent to which he had been affected by the French poets' experiments with handling language plastically, with the "color" and weight" no less than the sound of words. He spoke of wanting to capture the "illogical impingements" of connotations, and of depending only upon "the logic of metaphor." He aimed to express the kind of heightened consciousness that he evoked in "Wine Menagerie," the ecstasy that hovered between music and drunkenness. The resulting poems were very dense and obscure, though some of them, like his elegy "Praise for an Urn," were sustained by a compelling rhetoric. In his series of "Voyages" this rhetoric took on a deep sonority in response to his feeling for the sea and for Melville.

In "The Marriage of Faustus and Helen" (1922–1923) he showed the effect of Eliot's interpenetration of past and present by recasting the myth in jazz rhythms, in what he called a "symphonic" form. But he was already concerned with "an almost complete reverse" of Eliot's direction. Instead of disillusion and renunciation he was bent upon "a more positive goal," and he defied his skeptical generation by affirming his belief in "ecstatic vision." *The Bridge,* upon which he worked intermittently for half a dozen years, was designed to be his most important refutation of *The Waste Land*. Convinced of the necessity for poets to repossess the amplitude of myth, his was to be "the myth of America" from our earliest history. The content of his poem was to be an "organic panorama, showing the continuous and living evidence of the past in the inmost vital substance of the present," and its title was meant to suggest an equally vital span into the future. His declared master was Whitman, since Crane wanted an expansive identification with our life in order to be able to make his "mystical synthesis."

But his immense difficulty in finishing this poem, and the stylistic inequality between its parts, betray how much of it was a mere act of will and not a product of his deepest consciousness. His awareness of American history was hardly more than of a romantic spectacle. He had taken the leap from the time of "Powhatan's daughter" into modern New York with nothing to sustain him. What affirmation could he make when he knew only the breakdown of his family, and no community except a shifting metropolis? Cast off by his father, who disapproved of his being a poet, he often had lived on the ragged edge of poverty. Partly in consequence of his early emotional insecurity, he was a homosexual. Unlike Rimbaud, as Allen Tate remarked, Crane did not cultivate "derangement"; his disorder was ingrained and almost inescapable. No matter how strong his admiration for Whitman, his tortured sensibility was far more akin to Poe's, whose ghost he invoked in his hallucinated passage portraying the subway.

He knew that the modern poet needs "gigantic assimilative capacities," and he struggled hard over his structure. But he came to depend more and more on an exaltation difficult to capture. He managed to possess it during some summer weeks in the Caribbean in 1926. "I feel an absolute music in the air again," he said, "and some tremendous rondure floating somewhere." He attained his single fullest interval of production, but was again dispersed as soon as he got back to New York. *The Bridge,* when finally published, was far less of a whole than *The Waste Land.* It veered from passages of the purest poetic energy, as in the proem to Brooklyn Bridge, "The Harbor Dawn" and "The River," to other passages of sentimental tawdriness. In one of the most perceptive essays by one of our poets about another, Tate, while recognizing Crane's immense gifts, pointed out his utter failure to rise, in his conclusion, "Atlantis," to the passage from the *Paradiso* which is his source. Crane's failure was that of the romantic ego to find any sanctions outside itself. His "vision" had degenerated into sensationalism.

With the depression Crane did not share in the growing social and economic interests of many of his friends. He felt those interests to be largely a substitute for creative work. But he was unable to settle to anything sustained. He went to Mexico on a fellowship, but he dissipated there even more heavily. On the boat home, after a year with nothing done, and following a night of drinking, he committed suicide by jumping overboard. He felt, in his terrible violent restlessness, that he had reached a dead end. But despite his disintegration he had never given up his belief that "a real work of art" is "simply a communication between man and man, a bond of understanding and human enlightenment." In such lyric passages as his evocation of the Mississippi, at the close of "The River," he had attained his "absolute music," and an eloquence which has been rivaled in magnificence by few American poets.

Diametrically opposed to Crane's promiscuous immersion in the modern city are the exponents of Southern regionalism. As Tate argued: "Only a return to the provinces, to the small self-contained centers of life, will put the all-destroying abstraction, America, safely to rest." Such a line of argument separates the Nashville agrarians from Middle Western regionalists like Sandburg and Lindsay, who were largely followers of Whitman. Another feature, which distinguishes them from any recent talents in New England, is that for many years, beginning with their magazine the *Fugitive* (1922–1925), they worked together as a group and issued such joint pronouncements as *I'll Take My Stand* (1930). Some of the values that they held in common were their preference for the concrete and the localized as against the abstract and the generalized; and when they spoke in philosophical terms they dwelt on the necessity to offset the domination of a dehumanized scientific rationalism by the richer resources of imagination. Their politics were devoted to the preservation of tradition, and seeing the local menaced by the national, particularly through industrialization, they protested against the machine and against money values as the causes of modern rootlessness. Tate called himself a "reactionary," and some of the less clear minds of the group, taking their stand even against the racial reforms of the New Deal, drifted dangerously close to native Fascism.

Wholly free from such implications is John Crowe Ransom, who as a teacher of literature at Vanderbilt University was the moving force behind the *Fugitive*. Ransom is a poet of very limited production, the bulk of whose verse appeared in *Chills and Fever* (1924) and *Two Gentlemen in Bonds* (1927). If he could have managed to write poetry of so much suavity and elegance in any previous period of our history, he would be known by now as the kind of artist of whom we have had too few, the minor poet, not of promise but of a remarkably integrated and mature performance within his limitations. He is a serious wit in a sense akin to the seventeenth century poets, though he seems to have shaped his style independently of their revival, and to have received the impetus for his character studies rather from Hardy's *Satires of Circumstance*. He reflected on how a living tradition may make its adjustment to the Southern past in poems like "Antique Harvesters," where his diction is properly both slightly archaic and conversational. But his main theme is that of the divided sensibility, torn between reason and imagination, between science and faith. As he says in "Man Without Sense of Direction," he concentrates primarily on portraying the kind of character "who cannot fathom nor perform his nature." To the exposure of such states of consciousness he brings his most distinguishing gift, an irony which, as R. P. Warren pointed out, differs basically from all our familiar variants of romantic irony, since it is not used as a means of escape from an individual's predicament. Ransom's irony, in its experienced acceptance of human limitations, is an inheritance from Socratic irony, and is a device for gaining knowledge by offsetting any abstract ideal against a concrete actual. His poems, avoiding thereby any oversimplified statements, possess a remarkable fullness of body.

Allen Tate, growing up in the period when Eliot's criticism was making its first impact, shows in much of his verse the kind of intellectualization from which Eliot's richer lyrical impulse saved him, the intellectualization of a mind in which the analytical function outruns the creative. Despite Tate's objection to the limiting abstractness of so much modern knowledge, many of his poems are conceived very abstractly. He indicates his kinship with Ransom in remarking: "I often think of my poems as commentaries on those human situations from which there is no escape." In "The Last Days of Alice" he presents his version of the difficulty of belief in a mathematician's age; in "The Wolves" he probes to the sources of recent neurotic fear. In his best known poem, "Ode to the Confederate Dead," he deliberately contrasts the "active faith" of the Southern past with the contemporary "solipsism . . . that denotes the failure of the human personality to function properly in nature and society." Despite too numerous echoes of Eliot and Valéry, Tate's structure and rhythm have attained here a rare elevation and dignity.

If Tate's poetry reveals the results of tastes formed closely upon Eliot's, that of Robert Penn Warren, the youngest of the Fugitive group, furnishes the fullest evidence of what it meant to begin writing verse when the metaphysical poets had just been revived as a central influence upon creative activity. Some of Warren's early poems, especially "The Garden" and "Love's Parable," are thorough responses to the possibilities of reintroducing techniques like those of Marvell. Warren paid the price of his preoccupation with intellectual complexity by sacrificing almost any audience for his poetry except other poets and critics. But just after 1940 he was to start breaking away from such tight organization as he had used in poems of great moral weight like "Original Sin" and "Terror." In his "Ballad of Billie Potts" he renewed his approach to Southern history and made an attempt to combine what Yeats called "the poetry of the folk" and "the poetry of the coteries."

5

The diversity of the poetry of this time and the impossibility of arranging it into any single pattern may be sufficiently indicated by noting that Robinson Jeffers was born only a year before both Ransom and Eliot. His purposes are as far removed from either of theirs as the six thousand miles that separate Carmel and London. Born in Pittsburgh, the son of a Presbyterian theologian, he was educated partly in Europe, and manifested a range of intellectual curiosity by making some study of medicine, forestry, and zoology in various institutions on the Pacific coast. His first volume of poems, *Flagons and Apples* (1912), is as conventionally romantic as it sounds. He registered no response to any of the new poetic movements, and not until a dozen years later, in his narrative poem *Tamar,* did he find a voice of his own. In *The Tower Beyond Tragedy, Roan Stallion* (1925), and *The Women at Point Sur* (1927), he established both his content and his philosophy.

The plots of his long poems are of an unrelieved violence, presenting incest, rape, and murder, usually against the background of the bare California headlands and valleys. He chose this material deliberately. He insisted that since the First World War physical violence was no longer "anachronistic" in our lives; and he justified his treatment of sexual perversions on the ground that he wanted to "strip everything but its natural ugliness from the unmorality." Beyond that he developed his stories to present a thesis: "There is no health for the individual whose attention is taken up with his own mind and processes; equally there is no health for the society that is always introverted on its own members." That thesis would seem to rest on a basic confusion between psychology and politics, since the normal way for an individual to escape from excessive introversion is through a more outgoing interest in human society. But Jeffers holds, "Humanity is the mold to break away from, the atom to be split," and he carries his inhumanity to the point of announcing that "the unsocial birds are a greater race." In the light of such views it is no wonder that he possesses very little ability to represent dramatic action, since his characters exist only as symbols and stereotypes.

Some of his shorter poems are far more moving, since he has a broad descriptive mastery of his spectacular coast of granite and cypress, and his other interest in the exact processes of science enables him to give almost clinical accounts of moments of death—of man as well as of the "nobler" hawk. The form that he devised may superficially suggest Whitman, but though he believes that "a tidal recurrence is the one essential quality of the speech of poetry," he went far beyond Whitman in his understanding of the possibilities of accentual prosody, and of the "quantitative" value of his unstressed syllables. His handling of such verse, though monotonous in long stretches, is capable of passages of a grave majesty.

His view of the future of America is at the opposite pole from Whitman's. Jeffers' admirers have often spoken of him as universal, as beyond the restrictions of time or place, but he may best be understood as a peculiar kind of regionalist, a spokesman for the "continent's end" when the frontier movement was over, and the poet was aware of the oppressively luxuriant growth of Los Angeles and Hollywood. "Ascent to the Sierras," "Haunted Country," and "Apology for Bad Dreams" all offset primitive and austere nature against an overrich and soft civilization. In "Shine, Perishing Republic" (1926) he already dwelt on the decadence of American society, and revealed the extent to which he had been influenced by Spengler. With the depression and the advance of Fascism, he merely kept repeating that "civilization is a transient sickness." He declared that we had gutted and exploited a continent in our reckless western onrush, and that we deserved no better fate than to be oppressed by an imperialistic Caesar. He believed that in such times an individual must "isolate himself morally to a certain extent or else degenerate too." From his tower retreat at Carmel he averred that he was merely a "neutral" recorder of social decay. But he scorned the city proletariat, and insisted on the futility of any radical social reform. His irrationality also drove him to the length of announcing, despite his lifelong pacifism, that he preferred the greater dignity of "blind war" to any economic planning. In "Rearmament" he betrayed the unconscious worship of force to which his acceptance of Spengler had brought him by celebrating the "beauty" in "the disastrous rhythm . . . of the dream-led masses down the dark mountain."

6

In the years just at the end of the First World War when college undergraduates were more excited about contemporary American poetry than they had ever been before, such sinister thoughts were farthest from their minds. The popular taste of the twenties can be best caught in Edna St. Vincent Millay and Stephen Vincent Benét. Miss Millay's "Renascence" (1912) heralded her arrival at Vassar from Maine, and already contained the essence of what was to make her popular: an innocent freshness toward nature, which is none the less compounded out of the attitudes of the English romantic poets. She was soon to add the gamin boldness of the Greenwich Village Bohemian, and her quatrain about the candle burning at both its ends was hailed by the young anti-Victorians as their "Psalm of Life."

Her audience was increased by *Second April* (1921) and *The Harp-Weaver* (1923), and she was praised particularly by those who disliked the new intellectual poetry. The critical division over her work may be observed in the reception accorded *Fatal Interview* (1931). Some did not hesitate to liken this sonnet sequence to Shakespeare's. Others, upon more exacting scrutiny, insisted that even the most striking of these sonnets, such as "O sleep forever in the Latmian cave," did not wholly escape incoherence of feeling and blurred syntax. The fairest comparison for Miss Millay's qualities and limitations would be with the posthumous sonnet sequence by Elinor Wylie in *Angels and Earthly Creatures* (1929). Turning seriously to poetry only during the last decade of her life, Mrs. Wylie demonstrated how a romantic sensibility could be strengthened and purified by a taste for the metaphysicals, whereas, despite the phrase from Donne that forms her title, Miss Millay's sonnets remain enthusiastically but loosely Keatsian. Mrs. Wylie was the more mature craftsman, even though her personal distinction may have caused her friends to exaggerate her original force. As Morton Zabel said in reviewing her work: "In literature, as in life, there is room only for a few important experiences, but for many amenities." Her rewarding amenity is her deft and delicate control of her traditional medium, in contrast with most of Edna Millay's work. Miss Millay is at her best when freest from any emulation of other writers, in a poem like "The Return" (1934), the simplest kind of personal lyric. When she tried to go beyond lyrics, she showed little skill—though she produced, to be sure, in *The King's Henchman* (1926), a workmanlike libretto for an opera. She shared generously in the protest against the execution of Sacco and Vanzetti, but the poems she wrote on that occasion are hardly memorable. When she sought, under the growing pressures of the late thirties, to stir up an awareness of international problems, she fell into thin sentiment and hackneyed phrases.

Stephen Benét, as the son of an army officer, was brought up in various parts of the United States, and absorbed an interest in the American scene and its historical background. His precocious first poems gave evidence of another absorption, in the literary ballad as handled by William Morris and other late nineteenth century poets. He was to fuse these two interests in some of his best work, ballads using the material of American folklore and humor, of which "William Sycamore" (1923) is probably the most notable. Like Edna Millay he was also to participate in the gay revolt against the Victorians, particularly in the ebullience of "For All Blasphemers."

In *John Brown's Body* (1928) he solidified his gifts and produced the most widely read long poem of the period. In the view of some readers this work established Benét as the first national poet of the dimensions called for by Whitman; but Harriet Monroe characterized it as "a cinema epic." Composed within a couple of years, this full-length novel in a variety of verse forms testifies to its author's technical facility, as well as to his gusto for the personalities of the Civil War. But there are many slack pages, his fictional plots are rather expected, and most of his characters are two-dimensional. Such a work raises the problem of popular art in modern society. Benét's talents have not been considered as of anything like the first order by many other poets; and *John Brown's Body* has kept its largest following among readers under twenty. But such an audience is not to be scorned in a democracy, and Benét's share in reviving the bright colors of our heroic legends puts him squarely in the succession from Longfellow and Lindsay. The most striking defect of this poem is in its passages of reflection, which skip over grave problems with a delusive jauntiness. Benét had grown to understand more of our history when he wrote his "Ode to Walt Whitman" against the background of the depression; and in "Litany for Dictatorships" (1936) and "Nightmare at Noon" (1940), he looked ahead, much more affectingly than Miss Millay, to the menace of the war. In *Western Star,* the first section of a long poem on which he had been working for some years at his death, he still manifested the same warm feeling for the American land, if little advance in technique beyond his first attempted epic.

Archibald MacLeish, who was at Yale just ahead of Benét, performed another serviceable function by being a kind of middleman of taste between the experimenters and the general public. Reading his work from *The Pot of Earth* (1925) down to *America Was Promises* (1939) is to be presented with a chronicle of the dominant new influences in that period. He began writing verse as an undergraduate, but he dated his own poetic career from 1923, when he gave up the practice of law and went to live in France. At that time he reflected Eliot's interest in *The Golden Bough,* particularly in the theme of cyclical death and rebirth. He also utilized Eliot's technique of sudden contrasts to convey the broken rhythm of contemporary existence. A few years later, in "Land's End," he was bringing to American readers the wide-space imagery of Perse's *Anabase.* He demonstrated how much he had learned from Pound's versification in *Conquistador* (1932), and in its most successful portion, "Bernál Diaz' Preface to His Book," he extended the world-weary attitude of Gerontion. But he had returned to America by the end of the twenties, and was soon responding to the new mood of social protest. His *Frescoes for Mr. Rockefeller's City* (1933) was dedicated to Sandburg, and in *Public Speech* and his radio play, *The Fall of the City,* he caught up some of the tones and accents of the younger poets, particularly Auden. MacLeish was characterized throughout these years by generous enthusiasms, as well as by a sensitive ear, but he was too suggestible to possess a style quite his own. The conspicuous exception was in some of his short lyrics, like "The Too Late Born," or "You, Andrew Marvell," authentic expressions of his own elegiac emotion.

7

The period to which MacLeish served as a barometer was notable for a great deal more experimentation than can even be suggested here. Indeed, a leading aim of such an experimentalist as E. E. Cummings is to make it impossible to describe one of his poems or to do anything less than respond to its unique essence. His idiosyncratic treatment of punctuation and typography, which either excited or distracted his first readers, is his way of catching the eye and compelling attention. His content is actually very simple. He is a lyricist of romantic love, who is also a romantic anarchist in the New England tradition, and believes that a poem is an inspired moment breaking through the bars of syntax. His preoccupations hardly vary from the time of *Tulips and Chimneys* (1923). "Mostpeople" are frozen into conventional death, whereas "there's nothing as something as one"; the individual alone is alive, and that life is freshened by love, by "wonderful one times one." In his fleeting attention to "manunkind" in the mass, Cummings strikes a note of colloquial satire against some of its misleaders, particularly the advertiser and the warmonger.

Conrad Aiken, at Harvard with Eliot, is an experimentalist of a different sort from Cummings. His poems are not designed to startle and shock the reader into an awareness of life's potential freshness. On the contrary, Aiken lulls the reader with a seductive music, and transports him into the dreamworld of Freudian fantasy. He was skeptical from the outset of Amy Lowell's Imagists because of their lack of emotional force, and took exception to their content as merely "the semi-precious in experience." But his own double concern with music and psychology served unwittingly to rob most of his many long poems of any great energy. In evoking "the melody of chaos" his series of *Preludes* risked what Yvor Winters has called "the fallacy of imitative form." Their lines tended to deliquesce into a murmuring indefiniteness of language, into a realm where the consciousness is blurred and "the maelstrom has us all." Aiken escaped from this dilemma through the more concrete imagery of some of his poetry dealing with the impact of the city upon the sensitive observer. In "Discordants" and "Senlin" he was writing poems of this sort at the same time as Eliot's earliest work; and he returned to this genre, with very seasoned technical resources, in *Brownstone Eclogues,* at the beginning of the forties.

Two other experimentalists whose importance cannot be more than stated were both friends of Pound when he was a student at the University of Pennsylvania. William Carlos Williams was then in the medical school, while Marianne Moore was an undergraduate at Bryn Mawr. Williams, of mixed English, French, Spanish, and Jewish extraction, was to make his living as a doctor, mainly to the working class in Rutherford, New Jersey. That fact had a considerable effect on his work. Very responsive at first to the Imagists, he grew to see that their kind of poetry fell short because it lacked "structural necessity." Even more significant, his sensual delight, like Lawrence's, soon became grounded in the homeliest images of our common life. He defined "the classic" as "the local fully realized, words marked by a place"; and, diverging farthest from Pound, he added a warm sympathy with ordinary people to an ability to discover beauty in the midst of the impoverished and the sordid. Many—perhaps most—of his poems were far too casual, in the imagist mode which he never quite outgrew, but at his best, in "By the road to the contagious hospital" or "The Yachts," he reinforced his unfailingly vivid notations by impressive structures.

Marianne Moore drew attention to the genre to which her poetry belongs by calling one of her few books *Observations* (1924). When asked once what distinguished her, she answered: "Nothing; unless it is an exaggerated tendency to visualize; and on encountering manifestations of life—insects, lower animals, or human beings—to wonder if they are happy and what will become of them." She was called an "objectivist," as Williams had styled himself, and Kenneth Burke offered this definition for her kind of work: "In objectivism, though an object may be chosen for treatment because of its symbolic or subjective references, once it has been chosen it is to be studied in its own right." That helps account for the loving care with which she studied the jerboa or a fish or Peter the cat. She is feminine in a very rewarding sense, in that she makes no effort to be major.

Her versification, which was praised by both Eliot and Wallace Stevens, is like no one else's. She composes not by feet but by syllables: the result is not free verse but a formal, sometimes light, sometimes rigid pattern. She described her intentions by saying: "Over accent and over emphasis are to be avoided . . . and I feel that mathematics as we have it in music, can be of inestimable help to a poet." The danger in such deliberate work is always dryness, but Miss Moore devoted herself unremittingly to values. The titles of several of her poems, "When I Buy Pictures," "Critics and Connoisseurs," "Picking and Choosing," suggest how a poem for her is also an act of discrimination. In "Poetry" she indicated her desire to be, like Yeats, "a literalist of the imagination," and gave her best known definition of what authentic imagination must produce: "imaginary gardens with real toads in them."

Since the history of poetry is, in the last analysis, made up of poems and not of poets, no account of this period should fail to mention such impressive achievements as "The Ballad of a Strange Thing" (1927) by Phelps Putnam or "Ode to the Sea" (1937) by Howard Baker. Putnam was another New England romantic who projected, though he did not manage to complete, a highly personal handling of the American hero in search of experience. Baker, on the other hand, made the best fulfillment so far of the kind of classical revival sponsored by Yvor Winters at Stanford. His "Ode" may seem at first glance merely a formal exercise, but it cuts to the heart of our age when it proclaims: "Man is collective. Change is sure."

Such proclamations characterized the shift from the twenties into the thirties, but for the most part the new political and economic interests were more effectively expressed in novels and plays than in verse. Though Sandburg, as we have seen, made a renewed Whitmanesque affirmation in *The People, Yes,* no younger group emerged here at all comparable in quality to the new English poets surrounding Auden. Among the poets who began to be known in the thirties, Horace Gregory added to Crane's city a serious knowledge of our public issues, and Kenneth Fearing used the freest of rhythms for a harsh staccato satire, while Langston Hughes continued to contribute left-wing blues, and Muriel Rukeyser, among many others, brought warm social sympathies to an imperfect search for the proper form. In 1938 Delmore Schwartz produced *In Dreams Begin Responsibilities,* which was hailed as the most promising first book of the decade. Karl Shapiro, who was not to be generally known until after the outbreak of the Second World War, was by then just beginning to appear in the little magazines.

8

During the thirties Wallace Stevens had been cutting through all the conventional divisions between poetic generations, and was to prove himself another kind of artist of whom we have had too few instances in America, the one who is more fertile at sixty than at twenty-five. Stevens' life provides an extreme instance of the isolation of the American artist. Nearer to Frost than to Eliot in age, he studied at Harvard, and subsequently became an insurance lawyer in Hartford. He developed his talent apart from the stimulus of any group. His first poems did not appear in *Poetry* until he was thirty-five, and not until he was forty-four did he publish a book, *Harmonium* (1923). That unusual title, which signifies "a small reed organ," calls attention to Stevens' pervasive interest in music. He also spoke of "the essential gaudiness of poetry," and embodied in his lines an extraordinary brilliance of color, a flair for the exotic and the gorgeous, a fondness for ornamental words that he also relished for their unexpected connotations, a fondness too for "rosy chocolate and gilt umbrellas" and for "good, fat, guzzly fruit." His lushness was linked by some critics with the new material luxury of the twenties. He was also called "a dandy of eloquence" on the basis of such poems as "Le Monocle de mon oncle." The contrast with "Prufrock" is revelatory. Stevens once mentioned his debt to "the lightness, the grace, the sound and the color of the French," and he is more at his ease among such qualities than Eliot. His irony is much less stringent, and he did not feel the intellectual urgency that carried Eliot to the metaphysicals. Stevens also elaborated a rhetoric more traditionally formal in its periods than the dramatic speech Eliot wanted. His polish and elegance, again the attributes of the dandy, partly mask his graver concerns, but in "Sunday Morning" his epicureanism is aware of the problems encountered by modern man through the disappearance of the sanctions of the supernatural. His longest poem, "The Comedian As the Letter C" presents various stages of the artist in his struggles with reality.

He was to write very little during the next decade, and a reissue of *Harmonium* in the early thirties added hardly more than a dozen short poems. But with *Ideas of Order* (1935) he inaugurated a period of greatly increased productivity. Both the title and the contents of this new book puzzled some readers who had grown to expect from Stevens the heady flamboyance of "The Emperor of Ice Cream." But Horace Gregory had already discerned that Stevens was not merely a connoisseur of the senses, but also a trained observer of "the decadence that follows the rapid acquisition of wealth and power." Some of Stevens' longer meditations may betray by their diffuseness of structure and the inconclusiveness of their thought his lonely lack of interchange with other minds; but poems like "The Men That Are Falling" poise his matured resources against the growing menace of disorder.

His most persistent subject is the opposition between bare reality and what the imagination can make of it, a subject which he shares in part with Williams. But Stevens had thought more deeply upon the nature of art and celebrated

> The magnificent cause of being,
> The imagination, the one reality
> In this imagined world.

He worked out the implications of that paradox most thoroughly in *The Man with the Blue Guitar* (1937). By suggesting the example of Picasso, he insisted that art, even when seeming to distort reality, may actually bring us to a heightened awareness of it. Standing himself apart from political movements, Stevens made the nature of art the content of many poems, and thought of the activity of the poet as demanding resistance to pressures from without, pressures of too unrelieved fact. He knew that "a violent order is disorder," and he held that the imagination is in a sense an escape, but an escape to our proper domain. He believed that the poet's role "is to help people to lead their lives," but that he does so by transforming them into epicures, since the poet is a lover "of the world he contemplates and thereby enriches." When the greatest violence broke in 1939, Stevens went on to probe what basis for any humanism remained in his "Examination of the Hero in a Time of War." The contours of that examination were still to be extended, but whatever his resolved philosophy, Stevens had established himself as a poet of "the ultimate elegance: the imagined land." As the thirties drew to their close, he was increasingly regarded by younger poets as the man of richest sensibility who was writing poetry in America at that time.

Meanwhile Eliot had been running counter to the most widespread tendencies of the age, ever since he announced his conversion to Anglo-

Catholicism near the end of the twenties. The reasons for his decision were revealed indirectly in some remarks he made about Pascal:

I can think of no Christian writer, not Newman even, more to be commended to those who doubt, but who have the mind to conceive, and the sensibility to feel, the disorder, the futility, the meaninglessness, the mystery of life and suffering, and who can only find peace through a satisfaction of the whole being.

His declared position, at the same time, as "a royalist in politics," had far less reputable sanctions, since it seems to have been strongly affected by Charles Maurras and *L'Action française,* later to be thoroughly discredited for fascist sympathies. Eliot's discussion of politics was never very coherent, though his spiritual depth saved him from Pound's disasters. Some badly chosen sentences in *After Strange Gods* (1934) veered close to anti-Semitism, but after the rise of Hitler to power Eliot regarded the ethically inert and negative society of the democracies as better at least than positive evil. He made no more telling observation upon the relation of the individual to society than a comment on "the Catholic paradox: society is for the salvation of the individual and the individual must be sacrificed to society. Communism is merely a heresy, but a heresy is better than nothing."

Eliot's later poems, from *Ash Wednesday* (1930) through the *Four Quartets,* which were inaugurated by "Burnt Norton" in 1935, must be judged like any other poems, not on the basis of whether we accept or reject their theology, but of whether they have conveyed in moving rhythms the sense that, whatever their author's final beliefs, he is here reflecting perceptively and persuasively on human nature as we know it. By any such test, *Ash Wednesday* may well prove to be his most integrated long poem, as it certainly is a remarkable musical whole. Its themes are not calculated for popularity. They do not give voice to easy affirmation. Their realm is that of a Purgatorio, where suffering is made more acute by doubt, by "stops and steps of the mind" between skepticism and assurance. But their integrity to actual experience allows them to fulfill what Eliot believes to be one of the most valuable services of poetry, its power to make us "a little more aware of the deeper unnamed feelings which form the substratum of our being, to which we rarely penetrate; for our lives are mostly an evasion of ourselves."

In *Four Quartets* (1943) he illustrated his conviction that "the use of recurrent themes is as natural to poetry as to music." Looking back now over the past generation, he here finds our poetry to have been most characterized by its "search for a proper modern colloquial idiom." But he holds that we may be nearing another stage: "When we reach a point at which the poetic idiom can be stabilized, then a period of musical elaboration can follow." The

Quartets undertake such elaboration in a very different style from the witty paradoxes and conceits with which he formerly emulated the metaphysicals. Here he balances passages of meditative declaration against formal lyrics. His early work was difficult in its form, these poems are difficult in their thought. Their logic is sufficiently straightforward, but they present the reader with discourse largely unfamiliar to a secular age. The poet's reflections on time and memory return to his interest in Bergson, but Eliot is primarily occupied with the Christian conception of how man lives both "in and out of time," of how he is immersed in the flux and yet can penetrate to the eternal by apprehending timeless existence within time and above it. No less central to his mind is the doctrine of Incarnation, of God become man through the Savior, since Eliot holds that the nineteenth century substitution of Deification, of man becoming God through his own potentialities, led ineluctably through hero worship to dictatorship. Eliot had now found a more solid basis for his politics, as he demonstrated in his play, *Murder in the Cathedral* (1935), where he contrasted Christian law with violent usurpation of the fascist kind. It was easy to say that Eliot's religious poems were not widely representative of the age; but in a period of breakdown, moving into the shadow of war, they constituted some of the most sustained, if most somber, devotional poetry since the seventeenth century.

80. SUMMARY IN CRITICISM

THE function of literary criticism is perhaps rather to analyze and define the forces already at work in a living literature than to provide the impetus for new work. Yet, if it is good criticism, it should do both of these things, and the existence of an active, almost an organized, literary criticism in the years from 1925 to 1945—a criticism in working harmony with the best of contemporary creative writing—is perhaps the most convincing evidence of the ultimate importance of American literature during those years.

The writers of this criticism, no less than their fellow workers among novelists and poets, were continuators in several distinct lines of intention and method that had already declared themselves by 1925. Even though they yielded some of the larger conceptions of literature and art to specializations of technique, analysis, and social and moral thought, they retained the persistent Emersonian hope of a "liberation" for American literature as it had been revived in the decade 1910–1920 by such pioneers of the modern movement as Brooks, Bourne, and Mencken. They did not abandon the idea of the "new" —of aesthetic innovation, of moral and intellectual revision, of social and political adventure—so insistent in the first flush of literary radicalism in the earlier period. The conditions of 1915, however disturbed or distanced by ominous and destructive events, were still the conditions of 1945, and they were still shaping the literature and the criticism of that later day.

2

The description of modern literary criticism must therefore begin with recapitulation. The hazardous task of allocating a distinct character to the product of each of the three decades between 1915 and 1945 may be simplified as follows. The years from 1915 to 1925 were, as we have seen in an earlier chapter, devoted primarily to an attack on tradition, on conservatism, and on those vested interests—call them Idealism, Puritanism, "the genteel tradition," sentimentality, or whatever shibboleth was convenient at the time—that represented the time-lag, the forces of reaction, the "demon of the absolute," to the younger forces of insurgence and rebellion. It was a decade not only of a "new poetry," a "new novel," and a "new drama," but of a "new criticism" whose exponents fell generally into two groups: the realists and iconoclasts led by Brooks, Bourne, Mencken, Lewis Mumford, Ludwig Lewisohn, and Max Eastman; and the aesthetic rebels who, stepping forward from the ground prepared by Santayana, Huneker, Lewis Gates, and J. E. Spingarn, were now led by Ezra Pound and T. S. Eliot. The two groups differed in their artistic and technical principles, but they were allied in their resistance to a common enemy. They were fortunate in having the support of a new generation of American writers. They were, step by step, accompanied in the demonstration and defense of their tenets by actual literary production. They were able to carry through to successful public vindication the efforts of creative artists who were sharing their battle and reinforcing their attack. Yet in spite of their spirit of revolt and their apparent total newness, the presence in their thought and in their programs of some part of the traditional American idealism is as unmistakable as is the use of skeptical rather than prophetic, controversial rather than inspirational, methods of reestablishing it.

By the middle of the twenties, the campaign of these pioneers was generally won, both critically and popularly. A new sensibility was established in American writing. A new enthusiasm, in that decade of excited enthusiasms, had spread the contagion of irreverence, of realism, of "debunking," and of a fresh aesthetic spirit across the country. The first phase of modern criticism was an established event, with the *American Mercury* under Mencken's editorship its popular mouthpiece, the *Dial* its most important aesthetic journal, the *Nation* and the *New Republic* its chief weekly defenders, and writers of acceptably classic stature—Dreiser, Cather, Lewis, Robinson, Sandburg, Anderson, Pound, and Eliot—the witnesses to its variety and its vitality.

The following decade, dating roughly from 1925 to 1935 or a little beyond (some may prefer to date it from October, 1929, to September, 1939, for historical convenience), shows the altered character which any movement assumes when it has emerged from the heat of first encounters and begins to rest on established claims and achievements. Then, with immediate objectives gained, it meets its opposition on more serious terms and comes to grips with a more sober and serious challenge. Inevitably, this decade showed a sharper dividing of forces than the one which preceded it. It was obliged to put its claims to proof, and to subject its defiance to the tests of more serious issues in the moral and social realities of experience. It was a decade that brought forward a new kind of argument, and it was marked by at least two great controversies that took on the character of public, even political, contention.

The first of these controversies was the battle between the Humanists and the Realists. This conflict, already gathering strength during the preceding fifteen years, broke out in full mobilization in 1930 when Irving Babbitt and Paul Elmer More, accompanied by lieutenants like Norman Foerster, Robert Shafer, Gorham Munson, and Prosser Hall Frye, led the defense of traditional and conservative moral values, while a large phalanx of modernist critics—Edmund Wilson, Burton Rascoe, Malcolm Cowley, Kenneth Burke, Allen Tate, R. P. Blackmur, Lewis Mumford—reconciled their differences by defending the critical and creative insurgence.

For several years around 1930 the opposition of these two schools of literature filled the journals and magazines of America; their hostility was presented in full scale in the two anthologies which appeared in that year: *Humanism and America,* defending the Humanist position, and *The Critique of Humanism,* which stated the resistance. In these two books the two lines of thought that had descended from the nineteenth century were fully displayed: the ethical and moral arguments that had their roots in religious orthodoxy, on the one side; the social realism and liberal emancipation of Emerson's and Whitman's lineage, combined now with aesthetic rebellion, on the other. No public controversy in the entire history of American criticism has ever presented the divided inheritance of American literature more expressly. The Humanist controversy was the testing ground of a major antithesis, a radical division, in American beliefs. It acted as a climax of a long-prepared rivalry of forces in the native culture. It served as a watershed of critical energies and ideas. And when it was over, when the heat and considerable smoke of the hostilities had cleared from the air, there was no longer any possibility of mistaking the fundamental hiatus in contemporary critical thought, or of failing to recognize that when a new impulse asserted itself in American literature, the divided forces would find themselves not cleanly and simply divided, but complexly and inextricably involved in their purposes.

Curiously, an issue such as the Humanist controversy raised does not permit liberalism or insurgence to retain their earlier advantages. It insists on a consolidation of beliefs and arguments on both sides. After the Humanist orthodoxy had been checked and repudiated by the defenders of liberalism, these liberals themselves were propelled toward a solidification of their faith and toward an orthodoxy or dogmatism of their own. It was no longer permitted to espouse a free experimental realism, an enthusiastic democratic socialism, a negative skepticism, or an uninhibited iconoclasm such as had been possible in the days of Brooks and Mencken. It became necessary to show a more positive faith, an explicit program of social and realistic action; and this came to hand, during the thirties, in the tenets of Marxism. Thus the second major controversy of the thirties came into being, with Marxism and the dialectic materialism as its doctrine, and the world-wide economic depression and political disturbance of that decade as its incitement toward applying the responsibilities of literature to an immediate program of political action.

3

The Marxist position of these critics had been prepared, in the United States, during the preceding quarter-century. Forerunners like Thorstein Veblen, Floyd Dell, Upton Sinclair, Max Eastman, and V. F. Calverton had been active for fully three decades. Journals like the *Masses,* its successors the *Liberator* and the *New Masses,* were its chief organs, with newspapers like the *New Leader* and the *Socialist Call* carrying on the defense of socialist claims in both political and literary fields, and with more specialized organs like the *Partisan Review, Science and Society,* and *Politics* soon to represent the scholarly and sectarian positions which Marxist radicalism generated.

The necessity in criticism of socialist claims was nothing new. But it now appeared that the pioneers in this movement in the earlier years of the twentieth century had submitted too easily to the "malady" of the humanitarian ideal to satisfy their inheritors. They had accepted "the promise of American life" in too mystical and Whitmanian a spirit, compromising too easily with the hopes of rugged individualism or democratic culture, and holding aloof from committal to positive beliefs. The nineteenth and early twentieth century reformers most acceptable to American thinking had been acceptable because they left their revolutionary ardors at a mid-point of compromise, and stopped short of imposing the technical and forcible reforms of economic socialism. They were still adherents to the thinking of Whitman, Emerson, Howells, Henry George, and Edward Bellamy—the meliorists or gradualists of an older tradition. Books like Veblen's *The Theory of the Leisure Class* (1899), Upton Sinclair's *The Industrial Republic* (1907), V. F. Calverton's *The Newer Spirit* (1925) and *The Liberation of American Literature* (1932) asserted a more positive line of action. In 1931 Eastman's *The Literary Mind: Its Place in an Age of Science* joined science with socialism in disputing the liberal and aesthetic leniency of the foregoing generation.

But even more positive statements of socialist and communist orthodoxy now appeared. They came in Michael Gold's contributions to the *New Masses;* in Calverton's journal, the *Modern Monthly;* in the columns of the *New Republic* during its phase of Marxist sympathies. Malcolm Cowley's book of 1934, *Exile's Return,* described the conversion of an American expatriate, who had taken refuge in Paris in the years of the "lost generation," to social and economic realities. Joseph Freeman wrote a typical record of political conversion in his *American Testament* (1936). Waldo Frank wrote *The Re-Discovery of America* (1929) in terms of a discovery of the economic imperatives underlying cultural optimism. A series of American Writers' Congresses were staged in New York under the Marxist (or, as was claimed by dissidents, under Stalinist) auspices of the League of American Writers in 1935, 1937, and 1939. The division between Stalinists and Trotskyists became a major cleavage among Marxist radicals. Granville Hicks' book, *The Great Tradition* (1933, revised 1935), addressed itself to the task of bringing the later literary history of America into line with the Marxist propositions and historical claims. And a wide variety of critics, as often disagreeing as agreeing in their specific methods or allegiances, followed the Marxist line: Hicks, Gold, Edwin Berry Burgum, Joshua Kunitz, and Newton Arvin in general agreement with the official Communist position of that moment; Edmund Wilson, Kenneth Burke, Philip Rahv, James T. Farrell, Dwight Macdonald, William Phillips, and the contributors to the *Partisan Review* in terms of increasing dissent from the party program as its authoritarian and Stalinist dominance became increasingly apparent. When Bernard Smith published his *Forces in American Criticism* in 1939, he undertook, on a cue provided by Hicks' *Great Tradition,* to assess the whole American critical tradition in expressly Marxist terms, and thereby provided an occasion for disputing the value of economic or political "force" as a criterion of criticism that was to be further enhanced by a major historical event in the autumn of that year.

Critical controversy was now at active grips with party politics. The systematic form of the materialist dialectic taxed the defenders of the aesthetic approach to literature with matching its logic and consistency. Propaganda in literature became a continuous issue of debate. The economic and political distress of the times forced an agreement even among fiercely contending critical parties on the practical and moral ends of literature, spurred a critical examination of these ends, and established more firmly than ever before in American thought the necessity of seeing what constitutes the truth and integrity of a work of literature before it can hope to produce a desired effect in social or moral regeneration.

Obviously these benefits of dispute and responsibility soon became offset by corresponding evils. Critical activity became distracted by false simplifications and partisan bias. Its exponents readily substituted personal abuse for sober thinking and propaganda for logic. There appeared a heated warfare of terms and premises, in which debates over the "function" of art, "utility," "ideology," "mass consciousness," "bourgeois" values against "proletarian," and "autonomy" versus "propaganda," badly hindered the mere communication of intelligence about these issues, and permitted the discipline of realistic logic to lapse into dilemma and confusion. Hicks' book on *The Great Tradition* became a special and typical center of dispute. Its coherence of argument and its graphic dramatization of American social history were rendered suspect by the facility with which it accepted or dismissed the writers of American literature according to the degree to which they satisfied his highly simplified proposition on the interdependence of literature and economic law. This book was the particular stimulus that aroused another writer of Marxist sympathies, James T. Farrell, to write his *Note on Literary Criticism* (1936), in which he scored the lapses in valid argument and appreciation among the critics of the Left, reproved the dogmatists, and sketched the necessary corrections and qualifications of literal Marxism that were needed to preserve its values and methods for legitimate literary study.

Perhaps the central issue raised by Marxism was the issue of economic determinism as a conditioning force and value-principle in literature—a determinism that became a purely mechanical routine in the writings of dogmatic and inflexible believers. Max Eastman, of the older Socialist guard, published in 1934 his two studies called *Artists in Uniform: A Study of Literature and Bureaucratism* and *Art and the Life of Action,* both of them issuing from his own disillusionment with orthodox Marxism and Stalinism, and both serving as warnings against the official coercion of art in the service of the political state, of which Stalinism no less than totalitarian Fascism was, in his view, guilty. Younger defenders of Marxist thought—Rahv, Phillips, Farrell, Macdonald—sounded their warnings against the regimentation of art in a too literal Marxist spirit. Edmund Wilson, in an essay on "Marxism and Literature" (included in his collection *The Triple Thinkers* in 1938), refuted the Marxist orthodoxy among critics in a series of analyzed propositions. The old resistance of the individual to mass action or compulsion, so characteristic a trait of American political and literary liberalism, asserted itself with increasing emphasis.

Three statements made during the thirties illustrate this gradual correction of social and political extremism in criticism. One appeared in Newton Arvin's essay on "Individualism and American Writers":

The case for a proletarian literature is not always cogently stated or wisely defended—any more than the case against it. One must insist that to adopt the proletarian point of view does not mean, for a novelist, to deal solely with economic conflicts, or, for a poet, to be a voice only for protest, momentous as both these things are and *implicit* as they are bound to be. That a truly proletarian literature, for us in America at least, would mean a break with the mood of self-pity, with the cult of romantic separatism, with sickly subjectivism and melodramatic misanthropy—this much is almost too clear to deserve stating. But the duty of the critic is certainly not to file an order for a particular sort of fiction or poetry before the event; his duty is to clarify, as best he can, the circumstances in which fiction and poetry must take shape, and to rationalize their manifestations when they arrive. For the moment the important thing is that American criticism should define its position: in the midst of so much confusion, so much wasted effort, so much hesitation, this will itself be an advance.

Another appeared in Joseph Freeman's statement in 1935, in the anthology called *Proletarian Literature in America:*

No party resolution, no government decree, can produce art, or transform an agitator into a poet. A party card does not automatically endow a communist with artistic genius. Whatever it is that makes an artist, as distinguished from a scientist or man of action, it is something beyond the power of anyone to produce deliberately. But once the artist is there, once there is the man with the specific sensibility, the mind, the emotions, the images, the gift of language which makes the creative writer, he is not a creature in a vacuum.

A third was provided by Rahv and Phillips:

Unfortunately many misguided enthusiasts of revolution, effacing their own experience, take for their subject-matter the public philosophy as such, or attempt to adorn with rhetorical language conventionalized patterns of feeling and action. What they don't see is that these patterns are, in the final analysis, just as impersonal as the philosophy itself. . . . If there is to be an ever-fresh balance between the accent of the poet and the attitude he shares with other people, he must understand the connection between what is *real* to him as an individual and what is *real* to him as a partisan of some given philosophy.

The climax of ten years of Marxist controversy in American criticism arrived in the summer of 1939, when Stalin made his pact with Hitler on the eve of the outbreak of the Second World War in September. This event proved to be a violent and crucial test for those who had subscribed to the orthodox letter of the collaboration and interdependence of literature and political action. It provided, in fact, a date as crucial in the history of American critical thought as the Humanist controversy of 1930, the appearance of Van Wyck Brooks' *America's Coming-of-Age* in 1915, or, indeed, Emerson's Phi Beta Kappa address in 1837.

For some of the faithful the event had its logic and its explanation in the political ambiguities and cynicism of the preceding decade. But for many it meant a betrayal of faith, and the speed with which they resigned from the Communist Party or the Marxist cause (Granville Hicks, in his letter of resignation, provided the classic case of repudiation and eventual atonement to the American liberal principle) was perhaps in direct proportion to the obedient and blinkered docility of too many original conversions. Certain sympathizers whose ideas had been strongly stamped by the entire social-political issue— Edmund Wilson and Kenneth Burke chief among them—kept their minds flexible and receptive, and continued to adapt the Marxist analysis to their methods of formal analysis or social interpretation. But others were faced by absolute alternatives: repudiation or acceptance. Eloquence and mandatory dogmatism went out of the critical controversy swiftly. A more sober and considered critical balance was enforced among the thoughtful. Communism, during the succeeding years of the forties, was obliged, as a critical policy, to come to terms not only with historical and political fact but with aesthetic necessity and merit. Compromise, conciliation, and a sounder proportion of values asserted their usefulness, indeed their inevitability, in any literary program which is at all observant of the disparities that are bound to exist between theory and practice in art. Those disparities—the fact of them, but also the need of controlling or disciplining this wayward fact through a knowledge of aesthetic theory and of the recalcitrance of creative expression to theoretical abstractions—had meanwhile become the concern of another branch of American criticism, whose disputes provided a line of development that both corrected and paralleled that of Marxism in the criticism of the thirties.

4

If the political and social critics of the thirties can be described as descendants of an American line that brought the ideas of Emerson into conjunction with the claims of economic realism, the new aesthetic critics who were their contemporaries are recognizable as heirs of a similarly twofold evolution in American literary thought. It is an evolution whose salient traits appear in the concept of poetic "purity" as Poe sponsored it, and in the "moral necessity" of art as Henry James defined it. Whatever prominence these conceptions had arrived at in postclassical criticism in Europe, whatever hostilities or alliances they had engendered there during the nineteenth century, whatever actual indebtedness to the European masters these two American critics and their contemporaries showed, it was an expression definably American that they gave to their principles, and it is a peculiarly American version of the aesthetic-moralistic dualism that descended to their followers in the twentieth century. Aestheticism in the United States has always been more consciously and explicitly international in its tenets than the rival strain of social-realistic theory. The native defenders of artistic autonomy or privilege—Poe, Motley, Lowell, James, Brownell, Santayana, Gates, Huneker, Spingarn—have always invoked European precept or example more readily than exponents of social or humanitarian ideals, and some of them have taken their working principles directly from European sources: Coleridge, Schopenhauer, Arnold, Pater, France, or Croce. This continued to be the case when Ezra Pound and T. S

Eliot appeared on the scene around 1915 as sponsors of a new aesthetic approach to literary problems. But it proved inevitable that even the most extreme of these defenders of the aesthetic principle in the United States should arrive at a dualism of art and morality that carries the accent of an essentially American alliance of forces—an alliance that makes Pound and Eliot, as much as Henry James himself, unmistakably American characters when we consider them in the role of critic.

It is necessary to bring the critical work of James into any valid picture of contemporary American criticism. Not only was his final and greatest critical writing (the prefaces he wrote to his own books in 1907–1909) done in this century; but his importance as a critic was first fully recognized and assessed in America after the collection of these prefaces into book form as *The Art of the Novel* in 1934. His rank as a craftsman and creative thinker emerged in full scale only after his death in 1916, when his criticism was first read and studied; and it finally touched the thought of almost every serious American writer only by the time of the revival that accompanied the centenary of his birth in 1943. Pound and Eliot took him as their major American preceptor around 1915 as frankly as the social realists of that day took Emerson, Whitman, or Howells as theirs. This office of James' has increased during the ensuing three decades until today he holds almost undisputed rank as the greatest American school-maker in matters of formal craftsmanship and aesthetic discipline.

It was James who first saw clearly the modern creative problem in its two essential aspects: its oppression by social conflict and theories of scientific and moral determinism, and its acute subtilization by the defenses which the aesthetic techniques of the modern sensibility had set up against these oppressions. He saw modern criticism confronting the task of reconciling the real with the aesthetic, human experience in "its unprejudiced identity" with the form and laws of art. That task was nowhere more urgent than in America, and during the 1880's, when James still had the ambition of becoming the "American Balzac," he formulated his working principles as a critic. His critical doctrine showed three principal clauses. He argued for subtlety and plasticity in the critic's sympathy as a first condition. As a second, he demanded a tireless study of the vital experience upon which all art is based and its use as a test of material validity, since for him all art was "in basis moral." And he required finally a knowledge of how the intelligence of the artist stamps this material with its unmistakable impression of form and language, since that imprint constituted for James the "quality of mind" for which he looked in any valid work of art.

He defended the mean in both art and criticism. He had an American's native suspicion of cults and dogmas. He looked upon Gautier's "art for art" as an absurdity and upon Zola's naturalism as a "treacherous ideal." To him, aesthetic quality was as indispensable as realistic documentation; but to insist on the one without the other, or upon either without the harmonizing presence of a moral conception, was futile. Criticism must begin where a work of imagination begins: with experience tangibly perceived.

To lend himself, to project himself and steep himself, to feel and feel till he understands, and to understand so well that he can say, and to have perception at the pitch of passion and expression as embracing as the air, to be infinitely curious and incorrigibly patient, and yet plastic and inflammable and determinable, patient, stooping to conquer and yet serving to direct—these are fine chances for an active mind, chances to add the idea of independent beauty to the conception of success. . . . Just in proportion as he reacts and reciprocates and penetrates, is the critic a valuable instrument.

This was his plea for training in critical sensibility—a pioneer formulation of the impressionist principle. It alone leads the critic directly into contact with the work of art and with art's own sources. But we must not make the mistake of confusing what James said with what Pater taught, or with what later American exponents of French impressionism like Huneker, or of Crocean expressionism like Spingarn, advocated. Impressionism was at that time almost as unknown in America as it had been exaggerated in Europe, and it had a service to perform in bringing critics back to an intimate sense of art (as Lewis Gates, Huneker, and finally Eliot were to show). But James had no intention of subscribing literally to its methods. He was too thoroughly bred in ethical seriousness. When he declared, in *Partial Portraits* (1888), that "the deepest quality of a work of art will always be the quality of the mind of the producer," he meant that in both art and criticism "the moral sense and the artistic sense lie very close together." Only their combination will supply the abstract operations of the intellect with the vitality of a union that makes such "quality" possible. "The critic's judgment," he repeated, "being in the last analysis an estimate of the artist's quality of mind, is at once moral and aesthetic." The persistent linking of these terms runs like a motif through James' essays. To separate the moral from the aesthetic is to rob either of its vital complement. Genuine "unity of mind" exists in such "fusions and interrelations," with "every part of the stuff encircled in every other." That is the secret of aesthetic form, a writer's ultimate aim and achievement, just as its elucidation is the secret of the critic's success, his highest responsibility. These precepts stayed with James from his critical coming-of-age until he finally assayed his own achievement by their light when he wrote the prefaces for the New York Edition of his tales in the last decade of his life. They remain the clue to his role in modern American writing and to his part in the aesthetic thought that came to rival the social-realistic and the Humanist-moral schools in American criticism after 1925.

The exponents of aestheticism found themselves, in 1930, in a position somewhere midway between Humanism and Realism, and they continued to hold that difficult medial ground when Humanism gave way to moral dogmatism and Realism to Marxism, in the ensuing fifteen years. The aesthetic schools of the twenties had been obliged, in the face of both Humanism and the Marxist challenge, to consolidate their forces and to commit themselves to more positive ends and beliefs than had been allowed in the freer days of artistic experiment and rebellion. Where the realist critics of that earlier decade had moved toward social and economic values, the aesthetic critics now began to move toward values that may be variously defined as moral, ethical, and in some cases explicitly theological but, in any case, as formal and intellectual, as against the impressionism of the eclectic sensibility that had been the general rule when Santayana, Huneker, or the early Pound and Eliot dominated the scene. When Eliot in 1928, in the foreword to his book of essays called *For Lancelot Andrewes,* announced himself as a classicist in literature, a royalist in politics, and an Anglo-Catholic in religion, he startled many of his former admirers into repudiating his leadership; but actually he was only arriving at certain commitments which had been implicit in his New England heritage, his European sympathies, his historical principles, and his classical and formalist leanings (particularly as derived from T. E. Hulme, the English philosophical writer) from the beginning of his career. His announcement was symptomatic.

The aesthete, as much as the realist, was searching for a positive doctrine by which to confirm his faith in the discipline of art and intellect, an orthodoxy with which to buttress his identification of individual experience with the imperatives of moral responsibility and historical tradition. Eliot's books after 1930 indicated by their very titles the extra-aesthetic values to which he dedicated himself: *The Use of Poetry and the Use of Criticism* (1933), *After Strange Gods: A Primer of Modern Heresy* (1934), *Essays Ancient and Modern* (correlating traditional with modern standards in morals and art) (1936), *The Idea of a Christian Society* (1939), *The Classics and the Man of Letters* (1942), *The Man of Letters and the Future of Europe* (1944). His earlier argument that modern society would benefit by the establishment of a critical dictatorship, an élite of the intelligent, had (despite its echo of Matthew Arnold) ominous possibilities in an age of coercive cultural policies, but Eliot has been concerned to keep that principle both cautious and tentative in its practical application, while insisting that it be serious and responsible in its literary and moral workings. In the absence, among English-speaking countries, of a positively orthodox Christian or Thomistic school of aesthetics such as Jacques Maritain and Etienne Gilson were fostering in France, Eliot came to stand as the foremost representative of the league between aesthetic and moral ideas which has offered itself as one central synthesis of the critical forces of our century. His loyalty to the literary standard, despite his preoccupation with religious and ethical problems, was also explicitly emphasized in 1935, in his essay on "Religion and Literature," when he asserted that "the 'greatness' of literature cannot be determined solely by literary standards; though we must remember that whether it is literature or not can be determined only by literary standards."

To bring criticism into active collaboration with values, to assert the indispensability of technical and aesthetic evidences as the basis of genuine critical judgment, have thus become paramount in Eliot's critical work, making him, perhaps above every other practitioner, the dominating influence in aesthetic analysis after 1925—a major force among critics as diverse as Edmund Wilson, Kenneth Burke, John Crowe Ransom, Allen Tate, and R. P. Blackmur. But immediately behind Eliot in this effort stood, as a personal mentor, another American poet whose office as a critical school-maker is important in these developments. It was "active criticism" that Ezra Pound went abroad to study when he left America in 1907, beginning a thirty-five-year career in England, France, and Italy. In the early days of his apprenticeship Pound stood for a militantly aesthetic standard in experimentation, a rescue of art from the academic formulae and discreet moralism into which it had fallen in the United States of his youth. He was drawn toward critics and editors like Henry James, Rémy de Gourmont, W. B. Yeats, Ford Madox Hueffer, and T. E. Hulme—men who made less pretense of organizing a philosophic system out of their tastes and appreciations than of refreshing and extending these by constant study of the problems of form and style. He put himself to school, as poet and critic, among the experimental masters of the past and the nonconformist teachers of the present. On an eclectic principle he studied the Latin lyrists, the balladists of Provence and medieval Italy, the Elizabethan translators, the French symbolists, and the Chinese manuscripts he inherited from Ernest Fenollosa, all with the same zest he gave to the teachings of Gourmont in Paris or Hulme in London. His enthusiasm was so contagious that he himself was soon recognized as a leader in innovation and critical pedagogy.

From Gourmont he heard those conversations on style and aesthetic form which were expressed in an aphorism (later to be employed as an epigraph by Eliot) that gives focal expression to the liaison now set up between impressionism and the new formalism: "Ériger en lois ses impressions personnelles, c'est le grand effort d'un homme s'il est sincère." From Hulme he took up a protest against the romantic, the sentimental, the formally vague and subjective, the relative and the abstract, which the author of the fragmentary *Speculations* offered as his prophecy of a classical revival in modern literature.

This principle of form, however, had little to do with the revival of Aristotelian laws which was to appear in England and America among certain critics after 1930. When Eliot somewhat later (in *The Sacred Wood* in 1920) said, "One must be firmly distrustful of accepting Aristotle in a canonical spirit; this is to lose the whole living force of him," he was following Hulme's and Pound's directive. Pound gained his chief stimulation from his contemptuous opposition to the degenerate romanticism of late Victorian and Edwardian writers. For that reason he made a necessity of experiment, and his career became a continuous participation in unconventionality—in Imagism, in Vorticism, in the aesthetic laboratories of Paris, in Objectivism, in fact in any activity that satisfied his demand for freshness, exploration, invention, novelty. He repudiated critical systems: "Systems become tyrannies overnight." Despite his later political and economic alliances (Social Credit, Jeffersonian aristocratic thought, or later the political authoritarianism which came curiously to attract numerous modern writers and which led, in Pound's case, to his admiration of Fascism in Italy and to his eventual indictment as a traitor to his native country in the War of 1941–1945), Pound's purposes, in his best years as critic, were never primarily moral, except in the sense that aesthetic discipline demands an integrity beyond the formality of practical ethics. His book titles indicate his motives: *Instigations* (1920), *Irritations* (1922), *How to Read* (1931), *The A.B.C. of Reading* (1934), *Make It New* (1935). All these were writen less to persuade than to irritate and thus to apply the authority of creative literature itself as a critical instrument. When Pound defined his "categories" of criticism, he opposed the ineffectuality of abstract dogma with the dynamic value of the actual literary text.

Pound brought criticism back to an active study of texts more directly and unequivocally than impressionism aimed to do, and with none of the complexities of scientific method or formal analysis that I. A. Richards or the formalists after 1930 were to employ. His arguments suffered as much as his style from his exaggerated iconoclasm. His classifications often failed to classify, and his preferences were likely to confuse discrimination. But Pound's work, for all its violence, haphazardness, and shock tactics, had the virtues that go with these offenses: it was direct, energetic, experimental, seminal. It showed, in the years between 1910 and 1930, a virtue to which academic criticism and often social criticism cannot usually pretend: it was useful to writers. And in his role as a teacher of writers Pound's service was greatest, and his importance to aesthetic thought in the immediately future years second only to Eliot's.

The disciplining of the aesthetic experience, its substancing in moral values, which Eliot and Pound promoted, was to resort to other methods during the thirties. One of these appeared in the mature work of Yvor Winters, whose efforts to analyze the form of modern poetry, to define its processes, to find a critical methodology for them, and to rescue poetry from the disorder and confusion of aimless experimentation, led him toward more and more severely classical principles, these being partly influenced by the arguments of Irving Babbitt, partly by a personal contempt for the abuses and anti-intellectual tendencies of artistic experiments based on psychological and amoral motives —his dissension from the Humanist position being indicated, however, by his judgment on Babbitt: "His analysis of literary principles appears to me to be gravely vitiated by an almost complete ignorance of the manner in which the moral intelligence actually gets into poetry."

Another large-scale attempt to bring formal analysis into a working collaboration with social and human values appeared in the work of Kenneth Burke. Burke undertook a widely explorative study of literary form by using any technique that came to his hand—semantic research, psychological method, social analysis, structural analysis: projects that entailed investigations in the problems of communication, perception, agency, and instrumentation which culminated in books like *The Philosophy of Literary Form* (1941) and *A Grammar of Motives* (1945).

Still another method of aesthetic investigation appeared in the essays of R. P. Blackmur (*The Double Agent,* 1935; *The Expense of Greatness,* 1940), who, combining a naturalistic motive derived from Santayana with an analytical procedure comparable to that of I. A. Richards and William Empson in England, but always with overt indebtedness to James and Eliot, brought the evaluation of literary quality and effects down to a minute dissection of the style, form, diction, and structure in the poets and prose writers he studied.

A still more prominent case of aestheticism joining forces with a moral conception of literature appeared in the writers of the Southern school—the Regionalists and Traditionalists who had first appeared as early as 1922 in the pages of the magazine called the *Fugitive* in Nashville, Tennessee, and who then, during the thirtiees and forties, under the leadership of John Crowe Ransom and Allen Tate, included such critics as Cleanth Brooks, Robert Penn Warren, Donald Davidson, Randall Jarrell, and had as their organs the *Southern Review* (1935-1942), the *Kenyon Review* (beginning in 1939), and the renovated *Sewanee Review* (beginning in 1944). Here again the obligation of literary analysis to historical and moral tradition was asserted, specifically, in terms of the Southern inheritance in American life—an order of society based on classical conceptions of authority, value, and the aristocratic principle of intelligence, now posed anew against the competitive, aggressive, and experimental standards of the North. The essays of Tate and Ransom submitted their literary findings to the responsibility that a critic faces when he attempts to reconcile modernity or innovation with the formal order implicit in tradition. Tate called his first volume of essays *Reactionary Essays* (1936), indicating by that title the positive standard he made of a principle usually associated by modernists with inhibition and conservative negation; he called his second book of criticism *Reason in Madness* (1941), making its theme the opposition of moral order to eclectic license or utilitarian materialism in contemporary literature. And when Ransom announced the focal ambition of his work in the title of a characteristic essay, "Wanted: An Ontological Criticism," he showed himself to desiderate in modern art and criticism a metaphysic based on a total comprehension of reality, connecting literature with the essential nature, properties, and relations of things in their fullest possible coherence of mind and moral continuity.

Less committed to a conscious program of technique or moral values than these men was Edmund Wilson, one of the earliest disciples of the new criticism in the twenties, and continuing in 1946 to be one of the most influential practitioners of criticism in America. Wilson began as a student of the historical methods of nineteenth century French critics like Sainte-Beuve, Taine, Renan, and Anatole France. He wrote his brilliant first book of criticism, *Axel's Castle* (1931), a study of the Symbolist tradition in modern literature, as a study of "the productions of men of genius in the setting of the conditions that have shaped them." He took, in his future work, whatever he found valuable from the social and Marxist schools short of their dogmatic conclusions; from Freud and psychoanalysis his increasingly emphasized clue to effective expression in the psychic disability or social maladjustment of the artist; and from historical processes a drama of forces that continuously enlivens his reading of texts through his appreciation of the vitality and dynamism of social and moral experience (*The Triple Thinkers*, 1938; *To the Finland Station*, 1940; *The Wound and the Bow*, 1941).

It was the thoroughness of their stylistic investigations, the insight of their studies of literary patterns and structures, that lifted the best of these critics above the irresponsible conjurings of the impressionists, that made them conscious of what is involved in the creative process, and so brought them to resist, with a morality and orthodoxy of their own, the mechanism of social and political formulae. In them, the aesthetic procedure was at once rationalized and corrected, and utilitarian critical methods were revealed in their routine of inflexible prejudice and ineptitude. In them, moreover, the Marxist schools of the thirties found their most formidable resistance. This resistance was sometimes carried out so stubbornly and uncompromisingly that it led one chronicler, Alfred Kazin in *On Native Grounds* (1942), to describe the hostility of orthodoxies which he witnessed around him as "Criticism at the Poles." This resistance indicated a profound and fundamental division in the critical forces of the thirties, and it made that decade memorable for the decisions and commitments which will characterize it for future historians

5

This brings us to the latest phase of our survey: the criticism of the middle forties, which may be described as a movement toward assimilation and synthesis, an attempted compromise of methods, an effort to strike a reasonable balance and proportion among the values which thirty years of literary insurgence and critical research have turned up. Those three decades began, as we have seen, with protest and rebellion. They continued with experimentation and a free exploring of the techniques and resources of literature. Then they fell into doctrinaire schools and a hostile opposition of critical forces—liberals against traditionalists, realists against idealists, rebels against academicians, socialists against aesthetes, experimenters against dogmatists, with methods of argument or analysis borrowed from every possible field of modern research—semantics, the new psychologies of Freud and Jung, Marxism, theology, anthropology, history, sociology, philosophy. Now, perhaps, the moment had arrived for a more difficult task than is possible to sectarians, extremists, or insurgents; namely, the undertaking of a whole view of literature which admits the possible benefits of diverse intellectual and critical disciplines but insists on keeping the central integrity of literature intact, and holds in view the unity of art with the total sum of human experience and its moral values.

81. AMERICAN BOOKS ABROAD

THERE is the same difficulty in writing a history of American literature during the twentieth century that there is in picturing an object a few inches from the eyes: both are too close to be in focus. The observer of natural objects can change his position, but the historian who deals with contemporary life and letters has not the same privilege, being part of the process he is trying to describe. Not only his judgments but his selection of facts for record will have to be revised in later years. It can scarcely be doubted, however, on the evidence of the foregoing chapters, that a literary movement of power and character existed in the United States after about 1910, with its origins going back to the nineties. Nothing like it had occurred in our literature since the mid-years of the past century, when Emerson, Melville, and Whitman were in their prime.

The early statement of N. P. Willis, "The Atlantic is to us a century," applies with the same half-truth to the reverse of the situation he had in mind, for distance in space has somewhat the same effect as distance in time. Crossing the oceans is still a means by which the historian can step back to gain perspective. He can observe what happens when contemporary American writers are judged by the critical standards of other nations, and he can thereby reach another estimate of their importance; at the very least, he can learn to question local judgments.

It is not easy to follow American books around the world, especially since war and national jealousies have added the censorship of facts to our own capacity for disregarding them. For a long time any report from abroad is certain to be uneven and incomplete; yet we know enough already to reach a few suggestive conclusions. Perhaps the first of these is that American literature acquired a different international status during the last half-century; that it came to be regarded in Europe, in Latin America, and in the Orient as one of the major living world literatures. A second conclusion might be that the American writers most widely read on other continents are, in general, not the same as those most highly esteemed by our own critics. A third conclusion—among many others—is that the history of American books abroad has as many local variants as there are civilized countries.

As a general rule, American literary influence has followed one of two paths. Either it started in England, spread outward through the British Dominions (except Canada, which was influenced directly), and moved northeastward through Germany to Scandinavia; or else—for a smaller number of authors—it started in France, traveled eastward to the Slavic countries (though Russia after the Revolution followed her own taste in American books), then spread southward through the Mediterranean and finally southwestward to Latin America, which accepted the Paris standards rather than those of London or Madrid. Whitman and Poe are examples from our classical period of authors whose books followed these separate paths. Poe was so warmly adopted by the French that he came to be regarded as one of their Symbolist poets; and it was largely in Baudelaire's French translation that his stories were read in Eastern Europe and Latin America before the Slavic and Spanish worlds made sometimes very effective translations of their own. Whitman, on the other hand, had enthusiastic French and Latin American disciples, just as Poe had German disciples; but in the Latin countries there was never the wide popular audience for *Leaves of Grass* that existed in England and Germany.

The northern path is the one likely to be followed by sound historical romances, humorous works, and realistic novels conceived on a large scale; in a word, by books distinguished for scope as opposed to depth, for human warmth as opposed to emotional fire, for reasonableness as opposed to bitter logic. To list a few contemporary names, it is the path followed by the works of Dreiser, Hergesheimer, Lewis, Willa Cather, and Pearl Buck (all of whom were also published in France, though without being really naturalized there). Books that followed the southern path were more likely to be narrow, technically inventive (rather than polished), lyrical, intense, and even extravagant: they were, for example, the novels of Hemingway, Dos Passos (studied for his technical innovations), Faulkner (most highly praised of all), Erskine Caldwell, and John Steinbeck (except for his epical *Grapes of Wrath,* which was read in all countries). In both cases, it was the unsophisticated violence of American life that appealed to Europeans.

There were other books that followed both paths. Usually they were novels dealing with the wilderness, slavery, or the misdeeds of big business—in other words, with native American material that seemed fascinating and wildly foreign to Europeans of all nations. The Leatherstocking Tales, *Evangeline* (studied in both French and German schools), *Uncle Tom's Cabin, Tales of the Argonauts* (Bret Harte during his lifetime was more popular in the Latin countries than Mark Twain), *The Call of the Wild, The Jungle,* and *Gone with the Wind* are some of the books enjoyed almost universally.

2

England had welcomed the American writers of the classical period, and continued to read them for some time after they had begun to be neglected by the American public. In a middle-class English home about the year 1900, Emerson would stand on the shelves next to Carlyle, Longfellow next to Tennyson (with signs of being more frequently read) and Lowell next to Matthew Arnold. The new generation rejected them all, the Bostonians along with the native Victorians. To the younger English intellectuals of the time, the only transatlantic authors worth reading, except Whitman and Thoreau, were the new social realists, from Garland through Norris to Upton Sinclair. Dreiser's *Sister Carrie* was a critical success in London, when published there in 1901, although it had been arousing such a bitterly quiet condemnation in New York that the author—till then a successful journalist—found that his articles were being rejected by all the magazines.

The English were usually hospitable to American writers as persons, often more hospitable than they were to imported books. During the 1890's, there was a large American literary colony in what was still called the mother country: it included the aging Bret Harte, Henry James, Harold Frederic, Pearl Craigie from Boston (who wrote under the name John Oliver Hobbes), Howard Sturgis (author of the fine but neglected *Belchamber*), Henry Harland (who founded and edited the *Yellow Book*), and, for his last two years, Stephen Crane. Most of these authors had a more appreciative public in England than in the United States; for example, Bret Harte's new books continued to be read in their English editions long after most Americans had forgotten that he was still a living author. Stephen Crane, who could not complain of being neglected at home, could justly complain of being pursued there by scandals that the English found beneath their notice. Henry James, with no larger audience in London than in New York, at least found more of the happy few to understand his work. The same hospitality in later years would be shown to Ezra Pound, Conrad Aiken, Hilda Doolittle ("H. D."), and T. S. Eliot, the last of whom became a British subject in 1927, like James in 1915.

At the turn of the century, some of the larger American magazines were printing English editions; that of *Harper's* was edited by Andrew Lang and had a British circulation of 100,000. Many American books crossed the Atlantic. In the October, 1904, issue of *World's Work*, Chalmers Roberts broadly asserted that ten American books were being published in England where one had been published twenty years before. He was not surprised by the fondness of the English public for the genteel writings of James Lane Allen, a phenomenon remarked upon by many critics. What amazed him was the

English success of American rural novels like *David Harum, Eben Holden,* and *Mrs. Wiggs of the Cabbage Patch,* all of which he described as being "intensely foreign and full of detail quite unintelligible to the average Briton."

Shortly after 1910, however, the British public showed signs of losing interest in American fiction, except for commodities like the works of Zane Grey and Edgar Rice Burroughs (who afterward claimed that the globe-girdling adventures of Tarzan had been translated into fifty-six languages). American magazines discontinued their London editions. As for the serious American novelists, English critics learned to say that they were ten or twenty or fifty years behind the times. A few critics, however, had begun to discover the new American poets—Robinson, Masters, Sandburg, Lindsay—sometimes before they were known in the United States; for example, Robert Frost had his first two books published in London.

There were new American novelists, too, but they had few English readers during the First World War; one of its effects was to keep the two countries apart intellectually, even after they became allies. In 1920 the English publisher of *Main Street* was so little impressed by Sinclair Lewis' American success that he began by merely importing a few hundred sets of printer's sheets; it was not until later that he had the novel printed in England. *Main Street* was never popular there, although it was more generally liked in Australia, which, more than New Zealand, makes its own choice of American books. *Babbitt,* however, was the English best seller of 1922; and when its author next visited London he was received like the general of an Allied army. "England," Lewis told his hosts, with his redheaded gift for speaking his mind, "can no longer be the mother country to American literature, any more than she can be the mother country to American politics or American life." The English listened, protested, argued with one another, and came to believe that Lewis was right.

Babbitt was the beginning of a new era, during which American books were not only read but imitated. On their different literary levels, Hemingway, Edmund Wilson, James Thurber, Damon Runyon, and Dashiell Hammett each had English disciples, who sometimes improved on their various models. Graham Greene, for example, wrote English gangster novels that had a psychological depth lacking in his American precursors, except Hemingway. A younger Englishman, Peter Cheyney, stuck to his models closely, so much so that one of his stories was included (1945) in a French anthology of the new American writing. The editor had learned of Cheyney's nationality before the volume went to press, but had kept him with the others because of his American style. By this time, however, styles and influences were flying back and forth across the Atlantic; and the English imitators of the

American hard-boiled novelists—Graham Greene especially—were finding American imitators in their turn. Among poets the transatlantic relations were even closer. T. S. Eliot was the strongest early influence on the new English poets of the thirties such as Auden (before he came to live in the States), Spender, and MacNeice; while Auden in turn set the tone for American poets in the forties.

The American vogue continued year after year. In 1938 an English publisher reported that all the novels since *Babbitt* with a sale of more than 100,000 copies in England had been of American origin. American magazines were also read: especially *Time* (which had two English imitations), the *Reader's Digest* (with an English edition), and the *New Yorker*, which in the brighter circles, was quoted more often than *Punch*. In 1942 one quarter of the new trade books listed in English publishers' catalogues had been written in the States. By 1946, however, the percentage of transatlantic imports was beginning to decline.

3

In France it was still growing. Not only were the French translating or planning to translate dozens of the more prominent American novelists and the plays of Eugene O'Neill; they were also discovering and publishing, in the midst of a paper shortage, American books that had been largely neglected at home; for example, the fantastic *Miss Lonelyhearts,* by Nathanael West, which had been published here in 1933 and had promptly gone out of print. At the same time they showed a renewed interest in the American classics. The first French translation of *Moby Dick* appeared during the German occupation, together with a somewhat fictionalized biography of Melville by Jean Giono; and a translation of *The Scarlet Letter* was published in 1946.

The French had read most of the American classical authors when they first appeared, but had forgotten them sooner than the English. There were a few striking exceptions: notably Cooper and Poe, who were carried over bodily into French literature and remain an integral part of it. Among the Americans writing at the turn of the century, Henry James had a few careful French readers, and exercised a still undetermined influence on Marcel Proust. Jack London had a wider public; he inherited the French popularity of Bret Harte. Edith Wharton, who lived in France, had most of her books translated; they were praised in the terms that are usually applied to estimable but unexciting French novels. Most of the other living American writers were little known even in Paris; and their country was regarded, in general, as the literary home of cowboys, miners, trappers, and the inimitable Nick Carter, whose weekly adventures were then appearing in France, as in fifteen other foreign countries.

The First World War, which tended to separate us intellectually from the English, thus marking the end of what might be called the second colonial period in American letters, was an occasion for renewing old literary ties with the French. Much has been written about the flight of American writers to Paris during the twenties; it is not so generally known that there was a smaller but influential movement of French writers and scholars in the opposite direction. The migration began under French government auspices, with professors from the Sorbonne encouraged to make American tours and lecture at American universities. They were shortly followed by a selected group of French postgraduate students, some of whom carried home with them a wide knowledge of American authors. Chairs of American Civilization and Literature were founded at several of the French universities: at Paris (where Charles Cestre was the incumbent), Grenoble, Lille, Aix-Marseille, and elsewhere. French students working in the field produced what is probably the largest group of scholarly studies of American literature that exists in any foreign language.

But interest in American culture was also growing in a quite different circle, that of the younger avant-garde writers. Finding not much hope in Europe after the war, they were looking for new material, new ideas, new ways of life. A sort of romantic Americanism became the vogue among them after 1920: they were connoisseurs of American films, especially Westerns, they read the advertisements in the *Saturday Evening Post,* they dreamed of living in a New York skyscraper (though few of them, in life, got beyond making a single brief voyage), and they even dressed in what they thought was the American fashion, wearing belts instead of suspenders and shaving their upper lips; whereas the young Americans who were running off to France in those years were connoisseurs of French books and French wines and liked to wear little French mustaches. These were superficial signs on both sides, but they were an indication of tastes that proved to be lasting. The young American writers were deeply influenced by French literature in the Symbolist tradition; the young French writers were looking for American books that would express the picturesque qualities they found in American life; and when the books began to appear in translation, after 1930, they seized upon them enthusiastically.

The *Index Translationum,* published for eight years by the Institute of Intellectual Cooperation of the League of Nations, lists the titles and authors of all the books translated into the major European languages between 1932 and 1940. During that period there were 332 French translations of American books in the field of general literature. Jack London stands at the head of the list with twenty-seven titles, and James Oliver Curwood follows with twenty; both these adventure-story writers were old favorites with the French public, although their day was passing. Sinclair Lewis and Edgar Allan Poe have fourteen titles each; Ellery Queen has ten detective stories; Pearl Buck has nine of her books; Edgar Rice Burroughs, Louis Bromfield, and Henry James all have seven. Farther down the list are the new authors that the younger generation was reading: William Faulkner with five titles, Ernest Hemingway and Dashiell Hammett with four, John Dos Passos and Erskine Caldwell with three. None of these last reached the broadest French public, but all of them had what Lewis and Bromfield and Pearl Buck failed to achieve, that is, a direct influence on the style and content of the new French writing.

Faulkner, comparatively little known at home, had gained an amazingly deep and lasting French reputation. André Gide called him "one of the most important, perhaps *the* most important, of the stars in this new constellation"; and Jean-Paul Sartre was more extreme in his praise: "For young writers in France," he said in 1945, "Faulkner is a god." Many French critics were disturbed by what seemed to them the completely foreign quality of the new American novelists. The newspaper man in Gide's *Imaginary Interviews* says:

I grant you Hemingway, since he is the most European of them all. As for the others, I have to confess that their strangeness appals me. I thought I would go mad with pain and horror when I read Faulkner's *Sanctuary* and his *Light in August.* Dos Passos makes me suffocate. I laugh, it is true, when reading Caldwell's *Journeyman* or *God's Little Acre,* but I laugh on the wrong side of my mouth. . . . If one believes what they are saying, the American cities and countrysides must offer a foretaste of hell.

But if one believes what Flaubert said a hundred years ago French cities also must have been an abode of the damned. All these American novelists, except possibly Caldwell, were students of Flaubert; they had been applying methods learned from him to American materials. Now their books were being studied in turn by Flaubert's countrymen.

4

Most of the other European countries followed either the French or the British pattern in their choice of American books. A novel that was a best seller in England, like Kenneth Roberts' *Northwest Passage,* would also be a best seller in Germany and Scandinavia. An author admired by the French for his intensity or his technical discoveries would also be admired by other Latin nations. Almost everywhere there was a lack of interest in American literature during the years after 1900 and a birth or rebirth of interest at some moment after 1920. This new interest appeared earlier in the northern countries, because they liked Dreiser and Lewis, and later in the Latin countries, which showed more interest in younger writers like Hemingway and Faulkner. There were, however, national variations in the two general patterns; and in Russia after the Revolution the variations were so wide as to form a new pattern of their own.

Germany between 1890 and 1945 was another special case that has to be considered in some detail. In the Kaiser's Germany, Mark Twain had been by far the most popular American author; there were exactly 100 translations of his various works between 1890 and 1913. After him came Anna Katharine Green, the early detective-story writer, with eighty-one translations; then Bret Harte, Frances Hodgson Burnett, F. Marion Crawford, and Lew Wallace, the author of *Ben-Hur.* More than half the novels of American origin translated into German during the twenty-four years before the First World War were the work of these six writers. The most admired American poet was Walt Whitman, although his greatest popularity would come later, during the early years of the Weimar Republic. Emerson was the favorite American essayist.

After the war, the Germans were eager for books that dealt with American industry, the power by which they felt they had been defeated, and especially eager for anything that dealt with Henry Ford. What they looked for in American books was information first of all, but they were better pleased if the information was presented critically; therefore they liked Theodore Dreiser (who was for several years the most popular American author in the public libraries), Sinclair Lewis, Upton Sinclair, and, in general, all the critical realists. Hemingway was admired by the younger German writers who would later go into exile, but most of them were puzzled by his habit of understatement. When a German novelist wants to convey sadness or mild regret, he is likely to say that he was overwhelmed by waves of intolerable grief. When Hemingway wants to imply that his hero was overwhelmed by waves of intolerable grief, as at the end of *A Farewell to Arms,* he says that he "walked back to the hotel in the rain"; and the Germans did not know what to make of it. Thomas Wolfe, who never used a little word when he could find three big ones, was an author more to their taste. *Look Homeward, Angel* appealed to young people of all political faiths, before and after Hitler's coming to power. There were good as well as sinister qualities in the German youth movement, and some of the better ones were mirrored at a distance in Wolfe's hero.

The strength of the Socialist and Communist parties under the Weimar Republic helped to create a public for American authors with radical sym-

pathies: not only for Upton Sinclair and Jack London, but also for John
Dos Passos, whose books at one time had a larger circulation in Germany
than in the United States. Another writer admired by the German radicals
was Agnes Smedley, whose autobiography, *Daughter of Earth*, is comparatively little known in her own country, although it has been translated into
fourteen languages. In Germany, where it was called *Eine Frau Allein*, it was
especially popular among women seeking courage to lead independent lives.
Miss Smedley's various books on the Chinese Revolution were also widely
read until 1933, when they were all withdrawn from circulation. It was the
same with Dreiser, Sinclair, Dos Passos, and Hemingway, none of whose
works appeared in Germany between 1933 and 1946; they were the best
known of the many American authors who suffered from Hitler's burning
of the books.

Some of Sinclair Lewis' novels were also burned, but his new novels
continued to be published in spite of his having written the anti-Nazi *It
Can't Happen Here*. The *Index Translationum* shows that five of his novels
were translated into German between 1932 and 1940. There were eight translations of Pearl Buck during the same period, more than of any other serious
American author; perhaps her work was thought to be politically harmless
because it dealt with China and, unlike Agnes Smedley's, made no plea for
the Chinese Communists. Very few American books were published in
Hitler's Germany if they dealt with contemporary Europe or America in
any thoughtful fashion, no matter whether their authors were radical or
conservative. The German public was still curious about our literature, but
was offered, in general, only romance, adventure, mystery, and sentiment.

The *Index Translationum* lists 297 German translations from American
originals in the field of general literature, a figure not far from the French
total of 332. There is, however, a difference in quality. Nearly half the
German list consists of Westerns and detective stories, with Max Brand, a
mass purveyor of cowboy fiction, standing at the head of it with twenty-six
titles. Historical romances were popular as an escape from daily life under
a dictatorship: *Anthony Adverse, Northwest Passage,* and especially *Gone
with the Wind,* which by 1941 had achieved the huge German sale of 360,693
copies; then it disappeared from the bookstores with the demand for it still
unsatisfied. *Grapes of Wrath* was circulated with official approval after Pearl
Harbor, presumably on the ground that its picture of the Okies would serve
as anti-American propaganda. Instead, what it proved to most of its readers
was that American peasants at their most destitute could travel about the
country in automobiles, and that American writers were free to speak their
minds in epical novels, at a time when German literature was being stifled.
American books were read hungrily after the war ended, although few were

available. *Daughter of Earth* was republished and even serialized in a Berlin newspaper; Thornton Wilder's *The Skin of Our Teeth* was the hit of the German theaters.

5

In Sweden, and the other Scandinavian countries, there was not much interest in American literature before the middle twenties, although there was great interest in a few American writers. Mark Twain in particular enjoyed the same popularity as in Germany. The chief librarian of the Royal Swedish Library, Mr. O. H. Wieselgren, said in a letter that he was given the Swedish translation of *Huckleberry Finn* as a birthday present when he was ten years old.

I read the book [he continued] so that I learned it by heart. . . . *The Jungle,* by Upton Sinclair, was translated in 1906. Sinclair since that time has been very widely read, and his social views have a great importance for the working class in our country. *The Harbor,* by Ernest Poole, was translated in 1915 and met with great interest. But the most admired of all American authors in Sweden has been and is still Jack London. His first books came in translation in 1909–10, and since that time he has appeared in innumerable editions. In public libraries he is still the most sought-for American author.

Interest in American literature, as opposed to interest in particular writers, began with the visit to the United States of the influential critic G. Ruben Berg. On his return to Sweden in 1925, he published *Moderne Amerikaner,* in which he gave an account of the new authors who had appeared since 1910, with much space devoted to Sinclair Lewis. Most of the authors he mentioned were translated into Swedish during the years that followed, and in 1930 Lewis was the first American to win the Nobel Prize for literature, which is awarded by the Swedish Academy. Eugene O'Neill was the second, in 1936; he had always acknowledged his debt to Strindberg, and his plays were even more popular in Strindberg's country than in the rest of Europe. Pearl Buck, who won the prize in 1938, was also particularly liked in Sweden. Ten of her books appeared there between 1932 and 1940, more than were translated from any other American author during the years covered by the *Index Translationum.* In all, the *Index* lists 213 American books in the field of general literature that were published in Sweden: a curious selection from new and half-forgotten authors, with Louisa May Alcott rubbing elbows with Dashiell Hammett. "The 'hard-boiled' literature plays an important role for our younger authors," Mr. Wieselgren notes. "I think no literature has during the last decade been more important and more read here than the American."

The last statement would also apply to Norway and Denmark. In the latter country, Pearl Buck was the most popular American author from 1932 to 1939 (except for best sellers like *Anthony Adverse* and *Gone with the Wind*), but Hemingway and Steinbeck had succeeded her by 1940. Holland, however, was in a different situation. Sheltered from transatlantic winds by the British Isles, it received most of its American books indirectly, after they had first become popular in London. In general it made no distinction between British and American literature.

Under Mussolini the Italian censorship was in theory not very strict; the only two American novelists whose works are known to have been forbidden were Hemingway (after his description of the Italian retreat in *A Farewell to Arms*) and Upton Sinclair, whose books were removed by decree from public libraries. Still, the whole effect of Fascist policy was to discourage, in a quiet way, the translation of authors from the democratic countries. The Italian public heard little about the new American literature and, like the Dutch public, it made no sharp distinction between American books and English books—usually preferring the latter, just as it preferred French books to either. Even after the liberation, when the Italians set to work translating the foreign works they had missed for the previous twenty years, there were not many American authors in the early publishers' lists (Steinbeck, Vincent Sheean, Kenneth Roberts); more attention was paid to the new French and English poets and the classical Russian novelists.

In Spain, American books and American movies had a brief vogue under the Republic. There was a time when the younger Spanish poets, probably influenced by their French colleagues, wrote nostalgically about gangsters and skyscrapers and in some cases made pilgrimages to New York; that was also the time when the news stands in Barcelona and Madrid were full of American magazines; but the vogue ended with the civil war. American books were suspect in Franco's Spain; even *Gone with the Wind* was not published there until 1943.

6

But *Gone with the Wind,* which eventually appeared in all the other European countries and was read by both sides during the early years of the Second World War, was never published in Soviet Russia. In their choice of American books for translation, the Russians followed a pattern of their own, one that began to be discernible even before their Revolution. From the beginning they liked American books if they were realistic or humorous or heroic in treatment, if they were democratic in sentiment, if they dealt with life in a great city or, still better, with adventures on the frontier, and if the characters were representative of the American masses. Cooper was the first American author to win lasting favor in Russia; then came Harriet Beecher Stowe; then Bret Harte and Mark Twain; and then, in 1910, Jack London, whose popularity increased when he was universally regarded as a socialist writer after the 1917 Revolution—he was the author whom Krupskaya, Lenin's widow, read to her husband on his deathbed.

After 1918 there was a State Publishing House in Russia; but there were also commercial publishers until 1928, and they competed for books by American writers. Of these Jack London was still the most widely read: from 1918 to 1929 there were six editions of his collected works in twelve to thirty-volume sets. Upton Sinclair was almost as popular, his books being regarded as a mine of information about capitalistic society. There was such a scramble for the right to publish them that Lunacharsky, the People's Commissar of Education, put an end to it in 1925 by officially designating Sinclair as a Soviet classic, thus putting him on the same pinnacle as Tolstoy and Pushkin, and, incidentally, vesting the Russian copyright to his books in the State Publishing House.

O. Henry was another favorite, not only with the masses but also with many of the Soviet writers, who studied him for his technique (so that stories with an O. Henry twist were being published in Russia at a time when American short-story writers were imitating Chekhov). James Oliver Curwood was enough like London in his themes and settings to be liked for the same reasons; there were forty-two editions of his separate novels between 1925 and 1927. Other American authors published at about the same time were Sherwood Anderson (studied by serious Russian writers), Sinclair Lewis, Booth Tarkington (*Penrod*), Edna Ferber (*So Big* and *Show Boat*), Rex Beach, and Zane Grey. During all this period the general popularity of American books continued to increase. In six months of 1912, there had been seven American authors published in Russia as against twenty-two English authors; in six months of 1928, there were forty-two Americans and thirty-seven Englishmen.

In 1928, at the beginning of the first Five Year Plan, the state took over the whole Russian publishing trade. There was a change in the character of the books selected for translation: Rex Beach, Zane Grey, and other popular entertainers disappeared from the lists of the state-controlled publishing houses. In their place came several proletarian novelists of the American depression years: Michael Gold, Jack Conroy, Albert Halper, all of whom reached a Russian audience several times as large as their audience at home. A complete edition of Dreiser's works was published in 1930; it was called the literary event of the year. Dos Passos was the most widely read American author, in literary circles, from 1932 to 1934; at one time the Organization

Committee of Soviet Writers conducted a formal discussion of his work that lasted for three heated and dialectical evenings. From 1935 to 1939 or later, Hemingway occupied a similar position; he too was the subject of an organized discussion by Soviet writers, and his technical influence on them seems to have been more extensive and more lasting than that of Dos Passos (whose books, incidentally, continued to be published in Russia in spite of the strongly anti-Communist position which he took after 1935).

Hemingway was translated in full; and all his books reached a wide audience except *For Whom the Bell Tolls,* which had been set in type when the publishers became worried by a long passage attacking André Marty by name. Marty, the French Communist leader, was at that time a refugee in Russia, and a publishing house controlled by the state did not like to be put in the position of endorsing what it regarded as a slander against him. The result was that the volume never went to press, although the proof sheets were read attentively by most of the writers in Moscow. Erskine Caldwell and John Steinbeck are two other widely translated Americans whom the Russian writers admired. At the same time both men reached the general public, which also liked Pearl Buck, Richard Wright's *Native Son,* and, during the war years, John Hersey's *A Bell for Adano.*

Control of the publishing industry by the Soviet state kept many books out of Russia and promises to keep out many others during the postwar years of international tension. It also led to the translation of books with more political than commercial appeal; but apparently it had no deep effect on the literary preferences of the Russian people. They continued to like the American authors whom they liked from the beginning; and in general the state-controlled publishers supplied them with the books they demanded. The Russians are fond of exact figures: when they say that Jack London has been the most popular of all American authors in the Soviet Union, they support the statement by adding that his various books have been printed in 567 Russian editions, of which 10,367,000 copies were sold between 1918 and 1943. Mark Twain comes after him at a distance, with 3,100,000 copies sold during the same period, and Upton Sinclair comes third, with 2,700,000. In the twenty-five years that followed the Russian Revolution, there were 217 American authors translated into Russian—again the exact figure, furnished by the State Publishing House—and the total sale of their translated books was 36,788,900 copies.

7

There were not so many of our authors published in Latin America and, until the Second World War, their appearance was subject to long delays.

They had to make a double voyage across the Atlantic before reaching Argentina or Brazil; they traveled by way of Paris, and few of their books were admitted without a French visa of critical or popular approval. As in France, some of our Western and Northwestern story writers found a public easily: Rex Beach, James Oliver Curwood, Zane Grey. But the only serious North American author who exercised a direct influence in America Hispaña during the twenties was Waldo Frank. He lectured in all the capitals from Mexico City to Buenos Aires, he spoke a fluent literary Spanish, and he attacked Yankee imperialism while defending—and introducing to a sympathetic audience—the rebel American writers.

Early in 1941, a student of inter-American affairs went through a collection of the catalogues issued by Spanish-language publishers, almost all of whom have their headquarters in Santiago de Chile, Buenos Aires, or Mexico City. He found that they listed seven translations from Waldo Frank, more than from any other living North American writer. There were five translations from Sinclair Lewis, four from Steinbeck, and two each from Dos Passos and Upton Sinclair (though Sinclair had seven other books issued by smaller, chiefly socialistic, publishers who printed no catalogues); also the student found translations of best-selling novels like *The Good Earth, The Bridge of San Luis Rey, A Farewell to Arms,* and *Gone with the Wind*— in all, forty-three volumes from our current literature, exclusive of technical works, Westerns, and detective stories. He would have found many more North American books if he had examined the lists of the same publishers five years later, for there was a new interest in our literature after Pearl Harbor.

In part this interest resulted from the wartime activities of the Office of Inter-American Affairs, which sent several of our writers on lecture tours of South America and subsidized the publication of North American books that would not otherwise have appeared by paying for their translation into Spanish and Portuguese. Most of the books it subsidized were technical or historical; but the Office of Inter-American Affairs also arranged for the publication in Spanish of a two-volume anthology of contemporary North American writing, carefully edited by John Peale Bishop and Allen Tate There would have been a growing interest in our literature without such encouragement, for the Latin Americans were excited by our entrance into the war, they were receiving very few books from Europe, and they were hearing from many unofficial sources about the younger North American novelists and poets. Hemingway, Faulkner, Steinbeck, Katherine Anne Porter, and Hart Crane were among those admired by the Argentinian and Brazilian intellectuals.

It is hard to gather accurate information about American literature in the Orient, where, generally speaking, the laws of international copyright are not enforced. In Japan before the Second World War, they did not even exist, as regards American books: a treaty negotiated under the first Roosevelt gave the Japanese permission to translate any American work without notifying the author. Not even squatter's right was recognized, and there was nothing to prevent five Japanese publishers from presenting five differently garbled translations of the same novel, as happened in the case of *Gone with the Wind*. Of three Japanese versions of Whitman, who had a large following, only one is said to have had any literary merit. Poe also—his fiction rather than his verse—was inaccurately rendered and widely read.

After 1930 the ruling clique in Japan tried hard to discourage "decadent" American influences, including the new American fiction; but Japanese publishers kept racing to press with competing versions of American best sellers. *Main Street* was a success in Japan; so too was Pearl Buck's *The Good Earth*, which was followed by translations of her later books (even those like *The Patriot* in which she condemned the Japanese invasion of China); while *Gone with the Wind* was the greatest success of all, having a sale in its various translations of more than half a million copies. At least twenty-four books by Upton Sinclair were translated into Japanese. A correspondent told him in 1931, "A term now often on the lips of people interested in modern literature is *Sinkurea Jidai,* which means 'The Sinclair Era.'" Many of the American proletarian novelists who flourished in the thirties had larger sales in Japanese, as in Russian, than they had in their own language; and the censors at first were rather easy-going. Leafing through the proof sheets of translations about to be published, they looked chiefly for Japanese equivalents of three words, "revolution," "people's," and "social." If the dangerous words were present, at first they merely deleted them before approving the book for publication; but later they deleted the whole chapters in which they appeared and, still later, they began throwing the translators and publishers into jail. Hidemi Ozaki, who had translated Agnes Smedley's *Daughter of Earth,* was hanged in November, 1944, long after some of Sinclair's translators had preceded him to the scaffold. *Sinkurea Jidai* had ended.

There was also a Sinclair era in China, where at least seventeen of his books had been published by 1930. Six more were then in process of translation, but nobody in this country, it would seem, knows whether they appeared. In China the business of publishing foreign books is not only piratical, as it has been in Japan, but also completely unorganized. Any bookstore in Shanghai is likely to issue its own translations without notifying its rivals, let alone the American authors. Some of these authors have been widely read. There were, for example, at least three translations of *The Good Earth,* one of which was cut and garbled; the other two were widely discussed in the

Chinese press, where some of the reviewers—a minority, as might be expected—thought that Mrs. Buck had presented a true picture. *Gone with the Wind* appeared in one or more unauthorized translations. Lao Shaw, the author of *Rickshaw Boy,* reported for the Chinese writers born after 1910 that their chosen American author was Eugene O'Neill, who was also most influential with the educated public as a whole. Other favorites were Steinbeck and Saroyan.

In India the educated classes read many or most of their American books in the British colonial editions. Whitman, with what might be called his profound smattering of Eastern philosophy, has always had followers there; the greatest of these was Rabindranath Tagore. Gandhi read Thoreau, who contributed to his philosophy of nonviolent resistance; also, according to his nephew Narainadas Gandhi, he read "most if not all" of Upton Sinclair. No study has been made of recent translations into the various Indian languages; but it is known that *The Good Earth* was rendered at least into Bengali, and possibly into others as well, while various books by Sinclair have appeared in Bengali, Hindi, Gujarati, Tamil, Urdu, Telegu, Marathi, and Singhalese.

Beyond a doubt, Sinclair is the most widely translated novelist of the twentieth century not read for pure entertainment. By 1938 there had been 713 translations of his various books, which had then been published in forty-seven languages and thirty-nine countries. There are several reasons for Sinclair's international popularity. Shortly after he wrote *The Jungle,* which traveled round the world within two years of its American publication in 1906, he was adopted as a favorite author by the international working-class movement in both its main branches, the Menshevik and the Bolshevik, later the Social Democratic and the Communist. But his books were also read by the middle classes in most of the countries where they were allowed to circulate, partly because they all told straightforward, rapidly moving stories, but chiefly because each of his novels, besides being a story, was a well documented journalistic survey of some aspect of American life: an industry, a city, a political movement, or a celebrated trial. The world-wide interest in Upton Sinclair was also an interest in America as a whole.

8

From any survey of American books abroad, however incomplete it may be, we gain a somewhat different picture of American literature at home. We learn, for example, that it has been richer and more varied than most of us had suspected from merely reading our choice of each season's new fiction or factual reporting. The export of American literary works has not been standardized, like that of Detroit automobiles; instead each country has been choosing the American books that met its particular tastes. Sometimes these books have been the work of authors little known in the United States who achieved their widest fame in Europe or Asia. Sometimes American writers have been adopted and, as it were, given honorary citizenship by the different countries to which their minds appealed; so that Faulkner in France, Hemingway in Russia (like Jack London and Mark Twain before him), O'Neill and Pearl Buck in Scandinavia, Thomas Wolfe in Germany, Waldo Frank in Latin America, and Upton Sinclair in many parts of the world, but especially in the Orient, have come to be regarded as almost native authors.

At the same time, there are some American books that have swept across the world without pausing at national boundaries. Not a few of them were critical of American standards, and the reason for their popularity is not hard to explain: foreign readers like to be told that not everything is perfect in the land of the jukebox and the low-priced automobile. Most of the universally read books, however, were either adventure stories (a commercialized branch of fiction in which our writers have a long tradition of technical skill), or they were epical novels on the scale of *Gone with the Wind* and *Grapes of Wrath*—it did not matter, apparently, whether they dealt with the past or the present, from a conservative or a radical point of view, so long as they filled a canvas as big as the top of a covered wagon, and so long as they told a story that everyone could follow.

Story, or narrative, according to the English critic Lovat Dickson, is one of two qualities that distinguish recent American fiction. "To the outside observer," he said, "it seemed suddenly to become characteristic of all American entertainment and to mark it off quite sharply from the English equivalent. Story suddenly became of first-rate importance, and appreciation of narrative became a marked American characteristic." The other quality Dickson mentioned was gusto. "Today it seems to us in England," he said, "the essential, distinctive, and enviable quality of American fiction. Somewhere and somehow, in the American novel towards the end of the post-war decade, solemnity was miraculously shed and in its place appeared a new virility as mysteriously and suddenly as the works of Fielding, Sterne, and Smollett had appeared in eighteenth-century England."

French critics were more impressed by other qualities of American fiction (or by the same qualities under different names): they mentioned its intensity and singleness of emotion, its earthy dialogue, its delight in physical violence, and what they called its "pure exteriority," a term they applied to the practice common among American novelists of presenting character in terms of speech and action, without auctorial comments, as if they were writing for the stage. Russian and Czech critics were deeply impressed by the technical discoveries of our novelists, whom they studied very much as

American writers used to study Flaubert. Critics of all nations felt that they were dealing with a unified body of work. For that is our second impression after a survey of American books abroad: besides being immensely varied, they also possess a family resemblance that has not always been recognized at home. "American," said one French critic, "is not so much a nationality as a style."

During the first half of this century, the position of American literature in foreign countries has been completely transformed. It was still regarded, before 1900, as a department of English literature, a sort of branch factory that tried to duplicate the products of the parent firm. After 1930 it came to be regarded as one of the great world literatures in its own right, and perhaps, as regards contemporary work, the greatest of them all. But this transformed position was not merely a secondary result of the growth in economic and military power of the American nation; it was also an independent development that testified to a change in the literature itself. Europeans were not slow to recognize that there had been a literary revival here after 1910; and they showed the same hospitality to the new writers of the interwar period that they had shown, a century before, to the writers of the New York and New England renaissance.

82. END OF AN ERA

Because there had been a literary revival in the years immediately following World War I, many critics in 1945 confidently assumed that history would repeat its pattern and immediately offer a new generation of Fitzgeralds, Hemingways, and Eliots. What these critics did not seem to realize was that the temper of the young men who went into the second war was almost exactly the reverse of that of the young men of 1917. The crusade of 1914–1918 to make the world safe for democracy had not been repeated in 1939–1945, and an era of disillusionment and re-evaluation was not to be expected. The end of hostilities might bring time and opportunity for activity in literature and the other arts, but the kind of literature that appeared would be related to the whole cultural movement of the century rather than to the events of the four years of fighting.

Instead of the beginning, this was the end of an era. By 1952 it had become possible to demonstrate the reality of a second literary renaissance and to place its zenith at some time between 1920 and 1940. Whatever dismay and confusion of mind the social historians and moralists may have found in the interbellum period, the literary historian could now see it as a period in which the United States achieved, for the second time in its history, a cultural flowering. As the Republic once had reached its literary fulfillment in the movement of which Emerson, Melville, and Whitman were the leading spokesmen, so the Continental Nation now had found its mature expression in a dozen or more major writers from Dreiser and Frost to Eliot and Faulkner. In the generic sense, both movements were "romantic." Because many of the controlling ideas of the nineteenth century realists were opposed to those of the idealists, their thought has generally been treated as a reaction against romanticism; but as the second literary movement began to develop in the 1890's, it showed the faith in nature, the belief in emotion as against reason, the pride in religion and nation, and the searching for new forms and meanings that had characterized the earlier romanticism. "The literary movement of the nineties," as Mencken called it, supplied the central romantic drive for the literature of the twentieth century in America. In these terms, its rise and decline may be traced through the first half of that century.

The movement finally succeeded in breaking through resistance sometime between 1912 and 1915 with the major novels of Dreiser, Glasgow, and Cather, the first strong and original poetry of Frost, Sandburg, and Lindsay, and the call for a new literature by the "literary radicals" in criticism. At the same time, the founding of the "little" magazines, the beginning of an independent theater where O'Neill and others could find a hearing, and the establishment of new and experimental publishing houses created more direct means of reaching a rapidly growing public. After 1920, the generation of writers which had thus been somewhat belatedly discovered had had time to follow up their first successes and to compete with the next (the so-called "lost") generation, the young men who were just back from the armed services with the manuscripts of their first and bitter books. The years 1922–1925 seemed to mark a ripening of genius for both poets and novelists, with major works by Robinson, Frost, Dreiser, Glasgow, Stein, and most of the others of the older group. Meanwhile, Sinclair Lewis had appeared with three of his most effective satires, *Main Street, Babbitt,* and *Arrowsmith,* while F. Scott Fitzgerald, Wallace Stevens, John Dos Passos, Eugene O'Neill, Ernest Hemingway, and T. S. Eliot had offered books in which their challenge was first felt. With them, the movement became self-conscious enough to need new language, new symbols, new forms. Their technical experiments alone were enough to change the course of American literary history.

Much has been written about the changes in the temper of American life which were brought about by the stock-market collapse in 1929 and the subsequent years of depression and social reconstruction, but the flow of major writings in all forms seemed to have been little affected. Books of moral and social inventory rather than of radical challenge marked the early years of the decade of the 1930's, and the poetry, fiction, and drama of the "younger" generation deepened in meaning and broadened in theme as their authors approached their middle years. Thomas Wolfe, William Faulkner, Thornton Wilder, William Carlos Williams, and Clifford Odets, among others, had meanwhile made themselves heard. With the award of the Nobel Prize in Literature to Sinclair Lewis in 1930 and to Eugene O'Neill in 1936, American literature was for the second time in its history recognized as a world literature.

The violence in the work of most of these writers shocked their fellow Americans but aroused sincere curiosity and respect abroad. After 1925, American literature was translated, read, discussed, and imitated in France, Germany, Russia, and the Scandinavian countries as no earlier American literature had ever been. As Europe had once taught us to appreciate Poe, Emerson, and Whitman, it discovered particular virtues unseen by us in Hemingway, O'Neill, Pound, and Wolfe. We gradually learned to stop condemning these violent young men for not dispensing sweetness and light, and we were not startled as we once might have been by the high moral tone of the Stockholm address of the most violent of them all, William Faulkner. What had once seemed to be merely a criticism of American society was recognized now as a criticism of life, the ancient voices of tragedy and comedy in a modern language.

When Edmund Wilson described the history of symbolism in *Axel's Castle* (1931), he provided a text for his times as H. L. Mencken and Van Wyck Brooks had done for the 1910's and 1920's. It is in the daring, the vitality, and the overwhelming success of their symbolism that the great books of the early 1930's find their greatness. The years 1930 to 1936 alone saw Hart Crane's *The Bridge*, O'Neill's *Mourning Becomes Electra*, Macleish's *Conquistador*, Wolfe's *Of Time and the River*, Eliot's *Murder in the Cathedral*, Anderson's *Winterset*, Fitzgerald's *Tender is the Night*, Dos Passos' trilogy later assembled as *U.S.A.*, Nathanael West's *Miss Lonelyhearts*, and Faulkner's *Absalom, Absalom!* Steinbeck's *The Grapes of Wrath* (1939) was only one of many efforts during this decade to discover an American tradition, express it in American rhythms, and give it universal meaning by use of symbols. Whether turning with Eliot to the Christian myth, with Steinbeck and Wolfe to the Judaic, or with Anderson and O'Neill to the Hellenic, these writers were expressing in twentieth-century terms man's eternal defiance of his destiny. In either literature or politics, the period 1932–1939 in the United States, and in Western Europe as well, was one of an equilibrium of polarized violence. Such periods produce what De Quincey once called "the literature of power," a term which can be applied to these writings. The literature of the United States had reached its second romantic zenith.

2

Such a burst of literary energy would inevitably expend itself, for the young men would grow old and changing times would take their reckonings. The seeds of a conservative reaction had been sown in the critical movements of the interbellum period. After World War II, the so-called "New Criticism," already firmly established on the political, social, and religious conservatism of T. S. Eliot and on the intellectual challenges of Yvor Winters, Kenneth Burke, and R. P. Blackmur, found its rationale and its method in a closely wrought system of aesthetic analysis. When Archibald MacLeish in "Ars Poetica" (1926) wrote, "A poem should not mean / But be," he said far more than he himself intended or than the earliest phase of this movement was ready to accept. But even a decade earlier, the antiromantic influence of the English philosopher and critic T. E. Hume had been felt by Eliot and others, and the "Practical Criticism" of I. A. Richards had soon thereafter given his American followers a way of dealing with the meaning of a poem without reference to its source. With the widely influential textbook, *Understanding Poetry* (1938), by Cleanth Brooks and Robert Penn Warren, the academic study of literature made a fundamental shift from concern for a poem as an organic product of an author and his culture to its treatment as a complex organization of symbolic imagery, metaphor, irony, and paradox.

The influence of the Nashville "Fugitives" or "Southern Agrarians" had become a dominant national movement when John Crowe Ransom founded the *Kenyon Review* in Ohio (1939), Allen Tate took over the *Sewanee Review* (1944–1946) and Warren and others revived the *Southern Review* in Louisiana (1935–1942). With the moves of Tate, Warren, and later Cleanth Brooks to Minnesota and Yale, the analytical method of literary study, which had come to dominate the academy, was further formalized by such important works as René Wellek and Austin Warren's *Theory of Literature* (1949) and through massive historical studies: Wellek's *A History of Modern Criticism* (1955–1961) and W. K. Wimsatt and Brooks' *Literary Criticism: A Short History* (1957).

The New Critics, however, were not the only formalists of their day; others elaborated their distinct views of the autonomous character of all art. Thus, the Chicago school of neo-Aristotelians, comprising Ronald S. Crane, Elder Olson, W. R. Keast, and Richard McKeon, consolidated their achievement in a large anthology, *Critics and Criticism, Ancient and Modern* (1952). R. P. Blackmur, independent, intuitive, and dazzlingly dark, proved himself as a critic of enduring significance in *Language As Gesture* (1952) and *The Lion and the Honeycomb* (1954). And the Canadian scholar, Northrop Frye, offered in *The Anatomy of Criticism* (1957) an architectonic study of literature, based on exhaustive knowledge of myth, ritual, and archetype, which forced formalism beyond textual analysis.

Thus the new formal criticism became far more than a method. Underlying it was the revival of metaphysical poetry, signalized by Herbert J. C. Grierson's 1912 edition of the poems of John Donne and by an increasing interest on the parts of Pound and Eliot in French symbolism. Closely related to this trend was a focus on myth and symbol, fostered by the new developments in psychology and anthropology of Ernst Cassirer (*The Philosophy of Symbolic Forms*, 1923), Maud Botkin (*Archetypal Patterns of*

Poetry, 1934), and Bronislaw Malinowski (*Magic, Science and Religion*, 1948). Suzanne K. Langer (*Philosophy in a New Key*, 1942) and Richard Chase (*The Quest for Myth*, 1949) formulated in general terms the emphasis on metaphor and symbol which had become the index of literary meaning sought by the new analytical techniques. The result was a fulfillment of Eliot's dictum in 1922, "Poetry is not a turning loose of emotion, but an escape from emotion; it is not the expression of personality, but an escape from personality." In another twenty-five years this statement could be taken as a description of the mainstream as it then was, not only of American poetry, but of American literature in general.

One result of this trend toward intellectuality and conservatism was a reappraisal, after World War II, of the major poets of the interbellum period. The free-flowing naturalism and social involvement of Carl Sandburg, Edgar Lee Masters, and Robinson Jeffers gave way to the tight metaphorical and introspective poetry of their contemporaries, Wallace Stevens, William Carlos Williams, E. E. Cummings, Conrad Aiken, and Marianne Moore. Only Robert Frost of the elder bards survived into the new era because, as it later became apparent, there was a darker and more profound Frost, introspective and critical to the point of cynicism.

At the inauguration of President Kennedy in 1961, a startling new feature was introduced in the traditional ceremonies. By the President's invitation, a poet was asked to prepare a poem and read it from the platform. The poet chosen was inevitably Robert Frost, then in his eighty-seventh year and only two years before his death. The occasion was climactic and symbolic. Frost had long since become the most popular of American poets, not even Longfellow excepted. His readings of his poems interspersed with random comments on life and the making of poetry, were sell-out events year after year. More remarkable than this deserved popularity was Frost's artistic longevity. *A Masque of Reason* was published in 1945, and its companion, *A Masque of Mercy*, and *Steeple Bush* in 1947 when he was seventy-three; *In the Clearing* appeared in 1962. In these later poems Frost continued his dialogue with himself and meditated darkly on man's imminent end in this bomb-shadowed world.

The discovery of this later and deeply philosophical poet, particularly in the *Masques*, led to a critical re-reading of the New England nature verse of the earlier Frost who had seemed concerned mainly with farmhands, country walls, birches, and a snowy evening's stop by a wood. A fuller understanding of Frost's philosophical meanings resulted. The reappraisal which then set in led to biographical revelations which in turn chilled the genial warmth of his long-maintained public image. But each revelation merely disclosed a more and more complex person than had at first appeared, a mind and spirit in rapport with his troubled times, attempting to rescue his sanity in art. Frost's deceptive simplicity seems merely to have screened an underlying conservatism and a symbolism more akin to the work of Pound and Stevens than to that of the poets in the New England bardic tradition.

It was characteristic of Frost's humanity that he supported the movement for the release of Ezra Pound from St. Elizabeths, the Federal hospital for the insane. After the psychiatrists had declared in 1945 that Pound was mentally unfit to stand trial for treason and the jury had given its verdict of "unsound mind," Pound spent twelve years in St. Elizabeths. Here he continued to work on his Cantos and received many younger authors who made a cult of his writing. To Pound's earlier friends who deplored his anti-Semitism and his pro-Mussolini broadcasts during the war, his confinement seemed increasingly absurd. Since he had been judged unfit to stand trial for treason and so probably never would be tried, there was no reason, so his lawyers maintained, why he should not be released, as even convicted traitors had been, in his wife's care. In the summer of 1958 Pound and his wife left America to take up residence in a castle near Merano in the Italian Alps.

Meanwhile in the years of tribulation, Pound pressed on with the Cantos, his twentieth-century *Odyssey*; in 1948, *The Pisan Cantos, 74–84*; in 1956, *Section: Rock-Drill, 85–95 de los cantares*; in 1959, *Thrones 96–109 de los cantares*. In the fullness of time, so Pound averred and the cultists believed, the grand design of the Cantos would stand revealed. To those who were less hopeful, though they admired the Pound of the days when he was demanding that poets must "make it new," the newness now was in such occasional superb passages as the one from Canto LXXXI, which begins:

> The ant's a centaur in his dragon world,
> Pull down thy vanity, it is not man
> Made courage, or made order, or made grace,
>   Pull down thy vanity, I say pull down.

When T. S. Eliot published *The Waste Land* in 1922, he dedicated it to Ezra Pound, "il miglior fabbro." The posthumous publication in 1971 of the early drafts reveals why he thought Pound "the better maker." Pound's incisive revisions changed the nature of the poem and put the younger poet on a level of excellence that made him the leader of his generation. When Pound moved to Italy in 1925, Eliot became also their mentor as editor of the London *Criterion* from 1922 to 1939.

By 1950 one fact that all critics and literary historians could agree upon was Eliot's impressive influence in England, in the United States, and pretty much all over the world where poetry in English was read. Friend and foe alike began to speak of his "literary dictatorship," and to use his critical dicta as the gospel of literary judgment. Although his first important work in both poetry and criticism dates as far back as 1920, the full impact of his influence was not felt until the middle 1940's and bears conclusive testimony to the conservative phase of the literary movement of this era. Although born Thomas Stearns Eliot, of St. Louis, Missouri, and of the New England Eliots, he had long been a British subject; and his *Complete Poems and Plays, 1909–1950* (1952) was unquestionably the most historically important single literary work of the mid-century in both countries. Yet his poetical career had virtually come to an end when he collected his *Four Quartets* in 1943 and his later years were devoted mainly to lecturing and to writing of Christian comedy. He died in 1965; Pound in 1972.

However impressive it was, Eliot's conquest of British and American literature by 1950 did not go unchallenged. His authority was attacked by a "conservative" of another stamp, the poet Robert Hillyer, in the *Saturday Review* in the spring of 1950. Hillyer's protest was against the first award of the Bollingen Prize for Poetry to Ezra Pound's *Pisan Cantos* by the Fellows in American Letters of the Library of Congress, of which group Eliot was a member. A violent literary controversy resulted which later took many forms, for behind the rancor was the more important question, so some thought, of whether or not art could divorce itself from life and survive. Time softened if it did not settle this issue, for it was revived as late as 1972 when a committee of the American Academy of Arts and Sciences proposed Pound for the Emerson-Thoreau medal.

Eliot's protest against the "dissociation of sensibility" which, he thought, had occurred in the late seventeenth century and had led to the excesses of the romantic movement, had obvious kinship with the antiromantic "neohumanism" of his Harvard mentor, Irving Babbitt, and with the emphasis laid by J. E. Spingarn on the need for "a real philosophy of art" rather than the then current (1921) "disconnected body of literary theories." Eliot's own poetry had done much to demonstrate how this reassociation of sensibility might be brought about, how art might become again a kind of experience in its own right as it had been in the seventeenth-century English metaphysicals, rather than merely a halting and inadequate expression of the experience of "life," as organic poets from Wordsworth and Emerson to Frost and Masefield had assumed. The successful revolt against romanticism had been a long time coming, but when it came, it gave a confidence and authority to American literary thought that was recognized worldwide.

Meanwhile the poet who had become the major voice of this movement,

Wallace Stevens, continued to practice in his own way his belief in the integrity of art. Stevens transcended the bourgeois world not by living as a Bohemian but by the transfiguration of conventional experience in an aesthetic derived in part from his teacher at Harvard, George Santayana. The world is the *materia poetica* for this poet obsessed with "the idea of order," who "knew there never was a world" for his singer at Key West, "Except the one she sang, and singing, made." His *Collected Poems* in 1954, the year before his death, confirmed his supremacy in the field which he had early pre-empted for himself.

This was one of many such gatherings to appear in the early 1950s. Not only were the collected editions of Frost and Eliot brought up to date at this time, but new collections of Carl Sandburg, E. E. Cummings, Robinson Jeffers, William Carlos Williams, Archibald MacLeish, Conrad Aiken, and Marianne Moore contributed to the sense of a grand "summing-up" of the poetic achievements of a half-century. Several of these poets continued to be prolific, notably MacLeish, whose verse plays, *J.B.* (1957) and *Herakles* (1967) fulfilled a life-long effort to convert private poetry to "public speech." Williams completed his ambitious poem *Paterson* (1946–1958) well before his death in 1963, though notes and drafts for a sixth section were found among his papers.

Where *The Cantos* had taken all knowledge and most of history as their province, *Paterson* was purposely more parochial, scaling down Whitman's America to the local-color confines of one industrial town in New Jersey with its particular history, its particular moment. *Paterson* presents, as its epigraph states *in medias res*, "a local pride; spring, summer, fall and the sea; a confession; a basket; a reply to Greek and Latin with the bare hands; a gathering up; a celebration . . . a dispersal and a metamorphosis." The city, through a magnificently executed and believable pathetic fallacy, is embodied as a character, an individual, while the roar of the waterfall that powers its mills becomes the inchoate voice of experience which the author succeeds in purifying into poetry.

The backward glance that resulted from this achieved perspective discovered new strengths and beauty in others who had been too lightly dismissed as "coterie" or "minor" voices. John Crowe Ransom's career as a poet virtually ended in 1927 with his third volume, *Gentlemen in Bonds*. So rigorously did he prune in compiling his *Selected Poems* (1945) that less than half of his mature verse was retained. If we lost a poet, we gained a critic. In the *Kenyon Review*, which he founded in 1939, and the Kenyon School of English, he had a little "establishment" of his own. Allen Tate, Ransom's friend and fellow Fugitive, also showed the prevailing tendency of the critic to gain ascendency over the poet. But the poems in *The Winter Sea* volume of 1944 evince a new and terrifying beauty which owed much to Dante, whose influence is also seen in *Poems* (1960). Marianne Moore continued to issue periodically her usual slender but eagerly awaited volumes. After the *Collected Poems* of 1951 came *Like a Bulwark* (1956) and *O To Be a Dragon* (1959). From the beginning she was a poet's poet: Eliot introduced her *Selected Poems* of 1935 and those who wrote about her work were chiefly fellow poets. But Winthrop Sergeant's *New Yorker* profile of 1957 showed that a host of other admirers were making the trip across the East River to her Brooklyn apartment, which was crammed as full of significant oddities as her poems, and is now, after her death, preserved intact in the Rosenbach Museum in Philadelphia.

There has perhaps never been anything like it—the ability of these older and "difficult" poets to equal their best work when they passed the three-score bourne; but it was to the more sustained poems of the period, like Pound's later *Cantos*, Williams's *Paterson*, and Robert Penn Warren's *Brother to Dragons* that younger poets and critics looked, after 1965, for the summing up and the meaning of their predecessors.

3

The extraordinary flowering of American drama which took place in the years between 1915 and 1940 faded during the war years. By 1950 almost all of the older playwrights who made these years memorable in the American theater had disappeared from the scene. Death had claimed Sidney Howard in 1939 and Philip Barry in 1949. Robert Sherwood, who had been drawn into work for the Federal government during the war, died in 1955. Maxwell Anderson's power declined in his later poetic plays. George Kelly offered no new play after 1946. S. N. Behrman was busy adapting the work of others. Clifford Odets moved on to Hollywood, from which he made a few, not very successful, returns to Broadway. The Federal Theatre Project of 1935-1939 had left no progeny. And T. S. Eliot's three comedies, *The Cocktail Party* (1950), *The Confidential Clerk* (1954), and *The Elder Statesman* (1959) are so British in theme and mode as to have no place here except to complete the record of their author's career.

The greatly increased expense of production had much to do with the abrupt decline in the number of plays of literary merit which were seen each season. New York theaters are valuable real estate properties and the owners demand all the rent the traffic will bear. Costs increased so rapidly that if a play did not show signs of making a profit on Broadway in its first week, it was in danger of being closed. On the other hand, such huge returns were possible from successful musical shows that hopeful "angel" money flowed to these productions. The result was that producers played safe and usually ventured only with musical shows or plays adapted from successful novels or biographies. Experimentation was left to the new off-Broadway producers. Even they, in the first years of this movement, relied on the classics of the theater and plays by *avant-garde* European dramatists.

It is ironic, therefore, that the boldest experimenter of the earlier years, Eugene O'Neill, should have triumphed with three of his four plays produced in these Philistine years. If they had been written by a new dramatist, they might not have found a producer.

In the last years of his life O'Neill suffered from a crippling disease which made it almost impossible for him to write. (He could compose only in longhand.) Yet he worked as he could, particularly on two large cycles of plays to which he had given the encompassing titles of *A Tale of Possessors Self-Dispossessed* and *By Way of Obit*. The plays in the second series were to be one-acters. Before his death in 1953 one non-cycle play, *The Iceman Cometh*, was produced (1946). It was the first O'Neill play on Broadway in more than twelve years. The action, set in Harry Hope's saloon (Jimmie-the-Priest's of O'Neill's youth) is another variation on his favorite theme—that only in living by illusion can man be happy. Another non-cycle play, *A Moon for the Misbegotten*, based on the wasted life of O'Neill's brother Jamie, was headed for Broadway in 1947. Because of casting difficulties and poor notices in the tryout period, it was not given a New York production. When it was produced there ten years later, audiences realized that they had seen one of O'Neill's major plays. *A Touch of the Poet*, one of the plays in the *Tale of Possessors* cycle, was finished and could have been presented during the author's lifetime. O'Neill withheld it because he believed there was no contemporary actor who could play the part of the Irish braggart and ex-soldier Cornelius Melody. In the 1958 production, Eric Portman handled the role with distinction.

In 1944 O'Neill wantonly destroyed most of the scenarios and partly finished plays in the two cycles. From this slaughter two plays survive: *More Stately Mansions* and *Hughie*. One other non-cycle play, *Long Day's Journey into Night*, had been finished in 1941, but since it was intensely personal in its treatment of the lives of O'Neill's father, mother, brother, and the days of his own youth, he sealed the manuscript in the presence of his editors in 1945 and told them it was not to be published until twenty-five years after his death. Mrs. O'Neill, who controlled the rights of the play, disobeyed this injunction after the death of O'Neill's son, Eugene, Jr., and offered it for production in this country (it was first seen in Stockholm) to José Quintero. His production was the great event of the 1956 season. O'Neill had faced his dead at last—his hard-drinking and, to him, stingy and tyrannical father, his mother who suffered from drug addiction, his brother James who wasted his life in dissipation. He wrote himself into the play as the sensitive, tubercular, would-be poet Edmund.

Long Day's Journey into Night is undoubtedly O'Neill's greatest play. Now that we can see and read it and possess the circumstances of O'Neill's early life which it transmutes, we know that these agonizing family relationships played a larger part in O'Neill's writing than any other event, idea, or influence—his love of the sea, his beachcombing years, his lingering Catholicism, the philosophy of Nietzsche, the influence of the Greek dramatists and of Strindberg. As the Gelbs say in their biography (1962), the story of Eugene's family "was, indeed, born of tears and blood and was the key to O'Neill's tragic outlook on life and art."

With the exception of O'Neill, dramatists of the pre-war period produced little after 1945 to add to their reputations or to alter earlier critical judgments. Maxwell Anderson, S. N. Behrman, Clifford Odets, William Saroyan, and Thornton Wilder continued to build on their earlier successes, but the only one of the elder dramatists to add significantly to earlier work was Lillian Hellman. *The Children's Hour* (1934) had opened a career in which she proceeded effectively if somewhat uncertainly to chart a mid-course between tragedy and social message with *The Little Foxes* (1939), *Watch on the Rhine* (1941), and *Toys in the Attic* (1960). Meanwhile a new kind of drama was evolving in the early plays of Tennessee Williams, Arthur Miller, and Edward Albee.

4

It was said often enough after World War II that every writer who had seen combat carried in his barracks bag a war novel or plan for one. There must be some truth in this saying, for war novels appeared in abundance as soon as the fighting was over. It had been an all-out war and every household in the land was affected by it. Though such correspondents as John Gunther, William Shirer, Drew Middleton, and Ernie Pyle had reported it ably, the people who had stayed home wanted the novelists to tell all. What Cummings in *The Enormous Room*, Dos Passos in *Three Soldiers*, and Hemingway in *A Farewell to Arms* had done for their war the newer generation of novelists was expected to emulate.

But the literary climate of 1945 was very different from that of 1919 and the new young men were confronted by an older generation of established novelists who were still vigorous enough to command the center of critical and popular attention. In the context of the literary movements of the century, this was the late afternoon rather than the dawn. John Hersey, who had made his name as one of the most brilliant of the war correspondents, was thirty when he published *A Bell for Adano* (1944) and James A. Michener was a decade older when he offered his *Tales of the South Pacific* (1947), both of which showed more narrative skill than power.

The best of the war novels, *Guard of Honor* (1948) by James Gould Cozzens, was a study of private fortunes rather than of combat. This Pulitzer Prize winner was Cozzens' eleventh novel. Until it appeared he was known to only a small number of readers who had made something of a cult of his work.

The summing up was rather to be done by the once rebellious young men of the 1920's and 1930's, now the recognized masters in the field: Hemingway, Faulkner, and Dos Passos. Of the three, Hemingway, who had been silent since *For Whom the Bell Tolls* in 1940, now published least and his career came to an untimely end when he died, in the summer of 1961, of self-inflicted gunshot wounds. The rumor, for which he was apparently himself responsible, that he had a final and major novel nearing completion was symptomatic of the creative frustration he was suffering. All that had appeared by 1950 was *Across the River and into the Trees*—the title is derived from Stonewall Jackson's dying words—in which he pictured the stoic last days of Colonel Cantwell, veteran of two wars and an elderly Hemingway "hero," who holds death off until he can have one more fling at sport and love.

Two years later, in *The Old Man and the Sea*, Hemingway proved to those critics who were beginning to fear an approaching end to a distinguished career that he might still have that major novel in him. Again rumor which could be traced to the author himself suggested that this was but part of a much larger and more ambitious work. Even as it stood as a short tale, perfect in form and execution, it expressed better than Hemingway ever had before his faith in the sufficiency of life lived for itself. Old Santiago's triumphant struggle with his Fish, which results in a giant skeleton, underlines the moral: to have lived intensely is enough. For this, and for his earlier fiction, Hemingway received the 1954 Nobel Prize in literature, the sixth American-born writer to be so honored.

Two posthumous works, *A Moveable Feast* (1964), written in his Cuban retreat in 1957–1958, and *Islands in the Stream* (1970) served to complete the story of his life and works but did little to add to his reputation. The first, a series of nostalgic vignettes of life in Paris in the twenties recaptures the intimate charm of the younger Hemingway, while the second, the long-heralded "masterpiece," is a three-part epic of the adventures of a painter, Thomas Hunter, in the 1930's on the Island of Bimini in the Gulf Stream. The manuscript was pruned by Charles Scribner, Jr. and Mary Hemingway, but otherwise left in the last state that its author had struggled with, vigorous and vivid in spots, but still sprawling. Hunter's battles with himself, his family, war, rum, sex, and nature testify to the fact that here was one major American writer who was the same fighting romantic in the sixties that he had been in the twenties—now struggling against time with unwieldy and inexorable manuscripts. And still the legend grows.

A year and three days after Hemingway's death William Faulkner died of a heart attack in his home town of Oxford, Mississippi, the Jefferson of his novels and stories. Unlike Hemingway, he had published steadily in the years after World War II. At the time of his death his last novel, *The Reivers*, issued only a few weeks before, was making its way up the ladder of the bestseller lists. There was no novel in these years which equaled in complexity and depth such masterpieces as *The Sound and the Fury*, *Light in August*, and *Absalom, Absalom!*, though Faulkner had attempted in *A Fable* (1954) to write profound allegory based on events in the first war which were made to parallel the scenes of Christ's passion and crucifixion. *A Fable* did not clearly convey its message, but it called for a new reading of Faulkner's earlier work. Had a new Faulkner emerged? Was he trying to validate the lofty sentiments of his Stockholm Speech of 1950, in which he had affirmed his belief

. . . that man will not merely endure; he will prevail. He is immortal, not because he alone among creatures has an inexhaustible voice, but because he has a soul, a spirit capable of compassion and sacrifice and endurance. The poet's, the writer's duty is to write about these things. It is his privilege to help man endure by reminding him of the courage and honor and hope and pride and compassion and pity and sacrifice which have been the glory of his past.

In the earlier novels and stories Faulkner, so the legend went, had dealt in violence and brutality, squalor and misery. To his fellow Mississippians, he had seemed bent on persuading the rest of the nation that the deep South was decadent, its old families run to seed, and its yeoman stock ground down and brutalized.

But Faulkner had not changed. Compassion for man is thematic in his earlier work (Quentin Compson, Cash Bundren, Lena Grove, Joe Christmas). In his later work its expression is more overt, as in *Intruder in the Dust* (1948), whose hero, the Negro Lucas Beauchamp, is saved from lynching by the detective work of a white boy and an aristocratic old lady. Episodes in the later stories show Faulkner rehabilitating some of his disreputable characters. In *Requiem for a Nun* (1951), for instance, Temple Drake, the well-born slut of *Sanctuary*, is given a second chance. The stories which form the loosely integrated *The Hamlet* (1940) suggested that ever-breeding Snopes will soon descend on Jefferson like a cloud of seven-year locusts. They do swarm over the village in the other two parts of a new, comic trilogy, *The Town* (1957) and *The Mansion* (1959), but only Flem is down-right evil. Most of the time his rapacity is checked by Lawyer Stevens and V. K. Ratliff, the sewing-machine salesman-philosopher, two of Faulkner's later spokesman. His last novel, *The Reivers* (1962), was in the same vein. He had moved from the tragic irony of his major period to a kind of low-life novel of manners, but the Faulknerian compassion prevails in this phase as in the earlier, and the comic spirit finally triumphs over the tragic shadows.

At the time of his death Faulkner's career was inevitably compared to that of Henry James. Both were innovators in the art of fiction. Their writing had initially been too difficult for the common reader. Neither was diverted from the standards he set himself by failure or hostile criticism or occasional success. Faulkner's twenty-five volumes refuted the famous dictum of Van Wyck Brooks: "The blighted career, the arrested career, the diverted career are, with us, the rule." For with Faulkner, as with James, the exception proved (that is, tested) the rule. In the art of fiction, for his time he was supreme.

During these later years Dos Passos also kept steadily at work. In 1949 he published *The Grand Design*, the last novel in his second trilogy of which the first two were *Adventures of a Young Man* (1939) and *Number One* (1943); in 1952 the three parts were assembled under the title *District of Columbia*. There were ten works in the thirteen years between 1949 and 1961. Five of these were novels, two were travel books. The other three continued the task Dos Passos had set for himself in 1941 when he issued *The Ground We Stand On*, an exploration of the roots of American political and social idealism.

In this second trilogy Dos Passos intended to follow the fortunes of the Spotswood family (two sons and their father) through the Depression and into World War II. To expose Communist and Fascist forces was easy, but by the time Dos Passos began *The Grand Design*, he was so determined to show how President Roosevelt had subverted our freedoms, first through New Deal usurpations and then by taking us into war, that the Spotswood family almost sinks out of sight. In *Chosen Country* (1951), he made use of the past of his family and scenes from his own early years. In *Most Likely to Succeed* (1954) he was back at one of his now congenial tasks, ridiculing the American Communists. *The Great Days* (1958) reviews the war years as remembered by a correspondent who had got around and known the brass.

In 1961 Dos Passos attempted for a third time, in *Mid-Century*, the kind of large-scale, highly organized panoramic novel which he had invented in *U.S.A.*, but in this minute exploration of the labor movement from the days of the Wobblies on down, cynicism and despair outweigh hope. The novel points up what had happened to Dos Passos in the years between. In his deep concern over America's future, like Upton Sinclair he could not resist manipulating his characters for ideological ends. And in his last decade, he finally deserted fiction entirely for an assortment of personal, political, and historical excursions.

The lesson to be learned from the failure of these three masters to match their earlier performances is the obvious one that decline is itself a phase of life. The equilibrium of power and control that produced *Absalom, Absalom!*, *For Whom the Bell Tolls*, and *U.S.A.* could not be repeated. These writers had combined the challenge and possibilities of naturalism with the sensibility and control of art. They could not now top past successes by making explicit in word and symbol the meanings that had been intrinsic in their greatest works.

Although a latecomer to this group of major interbellum romantic naturalists, John Steinbeck had made a convincing entry with the social challenge of *In Dubious Battle* (1936) and his epic of the share-croppers *Grapes of Wrath* in 1939. His sense of tragic irony, however, had been early diluted by moral conviction and by a kind of fantasy that could only have a Gaelic origin somewhere. The gift of elfin and romantic humor, so appealing in *Tortilla Flat*, produced more earthy but somewhat less successful results in *Cannery Row* (1945) and *The Wayward Bus* (1947) as well as the pure folk poetry of *The Pearl* (1948), the year in which he was selected for the Nobel Prize. The epic scope and power of *In Dubious Battle* and *Grapes of Wrath* were recaptured to some degree in *East of Eden* (1952), a realistic and symbolic study of sin on the grand scale, in which humor is mixed with pathos, pathos with tragedy, and tragedy with too explicit a moral intention.

In December 1940, the year in which Scott Fitzgerald died, Nathanael West and his wife were killed in an automobile accident while returning to Hollywood from a weekend hunting excursion into Mexico. The event might almost be thought of as a symbolic end to the era of pure tragicomic irony in American fiction, for West's two short but impressive novels, *Miss Lonelyhearts* (1933) and *The Day of the Locust* (1939) had carried the agony of the human condition into passionate surrealism. There are those who feel that West was the most gifted writer of his day, but the very nature of his work, born as it was of spiritual pain and written in violence, seemed to presage an early death. Fate saw to it that neither he nor Fitzgerald had to adjust to the postwar phase of their contemporaries.

Others who had not quite attained these heights found it easier to continue along established courses of their own. It became the fashion after 1945, especially among formalist critics, to declare the decline and unlamented death of naturalism in American fiction, but a few non-reconstructed survivors of the mode, like James T. Farrell, Vardis Fisher, and Richard Wright, continued to find power in the ruthless honesty of its method and message, while Erskine Caldwell endlessly repeated his early successes in earthy comedy, and Thornton Wilder returned to fiction with *The Eighth Day* (1967).

Farrell in particular was faithful to the long chronicle which had started with *Studs Lonigan* but which had shifted its focus to the author's alter ego in the same gang, Danny O'Neill, and then to Danny's successor, the novelist Bernard Carr. As the tale moved relentlessly from volume to volume, Farrell left many of his earlier readers behind and failed to attract new critics of a mood sympathetic to his obvious mastery of the now-unfashionable medium to which he was so doggedly loyal.

If the comic spirit seemed to have come more into its own in the later work of Faulkner and Steinbeck, it failed to maintain its earlier high level of irony in the novels which Sinclair Lewis offered between 1945 and his death in 1951; but Lewis had, in his satires of the 1920's, demonstrated more clearly than was appreciated at the time that the novel of manners, which had always been one of the most persistent of American fictional genres, was now ready to respond to the challenge of American society on a broader front than the latest of practitioners in the mode, Edith Wharton, had been able to command.

From the vantagepoint of hindsight, it was possible in the late forties to realize that *All the King's Men* (1946) by Robert Penn Warren, *Guard of Honor* (1948) by James Gould Cozzens, *A Rage to Live* (1949) by John O'Hara, *Point of No Return* (1949) by John P. Marquand, and *The Great World and Timothy Colt* (1956) by Louis Auchincloss were birds of a feather—all masterly studies of the cultural patterns of a sophisticated American society, all attacks on the current mode of Hemingway, Faulkner, and Steinbeck by novelists who were more interested in the social environment than in the romantic ego as the principal shaper of the American destiny. This was the antiromantic kind of fiction that Cooper had struggled to achieve in his social novels from *The Pioneers* to *Satanstoe*, that Hawthorne and Melville had so carefully defined as the "novel" in contrast to their own "romance," that reached mature statements in Howells and James and then moved into new experimental forms with Sinclair Lewis and Scott Fitzgerald, and that finally persisted through the era of romantic naturalism of the twenties and thirties as a steady but largely submerged countercurrent of conservatism and satire. If further proof were needed of the essential conservatism of this "end of an era" period, it could be found in the critical recognition in the fifties and sixties of this almost forgotten group of major novelists, all of whom with the exception of Auchincloss, had established reputations by 1945.

Of them all, Marquand was the most typical and prolific, starting with the gentle New England satires, *The Late George Apley* (1937) and *Wickford Point* (1939) and moving to the more complex urban scene of New York City with *Point of No Return* (1949) where social status depends on money-power in contrast to the New England village of Clyde where only family position counts. The broader canvas does not disturb Marquand's central theme that, even in this country, rigid social forms and structures can coerce and crush the individual. For, like all successful novelists of manners, he loved and was a part of the society he so ruthlessly exposed.

The Pennsylvania town of Gibbsville (Pottsville) provided the principal locale for John O'Hara's Lantenengo County saga. A town of some 25,000 inhabitants, it was dominated by the middle-class aristocracy it had bred out of its own past. O'Hara's first novel, *Appointment in Samarra* (1934) gained a phenomenal success by irritating most critics of that day, but O'Hara knew what he wanted to do and went stubbornly ahead in his explorations of the hidden life of the country club set in his fictional Gibbsville, Port Johnson, and Fort Penn. From the beginning he was a popular novelist and short story writer. Born in 1905, the son of a doctor in Pottsville, he had worked at various odd jobs before he became a newspaper feature writer. He knew Hollywood from the inside and New York's theater and speakeasy café life and society. He grew up as a writer with the *New Yorker* and helped to formulate the typical slice-of-life short story which that magazine featured.

O'Hara's Lantenengo County saga, which began with *Samarra*, and embraced *A Rage to Live* (1949), *Ten North Frederick* (1955), and other novels and short stories down to his last, *The Lockwood Concern* (1965), suggests, as James Tuttleton has pointed out, "the density of an interrelated social world comprehensively imagined and precisely planned." If that plan is also superficial and somewhat marred by a cynical view of sex, it is at least thoroughly mastered by its chronicler, who has the intimate knowledge of detail and the technical control of his chosen medium to "tell it all."

The South too produced, in addition to Faulkner, its share of social critics in the serious and introspective vein. A younger member of the Nashville "Fugitive" group of poet-critics, Robert Penn Warren, had published two promising novels—*Night Rider* (1939) and *At Heaven's Gate* (1943)—before the end of World War II. His reputation was made secure by *All the King's Men* (1946), a popular as well as a critical success. Thereafter he seldom failed to score with the reading public. His popularity is not easy to explain, for the novels are subtle in theme and construction and are filled with symbolic meaning. Yet there is plenty of story interest and violent action, particularly so in *World Enough and Time* (1950) and *Band of Angels* (1955), and when the situation requires it, the language is bawdy.

Two themes are dominant in Warren's novels: the need for self-fulfillment, which can be achieved only through self-recognition, and the inevitability of contamination by the world when one steps out of the prison of self. Usually these themes are in conjunction. In *Night Rider*, Percy Munn is reluctantly drawn into the tobacco war, on the side of the growers, for the best of reasons. But as he becomes deeply involved, he commits acts which earlier would have horrified him. In the end he is annihilated, but not until he comes to some understanding of his selfhood. Similarly in *All the King's Men*, Jack Burden, close to the corrupting power of Willie Stark (modeled on Huey Long), attempts to understand the evil that flows from Willie and so discovers his own identity.

As a teacher and writer on the art of fiction, Warren became almost too much concerned in his later novels with experimental themes and technical mastery of structure, symbolism, and style. *Band of Angels* (1955), *The Cave* (1959) and *Flood* (1964) stretch the limits of reader credulity while skillfully answering to the requirements that the novelist has demanded of his art. Warren's return to major poetry in *Brother to Dragons* (1953) was welcomed by his critics.

But the social critic who most successfully raised the comedy of manners to the level of serious drama was James Gould Cozzens. Starting in a low key, with unsensational characters and plots and a style much heavier than that of O'Hara or Marquand, Cozzens was slow to gain acceptance by the reading public and the critics. Not until the publication of *The Last Adam* (1933) and *Men and Brethren* (1936) could one be certain of the kind of subject he would be likely to treat and the techniques he would use. He had changed course in each of the earlier works, of which there were five between 1924 and 1934.

In *The Last Adam*, Cozzens experimented with the kind of theme, social setting, and central character to which he would return in all of his subsequent novels except the semiautobiographical *Ask Me Tomorrow* (1940). The central character of *The Last Adam*, Dr. George Bull, dominates life in the small village of New Winton, often to the disgust of his fellow-townsmen. Here at last is the typical Cozzens pattern: at the center a man who is no paragon of virtue but whose professional competence and sense of responsibility serve the small community of which he has long been a member.

In *Men and Brethren* (1936), Cozzens looked at the ministry. The Reverend Ernest Cudlipp, Vicar of New York's Episcopal church of St. Ambrose (chapel of ease to wealthy Holy Innocents) is no ascetic and his calling is more prudential than mystical. But he is devoted, wise, sometimes worldly for churchly ends, and he usually knows the answer to the question which the Jews on the day of Pentecost put to Peter and the other Apostles: "Men and Brethren, what shall we do?"

In three later novels, Cozzens found his central figure in a lawyer's office. In the first of these, *The Just and the Unjust* (1942), the same sort of common-sense conscience battles with the ins and outs of technicalities which the textbooks only mention, the inside and the seamy side of the law. In *Guard of Honor* (1948), perhaps Cozzens's most satisfactory portrait of a strong character caught in "the culture's hum and buzz of implication," as Lionel Trilling has described the fictional context of a society, the central figure is a Judge, who, as Colonel Ross, has changed his gown for a uniform without escaping the central problem with which Cozzens is habitually concerned, the struggle of an individual to realize moral integrity within the rigid structures of a profession and a society. Without his good sense and knowledge of both the law and human nature, Ocanara Air Base would fall apart. The tense racial conflict might erupt into the scandal for which the press is greedy.

Nine years passed between *Guard of Honor* and the next novel, *By Love Possessed* (1957). Meanwhile Cozzens's reputation had grown and the new book was awaited with great interest. It proved to be his most ambitious novel and one in which he explores most fully his favorite theme of the moral dilemmas which the professional man of good conscience must face. A lawyer is again the central figure. Arthur Winner moves through the dooms which threaten clients and friends with the expertness of a disciplined moral navigator. In the end he too, having once been by unlawful love possessed, has to equivocate. The ironic conclusion is not intended to be a judgment. The reverberations of Shakespeare's *Julius Caesar* in the novel make it clear (if we need a hint) that Arthur Winner is a Brutus, brought low, not by patriotic zeal but by the love that possessed him.

Another reason why no great stir was made over Cozzens until late in his career is that he was not an innovator as Hemingway, Dos Passos, and Faulkner had been. Writing in the tradition of the novel of manners and morals, he seemed to be doing well what George Eliot and E. M. Forster had done in their time, and what Marquand and O'Hara were doing, in a lighter vein, beside him. Not until *Guard of Honor* appeared did critics begin to call attention to the flawless structure of the later novels, noting how subtly Cozzens uses the classical unities for his purpose. Each of these novels covers a crucial span of time (twenty-six hours for *Men and Brethren*, forty-nine for *By Love Possessed*). The action is confined to one small town, one airbase, one city parish. Though what happens is related objectively, we view the action from the angle of vision of the central character. These are usually men over forty, skilled in their professions, who keep their society from falling apart without gaining any lasting satisfaction for themselves. Cozzens had added a moral dimension to the contemporary novel of manners.

MID-CENTURY AND AFTER

83. THE NEW CONSCIOUSNESS

Since 1945, the world has undergone profound transformations. The United States, in particular, has experienced change more acutely, more rapidly, than other nations. Its special political and economic position in a world neither at peace nor at war, its ethnic character and technological resources, its very myths about itself, all conspired to strain its psychic life and alter its destiny. Perhaps the new consciousness of America was not single but multiple, a continuously changing consciousness of the new.

Survival was the tacit obsession of contemporary man. Yet in America —which ushered the nuclear age at Alamogordo in 1945, and sent Colonel Neil Armstrong to walk with giant steps on the moon, in 1969—the issues did not focus only on the doomsday bomb or the space program. A succession of wars from Korea to Vietnam; the explosion of the earth's population; ravages to the natural environment, renewed awareness of poverty and class distinctions in our society; continued discrimination by race. sex, and age; a crisis of historic American institutions, from Congress, the Presidency, and the Supreme Court on down; protest of every kind—all these perpetuated a mood that none could entirely ignore. Science and its extension in technology, accelerating all change, proved a vast boon and arch threat. Science could teach mankind how to reach quasars at the end of the universe and alter human genes, but remained silent concerning the ultimate moral and political decisions of the race. More immediately, technology pervaded the quotidian life of Americans, working miracles both for and against the quality of that life.

It became clear that the collapse of older values, older modes of behavior and awareness, left the world in the form of organized chaos, a bewildering mixture of anarchy and control. Increasingly, the public realm seemed ruled by a variety of fantasies, both comic and dreadful. Increasingly, too, the individual found himself driven toward apathy, violence, nihilism, which offered no true escape from the mass surrealism of the superstate. At the same time, as if the American Dream had suddenly become a universal dream, the promise of infinite human possibilities hung everywhere in the air. This, too, was part of the new consciousness.

The shifts in that consciousness were roughly reflected in the slogans, in the symbolic actions and qualities, of the Presidency. Roosevelt died in 1945, before the explosion at Hiroshima; Truman, who made the fateful decision, saw the war to a close. In the late forties, the Marshall Plan realized for a moment the large hope of linking and restoring broken nations. America was then preeminent in power and moral authority. But the Truman Doctrine soon certified the cold war; power politics begot caution and suspicion. During the Eisenhower years in the fifties, affluence and conformity were scarcely imperiled by McCarthyism on the one hand, or Beat revolt on the other; and the threat of massive retaliation hardly disrupted the quest of the "silent generation" for a good life in the suburbs. By the Inauguration of Kennedy in 1961, however, the country was eager for the spirit and style of the New Frontier. This spirit, thwarted by the assassination of the President in 1963, seemed to generate a new kind of national violence or insanity; the killers of Martin Luther King and Robert Kennedy struck in that same decade. Meanwhile, the Great Society of Johnson failed to materialize; America, wrenched by the Vietnam War, began to break out in dissent. The Berkeley Free Speech Movement of 1964 helped to foment rebellious movements of every kind: Students for a Democratic Society and Weathermen; Congress of Racial Equality and Black Panthers; Women's Lib and The Gay Liberation Front; Chicano and Red Power; Hippies and Yippies, Freaks and Crazies. Prefigured by the Beat Movement, a counterculture of the young flowered in the sixties. Its members imagined that they had discovered new versions of America in psychedelics, communes, occult literature, rock music, underground presses, body languages, and ecology. In the early seventies, however, a reaction against the frenetic activism of the immediate past was confirmed by the ethos of the Nixon Administration. The President journeyed to Peking and Moscow, devalued the dollar, and in January of 1973, officially withdrew from the nation's longest and most noxious war; but the national scandals and constitutional crises following the disclosures of Watergate brought the Presidency to a nadir of confidence. The future of America was open to any utopian or dystopian "scenario," as futurologists liked to say.

2

Political slogans and actions, however, cannot fully convey the changing temper of the postwar period. The very burden of self-awareness in a time of global anxiety drove men to seek more compelling formulations of their situation than politics can provide. These formulations, which drew on sociology and psychology, philosophy and theology, science and technology, criticism and *belles lettres*, amounted to a comprehensive view of man's relation to himself and the world. As such, they challenged the literary imagination and documented subtle shifts in the tenor of the years.

By the late forties, it became clear that America had developed a new kind of society. It was still possible for men of an earlier generation, like Lewis Mumford and Joseph Wood Krutch, to speak with the authority of a humane and unified cultural view. But the new "mass culture" seemed to rest on moral, economic, and technological premises of a different kind, seemed to express in new ways old psychic needs. This was evident in two highly controversial works, Alfred Kinsey's *Sexual Behavior of the American Male* (1948) and *Sexual Behavior of the American Female* (1953). Neutral in tone and heavy with statistics, these studies could still show marked changes in the American character, large discrepancies between practice and ideals. But the most influential work in that respect was David Riesman's *The Lonely Crowd* (1950). Its brilliant analysis of the emergent "other-directed" patterns of social behavior began a reconsideration of the historic individualism of America and its Protestant work ethic. Another challenge to the historic ideas of American democracy came from C. Wright Mills. In his two books, *White Collar* (1951) and *The Power Elite* (1956), Mills passionately exposed the invisible economic and political controls of a post-industrial nation. The list of cultural and sociological works that followed these books is long and varied; it includes numberless treatments of segments of American society as well as attempts to deal with the whole of it. By the late fifties, such anthologies as Bernard Rosenberg and David Maning White's *Mass Culture* (1957) or Eric Larrabee and Rolf Meyersohn's *Mass Leisure* (1958) began to have a familiar ring. Yet it would be an error to conclude that the sociological imagination exhausted itself in the first decade after the war. John Kenneth Galbraith, for instance, followed his earlier work, *The Affluent Society* (1958), with a probing analysis of America, *The New Industrial State* (1967); and Dwight Macdonald continued to delight and irritate with his sharp perceptions, in *Against the American Grain* (1962).

Complementing the sociological view, psychology also widened its claims on the American mind during the forties. Part of these claims concerned the study of myth, ritual, and archetype which the great modernist writers— Yeats and Eliot, Joyce and Faulkner—had stimulated decades earlier, and which certain critics continued to sponsor well into the fifties. Thus, such classics as Freud's *Totem and Taboo* (1918) and Frazer's *The Golden Bough* (1922), acquired new relevancy. Ritual and archetype, guilt and atonement, the cycles of the seasons, ceremonies of worship, were all perceived as fundamental descriptions of reality, of man's psyche in its primordial connections with the universe. Increasingly, psychology and anthropology met in the explorations of man's primitive heritage as the works of C. G. Jung, Otto Rank, and Geza Roheim showed. Increasingly, too, the efforts of such critics as Joseph Campbell, Francis Fergusson, Philip Wheelwright, Leslie Fiedler, and Northrop Frye elicited the implications of that heritage for various branches of literary studies.

The claims of psychoanalysis itself, however, were certainly as strong as those of mythography. Psychoanalysis created its own mode of discourse in urban America, its own fashionable chatter. Yet as Lionel Trilling brilliantly argued in *Freud and the Crisis of Our Culture* (1955), psychoanalysis also contained the elements of a philosophy of art, history, and human existence, all gloomily sketched in Freud's own *Civilization and Its Discontents* (1930). This last work was the point of departure for such original and vastly dissimilar psychoanalytic works as Erik Erikson's *Childhood and Society* (1950), Herbert Marcuse's *Eros and Civilization* (1955), and Norman O. Brown's *Life Against Death* (1959).

A more explicitly philosophical tendency emerged in the fifties. Opposition to complacencies of the period drew on the resources of secular existentialism, on man's awareness of himself as isolated and mortal. There was much, of course, in the American experience, willed, dangerous, and extreme as it often was, to nourish the sense of solitary self-reliance. Thus it came as no surprise when certain European thinkers, notably Jean-Paul Sartre and Albert Camus, became popular in America. Their readers here were also readers of such American novels as J. D. Salinger's *The Catcher in the Rye* (1951) and Ralph Ellison's *Invisible Man* (1952). Without being precisely existentialist, both works sought meaning in the most private gestures of irony, love, or rebellion. This search pervaded the broadly existential spirit of American literature during the fifties.

But the existential drive to meaning was not only secular in character; to a large extent, it was also religious. Hence the success of such works as Paul Tillich's *The Courage To Be* (1952), and the renewed interest in both formal theology and mystical experience. Spanning various faiths, this interest gave currency to the thought of Martin Buber, Nicolas Berdyaev, Gabriel Marcel, among religious existentialists, and of Reinhold Niebuhr and Karl Barth, among theologians. At times, however, the religious will implied more than self-transcendence; it implied an urgent criticism of the Western world, transcendence of civilization itself. Such was the motive of the Beat Movement which borrowed blissfully from Buddhist texts. In this revival of Oriental mysticism—it was to persist into the seventies—the philosophical works of D. T. Suzuki and Alan Watts played a crucial part.

Both strains of religious and secular existentialism met in an extraordinary work, Norman Mailer's essay, "The White Negro," collected in *Advertisements for Myself* (1959). The essay depicted the hipster, hero of the American night, living with instinct and the "rebellious imperatives" of the self. His existence in the jungles of cities embodied, and indeed preceded, all the formulations of European existentialists; his intense knowledge of magic, murder, and madness presaged a larger madness in the land. Coming at the end of a decade, Mailer's work seemed to mark a turning point in the sensibility of the age. For as the momentary openness of the forties had yielded to closure in the fifties, so did the latter break out into the tumults of the sixties. The various intellectual trends of earlier years continued in an era more apocalyptic, antinomian, and experimental in mood.

The mood of the sixties was reflected in the works of certain prophetic figures who became spokesmen of various movements or cults. Paul Goodman, of course, had begun to publish two decades earlier; but it was only in such works as *Growing Up Absurd* (1960) and *Utopian Essays and Practical Proposals* (1962) that his ideas became influential. These ideas concerned education, gestalt psychology, community anarchy, sexual ethics, and city planning, among many others. Mediating often between the Old Left and the New, Goodman seldom took the militant political stance of Herbert Marcuse. The latter sounded, in such works as *One Dimensional Man* (1964) and *An Essay on Liberation* (1969), the post-Marxist call to revolution which the New Left echoed around the world.

Approaching the same questions in a perspective at once more psychological and mystical than Marcuse's, Norman O. Brown followed his earlier, post-Freudian critiques of history with *Love's Body* (1966). In this original and hieratic work, composed mostly of aphorisms, Brown demanded the abolition of repressive reason and culture, of the reality principle itself. His complex, symbolic vision, however, was often pressed by epigones into the service of various religious and erotic cults. In sharp contrast with Brown, B. F. Skinner put his faith not in inner revelation but in outward regulation of behavior. His stilted utopian novel, *Walden Two* (1947), reached the height of its popularity two decades after its publication. His most controversial pronouncements appeared in *Beyond Freedom and Dignity* (1971), wherein Skinner argued that the old myth of individual liberty, of "autonomous man," would prove inadequate for human survival.

Politics, psychology, and religion could serve as agents of social transformation; science and technology could do so even more. Among the prophets of technology, the Canadian born Marshall McLuhan focused on the impact of various media on culture. In his central statement, *Understanding Media* (1964), McLuhan challenged the dominance of linear, visual, mechanical, and print-oriented culture, and predicted the emergence of the "global village," shaped by the invisible forces of computer technology and electric media. Buckminster Fuller went even farther in applying the principles of his "comprehensive, anticipatory design science" to the human situation. His many works, including *Nine Chains to the Moon* (1963) and *Utopia or Oblivion* (1969) declared a scientist's faith in man's capacity to conquer scarcity and conflict through technology, and indeed to reverse physical entropy through metaphysical organization of thought. The great appeal of Fuller's vision, naive as it sometimes seemed, rested on its rejection of violence and unreason, its avoidance of power politics, in proposing solutions to world problems. For the world, as Fuller insisted, was but a single spaceship called Earth.

There were, of course, many other trends in the sixties, trends more significant, perhaps, for their broad impact on culture than for their precise philosophic content. Foremost among these was the Black Power movement which drew on such disturbing statements as *The Autobiography of Malcolm X* (1965) and Eldridge Cleaver's *Soul on Ice* (1968). The student movement, originating in Berkeley, influenced both politics and pedagogy in far-flung places of the world. Betty Friedan's *The Feminine Mystique* (1963) gave the Women's Liberation movement a consciousness of itself that later works by Kate Millett, Gloria Steinem, and Germaine Greer further developed. The ecological concern, reverting to Rachel Carson's *Silent Spring* (1962), acquired international prestige as scientists and conservationists joined forces around the globe. The consumer movement also commanded the attention of both government and industry after Ralph Nader's indictment of Detroit car makers, *Unsafe at Any Speed* (1965). The new eroticism, sometimes frankly pornographic, throve on the relaxation of censorship laws; for the Grove Press had won in 1962 its legal right to republish Henry Miller's *Tropic of Cancer* (1931). At the same time, more precise knowledge of sexual behavior became widely available in such scientific studies as William H. Masters and Virginia E. Johnson's *Human Sexual Response* (1966). Somehow, the great rock festivals of 1969, at Woodstock and Altamont, seemed to epitomize the spirit of the sixties which Theodore Roszak described in *The Making of a Counter Culture* (1969), to epitomize its bright hopes and vicious lapses.

Yet the various tendencies of the sixties did not, of course, come to an abrupt end. Rather, they were modified by the sense of privacy, of restraint, or of outright lassitude, that became evident in the early seventies. Some former liberation movements became more spiteful and erratic before adapting themselves to the times, before finding a broader base for their appeal. Others, like the student movement, seemed quietly to fade. One thing was certain: the nation was experiencing a profound crisis of confidence. Henceforth, for better or for worse, America would never appear the same to others or to itself.

3

Criticism, *belles lettres* in general, also reflected changes in the consciousness of the postwar years. Despite its academic influence, the "New Criticism" and other kinds of formalism had exhausted their original powers by the late fifties; its exegetical enterprise had become too rarefied. Other approaches— mythographic, psychoanalytic, sociological—began to proliferate. The need was for a broader and more forceful critical vision, philosophic yet immediate, attentive to the literary qualities of the text yet quick in its cultural perceptions. This need was fulfilled in part by the works of Lionel Trilling, Leslie Fiedler, and Alfred Kazin. Dissimilar as they are, these men shared a certain moral and social intensity, and stood between the older generation of critics and the new.

Trilling's distinguished works, *The Liberal Imagination* (1950), *The Opposing Self* (1955), *Beyond Culture* (1965), revealed a subtle and profound knowledge of both the literary and social facts of the last two hundred years, a temper finely poised between the ideas of the Enlightenment and of Romanticism. His critique of the liberal tradition in America also contributed significantly to the revaluation of literary ideas in that period. Still, Trilling's aloofness from current literature, his excessive caution of the new culture, tended to limit his perspective and to qualify his intellectual authority on younger critics. By contrast, Leslie Fiedler appeared too polemic. He began his critical career with an obsessive interest in certain archetypes— the Jew, the Negro, the Indian, among others—which illuminate American life and literature. His major work, *Love and Death in the American Novel* (1960, 1966), explored the gothic, picaresque, and sentimental traditions of fiction in a perspective both mythic and social. His *Collected Essays* (1971), gathering the best of several earlier volumes, exhibited him as a courageous, sometimes erratic, more often inventive critic. Seldom inventive as a literary thinker, Alfred Kazin was still energetic as a reviewer and cultural critic; and his autobiographical works had a certain vividness and density of perception. But his essays in *Contemporaries* (1962) and *Bright Book of Life* (1973) showed an uncertain sensitivity to new authors. His best work remained *On Native Grounds* (1942), about the period between 1890 and 1940 in American letters.

Still younger critics, lacking the Marxist, Freudian, or New Criticism prejudices of the thirties and forties, proved highly attuned to shifting definitions of art and sensibility. Some felt that the concepts of art and culture themselves were under suspicion; "anti-art" and "post-culture" became current terms in the sixties and seventies. Others realized that honored literary quarterlies seldom sponsored new writing or thought. The establishment of letters seemed to disperse its influence through periodicals as curiously various as *The New Yorker, Evergreen Review, Ramparts, Playboy, The New York Review of Books*, and *Harper's*, as well as through many smaller academic journals and fugitive little magazines. Above all, many of the younger critics sensed that a distinct type of literature, postmodern rather than modern in its artistic and social character, had come into being in different parts of the world.

Among the first critics to treat postwar American fiction seriously, in *After the Lost Generation* (1951), John W. Aldridge also entered a major cultural controversy of the sixties, *In the Country of the Young* (1970). Another cultural critic, Benjamin De Mott, ranged over numerous topics in the lively, and at times coy, essays of *Hells and Benefits* (1962) and *Supergrow* (1969). The editors of two prestigious but no longer experimental magazines, *Commentary* and *Partisan Review*, Norman Podhoretz and Richard Poirier, respectively, wrote with deeper insights into the literary situation. Podhoretz's *Doings and Undoings* (1964) and Poirier's *The Performing Self* (1971) showed how much the energies of society and the idiom of criticism could change in the seven years that separated their publication. Susan Sontag was among the most brilliant, venturesome, and occasionally brittle, of the newer critics. Her analyses of camp, pornography, science fiction, cinema, happenings, and the new sensibility, in *Against Interpretation* (1966) and *Styles of Radical Will* (1969), were original contributions to the awareness of the period. The concern of Ihab Hassan, from *Radical Innocence* (1961) to *The Dismemberment of Orpheus* (1971), was with *avant-garde* movements of various kinds, particularly with the postmodern tendency of literature to subvert, parody, or transcend itself, a literature of silence. Youngest in this group, Richard Kostelanetz edited many works on emergent tendencies in arts and letters, and wrote himself *The Theatre of Mixed Means* (1968) and *Master Minds* (1969).

The direction of still another group of critics, also younger than the generation of Trilling, also antiformalist, could be discerned in the sixties. These critics include Geoffrey Hartman, J. Hillis Miller, Paul de Man, and Harold Bloom. They had in common a more theoretical approach to literature, a less immediate interest in new writing; and they shared their academic affiliation with Yale University during the seventies. Murray Krieger perceived in them a bias against the discrete analysis of texts, against the pretense of distance and objectivity in interpretation. That bias Krieger himself partly showed in such works as *The Play and Place of*

Criticism (1967). But the group had in common more than a bias: it combined a special understanding of Romantic myth and literature with a keen interest in European structuralism, linguistics, phenomenology, and hermeneutics. Hence its familiarity with such figures as Claude Lévi-Strauss, Jacques Lacan, Ferdinand de Saussure, Georges Poulet, Roland Barthes, Michel Foucault, and Jacques Derrida, shapers all of an intricate critical movement abroad. A strong awareness of that movement could be seen in Hartman's *Beyond Formalism* (1971), Miller's *Poets of Reality* (1965), de Man's *Blindness and Insight* (1971), and, more indirectly, in Bloom's original works, from Shelley's *Mythmaking* (1959) to *The Anxiety of Influence* (1973). These scholarly studies, which tended sometimes toward a certain involution of language, delimited a new area of literary consciousness in America.

Standing somewhat apart from these various circles of literary concern, Hugh Kenner gradually appeared as one of the most significant critical presences in America. His earlier works treated mainly such modernist figures as Joyce, Eliot, Pound, and Wyndham Lewis. But Kenner also wrote several books, among them *Samuel Beckett* (1961, 1968), *The Counterfeiters* (1968), and *Bucky* (1973), which clarified crucial aspects of the postmodern imagination. In the end, it was the quality of his elliptic mind, the ferocity of his learning, evidenced in *The Pound Era* (1971) that guaranteed his eminence more than any critical fashion or theory could.

Yet impressive as American criticism was in that period, another kind of writing possessed greater power or immediacy, certainly greater popularity, in the sixties and early seventies. The genre was a variant of the old belle lettristic essay, and went by the plain name of nonfiction or, more modishly, the "new journalism." Such writing often cut across traditional intellectual disciplines, compounding biography and analysis, anecdote and polemic, reportage and poetry. It revealed the inner stresses of culture in a way that permitted both author and reader to create a place for themselves, as *persons*, in the midst of current complexities. Significantly, some of the best examples of nonfiction came out of Black experience. Thus the essays of James Baldwin, from *Notes of a Native Son* (1955) to *No Name in the Street* (1972), seemed sometimes more impressive than his fiction. In a more stylish vein, Tom Wolfe dramatized the curious manners and morals of America in several works, including *The Kandy-Kolored Tangerine-Flake Streamline Baby* (1965) and *The Electric Kool-Aid Acid Test* (1968) which centered on novelist Ken Kesey and his Merry Pranksters. John Cage experimented with the format of the essay itself, regulating the typography on each page by computerized random operations derived mainly from the *I Ching*. An apostle of the *avant-garde* in various arts, Cage turned his extraordinary attention to social and human problems in *Silence* (1961) and *A Year From Monday* (1967). But it was Norman Mailer, of course, who captured the paramount questions of the moment magically, and pressed them on a larger public in forms that his heroic, clownish, and sagacious ego could devise. *The Armies of the Night* (1968), *Miami and the Siege of Chicago* (1968), *Of a Fire on the Moon* (1970) were less records than revelations of America's struggle with itself, in quest of new life.

There were, of course, many other gifted practitioners of nonfiction: Truman Capote, John Hersey, James Michener, Joan Didion, Jimmy Breslin. Yet few of them experimented with the genre itself, as did Cage, or possessed the power of Mailer. Curiously enough, the most remarkable instance of nonfiction may have been a collective effort, the series of *The Whole Earth Catalogue* (1968–1971), edited by Stewart Brand.

4

Since 1945, the changes in literature itself were more elusive than any analysis of social, intellectual, and critical trends could imply. Nonetheless, a certain pattern of literary history could be made from the passing years.

In the forties, younger writers were eager to escape the literary and political inheritance of the thirties, that is, escape both naturalism and socialism in their various hues. Thus they invoked ancestors of an earlier time— Eliot and Pound, Faulkner and Hemingway, O'Neill—whose shadow was to hang over the postwar scene. With the blessings of formalist critics, the new writers often favored mythic and complex symbolic forms. This was particularly true in the South where a renaissance of fiction, featuring Carson McCullers, Truman Capote, and Flannery O'Connor, seemed in progress. Yet many of the new writers had also shared the experience of total violence during the war. That experience maintained a certain tension in their work between artistic order and natural energy. The promise of the forties was rich: Norman Mailer, Saul Bellow, Theodore Roethke, Robert Lowell, Tennessee Williams, and Arthur Miller all began to publish then.

During the fifties, several tendencies appeared to coexist. Elegance and ceremony prevailed in a kind of literature that was soon labeled academic. By the mid-fifties, however, literary genres began to respond to a more jagged, roguish, or grotesque sense of reality. Leading the way, the novel veered toward existential or picaresque modes. Typically, its hero was a rebel-victim, a lone emissary of the Self in the repressive land of Culture, an ironic redeemer of reality. The lines that separated comedy from tragedy, satire from sentimentality, rigid from improvisational forms, blurred. To this antiformalist tendency, also labeled antiacademic, the San Francisco poets, including

Lawrence Ferlinghetti and Robert Duncan, the Black Mountain group surrounding Charles Olson, and the Beat writers, notably Allen Ginsberg and Jack Kerouac, gave their spontaneous energy. At once existential and mystic, the Beats in particular drew on the American traditions of rhapsodic dissent and transcendental affirmation. Brief in span and mixed in artistic quality, these related movements exerted, nevertheless, a critical influence on postwar literature. Before the end of the decade, two other movements had also gained recognition. Starting with the early works of Saul Bellow and Bernard Malamud, Jewish fiction appeared among the signal accomplishments of American literature. And the distinguished novel of Ralph Ellison, *Invisible Man*, preceded the urgent development of Black writing in decades to come.

In the sixties, literature showed increasing tolerance for fantasy and incongruity. Eroticism, gallows humor, comic surrealism, the absurdist manner, prevailed. Pop, op, funk, earth, minimal, and concept art, happenings, and mixed media affected literature by their antic and anarchic spirit; so did the guerrilla politics of the day. A playful postexistential vision, vaulting over various genres and subcultures, at once parodic and desperate, erudite and trivial, challenged the assumptions of art, of culture, of being. Literature was at times engaged in an epistemological quest of its own origin; at other times, it seemed to anticipate a sudden lexical death. But out of its own exhaustion, literature created striking new languages. In fiction, the work of William Burroughs, John Barth, Thomas Pynchon, gave evidence of this. In drama, the off-Broadway plays of Edward Albee and Jack Gelber, staged just before the turn of the decade, were superseded by the more radical theatre of still younger playwrights, like Sam Shepard, working off-off-Broadway. And in poetry, the major, independent voice of John Berryman articulated his own richly absurd idiom to conquer absurdity—as did the voice of Sylvia Plath—before suicide.

What the literary imagination would reveal of itself in the seventies was still uncertain. The future, which serious science fiction helped to dramatize, remained America's largest poem, daily revised. For the very idea of an elite *avant-garde*, presupposing a coherent bourgeois order subject to the norms of history, seemed to have become obsolete.

84. POETRY

"THE ARTIST," Ezra Pound observed long before World War II, "is the antenna of the race." Many implications of the new consciousness were anticipated but not fully developed in the poetry of the rebels of 1912—Pound himself, T. S. Eliot, William Carlos Williams, and Wallace Stevens—who expressed the profound dislocation of the present century from the past. At the same time the example of William Butler Yeats as well as the critical essays of Eliot insisted upon "the presence of the past in the present." American poetry since 1945 discloses both the tenacious hold of the historical imagination upon our poets and their explorations of irrational, unhistoried, and unexampled experiences.

"It is not meters, but a meter-making argument that makes a poem—a thought so passionate and alive that like the spirit of a plant or an animal it has an architecture of its own, and adorns nature with a new thing." So runs Emerson's revolutionary prophecy, which nobody but Whitman knew how to use in its own century. It might prove the motto for the best American poetry in ours. Is there another literature or time in which so many talented poets have in mid-career abandoned the conventions that formed the stance and syntax of their most successful poems, to re-create themselves in new personae, new styles, new prosodies? This has been true of Robert Penn Warren, Delmore Schwartz, Theodore Roethke, Robert Lowell, John Berryman, Karl Shapiro, W. S. Merwin, James Wright, and still others. Different as these poets are from one another, each has passed in his own way through a similar progress: early mastery of received forms and modes, the intensification of these traditional materials, then the struggle to free the tongue from accustomed language, the ear from familiar cadences, the eye from habitual ways of seeing, the sensibility from conventional responses.

Beyond these individual careers one can trace in contemporary American poetry a larger dialectic between classicism and romanticism, between formalist, organic, and aleatoric conceptions of art, between making traditions new and making new traditions. In the work of these poets is evident the shifting influence of the handful of modernist titans of an earlier generation. Now that Eliot, Pound, Stevens, Williams, and Auden are all dead, whoever would be king of the cats has debts to them all—as well as to Yeats and to Frost, the giants who tower behind *them*. In the years after World War II, for reasons at once literary, historical, and sociological, the weight of influence has shifted from Eliot's wartime ascendancy as the century's most powerful poet-critic, to the widening reputation of Wallace Stevens, with the unexpected resurgence of Pound and then of Williams as major examples to the younger poets. The lines of connection are overlapping and tangled, as different poets discovered these ancestors for themselves at their own convenience or through their own necessities.

2

The dominant aesthetic of the decade following World War II, as has been suggested in an earlier chapter, agreed with Eliot's definition of the historical tradition of English verse to which modern poetry belongs, and assumed the continuity of American verse with that tradition. The qualities of wit, metaphysical treatment of images, reliance upon mythic structures, and commitment to a Christian interpretation of life are readily evident. So are echoes and variations of Eliot's conceptions, announced in "Tradition and the Individual Talent," of the impersonality of the work of art, the objectivity of the poet, and the acceptance of the limits which the tradition and good taste impose upon appropriate subjects and diction. Poetry was accepted as a rational mode of discourse, syntactically and metrically conventional.

Such views deeply influenced the poetry of the forties and fifties. By the war's end the most promising poets, apart from Lowell, were Karl Shapiro, Randall Jarrell, John Berryman, and others who were influenced in varying degrees by the social concerns of W. H. Auden and the hieractic formality of Yeats. Among these were Delmore Schwartz, John Ciardi, Howard Moss, John Frederick Nims, John Malcolm Brinnin, Winfield Townley Scott, Howard Nemerov, William Meredith, and William Jay Smith. Most were characterized at the time as "University Wits," a designation which smudges their readily identifiable individual talents. What they shared was commitment to traditional versification in the metaphysical mode—in short, together they refracted their common influences, among which those of Eliot and the Fugitive poets John Crowe Ransom and Allen Tate loom largest, into a period style. This metaphysical or academic mode (both terms are misnomers) persisted in the work of younger poets. Some were merely accomplished, but others, like Anthony Hecht, John Hollander, Donald Justice, and W. D. Snodgrass, richly explored the possibilities of poetry which thinks as well as feels and feels as well as thinks.

If a particular style identifies a particular period, that period may yet have several styles. No sooner was Eliot's hegemony assured than it came under vehement attack. As early as 1947 Karl Shapiro, and in 1949 Delmore Schwartz, argued that the *obiter dicta* of Eliot's criticism no longer conformed to their sense of reality. To believe in the orderliness of the tradition, in historical continuity, in the rational structure of syntax, while experiencing the flux and chaos of contemporary life seemed to require an act of will which falsified their poetic responses. An alternative to the Eliot-New Criticism synthesis was readily at hand.

Eliot himself was on the jury which in 1949 awarded the Bollingen Prize to Ezra Pound: Apollo crowning Dionysus for *The Pisan Cantos*. It would be hard to conceive of a work more subversive of the period pieties described above. The relationship between Pound's career and Eliot's is one of tense symbiosis; both, as poets and as critics, were dedicated to conserving their separate conceptions of historic continuity while creating the modern consciousness by poetic means profoundly different from one another's, though they share much in common. Pound's *Pisan Cantos* records the flux of history—"The enormous tragedy of the dream in the peasant's bent shoulders"—at the same time that it recreates the stream of consciousness of an individual life, his own, that of an exiled, imprisoned, and deeply suffering man. Here is the artist as the hero of sensibility, the Romantic presentation of the self in opposition to Eliot's doctrine of "the extinction of personality." Pound's example would shortly influence a host of younger poets.

As Eliot's influence waned, Pound's waxed. During these years (until 1958) he was in St. Elizabeths Hospital in Washington, where his admirers sought him out and discussed with him his work and theirs. Soon vigorous defenses of Pound's enterprise were published by Hugh Kenner and other critics, while several groups of poets not in universities defiantly espoused one or another of his principles. His reconstruction of tradition elevated technical innovators like Arnaut Daniel and Cavalcanti above such established great reputations as Dante. "Make it new" became his slogan. In the Chinese ideogram he found a prototype for circumventing rational syntax in his effort to present the actual registration of psychological and mental processes. With its simultaneity of presentation, in its suppression of temporal linearity and of the artifice of completeness inherent in the normative sentence, Pound invented a new principle of presentation. His nonconsecutive lines, in which time, place, character, and incident flow into one another without connectives, engage the imagination of the reader, who must leap the spark gap from the terminals of the given to respond to the current of what is implied.

As Pound's reputation grew, so did that of another poet early associated with him. William Carlos Williams had by 1944 published twenty-three books of verse, fiction, and discursive prose, but he was still a poet with a minuscule following. Between 1946 and 1951 the four books of *Paterson* appeared (a fifth was published in 1958 and notes for a sixth posthumously in 1963), as did the two volumes of his *Collected Poems*. Quite suddenly Williams became a widely recognized major poet. His aesthetic of immediacy of perception and his technique of sensitively controlled improvisations free from traditional meters, forms, or modes made demands to which readers trained in academic verse and criticism were unprepared to acquiesce. But a new generation of readers was glad to accept the liberation from old constraints they found in his work. Like Pound, Williams emphasized innovative techniques, concentrating in his later years upon the need to use what he termed "the American foot," a three-stepped line which would free American poetry from dependency on the British iambic pentameter.

One result of Pound's and Williams' winning more readers among poets and more exegetes among scholars was the revival on a lesser scale of some of the other makers of the new poetry of the prewar period. The Objectivist school had flourished briefly in the thirties with Williams at its head; in the sixties there were republished the poems of Carl Rakosi and George Oppen, whose *Of Being Numerous*, his new work, won the Pulitzer Prize in 1969. Louis Zukofsky brought out sections of his long poem, "*A*" in several volumes in the late sixties and early seventies.

3

The most influential poet in the Pound-Williams axis was Charles Olson (1910–1970), rector of the experimental Black Mountain College in North Carolina in the early 1950's, when such artists and writers as Joseph Albers, John Cage, Robert Duncan, and Merce Cunningham were on the faculty. Their students numbered a whole generation of disciples, among them Robert Creeley, John Wieners, and Edward Dorn, while other poets such as Denise Levertov were influenced by Olson without having attended the college. Black Mountain was the antithesis of Kenyon College, where Ransom and Jarrell were on the faculty and Robert Lowell, Peter Taylor, Harry Brown, James Wright and Robert Mezey were students; or of Stanford, where Yvor Winters fostered neo-Augustan formalism.

Olson was a polymathic anti-intellectual intellectual, writer of a provocative study of Melville, *Call Me Ishmael* (1947), investigator of Mayan hieroglyphs in Yucatan, author of *The Maximus Poems*, and progenitor of the Projective or Open Field movement in poetry. In his essay, "Projective Verse" (1950), he opposes "(projectile (percussive (prospective vs. The NON-Projective," or what may be called " 'closed' verse, that verse which print bred and which is pretty much what we have had, in English & American, and have still got, despite the work of Pound & Williams." The typographic eccentricity is part of Olson's polemical effort to re-create sensibility by breaking up received assumptions.

Olson demands "COMPOSITION BY FIELD, as opposed to inherited line, stanza, over-all form." His theory derives from Gestalt psychology, but the prescriptive language, like Pound's, suggests mechanics: "A poem is energy transferred from where the poet got it . . . by way of the poem itself to, all the way over to, the reader. Okay. Then the poem itself must, at all points, be a high-energy construct, and, at all points, an energy-discharge." Form must be discovered in each occasion, not imposed upon it. Olson maintains that the reasons for abandoning "the conventions which logic has forced on syntax" as well as "the too set feet of the old line" are based on human physiology. He argues, further, that the typographical spacing made possible by the typewriter can "indicate exactly the breath, the pauses, the suspensions even of syllables, the juxtapositions even of parts of phrases" intended by the poet.

Olson's own poetry seems even more than his theories a belated flowering of the Class of 1912. His *Maximus Poems* (1953–1961) present a corporate hero, Maximus, and the history of Gloucester, Massachusetts, in the manner of *Paterson*, while the fluid treatment of time, the nonconsecutive versification and the attempted epical sweep suggest *The Cantos*. His Projectivist disciples mounted their coordinated assault against what they took to be the Establishment by founding their own magazines (*Black Mountain Review, Origen, Caterpillar*) and, as is the custom among members of a movement, by praising each other as though no other poets had claims to legitimacy.

Prominent among Olson's epigoni, in addition to those named above, are Paul Blackburn, Paul Carroll, Larry Eigner, and Jonathan Williams. The most accomplished of the Black Mountain Group are Denise Levertov, Duncan, and Creeley. It is Duncan whose work carries into a third generation the epical ambition and sweep of *The Cantos, Paterson*, and *Maximus*. Deeply influenced also by French Surrealism and the imagist technique and hermetic thought of H. D., Duncan projects the flow of history and myth through a single consciousness in his long work "Passages." Where Duncan is expansive, with Whitman-like inclusiveness, Creeley has made himself the master of the cameo effect, as in *For Love: Poems 1950–1960*.

A group which rivalled the Black Mountain poets as rebels against the academy arose in San Francisco in the mid-fifties. Writing in *Evergreen Review* (1957), Kenneth Rexroth reported the inessentiality to literature of "the world of poet-professors, Southern Colonels and ex-Left Social Fascists," and disclosed that in the freer climate of the Bay Area flourished a new poetry: Brother Antoninus (William Everson), Philip Lamantia, Jack Spicer, Lawrence Ferlinghetti, Jack Kerouac, and Allen Ginsberg were the first team for whom Rexroth campaigned. Later additions to the line-up included Gary Snyder, Michael McClure, Gregory Corso.

This group soon achieved notoriety for their Bohemian life styles, their mutually reinforcing use of one another as influences or dedicatees of one another's poems, and their appearance as characters in Kerouac's novels. They were photographed, written up and dubbed by *Life* magazine "the Beat generation." Their poems broke out of the gentility of the academic mode as their lives broke with the blandness of middle-class backgrounds. Many of these poets sought alternatives to the social and aesthetic conformity of the Eisenhower decade—sought them in Eastern religions, in drugs, in commune life, in other ways outside the organization world of instructorships, New York publishers, mortgages, and the nuclear family. They were among the pioneers of the social revolution of the sixties and seventies—doing it in the fifties. The most accomplished and ambitious of these poets were Allen Ginsberg and Gary Snyder.

Ginsberg's *Howl* (1956) was as incomprehensible to academic critics when it appeared as were the poems of Dr. Williams, who contributed a preface. If Ginsberg was denounced as a barbarian, that may be due to his reliance upon and continuance of traditions different from those commonly acknowledged at the time. His closest contemporary analogues are of course Williams and Pound, but his debt is greater than theirs to Whitman, whose rolling line and incantatory cataloguing manner he combines with an apocalyptic strain from the Hebrew prophets and the Hasidic zaddig. Blake and Christopher Smart make their contributions to his style, while, as he tells us in later poems in *Kaddish* (1960), he has levied debts on Artaud, Lindsay, Poe, Hart Crane, Blok, Mayakovsky, Tzara, Cendrars, Cocteau—a pantheon of the underground, revolutionary, prophetic, mad, disinherited poets of the Romantic movement. Their several contributions are welded into a personal idiom to express a deep personal anguish: the alienation, in *Howl*, of "the best minds of my generation" who are given to madness, drugs, and despair by the insanity of the world; and, in *Kaddish*, a searingly self-revealing autobiographical elegy for the poet's mother, Naomi, whose tragic paranoia is but an exaggeration of the sufferings of the Jews in the Europe she left behind. This extended portrait of personal and societal madness would seem to have been influenced to some degree by the opening up of such territory in Pound's *Pisan Cantos*. More vigorously than among the Projectivists, Ginsberg's poetry (and that of the other Beats) is based on oral and aural ryhthms. Its appeal is physical and immediate, and its language, in its day, was revolutionary. The acquittal of *Howl* in an obscenity trial in

San Francisco not only made the book and its author immediately famous but extended the doctrine, earlier promulgated in the case of James Joyce's *Ulysses* (in 1933), that regardless of its use of vulgar language, a true work of art has socially redeeming features. Henceforth the diction of American literature was uninhibited, nor did subsequent works require a parade of eminent academic critcs to assert their social value, as happened in the *Howl* case.

San Francisco brought them together but the poetic *données* of Ginsberg and Gary Snyder are a continent apart. Snyder, who studied anthropology at Reed College, fuses several disparate strains characteristic of the anti-Establishment West. He has lived among the American Indians and deeply respects their relationship to nature. He has worked as a forest ranger and logger and sees himself in the proletarian-anarchist tradition of the I.W.W. (as does Rexroth). Snyder looked Eastward for religious inspiration and for several years studied Zen in a Buddhist monastery in Japan. "As a poet," he has said, "I hold the most archaic values on earth. They go back to the late Paleolithic: the fertility of the soil, the magic of animals, the power-vision in solitude, the terrifying initiation and rebirth, the love and ecstasy of the dance, the common work of the tribe." These values inform his *Myths and Texts* (1960) and *The Back Country* (1968). Snyder is distinctively in the American grain with his free-flowing Ezratic versification, his alternation between demotic detail and transcendental illumination. His prose is collected in *Earth House Hold* (1969).

4

Quite apart from the contentions that divided American poetry into two camps was the achievement and the influence of Wallace Stevens. Although this poet had always had a devoted following among the *avant-garde*, not until the end of his life (he died in 1955, at the age of 76) did his work win wide readership and attract the emulation of younger contemporaries. Posthumously, his work has become firmly enshrined in the critical pantheon as scholars exegeticize his long philosophical poems and discover his themes to be restatements of those of the Romantic movement a century earlier. Stevens' insistent reliance upon the creative power of imagination in a world where "the death of one god was the death of all" sets his work in opposition to the Christian orthodoxy of Eliot, just as his contemplative aesthetic is opposed to Pound's *art engagé*. Yet Stevens' enthusiasts are more likely found among New Critics and traditional poets than among Beats or explorers of the Open Field.

As with Pound, Williams, or Eliot, Stevens' work yields different strains to different admirers. His early poetry, with its dazzling delight in "the gaiety of language," leads in one direction, while his intricately formal meditative late poems point in another. Although he early satirized "rationalists in square hats" and claimed for himself the exotic "sombrero," Stevens never abandoned intellectual organization or rational syntax. His influence may be read, along with that of Marianne Moore, between the lines of perhaps the most accomplished of the traditional poets, Richard Wilbur.

In his first book, *The Beautiful Changes* (1947), Wilbur had already assimilated these influences. He would withstand the pressures of the ensuing quarter-century to bend in the various directions outlined above. With meticulous craft he responded to the madness of the modern world by shutting it out from his verse. Wilbur's poems exhibit the hard-won excellence of a formality achieved by rigorous exclusions. This formalism is, however, a flexible instrument; he has never subscribed to the rigid Augustanism characteristic of Yvor Winters or J. V. Cunningham. His special intensity results from subjecting his romantic sensibility to the intellectual and spiritual decorum of his forms. His impulse is to impose an aesthetic coherence upon the incoherent. His brilliant essays on Poe suggest that Wilbur is at once tempted and repelled by the lure of *le poésie pur*; such titles as that of his first book and *Things of This World* (1956) recall him from the permanence of form to the flux of life. Responding to the violence of this world, he writes not of holocausts but on a scale the individual can grasp, in a pattern the mind can comprehend, as in "Mind" and "The Death of a Toad."

Another poet—very different from Wilbur—whose work is in the line of Stevens is A. R. Ammons. It is the exploration of reality in the late Stevens that Ammons's meditative poems resemble, though to be sure his more proximate derivations are from Emerson and Whitman, to whose work his own frequently alludes. In such poems as "Corsons Inlet" and "Essay on Poetics" he probes our knowledge of the natural world. Although his versification in its irregularity appears Projective on the page, Ammons is committed, through being "released from forms, / from the perpendiculars ... / of thought" to the transcendental discovery of "a direction of significance / running / like a stream through the geography of my work." His *Collected Poems 1951–1971* appeared in 1972.

5

Between the modernist masters and the postwar younger poets, there flourished a generation whose survivors are now the elder statesmen of American poetry. Richard Eberhart, Stanley Kunitz, Robert Penn Warren, Theodore Roethke, and Elizabeth Bishop defined their own aesthetics more or less independently of the still older poets so influential upon the University Wits, the Objectivists, Projectivists, and the Beats.

Although Richard Eberhart grew up in Minnesota, his work is stamped with New England transcendentalism. In such poems as "The Human Being Is a Lonely Creature" we see his tough-minded continuity with Emerson, whose "Ode to W. H. Channing" is echoed and transformed:

> Praise to harmony and love,
> They are best, all else is false.
> Yet even in love and harmony
> The human being is a lonely creature.

Eberhart has been singularly independent of the period styles, hewing tenaciously to his own way. From "If I Could Only Live at the Pitch that is Near Madness" (1942) to "Long Term Suffering" (in *Fields of Grace*, 1972), his concern, as the earlier poem affirms, is with "battalions of the race of mankind / Standing stolid, demanding a moral answer." This didactic impulse allies him with a greater New England poet, Frost. Eberhart's poems often show a Wordsworthian delight in an empathy with nature, while the paraphrasable argument of his lyrics is often deceptively subversive of their rational premises, as in Blake's "The Mental Traveller." His diction is very uneven, mingling undefined abstractions with gritty particulars. Eberhart's besetting flaw is a too-easy transcendental leap to the ideal, but his best work is gravely lyrical, informed with the conviction "that pain is essential" and that its transfiguration is possible.

Born in 1905, a year after Eberhart, Stanley Kunitz has published but four books of verse. In most of his work the style is firmly traditional but marked by an individuality which is spare, precise, and brooding. This poet has amalgamated into a personal idiom the influences of Hopkins, Yeats, the Blake of "Songs of Innocence" and "Songs of Experience" (rather than, as with more apocalyptic poets, the prophetic books) and especially the dark metaphysical introspection of the Jacobeans:

> Here at the monumental door,
> Carved with the curious legend of my youth,
> I brandish the great bone of my death,
> Beat once therewith and beat no more.

As in this stanza from "Open the Gates," his poems characteristically offer a fusion of dream, legend, and autobiography. Their special intensity reflects the great imaginative pressure under which they were written; they seem on the point of bursting out of the forms which so fittingly express them. Kunitz's *Selected Poems* appeared in 1958. His later work, in looser meters, appears in *The Testing Tree* (1971).

Robert Penn Warren, also born in 1905, emerged, after publication of his *Selected Poems* in 1944, as a boldly experimental poet who had moved far beyond the commitments of the Fugitive Group. Born in Kentucky and educated at Vanderbilt, Warren began as the youngest member of the South's most influential literary party. He shared their aesthetic which embodied the values of a presumed stable and hieratic society; a devotion to classical literature; the influence of metaphysical poetry; and the conception of verse as public discourse, formal in diction, traditional in meter, impersonal in tone. All this was changed in his later work, which explores an inward soulscape of memory in lines often unmetered but in looping rhythms effectively controlled. Here is the voice of memory, the somnambulist meditations of a ghost-haunted philosopher who cannot keep us from overhearing him. Warren is prepossessed by the problem of knowledge, by man's fallen nature, by the nature of truth amid the fluxions of time. His themes and their complex interweavings are boldly dramatized in *Brother to Dragons* (1953), a successful novel in verse. The guilt of the South is epitomized in the murder of an innocent slave; that of mankind in the Oedipal fixation of the murderer. As this fallible man is the nephew of Thomas Jefferson, the tale involves a questioning of that faith in human goodness on which our nation is founded.

The brooding violence and terror which striate this work characterize Warren's later poetry also. Unlike most of his contemporaries, Warren does not abjure narrative for the image, the symbol, or other discontinuous presentation. His language is alternately embellished and terse. In *Promises* (1957), *You, Emperors, and Others* (1960), and *Incarnations* (1968) he combines epiphany with expansiveness in serial poems, often based on his personal history. *Audubon: A Vision* (1969) is freely derived from an incident which the ornithologist-artist recorded in his journal; it is similar to that in Warren's earlier "Ballad of Billie Potts." Here murderous rapacity, violent frontier justice, and the revelation of character are framed in "a story of deep delight."

Theodore Roethke (1908–1963) in his first book, *Open House* (1941), reflected his childhood in the Michigan greenhouse of his father, a commercial flower-grower. This world of "urge, wrestle, resurrection of dry sticks" where "Even the dirt kept breathing a small breath" became the *terra poetica* in which his later work is rooted too, different though the later poetry is technically from his early adeptness in metered verse modeled on that of Léonie Adams and Louise Bogan. Roethke's obsessive theme, evident from *The Lost*

Son (1948) through his last book, *The Far Field* (1964), is the struggle of the soul to be born into self-knowledge. Bursting loose from the constraints of the period as to both style and subject, Roethke was a Romantic atavist, delving backwards and deep downwards into the unconscious, making the emergence of the self—*contra* Eliot—his great theme. His style divagates between allegiances to the long lyrical line and incantatory catalogues of Whitman and to a strict, end-stopped formality in metered stanzas—a debt he has acknowledged: "I take this cadence from a man named Yeats / I take it, and I give it back again." Roethke once described his effort to write long poems "which try in their rhythms to catch the very movement of the mind itself, to trace the spiritual history of a protagonist (not 'I,' personally), of all haunted and harried men, to make in this series . . . a true and not arbitrary order which will permit many ranges of feeling, including humor." With his self-knowledge buttressed by readings in Jung and Evelyn Underhill, and his unflinching honesty, Roethke is a poet of mystical affirmation.

Elizabeth Bishop (b. 1911) is often compared to Marianne Moore, and indeed her most frequently anthologized poems—"Roosters" and "The Fish" (from *North & South*, 1946)—do suggest the strong delicacy of phrasing, the wit, and the emblematic use of creatures while acknowledging their individuality, which characterized the older poet's work. But other modes and themes seem more truly characteristic of Miss Bishop. Born in Newfoundland, she lived for many years in Brazil, and the contrast between these two climates, suggested in the title of her first book, informs many of her poems. Her special stylistic quality is the assimilation of a seemingly casual conversational tone to the uses of the lyric or dramatic meditation, as in "At the Fishhouses" (in *A Cold Spring* 1955), "First Death in Nova Scotia" (in *Questions of Travel*, 1965), and many other poems. Robert Lowell has mentioned Elizabeth Bishop's work as one of the liberating influences upon his own.

6

The work of Robert Lowell (b. 1917), perhaps more than that of any other poet born in this century, embodies the troubled spirit of his time. His violent and powerful poetry has the broadest historical sense of any in the past quarter-century; it is instinct with personal experience, for Lowell is the chief actor in the drama of his own work. And that drama has been moved by potent themes—rebellion against family and inherited pieties; the force of his conversion to the Roman Catholic Church; conscientious objection in wartime; treatment in a mental hospital; unbearable crises in relationships with parents, with the government, with history, with God.

The poets of Lowell's generation or younger, discussed above, all have chosen to belong to either of the mutually exclusive movements to which he has applied Lévi-Strauss's division into "the cooked" and "the raw." There is, Lowell said, a poetry "laboriously concocted to be tasted . . . by a graduate seminar," and there is also the "raw, huge blood-dripping gobbets of unseasoned experience . . . that can only be declaimed." With great executive intelligence, Lowell first mastered the Eliot-New Critical tradition; then, wrenching himself out of it, he chose what were for him the needed aspects of the other. His raids on these competing traditions are not only stylistic but deeply involve his sense of history and of contemporaneity.

Lowell began as an admirer of Eliot and a student of Ransom; his first book, *Land of Unlikeness* (1944) has a preface by Allen Tate. In *Lord Weary's Castle* (1946) the tone is surer, though the tensions, unresolved in the earlier book, remain between son and father, between the poet's apocalyptic and imperious Catholic vision of perfection and his sense of the moral decay of his family's and country's Puritan tradition. In such poems as "Children of Light," "At the Indian Killer's Grave," and "The Quaker Graveyard at Nantucket," Lowell renders the severest judgment on the Puritan past made by any author since Hawthorne. His book is a thesaurus of received forms powerfully adapted to his modern occasions in a style of stark pentametric power. The manner of this learned poetry, however, became nearly Góngoristic in *The Mills of the Kavanaughs* (1951), a series of dramatic monologues. After this, a silence of eight years, during which Lowell ceased to be a Roman Catholic.

Visiting San Francisco, he heard the coffee-house declamations of Ginsberg and the other Beat poets, and found his own poems stilted, burdened by a "grand, ungrammatical, and . . . timeless hackneyed quality. All this was ended by reading Williams." Lowell wrote in 1961, "It's as if no poet except Williams had really seen America or heard its language." In Williams' style Lowell values the thrust, the "quick changes of tone, atmosphere and speed." A new colloquial diction and controlled casualness of rhythm inform the poems in *Life Studies* (1959). In subject as well as form they mark a new phase in Lowell's work. In these poems are remembered the ignominy of his father's botched career, the neurasthenia of his mother with her blighted ambitions, their deaths, and the disintegration of the class to which they belonged. Where his elegy to his uncle Arthur Winslow in *Lord Weary's Castle* had been strictly stanzaic, laden with mythological allusions, and had severely judged the materialism of its subject, in "My Last Afternoon with Uncle Devereux Winslow" (*Life Studies*) there are only the doomed young uncle and the child Robert Lowell, whose feelings in the presence of approaching death are rendered with economical imagery in spare free verse.

While Pound, Roethke, and Ginsberg had already opened up the exploration of madness in poetry, and, working within more conventional metrics, Kunitz, Shapiro, and Schwartz had broken away from Eliot's prescription of objectivity by writing of their own emotional crises, it was Lowell's *Life Studies* which came at the propitious moment when psychiatry had become a familiar of middle class American culture. This book seemed to inaugurate a new direction in the verse of younger poets.

Lowell's new, freer style is used more limberly and for more public utterance in *For the Union Dead* (1964). The title poem broodingly renders public issues—the Civil Rights struggle, the spoliation of the city and its past —in terms of personal memory and personal experience. The emotion of modern life is speared by the phrase, "a savage servility."

Near the Ocean (1967) revealed Lowell's turning away from improvisatory form. The three central poems here are based on the stanza used in Marvell's "The Garden." In the meantime Lowell had published *Imitations* (1961), a book of free adaptations from other languages, and several plays. These works are by no means tangential to his own poems. *Imitations* is an imperialistic conquest of the tradition of European poetry from Homer to Pasternak, with emphasis on Villon, Baudelaire, and Rimbaud; while the plays exert the sweep of Lowell's historical consciousness. Adapting Racine's *Phèdre* (1961), he found prototypes of the tragic greatness with which the classical world bore personal sufferings like those we cannot escape. In *The Old Glory* (1965) Lowell chose from Hawthorne and Melville tales that gave symbolic form to three of the most significant rebellions in our history: severance of the State from the Established Church in "Endicott and the Red Cross"; separation of the Colonies from the Crown in "My Kinsman, Major Molineux"; and the mutiny of Negro slaves in "Benito Cereno." The last play was the most successful, one of the few genuine tragedies for the modern stage and the most effective verse drama since Yeats.

With unabated energy Lowell has explored still another style. *Notebook 1967–1968* (1969, expanded as *Notebook* in 1970) attempts to subject all of the poet's experiences to the sinuous rigors of a single form, a nonrhymed sonnet stanza. Abrupt, surrealistic, these range in subject from the confessional to responses to day-to-day crises (Eugene McCarthy's presidential campaign, demonstrations against the Vietnam War, student uprisings at Columbia). One model is surely *The Pisan Cantos* with their similar juxtapositions of personal and literary memories against historical events. Another was doubtless John Berryman's "Dream Songs," which had begun to appear in magazines as early as 1959. Lowell has lived in England since 1970; his latest work is yet a further revision and expansion of *Notebook* into three volumes, published simultaneously in 1973: *History, For Lizzie and Harriet*, and *The Dolphin*.

The unresolved effort of John Berryman (1914-1972) was to discover or forge a style distinctively his own and adequate to all of his occasions. Like Lowell he went through several phases, but these seem in his case to divide rather than unify his *oeuvre*. In *Poems* (1942) and *The Dispossessed* (1948) he expertly practiced the period style, influenced more by Yeats and Auden than by Eliot. At this time he wrote what was published much later (1967) as *Berryman's Sonnets*, a baroque sequence analyzing a love affair in which are first evident the violent elisions of syntax and shifts of tone that would characterize his two other long poems. *Homage to Mistress Bradstreet* (1956) is Berryman's most sustained single work, an astonishing poem in which the poetess of three centuries earlier becomes his interlocutor, muse, and mistress as he blends his own consciousness and sensibility with hers. Not having to exorcise the ghosts of his own ancestors, as did Lowell, Berryman can recreate the earliest American experiences (subduing a "savage place," making poems in a wilderness, giving birth) without delivering a jeremiad against the Puritans. Yet his Mistress Bradstreet is isolated from her fellows, alienated by the prescience conferred by her sensibility. Like Hawthorne's Hester she transcends her time through her sufferings. In *Homage* begins Berryman's brooding relationship to God; a lapsed Catholic, this poet had no conversion but rather a painful struggle to regain his lost faith.

That loss is intricately related to another, his father's suicide when he was twelve. Berryman's was an anguished sensibility; much of his difficulty in defining his style seems to have resulted from unwillingness or inability to deal directly with his own painful experience. By a brilliant stroke he devised a means for doing so through a mask, a "human American man" he calls Henry, or Pussycat, or Mr. Bones in 77 *Dream Songs* (1964). These poems, by turns demotic and elevated, rhapsodic and satirical, searing and comic, are all cast in a loose form, normatively three six-line stanzas in each of his "sings," with occasional rhyme. The attempt to cram a life-time's daydreams, nightmares, ruminations, carnal joys, and sufferings into this repeated form is impressive. The models for *Dream Songs* are various; *The Cantos* is surely the chief, with its rapid shifts of tone and its historical-autobiographical sweep. Yeats' doctrine of the masks contributed much, and the character of Henry is constructed from the minstrel show tradition (the white man in blackface)—a device which frees the self to utter unseemly and libidinous fantasies. But the mask is forever slipping off, as "Cagey John" speaks in his own, or other, voices. His is the sophisticated sensibility which swiped the title of his subsequent dream song volume, *His Toy, His Dream, His Rest* (1968) from three pieces by Giles Farnaby (c. 1560-1600?) in *The Fitzwilliam Virginal Book*. Henry's name would seem to be borrowed from *The Red Badge of Courage* and *The Monster* by Stephen Crane, subject of Berryman's one critical study—a complicatedly Freudian biography which illuminates Berryman's work as much as it does Crane's.

After 385 *Dream Songs*, Berryman finally arrived at a style that treated his subjects directly—a flat, antilyrical, antipoetic style, prose lines in stanzas which in *Love & Fame* (1970) spread out confessional or autobiographical poems without benefit of the ventriloquism used heretofore. *Delusions, Etc.* (1972) continues this style in anguished devotions ("Opus Dei"), like Auden's *Nones* only in their use of the canonical hours. By the time this book appeared Berryman had taken his own life.

The confessional impulse, so strong in Lowell and Berryman, opened subjects which poets of differing metrical persuasions could explore. As poised and meticulous a poet as W. D. Snodgrass, writing poignantly rhymed quatrains in *Heart's Needle* (1959), recorded the effects of a divorce on a father and his three-year-old daughter. Sylvia Plath (1932–1963) broke out of the mold of verse conventions observed in *The Colossus* (1960) with the searing, savage concentration upon pain, suffering, and dying in *Ariel* (1965) and three subsequent posthumous volumes. Through the power of her work, and partly because of its exclusive focus on the suffering self as well as the notoriety of her suicide, Sylvia Plath became the center of a cult of readers and imitators. A third "confessional" poet, Anne Sexton, in *To Bedlam and Part Way Back* (1960) explored tortured relationships with parents and lovers and the experience of mental breakdown. All three of these poets began writing as students of Robert Lowell.

7

Confessional subjects were not the only means by which poets whose early work was conventional broke out into a new freedom. Existentialism and the deep image movement provided entries into new subjects and new attitudes for such poets as W. S. Merwin, Robert Bly, James Wright, and others. In Merwin's first three books (*A Mask for Janus*, 1952; *The Dancing Bears*, 1954; and *Green With Beasts*, 1956) the style has a high patina upon its baroque extensiveness, and if the Quest Hero appears as voyager and artist he wears the guises of Odysseus or Jason and celebrates Aphrodite in a dazzling array of ballads, cansos, songs, and other traditional forms and emblems. Merwin had early assimilated Stevens, Pound, and especially Robert Graves (whose children he tutored for a year on Mallorca). Lowell's *Life Studies* perhaps suggested the change evident in *The Drunk in the Furnace* (1960), in which for the first time Merwin writes anecdotally of grandparents and other relatives without invoking archetypal myths.

The Moving Target (1963) begins a third phase of Merwin's career, one which he is still developing. Here the world is stripped down to its existential bareness, a place of desolation in which memory gropes for shards of an irretrievable past to protect it from an unbearable future:

> At this moment I could believe in no change, . . .
> The sky vaulted as a heart
> Where I know the light will shatter like a cry
> Above a discovery:
> 'Emptiness.
> Emptiness! Look!'
> Look. This is the morning.

In this void things are animate, abstractions live, and form is perpetually revealed in the occasions of its own discovery.

Merwin is the first American to have profited from post-surrealist French poetry after World War II. Fluent in many languages, a distinguished translator, Merwin has taken hints from René Char and others, adopting the unpunctuated evasion of syntactical limits devised a generation earlier by Guillaume Apollinaire. The existential anguish in Merwin's work reflects also the responses to the disorientation of contemporary man from all traditional consolations, as expressed in the work of Samuel Beckett, Franz Kafka, and especially Jorge Luis Borges. Merwin's exploration of his evacuated world is surprisingly rich and protean in *The Lice* (1967), *The Carrier of Ladders* (1970), and *Writings to an Unfinished Accompaniment* (1973), and in a book of prose fables, *The Miner's Pale Children* (1970). His inscriptions upon the black slate of despair are not the result of his readings only; they reflect his deeply pessimistic concern for the fate of a civilization committed to nuclear explosions, exploitation, and irrational violence.

Such feelings of individual helplessness, compounded by the failure of our democratic institutions to respond to rational, humane efforts to abrogate the destructive imperialism of the economy and the polity, exacerbated the sense many writers had of the unavailability of rational means in art as well as in life. For those who, like Merwin, felt the present disconnected from history, reality was to be found not in the disorder of events but subjectively, in the inner life. One group of poets so motivated, and influenced by the writings of Jung, are those in the deep image movement. First proposed in 1950 by Jerome Rothenberg and Robert Kelly, this doctrine was refined in 1962 by Robert Bly and James Wright in *The Lion's Tale and Eyes*. They sought to reveal "the inward world" of "thoughts we have not thought," rather than define only what is already known. These notions are exemplified in Bly's *Silence in the Snowy Fields* (1962) and in Wright's

The Branch Will Not Break (1963) and *Shall We Gather at the River* (1968). The resulting poems have been purified of rhetoric and speak in limpid cadences of the discovery of his inner world by a persona who, as in Merwin's later work, is curiously baffled and passive. This poetry is emotionally highly charged, and by circumventing rhetoric and rational organization it partakes of the primitive, magical power of the verse of a preliterate tribe. Of the other poets who have mined the deep image—among them John Haines and Charles Simic—the most compelling is Mark Strand. He found his metier independently of Bly and Wright, a poetry of bare, proselike statements comprising fables (rather than descriptive images) in which an emotion is rendered as in a dream or hallucination. This spectral inwardness is delineated in *Reasons for Moving* (1968), *Darker* (1970), and *The Story of Our Lives* (1973).

In their subjectivity as in their existentialism, American poets moved outside the Anglo-American tradition to find examples and influences elsewhere, particularly among the symbolist and post-symbolist poets of the present century. Among the poets translated by several hands, including Merwin, are René Char, Yvan Goll, and St.-Jean Perse. The years since 1955 saw the translation also of Valéry Larbaud and Jules Laforgue by William Jay Smith; of Yves Bonnefoy by Galway Kinnell; and of Guillaume Apollinaire by William Meredith. Spanish and South American poets translated during these years include Pablo Neruda, César Vallejo, Federico Garcia Lorca, Blas de Otero, and Jorge Luis Borges. Thawing of the cold war permitted visits to this country of the Russian poets Yevgeny Yevtushenko and Andrei Voznesensky, both of whom were published here in translation, as were Vladimir Mayakowsky, Anna Akhmatova, Osip Mandelstam, and Joseph Brodsky, who has emigrated to this country. These and still other translations enlarged and internationalized the sense of contemporaneity of the American poets who made them.

8

From the late 1950's on there is evident in poetry a dichotomy in attitude to subject as well as to form. On the one hand there are the various movements based on the conception of *le poésie pur*—the New York School, aleatoric poetry, and concretism—and on the other, the poetry based on commitment to social action. Chief among practitioners of the latter are the poets who rallied opposition to the Vietnam War and the Black poets whose work expresses the rise of Black consciousness, Black pride, and in some cases the call for separatism.

Poets of the New York School were instrumental in adapting to verse the assumptions of Abstract Expressionism and Action painting. John Ashbery has described their aesthetic in his preface to Frank O'Hara's posthumous *Collected Poems* (1971) as influenced by "a modern tradition which is anti-literary and anti-artistic," that of Apollinaire, the Dadaists, and the collages of Braque and Picasso, as well as aleatoric music from Satie to Cage. Of his own poems Ashbery writes, "There are no themes or subjects in the usual sense, except . . . an individual consciousness confronting or confronted by a world of external phenomena." Structure and syntax are suppressed; in his own work, for example, *Some Trees* (1956), *The Tennis Court Oath* (1962), *Three Poems* (1972), texture is all. O'Hara's work is predominantly lyrical, that of Kenneth Koch often comic and satirical—*Ko*, (1959), *Thank You and Other Poems* (1962), *The Pleasures of Peace* (1969).

The aleatoric impulse is stronger in painting (Jackson Pollack) and in music (John Cage) than in poetry, but there are poets, including Cage himself (*Silence*, 1961; *A Year from Monday*, 1967) who are devoted to chance composition. Whether programmed by the *I Ching* or the fonts of a selectric typewriter, the total undermining of received structure has been attempted. Ted Berrigan, associated with the New York School, published *The Sonnets* (1964), intended to be read in any order. The aleatoric method would seem to commit the imitative fallacy compounded by solipsism. A more fruitful way of rendering the tension between chaos and form seems that devised by Donald Finkel, whose long poems *Answer Back* (1968) and *Adequate Earth* (1972), "about" cave exploration and Antarctica, respectively, are comprised of an intricate melange of voices, allusions, and quotations; the jigsaw puzzle effect is discovered and controlled by the poet. The background of these experiments is shadowed by Pound's *Cantos*, Mallarmé's *Un coup de dés*, and Apollinaire's *Calligrammes*.

The last of these is a possible point of departure, along with the work of E. E. Cummings, for yet another school which attacked structure, rhetoric, and the literary tradition. Indeed it dispensed with content as well as form. Concretism, an international movement, is, like the aleatoric and New York schools, allied with the visual arts; it expressed an effort, akin to that of minimal painting, to make the most concise statement possible, often in the form of a visual pun. Two anthologies by prominent concretists—Mary Ellen Solt's *Concrete Poetry: A World View* (1969) and Richard Kostelanetz's *Imaged Words & Worded Images* (1970)—have a sportiveness which all but compensates for their minim content.

No doubt much of the impetus toward these efforts to create a poetry devoid of public content is in reaction to the yoking of art to the chariot of whatever worthy cause. At the same time the practice of art as an autonomous activity during the years of the civil rights movement, growing opposition to the war in Vietnam, and the emergence of Black consciousness, may have spurred a reaction toward *le poésie engagé*. The problem of making good poetry from our arguments with others remains what it always has been: recent denunciations of racism and an imperialist war seem to have produced no better verses than did the proletarian poetry of the thirties. No one can fault the convictions of such works expressing revulsion against an unjustifiable war as Denise Levertov's *To Stay Alive* (1971) or Robert Bly's "The Teeth Mother Naked at Last," in *Sleepers Joining Hands* (1973), but perhaps the most effective indictment of the war in poetry is *Obscenities* (1972), by Michael Casey, a veteran whose work dramatizes the effects of Vietnam on the men who had to serve there.

Black poets have been caught in the same division between personal and social art. Until the civil rights movement, the assassinations of Malcolm X and Martin Luther King, and the riots in the city ghettos, Negro poets had worked within the traditions available to whites, which they used to express their special subject matter. This is true of Margaret Walker's Whitmanesque *For My People* (1942), Melvin B. Tolson's modernist *Libretto for the Republic of Liberia* (1953), Robert Hayden's *Selected Poems* (1966), and the early works of Gwendolyn Brooks, *A Street in Bronzeville* (1945), and *Annie Allen* (1949). In her interest in the urban life of her people Miss Brooks resembled Langston Hughes, whose work remained closer to the rhythms and idioms of his subjects.

A younger poet, LeRoi Jones, began writing as a Projectivist. Influenced by the revolutionary politics of Black America, he wrote savage plays (*Dutchman, The Toilet*) vehemently attacking whites and especially the Jews, joined the Nation of Islam, changed his name to Imamu Amiri Baraka, and became a political leader of the Black community in Newark, N.J. His verse has of course become as politicized as his actions (*Black Magic: Poetry 1961-1967*). Baraka's activism has energized a whole generation of younger Black poets, and Miss Brooks herself has joined their ranks. They include Don L. Lee, Nikki Giovanni, Clarence Major, and Larry Neal. Stephen Henderson argues on their behalf, in *Understanding the New Black Poetry* (1973), that such work is based on an aesthetic which white readers cannot share or understand. In their effort to forge the consciousness of their race many Black poets explore their own experiences in a discriminatory society, and explore also the resources of their Afro-American background—the argots and rhythms of jazz, blues, and ghetto life. Ishmael Reed, in *Conjure* (1972), constructs a Black alternative, Neo-Hoodoo, to the white traditions he rejects. A much less strident, more interiorized poetry is that of Michael S. Harper in *Dear John, Dear Coltrane* (1970) and *Song: I Want a Witness* (1972).

9

A number of poets whose work may prove among the most lasting of the period have joined no movements, issued no corporate manifestoes, but rather have written in the honorable American tradition of individualism. Their work is therefore harder to classify. What they share is an earned mastery of formal conventions; whether these are continued or replaced in their work with improvisatory forms, their poetry is distinguished by firmness of inner design and the imaginative energy of their language as experience is subsumed in a formal or visionary coherence. By not being self-categorized in any movement they are not limited to any particular proscriptive aesthetic. Among the poets whose work requires mention are Donald Justice, David Waggoner, William Stafford, Adrienne Rich, Philip Booth, M. L. Rosenthal, and Dabney Stuart; space precludes detailed discussion of their writings. Nor can the present historian with propriety summarize the work of Daniel Hoffman.

As the last quarter of the century begins it seems likely that its most interesting poets will be of the generation born between 1920 and 1930 and now in mid-career, at the height of their powers. A poet of extraordinary accomplishment is James Merrill, who in six books, from *First Poems* (1951) to *Braving the Elements* (1972), has followed the thread of memory in a way more reminiscent of Proust or Henry James than of his poetic contemporaries. His poetry is deeply personal, as in "The Thousand and Second Night" (*Nights and Days*, 1966) and "Days of 1935" (1972), yet the personal is framed by the larger world of public events. The inner life, summoned by reverberant images, asserts itself without this poet's abandoning the syntactical structure of experience.

Anthony Hecht, too, is a master of poetic convention. His work is at once elegant and intense (*The Hard Hours*, 1967). "Rites and Ceremonies," designedly structured to parallel Eliot's *Four Quartets*, is the most memorable poem by an American on the Jewish sacrifice in the Nazi holocaust. Hecht is an intellectual poet who, with stoicism and grace, imposes order upon his knowledge of suffering.

Beginning with his war poems, *The Arrivistes* (1949), and continuing through his poems to Walt Whitman and on the American sensibility in Europe (*At the End of the Open Road*, 1963), and those reminiscent of Voznesensky's treatment of Russia in *Adventures of the Letter I* (1972), Louis Simpson has written ambitiously, attempting to express the typical experience and emotion of his time. His last phase, a stripped-down bareness of style, is tangential to the Deep Image movement. Simpson's *Selected Poems* appeared in 1965.

Whitman is an avatar also of Galway Kinnell, whose first book, *What a Kingdom It Was* (1960) moved from formal lyricism into the apocalyptic with his long poem, "The Avenue Bearing the Initial of Christ into the New World." There is a fierce animism in "The Bear" (*Body Rags*, 1968) and, in *The Book of Nightmares* (1971), a vatic, incantatory encompassing of the life cycle, political satire, and a hermetic vision of universal truths.

In the work of James Dickey an early equilibrium between stability of form and violence of subject has been tipped toward power rather than finish. Dickey's long lines and stuttering rhythms express the gnawing guilt of the wartime pilot twenty years after in "The Firebombing"; and in "Falling" a stewardess swept out of an airliner merges with the universe in her flight toward death, becoming the unattainable goddess "desired by every sleeper in his dream." Dickey's *Selected Poems* was published in 1967.

Richard Howard deals with reality from a different tangent. An elegant and learned poet who accommodates the syllabic line, adapted from French, with an ease rivalling Auden's, Howard has reached around behind Pound's, Eliot's, and Yeats' masks to revive the dramatic monologue in a way at once objective and as revealing of the poet as the plaints of the confessional poets. In *Untitled Subjects* (1969) his characters from nineteenth-century England come to life with a genuine sense of the culture they bequeath us. Quite differently from Merrill, Howard too writes as a poetic heir of the late Henry James.

Another poet who wears much learning lightly is John Hollander. Formality is in a curiously poignant tension in his work with a thoroughly modern, indeed urban, sensibility. His life as a New Yorker is lovingly celebrated in the title poem of *Movie-Going* (1962), but it is his book-length *Visions from the Ramble* (1965) which best suggests his range. This meditative, reflective, autobiographical and lyrical poem demands comparison to Kinnell's Whitmanesque "The Avenue Bearing the Initial . . ." and with some of Lowell's discrete lyrics as the most powerful statement thus far of what it feels like to live amidst the tenacious memories and destructive energies of a modern American city.

If the past thirty years of American poetry have been rich with fulfillment, their promise has been, and remains, richer still. It may well be that from among the poets whose work is capsulized above some two or three will, in the coming decades, emerge with poems that will so powerfully express the emotions of both their society and their solitude, in forms appropriate to both our awareness of the traditions which have shaped our lives and the uniqueness of the life we know, that poetry will once again become a major art in our time.

85. DRAMA

Postwar drama in the United States may be said to have begun a few months before the war itself came to an end, when Tennessee Williams' *The Glass Menagerie* opened in New York on March 31, 1945. As with poetry, the new drama did not spring full-grown from the forehead of the *Zeitgeist*; it had ties, in manner and material, certainly in biography, with the prewar theater, and it was not until well into the sixties that any sense of a new consciousness began to be apparent.

Williams had had a disastrous pre-Broadway tryout of *Battle of Angels* in 1940, and *The Glass Menagerie*, although hardly a Depression play as that genre was known in the thirties, concerns a St. Louis family struggling to stay alive, actually and spiritually, just before the war. The play—a "memory play," as Williams calls it—is seen, however, from the vantage point of a narrator looking back, and Williams, in giving us that place to stand, was in fact looking forward to a new body of American drama. Williams became and remains—with Arthur Miller—one of the two most important American playwrights to emerge in the postwar theater. Aside from *Menagerie*, Williams' most important critical and commercial successes have been *A Streetcar Named Desire* (1947), *Cat on a Hot Tin Roof* (1955), and *The Night of the Iguana* (1961). It would be a mistake, however, to think of Williams primarily as the author of these four plays. Since 1945, he has averaged rather better than one play every two years and, despite a difference in quality among them, they form the body of work upon which his reputation rests.

Although there are shifts of emphasis in Williams' work—inevitably, since it reaches across a quarter century—and although he constantly experiments small ways with theatrical possibilities there is no sharp or sudden break in his creative continuity, no recognizable endings, no new beginnings. His work is obviously of a piece, a fact that can be seen by the kind of character who has preoccupied him since the beginning of his career. His "little company of the faded and frightened and difficult and odd and lonely," to use Alma's phrase from *The Eccentricities of a Nightingale* (1964) are men and women who, by virtue of their presumed difference from the norm, are forced to become outsiders, from which vantage point—one that Williams shares—they at least have a clear view of the world. That means, for Williams, that they can see the horror of it. These characters tend to fall into categories: (1) the artist, which includes not only real practitioners of the arts, mostly amateur or unsuccessful, but characters like Blanche in *Streetcar* who have a self-proclaimed refinement; (2) the cripple, which includes those with permanent or temporary physical disabilities or diseases, usually fatal; these include such characters as the single-breasted heroine of *The Mutilated* whose crippling is as much mental as physical, which means an overlap with (3) the insane, whose disturbances range from the certifiable to the pill-popping neurasthenia of so many Williams heroines; (4) the sexual specialists, from the virginal to the professional; and (5) the foreigners, who are usually native Americans of Latin origin.

In Williams' early work, his outsiders—his "fugitive kind," to borrow a phrase from *Battle of Angels*—are ordinarily set up in opposition to society —or to stronger, less sensitive characters, more at home in society—and, particularly in the plays of the late fifties, they are then destroyed: Val is lynched in *Orpheus Descending* (1957); Catharine is lobotomized in *Suddenly Last Summer* (1958), Chance is castrated in *Sweet Bird of Youth* (1959). This pattern was set as early as *A Streetcar Named Desire*, in which Blanche, raped by Stanley, goes mad, but there is an ambiguity in that play (Stanley is sometimes Blanche's victim, too) which prepares us for a later stage in Williams' treatment of the outsider. As it becomes more and more difficult to separate the victim from the victimizer in his plays, it is increasingly clear that, for Williams, the murderous "other" is time, which consumes us all, and an indifferent universe, which lets it happen. As *The Night of the Iguana* best illustrates, Williams' emphasis in the sixties has shifted to concern with and admiration for simple human survival.

Any attempt to compress Williams' recurring themes and characters into a few paragraphs necessarily gives a wrong impression of his work. His intention is serious and his presentation of it involves both theatrical shock and an emphatic sense of horror and pain. Even so, it is important to recognize that Williams is one of the most impressive comic writers in America. From *The Glass Menagerie* to *Small Craft Warnings* (1972), he has consistently created funny scenes, characters, and lines which have successfully shared stage space with the frightening and the pitiable.

Many of Williams' best scenes have been written in the realistic tradition— the one customarily accepted as the American theater's most vital style— but it is necessary to realize that, from the beginning, Williams has been essentially a nonrealistic dramatist; witness his use of significant names and obvious symbols, both verbal and visual. More important, he has consistently called for nonrealistic sets, designed to contribute to the mood and meaning of a piece; and he has increasingly made his characters larger than life in their grotesquerie and has asked them to break the frame of action, to step into a personal spotlight for a soliloquy or a direct address to the audience. His use of nonrealistic devices has lacked the revolutionary fervor of the twenties *avant-garde*; it has been simply a matter-of-fact acceptance of what was available and possible in a period in which realism has all but disappeared from our stage.

Arthur Miller's first postwar play and his first Broadway success, *All My Sons* (1947), was conventional in form, Ibsenism without Ibsen's complexity (in 1950, Miller adapted *An Enemy of the People* for Broadway), but he, too, works comfortably in nonrealistic drama as his most successful play, *Death of a Salesman* (1949), and his most controversial, the autobiographical *After the Fall* (1964), indicate. *Salesman* is probably the best wedding of expressionism with realism that the American stage has produced; in fact, it is one of the best plays to come out of the American theater.

If Williams is a product of the poverty-induced wanderlust of the 1930's —and a good case can be made for such a biographical reading of the man and his work—Miller is even more obviously a child of that decade. His youthful politics allied him with the American Left, for which drama has always been, if not a weapon, at least a diagnostic instrument designed to expose the ills of the system. Social criticism has always been and still is an important element in his work. Yet, like the best of the thirties social dramatists, he has avoided the narrowly propagandistic. At one level, *All My Sons* is an attack on the American business ethic, and *The Crucible* (1953), Miller's account of the Salem witch trials, is, among other things, the playwright's response to the McCarthyism of the fifties. Yet, even these, his most overtly political plays, are much richer than any ideological statement that can be distilled from them. They reflect the major theme of his work, the relationship between the individual and society; and their basic plots make use of perennial family situations that have been at the heart of drama since Aeschylus. *All My Sons* is a father-son confrontation and *The Crucible* is a triangle play. Most of Miller's plays make use of one or more of these domestic conflicts, or of a similar third possibility, the battle between two brothers; the latter is taken to its ultimate source in *The Creation of the World and Other Business* (1972), which, being a Biblical comedy, lets Miller use the great, first sibling rivalry between Cain and Abel. For Miller, then, social drama—which he calls "Whole Drama"—recognizes that man has a subjective and an objective existence, that he belongs to himself and his family as well as to the world. He is, then, a psychological as well as a social dramatist.

Miller's work divides, perhaps too neatly, into two related groups of plays, the four written between 1947 and 1956—*Sons, Salesman, Crucible*, and *A View from the Bridge* (1955, revised 1956)—and those written from 1964 on—*After the Fall, Incident at Vichy* (1964), *The Price* (1968) and *Creation*. In the eight years between *View* and *Fall*, Miller wrote a number of theoretical essays on his own plays and drama in general, and a film, *The Misfits* (1961), for Marilyn Monroe, who was then his wife. In the film and in his comments on *Salesman* in the Introduction to *Collected Plays* (1957), he came very close to espousing the reigning psychological cliché of the fifties Broadway stage, that love solves all problems, personal and social. Before and after his "silent" period, Miller dealt more seriously, much less sentimentally with the self in society. In the early plays, he was concerned with man and the image society tries to force upon him. His protagonists, all victim-heroes, either accept the societal image and die when they fail to realize it, or reject it and die in the process. Joe Keller, a good father and a "good" businessman, kills himself at the end of *All My Sons* when he recognizes that his son believes a man's duty extends beyond the well-being of his family. Willy Loman, Miller's most beautifully conceived character, dies at the end of *Death of a Salesman*, still believing in the American success myth which has killed him and infected his two sons. John Proctor, Miller's only romantic hero, dies at the end of *The Crucible*, refusing to sell his name to the witch hunters who expect him to embrace the communal guilt sweeping Salem. Eddie Carbone, having become an informer in *A View from the Bridge*, dies rather than live wearing his neighborhood's ugliest label of "informer." What the four characters have in common is that each of them, in his attempt to protect his name, is involved in a search for integrity; this is nowhere more obvious or more movingly presented than in Willy Loman, a consenting victim in a continual struggle against the truth that is smothering him.

Beginning with *After the Fall*, however, Miller's identity quest turned into a need for a workable definition. What Quentin in *After the Fall* and Von Berg in *Incident at Vichy* discover is a commonplace of contemporary psychology, that all men are guilty, that everyone shares in the evil, personal and social, walking the world. That idea informs the more recent plays as well. In his early plays, Miller wrote about the way society constructs images of man; in the later ones, he succumbed to one such image. The strength of the early plays lies in an implicit sense of man's possibility, the weakness of the later ones in an explicit statement of his limitations. The early ones, even at their most artificial, are rich with observation; the later ones—with the happy exception of *The Price*—are almost lost in concepts. This weakness can be seen most clearly in *The Creation of the World*, in which

Miller's attempt to mix comedy and philosophy results in a group of solemn cartoons. To criticize Miller's most recent work is not to dismiss him as a playwright of failed promise. If he had written nothing more than his early plays—in fact, if he had written only *Death of a Salesman*—he would be an important American dramatist. Both he and Williams have come under heavy attack for the plays they wrote during the sixties, but—as the career of Eugene O'Neill has taught us—no playwright of their stature need be counted out because of a string of less than major plays.

Williams and Miller, by virtue of their preeminence, are special cases, of course; yet even their work is a reflection of the Broadway theater in which they appeared. Miller's plays became a shade more psychological than social after *All My Sons*, and Williams, in the Broadway version of *Cat on a Hot Tin Roof* (the published play contains both third acts), edged toward the sex-as-salvation platitude of the fifties. The changing taste in drama implicit in the work of these two men can be seen more clearly in their lesser colleagues. In the years immediately following the war, Broadway was still awash with social conscience; it was as though the reformist impulse of the 1930's had survived the war and, somewhat attenuated, regained its foothold on the stage. This can be seen in its purest form, oddly enough, in a comedy like *Born Yesterday* (1946). Garson Kanin uses a Pygmalion fable in which a *New Republic* reporter educates a tough ex-chorus girl to turn against the junkyard millionaire who keeps her, a turn that is finally more public than private since the target expands to take in corrupt politics, corrupting capital, and the kind of indifference that allows both to flourish; the whole thing ends in a rather grand verbal gesture, the kind of liberal affirmation that was obligatory in the thirties. The more serious social plays of the period have less vitality, less staying power than the Kanin comedy, probably because none of them has characters as strongly theatrical as Billie Dawn and her junkman. One of the better serious plays of the period, Arthur Laurents' *Home of the Brave* (1945), is finally more interesting for what it portends than for what it is. Its subject matter—anti-Semitism—might have served a straightforward social play, but its plot, in which a paralyzed Jewish veteran is shocked into walking again, hinges on a psychological trick and points toward *A Clearing in the Woods* (1957), in which Laurents uses domesticated, post-*Salesman* expressionism to present his lonely heroine at four different ages.

Laurents, Robert Anderson (*Tea and Sympathy*, 1953), and Paddy Chayefsky (*Middle of the Night*, 1956) are fairly typical playwrights of the fifties. The best representative of that group, however, is William Inge, for as the audiences and the awards (the Pulitzer for *Picnic*, 1953) piled up, he began to seem, to some critics, a much more important playwright than he is. Inge's *The Dark at the Top of the Stairs* (1957) stands as an almost perfect example of Broadway seriousness in that decade. It is full of the kind of platitudinous self-analysis that passed for dialogue in the fifties and its characters all look as though they had just climbed out of some newspaper psychologist's column. It ends with the hero and his wife climbing hand in hand to face the dark at the top of the stairs, with the implied assumption that the sex act will smooth away their obvious incompatibility and their economic problems as well. Although this description is a fair one, so far as this play is concerned, it is a bit hard on Inge. His first play, *Come Back, Little Sheba* (1950), for all its flaws (the blatant symbolism, for instance) is genuinely touching on stage and it has in Lola a fully conceived character very unlike the casebook types that were to follow.

Although most of these playwrights are relatively young men, a new shift in public taste in the sixties cut them off from their admiring audiences, and their infrequent appearances in that decade made them seem like ghosts of a distant past. The saccharinity of the years in which they found their success can be seen at its most disadvantageous in the venemous essay, "Love, Love, Love," which Gore Vidal wrote for *Partisan Review* at the end of the decade (Fall 1959). The most portentous of the love-seeking plays remains Archibald MacLeish's *J.B.* (1958), which was once, wrongly, expected to bring verse back into the theater. Two plays which share the period's overriding concern with love and loneliness, but which stand out by virtue of their somewhat eccentric quality are Carson McCullers' *The Member of the Wedding* (1950), an adaptation of her own novel, and Jane Bowles' *In the Summer House* (1953).

It was during this period, too, that one of the most vigorous of the American popular dramatic forms—the wisecracking farce—all but disappeared from the stage. It was replaced by the standard Broadway comedy, usually a sentimental exercise in contained naughtiness, galloping euphemism, and the celebration of the status quo. Farce was to reemerge later, off-Broadway, in plays like Arthur Kopit's *Oh, Dad, Poor Dad, Mamma's Hung You in the Closet and I'm Feelin' So Sad* (1960) and in atypical Broadway plays usually commercial failures, like Saul Bellow's *The Last Analysis* (1964), which is so obviously superior to the more easily acceptable comedies of, say, Neil Simon. Oddly enough, while farce was declining, another popular dramatic form—the musical comedy—flourished. The integrated musical show, in which book and score really worked together, was firmly established and the genre began to get serious critical attention and to turn established playwrights into librettists. Arthur Laurents, for instance, did the books for two of the best musicals of the period, Leonard Bernstein's *West Side Story* (1957) and Jule Styne's *Gypsy* (1959), and his contributions to these shows are more effective, dramatically, than his straight plays. The musical comedy had, in Rodgers and Hammerstein, its equivalent of William Inge, but the first fifteen postwar years did produce a large number of significant shows, which range from *Regina* (1949), Marc Blitzstein's opera version of Lillian Hellman's *The Little Foxes*, to *Guys and Dolls* (1950), Frank Loesser's clever use of Damon Runyon's New York.

2

By the end of the fifties Broadway was largely given over to musicals, light comedies and European, mainly English, imports, but by that time the off-Broadway theater was firmly established as a rival—no, more an allied —production system in New York. A return to the little theater tradition of the twenties and thirties had begun right after the war in lofts and halls, converted movie houses and existing tiny theaters, and the impulse, more aesthetic than political, was to provide an antidote to Broadway. It became an alternative instead. There were a few producing organizations— the Circle in the Square, for instance—which retained some sense of their original artistic commitment, but by the mid-fifties, off-Broadway was, like Broadway, a loose collection of producers, working one show at a time and hoping for a lucrative long-run. As Broadway costs soared, the major advantage of an off-Broadway production was that a play could be staged for a relatively small investment, which meant that it was still possible to take risks with plays that were unlikely to appeal to the large audience necessary to keep a show open uptown. A theatrical advantage, of course, was that off-Broadway was not so firmly wed to the proscenium arch as Broadway was, and that the growing antirealist strain in American drama found a congenial home.

In the early days, the programs were heavy with modern classics, in revival or first production, and it was off-Broadway that introduced Americans to European playwrights—Jean Genet, Samuel Beckett, Eugène Ionesco— considered too special for the usual Broadway audience. From the beginning, however, one emphasis was on new American plays. Despite the auspices, most of these were no more experimental or daring than their Broadway counterparts, although some of them were plays of merit. For example, Alfred Hayes did an effective adaptation of his novel, *The Girl on the Via Flaminia* (1954), one of the best of the handful of plays that came directly out of the experience of Americans at war. At first, there was a general sense of scattered happy accident—an interesting play here, a promising playwright there. Then, suddenly, at the end of the fifties a number of playwrights emerged all at once, a sudden flowering of hope that so affected theater editors that they dubbed the young dramatists a group. Yet all that they had in common was a point in time. By then, the exchange between Broadway and off-Broadway was so established—performers, directors, playwrights moving from one to another—that their work sometimes appeared in one showcase, sometimes another. Even so, they remain off-Broadway's first sizable contribution to postwar American drama. They include Jack Gelber, whose *The Connection* (1959), a celebrated wedding of Pirandello games with naturalistic melodrama, is more conventional than it was originally thought to be; Arthur Kopit, who moved from the early playfulness of *Oh, Dad* to *Indians* (1968) a flawed but ambitious attempt to deal with the dark underside of American history in terms of show business; and Murray Schisgal, whose *Luv* (1963) mocked middle-class America's preoccupation with self-definition and did so in psychological clichés that suggest the cartoons of Jules Feiffer. With *Little Murders* (1967), Feiffer himself became an accomplished playwright. In some ways, Jack Richardson, the least successful commercially of the "group" is the most interesting, certainly the most intellectual. In one way or another, all of his plays—from *The Prodigal* (1960), his re-telling of the *Oresteia*, to his very black Broadway comedy, *Xmas in Las Vegas* (1965)—deal with ways of seeking or avoiding the kind of peace which is a rejection of life—both in its dangers and its vitality. His characters tend to be a bit fleshless and his lines often get tangled in actor-muzzling syntax, but despite these obviously antitheatrical attributes, his plays are fascinating in ways that some of the cleverer plays mentioned above never manage to be.

The first fine promise of the off-Broadway theater was never kept. Some of these writers—Richardson, for instance—seem to have dropped out of the theater completely; the others work infrequently and, with the possible exception of Kopit, their later work is inferior to their early plays. In contrast to them is Edward Albee, the most famous of their generation, who has worked steadily and well since *The Zoo Story* (1960) introduced him to the public. That play, which has become fair game for symbol hunters and myth-makers (it can be seen as a clash of cultures or a rebirth fable) is, more importantly, a favorite among small drama groups. The reasons—which are probably the reasons for Albee's theatrical staying power—are that the dramatic event, a confrontation in Central Park, has an electrifying immediacy on stage and that the dialogue, in the best theatrical tradition, is the embodiment of the event and not an explanation of it. These qualities remained with Albee when, after a number of successful short plays (*The American Dream*, 1960, despite its humor, showed that he could succumb to overdefinition), he moved on to *Who's Afraid of Virginia Woolf?* (1962), which is much longer than the conventional three-act play and which still commands the kind of attention from an audience that *The Zoo Story* gets. To some critics, *Virginia Woolf* has a family resemblance to the Inge-fifties-psychodramas described above. It does end with Martha and George heading into "the dark at the top of the stairs," arm in arm—an apparently upbeat ending—but there is a nice ambiguity to that action which grows not out of an extrinsic doubt about easy solutions to hard problems but out of the overpowering dramatic fact of Martha and George as a couple, bound to-gether in love and hate and a passion for survival games. More naturalistic than his other work, *Virginia Woolf* indicates that, even at his most idio-matic, Albee creates set stage speeches that are almost like arias both in their artifice and their effectiveness. This verbal talent, a kind of inspired artificiality, can be seen in all his work from *The Zoo Story* to *All Over* (1971). *Virginia Woolf* is still Albee's most important play, but his strength does not lie in a few best plays. Like Williams, he works at the writer's trade and, in the last dozen years, he has turned out a body of work which despite a wide variation in quality, identifies him as a major American play-wright.

Most of Albee's plays reflect a thematic preoccupation with a worst of all possible worlds in which, as Tobias says in *A Delicate Balance* (1966), "We do what we can." A playwright who returns insistently to situations which illustrate the accommodations forced on man by his condition and his society might be assumed to be suffering from that fashionable post-European disease, existential *Angst*. So Albee is, but there is a flicker of American optimism in him too; he is not capable of the comforting fifties happy endings, but his plays suggest that the latent reformer in him keeps whispering that there must be an exit from the void. The most interesting thing about Albee's work as a whole is not that he keeps writing about the same thing, but that he experiments with new styles. The most impressive—and most unsuccessful commercially—of his recent attempts is the connected pair of one-actors, *Box* and *Quotations from Chairman Mao Tse-Tung* (1968), known as *Box-Mao-Box*, since *Box*, a thirteen-minute monologue, is played at the beginning and the end of the other short play; built of fragments of dialogue and quotation, it appears to be a criticism—or at least a doubting examination—of Albee's own best style, that of *Virginia Woolf*.

3

During the sixties there were two important developments in the structure of the American theater, both of them already beginning to contribute to American repertory. The regional theater became increasingly strong with the growth of arts centers and professional acting companies all across the country; for the most part, the programs consist of classics and recent New York successes, but more and more frequently the regional groups are going their own way, rescuing undeserved New York failures, importing foreign plays that are too risky for commercial production in New York and, most important, introducing new plays and new playwrights. New York City is a region, too, of course, and some of the groups there—the American Place Theatre, Joseph Papp's Public Theater, the Repertory Theater of Lincoln Center—are less akin to commercial Broadway and off-Broadway production than to their counterparts around the country. The other theatrical development is primarily a New York phenomenon, the growth of off-off-Broadway as a reaction to the fact that off-Broadway had become a miniature version of Broadway. On a typical weekend there may be seventy-five to a hundred productions scattered around Manhattan, in store fronts, dance halls, churches and theaters. Many of them are scratched-together performances, often revivals, and many of them are awful, but there is a small, determined group of regular off-off-Broadway producers who do consistently interesting work and there is a growing list of playwrights who began (and frequently return to) off-off-Broadway.

Some of the new playwrights of the 1960's are established literary figures, like Robert Lowell. *The Old Glory* (1964), based on stories by Hawthorne and Melville, is a remarkable evocation of the American talent for mixing idealism and violence; it consists of three plays, connected by theme and symbol, but it was never played as a single work and its individual parts— particularly the excellent *Benito Cereno*—have made their way as separate one-act plays. A poet of quite a different kind, Kenneth Koch has written some very funny plays—*Bertha* (1959) and *George Washington Crossing the Delaware* (1962)—which suggest, as Gertrude Stein's plays do, the Dadaists reborn in American idiom. Most of the new playwrights are young men just beginning to make their way as dramatists, and they come to the theater carrying no reputation from another genre. Among the more interesting are Israel Horovitz (*The Indian Wants the Bronx*, 1968), Ronald Tavel (*Boy on the Straight-back Chair*, 1969), and David Rabe (*Sticks and Bones*, 1971).

Still more promising, at least at the moment, are two young playwrights, very different in style, who share only a superb sense of the stage—Ronald Ribman and Sam Shepard. Ribman is difficult to characterize because each of his plays is very different from the others. The first two do have their complexity and allusiveness in common. *Harry, Noon and Night* (1965) is a conventional psychological drama gone wild, a black comedy rich with social implications, and *The Journey of the Fifth Horse* (1966) is a fascinating adaptation of Turgenev's *The Diary of a Superfluous Man*, in which Ribman invents a publisher's reader to serve as unwilling analogue to Turgenev's diarist. After an intelligent but rather lifeless historical drama, *The Ceremony of Innocence* (1967), Ribman turned to the one-act play, but the three that make up *Passing Through From Exotic Places* (1969), despite the clever ideas on which they are built, show an attenuation unexpected after the richness of the first plays. His return to the full-length play, *A Break in the Skin* (1972), a comic lament on the triumph of technology, gives him room to let his theatrical imagination play, but saddles him with an end that is predictable, however surprising its details.

Sam Shepard began with short plays, a volume of which, *Five Plays*, was published in 1967, when the author was only twenty-four. This early work —of which *Red Cross* is the most impressive example—presents an image, an action, an event which has a tremendous dramatic validity, but which is almost impossible to understand in any of the conventional ways—as narration, symbol, allegory. The individual scenes that make up *Red Cross*, for instance, have a clear shape, dramatically and verbally, but the play as a whole teases more than it reveals and leaves the audience with a sense of unease. With *Melodrama Play*, the last of the *Five Plays*, plot line began to emerge more clearly and when Shepard went on to full-length plays— *La Turista* (1967), *Operation Sidewinder* (1970), and *The Tooth of Crime* (1972)—his wildly inventive theatrical imagination (too wild, some critics say) provided him with disparate scenes that suggest the one-acters, illuminated by a verifiable line of action and an apparent growing need to present, to elucidate, to satirize—perhaps to reform—the contemporary American scene.

One of the developments of the sixties which, if it became predominant, could have a marked influence on playwriting is the growth of companies in which the dramatist is reduced simply to one of the ensemble. The play, in such a theatrical context, emerges from a community effort, improvisation from a scenario, and words are generally of less importance—or of no more importance—than images that grow out of nonverbal sound, physical movement, spatial arrangement. The work of Jean-Claude van Itallie with Joseph Chaikin's Open Theatre, the best of the ensembles, is a good example. Although at least one of the three plays that make up *America Hurrah* (1966) developed out of open theatre exercises, it is a thematically unified collection of one-acters, not unlike many other such off-Broadway offerings. Its most imaginative segment, *Motel*, a violent and obscene puppet play, is certainly less close to the open theater work than, say, *Interview*, in which a handful of actors present the fragments of a great many characters, but even *Motel*, in which the mute dolls commit their destruction against a mechanical sound track, is primarily theatrical, almost nonexistent on the page. More characteristic is *The Serpent: A Ceremony* (1968), in which images of the Creation and the Fall constantly give way to contemporary counterparts. Van Itallie is credited with "words and structure," but the words are mostly banal and the show's strength is in its physicality. Both this movement, which has at least a sound theoretical base, and the more chaotic kind of theatricality, in which scripts are sacrificed to stage effects, flourished in the sixties, but, as noted earlier, the written play more than held its own.

It was also during the sixties that Black theater became important to American theater as a whole. It was Lorraine Hansberry's *A Raisin in the Sun* (1959), a conventional realistic play, a Broadway success, that launched the movement in the postwar years. *Raisin*, a very good play of its type, mixes a critique of the American success ethic with a "discovery of manhood" plot. The play came at the end of a decade that was optimistic about the solving of racial problems in this country, and, in its attitudes as well as its production context, *Raisin* reflected a sense of possibility that was soon to give way to the anger of the sixties. The new mood was reflected in James Baldwin's rather ponderous *Blues for Mr. Charlie* (1964) and, much more successfully, in Le Roi Jones's *Dutchman* (1964). The latter, a short play in which a murderous encounter between a white girl and a Black man on the subway becomes a symbolic statement without losing its power as a theatrical event, is still the most impressive play, dramatically, that the Black theater has produced. Such praise would mean little to Jones, however, for not long after the success of *Dutchman*, he turned his back on white criticism, began to see literature as a weapon, and, under his new name, Imamu Amiri Baraka, turned his attention to political and economic action.

In the late sixties, the Black theater movement flourished; theatrical groups sprang up all over the country, Black playwrights began to emerge in number, and aesthetic ideology raised its head. At first there were a large number of fairly simple propaganda plays (Baraka's post-*Dutchman* work reflects this), but it became quickly clear that the essential concern of most of the playwrights is to find ways of exploring Black experience, using Black idiom, and avoiding the kind of built-in footnotes that were once considered necessary for Black playwrights writing for a white audience. This artistic dilemma helps explain the split that exists among Black theater people, between those who think that they can be Black artists in a theatrical context in which whites are welcome and those who insist on Black plays by Black playwrights for Black audiences in Black neighborhoods, to avoid the presumed corruption of Black material by whites. Douglas Turner Ward

(*Happy Ending* and *Day of Absence*, 1965), one of the founders of the Negro Ensemble Company, is—as is his organization—representative of the former. Ed Bullins, whose reputation as a playwright was made through the American Place production of *The Electronic Nigger and Others* (1968), has become the strongest voice for the Black segregationist point of view, both as editor of *Black Theatre* and through his work with the New Lafayette Theatre in Harlem. Although Bullins implies that Black plays, like the Black experience, are so special that whites cannot properly respond to them, a play like his own *The Fabulous Miss Marie* (1971) looks startlingly like a standard genre play, just as *Ceremonies in Dark Old Men* (1969) by Lonnie Elder III, white-produced in a regular off-Broadway theater, suggests nothing so much as Black Odets. If one can cut through the rhetoric of the moment, what appears to be happening is that a growing Black audience and an interested white audience are increasing the chances for Black playwrights to be seen and heard. Right now, most of them seem to be working in familiar, even somewhat old-fashioned forms, although there is evidence of experimentation of various kinds—Ben Caldwell's *Riot Sale* (1968), Adrienne Kennedy's *Cities in Bezique* (1969). What presumably will happen is what has happened among white dramatists—the ordinary playwrights will continue to work in conventional forms of one kind or another and the best of them will find voices uniquely their own. In any case, it is clear that the Black playwright will never again be as peripheral to American drama as he was in the years before World War II.

86. FICTION

THE NEW CONSCIOUSNESS appeared more striking in the novels and stories of the postwar period than in other genres. Even before Hemingway and Faulkner, the two masters of modern American fiction, died in 1961 and 1962 respectively, a new generation of fiction writers had come into its own. Members of that generation began to publish during and after World War II; they were younger still than such authors as James Gould Cozzens, Robert Penn Warren, and John O'Hara who found their point of departure in the 1930's. But the postwar novelists, though they were far more susceptible to the influence of the twenties than of the thirties, were naturally determined to struggle against all their artistic ancestors.

Among older novelists, perhaps only Vladimir Nabokov was considered by some postwar writers as a liberator of fiction. Born in Russia in 1899, Nabokov came to the United States in 1940; and his best works, written originally in English, belong to a still later period: *Lolita* (1955, 1958), *Pale Fire* (1962), *Ada* (1969). Virtuoso word and chess player, magus of fantasy, cryptic lover of artifices, he created parodic patterns of memory, of sensuality, of dreams that satisfied self-delighting minds. His comic spirit was both learned and outlandish, his humor sometimes intellectually brittle. Writers who admired him most tended to be experimentalists, absurdists, or clever nihilists who found in the antics of Nabokov a reflection of their own void.

The spirit of Nabokovian play or fantasy asserted itself only later in the postwar era. This fact, however, underscored the essential difference between fiction in the fifties and in the sixties. Fiction shifted away from tragic naturalism toward mythic symbolism—and shifted again farther toward comic surrealism, black humor, pornography. It moved from an embattled existential ethos toward a cool, mock-structuralist outlook. It evolved from recognizable literary forms to elusive and intricate patterns vanishing in their own intricacies. Thus the novel ended by questioning itself at the very threshold of silence.

Yet fiction also acknowledged the enormous diversity of American culture, its stubborn facts and fluid fancies, its outer conformity and violence within. With a radical innocence, the fictional hero sought the sources of love and of freedom, the sources of being and of meaning. During the fifties, the search for love sometimes brought him to the edge of religious experience—Zen or Buddhist thought, Christian mysticism, the I-Thou encounter elucidated by Martin Buber. And the search for freedom sometimes immersed the hero in the destructive element—crime, anarchy, self-annihilation, the hipster's way of death. The two quests, starting from different points, often met in the figure of the rebel-victim, the holy goof, the saintly criminal, eternally the outsider, who incarnated in American literature the ancient dialectic of the primary "Yes" and the everlasting "No." Later, in the sixties, the character of the hero and the nature of his quest appeared to change, though perhaps only superficially so. Still the scapegoat redeemer, still the misfit hero, he became more knowing, campy, vaudevillian, a player-king in the lands of unreality. Yet despite the absurdity of his world, despite the chaos of his own motives, his perduring hope remained classic: the renewal of life through supreme fictions of the mind.

2

A closer view of postwar American fiction must begin in the forties with a complex phenomenon: the effort of the new writers to discover a new language, often in reaction to the naturalist legacy of the previous decade. This effort, sometimes equivocal, was manifest in the works of individual novelists: Nelson Algren, Wright Morris, and J. D. Salinger, among the oldest postwar writers. It was evident, too, in the war novel, the novel of manners, the Southern novel, and the Jewish novel among trends originating in the forties, evolving freely thereafter.

A Chicagoan, like James T. Farrell and Theodore Dreiser before him, Algren showed in *A Walk on the Wild Side* (1956) that the legacy of lurid naturalism did not suddenly disappear; the novel's language reflected a sentimental apprehension of life's defeats. Yet in his first and best novel, *The Man with the Golden Arm* (1949), Algren also proved that he could bring strong material under literary control. The violent underworld of drugs and gambling was given human meaning in the figure of Frankie Machine. Thus, Algren's work exemplified the renewed struggle between naturalism and symbolism in the early postwar years, a struggle that Edmund Wilson called crucial to all twentieth-century literature.

Wright Morris was perhaps more conscious of this struggle than Algren. In his brilliant study of American fiction, *The Territory Ahead* (1958), Morris explored the discrepancy between the richness of material and paucity of artistic resources in various novelists from Cooper to Hemingway. Morris came to fiction through the profession of photography, which left its imprint on his work. Beginning with his autobiographical novel of a Nebraska childhood, *My Uncle Dudley* (1942), and through more than a dozen works, Morris tried to impose the field of his inner vision on the vivid fragments of his Midwestern experience. At times tedious and opaque, Morris could still create such memorable fictions as *The Field of Vision* (1956) and *Ceremony in Lone Tree* (1960), in which memory and solitude mingled to render the pathos of unfulfilled life on the American prairie.

The contrasts between Algren and Morris, and between both and Salinger, marked a movement toward a compact, allusive idiom, a new artfulness in fiction. This was the idiom of Salinger's stories, deft, teasing, poignant, which began to appear in the forties. *Nine Stories* (1953), about children, adolescents, various misfits living in quiet or quixotic desperation, penetrated to the point where love and squalor met in American culture. But the true testament of a generation opposed to the spiritual vulgarity of that culture remained *The Catcher in the Rye* (1951). Innocent and experienced in the classic American manner, its adolescent hero roamed New York in search of love, truth, and simplicity. Recounted in the first person in the colloquial and tangy idiom of hurt innocence, this neo-picaresque novel created its own kind of terror and slapstick; it created a fashion. Suddenly, postwar American society could recognize its own character, its own self-betrayals, in the dejections of one boy, Holden Caulfield. In time, however, Salinger's religious interest in Zen Buddhism and Christian mysticism deepened; his language began to aspire to silence. His later novelettes, *Franny and Zooey* (1961) and *Raise High the Roof Beam, Carpenters* and *Seymour: An Introduction* (1963), reflected this interest as they reflected the extraordinary Glass family in a mirror darkly. Prolix and convoluted, full of jokes, allusions, and asides, these works shattered the story form in countless fragments; it was as if Salinger's purpose to atone for the "desecrations" of language could only thus be attained. Later still, Salinger secluded himself and ceased to write, emulating his own character, Seymour Glass, a holy suicide. The prophetic art of his best fiction survived both his silence and sentimentality.

The shift from naturalist to symbolist modes was perhaps even more striking in certain trends which began in the forties and evolved in subsequent decades. In the war novel, a genre understandably quick to possess the American imagination after 1945, the creative tension between these modes was precarious. Only the best, only the most inventive, war fictions endured. Thus, John Horne Burns' *The Gallery* (1947), and, better still, Norman Mailer's *The Naked and the Dead* (1948) succeeded in modifying the rawness of life and death with the cunning of art. The tendency toward fantasy became more pronounced with the years. Thus, John Hawkes' *The Cannibal* (1949) distilled violence into baleful poetry, and Joseph Heller's *Catch-22* (1961) conveyed violence in absurd humor.

But the exemplary war novelist was perhaps James Jones who remained throughout his career close to the sensibility of the forties. His best work was still his first, *From Here to Eternity* (1951), which depicted the loyalties and brutalities and dreams of soldiers in the "Pineapple Army" of Hawaii just before Pearl Harbor. Awkward or sentimental in parts, the work could still bring its characters angrily alive; the vision behind them was authentic. The realistic mode persisted in *The Thin Red Line* (1962). Shot with grisly humor, dense with detail, the novel denounced the illusions of romantic heroism in battle, denounced all forms of social cant.

If the strict naturalistic mode could no longer interpret the intricacies of contemporary life, neither could its opposite, the pure symbolist mode, satisfy the ambitions of the most energetic writers. For a time, in the late forties and early fifties, the novel of manners seemed to offer a way between these extremes. Brilliant and often satirical, it exposed the remaining enclaves of American society in a witty light. Thus, Mary McCarthy exposed cliques of leftist intellectuals in *The Oasis* (1949) and art colonists in *A Charmed Life* (1955). But the novel of manners also responded to the Jamesian precepts of style, structure, hidden implication; it cultivated an elegance of sensibility that the cerebral works of McCarthy often lacked. Jean Stafford's *Boston Adventure* (1944) and Frederick Buechner's *A Long Day's Dying* (1949) were examples of the new elegance. The manners of the drawing room as of the bedroom became the medium of fine moral discriminations. In these works, as in various Southern novels, fiction acquired a poetic and mythical texture; it made use of the archetypes of quest and romance. It also tended to become at once too delicate and bizarre.

To some extent, this tendency was always latent in the new Southern novel which also began to make its impact in the forties. The Gothic tradition of Southern fiction went back, of course, to Charles Brockden Brown and Edgar Allan Poe; but it was Faulkner's great myth of Yoknapatawpha County that gave it shape in the twentieth century. Rural, hence largely conservative, tragic in its sense of destiny, rich in legend and the cadences of living speech, acquainted deeply with both violence and ceremony, the South inspired a certain kind of literary imagination. At its best, Southern fiction contained its contradictions in Gothic, mythic, or grotesque forms; at its worst, it appeared merely precious or exotic.

Among the best Southern writers, Eudora Welty caught the concrete quality of life in her native Mississippi. The wistful, the monstrous, and the comic blended with both ease and originality in such novels as *Delta Wed-*

ding (1946) and *The Ponder Heart* (1954), as well as in her many stories. Carson McCullers also distinguished herself early as a Southern writer with a unique poetic sensibility. Her conception of grotesques seeking to transcend their spiritual isolation in love was one of the haunting images of the times. Her novels included *The Heart Is a Lonely Hunter* (1940), her first, longest, and most socially specified work, and *The Ballad of the Sad Café* (1951), perhaps her best fiction, which Edward Albee later adapted to the stage. Flannery O'Connor, a Catholic writer, revealed with greater lucidity the contortions of spirit in worldly terms. Her collections of short stories, *A Good Man Is Hard to Find* (1955), contained some of the most accomplished and terrifying fictions of the postwar period. And her two religious novels, *Wise Blood* (1952) and *The Violent Bear It Away* (1960), enhanced her vision of human beings struggling insanely to attain grace. Her avowed interest did not lie in grotesques as such but rather in the disorders which create the grotesque in man. At once comic and precise, her style, much admired by surrealists like Hawkes, turned nightmare into inescapable statement.

It was fortuitous that three gifted Southern novelists proved to be women. Yet after Faulkner and Warren, the sensibility of Southern fiction gradually increased in refinement, in subtlety, in formal poise, and lost in original force. William Styron did write a powerful first novel, *Lie Down in Darkness* (1951). The book presented the disintegration of a Southern family, and by symbolic implication, the disintegration of a particular genteel society. Guilt and incest and loss of belief ended in self-destruction. Styron's rhetoric surged darkly; echoes of Sir Thomas Browne and Sigmund Freud mingled with the sounds of Faulkner's fury. But the passionate tone of the work was not representative of postwar Southern fiction. In his early works, Truman Capote chose a more exquisite idiom, nocturnal and terror-laden as in *Other Voices, Other Rooms* (1948), or wistful and ethereal as in *The Grass Harp* (1951); in later work, he outgrew his identification with the Southern style entirely. Authors younger still than Capote or Styron continued to publish remarkable fictions, such as Walker Percy's *The Moviegoer* (1961). But by the middle of the sixties, it became apparent that the postwar renaissance in the Southern novel had run its course.

The Jewish novel, on the other hand, showed no marks of decline, only of development. It was Northern and urban in origin, liberal or radical in politics, inward with the social experience of the ghetto, the moral burden of history, the wry humor of the Jewish joke. Irony and ambiguity often hedged its statements; and its heroes, *schlemiels* or *schlimazels*, were characters of mixed innocence and sophistication, caught between memories of holocausts abroad and anxieties of assimilation at home. In America, Jewish fiction derived from the works of Nathanael West in the thirties and later from Henry Roth, representing the density of fact and ferocity of fantasy between which it tried to mediate. The Yiddish works of Isaac Bashevis Singer sharpened its consciousness; translated into English, such novels as *Satan in Goray* (1955) and *The Magician of Lublin* (1960) helped to extend Singer's indirect influence. But it was Saul Bellow and Bernard Malamud who did most to heighten the Jewish imagination after the war. Bellow, who will be discussed later in this chapter, began his explorations of that theme in *The Victim* (1947); Malamud developed other aspects of it.

Although the characters of Bernard Malamud were nearly all Jews, they appeared always in a nexus of universal implication. Malamud's tough, sardonic, and compassionate vision proclaimed the endurance of man, and defined the responsibility of the novelist as an effort "to keep civilization from destroying itself." His first novel, *The Natural* (1952), was an obscure, ambitious, allegorical tale of a fallen baseball hero who becomes a mythic American figure. Malamud's central concern, moral regeneration, appeared next in the flawless form of *The Assistant* (1957). A grim grocery store idyll set in an urban milieu, the novel transformed poverty, ignorance, and alienation into a luminous image of human responsibility. Less impressive, *A New Life* (1961) developed its theme on a backward university campus. But with *The Fixer* (1966), which drew on a historical incident of Jewish persecution in czarist Russia, and in *The Tenants* (1971), which presented a parable of the modern "occluded self" in the confrontation between two artists, one Black and the other a Jew, Malamud displayed mastery in sharp focus. His stories, collected in *The Magic Barrel* (1958) and *Pictures of Fidelman* (1969), contained some of his best and worst writings. An experimentalist in fiction he was not. Yet his blazing insights into the aches and indignities of daily life, his steadfast moral imagination and his rigorous art, insured for Malamud a place among the finest postwar novelists.

The changes in Jewish fiction since the publication of Bellow's *The Victim* can scarcely be conveyed in a rubric. Such diverse writers as Edward Lewis Wallant, Bruce Jay Friedman, Stanley Elkin, and Daniel Stern were not united in a common artistic or racial purpose. Their novelistic manner included whimsical realism and black humor, allegory and city romance; their interests ranged from anti-Semitism to the betrayals of love, history, and conscience. Still, it was possible to note that the main tendency of the Jewish novel, like that of postwar fiction in general, was to evolve into more open, experimental, and fantastic modes.

This very tendency was explicit in the career of a single Jewish novelist: Philip Roth. His first work, *Goodbye Columbus* (1959), contained marvelous stories written in the taut, evocative style of the fifties; and *Letting Go*

(1962), packed with novelistic action and dialogue, rendered its sense of city life conventionally. In *Portnoy's Complaint* (1969), however, Roth created a ribald, dialectic fantasy of onanism and guilt, prurience and altruism, Gentile and Jew, a fantasy projected against the familiar and familial pieties of America. With *The Breast* (1972), Roth went even farther in devising a fable of metamorphosis, more surreal than Kafka's and more humorous, though not as deeply resonant. For despite his great verbal skill and genuine comic insight, Roth did not always avoid a certain triviality.

3

By the middle of the fifties, it became clear that the struggle against the extremes of naturalism and symbolism, or raw and rarefied fiction, had been largely won. The novel could now afford a new extravagance in picaresque forms—Bellow, Ellison, Kerouac—or a new spareness in poetic power—Hawkes, Purdy, Kosinski—without losing its hold on its artistic reality. New trends began to emerge: the existential novel, the Black novel. New writers also made themselves known.

The existential novel did not embody precisely any philosophy; rather, it passionately rendered the growing sense of alienation in the West. Its solitary hero found his values in extreme rebellion or victimization, or else gave himself to the void. The destiny of the American characters in Paul Bowles' *The Sheltering Sky* (1949) and *Let It Come Down* (1953), for instance, was often self-annihilation. Self-exiled in a stark and pitiless land, North Africa, they confronted extreme situations, without the comforts of culture, reason, and history. Thus Bowles' unfit pilgrims in quest of being became preys with no choice.

Existential but also mystical, Beat fiction flaunted its affiliation with ancient Oriental religions as well as its disaffiliation from modern Western society. The authors of Beat fiction emerged from the coffee houses of San Francisco, Venice West, or Greenwich Village, invoking Buddha and Christ, chanting the *Bhagavad-Gita* and *Leaves of Grass*, devising a life-style of their own which featured sex, drugs, jazz, and the freedom of the open road. The Grand Llama of Beat novelists was Jack Kerouac who, at his mawkish worst, could be subliterary. Yet Kerouac could also bring a live, sweet, American rhythm to his fiction, and a wide-eyed innocence or vulnerability that softened existential anguish. His experiments with "spontaneous prose" did not bear out the theoretical claims he made for them; they only served to loosen the syntax of language and maintain the natural flow of perceptions. His best novels, *On the Road* (1957) and *The Dharma Bums* (1958), celebrated the sadness, energy, and terror of America, its cities and wilderness, its ragged lovers.

The hipster hero, nastier than the Beat and more inward with crime, pushed his existential rebellion farther; his world had no sacramental sweetness or light. This was the world of William Burroughs, a world of addicts, homosexuals, killers, a world ruled by entropy, waiting for an obscene apocalypse. This was the world of *Naked Lunch* (1959), fiendishly comic, total in its satire of the human condition, coldly surreal. Among the most original works of the postwar era, its language broke into a lunatic montage of scenes reminiscent of Hieronymus Bosch. Yet Burroughs himself, an experimentalist in anti-literature, pretended to find words abhorrent. "To speak," he declared, "is to lie."

Later, in the sixties, new variations of the existential themes of choice, revolt, and affirmation appeared in fiction. Some works, like John Rechy's *City of Night* (1963) and Hubert Selby's *Last Exit to Brooklyn* (1964), presented images of sexual violence and perversion so excessive as to approach Burroughs'. Other novels, like Willian Styron's *Set This House on Fire* (1960) and, a finer fiction, Ken Kesey's *One Flew Over the Cuckoo's Nest* (1962), explored the redemptive effects of individual rebellion, the edge of creative violence. The idea of creative cruelty also informed Jerzy Kosinski's *Steps* (1968), a lucid novel about the estranged self, acting as a predator precisely in order to discover the limits of its own possibilities, and thus to escape itself. In all these works, American society, indeed culture itself, was perceived as the dead weight of custom, the repressive force of abstraction from which man must escape.

During the sixties, existential fiction also took a turn toward extravagant comedy; its heroes appeared as roguish, antic, or picaresque figures, amorous and fleet of mind, adepts of chicanery. The best example of the type was perhaps Sebastian Dangerfield, hero of J. P. Donleavy's *The Ginger Man* (1955, 1958, 1965). A scruffy sensualist, he improvised his life with gusto in the ubiquitous shadow of death; his skullduggery protested human mortality. Donleavy's subsequent works retained the distinctive, elliptic style of his first novel without surpassing its vitality. But the existential rogue had arrived in American fiction to stay.

By its very nature, Black experience in America was also existential. Living close to threats of violence, of material and moral deprivation, Blacks often lived "in the lion's mouth," as a character in Ellison's *Invisible Man* (1952) put it, and improvised their existence at the far brink of society. Richard Wright, father of the modern Black novel, had understood this in *Native Son* (1940). But Ellison's work went farther in discovering new intricacies of the subject. A seething novel, it was one of the earliest in the postwar period to fuse realism and surrealism, jokes and blues, in the form of an ironic picaresque. It also exhibited great energy of mind in its apprehension of history, ideology, and human nature. The question of identity that Ellison's *Invisible Man* faced was the crucial question of the times; the syncopated music of his assent and denial expressed the perplexities of white and Black alike.

With the rise of the Black Power Movement, however, the role of the writer became at once more urgent and complex. Caught between the demands of revolution, of art, and of personal identity, the Black writer was often compelled to create a new stance for himself, a new name. It was this very question that obsessed James Baldwin in many essays, burning with anger, anguish, and self-knowledge. His novels, though somewhat less impressive than his nonfiction, included the fine, autobiographical *Go Tell It on the Mountain* (1953), as well as *Another Country* (1962) and *Tell Me How Long the Train's Been Gone* (1968), in which Baldwin attempted to place racial and political issues in an erotic context.

Younger still than Baldwin, a number of talented Black novelists published actively in the sixties. Some, like William Demby and Ishmael Reed, favored experimental forms of fiction. Demby's *The Catacombs* (1965) appeared as a cubist pastiche of history, extending the modernist techniques of Gertrude Stein and Picasso, Joyce and Pirandello, into the postwar period. Less intellectual, such novels of Reed as *Yellow-Back Radio Broke Down* (1969) expressed a unique anarchic humor, mingling outrage and absurdity, a kind of "patarealism" that yoked the antics of Dada and "pataphysics" to the dangers of Black experience. Other novelists, however, were less concerned with literary experiment than with a redefinition of Black consciousness; their work, largely traditional in form, derived its intensity from the material. Thus, for instance, William Melvin Kelley's *A Different Drummer* (1962) and John A. Williams' *The Man Who Cried I Am* (1967) affirmed the dignity of the Black individual by reconceiving his relation to his community, his heritage. Indeed, Black fiction, whether experimental or traditional, amounted to a re-vision of America.

There were, of course, other novelists of the decade whose work fits into no preconceived tendency or pattern. Of these, John Hawkes and James Purdy were the most important. Their original work, which earned them critical recognition belatedly at the end of the fifties, shared only a vague affinity with the Gothic and poetic novels of the period.

Hawkes, like Djuna Barnes before him, sought to reclaim the nocturnal poetry of existence. Like Nathanael West, too, Hawkes was a satirist and surrealist both. His fascination with the power, mystery, and buffoonery of evil expressed itself in a prose that moved on the fringe of madness. His haunting novel, *The Cannibal*, compressed the history of three wars (1870, 1914, 1939) and the ancient rituals of murder and cannibalism into a single statement. The novel was followed by a series of enigmatic novelettes, of which *The*

Goose on the Grave (1954) was typical. More dramatic, less menacing, and still macabrely humorous, his later works included *Second Skin* (1964), possibly his best fiction. The action of the characters, perceived by an aging and richly alert narrator, moved between memory and desire, between Maine and the Pacific, finding its own free rhythm, testifying fantastically to the endurance of life among deathly circumstances. Hawkes took poetic fiction to the probable limits of the genre, though his concept of literature remained unaffected by post-modern complexities.

There was also poetry, crisp, broken, desperate, in the fiction of James Purdy. His first work, a collection of stories entitled *The Color of Darkness* (1957), revealed him as the master of a deceptively simple style, compounding elements of Kafka and Sherwood Anderson. Purdy's humor, at once diabolic and tender, disguised the deep wound of violated innocence, of betrayed love. In his best allegorical novel, *Malcolm* (1959), Purdy focused on a fatherless youth, endlessly available to experience, yet himself a blank around which grotesque and grasping society took shape. The marriage of Malcolm ushered him finally "into happiness—and death." Thus in postwar fiction the initiation of youth often ended in morbid defeat. Death was more violent in *Eustace Chisolm and the Works* (1967), a tale of erotic torments set in Chicago during the thirties. The novel demonstrated Purdy's gift for insinuating social satire, for discovering a cultural content even in the dangerous privacy of love. Written in a more realistic manner, *Jeremy's Version* (1970) portrayed life in a small Midwestern town with acid sympathy. Though Purdy's vision could be cramped, it was often precisely angled on terror; it penetrated the archetypal night.

4

Fiction in the sixties was perhaps more audacious and problematic than in previous decades. The novel of fantasy led both the nonfiction novel and science fiction among trends of the period. Writers as distinct and various as John Barth, Kurt Vonnegut, and John Updike also attained prominence in the same decade.

The novel of fantasy was an intimate of chaos, a strange mutation of comedy. Satire, burlesque, nightmare were elements of a form that claimed for itself the widest imaginative freedom. The authors drawn to that form were often geomancers of language, players and parodists to the bone. Their Nabokovian ironies, however, did not always conceal their desperation, their disgust with reality, or their obsession with death.

Among the earliest and most benign of these fantasists, John Cheever possessed a cunning narrative gift, an eye for the exact, satiric detail, best displayed in his humorous stories. Whimsically, fondly, he also celebrated the history of an amorous New England clan in *The Wapshot Chronicle* (1957) and *The Wapshot Scandal* (1964). His characters seemed sometimes deft caricatures, conveying the heartiness and generosity of American manners, the gaminess of life itself. Yet Cheever's exuberance had its blacker side: "Life in the United States in 1960 is Hell," he stated. The exuberance of Thomas Berger was also touched by a deeper sense of the absurdity, the recalcitrance, of experience. Reinhart, protagonist of three novels, starting with *Crazy in Berlin* (1958), acted as innocent fool, jocular lover, mock hero, and death defier; his task was to keep conscience alive amid the vital incongruities of postwar America. Berger also wrote philosophical travesties, spoofing such pop forms as the Western in *Little Big Man* (1964) and the mystery in *Killing Time* (1967).

Some fantasists, more intent on new dislocations in the forms of fiction, appeared more *avant-garde* than Cheever and Berger, and became more fashionable. Laconic, idyllic, curiously haunted by some pastoral vision of America, Richard Brautigan developed a unique, fragmentary style in such darkly playful works as *Trout Fishing in America* (1967) and *In Watermelon Sugar* (1968). The naive loves and fresh laughter of his characters concealed an intuition of death, some vast blankness, reminiscent of Hemingway. Mocking the conventions of the novel, Brautigan presented, as on a Japanese screen, scenes etched sharply against a white page. Donald Barthelme went still farther in his experiments with nonlinear narratives and absurdist techniques. His novels, such as *Snow White* (1967) and *Sadness* (1972), his stories in *City Life* (1970), included pictures, fragments, collages, questionnaires, captions of every kind, fictions of detritus, agile, witty, and trivial. In a famous digression, Barthelme wrote: "We like books that have a lot of *dreck* in them, matter which presents itself as not wholly relevant (or indeed at all relevant). . . ." *Dreck* was indeed the invisible writing, the code in much contemporary fiction.

A more sombre writer, Thomas Pynchon assimilated such irrelevance into his controlled and paranoiac allegories; he was the supreme artificer of esoteric plots, bizarre characters, and a Joycean style almost too luxurious. Learned in science and letters, his focus was decay and destruction in nature or language, in sex or politics; entropy was the motive, perhaps even the shaper, of fictions. In *V* (1963), Pynchon designed a labyrinthine quest leading nowhere, except to the abysmal center of our century. In *The Crying of Lot 49* (1966), he posed an epistemological conundrum in lyric form. And in *Gravity's Rainbow* (1973), his largest, densest, and most rigorous work, Pynchon created an apocalyptic fantasy, set in Europe during 1944–1945, gathering all his themes.

Yet among fantasists of the sixties, John Barth was the first to recognize the post-modern crisis of fiction. In a signal essay entitled "The Literature of Exhaustion," he spoke thus of the young novelist writing in the shadow of Nabokov, Beckett, and Borges: "His artistic victory . . . is that he confronts an intellectual dead end and employs it against itself to accomplish new human work." A master parodist, versatile in style and skeptical of temper, Barth found his home in a region which he called "Ultimacy"; there irony and fancy found their largest freedom in "articulation." His two earliest novels, *The Floating Opera* (1956, 1957) and *The End of the Road* (1958, 1967), dealt with the crippling excesses of consciousness in a world deprived of moral values. Questioning himself as author and narrator, Barth still managed to make art of a nihilistic theme. But it was in *The Sot-Weed Factor* (1960, 1967) and *Giles Goat-Boy* (1966), compendious fictions of the contemporary world in the forms of pastiche, mock history, and droll allegory, that Barth revealed his genius for complete articulation. His heroes were "cosmic amateurs," lovers of reality who attempted to discover, within the medium of a Protean language, some balm for the ache of consciousness. *Lost in the Fun House* (1968) and *Chimera* (1972) went farther in decreating the forms of fiction, and in reconstructing myth, literature, even technology, so as to reflect glimmers of values that a post-modern artist may still hold. Yet as a comic fabulist, Barth could also strain his credibility and pall on his readers.

The search for credible form in a world where truth was often more implausible than fantasy inspired authors of the nonfiction novel. Surrealism was in the street; no fact was innocent of fancy, no fancy devoid of fact; myths and dreams were the stuff of post-modern history. Thus fantasists pretended with great skill to serve as reporters. The term "nonfiction novel" itself was applied by Truman Capote to his work, *In Cold Blood* (1966), which centered on an actual mass murder in Kansas. Based on notes, tapes, innumerable interviews, the book presented a shattering indictment of American society, in a form artfully compassionate and morally oblique. William Styron preferred to call his *Confessions of Nat Turner* (1967) a "meditation on history," though some Black writers challenged the historical veracity of the work and resented its novelistic impersonation of Turner, Black leader of a slave rebellion. Speaking both as narrator and character, as personal witness and voice of the times, Norman Mailer entitled the two parts of *The Armies of the Night* (1968): "History as a Novel" and "The Novel as History." Fiction, then, had become not only a metaphor of reality but also a metaphor of itself, under the disguise of factual narrative.

Another kind of fiction addressed itself specifically to the possibilities of technology. Modern science fiction, of course, developed before the second

World War; Hugo Gernsback started *Amazing Stories* in 1926, and John W. Campbell founded *Astounding Stories* in 1938. But the staggering acceleration of science and its technics after the war opened new resources to the genre. Science Fiction created new myths for the machines of America, new models for its society, new visions for its destiny in the universe. As fable, as satire, and as prophecy, whether utopian or dystopian, the best science fiction began to draw the grudging attention of critics in the sixties. Such prolific and accomplished writers as Isaac Asimov, Alfred Bester, Ray Bradbury, Robert Heinlein, and Theodore Sturgeon reached a serious audience, particularly among the young. The genre also attracted fantasists of a different kind: William Burroughs, for instance, in *The Soft Machine* (1961, 1965), *The Ticket That Exploded* (1962, 1967) and *Nova Express* (1964), and Kurt Vonnegut in almost all of his work.

Though Vonnegut began to publish in the fifties, he was largely ignored until technological fantasy became rife. A satirist and sentimentalist, a comedian as well, he viewed the human condition with a mixture of whimsy, affection, and arch despair. His values were ultimately personal, infrangible; death and absurdity haunted his gnomic style. *Player Piano* (1952), an anti-utopian fiction, lacked the life and witty fabulation of *The Sirens of Titan* (1959) and *Cat's Cradle* (1963), in which Vonnegut exposed the misdeeds of earthlings against a background of galactic adventures. *Slaughterhouse-Five* (1969) focused on the dreadful fire-bombings of Dresden during the second World War; accusation and exorcism sustained an autobiographical narrative which broke into science fiction in parts. But Vonnegut's most powerful work was not in the latter genre. *Mother Night* (1961, 1966), a study of nihilism and totalitarianism in the modern world, of pretense and hatred in mankind, avoided the facility of his lesser fiction. Its hero, villain, and narrator was, by his own admission, "a man who served evil too openly and good too secretly, the crime of his times."

Standing somewhat apart from various trends of the sixties, John Updike quickly achieved prominence in that decade. He admired Nabokov, shared his wit and verbal art, though Updike lacked the bravura of the older writer. He was, in a sense, a classic satiric novelist of manners who delineated subtle middle-class matters. But he was also a Christian author, a religious novelist, concerned in some dry way with death and dread, the counterfeits of love, the slow atrophies of spirit. His crisp mastery of the short story revealed itself early in *The Same Door* (1959). His two novels, *The Poorhouse Fair* (1959) and *Of the Farm* (1965), though conventional in their ironic realism, probed narrowly the perplexities of age and childhood, religion and science, family and marriage. The ambitions of Updike acquired scope in *The Centaur* (1963), an elaborate mythological fiction centering on a modern school teacher, Caldwell, who plays the part of Chiron, self-sacrificer, expiator of Promethean sins. But Updike's most impressive works remained *Rabbit Run* (1960) and its sequel, *Rabbit Redux* (1971). Their bungling, all-too-human, and still striving hero carried the burden of spiritual awareness in American culture, a culture of drugged feelings, sudden terrors, and stubborn renewals. Adroit in language as in perception, Updike's vision remained cerebral; in some odd way, he refused the implications of his largest themes.

5

The trends of former decades continued to develop in the seventies as new authors or new conditions appeared to give them shape. The experimental impulse in fiction, released earlier by such writers as Burroughs, Barth, Barthelme, and Pynchon, and by William Gaddis in his huge novel, *The Recognitions* (1955), took new directions in certain works. These included Robert Coover's *The Universal Baseball Association* (1968), Rudolph Wurlitzer's *Flats* (1970), Raymond Federman's *Double or Nothing* (1971), William H. Gass' *Omensetter's Luck* (1966), and Ronald Sukenick's *Out* (1973).

In the end, however, the symbolic stature and presence of postwar American fiction was gauged by its two major authors: Saul Bellow and Norman Mailer. Their energy, their imagination, their apprehensions of changing American realities, enhanced the possibilities of fiction both here and abroad.

Bellow wrote in the main, intelligent tradition of the novel; in his work the European realism of Balzac, Dickens, and Tolstoy was modified by the greater liberty of native fable and romance. His central concerns were freedom and love: freedom as the interplay between what is given and what is made in the life of man, and love as the interplay between man's identity and his completion in others. Insistently, he asked what it meant to be human in the contemporary world; insistently, he sought the "axial lines of existence." His urban, Jewish characters recalled their heritage at the same time that they embodied the perplexities of the Jew in America; their comic and painful quests adduced dignity to all men. The versatility of Bellow was evident in the differences between his earlier and later work: between the ironic and compact *Dangling Man* (1944), a mordant, existential tale set in wartime America, or *The Victim*, a profound parable of Gentile and Jew, and such torrential narratives as *The Adventures of Augie March* (1953) and *Henderson the Rain King* (1958). The humorous and headlong picaresque adventures of Augie March, "free-style and Chicago-born," bared all the interstices of the American Dream; his voice restored wonder and mind to the language of fiction. Henderson's fabulous quests in Africa, his search for some viable ideal of service, gave an even deeper sense of the human endeavor. Bruised by truth and reality, Henderson raised illusion, action, and pain to the level of felt wisdom. *Seize the Day* (1956), a brief masterpiece concerning the human encounter with error and death, stood with *Henderson the Rain King* at the apogee of Bellow's career. But *Herzog* (1964), a quasi-epistolary novel bristling with ironies, ideas, and self-pity, and *Mr. Sammler's Planet* (1970), a parable of the humanist conscience caught between past and future, history and science fiction, did not expand Bellow's sense of life. It seemed as if Bellow, out of tune with the times, had preferred to retrench; his art appeared a little querulous; and his imagination, once unparagoned, waited upon new fulfillments.

By contrast, Mailer continued to engage American reality and to divine its fantasies. Ambitious, embattled, and sometimes improvident of his genius, his claim rested on the style and vitality of his encounters rather than on any masterpiece of fiction. His domain was the perilous self. There instinct and mind, mystery and history, sex and politics, magic and technology— yes, even the Devil and God—improvised their truce on the breath of style, on the turn of vision. Yet the romantic heroism of Mailer was larger than his egoism; the task was to wrest from the contradictions of existence a finer fate for man. In his brilliant war novel, *The Naked and the Dead*, Mailer showed how ideology and morality can be overwhelmed by nature or by power. Critics who acclaimed the work, a best-seller, also dismissed his two subsequent novels: *Barbary Shore* (1951), a gloomy fable concerning sex and madness, the far Left and far Right in politics; and *The Deer Park* (1955), an exposé of cowardice, hypocrisy, and nihilism, set in a promiscuous Hollywood colony. The period, however, marked Mailer's breakthrough to a new erotic and existential vision. *Advertisements for Myself* (1959) was the turning point. The book, which contained the famous manifesto of hipsterism entitled "The White Negro," had the scope, excess, and searing introspection of a major work. Mailer had found his voice, the right timbre of an apocalyptic imagination, the right stance for the jester and seer, the anarch and social critic in himself. And he had found the live prose form, both sensuous and witty, both public and personal, that was to amplify his voice through so many works, from *The Presidential Papers* (1963) to *Existential Errands* (1972). Yet Mailer wrote also two strikingly original novels: *An American Dream* (1965) and *Why Are We in Vietnam?* (1967). In the first, he impersonated the author of pop detective fiction, and succeeded in creating a myth darker than parody, bigger than a tall tale, a myth of the lone individual answering the challenge to his most intimate being. And in the second, he impersonated a white, youthful Texan or a Harlem "cripple

Spade"—we never know which—on an Alaskan hunt for grizzly, creating another myth of initiation into the mysteries of nature and self, into the knowledge of fear, friendship, and father betrayal. But like all myths, these stories were not merely personal; both exposed the psychic life of America to itself, exposed the lunacy and wonder of a land seemingly bent on denying its truest impulse. Standing in the early seventies, few critics could resist the conclusion that Norman Mailer, despite his postures and sad self-exposures, was the man of letters with the greatest presence, mastery, and amazement.

TABLE OF AUTHORS

Editor's Note: Most of the chapters in these volumes are the work of single contributors; a few are collaborations. In many cases, sentences and paragraphs have been added, usually at the beginnings and ends of chapters, to tie the book together and to emphasize dominant themes; occasionally passages designed for one chapter have found a more logical place in another; and extreme variations in style have been somewhat modified. Differences of opinion among authors have been allowed to stand.

Preface: the Editors and Associates
Address to the Reader: Henry Seidel Canby; the Editors and Associates

The Colonies
  1. The European Background: Howard Mumford Jones
  2. Colonial Literary Culture: Louis B. Wright
  3. Reports and Chronicles: Randolph G. Adams
  4. Writers of the South: Louis B. Wright
  5. Writers of New England: Kenneth B. Murdock
  6. Jonathan Edwards: Thomas H. Johnson
  7. Writers of the Middle Colonies: Frederick B. Tolles
  8. Benjamin Franklin: Carl Van Doren

The Republic
  9. Revolution and Reaction: John C. Miller
  10. The Making of the Man of Letters: Robert E. Spiller
      (with passages by Alexander Cowie)
  11. The War of the Pamphlets: J. H. Powell
  12. Philosopher-Statesmen of the Republic: Adrienne Koch
  13. Poets and Essayists: Lewis Leary
  14. The Beginnings of Fiction and Drama: Alexander Cowie
  15. The American Dream: Gilbert Chinard

The Democracy
  16. The Great Experiment: Tremaine McDowell
  17. Art in the Market Place: Robert E. Spiller (with passages by Odell
        Shepard, Luther S. Mansfield, and John D. Wade)
  18. Washington Irving: Stanley T. Williams
  19. James Fenimore Cooper: Stanley T. Williams
  20. Diversity and Innovation in the Middle States: Luther S. Mansfield
  21. In New England: Tremaine McDowell
  22. In the South: John D. Wade
  23. Edgar Allan Poe: F. O. Matthiessen

Literary Fulfillment
  24. Democratic Vistas: David Bowers
  25. Ralph Waldo Emerson: Robert E. Spiller
  26. Henry David Thoreau: Townsend Scudder
  27. Nathaniel Hawthorne: Stanley T. Williams
  28. Herman Melville: Willard Thorp
  29. Walt Whitman: Henry Seidel Canby

Crisis
  30. A House Divided and Rejoined: Dixon Wecter
  31. The People's Patronage: William Charvat
  32. The Historians: Eric F. Goldman
  33. The Orators: Harold F. Harding, Everett L. Hunt, and Willard
        Thorp
  34. Literature and Conflict: George F. Whicher
  35. The New England Triumvirate: Longfellow, Holmes, Lowell: Odell
        Shepard
  36. Minority Report: The Tradition of the Old South: Henry Nash Smith
  37. Heard from the New World: Harold Blodgett

Expansion
  38. The Widening of Horizons: Henry Nash Smith
  39. Literary Culture on the Frontier: Dixon Wecter
  40. The American Language: H. L. Mencken
  41. The Mingling of Tongues: Henry A. Pochmann (with the assistance
        of Joseph Rossi and others)
  42. The Indian Heritage: Stith Thompson
  43. Folklore: Arthur Palmer Hudson
  44. Humor: Harold W. Thompson (with passages by Henry Seidel
        Canby)

45. Western Chroniclers and Literary Pioneers: Henry Nash Smith
46. The West As Seen from the East: George R. Stewart
47. Abraham Lincoln: The Soil and the Seed: Carl Sandburg

The Sections
48. The Second Discovery of America: Henry Nash Smith
49. The Education of Everyman: Dixon Wecter
50. Defenders of Ideality: Willard Thorp
51. Pilgrims' Return: Willard Thorp
52. Delineation of Life and Character: Carlos Baker
53. Western Record and Romance: Wallace Stegner
54. Realism Defined: William Dean Howells: Gordon S. Haight
55. Experiments in Poetry: Emily Dickinson and Sidney Lanier: William M. Gibson and Stanley T. Williams
56. Mark Twain: Dixon Wecter

The Continental Nation
57. A World to Win or Lose: Ralph H. Gabriel
58. Literature As Business: William Charvat
59. The Literature of Ideas: Merle Curti
60. Fiction and Social Debate: Walter F. Taylor
61. The Emergence of the Modern Drama: Sculley Bradley
62. Toward Naturalism in Fiction: Robert E. Spiller
63. Henry James: Richard P. Blackmur
64. The Discovery of Bohemia: Harry T. Levin
65. Henry Adams: Robert E. Spiller

The United States
66. The Hope of Reform: Henry Steele Commager
67. Creating an Audience: Malcolm Cowley and Henry Seidel Canby
68. The Battle of the Books: Robert E. Spiller
69. Edwin Arlington Robinson: Stanley T. Williams
70. The "New" Poetry: Willard Thorp
71. Theodore Dreiser: Robert E. Spiller (based, with permission, on an article by James T. Farrell)
72. Fiction Sums Up a Century: Henry Seidel Canby
73. Eugene O'Neill: Joseph Wood Krutch

A World Literature
74. Between Wars: Allan Nevins
75. How Writers Lived: Malcolm Cowley

76. Speculative Thinkers: Brand Blanshard
77. A Cycle of Fiction: Maxwell Geismar
78. An American Drama: Joseph Wood Krutch
79. Poetry: F. O. Matthiessen
80. Summary in Criticism: Morton D. Zabel
81. American Books Abroad: Malcolm Cowley
82. End of an Era: Willard Thorp and Robert E. Spiller (with passages
    by Ihab Hassan and Daniel Hoffman)

Mid-century and After
83. The New Consciousness: Ihab Hassan
84. Poetry: Daniel Hoffman
85. Drama: Gerald Weales
86. Fiction: Ihab Hassan

Bibliography
Thomas H. Johnson and Richard M. Ludwig

BIBLIOGRAPHY

This is a reader's bibliography and is therefore highly selective. It is designed as a guide to material useful to anyone who wishes to read further in the subjects discussed in this *History*. To that end, periodical items and monograph studies are omitted, as well as technical and textual studies and bibliographies directed primarily at the specialists. Such listings can be consulted in the second volume of this work, the *Bibliography*. The reader will find there guides to resources; biliographies by period, type, movements, and influences; and 238 individual author bibliographies.

When they are collected, the complete works of major authors are listed. Reprints of individual works by these authors, particularly paperbound editions, are so numerous that it is not feasible to list them separately. The reader is directed to *Paperbound Books in Print*, published three times a year by R. R. Bowker Company, New York, as a helpful guide to selecting reprints.

In recent years, publishers have begun issuing series of paperbound critical studies aimed at the general reader rather than the specialist. These books are uneven in quality and scope, but they are inexpensive, concise introductions to their subjects. For critical biographies, see *Twayne's United States Authors Series* (College and University Press). Brief critical studies are available in *Pamphlets on American Writers* (University of Minnesota Press). Collections of essays by various critics are in *Critical Editions* (W. W. Norton), *Discussions of Literature* (D. C. Heath), *Literary Casebooks in American Literature* (Thomas Y. Crowell), and *Twentieth-Century Views* (Prentice-Hall).

GENERAL SURVEY: *The Literature and Culture of the United States*

This *History* adopts an organic view of literature as a record of the experience of a people, and a survey of writings dealing with that experience is appropriate. The study by Charles A. and Mary R. Beard, *The Rise of American Civilization* (Macmillan), 1927, 2 vols. (rev. and enl., 1933, with Vol. III added in 1939 and Vol. IV in 1942) is significant. It deals chiefly with the economic forces which have molded American society. Merle Curti, *The Growth of American Thought* (Harper), 1943, 3rd ed.,

1480

1964, is a social history of American thought from its beginnings; it contains full bibliographies for the general reader. A comprehensive one-volume intellectual history, from colonial times to the present, is *Paths of American Thought* (Houghton Mifflin), 1963, essays by twenty-six contributors, edited by Arthur M. Schlesinger and Morton G. White. Stimulating and informative also is Ralph H. Gabriel, *The Course of American Democratic Thought: An Intellectual History Since 1815* (Ronald), 1940, 2nd ed., 1956. One of the most ambitious studies in recent years is Max Lerner's huge one-volume survey, *America as a Civilization: Life and Thought in the United States Today* (Simon and Schuster), 1957. Special studies of literature as documentation for intellectual history are Henry S. Commager, *The American Mind: An Interpretation of American Thought and Character Since the 1880's* (Yale), 1950; Merle Curti, *Probing Our Past* (Harper), 1955; and Stow Persons, *American Minds: A History of Ideas* (Holt), 1958. A critical survey of ideologies in American culture is Oscar Cargill, *Intellectual America: Ideas on the March* (Macmillan), 1941. It treats European ideas with respect to American literature, chiefly during the twentieth century. Richard D. Mosier, *The American Temper: Patterns of Our Intellectual Heritage* (California), 1952, stresses four phases in the growth of an American climate of ideas: Puritan, Enlightenment, Romantic, Modern. By no means out of date is Vernon L. Parrington, *Main Currents in American Thought* (Harcourt, Brace), 1927, 1930. More recent important studies are Loren Baritz's *City on a Hill: A History of Ideas and Myths in America* (Wiley), 1964; John Morton Blum, *The Promise of America* (Houghton Mifflin), 1965; Richard Hofstadter, *Anti-Intellectualism in American Life* (Knopf), 1963; and Thomas D. Clark, *The Emerging South* (Oxford), 1968.

The Library of Congress Series in American Civilization (Harvard), 1951–1965, is a comprehensive survey of the American scene in the first half of the twentieth century. Ralph Henry Gabriel is the general editor of the twelve volumes. *A History of the South*, 9 vols. (Louisiana State), 1947–1967, is under the general editorship of Wendell Holmes Stephenson and E. Merton Coulter.

A comprehensive survey of social growth is *A History of American Life* (Macmillan), 1927–1948, 13 vols., edited by Arthur M. Schlesinger and Dixon Ryan Fox, each volume contributed by an authority. A balanced two-volume political history is Samuel E. Morison, Henry S. Commager, and William E. Leuchtenberg, *The Growth of the American Republic*, 6th ed., rev. and enl. (Oxford), 1969, 2 vols. A socio-political history is Harry J. Carman, Harold C. Syrett, and Bernard W. Wishy, *A History of the American People*, 3rd ed., rev. (Knopf), 1967, 2 vols. An anthology of source material, preponderantly economic, is Louis M. Hacker and Helene S. Zahler, eds., *The Shaping of the American Tradition* (Columbia), 1947, 2 vols. The fifth volume of

Joseph Dorfman's *The Economic Mind in American Civilization* (Viking) was published in 1959. His study now covers the years 1606–1933. See also Harold U. Faulkner's *American Economic History*, 8th ed. (Harper), 1960, and two volumes by John Kenneth Galbraith, *The Affluent Society* (Houghton Mifflin), 1958, rev. ed. 1969, and *The New Industrial State* (Houghton Mifflin), 1967.

The *Dictionary of American History*, edited by James T. Adams and others (Scribner's), rev. ed. 1946, 5 vols., was supplemented by an additional volume in 1961. Under the direction of Thomas C. Cochran it was issued in one volume as *The Concise Dictionary of American History*, 1962, edited by Wayne Andrews. *Encyclopedia of American History*, revised and enlarged by Richard B. Morris (Harper), 1970, and *The Oxford Companion to American History*, edited by Thomas H. Johnson (Oxford), 1966, are useful. Two standard bibliographies are *Harvard Guide to American History*, edited by Oscar Handlin and others (Harvard), 1954, and *A Guide to the Study of the United States of America* prepared by Donald H. Mugridge and Blanche P. McCrum (Library of Congress), 1960. The latter provides annotations and headnotes.

American life as viewed by contemporaries is described in *A Mirror for Americans: Life and Manners in the United States, 1790–1870, as Recorded by American Travelers*, edited by Warren S. Tryon (Chicago), 1952, 3 vols.: I. Life in the East; II. The Cotton Kingdom; III. The Frontier Moves West. A compact account of the way Americans have lived from colonial times to the present is offered in Nelson M. Blake, *A Short History of American Life* (McGraw-Hill), 1952. A graphic one-volume survey is Roger Butterfield, *The American Past: A History of the United States from Concord to Hiroshima, 1775–1945* (Simon and Schuster), 1947. An excellent pictorial history is Marshall B. Davidson, ed., *Life in America* (Houghton Mifflin), 1951, 2 vols. Oliver W. Larkin, *Art and Life in America* (Rinehart), 1949, rev. ed., 1960, relates art and architecture to the civilization that produced them, as does Richard McLanathan's profusely illustrated *The American Tradition in the Arts* (Harcourt, Brace), 1968. Good histories are James Marston Fitch, *American Building: The Forces That Shape It* (Houghton Mifflin), 1948; John Burchard and Albert Bush-Brown, *The Architecture of America: A Social and Cultural History* (Little, Brown), 1961; Wayne Andrew's photographic history, *Architecture in America* (Atheneum), 1960; Virgil Barker, *American Painting: History and Interpretation* (Macmillan), 1950; *American Painting* (Skira/World), 1969, Volume I: *From Its Beginning to the Armory Show*, by Jules David Prown, Volume II: *The Twentieth Century*, by Barbara Rose; and Wayne Craven, *Sculpture in America* (Crowell), 1968. A major city-planning study is John W. Reps, *The Making of Urban America* (Princeton), 1965. Critical surveys of the popular arts include Russel Nye's comprehensive *The Unembarrassed Muse* (Dial), 1970, and Barry Ulanov's *The Two Worlds of American Art* (Macmillan), 1965.

A standard general history of American philosophy is I[saac] Woodbridge Riley, *American Thought from Puritanism to Pragmatism and Beyond*, 2nd ed., (Holt), 1923. Herbert W. Schneider, *A History of American Philosophy*, 2nd ed. (Columbia), 1963, is a source book and a survey from early times to the present. See also Joseph L. Blau, *Men and Movements in American Philosophy* (Prentice-Hall), 1952; John E. Smith, *The Spirit of American Philosophy* (Oxford), 1963; Robert Clifton Whittemore, *Makers of the American Mind* (Morrow), 1964; and Morton G. White, *Science and Sentiment in America: Philosophical Thought from Jonathan Edwards to John Dewey* (Oxford), 1972. Two useful collections are Ralph B. Winn., ed., *American Philosophy* (Philosophical Library), 1955, and Max Black., ed., *Philosophy in America* (Cornell), 1965.

Surveys of religion, written for the intelligent layman, are Willard L. Sperry, *Religion in America* (Macmillan), 1946; William W. Sweet, *The Story of Religion in America*, 2nd rev. ed. (Harper), 1950, Edwin S. Gaustad, *A Religious History of America* (Harper), 1966; and Sydney E. Ahlstrom, *A Religious History of the American People* (Yale), 1972. Anson Phelps Stokes, *Church and State in the United States* (Harper), 1950, 3 vols., is a monumental and indispensable work. But the most ambitious study of American religion is edited by James Ward Smith and A. Leland Jamison, in four volumes. Called *Religion in American Life* (Princeton), 1961, it surveys: I. The Shaping of American Religion (nine contributors); II. Religious Perspectives in American Culture (ten contributors); and IV., in two parts, A Critical Bibliography of Religion in America (by Nelson R. Burr). Vol. III, Religious Thought and Economic Society, was announced but never published.

There are so many excellent anthologies of American literature that it is not feasible to list them here. Two dictionaries of authors, titles, and facts are James D. Hart, ed., *The Oxford Companion to American Literature*, 4th ed. (Oxford), 1965, and Max J. Herzberg, ed., *The Reader's Encyclopedia of American Literature* (Crowell), 1962.

Standard introductions to the history of fiction are Arthur H. Quinn, *American Fiction* (Appleton), 1936; Carl Van Doren, *The American Novel, 1789–1939*, rev. ed. (Macmillan), 1940; Alexander Cowie, *The Rise of the American Novel* (American Book), 1948; and Edward Wagenknecht, *Cavalcade of the American Novel* (Holt), 1952. Richard Chase, *The American Novel and Its Tradition* (Anchor), 1957, is more an essay in definition than a historical treatment. Leslie Fiedler's *Love and Death in the American Novel* (Criterion), 1960, is a highly individual psychological study of fiction from 1789 to 1959. An important collection of documents "that bear on our long-standing self-consciousness about the American novel" is *The Idea of an American Novel* (Crowell), 1961, edited by Louis D. Rubin, Jr., and John Rees Moore.

The history of American drama is most fully treated in Arthur H. Quinn, *A History of the American Drama from the Beginning to the Civil War*, 2nd ed. (Appleton), 1943, continued in *A History of the American Drama from the Civil War to the Present Day*, rev. ed. (Appleton), 1937, with ample bibliographies and play lists. A one-volume survey is Glenn Hughes, *A History of the American Theatre, 1700–1950* (Samuel French), 1951. Anthologies of American plays are Richard Moody, ed., *Dramas from the American Theatre, 1762–1909* (World), 1966; John Gassner and Clive Barnes, eds., *Fifty Best Plays of the American Theatre: From 1787 to the Present* (Crown), 1970, 4 vols., Robert W. Corrigan, ed., *New American Plays, I* (Hill and Wang), 1970; William M. Hoffman, ed., *New American Plays II* and *III* (Hill and Wang), 1970; and Michael Benedikt, ed., *Theatre Experiment* (Doubleday), 1968. Jordan Y. Miller combines ten twentieth-century American plays with chapters on the historical background of American drama in *American Dramatic Literature* (McGraw-Hill), 1961.

The history of American poetry is treated most fully in Hyatt H. Waggoner, *American Poetry from the Puritans to the Present* (Houghton Mifflin), 1968; Roy Harvey Pearce, *The Continuity of American Poetry* (Princeton), 1961; and Kenneth Rexroth, *American Poetry in the Twentieth Century* (Herder and Herder), 1971. The most comprehensive collections are *The Poet in America: 1650 to the Present* (Heath), 1973, edited by Albert Gelpi, and *American Poetry* (Harper), 1965, edited by Gay Wilson Allen, Walter B. Rideout, and James K. Robinson. Also useful are Louis Untermeyer, *Modern American Poetry*, new and enl. ed. (Harcourt, Brace), 1962; Donald Hall and others, eds., *The New Poets of England and America* (Meridian), 1957, rev. ed. (World), 1972; Donald M. Allen, ed., *The New American Poetry, 1945–1960* (Grove), 1960; John Malcolm Brinnin and Bill Read, eds., *Twentieth Century Poetry: American and British (1900–1970)* rev. ed. (McGraw-Hill), 1970; and Richard Ellmann and Robert O'Clair, eds., *The Norton Anthology of Modern Poetry* (Norton), 1973.

A comprehensive survey of our literary heritage is Arthur H. Quinn, Kenneth B. Murdock, Clarence Gohdes, and George F. Whicher, *The Literature of the American People: A Historical and Critical Survey* (Appleton), 1951. Van Wyck Brooks published a five-volume study, *Makers and Finders: A History of the Writer in America, 1800–1915* (Dutton), 1936–1952. Walter F. Taylor's *A History of American Letters*, 1936, was expanded and revised to *The Story of American Letters* (Regnery), 1956. Robert E. Spiller's short history, *The Cycle of American Literature: An Essay in Historical*

Criticism (Macmillan), 1955, rev. ed. 1967, develops a theory of a single organic movement in American letters. Rod W. Horton and Herbert W. Edwards, *Backgrounds of American Literary Thought*, 2nd ed. (Appleton), 1967, is an exposition of movements from Puritanism to existentialism. Willard Thorp surveys modern literature in *American Writing in the Twentieth Century* (Harvard), 1960. Jay B. Hubbell makes an encyclopedic study in *The South in American Literature, 1607–1900* (Duke), 1954. Two general historical studies by foreign scholars are of high quality and keen perception: Heinrich Straumann, *American Literature in the Twentieth Century* (Hutchinson), 1951, and Marcus Cunliffe, *The Literature of the United States* (Penguin), 1954. Specialized treatments of American literary history are F. O. Matthiessen, *American Renaissance: Art and Expression in the Age of Emerson and Whitman* (Oxford), 1941; Howard Mumford Jones, *The Theory of American Literature* (Cornell), 1948, rev. ed., 1965; Charles Feidelson, Jr., *Symbolism and American Literature* (Chicago), 1953; R.W.B. Lewis, *The American Adam: Innocence, Tragedy, and Tradition in the Nineteenth Century* (Chicago), 1955; Jay Martin, *Harvests of Change: American Literature, 1865–1914* (Prentice-Hall), 1967; and Richard Ruland, *The Rediscovery of American Literature* (Harvard), 1967, a study of "the premises of critical taste, 1900–1940."

I. THE COLONIES: *Importation and Adaptation*

The transfer of a mature civilization and culture to a primitive environment has been the theme of a large number of competent studies. Samuel Eliot Morison has begun a three-volume study with *The European Discovery of America: The Northern Voyages, A.D. 500–1600* (Oxford), 1971. Howard Mumford Jones traces the influence of the European Renaissance and the classical tradition on the American experience in *O Strange New World: American Culture: The Formative Years* (Viking), 1964. The fullest treatment, stressing political and economic development, is Charles M. Andrews, *The Colonial Period of American History* (Yale), 1934–1938, 4 vols. The standard short history is Louis B. Wright, *The Atlantic Frontier: Colonial American Civilization, 1607–1763* (Knopf), 1947, (Cornell), 1959, followed by *The Cultural Life of the American Colonies, 1607–1763* (Harper), 1957. Bernard De Voto, *The Course of Empire* (Houghton Mifflin), 1952, one of the clearest accounts, has a continental perspective and brings the story down to 1805. Two general histories of the period are Curtis P. Nettels, *The Roots of American Civilization: A History of American Colonial Life* (Appleton), 1938, and Daniel J. Boorstin, *The Americans: The Colonial Experience* (Random), 1958. More specialized but equally important is Carl Bridenbaugh, *Cities in the Wilderness: The First Century of Urban Life in America, 1625–1742* (Ronald), 1938. Richard N. Dorson edited two collections: *America Begins: Early American Writing* (Pantheon), 1950, and *America Rebels: Narratives of the Patriots* (Pantheon), 1953.

Authoritative studies of regional intellectual history are Thomas J. Wertenbaker, *Founding of American Civilization: The Middle Colonies* (Scribner's), 1938; Louis B. Wright, *The First Gentlemen of Virginia: Intellectual Qualities of the Early Colonial Ruling Class* (Huntington), 1940; Richard L. Morton, *Colonial Virginia*, 2 vols., (North Carolina), 1960; and three volumes by Perry Miller: *The New England Mind: The Seventeenth Century* (Macmillan), 1939, *The New England Mind: From Colony to Province* (Harvard), 1953, and *Errand into the Wilderness* (Harvard), 1956, which he calls "a rank of spotlights on the massive narrative of the movement of European culture into the vacant wilderness of America." The second edition of Samuel Eliot Morison's *The Puritan Pronaos*, 1936, was published in 1956 under the title *The Intellectual Life of Colonial New England* (New York University). Peter N. Carroll's *Puritanism and the Wilderness* (Columbia), 1969, focuses on "the intellectual significance of the New England frontier, 1629–1700." Peter Gay's *A Loss of Mastery: Puritan Historians in Colonial America* (Berkeley), 1966, analyzes chiefly the work of William Bradford, Cotton Mather, and Jonathan Edwards.

No collection of voyages has superseded Richard Hakluyt's famous *Principall Navigations, Voiages, and Discoveries of the English Nation*, first issued in London in 1589. Often reprinted, it is available in eight volumes in Everyman's Library (Dutton). A convenient one-volume edition of the monumental seventy-three-volume edition of *The Jesuit Relations* is that of Edna Kenton (Boni), 1925. Francis Parkman captured the epic drama of the whole colonial period in his histories, which drew not only upon his own travel observations but upon the *Jesuit Relations*. *France and England in North America*, in seven parts and running to 13 volumes in the collected editions, is Parkman's major work. A one-volume condensation has been edited by John Tebbel under the title *The Battle for North America* (Doubleday), 1948.

The classic account of immigrants in America is that of William Bradford. His *Of Plymouth Plantation, 1620–1647* is available in complete text, edited by Samuel Eliot Morison (Knopf), 1952, with notes and introduction.

The Voice of the Old Frontier, edited by R. W. G. Vail (Pennsylvania), 1949, lists and discusses most of the old travel records, available in such libraries as the John Carter Brown Library in Providence, R.I., and the William L. Clements Library in Ann Arbor, Michigan. A basic tool is Clarence Brigham's *History and Bibliography of American Newspapers, 1690–1820* (American Antiquarian Society), 1947, 2 vols. A reference source for everyday life during the period is William Matthews, *American Diaries: An Annotated Bibliography of American Diaries Written Prior to the Year 1861* (University of California Publications in English, Vol. 16), 1945.

Colonial architecture as an expression of the utilitarian imagination of the settlers is studied in S[idney] Fiske Kimball, *Domestic Architecture of the American Colonies and of the Early Republic* (Scribner's), 1922. A more recent study is Hugh Morrison, *Early American Architecture, From the First Colonial Settlements to the National Period* (Oxford), 1952. Both are well illustrated. Carl Bridenbaugh, *The Colonial Craftsman* (New York University), 1950, discusses the place of the artisan in this society. Colonial portrait painting is the subject of James T. Flexner, *First Flowers of Our Wilderness* (Houghton Mifflin), 1947, emphasizing the practical traits of the colonists. See also his *Short History of American Painting* (Houghton Mifflin), 1950, and *The Light of Distant Skies, 1760–1835* (Harcourt, Brace), 1954. The early sculptors are studied in Albert Ten Eyck Gardner, *Yankee Stonecutters: The First American School of Sculpture, 1800–1850* (Columbia), 1945.

Still standard as a detailed history of early American writing is Moses Coit Tyler, *A History of American Literature, 1607–1765* (Cornell), 1949, first published in two volumes in 1878. The best brief introduction to New England writers is Kenneth B. Murdock, *Literature and Theology in Colonial New England* (Harvard), 1949. The useful anthology, *The Puritans*, edited by Perry Miller and Thomas H. Johnson (American Book), 1938, with an introduction on Puritan culture and way of life, has been issued in a two-volume second edition (Torchbooks), 1963, with bibliographies brought up to date. See also *Colonial American Writing*, edited by Roy Harvey Pearce (Holt), 1969.

The most widely known colonial writer is Benjamin Franklin. A new edition of all of his writings and all significant communications addressed to him, *The Papers of Benjamin Franklin*, is in progress under the auspices of the American Philosophical Society and Yale University Press. The general editor, Leonard W. Labaree, has been succeeded by William B. Willcox; the first volume appeared in 1960. The best brief introduction is in a serviceable volume of selections such as Frank L. Mott and Chester E. Jorgenson, eds., *Benjamin Franklin: Representative Selections* (Hill and Wang), rev. ed., 1962; or Nathan G. Goodman, ed., *A Benjamin Franklin Reader* (Crowell), 1945. Reprintings of the *Autobiography* are, of course, numerous. The nonspecialist will want to use the Yale University Press edition, edited by Leonard W. Labaree and others, 1964; the specialist, Max Farrand's *Benjamin Franklin's Memoirs: Parallel Text Edition* (Berkeley), 1949. The fullest modern biography is Carl Van Doren, *Benjamin Franklin* (Viking), 1938. Important general studies are Verner W. Crane, *Benjamin Franklin and a Rising People* (Little, Brown), 1954; Alfred Owen Aldridge, *Benjamin Franklin: Philosopher and Man* (Lippincott), 1965; and Bruce Ingraham Granger, *Benjamin Franklin: An American Man of Letters* (Cornell), 1964.

The Yale University Press edition of *The Works of Jonathan Edwards* began with Paul Ramsey's 1957 edition of *Freedom of the Will*. A good introduction to Jonathan Edwards is Clarence H. Faust and Thomas H. Johnson, eds., *Representative Selections* (Hill and Wang), rev. ed., 1962. Perry Miller, *Jonathan Edwards* (Sloane), 1949, discusses mainly the inner life of his subject. A narrative biography is Ola E. Winslow, *Jonathan Edwards, 1703–1758* (Macmillan), 1940. Edward H. Davidson's *Jonathan Edwards: The Narrative of a Puritan Mind* (Harvard), 1968, concentrates on Edwards' spiritual pilgrimage. James Carse's *Jonathan Edwards and the Visibility of God* (Scribner's), 1967, is written from the perspective of Edwards' theory of faith.

The poetry of Edward Taylor remained in manuscript until 1937. The first gathering was edited by Thomas H. Johnson, *The Poetical Works of Edward Taylor* (Rockland Editions), 1939, (Princeton), 1943. Donald E. Stanford edited a more comprehensive collection in *The Poems of Edward Taylor* (Yale), 1960. The 1701–1703 sermons, *Edward Taylor's "Christographia"* (Yale), 1962, were edited by Norman S. Grabo. The first full-length introduction to Taylor's poetry is Norman S. Grabo's *Edward Taylor* (Twayne), 1961.

An abridgment of *Samuel Sewell's Diary* has been edited by Harvey Wish (Putnam), 1967. The full text of Sarah Kemble Knight's sprightly *Journal* is set forth in *The Puritans*, mentioned above. The definitive edition of William Byrd's *Histories of the Dividing Line Betwixt Virginia and North Carolina* is that of William K. Boyd (The North Carolina Historical Commission), 1929. A popular reprint is Mark Van Doren's edition of *The Journey to the Land of Eden and Other Papers* (Macy-Masius), 1928. The 1774 edition of *The Works of John Woolman* was reprinted with a foreword by William A. Beardslee (Garrett), 1970. *The Journal and Major Essays of John Woolman* (Oxford), 1971, was edited by Phillips P. Moulton. In 1928 Mark Van Doren condensed and edited William Bartram's very influential *Travels Through North and South Carolina* . . . , 1791, an edition reprinted in 1940 (Barnes and Noble, Facsimile Library). A brief account of the Bartrams is Ernest Earnest, *John and William Bartram* . . . (Pennsylvania), 1940.

II. THE REPUBLIC: *Inquiry and Imitation*

The best introduction to the democratic idea and the American experiment at the time the states became united is to be found in the recent bibliographies of Washington, Adams, Jefferson, and Madison. Frank Donovan edited *The George Washington Papers* (Dodd, Mead), 1964, a 300-page redaction, designed for the general reader, of many editions of Washington papers. Before his death in 1953, Douglas Southall Freeman completed six volumes of *George Washington, a Biography* (Scribner's), 1948–1954. The seventh and final volume, *George Washington: First in Peace* (Scribner's), 1957, was completed by his assistants, John Alexander Carroll and Mary Wells Ashworth. Richard Harwell prepared the abridged one-volume edition, *Washington* (Scribner's), 1968. James T. Flexner's 4-volume *George Washington* (Little, Brown), 1965–1972, is the most recent major study. A brief critical biography by a British scholar is Marcus Cunliffe, *George Washington, Man and Monument* (Little, Brown), 1958. Catherine Drinker Bowen, *John Adams and the American Revolution* (Little, Brown), 1950, carries the story through July, 1776. Lyman H. Butterfield was the first editor of The Adams Papers, an estimated 300,000 pages of material dated 1630–1920, to be published in a multiple series of volumes by Harvard University Press. The *Diary and Autobiography of John Adams* (Harvard), 1961, 4 vols., is the first series to appear. Dumas Malone has projected a 5-volume study, *Jefferson and His Time*, the first being *Jefferson the Virginian* (Little, Brown), 1948, covering the period through the Declaration of Independence, followed by *Jefferson and the Rights of Man* (Little, Brown), 1952, *Jefferson and the Ordeal of Liberty* (Little, Brown), 1962, and *Jefferson the President: First Term, 1801–1805* (Little, Brown), 1970. Adrienne Koch, *Jefferson and Madison: The Great Collaboration* (Knopf), 1950, stresses the interplay of ideas. Merrill D. Peterson extends biography into social history with *The Jefferson Image in the American Mind* (Oxford), 1960, and *Thomas Jefferson and the New Nation* (Oxford), 1970. *The Papers of Thomas Jefferson*, a multivolume edition edited by Julian P. Boyd, began appearing from Princeton University Press in 1950. Volume XIX was issued in 1973. Irving Brant has given the most complete account of Madison, in six volumes, beginning with *James Madison: The Virginia Revolutionist* (Bobbs-Merrill), 1941, and concluding with *James Madison: Commander-in-Chief* (Bobbs-Merrill), 1961. William T. Hutchinson and William M. E. Rachal began an edition of *The Papers of James Madison* at the University of Chicago. The first two volumes appeared in 1962.

Still basic as an analysis of the democratic experiment is Henry Adams, *History of the United States During the Administrations of Jefferson and Madison* (1884–1889). Reprinted with an introduction by Henry S. Commager (Boni), 1930, it was condensed by Herbert Agar into two volumes, *The Formative Years* (Houghton Mifflin), 1947. Surveys of the period include Edmund S. Morgan, *The Birth of the Republic, 1763–1789* (Chicago), 1956; Merrill Jensen, *The New Nation: A History of the United States*

During the Confederation, 1781-1789 (Knopf), 1950; John C. Miller, *The Federalist Era, 1789-1801* (Harper), 1960; and Wesley Frank Craven, *The Legend of the Founding Fathers* (New York University), 1956. John R. Alden deals with "things social, economic, political, military, and diplomatic" in *A History of the American Revolution* (Knopf), 1969. A social history of the period is Carl and Jessica Bridenbaugh, *Rebels and Gentlemen: Philadelphia in the Age of Franklin* (Reynal and Hitchcock), 1942. Talbot Hamlin, *Greek Revival Architecture in America* (Oxford), 1944, shows how consciously Jefferson and others sought to embody the ideals of the new republic in buildings of enduring simplicity.

Detailed treatment of the literature of this period is in Moses Coit Tyler, *The Literary History of the American Revolution, 1763-1783* (Putnam), 1897, 2 vols., (Lenox Hill-Burt Franklin), 1970, 2 vols. in one; in Vernon L. Parrington, *The Colonial Mind, 1620-1800* (Harcourt, Brace), 1927—Vol. I of his *Main Currents in American Thought*; in Arthur H. Quinn and others, *The Literature of the American People* (Appleton), 1951, and in Harold S. Jantz, *The First Century of New England Verse* (American Antiquarian Society, Worcester), 1944. Accounts of the early development of the American novel and drama are mentioned in the General Survey section above.

Three reprints have made the writings of Thomas Paine easily available: Harry H. Clark, ed., *Thomas Paine: Representative Selections* (American Book), 1944, revised in 1961 with updated bibliography (Hill and Wang); Howard Fast, ed., *The Selected Work of Tom Paine, Set in the Framework of His Life* (Duell, Sloan), 1945; and Philip S. Foner, ed., *The Complete Writings of Thomas Paine* (Citadel), 1945, 2 vols., arranged by subject, and containing material not in previous collections. The major study in recent years is Alfred Owen Aldridge, *Man of Reason: The Life of Thomas Paine* (Lippincott), 1959.

The Federalist, 1787-1788, constitutes the most impressive series of essays in support of the Constitution, and has been important as authority on the principles of American government. These eighty-five essays, written by Alexander Hamilton, James Madison, and John Jay, are easily available in the 1941 Modern Library edition. More recent editions are Jacob E. Cooke, ed., *The Federalist* (Wesleyan), 1961, and Benjamin F. Wright, ed., *The Federalist* (Harvard), 1961.

Poems of Freneau, edited by Harry H. Clark (Harcourt, Brace), 1929, is a selection, with introduction. *The Prose of Philip Freneau* was selected and edited by Philip M. Marsh (Scarecrow), 1955. The newest biography is Jacob Axelrod's *Philip Freneau, Champion of Democracy* (Texas), 1967. Two critical studies are Lewis Leary, *That Rascal Freneau: A Study in*

Literary Failure (Rutgers), 1941, and Nelson D. Adkins, *Philip Freneau and the Cosmic Enigma: The Religious and Philosophical Speculations of an American Poet* (New York University), 1949. Claude M. Newlin, *The Life and Writings of Hugh Henry Brackenridge* (Princeton), 1932, is authoritative. Daniel Marder's *Hugh Henry Brackenridge* (Pittsburgh), 1967, is the most recent study. A study of our first novelist is Harry R. Warfel, *Charles Brockden Brown, American Gothic Novelist* (Florida), 1949. St. Jean de Crèvecoeur, *Letters from an American Farmer* (1782), was edited by William P. Trent (Fox, Duffield), 1904. A good available edition is in Everyman's Library (Dutton). His *Sketches of Eighteenth Century America* (Yale), 1925, are further letters edited by Henri L. Bourdin, Ralph H. Gabriel, and Stanley T. Williams. Percy G. Adams translated Crèvecoeur's 1801 volume, *Eighteenth-Century Travels in Pennsylvania and New York* (Kentucky), 1961. For John Trumbull, Timothy Dwight, Joel Barlow, and David Humphreys, see Leon Howard, *The Connecticut Wits* (Chicago), 1943.

III. THE DEMOCRACY: *The Meaning of Independence*

The struggle between the culture of the traditional past and that of the insurgent frontier affected every American thought and act after 1800. Daniel J. Boorstin continues his history of the American people with a survey from the Revolution to the Civil War, *The Americans: The National Experience* (Random), 1965. Russel B. Nye's *The Cultural Life of the New Nation, 1776–1830* (Harper), 1960, covers "the transition from the age of Locke and Jefferson to the age of Coleridge and Emerson." A social history of the period is Robert E. Riegel, *Young America, 1830–1840* (Oklahoma), 1949. George Dangerfield, *The Era of Good Feelings* (Harcourt, Brace), 1952, is a study of political transition from Jeffersonian republicanism to Jacksonian democracy. Political-social histories of the Jacksonian era are numerous: Arthur M. Schlesinger, Jr., *The Age of Jackson* (Little, Brown), 1945; Harold C. Syrett, *Andrew Jackson: His Contribution to the American Tradition* (Bobbs-Merrill), 1953; John William Ward, *Andrew Jackson: Symbol for an Age* (Oxford), 1955, a study of the popular image; and Marvin Meyers, *The Jacksonian Persuasion: Politics and Belief* (Stanford), 1957. The classic account of American manners and civilization during these years was recorded by Count Alexis de Tocqueville. His *De la Démocratie en Amérique* was first published in Paris in four volumes, 1835–1840. The best edition is edited by Phillips Bradley, *Democracy in America* (Knopf), 1944, 2 vols.

Standard histories of fiction and drama for the period are named in the

General Survey section. The literary, social, and cultural life of the Middle Atlantic area is the subject of Van Wyck Brooks, *The World of Washington Irving* (Dutton), 1944.

There are many complete sets of Irving's writings. *Works of Washington Irving* (Putnam), 1910, 40 vols., is standard. In 1969, the University of Wisconsin Press began publication of a 28-volume edition of the *Complete Works* under the direction of Henry A. Pochmann, succeeded by Herbert L. Kleinfield. A verbatim reprint of the 1809 edition of *Knickerbocker's A History of New York* was edited, with critical introduction, by Stanley T. Williams and Tremaine McDowell (Harcourt, Brace), 1927. Henry A. Pochmann, ed., *Washington Irving: Representative Selections* (American Book), 1934, is an excellent introduction. The definitive biography is Stanley T. Williams, *The Life of Washington Irving* (Oxford), 1935, 2 vols. William L. Hedge's *Washington Irving: An American Study, 1802–1832* (Johns Hopkins), 1965, focuses on Irving's relation to his intellectual environment and his influence on other writers.

Of the many collected editions of Cooper, *The Works of James Fenimore Cooper* (Putnam), 1895–1900, 33 vols., is the most easily procurable. James Franklin Beard edited *The Letters and Journals of James Fenimore Cooper*, (Harvard), 1960–1968, 6 vols., and is directing the publication of a 48-volume edition of the *Writings of James Fenimore Cooper*, to be published by the State University of New York Press. A valuable collection of his nonfictional prose is Robert E. Spiller, ed., *James Fenimore Cooper: Representative Selections* (American Book), 1936. Spiller's biography, *Fenimore Cooper: Critic of His Times* (Minton, Balch), 1931, gives data on Cooper's relationship with his publishers, his European travels, and his social thought. James Grossman, *James Fenimore Cooper* (Sloane), 1949, outlines and analyzes thirty-two novels. More recent critical estimates are Thomas Philbrick, *James Fenimore Cooper and the Development of American Sea Fiction* (Harvard), 1961; George Dekker, *James Fenimore Cooper: The American Scott* (Barnes and Noble), 1967; and John P. McWilliams, *Political Justice in a Republic: James Fenimore Cooper's America* (California), 1972.

The most inclusive one-volume edition of Bryant's work is Henry C. Sturges and Richard Henry Stoddard, eds., *The Poetical Works of William Cullen Bryant* (Appleton), 1903, known as the Roslyn Edition. The best selected text is Tremaine McDowell, *William Cullen Bryant: Representative Selections* (American Book), 1935, containing all the well-known poems, as well as hitherto unpublished or unavailable selections from Bryant's poetry, reviews, editorials, and correspondence. The most recent life is Charles H. Brown's *William Cullen Bryant* (Scribner's), 1971. Equally important are

Allan Nevins's treatment of Bryant as editor, *The Evening Post: A Century of Journalism* (Boni and Liveright), 1922, and Harry Houston Peckham's *Gotham Yankee: A Biography* . . . (Vantage), 1950. A recent critical study is Albert F. McLean's *William Cullen Bryant* (Twayne), 1964.

For Poe the most nearly complete edition is that of James A. Harrison, *The Complete Works of Edgar Allan Poe* (Crowell), 1902, 17 vols., reprinted by AMS Press in 1965. Still dependable and also in print is *The Complete Poems and Stories of Edgar Allan Poe with Selections from His Critical Writings*, edited by Arthur H. Quinn and Edward H. O'Neill (Knopf), 1946, 2 vols. Usable one-volume selected editions are Margaret Alterton and Hardin Craig, eds., *Edgar Allan Poe: Representative Selections* (American Book), 1935, revised in 1962 with an updated bibliography (Hill and Wang); Hervey Allen, ed., *Complete Tales and Poems* . . . (Modern Library), 1938; Philip Van Doren Stern, ed., *Edgar Allan Poe* (Viking), 1945; and Floyd Stovall, ed., *The Poems of Edgar Allan Poe* (Virginia), 1965. John W. Ostrom has edited, in two volumes, *The Letters of Edgar Allan Poe* (Harvard), 1948, reissued with a 56-page supplement in 1962 (Gordian). Poe has always been a controversial figure, and there is a diverse body of critical biography: Hervey Allen, *Israfel: The Life and Times of Edgar Allan Poe* (Doran), 1926, 2 vols., and (Farrar), 1934, 1 vol.; Arthur H. Quinn, *Edgar Allan Poe: A Critical Biography* (Appleton-Century), 1941; and a short and sane life by William R. Bittner, *Poe: A Biography* (Little, Brown), 1962. The most comprehensive critiques are Edward H. Davidson, *Poe: A Critical Study* (Harvard), 1957, and Daniel Hoffman, *Poe Poe Poe Poe Poe Poe Poe* (Doubleday), 1972. See also Killis Campbell, *The Mind of Poe, and Other Studies* (Harvard), 1933, and N. Bryllion Fagin, *The Histrionic Mr. Poe* (Johns Hopkins), 1949. French criticism of Poe is treated by Patrick F. Quinn in *The French Face of Edgar Poe* (Southern Illinois), 1957.

The Collected Works of John Pendleton Kennedy (Putnam), 1871, 10 vols., includes the *Life* by Henry T. Tuckerman which for many years remained the only full-length study. Charles H. Bohner, *John Pendleton Kennedy: Gentleman from Baltimore* (Johns Hopkins), 1961, is a valuable reassessment. John C. Guilds is general editor of *The Centennial Edition of the Writings of William Gilmore Simms* to be published in fifteen volumes by the University of South Carolina Press. The first volume appeared in 1969. The *Letters* were collected and edited by Mary C. Simms Oliphant, Alfred Taylor Odell, and T. C. Duncan Eaves (South Carolina), 1952–1956, 5 vols., with an introduction by Donald Davidson and a biographical sketch by Alexander S. Salley.

IV. LITERARY FULFILLMENT

During the mid-nineteenth century the search for answers to the problem of good and evil achieved a literary fulfillment. The greatest of the writers gave dramatic expression to the age-old theme, especially as it was felt to apply to democratic man. The best definitions of transcendentalism, the way by which the search was organized, are in the works of Emerson, particularly in his *Nature* (1836), *The American Scholar* (1837), and his essays on transcendentalism. The finest study of this exploration is F. O. Matthiessen, *American Renaissance: Art and Expression in the Age of Emerson and Whitman* (Oxford), 1941. Among the important intellectual histories are Irving H. Bartlett, *The American Mind in the Mid-Nineteenth Century* (Crowell), 1967, and Clement Eaton, *The Mind of the Old South* (Louisiana State), 1964. Perry Miller has assembled selections from minor writers in *The Transcendentalists* (Harvard), 1950, with introduction and notes. Quentin Anderson concentrates on Emerson, Hawthorne, and Whitman in *The Imperial Self: An Essay in American Literary and Cultural History* (Knopf), 1971. Four provocative studies of the fiction of this period are Harry Levin, *The Power of Blackness: Hawthorne, Poe, Melville* (Knopf), 1958; Marius Bewley, *The Complex Fate* (Grove), 1954, reprinted (Gordian), 1967, followed by *The Eccentric Design* (Columbia), 1959; and Joel Porte, *The Romance in America* (Wesleyan), 1969. Vernon L. Parrington, *The Romantic Revolution in America, 1800-1860* (Harcourt, Brace), 1928—Vol. II of his *Main Currents*—stresses the intellectual contributions. Perry Miller describes the great vitality of these years in *The Raven and The Whale: The War of Words and Wits in the Era of Poe and Melville* (Harcourt, Brace), 1956. Two popular, general surveys are Van Wyck Brooks, *The Flowering of New England: 1815-1865* (Dutton), 1936, and *The Times of Melville and Whitman* (Dutton), 1947.

The standard text of Emerson's writings is the Centenary Edition: *The Complete Works of Ralph Waldo Emerson*, edited by Edward W. Emerson (Houghton Mifflin), 1903-1904, 12 vols. A new edition of the *Collected Works* in approximately twelve volumes will be published by Harvard University Press under the general editorship of Alfred R. Ferguson. *Nature, Addresses, and Lectures*, 1972, edited by Robert E. Spiller, is the first volume to appear. The *Journals*, first edited in ten volumes in 1909-1914, are being reedited by William H. Gilman and others, *The Journals and Miscellaneous Notebooks of Ralph Waldo Emerson* (Harvard). The first volume, 1960, will be followed by at least fifteen more. The one-volume edition, *The Heart of Emerson's Journals* (Houghton Mifflin), 1926, was edited by Bliss Perry. The three-volume edition of *The Early Lectures of Ralph Waldo Emerson, 1833-*

1842, edited by Stephen E. Whicher, Robert E. Spiller, and Wallace E. Williams (Harvard), 1959–1972, is now complete. An inclusive edition of the letters is Ralph L. Rusk, ed., *The Letters of Ralph Waldo Emerson* (Columbia), 1939, 6 vols. One-volume selections are available: Mark Van Doren, ed., *The Portable Emerson* (Viking), 1946; Alfred Kazin and Daniel Aaron, eds., *Emerson: A Modern Anthology* (Houghton Mifflin), 1959. The standard biography is Ralph L. Rusk, *The Life of Ralph Waldo Emerson* (Scribner's), 1949. The leading studies of Emerson as philosopher and critic are Henry D. Gray, *Emerson: A Statement of New England Transcendentalism as Expressed in the Philosophy of Its Chief Exponent* (Stanford), 1917; Sherman Paul, *Emerson's Angle of Vision* (Harvard), 1952; and Stephen E. Whicher, *Freedom and Fate: An Inner Life of Ralph Waldo Emerson* (Pennsylvania), 1953. The best study of Emerson's aesthetics is Vivian C. Hopkins, *Spires of Form* (Harvard), 1951. In addition to Frederic I. Carpenter's *Emerson Handbook* (Hendricks), 1953, all students of Emerson will want to see Perry Miller, *The Transcendentalists: An Anthology* (Harvard), 1950, and F. O. Matthiessen, *American Renaissance* (Oxford), 1941.

The standard text of Thoreau's works is the Walden Edition: *The Writings of Henry David Thoreau* (Houghton Mifflin), 1906, 20 vols., edited by Bradford Torrey. The *Journal* (1837–1861) occupies the last fourteen volumes. Perry Miller, *Consciousness in Concord* (Houghton Mifflin), 1958, prints the hitherto missing volume of the *Journal*. A new edition, *The Writings of Henry D. Thoreau* in approximately twenty-five volumes, was begun by Princeton University Press in 1971. Walter Harding, the general editor, has been succeeded by William L. Howarth. Odell Shepard, *The Heart of Thoreau's Journal* (Houghton Mifflin), 1927, rev. ed., 1961, is an excellent selection. Carl Bode edited the *Collected Poems of Henry Thoreau* (Packard), 1943, enl. ed. (Johns Hopkins), 1964. Walter Harding and Carl Bode edited *The Correspondence* . . . (New York University), 1958. The most fully annotated edition of *Walden* is Walter Harding, ed., *The Variorum Walden* (Twayne), 1962, but see also James Lyndon Shanley, *The Making of Walden, with the Text of the First Version* (Chicago), 1957. The best one-volume collections are Henry S. Canby, *The Works of Thoreau* (Houghton Mifflin), 1937; Brooks Atkinson, ed., *Walden and Other Writings* . . . (Modern Library), 1937; and Carl Bode, ed., *The Portable Thoreau* (Viking), 1947. Two valuable biographies are Henry S. Canby, *Thoreau* (Houghton Mifflin), 1939, and Walter Harding, *The Days of Henry Thoreau* (Knopf), 1965. Joseph Wood Krutch, *Henry David Thoreau* (Sloane), 1948, is a general critical study, focusing on Thoreau as naturalist. The most comprehensive critique is Sherman Paul, *The Shores of America: Thoreau's Inward Exploration* (Illinois), 1958. Thoreau's ideas on economics are discussed in Leo Stoller, *After Walden* (Stanford), 1957. Walter Harding further assists the student of Thoreau with *A Thoreau Handbook* (New York University), 1959, and *Thoreau: Man of Concord* (Holt), 1960.

The standard text of Hawthorne's writings is the Riverside Edition: *The Complete Works of Nathaniel Hawthorne* (Houghton Mifflin), 1882–1883, 12 vols., edited by G. P. Lathrop. In 1963, Ohio State University Press began publication of *The Centenary Edition of the Works of Nathaniel Hawthorne*, under the editorship of William Charvat, Claude M. Simpson, Roy Harvey Pearce, Matthew J. Bruccoli, and Fredson Bowers. Newton Arvin edited *The Heart of Hawthorne's Journals* (Houghton Mifflin), 1929. The editing of the notebooks was first undertaken by Mrs. Hawthorne. The most reliable editions are *The American Notebooks* (Yale), 1932, and *The English Notebooks* (Oxford), 1941, both edited by Randall Stewart. The French and Italian notebooks are still unedited, as is the complete collection of Hawthorne's letters. Good selected texts are Malcolm Cowley, ed., *The Portable Hawthorne* (Viking), 1948, and Mark Van Doren, *The Best of Hawthorne* (Ronald), 1951. Randall Stewart, *Nathaniel Hawthorne: A Biography* (Yale), 1948, is the culmination of years of study of the Hawthorne papers. Mark Van Doren combines a biographical with a critical reading in *Nathaniel Hawthorne* (Sloane), 1949. An early perceptive critical study is Henry James, *Hawthorne* (Harper), 1879. Among the best critical studies of this century are Newton Arvin, *Hawthorne* (Little, Brown), 1929; Richard H. Fogle, *Hawthorne's Fiction: The Light and the Dark* (Oklahoma), 1952, rev. ed., 1964, under the title *Hawthorne's Imagery: The "Proper Light and Shadow" in the Major Romances*; Hyatt H. Waggoner, *Hawthorne: A Critical Study* (Harvard), 1955; Roy R. Male, *Hawthorne's Tragic Vision* (Texas), 1957; and Frederick C. Crews, *The Sins of the Fathers: Hawthorne's Psychological Themes* (Oxford), 1966.

The Works of Herman Melville (Constable), 1922–1924, 16 vols., is being replaced by a fifteen-volume Northwestern University Press-Newberry Library edition of *The Writings of Herman Melville. Typee*, published in 1968, was the first to appear. Harrison Hayford, Herschel Parker, and G. Thomas Tanselle are the general editors. Carefully annotated and illustrated popular editions of *Moby-Dick* are the Oxford Press volume, 1947, edited by Willard Thorp, and the Bobbs-Merrill volume, 1964, edited by Charles Feidelson. The text of *Billy Budd* is finally established in Harrison Hayford and Merton M. Sealts, Jr., eds., *Billy Budd, Sailor: An Inside Narrative* (Chicago), 1962. Melville's journals have been edited by Eleanor Melville Metcalf, *Journal of a Visit to London and the Continent* (Harvard), 1948, and Howard C. Horsford, *Journal of a Visit to Europe and the Levant* (Princeton), 1955. *The Letters of Herman Melville* (Yale), 1960, have been edited by Merrell R. Davis and William H. Gilman. Good one-volume selections are Willard Thorp, ed., *Herman Melville: Representative Selec-*

tions (American Book), 1938; Jay Leyda, ed., *The Complete Stories . . .* (Random), 1949; and Jay Leyda, ed., *The Portable Melville* (Viking), 1952. Two interdependent biographies are Leon Howard's formal narrative, *Herman Melville* (California), 1951, and Jay Leyda's *The Melville Log: A Documentary Life* (Harcourt, Brace), 1951, 2 vols. An earlier well-balanced biography is William E. Sedgwick, *Herman Melville: The Tragedy of Mind* (Harvard), 1944. More interpretive biographies are Lewis Mumford, *Herman Melville* (Literary Guild), 1929, and Newton Arvin, *Herman Melville* (Sloane), 1950. In the past twenty years a score of good critical studies have appeared. These are broadly representative: Richard Chase, *Herman Melville: A Critical Study* (Macmillan), 1949; Lawrance Thompson, *Melville's Quarrel with God* (Princeton), 1952; Milton Stern, *The Fine Hammered Steel of Herman Melville* (Illinois), 1957; Merlin Bowen, *The Long Encounter* (Chicago), 1960; Warner Berthoff, *The Example of Melville* (Princeton), 1962; Paul Brodtkorb, Jr., *Ishmael's White World: A Phenomenological Reading of Moby-Dick* (Yale), 1965, and John D. Seelye, *Melville: The Ironic Diagram* (Northwestern), 1970. James E. Miller, Jr., has prepared *A Reader's Guide to Herman Melville* (Farrar), 1962.

The first extensive collection of Whitman's work is *The Complete Writings of Walt Whitman*, edited by Richard M. Bucke, Thomas B. Harned, and Horace L. Traubel (Putnam), 1902, 10 vols., now out of print. New York University Press began publication in 1961 of *The Collected Writings* in eighteen projected volumes under the general editorship of Gay Wilson Allen and Sculley Bradley. Five volumes of *The Correspondence . . . ,* edited by Edwin H. Miller, 1961–1969, have appeared. *Leaves of Grass: Comprehensive Reader's Edition*, ed. Harold W. Blodgett and Sculley Bradley (New York University), 1965, a volume in *The Collected Writings*, is the standard text. Other useful collections are Sculley Bradley, ed., *Leaves of Grass and Selected Prose* (Holt), 1949, and Harold W. Blodgett, ed., *The Best of Whitman* (Ronald), 1953. The fullest biography to date is Gay Wilson Allen's *The Solitary Singer* (Macmillan), 1955, 3rd edition revised, 1967, but also informative are Emory Holloway, *Whitman: An Interpretation in Narrative* (Knopf), 1926, and Henry S. Canby, *Walt Whitman, An American* (Houghton Mifflin), 1943. Two important foreign biographies, now translated, are Frederick Schyberg, *Walt Whitman* (Copenhagen), 1933, (New York), 1951, and Roger Asselineau, *The Evolution of Walt Whitman* (Paris), 1954, (Cambridge, Mass.), 1960–1962. Critical studies are numerous and varied. A good introduction is Gay Wilson Allen's *Walt Whitman: As Man, Poet, and Legend* (Southern Illinois), 1961, revised edition, 1969, coupled with his *Reader's Guide to Walt Whitman* (Farrar), 1970. In collaboration with Charles T. Davis, Allen edited *Walt Whitman's Poems* (New York University), 1955, a selection with detailed critical notes to each poem and general guidance in a full introduction to Whitman's poetry. See also James E. Miller, Jr., *A Critical Guide to Leaves of Grass* (Chicago), 1957, and Edwin Haviland Miller, *Walt Whitman's Poetry: A Psychological Journey* (New York University), 1969. Richard Chase's *Walt Whitman Reconsidered* (Sloane), 1955, places the poet among his nineteenth-century contemporaries.

V. CRISIS: *Conflict, Refinement, Success*

By mid-century, national expansion across a continent set up stresses which accentuated conflicting patterns of living in North and South. The intense idealism at the root of all American traditions since 1620 had followed different courses. The issue on both sides was a defense of tradition, and from crisis it passed to conflict. This theme is nowhere better set forth than in the four-volume study of the period by Allan Nevins, *Ordeal of the Union* (Scribner's), 1947, 2 vols., covering the years 1847–1857; and *Emergence of Lincoln*, 1950, 2 vols., which brings the story down to Lincoln's election. Students of American literature will also want to read Edmund Wilson's study of the literature of the Civil War, *Patriotic Gore* (Oxford), 1962.

The literature on Lincoln is vast. *The Collected Works of Abraham Lincoln* (Rutgers), 8 vols., 1953, was edited by Roy P. Basler and others. A one-volume redaction, *The Living Lincoln*, ed. Paul M. Angle and Earl Schenck Miers (Rutgers), appeared in 1955. For the general reader a good collection of his writings is Roy P. Basler, ed., *Abraham Lincoln: His Speeches and Writing* (World), 1946. James G. Randall's biography, *Lincoln the President: Springfield to Gettysburg* (Dodd, Mead), 2 vols., 1945, is completed in two more volumes, *Lincoln the President: Midstream* (Dodd, Mead), 1952, and, with the assistance of Richard N. Current, *Lincoln the President: Last Full Measure* (Dodd, Mead), 1955. An excellent one-volume study is Benjamin P. Thomas, *Abraham Lincoln, a Biography* (Knopf), 1952. Stefan Lorant, *Lincoln: A Picture Story of His Life* (Harper), 1952, revised in 1969, assembles 700 illustrations.

The great orators of the day, many of them closely associated with the theme of conflict, include Henry Clay, John C. Calhoun, Daniel Webster, Theodore Parker, and Edward Everett. The fullest selection and critical survey of American oratory is William N. Brigance, ed., *A History and Criticism of American Public Address* (McGraw-Hill), 1943, 2 vols., with chapters on individual orators contributed by specialists. The story of American oratory is told in Gerald W. Johnson, *America's Silver Age* (Harper), 1939. Historical studies are David Meade, *Yankee Eloquence in the Middle West: The Ohio Lyceum, 1850–1870* (Michigan State), 1951, and Carl Bode,

The American Lyceum: Town Meeting of the Mind (Oxford), 1956. Victoria Case and Robert Ormond Case, *We Called It Culture: The Story of Chautauqua* (Doubleday), 1948, is an informal treatment of this American phenomenon. Carl Bode discusses best-sellers among many other subjects in his miscellany, *The Half-World of American Culture* (Southern Illinois), 1965.

The leading historians of the period vividly reconstructed the past. David Levin's *History as Romantic Art: Bancroft, Prescott, Motley, and Parkman* (Stanford), 1959, is an excellent introduction. The Centenary Edition of *The Works of Francis Parkman* (Little, Brown), 1923–1925, 12 vols., is the most recent. *The Battle for North America*, edited by John Tebbel (Doubleday), 1948, is an abridgement of Parkman's *France and England in North America*. Mason Wade edited *The Journals of Francis Parkman* (Harper), 1947, 2 vols., recently discovered, intrinsically important as part of the Parkman canon and for study of Parkman as historian and man of letters. Wilbur R. Jacobs compiled *Letters of Francis Parkman* (Oklahoma), 1960, 2 vols. Collections are Wilbur L. Schramm, ed., *Francis Parkman: Representative Selections* (American Book), 1938, and Samuel Eliot Morison, ed., *The Parkman Reader* (Little, Brown), 1955. Mason Wade, *Francis Parkman, Heroic Historian* (Viking), 1942, is an interpretive biography based on careful study of sources. Howard Doughty, *Francis Parkman* (Macmillan), 1962, is not only a critical biography but also a close study of Parkman's style. The Montezuma Edition of *The Works of William H. Prescott* (Lippincott), 1904–1906, 22 vols., edited by Wilfred H. Munro, contains the *Life* by George Ticknor. The *Conquest of Mexico* and the *Conquest of Peru* were issued in one volume (Modern Library), 1936. The most serviceable selected text is William Charvat and Michael Kraus, eds., *William Hickling Prescott: Representative Selections* (American Book), 1943. C. Harvey Gardiner, *William Hickling Prescott* (Texas), 1969, is the first biographical study in more than sixty years. The Netherlands Edition of *The Writings of John Lothrop Motley* (Harper), 1900, 17 vols., was edited by George W. Curtis. A convenient reprint of selections is Chester P. Higby and Bradford T. Schantz, eds., *John Lothrop Motley: Representative Selections* (American Book), 1939. No definitive life of Motley has been published. Bancroft's *History of the United States* (Little, Brown), was completed in ten volumes in 1875. The first collection of letters was made in Mark A. DeWolfe Howe, *The Life and Letters of George Bancroft* (Scribner's), 1908, 2 vols. The best critical biography is Russel B. Nye, *George Bancroft: Brahmin Rebel* (Knopf), 1944.

The poet most fully identified with the cause of abolition is Whittier. The standard library edition of *The Writings of John Greenleaf Whittier* (Houghton Mifflin), 1894, 7 vols., was edited by Horace E. Scudder, and is the basis for Scudder's one-volume edition of *The Complete Poetical Works* issued in the same year. The most recent selection of the poems is *Whittier*, edited by Donald Hall (Dell), 1960. A biographical study is Whitman Bennett, *Whittier, Bard of Freedom* (North Carolina), 1941. More recent is Edward Wagenknecht, *John Greenleaf Whittier: A Portrait in Paradox* (Oxford), 1967.

Traditionalism in the South is definitively treated in Francis P. Gaines, *The Southern Plantation: A Study in the Development and the Accuracy of a Tradition* (Columbia), 1924. A more recent discussion, chiefly from a literary viewpoint, is William R. Taylor, *Cavalier and Yankee: The Old South and American National Character* (Braziller), 1961. Three comprehensive surveys by Clement Eaton are *A History of the Old South* (Macmillan), 1949; *A History of the Southern Confederacy* (Macmillan), 1954; and *The Growth of Southern Civilization, 1790–1860* (Harper), 1961. See also Howard R. Floan's *The South in Northern Eyes, 1831 to 1861* (Texas), 1958. Gregory Paine has edited *Southern Prose Writers* (American Book), 1947; selections from the poetry of Timrod, Hayne, and others can be found in *Southern Poets*, ed. by Edd W. Parks (American Book), 1936. Jay B. Hubbell, *The South in American Literature, 1607–1900* (Duke), 1954, is the most thorough treatment of the subject, especially for the Civil War period. The best recent anthology is *The Literature of the South*, edited by Richmond Croom Beatty, Floyd C. Watkins, and Thomas Daniel Young (Scott, Foresman), 1952. Willard Thorp compiled *A Southern Reader* (Knopf), 1955, a documentary survey of life in the South.

The cultural background of the period comes alive in Van Wyck Brooks, *New England: Indian Summer, 1865–1915* (Dutton), 1940. It is given further extension in E. Douglas Branch, *The Sentimental Years, 1838–1860* (Appleton-Century), 1934. The defense of traditions has always been closely associated with the names of Longfellow, Holmes, and Lowell. The Riverside Edition of *The Complete Poetical and Prose Works of Henry Wadsworth Longfellow* (Houghton Mifflin), 1886, appeared in eleven volumes. Horace E. Scudder edited *The Complete Poetical Works . . .* (Houghton Mifflin), 1893, in one volume. Andrew Hilen published four of his projected six volumes of *Letters of Henry Wadsworth Longfellow* (Harvard), 1966–1972. *Henry Wadsworth Longfellow: Representative Selections*, edited by Odell Shepard (American Book), 1934, reprints only poetry. Lawrance R. Thompson, *Young Longfellow, 1807–1843* (Macmillan), 1938, is a good analysis of the early years. More recent biographies are Edward Wagenknecht, *Longfellow: A Full-Length Portrait* (Longmans), 1955, and Newton Arvin, *Longfellow: His Life and Work* (Little, Brown), 1963.

The Riverside Edition of *The Complete Works of Oliver Wendell Holmes* (Houghton Mifflin), 1891–1892, 13 vols., is standard. It was reissued in 1896 in fifteen volumes, and includes J. T. Morse's *Life and Letters*. A one-volume edition of the poems is that edited by Horace E. Scudder, *The Complete Poetical Works* (Houghton Mifflin), 1895. S. I. Hayakawa and Howard Mumford Jones edited *Oliver Wendell Holmes: Representative Selections* (American Book), 1939, still the most serviceable collection. The best biographical study is Eleanor M. Tilton, *Amiable Autocrat: A Biography of Dr. Oliver Wendell Holmes* (Schuman), 1947.

The Elmwood Edition of *The Complete Writings of James Russell Lowell* (Houghton Mifflin), 1904, 16 vols., is edited by Charles Eliot Norton. *Representative Selections* (American Book), 1947, is edited by Harry Hayden Clark and Norman Foerster. For many years the standard life was that of Horace E. Scudder, *James Russell Lowell, A Biography* (Houghton Mifflin), 1901, 2 vols. Ferris Greenslet, *James Russell Lowell: His Life and Work* (Houghton Mifflin), 1905, is brief but reliable. The major biography, updating Scudder and concentrating on Lowell the man, is Martin B. Duberman's *James Russell Lowell* (Houghton Mifflin), 1966. Richmond Croom Beatty, *James Russell Lowell* (Vanderbilt), 1942, and Leon Howard, *Victorian Knight-Errant: A Study of the Early Literary Career of James Russell Lowell* (California), 1952, are critical appraisals.

VI. EXPANSION: *New Perspectives*

Physical expansion into and across the North American continent followed upon Jefferson's purchase of the vast Louisiana territory. Oscar Handlin edited a collection large in scope, *This Was America: True Accounts . . . by European Travelers to the Western Shore in the Eighteenth, Nineteenth and Twentieth Century* (Harvard), 1949. The definitive study of the Lewis and Clark expedition is Reuben C. Thwaites, ed., *Original Journals of the Lewis and Clark Expedition, 1804–1806* (Dodd, Mead), 1904–1905, 8 vols. The condensed one-volume version, *The Journals of Lewis and Clark* (Houghton Mifflin), 1953, is edited by Bernard De Voto. The mastery of the trans-Mississippi is told in Bernard De Voto, *Across the Wide Missouri* (Houghton Mifflin), 1947, and his *The Year of Decision: 1846* (Little, Brown), 1943. The first focuses upon the fur trading and the Mountain Men during the two decades 1820–1840, illustrated with the paintings of Catlin, Bodmer, and Miller; the second carries the story through the Mexican War and the opening up of California. These accounts can be supplemented by Ray Allen Billington, *Westward Expansion: A History of the American Frontier* (Macmillan), 1949, followed by *The Far Western Frontier, 1830–1860* (Harper), 1956; Walter LaFeber, *The New Empire: An Intepretation of American Expansion, 1860–1898* (Cornell), 1963; Norman A. Graebner, *Empire on the Pacific: A Study in American Continental Ex-

pansion (Ronald), 1955; Stewart H. Holbrook, *The Yankee Exodus: An Account of Migration from New England* (Macmillan), 1950; and Louis B. Wright, *Culture on the Moving Frontier* (Indiana), 1955. The emotional effect of the West upon the American imagination is told in Henry Nash Smith, *Virgin Land: The American West as Symbol and Myth* (Harvard), 1950, re-issued with a new preface (Harvard), 1970. More recent literary-historical studies are Edwin Fussell, *Frontier: American Literature and the American West* (Princeton), 1965; and Roderick Nash, *Wilderness and the American Mind* (Yale), 1967, rev. ed., 1973.

The great collection of western travel accounts is that assembled and edited by Reuben G. Thwaites, *Early Western Travels: 1748–1846* (A. H. Clark), 1904–1907, 32 vols. Among them are the journals of Zebulon Pike, Stephen Long, Henry M. Brackenridge, and Josiah Gregg. The reminiscences of the *Stevens Party of 1844*, first published in 1888, were edited by George R. Stewart, Jr., under the title, *The Opening of the California Trail . . .* (California), 1953. Stewart has also written *The California Trail: An Epic with Many Heroes* (McGraw-Hill), 1962. The flavor of mountain-man speech and western folkways is preserved in Lewis H. Garrard, *Wah-To-Yah, and the Taos Trail*, 1850, edited by Ralph P. Bieber (A. H. Clark), 1938. Dee Brown, *Trail Driving Days* (Scribner's), 1952, features some 200 frontier photographs taken in the cow towns during 1860–1880. Notable contemporary accounts of the Far West written by men of letters are in Cooper's *The Prairie*, 1827, Irving's *A Tour on the Prairies*, 1835, R. H. Dana's *Two Years Before the Mast*, 1840, and Parkman's *The Oregon Trail*, 1849. Mark Twain's *Roughing It*, 1872, and Clarence King's *Mountaineering in the Sierra Nevada*, 1872, represent the high-water mark of travel narrative that belongs properly to *belles-lettres*. Authentic fictional twentieth-century reconstructions can be found in the novels of A. B. Guthrie, Vardis Fisher, James Boyd, Wallace Stegner, and George R. Stewart, Jr., to name only a few writers. James Monaghan, *The Great Rascal: The Life and Adventures of Ned Buntline* (Little, Brown), 1952, is an account of the prolific writer of western dime novels.

Specialized studies are subdivided into twenty-three individual rubrics in the valuable bibliography of frontier history (a listing of over 600 titles) included in Nelson Klose's *Concise Study Guide to the American Frontier* (Nebraska), 1964.

An introduction to Indian culture can be found in John Collier, *The Indians of the Americas* (Norton), 1947; Ruth Murray Underhill, *Red Man's America: A History of the Indians in the United States* (Chicago), 1953; Roy Harvey Pearce, *The Savages of America: A Study of the Indian and the Idea of Civilization* (Johns Hopkins), 1953, revised in 1965 under the title *Savages and Civilization*; and Dee Brown, *Bury My Heart at Wounded*

Knee: An Indian History of the American West (Holt), 1971. Clark Wissler's *The American Indian: An Introduction to the Anthropology of the New World*, 1917, is in its third edition (Peter Smith), 1950. His *Indians of the United States: Four Centuries of Their History and Culture*, 2nd ed. (Doubleday), 1946, is equally authoritative and more popular in appeal. See also D'Arcy McNickle, *The Indian Tribes of the United States: Ethnic and Cultural Survival* (Oxford), 1962, and Fred Eggan, *The American Indian: Perspectives for the Study of Social Change* (Chicago), 1966. The standard compilation of Indian tales, with introduction and full bibliographies, is Stith Thompson, *Tales of the North American Indians* (Harvard), 1929. Specialized studies of individual tribes and areas are easily available in the Civilization of the American Indian Series, published by the University of Oklahoma Press. Begun in 1932, the list includes more than 100 titles.

Folklore and folkways in the United States have been the subject of an impressive body of writing. Accounts of major American folk heroes are in Walter Blair, *Folklore in America: A Legendary History of Our Humorous Heroes* (Coward-McCann), 1944, and Richard Dorson's topical survey, *American Folklore* (Chicago), 1959. Studies of such folk heroes as Davy Crockett, Mike Fink, and Paul Bunyan are numerous and can be found under the individual name. Important collections of early tales and humor are Harold W. Thompson, *Body, Boots, and Britches* (Lippincott), 1940; Ben C. Clough, ed., *The American Imagination at Work: Tall Tales and Folk Tales* (Knopf), 1947; Mody C. Boatright and others, eds., *Folk Travelers: Ballads, Tales, and Talk* (Southern Methodist), 1953; John T. Flanagan and Arthur Palmer Hudson, eds., *Folklore in American Literature* (A. S. Barnes), 1958. Langston Hughes and Arna Bontemps have edited a group of tales, poems, and songs in *The Book of Negro Folklore* (Dodd, Mead), 1958. See also the pages of the *Journal of American Folklore, Western Folklore*, and the *Southern Folklore Quarterly*.

The pioneer study of American humor is Constance Rourke, *American Humor: A Study of the National Character* (Harcourt, Brace), 1931. More recent surveys are Jesse Bier, *The Rise and Fall of American Humor* (Holt), 1968; Norris W. Yates, *The American Humorist: Conscience of the Twentieth Century* (Iowa State), 1964; and Stephen Becker, *Comic Art in America* (Simon and Schuster), 1959. A popular survey of folk humor on the frontier is Thomas D. Clark, *The Rampaging Frontier* (Bobbs-Merrill), 1939. Walter Blair, *Horse Sense in American Humor* (Chicago), 1942, deals with the cracker-barrel philosophers. Generous samplings of American humor can be found in Mody C. Boatright, ed., *Folk Laughter on the American Frontier* (Macmillan), 1949, both an anthology and an analysis; Kenneth S. Lynn, ed., *The Comic Tradition in America* (Anchor), 1958; Walter Blair, ed., *Native American Humor, 1800-1900*, 2nd ed. (Chandler), 1960; and

Hennig Cohen and William B. Dillingham, eds., *Humor in the Old South-west* (Houghton Mifflin), 1964.

The definitive study of the American language, so vastly enriched by frontier associations, is H. L. Mencken, *The American Language: An Inquiry into the Development of English in the United States* (Knopf), 4th ed., 1936, with its *Supplement One*, 1945, and *Supplement Two*, 1948, abridged in one volume by Raven I. McDavid, Jr., and David W. Maurer (Knopf), 1963. A more recent general study is Charlton Laird, *Language in America* (World), 1970. Mitford M. Mathews, *A Dictionary of Americanisms on Historical Principles* (Chicago), 1951, 2 vols., stresses the distinctive additions Americans have made to the English language. He published a shorter version under the title *Americanisms: A Dictionary of Selected Americanisms on Historical Principles* (Chicago), 1966.

VII. THE SECTIONS: *Tradition and Experiment*

The pragmatic attitude of regionalists and realists, reflecting the modes peculiar to a place and time, is especially associated with humor, with frontier tall tales, and with local traditions. The conscious literary adoption of such themes began after the Civil War and before the end of the century had reached fullest maturity in the writings of Mark Twain.

The best social history of the era is Allan Nevins, *The Emergence of Modern America, 1865-1878* (Macmillan), 1927, reprinted in 1971 (Scholarly Press), supplemented by Hodding Carter, *The Angry Scar: The Story of Reconstruction, 1865-1890* (Doubleday), 1959, and C. Vann Woodward, *Reunion and Reaction: The Compromise of 1877 and the End of Reconstruction* (Little, Brown), 1951. A study of regionalism is Howard W. Odum and Harry E. Moore, *American Regionalism: A Cultural-Historical Approach to National Integration* (Holt), 1938, with extensive bibliographies. Merrill Jensen edited *Regionalism in America* (Wisconsin), 1951, a symposium. The relation of regionalism to American literary and social culture is the subject of Donald Davidson, *The Attack on Leviathan: Regionalism and Nationalism in the United States* (North Carolina), 1938. Louis D. Rubin, Jr., and Robert D. Jacobs edited twenty-nine critical essays and a bibliography in *Southern Renascence: The Literature of the Modern South* (Johns Hopkins), 1953. In 1961, the same editors compiled a briefer and newer collection, *South: Modern Southern Literature and Its Cultural Setting* (Doubleday). The following regional anthologies are all good: Harrry R. Warfel and G. H. Orians, eds., *American Local Color Stories* (American Book), 1941; Claude Simpson, ed., *The Local Colorists: American Short Stories, 1857-1900* (Harper), 1960; Edd W. Parks, ed., *Southern Poets* (American Book), 1936; Gregory Paine, ed., *Southern Prose Writers* (American Book), 1947; Richmond Croom Beatty, Floyd C. Watkins, and Thomas Daniel Young, eds., *The Literature of the South* (Scott, Foresman), 1952, rev. ed., 1968; Richard Beale Davis, C. Hugh Holman, and Louis D. Rubin, Jr., eds., *Southern Writing, 1585–1920* (Odyssey), 1970; John T. Flanagan, *America Is West: An Anthology of Midwestern Life and Literature* (Minnesota), 1945; T. M. Pearce and Telfair Hendon, eds., *America in the Southwest: A Regional Anthology* (New Mexico), 1933; Levette J. Davidson and Forrester Blake, eds., *Rocky Mountain Tales* (Oklahoma), 1947; and Stewart H. Holbrook, ed., *Promised Land: A Collecton of Northwest Writing* (McGraw-Hill), 1945.

New England regionalism is best seen in the writing of Sarah Orne Jewett. Her *Stories and Tales* (Houghton Mifflin), 1910, are in seven volumes. Willa Cather edited *The Best Stories of Sarah Orne Jewett* (Houghton Mifflin), 1945. Carl J. Weber and Richard Cary edited, individually, volumes of letters. A biography is F. O. Matthiessen, *Sarah Orne Jewett* (Houghton Mifflin), 1929. Richard Cary's *Sarah Orne Jewett* (Twayne), 1962, is a full-length critical study. The best known of the Virginia realists is Thomas Nelson Page. His writings are gathered in *The Novels, Stories, Sketches and Poems of Thomas Nelson Page* (Scribner's), 1906–1918, 18 vols. Among the best dealing with the deep south are Harris and Cable. Julia C. Harris edited *Joel Chandler Harris, Editor and Essayist: Miscellaneous Literary, Political, and Social Writings* (North Carolina), 1931. A convenient collection is *The Favorite Uncle Remus*, edited by George Van Santvoord and Archibald C. Coolidge (Houghton Mifflin), 1948. A recent critical biography is Paul M. Cousins, *Joel Chandler Harris* (Louisiana State), 1968. Cable's works are being reprinted by the Garrett Press in nineteen volumes under the editorship of Arlin Turner. Kjell Ekström, *George Washington Cable* (Harvard), 1950. is a study of Cable's early life and work. Arlin Turner, *George W. Cable, a Biography* (Duke), 1956, and Louis D. Rubin, Jr., *George Washington Cable* (Pegasus), 1969, are the most recent full-length studies. Edward Eggleston has best portrayed the Midwesterner in *The Hoosier School-Master* (1871) and *The Hoosier School-Boy* (1883). William Peirce Randel's *Edward Eggleston* (Twayne)) 1963, is a critical biography. The standard study of Midwestern literature is Ralph L. Rusk, *The Literature of the Middle Western Frontier* (Columbia), 1925, 2 vols., with extensive bibliographies. Edwin W. Gaston, Jr. studies southwestern fiction in *The Early Novels of the Southwest* (New Mexico), 1961.

Bret Harte, who helped to introduce the West to the East with *The Luck of Roaring Camp*, 1868, is usually thought of as the first local colorist. *The Writings of Bret Harte* (Houghton Mifflin), 1896–1903, 19 vols., is the standard edition. Selections have been issued in *The Luck of Roaring Camp . . . and Selected Stories and Poems* (Macmillan), 1928, with an introduction by George R. Stewart, Jr. A serviceable collection is Joseph B. Harrison, ed., *Bret Harte: Representative Selections* (American Book), 1941. The authoritative life is George R. Stewart, Jr., *Bret Harte: Argonaut and Exile* (Houghton Mifflin), 1931.

Literary exploration of the new realism became evident in the poetic experimentation of Lanier and Dickinson. Charles R. Anderson is general editor of *The Centennial Edition of Sidney Lanier* (Johns Hopkins), 1945, 10 vols. *Selected Poems* (Scribner's), 1947, has a preface by Stark Young. A detailed biography is Aubrey H. Starke, *Sidney Lanier: A Biographical and Critical Study* (North Carolina), 1933.

The variorum edition of the poems of Emily Dickinson was edited by Thomas H. Johnson (Harvard), 1955, 3 vols. This work establishes finally a dependable text. Johnson published a one-volume edition from this text, *The Complete Poems of Emily Dickinson* (Little, Brown), 1960, as well as a selection, edited with an introduction, *Final Harvest: Emily Dickinson's Poems* (Little, Brown), 1962. *The Letters of Emily Dickinson* (Harvard), 1958, 3 vols., were edited by Thomas H. Johnson in association with Theodora Ward. The first reliable biography was George F. Whicher, *This Was a Poet* (Scribner's), 1938. Also important are Thomas H. Johnson, *Emily Dickinson: An Interpretive Biography* (Harvard), 1955; Jay Leyda, *The Years and Hours of Emily Dickinson* (Yale), 1960, 2 vols.; and Theodora Ward, *The Capsule of the Mind: Chapters in the Life of Emily Dickinson* (Harvard), 1961. Critical estimates are Charles R. Anderson, *Emily Dickinson's Poetry: Stairway of Surprise* (Holt), 1960; Clark Griffith, *The Long Shadow: Emily Dickinson's Tragic Poetry* (Princeton), 1964; Albert J. Gelpi, *Emily Dickinson: The Mind of the Poet* (Harvard), 1965; Ruth Miller, *The Poetry of Emily Dickinson* (Wesleyan), 1965; and Brita Lindberg-Seyersted, *The Voice of the Poet: Aspects of Style in the Poetry of Emily Dickinson* (Harvard), 1968.

The first realist in American letters was John William De Forest, and it was William Dean Howells who first recognized his significance. *Miss Ravenel's Conversion*, 1867, was reprinted, edited by Gordon S. Haight (Harper), in 1939; it contains one of the best critical estimates of De Forest. See also James F. Light, *John William De Forest* (Twayne), and Edmund Wilson's chapter on the novelist in *Patriotic Gore* (Oxford), 1962. More than forty reprints of De Forest's work are now available and two complete editions are in progress (Garrett Press and Bald Eagle Press). The Indiana University Press began publication in 1968, under the editorship of Ronald Gottesman and Edwin H. Cady, succeeded by Don L. Cook and David J. Nordloh, of a forty-one-volume *Selected Edition of W. D. Howells*. Walter J. Meserve edited *The Complete Plays of William Dean Howells* (New York University), 1960. Clara M. and Rudolf Kirk edited *William Dean Howells:*

Representative Selections (American Book), 1950. The fullest biography is Edwin H. Cady's interpretive study, *The Road to Realism: The Early Years, 1837–1885* . . . (Syracuse), 1956, and *The Realist at War: The Mature Years, 1885–1920* . . . (Syracuse), 1958. Kenneth S. Lynn's *William Dean Howells: An American Life* (Harcourt, Brace), 1971, is the most recent critical biography. Critical estimates are Everett Carter, *Howells and the Age of Realism* (Lippincott), 1954; Clara M. Kirk and Rudolf Kirk, *William Dean Howells* (Twayne), 1962; and Kermit Vanderbilt, *The Achievement of William Dean Howells* (Princeton), 1968.

Mark Twain's writings epitomize the epic of America moving west. The collected works are *The Writings of Mark Twain* (Wells), 1923–1925, 37 vols., edited by Albert B. Paine. Paine also edited the *Letters* (Harper), 1917, 2 vols.; the *Speeches* (Harper), 1923; the *Autobiography* (Harper), 1924, 2 vols.; and the important *Notebook* (Harper), 1935. In recent years, Paine's work has been corrected and supplemented by dozens of volumes. Chief among them are *The Love Letters of Mark Twain*, ed. Dixon Wecter (Harper), 1949; *The Correspondence of Samuel L. Clemens and William Dean Howells, 1872–1910*, ed. Henry Nash Smith and William M. Gibson (Harvard), 1960, 2 vols.; Bernard De Voto's *Mark Twain in Eruption* (Harper), 1940, in effect a third volume of the *Autobiography*; and De Voto's edition of *Letters from the Earth* (Harper), 1962, collected sketches by Mark Twain for many years suppressed and now published posthumously with a preface by Henry Nash Smith. The University of California Press has begun publication, under the editorship of Frederick Anderson, of a projected fourteen volumes from The Mark Twain Papers in the General Library at the University of California at Berkeley. The *Iowa-California Edition of the Works of Mark Twain*, in twenty-four volumes, under the editorship of John C. Gerber, is also being published by the University of California Press.

The authorized biography is Albert B. Paine, *Mark Twain, A Biography* (Harper), 1912, 3 vols., but far more perceptive are William Dean Howells, *My Mark Twain* (Harper), 1910, and DeLancey Ferguson, *Mark Twain, Man and Legend* (Bobbs-Merrill), 1943. Dixon Wecter's *Sam Clemens of Hannibal* (Houghton Mifflin), 1952, was published after the author's untimely death, the first volume of a projected multivolume biography. For the general reader, Justin Kaplan's *Mr. Clemens and Mark Twain* (Simon and Schuster), 1966, is essential. Van Wyck Brooks' *The Ordeal of Mark Twain* (Dutton), 1920, rev. 1933, argues that Twain was thwarted by the prudishness and commercialism of America and was wasted as a talent in the western frontier. Bernard De Voto's *Mark Twain's America* (Little, Brown), 1932, is aimed directly at refuting Brooks' thesis. In recent years, several critics have turned their attention to Twain's artistry: Bernard De Voto,

Mark Twain at Work (Harvard), 1942; Gladys Bellamy, *Mark Twain as a Literary Artist* (Oklahoma), 1950; Walter Blair, *Mark Twain and Huck Finn* (California), 1960; Henry Nash Smith, *Mark Twain: The Development of a Writer* (Harvard), 1962; and James M. Cox, *Mark Twain: The Fate of Humor* (Princeton), 1966.

VIII. THE CONTINENTAL NATION: *Disillusion, Reform, Definition*

Thinkers and writers turned to materialistic determinism at a time when American culture was becoming predominantly industrial. The idea of progress by way of natural selection dominated their thinking. The best brief introduction to evolution as a general point of view is Richard Hofstadter, *Social Darwinism in American Thought: 1860–1915* (Pennsylvania), 1944. Merle Curti, *The Growth of American Thought*, 3rd ed. (Harper), 1964, also discusses the subject. The religious and scientific controversies of the time are treated in Philip P. Wiener, *Evolution and the Founders of Pragmatism* (Harvard), 1949. The growth of industrialism after the Civil War is set forth in Thomas C. Cochran and William Miller, *The Age of Enterprise: A Social History of Industrial America* (Macmillan), 1942, and Arthur M. Schlesinger, *The Rise of Modern America, 1865–1951* (Macmillan), 1951. The effects of this growth are studied in A. Whitney Griswold, *The American Cult of Success* (Johns Hopkins), 1934.

One of the most wide-ranging cultural histories of the period is Howard Mumford Jones, *The Age of Energy: Varieties of American Experience, 1865–1915* (Viking), 1971. Excellent discussions of the attempts of liberal thinkers since 1865 to define the role of the state in the ordering of society are Eric F. Goldman, *Rendezvous with Destiny: A History of Modern American Reform* (Knopf), 1952, and Ray Ginger, *Age of Excess: The United States from 1877 to 1914* (Macmillan), 1965. Charles A. Madison, *Critics and Crusaders: A Century of American Protest* (Holt), 1947; and Christopher Lasch, *The New Radicalism in America, 1889–1963* (Knopf), 1965, deal with reformers and reform movements in the machine age. A study of progressivism is Daniel Aaron, *Men of Good Hope* (Oxford), 1951. Larzer Ziff's *The American 1890s* (Viking), 1966, concentrates on the literary work of a "lost" generation. Stewart Holbrook has written a popular history of the period, *The Age of the Moguls* (Doubleday), 1953, which supplements Matthew Josephson's earlier and perceptive study, *The Robber Barons: The Great American Capitalists, 1861–1901* (Harcourt, Brace), 1934.

Vernon L. Parrington, Jr., *American Dreams: A Study of American Utopias* (Brown University), 1947, has chapters on Edward Bellamy and his followers. Joseph Schiffman edited *Edward Bellamy: Selected Writings on Religion and Society* (Liberal Arts), 1955. Sylvia E. Bowman's *The Year 2000* (Twayne), 1958, is a critical biography.

The Work of Stephen Crane, edited by Wilson Follett (Knopf), 1925–1926, 12 vols., was reprinted in 1963 by Russell and Russell. The *University of Virginia Edition of the Works of Stephen Crane*, in ten volumes, is under the general editorship of Fredson Bowers, *Bowery Tales*, 1969, being the first published. Joseph Katz edited a much-needed collection of *The Poems of Stephen Crane* (Cooper Square Publishers), 1966. *The Red Badge of Courage and Selected Poetry and Prose*, edited by William M. Gibson, 3rd ed. (Holt), 1968, is the most generous one-volume text. Robert Stallman and Lillian Gilkes edited *Stephen Crane: Letters* (New York University), 1960. Edwin H. Cady edited, with an introduction, Corwin K. Linson's memoir, *My Stephen Crane* (Syracuse), 1958. Two biographies are Thomas Beer, *Stephen Crane: A Study in American Letters* (Knopf), 1923, and John Berryman, *Stephen Crane* (Sloane), 1950. Edwin Cady combines criticism and biography in his *Stephen Crane* (Twayne), 1962. Eric Solomon places Crane's work in its American cultural context in *Stephen Crane: From Parody to Realism* (Harvard), 1965. Daniel G. Hoffman's critical analysis, *The Poetry of Stephen Crane* (Columbia), 1957, published seventeen of the poems for the first time.

The writings of Frank Norris are collected in *The Complete Edition of Frank Norris* (Doubleday), 1928, 10 vols. Franklin Walker edited, in a limited edition, *The Letters of Frank Norris* (Book Club of California), 1956. The only full-length biography is Franklin Walker, *Frank Norris* (Doubleday), 1932. Recent critical studies are Warren French's *Frank Norris* (Twayne), 1962, and Donald Pizer's *The Novels of Frank Norris* (Indiana), 1966. There is no complete edition of the writings of Jack London. Philip S. Foner edited Jack London, *American Rebel: A Collection of His Social Writings Together with an Extensive Study of the Man and His Times* (Citadel), 1947. *Best Short Stories of Jack London* (Doubleday), appeared in 1953.

The writings of Henry Adams have not been collected in a uniform edition; but Elizabeth Stevenson has edited, with an introduction, *A Henry Adams Reader* (Doubleday), 1958, and there are three important gatherings of his letters: the standard is W. C. Ford, *Letters of Henry Adams, 1858–1918* (Houghton Mifflin), 1930, 1938, 2 vols.; Harold Dean Cater has edited *Henry Adams and His Friends: A Collection of His Unpublished Letters* (Houghton Mifflin), 1947; and Newton Arvin has compiled *The Selected Letters of Henry Adams* (Farrar), 1951, a volume that reveals the traveler and his brilliant insights into the life about him. Two biographies have appeared in recent years. Ernest Samuels' *Henry Adams*, in three volumes

(Harvard), 1948–1964, is standard. Elizabeth Stevenson's *Henry Adams* (Macmillan), 1955, is a lively one-volume portrait. A study combining biography with extensive critical analysis is J. C. Levenson, *The Mind and Art of Henry Adams* (Houghton Mifflin), 1957, reprinted (Stanford), 1968. Robert Mane, *Henry Adams on the Road to Chartres* (Harvard), 1971, is a definitive study of the "Virgin" aspect of Adams' thought.

The collected American edition of the writings of Henry James is *The Novels and Tales of Henry James* (Scribner's), 1907–1909, 24 vols., 1917, 2 posthumous vols. In 1961, Scribner's began republishing all twenty-six volumes in a uniform edition, now available from Kelley Publishers. Leon Edel edited the *Complete Tales* (Lippincott) in twelve volumes. Useful editions of the shorter work are Lyon N. Richardson, ed., *Henry James: Representative Selections* (American Book), 1941, revised by the editor (Illinois), 1966; *The American Novels and Stories of Henry James*, edited by F. O. Matthiessen (Knopf), 1947; and *The Portable Henry James*, edited by Morton D. Zabel (Viking), 1951, revised by Lyall H. Powers (Viking), 1968. His critical prefaces are available in Richard P. Blackmur, ed., *The Art of the Novel* (Scribner's), 1934; Leon Edel, ed., *The Future of the Novel* (Vintage), 1956; and James E. Miller, Jr., ed., *Theory of Fiction: Henry James* (Nebraska), 1972. The full story of James' connection with the theater and all his plays, including seven not before published, are Leon Edel, ed., *The Complete Plays of Henry James* (Lippincott), 1949. *The Notebooks of Henry James*, edited by F. O. Matthiessen and Kenneth B. Murdock (Oxford), 1947, provides a private history of a writer's creative life over a period of thirty years. The letters are available in Percy Lubbock, ed., *The Letters of Henry James* (Scribner's), 1920, 2 vols., and Leon Edel, ed., *Selected Letters of Henry James* (Farrar), 1955. A brief critical biography is Frederick W. Dupee, *Henry James* (Sloane), 1951. Leon Edel's definitive biography appeared in five volumes: *Henry James: The Untried Years* (Lippincott), 1953; *The Conquest of London* (Lippincott), 1962; *The Middle Years* (Lippincott), 1962; *The Treacherous Years* (Lippincott), 1969; and *The Master* (Lippincott), 1972. Critical volumes are numerous. Joseph Warren Beach, *The Method of Henry James* (Yale), 1918, enl. ed. (Saifer), 1954, is an early study but still important. Richard Poirier, *The Comic Sense of Henry James* (Oxford), 1960, treats the early novels; F. O. Matthiessen, *Henry James: The Major Phase* (Oxford), 1944, is a detailed analysis of the late novels. Equally important are Oscar Cargill, *The Novels of Henry James* (Macmillan), 1961; Dorothea Krook, *The Ordeal of Consciousness in Henry James* (Cambridge), 1962; and a collection of critical essays about James edited by Frederick W. Dupee, *The Question of Henry James* (Holt), 1945.

IX. THE UNITED STATES: *Confidence and Criticism*

Two studies in twentieth-century intellectual history furnish a good introduction to the period: Henry S. Commager, *The American Mind* (Yale), 1950, and Crane Brinton, *Ideas and Men* (Prentice-Hall), 1950. An analysis of social thinking is Morton G. White, *Social Thought in America: The Revolt Against Formalism* (Viking), 1949, with special attention to the ideas of O. W. Holmes the younger, Veblen, Dewey, Beard, and James Harvey Robinson. Richard Hofstadter edited excerpts from contemporaneous writing in *The Progressive Movement, 1900–1915* (Prentice-Hall), 1963. An important but more specialized study is Henry F. May, *The End of American Innocence: A Study of the First Years of Our Own Time, 1912–1917* (Knopf), 1959. A more comprehensive survey is Frank Freidel, *America in the Twentieth Century*, 3rd ed. (Knopf), 1971. Two surveys of the American spirit since 1900 are Frederick L. Allen, *The Big Change: America Transforms Itself, 1900–1950* (Harper), 1952, and Lloyd R. Morris, *Postscript to Yesterday: America—The Last Fifty Years* (Random), 1947. Two sociological studies of the impact of industrialism on a "typical" Midwest city are R. S. and H. M. Lynd, *Middletown* (Harcourt, Brace), 1929, and *Middletown in Transition* (Harcourt, Brace), 1937.

There is no better first-hand treatment of writers and writing in the decade of the twenties than Malcolm Cowley, *Exile's Return: A Literary Odyssey of the 1920's*, rev. ed. (Viking), 1951. Henry S. Canby, *American Memoir* (Houghton Mifflin), 1947, and Lincoln Steffens, *Autobiography* (Harcourt, Brace), 1931, offer personal records of the transition from the nineteenth to the twentieth century. Edmund Wilson collected his always lively opinions in *The Shores of Light: A Literary Chronicle of the Twenties and Thirties* (Farrar), 1952. With the benefit of hindsight, Frederick J. Hoffman studies the period in *The Twenties: American Writing in the Postwar Decade* (Viking), 1955. The best collection of literary criticism is Morton D. Zabel, ed., *Literary Opinion in America*, 3rd rev. ed. (Harper), 1962. Charles I. Glicksberg edited *American Literary Criticism, 1900–1950* (Hendricks), 1951.

Van Wyck Brooks, *America's Coming of Age* (Huebsch), 1915, defines the issues for one age; his *The Writer in America* (Dutton), 1953, for another, His five volumes of literary history, of which *The Confident Years, 1885–1915* (Dutton), 1951, deals with this period, are a re-creation of our "usable" past. The essays of Randolph Bourne were selected by James Oppenheim for *Untimely Papers* (Huebsch), 1919, and by Van Wyck Brooks for *History of a Literary Radical and Other Essays* (1920), reprinted (S. A. Russell), in 1956. Both volumes appeared after Bourne's death. H. L. Mencken's six series of *Prejudices* (Knopf), 1919–1927, have been culled for *Selected Prejudices* (Modern Library), 1930. *The Days of H. L. Mencken* (Knopf), 1947, is a one-volume edition of *Happy Days* (1940), *Newspaper Days* (1941), and *Heathen Days* (1943). Three biographies are William Manchester, *Disturber of the Peace: The Life of H. L. Mencken* (Harper), 1951; Charles Angoff, *H. L. Mencken, A Portrait from Memory* (Yoseloff), 1956; and Carl Bode, *Mencken* (Southern Illinois), 1969.

Two specialized historical studies of the poetry of the period are Stanley F. Coffman, Jr., *Imagism: A Chapter for the History of Modern Poetry* (Oklahoma), 1951, and John M. Bradbury, *The Fugitives: A Critical Account* (North Carolina), 1958. Louise Bogan surveys the first half-century briefly in *Achievement in American Poetry* (Regnery), 1951. A fuller but still not complete historical analysis is Horace Gregory and Marya Zaturenska, *A History of American Poetry, 1900–1940* (Harcourt, Brace), 1946.

Studies of early twentieth-century poets are numerous. *The Complete Poems of Edwin Arlington Robinson* (Macmillan), 1937, appeared two years after his death. Briefer volumes are *Selected Early Poems and Letters*, edited by Charles T. Davis (Rinehart), 1960, and *Selected Poems of Edwin Arlington Robinson*, edited by Morton Dauwen Zabel (Macmillan), 1965. Ridgely Torrence edited *Selected Letters* (Macmillan), 1940, and Denham Sutcliffe edited *Untriangulated Stars: Letters . . . to Harry DeForest Smith* (Harvard), 1947. Herman Hagedorn produced the first and still valuable biography, *Edwin Arlington Robinson* (Macmillan), 1938. Recent critical estimates are in Ellsworth Barnard, *Edwin Arlington Robinson: A Critical Study* (Macmillan), 1952; Louis Coxe, *Edwin Arlington Robinson: The Life of Poetry* (Pegasus), 1968; and Wallace Anderson, *Edwin Arlington Robinson* (Houghton Mifflin), 1967, (Harvard), 1968. Vachel Lindsay, *Collected Poems* (Macmillan), 1934, is the most nearly complete edition. Edgar Lee Masters, *Vachel Lindsay: A Poet in America* (Scribner's), 1935, is narrative and critical; Mark Harris, *City of Discontent* (Bobbs-Merrill), 1952, is an interpretive biography of Lindsay and Springfield, Illinois. Eleanor Ruggles, *The West-Going Heart: A Life of Vachel Lindsay* (Norton), 1959, is the most recent biography. The best collection of poems by Carl Sandburg is *Complete Poems* (Harcourt, Brace), 1950, rev. ed., 1970. North Callahan's *Carl Sandburg: Lincoln of Our Literature* (New York University), 1969, is the "authorized" biography. Richard Crowder's critical biography, *Carl Sandburg* (Twayne), 1964, is the best introduction to the poet's work. *The Poetry of Robert Frost*, ed. Edward Connery Lathem (Holt), 1969, is a comprehensive edition. The major biography is Lawrance Thompson, *Robert Frost: The Early Years* (Holt), 1966, and *The Years of Triumph* (Holt),

1970. A third volume is projected. Elizabeth Shepley Sergeant, *Robert Frost: The Trial by Existence* (Holt), 1960, is a one-volume life. Important critical studies are Reginald L. Cook, *The Dimensions of Robert Frost* (Rinehart), 1958; James F. Lynen, *The Pastoral Art of Robert Frost* (Yale), 1960; Reuben Brower, *The Poetry of Robert Frost: Constellations of Intention* (Oxford), 1963; and Radcliffe Squires, *The Major Themes of Robert Frost* (Michigan), 1963.

An interpretation of American prose literature, 1890–1940, is Alfred Kazin, *On Native Grounds* (Reynal and Hitchcock), 1942. Maxwell Geismar, *The Last of the Provincials: The American Novel, 1915-1925* (Houghton Mifflin), 1947, pays special attention to Lewis, Cather, Anderson, and Fitzgerald. Early accounts are in Joseph Warren Beach, *American Fiction, 1920–1940* (Macmillan), 1941, and in Frederick J. Hoffman, *The Modern Novel in America, 1900–1950* (Regnery), 1951. Specialized studies are Blanche Housman Gelfant, *The American City Novel* (Oklahoma), 1954; Walter B. Rideout, *The Radical Novel in the United States, 1900–1954* (Harvard), 1956; W. M. Frohock, *The Novel of Violence in America*, rev. and enl. ed. (Southern Methodist), 1957; Michael Millgate, *American Social Fiction: James to Cozzens* (Barnes and Noble), 1964; and James Tuttleton, *The Novel of Manners in America* (North Carolina), 1972.

The Works of James Branch Cabell (McBride), 1927–1930, is in eighteen volumes. The collections of Ellen Glasgow's writings are not complete. The latest is the Virginia Edition (Scribner's), 1938, 12 vols., with new prefaces by the author. Blair Rouse edited *Letters to Ellen Glasgow* (Harcourt, Brace), 1958. A full-length critical study is Frederick P. W. McDowell, *Ellen Glasgow and the Ironic Art of Fiction* (Wisconsin), 1960. There is no collected edition of Edith Wharton's writings, except *An Edith Wharton Treasury*, edited by Arthur H. Quinn (Appleton-Century), 1950, which contains two novels and ten stories; *The Collected Stories of Edith Wharton*, edited by R. W. B. Lewis, 2 vols., (Scribner's), 1968; and *The Edith Wharton Reader*, edited by Louis Auchincloss (Scribner's), 1965. The best critical analysis is Blake Nevius, *Edith Wharton: A Study of Her Fiction* (California), 1953. *The Novels and Stories of Willa Cather* (Houghton Mifflin), 1937–1941, 13 vols., is the Library Edition. *Willa Cather's Collected Short Fiction, 1892-1912*, edited by Mildred R. Bennett (Nebraska), 1965, was revised by Beatrice Slote, 1970. Biographical studies have been numerous since Cather's death. Leon Edel completed E. K. Brown's *Willa Cather: A Critical Biography* (Knopf), 1953. Edith Lewis provided *Willa Cather Living: A Personal Record* (Knopf), 1953, and Elizabeth Shepley Sergeant, *Willa Cather: A Memoir* (Lippincott), 1953. Recent critical studies are John H. Randall III, *The Landscape and the Looking Glass: Willa Cather's Search for Value* (Houghton Mifflin), 1960; Edwin A. Bloom and Lillian D. Bloom,

Willa Cather's Gift of Sympathy (Southern Illinois), 1962; and James Wood-
ress, *Willa Cather: Her Life and Art* (Pegasus), 1970. There is no collected
edition of Sinclair Lewis. Harry E. Maule and Melville H. Cane have edited
a Sinclair Lewis reader, *The Man from Main Street: Selected Essays and
Other Writings, 1904–1950* (Random), 1953. Harrison Smith compiled *From
Main Street to Stockholm: Letters, 1919–1930* (Harcourt, Brace), 1952. A
comprehensive critical biography is Mark Schorer, *Sinclair Lewis: An American Life* (McGraw-Hill), 1961. Sherwood Anderson's work has not been
collected. A good selection, edited by Paul Rosenfeld, is *The Sherwood
Anderson Reader* (Houghton Mifflin), 1947. Howard Mumford Jones and
Walter B. Rideout edited *Letters of Sherwood Anderson* (Little, Brown),
1953. Two critical biographies are Irving Howe, *Sherwood Anderson*
(Sloane), 1951, and James Schevill, *Sherwood Anderson: His Life and
Work* (Denver), 1951. A recent full-length critical study is David Anderson
(no relative), *Sherwood Anderson: An Introduction and Interpretation*
(Barnes and Noble), 1967.

Howard Fast has edited *The Best Short Stories of Theodore Dreiser*
(World), 1947. Robert H. Elias edited *Letters of Theodore Dreiser* (Penn-
sylvania), 1959, 3 vols. Of biographical interest is Helen Dreiser, *My Life with
Dreiser* (World), 1951. The nonliterary life of Dreiser the man is W. A.
Swanberg's *Dreiser* (Scribner's), 1965. Two critical biographies are Robert
H. Elias, *Theodore Dreiser: Apostle of Nature* (Knopf), 1949, and F. O.
Matthiessen, *Theodore Dreiser* (Sloane), 1951. More recent studies are
Charles Shapiro, *Theodore Dreiser: Our Bitter Patriot* (Southern Illinois),
1962; Philip L. Gerber, *Theodore Dreiser* (Twayne), 1964; and Ellen Moers,
Two Dreisers (Viking), 1969. Alfred Kazin and Charles Shapiro edited
*The Stature of Theodore Dreiser: A Critical Survey of the Man and His
Work* (Indiana), 1955.

A good introduction to modern drama, from Ibsen to the present, is
Eric Bentley, *The Playwright as Thinker* (Reynal), 1946. For American
theater alone, there is Joseph Wood Krutch, *The American Drama Since
1918*, rev. ed. (Braziller), 1957, and Alan S. Downer, *Fifty Years of American Drama: 1900–1950* (Regnery), 1951. Gerald Weales' *American Drama
Since World War II* (Harcourt, Brace), 1962, and *The Jumping-Off Place:
American Drama in the 1960's* (Macmillan), 1969, are useful discussions of
the theater's most recent developments.

The most nearly complete collection of the writings of Eugene O'Neill
is *The Plays of Eugene O'Neill* (Scribner's), 1934–1935, 12 vols. Five later
plays are published separately: *The Iceman Cometh* (Random), 1946; *A
Moon for the Misbegotten* (Random), 1952; *Long Day's Journey into Night*
(Yale), 1956; *A Touch of the Poet* (Yale), 1957; and *Hughie* (Yale), 1959.
Joseph Wood Krutch provided an introduction to *Nine Plays of Eugene*

O'Neill (Modern Library), 1941. The first comprehensive biography is Arthur and Barbara Gelb, *O'Neill* (Harper), 1962. Doris Alexander writes about O'Neill's early years in *The Tempering of Eugene O'Neill* (Harcourt, Brace), 1962, Louis Sheaffer in *O'Neill: Son and Playwright* (Little, Brown), 1968. Agnes Boulton, *Part of a Long Story* (Doubleday), 1958, is the memoirs of O'Neill's first wife. Full-length critical analyses are Edwin A. Engel, *The Haunted Heroes of Eugene O'Neill* (Harvard), 1953; Doris V. Falk, *Eugene O'Neill and the Tragic Tension* (Rutgers), 1958; John Henry Raleigh, *The Plays of Eugene O'Neill* (Southern Illinois), 1965; and Travis Bogard, *Contour in Time: The Plays of Eugene O'Neill* (Oxford), 1972. Oscar Cargill and others edited *O'Neill and His Plays: Four Decades of Criticism* (New York University), 1961.

X. A WORLD LITERATURE

After 1925, the literature of the United States was recognized here and abroad as a world literature. Trends in general and the work of individual authors became subjects for definitive studies and international critical discussion. Items specific to the intellectual and social history of the times are mentioned in Section IX preceding. Many there mentioned dealing with fiction, poetry, and drama also extend into the period of the thirties, forties, and fifties. The following studies treat authors and literary problems of the present and the immediate past.

Current literary forms are traced to their earlier origins in the anthology edited by Mark Schorer and others, *Criticism: The Foundations of Modern Literary Judgment* (Harcourt, Brace), 1948; and in *Modern Literary Criticism, 1900–1970*, edited by Lawrence I. Lipking and A. Walton Litz (Oxford), 1971. Sixteen essays discussing politics and literature are in Lionel Trilling, *The Liberal Imagination: Essays on Literature and Society* (Viking), 1950. Stanley Edgar Hyman, *The Armed Vision: A Study in the Methods of Modern Literary Criticism* (Knopf), 1948, devotes each chapter to one critic representative of one point of view. Walter E. Sutton's *Modern American Criticism* (Prentice-Hall), 1963, is a valuable outline and summary of five representative types. Benjamin T. Spencer, *The Quest for Nationality: An American Literary Campaign* (Syracuse), 1957, is a history of American literary criticism which also treats the changing pattern of American culture. Daniel Aaron's *Writers on the Left: Episodes in American Literary Communism* (Harcourt, Brace), 1961, covers the period from 1912 to the early 1940's.

Recent criticism, to some extent based on social and psychological premises, includes James T. Farrell, *Literature and Morality* (Vanguard), 1947; F. O. Matthiessen, *The Responsibilities of the Critic* (Oxford), 1952, a posthumous collection of essays; Allen Tate, *The Man of Letters in the Modern World* (Longmans), 1955; Frederick J. Hoffman, *Freudianism and the Literary Mind*, rev. ed. (Louisiana State), 1957; and Edmund Wilson, *Classics and Commercials: A Literary Chronicle of the Forties* (Farrar), 1950.

Studies of poetry that express a conservative view are R. P. Blackmur, *The Double Agent: Essays in Craft and Elucidation* (Arrow), 1935; and *Language as Gesture: Essays in Poetry* (Harcourt, Brace), 1952; Allen Tate, *Reactionary Essays on Poetry and Ideas* (Scribner's), 1936; and Cleanth Brooks, *Modern Poetry and the Tradition* (North Carolina), 1939. An attempt to provide a "bridge" to modern poetry for the lay reader is Lloyd Frankenberg, *Pleasure Dome: On Reading Modern Poetry* (Houghton Mifflin), 1949, with attention to such poets as Pound, Eliot, Cummings, Williams, and Auden.

Critical essays which, for the most part, treat individual poets are Randall Jarrell, *Poetry and the Age* (Knopf), 1953; A. Alvarez, *Stewards of Excellence* (Scribner's), 1958; Ralph J. Mills, Jr., *Contemporary American Poetry* (Random), 1965; M. L. Rosenthal, *The New Poets* (Oxford), 1967; and Richard Howard, *Alone with America* (Atheneum), 1969. More general analyses—historical, critical, and semantic—include Muriel Rukeyser, *The Life of Poetry* (A. A. Wyn), 1949, Babette Deutsch, *Poetry in Our Time* (Holt), 1952, rev. ed. (Doubleday), 1963; Stanley Burnshaw, *The Seamless Web: Language-Thinking, Creative-Knowledge, Art-Experience* (Braziller), 1970; and Edwin Fussell, *Lucifer in Harness: American Meter, Metaphor, and Diction* (Princeton), 1973. Provocative collections of critical essays are *Poets in Progress*, edited by Edward Hungerford (Northwestern), 1962, and *The Contemporary Poet as Artist and Critic*, edited by Anthony Ostroff (Little, Brown), 1964. A comprehensive guide to the craft of poetry is Babette Deutsch, *Poetry Handbook—A Dictionary of Terms* (Funk and Wagnalls), 3rd ed., 1969.

No collected edition of Ezra Pound's work exists, but the reader will find these volumes vital: *Personae: Collected Shorter Poems* (New Directions), 1956; *The Cantos: 1-117* (New Directions), 1970; and *Selected Prose, 1909-1965* (New Directions), 1973. D. D. Paige edited *The Letters of Ezra Pound, 1907-1941* (Harcourt, Brace), 1950, reissued as *Selected Letters . . .* (New Directions), 1971. The best biography is Noel Stock, *The Life of Ezra Pound* (Pantheon), 1970. Book-length studies are Hugh Kenner, *The Poetry of Ezra Pound* (New Directions), 1951; John J. Espey, *Ezra Pound's Mauberley: A Study of Composition* (California), 1955; George Dekker, *The Cantos of Ezra Pound* (Barnes and Noble), 1963; and Donald Davie, *Ezra Pound: Poet as Sculptor* (Oxford), 1964. For the reader new to the poet's work, M. L. Rosenthal's *Primer of Ezra Pound* (Macmillan), 1960, is a concise, perceptive introduction. Two collections of essays are Peter Russell, ed., *An Examination of Ezra Pound* (New Directions), 1950, and Walter Sutton, ed., *Ezra Pound: A Collection of Critical Essays* (Prentice-Hall), 1963. John Hamilton Edwards and William Vasse, Jr., compiled an *Annotated Index to the Cantos of Ezra Pound* (California), 1957, reprinted, 1971. Most vital of all, for readers familiar with the whole canon, is Hugh Kenner's brilliant synthesis, *The Pound Era* (Berkeley), 1971.

Eliot's poetry is gathered in *Collected Poems, 1909-1962* (Harcourt, Brace), 1963, and *Poems Written in Early Youth* (Farrar), 1967. *Selected Essays* (Harcourt, Brace), rev. ed., 1950; *On Poets and Poetry* (Farrar), 1957; and *To Criticize the Critic* (Farrar), 1965, are the important collections of essays. Biographical information can be found in Herbert Howarth's *Notes on Some Figures Behind T. S. Eliot* (Houghton Mifflin), 1964, and Bernard Bergonzi's *T. S. Eliot* (Macmillan), 1971. The first major critical study was F. O. Matthiessen, *The Achievement of T. S. Eliot* (Oxford), 1935. It has been revised twice; the third edition, published in 1958, has a chapter on Eliot's later work by C. L. Barber. Further useful studies are Elizabeth Drew, *T. S. Eliot: The Design of His Poetry* (Scribner's), 1949; Helen L. Gardner, *The Art of T. S. Eliot* (Dutton), 1950; Hugh Kenner, *The Invisible Poet: T. S. Eliot* (McDowell-Obolensky), 1959; and Kristian Smidt, *Poetry and Belief in the Work of T. S. Eliot*, rev. ed. (Humanities Press), 1961. Leonard Unger edited *T. S. Eliot: A Selected Critique* (Rinehart), 1948. Two detailed studies of individual poems are George Williamson, *A Reader's Guide to T. S. Eliot* (Noonday), 1953, and Grover Smith, Jr., *T. S. Eliot's Poetry and Plays: A Study in Sources and Meaning* (Chicago), 1956, enl. ed., 1960.

Waldo Frank edited *The Collected Poems of Hart Crane* (Liveright), 1933, reprinted 1958. Philip Horton, *Hart Crane: The Life of an American Poet* (Norton), 1937, is supplemented by Brom Weber, *Hart Crane: A Biographical and Critical Study* (Bodley), 1948, and John Unterecker, *Voyager: A Life of Hart Crane* (Farrar), 1969. *Letters, 1916-1932* (Hermitage), 1952, reprinted (Berkeley), 1965, is edited by Brom Weber. The first full-length study of Crane's major work is L. S. Dembo, *Hart Crane's Sanskrit Charge: A Study of The Bridge* (Cornell), 1960. R. W. B. Lewis, *The Poetry of Hart Crane* (Princeton), 1967, is a comprehensive explication of the whole canon.

The best edition to date of Archibald MacLeish's poetry is *The Human Season: Selected Poems, 1926-1972* (Houghton Mifflin), 1972. Edna St. Vincent Millay's poems are edited by Norma Millay in *Collected Poems* (Harper), 1956. E. E. Cummings's *Complete Poems, 1913-1962* (Harcourt, Brace), appeared in 1972. The last gathering of Robinson Jeffers' poems is *The Selected Poetry . . .* (Random), 1938. Conrad Aiken's *Collected Poems*

(Oxford), 1953, 2nd ed., 1970, is almost complete. *The Collected Later Poems of William Carlos Williams* (New Directions) appeared in 1950, *The Collected Earlier Poems . . .* (New Directions) in 1951, followed by *Pictures from Brueghel and Other Poems* (New Directions), 1962, and *Paterson: Books I-V* (New Directions) 1963. Marianne Moore's *Complete Poems* (Viking) appeared in 1967. *The Collected Poems of Wallace Stevens* (Knopf), 1954, was published to honor Stevens on his seventy-fifth birthday. Of his poems and essays in *Opus Posthumous* (Knopf), 1957, edited with an introduction by Samuel French Morse, about one-third are here published for the first time.

Studies of fiction, specific to the period, are John Aldridge, *After the Lost Generation: A Critical Study of the Writers of Two Wars* (McGraw-Hill), 1951; Frederick J. Hoffman, *The Modern Novel in America, 1900–1950* (Regnery), 1951; Ihab Hassan, *Radical Innocence: Studies in the Contemporary American Novel* (Princeton), 1961; Marcus Klein, *After Alienation: American Novels in Mid-Century* (World), 1964; Jonathan Baumbach, *The Landscape of Nightmare* (New York University), 1965; Tony Tanner, *City of Words: American Fiction, 1950–1970* (Harper), 1971; and Alfred Kazin, *Bright Book of Life: American Novelists and Storytellers from Hemingway to Mailer* (Atlantic-Little, Brown), 1973.

The Portable F. Scott Fitzgerald (Viking), 1945, was edited by Dorothy Parker, with an introduction by John O'Hara. Malcolm Cowley selected *The Stories of F. Scott Fitzgerald* (Scribner's), 1951. A useful reprinting is *Three Novels: The Great Gatsby* (with an introduction by Malcolm Cowley), *Tender Is the Night* (with the author's final revisions; edited by Malcolm Cowley), *The Last Tycoon: An Unfinished Novel* (edited by Edmund Wilson) (Scribner's), 1953. *Afternoon of an Author*, edited by Arthur Mizener (Princeton), 1957, is a selection of uncollected stories and essays. Edmund Wilson edited *The Crack-Up* (New Directions), 1945, a volume of uncollected pieces, notebooks, and unpublished letters. Andrew Turnbull edited *The Letters* (Scribner's), 1963, a partial collection. A narrative biography with acute critical assessments is Arthur Mizener, *The Far Side of Paradise* (Houghton Mifflin), 1951. A more sensitive interpretation of the biography is Andrew Turnbull, *Scott Fitzgerald* (Scribner's), 1962. James E. Miller, Jr., *The Fictional Technique of Scott Fitzgerald* (Martinus Nijhoff), 1957, expanded in 1964 under the title *F. Scott Fitzgerald: His Art and His Technique* (New York University), is a detailed analysis of the first three novels. The best introductions to the whole literary career are Kenneth Eble's *F. Scott Fitzgerald* (Twayne), 1963, and Robert Sklar's *F. Scott Fitzgerald: The Last Laocoön* (Oxford), 1967. Alfred Kazin edited a collection of critical essays by various hands, *F. Scott Fitzgerald: The Man and His Work* (World), 1951.

Maxwell Geismar edited *The Portable Thomas Wolfe* (Viking), 1946. *The Short Novels of Thomas Wolfe*, edited by C. Hugh Holman (Scribner's), appeared in 1961. Elizabeth Nowell's *Letters of Thomas Wolfe* (Scribner's), was published in 1956, her *Thomas Wolfe: A Biography* (Doubleday) in 1960. The most recent biography is Andrew Turnbull's *Thomas Wolfe* (Scribner's), 1967. Critical and interpretive studies are Louis D. Rubin, Jr., *Thomas Wolfe: The Weather of His Youth* (Louisiana State), 1955; Floyd C. Watkins, *Thomas Wolfe's Characters: Portraits from Life* (Oklahoma), 1957; and Bruce R. McElderry, *Thomas Wolfe* (Twayne), 1963. Richard S. Kennedy, *The Window of Memory: The Literary Career of Thomas Wolfe* (North Carolina), 1962, sets straight the publishing history of Wolfe's novels as well as offers critical insights. Two collections of briefer critical essays are Richard Walser, ed., *The Enigma of Thomas Wolfe* (Harvard), 1953, and C. Hugh Holman, ed., *The World of Thomas Wolfe* (Scribner's), 1962.

In 1953, Scribner's began issuing a uniform edition of the collected works of Ernest Hemingway. The Modern Library edition of *The Stories of Ernest Hemingway* (1942) contains forty-nine stories and the play, *The Fifth Column*. Malcolm Cowley selected *The Sun Also Rises*, twenty-five stories, and excerpts from three novels for *The Portable Hemingway* (Viking), 1944. Charles Poore edited *The Hemingway Reader* (Scribner's), 1953. The first biography is Carlos Baker's *Ernest Hemingway: A Life Story* (Scribner's), 1969. Lillian Ross, *Portrait of Hemingway* (Simon and Schuster), 1961, is a frank, journalistic treatment of the man. The major critical study is Carlos Baker, *Hemingway: The Writer as Artist* (Princeton), 1952, 4th ed., 1972. Briefer critical estimates are Philip Young, *Ernest Hemingway* (Rinehart), 1952, enlarged as *Ernest Hemingway: A Reconsideration* (Pennsylvania State University), 1966; Sheridan Baker, *Ernest Hemingway* (Barnes and Noble), 1967; and Richard B. Hovey, *Hemingway: The Inward Terrain* (University of Washington), 1968, a psychoanalytic study. Charles Fenton treats the early years in *The Apprenticeship of Ernest Hemingway* (Farrar), 1954.

There is no collected edition of William Faulkner, but almost all of the novels are in print. *Collected Stories* (Random) appeared in 1950, *The Faulkner Reader* (Random) in 1954. Malcolm Cowley's selections for *The Portable Faulkner* (Viking), 1946, are excellent; his introduction is an important critical essay. There is as yet no biography, but the first chapter of Michael Millgate's major critical study, *The Achievement of William Faulkner* (Random), 1966, serves as a valuable profile. Full-length critical estimates are Hyatt H. Waggoner, *William Faulkner: From Jefferson to the World* (Kentucky), 1959, Olga Vickery, *The Novels of William Faulkner* (Louisiana State), 1959, rev. ed., 1964; and Cleanth Brooks, *William*

Faulkner: The Yoknapatawpha Country (Yale), 1963. Warren Beck, *Man in Motion: Faulkner's Trilogy* (Wisconsin), 1961, treats the Snopes novels. Frederick J. Hoffman and Olga Vickery edited *William Faulkner: Three Decades of Criticism* (Michigan State), 1960.

Critical estimates of John Steinbeck are Peter Lisca, *The Wide World of John Steinbeck* (Rutgers), 1958, and Warren French, *John Steinbeck* (Twayne), 1961. E. W. Tedlock, Jr., and C. V. Wicker edited *Steinbeck and His Critics: A Record of Twenty-Five Years* (New Mexico), 1957. John H. Wrenn, *John Dos Passos* (Twayne), 1961, is a useful introduction. At this time there is no full-length study of James T. Farrell, but Edgar M. Branch provided an informative pamphlet, *James T. Farrell* (Minnesota), 1963.

For estimates of recent dramatists, see the section preceding. A collection of Maxwell Anderson's plays is in *Eleven Verse Plays, 1929–1939* (Harcourt, Brace), 1940. Clifford Odets's early plays have been collected in one volume: *Six Plays* (Modern Library), 1939. Likewise Thornton Wilder's *Three Plays* (Harper), 1957. Lillian Hellman's *Collected Plays* (Little, Brown) appeared in 1972.

The bibliographies of writers whose careers began after 1945 are implicit in the text of this *History*.

INDEX

Abbot, Francis Ellingwood, 975
Abolitionists. *See* Civil War
Achenwall, Gottfried, 679
Acrelius, Israel, 31
Adair, James, 759
Adams, Andy, 864, *872*
Adams, Brooks, 1095, 1096
Adams, Charles Francis (1807–1886), 509
Adams, Charles Francis (1835–1915), 1081, 1082–1083, 1095
Adams, Franklin P., 757, 1131
Adams, Henry, 81, 430, 507, 509, 539, 544, 615, 639, 794, *796–797*, 812, 948, 987, 1051, 1065, 1067, *1080–1103*, 1111, 1140, 1509; historical writings, 539, *1084–1088;* marriage, 1088–1089, 1090; medievalism, 1085, 1100; oriental influence, 1081, 1092–1093, 1094–1095, 1100, 1102; philosophy of history, 1085–1087, 1095, 1096, 1097, 1100; symbolism, *1091–1093*, 1100, 1101, 1102; unity and multiplicity, 1098, 1099, 1100, 1101, 1102; *Burr*, 1088; *The Degradation of the Democratic Dogma*, 1098; *Democracy*, 615, 1090–1091; *The Education of Henry Adams*, 1080, 1090, 1097, 1098, 1099, 1101–1102; *Essays in Anglo-Saxon Law*, 1085; *Esther*, 1090–1091, 1095; *History of the United States of America during the Administrations of Thomas Jefferson and James Madison*, 639, 1086–1088, 1489; *A Letter to American Teachers of History*, 1098; *Mont-Saint-Michel and Chartres*, 1080, 1090, 1096, 1097, 1099–1101; *Randolph*, 1088
Adams, Herbert B., 799, 804
Adams, John, 37, 98, 120, 132, 134, 137, *146–161*, 163, 167, 543, 1087, 1489; *A Dissertation on the Canon and Feudal Law*, 134; *Works*, 1083

Adams, John Quincy, 127, 158, 220, 558, 563, 668, 1087
Adams, Léonie, 1435
Adams, Samuel, 12, 116, 124
Addams, Jane, 949, 1113, 1255
Addison, Joseph, 19, 94, 124, 151
Ade, George, 750, 754
Adler, Karl, 683
Aestheticism, 1076, 1078, 1241, 1365, 1368, 1371. *See also* Bohemianism; Criticism, literary
Agrarian movement, 233, 760–762, 791. *See also* Grangers; Industrialism; Populism
Aiken, Conrad, 1173, *1352*, 1376, 1396, 1399, 1517
Akhmatova, Anna, 1442
Albee, Edward, 1425, *1454–1455*, 1468; *All Over*, 1455; *The American Dream*, 1454; *Box*, 1455; *The Ballad of the Sad Cafe*, 1464; *A Delicate Balance*, 1455; *Quotations from Chairman Mao Tse-Tung*, 1455; *Who's Afraid of Virginia Woolf?* 1454–1455; *Zoo Story*, 1454, 1455
Alcott, Amos Bronson, 229, 346, 374, 375, 388, 399, 405, 407, 409, 564, 566, 654
Alcott, Louisa May, 1383
Alden, Henry Mills, 805, 957
Aldington, Richard, 1174, 1184, 1187, 1188
Aldrich, Thomas Bailey, 809, *810*, 811, 812, 814, *823–825*, 833, 899, 1157; *The Story of a Bad Boy*, 746, 810, 930
Aldridge, John W., 1422
Aleichem, Shalom (Solomon Rabinowitz), 693
Alger, Horatio, 801
Algren, Nelson, 1461; *The Man with the Golden Arm*, 1461; *A Walk on the Wild Side*, 1461
Allan, John, 322
Allen, Ethan, 141

Allen, Hervey, 1267, 1382, 1384
Allen, James Lane, 850, 1376
Allen, Samantha, 828
Allen, Viola, 1012
Allen, William Francis, 648
Allouez, Claude, 28
Almanacs, 63
Alsop, George, 38, 42-43, 49
Alsop, Richard, 168
Alta California, 865, 866, 929
Altgeld, John P., 1107, 1108, 1255
American Antiquarian Society, 646
American Ethnological Society, 647
American Journal of Archaeology, 830
American Magazine, 52
American Magazine and Monthly Chronicle (1757-1758), 96, 97
American Mercury, 1144, 1359
American Museum, 127
American Philosophical Society, 23
American Speech, 670
Americanization. *See* Immigration
Ames, Nathaniel (1708-1764), 652
Ames, Nathaniel (d. 1835), 447
Ammons, A. R., 1433; *Collected Papers 1951-1971*, 1433
Anarchiad, The, 168
Anderson, Hugh, 48
Anderson, Maxwell, 1318, *1320-1323*, 1394, 1402, 1520; *Elizabeth the Queen*, 1320; *Gods of the Lightning*, 1321, 1322; *Key Largo*, 1321, 1322-1323; *Mary of Scotland*, 1321; *What Price Glory?* 1243, 1317, 1318, 1320; *Winterset*, 1321, 1322, 1394
Anderson, Robert, 1451; *Tea and Sympathy*, 1451
Anderson, Sherwood, 1120, *1229-1233*, 1234, 1236, 1296, 1359, 1385; bibliography, 1514; *Many Marriages*, 1231; *A Story Teller's Story*, 1229; *The Triumph of the Egg*, 1230, 1232; *Winesburg, Ohio*, 1230, 1232
Annuals and gift books, 235, 289
Anti-Jacobin, 620
Antin, Mary, 691
Antislavery writing. *See* Slavery
Antoninus, Brother (William Everson), 1431
Apollinaire, Guillaume, 1442, 1443
Appleton's Journal, 793

Archdale, John, 38
Ark, The, 1432
Armand (Friedrich A. Strubberg), 681
Arnold, Matthew, 230, 486, 818, 825, 1136
Arp, Bill (Charles Henry Smith), 571, 744
Art and architecture, bibliography of, 1482
Arthur, Timothy Shay, 226, 524
Arvin, Newton, 1362, 1363
Asbury, Francis, 225, 653
Asch, Sholem, 693
Ash, Thomas, 38
Ashbery, John, 1443; *Some Trees*, 1443, *The Tennis Court Oath*, 1443; *Three Poems*, 1443
Asimov, Isaac, 1472
Astor, John Jacob, 240
Athenaeum Magazine, 300, 620
Atherton, Gertrude, 688
Atlanta *Constitution*, 648
Atlantic Monthly, 238, 368, 503, 520, 527, 602, 648, 650, 689, 793, 794, 804, 810, 814, 824, 839, 866, 873, 887, 888, 892, 932, 933, 979, 1034, 1084
Auchincloss, Louis, 1407, 1513
Auden, W. H., 1312, 1378, 1427, 1516
Audubon, John James, 93, 394, 656
Aycock, Charles, 1108

Babbitt, Irving, 1136, *1148-1150*, 1151, 1360, 1371, 1398; *Democracy and Leadership*, 1149; *Humanism in America*, 1149; *Literature and the American College*, 1148; *The Masters of Modern French Criticism*, 1149; *The New Laokoon*, 1149; *Rousseau and Romanticism*, 1149
Bacheller, Irving, 752, 963, 1377
Bacon, Francis, 94, 368, 375, 380
Bacon, Nathaniel, 49
Bagby, George W., 848-849
Bailey, J. M., 828
Baker, Howard, 1353
Baker, Ray Stannard, 993, 1125
Baker, William Mumford, 571
Baldwin, James, 1423, 1458, *1468; Another Country*, 1468; *Blues for Mr. Charlie*, 1458; *Go Tell It on the Mountain*, 1468; *No Name in the Street*, 1423; *Notes of a Native Son*, 1423; *Tell Me How Long the Train's Been Gone*, 1468

Baldwin, Joseph G., 657, 741

Ballads, 705–715. *See also* Songs

Baltimore. *See* Cities and towns

Bancroft, George, 230, 527, 610, 645, 1086, bibliography, 1499

Bancroft, Hubert Howe, 661

Bandelier, Adolph, 647

Baraka, Imamu Amiri (LeRoi Jones), 1444, 1458; *Black Magic: Poetry 1961–1967,* 1444; *Dutchman,* 1444, 1458; *The Toilet,* 1444

Barker, James Nelson, *187–188,* 281

Barlow, Joel, 129, *166–168,* 169, 173, 197, 668, 1491; *Advice to the Privileged Orders,* 166; *The Columbiad,* 168, 620; *The Conspiracy of Kings,* 166; *Hasty Pudding,* 167; *The Vision of Columbus,* 167, 168, 197

Barnard, Henry, 226

Barnes, Djuna, 1468

Barry, Philip, 1006, *1324*

Barth, John, 1425, 1469, *1471; Chimera,* 1471; *The End of the Road,* 1471; *The Floating Opera,* 1471; *Giles Goat-Boy,* 1471; *Lost in the Fun House,* 1471; *The Sot-Weed Factor,* 1471

Barth, Karl, 1418

Barthelme, Donald, 1470; *City Life,* 1470; *Sadness,* 1470; *Snow White,* 1470

Bartlett, John Russell, 666, *669–670*

Bartol, C. A., 828

Bartram, John, 91, 1488

Bartram, William, *92–93,* 203, 1488

Battle of Brooklyn, The, 185

Baudelaire, Charles, 321, 324, 341, 630

Bay Psalm Book, 20, 63, 69

Beach, Rex, 1385, 1387

Beadle, Erastus, 291

Beard, Charles A., 1154, 1260, 1284

Beat movement, 1416, 1418, 1425, 1431, 1466

Beaufain, Adrian (William Gilmore Simms), 230, 239, 240, 308, *311–313, 316–317,* 318, 319, 320, 378, 567, 608, 610, 681

Beecher, Henry Ward, 239, 503, 519, 554, 556, 655, 800, 802, 975

Beecher, Lyman, 225, 581–582, 653

Beecroft, John, 1268

Beer, Thomas, 1066

Behrman, S. N., 1320, *1323–1326,* 1402; *Biography,* 1324–1325; *Brief Moment,* 1324;

Rain from Heaven, 1325–1326; *The Second Man,* 1324

Beissel, Conrad, 678

Belasco, David, 1000, 1004, *1008–1010,* 1015

Bell, Alexander Graham, 803

Bellamy, Edward, 795, 973, 986, 988, *989–992,* 999, 1361, 1508; *Equality,* 991; *Looking Backward,* 989–991

Bellow, Saul, 1425, 1452, 1465, *1473–1474; The Adventures of Augie March,* 1473; *Dangling Man,* 1473; *Henderson the Rain King,* 1473, 1474; *Herzog,* 1474; *The Last Analysis,* 1452; *Mr. Sammler's Planet,* 1474; *Seize the Day,* 1474; *The Victim,* 1465, 1473

Ben-Ami, Jacob, 693

Benchley, Robert, 756

Benedict, E. C., 829

Benét, Stephen Vincent, 716, 1349, *1350–1351; The Devil and Daniel Webster,* 722; *John Brown's Body,* 716, *1350; Western Star,* 1351

Benét, William Rose, 1172

Benezet, Anthony, 141

Bennett, James Gordon, 241

Benson, Eugene, 831

Bentley, William, 349

Benton, Thomas Hart, 557

Berdyaev, Nicolas, 1418

Berger, Thomas, 1470; *Crazy in Berlin,* 1470; *Killing Time,* 1470; *Little Big Man,* 1470

Berrigan, Ted, 1443; *The Sonnets,* 1443

Berkeley, Sir William, 49

Berryman, John, 1425, 1426, 1427, 1438, *1439–1440; Berryman's Sonnets,* 1439; *77 Dream Songs,* 1439; *385 Dream Songs,* 1440; *Delusions,* 1440; *The Dispossessed,* 1439; *His Toy, His Dream, His Rest,* 1439; *Homage to Mistress Bradstreet,* 1439; *Love & Fame,* 1440; *Poems,* 1439

Best, William, 49

Best sellers. *See* Literature as business

Bester, Alfred, 1472

Beveridge, Albert J., 560

Beverley, Robert, 38, *44,* 53, 116

Biddle, Nicholas, *763–764,* 772

Bierce, Ambrose, 633, 661, 755, 866, 1021, *1068–1070; Black Beetles in Amber,* 1068; *Can Such Things Be?* 1069; *Collected*

Works, 1068; *The Devil's Dictionary,* 1069; *The Monk and the Hangman's Daughter,* 1069; *Tales of Soldiers and Civilians,* 1069; *Write It Right,* 1068
Bigelow, John, 301
Bigelow, Sturgis, 1092
Billings, Josh (Henry Wheeler Shaw), 524, 744-745
Biörck, Tobias Erick, 31
Bird, Robert Montgomery, 239, 270, 276, 281, 282, 283, 1001, 1002
Birkbeck, Morris, 762
Bishop, Elizabeth, 1433, *1436; A Cold Spring,* 1436; *North & South,* 1436; *Questions of Travel,* 1436
Bitzaron, 692
Black, Jeremiah H., 558
Black consciousness, 1423, 1444, 1458-1459, 1467-1468
Black Mountain Group, 1425, 1429, 1430
Black Mountain Review, 1430
Black Power Movement, 1416, 1420, 1468
Black Theatre, 1459
Blackburn, Paul, 1430
Blackmur, R. P., 1155, 1360, 1369, *1371,* 1394, 1395, 1510
Blackwood's Magazine, 290, 620
Blaine, James G., 559, 790, 791
Blair, James, 43-44, 814
Blair, Robert, 296
Blitzstein, Marc, 1327, 1453; *Regina,* 1453
Bloom, Harold, 1422, *1423*
Bly, Robert, 1440, *1441-1442,* 1444; *The Lion's Tale and Eyes,* 1441; *Silence in the Snowy Fields,* 1441; *Sleepers Joining Hands,* 1444
Boas, Franz, 1284
Bodenheim, Maxwell, 1239
Bodin, Jean, 37
Bogan, Louise, 1435, 1512
Bohemianism, *1065-1079,* 1155
Bok, Edward William, 957, 960
Boker, George Henry, 238-239, 524, 809, *810,* 813, *823,* 825, 826, *1001-1003; Anne Boleyn,* 1002; *Book of the Dead,* 813, *823; Calaynos,* 1002; *Francesca da Rimini,* 238, 1002-1003; *Leonor de Guzman,* 1002; *Plays and Poems,* 823; *Poems of the War,* 823

Bollingen Prize for Poetry, 1398, 1428
Bonnefoy, Yves, 1442
Book collecting, 19
Book trade. *See* Literature as business
Bookman, 1067
Book-of-the-Month Club, 1267
Booksellers, 125, 239, 1121. *See also* Printing and publishing
Boone, Daniel, 737, 760
Booth, Edwin, 1000
Booth, Philip, 1445
Borges, Jorge Luis, 1442
Boston. *See* Cities and towns
Boston Athenaeum, 293
Boston *Courier,* 1084
Boston *Daily Advertiser,* 1084
Boston *Evening-Post,* 22
Boston *News-Letter,* 21
Botta, Carlo Giuseppe Guglielmo, 200
Botkin, Maud, 1395
Boucher, Jonathan, 137, 669
Boucicault, Dion, 514, *1003-1004,* 1007
Bourke, John G., 647
Bourne, Randolph, 1136, *1137-1138,* 1141, 1358, 1359; *The History of a Literary Radical,* 1138; *Untimely Papers,* 1138; *Youth and Life,* 1137
Bowles, Jane, 1452; *In the Summer House,* 1452
Bowles, Paul, *1466; Let It Come Down,* 1466; *The Sheltering Sky,* 1466
Bowles, Samuel, 770, 909
Boyd, Ernest, 1155
Boyd, James, 717
Boyesen, Hjalmar Hjorth, 689, 814, 988
Boyle, Kay, 1296, 1314
Brace, Charles Loring, 509
Brackenridge, Henry Marie, 764, 1502
Brackenridge, Hugh Henry, 95, 123, 143, 169, *178-180,* 640, 656, 730, 771, 1491; *Modern Chivalry,* 178-180, 190, 764; *The Rising Glory of America,* 95, 169
Bradbury, Ray, 1472
Bradford, Andrew, 22
Bradford, Roark, 721
Bradford, William (1590-1657), 34, 1486
Bradford, William (1663-1752), 21
Bradstreet, Anne, *63-64,* 65
Bradstreet, Simon, 63

Braithwaite, W. S., 1173
Brandeis, Louis D., 691, 1107, 1111, 1258, 1282
Brannan, Sam, 865
Brand, Stewart, 1424
Brautigan, Richard, 1470; *In Watermelon Sugar*, 1470; *Trout Fishing in America*, 1470
Bray, Thomas, 20
Brébeuf, Jean de, 28
Breitmann, Hans (Charles Godfrey Leland), 683, 752
Breslin, Jimmy, 1424
Bright, John, 502, 509
Brightman, Edgar Sheffield, 1288
Brinnin, John Malcolm, 1427, 1484
Bristed, Charles Astor, 669
Bristed, John, 206
Broadway Journal, 281
Brockett, Linus P., 792
Brodsky, Joseph, 1442
Bromfield, Louis, 1264, 1380
Brook Farm, 375, 416, 418, 646
Brooklyn *Daily Eagle*, 473, 474, 475
Brooks, Cleanth, 617, 1371, 1395, 1516
Brooks, Gwendolyn, 1444; *Annie Allen*, 1444; *A Street in Bronzeville*, 1444
Brooks, Van Wyck, 1136, 1137, *1138–1141*, 1155, 1358, 1359, 1360, 1397, 1484, 1492, 1500, 1507, 1511; *America's Coming of Age*, 1137, 1139, 1364, 1511; *Emerson*, 1140; *The Flowering of New England*, 1141, 1313; *New England: Indian Summer*, 1141, 1500; *The Ordeal of Mark Twain*, 1139–1140, 1507; *The Pilgrimage of Henry James*, 1140; *Sketches in Criticism*, 1140; *The Wine of the Puritans*, 1138; *The World of Washington Irving*, 1141, 1492; *The Writer in America*, 1511
Brown, Charles Brockden, 125, 127, 129, 175, *181–184*, 287, 620, 640, 1491; *Arthur Mervyn*, 181, 183; *Clara Howard*, 181, 183, 184; *Edgar Huntly*, 181, 183, 184, *Jane Talbot*, 181, 183; *Ormond*, 181, 183, 184; *Wieland*, 181, 182–183, 190, 274
Brown, Dee, 1502
Brown, John, 301, 406, 505
Brown, John Carter, 644
Brown, Norman O., 1418, *1419*

Brown, Solyman, 298
Brown, Sterling A., 749
Brown, William Hill, 177
Browne, Charles Farrar, 633, 729, 742–743, 784, 828, 921, 1130
Browne, Dunn, 828
Browne, Francis F., 568
Brownell, Henry Howard, 570
Brownell, William Crary, 1136, 1146–1148, 1152, 1365; *American Prose Masters*, 1146; *Criticism*, 1147; *Democratic Distinction in America*, 1147; *French Art*, 1146; *French Traits*, 1146; *The Genius of Style*, 1147; *Standards*, 1147; *Victorian Prose Masters*, 1146
Brownlow, William G., 508
Brownson, Orestes A., 375, 434
Brulé, Etienne, 28
Brunner, Emil, 1287
Bryan, William Jennings, 560, 1107, 1108, 1111, 1115
Bryant, Edwin, 768
Bryant, Peter, 294–295
Bryant, William Cullen, 130, 173, 176, 239, 240, 241, 284, 286, 287, 290, 294–305, 346, 378, 491, 569, 715, 775, 812, 822, bibliography, 1492–1493; *The Embargo*, 295, 296; *Iliad*, 822; *Letters from the East*, 302; *Letters of a Traveller*, 302; *A Library of Poetry and Song*, 302; *Poems*, 299
Bryce, James, 800, 1111
Buber, Martin, 1418
Buchanan, Scott, 1280
Büchile, Karl, 679
Buck, Pearl, 1262, 1266, 1296, 1375, 1380, 1382, 1383, 1384, 1386, 1388–1389
Buckminster, Joseph Stevens, 232
Budd, Thomas, 37–38
Buechner, Frederick, 1463; *A Long Day's Dying*, 1463
Bulkeley, John, 69
Bullins, Ed, *1459; The Electronic Nigger and Others*, 1459; *The Fabulous Miss Marie*, 1459
Bunyan, John, 420
Bunyan, Paul, 713, 720
Burgoyne, John, 186
Burgum, Edwin Berry, 1362
Burke, Edmund, 166

Burke, Fielding, 1313
Burke, Kenneth, 1360, 1362, 1364, 1369, 1371, 1394
Burnett, Frances Hodgson, 1381
Burns, John Horne, 1462; *The Gallery,* 1462
Burritt, Elihu, 226
Burroughs, Edgar Rice, 1377, 1380
Burroughs, John, 414, 873
Burroughs, William, 1425, *1467, 1472; Naked Lunch,* 1467; *Nova Express,* 1472; *The Soft Machine,* 1472, *The Ticket That Exploded, 1472*
Burwell Papers, 49
Byles, Mather, 69
Bynner, Witter, 1172
Byrd, William, 19, 41, 44, *45–46,* 48, 53, 1488; *A Discourse Concerning the Plague with Some Preservatives Against It,* 45; *History of the Dividing Line,* 45; *A Journey to the Land of Eden,* 46; *A Progress to the Mines in the Year 1732,* 46
Byron, George Gordon, 174, 287, 288, 291, 321, 322, 323, 324

Cabell, James Branch, 1078, 1218, *1219–1222,* 1236, 1296, 1513; *Beyond Life,* 1078; *Jurgen,* 1219–1220, 1221
Cable, George Washington, 678, 687, 791, *855–858,* 1505; *The Grandissimes,* 856, 857; *Old Creole Days,* 857
Cage, John, *1423–1424,* 1429, 1443; *Silence,* 1424, 1443; *A Year from Monday,* 1424, 1443
Cahan, Abraham, 691, 693
Cain, James M., 1314
Caldwell, Ben, 1459; *Riot Sale,* 1459
Caldwell, Erskine, 724, 1256, 1407
Calhoun, John C., 223, 227, 545, 551–553, 567, 1498
California. *See* West
California Star, 865
Calverton, Victor Francis, 1154, 1361
Calvinism, 74–77, 86, 87, 364
Cambridge. *See* Cities and towns
Campbell, John, 21
Campbell, Joseph, 1418
Campbell, Thomas, 176, 277
Camus, Albert, 1418
Canby, Henry Seidel, 1127, 1153

Canonge, Louis-Placide, 685
Capote, Truman, 1424, *1464, 1471; The Grass Harp,* 1464; *In Cold Blood,* 1471; *Other Voices, Other Rooms,* 1464
Carey, Mathew, 124, 125, 126
Caritat, William, 125
Carleton, Henry Guy, 1008
Carleton, Will, 716, 863, 865, 866, *871*
Carlyle, Thomas, 349, 367, 375, 376, 382, 383, 385, 390, 393, 399, 474, 1083
Carman, Bliss, 1067, 1171
Carnegie, Andrew, 805, 812, 949, 1109, 1110, 1111
Carroll, Paul, 1430
Carson, Kit, 768, 1258
Carson, Rachel, 1420
Carter, Robert, 53
Cartwright, Peter, 225
Caruthers, William Alexander, *310–311,* 610, 612
Carver, Jonathan, *759–760*
Casey, Michael, 1444; *Obscenities,* 1444
Casket, 237
Cason, Clarence, 1257
Cassirer, Ernst, 1395
Castañeda, Pedro, 26
Caterpillar, 1430
Cather, Willa, 678, 688, 863, 1120, *1212–1216,* 1217, 1218, 1219, 1222, 1223, 1227, 1229, 1236, 1314, 1359, 1375, 1393, 1505, bibliography, 1513–1514; *Death Comes for the Archbishop,* 1212, 1214; *A Lost Lady,* 1212, 1215; *My Ántonia,* 1212, 1214; *Not Under Forty,* 1213; *O Pioneers!* 1212, 1213, 1214, 1215
Catherwood, Mary Hartwell, 868
Catholicism, 14, 27–29, 56–57, 658, 687, 944, 970–971
Catlin, George, *646–647,* 771
Cawein, Madison, 1171
Cayton, Horace, 1315
Censorship, 21, 813, 953, 954, 1134
Century, 647, 793, 805, 953, 956, 957, 959, 964
Chalkley, Thomas, 84
Champlain, Samuel de, 26–27, 34
Chanler, Margaret, 1096
Channing, Edward Tyrrel, 234, 390
Channing, William Ellery (1780–1842), 86,

225, 226, 232, 284, 285, 286, 287, 292, 295, 298, 304, 334, 346, 347, 564, 621, 1091

Channing, William Ellery (1818–1901), 364, 365, 374, 388, 399, 405

Chanteys. *See* Ballads; Songs

Chap-Book, 1067

Char, René, 1441, 1442

Charleston. *See* Cities and towns

Charlevoix, Pierre François Xavier de, 758–759

Chase, Mary, 1332

Chase, Richard, 1396

Chase, Samuel, 142

Chase, Stuart, 1257

Chateaubriand, François René, Vicomte de, 203, 204, 760

Chautauqua movement, 798–799, 955, 1123

Chayevsky, Paddy, 1451; *Middle of the Night,* 1451

Cheever, John, *1469–1470; The Wapshot Chronicle,* 1470; *The Wapshot Scandal,* 1470

Chesnutt, Charles Waddell, 854–855

Chevalier, Michel, 213

Chicago. *See* Cities and towns

Child, Francis James, 648, 674, 705

Child, Lydia Maria, 292, *293,* 565

Chilton, Edward, 43

Chivers, Thomas Holley, 315–317, 449

Choate, Rufus, 558

Chopin, Kate, 687, *858–859*

Chronicles. *See* Frontier; Regionalism and local color; Reports and chronicles

Churchill, Winston, 610, 1118, 1122

Churchman, John, 84–85

Ciardi, John, 1427

Cities and towns, culture of: Baltimore, 306–309; Boston, 231–232, 284, 285, 286, 287, 294; Cambridge, 587–588; Charleston, 308, 311–313; Chicago, 796; Concord, 231–232, 416; New Orleans, 659, 678, 855–859; New York, 231, 271, 287; Philadelphia, 96; Plymouth, 34, 35; Salem, 417; San Francisco, 660–662

City Gazette, 311

Civil War, 227, 301, *501–512,* 568–572, 579; abolitionists, 226, 292, 293, 301, 563–568,

574–575, 583–584; oratory, 542, 545, 548, 558; songs, 709

Clark, Lewis Gaylord, 241, 252

Clark, William, *763–764,* 771, 772

Clarke, James Freeman, 802

Classicism, 284, 286

Classics, influence of, 41, 45, 96, 149, 160

Clay, Henry, 227, 302, 545, *546–548,* 1498

Cleaver, Eldridge, 1420

Clemens, Jeremiah, 571

Clemens, Samuel Langhorne, 341, 525, 609, 634–635, 650, 661, 662, 729, 742, 745, 748, 789, 792, 794, 800, 801, 806–807, 820, *837–838,* 858, 863, 864, 865, 880, 897, *917–939,* 943, 948, 999, 1016, 1080, 1096, 1130, 1139, 1381, 1385, 1386, 1390, bibliography, 1507–1508; *The American Claimant,* 928; *The Celebrated Jumping Frog of Calaveras County and Other Sketches,* 865, 921; *A Connecticut Yankee in King Arthur's Court,* 634, 838, 934, 935; *Following the Equator,* 926; *The Gilded Age,* 864, 918, 924, 926–928; *Huckleberry Finn,* 609, 650, 918, 928–934, 1383; *The Innocents Abroad,* 829, 837, 921; *Life on the Mississippi,* 897, 919, 928–934; *The Mysterious Stranger,* 938–939; *Personal Recollections of Joan of Arc,* 934, 935; *The Prince and the Pauper,* 934; *Pudd'nhead Wilson,* 920, 924, *936; Roughing It,* 919–920, 923, 924; *Tom Sawyer,* 745, 918, 928–933; *Tom Sawyer Abroad,* 933; *Tom Sawyer, Detective,* 933; *A Tramp Abroad,* 838, 919, 925, 926; *What Is Man?* 937

Clinton, George, 142

Clubs, literary and cultural, 23, 123, 129, 239, 374, 957, 1067

Cobb, Irvin S., 752–753

Cobden, Richard, 209

Cogswell, Mason Fitch, 168

Cohan, George M., 1318

Colden, Cadwallader, 89–90

Cole, Thomas, 302, 304

Coleridge, Samuel Taylor, 286, 287, 324, 328, 337, 349, 350, 369, 370, 374

Colfax, Schuyler, 770

Colleges. *See* Education

Collier's, 960, 965

Colonial life and culture, 16–23; reports and

chronicles, 24–39; in the South, 40–53; in New England, 54–70; in the Middle Colonies, 82–100; struggle for independence, 115–118; bibliography, 1485–1488

Columbian, 127

Columbus, Christopher, 25

Columnists, 1130–1132

"Comedians," 128

Commercial Advertiser, 300

Communism, 1110, 1116, 1255, 1265, *1360–1365,* 1368, 1372. *See also* Labor movement; Marx; Industrialism; Socialism

Communitarian experiments, 646, 676. *See also* Transcendentalism; Utopianism

Comptes Rendus, 687

Comte, Auguste, 947, 980, 1096

Concord. *See* Cities and towns

Concord School of Philosophy, 375, 972

Concretism, 1443

Confessional poets, 1440

Conkling, Roscoe, 790, 791

Connecticut Wits, 120, 128, 162, 168, 169, 287, 1491

Connelly, Marc, 717, 1243, 1331

Conrad, Robert T., 1001

Conroy, Jack, 1385

Constitution, Federal, 221

Constitutional Convention, 119. *See also* Democracy

Conwell, Russell H., 801

Cook, Ebenezer, 51, 730

Cook, George Cram, 1239

Cooke, John Esten, 128, *316,* 571, 608, 610, 613, 849

Cooke, Philip Pendleton, 316, 610, 613

Cooke, Rose Terry, 573, 844

Coolbrith, Ina, 661, 866

Cooper, James Fenimore, 123, 125, 126, 130, 168, 176, 181, 183, 188, 203–204, 236, 237, 239, 241, 243, *253–269,* 271, 284, 291, 302, 304, 610, *623–624,* 644, 646, 669, 677, 715, 718, 732, 761, *772–773,* 1096, 1378, 1385, bibliography, 1492; European reputation of, 203–204, 623–624; theme of the frontier, 253, 257, 258, 261, 266; theories about literature, 256–258; *Afloat and Ashore,* 267; *The Bravo,* 624; *The Deerslayer,* 264, 266, 267; *Gleanings in Europe,* 623; *The Last of the Mohicans,* 262–263; *Leatherstocking Tales,* 254, 269, 1375; *A Letter to His Countrymen,* 265; *Lionel Lincoln,* 262; *The Littlepage Manuscripts,* 267, 268–269; *Miles Wallingford,* 267–268; *Notions of the Americans,* 623; *The Pathfinder,* 264–266; *The Pilot,* 261–262; *The Pioneers,* 254, 260, 624; *The Prairie,* 264, *772–773; Precaution,* 254, 256, 261; *The Red Rover,* 264, 624; *Satanstoe,* 274; *The Spy,* 125, 261, 624; *The Water Witch,* 264; *The Wept of Wish-ton-Wish,* 264

Cooper, Myles, 137

Cooper, Thomas, 153

Cooper Union, 230

Coover, Robert, 1473; *The Universal Baseball Association,* 1473

Copyright, 126, 236–237, 238, 334, 523, 621–622, *807, 961–962,* 964, 966, 1000

Coronado, Francisco Vásquez, 26

Corso, Gregory, 1431

Cortez Hernando, 26, 33

Corwin, Thomas, 558

Costain, Thomas, 1268

Cotton, John, 55

Cousin, Victor, 349

Cowley, Malcolm, 1360, 1361

Cowper, William, 165, 296

Coxe, Tench, 143, 144, 145; *View of the United States,* 145

Coyner, David H., 771

Cozzens, James Gould, *1403, 1409–1410,* 1513; *Ask Me Tomorrow,* 1409; *By Love Possessed,* 1410, 1411; *Guard of Honor,* 1403, 1407, 1410; *The Just and the Unjust,* 1410; *The Last Adam,* 1409; *Men and Brethren,* 1409, 1410, 1411

Craddock, Charles Egbert (Mary Noailles Murfree), 791, 850–851

Craigie, Pearl, 1376

Cramoisy, Sébastien, 27

Crane, Hart, 1263, *1344–1345,* 1387, 1394, bibliography, 1517; *The Bridge,* 1344–1345; *White Buildings,* 1344

Crane, Ronald S., 1395

Crane, Stephen, 825, 1016, 1017, *1020–1026,* 1027, 1080, 1118, 1135, 1197, 1376, 1439, bibliography, 1509; *Active Service,* 1025; *The Black Riders,* 899; *George's Mother,*

1025; *Maggie*, 1022, 1023, 1118; *The Monster*, 1025; *The O'Ruddy*, 1025; *The Red Badge of Courage*, 635, 1021, *1022-1023*, 1078; *The Third Violet*, 1022; *War Is Kind*, 1157; *Whilomville Stories*, 746, 1025

Crashaw, Richard, 66

Crawford, F. Marion, *832*, 1017, 1381

Creeley, Robert, 1429, *1430; For Love: Poems 1950-1960*, 1430

Creoles, 684-687

Crèvecoeur, St. Jean de, 42, 196, 677, 1491

Criticism, literary, 290, 541-542, 893, 897, *1135-1156, 1358-1373*, 1515-1516. See also Aestheticism; Humanism; Ideality; Imagists; Naturalism; Realism; Romanticism; Vorticism

Crockett, Davy, 221, 651, *737-738*, 866, 1258

Croly, Herbert, 1107

Crothers, Rachel, 1006, 1011

Cullen, Countee, 749, 1314

Cummings, E. E., 1351-1352, 1396, 1399, 1443, 1516, 1517

Cunningham, J. V., 1433

Curtis, George William, 812, 833

Curwood, James Oliver, 1380, 1385, 1387

Cushing, Frank Hamilton, 647

Dablon, Claude, 28

Dahlberg, Edward, 1314

d'Ailly, Pierre, 9

Daly, Augustin, *1003, 1004, 1005*, 1010

Daly, T. A., 752

Dana, Richard Henry (1787-1879), 181, 284, *286-287*, 290, 294, 298, 299, 640

Dana, Richard Henry (1815-1882), *293-294*, 776, 865

Da Ponte, Lorenzo, 688

Darwin, Charles, 790, 802, 947, 948, 1021, 1096, 1278-1279

Darwinism, 648, 950, *969-970*, 973, 974, 975

Davidson, Donald, 617, 1371

Davis, Jefferson, 507, 558

Davis, John, 203

Davis, Rebecca Blaine Harding, 573, *880-881*

Davis, Richard Harding, 1026, 1029

Dawson, William, 52

Day, Clarence, 729, *755-756*

Dean, Henry Clay, *794-795*

De Bry, Theodore, 32

Debs, Eugene V., 1108, 1110, 1117

Declaration of Independence, 117, 150, 152

Deep Image movement, 1440, 1441-1442, 1445

De Forest, John William, 571, *840*, 879, *881-885*, 1020, 1506; *European Acquaintance*, 840; *Honest John Vane*, 883; *Kate Beaumont*, 883-884; *A Lover's Revolt*, 884; *Miss Ravenel's Conversion from Secession to Loyalty*, 882-883; *Oriental Acquaintance*, 840; *Overland*, 884; *Playing the Mischief*, 883; *Seacliff*, 882; *A Volunteer's Adventures*, 882; *Witching Times*, 881

Delano, Alonzo, 768

Dell, Floyd, 1235, 1239, 1361

de Man, Paul, 1422

Demby, William, *1468; The Catacombs*, 1468

Democracy, aristocracy in, 117, 118, 223, 610-612; free enterprise, 790, 970; free speech, 22, 301, 976; patronage of literature, 968; theory of, 152-158, 208, 347-349, 353, 799, 1261; world democracy, 1116-1117. See also Fascism, Political and economic philosophy

Democratic Review, 475

De Mott, Benjamin, 1422

Dennie, Joseph, 123, 127, 129, *175-176*, 180, 242, 640

Denton, Daniel, 37, 88

de Otero, Blas, 1442

de Pauw, Cornelius, 204

de Pradt, Dominique Dufour, 207

Derby, George Horatio, 661, 864

De Soto, Hernando, 25

Determinism, 947, 970, 982

Deutsch, Babette, 1516

de Vriers, David Pieterszoon, 30

Dew, Thomas R., 567

Dewey, John, 229, 951, *1277-1282*, 1284, 1285, 1295

Dial (1840-1844), 225, 238, 368, 375, 393, 394, 395; (1880-1929), 1359

Dialect Notes, 670

Dialects. See Language, American

Diaries, 33, 60, 69, 676

Diaz, Bernal, 33

Dickens, Charles, 230, 679, 1003, 1083

Dickey, James 1446; *Selected Poems*, 1446

Dickinson, Anna E., 800

Dickinson, Emily, 242, 378, 525, 825, 900, 903–917, 1080, 1135, 1158, 1160, bibliography, 1506–1507; *Bolts of Melody*, 904; *Further Poems*, 904; *Letters*, 904; *Letters of Emily Dickinson*, 904; *Poems*, 904; *Poems of Emily Dickinson*, 904; *The Single Hound;* 904; *Unpublished Poems*, 904

Dickinson, John, 115, 116, 127, 132, *135–137*, 143; *Letters from a Farmer in Pennsylvania*, 132, 135–136; *Letters of Fabius*, 136, 143

Dictionaries, 664, 666, 669, 670, 671, 1482, 1504

Didion, Joan, 1424

Dix, Dorothea, 226

Dollard, John, 1257

Don Quixote, 179, 180

Donck, Adriaen van der, 30

Doniphan, Alexander, 766

Donleavy, J. P., 1467; *The Ginger Man*, 1467

Donne, John, 42, 66

Donnelly, Ignatius, 1108

Dooley, Mr. (Finley Peter Dunne), 749–751

Doolittle, Hilda, 1174, 1184, *1188–1189*, 1376

Dorn, Edward, 1429

Dos Passos, John, 1264, 1296, *1302–1304*, 1306, 1308, 1312, 1375, 1380, 1382, 1387, 1393, 1394, 1405, 1406, bibliography, 1520; *Adventures of a Young Man*, 1405; *Chosen Country*, 1405; *District of Columbia*, 1405; *The Grand Design*, 1405; *The Great Days*, 1405; *The Ground We Stand On*, 1312, 1405; *Manhattan Transfer*, 1302; *Mid-Century*, 1405–1406; *Most Likely To Succeed*, 1405; *Number One*, 1405; *Rosinante to the Road Again*, 1302; *U.S.A.*, 1302, 1303, 1406

Dostoevski, Feodor, 631

Doughby, Ralph, 681

Douglas, Stephen A., 501, 505, 558, 783

Dougles, David, 48

Downing, Jack (Seba Smith), 651, 732–733

Drake, Joseph Rodman, 127, 174, 176, 277

Drake, St. Clair, 1315

Drama, in colonial days, 23, 127–129; during Revolutionary period, 185–191; from 1820 to 1850, 238–239, 281–283; folk plays, 722–724; from 1850 to 1920, *1000–1015*, 1323; from 1920 to 1945, 693, *1238–1239*, 1242, *1317–1334;* bibliography, 1484, 1514–1515. *See also* Shakespeare

Draper, John W., 802

Dred Scott Decision, 505

Dreiser, Theodore, 863, 1037, 1107, 1120, 1134, 1142, *1197–1207*, 1209, 1217, 1227, 1236, 1296, 1359, 1375, 1381, 1382, 1385, 1392, 1393, bibliography, 1514; *An American Tragedy*, 1087, 1153, 1198, 1199, *1203*, 1206; *The Bulwark*, 1198, *1204*, 1205; *The Financier*, 1107, 1201, 1202, 1205; *The "Genius,"* 1198, 1202; *Hey Rub-a-dub-dub*, 1142; *Jennie Gerhardt*, 1197, 1201; *Newspaper Days*, 1200; *Sister Carrie*, 1016, 1197, 1201, 1376; *The Stoic*, 1198, 1202; *The Titan*, 1201, 1202

Drummond, Henry, 802

Dryden, John, 49, 65, 68, 69, 94

Du Bois, W. E. B., 1314

Dudley, Thomas, 63

Duganne, Augustine J. H., 570

Dulany, Daniel, 132, 134–135

DuMaurier, George, 957, 1066

Dunbar, Paul Laurence, 748–749, 854–855

Duncan, Robert, 1425, 1429, *1430*

Dungleson, Robley, 669

Dunlap, William, 129, 165, 181, *188–190*, 238; *André*, 189; *The Father*, 189; *The Glory of Columbia*, 189; *History of the American Theatre*, 190; *The Italian Father*, 189

Dunne, Finley Peter, 749–751

Dutton, Clarence E., 864, *875*

Duyckinck Brothers, 451

Duyckinck, Evert A., 235, 239, 240, 241, 448

Dwight, Theodore, 168

Dwight, Timothy, 120, 129, *165–166*, 620, 1491

Eastman, Mary H., 567

Eastman, Max, 1141, 1174, 1359, 1361, 1363

Eaton, Peggy, 15

Ebeling, Christoph Daniel, 206

Eberhart, Richard, 1433, *1434;* *Fields of Grace*, 1434

Echo, 168

Economic philosophy. *See* Political and economic philosophy

Eddy, Mary Baker, 801

Eden, Richard, 25

Edgeworth, Maria, 290

Edinburgh Review, 209, 212, 620

Edmonds, Walter, 1314

Education, 17, 96, 122–123, 226, 228–229, 511, 516–519, 658, 803, 804, 829, 954–956, 1122–1124, 1263; adult, 518–519, 654–655, 798–800, 955, 980, 1123; frontier, 653–655, 661–662; colleges and universities, 17, 93, 122, 123, 229–230, 233, 517–518, 654, 661–662, 803–804, 954–956, 1122–1123, 1261, 1270–1271, 1281; school laws, 123, 803; illiteracy, 517, 521, 608, 803; of women, 230, 517; influence of John Dewey, 1279–1281; influence of Thomas Jefferson, 17, 123, 153, 229. *See also* Feminism

Edwards, Jonathan, 14, 69, *71–81,* 86, 242, 371, 419, 1091, 1486, 1488; *Freedom of the Will,* 76, 77; *The Great Christian Doctrine of Original Sin Defended,* 74, 77–78; *Religious Affections,* 74, 78–79

Eggleston, Edward, 748, 863, 865, *869–870,* 879, 1020, bibliography, 1505; *The Hoosier Schoolmaster,* 865, 870

Eigner, Larry, 1430

Elder, Lonnie, III, 1459; *Ceremonies in Dark Old Men,* 1459

Eliot, Charles W., 230, 804, 1084

Eliot, John, 63

Eliot, T. S., 426, 1120, 1155, 1156, *1186,* 1187, 1297, 1335, *1340–1343, 1355–1357,* 1359, 1365, 1366, *1368–1369,* 1370, 1371, 1376, 1378, 1392, 1393, 1394, 1395, 1397, *1398,* 1399, *1400,* 1426, 1428, 1437, 1516, bibliography, 1517; *After Strange Gods,* 1356; *Ash Wednesday,* 1356; *The Cocktail Party,* 1400; *Complete Poems and Plays, 1909–1950,* 1398; *The Confidential Clerk,* 1400; *The Elder Statesman,* 1400; *For Lancelot Andrewes,* 1368; *Four Quartets,* 1356–1357; *Murder in the Cathedral,* 1357; *Prufrock and Other Observations,* 1341; *The Waste Land,* 1343, 1397

Elkin, Stanley, 1465

Elliott, Jonathan, 644

Elliott, Stephen, 308

Ellison, Ralph, 1418, 1425, *1467–1468; Invisible Man,* 1425, *1467–1468*

Ely, Richard T., 799

Elzevir, Abraham, 30

Emancipation Proclamation, 508

Emerson, Ralph Waldo, 14, 70, 81, 176, 221, 225, 229, 231, 232, 236, 238, 239, 240, 241, 242, 286, 291, 292, 293, 345, 346, *350–357, 358–387,* 399, 409, 416, 419, 434, 442, 472, 475, 480, 481, 482, 483, 498, 501, 505, 507, 513, 514, 519, 524, 563, 564, 569, 625–626, 639, 682, 774, 800, 817, 820, 834, 915, 984, 1080, 1091, 1100, 1135, 1136, 1150, 1158, 1160, 1194, 1361, 1364, 1365, 1376, 1381, 1395, 1426, 1433, 1485, 1494, bibliography, 1494–1495; career in the ministry, 361–366; lecturer, 368, 372–373, 382–385; Phi Beta Kappa address, 372, 621, 1364; philosophy of, 345–357, 368–371; poet, 377–381; style, 375–377, 381, 383; and Thoreau, 388, 391, *392–395,* 401, 404, 405, 407, 411; *The American Scholar,* 621; *The Conduct of Life,* 377, 381, 385–386; *Divinity School Address,* 15; *English Traits,* 368, 377, 381, *383–384,* 834; *Essays,* 367, 374, 375–377, 625; *May-Day,* 377; *Nature,* 346, 367, 368, 391; *Poems,* 377; *Representative Men,* 377, 381–383; *Society and Solitude,* 386; *Young Emerson Speaks,* 364

Emerson-Thoreau Medal, 1398

Empiricism, 982

English influences. *See* Foreign attitudes and influences

Epoch, 816

Ericsson, Leif, 24

Erikson, Erik, 1418

Erskine, John, 1127

Erzählung, 681, 683

Espejo, Antonio de, 26

Essay. *See* Criticism, literary

European influence. *See* Foreign attitudes and influences; Travel

Evans, Lewis, 90–91

Evans, Nathaniel, 97

Evarts, William M., 558

Everett, Edward, 230, 239, 241, 285, 287, 301, 527, *555–556,* 779, 1498

Evergreen Review, 1422, 1430

Everson, William (Brother Antoninus), 1431

Existentialism, 1418, 1440, 1466, 1467

Farmer, John S., 670

Farnaby, Giles, 1439

Farrell, James T., 1257, 1314, *1315*, 1362, 1363, *1407*, 1515, 1520; *Studs Lonigan*, 1407

Fascism, 1116, 1255, 1260, 1261; and Ezra Pound, 1397. *See also* Democracy

Faulkner, William, 722, 1297, *1304–1306*, 1309, 1312, 1375, 1380, 1381, 1387, 1390, 1392, 1393, 1394, *1404–1406*, 1463, bibliography, 1519–1520; *Absalom, Absalom!* 1306, 1404; "The Bear," 722; *A Fable*, 1404; *The Hamlet*, 1405; *Intruder in the Dust*, 1404; *Light in August*, 1304–1305, 1404; *The Mansion*, 1405; *The Reivers*, 1404, 1405; *Requiem for a Nun*, 1404; *Sanctuary*, 1304, 1404; *The Sound and the Fury*, 1304, 1305, 1404; *The Town*, 1405; Nobel Prize acceptance speech (1950), 1404

Fearing, Kenneth, 1354

Federal Theater Project, 1327, 1331

Federal Writers' Project, 1265–1266, 1270, 1313

Federalist, 142, *144*, 149, 154, 1490

Federman, Raymond, 1473

Feiffer, Jules, 1454; *Little Murders*, 1454

Feminism, 226, 503, 511, 800, 956–957, 1123, 1255. *See also* Women's Liberation movement

Fénelon, François, 94, 165

Fenollosa, Ernest, 1092, 1338

Ferber, Edna, 1385

Fergusson, Francis, 1418

Fergusson, Harvey, 678, 688

Ferlinghetti, Lawrence, 1425, 1431

Fessenden, Thomas Greene, 175

Ficke, Arthur Davidson, 1172

Fiction. *See* individual authors and movements; Satire; Criticism, literary

Fiedler, Leslie, 1418, *1421*, 1483

Field, Eugene, 716, 750, 863

Fielding, Henry, 187

Fields, James T., 239, 241, 515

Filson, John, 653, 655, 760, 768

Finkel, Donald, 1443; *Adequate Earth*, 1443; *Answer Back*, 1443

First Republic, 639

Fisher, Dorothy Canfield, 1212

Fisher, Henry L., 683

Fisher, Vardis, 1407

Fiske, John, 539, 799, *974–975*, 980, 1111

Fitch, Clyde, 957, 1000, 1008, 1010, *1011–1013*, 1015, 1237, 1318

Fitzgerald, F. Scott, 1263, 1264, 1266, 1296, *1298–1299*, 1300, 1306, 1307, 1311, 1393, 1394, bibliography, 1518; *The Great Gatsby*, 1298, 1299; *The Last Tycoon*, 1299, 1312; *Tender Is the Night*, 1299; *This Side of Paradise*, 1118, 1235, 1298, 1299

Fitzhugh, George, 567, 614

Fitzhugh, William, 53

Flateyjarbók, 24

Flaubert, Gustave, 1016, 1022, 1042, 1047, 1213, 1214, 1215

Fletcher, John Gould, 1174, 1187

Flint, F. S., 1173, 1184, *1185–1186*, 1187

Flint, Timothy, 273, 761–762, 865

Flood, Henry, 198

Flower, Benjamin O., 1107

Foerster, Norman, 1145, 1360

Folk literature, 609, 648, *703–727*, 1503; Indian, 694–702. *See also* Drama; Ballads; Humor; Songs

Foote, Mary Hallock, 869

Force, Peter, 526, 644

Foreign attitudes and influences: European, 192–193, *203–205*, 208–209, *244–248*, 249, 285, 411, 502, *618–636*, 659; English, *3–15*, 19, 68–69, 96, 97, 125, 176, 284, 618–619, 668, *1376–1378*, 1390, 1442; French, 119, 120, 658–659, 1297, *1378–1380*, 1390; German, 247, 349, 645, 679–680, *1380–1383*; Italian, 1384; Oriental, 356, 633, 641, 1388–1389; Latin American, 630–631, 1262, *1386–1387*; Russian, 1384–1386; Spanish, 530–533, 1384

Foreign language literatures in the United States. *See* French-American; German-American; Italian-American; Jewish-American; Pennsylvania German; Scandinavian-American; Spanish-American; Yiddish

Formalism, 1395, 1407, 1421, 1424, 1429, 1433

Forrest, Edwin, 238, 241, 1000, 1001

Forster, Georg, 201

Fortier, Alcée, 687

Fosdick, Harry Emerson, 1289

Foster, Hannah, 178

Foster, Stephen Collins, 716, *853*

Foster, Thomas J., 800

Fox, George, 84

Fox, John, Jr., 1121

Frank Leslie's Illustrated, 520

Frank, Waldo, 691, 1136, 1141, 1235, 1361, 1387, 1390

Franklin, Benjamin, 19, 20, 22, 23, 59, 69, 80, 84, 96, *101–112*, 123, 124, 132, 152, 200–202, 205, 285, 292, 371, 527, 678, 715, 730, bibliography, 1487–1488; American Philosophical Society, 103; *Autobiography*, 104, *109–112*, 201; *General Magazine, and Historical Chronicle, for all the British Plantations in America*, 103; *Journal*, 102; *Pennsylvania Gazette*, 102; *Poor Richard*, 102, 104–107; *Some Account of the Pennsylvania Hospital*, 107; *The Way to Wealth*, 107, 202

Franklin, James, 20, 22

Frederic, Harold, 992, 1016, 1017, 1376; *The Damnation of Theron Ware*, 635, 992

Freeman, Joseph, 1361, 1364

Freeman, Mary Wilkins, 847–848

Freeman's Journal, 171

Frémont, John Charles, *767–768*, 771, 772, 774, 775, 777

French, Alice, 869, 988

French-American literature, 27–29, 684–687

French influence. *See* Foreign attitudes and influences

Freneau, Philip, 95, 121, 123, 137, 162, *168–175*, 176, 378, 640, 715, bibliography, 1490–1491; *The British Prison-Ship*, 171; *The Rising Glory of America*, 95, 169

Freud, Sigmund, 1284, 1373, 1417, 1418

Friedan, Betty, 1420

Friedman, Bruce Jay, 1465

Friends, Society of. *See* Quakers

Frontier, westward migration, 118, 221, 639, 640, 641, 676, 943, bibliography, 1501–1502; chronicles of, 676–677, *758–770*, 862; culture of, 16, *652–662*, 687; humor and folklore, 609, 703–704, 710, 719–720, 737–738; in Cooper's novels, 253, 258, 261, 266; in Willa Cather's novels, 1212. *See also* West

Frost, Robert, 716, 1120, 1174, *1189–1196*, 1377, 1392, 1393, *1396–1397*, 1398, 1434; *A Boy's Will*, 1189, 1191; *A Further Range*, 1192; *In the Clearing*, 1396; *A Masque of Mercy*, 1396; *A Masque of Reason*, 1396; *Mountain Interval*, 1191; *New Hampshire*, 1192; *North of Boston*, 1189, 1191; *Steeple Bush*, 1396; *West-Running Brook*, 1192

Frye, Northrop, 1395, 1418

Frye, Prosser Hall, 1360

Fugitive, 1346–1347, 1371

Fugitive poets, 616–617, 1395, 1427, 1435

Fuller, Buckminster, 1420

Fuller, Henry Blake, 1017

Fuller, Margaret, 230, 238, 367, 374, 375, 393, 394, 434, 435

Fulton, C. C., 831

Furnas, J. C., 1257

Gaddis, William, 1473; *The Recognitions*, 1473

Galaxy, 816

Galbraith, John Kenneth, 1417, bibliography, 1482

Gale, Zona, 800, 1211, 1243

Gallatin, Albert, 142, 646, 647, 1086, 1087

Galloway, Joseph, 132, 137

Garcia Lorca, Federico, 1442

Garden, Alexander, 53

Garland, Hamlin, 794, 795, 863, 978, 999, 1016, *1017–1020*, 1027, 1065, 1118, 1157, 1197, 1376; *Back-Trailers from the Middle Border*, 1019; *Boy Life on the Prairie*, 1018; *Crumbling Idols*, 1017; *A Daughter of the Middle Border*, 1019; *Forty Years of Psychic Research*, 1020; *Main-Travelled Roads*, 1018; *Prairie Folks*, 1018; *Rose of Dutcher's Coolly*, 1019; *The Shadow World*, 1020; *A Son of the Middle Border*, 1019; *A Spoil of Office*, 1118; *Trail-Makers of the Middle Border*, 1019

Garrard, Lewis H., 767

Garreau, Louis-Armand, 685

Garrison, Lucy McKim, 648

Garrison, Wendell Phillips, 648

Garrison, William Lloyd, 226, 504, 564, 565

Gascoigne, George, 131

Gass, William H., 1473, *Omensetter's Luck*, 1473

Gates, Lewis E., 1078, 1359, 1365, 1367
Gazette de France, 195
Geismar, Maxwell, 1513, 1519
Gelber, Jack, 1425, 1454; The Connection, 1454
Genre writers. See Regionalism and local color
Genteel tradition, 645, 1078
Gentleman's Magazine, 21, 316
George, Henry, 661, 795, 864, 866, 875, 977–979, 986, 1018, 1107, 1361; Progress and Poverty, 875, 977–979
George, Lloyd, 1258
German-American literature, 678–683
German influence. See Foreign attitudes and influences
German theater, 682–683
Gerry, Elbridge, 142
Gerstäcker, Friedrich, 679, 681
Gibbons, Phebe E., 684
Gibbs, Willard, 807, 1094
Gift books. See Annuals and gift books
Gilbert, Humphrey, 131
Gilder, Richard Watson, 791, 805, 811, 813, 965, 1112, 1157
Gildersleeve, Basil, 318
Gillette, William, 1007, 1008
Gilpin, William, 864, 875–876
Ginsberg, Allen, 1425, 1431–1432; Howl, 1431; Kaddish, 1431
Giovanni, Nikki, 1444
Girard, Stephen, 240, 680
Gladden, Washington, 946
Glasgow, Ellen, 1197, 1210, 1211, 1216–1219, 1227, 1236, 1296, 1314, 1393, bibliography, 1513; Barren Ground, 1217, 1218, 1219; The Battle Ground, 1217, 1218; A Certain Measure, 1216; The Romantic Comedians, 1217, 1218
Glaspell, Susan, 1239
Glass, Montague, 751
Godey's Lady's Book, 226, 238, 335
Godfrey, Thomas, 96, 97–98, 185
Godkin, E. L., 790, 806, 976–977, 983
Godwin, William, 165, 166, 182, 286, 291
Goethe, Johann Wolfgang von, 173, 206, 375, 645, 822
Gold, Michael, 1239, 1361, 1385
Golden Era, 866
Goldenweiser, Alexander, 1284

Goll, Yvan, 1442
Gombo, 686
Gompers, Samuel, 560–561
Goodman, Paul, 1419
Goodrich, Samuel G., 228, 229, 418
Goodwin, Nat, 1010
Gooch, Governor, 51–52
Gordin, Jacob, 693
Gordon, Caroline, 617
Gough, John B., 226
Gourmont, Rémy de, 1185
Grady, Henry W., 560, 615, 791
Graham's Magazine, 237, 238, 239, 333, 334
Grangers, 946, 1110
Grant, Robert, 988
Grant, Ulysses S., 509, 791
Graves, Robert, 1440
Gray, Thomas, 96, 165, 174
Grayson, William John, 318, 567
Greeley, Horace, 230, 241, 395, 514, 769
Green, Anna Katharine, 1381
Green, Joseph, 69
Green, Paul, 724, 1257
Green, Samuel, 20
Greenough, Horatio, 817
Greenwood, Grace (Sara Jane Lippincott), 830
Gregg, Josiah, 765–766, 771, 1502
Gregory, Horace, 1354
Grey, Zane, 1377, 1385, 1387
Grierson, Herbert J. C., 1395
Grile, Dod, 1068. See also Bierce
Grimké, Angelina, 558
Griswold, Rufus W., 235, 238, 239, 321, 335, 336
Gronlund, Laurence, 895, 896
Guiney, Louise Imogen, 1157
Gunther, John, 1402

Hackett, James H., 238, 1003
Hadoar, 692
Haeckel, Ernst, 948, 1021
Haines, John, 1442
Hakluyt, Richard, 3, 4, 5, 26, 31, 1486
Hale, Edward Everett, 830
Haliburton, Thomas Chandler, 651, 734–735
Hall, G. Stanley, 799
Hall, James, 647, 761, 865
Hallam, Lewis, 128

Halleck, Fitz-Greene, 127, 130, 174, 270, 277–279, 378; *The Croaker Papers*, 127, 277

Hallesche Nachrichten, 679

Halper, Albert, 1257, 1313, 1385

Halpine, Charles G., 571

Hamilton, Alexander, 119, 120, 121, 132, 142, 143, 144, *146–160*, 180, bibliography, 1490; *First Report on the Public Credit*, 155; *Report on Manufactures*, 155

Hammett, Dashiell, 1313, 1377, 1380, 1383

Hammond, John, 38, 41–42

Hamor, Ralph, 33

Hanna, Mark, 790

Hansberry, Lorraine, *1458; A Raisin in the Sun*, 1458

Hansen, Marcus Lee, 677

Harbaugh, Henry, 683

Hardman, Frederick, 681

Hariot, Thomas, 31–32

Harland, Henry, 1066, 1376

Harper and Brothers, 126, 959

Harper, Michael S., 1444; *Dear John, Dear Coltrane*, 1444; *Song: I Want a Witness*, 1444

Harper, William Rainey, 567, 799, 955

Harper's Magazine, 258, 516, 520, 805, 953, 956, 964, 1070, 1376

Harper's Weekly, 516, 520, 806

Harrigan, Edward, 1003

Harris, George Washington, 741

Harris, Joel Chandler, 25, 648, *748*, 791, *851–854*, 1505; *The Chronicles of Aunt Minervy Ann*, 748; *Free Joe and Other Georgian Sketches*, 852; *Mingo*, 852; *Uncle Remus*, 648, 748, 851, 853, 854

Harris, William T., 972–973

Harte, Bret, 301, 651, 661, 662, 715, 745, 748, 792–793, 794, 825, 863, 865, 866–867, 879, 1376, 1378, 1381, 1385, bibliography, 1505–1506; European reception of, 633–634; *Condensed Novels*, 866; *"Luck of Roaring Camp" and Other Sketches*, 865, 867; *Tales of the Argonauts*, 634, 1375

Harte, Walter Blackburn, 1077

Hartford Wits, 120, 128, 162, 168, 169, 287, 1491

Hartman, Geoffrey, 1422, *1423*

Hartwell, Henry, 43

Harvard, John, 19

Harvard Magazine, 1083

Hassan, Ihab, *1422*, 1518

Hatoren, 692

Hauksbók, 24

Hawkes, John, *1463, 1468–1469; The Cannibal*, 1463, 1468; *The Goose on the Grave*, 1468–1469; *Second Skin*, 1469

Hawthorne, Nathaniel, 81, 91, 175, 181, 188, 238, 239, 240, 242, 243, 248, 333, 345, 346, 350–355, 374, 395, *416–440*, 441, 442, 483, 524, 620, 626–627, 646, 718, 812, 820, *835–836*, 1038, 1378, 1494, bibliography, 1496; marriage, 417; and Melville, 464; and Puritanism, 419–421; treatment of problem of evil, 351; *American Notebooks*, 422; *The Ancestral Footstep*, 418, 438, 836; *The Blithedale Romance*, 416, 431, 433–435; *Dr. Grimshaw's Secret*, 418, 439, 836; *The Dolliver Romance*, 418, 439; *English Notebooks*, 418, 836; *Fanshawe*, 417, 421; *The House of the Seven Gables*, 418, 421, 422, 426, *431–433*, 627; *Italian Notebooks*, 830; *Life of Franklin Pierce*, 431; *The Marble Faun*, 418, 421, *434–438*, 627, 830; *Mosses from an Old Manse*, 423; *Our Old Home*, 627, 836; *The Scarlet Letter*, 15, 239, 418, 422, *425–431*, 627, 776; *Septimius Felton*, 418, 439; *The Snow Image*, 423; *The Spectator*, 416; *Twice-Told Tales*, 239, 417, 423, 627; *The Wonder Book for Boys and Girls*, 431, 627

Hay, John, 715, 794, 833, 866, *870–871*, 988, 1093–1094

Hayden, Robert, 1444; *Selected Poems*, 1444

Haydon, Eustace, 1285

Hayes, Alfred, 1453; *The Girl on the Via Flaminia*, 1453

Hayley, William, 166

Hayne, Paul Hamilton, *318–320*, 569, 811, 825, 1500

Hayne, Robert Y., 558

Hearn, Lafcadio, 686, 687, *1070–1072*, 1092; *Chita: A Memory of Last Island*, 1071; *Diary of an Impressionist*, 1072; *Glimpses of Unfamiliar Japan*, 1072; *Japan: An Attempt at Interpretation*, 1072; *Kokoro*, 1072; *Kwaidan*, 1072

Hearst, William Randolph, 1068

Hearth and Home, 870

Hebrew language, 690, 692–693

Hecht, Anthony, 1427, *1445;* *The Hard Hours,* 1445

Hecker, Isaac Thomas, 679

Hedge, Frederick Henry, 232

Hegel, Georg Wilhelm Friedrich, 214, 349, 474, 972

Hegelianism, 642, 972

Heinlein, Robert, 1472

Heinzen, Karl Peter, 679

Heller, Joseph, 1463; *Catch 22,* 1463

Hellman, Lillian, *1402,* 1521; *The Children's Hour,* 1402; *The Little Foxes,* 1402, 1453; *Toys in the Attic,* 1402; *Watch on the Rhine,* 1402

Helper, Hinton R., 504, 567

Hemingway, Ernest, 1262, 1263, 1264, 1296, 1297, *1300–1302,* 1304, 1375, 1377, 1380, 1381, 1382, 1384, 1393, 1394, *1403–1404,* 1406, bibliography, 1519; *Across the River and into the Trees,* 1403; *Death in the Afternoon,* 1301; *A Farewell to Arms,* 1300, 1387; *For Whom the Bell Tolls,* 1312; *In Our Time,* 1300; *Islands in the Stream,* 1403; *A Moveable Feast,* 1403; *The Old Man and the Sea,* 1403; *To Have and Have Not,* 1301; Nobel Prize, 1403

Henderson, Alice Corbin, 1174

Henderson, Stephen, 1444

Hendrick, Burton J., 1111

Hennepin, Louis, 28–29

Henry, O. (William Sydney Porter), 755, 1385

Henry, Patrick, 124, 132, 142

Herbert, Henry William, 238

Hergesheimer, Joseph, *1235–1236,* 1296, 1375

Herne, James A., 1000, 1001, 1004–1005, 1011, 1015, 1318

Herrick, Robert, 989, 994–995

Herron, George D., 795

Hersey, John, 1402–1403, 1424; *A Bell for Adano,* 1403

Hesperian, 643

Heyward, DuBose, 717, 724, 1235

Hicks, Elias, 481

Hicks, Granville, 1362, 1364

Higginson, Thomas Wentworth, 503, 565, 570, 648, 791, 904, 905, 914, 916

Hildreth, Richard, 528, 566, 645

Hillard, G. S., 829

Hillhouse, James Abraham, 287–288

Hillyer, Robert, 1398

Himes, Chester, 1315

Historians, mid-nineteenth century, 526–540, 1499

Historical societies, 644

Hocking, William Ernest, 1291–1292

Hoffman, Charles Fenno, 277

Hoffman, Daniel G., 1445, 1493

Hogue, Wayman D., 721

Holbrook, Josiah, 231

Holland, J. G., 791

Hollander, John, 1427, *1446; Movie-Going,* 1446; *Visions for the Ramble,* 1446

Holley, Sallie, 558

Holm, Campanius, 31

Holm, Saxe (Helen Hunt Jackson), 90, 681, 914

Holm, Tomas Campanius, 30

Holmes, George Frederick, 614

Holmes, Oliver Wendell (1809–1894), 81, 239, 294, 372, 378, 381, 506, 569, 587–589, *596–601,* 649, 715, 754, 795, 811, 812, bibliography, 1501; *The Autocrat of the Breakfast Table,* 599–600; *Elsie Venner,* 598; *The Guardian Angel,* 598; *A Mortal Antipathy,* 598; *The Poet at the Breakfast-Table,* 599; *The Professor at the Breakfast-Table,* 599

Holmes, Oliver Wendell (1841–1935), 1110, 1111, *1282–1283*

Holmes, W. H., 874

Hood's *Fun,* 63?

Hooker, Thomas, 61, 62

Hooper, Johnson Jones, 740–741

Hopkins, Arthur, 1317

Hopkins, Lemuel, 129, 168

Hopkinson, Francis, 96, 97, *98–100,* 137, 171, 271

Horowitz, Israel, 1456; *The Indian Wants the Bronx,* 1456

Hovey, Richard, 1067, 1171

Howard, Bronson, 1001, 1004, *1005–1007,* 1010, 1011

Howard, Leon, 1491

Howard, Richard, 1446; *Untitled Subjects,* 1446

Howard, Sidney, 1243, 1317, 1318, 1327

Howe, E. W., 794, 1016, 1017, 1018, 1020

Howe, Julia Ward, 568, 828

Howe, Samuel Gridley, 226

Howells, William Dean, 341, 496, 689, 793, 794, 795, 805, 814, 817, *839-840*, 879, 880, 884, *885-898*, 903, 921, 929, 930, 944, 953, 964, 978, 979, 999, 1017, 1020, 1027, 1066, 1090, 1122, 1135, 1139, 1361, 1366, bibliography, 1506, 1507; *Annie Kilburn*, 894; *A Boy's Town*, 930; *A Chance Acquaintance*, 839, 889; *Criticism and Fiction*, 893, 1017; *Dr. Breen's Practice*, 891; *A Foregone Conclusion*, 887, 889; *A Hazard of New Fortunes*, 895; *Indian Summer*, 892-893; *Italian Journeys*, 839; *The Kentons*, 897; *The Lady of the Aroostook*, 889-890; *The Landlord at Lion's Head*, 896-897; *Life of Abraham Lincoln*, 887; *Literary Friends and Acquaintances*, 887; *Literature and Life*, 893; *A Little Swiss Sojourn*, 839, 840; *The Minister's Charge*, 894; *Mrs. Farrell*, 890; *A Modern Instance*, 891; *My Literary Passions*, 886; *The Rise of Silas Lapham*, 892; *The Son of Royal Langbrith*, 897; *Suburban Sketches*, 888; *Their Wedding Journey*, *839*, 888-889; *Through the Eye of the Needle*, 896; *A Traveller from Altruria*, 896; *Tuscan Cities*, 839, 840; *The Undiscovered Country*, 890-891; *Venetian Life*, 839, 840, 888; *The World of Chance*, 895-896; *Years of My Youth*, 885, 887

Hoyt, Charles, 1318

Hubbard, Elbert, 800, 1067

Hubbard, Frank McKinney, 753

Hubbard, William, 36

Hudson, Henry, 29

Huebsch, B. W., 1132

Hughes, Hatcher, 1243

Hughes, John T., 766-767

Hughes, Langston, 749, 1354, 1503

Hulme, T. E., 1184-1185, 1188, 1369, 1395

Humanism, 146, 1145, 1153, 1285, 1286, 1359-1361, 1368

Humanitarianism, 85, 118, 225, 292, 293, 790, 795, 949, 1260. *See also* Philosophy; Socialism and socialization

Humor, 609, 651, 657, 683, 725, *728-757*, 1503-1504. *See also* Folk literature

Humphreys, David, 129, 164, 165, 168, 171, 669, 1491

Huneker, James G., *1074-1077*, 1135, 1155, 1359, 1365, 1367, 1368; *Chopin, the Man and His Music*, 1075; *Egoists: A Book of Supermen*, 1076; *Iconoclasts: A Book of Dramatists*, 1076; *Ivory Apes and Peacocks*, 1076; *Melomaniacs*, 1076; *Mezzotints in Modern Music*, 1075; *The New Cosmopolis*, 1075; *Old Fogy*, 1075; *Painted Veils*, 1076; *The Pathos of Distance*, 1076; *Promenades of an Impressionist*, 1075; *Steeplejack*, 1075; *Unicorns*, 1076; *Variations*, 1075; *Visionaries*, 1076

Hunt, Richard, 796

Hunter, Richard, 127

Huntington, Collis P., 812

Hurewitz, Israel (Solomon Libin), 693

Hurston, Zora Neale, 749, 1315

Hutchins, Robert Maynard, 1280

Hutchinson, Anne, 14

Hutchinson, Thomas, 36, 90

Huxley, Thomas H., 814

Idealism, 86, *345-357*, 973-974, 1142, 1273, 1286, *1291-1293*

Ideality, 639, 792, 809, *813-814*, 817

Imagists, 824, *1185-1189*, 1336, 1337, 1370

Imlay, Gilbert, 760-761

Immigration, 642-644, 676-678, 690, 796, 1261. *See also* Labor movement

Independent, 870, 1112

Independent Whig, 94

Index Translationum, 1379, 1382, 1383

Indians and Indian literature, 42, 44, 47, 88, 89, 90, 92, 187, 263, 646-647, 665-666, 685, 686, *694-702*, 772, 1502-1503

Individualism, 350, 948-950, 969, 970, 971, 972, 974, 975, 976, 983, 984, 1116, 1255, 1258. *See also* Democracy; Socialism

Industrialism, 223, 302, 511, 515, 613-614, 615, 639, 641, 642, 789, 790, 791, 795, 796, 797, 944, 969, 971, *972-973*, 977, 978, *981*, 1253, 1255, 1256, 1257, 1259, 1307, 1308. *See also* Agrarian movement; Labor movement; Socialism

Inge, William, 1451-1452; *Come Back Little Sheba*, 1452; *The Dark at the Top of the*

Stairs, 1452; *Picnic*, 1451; Pulitzer Prize, 1451

Ingersoll, Robert G., 561

Inner light, doctrine of the, 347, 476

Instrumentalism, 951–952, *1278–1280*

Iredell, James, 143

Irving, Peter, 129

Irving, Washington, 125, 127, 129, 130, 171, 175, 176, 191, 235, 239, 240, 241, 242–252, 271, 284, 287, 302, 303, 304, 346, 420, 424, 621, 622–623, 644, 677, 731, 732, 772, *773–774*, 1083, bibliography, 1492; *The Alhambra*, 248, 249, 623; *Astoria*, 773, 774; *Bracebridge Hall*, 244, 248, 622, 827; *Captain Bonneville*, 773, 774; *Collected Works*, 622; *The Conquest of Granada*, 249, 623; *Diedrich Knickerbocker's A History of New York*, 243, 244, 622; *A History of the Life and Voyages of Columbus*, 249, 623; *The Letters of Jonathan Oldstyle, Gent.*, 244; *Life of Washington*, 251; *Rip Van Winkle*, 1005; *Salmagundi* essays, 127, 244, 622; *Sketch Book*, 127, 235, 242, *245–248*, 622, 827; *Tales of a Traveller*, 244, 249, 622; *A Tour on the Prairies*, 250, 772, 773

Irving Place Theater, 682

Italian-American literature, 688

Italian influences. *See* Foreign attitudes and influences

"Jack Downing" Papers, 732–734

Jackson, Andrew, 15, 119, 221, 224, 227, 480, 1491

Jackson, Helen Hunt, 90, 681, *869*, 914

James, Edwin, 765

James, Henry (1811–1882), 1045

James, Henry (1843–1916), 91, 183, 321, 341, 420, 421, 426, 439, 789, 814, 828, 832, 839, *840–842*, 879, 897, 1023, *1039–1064*, 1090, 1122, 1135, 1140, 1152, 1208, 1209, 1210, *1365–1368*, 1369, 1371, 1376, 1378, 1380, bibliography, 1510; argument against naturalism, 1059; concept of the novel, 1061; function of the artist and society, 1049–1056; international theme, 1046, 1049, 1055–1058; playwright, 1043; *The Ambassadors*, 1043, 1047, 1051, 1058, 1062; *The American*, 1056; *The American Scene*, 1042,

1058; *The Awkward Age*, 1055; *The Bostonians*, 615, 1059, 1060; *Daisy Miller*, 1049; *The Finer Grain*, 1043, 1063; *The Golden Bowl*, 1043, 1046, 1048, 1056, 1058, 1061; *The Ivory Tower*, 1043; *A Little Tour in France*, 840–841; *The Portrait of a Lady*, 1042, 1043, 1046, 1051, 1052, 1056, 1058; *Portraits of Places*, 841; *The Princess Casamassima*, 1059, 1060; *The Sacred Fount*, 1058, 1060–1061; *The Sense of the Past*, 1043; *The Spoils of Poynton*, 1042, 1051, 1059; *The Tragic Muse*, 1051, 1052; *Transatlantic Sketches*, 840; *Washington Square*, 1049, 1052, 1053; *What Maisie Knew*, 1055; *The Wings of the Dove*, 1043, 1046, 1049, 1056, 1058

James, William, 78, 371, 799, 951, *982–985*, 1044, 1094, 1282; *Essays in Radical Empiricism*, 982; *A Pluralistic Universe*, 982; *Pragmatism*, 982; *Principles of Psychology*, 983; *The Varieties of Religious Experience*, 982; *The Will to Believe*, 951, 982

Jarrell, Randall, 1371, 1427, 1516

Jarves, James Jackson, 829, 836–837

Jay, John, 142, 143, 144, 1490

Jeffers, Robinson, 1290, 1347–1349, 1399, 1517

Jefferson, Joseph, 1003

Jefferson, Thomas, 18, 41, 48, 117, 119, 121, 123, 132, 139, *146–161*, 169, 172, 205, 207, *208–209*, 220, 480, 504, 668, 688, 779, 976, 1086, 1087, 1261, bibliography, 1489; ideas on education, 18, 123, 153, 229; *Notes on the State of Virginia*, 41, 153, 208

Jesuit Relations, The, 27–28

Jewett, Sarah Orne, 845–847, 848, bibliography, 1505

Jewish-American literature, 690–692, 1425, 1464–1466, 1473

John Street Theater, 128

Johnson, Andrew, 224, 510

Johnson, Edward, 35, 65

Johnson, James Weldon, 749, 1314

Johnson, Samuel (1696–1772), 86–87, 123

Johnson, Samuel (1709–1784), 91, 96, 664

Johnson, Thomas H., 904, 1488, 1506

Johnson, Virginia E., 1420

Johnston, Mary, 610, 1119

Johnston, Richard Malcolm, 851–852

Jones, Hugh, 47

Jones, James, 1463; *From Here to Eternity*, 1463; *The Thin Red Line*, 1463

Jones, John Beauchamp, 567, 570

Jones, LeRoi (Imamu Amiri Baraka), 1444, 1458; *Black Magic: Poetry 1961–1967*, 1444; *Dutchman*, 1444; *The Toilet*, 1444

Jones, Robert Edmond, 1239

Jones, Rufus, 1288–1289

Josselyn, John, 35, 391

Journal of Speculative Philosophy, 642

Journalism. *See* Newspapers and magazines

Joyce, James, 1134, 1152

Judge, 754

Juet, Robert, 29

Jung, Carl Gustav, 1418, 1436

Justice, Donald, 1427, 1445

Kanin, Garson, *1451*; *Born Yesterday*, 1451

Kant, Immanuel, 972

Karlsefne, Thorfinn, 24

Kaufman, George S., 1243, 1319

Kazin, Alfred, 1372, 1421, 1513, 1514, 1518

Keast, W. R., 1395

Keayne, Robert, 20

Kelley, William Melvin, 1468; *A Different Drummer*, 1468

Kelly, George, 1243

Kelly, Myra, 751

Kelly, Robert, 1441

Kelpius, Johann, 678

Kendall, George W., 766

Kennedy, Adrienne, 1459; *Cities in Bezique*, 1459

Kennedy, John Pendleton, 241, 245, *307–308*, 309–310, *314*, 315, 320, 327, 610, 612, 613, bibliography, 1494; *Horse Shoe Robinson*, 314; *Letters of Mr. Paul Ambrose on the Great Rebellion in the United States*, 320; *Quodlibet*, 314; *Rob of the Bowl*, 314; *Swallow Barn*, 309, 613

Kenner, Hugh, *1423, 1428*, 1516

Kennerley, Mitchell, 1132, 1171

Kenyon Review, 617, 1371, 1395, 1399

Kerouac, Jack, 1425, 1431, 1466; *The Dharma Bums*, 1466; *On the Road*, 1466

Kerr, Orpheus C. (Robert H. Newell), 571, 784

Kesey, Ken, 1423, *1467*; *One Flew over the Cuckoo's Nest*, 1467

Kierkegaard, Soren, 1287

King, Clarence, 661, 794, 864, 865, 866, *873*, *1093–1094*

King, Edward, 642

King, Grace, 687, 858

Kinnell, Galway, 1442, *1446*; *Body Rags*, 1446; *The Book of Nightmares*, 1446; *What a Kingdom It Was*, 1446

Kinsey, Alfred, 1417

Kirkland, Caroline, 763

Kirkland, Joseph, 794, 1018

Knickerbocker Magazine, 316

Knight, Sarah Kemble, 1488

Knopf, Alfred A., 1132

Koch, Frederick H., 724

Koch, Kenneth, *1443, 1456*; *Bertha*, 1456; *George Washington Crossing the Delaware*, 1456; *The Pleasures of Peace*, 1443; *Thank You and Other Poems*, 1443

Kopit, Arthur, *1452, 1454*; *Indians*, 1454; *Oh, Dad, Poor Dad, Mamma's Hung You in the Closet and I'm Feelin' So Sad*, 1452, 1454

Körner, Gustav Philipp, 679

Kosinski, Jerzy, 1467; *Steps*, 1467

Kostelanetz, Richard, 1422, 1443

Kreymborg, Alfred, 1120, 1239

Krieger, Murray, 1422

Krutch, Joseph Wood, 1417

Kunitz, Joshua, 1362

Kunitz, Stanley, 1433, *1434–1435*; *Selected Poems*, 1435; *The Testing Tree*, 1435

Kürnberger, Ferdinand, 679

Labor movement, 301, 503, 946, 950, 971, 1116, 1254, 1258. *See also* Industrialism; Socialism

Ladd, Joseph Brown, 173

Ladies' Home Journal, 957

Laet, Johann de, 30

La Farge, John, 1088, *1094–1095*

La Follette, Robert M., 1108, 1115, 1117, 1255

Laforgue, Jules, 1442

Lahontan, Louis-Armand, Baron de, 29

Lamantia, Philip, 1431

Lamartine, Alphonse Marie Louis de, 198

Langer, Suzanne K., 1396

Language, American, 89, 123, *663-675*, 1298, 1504; bilingual writers, *676-693;* dialects and slang, 675, 683, 860, 953; vernacular in literature, 649-651. *See also* Spelling

Lanier, Sidney, 318, 506, 510, 574, 616, 715, 791, *899-903,* 1194, bibliography, 1506; *The Science of English Verse,* 900, 901, 902, 903; *Tiger-Lilies,* 568, 900

Larbaud, Valéry, 1442

Larcom, Lucy, 239

Lardner, Ring, 755, 756, 1131, *1233-1235,* 1236; *How To Write Short Stories,* 1235; *The Love Nest,* 1235

Lark, 1067

Larrabee, Eric, 1417

Las Casas, Bartolomé de, 193

Latin-American influences. *See* Foreign attitudes and influences; Spanish-American literature

Laudonnière, René Goulaine de, 32

Laurents, Arthur, 1451; *A Clearing in the Woods,* 1451; *Gypsy,* 1452; *Home of the Brave,* 1451; *West Side Story,* 1452

Lawrence, D. H., 1174

Lawson, John, 46-47

Lawson, John Howard, 1243, 1317, 1319, 1327, 1331

Lazarus, Emma, 690, 691

League of American Writers, 1265

Leatherstocking Series. *See* Cooper, James Fenimore

Le Clercq, Chrétien, 28

Lectures, 230-231, 513, 518-519, 800

Lederer, John, 38

Ledyard, John, 285

Lee, Don L., 1444

Lee, Richard Henry, 142-143

Lee, Robert E., 509, 511

Legaré, Hugh Swinton, 308, 567

Legaré, James Mathewes, 308

Leland, Charles Godfrey, 683, 752

Lenau, Nikolaus, 679

Lenox, James, 644

Levertov, Denise, 1429, 1430, 1444; *To Stay Alive,* 1444

Lévi-Strauss, Claude, 1423

Lewis and Clark, bibliography, 1502

Lewis, Alfred Henry, 864, 872

Lewis, Henry T., 741

Lewis, Meriwether, 763-764, 771, 772

Lewis, Richard, 51

Lewis, Sinclair, 820, 863, 1151, 1217, *1222-1229,* 1236, 1256, 1359, 1375, *1377,* 1380, 1381, 1382, 1383, 1385, 1387, 1393, bibliography, 1514; *Arrowsmith,* 1222, *1227,* 1236, *1393; Babbitt,* 1222, *1225-1227,* 1393; *Cass Timberlane,* 1227, 1228; *Dodsworth,* 1228; *Elmer Gantry,* 1228; *Main Street,* 1222, 1223, *1224-1225,* 1228, 1388, 1393; *The Man Who Knew Coolidge,* 1228; Nobel Prize, 1393

Lewisohn, Ludwig, 691, 1141, 1359

Liberator, 564

Libin, Solomon, 693

Libraries, 18-19, 20, 230, 655, 661, 803, *805,* 806, *955-956, 1124-1125*

Lieber, Francis, 507

Life (1883-1936), 754

Life Illustrated, 485

Lincoln, Abraham, 161, 301, 486, 488, 489, 503, 505, 506, 507, 508, 509, 510, 511, *553-555,* 729, 745, *778-786,* 794, 1181, 1313, bibliography, 1498; *Cooper Union Speech,* 783; *Gettysburg Speech,* 778, 779, 780, 782; *House Divided Speech of 1858,* 783; *Letter to Mrs. Bixby,* 778-779, 780, 782; *Message to Congress, December 1, 1862,* 780-781, 786; *Second Inaugural,* 778, 780, 782

Lindeström, Peter Mårtensson, 30

Lindsay, Vachel, 716, 1120, 1172, 1174, 1175-1179, *1377,* 1393, bibliography, 1512; *General William Booth Enters into Heaven and Other Poems,* 1174, 1177, 1178; *The Tree of Laughing Bells,* 1176

Lippincott, Sara Jane, 830

Lippmann, Walter, 1107, 1120, *1127, 1285-1286*

Literary Gazette, 620

Literary Guild, 1267-1268

Literature, as business, 953-968; book trade, 17, 19, 124, 127, 234-241, 514, 521-523; writing as a profession, 1119-1121, 1263-1264; author's income, 522, 1119, 1264-1266, 1269-1271; translations, 1378-1389. *See also* Printing and publishing

Little magazines, 1067

Little theater movement, 1124, 1237, 1242–1243, 1318

Littleton, Mark (John Pendleton Kennedy), 241, *307–308*, 309–310, *314*, 320, 610, 612, 613

Livingston, William, 93–95

Lloyd, Henry Demarest, 979–980, 1107, 1109; *Wealth Against Commonwealth*, 980

Local color. *See* Regionalism and local color

Locke, David Ross, 571, *743–744*, 784, 800, 828, 1130

Loesser, Frank, 1453; *Guys and Dolls*, 1453

Logan, James, 19, 96

London, Jack, 1016, 1029, *1033–1037*, 1120, 1121, 1197, 1378, 1379, 1382, 1383, 1385, 1386, 1390, bibliography, 1509; *The Call of the Wild*, 1034, *1036*, 1121, 1375; *The Iron Heel*, 1037; *John Barleycorn*, 1036; *The Kempton-Wace Letters*, 1035; *The Little Lady of the Big House*, 1036; *Martin Eden*, 1034, 1035, 1036; *The People of the Abyss*, 1037; *The Sea Wolf*, 1030, 1036; *The Son of the Wolf*, 1034; *White Fang*, 1036

Long, Stephen Harriman, 772, 1502

Longfellow, Henry Wadsworth, 15, 25, 122, 176, 188, 230, 238, 240, 289, 303, 333, 334, 378, 417, 483, 491, 508, 564, 569, *587–596*, 621, 628–629, 645, 681, 715, 775, 795, 811, 812, 820, 1261, 1375, bibliography, 1500; *Ballads and Other Poems*, 591; *The Belfry of Bruges and Other Poems*, 592; *Christus: A Mystery*, 594; *The Courtship of Miles Standish*, 593, 629; *Dante*, 822; *Evangeline*, 592, 629, 651, 681, 682, 775; *The Golden Legend*, 629, 645; *Hyperion*, 591, 645, 827; *In the Harbor*, 595; *Kavanagh*, 593; *Poems on Slavery*, 566, 593; *The Song of Hiawatha*, 593, 629, 647, 651, 682; *Tales of a Wayside Inn*, 593; *Ultima Thule*, 595; *Voices of the Night*, 591

Longstreet, Augustus Baldwin, 310, 649, 651, 657, 739, 762, 866

Loos, Anita, 755

Lord, Otis P., 914–915

Lorentz, Pare, 1314

"Lost" generation, 1393

Lovejoy, Arthur O., 1290

Lovejoy, Elijah Parish, 564

Lowell, Amy, 1120, 1174, *1186–1188*

Lowell, James Russell, 230, 239, 240, 294, 301, 303, 333, 372, 378, 389, 401, 409, 461, 502, 503, 507, 509, 510, 563, 564, 566, 569, 587–589, *601–606*, 649, 663, 715, *735–737*, 795, 804, 811, 812, 814, 816, 1135, 1136, 1365, 1376, bibliography, 1501; *Bigelow Papers*, 505, 507, 566, 602, 605, 649, 651, *735–737*; *The Cathedral*, 603, 604; *My Study Windows*, 603; *Ode Recited at the Harvard Commemoration*, 602; *Under the Willows*, 812; *The Vision of Sir Launfal*, 602, 604

Lowell, Robert, 1426, 1427, *1436–1438*, 1440, *1456*; *The Dolphin*, 1438; *For Lizzie and Harriet*, 1438; *For the Union Dead*, 1438; *History*, 1438; *Imitations*, 1438; *Land of Unlikeness*, 1437; *Life Studies*, 1437, 1438; *Lord Weary's Castle*, 1437; *The Mills of the Kavanaughs*, 1437; *Near the Ocean*, 1438; *Notebook*, 1438; *The Old Glory*, 1438, 1456; Racine's *Phèdre*, 1438

Lowell Institute, 230

Lowell Offering, 223

Lundy, Benjamin, 564

Lussan, Auguste, 685

Lyceum movement, *230–231*, 518, 800, 1123

Lyell, Sir Charles, 1094, 1103

Lyon, Mary, 226

Lyric Year, 1171–1172

Mabie, Hamilton Wright, 819, 820

Macaulay, Thomas B., 1083

McCarthy, Mary, 1463; *A Charmed Life*, 1463; *The Oasis*, 1463

McClure, Michael, 1431

McClure, S. S., 993

McCosh, James, 975

McCullers, Carson, 1424, 1452, *1464*; *The Ballad of the Sad Cafe*, 1464; *The Heart Is A Lonely Hunter*, 1464; *The Member of the Wedding*, 1452

Macdonald, Dwight, 1362, 1363, 1417

McGuffey, William Holmes, 654

McKay, Claude, 1314

MacKaye, Percy, 723, 1171

MacKaye, Steele, 1005

McKeon, Richard, 1395

MacLeish, Archibald, 1351, 1394–1395, 1517;
     Conquistador, 1394; Herakles, 1399; J.B.,
     1399, 1452
McLuhan, Marshall, 1419
McMaster, John Bach, 538
Macy, John A., 1137
Madison, James, 95, 142, 144, 146, 148–161,
     169, 220, 1086, 1087, 1489, 1490
Maeterlinck, Maurice, 1261
Magazines. See Newspapers and magazines
Mahan, Alfred Thayer, 977
Mailer, Norman, 1419, 1424, 1462, 1471,
     1474–1475; Advertisements for Myself,
     1419, 1474; An American Dream, 1474;
     The Armies of the Night, 1424, 1471;
     Barbary Shore, 1474; The Deer Park,
     1474; Existential Errands, 1474; Miami and
     the Siege of Chicago, 1424; The Naked and
     the Dead, 1462; Of a Fire on the Moon,
     1424; The Presidential Papers, 1474; Why
     Are We in Vietnam, 1474
Major, Clarence, 1444
Malamud, Bernard, 1425, 1465; The Assistant,
     1465; The Fixer, 1465; The Magic Barrel,
     1465; The Natural, 1465; A New Life,
     1465; Pictures of Fidelman, 1465; The
     Tenants, 1465
Malcolm X, 1420
Malinowski, Bronislaw, 1396
Maltz, Albert, 1313
Mandelstam, Osip, 1442
Mann, Horace, 226, 229, 292
Marcel, Gabriel, 1418
March, Francis A., 674
Marcuse, Herbert, 1418, 1419
Markham, Edwin, 1157, 1172
Marquand, John P., 1407, 1408; The Late
     George Apley, 1408; Point of No Return,
     1407, 1408; Wickford Point, 1408
Marquette, Jacques, 28
Marquis, Don, 755, 1131
Marryat, Frederick, 771
Martin, Helen Reimensnyder, 684
Marx, Karl, 502, 509, 950, 973, 1096, 1142,
     1360–1365, 1368, 1372
Massachusetts Historical Society, 1086
Massachusetts Magazine, 127
Masses, 1078, 1361
Masters, Edgar Lee, 1120, 1174, 1179–1181,

1377; Spoon River Anthology, 1179, 1180–
     1181
Masters, William H., 1420
Materialism, 946, 970, 1275–1276
Mather, Cotton, 13, 17, 18, 19, 36, 40, 59–
     60, 64, 69, 349, 1486; Bonifacius 59;
     Christian Philosopher, 59; Magnalia Christi
     Americana, 59, 64; Manuductio ad Minister-
     ium, 69; Political Fables, 59
Mather, Increase, 60
Mather, Richard, 63
Mathews, Cornelius, 281, 282
Mayakowsky, Vladimir, 1442
Mayhew, Jonathan, 134
Mazzei, Filippo, 197, 688
Meiklejohn, Alexander, 1280
Melville, Herman, 81, 240, 255, 293, 294, 346,
     350, 351, 352, 354, 355, 420, 430, 439, 440,
     441–471, 472, 524, 525, 572, 615, 621,
     627–628, 641, 776, 899, 1038, 1096, 1494;
     bibliography, 1496–1497; Battle Pieces,
     465–466, 571–572; Billy Budd, Foretopman,
     444, 468, 469–471; Clarel, 466–468, 615–
     616; The Confidence Man, 460, 461, 462,
     463–464; Israel Potter, 460, 461; Mardi,
     255, 271, 449–452, 628; Moby-Dick, 294,
     441, 449, 452–456, 628, 776, 1081, 1378;
     Omoo, 445–446, 628, 641; The Piazza
     Tales, 460, 461; Pierre, 456–459, 628;
     Redburn, 442, 448–449, 628; Typee, 294,
     443, 444–445, 628, 641; White-Jacket, 255,
     444, 446–448, 628
Mencken, H. L., 1075, 1078, 1127, 1136,
     1138, 1142–1145, 1153, 1154, 1256, 1297,
     1307, 1358, 1359, 1360, 1504, bibliography,
     1512; The American Language, 1144, 1145;
     Notes on Democracy, 1144, 1307; The Phi-
     losophy of Nietzsche, 1142–1143; Prej-
     udices, 1144, 1297
Mercier, Alfred, 686–687
Meredith, William, 1427, 1442
Merrill, James, 1445; Braving the Elements,
     1445; First Poems, 1445; Nights and Days,
     1445
Merrill, Stuart F., 1066
Merwin, W. S., 1426, 1440–1441; The Car-
     rier of Ladders, 1441; The Dancing Bears,
     1440; The Drunk in the Furnace, 1440;
     Green With Beasts, 1440; The Lice, 1441;

A Mask for Janus, 1440; *The Miner's Pale Children*, 1441; *The Moving Target*, 1440; *Writings to an Unfinished Accompaniment*, 1441

Meyersohn, Rolf, 1417

Michener, James A., 1403, 1424; *Tales of the South Pacific*, 1403

Middle Atlantic States: Maryland, 41, 42, 49; New Jersey, 82; New York, 37, 82, 87, 270; Pennsylvania, 82, 87, 88, 194, 270

Middle West, 515, 758-760, 820, 862-865, 870, 871, 1174, 1222-1223

Middleton, Drew, 1402

Millay, Edna St. Vincent, 1172, 1239, 1298, 1312, *1349-1350*, 1517

Miller, Arthur, 1424, *1449-1451*; *After the Fall*, 1449, 1450; *All My Sons*, 1449, 1450; *The Creation of the World and Other Business*, 1449, 1450; *The Crucible*, 1449, 1450; *Death of a Salesman*, 1449, 1450, 1451; *An Enemy of the People*, 1449; *Incident at Vichy*, 1450; *The Misfits*, 1450; *The Price*, 1450; *A View from the Bridge*, 1450

Miller, Henry, 1420

Miller, J. Hillis, 1422, 1423

Miller, Joaquin, 633, 661, 792, 793, 794, 863, 865, 866, *868*

Miller, William, 225

Millett, Kate, 1420

Mills, C. Wright, 1417

Milton, John, 94, 96, 164, 296, 420, 493

Minstrel shows, 722-723

Mitchell, Langdon, 1012, 1013, 1237

Mitchell, Margaret, 1267, 1375, 1382, 1384, 1387, 1388, 1389, 1390

M'lle New York, 1067, 1077

Möllhausen, Heinrich Balduin, 681-682

Monroe, Harriet, 1128, *1172-1173*, 1336

Monroe, James, 219, 220

Montague, William Pepperell, 1290

Montaigne, Michel de, 375, 1103

Montesquieu, Baron de la Brède et de, 29, 94

Moody, William Vaughn, 1000, *1013-1015*, *1157-1158*, 1237, 1318; *The Death of Eve*, 1014, 1158; *The Faith Healer*, 1014-1015, 1158; *The Fire Bringer*, 1014, 1158; *The Great Divide*, 1010, 1014, 1158; *Masque of Judgment*, 1013-1014, 1158

Moore, Marianne, 1174, 1352, 1353, 1396, 1399, 1400, 1433, 1518; *Collected Poems*, 1400; *Like a Bulwark*, 1400; *O To Be a Dragon*, 1400; *Selected Poems*, 1400

Moore, Thomas, 174

More, Paul Elmer, 1076, 1136, 1148, *1150-1152*, 1360; *A Century of Indian Epigrams*, 1150; *The Demon of the Absolute*, 1151; *Shelburne Essays*, 1150-1151

Morley, Christopher, 1131-1132

Morris, Gouverneur, 285

Morris, Wright, 1461-1462; *Ceremony in Lone Tree*, 1462; *The Field of Vision*, 1462; *My Uncle Dudley*, 1462

Morse, Jedidiah, 122, 123, 228, 654

Morton, Nathaniel, 35

Morton, Sarah Wentworth, 173

Morton, Thomas, 35, 36

Moss, Howard, 1427

Motion pictures, 672-673, 1124, 1266, 1270

Motley, John Lothrop, 526, 527, 528-529, 533-535, 540, 645, 1365, 1499, bibliography, 1499; *Rise of the Dutch Republic*, 534-535, 645

Mott, Lucretia, 230, 503

Moulton, Louise Chandler, 811

Mourt's Relation, 34

Mowatt, Anna Cora, 281

Muckraking movement, 946, 954, 965, 979, 992-995, 996-998, 1036, 1111

Muir, John, 661, 864, *873-874*; *The Mountains of California*, 874; *Our National Parks*, 874; *The Story of My Boyhood and Youth*, 874; *Travels in Alaska*, 874

Mulford, Prentice, 661, 866

Mumford, Lewis, 1136, 1141, 1154, 1257, 1359, 1360

Munchausen, Karl F. H., 728-729

Munson, Gorham, 1360

Murfree, Mary Noailles, 791, 850-851

Murray, John, 252

Musical Courier, 1075

Mysticism, 1288, 1292

Nabokov, Vladimir, 1460; *Ada*, 1460; *Lolita*, 1460; *Pale Fire*, 1460

Nader, Ralph, 1420

Nasby, Petroleum V. (David Ross Locke), 571, 743-744, 784, 800, 828, 1130

Nashville Fugitives. *See* Fugitive poets

Nast, Thomas, 806

Nathan, George Jean, 691, 1127

Nation, 790, 806, 814, 976, 1112, 1117, 1359

National Gazette, 172

National Youth Administration, 1260

Nationalism, 123, 147, 157, 219–220, 285, 290, 291, 298, 345, 595, 644, 677–678, 679, 946, 1107, 1119, 1255, 1262. *See also* Provincialism

Naturalsim, 847, 1016–1017, 1037–1038, 1087, 1136, 1142, 1200, 1286; in fiction, 1016–1038, 1407; in drama, 1321

Nature and nature writers, 93, 286, 413–414, 872–875, 1190–1194. *See also* individual authors

Neal, John, *290–291,* 292, 304, 620

Neal, Larry, 1444

Negroes, 511, 565, 583, 648, *714–715, 722–723, 748–749, 791, 851–855,* 1314–1315. *See also* Black consciousness

Neighborhood Playhouse, 1242

Nemerov, Howard, 1427

Neruda, Pablo, 1442

New Criticism, the, 1394, 1421, 1428

New England, 34–35, 54, 232, 233–234, 285, 289, 290, 292, 512, 587, 795, *843–848,* 1189–1190

New England Courant, 22

New England Magazine, 237

New England Weekly Journal, 22

New Jersey, 82

New Journalism, the, 1423

New Orleans. *See* Cities and towns

New Republic, 1107, 1117, 1261, 1359, 1361

New York. *See* Middle Atlantic States

New York City. *See* Cities and towns

New York *Evening Post,* 300, 320, 976

New York *Herald Tribune Books,* 1152

New York, *Ledger,* 520

New York Magazine, 127

New York *Mirror,* 238, 280, 827

New York Review, 300, 308

New York School poets, 1442–1443

New York Society Library, 125

New York *Sun,* 1075

New York *Sunday Mercury,* 520

New York *Times,* 1075, *1084*

New York *Tribune,* 514, 519, 769, 810, 811, 873

New York *World,* 1075

New Yorker, 751, 756, 1378

Newell, Robert Henry, 571, 784

Newspapers and magazines, 21–22, 23, 175, 237–238, 302, 519–521, 644, 656, 677, 688, 692, *805–806,* 953–954, 956, 964–965, *1125–1132,* 1269. *See also* Printing and publishing

Newton, Isaac, 86, 94, 948, 1096, 1099

Niblo, William, 241

Nichols, Anne, 1005

Nicholson, Meredith, 871–872

Niebuhr, Barthold, 1083

Niebuhr, Reinhold, 1287–1288, 1418

Niebuhr, Richard, 1287

Nietzsche, Friedrich Wilhelm, 948

Nims, John Frederick, 1427

Noah, Mordecai Manuel, 690, 691

Nobel Prize, 1393, 1403

Nordau, Max, 1079

Norris, Frank, 968, 978, 999, 1016, *1026–1033,* 1102, 1135, 1197, 1376, bibliography, 1509; *Blix,* 1030; *A Man's Woman,* 1031; *McTeague,* 635, 1026, 1029; *Moran of the Lady Letty,* 1030, 1036; *The Octopus,* 978, 1031–1033, 1102; *The Pit,* 989, 1033; *Vandover and the Brute,* 1029–1030; *Yvernelle,* 1028

North American Review, 176, 237, 284, 285, 286, 287, 295, 297, 298, 299, 303, 527, 814, 815, 1084, 1094, 1125

North-West Ordinance, 143

Northern Californian, 866

Norton, Charles Eliot, 507, 795, 830

Norton, John, 60

Norwegian-American literature. *See* Scandinavian-American literature

Novels. *See* individual authors and movements

Noyes, John Humphrey, 225

Núñez Cabeza de Vaca, Alvar, 25

Oakes, Urian, 65

Objectivist school, 1429

O'Connor, Flannery, 1424, 1464; *A Good Man Is Hard To Find,* 1464; *The Violent Bear It Away,* 1464; *Wise Blood,* 1464

Odets, Clifford, 1314, 1320, *1327–1330,* 1393,

1402, 1520; *Awake and Sing*, 1327–1329; *Golden Boy*, 1329; *Paradise Lost*, 1329; *Rocket to the Moon*, 1329; *Waiting for Lefty*, 1328

Odum, Howard W., 721, 1257

Off-Broadway theater, 1452, 1453, 1454, 1456

Oglethorpe, James, 48

O'Hara, Frank, 1443; *Collected Poems*, 1443

O'Hara, John, 1407, *1408*, 1518; *Appointment in Samarra*, 1408; *The Lockwood Concern*, 1408; *A Rage to Live*, 1408; *Ten North Frederick*, 1408

Olson, Charles, 1425, *1429–1430; Call Me Ishmael*, 1429; *The Maximus Poems*, 1429, 1430

Olson, Elder, 1395

O'Neill, Eugene, 1015, 1096, *1237–1250*, 1320, 1323, 1383, 1389, 1390, 1393, 1394, *1401–1402*, bibliography, 1514–1515; *Ah Wilderness!* 1244; *All God's Chillun Got Wings*, 1239, 1240; *Anna Christie*, 1240; *Beyond the Horizon*, 1240; *Bound East for Cardiff*, 1238, 1240; *By Way of Obit*, 1401; *Days Without End*, 1244; *Desire Under the Elms*, 1244, 1245, 1246–1247; *Diff'rent*, 1240; *Dynamo*, 1244; *The Emperor Jones*, 724, 1239, 1240; *The Great God Brown*, 1244, 1245, 1246, 1247; *The Hairy Ape*, 1239, 1240–1241, 1242; *Hughie*, 1401; *The Iceman Cometh*, 1249, 1401; *Long Day's Journey into Night*, 1401, 1402; *Marco Millions*, 1243; *A Moon for the Misbegotten*, 1401; *More Stately Mansions*, 1401; *Mourning Becomes Electra*, 1244, 1245, 1246, 1248–1249, 1394; *Strange Interlude*, 1244, 1245, 1246, 1247–1248, 1249; *A Tale of Possessors Self-Dispossessed*, 1401; *A Touch of the Poet*, 1401

Open Field movement, 1429–1430

Oppen, George, 1429; *Of Being Numerous*, 1429; Pulitzer Prize, 1429

Oratory, 93, *541–562*, 657, bibliography, 1498. *See also* Radio

Oregon Trail, 660, 767–768

O'Reilly, John Boyle, 1066

Oriental influence. *See* Foreign attitudes and influences

Origen, 1430

Otis, James, 132, *133–134*, 1086

Ottley, Roi, 1315

Otto, Max, 1285

Outlook, 819

Overland Monthly, 866, 870, 873, 1034

Overland Trail, 640

Pacifism, 1261

Page, Thomas Nelson, 613, 791, *849–850*, bibliography, 1505

Paine, Albert Bigelow, 929

Paine, Robert Treat, 173

Paine, Thomas, 117, 120, 127, 132, *138–141*, 144, 167, 169, 196, 208, 978, 1490; *The Age of Reason*, 141; *Agrarian Justice*, 141; *The American Crisis*, 140; *Common Sense*, 132, 138, 139, 144; *The Rights of Man*, 120, 141

Palmer, George Herbert, 799

Palmer, Joel, 660

Pamphlets, 131–145

Parke-Custis, George Washington, 281

Parker, Dorothy, 756, 1296, 1313, 1518

Parker, Lottie Blair, 1005

Parker, Samuel, 660

Parker, Theodore, 225, 226, 375, *556–557*, 564, 642, 1498

Parkman, Francis, 28, 29, 502, 503, 508, 526, 528, 529, *535–538*, 540, 567, 645, 776, bibliography, 1499; *California and Oregon Trail*, 535, 776; *France and England in North America*, 536–538; *The Jesuits in North America*, 28

Parks, William, 51

Parley, Peter (Samuel G. Goodrich), 228, 229, 418

Partisan Review, 1361, 1362

Pascal, Blaise, 375, 1103

Pastorius, Francis Daniel, 678

Pater, Walter, 818

Patten, Simon, 950

Pattie, James, 771

Pauck, Wilhelm, 1287

Paulding, James Kirke, 127, 175, 188, 238, 244, 270, *271–276*, 280, 291, 567, 738; *The Backwoodsman*, 272; *The Book of St. Nicholas*, 275; *The Bucktails*, 272, 274, 282; *The Dutchman's Fireside*, 273, 274; *The History of Uncle Sam and His Boys*, 272; *John Bull in America*, 272; *Koningsmarke*,

273; *The Lion of the West*, 272, 275, 282; *The Old Continental*, 273; *The Puritan and His Daughter*, 273; *Salmagundi*, 175, 271, 272; *Westward Ho!* 273, 274
Payne, John Howard, 191, 244, 281, 282
Payne, Will, 988, 989
Peabody, Elizabeth, 230, 374, 375
Peabody, George, 511
Peabody, Josephine, 1172
Peale, Charles Wilson, 122
Pearson, Karl, 1094
Peck, George W., 930
Peeples, Edwin, 1315
Peirce, Charles S., 951, 982
Pendleton, George, 795
Penn, William, 37, *83*, 84, 88, 96, 194; *Frame of Government*, 37; *Fruits of a Father's Love*, 83; *Further Account*, 37; *A letter from William Penn*, 37; *Letter to the Free Society of Traders*, 88; *Some account of the province of Pennsylvania*, 37; *Some Fruits of Solitude*, 83
Pennell, Joseph, 832
Pennsylvania. *See* Middle Atlantic States
Pennsylvania Gazette, 22
Pennsylvania German literature, 678, 683–684
Pennsylvania Journal and Weekly Advertiser, 140, 667
Percival, James Gates, 288–289
Percy, Thomas, 288
Percy, Walker, 1464; *The Moviegoer*, 1464
Periodicals. *See* Newspapers and magazines
Perry, Ralph Barton, 1290
Perse, St.-Jean, 1442
Peters, Paul, 1327
Philadelphia. *See* Cities and towns
Philadelphia Centennial Exposition of 1876, 796
Philadelphia Staatsbote, 679
Phillips, David Graham, 993, 1118
Phillips, Wendell, 504, 545, 558, 564
Phillips, William, 1362, 1363, 1364
Philosopher-statesmen, 146–161
Philosophy. *See* Determinism; Empiricism; Hegelianism; Humanism; Humanitarianism; Idealism; Instrumentalism; Materialism; Mysticism; Naturalism; Plato and Platonism; Positivism; Pragmatism; Rationalism; Relativism; Science; Transcendentalism

Phoenix, John (George Horatio Derby), 661, 864
Physiocrats, 978
Picayune, 766
Pickering, John, 666, 668–669
Pickering, Timothy, 142, 1086
Pierpont, John, 290, 292–293
"Pike," 864–866, 873
Pike, Nicholas, 654
Pike, Zebulon Montgomery, 764–765, 771, 1502
Pinckney, Eliza Lucas, 53
Pinero, Arthur Wing, 1009
Pingree, Hazen, 1108
Pinkney, Edward Coote, 307
Pinkney, William, 290, 307, 688
Pitkin, Walter B., 1290
Plantation aristocracy, 511
Plantation in literature, 612–613
Plath, Sylvia, 1425, *1440; Ariel*, 1440; *The Colossus*, 1440
Plato and Platonism, 147, 356, 972
Plattdeutsch, 683
Plays and playwrights. *See* Drama
Plutarch, 11
Plymouth. *See* Cities and towns
Pocahontas, 33, 187
Podhoretz, Norman, 1422
Poe, Edgar Allan, 130, 181, 183, 236, 238, 239, 240, 245, 248, 280, 287, 291, 303, 310, 315, 316, *321–342*, 378, 420, 424, 439, 483, 608, *629–631*, 682, 715, 774, 776, 816, 817, 820, 1038, 1065, 1135, 1152, 1365, 1375, 1378, 1380, 1388, bibliography, 1493; *Al Aaraaf*, 323; "Eldorado," 776; *Eureka*, 336–337; "Journal of Julius Rodman," 774, 777; "A Manuscript Found in a Bottle," 310; *Marginalia*, 337, 339; *Narrative of A. Gordon Pym*, 329, 774; *Poems*, 324–325; *Tales of the Folio Club*, 326, 327, 329; *Tales of the Grotesque and Arabesque*, 329–330; *Tamerlane and Other Poems*, 323; "Ulalume," 777
Poetry, 813, *899–916*, 1185–1189, 1353, 1426–1446. *See also* Criticism, literary; individual authors and movements
Poetry: A Magazine of Verse, 1128, *1172–1174*, 1180, 1181, 1184, 1185, 1189, 1336, 1337, 1340, 1354

Poirier, Richard, 1422

Political and economic philosophy, 146–161; economic determinism, 1087; imperialism, 639, 977; isolationism, 1255, 1256, 1262; *laissez faire*, 950, 975, 976, 980, 983, 1255; Manifest Destiny, 221, 761, 767, 877; popular sovereignty, 196–197, 220; radicalism, 977; reform movements, 226, 292, 1108–1113, 1115. *See also* Agrarian movement; Democracy; Industrialism

Political Greenhouse, 168

Political literature, 146–161

Political parties: Democratic, 480; Federalist, 118, 119; Free Soilers, 301; Know-Nothings, 502–503, 643, 830; Progressive, 1112, 1115; Republican, 119, 301, 505, 789, 790, 794; Whig, 227

Pollard, Percival, 1077

Pomfret, John, 94

Poole, Ernest, 1235, 1383

Pope, Alexander, 49, 68, 94, 124, 164, 165, 284, 286, 295, 296, 598

Population studies, 205–207, 222

Populism, 792, 794, 950, 952, 981, 1107, 1109, 1110

Port Folio, 127, 129, 175, 176, 640, 650

Porter, Gene Stratton, 1119, 1121

Porter, Katherine Anne, 1297, 1314, 1387

Porter, William Sydney, 755, 1385

Porter, William Trotter, 739

Porteus, Beilby, 296

Portico, 290

Positivism, 817, 947

Postl, Karl Anton (Charles Sealsfield), 679–681, 771

Pound, Ezra, *1173,* 1184, 1185, 1186, 1187, *1335–1340,* 1343, 1359, 1365, 1368, 1369–1370, 1376, 1395, *1397,* 1398, 1399, 1426, 1427, *1428,* 1429, 1431, 1440, 1516, bibliography, 1517; *Cantos,* 1339, 1343; *Cathay,* 1338; *Hugh Selwyn Mauberley,* 1338; *A Lume Spento,* 1336; *Lustra,* 1337; *Odyssey,* 1397; *Personae,* 1337; *The Pisan Cantos,* 1397, 1428; *Section: Rock-Drill, 85–95 de los cantares,* 1397; *The Spirit of Romance,* 1336; *Thrones, 96–109 de los cantares,* 1397; Bollingen Prize for Poetry, 1398

Poussin, Guillaume Tell, 213, 214

Powdermaker, Hortense, 1257

Powell, Adam Clayton, 1315

Powell, John Wesley, 647, 794, 864, *874, 876–877*

Pownall, Thomas, 195

Pragmatism, *951–952,* 982, 983, 1111, 1278, 1281, 1283, 1285

Prentiss, Seargent S., 558

Prescott, William Hickling, 239, 251, 526, *529–533,* 540, bibliography, 1499

Preston, Margaret Junkin, 570

Price, Richard, 197

Priestley, Joseph, 166

Prince, Thomas, 19, 36

Printing and publishing, 20–21, 51, 125–126, 234–237, 239–241, 516, 521–523, 621–622, 655–656, 657, 678, 803, 954, 955, 958–961, 963, 1132–1134, 1266, 1268, 1270. *See also* Literature as business; Newspapers and magazines

Progress, idea of, 945, 947

Progressive Movement, 947, 950, 1114

Projectivism. *See* Open Field movement

Prokosch, Frederick, 1314

Proletarierbund, 502

Protestantism, 12, 14–15, 225, 950–951, 958, 1288

Proud, Robert, 137

Proverb literature, 724–725

Provincetown Playhouse, 1238–1239. *See also* Drama

Provincialism, 285. *See also* Nationalism

Publick Occurrences, 21

Publishers. *See* Printing and publishing

Puck, 754

Pujo Committee, 1107

Pulitzer Prize, 1403, 1429, 1451

Purdy, James, 1468, *1469; The Color of Darkness,* 1469; *Eustace Chisolm and the Works,* 1469; *Jeremy's Version,* 1469; *Malcolm,* 1469

Pumpelly, Raphael, 1094

Punch, 633

Purchas, Samuel, 30, 31

Puritanism, 12, 34, *54–70,* 347, 419–421, 424, 542, 1138–1139, 1274–1275

Putnam, George Palmer, 236, 237, 239, 241, 516

Putnam, Phelps, 1353

Putnam's Magazine, 515, 516, 722

Put's Golden Songster, 866

Pyle, Ernie, 1402

Pynchon, Thomas, 1425, *1470; The Crying of Lot 49*, 1470; *Gravity's Rainbow*, 1470; *V*, 1470

Quakers, 82, 83–87, 88, 90–92, 195, 481, 482, 577–578. *See also* Transcendentalism

Quarterly Review, 212, 620

Queen, Ellery, 1380

Quincy, Edmund, 564, 565

Quinet, Edgar, 214

Rabe, David, 1456; *Sticks and Bones*, 1456

Rabinowitz, Solomon, 693

Radio, 562, 1124

Rahv, Philip, 1362, 1363, 1364

Rakosi, Carl, 1429

Ramus, Peter, 57

Randall, John Merman, 1285

Randolph, Edmund, 143

Randolph, John, 48

Rank, Otto, 1418

Ransom, John Crowe, 616, 617, 1155, *1346–1347*, 1369, 1371, 1372, 1395, 1399, 1427, 1437; *Gentlemen in Bonds*, 1399; *Selected Poems*, 1399

Raper, Arthur, 1257

Rascoe, Burton, 1360

Rastell, John, 3

Rationalism, 86, 87

Raumer, Friedrich L. von, 214

Rauschenbusch, Walter, 951

Rawlings, Marjorie Kinnan, 722, 1257

Raynal, Abbé, 195

Read, Opie, 721

Read, Thomas Buchanan, 239, 811

Reader's Digest, 1269, 1378

Realism, 59–62, 86, 87, 645, 794, 813, *878–898*, 1011, 1200, 1289–1290, 1359–1361, 1368

Rechy, John, 1467; *City of Night*, 1467

Reconstruction Finance Corporation, 1254

Reconstruction period, 510, 511, 641, 790, 969

Redpath, James, 800, 801

Redwood, Abraham, 20

Reed, Ishmael, 1444, *1468; Yellow-Back Radio Broke Down*, 1468

Reed, John, 1141, 1239

Reed, Sampson, 370

Reed, Walter, 947

Reedy's Mirror, 1078, 1179

Reese, Lizette W., 1157

Regional theater, 1455–1456

Regionalism and local color, 223, 227, 609, 650, 651, 704, 715, 716, 748, 769–770, 793, *843–861*, 863–864, 868–872, 946, 973, 1236. *See also* Cities and towns; Middle Atlantic States; Middle West; New England; South; West

Reicher, Emmanuel, 693

Reid, Mayne, 681

Reitzel, Robert, 682

Relativism, 951, 1285

Religion. *See* Calvinism; Catholicism; Philosophy; Protestantism; Puritanism; Quakers; Religious sects; Science; Social gospel; Theology; Unitarianism

Religious sects, 224, 225, 286, 641, 653, 958

Renaissance and the New World, 3–15

Reports and chronicles, 24–39, 87–91

Revolution, American, 118, 171, 172, 196, 197–198, 543–544, 610, 730

Revue des Deux Mondes, 212, 214, 628

Rexroth, Kenneth, 1430, 1431, 1484

Rhodes, Eugene Manlove, 872

Ribman, Ronald, 1456–1457; *A Break in the Skin*, 1457; *The Ceremony of Innocence*, 1457; *Harry, Noon and Night*, 1456; *The Journey of the Fifth Horse*, 1456; *Passing Through From Exotic Places*, 1457

Rice, Alice Hegan, 1377

Rice, Elmer, 691, 1243, 1317, 1319, 1326, 1327

Rich, Adrienne, 1445

Richards, I. A., 1395

Richardson, Jack, 1454; *The Prodigal*, 1454; *Xmas in Las Vegas*, 1454

Richardson, Samuel, 178, 182

Riddles, 725–726

Riesman, David, 1417

Riggs, Lynn, 717

Riis, Jacob, 949, 1107, 1113, 1255

Riley, James Whitcomb, 716, 748, 825, 863, *871*, 1122, 1157

Ripley, Ezra, 232

Ripley, George, 374

Roberts, Elizabeth Madox, 717, 1314

Roberts, Kenneth, 759, 1380, 1382, 1384

Robinson, Edwin Arlington, 716, 1120, 1135, *1157-1170*, 1359, 1377, 1393, bibliography, 1512; *Captain Craig,* 1159, 1162, *1163; The Children of the Night,* 1157, 1158, 1159, *1160-1162; Lancelot,* 1160, 1167, 1168; *The Man Against the Sky,* 1159, 1164; *Merlin,* 1160, 1165, 1167, 1168; *The Town Down the River,* 1159, 1163; *Tristram,* 1160, 1167, 1168

Robinson, James Harvey, 1283, 1284

Robinson, Rowland, 847

Rockefeller, John D., 1258, 1259

Roethke, Theodore, 1426, 1433, *1435-1436; The Far Field,* 1436; *The Lost Son,* 1435; *Open House,* 1435

Rogers, Henry H., 936

Rogers, Will, 753

Roheim, Geza, 1418

Rolfe, John, 44

Rölvaag, O. E., 689-690

Roman, Anton, 866

Romanticism, 91-93, 96-98, 284, 286, 287, 288, 292, 349, 355, 777, 791

Roosevelt, Franklin D., 562, 1111, 1253, 1258, 1259, 1262

Roosevelt, Theodore, 539, 560, 677, *945-946,* 952, 1107, 1108, 1110, 1111, 1112, *1113-1114,* 1115, 1255

Root, Elihu, 1255

Rosenberg, Bernard, 1417

Rosenfeld, Jonah, 693

Rosenthal, M. L., 1445, **1516**

Ross, Harold, 756

Rossetti, William M., 486, 816

Rosten, Leo C., 752

Roszak, Theodore, 1420

Roth, Philip, 1465-1466; *The Breast,* 1466; *Goodbye Columbus,* 1465; *Letting Go,* 1465-1466; *Portnoy's Complaint,* 1466

Rothenberg, Jerome, 1441

Rouquette, Adrien-Emmanuel, 685, 686, 1071

Rouquette, François-Dominique, 685-686

Rousseau, Jean Jacques, 29, 286

Rowson, Susanna, 177-178

Royce, Josiah, 946, 948, 973-974

Rukeyser, Muriel, 1312, 1354, 1516

Runyon, Damon, 755, 1377

Ruppius, Otto, 681

Rush, Benjamin, 142, 153

Rush, Richard, 127

Ruskin, John, 841

Russell, Bertrand, 1293, 1295

Russell, Irwin, 716, 853

Russell, Lord John, 1103

Russell's Magazine, 318

Russian interest in contemporary writers, 1384-1386

Russian Revolution, 981

Russophiles, 1261

Ruxton, George, 771

Sabin, Joseph, 32

Sagard, Gabriel, 28

Saint-Gaudens, Augustus, 957, 1091, 1092, 1094

Salem, Massachusetts. *See* Cities and towns

Salinger, J. D., 1418, *1462; The Catcher in the Rye,* 1418, 1462; *Franny and Zooey,* 1462; *Nine Stories,* 1462; *Raise High the Roof Beam, Carpenters,* 1462; *Seymour, An Introduction,* 1462

Salmagundi essays, 127

Saltus, Edgar, 1072-1074

San Francisco. *See* Cities and towns

San Francisco poets, 1424, 1430-1431. *See also* Beat movement

Sand, George, 474

Sandburg, Carl, 716, 863, 1120, 1174, *1181-1184,* 1296, 1359, 1377, 1393, 1399, bibliography, 1512; *Chicago Poems,* 1182; *Good Morning, America,* 1182, 1183; *Lincoln,* 1181, 1313; *The People, Yes,* 1183-1184

Sandys, George, 41

Santayana, George, *1273-1277,* 1359, 1365, 1368, 1399; *The Last Puritan,* 1274; *The Life of Reason,* 1275; *The Middle Span,* 1274; *Persons and Places,* 1274; *The Realms of Being,* 1275-1276

Sargent, Lucius M., 568

Saroyan, William, 1314, 1331, *1332-1333,* 1402

Sartre, Jean-Paul, 1418

Satire, 163-164, 178-180, 1222, 1224, 1225. *See also* individual authors

Saturday Review of Literature, 1153

Scandinavian-American literature, 24, 30-31, 689-690, 1383-1384

Schelling, Friedrich Wilhelm Joseph von, 286, 349

Schiller, F. C. S., 1279

Schisgal, Murray, 1454; *Luv*, 1454

Schleiermacher, Friedrich Ernst Daniel, 349

Schoolcraft, Henry Rowe, 647, 655, 694, 762

Schopf, Johann David, 679

Schurz, Carl, 1085

Schwartz, Delmore, 1354, 1426, 1427, 1428

Schwartz, Maurice, 693

Science, 353, 647-649, 799, 802, 947, 970, 974-976, 980, 1292-1293

Science fiction, 1471-1472

Scollard, Clinton, 1172

Scott, Walter, 174, 474, 530, 677, 685, 1083

Scott, Winfield Townley, 1427

Scribner's Monthly, 642, 816, 953, 959

Seabury, Samuel, 132, 137

Sealsfield, Charles, 679-681, 771

Sedgwick, Catharine Maria, 290, 291, 298, 304

Selby, Hubert, 1467; *Last Exit to Brooklyn*, 1467

Sergeant, Winthrop, 1400

Service, Robert W., 716

Sewall, Samuel, 60, 69, 127, 1488

Sewanee Review, 1371, 1395

Seward, William Henry, 506, 558, 1103

Sexton, Anne, 1440; *To Bedlam and Part Way Back*, 1440

Shafer, Robert, 1360

Shakespeare, William, 128, 189, 491

Shaler, Nathaniel S., 796

Shapiro, Karl, 1354, 1426, 1427, 1428

Sharpe, John, 20

Shaw, Henry Wheeler, 744-745

Shaw, Lao, 1389

Sheean, Vincent, 1263, 1384

Sheldon, Charles M., 801

Sheldon, Edward, 1237

Shellabarger, Samuel, 1268

Shepard, Sam, 1425, 1457; *La Turista*, 1457; *Melodrama Play*, 1457; *Operation Sidewinder*, 1457; *Red Cross*, 1457; *The Tooth of Crime*, 1457

Shepard, Thomas, 58, 70

Sheridan, Richard B., 186

Sherman, Stuart P., 1127, 1142, 1145, *1152-1153*

Sherwood, Adiel, 670

Sherwood, Robert, 1319, 1330

Shillaber, Benjamin P., 651

Shirer, William, 1402

Sigourney, Lydia Huntley, 226, *289*, 292

Sill, Edward Rowland, 661, 811

Silliman, Benjamin, 827

Simic, Charles, 1442

Simon, Neil, 1452

Simms, William Gilmore, 230, 239, 240, 308, *311-313*, 315, 316-317, 318, 319, 320, 378, 567, 608, 610, 681, bibliography, 1493; *Atalantis*, 312; *Beauchamps*, 312; *Charlemont*, 312; *Count Julian*, 312; *Guy Rivers*, 311, 312, 681; *Martin Faber*, 312; *The Partisan*, 312; *Pelayo, a Story of the Goth*, 312; *The Yemassee*, 312

Simpson, Louis, 1445; *Adventures of the Letter I*, 1445; *The Arrivistes*, 1445; *At the End of the Road*, 1445; *Selected Poems*, 1445

Sinclair, Upton, 978, 995-999, 1118, 1361, 1375, 1381, 1382, 1383, 1384, 1385, 1386, 1387, 1388, 1389; *American Outpost*, 998; *Boston*, 998; *Dragon's Teeth*, 998; *The Jungle*, 996-997, 1118, 1375, 1383; *Love's Pilgrimage*, 997; *Manassas*, 996; *Oil!* 998; *World's End*, 998

Singer, Isaac Bashevis, 1465; *The Magician of Lublin*, 1465; *Satan in Goray*, 1465

Single tax, 795, 973, 978-979

Singmaster, Elsie, 684

Skinner, B. F., 1419

Skinner, Otis, 1001, 1007, 1012

Sklar, George, 1327

Slavery, 85, 226, 227, 293, 301, 504-506, 511, 545, 563-568, 575-577, 583-584, 608-609. See also Civil War

Slick, Sam (Thomas Chandler Haliburton), 734-735

Slosson, Annie Trumbull, 844

Smart Set, 1078, 1144

Smedley, Agnes, 1382, 1383, 1388

Smith, Bernard, 1362

Smith, Charles Henry, 571, 744

Smith, William Jay, 1427, 1442

Smith, Elihu Hubbard, 129, 168, 181

Smith, Elizabeth Oakes, 282

Smith, F. Hopkinson, 832, 988

Smith, Jedediah S., 777

Smith, John, 3, 7, 10, 11, *32-33*, 44, 48, 187

Smith, Joseph, 225

Smith, Seba, 651, 732-733

Smith, William (1727-1803), 87, 93, 96, 97-98

Smith, William (1728-1793), 89-90

Smith, Winchell, 1005

Smithsonian Institution, 230, 647, 682

Snodgrass, W. D., 1427, *1440; Heart's Needle,* 1440

Snyder, Gary, 1431, *1432; The Back Country,* 1432; *Earth House Hold,* 1432; *Myths and Texts,* 1432

Social debate and fiction, 986-999

Social gospel, 649, 795, 951

Social security, 1254, 1257-1259

Socialism and socialization, 895, 896, 950, 969, 970, 971, 973, 977, 984, 1107, 1108, 1255, 1256, 1270-1272. *See also* Communism; Industrialism; Labor movement; Single tax; Social security

Sociology, 980

Solt, Mary Ellen, 1443

Songs, 648, 707-715

Sontag, Susan, 1422

Sothern, E. H., 1007

South, 38, 40, 41, 48, 49-52, *306-320*, 504, 510, 512, *607-617*, 641, 684-687, 791, 848-859, 949, 1216, 1256, 1257, 1304-1306, 1309, 1314, *1346-1347*, 1371, 1500

South Carolina Gazette, 22

Southern Agrarians. *See* Fugitive poets

Southern Literary Messenger, 237, 309, 310, 313, 314, 316, 317, 318, 326, 327, 328, 515, 774

Southern Quarterly Review, 317

Southern Review (1828-1832), 237, 308, 311, 608, 1395

Southern Review (1935-1942), 1371

Southern and Western Monthly Magazine and Review, 317

Southey, Robert, 296

Spalding, John Lancaster, 970-971

Spanish-American literature, 25-26, 659, 678, 687-688

Spanish influence. *See* Foreign attitudes and influences; Folk literature

Spargo, John, 1111, 1255

Sparks, Jared, *285*, 286, 527, 645

Spectator, 624

Spelling, American, 670, 674

Spencer, Herbert, 790, 947, 970, 974, 978, 980, 1018, 1021

Spender, Stephen, 1378

Spenser, Edmund, 420

Spicer, Jack, 1431

Spingarn, J. E., 1137, *1154-1156*, 1359, 1365, 1367, 1398

Spirit of the Times, 739, 741, 866

Springfield *Republican,* 770, 828

Stafford, Jean, 1463; *Boston Adventure,* 1463

Stafford, William, 1445

Stallings, Laurence, 1243, 1317, 1318

Standard Oil Company, 979

Standish, Myles, 11, 35

Stanton, Daniel, 84

Stanton, Elizabeth Cady, 503

Stedman, Edmund Clarence, 524, 795, 809, 811, 812, 813, 814, *815-818*, 819, 825, 900, 1136, 1157; *American Anthology,* 815; *Blameless Prince,* 825; *The Nature and Elements of Poetry,* 815, 816-817; *Victorian Anthology,* 815; *Victorian Poets,* 815, 816

Steele, Richard, 19, 151

Steele, Wilbur Daniel, 1239

Steere, Richard, 65

Steffens, Lincoln, 993, 1125

Stein, Gertrude, 1297, 1300, 1393

Stein, Kurt M., 683

Steinbeck, John, 688, 1256, 1265, *1312*, 1314, 1375, 1382, 1384, 1386, 1387, 1390, 1394, *1406*, bibliography, 1520; *Cannery Row,* 1406; *East of Eden,* 1406; *Grapes of Wrath,* 1256, 1312, 1382, 1390, 1406; *In Dubious Battle,* 1406; *The Pearl,* 1406; *Tortilla Flat,* 1406; *The Wayward Bus,* 1406

Steinem, Gloria, 1420

Stephens, Alexander H., 558

Sterling, James, 52

Stern, Daniel, 1465

Stevens, Thaddeus, 508

Stevens, Wallace, 1120, 1174, *1354-1355*, 1393, 1396, *1399*, 1426, 1427, *1432-1433*, 1440, bibliography, 1518; *Collected Poems,*

1399; *Harmonium,* 1354; *Ideas of Order,* 1355; *The Man with the Blue Guitar,* 1355
Stevenson, Robert Louis, 832, 1008
Stewart, Charles S., 444
Stimson, Henry L., 1262
Stith, William, 38, *47-48,* 53
Stockton, Frank R., 753-754
Stoddard, Charles Warren, 661, 866, 1067
Stoddard, Elizabeth Drew Barstow, 825, 880
Stoddard, John L., 800
Stoddard, Richard Henry, 239, 795, *809-810,* 811, 812, 815, *818-819,* 824, 825, 826
Stolberg, Benjamin, 1257
Stone, John A., 281, 282, 1000
Stone, Lucy, 503, 558
Storey, Moorfield, 1111, 1112
Storm, Hans Otto, 1314
Story, William Wetmore, 828, 831
Stowe, Calvin Ellis, 653
Stowe, Harriet Beecher, 239, 503, 504, 505, 522-523, 563, *581-586,* 608, *843-844,* 1385; *Dred,* 583, 624; *Minister's Wooing,* 584; *Oldtown Fireside Stories,* 844; *Oldtown Folks,* 584, 843; *The Pearl of Orr's Island,* 584, 843; *Poganuc People,* 844; *Sunny Memories of Foreign Lands,* 830; *Uncle Tom's Cabin,* 293, 505, 515, 563, 583, 624-625, 843, 1003, 1375
Strand, Mark, 1442; *Darker,* 1442; *Reasons for Moving,* 1442; *The Story of Our Lives,* 1442
Streit, Clarence, 1262
Stribling, T. S., 1296
Strong, Josiah, 977
Strubberg, Friedrich Armand, 681
Stuart, Dabney, 1445
Sturgeon, Theodore, 1472
Sturgis, Caroline, 367
Sturgis, Howard O., 1376
Stuyvesant, Petrus, 30
Styron, William, *1464, 1467, 1471;* *Confessions of Nat Turner,* 1471; *Lie Down in Darkness,* 1464; *Set This House on Fire,* 1467
Suggs, Simon (Johnson Jones Hooper), 740-741
Sullivan, Louis H., 818
Sumner, Charles, 239, 508, 558, 564

Sumner, William Graham, 944, 950, 975-977, 980, 1258
Suzuki, D. T., 1418
Swedenborgianism, 368, 369, 370, 380, 382
Swedish-American literature. *See* Scandinavian-American literature
Swift, Jonathan, 48, 69, 94
Swinburne, Algernon Charles, 815, 816, 818
Swing, Raymond, 562
Szold, Henrietta, 690

Tablet, 311
Taft, William Howard, 1114, 1255
Tagore, Rabindranath, 1173
Tailfer, Patrick, 48-49
Taine, Hippolyte Adolphe, 870, 1018
Tall tales. *See* Folk literature
Talmud, 692
Tarbell, Ida M., 993, 1111
Tarkington, Booth, *746-748,* 871, 1008, 1385
Tate, Allen, 617, 1155, 1345, 1346, *1347,* 1360, 1369, 1371, *1372,* 1395, *1399-1400,* 1427, 1437, 1516; *Poems,* 1400; *The Winter Sea,* 1399
Taussig, F. W., 796
Tavel, Ronald, 1456; *Boy on the Straight-Back Chair,* 1456
Taylor, Bayard, 239, 240, 513, 519, 524, 769, 809, *810,* 811, 812, 819, *821-823,* 824, 831, 864, 1066; *El Dorado,* 769; *Faust,* 822-823; *Home Pastorals,* 821; *The Picture of St. John,* 821; *Poems of the Orient,* 821; *Prince Deukalion,* 821-822; *Views A-foot,* 810, 831
Taylor, Edward, 65-68, 1488
Teasdale, Sara, 1172
Temperance movement, 226
Tennyson, Alfred, 493, 813
Testut, Charles, 685
Thackeray, William Makepeace, 200, 230, 1083
Thalia Theater, 682
Thanet, Octave (Alice French), 869, 988
Thaxter, Celia, 847
Theater. *See* Drama
Theology, 18, 83, 86, 648-649, 801, 802, 957, 1116
Thomas, Augustus, 1000, *1010-1011,* 1015, 1237

Thomas, Gabriel, 88
Thomas, Isaiah, 124
Thompson, Benjamin, 65
Thompson, Daniel Pierce, 284, 289
Thompson, Denman, 1005
Thompson, John Reuben, 317, 320
Thompson, Maurice, 610, 869
Thompson, Vance, 1077
Thompson, William T., 651, 740
Thomson, Charles, 90
Thoreau, Henry David, 229, 230, 293, 345, 346, 350, 351, 352, 353, 354, 355, 356, 367, 374, 375, 377, *388–415*, 419, 421, 441, 475, 482, 483, 505, 507, 566, *626–627*, 682, 774, 800, 1376, 1389, bibliography, 1495–1496; and Emerson, 391, 392–396, 404; journals, 397–399; life at Walden Pond, 396–400, 401; as naturalist, 413–414; philosophy of, 345–357; place in literature, 411–412, 415; poetry, 393, 410–411; and slavery, 398–399, 405–406; style, 394, 412–413; "Civil Disobedience," 388, 401; *Excursions*, 408; *The Maine Woods*, 408; *Poems of Nature*, 410; *Walden*, 388, 389, 403, *404–405*, 626, 627; *A Week on the Concord and Merrimack Rivers*, 388, 399–400, 401, *402–403*
Thornton, Richard H., 670–671
Thorpe, T. B., 649, 741
Thurber, James, *756–757*, 1377
Thwaites, Reuben G., 28
Ticknor, Francis, 506
Ticknor, George, 122, 230, 285, 295, 530, 567, 645, 1261
Tillich, Paul, 1418
Time, 1378
Time-Piece, 173
Timothy, Lewis, 21, 53
Timrod, Henry, 318–320, 506, 569, 1500
Tocqueville, Alexis de, 210–214, 655, 1086, 1111, 1491
Tolson, Melvin B., 1444; *Libretto for the Republic of Liberia*, 1444
Tolstoy, Leo Nikolaevich, 894, 1021
Tooke, Horne, 166
Tourgée, Albion W., 573–574
Transcendentalism, 225, *346–352*, *355–357*, 374–375, 416, 433–434, *481–483*, 645, 774–775, 790, 915, 972, bibliography, 1494. *See also* Idealism

Translations, 1378–1389
Travel in America, 24, 649, 676, 771; in Europe, 827–842
Trilling, Lionel, *1418, 1421,* 1515
Trumbull, John, 129, 137, *162–164,* 170, 620, 731, 1491
Tucker, George, 306
Tucker, Nathaniel Beverley, 314, 315, 317, 610–613
Tucker, St. George, 175
Tuckerman, Frederick Goddard, 899
Tudor, William, 285, 295
Turnbull Lectures, 812, 816, 818
Turner, Frederick Jackson, 761, 795, 984, 1087, 1154
Twain, Mark. *See* Samuel Langhorne Clemens
Tyler, Royall, *186–187,* 188, 281

Unitarianism, 286, 347, 348
United Nations, 1261
United States, literary influence abroad, 618–636, 1374–1391
United States Literary Gazette, 299
United States Magazine and Democratic Review, 237
"University Wits," 1427
Updike, John, 1469, *1472–1473; The Centaur,* 1472; *Of the Farm,* 1472; *The Poorhouse Fair,* 1472; *Rabbit Redux,* 1473; *Rabbit Run,* 1473
Usher, Hezekiah, 17
Utopianism, 215, 646, 1108. *See also* Communitarian experiments

Vail, Eugène A., 212
Vallejo, César, 1442
Van Doren, Carl, 1127
Van Doren, Mark, 1280
van Dyke, Henry, 815, 819, *820*
Van Itallie, Claude, 1457–1458; *America Hurrah (Motel, Interview,* and *The Serpent: A Ceremony),* 1457–1458
van Meteren, Emanuel, 29
van Rensselaer, Kiliaen, 30
Van Vechten, Carl, 1235
Veblen, Thorstein, 945, 956, 979, *981–982,* 1074, 1111, 1361; *The Theory of Business Enterprise,* 981; *The Theory of the Leisure Class,* 981

Vere, Maximilien Schele de, 670

Verplanck, Gulian, 299, 302

Verrazano, Giovanni da, 29, 31

Very, Jones, 374

Vielé-Griffin, Francis, 1066

Vietnam War protest literature, 1416, 1444

Villard, Oswald Garrison, 1107, 1126

Villiers de l'Isle-Adam, 200, 202, 630

Vimont, Barthélemy, 28

Vincent, John H., 798

Virginia, in Southern literature, 309, 311

Virginia Gazette, 22, 51, 688

Voltaire (François Marie Arouet), 166, 195, 530, 1103

Vonnegut, Kurt, 1469, *1472; Cat's Cradle,* 1472; *Mother Night,* 1472; *Player Piano,* 1472; *The Sirens of Titan,* 1472; *Slaughter-house-Five,* 1472

Vorse, Mary Heaton, 1239

Vorticism, 1187, 1370

Vorwärts, 693

Voznesensky, Andrei, 1442

Wadsworth, Charles, 905, 909, 910, 915

Waggoner, David, 1445

Walker, Margaret, 1444; *For My People,* 1444

Wallace, Henry A., 1262

Wallace, Horace Binney, 829–830

Wallace, Lew, 966, 1007, 1381

Wallace, William Ross, 568

Wallack, James William, 238

Wallant, Edward Lewis, 1465

Walter, Eugene, 1239

Ward, Artemus (Charles Farrar Browne), 633, 729, *742–743,* 784, 828, 921, 1130

Ward, Douglas Turner, 1458; *Day of Absence,* 1459; *Happy Ending,* 1459

Ward, Lester Frank, 944, *950, 980–981,* 1111

Ward, Nathaniel, *58–59,* 69

Ward, Samuel Gray, 367

Ward, Theodora, 904; 1506

Warden, David Baillie, 212

Ware, Henry, 364

Warner, Charles Dudley, 795, 833, 875, *926–927,* 988

Warren, Austin, 1395

Warren, Mercy Otis, 133, 186

Warren, Robert Penn, 617, 1314, 1346, *1347,* 1371, 1395, 1400, *1408–1409,* 1426, 1433,

1435; All the King's Men, 1407, 1409; *At Heaven's Gate,* 1408; *Audubon: A Vision,* 1435; *Band of Angels,* 1409; *Brother to Dragons,* 1400, 1409, 1435; *The Cave,* 1409; *Flood,* 1409; *Incarnations,* 1435; *Night Rider,* 1408, 1409; *Promises,* 1435; *World Enough and Time,* 1409; *You, Emperors, and Others,* 1435

Washington, Booker T., 560

Washington, George, 129, 153, 172, 186, *198–200,* 245, 779, 1489

Washington Square Players, 1242

Watson, Thomas E., 1109, 1111

Watterson, Henry, 851

Watts, Alan, 1418

Watts, Isaac, 68, 94

Wave, 1026, 1028

Webster, Charles L., 936

Webster, Daniel, 302, 544, *549–551,* 1498

Webster, Noah, 122, 123, 126, 129, 143, 167, 168, 175, 228, 650, 654, 668, 670

Weems, Mason Locke, 126

Weissen, Abraham, 693

Weld, Isaac, 203

Welde, Thomas, 63

Wellek, René, 1395

Wells, H. G., 1112

Welty, Eudora, 1463–1464; *Delta Wedding,* 1463–1464; *The Ponder Heart,* 1464

Wendell, Barrett, 815, 819, 820

Wescott, Glenway, 1264, 1296, 1314

Wesley, John, 49, 53

West, 250–251, 512, 609, 940, 660–662, 687, 710–711, *758–770, 771–777, 792–794, 862–877*

West, Benjamin, 96, 122

West, Nathaniel, 1378, *1406,* 1465; *The Day of the Locust,* 1406; *Miss Lonelyhearts,* 1406

Westcott, Edward Noyes, 751, 752, 963, 1377

Western Messenger, 656

Western Review, 655

Westminster Review, 620

Wharton, Edith, 1043, 1048, 1197, *1209–1211,* 1236, 1378, bibliography, 1513; *The Age of Innocence,* 1209–1210; *Ethan Frome,* 1211; *The House of Mirth,* 1209; *Hudson River Bracketed,* 1211; *The Old Maid,* 1211

Wheelwright, Philip, 1418

Whipple, E. P., 814

Whitaker, Alexander, 40, 41

White, Andrew Dickson, 802, 950

White, David Manning, 1417

White, E. B., 756

White, John, 32

White, Richard Grant, 811, 816

White, William Allen, 1111, 1117

Whitefield, George, 53

Whitehead, Alfred North, 1293–1295

Whitlock, Brand, 978, 1255

Whitman, Marcus, 660

Whitman, Walt, 81, 169, 176, 293, 304, 341, 345, 346, 350, 351, 352, 353, 354, 355, 378, 379, 398, 413, 441, 472–498, 501, 505, 510, 525, 571, 631–633, 650, 715, 814, 816, 818, 825, 899, 900, 917, 946, 984, 1065, 1080, 1087, 1091, 1135, 1152, 1181, 1209, 1211, 1361, 1366, 1381, 1388, 1389, 1431, 1433, 1436, 1445, 1446, 1485, 1494, bibliography, 1497–1498; and the common man, 473, 476, 480; imagery, 493–494; notebooks, 474, 475–476; place in literary history, 495–498; philosophy of, 345–357; Quaker, 481–483; self-dramatization, 479, 482; sensuality, 483–485; style, 491–493; symbolism, 493–494; transcendentalism, 481–483; "By Blue Ontario's Shore," 495; Democratic Vistas, 495–496, 621; Drumtaps, 486, 487, 571–572; Leaves of Grass, 379, 473–475, 476–488, 495, 632, 650, 682, 899; "Song of Myself," 477–480, 481–482, 483, 484, 485, 492; Specimen Days and Collect, 488; The Wound Dresser, 488

Whitney, W. D., 674

Whittier, John Greenleaf, 181, 303, 378, 505, 507, 563, 566, 575–581, 715, 811, 812, bibliography, 1499–1500; Snow-Bound, 578, 579–580, 682

Wieners, John, 1429

Wiggin, Kate Douglas, 1121

Wigglesworth, Michael, 63, 65, 69

Wilbur, Richard, 1433; The Beautiful Changes, 1433; Things of This World, 1433

Wilcox, Ella Wheeler, 1121

Wilde, Richard Henry, 309

Wilder, Thornton, 1263, 1264, 1331, 1332, 1383, 1387, 1393, 1402, 1407, 1520

Wilkes, Charles, 641

Wilkins, Mary E. (Mrs. Mary Wilkins Freeman), 847–848

Willard, Emma, 226, 230

Willard, Samuel, 61

Williams, John A., 1468; The Man Who Cried I Am, 1468

Williams, Jonathan, 1430

Williams, Roger, 14, 60

Williams, Tennessee, 1447–1449, 1451; Battle of Angels, 1447; Cat on a Hot Tin Roof, 1447, 1451; The Eccentricities of a Nightingale, 1447; The Glass Menagerie, 1447; The Mutilated, 1448; The Night of the Iguana, 1447, 1448; Orpheus Descending, 1448; Small Craft Warnings, 1448; Sweet Bird of Youth, 1448; A Streetcar Named Desire, 1448; Suddenly Last Summer, 1448

Williams, William Carlos, 1120, 1174, 1352, 1393, 1396, 1399, 1400, 1426, 1427, 1428–1429, 1516, 1518; Collected Poems, 1429; Paterson, 1399, 1400, 1429

Williamson, Hugh, 143

Willis, Nathaniel Parker, 238, 240, 241, 270–271, 279–281, 818; A l'Abri, 280; Bianca Visconti, 281, 282; The Convalescent, 280; Paul Fane, 280–281; Pencillings by the Way, 271, 280, 827; Tortesa the Usurer, 281, 282

Willkie, Wendell, 1262

Wilson, Edmund, 1078, 1360, 1362, 1363, 1364, 1369, 1372, 1377, 1394, 1498, 1511, 1516, 1518; The Crack-Up, 1518; Patriotic Gore, 1498; The Shores of Light, 1511

Wilson, James, 143

Wilson, John, 64–65

Wilson, Woodrow, 371, 561, 1107, 1108, 1109, 1111, 1114–1115, 1255, 1262

Wimsatt, W. K., 1395

Wingfield, Edward M., 33

Winslow, Edward, 34, 35

Winter, William, 811

Winters, Yvor, 1353, 1371, 1394, 1429

Winthrop, John, 34, 35

Winthrop, Theodore, 570, 865

Wirt, William, 175, 306–307

Wise, John, 69, 116

Wise, John S., 573

Wissler, Clark, 1284

Wister, Owen, 864, 872

Witherspoon, John, 87, 95, 667–668, 675

Wolcott, Roger, 68, 69

Wolfe, Thomas, 717, 1263, 1264, 1309–1311, 1312, 1381, 1390, 1393, 1394, 1423, bibliography, 1519; Look Homeward, Angel, 1309, 1310; Of Time and the River, 1309, 1310, 1394; The Web and the Rock, 1309, 1310; You Can't Go Home Again, 1309, 1310

Wolfert, Ira, 1314

Wolley, Charles, 37

Wollstonecraft, Mary, 166, 286

Women's Liberation movement, 1416, 1420. See also Feminism

Women's rights. See Feminism

Wood, William, 35

Woodberry, George Edward, 815, 819–820, 1136, 1155

Woollcott, Alexander, 756, 1132

Woolman, John, 15, 84, 85–86, 1488; Conversations on the True Harmony of Mankind, 85; Journal, 15, 85; Plea for the Poor, 85; Some Considerations on the Keeping of Negroes, 85

Woolson, Constance Fenimore, 868

Wordsworth, William, 286, 287, 288, 297, 300, 375, 486

Works Progress Administration, 1260

Wright, Frances, 480, 558

Wright, Frank Lloyd, 818

Wright, Harold Bell, 1121

Wright, James, 1426, 1440, 1441–1442; The Branch Will Not Break, 1442; The Lion's Tale and Eyes, 1441; Shall We Gather at the River, 1442

Wright, Richard, 1314, 1315, 1386, 1407, 1467; Native Son, 1467

Wurlitzer, Rudolph, 1473; Flats, 1473

Wylie, Elinor, 1296, 1349–1350

Yancey, William L., 558, 567

Yankee, 290

Yeats, William Butler, 1426, 1427, 1436, 1439

Yellow Book, 1065, 1066

Yevtushenko, Yevgeny, 1442

Yiddish, 690, 692–693

Yiddish Art Theater, 693

Youmans, Edward L., 802

Young, William, 1007

Zangwill, Israel, 677

Zenger, John Peter, 22

Zionism, 690–691

Zola, Emile, 814, 1016, 1017, 1022, 1028, 1039, 1200

Zorach, Margaret, 1239

Zugsmith, Leane, 1313

Zukofsky, Louis, 1429